S0-AWG-325

PROPERTY LAW

Aspen Casebook Series

PROPERTY LAW

Rules, Policies, and Practices

Sixth Edition

JOSEPH WILLIAM SINGER
Bussey Professor of Law, Harvard Law School

BETHANY R. BERGER
Thomas F. Gallivan, Jr. Professor of Real Property Law,
University of Connecticut School of Law

NESTOR M. DAVIDSON
Professor of Law, Fordham University School of Law

EDUARDO MOISÉS PEÑALVER
John P. Wilson Professor of Law, University of Chicago Law School

Law & Business

Published by Wolters Kluwer Law & Business in New York.

Wolters Kluwer Law & Business serves customers worldwide with CCH, Aspen Publishers, and Kluwer Law International products. (www.wolterskluwerlb.com)

To contact Customer Service, e-mail customer.service@wolterskluwer.com, call 1-800-234-1660, fax 1-800-901-9075, or mail correspondence to:

Wolters Kluwer Law & Business
Attn: Order Department
PO Box 990
Frederick, MD 21705

Printed in the United States of America.

1 2 3 4 5 6 7 8 9 0

ISBN 978-1-4548-3761-9

Library of Congress Cataloging-in-Publication Data

Property law : rules, policies, and practices / Joseph William Singer, Bussey Professor of Law, Harvard Law School, Bethany R. Berger, Thomas F. Gallivan, Jr. Professor of Real Property Law, University of Connecticut School of Law, Nestor M. Davidson, Professor of Law, Fordham University School of Law, Eduardo Moisés Peñalver, John P. Wilson Professor of Law, University of Chicago Law School. — Sixth edition.

p. cm.

Revised edition of: Property law / Joseph William Singer. 5th edition. c2010.

Includes bibliographical references and index.

ISBN 978-1-4548-3761-9 (alk. paper)

1. Property—United States—Cases. I. Singer, Joseph William, 1954- author II. Berger, Bethany R., author III. Davidson, Nestor M., author

KF560.S56 2014

346.7304—dc23

2013045071

Certified Chain of Custody
Promoting Sustainable Forestry
www.sfiprogram.org
SFI-01042

SFI label applies to the text stock

About Wolters Kluwer Law & Business

Wolters Kluwer Law & Business is a leading global provider of intelligent information and digital solutions for legal and business professionals in key specialty areas, and respected educational resources for professors and law students. Wolters Kluwer Law & Business connects legal and business professionals as well as those in the education market with timely, specialized authoritative content and information-enabled solutions to support success through productivity, accuracy and mobility.

Serving customers worldwide, Wolters Kluwer Law & Business products include those under the Aspen Publishers, CCH, Kluwer Law International, Loislaw, ftwilliam.com and MediRegs family of products.

CCH products have been a trusted resource since 1913, and are highly regarded resources for legal, securities, antitrust and trade regulation, government contracting, banking, pension, payroll, employment and labor, and healthcare reimbursement and compliance professionals.

Aspen Publishers products provide essential information to attorneys, business professionals and law students. Written by preeminent authorities, the product line offers analytical and practical information in a range of specialty practice areas from securities law and intellectual property to mergers and acquisitions and pension/benefits. Aspen's trusted legal education resources provide professors and students with high-quality, up-to-date and effective resources for successful instruction and study in all areas of the law.

Kluwer Law International products provide the global business community with reliable international legal information in English. Legal practitioners, corporate counsel and business executives around the world rely on Kluwer Law journals, looseleafs, books, and electronic products for comprehensive information in many areas of international legal practice.

Loislaw is a comprehensive online legal research product providing legal content to law firm practitioners of various specializations. Loislaw provides attorneys with the ability to quickly and efficiently find the necessary legal information they need, when and where they need it, by facilitating access to primary law as well as state-specific law, records, forms and treatises.

ftwilliam.com offers employee benefits professionals the highest quality plan documents (retirement, welfare and non-qualified) and government forms (5500/PBGC, 1099 and IRS) software at highly competitive prices.

MediRegs products provide integrated health care compliance content and software solutions for professionals in healthcare, higher education and life sciences, including professionals in accounting, law and consulting.

Wolters Kluwer Law & Business, a division of Wolters Kluwer, is headquartered in New York. Wolters Kluwer is a market-leading global information services company focused on professionals.

For Martha Minow
who has made all the difference
JWS

For Caleb Berger
who because of this project has been flipping through
property books since before he could talk
BB

For Clare Huntington
who always keeps me climbing higher
NMD

For my grandmother, Yolanda Grave de Peralta Peñalver,
whose loss of property
sparked my interest in the subject
EMP

In memory of
Mary Joe Frug
ז"ל

*Property rights serve human values.
They are recognized to that end,
and are limited by it.*

Chief Justice Joseph Weintraub
Supreme Court of New Jersey, 1971

SUMMARY OF CONTENTS

CONTENTS

Chapter 11
Leaseholds 809

PREFACE TO THE SIXTH EDITION

This Sixth Edition has undergone some major changes, the main one being the addition of three co-authors. Bethany R. Berger, Nestor M. Davidson, and Eduardo Moisés Peñalver are not only accomplished scholars of property law, they also have deep experience and knowledge of legal practice and the real world contexts in which property law operates.

The Sixth Edition has been thoroughly updated throughout, evidence that property law continues to change with surprising regularity for an area one might have thought settled in a mature, free market economy. As in the earlier editions, we have attempted to ensure that students and professors can get a clear and accurate picture of the current law, as well as a thorough understanding of the many disagreements among the states on the applicable rules in force. Some of the rules governing property are arcane and complex, and students should be able to learn them without reading a treatise on the side. At the same time, many of the cases have dissents, and almost all have policy discussion justifying the court's approach. Where no dissents are present and the states disagree about the law, we have made this clear in the note material.

In this edition, as in the past, we have included statutory and regulatory text as principal readings throughout the book. It is critical for first-year students to understand that the law is as much a creature of legislatures and agencies as it is of courts, and this is as true in property as in other areas of the law. We have also presented problems that place students in real lawyering roles so that they can use the materials in the book (principal cases, subsidiary cases, textual explanation of the doctrine, and policy concerns) to make arguments on both sides of hard cases and to learn both to justify their judgments and to criticize the results reached by the courts and legislatures.

For some of the principal cases, we have listed the exact or approximate address of the property considered in the case. Here is an example, from *Glavin v. Eckman* in Chapter 1:

Map: Aquinnah, Martha's Vineyard, Massachusetts

This will allow students and professors to go to an Internet map service, such as Google Maps (*http://maps.google.com*) or Bing Maps (*http://www.bing.com/maps/*) to view the property in question. Both Google and Bing Maps have satellite or aerial views that help give a sense of how the property is situated, as well as the surrounding terrain, and Google Earth has other features as well. Some of us project satellite images on a screen in the front of the classroom as we teach these cases, and it seems to help give students a sense of the lay of the land and the relations among the neighboring parcels. It is particularly helpful in understanding cases that involve land use conflicts among neighbors.

Note that cases throughout the book have been edited for succinctness and to focus students on the most relevant discussions. Some deletions of text within cases are noted by an ellipsis (. . .), but the bulk of our elisions in the text, as well as internal case citations and most footnotes, have been deleted without notation. When footnotes are retained in cases, they are renumbered so that footnotes are consecutively numbered in each chapter.

As with any new edition, especially one as thoroughly updated as this one has been, some mistakes surely have crept in. We would be delighted to hear about them or about any other feedback from faculty and students who use this book. Such feedback motivated many of the changes in this edition, and we welcome future suggestions from users of the Sixth Edition. Feel free to write to us at bethany.berger@law.uconn.edu; ndavidson@law.fordham.edu; penalver@uchicago.edu; and jsinger@law.harvard.edu.

Joseph William Singer
Cambridge, Massachusetts

Bethany R. Berger
Hartford, Connecticut

Nestor M. Davidson
New York, New York

Eduardo Moisés Peñalver
Chicago, Illinois

5774/2014

A GUIDE TO THE BOOK

Organization of the Book

The book is organized around six broad themes. In Part One, we introduce a basic framework for understanding the balance of rights, limitations, and duties inherent in ownership, using the example of tensions between the right to exclude and the right of access. We then address the primary justifications that have traditionally been invoked to justify property rights, including sovereignty, reward for labor, distributive justice, efficiency, recognition of relationships, possession, and personhood. Part Two explores the outer boundaries of ownership by examining how the legal system mediates a variety of resources other than real estate and personal goods, notably ideas, culture, human beings, and human bodies. Many of the most important doctrines in property law focus on relationships between neighbors and Part Three explores adverse possession, nuisance, zoning, and private agreements between owners (called servitudes) as examples. In Part Four, we explore the myriad ways the law allows property to be divided and shared, both concurrently and over time. These forms of ownership in common include concurrent tenancies, family property, corporate and other entity property, leaseholds, as well as the complex system of estates and future interests we have inherited from early English law. Part Five explores two fundamental aspects of the market for real estate, the role of property law and property lawyers in sales and financing and the importance of antidiscrimination law. Finally, the book concludes in Part Six with two chapters that highlight the fundamental tension between the role of the state in both defining and defending property rights. The constitutional law of property, including equal protection, due process, and takings, is a fitting way to return to the themes explored throughout these materials. In all of this, we seek to present a contemporary introduction to the law of property, focusing on various pressing issues of current concern as well as the basic rules governing the property system.

What Is Property?

Property rights concern relations among people regarding control of valued resources. Property law gives owners the power to control things, and it does this by placing duties on non-owners. For example, owners have the right to exclude non-owners from their property; this right imposes a duty on others not to enter property without the owner's consent. Property rights are relational; ownership is not just power over things but entails relations among people. This is true not only of the right to exclude but of the privilege to use property. An owner who operates a business on a particular parcel may benefit the community by creating jobs and providing needed services, and she may harm the community by increasing traffic or causing pollution. Development of a subdivision may affect drainage patterns and cause flooding on neighboring land. Property use makes others vulnerable to the effects of that use, for better or for worse. Power over things is actually power over people.

Property rights are *not absolute*. The recognition and exercise of a property right in one person often affects and may even conflict with the personal or property rights of others. To give one person an absolute legal entitlement would mean that others could not exercise similar entitlements. Property rights are therefore limited to ensure that property use and ownership do not unreasonably harm the legitimate, legally protected personal or property interests of others. The duty to exercise property rights in a manner compatible with the legal rights of others means that *owners have obligations as well as rights.*

Owners of property generally possess a *bundle of entitlements.* The most important are the privilege to use the property, the right to exclude others, the power to transfer title to the property, and immunity from having the property taken or damaged without their consent. These entitlements may be disaggregated—an owner can give up some of the sticks in the bundle while keeping others. Landlords, for example, grant tenants the right to possess their property in exchange for periodic rental payments while retaining the right to regain possession at the end of the leasehold. Because property rights are limited to protect the legitimate interests of others and because owners have the power to disaggregate property rights, entitlements in a particular piece of property are more often shared than unitary. It is almost always the case that more than one person will have something to say about the use of a particular piece of property. Property law therefore cannot be reduced to the rules that determine ownership; rather, it comprises rules that allocate particular entitlements and define their scope.

Property is owned in a *variety of forms.* An infinite number of bundles of rights can be created from the sticks in the bundle that comprise full ownership. However, some bundles are widely used and they comprise the basic forms or models of ownership. Some forms are used by individuals while others are used by couples (married or unmarried) or families. Other forms are used by groups of unrelated owners. Differences exist between forms that give owners management powers and those that separate ownership from management. Further distinctions exist between residential and commercial property and between nonprofit organizations and for-profit businesses. Within each of these categories are multiple subcategories, such as the distinction between partnerships and corporations or between male-female couples and same-sex couples. Particular models of property ownership have been created for different social contexts and types of property. Each model has a different way of bundling and dispersing the rights and obligations of ownership among various persons. Understanding property requires knowledge both of the individual sticks in the bundle of property rights and the characteristic bundles that characterize particular ownership forms.

Property is a *system* as well as an *entitlement*. A property right is a legal entitlement granted to an individual or entity but the extent of the legal right is partly determined by rules designed to ensure that the property system functions effectively and fairly. Many property law rules are geared not to protecting individual entitlements, but to ensuring that the environment in which those rights are exercised is one that maximizes the benefits of property ownership for everyone and is compatible with the norms underlying a free and democratic society. Some rules promote efficiency, such as the rules that facilitate the smooth operation of the real estate market. Other rules promote fairness or distributive justice, such as the fair housing laws that prohibit owners from denying access to property on the basis of race, sex, religion, or disability.

Tensions Within the Property System

In 1990, roughly a year after his nation was freed from Soviet domination, the foreign minister of Czechoslovakia, Jiri Dienstbier, commented that "[i]t was easier to make a revolution than to write 600 to 800 laws to create a market economy."[1] If anything, he understated the case. Each of the basic property entitlements is limited to ensure that the exercise of a property right by one person is compatible with the property and personal rights of others. The construction of a property system requires property law to adjudicate characteristic core tensions in the system.

Right to exclude versus right of access. It is often said that the most fundamental right associated with property ownership is the right to exclude non-owners from the property. If the right to exclude were unlimited, owners could exclude non-owners based on race or religion. Although at one time owners were empowered (and in some states required) to do this, current law prohibits discrimination on the basis of race, sex, national origin, religion, or disability in public accommodations, housing, and employment. Although individuals are free to choose whom to invite to their homes for dinner, market actors are regulated to ensure that access to property is available without regard to invidious discrimination. Property therefore entails a tension between privacy and free association norms on one side and equality norms on the other. Sometimes the right of access will take precedence over the right to exclude. The tension between these claims is one that property law must resolve.

Privilege to use versus security from harm. Owners are generally free to use their property as they wish, but they are not free to harm their neighbors' property substantially and unreasonably. A factory that emits pollutants into the air may be

1. William Echikson, *Euphoria Dies Down in Czechoslovakia*, Wall St. J., Sept. 18, 1990, at A-26, 1990 WL-WSJ 56114.

regulated to prevent the use of its property in ways that will destroy the individual property rights of others and common resources in air and water. Many uses of property impose "externalities" or spillover effects on other owners and on the community as a whole. Because owners are legally entitled to have their own property protected from pollutants dispatched to their property by others, owners' freedom to use their property is limited to ensure that their property use does not cause such unreasonable negative externalities.

Power to transfer versus powers of ownership. Owners are generally free to transfer their property to whomever they wish, on whatever terms they want. Freedom of disposition gives them the power to sell it, give it away, or write a will identifying who will get it when they die. They are also free to contract with others to transfer particular sticks in the bundle of sticks comprising full ownership to others while keeping the rest for themselves. Owners may even place conditions on the use of property when they sell it, limiting what future owners may do with it. They may, for example, limit the property to residential purposes by including a restriction in the deed limiting the property to such uses. Although owners are free to disaggregate property rights in various ways, and to impose particular restrictions on the use and ownership of land, that freedom is not unlimited. Owners are not allowed to impose conditions that violate public policy or that unduly infringe on the liberty interests of future owners. For example, an owner could not impose an enforceable condition that all future owners agree to vote for the Democratic candidate for president; this condition infringes on the liberty of future owners and wrongfully attempts to tie ownership of the land to membership in a particular political party. Nor are owners allowed to limit the sale of the property to persons of a particular race. Similarly, restrictions limiting the transfer of property will ordinarily not be enforced, both to protect the freedom of owners to move and to promote the efficient transfer of property in the marketplace. The freedom of an owner to restrict the future use or disposition of property must be curtailed to protect the freedom of future owners to use their property as they wish. The law limits freedom of contract and freedom of disposition to ensure that owners have sufficient powers over the property they own.

Immunity from loss versus power to acquire. Property owners have the right not to have their property taken or damaged by others against their will. However, it is often lawful to interfere with the property interests of others. For example, an owner who builds a house on a vacant lot may block a view enjoyed by the neighbor for many years. A new company may put a prior company out of business or reduce its profits through competition. Property rights must be limited to ensure that others can exercise similar rights in acquiring and using property. In addition, immunity from forced seizure or loss of property rights is not absolute when the needs of the community take precedence. To construct a new public highway or municipal building, for example, the government may exercise its eminent power to take private property for public uses with just compensation.

Recurring Themes

A number of important themes will recur throughout this book. They include the following:

Social context. Social context matters in defining property rights. We have different typical models of property depending on whether it is owned individually or jointly, among family members or non-family members, by a private or a governmental entity, devoted to profitable or charitable purposes, for residential or commercial purposes, open to public use or limited to private use.

Formal versus informal sources of rights. Property rights generally have their source in some formal grant, such as a deed, a will, a lease, a contract, or a government grant. However, property rights also arise informally, by an oral promise, a course of conduct, actual possession, a family relationship, an oral gift, longstanding reliance, and social customs and norms. Many of the basic rules of property law concern contests between formal and informal sources of property rights. While the law usually insists on formality to create property rights, it often protects informally created expectations over formally created ones. Determining when expectations based on informal arrangements should prevail over formal ones is a central issue in property law.

The alienability dilemma. It is a fundamental tenet of the property law system that property should be "alienable," meaning that it should be transferable from one person to another. Transferability allows a market to function and enables efficient transactions and property use to occur. It also promotes individual autonomy by allowing owners to sell or give away property when they please on terms they have chosen. This suggests that the law should allow owners to disaggregate property rights as they please. However, if owners are allowed to disaggregate property rights at will, it may be difficult to reconsolidate those rights. If property is burdened by obsolete restrictions, it may be expensive or impossible to get rid of them. Similarly, if property is disaggregated among too many owners, transaction costs may block agreements to reconsolidate the interests and make the property useable for current needs. The property may therefore be rendered inalienable.

Many rules of property law limit contractual freedom to ensure that particular bundles of property rights are consolidated in the same person—the "owner." Consolidating power in an "owner" ensures that resources can be used for current purposes and current needs and allows property to be freely transferred in the marketplace. We therefore face a tension between promoting alienability by consolidating rights in owners and promoting alienability by allowing owners to disaggregate their rights into unique bundles constructed by them.

Contractual freedom and minimum standards. Individuals want to be free to develop human relationships without having government dictate the terms of their association with others. Having the ability to rearrange property rights to create desirable packages of entitlements will help enable various relationships to flourish. However, there are also bounds to what is acceptable; this is why the law imposes certain minimum standards on contractual relationships. For example, although landlords are entitled to evict residential tenants who do not pay rent, the law in almost every state requires landlords to use court eviction proceedings to dispossess defaulting tenants. These proceedings give tenants a chance to contest the landlord's possessory claim and to have time to find a new place to live, rather than having their belongings tossed on the street and being dispossessed overnight. These limitations on free contract protect basic norms of fair dealing and promote the justified expectations of individuals who enter market transactions.

Social welfare. Granting owners power over property ensures that they can obtain resources to satisfy human needs. It also promotes social welfare by encouraging productive activity and by granting security to those who invest in economic projects. Clear property rights facilitate exchange and lower the costs of transactions by clarifying who owns what. At the same time, owners may use their property in socially harmful ways, and clear property rights may promote harmful, as well as beneficial, actions. Property rights must be limited to ensure that conflicting uses are accommodated to minimize the costs of desirable development on other owners and on the community. Moreover, rigid property rights may inhibit bargaining rather than facilitate it by granting owners the power to act unreasonably, thereby encouraging litigation to clarify the limits on the owner's entitlements. Reasonableness requirements, while less predictable than clear rules, may promote efficient bargaining by encouraging competing claimants to compromise in ways that minimize the costs of property use on others. We need to design rules of ownership and transfer that promote efficiency and social welfare by decreasing the costs of using and obtaining property while maximizing its benefits both to individual owners and to society as a whole.

Justified expectations. In a famous phrase, Jeremy Bentham wrote that "[p]roperty is nothing but a basis of expectation; the expectation of deriving certain advantages from a thing which we are said to possess, in consequence of the relation in which we stand towards it."[2] Owners justifiably expect to use their own property for their own purposes and to transfer it on terms chosen by them. However, because the property use often affects others, it must be limited to protect the expectations of others. Property law protects justified expectations. A central function of property law is to determine what the parties' actual expectations are and when they are, and are not, justified.

Distributive justice. Property rights are the legal form of wealth. Wealth takes many forms, including the right to control tangible assets, such as land and buildings, and intangible assets, such as stocks that give the holder the right to control and derive profit from a business enterprise. In fact, any legal entitlement that benefits the right holder may be viewed as a species of property. The rules of property law, like the rules

---

2. 1 Jeremy Bentham, *Theory of Legislation* 137 (Boston: Weeks, Jordan & Co., R. Hildreth trans. 1840).

of contract, family, and tax law, play an enormous role in determining the distribution of both wealth and income.

How well is property dispersed in the United States? One expert has noted that "[b]y several measurements, the United States in the late twentieth century led all other major industrial countries in the gap dividing the upper fifth of the population from the lower—in the disparity between top and bottom."[3]

One indicator of the distribution of property is income. Since 1967, income distribution has become increasingly unequal in the United States. In 2011, the Census Bureau reported that the share of total income going to the top fifth of American households increased from 43.6 percent in 1967 to 51.1 percent in 2011.[4] Within the top fifth of the population, the bulk of this increase was obtained by those at the very top. A 2010 white paper showed that between 1982 and 2006, the real incomes of the top 1 percent of families rose 127 percent, whereas the bottom 80 percent of families saw increases of only 13 percent or less in real income.[5]

The distribution of income also varies according to race, gender, and age. The median income of households in the United States was $50,054 in 2011; half of all households received more and half less than that amount. However, differences are substantial along racial lines. While the median income of white, non-Hispanic families was $55,412 in 2011, the median income for African American households was only $32,229 and that of Latino households was $38,624. The median household income of American Indians and Native Alaskan households in 2010 was $35,062.

Poverty is similarly unequally distributed by race. While 15 percent of all persons were poor by federal standards in 2011, only 9.8 percent of non-Hispanic whites were poor; by comparison, 27.6 percent of African Americans and 25.3 percent of Latinos fell below the poverty line. Data from 2010 show that 28.4 percent of American Indians and Native Alaskans were poor by official standards.

Although the gap in incomes between men and women has narrowed over the last quarter-century, men still earn more than women on average. In 2011, men who worked full time earned an average of $48,202 while women who worked full time earned only $37,118, or 77 percent of male earnings.

Children are more likely to be poor than adults, and some children are very likely to be poor. Although 13.5 percent of the population fell below the poverty line in 2011, 21.9 percent of children did so; moreover, 38.8 percent of African American children

---

3. Kevin Phillips, *The Politics of Rich and Poor: Wealth and the American Electorate in the Reagan Aftermath* 8 (1990).

4. Data in this section come from Carmen DeNavas-Walt, Bernadette D. Proctor & Jessica C. Smith, U.S. Census Bureau, *Income, Poverty, and Health Insurance Coverage in the United States: 2011* (Sept. 2012), *available at http://www.census.gov/prod/2012pubs/p60-236.pdf.* Data for 2010 come from U.S. Census Bureau, *Facts for Features: American Indian and Alaska Native Heritage Month: November 2011*, CB11-FF.22 (Nov. 2011), *available at http://www.census.gov/newsroom/releases/archives/facts_for_features_special_editions/cb11-ff22.html.*

5. Edward N. Wolff, *Recent Trends in Household Wealth in the United States: Rising Debt and the Middle-Class Squeeze — An Update to 2007*, 14 (Levy Economics Institute Working Paper No. 589, Mar. 2010), *available at http://www.levyinstitute.org/pubs/wp_589.pdf.*

and 34.1 percent of Hispanic children were living in poverty. Children who live in households without an adult male are extremely likely to be poor. While only 6.2 percent of children in families of married couples were poor in 2011, 31.2 percent of children living in female-headed households were poor. More than half of all children under six living in female-headed households (57.2 percent) were poor. Although 23.8 percent of white, non-Hispanic, female-headed households were poor, 42.3 percent of African American, female-headed households and 44 percent of Hispanic, female-headed households were poor. While the median income of married couples was $74,130, the median income of female-headed households was only $33,637, and the median income of male-headed households was $49,567.

Inequalities of both income and wealth are somewhat alleviated by transfer payments in the form of public assistance. Until the 1970s, elderly persons were more likely to be poor than the non-elderly. By 1990, however, the poverty rate for persons over 65 was less than that for the rest of the population, and relatively few elderly persons are among the homeless and extremely poor. This change in the position of the elderly was the result of public spending in the form of Social Security pensions, Medicare, and housing subsidies.[6] In 2011, the poverty rate for those 65 and older was 8.7 percent compared to 13.7 percent for those between 18 and 64.[7]

Wealth data show even greater inequality than income data. Far more than income, wealth determines financial security and economic prospects in the United States.[8] In 2007, the top 1 percent of U.S. households owned 34.6 percent of U.S. family net wealth while the top 5 percent owned well over half of all net wealth (62 percent). The top quintile owned 86 percent of wealth while the bottom 40 percent of the population owned 2 percent of net wealth.[9] The racial disparities are equally stark. In 2011, the median net worth of African American households was only 5.7 percent that of non-Hispanic white households, while the median net worth of Hispanic households was only 6.9 percent.[10] These racial disparities are essentially unchanged since 1983.[11] The 2008 recession and uneven recovery exacerbated wealth inequality. Declines in jobs and property values hit the primary sources of wealth for most Americans. Wealthy Americans, however, have a greater proportion of their assets invested in financial markets. The rebound in financial markets and sluggish recovery in jobs and home

---

6. Peter H. Rossi, *Down and Out in America: The Origins of Homelessness* 193 (1989).

7. U.S. Census Bureau, *Income, Poverty, and Health Insurance Coverage, supra* note 4.

8. Alfred Gottschalck, Marina Vornovytskyy & Adam Smith, U.S. Census Bureau, *Household Wealth in the U.S.: 2000 to 2011* (2013).

9. Wolff, *supra* note 5 (analyzing 2007 census data). *See also* Marco Cagetti & Mariacristina De Nardi, *Wealth Inequality: Data and Models* (Federal Reserve Bank of Chicago Working Paper No. 2005-10, Aug. 17, 2005), *available at http://papers.ssrn.com/sol3/papers.cfm?abstract_id=838325*; Lisa A. Keister, *Wealth in America* 64 (2000); Kevin Phillips, *supra* note 3, at 1-13.

10. U.S. Census Bureau, *Median Value of Assets for Households, by Type of Asset Owned and Other Selected Characteristics: 2011* (2013), *available at http://www.census.gov/people/wealth/.*

11. *Wolff, supra* note 5 (providing historical data).

values meant that although 93 percent of households saw their net worth decline between 2009 and 2011, the top 7 percent saw their net worth rise significantly.[12]

Individual versus shared ownership. Property may be owned and controlled by individuals; the history of the development of land law in England, for example, may be described as a shift from control over property by feudal lords and family inheritance restrictions to control by individual owners. But shared ownership continues to characterize property, perhaps increasingly so. In marriages and other intimate relationships, for example, ownership of homes and bank accounts is typically in the name of both partners. The assets of Americans, moreover, increasingly consist of investments in corporate stocks and ownership of condominiums or other common interest developments, both forms of property in which ownership and control are shared with many individuals. In addition, because ownership rights affect others, both statutory and common law recognize rights in the community to control property to some degree. The recognition of shared rights in property may differ in different cultures and legal systems. Compared to U.S. property law, for example, continental European systems may do more to recognize and facilitate common ownership, while English and Scottish legal systems recognize greater rights in the community to traverse and enjoy private lands.[13]

One persistent conflict between shared and individualist conceptions of property concerns American Indian nations, the original possessors of land in the United States. With more than 550 federally recognized tribes and scores of unrecognized tribes, it is difficult to generalize about American Indian land use systems, either in the past or the present. Nonetheless, many Native peoples recognized shared and community ownership more explicitly than did European American settlers. Native individuals and families did own property and land was bought and sold, but indigenous property systems often had a robust concept of shared use rights. While a particular family might use a piece of land to plant crops, for example, this would not preclude other tribal members from entering or gathering nonagricultural food on such lands. Much land, moreover, was considered to be owned by a tribe in common, and open to hunting, fishing, or the like by the tribe as a whole. (Note, however, that this sense of shared rights is not so different from rights of villagers to graze on common or uncultivated lands in early England, discussed in Chapter 8, §2.1, or the "right to roam" on unfenced land recognized for much of American history, discussed in Chapter 1, §1.)

More radically, for most indigenous peoples, land was not fungible—it could not simply be replaced with similar land elsewhere. Rather, specific areas were deeply connected to the history and spiritual identity of a tribe. For many Native peoples even

---

12. Richard Fry & Paul Taylor, Pew Research Center, *An Uneven Recovery, 2009-2011: A Rise in Wealth for the Wealthy, Declines for the Lower 93%* (2013), *available at http://www.pewsocialtrends.org/2013/04/23/a-rise-in-wealth-for-the-wealthydeclines-for-the-lower-93.*

13. *See* Michael Heller & Hanoch Dagan, *The Liberal Commons*, 110 Yale L.J. 549, 610-611 (2001); John A. Lovett, *Progressive Property in Action: The Land Reform (Scotland) Act 2003*, 89 Neb. L. Rev. 739 (2011); Jerry L. Anderson, *Britain's Right to Roam: Redefining the Landowner's Bundle of Sticks*, 19 Geo. Intl. Envtl. L. Rev. 375 (2007).

today, particular areas may be "the source of spiritual origins and sustaining myth which in turn provides a landscape of cultural and emotional meaning. The land often determines the values of the human landscape."[14] The community, therefore, could not be excluded from such areas without doing violence to the tribe and its identity. These differences in emphasis on shared versus individual rights in U.S. and Indian property systems were the source of much conflict, as well as repeated efforts by the federal government to inculcate a love of individual property as a tool to encourage tribal assimilation and dissolution.[15]

Normative Approaches

How should courts and legislatures adjudicate conflicting property claims? Various approaches can be used to conceptualize property rights and to adjudicate conflicts among property claimants.[16] Here is a brief description of the most common approaches.[17]

Positivism and legal realism. Positivist theories identify law with the "commands of the sovereign" or the rules promulgated by authoritative government officials for reasons of public policy.[18] Those rules may be intended to protect individual rights, promote the general welfare, increase social wealth, or maximize social utility. Judges are therefore directed to apply the law, as promulgated by authoritative government lawmakers, and to exercise discretion where there are gaps, conflicts, or ambiguities in the law while respecting the need for consistency with the letter and spirit of preexisting laws. Jeremy Bentham wrote that the "idea of property consists in an established expectation . . . of being able to draw . . . an advantage from the thing possessed."[19] He believed that "this expectation, this persuasion, can only be the work of law. It is only through the protection of law that I am able to inclose a field, and to

---

14. Frank Pommersheim, *The Reservation as Place: A South Dakota Essay*, 34 S.D. L. Rev. 246, 250 (1989); *see also* Rebecca Tsosie, *Land, Culture and Community: Reflections on Native Sovereignty and Property in America*, 34 Ind. L. Rev. 1291, 1302-1303 (2001).

15. *See, e.g.,* Chapter 15, §5.1 (cases and materials on the allotment policy, through which the United States forcibly divided tribal land among individual households).

16. For collections of scholarly approaches to property, *see Perspectives on Property Law* (Robert C. Ellickson, Carol M. Rose & Bruce A. Ackerman eds. 3d ed. 2002); *A Property Anthology* (Richard H. Chused ed. 2d ed. 1997).

17. Many, if not most, scholars combine various approaches. *See, e.g.,* Stephen R. Munzer, *A Theory of Property* (1990) (adopting a pluralist perspective including justice and equality, desert based on labor, and utility and efficiency); Carol M. Rose, *Property and Persuasion: Essays on the History, Theory, and Rhetoric of Ownership* (1994) (combining economic analysis, justice-based arguments, and feminist legal theory); Joseph William Singer, *Entitlement: The Paradoxes of Property* (2000) (using both justice and utilitarian considerations, as well as narrative theory, feminism, critical race theory, and critical legal studies).

18. John Austin, *Lectures of Jurisprudence* (1861-1863); H.L.A. Hart, *The Concept of Law* (1961).

19. Bentham, *supra* note 2, at 138.

give myself up to its cultivation with the sure though distant hope of harvest . . . . "[20] Property exists to the extent the law will protect it. "Property and law are born together, and die together. Before laws were made there was no property; take away laws, and property ceases."[21]

Positivists separate law and morals; they emphasize that, although moral judgments may underlie rules of law, they are not fully or consistently enforced by legal sanctions. Positivism was adopted by Progressive-era judges and scholars such as Oliver Wendell Holmes, who suggested analyzing legal rules in the way a "bad man" would. Such a person would not be interested in the moral content of the law but would simply want to predict what legal sanctions would be imposed on him if he engaged in prohibited conduct.[22] This approach was adopted by legal realist scholars of the 1920s and 1930s such as Karl Llewellyn, who argued that the law is what officials will do in resolving disputes.[23]

All lawyers are positivists in some sense because the job of advising clients necessarily entails identifying the rules of law that have been explicitly or implicitly adopted by authoritative lawmakers and predicting how those rules will be applied to the client's situation. Judges may also see their jobs as the enforcement of existing law and leave the job of amending law to legislatures. On the other hand, determining whether an existing rule was intended to apply to a particular situation requires judgment, as well as techniques of *statutory interpretation* and analysis of *precedent*, and a conception about the proper role of courts in the lawmaking process.

Justice and fairness. Positivism has been criticized by scholars who argue that ambiguities in existing laws must be filled in by judges, and that judges should not exercise untrammeled discretion in doing so. Rather, they should interpret gaps, conflicts, and ambiguities in the law in a manner that protects individual rights, promotes fairness, or ensures justice.

Rights theorists attempt to identify individual interests that are so important from a moral point of view that they not only deserve legal protection but may count as "trumps" that override more general considerations of public policy by which competing interests are balanced against each other. Such individual rights cannot legitimately be sacrificed for the good of the community.[24] Some *natural rights* theorists argue that rights have roots in the nature of human beings or that they are natural in the sense that people who think about human relationships from a rational and moral point of view are bound to understand particular individual interests

---

20. *Id.*

21. *Id.* at 139.

22. *See* Oliver Wendell Holmes, *The Path of the Law*, 8 Harv. L. Rev. 1 (1894).

23. Karl Llewellyn, *The Bramble Bush* (1930).

24. Ronald Dworkin, *Law's Empire* (1986); Ronald Dworkin, *Taking Rights Seriously* (1978); Charles Fried, *Right and Wrong* (1978); Allan Gewirth, *The Community of Rights* (1996); Jeremy Waldron, *The Right to Private Property* (1998).

as fundamental.[25] Other scholars, building on Immanuel Kant, ask whether a claim that an interest should be protected could be *universalized* such that every person in similar circumstances would be entitled to similar protection. Still others build on the *social contract* tradition begun by John Locke and Thomas Hobbes and ask whether individuals would choose to protect certain interests if they had to come to agreement in a suitably defined decision-making context. John Rawls, for example, asks what principles of justice would be adopted by individuals who did not know morally irrelevant facts about themselves, such as their race or sex.[26]

Some theorists focus on *desert*. John Locke argued that labor is the foundation of property. "Whatsoever then he removes out of the state that nature has provided and left it in, he has mixed his labor with, and joined to it something that is his own, and thereby makes it his property."[27] Other theorists focus on the role that property rights play in developing individual *autonomy*.[28] Hegel believed that property was a way that human beings constituted themselves as people by extending their will to manipulate the objects of the external world.[29] Professor Margaret Jane Radin, for example, has argued that "to be a *person* . . . an individual needs some control over resources in the external environment."[30] She distinguishes between forms of property that are important for the meaning they have to individuals (personal property such as a wedding ring) and property that is important solely because it can be used in exchange (fungible property such as money and investments).[31]

Other scholars focus on satisfying *human needs* or ensuring *distributive justice*. Nancy Fraser has argued that an important way to think about property rights is to focus on the ways we define people's needs and the ways in which the legal system does or does not meet those needs.[32] Frank Michelman has similarly argued that a system of private property requires, by its very nature, that property be widely dispersed. If all property were owned by one person, that person would be a dictator. Private property implies wide availability. It therefore entails a compromise between the principle of protecting possession and promoting widespread distribution.[33]

---

25. *See* Robert Nozick, *Anarchy, State, and Utopia* (1974); Judith Jarvis Thompson, *The Realm of Rights* (1990).

26. John Rawls, *A Theory of Justice* (1971). *See also* Thomas M. Scanlon, *What We Owe Each Other* (1998).

27. John Locke, *Second Treatise of Government* 17-18 (Bobbs-Merrill ed. 1952) (originally published in 1960).

28. Richard A. Epstein, *Simple Rules for a Complex World* 53-70 (1995).

29. Georg Wilhelm Friedrich Hegel, *Philosophy of Right* 40-41 (T. Knox trans. 1942).

30. Margaret Jane Radin, *Property and Personhood*, 34 Stan. L. Rev. 957 (1982).

31. Margaret Jane Radin, *Market-Inalienability*, 100 Harv. L. Rev. 1849 (1987). *See also* Margaret Jane Radin, *Contested Commodities: The Trouble with Trade in Sex, Children, Body Parts, and Other Things* (1996); Margaret Jane Radin, *Reinterpreting Property* (1993).

32. Nancy Fraser, *Unruly Practices, Power, Discourse, and Gender in Contemporary Social Theory* (1989).

33. Frank Michelman, *Possession and Distribution in the Constitutional Idea of Property*, 72 Iowa L. Rev. 1319 (1987). *See also* Waldron, *supra* note 24.

Utilitarianism, social welfare, and efficiency. Utilitarians focus on the *consequences* of alternative legal rules. They compare the costs and benefits of alternative property rules or institutions with the goal of adopting rules that will maximize *social utility* or *welfare*. Some scholars in the law and economics school of thought measure social utility by the concept of economic *efficiency*. Efficiency theorists measure costs and benefits by reference to what people are willing and able to pay for entitlements, given their resources.[34]

Individual property rights are thought to increase efficiency by encouraging productive activity and by granting security to those who invest in economic projects. Clear property rights also facilitate exchange by clarifying who owns what. They therefore create incentives to use resources efficiently.[35] On the other hand, Carol Rose has argued that clear definitions of property rights may be overly rigid, upsetting settled expectations and reliance interests.[36] This is why property rights are often defined by flexible standards, such as a reasonableness requirement, that adjust the relations of the parties to achieve a fair and efficient result. Rose has also argued that common ownership is sometimes the most efficient way to manage property.[37] Frank Michelman and Duncan Kennedy have also argued that efficiency requires a mixture of private property, sharing, and deregulation.[38] Cass Sunstein has noted that preferences are partially shaped by law and that cognitive biases may affect individuals' perceptions of their preferences.[39]

Social relations. Social relations approaches analyze property rights as relations among persons regarding control of valued resources. Legal rights are correlative; every legal entitlement in an individual implies a correlative vulnerability in someone else, and every entitlement is limited by the competing rights of others.[40] This analysis was developed by pragmatic legal scholars—called "legal realists"—from the 1920s through the 1930s. Property rights are interpreted as delegations of sovereign power to individuals by the state; these rights should therefore be defined to accommodate the

---

34. *See generally* Richard A. Posner, *Economic Analysis and Law* (7th ed. 2007); Steven Shavell, *Foundations of Economic Analysis of Law* (2004).

35. Shavell, *supra* note 34, at 11-23. *See also* Garrett Hardin, *The Tragedy of the Commons*, reprinted in *Economic Foundations of Property Law* 4 (Bruce Ackerman ed. 1975); Harold Demsetz, *Toward a Theory of Property Rights*, 57 Am. Econ. Rev. 347 (1967).

36. Carol Rose, *Crystals and Mud in Property Law*, 40 Stan. L. Rev. 577 (1988).

37. Carol Rose, *The Comedy of the Commons: Customs, Commerce, and Inherently Public Property*, 53 U. Chi. L. Rev. 711 (1986). *See also* Frank Michelman, *Ethics, Economics, and the Law of Property*, 24 Nomos: Ethics, Economics, and the Law 3 (1982) (arguing that the institution of property, by its nature, requires a large amount of cooperative activity).

38. Duncan Kennedy & Frank Michelman, *Are Property and Contract Efficient?*, 8 Hofstra L. Rev. 711 (1980).

39. Cass R. Sunstein, *Free Markets and Social Justice* (1997).

40. Wesley Hohfield, *Some Fundamental Legal Conception as Applied in Judicial Reasoning*, 28 Yale L.J. 16 (1913).

conflicting interests of social actors.[41] Current social relations theorists have broadened the scope of this analysis by examining the role property rights play in structuring social relations and the ways in which social relations shape access to property.[42] These approaches include feminist legal theory, critical race theory, critical legal studies, communitarianism, law and society, deconstruction and cultural studies.

Feminists such as Martha Minow argue that our identities, values, and needs are developed in relation to and in connection with others. The legal system relies on implicit conceptions of social relations and often implicitly treats certain groups or individuals as the norm and others as the exception. She argues that we must become conscious of the ways those underlying assumptions function in both social relations and the legal system.[43] Elizabeth V. Spelman similarly analyzes the implicit assumptions underlying conceptions of human relations. In particular, she focuses on the role that race, class, and gender play in shaping the concepts with which we understand human relations.[44]

These new insights have permeated recent discussions of property law. Property has traditionally been associated with the idea of autonomy within boundaries; for example, we assume that people are generally free to do what they like within the borders of their land. Yet Jennifer Nedelsky has argued that "[w]hat makes human autonomy possible is not isolation but relationship" with others.[45] She proposes that we replace the idea of *boundary* as the central metaphor for property rights with the idea of *relationships*.[46] Social relations approaches assume that people are situated in a complicated network of relationships with others, from relations among strangers, to relations among neighbors, to continuing relations in the market, to intimate relations in the family. Moreover, many of the legal developments of the twentieth century can be described as recognition of obligations that emerge over time out of relationships of interdependence.[47] The relational approach shifts our attention from asking who the owner is to the question of what relationships have been established.[48]

---

41. Walter Wheeler Cook, *Privileges of Labor Unions in the Struggle for Life,* 27 Yale L.J. 779 (1918); Robert Hale, *Bargaining, Duress, and Economic Liberty,* 43 Colum. L. Rev. 603 (1943); Morris Cohen, *Property and Sovereignty,* 13 Cornell L.Q. 8 (1927).

42. Gregory S. Alexander, *Commodity and Propriety: Competing Visions of Property in American Legal Thought, 1776-1970* (1997); C. Edwin Baker, *Property and Its Relation to Constitutionally Protected Liberty,* 134 U. Pa. L. Rev. 741 (1986).

43. Martha Minow, *Making All the Difference: Inclusion, Exclusion, and American Law* (1990).

44. Elizabeth V. Spelman, *Inessential Woman: Problems of Exclusion in Feminist Thought* (1989).

45. Jennifer Nedelsky, *Law, Boundaries, and the Bounded Self,* 30 Representations 162, 169 (1990).

46. *Id.* at 171-184. *See also* Jennifer Nedelsky, *Reconceiving Rights as Relationships,* 1 Rev. Const. Studies/Revue d'etudes Constitutionelles 1 (1993); Singer, *supra* note 17.

47. Roberto Mangabeira Unger, *The Critical Legal Studies Movement* 83-84 (1983).

48. Joseph William Singer, *The Reliance Interest in Property,* 40 Stan L. Rev. 611, 657 (1988).

Feminists[49] and critical race theorists have explored the relationship between race, sex, and property.[50] Patricia Williams has written eloquently about the social meaning of race and gender and their relation to power and to property law.[51] Keith Aoki has described the thinking that led to the alien land laws that denied property ownership to Japanese immigrants and provided the precursor to internment during World War II.[52] Alice Kessler-Harris and many other scholars have explored the social factors that determine the unequal wages paid to women and men as well as the relation between those factors and the distribution of property and power based on gender.[53]

Critical legal theorists have explored tensions or contradictions within property theory and law and used marginalized doctrines to argue for reform of property rules and institutions.[54] Communitarians and environmentalists emphasize the importance of community life as well as individual rights and argue that individuals have obligations as well as rights.[55] Law and society theorists investigate the "law in practice" rather than the "law on the books" to determine what norms actually govern behavior in the real world with respect to property.[56] Other scholars have used deconstruction, poststructuralism, or cultural theory to explore the unconscious assumptions underlying property law.[57]

Human flourishing. In recent years, some property theorists have begun to turn to the Aristotelian idea of human flourishing.[58] Human flourishing theories of property are self-consciously pluralist in their normative outlook. Like utilitarian theory, they view property as an institution that (like other legal institutions) ought to be structured to promote human well-being. Unlike utilitarianism, they understand well-being as comprised of a plurality of goods that are both objectively valuable and not fully commensurable with one another. These include goods like health, practical reason, sociability, personhood, and autonomy. These theorists draw on prior work

---

49. Martha Albertson Fineman, *The Illusion of Equality: The Rhetoric and Reality of Divorce Reform* (1991); Vicki Schultz, *Life's Work*, 100 Colum. L. Rev. 1881 (2000); Reva B. Siegel, *Home as Work: The First Women's Rights Claim Concerning Wives' Household Labor, 1850-1880,* 103 Yale L.J. 1073, 1077 (1994); Reva B. Siegel, *The Modernization of Marital Status Law: Adjudicating Wives' Rights to Earnings, (1860-1930),* 82 Geo. L.J. 2127 (1994); Joan Williams, *Unbending Gender: Why Family and Work Conflict and What to Do About It* (2000).

50. *Critical Race Theory: The Cutting Edge* (Richard Delgado ed. 1995).

51. Patricia Williams, *Fetal Fictions: An Exploration of Property Archetypes in Racial and Gendered Contexts,* 42 Fla. L. Rev. 81 (1990).

52. Keith Aoki, *No Right to Own? The Early Twentieth-Century "Alien Land Laws" as a Prelude to Internment,* 40 B.C. L. Rev. 37 (1998).

53. Alice Kessler-Harris, *A Woman's Wage* (1990).

54. Singer, *supra* note 17.

55. Mary Ann Glendon, *Rights Talk* (1991); Avishai Margalit, *The Decent Society* (1998); Jedediah Purdy, *For Common Things: Irony, Trust, and Commitment in America Today* (1999).

56. Robert C. Ellickson, *Order Without Law: How Neighbors Settle Disputes* (1991).

57. Jeanne Lorraine Schroeder, *The Vestal and the Fasces: Hegel, Lacan, Property, and the Feminine* (1998).

58. *See* Gregory S. Alexander & Eduardo Moisés Peñalver, *An Introduction to Property Theory,* ch. 5 (2012).

by economists and philosophers in the Aristotelian tradition, such as Amartya Sen and Martha Nussbaum.[59]

Libertarian and progressive approaches to property. Property is not only an intensely interesting subject but also an intensely debated one. As much or more than another subject typically covered in the first year of law school, property law is likely to elicit disagreement between libertarians who hope to minimize government regulation of property and progressives who hope to promote more equal opportunities to acquire property. The text will incorporate explicit considerations of these alternative perspectives, as well as the contrast between approaches focused on the normative idea of economic efficiency and approaches focused on norms of liberty, fairness, justice, and democracy. Those who would like background reading may look to Richard Epstein's books and the articles of Eric Claeys[60] for excellent introductions to the libertarian perspective and to the recent Symposium in the Cornell Law Review for an introduction to the progressive approach.[61]

---

59. *See, e.g.*, Martha C. Nussbaum, *Women and Human Development* (2000); Amartya Sen, *Development as Freedom* (1999); Amartya Sen, *Commodities and Capabilities* (1985).

60. *Compare* Epstein, *supra* note 28; Richard Epstein, *Takings: Private Property and the Power of Eminent* Domain (1985). Although he is a natural rights theorist and eschews the libertarian label, Professor Eric Claeys has written extensively, and in a sophisticated manner, in a vein that seeks to limit government interference with the rights of owners. *See, e.g.*, Eric R. Claeys, *Virtue and Rights in American Property Law*, 94 Cornell L. Rev. 889 (2009); Eric R. Claeys, *Takings, Regulations, and Natural Property Rights*, 88 Cornell L. Rev. 1549, 1669-1671 (2003).

61. Symposium*: Property and Obligation*, 94 Cornell L. Rev. 743 (2009), *including* Gregory S. Alexander, Eduardo Moisés Peñalver, Joseph William Singer & Laura S. Underkuffler, *A Statement of Progressive Property*, 94 Cornell L. Rev. 743 (2009); Gregory S. Alexander, *The Social-Obligation Norm in American Property Law*, 94 Cornell L. Rev. 745 (2009); Eduardo Moisés Peñalver, *Land Virtues*, 94 Cornell L. Rev. 821 (2009).

HOW TO BRIEF A CASE AND PREPARE FOR CLASS

Sources of Law

Legal rules are promulgated by a wide variety of government bodies in a hierarchical scheme. The major sources of law in that system include the following:

1. United States Constitution. The federal Constitution is the fundamental law of the land. It was adopted by state constitutional conventions, whose members were elected by (a small subset of) the people.[62] Constitutional amendments are generally passed by Congress and ratified by state legislatures. The Constitution determines the structure of the federal government, including the relations among the executive, legislative, and judicial branches of the federal government, and the relations between the federal government and the state governments. It also defines the powers of the federal government and limits the powers of both the federal government and the states to protect individual rights, including property rights and other rights such as freedom of speech, freedom from unreasonable searches and seizures, equal protection of the laws, and due process.

2. Federal statutes. Legislation is passed by the Congress of the United States and ratified by the president, or passed over the president's veto. Federal statutes address a wide variety of matters relating to property law; examples include the *Fair Housing Act of 1968,* the *Civil Rights Act of 1964,* the Internal Revenue Code, the *Sherman Antitrust Act,* and the *Worker Adjustment and Retraining Notification Act of 1988.*

3. Administrative regulations. Congress may pass legislation creating administrative agencies, such as the Environmental Protection Agency, the Equal Employment Opportunity Commission, the Federal Trade Commission, or the Internal Revenue Service; these agencies may have the power to promulgate regulations in a particular field (environmental protection, employment discrimination, or tax law).

---

62. It is important to note that when the United States Constitution was adopted in 1789, the voting population in the 13 states excluded women, African American men, American Indians, and white men who owned less than a certain amount of property.

4. State constitutions. Each state has its own constitution defining the structure of state government and defining certain fundamental individual rights against the state. In some instances, state constitutions grant greater protection to individual rights than does the federal constitution. For example, a search by the police that is allowed under the fourth amendment to the U.S. Constitution may be prohibited under the New Jersey constitution. Although state constitutions may not grant citizens less protection than provided by the federal constitution, they may grant their citizens more protection by going further than the U.S. Constitution in limiting the power of state officials.

5. State statutes. State statutes are passed by state legislatures with the consent of the governor (or by a supermajority vote over the governor's veto). Many state statutes deal with property law matters such as landlord-tenant legislation, recording acts, civil rights statutes, and regulation of family property on divorce.

6. State administrative regulations. State legislatures, like the federal Congress, may create administrative agencies that have the power to promulgate regulations in limited fields of law. The Massachusetts legislature, for example, has created a Building Code Commission endowed with the power to promulgate and enforce regulations on building construction and materials to protect the public from unsafe structures.

7. Common law. In the absence of any controlling statute or regulation, state courts adjudicate civil disputes by promulgating or applying rules of law. Judicial opinions explain and justify the rules adopted by judges to adjudicate civil disputes. During the first year of law school, most courses focus on common law rules and the process of common law decision making by judges, but property law is as much a statutory and regulatory topic as it is a product of common law decision making.

8. Local ordinances and bylaws. State legislatures delegate to local governments such as counties, cities, and towns the power to promulgate ordinances or bylaws in limited areas of law, including zoning, rent control, schools, traffic, and parking.

Lawyers' Skills

In reading materials and in preparing for class, you should keep in mind three basic tasks that lawyers perform.

1. Counseling. In advising clients, lawyers perform a variety of roles. First, they answer clients' questions about their legal rights. They do so by looking up the law in statutes, regulations, and judicial opinions. In so doing, they may or may not find legal rules that specifically address the question they need to answer. In either case, lawyers must predict how the courts would rule on the question if they had the opportunity to do so. This requires lawyers to make educated judgments about how prior case law will be applied to new fact situations. Second, lawyers counsel clients on how to conform their conduct to the dictates of the law and how to achieve their goals in a lawful manner. Third, lawyers draft legal documents for clients, including leases, deeds, purchase and sale agreements, bond documents, and employment contracts. Fourth, lawyers negotiate with other parties or their attorneys to settle disputes or to make deals.

2. Advocacy. If a dispute cannot be resolved amicably, one of the parties—called the "plaintiff"—may bring a lawsuit against the other party—called the "defendant"—claiming that the defendant engaged in wrongful conduct that violated the plaintiff's legal rights. To prevail in such a lawsuit, the plaintiff must be able to (a) prove in court by testimony, documentation, or other admissible evidence that the defendant engaged in the wrongful conduct and that the conduct caused the plaintiff's harm, and (b) demonstrate that the defendant's conduct violates a legally protected interest guaranteed to the plaintiff in a way that violates the plaintiff's legal rights. The parties will normally hire attorneys to conduct the lawsuit. Lawyers argue before judges about what the legal rules are governing the dispute. Sometimes the rules in force are clear. Often, however, the rule governing a particular situation is not clear. The rules contain numerous gaps, conflicts and ambiguities, and lawyers are experts in using the open texture of the law to develop plausible competing arguments about alternative possible rules of law to govern the situation. The attorneys for each side engage in advocacy of alternative possible rules of law, both in written arguments called "briefs" and in oral arguments before judges. In these settings, lawyers attempt to persuade judges to interpret existing rules or to create new legal rules in ways that favor their clients' interests. Lawyers must therefore learn the kinds of arguments judges find persuasive in interpreting and in modernizing the rules in force. Lawyers may also represent clients before legislative committees considering the passage of legislation.

3. Decision making. Finally, it is important to remember that the judges who decide cases are also lawyers. Their role is to adjudicate the cases before them by choosing the applicable legal rules to govern the dispute and others like it in the future. Similarly, legislatures promulgate statutes regulating conduct and resolving conflicts among competing interests. It is also important for you as a participant in the legal system to develop your own views about the wisdom and justice of our legal institutions and rules. Legal education teaches us to consider both sides of important contested questions of law before reaching a judgment about the proper outcome of the dispute. This does not mean we should be indifferent to what those outcomes are or that we should not criticize the rules in force. Your ability to argue for and against a position does not mean that you cannot make up your mind or present persuasive arguments to justify the result you reach; it means simply that your judgment about right and wrong should be true to the complexity of your own moral beliefs and that it is important to recognize what is lost, as well as what is gained, by any choice.

Reading Cases

Rules of law. In researching the law, attorneys might (1) find a rule of law that clearly defines the parties' respective rights; (2) find no rule of law directly on point (a gap in the law); (3) find a rule of law that does not clearly answer the question (an ambiguity in an existing rule); or (4) find two or more rules of law that arguably govern the dispute (a conflict among possibly applicable rules). Moreover, attorneys might find rules of law applying to situations that are arguably analogous to the case at hand. Lawyers find and exploit the gaps, conflicts, and ambiguities in the law to attempt to define the law in ways that benefit their clients.

In preparing for class, you should try to identify the rule of law—the general principle—each side in the case would like the court to promulgate. Ask yourself: What rule of law did the plaintiff urge the court to adopt? What rule of law did the defendant urge the court to adopt?

This is harder than it seems. Sometimes the parties' proposed rules of law are described in the judicial opinion, sometimes not. In either event, you must ask whether it would be wise to argue for a broad rule of law or a narrow one. For example, one might argue for a broad, rather vague, rule of law: "Non-owners are privileged to enter property when their activity will further a significant public policy." Or one might argue for a narrow rule of law, tied very closely to the facts of the case: "Lawyers and physicians working for agencies funded by the federal government may enter property to give professional assistance to migrant farmworkers." Similarly, an owner might argue for a broad rule of law granting owners the right to exclude non-owners under all circumstances, or she might argue for a narrower rule granting owners the right to exclude non-owners only if the owner can show just cause. It is up to you to identify the different ways each side might have framed its proposed rules of law.

Arguments

After identifying possible rules of law for each side, you should ask what arguments the parties might have given to justify adopting their proposed rules, as well as what arguments they could have given against the rule proposed by the other side. These arguments should include considerations about the fairness of the proposed rules to the parties: Which rule better protects individual rights? You should also consider the social consequences of the competing rules: Which rule better promotes the general welfare?

Briefing Cases

In preparing for class, at least at the beginning, you should brief your cases. This means writing an outline of the important elements of the decision. These elements include the following.

1. Facts. Who did what to whom? What is the relationship between the parties? What is the wrongful conduct the plaintiff claims the defendant engaged in, and how did it harm the plaintiff? What is the dispute between the parties about?

2. Procedural history. How did the courts below rule on the case? First, how did the trial court resolve the matter? Who won, and why? Did the party who lost in the trial court appeal an adverse ruling of law to an intermediate appellate court? If so, how did the appellate court rule, and why? Did one of the parties appeal the result in the appellate court to the state supreme court? What court issued the opinion you are reading—the state supreme court or some lower court? (Note that because cases in this and other casebooks have been edited, some portion of the procedural history may be omitted from the text reprinted in the book.)

3. Relief sought and judgment. What relief did the plaintiff seek? Did she ask for (a) a declaration of her rights (a declaratory judgment); (b) an injunction ordering the defendant to act or not to act in certain ways; or (c) damages to compensate the plaintiff for the harm? What was the judgment of the court issuing the opinion you are reading? Did it grant a declaratory judgment, issue an injunction, or order the payment of damages? Did it remand the case to a lower court for further proceedings, such as a new trial?

4. Legal question, or rule choice. What is the legal question or questions the court resolved? To answer this, you should determine what rule of law the plaintiff favored and what rule of law the defendant favored. What different legal rules did the court consider? What rules should it have considered? What rule of law would you propose if you were the plaintiff's attorney? The defendant's attorney?

5. Arguments and counterarguments. Place yourself in the position of the plaintiff's lawyer. What arguments would you give to persuade the court to adopt the rule of law favored by your client, and what arguments can you give against the rule of law favored by the defendant? Next, place yourself in the position of the defendant's lawyer. What arguments would you give to persuade the court to adopt the rule of law favored by your client, and what arguments can you give against the rule of law favored by the plaintiff?

a. Precedential arguments. These arguments appeal to existing rules of law. You may argue that an ambiguous rule of law—such as a rule creating a reasonableness standard of conduct—entitles your client to win. You may also argue that one of two conflicting rules of law governs the fact situation in your case or that a rule of law applies by analogy. To do either of these things, you must argue that a prior case establishes a principle of law that governs a situation that is identical—or sufficiently similar—to the case at hand such that the policies or principles that underlie and justify the earlier decision are applicable to the current case. Under these circumstances, you can argue that the prior case establishes a precedent that applies to your case. The lawyer on the other side will argue that the case at hand is different in important ways from the prior case and that because of those differences, the policies and principles underlying the earlier case do not apply to the case at hand. When the rule of law in the prior case does not apply to the case at hand, we say the lawyer has distinguished the precedent. What rules have you learned that can be applied either directly or by analogy to govern this case?

b. Statutory interpretation. The rights of the parties may be governed by a federal or state statute that regulates their conduct. Judges must interpret ambiguities in those statutes by reference to (1) the language of the statute; and (2) the legislative intent behind the statute, which may be elucidated by reference to the policies and purposes the legislation was intended to serve. How can you persuade the judge that your proposed interpretation of the statutory language or purposes best accords with the intent of the legislature? What counterarguments will the attorney on the other side make to answer your claims?

c. Policy arguments. These arguments appeal to a variety of considerations, including (1) fairness, individual and group rights, and justice in social relationships; and (2) the social consequences of alternative rules such that the choice of rules promotes social utility, efficiency, or the general welfare. What reasons can you give to persuade the judge that your proposed rule promotes both justice and social welfare? What counterarguments will the attorney on the other side make to answer your claims?

6. Holding. What rule of law did the court adopt, and how did it apply to the case? In identifying the holding of the case, it is important to consider several possibilities. Try to describe the rule of law in as broad a fashion as possible by (a) identifying a general category or a broad range of situations to which the rule would apply, and/or (b) appealing to general principles such as foreseeability, reasonableness, or promotion of alienability. Then try to describe the rule of law in as narrow a fashion as possible so as to limit the application of the rule to a narrow range of circumstances by (a) identifying the specific facts of the case as necessary to application of the rule, and/or (b) appealing to specific, rather than general, principles. For example, a possible broad holding of a case is that owners have an absolute right to exclude non-owners from their property unless the owner's act of exclusion violates public policy. An alternative narrow holding would be that owners of property open to the general public for business purposes have a right to exclude non-owners from their property unless those non-owners are engaging in expressive political activity that does not interfere with the operation of the business.

7. Reasoning of the court and criticism of that reasoning. What reasons did the court give for deciding the case the way it did? What problems can you find with the court's reasoning? Do you agree or disagree?

Reading Statutes and Regulations

Statutory interpretation can be the subject of entire law school courses, but it is important to become comfortable from the outset with statutory and regulatory language. This is because a great deal of legal practice involves statutory or regulatory questions that have not necessarily been ruled on by the courts.

There are examples of statutes and regulations throughout this book. The task in reading these legal texts is different than briefing cases for class discussion. The goal is to come to class with a broad-brush understanding of how the relevant statute or regulation works. As you prepare, pay attention to the details of the language and the structure of the text, note the kinds of issues the statute or regulation covers (and does not), what explicit exceptions or exemptions are set out, how the various parts of the text relate to each other, and ambiguities the language creates. It can be hard to master statutory or regulatory language in the absence of a specific conflict or question, but the basic exercise of careful reading will soon come naturally.

ACKNOWLEDGMENTS

Acknowledgments from Joseph William Singer

This book would not have been possible without the substantial help, suggestions, encouragement, and support of many people. I would like especially to thank Duncan Kennedy, whose imprint is evident throughout the book. He is responsible for some of the large structural components of the book, including the idea of organizing materials around the concept of consumer protection in the market for shelter, and many details, such as the inclusion of building code materials in the land use regulation section. He also developed the idea of systematizing legal arguments as a device for legal education. His personal, moral, and intellectual support over the years has been invaluable to me.

Jeremy Paul contributed in fundamental ways to the ideas about property and law school teaching represented in this book. The takings materials especially are shaped by his perspective. I want to thank Jack Beermann for getting me to write this book. His encouragement and intellectual support over the years buoyed me tremendously. Elizabeth V. Spelman has been essential in teaching me to "think about thinking" and to explore gender, race, and class issues in social relations. I would like also to thank Williamson Chang and Robert A. Williams, Jr., for prompting my interest in the legal relations between the United States and American Indian nations and between the United States and Native Alaskans and Native Hawaiians. Their personal insights and scholarly contributions on the property rights of Native American peoples contributed significantly to my own intellectual development and to various aspects of this book.

Various colleagues and friends who have provided detailed suggestions include Kathy Abrams, Greg Alexander, Keith Aoki, David Barron, Jack Beermann, Bethany Berger, Robert Brauneis, Betsy Clark, Alan Feld, Tamar Frankel, Louise Halper (ז"ל), James Holmes, Ian Haney López, Allan Macurdy, Martha Mahoney, Robert Merges, Ron Meyer, Frank Michelman, Nell Jessup Newton, Eduardo Peñalver, John Powell, John Rattigan, Aviam Soifer, Debra Pogrund Stark, Nomi Stoltzenberg, Gerald Torres, Robert Tuttle, Laura Underkuffler, André van der Walt, Johan van der Walt, and Kelly Weisberg.

Though they may not know it, a number of colleagues have especially influenced my understanding of property, including, but not limited to, Adeno Addis, Bob Anderson, Derrick Bell, Bethany Berger, James Boyle, Victor Brudney, Clark Byse, William W. Fisher III, William Forbath, Jerry Frug, Mary Joe Frug (ז"ל), Mary Ann Glendon, Carole Goldberg, Robert Gordon, Neil Gotanda, Kent Greenfield, Morton Horwitz, Karl Klare, John LaVelle, Charles Lawrence, Mari Matsuda, Gary Minda, Martha Minow, Nell Newton, Frances Olsen, Jennifer Nedelsky, Margaret Jane Radin, Carol Rose, Judy Royster, Katherine Stone, Rennard Strickland, Cass Sunstein, Lucie White, and Patricia Williams. Any failings in this book cannot be attributed to anyone in this disparate group.

The library reference staffs at Boston University School of Law and Harvard Law School made my life wonderfully easy and contributed enormously to the research necessary to this project. Special thanks go to Daniel Freehling, Marlene Alderman, Kim Dulin, Cynthia Murphy, Kristin Cheney, Jon Fernald, Naomi Ronen, and Janet Katz. William Kaleva, Carol Igoe, Holly Escott, and Patricia Fazzone provided cheerful and dedicated administrative assistance, at various times performing feats I would have thought impossible for human beings.

I would like to thank Deans Martha Minow, Elena Kagan, and Robert Clark of Harvard Law School and Dean Ronald Cass of the Boston University School of Law for financial support for research. Many aspects of the book would have been less developed were it not for a slew of research assistants who labored over the years, including Vanessa Antoinette, Mekonnen Ayano, Benjamin Beasley, Alanna Buchanan, Ariane Buglione, David Bunis, Andrew Crespo, Jeffrey Engelsman, Joel Freedman, Jonathan Gingerich, Rachel Gonzalez, Steven Gould, Margaret Guzman, Ulcca Hannsen, Joseph Harrington, Rebecca Haw, Philander Huynh, Gregory Ikonen, Laura Kershner, Vikas Khanna, Brian Korchin, Sara Madge, Stacey Moore, Garrett Moritz, Pablo Ormachea, Amanda Phillips, Neil Shah, Edward Tumavicus, Loren Washburn, David Wiseman, Ben Wizner, and Alithea Zymaris.

I would like to thank the staff at Aspen for their invaluable help in preparing and editing this book. I am also grateful to the anonymous reviewers whose suggestions have been incorporated into the final product. I continue to be amazed by the wonders of WESTLAW and LEXIS. The availability of computer research techniques and the ability to download cases and statutes shortened by years the time needed to write this book.

Lila Singer has taught me about teaching and social action. Max Singer (ז"ל) has inspired me with his work on low-income housing and hunger. I want to thank them for my education and for their example of how to live—my greatest inheritance. Robert Singer and Anne Rayman have both taught me about caretaking, and Adam and Rachel have shown me how to take care of those who take care of you. Gale Singer Adland and Peter Adland have taught me about making a home, and Ari, Jesse, and Naomi have shown me how to grow up.

Newton Minow has taught me to look at the real world and to figure out what works so that valuable resources are not wasted. Josephine Minow has taught me about attentiveness to others, involvement in causes, and how to get things done. Nell Minow and David Apatoff have taught me about the government of business and the business of government, and Benjamin and Rachel have shown me how to get totally and fanatically engrossed in something. Mary Minow and James Robenolt have taught me about getting information and how to use it once I have gotten it.

I would like also to thank the late Justice Morris Pashman (ז"ל) of the Supreme Court of New Jersey for teaching me about the art of judging. It is impossible to define exactly what good judgment entails, but it can be understood, at least partly, through example. Justice Pashman's sensitivity to the perspectives of each litigant epitomizes, for me, the preconditions for justice. When I try to imagine how a good judge would react to a particular problem, I turn to his example.

I wish I could show this book to Marcel Pallais Checa (ז"ל). Marcel taught me what it meant to be a committed intellectual and how to tie one's spiritual life to one's political commitments. He taught me that a philosopher could also be an economist. His assassination reminds me of both the value and the limits of the rule of law.

On May 31, 1992, Mira Judith Minow Singer made her astonishing entry into this world, voicing strong opinions, questioning authority, and generally sticking up for herself. She has increased my respect and admiration for parents generally and made me wonder how single parents manage. Her presence has reminded me that one out of every five children in the United States lives below the poverty line, and that almost half of all African American children do so. I wonder how we could take good care of her if we did not have a home. Mira has caused me to ponder anew the fact that we reward only some kinds of work with property while other kinds are not so rewarded, despite their social value, and the resultant inequalities that go along with such distinctions.

This book is doubly (in both senses of the word) dedicated to Martha Minow and Mary Joe Frug (ז"ל).

Mary Joe Frug's scholarship on gender issues in contracts casebooks heavily influenced both the content and the structure of this book. From her I learned about hidden messages—often unintended—and how to ask who was left out of a seemingly comprehensive treatment of a subject. Her work encouraged me to ask whether there were entitlements important to women that are not traditionally included in introductory property courses. Addressing this question prompted me to include materials in this casebook on public accommodations statutes applicable to "private" clubs that discriminate against women, child support, AFDC, domestic violence restraining-order statutes, unemployment benefits for women who leave work to take care of children or to be with a loved one, enforceability of restraints on marriage, statutes prohibiting discrimination on the basis of marital status, statutes prohibiting discrimination against families with children, the relationship between sex and race discrimination, statutes prohibiting discrimination on the basis of sexual orientation, equitable distribution, community property, property rights of unmarried couples, and nontraditional family relationships. Her work also encouraged me to look for cases that included women as central actors, including opinions written by female judges and cases involving women in a variety of roles, as both landlords and tenants, business executives and housekeepers, victims and villains.

Like dozens of other people, I had set up a date to talk with Mary Joe. I hoped to get further advice from her about this casebook. Our conversation setting up our date took place several days before her death. I have been playing out the conversation we might have had ever since. I hope that some of her appears in this book.

This book is dedicated also to Martha Minow. Martha has taught me about multiplicity—the properties of family and the families of property—and the way it all looks from the differing perspectives of different people in their different situations. She has taught me to ask what difference an argument or practice makes to real people in real relationships in the real world. In her hands, abstract concepts become relations among people; real estate is not a lifeless thing, but a *setting* in which people have families, engage in work and commerce, make a home. It is those relationships that matter.

Imagine a walled city bursting at its seams; with too many people, the constraints of the wall cause division among the inhabitants and the possibility of oppression—the powerful are inclined to exclude the weak. Where others see constraints, scarcity, and frustration, Martha thinks about how to break the wall down or how to create openings in it; if these things cannot be done—for now—she imagines how relationships among people in the city might be restructured so that this artificial constraint becomes understood as everyone's problem and not just the problem of minority groups. She embodies possibility; when everything seems hopeless, she opens doors to the land of change. In ways too many to count, to me and to many other people, she has made all the difference.

Special Acknowledgments for the Sixth Edition

Outstanding research assistance was provided by Melissa Friedman, Kylie Chiseul Kim, Lerae Kroon, and Michael Qin. Patricia Fazzone provided administrative assistance and continues to remind me about the connections between professional and spiritual work.

Acknowledgments from Bethany R. Berger

Thanks go to Nell Newton and Jeremy Paul for first telling me to use Joe's book, to Alexander Pearl and Allison Tirres for advice and suggestions throughout, and to the University of Connecticut Law School Foundation for supporting this work. Mariah Gleaton and Ryan Cook provided excellent research assistance, and Joan Wood was invaluable in formatting draft chapters before I distributed them to my classes.

Acknowledgments from Nestor M. Davidson

For their wonderful suggestions for the Sixth Edition, I want to thank William Boyd, Bill Callison, Bob Schwemm, and the person I know who is closest to a national monument himself, Charles Wilkinson. Over the past two years, I have also had invaluable research assistance from Tim Fitzmaurice, Max Meadows, Tim Polmateer, and Brittany Robbins.

Acknowledgments from Eduardo Moisés Peñalver

Thanks first to Joe Singer for including me in the Sixth Edition of his superb casebook and for being so gracious about all of our changes. I hope they have only sharpened (and not obscured) what is so special and distinctive about Joe's vision. Thanks also to Bethany and Nestor for being such exemplary co-authors, and to Oskar Liivak, Kali Murray, and Peter Karol for their advice and suggestions. Finally, thanks to Jessica Chung for her excellent research assistance.

Copyright Permissions

Kennedy, Duncan, *Form and Substance in Private Law Adjudication,* 89 Harv. L. Rev. 1687 (1976). Reprinted by permission of Duncan Kennedy and Harvard Law Review.

Laufer-Ukeles, Pamela, *Mothering for Money: Regulating Commercial Intimacy,* 88 Ind. L.J. 1223 (2013).

Merryman, John Henry, *Thinking About the Elgin Marbles,* 83 Mich. L. Rev. 1881 (1985).

Nash, Diane, photograph, provided courtesy of *The Tennessean.*

Postrel, Virginia, *With Functioning Kidneys for All,* The Atlantic, July 9, 2009.

Shelley family, photograph by George Harris, provided courtesy of Black Star Agency.

Waldman, Carl, maps from *Atlas of the North American Indian* (3d ed. 2009).

Waldron, Jeremy, *Homelessness and the Issue of Freedom,* 39 UCLA L. Rev. 295 (1991). Copyright © 1991 by The Regents of the University of California. All rights reserved. Reprinted by permission of Jeremy Waldron, UCLA Law Review, and William S. Hein & Co., Inc.

Williams, Patricia J., *Spirit-Murdering the Messenger: The Discourse of Fingerpointing as the Law's Response to Racism,* 42 U. Miami L. Rev. 127 (1987). Reprinted by permission of the University of Miami Law Review.

Williams, Walter E., *The Intelligent Bayesian,* in *Symposium, The Jeweler's Dilemma,* The New Republic, Nov. 10, 1986, at 18. Copyright © 1986 by Walter E. Williams. Reprinted by permission of Walter E. Williams.

PROPERTY LAW

PART ONE

PROPERTY IN A FREE AND DEMOCRATIC SOCIETY

CHAPTER 1

Trespass: The Right to Exclude and Rights of Access

§1 TRESPASS

Many rights go along with ownership or possession of property. Legal scholars have compiled lists of the standard property rights or "incidents of ownership," often derived in some way from Roman law. The following list, by professor and Harvard Law School dean Roscoe Pound, is typical: the right to possess, the right to exclude, the right to alienate, the right to use, the right to enjoy the fruits or profits, and the right to destroy. *See* Roscoe Pound, *The Law of Property and Recent Juristic Thought*, 25 A.B.A. J. 993, 997 (1939). Competing lists might be longer or shorter. But on virtually any telling, one of the central rights of ownership is the *right to exclude* others from one's property. The law of trespass both defines and protects the owner's right to exclude.

A **trespass** under the common law is an *unprivileged intentional intrusion on property possessed by another*. The **intent** requirement is met if the defendant engaged in a voluntary act, such as walking onto the property. It is not necessary that the trespasser intended to violate the owner's legal rights; mistaken entry on the land of another does not relieve the trespasser of liability. The intent requirement is not met if, for example, someone carries the trespasser onto the property against her will. The **intrusion** occurs the moment the non-owner enters the property. "The gist of an action of trespass is infringement on the right of possession." *Walker Drug Co. v. La Sal Oil Co.*, 972 P.2d 1238 (Utah 1998). An intrusion may occur upon physical entry by a person, an agent such as an employee, or an object such as a building that extends over the boundary onto a neighbor's property. A trespass may occur either above or below the surface. For example, a well dug on one's property that slants to an area underneath the neighbor's property constitutes a trespass. Similarly, a second-story porch that overhangs the neighbor's property also qualifies as a trespass.

A trespass is **privileged**, and thus not wrongful, if (1) the entry is done with the **consent** of the owner;[1] (2) the entry is justified by the **necessity** to prevent a more serious harm to persons or property; or (3) the entry is otherwise encouraged by **public policy**. Entry on property of another may be privileged, for example, if one is doing so to stop a crime or to help someone out of a burning house.

§1.1 Public Policy Limits on the Right to Exclude

The right to exclude protected by trespass law is very broad, but it is not absolute. In a variety of circumstances, legal rules limit the possessor's right to exclude non-owners from the property. In such cases, non-owners may have a right of access to the property. These rights of access are created by different sources of law, including common law, federal and state public accommodations statutes and labor relations statutes, and federal and state constitutional guarantees of freedom of speech. The cases in this chapter explore the contours of these competing rights in different contexts.

State v. Shack

277 A.2d 369 (N.J. 1971)

JOSEPH WEINTRAUB, C.J.

Defendants entered upon private property to aid migrant farmworkers employed and housed there. Having refused to depart upon the demand of the owner, defendants were charged with violating N.J. Stat. §2A:170-31[2] which provides that "[a]ny person who trespasses on any lands . . . after being forbidden so to trespass by the owner . . . is a disorderly person and shall be punished by a fine of not more than $50." Defendants were convicted in the Municipal Court of Deerfield Township.

Complainant, Tedesco, a farmer, employs migrant workers for his seasonal needs. As part of their compensation, these workers are housed at a camp on his property. Defendant Tejeras is a field worker for the Farm Workers Division of the Southwest Citizens Organization for Poverty Elimination, known by the acronym SCOPE, a non-profit corporation funded by the Office of Economic Opportunity pursuant to an act of Congress, 42 U.S.C.A. §§2861-2864.[3] The role of SCOPE includes providing for the "health services of the migrant farm worker." Defendant Shack is a staff attorney with the Farm Workers Division of Camden Regional Legal Services, Inc., known as "CRLS," also a nonprofit corporation funded by the Office of Economic Opportunity pursuant to an act of Congress, 42 U.S.C.A. §2809(a)(3). The mission of CRLS includes legal advice and representation for these workers.

1. One who enters property with the permission of the owner or possessor is called a *licensee* and has a property interest called a *license*. If the owner revokes the license, the non-owner must leave the land within a reasonable time; failure to do so will constitute a trespass.

2. This statute has been superseded by N.J. Stat. §2C:18-3. — EDS.

3. This statute, as well as the subsequently referenced statute, 42 U.S.C.A. §2809(a)(3), have been repealed. *See* Pub. L. No. 95-568, §8(a)(2), 92 Stat. 2428 (1978); Pub. L. No. 97-35, tit. VI, §683(a), 95 Stat. 519 (1981). — EDS.

Differences had developed between Tedesco and these defendants prior to the events which led to the trespass charges now before us. Hence when defendant Tejeras wanted to go upon Tedesco's farm to find a migrant worker who needed medical aid for the removal of 28 sutures, he called upon defendant Shack for his help with respect to the legalities involved. Shack, too, had a mission to perform on Tedesco's farm; he wanted to discuss a legal problem with another migrant worker there employed and housed. Defendants arranged to go to the farm together. Shack carried literature to inform the migrant farmworkers of the assistance available to them under federal statutes, but no mention seems to have been made of that literature when Shack was later confronted by Tedesco.

Defendants entered upon Tedesco's property and as they neared the camp site where the farmworkers were housed, they were confronted by Tedesco who inquired of their purpose. Tejeras and Shack stated their missions. In response, Tedesco offered to find the injured worker, and as to the worker who needed legal advice, Tedesco also offered to locate the man but insisted that the consultation would have to take place in Tedesco's office and in his presence. Defendants declined, saying they had the right to see the men in the privacy of their living quarters and without Tedesco's supervision. Tedesco thereupon summoned a State Trooper who, however, refused to remove defendants except upon Tedesco's written complaint. Tedesco then executed the formal complaints charging violations of the trespass statute.

I

The constitutionality of the trespass statute, as applied here, is challenged on several scores.

It is urged that the First Amendment rights of the defendants and of the migrant farmworkers were thereby offended. Reliance is placed on *Marsh v. Alabama*, 326 U.S. 501 (1946), where it was held that free speech was assured by the First Amendment in a company-owned town which was open to the public generally and was indistinguishable from any other town except for the fact that the title to the property was vested in a private corporation. Hence a Jehovah's Witness who distributed literature on a sidewalk within the town could not be held as a trespasser. Later, on the strength of that case, it was held that there was a First Amendment right to picket peacefully in a privately owned shopping center which was found to be the functional equivalent of the business district of the company-owned town in Marsh. *Amalgamated Food Employees Union Local 590 v. Logan Valley Plaza, Inc.*, 391 U.S. 308 (1968). [*Logan Valley* rests] upon the fact that the property was in fact opened to the general public.[4] There may be some migrant camps with the attributes of the company town in *Marsh* and of course they would come within its holding. But there is nothing of that character in the case before us, and hence there would have to be an extension of *Marsh* to embrace the immediate situation.

4. *Logan Valley* was substantially limited in application by the Supreme Court in *Lloyd Corp., Ltd. v. Tanner*, 407 U.S. 551 (1972) and substantially overruled in *Hudgens v. National Labor Relations Board*, 424 U.S. 507 (1976). *See infra* §3. — Eds.

Defendants also maintain that the application of the trespass statute to them is barred by the Supremacy Clause of the United States Constitution, Art. VI, cl. 2,[5] and this on the premise that the application of the trespass statute would defeat the purpose of the federal statutes, under which SCOPE and CRLS are funded, to reach and aid the migrant farmworker. The brief of the United States, amicus curiae, supports that approach. Here defendants rely upon cases construing the *National Labor Relations Act*, 29 U.S.C.A. §§151 *et seq.*, and holding that an employer may in some circumstances be guilty of an unfair labor practice in violation of that statute if the employer denies union organizers an opportunity to communicate with his employees at some suitable place upon the employer's premises.

These constitutional claims are not established by any definitive holding. We think it unnecessary to explore their validity. The reason is that we are satisfied that under our State law the ownership of real property does not include the right to bar access to governmental services available to migrant workers and hence there was no trespass within the meaning of the penal statute. The policy considerations which underlie that conclusion may be much the same as those which would be weighed with respect to one or more of the constitutional challenges, but a decision in nonconstitutional terms is more satisfactory, because the interests of migrant workers are more expansively served in that way than they would be if they had no more freedom than these constitutional concepts could be found to mandate if indeed they apply at all.

II

Property rights serve human values. They are recognized to that end, and are limited by it. Title to real property cannot include dominion over the destiny of persons the owner permits to come upon the premises. Their well-being must remain the paramount concern of a system of law. Indeed the needs of the occupants may be so imperative and their strength so weak, that the law will deny the occupants the power to contract away what is deemed essential to their health, welfare, or dignity.

Here we are concerned with a highly disadvantaged segment of our society. We are told that every year farmworkers and their families numbering more than one million leave their home areas to fill the seasonal demand for farm labor in the United States. The migrant farmworkers come to New Jersey in substantial numbers.

The migrant farmworkers are a community within but apart from the local scene. They are rootless and isolated. Although the need for their labors is evident, they are unorganized and without economic or political power. It is their plight alone that summoned government to their aid. In response, Congress provided under Title III-B of the *Economic Opportunity Act of 1964* (42 U.S.C.A. §§2701 *et seq.*) for "assistance for migrant and other seasonally employed farmworkers and their families." Section 2861 states "the purpose of this part is to assist migrant and seasonal farmworkers and

---

5. That clause states: "This Constitution, and the Laws of the United States which shall be made in Pursuance thereof; and all Treaties made, or which shall be made, under the Authority of the United States, shall be the supreme Law of the Land; and the Judges in every State shall be bound thereby, any Thing in the Constitution or laws of any State to the Contrary notwithstanding." — Eds.

their families to improve their living conditions and develop skills necessary for a productive and self-sufficient life in an increasingly complex and technological society." Section 2862(b)(1) provides for funding of programs "to meet the immediate needs of migrant and seasonal farmworkers and their families, such as day care for children, education, health services, improved housing and sanitation (including the provision and maintenance of emergency and temporary housing and sanitation facilities), legal advice and representation, and consumer training and counseling." As we have said, SCOPE is engaged in a program funded under this section, and CRLS also pursues the objectives of this section although, we gather, it is funded under §2809(a)(3), which is not limited in its concern to the migrant and other seasonally employed farmworkers and seeks "to further the cause of justice among persons living in poverty by mobilizing the assistance of lawyers and legal institutions and by providing legal advice, legal representation, counseling, education, and other appropriate services."

These ends would not be gained if the intended beneficiaries could be insulated from efforts to reach them. It is in this framework that we must decide whether the camp operator's rights in his lands may stand between the migrant workers and those who would aid them. The key to that aid is communication. Since the migrant workers are outside the mainstream of the communities in which they are housed and are unaware of their rights and opportunities and of the services available to them, they can be reached only by positive efforts tailored to that end. The *Report of the Governor's Task Force on Migrant Farm Labor* (1968) noted that "One of the major problems related to seasonal farm labor is the lack of adequate direct information with regard to the availability of public services," and that "there is a dire need to provide the workers with basic educational and informational material in a language and style that can be readily understood by the migrant." The report stressed the problem of access and deplored the notion that property rights may stand as a barrier, saying "In our judgment, 'no trespass' signs represent the last dying remnants of paternalistic behavior."

A man's right in his real property of course is not absolute. It was a maxim of the common law that one should so use his property as not to injure the rights of others. [*Sic utere tuo ut alienum non laedas.*] Although hardly a precise solvent of actual controversies, the maxim does express the inevitable proposition that rights are relative and there must be an accommodation when they meet. Hence it has long been true that necessity, private or public, may justify entry upon the lands of another.

The subject is not static. As pointed out in 5 Powell, *Real Property* §745, at 493-494 (Rohan 1970), while society will protect the owner in his permissible interests in land, yet

> such an owner must expect to find the absoluteness of his property rights curtailed by the organs of society, for the promotion of the best interests of others for whom these organs also operate as protective agencies. The necessity for such curtailments is greater in a modern industrialized and urbanized society than it was in the relatively simple American society of fifty, 100, or 200 years ago. The current balance between individualism and dominance of the social interest depends not only upon political and social ideologies, but also upon the physical and social facts of the time and place under discussion.

Professor Powell added in §746, at 494-496:

> As one looks back along the historic road traversed by the law of land in England and in America, one sees a change from the viewpoint that he who owns may do as he pleases with what he owns, to a position which hesitatingly embodies an ingredient of stewardship; which grudgingly, but steadily, broadens the recognized scope of social interests in the utilization of things.
>
> To one seeing history through the glasses of religion, these changes may seem to evidence increasing embodiments of the golden rule. To one thinking in terms of political and economic ideologies, they are likely to be labeled evidences of "social enlightenment" or of "creeping socialism" or even of "communistic infiltration," according to the individual's assumed definitions and retained or acquired prejudices. With slight attention to words or labels, time marches on toward new adjustments between individualism and the social interests.

This process involves not only the accommodation between the right of the owner and the interests of the general public in his use of his property, but involves also an accommodation between the right of the owner and the right of individuals who are parties with him in consensual transactions relating to the use of the property. Accordingly substantial alterations have been made as between a landlord and his tenant.

The argument in this case understandably included the question whether the migrant worker should be deemed to be a tenant and thus entitled to the tenant's right to receive visitors, *Williams v. Lubbering,* 63 A. 90 (N.J. Sup. Ct. 1906), or whether his residence on the employer's property should be deemed to be merely incidental and in aid of his employment, and hence to involve no possessory interest in the realty. *See Scottish Rite Co. v. Salkowitz,* 197 A. 43 (N.J. 1938). These cases did not reach employment situations at all comparable with the one before us. Nor did they involve the question whether an employee who is not a tenant may have visitors notwithstanding the employer's prohibition. Rather they were concerned with whether notice must be given to end the employee's right to remain upon the premises, with whether the employer may remove the discharged employee without court order, and with the availability of a particular judicial remedy to achieve his removal by process. We of course are not concerned here with the right of a migrant worker to remain on the employer's property after the employment is ended.

We see no profit in trying to decide upon a conventional category and then forcing the present subject into it. That approach would be artificial and distorting. The quest is for a fair adjustment of the competing needs of the parties, in the light of the realities of the relationship between the migrant worker and the operator of the housing facility.

Thus approaching the case, we find it unthinkable that the farmer-employer can assert a right to isolate the migrant worker in any respect significant for the worker's well-being. The farmer, of course, is entitled to pursue his farming activities without interference, and this defendants readily concede. But we see no legitimate need for a right in the farmer to deny the worker the opportunity for aid available from federal, state, or local services, or from recognized charitable groups seeking to assist him. Hence representatives of these agencies and organizations may enter upon the premises to seek out the worker at his living quarters. So, too, the migrant worker must be allowed to receive visitors there of his own choice, so long as there is no behavior hurtful to others, and members of the press may not be denied reasonable access to workers who do not object to seeing them.

It is not our purpose to open the employer's premises to the general public if in fact the employer himself has not done so. We do not say, for example, that solicitors or peddlers of all kinds may enter on their own; we may assume for the present that the employer may regulate their entry or bar them, at least if the employer's purpose is not to gain a commercial advantage for himself or if the regulation does not deprive the migrant worker of practical access to things he needs.

And we are mindful of the employer's interest in his own and in his employees' security. Hence he may reasonably require a visitor to identify himself, and also to state his general purpose if the migrant worker has not already informed him that the visitor is expected. But the employer may not deny the worker his privacy or interfere with his opportunity to live with dignity and to enjoy associations customary among our citizens. These rights are too fundamental to be denied on the basis of an interest in real property and too fragile to be left to the unequal bargaining strength of the parties.

It follows that defendants here invaded no possessory right of the farmer-employer. Their conduct was therefore beyond the reach of the trespass statute. The judgments are accordingly reversed and the matters remanded to the County Court with directions to enter judgments of acquittal.

Desnick v. American Broadcasting Companies, Inc.

44 F.3d 1345 (7th Cir. 1995)

RICHARD POSNER, Chief Judge.

The plaintiffs — an ophthalmic clinic known as the "Desnick Eye Center" after its owner, Dr. Desnick, and two ophthalmic surgeons employed by the clinic, Glazer and Simon — appeal from the dismissal of their suit against the ABC television network, a producer of the ABC program *Primetime Live* named Entine, and the program's star reporter, Donaldson. The suit is for trespass, defamation, and other torts arising out of the production and broadcast of a program segment of *Primetime Live* that was highly critical of the Desnick Eye Center.

In March of 1993 Entine telephoned Dr. Desnick and told him that *Primetime Live* wanted to do a broadcast segment on large cataract practices. The Desnick Eye Center has 25 offices in four midwestern states and performs more than 10,000 cataract operations a year, mostly on elderly persons whose cataract surgery is paid for by Medicare. The complaint alleges — and in the posture of the case we must take the allegations to be true, though of course they may not be — that Entine told Desnick that the segment would not be about just one cataract practice, that it would not involve "ambush" interviews or "undercover" surveillance, and that it would be "fair and balanced." Thus reassured, Desnick permitted an ABC crew to videotape the Desnick Eye Center's main premises in Chicago, to film a cataract operation "live," and to interview doctors, technicians, and patients. Desnick also gave Entine a videotape explaining the Desnick Eye Center's services.

Unbeknownst to Desnick, Entine had dispatched persons equipped with concealed cameras to offices of the Desnick Eye Center in Wisconsin and Indiana. Posing as patients, these persons — seven in all — requested eye examinations. Plaintiffs Glazer and Simon are among the employees of the Desnick Eye Center who were secretly videotaped examining these "test patients."

The program aired on June 10. Donaldson introduces the segment by saying, "We begin tonight with the story of a so-called 'big cutter,' Dr. James Desnick. . . . In our undercover investigation of the big cutter you'll meet tonight, we turned up evidence that he may also be a big charger, doing unnecessary cataract surgery for the money." Brief interviews with four patients of the Desnick Eye Center follow. One of the patients is satisfied ("I was blessed"); the other three are not — one of them says, "If you got three eyes, he'll get three eyes." Donaldson then reports on the experiences of the seven test patients. The two who were under 65 and thus not eligible for Medicare reimbursement were told they didn't need cataract surgery. Four of the other five were told they did. Glazer and Simon are shown recommending cataract surgery to them. Donaldson tells the viewer that *Primetime Live* has hired a professor of ophthalmology to examine the test patients who had been told they needed cataract surgery, and the professor tells the viewer that they didn't need it — with regard to one he says, "I think it would be near malpractice to do surgery on him." Later in the segment he denies that this could just be an honest difference of opinion between professionals.

[Plaintiff claims] that the defendants committed a trespass in insinuating the test patients into the Wisconsin and Indiana offices of the Desnick Eye Center, that they invaded the right of privacy of the Center and its doctors at those offices (specifically Glazer and Simon), that they violated federal and state statutes regulating electronic surveillance, and that they committed fraud by gaining access to the Chicago office by means of a false promise that they would present a "fair and balanced" picture of the Center's operations and would not use "ambush" interviews or undercover surveillance.

To enter upon another's land without consent is a trespass. The force of this rule has, it is true, been diluted somewhat by concepts of privilege and of implied consent. But there is no journalists' privilege to trespass. And there can be no implied consent in any nonfictitious sense of the term when express consent is procured by a misrepresentation or a misleading omission. The Desnick Eye Center would not have agreed to the entry of the test patients into its offices had it known they wanted eye examinations only in order to gather material for a television exposé of the Center and that they were going to make secret videotapes of the examinations. Yet some cases deem consent effective even though it was procured by fraud. There must be *something* to this surprising result. Without it a restaurant critic could not conceal his identity when he ordered a meal, or a browser pretend to be interested in merchandise that he could not afford to buy. Dinner guests would be trespassers if they were false friends who never would have been invited had the host known their true character, and a consumer who in an effort to bargain down an automobile dealer falsely claimed to be able to buy the same car elsewhere at a lower price would be a trespasser in the dealer's showroom. Some of these might be classified as privileged trespasses, designed to promote competition.

Others might be thought justified by some kind of implied consent—the restaurant critic for example might point by way of analogy to the use of the "fair use" defense by book reviewers charged with copyright infringement and argue that the restaurant industry as a whole would be injured if restaurants could exclude critics. But most such efforts at rationalization would be little better than evasions. The fact is that consent to an entry is often given legal effect even though the entrant has intentions that if known to the owner of the property would cause him for perfectly understandable and generally ethical or at least lawful reasons to revoke his consent.

The law's willingness to give effect to consent procured by fraud is not limited to the tort of trespass. The *Restatement* gives the example of a man who obtains consent to sexual intercourse by promising a woman $100, yet (unbeknownst to her, of course) he pays her with a counterfeit bill and intended to do so from the start. The man is not guilty of battery, even though unconsented-to sexual intercourse is a battery. *Restatement (Second) of Torts* §892B, illustration 9, pp. 373-374 (1979). Yet we know that to conceal the fact that one has a venereal disease transforms "consensual" intercourse into battery. *Crowell v. Crowell,* 105 S.E. 206 (N.C. 1920). Seduction, standardly effected by false promises of love, is not rape; intercourse under the pretense of rendering medical or psychiatric treatment is, at least in most states. It certainly is battery. Trespass presents close parallels. If a homeowner opens his door to a purported meter reader who is in fact nothing of the sort—just a busybody curious about the interior of the home—the homeowner's consent to his entry is not a defense to a suit for trespass. *See State v. Donahue,* 762 P.2d 1022, 1025 (Or. Ct. App. 1988); *Bouillon v. Laclede Gaslight Co.,* 129 S.W. 401, 402 (Mo. Ct. App. 1910). And likewise if a competitor gained entry to a business firm's premises posing as a customer but in fact hoping to steal the firm's trade secrets. *Rockwell Graphic Systems, Inc. v. DEV Industries, Inc.,* 925 F.2d 174, 178 (7th Cir. 1991); *E.I. duPont deNemours & Co. v. Christopher,* 431 F.2d 1012, 1014 (5th Cir. 1970).

How to distinguish the two classes of case—the seducer from the medical impersonator, the restaurant critic from the meter-reader impersonator? The answer can have nothing to do with fraud; there is fraud in all the cases. It has to do with the interest that the torts in question, battery and trespass, protect. The one protects the inviolability of the person, the other the inviolability of the person's property. The woman who is seduced wants to have sex with her seducer, and the restaurant owner wants to have customers. The woman who is victimized by the medical impersonator has no desire to have sex with her doctor; she wants medical treatment. And the homeowner victimized by the phony meter reader does not want strangers in his house unless they have authorized service functions. The dealer's objection to the customer who claims falsely to have a lower price from a competing dealer is not to the physical presence of the customer, but to the fraud that he is trying to perpetuate. The lines are not bright—they are not even inevitable. They are the traces of the old forms of action, which have resulted in a multitude of artificial distinctions in modern law. But that is nothing new.

There was no invasion in the present case of any of the specific interests that the tort of trespass seeks to protect. The test patients entered offices that were open to anyone expressing a desire for ophthalmic services and videotaped physicians engaged in professional, not personal, communications with strangers (the testers themselves). The activities of the offices were not disrupted. Nor was there any "inva[sion of] a person's private space," as in our hypothetical meter-reader case, as in the famous case of *De May v. Roberts,* 9 N.W. 146 (Mich. 1881) (where a doctor, called to the plaintiff's home to deliver her baby, brought along with him a friend who was curious to see a birth but was not a medical doctor, and represented the friend to be his medical assistant), as in *Dietemann v. Time, Inc.,* 449 F.2d 245 (9th Cir. 1971), on which the plaintiffs in our case rely. *Dietemann* involved a home. True, the portion invaded was an office, where the plaintiff performed quack healing of nonexistent ailments. The parallel to this case is plain enough, but there is a difference. Dietemann was not in business, and did not advertise his services or charge for them. His quackery was private.

No embarrassingly intimate details of anybody's life were publicized in the present case. There was no eavesdropping on a private conversation; the testers recorded their own conversations with the Desnick Eye Center's physicians. There was no violation of the doctor-patient privilege. There was no theft, or intent to steal, trade secrets; no disruption of decorum, of peace and quiet; no noisy or distracting demonstrations. Had the testers been undercover FBI agents, there would have been no violation of the Fourth Amendment, because there would have been no invasion of a legally protected interest in property or privacy. *United States v. White,* 401 U.S. 745 (1971); *Northside Realty Associates, Inc. v. United States,* 605 F.2d 1348, 1355 (5th Cir. 1979). "Testers" who pose as prospective home buyers in order to gather evidence of housing discrimination are not trespassers even if they are private persons not acting under color of law. The situation of the defendants' "testers" is analogous. Like testers seeking evidence of violation of antidiscrimination laws, the defendants' test patients gained entry into the plaintiffs' premises by misrepresenting their purposes (more precisely by a misleading omission to disclose those purposes). But the entry was not invasive in the sense of infringing the kind of interest of the plaintiffs that the law of trespass protects; it was not an interference with the ownership or possession of land. We need not consider what if any difference it would make if the plaintiffs had festooned the premises with signs forbidding the entry of testers or other snoops. Perhaps none, but that is an issue for another day.

Notes and Questions

1. **Criminal trespass.** Shack and Tejeras were charged with **criminal trespass** as defined by the New Jersey statute, N.J. Stat. §2A:170-31.[6] Tedesco invoked the criminal system by calling the police and filing a criminal complaint against Shack and

---

6. This law has been superseded by N.J. Stat. §2C:18-3, which provides, at §2C:18-3(b), that a "person commits a petty disorderly persons offense if, knowing that he is not licensed or privileged to do so, he enters or remains in any place as to which notice against trespass is given by: (1) Actual communication to the actor; or (2) Posting in a manner prescribed by law or reasonably likely to come to the attention of intruders; or (3) Fencing or other enclosure manifestly designed to exclude intruders."

Tejeras. Criminal proceedings are generally initiated by federal, state, or local government officials rather than by private citizens, and their purpose is to deter wrongful activities and to punish those who engage in them. These proceedings may include arrest, criminal complaint, or indictment by the prosecutor, arraignment (bringing formal charges against the accused in court), plea bargaining, and trial. Punishment may include imposition of a fine payable to the state, probation (continued supervision), and incarceration. How did the charge of criminal trespass in *Shack* differ from the common law definition of trespass?

2. **Legal basis for decision.** Did the court in *Shack* rest its ruling on the U.S. Constitution, a federal statute, a state statute, or the state common law? If the court rested its opinion on only one of these sources of law, what role did the others play in determining the outcome of the case?

3. *Ad coelum, ad inferos.* What are the spatial dimensions of the owner's land protected by the law of trespass? Does an airplane flying 30,000 feet above the parcel make an entry (privileged or otherwise)? A satellite orbiting the earth? What about someone tunneling a mine shaft thousands of feet below the surface? For centuries, the common law's short response to the question of the dimensions of an owner's parcel was the maxim that "*cujus est solum ejus est usque ad coelum et ad inferos*"—whoever owns the soil also owns up to the heavens and down to the depths (literally, "down to hell"). Applying this principle, courts have conceived of land ownership as ownership of a column of space (really a cone) extending from the center of the earth up to the sky. Although, on its own terms, the *ad coelum* maxim speaks in terms of ownership rather than exclusion of trespass, courts and commentators alike have sometimes used the maxim to argue that anything that penetrates the column is ostensibly an unprivileged entry onto the owner's land.

The *ad coelum* maxim is usually said to have made its way into the common law through the English jurist Sir Edward Coke in the seventeenth century, who included the principle in his influential *Institutes of the Lawes of England.* 1 Coke, *Institutes,* 19th ed. 1832, ch. 1 §1(4a); *see also* William Blackstone, *Commentaries on the Laws of England* 18 (Univ. of Chicago reprint 1979) (1768). For trespasses near the surface, the doctrine accurately describes how the law defines an entry. *See, e.g., Hannabalson v. Sessions,* 116 Iowa 457 (1902) (thrusting one's arm over a property boundary constitutes an entry); *Puerto v. Chieppa,* 78 Conn. 401 (1905) (a board attached to defendant's building and overhanging plaintiff's land constitutes an entry); *509 Sixth Avenue Corp. v. New York City Transit Authority,* 15 N.Y.2d 48 (1964) (encroachment by subway line 30 feet below surface constitutes an entry).

Far from the surface in either direction, the *ad coelum* maxim has come under increasing pressure within trespass law in recent years as a result of activities that Lord Coke (as he is sometimes called) could not possibly have anticipated. Consider aircraft overflights. After a debate during the early years of the aviation age, *see, e.g., Swetland v. Curtiss Airports Corp.,* 41 F.2d 929 (N.D. Ohio 1930), it is now settled doctrine that airplane overflights that do not interfere with the surface owner's use of the land do not give rise to a cause of action for trespass. *See Hinman v. Pacific Air Transport,*

84 F.2d 755 (9th Cir. 1936) ("This formula 'from the center of the earth to the sky' was invented at some remote time in the past when the use of space above land actual or conceivable was confined to narrow limits, and simply meant that the owner of the land could use the overlying space to such an extent as he was able, and that no one could ever interfere with that use."). Near the surface, courts are more willing to find airplane overflights to violate the rights of owners. *See, e.g., United States v. Causby,* 328 U.S. 256 (1946); *Griggs v. Allegheny County,* 369 U.S. 84 (1962); *Brenner v. New Richmond Regional Airport Commission,* 816 N.W.2d 291 (Wis. 2012); *see also* Stuart Banner, *Who Owns the Sky?* (2008).

The situation has similarly become more complicated far below the surface. As the law had traditionally operated, entering below someone's land constitutes a (subterranean) trespass. *See, e.g., Lewey v. H.C. Fricke Coke Co.,* 166 Pa. 536 (1895). New oil and gas drilling techniques, such as hydraulic fracturing (or "fracking," as it is called for short), have put pressure on traditional assumptions. Fracking involves the use of directional drilling to create a well bore through porous rock formations that contain isolated pockets of oil or gas. Fluids under very high pressure are then pumped into the bore hole. This high-pressure fluid creates cracks in the adjoining rock, allowing the pockets or oil and gas to escape to the surface. Those cracks can extend thousands of feet from the bore hole. Along with the fracking fluid, sand or even small beads are also pumped into the bore hole as "proppants" to prop the rock fissures open and prevent the cracks from closing on themselves once the fluid pressure is removed. The direction and length of the cracks that form as a result of the fluid pressure are impossible to control with any precision. As a result, they occasionally cross property boundaries. Applying the traditional *ad coelum* principle, injecting the fracking fluid and proppants into the column of space underlying the surface property of another person (even several miles down) would seem to constitute an entry. But, as the Texas Supreme Court put it, "the law of trespass need no more be the same two miles below the surface than two miles above." *Coastal Oil & Gas Corp. v. Garza Energy Trust,* 268 S.W.3d 1, 10 (Tex. 2008). As a general matter, law professor John Sprankling says, "when courts directly confront the scope of deep subsurface rights, they usually soften or ignore the [*ad coelum*] approach to the point where the exceptions swallow any supposed rule." John G. Sprankling, *Owning the Center of the Earth,* 55 UCLA L. Rev. 979, 1004 (2008).

Do the examples of airplane overflights and drilling deep underground show that, in the modern world, the *ad coelum* maxim is outmoded? Can we reconcile the results in these cases with continued adherence to the *ad coelum* understanding of the dimensions of an owner's property? In answering the question, it is important to remember that the issue of whether there has been an entry is just the first step in evaluating whether there has been an actionable trespass.

4. The significance of the right to exclude. In recent years, a number of leading legal scholars (and some courts) have argued that the right to exclude is not just one of the most important rights but is in fact a defining feature of the very concept of property. Thomas W. Merrill, *Property and the Right to Exclude,* 77 Neb. L. Rev. 730,

730 (1998); J.E. Penner, *The Idea of Property in Law* 71 (2000) ("[T]he right to property is a right to exclude others from things which is grounded by the interest we have in the use of things."); *see also Loretto v. Teleprompter Manhattan CATV Corp.*, 458 U.S. 419, 434 (1982) (describing "the right to exclude" as one of the most "treasured" and "important" sticks in the owner's "bundle of rights"); *Kaiser Aetna v. United States*, 444 U.S. 164, 179 (1979) (same).

In a similar vein, some scholars have suggested that the right to exclude—and therefore the law of trespass—is uniquely important for how property operates as a legal institution. Protecting the right to exclude with a relatively simple law of trespass, they argue, creates a broad zone of discretion for owners to choose what to do with their property. This ensures that owners are empowered to put their property to its most productive use. In addition, a clear law of trespass also economizes on "information costs" by sending a relatively simple message to people other than the owner, making it easy for them to navigate through a world of privately owned property without violating the rights of others. *See, e.g.*, Thomas W. Merrill & Henry E. Smith, *What Happened to Property in Law and Economics?*, 111 Yale L.J. 357, 389 (2001). As Thomas Merrill and Henry Smith put it, "messages about everyday property must be very simple—messages such as 'keep off' or 'don't touch'—couched in concepts readily comprehensible to remote people with little special legal or asset-specific information." Thomas W. Merrill & Henry E. Smith, *Making Coasean Property More Coasean*, 54 J.L. & Econ. 77, 90 (2011).

Other scholars have criticized the notion that the right to exclude has a privileged place within the concept or operation of property. Professor Larissa Katz, for example, argues that the heart of the concept of property is the owner's authority to determine its use, not the right to exclude. *See* Larissa Katz, *Exclusion and Exclusivity in Property Law*, 58 U. Toronto L.J. 275 (2008). Does the law of airplane overflights support her view? The rules governing aircraft navigation require all airplanes to stay 500 feet above the surface except when landing and to stay at least 500 feet away from any structures. *See* 14 C.F.R. §91.119. Is a landowner who cannot exclude an airplane from flying over her property at 500 feet still an owner of that space in a meaningful sense? Does the rule governing aircraft access prevent an owner from doing anything with her property that she might otherwise be able (or want) to do?

As long as non-owners (like the aircraft pilot navigating over privately owned land) must accommodate their activities to the owner's use decisions (*e.g.*, by keeping their distance from whatever buildings an owner happens to put up), qualifying the right to exclude does not by itself seem to undermine an owner's power to put the property to its most productive use. As for the cost of navigating through a world of owned property, placing too much importance on the law of trespass may cloud the issue. After all, trespassing is just one way of violating the property rights of others. And many owners wish to convey messages other than "keep off!" or "don't touch!" In particular, the owners of commercial property often want to say "come in! take a look!" Giving owners too much discretion with respect to the content of their "come in" messages may drive up information costs for non-owners rather than reducing them. *See* Gregory S. Alexander & Eduardo M. Peñalver, *An Introduction to Property Theory* 138 (2012).

5. The right to roam. At one time in the United States, most unenclosed and undeveloped land was open to the public for the purpose of hunting, gathering kindling and berries, and walking. Eric Freyfogle, *The Lost Right to Roam,* in *On Private Property: Finding Common Ground on the Ownership of Land* 29 (2007); Brian Sawers, *The Right to Exclude from Unimproved Land,* 83 Temp. L. Rev. 665, 675-679 (2011). Today, about half the states still allow hunting on private land unless the owner has posted "no trespassing" signs. Mark R. Sigmon, *Hunting and Posting on Private Land in America,* 54 Duke L.J. 549 (2004). Moreover, owners who wanted to protect their fields from wandering cattle originally had to fence them out; they had no right to complain that a trespass had occurred when cattle wandered onto their property. Nor could railroads insist that cattle owners prevent them from intruding on train tracks. *See, e.g.,* Sawers, *supra,* at 677 ("Free-roaming hogs and cattle were an important source of meat and income for farmers, particularly smaller farmers."); *Nashville & Chattanooga Railroad Co. v. Peacock,* 25 Ala. 229 (1854); *Macon & Western Railroad Co. v. Lester,* 30 Ga. 911 (1860). Over time, the rules changed to place liability on cattle owners for damage to crops on the neighbors' property and denied cattle owners remedies if their cattle wandered onto railroad tracks, effectively changing to a fencing-in system by which owners had the duty to keep their cattle from invading neighboring property.

The *right to roam* has long been recognized in Finland, Norway, and Sweden. Known as the *allemansraat* ("everyman's right") in Sweden, it entitles everyone to hike across or camp in the countryside on the property of another as long as they do not damage the land, interfere with the owner's use, or intrude on the privacy of owners and occupants.[7] In 2000, the United Kingdom adopted the *Countryside and Rights of Way Act 2000,* Acts of 2000, ch. 37, guaranteeing public rights of access for recreational purposes (mainly walking) to certain categories of uncultivated countryside in England and Wales.[8] Scotland adopted an even broader right-to-roam law in 2003.[9] *See* John A. Lovett, *Progressive Property in Action: The Land Reform (Scotland) Act 2003,* 89 Neb. L. Rev. 739 (2011); Jerry L. Anderson, *Britain's Right to Roam: Redefining the Landowner's Bundle of Sticks,* 19 Geo. Intl. Envtl. L. Rev. 375 (2007).

6. Graves. Individuals may have rights of access to cemeteries to visit the graves of their loved ones even if those graves are located on private property that has been sold to a subsequent owner. *Kentucky Department of Fish & Wildlife Resources v. Garner,* 896 S.W.2d 10 (Ky. 1995) (cemetery on public land has duty to give a key to the locked gate to an individual for his use and that of his heirs to visit the graves of their family members); *David v. May,* 135 S.W.2d 747 (Tex. Ct. App. 2003) (plaintiff has the

7. For information on Sweden, *see* Swedish Environmental Protection Agency, The Right of Public Access, *http://www.naturvardsverket.se/en/Enjoying-nature/The-Right-of-Public-Access/* (last visited Mar. 12, 2013).

8. *See Countryside and Rights of Way Act of 2000, available at http://www.legislation.gov.uk/ukpga/2000/37/contents* (last visited Mar. 12, 2013). The Ramblers Association "campaigns to increase and protect public access to the countryside." *See http://www.ramblers.org.uk/freedom/* (last visited Mar. 12, 2013).

9. *See Scottish Outdoor Access Code* (2003), *available at http://www.outdooraccess-scotland.com/outdoors-responsibly/access-code-and-advice/soac/* (last visited Mar. 12, 2013).

right of access to land to visit the graves of her grandparents). *See* Alfred L. Brophy, *Grave Matters: The Ancient Rights of the Graveyard,* 2006 BYU L. Rev. 1469.

7. **Investigative journalism.** In a case somewhat similar to *Desnick, Food Lion, Inc. v. Capital Cities/ABC, Inc.,* 194 F.3d 505 (4th Cir. 1999), *aff'g in part and rev'g in part* 887 F. Supp. 811 (M.D.N.C. 1995), the *Primetime Live* show sent two ABC television reporters to use false résumés to get jobs at Food Lion supermarkets. While working there, they secretly videotaped "what appeared to be unwholesome food handling practices" for later broadcast on television. Food Lion sued ABC, claiming, among other things, that ABC had committed the tort of fraud, that it had violated the duty of loyalty owed by employees to employers, and that its intrusion onto Food Lion's property constituted a trespass. The trial court held that ABC had committed a trespass when its reporters had entered the property because defendants had engaged in "wrongful conduct which could negate any consent to enter given by Food Lion." 887 F. Supp. at 820. Finding ABC liable for both fraud and trespass, the jury awarded Food Lion $1 nominal damages for trespass and $1 for violation of the duty of loyalty. It imposed $1,400 damages for the tort of fraud and a whopping $5,545,750 in punitive damages to punish and deter ABC from engaging in this kind of fraudulent deception in the future. The trial judge reduced the punitive damages to $315,000.

The Fourth Circuit reversed in part, agreeing with *Desnick* that the initial entry was consensual despite having been obtained by fraud so no trespass occurred when the reporters initially entered the property. However, the court found that a trespass had occurred *after* the initial entry when the reporters secretly videotaped the meat-packing process because this action exceeded the scope of the initial invitation. The court threw out the fraud claim. Although the fraud had caused Food Lion to hire the employees, it could not demonstrate any harm resulting from the hirings themselves. As at-will employees, they could leave at any time and had made no promises to work for any particular length of time. Thus Food Lion could not complain that they stayed for only two weeks. Any harm to Food Lion was caused by the broadcast and not by the fraud. The first amendment generally protects the right to publish truthful information, allowing remedies only for defamation — false statements that injure reputation — and even then, only in restricted circumstances. Because the punitive damages judgment had been premised on the fraud, and the fraud claim had now been thrown out, the Fourth Circuit also threw out the punitive damages judgment, leaving defendants with a nominal damages judgment of $2. *Accord, American Transmission, Inc. v. Channel 7 of Detroit, Inc.,* 609 N.W.2d 607 (Mich. Ct. App. 2000) (agreeing with *Desnick* and holding that despite the existence of fraudulent misrepresentations by employees of television station investigating dishonest practices in transmission repair shops, the shop owners had validly consented to the investigators' presence on their premises and that no specific interests relating to the peaceable possession of land were invaded). *But see Medical Laboratory Management Consultants v. ABC, Inc.,* 30 F. Supp. 2d 1182 (D. Ariz. 1998); *Shiffman v. Empire Blue Cross & Blue Shield,* 681 N.Y.S.2d 511, 512 (App. Div. 1998) (reporters who gained entry to medical offices by posing as potential patients could not assert consent as defense to trespass claim "since consent obtained by misrepresentation or fraud is invalid"); *Restatement (Second) of Torts* §892B(2) (1965) ("if the person consenting to the conduct of another . . . is induced [to consent] by the other's misrepresentation, the consent is not effective for the unexpected invasion or harm").

8. Trespass to computer systems. Trespass is usually a doctrine that concerns intrusions to real property. A version of the doctrine, called **trespass to chattels**, applies to personal property. The tort of trespass to chattels allows owners of personal property to recover damages for intentional interferences with the possession of personal property. The owner is entitled to injunctive relief stopping any such interference with the chattel. Mere touching of the object is usually not sufficient to constitute trespass; the plaintiff must either allege some injury to the property or show either dispossession or intentional "using or intermeddling" with it. *Restatement (Second) of Torts* §218 (1965).

In *Intel Corp. v. Hamidi*, 71 P.3d 296 (Cal. 2003), a former employee sent numerous e-mails to his former co-employees criticizing the employer. The e-mails breached no security barriers nor disrupted the employer's e-mail system. The lower courts held that the former employee had committed trespass to chattels on the ground that the former employee was "disrupting [the employer's] business by using its property." *Id.* at 302. The California Supreme Court reversed, holding that no trespass could be shown in the absence of dispossession unless the communication damaged the recipient's computer system or impaired its functioning. *Accord, CompuServe v. Cyber Promotions, Inc.*, 962 F. Supp. 1015, 1022 (S.D. Ohio 1997). *Cf. eBay, Inc. v. Bidder's Edge, Inc.*, 100 F. Supp. 2d 1058, 1071 (N.D. Cal. 2000) (finding damage when defendant Bidder's Edge's Internet-based auction aggregation site sent 80,000 to 100,000 information requests per day to eBay's auction trading site by "diminish[ing] the quality or value of eBay's computer systems [by consuming] at least a portion of [eBay's] bandwidth and server capacity").

9. Trespass and government searches. The fourth amendment of the United States Constitution says that "[t]he right of the people to be secure in their persons, houses, papers, and effects, against unreasonable searches and seizures, shall not be violated." But what is a search? After the U.S. Supreme Court's landmark decision in *Katz v. United States*, 389 U.S. 347 (1967), it seemed that whether a particular government action would be deemed a "search" depended on whether the defendant had a "reasonable expectation of privacy" that was violated by the government's activity. In *United States v. Jones*, 123 S. Ct. 945 (2012), however, the Court seemed to change gears, turning towards the law of trespass for an alternative definition of searches. The case involved a defendant who had been convicted of possessing several kilograms of cocaine with the intent to distribute. Part of the evidence used against the defendant came from a small GPS tracking device that federal agents attached to the underside of the defendant's wife's car. At trial, data from the GPS device was used to link the defendant to the location of a drug stash house. Instead of looking into the defendant's expectations of privacy (with regard to either the exterior of the vehicle or his presence on public streets), the Supreme Court asked whether the government's behavior constituted a trespass (to chattels). "The text of the Fourth Amendment," Justice Scalia wrote for the Court, "reflects its close connection to property. . . ." *Id.* at 950. Although the Court conceded its more recent cases had "deviated from that exclusively property-based approach, . . . for most of our history the Fourth Amendment was understood to embody a particular concern for government trespass upon the areas ('persons, houses, papers and effects') it enumerates." *Id.* Because, in *Jones*, "[t]he Government physically occupied private property," its actions constituted a trespass on an enumerated category of property, and because it did so to obtain information, its actions amounted to a search within the meaning of the fourth amendment. After *Jones*, actions that are not a trespass might still implicate the fourth amendment under a *Katz* expection-of-privacy analysis. And police action that would appear to involve trespass, but that occurs on categories of property not enumerated within the fourth amendment (such as "open fields"), might not violate the fourth amendment. *See Hester v. United States*, 265 U.S. 57 (1924). But, with respect to enumerated property ("houses, papers, and effects"), trespass provides a minimal threshold of fourth amendment protection.

The Court in *Jones* assumes that attaching a GPS device to a car is an obvious case of trespass to chattels. Do you agree? As Justice Alito noted in his concurring opinion in *Jones*, most courts would require some damage to the chattel in order to find a trespass. "Attaching to the bottom of a car a small, light object that does not interfere in any way with the car's operation . . . is generally regarded as so trivial that it does not provide a basis for recovery under modern [trespass] law." *Id.* at 961 (Alito, J., concurring in the judgment). Do you agree with Justice Alito that attaching a GPS device to a car does not harm the owner's interest in use or possession of the vehicle? Or do you think a car owner would be able to obtain an injunction to remove a GPS tracker installed on her car by a private party against her wishes, even if the tracker did not physically damage the car or interfere with its operation?

In *Florida v. Jardines*, 133 S. Ct. 1409 (2013), the Court considered a challenge to a "search" in which police officers (acting on an anonymous tip and without a warrant) brought a drug-sniffing dog onto the front porch of the defendant's home. In finding the act of bringing a drug dog onto the front porch to constitute a search, the Court acknowledged that an invitation to approach the front door "may be implied from the habits of the country." Id. at 1415. Notwithstanding this implicit license, the Court ruled out the notion that the police were acting under such an implicit license to approach the defendant's front door, since there is no customary invitation to bring a drug dog onto the front porch to sniff for contraband. Applying this logic, could a police officer approach the front door, knock, and ask the defendant a few questions without first obtaining a warrant? If the law of trespass defines (in part) the scope of fourth amendment protection, to whose law should courts look in order to determine whether some government action constitutes a trespass (and therefore a fourth amendment search)? The law of the jurisdiction where the putative search occurs? The law of the jurisdiction in which the criminal charges are brought? Some federal "constitutional common law" standard of trespass? What if different jurisdictions reach different conclusions about whether a particular sort of activity constitutes a common law trespass or instead falls within an implicit license?

Problems

1. A tenant in a three-unit apartment building allows his girlfriend to move into the apartment with him. The landlord, who occupies one of the three apartments, objects. Stating that she rented to him alone and not to his girlfriend, she asks him to have the girlfriend leave. After he refuses, the landlord sues to evict him. He argues that, like all other tenants, he has the right to receive visitors, *see Commonwealth v. Nelson,* 909 N.E.2d 42 (Mass. App. Ct. 2009); *State v. DeCoster,* 653 A.2d 891, 894 (Me. 1995), and that this right encompasses the right to choose to have family members or intimate associates stay with him at his home. What arguments can you make on both sides of this question? What rule of law would you promulgate if you were the judge?

2. Were *Desnick* and *Food Lion* decided correctly?

a. **Consent.** Should fraudulently obtained consent be a defense to a trespass claim as *Desnick* held, or should such consent be ineffective as a defense to a trespass claim as *Shiffman* held? Was the Fourth Circuit in *Food Lion* correct to find a trespass when the reporters exceeded the scope of the invitation by secretly videotaping, or was *Desnick* correct to find no trespass based on the secret videotaping?

b. **Public policy.** Should trespasses by investigative journalists be privileged because they further a strong public policy of protecting consumers from harmful products and services?

c. **Punitive damages.** If a trespass can be shown either because entry is obtained by fraud or because secret videotaping exceeds the scope of the permission to enter, should punitive damages be available for trespass to deter investigative journalists from entering property on false pretenses and thus obtaining embarrassing information they can broadcast to the world? Punitive damages are generally to punish and deter "outrageous" or "egregious" conduct, including conduct that displays a willful or reckless disregard of the rights of others. *JCB, Inc. v. Union Planters Bank, NA,* 539 F.3d 862, 872-877 (8th Cir. 2008). Does intentional trespass rise to that level? Did the conduct in *Desnick* and *Food Lion* rise to that level? If the actual damages are only $1, is a $100,000 punitive award excessive in relation to the harm?

3. Imagine that instead of attaching a GPS unit directly to the defendant's car, as in *Jones,* the government had hidden the GPS device inside a tire that the defendant purchased from a store that (prior to sale of the tire) had allowed the government to install the device. Should the defendant's consent to the presence of the tire on his car (without knowledge of the GPS device) shield the government from a finding that it had committed a trespass/search? *See United States v. Karo,* 468 U.S. 705 (1984) (installing a tracker in a can of ether sold to the defendant and then tracking that can to a locker in a public warehouse did not violate the fourth amendment).

§1.2 Limits on the Right to Exclude from Property Open to the Public

Uston v. Resorts International Hotel, Inc.

445 A.2d 370 (N.J. 1982)

Map: 1133 Boardwalk,
Atlantic City, New Jersey

MORRIS PASHMAN, J.

Since January 30, 1979, appellant Resorts International Hotel, Inc. (Resorts) has excluded respondent, Kenneth Uston, from the blackjack tables in its casino because Uston's strategy increases his chances of winning money. Uston concedes that his strategy of card counting can tilt the odds in his favor under the current blackjack rules promulgated by the Casino Control Commission (Commission). However, Uston contends that Resorts has no common law or statutory right to exclude him because of his strategy for playing blackjack.

CONTEXT

Blackjack is the only casino game played against the house in which the odds sometimes favor players. If a player can keep track of how many low-value cards have already been dealt (the goal of card counting), she can identify periods during which the odds are most favorable to her and increase her bets accordingly. The story of one famous card-counting team of MIT students is the subject of the 2003 book *Bringing Down the House*, by Ben Mezrich, as well as a (pretty bad) 2008 feature film entitled "21."

Kenneth Uston is a renowned teacher and practitioner of a complex strategy for playing blackjack known as card counting. Card counters keep track of the playing cards as they are dealt and adjust their betting patterns when the odds are in their favor. When used over a period of time, this method allegedly ensures a profitable encounter with the casino.

"[T]he statutory and administrative controls over casino operations established by the [Casino Control] Act are extraordinarily pervasive and intensive." *Knight v. Margate*, 86 *N.J.* 374, 380-81, 431 A.2d 833 (1981). The almost 200 separate statutory provisions "cover virtually every facet of casino gambling and its potential impact upon the public." *Id.* at 381, 431 A.2d 833. These provisions include a preemption clause, stating that the act prevails over "any other provision of law" in conflict or inconsistent with its provisions. *N.J.S.A.* 5:12-133(b). Moreover, the act declares as public policy of this State "that the institution of licensed casino establishments in New Jersey be strictly regulated and controlled." *N.J.S.A.* 5:12-1(13).

At the heart of the Casino Control Act are its provisions for the regulation of licensed casino games. *N.J.S.A.* 5:12-100 provides:

> e. All gaming shall be conducted according to rules promulgated by the commission. All wagers and pay-offs of winning wagers at table games shall be made according to rules promulgated by the commission, which shall establish such minimum wagers

> and other limitations as may be necessary to assure the vitality of casino operations and fair odds to and maximum participation by casino patrons.

The ability of casino operators to determine how the games will be played would undermine this control and subvert the important policy of ensuring the "credibility and integrity of the regulatory process and of casino operations." *N.J.S.A.* 5:12-1(b). The Commission has promulgated the blackjack rules that give Uston a comparative advantage, and it has sole authority to change those rules. There is no indication that Uston has violated any Commission rule on the playing of blackjack. *N.J.A.C.* 19:47-2.1 to -2.13. Put simply, Uston's gaming is "conducted according to rules promulgated by the Commission." *N.J.S.A.* 5:12-100(e).

The right of an amusement place owner to exclude unwanted patrons and the patron's competing right of reasonable access both have deep roots in the common law. In this century, however, courts have disregarded the right of reasonable access in the common law of some jurisdictions at the time the *Civil War Amendments* and *Civil Rights Act of 1866* were passed.

As Justice Goldberg noted in his concurrence in *Bell v. Maryland,* 378 U.S. 226 (1964):

> Underlying the congressional discussions and at the heart of the Fourteenth Amendment's guarantee of equal protection, was the assumption that the State by statute or by "the good old common law" was obligated to guarantee all citizens access to places of public accommodation. [378 U.S. at 296, Goldberg, J., concurring.]

See, e.g., Ferguson v. Gies, 46 N.W. 718 (Mich. 1890) (after passage of the Fourteenth Amendment, both the civil rights statutes and the common law provided grounds for a non-white plaintiff to recover damages from a restaurant owner's refusal to serve him, because the common law as it existed before passage of the civil rights laws "gave to the white man a remedy against any unjust discrimination to the citizen in all public places"); *Donnell v. State,* 48 Miss. 661 (1873) (state's common law includes a right of reasonable access to all public places).

The current majority American rule has for many years disregarded the right of reasonable access,[10] granting to proprietors of amusement places an absolute right arbitrarily to eject or exclude any person consistent with state and federal civil rights laws.

At one time, an absolute right of exclusion prevailed in this state, though more for reasons of deference to the noted English precedent of *Wood v. Leadbitter,* 153 Eng. Rep. 351 (Ex. 1845), than for reasons of policy. In *Shubert v. Nixon Amusement Co.,* 83 A. 369 (N.J. Sup. Ct. 1912), the former Supreme Court dismissed a suit for damages resulting from plaintiff's ejection from defendants' theater. Noting that plaintiff made no

---

10. The denial of freedom of reasonable access in some States following passage of the Fourteenth Amendment, and the creation of a common law freedom to arbitrarily exclude following invalidation of segregation statutes, suggest that the current majority rule may have had less than dignified origins. *See Bell v. Maryland, supra.*

allegation of exclusion on the basis of race, color or previous condition of servitude, the Court concluded:

> In view of the substantially uniform approval of, and reliance on, the decision in *Wood v. Leadbitter* in our state adjudications, it must fairly be considered to be adopted as part of our jurisprudence, and whatever views may be entertained as to the natural justice or injustice of ejecting a theater patron without reason after he has paid for his ticket and taken his seat, we feel constrained to follow that decision as the settled law. 83 A. at 371.

It hardly bears mention that our common law has evolved in the intervening 70 years. In fact, *Leadbitter* itself was disapproved three years after the *Shubert* decision by *Hurst v. Picture Theatres Limited,* 1 K.B. 1 (1914). Of far greater importance, the decisions of this Court have recognized that "the more private property is devoted to public use, the more it must accommodate the rights which inhere in individual members of the general public who use that property." *State v. Schmid,* 423 A.2d 615, 629 (N.J. 1980).

State v. Schmid involved the constitutional right to distribute literature on a private university campus. The Court's approach in that case balanced individual rights against property rights. It is therefore analogous to a description of the common law right of exclusion. Balancing the university's interest in controlling its property against plaintiff's interest in access to that property to express his views, the Court clearly refused to protect unreasonable exclusions. Justice Handler noted that

> Regulations . . . devoid of reasonable standards designed to protect both the legitimate interests of the University as an institution of higher education and the individual exercise of expressional freedom cannot constitutionally be invoked to prohibit the otherwise noninjurious and reasonable exercise of [First Amendment] freedoms. *Id.* at 632.

In *State v. Shack,* 277 A.2d 369 (N.J. 1971), the Court held that although an employer of migrant farmworkers "may reasonably require" those visiting his employees to identify themselves, "the employer may not deny the worker his privacy or interfere with his opportunity to live with dignity and to enjoy associations customary among our citizens." The Court reversed the trespass convictions of an attorney and a social services worker who had entered the property to assist farmworkers there.

Schmid recognizes implicitly that when property owners open their premises to the general public in the pursuit of their own property interests, they have no right to exclude people unreasonably. On the contrary, they have a duty not to act in an arbitrary or discriminatory manner toward persons who come on their premises. That duty applies not only to common carriers, innkeepers, owners of gasoline service stations, or to private hospitals, but to all property owners who open their premises to the public. Property owners have no legitimate interest in unreasonably excluding particular members of the public when they open their premises for public use.

No party in this appeal questions the right of property owners to exclude from their premises those whose actions "disrupt the regular and essential operations of the [premises]," or threaten the security of the premises and its occupants. In some circumstances, proprietors have a duty to remove disorderly or otherwise dangerous persons from the premises. These common law principles enable the casino to bar from its entire facility, for instance, the disorderly, the intoxicated, and the repetitive petty offender.

Whether a decision to exclude is reasonable must be determined from the facts of each case. Respondent Uston does not threaten the security of any casino occupant. Nor has he disrupted the functioning of any casino operations. Absent a valid contrary rule by the Commission, Uston possesses the usual right of reasonable access to Resorts International's blackjack tables.

Notes and Questions

1. **Historical background.** *Uston* is an outlier. Most modern courts have come out the other way, affirming the right of owners to exclude others from their commercial property for any reason not specifically prohibited by, for example, civil rights laws. *See Madden v. Queens County Jockey Club, Inc.*, 72 N.E.2d 697 (N.Y. 1947). This was not always the case. Before the Civil War, it was well established that certain business owners had a duty to serve anyone who sought their services and was able to pay.

The reach of this duty is a matter of some confusion. Blackstone noted in 1765 that "if an inn-keeper, or other victualler, hangs out a sign and opens his house for travelers, it is an implied engagement to entertain all persons who travel that way; and upon this universal *assumpsit* an action on the case will lie against him for damages, if he without good reason refuses to admit a traveler." 3 William Blackstone, *Commentaries on the Laws of England* 164 (Univ. of Chicago reprint 1979) (1768). For centuries, this duty applied to "anyone who held himself out [as open to the public] to serve all who might apply," and any such business was liable if, having so held itself out as open to the public, it refused to serve any member of the public who applied. *See* Charles K. Burdick, *The Origin of the Peculiar Duties of Public Service Companies*, 11 Colum. L. Rev. 514, 515-516 (1911); *see also* Norman F. Arterburn, *The Origin and First Test of Public Callings*, 75 U. Pa. L. Rev. 411, 421 (1927) (describing fourteenth-century laws, enacted in the wake of the Black Death, requiring all to work who were able, at a reasonable rate, and that none could refuse to practice his calling to whomever applied). The duty to serve extended beyond the modern categories of common carriers and innkeepers and encompassed other businesses as well. *See* Burdick, *supra*, at 514-516, 522 (describing farriers, tailors, and even surgeons as potentially "common" in the relevant sense of being subject to a duty to serve the general public). Early U.S. cases affirmed the obligation on public accommodations to serve the public. *Adams v. Freeman,* 12 Johns. 408 (N.Y. Sup. Ct. 1815). The usual justification for this obligation was the assumption underlying the traditional law of "common callings" that an owner assumes certain duties when he holds himself out as open to the public. *See* Joseph William Singer, *No Right to Exclude: Public Accommodations and Private Property,* 90 Nw. U. L. Rev. 1283, 1315-1316 (1996).

The limitation of the duty to serve to the categories of innkeepers and common carriers is a later development. The first case to clearly assert that places of entertainment holding themselves out as open to the general public had no common law duty to serve the public was decided in 1858 in Massachusetts. The court held that the Howard Athenæum, a well-known lecture hall near the State House, had the power to exclude African Americans. *McCrea v. Marsh,* 78 Mass. 211 (1858); *see also Burton v. Scherpf,* 83 Mass. 133 (1861) (allowing an African American to be ejected from a theater after he had bought a ticket). The apparent connection between the (relatively recent) narrowing of the duty to serve and the motive to exclude free African Americans led the New Jersey Supreme Court to comment in a footnote in *Uston* that the "the current majority rule may have less than dignified origins." 445 A.2d at 374. After the Civil War, most southern states adopted public accommodations laws prohibiting exclusion on the basis of race, but those laws were repealed when Reconstruction ended. The repeals began a long period of racial segregation in many states that ended only with passage of the federal public accommodations law in 1964. *See below* §2.1.

2. **Current law.** Although *Uston* follows the early common law rule in affirming that members of the public enjoy a right of reasonable access to all businesses that hold themselves out as open to the public, this is now a minority position. By the late nineteenth century, the right of access had been narrowed to innkeepers and common carriers (planes, trains, and buses). Most states continue to adhere to the newer version of the rule, recognizing an absolute right by owners to exclude without cause and limiting the duty to serve the public (the right of reasonable access) to innkeepers and common carriers. For example, five years before the New Jersey Supreme Court's decision in *Uston v. Resorts International,* Kenneth Uston had filed an almost identical case against a casino in Las Vegas, Nevada. The U.S. Court of Appeals for the Ninth Circuit, applying Nevada law, upheld the casino's right to exclude card counters. Confining the businesses with a duty to serve to innkeepers and common carriers, it observed that "the relationship [between the casino and Uston] was not one of innkeeper and patron, but rather one of casino owner and prospective gambler. The policies upon which the innkeeper's special common law duties rested are not present in such a relationship." *Uston v. Airport Casino, Inc.,* 564 F.2d 1216, 1217 (9th Cir. 1977).

The leading case affirming the majority rule is *Madden v. Queens County Jockey Club, Inc.,* 72 N.E.2d 697 (N.Y. 1947). In that case, the defendant barred the plaintiff "Coley" Madden from attending races at its racetrack on the mistaken belief that he was "Owney" Madden, a well-known bookmaker. Plaintiff sued the racetrack, claiming that he had a right "as a citizen and a taxpayer — upon paying the required admission price — to enter the race course and patronize the pari-mutuel betting there conducted." *Id.* at 698. The court concluded that places of amusement and resort enjoyed "an absolute power to serve whom they pleased." *Id.* Although New York's *Civil Rights Law* prohibited discrimination on account of race, creed, color, or national origin, because Coley Madden was not excluded for any of these reasons he had no right of access, and the defendant did not need to explain why it excluded him.

3. Policy. The court in *Uston* gave a series of policy arguments for extending the right of access to all businesses open to the public rather than limiting this obligation to innkeepers and common carriers. What policies could justify the majority rule, imposing a duty to serve the public on innkeepers and common carriers but granting most businesses a broad right to exclude?

Three justifications have traditionally been offered for the special obligations on innkeepers and common carriers. First, inns and common carriers were more likely to be monopolies than other businesses, so denial of service was tantamount to denying the ability to travel or to find a place to sleep away from home. Second, these businesses provided necessities whose denial would place individuals in risk from the elements or bandits on the highway. Third, innkeepers and common carriers hold themselves out as ready to serve the public and the public relies on this representation. Joseph William Singer, *No Right to Exclude: Public Accommodations and Private Property,* 90 Nw. U. L. Rev. 1283, 1305-1331 (1996). Do these rationales distinguish innkeepers and common carriers from other businesses, such as retail stores?

In *Brooks v. Chicago Downs Association, Inc.*, 791 F.2d 512, 517, 518-519 (7th Cir. 1986), the Seventh Circuit Court of Appeals explained the basis for the modern doctrine as follows:

> [P]roprietors of amusement facilities, whose very survival depends on bringing the public into their place of amusement, are reasonable people who usually do not exclude their customers unless they have a reason to do so. What the proprietor of a race track does not want to have to do is *prove* or *explain* that his reason for exclusion is a *just* reason. He doesn't want to be liable to [an excluded patron] solely because he mistakenly believed he was a mobster. The proprietor wants to be able to keep someone off his private property even if they only *look like* a mobster. As long as the proprietor is not excluding the mobster look-alike because of his national origin (or because of race, color, creed, or sex), then the common law, and the law of Illinois, allows him to do just that.
>
> [I]t is arguably unfair to allow a place of amusement to exclude for any reason or no reason, and to be free of accountability, except in cases of obvious discrimination. In this case, the general public is not only invited but, through advertising, is encouraged to come to the race track and wager on the races' outcome. But the common law allows the race track to exclude patrons, no matter if they come from near or far, or in reasonable reliance on representations of accessibility. We may ultimately believe that market forces would preclude any outrageous excesses — such as excluding anyone who has blond hair, or (like the plaintiffs) who is from Pennsylvania, or (even more outrageous) who has $250,000 to spend in one day of betting. But the premise of the consumer protection laws [is] that the reality of an imperfect market allows numerous consumer depredations. Excluding a patron simply because he is named Adam Smith arguably offends the very precepts of equality and fair dealing expressed in everything from the antitrust statutes to the Illinois Consumer Fraud and Deceptive Business Practices Act.
>
> But the market here is not so demonstrably imperfect that there is a monopoly or any allegation of consumer fraud. Consequently, there is no such explicit legislative

directive in the context of patrons attending horse races in Illinois — so the common law rule, relic though it may be[11] still controls.

Does this argument from competition distinguish innkeepers and common carriers from other businesses in the modern economy? If not, can you imagine a better distinction? If there is no reasonable distinction between those businesses with a duty to serve the public and those that have no such duty, what should the rule be? Should businesses have a duty to serve the public without unjust discrimination, or should they have an absolute right to exclude? Do proprietors in a competitive market have an incentive to act on the dominant prejudices of the majority? *Cf.* Joel Waldfogel, *The Tyranny of the Market* (2007) (arguing businesses with high fixed costs will — rationally — target their production at majority preferences). What factors would a hypothetical proprietor seeking to exclude "mobsters" employ when deciding whether a potential customer "look[s] like a mobster" (to use the Seventh Circuit's example in *Brooks*)? If the proprietor does rely on national origin (*e.g.*, the customer "looks Italian"), what effect (if any) does recognizing a right to exclude without having to offer reasons have on the ability of the customer to prove that he was the victim of unlawful discrimination?

4. Impact of the access/exclusion choice. Professor Patricia J. Williams wrote about an incident in which she was denied entry to a clothing store in New York City. *See* Patricia J. Williams, *Spirit-Murdering the Messenger: The Discourse of Fingerpointing as the Law's Response to Racism,* 42 U. Miami L. Rev. 127 (1987). The store was locked and equipped with a buzzer allowing the clerk inside to determine whether to allow customers into the store. Williams writes, "Two Saturdays before Christmas, I saw a sweater that I wanted to purchase for my mother. I pressed my brown face to the store window and my finger to the buzzer, seeking admittance." The clerk looked at her and mouthed "We're closed," even though it was one o'clock in the afternoon and several white customers were in the store. She continues,

> I was enraged. At that moment I literally wanted to break all of the windows in the store and *take* lots of sweaters for my mother. In the flicker of his judgmental grey eyes, that sales child had reduced my brightly sentimental, joy-to-the-world, pre-Christmas spree to a shambles. He had snuffed my sense of humanitarian catholicity, and there was nothing I could do to snuff his, without simply making a spectacle of myself.
>
> I am still struck by the structure of power that drove me into such a blizzard of rage. There was almost nothing I could do, short of physically intruding upon him, that would humiliate him the way he humiliated me. No words, no gestures, no prejudices of my own would make a bit of difference to him. His refusal to let me into the store was an outward manifestation of his never having let someone like me into the realm of his reality. He had no connection, no compassion, no remorse, no reference to me, and no desire to acknowledge me even at the estranged level of arm's length transactor. He saw me only as one who would take his money and therefore could not conceive that I was there to give him money.

---

11. As the New Jersey Supreme Court noted in *Uston*, the rise of the American common law right to exclude without cause alarmingly corresponds to the fall of the old segregation laws. . . .

> The violence of my desire to have burst into that store is probably quite apparent to the reader. I wonder if the violence and the exclusionary hatred are equally apparent in the repeated public urging that blacks put themselves in the shoes of white store owners, and that, in effect, blacks look into the mirror of frightened white faces to the reality of their undesirability; and that then blacks would "just as surely conclude that [they] would not let [themselves] in under similar circumstances."

Id. at 129. Is the use of buzzers consistent with the New Jersey Supreme Court's decision in *Uston*?

Consider Walter E. Williams's defense of the practice of store owners' racial profiling of customers:

> Imagine you are challenged to a basketball game and must select five out of 20 people who appear to be equal in every respect except race and sex. There are five black and five white females, five black and five white males. You have no information about their basketball proficiency. There is a million-dollar prize for the contest. How would you choose a team? If you thought basketball skills were randomly distributed by race and sex, you would randomly select. Most people would perceive a strong associative relationship between basketball skills on the one hand, and race and sex on the other. Most would confine their choice to males, and their choice would be dominated by black males.
>
> Can we say such a person is a sexist/racist? An alternative answer is that he is behaving like an intelligent Bayesian (Sir Thomas Bayes, the father of statistics). Inexpensively obtained information about race and sex is a proxy for information that costs more to obtain, namely, basketball proficiency.
>
> There is a large class of human behavior that generally falls into the same testing procedures. Doctors can predict the probability of hypertension by knowing race, and osteoporosis by knowing sex. A white jeweler who does not open his door to young black males cannot be labeled a racist any more than a black taxi driver who refuses to pick up young black males at night. Black females and white females and white males commit holdups, but in this world of imperfect information cab drivers and jewelers play the odds. To ask them to behave differently is to disarm them.

Walter E. Williams, *The Intelligent Bayesian,* The New Republic, Nov. 10, 1986, at 18. Is there a principled difference between considering race in choosing a basketball team and using race in deciding who to admit to a store or who to search?

5. Rules vs. standards. Scholars have long observed that property doctrine sometimes allocates property rights through rigid rules and sometimes through flexible standards. *See, e.g.,* Carol Rose, *Crystals and Mud in Property Law,* 40 Stan. L. Rev. 577 (1988). Trespass law in most jurisdictions operates as a rigid rule — owners have virtually absolute discretion to exclude from privately owned property for any reason not specifically prohibited by law. In New Jersey, on the other hand, trespass operates more like a standard, at least for commercial properties — owners who voluntarily open up their land to the public for the operation of a business open to all comers may only exclude on grounds that are commercially reasonable.

Rigid rules carry two advantages. First, they clarify who has the power to control a particular resource, thus quickly settling disputes. Second, they promote transactions by identifying who owns a particular set of rights in land, thereby clarifying who has the power to sell it. Without such clear rules, negotiations may be more drawn out and costly; the parties may spend time fighting about who really owns the entitlements about which they are supposed to be bargaining.

To legislatures and courts, rigid rules often look good at the planning stage. When an actual dispute arises, however, rigid rules often bring unanticipated, and substantial, injustice. Time and again, confronted with an actual conflict in which the application of the rigid rule seems unfair, courts have shown themselves to be unwilling to mechanically apply the rule. These courts often adjust relationships in ways that more closely approach the judges' intuitions about the just results in particular cases. They often do so by introducing standards, such as reasonableness, that increase flexibility.

Some scholars argue that the law of property cycles back and forth between rules and standards as judges and (especially) legislatures periodically try to clarify the law, which judges then muddy up with standards and exceptions. *See* Rose, *supra*. Others see in the modern law of property a steady shift from rules to standards as society becomes more complex and property rights more frequently butt up against each other. *See* Joseph Wiiliam Singer, *The Rule of Reason in Property Law*, 46 U.C. Davis L. Rev. 1375 (2013). Is it possible to generalize about when rules (or standards) are likely to be appropriate? *See, e.g.*, Felix Cohen, *Dialogue on Private Property*, 9 Rutgers L. Rev. 357 (1954) (suggesting that clear rules are likely to arise in property law when numerous normative considerations line up in favor of a particular outcome).

Problems

1. **Homeless persons.** A large department store located in downtown Boston has become a hangout for homeless persons during winter months when it is freezing outside. The store begins excluding any person who appears to be homeless. Massachusetts has the majority rule that imposes a duty to serve the public on innkeepers and common carriers but not on retail stores. Should Massachusetts adopt the New Jersey rule? What are the arguments on both sides? If Massachusetts does adopt the New Jersey rule, would exclusion of homeless persons be reasonable? What factors would go into such a determination?

2. **Teenagers.** A suburban mall has turned into a hangout for teenagers, some of whom block the entrance to shops and act in a manner the customers consider obnoxious. The mall manager institutes an anti-loitering policy, asking teenagers to leave if they are not in the mall to shop. Should the mall owner have the right to exclude the teenagers?

3. **Racially discriminatory surveillance.** A retail clothing store routinely has its employees follow African American customers around the store. One such customer is stopped and loudly accused of stealing the shirt he is wearing. He had purchased the shirt in the store several days earlier and, by some miracle, even has the receipt in his pocket to prove it. He sues the store, claiming that he was subjected to discriminatory

surveillance because of his race and that the store's practice of giving greater scrutiny to African American customers than to other customers denies his right of reasonable access to a place of public accommodation. The store defends the claim by noting that it is not a public accommodation because it is neither a common carrier nor an innkeeper, and that even if it is a common carrier, it did not deny him reasonable access to the store.[12] Are retail stores places of public accommodation with the duty to serve the public? If they are subject to this duty, is racially discriminatory surveillance a violation of the right of reasonable access under the common law of property?

§1.3 Trespass Remedies

Injunctions are available to remedy a trespass where the trespass is continuous in nature. *See, e.g., Cowles v. Shaw*, 2 Clarke 496 (Iowa 1856). A trespass is continuing where someone is personally present on the land of another or where they leave some object (such as a structure) on the land. Sometimes, courts will grant injunctions for trespasses that, while not strictly continuous, are so repetitious that it would put an unfair burden on the landowner to require her to bring repeated lawsuits. *See, e.g., Planned Parenthood of Mid-Iowa v. Maki*, 478 N.W.2d 637, 639-640 (Iowa 1991); *Theros v. Phillips*, 256 N.W.2d 852 (Minn. 1977). The law occasionally departs from the presumption in favor of injunctive relief, even for continuing trespasses. *See* Chapter 5, §4.1. What if the trespass alters the land in some way? How should the law make the injured landowner whole? What happens when a trespass does not alter the land, is a one-off event, and is not likely to be repeated? Is the owner without a remedy? Consider the following cases.

Glavin v. Eckman

881 N.E.2d 820 (Mass. App. Ct. 2008)

Map: Aquinnah, Martha's Vineyard, Massachusetts

Joseph Grasso, J.

Looking to enhance their view of the ocean, Bruce and Shelly Eckman hired Jon R. Fragosa and his landscaping company, Three Trees, Ltd. (Fragosa), to top and remove the trees that stood in the way. Fragosa improved the Eckmans' view by cutting down ten large, mature oak trees standing on the property of a neighbor, James A. Glavin, without Glavin's permission.

12. This problem is loosely based on a real case. *See* Reuters, *Eddie Bauer Settles Suit Based on Race,* N.Y. Times, Nov. 26, 1998, at A-26.

After trial on Glavin's claim against the Eckmans and Fragosa for the wrongful cutting of his trees, see Mass. Gen. Laws ch. 242, §7,[13] a jury rendered a special verdict in favor of Glavin. The jury found that (1) Fragosa wilfully cut trees on Glavin's land; (2) Fragosa did not have good reason to believe that he was lawfully authorized to cut the trees on Glavin's land; (3) the Eckmans wilfully cut trees on Glavin's land by directing Fragosa to do so; and (4) the Eckmans did not have good reason to believe that they were lawfully authorized to cut the trees on Glavin's land. The jury assessed $30,000 in damages as "the reasonable cost of restoring the property as nearly as reasonably possible to its original condition." The judge trebled those damages as required by the statute.

On appeal, the issues before us are whether . . . the restoration cost is an appropriate measure of damages [and whether] trebling of the restoration cost damages renders such damages unreasonable. Separately, we consider the Eckmans' contention that they cannot be held liable for the acts of Fragosa, an independent contractor. We affirm.

1. *Facts.* From the evidence at trial, the jury could have found the following. Glavin, the Eckmans, and a third individual, named Bea Gentry, own four roughly parallel rectangular parcels of land in the Aquinnah section of Martha's Vineyard, a place of natural beauty. Glavin owns the two westernmost lots. The Eckmans own the most easterly lot. Between the Glavin and Eckman lots is the lot owned by Gentry. By virtue of its greater elevation, the Eckmans' lot has a southwest view to the ocean across the adjacent lots.

Glavin lives with his wife and children in a house that he built on the westernmost lot in 1985. In 1990, he bought the adjoining 1.7-acre lot directly to the east of his house lot. A significant feature of the adjoining lot was a wetland about one-half acre in size that rose to a knoll containing a stand of ten large oak trees that were ideally situated to provide shade and serve as a backdrop to a pond that Glavin planned to restore at the edge of the wetland. A general contractor of considerable experience, Glavin had previously converted wetlands into ponds at least a half dozen times.

When building their vacation home in 1996, the Eckmans asked Glavin for permission to cut the stand of trees on Glavin's property to enhance their view of the ocean. Glavin refused their request, indicating that he had personal reasons for not cutting the trees. Subsequently, in 2001, the Eckmans hired Fragosa to trim or cut down the trees that blocked their view of the ocean. They directed Fragosa to clear as much as possible to enhance their water view, a job that Fragosa characterized as opening the view "to the max." When discussing the job, the Eckmans and Fragosa did not walk

---

13. Mass. Gen. Laws ch. 242, §7 provides:

> A person who without license wilfully cuts down, carries away, girdles or otherwise destroys trees, timber, wood or underwood on the land of another shall be liable to the owner in tort for three times the amount of the damages assessed therefor; but if it is found that the defendant had good reason to believe that the land on which the trespass was committed was his own or that he was otherwise lawfully authorized to do the acts complained of, he shall be liable for single damages only.

the Eckmans' property, but stood on the Eckmans' back deck overlooking the area to be trimmed.

It was readily apparent that most of the trees the Eckmans wanted removed were not on their property. When setting about the job, Fragosa inquired of Gentry, who granted him permission to cut and trim trees on her lot. Although Fragosa obtained Gentry's permission, he did not ascertain the boundaries of her property relative to the Eckman or Glavin properties, nor did he seek permission from Glavin or any other property owners in the area.

In cutting down the trees necessary to open the Eckmans' view, Fragosa strayed fifty to one hundred feet across the unmarked boundary between the Gentry and Glavin lots and cut the stand of mature oaks on Glavin's lot. The trees that Fragosa cut ranged from eleven to thirty inches in diameter at the stumps.

2. *The Eckmans' liability.* Fragosa does not contest the jury's findings of liability against him. The Eckmans, however, contend that Fragosa was an independent contractor for whose acts they cannot be held liable absent a finding that they directed him to cut down the trees. They maintain that the evidence was insufficient for the jury to conclude that they so directed Fragosa.

We disagree. The jury could permissibly conclude that the Eckmans, not Fragosa, defined the scope of the work to be performed by virtue of their retaining Fragosa to cut trees so as to maximize their view to the ocean. While Fragosa retained control over the manner in which the trees would be cut — whether by ax, hand saw, chain saw or other method — the Eckmans retained the ultimate control over the scope of Fragosa's work, cutting those trees that impeded the Eckmans' view. Photographs taken from the Eckmans' deck after the cutting and admitted in evidence show a distinct gap in the treetops that Glavin identified as the area where his trees had stood prior to being cut by Fragosa. The jury were free to disbelieve the Eckmans' and Fragosa's testimony that no direction was given to cut those particular trees. Indeed, in light of the strong evidence that Glavin's trees were the chief impediment to the Eckmans' view, and the undisputed evidence that the Eckmans had previously requested and been denied permission from Glavin to remove the trees that impeded their view, the jury could permissibly infer that the Eckmans had directed Fragosa, explicitly or implicitly, to cut down those particular trees regardless of whether the trees stood on Glavin's land or elsewhere. The jury could also permissibly conclude that having been denied permission from Glavin, the Eckmans decided to resort to self-help and enlisted Fragosa as a dupe or a willing accomplice.

3. *Restoration costs as a measure of damages.* The defendants maintain that the judge erred in permitting the jury to award a restoration cost measure of damages, rather than damages measured by the value of the timber wrongfully cut, or by the diminution in market value of the property as a result of the cutting. We disagree.

General Laws ch. 242, §7, specifies that one who wilfully and without license cuts the trees of another shall be liable in tort "for three times the amount of the damages assessed therefor." "The statute does not prescribe how the damages shall be measured." *Larabee v. Potvin Lumber Co.*, 459 N.E.2d 93, 98 (Mass. 1983). While the most common measures of damages are (1) the value of timber wrongfully cut, or (2) the diminution in value of the property as a result of the cutting, we discern no limitation in the statute to these measures of damages. Indeed, to limit damages to these measures would encourage, rather than deter, wrongdoers from engaging in self-help in circumstances such as when an ocean or other view is desired. The timber wrongfully removed may amount to no more than a single tree; and its removal may even improve, not diminish, the market value of the property. Yet the wrongful cutting may represent a significant loss to the property owner and a significant gain to the wrongdoer even where the value of the timber cut is negligible, or the diminution in value of the property owing to the cutting is minimal or nonexistent. So to limit the damages would permit a wrongdoer to rest assured that the cost of his improved view would be no more than treble the value of the timber cut even where the change wrought to his neighbor's property by the wrongful cutting, as here, is significant. The statute does not so confine a property owner's redress for the wrongdoing of an overreaching neighbor.

Although diminution in market value is one way of measuring damages, "market value does not in all cases afford a correct measure of indemnity, and therefore is not therefore 'a universal test.' " *Trinity Church v. John Hancock Mut. Life Ins. Co.*, 502 N.E.2d 532, 536 (Mass. 1987). Accordingly, "[r]eplacement or restoration costs have also been allowed as a measure of damages . . . where diminution in market value is unavailable or unsatisfactory as a measure of damages." *Id.* This is but another way of recognizing "that more complex and resourceful methods of ascertaining value must be used where the property is unusual . . . and where ordinary methods will produce a miscarriage of justice." *Id.*

The judge, as gatekeeper, has broad discretion to determine whether evidence other than fair market value is relevant to the question of damages. Here, the judge did not abuse that discretion in concluding that diminution in market value was not a fair and adequate measure of the damages that Glavin suffered by the wrongful cutting of his trees. Glavin had no desire to sell the property. Indeed, his plan was to hold on to the lot and utilize its mature oak trees to provide shade for a pond he planned to create from the existing wetlands, and as a backdrop to a tranquil view from his house lot. Regardless whether the planned restoration would increase the value of the lot as a building site and regardless whether the wrongful cutting had an impact on the market value of the lot, elimination of the trees wrought a significant change to Glavin's property. The trees represented decades of natural growth that could not easily be replicated. Moreover, any diminution in market value arising from the wrongful cutting was of less importance than was the destruction of the special value that the land and its stand of mature oak trees held for Glavin.

In such circumstances, the evidence supported the inference that diminution in market value was not

> **CONTEXT**
>
> Glavin had to take out loans to cover his $100,000 legal bill. He told the *Boston Herald* that he "never started this off for the money. I really saw something evil going on that had to be addressed." The paper also reported that "'view greed'—attempts to get better ocean views at all costs," is a longstanding problem on Martha's Vineyard. "Neighbors sometimes poison each others' trees," one resident told the paper, because "everyone knows what a chainsaw sounds like." Jerry Kronenberg, *Taking a Stand*, Boston Herald, Mar. 6, 2008.

a fair and adequate measure of Glavin's damages, and the judge did not err in permitting the jury to award restoration costs as an adequate measure of damages. A plaintiff may opt for either the value of the timber cut or the diminution in value of his property as the measure of damages under the statute, and when the latter measure does not fairly measure his damages, he may permissibly opt for restoration cost damages.

When applying a restoration cost measure of damages, a test of reasonableness is imposed. "Not only must the cost of replacement or reconstruction be reasonable, the replacement or reconstruction itself must be reasonably necessary in light of the damage inflicted by a particular defendant." *Id.* Here, the evidence supported the inference that restoration of Glavin's lot to its predamaged condition was reasonable and reasonably necessary in light of the damage inflicted by the defendants. The cutting down of ten mature oak trees was not a slight injury, and was wilfully undertaken by the defendants to achieve a previously denied view from their property to the ocean. The cost of restoring the lot, while substantial, was not a "very large and disproportionate expense to relieve from the consequences of a slight injury." See *id.* Glavin's use of his property was neither uneconomical nor improper. Likewise, restoration of the property to its predamaged condition was neither uneconomical nor improper.

We also cannot say as matter of law that the jury erred in concluding that because direct restoration of the affected area was either physically impossible or so disproportionately expensive that it would not be reasonable to undertake such a remedy, $30,000 was "the reasonable cost of restoring the property as nearly as reasonably possible to its original condition" (emphasis omitted). *Id.* The jury's award was a reasonable determination from the evidence presented. As discussed further below, this was a case where making an *actual* restoration would be uneconomical. The assessment of damages is traditionally a factual undertaking appropriate for determination by a jury as the representative voice of the community. Likewise, the jury are equipped to evaluate and eliminate any claimed damages that appear excessive. So long as the damages assessed represent a reasoned weighing of the evidence by the jury, fairly compensate the plaintiff for the loss incurred, and do not penalize the wrongdoer, the object of compensatory damages is accomplished. Given the unique value of the trees to Glavin, their integral role in his intended landscaping project, and the expert evidence as to the restoration costs, the jury's award cannot be said to be unreasonable.

We disagree with the defendants that the restoration cost damages awarded by the jury provided Glavin with a windfall. The defendants' tortious actions resulted in the elimination of ten large mature trees and effectively deprived Glavin of this feature of his property for his lifetime. Far from being a windfall, the damages were, at best, a necessary substitute for what nature would require decades to replace.

5. *Trebling damages under G.L. ch. 242, §7.* The defendants argue that even were we to conclude that the damages awarded by the jury were reasonable, when trebled under Mass. Gen. Laws ch. 242, §7, such damages are unreasonable. As noted previously, the restoration cost damages awarded by the jury fall within the range of what is reasonable. The trebling of those damages "ineluctably flows from the plain language of the statute," *Brewster Wallcovering Co. v. Blue Mountain Wallcoverings, Inc.,* 864 N.E.2d 518, 540 (Mass. Ct. App. 2007), and does not render the damages unreasonable.

The mandated trebling of damages represents a legislative judgment as to the punitive measure required to dissuade wrongdoers. A court should not interfere in that determination.

Jacque v. Steenberg Homes, Inc.

563 N.W.2d 154 (Wis. 1997)

Map: (Wilke's Lake) Schleswig, Wisconsin

William A. Bablitch, J.

Steenberg Homes had a mobile home to deliver. Unfortunately for Harvey and Lois Jacque (the Jacques), the easiest route of delivery was across their land. Despite adamant protests by the Jacques, Steenberg plowed a path through the Jacques' snow-covered field and via that path, delivered the mobile home. Consequently, the Jacques sued Steenberg Homes for intentional trespass. At trial, Steenberg Homes conceded the intentional trespass, but argued that no compensatory damages had been proved, and that punitive damages could not be awarded without compensatory damages. Although the jury awarded the Jacques $1 in nominal damages and $100,000 in punitive damages, the circuit court set aside the jury's award of $100,000. The court of appeals affirmed, reluctantly concluding that it could not reinstate the punitive damages because it was bound by precedent establishing that an award of nominal damages will not sustain a punitive damage award. We conclude that when nominal damages are awarded for an intentional trespass to land, punitive damages may, in the discretion of the jury, be awarded. We further conclude that the $100,000 awarded by the jury is not excessive. Accordingly, we reverse and remand for reinstatement of the punitive damage award.

¶2 The relevant facts follow. Plaintiffs, Lois and Harvey Jacques, are an elderly couple, now retired from farming, who own roughly 170 acres near Wilke's Lake in the town of Schleswig. The defendant, Steenberg Homes, Inc. (Steenberg), is in the business of selling mobile homes. In the fall of 1993, a neighbor of the Jacques purchased a mobile home from Steenberg. Delivery of the mobile home was included in the sales price.

¶3 Steenberg determined that the easiest route to deliver the mobile home was across the Jacques' land. Steenberg preferred transporting the home across the Jacques' land because the only alternative was a private road which was covered in up to seven feet of snow and contained a sharp curve which would require sets of "rollers" to be used when maneuvering the home around the curve. Steenberg asked the Jacques on several separate occasions whether it could move the home across the Jacques' farm field. The Jacques refused. The Jacques were sensitive about allowing others on their land because they had lost property valued at over $10,000 to other neighbors in an adverse possession action in the mid-1980's. Despite repeated refusals from the Jacques, Steenberg decided to sell the mobile home, which was to be used as a summer cottage, and delivered it on February 15, 1994.

¶4 On the morning of delivery, Mr. Jacque observed the mobile home parked on the corner of the town road adjacent to his property. He decided to find out where the movers planned to take the home. The movers, who were Steenberg employees, showed Mr. Jacque the path they planned to take with the mobile home to reach the neighbor's lot. The path cut across the Jacques' land. Mr. Jacque informed the movers that it was the Jacques' land they were planning to cross and that Steenberg did not have permission to cross their land. He told them that Steenberg had been refused permission to cross the Jacques' land.

¶5 One of Steenberg's employees called the assistant manager, who then came out to the Jacques' home. In the meantime, the Jacques called and asked some of their neighbors and the town chairman to come over immediately. Once everyone was present, the Jacques showed the assistant manager an aerial map and plat book of the township to prove their ownership of the land, and reiterated their demand that the home not be moved across their land.

¶6 At that point, the assistant manager asked Mr. Jacque how much money it would take to get permission. Mr. Jacque responded that it was not a question of money; the Jacques just did not want Steenberg to cross their land. Mr. Jacque testified that he told Steenberg to "[F]ollow the road, that is what the road is for." Steenberg employees left the meeting without permission to cross the land.

¶7 At trial, one of Steenberg's employees testified that, upon coming out of the Jacques' home, the assistant manager stated: "I don't give a— —what [Mr. Jacque] said, just get the home in there any way you can."

¶9 When a neighbor informed the Jacques that Steenberg had, in fact, moved the mobile home across the Jacques' land, Mr. Jacque called the Manitowoc County Sheriff's Department. After interviewing the parties and observing the scene, an officer from the sheriff's department issued a $30 citation to Steenberg's assistant manager.

¶14 Steenberg argues that, as a matter of law, punitive damages could not be awarded by the jury because punitive damages must be supported by an award of compensatory damages and here the jury awarded only nominal and punitive damages.

The Jacques argue that both the individual and society have significant interests in deterring intentional trespass to land, regardless of the lack of measurable harm that results. We agree with the Jacques.

¶21 We turn first to the individual landowner's interest in protecting his or her land from trespass. The United States Supreme Court has recognized that the private landowner's right to exclude others from his or her land is "one of the most essential sticks in the bundle of rights that are commonly characterized as property." *Dolan v. City of Tigard,* 512 U.S. 374, 384 (1994) (quoting *Kaiser Aetna v. United States,* 444 U.S. 164, 176 (1979)).

¶22 Yet a right is hollow if the legal system provides insufficient means to protect it. Felix Cohen offers the following analysis summarizing the relationship between the individual and the state regarding property rights:

> [T]hat is property to which the following label can be attached:
> To the world:
> Keep off X unless you have my permission, which I may grant or withhold.
> Signed: Private Citizen
> Endorsed: The state

Felix S. Cohen, *Dialogue on Private Property,* 9 Rutgers L. Rev. 357, 374 (1954). Harvey and Lois Jacque have the right to tell Steenberg Homes and any other trespasser, "No, you cannot cross our land." But that right has no practical meaning unless protected by the State.

¶23 Because a legal right is involved, the law recognizes that actual harm occurs in every trespass. The law infers some damage from every direct entry upon the land of another. The law recognizes actual harm in every trespass to land whether or not compensatory damages are awarded.

¶25 In sum, the individual has a strong interest in excluding trespassers from his or her land. Although only nominal damages were awarded to the Jacques, Steenberg's intentional trespass caused actual harm. We turn next to society's interest in protecting private property from the intentional trespasser.

Society has an interest in punishing and deterring intentional trespassers beyond that of protecting the interests of the individual landowner. Society has an interest in preserving the integrity of the legal system. Private landowners should feel confident that wrongdoers who trespass upon their land will be appropriately punished. When landowners have confidence in the legal system, they are less likely to resort to "self-help" remedies.

¶27 People expect wrongdoers to be appropriately punished. The $30 forfeiture was certainly not an appropriate punishment for Steenberg's egregious trespass in the eyes of the Jacques. If punitive damages are not allowed in a situation like this, what punishment will prohibit the intentional trespass to land? Moreover, what is to stop Steenberg Homes from concluding, in the future, that delivering its mobile homes via an intentional trespass and paying the resulting Class B forfeiture, is not more profitable than obeying the law? Steenberg Homes plowed a path across the Jacques' land and dragged the mobile home across that path, in the face of the Jacques' adamant refusal. A $30 forfeiture and a $1 nominal damage award are unlikely to restrain Steenberg Homes from similar conduct in the future. An appropriate punitive damage award probably will.

¶52 Our concern for deterrence is guided by our recognition of the nature of Steenberg's business. Steenberg sells and delivers mobile homes. It is, therefore, likely that they will again be faced with what was, apparently for them, a dilemma. Should they trespass and pay the forfeiture, which in this case was $30? Or, should they take the more costly course and obey the law? Today we alleviate the uncertainty for Steenberg Homes. We feel certain that the $100,000 will serve to encourage the latter course by removing the profit from the intentional trespass.

¶53 Punitive damages, by removing the profit from illegal activity, can help to deter such conduct. In order to effectively do this, punitive damages must be in excess of the profit created by the misconduct so that the defendant recognizes a loss. It can hardly be said that the $30 forfeiture paid by Steenberg significantly affected its profit for delivery of the mobile home. One hundred thousand dollars will.

Notes and Questions

1. **How robust is the right to exclude?** The Jacques said that the reason they were reluctant to give Steenberg Homes the right to cross their land was because they had lost land to adverse possession and wanted to guard their property rights carefully. Adverse possession is a doctrine that allows a longtime occupant of someone else's land to obtain title to it; the usual case is a border dispute in which both parties mistakenly place the boundary in a place different from that notated in the deeds to their parcels. *See* Chapter 5, §4.2. But permission is a defense to an adverse possession claim; the Jacques were in little danger of losing any of their property rights by this neighborly gesture. Should their reasons for refusing access matter? Suppose the request was to drive the mobile home over a road on the Jacques' land, causing no damage to it, and the cost to the neighbor of using a different route was $15,000 because a structure on the land had to be removed to bring the mobile home in. Should the Jacques have an obligation to allow access? Or does their status as owners give them the absolute power to exclude others from their land regardless of the reason and regardless of the neighbor's need?

2. **Damages and deterrence.** Was the punitive damage award excessive in *Jacque*? Or was it necessary to deter future trespasses like this?

3. **Incomplete defense of necessity.** **Necessity** is a defense to a trespass claim. If someone takes refuge on your property to escape a flood, as happened in New Orleans during Hurricane Katrina, there is no trespass. If a trespasser damages the property, the law imposes on the trespasser a duty to compensate the owner for the damage, but does not require the trespasser to pay for the mere privilege of access. *See Restatement (Second) of Torts* §197 (1965). Thus, in *Ploof v. Putnam,* 71 A. 188 (Vt. 1908), a couple and their children moored a small sailboat to the dock of the defendant during a sudden storm that threatened to overturn the boat and placed them in fear of their lives. But the defendant's servant unmoored the boat, which was driven on the shore by the storm, destroying it and casting the occupants into the lake. The court held that necessity justifies a trespass when needed to save lives or property and that defendant committed a tort (a wrongful act) against the plaintiffs by unmooring the boat. In *Vincent v. Lake Erie Transportation Co.,* 124 N.W. 221 (Minn. 1910), however, the court held that a steamship moored to a private wharf to avoid a severe storm was required to pay for the damage when the wind thrust the ship onto the wharf.

Suppose a car driver swerves onto someone's front lawn to avoid hitting a child in the street and damages a fence. Should the driver be required to pay for damage caused if she entered the land to save someone else's life?

§1.4 Hohfeldian Terminology

What do we mean when we talk about "property rights." In a highly influential article published in 1913, Professor Wesley Hohfeld identified eight basic kinds of legal rights: four primary legal entitlements (rights, privileges, powers, and immunities) and their opposites (no-rights, duties, disabilities, and liabilities). Wesley Hohfeld, *Some Fundamental Legal Conceptions as Applied in Judicial Reasoning,* 23 Yale L.J. 16 (1913). **Rights** are claims, enforceable by state power, that others act in a certain manner in relation to the rightholder. **Privileges** are permissions to act in a certain manner without being liable for damages to others and without others being able to summon state power to prevent those acts. **Powers** are state-enforced abilities to change legal entitlements held by oneself or others, and **immunities** are security from having one's own entitlements changed by others.

The four negations or opposites of the primary legal entitlements refer to the absence of such entitlements. One has **no-right** if one does not have the power to summon the aid of the state to alter or control the behavior of others. **Duties** refer to the absence of permission to act in a certain manner. **Disabilities** are the absence of power to alter legal entitlements, and **liabilities** refer to the absence of immunity from having one's own entitlements changed by others.

The eight terms are arranged in two tables of correlatives and opposites that structure the internal relationships among the different fundamental legal rights.

Jural Opposites

right	privilege	power	immunity
no-right	duty	disability	liability

Jural Correlatives

right	privilege	power	immunity
duty	no-right	liability	disability

Hohfeld's concept of **opposites** conveys the message that one must have one or the other but not both of the two opposites. For example, with regard to any class of acts, one must either have a right that others act in a certain manner or no right. Similarly, one must have either a privilege to do certain acts or a duty not to do them.

The concept of **correlatives** is harder to grasp. Legal rights, according to Hohfeld, are not merely advantages conferred by the state on individuals. Any time the state confers an advantage on some citizen, it necessarily changes the situation of others. Legal rights are not simply entitlements but jural relations among people. The concept of correlatives expresses legal relations from the point of view of two parties, though they can be scaled up to incorporate larger groups. "[I]f *X* has a right against *Y* that he shall stay off the former's land, the correlative (and equivalent) is that *Y* is under a duty toward *X* to stay off the place." If *A* has a duty toward *B*, then *B* has a right against *A*. The expressions are equivalent. Similarly, privileges are the correlatives of no-rights. "[W]hereas *X* has a *right* or *claim* that *Y*, the other man, should stay off the land, he himself has the *privilege* of entering on the land; or in equivalent words, *X* does not have a duty to stay off." If *A* has no duty toward *B*, *A* has a privilege to act and *B* has no right against *A*. Thus, if *A* has the privilege to do certain acts or to refrain from doing those acts, *B* is vulnerable to the effects of *A*'s actions. *B* cannot summon the aid of the state to prevent *A* from acting in such a manner no matter how *A*'s actions affect *B*'s interests.

The concepts identified and systematized by Wesley Hohfeld are useful in analyzing property rights (and other legal rights) for two reasons. First, they serve as a reminder that legal rights entail relations among persons. *A*'s right not to be harmed in a certain way implies duties on others not to harm *A* in that way. *A*'s privilege to act implies that others have no right to prevent *A* from acting and therefore may be vulnerable to negative effects of *A*'s actions, so long as *A* keeps her conduct within the scope of her privilege. In thinking about legal rights, it is important to identify (a) who has the entitlement, (b) against which specific individuals does the entitlement run, and (c) what specific acts are encompassed by the entitlement.

Second, Hohfeld's concepts help disentangle bundles of rights into their constituent parts. For example, the owner of a restaurant has the privilege of entering the property; non-owners have no right to prevent the owner from so doing. Does the owner's privilege to enter also mean that the owner has the right to exclude non-owners from the property? Yes and no. We have seen that the owner has the right to exclude patrons for certain reasons. But (as we will see in the next section) federal civil rights statutes provide that the owner has no right to exclude patrons on account of their race; on the contrary, such persons have a privilege to enter the restaurant and be served. The owner's privilege to enter does not necessarily mean that others have a duty not to enter. Both the owner and the patron have a privilege to enter the restaurant — the owner to run the place and the patron under an implicit invitation to obtain the service the owner is offering.

§2 DISCRIMINATION AND ACCESS TO "PLACES OF PUBLIC ACCOMMODATION"

§2.1 The Antidiscrimination Principle

The common law right to exclude (as embodied in the law of trespass) is subject to modification by statute. The most prominent examples are prohibitions on owners using certain categorizations (such as race) in granting or denying access to their properties. Which owners are subject to civil rights statutes and which groupings receive such statutory protection are matters of disagreement. Different jurisdictions have reached various conclusions on both questions, resulting in a complicated mixture of federal, state and local law.

A. Federal Antidiscrimination Law

Civil Rights Act of 1964, Title II

42 U.S.C. §§2000a, 2000a-6

§2000a. Prohibition Against Discrimination or Segregation in Places of Public Accommodation

(a) *Equal access.* All persons shall be entitled to the full and equal enjoyment of the goods, services, facilities, privileges, advantages, and accommodations of any place of public accommodation, as defined in this section, without discrimination or segregation on the ground of race, color, religion, or national origin.

(b) . . . Each of the following establishments which serves the public is a place of public accommodation within the meaning of this subchapter if its operations affect commerce, or if discrimination or segregation by it is supported by State action:

(1) any inn, hotel, motel, or other establishment which provides lodging to transient guests, other than an establishment located within a building which contains not more than five rooms for rent or hire and which is actually occupied by the proprietor of such establishment as his residence;

(2) any restaurant, cafeteria, lunchroom, lunch counter, soda fountain, or other facility principally engaged in selling food for consumption on the premises, including, but not limited to, any such facility located on the premises of any retail establishment; or any gasoline station;

(3) any motion picture house, theater, concert hall, sports arena, stadium or other place of exhibition or entertainment; and

(4) any establishment (A)(i) which is physically located within the premises of any establishment otherwise covered by this subsection, or (ii) within the premises of which is physically located any such covered establishment, and (B) which holds itself out as serving patrons of such covered establishments.

(e) *Private establishments.* The provisions of this subchapter shall not apply to a private club or other establishment not in fact open to the public, except to the extent that the facilities of such establishment are made available to the customers or patrons of an establishment within the scope of subsection (b) of this section.

§2000a-6. [A]ssertion of Rights Based on Other Federal or State Laws and Pursuit of Remedies for Enforcement of Such Rights . . .

(b) . . . [N]othing in this subchapter shall preclude any individual or any State or local agency from asserting any right based on any other Federal or State law not inconsistent with this subchapter, including any statute or ordinance requiring nondiscrimination in public establishments or accommodations, or from pursuing any remedy, civil or criminal, which may be available for the vindication or enforcement of such right.

Diane Nash (second from left), a leader of the movement to desegregate the lunch counters of Nashville's department stores, sits at an integrated lunch counter.[14]

Civil Rights Act of 1866

42 U.S.C. §§1981-1982

§1981. Equal Rights Under the Law

(a) *Statement of equal rights.* All persons within the jurisdiction of the United States shall have the same right in every State and Territory to make and enforce contracts, to sue, be parties, give evidence, and to the full and equal benefit of all laws and proceedings for the security of persons and property as is enjoyed by white citizens, and shall be subject to like punishment, pains, penalties, taxes, licenses, and exactions of every kind, and to no other.

(b) *"Make and enforce contracts" defined.* For purposes of this section, the term "make and enforce contracts" includes the making, performance, modification, and termination of contracts, and the enjoyment of all benefits, privileges, terms, and conditions of the contractual relationship.

(c) *Protection against impairment.* The rights protected by this section are protected against impairment by nongovernmental discrimination and impairment under color of State law.

§1982. Property Rights of Citizens

All citizens of the United States shall have the same right, in every State and Territory, as is enjoyed by white citizens thereof to inherit, purchase, lease, sell, hold, and convey real and personal property.

14. Reprinted by permission of the *Tennessean*.

Notes and Questions

1. **The *Civil Rights Act of 1964.*** The public accommodations provisions of Title II of the *Civil Rights Act of 1964*, 42 U.S.C. §§2000a to 2000a-6, directly addressed the problem of racial discrimination in motels, restaurants, lunch counters in department stores, gas stations, and theaters. It was intended to rectify some aspects of the enormous problem of racial segregation in the United States and was passed after a long period of struggle that included sit-ins, demonstrations, and litigation. Opponents of the law frequently criticized it as a violation of private property rights. *See* Eduardo M. Peñalver & Sonia K. Katyal, *Property Outlaws* ch.4 (2010). Passage of the act was followed by widespread resistance, including refusals by some public officials to enforce the law. Note that the statute regulates discrimination only on the basis of race, color, religion, and national origin. It does not prohibit discrimination on the basis of sex or sexual orientation. Nor does any other general federal statute regulating public accommodations.

Title II makes no provision for damages. An injured party may seek a court order requiring the defendant to stop discriminating in access to public accommodations covered by the act but may not seek damages. 42 U.S.C. §2000a-3(a). The plaintiff may be able to recover attorneys' fees from the defendant if the plaintiff prevails. §2000a-3(b).

2. **The *Civil Rights Act of 1866.*** Unlike the 1964 act, the *Civil Rights Act of 1866*, 42 U.S.C. §§1981 to 1982, regulates race discrimination only. Also, unlike the 1964 public accommodations law, damages are available for violations of the *Civil Rights Act of 1866.* Although §1981 was already in effect at the time the *Civil Rights Act of 1964* was passed, it had not yet been interpreted by the courts to regulate private conduct, such as the refusal by a restaurant owner to serve a patron. Rather, it was thought in 1964 that §1981 merely regulated *state* conduct, prohibiting (for example) state statutes that deprived black citizens of the capacity to enter binding contracts. In important opinions in 1968 and 1976, the Supreme Court held that the *Civil Rights Act of 1866* applied to private conduct as well as to legislation passed by state legislatures. *Jones v. Alfred Mayer Co.*, 392 U.S. 409 (1968) (holding that §1982 prohibits discrimination in the market for selling or leasing real property); *Runyon v. McCrary*, 427 U.S. 160 (1976) (holding that §1981 prohibits commercially operated, nonreligious schools from excluding qualified children solely on the basis of race). The Supreme Court reaffirmed the applicability of the *Civil Rights Act of 1866* to private conduct in *Patterson v. McLean Credit Union*, 491 U.S. 164 (1989). The *Civil Rights Act of 1991*, Pub. L. No. 102-166, tit. I, §101, 105 Stat. 1071 (1991), amended §1981 for the first time since 1870. This act approved the Supreme Court's interpretation of §1981 by providing that §1981 reaches private conduct, but the act also clarified §1981 by stating that it regulates the terms and conditions of contracts and not just the "right to make and enforce" contracts. As you will see in the notes that follow, courts continue to struggle with questions concerning the proper relationship between the *Civil Rights Act of 1866* and the *Civil Rights Act of 1964.*

3. What is a "place of public accommodation"? Is the list of covered establishments in the 1964 public accommodations law exhaustive or merely illustrative? *See Denny v. Elizabeth Arden Salons, Inc.*, 456 F.3d 427 (4th Cir. 2006) (holding that the list in §2000a is exhaustive). *Accord, Rhone v. Loomis*, 77 N.W. 31 (Minn. 1898) (holding that a state statute prohibiting discrimination in inns, taverns, restaurants, and places of "refreshment" did not prohibit a "saloon" from excluding an African American customer). *But see Sellers v. Philip's Barber Shop*, 217 A.2d 121 (N.J. 1966) (interpreting a state public accommodations statute providing that public accommodations "shall include" a long list of business establishments as covering barber shops even though they were not listed) *and In re Cox*, 474 P.2d 992 (Cal. 1970) (list of types of discrimination is illustrative).

Some courts have recently held that the *Civil Rights Act of 1866* regulates establishments that are not listed in the 1964 act, such as retail stores and service establishments, and that such stores may be liable for damages if they deny the right to contract under §1981 or the right to purchase property under §1982. *See Denny v. Elizabeth Arden Salons, Inc.*, 456 F.3d 427 (4th Cir. 2006) (§1981 would be violated if a salon refused service because it did not "do black people's hair"); *Perry v. Command Performance*, 913 F.2d 99 (3d Cir. 1990) (§1981 may have been violated when a salon refused to cut the hair of an African American woman); *Watson v. Fraternal Order of Eagles*, 915 F.2d 235, 240 (6th Cir. 1990) (noting that a "department store . . . is not directly covered by Title II but would be amenable to suit under §1981"); *Washington v. Duty Free Shoppers, Ltd.*, 710 F. Supp. 1288 (N.D. Cal. 1988) (§1981 prohibits retail store from refusing to serve customers because of race).

The Supreme Court has never addressed the question of whether the *Civil Rights Act of 1866* regulates the conduct of public accommodations such as restaurants, innkeepers, or retail stores. Although the refusal to serve a patron because of that person's race arguably comes within the language of both §1981 and §1982, it is important to know that a public accommodations law, much like the 1964 act, was passed in 1875. After doubts were expressed about the constitutionality of the *Civil Rights Act of 1866*, it was re-passed in 1870 after passage of the fourteenth amendment in 1868 with its prohibition against state deprivations of "equal protection of the laws." U.S. Const. art. XIV. Five years later, Congress passed the *Public Accommodations Act of 1875*, 18 Stat. 335, ch. 114, clearly regulating private actors. The Supreme Court struck down the *Public Accommodations Act* as unconstitutional in *The Civil Rights Cases*, 109 U.S. 3 (1883), on the ground that the fourteenth amendment authorized Congress to regulate state action but not private action by owners of private property, such as inns and restaurants. If the *Civil Rights Act of 1866* regulates the conduct of public accommodations, wouldn't this have made the 1875 statute superfluous and unnecessary? If §1981 or §1982 regulates public accommodations, why did Congress pass the 1875 statute?

Because of the holding of *The Civil Rights Cases* that the fourteenth amendment authorizes regulation of state action but not private action, Congress passed the *Civil Rights Act of 1964* pursuant to the commerce clause, which authorizes Congress to regulate "interstate commerce." *See Heart of Atlanta Motel, Inc. v. United States*, 379

U.S. 241 (1964); *Katzenbach v. McClung*, 379 U.S. 294 (1964) (both upholding the act as a valid exercise of Congress's power to regulate interstate commerce). Remember that the *Civil Rights Act of 1866* was not interpreted to apply to private conduct until 1968. But *what* private conduct is regulated by §§1981 and 1982? Can you think of a reason §§1981 and 1982 should be interpreted to regulate public accommodations when Congress passed a more specific statute regulating them in 1964—a statute that clearly omits any provision for damages?

4. Racially discriminatory surveillance. The courts appear to agree that the "right to make contracts" under §1981 includes the right to enter a store or other service provider. *Causey v. Sewell Cadillac-Chevrolet, Inc.*, 394 F.3d 285 (5th Cir. 2004); *Christian v. Wal-Mart Stores, Inc.*, 252 F.3d 862 (6th Cir. 2001); *Ackaa v. Tommy Hilfiger*, 1998 WL 136522 (E.D. Pa. 1998). Can you think of a way to interpret the language or purpose of §1981 in a way that would not view it as creating an obligation to allow individuals to enter retail stores to purchase goods or services? Assuming §1981 does require stores to allow individuals to enter without regard to race, does §1981 prohibit stores from discriminatorily following African American, Latino, or American Indian patrons around the store, searching them, and subjecting them to insults?

A minority of courts hold that such conduct violates the right to contract under §1981 and/or the right to purchase personal property under §1982. *Chapman v. Higbee*, 319 F.3d 825 (6th Cir. 2003) (equal benefits clause in §1981 gives right to equal treatment in seeking contract); *Phillip v. University of Rochester*, 316 F.3d 291 (2d Cir. 2003) (equal benefits clause of §1981 applies to private university whose security guards detained African American students but not their white friends in library lobby, calling police who arrested them and kept them detained overnight); *McCaleb v. Pizza Hut of America, Inc.*, 28 F. Supp. 2d 1043 (N.D. Ill. 1998) (family denied "full benefits" of the contract when denied utensils and harassed and threatened while at restaurant); *Nwakpuda v. Falley's, Inc.*, 14 F. Supp. 2d 1213 (D. Kan. 1998) (§1981 claim for store patron who was wrongfully detained because he was thought to be individual who had previously robbed the store); *Turner v. Wong*, 832 A.2d 340 (N.J. Super. Ct. App. Div. 2003).

However, most courts have interpreted the "right to make contracts" extremely narrowly, holding that this right is denied *only* when a patron is "actually prevented, and not merely deterred, from making a purchase or receiving service after attempting to do so." *Ackerman v. Food-4-Less*, 1998 WL 316084, at *2 (E.D. Pa. 1988). *Accord*, *Hampton v. Dillard Department Stores, Inc.*, 247 F.3d 1091 (10th Cir. 2001). These courts have denied relief when a patron was treated disrespectfully or refused assistance, *Arguello v. Conoco, Inc.*, 330 F.3d 355 (5th Cir. 2003) (no §1981 claim when clerk shouted obscenities and made racially derogatory remarks at Latino customer after she completed her purchase); *Wesley v. Don Stein Buick, Inc.*, 42 F. Supp. 2d 1192 (D. Kan. 1999); subjected to discriminatory surveillance, searches, or detention, *Gregory v. Dillard's Inc.*, 565 F.3d 464 (8th Cir. 2009) (no §1981 violation when store employees follow African Americans around the store and stand guard outside changing rooms when such customers try on clothes); *Morris v. Office Max, Inc.*, 89 F.3d 411 (7th Cir. 1996); removed from a store for discriminatory reasons after making a purchase, *Flowers v. TJX Cos.*, 1994 WL 382515 (N.D.N.Y. 1994); or put under surveillance and accused of shoplifting after purchasing items and leaving the store, *Garrett v. Tandy Corp.*, 295 F.3d 94 (1st Cir. 2002). Are these decisions consistent with the intent of the *Civil Rights Act of 1991*? Which interpretation of §1981 is correct?

5. Private clubs. What is the difference between a public accommodation and a private club? Courts generally look to see whether the organization is *selective* in its membership and has *limits* on the number of persons who can join. If the selection criteria track a statutory category, it is unlikely the group will be held to be a private club. A group that is limited to men, but has no other selection criteria and is unlimited in size, is likely to be held to be a public accommodation that is violating the law rather than a selective private club. Does it matter whether the organization is engaged in the sale of goods or services?

In *Watson v. Fraternal Order of Eagles*, 915 F.2d 235 (6th Cir. 1990), a private club was held to have violated §1981 when it refused to serve drinks to African American guests at a party held at the club. Because defendant was clearly a private club under 42 U.S.C. §2000a(e), its actions were not covered by the 1964 act. Nonetheless, Judge Merritt held that, although the defendant was immune from liability under that act, the plaintiff could bring an independent claim for relief under §1981. He noted that later, more specific statutes generally limit the interpretation of earlier, more general ones. Nonetheless, the earlier, broader statute continues in force if the legislature that passed the later act intended the general act to retain independent force.

However, in *Cornelius v. Benevolent Protective Order of the Elks*, 382 F. Supp. 1182 (D. Conn. 1974), Judge Blumenfeld held that an irrevocable conflict between a statute that authorizes conduct and one that prohibits it must be adjudicated by applying the later act. Thus §1981 could not be applied to a private club. Judge Blumenfeld argued that "the provisions of one statute which specifically focus on a particular problem will always, in the absence of express contrary legislative intent, be held to prevail over provisions of a different statute more general in its coverage." *Id.* at 1201. Moreover, when Congress passed the 1964 act, it believed it was enacting the first federal legislation prohibiting private discrimination in public accommodations. "Prior to *Jones v. Mayer*, 392 U.S. 409 (1968), sections 1981 and 1982 were thought to apply only to 'state action.' . . . Thus, the absence of express language in the 1964 Act limiting the 1866 Act is hardly evidence of an intention not to have that effect." *Id. Accord, Durham v. Red Lake Fishing & Hunting Club, Inc.*, 666 F. Supp. 954 (W.D. Tex. 1987). Should Congress's intent in 1964 with respect to the reach of Title II have decisive bearing on the proper interpretation of the 1866 law? Can you think of an argument that it should? That it should not?

6. Common carriers. Common carriers engaged in interstate commerce are regulated by the *Interstate Commerce Act* and are prohibited from all forms of unreasonable discrimination, not just discrimination based on race, religion, and national origin. 49 U.S.C. §§10741(b), 11101(a).

7. Unequal treatment and exclusion through "vibes." Civil rights laws require more than bare admission. They protect the rights of protected groups to equal treatment once admitted. A recent opinion of the Massachusetts Commission Against Discrimination, for example, found that a restaurant owner violated Massachusetts antidiscrimination law by requiring a black customer (who turned out to be an undercover police officer) to pay *before* receiving his food while not demanding payment in advance from the officer's white colleagues (who were also undercover). *See Massachusetts Commission Against Discrimination v. Capitol Coffee House,* No. 05-BPA-03196, Apr. 26, 2013.

Lior Strahilevitz has observed that owners often use indirect strategies to deter certain classes of people from even trying to enter an establishment. He describes owners who create "exclusionary vibes" (making people feel unwelcome by creating an environment unlikely to appeal to them) and "exclusionary amenities" (making people less likely to seek entry by bundling a product—say, housing in a particular community—with a product that members of a particular racial group are unlikely to want to consume—*e.g.*, mandatory membership in a community golf club). *See* Lior Jacob Strahilevitz, *Information Asymmetries and the Rights to Exclude,* 104 Mich. L. Rev. 1835, 1843 (2006); Lior Jacob Strahilevitz, *Exclusionary Amenities in Residential Communities,* 92 Va. L. Rev. 437 (2006). One bar in New York City, for example, has been investigated by the New York Human Rights Commission for enforcing a "no baggy jeans, no bling" dress code. *See* Douglas Quenqua, *Dress Codes in New York Clubs: Will This Get Me In?,* in N.Y. Times, July 27, 2011, at E-1. Would it violate the federal public accommodations law, 42 U.S.C. §2000a, to call a sports arena Redskins Stadium? *See* Note, *A Public Accommodations Challenge to the Use of Indian Team Names and Mascots in Professional Sports,* 112 Harv. L. Rev. 904 (1999) (arguing that it would). If it would violate the statute, does the first amendment's guarantee of free speech override the statute? Should the court hold that a statute that prohibits an owner from using the name *Redskins* is unconstitutional? *Compare Urban League of Rhode Island v. Sambo's of Rhode Island, Inc.,* File Nos. 79 PRA 074-06/06, 79 ERA 073-06/06, EEOC No. 011790461 (R.I. Commn. for Human Rights 1981) (restaurant violated state public accommodations law by using racially offensive name), *with Sambo's Restaurants, Inc. v. City of Ann Arbor,* 663 F.2d 686 (6th Cir. 1981) (holding that the first amendment's free speech clause protected the right to use the name *Sambo's*). What about a Ku Klux Klan themed restaurant with a white hooded mannequin inside and signs in front that make frequent use of racial epithets? *See* World Famous Georgia Peach Original Klan Bar, *http://www.gapeachbar.com/signs.html* (last visited Mar. 13, 2013).

Problems

1. Buzzers. Some stores in New York City lock their front doors and allow customers in after they have pressed a buzzer. The ostensible goal is to protect the store from armed robbery and other forms of theft and assault. Store owners and managers use the buzzer system to exclude selected members of the public from access to their stores. If a store installs a lock-and-buzzer system and allows entry only to patrons who the management or employees consider "safe," does the store come within the definition of a "place of public accommodation" under §2000a(b), or is it a "private establishment not in fact open to the public" under §2000a(e)? Are retail stores "places of public accommodation" as defined in §2000a(b)? If retail stores are generally covered by §2000a(b), do they "serve the public" if they install a buzzer and serve selected customers who show up on their doorsteps, or are they "not in fact open to the public" and thus exempt from the statute under §2000a(e)?

2. **National origin discrimination.** A night club in Boston that serves liquor requires all patrons to show a driver's license to prove they are over 21. The club refuses to allow a law student in when he shows his Puerto Rican driver's license on the (incorrect) ground that it is not a U.S. license. Has the club engaged in national origin discrimination in violation of the *Civil Rights Act of 1964*? What about a restaurant that refuses to serve patrons who cannot order in English?

B. State and Local Laws

New York Executive Law, Art. 15

§292 Definitions

9. The term "place of public accommodation, resort or amusement" shall include, except as hereinafter specified, all places included in the meaning of such terms as: inns, taverns, road houses, hotels, motels, whether conducted for the entertainment of transient guests or for the accommodation of those seeking health, recreation or rest, or restaurants, or eating houses, or any place where food is sold for consumption on the premises; buffets, saloons, barrooms, or any store, park or enclosure where spirituous or malt liquors are sold; ice cream parlors, confectionaries, soda fountains, and all stores where ice cream, ice and fruit preparations or their derivatives, or where beverages of any kind are retailed for consumption on the premises; wholesale and retail stores and establishments dealing with goods or services of any kind, dispensaries, clinics, hospitals, bath-houses, swimming pools, laundries and all other cleaning establishments, barber shops, beauty parlors, theatres, motion picture houses, airdromes, roof gardens, music halls, race courses, skating rinks, amusement and recreation parks, trailer camps, resort camps, fairs, bowling alleys, golf courses, gymnasiums, shooting galleries, billiard and pool parlors; garages, all public conveyances operated on land or water or in the air, as well as the stations and terminals thereof; travel or tour advisory services, agencies or bureaus; public halls and public elevators of buildings and structures occupied by two or more tenants, or by the owner and one or more tenants. Such term shall not include . . . any institution, club or place of accommodation which proves that it is in its nature distinctly private. In no event shall an institution, club or place of accommodation be considered in its nature distinctly private if it has more than one hundred members, provides regular meal service and regularly receives payment for dues, fees, use of space, facilities, services, meals or

beverages directly or indirectly from or on behalf of a nonmember for the furtherance of trade or business.

§296 Unlawful Discriminatory Practices

2. (a) It shall be an unlawful discriminatory practice for any person, being the owner, lessee, proprietor, manager, superintendent, agent or employee of any place of public accommodation, resort or amusement, because of the race, creed, color, national origin, sexual orientation, military status, sex, or disability or marital status of any person, directly or indirectly, to refuse, withhold from or deny to such person any of the accommodations, advantages, facilities or privileges thereof, including the extension of credit, or, directly or indirectly, to publish, circulate, issue, display, post or mail any written or printed communication, notice or advertisement, to the effect that any of the accommodations, advantages, facilities and privileges of any such place shall be refused, withheld from or denied to any person on account of race, creed, color, national origin, sexual orientation, military status, sex, or disability or marital status, or that the patronage or custom thereat of any person of or purporting to be of any particular race, creed, color, national origin, sexual orientation, military status, sex or marital status, or having a disability is unwelcome, objectionable or not acceptable, desired or solicited.

Notes and Questions

1. **Relation between federal and state public accommodations laws.** The federal public accommodations law was passed in 1964 as Title II of the *Civil Rights Act*. The statute applies across the country and, under the supremacy clause of the Constitution, prevails over any contrary state law.[15] Most states have also adopted public accommodations laws that apply within their borders. State statutes that are *inconsistent* with federal statutes are "preempted" by federal law and are unenforceable; state statutes not inconsistent with federal law are enforceable. State statutes and constitutional provisions may therefore go *further* than federal law in protecting individual rights. Is Article 15 of the New York Executive Law more protective than Title II?

For example, many state and local statutes prohibit discrimination in places of public accommodation on account of sex and sexual orientation; the federal statute, in contrast, does not prohibit discrimination in access to public places on either ground. State statutes may also be worded differently from the federal statute; they may therefore apply to more kinds of property or to more types of discriminatory acts than does federal law. Even when the wording in state and federal statutes is identical, the state statute may be interpreted by a state court to grant *more* protection against discrimination than does federal law. Because statutory interpretation involves interpreting

---

15. Article VI of the Constitution provides that the "Constitution, and the Laws of the United States which shall be made in Pursuance thereof . . . shall be the supreme Law of the Land; and the Judges in every State shall be bound thereby, any Thing in the Constitution or Laws of any State to the Contrary notwithstanding."

the intent of the legislature, a state court could conclude from the context surrounding passage of the state law that the legislature intended to grant greater protection than did Congress when it passed the federal statute.

2. *Dale v. Boy Scouts of America.* Courts have reached different results in considering whether state public accommodations statutes apply to membership organizations like the Boy Scouts or Jaycees that do not have a fixed place of operations. *Compare Dale v. Boy Scouts of America*, 734 A.2d 1196 (N.J. 1999), *rev'd on other grounds sub nom. Boy Scouts of America v. Dale*, 530 U.S. 640 (2000); *Quinnipiac Council, Boy Scouts of America, Inc. v. Commission on Human Rights & Opportunities*, 528 A.2d 352 (Conn. 1987) (both holding that the Boy Scouts is a public accommodation) *and United States Jaycees v. McClure*, 305 N.W.2d 764 (Minn. 1981), *aff'd sub nom. Roberts v. United States Jaycees*, 468 U.S. 609 (1984) (Jaycees held to be a "public accommodation") *with United States Jaycees v. Massachusetts Commission Against Discrimination*, 463 N.E.2d 1151 (Mass. 1984) (holding Jaycees not to be a place of public accommodation).

In *Dale v. Boy Scouts of America*, the New Jersey Supreme Court considered whether the Boy Scouts of America had violated New Jersey's law by excluding James Dale solely because of his sexuality. Dale was an "exemplary scout," earning over 25 merit badges, being honored as an Eagle Scout, then serving as an Assistant Scoutmaster. When he went away to college, he first acknowledged to himself and his friends and family that he was gay. After a local paper interviewed him as the "co-president of the Rutgers University Lesbian/Gay Alliance," Dale received a letter from the Boy Scouts Executive Office revoking his membership and asking him to "sever any relations [he] may have with the Boy Scouts of America." He was later told that the Boy Scouts did not "admit avowed homosexuals to membership."

Dale challenged the exclusion under New Jersey's *Law Against Discrimination* (LAD), which provides that "all persons shall have the opportunity . . . to obtain all the accommodations, advantages, facilities, and privileges of any place of public accommodation, . . . without discrimination because of . . . affectional or sexual orientation." N.J. Stat. §10:5-4. The New Jersey Supreme Court found that "place" was a "term of convenience, not of limitation." 734 A.2d at 1209. The court reasoned that any ambiguities should be decided in favor of broad application because the statute itself provided that it should be "liberally construed." *Id.* at 1208. Considering factors such as the Boy Scouts' broad solicitations to the public, its close relationships with federal government, schools, and other public accommodations, as well as its similarity to other organizations recognized as public accommodations, the court found that the organization was covered under the statute. The court also rejected the organization's claim that it was excluded as a "bona fide club, or place of accommodation, which is in its nature distinctly private," N.J. Stat. §10:5-5l, noting that it had over four million boys and one million adults as members at the time. The court then found that the Boys Scouts of America had denied Dale the privilege and advantage of being an Assistant Scoutmaster because of his sexuality, and had thereby violated the state law.

The U.S. Supreme Court reversed *Dale* in a 5-4 decision on the ground that prohibiting the Boy Scouts from excluding gay Scouts violated the first amendment's protections for freedom of association. *Boy Scouts of America v. Dale,* 530 U.S. 640 (2000). Writing for the Court, Chief Justice Rehnquist noted that the Boy Scouts "engaged in instilling its system of values in young people" and "that homosexual conduct is inconsistent with the values it seeks to instill." *Id.* at 643. "The forced inclusion of an unwanted person in a group infringes the group's freedom of expressive association if the presence of that person affects in a significant way the group's ability to advocate public or private viewpoints." *Id.* at 648. Although the Supreme Court of New Jersey had concluded that "New Jersey has a compelling interest in eliminating 'the destructive consequences of discrimination from our society,'" the Supreme Court found that the "state interests embodied in New Jersey's public accommodations law do not justify such a severe intrusion on the Boy Scouts' rights to freedom of expressive association." *Id.* at 647, 659.

In dissent, Justice Stevens questioned whether instilling the wrongfulness of homosexuality was really part of the Scouts' expressive purpose. He noted that nothing in the Scout Oath or Law "says the slightest thing about homosexuality" and Scoutmasters are directed "not [to] undertake to instruct Scouts, in any formalized manner, in the subject of sex and family life. The reasons are that it is not construed to be Scouting's proper area, and that you are probably not well qualified to do this." *Id.* at 669. Although the Boy Scouts issued policy statements on the question, nothing on homosexuality was placed in the Boy Scout or Scoutmaster Handbook. "[N]o lessons were imparted to Scouts; no change was made to BSA's policy on limiting discussion of sexual matters; and no effort was made to restrict acceptable religious affiliations to those that condemn homosexuality. In short, there is no evidence that this view was part of any collective effort to foster beliefs about homosexuality." *Id.* at 675. He criticized the majority for giving deference to the Boy Scouts' assertions regarding the nature of its expression. "To prevail in asserting a right of expressive association as a defense to a charge of violating an antidiscrimination law, the organization must at least show it has adopted and advocated an unequivocal position inconsistent with a position advocated or epitomized by the person whom the organization seeks to exclude." *Id.* at 687.

3. Evaluating the revised Boy Scouts of America policy under Article 15 of the New York Executive Law. In 2013, the Boy Scouts of America adopted a new policy admitting gay scouts but continuing to bar gay adults from staff and leadership positions. In the resolution adopting its new policy, the Boy Scouts made the following statement: "[T]he Boy Scouts of America does not have an agenda on the matter of sexual orientation, and resolving this complex issue is not the role of the organization, nor may any member use Scouting to promote or advance any social or political position or agenda." An Eagle Scout in New York turns 18 but is prohibited from becoming an Assistant Scoutmaster under the policy; he challenges it under Article 15 of the New York Executive Law, above. Should the New York courts find that the Boy Scouts are covered by the law? Would enforcing the New York law against the group violate its first amendment rights as articulated by the Supreme Court in *Dale*?

4. Gender discrimination. A health club for women refuses to admit a man for membership in New York City. Has it violated Article 15 of the New York Executive Law? *Compare LivingWell (North) Inc. v. Pennsylvania Human Relations Commission,* 606 A.2d 1287 (Pa. Commw. Ct. 1992) (suggesting no), *with Foster v. Back Bay Spas, Inc.,* 1997 WL 634354 (Mass. Super. Ct. 1997) (suggesting yes).

Problem

A 300-person country club has a "balanced" membership policy with no criteria for admission except that the club seeks to maintain an even balance of Christians and non-Christians (primarily Jews, but also a few Muslims). A club member must sponsor a prospective member. Anyone wanting to become a member of the club must find one person in the club willing to invite him or her to join. Applications are marked according to whether the applicant is a Jew, a Christian, a Muslim, or the member of another faith. Nonmembers are allowed to dine at the club only if accompanied by members. Members pay for the drinks and meals consumed by themselves or their guests on a quarterly basis. A Jewish man seeks to become a member but cannot because there is a two-year waiting list for Jews seeking membership. The only spots currently open are earmarked for Christians. Does he have a legal claim under Title II? Under Article 15 of the New York Executive Law? *See Mill River Club, Inc. v. New York State Division of Human Rights,* 59 A.D.3d 549 (2d Dept. 2009) (finding a claim under New York law).

§2.2 Discrimination Against Persons with Disabilities

The *Americans with Disabilities Act* (ADA), passed in 1990, and substantially amended in 2008, is one of the most important pieces of civil rights legislation approved by Congress since the *Civil Rights Act of 1964*. It differs in important respects from the prior civil rights laws. First, the broad diversity of disabilities it covers necessarily adds an enormous amount of complexity to the statute's operation. Second, while the statute superficially resembles those earlier statutes by prohibiting discrimination on the basis of disability in both employment and public accommodations, it defines discrimination to include the failure to take affirmative steps to facilitate access by the disabled. *See* 28 C.F.R. §§36.101 to 36.608; 42 U.S.C. §12183, 28 C.F.R. §§36.301 to 36.406.[16] What is required to comply with this mandate varies with the circumstances, such as whether the facility was in existence at the time the statute went into effect or was built after its enactment. The Justice Department has promulgated regulations implementing the statute and clarifying the scope of the obligations imposed on businesses, including modification of physical premises, policies, and practices. *See* 28 C.F.R. §§36.301-36.311.

---

16. In 1988, two years before passage of the ADA, Congress amended *Fair Housing Act of 1968,* 42 U.S.C. §§3601-3631, to prohibit discrimination on the basis of disability in the sale or rental of dwellings. *See* Chapter 13.

Americans with Disabilities Act of 1990, Title III — Public Accommodations and Services Operated by Private Entities

42 U.S.C. §§12102, 12181-12183, 12187, 12201, 12210, 12211

§12102. Definition of Disability

As used in this chapter:

(1) *Disability.* — The term "disability" means, with respect to an individual —

(A) a physical or mental impairment that substantially limits one or more major life activities of such individual;

(B) a record of such an impairment; or

(C) being regarded as having such an impairment (as described in paragraph (3)).

(2) *Major life activities.* —

(A) *In general.* — For purposes of paragraph (1), major life activities include, but are not limited to, caring for oneself, performing manual tasks, seeing, hearing, eating, sleeping, walking, standing, lifting, bending, speaking, breathing, learning, reading, concentrating, thinking, communicating, and working.

(B) *Major bodily functions.* — For purposes of paragraph (1), a major life activity also includes the operation of a major bodily function, including but not limited to, functions of the immune system, normal cell growth, digestive, bowel, bladder, neurological, brain, respiratory, circulatory, endocrine, and reproductive functions.

(3) *Regarded as having such impairment.* — For purposes of paragraph (1)(C):

(A) An individual meets the requirement of "being regarded as having such an impairment" if the individual establishes that he or she has been subjected to an action prohibited under this Act because of an actual or perceived physical or mental impairment whether or not the impairment limits or is perceived to limit a major life activity.

(B) Paragraph (1)(C) shall not apply to impairments that are transitory and minor. A transitory impairment is an impairment with an actual or expected duration of 6 months or less.

§12181. Definitions

(7) *Public accommodation.* — The following private entities are considered public accommodations for purposes of this title, if the operations of such entities affect commerce —

(A) an inn, hotel, motel, or other place of lodging, except for an establishment located within a building that contains not more than five rooms for rent or hire and that is actually occupied by the proprietor of such establishment as the residence of such proprietor;

(B) a restaurant, bar, or other establishment serving food or drink;

(C) a motion picture house, theater, concert hall, stadium, or other place of exhibition or entertainment;

(D) an auditorium, convention center, lecture hall, or other place of public gathering;

(E) a bakery, grocery store, clothing store, hardware store, shopping center, or other sales or rental establishment;

(F) a laundromat, dry-cleaner, bank, barber shop, beauty shop, travel service, shoe repair service, funeral parlor, gas station, office of an accountant or lawyer, pharmacy, insurance office, professional office of a health care provider, hospital or other service establishment;

(G) a terminal, depot, or other station used for specified public transportation;

(H) a museum, library, gallery, or other place of public display or collection;

(I) a park, zoo, amusement park, or other place of recreation;

(J) a nursery, elementary, secondary, undergraduate, or postgraduate private school, or other place of education;

(K) a day care center, senior citizen center, homeless shelter, food bank, adoption agency, or other social service center establishment; and

(L) a gymnasium, health spa, bowling alley, golf course, or other place of exercise or recreation.

(9) *Readily achievable.* — The term "readily achievable" means easily accomplishable and able to be carried out without much difficulty or expense. In determining whether an action is readily achievable, factors to be considered include —

(A) the nature and cost of the action needed under this chapter;

(B) the overall financial resources of the facility or facilities involved in the action; the number of persons employed at such facility; the effect on expenses and resources, or the impact otherwise of such action upon the operation of the facility;

(C) the overall financial resources of the covered entity; the overall size of the business of a covered entity with respect to the number of its employees; the number, type, and location of its facilities; and

(D) the type of operation or operations of the covered entity, including the composition, structure, and functions of the workforce of such entity; the geographic separateness, administrative or fiscal relationship of the facility or facilities in question to the covered entity.

§12182. Prohibition of Discrimination by Public Accommodations

(a) *General rule.* — No individual shall be discriminated against on the basis of disability in the full and equal enjoyment of the goods, services, facilities, privileges, advantages, or accommodations of any place of public accommodation by any person who owns, leases (or leases to), or operates a place of public accommodation.

(b) *Construction*

(1) *General prohibition*

(A) *Activities*

(i) *Denial of participation.* It shall be discriminatory to subject an individual or class of individuals on the basis of a disability or disabilities of such individual or class, directly, or through contractual, licensing, or other arrangements, to a denial of the opportunity of the individual or class to participate in or benefit from the goods, services, facilities, privileges, advantages, or accommodations of an entity.

(ii) *Participation in unequal benefit.* It shall be discriminatory to afford an individual or class of individuals, on the basis of a disability or disabilities of such individual or class, directly, or through contractual, licensing, or other arrangements with the opportunity to participate in or benefit from a good, service, facility, privilege, advantage, or accommodation that is not equal to that afforded to other individuals.

(iii) *Separate benefit.* It shall be discriminatory to provide an individual or class of individuals, on the basis of a disability or disabilities of such individual or class, directly, or through contractual, licensing, or other arrangements with a good, service, facility, privilege, advantage, or accommodation that is different or separate from that provided to other individuals, unless such action is necessary to provide the individual or class of individuals with a good, service, facility, privilege, advantage, or accommodation, or other opportunity that is as effective as that provided to others.

(iv) *Individual or class of individuals.* For purposes of clauses (i) through (iii) of this subparagraph, the term "individual or class of individuals" refers to the clients or customers of the covered public accommodation that enters into the contractual, licensing or other arrangement.

(B) *Integrated settings.* Goods, services, facilities, privileges, advantages, and accommodations shall be afforded to an individual with a disability in the most integrated setting appropriate to the needs of the individual.

(C) *Opportunity to participate.* Notwithstanding the existence of separate or different programs or activities provided in accordance with this section, an individual with a disability shall not be denied the opportunity to participate in such programs or activities that are not separate or different.

(D) *Administrative methods.* An individual or entity shall not, directly or through contractual or other arrangements, utilize standards or criteria or methods of administration—

(i) that have the effect of discriminating on the basis of disability; or

(ii) that perpetuate the discrimination of others who are subject to common administrative control.

(E) *Association.* It shall be discriminatory to exclude or otherwise deny equal goods, services, facilities, privileges, advantages, accommodations, or other opportunities to an individual or entity because of the known disability of an individual with whom the individual or entity is known to have a relationship or association.

(2) *Specific prohibitions*

(A) *Discrimination.*—For purposes of subsection (a) of this section, discrimination includes—

(i) the imposition or application of eligibility criteria that screen out or tend to screen out an individual with a disability or any class of individuals with disabilities from fully and equally enjoying any goods, services, facilities, privileges, advantages, or accommodations, unless such criteria can be shown to be necessary for the provision of the goods, services, facilities, privileges, advantages, or accommodations being offered;

(ii) a failure to make reasonable modifications in policies, practices, or procedures, when such modifications are necessary to afford such goods, services, facilities, privileges, advantages, or accommodations to individuals with disabilities, unless the entity can demonstrate that making such modifications would fundamentally alter the nature of such goods, services, facilities, privileges, advantages, or accommodations;

(iii) a failure to take such steps as may be necessary to ensure that no individual with a disability is excluded, denied services, segregated or otherwise treated differently than other individuals because of the absence of auxiliary aids and services, unless the entity can demonstrate that taking such steps would fundamentally alter the nature of the good, service, facility, privilege, advantage, or accommodation being offered or would result in an undue burden;

(iv) a failure to remove architectural barriers, and communication barriers that are structural in nature, in existing facilities, and transportation barriers in existing vehicles and rail passenger cars used by an establishment for transporting individuals (not including barriers that can only be removed through the retrofitting of vehicles or rail passenger cars by the installation of a hydraulic or other lift), where such removal is readily achievable; and

(v) where an entity can demonstrate that the removal of a barrier under clause (iv) is not readily achievable, a failure to make such goods, services, facilities, privileges, advantages, or accommodations available through alternative methods if such methods are readily achievable.

(3) *Specific construction*

Nothing in this subchapter shall require an entity to permit an individual to participate in or benefit from the goods, services, facilities, privileges, advantages and accommodations of such entity where such individual poses a direct threat to the health or safety of others. The term "direct threat" means a significant risk to the health or safety of others that cannot be eliminated by a modification of policies, practices, or procedures or by the provision of auxiliary aids or services.

§12183. New Construction and Alterations in Public Accommodations and Commercial Facilities

(a) *Application of term.* Except as provided in subsection (b) of this section, as applied to public accommodations and commercial facilities, discrimination for purposes of section 12182(a) of this title includes —

(1) a failure to design and construct facilities for first occupancy later than 30 months after July 26, 1990, that are readily accessible to and usable by individuals with disabilities, except where an entity can demonstrate that it is structurally impracticable to meet the requirements of such subsection in accordance with standards set forth or incorporated by reference in regulations issued under this subchapter; and

(2) with respect to a facility or part thereof that is altered by, on behalf of, or for the use of an establishment in a manner that affects or could affect the usability of the facility or part thereof, a failure to make alterations in such a manner that, to the maximum extent feasible, the altered portions of the facility are readily accessible to and usable by individuals with disabilities, including individuals who use wheelchairs. Where the entity is undertaking an alteration that affects or could affect usability of or access to an area of the facility containing a primary function, the entity shall also make the alterations in such a manner that, to the maximum extent feasible, the path of travel to the altered area and the bathrooms, telephones, and drinking fountains serving the altered area, are readily accessible to and usable by individuals with disabilities where such alterations to the path of travel or the bathrooms, telephones, and drinking fountains serving the altered area are not disproportionate to the overall alterations in terms of cost and scope (as determined under criteria established by the Attorney General).

§12187. Exemptions for Private Clubs and Religious Organizations

The provisions of this subchapter shall not apply to private clubs or establishments exempted from coverage under title II of the *Civil Rights Act of 1964* (42 U.S.C. 2000-a(e)) [42 U.S.C.A. §2000a *et seq.*] or to religious organizations or entities controlled by religious organizations, including places of worship.

§12201. Construction

(b) *Relationship to other laws.* Nothing in this chapter shall be construed to preclude the prohibition of, or the imposition of restrictions on, smoking [in] . . . places of public accommodation covered by . . . this chapter.

§12210. Illegal Use of Drugs

(a) *In general.* For purposes of this chapter, the term "individual with a disability" does not include an individual who is currently engaging in the illegal use of drugs, when the covered entity acts on the basis of such use.

(b) *Rules of construction.* Nothing in subsection (a) of this section shall be construed to exclude as an individual with a disability an individual who . . .

(3) is erroneously regarded as engaging in such use, but is not engaging in such use.

§12211. Definitions

(a) *Homosexuality and bisexuality.*—For purposes of the definition of "disability" in section 3(2) [§12102(2)], homosexuality and bisexuality are not impairments and as such are not disabilities under this chapter.

Problems

1. Attendants. A man whose legs and arms are substantially paralyzed but who has some movement in his hands and lower arms, and in his neck and part of his upper torso, is admitted to law school. His wheelchair is motor-operated, and he can use his hands to move himself around in the wheelchair. He applies for and obtains a room in the law school dormitory that he can share with his trained full-time attendant. He needs to be constantly attended because he is on a respirator to enable him to breathe and may require immediate attention if something goes wrong with the breathing mechanism. The law school notifies him that he will have to pay rent (the dormitory fee) both for himself and his attendant, effectively doubling the rent he must pay, because the attendant takes a space that would otherwise go to another paying law student. Has the law school violated the public accommodations provisions of the ADA?

2. Building renovations. A law school library is being renovated. Right now the only access to the library is through an underground tunnel through the elevator, with the entrance to the library on the fourth floor. The library stacks are not accessible by wheelchair. The $20 million renovation project will move the library entrance to the first floor and create two wheelchair-accessible entrances on the south side of the building. Although these south entrances visually appear to be the "back doors" to the library, in fact 90 percent of the students enter the library through these south entrances. The north entrance has a grand staircase and is architecturally the main entrance to the building from a design standpoint, although only about 10 percent of the users enter the building this way. Installing a lift or a ramp at this northern entrance would cost $80,000 to $150,000. Is the school required by §12183 to make the north entrance accessible by wheelchair?

3. Stadium seating. A new movie theater has stadium-style seating at a sharp incline on steep stairs and provides spaces for wheelchairs only down on the lowest level in the front row just in front of the screen in a sloped area. These seats are always the last to fill up because individuals must crane their necks back to see the film and the picture is somewhat distorted at that angle. However, those seats are used by the general public when the theater is full. A Justice Department regulation under the ADA requires movie theaters and stadiums to provide "wheelchair areas" that are "an integral part of any fixed seating plan" and to ensure that they possess "lines of sight comparable to those for members of the general public." *ADA Accessibility Guidelines*, 28 C.F.R. pt. 36, app. A, §4.33.3.

a. Has the theater violated the ADA? *Compare Lara v. Cinemark USA, Inc.*, 207 F.3d 783 (5th Cir. 2000) (no violation), *with Oregon Paralyzed Veterans of America v. Regal Cinemas, Inc.*, 339 F.3d 1126 (9th Cir. 2003) (violation). *Cf. United States v. Hoyts Cinemas Corp.*, 380 F.3d 558 (1st Cir. 2004) (rejecting the holdings of both *Lara* and *Oregon Paralyzed Veterans* and remanding for factual findings on the angles of view and visual distortion in seat placements in the sloped area). *See* Felicia H. Ellsworth, *The Worst Seats in the House: Stadium-Style Movie Theaters and the Americans with Disabilities Act,* 71 U. Chi. L. Rev. 1109 (2004).

b. Must the theater reserve seats next to spots reserved for wheelchair users for companions who accompany them so that they can sit together, thereby requiring individuals who have taken those seats to move to other available seats in the theater? In *Fortyune v. American Multi-Cinema, Inc.*, 364 F.3d 1075 (9th Cir. 2004), the court held that a quadriplegic had the right to have his wife sit next to him because his condition made it necessary to have someone with him at all times, making a modification of the theater's policy both "necessary" for him to enjoy the services and a "reasonable modification" of the theater's policy that would not "fundamentally alter" the nature of the services being offered. It held that theaters must reserve companion seats near wheelchair spots until ten minutes before show time. *See* 28 C.F.R. pt. 36, app. A, §4.33.3 ("At least one companion fixed seat shall be provided next to each wheelchair seating area").

c. Must stadiums provide wheelchair locations that allow patrons to view sports events even when spectators in front of them stand up? Recently adopted regulations say that they do. *Compare Miller v. California Speedway Corp.*, 536 F.3d 1020 (9th Cir. 2008) (holding that a facility violated the ADA and §4.33.3 when it provided wheelchair seating that did not allow lines of sight to the racetrack over standing spectators); *with Caruso v. Blockbuster-SONY Music Entertainment Centre at the Waterfront*, 193 F.3d 730 (3d Cir. 1999) (holding that neither the ADA nor §4.33.3 required sightlines over standing spectators but merely dispersal of seating). Is this a proper interpretation of the statute?

4. Historic landmarks. The ADA requirements for alteration of existing facilities do not apply to buildings that have been designated historic landmarks under federal or state law if the alterations will "threaten or destroy the historic significance" of the building. 42 U.S.C. §12204(a); 28 C.F.R. §36.405. A building that is now listed as a historical landmark under the *National Historic Preservation Act*, 16 U.S.C. §470 *et seq.*, has been in continuous use as a law school classroom building since 1880. The ceilings are very high and the acoustics in the classrooms are terrible. Students have great difficulty hearing each other when they speak. The law school wants either to drop the ceilings, float panels hung from the ceiling in the rooms, or install microphones at every seat to rectify the situation. The local historic preservation board refuses to grant the school permission to do any of these things on the ground that they would impair the historical and architectural integrity of the building. How should a court reconcile the requirements of the ADA with the historic preservation laws that prohibit alterations of historic buildings that would impair their historic significance?

5. Modifying policies. In *PGA Tour, Inc. v. Martin*, 531 U.S. 1049 (2001), the Supreme Court ruled that the Professional Golf Association (PGA) violated the ADA when it refused to allow golfer Casey Martin to use a cart to travel between holes in a professional golf tournament, which the Court treated as a place of public accommodation. Martin has a degenerative circulatory disorder that causes pain when he walks too far, and he sought a "reasonable modification" of the policy prohibiting the use of golf carts in its competitions under §12182(b)(2)(A)(ii). The PGA claimed that this would "fundamentally alter the nature" of the game because walking induced fatigue and was an essential part of the game at the high level of competition the PGA represented. The Court found to the contrary, concluding that waiving the rule would neither give Martin a competitive advantage nor alter the "essential character of the game of golf," which had always been shot-making. Justice Stevens noted that the trial court had found that the fatigue from walking during the tournament was not significant, thereby finding the defendant's justification insubstantial. Justices Scalia and Thomas dissented. Justice Scalia argued that the ADA gives individuals a right to participate in whatever services a public accommodation offers, not to change the nature of those services.

A law school professor gives an eight-hour take-home exam to be picked up at 8:30 A.M. and returned at 4:30 P.M. A student with dyslexia asks to be allowed to add 24 hours to the exam, picking it up at 8:30 A.M. one day and returning it at 4:30 P.M. the next day. Is the school obligated to comply? If so, may the school note on the student's transcript that she was given extra time to do the exam?

A woman suffers from limb girdle muscular dystrophy, which makes it difficult for her to walk or stand from a seated position. She seeks permission to use a Segway in Walt Disney World, despite a policy against two-wheeled vehicles in the park. Disney refuses to make an exception to its policy. Does its refusal violate the ADA? *See Baughman v. Walt Disney World Co.*, 685 F.3d 1131 (9th Cir. 2012) (finding the requested exception to constitute a reasonable accommodation). What sorts of arguments would you make if you represented Disney in defense of the existing policy?

6. Virtual "places." Do the ADA public accommodations provisions apply to businesses that do not operate at specific physical locations but offer services over the phone, by mail, or through the Internet? *Compare Carparts Distribution Center, Inc. v. Automotive Wholesalers Association of New England,* 37 F.3d 12, 26 (1st Cir. 1994) (ADA applies to goods and services "sold over the telephone or by mail with customers never physically entering the premises of a commercial entity to purchase the goods or services"), *with Weyer v. Twentieth Century Fox Film Corp.,* 198 F.3d 1104, 1114 (9th Cir. 2000) (concluding that places of public accommodation are "actual, physical places"), *and Parker v. Metropolitan Life Insurance Co.,* 121 F.3d 1006 (6th Cir. 1997) (public accommodations provisions of ADA require access only to physical places). *See also National Federation of the Blind v. Target Corp.,* 452 F. Supp. 2d 946 (N.D. Cal. 2006) (web sites are subject to the ADA only to the extent they impede access to a physical store).

If virtual places are covered by the statute, must they be made accessible to the blind through computer protocols that vocally describe screen images and allow navigation by use of the keyboard rather than a mouse? *Contrast Cullen v. Netflix, Inc.*, 880 F. Supp. 2d 1017 (N.D. Cal. 2012) (web sites are not places of public accommodation); *with National Association of the Deaf v. Netflix, Inc.*, 869 F. Supp. 2d 196 (D. Mass. 2012) ("In a society in which business is increasingly conducted online, excluding businesses that sell services through the Internet . . . would severely frustrate Congress's intent that individuals with disabilities fully enjoy the goods, services, privileges and advantages, available indiscriminately to other members of the general public."); *see also*

Tara E. Thompson, *Locating Discrimination: Interactive Web Sites as Public Accommodations Under Title II of the Civil Rights Act,* 2002 U. Chi. Legal F. 409.

Does the ADA require health insurance companies to offer coverage for mental illness as well as physical illness? *See MacNeil v. Time Insurance Co.,* 205 F.3d 179, 186 (5th Cir. 2000) (insurance company does not violate ADA when it caps benefits for patients with AIDS because the ADA does not "regulate the content of goods and services that are offered"); *Ford v. Schering-Plough Corp.,* 145 F.3d 601 (3d Cir. 1998) (no ADA violation when insurance company capped benefits for mental but not physical disabilities).

§3 FREE SPEECH RIGHTS OF ACCESS TO PUBLIC AND PRIVATE PROPERTY

Lloyd Corporation, Ltd. v. Tanner

407 U.S. 551 (1972)

Mr. Justice Lewis Powell delivered the opinion of the Court.

Lloyd Corp., Ltd. (Lloyd), owns a large, modern retail shopping center in Portland, Oregon. Lloyd Center embraces altogether about 50 acres, including some 20 acres of open and covered parking facilities which accommodate more than 1,000 automobiles. It has a perimeter of almost one and one-half miles, bounded by four public streets. It is crossed in varying degrees by several other public streets, all of which have adjacent public sidewalks. Lloyd owns all land and buildings within the Center, except these public streets and sidewalks. There are some 60 commercial tenants, including small shops and several major department stores.

The Center embodies a relatively new concept in shopping center design. The stores are all located within a single large, multi-level building complex sometimes referred to as the "Mall." Within this complex, in addition to the stores, there are parking facilities, malls, private sidewalks, stairways, escalators, gardens, an auditorium, and a skating rink. Some of the stores open directly on the outside public sidewalks, but most open on the interior privately owned malls. Some stores open on both. There are no public streets or public sidewalks within the building complex, which is enclosed and entirely covered except for the landscaped portions of some of the interior malls.

The Center is open generally to the public, with a considerable effort being made to attract shoppers and prospective shoppers, and to create "customer motivation" as well as customer goodwill in the community. In this respect the Center pursues policies comparable to those of major stores and shopping centers across the country, although the Center affords superior facilities for these purposes. Groups and organizations are permitted, by invitation and advance arrangement, to use the auditorium and other facilities. Rent is charged for use of the auditorium except with respect to certain civic and charitable organizations, such as the Cancer Society and Boy and Girl Scouts. The Center also allows limited use of the malls by the American Legion to sell poppies for disabled veterans, and by the Salvation Army and Volunteers of

America to solicit Christmas contributions. It has denied similar use to other civic and charitable organizations. Political use is also forbidden, except that presidential candidates of both parties have been allowed to speak in the auditorium.

The Center had been in operation for some eight years when this litigation commenced. Throughout this period it had a policy, strictly enforced, against the distribution of handbills within the building complex and its malls. No exceptions were made with respect to handbilling, which was considered likely to annoy customers, to create litter, potentially to create disorders, and generally to be incompatible with the purpose of the Center and the atmosphere sought to be preserved.

On November 14, 1968, the respondents in this case distributed within the Center handbill invitations to a meeting of the "Resistance Community" to protest the draft and the Vietnam war. The distribution, made in several different places on the mall walkways by five young people, was quiet and orderly, and there was no littering. There was a complaint from one customer. Security guards informed the respondents that they were trespassing and would be arrested unless they stopped distributing the handbills within the Center. Respondents left the premises as requested "to avoid arrest" and continued the handbilling outside. Subsequently this suit was instituted in the District Court seeking declaratory and injunctive relief.

The District Court, emphasizing that the Center "is open to the general public," found that it is "the functional equivalent of a public business district." 308 F. Supp., at 130. That court then held that Lloyd's "rule prohibiting the distribution of handbills within the Mall violates . . . First Amendment rights." 308 F. Supp., at 131. In a *per curiam* opinion, the Court of Appeals . . . concluded that the decisions of this Court in *Marsh v. Alabama*, 326 U.S. 501 (1946), and *Amalgamated Food Employees Union Local 590 v. Logan Valley Plaza, Inc.*, 391 U.S. 308 (1968), compelled affirmance.

Marsh involved Chickasaw, Alabama, a company town wholly owned by the Gulf Shipbuilding Corp. The opinion of the Court, by Mr. Justice Black, described Chickasaw as follows:

> "Except for (ownership by a private corporation) it has all the characteristics of any other American town. The property consists of residential buildings, streets, a system of sewers, a sewage disposal plant and a 'business block' on which business places are situated. A deputy of the Mobile County Sheriff, paid by the company, serves as the town's policeman. Merchants and service establishments have rented the stores and business places on the business block and the United States uses one of the places as a post office from which six carriers deliver mail to the people of Chickasaw and the adjacent area. The town and the surrounding neighborhood, which can not be distinguished from the Gulf property by anyone not familiar with the property lines, are thickly settled, and according to all indications the residents use the business block as their regular shopping center. In short the town and its shopping district are accessible to and freely used by the public in general and there is nothing to distinguish them from any other town and shopping center except the fact that the title to the property belongs to a private corporation." 326 U.S., at 502-503.

A Jehovah's Witness undertook to distribute religious literature on a sidewalk near the post office and was arrested on a trespassing charge. In holding that First and

Fourteenth Amendment rights were infringed, the Court emphasized that the business district was within a company-owned town, an anachronism long prevalent in some southern States and now rarely found.

In *Logan Valley* the Court extended the rationale of *Marsh* to peaceful picketing [by a Union] of a store located in a large shopping center, known as Logan Valley Mall, near Altoona, Pennsylvania. The Court noted that . . . publicly owned streets, sidewalks, and parks are so historically associated with the exercise of First Amendment rights that access to them for purposes of exercising such rights cannot be denied absolutely. *Lovell v. Griffin,* 303 U.S. 444 (1938); *Hague v. CIO,* 307 U.S. 496 (1939); *Schneider v. State,* 308 U.S. 147 (1939); *Jamison v. Texas,* 318 U.S. 413 (1943). The Court then considered *Marsh v. Alabama* and concluded that: "The shopping center here is clearly the functional equivalent of the business district of Chickasaw involved in Marsh." *Logan Valley,* 391 U.S. at 318.

The Court also took specific note of the facts that the Union's picketing was "directed solely at one establishment within the shopping center," *Id.* at 321. *Logan Valley* was decided on the basis of this factual situation, and the facts in this case are significantly different.[17]

The basic issue in this case is whether respondents, in the exercise of asserted First Amendment rights, may distribute handbills on Lloyd's private property contrary to its wishes and contrary to a policy enforced against all handbilling. In addressing this issue, it must be remembered that the First and Fourteenth Amendments safeguard the rights of free speech and assembly by limitations on state action, not on action by the owner of private property used nondiscriminatorily for private purposes only. [T]his Court has never held that a trespasser or an uninvited guest may exercise general rights of free speech on property privately owned and used nondiscriminatorily for private purposes only. Even where public property is involved, the Court has recognized that it is not necessarily available for speaking, picketing, or other communicative activities.

Respondents contend, however, that the property of a large shopping center is "open to the public," serves the same purposes as a "business district" of a municipality, and therefore has been dedicated to certain types of public use. The argument reaches too far. The Constitution by no means requires such an attenuated doctrine of dedication of private property to public use. The closest decision in theory, *Marsh v. Alabama,* involved the assumption by a private enterprise of all of the attributes of a state-created municipality and the exercise by that enterprise of semiofficial municipal functions as a delegate of the State. In effect, the owner of the company town was performing the full spectrum of municipal powers and stood in the shoes of the State. In the instant case there is no comparable assumption or exercise of municipal functions or power.

17. In *Hudgens v. National Labor Relations Board,* 424 U.S. 507 (1976), the Supreme Court rejected even this narrow reading of *Logan Valley,* effectively overruling the case altogether. — Eds.

Nor does property lose its private character merely because the public is generally invited to use it for designated purposes. Few would argue that a free-standing store, with abutting parking space for customers, assumes significant public attributes merely because the public is invited to shop there. Nor is size alone the controlling factor. The essentially private character of a store and its privately owned abutting property does not change by virtue of being large or clustered with other stores in a modern shopping center.

Judgment reversed and case remanded.

Mr. Justice THURGOOD MARSHALL, with whom Mr. Justice WILLIAM O. DOUGLAS, Mr. Justice WILLIAM J. BRENNAN, and Mr. Justice POTTER STEWART join, dissenting.

. . . Lloyd Center is even more clearly the equivalent of a public business district than was Logan Valley Plaza. Lloyd Center invites schools to hold football rallies, presidential candidates to give speeches, and service organizations to hold Veterans Day ceremonies on its premises. The court also observed that the Center permits the Salvation Army, the Volunteers of America, and the American Legion to solicit funds in the Mall. Thus, the court concluded that the Center was already open to First Amendment activities, and that respondents could not constitutionally be excluded from distributing leaflets solely because Lloyd Center was not enamored of the form or substance of their speech.

On Veterans Day, Lloyd Center allows organizations to parade through the Center with flags, drummers, and color guard units and to have a speaker deliver an address on the meaning of Veterans Day and the valor of American soldiers. Presidential candidates have been permitted to speak without restriction on the issues of the day, which presumably include war and peace. The American Legion is annually given permission to sell poppies in the Mall because Lloyd Center believes that "veterans . . . deserves (*sic*) some comfort and support by the people of the United States."

Members of the Portland community are able to see doctors, dentists, lawyers, bankers, travel agents, and persons offering countless other services in Lloyd Center. They can buy almost anything that they want or need there. For many Portland citizens, Lloyd Center will so completely satisfy their wants that they will have no reason to go elsewhere for goods or services. If speech is to reach these people, it must reach them in Lloyd Center.

For many persons who do not have easy access to television, radio, the major newspapers, and the other forms of mass media, the only way they can express themselves to a broad range of citizens on issues of general public concern is to picket, or to handbill, or to utilize other free or relatively inexpensive means of communication. The only hope that these people have to be able to communicate effectively is to be permitted to speak in those areas in which most of their fellow citizens can be found. One such area is the business district of a city or town or its functional equivalent. And this is why respondents have a tremendous need to express themselves within Lloyd Center.

Petitioner's interests, on the other hand, pale in comparison. It is undisputed that some patrons will be disturbed by any First Amendment activity that goes on, regardless of its object. But, there is no evidence to indicate that speech directed to topics unrelated to the shopping center would be more likely to impair the motivation of customers to buy than speech directed to the uses to which the Center is put, which petitioner concedes is constitutionally protected under *Logan Valley*.

It would not be surprising in the future to see cities rely more and more on private businesses to perform functions once performed by governmental agencies. The advantage of reduced expenses and an increased tax base cannot be overstated. As governments rely on private enterprise, public property decreases in favor of privately owned property. It becomes harder and harder for citizens to find means to communicate with other citizens. Only the wealthy may find effective communication possible unless we adhere to *Marsh v. Alabama* and continue to hold that "(t)he more an owner, for his advantage, opens up his property for use by the public in general, the more do his rights become circumscribed by the statutory and constitutional rights of those who use it," 326 U.S. 276.

When there are no effective means of communication, free speech is a mere shibboleth. I believe that the First Amendment requires it to be a reality. Accordingly, I would affirm the decision of the Court of Appeals.

Notes

1. **State constitutions.** Most states interpret their state constitutional free speech guarantees in a manner similar to the federal constitution, thus granting shopping center owners the power to exclude people handing out leaflets or others seeking to engage in similar speech activities. *See, e.g., United Food & Commercial Workers Union, Local 919 v. Crystal Mall Associates, L.P.,* 852 A.2d 659 (Conn. 2004); *City of West Des Moines v. Engler,* 641 N.W.2d 803 (Iowa 2002) (no free speech access rights to shopping centers). However, California and New Jersey have interpreted their state constitutions in a manner that adopts the views of Justice Marshall's dissenting opinion in *Lloyd.* While states may not adopt laws that deny constitutional rights protected by the U.S. Constitution, they may grant more expansive rights than those guaranteed by federal law either by interpretation of their state constitutions or through state statutes. Thus California held that the state constitution protected the right to hand out leaflets protesting the United Nation's resolution defining "Zionism" as a form of racism, and the U.S. Supreme Court upheld its right to do so. *See Robins v. PruneYard Shopping Center,* 592 P.2d 341 (Cal. 1979), *aff'd, PruneYard Shopping Center v. Robins,* 447 U.S. 74 (1980), and the New Jersey Supreme Court affirmed state constitutional rights to hand out leaflets to protest the first Iraq war. *New Jersey Coalition Against War in the Middle East v. J.M.B. Realty Corp.,* 650 A.2d 757 (N.J. 1994). *See also Wood v. State,* 2003 WL 1955433 (Fla. Cir. Ct. 2003) (state constitution prohibits a private owner of a "quasi-public" place from using state trespass laws to exclude peaceful political activity); *State v. Schmid,* 423 A.2d 615, 629 (N.J. 1980) (state constitution protects right to distribute literature on a private university campus).

A small number of states have found state constitutional rights to enter shopping centers seeking signatures to place a political candidate's name on the ballot or to get an initiative or referendum question placed on the ballot, *Batchelder v. Allied Stores International, Inc.*, 445 N.E.2d 590 (Mass. 1983); *Alderwood Associates v. Washington Environmental Council*, 635 P.2d 108 (Wash. 1981).

2. **Statutory labor organizing access rights.** Although there is no federal constitutional right of access to property open to the public for free speech purposes under the first amendment, the *National Labor Relations Act* (NLRA), a federal statute governing employment relations between employees and employers, does provide for some rights of access for labor organizations. Sections 7 and 8 of the NLRA prohibit employers from engaging in certain enumerated "unfair labor practices" that interfere with the rights of employees to form unions and engage in collective bargaining and other types of concerted activities for "mutual aid or protection," including striking and picketing. 29 U.S.C. §§157, 158. The Supreme Court has held that under some circumstances it may constitute an unfair labor practice under the NLRA for an employer to deny a right of access to certain areas of her property for purposes of picketing that property owner herself or an employer who is a lessee of a portion of that property. *Hudgens v. National Labor Relations Board,* 424 U.S. 507 (1976). Employees who are on strike or involved in a labor dispute with their employer may want access to the employer's property to picket, communicating to the employer and the public their side in the controversy. Nonemployees may want access to the parking lot or cafeteria of a workplace to distribute information designed to encourage the employees to form or join a union. In determining whether a right of access should be provided, the courts must balance the employer's property rights against the employees' rights under §7 to be free of unfair labor practices. See *Lechmere v. National Labor Relations Bd.,* 502 U.S. 527 (1992) (holding that union organizers had no right to enter the parking lot of a shopping center to put leaflets on the windshields of cars when there were reasonably effective alternative means of communicating with the employees); *Seattle-First National Bank v. National Labor Relations Board,* 651 F.2d 1272 (9th Cir. 1980) (unfair labor practice for the owner of an office building to refuse to allow striking restaurant employees to picket in the foyer outside a restaurant on the forty-sixth floor of the building); *Scott Hudgens,* 230 N.L.R.B. 414 (1977) (finding that striking employees of a business located in a shopping mall had a right to enter the mall to picket in front of their employer's place of business).

3. **Gun rights on private property.** Georgia's concealed carry law prohibits the holder of a properly licensed concealed firearm from carrying the firearm into certain types of premises, such as bars and churches, without first reporting the firearm to the management of the property and following the management's directions concerning the firearm. A gun-rights group sued, arguing that the statute violated the second amendment right to bear arms. On appeal from the district court's dismissal of the claim, the U.S. Court of Appeals for the Eleventh Circuit held that a private property owner's right to exclude people from carrying firearms on private property trumps gun-owners' rights to carry their firearms where they want. Consequently, a law delegating to property owners the right to dictate the terms on which firearms will be allowed on their premises does not violate the second amendment. According to the

court, "[a]n individual's right to bear arms as enshrined in the Second Amendment, whatever its full scope, certainly must be limited by the equally fundamental right of a private property owner to exercise exclusive dominion and control over its land." *Georgiacarry.org, Inc. v. Georgia*, 687 F.3d 1244 (11th Cir. 2012).

Problems

1. A shopping mall allows members of the Republican Party to hand out leaflets urging customers to vote for Republican candidates for Congress and for the president but refuses to allow members of the Democratic Party to hand out leaflets. Assume you are in a state that has not interpreted its constitution to require owners of private property open to the public to grant rights of access for free speech purposes. A Democrat who is excluded from handing out leaflets sues the shopping center owner and claims that even though the owner has no duty to allow all members of the public to pass out leaflets, once the owner allows *some* members of the public to do this, it must allow others to do so on a nondiscriminatory basis. Argue both sides.

2. A large shopping mall in New Jersey is owned by a survivor of the Nazi concentration camps. The Ku Klux Klan begins peaceably handing out literature in the shopping center, praising the Nazi Party and urging shoppers to vote for a member of the KKK who is running for public office and who has stated that the United States should adopt Nazi methods to deal with African Americans, Latinos, Asian Americans, and American Jews. The owner ejects the KKK members from the mall. They subsequently sue and claim that the owner is violating their free speech rights under the state constitution, as defined in *New Jersey Coalition*. The owner defends by arguing that she has the right to prevent her property from being used as a base from which to hand out literature that preaches hatred against particular ethnic groups. What should the court do?

3. A major Internet search engine refuses to list among its search results web pages that criticize the third-world labor practices of the conglomerate that owns the search engine. The group that maintains the blocked pages complains that this violates their rights to free speech; they argue that since nearly all Internet users locate web pages using a few major search engines, these engines are the equivalent of a public square or a modern shopping mall: the central way to get a message to the public. The search engine company responds that a search engine is private property: the company can choose to make accessible whatever information it wants, and it must have this right if it is to exclude pages containing pornography from its database. The company also argues that storing information is expensive, and it must be able to exclude at will to prevent its database from growing too large. The Electronic Frontier Foundation, a nonprofit organization that promotes free speech on the Internet, proposes legislation prohibiting search engines from refusing to include any web page in their database if the page's owner requests inclusion. If you were a member of the legislature, how would you vote and why?

4. A couple of weeks before the United States invaded Iraq in March 2003, a father and son were ousted from a mall in New York State for wearing T-shirts that protested

the decision to go to war. The father's T-shirt said "Give Peace a Chance," while his son's shirt read "No War with Iraq" on one side and "Let Inspections Work" on the other. Winnie Hu, *A Message of Peace on 2 Shirts Touches Off Hostilities at a Mall,* N.Y. Times, Mar. 6, 2003, at B-1. As the father and son were eating lunch, security guards asked them to remove the shirts or to leave the premises. Although the son complied by removing his shirt, the father did not. It appears that he also refused to leave the premises. He was arrested and charged with criminal trespass. New York has not adopted the *PruneYard* rule, and no other New York law apparently limited the owner's decision to exclude under these circumstances. The director of operations of the mall explained that the father and son were interfering with other shoppers and that "[t]heir behavior, coupled with their clothing, to express to others their personal views on world affairs were disruptive of customers." *Id.* Should the law protect the owner's right to exclude in a case like this, or should the courts recognize a right based on either the common law or the state constitution that would prohibit exclusion under these circumstances?

§4 BEACH ACCESS AND THE PUBLIC TRUST

Matthews v. Bay Head Improvement Association

471 A.2d 355 (N.J. 1984)

Map: Bay Head, New Jersey

SIDNEY M. SCHREIBER, J.

The public trust doctrine acknowledges that the ownership, dominion and sovereignty over land flowed by tidal waters, which extend to the mean high water mark, is vested in the State in trust for the people. The public's right to use the tidal lands and water encompasses navigation, fishing and recreational uses, including bathing, swimming and other shore activities. *Borough of Neptune City v. Borough of Avon-by-the-Sea,* 294 A.2d 47 (N.J. 1972). In *Avon* we held that the public trust applied to the municipally owned dry sand beach immediately landward of the high water mark.[18] The major issue in this case is whether, ancillary to the public's right to enjoy the tidal lands, the public has a right to gain access through and to use the dry sand area not owned by a municipality but by a quasi-public body.

I. Facts

The Borough of Bay Head (Bay Head) borders the Atlantic Ocean. Adjacent to it on the north is the Borough of Point Pleasant Beach, on the south the Borough of

---

18. The dry sand area is generally defined as the land west (landward) of the high water mark to the vegetation line or where there is no vegetation to a seawall, road, parking lot, or boardwalk.

Mantoloking, and on the west Barnegat Bay. Bay Head consists of a fairly narrow strip of land, 6,667 feet long (about 1 1/4 miles). A beach runs along its entire length adjacent to the Atlantic Ocean. There are 76 separate parcels of land that border the beach. All except six are owned by private individuals. Title to those six is vested in the [Bay Head Improvement] Association [(the Association)].

The Association was founded in 1910 and incorporated as a nonprofit corporation in 1932. Its certificate of incorporation states that its purposes are the improving and beautifying of the Borough of Bay Head, New Jersey, cleaning, policing and otherwise making attractive and safe the bathing beaches in said Borough, and the doing of any act which may be found necessary or desirable for the greater convenience, comfort and enjoyment of the residents. Its constitution delineates the Association's object to promote the best interests of the Borough and "in so doing to own property, operate bathing beaches, hire life guards, beach cleaners and policemen."

Nine streets in the Borough, which are perpendicular to the beach, end at the dry sand. The Association owns the land commencing at the end of seven of these streets for the width of each street and extending through the upper dry sand to the mean high water line, the beginning of the wet sand area or foreshore. In addition, the Association owns the fee in six shore front properties, three of which are contiguous and have a frontage aggregating 310 feet. Many owners of beachfront property executed and delivered to the Association leases of the upper dry sand area. These leases are revocable by either party to the lease on thirty days' notice. Some owners have not executed such leases and have not permitted the Association to use their beaches. Some also have acquired riparian grants from the State extending approximately 1000 feet east of the high water line.

The Association controls and supervises its beach property between the third week in June and Labor Day. It engages about 40 employees who serve as lifeguards, beach police and beach cleaners. Lifeguards, stationed at five operating beaches, indicate by use of flags whether the ocean condition is dangerous (red), requires caution (yellow), or is satisfactory (green). In addition to observing and, if need be, assisting those in the water, when called upon lifeguards render first aid. Beach cleaners are engaged to rake and keep the beach clean of debris. Beach police are stationed at the entrances to the beaches where the public streets lead into the beach to ensure that only Association members or their guests enter. Some beach police patrol the beaches to enforce its membership rules.

Membership is generally limited to residents of Bay Head. Class A members are property owners. Class B are non-owners. Large families (six or more) pay $90 per year and small families pay $60 per year. Upon application residents are routinely accepted. Membership is evidenced by badges that signify permission to use the beaches. Members, which include local hotels, motels and inns, can also acquire badges for guests. The charge for each guest badge is $12. Members of the Bay Head Fire Company, Bay Head Borough employees, and teachers in the municipality's school system have been issued beach badges irrespective of residency.

Except for fishermen, who are permitted to walk through the upper dry sand area to the foreshore, only the membership may use the beach between 10:00 A.M. and

5:30 P.M. during the summer season. The public is permitted to use the Association's beach from 5:30 P.M. to 10:00 A.M. during the summer and, with no hourly restrictions, between Labor Day and mid-June.

No attempt has ever been made to stop anyone from occupying the terrain east of the high water mark. During certain parts of the day, when the tide is low, the foreshore could consist of about 50 feet of sand not being flowed by the water. The public could gain access to the foreshore by coming from the Borough of Point Pleasant Beach on the north or from the Borough of Mantoloking on the south.

Association membership totals between 4,800 to 5,000. The Association President testified during depositions that its restrictive policy, in existence since 1932, was due to limited parking facilities and to the overcrowding of the beaches. The Association's avowed purpose was to provide the beach for the residents of Bay Head.

There is also a public boardwalk, about one-third of a mile long, parallel to the ocean on the westerly side of the dry sand area. The boardwalk is owned and maintained by the municipality.

II. The Public Trust

In *Borough of Neptune City v. Borough of Avon-by-the-Sea,* 294 A.2d 47, 51 (N.J. 1972), Justice Hall alluded to the ancient principle "that land covered by tidal waters belonged to the sovereign, but for the common use of all the people." . . . This underlying concept was applied in New Jersey in *Arnold v. Mundy,* 6 N.J.L. 1 (Sup. Ct. 1821).

The defendant in *Arnold* tested the plaintiff's claim of an exclusive right to harvest oysters by taking some oysters that the plaintiff had planted in beds in the Raritan River adjacent to his farm in Perth Amboy. The oyster beds extended about 150 feet below the ordinary low water mark. The tide ebbed and flowed over it.

Chief Justice Kirkpatrick . . . concluded that all navigable rivers in which the tide ebbs and flows and the coasts of the sea, including the water and land under the water, are "common to all the citizens, and that each [citizen] has a right to use them according to his necessities, subject only to the laws which regulate that use." *Id.* at 93. Later in *Illinois Central R.R. v. Illinois,* 146 U.S. 387, 453 (1892), the Supreme Court, in referring to the common property, stated that "[t]he State can no more abdicate its trust over property in which the whole people are interested . . . than it can abdicate its police powers."

In *Avon,* Justice Hall reaffirmed the public's right to use the waterfront as announced in *Arnold v. Mundy.* He observed that the public has a right to use the land below the mean average high water mark where the tide ebbs and flows. These uses have historically included navigation and fishing. In *Avon* the public's rights were extended "to recreational uses, including bathing, swimming and other shore activities." 294 A.2d at 54. The Florida Supreme Court has held:

> The constant enjoyment of this privilege [bathing in salt waters] of thus using the ocean and its foreshore for ages without dispute should prove sufficient to establish it as an American common law right, similar to that of fishing in the sea, even if this right had not come down to us as a part of the English common law, which it undoubtedly has. It

> has been said that "[h]ealth, recreation and sports are encompassed in and intimately related to the general welfare of a well-balanced state." Extension of the public trust doctrine to include bathing, swimming and other shore activities is consonant with and furthers the general welfare. The public's right to enjoy these privileges must be respected. *White v. Hughes,* 190 So. 446, 449 (Fla. 1939).

In order to exercise these rights guaranteed by the public trust doctrine, the public must have access to municipally owned dry sand areas as well as the foreshore. The extension of the public trust doctrine to include municipally owned dry sand areas was necessitated by our conclusion that enjoyment of rights in the foreshore is inseparable from use of dry sand beaches. In *Avon* we struck down a municipal ordinance that required nonresidents to pay a higher fee than residents for the use of the beach. We held that where a municipal beach is dedicated to public use, the public trust doctrine "dictates that the beach and the ocean waters must be open to all on equal terms and without preference and that any contrary state or municipal action is impermissible." 294 A.2d at 54.

III. Public Rights in Privately Owned Dry Sand Beaches

In *Avon* . . . our finding of public rights in dry sand areas was specifically and appropriately limited to those beaches owned by a municipality. We now address the extent of the public's interest in privately owned dry sand beaches. This interest may take one of two forms. First, the public may have a right to cross privately owned dry sand beaches in order to gain access to the foreshore. Second, this interest may be of the sort enjoyed by the public in municipal beaches under *Avon* . . . , namely, the right to sunbathe and generally enjoy recreational activities.

Beaches are a unique resource and are irreplaceable. The public demand for beaches has increased with the growth of population and improvement of transportation facilities. Furthermore the projected demand for salt water swimming will not be met "unless the existing swimming capacities of the four coastal counties are expanded." Department of Environmental Protection, Statewide Comprehensive Outdoor Recreation Plan 200 (1977). The DEP estimates that, compared to 1976, the State's salt water swimming areas "must accommodate 764,812 more persons by 1985 and 1,021,112 persons by 1995."

Exercise of the public's right to swim and bathe below the mean high water mark may depend upon a right to pass across the upland beach. Without some means of access the public right to use the foreshore would be meaningless. To say that the public trust doctrine entitles the public to swim in the ocean and to use the foreshore in connection therewith without assuring the public of a feasible access route would seriously impinge on, if not effectively eliminate, the rights of the public trust doctrine. This does not mean the public has an unrestricted right to cross at will over any and all property bordering on the common property. The public interest is satisfied so long as there is reasonable access to the sea.

[T]he particular circumstances must be considered and examined before arriving at a solution that will accommodate the public's right and the private interests involved. Thus an undeveloped segment of the shore may have been available and used for access so as to establish a public right-of-way to the wet sand. Or there may be publicly owned property, such as in *Avon*, which is suitable. Or, as in this case, the public streets and adjacent upland sand area might serve as a proper means of entry. The test is whether those means are reasonably satisfactory so that the public's right to use the beachfront can be satisfied.

The bather's right in the upland sands is not limited to passage. Reasonable enjoyment of the foreshore and the sea cannot be realized unless some enjoyment of the dry sand area is also allowed. The complete pleasure of swimming must be accompanied by intermittent periods of rest and relaxation beyond the water's edge. The unavailability of the physical situs for such rest and relaxation would seriously curtail and in many situations eliminate the right to the recreational use of the ocean. This was a principal reason why in *Avon* and [*Van Ness v. Borough of Deal,* 393 A.2d 571 (N.J. 1978),] we held that municipally owned dry sand beaches "must be open to all on equal terms." *Avon,* 294 A.2d at 54. We see no reason why rights under the public trust doctrine to use of the upland dry sand area should be limited to municipally owned property. It is true that the private owner's interest in the upland dry sand area is not identical to that of a municipality. Nonetheless, where use of dry sand is essential or reasonably necessary for enjoyment of the ocean, the doctrine warrants the public's use of the upland dry sand area subject to an accommodation of the interests of the owner.

We perceive no need to attempt to apply notions of prescription, *City of Daytona Beach v. Tona-Rama, Inc.*, 294 So. 2d 73 (Fla. 1974), dedication, *Gion v. City of Santa Cruz,* 465 P.2d 50 (Cal. 1970), or custom, *State ex rel. Thornton v. Hay,* 462 P.2d 671 (Or. 1969), as an alternative to application of the public trust doctrine. Archaic judicial responses are not an answer to a modern social problem. Rather, we perceive the public trust doctrine not to be "fixed or static," but one to "be molded and extended to meet changing conditions and needs of the public it was created to benefit." *Avon,* 294 A.2d at 54.

Precisely what privately owned upland sand area will be available and required to satisfy the public's rights under the public trust doctrine will depend on the circumstances. Location of the dry sand area in relation to the foreshore, extent and availability of publicly owned upland sand area, nature and extent of the public demand, and usage of the upland sand land by the owner are all factors to be weighed and considered in fixing the contours of the usage of the upper sand.

Today, recognizing the increasing demand for our State's beaches and the dynamic nature of the public trust doctrine, we find that the public must be given both access to and use of privately owned dry sand areas as reasonably necessary. While the public's rights in private beaches are not co-extensive with the rights enjoyed in municipal beaches, private landowners may not in all instances prevent the public from exercising its rights under the public trust doctrine. The public must be afforded reasonable access to the foreshore as well as a suitable area for recreation on the dry sand.

V. The Beaches of Bay Head

The Bay Head Improvement Association, which services the needs of all residents of the Borough for swimming and bathing in the public trust property, owns the street-wide strip of dry sand area at the foot of seven public streets that extends to the mean high water line. It also owns the fee in six other upland sand properties connected or adjacent to the tracts it owns at the end of two streets. In addition, it holds leases to approximately 42 tracts of upland sand area. The question that we must address is whether the dry sand area that the Association owns or leases should be open to the public to satisfy the public's rights under the public trust doctrine. Our analysis turns upon whether the Association may restrict its membership to Bay Head residents and thereby preclude public use of the dry sand area.

The general rule is that courts will not compel admission to a voluntary association. Ordinarily, a society or association may set its own membership qualifications and restrictions. However, that is not an inexorable rule. Where an organization is quasi-public, its power to exclude must be reasonably and lawfully exercised in furtherance of the public welfare related to its public characteristics.

[A] nonprofit association that is authorized and endeavors to carry out a purpose serving the general welfare of the community and is a quasi-public institution holds in trust its powers of exclusive control in the areas of vital public concern. When a nonprofit association rejects a membership application for reasons unrelated to its purposes and contrary to the general welfare, courts have "broad judicial authority to insure that exclusionary policies are lawful and are not applied arbitrarily or [discriminatorily]." *Greisman v. Newcomb Hospital,* 192 A.2d 817, 820 (1963). That is the situation here.

Bay Head Improvement Association is a non-profit corporation whose primary purpose as stated in its certificate of incorporation is the "cleaning, policing and otherwise making attractive and safe the bathing beaches" in the Borough of Bay Head "and the doing of any act which may be found necessary or desirable for the greater convenience, comfort and enjoyment of the residents." . . .

The Association's activities paralleled those of a municipality in its operation of the beachfront. The size of the beach was so great that it stationed lifeguards at five separate locations. The beach serviced about 5,000 members. The lifeguards performed the functions characteristic of those on a public beach. When viewed in its totality—its purposes, relationship with the municipality, communal characteristic, activities, and virtual monopoly over the Bay Head beachfront—the quasi-public nature of the Association is apparent. The Association makes available to the Bay Head public access to the common tidal property for swimming and bathing and to the upland dry sand area for use incidental thereto, preserving the residents' interests in a fashion similar to *Avon.*

There is no public beach in the Borough of Bay Head. If the residents of every municipality bordering the Jersey shore were to adopt the Bay Head policy, the public would be prevented from exercising its right to enjoy the foreshore. The Bay Head residents may not frustrate the public's right in this manner. By limiting membership only to residents and foreclosing the public, the Association is acting in conflict with the public good and contrary to the strong public policy "in favor of encouraging and expanding public access to and use of shoreline areas." *Gion v. City of Santa Cruz,* 465 P.2d 50, 59 (Cal. 1970). Indeed, the Association is frustrating the public's right under the public trust doctrine. It should not be permitted to do so.

Accordingly, membership in the Association must be open to the public at large.

The Public Advocate has urged that all the privately owned beachfront property likewise must be opened to the public. Nothing has been developed on this record to justify that conclusion. We have decided that the Association's membership and thereby its beach must be open to the public. That area might reasonably satisfy the public need at this time. [I]f the Association were to sell all or part of its property, it may necessitate further adjudication of the public's claims in favor of the public trust on part or all of these or other privately owned upland dry sand lands depending upon the circumstances. However, we see no necessity to have those issues resolved judicially at this time since the beach under the Association's control will be open to the public and may be adequate to satisfy the public trust interests.

The record in this case makes it clear that a right of access to the beach is available over the quasi-public lands owned by the Association, as well as the right to use the Association's upland dry sand. It is not necessary for us to determine under what circumstances and to what extent there will be a need to use the dry sand of private owners who either now or in the future may have no leases with the Association. Resolution of the competing interests, private ownership and the public trust, may in some cases be simple, but in many it may be most complex. In any event, resolution would depend upon the specific facts in controversy.

We realize that considerable uncertainty will continue to surround the question of the public's right to cross private land and to use a portion of the dry sand as discussed above. Where the parties are unable to agree as to the application of the principles enunciated herein, the claim of the private owner shall be honored until the contrary is established.

Notes and Questions

1. Public trust. In *Illinois Central Railroad Co. v. Illinois,* 146 U.S. 387, 435 (1892), the Supreme Court held as follows:

> It is the settled law of this country that the ownership of and dominion and sovereignty over lands covered by tide waters, within the limits of the several states, belong to the respective states within which they are found, with the consequent right to use or dispose of any portion thereof, when that can be done without substantial impairment of the interest of the public in the waters, and subject always to the paramount right of Congress to control their navigation so far as may be necessary for the regulation of commerce with foreign nations and among the states.

Some courts have held that the state may extinguish public rights of access under the public trust doctrine by conveying property to private owners free of such rights. *See, e.g., Greater Providence Chamber of Commerce v. Rhode Island,* 657 A.2d 1038 (R.I.

1995). Other courts, however, have held that the rights encompassed by the public trust doctrine are inalienable and lands subject to those rights cannot be reduced to private property free from public trust obligations. *See, e.g., Glass v. Goeckel,* 473 Mich. 667 (Mich. 2005).

2. Uses encompassed by the public trust doctrine. The New Jersey Supreme Court notes its earlier holding that the public trust doctrine included the right to enjoy the lands over which the tides flowed (tidal lands) for a broad variety of purposes, including navigation, fishing, and recreation such as swimming. It further extended the doctrine to encompass public rights of access to the dry sand area adjacent to the tidal lands, inland from the tidal lands to the line where vegetation started on lands owned by the municipalities. *See also Raleigh Avenue Beach Association v. Atlantis Beach Club, Inc.,* 879 A.2d 112 (N.J. 2005) (private club that holds title to the only beach in the township could not exclude members of the public from access to the dry sand area of the beach beyond the high tide line and could not charge high fees designed to limit access). In the earlier case of *Borough of Neptune City v. Borough of Avon-by-the-Sea,* 294 A.2d 47, 54 (N.J. 1972), Justice Hall explained the extension of the public trust doctrine to recreational uses in the following way:

> We have no difficulty in finding that, in this latter half of the twentieth century, the public rights in tidal lands are not limited to the ancient prerogatives of navigation and fishing, but extend as well to recreational uses, including bathing, swimming and other shore activities. The public trust doctrine, like all common law principles, should not be considered fixed or static, but should be molded and extended to meet changing conditions and needs of the public it was created to benefit.

In contrast, the Supreme Judicial Court of Massachusetts has limited public access under the public trust doctrine to tidal lands (defined as the lands seaward of the mean high water line) rather than the dry sand area. The court also limited public use rights to navigation and fishing purposes, specifically excluding recreational uses such as walking along the beachfront or bathing. *Opinion of the Justices,* 313 N.E.2d 561 (Mass. 1974). The Massachusetts court rejected the idea that the uses encompassed by the public trust doctrine could change or expand over time as social values and conditions changed. Rather, the court held that a statute redefining the public trust doctrine to allow a right of way for the public to walk along the beach on tidal lands constituted a physical invasion of the property rights of beachfront owners and could not be constitutionally required without paying just compensation to those owners for the loss of their property rights. To allow an expansion of public access would infringe on the property owners' right to exclude. *Accord, Severance v. Patterson,* 370 S.W.3d 705 (Tex. 2012) (limiting the public trust doctrine to land seaward of the mean high tide line and suggesting that the extension of the public trust doctrine to adjacent dry sand areas would raise constitutional concerns); *Bell v. Town of Wells,* 557 A.2d 168 (Me. 1989); *Opinion of the Justices,* 649 A.2d 604, 609 (N.H. 1994). *See also Leydon v. Town of Greenwich,* 777 A.2d 552, 564 n.17 (Conn. 2001) (limiting the public trust doctrine to the land seaward of the mean high tide line); *State ex rel. Haman v. Fox,* 594 P.2d 1093 (Ind. 1979) (same).

Should it make a difference whether the public has customarily used the beachfront adjoining private property for recreational purposes? Does longstanding customary use justify recognizing rights of access in the public?

If there is no longstanding public use, should the courts interpret the public trust doctrine to be rigidly limited to those uses customarily enjoyed in colonial times? Or should the doctrine be interpreted to authorize uses needed by the public and considered legitimate under evolving community standards? If the common law changes over time, as we have seen in *State v. Shack* and *Uston v. Resorts International,* why should the public trust doctrine be frozen in its colonial form? Was the New Jersey Supreme Court wrong to change the law in *Shack* and *Uston* to adjust the balance between the right to exclude and the right of access?

3. Dedication, prescription, and custom. Justice Schreiber notes that state courts have relied on three common law doctrines besides public trust, to grant rights of access to beaches by the general public. The doctrines are dedication, prescription, and custom.

Dedication involves a gift of real property from a private owner to the public at large. It requires an offer by the owner and acceptance by the public. Such an offer generally must be made by some unequivocal act by the property owner giving clear evidence of an intent to dedicate the land to public use. Longstanding acquiescence in use of beachfront property by the public may be interpreted as an implied dedication by the property owner and acceptance by the public. *Gion v. City of Santa Cruz,* 465 P.2d 50 (Cal. 1970). However, *Gion* was effectively overturned by the California legislature, which prohibited acquisition of public rights by implied dedication, although allowing public rights of access to arise by prescription. Cal. Civ. Code §1009.

Some states grant public rights of access to tidelands or the dry sand area of beaches under the doctrine of **prescription**. If the public has used property possessed by another for a particular purpose for a long time (measured by the relevant state statute of limitations), the public can acquire such rights permanently even if they never had them originally or if they had previously been reduced to private ownership. The permanent right to do something on another's land is called an *easement.* Such rights are generally created by agreement. However, if the owner fails to exclude trespassers from her property, she may lose her right to sue them under the relevant statute of limitations. The public acquires what is called a *prescriptive easement* to continue using the property for this purpose. *City of Daytona Beach v. Tona-Rama, Inc.*, 294 So. 2d 73 (Fla. 1974); *Concerned Citizens of Brunswick County Taxpayers Association v. Rhodes,* 404 S.E.2d 677 (N.C. 1991). For more on prescriptive easements, see Chapter 5, §3.

Most courts traditionally refused to allow the public to obtain an easement by prescription. Today, most courts will recognize such easements. Jon Bruce and James W. Ely, Jr., *The Law of Easements and Licenses in Land* ¶5.09[1] (rev. ed. 1995). They did so partly because (a) it was difficult to show continuous use by the public at large; (b) prescription might apply only to the particular tract of land at issue in the case, necessitating cumbersome and expensive litigation about every disputed parcel along the oceanfront; and (c) when private land is used by the public, courts may infer that the use was permissive, thereby defeating an element needed for prescriptive rights to vest.

Perhaps to avoid these problems, the Oregon Supreme Court relied on the doctrine of **custom**, rather than prescription, to hold that longstanding, uninterrupted, peaceable, reasonable, uniform use of the beachfront by the public for recreational purposes conferred continuing rights of access.

> The dry-sand area in Oregon has been enjoyed by the general public as a recreational adjunct of the wet-sand or foreshore area since the beginning of the state's political history. The first European settlers on these shores found the aboriginal inhabitants using the foreshore for clam-digging and the dry-sand area for their cooking fires. The newcomers continued these customs after statehood. Thus, from the time of the earliest settlement to the present day, the general public has assumed that the dry-sand area was a part of the public beach, and the public has used the dry-sand area for picnics, gathering wood, building warming fires, and generally as a headquarters from which to supervise children or to range out over the foreshore as the tides advance and recede.

State ex rel. Thornton v. Hay, 462 P.2d 671, 674 (Or. 1969). Applying the doctrine, the court prevented beachfront owners from enclosing the dry-sand area of their property in an attempt to limit access to members of a private beach club. In a later case, however, the Oregon Supreme Court limited the doctrine to those beaches for which proof exists of actual use by the public in the past. *See McDonald v. Halvorson,* 780 P.2d 714 (Or. 1989).

Hawai`i has a unique legal system recognizing public access to all beaches up to the "stable vegetation line" in accord with traditional Hawaiian custom. *See Diamond v. State Board of Land & Natural Resources,* 145 P.3d 704, 712 (Haw. 2006); *In re Banning,* 832 P.2d 724 (Haw. 1992); *Application of Ashford,* 440 P.2d 76 (Haw. 1968). *Cf. Ka Pa`akai O Ka`aina v. Land Use Commission,* 7 P.3d 1068 (Haw. 2000); *Public Access Shoreline Hawaii (PASH) v. Hawaii County Planning Commission,* 903 P.2d 1246 (Haw. 1995) (recognizing customary gathering rights of native Hawaiians along the shoreline).

Problems

1. *Matthews* involved beachfront property owned by a nonprofit charitable organization. In *Raleigh Avenue Beach Association v. Atlantis Beach Club, Inc.,* 185 N.J. 40 (N.J. 2005), the Supreme Court of New Jersey extended the *Matthews* ruling to require the owner of a beach club to allow anyone to become a member and prohibited the club from charging exorbitant fees designed to limit membership. The private owner had previously allowed the public to use the beach and had only recently converted it to a private beach club accessible only by members upon payment of fees higher than necessary to pay for costs of operation. The court applied the *Matthews* factors and found that the public interests in access outweighed the private interests in exclusion when there were no publicly owned beaches in the township and demand for beach access was very high. Two judges dissented on the ground that a nearby hotel allowed the public to use its beach. Did the court reach the correct result?

2. Now suppose members of the public begin using the dry sand area between the mean high water mark and the vegetation line in an area next to a private home. The owner puts up a fence and signs warning against trespassing on the beach. A member of the public sues the beachfront owner and asks for declaratory and injunctive relief preventing the owner from interfering with the public's right of access to the dry sand area along the beach, arguing that the state should adopt the standards used in Hawai`i.

a. What arguments could you make for the plaintiff that the principle underlying the rule of *Matthews* applies to this case? What arguments could you make for the defendant that this case is distinguishable from *Matthews* and *Raleigh Avenue Beach Association* and that the plaintiff has no right of access to the beach adjoining a private home?

b. If you were the judge deciding this case, what rule of law would you promulgate and how would you justify it?

§5 THE RIGHT TO BE SOMEWHERE AND THE PROBLEM OF HOMELESSNESS

The American Civil Liberties Union brought a lawsuit in Miami, Florida, challenging the city's sweep of homeless people from city parks before the 1988 Orange Bowl parade. *Pottinger v. City of Miami*, 810 F. Supp. 1551 (S.D. Fla. 1992). Miami had many more homeless people than it could handle in shelters. On November 16, 1992, District Judge C. Clyde Atkins ordered the police to stop arresting homeless persons for "innocent, harmless, and inoffensive acts" such as sleeping, eating, bathing, and sitting down in public and ordered the city to establish two " 'safe zones' where homeless people who have no alternative shelter can remain without being arrested for harmless conduct such as sleeping or eating." *Id.* at 1584. The case presented a conflict between the "need of homeless individuals to perform essential, life-sustaining acts in public and the responsibility of the government to maintain orderly, aesthetically pleasing public parks and streets." *Id.* at 1554. Judge Atkins explained his ruling this way:

> As a number of expert witnesses testified, people rarely choose to be homeless. Rather, homelessness is due to various economic, physical or psychological factors that are beyond the homeless individual's control.
>
> Professor Wright testified that one common characteristic of homeless individuals is that they are socially isolated; they are part of no community and have no family or friends who can take them in. Professor Wright also testified that homelessness is both a consequence and a cause of physical or mental illness. Many people become homeless after losing their jobs, and ultimately their homes, as a result of an illness. Many have no home of their own in the first place, but end up on the street after their families or friends are unable to care for or shelter them. Dr. Greer testified that once a person is on the street, illnesses can worsen or occur more frequently due to a variety of factors such as the difficulty or impossibility of obtaining adequate health care, exposure to

the elements, insect and rodent bites, and the absence of sanitary facilities for sleeping, bathing, or cooking. Both Professor Wright and Dr. Greer testified that, except in rare cases, people do not choose to live under these conditions.

According to Professor Wright's testimony, joblessness, like physical and mental illness, becomes more of a problem once a person becomes homeless. This is so because of the barriers homeless individuals face in searching for a job. For example, they have no legal address or telephone. Also, they must spend an inordinate amount of time waiting in line or searching for seemingly basic things like food, a space in a shelter bed or a place to bathe.

In addition to the problems of social isolation, illness, and unemployment, homelessness is exacerbated by the unavailability of many forms of government assistance. Gail Lucy, an expert in the area of government benefits available to homeless people, testified that many homeless individuals are ineligible for most government assistance programs. For example, Supplemental Security Income is available only to people who are sixty-five years of age or more, who are blind or disabled, and who are without other resources. Social Security Disability Insurance is available only to workers who have paid into the Social Security fund for five of the past ten years prior to the onset of the disability. Aid to Families with Dependent Children is available only to low-income families with physical custody of children under the age of eighteen. The only benefit that is widely available to the homeless is food stamps.

Another notable form of assistance that is unavailable to a substantial number of homeless individuals is shelter space. Lucy testified that there are approximately 700 beds available in local shelters. However, approximately 200 of these are "program beds," for which one must qualify. In addition, some of these beds are set aside for families. Given the estimated 6,000 individuals who were homeless at the time of trial and the untold number of people left homeless by Hurricane Andrew, the lack of adequate housing alternatives cannot be overstated. The plaintiffs truly have no place to go.

In sum, class members rarely choose to be homeless. They become homeless due to a variety of factors that are beyond their control. In addition, plaintiffs do not have the choice, much less the luxury, of being in the privacy of their own homes. Because of the unavailability of low-income housing or alternative shelter, plaintiffs have no choice but to conduct involuntary, life-sustaining activities in public places. The harmless conduct for which they are arrested is inseparable from their involuntary condition of being homeless. Consequently, arresting homeless people for harmless acts they are forced to perform in public effectively punishes them for being homeless. [A]rresting the homeless for harmless, involuntary, life-sustaining acts such as sleeping, sitting or eating in public is cruel and unusual [punishment].

The City suggests, apparently in reference to the aftermath of Hurricane Andrew, that even if homelessness is an involuntary condition in that most persons would not consciously choose to live on the streets, "it is not involuntary in the sense of a situation over which the individual has absolutely no control such as a natural disaster which results in the destruction of one's place of residence so as to render that person homeless." The court cannot accept this distinction. An individual who loses his home as a result of economic hard times or physical or mental illness exercises no more control over these events than he would over a natural disaster. Furthermore, as was established at trial, the City does not have enough shelter to house Miami's homeless residents.

> Consequently, the City cannot argue persuasively that the homeless have made a deliberate choice to live in public places or that their decision to sleep in the park as opposed to some other exposed place is a volitional act. As Professor Wright testified, the lack of reasonable alternatives should not be mistaken for choice.

Id. at 1564-1565. *Accord Jones v. City of Los Angeles,* 444 F.3d 1118 (9th Cir. 2006), *opinion vacated due to settlement by* 505 F.3d 1006 (9th Cir. 2007); *Johnson v. City of Dallas,* 860 F. Supp. 344 (N.D. Tex. 1994), *rev'd on standing grounds,* 61 F.3d 442 (5th Cir. 1995). In 1998, Miami settled the *Pottinger* litigation, agreeing to expand its social services for the homeless and to refrain from arresting the homeless for "life-sustaining activities" without offering them an available bed in a shelter. In April 2013, the City of Miami's commissioners voted to go back to court to try to undo aspects of the *Pottinger* settlement in order to give the police greater latitude to arrest the homeless and dispose of their possessions. *See* Charles Rabin & Andres Viglucci, *Miami to Go to Federal Court to Undo Homeless-Protection Act,* Miami Herald, Apr. 11, 2013.

Consider the following argument by Jeremy Waldron.

> Everything that is done has to be done somewhere. No one is free to perform an action unless there is somewhere he is free to perform it.
>
> One of the functions of property rules, particularly as far as land is concerned, is to provide a basis for determining who is allowed to be where.
>
> A person who is homeless is, obviously enough, a person who has no home. One way of describing the plight of a homeless individual might be to say that there is no place governed by a private property rule where he is allowed to be.
>
> Our society saves the homeless from this catastrophe only by virtue of the fact that some of its territory is held as collective property and made available for common use. The homeless are allowed to be — provided they are on the streets, in the parks, or under the bridges. Some of them are allowed to crowd together into publicly provided "shelters" after dark (though these are dangerous places and there are not nearly enough shelters for all of them). But in the daytime and, for many of them, all through the night, wandering in public places is their only option.
>
> [There] is . . . increasing regulation of the streets, subways, parks, and other public places to restrict the activities that can be performed there. What is emerging — and it is not just a matter of fantasy — is a state of affairs in which a million or more citizens have no place to perform elementary human activities like urinating, washing, sleeping, cooking, eating, and standing around.
>
> For a person who has no home, and has no expectation of being allowed into something like a private office building or a restaurant, prohibitions on things like sleeping that apply particularly to public places pose a special problem. For although there is no general prohibition on acts of these types, still they are effectively ruled out altogether for anyone who is homeless and who has no shelter to go to. The prohibition is comprehensive in effect because of the cumulation, in the case of the homeless, of a number of different bans, differently imposed. The rules of property prohibit the homeless person from doing any of these acts in private, since there is no private place that he has a right to be. And the rules governing public places prohibit him from doing any of these acts

> in public, since that is how we have decided to regulate the use of public places. So what is the result? Since private places and public places between them exhaust all the places that there are, there is nowhere that these actions may be performed by the homeless person. And since freedom to perform a concrete action requires freedom to perform it at some place, it follows that the homeless person does not have the freedom to perform them. If sleeping is prohibited in public places, then sleeping is comprehensively prohibited to the homeless. If urinating is prohibited in public places (and if there are no public lavatories) then the homeless are simply unfree to urinate. These are not altogether comfortable conclusions, and they are certainly not comfortable for those who have to live with them.

Jeremy Waldron, *Homelessness and the Issue of Freedom,* 39 UCLA L. Rev. 295 (1991).

In contrast to *Pottinger*, the California Supreme Court upheld a municipal ordinance that banned camping and storage of personal property in public areas despite evidence that the number of available shelter beds was 2,500 less than the need. *Tobe v. City of Santa Ana*, 892 P.2d 1145 (Cal. 1995). The court merely sustained the ordinance from a facial challenge, however, finding that it did not inevitably conflict with constitutional prohibitions; the court did not rule on the question whether, as applied to the particular facts of the case, the ordinance had the effect of infringing on constitutionally protected rights. The court held that "Santa Ana has no constitutional obligation to make accommodations on or in public property available to the transient homeless to facilitate their exercise of the right to travel," and rejected the notion that the ordinance punished individuals for the "involuntary status of being homeless" because the ordinance regulated conduct, not merely status. *Id.* at 1166. Disagreeing with the analysis in *Pottinger*, the court concluded that "[a]ssuming arguendo the accuracy of the declarants' descriptions of the circumstances in which they were cited under the ordinance, it is far from clear that none had alternatives to either the condition of being homeless or the conduct that led to homelessness and to the citations." *Id.* at 1167. Concurring Justice Joyce Kennard emphasized that the ruling merely upheld the ordinance on its face and did not reject on the merits the claim accepted in *Pottinger* that "a homeless person may not constitutionally be punished for publicly engaging in harmless activities necessary to life, such as sleeping." *Id. Accord, Davison v. City of Tucson*, 924 F. Supp. 989 (D. Ariz. 1996). *But cf. Lavan v. City of Los Angeles*, 797 F. Supp. 2d 1005 (C.D. Cal. 2011) (finding that city violated constitutional rights of the homeless by seizing and destroying property stored on streets without notice and an opportunity to be heard).

Do you agree with the *Pottinger* ruling?

Problems

Seventy convicted sex offenders live under a causeway connecting the City of Miami to Miami Beach because local laws bar them from living within 2,500 feet of where children gather, and there is apparently no place that they are allowed to live in the city. On July 9, 2009, the American Civil Liberties Union sued Miami-Dade County, arguing that its 2,500-foot restriction is preempted by state law, which provides for only a 1,000-foot protective zone. *See* Damien Cave, *Roadside Camp for Miami Sex Offenders Leads to Lawsuit,* N.Y. Times, July 10, 2009. Assuming the local government has the power to enact the 2,500-foot ordinance, do the sex offenders have any remedy? If you were advising the county government, what advice would you give?

CHAPTER 2

Competing Justifications for Property Rights

Property serves many policy goals, and parties justify their claims with many arguments. Some of the core justifications for property claims include sovereign allocation of rights; efficiency or social welfare maximization; distributive justice or equality; settled expectations; labor and investment; and possession or occupancy of the property. You will see courts and litigants invoking various arguments along these lines throughout the materials in this book. In arguing for and evaluating legal claims, lawyers need to be able to identify and employ these arguments to support their legal assertions. This chapter provides an introduction to some of these justifications.

Justifications may point in different directions: one could argue that the first to occupy the property is not the one who will use it most efficiently, for example, or that the government-sanctioned distribution is unequal and therefore unjust. Different justifications may also support each other: awarding rights to the current possessor might encourage investment in the property; or correcting distributive inequalities may facilitate full and efficient use. Some may argue that particular justifications are more compelling than others. Today, for example, much scholarship focuses on economic efficiency, while early American common law placed more emphasis on protecting established expectations. But almost everyone recognizes multiple justifications for property rights. Although the sections below are divided among different kinds of arguments for property rights, you will see litigants and courts making multiple arguments within each section.

§1 PROPERTY AND SOVEREIGNTY

Property and sovereignty are inextricably linked. First, property is the product of sovereignty: without authoritative enforcement of rights to things — without, that is, a sovereign — many argue that there is no property. Second, property in effect delegates sovereign rights to owners — by creating control over use of valuable resources, property gives owners legal control over other individuals. Morris Cohen, *Property and Sovereignty*, 13 Cornell L.Q. 8 (1928).

What justifies sovereign power to allocate and set rules for control of valuable resources? What if there is conflict over which sovereign has that authority? What if the rules set by the sovereign violate justice, equality, efficiency, or expectations founded on other sources? As you will see, while sovereign allocation is a powerful source of property rights, governmental actors (whether judicial, legislative, or executive) sometimes enforce rights acquired in violation of official rules.

§1.1 United States and American Indian Sovereignty

In the United States, all land held by non-Indians theoretically can be traced to title ultimately derived from the U.S. government or a prior colonial power, which in turn obtained title from an American Indian nation. In the mid-fifteenth century, an estimated five to ten million native inhabitants occupied the land mass that is now the United States. By a process of cultural extermination and diseases such as measles and smallpox, the population of American Indians shrank to about 200,000 by 1910. Louise Erdrich notes that this "is proportionately as if the population of the United States were to decrease from its present level to the population of Cleveland." Louise Erdrich, *Where I Ought to Be: A Writer's Sense of Place*, N.Y. Times Book Rev., July 28, 1985, at 1, 23.

European nations colonizing the Americas initially distributed the land without regard to Indian property rights. Asserting divine authority, they granted charters to the Americas from sea to sea and pole to pole. But in North America, both colonial and British law soon required Indian consent to acquire rights in Indian lands. This "consent" was often coerced, forged, or misunderstood. Land acquisition created intense conflict, both between American Indian nations and settlers and among the settlers themselves, who disagreed both about whether a government could regulate their acquisition of Indian land and which government could do so.

Johnson v. M'Intosh, 21 U.S. (8 Wheat.) 543 (1823), involves a conflict between non-Indians over the acquisition of Indian land. The plaintiffs claimed to have obtained title directly from the Illinois and Piankeshaw Indians. The defendant was later granted title by the United States after the government entered into treaties with a number of Indian tribes. In adjudicating this dispute, the Supreme Court had the unenviable task of justifying the process by which American Indian nations were robbed of their ancestral lands. At the same time, Chief Justice John Marshall's opinion provided the basis for substantial legal protection of Indian possessions. How well did the Chief Justice do in attempting to reconcile the demands of justice and power?

Johnson v. M'Intosh

21 U.S. 543 (1823)

[Joshua Johnson and Thomas Graham sued to eject William M'Intosh from certain lands in Illinois. Johnson and Graham claimed the lands by purchase from the Piankeshaw Indians, and M'Intosh claimed it under a grant from the United States. The parties stipulated to the following facts.

The lands were within those that the King of England had originally granted the Virginia Company in 1609. At the time of the grant this territory was "held, occupied, and possessed, in full sovereignty, by various independent tribes or nations of Indians, who were the sovereigns of their respective portions of the territory, and the absolute owners and proprietors of the soil." In 1624, the Virginia Company was dissolved, and it and its lands became the British colony of Virginia.

On October 7, 1763, the King of England issued the Royal Proclamation, reserving for the Indians all lands west of the Appalachians, and forbidding British subjects from purchasing or settling on any of those lands. In 1773, chiefs of the Illinois Nation sold William Murray and others two tracts of land west of the Appalachians for 24,000 dollars. The lands were within the limits of Virginia, east of the Mississippi and northwest of the Ohio Rivers. In 1775, certain chiefs of the Piankeshaw Nation sold Louis Viviat and others lands in the same area for $31,000.

In 1776, the colony of Virginia declared its independence from Great Britain. In 1779, the new State of Virginia decreed that it had the sole right to purchase lands from the Indians within its territory, and that any past or future purchases by individuals from the Indians were void. In 1783, Virginia conveyed all its lands northwest of the Ohio River to the United States. The lands ultimately became part of the State of Illinois. In 1803 and 1809 treaties, the United States acquired parts of the same territory previously purchased by Murray and Viviat from various Indian tribes. In 1818, the United States sold 11,560 acres of this territory to William M'Intosh.

Joshua Johnson and Thomas J. Graham inherited a portion of the lands purchased from the Piankeshaw in 1775 from one of the original private grantees. Neither they nor any of the grantees claiming under the 1773 and 1775 sales had ever had actual possession of the lands. The private grantees had, between 1781 and 1816, repeatedly petitioned the Congress of the United States to acknowledge and confirm their title to those lands without success.]

On the part of the plaintiffs, it was contended,

1. That . . . the Piankeshaw Indians were the owners of the lands in dispute, at the time of executing the deed of October 10th, 1775, and had power to sell. But as the United States had [later] purchased the same lands of the same Indians, both parties claim from the same source. [The Indian] title by occupancy is to be respected, as much as that of an individual, obtained by the same right, in a civilized state. The circumstance, that the members of the society held in common, did not affect the strength of their title by occupancy. In short, all, or nearly all, the lands in the United States, is holden under purchases from the Indian nations; and the only question in this case must be, whether it be competent to individuals to make such purchases, or whether that be the exclusive prerogative of government.

2. That the British king's proclamation of October 7th, 1763, could not affect this right of the Indians to sell; because they were not British subjects, nor in any manner bound by the authority of the British government, legislative or executive. And, because, even admitting them to be British subjects, absolutely, or sub modo, they were still proprietors of the soil, and could not be devested of their rights of property, or any of its incidents, by a mere act of the executive government, such as this proclamation.

3. That the proclamation of 1763 could not restrain the purchasers under these deeds from purchasing. [T]he establishment of a government establishes a system of laws, and excludes the power of legislating by proclamation. The proclamation could not have the force of law within the chartered limits of Virginia. A proclamation, that no person should purchase land in England or Canada, would be clearly void.

4. That the act of Assembly of Virginia, passed in May, 1779, cannot affect the right of the plaintiffs, and others claiming under these deeds; because, on general principles, and by the constitution of Virginia, the legislature was not competent to take away private, vested rights, or appropriate private property to public use, under the circumstances of this case.

On the part of the defendants, it was insisted, that the uniform understanding and practice of European nations, and the settled law, as laid down by the tribunals of civilized states, denied the right of the Indians to be considered as independent communities, having a permanent property in the soil, capable of alienation to private individuals. They remain in a state of nature, and have never been admitted into the general society of nations. Even if it should be admitted that the Indians were originally an independent people, they have ceased to be so. A nation that has passed under the dominion of another, is no longer a sovereign state. The same treaties and negotiations, before referred to, show their dependent condition. Or, if it be admitted that they are now independent and foreign states, the title of the plaintiffs would still be invalid: as grantees from the Indians, they must take according to their laws of property, and as Indian subjects. The law of every dominion affects all persons and property situate within it; and the Indians never had any idea of individual property in lands. It cannot be said that the lands conveyed were disjoined from their dominion; because the grantees could not take the sovereignty and eminent domain to themselves.

. . . By the law of nature, [American Indians] had not acquired a fixed property capable of being transferred. The measure of property acquired by occupancy is determined, according to the law of nature, by the extent of men's wants, and their capacity of using it to supply them. It is a violation of the rights of others to exclude them from the use of what we do not want, and they have an occasion for. Upon this principle the North American Indians could have acquired no proprietary interest in the vast tracts of territory which they wandered over; and their right to the lands on which they hunted, could not be considered as superior to that which is acquired to the sea by fishing in it. The use in the one case, as well as the other, is not exclusive. According to every theory of property, the Indians had no individual rights to land; nor had they any collectively, or in their national capacity; for the lands occupied by each tribe were not used by them in such a manner as to prevent their being appropriated by a people of cultivators. All the proprietary rights of civilized nations on this continent are founded on this principle. . . .

Mr. Chief Justice John Marshall delivered the opinion of the Court.

The plaintiffs in this cause claim the land, in their declaration mentioned, under two grants, purporting to be made, the first in 1773, and the last in 1775, by the chiefs of certain Indian tribes, constituting the Illinois and the Piankeshaw nations; and the question is, whether this title can be recognized in the Courts of the United States?

The facts, as stated in the case agreed, show the authority of the chiefs who executed this conveyance, so far as it could be given by their own people; and likewise show, that the particular tribes for whom these chiefs acted were in rightful possession of the land they sold. The inquiry, therefore, is, in a great measure, confined to the power of Indians to give, and of private individuals to receive, a title which can be sustained in the Courts of this country.

As the right of society, to prescribe those rules by which property may be acquired and preserved is not, and cannot be drawn into question; as the title to lands, especially, is and must be admitted to depend entirely on the law of the nation in which they lie; it will be necessary, in pursuing this inquiry, to examine, not singly those principles of abstract justice, which the Creator of all things has impressed on the mind of his creature man, and which are admitted to regulate, in a great degree, the rights of civilized nations, whose perfect independence is acknowledged; but those principles also which our own government has adopted in the particular case, and given us as the rule for our decision.

On the discovery of this immense continent, the great nations of Europe were eager to appropriate to themselves so much of it as they could respectively acquire. Its vast extent offered an ample field to the ambition and enterprise of all; and the character and religion of its inhabitants afforded an apology for considering them as a people over whom the superior genius of Europe might claim an ascendency. The potentates of the old world found no difficulty in convincing themselves that they made ample compensation to the inhabitants of the new, by bestowing on them civilization and Christianity, in exchange for unlimited independence. But, as they were all in pursuit of nearly the same object, it was necessary, in order to avoid conflicting settlements, and consequent war with each other, to establish a principle, which all should acknowledge as the law by which the right of acquisition, which they all asserted, should be regulated as between themselves. This principle was, that discovery gave title to the government by whose subjects, or by whose authority, it was made, against all other European governments, which title might be consummated by possession.

The exclusion of all other Europeans, necessarily gave to the nation making the discovery the sole right of acquiring the soil from the natives, and establishing settlements upon it. It was a right with which no Europeans could interfere. It was a right which all asserted for themselves, and to the assertion of which, by others, all assented.

Those relations which were to exist between the discoverer and the natives, were to be regulated by themselves. The rights thus acquired being exclusive, no other power could interpose between them.

In the establishment of these relations, the rights of the original inhabitants were, in no instance, entirely disregarded; but were necessarily, to a considerable extent, impaired. They were admitted to be the rightful occupants of the soil, with a legal as well as just claim to retain possession of it, and to use it according to their own discretion; but their rights to complete sovereignty, as independent nations, were necessarily diminished, and their power to dispose of the soil at their own will, to whomsoever they pleased, was denied by the original fundamental principle, that discovery gave exclusive title to those who made it.

While the different nations of Europe respected the right of the natives, as occupants, they asserted the ultimate dominion to be in themselves; and claimed and exercised, as a consequence of this ultimate dominion, a power to grant the soil, while yet in possession of the natives. These grants have been understood by all, to convey a title to the grantees, subject only to the Indian right of occupancy.

The history of America, from its discovery to the present day, proves, we think, the universal recognition of these principles.

No one of the powers of Europe gave its full assent to this principle, more unequivocally than England. The documents upon this subject are ample and complete. So early as the year 1496, her monarch granted a commission to the Cabots, to discover countries then unknown to Christian people, and to take possession of them in the name of the king of England. Two years afterwards, Cabot proceeded on this voyage, and discovered the continent of North America, along which he sailed as far south as Virginia. To this discovery the English trace their title.

[A]ll the nations of Europe, who have acquired territory on this continent, have asserted in themselves, and have recognized in others, the exclusive right of the discoverer to appropriate the lands occupied by the Indians. Have the American States rejected or adopted this principle?

By the treaty which concluded the war of our revolution, Great Britain relinquished all claim, not only to the government, but to the "propriety and territorial rights of the United States," whose boundaries were fixed in the second article. By this treaty, the powers of government, and the right to soil, which had previously been in Great Britain, passed definitively to these States. We had before taken possession of them, by declaring independence; but neither the declaration of independence, nor the treaty confirming it, could give us more than that which we before possessed, or to which Great Britain was before entitled. It has never been doubted, that either the United States, or the several States, had a clear title to all the lands within the boundary lines described in the treaty, subject only to the Indian right of occupancy, and that the exclusive power to extinguish that right, was vested in that government which might constitutionally exercise it.

The States, having within their chartered limits different portions of territory covered by Indians, ceded that territory, generally, to the United States, on conditions expressed in their deeds of cession, which demonstrate the opinion, that they ceded the soil as well as jurisdiction, and that in doing so, they granted a productive fund to the government of the Union. The lands in controversy lay within the chartered limits of Virginia, and were ceded with the whole country northwest of the river Ohio.

The ceded territory was occupied by numerous and warlike tribes of Indians; but the exclusive right of the United States to extinguish their title, and to grant the soil, has never, we believe, been doubted.

The magnificent purchase of Louisiana, was the purchase from France of a country almost entirely occupied by numerous tribes of Indians, who are in fact independent.

Yet, any attempt of others to intrude into that country, would be considered as an aggression which would justify war.

Our late acquisitions from Spain are of the same character; and the negotiations which preceded those acquisitions, recognize and elucidate the principle which has been received as the foundation of all European title in America.

The United States, then, have unequivocally acceded to that great and broad rule by which its civilized inhabitants now hold this country. They hold, and assert in themselves, the title by which it was acquired. They maintain, as all others have maintained, that discovery gave an exclusive right to extinguish the Indian title of occupancy, either by purchase or by conquest; and gave also a right to such a degree of sovereignty, as the circumstances of the people would allow them to exercise.

The power now possessed by the government of the United States to grant lands, resided, while we were colonies, in the crown, or its grantees. The validity of the titles given by either has never been questioned in our Courts. It has been exercised uniformly over territory in possession of the Indians. The existence of this power must negative the existence of any right which may conflict with, and control it. An absolute title to lands cannot exist, at the same time, in different persons, or in different governments. An absolute, must be an exclusive title, or at least a title which excludes all others not compatible with it. All our institutions recognise the absolute title of the crown, subject only to the Indian right of occupancy, and recognise the absolute title of the crown to extinguish that right. This is incompatible with an absolute and complete title in the Indians.

We will not enter into the controversy, whether agriculturists, merchants, and manufacturers, have a right, on abstract principles, to expel hunters from the territory they possess, or to contract their limits. Conquest gives a title which the Courts of the conqueror cannot deny, whatever the private and speculative opinions of individuals may be, respecting the original justice of the claim which has been successfully asserted. The British government, which was then our government, and whose rights have passed to the United States, asserted title to all the lands occupied by Indians, within the chartered limits of the British colonies. It asserted also a limited sovereignty over them, and the exclusive right of extinguishing the title which occupancy gave to them. These claims have been maintained and established as far west as the river Mississippi, by the sword. The title to a vast portion of the lands we now hold, originates in them. It is not for the Courts of this country to question the validity of this title, or to sustain one which is incompatible with it.

Although we do not mean to engage in the defence of those principles which Europeans have applied to Indian title, they may, we think, find some excuse, if not justification, in the character and habits of the people whose rights have been wrested from them.

The title by conquest is acquired and maintained by force. The conqueror prescribes its limits. Humanity, however, acting on public opinion, has established, as a general rule, that the conquered shall not be wantonly oppressed, and that their condition shall remain as eligible as is compatible with the objects of the conquest. Most usually, they are incorporated with the victorious nation, and become subjects or citizens of the government with which they are connected. The new and old members of the society mingle with each other; the distinction between them is gradually lost, and they make one people. Where this incorporation is practicable, humanity demands, and a wise policy requires, that the rights of the conquered to property should remain unimpaired; that the new subjects should be governed as equitably as the old, and that confidence in their security should gradually banish the painful sense of being separated from their ancient connexions, and united by force to strangers.

When the conquest is complete, and the conquered inhabitants can be blended with the conquerors, or safely governed as a distinct people, public opinion, which not even the conqueror can disregard, imposes these restraints upon him; and he cannot neglect them without injury to his fame, and hazard to his power.

But the tribes of Indians inhabiting this country were fierce savages, whose occupation was war, and whose subsistence was drawn chiefly from the forest. To leave them in possession of their country, was to leave the country a wilderness; to govern them as a distinct people, was impossible, because they were as brave and as high spirited as they were fierce, and were ready to repel by arms every attempt on their independence.

What was the inevitable consequence of this state of things? The Europeans were under the necessity either of abandoning the country, and relinquishing their pompous claims to it, or of enforcing those claims by the sword, and by the adoption of principles adapted to the condition of a people with whom it was impossible to mix, and who could not be governed as a distinct society, or of remaining in their neighbourhood, and exposing themselves and their families to the perpetual hazard of being massacred.

Frequent and bloody wars, in which the whites were not always the aggressors, unavoidably ensued. European policy, numbers, and skill, prevailed. As the white population advanced, that of the Indians necessarily receded. The country in the immediate neighbourhood of agriculturists became unfit for them. The game fled into thicker and more unbroken forests, and the Indians followed. The soil, to which the crown originally claimed title, being no longer occupied by its ancient inhabitants, was parcelled out according to the will of the sovereign power, and taken possession of by persons who claimed immediately from the crown, or mediately, through its grantees or deputies.

That law which regulates, and ought to regulate in general, the relations between the conqueror and conquered, was incapable of application to a people under such circumstances. The resort to some new and different rule, better adapted to the actual state of things, was unavoidable. Every rule which can be suggested will be found to be attended with great difficulty.

However extravagant the pretension of converting the discovery of an inhabited country into conquest may appear; if the principle has been asserted in the first instance, and afterwards sustained; if a country has been acquired and held under it; if the property of the great mass of the community originates in it, it becomes the law of the land, and cannot be questioned. So, too, with respect to the concomitant principle, that the Indian inhabitants are to be considered merely as occupants, to be protected, indeed, while in peace, in the possession of their lands, but to be deemed incapable of transferring the absolute title to others. However this restriction may be opposed to natural right, and to the usages of civilized nations, yet, if it be indispensable to that system under which the country has been settled, and be adapted to the actual condition of the two people, it may, perhaps, be supported by reason, and certainly cannot be rejected by Courts of justice.

. . . The absolute ultimate title has been considered as acquired by discovery, subject only to the Indian title of occupancy, which title the discoverers possessed the exclusive right of acquiring. Such a right is no more incompatible with a seisin in fee, than a lease for years, and might as effectually bar an ejectment.

Another view has been taken of this question, which deserves to be considered. The title of the crown, whatever it might be, could be acquired only by a conveyance from the crown. If an individual might extinguish the Indian title for his own benefit, or, in other words, might purchase it, still he could acquire only that title. Admitting their power to change their laws or usages, so far as to allow an individual to separate a portion of their lands from the common stock, and hold it in severalty, still it is a part of their territory, and is held under them, by a title dependent on their laws. The grant derives its efficacy from their will; and, if they choose to resume it, and make a different disposition of the land, the Courts of the United States cannot interpose for the protection of the title. The person who purchases lands from the Indians, within their territory, incorporates himself with them, so far as respects the property purchased; holds their title under their protection, and subject to their laws. If they annul the grant, we know of no tribunal which can revise and set aside the proceeding. We know of no principle which can distinguish this case from a grant made to a native Indian, authorizing him to hold a particular tract of land in severalty.

As such a grant could not separate the Indian from his nation, nor give a title which our Courts could distinguish from the title of his tribe, as it might still be conquered from, or ceded by his tribe, we can perceive no legal principle which will authorize a Court to say, that different consequences are attached to this purchase, because it was made by a stranger. By the treaties concluded between the United States and the Indian nations, whose title the

CONTEXT

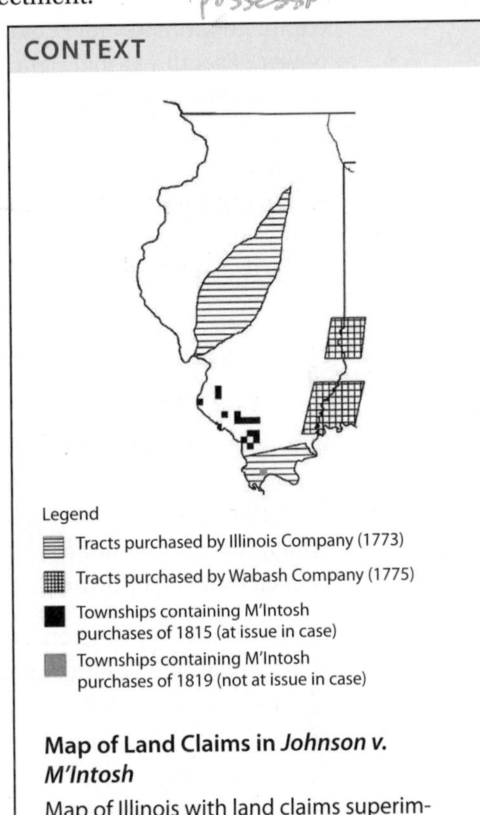

Map of Land Claims in *Johnson v. M'Intosh*

Map of Illinois with land claims superimposed, courtesy of Eric Kades, *History and Interpretation of the Great Case of Johnson v. M'Intosh*, 19 Law & Hist. Rev. 67 (2001). The striped and hatch marked areas are the Murray and Viviat purchases, and the black boxes represent the townships with M'Intosh's land at issue in the case. The plaintiffs' and defendant's lands are not within 50 miles of each other (the gray box at the tip of Illinois includes M'Intosh land not challenged in the case). Why then did they pursue the claim?

plaintiffs claim, the country comprehending the lands in controversy has been ceded to the United States, without any reservation of their title. These nations had been at war with the United States, and had an unquestionable right to annul any grant they had made to American citizens. Their cession of the country, without a reservation of this land, affords a fair presumption, that they considered it as of no validity. They ceded to the United States this very property, after having used it in common with other lands, as their own, from the date of their deeds to the time of cession; and the attempt now made, is to set up their title against that of the United States.

It has never been contended, that the Indian title amounted to nothing. Their right of possession has never been questioned. The claim of government extends to the complete ultimate title, charged with this right of possession, and to the exclusive power of acquiring that right.

After bestowing on this subject a degree of attention which was more required by the magnitude of the interest in litigation, and the able and elaborate arguments of the bar, than by its intrinsic difficulty, the Court is decidedly of opinion, that the plaintiffs do not exhibit a title which can be sustained in the Courts of the United States.

Notes and Questions

1. **Role of doctrine of discovery.** What was the purpose of the doctrine of discovery according to Justice Marshall? To whom did it apply?

2. **Indian property rights under doctrine.** What property rights did Indian nations have under the doctrine? What rights do they lack? Imagine, for example, that a non-Indian individual without federal consent forced an Indian off her land. Does the Indian have a cause of action to remove him? *See Fellows v. Blacksmith*, 60 U.S. 366 (1856) (deciding whether non-Indian state grantees have right to forcibly dispossess Seneca Indian landowners).

3. **United States property rights under doctrine.** What rights did the United States get in Indian lands under the doctrine of discovery? What property rights did they lack? Imagine, for example, that the United States grants an individual a right to lands subject to the Indian title of occupancy. What has to happen before the individual can legally move onto the land and start farming?

4. **The courts of the conqueror.** At the beginning of the opinion, the court reporter summarizes the arguments made by the parties. Note that the opinion does not adopt either of these arguments. Instead, Justice Marshall declared, "Conquest gives a title which the Courts of the conqueror cannot deny, whatever the private and speculative opinions of individuals may be, respecting the original justice of the claim which has been successfully asserted." What does this mean? Can you tell what Justice Marshall's "private and speculative opinion" is of the original justice of the loss of Indian property rights through the doctrine of discovery?

5. **Role of public opinion.** Justice Marshall states that "[h]umanity" has established "as a general rule" that the property rights of a conquered people remain unchanged after conquest, declaring that "public opinion, which not even the conqueror

can disregard, imposes these restraints upon him; and he cannot neglect them without injury to his fame, and hazard to his power." In *United States v. Percheman*, 32 U.S. 51 (1833), the Supreme Court followed this rule in interpreting various laws to validate titles to private citizens granted by Spain before the United States acquired Florida. Chief Justice Marshall's opinion explained, "The modern usage of nations, which has become law, would be violated; that sense of justice and of right which is acknowledged and felt by the whole civilized world would be outraged, if private property should be generally confiscated, and private rights annulled." *Percheman* at 86-87. Why does public opinion limit governmental actions? What are the costs to a government of ignoring public opinion? Why did the general rule not apply to Indian lands?

6. Later Supreme Court statements on Indian land. *Johnson v. M'Intosh* was among the earliest of many Supreme Court statements regarding Indian land. In 1831, Justice Marshall described the discovery doctrine in these words: "The extravagant and absurd idea, that the feeble settlements made on the sea coast, or the companies under whom they were made, acquired legitimate power by them to govern the people, or occupy the lands from sea to sea, did not enter the mind of any man. [All they gained] was the exclusive right of purchasing such lands as the natives were willing to sell." *Worcester v. Georgia*, 31 U.S. 515, 544-545 (1831). In 1835, the Court stated that "it [is] a settled principle, that [American Indians'] right of occupancy is considered as sacred as the fee simple of the whites." *Mitchel v. United States*, 34 U.S. 711, 746 (1835). Are these statements consistent with *Johnson v. M'Intosh*?

In *Tee-Hit-Ton Indians v. United States*, 348 U.S. 272 (1955), the Supreme Court rejected a claim by Alaska Native tribes against the United States for compensation for millions of acres of land. The Court held that although the fifth amendment provides that property shall not be taken without just compensation, U.S. Const., amdt. V, the Constitution did not protect tribal property unless the federal government had formally affirmed title to the land. The Court claimed to base its holding on "the rule derived from *Johnson v. M'Intosh* that the taking by the United States of unrecognized Indian title is not compensable under the Fifth Amendment":

> The line of cases adjudicating Indian rights on American soil leads to the conclusion that Indian occupancy, not specifically recognized as ownership by action authorized by Congress, may be extinguished by the Government without compensation. Every American schoolboy knows that the savage tribes of this continent were deprived of their ancestral ranges by force and that, even when the Indians ceded millions of acres by treaty in return for blankets, food and trinkets, it was not a sale but the conquerors' will that deprived them of their land.
>
> In the light of the history of Indian relations in this Nation, no other course would meet the problem of the growth of the United States. Our conclusion does not uphold harshness as against tenderness toward the Indians, but it leaves with Congress, where it belongs, the policy of Indian gratuities for the termination of Indian occupancy of Government-owned land rather than making compensation for its value a rigid constitutional principle.

In 1884 and 1900, laws for the acquisition and settlement of the Alaska Territory, the United States had provided that the Indians "shall not be disturbed in the possession of any lands actually in their use or occupation or now claimed by them," but the Court found these laws did not recognize any property rights in the Alaska Natives, but simply reserved the question for another day. Therefore the Alaska Natives had no legal protection — besides the "Indian gratuities" Congress was willing to provide — for the acquisition of the lands they had occupied for centuries. Is *Tee-Hit-Ton* consistent with *Johnson*?

§1.2 Competing Justifications for Property Rights

Johnson v. M'Intosh, together with the arguments of the parties at the beginning of the opinion, is a rich source of competing justifications for property rights. To help you spot and evaluate these arguments in the rest of the book, let's trace some of these competing justifications. (Note, however, that *Johnson* has been the subject of perhaps hundreds of articles and multiple full-length books: the list below is necessarily incomplete.)

1. First possession or occupancy. One of the most common arguments for property rights is that one is the first possessor or occupier of the property. *See* Carol Rose, *Possession as the Origin of Property*, 52 U. Chi. L. Rev. 73 (1985). What interests

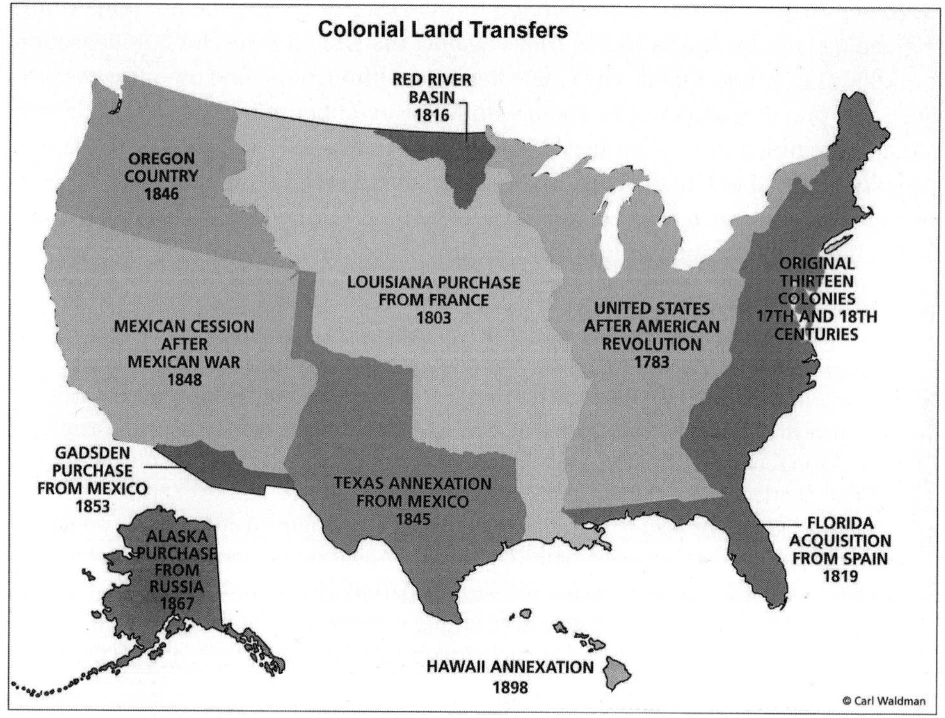

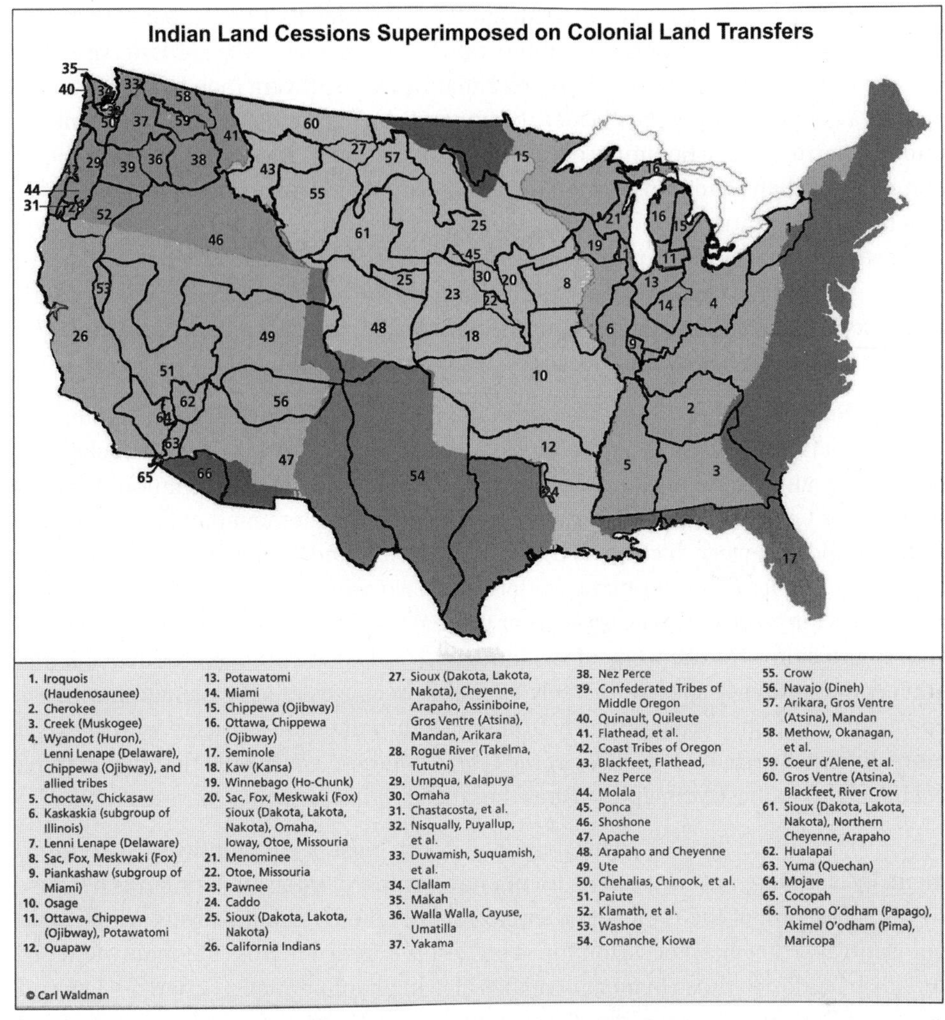

By superimposing official transfers of land from Indian nations over transfers from foreign nations, one can see that the United States recognized the need for consent from both. Maps by Carl Waldman, superimposed by Mira Singer.

does a rule according title to first possessors serve? Well, it might prevent disputes about title, by preventing latecomers from challenging those there first, and encourage individuals to quickly find and claim useful property. What objections can you think of to these justifications? More importantly, why don't these arguments work in *Johnson*? As the plaintiffs argue, the Indians were clearly the first occupants of the land in question. Justice Marshall acknowledges that "converting the discovery of an inhabited country into conquest" is an "extravagant pretension." So why don't the Indians have full property rights?

2. Labor and investment. The defendants counter that the Indians never acquired property rights because as hunters rather than farmers, "the lands occupied by each tribe were not used by them in such a manner as to prevent their being appropriated by a people of cultivators." Does this mean I can demand my neighbor's land if I intend to farm it, while he simply occasionally picnics on it? Recent scholarship shows that in fact Indians had transformed the North American landscape by their work before non-Indians arrived; and as the facts stipulate, neither of the parties in *Johnson* had ever set foot on the land. Regardless, Justice Marshall rejects that as a basis for deciding the case as well, saying, "We will not enter into the controversy, whether agriculturists, merchants, and manufacturers, have a right, on abstract principles, to expel hunters from the territory they possess, or to contract their limits."

3. Efficiency and maximization of social welfare. The farmers over hunters argument is also an efficiency argument that the farmers maximize overall social welfare by engaging in the most productive use of the land. Marshall's opinion does not turn on this argument, but he acknowledges it with his statement that part of the "excuse" for the discovery doctrine is that "[t]o leave [the Indians] in possession of their country, was to leave the country a wilderness." Two central tenets in efficiency-based arguments for property rules are (1) that property rights should be protected, to "assure to the cultivator the fruits of his industry," and so encourage productive labor, and (2) that property should be freely alienable because "[e]very alienation imports advantage" by transferring property from one who values it less to one who values it more. Jeremy Bentham, *Principles of the Civil Code*, chs. 3 & 19 (1802). Can you think of challenges to these principles? Does the rule in *Johnson* further these principles?

4. Distributive justice. The defendants also raise a distributive justice argument, by claiming that the Indians do not have property rights in their lands because "[i]t is a violation of the rights of others to exclude them from the use of what we do not want, and they have occasion for." The desire to prevent gross inequality and ensure distribution to those in great need has also been influential in American law and policy, influencing, for example, the passage of the *Homestead Act* in 1862, and the *Social Security Act* in 1934. Thomas Jefferson urged James Madison in 1785, "I am conscious that an equal division of property is impracticable. But the consequences of this enormous inequality producing so much misery to the bulk of mankind, legislators cannot invent too many devices for subdividing property." Does inequality justify redistribution of property? Under which circumstances, if any?

5. Sovereign authority or might makes right? That brings us back to Marshall's central point: the discovery doctrine is the law because the government in charge said so, and the government has to have the power to say who can acquire property rights and how. One could see this as a simple statement that property arises from law: in order to prevent constant insecurity of property rights and to facilitate transfers, we have agreed to governmental rules regarding what property rights are and how they are acquired. To settle a vast continent, and prevent settlers from getting the United States into wars it could not handle, the government needed authority over when Indian land was acquired and how.

For the Indians, however, the doctrine that they lacked rights to transfer their land based on the decree of foreigners who had never set foot on that land must have felt like a subtly different rule: that property rights are created by and favor those in power. U.S. history provides other support for such a perception. African slaves not only were property, but were prevented from owning property. *See, e.g., Graves v. Allan*, 52 Ky. 190 (Ky. App. 1852). *But see* Dylan C. Penningroth, *The Claims of Kinfolk: African American Property and Community in the Nineteenth-Century South* (2003) (describing the well-established ownership networks slaves developed with the consent of their masters). Married women's property became that of their husbands until the late nineteenth century. *See* Chapter 9, §3.1.B; Reva Siegel, *Home as Work: The First Women's Rights Claims Concerning Wives' Household Labor: 1850-1880*, Yale L.J. 1073, 1082 (1994) ("[A] wife negotiated marriage as a dependent: without property or the legal prerogative to earn it."). And "immigrants ineligible for citizenship," a category that included almost all Asian immigrants until well into the twentieth century, were prevented from owning property up and down the West Coast and in many other states. See Keith Aoki, *No Right to Own? The Early Twentieth-Century "Alien Land Laws" as a Prelude to Internment*, 40 B.C. L. Rev. 37 (1998); Rose Cuison Villazor, *Oyama v. California: At the Intersection of Property, Race, and Citizenship*, 87 Wash. U. L. Rev. 979 (2010). At the same time, these laws clashed with another fundamental precept of property: that the system works better when everyone can participate in property ownership.

§1.3 Past Wrongs, Present Remedies: Modern Indian Land Claims

In 1790, the year after the U.S. Constitution was ratified, Congress codified the prohibition on purchasing Indian land without federal consent. The *Trade and Intercourse Act*, also called the *Nonintercourse Act*, remains in effect with slight amendments today:

> No purchase, grant, lease, or other conveyance of lands, or of any title or claim thereto, from any Indian nation or tribe of Indians, shall be of any validity in law or equity, unless the same be made by treaty or convention entered into pursuant to the Constitution.

25 U.S.C. §177. Despite the statute, both states and private parties continued to acquire Indian land without federal consent. New York, for example, purchased most of the treaty lands of the Iroquois Nations of the Haudenosaunee Confederacy. Federal officials urged New York to comply with the *Nonintercourse Act*, but the state ignored them. Rather than enforcing the restriction, the United States tried to convince the tribes to exchange their remaining land for lands west of the Mississippi River. Although the tribes challenged the state purchases (including by arguing that they were fraudulent), procedural obstacles made it difficult for tribes to sue the states directly. State law prohibited tribes from bringing suit regarding Indian lands except through state-appointed guardians. Until 1875, federal courts lacked general jurisdiction to review questions of federal law. Even after 1875, state sovereign immunity barred suits

against the state to acquire their lands. *See* Robert N. Clinton & Margaret Tobey Hotopp, *Judicial Enforcement of the Federal Restraints on the Alienation of Indian Land: The Origins of the Indian Land Claims,* 31 Me. L. Rev. 17 (1979-1980); Joseph William Singer, *Nine-Tenths of the Law: Title, Possession & Sacred Obligations,* 38 Conn. L. Rev. 605 (2006). In the meantime, non-Indians bought and sold the acquired lands, cities and towns developed, and homes and businesses were built. The federal treaties guaranteeing the land to the Iroquois Nations seemed a thing of the past.

In 1966, however, the United States enacted a statute allowing tribes to bring actions against third parties in federal court without federal consent. In 1969, the Oneida Indian Nation of New York sued Oneida County seeking rent for occupation between 1968 and 1969 of 100,000 acres of land. The United States had guaranteed the land to the Oneidas in a 1794 treaty, but New York purchased the treaty land in 1795. In 1974, the Supreme Court held that the *Nonintercourse Act* granted the tribes a federal common law right to sue for violations of the act. *Oneida Indian Nation v. County of Oneida,* 414 U.S. 661 (1974) (*Oneida I*). On remand, the district court and court of appeals held that the 1795 purchase was void, and ordered the county to pay rent for the land. *Oneida Indian Nation v. Oneida County,* 719 F.2d 525 (2d Cir. 1983). The Supreme Court affirmed the decision, holding that no federal statute of limitations barred the tribal claims. *County of Oneida v. Oneida Indian Nation,* 470 U.S. 226 (1985) (*Oneida II*).

While this litigation was pending, the Oneidas brought an additional claim for possession of all of their original treaty land. Over the course of the 1970s, other tribes in New York, Maine, Massachusetts, Rhode Island, and Connecticut, brought *Nonintercourse Act* claims challenging state and private acquisitions of their land. Some of these claims were defeated or delayed by arguments that the plaintiffs were not really Indian tribes. Other claims were settled, usually with agreements that the tribe would cede most of its original land in exchange for the guarantee of some publicly owned lands as a reservation and funds to purchase additional reservation lands from willing sellers in a specified area. *E.g., Rhode Island Indian Claims Settlement Act,* 25 U.S.C. §1701 et seq.; *Maine Indian Claims Settlement Act,* 25 U.S.C. §1721 et seq.; *Mashantucket Pequot Indian Claims Settlement Act,* 25 U.S.C.A. §1751 et seq.; *Mohegan Nation (Connecticut) Land Claims Settlement Act,* 25 U.S.C. §1755 et seq. In order to secure the settlements, the tribes also agreed to significant state jurisdiction over the new lands.

But New York and the Iroquois Nations never settled. The ongoing litigation created concern among landowners, who feared ejectment from the land, and hostility against the tribes. Signs reading "no sovereign nation, no reservation" appeared along county roads. In 1999, in a case concerning land claims by the Cayuga Indian Nation, the U.S. district court held that the parties could not join private landowners to the litigation or seek to eject them, finding that such a remedy was impossible given the passage of time. *Cayuga Indian Nation of New York v. Cuomo,* 1999 U.S. Dist. LEXIS 10579 (N.D.N.Y. 1999). The district judge found that "the loss of their homeland has had an immeasurable impact upon the Cayuga culture and Cayuga society as a whole," *id.* at *77, and that the tribes had continuously tried to get back the land but that the "systems which theoretically should have assisted the Cayugas seemingly thwarted their efforts." *Id.* at *77 & *83. Nevertheless, ejectment of private landowners would "potentially displace literally thousands of private landowners and several public landowners" and would "prove all too vividly the old axiom: 'Two wrongs don't make a right.'" *Id.* at *90-*91; *see also Oneida Indian Nation of N.Y. v. County of Oneida,* 199 F.R.D. 61 (N.D.N.Y. 2000). In a later opinion, the court awarded the Cayuga Indian Nation approximately $247 million in damages for the lost rental value of their land, *Cayuga Indian Nation of New York v. Pataki,* 165 F. Supp. 2d 266 (N.D.N.Y. 2002), *rev'd,* 413 F.3d 266 (2d Cir. 2005), but, as you will see, the Second Circuit later held the Cayuga could not claim even that.

As the legal battle continued, the Oneida Indian Nation of New York bought back some of the lands within the boundaries laid out by its 1794 treaty with the United States. It began to operate businesses on the lands, arguing that because the treaty had never been legally terminated, the lands were part of a reservation and free from state taxation. The district court and Second Circuit agreed, but Supreme Court reversed. *Sherrill v. Oneida Indian Nation of New York,* 544 U.S. 197 (2005), held that laches, acquiescence, and impossibility barred the claim to freedom from state jurisdiction.

Laches is an equitable doctrine barring actions by those whose unreasonable delay in suing has resulted in prejudice to their opponents in defending the claim. *See* Kathryn E. Fort, *The New Laches: Creating Title Where None Existed,* 16 Geo. Mason L. Rev. 357 (2009). The Court did not discuss whether the Oneidas could have brought the suit earlier, or find that the passage of time would prejudice the defendants. Nevertheless, it held, laches applied because the state and counties had long exercised sovereignty over the territory, the Oneida Indian Nation had acquiesced in this state of affairs, and it would be disruptive now to alter the jurisdiction with respect to these parcels of land. The Second Circuit has applied the *Sherrill* decision to other ongoing land claims, reversing the aforementioned damages award in favor of the Cayugas as barred by laches as well. *Cayuga Indian Nation v. Pataki,* 413 F.3d 266 (2d Cir. 2005); *see also Oneida Indian Nation of N.Y. v. County of Oneida,* 617 F.3d 114 (2d Cir. 2010).

Notes and Questions

1. No one today argues that unauthorized state acquisitions of tribal lands were legal in 1795, and few still argue that they were justified at the time. But uncorrected injustice in allocations of property often leads to justifiable expectations by those who later purchase and improve the lands. How should these conflicting expectations — between Indian nations deprived of their homelands and those who later built homes and towns on those lands — be resolved? Do you agree with Judge McCurn that while states may be held liable today for the illegal acquisition of land, private landowners cannot be? Do you agree with the Supreme Court that even when tribes purchase land within their treaty boundaries from private sellers, it is too disruptive for tribes to assert immunity from state jurisdiction on those lands?

2. Many nations face the conflict between past injustice and present land possession. In South Africa, for example, apartheid segregated the races and concentrated all political and economic power in a white minority until the 1990s. Even after the formal

end of apartheid in 1994, the same white minority owned most of the productive land in the country. Although the country began a voluntary land distribution program, the program stalled because funds that might have been used to pay landowners were necessary for other social and economic programs. In addition, the existing landowners, who could take advantage of economies of scale and had far more capital and experience, were often more productive farmers. In the meantime, some landless black South Africans left desperately overcrowded townships to occupy lands they believed were unowned, or at least unneeded by their owners. *See* Sharon LaFraniere & Michael Wines, *Africa Quandary: Whites' Land v. the Landlessness of Blacks*, N.Y. Times, Jan. 6, 2004, at A-1.

In one case, over 40,000 squatters moved onto a portion of the Modderklip-Boerdery farm, building a makeshift town with thousands of shacks and streets. Although the lower courts granted Modderklip-Boerdery an order of eviction, when the residents refused to leave voluntarily, the sheriff demanded that Modderklip-Boerdery provide a deposit of 1.8 million rand (about 200,000 dollars) to cover the costs of the security firm the sheriff would need to hire to assist with the removal. The owner appealed, and the Supreme Court of Appeal of South Africa held that because government enforcement of property rights is an essential part of property, denying enforcement was therefore the equivalent of a taking of property. Eviction without provision of alternate housing, however, would violate the right to housing provided by the South African Constitution. The court found that Modderklip-Boerdery was entitled to damages for the loss of the land, and that the squatters were entitled to stay until the state provided them with other housing. *Modder East Squatters v. Modderklip Boerdery (PTY), Ltd.*, 2004 (8) BCLR 821 (SCA) (S. Afr.). How should the government respond to such conflicts? What are the potential costs of different courses of action?

§2 GOVERNMENT GRANT

§2.1 Homestead Acts and Land Grants

Once lands were taken from American Indian nations, they were held by the U.S. government as public lands. How were those lands distributed? The United States adopted a mixed strategy. Although the federal government retained a substantial amount, especially in the western states, it also sold or gave away millions of acres. "A whole continent was sold or given away — to veterans, settlers, squatters, railroads, states, colleges, speculators, and land companies." Lawrence M. Friedman, *A History of American Law* 231 (2d ed. 1985). The main reason for getting rid of the land was the promotion of the "basic postulate of American social structure. The ideal was a country of free citizens, small-holders living on their own bits of land." *Id.* at 232. Much of the land was granted as a gift under specific conditions rather than sold. A great deal of land was given to colleges and railroads, and other lands were granted to the state governments themselves. At least 130 million acres were granted to railroads. *Id.* at 415.

Beginning in 1796, land was sold in large tracts for relatively high prices. This policy provoked fears of land monopoly and seemed to favor speculators over farmers. Demands for cheaper, more available land prompted passage of an 1820 law reducing the price of land. Yet many settlers resisted federal policy, occupying federal lands before formally purchasing them. Bowing to settler demands, laws were repeatedly passed giving preferences (preemption rights) to actual settlers, including illegal settlers, culminating in a general law in 1841. That law gave the head of a family who had settled "in person" on land and "improved" it the first claim to buy the land, up to a maximum of 160 acres, at the minimum government price. *Id.* at 233-234.

After the Civil War, the *Morrill Act* of 1862 gave away vast tracts of land to the states: 30,000 acres for each senator and representative the state was entitled to under the 1860 census. The land was to be used to establish "Colleges for the Benefit of Agriculture and Mechanic Arts" — the land grant colleges existing in every state are the result. In addition, the *Homestead Act* of 1862 granted most heads of families, persons over 21, and veterans (except those who had "borne arms against the United States or given aid and comfort to its enemies") the right to "enter one quarter section or a less quantity of unappropriated public lands" if they would certify that they wanted the land for their own "exclusive use and benefit" and "for the purpose of actual settlement." *Id.* at 416. After five years of settlement, the government would issue a patent for the land. An actual settler who qualified could, however, buy up the land at the minimum price (generally $1.25 an acre) before the end of the five-year period.

The land laws were, in Friedman's words, "hopelessly inconsistent." A variety of policies were followed. "Some land was free for settlers; other land was for sale. The government proposed to sell some land to the highest bidder; proposed using other land to induce private enterprise to build railroads; gave other land to the state to fund their colleges." *Id.* at 417. The "homestead principle" of "giving land free to the landless poor" was the "weakest of all, and the first to go. The government continued to sell land for cash; and the best land was 'snapped up' by speculators." *Id.*

§2.2 Squatters

Despite emphasis on governmental allocation of property rights, individuals and groups often assert property rights inconsistent with the law, and perhaps more surprising, the government often recognizes these assertions by granting formal rights. Eduardo Moises Peñalver and Sonia K. Katyal note that "[t]ime and again, groups of people have intentionally violated property laws, and in a number of important instances, property law has responded by shifting to accommodate their demands, bringing them back within the fold of the law-abiding community." *Property Outlaws: How Squatters, Pirates, and Protesters Improve the Law of Property* (2010). Why does the government sometimes acquiesce to squatting? What does the excerpt below suggest?

James Willard Hurst, Law and the Conditions of Freedom in the Nineteenth-Century United States

3-5 (1956)

One day in February of 1836, in the scarce-born village of Pike Creek on the southeastern Wisconsin shore of Lake Michigan, Jason Lothrop — Baptist minister, schoolteacher, boarding house proprietor, and civic leader — set up on a stump a rude press of his own construction and with ink which he had made himself printed a handbill setting forth the record of the organizational meeting of "The Pike River Claimants Union . . . for the attainment and security of titles to claims on Government lands."

The settlers whose Union this was had begun to move into the lands about Pike Creek beginning in the summer of 1835. They were squatters; put less sympathetically, they were trespassers. They might not lawfully come upon the lands before the federal survey was made, and this was not completed in this area until about February 1, 1836; they might not make formal entry and buy until the President proclaimed a sale day, and Presidents Jackson and Van Buren withheld proclaiming these newly surveyed lands until 1839; they might not establish claims by pre-emption, for the existing pre-emption law expired by limitation in June, 1836, and was not immediately renewed because of objections to speculators' abuses.

Jason Lothrop recalled twenty years later: "Before the lands were surveyed, this often brought confusion and disputes with reference to boundary lines, and still greater confusion followed when the Government surveys were made in the winter of 1835-36. These contentions often led to bitter quarrels and even bloodshed."

The settlers met several times to discuss the need of a more orderly framework within which growth might go on. Finally their discussions produced a meeting at Bullen's store in Pike Creek on February 13, 1836, where they adopted the constitution of their Claimants Union[:]

> Whereas, a union and co-operation of all the inhabitants will be indispensably necessary, in case the pre-emption law should not pass, for the securing and protecting of our claims;
>
> And whereas, we duly appreciate the benefit which may result from such an association, not only in regulating the manner of making and sustaining claims, and settling differences in regard to them, but in securing the same to the holders thereof against speculators at the land sale; and being well aware that consequences the most dangerous to the interests of settlers will follow, if such a union be not formed; and as Government has heretofore encouraged emigration by granting pre-emption to actual settlers, we are assured that our settling and cultivating the public lands is in accordance with the best wishes of Government; and knowing that in some instances our neighbors have been dealt with in an unfeeling manner, driven from their homes, their property destroyed, their persons attacked, and their lives jeopardized, to satisfy the malignant disposition of unprincipled and avaricious men; and looking upon such proceedings as unjust, calculated to produce anarchy, confusion and the like among us, destroy our fair prospects, subvert the good order of society, and render our homes the habitations of terror and distrust — those homes, to obtain which we left our friends, deprived ourselves of the many blessings and privileges of society, have borne the expenses, and

encountered the hardships of a perilous journey, advancing into a space beyond the bounds of civilization, and having the many difficulties and obstructions of a state of nature to overcome, and on the peaceable possession of which our all is depending;

We, therefore, as well meaning inhabitants, having in view the promotion of the interest of our settlement, and knowing the many advantages derived from unity of feeling and action, do come forward this day, and solemnly pledge ourselves to render each other our mutual assistance, in the protection of our just rights.

From the survey Ordinance of 1785 on, squatters settled large areas of the public lands in defiance of law, ahead of official survey, without color of title other than that created by the impact of a popular feeling that would not be denied. At government auctions, they assembled in force unlawfully to frighten off free outside bidding and prevent competition from forcing any of their company to pay the public land office more than the legal minimum to regularize his holdings. But, as at Pike Creek, while they waited for the public sale day, these settlers all over the central and midwestern states set up local governments in the form of "claims associations," elected officers with whom to record their land claims and from whom to obtain decisions of conflicts, and then generally abided among themselves by these records and decisions. Often unlawful in origin, settlement nevertheless quickly brought effective demand for law.

§2.3 Freed Slaves

I and my children are now free! We are as free from the power of slaveholders as are the white people of the north; and though that, according to my ideas, is not saying a great deal, it is a vast improvement in *my* condition. The dream of my life is not yet realized. I do not sit with my children in a home of my own. I still long for a hearthstone of my own, however humble. I wish it for my children's sake far more than for my own.

—Harriet A. Jacobs[1]

Many freed slaves saw land ownership as a crucial element of freedom. As slave owners fled in advance of federal troops, their former slaves staked claims to the plantations as compensation for their years of unpaid labor. Yankee soldiers encouraged them, telling them they were entitled to 40 acres and a mule.

"My master has had me ever since I was seven years old, and never give me nothing," observed a twenty-one-year-old laborer in Richmond. "I worked for him twelve years, and I think something is due me." The day a South Carolina rice planter anticipated trouble was when one of his field hands told him that "the land ought to belong to the man who (alone) could work it," not to those who "sit in the house" and profit by the labor of others.

[P]lanters derived considerable comfort from the knowledge that Federal officials were prepared to confirm their property rights. Until the blacks acknowledged the futility of land expectations, the Freedmen's Bureau recognised how difficult it would be to stabilize agricultural operations. With that sense of priorities, the Bureau instructed its

1. Harriet A. Jacobs, *Incidents in the Life of a Slave Girl: Written by Herself* 201 (Harvard Univ. Press 1987) (1861).

> agents to do everything in their power to disabuse the ex-slaves of any lingering illusions about taking over their masters' lands.
>
> Rather than confirm the settlers in possession of the land they had cultivated and on which they had erected their homes, the government now proposed to return the plantations to those for whom they had previously labored as slaves.

Leon Litwack, *Been in the Storm So Long: The Aftermath of Slavery* 399-405 (1980). On May 29, 1865, President Andrew Johnson issued a Proclamation of Amnesty, pardoning most former Confederates and ordering their property returned. News of the proclamation helped fuel a rumor that the president had revoked the Emancipation Proclamation. Some refused to abandon their land. In Norfolk County, Virginia, ex-slave Richard Parker urged his fellow freedmen to fight to defend their lands together, arguing that "the white man had secured this land only by forcibly expelling the Indians and he suggested that they now exercise the same prerogative. After a pitched battle with county agents, the black settlers were finally driven off the land." *Id.* at 406.

Freedmen bureau officials and missionaries preached self-help instead of redistribution, telling the freedmen that if they worked hard and saved their wages, they would soon be able to buy land of their own. But many planters refused to sell or rent to blacks, for fear of losing a stable workforce and generating feelings of "impudence and independence." Litwack at 407. Labor contracts became new forms of peonage, criminalizing leaving before the contract was over or before debts to the landowner for seeds and supplies had been paid. *See* Aviam Soifer, *Status, Contract, and Promises Unkept*, 96 Yale L.J. 1916, 1944-51 (1987). Blacks who did manage to buy land of their own also often became the targets of extralegal violence and fraud.

Notes and Questions

1. **Contemporary implications.** *Johnson v. M'Intosh* discussed the acquisition of vast amounts of land from American Indian nations. A great deal of this land was given to the railroads for free. In the middle of the nineteenth century, land grants to railroads encompassed 155 million acres, "or more than one fourth of the Louisiana purchase, one ninth of what was then the nation's entire land area." Dee Brown, *Hear That Lonesome Whistle Blow* 176-177 (1977). Other land in the West was sold or distributed by the government at below-market prices. Still other land was sold at fair market value; some of this land went to speculators who resold it. James Willard Hurst notes that squatters often defeated federal land policies by trespassing on public lands; many of their claims were later recognized by the federal government. Leon Litwack recounts how freed slaves were denied not only access to land but also compensation for their years of unpaid labor; they were often constrained by economic necessity to continue working that same land, sometimes for the same master.

Together, these historical reports suggest an activist government taking and distributing land for a variety of purposes. They also suggest a fair amount of self-help and creation of law by communities of settlers who squatted on government land. What implications does such government policy have for us today?

2. Squatters on tribal land. A perennial problem was what to do about squatters who illegally entered tribal or federal lands without a permit from the federal government or a federal patent. Sometimes the United States used force to remove such trespassers. It might do so to ensure an orderly transfer of property and to give each person an equal chance to acquire the best lands. But politics often caused the government to look away when illegal settlements occurred. Pressure from illegal squatters also often led the United States to pressure tribes to sign new treaties giving up yet more land. The famous legal battle between the Cherokee Nation and the State of Georgia resulted from Cherokee refusal to bow to this pressure; the Cherokees won an initial legal victory in *Worcester v. Georgia*, 31 U.S. 515 (1831), but the United States ultimately forced the Cherokees off the land in what has become known as the Trail of Tears.

Problem

A group of homeless persons takes over abandoned property in a major city. The city has foreclosed on the property for failure to pay property taxes and has not yet resold it or begun looking for a buyer, since the property is dilapidated. The squatters claim a right to take over the abandoned property and point to the experience of the American West, where squatters took over property and interfered with land sales to others. More often than not, those squatters' claims were later confirmed by legislation. The city objects to random occupations of its property and hopes to develop a rational plan for the future use of the property.

1. As attorney for the city, what advice would you give the mayor?
2. As attorney for the squatters, what arguments would you make to persuade the city to allow your clients to claim possessory rights in abandoned city property? As attorney for the city, how would you respond to these arguments?

§2.4 Basic Needs Fulfillment

The constitutions of some countries, such as South Africa, contain a right to housing and basic welfare needs. *See, e.g.*, S. Afr. Const. ch. 2, §26 ("Everyone has the right to have access to adequate housing"); S. Afr. Const. ch. 2, §27(1) ("Everyone has the right to have access to a. health care services, including reproductive health care; b. sufficient food and water; and c. social security, including, if they are unable to support themselves and their dependants, appropriate social assistance"). The U.S. Constitution does not contain such a guarantee. In 1969, Professor Frank Michelman argued that the U.S. Constitution should be interpreted to require the states to provide minimum levels of government financial assistance sufficient to enable the poor to provide for their basic needs and to avoid severe deprivation. In effect, he suggested that individuals have a constitutional right to minimum protection to obtain access to the means necessary for human life. Frank Michelman, *Foreword: On Protecting the Poor Through the Fourteenth Amendment*, 83 Harv. L. Rev. 7 (1969); *see also* Frank

Michelman, *In Pursuit of Constitutional Welfare Rights: One View of Rawls' Theory of Justice,* 121 U. Pa. L. Rev. 962 (1973). No court in the United States has accepted this argument.

The New York Constitution requires provision of social welfare for the needy, but its enforcement is subject to legislative discretion. N.Y. Const. art. XVII, §1 ("The aid, care and support of the needy are public concerns and shall be provided by the state and by such of its subdivisions, and in such manner and by such means, as the legislature may from time to time determine"); *Tucker v. Toia,* 371 N.E.2d 449, 451 (N.Y. 1977) (although the legislature has the discretion to determine the means and amount of aid to the needy, the constitution prohibits the legislature from refusing to aid those it has classified as needy). Some courts have interpreted their state welfare statutes to impose obligations on the legislature to provide sufficient funding to enable families to live with their children and avoid placing their children in foster care. *See, e.g., Massachusetts Coalition for the Homeless v. Secretary of Human Services,* 511 N.E.2d 603 (Mass. 1987); *Jiggetts v. Grinker,* 553 N.E.2d 570 (N.Y. 1990); *Hodge v. Ginsberg,* 303 S.E.2d 245 (W. Va. 1983). Such rulings are subject to legislative amendment; the Massachusetts legislature overruled the *Massachusetts Coalition* case by inserting the words "subject to appropriation" in the statute. *See, e.g.,* Mass. Gen. Laws ch. 18, §2. Most state courts have agreed with a New Jersey court that ruled that "the extent to which funds are to be made available to meet the standard of need under New Jersey statutes is a political question to be decided by the representatives of the people." *In re Petitions for Rulemaking,* 538 A.2d 1302 (N.J. Super. Ct. App. Div. 1988).

At the time Professor Michelman wrote, federal welfare legislation guaranteed families with children an entitlement to a minimum level of government benefits. However, in 1996, Congress passed the *Personal Responsibility and Work Opportunity Act of 1996,* 42 U.S.C. §§601-619. This "welfare reform" bill abolished the old *Aid to Families with Dependent Children* (AFDC) program and replaced it with *Temporary Assistance to Needy Families* (TANF). The new law abolishes the welfare entitlement and replaces it with a more limited right to temporary assistance with a five-year lifetime limit on such government benefits and a requirement that recipients start working within two years in order to continue receiving benefits. States are empowered to apply even more stringent requirements, such as requiring recipients to go to work immediately, a policy that was originally adopted in Wisconsin. Wis. Stat. §49.141(2)(b) (repealed, 1999 Wis. Laws Act 9).

If a mother obtains a job paying the minimum wage, she is unlikely to be able to care for herself and her children and pay for housing, clothing, adequate childcare, and transportation without additional funding from some other source. Kathryn Edin & Laura Lein, *Making Ends Meet: How Single Mothers Survive Welfare and Low-Wage Work* (1997). Should individuals be entitled to minimum levels of assistance? Should parents be entitled to sufficient resources to live with their children? Consider the following story from the *New York Times.*

> The [welfare mother] had signed an agreement with the state to go to college, which she believed offered her the best route to a job that paid enough to support her three

> children. She was put on a waiting list. Her caseworker told her she would have to get a job in the meantime. A few weeks after she began working for $5.50 an hour, her 5-year-old got sick. The boy was running a fever and could not go to the day-care center. The worker then told the mother that the only acceptable excuse for missing work was a doctor's note saying that she herself was ill. So she left her son with a neighbor. When she came home, she found him alone and untended. She stayed home with him and was fired from her job. Her welfare benefits were then reduced because she had not done what her worker required. Unable to pay the rent, the family was evicted . . . and slept in a friend's car. Because of the family homelessness, one of the children's teachers reported them to child-protection services. The child-protection worker told the mother that her children would be placed in foster care if she could not provide for them.

Celia W. Dugger, *Iowa Plan Tries to Cut Off the Cash*, N.Y. Times, Apr. 7, 1995, at A-1, quoted in Joel F. Handler & Yeheskel Hasenfeld, *We the Poor People: Work, Poverty, and Welfare* 98 (1997).

Assume the mother sues the state, claiming that she has a constitutional right not to be separated from her children and that, if government assistance is needed to ensure this right, that she is constitutionally entitled to it so that she can raise her children in her own home. How would you decide the case?

§3 LABOR AND INVESTMENT

John Locke famously asserted that labor and investment were the basis for property rights: "Whatsoever then he removes out of the state that nature hath provided, and left it in, he hath mixed his labour with, and joined to it something that is his own, and thereby makes it his property." John Locke, *Second Treatise on Government*, ch. 5 §27 (1690). But labor only sometimes results in property rights. Even Locke immediately qualified his statement with the proviso that it would only apply "at least where there is enough, and as good, left in common for others." *Id.* What role should labor and investment play in claims to property? What kinds of labor are sufficient? Must the labor increase the objective value of the resource? How much does the individual's labor have to contribute to the final product as compared to the raw materials? Philosopher Robert Nozick, for example, asked whether someone who throws her can of tomato juice into the sea has gained ownership of the sea or simply lost her tomato juice? Robert Nozick, *Anarchy, State and Utopia* 175 (1974).

§3.1 Creative Labor

Questions of the effect of labor and investment are particularly pressing when the alleged property is not physical, but is instead the result of creation, invention, or, as in the next case, fact-gathering. Here, the useful product of the labor can be shared by many with very little additional effort. What are the arguments for and against creating property rights that prevent such sharing?

International News Service v. Associated Press

248 U.S. 215 (1918)

Mr. Justice MAHLON PITNEY delivered the opinion of the Court.

The parties are competitors in the gathering and distribution of news and its publication for profit in newspapers throughout the United States. The Associated Press, which was complainant in the District Court, is a co-operative organization, incorporated under the *Membership Corporations Law* of the state of New York, its members being individuals who are either proprietors or representatives of about 950 daily newspapers published in all parts of the United States. Complainant gathers in all parts of the world, by means of various instrumentalities of its own, by exchange with its members, and by other appropriate means, news and intelligence of current and recent events of interest to newspaper readers and distributes it daily to its members for publication in their newspapers. The cost of the service, amounting approximately to $3,500,000 per annum, is assessed upon the members and becomes a part of their costs of operation, to be recouped, presumably with profit, through the publication of their several newspapers. Under complainant's by-laws each member agrees upon assuming membership that news received through complainant's service is received exclusively for publication in a particular newspaper, language, and place specified in the certificate of membership, that no other use of it shall be permitted, and that no member shall furnish or permit any one in his employ or connected with his newspaper to furnish any of complainant's news in advance of publication to any person not a member. And each member is required to gather the local news of his district and supply it to the Associated Press and to no one else.

Defendant [International News Service] is a corporation organized under the laws of the state of New Jersey, whose business is the gathering and selling of news to its customers and clients, consisting of newspapers published throughout the United States, under contracts by which they pay certain amounts at stated times for defendant's service. It has widespread news-gathering agencies; the cost of its operations amounts, it is said, to more than $2,000,000 per annum; and it serves about 400 newspapers located in the various cities of the United States and abroad, a few of which are represented, also, in the membership of the Associated Press.

The parties are in the keenest competition between themselves in the distribution of news throughout the United States; and so, as a rule, are the newspapers that they serve, in their several districts.

Complainant in its bill, defendant in its answer, have set forth in almost identical terms the rather obvious circumstances and conditions under which their business is conducted. The value of the service, and of the news furnished, depends upon the promptness of transmission, as well as upon the accuracy and impartiality of the news; it being essential that the news be transmitted to members or subscribers as early or earlier than similar information can be furnished to competing newspapers by other news services, and that the news furnished by each agency shall not be furnished to newspapers which do not contribute to the expense of gathering it. And further, to quote from the answer:

> Prompt knowledge and publication of worldwide news is essential to the conduct of a modern newspaper, and by reason of the enormous expense incident to the gathering and distribution of such news, the only practical way in which a proprietor of a newspaper can obtain the same is, either through co-operation with a considerable number of other newspaper proprietors in the work of collecting and distributing such news, and the equitable division with them of the expenses thereof, or by the purchase of such news from some existing agency engaged in that business.

The bill was filed to restrain the pirating of complainant's news by defendant in three ways: First, by bribing employees of newspapers published by complainant's members to furnish Associated Press news to defendant before publication, for transmission by telegraph and telephone to defendant's clients for publication by them; second, by inducing Associated Press members to violate its by-laws and permit defendant to obtain news before publication; and, third, by copying news from bulletin boards and from early editions of complainant's newspapers and selling this, either bodily or after rewriting it, to defendant's customers.

The only matter that has been argued before us is whether defendant may lawfully be restrained from appropriating news taken from bulletins issued by complainant or any of its members, or from newspapers published by them, for the purpose of selling it to defendant's clients. Complainant asserts that defendant's admitted course of conduct in this regard both violates complainant's property right in the news and constitutes unfair competition in business. And notwithstanding [that] the case has proceeded only to the stage of a preliminary injunction, we have deemed it proper to consider the underlying questions, since they go to the very merits of the action and are presented upon facts that are not in dispute. As presented in argument, these questions are: (1) Whether there is any property in news; (2) Whether, if there be property in news collected for the purpose of being published, it survives the instant of its publication in the first newspaper to which it is communicated by the news-gatherer; and (3) Whether defendant's admitted course of conduct in appropriating for commercial use matter taken from bulletins or early editions of Associated Press publications constitutes unfair competition in trade.

. . . Complainant's news matter is not copyrighted. It is said that it could not, in practice, be copyrighted, because of the large number of dispatches that are sent daily; and, according to complainant's contention, news is not within the operation of the copyright act. Defendant, while apparently conceding this, nevertheless invokes the analogies of the law of literary property and copyright, insisting as its principal contention that, assuming complainant has a right of property in its news, it can be maintained (unless the copyright act be complied with) only by being kept secret and confidential, and that upon the publication with complainant's consent of uncopyrighted news of any of complainant's members in a newspaper or upon a bulletin board, the right of property is lost, and the subsequent use of the news by the public or by defendant for any purpose whatever becomes lawful.

In considering the general question of property in news matter, it is necessary to recognize its dual character, distinguishing between the substance of the information and the particular form or collocation of words in which the writer has communicated it.

No doubt news articles often possess a literary quality, and are the subject of literary property at the common law; nor do we question that such an article, as a literary production, is the subject of copyright by the terms of the act as it now stands.

But the news element — the information respecting current events contained in the literary production — is not the creation of the writer, but is a report of matters that ordinarily are *publici juris*; it is the history of the day. It is not to be supposed that the framers of the Constitution, when they empowered Congress "to promote the progress of science and useful arts, by securing for limited times to authors and inventors the exclusive right to their respective writings and discoveries" (Const. art. I, §8, par. 8), intended to confer upon one who might happen to be the first to report a historic event the exclusive right for any period to spread the knowledge of it.

We need spend no time, however, upon the general question of property in news matter at common law, or the application of the copyright act, since it seems to us the case must turn upon the question of unfair competition in business. And, in our opinion, this does not depend upon any general right of property analogous to the common-law right of the proprietor of an unpublished work to prevent its publication without his consent; nor is it foreclosed by showing that the benefits of the copyright act have been waived. We are dealing here not with restrictions upon publication but with the very facilities and processes of publication. The peculiar value of news is in the spreading of it while it is fresh; and it is evident that a valuable property interest in the news, as news, cannot be maintained by keeping it secret. Besides, except for matters improperly disclosed, or published in breach of trust or confidence, or in violation of law, none of which is involved in this branch of the case, the news of current events may be regarded as common property. What we are concerned with is the business of making it known to the world, in which both parties to the present suit are engaged. That business consists in maintaining a prompt, sure, steady, and reliable service designed to place the daily events of the world at the breakfast table of the millions at a price that, while of trifling moment to each reader, is sufficient in the aggregate to afford compensation for the cost of gathering and distributing it, with the added profit so necessary as an incentive to effective action in the commercial world. The service thus performed for newspaper readers is not only innocent but extremely useful in itself, and indubitably constitutes a legitimate business. The parties are competitors in this field; and, on fundamental principles, applicable here as elsewhere, when the rights or privileges of the one are liable to conflict with those of the other, each party is under a duty so to conduct its own business as not unnecessarily or unfairly to injure that of the other.

Obviously, the question of what is unfair competition in business must be determined with particular reference to the character and circumstances of the business. The question here is not so much the rights of either party as against the public but their rights as between themselves. And, although we may and do assume that neither party has any remaining property interest as against the public in uncopyrighted news matter after the moment of its first publication, it by no means follows that there is no remaining property interest in it as between themselves. For, to both of them alike, news matter, however little susceptible of ownership or dominion in the absolute sense, is stock in trade, to be gathered at the cost of enterprise, organization, skill, labor, and money, and to be distributed and sold to those who will pay money for it, as for any other merchandise. Regarding the news, therefore, as but the material out of which both parties are seeking to make profits at the same time and in the same field, we hardly can fail to recognize that for this purpose, and as between them, it must be regarded as *quasi* property, irrespective of the rights of either as against the public.

Not only do the acquisition and transmission of news require elaborate organization and a large expenditure of money, skill, and effort; not only has [news] an exchange value to the gatherer, dependent chiefly upon its novelty and freshness, the regularity of the service, its reputed reliability and thoroughness, and its adaptability to the public needs; but also, as is evident, the news has an exchange value to one who can misappropriate it.

The peculiar features of the case arise from the fact that, while novelty and freshness form so important an element in the success of the business, the very processes of distribution and publication necessarily occupy a good deal of time. Complainant's service, as well as defendant's, is a daily service to daily newspapers; most of the foreign news reaches this country at the Atlantic seaboard, principally at the city of New York, and because of this, and of time differentials due to the earth's rotation, the distribution of news matter throughout the country is principally from east to west; and, since in speed the telegraph and telephone easily outstrip the rotation of the earth, it is a simple matter for defendant to take complainant's news from bulletins or early editions of complainant's members in the eastern cities and at the mere cost of telegraphic transmission cause it to be published in western papers issued at least as early as those served by complainant. Besides this, and irrespective of time differentials, irregularities in telegraphic transmission on different lines, and the normal consumption of time in printing and distributing the newspaper, result in permitting pirated news to be placed in the hands of defendant's readers sometimes simultaneously with the service of competing Associated Press papers, occasionally even earlier.

Defendant insists that when, with the sanction and approval of complainant, and as the result of the use of its news for the very purpose for which it is distributed, a portion of complainant's members communicate it to the general public by posting it upon bulletin boards so that all may read, or by issuing it to newspapers and distributing it indiscriminately, complainant no longer has the right to control the use to be made of it; that when it thus reaches the light of day it becomes the common possession of all to whom it is accessible; and that any purchaser of a newspaper has the right to communicate the intelligence which it contains to anybody and for any purpose, even for the purpose of selling it for profit to newspapers published for profit in competition with complainant's members.

The fault in the reasoning lies in applying as a test the right of the complainant as against the public, instead of considering the rights of complainant and defendant, competitors in business, as between themselves. The right of the purchaser of a single newspaper to spread knowledge of its contents gratuitously, for any legitimate purpose not unreasonably interfering with complainant's right to make merchandise of it, may be admitted; but to transmit that news for commercial use, in competition with complainant — which is what defendant has done and seeks to justify — is a very different matter. In doing this defendant, by its very act, admits that it is taking material that has been acquired by complainant as the result of organization and the expenditure of labor, skill, and money, and which is salable by complainant for money, and that defendant in appropriating it and selling it as its own is endeavoring to reap where it has not sown, and by disposing of it to newspapers that are competitors of complainant's members is appropriating to itself the harvest of those who have sown. Stripped of all disguises, the process amounts to an unauthorized interference with the normal operation of complainant's legitimate business precisely at the point where the profit is to be reaped, in order to divert a material portion of the profit from those who have earned it to those who have not; with special advantage to defendant in the competition because of the fact that it is not burdened with any part of the expense of gathering the news. The transaction speaks for itself and a court of equity ought not to hesitate long in characterizing it as unfair competition in business.

The contention that the news is abandoned to the public for all purposes when published in the first newspaper is untenable. Abandonment is a question of intent, and the entire organization of the Associated Press negatives such a purpose. The cost of the service would be [prohibitive] if the reward were to be so limited. No single newspaper, no small group of newspapers, could sustain the expenditure. Indeed, it is one of the most obvious results of defendant's theory that, by permitting indiscriminate publication by anybody and everybody for purposes of profit in competition with the news-gatherer, it would render publication profitless, or so little profitable as in effect to cut off the service by rendering the cost prohibitive in comparison with the return.

It is to be observed that the view we adopt does not result in giving to complainant the right to monopolize either the gathering or the distribution of the news, or, without complying with the copyright act, to prevent the reproduction of its news articles, but only postpones participation by complainant's competitor in the processes of distribution and reproduction of news that it has not gathered, and only to the extent necessary to prevent that competitor from reaping the fruits of complainant's efforts and expenditure, to the partial exclusion of complainant, and in violation of the principle that underlies the maxim *sic utere tuo*, etc.

Mr. Justice Oliver Wendell Holmes, Jr., dissenting.

When an uncopyrighted combination of words is published there is no general right to forbid other people repeating them — in other words there is no property in the combination or in the thoughts or facts that the words express. Property, a creation of law, does not arise from value, although exchangeable — a matter of fact. Many exchangeable values may be destroyed intentionally without compensation. Property depends upon exclusion by law from interference, and a person is not excluded from using any combination of words merely because some one has used it before, even if it took labor and genius to make it. If a given person is to be prohibited from making the use of words that his neighbors are free to make some other ground must be found. One such ground is vaguely expressed in the phrase unfair trade. This means that the words are repeated by a competitor in business in such a way as to convey a misrepresentation that materially injures the person who first used them, by appropriating credit of some kind which the first user has earned. The ordinary case is a representation by device, appearance, or other indirection that the defendant's goods come from the plaintiff. But the only reason why it is actionable to make such a representation is that it tends to give the defendant an advantage in his competition with the plaintiff and that it is thought undesirable that an advantage should be gained in that way. Apart from that the defendant may use such unpatented devices and uncopyrighted combinations of words as he likes. The ordinary case, I say, is palming off the defendant's product as the plaintiff's but the same evil may follow from the opposite falsehood — from saying whether in words or by implication that the plaintiff's product is the defendant's, and that, it seems to me, is what has happened here.

Fresh news is got only by enterprise and expense. To produce such news as it is produced by the defendant represents by implication that it has been acquired by the defendant's enterprise and at its expense. When it comes from one of the great news collecting agencies like the Associated Press, the source generally is indicated, plainly importing that credit; and that such a representation is implied may be inferred with some confidence from the unwillingness of the defendant to give the credit and tell the truth. If the plaintiff produces the news at the same time that the defendant does, the defendant's presentation impliedly denies to the plaintiff the credit of collecting the facts and assumes that credit to the defendant. If the plaintiff is later in Western cities it naturally will be supposed to have obtained its information from the defendant. The falsehood is a little more subtle, the injury, a little more indirect, than in ordinary cases of unfair trade, but I think that the principle that condemns the one condemns the other. It is a question of how strong an infusion of fraud is necessary to turn a flavor into a poison. The dose seems to me strong enough here to need a remedy from the law. But as, in my view, the only ground of complaint that can be recognized without legislation is the implied misstatement, it can be corrected by stating the truth; and a suitable acknowledgment of the source is all that the plaintiff can require. I think that within the limits recognized by the decision of the Court the defendant should be enjoined from publishing news obtained from the Associated Press for hours after publication by the plaintiff unless it gives express credit to the Associated Press; the number of hours and the form of acknowledgment to be settled by the District Court.

Mr. Justice Louis D. Brandeis, dissenting.

There are published in the United States about 2,500 daily papers. More than 800 of them are supplied with domestic and foreign news of general interest by the Associated Press — a corporation without capital stock which does not sell news or earn or seek to earn profits, but serves merely as an instrumentality by means of which these papers supply themselves at joint expense with such news. Papers not members of the Associated Press depend for their news of general interest largely upon agencies organized for profit. Among these agencies is the International News Service which supplies news to about 400 subscribing papers. It has, like the Associated Press, bureaus and correspondents in this and foreign countries; and its annual expenditures in gathering and distributing news is about $2,000,000. Ever since its organization in 1909, it has included among the sources from which it gathers news, copies (purchased in the open market) of early editions of some papers published by members of the Associated Press and the bulletins publicly posted by them.

No question of statutory copyright is involved. The sole question for our consideration is this: Was the International News Service properly enjoined from using, or causing to be used gainfully, news of which it acquired knowledge by lawful means (namely, by reading publicly posted bulletins or papers purchased by it in the open market) merely because the news had been originally gathered by the Associated Press and continued to be of value to some of its members, or because it did not reveal the source from which it was acquired? . . .

An essential element of individual property is the legal right to exclude others from enjoying it. If the property is private, the right of exclusion may be absolute; if the property is affected with a public interest, the right of exclusion is qualified. But the fact that a product of the mind has cost its producer money and labor, and has a value for which others are willing to pay, is not sufficient to ensure to it this legal attribute of property. The general rule of law is, that the noblest of human productions — knowledge, truths ascertained, conceptions, and ideas — become, after voluntary communication to others, free as the air to common use. Upon these incorporeal productions the attribute of property is continued after such communication only in certain classes of cases where public policy has seemed to demand it. These exceptions are confined to productions which, in some degree, involve creation, invention, or discovery. But by no means all such are endowed with this attribute of property. The creations which are recognized as property by the common law are literary, dramatic, musical, and other artistic creations; and these have also protection under the copyright statutes. The inventions and discoveries upon which this attribute of property is conferred only by statute, are the few comprised within the patent law. There are also many other cases in which courts interfere to prevent curtailment of plaintiff's enjoyment of incorporeal productions; and in which the right to relief is often called a property right, but is such only in a special sense. In those cases, the plaintiff has no absolute right to the protection of his production; he has merely the qualified right to be protected as against the defendant's acts, because of the special relation in which the latter stands or the wrongful method or means employed in acquiring the knowledge or the manner in which it is used. Protection of this character is afforded where the suit is based upon breach of contract or of trust or upon unfair competition.

The knowledge for which protection is sought in the case at bar is not of a kind upon which the law has heretofore conferred the attributes of property; nor is the manner of its acquisition or use nor the purpose to which it is applied, such as has heretofore been recognized as entitling a plaintiff to relief.

Plaintiff . . . contended that defendant's practice constitutes unfair competition, because there is "appropriation without cost to itself of values created by" the plaintiff; and it is upon this ground that the decision of this court appears to be based. To appropriate and use for profit, knowledge and ideas produced by other men, without making compensation or even acknowledgment, may be inconsistent with a finer sense of propriety; but, with the exceptions indicated above, the law has heretofore sanctioned the practice. Thus it was held that one may ordinarily make and sell anything in any form, may copy with exactness that which another has produced, or may otherwise use his ideas without his consent and without the payment of compensation, and yet not inflict a legal injury; and that ordinarily one is at perfect liberty to find out, if he can by lawful means, trade secrets of another, however valuable, and then use the knowledge so acquired gainfully, although it cost the original owner much in effort and in money to collect or produce.

The unfairness in competition which hitherto has been recognized by the law as a basis for relief, lay in the manner or means of conducting the business; and the manner or means held legally unfair, involves either fraud or force or the doing of acts otherwise prohibited by law. That competition is not unfair in a legal sense, merely because the profits gained are unearned, even if made at the expense of a rival, is shown by many cases besides those referred to above. He who follows the pioneer into a new market, or who engages in the manufacture of an article newly introduced by another, seeks profits due largely to the labor and expense of the first adventurer; but the law sanctions, indeed encourages, the pursuit. . . .

The means by which the International News Service obtains news gathered by the Associated Press is also clearly unobjectionable. It is taken from papers bought in the open market or from bulletins publicly posted. No breach of contract or of trust, and neither fraud nor force, is involved. The manner of use is likewise unobjectionable. No reference is made by word or by act to the Associated Press, either in transmitting the news to subscribers or by them in publishing it in their papers. Neither the International News Service nor its subscribers is gaining or seeking to gain in its business a benefit from the reputation of the Associated Press. They are merely using its product without making compensation. That they have a legal right to do, because the product is not property, and they do not stand in any relation to the Associated Press, either of contract or of trust, which otherwise precludes such use. The argument is not advanced by characterizing such taking and use a misappropriation.

The great development of agencies now furnishing country-wide distribution of news, the vastness of our territory, and improvements in the means of transmitting intelligence, have made it possible for a news agency or newspapers to obtain, without paying compensation, the fruit of another's efforts and to use news so obtained gainfully in competition with the original collector. The injustice of such action is obvious. But to give relief against it would involve more than the application of existing rules

CONTEXT

Media mogul William Randolph Hearst created INS after the AP denied his papers membership. INS became dependent on AP stories about World War I after France and Great Britain refused it access to European wire and cable service because of Hearst's anti-war editorials. *See* Ben Procter, *William Randolph Hearst: The Later Years, 1911-1951*, 50 (2007).

of law to new facts. It would require the making of a new rule in analogy to existing ones. The unwritten law possesses capacity for growth; and has often satisfied new demands for justice by invoking analogies or by expanding a rule or principle. This process has been in the main wisely applied and should not be discontinued. Where the problem is relatively simple, as it is apt to be when private interests only are involved, it generally proves adequate. But with the increasing complexity of society, the public interest tends to become omnipresent; and the problems presented by new demands for justice cease to be simple. Then the creation or recognition by courts of a new private right may work serious injury to the general public, unless the boundaries of the right are definitely established and wisely guarded. In order to reconcile the new private right with the public interest, it may be necessary to prescribe limitations and rules for its enjoyment; and also to provide administrative machinery for enforcing the rules. It is largely for this reason that, in the effort to meet the many new demands for justice incident to a rapidly changing civilization, resort to legislation has latterly been had with increasing frequency.

The rule for which the plaintiff contends would effect an important extension of property rights and a corresponding curtailment of the free use of knowledge and of ideas; and the facts of this case admonish us of the danger involved in recognizing such a property right in news, without imposing upon news-gatherers corresponding obligations. A large majority of the newspapers and perhaps half the newspaper readers of the United States are dependent for their news of general interest upon agencies other than the Associated Press. The channel through which about 400 of these papers received, as the plaintiff alleges, "a large amount of news relating to the European war of the greatest importance and of intense interest to the newspaper reading public" was suddenly closed. The closing to the International News Service of these channels for foreign news (if they were closed) was due not to unwillingness on its part to pay the cost of collecting the news, but to the prohibitions imposed by foreign governments upon its securing news from their respective countries and from using cable or telegraph lines running therefrom. For aught that appears, all of the 400 subscribers of the International News Service would gladly have then become members of the Associated Press, if they could have secured election thereto.[2]

A Legislature, urged to enact a law by which one news agency or newspaper may prevent appropriation of the fruits of its labors by another, would consider such facts and possibilities and others which appropriate inquiry might disclose. Legislators might conclude that it was impossible to put an end to the obvious injustice involved in such appropriation of news, without opening the door to other evils, greater than that sought to be remedied. Or legislators dealing with the subject might conclude, that the right to news values should be protected to the extent of permitting recovery of damages for any unauthorized use, but that protection by injunction should be denied.

---

2. According to the by-laws of the Associated Press no one can be elected a member without the affirmative vote of at least four-fifths of all the members of the corporation or the vote of the directors.

Or again, a Legislature might conclude that it was unwise to recognize even so limited a property right in published news as that above indicated; but that a news agency should, on some conditions, be given full protection of its business; and to that end a remedy by injunction as well as one for damages should be granted, where news collected by it is gainfully used without permission. If legislators reached that conclusion, they would probably go further, and prescribe the conditions under which and the extent to which the protection should be afforded; and they might also provide the administrative machinery necessary for insuring to the public, the press, and the news agencies, full enjoyment of the rights so conferred.

Courts are ill-equipped to make the investigations which should precede a determination of the limitations which should be set upon any property right in news or of the circumstances under which news gathered by a private agency should be deemed affected with a public interest. Courts would be powerless to prescribe the detailed regulations essential to full enjoyment of the rights conferred or to introduce the machinery required for enforcement of such regulations. Considerations such as these should lead us to decline to establish a new rule of law in the effort to redress a newly disclosed wrong, although the propriety of some remedy appears to be clear.

Notes and Questions

1. **Copying and property.** The case for labor as a justification for property rights is easiest when the claimants claim ownership of tangible objects. But what if the competitor doesn't want the physical thing, but simply wants to copy the result? Generally, the law poses no obstacle. If my neighbor discovers through much experiment and research that a valuable food crop grows abundantly in the area, there is no barrier to me planting the same crop, with the same methods, next door. Indeed, at early common law, there would be nothing to stop anyone from copying the text of the *Harry Potter* series and selling the reproductions without giving J.K. Rowling a cent. *INS v. AP* discusses some of the policy tensions involved in the choice to give creators a right to consent to copying. What are the arguments in favor of giving creators the right to consent before others can copy their works? What are the arguments against giving creators rights?

2. **Property or unfair competition?** *INS v. AP* resolves these tensions by creating what has been called "quasi property." Note the limits on this protection. If I read an AP story in the newspaper, nothing prevents me from telling all my friends about what I just read. Nor does the holding prevent INS from using the facts reported in the story in another story published several months later. AP's rights extend only against competitors in the news business, and only for the limited time necessary to allow it to profit from its labor. Some have argued that the *INS v. AP* rule is not really about property at all, but is instead a rule against unfair competition. *See* Shyamkrishna Balganesh, *"Hot News": The Enduring Myth of Property in News*, 111 Colum. L. Rev. 419 (2011). One could also see the case as an example of the property doctrine of "relativity of title" — the question is not whether plaintiff would win against everyone in the world but only whether plaintiff's title is better than defendant's title.

3. Institutional competence. Justice Brandeis's dissent focuses less on what, if any, rights AP should have than on which institution, the legislature or the courts, should determine those rights. Why does he argue that this dispute is particularly ill-suited to judicial resolution? Are you convinced? If you were representing AP, how would you rebut his argument?

4. Which comes first—exchangeable value or exclusive rights to exchange? Justice Pitney suggests that there is a property right in fresh news because it has "exchange value, dependent on its novelty and freshness." *Id.* at 238. Because it is valuable, it should be protected as a property right with rules against misappropriation by a competitor. But Justice Pitney also states that the news will have no value unless it is legally protected; allowing INS to disseminate information collected by AP would render news collection "profitless, or so little profitable as in effect to cut off the service by rendering the cost prohibitive in comparison with the return." So is news valuable or isn't it?

Justice Holmes dissents, arguing that there is no property in fresh news. "Property, a creation of law, does not arise from value, although exchangeable—a matter of fact. Many exchangeable values may be destroyed intentionally without compensation. Property depends upon exclusion by law from interference." Well, yes, but this doesn't establish that there shouldn't be a property right in news. Do you see why?

Not all valuable interests are privately owned; many of the most valuable pieces of information, such as scientific truths or historical facts, are the common property of humankind. News does have value to many people. At the same time, its market value will vary depending on how much legal protection the courts grant for the news as against competitors. The greater the legal protection granted the plaintiff's interest, the more valuable the property interest to the plaintiff. Is there a way out of this circle?

5. The common law hot news tort. The precedential value of *INS v. AP* was abrogated by *Erie R.R. Co. v. Tompkins*, 304 U.S. 64 (1938), which held that federal courts could not create common law where state law created the rule of decision. But state courts have adopted the doctrine as a matter of state law. In *National Basketball Association v. Motorola, Inc.*, 105 F.3d 841 (2d Cir. 1997), the Second Circuit summarized New York's common law hot news tort as requiring the following:

> (i) a plaintiff generates or gathers information at a cost; (ii) the information is time-sensitive; (iii) a defendant's use of the information constitutes free riding on the plaintiff's efforts; (iv) the defendant is in direct competition with a product or service offered by the plaintiffs; and (v) the ability of other parties to free-ride on the efforts of the plaintiff or others would so reduce the incentive to produce the product or service that its existence or quality would be substantially threatened.

In that case, the NBA brought a complaint against the manufacturer of handheld pagers that provided "real-time" information about professional basketball games, including updated scores and statistics as the games were in process. How do the five factors above apply to the NBA claim? Why do you think the Second Circuit rejected it?

6. Intellectual property statutes. Part of the argument that the courts should not grant relief to AP is that federal statutes already provided significant protection for creative works, and those statutes did not prohibit the INS conduct. Copyright, patent, and trademark law are the core areas of federal intellectual property protection. Copyright and patent law are designed to fulfill the constitutional authorization to "promote the Progress of Science and the useful arts," U.S. Const. art. 1, §8, while trademark law is an outgrowth of common law protection. Chapter 3 provides a more detailed discussion of these laws.

a. Copyright. Copyright applies to "original works of authorship fixed in any tangible medium of expression," including literary, musical, dramatic, and pictorial works. 17 U.S.C. §102. It gives owners of the copyright the exclusive right to use or authorize the use of the work for a limited time. After that, the work enters the public domain and can be copied by anyone. Interestingly, John Locke, associated in property theory with the idea that labor gives rise to property rights, strongly advocated for time limits on the rights accorded by the Statute of Anne (1710), the original English copyright statute. The Statute of Anne granted authors rights for 14 years after publication, with the option of a single additional 14-year term; rights did not continue after the death of the author. In the United States, the period of exclusive copyright has progressively lengthened, and is now generally the author's life plus 70 years after the date of publication, or 95 years after publication or 120 years after creation for works made for hire. 17 U.S.C. §302.

Note that although AP could have copyrighted its articles, the law as it existed at the time required registration of the work, which was impracticable given the volume and time sensitivity of its articles. Copyright also would not have protected the news itself, only the "medium of expression," *i.e.*, the writing used to convey the news.

b. Patent. Patents may be issued to anyone who "invents or discovers any new and useful process, machine, manufacture, or composition of matter, or any new and useful improvement thereof." 35 U.S.C. §101. Unlike modern copyright law, protection in patent law depends on registration of the invention; before issuing a patent, the U.S. Patent and Trademark Office must determine that the subject of the patent is both new and non-obvious. (These decisions are sometimes questionable; in 2002, the PTO issued a patent to Ross E. Long, III for "an apparatus for use as a toy by an animal, for example a dog, to either fetch carry or chew . . . that resembles a branch in appearance . . . formed of any of a number of materials including . . . wood." U.S. Patent No. 6,360,693. That's right, he patented a stick for dogs.) Patents generally last 20 years from the date of issuance before they enter the public domain. 35 U.S.C. §154. What explains the shorter period for patent as opposed to copyright protection?

c. Trademark. Trademark law protects non-functional words, symbols, names, and devices used to identify one's goods and services. 15 U.S.C. §1127. Trademark does not bar uses of the mark that would not deceive consumers or dilute the value of the mark for the owner. 15 U.S.C. §1125. In particular, parodies and comparisons to existing products are fair game. 15 U.S.C. §1125(c)(3).

So Haute Diggity Dog did not infringe Louis Vuitton's trademark with its Chewy Vuiton plush chew toys, *Louis Vuitton Malletier, S.A. v. Haute Diggity Dog, LLC*, 507 F.3d 252 (4th Cir. 2007), nor did Saxony Products infringe Guerlain's trademark by telling consumers that its "Fragrance S" was like Shalimar (although it might have been liable for false advertising). *Saxony Products, Inc. v. Guerlain, Inc.*, 513 F.2d 716, 185 U.S.P.Q. 474 (9th Cir. 1975).

Problems

1. Several lawsuits have challenged practices of "media aggregators," web sites that provide snippets, photos, or links to content created by others. Most have settled without a reported decision. One that did not settle is *Barclays Capital v. Theflyonthewall .com*, 650 F.3d 876 (2d Cir. 2011). The plaintiffs were brokerage firms that engage in extensive research in order to advise their clients on the prospects of publicly traded companies and their industries. They wrote up this research and investment recommendations in reports that they provided to clients and prospective clients before the start of business, in hopes that recipients might purchase the recommended stocks using the firms' brokerage services. Theflyonthewall.com, which sends a daily e-mail with investment information to subscribers for a fee, obtained these reports and distributed the recommendations (but not the reports themselves) to their subscribers, often before the brokerage firms were able to do so. This reduced the investment advantage of the plaintiffs' clients, and made it less likely that they would use the plaintiffs' brokerage services. What result under the hot news test? *See Barclays Capital v. Theflyonthewall.com*, 650 F.3d 876 (2d Cir. 2011).

Compare a suit against Mario Lavandeira, who blogs about celebrities for perezhilton .com. X17, which owned the rights to many of the paparazzi photographs that Lavandeira posted, brought both copyright and hot news suits against him. The suit survived a motion to dismiss but ended in a private settlement. *X17, Inc. v. Lavandeira*, 563 F. Supp. 2d 1112 (C.D. Cal. 2007). Is this a stronger or weaker case than *Barclays*? Is the hot news claim here preempted by the *Copyright Act*?

§3.2 Commonly Owned Property: Tragedy or Comedy?

Without intellectual property rights, inventions and artistic creations are, in effect, common property. The physical manifestation of the creation may be owned, but the right to copy and use it belongs to everyone. Common property may be physical as well — public parks, oceans, and highways are in many respects also common property. Much of property law is organized around the idea that common ownership of property results in "tragedy." As described by ecologist Garrett Hardin,

> The tragedy of the commons develops in this way. Picture a pasture open to all. It is to be expected that each herdsman will try to keep as many cattle as possible on the commons. Such an arrangement may work reasonably satisfactorily for centuries because tribal wars, poaching, and disease keep the numbers of both man and beast well below the carrying capacity of the land. Finally, however, comes the day of reckoning, that is,

> the day when the long-desired goal of social stability becomes a reality. At this point, the inherent logic of the commons remorselessly generates tragedy.
>
> As a rational being, each herdsman seeks to maximize his gain. Explicitly or implicitly, more or less consciously, he asks, "What is the utility to me of adding one more animal to my herd?" This utility has one negative and one positive component.
>
> 1. The positive component is a function of the increment of one animal. Since the herdsman receives all the proceeds from the sale of the additional animal, the positive utility is nearly +1.
> 2. The negative component is a function of the additional overgrazing created by one more animal. Since, however, the effects of overgrazing are shared by all the herdsman, the negative utility for any particular decision-making herdsman is only a fraction of -1.
>
> Adding together the component partial utilities, the rational herdsman concludes that the only sensible course for him to pursue is to add another animal to his herd. And another; and another. . . . But this is the conclusion reached by each and every rational herdsman sharing a commons. Therein is the tragedy. Each man is locked into a system that compels him to increase his herd without limit — in a world that is limited. Ruin is the destination toward which all men rush, each pursuing his own best interest in a society that believes in the freedom of the commons. Freedom in a commons brings ruin to all.

Garrett Hardin, *The Tragedy of the Commons*, 162 Science 1243 (1968).

Although Hardin was an ecologist, tragedy of the commons arguments are common in law and economics analysis. Law and economics undertakes cost-benefit analysis of legal rules to determine whether a change from one legal rule to another will increase or decrease social wealth. Writing a year before Hardin, Harold Demsetz identified the same dynamic, arguing that "communal property results in great externalities. The full costs of the activities of an owner of a communal property right are not borne directly by him, nor can they be called to his attention easily by the willingness of others to pay him an appropriate sum." Harold Demsetz, *Toward a Theory of Property Rights*, 57 Am. Econ. Rev. 347, 354-358 (1967).

Hardin emphasized governmental controls as a solution to the tragedy of the commons. He even supported forcing individuals to "relinquish[] the freedom to breed" in order to limit the environmental impact of an increasing population. Law and economics scholars more frequently argue for property rights as a solution to the tragedy of the commons. Demsetz argued that creating individual property in valuable resources, where cost-effective, leads to more efficient use because individuals experience a greater share of the costs and benefits of their use. *See* Demsetz, *supra*, at 350-353. What are the advantages of property rights over governmental controls? What might the objection of an environmentalist be? More generally, what are the costs of individual property regimes? *See* Duncan Kennedy & Frank Michelman, *Are Property and Contract Efficient?*, 8 Cardozo L. Rev. 711 (1980).

Hardin, Demsetz, and classic economic analysis assumes that individuals are perfectly rational actors and that rational actors pursue the course of action that will yield them the greatest individual wealth. Contrary to this assumption, experimental studies have shown that people demonstrate far more cooperative and even altruistic behavior than the rational actor model would predict. Interestingly, for certain sorts of interactions, this deviation from self-interested behavior seems to be especially strong among those living in advanced capitalist economies. *See* Joseph Henrich et al., *The Weirdest People in the World,* 33 Behavioral and Brain Sciences 61 (2010). People living in such societies frequently demonstrate more cooperative and sharing behavior (at least with respect to certain tasks, such as dividing a pot of money) than those living in less economically developed societies. Why might that be? Henrich and his collaborators suggest that "norms and institutions for exchange in ephemeral interactions culturally coevolved with markets and expanding larger-scale sedentary populations."

What is the consequence of modifying the rational actor model for the predictions of the tragedy of the commons? Nobel Prize winning economist Elinor Ostrom and others have pointed out there are many instances of communally created and owned commons property, and that where they exist they are often more productive than neighboring individually owned property systems. *See* Elinor Ostrom, *Governing the Commons* (1990). Many of the fastest growing forms of property rely on common ownership and governance. Condominiums and residential subdivisions, where 62 million Americans now live, usually have significant common elements, such as lobbies, streets, and pools, and unit owners have the power to regulate these external elements of the development as a collective. Corporations and partnerships, important drivers of the modern economy, also depend on collective ownership of assets and profits. *See* Chapter 9, §4.

In *The Comedy of the Commons,* Carol Rose argued that for some kinds of property, open access actually increases its value. Rose identified a long history in English and American common law of recognizing public rights in private paths and roads, navigable waterways, and even recreational beaches or maypoles. These public access rights were justified in part by the danger of holdouts, or refusal to sell rights of access, and the difficulty of organizing a diffuse public to bargain with the property owner. More important, they reflected instances where use by more people actually increased the productivity of the property, by creating economies of scale and opportunities for trade and interaction with diverse individuals:

> Used in commerce, some property had qualities akin to infinite "returns to scale." Thus here, the commons was not tragic, but comedic, in the classical sense of a story with a happy outcome. And customary doctrines suggest that commerce might be thought a "comedy of the commons" not only because it may infinitely expand our wealth, but also, at least in part, because it has been thought to enhance the sociability of the members of an otherwise atomized society.

Carol Rose, *The Comedy of the Commons: Custom, Commerce, and Inherently Public Property,* 53 U. Chi. L. Rev. 711, 723 (1986); *see also* Anna di Robilant, *The Virtues of Common Ownership,* 91 B.U. L. Rev. 1359 (2011). Are there other kinds of resources in which use by the public generally is more comedy than tragedy?

§3.3 Ownership of Labor

John Locke rested his labor theory of acquisition on the grounds that although the resources of the world were given to humanity in common, each individual owned her own labor. In mixing the labor one owned with commonly owned natural resources, one made them one's own. But the relationship between labor and goods is rarely so direct. Locke himself quickly obscured the relationship between labor and property by asserting that "the grass my horse has bit; the turfs my servant has cut . . . [t]he labour that was mine . . . hath fixed my property in them." Locke, *Two Treatises on Government*, ch. 5, §29.

Today, most of us work to create goods or services for other individuals in exchange for money from yet other individuals, which we then exchange with other individuals for the goods and services we want. Most agree that, in general, this works out better for all concerned. Our clothes and cars, for example, are much more functional and plentiful than they would be if we had to make them for ourselves. Slavery is now illegal, so, in general, today's workers consent to this exchange. But given that few can be self-sufficient in an exchange-based economy, for most, the consent to work for others is made in the face of few meaningful alternatives. How much control do or should we have over the conditions of our labor? How much should the law intervene to regulate labor conditions?

In *Upton v. JWP Businessland,* 682 N.E.2d 1357 (Mass. 1997), an employer fired an at-will employee when she refused to work long hours because of her need to be with her young son. "The general rule is that an at-will employee may be terminated at any time for any reason or for no reason at all. Liability may be imposed on an employer, however, if an at-will employee is terminated for a reason that violates a clearly established public policy." *Id.* at 1358. Examples of such policies are being "terminated for asserting a legal right (*e.g.,* filing a workers' compensation claim), for doing what the law requires (*e.g.,* serving on a jury), or for refusing to disobey the law (*e.g.,* refusing to commit perjury)." *Id.* The question was whether refusing to work overtime in order to take care of one's child was a public policy that justified denying the employer the right to terminate the employee. The court held that it was not:

> There is no clearly established public policy which requires employers to refrain from demanding that their adult employees work long hours. Nor is any public policy directly served by an employee's refusal to work long hours. Because no public purpose is served by the conduct for which the plaintiff asserts she was discharged, this case is unlike those cases in which we have held that the employer may be liable for the discharge of an at-will employee.
>
> To advance her claim that her termination violated public policy, the plaintiff relies on the Commonwealth's strong policy favoring the care and protection of children. Her theory is that an employer may not properly discharge an employee whose refusal to work long hours is based on her sense of obligation to be with her young child. She argues that meeting the defendant's demands regarding work hours would cause her to neglect her child in contravention of public policy.

> There is no public policy which mandates that an employer must adjust its expectations, based on a case-by-case analysis of an at-will employee's domestic circumstances, or face liability for having discharged the employee. Construing the public policy exception to cover terminations of employees in the plaintiff's situation would tend to convert the general rule into a rule that requires just cause to terminate an at-will employee. Liability to an at-will employee for a discharge in violation of public policy must be based on general principles, and not on the special domestic circumstances of any particular employee.

The work of taking care of children in the home traditionally was uncompensated. It is still the case that more women than men engage in this uncompensated labor. This affects the ability of women to enter the workforce full time and is a primary reason for the continued disparity in incomes between men and women. In 2011, the median income of men who worked full time was $48,202, while the median income of women who worked full time was only $37,118, or 77 percent of male earnings. Carmen DeNavas-Walt, Bernadette D. Proctor & Jessica C. Smith, U.S. Census Bureau, *Current Population Reports, P60-243, Income, Poverty, and Health Insurance Coverage in the United States: 2011* (Sept. 2012), *available at http://www.census.gov/prod/2012pubs/p60-243.pdf.* Most women now work outside the home. The 1996 federal welfare reform statute, the *Personal Responsibility and Work Opportunity Act of 1996*, 42 U.S.C. §§601-619, requires most women with children to do so as a condition of receiving welfare benefits. Despite this fact, the organization of work remains hostile to parents and makes it difficult to meet the challenges of reconciling market work with care of one's children. Ann Crittenden, *The Price of Motherhood: Why the Most Important Job in the World Is Still the Least Valued* 4 (2001); Mary Joe Frug, *Securing Job Equality for Women: Labor Market Hostility to Working Mothers*, 59 B.U. L. Rev. 55 (1979); Meredith Johnson Harbach, *Outsourcing Childcare*, 24 Yale J.L. & Feminism 254, 258-270 (2012).

Joanna Upton would have been subject to criminal penalties if she had failed to support and protect her child or had otherwise neglected him. *Commonwealth v. Twitchell*, 617 N.E.2d 609 (Mass. 1993). She also could have lost custody. *In re Adoption of Greta*, 729 N.E.2d 273 (Mass. 2000). Why then was the duty to care for her children not deemed a "clearly established public policy"? Or should the case be decided on other grounds? To what extent should work in the home taking care of children affect the rules governing paid employment?

§4 FAMILIES

Much of our property comes not from our individual actions, but from our families. These familial endowments often determine our ability to get and keep other property. In an earlier time, economic status was largely determined by one's participation in the family business or residence in a family home; today, economic status is significantly determined by familial support for education and skill development. John Langbein, *The Twentieth-Century Revolution in Family Wealth Transmission*, 86

Mich. L. Rev. 722, 732-734 (1988). While most familial property transfers are voluntary, in many places the law sets a floor that relatives cannot sink below. Both custodial and noncustodial parents, for example, are required to support their children, at least to the age of majority, and all states require some division of property between spouses on divorce or death. The materials below concern debates about how far the obligation of familial support should extend.

§4.1 Child Support

Bayliss v. Bayliss

550 So. 2d 986 (Ala. 1989)

Gorman Houston, Justice.

We granted certiorari in this case to address the following issue: In Alabama, does a trial court have jurisdiction to require parents to provide post-minority support for college education to children of a marriage that has been terminated by divorce?

The trial court does have that jurisdiction. In a proceeding for dissolution of marriage or a modification of a divorce judgment, a trial court may award sums of money out of the property and income of either or both parents for the post-minority education of a child of that dissolved marriage, when application is made there for, as in the case at issue, before the child attains the age of majority. In doing so, the trial court shall consider all relevant factors that shall appear reasonable and necessary, including primarily the financial resources of the parents and the child and the child's commitment to, and aptitude for, the requested education. The trial court may consider, also, the standard of living that the child would have enjoyed if the marriage had not been dissolved and the family unit had been preserved and the child's relationship with his parents and responsiveness to parental advice and guidance.

Patrick Bayliss was born of the marriage of Cherry R. Bayliss ("mother") and John Martin Bayliss III ("father"). This marriage was terminated by divorce when Patrick was 12 years old. When Patrick was 18, his mother filed a petition to modify the final judgment of divorce, [asking the court to order her ex-husband to help pay for college for Patrick. She alleged that Patrick was interested in going to college and had the aptitude for it, that his father was wealthy and refused to contribute to his college education, and that both she and her ex-husband had attended college.]

Alabama Code 1975, §30-3-1, provides, in pertinent part: "Upon granting a divorce, the court may give the custody and *education of the children of the marriage* to either father or mother, *as may seem right and proper*." (Emphasis supplied.) . . .

We have found no early Alabama appellate court cases that even discussed whether a college education was a "necessary" that a divorced parent had to provide a *minor child*. The earliest case that we have found involving the question of whether a college education is a necessary is *Middlebury College v. Chandler*, 16 Vt. 683 (1844). In that case, which involved a suit brought by Middlebury College against the father of a minor college student for the student's tuition and other college expenses, the Vermont Supreme Court refused to hold that a college education was a necessary:

> The practical meaning of the term [necessaries] has always been in some measure relative, having reference as well to what may be called the conventional necessities of others in the same walks of life with the infant, as to his own pecuniary condition and other circumstances. Hence a good common school education, at the least, is now fully recognized as one of the necessaries for an infant.
>
> But it is obvious that the more extensive attainments in literature and science must be viewed in a light somewhat different. Though they tend greatly to elevate and adorn personal character, are a source of much private enjoyment, and may justly be expected to prove of public utility, yet in reference to men in general they are far from being necessary in a legal sense. The mass of our citizens pass through life without them. *Id.* at 538-539.

Beginning with the landmark case of *Esteb v. Esteb*, 244 P. 264 (Wash. 1926), courts have increasingly recognized a college education as a legal necessary for minor children of divorced parents. Justice Askren wrote:

> The rule in *Middlebury v. Chandler, supra* was clearly based upon conditions which existed at that time. An opportunity at that early date for a common school education was small, for a high school education less, and for a college education was almost impossible to the average family, and was generally considered as being only within the reach of the most affluent citizens. . . . But conditions have changed greatly in almost a century that has elapsed since that time. Where the college graduate of that day was the exception, today such a person may almost be said to be the rule. The law in an attempt to keep up with the progress of society has gradually placed minimum standards for attendance upon public schools, and even provides punishment for those parents who fail to see that their children receive at least such minimum education. It cannot be doubted that the minor who is unable to secure a college education is generally handicapped in pursuing most of the trades or professions of life, for most of those with whom he is required to compete will be possessed of that greater skill and ability which comes from such an education. 244 P. at 266-267.

Until *Ex parte Brewington*, 445 So. 2d 294 (Ala. 1983), our cases and the cases of the Court of Civil Appeals held that a trial court had no continuing equitable jurisdiction over the issues or parties to a divorce to require that a noncustodial parent provide support of any kind to any child that had reached the legislatively prescribed age of majority. In *Brewington*, we expanded our interpretation of the word "children" in the Alabama child support statute, to impose a duty on a divorced, noncustodial parent to support his children who continue to be disabled beyond the legislatively prescribed age of majority. We have previously interpreted the word "education" in the Alabama child support statute to include a college education as a necessary. We now expand the exception to the general rule — *i.e.*, the rule that a divorced, noncustodial parent has no duty to contribute to the support of his or her child after that child has reached the legislatively prescribed age of majority — beyond *Brewington, supra* (dealing with a physically or mentally disabled child) to include the college education exception.

The appellate courts of Florida have held that the noncustodial, divorced parent of an adult child cannot be required to pay college education expenses, in the absence of a disability or agreement. *Grapin v. Grapin*, 450 So. 2d 853 (Fla. 1984). It appears that the Courts in Missouri, Alaska, and possibly Vermont, have also so held. The father also relies on cases from North Carolina, Colorado, Nebraska, New Mexico, Ohio, New York, and Kentucky; however, it appears that these cases are not applicable to a decision under Alabama law, because of the particular language of the jurisdictional child support statutes of those states.

In expanding the exception to the general rule (that a divorced, noncustodial parent has no duty to support his child after that child reaches majority) to include the college education exception, we are merely refusing to limit the word "children" to minor children, because of what we perceive to be just and reasonable in 1989. The Latin phrase *stare decisis et non quieta movere* (stare decisis) expresses the legal principle of certainty and predictability; for it is literally translated as "to adhere to precedents, and not to unsettle things which are established." *Black's Law Dictionary* (5th ed. 1979). By this opinion, we are unsettling things that have been established by the appellate court of this State. However, we are persuaded that the ground or reason of those prior decisions by the Court of Civil Appeals would not be consented to today by the conscience and the feeling of justice of all those whose obedience is required by the rule on which the ratio decidendi of those prior decisions was logically based.

Therefore, we overrule that portion of cases that are inconsistent with this opinion.

Had the Bayliss family unit not been put asunder by divorce, would the father, who had attended college and was a man of significant means, have continued to provide a college education for Patrick (a young man who would be an Alpha Plus if this were Huxley's Brave New World) after Patrick reached 19 years of age? If so, the father's educational support obligations should not cease when Patrick reached 19 years of age.

This Court in *Ogle v. Ogle*, 156 So. 2d at 349 (Ala. 1963), quoted the following from *Pass v. Pass*, 118 So. 2d 769, 773 (Miss. 1960), with approval:

> [W]e are living today in an age of keen competition, and if the children of today . . . are to take their rightful place in a complex order of society and government, and discharge the duties of citizenship as well as meet with success the responsibilities devolving upon them in their relations with their fellow man, the church, the state and nation, it must be recognized that their parents owe them the duty to the extent of their financial capacity to provide for them the training and education which will be of such benefit to them in the discharge of the responsibilities of citizenship. It is a duty which the parent not only owes to his child, but to the state as well, since the stability of our government must depend upon a well-equipped, a well-trained, and well-educated citizenship. We can see no good reason why this duty should not extend to a college education. Our statutes do not prohibit it, but they are rather susceptible of an interpretation to allow it. The fact is that the importance of a college education is being more and more recognized in matters of commerce, society, government, and all human relations, and the college graduate is being more and more preferred over those who are not so fortunate. No parent should subject his worthy child to this disadvantage if he has the financial capacity to avoid it.

This is the public policy of our State. Since the normal age for attending college extends beyond the age of 19 years, under §30-3-1 courts have the right to assure that the children of divorced parents, who are minors at the time of the divorce, are given the same right to a college education before and after they reach the age of 19 years that they probably would have had if their parents had not divorced.

Notes and Questions

1. Courts generally hold that children of divorced parents are entitled "to be supported at least according to the standard of living to which they had grown accustomed prior to the separation of their parents." *Pascale v. Pascale*, 660 A.2d 485 (N.J. 1995). Does this include an obligation to pay for college? As a general rule, the duty to provide child support does not usually continue past the age of majority. Ironically, the age of majority was reduced from 21 to 18 just as college education was becoming more common. The reduction had nothing to do with family law, but instead was a response to the Vietnam War intended to ensure that 18-year olds subject to the draft could also vote on the leaders deciding war policy.

About 15 states permit judges to order noncustodial parents to pay for post-minority education expenses if they find that the parent would have paid for such expenses if not for the divorce. The rest do not permit involuntary orders of support for post-secondary education. Most of these will enforce orders resulting from stipulated agreements by the parents, but one state, New Hampshire, does not permit the courts to enforce even voluntary agreements. *See* Monica Hoff Wallace, *A Federal Referendum: Extending Child Support for Higher Education*, U. Kan. L. Rev. 665, 674-676 (2010). Even states that do not permit nonvoluntary orders of support for higher education, however, will often require child support past the age of majority if the child has significant disabilities that prevent economic self-sufficiency. *See, e.g., Hastings v. Hastings*, 841 So. 2d 484 (Fla. Ct. App. 2003) (holding that a 50-year-old whose disability was diagnosed when he was 8 could bring a support action against his father).

2. In holding that divorced parents have no legal duty to pay for their children's college education, the Florida Supreme Court explained that "[w]hile most parents willingly assist their adult children in obtaining a higher education that is increasingly necessary in today's fast-changing world, any duty to do so is a moral rather than a legal one." *Grapin v. Grapin*, 450 So. 2d 853, 854 (Fla. 1984). In Florida, the court noted, married parents have no legal obligation to pay for their children's college education; thus, the imposition of higher obligations on divorced parents would deny them equal protection under the law.

Should the law replicate the obligations of the parent or the expectations of the child in the absence of divorce? One longitudinal study found that although 88 percent of all college students received parental financial support, only 29 percent of college students with divorced parents received such support from either parent, and only 10 percent of noncustodial fathers provided such support. *See* Judith Wallerstein et al., *The Unexpected Legacy of Divorce: A 25 Year Landmark Study* 335-336 n.6 (2000). Another study found, in contrast, that divorced fathers did contribute to college expenses when they shared legal custody with the mother, but were far less likely to when they lacked legal custody. William V. Fabricius, *Listening to Children of Divorce:*

New Findings That Diverge from Wallerstein, Lewis and Blakelee, 52 Family Relations 385 (2003).

§4.2 Gifts and Inheritance

A gift is a transfer of property from one person to another without payment. *Inter vivos* gifts are transfers from one living person to another, while *testamentary transfers* are those effectuated at death through a valid will or inheritance.

The law of gifts requires (1) *intent* to transfer title, (2) *delivery* of the property, and (3) *acceptance* by the donee. *Westleigh v. Conger,* 755 A.2d 518, 519 (Me. 2000). Delivery generally requires physical transfer of the object itself. However, constructive or symbolic delivery might be sufficient. For example, constructive delivery would be recognized if the owner of a locked box gave the only key to the donee. Some courts, however, recognize constructive delivery only if physical delivery is inconvenient or impossible. Today, the delivery requirement may be accomplished by a writing rather than physical delivery. Many states allow a gift to be made through a formal deed or even a more informal writing that indicates a present intent to relinquish possession and to transfer title to the donee.

To make a gift, the donor must have a *present intent* to transfer ownership rights in the object. However, this does not mean that actual possession of the gift must be transferred to the donee. For example, a mother could give her daughter a piano but retain the right to keep it in her house until her death. In effect, the mother has retained a life estate in the piano and presently transferred a vested remainder to the daughter. *See Gruen v. Gruen,* 496 N.E.2d 869 (N.Y. 1986).

At death, people usually leave their property to a surviving spouse, although they may reserve a portion of the property for the children. If there is no surviving spouse, parents generally leave their property to surviving children with some portion reserved for charitable donations. Property is transferred either by a written will or, in the absence of a will, by the terms of state law, called the *intestacy statute.* Although the law allows individuals to determine who owns property after they die by writing a will, it limits their ability to completely disinherit a spouse. Laws in every state grant surviving spouses some portion of the property owned by the deceased spouse (called the *decedent*) at death. This topic is covered in Chapter 9, §3.2.B. However, the law in the United States allows parents to completely disinherit their children, leaving them nothing. Most European nations take a different tack, guaranteeing children some portion of the family assets when their parents die, thereby extending to children the same rights granted in the United States to surviving spouses.

Problems

1. Two people get engaged and exchange rings; they break off the engagement. Must they return the rings? Traditionally, donors were not allowed to impose conditions on gifts. Delivery of a gift with intent to transfer title would be held to be irrevocable. *Albinger v. Harris,* 48 P.3d 711, 719 (Mont. 2002). However, some courts have begun

to abandon this rule, and most will do so in the context of gifts given in contemplation of marriage. Because a wedding ring is clearly given under the understanding that the parties would be married, most courts will require the ring to be returned if the engagement is called off. *Lipton v. Lipton*, 514 N.Y.S.2d 158 (Sup. Ct. 1986); *Lindh v. Surman*, 742 A.2d 643 (Pa. 1999); *Crippen v. Campbell*, 2007 WL 2768076 (Tenn. Ct. App. 2007).

Should it matter whose fault it is that the marriage fell through? Some courts refuse to look into fault, *Aronow v. Silver*, 538 A.2d 851 (N.J. Super. Ct. Ch. Div. 1987); *Vigil v. Haber*, 888 P.2d 455 (N.M. 1994); *Cooper v. Smith*, 800 N.E.2d 372 (Ohio Ct. App. 2003), while others will not allow an individual to recover a ring if he broke off the engagement without justification, *Spinnell v. Quigley*, 785 P.2d 1149 (Wash. Ct. App. 1990) (fault relevant); *Heiman v. Parish*, 942 P.2d 631 (Kan. 1997) (fault should be a factor in extreme cases); *Curtis v. Anderson*, 106 S.W.3d 251, 256 (Tex. Ct. App. 2003) ("[A]bsent a written agreement a donor is not entitled to the return of an engagement ring if he terminates the engagement"). Which approach is better?

2. Two parties open a joint bank account. Should they each be entitled to use all the money in the account, or do they have an obligation not to withdraw excessive amounts of the money to ensure that some is left for their co-owner? Do the circumstances under which the money was deposited matter?

3. Should parents be entitled to completely disinherit their children, as is the law in the United States, or should children have a right to a portion of family assets owned by their parents at death, as is the law in most European states?

§5 POSSESSION

Possession is not really nine-tenths of the law (otherwise law school would be much shorter) but it is an important concept in property rights. The government has often distributed property based on possession even when possessors were violating prior law. Yet just as often, possessors' claims will be defeated in favor of a superior claim. What is necessary to legally possess a wild animal? A home run baseball? Oil or gas? The answers involve judgments about rewards for labor and investment, wealth maximization, justified expectations, and other policy concerns.

§5.1 Wild Animals

Pierson v. Post

2 Am. Dec. 264 (N.Y. 1805)

This was an action of trespass on the case commenced in a justice's court, by the present defendant against the now plaintiff.

The declaration stated that Post, being in possession of certain dogs and hounds under his command, did, "upon a certain wild and uninhabited, unpossessed and waste land, called the beach, find and start one of those noxious beasts called a fox," and whilst there hunting, chasing and pursuing the same with his dogs and hounds, and when in view thereof, Pierson, well knowing the fox was so hunted and pursued, did, in the sight of Post, to prevent his catching the same, kill and carry it off. A verdict having been rendered for the plaintiff below, the defendant there sued out a certiorari, and now assigned for error, that the declaration and the matters therein contained were not sufficient in law to maintain an action.

Daniel Tompkins, J., delivered the opinion of the court.

The question submitted by the counsel in this cause for our determination is, whether Lodowick Post, by the pursuit with his hounds in the manner alleged in his declaration, acquired such a right to, or property in, the fox, as will sustain an action against Pierson for killing and taking him away.

The cause was argued with much ability by the counsel on both sides, and presents for our decision a novel and nice question. It is admitted that a fox is an animal *ferae naturae* and that property in such animals is acquired by occupancy only. These admissions narrow the discussion to the simple question of what acts amount to occupancy, applied to acquiring right to wild animals?

If we have recourse to the ancient writers upon general principles of law, the judgment below is obviously erroneous. Justinian's Institutes, lib. 2, tit. 1, s.13, and Fleta, lib. 3, c.2, p.175, adopt the principle, that pursuit alone vests no property or right in the huntsman; and that even pursuit, accompanied with wounding, is equally ineffectual for that purpose, unless the animal be actually taken. The same principle is recognised by Bracton, lib. 2, c.1, p.8.

Puffendorf, lib. 4, c.6, s.2 and 10, defines occupancy of beasts *ferae naturae*, to be the actual corporal possession of them, and Bynkershoek is cited as coinciding in this definition. It is indeed with hesitation that Puffendorf affirms that a wild beast mortally wounded, or greatly maimed, cannot be fairly intercepted by another, whilst the pursuit of the person inflicting the wound continues. The foregoing authorities are decisive to show that mere pursuit gave Post no legal right to the fox, but that he became the property of Pierson, who intercepted and killed him.

It therefore only remains to inquire whether there are any contrary principles, or authorities, to be found in other books, which ought to induce a different decision.

Barbeyrac, in his notes on Puffendorf, does not accede to the definition of occupancy by the latter, but, on the contrary, affirms, that actual bodily seizure is not, in all cases, necessary to constitute possession of wild animals. He does not, however, *describe* the acts which, according to his ideas, will amount to an appropriation of such animals to private use, so as to exclude the claims of all other persons, by title of occupancy, to the same animals; and he is far from averring that pursuit alone is sufficient for that purpose. To a certain extent, and as far as Barbeyrac appears to me to go, his objections to Puffendorf's definition of occupancy are reasonable and correct. That is to say, that actual bodily seizure is not indispensable to acquire right to, or possession of, wild beasts; but that, on the contrary, the mortal wounding of such beasts, by one not abandoning his pursuit, may, with the utmost propriety, be deemed possession of him; since, thereby, the pursuer manifests an unequivocal intention of appropriating the animal to his individual use, has deprived him of his natural liberty, and brought him within his certain control. So also, encompassing and securing such animals with nets and toils, or otherwise intercepting them in such a manner as to deprive them of their natural liberty, and render escape impossible, may justly be deemed to give possession of them to those persons who, by their industry and labor, have used such means of apprehending them. Barbeyrac seems to have adopted, and had in view of his notes, the more accurate opinion of Grotius, with respect to occupancy. The case now under consideration is one of mere pursuit, and presents no circumstances or acts which can bring it within the definition of occupancy by Puffendorf, or Grotius, or the ideas of Barbeyrac upon that subject.

The case cited [*Keeble v. Hickeringill*], I think clearly distinguishable from the present; inasmuch as there the action was for maliciously hindering and disturbing the plaintiff in the exercise and enjoyment of a private franchise; and . . . that the ducks were in the plaintiff's decoy pond, and *so in his possession*, from which it is obvious that the court laid much stress in the opinion upon the plaintiff's possession of the ducks.

We are the more readily inclined to confine possession or occupancy of beasts *ferae naturae*, within the limits prescribed by the learned authors above cited, for the sake of certainty, and preserving peace and order in society. If the first seeing, starting, or pursuing such animals, without having so wounded, circumvented or ensnared them, so as to deprive them of their natural liberty, and subject them to the control of their pursuer, should afford the basis of actions against others for intercepting and killing them, it would prove a fertile source of quarrels and litigation.

However uncourteous or unkind the conduct of Pierson towards Post, in this instance, may have been, yet his act was productive of no injury or damage for which a legal remedy can be applied. We are of opinion the judgment below was erroneous, and ought to be reversed.

BROCKHOLST LIVINGSTON, J. My opinion differs from that of the court.

Whether a person who, with his own hounds, starts and hunts a fox on waste and uninhabited ground, and is on the point of seizing his prey, acquires such an interest in the animal, as to have a right of action against another, who in view of the huntsman and his dogs in full pursuit, and with knowledge of the chase, shall kill and carry him away?

This is a knotty point, and should have been submitted to the arbitration of sportsmen, without poring over Justinian, Fleta, Bracton, Puffendorf, Locke, Barbeyrac, or Blackstone, all of whom have been cited; they would have had no difficulty in coming to a prompt and correct conclusion. In a court thus constituted, the skin and carcass of poor *reynard* would have been properly disposed of, and a precedent set, interfering with no usage or custom which the experience of ages has sanctioned, and which must be so well known to every votary of Diana. But the parties have referred the question to our judgment, and we must dispose of it as well as we can, from the partial lights we possess, leaving to a higher tribunal, the correction of any mistake which we may be so unfortunate as to make. By the pleadings it is admitted that a fox is a "wild and noxious beast." Both parties have regarded him, as the law of nations does a pirate, *hostem humani generis*, and although *de mortuis nil nisi bonum*, be a maxim of our profession, the memory of the deceased has not been spared. His depredations on farmers and on barn yards have not been forgotten; and to put him to death wherever found, is allowed to be meritorious, and of public benefit. Hence it follows, that our decision should have in view the greatest possible encouragement to the destruction of an animal, so cunning and ruthless in his career. But who would keep a pack of hounds; or what gentleman, at the sound of the horn, and at peep of day, would mount his steed, and for hours together, *sub jove frigido*, or a vertical sun, pursue the windings of this wily quadruped, if, just as night came on, and his stratagems and strength were nearly exhausted, a saucy intruder, who had not shared in the honours or labours of the chase, were permitted to come in at the death, and bear away in triumph the object of pursuit? Whatever Justinian may have thought of the matter, it must be recollected that his code was compiled many hundred years ago, and it would be very hard indeed, at the distance of so many centuries, not to have a right to establish a rule for ourselves. In his day, we read of no order of men who made it a business, in the language of the declaration in this cause, "with hounds and dogs to find, start, pursue, hunt and chase," these animals, and that, too, without any other motive than the preservation of Roman poultry; if this diversion had been then in fashion, the lawyers who composed his institutes would have taken care not to pass it by, without suitable encouragement. If any thing, therefore, in the digests or pandects shall appear to militate against the defendant in error, who, on this occasion, was the foxhunter, we have only to say *tempora mutantur*; and if men themselves change with the times, why should not laws also undergo an alteration?

It may be expected, however, by the learned counsel, that more particular notice be taken of their authorities. I have examined them all, and feel great difficulty in determining, whether to acquire dominion over a thing, before in common, it be sufficient that we barely see it, or know where it is, or wish for it, or make a declaration of our will respecting it; or whether, in the case of wild beasts, setting a trap, or lying in wait, or starting, or pursuing, be enough; or if an actual wounding, or killing, or bodily tact and occupation be necessary. Writers on general law, who have favoured us with their speculations on these points, differ on them all; but, great as is the diversity of sentiment among them, some conclusion must be adopted on the question immediately before us. After mature deliberation, I embrace that of Barbeyrac, as the most rational, and least liable to objection. If at liberty, we might imitate the courtesy of a certain emperor, who, to avoid giving offence to the advocates of any of these different doctrines, adopted a middle course, and by ingenious distinctions, rendered it difficult to say (as often happens after a fierce and angry contest) to whom the palm of victory belonged. He ordained, that if a beast be followed with *large dogs and hounds*, he shall belong to the hunter, not to the chance occupant; and in like manner, if he be killed or wounded with a lance or sword; but if chased with *beagles only*, then he passed to the captor, not to the first pursuer. If slain with a dart, a sling, or a bow, he fell to the hunter, if still in chase, and not to him who might afterwards find and seize him.

Now, as we are without any municipal regulations of our own, and the pursuit here, for aught that appears on the case, being with dogs and hounds of *imperial stature*, we are at liberty to adopt one of the provisions just cited, which comports also with the learned conclusion of Barbeyrac, that property in animals *ferae naturae* may be acquired without bodily touch or manucaption, provided the pursuer be within reach, or have a *reasonable* prospect (which certainly existed here) of taking, what he has *thus* discovered an intention of converting to his own use.

When we reflect also that the interest of our husbandmen, the most useful of men in any community, will be advanced by the destruction of a beast so pernicious and incorrigible, we cannot greatly err, in saying, that a pursuit like the present, through waste and unoccupied lands, and which must inevitably and speedily have terminated in corporal possession, or bodily *seisin*, confers such a right to the object of it, as to make any one a wrongdoer, who shall interfere and shoulder the spoil. The justice's judgment ought, therefore, in my opinion, to be affirmed.

Notes and Questions

1. **Fairness and justice.** The court suggested that Pierson's conduct in seizing the fox at the last moment was "uncourteous or unkind" but not unlawful. Was Pierson's conduct unfair? And if so, why should it be lawful? If it was not fair, what was unfair about it? Do you need to know more about the social customs of hunters to answer this question? Or can it be answered without looking into social practice?

Who do you think had a right to take possession of the fox? Suppose Post had been hunting the fox for a week, and Pierson had been outside for a few minutes before coming upon it and seizing it. Does the principle of rewarding labor suggest giving property rights to Post — who worked for a week toward the goal of getting the fox? Or does it suggest that one who took a week was a poor hunter and deserved to lose the fox to Pierson?

2. **Social utility.** What rule of law would best encourage productive labor? Justice Livingston notes that wild foxes were "noxious beasts" who preyed on barnyards. He suggested that the rules of law should encourage people to hunt them. How could you argue that the rule of law promulgated by the court in Justice Tompkins's opinion achieved that end? What reasons did Justice Livingston give for believing that his proposed rule would better serve this purpose? With current fears about extinction of species, how do we determine whether social welfare will be best advanced by promoting hunting of wild animals or by preserving them?

Fox-hunting, as Justice Livingston pictured it, cost hundreds of pounds and countless hours training dogs and horses. Andrea McDowell, *Legal Fictions in* Pierson v. Post, 105 Mich. L. Rev. 735, 752, 762-763 (2006). The town of Bridgehampton was interested in reducing the fox population, but only paid four shillings as a reward for dead foxes to encourage their extermination. Bethany R. Berger, *It's Not About the Fox: The Untold History of* Pierson v. Post, 55 Duke L.J. 1089, 1130 (2006). What does this suggest about Livingston's argument?

3. Certainty. Which rule of law — Tompkins's or Livingston's — creates the most certainty about ownership rights? What are the advantages of certainty in property rules? Will the simplest rule necessarily discourage litigation or quarrels between parties or result in the most predictable application by the courts? *See* Carol Rose, *Crystals and Mud in Property Law,* 40 Stan. L. Rev. 577 (1988); Joseph William Singer, *The Rule of Reason in Property Law,* 46 U.C. Davis L. Rev. 1375 (2013).

4. Trespassing. How would the case have been resolved if Pierson had caught the fox on Post's land? Should the rule of capture still apply? Would it make a difference if Pierson had begun hunting the fox on his own land and chased it onto Post's land to make the capture? *See* Chapter 1, §1.1 (discussing hunting on private land).

5. Custom. Justice Livingston's dissent declares that the dispute should have been "submitted to the arbitration of sportsmen" and decided according to the customs of "votaries of Diana," *i.e.,* hunters. What would be the advantages of applying the customs prevailing among hunters to resolve the dispute? What would be the potential risks? For an early empirical study examining the prevalence of custom over law in resolving trespass disputes between farmers and ranchers in California, *see* Robert Ellickson, *Of Coase and Cattle: Dispute Resolution Among Neighbors in Shasta County,* 38 Stan. L. Rev. 623 (1986).

In the nineteenth century, the customs of the whaling industry were used to resolve a series of cases involving rights to whales. In *Swift v. Gifford,* 23 F. Cas. 558 (D. Mass. 1872), whalers on the ship *Rainbow* had harpooned a whale, and continued the chase after the whale broke free with the harpoon still in its side. Whalers on the ship *Hercules,* however, had spotted and killed the whale shortly before the *Rainbow* caught up with it. Following the custom that a whale belonged to those whose harpoon remained in the whale, so long as they continued the chase, the court awarded the whale to the *Rainbow.* In *Ghen v. Rich,* 8 F. 159 (D. Mass. 1881), the whale had been killed with a bomb lance and immediately sank to the bottom of the sea, rising a few days later to wash ashore on Cape Cod, where it was found and sold to others. In a dispute between the whalers and the finder, the court followed the Cape Cod custom to hold that the whale belonged to the ship that had shot it. Was it more appropriate to apply custom in such cases than to the dispute between Pierson and Post? Why or why not?

6. Why a lawsuit about a fox? The costs of suit alone would be greater than any possible recovery. Bethany Berger argues that the dispute was really about control of the village common. *See* Bethany R. Berger, *It's Not About the Fox: The Untold History of* Pierson v. Post, 55 Duke L.J. 1089 (2006). Although the New York Court of Appeals treated the land as "waste and unoccupied lands," the town of Southampton on Long Island had long endured conflicts over control of the common lands in the town and had attempted to solve them by dividing ownership among various interest groups. These included the investors in the original settlement, those who purchased land in the first decade of settlement, the Shinnecock Tribe that had reserved rights in the lands, and all the town residents. Pierson was among the "proprietors" who inherited from the town's original settlers special rights in undivided lands, while Post's father was a wealthy merchant who had profited from the West India trade after the Revolutionary War. Professor Berger argues that "Post's elaborate fox hunt over the commons would have been perceived as [a] display of conspicuous wealth, inimical to the town's agricultural traditions . . . of puritan thrift," and the lawsuit may have been "part of this growing conflict over who could regulate and use the common resources of the town, and over whether commerce and wealth would define its social organization." *Id.*[3]

Problems

1. *Fleet v. Hegeman*, 14 Wend. 42 (N.Y. 1934), applied the question of capture of wild animals to oysters. The plaintiff had placed small immature oysters in a marked bed in common waters open to all inhabitants of the town, and left them to mature for two years. The defendant then collected the oysters without the permission of the plaintiff. If you were representing the defendant, how could you use *Pierson* to support your client? If you were representing the plaintiff, how would you distinguish it? How should the case be resolved?

2. How would the rule of *Pierson v. Post* apply to other animals and other contexts? Imagine that rather than a fox in a rural area, the animal is a dog wandering in a city street. May you take the dog home and keep it? Now imagine that the animal is a tiger. If you shoot the tiger, may you claim its pelt? Or are you liable to a suit by the owner of the tiger from whose home it escaped?

§5.2 Baseballs

Popov v. Hayashi

2002 WL 31833731 (Cal. Super.)

McCarthy, J.

In 1927, Babe Ruth hit sixty home runs. That record stood for thirty four years until Roger Maris broke it in 1961 with sixty one home runs. Mark McGwire hit seventy in 1998. On October 7, 2001, at PacBell Park in San Francisco, Barry Bonds hit number seventy three. That accomplishment set a record which, in all probability, will remain un-broken for years into the future.

The event was widely anticipated and received a great deal of attention. The ball that found itself at the receiving end of Mr. Bond's bat garnered some of that attention. Baseball fans in general, and especially people at the game, understood the

3. As a capstone to the recent scholarship on *Pierson*, in 2008 Professor Angela Fernandez uncovered the original trial record of the case, long lost because it was catalogued under an alternative spelling of Jesse Pierson's name, Peirson rather than Pierson. The New York County Clerk's Division of Old Records had just begun cataloging its records under the second parties' name as well, so a search for Post turned up the case. Angela Fernandez, *The Lost Record of* Pierson v. Post, *the Famous Fox Case*, 27 Law & Hist. Rev. 149, 156-157 (2009).

importance of the ball. It was worth a great deal of money[4] and whoever caught it would bask, for a brief period of time, in the reflected fame of Mr. Bonds.

With that in mind, many people who attended the game came prepared for the possibility that a record setting ball would be hit in their direction. Among this group were plaintiff Alex Popov and defendant Patrick Hayashi. They were unacquainted at the time. Both men brought baseball gloves, which they anticipated using if the ball came within their reach.

Barry Bonds came to bat in the first inning. With nobody on base and a full count, Bonds swung at a slow knuckleball. He connected. The ball sailed over the right-field fence and into the arcade. When the seventy-third home run ball went into the arcade, it landed in the upper portion of the webbing of a softball glove worn by Alex Popov. While the glove stopped the trajectory of the ball, it is not at all clear that the ball was secure. Popov had to reach for the ball and in doing so, may have lost his balance.

Even as the ball was going into his glove, a crowd of people began to engulf Mr. Popov. He was tackled and thrown to the ground while still in the process of attempting to complete the catch. Some people intentionally descended on him for the purpose of taking the ball away, while others were involuntarily forced to the ground by the momentum of the crowd.

Eventually, Mr. Popov was buried face down on the ground under several layers of people. At one point he had trouble breathing. Mr. Popov was grabbed, hit and kicked. People reached underneath him in the area of his glove. Neither the tape nor the testimony is sufficient to establish which individual members of the crowd were responsible for the assaults on Mr. Popov.

The videotape clearly establishes that this was an out of control mob, engaged in violent, illegal behavior. Although some witnesses testified in a manner inconsistent with this finding, their testimony is specifically rejected as being false on a material point. At some point the ball left his glove and ended up on the ground. It is impossible to establish the exact point in time that this occurred or what caused it to occur.

Mr. Hayashi was standing near Mr. Popov when the ball came into the stands. He, like Mr. Popov, was involuntarily forced to the ground. He committed no wrongful act. While on the ground he saw the loose ball. He picked it up, rose to his feet and put it in his pocket.

We will never know if Mr. Popov would have been able to retain control of the ball had the crowd not interfered with his efforts to do so. Resolution of that question is the work of a psychic, not a judge

The deciding question in this case . . . is whether Mr. Popov achieved possession or the right to possession as he attempted to catch and hold on to the ball.

The parties have agreed to a starting point for the legal analysis. Prior to the time the ball was hit, it was possessed and owned by Major League Baseball. At the time it was hit it became intentionally abandoned property. The first person who came in possession of the ball became its new owner.

---

4. It has been suggested that the ball might sell for something in excess of $1,000,000.

The parties fundamentally disagree about the definition of possession. In order to assist the court in resolving this disagreement, four distinguished law professors participated in a forum to discuss the legal definition of possession. The professors also disagreed.

The disagreement is understandable. Although the term possession appears repeatedly throughout the law, its definition varies depending on the context in which it is used. Various courts have condemned the term as vague and meaningless.

While there is a degree of ambiguity built into the term possession, that ambiguity exists for a purpose. Courts are often called upon to resolve conflicting claims of possession in the context of commercial disputes. A stable economic environment requires rules of conduct which are understandable and consistent with the fundamental customs and practices of the industry they regulate. Without that, rules will be difficult to enforce and economic instability will result. Because each industry has different customs and practices, a single definition of possession cannot be applied to different industries without creating havoc.

[S]ome cases recognize possession even before absolute dominion and control is achieved. Those cases require the actor to be actively and ably engaged in efforts to establish complete control. Moreover, such efforts must be significant and they must be reasonably calculated to result in unequivocal dominion and control at some point in the near future.

This rule is applied in cases involving the hunting or fishing of wild animals or the salvage of sunken vessels.

These rules are contextual in nature. They are crafted in response to the unique nature of the conduct they seek to regulate. Moreover, they are influenced by the custom and practice of each industry. The reason that absolute dominion and control is not required to establish possession in the cases cited by Mr. Popov is that such a rule would be unworkable and unreasonable. The "nature and situation" of the property at issue does not immediately lend itself to unequivocal dominion and control. It is impossible to wrap ones arms around a whale, a fleeing fox or a sunken ship.

The opposite is true of a baseball hit into the stands of a stadium. Not only is it physically possible for a person to acquire unequivocal dominion and control of an abandoned baseball, but fans generally expect a claimant to have accomplished as much. The custom and practice of the stands creates a reasonable expectation that a person will achieve full control of a ball before claiming possession. There is no reason for the legal rule to be inconsistent with that expectation.

The central tenant of [the] Rule [advocated by Professor Brian Gray] is that the actor must retain control of the ball after incidental contact with people and things. Mr. Popov has not established by a preponderance of the evidence that he would have retained control of the ball after all momentum ceased and after any incidental contact with people or objects. Consequently, he did not achieve full possession.

That finding, however, does not resolve the case. The reason we do not know whether Mr. Popov would have retained control of the ball is not because of incidental contact. It is because he was attacked. His efforts to establish possession were interrupted by the collective assault of a band of wrongdoers.

As a matter of fundamental fairness, Mr. Popov should have had the opportunity to try to complete his catch unimpeded by unlawful activity. To hold otherwise would be to allow the result in this case to be dictated by violence. That will not happen.

A court sitting in equity has the authority to fashion rules and remedies designed to achieve fundamental fairness. Consistent with this principle, the court adopts the following rule. Where an actor undertakes significant but incomplete steps to achieve possession of a piece of abandoned personal property and the effort is interrupted by the unlawful acts of others, the actor has a legally cognizable pre-possessory interest in the property. That pre-possessory interest constitutes a qualified right to possession which can support a cause of action for conversion.

[T]his does not, however, address the interests of Mr. Hayashi. Mr. Hayashi was not a wrongdoer. He was a victim of the same bandits that attacked Mr. Popov. The difference is that he was able to extract himself from their assault and move to the side of the road. It was there that he discovered the loose ball. When he picked up and put it in his pocket he attained unequivocal dominion and control.

If Mr. Popov had achieved complete possession before Mr. Hayashi got the ball, those actions would not have divested Mr. Popov of any rights, nor would they have created any rights to which Mr. Hayashi could lay claim. Mr. Popov, however, was able to establish only a qualified pre-possessory interest in the ball. That interest does not establish a full right to possession that is protected from a subsequent legitimate claim.

An award of the ball to Mr. Popov would be unfair to Mr. Hayashi. It would be premised on the assumption that Mr. Popov would have caught the ball. That assumption is not supported by the facts. An award of the ball to Mr. Hayashi would unfairly penalize Mr. Popov. It would be based on the assumption that Mr. Popov would have dropped the ball. That conclusion is also unsupported by the facts.

Both men have a superior claim to the ball as against all the world. Each man has a claim of equal dignity as to the other. We are, therefore, left with something of a dilemma. Thankfully, there is a middle ground.

The concept of equitable division was fully explored in a law review article authored by Professor R.H. Helmholz in the December 1983 edition of the Fordham Law Review. As Helmholz points out, it is useful in that it "provides an equitable way to resolve competing claims which are equally strong." Moreover, "[i]t comports with what one instinctively feels to be fair."

Mr. Hayashi's claim is compromised by Mr. Popov's pre-possessory interest. Mr. Popov cannot demonstrate full control. Albeit for different reasons, they stand before the court in exactly the same legal position as did the five boys [in *Keron v. Cashman*, 33 A. 1055 (N.J. 1896), who found an old sock and played with the sock together until it broke open, spilling out $775. Here, as in *Keron*, Popov and Hayashi's] legal claims are of equal quality and they are equally entitled to the ball.

The court therefore declares that both plaintiff and defendant have an equal and undivided interest in the ball. Plaintiff's cause of action for conversion is sustained only as to his equal and undivided interest. In order to effectuate this ruling, the ball must be sold and the proceeds divided equally between the parties.

Notes and Questions

1. Aftermath. The full story of the battle for Barry Bonds's home run ball is captured in the documentary *Up for Grabs*. The ball ultimately sold only for $450,000, far less than was expected. (The same collector had purchased Mark McGwire's record-breaking ball for $3.2 million in 1999.) Popov's lawyer later sued Popov for his attorneys' fees, which he claimed at an hourly rate amounted to $473,000. Hayashi, who was an engineering student at the time of the suit, had retained his attorney on a contingency basis and so did not have a legal bill that dwarfed his gains. David Kravets, *Lawyer Sues Client Who Caught Bond's Ball: Fan Owes $473,000*, National Journal (Canada), July 9, 2003.

2. Custom. Ownership of the ball was only up for grabs because the original owner, Major League Baseball, had a policy of intentionally abandoning any balls hit into the stands. Major League Baseball only provides balls in games that are likely to have record-breaking hits, but home teams provide balls for other games and universally follow the same fan-friendly policy. This policy has been a matter of custom and practice for more than 60 years. Could a ball club reverse this policy? In 2001, Raphael Vasquez caught Mike Piazza's three-hundredth career home run and gave it to his six-year old daughter, Denise. Mets security guards surrounded the father and daughter and forced them to give up the ball, apparently because Piazza wanted it as a souvenir. Could Vasquez successfully sue the ball club?

What about balls that stay in the field? In 2004, backup Boston Red Sox first baseman Doug Mientkiewicz caught the ball that won the World Series for the team, breaking the "curse of the Bambino" of Red Sox lore. When he kept the ball, the Red Sox sued, claiming that Mientkiewicz's possession was only the result of his employment for the team. Who should win? Does it matter that the stadium was owned by the St. Louis Cardinals, which also supplied the ball? The suit was ultimately settled with the agreement that the ball would go to the National Baseball Hall of Fame. For more on ball ownership, *see* Paul Finkelman, *Fugitive Baseballs and Abandoned Property: Who Owns the Home Run Ball?*, 23 Cardozo L. Rev. 1609 (2002). For its surprisingly complicated tax consequences, *see* Andrew Appleby, *Ball Busters: How the IRS Should Tax Record-Setting Baseballs and Other Found Property Under the Treasure Trove Regulation*, 33 Vt. L. Rev. 43 (2008).

3. Constructive possession. What would have happened had Popov been able to prove that he got the ball firmly in his glove and was walking away, but the "gang of bandits" subsequently made him lose it? He would win against Hayashi. This illustrates that the doctrine of acquisition by possession does not require continual possession, but rather clear marking of ownership without abandonment of the property. Major League Baseball having abandoned the ball, once Popov had reduced it to his possession it remained in his constructive possession, and he could claim it against all others.

4. Equitable division. Scholars have advocated equitable division resolutions to different categories of cases. A 2007 article advocates their use in the case of what the authors call "windfalls," gains or losses that neither party could reasonably predict, so that the possibility of the windfall would not change the behavior of either party. In such cases, they assert, equitable division is efficient, because a normally risk-averse person would ex ante choose the equal division remedy as insurance against total loss; it is more just because it does not place the unforeseen loss entirely on any one party; and it furthers judicial integrity because it does not force courts into judicial contortions to justify choosing one party or the other. *See* Gideon Parchomovsky, Peter Siegelman & Steve Thel, *Of Equal Wrongs and Half Rights*, 82 N.Y.U. L. Rev. 738 (2007). Is this correct? If it is, why aren't split-the-difference remedies more common?

§5.3 Capture of Natural Resources

The law of capture has also been applied to disputes over ownership of oil and gas as well as water. How is an oil pool beneath your and your neighbor's land like a wild animal? How is it different? What about the water in a stream that flows past your land and your neighbor's? How do these similarities and differences affect the legal tests that should govern ownership of these resources? The materials below consider the rule of capture and oil and gas; rights and duties regarding water are covered in Chapter 7, §8.

Elliff v. Texon Drilling Co.

210 S.W.2d 558 (Tex. 1948)

A.J. FOLLEY, Justice.

This is a suit by the petitioners, Mrs. Mabel Elliff, Frank Elliff, and Charles C. Elliff, against the respondents, Texon Drilling Company, a Texas corporation, Texon Royalty Company, a Texas corporation, Texon Royalty Company, a Delaware corporation, and John L. Sullivan, for damages resulting from a "blowout" gas well drilled by respondents in the Agua Dulce Field in Nueces County.

The petitioners owned the surface and certain royalty interests in 3054.9 acres of land in Nueces County, upon which there was a producing well known as Elliff No. 1. They owned all the mineral estate underlying the west 1500 acres of the tract, and an undivided one-half interest in the mineral estate underlying the east 1554.9 acres. Both tracts were subject to oil and gas leases, and therefore their royalty interest in the west 1500 acres was one-eighth of the oil or gas, and in the east 1554.9 acres was one-sixteenth of the oil and gas.

It was alleged that these lands overlaid approximately fifty per cent of a huge reservoir of gas and distillate and that the remainder of the reservoir was under the lands owned by Mrs. Clara Driscoll, adjoining the lands of petitioners on the east. Prior to November 1936, respondents were engaged in the drilling of Driscoll-Sevier No. 2 as an offset well at a location 466 feet east of petitioners' east line. On the date stated, when respondents had reached a depth of approximately 6838 feet, the well blew out, caught fire and cratered. Attempts to control it were unsuccessful, and huge quantities of gas, distillate and some oil were blown into the air, dissipating large quantities from

the reservoir into which the offset well was drilled. When the Driscoll-Sevier No. 2 well blew out, the fissure or opening in the ground around the well gradually increased until it enveloped and destroyed Elliff No. 1. The latter well also blew out, cratered, caught fire and burned for several years. Two water wells on petitioners' land became involved in the cratering and each of them blew out. Certain damages also resulted to the surface of petitioners' lands and to their cattle thereon. The cratering process and the eruption continued until large quantities of gas and distillate were drained from under petitioners' land and escaped into the air, all of which was alleged to be the direct and proximate result of the negligence of respondents in permitting their well to blow out. The extent of the emissions from the Driscoll-Sevier No. 2 and Elliff No. 1, and the two water wells on petitioners' lands, was shown at various times during the several years between the blowout in November 1936, and the time of the trial in June 1946. There was also expert testimony from petroleum engineers showing the extent of the losses from the underground reservoir, which computations extended from the date of the blowout only up to June 1938. It was indicated that it was not feasible to calculate the losses subsequent thereto, although lesser emissions of gas continued even up to the time of the trial. All the evidence with reference to the damages included all losses from the reservoir beneath petitioners' land without regard to whether they were wasted and dissipated from above the Driscoll land or from petitioners' land.

The jury found that respondents were negligent in failing to use drilling mud of sufficient weight in drilling their well, and that such negligence was the proximate cause of the well blowing out.

On the findings of the jury the trial court rendered judgment for petitioners for $154,518.19, which included $148,548.19 for the gas and distillate, and $5970 for damages to the land and cattle. The Court of Civil Appeals reversed the judgment and remanded the cause.

The reversal by the Court of Civil Appeals rests [on the ground] that since substantially all of the gas and distillate which was drained from under petitioners' lands was lost through respondents' blowout well, petitioners could not recover because under the law of capture they had lost all property rights in the gas or distillate which had migrated from their lands.

[T]he sole question [is] whether the law of capture absolves respondents of any liability for the negligent waste or destruction of petitioners' gas and distillate, though substantially all of such waste or destruction occurred after the minerals had been drained from beneath petitioners' lands.

In the more recent trend of the decisions of our state, with the growth and development of scientific knowledge of oil and gas, it is now recognized "that when a[n] oil field has been fairly tested and developed, experts can determine approximately the amount of oil and gas in place in a common pool, and can also equitably determine the amount of oil and gas recoverable by the owner of each tract of land under certain operating conditions." *Brown v. Humble Oil & Refining Co.*, 83 S.W.2d 935, 940 (Tex. 1935).

In our state the landowner is regarded as having absolute title in severalty to the oil and gas in place beneath his land. The only qualification of that rule of ownership is that it must be considered in connection with the law of capture and is subject to police regulations. The oil and gas beneath the soil are considered a part of the realty. Each owner of land owns separately, distinctly and exclusively all the oil and gas under his land and is accorded the usual remedies against trespassers who appropriate the minerals or destroy their market value.

The conflict in the decisions of the various states with reference to the character of ownership is traceable to some extent to the divergent views entertained by the courts, particularly in the earlier cases, as to the nature and migratory character of oil and gas in the soil. In the absence of common law precedent, and owing to the lack of scientific information as to the movement of these minerals, some of the courts have sought by analogy to compare oil and gas to other types of property such as wild animals, birds, subterranean waters and other migratory things, with reference to which the common law had established rules denying any character of ownership prior to capture. However, as was said by Professor A.W. Walker, Jr., of the School of Law of the University of Texas: "There is no oil or gas producing state today which follows the wild-animal analogy to its logical conclusion that the landowner has no property interest in the oil and gas in place." 16 Tex. L. Rev. 370, 371. In the light of modern scientific knowledge these early analogies have been disproven, and courts generally have come to recognize that oil and gas, as commonly found in underground reservoirs, are securely entrapped in a static condition in the original pool, and, ordinarily, so remain until disturbed by penetrations from the surface. It is further established, nevertheless, that these minerals will migrate across property lines towards any low pressure area created by production from the common pool. This migratory character of oil and gas has given rise to the so-called rule or law of capture. That rule simply is that the owner of a tract of land acquires title to the oil or gas which he produces from wells on his land, though part of the oil or gas may have migrated from adjoining lands. He may thus appropriate the oil and gas that have flowed from adjacent lands without the consent of the owner of those lands, and without incurring liability to him for drainage. The non-liability is based upon the theory that after the drainage the title or property interest of the former owner is gone. This rule, at first blush, would seem to conflict with the view of absolute ownership of the minerals in place, but it was otherwise decided in the early case of *Stephens County v. Mid-Kansas Oil & Gas Co.*, 254 S.W. 290 (Tex. 1923). Mr. Justice Greenwood there stated, 254 S.W. at 292: "The objection lacks substantial foundation that gas or oil in a certain tract of land cannot be owned in place, because subject to appropriation, without the consent of the owner of the tract, through drainage from wells on adjacent lands. If the owners of adjacent lands have the right to appropriate, without liability, the gas and oil underlying their neighbor's land, then their neighbor has the correlative right to appropriate, through like methods of drainage, the gas and oil underlying the tracts adjacent to his own."

Thus it is seen that, notwithstanding the fact that oil and gas beneath the surface are subject both to capture and administrative regulation, the fundamental rule of absolute ownership of the minerals in place is not affected in our state. In recognition of such ownership, our courts, in decisions involving well-spacing regulations of our Railroad Commission, have frequently announced the sound view that each landowner should be afforded the opportunity to produce his fair share of the recoverable oil and gas beneath his land, which is but another way of recognizing the existence of correlative rights between the various landowners over a common reservoir of oil or gas.

It must be conceded that under the law of capture there is no liability for reasonable and legitimate drainage from the common pool. The landowner is privileged to sink as many wells as he desires upon his tract of land and extract therefrom and appropriate all the oil and gas that he may produce, so long as he operates within the spirit and purpose of conservation statutes and orders of the Railroad Commission. These laws and regulations are designed to afford each owner a reasonable opportunity to produce his proportionate part of the oil and gas from the entire pool and to prevent operating practices injurious to the common reservoir. In this manner, if all operators exercise the same degree of skill and diligence, each owner will recover in most instances his fair share of the oil and gas. This reasonable opportunity to produce his fair share of the oil and gas is the landowner's common law right under our theory of absolute ownership of the minerals in place. But from the very nature of this theory the right of each land holder is qualified, and is limited to legitimate operations. Each owner whose land overlies the basin has a like interest, and each must of necessity exercise his right with some regard to the rights of others. No owner should be permitted to carry on his operations in reckless or lawless irresponsibility, but must submit to such limitations as are necessary to enable each to get his own.

While we are cognizant of the fact that there is a certain amount of reasonable and necessary waste incident to the production of oil and gas to which the non-liability rule must also apply, we do not think this immunity should be extended so as to include the negligent waste or destruction of the oil and gas.

In 85 A.L.R. 1156, . . . the annotator states: ". . . The fact that the owner of the land has a right to take and to use gas and oil, even to the diminution or exhaustion of the supply under his neighbor's land, does not give him the right to waste the gas. His property in the gas underlying his land consists of the right to appropriate the same, and permitting the gas to escape into the air is not an appropriation thereof in the proper sense of the term."

In like manner, the negligent waste and destruction of petitioners' gas and distillate was neither a legitimate drainage of the minerals from beneath their lands nor a lawful or reasonable appropriation of them. Consequently, the petitioners did not lose their right, title and interest in them under the law of capture. At the time of their removal they belonged to petitioners, and their wrongful dissipation deprived these owners of the right and opportunity to produce them. That right is forever lost, the same cannot be restored, and petitioners are without an adequate legal remedy unless we allow a recovery under the same common law which governs other actions for damages and under which the property rights in oil and gas are vested. This remedy should not be denied.

In common with others who are familiar with the nature of oil and gas and the risks involved in their production, the respondents had knowledge that a failure to use due care in drilling their well might result in a blowout with the consequent waste and dissipation of the oil, gas and distillate from the common reservoir. In the conduct of one's business or in the use and exploitation of one's property, the law imposes upon all persons the duty to exercise ordinary care to avoid injury or damage to the property of others. Thus under the common law, and independent of the conservation statutes, the respondents were legally bound to use due care to avoid the negligent waste or destruction of the minerals imbedded in petitioners' oil and gas-bearing strata. This common-law duty the respondents failed to discharge. For that omission they should be required to respond in such damages as will reasonably compensate the injured parties for the loss sustained as the proximate result of the negligent conduct. The fact that the major portion of the gas and distillate escaped from the well on respondents' premises is immaterial. Irrespective of the opening from which the minerals escaped, they belonged to the petitioners and the loss was the same. They would not have been dissipated at any opening except for the wrongful conduct of the respondents. Being responsible for the loss they are in no position to deny liability because the gas and distillate did not escape through the surface of petitioners' lands.

We are therefore of the opinion the Court of Civil Appeals erred in holding that under the law of capture the petitioners cannot recover for the damages resulting from the wrongful drainage of the gas and distillate from beneath their lands.

Notes and Questions

Continuing impact of the rule of capture in oil and gas production. Although oil and gas production are subject to extensive regulation to prevent waste and protect the environment, the rule of capture generally remains the law. *See Browning Oil Co., Inc. v. Luecke*, 38 S.W.3d 625 (Tex. Ct. App. 2000); 6 *Thompson on Real Property, Second Thomas Editions* §49.02. Is the rule fair? Does it promote or inhibit investment in producing oil and gas? The effect of the rule has been diminished by the correlative rights recognized in cases like *Elliff* as well as spacing and drilling regulations designed to conserve the resource. In some situations, these regulations may involve *compulsory unitization*, or coordination between all surface owners to ensure maximum recovery from the common pool. *Thompson, supra*, at §49.02(d).

Problems

1. Plaintiff Corporation invests $1 million in exploring for oil on its property. After it discovers oil and begins to extract it for sale, its neighboring landowner, Defendant Corporation, begins to do likewise. Because the oil is part of a common pool underlying the neighboring pieces of property, the defendant is able to extract oil from the same pool discovered by the plaintiff. Defendant's costs are much less than plaintiff's because it does not have to undergo the expense of searching for the oil. This gives the defendant a competitive advantage. Plaintiff sues defendant, asking for an injunction ordering defendant to stop exploiting oil discovered by plaintiff's investment and labor. Defendant claims a right to extract oil from beneath its own property.

a. As plaintiff's attorney, what rule of law would you advocate that the court adopt? How would you justify that rule in terms of both fairness and social utility?

b. As defendant's attorney, what rule of law would you advocate that the court adopt? How would you justify that rule in terms of both fairness and social utility?

c. As the judge deciding the case, what rule of law would you adopt, and why?

2. The Exxon Valdez ran aground off the coast of Alaska in 1989, resulting in one of the largest oil spills in United States history. A lawsuit was filed against Exxon representing a class of tens of thousands of individuals who made their livelihood through commercial and subsistence fishing in the area. *Exxon Valdez v. Hazelwood*, 270 F.3d 1215 (9th Cir. 2001). The suit sought damages for the destruction of the fish supply. Use *Pierson v. Post* and *Eliff v. Texon* to argue for the plaintiffs or the defendants.

§5.4 Possession and the Presumption of Title

In the earlier cases, capture *creates* title to the property. But possession, even without evidence of capture or how the possession arose, may also create a presumption of legal title that will continue unless rebutted. Why does the law create this presumption? What functions does it serve? See the next case.

Willcox v. Stroup

467 F.3d 409 (4th Cir. 2006)

J. HARVIE WILKINSON III, Circuit Judge.

[Plaintiff Thomas Law Willcox found 444 documents from the administrations of two governors of South Carolina during the Civil War in a shopping bag in a closet at his late stepmother's home. The documents concern Confederate military reports, correspondence, and telegrams between various Confederate generals, officers, servicemen, and government officials, and related materials and have an appraised value of $2.4 million. Willcox allowed the papers to be microfilmed for the state archives. When he tried to sell the papers, Rodger Stroup, director of the South Carolina Department of Archives and History, obtained a temporary restraining order preventing the sale. Willcox then sued Stroup and the State of South Carolina for a declaratory judgment that he owned the papers.]

The papers seem to have come into Willcox's family through his great-great-uncle, Confederate Major General Evander McIver Law, who most likely came into possession of them during the February 1865 attack on the South Carolina capital by Union General William Tecumseh Sherman. On February 15, 1865, in anticipation of imminent attack, Governor A.G. Magrath declared martial law in Columbia and appointed General Law the Provost Marshal of the city. On February 16, 1865, a large number of State archives and records were removed from Columbia for safekeeping. On February 17, 1865, General Law was relieved of his duties as Provost Marshal, and General Sherman took control of Columbia. The parties submit no direct evidence of how General Law came into possession of the papers, nor is there any suggestion that he did so illegally.

On February 16, 1896, General Law wrote a letter to a New York book dealer regarding the sale of some letters which, both parties agree, appear to belong to the collection at issue here. By the 1940s, Mrs. Annie J. Storm, the granddaughter of General Law, was in possession of the papers and attempted to sell them to both the University of North Carolina at Chapel Hill ("UNC") and the South Caroliniana Library of the University of South Carolina. Mrs. Storm described the documents as "original State House papers entrusted to [her] grandfather at the time of the surrender." No sale resulted, but the papers were placed on microfilm at the Southern Historical Collection at UNC.

No evidence has been submitted of the papers' movements between the time of the Storm correspondence and plaintiff Willcox's discovery more than fifty years later. The point for present purposes is simply that, while the precise route by which Civil War-era gubernatorial papers arrived in a shopping bag in Thomas Law Willcox's stepmother's closet remains a mystery, it appears that the papers have been in the possession of the Law and Willcox families for over one hundred and forty years.

The exceptional nature of the papers in dispute—their early vintage, their unknown history—presents issues distinct from those of the typical personal property case. Without the benefit of clear chain of title, evidence of original ownership, eyewitness testimony, and any number of documentary aids usually helpful in the determination of ownership, the court must utilize the legal tools that remain at its disposal. In this situation, tenets of the common law that usually remain in the background of ownership determinations come to the forefront, their logic and utility revealed anew.

That possession is nine-tenths of the law is a truism hardly bearing repetition. The importance of possession gave rise to the principle that "[p]ossession of property is indicia of ownership, and a rebuttable presumption exists that those in possession of property are rightly in possession." 73 C.J.S. *Property* §70 (2004). The common law has long recognized that "actual possession is, prima facie, evidence of a legal title in the possessor." William Blackstone, 2 *Commentaries* *196. *See, e.g.,* Edward Coke, 1 *Commentary upon Littleton* 6.b. (19th ed. 1832) (strong presumption of ownership created by "continuall and quiet possession"); *Jeffries v. Great W. Ry. Co.* (1856) 119 Eng. Rep. 680 (K.B.) ("[T]he presumption of law is that the person who has possession has the property.").

This presumption has been a feature of American law almost since its inception. "Undoubtedly," noted the Supreme Court, "if a person be found in possession . . . it is prima facie evidence of his ownership." *Ricard v. Williams,* 20 U.S. 59, 105 (1822). Almost eighty years later, the Court reaffirmed, "If there be no evidence to the contrary, proof of possession, at least under a color of right, is sufficient proof of title." *Bradshaw v. Ashley,* 180 U.S. 59, 63 (1901). In this case, the possession of the Law and Willcox families triggers the presumption of their ownership of the papers.

The . . . unusual circumstances of this case . . . provide a notable illustration of why such a presumption exists in the first place.

First and foremost, the presumption operates to resolve otherwise impenetrable difficulties. Where neither party can establish title by a preponderance of the evidence, the presumption cuts the Gordian knot, determining ownership in favor of the possessor. This case shows the need for such a default rule. It presents questions the answers to which remain a mystery. Little is known of the papers' whereabouts, status, or movements from their creation to their acquisition by General Law. There is no evidence of how General Law acquired the papers. Not even the chain of possession within the Law and Willcox families has yet been determined with any certainty. In fact, in over one hundred and forty years of existence, these papers have apparently surfaced in the historical record only three times: in General Law's 1896 correspondence, in Annie Storm's 1940's correspondence, and in the current litigation.

This case thus poses questions which we are ill equipped to answer. Fortunately, however, the common law reveals its usefulness even in the acknowledgment of its limitations. The presumption of ownership from possession locates the parties' burdens. Where the party not in possession is able to establish superior title by satisfactory evidence, the presumption gives way in favor of this evidence. But where no such evidence is produced—where, as here, the events at issue are impossible to reconstruct—the presumption recognizes and averts the possibility of a court's presiding over a historical goose chase.

Second, the presumption of ownership in the possessor promotes stability. The presumption of ownership from possession is one of an array of legal principles designed to this end. The presumption means that, absent proof to the contrary, settled distributions and expectations will continue undisturbed. Even where evidence overcomes the presumption, other principles work to protect settled expectations, including the statute of limitations, the doctrine of adverse possession, and equitable defenses such as laches, staleness, abandonment, and waiver.

Such principles, working in concert, favor status-quo distributions over great upsets in property rights. At the most basic level, this fosters "the policy of protecting the public peace against violence and disorder." *See Sabariego v. Maverick,* 124 U.S. 261, 297 (1888). In contemporary commercial society, it protects the expectations of those in possession, thus encouraging them to make improvements that increase social wealth. *See, e.g.,* Richard A. Posner, *Economic Analysis of Law* 80-84 (6th ed. 2003); Thomas W. Merrill & Henry E. Smith, *What Happened to Property in Law and Economics?,* 111 Yale L.J. 357, 398 (2001) ("[T]he refined problems of concern in advanced economies exist at the apex of a pyramid, the base of which consists of the security of property rights."). Without rules such as the presumption of ownership, whether public or private, such valuable goals would give way to uncertainty.

In this case, the resulting confusion is not difficult to imagine. If the State were not required to defeat the presumption in order to gain title, a whole system of archival practice could be thrown into question. The State could claim ownership of other papers of Governors Pickens and Bonham held by the Library of Congress and Duke University, as well as papers of other South Carolina governors currently at institutions other than the State Archives. The result would be immense litigation over papers held by private owners, universities, historical societies, and federal depositories. It would upset settled archival arrangements and the expectations of institutions and historical scholars alike. Disregard of possession as presumptive evidence of ownership would throw the whole of this important area into turmoil.

Finally, while it has never been the practice of federal courts to ignore the law in favor of equitable considerations, it is worth noting that the employment of the presumption in this case in no way frustrates the public interest. Here, private possession does not shut the papers off from access by scholars or, indeed, by the interested public. They have been available for study for decades on microfilm at the University of North Carolina at Chapel Hill, and through the permission of plaintiff Willcox the South Carolina Department of Archives and History now also has a copy on microfilm. The papers are thus freely available for perusal and study regardless of who owns the originals. And, of course, if the State values possession of the original documents, it may acquire them on the open market.

In short, the common law, through the presumption of ownership in the possessor, resolves otherwise insoluble historical puzzles in favor of longstanding distributions and long-held expectations. Such a rule both protects the private interests of longtime possessors and increases social utility. Of course, this presumption will not always cut in one direction. In many instances, the State will possess the papers, and it will then be entitled to the strong presumption that the private party claims here. In this case, however, where the Law and Willcox families have been in possession for well over a century, the presumption favors plaintiff Willcox.

Having recognized the presumption in favor of Willcox's ownership, the court must consider whether the State has rebutted this presumption. In this case, the State has been unable to provide such evidence. There is no documentary evidence of the State's title, nor is there evidence of its recent possession. While there is no suggestion that the Law and Willcox families are bona fide purchasers, since no purchase was involved, there is also no indication that they acquired the papers in bad faith. In any case, the State's burden may not be met by challenging the sufficiency of the possessor's title but only by proving the superior strength of its claim.

Given the insufficient factual evidence, the State's remaining argument for ownership is that, under the law at the time of the documents' creation (1860-64) or their acquisition by General Law (1865), they were public property. South Carolina law of the relevant time period provides no basis for the State's claim of ownership.

[T]he practice in South Carolina accords with common law practice more generally. Presidential papers, for example, were considered private property from the time of George Washington, who following his second term removed his papers to Mount Vernon and bequeathed them in his will to his nephew, Supreme Court Justice Bushrod Washington. *See Nixon v. United States,* 978 F.2d 1269, 1278 (D.C. Cir. 1992). Jefferson, Madison, and Monroe also bequeathed their papers as private property by will. *See id.* When Congress first provided public funding for presidential libraries, such libraries depended upon former presidents to deposit their papers voluntarily. *See Presidential Libraries Act of 1955,* Pub. L. No. 84-373, 69 Stat. 695 (*codified as amended* at 44 U.S.C. §2112 (2000)).

For Congress to change this private ownership regime required a law prospectively granting the United States "complete ownership, possession, and control" of official presidential records. *See Presidential Records Act of 1978,* 44 U.S.C. §2201 *et seq.* (implementing process for archiving records and making them publicly available as soon as possible, subject to exceptions for confidential and privileged materials). A previous l aw, the *Presidential Records and Materials Preservation Act of 1974,* Pub. L. 93-526, 88 Stat. 1695, which exerted federal control over former President Nixon's papers in the wake of the Watergate scandal, was determined to have effected a per se taking of President Nixon's property interest in his papers. *See Nixon,* 978 F.2d at 1284.

We conclude that the State has failed to establish that South Carolina law at the relevant time treated gubernatorial papers as public property. This conclusion leaves the State with no basis upon which to rebut the strong presumption of possession in the Law and Willcox families and no basis upon which to claim title superior to that of plaintiff Willcox.

§6 RELATIVITY OF TITLE

Property does not just concern things, it concerns relationships among people with respect to things. Blackstone famously wrote that property conveys rights against "any other individual in the universe." This image conveys an important insight: unlike most contract rights, many property rights are not simply good against those we have entered into agreement with, but against a wide array of perfect strangers. *See* Thomas W. Merrill & Henry E. Smith, *The Property/Contract Interface,* 101 Colum. L. Rev. 773, 780-790 (2001). But it hides an important truth as well: property rights are often *relative*, good against most in most circumstances, but not against others. Rights to exclude, for example, do not hold in the face of emergency; it is not trespass to crash your plane on the land of another. *See* Chapter 1, §1.3. More important here, finding lost property or possessing land, even without official title to the property, will create rights against subsequent possessors, but not against the title owner. This concept, illustrated in materials below, is called **relativity of title**.

§6.1 Finders

The law of finders is a common illustration of the relativity of title. As illustrated dramatically in the cases below, who is entitled to keep found property depends on whether the conflict is with the original owner or possessor of the property, a subsequent possessor, or the owner of the land on which the property is found, and on whether the property is considered lost, mislaid, or abandoned.

Armory v. Delamirie

93 Eng. Rep. 664 (K.B. 1722)

The plaintiff being a chimney sweeper's boy found a jewel and carried it to the defendant's shop (who was a goldsmith) to know what it was, and delivered it into the hands of the apprentice, who under pretence of weighing it, took out the stones, and calling to the master to let him know it came to three halfpence, the master offered the boy the money, who refused to take it, and insisted to have the thing again; whereupon the apprentice delivered him back the socket without the stones. And now in trover against the master these points were ruled:

> **Terms:**
> **Trover** was an action for damages for wrongful interference with personal property. Why did the chimney sweeper's boy not sue in **replevin**, which was an action for return of the property?

That the finder of a jewel, though he does not by such finding acquire an absolute property or ownership, yet he has such a property as will enable him to keep it against all but the rightful owner, and subsequently may maintain trover.

That the action well lay against the master, who gives a credit to his apprentice, and is answerable for his neglect.

As to the value of the jewel several of the trade were examined to prove what a jewel of the finest water that would fit the socket would be worth; and the Chief Justice directed the jury, that unless the defendant did produce the jewel, and shew it not to be of the finest water, they should presume the strongest case against him, and make the value of the best jewels the measure of their damages: which they accordingly did.

Notes and Questions

1. **Conflicts between finders and subsequent possessors.** *Armory v. Delamirie* illustrates the basic rule: finders will generally prevail against all subsequent possessors of property. What justifies the rule? Is it intended to reward the finder? But the chimney sweep did not go down the chimney in hopes of finding a "jewel of the finest water," any more than most of us walk down the street in hopes of finding a stray hundred dollar bill. What behaviors, by the finder or others, does the rule encourage or discourage?

2. **Conflicts between finders and "rightful owners."** "Finders keepers, losers weepers," may be the law on the playground, but it is not the law anywhere else. Instead, conflicts between finders and original owners will be decided according to whether the property is considered lost, mislaid, or abandoned. Property is **lost** when the owner accidentally misplaced it; it is **mislaid** when the owner intentionally left it somewhere—and then forgets where she put it; it is **abandoned** when the owner forms an intent to relinquish all rights in the property. Property that has been lost or mislaid may subsequently be abandoned if the owner intends to give up any claim to the property. Finders will lose against original owners of lost or mislaid property; but will win against original owners of abandoned property since the original owner relinquished her rights to it.

Are rights against finders confined to "rightful owners" as *Armory v. Delamirie* states? Imagine that our chimney sweep forgets the bag with the jewel in it in the fireplace at his next job—can the maid who finds it while sweeping the grate claim it from him? No. The doctrine is not confined to those who have "true" title, but rather those who have better title. Even thieves of personal property may prevail against those who wrongfully take it from them. One recent decision held that a man who had taken $3,000 from his cousin's bank account to purchase a car fraudulently using his cousin's name could sue the car dealership for return of the stolen down payment, stating "the well-settled common-law rule that a thief in possession of stolen goods has an ownership interest superior to the world at large, save one with a better claim to the property." *Payne v. TK Autowholesalers*, 911 A.2d 747, 751 (Conn. App. 2006) (citations omitted).

3. Conflicts between the finder and the owner of the premises where the property was found. What happens if a person finds a lost, mislaid, or abandoned object on someone else's property? In a dispute between the landowner and the finder, the landowner will win if the finder was trespassing at the time she found the object.

If the finder is on the property with the landowner's permission, the courts are wildly divided. If an object is found in a private home, it is ordinarily awarded to the homeowner, but if the object is found in a place open to the public, some courts grant ownership to the finder and others to the landowner. Many courts distinguish between lost and mislaid property, awarding lost property to the finder and mislaid property to the owner of the premises, considering the landowner to have been unknowingly entrusted with the property by the person that mislaid it. The rule has been criticized for making much rest on determinations of the unknown owner's intent, and on perverse incentives it may create for finders. In *Benjamin v. Lindner Aviation*, a mechanic found $18,000 in old bills carefully rolled up and hidden in the wing of the plane, and turned it in to the police in hopes of claiming it if the owner did not appear, or recovering a statutory finders' fee. The court, however, found that the money was mislaid, and not lost, and therefore belonged to the bank that had repossessed the plane, and was not covered by the finders' fee statute. 534 N.W.2d 400 (Iowa 1995); *see also Terry v. Lock Hospitality, Inc.*, 37 S.W.3d 202 (Ark. 2001) (motel owners, rather than renovators, were entitled to $38,000 in old currency found by renovators in the ceiling tiles). Which rule, one that awarded the money to the finder or to the bank, is more likely to generate return of the money to the true owner? Why were these finds deemed mislaid rather than lost or abandoned?

If personal property is found **embedded** in the soil, courts ordinarily award the property—whether lost, mislaid, or abandoned—to the landowner rather than the finder, in the absence of agreement or statute to the contrary, on the ground that it is, in effect, part of the real property. *See United States v. Shivers*, 96 F.3d 120 (5th Cir. 1996) (old metal tokens found at an old mill site in Angelina National Forest belonged to the United States, not the coin collector who found them); *Klein v. Unidentified Wrecked and Abandoned Sailing Vessel*, 758 F.2d 511 (11th Cir. 1985) (holding that eighteenth-century shipwreck found in Biscayne National Park belonged to United States, rather than diver who found it). A possible exception to this principle applies to so-called **treasure trove**, gold, silver, or money intentionally buried more than a century before it is found. In England, ownership of treasure trove was historically given to the Crown, while in the United States ownership was given to the finder rather than the owner of the land, as long as the finder was not trespassing at the time it was found.

4. Restating the rule. The court in *Armory v. Delamirie* states that a finder gains "such a property as will enable him to keep it against all but the rightful owner." Is this an accurate statement of the doctrine? How would you rephrase it?

5. Finders statutes. Many states have legislation concerning lost property. These laws seek to get rid of the distinction between lost, mislaid, and abandoned property. They generally require the finder to report the find to the police and generally award the property to the finder if it is not claimed after a reasonable period, often requiring the true owner to pay some percentage of the object's value as a reward to the finder. *See, e.g.*, Fla. Stat. §§705.102-705.104 (awarding lost or abandoned property to finder after 90 days if true owner unidentified); Del. Code tit. 11, §8307(c) (lost money is returned to finder, if, after reasonable efforts, police are unable to locate owner). *But see* Del. Code tit. 11, §8307(a) (property other than money that comes to the police is sold after one year for police benefit). These statutes, however, are little understood and haphazardly implemented, and only a tiny fraction of lost property is turned in to the police or claimed there. In contrast, Japan has extremely high rates of return of lost property via the police. One author explains this phenomenon as a result of well-known policies, including a guaranteed reward from the true owner, effective institutions for implementation, and criminalizing failure to report found property. Mark D. West, *Losers: Recovering Lost Property in Japan and the United States*, 37 Law & Socy. Rev. 369 (2003).

Charrier v. Bell

496 So. 2d 601 (La. Ct. App. 1986)

ELVEN PONDER, Judge, retired.

Plaintiff is a former Corrections Officer at the Louisiana State Penitentiary in Angola, Louisiana, who describes himself as an "amateur archeologist." After researching colonial maps, records and texts, he concluded that Trudeau Plantation, near Angola, was the possible site of an ancient village of the Tunica Indians. He alleges that in 1967 he obtained the permission of Mr. Frank Hoshman, Sr., who he believed was the owner of Trudeau Plantation, to survey the property with a metal detector for possible burial locations. After locating and excavating approximately 30 to 40 burial plots lying in a circular pattern, plaintiff notified Mr. Hoshman that he had located the Tunica village. Although the evidence is contradictory, plaintiff contends that it was at that time that Mr. Hoshman first advised that he was the caretaker, not the owner, of the property.

Plaintiff continued to excavate the area for the next three years until he had located and excavated approximately 150 burial sites containing beads, European ceramics, stoneware, glass bottles; iron kettles, vessels and skillets; knives, muskets, gunflints, balls and shots; crucifixes, rings and bracelets; and native pottery. The excavated artifacts are estimated to weigh two to two and one-half tons.

In search of a buyer for the collection, plaintiff talked to Dr. Robert S. Neitzel of Louisiana State University, who, in turn, informed Dr. Jeffrey D. Brain of Harvard

Quick Review:
If the Tunica-Biloxi Tribe had not intervened, who should have won the suit under the rules of finders, Charrier or the owners of the Trudeau Plantation?

University. Dr. Brain, who was involved in a survey of archeology along the lower Mississippi River, viewed the artifacts and began discussions of their sale to the Peabody Museum of Harvard University. The discussions resulted in the lease of the artifacts to the Museum, where they were inventoried, catalogued and displayed.

Plaintiff initially informed Dr. Neitzel and Dr. Brain that he had found the artifacts in a cave in Mississippi, so as to conceal their source; later he did disclose the actual site of the find to Dr. Brain, who had expressed his concern over the title of the artifacts. Dr. Brain then obtained permission from the landowners to do further site testing and confirmed that it was the true source of the artifacts.

Confronted with the inability to sell the collection because he could not prove ownership, plaintiff filed suit against the six nonresident landowners of Trudeau Plantation, requesting declaratory relief confirming that he was the owner of the artifacts. Alternatively, plaintiff requested that he be awarded compensation under the theory of unjust enrichment for his time and expenses.

The State of Louisiana intervened in the proceeding on numerous grounds, including its duty to protect its citizens in the absence of the lawful heirs of the artifacts. In 1978, the State purchased Trudeau Plantation and the artifacts from the six landowners and agreed to defend, indemnify and hold the prior owners harmless from any and all actions.

In 1981 the Tunica and Biloxi Indians were recognized as an American Indian Tribe by the Bureau of Indian Affairs of the Department of the Interior.

The trial judge held that the Tunica-Biloxi Tribe is the lawful owner of the artifacts, finding that plaintiff was not entitled to the artifacts under La. Civ. Code art. 3423 as it read prior to amendment by Act No. 187 of 1982, which required discovery "by chance." The judge also found that plaintiff had no claim to the artifacts on the basis of abandonment under La. Civ. Code art. 3421, as it read prior to the amendment by Act No. 187 of 1982, because the legal concept of abandonment does not extend to burial goods.

The trial court also denied relief under the theory of unjust enrichment, finding that any impoverishment claimed by plaintiff was a result of his attempts "for his own gain" and that his presence and actions on the property of a third party placed him in a "precarious position, if not in legal bad faith."

The issues before this court are the adequacy of proof that the Tunica-Biloxi Indians are descendants of the inhabitants of Trudeau, the ownership of the artifacts, and the applicability of the theory of unjust enrichment.

Plaintiff first argues that the evidence that the members of the Tunica-Biloxi Indians of Louisiana, Inc., are legal descendants of the inhabitants of Trudeau Plantation was insufficient to entitle them to the artifacts.

The fact that members of other tribes are intermixed with the Tunicas does not negate or diminish the Tunicas' relationship to the historical tribe. Despite the fact that the Tunicas have not produced a perfect "chain of title" back to those buried at Trudeau Plantation, the tribe is an accumulation of the descendants of former Tunica Indians and has adequately satisfied the proof of descent.

Plaintiff next argues that the Indians abandoned the artifacts when they moved from Trudeau Plantation, and the artifacts became *res nullius* until found and reduced to possession by plaintiff who then became the owner.

Plaintiff contends that he has obtained ownership of the property through occupancy, which is a "mode of acquiring property by which a thing which belongs to nobody, becomes the property of the person who took possession of it, with the intention of acquiring a right of ownership upon it." La. Civ. Code art. 3412.

One of the five methods of acquiring property by occupancy is "By finding (that is, by discovering precious stones on the sea shore, or things abandoned, or a treasure)." La. Civ. Code art. 3414. Plaintiff contends that the artifacts were abandoned by the Tunicas and that by finding them he became the owner.

[T]he fact that the descendants or fellow tribesmen of the deceased Tunica Indians resolved, for some customary, religious or spiritual belief, to bury certain items along with the bodies of the deceased, does not result in a conclusion that the goods were abandoned. While the relinquishment of immediate possession may have been proved, an objective viewing of the circumstances and intent of the relinquishment does not result in a finding of abandonment. Objects may be buried with a decedent for any number of reasons. The relinquishment of possession normally serves some spiritual, moral, or religious purpose of the descendant/owner, but is not intended as a means of relinquishing ownership to a stranger. Plaintiff's argument carried to its logical conclusion would render a grave subject to despoliation either immediately after interment or definitely after removal of the descendants of the deceased from the neighborhood of the cemetery.

Although plaintiff has referred to the artifacts as *res nullius*, under French law, the source of Louisiana's occupancy law, that term refers specifically to such things as wild game and fish, which are originally without an owner. The term *res derelictae* refers to "things voluntarily abandoned by their owner with the intention to have them go to the first person taking possession." P. Esmein, Aubry & Rau, *Droit Civil Francais*, Vol. II, §168, at 46 (7th ed. 1966). Some examples of *res derelictae* given by Aubry and Rau include things left on public ways, in the cities or to be removed by garbage collectors.

The artifacts fall into the category of *res derelictae*, if subject to abandonment. The intent to abandon *res derelictae* must include the intent to let the first person who comes along acquire them. Obviously, such is not the case with burial goods.

French sources have generally held that human remains and burial goods located in cemeteries or burial grounds are not "treasure" under article 716 of the French Civil Code and thereby not subject to occupancy upon discovery. The reasoning has been that any contrary decision would lead to and promote commercial speculation and despoilment of burial grounds. The French commentator Demolombe noted the special treatment that should be given to burial goods, stating that such objects "have not been placed underground with the same intention which informs the deposit of what is called treasure, which in the latter case is, for a temporary period. Rather, they are an emplacement for a perpetual residence therein." 13 C. Demolombe, *Cours de Code Napoleon* §37, at 45-46 (2d ed. 1862).

The same reasoning that the French have used to treat burial goods applies in determining if such items can be abandoned. The intent in interring objects with the deceased is that they will remain there perpetually, and not that they are available for someone to recover and possess as owner.

For these reasons, we do not uphold the transfer of ownership to some unrelated third party who uncovers burial goods. The trial court concluded that La. Civ. Code art. 3421 was not intended to require that objects buried with the dead were abandoned or that objects could be acquired by obtaining possession over the objections of the descendants. We agree with this conclusion.

Plaintiff next argues that he is entitled to recover a sum of money to compensate his services and expenses on the basis of an *actio de in rem verso*.

The five criteria of such a claim *de in rem verso* are: (1) there must be an enrichment, (2) there must be an impoverishment, (3) there must be a connection between the enrichment and resulting impoverishment, (4) there must be an absence of justification or cause for the enrichment and impoverishment, and (5) there must be no other remedy at law available to plaintiff.

We first question whether there has been an enrichment. While the nonresident landowners were "enriched" by the sale of the property to the state, the ultimate owners of the artifacts presented substantial evidence that the excavation caused substantial upset over the ruin of "ancestrial burial grounds," rather than any enrichment.

Even if the Indians have been enriched, plaintiff has failed to prove that he has sustained the type [of] impoverishment for which *de in rem verso* may be used. His alleged loss resulted from the hours he spent excavating the artifacts, the greater portion of which activity was done at a time when plaintiff knew he was on property without the consent of the landowner. While contradictory testimony was presented regarding whether plaintiff initially had permission to go on the property, and whether that permission was adequate, by his own admission, plaintiff was informed by Hoshman that he did not own the property before the cessation of the excavating. Plaintiff's knowledge is further evidenced by his attempts to keep the location of his work secret; he did not identify Trudeau Plantation as the location of the find for almost five years after his discovery and he failed to seek out the landowners of the property until it was required for sale negotiations, although he removed two and one half tons of artifacts from their property. Plaintiff further acknowledges that he knew that the Tunica Indians might object to his excavations.

The impoverishment element in French law is met only when the factual circumstances show that it was not a result of the plaintiff's own fault or negligence or was not undertaken at his own risk. Obviously the intent is to avoid awarding one who has helped another through his own negligence or fault or through action taken at his own risk. Plaintiff was acting possibly out of his own negligence, but more probably knowingly and at his own risk. Under these circumstances, plaintiff has not proven the type of impoverishment necessary for a claim of unjust enrichment.

Additionally, plaintiff has failed to show that any enrichment was unjustified, entitling him to an action to recover from the enriched party. An enrichment will be unjustified "only if no legal justification for it exists." . . . Any enrichment received by the Tribe was justified.

For these reasons the judgment of the trial court is affirmed at appellant's costs.

Notes and Questions

1. **Aftermath.** The 1989 return of the artifacts to the Tunica-Biloxi Tribe should have been a joyous homecoming. Instead it was a shock. Harvard had transferred the collection to the State of Louisiana in 1981. Rather than preserving the centuries-old ceramics in a climate-controlled setting, the state had stored them carelessly in cardboard boxes, even keeping them in historic cabins behind the old French Quarter. The tribe was told it would cost $1.5 to 2 million to restore the collection. Patching together grants and donations, the tribe purchased two refrigerated trucks and slowly began the process. Profits from the tribe's Grand Casino Avoyelles, opened in 1991, funded completion of the restoration. *See* Jefferson Hennessy, *The Legend of the Tunica Treasure*, May 7, 2005, available at *http://jeffersonhennessy.blogspot.com/2005/05/legend-of-tunica-treasure.html.* Today, the goods are displayed in a museum in the Tunica-Biloxi Cultural and Educational Resources Center. The center is designed to resemble a sixteenth-century Tunica burial mound.

2. ***Native American Graves Protection and Repatriation Act of 1990.*** The casual pillaging of Tunica graves was one of many stories that contributed to passage of the *Native American Graves Protection and Repatriation Act of 1990* (NAGPRA), discussed further in Chapter 3, §7.2. Although criminal and common law protections in all states punish grave desecration, many states limit such protections to clearly bounded cemeteries, or restrict standing to enforce the protection to a limited set of relatives. *See, e.g., Hairston v. General Pipeline Construction, Inc.*, 704 S.E.2d 663 (W. Va. 2010) (common law only protected "clearly marked" cemeteries and only relatives designated by state intestacy statutes could enforce rights); Danny R. Veilleux, *Liability for Desecration of Graves and Tombstones*, 77 A.L.R.4th 108 (1990). While public sentiment generally condemns grave desecration, such sentiments only protected some burial grounds. Cities filled in and paved over slave burial grounds with little hesitation. Digging up and collecting bones and burial goods from Native American graves was almost a national pastime, avidly engaged in by Thomas Jefferson among many others. NAGPRA seeks to correct the gaps in law and morality that left Native American graves unprotected.

NAGPRA prevents removal or disturbance of Native human remains and burial goods from federal or tribal land without tribal consent. 25 U.S.C. §3002. It also requires federal agencies and museums receiving federal funds to repatriate such objects to the lineal descendants of the Native individuals or, if the descendants cannot be identified, to the tribe with a connection to the objects. 25 U.S.C. §§3002-3005. NAGPRA's prohibition on grave disturbance only applies on federal and tribal land. Many states also now have laws that prohibit knowing disturbance of Native burial grounds, but these laws vary widely.

3. **Cultural property.** The claims of the Tunica-Biloxi bear resemblance to demands for return of culturally important artifacts by nations across the world. Casual

acquisition of such objects by foreign collectors—whether sarcophagi from Egypt or Khmer statues in Cambodia—has long been the norm. The international and domestic laws governing such claims are discussed in Chapter 3, §6.1.

Problems

1. Revisit the facts of *Armory v. Delamirie.* What if the owner of the building in whose chimney the jewel was found asserts a claim against the chimney sweep's boy? Who should win? Should the answer depend on whether the jewel was lost, mislaid, or abandoned, and if so, which category does the jewel fall in? Now assume that the chimney sweep who employed the boy claims the jewel. Who should win?

2. In nineteenth-century Stamford, Connecticut, an enterprising individual, recognizing the value of the manure left behind by horses on the public street, hired two workers to scrape it into large piles one evening, intending to take it to fertilize his own land. The next day, before he could remove the piles, another person notices them and, unable to find their owner, took them away himself. In a contest over the manure between the individual that first scraped up the piles and the individual that took it away, who should win? What alternative arguments could you make? *See Haslem v. Lockwood,* 37 Conn. 500 (1871). What if the local hackney cab company, which can show that it owns half of the horses that walk along the street, intervenes to claim half the manure? What if the Borough of Stamford claims it as well?

§6.2 Real Property

Relativity of title does not apply just with respect to the relatively unique category of found property, but to land as well. What interests does the doctrine serve in the context of land?

Christy v. Scott

55 U.S. 282 (1852)

Mr. Justice Curtis delivered the opinion of the court.

The plaintiff in error filed a petition, in which he avers, that on the 1st day of June, 1839, he was seised in his demesne as of fee of three tracts of land, described in the petition by metes and bounds, and that the defendant, with force of arms, ejected him therefrom, and has thenceforward kept him out of possession thereof; and he prays judgment for damages and costs, and for the lands described. The defendant filed [a] substantive defence. The plaintiff demurred. There was no joinder in demurrer by the defendant, but the District Court treated the demurrers as raising issues in law, and gave judgment thereon for the defendant. The plaintiff has brought the record here by a writ of error.

> **Terms:**
> The claim that the plaintiff was **seised in his demesne as of fee** meant that he had actual possession and ownership of a fee simple estate, as opposed to ownership without possession, or possession without full ownership.

Upon this record, questions of great difficulty, and understood to affect the titles to large quantities of land, have been elaborately argued at the bar. These questions involve and depend upon the interpretation of the Colonization Laws of the Republic of Mexico, and their practical administration; the relative rights and powers of the central government, and of the State of Coahuila and Texas, in reference to the public domain; the modes of declaring and vindicating those rights, and exercising those powers under the constitution of the Mexican Republic; the effect of the separation of the State of Coahuila and Texas from Mexico, by the revolution of 1836, upon titles made by the State authorities before the revolution, and alleged to be defective for want of the sanction of the central government; as well as several important laws of the Republic of Texas, framed for the protection of the public domain, and for the repose of titles in that country.

It is impossible that the court should approach an adjudication of a case, involving elements so new and difficult, without much anxiety, lest they should have failed entirely to comprehend and fitly to apply them. And it is obvious, that before it is possible to do so, all the facts constituting the title of each party, and essential to a complete view of the case, and especially the documentary evidences of those titles, should be placed before us, in a determinate form.

This record is far from being sufficient in these substantial, and, indeed, necessary particulars. The petition avers a seisin in fee, on a particular day, and an ouster by the defendant. The defendant shows no title in himself to the land demanded, but asserts that the plaintiff claims title by a pretended grant, made on the 20th day of September, 1835; that the land was within the twenty frontier leagues bordering on the United States; that the approbation of the executive of the national government of Mexico was not given; and, in other pleas, avers other facts, to show that if any such grant had been made it would not have been valid.

According to the settled principles of the common law, this is not a defence to the action. The plaintiff says he was seised in fee, and the defendant ejected him from the possession. The defendant, not denying this, answers, that if the plaintiff had any paper title, it was under a certain grant which was not valid. He shows no title whatever in himself. But a mere intruder cannot enter on a person actually seised, and eject him, and then question his title, or set up an outstanding title in another. The maxim that the plaintiff must recover on the strength of his own title, and not on the weakness of the defendant's, is applicable to all actions for the recovery of property. But if the plaintiff had actual prior possession of the land, this is strong enough to enable him to recover it from a mere trespasser, who entered without any title.

Assuming what we do not decide, that [plaintiff's] title is not good as against the State of Texas, still it is not a defence, because no title in the defendant is shown. If the plaintiff, as his petition avers, was actually seised, and the defendant being a mere intruder, ejected him, it was an unlawful act, and the action is maintainable, notwithstanding the State of Texas may have the true title, or may have granted it to another.

For these reasons, we are of opinion the demurrer to each of these pleas must be sustained, the judgment of the District Court reversed, and the cause remanded.

Notes and Questions

Christy v. Scott involved complicated questions of whose laws — the Republic of Mexico after independence from Spain in 1824, the Mexican state of Coahuila and Texas, or the Republic of Texas after its 1836 revolt against Mexico — should govern acquisition of property in Texas once the United States acquired the land, and how those laws should be interpreted. The Supreme Court avoided deciding these questions by following the principle of relativity of title: one who does not have legal title to the land may still protect her rights against a later intruder. What justifies the doctrine? A Kentucky case adopting this principle explained it as follows:

> [S]urely it is not accordant with the principles of justice, that he who wrongfully ousts a previous possession, should be permitted to defend his wrongful possession against the claim of restitution merely by showing that a stranger, and not the previous possessor whom he had ousted, was entitled to the possession. The law protects a peaceable possession, against all except him who has the actual right to the possession, and no other can rightfully disturb or intrude upon it. [I]f the claimant . . . attempt to gain the possession by entering upon, and ousting, the existing peaceable possession, he does not thereby acquire a rightful or a peaceable possession. The law does not protect him against the prior possessor.

Sowder v. McMillan's Heirs, 4 Dana 456, 34 Ky. 456 (Ky. App. 1836).

Problems

1. Two law students rent an apartment under a one-year lease. The lease contains a "no subletting" clause preventing the tenants from granting possession of any part of the premises to another person during the lease term. Two months into the school year, one of the roommates has to return to her home in another state to take care of her sick mother. The remaining roommate, *A*, cannot afford to pay the rent by herself. She decides, therefore, to violate the terms of the lease by asking a new roommate, *B*, to move in. *B* makes an oral contract with *A* to pay one-third of the rent for the rest of the year.

B moves in but has unpleasant quarrels with *A*. After a few weeks, *A* finds a friend, *C*, to take *B*'s place. She tells *B* it is not working out and she will have to move out. *B* protests that she wants to stay. One day during school, *A* changes the lock on the door of the apartment and carries *B*'s belongings to the basement of the building to a storage area. *C* moves in and takes *B*'s place. *B* sues *A* and *C*, and asks the court to order *C* to vacate the premises and allow *B* to return. *A* and *C* defend by claiming that *B* never had a legal right to be in the apartment to begin with. You are the judge charged with deciding the case. What would you do?

2. In Florida, Mark Guerette identified 20 abandoned foreclosed homes designated as "public nuisances" by the municipalities because of lack of maintenance.

Catherine Skipp & Damien Cave, *At Legal Fringe, Empty Houses Go to the Needy,* N.Y. Times, Nov. 8, 2010. He begins paying taxes on the properties, fixes them up, and rents them to homeless families for a small charge, explaining to them what he has done. He is arrested and charged with fraud. Has Guerette provided anything of value to the families by letting them live there?

§6.3 Transfer of Stolen Property

Suppose *O* leaves his car with *A* to be repaired and then *A* sells the property to *B*, an innocent party who does not know that *A* was not entitled to sell it, before *O* can sue to get it back. *A* then absconds to a foreign jurisdiction. *O* sues *B* to get his car back. Although *O* would have had the right to get the car back from *A*, does *O* have the right to get the car back from *B*? The law resolves this conflict between two innocent persons by sometimes vesting title in the original "true owner" and sometimes granting title to the innocent or "bona fide" purchaser. This result again illustrates the concept of the relativity of title — *O* may have title as against *A*, but not as against *B*.

You can convey to someone else only what you own. If someone does not own Radio City Music Hall but attempts to sell it to you by granting you a deed, you get exactly what your "grantor" had — nothing. Similarly, if I steal your personal property and then resell it to an innocent purchaser who has no knowledge that the property is stolen (a "bona fide purchaser"), the innocent buyer generally is out of luck. A thief ordinarily has no right to transfer title to a third party. In *Autocephalous Greek-Orthodox Church of Cyprus v. Goldberg & Feldman Fine Arts, Inc.*, 717 F. Supp. 1374 (S.D. Ind. 1989), some valuable Christian mosaics were stolen from a church on the island of Cyprus after it was invaded by Turkey. Years later, they wound up, through a series of transactions, in the hands of defendant art dealers. The court held that "a thief never obtains title to stolen items, and one can pass no greater title than one has. Therefore, one who obtains stolen items from a thief never obtains title to or right to possession of the item." *Id.* at 1398. The thief "cannot pass any title to any subsequent transferees, including subsequent purchasers" even if they are bona fide purchasers who have no notice of the theft. *Id.*[5] *See also* Ray Andrews Brown, *The Law of Personal Property* §9.4, at 194 (3d ed. 1975).

When an owner voluntarily entrusts another with possession of her property, the law sometimes gives the grantee the power to transfer title to a bona fide purchaser. When a possessor has the power to transfer title to a bona fide purchaser, we say the possessor has "voidable title"; although the true owner has the right to recover property from someone to whom she entrusted the property, the law may give that possessor the power to divest the true owner of title by transferring title to a bona fide purchaser.

For example, in *Carlsen v. Rivera*, 382 So. 2d 825 (Fla. Dist. Ct. App. 1980), Coradino Rivera, owner of a Canadian car rental agency, leased a car to James McEnroe, who forged a title to the car in the name of a business he owned and sold it to a third party

5. A non-owner *may* be able to obtain title by adverse possession. *See* Chapter 5.

who obtained a facially valid title certificate in Florida. The car was then sold again to a fourth party, who finally sold it to defendant Carlsen. Rivera sued Carlsen to get his car back. The court applied the Florida version of the *Uniform Commercial Code*, U.C.C. §2-403(2), which provides that a bona fide purchaser will prevail over the true owner when the true owner has entrusted the property to a merchant who regularly deals in such goods. Fla. Stat. §672.403. Similarly, if an owner is induced to sell his property by fraud or duress, the seller may recover the property from the buyer unless the buyer has subsequently transferred the property to a bona fide purchaser. U.C.C. §2-403(1). On the other hand, when a thief takes property away from an owner, such that the initial transfer of possession is involuntary, neither the thief nor subsequent purchasers are entitled to keep title as against the true owner from whom the property was stolen even if those later possessors are bona fide purchasers. *Candela v. Port Motors, Inc.*, 617 N.Y.S.2d 49 (App. Div. 1994).

What justifies a rule of law that prevents the true owner of stolen property from recovering it from a bona fide purchaser just because the thief who wrongfully arranged for the sale "deals in goods of that kind"?

Problem

Plaintiff lent his car to a friend. The friend turns out not to be such a true friend, forges a title to the car, and sells it to a bona fide purchaser. Since the friend is not a merchant, the common law rule, rather than the *Uniform Commercial Code*, applies, enabling the plaintiff to recover the car from the bona fide purchaser on the grounds that a thief cannot transfer good title. Defendant argues that the common law should be changed to protect the rights of bona fide purchasers to obtain title to property even when the true owner did not entrust the property to a merchant.

a. What arguments can you make for the defendant's proposed rule of law? What can you say on the plaintiff's behalf? In answering these questions, consider whether it makes sense to distinguish merchants from other persons who wrongfully transfer title to stolen goods. How should the court rule?

b. Assume now that the car was stolen from the plaintiff's driveway rather than entrusted to a false friend. Does this make any difference in the analysis?

§7 PROPERTY FORMATION IN EVERYDAY LIFE

Enforceable rights to places, objects, and resources are not simply a creature of law. Individuals frequently claim such rights in daily life. Although parking on public streets is usually first come first served, for example, after a big snowstorm it is not uncommon to see individuals blocking off the places they have dug out with chairs and traffic cones. Most people will respect the claim to the parking space, at least for a reasonable time. Sociologist Erving Goffman discusses a similar phenomenon in his book *Asylums*, which considers the behavior of mental patients and other residents of what he called "total institutions," institutions that become worlds in themselves.

Erving Goffman, Asylums: Essays on the Social Situation of Mental Patients and Other Inmates

18-21, 243-253 (1967)

The admission procedure can be characterized as a leaving off and a taking on, with the midpoint marked by physical nakedness. Leaving off of course entails a dispossession of property, important because persons invest self feelings in their possessions. Perhaps the most significant of these possessions is not physical at all, one's full name; whatever one is thereafter called, loss of one's name can be a great curtailment of the self.

Once the inmate is stripped of his possessions, at least some replacements must be made by the establishment, but these take the form of standard issue uniform in character and uniformly distributed. These substitute possessions are clearly marked as really belonging to the institution and in some cases are recalled at regular intervals to be, as it were, disinfected of identifications. With objects that can be used up — for example, pencils — the inmate may be required to return the remnants before obtaining a reissue. Failure to provide inmates with individual lockers and periodic searches and confiscations of accumulated personal property reinforce property dispossession. Religious orders have appreciated the implications for self of such separation from belongings. Inmates may be required to change their cells once a year so as not to become attached to them. The Benedictine Rule is explicit:

> For their bedding let a mattress, a blanket, a coverlet, and a pillow suffice. These beds must be frequently inspected by the Abbot, because of private property which may be found therein. If anyone be discovered to have what he has not received from the Abbot, let him be most severely punished. And in order that this vice of private ownership may be completely rooted out, let all things that are necessary be supplied by the Abbot: that is, cowl, tunic, stockings, shoes, girdle, knife, pen, needle, handkerchief, and tablets; so that all plea of necessity may be taken away. And let the Abbot always consider that passage in the Acts of the Apostles: "Distribution was made to each according as anyone had need."

One set of the individual's possessions has a special relation to self. The individual ordinarily expects to exert some control over the guise in which he appears before others. For this he needs cosmetic and clothing, supplies, tools for applying, arranging, and repairing them, and an accessible, secure place to store these supplies and tools — in short, the individual will need an "identity kit" for the management of his personal front. He will also need access to decoration specialists such as barbers and clothiers.

On admission to a total institution, however, the individual is likely to be stripped of his usual appearance and of the equipment and services by which he maintains it, thus suffering a personal defacement. The impact of this substitution is described in a report on imprisoned prostitutes:

> First, there is the shower officer who forces them to undress, takes their own clothes away, sees to it that they take showers and get their prison clothes — one pair of black

> oxfords with Cuban heels, two pairs of much-mended ankle socks, three cotton dresses, two cotton slips, two pairs of panties, and a couple of bras. Practically all the bras are flat and useless. No corsets or girdles are issued.
>
> There is not a sadder sight than some of the obese prisoners who, if nothing else, have been managing to keep themselves looking decent on the outside, confronted by the first sight of themselves in prison issue.

There remains private claim on space, where the individual develops some comforts, control, and tacit rights that he shares with no other patients except by his own invitation. I shall speak here of *personal territory*. A continuum is involved, with a veritable home or nest at one extreme, and at the other a mere location or refuge site in which the individual feels as protected and satisfied as is possible in the setting.

In mental hospitals and similar institutions the basic kind of personal territory is, perhaps, the private sleeping room, officially available to around five or ten per cent of the ward population. In Central Hospital such a room was sometimes given in exchange for doing ward work. Once obtained, a private room could be stocked with objects that could lend comfort, pleasure, and control to the patient's life. Pin-up pictures, a radio, a box of paper-back detective stories, a bag of fruit, coffee-making equipment, matches, shaving equipment — these were some of the objects, many of them illicit, that were introduced by patients.

Patients who had been on a given ward for several months tended to develop personal territories in the day room, at least to the degree that some inmates developed favorite sitting or standing places and would make some effort to dislodge anybody who usurped them. Thus, on one continued treatment ward, one elderly patient in contact was by mutual consent accorded a free-standing radiator; by spreading paper on top, he managed to be able to sit on it, and sit on it he usually did. Behind the radiator he kept some of his personal effects, which further marked off the area as his place. A few feet from him, in a corner of the room, a working patient had what amounted to his "office," this being the place where staff knew they could find him when he was wanted. He had sat so long in this corner that there was a soiled dent in the plaster wall where his head usually came to rest. On the same ward, another patient laid claim to a chair that was directly in front of the TV set; although a few patients would contest this place, he generally could sustain his claim upon it.

Territory formation on wards has a special relation to mental disorder. In many civilian situations an equalitarian rule such as "first come, first served" prevails, and some disguise conceals another organizing principle, "strongest takes what he wants." This last rule operated to some extent on bad wards, just as the first rule did on good wards. Another dimension must be introduced, however. The alignment to ward life that many back-ward patients took, for whatever voluntary reason or from whatever involuntary cause, led them to remain silent and unprotesting and to move away from any commotion involving themselves. Such a person could be dislodged from a seat or place regardless of his size or strength. Hence, on the bad wards, a special pecking order of a sort occurred, with vocal patients in good contact taking favorite chairs and benches from those not in contact. This was carried to a point where one patient might force a mute one off a footrest, leaving the vocal patient with a chair and a footrest, and the mute patient with nothing at all — a difference that is not negligible considering the fact that except for breaks at mealtime some patients spent the whole of the day on these wards doing nothing but sitting or standing in one place.

Perhaps the minimum space that was built into a personal territory was that provided by a patient's blanket. In some wards, a few patients would carry their blankets around with them during the day and, in an act thought to be highly regressive, each would curl up on the floor with his blanket completely covering him; within this covered space each had some margin of control.

As may be expected, a personal territory can develop within a free place or group territory. For example, in the recreation room of a chronic male service one of the two large wooden armchairs favorably situated close to the light and the radiator was regularly taken by an elderly respected patient, both patients and staff recognizing his right to it.

In some cases, an assignment provided a personal territory. For example, the working patients who looked after their ward's clothing and supply room were allowed to stay in this room when no chores were to be done; and there they could sit or lie on the floor away from the alterations of commotion and pall in the day room.

In everyday life, legitimate possessions employed in primary adjustments are typically stored, when not in use, in special places of safekeeping which can be gotten to at will. When patients entered Central Hospital, especially if they were excited or depressed on admission, they were denied a private, accessible place to store things. If people were selfless, or were required to be selfless, there would of course be a logic to having no private storage place. But all have some self. Given the curtailment implied by loss of places of safekeeping, it is understandable that patients in Central Hospital developed places of their own.

It seemed characteristic of hospital life that the most common form of stash was one that could be carried on one's person wherever one went. One such device for female patients was a large handbag; a parallel technique for a man was a jacket with commodious pockets, worn even in the hottest weather. While these containers are quite usual ones in the wider community, there was a special burden placed upon them in the hospital: books, writing materials, washcloths, fruit, small valuables, scarves, playing cards, soap, shaving equipment (on the part of men), containers of salt, pepper, and sugar, bottles of milk — these were some of the objects sometimes carried in this manner. So common was this practice that one of the most reliable symbols of patient status in the hospital was bulging pockets. Another portable storage device was a shopping bag lined with another shopping bag. (When partly full, this frequently employed stash also served as a cushion and back rest.) Among men, a small stash was sometimes created out of a long sock: by knotting the open end and twisting this end around his belt, the patient could let a kind of moneybag inconspicuously hang down inside his trouser leg. Individual variations of these portable containers were also found. One young engineering graduate fashioned a purse out of a discarded oilcloth, the purse being stitched into separate, well-measured compartments for comb, toothbrush, cards, writing paper, pencil, soap, small face cloth, toilet paper — the whole attached by a concealed clip to the underside of his belt. The same patient had also sewn an extra pocket on the inside of his jacket to carry a book. Another male patient, an avid newspaper reader, invariably wore a suit jacket, apparently to conceal his newspapers, which he carried folded over his belt. Still another made effective use of a cleaned-out tobacco pouch for transporting food; whole fruit, unpeeled, could easily be put in one's pocket to be taken back to the ward from the cafeteria, but cooked meat was better carried in a grease-proof stash.

Notes and Questions

1. **Functions of property.** Why do total institutions strip inmates of their property? What are some of the most important kinds of property that inmates lose on entering the institution? What does the excerpt reveal about the various functions or roles of property?

2. **"Property" formation.** What are the various ways that inmates seek to replace some of the property that they have lost? What makes other inmates and staff members recognize these rights? What characteristics do these rights share with property as you understand it?

3. **Personhood and property.** Goffman writes, "If people were selfless . . . there would of course be a logic to having no private storage place." But because "all have some self" they needed to create private stashes. What does this mean? Is that really why people create stashes?

Scholars have argued that one justification for property rights is the importance of property to people's sense of self and their identity. *See* Margaret Jane Radin, *Property and Personhood*, 34 Stan. L. Rev. 957 (1982). Professor Radin argues that the legal system can distinguish between property that is "bound up with the holder," such as a wedding ring or a home, and more fungible property that is held "for purely instrumental reasons." *Id.* at 959-960. Just as rewarding labor and recognizing possession influence the texture of property rights, the legal system might likewise provide greater protection for property that is more constitutive of people's identity. Do you agree? What concerns might this justification for property rights raise?

4. **Property formation in your life.** Goffman pioneered sociological research through the close study of everyday interactions. What aspects of property formation do you see in your life? Consider your regular seat in your Property classroom. Do you have some kind of property right in it? What would be the sources of your claim?

5. **Property and homelessness.** Like Goffman's mental patients, homeless people lack a private place to store things. The City of Los Angeles has lost several lawsuits challenging its practice of seizing and destroying the belongings of homeless people on city sidewalks. In the most recent case, *Lavan v. City of Los Angeles*, 797 F. Supp. 2d 1005 (C.D. Cal. 2011), the court rejected claims that the contents of unattended shopping carts and other belongings were "abandoned," and found that it was unconstitutional to destroy them without providing notice and an opportunity to be heard. Several years before, neighborhood business owners had organized a warehouse for

homeless people to securely store their belongings, but many individuals were unable to manage its simple rules:

> Everything from toasters to typewriters is piled high on a Skid Row sidewalk under the watchful eye of a woman who calls herself Mercedes Benz.
>
> The sidewalk is public property, but the possessions are hers and her neighbors, setting up a conflict between the homeless and a city trying to bring order where chaos reigns. Since a federal judge ordered the city four months ago to stop seizing property from Skid Row streets, sidewalks already teeming with people are now crammed with stuff.
>
> For Benz, who's been homeless for three years, keeping track of her belongings, along with her health and legal problems, has been overwhelming.
>
> Benz, who said she receives disability for Agent Orange exposure, lost all her belongings in a street sweep earlier this year while she used the bathroom at a mission, but acknowledged she was warned the day before by a police officer to remove her stuff. "I just couldn't think carefully enough as to the next step," she said.
>
> The loss of court papers, clothes and other items was devastating. "I came out and thought I was on the wrong street. You know, what I did? I actually cried," she said. "I became lost outside all over again."

Christina Hoag, *LA Struggles to Cope with Possessions of Homeless*, Associated Press, Oct. 29, 2011.

PART TWO

WHAT CAN BE OWNED?

CHAPTER 3

Intellectual and Cultural Property

§1 INTRODUCTION

§1.1 Intangible Property

Traditionally, the most important property rights concerned tangible objects—most notably, land. Wealth is increasingly embodied in less tangible resources, such as financial assets. The least tangible thing imaginable is an idea. Can one own an idea? Ideas are free for public use, but the law grants some expressions of ideas, as well as some inventions and commercial marks, the status of limited property rights. Intellectual property law regulates control over the products of intellectual effort. It is one of the fastest growing areas of property law and of legal practice.

The core subjects of intellectual property law—copyrights and patents—are governed by federal statutes. The U.S. Constitution authorizes Congress to "promote the progress of science and useful arts, by securing for limited times to authors and inventors the exclusive right to their respective writings and discoveries." U.S. Const. art. I, §8, cl. 8. Pursuant to this clause, Congress has passed legislation protecting both copyrights and patents. Copyright law grants exclusive rights in literary and artistic works, including books, poetry, song, dance, dramatic works, computer programs, movies, sculpture, and paintings. Patent law grants exclusive rights in inventions, including processes, machines, and compositions of matter.

A third major area of intellectual property law is trademark law. Trademark law grants exclusive rights in symbols that indicate the source of goods or services. Unlike copyright and patent law, trademark law originated in state common law; federal legislation generally supplements, but does not displace, the common law in these areas. Trademark law grew out of the law of unfair competition and misappropriation, which prohibits companies from using information obtained from competitors in ways that unfairly appropriate the products of their competitors' efforts.

State common law has recently developed "publicity rights" to protect the ability of individuals to control the commercial use of their names or images. Limited protection has also emerged for "moral rights" that give artists the ability to prevent their works from being mutilated or misrepresented by subsequent owners. Cultural property is closely related to intellectual property and, as its name suggests, provides legal protection for certain important aspects of culture, such as antiquities and Native American funerary objects.

§1.2 Theories of Intellectual Property

Intellectual property law is beset by internal tensions. Once disclosed, ideas are generally not subject to ownership. We must be free to use ideas, our own and others,' in order to engage in all human activity. Too much private property in ideas would limit our autonomy and block desirable economic activity by creating insuperable transaction costs. At the same time, exclusive control over certain intellectual products enhances the autonomy of authors and inventors. Property rights can also protect the ability of creators to get credit for their works and create economic incentives to spur intellectual inquiry. Determining when the products of human effort should be subject to the creator's control and when they should become the common property of humankind is the core problem of intellectual property law.

Intellectual property scholars have justified intellectual property rights using many of the same theories we have already seen in the context of tangible property. *See* Chapter 2. The three dominant theories at work in intellectual property discussions are (1) utilitarian/economic theories; (2) Lockean natural rights theories; and (3) Hegelian/personhood theories. *See* Robert Merges, Peter S. Menell & Mark A. Lemley, *Intellectual Property in the New Technological Age* 2-22 (6th ed. 2012); *see also* Robert P. Merges, *Justifying Intellectual Property* (2010).

Utilitarian/economic theories. Utilitarian and economic theories of intellectual property, like Harold Demsetz's theory of property and Garrett Hardin's discussion of the "tragedy of the commons," focus on the problem of externalities. Both of those discussions, which focused on tangible resources, emphasized *negative* externalities (costs not included in the resource-user's cost-benefit analysis) that tended to lead the user to overconsume. *See* Chapter 2, §3.2. In contrast, within intellectual property discussions, the focus is on the uncompensated *positive* externalities produced by creative or inventive activities.

Public goods are resources that are consumed **nonrivalrously** and from which it is impossible to exclude others. Just as the behavioral assumptions of economic theory predict that people will engage in too much of the harm-producing activities, such as consumption of open-access commons, when those harms are shared with others, the same assumptions predict that people will decline to engage in activities, such as the creation of public goods, when the activities themselves are costly and the benefits of those activities are shared with others. Because others cannot be prevented from freely enjoying the benefits of public goods, self-interested actors have an incentive to sit back and take a **free ride** on the (costly) productive

Terms:
Nonrivalrous consumption occurs when consumption of a good by one person does not interfere with or impair consumption of the same good by someone else.

behavior of others rather than bear the costs of engaging in producing public goods themselves. If everyone adopts the same strategy, public goods will not be produced. To overcome this free-rider problem, economists favor taking affirmative steps to encourage the production of public goods. Where creating mechanisms to facilitate the prevention of free riding is costly or undesirable, government provision is a common solution. Classic examples of government-provided public goods are national defense or the network of public roads.

Innovation often has the features of a public good. It is costly to produce, both in terms of time and resources, but once an innovative idea is produced and disseminated, it is difficult (in the absence of some collective action) to prevent others from copying it. Because copyists do not have to pay for the (sunk) costs of innovation, they can profitably sell the innovative product for close to its marginal cost of production (the cost of producing an additional unit of the good, excluding sunk costs, such as the cost of innovation). Where innovation is costly and copying is cheap and easy, economic theory predicts that innovation will tend to be underproduced in the absence of some mechanism to empower actors to recoup their investment in innovation. One such mechanism is to create a legal monopoly that enables the innovator to prohibit others from copying her invention. This is the most common utilitarian explanation for the institution of intellectual property in the domains of copyright and patent law. *See* Richard A. Posner, *The Economic Analysis of Law* §3.3 (6th ed. 2003).[1] Is government provision another possibility? What would it look like as a tool for overcoming the free-rider problem in the innovation context?

It is important to understand the limits of this utilitarian argument for intellectual property. It does not rely on the notion that creators are morally entitled to capture the benefits they create. As in the tangible property context, utilitarian arguments for intellectual property are forward-looking and based on incentives to act in ways that enhance social welfare; they are not based on notions of individual desert. Where copying is not easy, or where innovators can recapture the value of their investment through the market advantages of being the **first mover**, the utilitarian argument does not offer much support for intellectual property rights. Indeed, where innovators can recover the costs of their innovation, the existence of copyists can be socially beneficial, since they help to propagate the innovation and foster competition. Their presence may even help to generate more innovation, as creators seek to stay one step ahead of the copyists. This is what seems to happen in the fashion industry. Fashion designs are not protected by intellectual property in the United States, and copying is rampant. But this does not seem to have harmed the industry, with its rapid cycle of innovation and its robust market in knock-off designs. *See* Kal Raustiala & Christopher Sprigman, *The Piracy Paradox: Innovation and Intellectual Property in Fashion Design*, 92 Va. L. Rev. 1688 (2006).

---

1. Trademark law, which aims to prevent consumer confusion about the origin of goods, relies on different utilitarian arguments having to do with the need to ensure the integrity of markets. *See* Merges, Menell & Lemley, *supra*, at 11.

The utilitarian argument does not assert that all positive externalities must be internalized. After all, as Demsetz observed, the creation of intellectual property rights, like the creation of property rights more generally, generates costs of its own. First, since all innovation must rely upon the storehouse of prior knowledge, increasing the cost of using that prior knowledge (*e.g.*, by protecting at least some of it as intellectual property) drives up the cost of innovation for creators. This suggests that, applying the assumptions of economic theory, the interaction between intellectual property protection and the speed of innovation will be complex. The creation of intellectual property rights that are too robust might even have the perverse effect of deterring innovation. Where too many people have intellectual property rights over inputs necessary to create a useful product, transaction costs can make it extremely expensive to gather the permissions necessary to bring the product to market. Michael Heller has called this situation — high transaction costs generated by a large number of property-based veto rights — the "tragedy of the anticommons." Michael A. Heller, *The Tragedy of the Anticommons*, 111 Harv. L. Rev. 621 (1998).

Another cost of creating intellectual property is that preventing free riders from competing with innovators in the marketplace (by granting the inventor a monopoly) drives up the price of the invention for consumers. Monopoly pricing will usually result in reduced consumption of the invention by consumers willing to pay more than the marginal cost of producing the good. Economists refer to this forgone consumption as "deadweight loss." Finally, because intellectual property protects its owners from competition, the creation of intellectual property encourages those who wish to escape from competition to lobby for the creation of intellectual property even where it will not be socially beneficial. This kind of behavior — what economists call "rent seeking" — is wasteful in its own right. *See* Mark A. Lemley, *Property, Intellectual Property, and Free Riding*, 83 Tex. L. Rev. 1031, 1064 (2005). How to calibrate intellectual property rights to optimize the balance of the various costs and benefits of intellectual property is a difficult problem that is the subject of a great deal of debate among courts, politicians, interest groups, and scholars.

CONTEXT

In their 2006 article, *The Piracy Paradox*, Kal Raustiala and Christopher Sprigman describe how the lack of IP protection for fashion actually increases the rate of innovation in the industry:

> The fashion cycle has long been familiar. What is less commonly appreciated is the role of IP law in fostering the cycle. We argue that fashion's low-IP regime is paradoxically advantageous for the industry. IP rules providing for free appropriation of fashion designs accelerate the diffusion of designs and styles. We call this process "induced obsolescence." If copying were illegal, the fashion cycle would occur very slowly. Instead, the absence of protection for creative designs and the regime of free design appropriation speeds diffusion and induces more rapid obsolescence of fashion designs. As Miucci Prada put it recently, "We let others copy us. And when they do, we drop it." The fashion cycle is driven faster, in other words, by widespread design copying, because copying erodes the positional qualities of fashion goods. Designers in turn respond to this obsolescence with new designs. In short, piracy paradoxically benefits designers by inducing more rapid turnover and additional sales.

Might the same dynamic arise in other property contexts where owners are confronted with positive externalities?

Lockean theories. As we saw in Chapter 2, John Locke's theory of property builds from twin premises of self-ownership and the original common endowment of the world's resources to the conclusion that people should be entitled to the products of their own labor, except where doing so would make others worse off by failing to leave them "enough and as good" of the common resources. *See* John Locke, *Second Treatise of Government*, ch. V (1698). Although Locke did not have much to say about the ownership of ideas, contemporary scholars have argued that his theory applies with special force in the context of intellectual production. Innovative ideas, the argument goes, are the products of the inventor's (intellectual) labor, and because they constitute something genuinely new, their protection as intellectual property cannot be thought to make anyone else worse off by taking anything out of the original common endowment. *See* Lawrence C. Becker, *Deserving to Own Intellectual Property*, 68 Chi.-Kent L. Rev. 609 (1993); Justin Hughes, *The Philosophy of Intellectual Property*, 77 Geo. L.J. 287 (1988).

As with utilitarian theories of intellectual property, however, Lockean theories suffer from tensions of their own. The most intractable problems for Lockean theories concern the difficulty of disentangling an innovator's contribution to an invention from the contribution of the intellectual "raw materials" supplied by prior knowledge. Rewarding an innovator with an exclusive right to her creation requires some way of defining that creation so to give the innovator her due while acknowledging that almost all individual creation draws on the work of others. Consider the challenge of defining with any precision the contribution of a writer who pens a novel that draws on prior tropes but also pushes the boundaries of literature in new directions.

Finally, note that the focus of the Lockean theory is on the relationship between the innovator and her creation. It simply asks whether the creation comes from the innovator's productive labor. Thus, it would seem to justify protecting intellectual property rights for all independent creators, even those who are not the first to discover an invention. Although copyright protects such independent creation, American patent law traditionally has not.

Hegelian/personhood theories. Hegelian personhood theory, which we also first encountered in Chapter 2, §7, has also been influential in discussions of intellectual property, particularly copyright and publicity rights. The idea is that through the creative process, the inventor or creator's very identity becomes bound up with the invention or creation. This bond between the creator and her creation gives rise to an entitlement to control the dissemination and use of the created work. The theory seems to have the most intuitive appeal when applied to highly individualized acts of creation — the inventor toiling away in her basement, or the artist or author at work in her studio. For discussions of personhood theories of intellectual property, *see* Hughes, *supra*, at 350-353; *Linda J. Lacey, Of Bread and Roses and Copyrights*, 1989 Duke L.J. 1532; Neil Netanel, *Copyright Alienability Restrictions and the Enhancement of Author Autonomy: A Normative Evaluation*, 24 Rutgers L.J. 347 (1993). Again, personhood theory seems to generate its own tensions for intellectual property rights. The same ambiguities surrounding intellectual borrowing that bedevil Lockean theories apply in the personhood context. Moreover, the identity of others besides the original creator can become tied up with an intellectual creation. To take an extreme example, fans can become "consumed" by their identification with works created by another person. *See* Christopher S. Yoo, *Copyright and Personhood Revisited* (Sept. 28, 2012), working paper, electronic copy *available at http://ssrn.com/abstract=2160441*.

Notes and Questions

1. **Tangible and intangible property theories.** How readily do the theories of tangible property apply to the problems posed by intellectual property? Are the complications posed by intellectual property different in kind from those that arise in the context of tangible property? Which theory or theories do you find most convincing? Least convincing? Does it matter whether we consider intellectual property as a kind of "property" or, instead, as a kind of regulation? *See, e.g.*, Mark A. Lemley, *Property, Intellectual Property, and Free Riding*, 83 Tex. L. Rev. 1031 (2005) (arguing that treating intellectual property as a kind of property lends itself to a counterproductive kind of intellectual property maximalism).

2. **What motivates creation?** Are economic theorists of intellectual property right to assume (as they typically do) that people uniformly need extrinsic incentives, such as the opportunity to profit, in order to engage in creative labor? Are there specific contexts where people are more or less likely to require those incentives? How would you describe those contexts? For an argument that production of cultural and informational products in the Internet age is often undertaken for reasons other than the desire for pecuniary gain — and so may not respond to incentives in the ways predicted by economic theory — *see* Yochai Benkler, *The Wealth of Networks* (2006).

§2 UNFAIR COMPETITION AND MISAPPROPRIATION

See Chapter 2, §3 Labor and Investment, at pages 107-124.

§3 TRADEMARK LAW

A trademark is a name, symbol, or type of packaging that identifies the producer of a good or service. Unlike copyright and patent law, trademark law is primarily based on state common law, not federal statute. The patent and copyright clause of the U.S. Constitution authorizes Congress to provide protection for original works of authorship and inventions. U.S. Const. art. I, §8, cl. 8. The Supreme Court struck down the first trademark laws, passed by Congress in 1870 and 1876, because they applied without regard to originality or novelty, crucial requirements for copyrights and patents. *United States v. Steffens* (*The Trade-Mark Cases*), 100 U.S. 82 (1879). Congress does, however, have the power to regulate interstate commerce. U.S. Const. art. I, §8, cl. 3. Because the Court considered trademarks to be a form of property within the purview of state regulation, Congress responded by passing statutes in 1881 and 1905 that addressed the interstate use of trademarks. The current federal trademark act, called the *Lanham Act*, 15 U.S.C. §§1051-1127, provides for the registration of trademarks created by state law, along with some rights that may supplement or displace state law.

Trademark law gives the owner of the "mark" the exclusive right to use it in connection with the sale of a particular good or service in a particular area. This protects consumers from the *confusion* resulting from different companies using the same or similar names. *See Jordache Enterprises, Inc. v. Levi Strauss & Co.*, 841 F. Supp. 506 (S.D.N.Y. 1993) (holding that "Jordache Basics 101" may be confusingly similar to "Levi's 501" jeans). However, trademark law does not give consumers a legal claim. Only a company that is using the mark may sue to prevent competitors from appropriating the goodwill associated with its mark. Trademark law grows out of state unfair competition law that prohibits "palming off" one's products as those of another. It therefore protects the goodwill associated with a particular company or product line from unfair competition.

> **Terms:**
> **Abandonment** is a term of art in trademark law and does not always mean the same thing as it does in other contexts. As with tangible property, mere nonuse of a trademark does not constitute abandonment. Intent to abandon is also required. But failure to use a trademark for an extended period will, by itself, constitute evidence of intent to abandon the mark. The *Lanham Act* treats nonuse for two years as prima facie evidence of abandonment. *See* 15 U.S.C. §1127.

Unlike copyright and patents, trademarks garner protection only if they are used in commerce to sell goods or services. Failure to use a mark for a long time may constitute **abandonment** of it. The first to use the mark in connection with a business establishes the mark and will prevail over a later user. The trademark's value, of course, is much more than just ease of identification. Once customers develop loyalty to a brand name, the trademark itself has substantial value. A name can become associated with quality, and this goodwill is a substantial property interest. For this reason, a trademark infringement will be found if confusion may result from a competitor's later use of a mark.

Words that describe goods generally (**generic** names) cannot be trademarked both because they are unlikely to signal a particular maker and because competitors are likely to need to use those words to sell their goods. Names that began by representing particular companies may become generic over time if people start using the trade name to mean the product itself, such as Scotch tape or Kleenex tissues. *See America Online v. AT&T Corp.*, 243 F.3d 812 (4th Cir. 2001) ("instant messaging" and "you have mail" cannot be trademarked because they are generic terms; however, "Buddy List" may not be generic in the eyes of the public).

The *Lanham Act* provides notice of trademarks by allowing them to be registered with the federal Patent and Trademark Office. 15 U.S.C. §1072. Those wishing to register a mark must assert that they are currently using the mark in connection with a business or that they intend to do so shortly; use must commence within 24 months at the latest. Like the recording system for deeds, *see* Chapter 12, §5, registration places the whole world on actual or constructive notice of existing trademarks. Later users of a mark cannot claim to have used it in good faith or without knowledge of its prior use. A trademark may not be registered if it was in prior use by another (unless that use has been abandoned) or if there is a likelihood of confusion.

Qualitex Co. v. Jacobson Products Co.

514 U.S. 159 (1995)

Justice STEPHEN BREYER delivered the opinion of the Court.

The question in this case is whether the *Trademark Act of 1946* (*Lanham Act*), 15 U.S.C. §§1051-1127, permits the registration of a trademark that consists, purely and simply, of a color. We conclude that, sometimes, a color will meet ordinary legal trademark requirements. And, when it does so, no special legal rule prevents color alone from serving as a trademark.

The case before us grows out of petitioner Qualitex Company's use (since the 1950's) of a special shade of green-gold color on the pads that it makes and sells to dry cleaning firms for use on dry cleaning presses. In 1989, respondent Jacobson Products (a Qualitex rival) began to sell its own press pads to dry cleaning firms; and it colored those pads a similar green-gold. In 1991, Qualitex registered the special green-gold color on press pads with the Patent and Trademark Office as a trademark. Qualitex subsequently added a trademark infringement count, 15 U.S.C. §1114(1), to an unfair competition claim, §1125(a), in a lawsuit it had already filed challenging Jacobson's use of the green-gold color.

The *Lanham Act* gives a seller or producer the exclusive right to "register" a trademark, 15 U.S.C. §1052, and to prevent his or her competitors from using that trademark, §1114(1). Both the language of the Act and the basic underlying principles of trademark law would seem to include color within the universe of things that can qualify as a trademark. The language of the *Lanham Act* describes that universe in the broadest of terms. It says that trademarks "include any word, name, symbol, or device, or any combination thereof." §1127. Since human beings might use as a "symbol" or "device" almost anything at all that is capable of carrying meaning, this language, read literally, is not restrictive. The courts and the Patent and Trademark Office have authorized for use as a mark a particular shape (of a Coca-Cola bottle), a particular sound (of NBC's three chimes), and even a particular scent (of plumeria blossoms on sewing thread). If a shape, a sound, and a fragrance can act as symbols why, one might ask, can a color not do the same?

A color is also capable of satisfying the more important part of the statutory definition of a trademark, which requires that a person "use" or "intend to use" the mark "to identify and distinguish his or her goods, including a unique product, from those manufactured or sold by others and to indicate the source of the goods, even if that source is unknown." 15 U.S.C. §1127.

True, a product's color is unlike "fanciful," "arbitrary," or "suggestive" words or designs, which almost *automatically* tell a customer that they refer to a brand. The imaginary word "Suntost," or the words "Suntost Marmalade," on a jar of orange jam immediately would signal a brand or a product "source"; the jam's orange color does not do so. But, over time, customers may come to treat a particular color on a product or its packaging (say, a color that in context seems unusual, such as pink on a firm's insulating material or red on the head of a large industrial bolt) as signifying a brand. And, if so, that color would have come to identify and distinguish the goods—*i.e.*, "to indicate" their "source" — much in the way that descriptive words on a product (say, "Trim" on nail clippers or "Car-Freshner" on deodorizer) can come to indicate a product's origin. In this circumstance, trademark law says that the word (*e.g.*, "Trim"), although not inherently distinctive, has developed "secondary meaning." *See Inwood Laboratories, Inc. v. Ives Laboratories, Inc.*, 456 U.S. 844, 851, n.11 (1982) ("Secondary meaning" is acquired when "in the minds of the public, the primary significance of a product feature . . . is to identify the source of the product rather than the product itself").

We cannot find in the basic objectives of trademark law any obvious theoretical objection to the use of color alone as a trademark, where that color has attained "secondary meaning" and therefore identifies and distinguishes a particular brand (and thus indicates its "source"). In principle, trademark law, by preventing others from copying a source-identifying mark, "reduce[s] the customer's costs of shopping and making purchasing decisions," 1 J. McCarthy, *McCarthy on Trademarks and Unfair Competition* §2.01[2], pp. 2-3 (3d ed. 1994), for it quickly and easily assures a potential customer that *this* item — the item with this mark — is made by the same producer as other similarly marked items that he or she liked (or disliked) in the past. At the same time, the law helps assure a producer that it (and not an imitating competitor) will reap the financial, reputation-related rewards associated with a desirable product. The law thereby "encourage[s] the production of quality products," and simultaneously discourages those who hope to sell inferior products by capitalizing on a consumer's inability quickly to evaluate the quality of an item offered for sale. It is the source-distinguishing ability of a mark — not its ontological status as color, shape, fragrance, word, or sign — that permits it to serve these basic purposes. And, for that reason, it is difficult to find, in basic trademark objectives, a reason to disqualify absolutely the use of a color as a mark.

Neither can we find a principled objection to the use of color as a mark in the important "functionality" doctrine of trademark law. The functionality doctrine prevents trademark law, which seeks to promote competition by protecting a firm's reputation, from instead inhibiting legitimate competition by allowing a producer to control a useful product feature. It is the province of patent law, not trademark law, to encourage invention by granting inventors a monopoly over new product designs or functions for a limited time, 35 U.S.C. §§154, 173, after which competitors are free to use the innovation. If a product's functional features could be used as trademarks, however, a monopoly over such features could be obtained without regard to whether they qualify as patents and could be extended forever (because trademarks may be renewed in perpetuity). . . . This Court consequently has explained that, "in general terms, a product feature is functional," and cannot serve as a trademark, "if it is essential to the use or purpose of the article or if it affects the cost or quality of the article," that is, if exclusive use of the feature would put competitors at a significant non-reputation-related disadvantage. *Inwood Laboratories, Inc., supra*, at 850, n.10. Although sometimes color plays an important role (unrelated to source identification) in making a product more desirable, sometimes it does not. And, this latter fact — the fact that sometimes color is not essential to a product's use or purpose and does not affect cost or quality—indicates that the doctrine of "functionality" does not create an absolute bar to the use of color alone as a mark.

It would seem, then, that color alone, at least sometimes, can meet the basic legal requirements for use as a trademark. It can act as a symbol that distinguishes a firm's goods and identifies their source, without serving any other significant function. Indeed, the District Court, in this case, entered findings . . . that show Qualitex's green-gold press pad color has met these requirements. The green-gold color acts as a symbol. Having developed secondary meaning (for customers identified the green-gold color as Qualitex's), it identifies the press pads' source. And, the green-gold color serves no other function. Accordingly, unless there is some special reason that convincingly militates against the use of color alone as a trademark, trademark law would protect Qualitex's use of the green-gold color on its press pads.

Respondent Jacobson Products says that there are . . . special reasons why the law should forbid the use of color alone as a trademark. We shall explain, in turn, why we, ultimately, find them unpersuasive.

First, Jacobson says that, if the law permits the use of color as a trademark, it will produce uncertainty and unresolvable court disputes about what shades of a color a competitor may lawfully use. Because lighting (morning sun, twilight mist) will affect perceptions of protected color, competitors and courts will suffer from "shade confusion" as they try to decide whether use of a similar color on a similar product does, or does not, confuse customers and thereby infringe a trademark. Jacobson adds that the "shade confusion" problem is "more difficult" and "far different from" the "determination of the similarity of words or symbols."

We do not believe, however, that color, in this respect, is special. Courts traditionally decide quite difficult questions about whether two words or phrases or symbols are sufficiently similar, in context, to confuse buyers. They have had to compare, for example, such words as "Bonamine" and "Dramamine" (motion-sickness remedies); "Huggies" and "Dougies" (diapers); "Cheracol" and "Syrocol" (cough syrup); "Cyclone" and "Tornado" (wire fences); and "Mattres" and "1-800-Mattres" (mattress franchisor telephone numbers).

Second, Jacobson argues, as have others, that colors are in limited supply. Jacobson claims that, if one of many competitors can appropriate a particular color for use as a trademark, and each competitor then tries to do the same, the supply of colors will soon be depleted. . . . [I]n the context of a particular product, only some colors are usable. By the time one discards colors that, say, for reasons of customer appeal, are not usable, and adds the shades that competitors cannot use lest they risk infringing a similar, registered shade, then one is left with only a handful of possible colors. And, under these circumstances, to permit one, or a few, producers to use colors as trademarks will "deplete" the supply of usable colors to the point where a competitor's inability to find a suitable color will put that competitor at a significant disadvantage.

This argument is unpersuasive, however, largely because it relies on an occasional problem to justify a blanket prohibition. When a color serves as a mark, normally alternative colors will likely be available for similar use by others. Moreover, if that is not so—if a "color depletion" or "color scarcity" problem does arise—the trademark doctrine of "functionality" normally would seem available to prevent the anticompetitive consequences that Jacobson's argument posits, thereby minimizing that argument's practical force.

The functionality doctrine . . . forbids the use of a product's feature as a trademark where doing so will put a competitor at a significant disadvantage because the feature is "essential to the use or purpose of the article" or "affects [its] cost or quality." The functionality doctrine thus protects competitors against a disadvantage (unrelated to recognition or reputation) that trademark protection might otherwise impose, namely their inability reasonably to replicate important non-reputation-related product features.

Notes and Questions

1. **Dilution.** In 1996, the *Lanham Act* was amended to protect owners of "famous marks" against "dilution of the distinctive quality of the mark" by giving them the right to obtain injunctive relief against competing uses even in the absence of consumer confusion. 15 U.S.C. §1125(c) (codifying the *Federal Trademark Dilution Act of 1995*, Pub. L. No. 104-374, §3 (1996)). The statute explicitly allows use of a mark in "comparative commercial advertising." *Id.* §1125(c)(4)(A). State antidilution laws continue to apply to "nonfamous" marks.

A mark may be diluted either because of **tarnishment** or **blurring**. Tarnishment occurs if a company sells inferior quality products. For example, the Singer name is commercially associated with sewing machines. If a business starts selling Singer vacuum cleaners, and they are of inferior quality, the Singer name might come to be associated with shoddy products and the value of the Singer name associated with sewing machines might decrease.

Blurring occurs when a distinctive mark begins to lose its association with a particular company. For example, Pepperidge Farm obtained an injunction ordering Nabisco to stop selling goldfish-shaped cheddar cheese-flavored crackers because this particular product was strongly associated with Pepperidge Farm, and sale of similar products by Nabisco would dilute the distinctive quality of Pepperidge Farm's mark. *Nabisco, Inc. v. PF Brands, Inc.*, 191 F.3d 208 (2d Cir. 1999).

One issue is whether injunctive relief should be granted in the absence of proof of actual economic harm. Some courts allowed relief based solely on the possibility of blurring while others held that dilution could be established only by showing actual economic harm resulting from the competing product. Congress answered this question in 2006 by amending the *Federal Trademark Dilution Act* to provide for relief when a mark is "likely to cause dilution." 15 U.S.C. §1125(c)(1).

2. **Cybersquatting and gripe web sites.** In the early years of the Internet, some people obtained web site domain names for the sole purpose of selling them to existing trademark holders, a practice that came to be known as "cybersquatting." Often no confusion resulted from this because anyone accessing the web site would know immediately that it was not owned by the company in question. However, in the spirit of the *Federal Trademark Dilution Act of 1995*, Congress passed the *Anticybersquatting Consumer Protection Act* (ACPA), 15 U.S.C. §1125(d), in 1999. This law prohibits

anyone from registering or using a domain name "with bad faith intent to profit from another's trademark." Anyone who obtains a domain name with the intent of selling it to the relevant company or somehow profiting from the traffic the famous trademark name generates would almost certainly violate the act. *See, e.g., PETA v. Doughney,* 263 F.3d 359 (4th Cir. 2001) (registration of the domain name "peta.org" allegedly on behalf of a fictional "People Eating Tasty Animals" violates the ACPA where used in bad faith to attempt to extract payment from the organization People for the Ethical Treatment of Animals); *Virtual Works, Inc. v. Volkswagen of America, Inc.*, 238 F.3d 264 (4th Cir. 2001) (*www.vw.net* domain name violates ACPA when registered by Virtual Works, Inc. because the company intended to profit from the name recognition attached to the common abbreviation for Volkswagen). Is "cybersquatting" any different than strategically buying a piece of land that another person is trying to acquire (say, as part of an effort to assemble a larger parcel) in order to profit by selling it to them? Why do you think Congress intervened in these disputes between "cybersquatters" and trademark owners? Is the law aptly named?

Disagreements have arisen among courts about gripe web sites that intend to criticize a company by using its name or its name plus a disparaging word such as "sucks." Although it has been argued that this is a noncommercial use outside the scope of the ACPA and that the first amendment protects such usages, one court has granted relief on behalf of a trademark owner against such a site when the site sought to "get even" with the trademark owner. *Morrison & Foerster v. Wick,* 94 F. Supp. 2d 1125 (D. Colo. 2000). Most courts, however, have held that use of a company's trademarked name in a web site address violates neither the ACPA nor the *Lanham Act* when the name is not used for commercial purposes or in a manner that would confuse potential customers. *See, e.g., Lamparello v. Falwell,* 420 F.3d 309 (4th Cir. 2005) (web site using the misspelled domain name fallwell.com and dedicated to criticizing Jerry Falwell's views on homosexuality did not constitute infringement or cybersquatting); *Aviva USA Corp. v. Vazirani,* 902 F. Supp. 2d 1246 (D. Ariz. 2012); *see also Bosley Medical Institute, Inc. v. Kremer,* 403 F.3d 672 (9th Cir. 2005). Nevertheless, such uses may still violate the ACPA if they are done "with bad faith intent to profit" from the trademarked name.

Problems

1. Section 2(a) of the *Lanham Act,* 15 U.S.C. §1052(a), prohibits the PTO from registering a trademark if it "[c]onsists of or comprises immoral, deceptive, or scandalous matter; or matter which may disparage or falsely suggest a connection with persons, living or dead, institutions, beliefs, or national symbols, or bring them into contempt or disrepute." Does the term "Redskins" fall within this prohibition? Does the first amendment's protection for free speech protect the trademark owner's right to use the name?

2. Christian Louboutin produces high-end footwear. Louboutin's shoes nearly always feature a bright-red lacquered outsole, usually accompanied by an upper portion of the shoe with a different color. In 2008, Louboutin received a trademark for the red sole. In 2011, Yves Saint Laurent (YSL) released a series of monochrome

shoes using various colors, including red. Louboutin sues, arguing that YSL's use of red soles infringed on Louboutin's trademark. YSL argues, among other things, that color is functional in fashion and that, as a result, *Qualitex* should not be controlling. Does the functionality of color vary by industry? Who should prevail in this case? *See Christian Louboutin S.A. v. Yves Saint Laurent America Holding, Inc.*, 696 F.3d 206 (2d Cir. 2012) (holding that a single color trademark is permissible in the fashion industry and that Louboutin's red sole had become a distinctive symbol for the brand but only when accompanied by an upper portion of a different color).

§4 COPYRIGHT LAW

§4.1 Original Works of Authorship

Copyright law is regulated by a federal statute that substantially preempts state law on the subject. 17 U.S.C. §101 *et seq.* The *Copyright Act* grants owners of "original works of authorship" that are fixed in a "tangible medium of expression," §102, exclusive rights to copy, distribute, perform, or display those works publicly and to make derivative works from them, §106. Ideas and facts cannot be copyrighted; only original *expressions* of ideas can be protected by copyright law. Authors own what they create unless they performed "work for hire"; such works are owned by the author's employer. §201(b). Copyright protection lasts for the life of the author plus 70 years, after which time the work becomes part of the public domain. With respect to works for hire, the copyright lasts for 95 years from the date of first publication or 120 years from the date of creation, whichever expires first. §302(c). Copyright protection is created automatically, with no need by the author or creator to take any affirmative steps, although authors need to register their copyrights before suing for infringement.

A. The *Copyright Act*

Copyright Act of 1976

17 U.S.C. §§102, 106, 107

§102. Subject matter of copyright: In general

(a) Copyright protection subsists, in accordance with this title, in original works of authorship fixed in any tangible medium of expression, now known or later developed, from which they can be perceived, reproduced, or otherwise communicated, either directly or with the aid of a machine or device. Works of authorship include the following categories:

(1) literary works;
(2) musical works, including any accompanying words;
(3) dramatic works, including any accompanying music;
(4) pantomimes and choreographic works;
(5) pictorial, graphic, and sculptural works;

(6) motion pictures and other audiovisual works;
(7) sound recordings; and
(8) architectural works.

(b) In no case does copyright protection for an original work of authorship extend to any idea, procedure, process, system, method of operation, concept, principle, or discovery, regardless of the form in which it is described, explained, illustrated, or embodied in such work.

§106. Exclusive rights in copyrighted works

Subject to sections 107 through 122, the owner of copyright under this title has the exclusive rights to do and to authorize any of the following:

(1) to reproduce the copyrighted work in copies or phonorecords;

(2) to prepare derivative works based upon the copyrighted work;

(3) to distribute copies or phonorecords of the copyrighted work to the public by sale or other transfer of ownership, or by rental, lease, or lending;

(4) in the case of literary, musical, dramatic, and choreographic works, pantomimes, and motion pictures and other audiovisual works, to perform the copyrighted work publicly;

(5) in the case of literary, musical, dramatic, and choreographic works, pantomimes, and pictorial, graphic, or sculptural works, including the individual images of a motion picture or other audiovisual work, to display the copyrighted work publicly; and

(6) in the case of sound recordings, to perform the copyrighted work publicly by means of a digital audio transmission.

§107. Limitations on exclusive rights: Fair use

Notwithstanding the provisions of sections 106 . . . , the fair use of a copyrighted work, including such use by reproduction in copies or phonorecords or by any other means specified by that section, for purposes such as criticism, comment, news reporting, teaching (including multiple copies for classroom use), scholarship, or research, is not an infringement of copyright. In determining whether the use made of a work in any particular case is a fair use the factors to be considered shall include—

(1) the purpose and character of the use, including whether such use is of a commercial nature or is for nonprofit educational purposes;

(2) the nature of the copyrighted work;

(3) the amount and substantiality of the portion used in relation to the copyrighted work as a whole; and

(4) the effect of the use upon the potential market for or value of the copyrighted work.

The fact that a work is unpublished shall not itself bar a finding of fair use if such finding is made upon consideration of all the above factors.

B. "Original" Works

Only "original" works of "authorship" are protected under the *Copyright Act*. The following case considers what this means.

Feist Publications, Inc. v. Rural Telephone Service Co.

499 U.S. 340 (1991)

Justice SANDRA DAY O'CONNOR delivered the opinion of the Court.

This case requires us to clarify the extent of copyright protection available to telephone directory white pages.

Rural Telephone Service Company, Inc., is a certified public utility that provides telephone service to several communities in northwest Kansas. It is subject to a state regulation that requires all telephone companies operating in Kansas to issue annually an updated telephone directory. Accordingly, as a condition of its monopoly franchise, Rural publishes a typical telephone directory, consisting of white pages and yellow pages. The white pages list in alphabetical order the names of Rural's subscribers, together with their towns and telephone numbers. The yellow pages list Rural's business subscribers alphabetically by category and feature classified advertisements of various sizes. Rural distributes its directory free of charge to its subscribers, but earns revenue by selling yellow pages advertisements.

Feist Publications, Inc., is a publishing company that specializes in area-wide telephone directories. Unlike a typical directory, which covers only a particular calling area, Feist's area-wide directories cover a much larger geographical range, reducing the need to call directory assistance or consult multiple directories. The Feist directory that is the subject of this litigation covers 11 different telephone service areas in 15 counties and contains 46,878 white pages listings — compared to Rural's approximately 7,700 listings. Like Rural's directory, Feist's is distributed free of charge and includes both white pages and yellow pages. Feist and Rural compete vigorously for yellow pages advertising.

As the sole provider of telephone service in its service area, Rural obtains subscriber information quite easily. Persons desiring telephone service must apply to Rural and provide their names and addresses; Rural then assigns them a telephone number. Feist is not a telephone company, let alone one with monopoly status, and therefore lacks independent access to any subscriber information. To obtain white pages listings for its area-wide directory, Feist approached each of the 11 telephone companies operating in northwest Kansas and offered to pay for the right to use its white pages listings.

Of the 11 telephone companies, only Rural refused to license its listings to Feist. Rural's refusal created a problem for Feist, as omitting these listings would have left a gaping hole in its area-wide directory, rendering it less attractive to potential yellow pages advertisers. . . .

Unable to license Rural's white pages listings, Feist used them without Rural's consent. Feist began by removing several thousand listings that fell outside the geographic range of its area-wide directory, then hired personnel to investigate the 4,935 that remained. These employees verified the data reported by Rural and sought to obtain additional information. As a result, a typical Feist listing includes the individual's street address; most of Rural's listings do not. Notwithstanding these additions, however, 1,309 of the 46,878 listings in Feist's 1983 directory were identical to listings in Rural's 1982-1983 white pages. Four of these were fictitious listings that Rural had inserted into its directory to detect copying.

Rural sued for copyright infringement in the District Court for the District of Kansas taking the position that Feist, in compiling its own directory, could not use the information contained in Rural's white pages. Rural asserted that Feist's employees were obliged to travel door-to-door or conduct a telephone survey to discover the same information for themselves. Feist responded that such efforts were economically impractical and, in any event, unnecessary because the information copied was beyond the scope of copyright protection.

This case concerns the interaction of two well-established propositions. The first is that facts are not copyrightable; the other, that compilations of facts generally are.

There is an undeniable tension between these two propositions. Many compilations consist of nothing but raw data — *i.e.*, wholly factual information not accompanied by any original written expression. . . . The key to resolving the tension lies in understanding why facts are not copyrightable. The *sine qua non* of copyright is originality. To qualify for copyright protection, a work must be original to the author. Original, as the term is used in copyright, means only that the work was independently created by the author (as opposed to copied from other works), and that it possesses at least some minimal degree of creativity. Originality does not signify novelty; a work may be original even though it closely resembles other works so long as the similarity is fortuitous, not the result of copying. To illustrate, assume that two poets, each ignorant of the other, compose identical poems. Neither work is novel, yet both are original and, hence, copyrightable.

Originality is a constitutional requirement. The source of Congress' power to enact copyright laws is Article I, §8, cl. 8, of the Constitution, which authorizes Congress to "secure for limited Times to Authors . . . the exclusive Right to their respective Writings." In two decisions from the late 19th century — *The Trade-Mark Cases*, 100 U.S. 82 (1879); and *Burrow-Giles Lithographic Co. v. Sarony*, 111 U.S. 53 (1884) — this Court defined the crucial terms "authors" and "writings." In so doing, the Court made it unmistakably clear that these terms presuppose a degree of originality.

It is this bedrock principle of copyright that mandates the law's seemingly disparate treatment of facts and factual compilations. "No one may claim originality as to facts." This is because facts do not owe their origin to an act of authorship. The distinction is one between creation and discovery: The first person to find and report a particular fact has not created the fact; he or she has merely discovered its existence.

Factual compilations, on the other hand, may possess the requisite originality. The compilation author typically chooses which facts to include, in what order to place them, and how to arrange the collected data so that they may be used effectively by readers. These choices as to selection and arrangement, so long as they are made independently by the compiler and entail a minimal degree of creativity, are sufficiently original that Congress may protect such compilations through the copyright laws. Thus, even a directory that contains absolutely no protectible written expression, only facts, meets the constitutional minimum for copyright protection if it features an original selection or arrangement.

This protection is subject to an important limitation. The mere fact that a work is copyrighted does not mean that every element of the work may be protected. Originality remains the *sine qua non* of copyright; accordingly, copyright protection may extend only to those components of a work that are original to the author. Thus, if the compilation author clothes facts with an original collocation of words, he or she may be able to claim a copyright in this written expression. Others may copy the underlying facts from the publication, but not the precise words used to present them. Where the compilation author adds no written expression but rather lets the facts speak for themselves, the expressive element is more elusive. The only conceivable expression is the manner in which the compiler has selected and arranged the facts. Thus, if the selection and arrangement are original, these elements of the work are eligible for copyright protection. No matter how original the format, however, the facts themselves do not become original through association.

This inevitably means that the copyright in a factual compilation is thin. Notwithstanding a valid copyright, a subsequent compiler remains free to use the facts contained in another's publication to aid in preparing a competing work, so long as the competing work does not feature the same selection and arrangement.

It may seem unfair that much of the fruit of the compiler's labor may be used by others without compensation. As Justice Brennan has correctly observed, however, this is not "some unforeseen byproduct of a statutory scheme." *Harper & Row, Publishers, Inc. v. Nation Enterprises*, 471 U.S. 539, 589 (1985) (dissenting opinion). It is, rather, "the essence of copyright," and a constitutional requirement. The primary objective of copyright is not to reward the labor of authors, but "to promote the Progress of Science and useful Arts." Art. I, §8, cl. 8. To this end, copyright assures authors the right to their original expression, but encourages others to build freely upon the ideas and information conveyed by a work. This principle, known as the idea/expression or fact/expression dichotomy, applies to all works of authorship. As applied to a factual compilation, assuming the absence of original written expression, only the compiler's selection and arrangement may be protected; the raw facts may be copied at will. This result is neither unfair nor unfortunate. It is the means by which copyright advances the progress of science and art.

In enacting the *Copyright Act of 1976*, 17 U.S.C. §101 *et seq.*, Congress [reaffirmed the view that copyright law protects only original works rather than the "sweat of the brow" by dropping] reference to "all the writings of an author" and replac[ing] it with the phrase "original works of authorship." 17 U.S.C. §102(a). . . . [The 1976 *Copyright Act* made clear] that compilations [are] not copyrightable *per se*. . . . The definition of "compilation" is found in §101 of the 1976 Act. It defines a "compilation" in the copyright sense as "a work formed by the collection and assembling of preexisting materials or of data *that* are selected, coordinated, or arranged *in such a way that* the resulting work as a whole constitutes an original work of authorship" (emphasis added).

The purpose of the statutory definition is to emphasize that collections of facts are not copyrightable *per se*. [A] compilation, like any other work, is copyrightable only if it satisfies the originality requirement ("an *original* work of authorship"). Although

§102 states plainly that the originality requirement applies to all works, the point was emphasized with regard to compilations to ensure that courts would not repeat the mistake of the [courts that had protected the "sweat of the brow" in the absence of originality].

In summary, the 1976 revisions to the *Copyright Act* leave no doubt that originality, not "sweat of the brow," is the touchstone of copyright protection in directories and other fact-based works. . . . The revisions explain with painstaking clarity that copyright requires originality, §102(a); that facts are never original, §102(b); that the copyright in a compilation does not extend to the facts it contains, §103(b); and that a compilation is copyrightable only to the extent that it features an original selection, coordination, or arrangement, §101.

The question is whether . . . Feist, by taking 1,309 names, towns, and telephone numbers from Rural's white pages, cop[ied] anything that was "original" to Rural[.] Certainly, the raw data does not satisfy the originality requirement. Rather, these bits of information are uncopyrightable facts.

The question that remains is whether Rural selected, coordinated, or arranged these uncopyrightable facts in an original way. The selection, coordination, and arrangement of Rural's white pages do not satisfy the minimum constitutional standards for copyright protection. In preparing its white pages, Rural simply takes the data provided by its subscribers and lists it alphabetically by surname. The end product is a garden-variety white pages directory, devoid of even the slightest trace of creativity.

Rural's selection of listings could not be more obvious: It publishes the most basic information — name, town, and telephone number — about each person who applies to it for telephone service. This is "selection" of a sort, but it lacks the modicum of creativity necessary to transform mere selection into copyrightable expression. Rural expended sufficient effort to make the white pages directory useful, but insufficient creativity to make it original.

Nor can Rural claim originality in its coordination and arrangement of facts. The white pages do nothing more than list Rural's subscribers in alphabetical order. This arrangement may, technically speaking, owe its origin to Rural [b]ut there is nothing remotely creative about arranging names alphabetically in a white pages directory. It is not only unoriginal, it is practically inevitable. This time-honored tradition does not possess the minimal creative spark required by the *Copyright Act* and the Constitution.

We conclude that the names, towns, and telephone numbers copied by Feist were not original to Rural and therefore were not protected by the copyright in Rural's combined white and yellow pages directory. . . . Because Rural's white pages lack the requisite originality, Feist's use of the listings cannot constitute infringement. This decision should not be construed as demeaning Rural's efforts in compiling its directory, but rather as making clear that copyright rewards originality, not effort. As this Court noted more than a century ago, " 'great praise may be due to the plaintiffs for their industry and enterprise in publishing this paper, yet the law does not contemplate their being rewarded in this way.' " *Baker v. Selden*, 101 U.S. 99, 105 (1880).

Notes and Questions

1. **Infringement and contributory infringement.** A person is liable for infringing a copyright when she "violates any of the exclusive rights of the copyright owner as provided by sections 106 through 121." *See* 17 U.S.C. §501(a). A person can be liable for **contributory infringement** when "with the knowledge of the infringing activity [by others, she] induces, causes, or materially contributes" to it. *Gershwin Publishing Corp. v. Columbia Artists Management*, 443 F.2d 1159, 1162 (2d Cir. 1971). When video cassette recorders (VCRs) first became available to home consumers in the 1970s, movie studios feared they would lead to widespread copyright piracy. Two studios sued Sony, a manufacturer of VCRs, alleging that Sony was liable for the infringing activities of VCR users. The Supreme Court held that a device maker is not liable for contributory infringement where its product is "capable of substantial non-infringing uses." *Sony Corp. v. Universal City Studios*, 464 U.S. 417, 442 (1984). Because the VCR is capable of substantial noninfringing uses, the Court reasoned, Sony was not liable just because some people put its product to infringing uses. *See id.* In *Metro-Goldwyn Mayer Studios, Inc. v. Grokster, Ltd.*, 545 U.S. 913 (2005), the Court considered a lawsuit by a group of copyright owners (including movie studios, recording companies, songwriters, and others) against Grokster, Inc. and StreamCast Networks, Inc., distributors of software products that allowed computer users to share electronic files (including copyrighted content) through networks in which users' computers communicate directly with one another. A unanimous Supreme Court held that, even though such peer-to-peer file-sharing software might be capable of substantial noninfringing uses, the device makers could not take advantage of the Court's holding in *Sony* since they distributed their products with the purpose of affirmatively promoting infringing uses. The Court pointed to numerous statements by Grokster and StreamCast in marketing materials suggestive of an intent to facilitate the sharing of copyrighted content. Would the holding in *Grokster* apply to a company marketing a similar product that did not make such statements?

Are web sites, such as YouTube, that permit users to post and share their own content liable for contributory infringement if users post infringing content? In 1998, Congress enacted the *Digital Millennium Copyright Act* (DMCA) that aimed to curb copyright infringement over the Internet. Title II of the DMCA (separately titled the *Online Copyright Infringement Liability Limitation Act* (OCILLA)), included a series of safe harbors insulating on-line service providers, storage providers, and location tools (such as search engines) from liability for users' copyright infringement. *See* 17 U.S.C. §512(a)-(d). The statute imposes a complex system of criteria for determining who is covered by the safe harbors, with web sites that serve as mere passive conduits of user content enjoying protection, provided they do not know of the infringement and are sufficiently responsive when notified of the presence of infringing content on their servers. The precise dimensions of these safe harbors, however, are a matter of continuing litigation. *See UMG Recordings v. Shelter Capital Partners LLC*, 718 F.3d 1006 (9th Cir. 2013); *Columbia Pictures Industry, Inc. v. Fung*, 710 F.3d 1020 (9th Cir. 2013); *Viacom International, Inc. v. YouTube*, 676 F.3d 19 (2d Cir. 2012).

2. Copying in the digital age. One of the core exclusive rights protected by copyright law is the right "to reproduce the copyrighted work in copies." *See* 17 U.S.C. §106. Section 101 defines "copies" as "material objects . . . in which a work is fixed by any method now known or later developed" and it defines "fixed" as a form that is "sufficiently permanent or stable to permit it to be perceived, reproduced, or otherwise communicated for a period of more than a transitory duration." In the age of cassette tapes and paper books, a copy was easy enough to recognize. But what about today, when music and literature are frequently consumed in digital form? What does it mean to make a copy of a digital music file? What if, every time you play the song on your computer, the computer copies the digital file from your hard drive into the computer's working memory? Is that file in the working memory a copy of the song? *See MAI Systems Corp. v. Peak Computer, Inc.*, 991 F.2d 511 (9th Cir. 1993) (transferring program from a computer's hard drive to its RAM, where it becomes perceptible to users until the computer is turned off, creates a copy of the program within the meaning of 17 U.S.C. §101); *but see Cartoon Network LP v. CSC Holdings, Inc.*, 536 F.3d 121 (2d Cir. 2008) (reading *MAI Systems* narrowly and holding that the transfer of a digital video file into a "buffer" where it was only present for a fleeting period of time did not create a copy within the meaning of §101); *CoStar Group, Inc. v. LoopNet, Inc.*, 373 F.3d 544 (4th Cir. 2004) (transitory copies made by conduits of information, such as Internet service providers, are not copies).

CONTEXT

Copyright lasts for a long time. It was not always this way. As recently as 1976, copyright lasted only 28 years, with an option to renew the copyright for an additional 28 years if the creator took the affirmative step of registering for the extension. Among the more famous works still (allegedly) protected by copyright is the famous "Happy Birthday" song. Rights to the song, which was written in the late nineteenth century by sisters Patty and Mildred Hill, passed through various entities over the years, ending up in the hands of Warner Music Group in 1998. Warner has aggressively policed its copyright in the song, demanding significant licensing fees for the rights to use of the song in films and on television. The result is that, while the song is ubiquitous in public life, it is less frequently sung on the big or small screen. Warner collects at least $2 million a year in licensing fees for the song. *See* Bernard Vaughan, *"Happy Birthday to You" Belongs to Us All, Lawsuit Says,* Reuters, June 13, 2013. Warner Music's entitlement to the song has not gone unchallenged, however. In a recent article, Professor Robert Brauneis says he could find no evidence of an actual copyright for the lyrics of "Happy Birthday to You" sung to the usual tune. *See* Robert Brauneis, *Copyright and the World's Most Popular Song*, 56 J. Copyright Socy. of the U.S.A. 335 (2009). Warner's rights are currently the subject of a legal challenge brought by a filmmaker. If Brauneis is right about the dubious status of the song under copyright law, why do you think it has taken so long for someone to mount a lawsuit challenging Warner's entitlement to licensing fees?

3. Copyfraud and orphan works. Copyright's long duration and automatic application to qualifying works generate a number of problems. Assertions of copyright over long-existing works have at least *prima facie* credibility. And yet the expense of determining the facts of the matter — or the statutory damages imposed for simply ignoring what turns out to be a meritorious demand — can easily exceed the price demanded by the person asserting the copyright. This mix of costs and benefits creates the potential for what Jason Mazzone has dubbed "copyfraud," the bad faith or fraudulent assertion of copyright in order to extract unmerited licensing fees. *See* Jason Mazzone, *Copyfraud and Other Abuses of Intellectual Property Law* (2011).

A second problem arises from the fact that most works subject to copyright protection do not enjoy much commercial success. Since most works generate almost no revenue for their owners, most owners have no interest in policing their works' use by others. And yet those works remain subject to (automatic) copyright protection. Tracking down the owner of the copyright many years after the work's creation can be a difficult task, particularly after the original creator has died and the copyright has passed to the creator's heirs, who may not even be aware that they own the copyright. But using the work in certain ways without the current copyright owner's express permission could subject the user to significant inconvenience, not to mention costly statutory penalties, should an unhappy owner eventually surface. The existence of **orphan works** (works that are subject to copyright but lack an easily identifiable owner) has been an obstacle to efforts to build comprehensive digital libraries, such as Google's plan to create a text-searchable database of millions of books. After Google announced its plans, a group of authors and publishers sued Google and several libraries participating in Google's digitization project, alleging that the creation of repositories of digital copies of books currently covered by copyright violates the rights of copyright owners, including the owners of orphan works. In late 2013, the district court concluded that Google's digitization was a transformative "fair use" and granted Google's motion for summary judgment. In doing so it noted that Google's project was likely to enhance the value of the copyrighted works included in the database. *See Authors Guild, Inc. v. Google Inc.*, No. 05 Civ. 8136 (DC), ___ F. Supp. 2d ___ (Nov. 14, 2013).

§4.2 Fair Use

Suntrust Bank v. Houghton Mifflin Co.

268 F.3d 1257 (11th Cir. 2001)

STANLEY F. BIRCH, JR., Circuit Judge:

In this opinion, we decide whether publication of *The Wind Done Gone* ("TWDG"), a fictional work admittedly based on Margaret Mitchell's *Gone with the Wind* ("GWTW"), should be enjoined from publication based on alleged copyright violations. The district court granted a preliminary injunction against publication of TWDG. . . . We vacate the injunction and remand for consideration of the remaining claims.

I. Background

SunTrust is the trustee of the Mitchell Trust, which holds the copyright in GWTW. Since its publication in 1936, GWTW has become one of the best-selling books in the world, second in sales only to the Bible. The Mitchell Trust has actively managed the copyright, authorizing derivative works and a variety of commercial items. It has entered into a contract authorizing, under specified conditions, a second sequel to GWTW to be published by St. Martin's Press. The Mitchell Trust maintains the copyright in all of the derivative works as well.

Alice Randall, the author of TWDG, persuasively claims that her novel is a critique of GWTW's depiction of slavery and the Civil-War era American South. To this end, she appropriated the characters, plot and major scenes from GWTW into the first half of TWDG.

After discovering the similarities between the books, SunTrust asked Houghton Mifflin to refrain from publication or distribution of TWDG, but Houghton Mifflin refused the request. Subsequently, SunTrust filed an action alleging copyright infringement, violation of the *Lanham Act,* and deceptive trade practices, and immediately filed a motion for a temporary restraining order and a preliminary injunction.

II. Discussion

Our primary focus at this stage of the case is on the appropriateness of the injunctive relief granted by the district court. In our analysis, we must evaluate the merits of SunTrust's copyright infringement claim, including Houghton Mifflin's affirmative defense of fair use. As we assess the fair-use defense, we examine to what extent a critic may use a work to communicate her criticism of the work without infringing the copyright in that work. To approach these issues in the proper framework, we should initially review the history of the Constitution's Copyright Clause and understand its relationship to the First Amendment.

A. History and Development of the Copyright Clause

The Copyright Clause finds its roots in England, where, in 1710, the Statute of Anne "was designed to destroy the booksellers' monopoly of the book trade and to prevent its recurrence." L. Ray Patterson, *Understanding the Copyright Clause,* 47 J. Copyright Soc'y USA 365, 379 (2000). This Parliamentary statute assigned copyright in books to authors, added a requirement that only a new work could be copyrighted, and limited the duration, which had been perpetual, to two fourteen-year terms. It is clear that the goal of the Statute of Anne was to encourage creativity and ensure that the public would have free access to information by putting an end to "the continued use of copyright as a device of censorship." Patterson at 379. The Framers of the U.S. Constitution relied on this statute when drafting the Copyright Clause of our Constitution, which reads, "The Congress shall have Power . . . to promote the Progress of Science . . . by securing for limited Times to Authors . . . the exclusive Right to their respective Writings. . . . " U.S. Const. art. 1, §8, cl. 8. Congress directly transferred the principles from the Statute of Anne into the copyright law of the United States in 1783, first through a recommendation to the states to enact similar copyright laws, and then in 1790, with the passage of the first American federal copyright statute.

The Copyright Clause was intended "to be the engine of free expression." *Harper & Row Publishers, Inc. v. Nation Enters.,* 471 U.S. 539, 558 (1985). To that end, copyright laws have been enacted to achieve the three main goals: the promotion of learning, the protection of the public domain, and the granting of an exclusive right to the author.

1. Promotion of Learning

In the United States, copyright has always been used to promote learning by guarding against censorship. Throughout the nineteenth century, the copyright in literature was limited to the right "to publish and vend books." Patterson, at 383. The term "copy" was interpreted literally; an author had the right only to prevent others from copying and selling her particular literary work. This limited right ensured that a maximum number of new works would be created and published. It was not until the 1909 Act, which codified the concept of a derivative work, that an author's right to protect his original work against imitation was established.

As a further protection of the public interest, until 1976, statutory copyright law required that a work be published before an author was entitled to a copyright in that work. Therefore, in order to have the sole right of publication for the statutory period, the author was first required to make the work available to the public. In 1976, copyright was extended to include any work "fixed in any tangible medium of expression" in order to adapt the law to technological advances. *Copyright Act of 1976*, 17 U.S.C. §102(a). Thus, the publication requirement was removed, but the fair use right was codified to maintain the constitutionally mandated balance to ensure that the public has access to knowledge.

The *Copyright Act* promotes public access to knowledge because it provides an economic incentive for authors to publish books and disseminate ideas to the public. Without the limited monopoly, authors would have little economic incentive to create and publish their work. Therefore, by providing this incentive, the copyright law promotes the public access to new ideas and concepts.

2. Protection of the Public Domain

The second goal of the Copyright Clause is to ensure that works enter the public domain after an author's rights, exclusive, but limited, have expired. Parallel to the patent regime, the limited time period of the copyright serves the dual purpose of ensuring that the work will enter the public domain and ensuring that the author has received "a fair return for [her] labors." *Harper & Row*, 471 U.S. at 5463. This limited grant "is intended to motivate the creative activity of authors . . . by the provision of a special reward, and to allow the public access to the products of their genius after the limited period of exclusive control has expired." *Sony Corp. of America v. Univ. City Studios, Inc.*, 464 U.S. 417, 429 (1984). The public is protected in two ways: the grant of a copyright encourages authors to create new works, . . . and the limitation ensures that the works will eventually enter the public domain, which protects the public's right of access and use.

3. Exclusive Rights of the Author

Finally, the Copyright Clause grants the author limited exclusive rights in order to encourage the creation of original works. Before our copyright jurisprudence developed, there were two separate theories of copyright in England — the natural law copyright, which was the right of first publication, and the statutory copyright, which was the right of continued publication. The natural law copyright, which is not a part of our system, implied an ownership in the work itself, and thus was preferred by the booksellers and publishers striving to maintain their monopoly over literature as well as by the Crown to silence "seditious" writings. Even after passage of the Statute of Anne, the publishers and booksellers resisted the loss of their monopoly in the courts for more than sixty years. Finally, in 1774, the House of Lords ruled that the natural law copyright, that is, the ownership of the work itself, expires upon publication of the book, when the statutory copyright attaches.

This bifurcated system was carried over into our copyright law. As of the 1909 Act, an author had "state common law protection [that] persisted until the moment of general publication." *Estate of Martin Luther King, Jr. v. CBS, Inc.*, 194 F.3d 1211, 1214 (11th Cir. 1999). After the work was published, the author was entitled to federal statutory copyright protection if she had complied with certain federal requirements (i.e. publication with notice). If not, the work was released into the public domain. The system illustrates that the author's ownership is in the copyright, and not in the work itself, for if the author had an ownership interest in the work itself, she would not lose that right if she published the book without complying with federal statutory copyright requirements. Compliance with the copyright law results in the guarantee of copyright to the author for a limited time, but the author never owns the work itself.

This has an important impact on modern interpretation of copyright, as it emphasizes the distinction between ownership of the work, which an author does not possess, and ownership of the copyright, which an author enjoys for a limited time. In a society oriented toward property ownership, it is not surprising to find many that erroneously equate the work with the copyright in the work and conclude that if one owns the copyright, they must also own the work.

B. The Union of Copyright and the First Amendment

The Copyright Clause and the First Amendment,[2] while intuitively in conflict, were drafted to work together to prevent censorship; copyright laws were enacted in part to prevent private censorship and the First Amendment was enacted to prevent public censorship. There are "conflicting interests that must be accommodated in drawing a definitional balance" between the Copyright Clause and the First Amendment. 1 Melville B. Nimmer & David Nimmer, *Nimmer on Copyright* §1.10[B][1] (2001). In establishing this balance "on the copyright side, economic encouragement for creators must be preserved and the privacy of unpublished works recognized. Freedom of speech[, on the other hand,] requires the preservation of a meaningful public or democratic dialogue, as well as the uses of speech as a safety valve against violent acts, and as an end in itself." *Id.*

In copyright law, the balance between the First Amendment and copyright is preserved, in part, by the idea/expression dichotomy and the doctrine of fair use.

1. The Idea/Expression Dichotomy

Copyright cannot protect an idea, only the expression of that idea. The result is that "copyright assures authors the right to their original expression, but encourages others to build freely upon the ideas and information conveyed by the work." *Feist Publications, Inc. v. Rural Tel. Serv. Co.*, 499 U.S. 340, 349-350 (1991). It is partly through this idea/expression dichotomy that copyright law embodies the First Amendment's

2. "Congress shall make no law . . . abridging the freedom of speech . . ." U.S. Const. amend. I.

underlying goal of encouraging open debate and the free exchange of ideas. Holding an infringer liable in copyright for copying the expression of another author's ideas does not impede First Amendment goals because the public purpose has been served — the public already has access to the idea or the concepts. A new author may use or discuss the idea, but must do so using her own original expression.

2. *Fair Use*

First Amendment privileges are also preserved through the doctrine of fair use.[3] Until codification of the fair-use doctrine in the 1976 Act, fair use was a judge-made right developed to preserve the constitutionality of copyright legislation by protecting First Amendment values. Had fair use not been recognized as a right under the 1976 Act, the statutory abandonment of publication as a condition of copyright that had existed for over 200 years would have jeopardized the constitutionality of the new Act because there would be no statutory guarantee that new ideas, or new expressions of old ideas, would be accessible to the public. Included in the definition of fair use are "purposes such as criticism, comment, news reporting, teaching . . . , scholarship, or research." §107. The exceptions carved out for these purposes are at the heart of fair use's protection of the First Amendment, as they allow later authors to use a previous author's copyright to introduce new ideas or concepts to the public. Therefore, within the limits of the fair-use test, any use of a copyright is permitted to fulfill one of the important purposes listed in the statute.

Because of the First Amendment principles built into copyright law through the idea/expression dichotomy and the doctrine of fair use, courts often need not entertain related First Amendment arguments in a copyright case.

The case before us calls for an analysis of whether a preliminary injunction was properly granted against an alleged infringer who, relying largely on the doctrine of fair use, made use of another's copyright for comment and criticism. As discussed herein, *copyright does not immunize a work from comment and criticism*. Therefore, the narrower question in this case is to what extent a critic may use the protected elements of an original work of authorship to communicate her criticism without infringing the copyright in that work. As will be discussed below, this becomes essentially an analysis of the fair use factors. As we turn to the analysis required in this case, we must remain cognizant of the First Amendment protections interwoven into copyright law.

C. *Appropriateness of Injunctive Relief*

SunTrust is not entitled to relief in the form of a preliminary injunction unless it has proved each of the following four elements: "(1) a substantial likelihood of success on the merits, (2) a substantial threat of irreparable injury if the injunction were not granted, (3) that the threatened injury to the plaintiff outweighs the harm an injunction may cause the defendant, and (4) that granting the injunction would not disserve

---

3. §107 ("Fair use of a copyrighted work . . . for purposes such as criticism [or] comment . . . is not an infringement of copyright.").

the public interest." *Am. Red Cross v. Palm Beach Blood Bank, Inc.*, 143 F.3d 1407, 1410 (11th Cir. 1998).

1. Substantial Likelihood of Success on the Merits

a. Prima Facie Copyright Infringement.

The first step in evaluating the likelihood that SunTrust will succeed on merits is to determine whether it has established the prima facie elements of a copyright infringement claim: (1) that SunTrust owns a valid copyright in GWTW and (2) that Randall copied *original* elements of GWTW in TWDG.

The first element, SunTrust's ownership of a valid copyright in GWTW, is not disputed. Houghton Mifflin does assert, however, that SunTrust did not establish the second element of infringement, that TWDG appropriates copyright-protected expression from GWTW. In order to prove copying, SunTrust was required to show a "substantial similarity" between the two works such that "an average lay observer would recognize the alleged copy as having been appropriated from the copyrighted work." Not all copying of a work is actionable, however, for, . . . "no author may copyright facts or ideas. The copyright is limited to those aspects of the work-termed 'expression' that display the stamp of the author's originality." *Harper & Row*, 471 U.S. at 547. Thus, we are concerned with substantial similarities between TWDG and GWTW only to the extent that they involve the copying of original, protected expression.

There is no bright line that separates the protectable expression from the nonprotectable idea in a work of fiction. . . . At one end of the spectrum, *scenes a faire*—the stock scenes and hackneyed character types that "naturally flow from a common theme"—are considered "ideas," and therefore are not copyrightable. But as plots become more intricately detailed and characters become more idiosyncratic, they at some point cross the line into "expression" and are protected by copyright.

Our own review of the two works reveals substantial use of GWTW. TWDG appropriates numerous characters, settings, and plot twists from GWTW. For example, Scarlett O'Hara, Rhett Butler, Bonnie Butler, Melanie Wilkes, Ashley Wilkes, Gerald O'Hara, Ellen O'Hara, Mammy, Pork, Dilcey, Prissy, Belle Watling, Carreen O'Hara, Stuart and Brenton Tarleton, Jeems, Philippe, and Aunt Pittypat, all characters in GWTW, appear in TWDG. Many of these characters are renamed in TWDG: Scarlett becomes "Other," Rhett Butler becomes "R.B.," Pork becomes "Garlic," Prissy becomes "Miss Priss," Philippe becomes "Feleepe," Aunt Pittypat becomes "Aunt Pattypit," etc. In several instances, Randall renamed characters using Mitchell's descriptions of those characters in GWTW: Ashley becomes "Dreamy Gentleman," Melanie becomes "Mealy Mouth," Gerald becomes "Planter." The fictional settings from GWTW receive a similarly transparent renaming in TWDG: Tara becomes "Tata," Twelve Oaks Plantation becomes "Twelve Slaves Strong as Trees." TWDG copies, often in wholesale fashion, the descriptions and histories of these fictional characters and places from GWTW, as well as their relationships and interactions with one another. TWDG appropriates or otherwise explicitly references many aspects of GWTW's plot as well, such as the scenes in which Scarlett kills a Union soldier and the scene in which Rhett stays in the room with his dead daughter Bonnie, burning candles. After carefully comparing the two works, we agree with the district court that, particularly in its first half, TWDG is largely "an encapsulation of [GWTW] [that] exploits its copyrighted characters, story lines, and settings as the palette for the new story."

b. Fair Use.

Randall's appropriation of elements of GWTW in TWDG may nevertheless not constitute infringement of SunTrust's copyright if the taking is protected as a "fair use." The codification of the fair-use doctrine in the Copyright Act provides:

> Notwithstanding the provisions of sections 106 and 106A, the fair use of a copyrighted work . . . for purposes such as criticism, comment, news reporting, teaching (including multiple copies for classroom use), scholarship, or research, is not an infringement of copyright. In determining whether the use made of a work in any particular case is a fair use the factors to be considered shall include —
>
> (1) the purpose and character of the use, including whether such use is of a commercial nature or is for nonprofit educational purposes;
>
> (2) the nature of the copyrighted work;
>
> (3) the amount and substantiality of the portion used in relation to the copyrighted work as a whole; and
>
> (4) the effect of the use upon the potential market for or value of the copyrighted work.

§107. In assessing whether a use of a copyright is a fair use under the statute, we bear in mind that the examples of possible fair uses given are illustrative rather than exclusive, and that "all [of the four factors] are to be explored, and the results weighed together in light of the purposes of copyright." *Campbell v. Acuff-Rose Music, Inc.*, 510 U.S. 569, 557-578 (1994). [O]ne of the most important purposes to consider is the free flow of ideas — particularly criticism and commentary.

Houghton Mifflin argues that TWDG is entitled to fair-use protection as a parody of GWTW. In *Campbell*, the Supreme Court held that parody, although not specifically listed in §107, is a form of comment and criticism that may constitute a fair use of the copyrighted work being parodied. Parody, which is directed toward a particular literary or artistic work, is distinguishable from satire, which more broadly addresses the institutions and mores of a slice of society. Thus, "parody needs to mimic an original to make its point, and so has some claim to use the creation of its victim's . . . imagination, whereas satire can stand on its own two feet and so requires justification for the very act of borrowing."

Before considering a claimed fair-use defense based on parody, however, the Supreme Court has required that we ensure that "a parodic character may reasonably be perceived" in the allegedly infringing work. The Supreme Court's definition of parody in *Campbell*, however, is somewhat vague. On the one hand, the Court suggests that the aim of parody is "comic effect or ridicule," but it then proceeds to discuss parody more expansively in terms of its "commentary" on the original. In light of the admonition in *Campbell* that courts should not judge the quality of the work or the success of the attempted humor in discerning its parodic character, we choose to take the broader view. For purposes of our fair-use analysis, we will treat a work as a parody if its aim is to comment upon or criticize a prior work by appropriating elements of the original in creating a new artistic, as opposed to scholarly or journalistic, work. Under this definition, the parodic character of TWDG is clear. TWDG is not a general commentary upon the Civil-War-era American South, but a specific criticism of and rejoinder to the depiction of slavery and the relationships between blacks and whites in GWTW. The fact that Randall chose to convey her criticisms of GWTW through a work of fiction, which she contends is a more powerful vehicle for her message than a scholarly article, does not, in and of itself, deprive TWDG of fair-use protection. We therefore proceed to an analysis of the four fair-use factors.

i. Purpose and Character of the Work

The first factor in the fair-use analysis, the purpose and character of the allegedly infringing work, has several facets. The first is whether TWDG serves a commercial purpose or nonprofit educational purpose. §107(1). Despite whatever educational function TWDG may be able to lay claim to, it is undoubtedly a commercial product. . . . The fact that TWDG was published for profit is the first factor weighing against a finding of fair use.

However, TWDG's for-profit status is strongly overshadowed and outweighed in view of its highly transformative use of GWTC's copyrighted elements. "The more transformative the new work, the less will be the significance of other factors, like commercialism, that may weigh against a finding of fair use." *Campbell*, 510 U.S. at 579. "The goal of copyright, to promote science and the arts, is generally furthered by the creation of transformative works." *Id.* A work's transformative value is of special import in the realm of parody, since a parody's aim is, by nature, to transform an earlier work.

The second factor in the "purpose and character" analysis relevant to this case is to what extent TWDG's use of copyrighted elements of GWTW can be said to be "transformative." The inquiry is "whether the new work merely supersedes the objects of the original creation, or instead adds something new, with a further purpose or different character, altering the first with new expression, meaning, or message." *Campbell*, 510 U.S. at 579. The issue of transformation is a double-edged sword in this case. On the one hand, the story of Cynara and her perception of the events in TWDG certainly adds new "expression, meaning, [and] message" to GWTW. From another perspective, however, TWDG's success as a pure work of fiction depends heavily on copyrighted elements appropriated from GWTW to carry its own plot forward.

However, as noted above, TWDG is more than an abstract, pure fictional work. It is principally and purposefully a critical statement that seeks to rebut and destroy the perspective, judgments, and mythology of GWTW. Randall's literary goal is to explode the romantic, idealized portrait of the antebellum South during and after the Civil War. In the world of GWTW, the white characters comprise a noble aristocracy whose idyllic existence is upset only by the intrusion of Yankee soldiers, and, eventually, by the liberation of the black slaves. Through her characters as well as through direct narration, Mitchell describes how both blacks and whites were purportedly better off in the days of slavery: "The more I see of emancipation the more criminal I think it is. It's just ruined the darkies," says Scarlett O'Hara. Free blacks are described as "creatures of small intelligence . . . like monkeys or small children turned loose among treasured objects whose value is beyond their comprehension, they ran wild — either from perverse pleasure in destruction or simply because of their ignorance." Blacks elected to the legislature are described as spending "most of their time eating goobers and easing their unaccustomed feet into and out of new shoes."

As the district court noted: "The earlier work is a third-person epic, whereas the new work is told in the first-person as an intimate diary of the life of Cynara. Thematically, the new work provides a different viewpoint of the antebellum world." While told from a different perspective, more critically, the story is transformed into a very different tale, albeit much more abbreviated. Cynara's very language is a departure from Mitchell's original prose; she acts as the voice of Randall's inversion of GWTW. She is the vehicle of parody; she is its means — not its end. It is clear within the first fifty pages of Cynara's fictional diary that Randall's work flips GWTW's traditional race roles, portrays powerful whites as stupid or feckless, and generally sets out to demystify GWTW and strip the romanticism from Mitchell's specific account of this period of our history. Approximately the last half of TWDG tells a completely new story that, although involving characters based on GWTW characters, features plot elements found nowhere within the covers of GWTW.

Where Randall refers directly to Mitchell's plot and characters, she does so in service of her general attack on GWTW. In GWTW, Scarlett O'Hara often expresses disgust with and condescension towards blacks; in TWDG, Other, Scarlett's counterpart, is herself of mixed descent. In GWTW, Ashley Wilkes is the initial object of Scarlett's affection; in TWDG, he is homosexual. In GWTW, Rhett Butler does not consort with black female characters and is portrayed as the captain of his own destiny. In TWDG, Cynara ends her affair with Rhett's counterpart, R., to begin a relationship with a black Congressman; R. ends up a washed out former cad. In TWDG, nearly every black character is given some redeeming quality — whether depth, wit, cunning, beauty, strength, or courage — that their GWTW analogues lacked.

In light of this, we find it difficult to conclude that Randall simply tried to "avoid the drudgery in working up something fresh." *Campbell*, 510 U.S. at 580. It is hard to imagine how Randall could have specifically criticized GWTW without depending heavily upon copyrighted elements of that book. A parody is a work that seeks to comment upon or criticize another work by appropriating elements of the original. "Parody needs to mimic an original to make its point, and so has some claim to use the creation of its victim's (or collective victims') imagination." *Campbell*, 510 U.S. at 580-581. Thus, Randall has fully employed those conscripted elements from GWTW to make war against it. Her work, TWDG, reflects transformative value because it "can provide social benefit, by shedding light on an earlier work, and, in the process, creating a new one." *Campbell*, 510 U.S. at 579.

While "transformative use is not absolutely necessary for a finding of fair use, . . . the more transformative the new work, the less will be the significance of other factors." *Id.* In the case of TWDG, consideration of this factor certainly militates in favor of a finding of fair use, and, informs our analysis of the other factors, particularly the fourth, as discussed below.

ii. Nature of the Copyrighted Work

The second factor, the nature of the copyrighted work, recognizes that there is a hierarchy of copyright protection in which original, creative works are afforded greater protection than derivative works or factual compilations. GWTW is undoubtedly entitled to the greatest degree of protection as an original work of fiction. This factor is given little weight in parody cases, however, "since parodies almost invariably copy publicly known, expressive works." *Campbell,* 510 U.S. at 586.

iii. Amount and Substantiality of the Portion Used

The third fair-use factor is "the amount and substantiality of the portion used in relation to the copyrighted work as a whole." §107(3). It is at this point that parody presents uniquely difficult problems for courts in the fair-use context, for "parody's humor, or in any event its comment, necessarily springs from recognizable allusion to its object through distorted imitation. . . . When parody takes aim at a particular original work, the parody must be able to 'conjure up' at least enough of that original to make the object of its critical wit recognizable." *Campbell,* 510 U.S. at 588. Once enough has been taken to "conjure up" the original in the minds of the readership, any further taking must specifically serve the new work's parodic aims.

GWTW is one of the most famous, popular, and enduring American novels ever written. Given the fame of the work and its primary characters, SunTrust argues that very little reference is required to conjure up GWTW. As we have already indicated in our discussion of substantial similarity, TWDG appropriates a substantial portion of the protected elements of GWTW. Houghton Mifflin argues that TWDG takes nothing from GWTW that does not serve a parodic purpose, the crux of the argument being that a large number of characters had to be taken from GWTW because each represents a different ideal or stereotype that requires commentary, and that the work as a whole could not be adequately commented upon without revisiting substantial portions of the plot, including its most famous scenes.

There are numerous instances in which TWDG appropriates elements of GWTW and then transforms them for the purpose of commentary. TWDG uses several of GWTW's most famous lines, but vests them with a completely new significance. For example, the final lines of GWTW, "Tomorrow, I'll think of some way to get him back. After all, tomorrow is another day," are transformed in TWDG into "For all those we love for whom tomorrow will not be another day, we send the sweet prayer of resting in peace."

On the other hand, however, we are told that not all of TWDG's takings from GWTW are clearly justified as commentary. We have already determined that TWDG is a parody, but not every parody is a fair use. SunTrust contends that TWDG, at least at the margins, takes more of the protected elements of GWTW than was necessary to serve a parodic function.

For example, in a sworn declaration to the district court, Randall stated that she needed to reference the scene from GWTW in which Jeems is given to the Tarleton twins as a birthday present because she considers it "perhaps the single most repellent paragraph in Margaret Mitchell's novel: a black child given to two white children as a birthday present . . . as if the buying and selling of children thus had no moral significance." Clearly, such a scene is fair game for criticism. However, in this instance, SunTrust argues that TWDG goes beyond commentary on the occurrence itself, appropriating such nonrelevant details as the fact that the twins had red hair and were killed at Gettysburg. There are several other scenes from GWTW, such as the incident in which Scarlett threw a vase at Ashley while Rhett was hidden on the couch, that are retold or alluded to without serving any apparent parodic purpose. Similar taking of the descriptions of characters and the minor details of their histories and interactions that arguably are not essential to the parodic purpose of the work recur throughout. . . . But we must determine whether the use is fair. In doing so, we are reminded that literary relevance is a highly subjective analysis ill-suited for judicial inquiry. Thus we are presented with conflicting and opposing arguments relative to the amount taken and whether it was too much or a necessary amount.

The Supreme Court in *Campbell* did not require that parodists take the bare minimum amount of copyright material necessary to conjure up the original work. Parody "must be able to conjure up *at least* enough of [the] original to make the object of its critical wit recognizable." *Campbell*, 510 U.S. at 588.

A use does not necessarily become infringing the moment it does more than simply conjure up another work. Rather, "once enough has been taken to assure identification, how much more is reasonable will depend, say [1] on the extent to which the [work's] *overriding purpose and character is to parody* the original or, in contrast [2] the likelihood that the parody may serve as *a market substitute* for the original." *Campbell*, 510 U.S. at 588. As to the first point, it is manifest that TWDG's *raison d'etre* is to parody GWTW. The second point indicates that any material we suspect is "extraneous" to the parody is unlawful only if it negatively effects the potential market for or value of the original copyright. Based upon this record at this juncture, we cannot determine in any conclusive way whether " 'the quantity and value of the materials used' are reasonable in relation to the purpose of the copying." *Id.* at 586.

iv. Effect on the Market Value of the Original

The final fair-use factor requires us to consider the effect that the publication of TWDG will have on the market for or value of SunTrust's copyright in GWTW, including the potential harm it may cause to the market for derivative works based on GWTW. . . . "The only harm to derivatives that need concern us . . . is the harm of market substitution. The fact that a parody may impair the market for derivative uses by the very effectiveness of its critical commentary is no more relevant under copyright that the like threat to the original market." *Campbell*, 510 U.S. at 593.

As for the potential market, SunTrust proffered evidence in the district court of the value of its copyright in GWTW. Several derivative works of GWTW have been authorized, including the famous movie of the same name and a book titled *Scarlett: The Sequel.* GWTW and the derivative works based upon it have generated millions of dollars for the copyright holders. SunTrust has negotiated an agreement with

> **CONTEXT**
>
> In the Woody Allen film *Midnight in Paris*, the main character, Gil Pender, quotes a line from William Faulkner's book, *Requiem for a Nun*. In the book, the attorney Gavin Stevens at one point says: "The past is never dead. In fact it's not even past." In the film, Pender says: "The past is not dead. Actually, it's not even past. You know who said that? Faulkner, and he was right. I met him too. I ran into him at a dinner party." The owner of the Faulkner literary rights sued Sony Picture Classics, the studio behind *Midnight in Paris*, for copyright infringement. The federal district court granted Sony's motion to dismiss, holding that the film's quotation constituted fair use. "How Hollywood's flattering and artful use of literary allusion is a point of litigation, not celebration, is beyond this court's comprehension. The court, in its appreciation for both William Faulkner as well as the homage paid him in Woody Allen's film, is more likely to suppose that the film indeed helped the plaintiff and the market value of *Requiem* if it had any effect at all." *Faulkner Literary Rights, LLC v. Sony Pictures Classics*, ___ F. Supp. 2d ___ (N.D. Miss. 2013).

St. Martin's Press permitting it to produce another derivative work based on GWTW, a privilege for which St. Martin's paid "well into seven figures." Part of this agreement was that SunTrust would not authorize any other derivative works prior to the publication of St. Martin's book.

An examination of the record, with its limited development as to relevant market harm due to the preliminary injunction status of the case, discloses that SunTrust focuses on the value of GWTW and its derivatives, but fails to address and offers little evidence or argument to demonstrate that TWDG would supplant demand for SunTrust's licensed derivatives. However, the Supreme Court and other appeals courts have made clear that, particularly in cases of parody, evidence of harm to the potential market for or value of the original copyright is crucial to a fair use determination. . . .

In contrast, the evidence proffered in support of the fair use defense specifically and correctly focused on market substitution and demonstrates why Randall's book is unlikely to displace sales of GWTW. Thus, we conclude, based on the current record, that SunTrust's evidence falls far short of establishing that TWDG or others like it will act as market substitutes for GWTW or will significantly harm its derivatives. Accordingly, the fourth fair use factor weighs in favor of TWDG.

c. *Summary of the Merits.*

We reject the district court's conclusion that SunTrust has established its likelihood of success on the merits. To the contrary, based upon our analysis of the fair use factors we find, at this juncture, TWDG is entitled to a fair-use defense.

Problems

1. Research articles. In *American Geophysical Union v. Texaco Inc.*, 60 F.3d 913 (2d Cir. 1994), the Second Circuit found that Texaco had not engaged in a fair use when it photocopied articles in scientific journals for use by its 400 to 500 research scientists. The scientists would review copies of journals and arrange to photocopy whole articles to be placed in file drawers until needed. The court determined that, although scholars generally are not paid for the articles they produce in scholarly journals, the journals themselves lost income they would have garnered had Texaco negotiated licensing fees with the journal publishers or purchased enough copies for use by its scientists who wanted to archive copies. Although the court considered Texaco's for-profit nature to be relevant, it did not view this fact alone to be determinative of the outcome of the case. Universities and law schools routinely arrange to photocopy or scan scholarly articles for both archival and current use by faculty members. Does this constitute a fair use?

2. **Space shifting.** If you have a music file on your computer's hard drive, downloading it to your iPhone requires making a new digital file for storage on the device. This is plainly making a copy of the song within the meaning of the Copyright Act. Is such **space shifting** copyright infringement or protected fair use? *See Recording Industry Associates of America v. Diamond Multimedia System*, 180 F.3d 1072, 1079 (9th Cir. 1999) (finding space shifting among a single user's multiple devices to constitute a form of copying that is protected as fair use).

3. **Fan fiction.** Many fans of particular books, movies, or television shows like to write stories involving the characters and/or the worlds created by the authors of those works. Some of these works are parodies, but many are more a form of homage to the original work. This work is sometimes published on the Internet and shared among amateurs. A major center of this work is *http://www.fanfiction.net*, a web site that publishes this fiction and, like so many web sites, contains advertisements for products. Copyright extends to "derivative works," 17 U.S.C. §§103, 106, which are defined as "work based upon one or more preexisting works, such as a translation, musical arrangement, dramatization, fictionalization, motion picture version, sound recording, art reproduction, abridgment, condensation, or any other form in which a work may be recast, transformed, or adapted," *id.* §101. Fan fiction may be a derivative work and may well violate the *Copyright Act. But see Litchfield v. Spielberg*, 736 F.2d 1352 (9th Cir. 1984) (a work is not derivative unless the amount of copying from the original is substantial). Some authors vigilantly police such uses while others are happy to have their fans imagine new stories involving the worlds and characters they created.

a. When these derivative works are published on a web site like Fanfiction.net, do they constitute a fair use of the copyrighted work? *See* Aaron Schwabach, *The Harry Potter Lexicon and the World of Fandom: Fan Fiction, Outsider Works, and Copyright*, 70 U. Pitt. L. Rev. 387 (2009) (exploring this question); Rebecca Tushnet, *Using Law and Identity to Script Cultural Production: Legal Fictions: Copyright, Fan Fiction, and a New Common Law*, 17 Loy. L.A. Ent. L.J. 651 (1997) (arguing that fan fiction should be legally protected as fair use).

b. In 2000, a fan of the *Harry Potter* series, Steven Vander Ark, created an online encyclopedia about the *Harry Potter* books, called *The Harry Potter Lexicon*, *http://www.hp-lexicon.org*. Although J.K. Rowling was a fan of the web site, when Vander Ark made plans to publish the encyclopedia in book form, as an A-to-Z guide to the creatures, characters, objects, events, and places that exist in the world of *Harry Potter*, she sued to enjoin the publication because she was planning to publish her own encyclopedia about the series. The court found the encyclopedia to violate Rowling's copyright because it copied so much of the original works. "Most of the Lexicon's 2,437 entries contain direct quotations or paraphrases, plot details, or summaries of scenes from one or more of the *Harry Potter* novels. Although hundreds of pages or thousands of fictional facts may amount to only a fraction of the seven-book series, this quantum of copying is sufficient to support a finding of substantial similarity where the copied expression is entirely the product of the original author's imagination and creation." *Warner Bros. Entertainment, Inc. & J.K. Rowling v. RDR Books*, 575 F. Supp. 2d 513, 535 (S.D.N.Y. 2008). The court found the encyclopedia not to be a derivative work because it does not "retell the story of *Harry Potter,* but instead gives the copyrighted material another purpose," and thus does not "represent the original works of authorship." *Id.* at 539. However, the court found the encyclopedia not to constitute a fair use. Although the "purpose and character" of the encyclopedia were "transformative," the "commercial nature" of the intended publication counted heavily against finding a fair use, and it often copied more than necessary for its informative purposes and thus "appropriates too much of Rowling's creative work for its purposes as a reference guide." *Id.* at 553. Did the court decide the case correctly? When is an encyclopedia like the *Harry Potter Lexicon* a legitimate "fair use"?

§4.3 Moral Rights

In many European countries, artists have the right to prevent the mutilation or alteration of their artworks after the works have been sold. This legally protected interest is called **moral right**, or *droit moral.* Artworks protected by moral rights are effectively encumbered by a covenant, which "runs with" the artwork when it is sold, creating an obligation on the part of the owner not to mutilate the artwork so as to destroy the artist's vision. Such rights are generally inalienable; they interpret the interest in preserving the artist's vision as a collective good that benefits the community and that cannot be traded away.

Until recently, moral rights were not recognized in the United States. *See, e.g., Vargas v. Esquire*, 164 F.2d 522 (7th Cir. 1947); *Crimi v. Rutger's Presbyterian Church*, 89 N.Y.S.2d 813 (Sup. Ct. 1949). In 1979, however, California passed the *California Art Preservation Act*, Cal. Civ. Code §§987-989, which permits injunctive relief, damages, and attorneys' fees for intentional or threatened mutilation or alteration of an artist's work. A bill was passed in New York in 1983 prohibiting alterations that would harm the artist's reputation. *New York Artists' Authorship Rights Act*, N.Y. Arts & Cult. Aff. Law §14.03(1). Moral rights legislation has been passed in at least nine states. *See, e.g.*, Conn. Gen. Stat. §42-116; Mass. Gen. Laws ch. 231, §85S; Pa. Stat. tit. 73, §§2101-2110; R.I. Gen. Laws §5-62-2(e); 3 M. Nimmer & D. Nimmer, *Nimmer on Copyright* §8D.02[A] (2011).

In 1990, Congress passed the *Visual Artists Rights Act* (VARA), 17 U.S.C. §§101, 106a, and 113, granting living artists rights to protect "works of visual art" unless the works are "made for hire," *id.* §101(B), or are "applied art," meaning "ornamentation or decoration that is affixed to otherwise utilitarian objects," *Carter v. Helmsley-Spear, Inc.*, 71 F.3d 77, 84-85 (2d Cir. 1995). The statute grants the artist the right to prevent "any intentional distortion, mutilation, or other modification of [the] work which would be prejudicial to his or her honor or reputation," 17 U.S.C. §106a(a)(3)(A), and to prevent any intentional or grossly negligent destruction of a work of "recognized stature," *id.* §106a(a)(3)(B). Owners of buildings can remove works of art, such as murals, floor mosaics, or architectural components, if they can do so without destroying or mutilating them, so long as they make a good faith effort to notify the artist. *Id.* §113(d)(2). The artist's right to prevent mutilation of the work that is part of a building is lost if the artist fails to remove the work or pay for its removal. If the artwork cannot be removed without destroying it, the artist who has not waived her right to do so may have the power to prevent destruction of the work and therefore may have the extraordinary power to control whether the building is renovated, destroyed, or redeveloped. Building developers ordinarily require artists to waive their rights to prevent destruction of the work when they are embedded in a building such that they cannot be removed without destroying them. Note that only works of "recognized stature" are protected from destruction. *Cf. Phillips v. Pembroke Real Estate, Inc.*, 288 F. Supp. 2d 89 (D. Mass. 2003) (VARA does not prevent removal of sculptures from a public park, even though they were specifically designed for that terrain and location, and the artist thought separation from the setting would destroy the artistic integrity of the sculptures); *Phillips v. Pembroke Real Estate, Inc.*, 819 N.E.2d 579 (Mass. 2004) (same result under *Massachusetts Art Preservation Act*, Mass. Gen. Laws ch. 231, §85S).

§5 PATENT LAW

Patent law grants inventors of processes, machines, and compositions of matter a monopoly over their inventions for up to 20 years. 35 U.S.C. §101 *et seq.* Unlike copyrights, which exist from the moment a work is first fixed into a tangible form, patents are granted by a government agency, the Patent and Trademark Office (PTO), after application by the inventor. The patent will be granted only if five requirements are met: (1) the subject matter of the invention must be patentable, *i.e.*, a "machine," method of "manufacture," or "composition of matter," 35 U.S.C. §101; and the invention must be (2) novel, 35 U.S.C. §102; (3) nonobvious, 35 U.S.C. §103; (4) useful, 35 U.S.C §101; and (5) fully and particularly described, 35 U.S.C. §112.

§5.1 Patentability

Association for Molecular Pathology v. Myriad Genetics, Inc.

133 S. Ct. 2107 (U.S. 2013)

Justice Clarence Thomas delivered the opinion of the Court.

I.

The human genome consists of approximately 22,000 genes packed into 23 pairs of chromosomes. Each gene is encoded as DNA, which takes the shape of the familiar "double helix" that Doctors James Watson and Francis Crick first described in 1953. Each "cross-bar" in the DNA helix consists of two chemically joined nucleotides. The possible nucleotides are adenine (A), thymine (T), cytosine (C), and guanine (G), each of which binds naturally with another nucleotide: A pairs with T; C pairs with G. The nucleotide cross-bars are chemically connected to a sugar-phosphate backbone that forms the outside framework of the DNA helix. Sequences of DNA nucleotides contain the information necessary to create strings of amino acids, which in turn are used in the body to build proteins. Only some DNA nucleotides, however, code for amino acids; these nucleotides are known as "exons." Nucleotides that do not code for amino acids, in contrast, are known as "introns."

Creation of proteins from DNA involves two principal steps, known as transcription and translation. In transcription, the bonds between DNA nucleotides separate, and the DNA helix unwinds into two single strands. A single strand is used as a template to create a complementary ribonucleic acid (RNA) strand. The nucleotides on the DNA strand pair naturally with their counterparts, with the exception that RNA uses the nucleotide base uracil (U) instead of thymine (T). Transcription results in a single strand RNA molecule, known as pre-RNA, whose nucleotides form an inverse image of the DNA strand from which it was created. Pre-RNA still contains nucleotides corresponding to both the exons and introns in the DNA molecule. The pre-RNA is then naturally "spliced" by the physical removal of the introns. The resulting product is a strand of RNA that contains nucleotides corresponding only to the exons from the original DNA strand. The exons-only strand is known as messenger RNA (mRNA), which creates amino acids through translation. In translation, cellular structures known as ribosomes read each set of three nucleotides, known as codons, in the mRNA. Each codon either tells the ribosomes which of the 20 possible amino acids to synthesize or provides a stop signal that ends amino acid production.

DNA's informational sequences and the processes that create mRNA, amino acids, and proteins occur naturally within cells. Scientists can, however, extract DNA from cells using well known laboratory methods. These methods allow scientists to isolate specific segments of DNA — for instance, a particular gene or part of a gene — which can then be further studied, manipulated, or used. It is also possible to create DNA synthetically through processes similarly well known in the field of genetics. One such method begins with an mRNA molecule and uses the natural bonding properties of nucleotides to create a new, synthetic DNA molecule. The result is the inverse of the mRNA's inverse image of the original DNA, with one important distinction: Because the natural creation of mRNA involves splicing that removes introns, the synthetic DNA created from mRNA also contains only the exon sequences. This synthetic DNA created in the laboratory from mRNA is known as complementary DNA (cDNA).

This case involves patents filed by Myriad. Myriad discovered the precise location and sequence of what are now known as the BRCA1 and BRCA2 genes. Mutations in these genes can dramatically increase an individual's risk of developing breast and ovarian cancer. The average American woman has a 12- to 13-percent risk of developing breast cancer, but for women with certain genetic mutations, the risk can range between 50 and 80 percent for breast cancer and between 20 and 50 percent for ovarian cancer. Before Myriad's discovery of the BRCA1 and BRCA2 genes, scientists knew that heredity played a role in establishing a woman's risk of developing breast and ovarian cancer, but they did not know which genes were associated with those cancers.

Myriad identified the exact location of the BRCA1 and BRCA2 genes on chromosomes 17 and 13. That information, in turn, enabled Myriad to develop medical tests that are useful for detecting mutations in a patient's BRCA1 and BRCA2 genes and thereby assessing whether the patient has an increased risk of cancer.

Once it found the location and sequence of the BRCA1 and BRCA2 genes, Myriad sought and obtained a number of patents. Myriad's patents would, if valid, give it the exclusive right to isolate an individual's BRCA1 and BRCA2 genes (or any strand of 15 or more nucleotides within the genes) by breaking the covalent bonds that connect the DNA to the rest of the individual's genome. The patents would also give Myriad the exclusive right to synthetically create BRCA cDNA. In Myriad's view, manipulating BRCA DNA in either of these fashions triggers its "right to exclude others from making" its patented composition of matter under the Patent Act. 35 U.S.C. §154(a)(1); see also §271(a) ("[W]hoever without authority makes . . . any patented invention . . . infringes the patent").

But isolation is necessary to conduct genetic testing, and Myriad was not the only entity to offer BRCA testing after it discovered the genes. The University of Pennsylvania's Genetic Diagnostic Laboratory (GDL) and others provided genetic testing services to women. Petitioner Dr. Harry Ostrer, then a researcher at New York University School of Medicine, routinely sent his patients' DNA samples to GDL for testing. After learning of GDL's testing and Ostrer's activities, Myriad sent letters to them asserting that the genetic testing infringed Myriad's patents. In response, GDL agreed to stop testing and informed Ostrer that it would no longer accept patient samples. Myriad also filed patent infringement suits against other entities that performed BRCA testing, resulting in settlements in which the defendants agreed to cease all allegedly infringing activity. Myriad, thus, solidified its position as the only entity providing BRCA testing.

Some years later, petitioner Ostrer, along with medical patients, advocacy groups, and other doctors, filed this lawsuit seeking a declaration that Myriad's patents are invalid under 35 U.S.C. §101.

II

Section 101 of the Patent Act provides:

> "Whoever invents or discovers any new and useful . . . composition of matter, or any new and useful improvement thereof, may obtain a patent therefor, subject to the conditions and requirements of this title." 35 U.S.C. §101.

We have "long held that this provision contains an important implicit exception[:] Laws of nature, natural phenomena, and abstract ideas are not patentable." *Mayo*, 566 U.S., at ___ (slip op., at 1) (internal quotation marks and brackets omitted). Rather, "'they are the basic tools of scientific and technological work'" that lie beyond the domain of patent protection. *Id.*, at ___ (slip op., at 2). As the Court has explained, without this exception, there would be considerable danger that the grant of patents would "tie up" the use of such tools and thereby "inhibit future innovation premised upon them." *Id.*, at ___ (slip op., at 17). This would be at odds with the very point of patents, which exist to promote creation. *Diamond v. Chakrabarty,* 447 U.S. 303 (1980) (Products of nature are not created, and " 'manifestations . . . of nature [are] free to all men and reserved exclusively to none' ").

The rule against patents on naturally occurring things is not without limits, however, for "all inventions at some level embody, use, reflect, rest upon, or apply laws of nature, natural phenomena, or abstract ideas," and "too broad an interpretation of this exclusionary principle could eviscerate patent law." 566 U.S., at ___ (slip op., at 2). As we have recognized before, patent protection strikes a delicate balance between creating "incentives that lead to creation, invention, and discovery" and "imped[ing] the flow of information that might permit, indeed spur, invention." *Id.*, at ___ (slip op., at 23). We must apply this well-established standard to determine whether Myriad's patents claim any "new and useful . . . composition of matter," §101, or instead claim naturally occurring phenomena.

It is undisputed that Myriad did not create or alter any of the genetic information encoded in the BRCA1 and BRCA2 genes. The location and order of the nucleotides existed in nature before Myriad found them. Nor did Myriad create or alter the genetic structure of DNA. Instead, Myriad's principal contribution was uncovering the precise location and genetic sequence of the BRCA1 and BRCA2 genes within chromosomes 17 and 13. The question is whether this renders the genes patentable.

Myriad recognizes that our decision in *Chakrabarty* is central to this inquiry. In *Chakrabarty,* scientists added four plasmids to a bacterium, which enabled it to break down various components of crude oil. The Court held that the modified bacterium was patentable. It explained that the patent claim was "not to a hitherto unknown natural phenomenon, but to a nonnaturally occurring manufacture or composition of matter—a product of human ingenuity 'having a distinctive name, character [and] use.' " The *Chakrabarty* bacterium was new "with markedly different characteristics from any found in nature," 447 U.S., at 310, due to the additional plasmids and resultant "capacity for degrading oil." In this case, by contrast, Myriad did not create anything. To be sure, it found an important and useful gene, but separating that gene from its surrounding genetic material is not an act of invention.

Groundbreaking, innovative, or even brilliant discovery does not by itself satisfy the §101 inquiry. In *Funk Brothers Seed Co. v. Kalo Inoculant Co.*, 333 U.S. 127 (1948), this Court considered a composition patent that claimed a mixture of naturally occurring strains of bacteria that helped leguminous plants take nitrogen from the air and fix it in the soil. *Id.*, at 128-129. The ability of the bacteria to fix nitrogen was well known, and farmers commonly "inoculated" their crops with them to improve soil nitrogen levels. But farmers could not use the same inoculant for all crops, both because plants use different bacteria and because certain bacteria inhibit each other. *Id.*, at 129-130. Upon learning that several nitrogen-fixing bacteria did not inhibit each other, however, the patent applicant combined them into a single inoculant and obtained a patent.

Id., at 130. The Court held that the composition was not patent eligible because the patent holder did not alter the bacteria in any way. *Id.*, at 132 ("There is no way in which we could call [the bacteria mixture a product of invention] unless we borrowed invention from the discovery of the natural principle itself"). His patent claim thus fell squarely within the law of nature exception. So do Myriad's. Myriad found the location of the BRCA1 and BRCA2 genes, but that discovery, by itself, does not render the BRCA genes "new . . . composition[s] of matter," §101, that are patent eligible.

Many of Myriad's patent descriptions simply detail the "iterative process" of discovery by which Myriad narrowed the possible locations for the gene sequences that it sought.[4] Myriad seeks to import these extensive research efforts into the §101 patent-eligibility inquiry. But extensive effort alone is insufficient to satisfy the demands of §101.

Nor are Myriad's claims saved by the fact that isolating DNA from the human genome severs chemical bonds and thereby creates a nonnaturally occurring molecule. Myriad's claims are simply not expressed in terms of chemical composition, nor do they rely in any way on the chemical changes that result from the isolation of a particular section of DNA. Instead, the claims understandably focus on the genetic information encoded in the BRCA1 and BRCA2 genes. If the patents depended upon the creation of a unique molecule, then a would-be infringer could arguably avoid at least Myriad's patent claims on entire genes by isolating a DNA sequence that included both the BRCA1 or BRCA2 gene and one additional nucleotide pair. Such a molecule would not be chemically identical to the molecule "invented" by Myriad. But Myriad obviously would resist that outcome because its claim is concerned primarily with the information contained in the genetic sequence, not with the specific chemical composition of a particular molecule.

cDNA does not present the same obstacles to patentability as naturally occurring, isolated DNA segments. As already explained, creation of a cDNA sequence from mRNA results in an exons-only molecule that is not naturally occurring. Petitioners concede that cDNA differs from natural DNA in that "the non-coding regions have been removed." They nevertheless argue that cDNA is not patent eligible because "[t]he nucleotide sequence of cDNA is dictated by nature, not by the lab technician." That may be so, but the lab technician unquestionably creates something new when cDNA is made. cDNA retains the naturally occurring exons of DNA, but it

CONTEXT

Immediately after the Supreme Court's decision in *Myriad*, several companies announced plans to offer their own BRCA tests at prices substantially lower than Myriad's $4,040. One company, Gene by Gene, Ltd., offered tests priced at $995. Myriad responded by suing the companies under patent claims that had not been at issue in the Supreme Court litigation. Some commentators saw the move as a delaying tactic that might allow Myriad to enjoy a few more months of monopoly pricing.

4. Myriad first identified groups of relatives with a history of breast cancer (some of whom also had developed ovarian cancer); because these individuals were related, scientists knew that it was more likely that their diseases were the result of genetic predisposition rather than other factors. Myriad compared sections of their chromosomes, looking for shared genetic abnormalities not found in the general population. It was that process which eventually enabled Myriad to determine where in the genetic sequence the BRCA1 and BRCA2 genes reside.

is distinct from the DNA from which it was derived. As a result, cDNA is not a "product of nature" and is patent eligible under §101, except insofar as very short series of DNA may have no intervening introns to remove when creating cDNA. In that situation, a short strand of cDNA may be indistinguishable from natural DNA.[5]

III

It is important to note what is not implicated by this decision. First, there are no method claims before this Court. Had Myriad created an innovative method of manipulating genes while searching for the BRCA1 and BRCA2 genes, it could possibly have sought a method patent. But the processes used by Myriad to isolate DNA were well understood by geneticists at the time of Myriad's patents "were well understood, widely used, and fairly uniform insofar as any scientist engaged in the search for a gene would likely have utilized a similar approach," 702 F. Supp. 2d, at 202-203, and are not at issue in this case.

Similarly, this case does not involve patents on new applications of knowledge about the BRCA1 and BRCA2 genes. Judge Bryson aptly noted that, "[a]s the first party with knowledge of the [BRCA1 and BRCA2] sequences, Myriad was in an excellent position to claim applications of that knowledge. Many of its unchallenged claims are limited to such applications." 689 F.3d, at 1349.

Nor do we consider the patentability of DNA in which the order of the naturally occurring nucleotides has been altered. Scientific alteration of the genetic code presents a different inquiry, and we express no opinion about the application of §101 to such endeavors. We merely hold that genes and the information they encode are not patent eligible under §101 simply because they have been isolated from the surrounding genetic material.

Juicy Whip, Inc. v. Orange Bang, Inc.

185 F.3d 1364 (Fed. Cir. 1999)

WILLIAM C. BRYSON, Circuit Judge.

The district court in this case held a patent invalid for lack of utility on the ground that the patented invention was designed to deceive customers by imitating another product and thereby increasing sales of a particular good. We reverse and remand.

I

Juicy Whip, Inc., is the assignee of United States Patent No. 5,575,405, which is entitled "Post-Mix Beverage Dispenser With an Associated Simulated Display of Beverage." A "post-mix" beverage dispenser stores beverage syrup concentrate and water in separate locations until the beverage is ready to be dispensed. The syrup and water are mixed together immediately before the beverage is dispensed, which is usually after the consumer requests the beverage. In contrast, in a "pre-mix" beverage

5. We express no opinion whether cDNA satisfies the other statutory requirements of patentability. *See, e.g.,* 35 U.S.C. §§102, 103, and 112.

dispenser, the syrup concentrate and water are pre-mixed and the beverage is stored in a display reservoir bowl until it is ready to be dispensed. The display bowl is said to stimulate impulse buying by providing the consumer with a visual beverage display. A pre-mix display bowl, however, has a limited capacity and is subject to contamination by bacteria. It therefore must be refilled and cleaned frequently.

The invention claimed in the '405 patent is a post-mix beverage dispenser that is designed to look like a pre-mix beverage dispenser. The claims require the post-mix dispenser to have a transparent bowl that is filled with a fluid that simulates the appearance of the dispensed beverage and is resistant to bacterial growth. The claims also require that the dispenser create the visual impression that the bowl is the principal source of the dispensed beverage, although in fact the beverage is mixed immediately before it is dispensed, as in conventional post-mix dispensers.

Juicy Whip sued defendants Orange Bang, Inc., and Unique Beverage Dispensers, Inc., (collectively, "Orange Bang") in the United States District Court for the Central District of California, alleging that they were infringing the claims of the '405 patent. Orange Bang moved for summary judgment of invalidity, and the district court granted Orange Bang's motion on the ground that the invention lacked utility and thus was unpatentable under 35 U.S.C. §101.

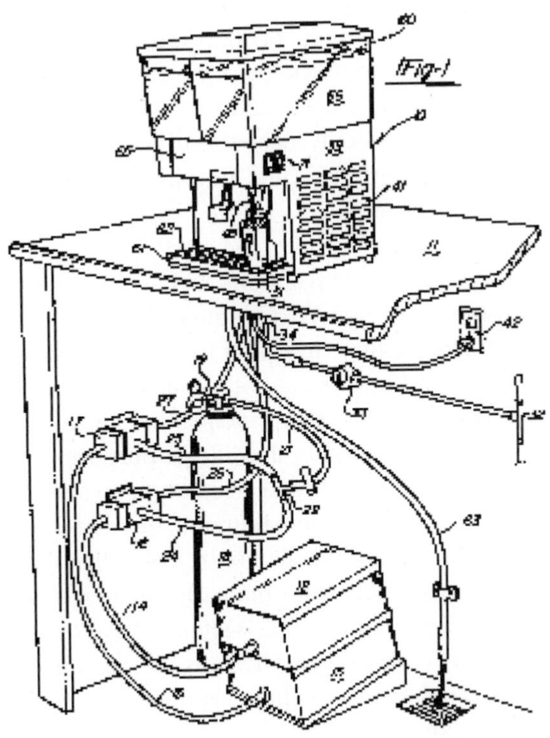

Fig. 1

The court concluded that the invention lacked utility because its purpose was to increase sales by deception, i.e., through imitation of another product. The court explained that the purpose of the invention "is to create an illusion, whereby customers believe that the fluid contained in the bowl is the actual beverage that they are receiving, when of course it is not." Although the court acknowledged Juicy Whip's argument that the invention provides an accurate representation of the dispensed beverage for the consumer's benefit while eliminating the need for retailers to clean their display bowls, the court concluded that those claimed reasons for the patent's utility "are not independent of its deceptive purpose, and are thus insufficient to raise a disputed factual issue to present to a jury." The court further held that the invention lacked utility because it "improves the prior art only to the extent that it increases the salability of beverages dispensed from post-mix dispensers"; an invention lacks utility, the court stated, if it confers no benefit to the public other than the opportunity for making a product more salable. Finally, the court ruled that the invention lacked utility because it "is merely an imitation of the pre-mix dispenser," and thus does not constitute a new and useful machine.

II

Section 101 of the Patent Act of 1952, 35 U.S.C. §101, provides that "[w]hoever invents or discovers any new and useful process, machine, manufacture, or composition of matter, or any new and useful improvement thereof," may obtain a patent on the invention or discovery. The threshold of utility is not high: An invention is "useful" under section 101 if it is capable of providing some identifiable benefit. *See Brooktree Corp. v. Advanced Micro Devices, Inc.*, 977 F.2d 1555, 1571 (Fed. Cir. 1992) ("To violate §101 the claimed device must be totally incapable of achieving a useful result"); *Fuller v. Berger*, 120 F. 274, 275 (7th Cir. 1903) (test for utility is whether invention "is incapable of serving any beneficial end").

To be sure, since Justice Story's opinion in *Lowell v. Lewis*, 15 F. Cas. 1018 (C.C.D. Mass. 1817), it has been stated that inventions that are "injurious to the well-being, good policy, or sound morals of society" are unpatentable. As examples of such inventions, Justice Story listed "a new invention to poison people, or to promote debauchery, or to facilitate private assassination." *Id.* at 1019. Courts have continued to recite Justice Story's formulation, but the principle that inventions are invalid if they are principally designed to serve immoral or illegal purposes has not been applied broadly in recent years. For example, years ago courts invalidated patents on gambling devices on the ground that they were immoral, but that is no longer the law.

In holding the patent in this case invalid for lack of utility, the district court relied on two Second Circuit cases dating from the early years of this century, *Rickard v. Du Bon*, 103 F. 868 (2d Cir. 1900), and *Scott & Williams v. Aristo Hosiery Co.*, 7 F.2d 1003 (2d Cir. 1925). In the *Rickard* case, the court held invalid a patent on a process for treating tobacco plants to make their leaves appear spotted. At the time of the invention, according to the court, cigar smokers considered cigars with spotted wrappers to be of superior quality, and the invention was designed to make unspotted tobacco leaves appear to be of the spotted—and thus more desirable—type. The court noted that the invention did not promote the burning quality of the leaf or improve its quality in any way; "the only effect, if not the only object, of such treatment, is to spot the tobacco, and counterfeit the leaf spotted by natural causes." 103 F. at 869.

The *Aristo Hosiery* case concerned a patent claiming a seamless stocking with a structure on the back of the stocking that imitated a seamed stocking. The imitation was commercially useful because at the time of the invention many consumers regarded seams in stockings as an indication of higher quality. The court noted that the imitation seam did not "change or improve the structure or the utility of the article," and that the record in the case justified the conclusion that true seamed stockings were superior to the seamless stockings that were the subject of the patent. *See Aristo Hosiery*, 7 F.2d at 1004. "At best," the court stated, "the seamless stocking has imitation marks for the purposes of deception, and the idea prevails that with such imitation the article is more salable." *Id.* That was not enough, the court concluded, to render the invention patentable.

We decline to follow *Rickard* and *Aristo Hosiery*, as we do not regard them as representing the correct view of the doctrine of utility under the Patent Act of 1952. The fact that one product can be altered to make it look like another is in itself a specific benefit sufficient to satisfy the statutory requirement of utility.

It is not at all unusual for a product to be designed to appear to viewers to be something it is not. For example, cubic zirconium is designed to simulate a diamond, imitation gold leaf is designed to imitate real gold leaf, synthetic fabrics are designed to simulate expensive natural fabrics, and imitation leather is designed to look like real leather. In each case, the invention of the product or process that makes such imitation possible has "utility" within the meaning of the patent statute, and indeed there are numerous patents directed toward making one product imitate another. *See, e.g.*, U.S. Pat. No. 5,762,968 (method for producing imitation grill marks on food without using heat); U.S. Pat. No. 5,899,038 (laminated flooring imitating wood); U.S. Pat. No. 5,571,545 (imitation hamburger). Much of the value of such products resides in the fact that they appear to be something they are not. Thus, in this case the claimed post-mix dispenser meets the statutory requirement of utility by embodying the features of a post-mix dispenser while imitating the visual appearance of a pre-mix dispenser.

The fact that customers may believe they are receiving fluid directly from the display tank does not deprive the invention of utility. Orange Bang has not argued that it is unlawful to display a representation of the beverage in the manner that fluid is displayed in the reservoir of the invention, even though the fluid is not what the customer will actually receive. Moreover, even if the use of a reservoir containing fluid that is not dispensed is considered deceptive, that is not by itself sufficient to render the invention unpatentable. The requirement of "utility" in patent law is not a directive to the Patent and Trademark Office or the courts to serve as arbiters of deceptive trade practices. Other agencies, such as the Federal Trade Commission and the Food and Drug Administration, are assigned the task of protecting consumers from fraud and deception in the sale of food products.

Of course, Congress is free to declare particular types of inventions unpatentable for a variety of reasons, including deceptiveness. *Cf.* 42 U.S.C. §2181(a) (exempting from patent protection inventions useful solely in connection with special nuclear material or atomic weapons). Until such time as Congress does so, however, we find no basis in section 101 to hold that inventions can be ruled unpatentable for lack of utility simply because they have the capacity to fool some members of the public. The district court therefore erred in holding that the invention of the '405 patent lacks utility because it deceives the public through imitation in a manner that is designed to increase product sales.

Notes and Questions

1. Patents in living things. As the Court reaffirmed in *Myriad*, it is possible to obtain a patent in living things, such as bacteria or plant varieties. The key is that the organism not be naturally occurring. It must instead be the product of human manipulation and satisfy the general requirements of patentability. *See Diamond v. Chakrabarty*, 447 U.S. 303 (1980) (allowing a patent in genetically modified bacteria).

2. Natural phenomena, laws of nature, and abstract ideas. Why should the question whether a substance (or organism) is naturally occurring be decisive for the question of patentability? Does the distinction make sense for a Lockean theory of intellectual property? A utilitarian theory? A Hegelian theory? In addition to naturally occurring substances ("natural phenomena"), abstract principles and laws of nature are also not patentable, even when discovering them requires the investment of substantial resources and effort. *See Mayo Collaborative Services v. Prometheus Laboratories, Inc.*, 132 S. Ct. 1289 (2012). Which principles, if any, do these exclusions from patentability all share?

3. Deceptive patents. Are you convinced by the Federal Circuit's reasoning in *Juicy Whip*? If you were the lawyer for Orange Bang, how would you distinguish the examples of cubic zirconium, imitation gold leaf, and synthetic fabrics? Is the sole purpose of those products to fool consumers? Might a consumer, informed of the nature of those products, nonetheless have reasons for wanting to purchase them? Do the products in *Rickard* and *Aristo Hosiery* have more in common with the Juicy Whip machine in being aimed solely at fooling consumers? Is the shift away from Justice Story's moral approach to utility a salutary one? Is it the proper role of the PTO to evaluate whether an invention promotes "sound morals"? Is it a proper role for Congress?

4. Business methods. Until recently, it was not possible to patent a "business method" because most business and financial innovations were either considered not to be "novel" or to be unpatentable because they did not involve physical processes. However, after the Federal Circuit decided that business methods are patentable, *State Street Bank & Trust Co. v. Signature Financial Group*, 149 F.3d 1368 (Fed. Cir. 1998), the Patent Office has issued hundreds of patents covering methods of doing business.

What constitutes a "novel" and "nonobvious" business method is hard to sort out. For example, in *Amazon.com, Inc. v. Barnesandnoble.com, Inc.*, 73 F. Supp. 2d 1228 (W.D. Wash. 1999), *rev'd*, 239 F.3d 1343 (Fed. Cir. 2001), Amazon.com sued Barnesandnoble.com alleging infringement of Amazon.com's patent for a "one-click" method for placing purchase orders over the Internet. This method allowed users to place personal information with the company that it could access on later visits to allow the buyer to complete a purchase by one computer mouse click on a "buy" button. Defendant argued that the patent was invalid because the invention of this method was neither novel nor non-obvious. The trial court granted plaintiff a preliminary injunction ordering defendant to cease using a similar one-click method on its web site without plaintiff's consent. The Ninth Circuit reversed, finding that several prior methods of Internet purchasing *did* anticipate the one-click method, making it neither novel nor nonobvious. The court therefore denied a preliminary injunction and remanded the case to the trial court.

The difficulty of applying the criteria of patentability to business methods, the vagueness of many business methods patents, and questions about whether businesses really need the incentive of a patent in order to generate innovative business models has led to a great deal of dissatisfaction with business methods patents. *See, e.g.,* David S. Olson, *Taking the Utilitarian Basis for Patent Law Seriously,* 82 Temp. L. Rev. 181, 227-236 (2009). In *Bilski v. Kappos,* 130 S. Ct. 3218 (2010), the Supreme Court considered an appeal from a patent applicant whom the PTO had denied a patent for a method of hedging risk in the field of commodities trading in energy markets. The PTO had rejected the application based on the lack of patentable subject matter under §101 of the Patent Act. The Federal Circuit heard the applicant's appeal en banc and affirmed the PTO's rejection of the application. In its decision, the Federal Circuit appeared to try to hem in the business methods patent category by holding that a process would only be patentable if it (1) is tied to a particular machine or apparatus, or (2) if it transforms a particular article into a different state or thing. *See In re Bilski,* 545 F.3d 943, 959-960 (Fed. Cir. 2008). The U.S. Supreme Court rejected the Federal Circuit's exclusive "machine-or-transformation" test, concluding that it constituted an improper attempt to cabin the broad language defining the subject matter scope of patentability under §101. "Congress took this permissive approach to patent eligibility to ensure that ingenuity should receive a liberal encouragement." 130 S. Ct. at 3225 (internal quotation marks omitted). Only the longstanding (though judicially created) prohibitions on patenting "laws of nature, physical phenomena, and abstract ideas" properly limit the broad reach of §101. *See id.* Nevertheless, the Court affirmed the denial of the patent application, holding that it represented an impermissible effort to patent the abstract idea of hedging. In a sweeping and exhaustively researched opinion concurring in the judgment, Justice Stevens recounted the history and policy of patent law and argued that business methods should not be patentable at all. "The[] many costs of business method patents not only may stifle innovation," he argued, "but they are also likely to stifle competition." *Id.* at 3256-3257 (Stevens, J., concurring in the judgment).

§5.2 Patent Remedies

eBay Inc. v. MercExchange, L.L.C.

547 U.S. 388 (2006)

Justice CLARENCE THOMAS delivered the opinion of the Court.

Petitioner eBay operates a popular Internet Web site that allows private sellers to list goods they wish to sell, either through an auction or at a fixed price. Petitioner Half.

com, now a wholly owned subsidiary of eBay, operates a similar Web site. Respondent MercExchange, L.L.C., holds a number of patents, including a business method patent for an electronic market designed to facilitate the sale of goods between private individuals by establishing a central authority to promote trust among participants. *See* U.S. Patent No. 5,845,265. MercExchange sought to license its patent to eBay and Half.com, as it had previously done with other companies, but the parties failed to reach an agreement. MercExchange subsequently filed a patent infringement suit against eBay and Half.com in the United States District Court for the Eastern District of Virginia. A jury found that MercExchange's patent was valid, that eBay and Half.com had infringed that patent, and that an award of damages was appropriate.

Following the jury verdict, the District Court denied MercExchange's motion for permanent injunctive relief. 275 F. Supp. 2d 695 (2003). The Court of Appeals for the Federal Circuit reversed, applying its "general rule that courts will issue permanent injunctions against patent infringement absent exceptional circumstances." 401 F.3d 1323, 1339 (2005). We granted certiorari to determine the appropriateness of this general rule. 546 U.S. 1029 (2005).

According to well-established principles of equity, a plaintiff seeking a permanent injunction must satisfy a four-factor test before a court may grant such relief. A plaintiff must demonstrate: (1) that it has suffered an irreparable injury; (2) that remedies available at law, such as monetary damages, are inadequate to compensate for that injury; (3) that, considering the balance of hardships between the plaintiff and defendant, a remedy in equity is warranted; and (4) that the public interest would not be disserved by a permanent injunction. *See, e.g., Weinberger v. Romero-Barcelo,* 456 U.S. 305, 311-313 (1982); *Amoco Production Co. v. Gambell,* 480 U.S. 531, 542 (1987). The decision to grant or deny permanent injunctive relief is an act of equitable discretion by the district court, reviewable on appeal for abuse of discretion. *See, e.g., Romero-Barcelo,* 456 U.S., at 320.

These familiar principles apply with equal force to disputes arising under the Patent Act. As this Court has long recognized, "a major departure from the long tradition of equity practice should not be lightly implied." *Id.* Nothing in the Patent Act indicates that Congress intended such a departure. To the contrary, the Patent Act expressly provides that injunctions "may" issue "in accordance with the principles of equity." 35 U.S.C. §283.

To be sure, the Patent Act also declares that "patents shall have the attributes of personal property," §261, including "the right to exclude others from making, using, offering for sale, or selling the invention," §154(a)(1). According to the Court of Appeals, this statutory right to exclude alone justifies its general rule in favor of permanent injunctive relief. 401 F.3d, at 1338. But the creation of a right is distinct from the provision of remedies for violations of that right. Indeed, the Patent Act itself indicates that patents shall have the attributes of personal property "[s]ubject to the provisions of this title," 35 U.S.C. §261, including, presumably, the provision that injunctive relief "may" issue only "in accordance with the principles of equity," §283.

This approach is consistent with our treatment of injunctions under the Copyright Act. Like a patent owner, a copyright holder possesses "the right to exclude others from using his property." *Fox Film Corp. v. Doyal*, 286 U.S. 123, 127 (1932); *see also id.* at 127-128 ("A copyright, like a patent, is at once the equivalent given by the public for benefits bestowed by the genius and meditations and skill of individuals and the incentive to further efforts for the same important objects" (internal quotation marks omitted)). Like the Patent Act, the Copyright Act provides that courts "may" grant injunctive relief "on such terms as it may deem reasonable to prevent or restrain infringement of a copyright." 17 U.S.C. §502(a). And as in our decision today, this Court has consistently rejected invitations to replace traditional equitable considerations with a rule that an injunction automatically follows a determination that a copyright has been infringed.

Neither the District Court nor the Court of Appeals below fairly applied these traditional equitable principles in deciding respondent's motion for a permanent injunction. Although the District Court recited the traditional four-factor test, 275 F. Supp. 2d, at 711, it appeared to adopt certain expansive principles suggesting that injunctive relief could not issue in a broad swath of cases. Most notably, it concluded that a "plaintiff's willingness to license its patents" and "its lack of commercial activity in practicing the patents" would be sufficient to establish that the patent holder would not suffer irreparable harm if an injunction did not issue. *Id.*, at 712. But traditional equitable principles do not permit such broad classifications. The court's categorical rule is also in tension with *Continental Paper Bag Co. v. Eastern Paper Bag Co.*, 210 U.S. 405, 422-430 (1908), which rejected the contention that a court of equity has no jurisdiction to grant injunctive relief to a patent holder who has unreasonably declined to use the patent.

In reversing the District Court, the Court of Appeals departed in the opposite direction from the four-factor test. The court articulated a "general rule," unique to patent disputes, "that a permanent injunction will issue once infringement and validity have been adjudged." 401 F.3d, at 1338. Just as the District Court erred in its categorical denial of injunctive relief, the Court of Appeals erred in its categorical grant of such relief.

Because we conclude that neither court below correctly applied the traditional four-factor framework that governs the award of injunctive relief, we vacate the judgment of the Court of Appeals, so that the District Court may apply that framework in the first instance.

Chief Justice John Roberts, with whom Justice Antonin Scalia and Justice Ruth Bader Ginsburg join, concurring.

I agree with the Court's holding that "the decision whether to grant or deny injunctive relief rests within the equitable discretion of the district courts, and that such discretion must be exercised consistent with traditional principles of equity, in patent disputes no less than in other cases governed by such standards," ante, and I join the opinion of the Court. That opinion rightly rests on the proposition that "a major departure from the long tradition of equity practice should not be lightly implied." *Weinberger v. Romero-Barcelo*, 456 U.S. 305, 320 (1982).

From at least the early 19th century, courts have granted injunctive relief upon a finding of infringement in the vast majority of patent cases. This "long tradition of equity practice" is not surprising, given the difficulty of protecting a right to exclude through monetary remedies that allow an infringer to use an invention against the patentee's wishes — a difficulty that often implicates the first two factors of the traditional four-factor test. This historical practice, as the Court holds, does not entitle a patentee to a permanent injunction or justify a general rule that such injunctions should issue. At the same time, there is a difference between exercising equitable discretion pursuant to the established four-factor test and writing on an entirely clean slate. "Discretion is not whim, and limiting discretion according to legal standards helps promote the basic principle of justice that like cases should be decided alike." *Martin v. Franklin Capital Corp.*, 546 U.S. 132, 139 (2005). When it comes to discerning and applying those standards, in this area as others, "a page of history is worth a volume of logic." *New York Trust Co. v. Eisner*, 256 U.S. 345, 349 (1921) (opinion for the Court by Holmes, J.).

Justice ANTHONY KENNEDY, with whom Justice JOHN PAUL STEVENS, Justice DAVID SOUTER, and Justice STEPHEN BREYER join, concurring.

The Court is correct, in my view, to hold that courts should apply the well-established, four-factor test — without resort to categorical rules — in deciding whether to grant injunctive relief in patent cases. The Chief Justice is also correct that history may be instructive in applying this test. The traditional practice of issuing injunctions against patent infringers, however, does not seem to rest on "the difficulty of protecting a right to exclude through monetary remedies that allow an infringer to use an invention against the patentee's wishes." Both the terms of the Patent Act and the traditional view of injunctive relief accept that the existence of a right to exclude does not dictate the remedy for a violation of that right. To the extent earlier cases establish a pattern of granting an injunction against patent infringers almost as a matter of course, this pattern simply illustrates the result of the four-factor test in the contexts then prevalent. The lesson of the historical practice, therefore, is most helpful and instructive when the circumstances of a case bear substantial parallels to litigation the courts have confronted before.

In cases now arising trial courts should bear in mind that in many instances the nature of the patent being enforced and the economic function of the patent holder present considerations quite unlike earlier cases. An industry has developed in which firms use patents not as a basis for producing and selling goods but, instead, primarily for obtaining licensing fees. For these firms, an injunction, and the potentially serious sanctions arising from its violation, can be employed as a bargaining tool to charge exorbitant fees to companies that seek to buy licenses to practice the patent. When the patented invention is but a small component of the product the companies seek to produce and the threat of an injunction is employed simply for undue leverage in negotiations, legal damages may well be sufficient to compensate for the infringement and an injunction may not serve the public interest. In addition injunctive relief may have different consequences for the burgeoning number of patents over business methods, which were not of much economic and legal significance in earlier times. The potential vagueness and suspect validity of some of these patents may affect the calculus under the four-factor test.

The equitable discretion over injunctions, granted by the Patent Act, is well suited to allow courts to adapt to the rapid technological and legal developments in the patent system.

Notes and Questions

1. **Injunctions and property.** Is there a connection between the value (to owners) of the right to exclude and the presumptive availability of injunctive relief? Does it matter what kind of property we are considering (e.g., whether it is valuable to its owner primarily because of the income it might generate or whether instead it has some noncommercial value to the owner)? What was Chief Justice Roberts trying to accomplish with his separate opinion?

2. **Patent trolls.** Justice Kennedy laments that "[a]n industry has developed in which firms use patents not as a basis for producing and selling goods but, instead, primarily for obtaining licensing fees." **Patent trolls** (also referred to somewhat more respectfully as "patent assertion entities") make money by purchasing patents, waiting for industries to develop around the technology arguably covered by the patent, and then approaching industry participants to demand licensing fees in exchange for a promise not to sue for patent infringement. *See* Mark A. Lemley, *Are Universities Patent Trolls?*, 18 Fordham Intell. Prop. Media & Ent. L.J. 611, 613 (2008). Justice Kennedy connects the rise of the patent assertion industry with the easy availability of injunctive relief. How might the test the Supreme Court articulated for injunctions in *eBay* alter the balance of negotiating power between patent owners and potential infringers? *See* Rebecca A. Hand, eBay v. MercExchange: *Looking at the Cause and Effect of a Shift in the Standard for Issuing Patent Injunctions,* 25 Cardozo Arts & Ent. L.J. 461 (2007).

§6 PUBLICITY RIGHTS

Martin Luther King, Jr. Center for Social Change v. American Heritage Products

296 S.E.2d 697 (Ga. 1982)

HAROLD N. HILL, JR., Presiding Justice:

The plaintiffs are the Martin Luther King, Jr. Center for Social Change (the Center),[6] Coretta Scott King, as administratrix of Dr. King's estate, and Motown Record Corporation, the assignee of the rights to several of Dr. King's copyrighted speeches. Defendant James F. Bolen is the sole proprietor of a business known as B & S Sales, which manufactures and sells various plastic products as funeral accessories. Defendant James E. Bolen, the son of James F. Bolen, developed the concept of marketing a plastic bust of Dr. Martin Luther King, Jr., and formed a company, B & S Enterprises, to sell

6. The Center is a nonprofit corporation that seeks to promote the ideals of Dr. King.

the busts, which would be manufactured by B & S Sales. B & S Enterprises was later incorporated under the name of American Heritage Products, Inc.

Although Bolen sought the endorsement and participation of the Martin Luther King, Jr. Center for Social Change, Inc., in the marketing of the bust, the Center refused Bolen's offer. Bolen pursued the idea, nevertheless, hiring an artist to prepare a mold and an agent to handle the promotion of the product. Defendant took out two half-page advertisements in the November and December 1980 issues of Ebony magazine, which purported to offer the bust as "an exclusive memorial" and "an opportunity to support the Martin Luther King, Jr. Center for Social Change." The advertisement stated that "a contribution from your order goes to the King Center for Social Change." Out of the $29.95 purchase price, defendant Bolen testified he set aside 3% or $.90, as a contribution to the Center. The advertisement also offered "free" with the purchase of the bust a booklet about the life of Dr. King entitled "A Tribute to Dr. Martin Luther King, Jr."

In addition to the two advertisements in Ebony, defendant published a brochure or pamphlet which was inserted in 80,000 copies of newspapers across the country. The brochure reiterated what was stated in the magazine advertisements, and also contained photographs of Dr. King and excerpts from his copyrighted speeches. The brochure promised that each "memorial" (bust) is accompanied by a Certificate of Appreciation "testifying that a contribution has been made to the Martin Luther King, Jr. Center for Social Change."

On November 21, 1980, and December 19, 1980, the plaintiffs demanded that the Bolens cease and desist from further advertisements and sales of the bust, and on December 31, 1980, the plaintiffs filed a complaint in the United States District Court for the Northern District of Georgia. . . . The motion for an injunction sought (1) an end to the use of the Center's name in advertising and marketing the busts, (2) restraint of any further copyright infringement and (3) an end to the manufacture and sale of the plastic busts. The defendants agreed to discontinue the use of the Center's name in further promotion. Therefore, the court granted this part of the injunction. The district court found that the defendants had infringed the King copyrights and enjoined all further use of the copyrighted material.

In ruling on the third request for injunction, the court confronted the plaintiffs' claim that the manufacture and sale of the busts violated Dr. King's right of publicity which had passed to his heirs upon Dr. King's death. The defendants contended that no such right existed, and hence, an injunction should not issue.

[T]he Eleventh Circuit Court of Appeals has certified the following questions:

(1) Is the "right of publicity" recognized in Georgia as a right distinct from the right of privacy?
(2) If the answer to question (1) is affirmative, does the "right to publicity" survive the death of its owner? Specifically, is the right inheritable and devisable?
(3) If the answer to question (2) is also affirmative, must the owner have commercially exploited the right before it can survive his death?

(4) Assuming the affirmative answers to questions (1), (2) and (3), what is the guideline to be followed in defining commercial exploitation and what are the evidentiary prerequisites to a showing of commercial exploitation?

The right of publicity may be defined as a celebrity's right to the exclusive use of his or her name and likeness. The right is most often asserted by or on behalf of professional athletes, comedians, actors and actresses, and other entertainers. This case involves none of those occupations. As is known to all, from 1955 until he was assassinated on April 4, 1968, Dr. King, a Baptist minister by profession, was the foremost leader of the civil rights movement in the United States. He was awarded the Nobel Prize for Peace in 1964. Although not a public official, Dr. King was a public figure, and we deal in this opinion with public figures who are neither public officials nor entertainers. Within this framework, we turn to the questions posed.

1. Is the "right of publicity" recognized in Georgia as a right distinct from the right of privacy?

Georgia has long recognized the right of privacy. In *Pavesich v. New England Life Ins. Co.*, 50 S.E. 68 (Ga. 1905), the picture of an artist was used without his consent in a newspaper advertisement of the insurance company. Analyzing the right of privacy, this court held: "The publication of a picture of a person, without his consent, as a part of an advertisement, for the purpose of exploiting the publisher's business, is a violation of the right of privacy of the person whose picture is reproduced, and entitles him to recover without proof of special damage." If the right to privacy had not been recognized, advertisers could use photographs of private citizens to promote sales and the professional modeling business would not be what it is today.

In the course of its opinion the *Pavesich* court said several things pertinent here. It noted that the commentators on ancient law recognized the right of personal liberty, including the right to exhibit oneself before the public at proper times and places and in a proper manner. As a corollary, the court recognized that the right of personal liberty included the right of a person not to be exhibited before the public, saying: "The right to withdraw from the public gaze at such times as a person may see fit, when his presence in public is not demanded by any rule of law is also embraced within the right of personal liberty. Publicity in one instance and privacy in the other is each guaranteed. If personal liberty embraces the *right of publicity*, it no less embraces the correlative right of privacy; and this is no new idea in Georgia law." (Emphasis supplied.)

Recognizing the possibility of a conflict between the right of privacy and the freedoms of speech and press, this court said: "There is in the publication of one's picture for advertising purposes not the slightest semblance of an expression of an idea, a thought, or an opinion, within the meaning of the constitutional provision which guarantees to a person the right to publish his sentiments on any subject." The defendants in the case now before us make no claim under these freedoms and we find no violation thereof.

Observing in dicta that the right of privacy in general does not survive the death of the person whose privacy is invaded, the *Pavesich* court said: "While the right of privacy is personal, and may die with the person, we do not desire to be understood as assenting to the proposition that the relatives of the deceased can not, in a proper case, protect the memory of their kinsman, not only from defamation, but also from an invasion into the affairs of his private life after his death. This question is not now involved, but we do not wish anything said to be understood as committing us in any way to the doctrine that against the consent of relatives the private affairs of a deceased person may be published and his picture or statue exhibited." 50 S.E. at 76.

Finding that Pavesich, although an artist, was not recognized as a public figure, the court said: "It is not necessary in this case to hold, nor are we prepared to do so, that the mere fact that a man has become what is called a public character, either by aspiring to public office, or by holding public office, or by exercising a profession which places him before the public, or by engaging in a business which has necessarily a public nature, gives to everyone the right to print and circulate his picture." 50 S.E. at 79-80. Thus, although recognizing the right of privacy, the *Pavesich* court left open the question facing us involving the likeness of a public figure.

On the other hand, in *Waters v. Fleetwood*, 91 S.E.2d 344 (Ga. 1956), it was held that the mother of a 14-year-old murder victim could not recover for invasion of the mother's privacy from a newspaper that published and sold separately photographs of her daughter's body taken after it was removed from a river. There the court found that publication and reproduction for sale of a photograph incident to a matter of public interest or to a public investigation could not be a violation of anyone's right of privacy.

The right to publicity is not absolute. In *Hicks v. Casablanca Records*, 464 F. Supp. 426 (S.D.N.Y. 1978), the court held that a fictional novel and movie concerning an unexplained eleven-day disappearance by Agatha Christie, author of numerous mystery novels, were permissible under the first amendment. On the other hand, in *Zacchini v. Scripps-Howard Broadcasting Co.*, 433 U.S. 562 (1977), a television station broadcast on its news program plaintiff's 15-second "human cannonball" flight filmed at a local fair. The Supreme Court held that freedom of the press does not authorize the media to broadcast a performer's entire act without his consent, just as the media could not televise a stage play, prize fight or baseball game without consent. Quoting from Kalven, *Privacy in Tort Law—Were Warren and Brandeis Wrong?*, 31 Law & Contemp. Prob. 326, 332 (1966), the Court said: "The rationale for [protecting the right of publicity] is the straight-forward one of preventing unjust enrichment by the theft of good will. No social purpose is served by having the defendant get free some aspect of the plaintiff that would have market value and for which he would normally pay."

[T]he courts in Georgia have recognized the rights of private citizens, as well as entertainers, not to have their names and photographs used for the financial gain of the user without their consent, where such use is not authorized as an exercise of freedom of the press. We know of no reason why a public figure prominent in religion and civil rights should be entitled to less protection than an exotic dancer or a movie actress. Therefore, we hold that the appropriation of another's name and likeness, whether such likeness be a photograph or sculpture, without consent and for the financial gain of the appropriator is a tort in Georgia, whether the person whose name and likeness is used is a private citizen, entertainer, or as here a public figure who is not a public official.

. . . We conclude that while private citizens have the right of privacy, public figures have a similar right of publicity, and that the measure of damages to a public figure for violation of his or her right of publicity is the value of the appropriation to the user. As thus understood the first certified question is answered in the affirmative.

2. Does the "right of publicity" survive the death of its owner (*i.e.*, is the right inheritable and devisable)?

The right of publicity is assignable during the life of the celebrity, for without this characteristic, full commercial exploitation of one's name and likeness is practically impossible. That is, without assignability the right of publicity could hardly be called a "right."

The courts that have considered the problem are not . . . unanimous. . . . In *Factors Etc., Inc. v. Pro Arts, Inc.*, 579 F.2d 215 (2d Cir. 1978),[7] Elvis Presley had assigned his right of publicity to Boxcar Enterprises, which assigned that right to Factors after Presley's death. Defendant Pro Arts published a poster of Presley entitled "In Memory." In affirming the grant of injunction against Pro Arts, the Second Circuit Court of Appeals said:

> The identification of this exclusive right belonging to Boxcar as a transferable property right compels the conclusion that the right survives Presley's death. The death of Presley, who was merely the beneficiary of an income interest in Boxcar's exclusive right, should not in itself extinguish Boxcar's property right. Instead, the income interest, continually produced from Boxcar's exclusive right of commercial exploitation, should inure to Presley's estate at death like any other intangible property right. To hold that the right did not survive Presley's death, would be to grant competitors of Factors, such as Pro Arts, a windfall in the form of profits from the use of Presley's name and likeness. At the same time, the exclusive right purchased by Factors and the financial benefits accruing to the celebrity's heirs would be rendered virtually worthless.

In *Lugosi v. Universal Pictures*, 603 P.2d 425 (Cal. 1979), the Supreme Court of California, in a 4 to 3 decision, declared that the right of publicity expires upon the death of the celebrity and is not descendible. Bela Lugosi appeared as Dracula in Universal Picture's movie by that name. Universal had acquired the movie rights to the novel by Bram Stoker. Lugosi's contract with Universal gave it the right to exploit Lugosi's name and likeness in connection with the movie. The majority of the court held that Lugosi's heirs could not prevent Universal's continued exploitation of Lugosi's portrayal of

CONTEXT

After the *Lugosi* case, California's legislature overruled the decision. In 1984, it enacted a statute making publicity rights in that state descendible and transferable for 70 years after the celebrity's death. *See* Cal. Civ. Code §3344.1. Courts initially held that the statute did not apply to celebrities who died before it went into effect, a group that included celebrities like Marilyn Monroe, whose publicity rights still had significant commercial value. *See, e.g., Shaw Family Archives Ltd. v. CMG Worldwide, Inc.*, 486 F. Supp. 2d 309 (S.D.N.Y. 2007). Soon thereafter, the California legislature went back to the drawing board and amended the statute to retroactively cover celebrities who died before 1985. *See* Cal. Civ. Code 3344.1(b).

7. *But see Pirone v. MacMillan*, 894 F.2d 579 (2d Cir. 1990) (holding that publicity rights are solely based on statutory law in New York and that the right of publicity was not descendible). — Eds.

Count Dracula after his death. The court did not decide whether Universal could prevent unauthorized third parties from exploitation of Lugosi's appearance as Dracula after Lugosi's death.

In *Memphis Development Foundation v. Factors Etc., Inc.*, 616 F.2d 956 (6th Cir. 1980), Factors, which had won its case against Pro Arts in New York (see above), lost against the Memphis Development Foundation under the Court of Appeals for the Sixth Circuit's interpretation of Tennessee law. There, the Foundation, a non-profit corporation, planned to erect a statue of Elvis Presley in Memphis and solicited contributions to do so. Donors of $25 or more received a small replica of the proposed statue. The Sixth Circuit reversed the grant of an injunction favoring Factors, holding that a celebrity's right of publicity was not inheritable even where that right had been exploited during the celebrity's life.[8] The court reasoned that although recognition of the right of publicity during life serves to encourage effort and inspire creative endeavors, making the right inheritable would not.

For the reasons which follow we hold that the right of publicity survives the death of its owner and is inheritable and devisable. Recognition of the right of publicity rewards and thereby encourages effort and creativity. If the right of publicity dies with the celebrity, the economic value of the right of publicity during life would be diminished because the celebrity's untimely death would seriously impair, if not destroy, the value of the right of continued commercial use. Conversely, those who would profit from the fame of a celebrity after his or her death for their own benefit and without authorization have failed to establish their claim that they should be the beneficiaries of the celebrity's death. Finally, the trend since the early common law has been to recognize survivability, notwithstanding the legal problems which may thereby arise. We therefore answer question 2 in the affirmative.

3. Must the owner of the right of publicity have commercially exploited that right before it can survive?

Exploitation is understood to mean commercial use by the celebrity other than the activity which made him or her famous, *e.g.*, an inter vivos transfer of the right to the use of one's name and likeness. The cases which have considered this issue . . . involved entertainers. The net result of following them would be to say that celebrities and public figures have the right of publicity during their lifetimes (as others have the right of privacy), but only those who contract for bubble gum cards, posters and tee shirts have a descendible right of publicity upon their deaths. That we should single out for protection after death those entertainers and athletes who exploit their personae during life, and deny protection after death to those who enjoy public acclamation but did not exploit themselves during life, puts a premium on exploitation. Having found that there are valid reasons for recognizing the right of publicity during life, we find no reason to protect after death only those who took commercial advantage of their fame.

---

8. The Second Circuit has now accepted the Sixth Circuit's interpretation of Tennessee law. *Factors Etc., Inc. v. Pro Arts, Inc.*, 652 F.2d 278 (2d Cir. 1981).

Perhaps this case more than others brings the point into focus. A well-known minister may avoid exploiting his prominence during life because to do otherwise would impair his ministry. Should his election not to take commercial advantage of his position during life *ipso facto* result in permitting others to exploit his name and likeness after his death? In our view, a person who avoids exploitation during life is entitled to have his image protected against exploitation after death just as much if not more than a person who exploited his image during life.

Without doubt, Dr. King could have exploited his name and likeness during his lifetime. That this opportunity was not appealing to him does not mean that others have the right to use his name and likeness in ways he himself chose not to do. Nor does it strip his family and estate of the right to control, preserve and extend his status and memory and to prevent unauthorized exploitation thereof by others. Here, they seek to prevent the exploitation of his likeness in a manner they consider unflattering and unfitting. We cannot deny them this right merely because Dr. King chose not to exploit or commercialize himself during his lifetime.

Question 3 is answered in the negative, and therefore we need not answer question 4.

CHARLES L. WELTNER, Justice, concurring specially.

[I]n proclaiming this new "right of publicity," we have created an open-ended and ill-defined force which jeopardizes a right of unquestioned authenticity—free speech. It should be noted that our own constitutional provision, Art. I, Sec. I, Par. IV, Constitution of Georgia, traces its lineage to the first Constitution of our State, in 1777, antedating the First Amendment by fourteen years. Its language is plain and all-encompassing: "No law shall ever be passed to curtail, or restrain the liberty of speech, or of the press; any person may speak, write and publish his sentiments, on all subjects, being responsible for the abuse of that liberty."

But the majority says that the fabrication and commercial distribution of a likeness of Dr. King is not "speech," thereby removing the inquiry from the ambit of First Amendment or Free Speech inquiries. To this conclusion I most vigorously dissent. When our Constitution declares that anyone may "speak, write and publish his sentiments, on all subjects" it does not confine that freedom exclusively to verbal expression. Art. I, Sec. I, Par. IV, Constitution of Georgia. Human intercourse is such that oft times the most powerful of expressions involve no words at all, *e.g.*, Jesus before Pilate; Thoreau in the Concord jail; King on the bridge at Selma.

Do not the statues of the Confederate soldiers which inhabit so many of our courthouse squares express the sentiments of those who raised them? Are not the busts of former chief justices, stationed within the rotunda of this very courthouse, expressions of sentiments of gratitude and approval? Is not the portrait of Dr. King which hangs in our Capitol an expression of sentiment? Manifestly so. If, then, a two-dimensional likeness in oil and canvas is an expression of sentiment, how can it be said that a three-dimensional likeness in plastic is *not*?

But, says the majority, our new right to publicity is violated only in cases involving financial gain. Did the sculptors of our Confederate soldiers, and of our chief justices, labor without gain? Was Dr. King's portraitist unpaid for his work? If "financial gain" is to be the watershed of violation *vel non* of this new-found right, it cannot withstand scrutiny. It is rare, indeed, that any expression of sentiment beyond casual conversation is not somehow connected, directly or indirectly, to "financial gain." For example, a school child wins a $25 prize for the best essay on Dr. King's life. Is this "financial gain"? Must the child then account for the winnings? The essay, because of its worth, is reprinted in a commercial publication. Must the publisher account? The publication is sold on the newsstand. Must the vendor account?

The majority will say "free speech." Very well. The same child wins a $25 prize in the school art fair. His creation — a bust of Dr. King. Must he account? The local newspaper prints a photograph of the child and of his creation. Must it account? The school commissions replicas of the bust to raise money for its library. Must it account? UNICEF reproduces the bust on its Christmas cards. Must it account? Finally, a purely commercial venture undertakes to market replicas of the bust under circumstances similar to those of this case. Must it account?

Obviously, the answers to the above questions will vary, and properly so, because the circumstances posited are vastly different. The dividing line, however, cannot be fixed upon the presence or absence of "financial gain." Rather, it must be grounded in the community's judgment of what, *ex aequo et bono*, is unconscionable.

Were it otherwise, this "right of publicity," fully extended, would eliminate scholarly research, historical analysis, and public comment, because food and shelter, and the financial gain it takes to provide them, are still essentials of human existence. Were it otherwise, no newspaper might identify any person or any incident of his life without accounting to him for violation of his "right to publicity." Were it otherwise, no author might refer to any event in history wherein his reference is identifiable to any individual (or his heirs!) without accounting for his royalties.

Each lawful restraint [on speech] finds its legitimacy, then, *not* because it is laid against some immutable rule (like the weights and measures of the Bureau of Standards) but because it is perceived that it would be irresponsible to the interest of the community — to the extent of being *unconscionable* — that such conduct go unrestrained. The doctrine of unjust enrichment finds its genesis in such a reckoning. It can be applied to just such a matter as that before us. Were we to do so, we could avoid entering the quagmire of combining considerations of "right of privacy," "right of publicity," and considerations of *inter vivos* exploitation. We would also retain our constitutional right of free speech uncluttered and uncompromised by these new impediments of indeterminate application. And we could sanction relief *in this case* — where relief is plainly appropriate.

Notes and Questions

1. **Imitators.** A recent version of the right of publicity has been used to challenge advertisements that *imitate* artists as a way to appropriate their image. The singer and actress Bette Midler brought a lawsuit against Young & Rubicam, an advertising agency that had hired one of her former backup singers to imitate Midler's rendition

of her 1973 hit "Do You Want to Dance?" to promote Ford Motor Co.'s Mercury Sable car. Midler claimed that the agency had stolen her voice. The U.S. Court of Appeals for the Ninth Circuit agreed, holding that "when a distinctive voice of a professional singer is widely known and deliberately imitated in order to sell a product, the sellers have appropriated what is not theirs and have committed a tort in California." *Midler v. Ford Motor Co.*, 849 F.2d 460, 463 (9th Cir. 1988). *Accord, Waits v. Frito-Lay, Inc.*, 978 F.2d 1093 (9th Cir. 1992) (singer Tom Waits obtains $375,000 in compensatory damages and $2 million in punitive damages against company that imitated his distinctive voice and singing style in a radio commercial).

Does prohibition of imitation go too far? In *White v. Samsung Electronics America, Inc.*, 971 F.2d 1395 (9th Cir. 1992), the court held that a copyright violation might well be established when a company used a robot in advertising that was intended to evoke images of Vanna White and the game show in which she became famous. Samsung was clearly using her image to sell its products without her consent in a way that might have created confusion as to whether White had agreed to allow her image to be used by the company. However, in a dissent to a decision denying a petition for rehearing, 989 F.2d 1512, 1513 (9th Cir. 1993), Judge Kozinski criticized the ruling.

> Saddam Hussein wants to keep advertisers from using his picture in unflattering contexts. Clint Eastwood doesn't want tabloids to write about him. Rudolf Valentino's heirs want to control his film biography. The Girl Scouts don't want their image soiled by association with certain activities. George Lucas wants to keep Strategic Defense Initiative fans from calling it "Star Wars." Pepsico doesn't want singers to use the word "Pepsi" in their songs. Guy Lombardo wants an exclusive property right to ads that show big bands playing on New Year's Eve. Uri Geller thinks he should be paid for ads showing psychics bending metal through telekinesis. Paul Prudhomme, that household name, thinks the same about ads featuring corpulent bearded chefs. And scads of copyright holders see purple when their creations are made fun of.
>
> Something very dangerous is going on here. Private property, including intellectual property, is essential to our way of life. It provides an incentive for investment and innovation; it stimulates the flourishing of our culture; it protects the moral entitlements of people to the fruits of their labors. But reducing too much to private property can be bad medicine. Private land, for instance, is far more useful if separated from other private land by public streets, roads and highways. Public parks, utility rights-of-way and sewers reduce the amount of land in private hands, but vastly enhance the value of the property that remains.
>
> So too it is with intellectual property. Overprotecting intellectual property is as harmful as underprotecting it. Creativity is impossible without a rich public domain. Nothing today, likely nothing since we tamed fire, is genuinely new: Culture, like science and technology, grows by accretion, each new creator building on the works of those who came before. Overprotection stifles the very creative forces it's supposed to nurture.
>
> The panel's opinion is a classic case of overprotection. Concerned about what it sees as a wrong done to Vanna White, the panel majority erects a property right of remarkable and dangerous breadth: Under the majority's opinion, it's now a tort for advertisers to *remind* the public of a celebrity. Not to use a celebrity's name, voice, signature or

> likeness; not to imply the celebrity endorses a product; but simply to evoke the celebrity's image in the public's mind. This Orwellian notion withdraws far more from the public domain than prudence and common sense allow. It conflicts with the *Copyright Act* and the Copyright Clause. It raises serious First Amendment problems. It's bad law, and it deserves a long, hard second look.

The Ninth Circuit found a likely violation of publicity rights when licensed airport Cheers bars used animatronic robots that resembled two characters from the *Cheers* television show. Although the actors had no right to prevent dissemination of the show itself, they had the right to prevent use of their images to sell products related to the show. *Wendt v. Host International*, 125 F.3d 806 (9th Cir. 1997) (applying California law). Does this distinction make sense?

2. **Free speech.** Does the right of publicity interfere with the right of free speech? *See Parks v. La Face Records*, 329 F.3d 437 (6th Cir. 2003) (grappling with the conflict between free speech rights and property rights in one's name); *Comedy III Productions, Inc. v. Gary Saderup, Inc.*, 21 P.3d 797 (Cal. 2001) (balancing publicity rights against the first amendment rights of an artist who sold lithographic print and silk-screened t-shirt reproductions of his drawings of the Three Stooges). After playwright Susan Ross wrote a play based on the life of the singer Janis Joplin, she was sued by Joplin's family and Manny Fox, a New York producer who owns the rights to make a film and play based on Joplin's life, on the ground that Ross had wrongly appropriated the plaintiffs' right of publicity in Joplin's image without obtaining the consent of Joplin's estate. The family claimed "the exclusive right to exploit stage productions, theatrical films and television productions based on the life and times of Janis Joplin." Judge Coughenour held that the play was a protected form of expression under the first amendment and that Joplin's family could not control artistic expressions based on her life. *Joplin Enterprises v. Allen*, 795 F. Supp. 349 (W.D. Wash. 1992). *See also ETW Corp. v. Jireh Publishing, Inc.*, 332 F.3d 915 (6th Cir. 2003) (first amendment prevents assertion of publicity right against an artist who painted Tiger Woods's victory at 1997 Master Tournament); *Matthews v. Wozencraft*, 15 F.3d 432 (5th Cir. 1994) (despite publicity right, defendant is entitled to produce a fictionalized biography without plaintiff's consent). Do you agree with the majority or dissenting opinions in the *Martin Luther King* case?

3. ***Lanham Act.*** Section 43(a) of the federal *Lanham Act*, 15 U.S.C. §1125, may support a publicity rights claim because it creates a civil claim against any person who identifies his product so to deceive consumers as to the association of the product's producer with another person or to cause consumers to falsely believe that other person has sponsored or approved of the product. *See ETW Corp. v. Jireh Publishing, Inc.*, 332 F.3d 915, 924 (6th Cir. 2003) ("The elements of a Lanham Act false endorsement claim are similar to the elements of a right of publicity claim under Ohio law." (citing Bruce P. Keller, *The Right of Publicity: Past, Present, and Future,* 1207 PLI Corp. Law and Prac. Handbook 159, 170 (October 2000))). In contrast, to show infringement of the common law right of publicity, the claimant need not show

a possibility of confusion; all that is required is unauthorized use. *Cf. Tyne v. Time Warner Entertainment Co.*, 901 So. 2d 802 (Fla. 2005) (state statute prohibiting use of a person's name or likeness for "commercial purposes" does not apply to a movie like *The Perfect Storm* that dramatizes real events and persons and does not directly promote a good or service).

4. Cultural icons. The images of famous people become part of popular culture—a common asset of the community. Absolute protection of someone's image would prevent others from commenting on or referring to the image without permission from the owner. At the same time, commercial exploitation of someone's image may harm an individual by associating her with a product with which she does not want to be associated. Such exploitation could also limit a celebrity's ability to derive commercial benefit from her own popularity. Should it make a difference if someone is simply trying to make money from a person's image—for example, using her to sell a product—or using her image in an artistic or literary fashion? *Compare Groucho Marx Productions, Inc. v. Day & Night Co.*, 689 F.2d 317 (2d Cir. 1982) (right of publicity does not survive the death of the owner; producers of a play mimicking the Marx Brothers could not be held liable to his heirs), *with John W. Carson v. Here's Johnny Portable Toilets, Inc.*, 698 F.2d 831 (6th Cir. 1983) (holding that defendant could not imitate Ed McMahon's introduction of Johnny Carson— "Here's Johnny!" —to sell its portable toilets). *See also* Cal. Civ. Code §§3344, 3344.1; Fla. Stat. §540.08; Tenn. Code §§47-25-1101 to 47-25-1108 (protecting the right of publicity).

5. Titles. In *Rogers v. Grimaldi*, 875 F.2d 994 (2d Cir. 1989), dancer and film star Ginger Rogers sued filmmaker Federico Fellini for using her name in a movie called *Ginger and Fred*. That movie was about two cabaret dancers who became known to their fans as Fred and Ginger because they imitated Fred Astaire and Ginger Rogers in their act. The court held that the use of a title is protected by the first amendment unless it has "no artistic relevance" to the underlying work, or if there is artistic relevance, that the title "explicitly misleads as to the source of the content of the work." *Id.* at 999. Applying this test, the court concluded that use of Ginger Rogers's name in the title was protected by the first amendment and thus barred claims based on either publicity rights or the *Lanham Act*. In contrast, the court in *Parks v. La Face Records*, 329 F.3d 437 (6th Cir. 2003), granted civil rights leader Rosa Parks the right to go forward with publicity rights and *Lanham Act* claims against the band OutKast and record producer LaFace Records for using her name as the title for a song. The district court had concluded that the title was artistically relevant to the song lyrics because the lyrics contain the phrase "Everybody move to the back of the bus" —a phrase obviously related to Parks. The Sixth Circuit reversed, holding that a jury could conclude that the song was not about Rosa Parks in any way. The "back of the bus" phrase was used to suggest that competitors to OutKast should get back and let OutKast get out front. This use starkly contrasts, for example, with the song "Rosa, Rosa" by blues artist Otis Taylor, which is clearly a tribute to Rosa Parks. Were the *Rogers* and *Parks* cases correctly decided?

Problems

Do companies have a free speech right to the commercial use of the name of a famous person who has been dead more than 100 years? Although some states refuse to extend the right of publicity after death, *see* N.Y. Civ. Rights §50, most states, like Georgia, do recognize such rights and sometimes provide time limits, *see* Cal. Civ. Code §3344.1 (70 years after death); Tenn. Code §47-25-1104 (10 years after death if not exploited; if commercially exploited, the rights ends 2 years after the use ceases); Tex. Prob. Code §§26.001-26.002 (50 years after death).

A surviving relative of Tasunke Witko (known in English as Crazy Horse) sought to prevent a beer company from selling "Crazy Horse Malt Liquor" on the ground that the law of the Rosebud Sioux Nation recognized a form of publicity right that was descendible and still in existence more than a century after the death of Crazy Horse. Crazy Horse was a spiritual leader of the Sioux people and opposed the use of liquor in any form. The Rosebud Sioux Trial Court strongly suggested that tribal law would recognize such a right but found no jurisdiction in tribal court because the beer was not sold on the reservation. Although the Rosebud Sioux Supreme Court reversed on the jurisdictional finding, a subsequent ruling by a federal judge held that the trial court had no jurisdiction over the claim. *In the Matter of the Estate of Tasunke Witko v. G. Heileman Brewing Co.* (Civ. No. 93-204) (Rosebud Sioux Tr. Ct., Oct. 25, 1994), *rev'd* (Rosebud Sioux Sup. Ct., May 1, 1996), *judgment vacated by Hornell Brewing Co. v. Rosebud Sioux Tribal Court*, 133 F.3d 1087 (8th Cir. 1998).

1. Suppose a suit is brought in state court in a state where the beer is sold seeking an injunction against the use of Crazy Horse's name in connection with the sale of liquor. Assume that the state in which suit is brought recognizes publicity rights but does not allow them to be inherited, at least where the individual did not take advantage of commercial use of the name during his lifetime. Plaintiff claims that publicity rights are a form of personal property and that the law of the domicile of a person at the time of death ordinarily applies to determine who inherits such property at death. Because Crazy Horse was domiciled on the Rosebud Sioux Reservation at his death, Rosebud law should apply to govern the case. Defendant beer company argues that such cases concern the regulation of business enterprises, and the law of the place where goods are sold should control the case. Which law should apply?

2. Assume now that the court has decided to apply its own law (the law of the place of sale) and is asked by plaintiff to allow publicity rights to be inherited whether or not they were exploited during life, citing *Martin Luther King, Jr.* Defendant argues that publicity rights should not be inherited. Alternatively, if they are inherited, they should lapse at some point after death—certainly after 100 years have passed. How should this issue be resolved?

3. Defendant now argues that it has a first amendment free speech right to use the name of a deceased public figure to sell its product. Argue both sides of this legal issue. How should it be resolved?

§7 CULTURAL PROPERTY

§7.1 The International Market in Cultural Property

United States v. Schultz

178 F. Supp. 2d 445 (S.D.N.Y. 2002)

JED S. RAKOFF, District Judge.

The marvelous artifacts of ancient Egypt, so wondrous in their beauty and in what they teach of the advent of civilization, inevitably invite the attention, not just of scholars and aesthetes, but of tomb-robbers, smugglers, black-marketeers, and assorted thieves. Every pharaoh, it seems, has a price on his head (at least if the head is cast in stone); and if the price is right, a head-hunter will be found to sever the head from its lawful owner. So, at least, is the theory of the instant indictment, which alleges, in effect, that the defendant and one or more co-conspirators arranged to steal highly valuable ancient Egyptian artifacts — including a million-dollar head of Amenhotep III — and "fence" them in New York. This, says the indictment, makes the defendant guilty of conspiracy to violate section 2315 of Title 18, United States Code, which provides, in pertinent part, that "[w]hoever receives, possesses, conceals, stores, barters, sells, or disposes of any goods, wares, or merchandise . . . which have crossed a State or United States boundary after being stolen . . . knowing the same to have been stolen . . . [is guilty of a crime]."

The defendant has pleaded not guilty and is presumed innocent. For purposes of this pre-trial motion [to dismiss his indictment], however, he assumes the facts as stated in the indictment and maintains that the indictment nonetheless fails to state a conspiracy to violate section 2315 because it presupposes, wrongly in his view, that someone who conspires to smuggle ancient artifacts out of Egypt is thereby guilty of, among other things, dealing in stolen goods, by virtue of Egyptian Law 117. That law provides that, as of 1983, all Egyptian "antiquities" — that is, objects over a century old having archeological or historical importance (Law 117, Art. 1) — "are considered to be public property," that is, property of the state. The defendant principally argues: (i) that Law 117, despite its assertion of state ownership, is really more in the nature of a licensing and export regulation, the violation of which does not constitute theft of property in the sense covered by section 2315; [and] (ii) that, assuming Law 117 really does work an expropriation of property by Egypt, the special kind of property thereby vested in that foreign state does not give rise to interests entitled to protection under United States law.

The primary problem with defendant's first argument — that Law 117 is really regulatory in nature — is the language of the law itself, which unequivocally asserts state ownership of all antiquities (Art. 6), requires their recording by the state (Art. 26), prohibits (with certain practical exceptions) private ownership, possession, or disposal of such antiquities (Arts. 6-8), and requires anyone finding or discovering a new antiquity to promptly notify the Antiquities Authority (Arts. 23-24), which, in the case of movable antiquities, then takes physical possession and stores the antiquities in the museums and storage facilities of the Authority (Art. 28). Thus, so far as Egyptian antiquities are concerned, Law 117 on its face vests with the state most, and perhaps all, the rights ordinarily associated with ownership of property, including title, possession, and right to transfer. This, on its face, is far more than a licensing scheme or export regulation.

To be sure, Law 117 qualifies certain aspects of state ownership where obvious practicalities so require. For example, while every newly-discovered but immovable antiquity is still deemed state owned, nonetheless "where the find is located on private property, the Authority shall decide within three months whether to remove the find, to initiate measures for expropriating the land upon which it is located, or to leave the antiquity in its place and register it in accordance with the provisions of this law." (Art. 23). Similarly, pre-1983 owners or possessors of antiquities, though now required to register their antiquities with the state if they have not already done so, may in certain circumstances maintain possession or even dispose of their antiquities, but only with permission of the Authority. *See, e.g.*, Arts. 7, 8, 9, 13. These adjustments to physical and historical circumstances only serve to confirm, however, that the statute's primary purpose is to transfer ownership to the state to the extent reasonably practicable.

Despite the plain language of Law 117, however, defendant argues that, in practice, even those antiquities discovered after 1983 have been left in the hands of their discoverers or other private transferees and that the law in operation really works more like a licensing or export regulation than like a transfer of property. But when, in response to these and other defense assertions, the Court convened an evidentiary hearing, pursuant to Rule 26.1 of the Federal Rules of Criminal Procedure, the defendant was unable to adduce any material, let alone persuasive evidence to support this contention. The most he could offer in this respect was the opinion of Professor Abou El Fadl, a professor of Islamic and Middle Eastern law at UCLA Law School, to the effect that nothing in Law 117 definitively prevents the Antiquities Authority from leaving physical possession of even an antiquity discovered after 1983 in the hands of a private finder, so long as the private finder promptly notifies the Authority of his find.

In response to this purely hypothetical opinion, the Government presented, among much else, the testimony of Dr. Gaballa Ali Gaballa, Secretary General to the Supreme Council of Antiquities, that in fact the state takes immediate physical custody of newly discovered antiquities, sometimes by the tens of thousands. Another Government witness, General Ali Sobky, Director of Criminal Investigations for the Antiquities Police (which employs more than 400 police officers), testified that his department regularly investigates and prosecutes dozens of serious violations of Law 117, of which relatively few are for smuggling and most are for trafficking within Egypt (including unlawfully possessing and disposing of state-owned antiquities). General Sobky also testified that even in the case where someone is acquitted of stealing a newly discovered antiquity, the antiquity is confiscated by the state as the lawful owner.

It is clear, therefore, that Law 117, far from being a disguised licensing scheme or export regulation, is precisely what it purports to be: a transfer of ownership of Egyptian antiquities to the state, effective 1983.

As for defendant's second argument—to the effect that American law does not, or should not, recognize the kind of "special" property interest created by "patrimony" laws like Law 117—it should first be noted that section 2315, which expressly refers to foreign commerce, has consistently "been applied to thefts in foreign countries and subsequent transportation into the United States," *United States v. McClain*, 545 F.2d 988, 994 (5th Cir. 1977) (citing cases): an implicit recognition of the interest of the United States in deterring its residents from dealing in the spoils of foreign thefts. In effectuating this policy, why should it make any difference that a foreign nation, in order to safeguard its precious cultural heritage, has chosen to assume ownership of those objects in its domain that have historical or archeological importance, rather than leaving them in private hands?[9] If an American conspired to steal the Liberty Bell and sell it to a foreign collector of artifacts, there is no question he could be prosecuted under section 2315. *Mutatis mutandis,* the same is true when, as here alleged, a United States resident conspires to steal Egypt's antiquities.

To be sure, even if the Government proves the defendant knew he was importing antiquities that were smuggled out of Egypt—an act that may not be inherently violative of United States law and policy—there may still be a jury question as to whether he knew he was dealing in stolen goods, an essential element of a section 2315 violation. But the indictment alleges he possessed such knowledge, and the Government asserts that it will prove, inter alia, that the defendant knew that at least two of the items he conspired to import had been stolen from the Antiquities Police. This is more than sufficient for purposes of the present motion.

While defendant raises still other arguments in support of his motion to dismiss the indictment, the Court finds them sufficiently meritless as not to warrant discussion here.

Accordingly, the Court, confirming its Order of December 27, 2001, hereby denies defendant's motion to dismiss the indictment.

Notes and Questions

1. **Legal protection of cultural property.** In 1970, the United Nations approved the *Convention on the Means of Prohibiting and Preventing the Illicit Import, Export and Transfer of Ownership of Cultural Property,* Nov. 14, 1970, 823 U.N.T.S. 231, 232-234. The law has spurred adoption of rules to prevent import and export of cultural property, and efforts to enforce older national laws prohibiting removal of artifacts. Museum guidelines promulgated in 2008, for example, discourage acquisition of any cultural artifacts without proof of removal from their country of origin before 1970, or removal with the consent of the country after that year. In a 2009 article in the

9. Egyptian law, like United States law, requires just compensation for takings. Accordingly, Law 117 expressly provides for full compensation to those who owned Egyptian antiquities prior to the state's assumption of ownership in 1983 or, even thereafter, to those whose land the state chooses to take by eminent domain in order to preserve the immovable antiquities upon it. Furthermore, even those persons who discover antiquities after 1983 and are therefore on notice of the state's ownership qualify, in the discretion of the Antiquities Authority, for financial rewards for their efforts.

Yale Law Journal,[10] Kristen Carpenter, Sonia Katyal, and Angela Riley observe that the growing tendency to speak about cultural heritage in property terms has sparked something of a backlash:

> In a recent *New York Times* column, Edward Rothstein complained that cultural property laws had engendered "a new form of protection, philistinism triumphing in the name of enlightened ideas." Legal scholars in particular — including those who typically align themselves with progressive causes — strongly criticize indigenous peoples' efforts to assert ownership and autonomy over their tangible and intangible traditional resources, arguing that culture is and must remain part of an entitlement-free commons. In one recent article, for example, Naomi Mezey contends that "the idea of property has so colonized the idea of culture that there is not much culture left in cultural property." For Mezey, the notion of indigenous cultural property raises the likelihood that once indigenous peoples obtain title to cultural property, they will use it to exclude others — a practice that would inevitably limit the free flow of culture.

Carpenter, Katyal, and Riley defend the use of the language of property as a tool for protecting indigenous cultural heritage. Building on the personhood theory of property elaborated by Margaret Jane Radin, they develop "a model of property and peoplehood, and in so doing articulate[] a justification for group-oriented legal claims to indigenous cultural property." "Peoplehood," they argue, "dictates that certain lands, resources, and expressions are entitled to legal protection as cultural property because they are integral to the group identity and cultural survival of indigenous peoples."

2. **Cultural patrimony versus cultural internationalism.** In recent years, there have been a number of high profile cases in which museums have returned antiquities and other cultural property to their places of origin. In 2007, for example, after lengthy negotiations, Yale University returned hundreds of Incan stone, metal, and ceramic artifacts to Peru. That same year, the Getty Museum in Los Angeles returned 40 items to Italy. Among them was the Morgantina Venus, which the museum had purchased in 1988 for $18 million. When the Getty acquired it, the statue was an "orphan," meaning that no one knew exactly where it came from and whether it had been looted from Italy. The Getty therefore knew it was taking a risk when it purchased the statue. In 2006, the museum adopted stricter acquisition policies in response to criticism that it was not complying with international norms.

Perhaps the longest running, and certainly among the highest profile, conflicts over cultural property involves sculptures removed by Thomas Bruce, 7th Earl of Elgin, from the Parthenon in Athens and sold to the British Museum in 1816, where they are still displayed as the "Elgin Marbles." Since 1983, the Greek government has been seeking the return of these sculptures, which the British Museum has resisted. Professor John Henry Merryman, in an article called *Thinking About the Elgin Marbles*, 83 Mich. L. Rev. 1881 (1985), notes that international law in 1801, when Elgin removed the Marbles, appears to have validated the transfer, as Elgin obtained permission from

10. Kristen A. Carpenter, Sonia K. Katyal & Angela R. Riley, *In Defense of Property*, 118 Yale L.J. 1022 (2009).

officials of the Ottoman Empire, which had ruled Greece for nearly four centuries at that point. That permission, however, did not resolve the question whether the British were somehow morally obligated to return the Marbles. Professor Merryman describes the argument for their return as cultural nationalism:

> The most obvious argument is that the Marbles belong in Greece because they are Greek. They were created in Greece by Greek artists for the civic and religious purposes of the Athens of that time. The appealing implication is that, being in this sense Greek, they belong among Greeks, in the place (the Acropolis of Athens) for which they were made. This argument, which I will call the argument from cultural nationalism, requires careful examination, since it is basic to the Greek position and because arguments like it are frequently made by other governments calling for the return of cultural property (and is strongly implied in their use of the term "repatriation").
>
> In its truest and best sense, cultural nationalism is based on the relation between cultural property and cultural definition. For a full life and a secure identity, people need exposure to their history, much of which is represented or illustrated by objects. Such artifacts are important to cultural definition and expression, to shared identity and community. They tell people who they are and where they come from. A people deprived of its artifacts is culturally impoverished.
>
> The difficulty comes in relating the notion of cultural deprivation to the physical location of the Marbles. By their removal to London and exposure in the British Museum, they have brought admiration and respect for the Greek achievement. Still, the argument for possession as an aspect of cultural nationalism has an instinctive appeal.
>
> The final component of the nationalism argument is political: the belief that the presence of the Marbles in England, or in any place other than Greece, is an offense to Greeks and to the Greek nation. The weight one gives to this kind of argument for the return of the Marbles depends to a large extent on one's attitude toward political nationalism itself. [I]f one sees it as at best a dubious good, with large elements of superstition and prejudice, with an unsavory record as the religion of the state, and as a source of international economic, social, political, and armed conflict, then the nationalist argument becomes an uncomfortable one to sustain.

Merryman dismisses this argument for several reasons: "it expresses values not clearly entitled to respect (political nationalism)," "it is founded on sentiment and mysticism rather than reason," and "it is a two-edged argument that is equally available to the British." Merryman calls the argument on the other side cultural internationalism:

> The Hague Convention for the Protection of Cultural Property in the Event of Armed Conflict of May 14, 1954, states in its preamble that "cultural property belonging to any people whatsoever" is "the cultural heritage of all mankind." [I]f the legal and moral arguments are treated as evenly balanced, and if the argument from nationalism is also inconclusive, are there considerations from the point of view of cultural internationalism (which the Hague Convention language expresses) that indicate the proper way to allocate the Marbles?
>
> Preservation takes priority for obvious reasons. [I]f one compares the record of care for works on the Acropolis and in the British Museum since 1816, it is clear where the greater danger has lain. The sculptural reliefs remaining on the Parthenon and the

> Caryatids on the Erechtheion have all been badly eroded by exposure to a variety of hazards, including the smog of Athens. The Marbles in the British Museum have fared much better. Under present conditions, the preservation concern favors leaving the Marbles in the British Museum.
>
> The other international interest is distributional; a concern for an appropriate international distribution of the common cultural heritage, so that all of mankind has a reasonable opportunity for access to its own and other people's cultural achievements. There is a tendency for works of art to flow from the poor to the wealthy nations, and one can imagine the unpleasant extreme of a Third World denuded of cultural property in order to stock the museums and the private collections of a few wealthy nations.
>
> It is true that Greek antiquities can be found in major museums and private collections throughout the world and that some of the greatest Greek antiquities are found abroad. But it is difficult to argue that Greece itself is in this sense impoverished. One of the reasons people go to Greece is to enjoy its wealth of antiquities. [I]t seems difficult to argue convincingly for the return of the Marbles to Athens on distributional grounds. If we focus instead on the question of access, there seems little reason to suppose that the Marbles would be more accessible to the world's peoples in Athens than they are in London.

Which side in this debate do you find more convincing?

3. Which law? In *Schultz*, the United States District Court applies the law of Egypt in determining that removal of antiquities from Egypt, if proven to have occurred as alleged by the government, constituted "theft" and therefore made the defendant liable for prosecution in the United States for importing antiquities into the United States. Is that appropriate? What interest does the United States have in enforcing Egyptian law governing antiquities?

In his discussion of the legality of the Marbles' removal, Merryman applies international law at the time of their removal, a time during which the Greek people were under the rule of Ottoman Empire. Is that the right law to apply? Or should we evaluate the legality of the Marbles' removal in terms of contemporary international law?

§7.2 Native American Cultural Property

Wana the Bear v. Community Construction, Inc.

180 Cal. Rptr. 423 (Ct. App. 1982)

Map: Stockton, California

COLEMAN BLEASE, Associate Justice.

Plaintiff Wana the Bear, a direct descendant of the Bear People Lodge of the Miwok Indians, seeks reversal of a judgment that the Native American burial ground under development by defendant Community Construction, Inc., is not a cemetery entitled to protection under the California cemetery law.

This case comes to us shrouded in the history of an ancient Indian people whose remains, bulldozed from their resting place, stir the anguish of their descendants. But there is no succor for these profound sensitivities in the law to which plaintiff appeals, the sepulchral confines of the California cemetery law.

On August 6, 1979, a final subdivision map was approved by the Stockton City Council and defendant went about excavating the subject property in the course of developing a residential tract. In the fall of 1979, defendant uncovered human remains on the property. Defendant continued developing the property, disinterring the remains of over 200 human beings. The burial ground had been used by the Miwok Indians until they were driven out of the area between 1850 and 1870. The site is known to be a burial ground and has been the subject of numerous archeological studies. The site still contains the remains of six or more persons. Plaintiff, a descendant of the Bear People Lodge of the Miwok Indians and related to some or all of the persons whose remains lie there, brought suit to enjoin further excavation and other "desecration" of the property on July 1, 1980.

The central issue in this case is whether the burial ground achieved a protectable status as a public cemetery under the 1872 cemetery law by virtue of its prior status as a public grave yard. We hold that it did not.

Plaintiff seeks enforcement by injunction of Health and Safety Code section 7052, which makes criminal the disinterment of human remains without authority of law. He argues that the section protects a cemetery, as defined by Health and Safety Code section 8100: "Six or more human bodies being buried at one place constitute the place a cemetery." He alleges, and we take it as true, that six or more human bodies are buried on the burial site. In order to escape the problem that the burial site does not comply with either of the two methods of creating a public cemetery, dedication or prescriptive use, plaintiff argues that section 8100, by virtue of its derivation from the 1854 cemetery law, applies to burial sites created prior to 1873 which, he claims, became public cemeteries, by the law of 1854, without dedication or prescriptive use.

The 1854 law made punishable the mutilation of any public grave yard and the disinterment of any deceased person in any grave yard. It defined a public grave yard as follows: "Where the bodies of six or more persons are buried, it is . . . a public grave yard." In 1872, this statute was replaced by chapter V of the new Political Code. It enacted the two means for creating a public cemetery, dedication and prescriptive use. Section 3106 of the Political Code read essentially as Health and Safety Code section 8100 does now: "Six or more human bodies being buried at one place constitutes the place a cemetery." Section 3105 vested title to lands "used as a public cemetery or graveyard, situated in or near to any city, town, or village, and used by the inhabitants thereof continuously, without interruption, as a burial-ground for five years" in the inhabitants and prohibited use of the lands "for any other purpose than a public cemetery." Section 3107 delineated the manner of dedicating public lands to "cemetery" or burial purposes. When the Health and Safety Code was created in 1939, these provisions were carried over into the present law.

Plaintiff claims that the presence of six or more bodies at the burial site in the period between 1854 and the time when the Miwoks were driven out (sometime between

1850 and 1870) rendered the burial ground a "public grave yard," indelibly impressing it with such character. But the 1854 law was not incorporated into the 1872 and subsequent law as claimed by plaintiff. The 1872 law did not simply reenact section 4 of the 1854 act (making a place where six bodies were buried a "public grave yard"). It added a prescriptive use condition, vesting title of the grave yard in the city or village using it only when the land was "used as a public cemetery . . . continuously, without interruption, as a burial-ground for five years." It further declared that "[n]o part of (the code was) retroactive unless expressly so declared." The Miwoks were no longer using the burial ground in 1873, when chapter V of the Political Code replaced the 1854 law; therefore, the burial ground was not made a cemetery by the operation of new section 3106.

Plaintiff finally makes a claim that public policy protects places where the dead are buried. There is indeed such a policy, but it is codified in the statutes governing the disposition of human remains. But they also establish the limits of the policy chosen by the Legislature. The legislative judgment is binding on us in the absence of a supervening constitutional right and none has been claimed.

The judgment is affirmed.

Notes and Questions

1. **What's at stake.** In his 1989 novel, *Talking God,* Tony Hillerman describes a dispute concerning control over American Indian human remains held by a national museum. The museum's public relations director defends keeping the remains because they are "a potentially important source of anthropological information" and because the "public has the right to expect authenticity and not to be shown mere reproductions." One morning, she finds a package on her desk. When she opens it, she sees arm and leg bones with a note explaining that "[y]ou won't bury the bones of our ancestors because you say the public has the right to expect authenticity in the museum when it comes to look at skeletons. Therefore I am sending you a couple of authentic skeletons of ancestors [from] the cemetery in the woods behind the Episcopal Church of Saint Luke." The note goes on: "[T]o make sure they would be perfectly authentic, I chose two whose identities you can personally confirm yourself." The note concludes by explaining that the remains in the box are those of her grandparents. Tony Hillerman, *Talking God* 1-6 (1989).

2. **Reburial of American Indian human remains found on private property.** *Wana the Bear* was partly overturned by California legislation expressly protecting American Indian burial sites. Cal. Govt. Code §6254(r); Cal. Health & Safety Code §7050.5; Cal. Pub. Res. Code §§5097.94, 5097.98, 5097.99. The legislation requires property owners who discover American Indian human remains on their property to notify public officials and to negotiate with representatives of the affected tribe for reburial of the remains and associated objects. *See People v. Van Horn,* 267 Cal. Rptr. 804 (Ct. App. 1990) (upholding the constitutionality of the statute and requiring an archaeologist to return two objects found in a site he excavated on private land while making a survey for the city of Vista, California, which was in the process of determining

whether to buy the land); Thomas Boyd, *Disputes Regarding the Possession of Native American Religious and Cultural Objects and Human Remains: A Discussion of the Applicable Law and Proposed Legislation,* 55 Mo. L. Rev. 883 (1990); Walter Echo-Hawk, *Museum Rights vs. Indian Rights: Guidelines for Assessing Competing Legal Interests in Native Cultural Resources,* 14 N.Y.U. Rev. L. & Soc. Change 437 (1986).

At least 13 states have passed legislation to protect all unmarked graves, including American Indian burial sites on private land owned by non-Indians. *See, e.g.,* Ala. Code §§41-3-1 to 41-3-6; Idaho Code §§27-501 to 27-504; Ill. Stat. ch. 20, §§3440/1 to 3440/16; Neb. Stat. §§12-1202 to 12-1212; Okla. Stat. tit. 21, §§1168-1168.6, tit. 53, §361; Wash. Rev. Code §§27.44.020 to 27.44.901, 27.53.060, 68.60.040 *et seq.*

It is well settled that the descendants of persons who are buried in a recognized cemetery may acquire an implied easement of access to the land where their ancestors are buried. They also may be entitled to an injunction preventing the owner of the land from defacing the graves or interfering with the "reverential character" of the graves. *Bogner v. Villiger,* 796 N.E.2d 679 (Ill. App. Ct. 2003). *Accord, Mallock v. Southern Memorial Park, Inc.,* 561 So. 2d 330 (Fla. Dist. Ct. App. 1990) (discussing a Florida statute that creates such rights); *Sanford v. Vinal,* 552 N.E.2d 579 (Mass. App. Ct. 1990) (discussing abandonment of such an easement).

3. **American Indian human remains and funerary objects found on federal and tribal land.** The *Native American Graves Protection and Repatriation Act* (NAGPRA), 25 U.S.C. §§3001-3013, 18 U.S.C. §1170, provides that American Indian and Native Hawaiian human remains and funerary objects placed with the body upon burial that are found on tribal or federal lands after the effective date of the statute belong to the lineal descendants of the person buried with the items. If such descendants cannot be found, the items belong to the tribe on whose tribal land they were found or to the tribe having the closest cultural affiliation with them. 25 U.S.C. §3002(a).

4. **Return of human remains held by museums.** As of 1991, the Smithsonian Institution and other institutions in the United States held tens of thousands of human remains of American Indians; the number may have been as high as 300,000. Margaret B. Bowman, *The Reburial of Native American Skeletal Remains: Approaches to the Resolution of a Conflict,* 13 Harv. Envtl. L. Rev. 147, 149 (1989). In addition to regulating human remains and funerary objects found on tribal and federal lands, NAGPRA provides that human remains and cultural items held by federal agencies and museums receiving federal funds shall be turned over to lineal descendants or to the appropriate American Indian tribe or Native Hawaiian organization. 25 U.S.C. §3005(a). The statute makes an exception to this rule when "the items are indispensable for completion of a specific scientific study, the outcome of which would be of major benefit to the United States." 25 U.S.C. §3005(b). Such items shall be returned within 90 days of the completion of the scientific study. Although the Smithsonian Institution is expressly excluded from coverage by the statute, 25 U.S.C. §3001(4) and (8), it is required to return those remains by the *National Museum of the Indian Act,* 20 U.S.C. §§80q to 80q-15. This statute requires the Smithsonian to return "any Indian human remains . . . identified by a preponderance of the evidence as those of a

particular individual or as those of an individual culturally affiliated with a particular Indian tribe, . . . upon the request of the descendants of such individual or of the Indian tribe." 20 U.S.C. §80q-9(c). It therefore allows the museum to retain any human remains for study that cannot be proven to have a connection to an identifiable tribe. As between the museum and American Indian nations, who has a stronger claim to the unidentified human remains held by the Smithsonian?

5. Native American artifacts. Under NAGPRA, sacred objects "needed by traditional Native American religious leaders for the practice of traditional Native American religions by their present day adherents" (25 U.S.C. §3001(3)(C)) and "objects of cultural patrimony" that have "ongoing historical, traditional or cultural importance central to the Native American group or culture" discovered on federal or tribal lands after the effective date of the law belong to the tribe on whose land they are found or to the tribe having the closest affiliation with the objects. 25 U.S.C. §3002(a). This provision of NAGPRA does not apply to items found on private or state land. As to sacred items or objects of cultural patrimony discovered prior to the effective date of the law and now in the hands of federal agencies or museums that receive federal funding, those objects must be returned (upon request) to tribes that can successfully establish a cultural affiliation with them. *See* 25 U.S.C. §3005. The agency or museum will not have to return the item if it can establish that it acquired the item from someone authorized to convey them or that the items are essential to important scientific research. *See id.* If the latter exception applies, the agency or museum must return the item when the research is completed. *See id.*; *see also* 43 C.F.R. §10.10.

Problems

1. A museum subject to NAGPRA has been asked to return its human remains. The museum argues that the remains are needed for a scientific study to extract DNA material from the bones for the purpose of genetically tracing which tribes evolved from other tribes and where their ancestors originated. It is hoped that the study will teach a great deal about migration patterns and the prehistory of America.

   a. Is this study "specific," as required by §3005(b)?

   b. Is it "of major benefit to the United States," as required by §3005(b)? Is other information needed to answer this question?

2. In the 1800s, J.S. Emerson took a number of Native Hawaiian artifacts from a cave on the Big Island. He put labels with his name on the items and sold several of them to the Bishop Museum in Honolulu and the Peabody Essex Museum in Massachusetts. In 2003, those items were repatriated from the museums and reburied in the cave. It is not clear whether the items were repatriated pursuant to NAGPRA — that is, whether they were affiliated with any Native Hawaiian organization. In 2004, Daniel Taylor, the owner of an antiquities store in Hawai`i, learned of the objects' reburial through a friend. He found the cave, which is on state land, pushed aside a stone that had been placed in front of the entrance, and found the artifacts, some of which still

had Emerson's labels affixed to them. Taylor took about 157 artifacts valued at between \$800,000 and \$1.2 million and tried to sell them. A grand jury in Hawai`i indicted Taylor for first-degree theft, a class B felony. To be guilty of theft under Hawai`i law, a defendant must intend to "obtain or exert control over the property of another." Taylor moved for the dismissal of his indictment, arguing that the state did not present the grand jury with evidence sufficient to establish that the property he took was "the property of another." Does NAGPRA answer the question of who owns the items Taylor took? Does state property law? What is the relevance, if any, of the law of Native Hawaiians who claim an affiliation with the items? *See State v. Taylor*, 269 P.2d 740 (Haw. 2011).

3. In a famous case, human remains more than 9,000 years old were found on federal land in Washington State. When the Army Corps of Engineers sought to return the remains of the "Kennewick man" to a group of Columbia River tribes, a group of scientists objected on the ground that the physiological features of the Kennewick man meant that he was Caucasian rather than Indian, that he could not be a lineal ancestor of the tribes in the area, and that examination of the remains was essential for scientific purposes. They were very eager to study the remains for scientific purposes because the presence of a Caucasian in the area at that time would change anthropologists' views of human biological and social history. The tribes contended that his genetic makeup was irrelevant and that if he had died in that spot 9,000 years ago, then he was on tribal land and within the jurisdiction of the tribe, and it would violate their religious beliefs not to rebury his remains. They also claimed a right to rebury him and a religious claim to prevent him from being prodded by scientists. The Ninth Circuit sided with the scientists on the ground that the Kennewick man was not a Native American and that the tribes could not prove they were related to him. The statute defines "Native American" as "relating to, a tribe, people, or culture *that is* indigenous to the United States," 25 U.S.C. §3001(9) (emphasis added), and the court determined that the use of the present tense implied that to take control of the remains, the tribe must prove they are related to a currently existing tribe or culture rather than asserting a relation between a past tribe or culture. Given his age, it was impossible to do that, and the tribes lost because they could not meet that burden. *Bonnichsen v. United States Department of Army*, 367 F.3d 864 (9th Cir. 2004). *See* Rebecca Tsosie, *Privileging Claims to the Past: Ancient Human Remains and Contemporary Cultural Values*, 31 Ariz. St. L.J. 583 (1999). Did the court interpret the statute correctly? Did it do the right thing? The secretary of the interior has promulgated rules under NAGPRA that regulate the disposition of Native American human remains that cannot be associated with a particular current federally recognized tribe by requiring repatriation to the tribe on whose land the remains were found. 43 C.F.R. §10.11.

4. The California legislation adopted after *Wana the Bear* required reburial of human remains on other land. Suppose the Miwok Indians had argued before the California legislature that the bodies of their ancestors had to remain where they were found because moving the bodies would disturb their souls. The Miwoks further argued that the ground where the ancestors were found was holy land. They therefore sought legislation that would prohibit removal and reburial of human remains from ground deemed to be holy by the tribe most closely affiliated with the persons whose remains were found.

a. What arguments could you make in favor of the legislation?
b. What arguments could you make against it?
c. What is the right thing to do?

CHAPTER 4

Human Beings and Human Bodies

§1 PROPERTY RIGHTS IN HUMAN BEINGS

What limits should the legal system impose on the conversion of human interests into exchangeable property rights? Does it make sense to use the vocabulary of property and market exchange to describe interests in human bodies and in people themselves? Is anything lost by using the imagery of property to evaluate these kinds of issues? Should there be a presumption that all interests are exchangeable? In recent years, law and economics scholars have used market and property images to analyze almost every imaginable legal problem. *See* Richard Posner, *Economic Analysis of Law* (7th ed. 2007). Professor Margaret Jane Radin has argued that the use of market rhetoric to analyze all legal issues has the effect of wrongfully "commodifying" human experience by conceptualizing all human relationships in terms of market exchange. She argues that certain types of property interests are so crucial to individual dignity, self-fulfillment, the ability to form essential human relationships, and the ability to participate as a member of political society, that they should be treated as personal rights rather than as exchangeable interests in a market. Margaret Jane Radin, *Market-Inalienability*, 100 Harv. L. Rev. 1849 (1987).

Market rhetoric is extremely useful, but it may be inappropriate in some cases. The materials in this chapter explore this issue by addressing a variety of interests in controlling people and human bodies, including the issues of slavery, children, body parts and human genes, and frozen embryos.

§2 SLAVERY

Dred Scott v. Sanford

60 U.S. 393 (1857)

Mr. Chief Justice ROGER B. TANEY delivered the opinion of the court.

[Dred Scott, once a slave but now claiming to be a citizen of the State of Missouri, sued John Sanford,[1] a citizen of New York, to obtain his freedom. Scott based federal jurisdiction on diversity of citizenship between the parties, raising the question in the court's mind whether Scott was in fact a citizen of Missouri. In 1834, Scott's former owner had taken him from Missouri, a slave state, to Illinois, a free state, where they lived for two years before moving to Minnesota, then part of the Louisiana Territory, before returning to Missouri in 1838. Scott was then sold to Sanford. Slavery was illegal in Illinois under state law and in Minnesota under the federal statute called the *Missouri Compromise*, Act of March 6, 1820, 3 Stat. 545. Sanford argued that Scott was not a citizen of Missouri and hence could not bring a lawsuit in federal court based on diversity of citizenship. Scott claimed to be both a Missouri citizen and a free man, based on his having obtained freedom by domicile for a long period in a state and a territory that did not recognize the status of slavery for its domiciliaries. Sanford claimed that neither Illinois nor the *Missouri Compromise* could constitutionally act to deprive him of his property interest in Scott when they returned to a state that recognized property interests in slaves.]

I

The plaintiff in error, who was also the plaintiff in the court below, was, with his wife and children, held as slaves by the defendant, in the State of Missouri; and he brought this action in the Circuit Court of the United States for that district, to assert the title of himself and his family to freedom.

[The first question concerned whether the court had jurisdiction to hear the case. Such jurisdiction existed in federal court over suits between "Citizens of different States," U.S. Const. art. III, §2, cl. 1. Plaintiff Dred Scott claimed that he was a citizen of Missouri and defendant Sanford a citizen of New York. The issue that had to be decided was whether the plaintiff was a "citizen" as defined in the Constitution.]

The question simply is this: Can a negro, whose ancestors were imported into this country, and sold as slaves, become a member of the political community formed and brought into existence by the Constitution of the United States, and as such become entitled to all the rights, and privileges, and immunities, guarantied by that instrument to the citizen? One of which rights is the privilege of suing in a court of the United States in the cases specified in the Constitution.

It will be observed, that the plea applies to that class of persons only whose ancestors were negroes of the African race, and imported into this country, and sold and held as slaves. The only matter in issue . . . is, whether the descendants of such slaves,

1. The case report misspells Sanford's name as Sandford. — EDS.

when they shall be emancipated, or who are born of parents who had become free before their birth, are citizens of a State, in the sense in which the word "citizen" is used in the Constitution of the United States.

The words "people of the United States" and "citizens" are synonymous terms, and mean the same thing. They both describe the political body who, according to our republican institutions, form the sovereignty, and who hold the power and conduct the Government through their representatives. They are what we familiarly call the "sovereign people," and every citizen is one of this people, and a constituent member of this sovereignty. The question before us is, whether the class of persons described in the plea in abatement compose a portion of this people, and are constituent members of this sovereignty? We think they are not, and that they are not included, and were not intended to be included, under the word "citizens" in the Constitution, and can therefore claim none of the rights and privileges which that instrument provides for and secures to citizens of the United States. On the contrary, they were at that time considered as a subordinate and inferior class of beings, who had been subjugated by the dominant race, and, whether emancipated or not, yet remained subject to their authority, and had no rights or privileges but such as those who held the power and the Government might choose to grant them.

[W]e must not confound the rights of citizenship which a State may confer within its own limits, and the rights of citizenship as a member of the Union. [P]revious to the adoption of the Constitution of the United States, every State had the undoubted right to confer on whomsoever it pleased the character of citizen, and to endow him with all its rights. But this character of course was confined to the boundaries of the State, and gave him no rights or privileges in other States beyond those secured to him by the laws of nations and the comity of States.

It is very clear, therefore, that no State can, by any act or law of its own, passed since the adoption of the Constitution, introduce a new member into the political community created by the Constitution of the United States. It cannot make him a member of this community by making him a member of its own. And for the same reason it cannot introduce any person, or description of persons, who were not intended to be embraced in this new political family, which the Constitution brought into existence, but were intended to be excluded from it.

The question then arises, whether the provisions of the Constitution, in relation to the personal rights and privileges to which the citizen of a State should be entitled, embraced the negro African race, at that time in this country, or who might afterwards be imported, who had then or should afterwards be made free in any State; and to put it in the power of a single State to make him a citizen of the United States, and endue him with the full rights of citizenship in every other State without their consent? Does the Constitution of the United States act upon him whenever he shall be made free under the laws of a State, and raised there to the rank of a citizen, and immediately clothe him with all the privileges of a citizen in every other State, and in its own courts?

The court thinks the affirmative of these propositions cannot be maintained.

In the opinion of the court, the legislation and histories of the times, and the language used in the Declaration of Independence, show, that neither the class of persons who had been imported as slaves, nor their descendants, whether they had become free or not, were then acknowledged as a part of the people, nor intended to be included in the general words used in that memorable instrument.

[African Americans] had for more than a century before been regarded as beings of an inferior order, and altogether unfit to associate with the white race, either in social or political relations; and so far inferior, that they had no rights which the white man was bound to respect; and that the negro might justly and lawfully be reduced to slavery for his benefit. He was bought and sold, and treated as an ordinary article of merchandise and traffic, whenever a profit could be made by it. This opinion was at that time fixed and universal in the civilized portion of the white race. It was regarded as an axiom in morals as well as in politics, which no one thought of disputing, or supposed to be open to dispute; and men in every grade and position in society daily and habitually acted upon it in their private pursuits, as well as in matters of public concern, without doubting for a moment the correctness of this opinion.

The language of the Declaration of Independence . . . would seem to embrace the whole human family, and if they were used in a similar instrument at this day would be so understood. But it is too clear for dispute, that the enslaved African race were not intended to be included, and formed no part of the people who framed and adopted this declaration; for if the language, as understood in that day, would embrace them, the conduct of the distinguished men who framed the Declaration of Independence would have been utterly and flagrantly inconsistent with the principles they asserted; and instead of the sympathy of mankind, to which they so confidently appealed, they would have deserved and received universal rebuke and reprobation.

Yet the men who framed this declaration were great men—high in literary acquirements—high in their sense of honor, and incapable of asserting principles inconsistent with those on which they were acting. They perfectly understood the meaning of the language they used, and how it would be understood by others; and they knew that it would not in any part of the civilized world be supposed to embrace the negro race, which, by common consent, had been excluded from civilized Governments and the family of nations, and doomed to slavery. They spoke and acted according to the then established doctrines and principles, and in the ordinary language of the day, and no one misunderstood them. The unhappy black race were separated from the white by indelible marks, and laws long before established, and were never thought of or spoken of except as property, and when the claims of the owner or the profit of the trader were supposed to need protection.

This state of public opinion had undergone no change when the Constitution was adopted.

[T]here are two clauses in the Constitution which point directly and specifically to the negro race as a separate class of persons, and show clearly that they were not regarded as a portion of the people or citizens of the Government then formed.

One of these clauses reserves to each of the thirteen States the right to import slaves until the year 1808, if it thinks proper. And the importation which it thus sanctions was unquestionably of persons of the race of which we are speaking, as the traffic in slaves in the United States had always been confined to them. And by the other provision the States pledge themselves to each other to maintain the right of property of the master, by delivering up to him any slave who may have escaped from his service, and be found within their respective territories. By the first above-mentioned clause, therefore, the right to purchase and hold this property is directly sanctioned and authorized for twenty years by the people who framed the Constitution. And by the second, they pledge themselves to maintain and uphold the right of the master in the manner specified, as long as the Government they then formed should endure. And these two provisions show, conclusively, that neither the description of persons therein referred to, nor their descendants, were embraced in any of the other provisions of the Constitution; for certainly these two clauses were not intended to confer on them or their posterity the blessings of liberty, or any of the personal rights so carefully provided for the citizen.

And upon a full and careful consideration of the subject, the court is of opinion, that, upon the facts stated in the plea in abatement, Dred Scott was not a citizen of Missouri within the meaning of the Constitution of the United States, and not entitled to sue in its courts.

II

The act of Congress, upon which the plaintiff relies, declares that slavery and involuntary servitude, except as a punishment for crime, shall be forever prohibited in all that part of the territory ceded by France, under the name of Louisiana, which lies north of thirty-six degrees thirty minutes north latitude, and not included within the limits of Missouri. And the difficulty which meets us at the threshold of this part of the inquiry is, whether Congress was authorized to pass this law under any of the powers granted to it by the Constitution; for if the authority is not given by that instrument, it is the duty of this court to declare it void and inoperative, and incapable of conferring freedom upon any one who is held as a slave under the laws of any one of the States.

[The] power of Congress over the person or property of a citizen can never be a mere discretionary power under our Constitution and form of Government. The powers of the Government and the rights and privileges of the citizen are regulated and plainly defined by the Constitution itself.

[An] act of Congress which deprives a citizen of the United States of his liberty or property, merely because he came himself or brought his property into a particular Territory of the United States, and who had committed no offence against the laws, could hardly be dignified with the name of due process of law.

[The] right of property in a slave is distinctly and expressly affirmed in the Constitution. The right to traffic in it, like an ordinary article of merchandise and property, was guarantied to the citizens of the United States, in every State that might desire it, for twenty years. And the Government in express terms is pledged to protect it in all future time, if the slave escapes from his owner. This is done in plain words — too plain to be misunderstood. And no word can be found in the Constitution which gives Congress a greater power over slave property, or which entitles property of that kind to less protection than property of any other description. The only power conferred is the power coupled with the duty of guarding and protecting the owner in his rights.

Upon these considerations, it is the opinion of the court that the act of Congress which prohibited a citizen from holding and owning property of this kind in the territory of the United States north of the line therein mentioned, is not warranted by the Constitution, and is therefore void; and that neither Dred Scott himself, nor any of his family, were made free by being carried into this territory; even if they had been carried there by the owner, with the intention of becoming a permanent resident.

[The Court then answered Scott's contention that his sojourn in Illinois and Minnesota had rendered him free by holding that his status was to be determined by Missouri law, his current domicile, and that under Missouri law, he remained a slave.]

Notes and Questions

1. ***Dred Scott* as constitutional interpretation.** *Dred Scott* was only the second decision in U.S. history (the first being *Marbury v. Madison*, 5 U.S. 137 (1803)) in which the Supreme Court held an act of Congress unconstitutional. *Dred Scott* is known for invalidating the **Missouri Compromise**, which had outlawed slavery in the territories, and for Chief Justice Taney's conclusion that African Americans were not "citizens" as defined in the federal Constitution.

What were Chief Justice Taney's reasons for his conclusion? Did these arguments apply to free African Americans, who were not descended from slaves? Was citizenship tied to free status or merely to race? Chief Justice Taney argues that the language of equality and freedom in the Declaration of Independence could not have been intended to include African Americans because then "the conduct of the distinguished men who framed the Declaration of Independence would have been utterly and flagrantly inconsistent with the principles they asserted." What follows from this inconsistency?

Chief Justice Taney emphasizes the constitutional clauses that explicitly recognize and protect slavery: the right to import slaves until 1808 and the fugitive slave clause, requiring all states to return slaves to their masters. Those clauses state:

> The Migration or Importation of Such Persons as any of the States now existing shall think proper to admit, shall not be prohibited by the Congress prior to the Year one thousand eight hundred and eight, but a Tax or duty may be imposed on such Importation, not exceeding ten dollars for each Person. [U.S. Const. art. I, §9, cl. 1.]
>
> No Person held to Service of Labour in one State, under the Laws thereof, escaping into another, shall, in Consequence of any Law or Regulation therein, be discharged from such Service or Labour, but shall be delivered up on Claim of the Party to whom such Service or Labour may be due. [U.S. Const. art. IV, §2, cl. 3.]

What arguments could Chief Justice Taney have made to interpret the Constitution—despite these clauses—to conclude that African Americans were in fact "citizens" as defined in the Constitution?

2. **The morality of slavery and the duty of the law.** When a pirate ship captured three vessels (one each from the United States, Spain, and Portugal) off the coast of Africa and took Africans from each ship, and one of those vessels was later captured off

the coast of the United States with many of the captured Africans aboard, the Supreme Court had to determine whether to treat the captured Africans as slaves and return them to their "owners" or to treat them as free persons. Because the United States had outlawed the slave trade (but not slavery) in 1808, the Court in *The Antelope*, 23 U.S. 66 (1825), ruled that the persons taken from the American ship should be freed. No owner claimed the Africans aboard the Portuguese ship, so they were freed as well. But the Court ordered the persons aboard the Spanish ship to be returned to their owners if they could prove their claims of title.

Chief Justice John Marshall explained that this was a case "in which the sacred rights of liberty and of property come in conflict with each other." *Id.* at 114. Quoting John Locke, Marshall easily concluded that slavery violated natural law. "That it is contrary to the law of nature will scarcely be denied. That every man has a natural right to the fruits of his own labour, is generally admitted; and that no other person can rightfully deprive him of those fruits, and appropriate them against his will, seems to be the necessary result of this admission." *Id.* at 120. However, the slave trade had long been engaged in by the "Christian and civilized nations of world" and "claimed all the sanction which could be derived from long usage, and general acquiescence." *Id.* at 115. The Court thus concluded that the slave trade was not contrary to the law of nations. Given a conflict between natural law and the positive law adopted by the nations of the world, the Court held that the positive law must prevail. "Slavery, then, has its origin in force; but as the world has agreed that it is a legitimate result of force, the state of things which is thus produced by general consent, cannot be pronounced unlawful." *Id.* at 121. Marshall explained, *id.* at 121-122:

> Whatever might be the answer of a moralist to this question, a jurist must search for its legal solution, in those principles of action which are sanctioned by the usages, the national acts, and the general assent, of that portion of the world of which he considers himself as a part, and to whose law the appeal is made. If we resort to this standard as the test of international law, the question, as has already been observed, is decided in favour of the legality of the trade. Both Europe and America embarked in it; and for nearly two centuries, it was carried on without opposition, and without censure. A jurist could not say, that a practice thus supported was illegal, and that those engaged in it might be punished, either personally, or by deprivation of property.

Recall that Marshall had similarly concluded in 1823 in reference to colonial claims of title over Indian lands that "[c]onquest gives a title which the Courts of the conqueror cannot deny, whatever the private and speculative opinions of individuals may be, respecting the original justice of the claim which has been successfully asserted." *Johnson v. M'Intosh*, 21 U.S. 543 (1823).

Did the Supreme Court do the right thing in *The Antelope*? What is the judge's appropriate role if a judge believes that the law violates fundamental norms of justice? *See* Robert M. Cover, *Justice Accused: Antislavery and the Judicial Process* (1975) (criticizing antislavery judges who felt bound by "the law" to return slaves to their purported masters).

§3 CHILDREN

In the Matter of Baby M

537 A.2d 1227 (N.J. 1988)

ROBERT N. WILENTZ, C.J.

In February 1985, William Stern and Mary Beth Whitehead entered into a surrogacy contract. It recited that Stern's wife, Elizabeth, was infertile, that they wanted a child, and that Mrs. Whitehead was willing to provide that child as the mother with Mr. Stern as the father.

The contract provided that through artificial insemination using Mr. Stern's sperm, Mrs. Whitehead would become pregnant, carry the child to term, bear it, deliver it to the Sterns, and thereafter do whatever was necessary to terminate her maternal rights so that Mrs. Stern could thereafter adopt the child. Mrs. Whitehead's husband, Richard, was also a party to the contract; Mrs. Stern was not. Although Mrs. Stern was not a party to the surrogacy agreement, the contract gave her sole custody of the child in the event of Mr. Stern's death. Mrs. Stern's status as a nonparty to the surrogate parenting agreement presumably was to avoid the application of the baby-selling statute to this arrangement. N.J. Stat. §9:3-54.[2]

Mr. Stern, on his part, agreed to attempt the artificial insemination and to pay Mrs. Whitehead $10,000 after the child's birth, on its delivery to him. In a separate contract, Mr. Stern agreed to pay $7,500 to the Infertility Center of New York ("ICNY").

[The Sterns entered the arrangement because Mrs. Stern learned that she might have multiple sclerosis and feared that pregnancy] might precipitate blindness, paraplegia, or other forms of debilitation. Based on the perceived risk, the Sterns decided to forego having their own children. The decision had special significance for Mr. Stern. Most of his family had been destroyed in the Holocaust. As the family's only survivor, he very much wanted to continue his bloodline.

Initially the Sterns considered adoption, but were discouraged by the substantial delay apparently involved and by the potential problem they saw arising from their age and their differing religious backgrounds. They were most eager for some other means to start a family.

Mrs. Whitehead's [willingness to act as a "surrogate mother"] apparently resulted from her sympathy with family members and others who could have no children (she stated that she wanted to give another couple the "gift of life"); she also wanted the $10,000 to help her family.

Mrs. Whitehead realized, almost from the moment of birth, that she could not part with this child. She had felt a bond with it even during pregnancy. Some indication of the attachment was conveyed to the Sterns at the hospital when they told Mrs. Whitehead what they were going to name the baby. She apparently broke into tears and

---

2. This statute has been repealed, 1993 N.J. Laws ch. 345, §20. *See* Lisa J. Trembly, *Untangling the Adoption Web: New Jersey's Move to Legitimize Independent Adoptions*, 18 Seton Hall Legis. J. 371 (1993). — EDS.

indicated that she did not know if she could give up the child. She talked about how the baby looked like her other daughter, and made it clear that she was experiencing great difficulty with the decision.

Nonetheless, Mrs. Whitehead was, for the moment, true to her word. Despite powerful inclinations to the contrary, she turned her child over to the Sterns on March 30 at the Whiteheads' home.

Later in the evening of March 30, Mrs. Whitehead became deeply disturbed, disconsolate, stricken with unbearable sadness. She had to have her child. She could not eat, sleep, or concentrate on anything other than her need for her baby. The next day she went to the Sterns' home and told them how much she was suffering.

The depth of Mrs. Whitehead's despair surprised and frightened the Sterns. She told them that she could not live without her baby, that she must have her, even if only for one week, that thereafter she would surrender her child. The Sterns, concerned that Mrs. Whitehead might indeed commit suicide, not wanting under any circumstances to risk that, and in any event believing that Mrs. Whitehead would keep her word, turned the child over to her. It was not until four months later, after a series of attempts to regain possession of the child, that Melissa was returned to the Sterns, having been forcibly removed from the home where she was then living with Mr. and Mrs. Whitehead, the home in Florida owned by Mary Beth Whitehead's parents.

The struggle over Baby M began when it became apparent that Mrs. Whitehead could not return the child to Mr. Stern. Due to Mrs. Whitehead's refusal to relinquish the baby, Mr. Stern filed a complaint seeking enforcement of the surrogacy contract. . . . [The court issued an ex parte order to Mrs. Whitehead to hand the child over to the Sterns. When the Sterns appeared at the Whiteheads' house with the process server and the police to enforce the order,] Mr. Whitehead fled with the child, who had been handed to him through a window while those who came to enforce the order were thrown off balance by a dispute over the child's current name.

Eventually the Sterns discovered where the Whiteheads were staying, commenced supplementary proceedings in Florida, and obtained an order requiring the Whiteheads to turn over the child. Police in Florida enforced the order, forcibly removing the child from her grandparents' home. She was soon thereafter brought to New Jersey and turned over to the Sterns.

[Trial Court Judge Sorkow] held that the surrogacy contract was valid; ordered that Mrs. Whitehead's parental rights be terminated and that sole custody of the child be granted to Mr. Stern; and, after hearing brief testimony from Mrs. Stern, immediately entered an order allowing the adoption of Melissa by Mrs. Stern, all in accordance with the surrogacy contract.

II. Invalidity and Unenforceability of Surrogacy Contract

We have concluded that this surrogacy contract is invalid. Our conclusion has two bases: direct conflict with existing statutes and conflict with the public policies of this State, as expressed in its statutory and decisional law.

A. *Conflict with Statutory Provisions*

The surrogacy contract conflicts with: (1) laws prohibiting the use of money in connection with adoptions; (2) laws requiring proof of parental unfitness or abandonment before termination of parental rights is ordered or an adoption is granted; and (3) laws that make surrender of custody and consent to adoption revocable in private placement adoptions.

(1) Our law prohibits paying or accepting money in connection with any placement of a child for adoption. N.J. Stat. §9:3-54a. Violation is a high misdemeanor. N.J. Stat. §9:3-54c. Excepted are fees of an approved agency (which must be a non-profit entity, N.J. Stat. §9:3-38a) and certain expenses in connection with childbirth. N.J. Stat. §9:3-54b.7.

Mr. Stern knew he was paying for the adoption of a child; Mrs. Whitehead knew she was accepting money so that a child might be adopted; the Infertility Center knew that it was being paid for assisting in the adoption of a child. The actions of all three worked to frustrate the goals of the statute.

The evils inherent in baby-bartering are loathsome for a myriad of reasons. The child is sold without regard for whether the purchasers will be suitable parents. The natural mother does not receive the benefit of counseling and guidance to assist her in making a decision that may affect her for a lifetime. In fact, the monetary incentive to sell her child may, depending on her financial circumstances, make her decision less voluntary.

Baby-selling potentially results in the exploitation of all parties involved. Conversely, adoption statutes seek to further humanitarian goals, foremost among them the best interests of the child. The negative consequences of baby-buying are potentially present in the surrogacy context, especially the potential for placing and adopting a child without regard to the interest of the child or the natural mother.

(2) The termination of Mrs. Whitehead's parental rights, called for by the surrogacy contract and actually ordered by the court, fails to comply with the stringent requirements of New Jersey law. Our law, recognizing the finality of any termination of parental rights, provides for such termination only where there has been a voluntary surrender of a child to an approved agency or to the Division of Youth and Family Services ("DYFS"), accompanied by a formal document acknowledging termination of parental rights, N.J. Stat. §§9:2-16, -17; N.J. Stat. §9:3-41; N.J. Stat. §30:4C-23, or where there has been a showing of parental abandonment or unfitness.

In this case a termination of parental rights was obtained not by proving the statutory prerequisites but by claiming the benefit of contractual provisions. [A] contractual agreement to abandon one's parental rights, or not to contest a termination action, will not be enforced in our courts. The Legislature would not have so carefully, so consistently, and so substantially restricted termination of parental rights if it had intended to allow termination to be achieved by one short sentence in a contract.

Since the termination was invalid, it follows, as noted above, that adoption of Melissa by Mrs. Stern could not properly be granted.

(3) The provision in the surrogacy contract stating that Mary Beth Whitehead agrees to "surrender custody . . . and terminate all parental rights" contains no clause

giving her a right to rescind. It is intended to be an irrevocable consent to surrender the child for adoption — in other words, an irrevocable commitment by Mrs. Whitehead to turn Baby M over to the Sterns and thereafter to allow termination of her parental rights.

[New Jersey statutes provide that no surrender of the custody of a child shall be valid unless the surrender is made to a state agency, is in writing and conforms to particular requirements, declares the person's desire to relinquish custody, acknowledges termination of parental rights to the state agency, and acknowledges full understanding of the effect of the surrender. N.J. Stat. §§9:2-14, 9:2-16, 9:2-17.]

It is clear that the Legislature so carefully circumscribed all aspects of a consent to surrender custody — its form and substance, its manner of execution, and the agency or agencies to which it may be made — in order to provide the basis for irrevocability. It seems most unlikely that the Legislature intended that a consent not complying with these requirements would also be irrevocable, especially where, as here, that consent falls radically short of compliance.

These strict prerequisites to irrevocability constitute a recognition of the most serious consequences that flow from such consents: termination of parental rights, the permanent separation of parent from child, and the ultimate adoption of the child. Because of those consequences, the Legislature severely limited the circumstances under which such consent would be irrevocable. The legislative goal is furthered by regulations requiring approved agencies, prior to accepting irrevocable consents, to provide advice and counseling to women, making it more likely that they fully understand and appreciate the consequences of their acts. N.J. Admin. Code tit. 10 §121A-5.4(c).

The provision in the surrogacy contract, agreed to before conception, requiring the natural mother to surrender custody of the child without any right of revocation is one more indication of the essential nature of this transaction: the creation of a contractual system of termination and adoption designed to circumvent our statutes.

B. Public Policy Considerations

The surrogacy contract's invalidity, resulting from its direct conflict with the above statutory provisions, is further underlined when its goals and means are measured against New Jersey's public policy. The contract's basic premise, that the natural parents can decide in advance of birth which one is to have custody of the child, bears no relationship to the settled law that the child's best interests shall determine custody.

The surrogacy contract violates the policy of this State that the rights of natural parents are equal concerning their child, the father's right no greater than the mother's. "The parent and child relationship extends equally to every child and to every parent, regardless of the marital status of the parents." N.J. Stat. §9:17-40. . . . The whole purpose and effect of the surrogacy contract was to give the father the exclusive right to the child by destroying the rights of the mother.

The only legal advice Mary Beth Whitehead received regarding the surrogacy contract was provided in connection with the contract that she previously entered into with another couple. Mrs. Whitehead's lawyer was referred to her by the Infertility

Center, with which he had an agreement to act as counsel for surrogate candidates. His services consisted of spending one hour going through the contract with the Whiteheads, section by section, and answering their questions. Mrs. Whitehead received no further legal advice prior to signing the contract with the Sterns.

Under the contract, the natural mother is irrevocably committed before she knows the strength of her bond with her child. She never makes a totally voluntary, informed decision, for quite clearly any decision prior to the baby's birth is, in the most important sense, uninformed, and any decision after that, compelled by a pre-existing contractual commitment, the threat of a lawsuit, and the inducement of a $10,000 payment, is less than totally voluntary. Her interests are of little concern to those who controlled this transaction.

Worst of all, however, is the contract's total disregard of the best interests of the child. There is not the slightest suggestion that any inquiry will be made at any time to determine the fitness of the Sterns as custodial parents, of Mrs. Stern as an adoptive parent, their superiority to Mrs. Whitehead, or the effect on the child of not living with her natural mother.

This is the sale of a child, or, at the very least, the sale of a mother's right to her child, the only mitigating factor being that one of the purchasers is the father. Almost every evil that prompted the prohibition on the payment of money in connection with adoptions exists here.

The differences between an adoption and a surrogacy contract should be noted, since it is asserted that the use of money in connection with surrogacy does not pose the risks found where money buys an adoption.

First, and perhaps most important, all parties concede that it is unlikely that surrogacy will survive without money. Despite the alleged selfless motivation of surrogate mothers, if there is no payment, there will be no surrogates, or very few. That conclusion contrasts with adoption; for obvious reasons, there remains a steady supply, albeit insufficient, despite the prohibitions against payment. The adoption itself, relieving the natural mother of the financial burden of supporting an infant, is in some sense the equivalent of payment.

Second, the use of money in adoptions does not produce the problem—conception occurs, and usually the birth itself, before illicit funds are offered. With surrogacy, the "problem," if one views it as such, consisting of the purchase of a woman's procreative capacity, at the risk of her life, is caused by and originates with the offer of money.

Third, with the law prohibiting the use of money in connection with adoptions, the built-in financial pressure of the unwanted pregnancy and the consequent support obligation do not lead the mother to the highest paying, ill-suited, adoptive parents. She is just as well-off surrendering the child to an approved agency. In surrogacy, the highest bidders will presumably become the adoptive parents regardless of suitability, so long as payment of money is permitted.

Fourth, the mother's consent to surrender her child in adoptions is revocable, even after surrender of the child, unless it be to an approved agency, where by regulation there are protections against an ill-advised surrender. In surrogacy, consent occurs so early that no amount of advice would satisfy the potential mother's need, yet the consent is irrevocable.

In the scheme contemplated by the surrogacy contract in this case, a middleman, propelled by profit, promotes the sale. Whatever idealism may have motivated any of the participants, the profit motive predominates, permeates, and ultimately governs the transaction. The demand for children is great and the supply small. The availability of contraception, abortion, and the greater willingness of single mothers to bring up their children has led to a shortage of babies offered for adoption. The situation is ripe for the entry of the middleman who will bring some equilibrium into the market by increasing the supply through the use of money.

Intimated, but disputed, is the assertion that surrogacy will be used for the benefit of the rich at the expense of the poor. *See, e.g.*, Margaret Jane Radin, *Market-Inalienability*, 100 Harv. L. Rev. 1849, 1930 (1987). In response it is noted that the Sterns are not rich and the Whiteheads not poor. Nevertheless, it is clear to us that it is unlikely that surrogate mothers will be as proportionately numerous among those women in the top twenty percent income bracket as among those in the bottom twenty percent. Put differently, we doubt that infertile couples in the low-income bracket will find upper income surrogates.

The point is made that Mrs. Whitehead agreed to the surrogacy arrangement, supposedly fully understanding the consequences. Putting aside the issue of how compelling her need for money may have been, and how significant her understanding of the consequences, we suggest that her consent is irrelevant. There are, in a civilized society, some things that money cannot buy. In America, we decided long ago that merely because conduct purchased by money was "voluntary" did not mean that it was good or beyond regulation and prohibition. Employers can no longer buy labor at the lowest price they can bargain for, even though that labor is "voluntary," 29 U.S.C. §206 (1982), or buy women's labor for less money than paid to men for the same job, 29 U.S.C. §206(d), or purchase the agreement of children to perform oppressive labor, 29 U.S.C. §212, or purchase the agreement of workers to subject themselves to unsafe or unhealthful working conditions, 29 U.S.C. §§651 to 678 (*Occupational Safety and Health Act of 1970*). There are, in short, values that society deems more important than granting to wealth whatever it can buy, be it labor, love, or life. Whether this principle recommends prohibition of surrogacy, which presumably sometimes results in great satisfaction to all of the parties, is not for us to say. We note here only that, under existing law, the fact that Mrs. Whitehead "agreed" to the arrangement is not dispositive.

The surrogacy contract is based on principles that are directly contrary to the objectives of our laws. It guarantees the separation of a child from its mother; it looks to adoption regardless of suitability; it totally ignores the child; it takes the child from the mother regardless of her wishes and her maternal fitness; and it does all of this, it accomplishes all of its goals, through the use of money.

Beyond that is the potential degradation of some women that may result from this arrangement. In many cases, of course, surrogacy may bring satisfaction, not only to the infertile couple, but to the surrogate mother herself. The fact, however, that many women may not perceive surrogacy negatively but rather see it as an opportunity does not diminish its potential for devastation to other women.

In sum, the harmful consequences of this surrogacy arrangement appear to us all too palpable. In New Jersey the surrogate mother's agreement to sell her child is void. Its irrevocability infects the entire contract, as does the money that purports to buy it.

Notes and Questions

1. **Baby-selling.** The contract in *Baby M* raises a host of legal questions. It is important to distinguish several issues. One question is whether the arrangement constitutes a criminal act in violation of state law prohibiting baby-selling. If it does, the mere fact of entering the contractual arrangement may subject the parties to criminal penalties. A second, and quite different, question is whether the contract is enforceable. It may very well be that the legislature did not intend to impose criminal penalties for surrogacy arrangements — such as those imposed on persons who buy and sell drugs or controlled substances — but that these agreements were unenforceable as a matter of contract law. As the law currently stands, the states do not seem to be treating surrogacy as a crime that would subject the parties to punishment by fine or imprisonment.

2. **Enforcement of surrogacy agreements.** The enforceability of surrogacy contracts raises a series of issues.

   a. **Void or voidable?** One possibility is that the courts could hold the contract **void as against public policy**. This is what the Supreme Court of New Jersey did in *Baby M*. Under this approach, the court approaches the case as if there were no agreement; the standard rule for settling a custody dispute is "the best interests of the child." A second possibility is to hold the contract **voidable** by the birth mother rather than absolutely void. Under this approach, the birth mother — but not the biological father — has the right to reject the contract. If she rejects the contract, custody is determined by the best interests of the child. A mother who was willing to hand over her child pursuant to the surrogacy agreement would be able to do so and would be able to obtain a court judgment ordering the contract parents to pay her the money owed on the agreement.

   b. **Damages or specific performance?** If the contract is enforceable, then the appropriate remedy for breach must be determined. One possibility is **specific performance** through an injunction ordering the mother to hand over the child in accordance with the contract terms. Such a result might comport with traditional law in that specific performance is often ordered when an item being sold is unique, such as land or artwork. Children are obviously unique, but should they be considered items for sale? If specific performance is denied, courts may enforce the contract by damages only.

3. **Disagreement in the courts.** Like the Supreme Court of New Jersey, other state courts have refused to enforce surrogacy arrangements. *See Doe v. Kelley*, 307 N.W.2d 438 (Mich. Ct. App. 1981) (interpreting the *Michigan Adoption Law* to prohibit the

exchange of money for surrogacy); *R.R. v. M.H.*, 689 N.E.2d 790 (Mass. 1998) (contract is void to the extent that it provides compensation to surrogate beyond costs incurred in pregnancy and surrogate's consent to relinquish parental rights not valid until time for effectively granting consent to adoption, four days after the child's birth).

Other courts have held that surrogacy contracts are voidable rather than void per se. The Supreme Court of Kentucky has held that the birth mother in a surrogacy arrangement has the right to void the contract if she changes her mind during pregnancy or immediately after birth. *Surrogate Parenting Associates v. Commonwealth ex rel. Armstrong*, 704 S.W.2d 209 (Ky. 1986). *See also Matter of Adoption of Baby Girl, L.J.*, 505 N.Y.S.2d 813 (Surr. Ct. 1986) (holding that surrogate parenting agreements are not void but are voidable if they do not conform with state adoption statutes).

The Supreme Court of California has held, in contrast, that surrogate mother contracts are specifically enforceable, at least where both the egg and sperm are donated by individuals other than the surrogate mother who bears the child. *Johnson v. Calvert*, 851 P.2d 776 (Cal. 1993). More broadly, however, the court held that "she who intended to procreate the child — that is, she who intended to bring about the birth of a child that she intended to raise as her own — is the natural mother under California law," suggesting that such contracts might be enforceable even if the egg were that of the surrogate mother. *Id.* at 782; *see also In re F.T.R.*, 833 N.W.2d 634 (Wis. 2013) (enforcing — in a case involving a surrogate who was also the egg donor — custody provisions of surrogacy contract, declining to enforce provisions of contract terminating surrogate's parental rights, and pleading with the Wisconsin state legislature to address the issue of surrogacy); *Doe v. Roe*, 717 A.2d 706 (Conn. 1998) (enforcing surrogacy contract over objections of surrogate who was not the egg donor). Should surrogacy arrangements be enforced? If so, by specific performance or by damages? If they should not be enforced, should they be void or voidable? Does the increasing acceptance of same-sex marriage have any bearing on the debate over surrogacy?

4. Surrogacy statutes. A number of states have adopted statutes concerning surrogacy agreements. Some states criminalize the agreements, particularly where they involve the payment of money. *See, e.g.*, Mich. Comp. Laws §722.859 (prohibiting surrogacy contracts and making it a felony for anyone other than the participating parties to assist in the formation of the contract); *see also* D.C. Code Ann. §§16-401 to -402; N.Y. Dom. Rel. L. §§121-124 (providing civil penalties for commercial surrogacy contracts); Wash. Rev. Code. §§26.26.101, .210-.260. Numerous countries also ban the practice, including Australia, China, the Czech Republic, Denmark, France, Germany, Italy, Mexico, Spain, Switzerland, Taiwan, and Turkey. *See* Pamela Laufer-Ukeles, *Mothering for Money: Regulating Commercial Intimacy*, 88 Ind. L.J. 1223, 1225 n.11 (2013). Some statutes merely declare the contracts voidable. *See, e.g.*, N.D. Code §13-18-05. Finally, other states permit the practice, but they typically regulate it very tightly. *See, e.g.*, Fla. Stat. §63.213 (permitting surrogacy contracts but limiting surrogate to reimbursement for expenses, including living expenses during pregnancy, and permitting surrogate to void promise to give up custody during the 48 hours after birth); N.H. Stat. §§168-B:1-32; Va. Code §20-156. For a comprehensive survey of state surrogacy laws, *see* Darra L. Hofman, *Mama's Baby, Daddy's Maybe*, 35 Wm. Mitchell L. Rev. 449 (2009).

5. Policy considerations and gestational surrogacy. In *Johnson, supra*, the majority opinion stated:

> Anna [Johnson] and some commentators have expressed concern that surrogacy contracts tend to exploit or dehumanize women, especially women of lower economic status. Anna's objections center around the psychological harm she asserts may result from the gestator's relinquishing the child to whom she has given birth. Some have also cautioned that the practice of surrogacy may encourage society to view children as commodities, subject to trade at their parents' will.
>
> We are unpersuaded that gestational surrogacy arrangements are so likely to cause the untoward results Anna cites as to demand their invalidation on public policy grounds. Although common sense suggests that women of lesser means serve as surrogate mothers more often than do wealthy women, there has been no proof that surrogacy contracts exploit poor women to any greater degree than economic necessity in general exploits them by inducing them to accept lower-paid or otherwise undesirable employment. We are likewise unpersuaded by the claim that surrogacy will foster the attitude that children are mere commodities; no evidence is offered to support it. The limited data available seem to reflect an absence of significant adverse effects of surrogacy on all participants.
>
> The argument that a woman cannot knowingly and intelligently agree to gestate and deliver a baby for intending parents carries overtones of the reasoning that for centuries prevented women from attaining equal economic rights and professional status under the law. To resurrect this view is both to foreclose a personal and economic choice on the part of the surrogate mother, and to deny intending parents what may be their only means of procreating a child of their own genetic stock. Certainly in the present case it cannot seriously be argued that Anna, a licensed vocational nurse who had done well in school and who had previously borne a child, lacked the intellectual wherewithal or life experience necessary to make an informed decision to enter into the surrogacy contract.

Terms:
Gestational surrogacy occurs when the surrogate carries a fetus to which she has no genetic relationship (because the egg is from the intended mother or donated by a third party). Today, 95 percent of surrogates are of the gestational variety. *See* J. Herbie Difonzo & Ruth C. Stern, *The Children of* Baby M., 39 Cap. U. L. Rev. 345, 355 (2011). When the surrogate also provides the egg, the arrangement is often referred to as **traditional surrogacy**.

851 P.2d at 785. However, Justice Joyce Kennard, the lone dissenting judge and the only woman on the court at the time, argued that a pregnant woman is "more than a mere container or breeding animal; she is a conscious agent of creation no less than the genetic mother." *Id.* at 797-798. Justice Kennard would have granted custody based on the best interests of the child.

Some analysts have supported the decision in *Baby M.* Martha A. Field, *Surrogate Motherhood: The Legal and Human Issues* 151 (1990) (arguing that either surrogate mother contracts should not be enforceable at all or the surrogate mother should have a right to change her mind for some time after the child is born); Patricia J. Williams, *The Alchemy of Race and Rights* 217-219, 224-226 (1991) (arguing that enforcing a contract signed at a discrete point of time may wind up "enslav[ing]" the one who signed it by depriving a surrogate mother of the power to exit an arrangement she comes to understand as extraordinarily harmful to her).

Others have argued that such contracts should be presumptively enforceable. For example, Professor Pamela Laufer-Ukeles has offered a qualified defense of surrogacy arrangements:

> [T]he vast majority of surrogate mothers do not attest to bonding with the babies they gestate to the extent that many predicted and was evident in the case of Baby M. While most surrogates assert that parting with the baby is a difficult separation, it does not appear to be as traumatic as expected. Indeed, given the thousands of surrogacy contracts that are entered into each year, " 'the lack of litigation is remarkable.' " When asked, surrogate mothers do not generally indicate that the babies belong to them; rather, they feel they are providing a meaningful and valuable service for the intended parents. While this appears to be true for both gestational and traditional surrogates, it seems especially true for gestational surrogates who do not have a genetic connection to the fetus. Gestational surrogates report to heavily emphasize genetics and consider the baby in the womb to be someone else's based on genetic affiliation. Whether or not one believes that genetic affiliation between intended parents and the baby does or should make a significant difference in the permissibility of surrogacy or in identifying legal motherhood, studies suggest that the lack of genetic affiliation matters to gestational surrogates (but apparently not to traditional surrogates) and facilitates the process for them. . . .
>
> Selling one's gestational services seems to be . . . more personal, involved, and implicating of bodily integrity than housekeeping, but not as potentially harmful as agreeing to undergo unproven drug therapies for high levels of compensation. Gestation is a condition, not an irreplaceable body part. And, with modern medicine, gestation is no more dangerous than many other activities that are legal. Still, it is a commitment of a bodily function, long-term and involved, that does not mirror typical jobs. Thus, there is room to be concerned about the autonomy of the surrogate without paternalistically denying her right to engage in their services altogether.

Pamela Laufer-Ukeles, *Mothering for Money: Regulating Commercial Intimacy*, 88 Ind. L.J. 1223, 1230-1231, 1249 (2013). *Accord*, Marjorie Maguire Shultz, *Reproductive Technology and Intent-Based Parenthood: An Opportunity for Gender Neutrality*, 1990 Wis. L. Rev. 297, 302-303; Lori B. Andrews, *Surrogate Motherhood: The Challenge for Feminists*, 16 Law Med. & Health Care 72 (1988); Carmel Shalev, *Birth Power: The Case for Surrogacy* (1989). Judge Richard Posner has argued that surrogacy contracts should be specifically enforced because (a) they are mutually beneficial to the parties; (b) they benefit the child because without them the child would not have been born; (c) there is no evidence that women, in general, misunderstand the distress they will feel at having to give up the baby; (d) poor women are better off if they have the choice to enter such agreements to make money; (e) women are competent to make voluntary and informed choices and it is paternalistic to assume that they are not competent to do so; and (f) commodification of the surrogacy relation is unlikely to affect social norms or attitudes toward the sanctity of human life. Richard Posner, *The Ethics and Economics of Enforcing Contracts of Surrogate Motherhood*, 5 J. Contemp. Health L. & Poly. 21 (1989); *see also* Richard A. Epstein, *Surrogacy: The Case for Full Contractual*

Enforcement, 81 Va. L. Rev. 2377 (1995). For a recent summary of the evolving debate, *see* Elizabeth Scott, *Surrogacy and the Politics of Commodification*, 72 Law & Contemp. Probs. 109 (2009).

Should it make a difference for the law's treatment of these arrangements whether the surrogate is also the donor of the ovum used to create the embryo or whether the contract involves so-called gestational surrogacy? *See A.G.R. v. D.R.H.*, Slip Op., Docket No. FD-09-1838-07 (N.J. Super. Ct. Hudson Cty., Dec. 23, 2009) (*available at http://graphics8.nytimes.com/packages/pdf/national/20091231_SURROGATE.pdf*) (rejecting the argument that the *Baby M* decision applied only when the surrogate is genetically related to the infant). Some of the states that permit surrogacy do so only for gestational surrogates. *See, e.g.*, 750 Ill. Comp. Stat. 47/1-47/75; N.D.C.C. §14-18-08.

§4 FROZEN EMBRYOS

In vitro fertilization techniques can enable couples with fertility problems to have children. Because the failure rate of the procedure is very high, the practice is to attempt to fertilize a number of eggs, allow them to begin dividing, and to implant some of the fertilized ova. Those that are not used initially are preserved for later use if the current implantation fails to result in a pregnancy. Disputes over the disposition of these fertilized ova have generated a host of difficult legal issues.

Are preembryos persons or property? In *Davis v. Davis*, 842 S.W.2d 588 (Tenn. 1992), Mary Sue Davis and Junior Davis disagreed over the use of seven of Mary Sue's preserved ova, fertilized by Junior's sperm. After the couple divorced, Mary Sue sought to have some of these frozen embryos implanted so that she could have a child. Junior objected. In an opinion by Judge W. Dale Young, the trial court held that "life begins at conception," that "human embryos are not property" but children, that it was in the best interests of those children to be available for implantation, and that "custody" of the children should be awarded to Mary Sue. *Id.* at 594. If this is correct, could Mary Sue Davis be vulnerable to a charge of child neglect or reckless abandonment if she chose *not* to implant the fertilized embryos?

> **Terms:**
> Courts variously characterize the fertilized ova as **embryos**, **frozen embryos**, **preembryos**, and **prezygotes**. In this context, the terms are interchangeable, although they may have different connotations and rhetorical effects.

The court of appeals reversed, noting that fetuses are not "persons" for a variety of purposes under Tennessee law. For example, the state's wrongful death statute does not allow a wrongful death for a viable fetus that is not first born alive; moreover, abortions were lawful in the state under a scheme that granted fetuses more protection as they developed. Consequently, the court held that the parties "share an interest in the seven fertilized ova" and therefore have the right to joint control with equal voice over their disposition.

The Tennessee Supreme Court agreed with the court of appeals that frozen embryos were not "persons" under Tennessee law, but did not categorize them as "property" either, *id.* at 597:

> [P]reembryos are not, strictly speaking, either "persons" or "property," but occupy an interim category that entitles them to special respect because of their potential for human life. It follows that any interest that Mary Sue Davis and Junior Davis have in the preembryos in this case is not a true property interest. However, they do have an interest in the nature of ownership, to the extent that they have decision-making authority concerning disposition of the preembryos, within the scope of policy set by law.

In contrast, in *Kass v. Kass*, 1995 WL 110368 (N.Y. Sup. Ct. 1995), a New York trial judge held that preembryos were "in the nature of a property interest." *Id.* at *1. However, the appellate division reversed on contractual grounds, sidestepping the issue of whether embryos are persons or property under New York law. 663 N.Y.S.2d 581, 585 (App. Div. 1997), *aff'd*, 696 N.E.2d 174 (N.Y. 1998). Should preembryos be categorized as persons, property, or something in between? Does attempting this categorization even make sense? What is at stake in the categorization decision?

Competing rights. Courts that have ruled on the matter usually characterize disputes over preembryos as conflicts between the right of one party to procreate and the right of the other party not to be forced to become a parent against his or her will. The latter right usually trumps. However, in dicta, some courts have expressed willingness to carve out an exception when the party seeking to implant the preembryos could not procreate any other way.

In *Davis*, the court of appeals reversed on rights grounds. "It would be repugnant and offensive to constitutional principles to order Mary Sue to implant these fertilized ova against her will. It would be equally repugnant to order Junior to bear the psychological, if not the legal, consequences of paternity against his will." 1990 WL 130807, at *3 (Tenn. Ct. App. 1990). Do you agree that it would be *equally* repugnant?

By the time *Davis* reached the Tennessee Supreme Court, Mary Sue Davis (now Mary Sue Stowe) had remarried and no longer wanted to use the preembryos herself but sought authority to donate them to a childless couple. Her ex-husband, also now remarried, vehemently opposed such a donation and preferred to see the preembryos destroyed. Agreeing with the appeals court's resolution of the conflict between the right to procreate and the right to avoid procreation, the court held that Junior Davis's interest in avoiding unwanted parenthood should prevail over Mary Sue Stowe's interest in donating the preembryos to avoid the burden of knowing that the lengthy and invasive procedures she had undergone were futile. The court further noted that the case would be closer if she were seeking to use the preembryos herself, "but only if she could not achieve parenthood by any other reasonable means." The court concluded, 842 S.W.2d at 604:

> Ordinarily, the party wishing to avoid procreation should prevail, assuming that the other party has a reasonable possibility of achieving parenthood by means other than use of the preembryos in question. If no other reasonable alternatives exist, then the argument in favor of using the preembryos to achieve pregnancy should be considered. However, if the party seeking control of the preembryos intends merely to donate them to another couple, the objecting party obviously has the greater interest and should prevail.

In *J.B. v. M.B.*, 751 A.2d 613 (N.J. Super. Ct. App. Div. 2000), the ex-husband in a divorce proceeding sought control of preembryos for the purpose of impregnating a woman if he later developed a new relationship or for donation to an infertile couple. The ex-wife objected and wanted the preembryos destroyed. In ruling for the ex-wife, the court relied on a rights analysis mirroring that in *Davis, id.* at 618-619:

> In the present case, the wife's right not to become a parent seemingly conflicts with the husband's right to procreate. The conflict, however, is more apparent than real. Recognition and enforcement of the wife's right would not seriously impair the husband's right to procreate. Though his right to procreate using the wife's egg would be terminated, he retains the capacity to father children.
>
> On the other hand, enforcing the husband's right to procreate using the embryos at issue in this case could result in the birth of the wife's biological child. Even if the wife were relieved of the financial and custodial responsibility for her child, the fact that her biological child would exist in an environment controlled by strangers is understandably unacceptable to the wife.

On review, 783 A.2d 707 (N.J. 2001), the New Jersey Supreme Court affirmed the lower court's rights analysis, *id.* at 717:

> M.B.'s right to procreate is not lost if he is denied an opportunity to use or donate the preembryos. M.B. is already a father and is able to become a father to additional children, whether through natural procreation or further in vitro fertilization. In contrast, J.B.'s right not to procreate may be lost through attempted use or through donation of the preembryos. Implantation, if successful, would result in the birth of her biological child and could have life-long emotional and psychological repercussions.

Unlike the courts in *Davis* and *J.B.*, the trial court in *Kass* expressed a different conception of the rights involved. Under this analysis, the woman would always have control of the preembryos in a divorce proceeding despite her husband's objection, on the ground that once the eggs were fertilized, the husband had no right to force the wife to stop the pregnancy, *id.* at *3:

> Just as an in vivo husband's "right to avoid procreation" is waived and ceases to exist after intercourse in a coital reproduction, such right should be deemed waived and non-existent after his participation in an in vitro program. Upon entering he knows, or should have known, that technology is such that the possibility and probability of a delayed implantation are very real. Absent some indication of a contrary intent, the agreement to participate, if it does not expressly provide for such an eventuality, must be deemed an agreement to permit a delayed implantation.

In reversing, the appellate division stated that the trial court "committed a fundamental error in equating a prospective mother's decision whether to undergo implantation of prezygotes which are the product of her participation in an [in vitro fertilization] procedure with a pregnant woman's right to exercise exclusive control over the fate of her []fetus." 663 N.Y.S.2d 581, 585 (App. Div. 1997), *aff'd*, 696 N.E.2d 174 (N.Y. 1998). Which rights analysis do you agree with? Can you think of an alternative way to frame the issue?

Biological parenthood is central to the prevailing rights analysis described above. For instance, in *Litowitz v. Litowitz*, 10 P.3d 1086 (Wash. Ct. App.), *rev'd*, 48 P.3d 261 (Wash. 2000), Becky Litowitz could not provide the eggs herself because of a hysterectomy. The couple hired a third party to donate eggs, subsequently fertilized by David Litowitz's sperm. After a divorce, Becky sought to have the eggs implanted in a surrogate to produce a child she would raise. However, the court awarded control to David, who wanted to donate the eggs to an infertile couple in another state. Because Becky's own eggs had not been used to produce the preembryos, the court reasoned that David's disposing of the preembryos as he wished would not infringe on her right not to procreate. Conversely, the court ruled that Becky's desired implantation of the preembryos in a surrogate to produce a child Becky would raise *would* infringe on David's right not to procreate. Do you agree with this result? Is it fair to allow one party to invoke his or her right not to procreate to prevent the other party from using the preembryos to beget a child, and then donate the preembryos to a couple in another state? Should the right not to procreate govern only when the party invoking it actually seeks *not* to procreate, rather than to procreate elsewhere? What rights should the woman who donated the eggs have if she chooses to assert them? Note that the trial court's decision was reversed on appeal because the parties' contract with the agency provided for destruction of the preembryos if they were not implanted within five years.

Contracts regarding preembryos. If the parties sign an agreement regarding disposition of the preembryos in the event of a dispute, should the agreement be enforced? Courts have generally held that the wishes of the parties should be honored if ascertainable. *See, e.g., Kass*, 663 N.Y.S.2d at 590 ("where the parties have indicated their mutual intent regarding the disposition of the pre-zygotes in the event of the occurrence of a contingency that decision must be scrupulously honored"); *In re Litowitz*, 48 P.3d 261 (Wash. 2002) (enforcing contract between husband and wife that fertilized embryos would be thawed out and destroyed if they were not implanted within five years); *Roman v. Roman*, 193 S.W.3d 40 (Tex. Ct. App. 2006) (enforcing an agreement to dispose of frozen embryos entered into by a divorcing couple before they created the embryos and refusing to allow the wife to keep the embryos as part of the division of community property).

Does it make sense to "scrupulously honor" the intent of the parties in this context? Is the court truly refraining from interfering with the parties' expressed wishes? Isn't the court interfering with one party's wishes no matter how it decides? Would the court have ruled the same way if the agreement gave one party a right to procreate over the other's objection?

In *A.Z. v. B.Z.*, 725 N.E.2d 1051 (Mass. 2000), the Supreme Judicial Court of Massachusetts held an agreement granting ultimate control of fertilized ova to the wife unenforceable because it violated a public policy against forcing a person to become a parent against his or her will. *Accord, In re Witten*, 672 N.W.2d 768 (Iowa 2003). Should all contracts regarding the disposition of preembryos be invalid? Or should they be enforced when they do not result in one party becoming a parent against his or her will?

Although a lower New Jersey court agreed with the Massachusetts rule, *J.B. v. M.B.*, 751 A.2d 613 (N.J. Super. Ct. App. Div. 2000), the Supreme Court of New Jersey modified, announcing that the "better rule, and the one we adopt, is to enforce agreements entered into at the time in vitro fertilization is begun, subject to the right of either party to change his or her mind about disposition up to the point of use or destruction of any stored preembryos." 783 A.2d at 719. How is this rule different from the one promulgated in *A.Z. v. B.Z.*? Is the "right of either party to change his or her mind" tantamount to a blanket invalidation of all contracts regarding the disposition of preembryos?

As with surrogacy contracts, some states have stepped in with legislation. A few states prohibit the sale of human embryos under any circumstances. *See* Fla. Stat. §873.05; Ind. Stat. §35-46-5-3(a); La. Stat. §122. Others single out the sale of embryos for research for legal prohibition. *See* Conn. Stat. §19a-32d; Mass. Gen. Laws §111L-8. Why might a state prohibit the sale of embryos for research but allow their sale for other purposes? A number of states also have enacted statutes that attempt to prevent disputes over preembryos. *See, e.g.*, Cal. Health & Safety Code §125315 (requiring fertility treatment providers to present patients with a form setting forth options for the disposition of stored embryos in the event of, for example, death or divorce); Tex. Fam. Code §160.706; Fla. Stat. §742.17; N.H. Rev. Stat. §168-B:15.

Differing approaches or underlying unity? Since only a handful of courts have spoken on the issue of in vitro fertilization disputes, the law in most states remains uncertain. The few courts that have approached the issue have done so in several different ways. In what ways do these approaches conflict? Is the law in this area simply an unsettled mess? Consider the fact that the *result* in all the cases is the same: none of the courts have allowed preembryos to be implanted over the objection of a party who wants the preembryos discarded. Are the courts using different arguments to achieve the same result? Is there some underlying or hidden reason for this uniform result? Or is the uniformity of result a coincidence?

§5 BODY PARTS

§5.1 Are Body Parts Property?

Moore v. Regents of the University of California

793 P.2d 479 (Cal. 1990)

EDWARD A. PANELLI, Justice.

The plaintiff is John Moore (Moore), who underwent treatment for hairy-cell leukemia at the Medical Center of the University of California at Los Angeles (UCLA Medical Center). The five defendants are: (1) Dr. David W. Golde (Golde), a physician who attended Moore at UCLA Medical Center; (2) the Regents of the University of California (Regents), who own and operate the university; (3) Shirley G. Quan [(Quan)], a researcher employed by the Regents; (4) Genetics Institute, Inc. (Genetics

Institute); and (5) Sandoz Pharmaceuticals Corporation and related entities (collectively Sandoz).

Moore first visited UCLA Medical Center on October 5, 1976, shortly after he learned that he had hairy-cell leukemia. After hospitalizing Moore and "withdraw[ing] extensive amounts of blood, bone marrow aspirate, and other bodily substances," Golde confirmed that diagnosis. At this time all defendants, including Golde, were aware that "certain blood products and blood components were of great value in a number of commercial and scientific efforts" and that access to a patient whose blood contained these substances would provide "competitive, commercial, and scientific advantages."

On October 8, 1976, Golde recommended that Moore's spleen be removed. Golde informed Moore "that he had reason to fear for his life, and that the proposed splenectomy operation . . . was necessary to slow down the progress of his disease." Based upon Golde's representations, Moore signed a written consent form authorizing the splenectomy.

Before the operation, Golde and Quan "formed the intent and made arrangements to obtain portions of [Moore's] spleen following its removal" and to take them to a separate research unit. Golde gave written instructions to this effect on October 18 and 19, 1976. These research activities "were not intended to have . . . any relation to [Moore's] medical . . . care." However, neither Golde nor Quan informed Moore of their plans to conduct this research or requested his permission. Surgeons at UCLA Medical Center, whom the complaint does not name as defendants, removed Moore's spleen on October 20, 1976.

Moore returned to the UCLA Medical Center several times between November 1976 and September 1983. He did so at Golde's direction and based upon representations "that such visits were necessary and required for his health and well-being, and based upon the trust inherent in and by virtue of the physician-patient relationship. . . ." On each of these visits Golde withdrew additional samples of "blood, blood serum, skin, bone marrow aspirate, and sperm." On each occasion Moore travelled to the UCLA Medical Center from his home in Seattle because he had been told that the procedures were to be performed only there and only under Golde's direction.

[The court then quoted plaintiff's complaint:] "In fact, [however,] throughout the period of time that [Moore] was under [Golde's] care and treatment, . . . the defendants were actively involved in a number of activities which they concealed from [Moore]. . . ." Specifically, defendants were conducting research on Moore's cells and planned to "benefit financially and competitively . . . [by exploiting the cells] and [their] exclusive access to [the cells] by virtue of [Golde's] on-going physician-patient relationship. . . ."

Sometime before August 1979, Golde established a cell line from Moore's T-lymphocytes. On January 30, 1981, the Regents applied for a patent on the cell line, listing Golde and Quan as inventors. "[B]y virtue of an established policy . . . , [the] Regents, Golde, and Quan would share in any royalties or profits . . . arising out of [the] patent." The patent issued on March 20, 1984, naming Golde and Quan as the inventors of the cell line and the Regents as the assignee of the patent. (U.S. Patent No. 4,438,032 (Mar. 20, 1984).)

The Regents' patent also covers various methods for using the cell line to produce lymphokines. Moore admits in his complaint that "the true clinical potential of each of the lymphokines . . . [is] difficult to predict, [but] . . . competing commercial firms in these relevant fields have published reports in biotechnology industry periodicals predicting a potential market of approximately 3.01 Billion Dollars by the year 1990 for a whole range of [such lymphokines]. . . ."

With the Regents' assistance, Golde negotiated agreements for commercial development of the cell line and products to be derived from it. Under an agreement with Genetics Institute, Golde "became a paid consultant" and "acquired the rights to 75,000 shares of common stock." Genetics Institute also agreed to pay Golde and the Regents "at least $330,000 over three years, including a pro-rata share of [Golde's] salary and fringe benefits, in exchange for . . . exclusive access to the materials and research performed" on the cell line and products derived from it. On June 4, 1982, Sandoz "was added to the agreement," and compensation payable to Golde and the Regents was increased by $110,000. "[T]hroughout this period, . . . Quan spent as much as 70 [percent] of her time working for [the] Regents on research" related to the cell line.

III. Discussion

A. Breach of Fiduciary Duty and Lack of Informed Consent

Moore repeatedly alleges that Golde failed to disclose the extent of his research and economic interests in Moore's cells before obtaining consent to the medical procedures by which the cells were extracted. These allegations, in our view, state a cause of action against Golde for invading a legally protected interest of his patient. This cause of action can properly be characterized either as the breach of a fiduciary duty to disclose facts material to the patient's consent or, alternatively, as the performance of medical procedures without first having obtained the patient's informed consent.

B. Conversion

Moore also attempts to characterize the invasion of his rights as a conversion — a tort that protects against interference with possessory and ownership interests in personal property. He theorizes that he continued to own his cells following their removal from his body, at least for the purpose of directing their use, and that he never consented to their use in potentially lucrative medical research. Thus, to complete Moore's argument, defendants' unauthorized use of his cells constitutes a conversion. As a result of the alleged conversion, Moore claims a proprietary interest in each of the products that any of the defendants might ever create from his cells or the patented cell line.

1. Moore's Claim Under Existing Law

Since Moore clearly did not expect to retain possession of his cells following their removal, to sue for their conversion he must have retained an ownership interest in them.

Moore relies, as did the Court of Appeal, primarily on decisions addressing privacy rights. One line of cases involves unwanted publicity. These opinions hold that every person has a proprietary interest in his own likeness and that unauthorized, business use of a likeness is redressible as a tort.

Moore . . . argues that "[i]f the courts have found a sufficient proprietary interest in one's persona, how could one not have a right in one's own genetic material, something far more profoundly the essence of one's human uniqueness than a name or a face?" However, . . . the goal and result of defendants' efforts has been to manufacture lymphokines. Lymphokines, unlike a name or a face, have the same molecular structure in every human being and the same, important functions in every human being's immune system. Moreover, the particular genetic material which is responsible for the natural production of lymphokines, and which defendants use to manufacture lymphokines in the laboratory, is also the same in every person; it is no more unique to Moore than the number of vertebrae in the spine or the chemical formula of hemoglobin.

[Moore also appeals to privacy cases holding that patients have the right to refuse medical treatment because each person has a right to determine what shall be done with his or her own body. However, we can protect privacy and personal dignity by requiring disclosure under fiduciary duty and informed consent doctrines, rather than] accepting the extremely problematic conclusion that interference with those interests amounts to a conversion of personal property.

The next consideration that makes Moore's claim of ownership problematic is California statutory law, which drastically limits a patient's control over excised cells [by regulating disposal of human tissues to protect public health and safety. *Cal. Health & Safety Code* §§7001, 7054.4]. By restricting how excised cells may be used and requiring their eventual destruction, the statute eliminates so many of the rights ordinarily attached to property that one cannot simply assume that what is left amounts to "property" or "ownership" for purposes of conversion law.

Finally, the subject matter of the Regents' patent — the patented cell line and the products derived from it — cannot be Moore's property. This is because the patented cell line is both factually and legally distinct from the cells taken from Moore's body. Federal law permits the patenting of organisms that represent the product of "human ingenuity," but not naturally occurring organisms. *Diamond v. Chakrabarty*, 447 U.S. 303, 309-310 (1980). Human cell lines are patentable because "[l]ong-term adaptation and growth of human tissues and cells in culture is difficult — often considered an art . . . ," and the probability of success is low. It is this inventive effort that patent law rewards, not the discovery of naturally occurring raw materials. Thus, Moore's allegations that he owns the cell line and the products derived from it are inconsistent with the patent, which constitutes an authoritative determination that the cell line is the product of invention.

2. *Should Conversion Liability Be Extended?*

Of the relevant policy considerations, two are of overriding importance. The first is protection of a competent patient's right to make autonomous medical decisions. . . .

This policy weighs in favor of providing a remedy to patients when physicians act with undisclosed motives that may affect their professional judgment. The second important policy consideration is that we not threaten with disabling civil liability innocent parties who are engaged in socially useful activities, such as researchers who have no reason to believe that their use of a particular cell sample is, or may be, against a donor's wishes.

Research on human cells plays a critical role in medical research. This is so because researchers are increasingly able to isolate naturally occurring, medically useful biological substances and to produce useful quantities of such substances through genetic engineering. These efforts are beginning to bear fruit. Products developed through biotechnology that have already been approved for marketing in this country include treatments and tests for leukemia, cancer, diabetes, dwarfism, hepatitis-B, kidney transplant rejection, emphysema, osteoporosis, ulcers, anemia, infertility, and gynecological tumors, to name but a few.

The extension of conversion law into this area will hinder research by restricting access to the necessary raw materials. Thousands of human cell lines already exist in tissue repositories, such as the American Type Culture Collection and those operated by the National Institutes of Health and the American Cancer Society. These repositories respond to tens of thousands of requests for samples annually. Since the patent office requires the holders of patents on cell lines to make samples available to anyone, many patent holders place their cell lines in repositories to avoid the administrative burden of responding to requests. At present, human cell lines are routinely copied and distributed to other researchers for experimental purposes, usually free of charge. This exchange of scientific materials, which still is relatively free and efficient, will surely be compromised if each cell sample becomes the potential subject matter of a lawsuit.

To expand liability by extending conversion law into this area would have a broad impact. The House Committee on Science and Technology of the United States Congress found that "49 percent of the researchers at medical institutions surveyed used human tissues or cells in their research." Many receive grants from the National Institutes of Health for this work. In addition, "there are nearly 350 commercial biotechnology firms in the United States actively engaged in biotechnology research and commercial product development and approximately 25 to 30 percent appear to be engaged in research to develop a human therapeutic or diagnostic reagent. . . . Most, but not all, of the human therapeutic products are derived from human tissues and cells, or human cell lines or cloned genes."

If the scientific users of human cells are to be held liable for failing to investigate the consensual pedigree of their raw materials, we believe the Legislature should make that decision. Complex policy choices affecting all society are involved, and "[l]egislatures, in making such policy decisions, have the ability to gather empirical evidence, solicit the advice of experts, and hold hearings at which all interested parties present evidence and express their views. . . ." *Foley v. Interactive Data Corp.*, 765 P.2d 373, 397 n.31 (Cal. 1988).

For these reasons, we hold that the allegations of Moore's third amended complaint state a cause of action for breach of fiduciary duty or lack of informed consent, but not conversion.

ARMAND ARABIAN, Justice, concurring.

Plaintiff has asked us to recognize and enforce a right to sell one's own body tissue for profit. He entreats us to regard the human vessel — the single most venerated and protected subject in any civilized society — as equal with the basest commercial commodity. He urges us to commingle the sacred with the profane. He asks much.

I share Justice Mosk's sense of outrage [at defendants' conduct], but I cannot follow its path. His eloquent paean to the human spirit illuminates the problem, not the solution. Does it uplift or degrade the "unique human persona" to treat human tissue as a fungible article of commerce? Would it advance or impede the human condition, spiritually or scientifically, by delivering the majestic force of the law behind plaintiff's claim? I do not know the answers to these troubling questions, nor am I willing — like Justice Mosk — to treat them simply as issues of "tort" law, susceptible of judicial resolution.

Where then shall a complete resolution be found? Clearly the Legislature, as the majority opinion suggests, is the proper deliberative forum.

ALLEN BROUSSARD, Justice, concurring and dissenting.

If defendants had informed plaintiff, prior to removal, of the possible uses to which his body part could be put and plaintiff had authorized one particular use, it is clear . . . that defendants would be liable for conversion if they disregarded plaintiff's decision and used the body part in an unauthorized manner for their own economic benefit. Although in this case defendants did not disregard a specific directive from plaintiff with regard to the future use of his body part, the complaint alleges that, before the body part was removed, defendants intentionally withheld material information that they were under an obligation to disclose to plaintiff and that was necessary for his exercise of control over the body part; the complaint also alleges that defendants withheld such information in order to appropriate the control over the future use of such body part for their own economic benefit. If these allegations are true, defendants clearly improperly interfered with plaintiff's right in his body part at a time when he had the authority to determine the future use of such part, thereby misappropriating plaintiff's right of control for their own advantage. Under these circumstances, the complaint fully satisfies the established requirements of a conversion cause of action.

[T]he majority's fear that the availability of a conversion remedy will restrict access to existing cell lines is unrealistic. In the vast majority of instances the tissues and cells in existing repositories will not represent a potential source of liability because they will have come from patients who consented to their organ's use for scientific purposes under circumstances in which such consent was not tainted by a failure to disclose the known valuable nature of the cells.

Furthermore, even in the rare instance — like the present case — in which a conversion action might be successfully pursued, the potential liability is not likely "to destroy the economic incentive to conduct important medical research," as the majority asserts. If, as the majority suggests, the great bulk of the value of a cell line patent and derivative products is attributable to the efforts of medical researchers and drug companies, rather than to the "raw materials" taken from a patient, the patient's damages will be correspondingly limited, and innocent medical researchers and drug manufacturers will retain the considerable economic benefits resulting from their own work.

Justice Arabian's concurring opinion suggests that the majority's conclusion is informed by the precept that it is immoral to sell human body parts for profit. But the majority's rejection of plaintiff's conversion cause of action does not mean that body parts may not be bought or sold for research or commercial purposes or that no private individual or entity may benefit economically from the fortuitous value of plaintiff's diseased cells. Far from elevating these biological materials above the marketplace, the majority's holding simply bars plaintiff, the source of the cells, from obtaining the benefit of the cells' value, but permits defendants, who allegedly obtained the cells from plaintiff by improper means, to retain and exploit the full economic value of their ill-gotten gains free of their ordinary common law liability for conversion.

STANLEY MOSK, Justice, dissenting.

[T]he concept of property is often said to refer to a "bundle of rights" that may be exercised with respect to that object—principally the rights to possess the property, to use the property, to exclude others from the property, and to dispose of the property by sale or by gift. . . . But the same bundle of rights does not attach to all forms of property. For a variety of policy reasons, the law limits or even forbids the exercise of certain rights over certain forms of property. For example, both law and contract may limit the right of an owner of real property to use his parcel as he sees fit. Owners of various forms of personal property may likewise be subject to restrictions on the time, place, and manner of their use. Limitations on the disposition of real property, while less common, may also be imposed. Finally, some types of personal property may be sold but not given away,[3] while others may be given away but not sold,[4] and still others may neither be given away nor sold.[5]

In each of the foregoing instances, the limitation or prohibition diminishes the bundle of rights that would otherwise attach to the property, yet what remains is still deemed in law to be a protectible property interest. [Moore] at least had the right to do with his own tissue whatever the defendants did with it: *i.e.*, he could have contracted with researchers and pharmaceutical companies to develop and exploit the vast commercial potential of his tissue and its products. Defendants certainly believe that their right to do the foregoing is not barred by section 7054.4 and is a significant property right. . . . The Court of Appeal summed up the point by observing that "Defendants'

3. A person contemplating bankruptcy may sell his property at its "reasonably equivalent value," but he may not make a gift of the same property. (*See* 11 U.S.C. §548(a).)

4. A sportsman may give away wild fish or game that he has caught or killed pursuant to his license, but he may not sell it. (*Fish & Game Code*, §§3039, 7121.) The transfer of human organs and blood is a special case that I discuss below.

5. *E.g.*, a license to practice a profession, or a prescription drug in the hands of the person for whom it is prescribed.

position that plaintiff cannot own his tissue, but that they can, is fraught with irony." It is also legally untenable.

[Nor does the patent on the cell line preclude plaintiff's property claim.] To be sure, the patent granted defendants the exclusive right to make, use, or sell the invention for a period of 17 years. But Moore does not assert any such right for himself. Rather, he seeks to show that he is entitled, in fairness and equity, to some share in the profits that defendants have made and will make from their commercial exploitation of the Mo cell line. I do not question that the cell line is primarily the product of defendants' inventive effort. Yet likewise no one can question Moore's crucial contribution to the invention — an invention named, ironically, after him: but for the cells of Moore's body taken by defendants, there would have been no Mo cell line.

[E]very individual has a legally protectible property interest in his own body and its products. First, our society acknowledges a profound ethical imperative to respect the human body as the physical and temporal expression of the unique human persona. One manifestation of that respect is our prohibition against direct abuse of the body by torture or other forms of cruel or unusual punishment. Another is our prohibition against indirect abuse of the body by its economic exploitation for the sole benefit of another person. The most abhorrent form of such exploitation, of course, was the institution of slavery. Lesser forms, such as indentured servitude or even debtor's prison, have also disappeared. Yet their specter haunts the laboratories and boardrooms of today's biotechnological research-industrial complex. It arises wherever scientists or industrialists claim, as defendants claim here, the right to appropriate and exploit a patient's tissue for their sole economic benefit — the right, in other words, to freely mine or harvest valuable physical properties of the patient's body: ". . . Such research tends to treat the human body as a commodity — a means to a profitable end. The dignity and sanctity with which we regard the human whole, body as well as mind and soul, are absent when we allow researchers to further their own interests without the patient's participation by using a patient's cells as the basis for a marketable product." Danforth, *Cells, Sales, & Royalties: The Patient's Right to a Portion of the Profits,* 6 Yale L. & Pol'y Rev. 179, 190 (1988).

A second policy consideration adds notions of equity to those of ethics. Our society values fundamental fairness in dealings between its members, and condemns the unjust enrichment of any member at the expense of another. This is particularly true when, as here, the parties are not in equal bargaining positions. We are repeatedly told that the commercial products of the biotechnological revolution "hold the promise of tremendous profit." In the case at bar, for example, the complaint alleges that the market for the kinds of proteins produced by the Mo cell line was predicted to exceed $3 billion by 1990. These profits are currently shared exclusively between the biotechnology industry and the universities that support that industry.

There is, however, a third party to the biotechnology enterprise — the patient who is the source of the blood or tissue from which all these profits are derived. While he may be a silent partner, his contribution to the venture is absolutely crucial: . . . but for the cells of Moore's body taken by defendants there would have been no Mo cell line at all. Yet defendants deny that Moore is entitled to any share whatever in the proceeds of this cell line. This is both inequitable and immoral.

Notes and Questions

1. **Relatives as owners of deceased family-members' bodies and body parts.** In *Brotherton v. Cleveland*, 923 F.2d 477 (6th Cir. 1991), plaintiff Deborah Brotherton alleged that defendants, in the course of performing an autopsy, removed her deceased husband's corneas for use as anatomical gifts without her consent. The court noted that "Ohio Rev. Code §2108.02(B), as part of the *Uniform Anatomical Gift Act* governing gifts of organs and tissues for research or transplants, granted her the right to control the disposal of Steven Brotherton's body." It held that "the aggregate of rights granted by the state of Ohio to Deborah Brotherton rises to the level of a 'legitimate claim of entitlement' in Steven Brotherton's body, including his corneas," and that this was sufficient to establish a property interest protected by the fourteenth amendment's prohibition on deprivations of property without due process of law. *See also Whaley v. County of Tuscola*, 58 F.3d 1111 (6th Cir. 1991) (recognizing a property interest in body parts and refusing to dismiss lawsuits by relatives of deceased persons whose eyeballs and corneas had been removed without permission by a pathology assistant at a county hospital). Suppose these events had occurred in California. Would the California Supreme Court reach the same result as the Sixth Circuit? *Cf. Perryman v. County of Los Angeles*, 153 Cal. App. 4th 1189 (2007) (relying on *Moore* and holding that the relatives of a murder victim did not have a property interest in the victim's body for the purposes of a claim that the county coroner mishandled the remains), *vacated and remanded for reconsideration by* 208 P.3d 622 (Cal. 2009). *But see Newman v. Sathyavaglswaran*, 287 F.3d 786 (9th Cir. 2002) (assessing California law and holding that parents had a constitutionally protected property interest in deceased children's corneas removed by county workers without their consent).

2. **Cell lines and the rights of descendants.** In 1951, Henrietta Lacks died of cervical cancer. Doctors removed some cells from her tumors and used them to start a number of cell lines. In the decades since her death, those cell lines have been used around the world in tens of thousands of studies. Lacks's surviving family members were not told about the use of her cells, and did not even discover that the cells were in widespread use until two decades later. Lacks's entire genetic code was even sequenced and published without the knowledge or approval of surviving family members. In 2013, the family entered into an agreement with the National Institutes of Health that would give family members a greater say over how Lacks's cells are used. *See* Carl Zimmer, *A Family Consents to a Medical Gift, 62 Years Later*, N.Y. Times, Aug. 7, 2013. For more on the story of Lacks's case, *see* Rebecca Skloot's 2010 book, *The Immortal Life of Henrietta Lacks.* Should surviving family members be entitled to a share of any profits earned from Lacks's cell lines?

3. **Informed consent.** Suppose that before Moore's operation Golde had informed Moore of his intent to use Moore's cells to create a cell line. Would the case have come out the same way? If Golde and Moore had signed a contract in which Golde agreed to pay Moore a percentage of the earnings from the cell line, would such a contract be enforceable under the majority's analysis in *Moore*? If Golde did not

commit the tort of conversion (an unprivileged appropriation of Moore's property), is Moore free to treat his body parts or cells as property that he can sell for the use of another?

Problem

A man who is sick with cancer deposits his sperm in a sperm bank for the purpose of impregnating his fiancée through in vitro fertilization. He dies before they are married and before the procedure can be completed, having left a will bequeathing all his "personal property" to his two adult children. The children claim the sperm are their property and want them to be destroyed, while the fiancée wants to try to have a child using the sperm. What should the court do? *See Hecht v. Superior Court*, 59 Cal. Rptr. 2d 222, 226 (Ct. App. 1996) (wrestling with the question of whether sperm should be treated as "property" and deciding in the negative).

§5.2 Markets in Body Parts

The *National Organ Transplant Act*, 42 U.S.C. §274e, makes it a federal crime "to knowingly acquire, receive, or otherwise transfer any human organ for valuable consideration for use in human transplantation if the transfer affects interstate commerce." It defines organs as "the human (including fetal) kidney, liver, heart, lung, pancreas, bone marrow, cornea, eye, bone, and skin or any subpart thereof and any other human organ (or any subpart thereof, including that derived from a fetus) specified by the Secretary of Health and Human Services by regulation." *Id.* Thus, blood is not an "organ" and so can be donated in exchange for valuable consideration. It is common for blood donors to receive cash and other incentives in exchange for their donation. Is it reasonable for the law to treat blood differently than other organs? Consider the following case.

Flynn v. Holder

684 F.3d 852 (9th Cir. 2012)

Andrew Kleinfeld, Senior Circuit Judge:

I. Facts

The complaint challenges the constitutionality of the ban on compensation for human organs in the National Organ Transplant Act, as applied to bone marrow transplants.

Some plaintiffs are parents of sick children who have diseases such as leukemia and a rare type of anemia, which can be fatal without bone marrow transplants. Another plaintiff is a physician and medical school professor, and an expert in bone marrow transplantation. He says that at least one out of five of his patients dies because no matching bone marrow donor can be found, and many others have complications when scarcity of matching donors compels him to use imperfectly matched donors.

One plaintiff is a parent of mixed race children, for whom sufficiently matched donors are especially scarce, because mixed race persons typically have the rarest marrow cell types. One plaintiff is an African-American man suffering from leukemia who received a bone marrow transplant from his sister. She was an imperfect match and, though the transplant saved his life, he continues to suffer from life-threatening and disabling complications on account of the slight genetic mismatch.

Another plaintiff is a California nonprofit corporation that seeks to operate a program incentivizing bone marrow donations. The corporation proposes to offer $3,000 awards in the form of scholarships, housing allowances, or gifts to charities selected by donors, initially to minority and mixed race donors of bone marrow cells, who are likely to have the rarest marrow cell type. The corporation, MoreMarrowDonors.org, alleges that it cannot launch this program because the National Organ Transplant Act criminalizes payment of compensation for organs, and classifies bone marrow as an organ.

We generally use the word "marrow" to refer to the soft, fatty material in the central cavities of big bones, what some people suck out of beef bones. Bone marrow is the body's blood manufacturing factory. Bone marrow transplants enable sick patients, whose own blood cells need to be killed to save their lives, to produce new blood cells. For example, patients with leukemia, which is cancer of the blood or bone marrow, may need chemotherapy or radiation to kill the cancer cells in their blood. The treatments kill the white blood cells essential to their immune systems. The patients will die if the killed cells are not quickly replaced with healthy cells. And they cannot be replaced without the stem cells, which we describe below, that can mature into white blood cells. These stem cells can only be obtained through bone marrow transplants.

Until about twenty years ago, bone marrow was extracted from donors' bones by "aspiration." Long needles, thick enough to suck out the soft, fatty marrow, were inserted into the cavities of the anesthetized donor's hip bones. These are large bones with big central cavities full of marrow. Aspiration is a painful, unpleasant procedure for the donor. It requires hospitalization and general or local anesthesia, and involves commensurate risks.

Most blood stem cells stay in the bone marrow cavity and grow into mature blood cells there, before passing into the blood vessels. But some blood stem cells flow into and circulate in the bloodstream before they mature. These are called "peripheral" blood stem cells, "peripheral" meaning outside the central area of the body. [A] new bone marrow donation technique, developed during the past twenty years, is called "peripheral blood stem cell apheresis." "Apheresis" means the removal or separation of something. [W]ith no need for sedatives or anesthesia, a needle is inserted into the donor's vein. Blood is withdrawn from the vein and filtered through an apheresis machine to extract the blood stem cells. The remaining components of the blood are returned to the donor's vein. The blood stem cells extracted in the apheresis method are replaced by the donor's bone marrow in three to six weeks. Complications for the donor are exceedingly rare.

The main difference between an ordinary blood donation and apheresis is that instead of just filling up a plastic bag with whole blood, the donor sits for some hours in a recliner while the blood passes through the apheresis machine. When used to separate out and collect hematopoietic stem cells from the donor's bloodstream, apheresis is called "peripheral blood stem cell apheresis" or a "bone marrow donation."

All donations from another person, except for one's identical twin, produce at least some graft-versus-host disease in the recipient, but the closer the genetic match, the less disease. Matching is easy in ordinary blood transfusions, because there are only four basic blood types. But there are millions of marrow cell types, so good matches are hard to find. The more diverse the patient's genetic heritage, the rarer the match. For example, African-Americans have especially great difficulty finding a compatible unrelated donor, as they tend to have a mix of African, Caucasian, and Native-American genes, and fewer potential donors are registered in the national civilian registry.

The establishment of this registry, the National Marrow Donor Program, which is funded by the federal government to assist in finding matches, was an important aspect of the statute at issue here. But even with this registry, good matches often cannot be found. And even when a good match is found in the registry, tracking down the potential donor from what may be an outdated address may be impossible to accomplish in time to save the patient's life—assuming the potential donor is willing to go through with the process when found.

The plaintiff nonprofit proposes to mitigate this matching problem by using a financial incentive. The idea is that the financial incentive will induce more potential donors to sign up, stay in touch so that they can be located when necessary, and go through with the donations. The nonprofit plans to focus its attention initially on minority and mixed race donors, because their marrow cell types are rarer. The financial incentives would be $3,000 in scholarships, housing allowances, or gifts to charities of the donor's choice, which the nonprofit acknowledges would be "valuable consideration" under the statutory prohibition.

Plaintiffs argue that the National Organ Transplant Act, as applied to MoreMarrowDonors.org's planned pilot program, violates the Equal Protection Clause.

II. Analysis

The core of plaintiffs' argument is that there is no rational basis for allowing compensation for blood, sperm, and egg donations, while disallowing compensation for bone marrow donations, because bone marrow donations can now be accomplished through apheresis without removing marrow, and the donor's body quickly regenerates the donated stem cells. Since the distinction, they argue, is without a rational basis, it violates the Equal Protection Clause, despite highly deferential "rational basis" review.

The Attorney General responds that the statute plainly classifies "bone marrow" as an organ for which compensation is prohibited, and that the congressional determination is indeed rational. The statute makes it a felony "to knowingly acquire, receive, or otherwise transfer any human organ for valuable consideration for use in human transplantation." And it defines the term "human organ" to include "bone marrow." Ergo, the statute expressly prohibits compensating bone marrow donors. According to the government's brief, Congress took the view that "human body parts should not be viewed as commodities," and had several policy reasons for disallowing compensation to donors, which suffice to serve as a rational basis for the prohibition.

Plaintiffs address their arguments largely to the peripheral blood stem cell apheresis method of extracting hematopoietic stem cells, but their complaint appears to challenge the prohibition on bone marrow transplants regardless of method. They do not, in their complaint or their brief, confine their challenge to transplants by means of apheresis. They apparently propose to give compensated donors the choice between aspiration and apheresis. To the extent that plaintiffs challenge the constitutionality of the compensation ban on bone marrow donation by the old aspiration method — where a long needle is inserted into the cavity of the hip bone to extract the soft, fatty marrow — the challenge must fail.

The statute says that the term "human organ" includes "bone marrow." It is irrelevant that the legislative history indicates that Congress viewed certain types of regenerable tissue, such as blood, as falling outside the statutory definition of "human organ." [T]he statute does not say that compensation is permitted for organs or body parts that regenerate and prohibited for those that do not. Nor is the statute consistent with such a construction. The statute defines the liver "or any subpart thereof" as an organ for which compensation is prohibited. The drafters doubtless knew that a partial resection of a liver can yield a donation that will save the recipient's life, and that the donor's liver will grow back. So the statute does expressly prohibit compensation for at least one explicitly denoted "human organ" that will regenerate.

As for whether the distinction between the organs or other body substances for which compensation is permitted and those for which it is prohibited has a rational basis, there are two classes of rational basis here: policy concerns and philosophical concerns. The policy concerns are obvious. Congress may have been concerned that if donors could be paid, rich patients or the medical industry might induce poor people to sell their organs, even when the transplant would create excessive medical risk, pain, or disability for the donor. Or, looking from the other end, Congress might have been concerned that every last cent could be extracted from sick patients needful of transplants, by well-matched potential donors making "your money or your life" offers. The existing commerce in organs extracted by force or fraud by organ thieves might be stimulated by paying for donations. Compensation to donors might also degrade the quality of the organ supply, by inducing potential donors to lie about their medical histories in order to make their organs marketable. Plaintiffs argue that a $3,000 housing subsidy, scholarship, or charitable donation is too small an amount to create a risk of any of these evils, but for a lot of people that could amount to three to six months' rent.

Congress may have had philosophical as well as policy reasons for prohibiting compensation. People tend to have an instinctive revulsion at denial of bodily integrity, particularly removal of flesh from a human being for use by another, and most particularly "commodification" of such conduct, that is, the sale of one's bodily tissue. While there is reportedly a large international market for the buying and selling of human organs, in the United States, such a market is criminal and the commerce is generally seen as revolting. Leon Kass examines the philosophical issue of commodification with his observation that nonprofit hospitals, donor registries, and physicians are permitted to make a lot of money from organ transplants, and the only people who get nothing are those whose organs are donated:

> [A]lthough we allow no commerce in organs, transplant surgeons and hospitals are making handsome profits from the organ-trading business, and even the not-for-profit transplant registries and procurement agencies glean for their employees a middleman's livelihood. Why . . . should everyone be making money from this business except the person whose organ makes it possible? Could it be that [the] real uneasiness [lies] with organ donation or with transplantation itself, for if not, what would be objectionable about its turning a profit?

Leon R. Kass, *Life, Liberty and the Defense of Dignity: The Challenge for Bioethics* 177 (2002). Kass suggests that the revulsion for commodification of human flesh is reflected in our language, *see id.* at 195: we call donors who are paid for their organs "donors" rather than "sellers" or "vendors." To account for why most of us are revolted by the notion of a poor person selling a kidney to feed his family, Kass cites the taboos we have against cannibalism, defilement of corpses, and necrophilia. *Id.* at 183. Kass points to the idea of "psychophysical unity, a position that regards a human being as largely, if not wholly, self-identical with his enlivened body," so that, as Kant put it, to " 'dispose of oneself as a mere means to some end of one's own liking is to degrade the humanity in one's person.' "*Id.* at 181-82, 185. In this view, "organ transplantation . . . is — once we strip away the trappings of the sterile operating rooms and their astonishing technologies — simply a noble form of cannibalism." *Id.* at 185.

These reasons are in some respects vague, in some speculative, and in some arguably misplaced. There are strong arguments for contrary views. But these policy and philosophical choices are for Congress to make, not us. The distinctions made by Congress must have a rational basis, but do not need to fit perfectly with that rational basis, and the basis need merely be rational, not persuasive to all. Here, Congress made a distinction between body material that is compensable and body material that is not. The distinction has a rational basis, so the prohibition on compensation for bone marrow donations by the aspiration method does not violate the Equal Protection Clause.

C. *Bone Marrow Transplants by Apheresis*

The focus, though, of plaintiffs' arguments is compensation for "bone marrow donations" by the peripheral blood stem cell apheresis method. For this, we need not answer any constitutional question, because the statute contains no prohibition. Such donations of cells drawn from blood flowing through the veins may sometimes anachronistically be called "bone marrow donations," but none of the soft, fatty marrow is donated, just cells found outside the marrow, outside the bones, flowing through the veins.

Congress could not have had an intent to address the apheresis method when it passed the statute, because the method did not exist at that time. We must construe the words of the statute to see what they imply about extraction of hematopoietic stem cells by this method. This issue has not been addressed by any of our sister circuits.

Since payment for blood donations has long been common, the silence in the National Organ Transplant Act on compensating blood donors is loud. The statute says "human organ" is defined as a human "kidney, liver, heart, lung, pancreas, bone marrow, cornea, eye, bone, and skin or any subpart thereof and any other human organ . . . specified by the Secretary of Health and Human Services by regulation." 42 U.S.C. §274e(c)(1). The government concedes that the common practice of compensating blood donors is not prohibited by the statute.

The government argues that hematopoietic stem cells in the veins should be treated as "bone marrow" because "bone marrow" is a statutory organ, and the statute prohibits compensation not only for donation of an organ, but also "any subpart thereof." We reject this argument, because it proves too much, and because it construes words to mean something different from ordinary usage. If the government's argument that what comes from the marrow is a subpart of the marrow were correct, then the statute would prohibit compensating blood donors. The red and white blood cells that flow through the veins come from the bone marrow, just like hematopoietic stem cells. But the government implicitly concedes that these red and white blood cells are not "subparts" of bone marrow under the statute, because it explicitly concedes that the statute does not prohibit compensation for blood donations.

As for ordinary usage, the bloodstream consists of plasma containing red cells, white cells, platelets, stem cells that will mature into one of these, and other material. We call this liquid as a whole "blood." No one calls it "bone marrow," even though these cells come from the marrow. There is no reason to think that Congress intended "bone marrow" to mean something so different from ordinary usage.

Likewise, every blood draw includes some hematopoietic stem cells. The word "subpart" refers to the organ from which the material is taken, not the organ in which it was created. Taking part of the liver for a liver donation would violate the statute because of the "subpart thereof" language. But taking something from the blood that is created in the marrow takes only a subpart of the blood.

III. Conclusion

It may be that "bone marrow transplant" is an anachronism that will soon fade away, as peripheral blood stem cell apheresis replaces aspiration as the transplant technique, much as "dial the phone" is fading away now that telephones do not have dials. Or it may live on, as "brief" does, even though "briefs" are now lengthy arguments rather than, as they used to be, brief summaries of authorities. Either way, when the "peripheral blood stem cell apheresis" method of "bone marrow transplantation" is used, it is not a transfer of a "human organ" or a "subpart thereof" as defined by the statute and regulation, so the statute does not criminalize compensating the donor.

Notes and Questions

1. Markets in organs. Consider the following argument in favor of allowing sales of at least some organs by Virginia Postrel:

> Outlawing payments to donors is ostensibly a way to keep the system fair, giving rich and poor an equally lousy chance of getting a kidney. But wealthier people can already more easily register at distant centers with short lists. They're also more likely to have friends and relatives who can afford the nonmedical expenses that living donation often entails, including time off from work, child care, hotel rooms, or cross-country travel. (It is legal for recipients or third parties to pay such expenses, but, unlike medical costs, they are not covered by insurance.)
>
> Patients with enough money and the right networks have yet another option. They can go abroad, to countries where the authorities sanction or ignore payments to living donors.
>
> Such "transplant tourism" is growing. Laparoscopic surgery is a First World luxury, as are desk jobs to which donors can safely return soon after surgery. With few protections beyond the surgeon's need to maintain a good reputation among potential donors, kidney vendors may not receive the full payments they're promised. In China[,] organs may come not only from paid living vendors but also from executed prisoners. Transplant tourism is, in short, an ethical morass.
>
> It is also a completely predictable byproduct of the current system, willed into being by policy makers who ignore the plight of kidney patients and by doctors who see above-board payments—and the protections of contract and malpractice law that would go with them—as pollution. Living donation is a low-risk procedure for the donor that offers life-changing rewards for the recipient. Yet the donor is the only person involved in the process who receives no compensation. To people who like to celebrate living donors as heroes, payment seems terribly crass. But the vicarious thrill of someone else's altruism comes at a terrible cost.

Virginia Postrel, *With Functioning Kidneys for All*, The Atlantic, July 9, 2009. Who do you think has the stronger argument concerning organ sales? How are the considerations the same as those at issue with surrogacy and preembryos? How are they different?

2. **The impact of markets.** In defending the rationality of Congress's distinction between blood and organs, the court in *Flynn* notes that "[c]ompensation to donors might also degrade the quality of the organ supply, by inducing potential donors to lie about their medical histories in order to make their organs marketable." The court may have had in mind a famous argument by Richard Titmuss that, because blood donation is altruistic behavior, offering to pay for it discourages those motivated by altruism from donating, leading to a degradation in both quantity and quality of blood donated. *See* Richard Titmuss, *The Gift Relationship* (1970).

Economists find this claim puzzling, because, in their view, offering a financial incentive should attract those who would not donate absent the incentive without changing the cost-benefit calculus of those who are willing to donate without the incentive. But social scientists have found that monetary incentives can sometimes change the social meaning of a civic or charitable act into a commercial one. This deprives altruists of the benefit of acting for the sake of duty and may cause the incentive to backfire. *See, e.g.*, Uri Gneezy & Aldo Rustichini, *A Fine Is a Price*, 29 J. Legal Stud. 1 (2000) (finding that the introduction of a fine for late pick-ups at an Israeli daycare increased late pickups); Bruno S. Frey & Felix Oberholzer-Gee, *The Cost of*

Price Incentives: An Empirical Investigation of Motivation Crowding Out, 87 Am. Econ. Rev. 746, 749-750 (1997). The economist Fred Hirsch calls this transformation of social meaning the "commercialization effect." Michael Sandel, *What Money Can't Buy* 120 (2012) (citing Fred Hirsch, *The Social Limits to Growth* (1976)).

For decades, the World Health Organization has affirmed Titmuss's views about the superior safety of donated blood, arguing that all blood donation should be uncompensated. *See* World Health Organization, *Towards 100% Voluntary Blood Donation* (2010) (*available at http://www.who.int/bloodsafety/publications/9789241599696_eng.pdf*). But recent empirical studies have tended to contradict Titmuss. According to a recent summary of the research in the journal *Science*, the availability of incentives for blood donation increases both the overall quantity and quality of donated blood. *See* Nicola Lacetera et al., *Economic Rewards to Motivate Blood Donations*, 340 Science 927 (May 24, 2013); *see also* Lorenz Goette & Alois Stutzer, *Blood Donations and Incentives*, IZA Working Paper 3580, July 2008 (*available for download at http://papers.ssrn.com/sol3/papers.cfm?abstract_id=1158977*). Others have found differences in how men and women respond to incentives, with women displaying a greater "crowding out" effect. *See* Carl Mellstrom & Magnus Johannesson, *Crowding Out in Blood Donation*, 6 J. Eur. Econ. Assn. 845 (2010). Does this argument about crowding out relate to the distinction between blood and organs? If Titmuss was wrong, might there still be reasons to oppose the sale of organs?

3. Paired donations. Under the *National Organ Transplant Act*, 42 U.S.C. §274e, it is legal to make a gift of an organ to a specific individual. It is also legal to engage in a "paired donation." In a **paired donation**, the first donor is incompatible with the person to whom she wants to donate her organ but is compatible with another person who has a willing donor who is compatible with the first donor's recipient. The statute exempts from its coverage an agreement between the two donor/recipient pairs to swap organs (giving the second donor's organ to the first recipient and the first donor's organ to the second recipient). The law also allows for several pairs of donors and recipients to link together in a daisy chain of "paired donations" in order to move organs from donors to compatible recipients. Although paired donations began in 2000, Congress amended the law in 2007 to make it clear that they are legal. Do you see why the express exemption for paired donations was necessary?

CONTEXT

Since the first paired donation in 2000, the number has steadily grown, reaching 443 in 2012. *See* Virginia Postrel, *An Economics Nobel for Saving Lives*, Bloomberg.com (Oct. 16, 2012), http://www.bloomberg.com/news/2012-10-16/an-economics-nobel-for-saving-lives.html.

PART THREE

RELATIONS AMONG NEIGHBORS

CHAPTER 5

Adverse Possession

§1 TITLE VERSUS POSSESSION

An unprivileged entry on land possessed by another is a trespass.[1] When, however, one possesses another's land in a manner that is exclusive, visible ("open and notorious"), continuous, and without the owner's permission ("adverse or hostile") for a period defined by state statute, this action transfers title from the "true" (or "record") owner to the adverse possessor. In this way, adverse possession doctrine transforms trespassers into owners. The following materials address the circumstances under which this occurs and the justifications for it.

§1.1 Border Disputes

Brown v. Gobble

474 S.E.2d 489 (W. Va. 1996)

FRANKLIN D. CLECKLEY, Justice:

This case involves the doctrines of adverse possession and tacking. David L. Gobble and Sue Ann Gobble, appellants/defendants below, appeal from a final order of the Circuit Court of Mercer County. At the conclusion of a bench trial the circuit court granted judgment for a strip of land to Gary S. Brown and Mitzi Brown, appellees/plaintiffs below.

I. Factual and Procedural Background

The plaintiffs instituted this action by filing a complaint on August 25, 1994. The complaint sought to have the defendants enjoined from interfering with the plaintiffs' intended use of a two-feet-wide tract of land that formed a boundary running between

1. *See* Chapter 1 for further discussion of trespass law.

the adjoining properties of the parties. The defendants answered the complaint and filed a counterclaim alleging ownership to the tract of land by adverse possession.

The record reveals that the defendants purchased their property by deed dated April 24, 1985. At the time of this land purchase a fence was in place which ran along the rear boundary of defendants' property. The two-feet-wide tract of land in question here was enclosed by the fence and visually appeared to be part of the defendants' property. When the defendants bought their land, they were informed by their real estate agent that their property ran up to and included the fence. The call references in their deed "read" as though the two-feet-wide tract of land was part of the conveyance.[2] The defendants believed the two-feet-wide tract of land was part of their property, and utilized it consistent with ownership rights up until the filing of this law suit.

The plaintiffs purchased their property by deed dated April 28, 1989. Shortly before making this purchase, the plaintiffs had a survey of the property done. The survey revealed that the fenced-in two-feet-wide tract of land was part of plaintiffs' property. Although the plaintiffs were aware at the time of the purchase of their property that the two-feet-wide tract of land was, in fact, theirs, they did nothing to show ownership to the tract until around August, 1994. It was in August of 1994, that the plaintiffs decided to build a road along the two-feet-wide tract of land. To do this meant cutting down several trees that were along the tract. The defendants apparently attempted to prevent the plaintiffs from building the road by asserting that they owned the tract of land. The plaintiffs thereafter instituted the present suit. The trial of this matter was held by the circuit court, sitting as fact finder, on December 13, 1994. The trial court made findings of fact and conclusions of law, wherein it held that "the defendants have failed to show by clear and convincing evidence their ownership by way of adverse possession[.]"

II. Discussion

We note at the outset that the standard of review for judging a sufficiency of evidence claim is not appellant friendly. Following a bench trial, the circuit court's findings, based on oral or documentary evidence, shall not be overturned unless clearly erroneous, and due regard shall be given to the opportunity of the circuit judge to evaluate the credibility of the witnesses. We will disturb only those factual findings that strike us wrong with the "force of a five-week-old, unrefrigerated dead fish."

A. Standard of Proof for Adverse Possession Claims

The first argument raised by the defendants is that the circuit court committed error by requiring them to prove adverse possession by clear and convincing evidence.

---

2. The pertinent call references of defendants' deed provide:

thence leaving the said Willowbrook Road N 71 degrees 28" E 184.80 feet *to a fence post* in the line of said private driveway, thence S 32 degrees 33" E 133.80 feet to a fence post in the line of said driveway, thence S 17 degrees 04" W 13 feet to a fence post in the line of said private driveway[.] [Emphasis added.]

There is a minority view that a preponderance of the evidence is sufficient to establish adverse possession. There is little reason given for adopting this standard other than it is the usual rule in civil cases.

On the other hand, the view adopted by a majority of jurisdictions is that adverse possession must be shown by clear and convincing evidence. It is appropriate, in our opinion, that adverse possession be proved by a more stringent standard than a mere preponderance of the evidence.

While the preponderance standard applies across the board in civil cases, a higher standard is needed where fairness and equity require more persuasive proof. Although the standard clear and convincing is less commonly used, it nonetheless is no stranger to West Virginia civil cases. In *Wheeling Dollar Sav. & Trust Co. v. Singer*, 250 S.E.2d 369, 374 (W. Va. 1978), this Court stated that "clear and convincing" is the measure or degree of proof that will produce in the mind of the fact finder a firm belief or conviction as to the allegations sought to be established. It should be the highest possible standard of civil proof. The interest at stake in an adverse possession claim is not the mere loss of money as is the case in the normal civil proceedings. Rather, it often involves the loss of a homestead, a family farm or other property associated with traditional family and societal values. To this extent, most courts have used the clear and convincing standard to protect these important property interests. Adopting the clear and convincing standard of proof is more than a mere academic exercise. At a minimum, it reflects the value society places on the rights and interests being asserted.

B. The Sufficiency of the Evidence

The next argument raised by the defendants is that their evidence was sufficient to establish adverse possession under the clear and convincing evidence standard. Regarding the doctrine of adverse possession, we stated in *Naab v. Nolan,* 327 S.E.2d 151, 153-54 (W. Va. 1985), the following: The doctrine of adverse possession is firmly established in our property law and accompanies W. Va. Code §55-2-1 in settling land disputes equitably and efficiently.[3] This doctrine enables one who has been in possession of a piece of real property for more than ten years to bring an action asserting that he is now the owner of that piece of property even when title rests in another. In Syllabus Point 3 of *Somon v. Murphy Fabrication and Erection Co.,* 232 S.E.2d 524 (W. Va. 1977) this Court stated:

> One who seeks to assert title to a tract of land under the doctrine of adverse possession must prove each of the following elements for the requisite statutory period: (1) That he has held the tract adversely or hostilely; (2) That the possession has been actual; (3) That it has been open and notorious (sometimes stated in the cases as visible and notorious); (4) That possession has been exclusive; (5) That possession has been continuous; (6) That possession has been under claim of title or color of title.

3. W. Va. Code §55-2-1 states: "No person shall make an entry on, or bring an action to recover, any land, but within ten years next after the time at which the right to make such entry or to bring such action shall have first accrued to himself or to some person through whom he claims." —Eds.

We also held in Syllabus Point 4 of *Somon*, that: "Where one by mistake occupies land up to a line beyond his actual boundary, believing it to be the true line, such belief will not defeat his right to claim that he holds such land adversely or hostilely under the doctrine of adverse possession."[4] In addition to recognizing the common law doctrine of adverse possession, we have long recognized the principle of "tacking." In Syllabus Point 3 of *Jarrett v. Stevens*, 15 S.E. 177 (W. Va. 1892), we stated that, "[t]o tack different adverse possessions to make up the period of bar the persons holding such possessions must be connected by privity of title or claim."

With the above principles of law in view, we now turn to the evidence presented below.

The defendants do not contend that they are the lawful owners of the two-feet-wide tract of boundary land as a result of call references in their deed. That is, they do not claim possession under color of title. They have alleged ownership through claim of title or right. The defendants also do not contend that they have personally possessed the two-feet-wide tract for the requisite ten-year period. Instead, they contend that they have established adverse possession by tacking on the time periods that their predecessors in title claimed the two-feet-wide tract. We have held that "tacking" permits adding together the time period that successive adverse possessors claim property, and that should this period of time added together be more than ten years, adverse possession may be allowed.

To establish the element of "tacking" the defendants presented evidence that Edward and Virgie Blevins (the "Blevins") were the original owners of the property they purchased in 1985. The Blevins owned the property as far back as 1937, and during the entire time of their ownership they believed the two-feet-wide tract was part of their land, and they exercised dominion and control over the tract consistent with ownership rights. The Blevins sold their property on October 30, 1978, to Norman and Martha Fletcher (the "Fletchers"), believing that they were also conveying the two-feet-wide tract. Mr. Fletcher testified that when they bought the property they believed that they had purchased the two-feet-wide tract, and possessed it consistent with ownership rights. The defendants testified that they bought their property from the Fletchers in 1985, and believed their land purchase included the two-feet-wide tract of boundary land, and that they possessed it consistent with ownership rights, up until the filing of this law suit. Based upon this tacking evidence, the defendants contend that they are entitled as a matter of law to add the period 1937-1985, to their nine-and-a-half

4. Thus, the law in West Virginia is that where a person, acting under a mistake as to the true boundary lines between his or her land and that of another, takes possession of land believing it to be his or her own, up to the mistaken line, claims a prescriptive right to it and so holds, the holding is adverse, and, if continued for the requisite period may ripen into adverse possession. The fact that the one who takes possession under these circumstances had no intention of taking what did not belong to him or her, does not affect the operation of this rule. In all cases, the intention and not the mistake is the test by which the character of the possession is determined.

year claim to the two-feet-wide tract, which would give them far in excess of ten years adverse possession of the tract.[5]

To establish the element of "hostile" or "adverse" possession by tacking, the defendants called several witnesses who testified that the two-feet-wide tract was fenced off as far back as 1937, that the Blevins placed the fence along the tract, and that the Blevins claimed the tract as theirs.[6] Evidence was presented to show that the Fletchers maintained the fence along the two-feet-wide tract, and that the fence remained in place throughout their ownership of the property. The defendants testified that they purchased their property from the Fletchers in 1985, and that they claimed ownership of the two-feet-wide tract, and that it remained fenced off up until the start of the instant law suit.

To establish the element of "actual" possession by tacking, the defendants called several witnesses who testified that the Blevins periodically repaired the fence surrounding the two-feet-wide tract, that they routinely planted a garden along the tract, and that the Blevins constructed and maintained a shed along a portion of the tract. Mr. Fletcher testified that he regularly planted a garden along the tract, that he routinely removed weeds from along the tract and fence, and that he picked blackberries from the area and walnuts from trees that had grown along the tract.[7] The defendants testified that they planted gardens along the tract, that they built a treehouse in one of the trees that had grown along the tract, and that they regularly mowed the grass and weeds in the area.

To establish the element of "open and notorious" possession by tacking, the defendants called several witnesses who testified that during the period that the Blevins owned the defendants' property, the reputation of the two-feet-wide tract in the community was that it belonged to the Blevins.[8] Mr. Fletcher testified that the reputation

5. Based upon the evidence the defendants presented regarding the Belvins and Fletchers, the defendants actually misunderstand the import of their evidence. The evidence seems to suggest that the Blevins may very well have established adverse possession to the two-feet-wide tract, because they maintained the tract for over ten years. The Blevins conveyed their adversely possessed property to the Fletchers, and the Fletchers in turn conveyed the same to the defendants. Therefore the tacking involved here does not require analysis of the defendants' period of ownership, unless it is established that the Blevins did not in fact acquire adverse possession. If it is determined that the Blevins acquired adverse possession of the two-feet-wide tract, the issue then merely becomes whether the Blevins intended to convey the two-feet-wide tract to the Fletchers, and whether the Fletchers intended to convey the two-feet-wide tract to the defendants. The period of ownership by the defendants becomes irrelevant under this scenario. It is only if a determination is made that the Blevins did not establish adverse possession that the defendants' period of ownership becomes relevant for tacking on the time period of the Fletchers.

6. We have held that to establish "hostile" or "adverse" possession, evidence must be presented which shows that possession of disputed property was against the right of the true owner and is inconsistent with the title of the true owner for the entire requisite ten-year period.

7. We have held that to establish "actual" possession, evidence must be presented which shows that possession of disputed property was used for enjoyment, cultivation, residence or improvements for the entire requisite ten-year period.

8. We have held that to establish "open and notorious" possession, evidence must be presented which shows that possession of disputed property was in such a manner as to give notice to the true owner that the property is being claimed by another for the entire requisite ten-year period.

in the community was that the two-feet-wide tract was part of his property. The defendants testified that the reputation in the community was that the two-feet-wide tract was part of their property.

To establish the element of "exclusive" possession by tacking, the defendants presented testimony by two of the original owners of plaintiffs' property.[9] These two witnesses testified that neither the Blevins' nor the Fletchers' claim to the two-feet-wide tract was ever objected to by them or those who owned the property with them. The defendants also presented evidence to show that only the Blevins and Fletchers respectively had control and dominion over the two-feet-wide tract. The defendants also testified that they had exclusive control and dominion over the two-feet-wide tract up until the time of this law suit.

To establish the element of "continuous" possession the defendants presented testimony that the Blevins enclosed, maintained, cultivated and claimed ownership of the two-feet-wide tract up until they sold their property to the Fletchers. Mr. Fletcher testified that he maintained, cultivated and claimed ownership of the two-feet-wide tract up until he sold the property to the defendants. The defendants testified that they maintained, cultivated and claimed ownership of the two-feet-wide tract up until the instant law suit.

To establish the element of "claim of title" the defendants presented evidence to show that neither the Blevins, Fletchers nor the defendants had actual title to the two-feet-wide tract, yet each claimed ownership of it pursuant to all of the above conduct, during their entire respective occupancy.

The trial court found that this evidence did not establish tacking or adverse possession by clear and convincing evidence. The trial court made this finding notwithstanding the fact that none of the defendants' tacking or adverse possession evidence was challenged or rebutted by the plaintiffs.

The findings made by the trial court are inadequate to allow this Court to find that all relevant factors were considered. Though helpful, the findings are not all-encompassing. Indeed, the findings of the circuit court ignored the central thrust of the defendants' evidence.

The circuit court either misunderstood or misapplied the theory of the defendants. The defendants do not claim that their actual possession of the property in question is sufficient to establish adverse possession. Rather, they contend that their predecessors in interest met all the necessary prerequisites of adverse possession and under the doctrine of tacking, the predecessors' interest was passed onto the defendants. The circuit court's findings never addressed this aspect of the defendants' case.

The upshot is that the circuit court failed to make any findings that would dispose of the defendants' tacking claim. [Accordingly, the judgment of the Circuit Court of Mercer County is reversed and remanded.]

9. We have held that to establish "exclusive" possession, evidence must be presented which shows that possession of disputed property was used only by the occupant and others were not permitted to use it or claim ownership during the entire requisite ten-year period.

Notes and Questions

1. **Adverse possession claims generate substantial litigation.** Each of the elements of adverse possession has caused problems of interpretation and application. Moreover, a significant number of states either add other elements to the standard list or identify multiple ways to acquire property by adverse possession. It is therefore crucial to examine carefully the version of the doctrine that has been adopted in your jurisdiction.

> ***ELEMENTS OF ADVERSE POSSESSION***
>
> The elements of a claim for adverse possession typically include (1) actual possession that is (2) open and notorious, (3) exclusive, (4) continuous, and (5) adverse or hostile (6) for the statutory period. Most states agree on this list of elements. Some states have enacted shorter statutes of limitation depending on whether the possessor has acted under (7) "color of title" or has (8) paid property taxes on the land.

Adverse possession doctrine allows a non-owner to acquire full ownership rights in real property if the non-owner "actually possesses" property without permission by the "true" owner (meaning the formal title holder) in a visible manner for the period of time established by statute. Adverse possession claims may be brought by the adverse possessor herself in a lawsuit against the record owner to **quiet title**. This kind of claim asks the court to grant a declaratory judgment that the adverse possessor has become the owner of the disputed property through adverse possession. Adverse possession claims may also arise as *defenses* to trespass or ejectment claims by record owners. In ejectment lawsuits, the record owner claims that the adverse possessor is wrongfully occupying her property and seeks a court order ejecting the adverse possessor from the property; the adverse possessor defends by asserting that he has acquired title by adverse possession and that plaintiff therefore has no right to eject him. In trespass cases, the plaintiff alleges an intentional intrusion on her property, while the adverse possessor defends by alleging that he is not trespassing because he has acquired ownership of the property by adverse possession.

2. **Actual possession.** The adverse possessor must physically occupy the property in some manner. Some states have statutes that identify which types of actions are required to establish "actual" possession. Cal. Code Civ. Proc. §323; Fla. Stat. §95.16; N.Y. Real Prop. Acts. §522. In the absence of a statute, "[a]ctual occupancy means the ordinary use to which the land is capable and such as an owner would make of it." *Smith v. Hayden,* 772 P.2d 47, 55 (Colo. 1989). This may be shown by enclosing the property by a fence and treating it as one's own. *Krosmico v. Pettit,* 968 P.2d 345 (Okla. 1998). *But see Hovendick v. Ruby,* 10 P.3d 1119 (Wyo. 2000) ("fence of convenience" designed to contain or keep out animals gives rise to a presumption of permissive use while a boundary fence gives rise to a presumption of adverse possession); N.Y. Real Prop. Acts. §543 (stating that enclosure of land by a fence or hedge is not sufficient for adverse possession). In the absence of a fence, one must demonstrate actual possession by engaging in significant activities on the land, such as building on the land and/or living or conducting a business there. Other actions that are often sufficient to show actual possession are farming, clearing the land, and planting shrubs. *Harris v. Lynch,* 940 S.W.2d 42 (Mo. Ct. App. 1997). The touchstone is

proof the possessor treated the land as an "average owner" would. *Jarvis v. Gillespie,* 587 A.2d 981, 985 (Vt. 1991).

An adverse possessor who has a deed that purports to transfer the land in question but is ineffective to transfer title because of a defect in the deed (such as lack of a signature) or a defect in the process by which the deed was issued (lack of notice to the owner when the property is sold for failure to pay property taxes, for example) has **color of title** to the property. In that case, occupation of any portion of the land described in the defective title is generally deemed to be actual possession of the whole lot described in the void deed. *See* §1.2, *infra.*[10]

3. Open and notorious. Courts generally agree that the possessory acts must be sufficiently visible and obvious to put a reasonable owner on notice that her property is being occupied by a non-owner. *Lawrence v. Town of Concord,* 788 N.E.2d 546, 551-552 (Mass. 2003); *Grappo v. Blanks,* 400 S.E.2d 168 (Va. 1991). The adverse possessor need not demonstrate that the "true owner" (the formal title holder) observed or knew about the adverse possessor's use of the property; rather, the true owner is "charged with seeing what reasonable inspection would disclose." William B. Stoebuck & Dale A. Whitman, *The Law of Property* §11.7, at 856 (3d ed. 2000). *Accord, Lawrence v. Town of Concord,* 788 N.E.2d at 552 (adverse possession available even when record owner did not know it owned the property in question).

A great deal of litigation has been generated over which acts are sufficient to put owners on notice. Enclosing land by a fence or a wall, as in *Brown v. Gobble,* is universally recognized as sufficiently open and notorious. *Smith v. Tippett,* 569 A.2d 1186 (D.C. 1990). Other acts deemed sufficient include building a structure, *Smith v. Hayden, supra* (garage located on neighboring property); clearing the land, laying down a driveway, mowing grass, and using the strip for parking, storage, garbage removal, and picnicking, *Chaplin v. Sanders,* 676 P.2d 431 (Wash. 1984); and planting and harvesting crops, *Cheek v. Wainwright,* 269 S.E.2d 443 (Ga. 1980). *Cf. Rhodes v. Cahill,* 802 S.W.2d 643 (Tex. 1990) (holding that isolated and selective clearing of trees for timber or grazing purposes and grazing cattle and goats without enclosing the land are insufficient to show adverse possession over a ten-year period).

4. Exclusive. The exclusivity requirement does not mean that no one but the owner used the property for the statutory period. Owners routinely allow others to enter their property for various purposes. **Exclusivity** generally means that the use "is of a type that would be expected of a true owner of the land in question" and that "the adverse claimant's possession cannot be shared with the true owner." *Smith v. Tippett,* 569 A.2d at 1190. Proving that possession was not shared with the true owner may require a showing that "the record owner has been effectively excluded," *Smith v. Hayden,* 772 P.2d at 52, although occasional entry by the true owner may not defeat

---

10. Cases involving mistaken boundaries may generate claims of either adverse possession or what are called prescriptive easements, which involve rights of access but not ownership. Prescriptive easements are discussed in detail in §3, *infra.* Border disputes may also be resolved by a variety of other doctrines, such as oral agreement, acquiescence, estoppel, and laches. *See* §4, *infra.*

the claim. *Id.* at 53. Two adverse possessors who possess property jointly may acquire joint ownership rights as co-owners.[11]

5. Continuous (tacking doctrine). The requirement that the adverse possessor's use be continuous does not mean that she must be on the property 24 hours a day. Nor does it mean that the owner may never leave the property for extended periods of time. Depending on the type of property in question, even extended absences may not defeat the claim. In *Howard v. Kunto,* 477 P.2d 210 (Wash. Ct. App. 1970), for example, adverse possession was established over a parcel of land used seasonally as a summer cabin. The court held the continuity requirement to mean that the adverse possessor must exercise control over the property in the ways customarily pursued by owners of that type of property. "[T]he requisite possession requires such possession and dominion 'as ordinarily marks the conduct of owners in general in holding, managing, and caring for property of like nature and condition.'" *Id.* at 213-214.

What happens if someone adversely possesses property for less than the time period required by the relevant statute and sells the property — or, more precisely, *purports* to sell it — to another owner? The general rule is that the succeeding periods of possession by different persons may be added together; this is called **tacking**. Successors can add the original adverse possessor's holding period only if they are in **privity** with one another, meaning that the original adverse possessor purported to transfer title to the property to the successor. *Shelton v. Strickland,* 21 P.3d 1179, 1184 (Wash. Ct. App. 2001). If, however, the successor dispossessed the prior adverse possessor forcibly, the tacking doctrine does not apply.

6. Adverse or hostile. Of all the elements of adverse possession, the adverseness requirement has given rise to the most confused and varied treatment. The courts agree that the adverseness requirement means that the use is nonpermissive. A showing that the true owner has permitted the use will defeat the claim. Beyond this basic premise, however, much disagreement ensues. It is important to distinguish the requirements for the state of mind of the true owner from the requirements for the state of mind of the adverse possessor.

a. True owner's state of mind. If someone is occupying another's land with the owner's permission, the occupier cannot acquire the land by adverse possession. The court's question, therefore, is whether the true owner *permitted* the use; if so, this defeats an adverse possession claim. Although it is counterintuitive, the adverse possessor must show that her use was *nonpermissive* to obtain ownership by adverse possession. What evidence is sufficient to prove that possession is nonpermissive? This is generally not a problem if the owner has expressly granted permission (through granting a license or lease, for example) or has expressly denied permission (by posting "No Trespassing" signs, for example). In many cases, however, the owner has said nothing either way. In such cases, the courts almost always hold that there is a *presumption* that possession of another's property is *nonpermissive. Robarge v. Willett*, 636 N.Y.S.2d 938 (App. Div. 1996). This means

11. They will own the property as tenants in common. *See* Chapter 9, §2.

that adverse possession can be established by longstanding, visible, continuous possession of another's land. No proof need be given on the question of adverseness; lack of permission is presumed. If all the elements are met, adverse possession can be claimed unless the true owner produces evidence to show that the use was permissive.

Co-owners of property, such as two sisters who own a house jointly or two roommates who share an apartment, are each legally entitled to possess the whole property. They work out actual usage informally between or among themselves. Use of the whole property by one of two co-owners is as of right because each is acting within her legal rights if she occupies the whole property. No permission is needed to possess the whole property so no trespass has occurred if an owner possesses the whole. To acquire adverse possession against a co-owner, one must make an explicit statement of intent to take possession of the entire property by adverse possession; this is called an **ouster**.[12]

Similarly, possession that begins as permissive will stay that way unless the owner explicitly revokes permission or the adverse possessor announces that she is ousting the true owner and claiming the property as her own. However, if the owner allows another to possess his property for a very long time and the possessor reasonably relies on that permission to invest in the land, she may be granted possessory rights on the ground that the owner is estopped from denying continued permission.[13]

b. Adverse possessor's state of mind. Four approaches exist. They include (i) an **objective test** based on possession (the rule in most states); and **subjective tests** based on (ii) a **claim of right**; (iii) **intentional dispossession**; and (iv) **good faith**. An objective test makes the adverse possessor's state of mind irrelevant, while a subjective test requires the adverse possessor to prove a particular attitude on her part *in addition* to showing that the true owner did not permit the possession.

i. Lack of permission. The first approach is an objective test, meaning that the adverse possessor's state of mind is irrelevant. All that matters is that the possessor *lacked permission* from the true owner. This is the law in the overwhelming majority of states. *See Yourik v. Mallonee,* 921 A.2d 869, 878 (Md. 2007) (adverse possessor wins, even though she knew she was occupying property owned by another).

ii. Claim of right. Some courts state that the adverse possessor must allege a "claim of right." This looks like a subjective test because it means "a possessor's intention to appropriate and use the land as his own to the exclusion of all others." *Grappo v. Blanks,* 400 S.E.2d at 171. However, in most states, this second test is actually a variant on the first. States that require a "claim of right" generally do not require proof of what the adverse possessor was thinking; all they require is that the adverse possessor act toward the land as an average

12. For rules about joint owners and the definition of ouster, *see* Chapter 9, §2.2.

13. *See* Chapter 8, §2.3.

owner would act. "That intention need not be expressed but may be implied by a claimant's conduct. Actual occupation, use, and improvement of the property by the claimant, as if he were in fact the owner, is conduct that can prove a claim of right." *Id.* This collapses the claim of right test into the "actual possession" test, automatically satisfying the claim of right if actual possession has been shown.

Some states, however, that require a showing of a claim of right will allow the presumption that actual possession is under a claim of right to be defeated if the evidence shows that the adverse possessor knew where the boundary was and never intended to claim property outside her borders as her own. *Petsch v. Widger,* 335 N.W.2d 254, 260 (Neb. 1983); *Mid-Valley Resources, Inc. v. Engelson,* 13 P.3d 118 (Or. Ct. App. 2000). Other courts will deny adverse possession even when the adverse possessor was unsure of where the boundary lay but testifies that she never intended to take over ownership of property that was not hers. *Ellis v. Jansing,* 620 S.W.2d 569 (Tex. 1981). In these states, the claim of right requirement is identical to the intentional dispossession test, discussed next.

iii. Intentional dispossession. Some states require a showing of intentional dispossession in certain cases. Under this test, the adverse possessor must be aware that she is occupying property owned by someone else and must intend to oust or dispossess the true owner. In these states, mistaken occupation of land cannot give rise to adverse possession if the adverse possessor has no intention of taking over property she does not own. As explained above, this test may be phrased as a claim of right. The courts that adopt this test ordinarily limit it to boundary disputes. *See, e.g., Ellis v. Jansing,* 620 S.W.2d 569 (Tex. 1981) (holding that adverse possession could not be established where the adverse possessor "never claimed or intended to claim any property other than that described in his deed . . . and he never intended to claim any property owned by the abutting property owner"). *Accord, McQueen v. Black,* 425 N.W.2d 203 (Mich. Ct. App. 1988); *Perry v. Heirs at Law & Distributees of Gadsden,* 449 S.E.2d 250 (S.C. 1994).

Most scholars and courts reject this test on the grounds that it rewards wrongdoers (intentional trespassers) and fails to protect innocent persons who have mistakenly occupied land belonging to another. It can seem perverse to deny protection to good faith possessors while granting repose to those who intended to invade and steal neighboring land. "To limit the doctrine of adverse possession to the latter type places a premium on intentional wrongdoing, contrary to fundamental justice and policy." *Smith v. Tippett,* 569 A.2d at 1191. One answer may lie in the type of disputes a jurisdiction wants to rule out. Border disputes between neighbors may be more likely to be based on mistakes. And yet they generate discord. Squatting, however, often enjoys support among neighbors when squatters improve property that owners have left to decay. *See* Eduardo M. Peñalver & Sonia K. Katyal, *Property Outlaws* 133-134 (2010). If a community plagued by underused property wants to encourage squatting (perhaps to punish absentee owners) but avoid discord among neighbors, it might conclude that intentional adverse possession should be allowed while adverse possession by mistake should not. *See id.* at 148-152 (defending intentional adverse possession under contexts of extreme economic inequality); *see also* Lee Anne Fennell, *Efficient Trespass: The Case for "Bad Faith" Adverse Possession,* 100 Nw. U. L. Rev. 1037 (2006).

iv. ***Good faith.*** Some states require the exact opposite of an intent to oust the true owner: instead, they require good faith occupation to prevail. In these jurisdictions, *only innocent* possessors — those who *mistakenly* occupy property owned by someone else — can acquire ownership by adverse possession. Colo. Rev. Stat. §38-41-101(3)(b)(II); Ga. Code §§44-5-161 to -162; N.M. Stat. §37-1-22; *Halpern v. Lacy Investment Corp.,* 379 S.E.2d 519 (Ga. 1989) (holding that those who knowingly occupy land of others are "trespassers" or "squatters" and cannot obtain title by adverse possession because they have not entered the land with a good faith claim of right); *Carpenter v. Ruperto,* 315 N.W.2d 782 (Iowa 1982) (no adverse possession because "claim of right" is essential element, and it cannot be established if the adverse possessor knew she was possessing land she did not own).

Some states provide a shorter statute of limitations if the possession was in good faith. *Compare* La. Civ. Code arts. 3473 and 3475 *with* art. 3486 (10-year period for prescription if possession was in good faith and 30-year period if possession was in bad faith). Professor Richard Helmholz has argued that even though most states reject a good faith test, they *in fact* grant adverse possession only to good faith possessors. They do this, he claims, by manipulating the other elements of the test, such as the open and notorious, exclusivity, or continuity requirements. Richard Helmholz, *Adverse Possession and Subjective Intent,* 61 Wash. U. L.Q. 331 (1983); Richard Helmholz, *More on Subjective Intent: A Response to Professor Cunningham,* 64 Wash. U. L.Q. 65 (1986). Professor Roger Cunningham has rejected Helmholz's claim, arguing instead that the courts do not in fact require good faith to prevail. Roger Cunningham, *Adverse Possession and Subjective Intent: A Reply to Professor Helmholz,* 64 Wash. U. L.Q. 1 (1986). Whoever is correct in this debate, it is clear that most courts have so far rejected the idea of adopting a good faith test as a formal element in adverse possession doctrine. *Chaplin v. Sanders,* 676 P.2d 431 (Wash. 1984).

7. **For the statutory period.** The statutory period varies widely from state to state. As of 2013, the periods include 5 years (3 states), 7 years (4 states), 10 years (16 states), 15 years (9 states), 18 years (1 state), 20 years (12 states), 21 years (2 states), 30 years (2 states), and 40 years (1 state). *See* 10 *Thompson on Real Property, Second Thomas Editions* §87.01. Some define different periods, depending on whether the adverse possessor has paid property taxes on the property in question or whether the adverse possessor had color of title.

Many states will **toll** the statute of limitations if the true owner is under a **disability** such as infancy, insanity, or incompetence (wardship), either providing that the statute begins running only after the disability ends, shortening the limitations period once the disability is removed, or providing a maximum period longer than the standard statute of limitations even if the disability has not terminated. Other categories may include imprisonment and absence from the state.

8. Claims against the government. Courts have traditionally held that adverse possession claims cannot prevail against government property. Thus, those who possess or use public property could never acquire prescriptive rights in that property. *Stickney v. City of Saco,* 770 A.2d 592, 603 (Me. 2001). However, a significant number of states have passed statutes limiting or abolishing governmental immunity from adverse possession. Paula R. Latovick, *Adverse Possession Against the States: The Hornbooks Have It Wrong,* 29 U. Mich. J.L. Reform 939 (1996). *See* Ky. Rev. Stat. §413.150; N.C. Gen. Stat. §1-35; N.D. Cent. Code §28-01-01; Wis. Stat. §893.29. Other states have limited the rule by common law, thereby allowing adverse possession claims against government owners if the property is not held for public use or is dedicated to commercial purposes or is otherwise not open to the public. *American Trading Real Estate Properties, Inc. v. Town of Trumbull,* 574 A.2d 796, 800 (Conn. 1990); *Devins v. Borough of Bogota,* 592 A.2d 199 (N.J. 1991). A federal statute allows adverse possession of federal lands in certain instances if a claimant has occupied the property for 20 years in good faith reliance on a claim or color of title and has either cultivated the land or constructed improvements. 43 U.S.C. §1068.

9. Effect on preexisting nonpossessory interests. Adverse possessors generally obtain ownership rights subject to preexisting liens, easements, restrictive covenants, and mineral interests. Unless the adverse possessor has acted in a manner inconsistent with those interests, they have been held to persist.

10. Border disputes. New York substantially changed its adverse possession law in 2008, effectively abolishing adverse possession in most border dispute cases. The law allows an adverse possessor to acquire property by building a permanent structure that encroaches on land owned by another but denies adverse possession by deeming "permissive and non-adverse" what the statute calls "de minimis non-structural encroachments" such as lawn mowing, plantings, fences, and sheds. N.Y. Real Prop. Acts. §543. Would you support passage of a similar law in your state?

11. Protecting the true owner. Once a record owner discovers that a neighbor has encroached on her land, what can that owner do to protect his interests?

§1.2 Color of Title

"An individual acquires color of title when a written conveyance appears to pass title but does not do so, either from want of title in the person making it, or the defective mode of conveyance." *Glaser v. Bayliff,* 1999 WL 34709, at *4 (Ohio Ct. App. 1999). The defective title may be void because the person who conveys it does not actually own the land it purports to convey; because the document lacks a signature, *Romero v. Garcia,* 546 P.2d 66 (N.M. 1976); because it contains mistaken or ambiguous descriptions of the land to be conveyed, *Quarles v. Arcega,* 841 P.2d 550 (N.M. Ct. App. 1992); or because it was procured through a faulty procedure, such as a deed granted at a tax sale when the sheriff failed to follow statutorily mandated procedures, *Green v. Dixon,* 727 So. 2d 781 (Ala. 1998) (color of title established by tax deed that was void because of lack of notice to the owner). What sort of document counts as providing a claimant with "color of title"? Consider the following case.

Romero v. Garcia

546 P.2d 66 (N.M. 1976)

DAN SOSA, JR., J.

Plaintiff-appellee Ida Romero, formerly Garcia, filed suit to quiet title against defendants-appellants Mr. and Mrs. Antonio Garcia, who are her former father-in-law and mother-in-law. The suit to quiet title was based upon adverse possession for more than ten years under color of title and payment of taxes. From judgment for the plaintiff, defendants appeal. We affirm the trial court.

The facts are the following: In 1947 plaintiff Ida Garcia Romero and her deceased husband Octaviano Garcia, son of the defendants, purchased the 13 acres in dispute for $290 from Octaviano's father, Antonio Garcia. Mrs. Antonio Garcia failed to join in the conveyance. The 13 acres were carved out of 165 acres Antonio Garcia had purchased in 1923. The plaintiff and her deceased husband entered into possession in 1947 and built a home on the land with the help of both defendants. The deed was recorded in May, 1950. Ida and Octaviano lived in their home until 1962, when he died, whereupon she moved to Colorado and subsequently remarried.

The main thrust of the appellants' argument concerns the deed. Appellants argue that (1) the void deed was inadequate for color of title and (2) the deed's description was inadequate for adverse possession because it failed to describe a specific piece of property. The first argument is clearly erroneous. A deed is sufficient for the purpose of color of title even though it is void because it lacks the signature of a member of the community.

> **CONTEXT**
>
> In community property states, property acquired by a married couple is held jointly as a "community." Both members of the community must sign a deed conveying community property. In *Romero*, the deed purporting to convey the parcel was void because it included only the signature of Octaviano's father, but not that of his mother. For more on community property, *see* Chapter 9, §3.2.

We move to the question of whether the deed was insufficient for adverse possession because it failed to describe adequately a parcel of land which can be ascertained on the ground. Since the deed in question was in Spanish, the court and the parties relied on the following English translation of the description:

> A piece of land containing 13 acres more or less, within the following description: NE 1/4 SE 1/4, S 1/2 SE 1/4 NE 1/4, Section 32, NW 1/4 SW 1/4, S 1/2 SW 1/4 NW 1/4, Section 33, Township 32 N. Range 7E N.M.P.M., said 13 acres are bounded as follows: East and South bounded by property of Antonio Garcia; on the North by the National Forest

> and on the West by property of Alfonso Marquez. The said 13 acres are in the NW corner of the ranch above described.

Not translated but part of the deed to the appellee's husband are the following words in Spanish: "Con derecho de agua del Sublet del Rio de Los Pinos," which translated mean "with water rights assigned from the Sublet [creek] of the Los Pinos river."

The description in the deed specified that the land is bounded on the north by the National Forest and on the west by Alfonso Marquez and on the south and east by the grantor. The deed also specified that there shall be water rights to the land from the Los Pinos River. The Los Pinos River is generally to the south of this property and at one point only some twenty feet from the alleged southern boundary. In *Richardson v. Duggar*, 525 P.2d 854, 857 (N.M. 1974) we held that the deed is not void for want of proper description if, with the deed and with extrinsic evidence on the ground, a surveyor can ascertain the boundaries.

In the case at bar we had testimony from the grantor that the fence line along the entire northern boundary had been there for over fifty years, and the fence line on the western boundary of the property which he conveyed to his son had also been there for more than fifty years. We therefore see that the northwest corner was adequately established as being the intersection of these two fence lines. The surveyor testified that the plaintiff showed him generally where the land was and pointed to the house that was built by the plaintiff and the defendants. The surveyor walked down the western boundary line and found a pipe in position; he established that pipe as the southwest corner. He shot an angle parallel to the northern boundary line and found a pile of rocks which he established as the southeastern corner. He then closed the parallelogram by shooting a line to the northern boundary parallel to the western fence. This parallelogram measured 12.95 acres; the deed granted "13 acres more or less." Thus, the land is in the shape of a parallelogram and is bounded by the National Forest on the north, by Alfonso Marquez (now lands of Mr. L. C. White) on the west, and on the south and east by the grantor. This parallelogram is also in close proximity to the river from which water could be used in accordance with the assignment of the water rights.

Mrs. Romero consistently identified this land as the property she and her deceased husband had purchased and which she thereafter possessed and from which she sold the hay for several years. Defendant failed to object to this testimony.

The trial court made the following findings of fact:

> 15. The land described in the complaint of the plaintiff herein, by virtue of the description of the said deed itself and the actions and understandings of the parties as to the boundaries of said land, is capable of determination as to the exact location of the boundaries of said land conveyed to Plaintiff's deceased husband.
>
> 16. The Northwest corner of the land conveyed is established by the intersection of a fence line extending along the entire northern boundary of said property from east to west, and the point where an existing fence line along the westerly boundary of said property intersected; the Southwest corner of said lands of the Plaintiff was marked by an iron pipe found in place by a surveyor, and the Southeast corner of said property

> conveyed was marked by a pile of rocks, and the Northeast corner of said tract was marked by an existing fence extending from East to West along the entire northerly boundary of said tract of land.

The court feels that when the evidence, with all reasonable inferences deducible therefrom, is viewed in the light most favorable in support of the findings, there was substantial evidence to support these findings of fact and others relevant to this issue.

The court in *Garcia v. Garcia,* 525 P.2d 863, 865 (N.M. 1974) stated that ". . . an indefinite and uncertain description may be clarified by subsequent acts of the parties," and found that:

> The evidence here is clear that subsequent acts of the parties in going upon and generally pointing out the boundaries of the lands to the surveyor, aided by other extrinsic evidence, enabled the surveyor to prepare the plat relied upon by all the parties. In fact, if it were not for the extrinsic evidence by which the surveyor was able to locate the lands, the 1968 deed from Nazario to plaintiffs would fail for lack of means by which to identify any lands.

In the case at bar the subsequent acts of the parties in erecting a house and pointing to the land were sufficient to ascertain the boundaries.

Finally, appellants argue that appellee failed to pay the tax continuously, for appellee had been in arrears several times, ranging from 1 1/2 to almost 4 years. However, appellee did pay the taxes in each case before a tax deed was issued to the state. Thus, we hold that appellee complied substantially with the continuous payment of taxes requirement of adverse possession under N.M. Stat. §23-1-22.

The judgment of the trial court will be affirmed.

Notes and Questions

1. **Legal consequences of color of title.** Some states lower the number of years required to obtain adverse possession when the owner has color of title. *Compare* Tex. Code §16.026 (10 years if no color of title) *with* Tex. Code §16.025 (5 years if cultivated, paid taxes, with registered deed) *and* Tex. Code §16.024 (3 years if under color of title). In a few states, adverse possession statutes treat color of title as a prerequisite for any successful adverse possession claim. *See, e.g.,* N.M. Stat. §37-1-22.

In all states, as noted above in §1.1, when color of title exists, courts use the land area described in the title as conclusive evidence of the property that is being adversely possessed. Actual possession of any portion of that land constitutes adverse possession of all the land described in the document providing color of title (except to the extent that some portion of the land described is actually occupied by the original title owner). In such a case of so-called constructive possession, color of title functions as fences often do to help the court determine the boundaries of the land being claimed by adverse possession.

2. **Color of title and permission.** As we discussed above, color of title sometimes exists because a technical defect in the deed conveying the property renders the

conveyance invalid. In those situations, the true owner intends to convey the property but fails to do so. Does this mean that the occupant takes possession with the owner's permission and therefore fails to satisfy the requirement of adversity? After all, in a sense, she enters the property with the true owner's (*i.e.*, the failed conveyor's) consent. On the other hand, she takes possession of the property as someone claiming ownership on her own behalf, not as someone entering by virtue of ongoing permission granted by the owner and (therefore) as someone subordinate to the owner's superior title. Where an adverse possessor enters the property as part of an intended (but somehow invalid) conveyance, courts typically deem the possession to be adverse to the owner. *See Polanski v. Town of Eagle Point*, 141 N.W.2d 281 (Wis. 1966) ("Where it is admitted that the present possession is the result of a conveyance by a former owner, it is obvious that there will be no forcible entry. However, the occupation of property pursuant to a deed is presumptively and in fact an act adverse to and in derogation of the former owner's title."); *cf. Hubbard v. Curtiss*, 684 P.2d 842 (Alaska 1984) ("The possession of a grantee is presumptively adverse to his grantor. This presumption is logical because once the grantor has purported to convey property neither he nor his grantee believe that the grantee's possession is subordinate to the grantor's title."); 3 Am. Jur. 2d *Adverse Possession* §192.

§1.3 Squatters

Nome 2000 v. Fagerstrom

799 P.2d 304 (Alaska 1990)

Map: Osborne Road, Nome, Alaska

WARREN MATTHEWS, JR., Chief Justice.

This appeal involves a dispute over a tract of land measuring approximately seven and one-half acres, overlooking the Nome River (hereinafter the disputed parcel). Record title to a tract of land known as mineral survey 1161, which includes the disputed parcel, is held by Nome 2000.

On July 24, 1987, Nome 2000 filed suit to eject Charles and Peggy Fagerstrom from the disputed parcel. The Fagerstroms counterclaimed that through their use of the parcel they had acquired title by adverse possession. The Fagerstroms counterclaimed that through their use of the parcel they had acquired title by adverse possession.

A jury trial ensued and, at the close of the Fagerstroms' case, Nome 2000 moved for a directed verdict on two grounds. First, it maintained that the Fagerstroms' evidence of use of the disputed parcel did not meet the requirements of the doctrine of adverse possession. Alternatively, Nome 2000 maintained that the requirements for adverse possession were met only as to the northerly section of the parcel and, therefore, the Fagerstroms could not have acquired title to the remainder. The trial court denied the motion. After Nome 2000 presented its case, the jury found that the Fagerstroms had adversely possessed the entire parcel.

The disputed parcel is located in a rural area known as Osborn. During the warmer seasons, property in Osborn is suitable for homesites and subsistence and recreational activities. During the colder seasons, little or no use is made of Osborn property.

Charles Fagerstrom's earliest recollection of the disputed parcel is his family's use of it around 1944 or 1945. At that time, he and his family used an abandoned boy scout cabin present on the parcel as a subsistence base camp during summer months. Around 1947 or 1948, they moved their summer campsite to an area south of the disputed parcel. However, Charles and his family continued to make seasonal use of the disputed parcel for subsistence and recreation.

In 1963, Charles and Peggy Fagerstrom were married and, in 1966, they brought a small quantity of building materials to the north end of the disputed parcel. They intended to build a cabin. In 1970 or 1971, the Fagerstroms used four cornerposts to stake off a twelve acre, rectangular parcel for purposes of a Native Allotment application.[14] The northeast and southeast stakes were located on or very near mineral survey 1161. The northwest and southwest stakes were located well to the west of mineral survey 1161. The overlap constitutes the disputed parcel. The southeast stake disappeared at an unknown time. Also around 1970, the Fagerstroms built a picnic area on the north end of the disputed parcel. The area included a gravel pit, beachwood blocks as chairs, firewood and a 50-gallon barrel for use as a stove.

About mid-July 1974, the Fagerstroms placed a camper trailer on the north end of the disputed parcel. The trailer was leveled on blocks and remained in place through late September. Thereafter, until 1978, the Fagerstroms parked their camper trailer on the north end of the disputed parcel from early June through September. The camper was equipped with food, bedding, a stove and other household items.

About the same time that the Fagerstroms began parking the trailer on the disputed parcel, they built an outhouse and a fish rack on the north end of the parcel. Both fixtures remained through the time of trial in their original locations. The Fagerstroms also planted some spruce trees, not indigenous to the Osborn area, in 1975-76.

During the summer of 1977, the Fagerstroms built a reindeer shelter on the north end of the disputed parcel. The shelter was about 8 × 8 feet wide, and tall enough for Charles Fagerstrom to stand in. Around the shelter, the Fagerstroms constructed a pen which was 75 feet in diameter and 5 feet high. The shelter and pen housed a reindeer for about six weeks and the pen remained in place until the summer of 1978.

During their testimony, the Fagerstroms estimated that they were personally present on the disputed parcel from 1974 through 1978, "every other weekend or so" and "[a] couple times during the week . . . if the weather was good." When present they used the north end of the parcel as a base camp while using the entire parcel for subsistence and recreational purposes. Their activities included gathering berries, catching

14. Federal law authorizes the Secretary of the Interior to allot certain non-mineral lands to Native Alaskans. As a result of her application, Peggy was awarded two lots (lots 3 and 12) which border the disputed parcel along its western boundary.

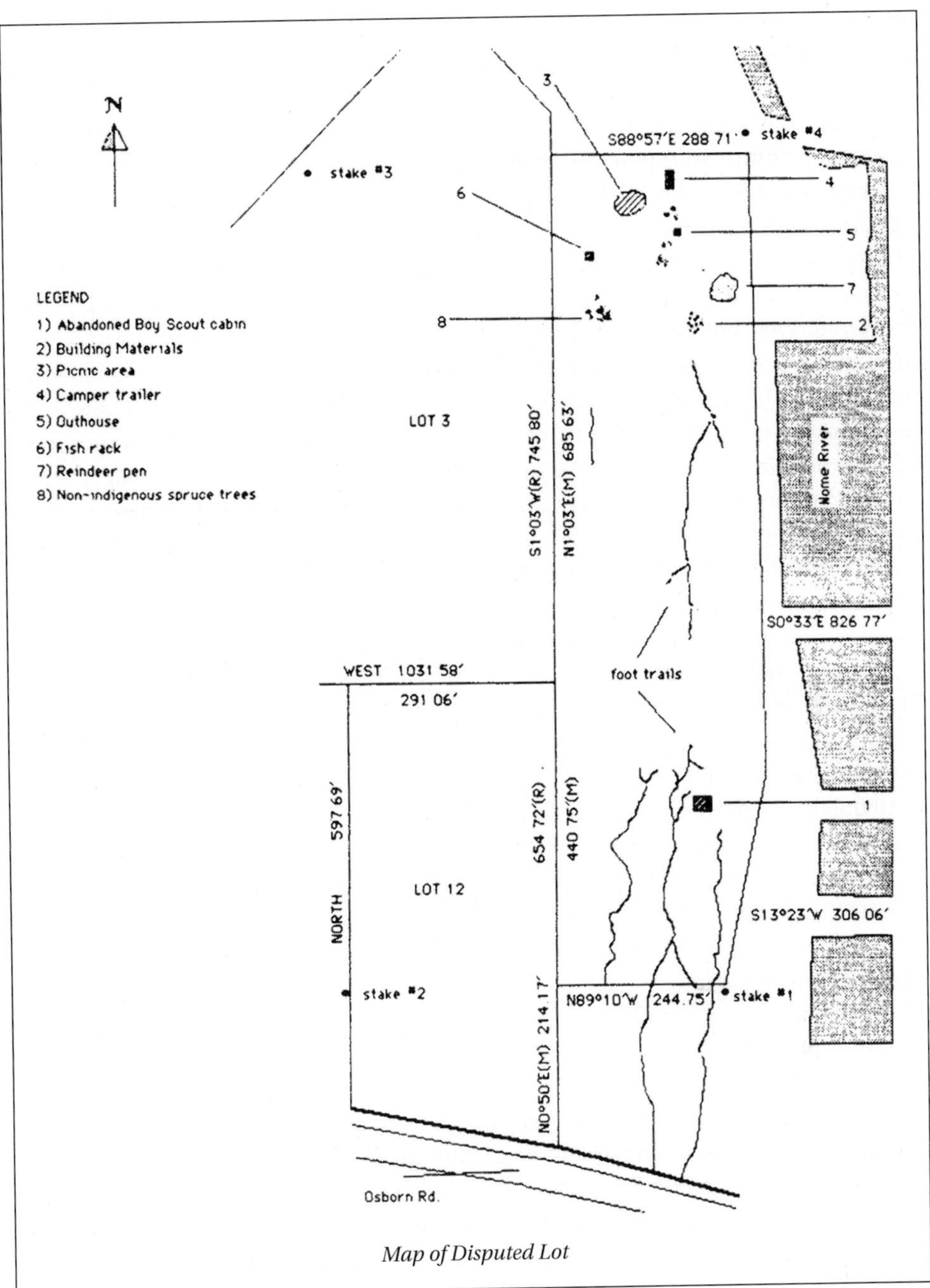

Map of Disputed Lot

and drying fish and picnicking. Their children played on the parcel. The Fagerstroms also kept the property clean, picking up litter left by others.

While so using the disputed parcel, the Fagerstroms walked along various paths which traverse the entire parcel. The paths were present prior to the Fagerstroms' use of the parcel and, according to Peggy Fagerstrom, were free for use by others in connection with picking berries and fishing. On one occasion, however, Charles Fagerstrom excluded campers from the land. They were burning the Fagerstroms' firewood.

Nome 2000 placed into evidence the deposition testimony of Dr. Steven McNabb, an expert in anthropology, who stated that the Fagerstroms' use of the disputed parcel was consistent with the traditional Native Alaskan system of land use. According to McNabb, unlike the non-Native system, the traditional Native system does not recognize exclusive ownership of land. Instead, customary use of land, such as the Fagerstroms' use of the disputed parcel, establishes only a first priority claim to the land's resources. The claim is not exclusive and is not a matter of ownership, but is more in the nature of a stewardship. That is, other members of the claimant's social group may share in the resources of the land without obtaining permission, so long as the resources are not abused or destroyed. McNabb explained that Charles' exclusion of the campers from the land was a response to the campers' use of the Fagerstroms' personal property (their firewood), not a response to an invasion of a perceived real property interest.

Nevertheless, several persons from the community testified that the Fagerstroms' use of the property from 1974 through 1977 was consistent with that of an owner of the property. For example, one Nome resident testified that since 1974 "[the Fagerstroms] cared for [the disputed parcel] as if they owned it. They made improvements on it as if they owned it. It was my belief that they did own it."

During the summer of 1978, the Fagerstroms put a cabin on the north end of the disputed parcel. Nome 2000 admits that from the time that the cabin was so placed until the time that Nome 2000 filed this suit, the Fagerstroms adversely possessed the north end of the disputed parcel. Nome 2000 filed its complaint on July 24, 1987.

The Fagerstroms' claim of title by adverse possession is governed by Alaska Stat. §09.10.030, which provides for a ten-year limitations period for actions to recover real property.[15] Thus, if the Fagerstroms adversely possessed the disputed parcel, or any portion thereof, for ten consecutive years, then they have acquired title to that property. Because the Fagerstroms' use of the parcel increased over the years, and because Nome 2000 filed its complaint on July 24, 1987, the relevant period is July 24, 1977 through July 24, 1987.

We recently described the elements of adverse possession as follows: "In order to acquire title by adverse possession, the claimant must prove, by clear and convincing evidence, . . . that for the statutory period 'his use of the land was continuous, open and notorious, exclusive and hostile to the true owner.'" *Smith v. Krebs,* 768 P.2d 124, 125 (Alaska 1989). The first three conditions—continuity, notoriety and exclusivity—describe the physical requirements of the doctrine. The fourth condition, hostility, is often imprecisely described as the "intent" requirement.

Nome 2000 argues that as a matter of law the physical requirements are not met absent "significant physical improvements" or "substantial activity" on the land. Thus,

---

15. A seven-year period is provided for by Alaska Stat. §09.25.050 when possession is under "color and claim of title." The Fagerstroms do not maintain that their possession was under color of title.

according to Nome 2000, only when the Fagerstroms placed a cabin on the disputed parcel in the summer of 1978 did their possession become adverse. For the prior year, so the argument goes, the Fagerstroms' physical use of the property was insufficient because they did not construct "significant structure[s]" and their use was only seasonal. Nome 2000 also argues that the Fagerstroms' use of the disputed parcel was not exclusive because "[o]thers were free to pick the berries, use the paths and fish in the area." We reject these arguments.

Whether a claimant's physical acts upon the land are sufficiently continuous, notorious and exclusive does not necessarily depend on the existence of significant improvements, substantial activity or absolute exclusivity. Indeed, this area of law is not susceptible to fixed standards because the quality and quantity of acts required for adverse possession depend on the character of the land in question. Thus, the conditions of continuity and exclusivity require only that the land be used for the statutory period as an average owner of similar property would use it. Where, as in the present case, the land is rural, a lesser exercise of dominion and control may be reasonable.

The character of the land in question is also relevant to the notoriety requirement. Use consistent with ownership which gives visible evidence of the claimant's possession, such that the reasonably diligent owner "could see that a hostile flag was being flown over his property," is sufficient. *Shilts v. Young*, 567 P.2d 769, 776 (Alaska 1977). Where physical visibility is established, community repute is also relevant evidence that the true owner was put on notice.[16]

Applying the foregoing principles to this case, we hold that the jury could reasonably conclude that the Fagerstroms established, by clear and convincing evidence, continuous, notorious and exclusive possession for ten years prior to the date Nome 2000 filed suit. We point out that we are concerned only with the first year, the summer of 1977 through the summer of 1978, as Nome 2000 admits that the requirements of adverse possession were met from the summer of 1978 through the summer of 1987.

The disputed parcel is located in a rural area suitable as a seasonal homesite for subsistence and recreational activities. This is exactly how the Fagerstroms used it during the year in question. On the premises throughout the entire year were an outhouse, a fish rack, a large reindeer pen (which, for six weeks, housed a reindeer), a picnic area, a small quantity of building materials and some trees not indigenous to the area. During the warmer season, for about 13 weeks, the Fagerstroms also placed a camper trailer on blocks on the disputed parcel. The Fagerstroms and their children visited the property several times during the warmer season to fish, gather berries, clean the premises, and play. In total, their conduct and improvements went well beyond "mere casual and occasional trespasses" and instead "evince[d] a purpose to exercise exclusive dominion over the property." *See Peters v. Juneau-Douglas Girl Scout Council*, 519 P.2d 826, 830 (Alaska 1974). That others were free to pick berries and fish is consistent with the conduct of a hospitable landowner, and undermines neither the

16. The function of the notoriety requirement is to afford the true owner an opportunity for notice. However, actual notice is not required; the true owner is charged with knowing what a reasonably diligent owner would have known.

continuity nor exclusivity of their possession. *See id.* at 831 (claimant "merely acting as any other hospitable landowner might" in allowing strangers to come on land to dig clams).

With respect to the notoriety requirement, a quick investigation of the premises, especially during the season which it was best suited for use, would have been sufficient to place a reasonably diligent landowner on notice that someone may have been exercising dominion and control over at least the northern portion of the property. Upon such notice, further inquiry would indicate that members of the community regarded the Fagerstroms as the owners. Continuous, exclusive, and notorious possession were thus established.

Nome 2000 also argues that the Fagerstroms did not establish hostility. It claims that "the Fagerstroms were required to prove that they intended to claim the property as their own." According to Nome 2000, this intent was lacking as the Fagerstroms thought of themselves not as owners but as stewards pursuant to the traditional system of Native Alaskan land usage. We reject this argument and hold that all of the elements of adverse possession were met.

What the Fagerstroms believed or intended has nothing to do with the question whether their possession was hostile. Hostility is instead determined by application of an objective test which simply asks whether the possessor "acted toward the land as if he owned it," without the permission of one with legal authority to give possession. *Hubbard v. Curtiss,* 684 P.2d 842, 848 (Alaska 1984). As indicated, the Fagerstroms' actions toward the property were consistent with ownership of it, and Nome 2000 offers no proof that the Fagerstroms so acted with anyone's permission. That the Fagerstroms' objective manifestations of ownership may have been accompanied by what was described as a traditional Native Alaskan mind-set is irrelevant. To hold otherwise would be inconsistent with precedent and patently unfair.

Having concluded that the Fagerstroms established the elements of adverse possession, we turn to the question whether they were entitled to the entire disputed parcel. Specifically, the question presented is whether the jury could reasonably conclude that the Fagerstroms adversely possessed the southerly portion of the disputed parcel.

Absent color of title,[17] only property actually possessed may be acquired by adverse possession. Here, from the summer of 1977 through the summer of 1978, the Fagerstroms' only activity on the southerly portion of the land included use of the pre-existing trails in connection with subsistence and recreational activities, and picking up litter. They claim that these activities, together with their placement of the corner-posts, constituted actual possession of the southerly portion of the parcel. Nome 2000 argues that this activity did not constitute actual possession and, at most, entitled the Fagerstroms to an easement by prescription across the southerly portion of the disputed parcel.

Nome 2000 is correct. The Fagerstroms' use of the trails and picking up of litter, although perhaps indicative of adverse use, would not provide the reasonably diligent

17. As noted above, the Fagerstroms do not claim the disputed parcel by virtue of [color of title].

owner with visible evidence of another's exercise of dominion and control. To this, the cornerposts add virtually nothing. Two of the four posts are located well to the west of the disputed parcel. Of the two that were allegedly placed on the parcel in 1970, the one located on the southerly portion of the parcel disappeared at an unknown time. The Fagerstroms maintain that because the disappearing stake was securely in place in 1970, we should infer that it remained for a "significant period." Even if we draw this inference, we fail to see how two posts on a rectangular parcel of property can, as the Fagerstroms put it, constitute "[t]he objective act of taking physical possession" of the parcel. The two posts simply do not serve to mark off the boundaries of the disputed parcel and, therefore, do not evince an exercise of dominion and control over the entire parcel. Thus, we conclude that the superior court erred in its denial of Nome 2000's motion for a directed verdict as to the southerly portion. This case is remanded to the trial court, with instructions to determine the extent of the Fagerstroms' acquisition in a manner consistent with this opinion.

> **CONTEXT**
>
> The plaintiff in *Nome 2000* claimed that the Fagerstroms had not acquired the property by adverse possession because they were Native Alaskans and their use did not establish sufficient "possessory" control as to constitute a claim of ownership protectable by adverse possession law. The court rejected this argument. Why? If you were the attorney for the true owner, what better argument could you have presented to support your client's position?

Notes and Questions

1. **Good faith.** Should an adverse possessor gain title to property if she knows she is occupying property belonging to another, as the Fagerstroms did? Would your opinion of the proper result in *Brown v. Gobble* change if you knew that the adverse possessors intentionally and knowingly built the fence in a manner that encroached several feet onto their neighbor's property?

In 2007, Richard McLean, a former judge and mayor of Boulder, Colorado, and his wife, attorney Edith Stevens, won a lawsuit against their neighbors Don and Susie Kirlin in which McLean and Stevens claimed a third of the Kirlins' land by adverse possession. The trial judge believed their evidence that they had taken over the property and occupied it for 25 years, more than the 18 years required by the statute of limitations. The case elicited a firestorm of protest because McLean and Stevens admitted that they knew they were trespassing on their neighbors' property the whole time. *See* Heath Urie, *Couple Will Appeal "Adverse Possession" Ruling,* Daily Camera Online, Nov. 15, 2007. This intentional "land grab" created an enormous backlash that led to Colorado amending its statutes in 2008 to allow adverse possession only if the adverse possessor "had a good faith belief [that he or she] was the actual owner of the property and the belief was reasonable under the particular circumstances." Colo. Rev. Stat. §38-41-101(3)(b)(II). Alaska similarly amended its law in 2003 to adopt a good faith requirement for border cases. Alaska Stat. §09.45.052 (adverse possessors can prevail in border disputes only if they have "a good faith but mistaken belief" that the property lay within the borders of their own land). And in 2008, New York amended its adverse possession statute to require the claimant to show "a reasonable basis for the belief that the property belongs to the adverse possessor." N.Y. Real Prop. Acts. §501.

Would you favor passing such a statute in your jurisdiction? Should border cases be treated any differently from those in which someone squats on another's land? What are the arguments for and against adopting a good faith requirement in these cases?

2. Rural land. When land is possessed in a rural area, on land that is wooded and/or unimproved, as in *Nome 2000,* some courts adopt different standards.

a. Actual possession. Some courts hold that actual possession can be established by lesser acts than would be required in an urban area. This is because the law requires the adverse possessor to use the land as an average owner would use it, and if land in the area is not used intensively, then actual possession may be shown with fewer acts on the land. However, other courts focus on the fact that the use must be "open and notorious" and that greater acts should be required in rural areas to ensure that a reasonable owner would be on notice of the occupation of her land. Most courts refuse to adopt a special rule for rural, wooded, or unimproved land. Which of these three approaches is best?

b. Adverse. Should the courts presume that possession of rural land is permissive rather than nonpermissive? The owner in *Nome 2000,* for example, may have had no objection to the Fagerstroms' use of the land because it did not, for the moment, interfere with any of the owner's interests. Should the presumption that land use is nonpermissive be reversed for unimproved land in areas that are wooded, remote, and unimproved?

3. Family. Should possession be presumed to be permissive when the adverse possessor and record title holder are in the same family or otherwise related to each other? *Compare Petch v. Widger,* 335 N.W.2d 254 (Neb. 1983) (yes), *with Totman v. Malloy,* 725 N.E.2d 1045 (Mass. 2000) (no).

4. Self-Help. As we discuss in Chapter 11, landlords are typically barred from engaging in self-help to remove defaulting tenants from their property. Should the law apply the same policy against self-help to conflicts between owners and adverse possessors? Between owners and squatters?

§2 JUSTIFICATIONS FOR ADVERSE POSSESSION: "ROOTS WHICH WE SHOULD NOT DISTURB" OR "LAND PIRACY"?

Robert Cooter and Thomas Ulen propose two economic justifications for adverse possession. First they argue that by quieting title and closing off stale claims, adverse possession "lowers the cost of establishing rightful ownership claims by removing the risk that ownership will be disputed on the basis of the distant past." Robert Cooter & Thomas Ulen, *Law and Economics* 155 (5th ed. 2007). Uncertainty inhibits transactions, or it raises their costs, thereby lowering their profitability. This is because people can sell only what they own; if it is unclear what people own, they will be inhibited from entering transactions because of the risk that they will not in fact be buying or selling what they are purporting to buy or sell. By defining who is the lawful owner in the case of boundary disputes, adverse possession doctrine both settles the dispute and allows further transactions to take place. *Id.*

It may be true that adverse possession settled boundary disputes before a recording system was in place; with both a recording system and the ability to use scientific surveying methods to fix the boundaries of property, however, it is almost always more efficient and economical to rely on the boundaries fixed in the record title to identify the record owner than it is to conduct a lawsuit to determine whether the complicated and confusing elements of adverse possession have been met. Even in cases of conflicting deeds—where two deeds purport to grant ownership to the same parcel or strip to different persons—it would be less expensive simply to rely on a rule that ownership vests in the person whose deed was recorded first.

Richard Epstein provides another explanation of how adverse possession lowers the costs of determining the title holder. He argues that it "shorten[s] the period during which prospective purchasers and lenders (both noted for their squeamishness) need examine the state of the title." Richard Epstein, *Past and Future: The Temporal Dimension in the Law of Property*, 64 Wash. U. L.Q. 667, 678 (1986). Of course, in the case of a record owner whose deed properly describes the land in question and an adverse possessor whose deed does *not* cover that land, this explanation is wanting. Rather than fixing the owner in a certain fashion, the rule tends to generate litigation. In this type of dispute, it would almost certainly be more predictable simply to fix title in the record owner. And in the case of conflicting deeds (two deeds whose land descriptions both cover the strip of property in question), it would almost certainly be less expensive simply to limit the time period (to 50 years or so) within which one must search the title records and then fix ownership in the person whose deed was recorded first.

The second explanation Cooter and Ulen advance for adverse possession is that it "prevents valuable resources from being left idle for long periods of time by specifying procedures for a productive user to take title from an unproductive user." Cooter & Ulen, *supra*, at 155. Those who do not use their property run the risk of losing that property to an adverse possessor. Cooter and Ulen do note, however, that using property is not always beneficial to society. Moreover, if the adverse possessor really values the property more than the true owner, why not require the adverse possessor to find out who the true owner is and offer to buy the property from him?

Justice Oliver Wendell Holmes offered a different explanation for adverse possession in a letter to William James. Holmes explained adverse possession as based on the desire to protect the expectations of the adverse possessor who has come to "shape his roots to his surroundings, and when the roots have grown to a certain size, cannot be displaced without cutting at his life." *Tioga Coal Co. v. Supermarkets General Corp.*, 546 A.2d 1, 5 (Pa. 1988) (quoting Holmes). This explanation rests on the desire to protect the settled expectations of the adverse possessor as against the true owner, who would regard recovery of the land as an unexpected windfall—like winning the lottery.

Judge Richard Posner of the United States Court of Appeals for the Seventh Circuit adopts Holmes's explanation but translates it into the language of wealth and utility. Posner argues:

> Over time, a person becomes attached to property that he regards as his own (is this a purely psychological phenomenon or can it be explained in economic terms?), and the deprivation of the property would be wrenching. Over the same period of time, as Holmes pointed out, a person loses attachment to property that he regards as no longer his own, and the restoration of the property would give him therefore only moderate pleasure. This is a point about diminishing marginal utility of income. The adverse possessor would experience the deprivation of the property as a diminution in his wealth; the original owner would experience the restoration of the property as an increase in *his* wealth. If they have the same wealth, their combined utility will be greater if the adverse possessor is allowed to keep the property.

Richard Posner, *Economic Analysis of Law* §3.12, at 97-98 (8th ed. 2011).

Stewart Sterk has similarly presented an economic defense of adverse possession. Like Posner and Cooter and Ulen, Sterk asserts that the adverse possessor is likely to value the property more than the true owner. Stewart Sterk, *Neighbors in American Land Law*, 87 Colum. L. Rev. 55 (1987). He explains that the true owner has "demonstrated virtually no concern with the possessor's occupation." *Id.* at 80. Because the encroaching adverse possessor has shown by her actions that she values the strip more, it is therefore wealth-maximizing to transfer ownership to her. If this is so, why not rely on private bargaining to do this? If the adverse possessor really values the strip more than the true owner, why shouldn't she *have* to offer the true owner enough money to induce the true owner to sell? After all, requiring a transaction will *test* the proposition that the adverse possessor is the most valued user.

Sterk answers that the costs of strategic bargaining may discourage such a wealth-maximizing transaction. In a two-person bargaining situation, each party must guess what the other party's bottom line is—how much time she has to bargain and what price she is willing to pay or accept—and what bargaining strategy the other side will adopt. "If the costs of transmitting offers and counteroffers are high, the bargainer may find that his best strategy is to eschew bargaining altogether." *Id.* at 72. If the adverse possessor usually values the strip more, and the costs of bargaining prohibit a transfer from the true owner to the adverse possessor, then adverse possession doctrine promotes efficiency by vesting ownership in the adverse possessor. Does this mean, however, that the transfer should not require compensation from the adverse possessor to the record owner?

As Sterk and others have noted, moreover, it is not a foregone conclusion that the adverse possessor places a higher value on the property than the true owner, at least if value is measured in terms of willingness to pay in a market transaction. "[T]he adverse possessor's offer price is likely to be lower, and may be much lower, than her asking price. The adverse possessor may not be able to come up with $10,000 in cash, or be willing to borrow $10,000 to buy the strip, but may be very willing to keep the strip rather than sell it to the true owner for the same price." Jack Beermann & Joseph William Singer, *Baseline Questions in Legal Reasoning: The Example of Property in Jobs*, 23 Ga. L. Rev. 911, 964-965 (1989).

But the inability of the cash- or credit-poor to come up with money to make a market offer may make "willingness to pay" a poor metric for measuring the degree to which an adverse possessor values the property. As Eduardo Peñalver and Sonia Katyal have argued, "[p]eople who have nothing (or very little) will have limited means to express in market offers the value they place on an item of property. . . . The adverse possessor's long-term use (and improvement) of the property, combined with the risk of civil and criminal sanctions, will in many cases constitute strong prima facie evidence that the lawbreaker places high value on the property." *See* Eduardo M. Peñalver & Sonia K. Katyal, *Property Outlaws* 128-129 (2010). Lee Fennell concurs that "[t]he law's harsh treatment of knowing trespassers before the statutory period has run amounts to a built-in test of the relative subjective values that the trespasser and the record owner place on the land." Lee Anne Fennell, *Efficient Trespass: The Case for "Bad Faith" Adverse Possession*, 100 Nw. U. L. Rev. 1037, 1043 (2006).

As a consequence of the operation of distortions on some adverse possessors' ability to express their valuation of the land in terms of offers to pay, determining who values the land more may differ according to which side is required to buy the land from the other. "Because of the difference between offer and asking prices, the result may differ depending on which party is declared the owner of the disputed strip." Beerman & Singer, *supra*, at 964-965. Under these circumstances, efficiency analysis based on "willingness to pay" becomes far less determinate.

Professor Margaret Jane Radin adopts Holmes's explanation for adverse possession but uses the language of justice and fairness rather than economics. Her approach centers on the significant distinction between personal and fungible property: an object is "fungible" if "it is perfectly replaceable with money"; it is "personal" if it "has become bound up with the personhood of the holder and is no longer commensurate with money." Radin argues that the adverse possessor's interest is "initially fungible" but "becomes more and more personal as time passes." Margaret Jane Radin, *Time, Possession, and Alienation*, 64 Wash. U. L.Q. 739, 748 n.26 (1986). "At the same time, the titleholder's interest fades from personal to fungible and finally to nothingness. At what point is the titleholder detached enough and the adverse possessor attached enough to make the switch? This [requires] a moral judgment." *Id.* at 748-749. One problem with this explanation, as Radin concedes, is that the personality theory does not always apply to corporations. *Id.* at 749.

Another moral basis for adverse possession lies in "the reliance interests that the possessor may have developed through longstanding possession of the property." Thomas Merrill, *Property Rules, Liability Rules, and Adverse Possession*, 79 Nw. U. L. Rev. 1122, 1131 (1984-1985). Thus, adverse possession may be justified by the moral principle of protecting reliance on relationships. The adverse possessor and the true owner develop a kind of relationship based on the true owner's acquiescence in having her property occupied by the adverse possessor. "The possessor comes to expect and may have come to rely on the fact that the true owner will not interfere with the possessor's use of the property . . . and the true owner has fed those expectations by her actions (or her failure to act)." Joseph William Singer, *The Reliance Interest in Property*, 40 Stan. L. Rev. 611, 666-667 (1988). The true owner has failed to interfere with the adverse possessor's use, thereby generating expectations of continued access on the part of the adverse possessor. For that reason, "[i]t is morally wrong for the true owner to allow a relationship of dependence to be established and then to cut off the dependent party." *Id.* at 667. Does this argument adequately account for the law's distinction between permissive use (which cannot generate a claim for adverse possession) and nonpermissive use (which can)?

Is there any way to justify the extension of adverse possession doctrine to the knowing trespasser — the land pirate who intentionally trespasses and occupies neighboring land, knowing that the neighbor is ignorant of the actual border? It seems perverse to reward such a person. Under this view, the law of adverse possession should always include a good faith standard, either as an element of the claim that must be proved by the adverse possessor or as a defense allowing the true owner to defeat a claim of adverse possession if the true owner can show the presence of bad faith.

Several arguments might justify granting protection to the land pirate. First, one purpose of the adverse possession doctrine is to create security by encouraging owners to rely on existing practical arrangements that have persisted for a long time. Resting title on something as difficult to prove as good faith (how can we easily determine someone's state of mind?) will make property rights too unpredictable and generate even more litigation, making ownership less stable, less certain, and less predictable than it now is.

Second, we might interpret the failure of the true owner to object to the presence of a squatter as tantamount to abandonment of the owner's rights. Finders generally become owners of abandoned goods. Adverse possession requires occupation to be open and notorious. An owner's failure to object to such an occupation may indicate a lack of concern about the encroachment. Strictly speaking, American law does not allow landowners to abandon ownership of their property, but for an owner who places no value on her rights — as evidenced by her failure to assert them within the lengthy adverse possession period — it might not be accurate to call the intentional trespasser a pirate or thief. After all, we do not think of finders of abandoned property in these terms.

Third, even if we view the land pirate as an immoral thief, one policy behind the statute of limitations is to give victims incentives to bring lawsuits within a reasonable time; when this is done, everyone has repose, knowing that she is not subject to lawsuits for actions undertaken long ago. The interest in repose is a strong one. Moreover, it is wrong for the victim to wait too long to vindicate her rights. One can argue about the amount of time that is appropriate, but at some point the failure to assert one's rights may become more blameworthy than the original wrong.

Finally, in situations of intentional adverse possession, the title owner may not be a hapless neighbor but a land speculator who is merely warehousing the property in the hope of being able to sell it and reap a profit should land prices rise. In the meantime, the property sits unused and decaying. During the recent foreclosure crisis, banks became the owners of large numbers of properties in hard-hit communities. Instead of quickly renting or selling these properties, some banks held them vacant for protracted periods of time. These vacant properties became unsightly magnets for crime. Under these circumstances, neighbors may judge a squatter who moves in and improves the property to be a sympathetic character who helps to remove the blight of empty housing from the community. *See* Peñalver & Katyal, *supra*, at 133-134; Ben Austen, *The Death and Life of Chicago*, N.Y. Times Magazine, May 29, 2013 (describing a movement of squatters in Chicago who, typically with the support of neighbors, occupy housing that has been foreclosed and held vacant by banks).

Because adverse possession doctrine employs relatively flexible standards, it allows substantial room for manipulation by decision makers and, in certain cases, significant uncertainty for property owners. To avoid such uncertainty, more rigid rules could be adopted to settle boundary and other possessory disputes. Yet adverse possession is one of the oldest rules of property law, and some version of it already exists in every jurisdiction. Most scholars continue to think that it both promotes justice and fulfills important social and individual needs.

§3 PRESCRIPTIVE EASEMENTS

If the scope of the non-owner's actions is limited to a narrow use of another's land rather than general possession of it, she may be granted a **prescriptive easement** rather than title by adverse possession. Easements are limited rights to use the property of another. They can be either **affirmative** (the right to engage in a particular use on another's land) or **negative** (the right to limit or block a particular use of another's land). The right to cross neighboring property—known as a **right of way**—is an example of an affirmative easement. The right to prevent a neighbor from adding an extra story onto her building is an example of a negative easement. *See* Chapter 8, §2. Affirmative easements, but not negative easements, may be acquired by prescription.

Community Feed Store, Inc. v. Northeastern Culvert Corp.

559 A.2d 1068 (Vt. 1989)

Map: Westminster Station, Vermont
[west of U.S. Route 5 at connection with Route 123]

Ernest W. Gibson III, Justice.

Plaintiff brought an action claiming a prescriptive easement over a portion of defendant's land. The trial court rejected the claim and, instead, entered judgment for defendant on its counterclaim for ejectment, from which plaintiff appeals. We reverse.

Plaintiff operates a small wholesale and retail animal feed business in Westminster Station, Vermont. Defendant is a neighboring business which owns the land adjacent to that upon which plaintiff's buildings stand. At issue is a parcel of land to the north of plaintiff's principal building (the "mill"), which testimony showed to be a rectangular area measuring approximately 60 × 90 feet, covered with gravel but not otherwise improved. Plaintiff owns that part of the gravel area extending approximately twenty-eight feet to the north of the mill; the remainder belongs to defendant.

The mill has loading areas on both the north and south sides: the north loading dock is used mostly by trucks delivering bag feed and by customers coming to pick up feed, while the southern area is where plaintiff receives shipments of feed in bulk. Testimony showed that vehicles using either loading area would use the gravel lot for turning and backing. Evidence tended to show that the suppliers' trucks as well as the customers' smaller vehicles used the gravel lot for this purpose.

Although defendant bought its land in 1956, it was not until a new survey was made in 1984 that it was conclusively established that the bulk of the gravel area used by plaintiff's vehicles actually belonged to defendant. Defendant then erected a barrier at approximately the location of the survey line to prevent cars and trucks from using its portion of the gravel area, precipitating plaintiff's lawsuit for declaration of a prescriptive easement.

The court, after making findings of fact, concluded that plaintiff's claim of a prescriptive easement failed for two reasons: first, plaintiff failed to prove with sufficient particularity the width and length of the easement; and second, any use of the area in question by plaintiff or its customers was made with the permission of the fee owner. Plaintiff claims that the court erred in these conclusions and in the findings of fact supporting them, and that the record as a whole supports the conclusion that a prescriptive easement exists.

Findings of fact will not be overturned on appeal unless they are clearly erroneous. The evidence must be viewed in the light most favorable to the prevailing party, and the findings will be upheld if supported by reasonable or credible evidence, even if contrary evidence exists. Despite this strict standard, a thorough review of the record leads us to the conclusion that plaintiff is correct in its claims that the court erred in making two findings of fact.

In Finding 18, the court held that although "all types of vehicles have turned and backed up to plaintiff's building for loading and unloading since the early 1920s," plaintiff had "failed to prove by the requisite measure of proof as to what portion, if any, of defendant's land" was used by plaintiff's vehicles. This finding, which entails both an issue of law (the measure of proof necessary to establish an easement) and an issue of fact, served as the basis for the court's first conclusion of law denying the claim for a prescriptive easement.

The elements necessary to establish a prescriptive easement and adverse possession are essentially the same under Vermont law: an adverse use or possession which is open, notorious, hostile and continuous for a period of fifteen years, and acquiescence in the use or possession by the person against whom the claim is asserted. The difference lies in the interest claimed. The term "prescription" applies to the acquisition of nonfee interests, while "adverse possession" indicates that the interest claimed is in fee.

Adverse possession may be asserted either under claim of title (where claimant took possession under a deed which is for some reason defective), or under a claim of right which arises from the open, notorious and hostile possession of the land at issue.[18] Where there is color of title, it is relatively simple to ascertain the extent of the possession claimed, since "actual and exclusive occupation of any part of the deeded premises carr[ies] with it constructive possession of the whole. . . ." In the absence of color of title, however, and where a lot has no definite boundary marks, adverse possession can only extend as far as claimant has actually occupied and possessed the land in dispute.

Where prescriptive use is claimed, our law requires proof similar to that needed to establish adverse possession under claim of right. In *Morse v. Ranno,* 32 Vt. 600, 607 (1860), this Court held that where a claim of prescriptive easement for a public highway over private land was made,

> the extent of the acquisition, the width of the road, must be determined by the extent of the actual occupation and use. There can be no constructive possession beyond the limits which are defined by the user upon the land, or by other marks or boundaries marking the extent of the claim.

See also Gore v. Blanchard, 118 A. 888, 894 (Vt. 1922) (width of highway acquired by user is determined by the extent of the actual use and occupation or by other marks and boundaries indicating the extent of the claim).

This approach to defining the extent of a prescriptive easement is reflected in the position taken by the drafters of the *Restatement of Property,* which states that "[t]he extent of an easement created by prescription is fixed by the use through which it was created." *Restatement of Property* §477 (1944).

> No use can be justified under a prescriptive easement unless it can fairly be regarded as within the range of the privileges asserted by the adverse user and acquiesced in by the owner of the servient tenement. Yet, no use can ever be exactly duplicated. If any practically useful easement is ever to arise by prescription, the use permitted under it must vary in some degree from the use by which it was created. Hence, the use under which a prescriptive easement arises determines the *general outlines* rather than the minute details of the interest. *Id.,* comment b (emphasis added).

In California, case law requires claimants to show prescriptive easements by "a definite and certain line of travel" for the statutory period. *Warsaw v. Chicago Metallic Ceilings, Inc.,* 676 P.2d 584, 587 (Cal. 1984). Despite the apparently restrictive nature of that standard, however, the *Warsaw* court, on facts almost identical to ours, found that an easement existed for the purpose of trucks turning around and positioning themselves at loading docks attached to plaintiff's building, stating that "[s]light deviations from the accustomed route will not defeat an easement, [only] substantial changes which break the continuity of the course of travel. . . ." *Id.*

From the case law cited above, it is clear that when a prescriptive easement is claimed, the extent of the user must be proved not with absolute precision, but only as to the general outlines consistent with the pattern of use throughout the prescriptive

18. The court here uses "claim of title" to mean "color of title." This is incorrect. Most courts use the term "claim of title" interchangeably with "claim of right," as distinct from "color of title," *i.e.*, a defective deed. — Eds.

period. We hold that where a claimant adduces enough evidence to prove those general outlines with reasonable certainty, it has met its burden on that issue.

In this case, the trial court had before it extensive evidence as to the nature and scope of the user claimed. Testimony showed that the gravel area at issue was approximately 60 by 90 feet long, extending from the northern end of the mill approximately to where a railroad call box (attached to what resembles a telephone pole) is located. Surveys were introduced showing the exact northern boundary of plaintiff's land, falling approximately twenty-eight feet to the north of the mill and, therefore, twenty-eight feet into the gravel area. Photographs were also admitted into evidence clearly showing the gravel area and the northern loading dock. In addition, plaintiff's president drew a diagram showing the use of the gravel area by trucks and cars, indicating the railroad call box as the north limit.

Under the standard discussed above, we conclude that plaintiff met its burden by establishing the general outlines of the easement with reasonable certainty.

The second—and in its own view, more important—basis upon which the court denied plaintiff's claim was its conclusion that any use made by plaintiff was with the fee owner's permission.

[T]he elements necessary to prove a prescriptive easement [are] open, notorious, hostile and continuous use over a fifteen-year period in which the fee owner has acquiesced. In its findings, the trial court found as fact that the area in dispute had been used by vehicles of all descriptions in a manner consistent with the claimed use since the 1920s. The record showed that this use continued uninterrupted, and in a manner substantially unchanged since then but for the modernization of the vehicles using the area, until the barrier was erected in 1984. On the facts as found by the court, this comprises "open, notorious and continuous" use of defendant's property.

ELEMENTS OF PRESCRIPTION

The elements for establishing a prescriptive easement are the same as those for adverse possession except that the claimant must show adverse "use" rather than adverse "possession." Most courts drop the exclusivity requirement, although some retain it. *See Hoffman v. United Iron & Metal Co.*, 671 A.2d 55, 64 (Md. Ct. Spec. App. 1996); *Rogers v. Marlin,* 754 So. 2d 1267, 1272 (Miss. Ct. App. 1999). A few states add the requirement that the true owner "acquiesce" in the adverse use.

The general rule is that open and notorious use will be presumed to be adverse. The trial court noted in its order (without further comment), and the defendant argues, that not this presumption but the presumption that public use of private property is by permission should apply. This case does not, however, involve . . . generalized public use.[19]

---

19. Defendant's reliance on *Plimpton v. Converse,* 44 Vt. 158 (1871), is misplaced. That case, which also enunciated the "public use" exception to the general presumption of adversity, involved one shopholder's claim of prescriptive easement as to passage, both for himself and his customers, over a neighboring shopholder's land. There, the Court found that because the second shopholder had already opened his land to general passage by his own customers, there was a presumption of permission to all public users, including the first shopholder and his customers. Those facts are distinguishable from the instant case, in which no showing was made that defendant had "thrown open" its land to general passage.

In order to prove the final element of its claim, the passing of the fifteen-year period set forth at Vt. Stat. tit. 12, §501, plaintiff proved the chain of title of its property from plaintiff's predecessors in interest from 1929 through the present, and showed through uncontradicted testimony that those predecessors had also made use of the gravel area now claimed by plaintiff as an easement by prescription. Under the doctrine of "tacking," plaintiff may add those previous periods of use to its own upon a showing that it has "assume[d] the use of the easement directly from his predecessor as a part of his receipt of the dominant estate." The record supports the conclusion that adverse use began no later than 1929, with the result that the prescriptive period expired in 1944. The record supports a conclusion that the claimed use was made in an open, notorious, continuous and adverse manner from 1929 until at least 1956.

Notes and Questions

1. **Burden of proof.** As with adverse possession, many courts require proof of adverse use for prescriptive easements by clear and convincing evidence, *McDonald v. Harris,* 978 P.2d 81 (Alaska 1999), while some require only that the claimant prove the elements by a preponderance of the evidence. *Stiefel v. Lindemann,* 638 A.2d 642, 649 n.8 (Conn. Ct. App. 1994).

Adverse possession claims result in a transfer of title to the adverse possessor while prescriptive easement claims result in the right to continue the kind and amount of use that persisted during the statutory period.

CONTEXT

As in adverse possession, occasional or sporadic use is likely to violate the continuity requirement for a prescriptive easement. *Barchowsky v. Silver Farms, Inc.,* 659 A.2d 347, 354 (Md. Ct. Spec. App. 1995). However, in *United States ex rel. Zuni Tribe of N.M. v. Platt,* 730 F. Supp. 318 (D. Ariz. 1990), the court recognized a prescriptive easement of passage in the Zuni Tribe, which had traversed a 110-mile path located on private lands every four years on a pilgrimage to a sacred site and probably had been doing so since 1540.

2. **Acquiescence.** As *Community Feed Store* demonstrates, a significant number of states require the prescriptive easement claimant to prove **acquiescence** by the true owner as one of the elements of the claim. This is a confusing term. How can the true owner both "acquiesce" in the use and "not permit" it?

The acquiescence requirement may have its origin in the theory that prescriptive easements are based not on adverse or nonpermissive use, but on a **lost grant**. Because statutes of limitation usually applied only to possessory claims in England, English law protected longstanding use on the premise that the use had a lawful origin. The device of choice was the fiction of a lost grant. This theory presumes initial permissive use and therefore contradicts the requirement of proving that use was adverse or nonpermissive.

For some courts today, acquiescence merely means that the owner did not assert her right to exclude by bringing a trespass action; this interpretation renders the requirement duplicative and unnecessary. For some courts, however, it does have independent significance; it means that the landowner must have *known* about the use and passively allowed it to continue without formally granting permission. *Sparling v.*

Fon du Lac Township, 745 N.E.2d 660 (Ill. App. Ct. 2001). Alternatively, it could mean that a reasonable owner would or *should* have known of the use; this meaning duplicates the requirement that the use be open and notorious because use is open and notorious only if it is sufficiently visible to put a reasonable owner on notice of it. *Hodgins v. Sales,* 76 P.3d 969, 973 (Idaho 2003); *Jones v. Cullen,* 1998 WL 811558, at *5 (Minn. Ct. App. 1998); *Lingvall v. Bartmess,* 982 P.2d 690, 694 (Wash. Ct. App. 1999).

3. Presumptions as to permission. Most states presume that a use that satisfies the other elements of prescription is nonpermissive, just as they do with adverse possession. *See, e.g., Harambasic v. Owens,* 920 P.2d 39, 40-41 (Ariz. Ct. App. 1996). However, a fair minority of courts presume that use, unlike possession, is presumptively permissive rather than adverse. *Johnson v. Coshatt,* 591 So. 2d 483, 485 (Ala. 1991); *McGill v. Wahl,* 839 P.2d 393, 397-398 (Alaska 1992). They do so because owners often do allow their neighbors to cross over their land as a "neighborly gesture," *Jones v. Cullen,* 1998 WL 811558, at *5 (Minn. Ct. App. 1998), and there may therefore be more warrant for assuming that limited uses are permissive than there is for presuming that occupation is permissive. *Johnson v. Stanley,* 384 S.E.2d 577, 579 (N.C. Ct. App. 1989). Some courts adopt a presumption that use is permissive only if it can be shown that there was a community custom to allow such uses on the land of others. *Warnack v. Coneen Family Trust,* 879 P.2d 715 (Mont. 1994). Finally, some states protect owners from prescriptive easements over large bodies of unenclosed land under a "neighborhood accommodation exception" where the owners could not reasonably know of passings over the land. *See Algermissen v. Sutin,* 61 P.3d 176, 182 (N.M. 2002) (describing but not applying this exception).

CONTEXT

Trees. A great deal of litigation has ensued between neighbors over encroaching trees. Owners are entitled to cut branches of their neighbors' trees that encroach over their land. *Lane v. W.J. Curry & Sons,* 92 S.W.3d 355, 360 (Tenn. 2002). Can a tree owner obtain a prescriptive easement allowing the tree's branches to remain over neighboring land? Almost all courts hold no, creating an important exception to the prescriptive easement doctrine. *Pierce v. Casady,* 711 P.2d 766 (Kan. Ct. App. 1985); *Koresko v. Farley,* 844 A.2d 607 (Pa. Commw. Ct. 2004). However, some courts may allow such rights to ripen into easements. *Garcia v. Sanchez,* 772 P.2d 1311 (N.M. Ct. App. 1989); *Jones v. Wagner,* 624 A.2d 166, 171 n.3 (Pa. Super. Ct. 1993).

4. The good faith problem. In *Community Feed Store,* one person mistakenly used his neighbor's property. In contrast, in *Warsaw v. Chicago Metallic Ceilings, Inc.,* 676 P.2d 584 (Cal. 1984), cited in *Community Feed Store,* the adverse user clearly knew that it was trespassing on neighboring property. In *Warsaw,* plaintiffs arranged for the construction of a large commercial building on their property but unfortunately left insufficient space between the edge of the building and their property line. The 40-foot driveway was "inadequate since the large trucks which carried material to and from plaintiffs' loading dock could not turn and position themselves at these docks without traveling onto the defendant's property," *id.* at 586, which they proceeded to do for the next seven years. When defendant developed plans to build on the portion of its property that had been used by plaintiffs to back up its delivery trucks, plaintiffs sued to establish a prescriptive easement over the 25-foot strip on the edge of defendant's property. Defendant unwisely continued construction over the disputed strip while litigation proceeded. Plaintiffs ultimately prevailed, obtaining a prescriptive easement since the relevant statute of limitations allowed a relatively short six-year period to establish such an easement.

5. Acquisition by the public. Many older cases and some modern cases hold that the public could not acquire an easement by prescription. *Mihalczo v. Borough of Woodmont,* 400 A.2d 270, 272 (Conn. 1978); *Forest Hills Gardens Corp. v. Baroth,* 555 N.Y.S.2d 1000, 1002 (Sup. Ct. 1990). This rule is based partly on the difficulty of proving continuity of use (how does one define the public?), partly on the difficulty of excluding the general public from certain areas, and partly on the presumption that public use of private property is permissive rather than adverse.

However, the strong trend of modern cases is to recognize that the public may acquire prescriptive easements, while often presuming that public access to private land is permissive in the absence of clear evidence to the contrary, thereby defeating the claim for prescription. *Houghton v. Johnson,* 887 N.E.2d 1073 (Mass. App. Ct. 2008) (evidence insufficient to prove public prescriptive easement over private beach); *Weidner v. State,* 860 P.2d 1205, 1209 (Alaska 1993) (holding that the state could acquire an easement by prescription); *Limestone Dev. Corp. v. Village of Lemont,* 672 N.E.2d 763, 768 (Ill. App. Ct. 1996); *Fears v. YJ Land Corp.,* 539 N.W.2d 306, 308 (N.D. 1995). This is the approach adopted by the *Restatement (Third) of Property (Servitudes)* §2.18 (2000). Some states have statutes providing that use by the public of a road for a certain amount of time creates a public highway. Idaho Code §40-202. A few states have used this doctrine to recognize prescriptive rights in the public to use beaches for recreational purposes. *City of Daytona Beach v. Tona-Rama, Inc.,* 294 So. 2d 73, 75 (Fla. 1974); *Villa Nova Resort, Inc. v. State,* 711 S.W.2d 120, 127 (Tex. Ct. Civ. App. 1986).

Problems

1. What arguments could you make for the plaintiff in *Community Feed Store* that use of another's property is presumptively nonpermissive? What arguments could you make for the defendant true owner that use of a neighbor's property in the context of the case should be held presumptively permissive (with the owner's implied consent) and thus not subject to prescription? Which presumption do you think the court should adopt? Why?

2. Assume the facts in *Warsaw v. Chicago Metallic Ceilings, supra,* in which the neighbor knew its trucks were trespassing on neighboring land. For each of the following questions, construct the strongest arguments on both sides, and then determine what the rule of law should be and justify it.

   a. **Should there be a good faith requirement?** The adverse user clearly knew that it was using someone else's property. To obtain an easement by prescription, should the adverse user be required to have good faith, that is, not to know that it is trespassing on someone else's property?

   b. **Should the adverse user lose when the problem is the result of its own negligence?** The adverse users in *Warsaw* negligently built their building too close to the property line. Their need to trespass on the true owner's property for the purpose of backing up their trucks is therefore the result of their own bad planning. Should the court adopt an exception to the prescriptive easement rules to deny the plaintiff a remedy when the plaintiff's trespassory activity is necessitated by the plaintiff's own negligent planning?

c. **Should there be compensation for the prescriptive easement when the adverse user acted in bad faith?** Adverse possessors and prescriptive easement claimants obtain property rights by prescription without obligation to compensate the true owner for the property rights lost by the true owner. In *Warsaw*, however, Justice Reynoso dissented, on the grounds that it was unfair to award a prescriptive easement to a bad faith trespasser — one who knew that she was trespassing on neighboring property — without requiring her to compensate the true owner for the property rights lost. What arguments can you make for and against this proposal? What rule of law should the court adopt? Should the same rule apply where the trespass is innocent?

§4 OTHER INFORMAL WAYS TO TRANSFER TITLE TO REAL PROPERTY

The Statute of Frauds generally requires a formal writing to transfer interests in real property. As adverse possession demonstrates, however, there are significant exceptions to this general principle. In boundary disputes, a variety of doctrines may result in transfers of ownership without the formalities that usually accompany property transfers. Unlike the case of adverse possession or prescriptive easements, these rules may apply even when non-owners have occupied the property in question with the true owner's permission.

§4.1 The Improving Trespasser

What happens when someone mistakenly invests a lot of money in building a structure that encroaches on a neighbor's property? If the structure *decreases* the value of the neighboring property, the owner ordinarily wishes it to be removed. Owners normally have the right to end a continuing trespass. But should the result be any different when the structure costs a substantial amount to build and causes only a negligible amount of harm to the property interests of the landowner? Should it matter that the owner of the land on which the encroachment was placed failed to object or intervene while the construction was occurring?

The converse problem occurs when the structure *improves* the value of the neighboring property. In this case, the landowner may wish to keep the structure; because it is on her property, the courts generally hold that she has a right to do so. But does the builder have a right to be compensated for the amount spent in the construction to avoid unjust enrichment to the landowner, or would this unjustly force the landowner to pay for something she never wanted or bargained for? If the structure merely encroaches on the neighboring land, should the builder have a right to purchase the land over which it sits, even if the landowner objects?

A. Removal of Encroaching Structures: Relative Hardship

Many courts, especially in older cases, hold that a property owner has an absolute right to an injunction ordering an encroaching structure removed, no matter what the cost involved or the relative value of the properties or the extent of the encroachment. This is most often done in the case of a fence or wall, driveway, or overhanging porch or fire escape, but some courts go so far as to order the removal of an encroaching building. For example, in *Bishop v. Reinhold,* 311 S.E.2d 298 (N.C. Ct. App. 1984), defendants partially erected their house on the adjoining, unimproved lot of the plaintiffs. The court held that the plaintiffs had an absolute right to have the part of the house that encroached on plaintiffs' property removed. *See, e.g., Geragosian v. Union Realty Co.*, 193 N.E. 726, 728 (Mass. 1935) ("The general rule is that the owner of land is entitled to an injunction for the removal of trespassing structures.").

The majority of states, however, now reject this rigid approach and instead adopt the **relative hardship** doctrine. *Urban Site Venture II Limited Partnership v. Levering Associates Limited Partnership,* 665 A.2d 1062 (Md. 1995); *Restatement of Property* §563 (1944). If the encroachment is innocent (the result of a mistake), the harm minimal, the interference in the true owner's property interests small, and the costs of removal substantial, the courts often refuse to grant an injunction ordering removal of the structure. Instead, they will either order the encroaching party to pay damages to the landowner to compensate for the decrease in market value of the owner's land or order a forced sale of the property from the landowner to the owner of the encroaching structure with damages equal to the value of the land taken and possibly a premium to compensate for the involuntary nature of the transfer in ownership. If, however, the cost of removal is not substantial or the interference with the neighbor's ability to use its property is substantial, removal will still be ordered. The North Carolina Court of Appeals explained the doctrine in *Williams v. South & South Rentals, Inc.,* 346 S.E.2d 665, 669 (N.C. Ct. App. 1986):

> Where the encroachment is minimal and the cost of removing the encroachment is most likely substantial, two competing factors must be considered in fashioning a remedy. On the one hand, without court intervention, a defendant may well be forced to buy plaintiff's land at a price many times its worth rather than destroy the building that encroaches. On the other hand, without the threat of a mandatory injunction, builders may view the legal remedy as a license to engage in private eminent domain. The process of balancing the hardships and the equities is designed to eliminate either extreme. Factors to be considered are whether the owner acted in good faith or intentionally built on the adjacent land and whether the hardship incurred in removing the structure is disproportionate to the harm caused by the encroachment. Mere inconvenience and expense are not sufficient to withhold injunctive relief. The relative hardship must be disproportionate.

When the encroachment is innocent, the remedy will depend both on the circumstances and on the views of the judge about the relative equities. Removal was ordered in *Leffingwell v. Glendenning,* 238 S.W.2d 942 (Ark. 1951), where a stone-and-cement wall encroached from three to four inches onto neighboring property. The court ordered removal of the encroachment on the ground that "the cost to appellees of removal is not disproportionate to the value appellant appears to place on the land." *Id.* at 944; *see also Storey v. Patterson,* 437 So. 2d 491, 495 (Ala. 1983) (ordering the defendant to remove the portion of her concrete driveway that encroached 12 feet onto a small neighboring lot because the encroachment "permanently impaired the [plaintiffs'] use and enjoyment of their property").

But courts will refuse to order the removal of a mistaken encroachment when the equities tilt strongly in favor of the encroacher. In *Yeakel v. Driscoll,* 467 A.2d 1342 (Pa. Super. Ct. 1983), the court declined to order the removal of a recently constructed fire wall that encroached two inches onto plaintiff's porch. The court invoked the maxim *de minimus non curat lex,* meaning "that the law will not concern itself with trifles. More specifically it means that a court will not grant equitable relief to a plaintiff who seeks a decree which will do him no good but which will work a hardship on another." *Id.* at 1344. *See Gilpin v. Jacob Ellis Realties,* 135 A.2d 204 (N.J. Super. Ct. App. Div. 1957) (denying an injunction removing an encroachment when the cost of removal was $11,500 and the damage to neighboring property was only $1,000); *Generalow v. Steinberger,* 517 N.Y.S.2d 22 (App. Div. 1987) (refusing to order removal of a driveway and wall that encroached 8.4 inches onto neighboring property and relegating plaintiff to damages); *Knuth v. Vogels,* 61 N.W.2d 301 (Wis. 1953) (refusing to order removal of a garage that encroached one to two feet onto plaintiff's property and giving the defendant trespasser the option of removing the structure or paying damages).

Where encroachment occurs in bad faith, however, courts refuse to consider arguments about relative hardship. For example, in *Warsaw v. Chicago Metallic Ceilings, Inc.,* 676 P.2d 584 (Cal. 1984), the defendant proceeded to build a structure that infringed on its neighbor's property, even though the defendant knew that plaintiff claimed that the structure would infringe on the plaintiff's property. The court ordered the structure removed. The court did not weigh relative hardship because "the defendant acted with a full knowledge" of the owner's asserted rights. *Id.* at 588. Because construction began while a lawsuit was pending regarding the parties' property rights, the court held that defendant "gambled on the outcome of the action and lost." *Id. Accord, Goulding v. Cook,* 661 N.E.2d 1322 (Mass. 1996) (ordering removal of septic tank built when builder knew land ownership was in dispute).

B. Enrichment versus Forced Sale

What happens when, rather than partially encroaching, an *entire structure* is built on land belonging to another? Are the situations meaningfully different? Traditionally, courts have held that the structure belongs to the owner of the land on which it sits. *Banner v. United States,* 238 F.3d 1348 (Fed. Cir. 2001). Does this result in unjust enrichment to the landowner? Or is it an appropriate result in light of the builder's negligence in building on someone else's land? If both parties were negligent in allowing the construction to happen, what should the court do? Should it order the landowner to pay for the building so that the landowner is not unjustly enriched? Or should the landowner be forced to sell the land to the builder? The following case deals with these questions.

Somerville v. Jacobs

170 S.E.2d 805 (W. Va. 1969)

Map: 1600 13th Street, Parkersburg, West Virginia

FRANK C. HAYMOND, President:

The plaintiffs, W.J. Somerville and Hazel M. Somerville, the owners of Lots 44, 45 and 46 in the Homeland Addition to the city of Parkersburg, in Wood County, believing that they were erecting a warehouse building on Lot 46 which they owned, [and in reliance on a surveyor's report and plat,] mistakenly constructed the building on Lot 47 owned by the defendants, William L. Jacobs and Marjorie S. Jacobs. Construction of the building was completed in January 1967 and by deed dated January 14, 1967 the Somervilles conveyed Lots 44, 45 and 46 to the plaintiffs Fred C. Engle and Jimmy C. Pappas who subsequently leased the building to the Parkersburg Coca-Cola Bottling Company, a corporation. Soon after the building was completed but not until then, the defendants learned that the building was on their property and claimed ownership of the building and its fixtures on the theory of annexation. The plaintiffs then instituted this proceeding for equitable relief in the Circuit Court of Wood County and in their complaint prayed, among other things, for judgment in favor of the Somervilles for $20,500.00 as the value of the improvements made on Lot 47, or, in the alternative, that the defendants be ordered to convey their interest in Lot 47 to the Somervilles for a fair consideration. The Farmers Building and Loan Association, a corporation, the holder of a deed of trust lien upon the land of the defendants, was on motion permitted to intervene and be made a defendant in this proceeding.

The controlling question for decision is whether a court of equity can award compensation to an improver for improvements which he has placed upon land not owned by him, which, because of mistake, he had reason to believe he owned, which improvements were not known to the owner until after their completion and were not induced or permitted by such owner, who is not guilty of any fraud or inequitable conduct, and require the owner to pay the fair value of such improvements or, in the alternative, to convey the land so improved to the improver upon his payment to the owner of the fair value of the land less the value of the improvements.

Though there are numerous decisions by this Court relating to improvements to land, the precise question here involved is one of first impression in this jurisdiction.

[T]he question has been considered by appellate courts in other jurisdictions and though the cases are conflicting the decisions in some jurisdictions, upon particular facts, recognize and sustain the jurisdiction of a court of equity to award compensation to the improver to prevent unjust enrichment to the owner and in the alternative to require the owner to convey the land to the improver upon his payment to the owner of the fair value of the land less the improvements.

In Section 625, Chapter 11, Volume 2, *Tiffany Real Property,* Third Edition, the text contains this language:

> Since the rule that erections or additions made by one who has no rights to land are fixtures, and therefore not removable by him, even though he made them in the belief that he was the owner of the land, is calculated to cause hardship to an innocent occupant of another's land, by giving the benefit of his labor and expenditures to the landowner, the courts of this country, without either imputing fraud or requiring proof of it, hold it inequitable to allow one to be enriched under such circumstances by the labor and expenditures of another who acted in good faith and in ignorance of any adverse claim or title. Applying this doctrine of "unjust enrichment," a court of equity will, on the principle that he who seeks equity must do equity, refuse its assistance to the rightful owner of land as against an occupant thereof unless he makes compensation for permanent and beneficial improvements, made by the latter without notice of the defect in his title.

From the foregoing authorities it is manifest that equity has jurisdiction to, and will, grant relief to one who, through a reasonable mistake of fact and in good faith, places permanent improvements upon land of another, with reason to believe that the land so improved is that of the one who makes the improvements, and that the plaintiffs are entitled to the relief which they seek in this proceeding.

The undisputed facts, set forth in the agreed statement of counsel representing all parties, is that the plaintiff W. J. Somerville in placing the warehouse building upon Lot 47 entertained a reasonable belief based on the report of the surveyor that it was Lot 46, which he owned, and that the building was constructed by him because of a reasonable mistake of fact and in the good faith belief that he was constructing a building on his own property and he did not discover his mistake until after the building was completed. It is equally clear that the defendants who spent little if any time in the neighborhood were unaware of the construction of the building until after it was completed and were not at any time or in any way guilty of any fraud or inequitable conduct or of any act that would constitute an estoppel. In short, the narrow issue here is between two innocent parties and the solution of the question requires the application of principles of equity and fair dealing between them.

It is clear that the defendants claim the ownership of the building. Under the common law doctrine of annexation, the improvements passed to them as part of the land. This is conceded by the plaintiffs but they assert that the defendants can not keep and retain it without compensating them for the value of the improvements, and it is clear from the testimony of the defendant William L. Jacobs in his deposition that the defendants intend to keep and retain the improvements and refuse to compensate the plaintiffs for their value. The record does not disclose any express request by the plaintiffs for permission to remove the building from the premises if that could be done without its destruction, which is extremely doubtful as the building was constructed of solid concrete blocks on a concrete slab, and it is reasonably clear, from the claim of the defendants of their ownership of the building and their insistence that certain fixtures which have been removed from the building be replaced, that the defendants will not consent to the removal of the building even if that could be done.

In that situation if the defendants retain the building and refuse to pay any sum as compensation to the plaintiff W.J. Somerville they will be unjustly enriched in the amount of $17,500.00, the agreed value of the building, which is more than eight and one-half times the agreed $2,000.00 value of the lot of the defendants on which it is located, and by the retention of the building by the defendants the plaintiff W.J. Somerville will suffer a total loss of the amount of the value of the building. If, however, the defendants are unable or unwilling to pay for the building which they intend to keep but, in the alternative, would convey the lot upon which the building is constructed to the plaintiff W.J. Somerville upon payment of the sum of $2,000.00, the agreed value of the lot without the improvements, the plaintiffs would not lose the building and the defendants would suffer no financial loss because they would obtain payment for the agreed full value of the lot and the only hardship imposed upon the defendants, if this were required, would be to order them to do something which they are unwilling to do voluntarily. Under the facts and circumstances of this case, if the defendants refuse and are not required to exercise their option either to pay W.J. Somerville the value of the improvements or to convey to him the lot on which they are located upon his payment of the agreed value, the defendants will be unduly and unjustly enriched at the expense of the plaintiff W.J. Somerville who will suffer the complete loss of the warehouse building which by bona fide mistake of fact he constructed upon the land of the defendants. Here, in that situation, to use the language of the Supreme Court of Michigan in *Hardy v. Burroughs,* 232 N.W. 200, "It is not equitable . . . that defendants profit by plaintiffs' innocent mistake, that defendants take all and plaintiffs nothing."

To prevent such unjust enrichment of the defendants, and to do equity between the parties, this Court holds that an improver of land owned by another, who through a reasonable mistake of fact and in good faith erects a building entirely upon the land of the owner, with reasonable belief that such land was owned by the improver, is entitled to recover the value of the improvements from the landowner and to a lien upon such property which may be sold to enforce the payment of such lien, or, in the alternative, to purchase the land so improved upon payment to the landowner of the value of the land less the improvements and such landowner, even though free from any inequitable conduct in connection with the construction of the building upon his land, who, however, retains but refuses to pay for the improvements, must, within a reasonable time, either pay the improver the amount by which the value of his land has been improved or convey such land to the improver upon the payment by the improver to the landowner of the value of the land without the improvements.

FRED CAPLAN, Judge, dissenting:

Respectfully, but firmly, I dissent from the decision of the majority in this case. Although the majority expresses a view which it says would result in equitable treatment for both parties, I am of the opinion that such view is clearly contrary to law and to the principles of equity and that such holding, if carried into effect, will establish a dangerous precedent.

I am aware of the apparent alarmist posture of my statements asserting that the adoption of the majority view will establish a dangerous precedent. Nonetheless, I believe just that and feel that my apprehension is justified. On the basis of unjust enrichment and equity, the majority has decided that the errant party who, without improper design, has encroached upon an innocent owner's property is entitled to equitable treatment. That is, that he should be made whole. How is this accomplished? It is accomplished by requiring the owner of the property to buy the building erroneously constructed on his property or by forcing (by court edict) such owner to sell his property for an amount to be determined by the court.

What of the property owner's right? The solution offered by the majority is designed to favor the plaintiff, the only party who had a duty to determine which lot was the proper one and who made a mistake. The defendants in this case, the owners of the property, had no duty to perform and were not parties to the mistake. Does equity protect only the errant and ignore the faultless? Certainly not.

It is not unusual for a property owner to have long range plans for his property. He should be permitted to feel secure in the ownership of such property by virtue of placing his deed therefor on record. He should be permitted to feel secure in his future plans for such property. However, if the decision expressed in the majority opinion is effectuated then security of ownership in property becomes a fleeting thing. It is very likely that a property owner in the circumstances of the instant case either cannot readily afford the building mistakenly built on his land or that such building does not suit his purpose. Having been entirely without fault, he should not be forced to purchase the building.

In my opinion for the court to permit the plaintiff to force the defendants to sell their property contrary to their wishes is unthinkable and unpardonable. This is nothing less than condemnation of private property by private parties for private use. Condemnation of property (eminent domain) is reserved for government or such entities as may be designated by the legislature. Under no theory of law or equity should an individual be permitted to acquire property by condemnation. The majority would allow just that.

I am aware of the doctrine that equity frowns on unjust enrichment. However, contrary to the view expressed by the majority, I am of the opinion that the circumstances of this case do not warrant the application of such doctrine. It clearly is the accepted law that as between two parties in the circumstances of this case he who made the mistake must suffer the hardship rather than he who was without fault.

I would remand the case to [the circuit] court with directions that the trial court give the defendant, Jacobs, the party without fault, the election of purchasing the building, of selling the property, or of requiring the plaintiff to remove the building from defendant's property.[20]

Notes and Questions

1. **Mistake.** When a builder mistakenly constructs an entire structure on land belonging to another, the courts generally rule that the landowner becomes the owner of the structure built on her land by another. Does this rule make sense, given the fact that the landowner stood by and allowed the construction to occur without intervening? Does the owner have any obligation to look out for her own rights? Does the landowner have to compensate the builder? The builder claims that failure to compensate will leave the landowner unjustly enriched by the builder's investment; moreover, both parties made a mistake — the builder by encroaching on neighboring property and the landowner by not noticing that someone was building on her own land and not taking action to prevent it. Which property claim should prevail?

Like the court in *Somerville v. Jacobs,* some courts hold that an innocent trespasser who improves property in the good faith belief that it was her own property has a right to compensation for the value of the improvements made when those improvements increase the value of the property. Some courts, however, hold that "trespassers cannot have the advantage of any benefits they have made to the property. Such improvements belong to the landowner, without compensation to trespassers for labor or materials." 9-64A *Powell on Real Property* §64A.05[5]. Do you agree with the majority or the dissenting opinion in *Somerville*?

2. **Betterment statutes.** Some states have **betterment statutes** that allow owners to choose between paying the builder the value of improvements built on their land or selling the land on which the improvement sits to the builder. They generally allow compensation only when the builder had color of title and believed in good faith that the land was hers. *See, e.g.,* Ark. Code §18-60-213; N.C. Gen. Stat. §§1-340 to 1-351. In effect, these statutes force owners to pay for unwanted improvements or give up to the builder land they otherwise would have owned. Should the burden be on the builder to make sure she is building on her own land, or should the landowner have an obligation to determine if someone else is building on her own land and act to stop the trespass?

Problem

In *Banner v. United States,* 238 F.3d 1348 (Fed. Cir. 2001), *aff'g* 44 Fed. Cl. 568 (Fed. Cl. 1999), title to most of the town of Salamanca, New York, was held by the Seneca Nation of Indians. In the 1870s, non-Indians began to settle on Seneca land

20. The West Virginia Supreme Court has acknowledged a change in the law measuring restitution damages, stating that the "measure of damages in an unjust enrichment claim is the greater of the enhanced market value of the property or the cost of the improvements to the property." *Realmark Developments, Inc. v. Ranson,* 588 S.E.2d 150 (W. Va. 2003). — Eds.

pursuant to leases granted them by the Seneca Nation. However, under federal Indian law,[21] those leases were not valid under federal law without the consent of the United States. An 1875 federal statute validated the leases and extended them for a number of years. Several statutes followed until Congress unilaterally extended those leases in an 1890 federal statute for 99 years. With no choice but to extend the leases, the Seneca Nation itself renewed the leases at nominal rents of $1 to $10 a year. Those rents were not raised over the entire period of the leases until they expired on February 1, 1991.

At that point the City of Salamanca created a public authority to negotiate a new arrangement with the Seneca Nation. That agreement provided that "(1) the United States and the state of New York would pay a combined $60 million to the Seneca Nation to remedy the severe value inequities of the 99-year leases, (2) the Seneca Nation would offer new leases to the then-existing lessees with a term of forty years, renewable for another forty years at fair market value. . . ." *Id.* The agreement left for the future the question of who would own the improvements on the land at the end of the leases if they ever expired and were not renewed. That agreement was ratified by Congress in legislation passed in 1990.

Because some individuals refused to accept the lease renewals, the United States brought suit against them on behalf of the Seneca Nation to eject them from Seneca lands. The court ruled that the tribe was not obligated to renew the leases and that ejectment was a proper remedy. The court also ruled that the Seneca Nation owned the improvements placed on the land. The ejected owners then brought a claim against the United States arguing that, by failing to provide compensation for the lost value of their dwellings, the United States had taken their property without just compensation. The Federal Circuit Court affirmed the ruling of the Court of Federal Claims that no such taking had occurred because the common law granted ownership of buildings built on land belonging to another to the owner of the land.

Were the courts correct to hold that the Seneca Nation owned the improvements built on their land? Does it matter that, in the past, the United States had consistently sided with the settlers and protected their interests when they conflicted with the interests of the Seneca Nation? Does it matter that Congress had several times passed statutes ratifying and extending the leases without regard to whether the Seneca Nation wanted the leases to be extended? Would it matter if the United States had, in the past, verbally assured the settlers that, at some point, the land would be transferred from the Seneca Nation to the non-Indian settlers?

What are the arguments for and against requiring the Seneca Nation or the United States to compensate the builders for the improvements placed on Seneca land? What are the arguments for a forced sale of the land from the Seneca Nation to the home builders who had lived on the land for more than 100 years?

21. For more on tribal title and federal Indian law, *see* Chapter 2, §1.

§4.2 Boundary Settlement

A. Oral Agreement

Courts may uphold **oral agreements** between neighbors that set the boundary between their properties if (1) both parties are uncertain where the true boundary lies or a genuine dispute exists over the location of the boundary, (2) the parties can prove the existence of an agreement setting the boundary, and (3) the parties take (and/or relinquish) possession to the agreed line. *Fogerty v. State,* 231 Cal. Rptr. 810 (Ct. App. 1986); *Shultz v. Johnson,* 654 So. 2d 567 (Fla. Dist. Ct. App. 1995); *Morrissey v. Haley,* 865 P.2d 961 (Idaho 1993); Lawrence Berger, *Unification of the Doctrines of Adverse Possession and Practical Location in the Establishment of Boundaries,* 78 Neb. L. Rev. 1, 7-11 (1999).

B. Acquiescence

Even without an oral agreement, the courts may nonetheless recognize longstanding **acquiescence** by both neighbors in a common boundary. William B. Stoebuck & Dale A. Whitman, *The Law of Property* §11.8, at 864 (3d ed. 2000). "(1) [A]djoining owners (2) who occupy their respective tracts up to a clear and certain line (such as a fence), (3) which they mutually recognize and accept as the dividing line between their properties (4) for a long period of time, cannot thereafter claim that the boundary thus recognized is not the true boundary." *Tresemer v. Albuquerque Public School District,* 619 P.2d 819, 820 (N.M. 1980). *Accord, Huntington v. Riggs,* 862 N.E.2d 1263 (Ind. Ct. App. 2007); *RHN Corp. v. Veibell,* 96 P.3d 935 (Utah 2004).

C. Estoppel

A boundary may be established by **estoppel** when one owner "erroneously represents to the other that the boundary between them is located along a certain line [and] the second, in reliance on the representations, builds improvements which encroach on the true boundary or takes other detrimental actions." Stoebuck & Whitman, *supra,* §11.8, at 866. The party who made the representations is then "estopped to deny them, and the boundary is in effect shifted accordingly." *Id.* Some states may find estoppel even when no explicit representation is made; they may infer a representation "from an owner's silence in the face of knowledge that his neighbor is building an encroaching structure." *Id.* §11.8, at 867.

D. Laches

An owner who delays in asserting a property interest may be barred from asserting the interest by the equitable doctrine of **laches**. Laches is "an equitable defense based primarily on circumstances which render inequitable the granting of relief to a dilatory plaintiff." *Rilley v. Quinlan,* 1999 Mich. App. LEXIS 2467 (1999). The doctrine applies when "there has been an unexcused or unexplained delay in commencing an action and a corresponding change of material condition, which results in prejudice." *Id.* Mere lapse of time is insufficient to support the defense of laches. "It must appear [that] the delay resulted in some prejudice to the party asserting laches which would make it inequitable to disregard the lapse of time and incidental consequences." *Id.* If an owner knows about an encroachment and does nothing to stop it, the delay in asserting the owner's rights may cause the encroacher to invest in reliance on the belief that the occupation is not wrongful. In that case, even if the statute of limitations has not run, the court may deny injunctive relief because of the unreasonable delay in asserting the owner's rights.

§4.3 Dedication

A **dedication** is a transfer of real property from a private owner to a government entity such as a city. A valid dedication requires an **offer** by the owner of the property and an **acceptance** by the public. The offer consists of words or conduct on the part of the owner that demonstrate an intent to turn the property over to the public. The offer may be made by a written or oral statement from the owner. The courts may also find an implied offer by one who invites or merely permits the public to use her land for a long period of time. The acceptance may be made formally by passing a city council resolution or informally by taking over maintenance of the area or ceasing to collect property taxes on the parcel. Finally, just as an offer may be implied from the owner's longstanding acquiescence in public use, an acceptance may be implied from long and substantial public use, even absent governmental action. Stoebuck & Whitman, *supra,* §11.6, at 846-850.

Most courts take seriously the idea that the owner must express an intent to make a gift of the property to the public, whether this is expressed through an oral statement or by conduct evidencing an intent to make a gift. *See, e.g., General Auto Service Station v. Maniatis,* 765 N.E.2d 1176 (Ill. App. Ct. 2002) (evidence insufficient to show either dedication or acceptance despite long public usage). Some courts, however, have found dedication when the owner has objected to public use but has made no serious effort to stop that use. In *Gion v. City of Santa Cruz,* 465 P.2d 50 (Cal. 1970), for example, the California Supreme Court found that the owners of a private beach had "dedicated" their property to the public by acquiescing in longstanding public use; the owners' efforts to stop the use were "half-hearted and ineffectual." Stoebuck & Whitman, *supra,* §11.6, at 848. This opinion proved controversial, however, and was effectively overturned by a subsequent California statute. *See* Cal. Civ. Code §§813, 1009.

§4.4 Riparian Owners: Accretion and Avulsion

Special rules have developed to govern changes in borders of "riparian property" located on a river or other body of water. Slow changes in buildup of land caused by slow deposit of silt or sand on the border of the land (**accretion**) belong to the owner of the land whose borders are thus enlarged; gradual losses of land caused by **erosion** shrink the owner's land rights. However, very sudden changes caused by events such as earthquakes and floods (referred to as **avulsion**) are generally held not to change the borders of property. *City of Long Branch v. Liu,* 833 A.2d 106 (N.J. Super. Ct. 2003) (avulsion found from government infusion of new sand).

§5 ADVERSE POSSESSION OF PERSONAL PROPERTY

The analog for trespass in the context of chattels is conversion. The statute of limitations for conversion begins to run when the property is wrongfully taken (converted) and the owner dispossessed of the property. *Songbyrd, Inc. v. Estate of Albert B. Grossman,* 23 F. Supp. 2d 219 (N.D.N.Y. 1998) (adverse possession of music recordings); *Vigilant Insurance Co. of America v. Housing Authority of the City of El Paso,* 660 N.E.2d 1121 (N.Y. 1995) (bonds). Without supplemental doctrines, the wrongful possessor would become immune from suit by the original owner upon the expiration of the statute of limitations. But the transfer of title to the possessor upon the expiration of the limitations period — as occurs with the adverse possession of land — would be harsher for chattel owners than it would be for landowners. Do you see why? As a result, courts have developed different rules that (under certain circumstances) work to extend the statute of limitations for conversion. Most jurisdictions follow one of two principal approaches: the discovery rule or the demand rule.

The leading case establishing the **discovery rule** is *O'Keeffe v. Snyder,* 416 A.2d 862 (N.J. 1980). In *O'Keeffe,* the painter Georgia O'Keeffe sued a New York gallery owned by Barry Snyder to recover three paintings stolen from her and purchased for $35,000 by Snyder from a third party, Ulrich A. Frank, who had inherited them from his father. Snyder claimed that he had acquired title to the paintings by adverse possession under New Jersey's six-year statute of limitations. Snyder claimed that the six-year period started to run when the paintings were stolen. In contrast, O'Keeffe argued that she had not known where the paintings were after they were stolen and thus could not reasonably have made a demand to have the paintings returned. Since she had sued the possessor within six years of discovering where the paintings were, her claim should not be barred. The court agreed, noting that a thief can never acquire good title and that no one can acquire good title from a thief; even a bona fide purchaser who is unaware that property was stolen will not ordinarily be able to retain ownership in a contest with the true owner. An exception to this principle is contained in the *Uniform Commercial Code,* which provides that entrusting possession of goods to a merchant who deals in that kind of goods gives the merchant the power to transfer all the rights of the entruster to a buyer in the ordinary course of business, thereby vesting good title in the buyer as against the original owner. *See* U.C.C. §2-403(2). The court held that if that section of the UCC did not apply, the statute of limitations for adverse possession (in someone other than the true owner) would start to run only when the true owner discovers, or reasonably should have discovered, where the stolen personal property was located. The question, therefore, was whether O'Keeffe had used due diligence to recover the paintings and whether the paintings had been concealed from her. *Accord, Charash v. Oberlin College,* 14 F.3d 291, 299 (6th Cir. 1994).

In contrast to the discovery rule for adverse possession of personal property, the New York Court of Appeals has promulgated a **demand rule** — one that is rather more protective of the interests of the true owner, at least when the artwork has been sold to a bona fide purchaser who was unaware of the theft. In *Solomon R. Guggenheim Foundation v. Lubell,* 569 N.E.2d 426 (N.Y. 1991), a Chagall gouache was stolen from the storeroom of the Guggenheim Museum in the late 1960s. However, the museum neither notified the police nor publicly announced the theft. The current possessor argued that the failure to attempt to recover the artwork meant that the museum's rights were barred by the three-year statute of limitations. The museum responded that this was a tactical decision "based upon its belief that to publicize the theft would succeed only in driving the gouache further underground and greatly diminishing the possibility that it would ever be recovered." The court rejected the discovery rule on the grounds that it was wrong to place a general obligation of due diligence on the true owner. Rather, the court held that "a cause of action for replevin against the good faith purchaser of a stolen chattel accrues when the true owner makes demand for return of the chattel and the person in possession of the chattel refuses to return it. Until demand is made and refused, possession of the stolen property by the good faith purchaser for value is not considered wrongful." The court explained, *id.* at 431:

> [O]ur decision today is in part influenced by our recognition that New York enjoys a worldwide reputation as a preeminent cultural center. To place the burden of locating stolen artwork on the true owner and to foreclose the rights of that owner to recover its property if the burden is not met would, we believe, encourage illicit trafficking in stolen art. Three years after the theft, any purchaser, good faith or not, would be able to hold onto stolen art work unless the true owner was able to establish that it had undertaken a reasonable search for the missing art. This shifting of the burden onto the wronged owner is inappropriate. In our opinion, the better rule gives the owner relatively greater protection and places the burden of investigating the provenance of a work of art on the potential purchaser.

Oddly, however, although the court rejected placing a due diligence obligation on the museum for the purpose of applying adverse possession doctrine, the court held that the museum might be precluded from recovering its property because of the equitable doctrine of laches. Under that rule of law, a plaintiff may not prevail if the plaintiff unreasonably delayed in asserting its rights and others were prejudiced by that delay. Does this doctrine impose a due diligence requirement through the back door?

Which rule is better — the discovery rule or the demand rule? *See also Autocephalous Greek-Orthodox Church of Cyprus v. Goldberg & Feldman Fine Arts, Inc.*, 717 F. Supp. 1374 (S.D. Ind. 1989) (theft and sale of Christian mosaics from Cyprus and application of the discovery rule).

Problem

An increasing amount of attention has focused on artworks confiscated by the Nazis from Jewish families during World War II. *See, e.g.*, Patricia Cohen, *Museums Faulted on Restitution of Nazi-Looted Art,* N.Y. Times, June 30, 2013. Some of these works were subsequently sold and purchased by good faith buyers. Others were donated to museums. In either case, disputes have arisen between current possessors and the heirs of the original owners over ownership of the works.

Assume a painting was taken from a Jewish family by the Nazi regime pursuant to its racially motivated policy of extermination. The painting winds up in the hands of a private family and is later sold to a museum in the United States in 1960. The painting is displayed for 40 years. The granddaughter of the couple who owned the painting discovers in January 2001 that it belonged to her grandparents and sues to obtain ownership of the painting. The statute of limitations for adverse possession is 30 years.

a. What is the plaintiff's argument for adopting the demand rule?
b. What is the defendant's argument for the discovery rule?
c. What should the court do?

CHAPTER 6

Nuisance: Resolving Conflicts Between Free Use and Quiet Enjoyment

§1 LAND USE CONFLICTS AMONG NEIGHBORS

We do not live alone, and the use of one's own property can affect the property and personal interests of others, even if we do not commit a trespass by physically intruding onto their land. Nontrespassory interferences with the property rights of others can occur when the use of *one's own property* harms the property interests of one's neighbors. Such conflicts may arise in a wide variety of situations, including pollution, noise, odors, criminal activity, excavation undermining lateral support of neighboring land, flooding, and blocking access to light and air.

Because use of one's land often affects other landowners, the privilege to use one's property is limited by the legal rights of other owners to be protected from uses that unreasonably harm their use or enjoyment of their own property. At the same time, the right to be secure from conduct that interferes with one's use or enjoyment of property is not absolute. Because interests in free use often clash with interests in security, we cannot provide absolute protection for either. As the *Restatement (Second) of Torts* notes, "[i]t is an obvious truth that each individual in a community must put up with a certain amount of annoyance, inconvenience and interference and must take a certain amount of risk in order that all may get on together." *Restatement (Second) of Torts* §822, cmt. g (1977). However, free use rights must be limited when "the harm or risk to one is greater than he ought to be required to bear under the circumstances, at least without compensation." *Id.*

Nuisance law is the principal means by which the common law of property addresses land use conflicts. Nuisance doctrine provides remedies for conduct that causes *unreasonable harm to the use and enjoyment of land*. Supplementing the basic nuisance analysis are a series of special rules that courts and legislatures have developed to govern conflicts over support obligations, water rights, and access to light and air.

The Reciprocal Nature of Conflicting Land Uses

When a factory spews smoke into the air and pollutes the environment for neighboring owners, we normally view the factory as causing harm to surrounding homeowners. But economist Ronald Coase notes that regulations that prevent a factory from polluting the air would limit the owner's freedom to operate the factory as it wishes and thus impose costs on the owner.

> The question is commonly thought of as one in which *A* inflicts harm on *B* and what has to be decided is: how should we restrain *A*? But this is wrong. We are dealing with a problem of a reciprocal nature. To avoid the harm to *B* would inflict harm on *A*. The real question that has to be decided is: should *A* be allowed to harm *B* or should *B* be allowed to harm *A*? The problem is to avoid the more serious harm.

Ronald Coase, *The Problem of Social Cost,* 3 J.L. & Econ. 1, 2 (1960). Coase cites the example of *Sturges v. Bridgman,* LR 11 Ch D 842 (1879), a famous case about a candy maker who uses noisy machinery that disturbs the work of a doctor next door.

> To avoid harming the doctor would inflict harm on the confectioner. The problem posed by this case was essentially whether it was worth while, as a result of restricting the methods of production which could be used by the confectioner, to secure more doctoring at the cost of a reduced supply of confectionery products.

Id. To determine whether to regulate the polluting factory or the confectioner requires comparing the costs and benefits of allowing the defendant to operate with the costs and benefits of prohibiting or regulating the defendant's operations.

In the context of land use disputes, one owner is seeking to be secure from harms caused by another owner's land use; the question is whether to protect the plaintiff's interest in security from harm or the defendant's interest in freedom of action. Regulating an activity harms those who wish to engage in it either by banning it or by making it more expensive. Failing to regulate an activity also has harmful consequences: It authorizes one owner to interfere with or even destroy the interests of others in the use and enjoyment of their property. Deciding not to protect property interests by failing to prohibit harmful use of land is as much a regulatory choice as choosing to prohibit or limit such uses.

Like most economists, Coase eschews moral judgment and attempts to remain studiously neutral as between the conflicting activities. The only question is which activity causes more harm. This suggests that the central question is the *magnitude* of the harms on both sides and not their *character*. This assumption seems innocuous when the two activities are equally legitimate, such as the conflict between the confectioner and the doctor or between the cattle rancher and the farmer. But is this assumption always warranted? Take the pollution example. It is true that regulation of the polluting activity may reduce the amount of the product created by that activity, and we would like to know what this cost is before we choose to regulate the conduct to avoid the pollution. This does not necessarily mean that we are — or should be — indifferent as between an economic activity that causes pollution and one that does not cause pollution. After all, other things being equal, we may prefer to live in a less-polluted environment.

In determining how serious these consequences of a land use are, as Coase asks us to do, we should be interested not only in the dollar value of production or income but also in the full range of values we care about— some of which are hard to put a dollar value on. We care, for example, about the distribution of costs and benefits; it is wrong to make some people bear a disproportionate share of the burdens necessary to promote social welfare. In addition, some values are more fundamental than others. For example, the law deems an unprivileged intrusion on property to be a trespass whether or not the benefits of entry outweigh the costs, giving individual interests in possession a privileged status. How do we determine which interests are fundamental? How should we evaluate costs and benefits that are hard to describe in monetary terms: Should we assign numbers to account for the magnitude of such costs and benefits, or should we evaluate those considerations in another way?

§2 NUISANCE

As with all legal questions, there are two distinct (though related) issues in all nuisance cases. The first question is which party has the basic entitlement. Does the plaintiff have a right to be secure from this kind of harm, or does the defendant have the right to engage in the activity? The second question has to do with the remedy used to vindicate the entitlement.

§2.1 Defining Unreasonable Interference

A **nuisance** is a substantial and unreasonable interference with the use or enjoyment of land. *San Diego Gas & Electric Co. v. Superior Court,* 920 P.2d 669, 696 (Cal. 1996); *Bargmann v. Soll Oil Co.,* 574 N.W.2d 478, 486 (Neb. 1998); *Schneider National Carriers, Inc. v. Bates,* 147 S.W.3d 264, 269 (Tex. 2004). Nuisance law is a flexible doctrine that has been applied in a variety of circumstances.

Typical nuisance cases involve activities that are "offensive, physically, to the senses and [which] by such offensiveness makes life uncomfortable [such as] noise, odor, smoke, dust, or even flies." *In re Chicago Flood Litigation,* 680 N.E.2d 265, 278 (Ill. 1997). Nuisances have been found in the case of vibration or blasting that damages a house; the emission of pollutants, such as smoke, dust, gas or chemicals; offensive odors; and noise. *See, e.g., Howard Opera House Association v. Urban Outfitters, Inc.,* 322 F.3d 125 (2d Cir. 2003) (applying Vermont law) (loud music in retail store that violates local noise ordinance constitutes nuisance against neighboring tenants); *Shutes v. Platte Chemical Co.,* 564 So. 2d 1382 (Miss. 1990) (toxic waste spilled at chemical factory seeps through the ground, killing vegetation on nearby parcels of land and depreciating the value of the property constitutes a nuisance); *Padilla v. Lawrence,* 685 P.2d 964 (N.M. Ct. App. 1984) (homeowners recover from manure processing plant for damage to property interests resulting from odors, dust, noise, and flies); *Bradley v. American Smelting & Refining Co.*, 709 P.2d 782 (Wash. 1985) (homeowner entitled to bring a claim for nuisance against copper smelting factory that emitted microscopic airborne particles of heavy metals in the manufacturing process).

Dobbs v. Wiggins

401 Ill. App. 3d 367 (2010)

Justice BRUCE D. STEWART delivered the opinion of the court:

The plaintiffs and the defendant all reside on a dead-end road, Triton Lane, in rural Jefferson County, Illinois. Larry and Frances Dobbs live on a parcel of property that is directly north of Wiggins's property, and Wayne and Lorena Richard lived on a parcel of property that lies north of the Dobbs property. The Dobbses and the Richards have lived on their property for approximately 30 years. Wiggins purchased his property on Triton Lane in 1995, built a home and dog kennels on the property, and began raising, training, and kenneling bird dogs. On November 19, 2007, the Dobbses and the Richards filed a complaint against Wiggins that alleged that barking dogs on the Wiggins property constituted a private nuisance.

The circuit court began a two-day bench trial on the plaintiffs' complaint on April 15, 2009. At the trial, Larry Dobbs testified that . . . Wiggins's property was directly south of his property line. Larry testified that he enjoyed working outside in his garden, in his flower bed, and around his fish pond, sitting outside on his deck, and hosting cookouts for family members. According to Larry, at first Wiggins "didn't have that many" dogs, and the dogs did not bark much. However, the noise from barking dogs kenneled on Wiggins's property grew worse over time. In an attempt to alleviate some of the noise, Larry planted a row of cedar trees on his property.

Larry told the court that his house was approximately 200 to 250 yards from a barn where Wiggins kenneled many of his dogs. Larry testified that the barking was constant, day and night. The dogs might bark for two straight hours, take a break, and start barking again, but there was never any extended period of time in which they completely quit barking. Larry stated that in 2007 the barking was at its worst. When he went outside to do chores, he did not spend any time outside enjoying his property like he had in the past. He used to enjoy having his windows at his home open, but he now keeps them shut because of the barking noise. According to Larry, the noise was worse during the summer months as compared to the winter months. Larry approached Wiggins sometime in August of 2007 to complain about the noise. [Larry] testified that the noise was less at the time of the trial than in July of 2007 because there were fewer dogs on Wiggins's property; however, the barking noise was still a problem that made it hard for him to enjoy his property. He testified that he could hear the barking from inside his house. Wiggins testified that on February 16, 2009, the parties inspected Wiggins's kennels in preparation for the trial, and at that time, he counted a total of 69 dogs on Wiggins's property. During the inspection, whenever someone arrived, the dogs barked for 20 to 30 minutes before quieting down. After the dogs quieted down, they could carry on a normal conversation in front of the kennels.

Frances testified that she had been married to Larry for 16 years and had lived on their property on Triton Lane since that time. Frances noticed the noise from Wiggins's barking dogs sometime after Wiggins purchased his property. Frances described the barking as "[e]xcessive, continuous, chronic barking." Frances testified: "I'm an early riser and sometimes I would be up five, six in the morning and they would be barking and continue barking for hours. Then, you know, they might quit for half an hour, couple of minutes. Sometimes I would think, oh, thank goodness, you know, they've quit barking and I'd step outside and here they go again and I would have to go back into the house." Prior to Wiggins kenneling dogs on his property, Frances liked to open the windows to her home in the springtime and let fresh air in. Now she no longer liked to open her windows because of Wiggins's barking dogs. Frances claimed that the barking could be heard inside and that she had to turn on a radio or television to drown out the noise. She testified that a lot of nights, she could not go to sleep because of the noise. [T]he barking noise had caused her stress and restricted her and Larry from enjoying any outside activities in their yard.

Wayne Richard testified that he had lived on Triton Lane with his wife for 30 years. Wayne testified that his house was 200 to 250 yards north of the Dobbs house. He estimated that his house was approximately 500 yards northwest of Wiggins's property. His house and the Dobbs house were the houses closest to Wiggins's property. Wayne testified that he liked to garden, mow, and race lawnmowers with his grandson in his yard. In the evenings, he liked to sit outside on his patio and listen to the sounds of nearby wildlife, including coyotes, turkeys, geese, and occasionally, nearby cattle. He testified that the coyotes howling would cause Wiggins's dogs to start barking.

According to Wayne, . . . the noise from the dogs on Wiggins's property gradually increased over time. He stated that it was noticeable in 2007 and became a "real nuisance" to him in 2007. He testified, "[W]e can't do anything outside without hearing the dogs." Wayne used to like having his windows open, but with the windows open, he could hear the dogs barking from everywhere in the house. He had to close his windows, and he usually turned on his television or his radio so he could not hear the barking. Wayne had been to the Dobbses' property and heard the dogs barking inside and outside of their house as well.

Wayne testified that he had two conversations about the dogs with Wiggins. According to Wayne, Wiggins stated that he wanted to be a good neighbor and had bought some device to quiet the dogs but that he was "within his rights" regardless of how many dogs were barking. Wiggins told Wayne that he moved to the country so he could raise the dogs, and Wayne responded that he moved to the country to get away from noise.

Wayne's wife, Lorena (Lori), testified that she enjoyed various activities outside, including gardening, reading, playing with kids, and cooking out. Now everything she did outside was "to the accompaniment of barking dogs." She did not invite people over for an outside activity very often anymore because of the noise. She used to like to keep the windows in her house open in the spring before it got too hot, but they did not open the windows as often because of the barking, and they no longer slept with the windows open. According to Lori, when Wiggins moved into the area, he started raising dogs and the noise began to escalate as he accumulated more dogs. Lori testified that, in 2006, she could no longer ignore the noise. Every time she was outside—morning, noon, and evening—she could hear the dogs barking, whining, howling, and yipping. The noise got worse in 2007 and continued through 2009 at the same frequency and intensity.

Mary McKowen lived in a house that was approximately 2 ¼ miles north of the Dobbs house, and she had lived there for approximately 40 years. She was a longtime friend of Larry Dobbs and his family. McKowen testified that when she and her husband, Nolan, were outside on their property, they could hear Wiggins's dogs barking to the south. During her visits at the Dobbs residence in 2007, McKowen could hear the dogs barking outside every time she visited, which she felt was very annoying.

Charles Downey lived on Triton Lane approximately one mile north of the Dobbs residence, and he had lived there for nearly 30 years. He had been to the Dobbs house at various times and had heard the dogs barking at the Dobbs home. Downey described the barking as "quite a bit louder" at the Dobbs property and testified that the barking would be annoying to listen to all the time. Downey testified that he also, from time to time, helped Wiggins at his property, including feeding his dogs and horses. In addition, Downey designed and built some of Wiggins's kennels. Downey estimated that in 2007 Wiggins had more than 100 dogs on his property.

Martin Boykin of the Jefferson County Animal Control testified that in January of 2008, he responded to Triton Lane in response to a complaint that a dog owned by the Dobbses was acting aggressively, trying to bite people, and not allowing the mail to be delivered. On that occasion, he spoke with both Wiggins and Larry Dobbs near their property line for at least a half an hour. In describing the barking coming from the Wiggins property during this visit, Boykin testified: "You could hear somewhat some barking but nothing to—you couldn't really tell, I mean, a number of dogs or anything like that. It wasn't nothing loud or, you know, anything that would disturb anyone, I would assume." He told the circuit court that he did not believe the barking level was "disturbing." He testified that he had not been to the property except on that one occasion.

Wiggins testified that he had been involved in raising and training bird dogs since he was a child helping his grandfather raise and train bird dogs. Wiggins testified that from 2002 to 2008, he has had a total income of $139,295 from selling his bird dogs. Wiggins testified that after he moved to his Triton Lane property and built his kennels, he asked Larry several times every year whether his dogs bothered him in any way. According to Wiggins, Larry always told him that the dogs were not a problem and that he could not hear them. Wiggins testified that he had hundreds of such conversations with Larry over the years. However, in a conversation on August 11, 2007, Larry told Wiggins that the barking was out of control and asked him to do something about it. According to Wiggins, that was the first time Larry had complained about the barking in the 15 years he had lived there. At that time, he owned approximately 100 dogs. After that conversation, Wiggins made attempts to reduce the noise level. Wiggins believed that because of these measures, the dogs were quieter at the time of the trial than they had been in 2007.

On July 21, 2009, the circuit court entered a judgment in favor of the plaintiffs. The court found that, although Wiggins's land was well-suited for a dog kennel, the barking dogs resulted in an invasion of the plaintiffs' interest in the use and enjoyment of their lands and that the gravity of the harm done to the plaintiffs outweighed the utility of Wiggins's dog kennels. The court ordered Wiggins to decrease the number of dogs in his possession to no more than six, to kennel his dogs in the southern region of his property, and to take all the steps necessary to adequately suppress any noise caused by any barking dogs. Wiggins filed a timely notice of appeal.

The first argument that Wiggins raises on appeal is that the circuit court's finding that his dogs constituted a nuisance was against the manifest weight of the evidence. We disagree.

"[A]n appellate court will defer to the findings of the circuit court unless they are against the manifest weight of the evidence." *Chicago Investment Corp. v. Dolins*, 481 N.E.2d 712 (Ill. 1985). Accordingly, in the present case, we will review the circuit court's finding that the barking dogs constituted a nuisance under the manifest-weight-of-the-evidence standard.

"A private nuisance is a substantial invasion of another's interest in the use and enjoyment of his or her land." *Willmschen v. Trinity Lakes Improvement Ass'n*, 840 N.E.2d 1275 (Ill. App. 2005). "The invasion must be either intentional or negligent, and unreasonable." *Id.* at 553. In determining whether particular conduct constitutes a nuisance, the standard is the conduct's effect on a reasonable person. The Illinois Supreme Court has frequently stated that a nuisance must be physically offensive to the senses to the extent that it makes life uncomfortable. An invasion constituting a nuisance can include noise, smoke, vibration, dust, fumes, and odors produced on the defendant's land and impairing the use and enjoyment of neighboring land. Whether the complained-of activity constitutes a nuisance is generally a question of fact. In an action to enjoin a private nuisance, the circuit court must balance the harm done to the plaintiffs against the benefit caused by the defendant's use of the land and the suitability of the use in that particular location.

In *Woods v. Khan*, 420 N.E.2d 1028 (Ill. App. 1981), the plaintiffs brought a lawsuit to enjoin the defendants' poultry business as a private nuisance. The plaintiffs lived within a mile of the defendants' poultry business in rural Godfrey, Illinois, and they had lived there before the defendants built their facility in the area. The neighborhood was zoned agricultural, and many of the plaintiffs raised livestock on their own property. The plaintiffs complained that the poultry facility resulted in bad odors and swarms of flies and that the intensity of both varied from day to day. Some of the plaintiffs were required to seal their houses when the odor and insects were at their worst, and some plaintiffs cut back on outdoor activities and quit inviting guests to their homes. Some plaintiffs complained of breathing difficulties, sore throats, and nausea.

In *Woods*, the court concluded "that the trial court properly determined that the odors and flies were sufficiently bothersome to justify injunctive relief." In weighing the gravity of the harm to the plaintiffs against the utility of the defendants' business and the suitability of its location, the court stated that the following questions had to be answered: "(1) Are the defendants engaged in a useful enterprise? (2) Is this area of rural Godfrey well suited for an egg production facility? (3) Which came first, the chickens or the plaintiffs? (4) Can the odors and flies be reduced? (5) Is modification of the facility practical?" The court concluded that although the poultry facility was a vital industry, the poultry facility was the "newcomer to the area" and was located too close to several residences.

As noted above, in order to prove an actionable nuisance, the plaintiffs had the burden of proving that barking dogs constituted an invasion that was substantial, intentional or negligent, and unreasonable. The plaintiffs presented sufficient evidence for the circuit court to find the elements necessary to conclude that the barking dogs from the Wiggins property constituted a nuisance.

First, the plaintiffs presented sufficient evidence for the circuit court to find that the barking noise emanating from the Wiggins property was substantial. In determining whether the noise was substantial, the circuit court had to consider the effect it would have on a normal person of ordinary habits and sensibilities. The circuit court found that the plaintiffs were not "unduly sensitive" and were not "delicate, fastidious, [or] pursuing a dainty way of life." This finding was not against the manifest weight of the evidence. Wiggins disputed the extent of the barking and presented conflicting evidence on that issue, but the circuit court, as the trier of fact, determined the credibility of the witnesses and the weight to be given to the evidence. We cannot say that the circuit court's finding of a substantial invasion of the plaintiffs' properties was unsupported by the facts presented at the trial.

Second, in order to constitute a nuisance, an invasion must be either intentional or negligent. The plaintiffs presented sufficient evidence for the circuit court to find that the noise invasion was intentional. For purposes of an intentional invasion, it is not necessary for the circuit court to find that Wiggins kenneled the dogs for the purpose of creating noise. Instead, an intentional invasion occurs when the defendant knows that an invasion of another's interest in the use or enjoyment of his or her land is resulting or is substantially certain to result. The circuit court found that Wiggins "knew that the barking dogs were an invasion of the Plaintiffs' lands or that it was substantially certain to result." This finding was not against the manifest weight of the evidence presented at the trial. Wiggins kenneled, at times, nearly 100 dogs on his property, knew that he had a few problem dogs that barked frequently, knew that wildlife in the area could set off the dogs, and knew that a few dogs barking often caused a chain reaction, resulting in many of the nearly 100 dogs barking simultaneously. Under these facts, we cannot conclude that it was against the manifest weight of the evidence for the circuit court to find that Wiggins knew that the constant barking noise was substantially certain to be invasive to his neighbors who were located approximately 250 yards away, across an open field.

Third, the circuit court found that the noise nuisance was unreasonable. The resolution of this question of fact required the circuit court to weigh the gravity of the harm done to the plaintiffs against the utility of Wiggins's kennels and the suitability of the location of his kennels. The circuit court found as follows:

> That although the Defendant is operating a small business on his property, the gravity of the harm done to the Plaintiffs outweighs the utility of the Defendant's business and the suitability of the location of that business. To make this finding the Court balanced the following:
>
> (a) Defendant is engaged in a useful business (raising bird dogs);
>
> (b) Defendant is located in an area of Jefferson County well-suited for a dog kennel;
>
> (c) Plaintiffs were located on their property before the Defendant started his dog kennel;
>
> (d) Although the Defendant has made efforts, the barking of the dogs cannot be reduced to a level that is not a substantial invasion of Plaintiffs' lands; and
>
> (e) There is no practical way to modify the Defendant's kennels to stop the dogs from barking.

The circuit court was charged with the task of balancing these conflicting interests to determine whether the intentional invasion of barking noise was an unreasonable invasion and, therefore, an actionable private nuisance. The circuit court heard enough evidence to conclude that 69 or more dogs kenneled on Wiggins's property caused an unreasonable noise invasion that interfered with the plaintiffs' use and enjoyment of their nearby land. The appellate court is not permitted to "substitute its judgment on questions of fact fairly submitted, tried, and determined from the evidence which did not greatly preponderate either way." *Maple v. Gustafson*, 603 N.E.2d 508 (Ill. 1992). Accordingly, we must affirm the circuit court's finding that the barking from the dogs kenneled on Wiggins's property constituted a private nuisance.

Wiggins argues, alternatively, that even if the plaintiffs sufficiently established that his dogs constituted a nuisance, the remedy issued by the circuit court was improper because it effectively terminated his business without affording him an opportunity to reduce or abate the nuisance. The granting of an injunction is within a trial court's discretion, and on appeal, the reviewing court will only reverse a circuit court's ruling when the circuit court manifestly abused its discretion. The mere existence of a nuisance does not automatically entitle the plaintiffs to injunctive relief against the nuisance. "Equity will not, as a matter of course, order relief in nuisance cases until all the circumstances and consequences of such action are considered." *Tamalunis v. City of Georgetown*, 542 N.E.2d 402 (Ill. App. 1989).

In the present case, the circuit court entered a permanent injunction requiring Wiggins to decrease the number of dogs in his possession to no more than six, to kennel the dogs only at a location in the southern region of his property, and to take all the steps necessary to adequately suppress any noise caused by the dogs barking. It was not against the manifest weight of the evidence for the circuit court to find that the number of dogs Wiggins kenneled on his property at the time of the trial, 69 dogs or more, constituted a private nuisance given the testimony concerning the noise level even after Wiggins attempted measures to reduce the noise. However, the evidence at the trial was insufficient to support a finding that Wiggins must reduce the number of dogs in his possession to six in order to abate the nuisance. Therefore, an injunction requiring him to reduce the number of dogs in his possession to six or less was an abuse of discretion under the facts presented at the trial.

The evidence at the trial suggested that Wiggins might be able to correct the nuisance by reducing the number of dogs to some number fewer than 69 but greater than 6. Wiggins began kenneling dogs on his property beginning in 1995, and he did so for more than 10 years without any complaints from his neighbors. The evidence at the trial included testimony describing several measures Wiggins took after August of 2007 to reduce the barking noise. The circuit court found that these measures were insufficient to abate the noise nuisance from the 69 or more barking dogs. However, the evidence presented at the trial was insufficient to determine the maximum number of dogs that could be maintained on the property without causing a private nuisance.

"The restraint imposed by an injunction should not be more extensive than is reasonably required to protect the interests of the party in whose favor it is granted[ ] and should not be so broad as to prevent defendant from exercising his rights." *People ex rel. Traiteur v. Abbott*, 327 N.E.2d 130 (Ill. App. 1975).

The circuit court found that Wiggins's canine business was a useful business located in an appropriate rural area, and we believe that further evidence is necessary for the circuit court to determine the proper scope of injunctive relief. The circuit court had insufficient evidence to consider all the circumstances and consequences of injunctive relief limiting Wiggins to six dogs, and we believe that the scope of the injunction was an abuse of discretion based on the evidence before the circuit court. Without further evidence, we cannot determine whether the circuit court's injunction was too broad in scope, creating an unnecessary hardship on Wiggins. We do not offer any opinion on the number of dogs Wiggins should be limited to kenneling on his property; we only conclude that the evidence presented at the trial was insufficient to determine the appropriate remedy. Accordingly, we remand this cause for further proceedings relevant to the scope of the injunctive relief necessary to abate the noise nuisance.

Page County Appliance Center, Inc. v. Honeywell, Inc.

347 N.W.2d 171 (Iowa 1984)

W.W. Reynoldson, Chief Justice.

Plaintiff Page County Appliance Center, Inc. (Appliance Center), sued Honeywell, Inc. (Honeywell), and ITT Electronic Travel Services, Inc. (ITT), for nuisance and tortious interference with business relations. Defendants appeal from judgment entered on jury verdicts awarding compensatory and punitive damages. Honeywell appeals from a judgment rendered against it on ITT's cross-claim for indemnification. We reverse and remand for new trial.

Appliance Center has owned and operated an appliance store in Shenandoah, Iowa, since 1953. . . . Before 1980, [the owner, John Pearson,] had no reception trouble with his display televisions. In early January 1980, however, ITT placed one of its computers with Central Travel Service in Shenandoah as part of a nationwide plan to lease computers to retail travel agents. Central Travel was separated by only one other business from the Appliance Center. This ITT computer was manufactured, installed, and maintained by Honeywell.

Thereafter many of Pearson's customers told him his display television pictures were bad; on two of the three channels available in Shenandoah he had a difficult time "getting a picture that was fit to watch." After unsuccessfully attempting several remedial measures, in late January 1980, he finally traced the interference to the operations of Central Travel's computer. Both defendants concede Pearson's problems were caused by radiation leaking from the Honeywell computer.

[After Pearson complained to Kay Crowell, owner of Central Travel,] Honeywell technicians made repeated trips to make various unsuccessful adjustments to the computer. They found the computer was operating properly; the interference-causing radiation was a design and not a service problem.

The Honeywell engineers effected a 70 percent improvement in the television reception by certain modifications of the computer in the fall of 1980. Pearson, still dissatisfied, started this action in December. While the suit was pending, Honeywell further modified the computer, finally alleviating Pearson's problems in May 1982.

At trial a Honeywell senior staff engineer admitted the technology to manufacture a non-radiation-emitting computer was available long before it developed this computer, but opined it would have been neither cost nor consumer effective to utilize that technology. He testified Honeywell believed it had corrected Pearson's problems in the fall of 1980.

The Appliance Center's case against Honeywell and ITT finally was submitted to the jury on the theories of nuisance and tortious interference with prospective business relations. It asked for only injunctive relief against Kay Crowell, doing business as Central Travel Service. The latter's motion for summary judgment was sustained. The jury found for the Appliance Center against the remaining defendants on both theories, and further found the Appliance Center should recover $71,000 in compensatory damages and $150,000 in exemplary damages. . . . Trial court awarded ITT full indemnity against Honeywell, in the amount of $221,000, together with attorney fees and costs. Both defendants appeal from the judgment in favor of Appliance Center; Honeywell additionally appeals from the judgment awarding ITT indemnity.

Our analysis of ITT's first contention must start with Iowa Code section 657.1, which in relevant part states:

> Whatever is . . . an obstruction to the free use of property, so as essentially to interfere with the . . . enjoyment of . . . property, is a nuisance, and a civil action by ordinary proceedings may be brought to enjoin and abate the same and to recover damages sustained on account thereof.

Narrowing our focus, we note the Appliance Center is alleging a "private nuisance," that is, an actionable interference with a person's interest in the private use and enjoyment of his or her property. It also is apparent that if Central Travel's computer emissions constitute a nuisance it is a "nuisance *per accidens*, or in fact"—a lawful activity conducted in such a manner as to be a nuisance.

Principles governing our consideration of nuisance claims are well established. One's use of property should not unreasonably interfere with or disturb a neighbor's comfortable and reasonable use and enjoyment of his or her estate. A fair test of whether the operation of a lawful trade or industry constitutes a nuisance is the reasonableness of conducting it in the manner, at the place, and under the circumstances shown by the evidence. Each case turns on its own facts and ordinarily the ultimate issue is one of fact, not law. The existence of a nuisance is not affected by the intention of its creator not to injure anyone. Priority of occupation and location — "who was there first" — is a circumstance of considerable weight.

When the alleged nuisance is claimed to be offensive to the person, courts apply the standard of "normal persons in a particular locality" to measure the existence of a nuisance. This normalcy standard also is applied where the use of property is claimed to be affected. "The plaintiff cannot, by devoting his own land to an unusually sensitive use, . . . make a nuisance out of conduct of the adjoining defendant which would otherwise be harmless." W. Prosser, *The Law of Torts* §87, at 579 (4th ed. 1971).

In the case before us, ITT asserts the Appliance Center's display televisions constituted a hypersensitive use of its premises as a matter of law, and equates this situation to cases involving light thrown on outdoor theater screens in which light-throwing defendants have carried the day. . . .

We cannot equate the rare outdoor theater screen with the ubiquitous television that exists, in various numbers, in almost every home. Clearly, the presence of televisions on any premises is not such an abnormal condition that we can say, as a matter of law, that the owner has engaged in a peculiarly sensitive use of the property. This consideration, as well as related considerations of unreasonableness, gravity of harm, utility of conduct, and priority of occupation, are factual determinations that should have been submitted to the jury in this case. We find no trial court error in refusing to direct a verdict on this ground.

ITT's second contention asserts trial court should have directed a verdict in its favor because it did not participate in the creation or maintenance of the alleged nuisance. We have noted ITT was engaged in a multimillion dollar, national program to lease computers to travel agencies. It owned this computer and leased it to Central Travel. It was to ITT that the agency first turned when the effect of the computer radiation became apparent. ITT continued to collect its lease payments; the computer did not operate for the benefit of Crowell alone. The jury could have found ITT evidenced some measure of its responsibility, as owner of the computer, in contacting Honeywell and making belated inquiries regarding Appliance Center's problems both to Pearson and Crowell.

An action for damages for nuisance need not be predicated on negligence. Nuisance ordinarily is considered as a condition, and not as an act or failure to act on the part of the responsible party. A person responsible for a harmful condition found to be a nuisance may be liable even though that person has used the highest possible degree of care to prevent or minimize the effect.

Where there is reasonable doubt whether one of several persons is substantially participating in carrying on an activity, the question is for the trier of fact. We hold such reasonable doubt existed on the record made in this case, and trial court did not err in refusing to direct a verdict on this ground.

Honeywell asserts trial court should have granted its motion for directed verdict because, even though it manufactured the computer, Central Travel and ITT were in control of the instrument at all relevant times; thus Honeywell did not have the legal right to terminate its use. Honeywell devotes ten and one-half pages of its brief to this thesis without mentioning that it had an ongoing contract to service and maintain the computer.

Much of what we have written [above] applies here. Again, the issue is one of material participation. Honeywell's design permitted radiation to escape this computer, although technology was available to minimize this effect. Apparently factors of cost and ease of service access weighed more in the design decision. Honeywell was the only party with the technological know-how to control the radiation leakage. Its maintenance contract with ITT clearly absolved it of any liability if anyone else made any alterations or additions to the equipment, and reserved the right to terminate the agreement should that occur. As with ITT, we think Honeywell's material participation was an issue for the finder of fact.

Trial court's instructions required Appliance Center to prove defendants "unreasonably" interfered with the Center's use and enjoyment of its property. Honeywell and ITT objected, in essence, that this permitted the jury to judge "unreasonableness" in a vacuum; that the instructions made no attempt to define the unreasonableness concept. Because reasonableness under our nuisance decisions ordinarily is a question for the jury, the court on retrial should provide more guidance for the jury.

In *Bates v. Quality Ready Mix Co.*, 154 N.W.2d 852, 857 (Iowa 1968), we noted that reasonableness is a function of the manner in which, and the place where, defendant's business is conducted, and the circumstances under which defendant operates. Additional factors . . . include priority of location, character of the neighborhood, and the nature of the alleged wrong. The "character and gravity of the resulting injury" is, in fact, "a major factor in determining reasonableness," *Montgomery v. Bremer County Board of Supervisors,* 299 N.W.2d 687, 697 (Iowa 1980). Balanced against the gravity of the wrong is the utility and meritoriousness of the defendant's conduct.

Another instruction given in this case stated that "[o]ne who contributes to the creation or continuance of a nuisance may be liable." ITT objected that neither this instruction nor any other informed the jury that a defendant's conduct must be a "substantial factor" in bringing about the alleged harm. Upon retrial the instructions should incorporate this requirement.

Both Honeywell and ITT objected because the court did not submit to the jury the issue whether Appliance Center was devoting its premises to an unusually sensitive use. The discussion in division I is relevant here. We hold defendants were entitled to have this question resolved by the jury.

We reverse and remand with instructions to set aside the judgment in favor of Appliance Center against Honeywell and ITT, and the judgment entered on ITT's cross-claim against Honeywell. Defendants shall be granted a new trial in conformance with this opinion.

Notes and Questions

1. **Unreasonable harm to the use and enjoyment of land.** How do the courts determine when an interference with the use and enjoyment of land is unreasonable? First, they must determine what interests are encompassed by the right to the "use and enjoyment of land." Those interests include freedom from pollution, noise, odors, and smoke. Is the market value of the plaintiff's property (by itself) such an interest? If not, why not? Second, they need to determine how serious the interference must be for a nuisance to be present. Traditionally, the court required the harm to be **substantial** before it could give rise to a nuisance claim. Third, if defendant has substantially interfered in the plaintiff's use and enjoyment of land, how do we determine whether that harm is **unreasonable**? For intentional nuisances, the focus of the reasonableness inquiry is on the impact of the defendant's conduct on the plaintiff. Courts ask whether the defendant's conduct creates consequences for the plaintiff that a typical landowner should not be expected to bear. The question is whether those consequences exceed a reasonable threshold beyond which the court will conclude that the defendant has created a nuisance. Was the harm to Wiggins's neighbors from the barking of his dogs substantial or a mere annoyance that people should have to bear?

> ***NUISANCE:***
>
> A harm that is 1) substantial and 2) unreasonable.
>
> **Factors Courts Consider in Finding Nuisance:**
>
> 1. The extent of the harm.
> 2. The character of the harm.
> 3. The economic and social value of the conflicting activities.
> 4. The suitability of the activities for the location.
> 5. The ability of either party to avoid the conflict and the practicability and fairness of making the party do so.
>
> *See, e.g., Restatement (Second) of Torts* §828 (1977).

In answering these questions, courts consider both fairness and welfare. On the fairness side, courts will consider:

a. **The character of the harm.** Aesthetic harms will be viewed as less serious than health or safety concerns.

b. **Distributive considerations.** Is it fair to make an individual owner bear the costs of defendant's socially beneficial activity, or should those costs be spread around to the owner causing the damage and its employees and customers?

c. **Fault.** Is one of the owners engaged in a disfavored activity? Is the conduct appropriate for the area? Did the plaintiff come to the nuisance?

On the welfare side, courts will consider:

d. **Costs and benefits.** The costs and benefits of allowing the harmful conduct must be compared with the costs and benefits of prohibiting it.

e. **Incentives.** What effects will liability or immunity have on incentives to engage in the respective activities? How will the distribution of the burdens and benefits of conflicting land uses affect incentives to invest in safety or to engage in desirable economic activities?

f. Lowest cost avoider. Which party can more cheaply avoid the cost? Should this party also bear the burden of paying that cost?

Malice may also be relevant to the court's evaluation of the defendant's conduct. For example, many states will grant injunctions against so-called **spite fences** constructed for the sole purpose of blocking their neighbors' light and air. When such fences serve no purpose other than the builders' desire to hurt their neighbors, some states will grant an injunction ordering the fence torn down. *See Wilson v. Handley*, 119 Cal. Rptr. 2d 263 (Ct. App. 2002) (*applying* Cal. Civ. Code §841.4); *DeCecco v. Beach*, 381 A.2d 543 (Conn. 1977) (*applying* Conn. Gen. Stat. §52-570); *Gertz v. Estes*, 879 N.E.2d 617 (Ind. Ct. App. 2008) (applying Ind. Code §§32-26-10-1 and -2). *But see Maioriello v. Arlotta*, 73 A.2d 374 (Pa. 1950) (refusing to enjoin a spite fence). Why should malice figure in the nuisance calculus?

2. Intentional nuisance, negligence, ultrahazardous activities, and nuisances *per se*. Intentional nuisance must be distinguished from **negligence**. Negligence law prohibits and provides remedies for unreasonable *conduct*; this implies a judgment that a reasonable person would have foreseen the harm and prevented it. Intentional nuisance focuses primarily on the *result* of the conduct rather than the conduct itself; the question is not whether the defendant's conduct was unreasonable but whether the interference suffered by the plaintiff is unreasonable. Such interference is unreasonable under nuisance law if it involves substantial harm that an owner should not have to bear for the good of society. Thus, conduct that is not negligent (because the defendant took due care to avoid the harm) may still constitute a nuisance (because the conduct in fact results in harm to the neighbors' property interests that is not justified by the social utility of the conduct causing it). Conversely, where the defendant's conduct is negligent, defendant may be liable under a negligence theory even if the impact on the plaintiff would not otherwise rise to the level of a substantial interference.

Most courts impose strict liability on landowners if they engage in **ultrahazardous activities** that cause harm to neighboring land. In such cases, nontrespassory conduct may result in liability without a need to prove either negligence or the unreasonableness and substantial harm requirements of nuisance doctrine. Some cases have imposed strict liability on landowners who have stored toxic waste on their property. *See, e.g., T & E Industries v. Safety Light Corp.*, 587 A.2d 1249 (N.J. 1991); *State v. Ventron Corp.*, 468 A.2d 150 (N.J. 1983).

Some activities may be so disfavored that they will be held to constitute nuisances no matter where they take place or what consequences they generate — so-called **nuisances *per se***. An example would be criminal activity such as property routinely used for illegal drug manufacture or sale. Other activities may constitute nuisances because they are "a right thing in a wrong place — like a pig in the parlor instead of the barnyard."[1]

1. *Village of Euclid v. Ambler Realty Co.*, 272 U.S. 365, 388 (1962).

3. Who can be sued? Can a manufacturer of a hazardous substance be sued for damages for nuisance when it leaks through the ground and causes harm to neighboring land? *Page County* adopts the general rule that imposes liability on any actor who "materially participated" in causing the harm. *See also Parks Hiway Enterprises, LLC v. CEM Leasing, Inc.*, 995 P.2d 657, 667 (Alaska 2000) (question is whether defendant's conduct was a "substantial factor" in causing the harm). What factors led the court to determine that the evidence showed that Honeywell contributed to the harm? Would Honeywell have been liable if its only participation was the design and sale of the computer? *Compare Hall v. Phillips*, 436 N.W.2d 139 (Neb. 1989) (manufacturer and distributor of herbicide liable for nuisance), *and New York v. Fermenta ASC Corp.*, 630 N.Y.S.2d 884 (Sup. Ct. 1995) (holding the manufacturer and distributor of a herbicide liable for trespass when it broke down in the soil after usage by customers and a chemical byproduct leached through the soil and invaded the public water supply), *with Parks Hiway Enterprises, supra* (gas producer not liable for nuisance merely because it produced the gas that bled into neighboring land).

4. When to sue?

a. Not too early. The doctrine of **anticipatory nuisance** governs lawsuits to bar a nuisance before the challenged use is actually in place. Most courts agree that a claimant seeking an injunction against a use that is not yet in place must prove with near certainty that the use, once in place, will constitute a nuisance. *See, e.g., Simpson v. Kollasch*, 749 N.W.2d 671 (Iowa 2008) ("An anticipated nuisance will not be enjoined unless it clearly appears a nuisance will necessarily result from the act."); *Duff v. Morgantown Energy Associates*, 421 S.E.2d 253 (W. Va. 1992) ("[T]o warrant injunctive relief as to a prospective nuisance, 'the fact that it will be a nuisance if so used must be made clearly to appear, beyond all ground of fair questioning.' "). However, once a nuisance-causing activity is built, the waste of dismantling the operation may weigh against finding a nuisance. How does the difficulty of obtaining an injunction on a theory of anticipatory nuisance affect the usefulness of nuisance law as a tool for regulating land use conflicts?

b. Not too late. Nuisance claimants must sue before the statute of limitations expires. Many courts distinguish between **temporary** and **permanent** nuisances. A permanent nuisance either irreparably injures the plaintiff's property or is of such a character that it is likely to continue indefinitely; in such a case, the statute of limitations for bringing a claim begins at the time the nuisance begins. In contrast, a temporary nuisance can be alleviated by changes in the defendant's conduct, and the claim "accrues anew upon each injury" or occurs intermittently. *Schneider National Carriers*, 147 S.W.3d at 270, 272.

5. Nuisance defenses. Two common defenses to nuisance claims are (1) that the defendant got there first and (2) that the plaintiff is too sensitive:

a. Temporal priority, and "coming to the nuisance." The fact that a harmful activity was established first will weigh in favor of the defendant. When the plaintiff comes to the nuisance, one can argue that she created the problem herself. An owner who builds a house next to a pig farm should not be surprised at the resulting odors. For this reason, in all states, it will be harder for a plaintiff to prevail in a nuisance case if she came to the nuisance. At the same time, coming to the nuisance is not an absolute defense; it may be wrong to continue operating a polluting activity once it becomes surrounded by numerous other homes and businesses. Some statutes do make it an absolute defense in certain cases that the plaintiff came to the nuisance.

> **CONTEXT**
>
> Many states have passed **right to farm** statutes that protect farmers from liability for nuisance if their farms were established before surrounding residential property was constructed. However, the Iowa Supreme Court found that one such statute unconstitutionally took away the right to sue for nuisance. *Bormann v. Board of Supervisors*, 584 N.W.2d 309 (Iowa 1998).

When owners come to the nuisance, the courts may enjoin the offending activity on the condition that those who came to the nuisance compensate the prior developer for the costs associated with shutting down and/or relocating. In *Spur Industries v. Webb*, 494 P.2d 700 (Ariz. 1972), for example, a developer built a residential community near a cattle ranch. Ordinarily, it would be possible to convince a court that the smells generated by a cattle ranch constitute a substantial and unreasonable interference in the use and enjoyment of residential property. However, because the homeowners "came to the nuisance," they had a much harder time convincing the court that the cattle feedlot should be shut down than they would have had if the residential community had been established first. This is probably why the court in *Spur* granted the plaintiffs an injunction only on the condition that they compensate the defendant for the costs that relocation would impose on him.

b. Unusual sensitivity. Unlike in negligence law, in the law of nuisance, even serious harms may be privileged if the plaintiff is **unusually sensitive** and the court concludes that it would be wrong to regulate the defendant's generally inoffensive activity or impose damages for the plaintiff's harm. *Jenkins v. CSX Transportation, Inc.*, 906 S.W.2d 460 (Tenn. Ct. App. 1995) (no remedy for plaintiff who had an extremely rare allergy to fumes from railroad ties near his land). Nuisance law aims to protect owners' reasonable interests in the use and enjoyment of their land. In *Page County*, the court considered but ruled out the argument that the defendant's conduct should not be judged a nuisance because the plaintiff was abnormally sensitive. Do you agree with its conclusion that the plaintiff was not abnormally sensitive to electromagnetic interference? If the plaintiff were a homeowner complaining that she suffered interference with her television reception due to the defendant's business, do you think the court would have found the harm to rise to the level of a nuisance? Would the answer change between the 1980s and today?

6. Aesthetic nuisance and stigma. Although most nuisance cases involve physical harm to land or discomfort or danger to persons, the doctrine is broad enough to encompass any conduct that causes unreasonable and substantial harm to the use and enjoyment of land. Thus, nuisance claims have been brought against owners who have allowed their property to be overrun by drug dealers, thereby interfering with the interests of landowners in the neighborhood. *Lew v. Superior Court*, 25 Cal. Rptr.

2d 42 (Ct. App. 1993). In several cases, homeowners have been enjoined from lavish displays of lights and loud Christmas music that drew an enormous influx of visitors to a residential neighborhood. *See, e.g., Osborne v. Power*, 908 S.W.2d 340 (Ark. 1995); *Rodrigue v. Copeland*, 475 So. 2d 1071 (La. 1985).

Courts have historically been reluctant to find visual annoyances, by themselves, to be nuisances in the absence of physical manifestations, such as foul odors, or threats to health or safety. Mere unsightliness, the usual account goes, was not enough to ground a nuisance claim. *See* Note, *Aesthetic Nuisance: An Emerging Cause of Action*, 45 N.Y.U. L. Rev. 1075, 1080-1087 (1970); Note, Dix W. Noel, *Unaesthetic Sights as Nuisances*, 25 Cornell L.Q. 1, 1-5, 8 (1939). In recent years, however, courts have been more willing to find a nuisance on the basis of mere visual harm. *See Rattigan v. Wile*, 841 N.E.2d 680, 689 (Mass. 2006) ("[T]he modern trend is toward recognition that aesthetic considerations may legitimately generate public and private concern."); *Foley v. Harris*, 286 S.E.2d 186, 190-191 (Va. 1982) (unsightly junked cars on lot were a nuisance); John Copeland Nagle, *Moral Nuisances*, 50 Emory L.J. 265, 286-287 (2001) (detecting a judicial trend in favor of recognizing aesthetic nuisances). *But see* Henry E. Smith, *Exclusion and Property Rules in the Law of Nuisance*, 90 Va. L. Rev. 965, 999-1000 (2004) (describing courts as continuing to reject claims of aesthetic nuisance). Despite this trend, courts remain reluctant to do so where the claim of harm is based on a mere difference in taste. They seem more likely to find a visual nuisance where there is some evidence of malice or spite. *See, e.g., Rattigan*, at 688-690. The general trend toward accepting nuisance claims based on aesthetic harm seems consistent with the basic premises of nuisance law, particularly where there are strong, widely shared norms against the particular type of land use that generates the visual harm.

In *DeSario v. Industrial Excess Land Fill Inc.*, No. 89-570 (Ohio Ct. Common Pleas 1994), a jury awarded the owners of noncontaminated property within two miles of a toxic waste dump $6.7 million in damages for the loss of their property value caused by the "stigma" of being near the dump. Natl. L.J., Jan. 16, 1995, at A13. *Accord, Scheg v. Agway, Inc.*, 645 N.Y.S.2d 687 (App. Div. 1996). Most courts deny such claims, even if the loss of market value of the land is substantial. For example, in *Adams v. Star Enterprises*, 51 F.3d 417 (4th Cir. 1995), the court refused to allow owners of property adjacent to land contaminated by a leak at an oil distribution facility to recover damages for mere fear of future health effects or for diminution in the value of their property absent a showing of detectable, physical encroachment on their property. *Accord, Smith v. Kansas Gas Service Co.*, 169 P.3d 1052, 1063 (Kan. 2007) (no nuisance when natural gas escaped from a facility in the absence of physical injury to properties or interference with use and enjoyment "distinct from the claim that the property's value has diminished because of marketplace fear or stigma"). Which approach is best?

7. Public nuisances. A public nuisance is "an unreasonable interference with a right common to the general public." *Restatement (Second) of Torts* §821B(1) (1977). The traditional example is obstruction of public highways. As it originated in England, the public nuisance doctrine covered a host of minor criminal offenses. It was extended to allow common law actions involving such claims as

> interference with the public health, as in the case of keeping diseased animals or the maintenance of a pond breeding malarial mosquitoes; with the public safety, as in the case of the storage of explosives in the midst of a city or the shooting of fireworks in the public streets; with the public morals, as in the case of houses of prostitution or indecent exhibitions; with the public peace, as by loud and disturbing noises; with the public comfort, as in the case of widely disseminated bad odors, dust and smoke; with the public convenience, as by the obstruction of a public highway or a navigable stream.

Id. §821B. Traditionally, public nuisances could be challenged only by public officials. Private landowners could obtain a remedy against a public nuisance only if they suffered some special damage different from that generally suffered by the public as a whole. The *Restatement (Second) of Torts,* however, provides that any member of the public affected by the activity should be able to bring a lawsuit, and this seems to represent the trend in the law. *Restatement (Second) of Torts* §821c (1979). Statutes may authorize individuals to bring claims to abate public nuisances. *See Kellner v. Capelini,* 516 N.Y.S.2d 827 (Civ. Ct. 1986) (applying an ordinance giving citizens the right to sue to shut down a public nuisance and granting an injunction ordering a landlord to evict tenants who used the property for illegal crack cocaine sales).

In the late twentieth century, the courts began to see an explosion of public nuisance litigation. It has been used to challenge liquor stores that sell liquor to minors, theaters or stores showing or selling pornographic materials, and motels that are used for prostitution. *See, e.g., City of Miami v. Keshbro, Inc.,* 717 So. 2d 601 (Fla. Dist. Ct. App. 1998) (motel closed for prostitution and drug use); *Bosarge v. State ex rel. Price,* 666 So. 2d 485 (Miss. 1995) (club closed for selling liquor to minors); *State ex rel. Bowers v. Elida Road Video & Books, Inc.,* 696 N.E.2d 668 (Ohio Ct. App. 1997) (adult bookstore closed because of sexual activity). Some cities have used public nuisance in an effort to abate harms caused when owners leave their buildings or land vacant for long periods of time. *See, e.g.,* Jonathan Oosting, *Michigan Approved for $100 Million in Federal Funding to Demolish Blighted Homes in 5 Cities,* June 6, 2013, *available at http://www.mlive.com/politics/index.ssf/2013/06/michigan_100_million_demolitio.html* (last checked July 9, 2013).

8. Climate change as a public nuisance. In 2004, several states (along with nonprofit land trusts) sued various electric utilities, arguing that their emission of greenhouse gases — and the resultant changes in the climate — constituted a public nuisance under state and federal law. The U.S. Supreme Court held that federal environmental laws preempted the plaintiffs' federal common law claims, but left open the possibility that the plaintiffs might have surviving nuisance claims under state law. *See American Electric Power Co. v. Connecticut,* 131 S. Ct. 2527 (2011). At least one federal court has subsequently held that state law nuisance claims are also preempted by federal environmental laws. *See Comer v. Murphy Oil USA, Inc.,* 839 F. Supp. 2d 849 (S.D. Miss. 2012).

9. Statutory and administrative regulation of land use. Although nuisance litigation retains significance, in recent years it has been eclipsed to a substantial extent by federal and state environmental protection legislation. In light of the difficulty of proving anticipatory nuisance and the costs of abating nuisances once they are in place, does this shift make sense? Federal legislation includes the *Clean Air Act,* 42 U.S.C. §§7401-7642; the *Clean Water Act,* 33 U.S.C. §§1251-1376; the *Comprehensive Environmental Response, Compensation, and Liability Act* (the *Superfund Act,* or *CERCLA*), 42 U.S.C. §§6901-9657; and the *Superfund Amendments and Reauthorization Act of 1986* (SARA), Pub. L. No. 99-499, 100 Stat. 1613. State environmental regulation may place more stringent limits on environmental pollution. In addition, local zoning law may regulate and separate incompatible neighboring land uses.

Environmental protection statutes ordinarily establish administrative agencies with powers to issue regulations having the force of law. Those agencies generally have enforcement powers, such as the power to impose fines on persons who violate the regulations or to obtain injunctive relief in court to compel compliance.

Problems

1. **Drug dealing.** A half-vacant apartment building is used by drug dealers and drug users. Some of the dealers are tenants in the building who sell crack cocaine in their apartments, while other dealers have entered the building without the owner's permission, using vacant apartments to conduct their business. The illegal activities have attracted a large number of drug buyers and users into the neighborhood, disrupting a formerly quiet neighborhood of brownstone homes and turning the area into a drug market. The landlord is a real estate company engaged in the business of renting housing. The landlord in no way encouraged or participated in the illegal activities, but has failed to do anything to remedy the problem. Twenty neighbors bring a lawsuit against the landlord claiming the landlord's use of its property constitutes a nuisance. They ask for damages and for an injunction ordering the landlord to stop the illegal activity.

In *Lew v. Superior Court,* 25 Cal. Rptr. 2d 42 (Ct. App. 1994), the court enforced a state statute providing that landlords could be held liable for nuisance when the landlords' apartments had become a hub of drug activity and landlords did not act reasonably in dealing with the problem. Commentators have disagreed about the fairness of imposing such obligations on landlords. *Compare* David C. Anderson, *How to Rescue a Crack House,* N.Y. Times, Feb. 8, 1993, at A-16, *with* Gideon Kanner, *California Makes Landlords Do the Police's Job,* Wall St. J., Jan. 27, 1993, at A-19; *see also City of Seattle v. McCoy,* 4 P.3d 159, 168 (Wash. Ct. App. 2000) (an innocent owner who does not cause and could not have reasonably prevented illegal drug use on the premises has not caused a nuisance). *Accord, Restatement (Second) of Torts* §838 (1977) ("A possessor of land upon which a third party carries on an activity that causes a nuisance is subject to liability for the nuisance if . . . (a) the possessor knows or has reason to know [of the activity] and (b) he consents to the activity or fails to exercise reasonable care to prevent the nuisance").

a. What arguments could you make on behalf of the plaintiffs for both damages and injunctive relief?

b. What arguments could you make on behalf of the defendant landlord that it is not responsible for criminal actions committed by its tenants and that it is certainly not responsible for the actions of trespassers and therefore is not liable for either damages or injunctive relief to abate the nuisance?

c. What should the court do? Explain your reasoning.

2. Secondhand smoke. A tenant living in a second-floor condominium unit in a three-story, six-unit building complains about cigarette smoke originating in the downstairs unit. The smoke enters the second-floor apartment through vents in the central cooling and heating system. The upstairs tenant cannot stand the smell of the smoke, and the smoke itself makes her cough and wheeze. The downstairs owner is a smoker who argues that she is entitled to smoke in her own home. Although smoking is now prohibited by law in most restaurants and workplaces in the jurisdiction, no law prohibits smoking at home. Should a judge rule that the smoking constitutes a nuisance? If so, should she grant an injunction ordering the condo owner to stop smoking at home? One state has a statute defining a nuisance to include "tobacco smoke that drifts into any residential unit a person rents, leases, or owns, from another residential or commercial unit." Utah Code §78B-6-1101(3). *Compare DeNardo v. Corneloup*, 163 P.3d 956 (Alaska 2007) (secondhand smoke drifting from one property to another is not a nuisance), *with Dworkin v. Paley*, 638 N.E.2d 636 (Ohio Ct. App. 1994) (tenant allowed to move out before the end of the lease term when downstairs tenant disturbed her quiet enjoyment by excessive smoking).

§2.2 Nuisance Remedies

As we noted above, nuisance cases always involve two questions: (1) the determination of the entitlement to engage in a use or to be free from the harm caused by someone else's use and (2) the choice of a remedy. As Guido Calabresi and A. Douglas Melamed observed in an extremely influential law review article, there are typically two types of remedies in the nuisance context: injunctions and damages, or in their terminology, "property rules" and "liability rules." *See* Guido Calabresi & A. Douglas Melamed, *Property Rules, Liability Rules, and Inalienability: One View of the Cathedral*, 85 Harv. L. Rev. 1089 (1972).

Property rules (injunctions) fix an absolute entitlement either to engage in the conduct (*no liability*) or to be secure from the harm (*injunctive relief ordering defendant to stop committing the harm*). With property rules, the parties are free to bargain to give up their rights to commit or be free from the harm. The price of the entitlement would therefore be fixed by private bargaining rather than by a court order.

Liability rules (damages), in contrast, prohibit one party from interfering with the interests of the other unless the party is willing to pay an amount determined by a court of law or some other authoritative third party. If the plaintiff is entitled to be protected from the harm by a liability rule, then defendant's failure to prevent the harm subjects the defendant to damages. Conversely, if defendant is entitled to engage in the harmful activity, protecting that entitlement with a liability rule means that the plaintiff will be able to obtain an injunction stopping that activity if it compensates the defendant for the economic losses associated with stopping the activity; this later remedy is called a **purchased** or **conditional injunction**. A plaintiff will be granted an injunction only if it pays damages to compensate defendant for its losses.[2]

Table 6-1 summarizes these rules.

Table 6-1 Entitlements

Remedies	Plaintiff's entitlement	Defendant's entitlement
Property rule	π can get an injunction ordering Δ to stop the harmful conduct; if Δ wants to commit the harm, Δ must offer π enough money to induce π to agree to give up π's right to be free from harm.* *(injunction)*	Δ has legal liberty to commit the harm without liability; if π wants to prevent the harm, π must offer Δ enough money to induce Δ to agree to stop the harmful conduct. *(no nuisance)*
Liability rule	π can get damages from Δ for committing the harm, but no injunction; Δ is free to commit the harm if Δ is willing to pay a damages judgment. *(damages)*	π can stop Δ's conduct if π is willing to pay damages as determined by a court to compensate Δ for Δ's loss of profits. *(purchased injunction)*

* π refers to plaintiff and Δ refers to defendant.

In a case like *Dobbs v. Wiggins*, where a plaintiff is seeking only injunctive relief, the two stages can seem to collapse into one. While this is understandable, the failure to keep the entitlement question separate from the remedial, balancing of utilities question is the source of some confusion in nuisance law. The *Restatement (Second) of Torts* §826(a), for example, appears to mix these two questions when it defines a land use as "unreasonable" (*i.e.*, a nuisance) where the "gravity of the harm [to the plaintiff] outweighs the utility of the actor's conduct." If the question at the entitlement stage were simply a matter of balancing the utilities, a defendant's actions would be allowed to impose enormous costs on its neighbors just because the defendant's use is a socially valuable one. If that were the law, what kinds of land uses would it favor?

Nuisance law permits the decision maker to consider the utility of the defendant's conduct at both stages, but the relevance of that utility will be different in the two stages. In determining whether to classify the defendant's conduct as a nuisance, courts weigh the utility of the defendant's conduct in the defendant's favor. That is,

---

2. The usual version is the *option* where plaintiffs have the power to shut down the offending activity by obtaining an injunction if they choose to pay damages. They have the option to force a sale of the entitlement from the defendant to them. An alternative version is the *put* whereby defendant can force the plaintiffs to purchase the injunction whether or not they wish to do so. *See, e.g.*, Ian Ayres, *Protecting Property with Puts*, 32 Val. U. L. Rev. 793 (1988).

a defendant whose behavior is socially beneficial gets more leeway to impose costs on its neighbors, but the focus remains on the impact of the defendant's conduct on the plaintiff. The fact that a defendant's conduct is socially valuable is not decisive. In contrast to the entitlement stage, where the focus is on the impact on the plaintiff, the costs and benefits of the defendant's conduct is a central consideration at the remedial stage.

Boomer v. Atlantic Cement Co.

26 N.Y.2d 219 (1970)

FRANCIS BERGAN, Judge.

Defendant operates a large cement plant near Albany. These are actions for injunction and damages by neighboring land owners alleging injury to property from dirt, smoke and vibration emanating from the plant. A nuisance has been found after trial, temporary damages have been allowed; but an injunction has been denied. The public concern with air pollution arising from many sources in industry and in transportation is currently accorded ever wider recognition accompanied by a growing sense of responsibility in State and Federal Governments to control it. Cement plants are obvious sources of air pollution in the neighborhoods where they operate.

But there is now before the court private litigation in which individual property owners have sought specific relief from a single plant operation. The threshold question raised by the division of view on this appeal is whether the court should resolve the litigation between the parties now before it as equitably as seems possible; or whether, seeking promotion of the general public welfare, it should channel private litigation into broad public objectives.

A court performs its essential function when it decides the rights of parties before it. Its decision of private controversies may sometimes greatly affect public issues. Large questions of law are often resolved by the manner in which private litigation is decided. But this is normally an incident to the court's main function to settle controversy. It is a rare exercise of judicial power to use a decision in private litigation as a purposeful mechanism to achieve direct public objectives greatly beyond the rights and interests before the court. Effective control of air pollution is a problem presently far from solution even with the full public and financial powers of government. In large measure adequate technical procedures are yet to be developed and some that appear possible may be economically impracticable.

It seems apparent that the amelioration of air pollution will depend on technical research in great depth; on a carefully balanced consideration of the economic impact of close regulation; and of the actual effect on public health. It is likely to require massive public expenditure and to demand more than any local community can accomplish and to depend on regional and interstate controls.

A court should not try to do this on its own as a by-product of private litigation and it seems manifest that the judicial establishment is neither equipped in the limited nature of any judgment it can pronounce nor prepared to lay down and implement an effective policy for the elimination of air pollution. This is an area beyond the circumference of one private lawsuit. It is a direct responsibility for government and should not thus be undertaken as an incident to solving a dispute between property owners and a single cement plant — one of many — in the Hudson River valley.

The cement making operations of defendant have been found by the court of Special Term to have damaged the nearby properties of plaintiffs in these two actions. That court, as it has been noted, accordingly found defendant maintained a nuisance and this has been affirmed at the Appellate Division. The total damage to plaintiffs' properties is, however, relatively small in comparison with the value of defendant's operation and with the consequences of the injunction which plaintiffs seek.

The ground for the denial of injunction, notwithstanding the finding both that there is a nuisance and that plaintiffs have been damaged substantially, is the large disparity in economic consequences of the nuisance and of the injunction. This theory cannot, however, be sustained without overruling a doctrine which has been consistently reaffirmed in several leading cases in this court and which has never been disavowed here, namely that where a nuisance has been found and where there has been any substantial damage shown by the party complaining an injunction will be granted.

The rule in New York has been that such a nuisance will be enjoined although marked disparity be shown in economic consequence between the effect of the injunction and the effect of the nuisance.

The court at Special Term also found the amount of permanent damage attributable to each plaintiff, for the guidance of the parties in the event both sides stipulated to the payment and acceptance of such permanent damage as a settlement of all the controversies among the parties. The total of permanent damages to all plaintiffs thus found was $185,000. This basis of adjustment has not resulted in any stipulation by the parties.

This result at Special Term and at the Appellate Division is a departure from a rule that has become settled; but to follow the rule literally in these cases would be to close down the plant at once. This court is fully agreed to avoid that immediately drastic remedy; the difference in view is how best to avoid it.[3]

One alternative is to grant the injunction but postpone its effect to a specified future date to give opportunity for technical advances to permit defendant to eliminate the nuisance; another is to grant the injunction conditioned on the payment of permanent damages to plaintiffs which would compensate them for the total economic loss to their property present and future caused by defendant's operations. For reasons which will be developed the court chooses the latter alternative.

If the injunction were to be granted unless within a short period — e.g., 18 months — the nuisance be abated by improved methods, there would be no assurance that any significant technical improvement would occur. Moreover, techniques to eliminate dust and other annoying by-products of cement making are unlikely to be

3. Respondent's investment in the plant is in excess of $45,000,000. There are over 300 people employed there.

developed by any research the defendant can undertake within any short period, but will depend on the total resources of the cement industry nationwide and throughout the world. The problem is universal wherever cement is made.

For obvious reasons the rate of the research is beyond control of defendant. If at the end of 18 months the whole industry has not found a technical solution a court would be hard put to close down this one cement plant if due regard be given to equitable principles. On the other hand, to grant the injunction unless defendant pays plaintiffs such permanent damages as may be fixed by the court seems to do justice between the contending parties. All of the attributions of economic loss to the properties on which plaintiffs' complaints are based will have been redressed.

The limitation of relief granted is a limitation only within the four corners of these actions and does not foreclose public health or other public agencies from seeking proper relief in a proper court. It seems reasonable to think that the risk of being required to pay permanent damages to injured property owners by cement plant owners would itself be a reasonable effective spur to research for improved techniques to minimize nuisance. The power of the court to condition on equitable grounds the continuance of an injunction on the payment of permanent damages seems undoubted. [P]ermanent damages are allowed where the loss recoverable would obviously be small as compared with the cost of removal of the nuisance.

Thus it seems fair to both sides to grant permanent damages to plaintiffs which will terminate this private litigation. The theory of damage is the "servitude on land" of plaintiffs imposed by defendant's nuisance. The judgment, by allowance of permanent damages imposing a servitude on land, which is the basis of the actions, would preclude future recovery by plaintiffs or their grantees. This should be placed beyond debate by a provision of the judgment that the payment by defendant and the acceptance by plaintiffs of permanent damages found by the court shall be in compensation for a servitude on the land.

The orders should be reversed, without costs, and the cases remitted to Supreme Court, Albany County to grant an injunction which shall be vacated upon payment by defendant of such amounts of permanent damage to the respective plaintiffs as shall for this purpose be determined by the court.

MATTHEW J. JASEN, Judge (dissenting).

I see grave dangers in overruling our long-established rule of granting an injunction where a nuisance results in substantial continuing damage. In permitting the injunction to become inoperative upon the payment of permanent damages, the majority is, in effect, licensing a continuing wrong. It is the same as saying to the cement company, you may continue to do harm to your neighbors so long as you pay a fee for it. Furthermore, once such permanent damages are assessed and paid, the incentive to alleviate the wrong would be eliminated, thereby continuing air pollution of an area without abatement.

It is true that some courts have sanctioned the remedy here proposed by the majority in a number of cases, but . . . [i]n those cases, the courts, in denying an injunction and awarding money damages, grounded their decision on a showing that the use to which the property was intended to be put was primarily for the public benefit. Here, on the other hand, it is clearly established that the cement company is creating a continuing air pollution nuisance primarily for its own private interest with no public benefit. This kind of inverse condemnation may not be invoked by a private person or corporation for private gain or advantage. The promotion of the interests of the polluting cement company has, in my opinion, no public use or benefit. Nor is it constitutionally permissible to impose servitude on land, without consent of the owner, by payment of permanent damages where the continuing impairment of the land is for a private use.

Notes and Questions

1. **Stage 1 and stage 2.** If the defendant's conduct was so valuable, why did the court in *Boomer* even find it to be a nuisance? Atlantic Cement's behavior was reasonable on the social level in the sense that it increased overall social utility, but the costs of the defendant's activity were not fairly distributed. The concentrated nature of the harm generated by the defendant's cement factory violated the individual plaintiff's right to security; the harm was greater than any individual should be forced to bear for the good of society. Requiring damages but not awarding an injunction, therefore, was consistent with a determination that the activity was efficient—it increased social utility to allow it to go forward because its overall benefits vastly outweighed its costs (the stage 2 nuisance inquiry)—but that the costs of the activity were unfairly distributed (the stage 1 nuisance inquiry)—the plaintiff's property interests were being unfairly sacrificed. Resorting to a damages remedy where the costs of an injunction would be too high (relative to the benefit it would generate) gives courts a way to recompense the wrong being perpetrated on the plaintiff while allowing a socially valuable use to continue.

2. **Responses to *Boomer*.** After the *Boomer* decision, the American Law Institute (partially) endorsed the court's approach in a revision of the *Restatement (Second) of Torts.* Section 826(b) of the *Restatement (Second)* supplements the (confusing) balancing test §826(a) with a test that provides for damages when "the harm caused by the conduct is serious and the financial burden of compensating for this and similar harm to others would not make the continuation of the conduct not feasible." Does the infeasibility of paying damages suggest that (taking into account the costs of the defendant's conduct for the plaintiff) the defendant's conduct is not cost effective? If so, why should the defendant escape paying damages if their payment would put it out of business? What about the possibility that the defendant's activities generate positive externalities—benefits that accrue to others and that are not reflected in the defendant's balance sheets?

3. **How much of an innovation?** Although injunctions are the most common remedy for nuisance, the law in most jurisdictions is that a plaintiff is not automatically entitled to injunctive relief just because the defendant's conduct constitutes a nuisance. Instead, the question whether to grant an injunction (and the proper scope of

that injunction) rests with the sound discretion of the trial court. The court in *Boomer* characterized its use of a damages remedy in that case as a dramatic innovation because it believed that the prior law *required* an injunction to issue automatically and without exception upon determining a defendant's conduct to constitute a nuisance. While there was at least one earlier case to that effect in New York, the usual practice once a nuisance has been found was (and continues to be) to balance the utilities before granting an injunction. Courts applied a presumption in favor of granting injunctive relief to successful plaintiffs but refused to do so where the cost of the injunction to the defendant dramatically outweighed the value of the injunction to the plaintiff. *See* Douglas Laycock, *The Neglected Defense of Undue Hardship (and the Doctrinal Train Wreck in* Boomer v. Atlantic Cement), 4 J. Tort L. 1, 7-19 (2012). Professor Laycock describes how the majority in *Boomer* distorted the legal landscape in New York, confusing generations of subsequent legal scholars. He concludes, "[T]he bottom line is that *Boomer* was no innovation. The opinion could have been written as a straightforward application of the undue hardship defense with only one or at most a few exceptional cases." *Id.*

§2.3 Nuisance or Trespass?

Johnson v. Paynesville Farmers Union Cooperative Oil Co.

817 N.W.2d 693 (Minn. 2012)

LORIE SKJERVEN GILDEA, Chief Justice.

This action involves alleged pesticide contamination of organic farm fields in central Minnesota. Appellant Paynesville Farmers Union Cooperative Oil Company ("Cooperative") is a member owned farm products and services provider that, among other things, applies pesticides to farm fields. Respondents Oluf and Debra Johnson ("Johnsons") are organic farmers. The Johnsons claim that while the Cooperative was spraying pesticide onto conventionally farmed fields adjacent to the Johnsons' fields, some pesticide drifted onto and contaminated the Johnsons' organic fields. The Johnsons sued the Cooperative on theories including trespass, nuisance, and negligence per se and sought damages and injunctive relief.

Before discussing the factual background of this case, it is helpful to briefly summarize the organic farming regulations at issue. American organic farming is regulated by the Organic Foods Production Act of 1990, 7 U.S.C. §§6501-6523 (2006) ("OFPA"), and the associated federal regulations in the National Organic Program, 7 C.F.R. §205 (2012) ("NOP"). Minnesota has adopted the OFPA and the NOP as its state organic farming law.

Under the OFPA and the NOP regulations, a producer cannot market its crops as "organic," and receive the premium price paid for organic products, unless the producer is "certified" by an organic certifying agent. Among numerous other requirements, the NOP provides that land from which crops are intended to be sold as organic must "[h]ave had no prohibited substances . . . applied to it for a period of 3 years immediately preceding harvest of the crop." 7 C.F.R. §205.202(b).[4] Under the NOP regulations, crops may not be sold as organic if the crops are shown to have a prohibited substance on them at levels that are greater than 5 percent of the Environmental Protection Agency's tolerance level for that substance. 7 C.F.R. §205.671.

In June 2007, the Johnsons filed a complaint with the Minnesota Department of Agriculture ("MDA"), alleging that the Cooperative had contaminated one of their transitional soybean fields[5] through pesticide drift. The subsequent MDA investigation verified that on June 15, 2007, a date when winds were blowing toward the Johnsons' fields at 9 to 21 miles per hour, the Cooperative sprayed Status (diflufenzopyr and dicamba) and Roundup Original (glyphosate) onto a conventional farmer's field immediately adjacent to one of the Johnsons' transitional soybean fields. The MDA informed the Johnsons that there was no tolerance for diflufenzopyr in soybeans (organic, transitional, or conventional) and that, pending chemical testing, the MDA would "determine if there [would] be any harvest prohibitions" on the Johnsons' soybeans. After receiving the results of the chemical testing, the MDA informed the parties that test results revealed that the chemical dicamba was present, but below detection levels. The MDA also reported that the chemicals diflufenzopyr and glyphosate were not present. Because only one of the three chemicals was present based on its testing, the MDA concluded that "it can not be proven if the detections were from drift." And even though the testing did not find diflufenzopyr, the MDA still required that the Johnsons plow down a small portion of the soybeans growing in the field because of "the presence of dicamba" and based on the "visual damage" observed to this crop. In response to this MDA directive, the Johnsons destroyed approximately 10 acres of their soybean crop.

The Johnsons also reported the alleged pesticide drift to their organic certifying agent, the Organic Crop Improvement Association (OCIA), as they were required to do under the NOP. In an August 27, 2007 letter, the OCIA stated that there may have been chemical drift onto a transitional soybean field and that chemical testing was being done. The Johnsons were also told that "[i]f the analysis indicate[d] contamination," they would have to "take this land back to the beginning of 36-month transition." Based on the OCIA's letter, and the dicamba found by the MDA, the Johnsons took the transitional soybean field back to the beginning of the 3-year transition process. In other words, the Johnsons did not market soybeans harvested from this field as organic for an additional 3 years.

On July 3, 2008, the Johnsons reported another incident of alleged contamination to the MDA. The MDA investigator did not observe any plant injury, but chemical testing revealed a minimal amount of glyphosate in the Johnsons' transitional alfalfa. The Johnsons reported another incident of drift on August 1, 2008. The MDA "did not observe any plant injury to the alfalfa field or plants, grass and weeds," but chemical

4. The parties agree that the pesticides the Cooperative sprayed are "prohibited substances" under the NOP.

5. A transitional field is one onto which prohibited substances are no longer being applied but has not yet been certified as organic.

testing revealed the presence, at minimal levels, of chloropyrifos. The MDA concluded that drift from the Cooperative's spraying caused both of the positive test results. After receiving these test results, the Johnsons took the affected alfalfa field out of organic production for an additional 3 years.

Based on the presence of pesticides in their fields, the Johnsons filed this lawsuit against the Cooperative, alleging trespass, nuisance, negligence per se, and battery.[6] They sought damages and a permanent injunction prohibiting the Cooperative from spraying pesticides within a half mile of the Johnsons' fields.

After a hearing, the district court granted the Cooperative summary judgment on all of the Johnsons' claims, denied the Johnsons' motion to amend, and vacated the temporary injunction. The district court concluded that the Johnsons' trespass claim failed as a matter of law, relying on the court of appeals decision in *Wendinger v. Forst Farms, Inc.*, 662 N.W.2d 546, 550 (Minn. App. 2003), which held that Minnesota does not recognize trespass by particulate matter.[7] The district court also concluded that all of the Johnsons' negligence per se and nuisance claims failed as a matter of law because the Johnsons lacked evidence of damages. This determination was based on the court's conclusion that because there was no evidence that any chemical on the Johnsons' crops exceeded the 5 percent tolerance level in 7 C.F.R. §205.671, the Johnsons could have sold their crops as organic and therefore the Johnsons did not prove damages. Because the Johnsons did not have any "evidence of damages based on the NOP regulations," the court concluded that all of the Johnsons' claims must be dismissed.

The court of appeals reversed and remanded. We granted the Cooperative's petition for review.

I.

We turn first to the question of whether, as the district court held, the Johnsons' trespass claim fails as a matter of law. The Johnsons assert that the Cooperative trespassed when it sprayed pesticide onto a neighboring conventional field and wind carried the pesticide, as particulate matter, onto the Johnsons' land. The Johnsons contend "that as long as there is damage to the land resulting from deposition of 'particulate matter' a viable claim for trespass exists." The Cooperative argues that the invasion of particulate matter does not, as a matter of law, constitute a trespass in Minnesota.

In Minnesota, a trespass is committed where a plaintiff has the "right of possession" to the land at issue and there is a "wrongful and unlawful entry upon such possession by defendant." *All Am. Foods, Inc. v. Cnty. of Aitkin*, 266 N.W.2d 704, 705 (Minn. 1978). Actual damages are not an element of the tort of trespass. In the absence of actual damages, the trespasser is liable for nominal damages. Finally, because trespass

---

6. The trial court dismissed the battery claim for lack of evidence of intent, and the Plaintiffs did not appeal that dismissal. — EDS.

7. The district court defined "particulate matter" as "'[m]aterial suspended in the air in the form of minute solid particles or liquid droplets, especially when considered as an atmospheric pollutant.'" (Quoting The American Heritage Dictionary of the English Language 1282 (4th ed. 2000)). For purposes of this opinion, we use the same definition.

is an intentional tort, reasonableness on the part of the defendant is not a defense to trespass liability.

We have not specifically considered the question of whether particulate matter can result in a trespass. The "gist of the tort" of trespass, however, is the "intentional interference with rights of exclusive possession." Dan B. Dobbs, The Law of Torts §50 at 95 (2000). In other words, the tort of trespass is committed when a person "intentionally enters or causes direct and tangible entry upon the land in possession of another." *Id.*, §50 at 95 (footnotes omitted). And the defendant's entry must be done "by means of some physical, tangible agency" in order to constitute a trespass. James A. Henderson, Jr. et al., The Torts Process 386 (7th ed. 2007). Our case law is consistent with this traditional formulation of trespass because we have recognized that a trespass can occur when a person or tangible object enters the plaintiff's land.

When people or tangible objects enter the plaintiff's land without permission, these entries disturb the landowner's right to exclusively possess her land. But the disruption to the landowner's exclusive possessory interest is not the same when the invasion is committed by an intangible agency, such as the particulate matter at issue here. Such invasions may interfere with the landowner's use and enjoyment of her land, but those invasions do not require that the landowner share possession of her land in the way that invasions by physical objects do.

The court of appeals forged new ground in this case and extended Minnesota trespass jurisprudence when it held that a trespass could occur through the entry of intangible objects, such as the particulate matter at issue here. The court looked outside Minnesota to support the holding it reached.

In *Bradley* [*v. Am. Smelting & Ref. Co.*, 709 P.2d 782 (1985)], the Washington Supreme Court held that particulate matter deposited on the plaintiff's land from the defendant's copper smelter could constitute a trespass. 709 P.2d at 784, 790. And in *Borland* [*v. Sanders Lead Co.*, 369 So. 2d 523 (Ala. 1979)], the Alabama Supreme Court upheld a trespass claim based on the defendant's "emission of lead particulates and sulfoxide gases" that the plaintiffs alleged accumulated on their property. 369 So. 2d at 525-26.

[T]he expansion of the tort of trespass in cases such as *Bradley* and *Borland* to include invasions by intangible matter potentially "subject[s] countless persons and entities to automatic liability for trespass absent any demonstrated injury." *John Larkin, Inc.* [*v. Marceau*], 959 A.2d 551, 555 (Vt. 2008). To guard against that result, the courts in both *Bradley* and *Borland* required that it be reasonably foreseeable that the intangible matter "result in an invasion of plaintiff's possessory interest," and that the invasion caused "substantial damages" to the plaintiff's property. *Borland*, 369 So. 2d at 529; *accord Bradley*, 709 P.2d at 791. This formulation of trespass, however, conflicts with our precedent defining the elements of trespass. Under Minnesota trespass law, entry upon the land that interferes with the landowner's right to exclusive possession results in trespass whether that interference was reasonably foreseeable or whether it caused damages.

Not only is the rule from the *Bradley* and *Borland* courts inconsistent with our trespass precedent, but the rule in those cases also blurs the line between trespass and nuisance. Traditionally, trespasses are distinct from nuisances: "[t]he law of nuisance deals with indirect or intangible interference with an owner's use and enjoyment of land, while trespass deals with direct and tangible interferences with the right to exclusive possession of land." Dobbs, *supra*, §50 at 96. But in cases like *Bradley* and *Borland*, the courts "call[ ] the intrusion of harmful microscopic particles" a trespass and not a nuisance, and then "us[e] some of the techniques of nuisance law to weigh the amount and reasonableness of the intrusion." Dobbs, *supra*, §50 at 96.

But the Johnsons argue that *Bradley* and *Borland* reflect the modern view of trespass and urge us to likewise abandon the traditional distinctions between trespass and nuisance when considering invasions by particulate matter. We decline the Johnsons' invitation to abandon the traditional distinctions between trespass and nuisance law. Our trespass jurisprudence recognizes the unconditional right of property owners to exclude others through the ability to maintain an action in trespass even when no damages are provable. The rule the Johnsons advocate, and that the court of appeals adopted, erodes this right because it imposes on the property owner the obligation to demonstrate that the invasion causes some consequence. Imposing this restriction on a trespass claim is inconsistent with our precedent that provides a remedy to a property owner "for any trivial trespass." *Romans* [*v. Nadler*], 14 N.W.2d 482, 486 (Minn. 1944). Moreover, it is not necessary for us to depart from our traditional understanding of trespass because other causes of action — nuisance and negligence — provide remedies for the type of behavior at issue in this case.

The Johnsons' claim is that the Cooperative's actions have prevented them from using their land as an organic farm, not that any action of the Cooperative has prevented the Johnsons from possessing any part of their land. The Johnsons' claim is one for nuisance, not trespass. We therefore hold that the district court did not err in concluding that the Johnsons' trespass claim failed as a matter of law.

II.

Having concluded that the Johnsons' trespass claim fails as a matter of law, we turn next to their nuisance and negligence per se claims. The Johnsons allege that the pesticide drift from the Cooperative's spraying constituted a nuisance because it caused an interference with their use and enjoyment of their land. The Johnsons also allege that the pesticide drift constitutes negligence per se, asserting that the Cooperative violated Minn. Stat. §18B.07 (2010) by "direct[ing] . . . pesticide[s] onto property beyond the boundaries of the target site," using the pesticides in a manner inconsistent with their labels, and endangering the Johnsons' agricultural products. The Johnsons seek loss of profits under both the nuisance and negligence per se claims based on their alleged inability to market their crops as organic under 7 C.F.R. §205.202(b). In addition, the Johnsons claim damages for actual crop losses, inconvenience, and adverse health effects.

The district court dismissed the Johnsons' nuisance and negligence per se claims because the court concluded that the Johnsons had not proven damages. Specifically, the court concluded that the Johnsons had no evidence of damages "from any alleged drift because there is no evidence said drift caused [the Johnsons] to lose their organic certification and there is no evidence that [the Johnsons] could not still sell their crops as organic since the levels of prohibited substances were below the applicable tolerance levels." Based on this conclusion, the court granted the Cooperative summary judgment and dismissed the Johnsons' nuisance and negligence per se claims.

A.

The Johnsons argue that they had to remove certain fields from organic production for 3 years because pesticides were "applied to" those fields in violation of 7 C.F.R. §205.202(b). As a result, the Johnsons claim they lost the ability to market crops from that field as organic, and therefore lost the opportunity to seek the premium prices commanded by organic products. For its part, the Cooperative argues that the phrase "applied to it" in 7 C.F.R. §205.202(b), unambiguously means that the organic farmer intentionally applied the prohibited substance to the field. Because the Johnsons did not apply pesticides to the field, the Cooperative argues that section 205.202(b) does not restrict the Johnsons' sale of organic products.

When we read the phrase "applied to it" in 7 C.F.R. §205.202(b), within the context of the OFPA's focus on regulating the practices of the producer of organic products, we conclude that this phrase unambiguously regulates behavior by the producer. In other words, in order for products to be sold as organic, the organic farmer must not have applied prohibited substances to the field from which the product was harvested for a period of 3 years preceding the harvest.

As the Johnsons read section 205.202(b), any amount of pesticide, no matter how it came into contact with the field, would require that the field be taken out of organic production for 3 years. [T]he OFPA and NOP would not need a provision allowing crops with minimum levels of pesticide on them (i.e., less than 5 percent) to be sold as organic because such crops would necessarily have been harvested from fields ineligible for organic production. We are not to adopt an interpretation that renders one section of the regulatory scheme a nullity. *See Markham v. Cabell,* 326 U.S. 404, 409 (1945).

Having concluded that "applied to it" refers to situations where the producer has applied prohibited substances to the field, we must consider whether the district court correctly dismissed the Johnsons' nuisance and negligence per se claims based on 7 C.F.R. §205.202(b). In other words, the question presented is whether the Johnsons created an issue for trial that the Cooperative's pesticide drift required the Johnsons to remove their field from organic production due to 7 C.F.R. §205.202(b). We conclude that they did not.

Construing the evidence in the light most favorable to the Johnsons, their certifying agent, OCIA, directed them to take their soybean fields out of organic production for 3 years. But any such directive was inconsistent with the plain language of 7 C.F.R. §205.202(b). It was also inconsistent with the OFPA because the Johnsons presented no evidence that any residue exceeded the 5 percent tolerance level in 7 C.F.R. §205.671. The certifying agent's erroneous interpretation of section 205.202(b) and the OFPA was the proximate cause of the Johnsons' injury, but the Johnsons cannot hold the Cooperative liable for the certifying agent's erroneous interpretation of the law. The Johnsons' remedy for the certifying agent's error was an appeal of that determination because it was "inconsistent with the" OFPA. 7 U.S.C. §6520(a)(2).

B.

Our conclusion that the district court properly dismissed the Johnsons' negligence per se and nuisance claims based on 7 C.F.R. §205.202(b), does not, however, end our analysis of those claims. [T]he Johnsons claim that the MDA required them to destroy a portion of their transitional soybeans affected by the alleged 2007 drift because of "the presence of dicamba" on and "visual damage" to the soybeans. The Johnsons argue that the Cooperative is liable, under nuisance and negligence per se theories, for damages resulting from the destruction of these soybeans. Because the district court failed to address whether there were any genuine issues of material fact on this aspect of the Johnsons' nuisance and negligence per se claims, we hold that the court erred when it dismissed these claims.

In addition, the Johnsons' nuisance claim alleges that pesticides below the recommended dosage can spur weed growth and that they have had to take extra measures to control weeds in 2007 and 2008 as a result of drift onto their fields from the Cooperative's actions. They also contend that the drift caused additional record-keeping and other burdens in connection with the operation of their farm. Finally, they allege that Oluf Johnson suffers from "cotton mouth, swollen throat and headaches" when exposed to pesticide drift. In *Highview North Apartments v. County of Ramsey*, we held that "disruption and inconvenience" caused by a nuisance are actionable damages. 323 N.W.2d 65, 73 (Minn. 1982). The "inconvenience" and adverse health effects the Johnsons allege are the type of claims contemplated in *Highview North Apartments*, and if proven, they may affect the Johnsons' ability to use and enjoy their land and thereby constitute a nuisance. *See* Minn. Stat. §561.01. Because the district court failed to address whether there are any genuine issues of material fact on this aspect of the Johnsons' nuisance claim, we hold that the court erred when it dismissed the nuisance claim.

Notes and Questions

Nuisance and trespass. Some harms that were traditionally not counted as trespasses clearly involve the physical invasion of land. For example, air pollution involves the physical invasion of land by smoke particles, but it has usually been characterized as a nuisance rather than a trespass. And courts have sometimes used principles drawn from nuisance law to analyze whether an injunction is the appropriate for repeated, low-grade trespasses. *See, e.g., Casteel v. Town of Afton*, 287 N.W. 245 (Iowa 1939).

Some courts have tried to distinguish trespass from nuisance by arguing that a trespass must be "direct," such as a bullet fired across land, and that smoke particles carried by the wind constitute an "indirect" invasion and therefore do not qualify as an intentional invasion. Other courts have sometimes held that trespass requires invasion by physical objects that are larger than microscopic particles. But the trend is to focus not so much on the size of the particles as on the nature of the interest the plaintiff is asserting. According to Prosser and Keeton,

> [T]respass is an invasion of the plaintiff's interest in the exclusive possession of his land, while nuisance is an interference with his use and enjoyment of it. The difference is that between walking across his lawn and establishing a bawdy house next door; between felling a tree across his boundary line and keeping him awake at night with the noise of a rolling mill.

Prosser & Keeton, Torts §87, at 622. In other words, the interest being protected by trespass law is the plaintiff's possessory interest in the land. Nuisance concerns one owner's use of her own land that interferes with her neighbor's use and enjoyment of his property. The interest being protected is not the right to exclusive possession but instead the right to quiet enjoyment of the land.

Under this interest-focused approach, we might conceivably understand the same invasion of a plaintiff's property by particles as both a trespass and a nuisance, or as either of the two. *See, e.g., Amaral v. Cuppels*, 831 N.E.2d 915 (Mass. App. 2005); *H.E. Stevenson et al. v. E.I. DuPont de Nemours,* 327 F.3d 400 (5th Cir. 2003) (applying Texas law); *Gill v. LDI*, 19 F. Supp. 2d 1188 (W.D. Wash. 1998); *Hoery v. United States*, 64 P.3d 214 (Colo. 2003); *New York v. Fermenta ASC Corp.*, 630 N.Y.S.2d 884 (Sup. Ct. 1995). For example, in *Bradley v. American Smelting & Refining Co.*, 709 P.2d 782 (Wash. 1985), which the court discussed in *Johnson*, the Washington Supreme Court allowed plaintiffs to proceed on both trespass and nuisance claims against a factory emitting arsenic and cadmium that fell on plaintiffs' land. However, the court in *Bradley* made two significant changes in trespass law as it applied to microscopic particles. It held, first, that a trespass could occur only if the particles fell to the ground and stayed there rather than dissipating through the air. Second, the court held that liability for trespass by such particles could be found only if plaintiffs could prove substantial damage. The court justified this change by arguing that a "reconciliation must be found between the interest of the many who are unaffected by the possible poisoning and the few who may be affected." 709 P.2d at 785. It further explained that "[n]o useful purpose would be served by sanctioning actions in trespass by every landowner within a hundred miles of a manufacturing plant. Manufacturers would be harassed and the litigious few would cause the escalation of costs to the detriment of the many." *Id.* at 791. *Accord, Public Service Co. of Colorado v. Van Wyck*, 27 P.3d 377, 390 (Colo. 2001) ("[I]n Colorado, an intangible intrusion may give rise to claim for trespass, but only if an aggrieved party is able to prove physical damage to the property caused by such intangible intrusion"). In light of these modifications of traditional trespass law by the court in *Bradley*, what is the benefit (if any) of characterizing a claim as a trespass by microscopic particles rather than as a traditional nuisance claim? Other courts, like the court in *Johnson*, reject the *Bradley* approach, holding instead that physical invasion by dust, noise, and vibration does not constitute a trespass, although it may well be a nuisance. *See, e.g., Adams v. Cleveland-Cliffs Iron Co.*, 602 N.W.2d 215 (Mich. Ct. App. 1999).

§3 LIGHT AND AIR

Fontainebleau Hotel Corp. v. Forty-Five Twenty-Five, Inc.

114 So. 2d 357 (Fla. Dist. Ct. App. 1959)

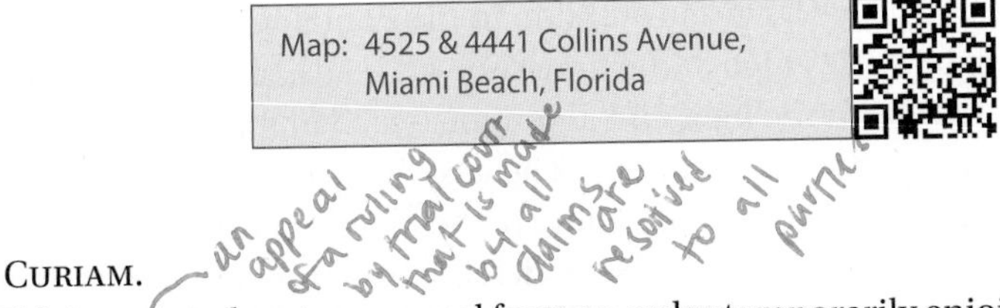

Map: 4525 & 4441 Collins Avenue,
Miami Beach, Florida

PER CURIAM.

This is an interlocutory appeal from an order temporarily enjoining the appellants from continuing with the construction of a fourteen-story addition to the Fontainebleau Hotel, owned and operated by the appellants. Appellee, plaintiff below, owns the Eden Roc Hotel, which was constructed in 1955, about a year after the Fontainebleau, and adjoins the Fontainebleau on the north. Both are luxury hotels, facing the Atlantic Ocean. The proposed addition to the Fontainebleau is being constructed twenty feet from its north property line, 130 feet from the mean high water mark of the Atlantic Ocean, and 76 feet 8 inches from the ocean bulkhead line. The 14-story tower will

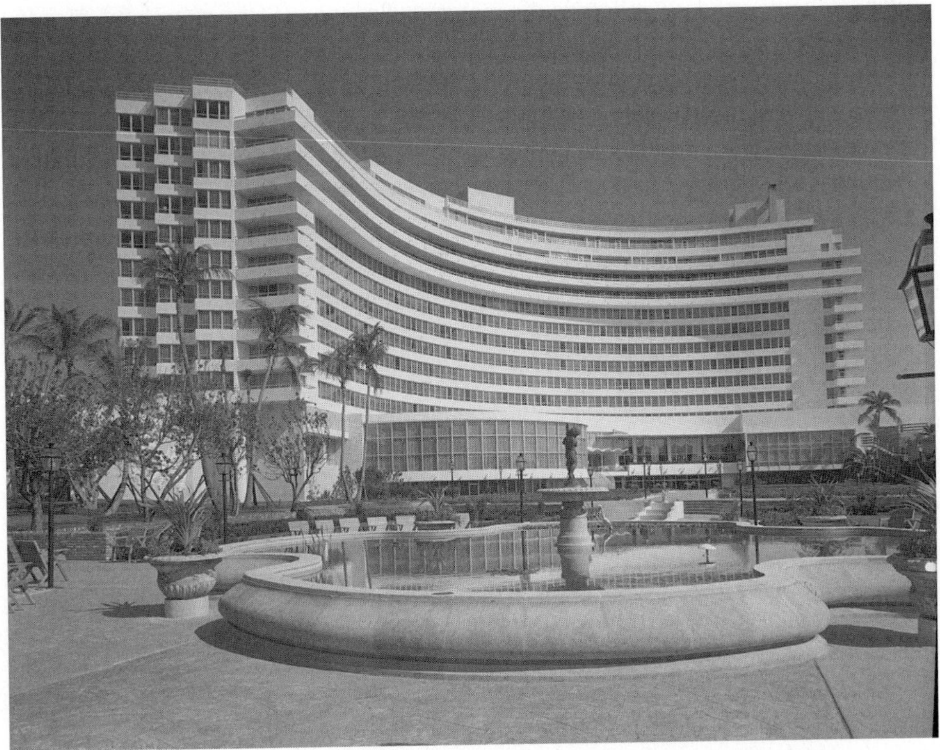

Figure 1 — Fontainebleau Hotel, photograph from the Library of Congress (1955)

extend 160 feet above grade in height and is 416 feet long from east to west. During the winter months, from around two o'clock in the afternoon for the remainder of the day, the shadow of the addition will extend over the cabana, swimming pool, and sunbathing areas of the Eden Roc, which are located in the southern portion of its property.

In this action, plaintiff-appellee sought to enjoin the defendants-appellants from proceeding with the construction of the addition to the Fontainebleau (it appears to have been roughly eight stories high at the time suit was filed), alleging that the construction would interfere with the light and air on the beach in front of the Eden Roc and cast a shadow of such size as to render the beach wholly unfitted for the use and enjoyment of its guests, to the irreparable injury of the plaintiff; further, that the construction of such addition on the north side of defendants' property, rather than the south side, was actuated by malice and ill will on the part of the defendants' president toward the plaintiff's president; and that the construction was in violation of a building ordinance requiring a 100-foot setback from the ocean. It was also alleged that the construction would interfere with the easements of light and air enjoyed by plaintiff and its predecessors in title for more than twenty years and "impliedly granted by virtue of the acts of the plaintiff's predecessors in title, as well as under the common law and the express recognition of such rights by virtue of Chapter 9837, Laws of Florida 1923. . . ." Some attempt was also made to allege an easement by implication in favor of the plaintiff's property, as the dominant, and against the defendants' property, as the servient, tenement.

The defendants' answer denied the material allegations of the complaint, pleaded laches and estoppel by judgment.

The chancellor heard considerable testimony on the issues made by the complaint and the answer and, as noted, entered a temporary injunction restraining the defendants from continuing with the construction of the addition. His reason for so doing was stated by him, in a memorandum opinion, as follows:

> [N]o one has a right to use his property to the injury of another. In this case it is clear from the evidence that the proposed use by the Fontainebleau will materially damage the Eden Roc. There is evidence indicating that the construction of the proposed annex by the Fontainebleau is malicious or deliberate for the purpose of injuring the Eden Roc, but it is scarcely sufficient, standing alone, to afford a basis for equitable relief.

This is indeed a novel application of the maxim *sic utere tuo ut alienum non laedas.* This maxim does not mean that one must never use his own property in such a way as to do any injury to his neighbor. It means only that one must use his property so as not to injure the lawful *rights* of another. In *Reaver v. Martin Theatres*, 52 So. 2d 682, 683 (Fla. 1951), under this maxim, it was stated that "it is well settled that a property owner may put his own property to any reasonable and lawful use, so long as he does not thereby deprive the adjoining landowner of any right of enjoyment of his property *which is recognized and protected by law, and so long as his use is not such a one as the law will pronounce a nuisance.*" [Emphasis supplied.]

No American decision has been cited, and independent research has revealed none, in which it has been held that—in the absence of some contractual or statutory obligation — a landowner has a legal right to the free flow of light and air across the adjoining land of his neighbor. Even at common law, the landowner had no legal right, in the absence of an easement or uninterrupted use and enjoyment for a period of 20 years, to unobstructed light and air from the adjoining land. And the English doctrine of "ancient lights" has been unanimously repudiated in this country.

There being, then, no legal right to the free flow of light and air from the adjoining land, it is universally held that where a structure serves a useful and beneficial purpose, it does not give rise to a cause of action, either for damages or for an injunction under the maxim *sic utere tuo ut alienum non laedas*, even though it causes injury to another by cutting off the light and air and interfering with the view that would otherwise be available over adjoining land in its natural state, regardless of the fact that the structure may have been erected partly for spite.

We see no reason for departing from this universal rule. If, as contended on behalf of plaintiff, public policy demands that a landowner in the Miami Beach area refrain from constructing buildings on his premises that will cast a shadow on the adjoining premises, an amendment of its comprehensive planning and zoning ordinance, applicable to the public as a whole, is the means by which such purpose should be achieved. . . . But to change the universal rule — and the custom followed in this state since its inception — that adjoining landowners have an equal right under the law to build to the line of their respective tracts and to such a height as is desired by them (in the absence, of course, of building restrictions or regulations) amounts, in our opinion, to judicial legislation.

Since it affirmatively appears that the plaintiff has not established a cause of action against the defendants by reason of the structure here in question, the order granting a temporary injunction should be and it is hereby reversed with directions to dismiss the complaint.

Prah v. Maretti

321 N.W.2d 182 (Wis. 1982)

SHIRLEY S. ABRAHAMSON, Justice.

This appeal from a judgment of the circuit court for Waukesha county, Max Raskin, circuit judge, was certified to this court by the court of appeals, as presenting an issue of first impression, namely, whether an owner of a solar-heated residence states a claim upon which relief can be granted when he asserts that his neighbor's proposed construction of a residence (which conforms to existing deed restrictions and local ordinances) interferes with his access to an unobstructed path for sunlight across the neighbor's property. This case thus involves a conflict between one landowner (Glenn Prah, the plaintiff) interested in unobstructed access to sunlight across adjoining property as a natural source of energy and an adjoining landowner (Richard D. Maretti, the defendant) interested in the development of his land.

According to the complaint, the plaintiff is the owner of a residence which was constructed during the years 1978-1979. The complaint alleges that the residence has a solar system which includes collectors on the roof to supply energy for heat and hot water and that after the plaintiff built his solar-heated house, the defendant purchased the lot adjacent to and immediately to the south of the plaintiff's lot and commenced planning construction of a home. The complaint further states that when the plaintiff learned of defendant's plans to build the house he advised the defendant that if the house were built at the proposed location, defendant's house would substantially and adversely affect the integrity of plaintiff's solar system and could cause plaintiff other damage. Nevertheless, the defendant began construction. The complaint further alleges that the plaintiff is entitled to "unrestricted use of the sun and its solar power" and demands judgment for injunctive relief and damages.

Plaintiff's home was the first residence built in the subdivision, and although plaintiff did not build his house in the center of the lot it was built in accordance with applicable restrictions. Plaintiff advised defendant that if the defendant's home were built at the proposed site it would cause a shadowing effect on the solar collectors which would reduce the efficiency of the system and possibly damage the system. To avoid these adverse effects, plaintiff requested defendant to locate his home an additional several feet away from the plaintiff's lot line, the exact number being disputed. Plaintiff and defendant failed to reach an agreement on the location of defendant's home before defendant started construction.

We consider first whether the complaint states a claim for relief based on common law private nuisance. This state has long recognized that an owner of land does not have an absolute or unlimited right to use the land in a way which injures the rights of others. The rights of neighboring landowners are relative; the uses by one must not unreasonably impair the uses or enjoyment of the other. When one landowner's use of his or her property unreasonably interferes with another's enjoyment of his or her property, that use is said to be a private nuisance.

The private nuisance doctrine has traditionally been employed in this state to balance the rights of landowners, and this court has recently adopted the analysis of private nuisance set forth in the *Restatement (Second) of Torts.* The *Restatement* defines private nuisance as "a nontrespassory invasion of another's interest in the private use and enjoyment of land." *Restatement (Second) of Torts* §821D (1977). The phrase "interest in the private use and enjoyment of land" as used in §821D is broadly defined to include any disturbance of the enjoyment of property.

Although the defendant's obstruction of the plaintiff's access to sunlight appears to fall within the *Restatement*'s broad concept of a private nuisance as a nontrespassory invasion of another's interest in the private use and enjoyment of land, the defendant asserts that he has a right to develop his property in compliance with statutes, ordinances and private covenants without regard to the effect of such development upon the plaintiff's access to sunlight. In essence, the defendant is asking this court to hold that the private nuisance doctrine is not applicable in the instant case and that his right to develop his land is a right which is *per se* superior to his neighbor's interest in access to sunlight. This position is expressed in the maxim "cujus est solum, ejus est usque ad coelum et ad inferos," that is, the owner of land owns up to the sky and down to the center of the earth. The rights of the surface owner are, however, not unlimited.

The defendant is not completely correct in asserting that the common law did not protect a landowner's access to sunlight across adjoining property. At English common law a landowner could acquire a right to receive sunlight across adjoining land by both express agreement and under the judge-made doctrine of "ancient lights." Under the doctrine of ancient lights if the landowner had received sunlight across adjoining property for a specified period of time, the landowner was entitled to continue to receive unobstructed access to sunlight across the adjoining property. Under the doctrine the landowner acquired a negative prescriptive easement and could prevent the adjoining landowner from obstructing access to light.[8]

Although American courts have not been as receptive to protecting a landowner's access to sunlight as the English courts, American courts have afforded some protection to a landowner's interest in access to sunlight. American courts honor express easements to sunlight. American courts initially enforced the English common law doctrine of ancient lights, but later every state which considered the doctrine repudiated it as inconsistent with the needs of a developing country. Indeed, for just that reason this court concluded that an easement to light and air over adjacent property could not be created or acquired by prescription and has been unwilling to recognize such an easement by implication.

Many jurisdictions in this country have protected a landowner from malicious obstruction of access to light (the spite fence cases) under the common law private nuisance doctrine. If an activity is motivated by malice it lacks utility and the harm it causes others outweighs any social values. . . . Thus a landowner's interest in sunlight has been protected in this country by common law private nuisance law at least in the narrow context of the modern American rule invalidating spite fences.

This court's reluctance in the nineteenth and early part of the twentieth century to provide broader protection for a landowner's access to sunlight was premised on three policy considerations. First, the right of landowners to use their property as they wished, as long as they did not cause physical damage to a neighbor, was jealously guarded.

Second, sunlight was valued only for aesthetic enjoyment or as illumination. Since artificial light could be used for illumination, loss of sunlight was at most a personal annoyance which was given little, if any, weight by society.

Third, society had a significant interest in not restricting or impeding land development. This court repeatedly emphasized that in the growth period of the nineteenth and early twentieth centuries change is to be expected and is essential to property and that recognition of a right to sunlight would hinder property development.

Considering these three policies, this court concluded that in the absence of an express agreement granting access to sunlight, a landowner's obstruction of another's access to sunlight was not actionable. These three policies are no longer fully accepted or applicable. They reflect factual circumstances and social priorities that are now obsolete.

First, society has increasingly regulated the use of land by the landowner for the general welfare.

---

8. No American common law state recognizes a landowner's right to acquire an easement of light by prescription.

Second, access to sunlight has taken on a new significance in recent years. In this case the plaintiff seeks to protect access to sunlight, not for aesthetic reasons or as a source of illumination but as a source of energy. Access to sunlight as an energy source is of significance both to the landowner who invests in solar collectors and to a society which has an interest in developing alternative sources of energy.

Third, the policy of favoring unhindered private development in an expanding economy is no longer in harmony with the realities of our society. The need for easy and rapid development is not as great today as it once was, while our perception of the value of sunlight as a source of energy has increased significantly.

Courts should not implement obsolete policies that have lost their vigor over the course of the years. The law of private nuisance is better suited to resolve landowners' disputes about property development in the 1980's than is a rigid rule which does not recognize a landowner's interest in access to sunlight. As we said in *Ballstadt v. Pagel*, 232 N.W. 862 (Wis. 1930), "What is regarded in law as constituting a nuisance in modern times would no doubt have been tolerated without question in former times." We read *State v. Deetz*, 224 N.W.2d 407 (Wis. 1974), as an endorsement of the application of common law nuisance to situations involving the conflicting interests of landowners and as rejecting per se exclusions to the nuisance law reasonable use doctrine.

In *Deetz* the court abandoned the rigid common law common enemy rule with respect to surface water and adopted the private nuisance reasonable use rule, namely that the landowner is subject to liability if his or her interference with the flow of surface waters unreasonably invades a neighbor's interest in the use and enjoyment of land. *Restatement (Second) of Torts*, §§822, 826, 829 (1977). This court concluded that the common enemy rule which served society "well in the days of burgeoning national expansion of the mid-nineteenth and early-twentieth centuries" should be abandoned because it was no longer "in harmony with the realities of our society." *Deetz, supra*, 224 N.W.2d 407. We recognized in *Deetz* that common law rules adapt to changing social values and conditions.

Yet the defendant would have us ignore the flexible private nuisance law as a means of resolving the dispute between the landowners in this case and would have us adopt an approach, already abandoned in *Deetz*, of favoring the unrestricted development of land and of applying a rigid and inflexible rule protecting his right to build on his land and disregarding any interest of the plaintiff in the use and enjoyment of his land. This we refuse to do.[9]

9. Defendant's position that a landowner's interest in access to sunlight across adjoining land is not "legally enforceable" and is therefore excluded *per se* from private nuisance law was adopted in *Fontainebleau Hotel Corp. v. Forty-Five Twenty-Five, Inc.*, 114 So. 2d 357 (Fla. App. 1959). . . .

We do not find the reasoning of *Fountainebleau* persuasive. . . . The court did not explain why an owner's interest in unobstructed light should not be protected or in what manner an owner's interest in unobstructed sunlight differs from an owner's interest in being free from obtrusive noises or smells or differs from an owner's interest in unobstructed use of water. The recognition of a *per se* exception to private nuisance law may invite unreasonable behavior.

Private nuisance law, the law traditionally used to adjudicate conflicts between private landowners, has the flexibility to protect both a landowner's right of access to sunlight and another landowner's right to develop land. Private nuisance law is better suited to regulate access to sunlight in modern society and is more in harmony with legislative policy and the prior decisions of this court than is an inflexible doctrine of non-recognition of any interest in access to sunlight across adjoining land.

We therefore hold that private nuisance law, that is, the reasonable use doctrine as set forth in the *Restatement*, is applicable to the instant case. Recognition of a nuisance claim for unreasonable obstruction of access to sunlight will not prevent land development or unduly hinder the use of adjoining land. It will promote the reasonable use and enjoyment of land in a manner suitable to the 1980's. That obstruction of access to light might be found to constitute a nuisance in certain circumstances does not mean that it will be or must be found to constitute a nuisance under all circumstances. The result in each case depends on whether the conduct complained of is unreasonable.

Accordingly we hold that the plaintiff in this case has stated a claim under which relief can be granted. Nonetheless we do not determine whether the plaintiff in this case is entitled to relief. In order to be entitled to relief the plaintiff must prove the elements required to establish actionable nuisance, and the conduct of the defendant herein must be judged by the reasonable use doctrine.

The circuit court concluded that because the defendant's proposed house was in conformity with zoning regulations, building codes and deed restrictions, the defendant's use of the land was reasonable. This court has concluded that a landowner's compliance with zoning laws does not automatically bar a nuisance claim.

[O]ur examination of the record leads us to conclude that the record does not furnish an adequate basis for the circuit court to apply the proper legal principles on summary judgment. The application of the reasonable use standard in nuisance cases normally requires a full exposition of all underlying facts and circumstances. Too little is known in this case of such matters as the extent of the harm to the plaintiff, the suitability of solar heat in that neighborhood, the availability of remedies to the plaintiff, and the costs to the defendant of avoiding the harm. Summary judgment is not an appropriate procedural vehicle in this case when the circuit court must weigh evidence which has not been presented at trial.

Because the plaintiff has stated a claim of common law private nuisance upon which relief can be granted, the judgment of the circuit court must be reversed.

William Callow, Justice, dissenting.

The majority concludes that this court's past reluctance to extend protection to a landowner's access to sunlight beyond the spite fence cases is based on obsolete policies which have lost their vigor over the course of the years. The three obsolete policies cited by the majority are: (1) Right of landowners to use their property as they desire as long as no physical damage is done to a neighbor; (2) In the past, sunlight was valued only for aesthetic value, not a source of energy; and (3) Society has a significant interest in not impeding land development. . . . The majority has failed to convince me that these policies are obsolete.

I firmly believe that a landowner's right to use his property within the limits of ordinances, statutes, and restrictions of record where such use is necessary to serve his legitimate needs is a fundamental precept of a free society which this court should strive to uphold.

In the instant case, we are dealing with an action which seeks to restrict the defendant's private right to use his property, notwithstanding a complete lack of notice of restriction to the defendant and the defendant's compliance with applicable ordinances and statutes. The plaintiff who knew of the potential problem before the defendant acquired the land seeks to impose such use restriction to accommodate his personal, private benefit—a benefit which could have been accommodated by the plaintiff locating his home in a different place on his property or by acquiring the land in question when it was for sale prior to its acquisition by the defendant.

The right of a property owner to lawful enjoyment of his property should be vigorously protected, particularly in those cases where the adjacent property owner could have insulated himself from the alleged problem by acquiring the land as a defense to the potential problem or by provident use of his own property.

The majority concludes that sunlight has not heretofore been accorded the status of a source of energy, and consequently it has taken on a new significance in recent years. Solar energy for home heating is at this time sparingly used and of questionable economic value because solar collectors are not mass produced, and consequently, they are very costly. Their limited efficiency may explain the lack of production.

Regarding the third policy the majority apparently believes is obsolete (that society has a significant interest in not restricting land development) . . . , I concede the law may be tending to recognize the value of aesthetics over increased volume development and that an individual may not use his land in such a way as to harm the public. The instant case, however, deals with a private benefit. [At the same time, it] is clear that community planners are acutely aware of the present housing shortages, particularly among those two groups with limited financial resources, the young and the elderly. While the majority's policy arguments may be directed to a cause of action for public nuisance, we are presented with a private nuisance case which I believe is distinguishable in this regard.

I would submit that any policy decisions in this area are best left for the legislature. "What is 'desirable' or 'advisable' or 'ought to be' is a question of policy, not a question of fact. What is 'necessary' or what is 'in the best interest' is not a fact and its determination by the judiciary is an exercise of legislative power when each involves political considerations." *In re City of Beloit,* 155 N.W.2d 633, 636 (Wis. 1968). . . . I would concur with these observations of the trial judge: "While temptation lingers for the court to declare by judicial fiat what is right and what should be done, under the facts in this case, such action under our form of constitutional government where the three branches each have their defined jurisdiction and power, would be an intrusion of judicial egoism over legislative passivity."

In order for a nuisance to be actionable in the instant case, the defendant's conduct must be "intentional and unreasonable." It is impossible for me to accept the majority's conclusion that Mr. Maretti, in lawfully seeking to construct his home, may be intentionally and unreasonably interfering with the plaintiff's access to sunlight.

I conclude that plaintiff's solar heating system is an unusually sensitive use. In other words, the defendant's proposed construction of his home, under ordinary circumstances, would not interfere with the use and enjoyment of the usual person's property. . . . "The plaintiff cannot, by devoting his own land to an unusually sensitive use, such as a drive-in motion picture theater easily affected by light, make a nuisance out of conduct of the adjoining defendant which would otherwise be harmless."

I further believe that the majority's conclusion that a cause of action exists in this case thwarts the very foundation of property law. Property law encompasses a system of filing and notice in a place for public records to provide prospective purchasers with any limitations on their use of the property. Such a notice is not alleged by the plaintiff. Only as a result of the majority's decision did Mr. Maretti discover that a legitimate action exists which would require him to defend the design and location of his home against a nuisance suit, notwithstanding the fact that he located and began to build his house within the applicable building, municipal, and deed restrictions.

I believe the facts of the instant controversy present the classic case of the owner of a solar collector who fails to take any action to protect his investment. There is nothing in the record to indicate that Mr. Prah disclosed his situation to Mr. Maretti prior to Maretti's purchase of the lot or attempted to secure protection for his solar collector prior to Maretti's submission of his building plans to the architectural committee. Such inaction should be considered a significant factor in determining whether a cause of action exists.

I do not believe that an adjacent lot owner should be obliged to experience the substantial economic loss resulting from the lot being rendered unbuildable by the contour of the land as it relates to the location and design of the adjoining home using solar collectors.

Notes and Questions

1. **Light and air.** The vast majority of courts in the United States would hold that, in the absence of an agreement to the contrary, owners have absolute rights to develop their property without liability for any interference with their neighbor's interests in light and air. *See also* Sara C. Bronin, *Solar Rights*, 89 B.U. L. Rev. 1217, 1250-1257 (2009) (describing general failure of nuisance claims to permit solar power). This is often expressed by saying that no easement for light and air exists unless a contract creates it. One exception to this principle is that some courts will enjoin "spite fences" — structures that are erected for the *sole purpose* of maliciously harming the neighbor by interfering with her access to sunlight. *DeCecco v. Beach,* 381 A.2d 543 (Conn. 1977) (applying Conn. Gen. Stat. §52-570); *Gertz v. Estes*, 879 N.E.2d 617 (Ind. Ct. App. 2008) (applying Ind. Code §§32-26-10-1 and -2). *But see Maioriello v. Arlotta*, 73 A.2d 374 (Pa. 1950) (holding that owners may build so as to obstruct light, air, and view of adjoining landowners, even though the structure serves no useful purpose and is erected solely to annoy the adjoining owner).

Another state that has joined the Wisconsin Supreme Court in using nuisance doctrine to adjudicate conflicts over light and air in some instances is New Hampshire. In *Tenn v. 889 Associates, Ltd.*, 500 A.2d 366 (N.H. 1985), for example, Justice David Souter applied nuisance law to a claim that construction of a building would interfere with light and air of the building next to it. Explicitly rejecting the rule in *Fontainebleau,* Justice Souter wrote:

> The present defendant urges us to adopt the *Fontainebleau* rule and thereby to refuse any common law recognition to interests in light and air, but we decline to do so. If we were so to limit the ability of the common law to grow, we would in effect be rejecting one of the wise assumptions underlying the traditional law of nuisance: that we cannot anticipate at any one time the variety of predicaments in which protection of property interests or redress for their violation will be justifiable. For it is just this recognition that has led the courts to avoid rigid formulations for determining when an interference with the use of property will be actionable, and to rest instead on the flexible rule that actionable, private nuisance consists of an unreasonable as well as a substantial interference with another person's use and enjoyment of his property. That is, because we have to anticipate that the uses of property will change over time, we have developed a law of nuisance that protects the use and enjoyment of property when a threatened harm to the plaintiff owner can be said to outweigh the utility of the defendant owner's conduct to himself and to the community.

Id. at 370. At the same time, the court upheld the lower court's determination that construction of the building would *not* constitute a nuisance since the plaintiff's building would continue to receive sufficient light characteristic of an urban area where buildings often buttress and block the sides of adjacent structures.

2. Solar shade statutes. California has passed a statute called the *Solar Shade Control Act,* Cal. Pub. Res. §§25980-25986, which provides that "[a]fter the installation of a solar collector, a person owning or in control of another property shall not allow a tree or shrub to be placed or, if placed, to grow on that property so as to cast a shadow greater than 10 percent of the collector absorption area upon that solar collector surface at any one time between the hours of 10 A.M. and 2 P.M., local standard time." *Id.* §25982. The statute was amended in 2008 (after a highly publicized controversy that resulted in the destruction of eight redwoods) to ensure that the statute would no longer apply to trees planted prior to installation of the solar collector. Felicity Barringer, *Trees Block Solar Panels, and a Feud Ends in Court,* N.Y. Times, Apr. 7, 2008, at A-14; *see also* Troy A. Rule, *Airspace in a Green Economy,* 59 UCLA L. Rev. 270 (2011) (advocating increased use of options and liability rules to facilitate alternative energy while respecting owners' interests under existing law).

Law and Economics Analysis of Nuisance

1. Externalities. Economic analysis of law seeks to identify the most efficient rule of law, generally by evaluating the costs and benefits of different alternatives. Traditional analysis of efficiency in nuisance cases starts from the notion of externalities. **Externalities** are costs imposed on third parties that are not taken into account in the actor's own cost-benefit determinations. The factory owner in *Boomer*, for example, harms neighboring homeowners by causing pollution. This harm is a cost of the factory's economic activity; it is a loss that must be borne by society as a consequence of operation of the factory. Yet, unless the law intervenes, the factory's owner will not take account of this cost in determining whether its operations are profitable; a rationally self-interested factory will go forward with the activity even if the net social costs of its activity outweigh the benefits. Classical economic analysis of nuisance sought to make the factory to pay for and thereby **internalize** the external harms that its operation causes. By requiring the company to account to society for the harm it caused, the factory's private cost-benefit calculations would be made congruent with the social cost-benefit calculation; its decisions about the level and manner of operation will therefore promote social welfare.

Terms:
Economists recognize different definitions of the term **efficiency**. An action is **Pareto efficient** if it makes someone better off without making anyone worse off. Perfectly voluntary transactions are considered Pareto efficient. Economic analysis of law, however, often uses **Kaldor-Hicks efficiency**, which defines an action as efficient if its benefits outweigh its costs, even if someone is made worse off.

2. **Coase Theorem.** In his famous article *The Problem of Social Cost*, 3 J.L. & Econ. 1 (1960), Ronald Coase criticized the argument that property owners should necessarily be required to internalize their external costs.

a. **Joint costs.** As discussed in §1, Coase observed that externalities are reciprocal. In *Boomer*, for example, if the houses were not located near the factory, there would be no problem. It therefore is not obvious that the factory must internalize the costs it imposes. It could as easily be said that the homeowners should internalize the costs of engaging in a sensitive use like homeowning by compensating the factory for its losses associated with shutting down or installing pollution control devices. A better way to understand the situation, Coase argued, is to consider the problem as involving *joint costs* that each activity imposes on the other. The problem is to determine who should bear the burden of avoiding it.

b. **Subsequent bargains.** Another crucial part of Coase's analysis is that parties are free to bargain around any legal allocation of entitlements. Even if the court rules that the homeowners have the right to an injunction ordering the factory to stop operating, the factory will not necessarily shut down. Rather, the factory may offer the homeowners a money payment to induce them to sell their property right to enjoin the nuisance. If the factory values the right to pollute more than the homeowners value the right to be free from pollution, the factory owner will be able to offer the homeowners enough to persuade them to forgo their right to be free from pollution. Similarly, if the court rules that the factory operation is not a nuisance, the homeowners may attempt to pay the factory owner to induce it not to exercise its right to operate the factory. They will succeed if they value the right to be free from pollution more highly than the factory owner values the right to pollute.

If the costs of transacting are zero, then the choice of legal rules or the allocation of the entitlement in question will arguably have no effect on allocative efficiency.

Whoever values the entitlement more will either keep it—if they already own it—or will buy it from the other party. This is part I of the Coase Theorem: *If there are no transaction costs, it does not matter which legal rule is chosen because any legal rule will produce an efficient result.*

Take the case of *Fontainebleau Hotel Corp. v. Forty-Five Twenty-Five, Inc.* The legal issue is whether the Fontainebleau Hotel has a legal liberty to build an addition onto its hotel that would cast a shadow over the swimming pool of the Eden Roc. Either the Fontainebleau has an entitlement to build freely, without liability to its neighbor, or the Eden Roc has an entitlement to be free from wrongful interference with its light and air. Assume the Fontainebleau Hotel anticipates that its profits will rise if it builds the addition both because it can accommodate more people and because it will increase the demand for rooms at the Fontainebleau by decreasing the number of people willing to take rooms at the Eden Roc. This anticipated rise in profits translates into a $10 million increase in the market value of the Fontainebleau's property. At the same time, if the addition is built, the Eden Roc will suffer a decrease of $6 million in the market value of its property. Assuming that no third parties are affected by this decision (an unrealistic but simplifying assumption), social wealth will be increased by allowing the addition to be built. It will cause $10 million of benefit and only $6 million of harm, making society better off overall by $4 million.

If the transaction costs are zero, the Fontainebleau will go ahead and build the addition. If the court holds that the addition is a nuisance and that the Eden Roc has the right to an injunction stopping the addition, the parties will bargain around this result, since the Fontainebleau stands to gain $10 million if the addition is built while the Eden Roc will lose only $6 million. If the Fontainebleau offers the Eden Roc any amount over $6 million, the Eden Roc will be better off accepting the money and selling to the Fontainebleau the right to build without liability than it would be by blocking the addition. A payment of more than $6 million will fully compensate the Eden Roc for the losses associated with the addition; in theory, there should be no difference between not having the addition built and having the addition built with a $6 million payment. Any money offered over $6 million will leave the Eden Roc better off than before.

At the same time, so long as the Fontainebleau makes a payment under $10 million, it will be better off building the addition while paying the Eden Roc to induce it to give up its nuisance claim than not going ahead with the project. The costs of paying off the Eden Roc will be less than the benefits of constructing the addition. Thus, in the absence of transaction costs, the parties will agree for some sum between $6 million and $10 million to allow the project to go forward.

If the court holds that the addition is not a nuisance, the project will similarly go forward. In this case, the Eden Roc would be willing to offer the Fontainebleau up to $6 million to prevent the building of the addition. Any amount over $6 million would be irrational; the Eden Roc would be worse off than if it paid nothing. It would make no sense to pay $7 million to avoid a $6 million harm. At the same time, the Fontainebleau would not accept any payment under $10 million to give up its right to build. Any payment under $10 million would leave it worse off than if it built the project. Thus, in the absence of transaction costs, the efficient allocation of entitlements is achieved no matter how the court rules.

c. Distributive issues. Even if the choice of legal rule has no effect on efficiency in the absence of transaction costs, it has an enormous effect on the distribution of wealth between the parties. Efficiency analysis may tell us whether an activity should go forward, but it is not decisive as to who should pay for this outcome. In our example, we have assumed that the project is wealth maximizing because it creates benefits of $10 million and costs of only $6 million; we therefore conclude that the project is efficient and should go forward despite the losses it will inflict on the Eden Roc.[10] But efficiency analysis does not tell us who should bear the $6 million cost of obtaining this $10 million benefit. The court could choose to impose the cost either on the plaintiff Eden Roc, by denying the plaintiff any remedy, or on the Fontainebleau, by requiring it to pay damages of $6 million to the Eden Roc. As long as damages are calculated correctly,[11] allowing the plaintiff to receive damages, but not an injunction, will achieve the efficient result because the project will go forward (the cost of the damages are less than the expected profits); at the same time, such a result will achieve the distributive goal of placing the burden on the party that profits from the activity.

Similarly, if the numbers were reversed and the project was inefficient, the court could choose who should bear the economic costs of forgoing the project. Assume the benefits to the Fontainebleau are $6 million and the costs to the Eden Roc are $10 million. In this case, the losses outweigh the benefits and the project will decrease, rather than increase, social wealth; it should therefore be enjoined. Granting the plaintiff an injunction stopping the project will achieve the efficient result. Again, efficiency analysis cannot give us a conclusive answer as to who should pay the costs associated with the injunction. The court could choose to impose the burden on the Fontainebleau by granting the plaintiffs a simple injunction, thereby denying the Fontainebleau the opportunity to make $6 million. Or, the court could impose the cost on the plaintiff by granting the Eden Roc a purchased injunction, conditioning the injunction on the Eden Roc's compensating the Fontainebleau for the $6 million loss the injunction imposes on it. Only an analysis of distributive justice can tell us who should bear the cost.

d. Transaction costs. The observation that the choice of legal rules has no effect on allocative efficiency depends on the assumption that there are no **transaction costs**, or costs to the parties in reaching an agreement. But there are always transaction costs, as Coase well understood. The legal rule chosen by the court may therefore affect the outcome. If the court chooses the wealth-maximizing

---

10. The example assumes that the Fontainebleau cannot avoid the harm by relocating its construction project.

11. This is a big "if." *See* James E. Krier & Stewart J. Schwab, *Property Rules and Liability Rules: The Cathedral in Another Light*, 70 N.Y.U. L. Rev. 440 (1995) (questioning the ability of courts to calculate damages accurately).

entitlement, all well and good from an efficiency standpoint; but if the court chooses the inefficient entitlement, transaction costs may be so high as to prevent the parties from correcting the mistake by a subsequent bargain.

Suppose an agreement between the Fontainebleau and the Eden Roc costs $5 million to reach. This sum includes the cost of conducting the negotiations, hiring attorneys, getting financing to buy off the other party, and bringing into the talks third parties who might be benefited or harmed by construction of the project. If the court grants the Fontainebleau the right to build by holding that the project is not a nuisance, the Fontainebleau will go ahead and build, thereby achieving the efficient result. If, however, the court rules the project a nuisance, thereby assigning the entitlement to the Eden Roc, the project will not go forward: The Eden Roc will not accept less than $6 million to give up its rights to stop the project, and the cost of arranging such a deal is $5 million. The total cost of buying the right to build is therefore $6 million plus $5 million, or $11 million. But the Fontainebleau stands to gain only $10 million by building the addition. It will not pay $11 million to get a $10 million gain; it would be better off not building. This result is inefficient since the benefits to society of the project are greater than the costs. This, then, is part II of the Coase Theorem: *In the presence of transaction costs, the choice of entitlements by the courts may have an effect on efficiency. The courts may increase efficiency by assigning entitlements to the parties who would purchase them in the absence of transaction costs.*

There are several kinds of transaction costs.[12] One of the most basic is **bargaining costs**, costs incurred in finding and negotiating with others. These include the time spent in negotiating and reaching agreement, the cost of getting advice necessary to complete the agreement (such as legal and financial advice), and the costs of generating information necessary to determine whether to go ahead with the deal. They may also include the cost of litigation; as part of the bargaining process, one party may file suit as a way to pressure the other party into reaching an agreement.

Strategic bargaining costs, including holdout and free rider problems, may also increase the costs of agreement. Strategic bargaining arises when each party attempts to get as much as possible out of the other party by stalling or waiting or otherwise trying to capture the most gains from the deal. **Holdout** problems arise when one party holds out for more money on the wrongful assumption that the other party is willing to pay more; imperfect information about the other party's desires may squelch a deal that would be to both parties' advantage. **Free rider** problems arise when one party waits for others to take care of the problem; a party may not bring a nuisance suit because it wrongly assumes or hopes that others will bring the suit and pay the costs. Free rider problems are common in fund-raising drives by public television and radio stations; many listeners fail to make a donation because they assume others will do so, thereby enabling the free riders to

---

12. Both what counts as a transaction cost and whether transaction costs should be central to analysis of property rules are contested questions. *See, e.g.,* Lee Anne Fennell, *The Problem of Resource Access*, 126 Harv. L. Rev. 1471, 1479 (2013) (noting that there is no agreed-upon definition of the term, and arguing that focus on transaction costs misdirects property scholars).

get something for nothing. Other commonly discussed transaction costs include **administrative costs** (the costs of litigation or enforcement or even of maintaining a system of property) and **agency costs** (the costs associated with hiring other people to carry out a task, including the possibility that they may not carry out the employer's purposes accurately and diligently).

Transaction costs are likely to be high if the transaction involves a large number of parties. So far, we have assumed that the Eden Roc and the Fontainebleau are the only legal actors affected by the decision to build the addition to the Fontainebleau. This is clearly a false assumption. Whichever way the decision goes, there are many people who will be affected by it, both positively and negatively. Those who will benefit by construction of the addition may include present and future employees and shareholders of the Fontainebleau, the city government (if the project has the effect of increasing tourism and therefore increasing the tax base of the city), other businesses in the city that will provide services to the Fontainebleau and its customers, and the families of all the persons benefited by the Fontainebleau's operations. Those who may be harmed by the project include the shareholders and employees of the Eden Roc (assuming none benefits from the Fontainebleau's renewed prosperity) and their families, the city government (if the net effect of the project is negatively affecting tax revenues), and citizens who may lose access to part of the beach. The cost of finding all the individuals affected by this dispute, getting them involved in negotiations on one side or the other, and reaching agreement are enormous.

Transaction costs can also be high when numbers are small. Focus again on just Fontainebleau and Eden Roc. If either party wants to reverse an entitlement awarded by the court, they each have only one party with whom to bargain. If the court awards the entitlement to Eden Roc, the only way for Fontainebleau to get the right to build is to buy it from Eden Roc (and no one else). And, conversely, the only party to whom Eden Roc can sell that entitlement (if it is so inclined) is Fontainebleau, and no one else. Parties in this situation are said to be locked into a **bilateral monopoly**.[13] Although the number of people involved in these negotiations may be small (only two), the bilateral monopoly may generate high transaction costs that make it hard for parties to bargain toward an efficient solution. Each party has an incentive to try to leverage its monopoly position to extract as hard a bargain as it can from the other. In the absence of market competition to discipline these ambitions, the result can be paralysis.

Transaction costs may therefore prevent parties from making mutually beneficial exchanges. Because of the prevalence of these costs, the courts may be able to improve efficiency by paying attention to these and other impediments to bargaining. If the court can both identify relevant transaction costs and make fairly accurate judgments about which party would purchase the entitlement in the absence of these impediments to agreement, it can increase social wealth by assigning the entitlement to the party that would purchase it in the absence of these transaction costs.

---

13. Technically, the seller is trapped in a **monopsony**, a situation in which there is only one buyer.

e. Lowest cost avoider. Often the court itself lacks perfect information concerning the wants of the parties. This is because parties have strong incentives to misstate their true valuation of a particular entitlement. Courts attempting to choose legal rules in a way that promotes efficiency therefore may resort to second-best solutions. One is to look to objective measures of value, such as the value of an entitlement on the open market. But claimants may value the entitlement in question more highly than the fair market value. In light of the difficulties of answering the valuation question, a common solution proposed by law and economics scholars is to place the burden either on the party that has access to the best information and the greatest incentives to make a general social cost-benefit analysis or on the party that can avoid the harm at the lowest cost (the so-called lowest cost avoider). This is an imperfect solution because the cost of avoiding a harm can be difficult to ascertain in advance.

Recall Calabresi and Melamed's distinction between property rules and liability rules, discussed above in §2.2. The concept of transaction costs is relevant to their distinction. If a court can measure damages caused by a behavior more accurately than it can obtain information about who values an entitlement more highly, it can encourage the efficient result by resorting to a liability rule (damage) remedy over a property rule (injunction) remedy. *See* 85 Harv. L. Rev. 1107-1109. On this assumption, even if the court assigns the entitlement incorrectly, a party who values the entitlement more highly will simply pay the damages remedy and proceed. *See id.* at 1120. As we have already observed, the liability rule remedy may also have desirable distributive consequences by forcing the party who ultimately gets the entitlement to share the benefits with those who are harmed as a result. Of course, courts cannot be sure that they are measuring harms accurately, and so the possibility of inefficiency still looms large.

3. Critiques of (some kinds of) efficiency analysis. Certain common forms of economic analysis of law have been subject to a number of challenges. Below we will examine some of the most important objections.

a. Efficiency is a function of the initial distribution of wealth. Much economic analysis defines value by reference to willingness and ability to pay. This means, of course, that the preference of those who have more wealth count more in the analysis since their ability to pay is greater than those with less wealth. Determinations of efficiency therefore become a function of the distribution of wealth.

Judge Richard Posner of the Seventh Circuit Court of Appeals is one of the inventors and most influential proponents of the economic analysis of law. Although he justifies the use of wealth maximization as a measure of both social welfare and justice, he notes that reliance on "willingness to pay" as a criterion of value may sometimes conflict with achieving a result that maximizes social utility. He gives an example of a poor person desperately in need of an expensive medicine being outbid by a rich person who will benefit marginally from the medicine but who does not really need it. "In the sense of value used in this book, the pituitary extract is more valuable to the rich family than to the poor one, because value is measured by willingness to pay; but the extract would confer greater happiness in the hands of the poor family than in the hands of the rich one." Richard Posner, *Economic Analysis of Law* §1.2 at 16 (8th ed. 2011). Judge Posner notes that because value (as economic analysis defines it) is a function of ability to pay, efficiency "has limitations as an ethical criterion of social decisionmaking." *Id.*

Since efficiency when measured in terms of willingness to pay is a function of the distribution of wealth, it is incomplete as a criterion of justice without a defense of the existing distribution of wealth. Yet economic analysis cannot itself provide such a justification since it determines value by willingness and ability to pay, which in turn is determined by an initial distribution of wealth. For this reason, the initial distribution of wealth or property rights must be justified on other grounds, such as a political theory of justice.

One response to the impact of the existing distribution on willingness to pay is to structure our cost-benefit analysis to weigh costs or benefits felt by the worst-off more heavily than those felt by the best-off. Known as "prioritarianism," *see, e.g.*, Matthew D. Adler, *Well Being and Fair Distribution* 360-367 (2012), this tipping of the scales in favor of the worst-off could generate efficiency judgments that diverge dramatically based on who is affected by a particular activity. If the owners of a factory tend to be well off, and those who live near a factory (and suffer most from its activities) tend to be worse off, a prioritarian standard of efficiency might suggest awarding the entitlement to be free from pollution to the neighbors, even when we are confident that the owners of the factory are willing to pay more for the right to pollute.

b. Offer-asking problem. Transaction cost analysis depends on the assumption that it is possible, in most cases, to generate a single answer to the question who values the entitlement more by asking who is likely to end up with it after a bargaining process in the absence of transaction costs. This analysis assumes that, in the absence of transaction costs, the same party will end up with the entitlement no matter who owned the entitlement at the start of the bargaining. Whoever values the entitlement more will either keep it (if she is the initial owner) or buy it (if she is initially the non-owner). This prediction depends on the assumption that offer and asking prices are unlikely to differ very much.

Many scholars argue that this assumption is unwarranted. They suggest that, in many cases, how much a person values an entitlement will depend on which party is given the entitlement initially. *See* Duncan Kennedy, *Cost-Benefit Analysis of Entitlement Problems: A Critique*, 33 Stan. L. Rev. 387 (1981). This is true because, for a variety of reasons, offer prices will often be lower, and in some situations much lower, than asking prices. In some cases, this objection reinforces the concern about the distribution of wealth, which we have already discussed. For example, in *Boomer v. Atlantic Cement Co.*, suppose the factory is given the right to pollute. To apply transaction cost analysis, we compare the factory's asking price (to give up its freedom of action) with the homeowners' offer price (to obtain security from infliction of the harm). The homeowners' offer price is limited by their wealth, including the amount of money and other assets they currently own and the amount they would be willing and able to borrow. This amount is likely to be low and may very well be less than the amount of lost profits the factory owner would demand to shut down the factory or install pollution control devices. Assume that 50 homeowners could offer the company $50,000 ($1,000 each), but the lowest cost method of avoiding the harm by installing pollution control devices would cost the factory $500,000. The cost of avoiding the harm ($500,000) is 10 times greater than the value of avoiding it ($50,000). If this is the case, the efficient solution is to let the factory operate freely.

On the other hand, suppose we initially grant the homeowners an entitlement to be free from pollution. We then compare the homeowners' asking price and the factory owner's offer price. For purposes of simplicity, assume the cost of avoiding the harm is still $500,000 and that the factory owner is willing and able to pay any amount less than this to avoid the $500,000 expense. Assume also that each of the homeowners equally opposes operation of the factory. The most the factory owner would offer each homeowner to avoid installing the pollution control devices is $500,000 divided by 50, or $10,000. Although each of the homeowners would not be able to offer the company more than $1,000 to induce it to stop polluting, $10,000 may not be acceptable as a payment for either relocating or living with the grime, dirt, and health problems produced by the pollution. Each homeowner's asking price, in other words, may be higher than $10,000.

Mark Kelman gives several examples of asking-offer divergence:

> A fully rational individual, a professor at a business school, buys a bottle of imported wine for $5. After its value increases, a wine dealer with whom he regularly deals offers him $100 for the bottle of wine. Although he has never purchased a bottle of wine for $100, in fact, he has never paid more than $35 for one and would not do so now, the professor drinks the wine rather than sell it. . . . A consumer buys a new color television and decides to keep his old black and white set for which he could *realize* $50 [if he sold it]. If that second television were destroyed, he would not pay $50 for a second television. [In a business school class, students] were asked what they would pay to be able to see a mountain view that had been blocked off for some time by factory smoke, and what one would have to pay them to block off the view if it were not currently blocked. Again, answers invariably followed the same pattern: People would pay out a lower order magnitude of money to clear an obstructed view than they would demand to allow the factory smoke to block it.

Mark Kelman, *Consumption Theory, Production Theory, and Ideology in the Coase Theorem*, 52 S. Cal. L. Rev. 669, 678-679, 681-682 (1979). In the wine example, the professor's offer price would be $35 or less, but his asking price is over $100; in the television example, the consumer's offer price would be nothing (he would not pay for a second television), but his asking price is more than $50, while in the pollution example, the offer price would be many times lower than the asking price.

Why might we see a divergence between offer and asking prices? One reason may be practical. The homeowners in our example may, as a subjective matter, be willing to pay a lot more than $1,000 to stop the pollution, but their wealth or access to credit places an upper limit on the offer they can realistically make. These same practical limitations do not impose the same constraints on what they can demand in order to give up the entitlement.

Another possible reason for offer-asking differences is the impact of the initial allocation of the entitlement on the distribution of wealth. With asking prices, the homeowners already *own* the entitlement to prevent the pollution. They are therefore richer than they were when the entitlements are reversed. If wealth has a declining marginal utility, then making people wealthier (by granting them an entitlement) should increase what they demand to part with it.

Second, in the context of many common land use disputes involving large numbers of people affected by industrial activities, transaction costs can work to drive down offer prices because of free-rider problems, and drive up asking prices, because of hold-outs. Suppose, for example, the Eden Roc Hotel was not a private concern but a municipally owned beach open to the public. The harm caused by the building of the addition to the Fontainebleau would be borne by all the residents who used the public beach or otherwise benefited from its availability. Transaction costs would certainly prevent all parties affected by the dispute from participating in a massive negotiation. Moreover, in estimating the value of keeping the public beach sunny to the third parties affected by the project, the decision maker could use either their offer prices or their asking prices. Their offer prices are likely to be much lower than their asking prices. Because of free riders, they are likely to offer very little money to keep the Fontainebleau project from being built. If, however, we consider how much the Fontainebleau would have to pay them to give up their right to have a sunny public beach, the number is likely to be considerably higher, not least because of the potential for individuals to hold out to try to capture as high a payment as possible.

Another possible explanation for observed gaps between asking prices and offers is a psychological one. We may value what we have more than what we could have. *See* Richard Thaler, *Toward a Positive Theory of Consumer Choice,* 1 J. Econ. Behav. & Org. 39, 44 (1980). This phenomenon has become known as the **endowment effect**. One explanation for the phenomenon is provided by **prospect theory,** which asserts that people measure their well-being by reference to their current entitlements or endowments, and are *risk averse* in that they seek to avoid loss more than they seek to acquire gains of the same magnitude. *See* Amos Tversky & Daniel Kahneman, *Prospect Theory: An Analysis of Decision Under Risk,* 47 Econometrica 263 (1979).

Scores of experiments by economists and psychologists have found evidence of the endowment effect. *See, e.g.,* Colin Camerer, *Individual Decision Making,* in *The Handbook of Experimental Economics* 587, 665-670 (John H. Kagel & Alvin E. Roth eds. 1995); Daniel Kahneman et al., *Experimental Tests of the Endowment Effect and the Coase Theorem,* 98 J. Pol. Econ. 1325 (1990). One classic experiment involved students in an advanced undergraduate Law and Economics course at Cornell. Half of the class was given Cornell mugs (easily available at the campus bookstore) and the other group was given an opportunity to buy them.

> The students who were assigned mugs had a strong tendency to keep them. Whereas the Coase Theorem would have predicted that about half the mugs would trade (since transaction costs had been shown to be essentially zero in the token experiments, and mugs were randomly distributed), instead only fifteen percent of the mugs traded. And those who were endowed with mugs asked more than twice as much to give up a mug as those who didn't get a mug were willing to pay.

Christine Jolls, Cass R. Sunstein & Richard Thaler, *A Behavioral Approach to Law and Economics*, 50 Stan. L. Rev. 1471, 1484 (1998).

The endowment effect's deviation from the simplified behavioral model at the heart of classical economic theory has given the phenomenon a central place in efforts to create a field of **behavioral law and economics,** an economic analysis of law that is based on more complex, empirically grounded models of human behavior. Some scholars have called the endowment effect "the most significant single finding from behavioral economics for legal analysis to date." Russell Korobkin, *The Endowment Effect and Legal Analysis*, 97 Nw. U. L. Rev. 1227, 1229-1230 (2003); Herbert Hovenkamp, *The Limits of Preference-Based Legal Policy*, 89 Nw. U. L. Rev. 4, 55 (1994). Nevertheless, the notion (central to most discussions of the endowment effect) that, apart from wealth effects or other transaction costs, mere ownership of an object changes people's valuation of it remains controversial. A number of studies have failed to identify a pure endowment effect, leading some scholars to argue that its observation is an artifact of flawed experimental design. *See, e.g.*, Charles R. Plott & Kathryn Zeiler, *Exchange Assymetries Incorrectly Interpreted as Evidence of Endowment Theory and Prospect Theory?*, 97 Am. Econ. Rev. 1449 (2007).

Whether caused by practical constraints, wealth effects, transaction costs, or an endowment effect, gaps between asking and offer prices remain an important consideration for efficiency analysis of the law based on willingness to pay. If asking prices are likely to be higher than offer prices, we may arrive at conflicting definitions of which allocation of entitlements is efficient or wealth maximizing. In cases like this, efficiency analysis becomes indeterminate. We need some other criterion to tell us which starting place is appropriate.

c. The difficulty of defining a "voluntary" exchange. Voluntary exchanges increase social wealth by making both parties better off in their own terms. In contrast, involuntary or coerced exchanges do not make both parties better off; someone who is coerced may agree to an arrangement that leaves her worse off. To apply transaction cost analysis, it is necessary to define clearly what is and is not a voluntary exchange. But this is not easy to do; people with differing political views and theories of justice will disagree substantially on this question, particularly in their attitudes toward the problem of unequal bargaining power.

We could define coercion narrowly to include only physical duress (arm twisting) or physical threats (pressing a gun to the head); or we could define it more broadly to include economic duress caused by unequal bargaining power. There is no purely logical answer to this question.

Suppose you have fallen into a deep pit filled with poisonous snakes. I come along and observe you in the pit. I am not responsible for your predicament and have no legal duty to help you. I offer to sell you a ladder in exchange for half your future earnings. You agree to buy; I agree to sell. It is a Pareto superior exchange; you are happier with your life and half your future earnings than the alternative; I am happier as well with this outcome. Is the contract voluntary? There is no simple answer to this question. You obviously felt forced to agree; you paid an awful lot for the ladder. But you also benefited substantially by the deal. Is the contract fair? The terms are onerous for you, but so was the alternative. We could, consistent with a regime of freedom of contract, enforce this contract (because it was the result of voluntary choice and was mutually beneficial) or not enforce it (because it was the result of coerced choice and its terms are unconscionable).

d. Efficiency has a conservative bias. Many critics of economic analysis have suggested that it has a conservative bias, partly because it gives greater weight to the interests of the wealthy and the large corporations that currently wield substantial economic power. Because value is defined by reference to willingness and ability to pay, and because of the offer-asking problem, the analysis tends to privilege the interests of property owners over the interests of non-owners. To the extent that property owners are content with the fact that they own property, the analysis is likely to lead unavoidably to outcomes that differ only in marginal ways from current arrangements.

A second indication of a conservative bias in the analysis is its requirement that the analyst hold everything constant but the particular entitlement in question. The *Fontainebleau* analysis, for example, assumed that both the existing distribution of wealth and *all other legal rules* remained the same. This assumption is necessary to simplify the analysis and produce an answer. If, instead of holding everything else constant, we were to put more than one rule up for grabs at a time — for example, by suggesting changes to the tax system, the antitrust laws, the bankruptcy laws, or the rules about what constitutes unfair competition — the analysis becomes much more difficult. This is because every choice depends on the background set of legal entitlements that define the market context in which the parties bargain. It is only when we pay attention to the market and institutional structures within which bargains take place that we can imagine alternative ways of operating a decentralized market system. In contrast, the method of holding everything constant but the one entitlement in question makes consideration of alternative market structures impossible. *See* Arthur Leff, *Economic Analysis of Law: Some Realism About Nominalism,* 60 Va. L. Rev. 451 (1974); Lee Anne Fennell, *The Problem of Resource Access*, 126 Harv. L. Rev. 1471 (2013); Kennedy, *supra.*

e. Commodification. A final critique comes from Professor Margaret Jane Radin. Radin has argued that certain kinds of valued resources should not be traded in the market or otherwise treated as if they were commodities for sale; these interests are taken out of the market system (partly or totally) and effectively made inalienable. For example, we regulate safety conditions in the workplace to protect individual workers from being killed or maimed on the job, and we will not let people bargain away their right to a safe workplace. Protecting workers from unreasonably dangerous conditions may benefit the public by lowering costs, but it is also fundamentally designed to protect individual dignity. Margaret Jane Radin, *Market-Inalienability,* 100 Harv. L. Rev. 1849 (1987). Some issues are simply discussed more appropriately in nonmarket language, that is, in terms of justice and rights rather than wealth and efficiency. For example, Calabresi and Melamed argue that slavery may be inefficient because observing the plight of slaves makes "sensitive" people "unhappy." Guido Calabresi & A. Douglas Melamed, *Property Rules, Liability Rules, and Inalienability: One View of the Cathedral,* 85 Harv. L. Rev. 1089, 1111-1112 (1972). This is a pretty feeble way to condemn the institution of slavery. Do we really want to say that the reason slavery is bad is because it is inefficient, or would it be better to be able to say that it is evil and an affront to the values of liberty and equality? The language of efficiency simply cannot capture much of what we mean when we talk about justice and fairness in social relationships. *See also* Margaret Jane Radin, *Residential Rent Control,* 15 Phil. & Pub. Aff. 350 (1986).

Professor Jane Cohen has criticized a proposal by Judge Posner to introduce more free market elements into the adoption process, effectively allowing people greater freedom to buy and sell children. Cohen imagines and describes the social context within which such market transactions would take place. Her description leaves substantial doubt about whether Posner's proposal would make our society better off than before. Jane Maslow Cohen, *Posnerism, Pluralism, Pessimism,* 67 B.U. L. Rev. 105 (1987). Professors Frances Miller and Tamar Frankel have similarly argued that market theory constitutes a wholly inappropriate model for public policy decisions about adoption. Frances Miller & Tamar Frankel, *The Inapplicability of Market Theory to Adoptions,* 67 B.U. L. Rev. 99 (1987).

Even focusing narrowly on the consequences of treating certain goods as commodities, property and market solutions may backfire if they change the social meaning of practices. The economist Fred Hirsch calls this transformation of social meaning the "commercialization effect." Michael Sandel, *What Money Can't Buy* 120 (2012) (citing Fred Hirsch, *The Social Limits to Growth* (1976)).

§4 WATER RIGHTS

§4.1 Diffuse Surface Water: Flooding Problems

Armstrong v. Francis Corp.

120 A.2d 4 (N.J. 1956)

Map: (Milton Lake) Lake Avenue, Rahway, New Jersey

WILLIAM J. BRENNAN JR., J.

A small natural stream rose in Francis [Corporation's] 42-acre tract, which lies immediately south of Lake Avenue in Rahway. The stream flowed in a northerly direction

1200 feet across the Francis lands through a seven-foot box culvert under Lake Avenue and emptied into Milton Lake, 900 feet north of the avenue. It was the natural drainway for the larger 85-acre area south of Lake Avenue which includes the Francis tract.

Francis stripped its tract and erected 186 small homes thereon in a development known as Duke Estates, Section 2. It also built some 14 houses on an adjacent small tract known as Duke Estates, Section 1, lying in another drainage area. It constructed a drainage system of streets, pavements, gutters, ditches, culverts and catch basins to serve both developments. The system emptied into a corrugated iron pipe laid by Francis below the level of the natural stream bed on its lands. The pipe followed the course of the stream bed to the box culvert under Lake Avenue, although deviating from the course at some places. The pipe was covered with fill on Francis' tract and all evidence of the natural stream there has disappeared.

The drainage of the original 85 acres was thus augmented not only by the drainage of some 2 acres of the Duke Estates, Section 1, but also by waters percolating into the joints of the pipe where it lay below the level of the water table of the Francis tract. The pipe joints were expressly designed to receive such percolating waters, and, to the extent that the percolation lowered the level of the water table, the result was to provide a drier terrain more suitable to housing development.

Where the stream passes north of Lake Avenue en route to Milton Lake after leaving the box culvert it remains largely in its natural state and forms the boundary line between the residential tracts of the plaintiffs Armstrong and the defendants Klemp. The Klemps were made parties defendant by Francis' cross-claim but prevailed thereon and were allowed the same relief as the Armstrongs. The stream passes through a 36-inch culvert under the Klemp driveway and thence, across lands of the Union County Park Commission, to the Lake. The Francis improvement resulted in consequences for the Armstrongs and the Klemps fully described by Judge Sullivan in his oral opinion as follows:

> Now the stream as it emerges from the underground pipe goes under Lake Avenue and then flows past and through the Armstrong and Klemp properties is no longer the "babbling brook" that Mr. Klemp described. Now there is a constant and materially increased flow in it. The stream is never dry. The water is now discolored and evil smelling and no longer has any fish in it. A heavy deposit of silt or muck up to eighteen inches in depth now covers the bottom of the stream. After a heavy rainstorm the stream undergoes a remarkable change for several hours. All of the upstream rain water that used to be absorbed or held back is now channeled in undiminished volume and at great speed into this stream. This causes a flash rise or crest in the stream, with a tremendous volume of water rushing through at an accelerated speed. As a result, the stream has flooded on several occasions within the last year, although this was unheard of previously. More distressing, however, is the fact that during these flash situations the body of water moving at the speed it does tears into the banks of the brook particularly where the bed may turn or twist. At a point even with the plaintiff's [Armstrong's] house the stream makes a sharp bend. Here the effect of the increased flow of water is most apparent since the bank on plaintiff's side of the stream has been eaten away to the extent of about ten feet. This erosion is now within fifteen feet of the Armstrong septic tank

> system. It is difficult to say where it will stop, where the erosion will stop. The silting has, of course, raised the bed of the stream up to eighteen inches in places and the raising of the stream results in water action against different areas of the bank so that the erosion problem while unpredictable is ominous. The eating away of the banks in several places has loosened rocks or boulders which have been rolled downstream by the force of the water. Those stones, however, as they rolled through the Klemp culvert cracked and broke the sides and bottom of the culvert and the water is now threatening to undermine the entire masonry. There is no doubt but that the defendant's activities have caused all of the condition just related.
>
> A matter of some concern is that defendant's housing development occupies only about one-half of the area which drains into this brook. At the present time there is a forty acre undeveloped section to the south of the defendant and it is reasonable to assume that it, too, will be improved and built upon at some future time. Defendant's underground trunk sewer was built to accommodate any possible runoff from this tract. If and when that section is developed, Armstrong and Klemp will have that much more erosion, silting and flooding to deal with.

Judge Sullivan concluded that the Armstrongs and the Klemps were plainly entitled to relief in these circumstances and "that the only sensible and permanent solution to the problem is to pipe the rest of the brook," that is, from the culvert outlet at Lake Avenue the entire distance to Milton Lake. A plan for that purpose had been prepared by Francis' engineer and approved by the Armstrongs and the Klemps at a time when efforts were being made to compromise the dispute before the trial. The final judgment orders Francis, at its expense, forthwith to proceed with and complete within 60 days the work detailed on that plan. The Union County Park Commission has given its formal consent to the doing of the work called for by the plan on its lands.

> **Terms:**
> ***Damnum absque injuria*** means damage without a wrongful act. It is a harm that someone suffers that does not give rise to a legal cause of action.

The important legal question raised by the appeal is whether the damage suffered by the Armstrongs and the Klemps is ***damnum absque injuria***, namely, merely the non-actionable consequences of the privileged expulsion by Francis of waters from its tract as an incident to the improvement thereof.

The casting of surface waters from one's own land upon the land of another, in circumstances where the resultant material harm to the other was foreseen or foreseeable, would appear on the face of it to be tortious conduct, as actionable where the consequences of an unreasonable use of the possessor's land, as in the case of the abstraction or diversion of water from a stream which unreasonably interferes with the use of the stream below, and as in the case of the unreasonable use of percolating or subterranean waters, and as in the case of artificial construction on one's land which unreasonably speeds the waters of a stream past one's property onto that of an owner below, causing harm. Yet only the courts of the states of New Hampshire and Minnesota have expressly classified the possessor's liability, where imposed, for harm by the expulsion of surface waters to be a tort liability. Those courts have evolved the "reasonable use" rule laying down the test that each possessor is legally privileged to make a reasonable use of his land, even though the flow of surface waters is altered thereby and causes some harm to others, but incurs liability when his harmful interference with the flow of surface waters is unreasonable. *Franklin v. Durgee*, 51 A. 911 (N.H. 1901); *Sheehan v. Flynn*, 61 N.W. 462 (Minn. 1894).

All other states have treated the legal relations of the parties as a branch of property law — that is, have done so, if we emphasize only the language of the decisions and ignore the actual results reached. Two rules have been evolved which, in their statement, are directly opposed, for under one the possessor would not be liable in any case and under the other he would be liable in every case. But an analysis of the results reached under both rules shows that neither is anywhere strictly applied. The first rule, purportedly applicable in our own State, stems from the view that surface waters are the common enemy. The "common enemy" rule emphasizes the possessor's privilege to rid his lands of surface waters as he will. That rule "is, in substance, that a possessor of land has an unlimited and unrestricted legal privilege to deal with the surface water on his land as he pleases, regardless of the harm which he may thereby cause others." The other rule, borrowed from the civil law of foreign nations and called the "civil law" rule, emphasizes not the privileges of the possessor but the duties of the possessor to other landowners who are affected by his expulsion of surface waters from his lands. That rule is to the effect that "a person who interferes with the natural flow of surface waters so as to cause an invasion of another's interests in the use and enjoyment of his land is subject to liability to the other."

[T]he courts here and elsewhere, in terms of results, have actually come out at the "reasonable use" doctrine. Professor Kinyon and Mr. McClure have summarized the course of the decisions as follows:

> From the rationale of the common enemy rule, it would seem that a possessor of land has an unlimited privilege to rid his land of the surface water upon it or to alter its course by whatever means he wishes, irrespective of the manner of doing it or the harm thereby caused to others. However, in substantially all of the jurisdictions purportedly committed to that rule, the courts have refused to go that far. Most of these courts have developed a qualifying rule which is, in substance, that a possessor of land is not privileged to discharge upon adjoining land, by artificial means, large quantities of surface water in a concentrated flow otherwise than through natural drainways, regardless of the means by which the surface water is collected and discharged. The scope of this qualifying rule varies from jurisdiction to jurisdiction, but it has been adopted in one form or another. . . .
>
> In jurisdictions purportedly committed to the civil law rule, one would expect from the rationale of that rule to find that a possessor has no privilege, under any circumstances, to interfere with the surface water on his land so as to cause it to flow upon adjoining land in a manner or quantity substantially different from its natural flow. An examination of the cases in these jurisdictions, however, reveals that the courts have refused to follow the rationale of the rule to that extent. In most of these jurisdictions the courts have recognized that a possessor must have a privilege, under certain circumstances, to make minor alterations in the natural flow of surface water where necessary to the normal use and improvement of his land, even though such alterations cause the surface water to flow upon adjoining land in a somewhat unnatural manner. This is especially true where the possessor disposes of the surface water by depositing it in existing natural drainways. Consequently, the courts . . . , with variations from state to

> state, have held that a possessor has a limited privilege to discharge surface water on other lands, by artificial means in a non-natural manner. . . . Kinyon & McClure, *Interferences with Surface Waters*, 24 Minn. L. Rev. 899, 916, 920, 913 (1940).

The authors conclude:

> [Thus] even though the broad principle of reasonable use has not made much headway as an articulate basis of decision, substantially all of the jurisdictions which purport to follow the civil law or common enemy rules have engrafted upon them numerous qualifications and exceptions which, in actual result, produce decisions which are not as conflicting as would be expected, and which would generally be reached under the reasonable use rule.

We therefore think it appropriate that this court declare, as we now do, our adherence in terms to the reasonable use rule and thus accord our expressions in cases of this character to the actual practice of our courts. [I]t is significant of the true state of the law that the *Restatement* [*(Second)*] *of Torts* §833, has adopted the reasonable use test as the rule actually prevailing.

The rule of reasonableness has the particular virtue of flexibility. The issue of reasonableness or unreasonableness becomes a question of fact to be determined in each case upon a consideration of all the relevant circumstances, including such factors as the amount of harm caused, the foreseeability of the harm which results, the purpose or motive with which the possessor acted, and all other relevant matter. It is, of course, true that society has a great interest that land shall be developed for the greater good. It is therefore properly a consideration in these cases whether the utility of the possessor's use of his land outweighs the gravity of the harm which results from his alteration of the flow of surface waters. But while today's mass home building projects, of which the Francis development is typical, are assuredly in the social good, no reason suggests itself why, in justice, the economic costs incident to the expulsion of surface waters in the transformation of the rural or semi-rural areas of our State into urban or suburban communities should be borne in every case by adjoining landowners rather than by those who engage in such projects for profit. Social progress and the common well-being are in actuality better served by a just and right balancing of the competing interests according to the general principles of fairness and common sense which attend the application of the rule of reason.

Notes and Questions

1. **Diffuse surface water.** Diffuse surface water is "drainage water from rain, melting snow, and springs that runs over the surface of the earth . . . but does not amount to a stream." William B. Stoebuck & Dale A. Whitman, *The Law of Property* §7.6, at 430 (3d ed. 2000). Such water may coalesce into a pool or marsh but is not stable enough to constitute a lake or stream. Surface water is generally considered a nuisance, and most property owners are anxious to get rid of it.

The power to withdraw surface water is subject to substantial regulation, even if no other owners are harmed through flooding or discharge of water onto their lands.

Federal and state environmental laws regulate drainage of "wetlands" and the ability of owners to fill in such lands for development purposes. The federal *Clean Water Act*, 33 U.S.C. §1344, for example, has been interpreted to place limits on the ability of owners to drain and fill in wetlands for development purposes, and many states regulate such development to protect the environment. *See, e.g., Massachusetts Water Management Act*, Mass. Gen. Laws ch. 21G, §§1-19.

Disputes arise when property owners attempt to drain surface water off their property through pipes and drainage systems that may cause flooding or other water damage to neighboring property. Damage may also occur because development of property naturally changes drainage patterns and may cause increased runoff of surface water, even if no drainage system is installed. Property owners on lower land object to the intentional or unintentional flooding of their property by development elsewhere. As Justice Brennan explains, state courts have followed three different rules.

a. Common enemy rule. The *common enemy* doctrine allows property owners the absolute freedom to develop their property without liability for any resulting damage to neighbors caused by increased runoff of surface water. This doctrine adopts the *damnum absque injuria* solution to land use conflicts: The defendant is privileged to develop its property and to expel unwanted surface water without liability for any resultant damage to the neighbors' property. This rule may be the law in about 17 states. Stoebuck & Whitman, *supra*, at 431. Most courts adopting this rule have substantially modified it. Some impose liability for negligence, allowing damages for harm caused by conduct that foreseeably causes unreasonable harm to neighbors. Many impose liability on the developing property owner if she installs pipes or drainage devices designed to collect and expel water in greater quantity or with greater force than would naturally occur or in a different direction than the natural drainage patterns of the land. *See Haith v. Atchison County*, 793 S.W.2d 151 (Mo. Ct. App. 1990); *Halverson v. Skagit County*, 983 P.2d 643 (Wash. 1999). *Cf. Lucas v. Rawl Family Limited Partnership*, 598 S.E.2d 712 (S.C. 2004) (common enemy rule unless defendant's actions constitute a nuisance *per se*).

b. Natural flow rule. At the other extreme is the *natural flow* or *civil law* doctrine, which grants the injured property owner absolute security against injury from flooding caused by a neighboring property owner's development of her property. Owners are entitled to discharge water through natural drainage pathways, but any development that alters the amount, force of flow, or direction of the natural drainage will result in liability for any resulting harm to neighboring land. This doctrine adopts the *strict liability* or *veto rights* solution to land use conflicts; the injured plaintiff has the legal right to stop the defendant's activity and to recover damages for harm already inflicted. *See* S.D. Codified Laws §46A-10A-70; *Powers v. Judd*, 553 A.2d 139 (Vt. 1988).

Until recently, the natural flow rule was the law in roughly half the states. Today it persists in only a few states. The natural flow doctrine might inhibit land development because most development will change drainage patterns. To encourage development, most states following this rule have adopted exceptions to allow minor increases in the natural flow of surface water. Other states limit application of the natural flow doctrine to rural land and apply the reasonable use test to urban land. *See First Lady, LLC v. JMF Properties, LLC,* 681 N.W.2d 94 (S.D. 2004) (natural flow applicable except in urban settings, where reasonable use test applies); Stoebuck & Whitman, *supra,* at 432. Of course, development is possible even with strict liability on developers for harm caused by their development; they simply must compensate those property owners harmed by their development. If the development is profitable enough, the project may well go forward despite liability for resulting damage or for investment to prevent flooding.

c. Reasonable use test. The New Jersey Supreme Court in *Armstrong* adopted a middle position, the *reasonable use* test. This rule requires the decision maker to determine in specific cases whether the defendant's conduct caused unreasonable interference with the neighbors' use of their land. This determination involves balancing the social benefit derived from development of defendant's property, the availability of cost-effective means to avoid or mitigate the harm, and the gravity of the harm to plaintiff's property. Substantial harm to neighboring property is likely to be found to be unreasonable, even if the value of defendant's conduct far outweighs the value of the plaintiff's property. It is a separate question whether the plaintiff will be limited to damages for the harm or may get an injunction stopping the harmful development from occurring. This test has rapidly gained adherents and is now the majority rule. *See, e.g., Locklin v. City of Lafayette,* 867 P.2d 724 (Cal. 1994); *Westland Skating Center v. Gus Machado Buick, Inc.,* 542 So. 2d 959 (Fla. 1989); *Heins Implement Co. v. Missouri Highway & Transportation Commission,* 859 S.W.2d 681 (Mo. 1993).

2. Policy considerations. What reasons did the court give in *Armstrong* for adopting the reasonable use test? Are you persuaded? What are the disadvantages of the reasonable use test? What arguments could you make that the common enemy rule is preferable? What arguments could you make that the natural flow rule is better than both of the other rules?

Policy Arguments and Counterarguments

Justice Brennan appealed to a number of policy considerations in his opinion in *Armstrong.* Lawyers appeal to policy arguments to persuade the court to adopt a rule of law that favors their client's interests. It is essential for you to understand and master these arguments so that you can become an effective advocate for a client on either side of a dispute. Policy arguments appeal to values that are widely shared. However, they also demonstrate that many values we hold may conflict. The fact that it is almost always possible to generate plausible, conventional legal arguments on both sides of a case in which both parties have intuitively attractive claims does not mean that it is impossible to resolve legal disputes. It simply means that decision makers must accommodate these conflicting moral impulses to make considered judgments about the relative strength of competing claims in particular social contexts.

This compilation of arguments is not meant to be exclusive. You will see these arguments and others in legal analysis in both judicial opinions and legal scholarship. You will invent or construct new arguments yourself.

Rights: Freedom of Action versus Security

1. Justice in social relationships. Rights arguments appeal to fairness or justice in social relationships. Those relationships sometimes involve conflicting interests, and it is the job of both courts and legislatures to take those interests into account, accommodating them when possible and choosing between them when necessary. Justice Shirley Abrahamson of the Wisconsin Supreme Court explains that the "rights of neighboring landowners are relative; the uses of one must not unreasonably impair the uses or enjoyment of the other." *Prah v. Maretti*, 321 N.W.2d 182, 187 (Wis. 1982). Although landowners are free to use their property as they wish, they do "not have an absolute or unlimited right to use the land in a way that injures the rights of others." *Id.*

2. Rights as freedom of action. On one hand, landowners may claim the "right . . . to use their property as they wish[]," or the "right to develop [their] property . . . without regard to the effect of such development upon [others]." *Id.* at 189, 188. As Justice William Callow, also a member of the Wisconsin Supreme Court, stated, "I firmly believe that a landowner's right to use his property within the limits of ordinances, statutes, and restrictions of record where such use is necessary to serve his legitimate needs is a fundamental precept of a free society. . . ." *Id.* at 194 (Callow, J., dissenting). We can refer to the right to control the use of one's property as a right of freedom of action. For example, the defendant in *Armstrong* claimed a right to develop its property without having to take into account the possibility of increased surface flooding on neighboring property. To require the developer to foresee and prevent all damage from surface water drainage to other property or to compensate for any losses caused by development would arguably interfere too much with the developer's freedom to develop its own property.

3. Rights as security. The converse of the right to use one's property is the right to have one's property protected from harm. Justice Abrahamson explains that property holders have a right to be protected from land use by a neighbor who "unreasonably interferes with another's enjoyment of his or her property. . . ." *Id.* at 187. The freedom to use property is limited to the extent necessary to protect other property holders' rights of security. Similarly, Justice Brennan argues in *Armstrong* that while development is "in the social good, no reason suggests itself why, in justice, the economic costs incident [to development] should be borne in every case by adjoining landowners rather than by those who engage in such projects for profit." 120 A.2d at 10.

4. Value judgments. Each case in this chapter raises the question where to draw the line between one possessor's right to use her property freely and another possessor's right to security. The best solution may be one that protects the legitimate interests of both parties to some extent. The issue requires careful reflection on the social context in which the dispute arises and value judgments about the merits of the competing claims. These judgments include determining whether the interests asserted are legitimate, just claims and deciding which should prevail when conflict between legitimate claims cannot be avoided.

Social Utility: Competition versus Secure Investment

1. Promoting the general welfare by enacting appropriate incentives. Social utility arguments appeal to the goal of generating rules of law that promote socially desirable conduct and deter socially harmful conduct. Most conduct has both beneficial and harmful effects. When two legitimate activities conflict, it becomes necessary to choose which activity should prevail. Legal rules may authorize or even encourage particular kinds of land use by declaring that use privileged, freeing the possessor to engage in the activity without fear of liability to others. The rules in force also may discourage or prohibit other kinds of land use by granting those injured by the activity the right to obtain damages or an injunction to limit or even terminate the activity.

Social utility arguments have two components. First, they assert that particular legal rules create specified incentives that encourage or discourage certain kinds of behavior. Second, they evaluate that behavior by asserting that a particular rule is better than the alternatives either because it promotes socially desirable conduct — behavior that has greater social benefits than social costs — or because it discourages socially harmful conduct — an activity whose costs outweigh its benefits.

2. Promoting competition. Lawyers often argue that social welfare is maximized when the government deregulates economic activity by freeing property holders to develop their property as they see fit. Justice William Callow argued that "society has a significant interest in not restricting land development." 321 N.W.2d at 194 (Callow, J., dissenting). Rules governing land use should be chosen in a way that promotes "land improvement and development" by protecting landowners from ruinous liability. *Id.* at 195. Shielding property holders from liability encourages investment in socially beneficial economic activities. Every use of land has potential effects on neighbors and the community as a whole, some positive and some negative. For example, building a house or factory may increase traffic and congestion in an area or block a beautiful view; requiring the developer to compensate those who suffer these negative effects may stifle desirable economic development.

3. Protecting the security of investment. The converse argument is that no one will invest to develop property if the investment is not secure. The basis of the institution of property is to provide security for justified expectations. Why take the risk of building a house if your neighbor is free to flood your property and destroy the value of your investment? Providing this kind of security requires legal rules that give developers incentives to use their property in ways that minimize the harm to other property owners. Development generally should be encouraged, but not to the extent that its harmful effects outweigh its benefits. As Justice Abrahamson noted in *Prah,* "unrestricted development of land" may cause more harm than good. 321 N.W.2d at 190.

The goal should be to promote only "reasonable" development (whose social benefits outweigh its social costs) and to discourage "unreasonable" development. *Id.* at 191.

Land development benefits society, but it also may negatively affect neighboring property. If the developer does not have to pay for these negative effects, a divergence arises between the private costs of the project (the costs of building the homes) and the total social costs of the project (the costs to the developer of building the homes plus the external harmful effects on neighbors). Here the private benefits of the project will outweigh its private costs, even though the total social costs of the project may be higher than its total social benefits. Requiring the developer to compensate those burdened by the development induces the developer to take the external costs into account or to internalize them. By bringing private costs in line with social costs, the rules in force can encourage activity whose social benefits outweigh its social costs and discourage activity whose total social costs outweigh its social benefits.[14]

4. **Balancing interests.** Assessing social utility arguments requires a judgment about how people will actually respond to alternative legal rules; it also involves predicting and evaluating the relative costs and benefits of alternative legal rules. This is often expressed in judicial opinions by stating that it is necessary to "balance the interests" of the parties to determine which rule of law should be adopted.

Formal Realizability or Administrability: Rigid Rules versus Flexible Standards

1. **Predictability versus justice in the individual case.** While rights and social utility considerations appeal to the substantive justice or wisdom of legal rules, formal considerations concern the manner in which rules are expressed and implemented.

2. **Rules.** Legal rules are sometimes defined in a way that allows mechanical application. For example, the rigid rule allowing 18-year olds to vote cleanly answers the question whether a 17-year old may vote — the answer is no. No need for interpretation or judgment arises. Duncan Kennedy notes that "the two great social virtues of formally realizable rules, as opposed to standards or principles, are the restraint of official arbitrariness and certainty." Duncan Kennedy, *Form and Substance in Private Law Adjudication*, 89 Harv. L. Rev. 1687, 1688 (1976). Rules offer certainty or predictability because each citizen knows her rights and obligations. The rules also control arbitrary judicial discretion, with the propitious result that like cases are treated alike and judges are prevented from deciding cases by reference to impermissible and perhaps unconscious biases. "[I]f private actors can know in advance the incidence of official intervention, they will adjust their activities in advance to take account of them. From the point of view of the state, this increases the likelihood that private activity

14. Note that property development has *external benefits* as well as *external costs*: It may create jobs, expand the tax base, or provide needed housing. Requiring the developer to pay the internal and external costs of the project may not result in the best result from the standpoint of society as a whole if the total social benefits of the project substantially exceed the private profits to the developer.

will follow a desired pattern. From the point of view of the citizenry, it removes the inhibiting effect on action that occurs when one's gains are subject to sporadic legal catastrophe." *Id.* at 1688-1689.

Rigid rules, do, however, have distinct disadvantages. By definition, they require particular results, even if those results seem unfair under the circumstances. An 18-year-old-voter rule is both over- and underinclusive. Some persons younger than 18 are mature enough to vote but are not allowed to do so; some persons older than 18 are not mature enough to vote but are allowed to do so. "From the point of view of the purpose of the rules, this combined over- and underinclusiveness amounts not just to licensing but to requiring official arbitrariness. If we adopt the rule, it is because of a judgment that this kind of arbitrariness is less serious than the arbitrariness and uncertainty that would result from empowering the official to apply [a standard] directly to the facts of each case." *Id.* at 1689.

3. Standards. In contrast to rigid rules, legal doctrines are sometimes flexible. Such doctrines take the form of standards or principles. Sometimes standards "refer directly to one of the substantive objectives of the legal order, such as good faith, due care, fairness, unconscionability, unjust enrichment, and reasonableness." *Id.* at 1688. Other times, standards take the form of lists of "factors" that are to be considered in adjudicating a case. Flexible standards have the benefit of obtaining justice in the individual case by allowing the decision maker to take account of all relevant circumstances. Because they cannot be mechanically applied, however, they may offer less predictability to citizens or guidance to judges and juries in adjudicating cases.

4. Formal realizability and social utility. Kennedy notes that the choice between rules and standards is affected by the substantive goal of developing rules that have desirable social effects. If rules are more predictable than standards, they may promote social welfare because they enable people to plan and because they induce actors to look out for their own interests knowing when the law will, and will not, protect them. However, because of their rigidity, rules are almost certain to be either over- or underinclusive, or both. Using rules means that "sometimes perfectly innocent behavior will be punished, and that sometimes plainly guilty behavior will escape sanction. These costs of mechanical over- and underinclusion are the price of avoiding the potential arbitrariness and uncertainty of a standard." *Id.* at 1695.

Standards may therefore sometimes promote social welfare better than rules because the very uncertainty of how the law will apply to one's actions will discourage socially undesirable conduct. Actors will imagine whether they can justify their actions to a jury, and this worry may deter them from engaging in socially harmful conduct. Rules, in contrast, "allow the proverbial 'bad man' to 'walk the line,' that is, to take conscious advantage of underinclusion to perpetuate [wrongs] with impunity." *Id.* at 1696. Conversely, confidence that a jury of one's peers would find one's conduct reasonable would induce the actor to go forward, when a rigid rule might deter such socially valuable conduct.

A standard counterargument in favor of rules is that rules are indeed more predictable than standards, and the benefits achieved by predictability far outweigh any loss to social welfare due to the imprecision of rules. A standard response to that argument is that it is not at all clear that rules are more predictable than standards. After all, standards become more predictable over time as their application is elaborated through case law. And rules cannot be mechanically applied because they do not determine the scope of their own application. The common law system works by *distinguishing* cases. A rule that grants husbands the right to inherit the family home upon death of their wives is not likely to be applied if the husband murders his wife. Owners have the right to exclude non-owners from their property, but restaurants cannot exclude people based on their race. Because we must determine the fact situations to which rules apply, it cannot be the case that their application is purely mechanical. Thus, the advantages of rules over standards in terms of predictability may well be overstated.

Judicial Role and Institutional Competence

Judicial role and institutional competence arguments are concerned with the proper spheres of authority of legal institutions and the proper relations among separate branches of government in the legal system. Arguments about the spheres of authority of different governmental actors revolve around the question of which government officials may appropriately modernize or change existing rules of law or patterns of social practice.

Judicial role arguments address the following questions: What is the proper role of the courts as lawmakers? What is the proper division of lawmaking authority between the courts and the legislature? What is the proper way for courts to interpret and implement legislative enactments? These "judicial role" arguments typically focus on the democratic legitimacy of legislatures and the relative illegitimacy of courts, particularly unelected federal courts. Arguments about the proper method of statutory interpretation, judicial activism, and judicial restraint are usually rooted in assumptions or arguments about the proper judicial role.

Institutional competence arguments rely on stylized descriptions of how courts (or legislatures or administrative agencies) go about making decisions, and how those processes might offer particular advantages or disadvantages when resolving specific sorts of questions. For example, lawyers will often observe that courts are more passive decision makers than legislatures. They must wait for cases to come to them and they must accept the information that litigants (with varying resources and different quality of representation) bring to them. These limitations appear to restrict the competence of judges to craft broad rules or administer remedies that will require long-term supervision. On the other hand, legislatures and administrative agencies may be subject to lobbying and capture by interest groups with the resources to involve themselves in the lawmaking or rulemaking process. Somewhat differently, they may be particularly vulnerable to political pressure to reach decisions that are likely to appeal to majorities at the expense of minorities. The structured formality of litigation, someone might argue, makes courts more resistant to each of these sorts of pressures. Our point here is not to endorse the accuracy of any of these empirical claims, but just to introduce you to this style of argument.

Problem

Assume that the defendant in *Armstrong* advocated the common enemy rule, while the plaintiff advocated the reasonable use test. Assume also that, based on earlier court decisions, the jurisdiction had previously applied the common enemy rule.

1. Construct defendant's arguments in favor of the common enemy rule based on (a) rights, (b) social utility, (c) formal realizability, and (d) institutional role.

2. Construct plaintiff's arguments in favor of the reasonable use test based on (a) rights, (b) social utility, (c) formal realizability, and (d) institutional role.

§4.2 Ownership of Water

See Chapter 7, §8.2, at pages 500-510.

§5 SUPPORT RIGHTS

Landowners own both the surface and the earth beneath the surface unless they have sold the subsurface to others in the form of mineral rights.[15] The subsurface is needed to support both the surface of the land and structures built on it. Excavation or construction on a particular parcel may have the unwanted effect of undermining the support for neighboring land. For example, if an owner excavates all the way up to the property line, the neighboring land may be insufficiently strong to stand up by itself; some of it may fall into the hole created by the excavation. The excavation has undermined the **lateral support** for the neighboring land by taking away the land along the side of the neighbor's subsurface that held it up. Alternatively, an owner may excavate and dig a well to draw water from underneath his own land. Since groundwater beneath the surface is diffused throughout it, the withdrawal of water may draw some water from beneath neighboring property. If enough water is withdrawn, the neighbor's subsurface may collapse, undermining support for the surface from underneath and depriving the neighbor of **subjacent support**. The materials in this section address the rules governing conflicts between neighbors whose activities undermine support for land and structures on it.

15. Mineral rights include the right to extract minerals from beneath the surface of the land.

§5.1 Lateral Support

Noone v. Price

298 S.E.2d 218 (W. Va. 1982)

Map: Glen Ferris, West Virginia

RICHARD NEELY, Justice.

In 1960 the plaintiffs below, and appellants in this Court, Mr. and Mrs. William H. Noone, bought a house located on the side of a mountain in Glen Ferris, West Virginia. This house had been constructed in 1928 or 1929 by Union Carbide, and in 1964, four years after plaintiffs purchased the house, plaintiffs became aware that the wall under their front porch was giving way and that the living room plaster had cracked.

The defendant below, appellee in this Court, Mrs. Marion T. Price, lived directly below the plaintiffs at the foot of the hill in a house that was built in 1912. Sometime between 1912 and 1919 a wall of stone and concrete was constructed along the side of the hill, ten to twelve feet behind the defendant's house. This wall was a hundred to a hundred and twenty-five feet long, approximately four feet high, and of varying degrees of thickness. The wall lay entirely on the defendant's property, and was approximately ten to twelve feet from the property line that divided the defendant's property from the plaintiffs' property. The defendant purchased her house in 1955 and lived there until 1972, when she sold the property. Before the defendant's purchase, the wall had fallen into disrepair.

When the plaintiffs discovered that their house was slipping down the hill, they complained to the defendant that their problem was the result of deterioration in the defendant's retaining wall. The defendant did nothing to repair the wall and the plaintiffs repaired the damage to their house at a cost of approximately $6,000.

The action before us now was filed in 1968 for damages of $50,000 for failure of the defendant to provide lateral support for the plaintiffs' land, and her negligent failure to provide lateral support for their house. Plaintiffs alleged that the wall was constructed to provide support to the slope upon which their house was built, and that the disrepair and collapse of the wall caused the slipping and eventual damage to their property.

The defendant denied that the wall on her property provided support to the slope, or that the condition of her wall caused the slipping and damage to the plaintiffs' property. In addition, the defendant asserted that the plaintiffs were negligent in failing to take reasonable precautions to protect their own property and were estopped from suing her because the wall on her property was erected by her predecessor in title and the plaintiffs had purchased their property with knowledge of the wall's deteriorating condition.

I

This case provides an opportunity that we have not had for many years to address the obligations of adjoining landowners to provide lateral support to each other's land. Support is lateral when the supported and supporting lands are divided by a vertical plane. The withdrawal of lateral support may subject the landowner withdrawing the support to strict liability or to liability for negligence. We have recognized both forms of liability in *Walker v. Strosnider*, 67 S.E. 1087 (W. Va. 1910) and this case, remarkably enough, is still in harmony with the modern weight of authority as articulated in the *Restatement (Second) of Torts*.

> **Terms:**
> ***Ex jure naturae*** means "by natural law." This term described rights that were thought to inhere in ownership of land and did not have to be obtained by a separate bargain and contract with one's neighbor.

As a general rule, "[a] landowner is entitled, ***ex jure naturae***, to lateral support in the adjacent land for his soil." Point 2, syllabus, *McCabe v. City of Parkersburg*, 79 S.E.2d 87 (W. Va. 1953). Therefore, as we said in syllabus point 2 of *Walker, supra*:

> An excavation, made by an adjacent owner, so as to take away the lateral support, afforded to his neighbor's ground, by the earth so removed, and cause it, of its own weight, to fall, slide or break away, makes the former liable for the injury, no matter how carefully he may have excavated. Such right of support is a property right and absolute.

An adjacent landowner is strictly liable for acts of commission and omission on his part that result in the withdrawal of lateral support to his neighbor's property. This strict liability, however, is limited to land in its natural state; there is no obligation to support the added weight of buildings or other structures that land cannot naturally support. However, the majority of American jurisdictions hold that if land in its natural state would be capable of supporting the weight of a building or other structure, and such building or other structure is damaged because of the subsidence of the land itself, then the owner of the land on which the building or structure is constructed can recover damages for both the injury to his land and the injury to his building or structure. The West Virginia cases are largely consistent with this position, although none has expressly so held.

The converse of the preceding rule is also the law: where an adjacent landowner provides sufficient support to sustain the weight of land in its natural state, but the land slips as a direct result of the additional weight of a building or other structure, then in the absence of negligence on the part of the adjoining landowner, there is no cause of action against such adjoining landowner for damage either to the land, the building, or other structure.

The issue in the case before us concerns the proper application of the strict liability rule. The circuit court improperly awarded summary judgment because the plaintiffs should have been allowed to prove that their land was sufficiently strong in its natural state to support the weight of their house, and that their house was damaged as a result of a chain reaction that began when the land in its natural state, toward the bottom of the hill, slipped as a result of the withdrawal of lateral support occasioned by the deterioration of the retaining wall, causing, in turn, successive parts of the hillside to subside until the ripple effect reached the foundation of the plaintiffs' house.

The cases recognize that lateral support sufficient to hold land in its natural state may be insufficient to support the additional weight of a building or other structure. If, therefore, as a result of the additional weight of a building or other structure, so much strain is placed upon existing natural or artificial lateral support that the support will no longer hold, then in the absence of negligence, there is no liability whatsoever on the part of an adjoining landowner. In the case before us, this means that if the weight of the plaintiffs' house placed so much pressure on the soil that the house itself caused the subsidence, and the land would not have subsided without the weight of the house, then the plaintiffs cannot recover.

II

A theoretical problem that presents itself in all of these cases is the extent to which the obligation of support runs with the land. The weight of authority appears to be that where an actor, whether he be an owner, possessor, lessee, or third-party stranger, removes necessary support he is liable, and an owner cannot avoid this liability by transferring the land to another. Nevertheless, when an actor who removes natural lateral support substitutes artificial support to replace it, such as a retaining wall, the wall then becomes an incident to and a burden on the land upon which it is constructed, and subsequent owners and possessors have an obligation to maintain it.

In the case *sub judice*, the plaintiffs' land had no buildings erected on it at the time the defendant's predecessor in title built the retaining wall on his property; therefore, he needed only to erect a retaining wall sufficient to provide support for their soil. He was not required to furnish a wall sufficient to support any structure which they might erect upon their property. The defendant, as his successor, merely had the obligation to maintain the wall to support the plaintiffs' land in its natural condition. Defendant was not required to strengthen the wall to the extent that it would provide support for the weight of plaintiffs' buildings.

III

Since the pleadings in the case before us make reference to negligence, it is appropriate here to address the scope of a negligence theory. In general, it has been held that while an adjoining landowner has no obligation to support the buildings and other structures on his neighbor's land, nonetheless, if those structures are actually being supported, a neighbor who withdraws such support must do it in a non-negligent way. In an action predicated on strict liability for removing support for the land in its natural state, the kind of lateral support withdrawn is material, but the quality of the actor's conduct is immaterial; however, in a proceeding based upon negligence, the kind of lateral support withdrawn is immaterial, and the quality of the actor's conduct is material. Comment e, *Restatement (Second) of Torts* §819 succinctly explains the nature of liability for negligence.

> The owner of land may be unreasonable in withdrawing lateral support needed by his neighbor for artificial conditions on the neighbor's land in either of two respects. First, he may make an unnecessary excavation, believing correctly that it will cause his neighbor's land to subside because of the pressure of artificial structures on the

neighbor's land. If his conduct is unreasonable either in the digging or in the intentional failure to warn his neighbor of it, he is subject to liability to the neighbor for the harm caused by it. The high regard that the law has by long tradition shown for the interest of the owner in the improvement and utilization of his land weighs heavily in his favor in determining what constitutes unreasonable conduct on his part in such a case. Normally the owner of the supporting land may withdraw lateral support that is not naturally necessary, for any purpose that he regards as useful provided that the manner in which it is done is reasonable. But all the factors that enter into the determination of the reasonableness or unreasonableness of the actor's conduct must be considered, and in a particular case the withdrawal itself may be unreasonable. Thus, if the actor's sole purpose in excavating his land is to harm his neighbor's structures, the excavation itself is unreasonable. Furthermore, although for the purpose of permanently leveling the land it may be reasonable to withdraw support that is not naturally necessary, it may be unreasonable to make an excavation for a building that will itself require a foundation, without providing for the safeguarding of the neighbor's structures during the progress of the work. Likewise it is normally unreasonable not to notify an adjacent landowner of excavations that certainly will harm his structures, unless the neighbor otherwise has notice.

Secondly, the owner of land may be negligent in failing to provide against the risk of harm to his neighbor's structures. This negligence may occur either when the actor does not realize that any harm will occur to his neighbor's structures or when the actor realizes that there is a substantial risk to his neighbor's land and fails to take adequate provisions to prevent subsidence, either by himself taking precautions or by giving his neighbor an opportunity to take precautions. Although the law accords the owner of the supporting land great freedom in withdrawing from another's land support that is not naturally necessary in respect to the withdrawal itself, it does not excuse withdrawal in a manner that involves an unreasonable risk of harm to the land of another. The owner in making the excavation is therefore required to take reasonable precautions to minimize the risk of causing subsidence of his neighbor's land. In determining whether a particular precaution is reasonably required, the extent of the burden that the taking of it will impose upon the actor is a factor of great importance.

In the case of *Walker v. Strosnider, supra*, Judge Poffenbarger, speaking for a unanimous court, explained the law of West Virginia in a way completely in accord with the modern *Restatement*. He summarized the cause of action for negligence as follows:

[An owner] may use his property, but he must use it in a lawful, that is, careful, manner. In other words, he must execute the work, as far as is reasonably practicable, and not unduly burdensome, with a view to the safety of the buildings on the adjacent property. But for this rule, he might go at any hour of the day or night, without having given notice to the adjoining owner, indicating when, how or to what extent he intended to alter the condition of his property, and make an excavation for a cellar along the entire wall of a heavy valuable building, knowing it would fall in consequence thereof, and yet intending to replace, the earth removed by a wall. He would be under no duty to vary the mode or manner of his work in the slightest degree, in respect to the time thereof or otherwise, in the interests of the safety of the building. Having thus made the excavation, he could build his wall at his leisure and would be under no duty to prosecute the work diligently even though it should be apparent that delay in this part

> of the work would endanger the building. Such conduct would be reckless, careless and wanton, in view of the ease with which the mode of work could be varied, in respect to time and manner, and previous notice given of the intention to alter the condition of the property, the extent of the alteration, the manner in which it is to be done and the time, so as to afford the owner of the building an opportunity to take such measures for its protection, as he might see fit to adopt. . . . 67 S.E. at 1090.

IV

It would appear that the case before us either stands or falls on a question of strict liability. It is admitted that the retaining wall on the defendant's property was constructed at least sixty years ago, before the construction of the plaintiffs' house, and that all parties to this action were aware of the condition of the wall. Furthermore, there is no allegation that the defendant did anything to cause the collapse of the wall, but rather only failed to keep it in repair. Therefore, if the plaintiffs can recover, they must do so by proving that the disrepair of the retaining wall would have led ineluctably to the subsidence of their land in its natural condition. If, on the other hand, the land would not have subsided but for the weight of the plaintiffs' house, then they can recover nothing.

Notes and Questions

1. Easements and servitudes. An **easement** is a limited right to do something on, or to control the use of, someone else's property. An **affirmative easement** is a right to do something on *someone else's* property. The right to cross someone else's property, for example, is called a **right of way**. A **negative easement** is a right to prevent someone else from using her *own* property in a certain way. Modern terminology confines the term easement to affirmative easements and uses the word *servitude* to describe restrictions on land use, including negative easements. *See* Chapter 8, §1. Most easements and servitudes are created by agreement among neighbors. Some, like the **servitude for lateral support of land**, are created by the common law. Each owner has an obligation to maintain lateral support for neighboring land; conversely, each owner has a right to prevent her neighbors from excavating on their property to remove lateral support for her land.

2. Land versus structures. Courts have often distinguished lateral support of land from lateral support of buildings or other structures built on the land. The common law grants each landowner a servitude for lateral support of land in its natural condition. Owners who withdraw lateral support for neighboring land are strictly liable for any resulting damage to the land. On the other hand, owners have no duty to support structures on their neighbors' land. They do have a duty not to excavate in a negligent manner; they have a duty to act as a reasonably prudent person would — they cannot use unreasonably dangerous engineering methods or create unnecessary risks to adjoining property. They are also obligated to provide temporary support for neighboring land during excavation and to notify the neighbors if their excavation poses a risk to neighboring structures. *Spall v. Janota*, 406 N.E.2d 378 (Ind. Ct. App. 1980);

Klebs v. Yim, 772 P.2d 523 (Wash. Ct. App. 1989) (both holding that there is an absolute right of lateral support for land but only a duty to refrain from negligent injury to adjoining structures). However, the obligation to avoid negligence does not mean that owners have a duty to avoid foreseeable harm to neighboring structures if the land in its natural condition, in combination with the underlying foundation of the structures, would not have been sufficient to support those structures.

What happens if the land in its natural condition is sufficient to support a structure on neighboring land and the removal of support for the land causes a chain reaction resulting in damage to the building? Older law, retained in some states, denied a remedy to the owner of the building. *Thurston v. Hancock*, 12 Mass. 220 (1815). However, the modern approach adopted in *Noone* imposes damages for harm both to the land and to the building if the harm to the building was caused by removal of lateral support for the land. The damages to the building are **consequential damages** resulting from breach of a legal duty to support the land. If, on the other hand, the neighboring building was built negligently with inadequate support so that it would have been damaged eventually even if the defendant did not withdraw lateral support for the land, then plaintiff can recover no damages for harm to the building resulting from the withdrawal of lateral support, under either the older or the modern approach.

Why is the standard of care different for land and structures? This distinction can be traced in U.S. law to an early Massachusetts case, *Thurston v. Hancock, supra.* In *Thurston*, the plaintiff had built a brick house with its rear wall within two feet of the boundary of his land. In 1811, the defendants began digging a foundation on their own land within six feet of the rear of the plaintiff's house, causing part of the earth on the surface of the plaintiff's land to slide onto the defendant's land, and rendering the foundations of the plaintiff's house insecure so that he had to abandon it. The Massachusetts Supreme Judicial Court held that the plaintiff could recover only for the damage to the soil, not to the house. Chief Justice Parker, in delivering judgment said:

> It is a common principle of the civil and of the common law, that the proprietor of land, unless restrained by covenant or custom, has the entire dominion, not only of the soil, but of the space above and below the surface, to any extent he may choose to occupy it. The law, founded upon principles of reason and common utility, has admitted a qualification to this dominion, restricting the proprietor so to use his own, as not to injure the property or impair any actual existing rights of another. *Sic utere tuo ut alienum non laedas.* But this subjection of the use of a man's own property to the convenience of his neighbor is founded upon a supposed preexisting right in his neighbor to have and enjoy the privilege which by such act is impaired. A man, in digging upon his own land, is to have regard to the position of his neighbor's land, and the probable consequences to his neighbor, if he digs too near his line; and if he disturbs the natural state of the soil, he shall answer in damages; but he is answerable only for the natural and necessary consequences of his act, and not for the value of a house put upon or near the line by his neighbor. The plaintiff built his house within two feet of the western line of the lot, knowing that the town, or those who should hold under it, had a right to build equally near to the line, or to dig down into the soil for any other lawful purpose. He

> knew also the shape and nature of the ground, and that it was impossible to dig there without causing excavations. He built at his peril; for it was not possible for him, merely by building upon his own ground, to deprive the other party of such use of his as he should deem most advantageous. . . . It is, in fact, *damnum absque injuria.*

Id. at 224, 229. Does this explanation make sense?

3. **Retaining walls.** If a retaining wall was built on defendant's land for the purpose of maintaining lateral support for plaintiff's land, defendant has a strict obligation to keep the wall in good repair to avoid loss of lateral support for the plaintiff's land. This obligation **runs with the land** and is binding on subsequent owners of the property. *Salmon v. Peterson,* 311 N.W.2d 205, 206-207 (S.D. 1981). However, the obligation extends only to such support as is needed to support the neighbor's land in its natural condition. In the absence of statute, an owner of a retaining wall has no obligation to keep it strong enough also to support the added weight of the neighbor's building. In practice, how do you think courts are likely to go about assessing whether a defendant's behavior satisfies the obligation to support the land in its natural condition? *See Klebs v. Yim,* 772 P.2d 523 (Wash. Ct. App. 1989) (defendant had "a duty to maintain an existing retaining wall on [defendant's] property" and was liable for failure to maintain the wall but was not liable for damage to plaintiff's property attributable to the additional weight imposed by plaintiff's swimming pool). If a retaining wall on defendant's land is actually supporting the buildings on plaintiff's land, defendant does have a duty to act non-negligently in withdrawing that support, by notifying the plaintiff of any changes so that plaintiff can take steps to support her own structure.

4. **Natural conditions.** Do owners have obligations to take reasonable steps to prevent natural conditions on their land from harming neighboring owners? Some courts have held that an owner who reasonably should know that her property is subject to landslides should take reasonable steps to protect property downhill from her. *Sprecher v. Adamson,* 636 P.2d 1121 (Cal. 1981). However, other courts have taken the position that owners are not liable for harms caused by the natural condition of their land, although they may be liable for conditions caused by their development of their own land. *Price ex rel. Estate of Price v. City of Seattle,* 24 P.3d 1098 (Wash. Ct. App. 2001).

5. **Measurement of damages.** Courts have used a variety of approaches to measure damages for injury to lateral support. Those approaches include (a) the cost of restoration; (b) the diminution in value of the property; and (c) in the case of liability for damage to a building, the value of the lost use of the building plus an amount representing permanent depreciation in the building's value. 9-64A *Powell on Real Property* §64A.05.

6. **Building codes and private rights of action.** In addition to common law rules regulating land use, every state has passed statutes regulating both land use and building construction. We discuss these statutes at greater length in the next chapter.

Massachusetts State Building Code

Mass. Gen. Laws ch. 143, §§3A, 57, 59, 94

§3A. [T]he local inspector shall enforce the state building code as to any building or structure within the city or town from which he is appointed.

§57. The . . . superior court shall have jurisdiction in equity to enforce . . . the state building code . . . , the enforcement of which . . . is the responsibility of [the] local inspector.

§59. The . . . superior court may, upon the application of the . . . local inspector, enforce by any suitable process or decree . . . the state building code.

§94. Whoever violates any provision of the state building code . . . shall be punished by a fine of not more than one thousand dollars or by imprisonment for not more than one year, or both, for each such violation. Each day during which a violation exists shall constitute a separate offense.

International Building Code §3307

Adopted by 780 Code of Massachusetts Regulations ch. 33

3307.1 Protection required. Adjoining public and private property shall be protected from damage during construction, remodeling and demolition work. Protection must be provided for footings, foundations, party walls, chimneys, skylights and roofs. Provisions shall be made to control water runoff and erosion during construction or demolition activities. The person making or causing an excavation to be made shall provide written notice to the owners of adjoining buildings advising them that the excavation is to be made and that the adjoining buildings should be protected. Said notification shall be delivered not less than 10 days prior to the scheduled starting date of the excavation.

Notes and Questions

Effect of statutory provisions. The regulations promulgated by the Massachusetts state building code commission apparently require all landowners to protect neighboring structures. If an owner violates the building code by undermining lateral support for a neighboring building, is the violator financially liable to the injured property owner for any resulting damage?

Three questions must be considered. First, do the regulations create a private right of action, *i.e.*, a right to sue the neighbor for damages? The right may be express or implied. It is express if the text of the laws clearly creates a right to sue and implied if the court infers such a right from the text by reference to the purposes the regulations were intended to achieve or the policies underlying the regulations. Second, if no such right was created, are the remedies included in the statute (criminal penalties including fines and imprisonment and civil claims by the local inspector) intended to be exclusive or nonexclusive? If those remedies are exclusive, a private owner cannot seek a remedy under the common law. If they are nonexclusive, we reach the third question. Should the common law be changed to promote the policies underlying the statute and regulations, or should the legislature's failure to alter the common law rule induce the court to retain it until changed by the legislature?

Problem

A building in an urban downtown area is demolished to make way for a new structure. The demolition of the building and excavation of the land underneath it undermine lateral support for a neighboring structure, causing damage to the foundation of the neighboring building. It seems that the foundation of the demolished building had been providing needed support for the neighboring structure. The owner of the damaged building sues the neighbor for damages to recoup the cost of fixing her building.

1. Applying the Massachusetts laws and building code excerpted above, what is plaintiff's argument that the law entitles her to recover such damages, either expressly or implicitly? What is defendant's argument in response?

2. If the state law does not provide a private right of action for non-negligent harm to buildings on neighboring land, what is plaintiff's argument that the common law should be changed to provide such a remedy? What is defendant's argument that the common law negligence standard should be retained?

§5.2 Subjacent Support

Friendswood Development Co. v. Smith-Southwest Industries, Inc.

576 S.W.2d 21 (Tex. 1978)

PRICE DANIEL, J.

The question in this case is whether landowners who withdrew percolating ground waters from wells located on their own land are liable for subsidence which resulted on lands of others in the same general area.

Smith-Southwest Industries and other landowners located in the Seabrook and Clear Lake area of Harris County brought this class action in 1973 against Friendswood Development Company and its corporate parent, Exxon Corporation, alleging that severe subsidence of their lands was caused by the defendants' past and continuing withdrawals of vast quantities of underground water from wells on defendants' nearby lands.

Allegations and Summary Judgment Proof

[Plaintiff landowners alleged that defendant Friendswood had pumped large amounts of subsurface waters from its own property for sale primarily to industrial users.] These wells were drilled from 1964 through 1971, even though previous engineering reports to defendants showed that production therefrom would result in a certain amount of land subsidence in the area. Plaintiffs alleged that the wells were negligently spaced too close together, too near the common boundary of lands owned by plaintiffs and defendants, and that excessive quantities were produced with knowledge that this would cause subsidence and flooding of plaintiffs' lands. Plaintiffs alleged that this extensive withdrawal of ground water proximately caused the sinking and loss of elevation above mean sea level of their property and the property of others similarly situated along the shores of Galveston Bay and Clear Lake, resulting in the erosion and flooding of their lands and damage to their residences, businesses and improvements. Plaintiffs further allege that the manner in which Friendswood Development Company continues to use its property for the withdrawal and sale of large amounts of fresh water to commercial users on other lands constitutes a continuing nuisance and permanent loss and damage to their property.

Plaintiffs concede that subsidence in the area complained of was known to be a "potential problem" before defendants' operations began, but they allege that Friendswood and Exxon knew that the problem "would be severely aggravated" by the withdrawals which the companies contemplated. There was summary judgment proof of such knowledge and aggravation.

Reports in the record and publications of official agencies reflect that land subsidence in Harris County is not peculiar to or confined within the Galveston Bay and Clear Creek areas described in plaintiffs' petition. Rather it is a problem which has existed for many years in Harris and Galveston Counties. Harris County alone had 2,635 ground water wells in the inventory compiled by the U.S. Geological Survey in cooperation with the Texas Water Development Board in 1972. The Chicot and Evangeline aquifers underlie the Houston-Galveston region, which includes all of Harris and Galveston Counties and parts of adjacent counties. These two aquifers furnish all of the ground water pumped in the Houston-Galveston region, according to the U.S. Geological Report prepared by R. K. Gabrysch and C. W. Bonnet in 1974. This report states that water level declines of as much as 200 feet have resulted in wells completed in the Chicot aquifer and as much as 325 feet in the Evangeline aquifer during 1943-73, and "the declines in artesian pressures have resulted in a pronounced regional subsidence of the land surface." It states that the area in which there has been subsidence of one foot or more has increased from 350 square miles in 1954 to about 2,500 square miles in 1973. The contour lines of this area encompass practically all of Harris and Galveston Counties and include all of the principal areas of ground water withdrawals. Maps in the report indicate that the land and wells involved in this suit are in or near the "Johnson Space Center Area," where the land surface subsided about 2.12 feet between 1964 and 1973.

The general and widespread problem of subsidence in Harris and Galveston Counties has been considered in numerous other writings, and more notably by action of the Legislature, which created the Harris-Galveston Coastal Subsidence District in 1975. This is a comprehensive measure "to provide for the regulation of the withdrawal of ground water within the boundaries of the district for the purpose of ending subsidence which contributes to or precipitates flooding, inundation, or overflow of any area within the district." It includes all of Harris and Galveston Counties and provides for a board of fifteen members with the power to grant or decline permits for new wells, regulate spacing and production, require metering devices, and adopt any rules necessary to prevent further subsidence.

Nature of Plaintiffs' Action

Plaintiffs have alleged an action in tort based upon the general rule that a landowner has a duty not to use his property so as to injure others. *Sic utere tuo ut alienum non laedas.* [However, this court has held that this general rule does not apply to withdrawals of underground water. Rather, this court has] adopted the common law rule that such rights are not correlative, but are absolute, and thus are not subject to the conflicting "reasonable use" rule. *Houston & T. C. Ry. Co. v. East*, 81 S.W. 279 (Tex. 1904).

Plaintiffs [contend] that the "reasonable use" doctrine should apply to ground water the same as it does to other real property.

In [*East*,] the railroad company, with full knowledge of the long existence of Mr. East's small shallow well on his homestead, dug a well twenty feet in diameter and 66 feet deep on its own adjacent property, from which it pumped 25,000 gallons of water per day. This resulted in lowering the water level on plaintiff's land and drying up his well. [The plaintiff argued for the "reasonable use" or "American rule," which held that the right of a landowner to draw underground water from his land was not absolute, but limited to the amount necessary for the reasonable use of his land, and that the rights of adjoining landowners are correlative and limited to reasonable use. The defendant argued for the contrary English doctrine laid down in *Acton v. Blundell*, 152 Eng. Rep. 1223 (Ex. 1843), that, "if a man digs a well on his own field and thereby drains his neighbor's, he may do so unless he does it maliciously."]

II. Adoption of the Common Law Rule of Absolute Ownership

Thus, on the appeal of the *East* case to this Court, the conflicting aspects of the "reasonable use" rule and the common law rule, later referred to as the "English rule" or "absolute ownership rule," were clearly presented. This Court discussed both rules and made a deliberate choice of the common law rule as announced in *Acton v. Blundell, supra.*[16]

In holding that the owner may withdraw water from beneath his land without liability for lowering the water table and thus damaging his neighbor's well and land, the Court mentioned only waste and malice as possible limitations to the rule. Absent these, the Court clearly embraced the doctrine stated in *Acton v. Blundell, supra*, that this type of damage "falls within the description *damnum absque injuria*, which cannot become the ground of action." This legal maxim denotes a loss without injury in

16. The public policy considerations were said to be (1) "because the existence, origin, movement and course of such waters, . . . are so secret, occult and concealed that an attempt to administer any set of legal rules in respect to them would be involved in hopeless uncertainty, and would, therefore, be practically impossible"; and (2) "because any such recognition of correlative rights would interfere, to the material detriment of the commonwealth, with drainage and agriculture, mining, . . ." etc. 81 S.W. 279, 281.

the legal sense, that is, without the invasion of a legal right or the violation of a legal duty.

The English rule of so-called "absolute ownership" was applied by this Court in *Texas Co. v. Burkett*, 296 S.W. 273 (Tex. 1927), which held that a landowner has the absolute right to sell percolating ground water for industrial purposes off the land. At a time when the trend in other jurisdictions was away from the English rule and toward the "reasonable use" rule, the English rule was reaffirmed by this Court in *City of Corpus Christi v. City of Pleasanton*, 276 S.W.2d 798 (Tex. 1955).

Subsidence Cases Under the Common Law Rule

Although the *East*, *Corpus Christi*, and *Williams*[17] cases involved damages to wells and lands of the plaintiffs because the water tables beneath their lands were lowered by ground water withdrawals of the defendants, none of these nor any other Texas case has dealt specifically with land subsidence resulting from such pumping of underground waters. In other jurisdictions adhering to the English ground water rule, liability for neighboring land subsidence has been denied.

On the basis of the earlier decisions cited above, the *Restatement of Torts* §818 (1939), adopted the following rule:

> §818. Withdrawing Subterranean Water
>
> To the extent that a person is not liable for withdrawing subterranean waters from the land of another, he is not liable for a subsidence of the other's land which is caused by the withdrawal.

We have found nothing in our Constitution, laws, or decisions inconsistent with the common law rule.

Stare Decisis

We agree that some aspects of the English or common law rule as to underground waters are harsh and outmoded, and the rule has been severely criticized since its reaffirmation by this Court in 1955. Most of the critics, however, recognize that it has become an established rule of property law in this State, under which many citizens own land and water rights. The rule has been relied upon by thousands of farmers, industries, and municipalities in purchasing and developing vast tracts of land overlying aquifers of underground water. Approximately 50,000 wells are used to irrigate 2,800,000 acres in the thirteen county High Plains area of West Texas. As shown in the official reports cited earlier in this opinion, over 2,600 water wells have been drilled in Harris County alone while this rule of immunity from liability was in effect. The very wells which brought about this action were drilled after the English rule had been reaffirmed by this Court in 1955.

On this subject, we are not writing on a clean slate. Even though good reasons may exist for lifting the immunity from tort actions in cases of this nature, it would

17. *Pecos County Water Control & Improvement District 1 v. Williams*, 271 S.W.2d 503 (Tex. Ct. App. 1954). — Eds.

be unjust to do so retroactively. The doctrine of *stare decisis* has been and should be strictly followed by this Court in cases involving established rules of property rights. It is for this reason that, as to past actions complained of in this case, we follow the English rule and *Restatement of Torts* §818 (1939) in holding that defendants are not liable on plaintiff's allegations of nuisance and negligence.

As to Future Wells and Subsidence

[T]he Legislature has entered the field of regulation of ground water withdrawals and subsidence. This occurred after geologists, hydrologists, and engineers had developed more accurate knowledge concerning the location, source, and measurement of percolating underground waters, and after legislators became aware of the potential conflicts inherent in the unregulated use of ground water under the English rule of ownership. With a rule that recognizes ownership of underground water by each individual under his own land, but with no limitation on the manner and amount which another individual landowner might produce (absent willful waste and malicious malice [*sic*]), legislative action was essential in order to provide for conservation and protection of public interests.

The legislative policy contained in Chapter 52 of the Texas Water Code is designed to limit the exercise of that portion of the English rule which has been interpreted as giving each landowner the right to take all the water he pleases without regard to the effect on other lands in the same area. For instance, §52.117 of the Water Code, applicable to Underground Water Conservation Districts, provides:

> §52.117. Regulation of Spacing and Production[18]
>
> In order to minimize as far as practicable the drawdown of the water table or the reduction of artesian pressure, to control subsidence, or to prevent waste, the district may provide for the spacing of water wells and may regulate the production of wells.

Ten of these Underground Water Conservation Districts are active in an area embracing much of West Texas. The need for additional legislation for creation of districts to cover unregulated ground water reservoirs and to solve other conflicts which may arise in this area of water law and subsidence seems to be inevitable. Providing policy and regulatory procedures in this field is a legislative function. It is well that the Legislature has assumed its proper role, because our courts are not equipped to regulate ground water uses and subsidence on a suit-by-suit basis.

This case, however, gives the Court its first opportunity to recognize, and to encourage compliance with, the policy set forth by the Legislature and its regulatory agencies in an effort to curb excessive under groundwater withdrawals and resulting land subsidence. It also affords us the opportunity to discard an objectionable aspect of the court-made English rule as it relates to subsidence by stating a rule for the future which is more in harmony with expressed legislative policy. We refer to the past immunity from negligence which heretofore has been afforded ground water producers solely because of their "absolute" ownership of the water.

---

18. This section was replaced in 1995 by Tex. Water Code §36.116. — Eds.

As far as we can determine, there is no other use of private real property which enjoys such an immunity from liability under the law of negligence. This ownership of underground water comes with ownership of the surface; it is part of the soil. Yet, the use of one's ground-level surface and other elements of the soil is without such insulation from tort liability. Our consideration of this case convinces us that there is no valid reason to continue this special immunity insofar as it relates to future subsidence proximately caused by negligence in the manner which wells are drilled or produced in the future. It appears that the ownership and rights of all landowners will be better protected against subsidence if each has the duty to produce water from his land in a manner that will not negligently damage or destroy the lands of others.

Therefore, if the landowner's manner of withdrawing ground water from his land is negligent, willfully wasteful, or for the purpose of malicious injury, and such conduct is a proximate cause of the subsidence of the land of others, he will be liable for the consequences of his conduct. The addition of negligence as a ground of recovery shall apply only to future subsidence proximately caused by future withdrawals of ground water from wells which are either produced or drilled in a negligent manner after the date this opinion becomes final.

While this addition of negligence as a ground of recovery in subsidence cases applies to future negligence in producing water from existing wells and those drilled or produced in a negligent manner in the future, it has been suggested that this new ground of recovery should be applied in the present cause of action. This is often done when a court writes or adds a new rule applicable to personal injury cases, but seldom when rules of property law are involved. This is because precedent is necessarily a highly important factor when problems regarding land or contracts are concerned. In deeds, property transactions, and land developments, the parties should be able to rely on the law which existed at the time of their actions.

JACK POPE, J., dissenting.

I respectfully dissent. The court has decided this cause upon the mistaken belief that the case is governed by the ownership of ground water. Plaintiffs assert no ownerships to the percolating waters pumped and extracted from the ground by defendants. They make no complaint that their own wells have been or will be pumped dry. They seek no damages for the defendants' sale of the water. Plaintiffs' action calls for no change in nor even a review of the English rule of "absolute ownership" of ground water, the American rule of "reasonable use" of ground water, nor the Texas rule of "nonwasteful" use of ground water. They claim no correlative rights in the water. The Texas law of percolating waters is not put in issue by this suit, and there is no occasion to overrule that law either now or prospectively.

Plaintiffs' complaint is that defendants are causing subsidence of their land. They assert an absolute right to keep the surface of their land at its natural horizon. The landowners' right to the subjacent support for their land is the only right in suit, and this is a case of original impression. . . . It is no more logical to say that this is a case concerning the right to ground water than it would be correct in a case in which an adjoining landowner removed lateral support by a caterpillar to say that the case would be governed by the law of caterpillars. In making this decision about one's right to subjacent support, I would use as analogies other kinds of cases concerning support, such as the right to lateral support.

A landowner's right to lateral support for his land is an absolute right. The instrument employed in causing land to slough off, cave in or wash away is not the real subject of inquiry. The inquiry is whether the adjoining owner actually causes the loss of support. Whether the support is destroyed by excavation, ditching, the flowing of water, the pumping of water, unnatural pressure, unnatural suction, or explosives, the right to support is the same, and it is an absolute right.

A second analogous rule which protects one's subsurface from damage by an operator on other lands is found in *Gregg v. Delhi-Taylor Oil Corp.*, 344 S.W.2d 411, 416 (Tex. 1961). Mr. Gregg, in the development of his mineral lease, was preparing to use a sand fracturing technique to open cracks and veins extending some distance from his lease and to alter the substructure of neighboring land. By use of hydraulic pressure the ruptures of the subsurface formations would free greater quantities of gas. The rupture beneath the Delhi-Taylor's lands would create only small veins about one-tenth of an inch in diameter. This court regarded the creation of fissures on another's land as an invasion of property rights. . . . This court denied one landowner the right to interfere with the subsurface of lands beyond his own lease boundaries. The same principle was applied in *Gregg v. Delhi-Taylor Oil Corp.*, 344 S.W.2d 411 (Tex. 1961), and in *Delhi-Taylor Oil Corp. v. Holmes*, 344 S.W.2d 420 (Tex. 1961). In my judgment, the examples are indistinguishable from the present case.

Elliff v. Texon Drilling Co., 210 S.W.2d 558 (Tex. 1948), was another example in which this court looked at the damage done [to] a neighbor's subsurface estate by an oil driller who had the right to capture oil through the wellbore on his own lease. This court expressly rejected holdings by the Louisiana Supreme Court which held that an adjoining owner has no action against one who negligently destroys a reservoir. This court also rejected the defense that one's right to capture the oil rendered him immune from damages for his negligence in wasting it.

We thus reach the end result. Under our prior holdings compared with today's, one who mines for oil may not destroy his neighbor's subjacent geology; but the right to pump water, we inconsistently say, is the right to destroy the subsurface geology, the subjacent support and even the surface of the land. Defendants may pump the plaintiffs' land to the bottom of Galveston Bay.

The error of the majority is its narrow focus upon the right of the defendants to pump ground water. We should enlarge our vision so we can see what this lawsuit is about. I do not believe it is sound law that the right to pump water is the power to destroy the surface of surrounding landowners. If defendants argue that they have an absolute right to pump groundwater, plaintiffs reply that they too have an absolute right to the support of their natural surface.

There is yet another legal principle that we should observe. Many things, though lawful, when done to excess, become remediable. Church bells may toll the knell of parting day or announce the time for solemn services, but when bells continuously clang without interruption for many days, the rights of others spring into being. What we do cannot be understood except in relation to those we touch. We have in this case the pleadings and showing that the defendants have abused their right to pump water to the point that property and the rights of others are ignored and destroyed.

Finally, and importantly, I dissent from the majority's holding that landowners in the future may prosecute a suit for damages for the destruction of their property if, and only if the action is one for negligence, willful waste, or malicious injury. I rather assume that pumpers of ground water will carefully do so, will not waste their water, and will bear no ill will toward those whose property they are destroying. I would hold that an owner of land may assert an action against one who destroys the lateral or subjacent support to his land in its natural state when: (1) he engages in conduct knowing that it will cause damages to another's land by loss or destruction of the subjacent support, or (2) the plaintiff proves negligence, or (3) the plaintiff proves a nuisance, and here a balancing will be a factor.

I also dissent from the court's denial of rights to the plaintiffs, while acknowledging that future landowners may have an action at least in negligence. This court, in recent years, has recognized a number of new actions, and each time, the successful party was allowed the victory.... In my opinion, it is basically unfair to treat the plaintiffs in this case unequally by recognizing that they possess an action, but by denying them the remedy.

Notes and Questions

1. **Rule of capture or right to support.** The majority, in effect, reads its past cases as holding that the absolute nature of the rule of capture for groundwater protects those who remove groundwater from liability for the subsidence caused by their actions. The dissent accuses the majority of making a category mistake — applying a rule of acquisition (the rule of capture) to resolve a dispute about the duties that owners owe to one another (the duty not to cause subsidence). Who has the better of the argument?

2. **Current law.** Some courts agree with the majority in *Friendswood*, imposing liability for undermining subjacent support only when negligence can be shown. Other courts extend the absolute duty to provide lateral support for land to the context of subjacent support, imposing strict liability for removal of subjacent support. *See Los Osos Valley Associates v. City of San Luis Obispo*, 36 Cal. Rptr. 2d 758, 763 (Ct. App. 1994); *Muskatell v. City of Seattle*, 116 P.2d 363 (Wash. 1941); *Restatement (Second) of Torts* §818 illus. 1 & 2 (1977) (adopting this approach).

3. **Separation of the surface from the mineral estate.** One exception to the rule that there is no duty to provide subjacent support in the absence of negligence occurs when ownership of the minerals beneath the surface is separated from ownership of the surface. In the absence of agreement to the contrary, the owner of the surface has an absolute right not to have its subjacent support undermined by the owner of the mineral estate. In *Large v. Clinchfield Coal Co.*, 387 S.E.2d 783 (Va. 1990), the plaintiffs, George and Betty Large, sought to prevent the defendant, Clinchfield Coal Company,

from engaging in "longwall mining," a practice that involves removing coal without leaving any supporting pillars of coal, resulting in subsidence of the land surface. The court held that any appreciable damage to the surface or a diminution in its usability by the owner of the mineral estate will be sufficient to sustain a finding of liability without a need for a showing of negligence or unreasonableness. *Accord, Platts v. Sacramento Northern Railway*, 253 Cal. Rptr. 269 (Ct. App. 1988) (holding that a surface estate owner has an absolute right to subjacent support from the owner of a subsurface estate but that the obligation did not run with the land; the mineral estate owner who took possession of the property after the act causing the removal of the surface support was not responsible for the damage).

4. Retroactivity. The majority opinion in *Friendswood* argues that it is wrong to apply a new rule of law retroactively. What exactly does this mean? Does retroactivity constitute a particularly salient concern for property law? Although the opinion is confusingly worded, the majority sought to apply the new negligence rule both to new wells drilled after the date the opinion in *Friendswood* was issued and to withdrawals of water from existing wells that were drilled before the opinion was issued. Doesn't application of the new rule to withdrawal of water from existing wells constitute a retroactive application of the new rule? After all, investments were arguably made in digging existing wells based on an expectation that the developer would be free from liability for any resulting harm.

What arguments does the court give to justify refusing to apply the new rule retroactively to withdrawals of water that occurred in the past? What arguments could you make on behalf of the plaintiffs for retroactive application of the new rule? How could you argue that even if the new rule is applied prospectively as to all other landowners, it should be applied retroactively to benefit the plaintiffs who brought this particular lawsuit? Was the court correct to apply its new rule to future withdrawals of water from existing wells?

5. Precedent. The judges in *Friendswood* addressed a variety of policy arguments concerning the wisdom and justice of the competing rules advocated by the parties. They also interpreted earlier decisions to determine whether prior law answered the question, directly or indirectly. The majority opinion concluded that the case was governed by the previously established rule that owners have the absolute right to withdraw groundwater from their property, even if this has the effect of withdrawing groundwater from beneath other land. The court then chose to overrule the cases that established the existing rule and to apply the new rule prospectively. In contrast, the dissenting judge argued that the issue in *Friendswood* was not governed by the rule about withdrawal of groundwater at all; instead, the dissenting opinion distinguished the prior cases establishing that rule and argued that the case was one of first impression, meaning that the specific issue before the court had never been precisely addressed by a prior case. In addition, each of the opinions referred to prior cases that established a variety of rules of law by arguing that those cases are analogous to the case at hand and that, therefore, the principles established in those prior cases should extend to the situation before the court.

In applying precedent, the lawyers for each side look for precedents that help them. The plaintiff's attorney, for example, may argue that a prior case stands for a broad rule of law that applies to the current case as well. To do this, the attorney must describe the holding of the earlier case — the rule of law for which it stands — in a way that encompasses both cases. The defendant's attorney must attempt to distinguish the earlier case by arguing that the factual context in the earlier case is different in significant ways from the case at hand and that there are good reasons of policy or justice to adjudicate this case differently from the earlier case. Note that two steps are necessary in distinguishing a precedent: (a) identifying significant factual differences between the prior case and the case at hand, and (b) explaining why, as a matter of social policy, the cases should be handled differently. The plaintiff's attorney must counter this argument by explaining why the case at hand is indistinguishable from the earlier case. This requires arguing that (a) the factual differences between the two cases are not important, and (b) the policies justifying the result in the earlier case apply to the current case as well.

What precedents did the majority and dissenting opinions rely on to decide the case in *Friendswood*? Which rules of law did the opinions mention?

6. The complex range of solutions for land use conflicts. We have seen that some kinds of land use disputes between neighbors, such as conflicts over lateral and subjacent support, water rights, and light and air, are governed by specific sets of legal rules. Land use disputes not covered by these specific rules are governed by the general law of nuisance.

The courts have adopted various approaches to settle land use disputes. At one extreme are the doctrines granting the victim absolute security from harm to certain property interests; when courts grant veto rights, they impose liability if the plaintiff can show that the defendant caused the harm. At another extreme are the doctrines granting the defendant an absolute privilege to engage in the activity without liability of any kind. In the middle are doctrines regulating the defendant's conduct only if it is deemed unreasonable; the standard of what conduct is reasonable or unreasonable may be defined by a general "reasonableness" requirement, negligence, and nuisance.

Strict liability rules	Reasonableness doctrines	Free use rules
• easement for lateral support of land • prior appropriation of water (veto rights in first user) • natural flow doctrine for diffuse surface water	• nuisance doctrine • negligence (lateral support of structures) • reasonable use doctrine for water • malice doctrine for spite fences	• common enemy rule for diffuse surface water • no easement for light and air • free use or absolute ownership of groundwater

Problem

You practice in a jurisdiction that has no precedent on the question of whether an owner can excavate on her property and withdraw water in a way that undermines subjacent support for property located some distance away. At least two prior cases, however, are relevant. Your jurisdiction has adopted the reasonable use test to govern conflicts over flooding caused by diffuse surface water, as established in *Armstrong v. Francis*: Owners have a duty to act reasonably in developing their property to avoid causing unreasonable harm to neighboring owners that results from the runoff of diffuse surface water. Your jurisdiction has also adopted the free use or absolute ownership test to govern disputes over groundwater, as established in *Acton v. Blundell*, 152 Eng. Rep. 1223 (Exch. 1843), and *Houston & T.C. Railway Co. v. East*, 81 S.W. 279 (Tex. 1904). Landowners may withdraw as much groundwater as they wish, unless they waste the water, even if the effect is to withdraw groundwater from beneath the plaintiff's land. In addition, your jurisdiction has adopted the common law rule concerning lateral support of land: an absolute duty to support neighboring land in its natural condition but only a duty not to act negligently in withdrawing support from neighboring structures.

1. Make an argument for the plaintiffs that precedent justifies giving them a right to stop the subsidence and get damages for past subsidence.

2. Make an argument for the defendants that precedent gives them freedom to withdraw the water without any liability.

CHAPTER 7

Land Use and Natural Resources Regulation

§1 LAND USE REGULATION: ORIGINS, AUTHORITY, AND PROCESS

§1.1 The Roots and Structure of Zoning

Public planning and the regulation of land use in the United States have origins that trace to colonial history. Public officials planned early towns, such as Annapolis and Williamsburg, as well as cities such as Philadelphia and Washington, D.C. As the nation grew, frontier settlements were regularly laid out in orderly fashion, with provisions for specific types of development, street grids, and public infrastructure. *See generally* James D. Kornwolf, *Architecture and Town Planning in Colonial North America* (2003). By the time of the Founding, it was common to have laws that, for example, mandated the development of underutilized land, directed such lands to specific uses such as mills, compelled the draining of wetlands, set fencing requirements to prevent animals from wandering, and required the removal of noxious plants. Other land use laws created specific residential areas in towns, regulated the height and materials, as well as the aesthetics, of buildings, and imposed a variety of affirmative obligations on urban land owners. *See* John F. Hart, *Colonial Land Use Law and Its Significance for Modern Takings Doctrine*, 109 Harv. L. Rev. 1252, 1259-1281 (1996).

As cities grew rapidly in the nineteenth century, fueled by immigration and widespread industrialization after the Civil War, the need for planning and land use regulation grew. Between 1840 and 1880, the number of American cities with populations over 100,000 grew from 3 to 77. Julian Conrad Juergensmeyer & Thomas E. Roberts, *Land Use Planning and Development Regulation Law* §1.3, at 5 (3d ed. 2013). After the Chicago World's Fair of 1893, the City Beautiful Movement spread the ideal of civic improvement, and local governments responded with infrastructure investments and an era of grand public architecture.

At the turn of the twentieth century, urban planning began to develop as a profession. The architect Daniel H. Burnham, who is famously (although perhaps apocryphally) attributed with the saying "make no small plans, they have no magic to stir men's blood," was the mastermind behind the 1911 General Plan of Chicago, which was the first adopted comprehensive city plan. The Plan of Chicago was a sweeping vision for the city's development, outlining future parks, boulevards, monuments, a civic center, and other improvements, and sparked broad interest in urban planning. *See* Carl Smith, *The Plan of Chicago: Daniel Burnham and the Remaking of the American City* 86-87 (2006).

As comprehensive planning was gaining acceptance, local governments were also experimenting with new approaches to land use regulation. In 1904 and 1905, Boston enacted ordinances that divided the city into distinct height districts, a practice that the Supreme Court upheld in *Welch v. Swasey*, 214 U.S. 91 (1909). Los Angeles passed the first modern zoning code in 1909, a city-wide ordinance that separated residential from industrial uses. New York City in 1916 enacted a comprehensive zoning code that defined commercial, retail, and residential uses. And in the 1920s, the federal government began promoting zoning as a tool for economic development, promulgating legislation that included a model state statute to enable local governments to zone.

§1.2 Zoning Authority and Validity

As zoning spread in the 1920s, the issue of the constitutionality of this regulatory approach to land use reached the Supreme Court. How the Court addressed the authority for, and validity of, comprehensive zoning set the legal terms of land use regulation for much of the subsequent nine decades.

Village of Euclid v. Ambler Realty Co.

272 U.S. 365 (1926)

Map: Euclid Avenue, Euclid, Ohio

Mr. Justice George Sutherland delivered the opinion of the Court.

The village of Euclid is an Ohio municipal corporation. It adjoins and practically is a suburb of the city of Cleveland. Its estimated population is between 5,000 and 10,000, and its area from 12 to 14 square miles, the greater part of which is farm lands or unimproved acreage.

Appellee is the owner of a tract of land containing 68 acres, situated in the westerly end of the village, abutting on Euclid Avenue to the south and the Nickel Plate Railroad to the north. Adjoining this tract, both on the east and on the west, there have been laid out restricted residential plats upon which residences have been erected.

On November 13, 1922, an ordinance was adopted by the village council, establishing a comprehensive zoning plan for regulating and restricting the location of trades, industries, apartment houses, two-family houses, single family houses, etc., the lot area to be built upon, the size and height of buildings, etc.

the general public interest would so far outweigh the interest of the municipality that the municipality would not be allowed to stand in the way.

We find no difficulty in sustaining restrictions of the kind thus far reviewed. The serious question in the case arises over the provisions of the ordinance excluding from residential districts apartment houses, business houses, retail stores and shops, and other like establishments. This question involves the validity of what is really the crux of the more recent zoning legislation, namely, the creation and maintenance of residential districts, from which business and trade of every sort, including hotels and apartment houses, are excluded.

The matter of zoning has received much attention at the hands of commissions and experts, and the results of their investigations have been set forth in comprehensive reports. These reports which bear every evidence of painstaking consideration, concur in the view that the segregation of residential, business and industrial buildings will make it easier to provide fire apparatus suitable for the character and intensity of the development in each section; that it will increase the safety and security of home life, greatly tend to prevent street accidents, especially to children, by reducing the traffic and resulting confusion in residential sections, decrease noise and other conditions which produce or intensify nervous disorders, preserve a more favorable environment in which to rear children, etc. With particular reference to apartment houses, it is pointed out that the development of detached house sections is greatly retarded by the coming of apartment houses, which has sometimes resulted in destroying the entire section for private house purposes; that in such sections very often the apartment house is a mere parasite, constructed in order to take advantage of the open spaces and attractive surroundings created by the residential character of the district. Moreover, the coming of one apartment house is followed by others, interfering by their height and bulk with the free circulation of air and monopolizing the rays of the sun which otherwise would fall upon the smaller homes, and bringing, as their necessary accompaniments, the disturbing noises incident to increased traffic and business, and the occupation, by means of moving and parked automobiles, of larger portions of the streets, thus detracting from their safety and depriving children of the privilege of quiet and open spaces for play, enjoyed by those in more favored localities — until, finally, the residential character of the neighborhood and its desirability as a place of detached residences are utterly destroyed. Under these circumstances, apartment houses, which in a different environment would be not only entirely unobjectionable but highly desirable, come very near to being nuisances.

If these reasons, thus summarized, do not demonstrate the wisdom or sound policy in all respects of those restrictions which we have indicated as pertinent to the inquiry, at least, the reasons are sufficiently cogent to preclude us from saying, as it must be said before the ordinance can be declared unconstitutional, that such provisions are clearly arbitrary and unreasonable, having no substantial relation to the public health, safety, morals, or general welfare.

It is true that when, if ever, the provisions set forth in the ordinance in tedious and minute detail, come to be concretely applied to particular premises, including those of the appellee, or to particular conditions, or to be considered in connection with specific complaints, some of them, or even many of them, may be found to be clearly arbitrary and unreasonable. But where the equitable remedy of injunction is sought, as it is here, not upon the ground of a present infringement or denial of a specific right, or of a particular injury in process of actual execution, but upon the broad ground that the mere existence and threatened enforcement of the ordinance, by materially and adversely affecting values and curtailing the opportunities of the market, constitute a present and irreparable injury, the court will not scrutinize its provisions, sentence by sentence, to ascertain by a process of piecemeal dissection whether there may be, here and there, provisions of a minor character, or relating to matters of administration, or not shown to contribute to the injury complained of, which, if attacked separately, might not withstand the test of constitutionality.

Under these circumstances, therefore, it is enough for us to determine, as we do, that the ordinance in its general scope and dominant features, so far as its provisions are here involved, is a valid exercise of authority, leaving other provisions to be dealt with as cases arise directly involving them.

Notes and Questions

1. **A "fairly helpful clew"?** The Supreme Court in *Euclid* invokes the maxim *sic utere tuo ut alienum non laedas* to explain the scope of legitimate authority to zone. The village of Euclid's zoning code, as the Court discussed, separated apartment buildings from single-family homes (and two-family homes from one-family homes). In those residential zones, apartment buildings could be "a mere parasite," the Court stated, and "come very near to being nuisances." What harms, specifically, did the Court contemplate this separation of uses preventing?

The District Court in *Euclid,* although striking down the statute, noted that the "blighting of property values and the congesting of population, whenever the colored or certain foreign races invade a residential section, are so well known as to be within the judicial cognizance." *Ambler Realty Co. v. Village of Euclid,* 297 F. 307, 313 (N.D. Ohio 1924). The Supreme Court in *Buchanan v. Warley,* 245 U.S. 60 (1917), struck down a Louisville, Kentucky statute that prohibited both white persons and African Americans from moving into and occupying a residence on a street that included a majority of owners of the opposite race. After *Buchanan,* local governments could not directly use zoning authority to regulate race, but a consistent critique of zoning since its inception has been its tendency to foster segregation. *See* Richard H. Chused, Euclid*'s Historical Imagery,* 51 Case W. Res. L. Rev. 597, 604-615 (2001). Constitutional and statutory constraints on discriminatory and exclusionary zoning are discussed below in §5.

2. **Judicial deference.** The Court in *Euclid* stated that "[i]f the validity of the legislative classification for zoning purposes be fairly debatable, the legislative judgment must be allowed to control." Courts regularly invoke this deference to legislative judgment when reviewing zoning ordinances. As we will see, however, there are a number of circumstances where courts take a more searching, less deferential, approach to challenges to zoning ordinances. *See* §3.

3. Zoning legislation and the planning process. State governments, as the Supreme Court alluded to in *Euclid*, are the ultimate repositories of the **police power**, the authority to regulate for health, welfare, and safety. One of the major ways states regulate property is by delegating power to local governments to regulate land use. States delegate zoning power through legislation, often called **zoning enabling acts**. The acts define both the scope of the powers delegated to local governments and the procedures by which the zoning process operates.

Voters in the local government elect a governing body, such as a **city council** or **county board of commissioners**. (Many smaller communities in New England have a **town meeting** form of government that allows voters to attend regularly scheduled meetings and vote on local laws.) The governing body is the legislative branch of government and has the power to adopt local laws governing land use in the jurisdiction, usually called **zoning ordinances** or **by-laws**. Many local governments have an executive branch as well, under a **mayor**, **county executive**, **board of selectmen**, or other forms, and departments within the executive branch that enforce zoning codes.

Zones are meant to be established in accordance with a rational scheme for promoting development by separating incompatible uses; many zoning enabling acts also require local governments to establish a **comprehensive plan** for the jurisdiction as a whole. Such plans show the general divisions of the jurisdiction into residential, agricultural, commercial, and industrial uses and describe objectives, such as a certain level of residential growth, the preservation of specified open space, particular types of industrial development, and the like.

The comprehensive plan and the zoning ordinance itself are generally prepared by a **planning commission** before adoption by the local legislative body. Planning commissions are composed of community members appointed by the local legislative body. In addition to developing plans and codes, the planning commission holds public hearings, investigates and obtains relevant information, and recommends changes over time in the local zoning law or in standards for applying or administering it. The commission is often aided by a **planning department** composed of professional planners. If the local government is too small to have a planning department, it may hire a private planning firm to aid it in drafting a comprehensive plan and/or the zoning law itself.

The planning commission also receives petitions from particular landowners who are seeking amendments to the zoning law as it applies to their parcels. Although the planning commission has no power to pass a zoning law itself, it does hold public hearings on such petitions and makes recommendations to the city council or other legislative body to accept or reject such petitions, and its recommendations are often accepted by the lawmaking body.

Finally, most zoning enabling acts authorize municipalities to delegate power to an administrative agency, often called the **zoning board** or **board of adjustment**. This agency primarily serves to evaluate requests for administrative relief from zoning requirements, as discussed in detail below. *See* §4.

4. The mechanics of Euclidean zoning. Traditional "Euclidean" zoning, so called because of the *Euclid* case, not the ancient Greek mathematician, consists of both use and area zoning. **Use zoning** divides municipalities into districts and regulates the kinds of uses allowed within each district. For example, some areas may allow only agricultural uses; others may allow residential uses; still others may allow commercial uses (stores and restaurants); and, finally, others permit industrial uses. As in *Euclid,* such zoning is usually cumulative; the uses form a pyramidal structure, with the most intensive uses at the top. Single-family housing is often allowed in multi-family districts and residential housing can be allowed in industrial districts—if anyone is willing to place housing there. This pyramid generally does not work in the reverse; apartment buildings are not allowed in single-family districts, industry is excluded from residential areas, and so forth.

Area zoning, by contrast, regulates the size of lots, the height of buildings, requirements to set back structures a certain distance from property borders, and other aspects of the physical configuration of the property. In order for an owner to understand the range of what is allowed on her property under a zoning ordinance, it is necessary to examine use and area restrictions together.

In addition to statutory language specifying various use and area zones, zoning ordinances also generally include a **zoning map**. The map is necessary to show where specific zones are physically located in a given jurisdiction.[1] The portion of the 1922 zoning map for the Village of Euclid that contains Ambler Realty's parcel is reproduced on page 000. Zoning maps are available on municipal and county web sites in many communities. Can you find the zoning map for the neighborhood you grew up in? Where you go to law school?

5. Motivations for zoning. Zoning is often justified, as it was in *Euclid,* as a means of prospectively limiting the harms that might arise from the proximity of incompatible land uses. Is zoning a better tool for this purpose than nuisance law? Than agreements between neighboring owners? What are the best arguments for distinguishing each of these approaches to controlling the uses of land? Are they necessarily mutually exclusive?

Land use regulation can also be understood as a tool that local governments use to influence the composition of their communities and the tax and budgeting implications that flow from that composition. Property taxes are a primary source of revenue for most local governments, which can shape zoning incentives. Can you see how?

---

1. Most zoning ordinances specify use and area districts and identify where they fit on the zoning map. Sometimes, however, more flexibility is desired. In some cases, municipalities create **planned unit developments** in which the zoning board or its planning staff work to establish overall density requirements and then work directly with developers of a particular area to construct a rational scheme that mixes uses (such as commercial and residential) in a desirable way. The plan is then approved by an administrative zoning board, usually after public hearings with public participation. Similarly, **floating zones** set forth detailed use requirements but are not attached to a specific location—hence they metaphorically "float"—until a specific proposal is brought forward and the zone is designated on the zoning map by the local legislative body.

William Fischel has argued that because homeowners tend to concentrate their assets in their homes, they are particularly politically aware of policies that may affect the value of those homes. *See* William Fischel, *The Homevoter Hypothesis: How Home Values Influence Local Government Taxation, School Finance, and Land-Use Policies* (2001). This creates a political incentive to respond to the policy preferences of these "homevoters," which can translate to zoning that tends to preserve the value of owner-occupied property. What kinds of land use regulations would you expect to follow from this? Who might this tend to exclude? *See* Edward L. Glaeser & Joseph Gyourko, *Zoning's Steep Price*, 25 Reg. 24 (2002) (arguing that zoning contributes to high housing costs).

§1.3 Other Land Use Regulatory Regimes

Zoning is only one of a number of related regulatory regimes that define the uses and development of land. Another prominent example is **subdivision regulation**. In many jurisdictions, an owner seeking to subdivide a large parcel, for example to build a neighborhood of single-family homes, must go through a rigorous review process to ensure, among other things, that the new subdivision will have sufficient infrastructure such as streets, sidewalks, and sewers, and that the subdivision will conform to legal requirements for lot sizes, open space, police and emergency vehicle access, and connection to the jurisdiction's street and utility grids. Even where a parcel is not being subdivided, large-scale development in many jurisdictions nonetheless requires a process of **site-plan review**. This process similarly focuses on whether there is sufficient infrastructure and services related to the new development. Subdivision control and site-plan review work with zoning, but can involve different officials and focus on different regulatory goals.

Another important regulatory regime involves housing, building, and development codes. These codes focus on structural safety, the quality of building materials, and public health concerns, such as ensuring sufficient light and air in residential buildings. These are often based on model codes that are adopted by local governments, at times with modifications. In recent years, building codes have increasingly focused on issues such as energy efficiency and sustainability.

§1.4 Modernizing Zoning

Euclidean zoning traditionally focused on separating uses in order to prospectively manage land use conflicts on a comprehensive basis. Although that remains an important aspect of most zoning codes, modern land use regulation has evolved significantly to encompass broader goals and new techniques. Zoning can now focus as much on development incentives, community aesthetics, combating so-called big box development, and historic preservation as it does on classifying land.

One criticism of traditional zoning is that it favors a distinctly suburban model of land use that fosters sprawling development and a privatized approach to community through the kind of residential zones upheld in *Euclid*. In response, "smart growth" or growth management laws limit and channel the overall development in a jurisdiction, seeking to utilize existing urban infrastructure, preserve open space, reduce car-dependency, and promote public health. They do so through a combination of regulations that promotes the mixing, rather than the separation, of land uses, emphasizes a scale and density of development that facilitates transportation options such as transit and walking, and caps the pace or footprint of new development. Growth management laws have generated legal challenges, which will be explored in §5.

New Urbanism similarly approaches development regulation with an emphasis on compact, mixed-used communities that favor walkability and transit. The heart of the new-urbanist critique of Euclidean zoning is that its approach to land use regulation stands in stark tension with an older tradition of urbanism that facilitated human-scale community. *See* Andres Duany, Elizabeth Plater-Zyberk & Jeff Speck, *Suburban Nation: The Rise of Sprawl and the Decline of the American Dream* (2001). **Form-based codes** are an increasingly popular zoning technique to advance New Urbanism. Such codes generally describe an allowable building envelope and the aesthetics of new development, leaving the specific uses of a given building largely unregulated. These codes often regulate through illustrations enacted into law as opposed to the text and map approach of traditional zoning. The idea is to focus on the experience of the streetscape and the form of the community rather than on potential conflicts between incompatible uses.[2]

These modern approaches to land use regulation place more emphasis on sustainability and equity, with a greater recognition of the environmental and social costs of traditional zoning.

§1.5 Patterns in Land Use Litigation

Disputes over land use regulation tend to follow two broad patterns. In the first, a property owner who is aggrieved about a land use restriction challenges a given action by the relevant local government agency. This can involve situations where the initial imposition of zoning or other land use regulation interferes with an existing use or with an owner's plans for her property. This kind of dispute, however, more often involves owners' challenges to unfavorable decisions when owners seek to rezone their property, to obtain discretionary relief from zoning, or to obtain other required approvals for new development.

In the second common pattern of litigation, an owner is granted the right to do something with her property that neighbors or other community members object to, and those neighbors challenge the local government's decision. In these cases, there can be questions of **standing**, or entitlement to litigate, given that neighbors and

2. Form-based codes bear some resemblance to **performance zoning**, which has been an important part of zoning for the past half-century. Performance zoning shifts the focus of regulation from classifying uses to establishing standards for the impacts of kinds of development. Industrial performance zoning, for example, might set limits on issues such as emissions or noise, and only allow uses that meet these standards. Julian Conrad Juergensmeyer & Thomas E. Roberts, *Land Use Planning and Development Regulation Law* §4.19, at 90 (3d ed. 2013).

others may be affected by, but not directly subject to, a zoning decision. Decisions on standing usually turn on a fact-specific combination of legislative authorization under the relevant zoning code and an analysis of the extent of the injury to the aggrieved party. *Compare, e.g., Ray v. Mayor and City Council of Baltimore*, 59 A.3d 545 (Md. 2013) (residents who lived more than 1,000 feet from a site that was approved for rezoning lacked sufficient particular aggrievement for standing), *with Heffernan v. Missoula City Council*, 255 P.3d 80, 90-96 (Mont. 2011) (neighbors had standing because they fell within the statutory definition of parties entitled to challenge land use regulatory decisions and met the state constitutional requirement of alleging "a past, present, or threatened injury to a property or civil right").

Public opinion and citizens associations are quite powerful in zoning practice. Organized citizen groups may affect both the general shape of the zoning law and individual zoning board decisions on particular development proposals. Property developers must contend with neighborhood opposition to particular projects and may need to negotiate with citizens organizations to obtain their consent or acquiescence. These negotiations can lead to **community benefit agreements** that specify certain obligations for developers regarding issues such as affordable housing, local jobs, and development-impact mitigation. Zoning boards and city councils may also block particular developments until changes are made so as to address the concerns of neighbors and community activists. Perhaps not surprisingly, land use regulation, at least when it involves large-scale development, has increasingly shifted toward a model of negotiation. This shift may have the advantage of producing zoning rules that more carefully balance the needs of the owner and the community in the context of a given development proposal. Striking such a balance, however, can pose a challenge to the model of neutral, even-handed, prospective rational planning. *See* Carol Rose, *Planning and Dealing: Piecemeal Land Controls as Problem of Local Legitimacy*, 71 Cal. L. Rev. 837 (1983).

Facing opposition from community groups over development or from environmental groups who fear the adverse environmental effects of particular projects, some developers have struck back by bringing lawsuits against community groups to intimidate them into dropping their opposition. The most common action brought is a claim of defamation, in which the developer alleges that defendants have made false statements intended to harm the developer's reputation. Most courts have dismissed these lawsuits, on the grounds that (1) defendants have free speech rights to petition the government, or (2) the statements alleged to have been made by defendants constitute opinions, not statements of fact, and thus cannot be true or false. These cases have been characterized as **SLAPP suits**, a term that stands for "strategic lawsuits against public participation." *See* Penelope Canan & George W. Pring, *SLAPPs: Getting Sued for Speaking Out* (1996).

Defendants in SLAPP suits have several avenues of recourse. They may bring a countersuit (called a "SLAPP-back") for the tort of malicious prosecution, claiming that the lawsuit against them is frivolous, without substantial basis, and motivated by malice. They may seek sanctions against the plaintiff's attorney through the state board of bar overseers, on the grounds that the plaintiff's attorney has violated state ethical guidelines against bringing litigation for the sole purpose of harassment. If the suit was brought in federal court, they may ask for Rule 11 sanctions, on the grounds that the claim lacks any basis in law. Some states have also regulated SLAPP suits by statute. *See, e.g.,* Mass. Gen. Laws. ch. 231, §59H; Cal. Civ. Proc. §425.16; N.Y. Civ. Rights Law §§70-a & 76-a; N.Y.C.P.L.R. §§3211(g) & 3212(h).

§2 CONSTRAINTS ON ZONING AUTHORITY TO PROTECT PREEXISTING PROPERTY RIGHTS

When municipalities enact zoning codes, the legislation tends to follow existing land use patterns. This means that owners who are using their property in a certain way, such as for single-family homes or farmland, are able to continue doing so. However, zoning may also require owners to phase out or change existing uses, or may impose new rules in the middle of the development process, as local governments recognize new concerns (or respond to new pressures). Two doctrines in particular, prior nonconforming use and vested rights, can provide legal protection against newly enacted zoning or other land use regulation that surprises owners who had invested in reliance on prior law.

The source and status of these doctrines is unclear. They may constitute applications of the federal or state constitutional rules prohibiting uncompensated takings of property, or due process limitations on retroactive legislation. However, many cases applying these rules treat them as nonconstitutional doctrines, suggesting that they are based on an interpretation of the state's zoning enabling act or its administrative law code. *See generally* Christopher Serkin, *Existing Uses and the Limits of Land Use Regulations,* 84 N.Y.U. L. Rev. 1222 (2009).

§2.1 Prior Nonconforming Uses

Town of Belleville v. Parrillo's, Inc.

416 A.2d 388 (N.J. 1980)

Map: Harrison Street, Belleville, New Jersey

ROBERT L. CLIFFORD, J.

[S]ometime prior to 1955 Parrillo's operated as a restaurant and catering service on Harrison Street, Belleville. On January 1, 1955 the Town enacted a new zoning ordinance of which all provisions pertinent here are still in effect. The system created under that ordinance provided for zoning under which specific permitted uses for each zone were itemized. Uses not set forth for a particular zone were deemed prohibited. Parrillo's was situated in a "B" residence zone, which did not allow restaurants.

However, because it had been in existence prior to the effective date of the zoning ordinance, defendant's establishment qualified as a preexisting nonconforming use[3] and, under the terms of the ordinance, was allowed to remain in operation.

In 1978 defendant's owners made certain renovations in the premises. Upon their completion Parrillo's opened as a discotheque. We readily acknowledge that included among those for whom the term "discotheque" has not, at least until this case, found its way into their common parlance are some members of this Court; and on the assumption that there may be others whose experience has denied them an intimate familiarity with the term and the milieu to which it applies, we pause to extend the benefit of definition. *Webster's Third New International Dictionary* 63a (1976) informs us that a discotheque is a "small intimate nightclub for dancing to recorded music; broadly: a nightclub often featuring psychedelic and mixed-media attractions (as slides, movies, and special lighting effects)." "Disco" appears to be an accepted abbreviation. Defendant's operation is closer to the broad definition above than it is to a small or intimate cabaret.

Shortly after they had opened under the new format, Parrillo's owners applied for a discotheque license as required by the Town's ordinance regulating dancehalls. Although the application was denied, defendant continued business as usual. Thereupon the municipal construction code official filed the charges culminating in the conviction under review. The municipal court imposed a fine of $250.00.

On a trial *de novo* after defendant's appeal to the Superior Court, Law Division, the defendant was again found guilty. The Appellate Division reversed.

Superior Court Judge Joseph Walsh made extensive and specific findings of fact. They are amply supported by the record and are as follows:

The business was formerly advertised as a restaurant; it is now advertised as a "disco." It was formerly operated every day and now it is open but one day and three evenings. The primary use of the dance hall was incidental to dining; now it is the primary use. The music was formerly provided by live bands and now it is recorded and operated by a so-called "disc-jockey." An admission charge of $3.00 on the Wednesday opening and $5.00 on the Friday and Saturday openings is now mandatory as opposed to any prior entry charge. There is no charge for Sunday. Formerly there was but one bar; now there are several.

During the course of the testimony it was admitted that the business is operated as a "disco." Normal lighting in the premises was altered to psychedelic lighting, colored and/or revolving, together with mirrored lighting. The premises were crowded and there were long lines waiting to enter. There are now fewer tables than the prior use required and on one occasion there were no tables. The music was extremely loud and the premises can accommodate 431 persons legally. There have been numerous complaints from residents adjacent to the area. During the course of the testimony

3. N.J. Stat. §40:55D-5 defines a "nonconforming use" as "a use or activity which was lawful prior to the adoption, revision or amendment of a zoning ordinance, but which fails to conform to the requirements of the zoning district in which it is located by reason of such adoption, revision, or amendment." — EDS.

"disco" dancing was described by the owners as dancing by "kids" who "don't hold each other close." The bulk of the prior business was food catering; now there is none. The foods primarily served at the present time are "hamburgers" and "cheeseburgers," although there are other selections available to people who might come in earlier than the "disco" starting time.

On the basis of these findings Judge Walsh concluded that there had been a prohibited change in the use of the premises. He found to be dispositive the straightforward proposition that "a 'disco' is a place wherein you dance and a restaurant a place wherein you eat. It is as simple as that"—an unvarnished exercise in reductionism, perhaps, but one fully justified in this case. He concluded that the defendant had "abandoned all the pretenses of the continued existence of a restaurant as it was before." We agree with that conclusion.

Historically, a nonconforming use has been looked upon as "a use of land, buildings or premises that lawfully existed prior to the enactment of a zoning ordinance and which is maintained after the effective date of such ordinance even though it does not comply with the use restrictions applicable to the area in which it is situated." 6 R. Powell, *The Law of Real Property*, ¶871 (Perm. ed. 1979). Under the Municipal Land Use Act, N.J. Stat. §§40:55D-1 *et seq.*, such property is deemed to have acquired a vested right to continue in such form, irrespective of the restrictive zoning provisions:

> Any nonconforming use or structure existing at the time of the passage of an ordinance may be continued upon the lot or in the structure so occupied and any such structure maybe restored or repaired in the event of partial destruction thereof. (N.J. Stat. §40:55D-68.)

This statutory guarantee against compulsory termination, however, is not without limit. Because nonconforming uses are inconsistent with the objectives of uniform zoning, the courts have required that consistent with the property rights of those affected and with substantial justice, they should be reduced to conformity as quickly as is compatible with justice. In that regard the courts have permitted municipalities to impose limitations upon nonconforming uses. Such restrictions typically relate to the change of use; the enlargement or extension of the repair or replacement of nonconforming structures; and limits on the duration of nonconforming uses through abandonment or discontinuance.

The method generally used to limit nonconforming uses is to prevent any increase or change in the nonconformity. Under that restrictive view our courts have held that an existing nonconforming use will be permitted to continue only if it is a continuance of substantially the same kind of use as that to which the premises were devoted at the time of the passage of the zoning ordinance. In that regard nonconforming uses may not be enlarged as of right except where the change is so negligible or insubstantial that it does not warrant judicial or administrative interference. Where there is doubt as to whether an enlargement or change is substantial rather than insubstantial, the courts have consistently declared that it is to be resolved against the enlargement or change.

In the instant case it is acknowledged by all parties that the former restaurant had constituted a proper preexisting nonconforming use. The issue then becomes whether the conversion from a restaurant to a discotheque represented a substantial change, and was thus improper. Fundamental to that inquiry is an appraisal of the basic character of the use, before and after the change.

Courts that have engaged in that appraisal have proceeded with a caution approaching suspicion. *Hantman v. Randolph Twp.*, 155 A.2d 554 (N.J. Super. Ct. App. Div. 1959), well illustrates the proper analysis for examining changes in nonconforming uses. In *Hantman*, the plaintiffs owned a commercial bungalow colony which was primarily dedicated to seasonal use. When the area in which the colony was situated was zoned for residential use, the plaintiffs' property was afforded preexisting nonconforming use status by the Township. In 1957 the plaintiffs attempted to convert the bungalows into dwellings suitable for year-round occupancy. That effort was challenged by the Township on the ground that the change would constitute an unlawful extension of the nonconforming use.

Reviewing the facts the court established that the plaintiffs' bungalows were in fact nonconforming uses. It then proceeded to address the question of whether permitting full-time occupancy would effect a substantial change in the premises. Answering in the affirmative, the court declared, "an increase in the time period during which a nonconforming use is operated may justifiably be the basis for finding an unlawful extension thereof, just as changes in the functional use of the land or increases in the area of use have been." Recognizing that nonconforming uses are disfavored, the Appellate Division emphasized the deleterious effect that year-round operation of the bungalows might have upon the general welfare of the municipality. Noting that where there is doubt as to the substantiality of the extension, it should be disapproved, the court found the proposed conversion represented a substantial, and therefore unlawful, change in the nonconforming property. We fully approve of and adopt the approach and analytical framework of the *Hantman* court.

We have already expressed our agreement with the municipal court and with Judge Walsh, presiding at the trial *de novo*, that defendant's conversion of the premises from a restaurant to a discotheque resulted in a substantial, and therefore impermissible, change. The entire character of the business has been altered. What was once a restaurant is now a dancehall. Measured by the zoning ordinance the general welfare of the neighborhood has been demonstrably affected adversely by the conversion of defendant's business. Our strong public policy restricting nonconforming uses requires reversal of the judgment below.

Notes and Questions

1. **Curtailing incompatible uses through amortization.** Even where zoning generally follows existing patterns of development, there can be isolated parcels that are being used in ways that are not compatible with the surrounding zone. In many instances, this can be non-controversial, as with a small grocery store in an otherwise residential neighborhood. But nonconforming uses can also undermine the public purposes of zoning and create a legislatively protected monopoly, if an owner has the exclusive right to conduct a business in the area. Early zoning codes generally assumed

that disfavored incompatible uses would largely fade away over time, but that turned out not to be the case for many such anomalies. (Can you see why?) Zoning codes thus have to balance the rights of owners whose established uses conflict with the orderly development of a community and the expectations of neighbors who may be relying on the general character of a neighborhood to be protected by zoning.

In most states, local governments may require nonconforming uses to be phased out through a process called **amortization**. With amortization, local governments give the nonconforming owner a limited period of time to continue the use. If this gives owners sufficient time to realize a reasonable return on their investment, that will balance the owner's reliance interest with the public's needs represented in the zoning code. Amortization periods can be fixed by statute, depending on the nature of the property. *See* Patricia E. Salkin, *Abandonment, Discontinuance and Amortization of Nonconforming Uses: Lessons for Drafters of Zoning Regulations*, 38 Real Est. L.J. 486 (2010) (citing local amortization statutes with periods ranging from 3 to 50 years). They can also be set on a case-by-case basis, looking at issues such as the depreciable value of the property and an owner's specific investment. Courts have upheld both methods, but in so doing, generally look to whether owners can obtain a reasonable return on their investment, weighing public gain against private loss. *See, e.g., Bugsy's, Inc. v. City of Myrtle Beach*, 530 S.E.2d 890, 895 (S.C. 2000).

In general, nonconforming uses may continue even where property has been transferred from one owner to another. However, in *Village of Valatie v. Smith*, 632 N.E.2d 1264 (N.Y. 1994), the court upheld a provision that provided the right to continue a nonconforming use would be terminated upon transfer of the property. The defendant had inherited a mobile home that was nonconforming because it was situated outside of a mobile home park. The village sought to have the mobile home removed, and the owner argued that pegging termination to the transfer had no relation either to the village's land use objectives or to the owner's investment and impermissibly zoned based on who owns the property, not on the use to which the property is being put. The court rejected these arguments under a general test that looked to the overall reasonableness of the amortization period.

2. Limiting changes for nonconforming uses. *Belleville v. Parrillo's* illustrates another way to balance an owner's interest in continuing a nonconforming use against the public interest in the zoning code, by strictly limiting the owner to the use that existed at the time zoning was imposed. An owner may then continue the nonconforming use indefinitely.

This right to continue a nonconforming use can raise a number of legal challenges. For example, is an owner allowed to increase the intensity of uses as business grows? *See, e.g., Piesco v. Hollihan*, 47 A.D.3d 938 (N.Y. App. Div. 2008) (nonconforming restaurant and marina allowed to increase the volume and intensity of the use). Can the owner of a nonconforming parcel expand to use more of a given parcel? *Compare, e.g., Shirley Wayside Ltd. Partnership v. Board of Appeals of Shirley*, 961 N.E.2d 1055 (Mass. 2012) (nonconforming mobile home park entitled to expand the area on the property that had mobile homes on it), *with Adams Outdoor Advertising, L.P. v. Board of Zoning Appeals*, 645 S.E.2d 271 (Va. 2007) (owner of nonconforming billboard denied the right to add an electronic message board because the addition increased the billboard's depth, even though its visible dimensions were unchanged). How should courts evaluate the extent to which a change to a nonconforming use is permissible?

3. Abandonment and destruction. Under many zoning ordinances, if a nonconforming use is abandoned or discontinued, the nonconforming status is lost, even if the owner later attempts to reestablish that use. The standard for abandonment or discontinuance is generally defined by the relevant zoning code, most of which are interpreted by courts to require proof of the owner's intent to abandon. *Compare, e.g., Gorgone v. D.C. Board of Zoning Adjustment*, 973 A.2d 692, 694 (D.C. 2009) (requiring a showing of an overt act or failure to act that implies abandonment as well as evidence of intent by the owner to abandon), *with Pike Indus., Inc. v. Woodward*, 999 A.2d 257, 261-262 (N.H. 2010) (zoning ordinance did not require evidence of intent to abandon where it provided that if "a non-conforming use has been discontinued for more than one year for any reason, such non-conforming use shall not thereafter be re-established"). If a nonconforming use is not abandoned, but substantially damaged or destroyed, for example in a fire, most zoning ordinances do not allow owners to rebuild.

§2.2 Vested Rights

Stone v. City of Wilton

331 N.W.2d 398 (Iowa 1983)

Map: Wilton, Iowa

ARTHUR MCGIVERIN, Justice.

Plaintiffs Alex and Martha Stone appeal from the dismissal of their petition for declaratory judgment, injunctive relief and damages in an action regarding defendant City of Wilton's rezoning from multi-family to single-family residential of certain real estate owned by plaintiffs. The issues raised by plaintiffs focus on the validity of the rezoning ordinance. We find no error in trial court's rulings and affirm its decision.

This appeal is a zoning dispute involving approximately six acres of land in the city of Wilton, Iowa. Plaintiffs purchased the undeveloped land in June 1979 with the intent of developing a low income, federally subsidized housing project. The project was to consist of several multi-family units; therefore, feasibility of the project depended upon multi-family zoning of the tract. At the time of purchase approximately one-fourth of plaintiffs' land was zoned R-1, single-family residential, and the remainder was zoned R-2, multi-family residential.

After the land was purchased, plaintiffs incurred expenses for architectural fees and engineering services in the preparation of plans and plats to be submitted to the city council and its planning and zoning commission. In addition, plaintiffs secured a Farmers' Home Administration (FHA) loan commitment for construction of the project.

In December 1979 plaintiffs filed a preliminary plat for the project with the city clerk. In March 1980, following a public meeting, the planning and zoning commission recommended to the city council that land in the northern part of the city be rezoned to single-family residential due to alleged inadequacies of sewer, water and electrical services. The rezoning recommendation affected all of plaintiffs' property plus tracts owned by two other developers. Plaintiffs' application on May 21, 1980, for a building permit to construct multi-family dwellings was denied due to the pending rezoning recommendation.

In May 1980, plaintiffs filed a petition against the city seeking a declaratory judgment invalidating any rezoning of their property, temporary and permanent injunctions to prohibit passage of any rezoning ordinance, and in the event of rezoning, $570,000 damages for monies expended on the project, anticipated lost profits and alleged reduction in the value of plaintiffs' land.

In accordance with the recommendation of the planning and zoning commission, the city council passed an ordinance rezoning the land from R-2 to R-1 in June 1980. Following the council's rezoning decision, the planning and zoning commission approved plaintiffs' preliminary plat.

[T]he inevitable restrictions on individual uses of property which accompany zoning normally do not constitute a taking. Plaintiffs, however, claim to have had a vested right in developing their property as subsidized, multi-family housing and, therefore, the rezoning allegedly amounted to a taking of this right. Consequently, they contend the zoning ordinance should be inapplicable to their project. We disagree.

The record shows that a factor in the Stones' choice of property was zoning which permitted multi-family residences. Immediately after purchasing the property in Wilton, plaintiffs made certain expenditures in preparation for obtaining the necessary government financing and in order to comply with city ordinances for platting and building permits. These expenditures totaled approximately $7,900, plus the time and effort expended personally by the plaintiffs.

The standard for determining if a property owner has vested rights in a zoning classification was set forth in *Board of Supervisors of Scott County v. Paaske*, 98 N.W.2d 827, 831 (Iowa 1959):

> It is impossible to fix a definite percentage of the total cost which establishes vested rights and applies to all cases. It depends on the type of the project, its location, ultimate cost, and *principally the amount accomplished under conformity*. Each case must be decided on its own merits, taking these elements into consideration. (Emphasis added.)

Prior to rezoning, Paaske purchased a parcel of land onto which he planned to move five houses. The county granted him a permit to move the houses. Paaske excavated the basements for four houses; placed a septic tank underground for the fifth house; laid concrete footings for the basement of two houses; entered into a contract for the building of the foundations under all five houses, and placed a substantial amount of building materials on the property before the land was rezoned. We concluded that Paaske's endeavors prior to rezoning were so substantial that he had a vested right in completing his project.

In the present case, one of the factors leading to the purchase of this land in Wilton was the fact that it was zoned for multi-family residences. Plaintiffs secured funding from the FHA and engaged the services of an architect and engineer who drew up plans and plats. But these were only the most preliminary steps towards construction. The architect's plans were not the working blueprints of a contractor. The trial court stated they were "the kind [of plans] that one could find in *Better Homes and Gardens* [magazine]." No construction bids were sought and no construction contracts were let. No materials were placed on the site and no construction or earth work was started. We agree with the trial court that plaintiffs' efforts and expenditures prior to rezoning were not so substantial as to create vested rights in the completion of the housing project on that particular tract of land in Wilton.

Under the facts of this case, plaintiffs had to prove they had a vested right to complete their intended project in order to argue that the rezoning constituted a taking. All that the rezoning did was to deprive plaintiffs of what they considered to be the land's most beneficial use. If, as we have found, the ordinance is a valid exercise of police power, the fact that it deprives the property of its most beneficial use does not render it an unconstitutional taking.

"In determining where a zoning regulation ends and a taking of property begins, the test is essentially one of reasonableness." C. Rhyne, *The Law of Local Government Operations*, §26.16 at 745 (1980). We do not believe that rezoning a portion of plaintiffs' property from R-2 to R-1 exceeded the bounds of reasonableness. The city council clearly could have reasonably believed that the general welfare interests of the community outweighed the Stones' investment interest in constructing subsidized, multi-family housing.

Even if the testimony of Stones' expert is accepted, the change in zoning resulted in, at most, a 42% decrease in value of their property. Such economic impact does not constitute a taking in light of the council's reasonable belief that the public welfare required a change in zoning. *See Euclid v. Ambler Realty Co.*, 272 U.S. 365 (1926) (75% diminution in value caused by zoning law did not constitute a taking). Other evidence, however, showed the rezoning to R-1 only slightly affected the fair market value of plaintiffs' land.

Plaintiffs' claim to a right to realize their investment expectations overlooks the fact that "rights granted by legislative action under police power can be taken away when in the valid exercise of its discretion the legislative body sees fit." [*Keller v. City of Council Bluffs*, 66 N.W.2d 113, 119 (Iowa 1954).] At most, the decision of the council "took" from plaintiffs a sizeable tax shelter. Because the reasonableness of the council's decision to rezone plaintiffs' property clearly is at least a fairly debatable question, we cannot substitute our view of reasonableness for that of the council.

We hold that the ordinance which rezoned an area of the city of Wilton that included a portion of plaintiffs' land is valid and applicable to plaintiffs' land and proposed project.

Notes and Questions

Most states agree with the standard in *Stone*: owners have vested rights to existing zoning law if they have invested substantially in good faith reliance on that law. A majority of courts will require an owner's substantial investment to be made based on a validly issued building permit or other approval. Julian Conrad Juergensmeyer & Thomas E. Roberts, *Land Use Planning and Development Regulation Law* §5.28, at 171 (3d ed. 2013). In some states, by contrast, developers can vest their rights if they incur substantial costs in reasonable reliance on existing law even in the absence of a building permit. *See Friends of Yamhill County, Inc. v. Board of Commissioners of Yamhill County*, 264 P.3d 1265, 1274 (Or. 2011); *see also* Va. Code §15.2-2307 (requiring extensive obligations or substantial expenditure in good faith reliance on a "significant affirmative governmental act" such as a rezoning or site plan approval).

The question of how to measure the necessary substantiality of the investment has divided the courts. In *Friends of Yamhill County*, the court noted that one approach has been to compare " 'the ratio of expenses incurred to the total cost of the project,' " measuring "those expenses that related 'exclusive[ly]' to the proposed development." 264 P.3d at 1275 (quoting *Town of Hempstead v. Lynne*, 222 N.Y.S.2d 526 (1961)). *Friends of Yamhill County* identified a broader approach, however, adding to the ratio analysis other factors that include:

> the good faith of the landowner, whether or not he had notice of any proposed zoning or amendatory zoning before starting his improvements, the type of expenditures, i.e., whether the expenditures have any relation to the completed project or could apply to various other uses of the land, the kind of project, the location and ultimate cost. Also, the acts of the landowner should rise beyond mere contemplated use or preparation, such as leveling of land, boring test holes, or preliminary negotiations with contractors or architects.

Id. (quoting *Clackamas Co. v. Holmes*, 508 P.2d 190 (Or. 1973) (citations omitted)).

A minority of states grants developers vested rights upon the filing of a valid and fully complete building permit application, without the need to demonstrate substantial expenditures. *See, e.g.*, *Abbey Road Group, LLC v. City of Bonney Lake*, 218 P.3d 180, 182-183 (Wash. 2009). This so-called early vesting approach is thought to promote certainty, because it identifies a moment in the development process when owners and the local government know that the land use rules in force will remain. Some states allow vesting if a developer obtains site-specific approval for development, such as a preliminary subdivision plan, even before a building permit is issued; New Jersey provides such protection. *See, e.g.*, N.J. Stat. §§40:55D-49 to 40:55D-52. Some states go so far as to grant developers vested rights to use their land in accordance with the zoning law in place at the time they *apply for* site-specific approval. Colo. Rev. Stat. §§24-68-101 to 24-68-106; Mass. Gen. Laws ch. 40A, §6; Tex. Loc. Gov't Code §§245.002-245.006; Wash. Rev. Code §§19.27.095, 58.17.033.

Problems

1. In *Cumberland Farms v. Town of Groton*, 719 A.2d 465 (Conn. 1998), land used as a gas station was rezoned for residential use. The gas station was allowed to continue operation as a prior nonconforming use. However, when the owner was required by federal environmental statutes to clean up pollution caused by leaking underground storage tanks on the property, the owner sought to open a little convenience store on the property along with the gas station to raise enough money to pay for the cleanup. Assume that the income from operation of the gas station is not sufficient to pay for the environmental cleanup but that the owner could sell the property at a very low price to someone who could clean up the property, demolish the gas station, and construct condominiums on the land. Such a sale would end the prior nonconforming use and clean up the property but the current owner would have lost his business and received very little in selling the land. The current owner cannot convert the property to condominiums himself because no bank would loan him the money for the project. The property has a viable economic use for another owner but the only economically viable use for the current owner is to open the convenience store and keep operating the gas station.

Is the current owner entitled to open a small convenience store on the gas station property under the prior nonconforming use doctrine?

2. A licensed day care center operates on a parcel of property that is rezoned for residential use. The day care use is allowed to continue as a prior nonconforming use. The cost of insurance rises so dramatically that it may no longer be profitable to operate the day care center. The site is suitable for a single-family dwelling, but the structure is not; the cost of renovating the day care center to convert it to a single-family home is roughly equivalent to the cost of tearing it down and building an entirely new structure. The owner of the day care center wishes to convert the property for use as classroom facilities for deaf high school students, who would take some classes at the center and other classes with hearing students at the high school. The building is suited to such a use.

a. **Prior nonconforming use.** Would this constitute an unlawful extension of a prior nonconforming use under the standards articulated in *Belleville v. Parrillo's*?

b. **Vested rights.** The owner gets the property rezoned for school purposes, begins plans to convert the building, hires and pays fees to an architect and signs a contract with a building contractor to renovate the day care center and a contract with the school board to provide classes in sign language for the deaf high school students in the school district. Both contracts are contingent on obtaining a building permit as required by the local zoning law. The owner applies for, but has not yet been granted, a building permit and has spent a total of $20,000. The neighbors organize opposition to the location of the project and successfully induce the city council to rescind its rezoning of the parcel, effectively returning the parcel to residential use. The owner of the parcel sues the city, claiming that the second rezoning interferes with her vested rights in the prior zoning classification. She argues that owners have vested rights to use property in accordance with existing zoning classifications if they invest substantial amounts of money (in addition to the purchase price of the parcel) in plans to build on the parcel in reasonable reliance on the existing classification. The city argues that no vested rights can arise until a building permit has actually issued, regardless of the sum the owner has spent in preparatory plans. Which rule should the court adopt?

§3 REZONING AND CHALLENGES TO ZONING CLASSIFICATIONS

Developers who want to build projects that are inconsistent with current zoning requirements may approach the planning board or the city council with a proposal to **rezone** the parcel in a manner that will authorize the project. Rezoning may be done for particular parcels or for whole districts or portions of districts. Rezoning can involve amendments to the text of the ordinance, which prospectively change the allowable uses or the permitted physical attributes of the development, or can involve map amendments, which change the geographical boundaries of existing zones. Some rezoning involves both text and map amendments.

Many state zoning enabling acts require any changes in the zoning ordinance to accord with the comprehensive plan. This does not mean the plan cannot be changed over time. It does mean, however, that zoning decisions are intended to be made with a broad, long-range view of how uses harmonize in the jurisdiction as a whole. Some courts will hold local legislatures strictly to the requirement that zoning proceed in accord with a general plan, striking down zoning amendments that are not sufficiently justified in light of comprehensive planning. *Riya Finnegan LLC v. Township Council of South Brunswick*, 962 A.2d 484, 489-491 (N.J. 2008). Many courts grant greater discretion to the governing body; some treat the zoning code itself as evidence of a master plan, and some courts, particularly in states that have no requirement for planning, may not require consistency with planning at all.

Review for consistency with a general plan is only one of several doctrines under which courts reviewing challenges to particularized zoning changes may take a less deferential approach than normally applied to economic and social regulation. This section reviews several of these doctrines: (1) contract and conditional zoning, (2) spot zoning, (3) the change or mistake doctrine, and (4) characterizing rezoning as a quasi-judicial, rather than legislative, act. These doctrines, which can overlap to some degree in practice, do not necessarily render rezoning invalid, but they can weaken the presumption of validity that generally applies to legislative acts.

This less deferential approach to judicial review may be justified by concerns about a breakdown in the political process through which a given land use law has been passed, or concerns about local corruption. Alternatively, courts may be seeking to reinforce the primacy of general, prospective, comprehensive zoning. As you read the material in this section, consider whether it is better for courts to defer to local legislatures when owners challenge zoning law or take a more active role in overseeing the local political process.

Durand v. IDC Bellingham, L.L.C.

793 N.E.2d 359 (Mass. 2003)

Map: Bellingham, Massachusetts

CORDY, ROBERT, J.

On May 28, 1997, residents attending the town of Bellingham's (town's) open town meeting voted to rezone a parcel of land located in the town. Three and one-half years later, several residents living near the parcel brought suit challenging the rezoning. The question before the court is whether the town meeting vote was invalid because the prospective owner of the parcel, IDC Bellingham, L.L.C. (IDC), had offered to give the town $8 million if the rezoning was approved and a power plant was built and operated on the site.

1. Background

The essential facts of this case are undisputed. In 1993, the town began to examine ways to increase its property tax base. An economic development task force was appointed by the town's board of selectmen (board) to study the issue. The task force prepared a report recommending that development of industrial land in the town be a priority. The report identified a parcel on the corner of Depot Street and Box Pond Road (locus), which abutted land that was already zoned for industrial use, as a candidate for rezoning from agricultural and suburban use to industrial use. Subsequently, at the town's May, 1995, town meeting, a zoning article proposing the rezoning of the locus and an adjacent parcel for industrial use fell eight votes short of the required two-thirds majority.

In 1997, IDC, which owned a power plant in the town, began discussions with town officials about the possibility of rezoning the locus so that a second plant might ultimately be built on it. These discussions included the subject of what public benefits and financial inducements IDC might offer the town with regard to the proposed plant. The town administrator told IDC officials that the town was facing an $8 million shortfall in its plans to construct a much needed new high school. Shortly thereafter, the president of IDC publicly announced that IDC would make an $8 million gift to the town if IDC (1) decided to build the plant; (2) obtained the financing and permits necessary to build the plant; and (3) operated the plant successfully for one year. The offer was made to generate support for the plant and became common knowledge in the town.

While the genesis of the offer was the need for a new high school, IDC made it clear that the town could use the money for any municipal purpose. The town's high school building committee, the town's finance committee, the town's master plan steering committee, and certain town officials voiced strong support for the plant and the zoning change required for its construction on the locus. Some committee members engaged in a campaign to get voters to the town meeting at which the rezoning was to be considered.

On May 28, 1997, the town held its open town meeting and a zoning article calling for the rezoning of the locus was introduced. IDC made a presentation of its proposed use of the locus for a second power plant and reiterated its offer of an $8 million gift to the town if the plant was built and became operational. The planning board and finance committee both recommended passage of the zoning article. There was some discussion of the zoning aspects of the proposal, as well as discussion regarding the offered gift. Residents for and against the proposal to build a plant on the site spoke, and IDC responded to their comments. The zoning article passed by more than the necessary two-thirds vote of the town meeting.

Between May, 1997, and January, 2001, IDC spent approximately $7 million to develop the locus for a power plant. At some point in the summer of 1998, the board learned that IDC was proposing to increase the size of the plant beyond what it had presented to the town meeting in 1997. Consequently, the board wrote a letter to the energy facilities siting board [whose approval is required prior to the construction of any "generating facility," *see* Mass. Gen. Laws ch. 164, §§69H-69J1/2] withdrawing its support for the plant. Shortly thereafter, representatives of IDC and the board met to negotiate a compromise. The outcome of those negotiations was an agreement by IDC to reduce the size of the plant and, in April, 1999, the execution of an "Agreement for Water/Wastewater Services" between IDC and the town. The agreement provided in part that:

> IDC shall provide funds ($8,000,000.00) to the Town for its various capital expenditures, municipal projects and municipal improvements. This Agreement is intended to memorialize, without duplicating the $8,000,000 commitment IDC and its affiliates previously made to the Town in connection with the Plant.

IDC submitted a request for five special permits to the town's zoning board of appeals on May 5, 2000, and the special permits were granted on January 2, 2001. On January 23, 2001, the plaintiffs, eight landowners located near the locus, filed suit in the Land Court against IDC, the town, the town zoning board of appeals, and the owner of the property. [Plaintiffs] seek declaratory judgment that the rezoning of the locus on May 28, 1997, was void because it constituted illegal "contract" zoning.

[T]he [trial] judge found that "contract zoning" had not occurred here, at least within the meaning he ascribed to that term. He then found that "there would be little doubt that the 1997 rezoning was valid" if the $8 million gift offer had not been made, and proceeded to discuss its implications. He viewed the offer of the gift as an "extraneous consideration," because it was not defended as being in mitigation of the impacts of the project, and therefore concluded that it was "offensive to public policy." He ultimately concluded that the fact that the offer was made was sufficient, without the necessity of finding that voting town meeting members were influenced by it, to nullify the rezoning vote. The defendants appealed. Because we conclude that the voluntary offer of public benefits beyond what might be necessary to mitigate the development of a parcel of land does not, standing alone, invalidate a legislative act of the town meeting, we reverse.

2. *Discussion*

The enactment of a zoning bylaw by the voters at town meeting is not only the exercise of an independent police power; it is also a legislative act carrying a strong presumption of validity. It will not normally be undone unless the plaintiff can demonstrate "by a preponderance of the evidence that the zoning regulation is arbitrary and unreasonable, or substantially unrelated to the public health, safety . . . or general welfare." *Johnson v. Edgartown*, 680 N.E.2d 37, 40 (Mass. 1997). If the reasonableness of a zoning bylaw is even "fairly debatable, the judgment of the local legislative body responsible for the enactment must be sustained." *Crall v. Leominster*, 284 N.E.2d 610, 615 (Mass. 1972). Such an analysis is not affected by consideration of the various possible motives that may have inspired legislative action. *See Boston v. Talbot*, 91 N.E. 1014, 1016-1017 (Mass. 1910). ("The diverse character of such motives, and the impossibility of penetrating into the hearts of men and ascertaining the truth, precludes all such inquiries as impracticable and futile").[4]

a. *State Law*

Municipal zoning procedure is governed by Mass. Gen. Laws ch. 40A. Section 5 dictates the process a municipality must follow in amending its zoning bylaws. In a town, such an amendment must be submitted to the board [of selectmen], which, within fourteen days, must then refer the amendment to the planning board for review. The planning board has sixty-five days during which to hold a public hearing, with notice provided beforehand, at which members of the public can offer their views on the amendment. Once the hearing has been held, the planning board has twenty-one days to provide its recommendation to the town meeting. Thereafter, the town meeting may adopt, reject, or amend the proposed amendment to the zoning bylaw. The town meeting must act, however, within six months of the planning board hearing. The amendment will not be enacted unless it receives a two-thirds vote from town meeting. Neither party claims that this process was not followed, and the record before us indicates that it was.

An agreement between a property owner and a municipality to rezone a parcel of land may cause the municipality to violate the process mandated by §5. Such an instance of "contract zoning," as we will refer to it, involving a promise by a municipality to rezone a property either before the vote to rezone has been taken or before the

4. *But see Pheasant Ridge Assocs. Ltd. P'ship v. Burlington*, 506 N.E.2d 1152, 1157 (Mass. 1987) (where undisputed evidence "requires" conclusion that town's exercise of eminent domain had been bad faith attempt to contravene State's affordable housing law, Mass. Gen. Laws ch. 40B, land taking could be invalidated). The *Pheasant Ridge* case, decided under a different statute intended to limit rather than grant municipal power, is inapposite to the question at hand.

required §5 process has been undertaken, evades the dictates of Mass. Gen. Laws ch. 40A, and may render the subsequent rezoning invalid. The Land Court judge correctly concluded that no such advance agreement existed in this case. IDC pledged that if the town were to rezone the locus for industrial use (and if other events occurred), IDC would pay the town $8 million. At no time before the May 28, 1997, town meeting were the voters of town meeting bound to approve the zoning change.[5] Because the town followed the procedures dictated by §5, the rezoning was not invalid on statutory grounds.[6]

b. *Validity of the Bylaw as Exercise of Legislative Police Power*

The judge found that absent the $8 million offer, the rezoning was substantively valid. We take that to mean that it was neither arbitrary nor unreasonable, and was substantially related to the public health, safety, or general welfare of the town. In other words, its adoption served a valid public purpose. The record fully supports this conclusion. The locus abutted land zoned for industrial use; a town-appointed task force (preceding and completely unrelated to the power plant development proposal) had recommended its rezoning after studying the town's tax base and the need for economic development;[7] and a previous rezoning attempt based on that recommendation had just barely failed to get the necessary two-thirds majority at the 1995 town meeting.

In sum, the enactment of the bylaw rezoning the locus was not violative of State law or constitutional provisions, and met the substantive requirements of a valid exercise of legislative police power. Nevertheless, the judge set it aside because he concluded that the $8 million offer was an "extraneous consideration," that is, an offer not "tied to the impacts of the project" and therefore "offensive to public policy." We must decide whether such a consideration, voluntarily offered as part of a campaign in support of a development project, constitutes an independent ground on which to set aside a legislative act, regardless of its otherwise valid nature. If it is, we must decide further whether the mere existence of an "extraneous consideration" invalidates the legislative act as a matter of law, regardless whether it is proved to have actually influenced the votes of the legislative body. Because we conclude that a voluntary offer of public

---

5. As the Land Court judge recognized, in the circumstance where the town meeting is the governmental body charged with the responsibility for approving or denying a zoning bylaw, it is difficult to imagine how there could be an agreement in advance of the vote to approve such an action.

6. A municipality's decision to amend its zoning bylaw is also constrained by the State's "reserved powers doctrine," which bars a legislative body from bargaining away its police powers. Some forms of "contract zoning" are "suspect because of the concern that a municipality will contract away its police power to regulate on behalf of the public in return for contractual benefits offered by a landowner whose interest is principally served by the zoning action." *McLean Hosp. Corp. v. Belmont*, 778 N.E.2d 1016, 1020 (Mass. App. Ct. 2002). There was no evidence, however, that the town bargained away its police power in this case. The town merely acted on an offer by IDC; its power to approve or reject the proposed zoning amendment remained unencumbered, as did its power to rezone the property in the future if circumstances made it necessary for the protection of the public health, safety, or general welfare to do so.

7. Promoting economic development is a proper basis for a town's exercise of its zoning power.

benefits is not, standing alone, an adequate ground on which to set aside an otherwise valid legislative act, we do not reach the second question.

In general, there is no reason to invalidate a legislative act on the basis of an "extraneous consideration," because we defer to legislative findings and choices without regard to motive. We see no reason to make an exception for legislative acts that are in the nature of zoning enactments, and find no persuasive authority for the proposition that an otherwise valid zoning enactment is invalid if it is in any way prompted or encouraged by a public benefit voluntarily offered. We conclude that the proper focus of review of a zoning enactment is whether it violates State law or constitutional provisions, is arbitrary or unreasonable, or is substantially unrelated to the public health, safety, or general welfare. In the absence of any infirmity other than the existence of a voluntary offer to make a gift to the town at some time in the future when the power plant became operational, we conclude that the judge erred in holding the zoning ordinance invalid and granting summary judgment to the plaintiffs.

FRANCIS X. SPINA, J. (concurring in part and dissenting in part, with whom IRELAND and COWIN, join).

A municipality may not relinquish its police power by contract. The zoning power of a municipality is among its police powers. There is no dispute here that the zoning change is valid on its face, but the issue that must be addressed is whether the town meeting entered into an unlawful agreement that called for it to relinquish its zoning power. In my view, there is no material fact in dispute, and the facts show that the town meeting improperly agreed to exercise its power to rezone land in exchange for a promise to pay money. The exercise of that power to approve the requested zoning change was a condition precedent to the promise of IDC Bellingham, L.L.C. (IDC Bellingham), to pay money under its agreement with the town of Bellingham (town).

The summary judgment record establishes that IDC Bellingham offered the town \$8 million, on condition that the town meeting approve the zoning change. The same request for a zoning change had failed two years earlier, and the only change in circumstances was the \$8 million offer. The town meeting accepted the offer and voted for the zoning change. The undisputed evidence indicates that the vote was not "a decision solely in respect of rezoning the locus." *Sylvania Elec. Prods. Inc. v. Newton*, 183 N.E.2d 118, 123 (Mass. 1962). The parties struck a bargain: the payment of money in return for a zoning change. Representatives from IDC Bellingham walked away from the town meeting with their zoning change and an unenforceable promise to pay \$8 million. There can be no doubt that were IDC Bellingham to default on its promise, the town would be left with a questionable contract claim based on a sale of its police power in reliance on a promise.

It was a sale of the police power because there is nothing in the record to legitimize the \$8 million offer as "intended to mitigate the impact of the development upon the town," or as "reasonably intended to meet public needs arising out of the proposed development." *Rando v. North Attleborough*, 692 N.E.2d 544, 548 (Mass. App. Ct. 1998). The record does not show that the money "bear[s] some identifiable relationship to the locus so that there can be assurance that the town's legislative body did not act for reasons irrelevant to the zoning of the site at issue." *McLean Hosp. Corp. v. Belmont,* 778 N.E.2d 1016, 1022 (Mass. App. Ct. 2002). This analysis is consistent with the law as applied to similar situations in other areas of zoning: towns may not exact hefty payments or require conditions unrelated to any aspect of a site in return for favorable government action. *See, e.g., Middlesex & Boston St. Ry. v. Aldermen of Newton,* 359 N.E.2d 1279, 1281-85 (Mass. 1977) (city could not condition special permit for garden apartments on developer's leasing five apartments to town's low income housing program). Considerations that are unrelated to the impacts of a proposed development are "extraneous" and may not provide the basis needed to justify an exercise of the police power. *Sylvania Elec. Prods. Inc. v. Newton, supra,* 183 N.E.2d at 123. Where extraneous considerations are shown to be the basis for an exercise of the police power, the operational vote may be "impeach[ed]." *Id.* Here, IDC's offer was unrelated to any aspect of the proposed development or any public need arising out of the zoning change, and therefore was not a legitimate basis for the vote. Sadly, these circumstances demonstrate government and private interests at their shameful worst, and are most likely to involve the most needy towns.

Notes and Questions

1. **Contract and conditional zoning.** In reviewing requests to rezone parcels, governing bodies often wish to mitigate negative externalities or to improve neighborhood amenities in connection with the change. They sometimes do so by negotiating with the owner and then allowing the rezoning subject to specified conditions designed to ensure that the development is not harmful to the neighbors or the community. These conditions may involve anything from special limitations on uses, to specially tailored height or bulk restrictions, to requiring dedication of land to the city to widen abutting public streets or maintain open space. This process is called **contract** or **conditional zoning**.

Contract zoning has often been challenged as (1) unauthorized by the zoning enabling act; (2) inconsistent with the comprehensive plan; or (3) illegal preferential "spot zoning." It has also been challenged as an unconstitutional form of lawmaking on the ground that laws should not be negotiated with a private party but should be adopted through open procedures that can be monitored by the public. *See, e.g., Mayor & Council of Rockville v. Rylyns Enterprises, Inc.,* 814 A.2d 469, 488 (Md. 2002); *cf. League of Residential Neighborhood Advocates v. City of L.A.,* 498 F.3d 1052, 1057 (9th Cir. 2007) (settlement agreement that allowed a synagogue in a neighborhood zoned residential only was invalid absent compliance with ordinary conditional use procedures). While a number of cases strike down contract zoning, others are increasingly approving the practice, with some state statutes now expressly authorizing it. *See, e.g.,* Ariz. Rev. Stat. §§9-462.01(E), 11-832. *See generally* Julian Conrad Juergensmeyer & Thomas E. Roberts, *Land Use Planning and Development Regulation Law* §5.11, at 141-146 (3d ed. 2013).

2. **Bilateral and unilateral agreements.** Some courts distinguish between so-called bilateral and unilateral arrangements. Bilateral agreements involve promises

on both sides, by the owner and by the local government. For example, a city may promise to rezone a lot in return for a promise by the owner to restrict the otherwise allowable development on her lot and perhaps to record the restrictions as covenants. Unilateral promises, by contrast, are commitments by the owner to agree to certain conditions (again, often recorded) in order to induce the municipality to rezone the land. Such arrangements protect the rights of the public to attend a public hearing on the rezoning proposal but still raise issues about whether such ad hoc decision making is desirable or promotes corruption and unfair deviations from the comprehensive plan. A handful of courts have held that unilateral conditional zoning is unlawful. *See, e.g., Dacy v. Village of Ruidoso*, 845 P.2d 793, 796-798 (N.M. 1992). However, when the restrictions on the rezoned property are agreed to voluntarily by the landowner as part of the rezoning process courts will often uphold the arrangement. *See, e.g., Massey v. City of Charlotte*, 550 S.E.2d 838, 844 (N.C. Ct. App. 2001). These unilateral restrictions are often called conditional (rather than contract) zoning because no promise is made by the governing body that bargains away the police power.[8]

In *Durand*, how did the court characterize the nature of the payment that IDC agreed to make to the town of Bellingham? What did IDC get in return? Was the majority in *Durand* correct to say that the promise of funds was "extraneous"? Why might the court have declined to second-guess the rezoning? Should it have?

3. Spot zoning. Spot zoning refers to selective rezoning by the local legislative body to favor a single parcel or small group of parcels. Spot zoning doctrine originated in state constitutional proscriptions on "special legislation," that is, government grants or benefits given to individual citizens that are not justified as measures intended to promote the general welfare. Some courts hold that spot zoning is invalid unless there is a "clear showing" of a "reasonable basis" for selective rezoning based on the comprehensive plan and the benefits of the change. *Good Neighbors of South Davidson v. Town of Denton*, 559 S.E.2d 768, 772 (N.C. 2002). A variation on this is "reverse" spot zoning, where a parcel or small group of parcels is singled out for more onerous restrictions. *See Helena Sand and Gravel, Inc. v. Lewis and Clark County Planning and Zoning Commission*, 290 P.3d 691, 699-700 (Mont. 2012). It is difficult to win spot or reverse spot zoning challenges; local governments generally have latitude to rezone individual parcels of land when this is deemed to be in the public interest. *See, e.g., Historic Charleston Foundation v. City of Charleston*, 734 S.E.2d 306 (S.C. 2012) (denying a spot zoning challenge to a municipal decision changing the zoning law to allow a portion of a site that had been limited to buildings of up to 55 feet to allow buildings up to 105 feet tall).

4. Change or mistake requirement. In some jurisdictions, rezoning of individual parcels may only be made to reflect changes in the character of a neighborhood since the original zoning code was enacted or mistakes in that zoning. *See, e.g.,*

8. Owners who disagree with conditions imposed or sought through a discretionary land use regulatory process may challenge such conditions as unconstitutional "exactions." For the standards that govern such challenges, *see* Chapter 15, §7.

Albuquerque Commons Partnership v. City Council of Albuquerque, 184 P.3d 411, 425-426 (N.M. 2008) (zoning map amendment not justified based on any change or mistake). As with spot zoning and conformity with a comprehensive plan, the change or mistake doctrine seeks to protect owners' justifiable reliance on existing zoning and the stability of the overall zoning code by limiting the types of individualized changes that may be made to a zoning ordinance over time. This doctrine can raise difficult questions of what constitutes a sufficient change or mistake, and courts often accord some latitude to legislative bodies in applying the relevant standards. *See, e.g., Thomas v. Board of Supervisors of Panola County*, 45 So. 3d 1173, 1182-1187 (Miss. 2010).

5. Characterizing rezoning as quasi-judicial. Finally, some jurisdictions temper the deference to local legislative bodies by characterizing statutes that rezone an individual parcel as **quasi-judicial** or administrative rather than legislative. In the famous case *Fasano v. Board of County Commissioners of Washington County*, 507 P.2d 23 (Or. 1973), the Oregon Supreme Court explained:

> [We] would be ignoring reality to rigidly view all zoning decisions by local governing bodies as legislative acts to be accorded a full presumption of validity and shielded from less than constitutional scrutiny by the theory of separation of powers. Local and small decision groups are simply not the equivalent in all respects of state and national legislatures. It is not a part of the legislative function to grant permits, make special exceptions, or decide particular cases. Such activities are not legislative but administrative, quasi-judicial, or judicial in character. To place them in the hands of legislative bodies, whose acts as such are not judicially reviewable, is to open the door completely to arbitrary government.
>
> Ordinances laying down general policies without regard to a specific piece of property are usually an exercise of legislative authority, are subject to limited review, and may only be attacked upon constitutional grounds for an arbitrary abuse of authority. On the other hand, a determination whether the permissible use of a specific piece of property should be changed is usually an exercise of judicial authority and its propriety is subject to an altogether different test.

Id. at 26.

In the minority of jurisdictions that follow the *Fasano* rule, the process of passing legislation to rezone individual parcels is treated more like an administrative process than a legislative one. This can result in parties having procedural rights, including the right to be heard by an impartial tribunal, to present and rebut evidence, and to findings based on a record. *Id.* at 30. Is it appropriate to treat local elected legislative bodies as "quasi-judicial" entities when they pass laws to amend zoning?

§4 ADMINISTRATIVE FLEXIBILITY: ZONING BOARDS

Zoning can be an inflexible tool because it governs entire municipalities and reflects conditions that may change over time. Municipalities can rezone, but that can be cumbersome if done for the entire community and open to a number of challenges when done for individual properties. From the earliest days of modern land use planning, however, administrative zoning boards have had authority to administer zoning laws in ways that increase their flexibility. In particular, zoning boards generally can grant variances or special exceptions from restrictions imposed by the zoning ordinance. A **variance** grants permission to use or develop a parcel in a way that otherwise violates the zoning ordinance in order to alleviate special hardship. A **special exception** is a permit to develop property in ways that the zoning ordinance authorizes only if specifically approved by the zoning board after meeting certain conditions. Each has distinct procedural and substantive requirements and each can be challenged, whether granted or denied, in court.

§4.1 Variances

Krummenacher v. Minnetonka

783 N.W.2d 721 (Minn. 2010)

Map: 17622 Ridgewood Road, Minnetonka, Minnesota

LORIE GILDEA, Justice.

This case involves the decision of respondent City of Minnetonka to grant a variance to respondent JoAnne Liebeler so that she could expand her nonconforming garage. Appellant Beat Krummenacher is Liebeler's neighbor and he challenges the City's decision. The district court upheld the City's variance, and the court of appeals affirmed. Because we conclude that the City applied the wrong standard to Liebeler's variance request, we reverse and remand to the City for reconsideration under the correct standard.

Liebeler owns property located in Minnetonka. Krummenacher is Liebeler's neighbor to the west. Liebeler's property consists of a 2.4-acre lot, which contains a 2,975-square-foot home and an attached two-car garage. The property also contains a detached flat-roofed garage that a previous owner constructed sometime in the 1940s. The City has an ordinance requiring that the detached garage be set back a minimum of 50 feet from the property's boundary line. Minnetonka City Code §300.10. Liebeler's garage was constructed before this ordinance went into effect, and it does not satisfy the setback requirement. Specifically, the garage is nonconforming because it is set back only 17 feet from the front yard lot line. Because the garage was constructed before the ordinance became effective, however, the garage is a permissible nonconformity.

On March 31, 2008, Liebeler applied for a variance to expand the detached garage by adding a pitched roof and a second-story room above the garage that could be used as a yoga studio and craft room. Liebeler's proposal was to renovate the garage itself, both to fix its leakage problems and improve its appearance, and also to expand the garage by adding a living space above it. Because adding a second story to the garage would result in a vertical expansion of a nonconforming structure, Liebeler was required, under the Minnetonka City Code, to apply for a variance from the City. *See* Minnetonka City Code §300.29.3(g). Liebeler's proposed addition would not alter the footprint of the garage and would comply with the City zoning requirements for a detached garage with respect to maximum height and size.

The City's Planning Commission held a public hearing on May 15, 2008, to consider Liebeler's request. Both Liebeler and Krummenacher had an opportunity to present their arguments at that hearing. Liebeler explained that she believed that the flat roof was causing leakage problems and that the structure itself needed to be updated. Krummenacher objected to Liebeler's proposed project, explaining that the added height of the garage would obstruct his view to the east.

The Planning Commission approved Liebeler's request for the variance. Krummenacher appealed the Planning Commission's decision to the Minnetonka City Council. The City Council held a public hearing on the variance request on June 30, 2008, at which both sides presented their arguments. After an examination of the record, the City Council upheld the Planning Commission's decision and findings. The City Council found that Liebeler's "proposal is reasonable and would meet the required standards for a variance." The council listed four requirements and found that the variance satisfied those requirements as follows:

> (1) Undue Hardship: there is an undue hardship due to the topography of the site, width of the lot, location of the driveway and existing vegetation.
> (2) Unique Circumstance: The existing, non-conforming setback is a circumstance that is not common to every similarly zoned property.
> (3) Intent of the Ordinance: The improvements would not increase the footprint of the garage, and would comply with the zoning ordinance requirements for a detached garage for maximum height and size.
> (4) Neighborhood Character: The garage improvements would not alter the character of the neighborhood. The improvements would visually enhance the exterior of the garage. There is also a detached garage on the property to the east that is set back 17 feet from [the street].

Krummenacher then brought suit in district court challenging, among other things, the City's finding of undue hardship.

[Krummenacher argues] that the City's decision must be set aside because it was arbitrary and capricious. Municipalities have "broad discretionary power" in considering whether to grant or deny a variance. We review such decisions "to determine whether the municipality "was within its jurisdiction, was not mistaken as to the applicable law, and did not act arbitrarily, oppressively, or unreasonably, and to determine whether the evidence could reasonably support or justify the determination." *In re Stadsvold*, 754 N.W.2d 323, 332 (Minn. 2008) (internal quotation omitted).

Krummenacher argues that the City's decision was arbitrary and capricious because the City did not apply the proper standard to determine whether Liebeler demonstrated "undue hardship" as defined in Minn. Stat. §462.357, subd. 6. This provision allows a city to grant a variance "from the literal provisions of the ordinance in instances where their strict enforcement would cause undue hardship because of circumstances unique to the individual property under consideration." Minn. Stat. §462.357, subd. 6.

Minnesota Statutes §462.357, subd. 6, provides a definition of "undue hardship," and that definition requires that three factors be met. Specifically, the statute defines "undue hardship" as meaning,

> the property in question cannot be put to reasonable use if used under conditions allowed by the official controls, the plight of the landowner is due to circumstances unique to the property not created by the landowner, and the variance, if granted, will not alter the essential character of the locality.

Id. To receive a variance, the applicant must show that he or she meets all of the three statutory requirements of the "undue hardship" test. *Id.* In addition to satisfying the "undue hardship" requirement, the statute allows municipalities to grant variances only "when it is demonstrated that such actions will be in keeping with the spirit and intent of the ordinance." *Id.* Krummenacher argues that Liebeler's application does not meet any of the requirements for "undue hardship."

The first factor a variance applicant must establish to satisfy the statute's definition of "undue hardship" is that "the property in question cannot be put to reasonable use if used under conditions allowed by the official controls." Minn. Stat. §462.357, subd. 6; *see also* Minnetonka City Code §300.07.1(a). Krummenacher argues that based on the plain and unambiguous language of the statute, a municipality may grant a variance only when the property cannot be put to any reasonable use without it. According to Krummenacher, Liebeler had a reasonable use for her garage without the addition of a yoga studio and craft room — its current use as a storage space for vehicles. Krummenacher argues therefore that the City did not have the statutory authority to grant the variance.

[In] *Rowell v. Board of Adjustment of Moorhead*, 446 N.W.2d 917 (Minn. Ct. App. 1989), *rev. denied* (Minn. Dec. 15, 1989), [the court] interpreted the "undue hardship" section of Minn. Stat. §462.357, subd. 6, as requiring a variance applicant to show that the "property owner would like to use the property in a reasonable manner that is prohibited by the ordinance." *Id.* at 922.

[T]he *Rowell* "reasonable manner" standard is the standard the City used in evaluating Liebeler's request for a variance. Specifically, as reflected in the City Council Resolution, the City found that "the proposal is reasonable" and with respect to "undue hardship," that "[t]here is an undue hardship due to the topography of the site, width of the lot, location of the driveway and existing vegetation."

The plain language of the statute and our precedent compel us to reject the City's invitation to adopt *Rowell*'s interpretation of "undue hardship." The statute provides that to prove "undue hardship," the variance applicant must show that "the property in question cannot be put to a reasonable use" without the variance. Minn. Stat. §462.357, subd. 6.

In addition, in formulating the "reasonable manner" standard, the court in *Rowell* appears to have relied on the "practical difficulties" standard. *See Rowell*, 446

N.W.2d at 922. But we have made a clear distinction between the "practical difficulties" standard and the "undue hardship" standard. In *Stadsvold*, we interpreted Minn. Stat. §394.27, subd. 7, which sets forth the statutory standard for county variances. This statute contains both the "practical difficulties" standard and a "particular hardship" standard. We distinguished the "less rigorous 'practical difficulties' " standard that applies to area variance applications from the more rigorous "particular hardship" standard that applies to use variance applications. *Stadsvold*, 754 N.W.2d at 330-31.[9]

Adopting the *Rowell* "reasonable manner" standard would be inconsistent with the distinction we made in *Stadsvold* between the "practical difficulties" and "hardship" standards. The legislature defined the "hardship" standard in the county statute the same way it defined the "undue hardship" standard in the municipal statute.[10] Because the legislature used the same language in both the county and city variance statutes when defining "hardship," our analysis in *Stadsvold* requires us to conclude that the "undue hardship" standard in Minn. Stat. §462.357, subd. 6, is more demanding than the "practical difficulties" standard the court of appeals appears to have relied on in *Rowell*, 446 N.W.2d at 922. *Rowell's* interpretation of the "undue hardship" standard, requiring only that the proposed use be "reasonable," would render the "undue hardship" standard in section 462.357 less stringent than the "practical difficulties" standard and much less stringent than the "particular hardship" standard in the county variance statute, which the "undue hardship" standard appears to parallel. *See Stadsvold*, 754 N.W.2d at 331. In short, our analysis in *Stadsvold* simply does not leave room for the *Rowell* "reasonable manner" standard.

We recognize that the standard we apply today, while followed elsewhere, is not the universal rule.[11] For example, in *Simplex Technologies, Inc. v. Town of Newington*, 145 N.H. 727, 766 A.2d 713 (2001), the New Hampshire Supreme Court provided a thorough and insightful review of the development of land use variance law, and its practical construction in modern times. The New Hampshire statute did not contain a specific definition of "unnecessary hardship," like our statute does, and the court concluded that its prior definition of the statutory term "unnecessary hardship" "ha[d] become too restrictive in light of the constitutional protections by which it must be

9. As we discussed in *Stadsvold*, "[t]here are two types of variances: use variances and area variances. 'A use variance permits a use or development of land other than that prescribed by zoning regulations.' An area variance controls 'lot restrictions such as area, height, setback, density and parking requirements.' " 754 N.W.2d at 329.

10. " 'Hardship' as used in connection with the granting of a variance means the property in question cannot be put to a reasonable use if used under the conditions allowed by the official controls; the plight of the landowner is due to circumstances unique to the property not created by the landowner; and the variance, if granted, will not alter the essential character of the locality." Minn. Stat. §394.27, subd. 7.

11. While most jurisdictions use the phrase "unnecessary hardship" rather than "undue hardship" as the applicable standard, many jurisdictions appear to require that the variance applicant establish real hardship if the variance is denied rather than simply requiring that the applicant show the reasonableness of the proposed use.

tempered." *Id.* at 717. The New Hampshire Supreme Court framed the issue in the following terms:

> Inevitably and necessarily there is a tension between zoning ordinances and property rights, as courts balance the right of citizens to the enjoyment of private property with the right of municipalities to restrict property use. In this balancing process, constitutional property rights must be respected and protected from unreasonable zoning restrictions.

Id. at 716-17. In light of these considerations, the New Hampshire Supreme Court said that "unnecessary hardship" would, in the future, be established when a landowner showed that (1) a zoning restriction as applied interferes with a reasonable use of the property, considering the unique setting of the property in its environment; (2) no fair and substantial relationship exists between the general purposes of the zoning ordinance and the specific restriction on the property; and (3) the variance would not injure the public or private rights of others. *Id.* at 717.

Had the Minnesota Legislature not defined "undue hardship" in Minn. Stat. §462.357, subd. 6, we might consider the approach articulated in *Simplex.* A flexible variance standard allows municipalities to make modest adjustments to the detailed application of a regulatory scheme when a zoning ordinance imposes significant burdens on an individual, and relief can be fashioned without harm to the neighbors, the community, or the overall purposes of the ordinance. *See* David W. Owens, *The Zoning Variance: Reappraisal and Recommendations for Reform of a Much-Maligned Tool,* 29 Colum. J. Envtl. L. 279, 317 (2004) ("If the variance power is to be used both as a constitutional safeguard and as a tool for flexibility, zoning enabling acts and local ordinances should be amended to delineate these two purposes and set different standards for each. The failure to make such a distinction underlies much of the past controversy regarding variances. Courts and commentators have traditionally viewed the variances as the former — a very limited tool for avoidance of constitutional infirmity in extraordinary cases. Most variance petitions, and consequently most board of adjustment decision-making, have viewed the variances as the latter — a tool to provide flexible implementation rather than constitutional infirmity.").

We recognize that the *Rowell* "reasonable manner" standard represents a longstanding interpretation of the undue hardship standard in Minn. Stat. §462.357, subd. 6, and that Minnesota municipalities have been granting variances under the "reasonable manner" standard for many years. We also recognize that our decision will result in a restriction on a municipality's authority to grant variances as compared with the "reasonable manner" standard. But whatever value we may find in a more flexible standard, particularly with regard to area variances, we cannot ignore the plain language of the statute.

[A] property owner is entitled to have his or her variance application heard under the correct legal standard, which supports a remand in this case. We reverse and remand the matter to the City for renewed consideration of Liebeler's variance request in light of our rejection of the "reasonable manner" standard from *Rowell.*

Notes and Questions

1. **Variance law on the books versus law in action.** *Krummenacher* illustrates a common phenomenon in the application of variance standards where the nominal standard may not be what a city council or zoning board actually applies. Most states allow officials to grant variances only when application of zoning to a particular owner results in some variation of an **undue** or **unnecessary hardship**, and the test for this can be quite strict.

A variance generally will not be granted where the hardship is self-imposed, *Board of Adjustment v. Verleysen*, 36 A.3d 326, 332 (Del. 2012), leading some courts to hold that the owner's refusal to sell the property for fair market value to a neighbor who is willing and able to buy constitutes a self-imposed hardship. *Commons v. Westwood Zoning Board of Adjustment*, 410 A.2d 1138, 1142 (N.J. 1980); *see also Sciacca v. Caruso*, 769 A.2d 578 (R.I. 2001) (no variance when hardship was self-imposed because of the owner's acts in separating the property into different parcels that caused the problem). In addition, hardship will often not be found unless there is no economically viable use of the property (or no reasonable return on the owner's investment) if the zoning law is enforced. *See, e.g., Lewis v. Town of Rockport*, 870 A.2d 107 (Me. 2005) (grant of a variance reversed where owner did not demonstrate "practical loss of all beneficial use of land"). *But see Simplex Technologies v. Town of Newington*, 766 A.2d 713 (N.H. 2001) ("unnecessary hardship" standard requires showing that zoning restriction interferes with an owner's "reasonable use of the property, considering the unique setting of the property in its environment"). Many states have added the requirement that the property must be different in some unique way from surrounding property, such as having an unduly narrow frontage or an odd shape or elevation, and that the hardship arise out of this condition.

As *Krummenacher* discusses, however, zoning boards routinely grant variances on a somewhat a lower standard. This is especially the case where the requested variance is not a dramatic change in the structure and if no one (especially abutting neighbors) objects to the granting of the variance, although even when neighbors object, boards sometimes choose to favor development over such objections. In effect, zoning boards often ignore the law and grant variances when there is no showing that the owner has met the standard for undue hardship. Julian Conrad Juergensmeyer & Thomas E. Roberts, *Land Use Planning and Development Regulation Law* §5.14, at 150-152 (3d ed. 2013); Jesse Dukeminier, Jr. & Clyde L. Stapleton, *The Zoning Board of Adjustment: A Case Study in Misrule*, 50 Ky. L.J. 273 (1962).

If no neighbor objects to a grant of a variance on less than a strict application of the hardship standard, there is little chance the grant of the variance will be challenged in court. On the other hand, if a board grants a variance when the standard for hardship is

FACTORS

Although different jurisdictions establish different factors, in evaluating challenges to variances, most courts look to whether:

1. the property is unusual, exceptional, or unique;
2. the owner created the hardship at issue;
3. without a variance, zoning restriction imposes undue hardship or practical difficulties; and
4. the variance will significantly undermine public good or the zoning plan.

absent, and aggrieved neighbors challenge the grant, the board's decision is likely to be reversed.

2. **Variations in the standards for variances.** Some states allow variances to be granted on a lesser showing of **practical difficulties**. *See, e.g.*, Ind. Code §36-7-4-918.5; Juergensmeyer & Roberts, *supra*, §5.23, at 163-164. To show practical difficulties, the owner must prove significant economic injury from enforcement of the zoning ordinance. Some states interpret the "practical difficulties" test to mean the same thing as the unnecessary hardship test. The zoning enabling acts in some states require a showing of *both* unnecessary hardship and practical difficulties; others allow a variance if *either* of these tests is met. Some states go further and allow variances to be issued in unusual circumstances if this will provide a significant public benefit and the variance can be granted "without substantial detriment to the public good and will not substantially impair the intent and purpose" of the zoning ordinance. N.J. Stat. §40:55D-70(d), *interpreted in Cell South of N.J., Inc. v. Zoning Board of Adjustment*, 796 A.2d 247 (N.J. 2002).

After the *Krummenacher* decision, Minnesota amended the statutory standard for variances from "undue hardship" to "practical difficulties." *See* Minn. Stat. §394.27(7). How might Liebeler's variance application come out on remand if the practical difficulties standard was applied?

3. **Area versus use variances.** As *Krummenacher* noted, variances can be "area," which relax lot and building restrictions, or "use," which lift restrictions on the purposes to which a property can be put. Some states expressly prohibit use variances entirely. Cal. Govt. Code §65906. Other states prohibit use variances from being granted by zoning boards on the ground that they are effectively rezonings that should be voted on by the city council (or other lawmaking body) and not granted by an administrative agency such as the zoning board. Some states allow use variances to be granted upon a showing of unnecessary hardship while allowing area variances to be granted on the lower standard of demonstration of practical difficulties. Juergensmeyer & Roberts, *supra*, §5.15, at 152-154.

§4.2 Special Exceptions

Unlike a variance, which grants the property owner the right to do something ordinarily prohibited by the zoning law to avoid undue hardship, a **special exception**, which can also be called a **special permit** or a **conditional use**, describes a type of land use that is permitted by the zoning law but subject to administrative approval before it may be allowed. The uses subject to the special exception process are often particularly sensitive or may pose the risk of particular harms. Typical examples include gas stations, parking lots, landfills, airports, hospitals, and halfway houses. The special exception process can also apply to more benign uses that nonetheless require evaluation on an individual basis before they are sited because of their potential impact on traffic and parking, such as recreation facilities, schools, and churches. Unlike variances, there is a presumption that the owner can engage in the permitted use so long as the established conditions are met. *National Cathedral Neighborhood Association v. D.C. Board of Zoning Adjustment*, 753 A.2d 984, 986 n.1 (D.C. 2000). The special exception process generally allows zoning boards to grant permission subject to specific, reasonable conditions that might mitigate negative impacts.

Courts regularly uphold decisions by zoning boards to deny special exceptions, *see, e.g., Montgomery County v. Butler*, 9 A.3d 824 (Md. 2010) (upholding the denial of a special exception for a landscaping contractor based on a standard of "non-inherent adverse effects," specifically noise from trucks). Courts, however, will reverse such denials if an owner meets the legislative standards or if zoning boards apply factors that are not in the special exception statute. For example, in *New Cingular Wireless PCS v. Sussex County Board of Adjustment*, 65 A.3d 607 (Del. 2013), a telephone company sought to build a cellular telephone tower in a commercial zone, on a parcel that also included a gas station, a fast food restaurant, and a convenience store. Because there was a condominium next door, the company was required to obtain a special exception from the county Board of Adjustment. The Board denied the application, finding that the company had failed to show that the cell tower "would not affect adversely the uses of the adjacent properties." The Delaware Supreme Court reversed because the statutory standard required a finding that the proposed use will not "*substantially* affect adversely the uses of adjacent and neighboring property." *Id.* at 611. As the court noted, the Board had impermissibly imposed a much heavier burden on the company. *Id.* at 611-612.

Special exceptions generally require sufficient direction to the zoning board. Vague conditions may be struck down as improper delegations of legislative power from the municipal governing body to the administrative zoning board. *Kosalka v. Town of Georgetown*, 752 A.2d 183, 187 (Me. 2000) (finding a condition that all proposed developments in a shore area "conserve natural beauty" an unconstitutional delegation because it lacked cognizable, quantitative standards). In *Cope v. Inhabitants of the Town of Brunswick*, 464 A.2d 223 (Me. 1983), a zoning law gave the zoning board the power to grant an exception to allow multi-unit apartment buildings in a certain area, so long as this would "not adversely affect the health, safety, or general welfare of the public." After the zoning board denied the owner's request for the special exception, the owner challenged the board's action in court, which struck down the condition relating to public welfare on the ground that it did not give sufficient guidance to the board and effectively delegated legislative power to an unelected administrative agency. As a remedy, the court ordered the town to grant the permit since, by establishing the exception, the enacting legislative body had already determined that the use would ordinarily not be detrimental to the community.

In contrast, the Colorado Supreme Court upheld a zoning law that provided that certain uses were "permitted" within an identified district but retained in the zoning agency the right to review each proposed use on the basis of "neighborhood compatibility." *City of Colorado Springs v. SecurCare Self Storage, Inc.*, 10 P.3d 1244 (Colo. 2000). *See also Fordham v. Butera*, 876 N.E.2d 397 (Mass. 2007) (ordinance delegating authority to zoning board of appeals to allow business storage activities provided constitutionally sufficient standards).

§5 THE PROBLEM OF EXCLUSIONARY ZONING

Southern Burlington County NAACP v. Township of Mount Laurel

336 A.2d 713 (N.J. 1975)

FREDERICK W. HALL, J.

This case attacks the system of land use regulation by defendant Township of Mount Laurel on the ground that low and moderate income families are thereby unlawfully excluded from the municipality.

There is not the slightest doubt that New Jersey has been, and continues to be, faced with a desperate need for housing, especially of decent living accommodations economically suitable for low and moderate income families. Plaintiffs represent the minority group poor (black and Hispanic) seeking such quarters. But they are not the only category of persons barred from so many municipalities by reason of restrictive land use regulations. We have reference to young and elderly couples, single persons and large, growing families not in the poverty class, but who still cannot afford the only kinds of housing realistically permitted in most places — relatively high-priced, single-family detached dwellings on sizeable lots and, in some municipalities, expensive apartments. We will, therefore, consider the case from the wider viewpoint that the effect of Mount Laurel's land use regulation has been to prevent various categories of persons from living in the township because of the limited extent of their income and resources.

I. The Facts

Mount Laurel is a flat, sprawling township, 22 square miles, or about 14,000 acres, in area, on the west central edge of Burlington County. Under the present ordinance, 29.2% of all the land in the township, or 4,121 acres, is zoned for industry. At the time of trial no more than 100 acres were actually occupied by industrial uses. The rest of the land so zoned has remained undeveloped. [As] happens in the case of so many municipalities, much more land has been so zoned than the reasonable potential for industrial movement or expansion warrants. At the same time, however, the land cannot be used for residential development under the general ordinance.

The amount of land zoned for retail business use under the general ordinance is relatively small — 169 acres, or 1.2% of the total. The balance of the land area, almost 10,000 acres, has been developed until recently in the conventional form of major subdivisions. The general ordinance provides for four residential zones, designated R-1, R-1D, R-2 and R-3. All permit only single-family, detached dwellings, one house per lot — the usual form of grid development. Attached townhouses, apartments (except on farms for agricultural workers) and mobile homes are not allowed anywhere in the township under the general ordinance. The dwellings are substantial; the average value in 1971 was $32,500 and is undoubtedly much higher today.

The general ordinance requirements, while not as restrictive as those in many similar municipalities, nonetheless realistically allow only homes within the financial reach of persons of at least middle income. The R-1 zone requires a minimum lot area of 9,375 square feet, a minimum lot width of 75 feet at the building line, and a minimum dwelling floor area of 1,100 square feet if a one-story building and 1,300 square feet if one and one-half stories or higher. The R-2 zone, comprising a single district of 141 acres in the northeasterly corner, has been completely developed. While it only required a minimum floor area of 900 square feet for a one-story dwelling, the minimum lot size was 11,000 square feet; otherwise the requisites were the same as in the R-1 zone.

The general ordinance places the remainder of the township, outside of the industrial and commercial zones and the R-1D district (to be mentioned shortly), in the R-3 zone. This zone comprises over 7,000 acres—slightly more than half of the total municipal area [and requires a minimum lot size of about one-half acre (20,000 square feet), and the lot width at the building line must be 100 feet].

The R-1D district [reduces] the minimum lot area from 20,000 square feet required in the R-3 zone to 10,000 square feet (12,000 square feet for corner lots) but with the proviso that one-family houses—the single permitted dwelling use—"shall not be erected in excess of an allowable development density of 2.25 dwelling units per gross acre." The minimum lot width at the building line must be 80 feet and the minimum dwelling floor area is the same as in the R-3 zone.

A variation from conventional development has recently occurred in some parts of Mount Laurel, as in a number of other similar municipalities, by use of the land use regulation device known as "planned unit development" (PUD). This scheme differs from the traditional in that the type, density and placement of land uses and buildings, instead of being detailed and confined to specified districts by local legislation in advance, is determined by contract, or "deal," as to each development between the developer and the municipal administrative authority, under broad guidelines laid down by state enabling legislation and an implementing local ordinance. The stress is on regulation of density and permitted mixture of uses within the same area, including various kinds of living accommodations with or without commercial and industrial enterprises.

[Mt. Laurel approved four PUD projects before the state enabling legislation was repealed in 1977.] While multi-family housing in the form of rental garden, medium rise and high rise apartments and attached townhouses is for the first time provided for, as well as single-family detached dwellings for sale, it is not designed to accommodate and is beyond the financial reach of low and moderate income families, especially those with young children. The aim is quite the contrary; as with the single-family homes in the older conventional subdivisions, only persons of medium and upper income are sought as residents.

Still another restrictive land use regulation was adopted by the township through a supplement to the general zoning ordinance enacted in September 1972 creating a new zone, R-4, Planned Adult Retirement Community (PARC). The enactment recited a critical shortage of adequate housing in the township suitable "for the needs and desires of senior citizens and certain other adults over the age of 52." The permission was essentially for single ownership development of the zone for multi-family housing (townhouses and apartments), thereafter to be either rented or sold as cooperatives or condominiums. The extensive development requirements detailed in the ordinance make it apparent that the scheme was not designed for, and would be beyond the means of, low and moderate income retirees.

All this affirmative action for the benefit of certain segments of the population is in sharp contrast to the lack of action, and indeed hostility, with respect to affording any opportunity for decent housing for the township's own poor living in substandard accommodations, found largely in the section known as Springville (R-3 zone). The 1969 Master Plan Report recognized it and recommended positive action. The continuous official reaction has been rather a negative policy of waiting for dilapidated premises to be vacated and then forbidding further occupancy. An earlier non-governmental effort to improve conditions had been effectively thwarted. In 1968 a private non-profit association sought to build subsidized, multi-family housing in the Springville section with funds to be granted by a higher level governmental agency. Advance municipal approval of the project was required. The Township Committee responded with a purportedly approving resolution, which found a need for "moderate" income housing in the area, but went on to specify that such housing must be constructed subject to all zoning, planning, building and other applicable ordinances and codes. This meant single-family detached dwellings on 20,000 square foot lots. (Fear was also expressed that such housing would attract low income families from outside the township.) Needless to say, such requirements killed realistic housing for this group of low and moderate income families.[12]

The record thoroughly substantiates the findings of the trial court that over the years Mount Laurel "has acted affirmatively to control development and to attract a selective type of growth" and that "through its zoning ordinances has exhibited economic discrimination in that the poor have been deprived of adequate housing and the opportunity to secure the construction of subsidized housing, and has used federal, state, county and local finances and resources solely for the betterment of middle and upper-income persons."

There cannot be the slightest doubt that the reason for this course of conduct has been to keep down local taxes on *property* (Mount Laurel is not a high tax municipality) and that the policy was carried out without regard for non-fiscal considerations with respect to *people*, either within or without its boundaries. This conclusion is demonstrated not only by what was done and what happened, as we have related, but also by innumerable direct statements of municipal officials at public meetings over the years which are found in the exhibits.

This policy of land use regulation for a fiscal end derives from New Jersey's tax structure, which has imposed on local real estate most of the cost of municipal and

12. The record is replete with uncontradicted evidence that, factually, low and moderate income housing cannot be built without some form of contribution, concession or incentive by some level of government. Such, under various state and federal methods, may take the form of public construction or some sort of governmental assistance or encouragement to private building. Multi-family rental units, at a high density, or, at most, low cost single-family units on very small lots, are economically necessary and in turn require appropriate local land use regulations.

county government and of the primary and secondary education of the municipality's children. The latter expense is much the largest, so, basically, the fewer the school children, the lower the tax rate. Sizeable industrial and commercial ratables are eagerly sought and homes and the lots on which they are situated are required to be large enough, through minimum lot sizes and minimum floor areas, to have substantial value in order to produce greater tax revenues to meet school costs. Large families who cannot afford to buy large houses and must live in cheaper rental accommodations are definitely not wanted, so we find drastic bedroom restrictions for, or complete prohibition of, multi-family or other feasible housing for those of lesser income.

Terms:
Ratable is a term used by local officials and planners to mean property subject to assessment and taxation. **Good ratables**, like industrial and commercial uses, are those that generate tax revenue with relatively less demand for services.

This pattern of land use regulation has been adopted for the same purpose in developing municipality after developing municipality. Almost every one acts solely in its own selfish and parochial interest and in effect builds a wall around itself to keep out those people or entities not adding favorably to the tax base, despite the location of the municipality or the demand for varied kinds of housing. There has been no effective intermunicipal or area planning or land use regulation. All of this is amply demonstrated by the evidence in this case as to Camden, Burlington and Gloucester counties. One incongruous result is the picture of developing municipalities rendering it impossible for lower paid employees of industries they have eagerly sought and welcomed with open arms (and, in Mount Laurel's case, even some of its own lower paid municipal employees) to live in the community where they work.

The other end of the spectrum should also be mentioned because it shows the source of some of the demand for cheaper housing than the developing municipalities have permitted. Core cities were originally the location of most commerce and industry. Many of those facilities furnished employment for the unskilled and semi-skilled. These employees lived relatively near their work, so sections of cities always have housed the majority of people of low and moderate income, generally in old and deteriorating housing. Despite the municipally confined tax structure, commercial and industrial ratables generally used to supply enough revenue to provide and maintain municipal services equal or superior to those furnished in most suburban and rural areas.

The situation has become exactly the opposite since the end of World War II. Much industry and retail business, and even the professions, have left the cities. Camden is a typical example. The testimonial and documentary evidence in this case as to what has happened to that city is depressing indeed. For various reasons, it lost thousands of jobs between 1950 and 1970, including more than half of its manufacturing jobs (a reduction from 43,267 to 20,671, while all jobs in the entire area labor market increased from 94,507 to 197,037). A large segment of retail business faded away with the erection of large suburban shopping centers. The economically better situated city residents helped fill up the miles of sprawling new housing developments, not fully served by public transit. In a society which came to depend more and more on expensive individual motor vehicle transportation for all purposes, low income employees very frequently could not afford to reach outlying places of suitable employment and they certainly could not afford the permissible housing near such locations. These people have great difficulty in obtaining work and have been forced to remain in housing which is overcrowded, and has become more and more substandard and less and less tax productive. There has been a consequent critical erosion of the city tax base and inability to provide the amount and quality of those governmental services—education, health, police, fire, housing and the like—so necessary to the very existence of safe and decent city life. This category of city dwellers desperately needs much better housing and living conditions than is available to them now, both in a rehabilitated city and in outlying municipalities. They make up, along with the other classes of persons earlier mentioned who also cannot afford the only generally permitted housing in the developing municipalities, the acknowledged great demand for low and moderate income housing.

How this tax structure screws the poor

II. The Legal Issue

The legal question before us, as earlier indicated, is whether a developing municipality like Mount Laurel may validly, by a system of land use regulation, make it physically and economically impossible to provide low and moderate income housing in the municipality for the various categories of persons who need and want it and thereby, as Mount Laurel has, exclude such people from living within its confines because of the limited extent of their income and resources.

We conclude that every such municipality must, by its land use regulations, presumptively make realistically possible an appropriate variety and choice of housing. More specifically, presumptively it cannot foreclose the opportunity of the classes of people mentioned for low and moderate income housing and in its regulations must affirmatively afford that opportunity, at least to the extent of the municipality's fair share of the present and prospective regional need therefor. These obligations must be met unless the particular municipality can sustain the heavy burden of demonstrating peculiar circumstances which dictate that it should not be required so to do.[13]

We reach this conclusion under state law and so do not find it necessary to consider federal constitutional grounds urged by plaintiffs. We begin with some fundamental principles as applied to the scene before us.

> **CONTEXT**
>
> Until the 1950s, Mount Laurel was largely agricultural. The town had a stable African American population that included families whose ancestors had arrived as slaves before 1800, and had been a stop on the Underground Railroad. After World War II, however, the town became a suburb for Philadelphia and Camden. Farmers sold the land on which blacks had been tenant farmers, and blacks were relegated to shacks in Springville. The *Mount Laurel* litigation was catalyzed when the town blocked efforts to build apartment buildings to replace Springville's dilapidated housing. David Kirp, *Our Town: Race, Housing and the Soul of Suburbia* 43-47 (1995).

13. While, as the trial court found, Mount Laurel's actions were deliberate, we are of the view that the identical conclusion follows even when municipal conduct is not shown to be intentional, but the effect is substantially the same as if it were.

Land use regulation is encompassed within the state's police power. It is required that, affirmatively, a zoning regulation, like any police power enactment, must promote public health, safety, morals or the general welfare.

[A central issue is] *whose* general welfare must be served or not violated in the field of land use regulation. Frequently the decisions in this state have spoken only in terms of the interest of the enacting municipality, so that it has been thought, at least in some quarters, that such was the only welfare requiring consideration. It is, of course, true that many cases have dealt only with regulations having little, if any, outside impact where the local decision is ordinarily entitled to prevail. However, it is fundamental and not to be forgotten that the zoning power is a police power of the state and the local authority is acting only as a delegate of that power and is restricted in the same manner as is the state. So, when regulation does have a substantial external impact, the welfare of the state's citizens beyond the borders of the particular municipality cannot be disregarded and must be recognized and served.

This brings us to the relation of housing to the concept of general welfare just discussed and the result in terms of land use regulation which that relationship mandates. There cannot be the slightest doubt that shelter, along with food, are the most basic human needs.

It is plain beyond dispute that proper provision for adequate housing of all categories of people is certainly an absolute essential in promotion of the general welfare required in all local land use regulation. Further, the universal and constant need for such housing is so important and of such broad public interest that the general welfare which developing municipalities like Mount Laurel must consider extends beyond their boundaries and cannot be parochially confined to the claimed good of the particular municipality. It has to follow that, broadly speaking, the presumptive obligation arises for each such municipality affirmatively to plan and provide, by its land use regulations, the reasonable opportunity for an appropriate variety and choice of housing, including, of course, low and moderate cost housing, to meet the needs, desires and resources of all categories of people who may desire to live within its boundaries. Negatively, it may not adopt regulations or policies which thwart or preclude that opportunity.

It is also entirely clear, as we pointed out earlier, that most developing municipalities, including Mount Laurel, have not met their affirmative or negative obligations, primarily for local fiscal reasons.

In sum, we are satisfied beyond any doubt that, by reason of the basic importance of appropriate housing and the longstanding pressing need for it, especially in the low and moderate cost category, and of the exclusionary zoning practices of so many municipalities, conditions have changed, and judicial attitudes must be altered to require, as we have just said, a broader view of the general welfare and the presumptive obligation on the part of developing municipalities at least to afford the opportunity by land use regulations for appropriate housing for all.

We turn to application of these principles in appraisal of Mount Laurel's zoning ordinance, useful as well, we think, as guidelines for future application in other municipalities.

The township's general zoning ordinance (including the cluster zone provision) permits, as we have said, only one type of housing — single-family detached dwellings. This means that all other types — multi-family including garden apartments and other kinds housing more than one family, town (row) houses, mobile home parks — are prohibited. Concededly, low and moderate income housing has been intentionally excluded. While a large percentage of the population living outside of cities prefers a one-family house on its own sizeable lot, a substantial proportion do not for various reasons. Moreover, single-family dwellings are the most expensive type of quarters and a great number of families cannot afford them. Certainly they are not pecuniarily feasible for low and moderate income families, most young people and many elderly and retired persons, except for some of moderate income by the use of low cost construction on small lots.

As previously indicated, Mount Laurel has allowed some multi-family housing by agreement in planned unit developments, but only for the relatively affluent and of no benefit to low and moderate income families. And even here, the contractual agreements between municipality and developer sharply limit the number of apartments having more than one bedroom. The design of such limitations is obviously to restrict the number of families in the municipality having school age children and thereby keep down local education costs. Such restrictions are so clearly contrary to the general welfare as not to require further discussion.

Mount Laurel's zoning ordinance is also so restrictive in its minimum lot area, lot frontage and building size requirements, earlier detailed, as to preclude single-family housing for even moderate income families. Required lot area of at least 9,375 square feet in one remaining regular residential zone and 20,000 square feet (almost half an acre) in the other, with required frontage of 75 and 100 feet, respectively, cannot be called small lots and amounts to low density zoning, very definitely increasing the cost of purchasing and improving land and so affecting the cost of housing. As to building size, the township's general requirements of a minimum dwelling floor area of 1,100 square feet for all one-story houses and 1,300 square feet for all of one and one-half stories or higher is without regard to required minimum lot size or frontage or the number of occupants. Again it is evident these requirements increase the size and so the cost of housing. The conclusion is irresistible that Mount Laurel permits only such middle and upper income housing as it believes will have sufficient taxable value to come close to paying its own governmental way.

Akin to large lot, single-family zoning restricting the population is the zoning of very large amounts of land for industrial and related uses. Mount Laurel has set aside almost 30% of its area, over 4,100 acres, for that purpose; the only residential use allowed is for farm dwellings. In almost a decade only about 100 acres have been developed industrially. Despite the township's strategic location for motor transportation purposes, as intimated earlier, it seems plain that the likelihood of anywhere near the whole of the zoned area being used for the intended purpose in the foreseeable future is remote indeed and that an unreasonable amount of land has thereby been removed from possible residential development, again seemingly for local fiscal reasons.

Without further elaboration at this point, our opinion is that Mount Laurel's zoning ordinance is presumptively contrary to the general welfare and outside the intended scope of the zoning power in the particulars mentioned. A facial showing of invalidity is thus established, shifting to the municipality the burden of establishing valid superseding reasons for its action and non-action. We now examine the reasons it advances.

The township's principal reason in support of its zoning plan and ordinance housing provisions, advanced especially strongly at oral argument, is the fiscal one previously adverted to, *i.e.*, that by reason of New Jersey's tax structure which substantially finances municipal governmental and educational costs from taxes on local real property, every municipality may, by the exercise of the zoning power, allow only such uses and to such extent as will be beneficial to the local tax rate. In other words, the position is that any municipality may zone extensively to seek and encourage the "good" tax ratables of industry and commerce and limit the permissible types of housing to those having the fewest school children or to those providing sufficient value to attain or approach paying their own way taxwise.

We have no hesitancy in now saying, and do so emphatically, that, considering the basic importance of the opportunity for appropriate housing for all classes of our citizenry, no municipality may exclude or limit categories of housing for that reason or purpose. While we fully recognize the increasingly heavy burden of local taxes for municipal governmental and school costs on homeowners, relief from the consequences of this tax system will have to be furnished by other branches of government. It cannot legitimately be accomplished by restricting types of housing through the zoning process in developing municipalities.

III. *The Remedy*

The township is granted 90 days from the date hereof, or such additional time as the trial court may find it reasonable and necessary to allow, to adopt amendments to correct the deficiencies herein specified. It is the local function and responsibility, in the first instance at least, rather than the court's, to decide on the details of the same within the guidelines we have laid down. If plaintiffs desire to attack such amendments, they may do so by supplemental complaint filed in this cause within 30 days of the final adoption of the amendments.

The municipality should first have full opportunity to itself act without judicial supervision. We trust it will do so in the spirit we have suggested, both by appropriate zoning ordinance amendments and whatever additional action encouraging the fulfillment of its fair share of the regional need for low and moderate income housing may be indicated as necessary and advisable. (We have in mind that there is at least a moral obligation in a municipality to establish a local housing agency pursuant to state law to provide housing for its resident poor now living in dilapidated, unhealthy quarters.) Should Mount Laurel not perform as we expect, further judicial action may be sought by supplemental pleading in this cause.

Notes and Questions

1. **Property and regulation.** Does the limitation on exclusionary zoning imposed by the court in *Mount Laurel* infringe on property rights, or does it protect them? Does it regulate the market for real property, or does it constitute a form of deregulation?

2. **Why not federal law?** The New Jersey Supreme Court in *Mount Laurel* relied on the New Jersey Constitution as the basis for its decision. Why didn't the court decide the case under the federal Constitution or under the federal *Fair Housing Act*, 42 U.S.C. §3601 *et seq.*, which prohibits discrimination in land use regulation by local governments? *See* Chapter 13. One reason might have been that the Supreme Court has interpreted the federal due process and equal protection clauses to afford great latitude to local governments in the absence of intentional discrimination. *See* §1.2, *supra*. As to the federal *Fair Housing Act*, the analysis of claims that land use regulations have a discriminatory effect proceed under a doctrinal analysis that likewise gives a fair measure of deference to local authority, and that may have been difficult to support the sweeping remedy the *Mount Laurel* court adopted. *See* Peter H. Schuck, *Judging Remedies: Judicial Approaches to Housing Segregation*, 37 Harv. C.R.-C.L. L. Rev. 289, 318 (2002) (arguing that deferential standards under federal constitutional and statutory law best explains the decision by advocates and the New Jersey Supreme Court to focus on income rather than race). Keep in mind as well that any decision by the New Jersey Supreme Court based on federal law would have been reviewable by the U.S. Supreme Court.

3. **Regionalism and land use regulation.** In *Euclid v. Ambler Realty*, one argument against Euclid's zoning code was that it impeded the natural industrial development of the larger Cleveland region of which the village was a part. The Supreme Court rejected this argument, stating that the village of Euclid was "politically a separate municipality, with powers of its own and authority to govern itself as it sees fit." 272 U.S. 365, 389 (1926). In so doing, however, the Court noted that it was not excluding "the possibility of cases where the general public interest would so far outweigh the interest of the municipality that the municipality would not be allowed to stand in the way." *Id.* at 390. How did the Supreme Court of New Jersey in *Mount Laurel* approach the balance between local autonomy and "the general public interest" in evaluating the scale at which authority over land use should be exercised?

4. ***Mount Laurel II.*** In *Mount Laurel I*, the Supreme Court of New Jersey ordered the township of Mount Laurel to amend its zoning law to remove unconstitutional restrictions on the development of low- and moderate-income housing. This remedy depended, to some extent, on trusting the presumed good faith of municipal officials. That trust turned out to be unwarranted. Many municipalities, including Mount Laurel, evaded or ignored the constitutional mandate in *Mount Laurel I*. Mount Laurel, for example, responded by rezoning 20 acres of land for low-income housing—less than

one-quarter of 1 percent of the town's entire area — on which, for various reasons, it was exceedingly unlikely that low-income housing would ever be built. Other communities similarly failed to comply with the constitutional mandate.

New challenges were brought against the zoning ordinances of many municipalities, including a second case against Mount Laurel itself. Six of these cases were consolidated in a single appeal to the New Jersey Supreme Court, which issued a second *Mount Laurel* opinion in 1983. *South Burlington County NAACP v. Township of Mount Laurel*, 456 A.2d 390 (N.J. 1983) (*Mount Laurel II*). Chief Justice Robert Wilentz's 120-page opinion in *Mount Laurel II* took more than two years to produce. Under *Mount Laurel II*, the obligation to provide a realistic opportunity for decent housing for a municipality's *resident* poor was extended to cover every municipality in the state rather than being limited to "developing" communities, as under *Mount Laurel I*. In addition, the court in *Mount Laurel II* authorized affirmative remedies to encourage the construction of low- and moderate-income housing. For example, the court provided for the appointment of three "regional" trial judges to handle all cases involving challenges to exclusionary zoning ordinances in the northern, central, and southern regions of New Jersey. This arrangement was intended to generate consistent definitions of "regions," and the housing needs of each region, to determine each community's fair share of the regional housing need in an orderly way.

The *Mount Laurel II* court required municipalities to take affirmative steps to encourage the development of housing for low- and moderate-income persons if the *Mount Laurel* obligations could not otherwise be met. If municipalities failed to comply with the constitutional mandate, courts were empowered to order affirmative remedies, including government subsidies, incentives for private developers to set aside a portion of their developments for low- and moderate-income residents by relaxing various zoning restrictions, and mandatory set-asides for developers. The court also authorized a "builder's remedy," which would order a municipality to allow a developer to construct a particular project that includes a substantial amount of lower-income housing unless the "municipality establishes that because of environmental or other substantial planning concerns, the plaintiff's proposed project is clearly contrary to sound land use planning." Ultimately, if all of this failed, a special master could be appointed to rewrite the zoning ordinance to comply with the jurisdiction's constitutional obligations under *Mount Laurel*.

5. Subsequent legislation. The *Mount Laurel II* opinion openly invited the New Jersey legislature to enact legislation implementing the constitutional obligation to prevent exclusionary zoning practices. The legislature responded by enacting the *Fair Housing Act of 1985*, N.J. Stat. §§52:27D-301 to 52:27D-329 (1986), which transferred authority over *Mount Laurel* cases to a state administrative agency called the Council on Affordable Housing (COAH). The act placed a temporary moratorium on the controversial builder's remedy; it also allowed municipalities to buy their way out of the *Mount Laurel* obligation by paying neighboring communities to absorb up to half of their fair-share obligation in what were called "regional contribution agreements." The *Fair Housing Act* was upheld by the New Jersey Supreme Court in *Hills Development*

Co. v. Bernards Township, 510 A.2d 621 (N.J. 1986) (often called *Mount Laurel III*). The provision of the act allowing for regional cooperation agreements was eliminated from the statutory regime in 2008. *See In re Denial of Regional Contribution Agreement Between Galloway Township and City of Bridgeton*, 12 A.3d 232 (N.J. App. Div. 2011). The builder's remedy survives, however, and is available when the municipality fails to comply fully with its statutory obligations. *Toll Brothers, Inc. v. Township of West Windsor*, 803 A.2d 53 (N.J. 2002).[14]

6. **Constitutional versus statutory approaches to exclusionary zoning.** Although much heralded, the *Mount Laurel* doctrine is a minority rule, as few states have explicitly interpreted their state constitutions to limit exclusionary zoning. Several states, however, have addressed exclusionary zoning, as New Jersey eventually did, by statute. *See* James Kushner, *Affordable Housing as Infrastructure in the Time of Global Warming*, 42/43 Urb. Law. 179, 189 (2011) (noting that at least 16 states have some form of proscription or planning requirement related to exclusionary zoning).

For example, California, Massachusetts, and Oregon have adopted legislation to limit exclusionary zoning. Cal. Govt. Code §§65580-65589.8; Mass. Gen. Laws ch. 40B, §§20-23; Or. Rev. Stat. §§197.005-197.850. California's statute, which resembles the *New Jersey Fair Housing Act*, mandates comprehensive planning by a state agency to ensure that local zoning laws take into account each municipality's fair share of the regional low-income housing need. Both New Jersey and California employ "inclusionary" zoning techniques such as set-asides and density bonuses. In contrast, Massachusetts enacted a statute known as the *Anti-Snob Zoning Act*, empowering developers to challenge local permit denials by appealing unfavorable local zoning board decisions to a state review board, which is authorized to overturn local board decisions that exclude low-income housing needed in the municipality. Oregon, like Massachusetts, prevents local governments from excluding low-cost housing. Harold McDougall, *From Litigation to Legislation in Exclusionary Zoning*, 22 Harv. C.R.-C.L. L. Rev. 623 (1987). *See also Britton v. Town of Chester*, 595 A.2d 492 (N.H. 1991) (adopting a variation of the *Mount Laurel* doctrine as an interpretation of the state zoning enabling act).

7. **Efficiency.** In recent years, many municipalities have adopted linkage ordinances that condition real estate development on either providing a certain percentage of housing units for low-income persons or paying a tax to a municipal fund for this purpose. Do these inclusionary zoning techniques have positive or negative effects on social welfare? Some scholars have argued that inclusionary zoning likely will be inefficient. Professor Robert Ellickson has argued that such zoning effectively imposes a tax on new construction because some units that would not otherwise be profitable must be included in the development, thereby raising the costs of providing

14. In 2011, the governor of New Jersey attempted to abolish COAH, the agency responsible for overseeing New Jersey's *Fair Housing Act*, but the New Jersey Supreme Court held that the governor's authority over the state's executive branch does not extend that far. *See In re Plan for Abolition of Council on Affordable Housing*, 70 A.3d 559 (N.J. 2013).

new housing. When the cost of new housing is artificially raised by government regulation, less will be provided, thereby exacerbating the already existing shortage of low-income housing and interfering with the filtering mechanism by which wealthy homeowners move to better housing and leave their prior residences for less wealthy consumers. Robert C. Ellickson, *The Irony of "Inclusionary Zoning,"* 54 S. Cal. L. Rev. 1167 (1981).

Other scholars, however, contend that such techniques are likely to *restore* the efficient use of land by removing inefficient restrictions on development contained in existing exclusionary zoning laws. Laws that exclude low-income housing from the community arguably decrease social welfare by attempting to create protected enclaves without accounting for the externalities of limiting low-income housing to urban areas. They may also artificially increase the cost of low-income housing by excluding it from areas in which developers could otherwise profitably build it. Andrew G. Dietderich, *An Egalitarian's Market: The Economics of Inclusionary Zoning Reclaimed*, 24 Fordham Urb. L.J. 23 (1996).

8. Has inclusionary zoning worked? The evidence on the effectiveness of inclusionary zoning is mixed, and much depends on the details of any given program. There is some indication that longer-standing programs have stimulated the production of new low-income housing construction. *See* Jenny Schuetz, Rachel Meltzer & Vicki Been, *Silver Bullet or Trojan Horse? The Effects of Inclusionary Zoning on Local Housing Markets in the United States*, 14 Urb. Stud. 297 (2011) (collecting empirical studies and indicating, based on programs in suburban Boston and the San Francisco metropolitan area, that production increases were modest and impact on housing prices mixed). There is good evidence that *Mount Laurel* and the process it created has led to significant new production of low- and moderate-income housing. *See* Alan Mallach, *The* Mount Laurel *Doctrine and the Uncertainties of Social Policy in a Time of Retrenchment*, 63 Rutgers L. Rev. 849, 851 (2011). However, there are genuine questions about whether even *Mount Laurel* has actually generated social mobility. *Id.* at 861.

9. Growth controls. Growth controls and, more recently, "smart growth," ordinances raise concerns about exclusionary consequences. In the famous case of *Golden v. Planning Board of the Town of Ramapo*, 285 N.E.2d 291 (N.Y. 1972), the New York Court of Appeals upheld a provision that limited growth based on the availability of adequate municipal services. The town had undertaken an in-depth study of existing land uses, infrastructure, and likely residential, commercial, and industry development and had drafted a master plan based on that study. It then passed amendments to its zoning code that limited the approval of new subdivisions in order to sequence new residential development with planned public improvements. In approving this process, the Court indicated that it would "not countenance . . . under any guise . . . community efforts at immunization or exclusion." *Id.* at 302. The Court found, nonetheless, that "far from being exclusionary, the present amendments merely seek, by the implementation of sequential development and timed growth, to provide a balanced cohesive community dedicated to the efficient utilization of land." *Id.*

Growth controls, however, remain controversial. In *Zuckerman v. Town of Hadley*, 813 N.E.2d 843, 849 (Mass. 2004), for example, the Massachusetts Supreme Judicial Court held that a town's permanent limit on the number of building permits that can be issued annually for single-family homes designed to limit the number of children in public school "is inherently and unavoidably detrimental to the public welfare, and therefore not a legitimate zoning purpose" and thus unconstitutional. Justice Cordy explained: "Despite the perceived benefits that enforced isolation may bring to a town facing a new wave of permanent home seekers, it does not serve the general welfare of the Commonwealth to permit one particular town to deflect that wave onto its neighbors." *Id.* at 850.

§6 EXPRESSION, SPEECH, AND RELIGION IN LAND USE

§6.1 Aesthetic Zoning, Expression, and Discretion

Anderson v. City of Issaquah

851 P.2d 744 (Wash. Ct. App. 1993)

Map: 145 Gilman Boulevard, Issaquah, Washington

FAYE COLLIER KENNEDY, Judge.

Appellants M. Bruce Anderson, Gary D. LaChance, and M. Bruce Anderson, Inc. (hereinafter referred to as Anderson), challenge the denial of their application for a land use certification, arguing, *inter alia,* that the building design requirements contained in Issaquah Municipal Code (IMC) 16.16.060 are unconstitutionally vague.

Facts

Anderson owns property located at 145 N.W. Gilman Boulevard in the City of Issaquah (City). In 1988, Anderson applied to the City for a land use certification to develop the property. The property is zoned for general commercial use. Anderson desired to build a 6800 square foot commercial building for several retail tenants.

After obtaining architectural plans, Anderson submitted the project to various City departments for the necessary approvals. The process went smoothly until the approval of the Issaquah Development Commission (Development Commission) was sought. This commission was created to administer and enforce the City's land use regulations. It has the authority to approve or deny applications for land use certification.

Chapter 16.16.060 of the IMC enumerates various building design objectives which the Development Commission is required to administer and enforce. Insofar as is relevant to this appeal, the Development Commission is to be guided by the following criteria:

IMC 16.16.060(B). Relationship of Building and Site to Adjoining Area.

1. Buildings and structures shall be made compatible with adjacent buildings of conflicting architectural styles by such means as screens and site breaks, or other suitable methods and materials.

2. Harmony in texture, lines, and masses shall be encouraged.

IMC 16.16.060(D). Building Design.

1. Evaluation of a project shall be based on quality of its design and relationship to the natural setting of the valley and surrounding mountains.

2. Building components, such as windows, doors, eaves and parapets, shall have appropriate proportions and relationship to each other, expressing themselves as a part of the overall design.

3. Colors shall be harmonious, with bright or brilliant colors used only for minimal accent.

4. Design attention shall be given to screening from public view all mechanical equipment, including refuse enclosures, electrical transformer pads and vaults, communication equipment, and other utility hardware on roofs, grounds or buildings.

5. Exterior lighting shall be part of the architectural concept. Fixtures, standards and all exposed accessories shall be harmonious with the building design.

6. Monotony of design in single or multiple building projects shall be avoided. Efforts should be made to create an interesting project by use of complimentary details, functional orientation of buildings, parking and access provisions and relating the development to the site. In multiple building projects, variable siting of individual buildings, heights of buildings, or other methods shall be used to prevent a monotonous design.

As initially designed, Anderson's proposed structure was to be faced with off-white stucco and was to have a blue metal roof. It was designed in a "modern" style with an unbroken "warehouse" appearance in the rear, and large retail style windows in the front. The City moved a Victorian-era residence, the "Alexander House," onto the neighboring property to serve as a visitors' center. Across the street from the Anderson site is a gasoline station that looks like a gasoline station. Located nearby and within view from the proposed building site are two more gasoline stations, the First Mutual Bank Building built in the "Issaquah territorial style," an Elk's hall which is described in the record by the Mayor of Issaquah as a "box building," an auto repair shop, and a veterinary clinic with a cyclone fenced dog run. The area is described in the record as "a natural transition area between old downtown Issaquah and the new village style construction of Gilman [Boulevard]."

The Development Commission reviewed Anderson's application for the first time at a public hearing on December 21, 1988. Commissioner Nash commented that "the facade did not fit with the concept of the surrounding area." Commissioner McGinnis agreed. Commissioner Nash expressed concern about the building color and stated that he did not think the building was compatible with the image of Issaquah. Commissioner Larson said that he would like to see more depth to the building facade. Commissioner Nash said there should be some interest created along the blank back wall. Commissioner Garrison suggested that the rear facade needed to be redesigned.

At the conclusion of the meeting, the Development Commission voted to continue the hearing to give Anderson an opportunity to modify the building design.

On January 18, 1989, Anderson came back before the Development Commission with modified plans which included changing the roofing from metal to tile, changing the color of the structure from off-white to "Cape Cod" gray with "Tahoe" blue trim, and adding brick to the front facade. During the ensuing discussion among the commissioners, Commissioner Larson stated that the revisions to the front facade had not satisfied his concerns from the last meeting. In response to Anderson's request for more specific design guidelines, Commissioner McGinnis stated that the Development Commission had "been giving direction; it is the applicant's responsibility to take the direction/suggestions and incorporate them into a revised plan that reflects the changes." Commissioner Larson then suggested that "[t]he facade can be broken up with sculptures, benches, fountains, etc." Commissioner Nash suggested that Anderson "drive up and down Gilman and look at both good and bad examples of what has been done with flat facades."

As the discussion continued, Commissioner Larson stated that Anderson "should present a [plan] that achieves what the Commission is trying to achieve through its comments/suggestions at these meetings" and stated that "architectural screens, fountains, paving of brick, wood or other similar method[s] of screening in lieu of vegetative landscaping are examples of design suggestions that can be used to break up the front facade." Commissioner Davis objected to the front facade, stating that he could not see putting an expanse of glass facing Gilman Boulevard. "The building is not compatible with Gilman." Commissioner O'Shea agreed. Commissioner Nash stated that "the application needs major changes to be acceptable." Commissioner O'Shea agreed. Commissioner Nash stated that "this facade does not create the same feeling as the building/environment around this site."

Commissioner Nash continued, stating that he "personally like[d] the introduction of brick and the use of tiles rather than metal on the roof." Commissioner Larson stated that he would like to see a review of the blue to be used: "Tahoe blue may be too dark." Commissioner Steinwachs agreed. Commissioner Larson noted that "the front of the building could be modulated [to] have other design techniques employed to make the front facade more interesting."

With this, the Development Commission voted to continue the discussion to a future hearing.

On February 15, 1989, Anderson came back before the Development Commission. In the meantime, Anderson's architects had added a 5-foot overhang and a 7-foot accent overhang to the plans for the front of the building. More brick had been added to the front of the building. Wood trim and accent colors had been added to the back of the building and trees were added to the landscaping to further break up the rear facade.

Anderson explained the plans still called for large, floor to ceiling windows as this was to be a retail premises: "[A] glass front is necessary to rent the space. . . ." Commissioner Steinwachs stated that he had driven Gilman Boulevard and taken notes. The following verbatim statement by Steinwachs was placed into the minutes:

"My General Observation From Driving Up and Down Gilman Boulevard."

> I see certain design elements and techniques used in various combinations in various locations to achieve a visual effect that is sensitive to the unique character of our Signature Street. I see heavy use of brick, wood, and tile. I see minimal use of stucco. I see colors that are mostly earthtones, avoiding extreme contrasts. I see various methods used to provide modulation in both horizontal and vertical lines, such as gables, bay windows, recesses in front faces, porches, rails, many vertical columns, and breaks in roof lines. I see long, sloping, conspicuous roofs with large overhangs. I see windows with panels above and below windows. I see no windows that extend down to floor level. This is the impression I have of Gilman Boulevard as it relates to building design.

Commissioner Nash agreed stating, "[T]here is a certain feeling you get when you drive along Gilman Boulevard, and this building does not give this same feeling." Commissioner Steinwachs wondered if the applicant had any option but to start "from scratch." Anderson responded that he would be willing to change from stucco to wood facing but that, after working on the project for 9 months and experiencing total frustration, he was not willing to make additional design changes.

At that point, the Development Commission denied Anderson's application, giving four reasons:

> 1. After four [sic] lengthy review meetings of the Development Commission, the applicant has not been sufficiently responsive to concerns expressed by the Commission to warrant approval or an additional continuance of the review.
>
> 2. The primary concerns expressed relate to the building architecture as it relates to Gilman Boulevard in general, and the immediate neighborhood in particular.
>
> 3. The Development Commission is charged with protecting, preserving and enhancing the aesthetic values that have established the desirable quality and unique character of Issaquah, reference IMC 16.16.010C.
>
> 4. We see certain design elements and techniques used in various combinations in various locations to achieve a visual effect that is sensitive to the unique character of our Signature Street. On Gilman Boulevard we see heavy use of brick, wood and tile. We see minimal use of stucco. We see various methods used to provide both horizontal and vertical modulation, including gables, breaks in rooflines, bay windows, recesses and protrusions in front face. We see long, sloping, conspicuous roofs with large overhangs. We see no windows that extend to ground level. We see brick and wood panels at intervals between windows. We see earthtone colors avoiding extreme contrast.

Anderson, who by this time had an estimated $250,000 into the project, timely appealed the adverse ruling to the Issaquah City Council (City Council). After a lengthy hearing and much debate, the City Council decided to affirm the Development Commission's decision by a vote of 4 to 3.

The City Council considered formal written findings and conclusions on April 3, 1989. The City Council verbally adopted its action on that date but required that certain changes be made to the proposed findings and conclusions. Those changes were made and the final findings and conclusions were signed on April 5, 1989 (backdated to April 3). On April 5, a notice of action was issued to Anderson, stating that he had

14 days *from the date of that notice* in which to file any appeal. Thirteen days later, on April 18, 1989, Anderson filed a complaint in King County Superior Court.

Discussion

[A] statute which either forbids or requires the doing of an act in terms so vague that men [and women] of common intelligence must necessarily guess at its meaning and differ as to its application, violates the first essential of due process of law. *Connally v. General Constr. Co.*, 269 U.S. 385, 391 (1926). In the area of land use, a court looks not only at the face of the ordinance but also at its application to the person who has sought to comply with the ordinance and/or who is alleged to have failed to comply. The purpose of the void for vagueness doctrine is to limit arbitrary and discretionary enforcements of the law.

Looking first at the face of the building design sections of IMC 16.16.060, we note that an ordinary citizen reading these sections would learn only that a given building project should bear a good relationship with the Issaquah Valley and surrounding mountains; its windows, doors, eaves and parapets should be of "appropriate proportions"; its colors should be "harmonious" and seldom "bright" or "brilliant"; its mechanical equipment should be screened from public view; its exterior lighting should be "harmonious" with the building design and "monotony should be avoided." The project should also be "interesting." IMC 16.16.060(D)(1)-(6). If the building is not "compatible" with adjacent buildings, it should be "made compatible" by the use of screens and site breaks "or other suitable methods and materials." "Harmony in texture, lines, and masses [is] encouraged." The landscaping should provide an "attractive . . . transition" to adjoining properties. IMC 16.16.060(B)(1)-(3).

As is stated in the brief of amici curiae, we conclude that these code sections "do not give effective or meaningful guidance" to applicants, to design professionals, or to the public officials of Issaquah who are responsible for enforcing the code. Brief of Amici Curiae, at 1. Although it is clear from the code sections here at issue that mechanical equipment must be screened from public view and that, probably, earth tones or pastels located within the cool and muted ranges of the color wheel are going to be preferred, there is nothing in the code from which an applicant can determine whether his or her project is going to be seen by the Development Commission as "interesting" versus "monotonous" and as "harmonious" with the valley and the mountains. Neither is it clear from the code just what else, besides the valley and the mountains, a particular project is supposed to be harmonious with, although "[h]armony in texture, lines, and masses" is certainly encouraged. IMC 16.16.060(B)(2).

In attempting to interpret and apply this code, the commissioners charged with that task were left with only their own individual, subjective "feelings" about the "image of Issaquah" and as to whether this project was "compatible" or "interesting." The commissioners stated that the City was "making a statement" on its "signature street" and invited Anderson to take a drive up and down Gilman Boulevard and "look at good and bad examples of what has been done with flat facades." One commissioner drove up and down Gilman, taking notes, in a no doubt sincere effort to define that which is left undefined in the code.

The point we make here is that neither Anderson nor the commissioners may constitutionally be required or allowed to guess at the meaning of the code's building design requirements by driving up and down Gilman Boulevard looking at "good and bad" examples of what has been done with other buildings, recently or in the past. We hold that the code sections here at issue are unconstitutionally vague on their face. The words employed are not technical words which are commonly understood within the professional building design industry. Neither do these words have a settled common law meaning.

As they were applied to Anderson, it is also clear the code sections at issue fail to pass constitutional muster. Because the commissioners themselves had no objective guidelines to follow, they necessarily had to resort to their own subjective "feelings." The "statement" Issaquah is apparently trying to make on its "signature street" is not written in the code. In order to be enforceable, that "statement" must be written down in the code, in understandable terms. The unacceptable alternative is what happened here. The commissioners enforced not a building design code but their own arbitrary concept of the provisions of an unwritten "statement" to be made on Gilman Boulevard. The commissioners' individual concepts were as vague and undefined as those written in the code. This is the very epitome of discretionary, arbitrary enforcement of the law.

[A]esthetic standards are an appropriate *component* of land use governance. Whenever a community adopts such standards they can and must be drafted to give clear guidance to all parties concerned. Applicants must have an understandable statement of what is expected from new construction. Design professionals need to know in advance what standards will be acceptable in a given community. It is unreasonable to expect applicants to pay for repetitive revisions of plans in an effort to comply with the unarticulated, unpublished "statements" a given community may wish to make on or off its "signature street." It is equally unreasonable, and a deprivation of due process, to expect or allow a design review board such as the Issaquah Development Commission to create standards on an *ad hoc* basis, during the design review process.

It is not disputed that Anderson's project meets all of the City's land use requirements except for those unwritten and therefore unenforceable requirements relating to building design which the Development Commission unsuccessfully tried to articulate during the course of several hearings. We order that Anderson's land use certification be issued, provided however, that those changes which Anderson agreed to through the hearing before the City Council may validly be imposed.

Notes and Questions

1. **Aesthetic zoning.** Aesthetic zoning is a common aspect of contemporary land use regulation. Common examples include the kind of architecture or design review the court reviewed in *Anderson*, as well as limitations on billboards and other signs, and regulations of particularly unsightly land uses such as junkyards.

Courts were initially suspicious of aesthetic zoning as a valid object of the police power, *see, e.g., Spann v. Dallas*, 235 S.W. 513, 516 (1921) ("[I]t is not the law . . . that a man may be deprived of the lawful use of his property because his tastes are not in accord with those of his neighbors"), and some courts continue to echo *Anderson*'s grudging acceptance. In *Berman v. Parker*, 348 U.S. 26, 33 (1954), a case that involved the use of eminent domain for urban renewal, the Supreme Court stated that:

> The concept of the public welfare is broad and inclusive. The values it represents are spiritual as well as physical, aesthetic as well as monetary. It is within the power of the legislature to determine that the community should be beautiful as well as healthy, spacious as well as clean, well-balanced as well as carefully patrolled.

Since *Berman*, courts have generally accepted aesthetics as a legitimate aspect of zoning, and litigation challenges now focus primarily on the kinds of due process vagueness concerns that *Anderson* addressed.

2. Aesthetics and the first amendment. Aesthetic regulations have raised first amendment concerns, particularly in the context of signage regulations. *See, e.g., Metromedia, Inc. v. City of San Diego*, 453 U.S. 490 (1991). In *City of Ladue v. Gilleo*, 512 U.S. 43 (1994), a homeowner had placed a sign on her front lawn in December 1990 that read "Say No to War in the Persian Gulf, Call Congress Now." After her sign disappeared and a replacement was knocked down, the homeowner complained to the police, only to be informed that the city prohibited such signs. Reviewing the constitutionality of this prohibition, the Court began by noting that although signs

> are a form of expression protected by the Free Speech Clause, they pose distinctive problems that are subject to municipalities' police powers. Unlike oral speech, signs take up space and may obstruct views, distract motorists, displace alternative uses for land, and pose other problems that legitimately call for regulation. It is common ground that governments may regulate the physical characteristics of signs—just as they can, within reasonable bounds and absent censorial purpose, regulate audible expression in its capacity as noise.

Id. at 48. Notwithstanding Ladue's valid interest "minimizing the visual clutter associated with signs," *id.* at 54, the Court found that the ban impermissibly

> foreclosed [the lawn sign] medium to political, religious, or personal messages. Signs that react to a local happening or express a view on a controversial issue both reflect and animate change in the life of a community. Often placed on lawns or in windows, residential signs play an important part in political campaigns, during which they are displayed to signal the resident's support for particular candidates, parties, or causes. They may not afford the same opportunities for conveying complex ideas as do other media, but residential signs have long been an important and distinct medium of expression.

Id. at 54-55. This elimination of an entire medium of communication, moreover, could not be justified as a valid regulation of time, place, or manner of speech, particularly where the regulation interfered with the long-recognized "special respect for individual liberty in the home." *Id.* at 58.

Problem

If you were asked to rewrite the relevant provisions of Issaquah's design ordinance to meet the standards the *Anderson* court articulated, how would you do so? What kinds of substantive and procedural protections for owners going through the design-review process would you add? What considerations would be important to preserve for the community?

§6.2 Restrictions on Free Speech in Land Use Regulation

Local governments frequently seek to regulate unpopular types of expression, such as adult book stores and nude dancing establishments. In *City of Los Angeles v. Alameda Books*, 535 U.S. 425 (2002), the Supreme Court attempted to clarify the standards that apply to such regulations. Los Angeles sought to prevent the grouping of adult uses through an ordinance that barred such uses within 1,000 feet of each other and also required such uses to be more than 500 feet from any religious institution, school, or public park. The ordinance, however, inadvertently allowed multiple adult businesses in a single building. After Los Angeles amended its code to close that loophole, two adult bookstores operating in the same establishment filed suit. In all of this, the city had relied on an old 1977 study that indicated that the concentration of adult uses was associated with higher rates of certain crimes in surrounding areas.

Justice O'Connor, in a plurality opinion, described the framework for evaluating land use regulations that target speech established in *Renton v. Playtime Theatres, Inc.*, 475 U.S. 41 (1986), which concerned an ordinance banning adult movie theaters from locating within 1,000 feet of a residential zone, family dwelling, church, park, or school. First, the Court considers whether the ordinance bans the form of expression altogether. If it does not, the ordinance will be analyzed as "a time, place, and manner regulation." The Court next considers whether the restriction is "content neutral or content based. If the regulation were content based, it would be considered presumptively invalid and subject to strict scrutiny." In *Renton*, the Court found the ordinance to be content-neutral, because it "was aimed not at the content of the films shown at adult theaters, but rather at the secondary effects of such theaters on the surrounding community, namely, at crime rates, property values, and the quality of the city's neighborhoods." If content-neutral, an ordinance would be upheld so long as it "was designed to serve a substantial government interest and that reasonable alternative avenues of communication remained available." The Court in *Renton* found that the city met this burden. 535 U.S. at 433-434.

In *Alameda Books*, the court of appeals had rejected the relevance of the 1977 study because it focused on the concentration of businesses within a neighborhood but not within a given building. To the *Alameda Books* plurality, however, this was too high a burden. Instead, it opined, local governments are entitled "rely on any evidence that is 'reasonably believed to be relevant' for demonstrating a connection between speech and a substantial, independent government interest." *Id.* at 436 (quoting *Renton*, 475 U.S. at 51-52).

Justice Kennedy concurred, framing the conflict at issue as follows:

> Speech can produce tangible consequences. It can change minds. It can prompt actions. These primary effects signify the power and the necessity of free speech. Speech can also cause secondary effects, however, unrelated to the impact of the speech on its audience. A newspaper factory may cause pollution, and a billboard may obstruct a view. These secondary consequences are not always immune from regulation by zoning laws even though they are produced by speech.
>
> Municipal governments know that high concentrations of adult businesses can damage the value and the integrity of a neighborhood. The damage is measurable; it is all too real. The law does not require a city to ignore these consequences if it uses its zoning power in a reasonable way to ameliorate them without suppressing speech.

Id. at 444. Justice Kennedy argued that "[t]hese ordinances are content based, and we should call them so," but that the *Renton* analysis should control nonetheless. On that analysis, Justice Kennedy argued, it is not enough to examine secondary effects in isolation in evaluating the evidence a jurisdiction relies on to justify restricting adult speech; instead a court must evaluate "how speech will fare" under the law. If the effect of the ordinance is to reduce secondary effects by reducing (rather than merely dispersing) speech, then it is impermissible. *Id.* at 450-451.

State constitutional law can be more protective of speech than the federal Constitution. In *City of Erie v. Pap's A.M.*, 529 U.S. 277 (2000), the Supreme Court upheld the constitutionality of a zoning ordinance that effectively banned nude dancing, finding the law a valid content-neutral regulation of conduct rather than expression, geared to protecting the people from the secondary effects of adult entertainment establishments. *Accord*, *Barnes v. Glen Theatre, Inc.*, 501 U.S. 560, 570 (1991) (government has legitimate interest in preventing public nudity that is "unrelated to the suppression of free expression"). However, in *Mendoza v. Licensing Board of Fall River*, 827 N.E.2d 180 (Mass. 2005), the state supreme court interpreted its state constitutional free speech guarantee more broadly and found that, while the city could regulate the time, place, and manner of the practice, the city could not completely ban nude dancing from anywhere in the city.

§6.3 Freedom of Religion and Religious Land Uses

Westchester Day School v. Village of Mamaroneck

504 F.3d 338 (2d Cir. 2007)

RICHARD J. CARDAMONE, Circuit Judge:

For nearly 60 years Westchester Day School (plaintiff, WDS, day school, or school) has been operating an Orthodox Jewish co-educational day school with classes from pre-school to eighth grade. Believing it needed to expand, the school submitted construction plans to the Village of Mamaroneck and an application for the required special permit. When the village zoning board turned the application down, the present litigation ensued.

Westchester Day School is located in the Orienta Point neighborhood of the Village of Mamaroneck, Westchester County, New York. Its facilities are situated on 25.75 acres of largely undeveloped land (property) owned by Westchester Religious Institute. The Mamaroneck Village Code permits private schools to operate in "R-20 Districts" if the Zoning Board of Appeals of the Village of Mamaroneck (ZBA or zoning board) grants them a special permit.

As a Jewish private school, Westchester Day School provides its students with a dual curriculum in Judaic and general studies. Even general studies classes are taught so that religious and Judaic concepts are reinforced. Thus, the school strives to have every classroom used at times for religious purposes, whether or not the class is officially labeled Judaic. A Jewish day school like WDS exists, at least in part, because Orthodox Jews believe it is the parents' duty to teach the Torah to their children. Since most Orthodox parents lack the time to fulfill this obligation fully, they seek out a school like WDS.

By 1998 WDS believed its current facilities inadequate to satisfy the school's needs. The district court's extensive findings reveal the day school's existing facilities are deficient and that its effectiveness in providing the education Orthodox Judaism mandates has been significantly hindered as a consequence. In October 2001 the day school submitted to the zoning board an application for modification of its special permit to enable it to proceed with this $12 million expansion project. On February 7, 2002 the ZBA voted unanimously to issue a "negative declaration," which constituted a finding that the project would have no significant adverse environmental impact and thus that consideration of the project could proceed. After the issuance of the negative declaration, a small but vocal group in the Mamaroneck community opposed the project. As a result of this public opposition, on August 1, 2002 the ZBA voted 3-2 to rescind the negative declaration. [After earlier litigation on this issue, the ZBA] proceeded to conduct additional public hearings to consider the merits of the application. The ZBA had the opportunity to approve the application subject to conditions intended to mitigate adverse effects on public health, safety, and welfare that might arise from the project. Rather, on May 13, 2003 the ZBA voted 3-2 to deny WDS's application in its entirety.

The stated reasons for the rejection included the effect the project would have on traffic and concerns with respect to parking and the intensity of use. Many of these grounds were conceived after the ZBA closed its hearing process, giving the school no opportunity to respond. The district court found the stated reasons for denying the application were not supported by evidence in the public record before the ZBA, and were based on several factual errors. It surmised that the application was in fact denied because the ZBA gave undue deference to the public opposition of the small but influential group of neighbors who were against the school's expansion plans. It also noted that the denial of the application would result in long delay of WDS's efforts to remedy the gross inadequacies of its facilities, and substantially increase construction costs.

On May 29, 2003 the school filed [a complaint raising claims under the Religious Land Use and Institutionalized Persons Act (RLUIPA), 42 U.S.C. §2000cc *et seq.*, and other statutes]. A seven-day bench trial began on November 14, 2005 and resulted in the March 2006 judgment. The district court ordered the Village to issue WDS's special permit immediately.

Application of RLUIPA

RLUIPA prohibits the government from imposing or implementing a land use regulation in a manner that

> imposes a substantial burden on the religious exercise of a person, including a religious assembly or institution, unless the government demonstrates that imposition of the burden on that person, assembly, or institution (A) is in furtherance of a compelling governmental interest; and (B) is the least restrictive means of furthering that compelling governmental interest. 42 U.S.C. §2000cc(a)(1).

A. Religious Exercise

Religious exercise under RLUIPA is defined as "any exercise of religion, whether or not compelled by, or central to, a system of religious belief." §2000cc-5(7)(A). Further, using, building, or converting real property for religious exercise purposes is considered to be religious exercise under the statute. §2000cc-5(7)(B). To remove any remaining doubt regarding how broadly Congress aimed to define religious exercise, RLUIPA goes on to state that the Act's aim of protecting religious exercise is to be construed broadly and "to the maximum extent permitted by the terms of this chapter and the Constitution." §2000cc-3(g).

[T]o get immunity from land use regulation, religious schools need to demonstrate more than that the proposed improvement would enhance the overall experience of its students. For example, if a religious school wishes to build a gymnasium to be used exclusively for sporting activities, that kind of expansion would not constitute religious exercise. Or, had the ZBA denied the Westchester Religious Institute's 1986 request for a special permit to construct a headmaster's residence on a portion of the property, such a denial would not have implicated religious exercise. Nor would the school's religious exercise have been burdened by the denial of a permit to build more office space.

[The] district court made careful factual findings that each room the school planned to build would be used at least in part for religious education and practice, finding that Gordon Hall and the other facilities renovated as part of the project, in whole and in all of their constituent parts, would be used for "religious education and practice." In light of these findings, amply supported in the record, the expansion project is a "building [and] conversion of real property for the purpose of religious exercise" and thus is religious exercise under §2000cc-5(7)(B).

B. Substantial Burden

Supreme Court precedents teach that a substantial burden on religious exercise exists when an individual is required to "choose between following the precepts of her religion and forfeiting benefits, on the one hand, and abandoning one of the precepts of her religion . . . on the other hand." *Sherbert v. Verner*, 374 U.S. 398, 404 (1963). A number of courts use this standard as the starting point for determining what is a substantial burden under RLUIPA. When a municipality denies a religious institution the right to expand its facilities, it is difficult to speak of substantial pressure to change religious behavior, because in light of the denial the renovation simply cannot proceed. Accordingly, when there has been a denial of a religious institution's building application, courts appropriately speak of government action that directly *coerces* the religious institution to change its behavior, rather than government action that forces the religious entity to choose between religious precepts and government benefits. *See, e.g.*, [*Midrash Sephardi, Inc. v. Town of Surfside*, 366 F.3d 1214, 1227 (11th Cir. 2004)] ("[A] substantial burden is akin to significant pressure which directly coerces the religious adherent to conform his or her behavior accordingly."). Here, WDS contends that the denial of its application in effect coerced the day school to continue teaching in inadequate facilities, thereby impeding its religious exercise.

Yet, when the denial of a religious institution's application to build is not absolute, such would not necessarily place substantial pressure on the institution to alter its behavior, since it could just as easily file a second application that remedies the problems in the first. As a consequence, rejection of a submitted plan, while leaving open the possibility of approval of a resubmission with modifications designed to address the cited problems, is less likely to constitute a "substantial burden" than definitive rejection of the same plan, ruling out the possibility of approval of a modified proposal. Of course, a conditional denial may represent a substantial burden if the condition itself is a burden on free exercise, the required modifications are economically unfeasible, or where a zoning board's stated willingness to consider a modified plan is disingenuous. However, in most cases, whether the denial of the application was absolute is important; if there is a reasonable opportunity for the institution to submit a modified application, the denial does not place substantial pressure on it to change its behavior and thus does not constitute a substantial burden on the free exercise of religion.

We recognize further that where the denial of an institution's application to build will have minimal impact on the institution's religious exercise, it does not constitute a substantial burden, even when the denial is definitive. There must exist a close nexus between the coerced or impeded conduct and the institution's religious exercise for such conduct to be a substantial burden on that religious exercise. Imagine, for example, a situation where a school could easily rearrange existing classrooms to meet its religious needs in the face of a rejected application to renovate. In such case, the denial would not substantially threaten the institution's religious exercise, and there would be no substantial burden, even though the school was refused the opportunity to expand its facilities.

Note, however, that a burden need not be found insuperable to be held substantial. When the school has no ready alternatives, or where the alternatives require substantial "delay, uncertainty, and expense," a complete denial of the school's application might be indicative of a substantial burden.

We are, of course, mindful that the Supreme Court's free exercise jurisprudence signals caution in using effect alone to determine substantial burden. This is because an effect focused analysis may run up against the reality that "[t]he freedom asserted by [some may] bring them into collision with [the] rights asserted by" others and that "[i]t is such conflicts which most frequently require intervention of the State to determine where the rights of one end and those of another begin." *Braunfeld v. Brown*, 366 U.S. 599, 604 (1961). Accordingly, the Supreme Court has held that generally applicable burdens, neutrally imposed, are not "substantial." *See Jimmy Swaggart Ministries v. Bd. of Equalization*, 493 U.S. 378, 389-91 (1990).

This reasoning helps to explain why courts confronting free exercise challenges to zoning restrictions rarely find the substantial burden test satisfied even when the resulting effect is to completely prohibit a religious congregation from building a church on its own land. A number of our sister circuits have applied this same reasoning in construing RLUIPA's substantial burden requirement. For example, the Seventh Circuit has held that land use conditions do not constitute a substantial burden under RLUIPA where they are "neutral and traceable to municipal land planning goals" and where there is no evidence that government actions were taken "*because* [plaintiff] is a *religious* institution." *Vision Church v. Vill. of Long Grove*, 468 F.3d 975, 998-99 (7th Cir. 2006). Similarly, the Ninth Circuit has held that no substantial burden was imposed, even where an ordinance "rendered [plaintiff] unable to provide education and/or worship" on its property, because the plaintiff was not "precluded from using other sites within the city" and because "there [is no] evidence that the City would not impose the same requirements on any other entity." [*San Jose Christian College v. City of Morgan Hill*, 360 F.3d 1024, 1035 (9th Cir. 2004).] The Eleventh Circuit has also ruled that "reasonable 'run of the mill' zoning considerations do not constitute substantial burdens." *Midrash Sephardi*, 366 F.3d at 1227-28 & n.11.

The same reasoning that precludes a religious organization from demonstrating substantial burden in the neutral application of legitimate land use restrictions may, in fact, support a substantial burden claim where land use restrictions are imposed on the religious institution arbitrarily, capriciously, or unlawfully. The arbitrary application of laws to religious organizations may reflect bias or discrimination against religion. Where the arbitrary, capricious, or unlawful nature of a defendant's challenged action suggests that a religious institution received less than even-handed treatment, the application of RLUIPA's substantial burden provision usefully "backstops the explicit prohibition of religious discrimination in the later section of the Act." [*Saints Constantine & Helen Greek Orthodox Church, Inc. v. City of New Berlin*, 396 F.3d 895, 900 (7th Cir. 2005).]

Accordingly, we deem it relevant to the evaluation of WDS's particular substantial burden claim that the district court expressly found that the zoning board's denial of the school's application was "arbitrary and capricious under New York law because the purported justifications set forth in the Resolution do not bear the necessary substantial relation to public health, safety or welfare," and the zoning board's findings are not supported by substantial evidence. Although the Village disputes this finding, we conclude that it is amply supported by both the law and the record evidence.

[T]he zoning board denied WDS's application based, in part, on an accusation that the school made "a willful attempt" to mislead the zoning board. In fact, the accusation was unsupported by the evidence and based on the zoning board's own error with respect to certain relevant facts. The ZBA's allegations of deficiencies in the school's traffic study were also unsupported by the evidence before it. The concern about lack of adequate parking was based on the zoning board's own miscalculation. In each of these instances, the ZBA's assumptions were not only wrong; they were unsupported by its own experts.

[T]wo other factors drawn from our earlier discussion must be considered in reaching such a burden determination: (1) whether there are quick, reliable, and financially feasible alternatives WDS may utilize to meet its religious needs absent its obtaining the construction permit; and (2) whether the denial was conditional. These two considerations matter for the same reason: when an institution has a ready alternative — be it an entirely different plan to meet the same needs or the opportunity to try again in line with a zoning board's recommendations — its religious exercise has not been substantially burdened.

Here, the school could not have met its needs simply by reallocating space within its existing buildings. The architectural firm it hired determined that certain essential facilities would have to be incorporated into a new building, because not enough space remained in the existing buildings to accommodate the school's expanding needs. Further, experts hired by WDS determined that the planned location for Gordon Hall was the only site that would accommodate the new building.

In examining the second factor we believe the denial of WDS's application was absolute. First, we observe that the ZBA could have approved the application subject to conditions intended to mitigate adverse effects on public health, safety, and welfare. Yet the ZBA chose instead to deny the application in its entirety. Second, were WDS to prepare a modified proposal, it would have to begin the application process anew. This would have imposed so great an economic burden as to make the option unworkable. Third, the district court determined that ZBA members were not credible when they testified they would give reasonable consideration to another application by WDS. When the board's expressed willingness to consider a modified proposal is insincere, we do not require an institution to file a modified proposal before determining that its religious exercise has been substantially burdened.

C. *Least Restrictive Means to Further a Compelling State Interest*

Under RLUIPA, once a religious institution has demonstrated that its religious exercise has been substantially burdened, the burden of proof shifts to the municipality to prove it acted in furtherance of a compelling governmental interest and that its action is the least restrictive means of furthering that interest. §2000cc-2(b). Compelling state interests are "interests of the highest order." *Church of the Lukumi Babalu Aye, Inc. v. City of Hialeah*, 508 U.S. 520, 546 (1993). The Village claims that it has a compelling interest in enforcing zoning regulations and ensuring residents' safety through traffic regulations. However, it must show a compelling interest in imposing the burden on religious exercise in the particular case at hand, not a compelling interest in general.

The district court's findings reveal the ZBA's stated reasons for denying the application were not substantiated by evidence in the record before it. The court stated the application was denied not because of a compelling governmental interest that would adversely impact public health, safety, or welfare, but was denied because of undue deference to the opposition of a small group of neighbors.

Further, even were we to determine that there was a compelling state interest involved, the Village did not use the least restrictive means available to achieve that interest. The ZBA had the opportunity to approve the application subject to conditions, but refused to consider doing so.

Notes and Questions

1. **Congress versus the courts on religious freedom.** The first and fourteenth amendments to the U.S. Constitution protect the "free exercise" of religion. In *Employment Division v. Smith*, 494 U.S. 872 (1990), the Supreme Court held that no violation of the free exercise clause occurs when a neutral and generally applicable regulatory law places a burden on an individual's religion. With several narrow exceptions, only laws that prohibit specific religious practices or coerce individuals to engage in religious practices raise constitutional issues of free exercise. Responding to *Smith*, in 1993 Congress passed the *Religious Freedom Restoration Act* (RFRA), 42 U.S.C. §§2000bb-1 to 2000bb-3, granting exemptions from government regulations that substantially burden the free exercise of religion unless the government could show a compelling governmental interest for the regulation and that the interest could not be achieved in a manner less restrictive of religious practice. In 1997, the Supreme Court held RFRA unconstitutional as applied to state governments because Congress's power under the fourteenth amendment to regulate the states to protect religious "liberty" could not go beyond the protections afforded by the first amendment. *City of Boerne v. Flores*, 521 U.S. 507 (1997). Because Congress was, in effect, trying to expand federal protection for religious freedom beyond what the Court believed was encompassed by the first amendment, and because it was attempting to regulate the states, it exceeded its powers.[15]

City of Boerne generated a number of legislative responses. At the state level, a number of states enacted their own versions of RFRA. Alabama, for example, amended its constitution to do so. Ala. Const. amend. 622, §V. Other states that passed such laws by statute include Arizona, Ariz. Stat. §41-1493.01; Connecticut, Conn. Gen. Stat. §52-571b; Florida, Fla. Stat. §§761.01-761.05; Idaho, Idaho Code §73-402; Illinois, 775 Ill. Comp. Stat. 35/1-99; New Mexico, N.M. Stat. §§28-22-1 to 28-22-5; Oklahoma, Okla. Stat. tit. 51, §§251-258; Rhode Island, R.I. Gen. Laws §§42-80.1-1 to 42-80.1-4; South Carolina, S.C. Code §§1-32-10 to 1-32-60; and Texas, Tex. Civ. Prac. & Rem. Code §§110.001-110.012.

At the federal level, Congress responded by passing the *Religious Land Use and Institutionalized Persons Act of 2000* (RLUIPA), 42 U.S.C. §§2000cc to 2000cc-5. More limited in scope, RLUIPA protects the religious exercise rights of prisoners and prohibits

---

15. RFRA may still be constitutional as applied to federal statutes and administrative actions. *See, e.g., Hankins v. Lyght*, 441 F.3d 96, 109 (2d Cir. 2006).

governments from "impos[ing] or implement[ing] a land use regulation in a manner that imposes a substantial burden on the religious exercise of a person, including a religious assembly or institution" unless the regulation furthers "a compelling governmental interest" and "is the least restrictive means of furthering that compelling governmental interest." 42 U.S.C. §2000cc.

To meet the constitutional requirements set out in *City of Bourne*, the statute applies only if (a) the affected activity receives federal funds, (b) either the substantial burden or the removal of the burden would affect "interstate commerce," or (c) the burden is imposed in the course of governmental procedures that involve "individualized assessments of the proposed uses for the property involved." *Id.* §2000cc(a)(2). The statute further provides that no government "shall impose or implement a land use regulation that (A) totally excludes religious assemblies from a jurisdiction; or (B) unreasonably limits religious assemblies, institutions, or structures within a jurisdiction." *Id.* §2000cc(b)(3).

The Supreme Court has held that the "institutionalized persons" aspects of RLUIPA do not violate the constitution's establishment clause, *see Cutter v. Wilkinson*, 544 U.S. 709 (2005), but has yet to address the act's land use provisions.

2. Religious exercise. *Westchester Day School* noted how broadly Congress defined religious exercise under §§2000cc-5(7) and 3(g), but nonetheless gave several examples of uses related to the religious school that would not have qualified, such as a gymnasium for students or a residence for the headmaster. Do you agree with this interpretation? Why does a given portion of a facility have to be directly used for religious education to constitute "religious exercise"? What if a church believes that part of its ministry includes social gatherings for its members and seeks to build a facility that is used for gatherings, but not worship?

Many faiths include strictures relating to relieving suffering and alleviating poverty and, as a result, many religious institutions offer social services, such as soup kitchens, homeless shelters, and housing. If a religious institution offers a social service or a service that looks like a commercial activity as part of its mission, is this the "exercise of religion"? *See, e.g., Greater Bible Way Temple v. City of Jackson*, 733 N.W.2d 734 (Mich. 2007) (proposed assisted living facility for elderly and disabled people claimed to be part of a church's mission was not considered religious exercise). Why might courts limit the scope of the kinds of services that might constitute religious exercise?

Courts can also take a narrow view of claims that uses that *support* a religious mission are themselves the exercise of religion. *See, e.g., Cathedral Church of the Intercessor v. Village of Malverne*, 353 F. Supp. 2d 375 (E.D.N.Y. 2005) (no RLUIPA claim when expansion of church's administrative offices was blocked); *Scottish Rite Cathedral v. City of L.A.*, 67 Cal. Rptr. 3d 207, 215-216 (Ct. App. 2007) (holding that "a burden on a commercial enterprise used to fund a religious organization does not constitute a substantial burden on 'religious exercise' within the meaning of RLUIPA").

3. How substantial does the burden have to be? As *Westchester Day School* pointed out, some courts hold that land use restrictions are not a substantial burden where such conditions are "neutral and traceable to municipal land planning goals."

Vision Church v. Village of Long Grove, 468 F.3d 975, 998-999 (7th Cir. 2006). In passing RLUIPA, Congress was responding to the Supreme Court's holding in *Smith* that the free exercise clause is not violated when a neutral and generally applicable regulatory law burdens an individual's religion. Does that suggest that even neutral and generally applicable zoning laws might create a substantial burden on religious exercise?

Courts have taken varying approaches to evaluating whether a land use regulation constitutes a substantial burden on religious exercise. In contrast to the standard the Second Circuit applied in *Westchester Day School*, for example, the Seventh Circuit has held that "a land-use regulation that imposes a substantial burden on religious exercise is one that necessarily bears direct, primary, and fundamental responsibility for rendering religious exercise—including the use of real property for the purpose thereof within the regulated jurisdiction generally—effectively impracticable." *City League of Urban Believers v. Chicago*, 342 F.3d 752, 761 (7th Cir. 2003). For a discussion of the primary factors that courts have looked to in approaching the question of substantial burden, *see* Karla L. Chaffee & Dwight H. Merriam, *Six Fact Patterns of Substantial Burden in RLUIPA: Lessons for Potential Litigants*, 2 Alb. Gov't L. Rev. 437, 453-474 (2009) (noting that courts evaluate, among other factors, the level of financial hardship and inconvenience imposed by a regulation, whether current facilities are adequate for religious exercise or other property is available, and whether a regulation treats religious institutions differently than secular ones).

4. Compelling governmental interest. One of the more difficult questions RLUIPA poses is what constitutes a "compelling governmental interest" in the zoning context. In *Westchester Day School*, the court avoided this question by holding that the interest asserted was disingenuous. Other courts approach this question by focusing on whether a purported interest is being advanced by the least restrictive means. *See, e.g., Covenant Christian Ministries, Inc. v. City of Marietta*, 654 F.3d 1231 (11th Cir. 2011) (complete prohibition on religious assemblies in residential zones is not the least restrictive means). But are traditional land use policy rationales such as the separation of incompatible uses, orderly development, and pedestrian and traffic safety "compelling"?

In *International Church of the Foursquare Gospel v. City of San Leandro*, 634 F.3d 1037 (9th Cir. 2011), a municipality justified its denial of rezoning and a conditional use permit to a church on the ground that the parcel at issue was located in an industrial park zoning district that did not allow for any "assembly uses" such as churches, clubs, and lodges. The parcel was also situated in a "focus area" designated by the city's general plan for industrial and technological activity, and the area contained several manufacturing plants and other industrial and light-industrial uses that brought a present and future presence of hazardous materials and activities. The Ninth Circuit held that preserving the land for industrial or technology uses was not a compelling governmental interest. *Id.* at 1048-1049.

If keeping large congregations from regularly gathering in the middle of an active industrial zone that is in the vicinity of hazardous wastes is not a "compelling governmental interest" under RLUIPA, would any of the kinds of separation of uses cited by the Supreme Court in *Euclid v. Ambler Realty, see* §1.2, *supra,* qualify? Is this a justifiable limitation on local-government authority? How should courts decide which public purposes in land use regulation are "compelling"?

5. Discrimination and exclusion claims. In addition to the prohibition on placing a substantial burden on religious exercise in 42 U.S.C. §2000cc(a), RLUIPA also prohibits "[d]iscrimination and exclusion" in §2000cc(b). This encompasses three distinct provisions:

> (1) Equal terms. No government shall impose or implement a land use regulation in a manner that treats a religious assembly or institution on less than equal terms with a nonreligious assembly or institution.
>
> (2) Nondiscrimination. No government shall impose or implement a land use regulation that discriminates against any assembly or institution on the basis of religion or religious denomination.
>
> (3) Exclusions and limits. No government shall impose or implement a land use regulation that—
>
> (A) totally excludes religious assemblies from a jurisdiction; or
>
> (B) unreasonably limits religious assemblies, institutions, or structures within a jurisdiction.

Much recent RLUIPA litigation has focused on the equal terms provision, which tends to arise in instances where a church or other religious institution can point to some nonreligious use, such as secular meeting hall, that has received more favorable treatment. The circuit courts have divided in interpreting this provision. *See Centro Familiar Cristiano Buenas Nuevas v. City of Yuma,* 651 F.3d 1163, 1169 n.25 (9th Cir. 2011). Most circuits have held that the appropriate focus is whether a religious institution is similarly situated to a nonreligious institution in terms of the given regulatory purpose of the land use provision at issue. *See id.* at 1172-1173. In *Kingdom Ministries v. Village of Hazel Crest,* 611 F.3d 367 (7th Cir. 2010) (en banc), the court added the caveat that the comparison must be made with respect to "accepted zoning criteria," but found that a restriction on churches allegedly intended to reserve a commercial area for revenue-generating businesses met the test because secular businesses that did not generate revenue, such as libraries and community centers, were banned as well. The Eleventh Circuit, by contrast, has held that if a statute or zoning ordinance facially differentiates between religious and nonreligious assemblies or institutions, it must survive strict scrutiny. *Midrash Sephardi, Inc. v. Town of Surfside,* 366 F.3d 1214 (11th Cir. 2004).

6. Remedies under RLUIPA. Under RLUIPA, a litigant "may assert a violation of this chapter as a claim or defense in a judicial proceeding and obtain appropriate relief against a government." §2000cc-2(a). The Supreme Court has held that "appropriate relief" does not include money damages in suits by prisoners against states because Congress did not abrogate state sovereign immunity. *Sossamon v. Texas,* 131 S. Ct. 1651, 1655 (2011). Justice Sotomayor pointed out in dissent, however, that the land use provisions of the statute may yield a different conclusion. *Id.* at 1668 n.5. Several circuit courts have held that money damages are available under RLUIPA against *local* *governments,* such as municipalities and counties, which do not share the same immunity as states. *See, e.g., Centro Familiar,* 651 F.3d at 1168-1169; *Lighthouse Institute for Evangelism, Inc. v. City of Long Branch,* 510 F.3d 253, 260-261 (3d Cir. 2007).

7. **Disaster relief and religious land uses.** In the wake of Hurricane Sandy, a 2012 storm that devastated wide areas of New Jersey, New York, Connecticut, and other northeastern states, the U.S. House of Representatives passed a bill that would allow federal disaster relief to be provided to churches, synagogues, mosques, temples, and other religious establishments. *See* H.R. 592 (2013). Currently, under the *Robert T. Stafford Disaster Relief and Emergency Assistance Act,* 42 U.S.C. §5121 *et seq.*, disaster aid can be provided to religious entities that are performing "essential services of governmental nature." 42 U.S.C. §§5122(11)(B), 5172(a)(3); *see also* Federal Emergency Management Agency, Disaster Assistance Policy 9521.3(7)(4)(3) ("Space dedicated to or primarily used for religious, political, athletic, recreational, or vocational purposes, is not eligible for Public Assistance Program assistance under the governing statutes and regulations."). The case law on whether governmental grants to religious institutions violate the establishment clause is complicated, but in general, the Supreme Court has allowed funding to flow to religious entities through neutral programs that do not single out such organizations. *See, e.g., Zelman v. Simmons-Harris,* 536 U.S. 639 (2002) (educational voucher program that allowed recipients to attend religiously affiliated schools did not violate establishment clause); *Mitchell v. Helms,* 530 U.S. 793, 836 (O'Connor, J., concurring) (2000) (federal and state school aid programs that applied to parochial schools did not violate the establishment clause). Do disaster relief funds provided to houses of worship that are not tied to specific services those facilities provide violate the establishment clause? What are the best arguments on both sides?

Problems

1. A city zoning law prohibits structures more than two stories tall in a residential subdivision otherwise composed entirely of single-family homes. A church seeks to renovate its facility to obtain more space. It plans to construct a seven-story tower to accommodate both its religious services and other activities, including a soup kitchen and a homeless shelter that will accommodate 30 people. Is the church entitled to do this under the terms of RLUIPA?

2. A church allows homeless persons to sleep on its landing and front steps. The city seeks to prevent this on the ground that it provides shelters for the homeless where they will be safer than they would be sleeping outside. Some homeless persons refuse to go to the shelters either because the shelters are dangerous or because they value the freedom of being outside a facility. The church claims that it has a first amendment right to the free exercise of religion that allows it to grant sanctuary to the poor. *See Fifth Avenue Presbyterian Church v. City of New York,* 293 F.3d 570 (2d Cir. 2002) (holding that there may be such a right). If the city had an ordinance requiring homeless shelters to obtain permits to operate and denied the church the power to allow

people to sleep on its steps in violation of local anti-loitering ordinances, does the church have a right under RLUIPA to continue its practices?

3. A church seeks a special use permit to build a large structure to enable it to expand its operations to both operate a day care center and to create a new kindergarten to eighth grade religious elementary school. The town denies the permit because it insists on reducing the size of the structure and the number of students attending the school. The church has to shut down its day care center because it does not have enough space for it along with its other activities. Is the denial of the special use permit a "substantial burden" on the church's religious exercise under RLUIPA?

4. A religious organization seeks to build a Sikh temple on land zoned for residential purposes. The city refuses to grant a conditional use permit based on citizens' voiced fears that noise and traffic would interfere with the surrounding neighborhood. The organization seeks a second permit to build the facility on land zoned for agricultural purposes. Neighbors again complained, and the permit was denied. Another Sikh temple exists in the community. Has the city placed a "substantial burden" on the organization's "religious exercise"? As attorney for the Sikh organization, what questions would you ask your client to attempt to show a substantial burden? As attorney for the city, how would you respond to those claims?

§7 ENVIRONMENTAL REGULATIONS AND LAND USE

The use of real property is regulated not only by local zoning laws but also by a variety of state and federal laws, many of which seek to protect the environment. The interplay between environmental law and land use regulation raises a host of legal and practical issues and real property lawyers are increasingly becoming experts in areas of law that include wetlands regulation, protection for endangered species, air quality standards, clean water, and others. This section addresses three examples of this interplay: liability for hazardous wastes, environmental impact assessment, and planning for climate change.

§7.1 Owner Liability for Hazardous Wastes

CERCLA. In 1980, Congress passed the *Comprehensive Environmental Response, Compensation and Liability Act* (CERCLA), and in 1986 followed with the *Superfund Amendments and Reauthorization Act* (SARA), 42 U.S.C. §§9601-9675. These statutes authorize the Environmental Protection Agency (EPA) to respond to or to require others to respond to imminent and substantial danger to the public health or welfare or the environment caused by release of a hazardous substance from a facility. CERCLA imposes liability on persons who either owned or operated a facility when hazardous substances were released and on some present owners and operators of such facilities. This liability is strict, meaning that fault is not at issue. Courts have also held that liability under CERCLA is joint and several where harm cannot be accurately apportioned, and the Supreme Court has indicated triggering this apportionment requires only a reasonable estimate of each party's share. *See Burlington North & Santa Fe Railway Co. v. United States*, 556 U.S. 599 613-619 (2009). Each person found liable may go after other potential defendants to share the cost of the cleanup, but if other responsible parties cannot be found, or their companies have dissolved or are insolvent, and it is not feasible to apportion harms, then any responsible party may be saddled with the entire cost.

Defenses under CERCLA are minimal. Parties are not responsible for (1) acts of God; (2) acts of war; and (3) acts or omissions of third parties with whom the defendant had no contractual relationship, if the defendant shows that it exercised due care and took all reasonable precautions against foreseeable acts of the third party. SARA and the *Small Business Liability Relief and Brownfields Revitalization Act,* Pub. L. No. 107-118, 115 Stat. 2356 (2002), commonly known as the *Brownfields Act,* clarified the so-called innocent owner defense. To claim this defense, which is based on the theory that contamination is the result of third-party acts or omissions, an owner must have made good faith efforts to determine whether the land was polluted and must not have discovered any preexisting hazardous substances before purchasing the property. As a result, environmental assessment has become a standard aspect of most large-scale land acquisitions. If the owner later discovers that the property is contaminated, the owner may not transfer the property without disclosing this fact to the purchaser. Failure to disclose causes the seller to be liable for the cleanup even if the seller did not cause the contamination.

State hazardous waste statutes. Most states have adopted legislation designed to encourage or compel property owners to clean up toxic waste sites. Some states require that the presence of hazardous waste be made known to buyers, allowing the sale to be rescinded if notice is not provided. Ind. Code §13-25-3-2. Other states impose strict liability on property owners to clean up their property or to reimburse the state for cleanup costs. To ensure payment for the cleanup, these states impose a "superlien" on the property, which takes priority over all or most other debts. New Jersey's *Industrial Site Recovery Act,* the most stringent in the country, prohibits certain owners from transferring their property until they either *certify* that no hazardous substances remain on the property or execute an approved cleanup plan. N.J. Stat. §13:1k-6 *et seq.*

Brownfield redevelopment and environmental covenants. CERCLA and related federal and state statutes have focused attention on reclaiming contaminated property, often called **brownfields**, for productive use. Fear of liability can be a significant deterrent to the redevelopment of sites, particularly in urban areas that have an industrial history but are ripe for productive use. In many instances, it would not be feasible or cost effective to eliminate all hazardous wastes, but it can make sense to perform a limited cleanup as long as the use of the site will be controlled in the future. Thus, a retail store on a former industrial site might require less remediation than a future playground or subdivision. This approach is known as "risk-based" cleanup because the level of remediation is tied to an assessment of the likelihood of harm in the future, rather than absolute safety. *See* Roger D. Schwenke, *Applying and Enforcing Institutional Controls in the Labyrinth of Environmental Requirements — Do We Need More Than the Restatement of Servitudes to Turn Brownfields Green?*, 38 Real Prop., Prob. & Trust J. 295 (2003).

Brownfield sites are thus increasingly being reclaimed subject to institutional controls that are meant to limit future uses and put the public on notice of the extent — and limits — of any remediation that has been done on the site. Environmental covenants have become a common technique for these purposes. Such covenants are recorded and intended to bind future owners.

Questions of the status and enforceability of environmental covenants led the National Conference of Commissioners on Uniform State Laws to adopt the Uniform Environmental Covenants Act (UECA) in 2003. The UECA, which has been adopted in about 25 jurisdictions, is intended to make clear that notwithstanding potential state common law impediments to the contrary, environmental covenants that involve responsible public agencies are enforceable and will not be eliminated through tax lien foreclosures, adverse possession, or the application of marketable title statutes.[16] (Prior interests will take priority, unless subordinated.) The UECA does not change the substantive standards for liability and remediation, but does provide a tool to allow owners, regulators, purchasers, and the public to record and enforce controls on brownfield sites.

§7.2 Environmental Impact Assessment

Environmental assessment. Modeled after the *National Environmental Policy Act of 1969*, 42 U.S.C. §4321 (NEPA), a number of states have passed environmental policy acts designed to provide information to allow policymakers to evaluate the environmental impact of policy decisions. These state statutes are generally referred to as **little NEPAs** or **SEPAs**. NEPA applies to actions by the federal government but many of the state analogues apply to *private* development if there are discretionary state or local actions involved in approving such development. *See Friends of Mammoth v. Board of Supervisors*, 502 P.2d 1049 (Cal. 1972) (establishing the application of the *California Environmental Quality Act of 1970* to private projects).

---

16. To cover a variety of bases, §5(b) of the UECA provides that "[a]n environmental covenant that is otherwise effective is valid and enforceable even if:

(1) it is not appurtenant to an interest in real property;

(2) it can be or has been assigned to a person other than the original holder;

(3) it is not of a character that has been recognized traditionally at common law;

(4) it imposes a negative burden;

(5) it imposes an affirmative obligation on a person having an interest in the real property or on the holder;

(6) the benefit or burden does not touch or concern real property;

(7) there is no privity of estate or contract;

(8) the holder dies, ceases to exist, resigns, or is replaced; or

(9) the owner of an interest subject to the environmental covenant and the holder are the same person."

SEPAs require proponents of a project to identify the project's effects, evaluate the costs and benefits of alternative approaches, and consider ways to mitigate the identified environmental impact. These statutes are primarily procedural, rather than substantive, which is to say that they do not dictate the outcome of a given land use decision or policy, but instead seek to improve decision making by making information available that would otherwise get less attention.

The details of the process under SEPAs vary from state to state, but generally involve two stages. In the first, officials have to determine whether a given project is even subject to environmental assessment. Many kinds of routine or small-scale projects are exempt, so that, for example, a homeowner doing a renovation will not have to go through any kind of environmental review when she applies for a building permit. For much larger-scale development, however, an initial **environmental assessment (EA)** will be required to determine whether the project's impact will be significant. If it is determined that a project will likely have significant impact on the environment, then a full **environmental impact statement** or **report** (**EIS** or **EIR**) will be required.

Courts are regularly confronted with cases that challenge compliance with SEPA requirements at each of these stages. For example, many cases involve the question whether a determination that a project will not have a significant impact, and thus will not have to undertake an EIS, was properly made by the relevant agency. *See, e.g., Communities for a Better Environment v. South Coast Air Quality Management District*, 226 P.3d 985 (Cal. 2010). Opponents of development frequently challenge the sufficiency of the EIS itself, on the ground that particular required elements were left out or that what was included in the EIS was not adequate. *See, e.g., Develop Don't Destroy (Brooklyn), Inc. v. Empire State Development Corp.*, 94 A.D.3d 508 (N.Y. App. Div. 2012) (rejecting the final environmental impact statement for the Atlantic Yards Arena Redevelopment Project, which includes a sports arena and 16 high-rise buildings, because it erroneously assumed a 10-year build-out rather than the 25 years the developer contemplated to complete the project).

What does the requirement for environmental impact assessment suggest about the potential shortcomings of the process through which real estate development otherwise takes place?

Physical versus non-physical impacts. Some state environmental policy acts define "environment" very broadly to include the impact of a proposed project on social and economic conditions. In the seminal case *Chinese Staff & Workers Association v. City of New York*, 502 N.E.2d 176 (N.Y. 1986), New York's highest court evaluated the sufficiency of a decision that a proposed high-rise luxury condominium in a low-income neighborhood would have no significant effect on the environment. The agencies that reviewed the special permit application had evaluated the project's impact on the *physical environment* and indicated that if certain mitigating steps were taken, the developer would not have to undertake a full EIS. New York's SEPA defined "environment" as "'the physical conditions which will be affected by a proposed action, including land, air, water, minerals, flora, fauna, noise, objects of historic or aesthetic significance, existing patterns of population concentration, distribution, or growth, and existing community or neighborhood character.'" *Id.* at 179 (quoting ECL 8-0105[6]; CEQR 1[f]). In light of this definition, the court held that "the potential displacement of local residents and businesses is an effect on population patterns and neighborhood character which must be considered in determining whether the requirement for an EIS is triggered." *Id.* at 180.

NIMBYs, LULUs, and process. One recurring challenge in land use regulation is finding a balance between the need for meaningful public participation and the reality that communities can sometimes oppose unpopular, but necessary, projects under the banner of "not in my backyard" (**NIMBY**). Environmental review has been a particular flashpoint in controversies over this balance. Proponents highlight environmental review's ability to force decision makers to consider the ecological and social costs of development and the leverage such review can provide for public input. Critics, on the other hand, voice concerns about approval processes raising the costs of development and replicating dynamics where communities with more resources can avoid locally undesirable land uses (or **LULUs**), such as affordable housing and environmentally hazardous projects, making LULUs more likely to be sited in low-income areas, particularly in communities of color.

§7.3 Climate Change and Land Use Planning: Mitigation and Adaptation

Perhaps the most significant emerging development in terms of the intersection of land use regulation and environmental law is a growing focus by planners, local government officials, and advocates on climate change. *See* John R. Nolon, *Land Use for Energy Conservation and Sustainable Development: A New Path Toward Climate Change Mitigation*, 27 J. Land Use & Envtl. L. 295 (2012). Residential and commercial buildings account for over 40 percent of energy consumption in the United States, *id.* at 299. A significant portion of remaining greenhouse gas production is influenced by the density and location of development, which influences the need for transportation, particularly with automobiles.

Land use regulation relating to climate change falls into two broad categories: mitigation and adaptation. **Mitigation** involves efforts to reduce greenhouse gas emissions through changes to the built environment. Examples include building codes that seek to limit energy use, reduce water consumption, and the generation of wastes in new developments. Mitigation can also involve planning and land use regulatory approaches that increase density and reduce the need for transportation.

By contrast, **adaptation** involves efforts to respond to changes in the environment unleashed by climate change. These can include strengthening building codes to respond to the rise in weather events once considered extreme as well as changes to siting and other land use decisions to take development out of the path of disaster. *See* Tara Siegel Bernard, *Rebuilding After Sandy, but with Costly New Rules*, N.Y. Times, May 11, 2013, at B-1.

At the federal level, the Environmental Protection Agency has authority under the *Clean Air Act*, 42 U.S.C. §7521, to regulate greenhouse gases, *see Massachusetts v. Environmental Protection Agency*, 549 U.S. 497 (2007), but much of the regulatory response so far has taken place at the state and local level. For example, California in 2006 passed AB 32, the *Global Warming Solutions Act*, codified at Cal. Health & Safety Code §38501 *et seq*. The statute seeks to reduce the state's emissions of greenhouse gases such as carbon dioxide to 1990 levels by 2020. One element of the regulatory regime it introduced focuses on reducing vehicle miles traveled. A later companion statute, Stats. 2008, c.728 (S.B.375), §2, requires regions in California to plan for more compact development in line with regional targets for emissions reductions. Regulations under the act also now provide guidance for evaluating greenhouse gas emissions and formulating feasible mitigation measures to reduce their impacts for purposes of the *California Environmental Quality Act*. Cal. Code Regs., tit. 14, §15064.4, 15126.4. *Cf. Rialto Citizens for Responsible Growth v. City of Rialto*, 146 Cal. Rptr. 3d 12, 44-45 (Ct. App. 2012).

§8 NATURAL RESOURCES REGULATION

§8.1 Regulating Property in Natural Resources

Land is an important resource, but the use and exploitation of a range of other natural resources are regulated as well. "Natural resources" is a capacious concept that can encompass almost any product of nature, *In re Tortorelli*, 66 P.3d 606, 610 (Wash. 2003), including water, oil, gas, minerals, forests, rangelands, wildlife, wetlands, and other aspects of the natural landscape. Like land, natural resources more broadly are governed by a combination of common law doctrines and federal, state, and local statutes and regulations. This body of law for many natural resource conflicts reflects the inherently public aspects of such resources given our common interests in their preservation and wise management. *See* Joseph Sax, *The Public Trust Doctrine in Natural Resource Law: Effective Judicial Intervention*, 68 Mich. L. Rev. 471 (1970); Michael C. Blumm & Aurora Paulsen, *The Public Trust in Wildlife*, 2103 Utah L. Rev. (forthcoming 2013). Scale is also an important aspect of natural resources regulation, with natural systems rarely conforming to political jurisdictions.

Just as property in intangibles reflects certain characteristics that are inherent to ideas and information, *see* Chapter 3, §1.1, the law of natural resources has been shaped by the nature of the relevant resources it governs. The rules for the ownership and use of water, for example, have a lot to do with the fact that water moves and can be reused by many claimants. By contrast, the rules for trees and many kinds of hard-rock minerals reflect the fact that they begin fixed in a certain place and tend to be exhausted when used. For every natural resource, however, some common questions arise: How should the law balance productive use and conservation, protect investment and expectations while preventing monopoly, and distribute rights fairly between multiple owners with competing interests?

These are difficult values to balance, and our legal system has traditionally preferred consumption over sustainability. As Professor Joseph Sax has written:

> For two centuries [in the development of the American continent], virtually nothing of the economy of nature was intentionally saved. That is well known. What is perhaps not so well recognized (though it has been extensively documented by legal historians), is that the law was constructed and reconstructed to drive this process forward. The rules of landownership were shaped in order to incentivize transformation to the new economy and to discourage retention of nature's economy. For example, there was no economic reason to leave water in a river, or to refrain from damming it, nor was there any such reason to leave land unfenced so as to permit the passage of wildlife or to leave land uncultivated as habitat. On the contrary, leaving water in a river was considered waste. Even those who wanted to obtain a right to keep waters flowing in-stream were prevented from doing so. The old preindustrial rules mandating retention of the natural flow of rivers were abolished so that rivers could be dammed to generate hydropower, the open range fenced, and bounties paid to exterminate predators such as wolves. That was the logic of the transformative economy, and the law of property rights was its obedient servant.

Joseph L. Sax, *Ownership, Property, and Sustainability*, 31 Utah Envtl. L. Rev. 1, 6 (2011); *see also* John G. Sprankling, *The Antiwilderness Bias in American Property Law*, 63 U. Chi. L. Rev. 519 (1996).

Although still highly contested terrain, contemporary perspectives about natural resources regulation are beginning to reflect ideas of stewardship and an ethos that values wilderness for its own sake. *Cf.* Aldo Leopold, *A Sand County Almanac and Sketches Here and There* 224-225 (1949) (advocating for a "land ethic" that holds that an action is right if it "tends to preserve the integrity, stability, and beauty of the biotic community" and "wrong when it tends otherwise"). This perspective has deep roots in American law as well, and has begun to gain greater recognition in our legal system with the rise of the conservation movement and increasing ecological awareness. Eric T. Freyfogle, *The Land We Share: Private Property and the Common Good* (2003). As with every other aspect of property law, moreover, climate change is beginning to alter the landscape of natural resources regulation, a trend that is likely to accelerate as the effects of climate change deepen. A. Dan Tarlock, *Takings, Water Rights, and Climate Change*, 36 Vt. L. Rev. 731 (2012).

Natural resources and environmental protection. A number of federal and state statutes regulate specific natural resources in order to limit pollution. Among the most prominent of these regimes are the *Clean Air Act*, 42 U.S.C. §7401 *et seq.* (CAA), and the *Clean Water Act*, 33 U.S.C. §1251 *et seq.* (CWA). The Environmental Protection Agency (EPA) is empowered by the CWA and the CAA to restrict pollution in order to improve air and water quality. *See* 42 U.S.C. §7401(b)-(c); 33 U.S.C. §1251. This authority impacts natural resources by defining air quality criteria and control techniques, *e.g.*, 42 U.S.C. §§7408-7409, which States must implement in plans submitted to the EPA, 42 U.S.C. §7410, and creating water quality surveillance systems, 33 U.S.C. §1254(a)(5). Despite an express disavowal in the CAA against infringement of local government authority over land use, 42 U.S.C. §7431, controlling pollution necessarily limits the exploitation of natural resources.

The federal *Endangered Species Act*, 16 U.S.C. §1531 *et seq.* (ESA), protects animals and plants that are either endangered or threatened. "Endangered" means that a species is in danger of extinction, while a "threatened" species is one that is likely to become endangered. *Id.* §§1532(6), (20). The ESA makes it illegal to "take" endangered species, *id.* §1538(a)(1)(B), and the meaning of take includes "harm," *id.* §1532(19). Harm, in turn, encompasses "significant habitat modification or degradation where it actually kills or injures wildlife by significantly impairing essential behavioral patterns, including breeding, feeding, or sheltering." 50 C.F.R. 17.3; *see also Babbitt v. Sweet Home Chapter of Communities for a Great Oregon*, 515 U.S. 687 (1995) (upholding the regulatory definition of "take" to include habitat modification). As a result, the ESA can have significant impacts on land use and natural resource regulation, which has generated a great deal of litigation, both challenging federal enforcement of the act as well as challenging federal agencies to do more to protect endangered species, sometimes in the same case. *See, e.g., In re Polar Bear Endangered Species Act Listing and Section 4(d) Rule Litig.—MDL No. 1993*, 709 F.3d 1 (D.C. Cir. 2013).

Public lands and planning for natural resource management. The federal government holds title to about 28 percent of the land in the United States, a landmass of roughly 635 to 640 million acres, and subsurface rights to hundreds of millions of acres more. *See* Ross W. Gort et al., Congressional Research Service, *Federal Land Ownership: Overview and Data Summary* (2012). Individual states have large holdings as well, forming a mosaic of public lands that contains a significant portion of the nation's natural resources.

Federal public lands are managed primarily by four federal agencies, the Bureau of Land Management (BLM), the National Park Service (NPS), the U.S. Forest Service (USFS), and the U.S. Fish and Wildlife Service's National Wildlife Refuge (NWR).[17] Each of these agencies operates under statutes that balance in distinctive ways competing interests in the use of the resources they manage, including extraction, recreation, and preservation. Among the more important of these framework regimes are the *Federal Land Policy Management Act of 1976*, 43 U.S.C. §1701 *et seq.* (FLPMA), which governs BLM lands; the *National Forest Management Act of 1976*, 16 U.S.C. §1600 *et seq.*, which governs USFS land; and, for the NPS, a series of individual park organic statutes, *see, e.g.,* 16 U.S.C. §§221-228j (establishing the Grand Canyon National Park); 16 U.S.C. §21 (establishing Yellowstone National Park). A number of statutes designate particularly sensitive or important public lands for protection, including the *Wilderness Act of 1964*, 16 U.S.C. §1131 *et seq.*, which created the National Wilderness Preservation System; the *Antiquities Act of 1906*, 16 U.S.C. §431 *et seq.*, which allows the president to designate National Monuments; as well as the *National Wild and Scenic Rivers Act*, 16 U.S.C. §1271 *et seq.*, the *National Scenic Trails Act*, 16 U.S.C. §1244, and National Con-

17. The U.S. Department of Defense oversees roughly 19 million acres of land owned by the federal government. Gort et al., *supra*.

servation Areas designated by individual statutes, *see, e.g.*, Red Cliffs National Conservation Area, 16 U.S.C. §460www; Beaver Dam Wash National Conservation Area, 16 U.S.C. §460xxx.

As with land use, planning is central to the management of natural resources on public lands. Some federal lands have a primary purpose, as with wilderness areas and military bases; most public lands, however, are multi-use and federal statutes prescribe the process through which agencies have to plan for balancing those often conflicting uses. For example, FLPMA directs the BLM to manage public lands to:

> protect the quality of scientific, scenic, historical, ecological, environmental, air and atmospheric, water resource, and archaeological values; that, where appropriate, will preserve and protect certain public lands in their natural condition; that will provide food and habitat for fish and wildlife and domestic animals; and that will provide for outdoor recreation and human occupancy and use.

43 U.S.C. §1701(a)(8). To meet this mandate, FLPMA requires the BLM to "prepare and maintain . . . an inventory of all public lands and their resource and other values (including, but not limited to, outdoor recreation and scenic values), giving priority to areas of critical environmental concern." *Id.* §1711(a). Based on this inventory, the BLM develops and maintains plans for each BLM area under a principle of "multiple use and sustained yield." *Id.* §§1712(a), 1712(c)(1), 1732(a). The agency has wide discretion in implementing these plans, *Norton v. Southern Utah Wilderness Alliance*, 542 U.S. 55 (2004), but this statutory planning regime attempts to bring public participation and transparency to the process of prioritizing often deeply contentious conflicts over the use of natural resources.

§8.2 Water Law

Water has attributes that make it as much a common resource as the subject of individual ownership. A single river, as it snakes from high mountains to the ocean, can supply water for fishing, white water rafting, farming, generating hydroelectric power, flushing industrial wastes, and filling the many needs of small towns and big cities. It can also support the biodiversity of the fish that live in it, the plants that border it, and the ecosystems that depend on it. Similarly, aquifers — underground water reservoirs — can hold vast quantities of water beneath the lands of hundreds or thousands of surface owners putting that water to any number of uses. The Ogallala Aquifer, one of the world's largest, stretches under roughly 174,000 square miles from Texas up to South Dakota, and is estimated to hold nearly three billion acre-feet of water.[18] V.L. McGuire, U.S. Geological Survey, *Water-Level and Storage Changes in the High Plains Aquifer, Predevelopment to 2011 and 2009-11* (2013).

Water law combines common law doctrines with constitutional, statutory, and administrative regulations. Generally, water rights can be established by a diversion of

18. One "acre foot" is the amount of water that would cover an acre of surface area, one foot deep, and represents about 325,851 gallons of water.

water, an administrative permit, or a court decree. Much of the law of water governs competing claims to water as conditions or the needs of users change. Consider the following case.

State Department of Ecology v. Grimes

852 P. 2d 1044 (Wash. 1993)

Map: Marshall Lake, Pend Oreillè County, Washington

CHARLES Z. SMITH, Justice.

This matter is before the court upon direct review, raising the question of the legal definition of "reasonable use" of water as an element of "beneficial use" under the Water Code of 1917, Wash. Rev. Code §90.03, the Water Resources Act of 1971, Wash. Rev. Code §90.54, and other related statutes. Appellants Clarence E. and Peggy V. Grimes (Grimeses) appeal from a decree adjudicating water rights pursuant to Wash. Rev. Code §90.03.200 entered by the Pend Oreille County Superior Court. Respondents are Leonard B. and Elsie E. Magart and the State of Washington Department of Ecology (Ecology). We affirm the Superior Court.

In September 1981, the Department of Ecology filed a petition in the Pend Oreille County Superior Court for clarification of existing rights to divert, withdraw, or otherwise make beneficial use of the surface and ground waters of the Marshall Lake and Marshall Creek drainage basin (Marshall Lake basin). Ecology investigated the Marshall Lake basin and the locality served by it and found that the interests of the public and users of the surface and ground waters would be served by an adjudication and determination of the relative rights of all claimants to the use of these waters.

Donald W. Moos, Director of Ecology, appointed William R. Smith as referee to take testimony and report his recommendations to the Superior Court. The Grimeses [filed a] claim for the use of waters for domestic supply, irrigation and recreational purposes. The Grimeses requested an instantaneous flow rate of 3 cubic feet per second (c.f.s.) for irrigation purposes, and a storage right of 1,520 acre feet of water in the Marshall Lake reservoir. The referee recommended that this claim be confirmed, but limited it to an instantaneous flow of 1.5 c.f.s. during irrigation season, and a storage right of 183 acre feet plus 737 acre feet for evaporative loss, for a total storage right of 920 acre feet.

[T]he Grimeses filed exceptions to the report of the referee in the superior court [relating to] (1) the right to store 183 acre feet of water and the period of storage in Marshall Lake; and (2) the establishment of a minimum level of Marshall Lake for measuring waters to be stored under the Grimeses' storage right. On January 5, 1990, the Superior Court entered its "Decree Adjudicating Water Rights Pursuant to [Wash. Rev. Code §]90.03.200." Based upon stipulations between the parties, the decree stated that the natural level of Marshall Lake, for the purposes of a measurement of the storage right, is 2,722.62 feet above mean sea level, rather than 2,720 as recommended by the referee.

[The Grimeses appealed. The Court of Appeals issued an order of certification, which allows an appeal directly to the Supreme Court, stating that "[t]he decision of this [case] is of broad public import as it will impact at least 35 irrigation districts, water companies and municipalities who in turn represent thousands of water users in the Yakima River basin."]

General Adjudication

A general adjudication is a special form of quiet title action to determine all existing rights to the use of water from a specific body of water. The provisions for adjudication in the Water Code, Wash. Rev. Code §90.03.110-.245, may not be used to lessen, enlarge or modify existing water rights. An adjudication of water rights is only for the purpose of determining and confirming those rights. The surface water rights of the Grimeses in this case are pre-1917 rights, established 11 years before adoption of the Water Code of 1917 and 65 years before adoption of the Water Resources Act of 1971. To confirm existing rights, the referee must determine two primary elements of a water right: (1) the amount of water that has been put to beneficial use and (2) the priority of water rights relative to each other.

The Doctrine of Prior Appropriation[19]

The law of prior appropriation was established in this state by the Territorial Legislature in 1873 and recognized by this court in 1897. *Benton v. Johncox*, 49 P. 495 (Wash. 1897). This court in *Neubert v. Yakima-Tieton Irrigation District*, 814 P.2d 199, 201 (Wash. 1991), said that "[t]he appropriated water right is perpetual and operates to the exclusion of subsequent claimants." In that case we said appropriative water rights require that:

> Once appropriated, the right to use a given quantity of water becomes appurtenant to the land. The appropriated water right is perpetual and operates to the exclusion of subsequent claimants. The key to determining the extent of plaintiffs' vested water rights is the concept of "beneficial use". . . . An appropriated water right is established and maintained by the purposeful application of a given quantity of water to a beneficial use upon the land. [*Id.* at 201-202.]

Beneficial use refers to the quantity of water diverted by the appropriator, not to its availability in the source of supply. "The underlying reason for all this constitutional, legislative and judicial emphasis on beneficial use of water lies in the relation of available water resources to the ever-increasing demands made upon them." [1 *Waters and Water Rights* §19.2, at 87 (R. Clark ed. 1967).]

---

19. The Grimeses argue that they are entitled to their claimed water rights on the basis of their riparian ownership. Each of their original claims, however, were based on appropriation law. Because of this, we need not decide whether riparian rights to Marshall Lake have been eliminated because of its artificial elevation.

"Beneficial use" is a term of art in water law, and encompasses two principal elements of a water right. First, it refers to the purposes, or type of activities, for which water may be used. Use of water for the purposes of irrigated agriculture is a beneficial use. The Grimeses' use of water to irrigate alfalfa fields is not at issue in this case. Second, beneficial use determines the measure of a water right. The owner of a water right is entitled to the amount of water necessary for the purpose to which it has been put, provided that purpose constitutes a beneficial use. To determine the amount of water necessary for a beneficial use, courts have developed the principle of "reasonable use." Reasonable use of water is determined by analysis of the factors of water duty and waste.

In his findings establishing the measure of the Grimeses' water right, the referee stated that:

> [A] valid right for irrigation purposes only exists for the benefit of these claimants and such right is derived from the original 1906 Linsley notice. It is, therefore, recommended that a right be confirmed to these defendants, with a July 13, 1906 priority for the irrigation of 73 acres from Marshall Lake. Quantification of the amount of water to which this right is entitled creates somewhat of a problem in that there has been no direct testimony regarding the amount of water placed to beneficial use other than a reference in the state's investigatory report that 56 sprinklers are utilized in the system.... Therefore, the Referee will allow the standard duty of water which would be 1.2 cubic feet per second plus an additional 25 percent for transportation loss, thus making an aggregate amount of 1.5 cubic feet per second identified with this right....
>
> A second element concerning this right is the amount of storage of water to which these claimants are entitled.... [T]hese waters also have recreational benefits, not only to the riparian owners around the lake but also to the general public through the use of resort facilities located on the lake.... Therefore, the Referee recommends that a related but separate right be confirmed to these defendants for the storage of 920 acre-feet in Marshall Lake for irrigation and recreation purposes. The priority shall be fixed as of July 13, 1906. The period during which waters may be stored shall be identified as those periods of the year which do not include the April 1 to October 31 irrigation season.

The Grimeses challenge the referee's "consideration of the evidence" and his application of the law in making these findings.

Water Duty

"[Water duty is] that measure of water, which, by careful management and use, without wastage, is reasonably required to be applied to any given tract of land for such period of time as may be adequate to produce therefrom a maximum amount of such crops as ordinarily are grown thereon. It is not a hard and fast unit of measurement, but is variable according to conditions." *In re Steffens*, 756 P.2d 1002, 1005-06 (Colo. 1988).

The referee based his determination of the volume of water necessary for irrigation in the Marshall Lake basin on a Washington State University Research Bulletin entitled "Irrigation Requirements for Washington — Estimates and Methodology" (Irrigation Report), and on the expert testimony of Jim Lyerla, the District Supervisor for seven Eastern Washington counties, including Pend Oreille County, in the Water Resources Program of the Department of Ecology. Mr. Lyerla testified that as a part of his work in assigning water quantities to new water permittees, he relied on the Irrigation Report to determine the "water duty" for a proposed use of water. The Irrigation Report provides information for water requirements for specific crops, given in inches per acre per irrigation season, in 40 locations around the state, including Newport, Washington, 5 miles south of Marshall Lake.

Based on the testimony of Mr. Lyerla and the Irrigation Report, the referee determined that an irrigated alfalfa crop grown in the Marshall Lake area requires 21 inches or 1.75 acre feet of water per acre during the irrigation season. The referee then applied an efficiency factor and increased this water duty to 2.5 acre feet per acre per year. The referee found this water duty to be "approximately commensurate with the duty utilized by the Department of Ecology in its quantity allocations in this geographic area under the water right permit system."

Because water rights are characterized in both total yearly allowance and instantaneous flow, the referee also established the maximum rate of diversion at 0.0166 c.f.s. per acre under irrigation. The referee first calculated a standard flow of 1 c.f.s. of water per 60 acres as a reasonable instantaneous flow for alfalfa irrigation in the Marshall Lake basin. In considering the Grimeses' claim, he determined that the Grimeses were entitled to sufficient flow to irrigate 73 acres, or a minimum of 1.21 c.f.s. He then calculated in an efficiency factor to increase this flow by 25 percent and awarded the Grimeses an instantaneous flow of 1.5 c.f.s.

The referee observed that a larger water duty could be awarded to any claimant with specific information proving a right to a larger amount. The 2.5 acre feet/0.0166 c.f.s. water duty was applied when "quantitative evidence of the rate and volume of a right was neither submitted nor made clear during testimony." The referee also observed that "the use of water under all irrigation rights is, however, limited to the amount of water that can be beneficially applied to that number of acres identified in the water right." The referee did not indiscriminately award this water duty to any claim for an irrigation right, but required claimants to prove the number of acres historically irrigated.

The referee's determination of a generic water duty for irrigation of alfalfa in the Marshall Lake basin is supported by a preponderance of the evidence and will not be disturbed by this court.

Waste

From an early date, courts announced the rule that no appropriation of water was valid where the water simply went to waste. Those courts held that the appropriator who diverted more than was needed for the appropriator's actual requirements and allowed the excess to go to waste acquired no right to the excess. A particular use must not only be of benefit to the appropriator, but it must also be a reasonable and economical use of the water in view of other present and future demands upon the source of supply. The difference between absolute waste and economical use has been said to be one of degree only.

Appellant Clarence E. Grimes acknowledged in his testimony that his existing irrigation system required a water flow of up to 3 cubic feet per second in order to deliver 1 cubic foot per second to the field, and that this system was highly inefficient, causing one-half to two-thirds loss of water. Mr. Grimes also testified that uncertainties and ongoing litigation concerning the stability and safety of the irrigation dam had prevented continuous irrigation of his alfalfa acreage.

While an appropriator's use of water must be reasonably efficient, absolute efficiency is not required. The referee determined that, pursuant to Wash. Rev. Code §90.14.160, the uncertainties concerning the irrigation dam constituted sufficient cause not to find a complete abandonment of the Grimeses' water right. He resolved the conflicting testimony by limiting the irrigable acreage to the 73 acres recommended by Ecology. Relying on a standard efficiency factor for irrigation sprinkler systems found in the irrigation report, he confirmed in the Grimeses a water right with one-fourth conveyance loss for a total of 1.5 cubic feet per second. There was at least sufficient evidence for the referee to determine the maximum acreage to which the Grimeses' water right applied, and in limiting the allowable loss for system inefficiency in establishing their instantaneous flow.

The Reasonable Efficiency Test

In limiting the Grimeses' vested water right, the referee balanced several factors, including the water duty for the geographical area and crop under irrigation, the claimants' actual diversion, and sound irrigation practices. In his report, the referee described his method of calculating the Grimeses' water right as a "reasonable efficiency" test.

While the referee stated that he relied on this test, and while he did in fact consider some of its elements, he did not actually utilize the test in its entirety. Therefore, we will review the factors he did consider to determine whether his analysis remained within the boundaries of prior appropriation law. In his discussion of the basis for his recommendation concerning the Grimeses' claim, the referee stated that he would "balance [the water duty] against not only the actual amount of water diverted from the lake for irrigation purposes but also against the concepts of beneficial use of water and sound irrigation practices."

Amici curiae urge this court to hold that only "the established means of diversion and application according to the reasonable custom of the locality" may be considered in defining reasonable use. This court has consistently held that rights of users of water for irrigation purposes are vested rights in real property. Amici curiae assert that the "local custom" test has been employed historically to determine whether given applications of water are wasteful, within the meaning of beneficial use, and that courts should now apply it in the setting of general adjudications. This is the established law in this state.

Decisions of courts throughout the western states provide a basis for defining "reasonable efficiency" with respect to irrigation practices. While customary irrigation practices common to the locality are a factor for consideration, they do not justify waste of water. As this court stated in a case predating the Water Code of 1917:

> [W]hen rights in such an important element as water is in the arid regions are to be measured by the courts, we cannot lay down a rule that would give to the user an arbitrary right to use water at will. [An irrigator's] rights are to be measured by his necessities . . . and not by any fanciful notion of his own. . . .
>
> . . . [C]ustom can fix the manner of use of water for irrigation only when it is founded on necessity . . . [and] an irrigator is entitled to use only so much as he can put to a beneficial use, for the public policy of the people of the United States will not tolerate waste of water in the arid regions. [*Shafford v. White Bluffs Land & Irrigation Co.*, 114 P. 883, 884-886 (1911).]

Local custom and the relative efficiency of irrigation systems in common use are important elements, but must be considered in connection with other statutorily mandated factors, such as the costs and benefits of improvements to irrigation systems, including the use of public and private funds to facilitate improvements.

In limiting the Grimeses' water use by a requirement of reasonable efficiency, the referee properly considered the irrigation report, the Grimeses' actual water use, and their existing irrigation system. The referee alluded to a test incorporating factors that consider impacts to the water source and its flora and fauna. While consideration of these impacts is consonant with the State's obligations under Wash. Rev. Code [§]§90.03.005 and 90.54.010(1)(a) and (2), these factors cannot operate to impair existing water rights. Other laws may, however, operate to define existing rights in light of environmental values.

There is some confusion in the record as to the legal standard used by the referee in determining beneficial use. [I]n a footnote [in his supplemental report,] the referee set forth a detailed "test of reasonable efficiency" which he purportedly used in determining beneficial use. That "test" is stated as follows:

> (1) [C]ustomary delivery and application practices in the area, (2) technology and "practices" improvements feasible and available to reduce water consumptions and financial needs associated with implementation thereof, and (3) impacts of improvements of existing facilities and practices, if initiated, upon (a) the water source from which the diversion takes place, (b) the existing flora and fauna within the area of diversion, conveyancy and actual uses, (c) other water rights from said water source, and (d) other water users on other water sources.

There is nothing in the record to support the referee's statement that he employed the reasonable efficiency test. Nowhere in the record does he discuss application of the elements of the so-called "test." If he had in fact applied the "test," it would be necessary for this court to reverse and remand. That test is without statutory authorization in an adjudication proceeding which relates exclusively to confirmation of water rights established or created under "other provisions of state law or under federal laws." The suggested test would be contrary to the vested rights of water users. Included in the vested rights is the right to diversion, delivery and application "according to the usual methods of artificial irrigation employed in the vicinity where such land is situated." Wash. Rev. Code §90.03.040.

While we reject use of the specific test suggested by the referee, we affirm because (1) there is no indication in the record that he in fact applied the factors stated in the "test," and (2) he applied the actual beneficial use made by Grimes, taking into account the actual needs and use and the methods of delivery and application in the vicinity. The adjudication and confirmation of a water right in an amount less than claimed by Grimes does not result from application of the so-called test. Rather, as the referee makes clear:

> Quantification of the amount of water to which this right is entitled creates somewhat of a problem in that there has been no direct testimony regarding the amount of water placed to beneficial use other than a reference in the state's investigatory report that 56 sprinklers are utilized in the system.

In the absence of such proof, the referee nevertheless confirmed the right by using a normal duty of water for the type of crops raised and specifically added 25 percent for transportation loss. Making the best of inadequate proof by the claimant, it appears from the record that the referee applied the usual methods of irrigation employed in the vicinity where the Grimeses' land is located.

Notes and Questions

1. **Water rights.** What rights did the Grimeses have in the Marshall Lake basin? How were these rights determined?

2. **Water law fundamentals.** There have historically been different rules for **surface water**, such as lakes, rivers, and streams, and **groundwater**, such as aquifers and percolating water. However, increasing understanding of the connections between these two water sources has led to some merging of the doctrines. Robert Haskell Abrams, *Legal Convergence of East and West in Contemporary Water Law*, 42 Envtl. L. 65, 69-80 (2012); *cf. Kobobel v. Department of Natural Resources*, 249 P.3d 1127 (Colo. 2011) (groundwater users had no takings claim against state for prohibiting withdrawal that would affect prior surface water users).

a. **Groundwater.** Rules for allocation of groundwater were initially adopted from England. Based in part on the difficulty of predicting the location and movement of groundwater, England followed an **absolute ownership** or **free use** rule, permitting all surface estate owners to withdraw as much groundwater as they could from their land, regardless of the harm to other owners above the aquifer. In *Acton v. Blundell*, 152 Eng. Rep. 1223, 1234 (Exch. 1843), for example, the court rejected the claims of a mill owner against his neighbor, whose excavations for coal depleted the common aquifer, leaving insufficient water to run his mill. The court justified its decision in the following way:

> [I]f the man who sinks the well in his own land can acquire by that act an absolute and indefeasible right to the water that collects in it, he has the power of preventing his neighbour from making any use of the spring in his own soil which shall interfere with the enjoyment of the well. Further, the advantage on one side, and the detriment to the other, may bear no proportion. The well may be sunk to supply a cottage, or a drinking-place for cattle; whilst the owner of the adjoining land may be prevented from winning metals and minerals of inestimable value.

While a few U.S. states still follow the absolute ownership rule, most have rejected it. In its stead, most states follow the **reasonable use** rule, considering both the interests of the surface estate owners and the interests of society as a whole, particularly given the risk of depletion and the effect of one owner's extraction on other owners. 6 Thompson on Real Property, Second Thomas Editions §50.11(f); *see also Restatement (Second) of Torts* §858 (1979) (liability for unreasonable harm to other surface owners). A few states follow the **correlative rights** doctrine, allowing each surface estate owner to withdraw an equitable ("fair and just") portion of the groundwater, perhaps in proportion to what percentage of the aquifer underlies their property. Still other states, particularly those in the arid West, have adopted the **prior appropriation** doctrine for groundwater, effectively allocating rights according to the point in time when property owners begin withdrawing the water.

In all jurisdictions, municipal and state governments increasingly intervene in water allocation to ensure predictable and fair allocation of rights, and conservation and protection of the resource. This regulation began early in the twentieth century, but has grown much more intensive in the face of greater competition for scarce resources, growing knowledge about the interconnectedness of water systems, and faster climatological change. What are the rights of owners in the existing water allocations? The Texas Supreme Court held that state deprivation of the right to use some of the groundwater under one's property could constitute a taking for which the U.S. and Texas constitutions require compensation. *Edwards Aquifer Authority v. Day*, 369 S.W.3d 814 (Tex. 2012). Texas is one of the few states to still follow the absolute ownership rule for groundwater. Would the issue be resolved differently under a reasonable use or correlative rights test?

b. Surface Water. In the United States, surface water has historically been allocated according one of two dominant rules. The **riparian** doctrine, adopted by most American jurisdictions, allocates those owning land bordered the body of water (the "**riparian owners**") rights to the water flowing past their land. Disputes between riparian owners are allocated according to a **reasonableness test** that takes into account the relative costs and benefits of the various uses, harms to competing claimants to the water, and other factors. Most western states, where water was scarce, adopted instead the **prior appropriation** or **appropriation** doctrine, prioritizing the rights of those first to make productive beneficial use of the water against later users. *See* 6 *Thompson on Real Property, Second Thomas Editions* §§50.08-50.09. Several states have "hybrid" systems that began as riparian but then shifted to appropriation. *Id.* §50.10. Appropriation was thought more appropriate for a "dry and thirsty land." *Yunker v. Nichols*, 1 Colo. 551, 553, 555 (1872).

Both systems propertize water to a certain extent, but do so quite differently, with riparian jurisdictions dividing rights among landowners and appropriation jurisdictions allocating rights based on priority of use. The trend in both jurisdictions, moreover, is to treat water as a common resource to be regulated by public agencies to ensure water is used in the common interest. A number of riparian jurisdictions have turned to **regulated riparianism**, administrative permit systems allocating time-limited licenses to use specified amounts of water for specified purposes. Abrams, *supra*, at 68; Joseph W. Dellapenna, *The Evolution of Riparianism in the United States*, 95 Marq. L. Rev 53 (2011). Similarly, statutes in appropriation jurisdictions explicitly declare water to be a public resource, and administer the priority system by agencies that consider public interest in regulating use, providing some protection for the interests of junior users, and preserving and efficiently using the water system. Abrams, *supra*, at 91.

3. Waste, abandonment, and stress on water rights. Traditionally, water rights in prior appropriation jurisdictions, once established, have been considered vested, but there are limitations to this principle. Two important limitations are **waste** and **abandonment**. As *Grimes* illustrated, a water right in a prior appropriation state is limited to beneficial use, *Joyce Livestock Co. v. United States,* 156 P.3d 502, 520 (2007) ("A water right does not constitute the ownership of the water; it is simply a right to use the water to apply it to a beneficial use"); this right, in turn, is limited by the requirement that the beneficial user not waste the water. *See, e.g., In re Application for Water Rights in Rio Grande County,* 53 P.3d 1165 (Colo. 2002). Abandonment, by contrast, involves the relinquishment of a water right, *see Okanogan Wilderness League, Inc. v. Town of Twisp,* 947 P.2d 732, 738 (Wash. 1997), and generally requires both non-use and the intent to abandon. Courts have also applied doctrines of non-use, forfeiture, and estoppels to terminate water rights acquired by appropriation.

Demand for water in the West is highly stressed and facing new demands, such as significantly increasing urban uses. *See* Marc Reisner, *Cadillac Desert: The American West and Its Disappearing Water* (1993). How would you expect this to change water doctrine?

4. Justifying prior appropriation. Some scholars argue that regimes such as prior appropriation developed in the West to privilege the efficient use of water, particularly through privatization and the protection of productive use. *See, e.g.,* Terry L. Anderson & P.J. Hill, *The Evolution of Property Rights: A Study of the American West,* 18 J.L. & Econ. 163, 177-178 (1975). By contrast, others argue that appropriation doctrine was primarily concerned with equity and distributive justice. *See, e.g.,* David Schorr, *The Colorado Doctrine: Water Rights, Corporations and Distributive Justice on the American Frontier* (2012). Focusing on the Colorado Supreme Court's landmark case of *Coffin v. Left Hand Ditch,* 6 Colo. 443 (1882), David Schorr notes that adopting a riparian regime in the western United States could have fostered monopolies and fueled speculation. In this way, appropriation was subsidiary to a "sufficiency" principle that actually limited use through doctrines such as beneficial use and forfeiture for non-use, to ensure the widespread distribution of water rights. Are economic efficiency and distributional accounts of the rejection of riparianism in the American West necessarily mutually exclusive?

Problem

Two neighboring farmers in a prior appropriation state each have rights to divert water from a nearby river through a series of ditches. If the first neighbor ceases beneficial use of the water to which he is entitled, and the second neighbor diverts that water to his own use, should the water rights go back to other users, or can the second neighbor claim title by adverse possession? *See Archuleta v. Gomez,* 200 P.3d 333 (Colo. 2009) (adverse possession of a water right requires a demonstration that the claimant "exclusively, hostilely, and adversely made an actual beneficial consumptive use of all or a portion of" another's "deeded irrigation water right interests" for the required period of 18 years; however if the original user of the water right abandoned the right, it would go back to the river for other uses).

CHAPTER 8

Servitudes: Rules Governing Contractual Restrictions on Land Use

§1 SERVITUDES

How can the law help coordinate use of different parcels of land? Owners can bring nuisance suits against each other. Governments can impose zoning laws to determine how land can be used. But what if owners want to make private agreements to restrict each other's uses, or to gain limited use or access rights for themselves? For example, neighbors may want to agree that they will only use their property for residential purposes, or one neighbor may want the right to pass over another's land to access a public road. More idiosyncratically, an owner using solar power may want to prevent her neighbors from developing their land so as to block sun to her solar panels. *Cf. Prah v. Maretti, supra,* Chapter 6, §3. Owners can of course enter contracts with each other, but how can they bind future possessors of the land? To do this, they need to create a servitude.

A **servitude** is a right or an obligation that "runs with the land," meaning that it automatically passes to subsequent owners or possessors of the land. *Restatement (Third) of Property (Servitudes)* §1.1 (2000). Servitudes are often necessary to enjoy and secure expectations with respect to land. Access to utilities, such as telephone, electricity, and cable service, may depend on granting utility companies rights to run lines over your property and the property of your neighbors. The utilities would not invest in those lines if, when you sold your property, the next owner could simply revoke the agreement. Similarly, the explosion of condominiums and other common interest residential communities depends upon numerous determinations as to how the owners will use their property and contribute to the maintenance of common elements like landscaping and recreation facilities.

Servitudes may be either affirmative or negative. **Affirmative servitudes** are rights to use another's land for a limited purpose. Affirmative servitudes are usually called **easements**. The most common kind of easement is the **right of way**, the right to use another's land for ingress or egress. Examples include the right of a railroad to run tracks over land, or the right of a landowner to cross over neighboring land to access a public road, body of water, or other amenity. Another distinctive form of easement, the **profit à prendre**, or **profit**, allows non-owners to collect resources from the land, such as coal, water, or timber.

Negative servitudes are restrictions with respect to what owners can do with their own land. Residential property may be subject to servitudes not to use the property for commercial or multifamily purposes; commercial property may be subject to servitudes not to use the property for businesses that compete with the servitude's beneficiary; undeveloped or agricultural land may be subject to servitudes to keep the land in its undeveloped state. Negative servitudes go by many names — *e.g.*, negative easements, real covenants, and equitable servitudes — but the modern trend is to call all negative servitudes **covenants**. Courts originally viewed negative servitudes with suspicion, resulting in significant restrictions on their creation and enforcement. As negative servitudes have become more common, and indeed essential to many modern forms of ownership, these restrictions have eased. A number of traditional restrictions still remain, however, and legislatures are creating new restrictions to deal with new problems.

The resulting law of servitudes is confusing. Professor Susan French, the Reporter for the American Law Institute's *Restatement (Third) of Property (Servitudes)*, has called it "the most complex and archaic body of American property law remaining in the twentieth century. Others have described it more colorfully 'as an unspeakable quagmire,' 'confounding intellectual experiences,' and an area of the law full of 'rigid categories, silly distinctions, and unreconciled conflicts over basic values.'" Susan French, *Servitudes Reform and the New Restatement of Property: Creation Doctrines*

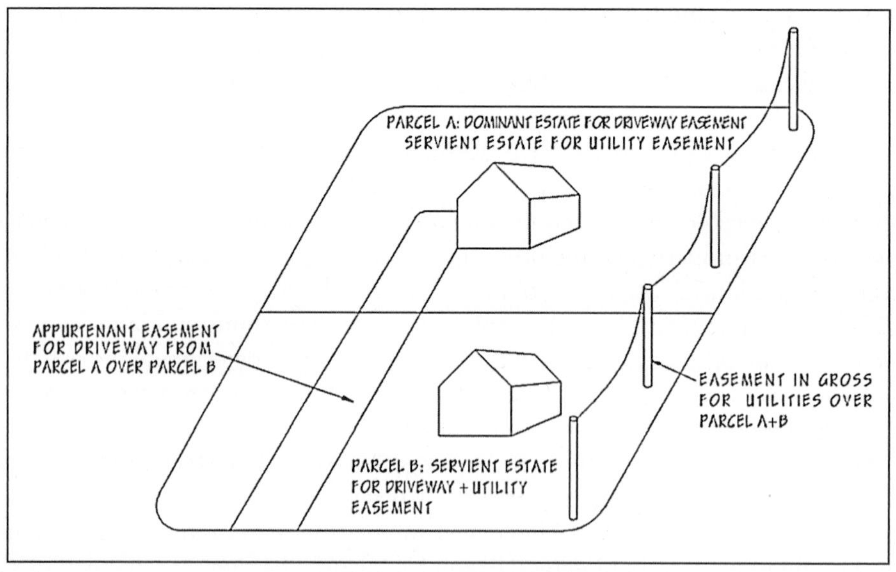

Servitudes diagram (drafted by Katya Stassen)

and Structural Simplification, 73 Cornell L. Rev. 928 (1988). Don't be discouraged. The problem is not with you; it lies in the confused doctrines.

Affirmative and negative servitudes share some common vocabulary. Land subject to the burden of a servitude is called the **burdened** or **servient** estate. If the right to benefit from a servitude automatically passes to the owners of a particular parcel of land, that land is called the **benefited** or **dominant** estate. If there is a benefited estate, the servitude is known as an **appurtenant** easement. Many servitudes are appurtenant; the right to cross over a parcel of land from another parcel of land, for example, is generally appurtenant, as is the right of one neighbor to prevent certain uses of neighboring land. Servitudes may also be **in gross**, meaning that the benefit of the servitude is held by a particular individual or entity rather than running with a parcel of land. Servitudes to run utility lines on land, for example, are typically in gross. The utility company that owns the benefit of the servitude may move its headquarters and still enjoy the servitude right.

Both traditional and modern servitude doctrines respond to a common set of problems. Servitudes allocate use and governance rights among owners and non-owners. As such, they can coordinate land use, secure expectations and identity interests in land, encourage investment, and encourage alienation of land. But they may also burden land with useless or outdated restrictions, undermine broader policy goals, or unfairly surprise and undermine expectations of new purchasers of the land. Servitudes may also result in new coordination problems, as holders of the benefit and burden of the servitude disagree as to how the land should be used.

One can evaluate servitude law according to how successfully it balances these conflicting policy concerns. Do *formal* requirements for creation of servitudes help ensure that the parties creating the servitude truly intend to bind the land and that future owners have notice of the servitude's existence? Do *rules for interpretation* of ambiguous servitudes further the presumed intent of the parties, prevent unfair surprise, and ensure that the land serves public interests? Do *substantive* restrictions on servitudes ensure that they increase land value and do not undermine other important policy goals? Finally, do rules for *termination* end servitudes that no longer serve party intent or other interests or that unduly burden the land? As you learn the rules that govern servitudes, consider whether the rules do serve these goals, and whether they do so effectively.

§2 EASEMENTS

§2.1 Definition and Background

Easements, or affirmative servitudes, are nonpossessory rights to use another's land that run with the land. Easements are likely as old as property law itself. Aspects of the English law of easements were borrowed from the laws of ancient Rome. Medieval English agriculture depended on a system of easements through which individuals had rights to grow crops on particular strips of land, but village residents as a whole had rights to graze their flock on the lands when not under cultivation.[1] Although enclosure of agricultural lands between the sixteenth and nineteenth centuries ended this open-field system, the idea of common access rights remained engrained in England, perhaps leading to the extensive public access rights to private lands still seen throughout Great Britain.[2]

Early English immigrants to North America brought the system of common pasturage with them; its remnants may be seen in town commons throughout New England. Although common pasturage is not a meaningful feature of modern law, easements for utilities burden virtually all property, and much other land is subject to rights of way allowing others to cross over it, and profits allowing easement holders to collect resources from the land.

Easements must be distinguished from **leases** and **licenses**. **Leases**, discussed further in Chapter 11, are possessory rights to use a defined space for all uses not explicitly or implicitly prohibited in the lease. Easements, however, are nonpossessory, meaning that they give the holder only the right to use the land for limited purposes, and the right need not be for a defined space.

Licenses are limited rights to enter or use land that do not run with the land and are usually revocable at will by the grantor. Possessors of real property constantly grant non-owners permission to enter their property; you do so every time you invite someone over for dinner. No writing is required to create a license, and many licenses are implied by the circumstances. For example, a store open to the public conveys a clear message that members of the public are invited to enter the property for the purpose of browsing or shopping. Entering a store during business hours would not be deemed a trespass because entry onto the property is based on implied consent. The entry becomes a trespass only when the licensee refuses to leave after being asked to do so. Revocable licenses are not transferable, they cannot be inherited or left by will, and they are not property interests protected by the takings clause of the U.S. Constitution or subject to the Statute of Frauds.

Although licenses may be created without a writing, while easements are subject to the Statute of Frauds, licenses are frequently formalized in writing and courts will recognize oral easements under certain circumstances. And while licenses are generally not transferrable, some licenses, such as movie or theater tickets, may be transferred to others. Finally, although licenses are frequently said to be revocable at will, revocation is limited in a number of circumstances. First, a license granted in return for consideration may become a contract, so that revocation is subject to damages and other contract remedies. Second, a license to enter land and remove personal property purchased by the license holder is a **license coupled with an interest**, and cannot be revoked for a reasonable time to permit the property to be removed. State

1. *See* Warren O. Ault, *Open-Field Farming in Medieval England: A Study of Village By-Laws* (1972); Henry E. Smith, *Semicommon Rights and Scattering the Open Fields*, 29 J. Leg. Stud. 131 (2000).

2. *See* John A. Lovett, *Progressive Property in Action: The Land Reform (Scotland) Act 2003*, 89 Neb. L. Rev. 739, 753-770 (2011) (discussing common law and statutory rights to roam in Scotland, England, and Wales).

and federal civil rights law may prohibit revocation of a license to enter property open to the public on the basis of a customer's race or other prohibited purposes.[3] In addition, as discussed in §2.3[A] when a license is granted under circumstances that would make it unfair to revoke it, courts may find it has become an **easement by estoppel**.

In other words, the features that are said to distinguish easements from licenses — penalties for revocation, transferability, creation in writing — are often present in licenses as well. The modern trend is to focus on whether the parties intended to create a temporary or permanent right and whether other policy considerations support or forbid creation of the easement; formal differences are important evidence in answering these questions. *Paul v. Blakeley*, 51 N.W.2d 405, 407 (Iowa 1952); *see also* Alfred F. Conard, *An Analysis of Licenses in Land*, 42 Colum. L. Rev. 809, 827-829 (1942).

§2.2 Creation by Express Agreement

Most easements are created by express agreement between the owners of the burdened and benefited land. Sometimes an easement is created by a deed that conveys the easement by itself; an owner, for example, may sell to his neighbor a right of way across the owner's own land. At other times, the easement is created at the same time a parcel of property burdened or benefited by the easement is sold; for example, the grantor may sell part of her land by a deed reciting that, in addition to granting ownership of the parcel to the grantee, the grantor also conveys to the grantee an easement of passage over the land remaining with the grantor.

A. Writing (Statute of Frauds)

As interests in land, the Statute of Frauds requires easements to be in writing to be enforceable.[4] Statutes of Frauds have been adopted in all 50 states. To satisfy the Statute of Frauds, the easement must be contained in a writing signed by the grantor and sufficiently describe the easement and the grantee. Some states also require the writing to state the consideration for transfer of the easement. Here are the real property portions of two typical state Statutes of Frauds:

California Statute of Frauds

West's California Civil Code §1624

(a) The following contracts are invalid, unless they, or some note or memorandum thereof, are in writing and subscribed by the party to be charged or by the party's agent:

. . .

3. *See* Chapter 1 §2.

4. Section 2.4 covers a number of exceptions to the Statute of Frauds respecting easements. Other exceptions to the Statute of Frauds include fraud and part performance. *See* Chapter 12, §2.1.

(3) An agreement for the leasing for a longer period than one year, or for the sale of real property, or of an interest therein; such an agreement, if made by an agent of the party sought to be charged, is invalid, unless the authority of the agent is in writing, subscribed by the party sought to be charged.

New York Statute of Frauds

McKinney's New York General Obligations Law §5-703

2. A contract for the leasing for a longer period than one year, or for the sale, of any real property, or an interest therein, is void unless the contract or some note or memorandum thereof, expressing the consideration, is in writing, subscribed by the party to be charged, or by his lawful agent thereunto authorized by writing.

B. Limits on Negative Easements

Restrictions held by another on what an owner can do with her land are sometimes called **negative easements**. Courts traditionally limited the negative easements that could be created by contract to three kinds: (1) the right to lateral support of one's building, (2) rights to prevent both light and air from being blocked by construction on neighboring land, and (3) the right to prevent interference with the flow of an artificial stream such as an aqueduct. The law of covenants, covered later in this chapter, developed to get around the limitations on negative easements. Negative easement language still appears in modern law, however, particularly in discussions of **conservation easements** (preventing development of land for environmental purposes), **historic preservation easements** (preventing destruction or alteration of buildings that have historical or architectural importance), and **solar easements** (to protect access to sunlight for solar energy). Most of these new easements have been created or recognized by statute. *See, e.g.*, Alaska Stat. §§34.17.010-34.17.060 (conservation easements). The Uniform Laws Commission chose to label conservation easements "easements" largely because lawyers were comfortable with easements, but a little scared of covenants. Prefatory Note, Uniform Conservation Easement Act of 1981. Because these servitudes are usually authorized by statute, they have properties that differ from both covenants and easements.

C. Running with the Land

As with all servitudes, a central question about easements concerns the circumstances under which they run with the land. This is really two separate questions. The first is whether the burden runs with the servient estate. Must a future owner of the land allow the easement owner continued access to or control over her land under the terms of the original easement? The second question is whether the *benefit* runs with the dominant estate. Is the easement owned by the person to whom it was originally granted or by whoever happens to own the parcel of land it was intended to benefit? If the benefit runs with a particular parcel of land, the easement is **appurtenant** to the land. If the benefit attaches to a person or entity rather than a parcel of land, the easement is **in gross**.[5] A common modern kind of easement in gross is a right of way for utility lines over property.

Easements created by an express agreement run with the land only if (1) the easement is in *writing*, (2) subsequent owners of the servient estate had *notice* of the easement at the time of purchase of the servient estate, and (3) the original grantor who created the easement *intended* the easement to run with the land.

ELEMENTS FOR EXPRESS EASEMENTS TO RUN WITH THE LAND

An express easement will run with the burdened or benefited estate if

1. It is in writing;
2. For the burden to run, there was notice to the servient estate holder of the easement; and
3. It was intended to run with that estate.

1. Writing. The required writing is the *original* writing creating the easement. The writing must be one complying with the Statute of Frauds. Sales literature, for example, will not satisfy this requirement, although it may, as we will see, provide evidence for an easement by implication or estoppel. *The easement does not have to be mentioned in subsequent deeds.* It is good legal practice, however, to include a specific reference to existing easements when either the dominant or servient estate is transferred.

2. Notice. Easements are binding on subsequent owners of the servient estate only if they have notice of them. Three kinds of notice exist. First, if the subsequent owners in fact know about the existence of the easement, they have **actual** notice. Second, if there are visible signs of use by non-owners, such as telephone poles, above-ground utility lines, or a path across the property, the owner may be put on **inquiry** notice. This means that a reasonable buyer would do further investigation to discover whether an easement exists. Third, if the deed conveying the easement is recorded in the proper registry of deeds in the proper place, and if a reasonable search of the registry would lead to discovery of the deed, then subsequent owners are deemed to be on **constructive** notice. This means that, whether they actually knew or did not know about the easement, they *should have known*.

3. Intent. Easements bind future owners of the servient estate (or benefit future owners of the dominant estate) only if the grantor intends them to be bound (or benefited). Intent may be clearly stated, as when the deed creating the easement states that the easement "is intended to run with the [benefited and/or burdened] land," or that the easement passes to the owner's "heirs and assigns." If the conveyance is ambiguous as to the grantor's intent, intent may be inferred from the circumstances. If, for example, the easement is one that is likely to have been intended to be limited to the two parties, such as a right given by a landowner to a friend to swim in a pond on

5. Easements in gross are also sometimes referred to as *personal easements,* as in *Green v. Lupo, infra.* This terminology is somewhat confusing since some courts have further subdivided easements in gross into two categories: (1) *commercial* easements used for business purposes, such as a right of way for utility lines, which can be sold or assigned; and (2) *personal* easements used for individual convenience or pleasure, such as a right to swim in a private lake, which cannot be.

her property, courts will typically hold that the benefit is limited to the friend and that it was not intended to bind future owners of the burdened parcel.

§2.3 Interpretation of Ambiguous Easements

A. Appurtenant or In Gross

What happens when a grantor's intent is not unambiguously stated in the deed? The next case deals with this question.

Green v. Lupo

647 P.2d 51 (Wash. Ct. App. 1982)

John A. Petrich, Acting Chief Judge.

The plaintiffs, Don Green and his wife Florence, initiated this suit to specifically enforce an agreement to grant an easement. From a decree which determined that the contemplated easement was personal rather than appurtenant to their land as claimed, plaintiffs appeal. We reverse.

The issue raised on appeal is whether parol evidence is admissible to construe an easement as personal to the grantees where the easement is agreed in writing to be for ingress and egress for road and utilities purposes but the writing does not expressly characterize the easement as either personal or appurtenant. We believe that parol evidence was properly admitted here but the conclusion that the easement is personal to plaintiffs was erroneous.

The parties involved are adjoining landowners. The plaintiffs, once the owners of the entire tract, now retain several acres located south of the defendants' property. The defendants purchased their parcel (the north tract) from the plaintiffs by real estate contract. While they were still paying on that contract, the defendants requested a deed release to a small section of the north tract to allow financing for the construction of a home. The plaintiffs agreed in return for the promise of an easement along the southern 30 feet of the north tract when the defendants eventually obtained title. The express terms of the promised easement were contained in a written agreement which was executed in the form required for the conveyance of an interest in real property. Wash. Rev. Code §64.04.

> Terms:
> **A real estate contract**, also called a **real estate installment contract**, is a contract for sale of real estate in which title remains in the seller until the full purchase price is paid. Without title, the Lupos could not use the land as collateral for a loan until the Greens agreed to transfer title to part of the property early.

The plaintiffs' development of their land for mobile home occupancy caused tension between the landowners. Apparently some of the occupants of plaintiffs' mobile home development used the easement as a practice runway for their motorcycles. When the defendants obtained title to the north tract they refused to formally grant the easement as promised. They also placed logs along the southern boundary of the easement to restrict access from the plaintiffs' property. The plaintiffs brought this action to obtain specific performance of the promise to grant an easement and to enjoin any interference with their use of the easement.

Evidence was admitted describing a single-family cabin or residence built by or for the plaintiffs in the northeast corner of the plaintiffs' tract. It was defendants' contention, and they so testified, that the purpose of the easement was to serve the plaintiffs in their personal use and occupancy of this cabin or home. They claimed the easement was not intended to serve the plaintiffs' entire tract, part of which had been developed as a mobile home site, and which had access by other existing roads.

The trial court concluded that an easement was granted for the use and benefit of the plaintiffs alone and could not be assigned or conveyed. The court ordered the plaintiffs' use to be limited to ingress and egress for their own home or cabin and prohibited the passage of motorcycles.

It was the duty of the court in construing the instrument which created the easement to ascertain and give effect to the intention of the parties. The intention of the parties is determined by a proper construction of the language of the instrument. Where the language is unambiguous other matters may not be considered; but where the language is ambiguous the court may consider the situation of the property and of the parties, and the surrounding circumstances at the time the instrument was executed, and the practical construction of the instrument given by the parties by their conduct or admissions. Simply stated parol evidence may always be used to explain ambiguities in written instruments and to ascertain the intent of the parties.

The pivotal issue in deciding the propriety of admitting parol evidence is whether the written instrument is ambiguous. A written instrument is ambiguous when its terms are uncertain or capable of being understood as having more than one meaning.

The written instrument promised the easement specifically to the plaintiffs, to "Don Green and Florence B. Green," and described the easement as "for ingress and egress for road and utilities [purposes]." The designation of named individuals as dominant owners evidences an intent that the easement be personal to the named parties. The grant of an easement for ingress, egress and utilities to the owners of adjacent land is evidence of an intent that the easement benefit the grantees' adjacent land. We find that the instrument was ambiguous as to whether the easement granted was personal to the plaintiffs or appurtenant to their land. We therefore conclude that parol evidence was properly admitted.

The trial court's findings of fact are supported by competent evidence and are not assigned as error; they must be considered as verities on appeal. The court's findings do not, however, support the conclusion that the easement was personal. The court found that the easement was granted for ingress, egress, for road and utilities purposes. As we have noted, the grant of such an easement supports the conclusion that the easement was intended to be an easement appurtenant. In addition, the trial court found "the use of the easement by the plaintiff was *to obtain access to the land*, retained by plaintiff, for the construction and habitation by plaintiff in a cabin." (Italics ours.) This finding also supports the conclusion that the easement was intended to benefit plaintiffs' land.

The trial court's conclusion that the easement was personal to the plaintiffs was erroneous. There is a strong presumption in Washington that easements are appurtenant to some particular tract of land; personal easements, easements in gross, are not favored. An easement is not in gross when there is anything in the deed or the situation of the property which indicates that it was intended to be appurtenant to land retained or conveyed by the grantor. Viewed in this light, the court's factual findings mandate the conclusion that the easement was intended to be appurtenant to plaintiffs' property.

Easements appurtenant become part of the realty which they benefit. Unless limited by the terms of creation or transfer, appurtenant easements follow possession of the dominant estate through successive transfers. The rule applies even when the dominant estate is subdivided into parcels, with each parcel continuing to enjoy the use of the servient tenement. The terms of the easement promised do not limit its transfer. The easement promised the plaintiffs is appurtenant to their property and assignable to future owners of that property.

The defendants request that equitable limitations be imposed on any easement granted. A servient owner is entitled to impose reasonable restraints on a right of way to avoid a greater burden on the servient owner's estate than that originally contemplated in the easement grant, so long as such restraints do not unreasonably interfere with the dominant owner's use.

Testimony presented at trial showed that youngsters who now live on the dominant estate use their motorcycles on the easement in a fashion that constitutes a dangerous nuisance which was not considered when the easement was created. This evidence supports the imposition of equitable restrictions on the dominant owners' use, restrictions which will not unreasonably interfere with that use.

The trial court enjoined the use of motorcycles on the easement. There is insufficient evidence on the record to assess the impact of a complete ban on motorcycle use on the dominant estate's owners. Motorcycles are a common means of transportation. On its face, the ban appears to unreasonably interfere with the dominant owners' use of the easement. Although an equitable solution to the motorcycle problem is necessary, the trial court abused its discretion in imposing a ban on motorcycles without proper consideration of the ban's effect on the dominant owners' use of the easement.

Reversed and remanded with directions to modify the decree so as to declare the easement for ingress and egress for road and utility purposes to be appurtenant to plaintiffs' property and to devise reasonable restrictions to assure that the easement shall not be used in such a manner as to create a dangerous nuisance.

Notes and Questions

1. **Running of the benefit.** Because the court finds the easement to be appurtenant, it can be used by anyone with a legal right to possess any part of the dominant estate — not just the Greens, but the youths with motorcycles residing in the mobile home park the Greens created. Do you think that was the Lupos' expectation when they agreed to transfer the easement? Why then does the court find that the easement is appurtenant?

2. **Distinguishing in gross from appurtenant easements.** How can you tell whether an easement is in gross or appurtenant? The primary criterion is the *intent of the grantor*. Clear language in the deed conveying the easement that describes it as in gross or appurtenant will ordinarily answer the question — unless surrounding circumstances admissible under the parol evidence rule show that the grantee was

misled or otherwise treated unfairly. What in the express language of the agreement between the Greens and the Lupos creates ambiguity about whether the easement was personal or appurtenant?

When the language in the deed is ambiguous, the court must look to surrounding circumstances and to policy considerations. If the easement is one that would be *useful* separate from ownership of neighboring land, such as a utility easement, the courts are likely to hold that it was intended to be in gross. Since utility easements, such as a right of way for telephone lines, would be useful to the utility company apart from ownership of neighboring property, they are likely to be deemed in gross. If the easement has little or no utility separate from ownership of neighboring land, and is useful to anyone who owns the parcel of land benefited by the easement — such as the right of way in *Green v. Lupo* — courts are likely to hold that the easement is appurtenant.

Courts often voice a constructional preference for appurtenant easements. They may say that there is a *presumption* that easements are appurtenant rather than in gross. *See Broadwater Development, L.L.C. v. Nelson,* 219 P.3d 492, 504 (Mont. 2009); *Nature Conservancy of Wisconsin, Inc. v. Altnau,* 756 N.W.2d 641, 647 (Wis. Ct. App. 2008). Courts have argued that appurtenant easements are preferable because they limit the number of persons with easements over the land to the number of neighboring parcels. They also argue that because appurtenant easements are limited to owners of neighboring or nearby property while easements in gross can be owned by anyone, easements in gross create more uncertainty about land use rights than appurtenant easements. One can check with the neighbors to see if any appurtenant rights exist, but it is harder to check with the general public to find owners of easements in gross. Can you think of a counterargument to this reasoning?

3. Severability from the land. The courts generally hold that an appurtenant easement cannot be *severed* from the land. An owner of the dominant estate who sells the land cannot retain the benefit of the servitude while giving up the land; nor can the beneficiary of the easement transfer the benefit of the easement to another while retaining ownership of the dominant estate. Appurtenant easements pass automatically to whomever owns the dominant estate and cannot be severed from ownership of that estate. *Cricklewood on the Bellamy Condominium Association v. Cricklewood on the Bellamy Trust,* 805 A.2d 427 (N.H. 2002).

4. Transferability of easements. Appurtenant easements are transferable by definition; when the dominant estate is sold or given away, the new owner also owns the appurtenant easement attached to the land. Easements in gross were traditionally not transferable but are generally held to be transferable now, especially if they are commercial in nature, such as utility easements. *Restatement (Third) of Property (Servitudes)* §5.8 (2000). Profits (rights to enter land to remove material such as minerals or timber) were always presumed to be alienable. If an easement in gross is for personal convenience or enjoyment — for example, a right to swim in a private lake — courts may rule that the grantor did not intend the easement to be transferable to others. Some states retain the older rule, holding that easements in gross are not transferable. *King v. Lang,* 42 P.3d 698, 702 (Idaho 2002); *Tupper v. Dorchester County,* 487 S.E.2d 187, 191 (S.C. 1997).

Problem

Bruce and Martin own neighboring tracts of land. Bruce's parcel borders a natural lake, Lake Pescatarian, but Martin's does not. At Martin's request, Bruce creates a deed providing as follows:

> I, Bruce, on behalf of myself and my heirs and assigns, transfer to my friend and neighbor, Martin, the right to enter my land to fish at Lake Pescatarian.

Martin dies, and his land is inherited by his obnoxious son, Charlie. Charlie wants to continue fishing at the lake; Bruce does not want to let him. What are the alternative arguments supporting their positions? Who will succeed? How could Bruce have drafted the easement to avoid this ambiguity?

B. Scope and Apportionment

Cox v. Glenbrook Co.

371 P.2d 647 (Nev. 1962)

GORDON THOMPSON, Justice.

In this case Glenbrook Company, a family corporation, by complaint, and Cox and Detrick, copartners, by answer and counterclaim, each request a declaratory judgment as to the scope and extent of a certain right-of-way herein referred to as the "Quill Easement," granted Henry Quill by the Glenbrook Company in 1938. The conveying instrument reads:

> That said grantor, in consideration of the sum of ten dollars ($10.00), lawful money of the United States of America, to it in hand paid by the grantee, receipt whereof is hereby acknowledged, does by these presents grant, bargain, sell and convey to the said grantee an easement and right-of-way, with full right of use over the roads of the grantor as now located or as they may be located hereafter (but such relocation to be entirely at the expense of the grantor) from the State Highway known as U.S. Route 50 to the following described property: [description of Quill property.] To have and to hold said right-of-way and easement unto the said grantee, his heirs and assigns forever.

1. The Facts

The relevant facts are not disputed. The Quill property contains 80 acres. Henry Quill died in 1943. In 1945 the administratrix of his estate sold the property, with appurtenances, to Kenneth F. Johnson for $8,600. In 1960 Johnson sold the property to Cox and Detrick for $250,000, $50,000 down, with the balance secured by trust deed and payable over an extended period.

Cox and Detrick propose to subdivide their property into parcels of one acre or more, resulting in a minimum of 40 or a maximum of 60 separate parcels. The building on each parcel is to be limited to a residence and a guesthouse. Permanent, as distinguished from seasonal, homes are planned. A commercial development of the property is not contemplated. Zoning will permit the proposed development. An advertising program to sell the individual parcels was commenced. Cox and Detrick anticipate a fully developed subdivision in ten years. The 80 acres are said to be surrounded on two sides by property owned by George Whittel, and on two sides by the property of Glenbrook Company. The Quill Easement is the only existing ingress to and egress from that tract.

The property of Glenbrook Company fronts on Glenbrook Bay, Lake Tahoe. For more than 25 years it has operated a resort business. Its facilities consist of a beach, approximately 30 guest cottages, a tennis court, riding stables, foot paths for hiking, horse trails for riding, a golf course, a post office, a rodeo area, a service station, a bar, and a dining room and lounge at the Glenbrook Inn. The golf course may be used by nonguests upon paying a higher green fee. The bar is open to the public, as is the dining room when not completely reserved by guests. There is no gambling. Glenbrook is operated on a seasonal basis from mid-June through September and is widely known as a beautiful summer vacation resort for families, many of whom return year after year. The atmosphere sought to be maintained is that of peace, seclusion and quiet. The roads through the property are generally unpaved except for the main road from U.S. Highway 50 to the golf course. At the entrance to the main road is a sign stating that permission to pass over is revocable at any time. The main road is the only way in or out from the Glenbrook properties. In years past, from time to time, Glenbrook Company has sold small parcels of its property to individuals. In each instance it has granted the purchaser a right-of-way for ingress and egress.

The following rough sketch will, perhaps, be of some assistance.

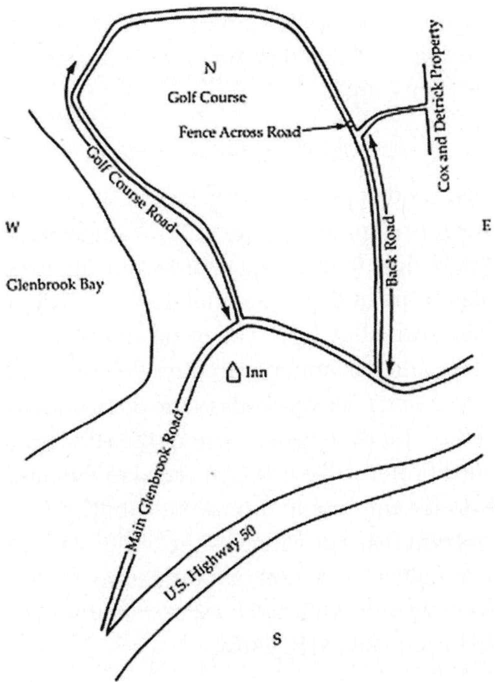

To get to the Cox and Detrick property one may take either the "golf course road" or the "back road." Before this action started, the "golf course road" was fenced off. A portion of the "back road" was built in 1936 to provide a way to water tanks which supplied water for the golf course. In the late 1930s it was extended to the Quill (now Cox and Detrick) properties. Glenbrook Company, because of friendship with Quill, supplied the tractor and blade used in so extending the road. The road was, and is, narrow and unpaved. In most places it is wide enough for only one car. Trees, rocks and manzanita generally border it. There is an occasional "turn out." A worker, who extended the road to the Quill property in the late 1930s, stated that Quill just wanted "a rough road, so that he could go on up with a car." Cox frankly stated that he would like to use the "back road" if it "were passable," and that he definitely wanted to widen the road. That road has seldom been used by anyone except the four or five families having homes along its course, and their guests.

2. *The Lower Court's Judgment*

After trial before the court without a jury, judgment was entered declaring that the Quill Easement is limited in three respects: (a) "to such uses as are and will be reasonably consistent with the use to which the servient property is employed, that is, a conservative, family, mountain resort operation, and is further limited, as to reasonable use, to the use contemplated in the original grant to Quill, that is, access to and egress from the entire dominant parcel by a single family in occupancy, and their guests"; (b) "to use of the Glenbrook roads as those roads are presently constructed and maintained, or as the Glenbrook Company by its own action or by mutual agreement with interested parties, may hereafter locate and construct roads in the Glenbrook estate"; and (c) that "The proposed use of the so-called Quill Easement by the defendants herein, that is, the use of the Glenbrook roads by purchasers of subdivided parcels of the former Quill property, would constitute an illegal and unjustified burden and surcharge upon the servient estate."

5. *Unwarranted Restrictions*

(A) We shall first discuss that portion of the judgment restricting the use to ingress to and egress from the entire dominant parcel "by a single family in occupancy and their guests." Such a restriction, in our view, destroys the appurtenant character of the easement. Yet, there can be no question but that the Quill Easement was appurtenant to the 80 acre tract then owned by him. The terms of the conveyance, "to have and to hold said right-of-way and easement unto the said grantee, his heirs and assigns forever," make it clear that one who succeeds to the possession of the dominant tenement, succeeds as well to the privileges of use of the servient tenement authorized by the conveyance. Furthermore, those who succeed to the possession of each of the parts into which the dominant tenement may be subdivided, also succeed to such privileges of use, unless otherwise provided by the terms of the conveyance. The Quill conveyance does not contain a restriction that the easement granted is to be appurtenant to the dominant estate only while such estate remains in single possession, and none may be imposed by judicial declaration.

(B) The judgment further restricts the use of the easement to "use of the Glenbrook roads as those roads are presently constructed and maintained." We are uncertain as to the precise meaning of this restriction. If such language prohibits the owner of the dominant estate from making any improvements or repairs of the way, it is too restrictive. As a general rule, the owner of an easement may prepare, maintain, improve or repair the way in a manner and to an extent reasonably calculated to promote the purposes for which it was created. The owner may not, however, by such action, cause an undue burden upon the servient estate, nor an unwarranted interference with the independent rights of others who have a similar right of use. The action of Cox and Detrick in leveling or "rough grading" the "back road," to the extent that it was confined to the area within the exterior borders of the road as they existed when the easement was originally granted, was an improvement reasonably calculated to promote the purposes for which the easement was created. Such leveling or rough grading as so confined, would not, in itself, cause an undue burden upon the servient estate, nor constitute an unwarranted interference with the easement rights of other private property owners.

However, their conduct in attempting to widen the way is another matter. A careful study of the record makes it clear that the ultimate intention of the subdividers is to widen the "back road" in order that two cars going in opposite directions may pass comfortably at all points along its course. The conveying instrument does not specify the width of the way expressly; it does, however, refer to the "roads as now located." The "back road" as it existed at the time of the grant of easement, was described as a "small road," and wide enough for just one car. The record does not disclose that the predecessors of Cox and Detrick ever sought or attempted to widen the "back road." There is no evidence tending to indicate that either Glenbrook Company or Henry Quill contemplated or intended a wider road than existed when the grant was made. When the width is not specified, the conveying instrument must be construed in the light of the facts and circumstances existing at its date and affecting the property, the intention of the parties being the object of inquiry. Indeed, it is sometimes held, as a matter of law, that where the width of a right-of-way is not specified in the grant, it is limited to the width as it existed at the time of the grant. We need not go that far. We believe that the intention of the parties at the time of the grant, when there is evidence to indicate such intention, controls as to width.

As already stated, the only evidence in the record with reference to the "back road" indicates that Henry Quill desired a way wide enough for one car; that such was the character of the "back road" at that time, with occasional "turn outs." We must conclude, therefore, that such was the parties' intention in 1938 when the grant was made. If the width of the way is what the lower court had in mind when it restricted the easement to "use of the Glenbrook roads as those roads are presently constructed and maintained" (the record revealing no substantial change from 1938 to time of trial, except for the work of Cox and Detrick before mentioned), then we find ourselves in accord.

7. *Area Wherein Judgment Is Premature*

The judgment entered also declared that the proposed use of the Quill Easement would constitute an illegal burden and surcharge upon the servient estate. The announced intention by the owners of the dominant estate as to their proposed future use of the easement does not, of itself, constitute an unreasonable burden upon the servient estate. When the facts concerning that use become known, an unreasonable burden upon the servient estate may, or may not result. That determination must await the presentation of evidence then in existence.

In our judgment the lower court erred in declaring that the proposed use of the Quill Easement would constitute an unreasonable burden upon the servient estate, in the absence of existing evidence. It should have done no more than to announce, in general terms, the applicable legal principle within which a subsequent factual determination could be made if occasion therefore arises.

10. Conclusions

From the foregoing it is apparent that the parties seek a declaration of rights in the following respects:

First: The privilege of use of the Glenbrook roads as located on January 7, 1938 (the date of the grant of easement) is not restricted by the terms of the grant, and is appurtenant to the dominant estate, and may be enjoyed by those who succeed to the possession of the dominant estate in its entirety or by those who succeed to the possession of the parts into which such estate may be subdivided.

Second: The owners of the easement may maintain, repair and improve the way in a manner reasonably calculated to promote the purposes for which the easement was created, provided, however, (a) such maintenance, repair or improvement is confined to the area within the exterior borders of the way as it existed on January 7, 1938 (the date of the grant of easement); (b) that such maintenance, repair, or improvement will not cause an undue burden upon the servient estate; (c) that such maintenance, repair or improvement will not cause an unwarranted interference with the independent rights of others who have a similar right of use.

Third: The owners of the easement may not widen the way, its width being limited, by reason of the evidence introduced, to the width of the way on January 7, 1938 (the date of the grant of easement); and, insofar as the portion of the way herein referred to as the "back road" is concerned, that width is sufficient only for one car with occasioned "turn outs."

Fourth: The owner of the servient estate has the right to relocate the way at its own expense, which right includes the right to barricade that portion of the existing way herein referred to as the "golf course road."

Fifth: The owners of the easement may not, by reason of their proposed subdivision development, or otherwise, cause an undue burden upon the servient estate, or an unwarranted interference with the independent rights of others who have a similar right of use. Whether such a burden or interference will occur cannot be conclusively declared upon existing evidence. In the event the owners of the easement proceed with their announced plan, their use of the way is limited to the extent herein noted. We believe it proper, however, at this time, to note that, should they proceed with their proposed plan, the trier of the facts in subsequent litigation, if it occurs, might or might not determine upon evidence then existing, that their use of the way causes an unreasonable burden upon the servient estate or an unwarranted interference with the independent rights of others who have a similar right of use; hence, any further action on their part to develop their property in the manner proposed is subject to such contingency.

Henley v. Continental Cablevision of St. Louis County, Inc.

692 S.W.2d 825 (Mo. Ct. App. 1985)

CARL R. GAERNTNER, Judge.

Pursuant to an indenture recorded on April 8, 1922, plaintiffs' predecessors as trustees, were expressly granted the right to construct and maintain electric, telephone and telegraphic service on or over the rear five feet of all lots in the subdivision, and to grant easements to other parties for the purposes of creating and maintaining such systems. In July, 1922 and August, 1922, respectively, the trustees conveyed an easement to Southwestern Bell Telephone Company to "construct, reconstruct, repair, operate and maintain its lines for telephone and electric light purposes" and similarly to Union Electric to "keep, operate and maintain its lines consisting of cables, manholes, wires, fixtures and appurtenances thereto." Subsequently, in 1981 and 1982, defendant [Continental Cablevision of St. Louis County, Inc.] exercised licenses acquired from both utilities to enter upon these easements, and erected cables, wires and conduits for the purpose of transmitting television programs.

Plaintiffs [as trustees of University Park subdivision] filed an action for an injunction on December 29, 1983, seeking not only to enjoin a continuing trespass and compel the removal of defendant's wires and cables, but also seeking $300,000 in damages and the reasonable value of the use of plaintiffs' property for defendant's profit based upon *quantum meruit.*

Both parties agree that the subject easements are easements in gross, *i.e.*, easements which belong to the owner independently of his ownership or possession of other land, and thus lacking a dominant tenement. The dispositive issue here is whether or not these easements are exclusive and therefore apportionable by the utilities to, in this case, defendant Continental Cablevision.

We believe the very nature of the 1922 easements obtained by both utilities indicates that they were intended to be exclusive and therefore apportionable. It is well settled that where the servient owner retains the privilege of sharing the benefit conferred by the easement, it is said to be "common" or non-exclusive and therefore not subject to apportionment by the easement owner. Conversely, if the rights granted are exclusive of the servient owners' participation therein, divided utilization of the rights granted are presumptively allowable. This principle stems from the concept that one who grants to another the right to use the grantor's land in a particular manner for a specified purpose but who retains no interest in exercising a similar right himself, sustains no loss if, within the specifications expressed in the grant, the use is shared by the grantee with others. On the other hand, if the grantor intends to participate in the use or privilege granted, then his retained right may be diminished if the grantee shares his right with others. Thus, insofar as it relates to the apportionability of an easement in gross, the term "exclusive" refers to the exclusion of the owner and possessor of the servient tenement from participation in the rights granted, not to the number of different easements in and over the same land.

Here, there is no claim that plaintiffs' predecessors had at the time the easements were granted, any intention to seek authority for, or any interest whatsoever in using the five foot strips for the construction and maintenance of either an electric power system or telephone and telegraphic service. Moreover, at no time during the ensuing sixty-three years have the trustees been authorized to furnish such services by any certificate of convenience and necessity issued by the Public Service Commission pursuant to Mo. Rev. Stat. §§392.260 and 393.170 (1978). Accordingly, the easements granted to Southwestern Bell and Union Electric were exclusive as to the grantors thereof and therefore apportionable.

Plaintiffs also argue defendant could acquire no rights from the utilities since their easements did not mention television cables, and that the cable attachments themselves constituted an extra burden on the property. We disagree. The owner of an easement may license or authorize third persons to use its right of way for purposes not inconsistent with the principal use granted. The 1922 easements granted to Union Electric expressly provided the right of ingress and egress by Union Electric, its successors and assigns, to "add to the number of and relocate all wires, cables, conduits, manholes, adding thereto from time-to-time." Similarly, the easement conveyed to Southwestern Bell expressly contemplated the construction and maintenance of "all poles, cables, wires, conduits, lateral pipes, anchor guys and all other fixtures and appurtenances deemed necessary at anytime by [Southwestern Bell], its successors and assigns." It can hardly be said that the addition of a single coaxial cable to the existing poles for the purpose of transmitting television images and sound by electric impulse increases the burden on the servient tenement beyond the scope of the intended and authorized use.

Although this is a case of first impression in Missouri, courts in other jurisdictions have addressed the legal effect of adding coaxial cables for television transmission to existing electric and telephone poles erected on easements without the consent of the owners of the fees. These courts have uniformly rejected arguments identical to those made by plaintiffs herein and have reached a conclusion similar to ours.

In *Jolliff v. Hardin Cable Television Co.*, 269 N.E.2d 588 (Ohio 1971), an easement granted to a power company for the transmission of electric power, including telegraph or telephone wires, was held to be an apportionable easement in gross by reason of the express language of the conveyance authorizing the grantee to lease some portion of its interest to third parties. In addressing the question of an additional burden on the servient tenements, the court noted that the attachment of a television coaxial cable to existing poles constituted no more of a burden than would installation of telephone wires, a burden clearly contemplated at the time of the grants.

In *Crowley v. New York Telephone Company*, 363 N.Y.S.2d 292 (Dist. Ct. 1975) it was held that the failure to make specific mention of cable television in a 1949 easement to locate telephone poles and wires on plaintiff's property could not be so narrowly interpreted as to prohibit the addition of television cables to the telephone poles. "Just as we must accept scientific advances, we must translate the rights of parties to an agreement in the light of such developments." 363 N.Y.S.2d at 294.

In *Hoffman v. Capitol Cablevision System, Inc.*, 383 N.Y.S.2d 674 (App. Div. 1976), the court concluded that the rights granted to two utilities were exclusive *vis-à-vis* the landowner, and were, therefore apportionable by the grantees. The addition of cable and equipment to already existing poles was held to constitute no additional burden since the defendant was doing only what the utilities were enabled to do. The court noted the general rule that easements in gross for commercial purposes are particularly alienable and transferable. For these reasons, the court held the failure to foresee and specifically refer to cable television in the grant was of no consequence.

The reasoning of the *Hoffman* court has recently been found persuasive by the California court in *Salvaty v. Falcon Cable Television*, 212 Cal. Rptr. 31 (Ct. App. 1985). The court stated:

> In the case at bench, the addition of cable television equipment on surplus space on the telephone pole was within the scope of the easement. Although the cable television industry did not exist at the time the easement was granted, it is part of the natural evolution of communications technology. Installation of the equipment was consistent with the primary goal of the easement, to provide for wire transmission of power and communication. We fail to see how the addition of cable equipment to a pre-existing utility pole materially increased the burden on appellant's property. 212 Cal. Rptr. at 34-35.

The unsurprising fact that the drafters of the 1922 easements did not envision cable television does not mandate the narrow interpretation of the purposes of the conveyance of rights and privileges urged by plaintiffs. The expressed intention of the predecessors of plaintiff trustees was to obtain for the homeowners in the subdivision the benefits of electric power and telephonic communications. Scientific and technological progress over the ensuing years have added an unforeseen dimension to such contemplated benefits, the transmission by electric impulse of visual and audio communication over coaxial cable. It is an inescapable conclusion that the intention of plaintiffs' predecessors was the acquisition and continued maintenance of available means of bringing electrical power and communication into the homes of the subdivision. Clearly, it is in the public interest to use the facilities already installed for the purpose of carrying out this intention to provide the most economically feasible and least environmentally damaging vehicle for installing cable systems.

Notes and Questions

1. **Scope.** Three issues arise in determining whether the owner of an easement is misusing it by going beyond the scope of activities contemplated by the grantor: (a) whether the use is of a *kind* contemplated by the grantor, (b) whether the use is so heavy that it constitutes an *unreasonable burden* on the servient estate not contemplated by the grantor, and (c) whether the easement can be *subdivided.*

2. **Kinds of uses encompassed by the easement.** Conflicts over use may concern what kinds of activities are encompassed by the easement. For example, can

a general right of way initially used for road purposes be used to place utility lines? Many courts hold that a general right of way may be used for any reasonable purpose. *Weeks v. Wolf Creek Industries, Inc.*, 941 So. 2d 263, 270 (Ala. 2006); *Cannata v. Berkshires Natural Resources Council*, 901 N.E.2d 1250, 1255 (Mass. App. 2009).

Where, as in *Henley*, the easement is for a particular purpose, the question is whether the use is reasonably included within that purpose. Absent clear evidence of the parties' intent, most courts will find that the manner of use of an easement may "change over time to take advantage of developments in technology and to accommodate normal development of the dominant estate or enterprise benefited by the servitude," so long as it does not unreasonably burden the servient estate. *Restatement (Third) of Property (Servitudes)* §4.10. Thus most courts will agree with *Henley* that an easement for electric and telephone purposes can be used for cable transmission. More recent decisions have reached similar results with respect to use of telephone and electricity easements for wireless telephone equipment and fiber optic cable. *See Zhang v. Omnipoint Communication Enterprises*, 866 A.2d 588 (Conn. 2005); *Municipal Electric Authority of Georgia v. Gold-Arrow Farms, Inc.*, 625 S.E.2d 57 (Ga. App. 2005). The Texas Supreme Court in *Marcus Cable Associates v. Krohn*, 90 S.W.3d 697, 699 (Tex. 2002), however, found that an easement for "an electric transmission or distribution line or system" did not allow the holder to install cable television lines. Courts have also differed on whether a utility easement acquired by prescription, which is fixed by the prescriptive use, may be used for cable purposes. *Compare Heydon v. MediaOne*, 739 N.W.2d 373 (Mich. App. 2007) (yes) *with Jackson v. City of Auburn*, 971 So. 2d 696 (Ala. App. 2006) (no).

Grantors retain whatever rights they do not give away, but the question is *what* rights the grantor gave away when it granted the initial easement. Should easements be interpreted broadly or narrowly? Should the owner of a general right of way who acquired the easement initially for road purposes be allowed to use the road for other purposes such as phone or electric utility lines? What result is most likely to effectuate the intent of the parties? What result is more likely to promote the alienability of property? Should alienability of property be the preeminent goal? If not, what should be? Note that had the easement not been found to include cable with *Henley*, Cablevision would have to negotiate with and compensate University Park rather than the utility companies in order to run its cable lines. Is anything wrong with that result?

3. Unreasonable additional burden. The owner of an easement may be clearly engaged in the kind of activity contemplated by the easement but the degree or intensity of use may still constitute an unreasonable burden. For example, the court in *Green v. Lupo*, although allowing motorcycle use over the road, stated that such use could be limited and regulated to protect the legitimate interests of the owner of the servient estate. Similarly, the court in *Cox* required the trial court to determine whether subdivision of the dominant estate would impose an unreasonable additional burden on the servient estate.

When the grantor's intent is ambiguous with respect to the changed use, courts must balance the interests of the easement owner in freedom to develop his property against the interests of the servient estate owners in security from having their property overly burdened in a way they should not have had to anticipate. *Compare Peterson v. Town of Oxford*, 459 A.2d 100 (Conn. 1983) (use of drainage easement for subdivision so that water from brook overflowed and eroded servient estate was unreasonable burden), *and Bassett v. Harrison*, 807 A.2d 695 (Md. App. 2002) (use of general right of way to haul sand and gravel was unreasonable burden), *and Davis v. Bruk*, 411 A.2d 660 (Me. 1980) (paving a country road would cause unreasonable burden by increasing speed and safety issue with cars near defendant's home), *with Hayes v. Aquia Marina, Inc.*, 414 S.E.2d 820 (Va. 1992) (expanding marina on dominant estate from 84 to 230 boat slips and paving road to the marina would not unreasonably burden servient estate).

4. Divisibility. The question of divisibility of appurtenant easements generally arises when the owner of the dominant estate subdivides the property and attempts to transfer to new owners rights to use the easement to obtain access to their property. Most courts hold that "the benefits of an appurtenant easement move to each portion of the dominant parcel upon its subdivision and transfer of the various pieces." Gerald Korngold, *Private Land Use Arrangements: Easements, Real Covenants, and Equitable Servitudes* §5.05, at 213 (2d ed. 2004). The first *Restatement on Property* notes:

> [D]ominant tenements are ordinarily divisible and their division is so common that it is assumed that the possibility of their division is contemplated in their creation. Hence, unless forbidden by the manner or terms of its creation, the benefit of an easement appurtenant accrues upon a subdivision of a dominant tenement to the benefit of each of the parts into which it is subdivided.

Restatement of Property §488 cmt. c (1944).The *Restatement (Third)* maintains this rule, §§4.6 & 5.9, but elsewhere suggests that using an easement over a 20-foot dirt road initially established between two farms for a 100-unit subdivision later built on the dominant estate would constitute an unreasonable burden on the servient estate. §4.10, illus. 26. Are these positions consistent?

5. Apportionability. With easements in gross, the question of divisibility of the easement is referred to as the issue of **apportionability**. When an easement in gross is **nonexclusive** — meaning the grantor, or owner of the servient estate, has reserved for herself the right to use the easement in conjunction with the grantee — the easement is generally held to be nonapportionable; the grantor herself could sell further rights to others so long as those new easements did not interfere with the use of the existing easement by the first grantee. The courts presume that under these circumstances, the grantor would want to retain the right to obtain the economic benefits of any future easements. When, however, the easement is **exclusive** — meaning the grantor has no right to use the easement in conjunction with the grantee — the easement is generally held to be apportionable. Since the grantor has no right to grant other easements, the grantee is not interfering with any rights the grantor might have to sell or lease use of the easement to others.

The *Restatement (Third)* provides instead that easements in gross can be divided unless this is contrary to the intent of the parties who created the easement or "unless the division unreasonably increases the burden on the servient estate." *Id.* §5.9. This appears to be consistent with the trend in the law, which is to answer the question by reference to the intent of the grantor. William B. Stoebuck & Dale A. Whitman, *The Law of Property* §8.11, at 465 (3d ed. 2000).

6. Width of the road. The court in *Cox* concludes that the grantor intended to allow the dominant estate to be subdivided but that the road was intended to be limited to a one-car width with existing "turn-abouts." Is this consistent? It is unlikely to be practicable to subdivide the dominant estate *unless* the easement is widened to at least two lanes. If the owner of the dominant estate has the right to subdivide his land, and each of his grantees will have a right to use the easement (so long as this collective use does not constitute an unreasonable additional burden on the servient estate), how can it be that the dominant estate owner has no right to a wider road? If the grantor could contemplate that the dominant estate would be subdivided, wouldn't the grantor also be able to foresee and contemplate the need for a wider road? How would Justice Thompson answer this question?

7. Changing location of the easement. Can the owner of the servient estate change the location of the easement? The traditional rule prevents this; the owner of the servient estate must obtain the consent of the easement holder to relocate it. *Herren v. Pettengill,* 538 S.E.2d 735 (Ga. 2000); *Koeppen v. Bolich,* 79 P.3d 1100 (Mont. 2003). However, some recent cases and the *Restatement (Third) of Property (Servitudes)* §4.8(3) (2000), allow the owner of the servient "reasonable changes in the location or dimensions of an easement, at the servient owner's expense, to permit normal use or development of the servient estate, but only if the changes do not (a) significantly lessen the utility of the easement, (b) increase the burdens on the owner of the easement in its use and enjoyment, or (c) frustrate the purpose for which the easement was created," *id.* §4.8(3); *see M.P.M. Builders, LLC v. Dwyer,* 809 N.E.2d 1053 (Mass. 2004). Several courts have adopted middle positions. One court allowed the servient estate owner to relocate the easement so long as damages were paid to the dominant estate owner, *Umphres v. J.R. Mayer Enterprises, Inc.,* 889 S.W.2d 86 (Mo. Ct. App. 1994), while another allowed relocation only after a court finding that relocation would not harm the easement owner, *Roaring Fork Club L.P. v. St. Jude's Co.,* 36 P.3d 1229 (Colo. 2001). Other courts, however, have rejected the *Restatement (Third)*'s position, calling it "a threat to the certainty of property rights and real estate transactions, as a catalyst for increased litigation, and as a means for purchasers of servient estates to reap a windfall at the expense of owners of dominant estates." *AKG Real Estate, LLC v. Kosterman,* 717 N.W.2d 835, 842 (Wis. 2006); *see Cottonwood Duplexes, LLC v. Barlow,* 149 Cal. Rptr. 3d 235 (Cal. App. 2012) (court could not reduce scope of easement from 60 feet to 15 feet although size of existing easement was not necessary for its purposes and inhibited development). What do you think?

8. Extension of the use. What if the easement holder wants to use the easement to obtain access to the dominant estate but also to reach a subsequently acquired lot on the other side of the dominant estate? The rule in most jurisdictions prohibits this extension of the use absent contrary evidence of the intent of the parties. *See Christensen v. City of Pocatello*, 124 P.3d 1008 (Idaho 2005); *Bateman v. Board of Appeals of Georgetown*, 775 N.E.2d 1276 (Mass. App. Ct. 2002). In adopting this rule, the *Restatement (Third)* comments that it "reflects the likely intent of the parties by setting an outer limit on the potential increase in use of an easement brought about by normal development of the dominant estate," and "avoids otherwise difficult litigation over the question whether increased use unreasonably increases the burden on the servient estate." *Restatement (Third)* §4.11 cmt. b. Should the rule be waived if the easement holder can prove it will cause no additional burden? *Cf. Brown v. Voss*, 715 P.2d 514 (Wash. 1986) (denying an injunction where the defendant sought to use the easement for a single-family house on the combined parcel).

Problems

1. Should the defendant owners of the dominant estate in *Cox* have the right to widen the road to accommodate a subdivision of 40 homes? Would this exceed the scope of the easement?

    a. What arguments could you make for the plaintiff that the width of the road should be set at the historical width existing at the time of the original conveyance?

    b. What arguments could you make for defendants that they have a right to widen the road to accommodate the subdivision of the dominant estate?

    c. How should the case be adjudicated, and why?

2. Assume now that the original easement was a two-lane road so there is no need to widen it. Would subdividing the dominant estate and building 40 homes constitute an unreasonable additional burden on the servient estate?

    a. What arguments could you make for the plaintiff that the subdivision would exceed the scope of the original easement and constitute an unreasonable additional burden on the servient estate?

    b. What arguments could you make for defendants that the subdivision would not constitute an unreasonable additional burden on the servient estate?

    c. How should the case be adjudicated, and why?

§2.4 Creation of Easements by Implication

The purposes of Statutes of Frauds are to protect individuals from fraudulent claims that they made oral promises, or false claims about the essentials of those promises. As applied to property, Statutes of Frauds also help protect later purchasers from unexpected claims regarding their land. When an oral promise has been made, however, the refusal to enforce it because it was not in writing effectively allows the promisor to perpetrate a fraud. Insisting on a writing may also violate expectations created in other ways. Courts have therefore recognized at least four ways in which easements may be created without being described in a writing complying with the Statute of Frauds.

1. **Easements by estoppel** may be found when a landowner grants the claimant permission to use the property, and the claimant so changes position in reasonable reliance on the continuation of the permission, that it would create substantial injustice to revoke it.

2. **Easements by prescription** are created through adverse and open use of the land continuously until the expiration of the statute of limitations for trespass. Jurisdictions vary on the kind of adversity and exclusivity required. *See* Chapter 5, §3.

3. **Easements implied by prior use** may be found when a parcel of land is divided or severed, and prior to severance one part of the estate used the other part of the estate, the use was obvious or apparent, and is reasonably necessary for enjoyment of the estate.

4. **Easements by necessity** may arise when an estate is severed and upon severance one part of the estate becomes landlocked, requiring a right of way over the other part of the severed estate to access a public road.

What different interests are served by these diverse exceptions to the writing requirement? Although the four forms of implied easements may appear quite different, plaintiffs often raise more than one of these theories to support their claims.

A. Easements by Estoppel

Lobato v. Taylor

71 P.3d 938 (Colo. 2002) (en banc)

Chief Justice MARY MULLARKEY delivered the Opinion of the Court.

The history of this property rights controversy began before Colorado's statehood, at a time when southern Colorado was part of Mexico; at a time when all of the parties' lands were part of the one million acre Sangre de Cristo grant, an 1844 Mexican land grant. Here, we determine access rights of the owners of farmlands in Costilla County to a mountainous parcel of land now known as the Taylor Ranch. As successors in title to the original settlers in the region, the landowners exercised rights to enter and use the Taylor Ranch property for over one hundred years until Jack Taylor fenced the land in 1960 and forcibly excluded them. These rights, they assert, derive from Mexican law . . . and an express or implied grant, and were impermissibly denied when the mountain land was fenced.

In 1844, the governor of New Mexico granted two Mexican nationals a one million-acre land grant, located mainly in present-day southern Colorado (Sangre de Cristo grant), for the purpose of settlement. The original grantees died during the war between the United States and Mexico. The land was not settled in earnest until after the cessation of the war, and Charles (Carlos) Beaubien then owned the grant.

In 1848, the United States and Mexico entered into the Treaty of Guadalupe Hidalgo, ending the war between the two countries. *Treaty of Peace, Friendship, Limits, and Settlement (Treaty of Guadalupe Hidalgo)*, February 2, 1848, U.S.-Mex., 9 Stat. 922. Pursuant to the treaty, Mexico ceded land to the United States, including all of

California, Nevada, and Utah; most of New Mexico and Arizona; and a portion of Colorado. The United States agreed to honor the existing property rights in the ceded territory. Congress confirmed Carlos Beaubien's claim to the Sangre de Cristo grant in the 1860 Act of Confirmation. 12 Stat. 71 (1860).

In the early 1850s, Beaubien successfully recruited farm families to settle the Colorado portion of the Sangre de Cristo grant. He leased a portion of his land to the United States government to be used to establish Fort Massachusetts and recruited farmers to settle other areas. The settlement system he employed was common to Spain and Mexico: strips of arable land called vara strips were allotted to families for farming, and areas not open for cultivation were available for common use. These common areas were used for grazing and recreation and as a source for timber, firewood, fish, and game.

In 1863, Beaubien gave established settlers deeds to their vara strips. That same year, Beaubien executed and recorded a Spanish language document that purports to grant rights of access to common lands to settlers on the Sangre de Cristo grant (Beaubien Document). In relevant part, this document guarantees that "all the inhabitants will have enjoyment of benefits of pastures, water, firewood and timber, always taking care that one does not injure another."

A year later, Beaubien died. Pursuant to a prior oral agreement, his heirs sold his interest in the Sangre de Cristo grant to William Gilpin, who was Colorado's first territorial governor. The sales agreement (Gilpin agreement) stated that Gilpin agreed to provide vara strip deeds to settlers who had not yet received them. The agreement further stated that Gilpin took the land on condition that certain "settlement rights before then conceded . . . to the residents of the settlements . . . shall be confirmed by said William Gilpin as made by him."

In 1960, Jack Taylor, a North Carolina lumberman, purchased roughly 77,000 acres of the Sangre de Cristo grant (mountain tract) from a successor in interest to William Gilpin. Taylor's deed indicated that he took the land subject to "claims of the local people by prescription or otherwise to right to pasture, wood, and lumber and so-called settlement rights in, to, and upon said land."

Despite the language in Taylor's deed, he denied the local landowners access to his land and began to fence the property. The current case began in 1981. In that year a number of local landowners filed suit in Costilla County District Court. The landowners asserted that they had settlement rights to the Taylor Ranch and that Taylor had impermissibly denied those rights.

After the trial, the court made a finding of fact that the landowners or their predecessors in title had "grazed cattle and sheep, harvested timber, gathered firewood, fished, hunted and recreated on the land of the defendant from the 1800s to the date the land was acquired by the defendant, in 1960." The trial court further found that the community referred to Taylor Ranch as "open range," and that prior to 1960, the landowners "were never denied access to the land." The court also stated that it did "not dispute" that the settlers could not have survived without use of the mountain area of the grant. Despite these findings, the court determined that the landowners had no rights in the Taylor Ranch. The court of appeals affirmed.

The parties, at various points in the voluminous briefing of this twenty-one year-old litigation, agree that the rights at issue are most appropriately characterized as profits à prendre. A profit à prendre — in modern parlance, a profit — "is an easement that confers the right to enter and remove timber, minerals, oil, gas, game, or other substances from land in the possession of another." *Restatement (Third) of Property: Servitudes* §1.2(2) (1998) [hereinafter Restatement]. Thus, a profit is a type of easement.

An easement can be in gross or appurtenant. An easement in gross does not belong to an individual by virtue of her ownership of land, but rather is a personal right to use another's property. An easement appurtenant, on the other hand, runs with the land. It is meant to benefit the property, or an owner by virtue of her property ownership. An easement is presumed to be appurtenant, rather than in gross.

In this case, the landowners allege that the settlement rights were to be used in connection with their land. They argue that the firewood was used to heat their homes, the timber to frame their adobe houses, and the grazing necessary to the viability of their farms. The landowners also assert that the settlement rights were granted to their predecessors in title by virtue of their interest in their vara strips and were in fact a necessary incentive for settlement in the area.

We conclude that the rights the landowners are claiming are best characterized as easements appurtenant to the land. We reach this conclusion from the evidence that under Mexican custom access to common land was given to surrounding landowners, the evidence that this access was used to benefit the use of the land, and the presumption in favor of appurtenant easements.

B. Sources of the Rights

The landowners argue that their settlement rights stem from three sources: Mexican law, prescription, and an express or implied grant from Beaubien.

Regarding the Mexican law claim, the landowners claim that community rights to common lands not only are recognized by Mexican law, but also are integral to the settlement of an area. The landowners further point out that in the Treaty of Guadalupe Hidalgo, the United States government agreed that the land rights of the residents of the ceded territories would be "inviolably respected."

[T]he landowners cannot claim rights under Mexican law. Their predecessors in title did not settle on the Sangre de Cristo grant until after the land was ceded to the United States and thus their use rights developed under United States law. Mexican land use and property law are highly relevant in this case in ascertaining the intentions of the parties involved, see *infra*. However, because the settlement of the grant occurred after the land was ceded to the United States, we conclude that Mexican law cannot be a source of the landowners' claims.

As evidence of a grant of rights from Carlos Beaubien, the landowners rely primarily on the Beaubien Document. The document was written by Beaubien in 1863, one year before his death.

One English translation of the document reads, in part:

> Plaza of San Luis de la Culebra, May 11, 1863.
>
> It has been decided that the lands of the Rito Seco remain uncultivated for the benefit of the community members (gente) of the plazas of San Luis, San Pablo and Los Ballejos and for the other inhabitants of these plazas. The vega, after the measurement of three acres from it in front of the chapel, to which they have been donated, will remain for the benefit of the inhabitants of this plaza and those of the Culebra as far as above the plaza of Los Ballejos. . . . Those below the road as far as the narrows will have the right to enjoy the same benefit. . . . [*No one may*] *place any obstacle or obstruction to anyone in the enjoyment of his legitimate rights*. . . . Likewise, each one should take scrupulous care in the use of water without causing damage with it to his neighbors nor to anyone. According to the corresponding rule, *all the inhabitants will have enjoyment of benefits of pastures, water, firewood and timber, always taking care that one does not injure another.*

(Emphases added.)

We agree that the Beaubien Document does not meet the formal requirements for an express grant of rights. However, we find that the document, when taken together with the other unique facts of this case, establishes a prescriptive easement, an easement by estoppel, and an easement from prior use.

A court can imply an easement created by estoppel when 1) the owner of the servient estate "permitted another to use that land under circumstances in which it was reasonable to foresee that the user would substantially change position believing that the permission would not be revoked," 2) the user substantially changed position in reasonable reliance on that belief, and 3) injustice can be avoided only by establishment of a servitude. Whether reliance is justified depends upon the nature of the transaction, including the sophistication of the parties.

An easement implied from prior use is created when 1) the servient and dominant estates were once under common ownership, 2) the rights alleged were exercised prior to the severance of the estate, 3) the use was not merely temporary, 4) the continuation of this use was reasonably necessary to the enjoyment of the parcel, and 5) a contrary intention is neither expressed nor implied. The rationale for this servitude is as follows:

> The rule stated in this section is not based solely on the presumed actual intent of the parties. It furthers the policy of protecting reasonable expectations, as well as actual intent, of parties to land transactions. Restatement, *supra*, §2.12 cmt. a.

[T]he court of appeals in this case rejected the land-owners' claims of an implied easement [finding] that, although easements in the form of access rights could be implied, easements in the form of profits could not. Although this court has not addressed implied profits for over thirty-five years, there is a modern trend to apply the same rules to easements of access and to profits.

The Restatement explains that, although some profits such as mineral and water rights have specific rules, generally as between easements in the form of access rights and easements in the form of profits, "there are no doctrinal differences between them." Restatement, *supra*, §1.2 reporter's note. Easements and profits are treated equally because the same public policy and practical considerations that underlie implied rights of access also underlie implied profits. A recognition that parties do not always comply with strict rules of express conveyance, a desire to effectuate the intent of the parties, and the aim of fairness apply equally to easements and profits.

i. Prescriptive Easement

Because Taylor's deed indicates that Taylor's ownership of the land is subject to the landowners' prescriptive rights, we begin with an application of the law of prescriptive easements. [The court found that the plaintiffs had established a prescriptive easement under the theory that a continuous use under an intended but ineffective grant is adverse. Easements by prescription are discussed more fully in Chapter 5, §3.]

ii. Easement by Estoppel

The landowners have . . . established every element of an easement by estoppel. First, Taylor's predecessors in title "permitted [the settlers] to use [the] land under circumstances in which it was reasonable to foresee that the [settlers] would substantially change position believing that the permission would not be revoked." *Restatement, supra*, §2.10. The settlers' reliance was reasonable because rights were expected, intended, and necessary. It was expected because of the Mexican settlement system discussed above. Also discussed above, this settlement system, combined with the actual practices and the deeds associated with the Taylor Ranch, show that rights were intended.

The rights were also necessary. The plaintiffs' expert, Dr. Marianne Stoller, testified that access to wood was necessary to heat homes, access to timber was necessary to build homes, and access to grazing was necessary for maintaining livestock.

The second element, that the user substantially change position in reasonable reliance on the belief, is easily found. The landowners' predecessors in title settled Beaubien's grant for him. They moved onto the land and established permanent farms.

The third element, the avoidance of injustice, is also undeniably present. The original Sangre de Cristo grant was given on the condition that it be settled. Indeed, under Mexican law, the grant would have been revoked if settlement did not succeed. The settlers, then, fulfilled the condition of the grant that made Beaubien fee owner of one million acres of land.

Beaubien attracted settlers to the area by convincing them that he would provide them with the rights they needed for survival. Beaubien knew that families would rely on his promises and leave their homes to travel hundreds of miles on foot or horseback to establish new homes.

A condition of the conveyance of Beaubien's land, from Gilpin down to Taylor, was that the owner honor these rights. Although these promised rights were exercised for over one hundred years, although these rights were necessary to the settlers' very existence, and although Taylor had ample notice of these rights, Taylor fenced his land over forty years ago. It is an understatement to say that this is an injustice.

The landowners have established each element of an easement by estoppel.

iii. *Easement from Prior Use*

Lastly, every element of an easement from prior use has been shown. First, both Taylor's and the landowners' lands were originally under the common ownership of Beaubien who owned the entire Sangre de Cristo grant before settlement.

Second, the rights were exercised prior to the severance of the estate. As discussed above, many of the rights the landowners claim were needed and expected for life in the San Luis Valley. This necessity existed from the first days of settlement—indicating that these rights were exercised prior to severance of title.

The third and fourth prongs—that the use was not merely temporary and is reasonably necessary to the enjoyment of the land—are also easily established. The trial court's findings of fact establish that the rights were exercised from the time of settlement until Taylor came on the scene. Moreover, as discussed above, the rights were reasonably necessary.

Lastly, no contrary intention is expressed or implied; thus, the fifth element is present. Custom, expectation, practice, and language in the documents and deeds surrounding the Taylor ranch property indicate not only that a contrary intention did not exist, but that the parties affirmatively intended for these rights to exist.

All five elements of an easement from prior use have been established.

C. *Extent of the Rights*

Having found that the landowners have implied profits in the Taylor Ranch, we now must address the scope of those rights. We imply the rights memorialized in the Beaubien Document. Accordingly, we hold that the landowners have implied rights in Taylor's land for the access detailed in the Beaubien Document—pasture, firewood, and timber. These easements should be limited to reasonable use—the grazing access is limited to a reasonable number of livestock given the size of the vara strips; the firewood limited to that needed for each residence; and the timber limited to that needed to construct and maintain residence and farm buildings located on the vara strips. We reject the landowners' claims for hunting, fishing, and recreation.

Justice Alex Martinez, dissenting only as to part II.C.

[T]his case involves the settlement rights of people who have been largely dispossessed of their rights in land when Taylor fenced the property. There is little dispute that the settlers enjoyed extensive rights in the lands that comprise the Taylor Ranch for about one hundred years. Rather, the dispute concerns the extent of the rights, if any, that survive when we construe settlement rights conceived in a different era pursuant to contemporary standards. In short, the difficulty of this case is that we must address the grave injustices imposed upon the settlers' successors in interest by interpreting documents from a different era, intended to reflect Beaubien's intent, through the perspective of modern property law. Nonetheless, equitable principles in our modern jurisprudence, properly construed and applied, permit us to recognize the rights of the settlers and their successors in interest.

I would apply the reasoning of the majority opinion . . . to conclude that the landowners have also established access rights for fishing, hunting, and recreation.

The trial court made strong findings that "[t]he plaintiffs' predecessors in title grazed cattle and sheep, harvested timber, gathered firewood, fished, hunted and recreated on the land of the defendant from the 1800s to the date the land was acquired by the defendant, in 1960." The trial court also found that, prior to 1960 when Taylor fenced the land, the landowners referred to that land as "open range" and that the landowners were "never denied access to the land for grazing of cattle, sheep, harvesting timber, gathering firewood, fishing, hunting, or recreating." My review of the record reveals that the trial court's findings of fact that fishing, hunting, and recreation were included in the settlement rights contemplated by the Beaubien document are correct.

Justice Rebecca Love Kourlis, dissenting.

Although I have great sympathy for the historic and present plight of the landowners in this action, I cannot support the majority opinion for two reasons. First, it is my view that in 1863 Charles Beaubien attempted to make a community grant for the benefit of the inhabitants of the plazas of San Luis, San Pablo, and Los Ballejos. The law in effect at the time did not recognize such a grant and instead required individual identification of grantees. Hence, the Beaubien Document had no legal effect.

There were two types of grants of land from the government [of Mexico]: private grants to individuals who would own the land and who could sell it after they met a requirement of establishing possession of the land; and community grants.[6]

In 1863, the year Charles Beaubien executed the Beaubien Document, under Colorado Territorial law, a document conveying any interest in real estate had to meet several formal requirements, including the requirements that it incorporate an accurate description of the property and the names of the grantees.

In 1863, the year Charles Beaubien executed the Beaubien Document, under Colorado Territorial law, a document conveying any interest in real estate had to meet several formal requirements, including the requirements that it incorporate an accurate description of the property and the names of the grantees:

> [T]he christian and surnames of the . . . grantees . . . and . . . an accurate description of the premises, or the interest in the premises intended to be conveyed, and shall be subscribed by the party or parties making the same, and be duly proved or acknowledged, before some officer authorized to take the proof or acknowledgment of deeds, or by his, her or their attorney in fact.

Territorial Laws of Colo., 1st Sess., An Act Concerning Conveyances of Real Estate, 64, 64, §2 (1861). The requirement that the document identify grantees by name is indicative of the territorial legislature's overt decision not to honor community grants that failed to mention specific grantees.

---

6. As one commentator notes, the themes found in the land tenure and law in Spain and Mexico are repeated in the southwestern United States in the nineteenth century: a tension between private land and communal land, and the importance of Spanish custom. Malcolm Ebright, Land Grants & Lawsuits in Northern New Mexico 21 (1994).

The Beaubien Document flatly fails to meet that requirement. The Beaubien Document does not give the christian and surnames of the grantees, instead only referring generally to the "community members" and "inhabitants" of specified villages.

[T]he Beaubien Document, like every other real property transfer, must be held to the standards of the law in effect at the time it was executed in order to protect the certainty and marketability of property interests. The Document does not comport with those laws, and it, therefore, has no validity as to the landowners here.

The Document intended to create a grant to the members of a community: such a grant was in contravention of the applicable statutes and was, therefore, invalid.

I would also decline to apply principles of easement by estoppel, because there is no showing here of misrepresentation or concealment of material facts by Beaubien or any of his successors in interest. . . . There has been no showing in this case that Beaubien or Gilpin either misrepresented material facts or intended the landowners to rely to their detriment upon a parol agreement. Indeed, to my knowledge, the only context in which such a doctrine has been applied to the acquisition of easements has involved ditches and ditch rights, an area in which rights are so firmly entrenched as to be included within the Colorado Constitution.

Notes and Questions

1. **Background and aftermath.** *Lobato v. Taylor* illustrates the power of running with the land. Here, rights allegedly acquired in the 1800s are found to pass down through several owners of the servient estate, the Mountain Tract and generations of owners of the dominant estate, the Costilla County residents, to still exist in 2002. The immediate conflict leading to *Lobato v. Taylor* began in 1960, when a North Carolina lumberman, Jack Taylor, purchased the 77,000-acre Mountain Tract for what he considered the bargain price of $500,000. Although the sellers warned him of the practices of the Costilla County residents, he enclosed it in barbed wire, hired guards to patrol the area, and confiscated rifles and other equipment from those he found on the land. Taylor also immediately filed a lawsuit seeking a judicial declaration that he had title to the land free from any other claims. Relying on diversity jurisdiction, he filed the action in federal district court some 200 miles away from the county. The federal court found for Taylor, holding that any rights that the county residents might have had under Mexican law were extinguished. *Sanchez v. Taylor*, 377 F.2d 733 (10th Cir. 1967).

ELEMENTS OF EASEMENTS BY ESTOPPEL

1. Permission from the owner to use the land;
2. Foreseeable and reasonable reliance on continuation of the permission;
3. Changed position by the claimant (usually through significant expenditures) in reliance on continuation; and
4. Finding an easement is necessary to prevent injustice.

The dispute continued, fueled in part by resentment of Taylor's "attitude," evidenced by television interviews in which Taylor dismissed the Latino county residents' opposition as the result of "an inferiority complex. They know they're not equal, mentally or physically to a white man, and that's why they stick together so." Calvin Trillin, *U.S. Journal, Costilla County: A Little Cloud on the Title*, The New Yorker 122, 128, Apr. 26, 1976. The federal judgment would usually have barred the later state action, but the Colorado Supreme Court found that Taylor failed to provide the Costilla residents with adequate notice, as he had served them only by publication of the federal action. *Lobato v. Taylor*, 70 P.3d 1152 (Colo. 2003). After remand, the Colorado Supreme Court held that the easement rights belonged to any resident who could trace title to the land of the original settlers under Beaubien.

2. **Communal land grants.** Although the majority holds that the Beaubien Grant was not legally effective in itself, it relies on the grant in finding that the plaintiffs had easements by estoppel. Justice Kourlis argues in dissent that the grant did not simply fail to comply with formalities; instead, it attempted to create a communal property right, something recognized under Mexican law but deliberately prohibited by the new Colorado Territory. Why might Colorado have forbidden the communal land grant system? If Justice Kourlis was correct that the territory did forbid communal land grants, what effect should that have on the recognition of informally created easements today?

3. **Easements by estoppel.** Easements by estoppel may be found in three different kinds of circumstances. Some courts may apply the doctrine to only some of these circumstances; some may even reject the doctrine entirely, rigidly enforcing the Statute of Frauds in this context. *See Kitchen v. Kitchen*, 641 N.W.2d 245 (Mich. 2002).

a. **Noncompliance with the Statute of Frauds.** In the first circumstance, the parties intended to create an easement but failed to comply with the requisite formalities, such as a writing, seal, or adequate description of the property. If the claimant substantially invested in reasonable reliance on the agreement, courts may find an easement by estoppel. *Restatement (Third)* §2.09; *see, e.g., Kluger v. Kubick*, 954 A.2d 262 (Conn. App. 2008) (plaintiff and defendant walked property line and agreed on location of new driveway before defendant built driveway running over plaintiff's property). This is consistent with the general equitable exception to the Statute of Frauds. In the absence of a writing, however, it is often difficult to determine whether the parties intended to create a permanent easement or a temporary license, so cases often turn on one of the other grounds for estoppel.

b. **Reasonable reliance on continuation of consent.** Courts also sometimes find estoppel even in the absence of proof of the grantor's intent to create an easement when "the owner or occupier permitted another to use that land under circumstances in which it was reasonable to foresee that the user would substantially change position believing that the permission would not be revoked, and the user did substantially change position in reasonable reliance on that belief." *Restatement (Third)* §2.10(1). The permission may either be express or implicit from acquiescence in the continued use.

In *Holbrook v. Taylor*, 532 S.W.2d 763 (Ky. 1976), for example, the alleged easement, an old mine road, was the only existing road to the appellees' property. The appellees re-graded the road, transported construction materials along it, and built their home in reliance on permission to use the road. Although there was no proof of express consent by the owner of the servient estate, the court found that an irrevocable easement by estoppel had been created. *Id.*; *see also Cleaver v. Kundiff*, 203 S.W.3d 373 (Tex. App. 2006) (finding "the jury could reasonably infer that the Armstrongs would not have built their house without some reliable means of access and would not have expended time and money maintaining a road over which they had no claim"). In contrast, the Maine Supreme Court found that a claimant simply had a temporary license to allow transportation of construction materials, even though the claimant paid to pave the turnaround, and building a driveway to the public road over the claimant's own property would be very difficult. *Woods v. Libby*, 635 A.2d 960 (Me. 1993).

c. **Fraud or misrepresentation.** Some courts will only find an easement by estoppel when there has been fraud or misrepresentation about the existence of or intent to grant an easement. *See Flaig v. Gramm*, 983 P.2d 396 (Mont. 1999) (no easement by estoppel where parties jointly invested in building and maintaining well based upon mistaken belief that it was on their common boundary); *Jones v. Stamper*, 297 S.W.3d 73, 77 (Ky. App. 2009) (no easement by estoppel after landowner's death although neighbors paid landowner $500 for agreement that they could access the highway over his land and then paid to construct a road over the land). This was the position Justice Kourlis advocated in dissent in *Lobato v. Taylor.* Even in jurisdictions where fraud is not a necessary element of the claim, fraud plus investment in reliance on the fraud is an alternate ground for finding an easement by estoppel. *See Restatement (Third)* §2.10(2).

Other courts find that letting an individual substantially invest in reliance on a reasonable belief that the permission to enter the land will be permanent is itself a kind of fraud. In *Stoner v. Zucker*, 83 P. 808 (Cal. 1906), for example, plaintiff granted defendant a revocable license to enter plaintiff's property to construct a ditch for carrying water. Defendant constructed the ditch at the expense of $7,000 (about $180,000 in today's dollars). The court found that "it would countenance a fraud to allow the plaintiff to revoke permission to use the ditch." *Id.* at 809-810. In contrast, *Harber v. Jensen*, 97 P.3d 57 (Wyo. 2004), held that expenditures in reliance on unwritten permission extending over 70 years was not evidence of fraud where the owners (the children of the original licensees) did not seek express permission and the defendants did not know that the expenditures were being made. Can you distinguish these cases?

4. **Constructive trust.** Rights to use land titled in another may also be created through a constructive trust. An express trust is an arrangement in which one person or entity, the **trustee**, has title to some property for the express benefit of another, the **beneficiary**. A constructive trust, in contrast, is an equitable exception to the Statute of Frauds. It may be found when "legal title to property has been obtained through actual fraud, misrepresentations, concealments, taking advantage of one's necessities, or under circumstances otherwise rendering it unconscionable for the holder of legal title to retain beneficial interest in property." *Snider v. Arnold*, 289 P.3d 43 (Idaho 2012) (finding constructive trust on cabin permitted in brother's name in favor of sister); *Goggin v. Goggin*, 267 P.3d 885, 892 (Utah 2011) (imposing constructive trust on horse farm titled in ex-husband's name that ex-wife had helped to develop under understanding of partnership). In *Rase v. Castle Mountain Ranch, Inc.*, 631 P.2d 680 (Mont. 1981), for example, the court imposed a constructive trust in favor of individuals who

had built cabins and summer cottages and used them for over 50 years with the written license from the ranch owner, who wanted company and extra security but did not want to sell title to the land because of concerns about water rights. When the ranch was sold, the purchaser asked the rancher to terminate the licenses, and he refused. The new owner then immediately notified the cabin owners that their licenses were terminated. The court found that the new owner, given its knowledge of the semi-permanent nature of the cabin owner's license, engaged in fraud in buying the land then terminating the cabin owner's rights. It imposed a constructive trust on the land in favor of the cabin owners, but only for 15 years after the sale.

Problem

In 1860, Peter Feeley purchased a family burial plot in Mount Auburn Cemetery in Cambridge, Massachusetts. Under existing law, the purchase of a burial plot in a cemetery owned by another was an easement for burial of one's dead. The purchase agreement was not impressed with a seal, which was necessary to create a formal easement under the Statute of Frauds at the time. Peter Feeley buried a child in the plot in 1860, and his wife there in 1898. After Mr. Feeley's death in 1904, the superintendent of the cemetery opened Mrs. Feeley's grave to ascertain who was in there, and then, finding that the grave was not deep enough to bury Mr. Feeley as well, "flattened down" Mrs. Feeley's casket and bones to make room. The Feeleys' surviving children learned about this after they found a plate that the superintendent had removed from their mother's grave and left lying on the ground. They brought a trespass action against the superintendent of the cemetery. Because licenses cannot give rise to an action for trespass and cannot usually be inherited, to succeed they had to show that Mr. Feeley had a burial easement in the plot. What exceptions to the Statute of Frauds for easements could they assert? Should they succeed? (Facts, but not solution, taken from *Feeley v. Andrews*, 77 N.E. 766 (Mass. 1906).)

B. Easements Implied from Prior Use

Granite Properties Limited Partnership v. Manns

512 N.E.2d 1230 (Ill. 1987)

Map: Area between Rou des Chateaux & S. Prairie Street & E. Bethalto Drive, Bethalto, Illinois

Justice Howard C. Ryan delivered the opinion of the court:

The plaintiff, Granite Properties Limited Partnership, brought this suit in the circuit court of Madison County, seeking to permanently enjoin the defendants, Larry and Ann Manns, from interfering with the plaintiff's use and enjoyment of two claimed easements over driveways which exist on the defendants' property. One driveway provides ingress to and egress from an apartment complex and the other to a shopping center. Both the apartment complex and the shopping center are situated on the plaintiff's property.

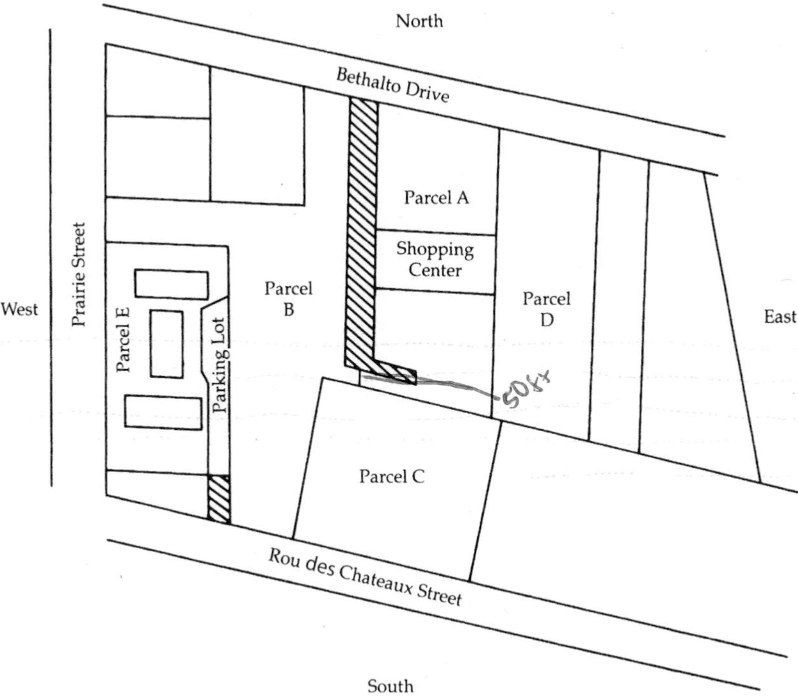

As indicated [in the map above] the parcels which are the subject of this appeal are adjoining tracts located to the south of Bethalto Drive and to the north of Rou des Chateaux Street in Bethalto, Illinois. The plaintiff and its predecessors in title owned all of the subject properties from 1963 or 1964 until 1982, at which time the parcel labeled "B" was conveyed by warranty deed to the defendants. The plaintiff currently owns the parcels labeled "A" and "E," which are on the opposite sides of parcel B. The shopping center situated on the parcel designated "A" extends from lot line to lot line across the east-west dimension of that property. To the north of the shopping center is an asphalt parking lot with approximately 191 feet of frontage on Bethalto Drive. To the east of the shopping center on the parcel labeled "D" is a separately owned health club. To the south of parcel A on the parcel denominated "C" are five four-family apartment buildings. The distance between the back of the shopping center and the property line of parcel C is 50 feet. The shopping center's underground utility facilities are located in this area. An apartment complex, known as the Chateau des Fleurs Apartments, is located on the parcel labeled "E." Both of the plaintiff's properties were developed prior to the time parcel B was sold to the defendants. Parcel B remains undeveloped.

The first claimed easement provides access to the rear of the shopping center which is located on parcel A. The center, which was built in 1967, contains several businesses, including a grocery store, a pharmacy, and doctors' offices. The rear of the center is used for deliveries, trash storage and removal, and utilities repair. To gain access to the rear of the shopping center for these purposes, trucks use a gravel driveway which runs along the lot line between parcel A and parcel B. A second driveway, located to the east of the shopping center on parcel D, enables the trucks to circle the shopping center without having to turn around in the limited space behind the stores.

Robert Mehann, the owner of the Save-A-Lot grocery store located in the shopping center, testified on direct examination that groceries, which are delivered to the rear of the store, are loaded by forklift on a concrete pad poured for that purpose. Mehann indicated that there are large, double steel doors in the back of the store to accommodate items which will not fit through the front door. Mehann testified that semitrailer trucks make deliveries to the rear of the grocery store four days a week, with as many as two or three such trucks arriving daily. An average of 10 to 12 trucks a day, including semitrailer trucks, make deliveries to the grocery store. Mehann further explained on direct examination that because the area behind the Save-A-Lot building extends only 50 feet to the rear property line, it would be difficult, if not impossible, for a semitrailer truck to turn around in the back and exit the same way it came in. In response to a question as to whether it would be feasible to have trucks make front-door deliveries, Mehann suggested that such deliveries would be very disruptive; pallets that would not fit through the front door would have to be broken down into parts, requiring extra work, and there would not be adequate space in the front of the store to do such work during business hours. Mehann admitted on cross-examination that he had not investigated the cost of installing a front door which would be big enough for pallets of groceries to be brought in by forklift. Further cross-examination revealed that there would not be enough space to manipulate the forklift around the front of the store, although it could be run between the shelves of food to the back of the store.

Also called as a witness for Granite Properties Limited Partnership was Darrell Layman, a limited partner. Layman noted that the shopping center had been in continuous operation since 1967 and that the pattern for deliveries had always been to the rear of the individual stores. When asked whether he had "ever seen a semi back up in the rear of the shopping center and go out the way it came in," Layman responded, "That would be impossible." On cross-examination, however, Layman admitted that, although it was very difficult, he had seen semitrailer trucks exit the same way they came in. Layman also acknowledged on cross-examination that he had not investigated the cost of expanding the size of the front doors of the building. He also claimed that it "would seem impossible" to him to put in any kind of a hallway or passageway which would allow equipment to bring supplies into the stores from the front. On redirect examination, Layman explained that the delivery trucks follow no set schedule and, therefore, their presence may overlap at times. He stated that he had seen as many as four or five delivery trucks backed up. Layman opined that there was "no way" the trucks could back up and turn around when there were multiple trucks present.

The other claimed easement concerns ingress and egress over a driveway which leads into the parking area of the apartment complex situated on parcel E. The complex, which was erected in the 1960s prior to the conveyance of parcel B to the defendants, consists of three buildings containing 36 units. The parking lot, which is situated to the rear of the buildings, provides 72 parking spaces. The only access to the parking lot is by a driveway from Rou des Chateaux, a public street located to the south of the properties. The driveway, which cuts across a small panhandle on the southwestern corner of parcel B, has been in existence since the apartment complex was constructed. The terrain around the apartment complex is flat, including the area in front of the buildings along Prairie Street to the west.

Limited partner Darrell Layman testified at trial that if the area in front of the apartment complex, measuring 300 feet along Prairie Street and 30 feet deep, were to be converted into a parking lot, then there would be room for only 30 parking spaces. He admitted on direct examination that he had not investigated the cost of rocking or asphalting this area for that purpose. Although there was a distance of 20 feet between the apartment buildings, Layman opined that it would not be enough "usable space" to accommodate a driveway from Prairie Street to the existing parking lot because such driveway would interfere with stairways which lead to the basement apartments. Although he admitted that he did not investigate the cost of installing a driveway either between the buildings or adjacent to the end building on the north, Layman concluded that, based on his experience in the layout and design of apartment buildings, "it would be a dangerous situation" for the tenants of the apartments if a driveway were to be run between the buildings or next to their sides. Layman concluded his testimony by claiming that the plaintiff was unaware of any easement problems as to the driveways in question at the time parcel B was deeded to the defendants; otherwise, he asserted, "it would not have been deeded."

The defendant, Larry Manns, stated that he purchased parcel B from the plaintiff in the summer of 1982. Shortly afterwards, he had a survey made of the property. The survey indicated possible encroachments by the plaintiff as to the driveways in question. Finding no recorded easements following a title search, Manns stated that he notified the plaintiff to discontinue its use of the driveways. On cross-examination, Manns admitted that he saw the two driveways before he bought the subject property.

The plaintiff contends in this court that it acquired, by implied reservation, easements over the driveways which provide access to the rear of the shopping center located on parcel A and to the parking lot of the apartment complex situated on parcel E. Plaintiff alleges that parcels A, B and E were held in common ownership by the plaintiff and its predecessors in title until 1982, at which time the defendants received a warranty deed to parcel B, that the driveways in question were apparent and obvious, permanent, and subject to continuous, uninterrupted, and actual use by the plaintiff and its predecessors in title until the time of severance of unity of ownership, and that the driveways are highly convenient and reasonably necessary for the beneficial use and enjoyment of the shopping center and the apartment complex. Therefore, the plaintiff maintains that, upon severance of unity of title, the defendants took parcel B subject to the servitudes then existing, as the parties are presumed to convey with reference to the existing conditions of the property.

On the merits, the crucial issue is whether, in conveying that portion of its property now owned by the defendants (parcel B), the plaintiff retained easements by implication over the driveways in question.

There are two types of implied easements—the easement by necessity and the easement implied from a preexisting use. The easement by necessity usually arises when an owner of land conveys to another an inner portion thereof, which is entirely surrounded by lands owned either by the grantor or the grantor plus strangers. Unless a contrary intent is manifested, the grantee is found to have a right-of-way across the retained land of the grantor for ingress to, and egress from, the landlocked parcel. Similarly, an easement is implied by way of necessity in the deed when the owner of lands retains the inner portion, conveying to another the balance.

The easement implied from a prior existing use, often characterized as a "quasi-easement," arises when an owner of an entire tract of land or of two or more adjoining parcels, after employing a part thereof so that one part of the tract or one parcel derives from another a benefit or advantage of an apparent, continuous, and permanent nature, conveys or transfers part of the property without mention being made of these incidental uses. In the absence of an expressed agreement to the contrary, the conveyance or transfer imparts a grant of property with all the benefits and burdens which existed at the time of the conveyance of the transfer, even though such grant is not reserved or specified in the deed. This court has stated on numerous occasions that an easement implied from a preexisting use is established by proof of three elements: first, common ownership of the claimed dominant and servient parcels and a subsequent conveyance or transfer separating that ownership; second, before the conveyance or transfer severing the unity of title, the common owner used part of the united parcel for the benefit of another part, and this use was apparent and obvious, continuous, and permanent; and third, the claimed easement is necessary and beneficial to the enjoyment of the parcel conveyed or retained by the grantor or transferor.

As the above discussion indicates, easements created by implication arise as an inference of the intention of the parties to a conveyance of land. This inference, which is drawn from the circumstances surrounding the conveyance alone, represents an attempt to ascribe an intention to parties who had not thought or had not bothered to put the intention into words, or to parties who actually had formed no intention conscious to themselves. To fill these common gaps resulting in incomplete thought, courts find particular facts suggestive of intent on the part of the parties to a conveyance. In the case of an easement implied from a preexisting use, proof of the prior use is evidence that the parties probably intended an easement, on the presumption that the grantor and the grantee would have intended to continue an important or necessary use of the land known to them that was apparently continuous and permanent in its nature. Where an easement by necessity is claimed, however, there is no requirement of proof of a known existing use from which to draw the inference of intention. This leaves proof of necessity alone to furnish the probable inference of intention, on the presumption that the grantor and the grantee do not intend to render the land unfit for occupancy.

This essentially is the position taken by the *Restatement of Property* §474 (1944). The *Restatement* operates on the basis of eight "important circumstances" from which the inference of intention [to create or reserve an easement] may be drawn: whether the claimant is the conveyor or the conveyee; the terms of the conveyance; the consideration given for it; whether the claim is made against a simultaneous conveyee; the extent of necessity of the easement to the claimant; whether reciprocal benefits result to the conveyor and the conveyee; the manner in which the land was used prior to its conveyance; and the extent to which the manner of prior use was or might have been known to the parties. *Restatement of Property* §476 (1944). These eight factors vary in their importance and relevance according to whether the claimed easement originates out of necessity or for another reason.

In applying the *Restatement*'s eight important circumstances to the present case, the fact that the driveways in question had been used by the plaintiff or its predecessors in title since the 1960s, when the respective properties were developed, that the driveways were permanent in character, being either rock or gravel covered, and that the defendants were aware of the driveways' prior uses before they purchased parcel B would tend to support an inference that the parties intended easements upon severance of the parcels in question. Although the prior uses which the plaintiff seeks to continue existed during the common ownership of the parcels in question, under circumstances where the defendants were fully informed by physical appearance of their existence, the defendants, nevertheless, argue that there are two factors which overwhelmingly detract from the implication of an easement: that the claimant is the conveyor and that the claimed easement can hardly be described as "necessary" to the beneficial use of the plaintiff's properties. Relying on the principle that a grantor should not be permitted to derogate from his own grant, the defendants urge this court to refuse to imply an easement in favor of a grantor unless the claimed easement is absolutely necessary to the beneficial use and enjoyment of the land retained by the grantor. The defendants further urge this court not to cast an unreasonable burden over their land through imposition of easements by implication where, as here, available alternatives affording reasonable means of ingress to and egress from the shopping center and the apartment complex allegedly exist.

While the degree of necessity required to reserve an easement by implication in favor of the conveyor is greater than that required in the case of the conveyee, even in the case of the conveyor, the implication from necessity will be aided by a previous use made apparent by the physical adaptation of the premises to it. Moreover, the necessity requirement will have a different meaning and significance in the case involving proof of prior use than it will in a case in which necessity alone supports the implication; otherwise, proof of prior use would be unnecessary. Thus, when circumstances such as an apparent prior use of the land support the inference of the parties' intention, the required extent of the claimed easement's necessity will be less than when necessity is the only circumstance from which the inference of intention will be drawn. While some showing of necessity for the continuance of the use must be shown where a prior use has been made, to the extent that the prior use strengthens the implication, the degree or extent of necessity requisite for implication is reduced. As one treatise concludes:

> If a previous use is continuous and apparent, an easement may be created by implication even though the need for the use to be made is not sufficiently great to meet the

> test of necessity as applied in the absence of such a previous use. Hence, the test is phrased in terms of *reasonable necessity* rather than in terms of unqualified necessity. A use is necessary, it is often said, when without it no effective use could be made of the land to be benefited by it. *Where, because of a continuous and apparent previous use, the test of necessity becomes that of reasonable necessity, it is said that a use is reasonably necessary when it is reasonably convenient to the use of the land benefited.* In fact, however, reasonable necessity too is a flexible test. *The more pronounced a continuous and apparent use is, the less the degree of convenience of use necessary to the creation of an easement by implication.* (Emphasis added.) 2 *American Law of Property* §8.43 (A.J. Casner ed. 1952).

Professor Powell . . . suggests that in a case with proof of prior use, the word "necessity" should be replaced by the phrase "important to the enjoyment of the conveyed quasi-dominant [or quasi-servient] parcel." 3 R. Powell, *The Law of Real Property* §411[2] (P. Rohan ed. 1987).

[T]he authorities agree that the degree or extent of necessity required to create an easement by implication differs in both meaning and significance depending on the existence of proof of prior use. Hence, given the strong evidence of the plaintiff's prior use of the driveways in question and the defendants' knowledge thereof, we must agree with the appellate court majority that the evidence in this case was sufficient to fulfill the elastic necessity requirement.

For the above reasons, the judgment of the appellate court is affirmed.

Notes and Questions

1. **Easements implied from prior use**, also called **quasi-easements** or **easements by implication**, permit a use to continue after severance of one parcel into two if the prior use was apparent before severance, and reasonably necessary or convenient for the enjoyment of the severed estate. *Stansbury v. MDR Development, L.L.C.*, 871 A.2d 612 (Md. 2005); *see Restatement (Third)* §2.12. The *Restatement (Third)* also provides that a use for underground utility or sewer lines may qualify for an easement by implication even when it is not visible to the parties. *Id.*; *see Villancourt v. Motta*, 986 A.2d 985 (R.I. 2009) (finding easement by implication for sewer lines under neighboring condominium). The general test is whether the parties had reason to expect that the use would continue despite severance of the parcel. In *Lobato v. Taylor*, the court finds an easement implied by prior use because the use for timber and grazing was necessary to support oneself on the land, so that when Carlos Beaubien divided the land into vara strips, Beaubien would already have been relying on the land for these purposes, and the settlers had reason to expect that the use would not terminate. As the attorney for Taylor, how could you challenge this finding?

ELEMENTS OF EASEMENTS IMPLIED FROM PRIOR USE

1. Two parcels were previously owned by a common grantor;
2. One parcel was previously used for the benefit of the other parcel in a manner that was apparent and continuous; and
3. The use is "reasonably necessary" or "convenient" for enjoyment of the dominant estate.

2. "Reasonably necessary" use. What kinds of uses are sufficiently "necessary" to continue after severance as an easement by implication from prior use? Most easements by implication are rights of way for the passage of people or vehicles to get to the property. But easements implied by prior use have also been found to give subdivision residents access to an artificial lake created by the developer, *Russakoff v. Scruggs*, 400 S.E.2d 529 (Va. 1991), to create direct access from the thirteenth to the fourteenth hole of a golf course, *Williams Island Country Club, Inc. v. San Simeon at the California Club, Ltd.*, 454 So. 2d 23 (Fla. App. 1984), and to give subdivision residents access to a boat ramp, *Polhemus v. Cobb*, 653 So. 2d 964 (Ala. 1995). The question is often whether the use is sufficiently apparent and significant to enjoyment of the property that the parties likely believed it was part of their bargain.

C. Easements by Necessity

Finn v. Williams

33 N.E.2d 226 (Ill. 1941)

FRANCIS S. WILSON, Justice.

February 16, 1895, Charles H. Williams owned a tract of land in Salisburg township, in Sangamon county, consisting of approximately 140 acres. On the day named, Williams conveyed 39.47 acres to Thomas J. Bacon. In 1937, the plaintiffs, Eugene E. Finn and Curtis Estallar Finn, acquired the title to this tract. The defendant, Zilphia Jane Williams, inherited the remaining 100 acres. By their complaint filed in the circuit court of Sangamon county, plaintiffs charge that the nearest and only available means of egress from and ingress to their land to a highway and to any market for their livestock and crops is by means of a right of way over defendant's tract immediately to the north; that their tract is not located or situated on any public highway and is entirely surrounded by land of strangers and the defendant's tract; that prior to and during all the time the 40 acres and the 100 acres constituted one tract and were owned by defendant's husband, the only means of ingress and egress to and from the single tract to a highway was by right of way in a northerly direction through a third tract of land north and adjacent to the present tract of defendant, and that this open road is still used by defendant as her only means of egress and ingress from and to the highway. The relief sought was the declaration of a right of way easement of necessity from the north line of plaintiffs' tract through the defendant's tract, to the beginning of the right of way road through the third tract mentioned. Answering, the defendant admitted that plaintiffs' land is not located or situated on any public highway but averred that since its severance from her land it is and has been located on a private road leading to the south to a public highway. This averment, plaintiffs denied.

Private permissive ways of ingress and egress over the land of strangers both to the east and to the south have been available to the successive owners, including plaintiffs, of the 40-acre tract since its severance from the 100-acre tract of the defendant in

1895, but each of the private ways over the lands of the adjoining strangers has been closed and, as defendant concedes, these permissive means of ingress and egress do not now exist. Two witnesses for defendant who had lived near the property in controversy for about sixty years testified to roads leading to the south and to the east from the 40-acre tract over the land of strangers. These roads were private roads over the property of strangers, and are now closed. Nathan Woodrum, defendant's son-in-law, testified that he had until recently lived on the 100-acre tract, and that a road through defendant's land connects with the road through the tract at the north, and that the road through this third tract is the only mode of access to the highway unless permission be obtained to go through the land of strangers. Since May, 1939, defendant has refused to permit plaintiff to travel further over the right of way through her tract. As a result of defendant's action, the plaintiffs have been unable to take their livestock and farm products to market, have had no means of egress from or ingress to their 40 acres on which they live, and have had to walk to the township highway, a distance of about three-quarters of a mile carrying such produce as they could.

Quick Review:
Between 1895 and 1939, the plaintiffs and their predecessors had accessed the road via other surrounding land. Could they claim an easement by prescription over the land? Why didn't they claim an easement by necessity over that land?

The evidence does not sustain defendant's averment that plaintiffs have the use of a private road leading to the south to a public highway and defendant, by her concession that a present necessity exists, has apparently abandoned this claim. She maintains, however, that the necessity has arisen by reason of changed circumstances since the severance of the two tracts. Firmly established principles control. Where an owner of land conveys a parcel thereof which has no outlet to a highway except over the remaining lands of the grantor or over the land of strangers, a way by necessity exists over the remaining lands of the grantor. If, at one time, there has been unity of title, as here, the right to a way by necessity may lay dormant through several transfers of title and yet pass with each transfer as appurtenant to the dominant estate and be exercised at any time by the holder of the title thereto. Plaintiffs' land is entirely surrounded by property of strangers and the land of the defendant from which it was originally severed. A right of way easement of necessity was necessarily implied in the conveyance severing the two tracts in 1895, and passed by *mesne* conveyances to plaintiffs in 1937. The fact that the original grantee and his successors in interest have been permitted ingress to and egress from the 40 acres over the land owned by surrounding strangers is immaterial. When such permission is denied, as in the present case, the subsequent grantees may avail themselves of the dormant easement implied in the deed severing the dominant and servient estates.

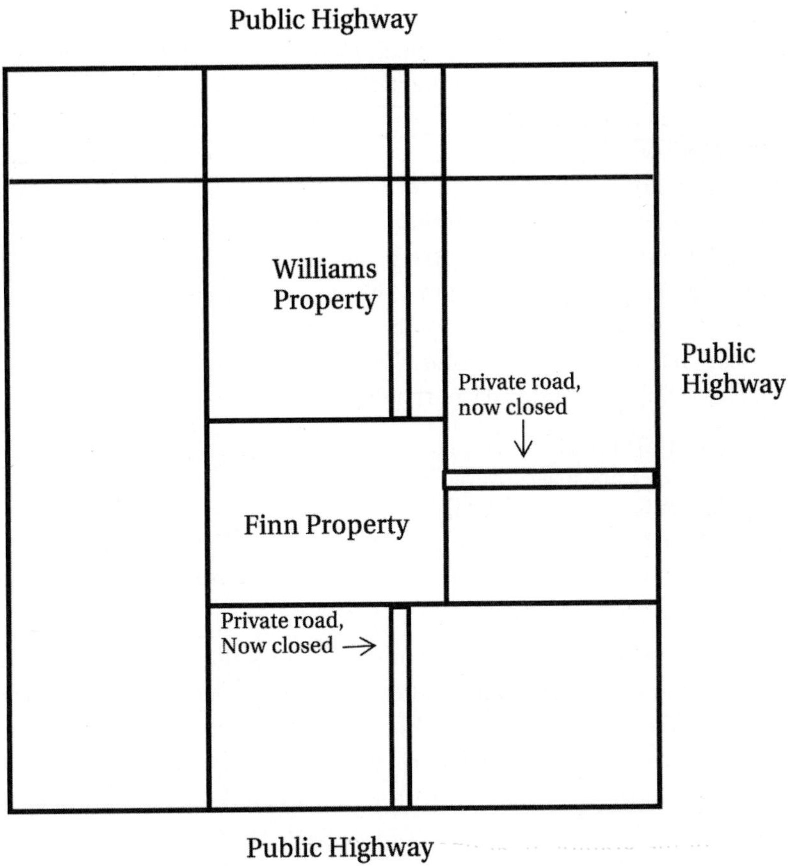

Public Highway

Williams Property

Private road, now closed

Public Highway

Finn Property

Private road, Now closed

Public Highway

Notes and Questions

> ***ELEMENTS FOR EASEMENTS BY NECESSITY***
>
> 1. The dominant and servient estates were formerly one parcel; and
> 2. At the time of severance the dominant estate became landlocked.

1. **Easements by necessity.** The policies underlying the doctrine of easement by necessity are (a) to effectuate the intent of the parties and (b) to promote the efficient utilization of property. Sometimes these policies go together. Ordinarily, we can expect buyers not to agree to buy landlocked property unless they have guaranteed access to it by an easement over neighboring land. Thus granting a right of access both promotes land utilization and the intent of the parties. As the Idaho Supreme Court explained in *Burley Brick and Sand Company v. Cofer*, 629 P.2d 1166, 1168 (Idaho 1981):

> A way of necessity is an easement arising from an implied grant or implied reservation; it is of common-law origin and is supported by the rule of sound public policy that lands should not be rendered unfit for occupancy or successful cultivation. Such a way is the result of the application of the presumption that whenever a party conveys property, he conveys whatever is necessary for the beneficial use of that property and retains whatever is necessary for the beneficial use of land he still possesses. Thus, the legal basis of a way of necessity is the presumption of a grant arising from the circumstances of the case.

Courts split, however, on what to do when these policies conflict. Many courts (perhaps most courts today) hold that the ultimate purpose of the rule is to effectuate the intent of the grantor. Thus no easement of necessity will be recognized if it is clear that the grantor intended to sell, and the grantee knew she was buying, a landlocked parcel. The *Restatement (Third)* takes this view. *Restatement (Third) of Property (Servitudes)* §2.15 (2000); *see also Murphy v. Burch*, 205 P.3d 289 (Cal. 2009) (no easement by necessity implied in favor of government when facts suggested it did not intend to create one); *Yellowstone River, LLC v. Meriwether Land Fund, LLC*, 264 P.3d 1065, 1079 (Mont. 2011) (public policy justification only supports easement by necessity where intent to create one can be inferred from the circumstances).

In contrast, in *Frederick v. Consolidated Waste Services, Inc.*, 573 A.2d 387, 389 (Me. 1990), the Maine Supreme Judicial Court held that

> An easement created by strict necessity [arises] when a grantor conveys a lot of land from a larger parcel, and that conveyed lot is "landlocked" by the grantor's surrounding land and cannot be accessed by a road or highway. Because of the strict necessity of having access to the landlocked parcel, an easement over the grantor's remaining land benefitting the landlocked lot is implied as a matter of law irrespective of the true intent of the common grantor.

573 A.2d at 389. The Vermont Supreme Court similarly held in *Traders, Inc. v. Bartholomew*, 459 A.2d 974, 978 (Vt. 1983), that easements by necessity "often thwart[] the intent of the original grantor or grantee," because "the demands of our society prevent any man-made efforts to hold land in perpetual idleness as would result if it were cut off from all access by being completely surrounded by lands privately owned." *Accord, Swan v. Hill*, 855 So. 2d 459, 464 (Miss. Ct. App. 2003) ("The concern of the court is only whether alternative routes exist.").

Which approach is better? Should an easement by necessity be granted to the buyer to prevent the buyer's land from becoming landlocked when it is clear that the grantor did not intend to grant such an easement over the grantor's retained land? What arguments can you make on both sides of this question?

2. Statutory regulation of landlocked parcels. Some states have enacted statutes empowering the owner of a landlocked parcel to obtain an easement over neighboring land for access to a public road by application to a public official and payment of compensation to the landowner whose property is burdened by the easement. Washington State's statute reads as follows:

> An owner . . . of land which is so situated with respect to the land of another that it is necessary for its proper use and enjoyment to have and maintain a private way of necessity . . . across, over or through the land of such other, . . . may condemn and take lands of such other sufficient in area for the construction and maintenance of such private way of necessity.

Wash. Rev. Code §8.24.010; *see also* Ala. Code §18-3-20; Ark. Stat. §27-66-401; Mass. Gen. Laws ch. 82, §24; Miss. Code §65-7-205; Or. Rev. Stat. §376.180. Recently, such statutes have faced challenges that they are unconstitutional on the grounds that they permit taking of property for private purposes rather than public use. *See In re Opening a Private Road ex rel. O'Reilly*, 5 A.3d 246 (Pa. 2010) (remanding to determine whether application for condemnation of private road to provide access from landlocked land served a public purpose sufficient to sustain its constitutionality); *Tolksdorf v. Griffith*, 626 N.W.2d 163 (Mich. 2001) (private roads act unconstitutional taking of property for a "predominantly private purpose" when it allowed owner to get access to landlocked parcel by buying easement over neighboring land).

Problems

1. Adam owns property bordered to the east by a river, to the west and north by private property, and to the south by a public road. Along the river is a one-lane public street. Adam divides the property into northern and southern parcels, selling the northern parcel to Barbara. After some years, increasingly violent storms begin causing regular flooding and destruction of the one-lane street. The government decides to stop maintaining and rebuilding it, and soon the street is no more. Barbara's parcel is now landlocked. Can she assert an easement by necessity over Adam's land?

2. The doctrine of easement by necessity applies when land has no access to a public road. Should it apply when property is physically located along a public road but the cost of creating useable access to that road is prohibitively expensive? *Compare Schwab v. Timmons*, 589 N.W.2d 1 (Wis. 1999) (no easement by necessity granted merely because the cost of building a road over a bluff to a public road was $700,000); *Harkness v. Butterworth Hunting Club*, 58 So. 3d 703 (Miss. Ct. App. 2011) (no easement by necessity where alternative access was available by building a road over several deep ravines) *abrogating Mississippi Power Co. v. Fairchild*, 791 So. 2d 262 (Miss. Ct. App. 2001) (power company entitled to easement by necessity if the only access to a public road was over a river because the cost of bridge construction would be prohibitive) *with Thompson v. Whinnery*, 895 P.2d 537 (Colo. 1995) ("great necessity" rather than absolute necessity, was the standard in Colorado, but standard was not met when part of parcel across canyon used for recreational and grazing purposes could be accessed by horseback).

3. Relatedly, what if the only access to the land is by water? In *Berge v. State*, 915 A.2d 189 (Vt. 2006), the court held that the fact that plaintiff could access a public road via boat from his property did not defeat an easement by necessity. Although the test in Vermont was that there must be "strict necessity," the majority found that "since the easement is based on social considerations encouraging land use, its scope ought to be sufficient for the dominant owner to have the reasonable enjoyment of his land for all lawful purposes." 915 A.2d at 192. Access by water did not allow a modern owner "reasonable enjoyment" of his land. The dissent argued that water access was reasonable for property such as the plaintiff's, which was used for seasonal outdoor recreation, and that the majority had forgotten that "[t]he public's interest in access to landlocked property must be balanced against the serious consequences inherent in granting one landowner an uncompensated interest in the property of a neighbor." 915 A.2d at 196 (Reinhardt, J. dissenting). Who is right?

§2.5 Modifying and Terminating Easements

Easements last forever unless they are terminated (1) by **agreement** in writing (release of the easement by the holder); (2) by their own terms — for example, if the deed conveying the easement expressly states that it is to last for ten years; (3) by **merger**, when the holder of the servient estate becomes the owner of the dominant estate; (4) by **abandonment**, if it can be shown that the owner of the easement, by her conduct, indicated an intent to abandon the easement; or (5) by **adverse possession** or **prescription** by the owner of the servient estate or by a third party.

Sometimes courts terminate easements (6) because of **frustration of purpose**. "Traditional doctrine terminates obsolete easements either by a liberal application of the abandonment principle, or by finding that the purpose of the easement has become impossible to accomplish, or that the easement no longer serves its intended purpose . . . ." *Restatement (Third) of Property (Servitudes)* §7.10 (2000). *See Boissy v. Chevron*, 33 A.3d 1109, 1114 (N.H. 2011) (easement to get water from well terminated once well could no longer be located). The *Restatement (Third)* proposes changing this doctrine by permitting modification rather than termination when modification would permit accomplishment of the purpose of the easement, *id.*, but few courts have as yet adopted this position.

Many states have enacted "marketable title acts," which may require that easements, along with other encumbrances on property interests, be re-recorded periodically (generally every 30 to 50 years) to be binding on future purchasers. The purpose of these statutes is to limit how far back a buyer must look in the chain of title to determine the validity of the seller's title and the existence of encumbrances on the land. However, they also have the effect of making unenforceable those interests that were put in place a long time ago and were of insufficient importance to anyone to be re-recorded in compliance with the statute. Failure to comply with the marketable title act by re-recording the easement may leave the easement owner unprotected from a subsequent purchaser of the servient estate who, depending on the language in the statute, may be entitled to buy the property free of the burden of the easement.

§3 COVENANTS

§3.1 Definition and Background

Negative servitudes, commonly called **covenants**, are restrictions on use of land or obligations regarding land held by one who does not own the land. For example, a neighbor may have the right to prevent you from building over a certain height on your land, or the right to require you to mow your grass regularly. Common law originally placed many restrictions on covenants running with the land; modern law generally eases these restrictions, but may create other restrictions to further public policy goals.

At early common law, restrictions on land held by others were called **negative easements**. But because a restriction on land use is not visible to a purchaser in the way an affirmative easement, like a driveway, might be, courts were concerned about notice to subsequent owners. In addition, because English law permitted negative easements to be acquired by prescription, there was concern that prescriptive rights in the status quo would prevent useful development of land. Therefore courts limited negative easements to three categories: (1) rights to lateral support of one's buildings; (2) rights to free flow of light and air; and (3) rights to water from an artificial stream.

Landowners entered into contractual arrangements to get around these limitations.[7] Contract rights, however, generally did not bind or benefit subsequent purchasers of the benefited or burdened parcels. Individuals had to be in **privity of contract**, or parties to the original contract, to be either bound by the contract or entitled to enforce its benefits. How could agreements regarding land benefit or burden future possessors of the land?

The concept of **real covenants** developed to address this problem. In *Spencer's Case,* 77 Eng. Rep. 72 (1583), the court held that an agreement would bind successors in interest to the land if it was (1) in **writing**, (2) **intended** to be binding on future tenants, (3) **touched and concerned** the land, meaning that it affected the use of the land itself, and (4) if there was **privity of estate**, or mutual ownership of land, between the covenanting parties. For the English courts, "privity of estate" meant **simultaneous privity**, that the parties had simultaneous interests in the same parcel of land. Landlords and tenants were in simultaneous privity because they had rights in the same parcel at the same time. But buyers and sellers of land were not; once the land was sold, the seller would not share a simultaneous interest in the land with the buyer.

However, England had two court systems: the law courts, which awarded damages, and the equity courts, which provided equitable injunctive or declaratory relief in cases in which the harsh common law rule would create injustice. In *Tulk v. Moxhay,* 41 Eng. Rep. 1143 (1848), the chancellor of the equity courts created the concept of **equitable servitudes**, covenants that could be enforced by injunction despite the lack of privity. If the covenant met the writing, intent, and touch and concern requirements, *and* the current owner had purchased with **notice** of the restriction, the owner of the burdened estate could be enjoined from violating the covenant. "Of course," the court opined, "the price would be affected by the covenant, and nothing could be more inequitable than that the original purchaser should be able to sell the property the next day for a greater price, in consideration of the assignee being allowed to escape from the liability which he himself had undertaken." *Id.* Real covenants and equitable servitudes thus differed both in the requirements for running with the land and in the remedies available to enforce them. A real covenant (requiring privity) was necessary to get damages, while an equitable servitude (requiring notice) was necessary for an injunction.

Courts in the United States adopted both real covenants and equitable servitudes law. The law of real covenants expanded the definition of privity. Some states did this by expanding the concept of simultaneous privity from the landlord-tenant relationship to situations in which one owner owns an easement in the property of the other and/or both owners have mutual easements in each other's property. Most courts

7. This historical material is taken from A.W.B. Simpson, *A History of the Land Law* (2d ed. 1986).

expanded the privity concept by adopting the doctrine of **instantaneous privity**, finding privity if a covenant was created during the legal transfer of land. Thus a covenant included in a deed of sale restricting use of the parcel might bind future owners of the property conveyed. The fiction was that at the moment the deed passes from seller to buyer, the parties have a fleeting simultaneous interest in the property.

Over the twentieth century, developers initiated vast expansions of the use of the covenant form. Large residential developments in which unit owners had common restrictions and privileges were a key part of the rise of suburbs in the wake of World War II. The proliferation of shopping plazas and shopping malls, in which numerous retail businesses share facilities bound by common rules, followed soon after. Private agreements regarding land use that ran with the land were no longer viewed as idiosyncratic obstacles to development, but as necessary aids to increasingly dense and interconnected land use. In addition, concerns about notice to subsequent buyers were never as significant in the United States, where registries of deeds had recorded restrictions on land since colonial times. Many courts relaxed restrictions on the covenant form, merging the law of real covenants and equitable servitudes, and modifying or even abolishing touch and concern and privity requirements.

The massive Levittown development, on Long Island, New York, was one of the most famous of the new subdivisions expanding the use of the covenant form in the wake of World War II. Tony Linck, for Life Magazine, Aerial View of Levittown, June 1948

Despite these trends, many courts still adhere to some of the traditional technical requirements and distinctions. It is therefore important to understand both the traditional rules for real covenants and their modern modifications. The table below sets forth the traditional rules for real covenants and equitable servitudes as well as the *Restatement (Third)* approach to help make the alternatives clearer. These elements are further discussed in the notes below. Remember, however, that most courts follow a doctrine somewhere between the traditional and *Restatement (Third)* rules.

Real Covenants (Damages)	**Equitable Servitude (Injunctive Relief)**	***Restatement (Third)***
1. Writing complying with Statute of Frauds	1. Writing complying with Statute of Frauds	1. Writing complying with Statute of Frauds
2. Intent to run (presumed if appurtenant)	2. Intent to run (presumed if appurtenant)	2. Intent to run (presumed if appurtenant)
3. Privity including both — a. Horizontal privity: covenant was created during transfer of burdened and benefited land; or parties are in lessor-lessee relationship or own mutual easements. b. Vertical privity: Current owners obtained land by legal transfer from original covenantors.	3. Actual, inquiry, or constructive notice to owner of servient estate; enforcer must be intended beneficiary of covenant.	3. Actual, inquiry, or constructive notice to owner of servient estate; enforcer is intended beneficiary. For affirmative obligations (*e.g.*, obligation to pay homeowners association fees, obligation to maintain lawn) burden will only run to tenant if makes more sense for tenant to perform, but benefit can be enforced by either tenant or landowner.
4. Touch and concern — direct effect on use or value of land. Both burden and benefit must touch and concern some land. Benefits in gross will not run against owners of servient estates unless held by governments or nonprofits.	4. Touch and concern (same test as for real covenants).	4. Enforceable unless "unreasonable": Covenant is not arbitrary, spiteful, capricious, does not unreasonably burden constitutional right, restrain alienation or restrain trade, and does not otherwise violate public policy. Benefits in gross can run so long as benefit holder has "legitimate interest" in covenant and is identifiable.

§3.2 Creation of Covenants

A. The Traditional Test

Neponsit Property Owners' Association v. Emigrant Industrial Savings Bank

15 N.E.2d 793 (1938)

IRVING LEHMAN, Judge.

[The plaintiff, the Neponsit Property Owners' Association, brought an action against defendant Emigrant Industrial Savings Bank to foreclose a lien created by a covenant on land owned by the Emigrant Industrial Savings Bank. The Neponsit Realty Company had developed the land as a residential community in 1911. In 1917, it sold property in the development to Robert and Charlotte Deyer. Emigrant Savings Bank bought the Deyers' land at a foreclosure sale in 1935. After selling the parcels, the Neponsit Realty Company assigned its rights under the covenant to the Neponsit Property Owners' Association. The deed to the Deyers included the following covenant:]

> And the party of the second part for the party of the second part and the heirs, successors and assigns of the party of the second part further covenants that the property conveyed by this deed shall be subject to an annual charge in such an amount as will be fixed by the party of the first part, its successors and assigns, not, however exceeding in any year the sum of four ($4.00) Dollars per lot 20x100 feet. The assigns of the party of the first part may include a Property Owners' Association which may hereafter be organized for the purposes referred to in this paragraph, and in case such association is organized the sums in this paragraph provided for shall be payable to such association. [S]aid charge shall . . . become a lien on the land and shall continue to be such lien until fully paid. Such charge shall be payable to the party of the first part or its successors or assigns, and shall be devoted to the maintenance of the roads, paths, parks, beach, sewers and such other public purposes as shall from time to time be determined by the party of the first part, its successors or assigns. And the party of the second part by the acceptance of this deed hereby expressly vests in the party of the first part, its successors and assigns, the right and power to bring all actions against the owner of the premises hereby conveyed or any part thereof for the collection of such charge and to enforce the aforesaid lien therefor.
>
> These covenants shall run with the land and shall be construed as real covenants running with the land until January 31st, 1940, when they shall cease and determine.

Every subsequent deed of conveyance of the property in the defendant's chain of title, including the deed from the referee to the defendant, contained, as we have said, a provision that they were made subject to covenants and restrictions of former deeds of record.

There can be no doubt that Neponsit Realty Company intended that the covenant should run with the land and should be enforceable by a property owners association against every owner of property in the residential tract which the realty company was then developing. The language of the covenant admits of no other construction. Regardless of the intention of the parties, a covenant will run with the land and will be enforceable against a subsequent purchaser of the land at the suit of one who claims the benefit of the covenant, only if the covenant complies with certain legal requirements. These requirements rest upon ancient rules and precedents. The age-old essentials of a real covenant, aside from the form of the covenant, may be summarily formulated as follows: (1) It must appear that grantor and grantee intended that the covenant should run with the land; (2) it must appear that the covenant is one "touching" or "concerning" the land with which it runs; (3) it must appear that there is "privity of estate" between the promisee or party claiming the benefit of the covenant and the right to enforce it, and the promisor or party who rests under the burden of the covenant.

The covenant in this case is intended to create a charge or obligation to pay a fixed sum of money to be "devoted to the maintenance of the roads, paths, parks, beach, sewers and such other public purposes as shall from time to time be determined by the party of the first part [the grantor], its successors or assigns." It is an affirmative covenant to pay money for use in connection with, but not upon, the land which it is said is subject to the burden of the covenant. Does such a covenant "touch" or "concern" the land? These terms are not part of a statutory definition, a limitation placed by the State upon the power of the courts to enforce covenants intended to run with the land by the parties who entered into the covenants. Rather they are words used by courts in England in old cases to describe a limitation which the courts themselves created or to formulate a test which the courts have devised and which the courts voluntarily apply. Cf. *Spencer's Case*, Coke, vol. 3, part 5, 16a; *Mayor of Congleton v. Pattison*, 10 East 130. In truth such a description or test so formulated is too vague to be of much assistance and judges and academic scholars alike have struggled, not with entire success, to formulate a test at once more satisfactory and more accurate. "It has been found impossible to state any absolute tests to determine what covenants touch and concern land and what do not. The question is one for the court to determine in the exercise of its best judgment upon the facts of each case." *Clark on Covenants and Interests Running with Land*, p. 76.

It has been suggested that a covenant which runs with the land must affect the legal relations — the advantages and the burdens — of the parties to the covenant, as owners of particular parcels of land and not merely as members of the community in general, such as taxpayers or owners of other land. That method of approach has the merit of realism. The test is based on the effect of the covenant rather than on technical distinctions. Does the covenant impose, on the one hand, a burden upon an interest in land, which on the other hand increases the value of a different interest in the same or related land?

A promise to pay for something to be done in connection with the promisor's land does not differ essentially from a promise by the promisor to do the thing himself, and both promises constitute, in a substantial sense, a restriction upon the owner's right to use the land, and a burden upon the legal interest of the owner. On the other hand, a covenant to perform or pay for the performance of an affirmative act disconnected with the use of the land cannot ordinarily touch or concern the land in any substantial degree. Thus, unless we exalt technical form over substance, the distinction between covenants which run with land and covenants which are personal must depend upon the effect of the covenant on the legal rights which otherwise would flow from ownership of land and which are connected with the land. The problem then is: Does the covenant in purpose and effect substantially alter these rights?

Looking at the problem presented in this case . . . it seems clear that the covenant may properly be said to touch and concern the land of the defendant and its burden should run with the land. True, it calls for payment of a sum of money to be expended for "public purposes" upon land other than the land conveyed by Neponsit Realty Company to plaintiff's predecessor in title. By that conveyance the grantee, however, obtained not only title to particular lots, but an easement or right of common enjoyment with other property owners in roads, beaches, public parks or spaces and improvements in the same tract. For full enjoyment in common by the defendant and other property owners of these easements or rights, the roads and public places must be maintained. In order that the burden of maintaining public improvements should rest upon the land benefited by the improvements, the grantor exacted from the grantee of the land with its appurtenant easement or right of enjoyment a covenant that the burden of paying the cost should be inseparably attached to the land which enjoys the benefit. It is plain that any distinction or definition which would exclude such a covenant from the classification of covenants which "touch" or "concern" the land would be based on form and not on substance.

Another difficulty remains. Though between the grantor and the grantee there was privity of estate, the covenant provides that its benefit shall run to the assigns of the grantor who "may include a Property Owners' Association which may hereafter be organized for the purposes referred to in this paragraph." The plaintiff has been organized to receive the sums payable by the property owners and to expend them for the benefit of such owners. Various definitions have been formulated of "privity of estate" in connection with covenants that run with the land, but none of such definitions seems to cover the relationship between the plaintiff and the defendant in this case. The plaintiff has not succeeded to the ownership of any property of the grantor. It does not appear that it ever had title to the streets or public places upon which charges which are payable to it must be expended. It does not appear that it owns any other property in the residential tract to which any easement or right of enjoyment in such property is appurtenant. It is created solely to act as the assignee of the benefit of the covenant, and it has no interest of its own in the enforcement of the covenant.

The arguments that under such circumstances the plaintiff has no right of action to enforce a covenant running with the land are all based upon a distinction between the corporate property owners association and the property owners for whose benefit the association has been formed. If that distinction may be ignored, then the basis of the arguments is destroyed.

The corporate plaintiff has been formed as a convenient instrument by which the property owners may advance their common interests. We do not ignore the corporate form when we recognize that the Neponsit Property Owners' Association, Inc., is acting as the agent or representative of the Neponsit property owners. As we have said in another case: when Neponsit Property Owners' Association, Inc., "was formed, the property owners were expected to, and have looked to that organization as the medium through which enjoyment of their common right might be preserved equally for all." *Matter of City of New York, Public Beach, Borough of Queens*, 269 N.Y. 64, 75, 199 N.E. 5, 9. Only blind adherence to an ancient formula devised to meet entirely different conditions could constrain the court to hold that a corporation formed as a medium for the enjoyment of common rights of property owners owns no property which would benefit by enforcement of common rights and has no cause of action in equity to enforce the covenant upon which such common rights depend. In substance if not in form the covenant is a restrictive covenant which touches and concerns the defendant's land, and in substance, if not in form, there is privity of estate between the plaintiff and the defendant.

[*Affirmed.*]

Notes and Questions

1. **Defining the issue.** *Neponsit Property Owners Association*, decided in 1938 just before the explosion of residential common interest developments, considered whether the Neponsit Property Owners Association could enforce a covenant to pay four dollars per lot annually for the maintenance of roads, parks, beach, and other public amenities of the Neponsit development against the Emigrant Savings Bank. Because neither the plaintiff nor the defendant was an original signatory to the covenant, the question is whether the covenant ran with the land to bind or benefit succeeding owners of the property. In holding that the covenant could be enforced, the court decided two enormously important questions for residential developments: first, whether affirmative covenants to pay fees for the benefit of common amenities in the development touched and concerned the land; and second, whether property owners associations (rather than individual owners themselves) were in privity of estate and could enforce the restrictions.

Let's first lay out the history of the covenants and the land. The Neponsit Realty Association owned and developed the area on Rockaway Peninsula as a 38-block, 1,600-home high-end residential community between 1910 and 1920. *See* Stewart E. Sterk, Neponsit Property Owners Association v. Emigrant Savings Bank, Property Stories 384 (2009). Robert and Charlotte Deyer purchased their home from the Realty Association in 1917. Their deed, like all others in the community, included numerous covenants, including the one at issue in the case. The Realty Association assigned its ability to enforce the covenants to the Neponsit Property Owners Association, to which all property owners in Neponsit automatically became members. In 1935, in the aftermath of the Great Depression, the Deyers lost their home to foreclosure, and Emigrant Savings Bank purchased it at a foreclosure sale.

> **CONTEXT**
>
> The residents of Neponsit have included well-known figures such as New York Mayor Abe Beame and, for a time, Judy Garland.

What would have happened if Deyer had stopped paying the maintenance fees before the transfer from Neponsit Realty to the Neponsit Property Owners? The answer is simple: Deyer is bound by normal contract law to Neponsit Realty. However, both owners transferred their interests. Two issues appear. First, are the original covenanting parties still bound and benefited by the promise? Second, are their successors bound and benefitted by the promise?

2. Rights and obligations of original covenanting parties. In general, the original parties to a covenant will no longer have rights or obligations under a covenant after they have sold the land the covenant concerns.

a. Benefit of covenants held in gross. First, does Neponsit Realty have the power to enforce the covenant once it sells all its land in the development? The answer is probably no for two reasons. First, a court will likely interpret the covenant to benefit the current owner of the land and not prior possessors, unless the agreement contains explicit language to the contrary. *Waikiki Malia Hotel, Inc. v. Kinkai Properties Limited Partnership*, 862 P.2d 1048, 1057-1059 (Haw. 1993).

Second, even when the language of the covenant is clear, courts have traditionally refused to impose the burden of a covenant on future owners of the servient estate if the benefit of the covenant is held in gross, meaning that it benefits an individual or entity rather than land. An important exception is that many jurisdictions, by common law or statute, permit enforcement of covenants in gross when the covenant is held by a government entity or by a charity, like a land conservation trust or a historic preservation trust. *See Uniform Conservation Easement Act* (adopted in more than 20 states); *Bennett v. Commissioner of Food & Agriculture*, 576 N.E.2d 1365 (Mass. 1991).

b. Enforceability against original covenantor after the land is transferred. Are the Deyers, the original promisors, still bound to ensure by the present performance of the covenant? The answer is almost certainly no. A prior owner is not legally responsible for the actions of the subsequent owners of the burdened land.

Had the Deyers simply leased the land to Emigrant Savings Bank, the answer would probably be yes. Leases are treated differently from sales because landlords may include the covenant in any lease and end the leasehold and evict the tenant if the tenant violates the lease. The landlord's failure to include such a covenant or to exercise the right to enforce such a covenant constitutes an independent breach of the covenant.

3. Obligations of successors in interest. Can the successor owners of the dominant estate (the owners of the other parcels in the Neponsit development) obtain relief against Emigrant Savings Bank, the subsequent possessor of the servient estate? The answer will be yes only if both the benefit and the burden run with the land. In addition, to determine what kind of relief is available, we must apply both the law of real covenants and the law of equitable servitudes. If the court follows traditional distinctions, damages are only available for real covenants, while injunctive relief is only available for equitable servitudes.

Under the law of **real covenants**, land use restrictions run with the land when (1) the covenant is in **writing**; (2) the grantor **intended** the restriction to run with the land on both sides, binding future owners of the servient estate and benefiting future owners of the dominant estate; (3) the restriction **touches and concerns** both the dominant and servient estates; and (4) **privity of estate** exists between the original covenanting parties (**horizontal privity**) and between those parties and succeeding owners (**vertical privity**). **Equitable servitudes** law contains most of these elements, but replaces privity of estate with **notice** of the covenant to the owner of servient estate. Notice was not originally required to enforce a real covenant, but almost all courts today require notice for enforcement of a real covenant as well. The *Restatement (Third),* which substantially modifies the privity and touch and concern requirements, is discussed separately in §3.2.B.

Four of the five requirements are *formalities,* while only one (the touch and concern test) is *substantive.* Formal requirements regulate the manner in which a right or obligation is created; individuals who wish to create the right or obligation may do so as long as they adhere to the formalities. They are not designed to prevent or discourage particular behavior; rather, they are rules designed to ensure that actors communicate their intentions clearly, both to each other and to the judges who are empowered to enforce their agreements. Duncan Kennedy, *Form and Substance in Private Law Adjudication,* 89 Harv. L. Rev. 1685, 1691 (1976). Substantive requirements, on the other hand, limit the ability of individuals to create certain rights. They "prevent people from engaging in particular activities because those activities are morally wrong or otherwise flatly undesirable." *Id.* No amount of careful planning will enable an owner to avoid such a requirement. We will start with the formal requirements (writing, notice, intent, and privity) and then discuss the substantive touch and concern test.

4. **Writing complying with the Statute of Frauds.** Like all transfers of property interests lasting more than a year, the covenant must be created in a writing signed by the grantor and otherwise complying with the Statute of Frauds to be valid. Once the covenant is created, the writing need not be repeated in subsequent transfers of the land. Here, the written covenant in the deed transferring the land from Neponsit Realty to the Deyers clearly satisfies the writing requirement.

Developers of residential subdivisions may also record a *declaration* of restrictions applicable to the entire subdivision and/or a *plat* (a detailed map showing the restrictions) before any lot is sold. Some states may require that the restriction be specifically mentioned in the deed or lease when individual lots are sold, even if only by reference to the earlier recorded declaration or plat. Most states, however, find that a covenant in a prior-recorded declaration or plat meets the writing requirement. *Citizens for Covenant Compliance v. Anderson,* 906 P.2d 1314 (Cal. 1995); *Arnold v. Chandler,* 428 A.2d 1235 (N.H. 1981).

As discussed earlier in this chapter, easements can be created by implication. Can covenants? The short answer is yes, but more rarely. Where a seller fraudulently promises that there are covenants on the land, and the buyers rely to their detriment on the promise, courts have sometimes applied the equitable doctrine of estoppel to enforce the false representations. *See, e.g., Prospect Development Co., Inc. v. Bershader,* 515 S.E.2d 291 (Va. 1999) (preventing development of wooded lot next to plaintiffs' home when developers' maps designated lot as "preserved land," charged a premium for lot next to land, repeatedly told buyers that lot would not be developed, and the bird-loving buyers had designed their home to get the best view of the wooded lot); *PMZ Oil Co. v. Lucroy*, 449 So. 2d 201 (Miss. 1984) (enjoining construction of townhouse condominiums in development when the developer had told all lot purchasers that its 16-lot subdivision would be restricted to "one quality single-family dwelling per lot" and showed them an unrecorded plat noting the restrictions). *But see Bennett v. Charles Corp.*, 226 S.E.2d 559 (W. Va. 1976) (allowing a developer to convert remaining unsold lots in a subdivided tract into a cemetery, despite violation of the developer's oral promise to develop a tract as a residential subdivision, finding no fraudulent or inequitable conduct).

5. **Notice.** The notice requirement is intended to protect the owner of the servient estate, so the question is whether the owner of the burdened estate knew or should have known the parcel was restricted when she purchased the land. Notice may be *actual, inquiry,* or *constructive.*

a. A buyer or lessee is on **actual notice** of the covenant if he was actually told about it or was otherwise made aware of it. In *Neponsit*, it is unclear whether Emigrant Savings Bank was on actual notice of the covenant when it purchased the property at a foreclosure sale.

b. The buyer or lessee is on **inquiry notice**, sometimes called *actual implied* notice, if the condition of the premises would make a reasonable purchaser inquire about the existence of a covenant. Inquiry notice of covenants is less likely than inquiry notice of easements, such as rights of way, which a buyer can often visually observe. Some courts have found, however, that a uniform pattern of residential development places a reasonable buyer on notice of the potential presence of restrictive covenants. *See, e.g., Sanborn v. McLean*, 206 N.W. 496 (Mich. 1925). In *Winn-Dixie Stores, Inc. v. Dolgencorp, Inc.*, 964 So. 2d 261 (Fla. Dist. Ct. App. 2007), the court found that a corporation with 7,800 stores in shopping plazas across America was on inquiry notice that the anchor tenant likely had a covenant preventing competing grocery stores in the plaza. Is this finding justified? In most cases, however, the primary inquiry is likely to be conducted by researching the registry of deeds to find any relevant recorded restrictions. That brings us to constructive notice.

c. A buyer or lessee is said to be on **constructive notice** if the restriction was recorded within the registry of deeds and could be found via a reasonable search of the records prior to sale. A reasonable purchaser is expected to search the title to find out whether the property is burdened by any land use restrictions. The facts of *Neponsit* state that every deed in Emigrant Savings Bank's chain of title provided that the conveyances were "subject to covenants and restrictions of former deeds of record," implying that the Deyer deed was recorded, so Emigrant Savings Bank was on constructive notice.

What if the covenant was recorded in the deed between the seller, Neponsit Realty, and a prior purchaser of adjoining land? Neponsit Realty might have, for example, pledged to a prior purchaser to restrict all its remaining land in the development to single-family residences, but only recorded the covenant with that purchaser's deed. States disagree on whether a subsequent purchaser is on notice of the covenant. The majority of courts hold that a reasonable record search includes all grants made by the original owner regarding nearby or contiguous land while the grantor owned the property. Because title searches in the United States are typically made by looking under the name of the grantor, rather than the specific location of the property, these courts hold that purchasers are on constructive notice of restrictions by the grantor recorded regarding other property. A substantial minority of courts, however, hold that the purchaser is only bound by those restrictions appearing in the chain of title for the burdened property itself.

6. **Intent to run with the land.** Intent to run with the land may be made explicit, as it is in the Neponsit deed, with language declaring that it is on behalf of the owner's "successors or assigns" or that the covenant "runs with the land." What happens if the deed or lease does not include such language? Courts generally hold that appurtenant covenants — those benefitting some land — are presumptively intended to run with the benefited and burdened land. *See Sun Oil Co. v. Trent Auto Wash, Inc.,* 150 N.W.2d 818 (Mich. 1967) (holding that a covenant prohibiting use of land to operate a gas station was intended to run with the land); *Runyon v. Paley,* 416 S.E.2d 177, 185-187 (N.C. 1992) (presuming that the benefit was intended to run with the land if it is clear the burden was intended to run with the land). However, some courts require clear evidence of intent to run. *Charping v. J.P. Scurry & Co.,* 372 S.E.2d 120 (S.C. 1988); *Tennsco Corp. v. Attea,* 2002 WL 1298808 (Tenn. Ct. App. 2002).

7. **Privity of estate.** The concept of privity of estate contains the core principle of servitudes law: one piece of property is burdened for the benefit of another (so-called **horizontal privity**) and these benefits and burdens run to succeeding owners of both parcels (**vertical privity**). At the same time, the law of privity developed maddeningly complicated technical limitations that were unrelated to any legitimate policy concerns. The modern trend is to relax or do away with the privity requirement, but a number of states still retain it. *See Beeren & Barry Investments, L.L.C. v. AHC, Inc.,* 671 S.E.2d 147 (Va. 2009); *Cunningham v. City of Greensboro,* 711 S.E.2d 477 (N.C. App. 2011). Although privity was not traditionally required to obtain injunctive relief for a covenant as an equitable servitude, courts that maintain the requirement may not make this distinction, or may require privity to enforce obligations to pay assessments, as in *Neponsit.*

a. **Horizontal privity.** Horizontal privity regulates the relationship between the original covenanting parties. Because land use restrictions both limit the free use of land and may make it less alienable, they were traditionally thought to be unjustified unless the burden on land was outweighed by a compensating benefit to some other property owner. The horizontal privity requirement served to promote this purpose.

Most courts in the United States adopted an **instantaneous privity** test, finding horizontal privity when the covenant is created at the moment the owner of one parcel sells or transfers rights in the other parcel. Thus, a covenant contained in a deed of sale transferring a property interest will satisfy the horizontal privity requirement. Similarly, a covenant in a lease (transferring a leasehold) or a mortgage (transferring a lien or right to foreclose) will satisfy the horizontal privity requirement.

What kinds of relationships does horizontal privity exclude? The two most important are (1) agreements between neighbors that are not part of a simultaneous conveyance of another property right; (2) agreements between grantors and grantees that are not made at the same time as the conveyance of the property interest burdened or benefited by the covenant.[8] An example of the first problem is a contract among all the owners in a neighborhood to restrict the property to residential uses. Because the neighbors already own their land, they are not in privity of estate. An example of the second problem is a covenant made one week after the sale of a parcel; this does not satisfy the privity requirement because at that moment the grantor no longer owns the property of the grantee.

b. Vertical privity. Vertical privity refers to the relationship between the original covenanting parties and subsequent owners of each parcel. **Strict vertical privity** required that the grantor did not retain any future interests in the land. Thus vertical privity is present when an owner sells her property but not when she leases it. **Relaxed vertical privity**, adopted by many courts, would allow the benefit and the burden to run to all subsequent possessors of the land in appropriate circumstances. Thus a tenant would be in vertical privity with the lessor, even though the lessor retains interests in the land.

Neponsit considers whether the Neponsit Property Owners Association is in vertical privity with Neponsit Realty. On the surface, it does not appear to be, because the association does not own any property in its own name. But the court moves past the corporate form to its substance, recognizing that the Neponsit Property Owners Association is composed of and exists to represent the owners of Neponsit homes. These owners all purchased their property from the Realty Association, and so are in vertical privity with it. *Neponsit* thus recognizes enforcement of covenants by organizations representing the property owners, a key feature of governance of modern common interest developments.

---

8. A third problem arises in the context of residential subdivisions when early buyers of lots try to enforce covenants entered into by later buyers. This topic is addressed at §4.3.

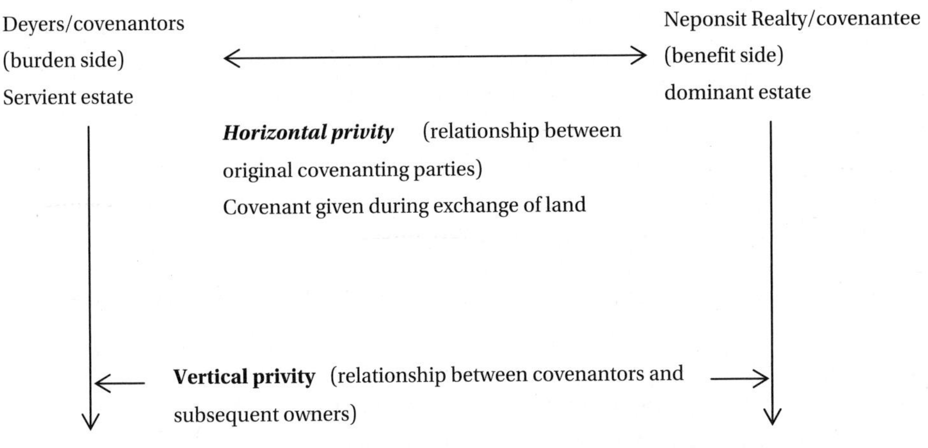

8. Substantive requirements: the "touch and concern" test. Courts have traditionally allowed covenants to run with the land only if they "touch and concern" the land, meaning that they affect the use or value of the land itself. The test is intended to identify the kinds of obligations that should attach to the land rather than the individuals making the agreement. "Where the burdens and benefits created by the covenant may exist independently from the parties' ownership interests in land, the covenant does not touch and concern the land and will not run with the land." *Runyon v. Paley*, 416 S.E.2d 177, 183 (N.C. 1992); *see Vulcan Materials Co. v. Miller*, 691 So. 2d 908, 914 (Miss. 1997) ("A covenant that imposes a burden on real property for the benefit of the grantor personally does not follow the land into the possession of an assignee"); 7 *Thompson on Real Property, Second Thomas Editions*, §61.04; *Restatement of Property* §537 (1944).

On the burden side, an obligation touches and concerns the burdened estate if it affects the use and enjoyment of the land. On the benefit side, an obligation touches and concerns a dominant estate if it improves enjoyment of that land or increases its market value. Restrictive covenants that limit land use, such as covenants limiting the land to residential purposes or prohibiting the sale of liquor on the land will generally touch and concern both the dominant and servient estates. They touch and concern the servient estate because they restrict the use of the land; they touch and concern the dominant estate because the restriction is intended to benefit the owners of the dominant estates whoever they happen to be and because most purchasers of the dominant estates would consider the right to enforce the covenant as increasing the value or attractiveness of the benefited land.

The traditional refusal to enforce covenants when the benefit is held in gross (note 2.a, *supra*) is an application of the touch and concern test. Covenants that restrict land use interfere with both the right of free use of property and the marketability of the property. This cost is thought to be justified if there is a sufficient compensating benefit to other land. But when no land is benefited this presumption falls away, and the autonomy interests of current owners trumps the power of the "dead hand" of prior owners to control the property. *See Garland v. Rosenshein*, 649 N.E.2d 756 (Mass. 1995); *Lakewood Racquet Club, Inc. v. Jensen*, 232 P.3d 1147 (Wash. App. 2010).

Affirmative obligations to pay fees, like that in *Neponsit*, have often caused problems for the courts. Payment of money may appear to be more in the realm of contract law than an obligation that should attach to the land itself. As the court recognized in *Neponsit*, however, when the fees are used to maintain the common elements of a community, it does touch and concern the land by preserving the value of the properties in a community.

Although the obligation to pay property owners association dues is now well established, other cases are more controversial. For example, in *Castlebrook, Limited v. Dayton Properties Limited Partnership*, 604 N.E.2d 808 (Ohio Ct. App. 1992), the court held that a covenant to return a tenant's security deposit did not touch and concern the land and hence was not binding on a successor landlord. In *Chesapeake Ranch Club, Inc. v. C.R.C. United Members, Inc.*, 483 A.2d 1334 (Md. Ct. Spec. App. 1984), the court held that a covenant to pay dues to belong to a recreational facility did not touch and concern the land. The current trend, however, is to enforce such obligations. *See Nickerson v. Green Valley Recreation, Inc.*, 265 P.3d 1108, 1115-1116 (Ariz. App. 2011) (enforcing covenant to pay membership fees and collecting similar cases). Should a homeowner in a subdivision be bound by a covenant that requires the owner to pay dues to a health club? Would your answer change if the club admits anyone as a member (not just homeowners in the neighborhood), is profitable, and charges $1,000 a year while the owner has no interest in using the facilities?

B. The *Restatement (Third)* and Its Influence

The *Restatement (Third) of Property (Servitudes)* was adopted by the American Law Institute (ALI) in 1998 and published in final form in 2000. Recognizing that covenants are now indispensable tools of land use development, it seeks to merge and simplify the law of covenants and easements and further the trend of easing restrictions on covenants running with the land. Restatements are not authoritative sources of law, but they are often cited in court opinions as persuasive indications of the direction in which courts are or should be moving. No jurisdiction has adopted the *Restatement (Third)* in its entirety, although several courts have relied on aspects of it.

The *Restatement (Third)* proposes to abolish the distinction between real covenants and equitable servitudes; abolish the privity requirement; permitting enforcement of covenants in gross; and replace the touch and concern test with a review for reasonableness that more explicitly incorporates policy concerns. As you will see, however, the substance of these factors still plays a limited role in the *Restatement (Third)*, and many courts continue to rely on traditional requirements.

1. Abolishing the distinction between negative easements, real covenants, and equitable servitudes. The *Restatement (Third)* drops the terms "real covenant" and "equitable servitudes" and "negative easement," encompassing all within the category of "covenants running with the land." §§1.2-1.4. Although some courts have embraced this change, *see Dunning v. Buending*, 247 P.3d 1145 (N.M. App. 2010), other courts still commonly use the terms "negative easement" and "equitable servitude." *See Nordbye v. BRCP/GM Ellington*, 266 P.3d 92, 102 (Or. App. 2011) (holding that if commitment to maintain property as low-income housing were not enforceable as a real covenant, it would be enforceable as an equitable servitude because owners had notice of the restriction); *Prospect Development Co., Inc. v. Bershader*, 515 S.E.2d 291 (Va. 1999) (analyzing development restrictions as "negative easements").

2. Abolishing the horizontal privity requirement. The *Restatement (Third) of Property* §2.4 (2000) would abolish the horizontal privity requirement entirely. The drafters argue that although the requirement may have helped to ensure intent and notice of the restriction, the intent and notice requirements serve these interests more directly. *Id.* The abolishment of the horizontal privity requirement followed several jurisdictions that were critical of the rule. Nevertheless, some courts continue to demand horizontal privity before finding an enforceable covenant. *See, e.g., Cunningham v. Greensboro*, 711 S.E.2d 477, 485-486 (N.C. App. 2011) (refusing to enforce utility agreements that were created without horizontal privity).

3. Abolishing the touch and concern requirement. The *Restatement (Third)* seeks to "permit innovative land-development practices using servitudes without the sometimes irrational impediments imposed by the touch and concern doctrine." *Supra* §3.2. The *Restatement* proposes abolishing the touch and concern requirement, and shifting the burden to those challenging enforcement to prove that the requirement violates public policy for reasons that include, but are not limited to, that the servitude (1) is arbitrary, spiteful, or capricious; (2) unreasonably burdens a fundamental constitutional right; (3) imposes an unreasonable restraint on alienation under §3.4 or §3.5; (4) imposes an unreasonable restraint on trade or competition under §3.6; or (5) is unconscionable under §3.7. *Id.* §3.1. In some places, however, the *Restatement (Third)* seems to reintroduce the touch and concern element through the back door by providing that burdens having "nothing to do with ownership, occupancy, or use of the land" may be invalidated as arbitrary or capricious, *id.* §3.2 cmt. e, or unreasonable indirect restraints on alienation of land. *Id.* §3.5. Similarly, the *Restatement (Third)* specifically provides that the benefit of covenants need not touch and concern the land, *id.* §2.6, but requires that the beneficiary of the covenant is reasonably identifiable, *id.* §7.13, and has a "legitimate interest" in enforcing it. *Id.* §8.1.

Despite the *Restatement (Third)*, many courts still retain some version of the touch and concern requirement. *Dunning v. Buending*, 247 P.3d 1145 (N.M. App. 2010) (covenant must touch and concern the land; restriction on subdividing lot did so); *Midsouth Golf v. Fairfield Harbourside Condominium Association*, 652 S.E.2d 378 (S.C. 2007) (recreation fees were invalid because they did not touch and concern the land); *Deep Water Brewing, LLC v. Fairway Resources Limited*, 215 P.3d 990 (Wash. App. 2009) (covenants must touch and concern both burdened and benefited land; height restriction to preserve view did so); *see also Nickerson v. Green Valley Athletic Association*, 265 P.3d 1108 (Ariz. App. 2011) (although 2008 statute appeared to abolish touch and concern requirement for covenants, requirement still applied to covenants created before its enactment). Quite a few states, however, have abolished or modified the prohibition on benefits in gross. *See, e.g., El Paso Refinery, LP v. TRMI*, 302 F.3d 343 (5th Cir. 2002) (finding it arguable that Texas has abandoned the requirement for the benefit of the covenant, but the burden must still touch and concern); *Wykeham Rise, LLC v. Federer*, 52 A.3d 702, 717 (Conn. 2012) ("It is clear that these benefits in gross may validly be created.").

4. Changing interpretive presumptions. Courts traditionally interpreted ambiguous covenants in the manner that would be the least burdensome to the free use of land. *Forster v. Hall*, 576 S.E.2d 746, 750 (Va. 2003) ("[R]estrictions of the free use of land . . . are disfavored by public policy and must be strictly construed"); *see also City of Bowie v. MIE Properties, Inc.*, 922 A.2d 509, 522 (Md. 2007) (stating that under "the general rule in favor of the unrestricted use of property . . . ambiguity in a restriction will be resolved against the party seeking its enforcement"). There is a longstanding trend, however, of recognizing that covenants may in fact enhance land value, and abandoning strict construction to interpret covenants to fulfill the intent of the parties. *See Powell v. Washburn*, 125 P.3d 373, 376-377 (Ariz. 2006) ("Arizona's rule that courts should enforce the intent of the parties to a restrictive covenant in the absence of ambiguity reaches back to the 1930s."); *Joslin v. Pine River Development Corp.*, 367 A.2d 599, 601 (N.H. 1976) ("The former prejudice against restrictive covenants which led courts to strictly construe them is yielding to a gradual recognition that they are valuable land use planning devices."); *Viking Properties, Inc. v. Holm*, 118 P.3d 322, 326 (Wash. 2005) (discussing abandonment of strict construction rule). The *Restatement (Third)* follows this trend, providing that covenants should be interpreted to further the intent of the parties, carry out their purposes, and avoid violating public policy. *Restatement (Third)* §4.1.

Problems

1. **Writing.**

a. A developer creates a residential subdivision and offers lots within it for sale. The brochures for the subdivision describe it as a "premier residential community," to have "restrictive covenants to fulfill the purposes of the community." Neither the deeds nor the recorded subdivision map, however, refer to any restrictive covenants. The developer sells some of the lots, but is unable to sell more to people interested in them for residential purposes, and sells the remainder to a buyer who plans to build a big box store. Is there a writing sufficient to create a restrictive covenant on the land?

b. In 1872, a developer recorded a subdivision map showing proposed lots and streets and parks in a seaside vacation community on Martha's Vineyard in Massachusetts. The map included three parcels labeled "Prospect Park," "Webster Park," and "Plaza." These parcels were about five times the size of the proposed residential lots, and were irregularly shaped. The rest of the parcels in the subdivision were sold to individual homeowners; the deeds did not mention any rights with respect to the park parcels specifically, but all referred to the recorded subdivision map. More than a hundred years later, the owners of the lots, the heirs of the original developer, sought to sell the undeveloped park parcels to buyers who wanted to build residences on them. Owners of other homes in the subdivision claim that the parcels are subject to an equitable servitude prohibiting development. Is there a sufficient writing to create a covenant preventing development? *Compare Reagan v. Brissey*, 844 N.E.2d 672 (Mass. 2006) *and Agua Fria Save the Open Space Association v. Rowe*, 255 P.3d 390 (N.M. 2011).

2. Intent to run. AHC, Inc., a developer of low-income housing, sells a home to a couple with financing. The financing agreement includes a deed of trust from the couple providing that "[i]n the event of Grantor's death or in the event that Grantor elects to sell the property secured hereby at any time within thirty (30) years from the date of the Trust, AHC, Inc., its successors or assigns shall have the option to purchase the property at the Purchase Price as hereinafter defined. . . ." The couple later refinances the home with Option One Mortgage, and defaults on the refinanced loan. Option One initiates a foreclosure sale on the property, at which an investment company purchases the home. Does the option to purchase run to subsequent owners like the investment company? What does the language suggest? Why might a developer of low-income housing include such an option? *Beeren & Barry Investments, L.L.C. v. AHC, Inc.*, 671 S.E.2d 147 (Va. 2009), discusses this problem.

3. Horizontal privity.

a. *A* sells land to *B*; the deed specifies that the land can only be used for residential purposes. Is there *simultaneous horizontal privity* (the old English test)? Is there *instantaneous horizontal privity* (the common American test)?

b. *A* and *B* are neighbors; *A* plans to install solar panels and wants to make sure *B* does not build to block them. *B* agrees to enter into a covenant restricting her from building so as to obstruct the flow of sunlight to the solar panels. Is there horizontal privity under the common American test? Assume that *C* purchases *B*'s land knowing of the covenant. May *A* enforce the covenant against *C*? Under traditional rules, what remedies may *A* seek?

4. Vertical privity. *A* sells land to *B* with a covenant that *B* may not block the flow of a natural stream from *B*'s land to *A*'s land. Is there vertical privity in the following situations? With or without vertical privity, should the covenant be enforceable by or against the subsequent owner of the land?

a. *A* sells his land to *C*.

b. *B*'s land is foreclosed and sold at a foreclosure sale to *D*.

c. *B* leases her land to *E*.

d. *B* loses her land by adverse possession to *F*.

e. *A* dies and *G* inherits his land.

5. Notice. *O* sells a residential lot to *A* within a subdivision. The deed, like all other deeds in the subdivision, provides that *A* can only paint the home in certain approved "southwestern" shades: sand, adobe, cactus, and sandia. The deed is recorded. *B* later purchases the home, without any actual knowledge of the restriction.

She paints the property hunter green. What different arguments can you make that she has legal notice of the restriction?

6. Touch and concern. Do the following covenants touch and concern the burdened land? Do they touch and concern some benefited land (*i.e.*, are these restrictions appurtenant or in gross)? Would they be upheld under *Restatement (Third)* public policy analysis?

a. The covenants for a condominium development provide that unit owners may not have dogs. How would the analysis change for a restriction preventing cats?

b. The deed for a historic house provides that the owners must always hang a portrait of the original owner.

c. An owner of two supermarkets two miles apart sells one with the covenant that the land may never be used for supermarket purposes.

d. The covenants upon sale of an oil refinery provide that the grantee "shall never, directly or indirectly, attempt to compel Grantor to clean up, remove or take remedial action or any other response with respect to any of the buried sludge sites, the waste pile site, the Active Hazardous Waste Storage Sites, the underground liquid petroleum and petroleum vapors (including, without limitation, any leaching therefrom or contamination of the air, ground or the ground water thereunder or any effects related thereto), or any and all waste water treatment ponds or treatment systems on or in the vicinity of said premises or seek damages therefor. This covenant shall run with the land and shall bind Grantee's successors, assigns and all other subsequent owners of the property." *See El Paso Refinery, LP v. TRMI*, 302 F.3d 343 (5th Cir. 2002). The court found that Texas law did not necessarily require that a covenant benefit land in order to run (*i.e.*, that covenants in gross were permissible) but that it must touch and concern the burdened land. Does the covenant touch and concern the burdened land?

C. Remedies

Should covenants normally be enforced by damages or injunctive relief? Traditional contract law holds that damages are the usual remedy for breach of contract while injunctions are awarded only when damages are inadequate. Property law, however, represents one of the most important areas in which damages are often thought inadequate because of the unique value attached to the *location* of land and the desire to use particular unique structures. The granting of an injunction, however, has always been discretionary.

Consider Judge Richard Posner's explanation for the predilection for injunctions in a case involving breach of an anticompetitive covenant. In *Walgreen Co. v. Sara Creek Property Co.*, 966 F.2d 273 (7th Cir. 1992), a shopping center landlord (Sara Creek) breached an anticompetitive covenant in a lease with a tenant pharmacy (Walgreens) by arranging for a department store containing a pharmacy (Phar-Mor) to replace an anchor tenant whose business was doing badly. The issue was whether the covenant could be enforced by an injunction ordering the landlord not to allow a competitor to operate in the center or whether an injunction would be denied and the plaintiff relegated to damages. The Seventh Circuit upheld the trial court's decision to issue an injunction.

Judge Posner explained that damages are normally the remedy for breach of contract because the promisee receives damages to compensate for losing the benefit of the bargain, making the promisee indifferent as between performance and breach, while the promisor who is relieved from the promise can obtain the benefit of a more profitable bargain with another party, thereby shifting resources to a more valuable use without harming the promisee. If "the value of Phar-Mor's occupancy of the anchor premises may exceed the cost to Walgreen of facing increased competition[, . . .] society will be better off if Walgreen is paid its damages, equal to that cost, and Phar-Mor is allowed to move in rather than being kept out by an injunction." *Id.* at 274. However, Judge Posner concluded that in this case, an injunction was more likely to achieve the efficient result than damages. First, he noted that injunctive relief ordering compliance with the covenant would not necessarily end the matter; the parties could bargain for a contrary result. In contrast, damages are set by the court or by a jury rather than by the parties through private bargaining. Unless transaction costs block private bargaining, a number reached by the parties is more likely to represent the actual value of the entitlements in question than a number reached by a third party. If the parties can reach an agreement at an amount chosen by them, both will be better off. "A battle of experts is a less reliable method of determining the actual cost to Walgreen of facing new competition than negotiations between Walgreen and Sara Creek over the price at which Walgreen would feel adequately compensated for having to face that competition." *Id.* at 276.

At the same time, Judge Posner noted that transaction costs might block negotiation between the parties since they were in a situation of "bilateral monopoly" in which "two parties can deal only with each other: the situation that an injunction creates. . . . Walgreen can 'sell' its injunctive right only to Sara Creek, and Sara Creek can 'buy' Walgreen's surrender of its right to enjoin the leasing of the anchor tenant's space to Phar-Mor only from Walgreen." *Id.*

> The lack of alternatives in bilateral monopoly creates a bargaining range, and the costs of negotiating to a point within that range may be high. Suppose the cost to Walgreen of facing the competition of Phar-Mor at the Southgate Mall would be $1 million, and the benefit to Sara Creek of leasing to Phar-Mor would be $2 million. Then at any price between those figures for a waiver of Walgreen's injunctive right both parties would be better off, and we expect parties to bargain around a judicial assignment of legal rights if the assignment is inefficient. R.H. Coase, *The Problem of Social Cost*, 3 J.L. & Econ. 1 (1960). But each of the parties would like to engross as much of the bargaining range as possible — Walgreen to press the price toward $2 million, Sara Creek to depress it toward $1 million. With so much at stake, both parties will have an incentive to devote substantial resources of time and money to the negotiation process. The process may even break down, if one or both parties want to create for future use a reputation as a hard bargainer; and if it does break down, the injunction will have brought about an inefficient result. All these are in one form or another costs of the injunctive process that can be avoided by substituting damages.

Id. at 276. Thus, both damages and injunctions have both costs and benefits. The benefits of an injunction are that the parties get to bargain to determine who values the entitlement the most and to set the appropriate price; they also avoid the time and expense of litigation and the inaccuracy of damage awards set by a third party who is less knowledgeable about the benefits of anticompetitive covenants and their value to the parties than the parties themselves. The benefits of damages are that litigation can produce a result where transaction costs might prevent the parties from bargaining to a mutually beneficial result; indeed, the possibility that a jury would determine the appropriate level of damages might be an incentive to get the parties to agree to an appropriate resolution, thereby promoting rather than discouraging bargaining. In any event, Judge Posner concluded that the trial judge appropriately determined that "the costs (including forgone benefits) of the damages remedy would exceed the costs (including forgone benefits) of an injunction." *Id.* at 278.

Professor Ward Farnsworth criticizes the kind of reasoning presented by Judge Posner by noting that in nuisance cases he examined, the parties never bargained to rearrange the results reached by the court both because the winning party believed it deserved to win and because of hard feelings generated by the dispute, making the parties unwilling to compromise and transfer property rights even if this would otherwise have been in their mutual best interest. Ward Farnsworth, *Do Parties to Nuisance Cases Bargain After Judgment? A Glimpse Inside the Cathedral,* 66 U. Chi. L. Rev. 373 (1999). This may suggest that significant transaction costs may bar bargaining between the owners of the servient and dominant estates.

Courts have also had trouble with affirmative covenants that require owners to continue particular uses, although some courts have enforced such covenants. *Compare Shalimar Association v. D.O.C. Enterprises, Inc.*, 688 P.2d 682 (Ariz. Ct. App. 1984) (requiring an owner to continue operating a golf course to comply with an affirmative covenant) *with Oceanside Community Associates v. Oceanside Land Co.,* 195 Cal. Rptr. 14 (Ct. App. 1983) (refusing to grant an injunction ordering an owner to renovate and operate a golf club but imposing a lien on the property for lost value to the dominant estates resulting from the failure to comply with the covenant).

§4 COVENANTS IN RESIDENTIAL SUBDIVISIONS, CONDOMINIUMS, AND OTHER MULTIPLE OWNER DEVELOPMENTS

The covenants typical under early English law were agreements between a few individual owners. Today, covenants may bind hundreds, thousands, and even tens of thousands of people. The power of these covenants in creating shared rights and obligations is reflected in the name of the developments they create — "common interest developments." Although they include commercial developments such as shopping centers, these materials will focus on residential developments. This expansion of the covenant form raises many new questions. What is necessary to bind unit owners to common covenants? What are the rights of unit owners to enforce the covenants against each other? What are the rights of the unit owners against the developer?

Finally, what are the boundaries on what either developers or unit owners can demand of an owner? The doctrine of implied reciprocal negative servitudes responds to some of these questions, while the statutes and common law that govern common interest developments respond to others. Finally, substantive limitations on the enforcement of covenants in general, discussed in §5, have had to adapt to the growth of common interest developments.

§4.1 Implied Reciprocal Negative Servitudes in Residential Subdivisions

An owner of a large tract of land wants to subdivide it and sell 100 lots. She wants to ensure that the lots are restricted to residential use and each lot to a single-family home. To accomplish this, she places covenants in each deed by which the purchaser agrees for herself, her heirs and assigns, to restrict the property to use as a single-family home. Does this accomplish her purpose under either the law of real covenants or equitable servitudes? For perhaps surprising reasons, the answer is no.

O sells to Buyer 1 Buyer 1 gives covenant to *O*	*O* sells to Buyer 2 Buyer 2 gives covenant to *O*
O sells to Buyer 3 Buyer 3 gives covenant to *O*	*O* sells to Buyer 4 Buyer 4 does not give a covenant

To illustrate this, imagine the following situation. *O* subdivides a parcel, and sells lots to Buyers 1, then Buyer 2, then Buyer 3, then Buyer 4. In the deeds with lots 1, 2, and 3, the buyers covenant to *O* to only use the land for residential purposes. The covenants are presumed to benefit *O*'s remaining land. Each buyer who purchases *O*'s land after the covenant is made, therefore, gets the benefit of the covenants already made benefitting O's land, and can enforce them against the earlier buyers. But earlier purchasers could not: *O* simply received a promise, but did not make a promise to restrict its remaining land. Buyer 3, for example, could prevent Buyer 1 from using the land for non-residential purposes, but Buyer 1 could not restrain Buyer 3. Nobody, moreover, could stop Buyer 4 from using that parcel as she wished, because the parcel was sold without a covenant.

The doctrine of **implied reciprocal negative servitudes** (also called implied reciprocal negative easements) solves both problems by implying that when a owner sells a number of parcels with evidence of intent to create a **common plan** or **scheme** of development then (1) covenants made to the seller benefit all parcels within the plan; and (2) all parcels within the plan are bound by the covenants. The courts reasoned that owners of other parcels within the common plan area were intended third-party beneficiaries of the agreements made with the developer, and that it would be unjust to permit owners to violate the covenants despite the lack of restrictions in their chain of title. As the cases below illustrate, the question then becomes what is sufficient evidence of intent to create a common plan, and what land comes within the plan.

Statutes and regulations in many states now require developers to file a **declaration** prior to selling individual lots subject to a common plan. The declaration describes the area covered by the common plan and recites the covenants applicable to the lots. Buyers are on constructive notice of the restrictions in the declaration if it is recorded prior to their purchase and are deemed to impliedly agree to abide by the restrictions; these grantee covenants are deemed to be made for the benefit of all lots in the plan. The declaration also constitutes a promise by the developer to restrict the remaining lots when they are sold; this constitutes a grantor covenant. If a declaration is filed, an earlier buyer who sues a later buyer for violating a covenant can base her claim on both the grantor covenant and the grantee covenant.

Evans v. Pollock

796 S.W.2d 465 (Tex. 1990)

Map: Hornsby Hill Road, Austin, Texas

C.L. Ray, Justice.

The doctrine of implied reciprocal negative easements applies when an owner of real property subdivides it into lots and sells a substantial number of those lots with restrictive covenants designed to further the owner's general plan or scheme of development. The central issue is usually the existence of a general plan of development. The lots retained by the owner, or lots sold by the owner from the development without express restrictions to a grantee with notice of the restrictions in the other deeds, are burdened with what is variously called an implied reciprocal negative easement, or an implied equitable servitude, or negative implied restrictive covenant, that they may not be used in violation of the restrictive covenants burdening the lots sold with the express restrictions. A reasonably accurate general statement of the doctrine has been given as follows:

> [W]here a common grantor develops a tract of land for sale in lots and pursues a course of conduct which indicates that he intends to inaugurate a general scheme or plan of development for the benefit of himself and the purchasers of the various lots, and by numerous conveyances inserts in the deeds substantially uniform restrictions, conditions and covenants against the use of the property, the grantees acquire by implication an equitable right, variously referred to as an implied reciprocal negative easement or an equitable servitude, to enforce similar restrictions against that part of the tract retained by the grantor or subsequently sold without the restrictions to a purchaser with actual or constructive notice of the restrictions and covenants. *Minner v. City of Lynchburg*, 129 S.E.2d 673, 679 (Va. 1963).

Facts

In September of 1947 Stanley and Sarah Agnes Hornsby (the Hornsbys), together with Charles and Bernice McCormick (McCormicks) platted a subdivision around Lake Travis from their commonly owned property in Travis County. They named the subdivision "Beby's Ranch Subdivision No. 1." The plat itself did not state any restrictions on land-use. The plat divided the property into seven blocks designated alphabetically "A" through "G." The plat did not further subdivide blocks C, D, E, and F, but blocks A, B, and G were divided into thirty-one lots. The subdivision is on a peninsula-like tract that extends into the lake, so that much of it has lake frontage. All of the platted lots are lakefront lots. Block G is located on the point of the peninsula. Block F is located on a hill and is surrounded by lakefront lots.

Block F is also referred to as the "hilltop."

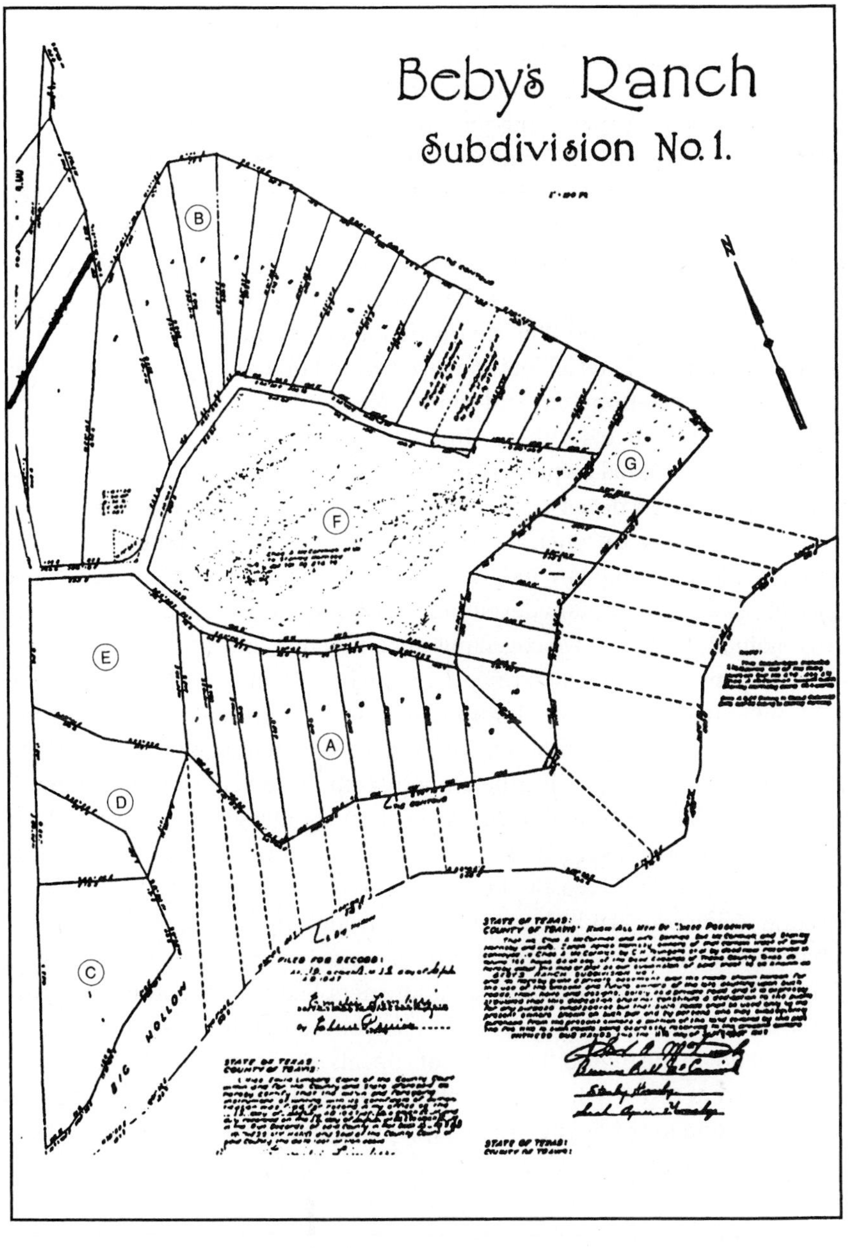

In October of 1947, before selling any lots other than two lots sold prior to the platting discussed below, the Hornsbys and McCormicks partitioned Beby's No. 1 between themselves. By partition deed the McCormicks received title to all of Blocks A, B, and C, and the Hornsbys got Blocks D, E, F, and G. Over the next several years, the Hornsbys and the McCormicks conveyed twenty-nine parcels of land from Beby's No. 1 to third parties or one another. Stanley Hornsby, a real estate attorney, and his law partner Louise Kirk, handled most of the legal work relating to the sale of lots, and the McCormicks made most of the sales. A real estate agent advertised some of the lakefront lots for sale in 1955, describing them as in "a restricted subdivision." Each deed from the Hornsbys and the McCormicks contained substantially the same restrictive covenants, including, among others, covenants: (1) prohibiting business or commercial use of the land conveyed; (2) restricting the land to residential use with only one dwelling per lot; and (3) providing that the restrictions could be changed by 3/4 of the property owners within the subdivision "voting according to front footage holdings on the 715 contour line" of the lake. In 1946 the McCormicks had conveyed two of the lakefront lots unburdened by any deed restrictions. When the original grantee conveyed the two lots to third parties in 1954, he had Hornsby draft the deeds. The deeds contained the restrictions that the property could not be used for any business or commercial purposes and that the restrictions could be altered by the "3/4 vote" along the 715 contour. Thus all lots conveyed ended up with substantially similar restrictions. All were lakefront lots, and voting rights under the restrictive covenants apparently were limited to lots with lake frontage.

The Hornsbys retained ownership of lots 4 through 8 in Block G and all of Block F. Both Hornsbys are now deceased, and the retained property passed to their devisees. The present dispute arose when the Hornsby devisees contracted to sell Thomas R. Pollock all of Block F and lots 4 and 5 in Block G for the purpose of building a marina, private club, and condominium development. Charles Evans and other owners whose deeds contained the restrictive covenants sued for equitable relief under the implied reciprocal negative easement doctrine. They sought declaration that the restrictive covenants enumerated above expressly imposed by deed upon their property were implied upon the Hornsby retained property. They further sought an injunction to prevent the Hornsby devisees from conveying the property without such deed restrictions.

Trial was to the court. The testimony sharply conflicted as to Stanley Hornsby's oral representations of his intentions for the retained property. The evidence ranged from testimony that could reasonably be interpreted to mean that Hornsby intended all the subdivision property to be restricted, to testimony lending itself to the conclusion that Hornsby intended the retained property to be unrestricted in all respects.

[The trial court held that the original subdividers, Stanley and Sarah Agnes Hornsby and Charles and Bernice McCormick, intended the restrictions to apply to all the lakefront lots but not to the hilltop. The court of appeals reversed, holding that none of the retained lots were restricted, on the ground that for the implied reciprocal negative easement doctrine to apply, the original grantors must have intended that the entire subdivision be similarly restricted.]

The Scope of a "Restricted District"

Provisions in restrictive covenants that the restrictions may be waived or modified by the consent of three-fourths of the lot owners constitute strong evidence that there is a general scheme or plan of development furthered by the restrictive covenants. The voting rights in the present case clearly attached only to lakefront lots. It was reasonable for the trial court to conclude that the restrictions were meant to apply only to the lakefront lots. The legal question is whether all the tracts in the development must be intended to be subject to the restrictions for the implied reciprocal negative easement doctrine to apply to any of the retained lots. We find it immaterial whether the question is phrased as whether the plan may be that some tracts are unrestricted while others are restricted, or whether the plan need only apply to certain similarly situated lots. We hold that the general plan or scheme may be that the restrictions only apply to certain well-defined similarly situated lots for the doctrine of implied reciprocal negative easements to apply as to such lots. Logical extensions of Texas decisions, as well as decisions from sister states, support our conclusion.

[Particularly] in point is the Kentucky case of *Bellemeade Co. v. Priddle*, 503 S.W.2d 734 (Ky. Ct. App. 1974). There the owners had platted and recorded sections I, II, III, IV and V of the Bellemeade subdivision. Sections I, II, III and IV had been marketed as restricted to one-family residential uses, but section V was a tract of approximately 12 acres adjacent to a major United States highway, different in character from the other sections. When the plat of section I went to record, there was a contract with the real estate firm marketing the subdivision which gave it the exclusive right to sell residential lots, but there was a separate provision giving those agents the exclusive right to sell, lease or develop section V as multi-family duplex housing, a shopping center and parking area. There was evidence of negotiations about section V with prospective buyers or developers for commercial enterprises both before and after the platting of the subdivision. After reviewing the marketing evidence, the court concluded there was no evidence that any lots in section V were offered for sale for residential purposes or evidence of confusion as to the developers' intent. The court held that the implied reciprocal negative easement doctrine applied as to retained lots in sections I through IV, but that section V was not part of the restricted area and could be sold for construction of a proposed Holiday Inn motel.

We have reviewed the record and find there is some evidence to support all trial court findings that were attacked in the court of appeals. Because there were factual sufficiency points raised in the court of appeals upon which that court has not ruled, we remand this cause to the court of appeals for further consideration consistent with this opinion.

Sanborn v. McLean, 206 N.W. 496 (Mich. 1925). Defendant Christina McLean owned land on which she and her husband sought to build a gas station. It would be located behind their house in a "high grade neighborhood" on Collingwood Avenue in Detroit, Michigan. All of the lots fronting on that portion of the road had once been owned by a single owner who imposed restrictive covenants on 53 of the 91 lots, limiting them to residential purposes. No restrictions appear in the chain of title to the McLean lot. The court held that the McLeans were on constructive notice of the restrictions in the deeds to neighboring properties and that the uniform residential character of the surrounding properties also put the McLeans on inquiry notice to determine whether there were restrictive covenants on neighboring lots that might be interpreted to create a plan to restrict the entire neighborhood to residential uses. Since a majority of the lots were restricted, the court inferred an intent to create a common plan even though a great number of the properties did not have restrictions in their line of title. Given evidence of an intent to create a common plan and constructive or inquiry notice on purchasers like the McLeans, the court imposed an implied reciprocal negative servitude restricting the McLean lot to residential purposes.

Riley v. Bear Creek Planning Committee, 551 P.2d 1213 (Cal. 1976). Ernest and Jewel Riley built a "snow tunnel" or "covered walkway" on their lot without first obtaining approval of the architectural control committee empowered by a recorded declaration to regulate land use in the area. The Rileys had purchased the first lot in the residential subdivision upon the representation of the seller that the properties would be subject to the recorded restrictions that they were given before buying the lot. However, the declaration containing the restrictions was not recorded until after they had purchased their lot; moreover, because of a mistake by the title company, their deed did not mention the restrictions. Although it appeared clear that buyers who purchased lots after the declaration was recorded were subject to the restrictions, the California Supreme Court ruled that the Rileys were not subject to the restrictions because there was no writing in their deed limiting the use of their land and the intent of the owner to impose those restrictions was not binding on them. Evidence of their knowledge of the grantor's intent to impose restrictions was not admissible under the parol evidence rule (which excluded admission of oral evidence that contradicts a writing in certain cases) and the Statute of Frauds (which required interests in land to be in writing to be enforceable), *id.* at 1221-1222:

> [There] is a practical consideration favoring the rule. The grantee of property subject to mutually enforceable restrictions takes not just a servient tenement but, as owner of a dominant tenement, acquires a property interest in all other lots similarly burdened for the benefit of his property. That fact significantly affects the expectations of the parties and inevitably enters into the exchange of consideration between grantor and grantee. Even though the grantor omits to include the mutual restrictions in deeds to parcels thereafter severed from the servient tenement, those who take such property with notice, actual or constructive, of the restrictions are bound thereby. Thus, the recording statutes operate to protect the expectations of the grantee and secure to him the full benefit of the exchange for which he bargained. Where, however, mutually enforceable equitable servitudes are sought to be created outside the recording statutes, the vindication of the expectations of the original grantee, and for that matter succeeding grantees, is hostage not only to the good faith of the grantor, but, even assuming good faith, to the vagaries of proof by extrinsic evidence of actual notice on the part of grantees who thereafter take a part of the servient tenement either from the common grantor or as

> successors in interest to his grantees. The uncertainty thus introduced into subdivision development would in many cases circumvent any plan for the orderly and harmonious development of such properties and result in a crazy-quilt pattern of uses frustrating the bargained-for expectations of lot owners in the tract.

Justice Matthew Tobriner dissented, *id.* at 1222:

> I cannot subscribe to the majority's conclusion that a buyer of a subdivision lot, who takes his deed with actual knowledge of a general plan of mutual restrictions applicable to the entire subdivision and who conducts himself for many years in a manner which demonstrates his belief that such restrictions apply to his property, thereafter violate all such restrictions with impunity simply because the restrictions were inadvertently omitted from his individual deed. Contrary to the majority's suggestion, we need not decree this inequitable result in order to prevent fraud to maintain security in land titles; the very antithesis — a ruling that a buyer with *actual knowledge* of restrictions is thereby bound — ensures fairness and promotes security in land transactions; it implements the intention of both the buyer and the seller.
>
> The majority's holding will permit plaintiffs in this case to ignore restrictions designed to preserve natural beauty and property values in a carefully planned residential community. Although the use of all other lots in the community will continue to be restricted, plaintiffs will be free to subdivide their land into any number of small building sites, construct apartments or rent commercial space, ignore building lines and obstruct views from neighboring lots, raise livestock, and strip the land by removing trees and shrubs.
>
> Common sense and substantive justice dictates that the plaintiffs should not be free to violate such restrictions. At the time of purchase plaintiffs had actual knowledge of those restrictions; the restrictions formed a part of the consideration exchanged by the parties. The restrictions continue to enhance the value of plaintiffs' individual lot because all other property owners in the subdivision are bound thereby.
>
> Accordingly, I would hold that the evidence offered by defendant committee is admissible to establish the existence of building restrictions binding upon plaintiffs.

Notes and Questions

1. **Implied reciprocal negative servitudes.** The doctrine of implied reciprocal negative servitudes, or reciprocal negative easements, was invented to deal with the intent, notice, and privity of estate issues that arise when a developer imposes grantee covenants on all lots in a residential subdivision and when the developer intentionally or inadvertently leaves those restrictions off some of the lots.

A common plan can be shown by various factors, such as the presence of restrictions in all or most deeds to property in the area, a recorded plat (map) showing the restrictions; the presence of restrictions in the last deed (since the grantor retains no land left to be benefited, the suggestion is that the intended beneficiaries of the promise are the other lots in the neighborhood); observance by owners of similar development of their land and conformity to the written restrictions; language stating that the covenants are intended to run with the land; and the recording of a declaration stating that the covenants are intended to be mutually enforceable. Gerald Korngold, *Private*

Land Use Arrangements: Easements, Real Covenants, and Equitable Servitudes §9.09, at 301-302 (1990). Evidence tending to show the absence of a common plan is that some deeds are unrestricted and that the restrictions are nonuniform.

Some courts, however, reject the doctrine of implied reciprocal negative servitudes applied in *Evans v. Pollock*, holding instead that reciprocal covenants will be enforced only if deeds in the chain of title themselves refer to the covenants or the developer records a declaration containing the restrictions prior to the sale of the properties sought to be burdened and benefited by them. *Citizens for Covenant Compliance v. Anderson*, 906 P.2d 1314, 1326 (Cal. 1995).

2. **The problem of unrestricted lots.** What happens if the developer fails to record a declaration or plat and imposes restrictive grantee covenants in most, but not all, of the deeds to property in the subdivision, and the grantor makes no promise to restrict the remaining lots? Can the owners of lots restricted by grantee covenants enforce them against buyers of the unrestricted lots? If the buyers of the remaining lots knew of the restriction and orally promised to comply with it, one might apply equitable estoppel doctrine in conjunction with third-party beneficiary doctrine to allow enforcement by prior and later buyers. But what if no oral statements are made by the buyers of the unrestricted lots promising to abide by the covenants?

Most courts hold that buyers of unrestricted lots are on constructive notice of covenants in other deeds in the vicinity sold by the same grantor. *Roper v. Camuso*, 829 A.2d 589, 595 (Md. 2003). *Sanborn v. McLean* went so far as to argue that a buyer in a residential neighborhood should be on inquiry notice if there is a uniform pattern of development that might suggest the existence of a common plan.

What evidence is sufficient to show a common plan? If too many of the lots in the subdivision are sold without restrictions, the court may find that no common scheme was in fact established, thus freeing all the unrestricted lots from the duty to comply with the covenants in their neighbors' deeds. *Petersen v. Beekmere, Inc.*, 283 A.2d 911 (N.J. Super. Ct. Ch. Div. 1971). *Sanborn v. McLean* imposed restrictive covenants on an entire neighborhood even though the covenants were included in only 53 of 91 deeds. Was this justified? *Compare Forster v. Hall*, 576 S.E.2d 746 (Va. 2003) (implied reciprocal negative servitude prohibiting mobile homes was enforced against unrestricted lots when 93 percent of lots were restricted).

What justifies limiting a property owner's right to develop his land when the deed he received from the seller neither had any restrictions in it nor referred to the restrictions in deeds previously granted to others in the subdivision? In *Riley*, the California Supreme Court rejected the ruling in *Sanborn* by holding a lot cannot be restricted unless those restrictions appear in the chain of title to that particular lot. Thus, the first buyers were not restricted because they purchased prior to the recordation of the declaration, even though they were on notice of the restrictions at the time they purchased. Do you agree with the court's ruling or with the dissenting opinion of Justice Tobriner?

In 1995, the California Supreme Court clarified *Riley* by holding that any buyer of a lot covered by a recorded declaration is bound by the restrictions in the declaration even if his deed nowhere mentions the declaration or the restrictions. *Citizens for Covenant Compliance v. Anderson*, 906 P.2d 1314 (Cal. 1995). The terms of a recorded declaration are impliedly included in the deeds to lots covered by the declaration. This leaves standing the ruling in *Riley* that exempts lots purchased before the declaration was recorded.

3. Lots retained by the grantor. Suppose all the covenants in the neighborhood contain grantee covenants restricting the property to single-family use. Moreover, the developer files a declaration to that effect describing all the property in the subdivision as restricted. The developer owns property across the street from this subdivision; the property is left undeveloped for several years after the subdivision is completed. The developer then seeks to build on this property in a manner inconsistent with the restrictions imposed on the subdivision. Can the developer do this? The question arises whether the neighboring tract should be treated as part of the common plan. If it was noted on the original plat, the courts are likely to hold that it was part of the common plan. But suppose it was never described on the plat or the declaration or orally as part of the development. May the developer sell to commercial users in a manner that does not constitute a common law nuisance but nonetheless interferes with the common residential scheme by substantially changing the environment? No promises of any kind were made to the buyers in the subdivision that the developer would not do this. Most courts hold that only parcels within the common scheme are restricted and that the grantor's intent to leave a tract or parcel out of the common scheme is determinative.

In *Duvall v. Ford Leasing Development Corp.*, 255 S.E.2d 470 (Va. 1979), a developer subdivided and built homes on a large tract in stages over a 25-year period. Each of the subdivisions was restricted to residential use. The developer then sold its remaining land, expressly providing in the deed that a portion of it would remain free of restrictions of any kind. The buyer of that land sold the unrestricted parcel to an owner who sought to establish a car sales and service business. Relying on the piecemeal development and the fact that it occurred over a long period of time, the court held that the development consisted of separate subdivisions and that the entire property was not subject to a single common plan. In contrast, the court in *Snow v. Van Dam*, 197 N.E. 224 (Mass. 1935), concluded that a lot across the street from the rest of a subdivision was intended to be in the same common plan, although it was sold more than 15 years after the first lot, because it was included in the description of the entire tract when it was registered and the delay in sale was caused by the inability to sell the property rather than an intent to exclude it from the restricted area.

When a developer that deliberately leaves some of its contiguous land out of the common scheme attempts to develop the retained land in a manner inconsistent with the common scheme, is there any argument for constraining the developer's ability to do this? Does it matter if the unrestricted lots are located outside but adjacent to the subdivision or inside it?

Problems

1. A developer sells 45 of 50 lots in a subdivision, with grantee covenants restricting uses to single-family homes. The developer orally assures the buyers that all the lots will be restricted. The developer, however, has trouble selling the last five lots located on the edge of the development. A buyer offers to purchase three of the lots if they can be combined and an apartment building constructed with 25 apartments. The price is lower than the developer hoped to get for the three properties, but no other buyers seem ready to purchase the lots for use as single-family homes at prices that would allow the developer to make a profit. Then another buyer comes along who offers an extremely high price for the last two lots so long as no covenant is included in the deed; this buyer wants to build a gas station. Several of the owners of the restricted lots sue the owners of the lots that are to be developed as an apartment building and a gas station.

   a. Can they enforce the restrictions against these owners under current law? Should they be able to do so?

   b. Now suppose the developer intended all along to sell the last five lots as unrestricted lots, and the buyers can prove that the developer intended to defraud them at the time of purchase, rather than merely changing her mind when the market went soft. Does this change your analysis?

2. A developer owns two large tracts located across the road from each other. The area is rural and undeveloped. The developer constructs a residential subdivision on one tract, with grantor and grantee covenants restricting the property to single-family homes. The developer also represents orally to the buyers that the area will be a pleasant residential neighborhood. All the lots contain the covenants, and uniform development occurs. Then the developer makes plans to turn the tract across the street into a shopping center. Can she do so?

§4.2 Common Interest Developments and Property Owners Associations

As of 2011, some 62 million Americans lived in settings in which multiple dwellings are joined by servitudes providing them with shared rights in common elements such as roads and recreational facilities, or shared obligations to contribute fees to an owners association that maintains the common elements, enforces the covenants, and (in some cases) enacts rules for the community. The *Restatement (Third)* and the Uniform Laws Commission have called such residential settings "common interest communities." *See Restatement (Third)* §6.2; U.L.A., *Uniform Common Interest Owners Bill of Rights* §2.6. The California Supreme Court calls them "common interest developments" and "community associations." *Nahrstedt v. Lakeside Village Condominium Association, Inc.*, 878 P.2d 1275 (Cal. 1994). Do these terms strike you as appropriate descriptions?

Part of the explosion of common interest developments in the 1970s was tied to federal tax changes that made ownership of rental properties less profitable, and gave unit owners tax credits similar to those for single-family housing. *See* Henry Hansmann, *Condominium and Cooperative Housing: Transactional Efficiency, Tax Subsidies, and Tenure Choice,* 20 J. Leg. Studies 25 (1991). Federal law still creates some differences between common interest developments and single-family homes. Hurricane Sandy drew attention to one: Common elements are generally not eligible for FEMA disaster assistance given to single-family homes, because property owners associations are considered businesses under the law.

This section discusses some of the kinds of residential common interest developments, and distinct legal and policy questions they pose.

A. Residential Subdivisions and Condominiums

Most common interest developments are either composed of separate houses in a planned subdivision or are **condominiums** — attached dwellings or units in an apartment building. The developer typically drafts the initial covenants or **CC&Rs** (conditions, covenants, and restrictions) for these communities and records them as a **declaration** or **master deed** with the local recording office or register of deeds prior to sale of the first unit. In buying their units, owners agree to abide by these covenants. Owners individually own and obtain financing for their own units, but they share ownership of the common elements of the community. Owners may vote to amend the initial covenants, although a supermajority vote of between 60 to 75 percent is usually required.

The declaration will typically create a **homeowners association** or **condominium association**. Each of the owners is a member of the association. Owners are empowered to vote for the members of a board, called the board of trustees or board of managers, to manage the association's common interests. In addition to enforcing covenants, homeowners associations may be empowered to collect dues and fees from the owners to maintain common areas such as roads and recreational facilities and rooftops and hallways of condominiums. They are also often empowered to promulgate bylaws or rules governing use of common areas and perhaps even the appearance and use of individual lots or units. Unpaid dues or fines for rule violations often constitute liens on the property empowering the owners association to foreclose.

In effect, these associations function like local governments, except that votes are not based on "one person-one vote" but are based on property ownership. Only owners have voting rights; tenants and other family members are not entitled to vote in board elections; and owners of more property in the community may have more votes. Just as shareholders of corporations generally have votes based on the number of shares they own, votes in homeowners associations may be unequal because they may be based on lot sizes (or, as seen in *Evans v. Pollock, supra,* lake frontage). Developers may also give themselves more than one vote for each unit they own. *See, e.g., Hughes v. New Life Development Corporation,* 387 S.W.3d 453 (Tenn. 2012) (upholding scheme in which developer had five votes per lot owned); Evan McKenzie, *Beyond Privatopia: Rethinking Residential Private Government* 11 (2011) (three votes per unsold lot is typical). Unlike governments, owners associations are generally not subject to federal or state constitutional restrictions. *But cf. Shelley v. Kraemer, infra* (holding that enforcement of a racially discriminatory covenant violated the fourteenth amendment).

State statutes regulate common interest developments by providing basic ground rules for their organization. These statutes may define the basic structure of the common interest development, requiring a declaration, bylaws, and supermajority votes for amendment of covenants and certain other decisions of the association.

B. Cooperatives

Condominiums must be distinguished from **cooperatives**. In a cooperative arrangement, the entire building is owned by a single nonprofit cooperative corporation. Individual owners buy shares in the corporation and then lease their individual units from the corporation. Since ownership is vested in the corporation, the costs of operating the cooperative, including payments for the building's mortgage (if there is one), will be financed by the corporation itself. The monthly payment by each owner (in the form of rent) covers that owner's share of the mortgage payment, as well as fees for upkeep and management. If an individual owner fails to make her monthly payment to the corporation, other owners must make up the difference in order to prevent foreclosure. Defaulting tenants can be evicted by the corporation and lose their stock. The greater financial interdependence of cooperative owners makes this a more fragile structure than the condominium structure; it is therefore much less common. Because of the financial interdependence of cooperative owners, cooperatives often assume the power to approve or veto sales of particular units to protect other cooperative members' collective financial stake in the building.

C. Community Land Trusts and Limited Equity Co-ops

Advocates for the poor have been creative in inventing new forms of landholding tailored to low-income persons. Two widely used forms are limited equity cooperatives and community land trusts. Although structured differently, the purpose of these ownership forms is "to remove land from the speculative market, create housing for low income people, and keep that housing affordable." Christopher Seeger, *The Fixed Price Preemptive Right in the Community Land Trust Lease: A Valid Response to the Housing Crisis or an Invalid Restraint on Alienation?*, 11 Cardozo L. Rev. 471 (1989); *see* James J. Kelly, *Land Trusts That Conserve Communities*, 59 DePaul L. Rev. 69 (2009).

Community land trusts. A community land trust is a nonprofit corporation that buys and holds title to property, ordinarily by acquiring inexpensive land located in a depressed area or land whose purchase is subsidized by government loans, loan guarantees, or subsidies. The trust retains title to the land, but sells residences on the land, whether as single-family homes or condominiums, to lower-income purchasers at below market rates. Although the purchasers own their units, they receive a **ground lease** for the land. Such ground leases separate land and unit ownership, and are common in commercial transactions involving large office buildings. The ground lease ordinarily lasts for a long time — often 99 years — and may be renewable.

A crucial aspect of the arrangement is that the lessee-unit owners agree to sell to either the community land trust, or another low-income purchaser, at a below-market price that splits the equity in the property between the landowner and the unit owner. This arrangement ensures that the property will remain low cost and therefore available to other low-income buyers. Community land trusts got their start in the 1960s as part of the Civil Rights Movement, but have multiplied in recent decades in response to rising property costs and federal and state recognition and support. *See* Sarah Iline Stein, *Wake Up, Fannie Mae, I Think I Got Something to Say to You: Financing Community Land Trust Homeowners Without Stripping Affordability Provisions*, 60 Emory L.J. 209 (2010); 42 U.S.C. §12773 (authorizing federal support for community land trusts).

Limited equity cooperatives. A limited equity cooperative has a purpose similar to a community land trust but is organized like a regular cooperative. The purchaser buys shares in the cooperative and obtains a lease to a particular unit. The contracts involved in this arrangement allow sale of the owner's shares at a fixed price, thus preventing the owner from benefiting from increases in the market value of the unit. Judith Bernstein-Baker, *Cooperative Conversion: Is It Only for the Wealthy? Proposals That Promote Affordable Cooperative Housing in Philadelphia,* 61 Temp. L. Rev. 393 (1988).

D. Competing Perspectives

The rise of the common interest development is a "quiet revolution in the structure of community organization, local government, land-use control, and neighbor relations." Stephen E. Barton & Carol J. Silverman, *Preface, Common Interest Communities* at xi (S. Barton & C. Silverman eds. 1994). Common interest developments are no longer simply a U.S. phenomenon, but have spread to every continent; in China, an estimated 250 million people live in privately governed communities. Evan McKenzie, *Beyond Privatopia: Rethinking Residential Private Government* x (2011). Developers often prefer them, because they can use less space by providing common recreational facilities rather than a yard for each home. But the phenomenon is no longer driven solely by the market. Many municipalities either explicitly or in practice require new construction to be bound by a property owners association in order to offload the costs of providing public goods. McKenzie, *supra*, at 6-7; Paula A. Franzese & Steven Siegel, *The Common Interest Community as Metaphor and Paradox*, 72 Mo. L. Rev. 1111, 1119-1121 (2004). In many of these developments, streets, infrastructure, parks, and recreation, are all privately paid for and controlled by CC&Rs and the owners associations that administer them. These developments also often perform police functions, employing private security officers. They may also close off their interior streets and erect walls or gates, becoming "gated communities." Governing associations, however, are not held to constitutional norms and their directors are volunteers who often have little training or support.

Some scholars laud this development. Proponents cite the explosion of this housing form as evidence that Americans desire its benefits, *see* Robert H. Nelson, *Private Neighborhoods and the Transformation of Local Government* 7-8 (2005), and emphasize the "perfectly voluntary nature of membership in a homeowners association." Robert C. Ellickson, *Cities and Homeowners Associations*, 130 U. Pa. L. Rev. 1519, 1520 (1982). Common interest developments, they argue, offer a voluntary, market-based alternative to coercive governments, putting "[p]rivate profit . . . at the service of devising a better system of local governance — at least from the viewpoint of the homebuyers themselves." Nelson, *supra*, at 14. Others praise the potential of the common interest development to create communities that counter the atomization of modern life. *See, e.g.*, Mark Fenster, *Community by Covenant, Process, and Design: Cohousing and the Contemporary Common Interest Community*, 15 J. Land Use & Envtl. L. 3 (1999) (critiquing the co-housing movement).

Others challenge the assertions of voluntariness and flexibility. They point out that common interest developments are the only housing available in many markets, claiming that their rise has been driven not by owner demand but by developers and municipal zoning requirements. Purchasers have no power to negotiate the restrictions on their homes, and may not read or understand the many pages of legal language that describes them. Critics also argue that the hoped-for diversity in housing options has not appeared. Despite developments like Celebration and "co-housing" communities that include cooperative elements, most CC&Rs are largely boilerplate, copied from one community to another. This boilerplate may be more restrictive than most purchasers would desire, as developers seek to reassure early purchasers and avoid adverse selection into the community by less desirable residents. Lee Anne Fennell, *Contracting Communities*, 2004 U. Ill. L. Rev. 829. Many scholars express concern about exclusionary conduct, oppressive micromanagement, and the privatization of governmental functions by homeowners associations. *See* Gerald E. Frug, *Cities and Homeowners Associations: A Reply*, 130 U. Pa. L. Rev. 1589 (1982); Ellickson, *supra*, at 1533 (proposing a takings clause for common interest developments); Stewart Sterk, *Minority Protection in Residential Private Governments*, 77 B.U. L. Rev. 273 (1997). Newspapers regularly publish horror stories about owners associations foreclosing on homes worth hundreds of thousands for unpaid dues of a few hundred dollars; filing lawsuits against owners who paint their mailboxes the wrong color, hang mezzuzahs on their doors, or park their pickup trucks in the driveway; and putting senior citizens in jail for failing to re-sod a brown lawn.

> **CONTEXT**
>
> **Celebration or Stepford life?**
>
> The Disney-built development of Celebration, Florida seeks to replicate a small town Main Street feel, paying employees to facilitate group activities, and making fake snow ("snoap") at Christmas. The development has won awards from the Urban Land Institute and seen property values skyrocket, although they've dipped significantly since the recession. Critics also abound, and they were morbidly gleeful at news of the first murder, followed soon after by an unrelated suicide, and stories of high divorce rates in the community.

So what do owners think? The Community Associations Institute, an industry group representing owners associations, regularly conducts a survey that finds that the overwhelming majority of owners like living in their common interest development and would choose to live in one again. Others critique the methodology of these surveys and point to an earlier survey conducted in California finding that 84 percent of residents would not choose to live a common interest development again. Barton & Silverman, *supra*, at 137. Groups of disgruntled owners have secured legislation in several states imposing state oversight and regulation over owners associations. Nevertheless, these developments continue to spread and people continue to buy into them. What do you think?

§4.3 Relationship Between Unit Owners and Developers

Appel v. Presley Cos.

806 P.2d 1054 (N.M. 1991)

Map: Vista Serena Lane SW,
Albuquerque, New Mexico

Gene E. Franchini, Justice.

Plaintiffs Daniel and Patricia Appel appeal from an order granting summary judgment to defendants The Presley Company of New Mexico (Presley) and Wolfe Company, Inc. (Wolfe). In their complaint, the Appels asserted three claims: breach of restrictive covenants; negligent and fraudulent misrepresentation; and unfair trade practices.

Facts

On January 3, 1979, Presley recorded with the Bernalillo County Clerk a replat for the Vista Del Sandia subdivision. On October 8, 1982, Presley recorded a set of restrictive covenants covering all the property shown on the replat, including a tract in the subdivision arroyo. The covenants regulated the land use, building type, quality, and size of the residential single-family dwellings that were to be placed on the subdivision property. In November 1982, the Appels met with Presley and its agents regarding the possible purchase of a lot in the subdivision. The Appels allege certain representations were made concerning lots in the subdivision and the purpose of the restrictive covenants. The Appels further allege that the restrictive covenants were used as a sales tool which they relied on in purchasing a lot and constructing their home. On April 25, 1984, the subdivision's Architectural Control Committee, consisting of three members who were all employees or officers of Presley, executed an amendment of the restrictive covenants. This amendment deleted nine lots from the effect of the restrictive covenants, including Lots 28-A and 30 which are involved in this appeal. Since the covenants were amended, some of the lots have been subdivided into smaller lots and townhouses have been constructed on them. Presley sold Lot 28-A to Wolfe in April

1988. Wolfe is replatting Lot 28-A into four lots for single family residences. No development plans exist for Lot 30, the arroyo lot.

I. Restrictive Covenants

The Appels filed their complaint to enjoin Wolfe's proposed replatting and construction and to enjoin the construction of any buildings on Lot 30. The following provisions contained in the restrictive covenants were relied on by the trial court to authorize the amendments:

> 15. *Architectural Control Committee:* At any time, the then record owners of the majority of the lots shall have the power, through a duly recorded written instrument, to change the membership of the Committee or to withdraw from the Committee, or restore to it any of its powers and duties.
>
> 17. *Terms of covenants:* These covenants are to run with the land and shall be binding on all parties and all persons claiming under them for a period of thirty (30) years from the date these covenants are recorded, after which time said covenants shall be automatically extended for successive periods of ten (10) years, unless an instrument signed by a majority of the then lot owners of the lots have been recorded, agreeing to change said covenants in whole or in part.
>
> 20. *Variance:* A majority of the Architectural Control Committee, may from time to time, make amendments and/or exceptions to these restrictions, covenants and reservations without the consent of any of the owners of any of the other lots in said subdivision.

In particular, the trial court emphasized the "amendments and/or exceptions to these restrictions" language of paragraph 20 in the restrictive covenants. The trial court found that the language was unambiguous and that the covenant permitted the Architectural Control Committee to make exceptions and remove individual lots from the covenants. This court has recognized the importance of enforcing protective covenants where the clear language of the covenants, as well as the surrounding circumstances, indicates an intent to restrict use of land. In *Montoya v. Barreras*, 473 P.2d 363 (N.M. 1970), we refused to allow an individual lot to be removed from the effect of a restrictive covenant in spite of a provision in the covenant allowing change by majority approval. We held: "To permit individual lots within an area to be relieved of the burden of such covenants, in the absence of a clear expression in the instrument so providing, would destroy the right to rely on restrictive covenants which has traditionally been upheld by our law of real property." *Id.* at 365. Here, the trial court found the "amendments and/or exceptions to these restrictions" language to be the clear expression required by *Montoya*.

We agree that the language permitted the Architectural Control Committee to make amendments or exceptions to the restrictive covenant. However, courts have determined that provisions allowing amendment of subdivision restrictions are subject to a requirement of reasonableness. As stated in 7 G. Thompson, *Real Property*, §3171 (repl. 1962), "A court of equity will not enforce restrictions where there are circumstances that render their enforcement inequitable."

In *Flamingo Ranch Estates, Inc. v. Sunshine Ranches Homeowners, Inc.*, 303 So. 2d 665 (Fla. Dist. Ct. App. 1974), the court addressed a similar clause reserving to the land developer the right to alter, amend, repeal, or modify restrictions at any time in his sole discretion. The court noted the inherent inconsistency between an elaborate set of restrictive covenants, designed to provide for a general scheme or plan of development, and a clause reserving in the grantor the power to change or abandon any part of it. The court reconciled the inconsistency by reading into the restrictive clause a requirement of reasonableness. Thus, the clause allowing the owners the right to alter, amend, repeal, or modify these restrictions at any time in its sole discretion is a valid clause so long as it is exercised in a reasonable manner so as not to destroy the general scheme or plan of development.

The Supreme Court of Alabama also imposed a test of reasonableness when a developer exercised his reserved right to cancel or modify any of the restrictive covenants. *Moore v. Megginson*, 461 So. 2d 993 (Ala. 1982). The court affirmed the trial court's finding that the developer's "exercise of his right to cancel or modify the restrictive covenants 'must be reasonable, with due regard for the property rights and investments of the persons who relied upon the residential covenants which were in full force at the time of their purchase.' " *Id.*

A determination of whether the exceptions were reasonably exercised or whether they essentially destroyed the covenants requires resolution of a factual matter and, therefore, the summary judgment must be reversed and testimony should be taken accordingly. Additionally, if it is found that the exceptions were applied in an unreasonable manner, thereby breaching the covenants, the trial court should apply the doctrine of relative hardships.

As we stated in *Cunningham* [*v. Gross*, 699 P.2d 1075 (N.M. 1985)], any request for injunctive relief is directed to the sound discretion of the trial court. "In determining whether such relief should issue, the court may consider a number of factors and should balance equities and hardships where required." 699 P.2d at 1077. Factors for the trial court to consider include, *id.* at 1078:

> (1) [T]he character of the interest to be protected, (2) the relative adequacy to the plaintiff of injunction in comparison with other remedies, (3) the delay, if any, in bringing suit, (4) the misconduct of the plaintiff if any, (5) the interest of third persons, (6) the practicability of granting and enforcing the order or judgment, and (7) the relative hardship likely to result to the defendant if an injunction is granted and to the plaintiff if it is denied.

In view of the foregoing, we reverse and remand on the trial court's order granting summary judgment on Claim I.

II. Misrepresentation and Unfair Trade Practices Act

The trial court erred . . . finding no material issue of fact regarding misrepresentation and violation of the *[Unfair] Trade Practices Act.* The trial court focused only on statements made by Presley representatives in 1982 about certain lots not being developable, ignoring other alleged misrepresentations concerning the effect of the covenants. The Appels produced sufficient evidence to raise factual questions as to whether Presley misrepresented that Lot 30 would remain open space and that the covenants would maintain the intended character of the subdivision. Whether or not the statements made to the Appels about Lots 28-A and 30 were true or false at the time made are issues of fact to be determined at trial, not by the court on summary judgment.

The order granting summary judgment by the trial court is reversed on all three claims and the cause is remanded for reinstatement for trial upon the court's docket.

Notes and Questions

1. **Developer control.** The developer of a condominium initially owns all the units and therefore controls the condominium association. Declarations also frequently give developers multiple votes per unsold unit or the right to appoint a majority of board members, permitting them to maintain control even after most of the units are sold. The *Uniform Common Interest Ownership Act* §3-103, as well as the laws of a number of states that have not adopted the act, provide that developers must turn over control to unit owners once 75 percent of the units are sold or two years after units stop being sold in the ordinary course of business. *See also Restatement (Third) of Property (Servitudes)* §6.19. Even these protections, however, may leave a substantial period where the developer can dominate the property owners association and govern the interests of unit owners.

2. **Developer power to amend the declaration.** The *Restatement (Third)* §6.21 provides: "A developer may not exercise a power to amend or modify the declaration in a way that would materially change the character of the development or the burdens on the existing community members unless the declaration fairly apprises purchasers that the power could be used for the kind of change proposed." In a case similar to *Appel,* a Kansas court adopted this *Restatement* rule, holding that a developer's power to "amend" the covenants limiting land to single-family or duplex homes did not include the power to "revoke" them entirely and build four-unit housing. *North Country Villas Homeowners Association v. Kokenge,* 163 P.3d 1247 (Kan. Ct. App. 2007). The court noted that it was not applying a "reasonableness test," but holding that such an amendment "would violate notice principles by materially changing the general development plan of the subdivision without fair warning to purchasers." *Id.* at 1254.

Hughes v. New Life Development Corp., 387 S.W.3d 453 (Tenn. 2012), reached the opposite result. As in *Appel* and *North Country Villas,* the power to change the master plan was included in the original declaration, which also provided developer with five votes for each unsold unit it owned. Replacing the original developer after half of the platted units had been sold, the new developer used its supermajority

CONTEXT

The recession highlighted the issue of developer control in the event of developer bankruptcy—a particularly significant problem when the unit owners want to sue the developer through their (developer controlled) owners association. Some jurisdictions respond to this issue by interpreting filing for bankruptcy as a de facto turnover of control. Larry Woodard, *Representing a Homeowners Association Facing Developer Bankruptcy,* 24-AUG Prob. & Prop. 36 (2010).

of votes to amend the declaration to change a planned 80-residence community with wilderness preserves and hiking into a 650-residence golf resort. The Tennessee Supreme Court upheld these actions: "Contract law in Tennessee plainly reflects the public policy allowing competent parties to strike their own bargains. These contract principles, applied in the context of a private residential development with covenants that are expressly subject to amendment without substantive limitation, yield the conclusion that a homeowner should not be heard to complain when, as anticipated by the recorded declaration of covenants, the homeowners' association amends the declaration." *Id.* at 475-476.

3. Management contracts. Developers may use their period of control to arrange for management or other contracts in which the condominium hires the developer to provide services in exchange for management fees. Owners often have found these contracts are unfair either because the fees charged by the developer-manager are exorbitant or because the contracts last for so long that they prevent the unit owners from hiring someone else if they become dissatisfied with the way the place is being run.

The *Condominium and Cooperative Conversion Protection and Abuse Relief Act,* 15 U.S.C. §§3601-3616, authorizes condominiums and cooperatives, by a two-thirds vote, to terminate without penalty management contracts of more than three years entered into while the developer had majority control of the condominium or cooperative. *Id.* §3607(a). Many states have also passed statutes regulating developer-created contracts, often providing that they can be rejected by a supermajority vote. *See, e.g., Comcast of Florida v. L'Ambiance Beach Condominium Association, Inc.*, 17 So. 3d 839 (Fla. App. 2009) (applying a Florida statute that allowed 75 percent or more of the unit ownership rights to repudiate a contract permitting Comcast to provide and manage cable services to the units).

4. Developer's power to enforce covenants after sale of all units. Recall the rule restricting the enforceability of covenants when the benefit is held in gross. The declaration may give the developer the power to enforce the covenants by bringing a lawsuit to compel compliance. When the developer of a subdivision attempts to continue to enforce the covenant after the last parcel is sold, the courts may deny the developer standing to bring a suit to enforce the covenants because of the policies underlying the rule prohibiting the benefit of covenants to be held in gross. The developer's legitimate interest in retaining control over development in the subdivision is to increase the marketability of the lots; assuring prospective buyers that the subdivision is restricted to residential use, or even single-family homes, may increase the market value of the property and attract buyers. Once the developer leaves, however, she is an outsider whose legitimate interests have already been satisfied; continued control by the developer is seen as meddling. There is therefore a strong, although not universal, presumption against continued enforcement by absentee developers who no longer own property in the neighborhood. *Garland v. Rosenshein*, 649 N.E.2d 756 (Mass. 1995) (benefit of covenant held in gross cannot be enforced); *Smith v. First Savings of Louisiana*, 575 So. 2d 1033 (Ala. 1991) (refusing to allow the developer to retain control of the architectural review commission empowered to approve building changes in the subdivision once the last parcel was sold); *Armstrong v. Roberts*, 325 S.E.2d 769 (Ga. 1985) (developer cannot waive a covenant after all parcels are sold and it has no economic interest in the subdivision).

Some courts have allowed developers to continue to enforce covenants when the declaration allows this, at least where the owners have the power to amend the declaration and there is no showing that the developer "retained unreasonable or imperious control over . . . decisions of homeowners long after having completed the subdivision." *B.C.E. Development, Inc. v. Smith*, 264 Cal. Rptr. 55, 61 (Ct. App. 1989). *Accord, Christiansen v. Casey*, 613 S.W.2d 906 (Mo. Ct. App. 1981). Although the *Restatement (Third)* makes covenants enforceable when the benefit is held in gross, *id.* §2.6(b), it still requires a legitimate interest in the party who seeks enforcement, *id.* §2.6 cmt. d. What legitimate reasons, if any, could a developer have for retaining the power to enforce the covenants once the last unit is sold?

5. Private transfer fees. In recent years, a growing number of developers and homeowners associations have inserted covenants requiring owners to pay them a private transfer fee when the property is sold. The fee may encumber the property for as long as 99 years and is typically set at about 1 percent of the sale price. Developers claim that these fees create an alternative source of financing, allowing them to create developments less expensively, and that the savings are passed on to purchasers. Because these fees are often not assessed against the original purchaser, owners may not realize that they are in place. More than half of the states now ban private transfer fees by statute and a 2012 federal regulation prohibits Fannie Mae from purchasing loans on properties burdened by such fees. 12 C.F.R. Part 1228. These laws exempt private transfer fees to homeowners association if the fee is dedicated to homeowners association activities, and they do not generally apply to private transfer fees recorded before the laws were promulgated.

Problems

1. A famous architect develops a subdivision of 50 homes with an unusual design for the houses. The design is popular, and the properties are sold for high prices. Before the first home was sold, the developer recorded a declaration that contained restrictive covenants preventing any external changes to the structures or landscaping without consent of the architectural review commission. The developer was identified by name in the declaration as the sole member of the architectural review commission. Every deed refers to the declaration.

a. Five years after the last home was sold, a homeowner seeks to change the color of her house and to add a sunroom. The architect refuses to allow the changes, although none of the neighbors objects to them. The owner sues the architect, claiming that the covenant granting the architect continued control of the architectural review commission after the last unit was sold is unenforceable. The architect claims that the design of the houses is akin to a work of art, that she has a right to artistic control of the houses, and that the plaintiff voluntarily consented to this arrangement. Some of the neighbors support the architect's position in order to maintain the value of their homes. Who should win? Would your answer change if the problem arose 50 years after the last house was sold? Suppose the architect wrote a will leaving her right of enforcement to her daughter at her death. Could the daughter enforce the covenant?

b. Now suppose the declaration grants the architect complete control of interior design, including furniture. A resident is paralyzed in an automobile accident and wants to change the furniture and the kitchen to make them wheelchair accessible. The architect refuses to agree to the change. No owner in the neighborhood objects to her proposed changes. The homeowner argues that the benefit of the covenant cannot be held in gross. Who should win? Is there another basis to invalidate the covenant? Should it be enforced?

2. On September 23, 2012, New York became the 37th state to ban private transfer fees. The law finds that private transfer fees violate the public policy of the state by "impairing the marketability and transferability of real property and by constituting an unreasonable restraint on alienation." N.Y. Real Prop. Law §471. However, the law declares that the ban on enforcement of such fees "shall not apply to a private transfer fee obligation recorded or entered into prior to the effective date of this section. This section shall not be deemed to require that a private transfer fee obligation recorded, filed or entered into in this state before the effective date of this section is presumed valid and enforceable. It is the public policy of this state that no private transfer fee obligation shall be valid or enforceable whenever entered into, recorded or filed." *Id.* §473.

The law resonates with an early New York case, *De Peyster v. Michael*, 6 N.Y. 467 (1852), which invalidated a requirement that the owner provide the original lessor of the land one quarter of the purchase price upon every sale. The court held that the requirement was an invalid restraint on alienation prohibited by New York's rejection of feudalism:

> If the continuance of the estate can be made to depend on the payment of a tenth, or a sixth, or a fourth part of the value of the land at every sale, it may be made to depend on the payment of nine-tenths, or the whole of the sale money. It would be a bold assertion to say that the adoption of such a principle would not operate as a fatal restraint upon alienation.
>
> Restraints upon alienation of lands held in fee simple were of feudal origin. A feoffment in fee did not originally pass an estate in the sense in which we now understand it. The purchaser took only an usufructuary interest, without the power of alienation in prejudice of the heir or of the lord. In default of heirs the tenure became extinct and the land reverted to the lord. This restraint on alienation was a violent and unnatural state of things, contrary to the nature and value of property, and the inherent and universal love of independence.
>
> [A]fter a careful examination of the grounds on which these restraints on alienations in fee were originally sustained in England; of the change in the law there by statute nearly 600 years ago; of the mode in which that change was wrought; and finding that the same change has taken place here by our own statutes, we cannot entertain a doubt

> that the condition to pay sale money on leases in fee, is repugnant to the estate granted, and therefore void in law.

6 N.Y. at 496-498, 505. A developer seeks to enforce a 1 percent private transfer fee to the developer included in a covenant signed and recorded long before the New York statute was enacted. What arguments can you make for the developer? For the owner?

§5 SUBSTANTIVE LIMITATIONS ON CREATION AND ENFORCEMENT OF COVENANTS

Covenants give private individuals and associations significant power over how others use their land. While early covenant law often restricted this power, today courts and legislatures generally permit and encourage such agreements to allow people to structure land use to best meet their needs. But enforcement of covenants may undermine other societal or individual interests. This section considers different grounds for challenging covenants: first, general review for reasonableness and public policy violations; second, assertion of constitutional violations; third, claims of discrimination under the *Fair Housing Act*; fourth, review of restrictions on alienability; and fifth, claims of unreasonable restraint of trade.

§5.1 Review for Reasonableness and Public Policy Violations

A. Covenants

Public policy concerns have always been a part of covenant law, particularly for injunctive relief, which is an equitable remedy. Although the overriding policy concern was that covenants violated a policy favoring free use of land, more specific concerns also came into play. The touch and concern test was often used as the way to invalidate covenants, even those like restrictions on competing uses by a neighboring business that clearly touched and concerned the land. In 1988, Susan French noted, "When a court invalidates a covenant obligation on the ground that it does not touch and concern the land, it makes a substantive judgment that the obligation should not be permitted to run with the land. The real reasons for the invalidation are seldom, if ever given." Susan French, *Servitudes Reform and the New Restatement of Property: Creation Doctrines and Structural Simplification,* 73 Cornell L. Rev. 928, 939-940 (1988).

Modern law tends to address public policy concerns more directly, invalidating covenants that are "unreasonable." Rules and bylaws enacted by common interest development associations may also be reviewed for reasonableness. Reasonableness is a deliberately flexible standard, taking into account and balancing many factors. Will a reasonableness standard be more likely to find covenants valid or invalid than the traditional touch and concern test? See the next cases.

Davidson Brothers, Inc. v. D. Katz & Sons, Inc.

643 A.2d 642 (Super. Ct. App. Div. 1994),
on remand from 579 A.2d 288 (N.J. 1990)

Map: 263-271 George Street; Elizabeth Street, New Brunswick, New Jersey 

WILLIAM M. D'ANNUNZIO, J.A.D.

Plaintiff Davidson Bros., Inc. (Davidson) appeals from a trial court judgment entered after a bench trial held on remand from the Supreme Court. *Davidson Bros., Inc. v. D. Katz & Sons, Inc.*, 579 A.2d 288 (N.J. 1990). Applying the reasonableness test formulated by the Supreme Court, the trial court determined that a covenant prohibiting the use as a supermarket of a property in downtown New Brunswick, New Jersey, was unenforceable. We now affirm.

Davidson operated a number of supermarkets in New Jersey. In 1952, it opened a supermarket of 10,000 square feet on George Street in downtown New Brunswick. In June 1978, Davidson took over an existing supermarket located at Elizabeth Street, also in New Brunswick but approximately two miles from the George Street store (hereinafter George Street), near the border with North Brunswick. Davidson paid $315,000 for the assets of the Elizabeth Street store (hereinafter Elizabeth Street), not including inventory, and made a substantial additional investment for improvements. Davidson leased the Elizabeth Street real property.

Davidson closed George Street in February 1979 because its volume had decreased after Davidson acquired Elizabeth Street. It sold George Street in September 1980 to defendant D. Katz & Sons, Inc. (Katz), a rug merchant. The deed to Katz contained the covenant in issue:

> The lands and premises described herein and conveyed hereby are conveyed subject to the restriction that said lands and premises shall not be used as and for a supermarket or grocery store of a supermarket type, however designated, for a period of forty (40) years from the date of this deed. This restriction shall be a covenant attached to and running with the lands.

The closing of George Street as a supermarket created a hardship for downtown residents, most of whom did not own or have ready access to motor vehicles. In response to their plight, the city government sought to attract another supermarket operator to the downtown area. The city's efforts culminated in the acquisition of George Street from Katz by the defendant New Brunswick Housing Authority, and the leasing of the property, for one dollar a year, to defendant C-Town, on condition that C-Town invest at least $10,000 for improvements and operate George Street as a supermarket.

Davidson commenced this action to enforce the covenant. Davidson appealed from an adverse summary judgment and we affirmed in an unreported opinion, utilizing traditional "touch and concern" analysis applicable to covenants alleged to run with the land.

Our Supreme Court granted Davidson's petition for certification and reversed and remanded for a trial. In doing so, the Court determined that "rigid adherence" to the "touch and concern" requirement was no longer warranted. It held that enforceability of a covenant would depend on its reasonableness, and that the principle of "touch and concern" is "but one of the factors." The Court then described eight factors to be considered in resolving the reasonableness issue:

1. The intention of the parties when the covenant was executed, and whether the parties had a viable purpose which did not at the time interfere with existing commercial laws, such as antitrust laws, or public policy.
2. Whether the covenant had an impact on the considerations exchanged when the covenant was originally executed. This may provide a measure of the value to the parties of the covenant at the time.
3. Whether the covenant clearly and expressly sets forth the restrictions.
4. Whether the covenant was in writing, recorded, and if so, whether the subsequent grantee had actual notice of the covenant.
5. Whether the covenant is reasonable concerning area, time or duration. Covenants that extend for perpetuity or beyond the terms of a lease may often be unreasonable.
6. Whether the covenant imposes an unreasonable restraint on trade or secures a monopoly for the covenantor. This may be the case in areas where there is limited space available to conduct certain business activities and a covenant not to compete burdens all or most available locales to prevent them from competing in such an activity.
7. Whether the covenant interferes with the public interest.
8. Whether, even if the covenant was reasonable at the time it was executed, "changed circumstances" now make the covenant unreasonable.

On remand, Davidson no longer sought injunctive relief. [Davidson sold its] Elizabeth Street store to another supermarket operator in 1989 for $687,500. Davidson limited its claim to damages consisting of lost sales and profits during the two year period it competed with C-Town, and the reduced value of its Elizabeth Street store due to C-Town's competition.

Quick Review:
If the covenant was analyzed under traditional tests, would it pass? Was there notice? Privity? Intent to run? Did it touch and concern the burdened land? Did it touch and concern or benefit other land? Could Davidson Bros. get an injunction and/or damages against the New Brunswick Authority? Against C-Town?

Davidson's accountant testified that sales at Elizabeth Street for 1988 and 1989 were $1,452,000 less than they would have been had the George Street store not reopened. He calculated the lost profit on those sales to be $350,000. He also opined that due to the lower sales volume, Davidson sold the Elizabeth Street store for $567,000 less than it should have sold for.

Defendants' accountant disagreed. He testified that although Elizabeth Street may have lost sales due to C-Town's operation of George Street, those lost sales would not have been profitable. Defendants' accountant also testified that the Elizabeth Street store did not lose value as a result of C-Town's competition.

After a lengthy trial, the trial court rendered an oral opinion. Applying the eight factors announced by the Supreme Court, the court found that the 40-year term was unreasonably long (factor 5); that the covenant imposed an unreasonable restraint of trade (factor 6); and that it was contrary to the public interest (factor 7). Regarding factor seven, the court ruled that the covenant adversely impacted the public interest because "there is a substantial public need for the supermarket under the circumstances of this case."

The trial court deemed the damages issue to be moot because of its determination that the covenant was unreasonable and unenforceable. However, the court announced that it was unable to determine from the evidence that Davidson had sustained damages due to C-Town's competition.

We now affirm on the ground that the covenant was so contrary to public policy that it should not be recognized as a valid, enforceable obligation.

The proofs established that New Brunswick is a small city which continues to suffer from many of the maladies affecting the larger cities of New Jersey and the nation, especially in its core downtown area. This area, where George Street is located, has been the focus of a large scale redevelopment and revitalization effort measured in decades. Although this effort's emphasis has been on commercial projects primarily, the downtown area is also the site of many low to moderate income housing projects of the New Brunswick Housing Authority. These were federally funded projects, and many of their residents depended on George Street for their shopping requirements before Davidson closed the store. George Street is within two blocks of four of those housing projects with a total of 726 units.

The testimony of New Brunswick's Director of Policy, Planning and Economic Development, and his report which was introduced into evidence, provided a demographic profile of the city. There are a total of 3,148 households in the downtown area. Twenty-six percent of those households are below the poverty level, compared with seventeen percent in the balance of the city. Of the "family households" downtown, twenty-eight percent are female householders with children, compared with fourteen percent in the balance of the city. Of the female headed households, fifty-four percent are below the poverty level, which is consistent with the balance of the city. Thirty-seven percent of the downtown housing units have no vehicle, almost twice as many as the balance of the city. Seven hundred and forty-three downtown units are occupied by persons sixty-five years and older; twenty-one percent of those seniors are below the poverty level, almost double the proportion in the rest of the city. The downtown area, therefore, contains the city's greatest concentration of disadvantaged persons.

Davidson's closing of George Street further disadvantaged them. No other supermarket was within walking distance. For those who lacked access to motor vehicles, buses, taxis and dependence on others replaced a walk to the supermarket. The problem was especially difficult for female heads of household who used to send their children to the store or have their children accompany them. With the elimination of George Street, getting to the supermarket was a particularly difficult exercise in logistics and child care.

But inconvenience was not the only cost. Dr. James J. O'Connor testified for defendants as an expert in food marketing and distribution. Dr. O'Connor's experience involved hands-on management of his family's wholesale and retail food businesses, followed by academic and government experience in food distribution issues. Shortly before his testimony in this case, Dr. O'Connor had completed a study for the United States Department of Agriculture regarding supermarkets in United States cities. According to Dr. O'Connor, the absence of a supermarket in a low income city neighborhood makes food more expensive and has a negative impact on diet and, therefore, on the inner city population's health.

Dr. O'Connor also stated that the absence of a supermarket contributes to inner city decay, because a supermarket is a retail anchor that attracts other retail operations. Withdrawal of a supermarket tends to force other merchants to leave the same neighborhood. The resulting vacuum is filled by convenience stores or "ma and pa" groceries. They are more expensive and lack variety. They rarely have produce and, if they do have it, it is of poor quality. Moreover, selection of poultry and fish is very limited and very expensive. Dr. O'Connor opined that there is a general lack of inner city supermarkets in the nation, which poses a significant social policy problem.

Dr. O'Connor's uncontradicted testimony is consistent with the conclusions reached by a congressional committee. House Select Comm. on Hunger, 100th Cong., 1st Sess., *Obtaining Food: Shopping Constraints on the Poor* (Comm. Print 1987) (hereinafter *Report*). The committee concluded that "low-income consumers are unable to maximize their limited expendable resources for a basic need — food — because of the barriers of the [sic] location and transportation. Hence, the grip of hunger and poverty tightens around the low-income consumer." *Id.* at 1.

The committee recognized the exacerbating impact of "supermarket migration" on this problem, *id.* at 4:

> During the late 1970's and early 1980's major supermarkets migrated away from the inner cities and low-income areas, toward the suburbs. Major reasons cited for the migration by the food industry include: high insurance rates, employment and security problems, and outmoded and understocked inner-city stores — conditions which keep profits low. The exodus to the suburbs provided cheaper land, better control over operational hazards and, in general, greater profits. According to the Food Marketing Institute, in 1981, 90 percent of the conventional grocery stores, located in low-income neighborhoods, [that] either closed voluntarily or went out of business, did so to relocate into the suburbs. These were the stores that had traditionally served low-income areas. During the same year, over one-half the new stores that opened were super stores locating in the suburbs and other higher-income areas.
>
> As these trends continue, low-income urban and rural consumers are faced with fewer food markets in the immediate vicinity of their homes and the greater expense in accessing reasonably priced foods. This migration has increased the economic drain on the urban and rural low-income consumer's already limited food budget, reducing, and in come cases, removing the opportunity for low-income households to shop competitively.

The committee also recognized the impact of the inner city consumers' limited shopping choices: "You have this perverse irony that the poorest have to pay more for a basic necessity of life." *Id.* at 3.

In its Report, the committee noted that experts and organizations addressing the problems of urban living recommended the provision of incentives to bring supermarkets back into the cities. The committee recommended, among other policy options, that "State and local governments should implement tax breaks and other incentives to . . . small- and medium-sized grocer[ies], and supermarket chains to encourage their expansion and/or relocation in low-income communities." *Id.* at 10.

New Brunswick's initial efforts to respond to the problem were unsuccessful. It attempted to provide and organize transportation, an option that proved to be ineffective. It also sought to find a downtown property easily adaptable to supermarket use and to attract another supermarket operator to run it. Other than the George Street store, however, there was none available.

Senator John Lynch, the Mayor of New Brunswick during the relevant period, testified that initial approaches to supermarket operators were unsuccessful because too much capital was required to rehabilitate and convert other buildings to supermarket use. According to Senator Lynch the "problem was making the bottom line work because of assembling the property, providing relocation costs, dealing with [environmental] laws, all of those things that add cost to the bottom line." Moreover, many properties that had conversion potential were unavailable or had other problems.

On the other hand, George Street, the former supermarket, was capable of being easily reconverted to supermarket use.

New Jersey courts have refused to enforce contracts that violate public policy. See *Vasquez v. Glassboro Service Ass'n, Inc.,* 415 A.2d 1156 (N.J. 1980) (contract requiring migrant farmworker to leave barracks immediately upon discharge violates public policy). "No contract can be sustained if it is inconsistent with the public interest or detrimental to the common good." *Id.* at 98.

"The sources of public policy include federal and state legislation and judicial decisions." *Id.* The rehabilitation of our inner cities is a public policy of this State often expressed in relevant legislation.

The *New Jersey Economic Development Authority Act* (EDA), N.J.S.A. 34:1B-1 to -21, is intended to promote economic development generally throughout the State. As part of the EDA, the Legislature determined that the "provision of buildings, structures and other facilities to increase opportunity for employment in manufacturing, industrial, commercial, recreational, retail and service enterprises in the State is in the public interest." N.J.S.A. 34:1B-2b. The Legislature also specifically addressed the developmental problems of inner cities when it found:

> By virtue of their architectural and cultural heritage, their positions as principal centers of communication and transportation and their concentration of productive and energy efficient facilities, many municipalities are capable of ameliorating the conditions of deterioration which impede sound community growth and development; and *that building a proper balance of housing, industrial and commercial facilities and increasing the attractiveness of such municipalities to persons of all income levels is essential*

> *to restoring such municipalities as desirable places to live, work, shop and enjoy life's amenities.*

[N.J.S.A. 34:1B-2f (emphasis added).]

Similarly, in enacting the *New Jersey Urban Enterprise Zones Act*, N.J.S.A. 52:27H-60 to -89, the Legislature determined that "there persist in this State, particularly in its urban centers, areas of economic distress characterized by high unemployment, low investment of new capital, blighted conditions, obsolete or abandoned industrial or commercial structures, and deteriorating tax bases." N.J.S.A. 52:27H-61a. The Legislature also noted that revitalization of those areas required "application of the skills and entrepreneurial vigor of private enterprise; and it is the responsibility of government to provide a framework within which *encouragement be given to private capital investment in these areas, disincentives to investment be removed or abated,* and mechanisms be provided for the coordination and cooperation of private and public agencies in restoring the economic viability and prosperity of these areas." N.J.S.A. 52:27H-61 (emphasis added).

In support of these objectives, the Legislature offered a rich variety of subsidies and incentives to businesses operating in a designated enterprise zone. The City of New Brunswick currently is eligible for Open Competitive Urban Enterprise Zone Designation.

Other laws, too numerous to describe in detail, reveal how urban rehabilitation is imbedded in public policy and the public interest.

Davidson's withdrawal from George Street caused difficulties and hardships of the nature mentioned earlier and made the downtown area a less hospitable and desirable place. Davidson had the right to terminate its George Street operation. In doing so, however, it imposed a restriction on the use of its former property designed to impede the relocation of another supermarket operation to the downtown area. The evidence supports the conclusion that the George Street store was peculiarly suited for supermarket use, and that there were no economically viable substitute locations. Consequently, the covenant, if enforced through injunctive relief or exposure to a judgment for damages, presented a formidable obstacle to remediation of the harm caused by Davidson's withdrawal. By harm, we mean the personal hardship caused by the withdrawal of a supermarket as well as the damage to the ongoing efforts of government and private enterprise to revitalize the city. We are persuaded, therefore, that, in the absence of any equivalent reciprocal benefit to the city, Davidson's scorched earth policy is so contrary to the public interest in these circumstances that the covenant is unreasonable and unenforceable.

Affirmed.

Nahrstedt v. Lakeside Village Condominium Association, Inc.

878 P.2d 1275 (Cal. 1994)

JOYCE L. KENNARD, Justice.

A homeowner in a 530-unit condominium complex sued to prevent the homeowners association from enforcing a restriction against keeping cats, dogs, and other animals in the condominium development. The owner asserted that the restriction, which was contained in the project's declaration recorded by the condominium project's developer, was "unreasonable" as applied to her because she kept her three cats indoors and because her cats were "noiseless" and "created no nuisance." Agreeing with the premise underlying the owner's complaint, the Court of Appeal concluded that the homeowners association could enforce the restriction only upon proof that plaintiff's cats would be likely to interfere with the right of other homeowners "to the peaceful and quiet enjoyment of their property."

Those of us who have cats or dogs can attest to their wonderful companionship and affection. Not surprisingly, studies have confirmed this effect. But the issue before us is not whether in the abstract pets can have a beneficial effect on humans. Rather, the narrow issue here is whether a pet restriction that is contained in the recorded declaration of a condominium complex is enforceable against the challenge of a homeowner. As we shall explain, the Legislature, in Civil Code section 1354, has required that courts enforce the covenants, conditions and restrictions contained in the recorded declaration of a common interest development "unless unreasonable."

Under this standard established by the Legislature, enforcement of a restriction does not depend upon the conduct of a particular condominium owner. Rather, the restriction must be uniformly enforced in the condominium development to which it was intended to apply unless the plaintiff owner can show that the burdens it imposes on affected properties so substantially outweigh the benefits of the restriction that it should not be enforced against any owner. Here, the Court of Appeal did not apply this standard in deciding that plaintiff had stated a claim for declaratory relief. Accordingly, we reverse the judgment of the Court of Appeal and remand for further proceedings consistent with the views expressed in this opinion.

I

Lakeside Village is a large condominium development in Culver City, Los Angeles County. It consists of 530 units spread throughout 12 separate 3-story buildings. The residents share common lobbies and hallways, in addition to laundry and trash facilities.

The Lakeside Village project is subject to certain covenants, conditions and restrictions (hereafter CC & R's) that were included in the developer's declaration recorded with the Los Angeles County Recorder on April 17, 1978, at the inception of the development project. Ownership of a unit includes membership in the project's homeowners association, the Lakeside Village Condominium Association (hereafter Association), the body that enforces the project's CC & R's, including the pet restriction, which provides in relevant part: "No animals (which shall mean dogs and cats), livestock, reptiles or poultry shall be kept in any unit."[9]

In January 1988, plaintiff Natore Nahrstedt purchased a Lakeside Village condominium and moved in with her three cats. When the Association learned of the cats'

9. The CC & R's permit residents to keep "domestic fish and birds."

presence, it demanded their removal and assessed fines against Nahrstedt for each successive month that she remained in violation of the condominium project's pet restriction.

Nahrstedt then brought this lawsuit against the Association, its officers, and two of its employees, asking the trial court to invalidate the assessments, to enjoin future assessments, to award damages for violation of her privacy when the Association "peered" into her condominium unit, to award damages for infliction of emotional distress, and to declare the pet restriction "unreasonable" as applied to indoor cats (such as hers) that are not allowed free run of the project's common areas. Nahrstedt also alleged she did not know of the pet restriction when she bought her condominium. [The Association demurred, and the trial court sustained the demurrer and dismissed Nahrstedt's complaint. A divided Court of Appeal reversed, finding that whether the restriction was "unreasonable" depended on the facts of her particular case.]

II

Today, condominiums, cooperatives, and planned-unit developments with homeowners associations have become a widely accepted form of real property ownership. These ownership arrangements are known as "common interest" developments. The owner not only enjoys many of the traditional advantages associated with individual ownership of real property, but also acquires an interest in common with others in the amenities and facilities included in the project. It is this hybrid nature of property rights that largely accounts for the popularity of these new and innovative forms of ownership in the 20th century.

[S]ubordination of individual property rights to the collective judgment of the owners association together with restrictions on the use of real property comprise the chief attributes of owning property in a common interest development. Notwithstanding the limitations on personal autonomy that are inherent in the concept of shared ownership of residential property, common interest developments have increased in popularity in recent years, in part because they generally provide a more affordable alternative to ownership of a single-family home. One significant factor in the continued popularity of the common interest form of property ownership is the ability of homeowners to enforce restrictive CC & R's against other owners (including future purchasers) of project units.

When restrictions limiting the use of property within a common interest development satisfy the requirements of covenants running with the land or of equitable servitudes, what standard or test governs their enforceability? In California, as we explained at the outset, our Legislature has made common interest development use restrictions contained in a project's recorded declaration "enforceable . . . *unless unreasonable*." (§1354, subd. (a), italics added.)

In states lacking such legislative guidance, some courts have adopted a standard under which a common interest development's recorded use restrictions will be enforced so long as they are "reasonable."

In *Hidden Harbour Estates v. Basso* (Fla. Dist. Ct. App. 1981) 393 So. 2d 637, the Florida court distinguished two categories of use restrictions: use restrictions set forth in the declaration or master deed of the condominium project itself, and rules promulgated by the governing board of the condominium owners association or the board's interpretation of a rule. (*Id.* at p. 639.) The latter category of use restrictions, the court said, should be subject to a "reasonableness" test, so as to "somewhat fetter the discretion of the board of directors." (*Id.* at p. 640.) Such a standard, the court explained, best assures that governing boards will "enact rules and make decisions that are reasonably related to the promotion of the health, happiness and peace of mind" of the project owners, considered collectively. (*Ibid.*)

By contrast, restrictions contained in the declaration or master deed of the condominium complex, the Florida court concluded, should not be evaluated under a "reasonableness" standard. (*Hidden Harbour Estates v. Basso, supra,* 393 So. 2d at pp. 639-640.) Rather, such use restrictions are "clothed with a very strong presumption of validity" and should be upheld even if they exhibit some degree of unreasonableness. (*Id.* at pp. 639, 640.) Nonenforcement would be proper only if such restrictions were arbitrary or in violation of public policy or some fundamental constitutional right. (*Id.* at pp. 639-640.)

Indeed, giving deference to use restrictions contained in a condominium project's originating documents protects the general expectations of condominium owners "that restrictions in place at the time they purchase their units will be enforceable." (Note, *Judicial Review of Condominium Rulemaking, supra,* 94 Harv. L. Rev. 647, 653); Ellickson, *Cities and Homeowners' Associations* (1982) 130 U. Pa. L. Rev. 1519, 1526-1527. This in turn encourages the development of shared ownership housing — generally a less costly alternative to single-dwelling ownership — by attracting buyers who prefer a stable, planned environment. It also protects buyers who have paid a premium for condominium units in reliance on a particular restrictive scheme.

III

In California, common interest developments are subject to the provisions of the *Davis-Stirling Common Interest Development Act* (hereafter Davis-Stirling Act or Act). (§1350 et seq.) The Act, passed into law in 1985, consolidated in one part of the Civil Code certain definitions and other substantive provisions pertaining to condominiums and other types of common interest developments.

Pertinent here is the Act's provision for the enforcement of use restrictions contained in the project's recorded declaration. That provision, subdivision (a) of section 1354, states in relevant part: "The covenants and restrictions in the declaration shall be enforceable equitable servitudes, *unless unreasonable,* and shall inure to the benefit of and bind all owners of separate interests in the development." (Italics added.)

The provision's express reference to "equitable servitudes" evidences the Legislature's intent that recorded use restrictions falling within section 1354 are to be treated as equitable servitudes. [W]hen enforcing equitable servitudes, courts are generally disinclined to question the wisdom of agreed-to restrictions. This rule does not apply, however, when the restriction does not comport with public policy. Equity will not enforce any restrictive covenant that violates public policy. (See *Shelley v. Kramer,* 334 U.S. 1 (1948).) Nor will courts enforce as equitable servitudes those restrictions that are arbitrary, that is, bearing no rational relationship to the protection, preservation, operation or purpose of the affected land.

With these principles of equitable servitude law to guide us, we now turn to section 1354. [U]nder subdivision (a) of section 1354 the use restrictions for a common interest development that are set forth in the recorded declaration are "enforceable equitable servitudes, unless unreasonable." In other words, such restrictions should be enforced unless they are wholly arbitrary, violate a fundamental public policy, or impose a burden on the use of affected land that far outweighs any benefit.

When courts accord a presumption of validity to all such recorded use restrictions and measure them against deferential standards of equitable servitude law, it discourages lawsuits by owners of individual units seeking personal exemptions from the restrictions. This also promotes stability and predictability in two ways. It provides substantial assurance to prospective condominium purchasers that they may rely with confidence on the promises embodied in the project's recorded CC & R's. And it protects all owners in the planned development from unanticipated increases in association fees to fund the defense of legal challenges to recorded restrictions.

Contrary to the dissent's accusations that the majority's decision "fray[s]" the "social fabric," we are of the view that our social fabric is best preserved if courts uphold and enforce solemn written instruments that embody the expectations of the parties rather than treat them as "worthless paper" as the dissent would. Our social fabric is founded on the stability of expectation and obligation that arises from the consistent enforcement of the terms of deeds, contracts, wills, statutes, and other writings. To allow one person to escape obligations under a written instrument upsets the expectations of all the other parties governed by that instrument (here, the owners of the other 529 units) that the instrument will be uniformly and predictably enforced.

IV

Under the holding we adopt today, the reasonableness or unreasonableness of a condominium use restriction that the Legislature has made subject to section 1354 is to be determined *not* by reference to facts that are specific to the objecting homeowner, but by reference to the common interest development as a whole. As we have explained, when, as here, a restriction is contained in the declaration of the common interest development and is recorded with the county recorder, the restriction is presumed to be reasonable and will be enforced uniformly against all residents of the common interest development *unless* the restriction is arbitrary, imposes burdens on the use of lands it affects that substantially outweigh the restriction's benefits to the development's residents, or violates a fundamental public policy.

We conclude, as a matter of law, that the recorded pet restriction of the Lakeside Village condominium development prohibiting cats or dogs but allowing some other pets is not arbitrary, but is rationally related to health, sanitation and noise concerns legitimately held by residents of a high-density condominium project such as Lakeside Village, which includes 530 units in 12 separate 3-story buildings.

Nahrstedt's complaint alleges no facts that could possibly support a finding that the burden of the restriction on the affected property is so disproportionate to its benefit that the restriction is unreasonable and should not be enforced. Also, the complaint's allegations center on Nahrstedt and her cats (that she keeps them inside her condominium unit and that they do not bother her neighbors), without any reference to the effect on the condominium development as a whole, thus rendering the allegations legally insufficient to overcome section 1354's presumption of the restriction's validity.

[*Reversed and remanded.*]

ARMAND ARABIAN, Justice, dissenting.

"There are two means of refuge from the misery of life: music and cats."[10]

I respectfully dissent. While technical merit may commend the majority's analysis, its application to the facts presented reflects a narrow, indeed chary, view of the law that eschews the human spirit in favor of arbitrary efficiency. In my view, the resolution of this case well illustrates the conventional wisdom, and fundamental truth, of the Spanish proverb, "It is better to be a mouse in a cat's mouth than a man in a lawyer's hands."

As explained below, I find the provision known as the "pet restriction" contained in the covenants, conditions, and restrictions (CC & R's) governing the Lakeside Village project patently arbitrary and unreasonable within the meaning of section 1354. Given the substantial benefits derived from pet ownership, the undue burden on the use of property imposed on condominium owners who can maintain pets within the confines of their units without creating a nuisance or disturbing the quiet enjoyment of others substantially outweighs whatever meager utility the restriction may serve in the abstract.

Both recorded and unrecorded history bear witness to the domestication of animals as household pets.[11] In addition to these historical and cultural references, the value of pets in daily life is a matter of common knowledge and understanding as well as extensive documentation. People of all ages, but particularly the elderly and the young, enjoy their companionship. Those who suffer from serious disease or injury and are confined to their home or bed experience a therapeutic, even spiritual, benefit from their presence. Animals provide comfort at the death of a family member or dear friend, and for the lonely can offer a reason for living when life seems to have lost its meaning. While pet ownership may not be a fundamental right as such, unquestionably it is an integral aspect of our daily existence, which cannot be lightly dismissed and should not suffer unwarranted intrusion into its circle of privacy.

What is gained from an uncompromising prohibition against pets that are confined to an owner's unit and create no noise, odor, or nuisance?

[T]he majority accept uncritically the proffered justification of preserving "health and happiness" and essentially consider only one criterion to determine enforceability:

10. Albert Schweitzer.

11. Archeologists in Israel found some of the earliest evidence of a domesticated animal when they unearthed the 12,000-year-old skeleton of a woman who was buried with her hand resting on the body of her dog.

> **CONTEXT**
>
> In 2000, the California legislature overturned the result in *Nahrstedt* by adopting a statute providing that "[n]o governing documents shall prohibit the owner of a separate interest within a common interest development from keeping at least one pet within the common interest development, subject to reasonable rules and regulations of the association." Cal. Civ. Code §1360.5. The statute does not apply to covenants entered into before its enactment.

was the restriction recorded in the original declaration? If so, it is "presumptively valid," unless in violation of public policy. Given the application of the law to the facts alleged and by an inversion of relative interests, it is difficult to hypothesize any CC & R's that would not pass muster. Such sanctity has not been afforded any writing save the commandments delivered to Moses on Mount Sinai, and they were set in stone, not upon worthless paper.

Moreover, unlike most conduct controlled by CC & R's, the activity at issue here is strictly confined to the owner's interior space; it does not in any manner invade other units or the common areas. Owning a home of one's own has always epitomized the American dream. More than simply embodying the notion of having "one's castle," it represents the sense of freedom and self-determination emblematic of our national character. Granted, those who live in multi-unit developments cannot exercise this freedom to the same extent possible on a large estate. But owning pets that do not disturb the quiet enjoyment of others does not reasonably come within this compromise. Nevertheless, with no demonstrated or discernible benefit, the majority arbitrarily sacrifice the dream to the tyranny of the "commonality."

Notes and Questions

1. **Reasonableness and public policy.** In *Davidson* and *Nahrstedt*, state courts adopt a reasonableness test rather than more traditional tests for evaluating covenants. But the test operates very differently in the hands of the two courts. The reasonableness test as described by the New Jersey Supreme Court adds additional tests on top of the traditional criteria: "We do not abandon the 'touch and concern' test," the New Jersey Supreme Court stated, "but rather hold that the test is but one of the factors a court should consider in determining the reasonableness of the covenant." *Davidson,* 579 A.2d at 295. As the court described, courts had previously engaged in "illogical and contorted applications of the 'touch and concern' rules . . . because courts have been pressed to twist the rules of 'touch and concern' in order to achieve a result that comports with public policy and a free market." *Id.* The New Jersey test seeks to make those public policy concerns explicit.

In contrast, the California test cloaks all covenants with a strong presumption of validity. Although the opinion construed a California statute, as the *Nahrstedt* court noted, a number of other courts adopted a similar test as a matter of common law.

Which test is better? Which better guarantees the stability and enforceability of agreements? Which better serves the public interest? Are there differences between commercial covenants and covenants governing common interest developments that justify the differences? How would the covenant in *Davidson* fare under the *Nahrstedt* test?

2. Restatement (Third). The *Restatement (Third)* adopts the position that servitudes are presumptively valid unless they are "illegal or unconstitutional or violate[] public policy." *Id.* §3.1. The comments note that this "applies the modern principle of freedom of contract to creation of servitudes. Rooted in the notion that it is in the public interest to recognize that individuals have broad powers to order their own affairs,' " the principle is that parties are generally free to " 'contract as they wish, and courts will enforce their agreements without passing on their substance.' " *Id.* §3.1 cmt. a.

At the same time, the *Restatement (Third)* retains a substantial role for the courts in regulating and invalidating covenants. In addition to covenants that constitute unreasonable restraints on alienation and competition, the *Restatement (Third)* provides that "[s]ervitudes that are invalid because they violate public policy include, but are not limited to" those that are "arbitrary, spiteful, or capricious" or "that unreasonably burden[] a fundamental constitutional right" or are "unconscionable." *Id.* §3.1. Determining when a covenant violates public policy requires consideration of a host of values.

> Resolving public policy claims requires balancing interests. Resolving claims that a servitude violates public policy requires assessing the impact of the servitude, identifying the public interests that would be adversely affected by leaving the servitude in force, and weighing the predictable harm against the interests in enforcing the servitude. Only if the risks of social harm outweigh the benefits of enforcing the servitude is the servitude likely to be held invalid. The policies favoring freedom of contract, freedom to dispose of one's property, and protection of legitimate expectation interests nearly always weigh in favor of the validity of voluntarily created servitudes. A host of other policies, too numerous to catalog, may be adversely impacted by servitudes. Policies favoring privacy and liberty in choice of lifestyle, freedom of religion, freedom of speech and expression, access to the legal system, discouraging bad faith and unfair dealing, encouraging free competition, and socially productive uses of land have been implicated by servitudes. Other policies that become involved may include those protecting family relationships from coercive attempts to disrupt them, and protecting weaker groups in society from servitudes that exclude them from opportunities enjoyed by more fortunate groups to acquire desirable property for housing or access to necessary services.

Id. §3.1 cmt. *l.* How would the supermarket covenant in *Davidson* fare under the *Restatement (Third)* test? How would *Nahrstedt*'s no pets covenant?

3. Remedies and the public interest. In the New Jersey Supreme Court ruling before remand in *Davidson Brothers,* Justice Pollock opined that because the covenant touched and concerned the land, it should be enforceable, but that equitable and public policy concerns suggested it should be enforced with damages rather than an injunction. On remand, the lower courts determined that the covenant should not be enforced at all. What are the arguments in favor of each position?

4. Retroactive impact of covenant changes. Further questions arise when covenants are amended or imposed after the owner purchases a unit. Could a no pets covenant be enforced against an owner with pets who purchased before it was in effect? Could a new no sex offenders covenant be enforced to prevent an existing owner from having her son move in with her? What about a no smoking covenant against an existing owner who is a smoker? What are the competing arguments?

5. Reasonableness in implementation. Courts often impose a reasonableness standard in implementation of covenants even where the covenant itself does not provide for one.

For example, some developers impose covenants requiring owners to obtain approval of an architectural review committee chosen by the homeowners association when they seek to make structural changes to their homes or even when they paint their shutters. In such cases, most courts hold such committees to a standard of reasonableness even if the covenants include no restrictions on the committee's discretion. *See, e.g., Portola Hills Community Association v. James*, 5 Cal. Rptr. 2d 580 (Ct. App. 1992) (holding that it would be unreasonable for a homeowners association to ban a satellite dish when the dish would be located in the backyard and would not be visible to the neighbors); *Smith v. Butler Mountain Estates Property Owners Association*, 367 S.E.2d 401 (N.C. Ct. App. 1988) (holding refusal to allow an owner to build a geodesic dome in a community of otherwise flat plane roofs was reasonable); *Riss v. Angel*, 934 P.2d 669, 677-679 (Wash. 1997) (holding that power to approve plans for new construction must be exercised "reasonably and in good faith"). In contrast, the Supreme Court of Oregon held that an architectural committee's decisions were subject only to review for fraud, bad faith, or lack of honest judgment when the covenants gave it "discretion" to make such decisions and specifically provided that it be the "sole judge of the suitability" of the height of improvements. *Valenti v. Hopkins*, 926 P.2d 813 (Or. 1996).

In a hopefully more *sui generis* case, a homeowners association ordered an elderly veteran with Hodgkin's disease to, among other things, "clear his bed of all paper and books," "not use his downstairs bathroom for storage," and suggested that he "throw out" or donate all "outdated clothes that had not been worn in five years" to comply. *Fountain Valley Chateau Banc Homeowner's Association v. Department of Veterans Affairs*, 79 Cal. Rptr. 2d 248, 251 (1998). (Would your bed or closet meet these requirements?) Although the applicable covenants required owners to maintain their properties in a "clean, sanitary, and attractive condition," the court found "it is virtually impossible to say the association acted reasonably," as the fire department had inspected the premises and found that they did not pose a health or fire hazard. *Id.* at 256. "If it is indeed true that homeowner's associations can often function 'as a second municipal government'; then we have a clear cut case of a 'nanny state'—nanny in almost a literal sense—going too far." *Id.* at 256.

Problems

1. A 2008 Arizona statute provides that all covenants are "valid and enforceable" so long as they do not violate any statutes or prior covenants, and the owners of the property consented. Ariz. Rev. Stat. §33-440. Can enforcement of a covenant be challenged on the grounds that it is unreasonable or violates public policy?

2. What would violate the *Nahrstedt* test? Natore Nahrstedt declared that her cats Boo Boo, Dockers, and Tulip "were like my children." Imagine that the covenant had actually prohibited children, and Natore had moved in only to discover her actual children could not live with her. Would the covenant be unreasonable under the *Nahrstedt* test?[12] What if the covenant prohibited watching television in one's home?

3. In *Mulligan v. Panther Valley Property Owners Association,* 766 A.2d 1186 (N.J. Super. Ct. App. Div. 2001), a homeowners association in a gated residential community of more than 2,000 homes (including single-family homes, townhouses, and condominium units) voted to amend applicable covenants to prohibit occupancy of any unit by a registered sex offender. Is the covenant unreasonable under the *Davidson* test?

4. When developers sell homes with rights to use commonly owned areas, such as a lake, recreational area, or road, there is normally a declaration creating a homeowners association with the power to impose assessments on owners to recover the costs of maintenance of those areas. If a developer fails to create such an association or the declaration does not initially give the association the power to tax owners to pay for maintenance of common areas or common easements, can the homeowners whose properties are appurtenant to the common areas or easements vote to create a homeowners association and/or impose assessments on owners who do not agree? The *Restatement (Third)* says yes (§6.3). *But compare Evergreen Highlands Association v. West,* 73 P.3d 1 (Colo. 2003) (association has power to add new declaration provisions including provisions requiring membership in the homeowners association and authorizing, for the first time, mandatory assessments to maintain common areas), *and Weatherby Lake Improvement Co. v. Sherman,* 611 S.W.2d 326 (Mo. Ct. App. 1980) (power to create a homeowners association to manage and maintain a commonly owned lake), *with Wendover Road Property Owners Association v. Kornicks,* 502 N.E.2d 226 (Ohio Ct. App. 1985) (owners cannot compel participation in the cost of improvements to commonly owned easements in the absence of a declaration creating a homeowners association with the power to impose such assessments). *Cf.* Okla. Stat. tit. 11, §42-106.1 (60 percent of owners subject to covenants can vote to create an association whose decisions will be binding on those who agree to it and on successors in interest of existing owners).

5. A covenant limiting property to residential use and barring any commercial use is interpreted to preclude operation of a family day care center. Given the need for affordable, convenient day care, does this covenant violate public policy? *See Terrien v. Zwit,* 648 N.W.2d 602 (Mich. 2002) (holding that it does not violate public policy, reversing lower court rulings to the contrary).

---

12. Restrictions on children violate the Fair Housing Act, 42 U.S.C. §§3604, 3607(b), except in senior housing. The question here is whether it violates the general test for covenants.

B. Rules and Bylaws

O'Buck v. Cottonwood Village Condominium Association, Inc.

50 P.2d 813 (Alaska 1988)

JAY A. RABINOWITZ, Chief Justice.

John and Janie O'Buck, plaintiffs and appellants in this case, purchased a unit in the Cottonwood Village Condominiums in June 1981. At that time, the unit was pre-wired for a central television antenna and for Visions, an antenna-based cable system. It is impossible to watch television in the unit without an outdoor antenna or cable because of bad reception. The availability of an antenna was an important consideration for the O'Bucks in deciding to purchase their unit because they have four televisions and frequently watch different programs.

In 1984, the Board of Directors of the Cottonwood Village Association ("the Board" or "the Association") had to address a serious problem of roof leakage in the condominiums. Among the several causes of leakage were badly mounted antennae and foot traffic on the roof related to the antennae. The Association paid $155,000 to have the roofs repaired. In order to do the work, the contractors removed all the antennae from the roofs. Before any of the antennae were reinstalled, the Board adopted a rule prohibiting the mounting of television antennae anywhere on the buildings. The purposes of this rule were to protect the roof and to enhance the marketability of the condominium units. The Board further decided to make the MultiVisions cable system available as an alternative to antennae. The Board rejected other alternatives such as a satellite dish or antennae mounted on the sides of the buildings. The Board offered to pay the fifteen dollar hookup fee to MultiVisions and to pay for the depreciated value of the old antennae. The O'Bucks were paid $284.20 for their antenna, which had been damaged when contractors removed it from the roof. The O'Bucks now have one television hooked up to MultiVisions. Their other sets have no reception, and it would cost ten dollars per month per set to hook them up.

The O'Bucks subsequently filed a complaint against the Association seeking damages and an injunction against enforcement of the rule.

The O'Bucks challenge the Board's authority to adopt the rule. We conclude that the Board had authority to enact a rule banning television antennae from buildings under either of two provisions in the Declaration of Condominium, the "constitution" of the Association. *See* Alaska Stat. §§34.07.010-.070.

First, article IX, section 4 of the Declaration authorizes the Board to adopt rules and regulations governing the use of the common areas, which include the roofs and walls of the buildings. That section provides:

> *Rules and Regulations.* Rules and regulations may be adopted by the Board of Directors concerning and governing the use of the general and limited common areas providing such rules and regulations shall be furnished to owners prior to the time they become effective and that such rules and regulations shall be uniform and nondiscriminatory.

Second, article XIX, section 1(d) of the Declaration authorizes the Board to require unit owners to take action to preserve a uniform exterior appearance to the buildings. That section provides:

> In order to preserve a uniform exterior appearance to the building, the Board may require the painting of the building, decks and balconies, and prescribe the type and color of paint, and *may prohibit*, require, or regulate *any modification* or decoration of the building, decks and balconies undertaken or proposed by any owner. This power of the Board extends to screens, doors, awnings, rails *or other visible portions of each condominium unit and condominium building*. The Board may also require use of a uniform color of draperies or drapery lining for all units. (Emphasis supplied.)

Given these two provisions, the Board had authority to ban antennae either on roof-protection grounds (under article IX, section 4) or on aesthetic grounds (under either section), both of which were given as reasons for the antennae rule.

The O'Bucks also cite several provisions of the Declaration and Bylaws which explicitly prohibit or authorize the prohibition of other things, such as pets, modification of buildings, and posting of bills. They reason that since there is no explicit authorization to prohibit antennae, and since the Declaration and Bylaws contemplate the existence of antennae, a right to have an antenna is reasonably inferred and cannot be taken away without amending the Declaration or Bylaws. They rely on *Beachwood Villas Condominium v. Poor,* 448 So. 2d 1143, 1145 (Fla. Dist. Ct. App. 1984), which held: "provided that a board-enacted rule does not contravene either an express provision of the declaration *or a right reasonably inferable therefrom,* it will be found valid, within the scope of the board's authority." (Emphasis supplied.)

We do not find the O'Bucks' arguments persuasive.

The absence of any provision explicitly authorizing the Board to ban antennae is not fatal to the Board's right to do so. As noted in *Beachwood Villas,* "[i]t would be impossible to list all restrictive uses in a declaration of condominium." 448 So. 2d at 1145. Thus, in that case the court upheld board-enacted rules regulating unit rentals and the occupancy of units by guests during the owner's absence. The court refused to find a reasonably inferable right and upheld the rules even in the absence of an express provision authorizing them.

For these reasons, we hold that the Declaration and Bylaws granted the Board the authority to enact the subject rule banning television antennae on buildings.

Both parties agree that a condominium association rule will not withstand judicial scrutiny if it is not reasonable. This standard of review is supported by case law and legal commentary.

The superior court found that roof-mounted television antennae were one of a number of causes of leaking roofs. This finding has ample support in the record. The architect engaged by the Association to make recommendations as to what to do about the problem testified that television antennae caused problems on each of the twenty-two roofs in the condominium project. Other problems causing the leaking were age of the condominiums, their poor design, and problems of poor workmanship which went into the construction of the condominium buildings. He also testified that it was important to limit foot traffic on the roofs, as many owners were apparently causing damage to the roofs when walking there to adjust their antennae. The repairs to the roof cost the Association $155,000. These facts clearly justified the Board's action to limit or prohibit television antennae and foot traffic on the roofs.

If the roof problems were the only justification for the rule, the O'Bucks would have a stronger argument that the rule was unreasonable. This is because they hired an architect who designed a method of installing antennae on the sides of the buildings rather than the roofs. This method would involve only brief work on the roof to connect the coaxial cable, and the rest of the work could be done from a ladder or hydraulically operated bucket. The availability of this relatively inexpensive alternative would cast some doubt on the reasonableness of a blanket prohibition on antennae if the only purpose of the rule was to protect the roofs.

However, it is clear that other legitimate considerations also motivated the antenna ban. As discussed above, the Declaration specifically authorized the prohibition of modifications or decorations to preserve a uniform exterior appearance to the buildings. Numerous witnesses testified that the Board was influenced by the unsightliness of the antennae. It was estimated that each of the 104 units in the twenty-two buildings had an antenna protruding from the roof. Witnesses testified that the Board felt that the elimination of the forest of antennae combined with the availability of a state-of-the-art cable system would enhance the marketability of the units. This evidence is adequate to support the superior court's conclusion that aesthetics and improved marketability were grounds for the antenna ban.

It is clear that the O'Bucks do not agree that the antenna ban improved the exterior appearance of the buildings. They describe this goal as "[nothing] more than a sop to personal prejudice or unarticulated personal values." However, this is a facet of the freedom they sacrificed when they bought into a condominium association.

> **CONTEXT**
>
> The Federal Communications Commission later prohibited condo rules like that in *O'Buck* pursuant to a 1996 congressional directive to "prohibit restrictions that impair a viewer's ability to receive video programming services through devices designed for over-the-air reception of television broadcast signals, multichannel multipoint distribution service, or direct broadcast satellite services." 47 U.S.C. §303 Note. Why would Congress enact such a directive? Hint: It wasn't because of the powerful couch potato lobby.

[C]ondominium owners consciously sacrifice some freedom of choice in their decision to live in this type of housing. Unit owners may not rely on the courts to strike down reasonable rules on the grounds of differences in aesthetic tastes.

In evaluating the reasonableness of a condominium association rule, it is necessary to balance the importance of the rule's objective against the importance of the interest infringed upon. In a case where a rule seriously curtails an important civil liberty—such as, for example, freedom of expression—we will look with suspicion on the rule and require a compelling justification. The antenna ban in the instant case curtails no significant interests. The only loss suffered is that the O'Bucks and the other owners must now pay a small monthly fee to receive television, and even this cost is offset to a degree by the savings from the lack of need to install and maintain an antenna. In some cases, we might consider a financial burden to be an important interest. However, the fee in this case is small in view of the wherewithal of the members of the Association.[13] For this reason, we find that the interests of the Association in improving the exterior appearance of the buildings and enhancing the marketability of the units more than adequately justify the small financial burden placed on the owners.

Neuman v. Grandview at Emerald Hills, Inc.

861 So. 2d 494 (Fla. Dist. Ct. App. 2003)

Map: 2800 N. 45th Avenue, Hollywood, Florida

MARTHA C. WARNER, J.

The issue presented in this case is whether a condominium association rule banning the holding of religious services in the auditorium of the condominium constitutes a violation of Fla. Stat. §718.123, which precludes condominium rules from unreasonably restricting a unit owner's right to peaceably assemble. We hold that the rule does not violate the statute and affirm.

Appellee Grandview is a condominium association with 442 members, appellants being two of the members. Appellants reside at Grandview condominium during the winter months. The common elements of the condominium include an auditorium that members can reserve for social gatherings and meetings. Grandview enacted a rule governing the use of the auditorium in 1982, which provided that the auditorium could be used for meetings or functions of groups, including religious groups, when at least eighty percent of the members were residents of Grandview condominium. Generally, the only reservations made for the auditorium on Saturdays were by individual members for birthday or anniversary celebrations.

In January 2001, several unit owners reserved the auditorium between 8:30 and noon on Saturday mornings. While they indicated they were reserving it for a party, they actually conducted religious services. Approximately forty condominium members gathered for the services.

Upon discovering that religious services were being conducted on Saturdays in the auditorium, several other members complained to the Board of Directors ("Board"). The Board met in February to discuss restrictions on the use of the auditorium and common elements for religious services and activities. The meeting became very confrontational between those members supporting the use of the auditorium for religious services and those opposing such use. Based upon the controversial nature of the issue, the Board's desire not to have a common element tied up for the exclusive use of a minority of the members on a regular basis, and to avoid conflicts between

13. The units were advertised at a cost of $97,000 in 1981.

different religious groups competing for the space, the Board first submitted the issue to a vote of the owners. Seventy percent of the owners voted in favor of prohibiting the holding of religious services in the auditorium. The Board then voted unanimously to amend the rule governing the use of the auditorium. The new rule provided that "no religious services or activities of any kind are allowed in the auditorium or any other common elements."

Appellants filed suit against Grandview seeking injunctive and declaratory relief to determine whether the rule violated their constitutional rights or was in violation of §718.123, and whether the rule was arbitrarily and capriciously enacted by the Board. Grandview answered, denying that the rule was arbitrary or violated appellants' statutory or constitutional rights. Appellants moved for a temporary injunction alleging that Grandview was not only preventing the owners from holding religious services, it was also prohibiting the use of the auditorium for holiday parties, including Christmas and Chanukah, based upon its prohibition against using the common elements "for religious activities of any kind." The court granted the motion as to the use of the auditorium for religious activities of any kind but denied it as it applied to the holding of religious services. Based upon the temporary injunction as to religious activities, Grandview amended its rule to limit the prohibition to the holding of religious services in the auditorium.

At a hearing on appellants' motion for a permanent injunction against the rule, the appellants relied primarily on §718.123, which prohibits condominium associations from unreasonably restricting the unit owners' rights to peaceable assembly. They argued that religious services fell into the category of a "peaceable assembly," and a categorical ban on the holding of religious services was per se unreasonable. Grandview maintained that it had the right to restrict the use of its common elements. Because the right of peaceable assembly did not mandate a right to conduct religious services, it had the right to poll its members and restrict the use based upon the majority's desires. As such, Grandview maintained the exercise of this right was reasonable.

In its final order denying the injunction, the court determined that because no state action was involved, the unit owners' constitutional rights of freedom of speech and religion were not implicated by Grandview's rule. The court determined that the rule did not violate §718.123, as the condominium association had the authority to enact this reasonable restriction on the use of the auditorium. Appellants challenge that ruling.

Chapter 718, Florida's "*Condominium Act*," recognizes the condominium form of property ownership and "establishes a detailed scheme for the creation, sale, and operation of condominiums." *Woodside Vill. Condo. Ass'n v. Jahren,* 806 So. 2d 452, 455 (Fla. 2002). Thus, condominiums are strictly creatures of statute. The declaration of condominium, which is the condominium's "constitution," creates the condominium and "strictly governs the relationships among the condominium units owners and the condominium association." *Id.* at 456. Under the declaration, the Board of the condominium association has broad authority to enact rules for the benefit of the community.

In *Hidden Harbour Estates, Inc. v. Norman*, 309 So. 2d 180, 181-82 (Fla. Dist. Ct. App. 1975), this court explained the unique character of condominium living which, for the good of the majority, restricts rights residents would otherwise have were they living in a private separate residence:

> It appears to us that inherent in the condominium concept is the principle that to promote the health, happiness, and peace of mind of the majority of the unit owners since they are living in such close proximity and using facilities in common, each unit owner must give up a certain degree of freedom of choice which he might otherwise enjoy in separate, privately owned property. Condominium unit owners comprise a little democratic sub society of necessity more restrictive as it pertains to use of condominium property than may be existent outside the condominium organization.

Section 718.123(*1*) recognizes the right of the condominium association to regulate the use of the common elements of the condominium (emphasis added):

> All common elements, common areas, and recreational facilities serving any condominium shall be available to unit owners in the condominium or condominiums served thereby and their invited guests for the use intended for such common elements, common areas, and recreational facilities, subject to the provisions of §718.106(4). *The entity or entities responsible for the operation of the common elements, common areas, and recreational facilities may adopt reasonable rules and regulations pertaining to the use of such common elements, common areas, and recreational facilities. No entity or entities shall unreasonably restrict any unit owner's right to peaceably assemble* or right to invite public officers or candidates for public office to appear and speak in common elements, common areas, and recreational facilities.

The statutory test for rules regarding the operation of the common elements of the condominium is reasonableness. The trial court found the rule preventing use of the auditorium for religious services was reasonable in light of the Board's concern for a serious potential for conflict of use which could arise among competing religious groups. Having polled the members and determined that a majority of the members approved the ban, the Board's rule assured that the auditorium was "available to unit owners in the condominium or condominiums served thereby and their invited guests for the use intended" in accordance with the statute. §718.123(*1*).

The appellants' main argument both at trial and on appeal suggests that because the statute mandates that the Board may not "unreasonably restrict any unit owner's right to peaceably assemble," §718.123(*1*), a categorical prohibition of all religious services exceeds the Board's powers, as the right to meet in religious worship would constitute the right to peaceably assemble. However, the right to peaceably assemble has traditionally been interpreted to apply to the right of the citizens to meet to discuss public or governmental affairs. *See United States v. Cruikshank*, 92 U.S. 542, 551-555 (1875). Assuming for purposes of this argument that the right to gather for religious worship is a form of peaceable assembly, the rule in question bans this particular form of assembly, but not all right to assemble. Certainly, a categorical ban on the right of members to use the auditorium for any gathering would be contrary to statute. However, the statute itself permits the reasonable regulation of that right. Prohibiting those types of assembly which will have a particularly divisive effect on the condominium community is a reasonable restriction. The Board found that permitting the holding of regular worship services and the competition among various religious groups for use of the auditorium would pose such conflict. Where the condominium association's regulations regarding common elements are reasonable and not violative of specific statutory limitations, the regulations should be upheld. The trial court found the restriction reasonable under the facts. No abuse of discretion has been shown.

The judgment of the trial court is affirmed.

Notes and Questions

1. **Within the scope of board authority.** To withstand review, bylaws and other board actions must not only be reasonable, but must be within the scope of the authority reasonably created by the declaration. As *O'Buck* shows, the authority need not explicitly speak to the particular rule. The determination of whether the restriction is within the scope of the authority created by the covenants is affected by whether the jurisdiction still interprets covenants strictly in favor of the free use of land or whether it interprets them broadly to achieve the intent of the parties, and whether court finds the bylaw affects an important right or reasonable reliance of the owner. *Compare Apple Valley Gardens Association v. MacHutta,* 763 N.W.2d 126 (Wis. 2009) (holding that because covenants mentioned but did not affirmatively permit renting of units, bylaw preventing leasing was permissible) *with Kiekel v. Four Colonies Homes Association,* 162 P.3d 57 (Kan. App. 2007) (finding that rental restriction had to be enacted by amendment to declaration rather than bylaw where declaration mentioned even if it did not affirmatively permit leasing), *and Apple Valley,* 763 N.W.2d at 134-139 (Prosser, J., dissenting) (given importance of and practice of leasing and rule that restrictions on property should be construed strictly, prohibition on leasing should not be accomplished via an amendment to the bylaws.)

2. **Standard of review.** Once they have deemed a board's actions to be authorized, most courts review them for reasonableness. Others, however, review board actions under the business judgment rule. *Compare Lamden v. La Jolla Shores Clubdominium Homeowners Association,* 980 P.2d 940, 950 (Cal. 1999) (review for whether judgment is reasonable and in good faith deferring to the board's "authority and presumed expertise") *with Committee for a Better Twin Rivers v. Twin Rivers Homeowners Association,* 929 A.2d 1060, 1074 (N.J. 2007) (business judgment rule). This business judgment rule was created in the context of actions against corporate boards and officers, and immunizes them from liability "so long as the court determines that the process employed was either rational or employed in a good faith effort to advance corporate interests." *In re Caremark International Inc. Derivative Litigation,* 698 A.2d 959, 967 (Del. Ch. 1996); *see* Chapter 10, §4. The leading case adopting the business judgment rule is *Levandusky v. One Fifth Avenue Apartment Corp.,* 553 N.E.2d 1317, 1321 (N.Y. 1990). In *Levandusky,* Chief Justice Judith Kaye acknowledged that "the broad powers of a cooperative board hold potential for abuse through arbitrary and

malicious decision-making, favoritism, discrimination and the like," but that generalized review for reasonableness was inappropriate:

> As this case exemplifies, board decisions concerning what residents may or may not do with their living space may be highly charged and emotional. A cooperative or condominium is by nature a myriad of often competing views regarding personal living space, and decisions taken to benefit the collective interest may be unpalatable to one resident or another, creating the prospect that board decisions will be subjected to undue court involvement and judicial second-guessing. Allowing an owner who is simply dissatisfied with particular board action a second opportunity to reopen the matter completely before a court, which—generally without knowing the property—may or may not agree with the reasonableness of the board's determination, threatens the stability of the common living arrangement.
>
> Moreover, the prospect that each board decision may be subjected to full judicial review hampers the effectiveness of the board's managing authority. The business judgment rule protects the board's business decisions and managerial authority from indiscriminate attack. At the same time, it permits review of improper decisions, as when the challenger demonstrates that the board's action has no legitimate relationship to the welfare of the cooperative, deliberately singles out individuals for harmful treatment, is taken without notice or consideration of the relevant facts, or is beyond the scope of the board's authority.

Id. at 1321. Do you agree? Are there other differences between the corporate setting and the property owner's association that influence your judgment?

3. American flag. Justice Clarence Thomas's father-in-law, Donald Lamp, hung an American flag outside the balcony of his condominium unit. The condominium association had passed a rule prohibiting any banners or flags outside units, including the American flag. It did so, it seems, for aesthetic reasons and to preserve a uniform appearance of the units. Lamp was asked to abide by the rule, but he refused. After nationwide publicity, the association amended its policy to make an exception for the American flag. In 2006, Congress passed the *Freedom to Display the American Flag Act*, 4 U.S.C. §5 note (Pub. L. No. 109-243, 120 Stat. 572 (2006)), which guarantees the right to fly the American flag on one's property, regardless of any condominium or homeowners association rule or covenant to the contrary. The statute appears to respond directly to the Lamp case and oddly does not confer a similar entitlement on tenants. *Cf.* Ark. Code §14-1-203 (granting a right to fly the American flag, but this right does not extend to residential tenants in buildings with fewer than 12 units). Imagine that a unit owner is prevented from flying the Puerto Rican flag—may she challenge the statute as impermissible content discrimination?

4. Political signs. Many association regulations restrict the signs owners can post outside their units. Such restrictions have almost universally been held not to constitute state action in violation of the U.S. Constitution. *See Committee for a Better Twin Rivers v. Twin Rivers Homeowners Association*, 929 A.2d 1060 (N.J. 2007). In *Twin Rivers*, dissident members of a homeowners association sought to engage in various kinds of speech activity to change the policies of the association. They sued for relief from a rule that prohibited the placement of more than one sign in a window and one sign in the front yard no more than three feet from the home. Although the Supreme Court of New Jersey ruled that the homeowners association was not a "state actor," the New Jersey constitution forbids private actions that unreasonably restrict speech. The court found, however, that as the owners could still post some signs, their rights were not unreasonably restricted. In a subsequent case, however, the court held that a similar prohibition on all signs other than for sale signs did violate the New Jersey constitution. *Mazdabrook Commons Homeowners' Association v. Khan*, 46 A.3d 507 (N.J. 2012). Would a similar blanket restriction be invalid in a state that did not have such a constitution?

Problems

1. Each unit in a five-story condominium complex has a porch. The condominium association passes a rule that provides that "no owner shall erect a structure on the porch." One owner builds a *sukkah*, a temporary structure used by Jews to celebrate the religious festival of Sukkot. The condominium association believes the ramshackle structure is unsightly and tells the owner to remove it and not to build any other structures like it in the future, even though it will be up for less than two weeks. The unit owner comes to you for advice. Is the restriction on use of the porch reasonable and enforceable?

2. A professional violinist purchases a condominium unit. Her neighbors complain that she disturbs them when she plays her violin. The violinist agrees not to play before 10 A.M. or after 7 P.M., but her neighbors are not satisfied. The condominium association passes a rule prohibiting all owners from playing musical instruments in their apartments. Is the rule reasonable and enforceable?

3. A homeowner installs a clothesline in her backyard to air dry her laundry. The bylaws of the association applicable to her property prohibit this, presumably for aesthetic reasons and because hanging laundry outdoors is thought to lower property values. The owner argues that she is an environmentalist who is trying to save energy by not using her clothes dryer. She also feels an obligation to do so because of the rolling blackouts experienced by California in recent memory. Is the bylaw reasonable? Should a court enforce it?[14] *See* Dusty Horwitt, *The Right to Dry: Laundry on the Line*, Legal Aff., Jan./Feb. 2004.

4. A co-op board in a building at 180 West End Avenue, New York City, banned all smoking inside the apartments by new owners. The rule allowed existing owners to smoke but put new owners on notice that they would not be free to smoke inside their own apartments. Is the ban reasonable? Would it be reasonable if it were applied to existing owners as well as new buyers? *See* Dennis Hevesi, *Co-Op Board Bans Smoking in Apartments by New Owners*, N.Y. Times, Apr. 30, 2002.

---

14. I owe this hypothetical to a *Doonesbury* cartoon by Garry Trudeau.

§5.2 Constitutional Limitations

Does the Constitution place limits on covenants? Although homeowners associations have been called "residential private governments," the U.S. Constitution only applies to covenant enforcement or actions by homeowners associations if state action is found. *Shelley v. Kraemer*, 334 U.S. 1 (1948), below, held that the fourteenth amendment prohibited homeowner enforcement of a racially restrictive covenant. Why did the Court find state action here?

Shelley v. Kraemer

334 U.S. 1 (1948)

Map: 4600 Labadie Avenue, St. Louis, Missouri

Mr. Chief Justice FRED VINSON delivered the opinion of the Court.

These cases present for our consideration questions relating to the validity of court enforcement of private agreements, generally described as restrictive covenants, which have as their purpose the exclusion of persons of designated race or color from the ownership or occupancy of real property. Basic constitutional issues of obvious importance have been raised.

The first of these cases comes to this Court on certiorari to the Supreme Court of Missouri. On February 16, 1911, thirty out of a total of thirty-nine owners of property fronting both sides of Labadie Avenue between Taylor Avenue and Cora Avenue in the city of St. Louis, signed an agreement, which was subsequently recorded, providing in part:

> [T]he said property is hereby restricted to the use and occupancy for the term of Fifty (50) years from this date, so that it shall be a condition all the time and whether recited and referred to as [sic] not in subsequent conveyances and shall attach to the land, as a condition precedent to the sale of the same, that hereafter no part of said property or any portion thereof shall be, for said term of Fifty-years, occupied by any person not of the Caucasian race, it being intended hereby to restrict the use of said property for said period of time against the occupancy as owners or tenants of any portion of said property for resident or other purpose by people of the Negro or Mongolian Race.

The entire district described in the agreement included fifty-seven parcels of land. The thirty owners who signed the agreement held title to forty-seven parcels, including the particular parcel involved in this case. At the time the agreement was signed, five of the parcels in the district were owned by Negroes. One of those had been occupied by Negro families since 1882, nearly thirty years before the restrictive agreement was executed. The trial court found that owners of seven out of nine homes on the south side of Labadie Avenue, within the restricted district and "in the immediate vicinity" of the premises in question, had failed to sign the restrictive agreement in 1911. At the time this action was brought, four of the premises were occupied by Negroes, and had been so occupied for periods ranging from twenty-three to sixty-three years. A fifth parcel had been occupied by Negroes until a year before this suit was instituted.

On August 11, 1945, pursuant to a contract of sale, petitioners Shelley, who are Negroes, for valuable consideration received from one Fitzgerald a warranty deed to the parcel in question. The trial court found that petitioners had no actual knowledge of the restrictive agreement at the time of the purchase.

Quick Review:
Does the covenant here meet the common law requirements? Is there horizontal privity? Vertical privity? Intent to run? Is there notice? Does it touch and concern the plaintiffs' land? Does it touch and concern the defendants' land? What do we have to assume to find that the covenant touches and concerns the land here?

On October 9, 1945, respondents, as owners of other property subject to the terms of the restrictive covenant, brought suit in Circuit Court of the city of St. Louis praying that petitioners Shelley be restrained from taking possession of the property and that judgment be entered divesting title out of petitioners Shelley and revesting title in the immediate grantor or in such other person as the court should direct. The trial court denied the requested relief on the ground that the restrictive agreement, upon which respondents based their action, had never become final and complete because it was the intention of the parties to that agreement that it was not to become effective until signed by all property owners in the district, and signatures of all the owners had never been obtained.

The Supreme Court of Missouri sitting en banc reversed and directed the trial court to grant the relief for which respondents had prayed. That court held the agreement effective and concluded that enforcement of its provisions violated no rights guaranteed to petitioners by the Federal Constitution. At the time the court rendered its decision, petitioners were occupying the property in question.

The second of the cases under consideration comes to this Court from the Supreme Court of Michigan. The circumstances presented do not differ materially from the Missouri case.

Petitioners have placed primary reliance on their contentions, first raised in the state courts, that judicial enforcement of the restrictive agreements in these cases has violated rights guaranteed to petitioners by the Fourteenth Amendment of the Federal Constitution and Acts of Congress passed pursuant to that Amendment.[15] Specifically, petitioners urge that they have been denied the equal protection of the laws, deprived of property without due process of law, and have been denied privileges and immunities of citizens of the United States. We pass to a consideration of those issues.

---

15. The first section of the Fourteenth Amendment provides: "All persons born or naturalized in the United States, and subject to the jurisdiction thereof, are citizens of the United States and of the State wherein they reside. No State shall make or enforce any law which shall abridge the privileges or immunities of citizens of the United States; nor shall any State deprive any person of life, liberty, or property, without due process of law; nor deny to any person within its jurisdiction the equal protection of the laws."

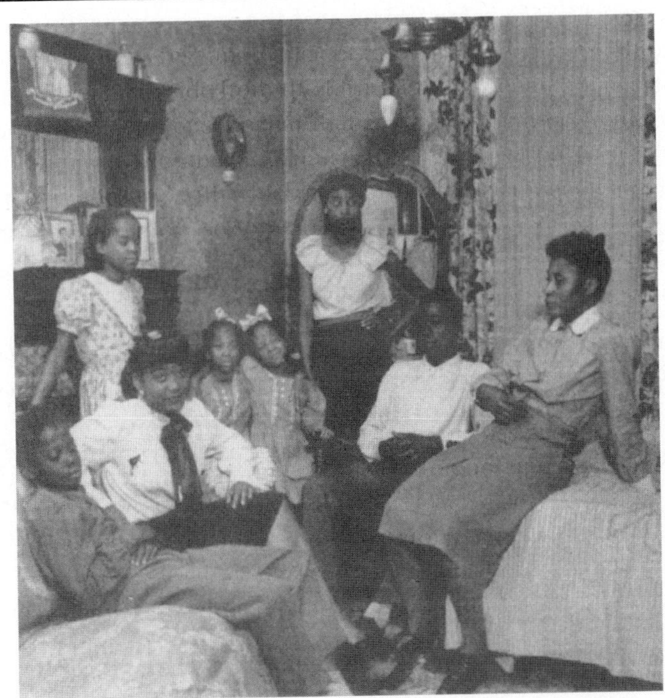

J.D. and Ethel Lee Shelley and their children. Photograph by George Harris. Reprinted by permission of Black Star Publishing.

I

It is well, at the outset, to scrutinize the terms of the restrictive agreements involved in these cases. In the Missouri case, the covenant declares that no part of the affected property shall be "occupied by any person not of the Caucasian race, it being intended hereby to restrict the use of said property . . . against the occupancy as owners or tenants of any portion of said property for resident or other purpose by people of the Negro or Mongolian Race." Not only does the restriction seek to proscribe use and occupancy of the affected properties by members of the excluded class, but as construed by the Missouri courts, the agreement requires that title of any person who uses his property in violation of the restriction shall be divested. The restriction of the covenant in the Michigan case seeks to bar occupancy by persons of the excluded class. It provides that "This property shall not be used or occupied by any person or persons except those of the Caucasian race."

It should be observed that these covenants do not seek to proscribe any particular use of the affected properties. Use of the properties for residential occupancy, as such, is not forbidden. The restrictions of these agreements, rather, are directed toward a designated class of persons and seek to determine who may and who may not own or make use of the properties for residential purposes. The excluded class is defined wholly in terms of race or color; "simply that and nothing more."[16]

It cannot be doubted that among the civil rights intended to be protected from discriminatory state action by the Fourteenth Amendment are the rights to acquire, enjoy, own and dispose of property. Equality in the enjoyment of property rights was regarded by the framers of that Amendment as an essential pre-condition to the realization of other basic civil rights and liberties which the Amendment was intended to guarantee. Thus, §1978 of the Revised Statutes, derived from §1 of the *Civil Rights Act of 1866* [now codified at 42 U.S.C. §1982] which was enacted by Congress while the Fourteenth Amendment was also under consideration, provides:

> All citizens of the United States shall have the same right, in every State and Territory, as is enjoyed by white citizens thereof to inherit, purchase, lease, sell, hold, and convey real and personal property.

It is likewise clear that restrictions on the right of occupancy of the sort sought to be created by the private agreements in these cases could not be squared with the requirements of the Fourteenth Amendment if imposed by state statute or local ordinance. We do not understand respondents to urge the contrary.

But the present cases, unlike those just discussed, do not involve action by state legislatures or city councils. Here the particular patterns of discrimination and the areas in which the restrictions are to operate, are determined, in the first instance, by the terms of agreements among private individuals. Participation of the State consists in the enforcement of the restrictions so defined. The crucial issue with which we are here confronted is whether this distinction removes these cases from the operation of the prohibitory provisions of the Fourteenth Amendment.

Since the decision of this Court in the *Civil Rights Cases*, 109 U.S. 3 (1883), the principle has become firmly embedded in our constitutional law that the action inhibited by the first section of the Fourteenth Amendment is only such action as may fairly be said to be that of the States. That Amendment erects no shield against merely private conduct, however discriminatory or wrongful.

We conclude, therefore, that the restrictive agreements standing alone cannot be regarded as a violation of any rights guaranteed to petitioners by the Fourteenth Amendment. So long as the purposes of those agreements are effectuated by voluntary adherence to their terms, it would appear clear that there has been no action by the State and the provisions of the Amendment have not been violated.

But here there was more. These are cases in which the purposes of the agreements were secured only by judicial enforcement by state courts of the restrictive terms of the agreements. The respondents urge that judicial enforcement of private agreements does not amount to state action; or, in any event, the participation of the State is so attenuated in character as not to amount to state action within the meaning of the Fourteenth Amendment. Finally, it is suggested, even if the States in these cases may be deemed to have acted in the constitutional sense, their action did not deprive

---

16. Buchanan v. Warley, 245 U.S. 60, 73 (1917).

petitioners of rights guaranteed by the Fourteenth Amendment. We move to a consideration of these matters.

II

That the action of state courts and of judicial officers in their official capacities is to be regarded as action of the State within the meaning of the Fourteenth Amendment, is a proposition which has long been established by decisions of this Court.

One of the earliest applications of the prohibitions contained in the Fourteenth Amendment to action of state judicial officials occurred in cases in which Negroes had been excluded from jury service in criminal prosecutions by reason of their race or color. These cases demonstrate, also, the early recognition by this Court that state action in violation of the Amendment's provisions is equally repugnant to the constitutional commands whether directed by state statute or taken by a judicial official in the absence of statute. Thus, in *Strauder v. West Virginia,* 100 U.S. 303 (1880), this Court declared invalid a state statute restricting jury service to white persons as amounting to a denial of the equal protection of the laws to the colored defendant in that case.

The action of state courts in imposing penalties or depriving parties of other substantive rights without providing adequate notice and opportunity to defend, has, of course, long been regarded as a denial of the due process of law guaranteed by the Fourteenth Amendment. *Brinkerhoff-Faris Trust & Savings Co. v. Hill,* 281 U.S. 673 (1930); *Pennoyer v. Neff,* 95 U.S. 714 (1878).

In numerous cases, this Court has reversed criminal convictions in state courts for failure of those courts to provide the essential ingredients of a fair hearing. [*Moore v. Dempsey,* 261 U.S. 86 (1923); *Frank v. Mangum,* 237 U.S. 309 (1915).]

But the examples of state judicial action which have been held by this Court to violate the Amendment's commands are not restricted to situations in which the judicial proceedings were found in some manner to be procedurally unfair. It has been recognized that the action of state courts in enforcing a substantive common-law rule formulated by those courts, may result in the denial of rights guaranteed by the Fourteenth Amendment, even though the judicial proceedings in such cases may have been in complete accord with the most rigorous conceptions of procedural due process. Thus, in *American Federation of Labor v. Swing,* 312 U.S. 321 (1941), enforcement by state courts of the common-law policy of the State, which resulted in the restraining of peaceful picketing, was held to be state action of the sort prohibited by the Amendment's guaranties of freedom of discussion.

The short of the matter is that from the time of the adoption of the Fourteenth Amendment until the present, it has been the consistent ruling of this Court that the action of the States to which the Amendment has reference, includes action of state courts and state judicial officials. Although, in construing the terms of the Fourteenth Amendment, differences have from time to time been expressed as to whether particular types of state action may be said to offend the Amendment's prohibitory provisions, it has never been suggested that state court action is immunized from the operation of those provisions simply because the act is that of the judicial branch of the state government.

III

Against this background of judicial construction, extending over a period of some three-quarters of a century, we are called upon to consider whether enforcement by state courts of the restrictive agreements in these cases may be deemed to be the acts of those States; and, if so, whether that action has denied these petitioners the equal protection of the laws which the Amendment was intended to insure.

We have no doubt that there has been state action in these cases in the full and complete sense of the phrase. The undisputed facts disclose that petitioners were willing purchasers of properties upon which they desired to establish homes. The owners of the properties were willing sellers; and contracts of sale were accordingly consummated. It is clear that but for the active intervention of the state courts, supported by the full panoply of state power, petitioners would have been free to occupy the properties in question without restraint.

These are not cases, as has been suggested, in which the States have merely abstained from action, leaving private individuals free to impose such discriminations as they see fit. Rather, these are cases in which the States have made available to such individuals the full coercive power of government to deny to petitioners, on the grounds of race or color, the enjoyment of property rights in premises which petitioners are willing and financially able to acquire and which the grantors are willing to sell. The difference between judicial enforcement and nonenforcement of the restrictive covenants is the difference to petitioners between being denied rights of property available to other members of the community and being accorded full enjoyment of those rights on an equal footing.

The enforcement of the restrictive agreements by the state courts in these cases was directed pursuant to the common-law policy of the States as formulated by those courts in earlier decisions. In the Missouri case, enforcement of the covenant was directed in the first instance by the highest court of the State after the trial court had determined the agreement to be invalid for want of the requisite number of signatures. In the Michigan case, the order of enforcement by the trial court was affirmed by the highest state court. The judicial action in each case bears the clear and unmistakable imprimatur of the State. We have noted that previous decisions of this Court have established the proposition that judicial action is not immunized from the operation of the Fourteenth Amendment simply because it is taken pursuant to the state's common-law policy. Nor is the Amendment ineffective simply because the particular pattern of discrimination, which the State has enforced, was defined initially by the terms of a private agreement. State action, as that phrase is understood for the purposes of the Fourteenth Amendment, refers to exertions of state power in all forms. And when the effect of that action is to deny rights subject to the protection of the Fourteenth Amendment, it is the obligation of this Court to enforce the constitutional commands.

Respondents urge, however, that since the state courts stand ready to enforce restrictive covenants excluding white persons from the ownership or occupancy of property covered by such agreements, enforcement of covenants excluding colored persons may not be deemed a denial of equal protection of the laws to the colored persons who are thereby affected. This contention does not bear scrutiny. The parties have directed our attention to no case in which a court, state or federal, has been called upon to enforce a covenant excluding members of the white majority from ownership or occupancy of real property on grounds of race or color. But there are more fundamental considerations. The rights created by the first section of the Fourteenth Amendment are, by its terms, guaranteed to the individual. The rights established are personal rights. It is, therefore, no answer to these petitioners to say that the courts may also be induced to deny white persons rights of ownership and occupancy on grounds of race or color. Equal protection of the laws is not achieved through indiscriminate imposition of inequalities.

Nor do we find merit in the suggestion that property owners who are parties to these agreements are denied equal protection of the laws if denied access to the courts to enforce the terms of restrictive covenants and to assert property rights which the state courts have held to be created by such agreements. The Constitution confers upon no individual the right to demand action by the State which results in the denial of equal protection of the laws to other individuals. And it would appear beyond question that the power of the State to create and enforce property interests must be exercised within the boundaries defined by the Fourteenth Amendment.

The historical context in which the Fourteenth Amendment became a part of the Constitution should not be forgotten. Whatever else the framers sought to achieve, it is clear that the matter of primary concern was the establishment of equality in the enjoyment of basic civil and political rights and the preservation of those rights from discriminatory action on the part of the States based on considerations of race or color. Seventy-five years ago this Court announced that the provisions of the Amendment are to be construed with this fundamental purpose in mind. Upon full consideration, we have concluded that in these cases the States have acted to deny petitioners the equal protection of the laws guaranteed by the Fourteenth Amendment. Having so decided, we find it unnecessary to consider whether petitioners have also been deprived of property without due process of law or denied privileges and immunities of citizens of the United States.

For the reasons stated, the judgment of the Supreme Court of Missouri and the judgment of the Supreme Court of Michigan must be reversed.

Notes and Questions

1. **Background on racially restrictive covenants.** Racially restrictive covenants were widely used to exclude African Americans from residential communities for much of the twentieth century. Covenants also prohibited sales or rentals to American Indians, Jews, Asian Americans, and Latinos. (Note that the covenant here excluded "people of the Negro or Mongolian Race." "Mongolian" was a term for Asians often used in discriminatory laws in this period. Missouri added a prohibition on marriages with Mongolians to its anti-miscegenation law in 1919, although Asians were only .02 percent of the state's population. Hrishi Karthikey & Gabriel J. Chin, *Preserving Racial Identity: Population Patterns and the Application of Anti-Miscegenation Statutes to Asian Americans, 1910-1950*, 9 Asian L.J. 1 (2002).)

Private individuals and realtor associations initiated creation of these covenants, a process that increased after the Supreme Court held that racially restrictive zoning was unconstitutional in 1917. *Buchanan v. Warley*, 245 U.S. 60 (1917). The United States, however, greatly encouraged their spread. The Federal Housing Administration (FHA), created by the National Housing Act of 1934, strongly encouraged such covenants. The FHA Underwriting Manual, describing the kinds of properties it would insure, declared, "If a neighborhood is to retain stability, it is necessary that properties shall continue to be occupied by the same social and racial classes." The FHA would not guarantee mortgages in integrated neighborhoods, and insisted on racially restrictive covenants in housing developments it financed. Because FHA guarantees transformed the mortgage market, these standards had tremendous influence on the availability of financing. Although the FHA stopped refusing to insure developments without such covenants after *Shelley* in 1948, it was not until 1962 that President Kennedy prohibited FHA guarantees for properties with such covenants. *See* Adam Gordon, Note, *The Creation of Homeownership: How New Deal Changes in Banking Regulation Simultaneously Made Homeownership Accessible to Whites and Out of Reach for Blacks*, 115 Yale L.J. 186 (2005).

Racially restrictive covenants helped to continue segregation long after they became legally unenforceable because such restrictions signaled racial exclusivity to potential buyers. *See* Richard Brooks & Carol Rose, *Saving the Neighborhood: Racially Restrictive Covenants, Law and Social Norms* (2013).

Today, covenants that prohibit sale or lease of dwellings to, or occupancy by, persons on the basis of race violate federal civil rights statutes, including the federal *Fair Housing Act* of 1968, 42 U.S.C. §3601 *et seq.*, and the *Civil Rights Act* of 1866, 42 U.S.C. §§1981, 1982. Before *Shelley*, however, only a minority of states, by common law or statute, declared such covenants unenforceable. *See, e.g., Gandolfo v. Hartman*, 49 F. 181 (S.D. Cal. 1892) (finding covenant restricting Chinese occupancy violated fourteenth amendment and Burlingame Treaty with China); *Corin v. Glenwood Cemetery*, 69 A. 1083 (N.J. Super. Ct. Ch. Div. 1908) (applying a state statute prohibiting racial discrimination by cemeteries).

2. State action and *Shelley v. Kraemer*. The fourteenth amendment provides: "[Nor] shall any State deprive any person of life, liberty, or property, without due process of law, nor deny to any person within its jurisdiction the equal protection of the laws." U.S. Const. amdt. XIV. In the *Civil Rights Cases*, 109 U.S. 3 (1883), the Supreme Court held that the fourteenth amendment regulates the conduct of state government and state officials but not the conduct of private or nongovernmental actors. Since then, courts have attempted to draw the line between public and private conduct — between those states of affairs legitimately attributable to the state and those for which the state cannot legitimately be held legally responsible.[17]

---

17. Note that this version of the public/private distinction is different from the version implicated in public accommodations statutes. *See* §1.2. There the question was whether private property had been sufficiently opened to the public to be considered in the business of serving the public in general in a nonselective manner, such that the owner would have no legitimate interest in discriminating against persons on an illegitimate basis.

Why does the Court hold that enforcing the covenant against the Shelleys would constitute state action? Does the decision mean that every judicial enforcement of a private agreement results in state action permitting constitutional scrutiny of its terms? Many legal scholars have criticized the opinion for failing to adequately distinguish a private sphere that is immune from control by the law. *See* Mark D. Rosen, *Was* Shelley v. Kraemer *Correctly Decided? Some New Answers*, 95 Cal. L. Rev. 451, 453-454 (2007).

Others respond that *Shelley* demonstrates the artificiality of the state action doctrine. The state is always involved in shaping, sanctioning, and facilitating private choices. This is particularly true with respect to property, in which recognizing a property right in one usually means denying it for another. In this case, for example, a decision that Kraemer's covenant is enforceable is also a decision that the Shelleys' deed is invalid because of their race. Because the state usually has the power to prevent discrimination, moreover, state inaction is also a decision to permit discrimination. Many scholars, therefore, have advocated scrapping the doctrine. *See* Erwin Chemerinsky, *Rethinking State Action*, 80 Nw. U. L. Rev. 503 (1985); Stephen Gardbaum, *The "Horizontal Effect" of Constitutional Rights*, 102 Mich. L. Rev. 387 (2003).

Scholars have also argued that *Shelley* is a case of state action in a more limited sense, focusing on governmental support for racially restrictive covenants, the distinctive judicial role in approval of covenants running with the land, or the resemblance between enforcement of private covenants and state zoning power. *See* Carol Rose, *Shelley v. Kraemer*, in *Property Stories* 169, 195 (Gerald Korngold & Andrew P. Morriss eds. 2004); Thomas P. Lewis, *The Meaning of State Action*, 60 Colum. L. Rev. 1083, 1115 (1960). For a symposium issue discussing these questions, *see Symposium on the State Action Doctrine of* Shelley v. Kraemer, 67 Wash. U. L.Q. 673 (1989).

3. Rise and fall of state action. *Shelley* was one of several cases finding state action in the actions of private parties between the 1940s and 1960s. *See, e.g., Terry v. Adams*, 345 U.S. 461 (1953) (holding fifteenth amendment prohibited pre-primary election procedures of private Democratic club); *Marsh v. Alabama*, 326 U.S. 501 (1946) (holding first amendment required private company town to permit leafleting by Jehovah's Witnesses); *Amalgamated Food Employees Union v. Logan Valley Plaza, Inc.*, 391 U.S. 308 (1968) (holding first amendment required private shopping mall to permit picketing by union workers on its premises). The Court has since retreated from expansive prior readings of the state action doctrine. While *Shelley v. Kraemer* has not been overruled, it is not clear what force it has outside of its facts. In *Evans v. Abney*, 396 U.S. 435 (1970) (Chapter 10, §4.3), for example, the Court considered Baconsfield Park, which was built by the city of Macon, Georgia on land willed to the city on condition that only white people be permitted to use it. In an earlier case, the Court had held that Baconsfield was effectively a city park, so continued segregation was unconstitutional state action. *Evans v. Newton*, 382 U.S. 296 (1966). The state courts then determined that because the original discriminatory condition of the will could not be fulfilled, the land reverted to the donor's heirs as a matter of state law. The Supreme Court held that there was no state action in closing of the park to fulfill the testator's discriminatory intent. *Evans v. Abney*, 396 U.S. 435 (1970).

4. Ducking the question. In *Rice v. Sioux City Memorial Park Cemetery*, 60 N.W.2d 110 (Iowa 1953), the court refused to impose damages against a private cemetery that refused to bury plaintiff's deceased husband, who was killed in combat on active duty in Korea, when they discovered during the funeral that he was a Winnebago Indian, and not "Caucasian" as required by a restrictive covenant in the contract of sale of the burial lot. The court refused to apply *Shelley* because, unlike the plaintiff in *Shelley*, the plaintiff in *Rice* had herself contractually agreed to the restriction. *Id.* at 115.[18]

The United States Supreme Court granted certiorari, and, because the Court was evenly divided on the matter, affirmed the state court without opinion. *Rice v. Sioux City Memorial Park Cemetery*, 348 U.S. 880 (1954). Mrs. Rice successfully petitioned the Court for rehearing before the full Court, but the Court then dismissed certiorari as improvidently granted because Iowa had enacted a statute prohibiting such restrictions in the future. *Rice v. Sioux City Memorial Park Cemetery*, 349 U.S. 70 (1955). Scholars attribute the unusual decision to twice take the case and then twice fail to rule to the Court's reluctance to further wade into the issue of desegregation after the uproar over *Brown v. Board of Education*. *See* Stephen L. Wasby et al., *Desegregation from* Brown *to* Alexander 137 (1977).

5. Constitutional violations under the *Restatement (Third)*. The *Restatement (Third)* provides that among the grounds for holding a covenant unenforceable is that "it unreasonably burdens a fundamental constitutional right." *Restatement (Third) on Property: Servitudes* §3.1(2). The comments make clear that this does not apply constitutional standards to restrictions whose enforcement would not otherwise constitute state action. Rather, it means that if a servitude would be unconstitutional if enforced by a state court, it is also invalid before enforcement as a matter of public policy. The drafters state, "Although there may seem to be little practical difference between an unenforceable servitude and an invalid one, recognizing the invalidity of a servitude that is not enforceable under any circumstances may facilitate its removal from the title or from the governing documents of a common-interest community." *Id.* cmt. (d).

6. Subsequent cases regarding covenants. Outside the context of racial discrimination, state action has rarely been found in enforcement of covenants. A number of cases have involved first amendment challenges to restrictions on posting signs on one's residence. These have generally failed. *See Committee for a Better Twin Rivers v. Twin Rivers Homeowners Association*, 929 A.2d 1060 (N.J. 2007); *Linn Valley Lakes Property Owners Association v. Brockway*, 824 P.2d 948 (Kan. 1992); *Midlake on Big*

18. After the Iowa Supreme Court decision, President Truman sent angry telegrams to the mayor of Sioux City and the director of the cemetery, and notified Evelyn Rice that her husband could be buried in Arlington National Cemetery. *Truman Sets Arlington Internment for Indian Denied "White" Burial*, N.Y. Times, Aug. 30, 1951, at 1, 2. In response to Truman's intervention, the cemetery apologized to Mrs. Rice and offered her a free lot anywhere in the cemetery; Mrs. Rice preferred the Arlington Cemetery offer, and Sgt. Rice was buried there with military honors on September 6, 1951. *Indian Hero Is Buried in Arlington Cemetery After Being Refused Internment in Sioux City*, N.Y. Times, Sept. 6, 1951, at 3.

Boulder Lake Condominium Association v. Cappuccio, 673 A.2d 340 (Pa. Super. Ct. 1996); *see also Goldberg v. 400 E. Ohio Condominium Association*, 12 F. Supp. 2d 820 (N.D. Ill. 1998) (enforcement of condominium rule prohibiting all canvassing except for political campaigning was not state action). A few cases have refused to enforce covenants on constitutional grounds, but these are outliers. *See, e.g., Gerber v. Longboat Harbour Condominium, Inc.*, 724 F. Supp. 884 (M.D. Fla. 1989), *aff'd in part and vacated in part*, 757 F. Supp. 1339 (M.D. Fla. 1991) (restriction on manner in which residents flew the American flag); *Gittleman v. Woodhaven Condominium Association, Inc.*, 972 F. Supp. 894 (D.N.J. 1997) (state action in enforcement of covenant that would prevent parking for disabled resident); *West Hill Baptist Church v. Abbate*, 261 N.E.2d 196 (Ohio Ct. Com. Pleas 1969) (restriction barring construction of a church would constitute impermissible state action). In some cases, state constitutions have also been found to create greater protection for speech rights. *See Mazdabrook Commons Homeowners' Association v. Khan*, 46 A.3d 507 (N.J. 2012) (holding prohibition on posting any political signs violated New Jersey constitution despite lack of state action); *Lamprecht v. Tiara at the Abbey Homeowners Association*, No. 12 JE-CC00227 (Mo. Cir. Ct. Oct. 13, 2013) (holding prohibition on all political signs invalid under Missouri constitution).

Problems

Is the argument for state action in the following cases stronger or weaker than in *Shelley v. Kraemer*? Should the court find state action in these cases?

1. Neighbors covenant with each other not to allow their properties to be occupied by non-Caucasians. Defendant breaches the covenant; plaintiff seeks damages for the breach. *See Barrows v. Jackson*, 346 U.S. 249 (1953) (discussing the issue).
2. African Americans seek to dine at a restaurant that has a whites-only policy and refuse, when asked, to leave. The owner calls the police to remove them as trespassers. *See generally* Christopher W. Schmidt, *The Sit-Ins and the State Action Doctrine*, 18 Wm. & Mary Bill Rts. J. 767 (2010).
3. An individual makes a substantial donation to a charity upon the agreement that it will be used for Jewish education. The organization decides instead to use the donation for general education. The donor sues to enforce the agreement.
4. A condo owners association enacts a rule providing that the common gathering room of the association cannot be used to conduct religious services. They file to collect fines against a group of owners who violate the rule.

§5.3 The *Fair Housing Act*

The *Fair Housing Act*, 42 U.S.C. §3601 et seq., is more fully reprinted and discussed in Chapter 13. Because it plays an important role in regulation of covenants and common interest developments, however, it is discussed briefly here. Key provisions of the *Fair Housing Act* make it unlawful

> (a) [t]o refuse to sell or rent after the making of a bona fide offer, or to refuse to negotiate for the sale or rental of, or otherwise make unavailable or deny, a dwelling to any person because of race, color, religion, sex, familial status, or national origin, [or]
>
> (b) [t]o discriminate against any person in the terms, conditions, or privileges of sale or rental of a dwelling, or in the provision of services or facilities in connection therewith, because of race, color, religion, sex, familial status, or national origin.

42 U.S.C. §3604.[19]

1. Unpleasant but not unavailable? The act clearly prohibits covenants like that in *Shelley v. Kramer* that restrict sale or rental of dwellings based on race or religion. Some courts, however, have held that covenants that make a residence less livable for particular groups but do not make the property *unavailable* do not violate the act unless it is shown that they were enacted to target that group. In a particularly egregious case, the Seventh Circuit considered a condominium association that interpreted a restriction prohibiting residents from placing "objects of any sort . . . outside Unit entrance doors" to prohibit residents from hanging mezuzot, rectangular boxes a few inches long containing a passage from the Torah, which Jews are commanded to hang on their lintels. The condo repeatedly removed the Blochs' mezuzot, including during Mr. Bloch's funeral (even though they left the coat rack the Blochs had rented in the hall). A panel of the Seventh Circuit rejected the FHA claim entirely; en banc, the court agreed that the condo had never made the property "unavailable" to the Blochs because they had never moved out, but remanded for determination of whether the condo intentionally discriminated against them. *Bloch v. Frischholz,* 587 F.3d 771 (7th Cir. 2009) (en banc). Is this the correct interpretation of the statute?

2. Conflict with religious practices. Neutral rules in common interest developments often conflict with the religious practices of residents. Restrictions on changes to exterior elements may prohibit not only mezuzot, but also Hindu jhandi flags, South Asian kolam drawings, Virgin Mary statues, and Jewish sukkot. *See* Angela C. Carmela, *Religion Free Environments in Common Interest Communities,* 38 Pepp. L. Rev. 57, 67-71 (2010). Prohibitions on using common areas for religious worship are also common. *Id.* at 71-72. While discriminating against a particular religion in enacting or enforcing such laws would violate the *Fair Housing Act,* courts uphold otherwise neutral laws, even those that discriminate against religion generally, finding that they do not make housing unavailable because of religion. *See Savanna Club Worship Service, Inc. v. Savanna Club Homeowners Association, Inc.*, 456 F. Supp. 2d 1223 (S.D. Fla. 2005) (upholding condo rule that prohibited use of common areas for worship); *Tien Tao Association Inc. v. Kingsbridge Park Community Association, Inc.*, 953 S.W.2d 525 (Tex. App. 1997) (FHA did not prohibit enforcement of covenants to prohibit use of dwellings as Tao place of worship or erection of 30-foot religious flagpoles).

---

19. The prohibition on discrimination based on familial status prohibits discrimination against families with children under 18; the prohibition does not apply in developments dedicated to senior housing. 42 U.S.C. §3607(b).

3. Reasonable accommodations for individuals with disabilities. In 1988, the *Fair Housing Act* was amended to prohibit discrimination against persons with disabilities. 42 U.S.C. §3604(f). Although intentional discrimination is clearly prohibited, so are practices that make it more difficult for individuals with disabilities to enjoy the property. Among other things, discrimination includes refusals to make "reasonable accommodation in rules, policies, practices, or services, when such accommodations may be necessary to afford such person equal opportunity to use and enjoy a dwelling." §3604(f)(3)(B). This provision has been interpreted to prohibit enforcement of covenants restricting property to single-family residential housing where those covenants were interpreted to prohibit group homes of people with disabilities living in a family-like setting. *Hill v. Community of Damien Malokai*, 121 N.M. 353 (N.M. 1994) (covenant could not be interpreted to prohibit group home for four unrelated adults with AIDS), to require amendments to rules and covenants to provide accessible parking, *Gittleman v. Woodhaven Condominium Association, Inc.*, 972 F. Supp. 894 (D.N.J. 1997), and to require that post-1988 construction be wheelchair accessible. *United States v. Quality Built Construction, Inc.*, 309 F. Supp. 2d 767 (E.D.N.C. 2003).

§5.4 Restraints on Alienation

The common law has long contained a strong presumption that property owners should be able to transfer their interests. This presumption may conflict with efforts by owners and developers to control ownership and occupancy of neighboring communities. Promoting alienability may allow property to shift easily to a more valued use, enhance freedom and flexibility for current owners, encourage dispersal of property to new owners, and prevent discriminatory exclusion. At the same time, restraints on alienation may enhance the value of units to be marketed and allow owners to create cohesive and congenial communities. Determining when restraints on alienation are and are not reasonable is therefore a core task of property law.

Northwest Real Estate Co. v. Serio

144 A. 245 (Md. 1929)

HAMMOND URNER, J.

A deed in fee simple for a lot of ground contained, in addition to various building and use restrictions, a provision that the land should not be subsequently sold or rented, prior to a designated date, without the consent of the grantor. The decisive question in this case is whether the restraint thus sought to be imposed upon the alienation of the property is void as being repugnant to the granted estate.

[The covenant in the 1927 deed states:]

> And for the purposes of maintaining the property hereby conveyed and the surrounding property as a desirable high class residential section for themselves[,] their successors, heirs, executors, administrators and assigns that until January 1, 1932, no owner of the land hereby conveyed shall have the right to sell or rent the same without the written consent of the grantor herein which shall have the right to pass upon the character[,] desirability and other qualifications of the proposed purchaser or occupant of the property.

On March 27, 1928, the grantees contracted in writing to sell the lot to Charles Serio and wife. The Northwest Real Estate Company declined to give its consent to the sale and transfer for which the contract provided. The purchaser then brought this suit against the vendors and the company to compel the specific performance of the agreement without the consent of the company, on the theory that the quoted covenant is void, or with the judicially enforced consent of the company, if the covenant should be held to be valid, the averment being made in the bill of complaint that the company's refusal to consent was arbitrary and unreasonable.

The restriction imposed by the deed of the Northwest Real Estate Company upon sales by its grantees and their successors was clearly repugnant to the fee-simple title which the deed conveyed. Its object was to deprive the grantees, until 1932, of the unrestrained power of alienation incident to the absolute ownership which the granting clause created.

CARROLL BOND, C.J., dissenting.

The restraint upon alienation included in the deed . . . seems clearly enough to be one intended merely to give the developer of a suburban area of land power to control the character of the development for a time long enough to secure a return of his capital outlay, and to give early purchasers of lots and buildings some security in their own outlay. In those objects there is nothing against the public interest. We can hardly hold that the modern method of developing city or suburban areas as single large enterprises is detrimental to the public. On the contrary, it seems to be often the only method by which such areas can be conveniently and economically opened, so that houses may be provided upon convenient terms, with all the neighborhood necessities of streets, sewers, and the like ready at the outset. The venture of capital for this purpose appears to be distinctly a public benefit rather than a detriment, one which it is to the public advantage to encourage and promote rather than to hinder. But we know that there are real, substantial dangers to be feared in such ventures, and that, under the modern conditions of rapid city growth and rapid shifts of city populations, one of the most important risks is probably that which comes from the chance of invasion into the new neighborhood of an element of the population which the people to whom the developer must look for the return of his outlay will regard as out of harmony with them. However fanciful may be the aversions which give rise to it, and however deplorable they may be, to the developer they and their consequences must be as real as destructive physical forces. And, if it is to the public interest that this method of development be encouraged rather than hindered, then practically there must be a public gain in removal or diminution of this deterring danger. And the temporary restraint on alienation which the parties here involved have adopted to that end must, I think, be viewed as in point of fact reasonable, and from the standpoint of the public interest actually desirable. And, if this is true, then I venture to think there is no substantial reason why the law should interfere with it, denying the parties the right to agree as they have agreed, or denying their agreement full validity.

Is *Serio* a case about restraints on alienation or about anti-discrimination policy? Should developers be able to exclude individuals consistent with their senses of the prospective buyers "aversions"?

Woodside Village Condominium Association, Inc. v. Jahren

806 So. 2d 452 (Fla. 2002)

Map: 4215 E. Bay Drive, Clearwater, Florida

HARRY LEE ANSTEAD, J.

At issue is the validity of amendments to the Declaration of Condominium adopted by the condominium owners which restrict the leasing of units in Woodside Village. Woodside Village is a condominium development located in Clearwater, Florida, consisting of 288 units. It was established in 1979 pursuant to Florida's "Condominium Act," chapter 718, Florida Statutes. Petitioner, Woodside Village Condominium Association, Inc. ("Association"), is the condominium association that was formed pursuant to the Declaration of Condominium of Woodside Village ("Declaration"), recorded in the public records of Pinellas County. Respondents, Adolph S. Jahren and Gary M. McClernan, each own residential condominium units in Woodside Village.

[Section 10.3 of the] original Declaration of Condominium for Woodside Village [permitted leasing of condominium units but required Board of Directors approval for initial leases lasting more than one year]. In addition, §10.3 was amended in 1995 to require that all leases and renewals receive prior approval from the Board of Directors.

In 1997 some owners became concerned that units were increasingly becoming non-owner occupied, and that such a condition would have a negative impact on the quality of life in Woodside Village and on the market value of units. Accordingly, [while keeping the requirement of Board approval for leases,] §10.3 was amended in March of 1997 to limit the leasing of units to a term of no more than nine months in any twelve-month period. A provision was also added prohibiting owners from leasing their units during the first twelve months of ownership. [Another provision prohibited owners from renting more than three of their units at any one time.] These amendments were adopted by a vote of at least two-thirds of the unit owners as required by the Declaration. The following year the Association notified respondents in writing that two of their respective units were not in compliance with the nine-month lease restriction set out in §10.3 as amended.

When the respondents failed to come into compliance with the leasing restrictions, the Association filed complaints in circuit court seeking injunctions to enforce compliance with the provisions of the Declaration. Respondents [denied] that compliance could be mandated under Florida law. In addition, respondents filed counterclaims for declaratory and injunctive relief asserting that the lease restriction was unreasonable, arbitrary, and capricious, and had no purpose other than to effectively ban all leasing of units. Respondents also asserted the lease restriction was confiscatory and deprived them of lawful uses which were permissible at the time of purchase. Accordingly, respondents sought an injunction prohibiting the Association from enforcing the lease restriction or, alternatively, requiring the Association to compensate respondents for the fair market value of their units.

Condominiums and the forms of ownership interests therein are strictly creatures of statute. *See* Flat. Stat. §§718.101-718.622. In Florida, Chapter 718, Florida Statutes, known as Florida's "Condominium Act," gives statutory recognition to the condominium form of ownership of real property and establishes a detailed scheme for the creation, sale, and operation of condominiums. Pursuant to §718.104(2), a condominium is created by recording a declaration of condominium in the public records of the county where the land is located.

The declaration, which some courts have referred to as the condominium's "constitution," strictly governs the relationships among the condominium unit owners and the condominium association. [B]ecause condominiums are a creature of statute courts must look to the statutory scheme as well as the condominium declaration and other documents to determine the legal rights of owners and the association.

From the outset, courts have recognized that condominium living is unique and involves a greater degree of restrictions upon the rights of the individual unit owners when compared to other property owners. For instance, in *White Egret Condominium, Inc. v. Franklin,* 379 So. 2d 346, 350 (Fla. 1979), we recognized that "reasonable restrictions concerning use, occupancy and transfer of condominium units are necessary for the operation and protection of the owners in the condominium concept." In *White Egret,* we quoted favorably from *Hidden Harbour Estates, Inc. v. Norman,* 309 So. 2d 180 (Fla. Dist. Ct. App. 1975), to further explain the restrictive nature of condominium ownership and living:

> Inherent in the condominium concept is the principle that to promote the health, happiness, and peace of mind of the majority of the unit owners since they are living in such close proximity and using facilities in common, each unit owner must give up a certain degree of freedom of choice which he might otherwise enjoy in separate, privately owned property. Condominium unit owners comprise a little democratic sub society of necessity more restrictive as it pertains to use of condominium property than may be existent outside the condominium organization.

Consistent with this analysis of condominium ownership, courts have acknowledged that "increased controls and limitations upon the rights of unit owners to transfer their property are necessary concomitants of condominium living." *Aquarian Foundation, Inc. v. Sholom House, Inc.,* 448 So. 2d 1166, 1167 (Fla. Dist. Ct. App. 1984). Indeed, section 718.104(5), Florida Statutes, expressly recognizes that a declaration of condominium may contain restrictions concerning the use, occupancy, and transfer of units. *See* §718.104(5).[20]

---

20. Fla. Stat. §718.104(5) provides: "The declaration as originally recorded or as amended under the procedures provided therein may include covenants and restrictions concerning the use, occupancy, and transfer of the units permitted by law with reference to real property. However, the rule against perpetuities shall not defeat a right given any person or entity by the declaration for the purpose of allowing unit owners to retain reasonable control over the use, occupancy, and transfer of units." —Eds.

Courts have also consistently recognized that restrictions contained within a declaration of condominium should be clothed with a very strong presumption of validity when challenged. The logic behind this presumption was explained in *Hidden Harbour Estates, Inc. v. Basso,* 393 So. 2d 637, 639-640 (Fla. Dist. Ct. App. 1981), wherein the court reasoned:

> There are essentially two categories of cases in which a condominium association attempts to enforce rules of restrictive uses. The first category is that dealing with the validity of restrictions found in the declaration of condominium itself. The second category of cases involves the validity of rules promulgated by the association's board of directors or the refusal of the board of directors to allow a particular use when the board is invested with the power to grant or deny a particular use.
>
> In the first category, the restrictions are clothed with a very strong presumption of validity which arises from the fact that each individual unit owner purchases his unit knowing of and accepting the restrictions to be imposed. Such restrictions are very much in the nature of covenants running with the land and they will not be invalidated absent a showing that they are wholly arbitrary in their application, in violation of public policy, or that they abrogate some fundamental constitutional right.

Significantly, Fla. Stat. §718.110 also provides broad authority for amending a declaration of condominium. In particular, section 718.110(1)(a) provides:

> If the declaration fails to provide a method of amendment, the declaration *may be amended as to all matters* except those listed in subsection (4) or subsection (8) if the amendment is approved by the owners of not less than two-thirds of the units. (emphasis added)

Based upon this broad statutory authority and the provisions for amendment set out in the declaration of condominium, courts have recognized the authority of condominium unit owners to amend the declaration on a wide variety of issues, including restrictions on leasing. Of course, §718.110(1)(a) itself contains some restrictions on the amendment process. For example, pursuant to subsections (4) and (8), all unit owners must consent to amendments which materially alter or modify the size, configuration or appurtenances to the unit, change the percentage by which the unit owner shares the common expenses and owns the common surplus of the condominium, or permit timeshare estates to be created in any unit of the condominium, unless otherwise provided in the declaration as originally recorded. *See* Fla. Stat. §718.110(4), (8). These provisions are not at issue here.

In *Seagate Condo. Ass'n, Inc. v. Duffy,* 330 So. 2d 484 (Fla. Dist. Ct. App. 1976), the court upheld an amendment to the declaration of condominium prohibiting leasing of any units, except for limited periods in cases of hardship. The trial court held that the amendment was both an unreasonable restriction and an unlawful restraint on alienation and awarded damages for lost rents to the unit owners who challenged the amendment. On appeal, the Fourth District reversed, and explained, *id.* at 486-487:

> The restriction . . . is reasonable. Given the unique problems of condominium living in general and the special problems endemic to a tourist oriented community in South Florida in particular, appellant's avowed objective — to inhibit transciency and

> to impart a certain degree of continuity of residence and a residential character to their community — is, we believe, a reasonable one, achieved in a not unreasonable manner by means of the restrictive provision in question. The attainment of this community goal outweighs the social value of retaining for the individual unit owner the absolutely unqualified right to dispose of his property in any way and for such duration or purpose as he alone so desires.

The district court upheld the amendment even as it was applied to unit owners who acquired their units prior to the amendments.

We note that the majority of courts in other jurisdictions have held that a duly adopted amendment restricting either occupancy or leasing is binding upon unit owners who purchased their units before the amendment was effective. *See Ritchey v. Villa Nueva Condo. Ass'n*, 146 Cal. Rptr. 695, 700 (Cal. Ct. App. 1978); *Apple II Condo. Ass'n v. Worth Bank & Trust Co.*, 659 N.E.2d 93 (Ill. App. Ct. 1995); *Breezy Point Holiday Harbor Lodge-Beachside Apartment Owners' Ass'n v. B.P. P'ship*, 531 N.W.2d 917, 920 (Minn. Ct. App. 1995); *McElveen-Hunter v. Fountain Manor Ass'n, Inc.*, 399 S.E.2d 112 (N.C. 1991); *Shorewood West Condo. Ass'n v. Sadri*, 992 P.2d 1008, 1012 (Wash. 2000); *but see 560 Ocean Club, L.P. v. Ocean Club Condo. Ass'n (In re 560 Ocean Club, L.P.)*, 133 B.R. 310, 320 (Bankr. D.N.J. 1991); *Breene v. Plaza Tower Ass'n*, 310 N.W.2d 730, 734 (N.D. 1981).

In *Apple II Condo. Ass'n v. Worth Bank & Trust Co.*, the Illinois appellate court [upheld] the validity of a declaration amendment which restricted leasing of units to no more than once during ownership, with no lease exceeding twelve months. In enforcing the amendment, the court declared, 659 N.E.2d at 97:

> In our view, neither the fact that there were no restrictions on the property when the Harmons purchased their unit nor the fact that the Harmons purchased the property for investment purposes is relevant to the proper resolution of the issues presented in this case. As purchasers of the condominium property, the Harmons are charged with knowledge of the Condominium Property Act and that the Declaration governing their unit was subject to amendment. Section 18.4(h) of the Act specifically recognizes that the Board may implement rules governing the "use of the property," so long as the restrictions do not impair those rights guaranteed by the First Amendment to the United States Constitution or the Free Speech provisions of the Illinois Constitution. In the absence of a provision either in the Amendment or in the original Declaration, condominium owners do not have vested rights in the *status quo ante*.

The court further reasoned that the approval of the amendment by the association's membership made the leasing restriction a "category one" restriction under *Basso*, thereby elevating the level of deference given by the court. Accordingly, the court concluded that when an amendment has been passed by an association's membership it would presume the restriction was valid and uphold it unless it was shown that the restriction was arbitrary, against public policy, or in violation of some fundamental constitutional right.

We agree with this reasoning. To hold otherwise, we would have to conclude that the right to amend a declaration of condominium is substantially limited, well beyond those limitations imposed by the Legislature in section 718.110(4) and (8). We would also be faced with the difficult task of deciding what subjects could be addressed by the amendment process, a task much better suited for the Legislature, as can be seen by its imposition of restrictions in section 718.110.

Respondents in this case purchased their units subject to the Declaration which expressly provides that it can be amended and sets forth the procedure for doing so. Section 14 of the Declaration generally provides that an amendment may be adopted by a supermajority of two-thirds of the owners.[21] Further, section 13 expressly states that each owner shall be governed by the Declaration as amended from time to time:

> 13. *Compliance and Default.* Each apartment owner shall be governed by and shall comply with the terms of this Declaration, the By-Laws and the Rules and Regulations adopted pursuant thereto, and Management Agreement, and said documents *as they may be amended from time to time.* Failure of the apartment owner to comply therewith shall entitle the Association or other apartment owners to the following relief in addition to other remedies provided in this Declaration and the Condominium Act.

(Emphasis added.) In addition, the legal description for each of respondents' units that were allegedly being used in violation of the lease restriction provides that the units are subject to the restrictions contained in the Declaration and subsequent amendments thereto.

Thus, we find that respondents were on notice that the unique form of ownership they acquired when they purchased their units in the Woodside Village Condominium was subject to change through the amendment process, and that they would be bound by properly adopted amendments.

We also conclude that the respondents have failed to demonstrate that the restriction, in and of itself, violates public policy or respondents' constitutional rights, at least as asserted herein. As discussed above, most such restrictions simply come with the unique territory of condominium ownership. Indeed, it is restrictions such as these that distinguish condominium living from rental apartments or single-family residences. Hence, persons acquiring units in condominiums are on constructive notice of the extensive restrictions that go with this unique, and some would say, restrictive, form of residential property ownership and living. Accordingly, we conclude the amendment is valid and enforceable against respondents.

We recognize the concerns that owners, such as respondents, who purchased their individual condominium units for investments have regarding the imposition of lease restrictions through subsequent declaration amendments without the consent of all unit owners. The question is, of course, how far can two-thirds of the condominium owners go in restricting leasing rights in the condominium units. The answer will

---

21. Section 14.5, however, provides in part that "no amendments shall discriminate against any apartment owner nor against any apartment or class or group of apartment owners unless the apartment owners so affected . . . consent; and no amendment shall change any apartment nor the share in the common elements, and other of its appurtenances nor increase the owner's share of the common expenses unless the owner of the apartments concerned . . . joins in the execution of the amendment."

usually be found in the legislative scheme creating and governing condominiums. Although we believe such concerns are not without merit, we are constrained to the view that they are better addressed by the Legislature. If condominium owners are to be restrained in their enactment of such lease restrictions, it is appropriate that such restraint be set out in the legislative scheme that created and regulates condominiums and condominium living. As noted above, the Legislature has demonstrated its awareness of the need for limitations on the authority of unit owners to amend a declaration by its enactment of section 718.110(1)(a), (4), and (8). However, as noted, in this instance no provision in the Condominium Act prohibits the adoption of an amendment imposing a lease restriction, nor does any provision require the consent of all unit owners to adopt such an amendment. To the contrary, the Condominium Act provides broad authority for amending a declaration of condominium. *See* Fla. Stat. §718.110(1)(a).

PEGGY A. QUINCE, J., specially concurring.

I concur in the majority's decision which quashes the decision by the Second District Court of Appeal. I write simply to urge the Legislature to seriously consider placing some restrictions on present and/or future condominium owners' ability to alter the rights of existing condominium owners. At the time the units in question here were purchased, the owners had the right to lease their property with relatively few restrictions. This valuable right may well have been the determinative factor for their decisions to buy these properties. As the district court suggested, there should at least be some type of "escape" provision for those "unit owners whose substantial property rights are altered by amendments to declarations adopted after they acquire their property."

Notes and Questions

1. **Direct and indirect restraints on alienation.** Total restraints on alienation of fee simple interests are uniformly held void and unenforceable. *Statham v. Kelly*, 584 S.E.2d 246 (Ga. 2003) (invalidating requirement that devisees use property as their personal residences); *R.H. Macy & Co. v. May Department Stores Co.*, 653 A.2d 461 (Md. 1995). Courts traditionally have held that an absolute restraint on alienation is "repugnant" to the nature of a "fee simple" interest in real property. *Statham*, 584 S.E.2d at 246. The argument seems to be that a fee simple is a property interest that is by definition alienable so a restraint on alienation cannot attach to it. This argument is formalistic and circular; it gives no *reason* for refusing to allow the property to be inalienable. The argument is not wholly without content, however; it appeals to the idea that owners should presumptively have full control over the property they own, and one of the central powers that owners want and need is the power to transfer the property on terms chosen by them. Absolute prohibitions on alienation thus seem to contradict the very notion of ownership. *See De Peyster v. Michael*, 6 N.Y. 467, 506 (1852).

Short of an absolute prohibition on alienation, however, most courts today hold that reasonable restraints or preconditions on alienation are valid, even if they attach to fee interests. *Restatement (Third) of Property (Servitudes)* §3.4 (2000). Reasonableness is determined by "weighing the utility of the restraint against the injurious consequences of enforcing the restraint." *Id.*; *see, e.g., Alby v. Banc One Financial*, 128 P.3d 81 (Wash. 2006) (upholding restriction on mortgaging or encumbering land during life of grantor, where land was sold by grantors to their daughter and son-in-law at far below market price).

Private controls on land use may also make property less alienable by eliminating buyers who do not want the land with the restrictions. Such restrictions may be challenged as **indirect restraints on alienation**, but these claims are very difficult to win if the restriction was voluntarily entered into and has some justification. *See, e.g., Wykeham Rise, LLC v. Federer*, 52 A.3d 702 (Conn. 2012) (reversing and remanding for factual development summary judgment finding of invalidity of covenant prohibiting any development on restricted land); *Lamar Advertising v. Larry & Vicki Nicholls, LLC*, 213 P.3d 641 (Wyo. 2009) (finding 15-year renewal on billboard lease was valid although the billboard prevented development of the property and rent on the billboard had been fixed at $400 since 1990); *Restatement (Third)* for example, invalidates indirect restraints only if they "lack[] a rational justification." *Id.* §3.5(2).

2. Consent to sell clauses. As *Serio* shows, covenants that require owners to obtain the consent of the grantor or developer of the subdivision or condominium are often struck down by the courts as unreasonable direct restraints on alienation. *See Camino Gardens Association, Inc. v. McKim*, 612 So. 2d 636 (Fla. Dist. Ct. App. 1993); *Kenney v. Morgan*, 325 A.2d 419 (Md. 1974). If the developer no longer owns any land in the development, the covenant will violate the traditional rule prohibiting the enforcement of a covenant when the benefit is held in gross. Even under the *Restatement (Third)* rule that benefits may be held in gross to achieve a legitimate interest, it is unclear what legitimate interest a developer who no longer owns land would retain in consenting to future sales. The dissenting opinion in *Serio* provides a policy argument in favor of enforcing covenants that give developers the power to consent to future sales while the developer still owns units, and perhaps for a short period afterward. The analysis in the majority opinion is based on the formalistic repugnancy thesis. Assume that the court would not imply a duty to act reasonably but would interpret the covenant to give the grantor full discretion to grant or withhold consent to any sale. Can you provide a better, policy-based justification for invalidating such a provision than that given by the majority opinion in *Serio* of Justice Urner? How would the dissenting judge respond to these new arguments?

In contrast to grantor/developer consent requirements, covenants that grant such powers to a homeowners or condominium association are ordinarily upheld either if they (a) require the association to act reasonably, *see Laguna Royale Owners Association v. Darger*, 174 Cal. Rptr. 136 (Ct. App. 1981) or (b) are in the form of *preemptive rights* that ensure that the owner can transfer the unit for its fair market value to the association or its members or that require the holder of the preemptive right to match any bona fide offers made by a third party. *Smith v. Mitchell*, 269 S.E.2d 608 (N.C. 1980). Discretionary powers over transfer are particularly likely to be upheld in the special case of *cooperatives* because of the greater financial interdependence of the owners. Mariah Carey, Barbara Streisand, Madonna, Rush Limbaugh, and Sheik Hamad bin Jassim bin Jaber Al-Thani, the prime minister of Qatar and owner of Harrod's, are all among the rich and famous rejected by co-op boards.

3. Limitations on leasing. As *Woodside Village* notes, most courts agree that leasing restrictions in condominium declarations can be retroactively imposed on owners who purchased units before those restrictions were adopted. *See also Cape May Harbor Village and Yacht Club Association, Inc. v. Sbraga*, 22 A.3d 158 (N.J. Super. Ct. App. Div. 2011). Courts differ, however, on whether such restrictions can be imposed by bylaw rather than amendments to the declaration. *Compare Apple Valley Gardens Association v. MacHutta*, 763 N.W.2d 126 (Wis. 2009) (upholding bylaw) *with Kiekel v. Four Colonies Homes Association*, 162 P.3d 57 (Kan. App. 2007) (invalidating bylaw). The Florida legislature effectively overruled *Woodside* by passing a statute to the contrary in 2004. Fla. Stat. §718.110(13) prohibits declaration amendments from imposing retroactive lease restrictions on nonconsenting owners. Is this fact relevant in determining whether the Florida Supreme Court correctly interpreted the Florida statute? If so, how?

The North Dakota Supreme Court held in *Breene v. Plaza Tower Association*, 310 N.W.2d 730 (N.D. 1981), that restrictions on leasing of condominium units cannot be imposed retroactively on owners who purchased before the declaration was amended to impose such restrictions. The court interpreted North Dakota statutes requiring a recorded declaration of restrictions prior to the conveyance of any units to require notice to prospective buyers. The court found that "a necessary corollary of this is that a restriction adopted after the purchase of a condominium unit would not be enforceable against the purchaser except through the purchaser's acquiescence." 310 N.W.2d at 310. Is this argument convincing? Can you make a better argument against retroactive application of leasing restrictions on condominium owners? How could you interpret the statutory language to authorize retroactive leasing restrictions?

The *Restatement (Third)* requires unanimous consent for declaration amendments that "prohibit or materially restrict the use or occupancy or units," §6.10(2), or "that deprive owners of significant property or civil rights," §6.10 cmt. g. However, it makes this rule disclaimable; if the declaration provides otherwise, it is enforceable unless a statute prohibits retroactive enforcement. If the Florida Supreme Court had adopted this interpretation of the common law, would it have changed the result in *Woodside*? Should the court adopt this approach?

4. Charities. Restraints on alienation are generally allowed when the holder of the property interest is a charity. Can you imagine what policies underlie this exception to the rule against unreasonable restraints on alienation?

5. Low-income housing. In recent years, charitable organizations called *community development corporations* (CDCs) have established housing for low-income families. To ensure that the housing remains available for such families, it is often subject to restraints on alienation that prohibit leasing the property or sale to a family that is not a low-income family. In *City of Oceanside v. McKenna*, 264 Cal. Rptr. 275 (Ct. App. 1990), Michael Shawn McKenna purchased a condominium in a development that had been sold by the city for less than its fair market value to a developer for the express purpose of creating housing affordable by low- and moderate-income persons. The units were subject to covenants that prohibited owners from renting their units out and from "failing to occupy the dwelling as the owner's principal place of residence for any period." McKenna got a new job in San Francisco and sought to rent his unit. The city sued him to enforce the covenant. The court noted that "[o]n determining whether a restraint on alienation is unreasonable, the court must balance the justification for the restriction against the quantum of the restraint. The greater the restraint, the stronger the justification must be to support it." *Id.* at 279. It held that the restriction on leasing was a reasonable restraint on alienation because "the provision of housing for low and moderate income persons is in keeping with the public policy of this state. Thus, the restrictions support rather than offend the policies of this state." *Id.* at 280.

§5.5 Anticompetitive Covenants

Anticompetitive covenants are enforceable under the common law only if they are "reasonable." In *Whitinsville Plaza v. Kotseas*, 390 N.E.2d 243 (Mass. 1979), the Massachusetts Supreme Judicial Court defined reasonable anticompetitive covenants as ones that are "reasonably limited in time and space [and product line] and consonant with the public interest" and that "serve a purpose of facilitating orderly and harmonious development for commercial use." This approach has been adopted by other courts as well. *See Davidson Brothers, Inc. v. D. Katz & Sons, Inc.*, 579 A.2d 288 (N.J. 1990); *Vermont National Bank v. Chittenden Trust Co.*, 465 A.2d 284 (Vt. 1983).

Most cases concerning anticompetitive covenants occur in the context of shopping center leases. Further, most claims proceed not on the basis of the common law reasonableness requirement but on the basis of federal antitrust policy contained in the *Sherman Antitrust Act*, 15 U.S.C. §1 et seq. This act prohibits all contracts "in restraint of trade." However, as the court explains in *Optivision, Inc. v. Syracuse Shopping Center Associates*, 472 F. Supp. 665, 674, 676, 679 (N.D.N.Y. 1979):

> If this provision were to be read literally, all commercial contracts would be regarded as violative of the Act since every agreement binds the contracting parties to its terms, and, accordingly, restrains their commercial dealings to a certain extent. Recognizing that it was not Congress' intention to prohibit all contracts nor even all contracts that cause an insignificant or attenuated restraint of trade, the Supreme Court adopted the rule of reason as the standard of analysis for scrutinizing most business relations under the *Sherman Act*. Under this rule, all the circumstances presented by a particular case must be evaluated by the trier of fact to determine whether the complained of conduct imposes an unreasonable restraint on competition.
>
> [T]he Court is unable to conclude that exclusivity clauses in shopping center leases are unreasonable in all possible circumstances. The competitive impact of such arrangements may vary considerably depending upon the availability of suitable alternate

> locations in the relevant market, and upon the strength of the remaining competition. In addition, there is a possible economic justification for a provision of this nature. In some situations, it may be necessary to include such a clause in a shopping center lease in order to attract to the center a certain type of store which might be unwilling to commit itself to a lease with high rentals if it knows that a competing store will be present in the center.
>
> If an exclusivity provision is necessary to attract [a particular type of] store, such a clause has a beneficial impact on competition that will have to be considered along with any adverse competitive effects.

In *Dunafon v. Delaware McDonald's Corp.*, 691 F. Supp. 1232 (W.D. Mo. 1988), an owner promised lessee McDonald's that it would not grant a lease "to any persons to engage in a carry-out fast food restaurant in which food and beverages are dispensed that is in direct competition with lessee within the mall shopping center." An owner of a Taco Bell restaurant sued both the lessor and lessee for a declaratory judgment that the covenant violated the federal antitrust law, known as the *Sherman Act*. The court held that such covenants were not per se unlawful but would constitute unreasonable restraints on trade only if they violate the "rule of reason."

The rule of reason requires the court to examine the circumstances to determine whether the operation of the covenant actually effectuates an unreasonable restraint on competition. The court will first define the relevant product (or service) market and the effective geographic area in which competition is likely to be present. *See Acme Markets, Inc. v. Wharton Hardware & Supply Corp.*, 890 F. Supp. 1230 (D.N.J. 1995). It will then compare the anticompetitive effect of the covenant with its pro-competitive effect. An anticompetitive covenant may increase competition because it provides security that induces a new competitor to enter the market, thereby generating new business and new competition. In *Dunafon*, the court determined that the covenant induced McDonald's to invest in creating a new restaurant and that the presence of this restaurant helped generate business for the shopping center. Because the area previously had little commercial property and few fast-service restaurants, the covenant may have had the effect of inducing new competition to emerge, rather than stifling it. Given the availability of nearby sites where competing fast food restaurants could locate, the court found that the pro-competitive effects of the covenant outweighed its anticompetitive effects and that it was therefore lawful and enforceable.

Problem

An entrepreneur seeking to open a deli leases property on the first floor of a large downtown office building. Seeking to protect her business, the entrepreneur convinces the landlord to include the following language in the lease: "Landlord covenants not to permit any other property in the building to be used for operation of a deli." The entrepreneur opens and begins operating a profitable deli. Later, a second entrepreneur rents space in the building and opens a sit-down restaurant. The restaurant does not harm the deli's business because it caters to a different clientele. However, after a year, the restaurant begins subletting some of its space to a cart that sells convenient, deli-style sandwiches at lunchtime. The deli's business suffers as people start buying from the cart. The deli owner sues the landlord, the restaurant, and the cart owner seeking to enforce the covenant. She argues that the cart is effectively a "deli" because it sells deli-style sandwiches. She also argues that she never would have invested so much money, time, and labor in the deli if she had known that the landlord was going to allow another tenant to breach the covenant. The defendants respond that there is no breach, since a cart is simply not a deli. They argue in the alternative that even if the cart is effectively a deli, enforcing such an anticompetitive covenant is void as against public policy, because the labor force downtown needs convenient places to eat and competition is desirable. Which side should win?[22]

§6 MODIFYING AND TERMINATING COVENANTS

§6.1 Changed Conditions

El Di, Inc. v. Town of Bethany Beach

477 A.2d 1066 (Del. 1984)

Daniel L. Herrmann, Chief Justice for the majority.

This is an appeal from a permanent injunction granted by the Court of Chancery upon the petition of the plaintiffs, The Town of Bethany Beach, et al., prohibiting the defendant, El Di, Inc. ("El Di") from selling alcoholic beverages at Holiday House, a restaurant in Bethany Beach owned and operated by El Di.

El Di purchased the Holiday House in 1969. In December 1981, El Di filed an application with the State Alcoholic Beverage Control Commission (the "Commission") for a license to sell alcoholic beverages at the Holiday House. On April 15, 1982, finding "public need and convenience," the Commission granted the Holiday House an on-premises license. The sale of alcoholic beverages at Holiday House began within 10 days of the Commission's approval. Plaintiffs subsequently filed suit to permanently enjoin the sale of alcoholic beverages under the license.

On appeal it is undisputed that the chain of title for the Holiday House lot included restrictive covenants prohibiting both the sale of alcoholic beverages on the property and nonresidential construction.[23] The same restriction was placed on property in Bethany Beach as early as 1900 and 1901 when the area was first under development.

---

22. This problem is based on *Kobayashi v. Orion Ventures, Inc.*, 678 N.E.2d 180 (Mass. App. Ct. 1997).

23. The restrictive covenant stated:

> This covenant is made expressly subject to and upon the following conditions: *viz.*, That no intoxicating liquors shall ever be sold on the said lot . . . ; a breach of which said condition [. . .] shall cause said lot to revert to and become again the property of the grantor, his heirs and assigns; and upon such breach of said conditions or restrictions, the same may be restrained or enjoined in equity by the grantor, his heirs or assigns, or by any co-lot owner in said plan or other party injured by such breach.

—Eds.

As originally conceived, Bethany Beach was to be a quiet beach community. The site was selected at the end of the nineteenth-century by the Christian Missionary Society of Washington, D.C. In 1900, the Bethany Beach Improvement Company ("BBIC") was formed. The BBIC purchased lands, laid out a development and began selling lots. To insure the quiet character of the community, the BBIC placed restrictive covenants on many plots, prohibiting the sale of alcohol and restricting construction to residential cottages. Of the original 180 acre development, however, approximately 1/3 was unrestricted.

The Town of Bethany Beach was officially incorporated in 1909. The municipal limits consisted of 750 acres including the original BBIC land (hereafter the original or "old-Town"), but expanded far beyond the 180 acre BBIC development. The expanded acreage of the newly incorporated Town, combined with the unrestricted plots in the original Town, left only 15 percent of the new Town subject to the restrictive covenants.

Despite the restriction prohibiting commercial building ("no other than a dwelling or cottage shall be erected . . ."), commercial development began in the 1920's on property subject to the covenants. This development included numerous inns, restaurants, drug stores, a bank, motels, a town hall, shops selling various items including food, clothing, gifts and novelties and other commercial businesses. Of the 34 commercial buildings presently within the Town limits, 29 are located in the old-Town originally developed by BBIC. Today, Bethany Beach has a permanent population of some 330 residents. In the summer months the population increases to approximately 10,000 people within the corporate limits and to some 48,000 people within a 4 mile radius. In 1952, the Town enacted a zoning ordinance which established a central commercial district designated C-1 located in the old-Town section. Holiday House is located in this district.

Since El Di purchased Holiday House in 1969, patrons have been permitted to carry their own alcoholic beverages with them into the restaurant to consume with their meals. This "brown-bagging" practice occurred at Holiday House prior to El Di's ownership and at other restaurants in the Town. El Di applied for a license to sell liquor at Holiday House in response to the increased number of customers who were engaging in "brown-bagging" and in the belief that the license would permit restaurant management to control excessive use of alcohol and use by minors. Prior to the time El Di sought a license, alcoholic beverages had been and continue to be readily available for sale at nearby licensed establishments including: one restaurant 1/2 mile outside the Town limits, 3 restaurants within a 4 mile radius of the Town, and a package store some 200-300 yards from the Holiday House.

In granting plaintiffs' motion for a permanent injunction, the Court of Chancery rejected defendant's argument that changed conditions in Bethany Beach rendered the restrictive covenants unreasonable and therefore unenforceable. The Chancery Court found that although the evidence showed a considerable growth since 1900 in both population and the number of buildings in Bethany Beach, "the basic nature of Bethany Beach as a quiet, family oriented resort has not changed." The Court also found that there had been development of commercial activity since 1900, but that this "activity is limited to a small area of Bethany Beach and consists mainly of activities for the convenience and patronage of the residents of Bethany Beach."

The Trial Court also rejected defendant's contention that plaintiffs' acquiescence and abandonment rendered the covenants unenforceable. In this connection, the Court concluded that the practice of "brown-bagging" was not a sale of alcoholic beverages and that, therefore, any failure to enforce the restriction as against the practice did not constitute abandonment or waiver of the restriction.

We find that the Trial Court erred in holding that the change of conditions was insufficient to negate the restrictive covenant.

A court will not enforce a restrictive covenant where a fundamental change has occurred in the intended character of the neighborhood that renders the benefits underlying imposition of the restrictions incapable of enjoyment. Review of all the facts and circumstances convinces us that the change, since 1901, in the character of that area of the old-Town section now zoned C-1 is so substantial as to justify modification of the deed restriction. We need not determine a change in character of the entire restricted area in order to assess the continued applicability of the covenant to a portion thereof.

It is uncontradicted that one of the purposes underlying the covenant prohibiting the sale of intoxicating liquors was to maintain a quiet, residential atmosphere in the restricted area. Each of the additional covenants reinforces this objective, including the covenant restricting construction to residential dwellings. The covenants read as a whole evince an intention on the part of the grantor to maintain the residential, seaside character of the community.

But time has not left Bethany Beach the same community its grantors envisioned in 1901. The Town has changed from a church-affiliated residential community to a summer resort visited annually by thousands of tourists. Nowhere is the resultant change in character more evident than in the C-1 section of the old-Town. Plaintiffs argue that this is a relative change only and that there is sufficient evidence to support the Trial Court's findings that the residential character of the community has been maintained and that the covenants continue to benefit the other lot owners. We cannot agree.

In 1909, the 180 acre restricted old-Town section became part of a 750 acre incorporated municipality. Even prior to the Town's incorporation, the BBIC deeded out lots free of the restrictive covenants. After incorporation and partly due to the unrestricted lots deeded out by the BBIC, 85 percent of the land area within the Town was not subject to the restrictions. Significantly, nonresidential uses quickly appeared in the restricted area and today the old-Town section contains almost all of the commercial businesses within the entire Town. Moreover, these commercial uses have gone unchallenged for 82 years.

The change in conditions is also reflected in the Town's decision in 1952 to zone restricted property, including the lot on which the Holiday House is located, specifically for commercial use. Although a change in zoning is not dispositive as against a private covenant, it is additional evidence of changed community conditions.

Time has relaxed not only the strictly residential character of the area, but the pattern of alcohol use and consumption as well. The practice of "brown-bagging" has continued unchallenged for at least twenty years at commercial establishments located on restricted property in the Town. On appeal, plaintiffs rely on the Trial Court finding that the "brown-bagging" practice is irrelevant as evidence of waiver inasmuch as the practice does not involve the sale of intoxicating liquors prohibited by the covenant. We find the "brown-bagging" practice evidence of a significant change in conditions in the community since its inception at the turn of the century. Such consumption of alcohol in public places is now generally tolerated by owners of similarly restricted lots. The license issued to the Holiday House establishment permits the El Di management to better control the availability and consumption of intoxicating liquors on its premises. In view of both the ready availability of alcoholic beverages in the area surrounding the Holiday House and the long-tolerated and increasing use of "brown-bagging" enforcement of the restrictive covenant at this time would only serve to subvert the public interest in the control of the availability and consumption of alcoholic liquors.

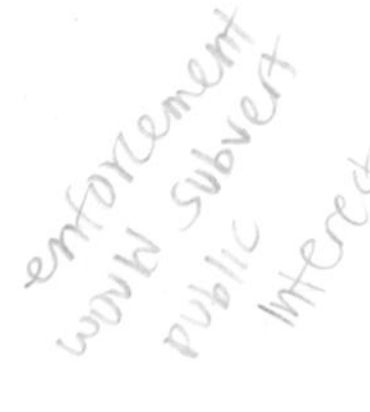

In view of the change in conditions in the C-1 district of Bethany Beach, we find it unreasonable and inequitable now to enforce the restrictive covenant. To permit unlimited "brown-bagging" but to prohibit licensed sales of alcoholic liquor, under the circumstances of this case, is inconsistent with any reasonable application of the restriction and contrary to public policy.

We emphasize that our judgment is confined to the area of the old-Town section zoned C-1. The restrictions in the neighboring residential area are unaffected by the conclusion we reach herein.

ANDREW CHRISTIE, Justice, with whom MOORE, Justice, joins, dissenting.

I respectfully disagree with the majority.

I think the evidence supports the conclusion of the Chancellor, as finder of fact, that the basic nature of the community of Bethany Beach has not changed in such a way as to invalidate those restrictions which have continued to protect this community through the years as it has grown. Although some of the restrictions have been ignored and a portion of the community is now used for limited commercial purposes, the evidence shows that Bethany Beach remains a quiet, family-oriented resort where no liquor is sold. I think the conditions of the community are still consistent with the enforcement of a restrictive covenant forbidding the sale of intoxicating beverages.

In my opinion, the toleration of the practice of "brown bagging" does not constitute the abandonment of a longstanding restriction against the sale of alcoholic beverages. The restriction against sales has, in fact, remained intact for more than eighty years and any violations thereof have been short-lived. The fact that alcoholic beverages may be purchased right outside the town is not inconsistent with my view that the quiet-town atmosphere in this small area has not broken down, and that it can and should be preserved. Those who choose to buy land subject to the restrictions should be required to continue to abide by the restrictions.

I think the only real beneficiaries of the failure of the courts to enforce the restrictions would be those who plan to benefit commercially.

I think that restrictive covenants play a vital part in the preservation of neighborhood schemes all over the State, and that a much more complete breakdown of the neighborhood scheme should be required before a court declares that a restriction has become unenforceable.

Notes and Questions

1. Changed conditions. Covenants will not be enforced if *conditions have changed so drastically* inside the neighborhood restricted by the covenants that enforcement will be of *no substantial benefit* to the dominant estates, *Restatement of Property* §564 (1944). The change "must be so radical as to defeat the essential purpose of the covenant or render the covenant valueless to the parties." *Dierberg v. Wills*, 700 S.W.2d 461, 467 (Mo. Ct. App. 1985). *See City of Bowie v. MIE Properties, Inc.*, 922 A.2d 509, 526, 527 (Md. 2007) (question is whether, "after the passage of a reasonable period of time," and because of a "dramatic change in the character of the neighborhood" or some other fact, "the continuing validity of the covenant cannot further the purpose for which it was formed in light of changed relevant circumstances."). The *Restatement (Third) of Property (Servitudes)* explains that very few cases result in application of the doctrine. "The test is stringent: Relief is granted only if the purpose of the servitude can no longer be accomplished." *Id.* §7.10 cmt. a. Some state statutes also require covenants to be of "actual and substantial benefit" in order to be enforceable. Mass. Gen. Laws ch. 184, §30; N.Y. Real Prop. Acts Law §1951.

The changed conditions doctrine may also apply when substantial changes have occurred *outside* the restricted subdivision. Lots located on the fringe of the restricted area, however, may not invoke the changed conditions doctrine, even if the adjacent property is engaged in activity contrary to the covenant, if it is still possible for the restrictions to create benefit within the subdivision. If lots on the border of the restricted area could easily free themselves from the covenant, it would quickly lose its effect over time as succeeding blocks of fringe lots succumbed to external changes. The changed conditions doctrine is likely to apply to changes outside the restricted subdivision only when those changes have so adversely affected so many lots in the subdivision that enforcement is pointless. *River Heights Associates L.P. v. Batten*, 591 S.E.2d 683 (Va. 2004) (refusing to apply the changed conditions doctrine to allow lots on the edge of a restricted subdivision that had been rezoned for commercial use to develop commercially in violation of the covenant). Traditionally, the changed conditions doctrine has not applied to easements.

As *El Di* shows, determining when a covenant is no longer of substantial benefit is not a precise science. In *Allemong v. Frendzel*, 363 S.E.2d 487 (W. Va. 1987), the property was similarly subject to a restraint on the sale of liquor. The current owners of the servient estate, Donald and Lillian Frendzel, operated a grocery convenience store and began to sell liquor. Within a three-mile radius of the property were located numerous sales outlets for beer, including two establishments located within a quarter of a mile of the Frendzels' store. Because the area immediately surrounding the restricted parcel was predominantly residential and agricultural, however, the court held that there had not been "a radical change or changes in the neighborhood . . . which would effectively destroy the objectives of the covenant and thus render it unenforceable." The court explained, *id.* at 492:

> We do not agree with the appellant that these commercial properties in the general vicinity of the restricted parcel significantly change the residential character of the immediate area. Even if we were to accept the appellant's contention, "every effort must be exerted to protect the unchanged portions of residential neighborhoods when businesses begin to encroach on the fringes." *Morris v. Nease*, 238 S.E.2d 844, 847 (W. Va. 1977).
>
> Based on the evidence, we believe that the nonresidential use of the property in the vicinity of the appellants' convenience store [has] not destroyed the essential objects and purposes of the restrictive covenant. We further believe that the benefits of the original plan envisioned by the grantor may be realized for that portion of the neighborhood which remains primarily residential and agricultural.

The *Restatement (Third)* alters the changed conditions doctrine in several crucial ways. First, it extends the doctrine to easements. Second, it uses termination rules to substitute for controls that had traditionally been applied through the touch and concern test. *Restatement (Third)* §7.10 cmt. a. Third, it suggests modification of the covenant in lieu of termination if modification will allow the covenant to serve its original purpose. Traditionally, a finding of changed conditions required invalidation of the covenant. Under the *Restatement* version of the test, however, termination is only allowed if modification is not feasible. *Id.* §7.10. Also, if the purpose of the servitude can be accomplished but "because of changed conditions the servient estate is no longer suitable for any use permitted by the servitude, a court may modify the servitude to permit other uses under conditions designed to preserve the benefits of the original servitude." *Id.* However, the *Restatement (Third)* cautions that a court should rarely intervene if a mechanism exists for terminating the covenant in a manner that does not require the unanimous consent of the beneficiaries, such as a supermajority vote of the members of a homeowners association. *Id.* §7.10 cmt. a.

2. Damages versus injunctive relief. As noted above, damages were traditionally not awarded for breach of a covenant unless privity of estate was present under real covenants law, while injunctive relief was available even in the absence of privity. Because most owners want enforcement by injunctive relief and because it makes little sense to make it harder to obtain damages than injunctive relief (the reverse is usually the case), the courts appear now to be ready to award either an injunction or damages for violation of a covenant running with the land whether or not strict vertical privity is present. Remedies are chosen on the basis of their appropriateness under the circumstances.

When it comes to modifying or terminating a covenant, an alternative to complete invalidation of a covenant under the changed conditions doctrine is to allow the violation of the covenant to occur upon the payment of compensatory damages to the owners of the dominant estates. *Restatement (Third) of Property (Servitudes)* §8.3 (2000); *Restatement of Property* §564 (1944). When might damages be an appropriate remedy in lieu of injunctive relief? Would they have been appropriate in *El Di*?

§6.2 Relative Hardship

Unlike the changed conditions doctrine, which focuses on whether the covenant remains of substantial benefit to the dominant estate, the *relative hardship* doctrine focuses on the servient estate. A covenant will not be enforced if the harm caused by enforcement, that is, the hardship to the owner of the servient estate, will be greater by a "considerable magnitude" than the benefit to the owner of the dominant estate, *Restatement of Property* §563 (1944). If the hardship is great and the benefit small, the courts may refuse to enforce the covenant. *Appel v. Presley Cos.*, 806 P.2d 1054 (N.M. 1991). If, however, the benefit of the covenant is substantial, the courts are unlikely to apply the doctrine even if the hardship to the servient estate is substantial.

For example, in *Lange v. Scofield*, 567 So. 2d 1299 (Ala. 1990), the court refused to enforce a covenant requiring that all owners of property adjoining or across the street from a parcel consent to the construction of a house on the parcel. One of the surrounding owners refused to give her consent, arguing that another house in the neighborhood would increase density and lower property values. The court found that construction would have no effect on property values and that any benefit received by the neighbor through enforcing the covenant would be negligible and far outweighed by the hardship that enforcement would cause the landowner who wished to construct the house.

The *Restatement (Third)* treats the relative hardship doctrine not as a basis for terminating or modifying servitudes, but, rather, as a factor to consider in determining the availability and selection of appropriate remedies. *Restatement (Third)* §8.3. If compliance with a covenant is unreasonable because the burden is great and the benefit small, the *Restatement (Third)* concludes that nonenforcement may be appropriate, but some amount of damages are probably appropriate to compensate the servitude beneficiary for the loss of the benefit of the covenant, small as it may be. *Id.* §8.3 cmts. a, h.

In *Shalimar Association v. D.O.C. Enterprises, Inc.*, 688 P.2d 682 (Ariz. Ct. App. 1984), the court enforced an equitable servitude requiring an owner to continue operating a golf course against a complaint by the current owner that such a use was not profitable. It refused to apply either the changed conditions or relative hardship doctrines. "A mere change in economic conditions rendering it unprofitable to continue the restrictive use is not alone sufficient to justify abrogating the restrictive covenant." *Id.* at 691. What might justify this result? What is the argument on the other side?

§6.3 Other Equitable Defenses

In addition to the changed conditions and relative hardship doctrines, the courts have identified a number of general equitable doctrines that may result in nonenforcement of a servitude.

Acquiescence, abandonment, or unclean hands. The complaining party may be barred from enforcing the covenant if he has tolerated or failed to object to other violations of the covenant. Toleration may indicate an intent to abandon the covenant, and the defendant may reasonably rely on the failure to enforce the covenant in investing in her property. *See Morris v. Nease*, 238 S.E.2d 844 (W. Va. 1977). This may occur if the plaintiff:

1. has violated the covenant himself (*unclean hands*), or
2. has tolerated previous violations of the covenant by the owner of the servient estate (*acquiescence*), or
3. has tolerated violations of the covenants by owners of other restricted parcels in the neighborhood covered by the covenant (*abandonment*).

Estoppel. An owner of a dominant estate who orally represents to the owner of a servient estate that she will not enforce the covenant may be estopped from asserting her interests in enforcing the covenant if the owner of the servient estate changes his position in reliance on the oral statement.

Laches. If the covenant has been ignored or breached for a substantial period of time — but less than the time necessary to establish prescriptive rights — the court may find that unexcused delay in enforcing the covenant prompted investment in reliance on the failure to object to the violation and that enforcement of the covenant would be unconscionable.

Marketable title acts. As with easements, many states have marketable title statutes that terminate restrictive covenants if they are not re-recorded after a specified period of time. *See, e.g.*, Mass. Gen. Laws ch. 184, §27.

Other ways to terminate covenants. Other ways to terminate covenants include the following:

1. *Language in instrument.* Many subdivisions or condominium associations are subject to covenants that terminate within a stated number of years unless they are periodically renewed by the homeowners association or condominium owners association.
2. *Merger.* As with easements, if the burdened and benefited estates come under the ownership of the same person, the covenants will terminate.
3. *Release.* All parties affected by the covenant — both burdened and benefited estates — may agree in writing to terminate the covenant or release the property from it.
4. *Prescription.* Open and notorious violation of the covenant without permission for the statutory period may terminate the covenant by operation of the statute of limitations.

§6.4 Statutes

A number of states have enacted statutes that regulate the enforceability of covenants and provide a variety of doctrines allowing those covenants to be removed over time. These statutes generally provide that covenants may not enforced unless they are of "actual and substantial benefit" to those enforcing the restriction, or the purpose of the restriction can no longer be fulfilled. *See, e.g.,* Cal. Civ. Code §885.040; Mass. Gen. Laws ch. 184, §30; Minn. Stat. §500.20(1); N.Y. Real Prop. Law §1951. The below case construes Massachusetts's particularly wide-ranging statute.

Blakeley v. Gorin

313 N.E.2d 903 (Mass. 1974)

Map: 13-15 Arlington Street; 2 Commonwealth Avenue; Public Alley 437, Boston, Massachusetts

EDWARD F. HENNESSEY, J.

The petitioners, owners of a parcel of land subject to certain restrictions known as the Commonwealth Restrictions, seek a determination and declaration that the restrictions are obsolete and unenforceable.

The Commonwealth Restrictions date from the middle of the last century. By 1850 the condition of the tidal flats which composed the area now known as the Back Bay had become a nuisance, largely due to drainage problems. The Commonwealth determined to fill in the area and sell lots for dwellings, subject to restrictions in conformity with a comprehensive land use plan.

With some exceptions and minor variations the same stipulations and agreements were inserted into all the deeds to land in the Back Bay district, from the Commonwealth as grantor to various private grantees, beginning in 1857.

General Laws ch. 184, §30, on which the petitioners rely, provides that no restriction shall be enforced or declared to be enforceable unless it is determined that the restriction is, at the time of the proceeding, of actual and substantial benefit to a person claiming rights of enforcement. Further, even if a restriction is found to be of such benefit, it shall not be enforced except by award of money damages if any of several enumerated conditions are found to exist.

The facts are as follows. The petitioners are the owners of two parcels of land separated by Public Alley No. 437; the first is known as 2, 4, 6, 8, and 10 Commonwealth Avenue and the second as 13-15 Arlington Street and 1, 3, and 5 Newbury Street. The former is presently a vacant lot; the latter is the site of the Ritz-Carlton Hotel. Both are subject to various of the Commonwealth Restrictions. The petitioners plan to build on the former lot a 285 foot high hotel-apartment building, with a twelve-story structure as a bridge over the alley, connecting it with the Ritz-Carlton. Plans call for the new building to contain such restaurant and shopping facilities as are usually incidental to the running of a large hotel, and an underground garage for off-street parking as required by the Boston Zoning Code.

The respondents are the owners of 12-14 Commonwealth Avenue, a parcel which is adjacent to the petitioners' vacant lot and backs on the same alley. This property contains an eight-story building with eight apartments on each floor except the first, half facing Commonwealth Avenue and half the alley in back, half (the corner apartments) being of two rooms and half efficiency apartments. The thirty-two rear apartments derive their principal light and air from one window in each apartment on the alley.

Among the restrictions contained in the original deeds to the [defendant's parcels] are the following:

> (a) That a passageway, sixteen feet wide, is to be laid out in the rear of the premises, the same to be filled in by the Commonwealth, and to be kept open and maintained by the abutters in common.

We note that the most difficult aspect of this case concerns the passageway. There will be no obstruction to the movements of persons or vehicles, since the bridge between the Ritz-Carlton building and the new building will start at a point thirteen feet above the ground. Nevertheless, the bridge will occupy most of the space between the two buildings for a height of twelve stories, with consequent effect on light and air. For this reason we have determined, as discussed later in this opinion, that damages are to be awarded for loss of light and air.

Equity does not invariably and automatically grant specific enforcement of such restrictions on the use of land. While the usual grounds for denying such enforcement in a case involving real property is *laches*, or other inequitable conduct by the party seeking to enforce the restriction, this need not always be the case. The *Restatement of Property* §563 (1944) would deny enforcement, apparently without compensation, if the "harm done by granting the injunction will be disproportionate to the benefit secured thereby." The official comments . . . suggest[] that the standard be a "disproportion . . . of considerable magnitude."

The . . . restriction . . . mandat[es] that the passageway behind the petitioners' lot, now Public Alley No. 437, shall "be kept open." The judge found, on evidence which clearly supports his findings, that the respondents have an actual and substantial benefit in the enforcement of this restriction and that the proposed building would violate it. However, his further findings that the restriction is obsolete and that the respondents are entitled to only nominal damages are plainly wrong. We nevertheless hold that, even though it is not obsolete, the restriction shall not be specifically enforced. In lieu of specific enforcement, damages are to be awarded.

Considerable and conflicting evidence was adduced at trial as to the potential effect that bridging the alley would have on the light and air available to the apartments in the rear of the respondents' building. It appears that all parties are in agreement that the "bridge" would decrease the direct sunlight available to the apartments; the dispute is as to the magnitude of the decrease. The testimony on ambient light and on available air was conflicting as to whether there would be an increase or a decrease. Clearly there would be some effect on the property. There was testimony to support a finding that the effect would not be *de minimis* but would be substantial.

There are several alternatives in [Mass. Gen. Laws] ch. 184, §30, which support the judge's decision to deny specific enforcement. On the evidence in this case, the petitioners have made a compelling case for such denial based on all of the following statutory grounds: "(1) changes in the character of the properties affected or their neighborhood [and] in applicable public controls of land use or construction, or in any other conditions or circumstances, [which] reduce materially the need for the restriction or the likelihood of the restriction accomplishing its original purposes . . . or (4) continuation of the restriction on the parcel against which enforcement is claimed . . . would impede reasonable use of land for purposes for which it is most suitable, and would tend to impair the growth of the neighborhood or municipality in a manner inconsistent with the public interest . . . or (5) enforcement, except by award of money damages, is for any other reason inequitable or not in the public interest."

Applying these criteria, we observe that the evidence shows, *inter alia,* that the properties and the neighborhood have drastically changed. Single-family residences have been replaced by moderately high-rise buildings for apartments and institutional use. We have found that the passageway restriction is of an actual and substantial benefit in its effect on light and air, but the proposed bridge will have only a modest impact in view of the drastic changes which have already occurred. In particular, an occupant of the respondents' building, in looking out a rear window of that structure, would see to his immediate left and across the passageway the high-rise Ritz-Carlton building. As to the petitioners' unused land to that viewer's immediate left, on the same side of the passageway, it seems inevitable that, even if the bridge were not permitted, a building higher than the respondents' building would at some time be constructed on it.

The record also clearly supports a conclusion that continued enforcement of the restriction would tend to impede reasonable use of the land for purposes for which it is most suitable. The uncontradicted evidence was that a free standing tower is economically unfeasible presumably because of the small size of the parcel, and that the plaintiffs' proposal for an apartment-hotel complex connected to the adjacent Ritz-Carlton is the most suitable use of the land.

The evidence supports a conclusion that the proposed bridge is not an arbitrary and unnecessarily large intrusion. The twelve stories of the bridge relate to twelve of the lower floors of the new building which are to be used as a hotel; above those floors there will be apartments. The hotel floors are feasible only if connected to the hotel services of the Ritz Carlton. Therefore, all considerations of equity, and the most suitable use of the property, support the planned bridge construction in size as well as purpose.

Weighing and comparing the interests of the parties and the public in accordance with the several provisions of §30 brings us almost inevitably to the conclusion that there should be no specific enforcement. In the words of provision (5) of the statute, which unquestionably confers the broadest discretion on the court, enforcement here would be inequitable and not in the public interest. The magnitude of the harm to the petitioners in specific enforcement of the restriction far exceeds that to the respondents in its denial. Moreover we are mandated by the statute to have due regard for the public interest in determining the manner of enforcement of a restriction. The land in question has been vacant for over a decade. We take judicial notice of the exceedingly high property tax rates current in the city of Boston and the beneficial effect on the tax base of the petitioners' plan to construct a multimillion dollar project of public usefulness on presently unutilized land. In the circumstances both the balance of equities between the parties and a consideration of the public interest require that the respondents accept money damages by way of enforcement of this restriction.

The final decree is reversed and the case is remanded to the Superior Court, where damages are to be assessed for the loss of benefit in light and air. Such further evidence as the judge deems to be necessary shall be heard on the issue of damages.

FRANCIS QUIRICO, Justice, dissenting, with whom REARDON, J., joins.

I agree with today's holding by the court that the restriction with respect to the passageway "was designed to preserve light and air to the properties it benefited," and that "[a]s this urban area has grown and become ever more congested in the century since this restriction was first imposed, light and air have become more, not less, valuable. The restriction securing the respondents' rights to them is certainly not obsolete."

The question then becomes what remedy or relief is available to the parties. This court holds that notwithstanding its findings that the passageway restriction is of actual and substantial benefit to the respondents and that it has not become obsolete, the petitioners have the right, under the terms of Mass. Gen. Laws ch. 184, §30, to compel the respondents to receive money damages in lieu of their right to specific enforcement of the restriction.

I do not agree with the ultimate conclusion that under §30 the respondents' relief should be limited to money damages rather than specific enforcement of the restriction relating to the open passageway.

The court relies in part on its conclusion that "the properties and the neighborhood have drastically changed (since the restrictions were imposed). Single family residences have been replaced by moderately high-rise buildings for apartments and institutional use." I do not consider this change to be drastic. It seems clear to me from the record that Commonwealth Avenue in the block between Arlington and Berkeley streets, with its unique architectural and physical features, is one of the few remaining residential boulevards in the city, providing a welcome oasis amidst the skyward push of Boston's newer commercial buildings. Contrary to the court's conclusion, I believe that the erection of a twelve-story bridging structure at the very entrance of this block does constitute "an arbitrary and unnecessarily large intrusion" which is not justified by any change in the character of the area.

Notes and Questions

The statute in *Blakeley* changed the common law by giving the court the option of damages rather than an injunction to enforce a covenant that was still of substantial benefit but violated the public interest. The majority found that the facts brought the court "almost ineluctably to the conclusion that there should be no specific performance." Do you agree that an injunction was inappropriate in this case? What are the arguments in favor and against granting an injunction?

PART FOUR

OWNERSHIP IN COMMON

CHAPTER 9

Concurrent, Family, and Entity Property

§1 VARIETIES OF COMMON OWNERSHIP

Property may be held by more than one person in many different ways. Property rights may be divided, with specific sticks in the bundle of rights that make up property allocated to different persons or groups, or with the right to all the sticks divided over time. Leaseholds provide an example of both divisions: the tenant has the right to possess and control the property during her lease, while the landlord has both the right to establish conditions for use during the lease period and the future right to possess the property after the lease ends. Property rights may be shared as well as divided. In other words, more than one person may have the right to control the same thing at the same time. This is called **concurrent ownership**. For example, a wife and husband may together own a condominium apartment in an urban building. In this arrangement each has a concurrent right to possess the entire condominium unit. They have to agree how the property will be used — whether they will live in the condominium or rent it out to others, how they will use each room, whom they will invite to dinner, and so on. They also share with other condominium owners the right to use common areas of the building. Disputes about the use and condition of common areas — such as whether to pay for a new roof — must be worked out in conjunction with the other condominium owners.

Family members often share property through one of the concurrent tenancies. But familial relationships also give rise to distinctive **family property** rights. Minor children, for example, have a right to support from their noncustodial parents. Marriage also has many consequences for property. In community property states, rights to most property individually acquired during marriage is shared equally with one's spouse. In separate property states, spouses have rights to each other's property on divorce and death. Such rules also raise questions of the property rights of people in family-like relationships that are not recognized by the state, whether same-sex couples, same- or opposite-sex unmarried cohabitants, or non-sexual long-time live-in companions.

Individuals also share property rights through **entity property**, in which beneficial use of the property is significantly divided from rights to govern the property. Perhaps the predominant form of entity property is the corporation, in which vast numbers of shareholders own shares in entities managed by others. Another important form of entity property is the common interest development, discussed in detail in Chapter 8, in which hundreds or thousands of individuals and families own units in developments managed by property owners associations. The growth and increasing influence of these forms of ownership require reconsideration of the meaning of property and the line between private and public action.

§2 CONCURRENT TENANCIES

§2.1 Forms of Concurrent Tenancies

The three common law concurrent tenancies are the **tenancy in common**, the **joint tenancy**, and the **tenancy by the entirety**.[1] In all concurrent tenancies each tenant, no matter how small her fractional interest, has the right to possess the entire parcel—unless all the co-tenants agree otherwise. Absent agreement, all co-tenants also have the right to share the profits from the property, such as rents and royalties, and the obligation to contribute to basic costs of maintaining the property, such as mortgage and property taxes. The three tenancies, however, differ in four key dimensions: first, how they are *created*; second, whether there is a *right of survivorship*, meaning that surviving co-tenants automatically inherit a deceased co-tenant's share of the property; third, whether tenants can unilaterally *sever* or *terminate* their tenancy; and fourth, whether tenants can unilaterally *encumber* the property, such as by leasing it, pledging it as security, or having it levied to pay a debt. A fourth form of concurrent ownership, the **partnership** for business purposes, is similar in some respects to the concurrent tenancies, but is now classified as a form of entity property and is discussed in §4 of this chapter.

A. Tenancy in Common

Tenancies in common may be created explicitly, by conveying property to more than one party as "tenants in common." Tenancies in common are also usually the default form of concurrent tenancy in face of ambiguity; if property is conveyed or devised to multiple owners, the law will presume that they are tenants in common. For example:

---

1. An additional common law concurrent tenancy, *coparceny*, is obsolete. It arose when property was inherited by multiple relatives. Because the traditional English heirship rule in most jurisdictions was primogeniture, meaning that a single male heir would inherit, it only arose when the decedent had no male heirs so that property would descend to multiple daughters or other female descendants.

O devises Blackacre to *A* and *B*.

O conveys Blackacre to *A*, *B*, and *C* as tenants in common, with a 1/4 undivided interest in *A*, a 1/4 undivided interest in *B*, and a 1/2 undivided interest in *C*.

Each co-tenant has the right to transfer or encumber the interest unilaterally and devise it or have it inherited in case of intestacy on death. Of course, each co-tenant only has the authority to transfer her own interest, and buyers may be unwilling to share ownership with a stranger. Tenants may also file to terminate the co-tenancy and divide the property or its proceeds by bringing an action for **partition**. In partition proceedings, a court may order the property physically divided among the co-owners. If this is not feasible or appropriate, the court will order the property to be sold and the proceeds divided among the co-owners in proportion to their ownership shares.

Tenancies in common are often used divide rights in timeshares or fractional interests in vacation property. The property is held in concurrent ownership, but the individual owners have contractual rights to exclusively occupy the property during their allocated time. Tenancies in common may also be used to create a less-regulated alternative to condominiums, in which the co-owners have contractual rights to exclusively occupy their units. Both kinds of tenancies in common are often financed by a single mortgage, which created a number of problems during the recent housing crisis. Individual financing of one's share has become more available today.

B. Joint Tenancy

The main difference between joint tenancy and tenancy in common is the **right of survivorship**. When a joint tenant dies, her property interest is immediately transferred to the remaining joint tenants in equal shares. Thus, in a joint tenancy owned by *A*, *B*, and *C*, each with a one-third undivided interest, *A*'s interest when she dies goes to *B* and *C* (that is, half to *B* and half to *C*). The result is that *B* and *C* own the property as joint tenants, each possessing a one-half undivided interest, in the property. If *A* tries to devise her one-third interest, her will would have no effect; she has no right to devise her interest. Although joint tenancies are no longer the default form of concurrent ownership, they continue to be popular, particularly for family property and joint bank accounts. The right of survivorship consolidates property among the parties, simplifying use and ownership. Importantly, it also avoids probate, which is expensive and can tie up property for long periods. For this reason, a joint tenancy with right of survivorship is sometimes called the "poor man's will."

Traditionally, joint tenancies could only be created if they shared the **four unities** of time, title, interest, and possession. This means that (1) the interest of each joint tenant must be created at the same moment in *time*; (2) all joint tenants must acquire title by the same instrument or *title* (joint tenancy does not ordinarily arise by intestate succession); (3) all joint tenants must possess equal fractional undivided *interests* in the property and their interest must last the same amount of time; and (4) all joint tenants must have the right to *possess* the entire parcel. Although the four unities remain in force in many states, others have rejected them in favor of a test considering the intent of the parties. *See In re Estate of Johnson*, 739 N.W.2d 493 (Iowa 2007) (adopting intent-based approach and discussing trend); R.H. Helmholz, *Realism and Formalism in Severance of Joint Tenancies*, 77 Neb. L. Rev. 1, 21-22 (1998) (discussing retreat from four unities when they contravene intent). Although a number of states have statutes that appear to abolish joint tenancies entirely, these states will often find joint tenancies with a right of survivorship if the intent to create them is clearly expressed. *See* 1 Joyce D. Palomar & Robert Wilcox, *Patton and Palomar on Land Titles* §223 (3d ed. 2003); *see, e.g., McLeroy v. McLeroy*, 40 S.W.2d 1027 (Tenn. 1931) (interpreting Tenn. Code §66-1-107). Because of the presumption against joint tenancy and survivorship in many states, however, drafters are well advised to be explicit:

> *O* conveys Blackacre to *A* and *B* as joint tenants with the right of survivorship.
> *O* devises Blackacre to *A*, *B*, and *C* as joint tenants and not as tenants in common.

In most states, the right of survivorship is highly contingent because a joint tenant who transfers her property interest can destroy the right of survivorship of her fellow owners with respect to her share. For example, if *A* and *B* own property as joint tenants, each owner has the right to obtain full ownership of the property when the other co-tenant dies (the right of survivorship). If *A* sells her one-half undivided interest to *C*, however, the joint tenancy is **severed**, and *B*'s right of survivorship is destroyed. The result is that *B* and *C* will own the property as tenants in common. As with tenancy in common, joint tenants may also file for partition of the property. A few states prohibit severance by statute. S.C. Code §27-7-40 (prohibiting unilateral severance of joint tenancy); Nev. Const. art. IV §30 (prohibiting conveyance of homestead property without consent of both husband and wife). Many states will also deem a joint tenancy to be converted to a tenancy in common if married co-tenants divorce. Courts have also held that a joint tenancy is converted to a tenancy in common and the right of survivorship destroyed if one joint tenant murders the other. *See In re Estate of Thomann*, 649 N.W.2d 1 (Iowa 2002) (interpreting effect of Iowa Code §633.535 on property rights after murder-suicide).

Can an owner sever a joint tenancy and destroy the right of survivorship by conveying her interest from herself as joint tenant to herself as tenant in common? Traditionally, this could not be done because it did not break the four unities, but most states now permit such "self-severance." *See Taylor v. Canterbury*, 92 P.3d 961 (Colo. 2004); *Sathoff v. Sutterer*, 869 N.E.2d 354 (Ill. Ct. App. 2007) (applying 765 Ill. Comp. Stat. 1005/1b); *In re Estate of Johnson*, 739 N.W.2d 493, 499 n.9 (Iowa 2007). The procedure creates the possibility of fraud. Consider a husband who secretly signs such a document and gives it to his daughter for safekeeping. If he survives his wife, he can claim her interest because the attempted severance was secret. If he predeceases her, however, his daughter can claim to inherit his 50-percent interest on the grounds that his wife's right of survivorship has been destroyed by severance. To address this possibility, some states require that conveyances be publicly recorded to sever a joint tenancy; this would prevent a co-tenant from benefiting from the right to survivorship after conveying the interest to himself. *See* Cal. Civ. Code §683.2(c); Colo. Rev. Stat.

§38-31-101 (5)(a); *see* John V. Orth, *The Perils of Joint Tenancies*, 44 Real Prop. Tr. & Est. L.J. 427 (2009).

Severance occurs only between the selling owner and the remaining owners; it does not change the relations of the remaining owners among themselves. *Sathoff*, 869 N.E.2d at 356-357. For example, if *A*, *B*, and *C* own property as joint tenants, and *A* conveys his interest to *D*, the result is that *D* owns a one-third interest as a tenant in common with *B* and *C*, who each own a one-third interest as joint tenants with each other. When *D* dies, her one-third interest will go to her heirs or devisees. However, when *B* dies, his interest goes to *C* as a surviving joint tenant, who will then own a two-thirds interest as a tenant in common with *D*.

In most states, joint tenants are free to encumber their interests during their lives, such as by renting them or pledging them as security for a debt. *But see* S.C. Code §27-7-40 (prohibiting unilateral encumbrance). So long the property is not actually sold, however, these encumbrances generally do not survive the death of the encumbering co-tenant.

Joint bank accounts. Many, perhaps most, personal joint bank accounts are joint tenancies with rights of survivorship. The right of survivorship is often provided by the bank's signature form and may even be presumed absent contrary evidence. *See Estate of Ostlund*, 918 A.2d 649, 656-658 (N.J. 2007) (despite evidence that ailing father added his son to his account so that he could pay his bills, the evidence did not clearly and convincingly rebut presumption of survivorship); *Uniform Probate Code* §6-212 (2010) (survivorship presumed absent clear and convincing evidence). The four unities are rarely required. Absent other evidence, during their lives tenants are usually entitled only to the right to withdraw funds according to their contributions to the account, although some states and the revised Uniform Probate Code provide that married couples are presumed to have contributed equally. *See Uniform Probate Code* §6-211; Lisa R. Mahle, *A Purse of Her Own: The Case Against Joint Bank Accounts*, 16 Tex. J. Women & Law 45 (2006). Much litigation concerns whether elderly people creating joint accounts intended to create a right of survivorship and *inter vivos* use of the account, or simply intended a "convenience account" to permit a child or other helper to write checks on their behalf during life.

Joint tenancy versus dual life estates with alternative contingent remainders. It is possible to create an indestructible right of survivorship if one uses the form of life estates and remainders. For example:

> *O* to *A* and *B* as life tenants, with a remainder in *A* if *A* survives *B*, and a remainder in *B* if *B* survives *A*.

This conveyance creates alternative contingent remainders in *A* and *B*. Whoever dies second will obtain the remainder and, hence, the property in fee simple absolute. A conveyance of *A*'s life estate will *not* destroy the contingent remainder. *See Albro v. Allen*, 454 N.W.2d 85 (Mich. 1990) (interpreting a joint life estate with alternative contingent remainders).

C. Tenancy by the Entirety

Tenancies by the entirety are available only to legally married couples. *See Baker v. Speaks*, 295 P.3d 847, 859-860 (Wyo. 2013) (whether the defendants had a tenancy by the entirety depended on whether they had contracted a common law marriage in another state). The tenancy by the entirety originated in the idea that the married couple was one legal person; it was linked to the doctrine of coverture, which gave the husband the sole power to manage and control his wife's property. As a result, many states abolished tenancies by the entirety when they abolished coverture. Today, however, the tenancy by the entirety is recognized in more than half the states and in the District of Columbia. 7 *Powell on Real Property* §52.01. Some of these states presume that conveyances to married couples are tenancies by the entirety absent contrary evidence, *see* Alaska Stat. §34.15.110; Ind. Code §32-17-3-1; *Beal Bank, SSB v. Almand & Associates*, 780 So. 2d 45 (Fla. 2001); *In re VanConett Estate*, 687 N.W.2d 167 (Mich. App. 2004), while others apply the usual presumption in favor of tenancies in common, Haw. Rev. Stat. §509-1; 4 *Thompson on Real Property, Second Thomas Editions* §33.06(e).

Like a joint tenancy, the tenancy by the entirety includes a right of survivorship. This right is much more stable than in a joint tenancy, however, because absent agreement of both parties the tenancy by the entirety is only severed on divorce or death.

Although the law varies from state to state, in most states, spouses cannot encumber their interest in property held by the entirety without each other's consent, and creditors cannot attach property held through tenancy by the entirety to satisfy debts of one of the spouses. *See Sawada v. Endo*, §2.2.D, below; *Beal Bank, SSB v. Almand & Associates, supra*; *Baker v. Speaks, supra*, at 859 (Wyo. 2013); *Bunker v. Peyton*, 312 F.3d 145 (4th Cir. 2002) (applying Virginia law). *But see United States v. Craft*, 535 U.S. 274 (2002) (an individual's interest in tenancy by the entirety property subject to federal tax lien for unpaid taxes).

Problems

1. *A*, owner of Greenacre, executes and delivers a deed conveying Greenacre "jointly to myself and my wife *B*." How will this conveyance be interpreted?

2. A mother and son acquire a parcel of land as "tenants by the entirety." How should a court interpret this conveyance?

3. An elderly father and his daughter from his first marriage open an account labeled a "joint bank account." The deposits in the account are most of the father's lifetime savings; the daughter does not contribute. During the father's life, the daughter draws from the account only to write checks for her father's rent, medical bills, and other expenses. When the father dies, $300,000 is left in the account. His will divides his estate equally among the daughter and his two children from his second marriage. The daughter claims that she is entitled to the proceeds of the account by right of survivorship. This would leave assets worth about $15,000 to be divided among the children under the will. What should the court do?

4. What should be the default in cases of intestacy? More than half of Americans die without a will; this proportion is much larger for African Americans, Latinos, and for middle- to lower-income people of all races. When individuals die intestate, their property goes to their intestate heirs. This frequently means shared ownership. For example, if the decedent leaves multiple children and no spouse, or a spouse who is not a parent of the children, the property will be divided among them. Following the usual default rule, the estate descends to the intestate heirs as tenants in common. If those heirs also die intestate, the property is divided among yet more heirs and so on exponentially. In a few generations, the number of co-tenants in such "heirs property" may become so large that joint management of the property is impossible. Two much-discussed examples of this dynamic involve African American farmers and Native Americans.

African American rural landownership dropped by more than 90 percent between 1920 and 1999 and continues to decline. There are many causes of this phenomenon—discrimination and violence against black landowners, African Americans' "Great Migration" to the North, and the general decline of small farms—but one cause may be the frequency of heirs property, estimated to constitute one-quarter to 40 percent of Black-owned rural property. A typical parcel of heirs property has eight or more co-owners but may have many more, and many of the co-owners live outside the Southeast where the property is located. Such property is harder to manage and vulnerable to loss through forced partition sale or foreclosure. *See* Thomas W. Mitchell, *From Reconstruction to Deconstruction: Undermining Black Landownership, Political Independence, and Community Through Partition Sales of Tenancies in Common*, 95 Nw. U. L. Rev. 505 (2001); Todd Lewan & Dolores Barclay, *Developers and Lawyers Use a Legal Maneuver to Strip Black Families of Land*, Associated Press, Dec. 30, 2001.

In the late nineteenth and early twentieth century, much tribal land was forcibly divided among individual Indians pursuant to the federal allotment acts. One impact of the acts was to apply state probate laws, including intestacy laws, to allotment holders who rarely made wills. As a result, by 1934 "[o]n allotted reservations, numerous cases exist where the shares of each individual heir from lease money may be 1 cent a month. Or one heir may own minute fractional shares in 30 or 40 different allotments. The cost of leasing, bookkeeping, and distributing the proceeds in many cases far exceeds the total income." 78 Cong. Rec. 11728 (1934) (Rep. Edgar Howard). By 2004, some interests amounted to only 0.0000001 percent, or 1/9 millionth, of the undivided allotment. Testimony of Ross O. Swimmer, Special Trustee for American Indians, House Resources Comm. Hearing on S. 1721 (AIPRA) (June 23, 2004). While much of this land is in trust and cannot be sold or foreclosed upon, this fractionation means that the owners get almost no value from their land.

One way to prevent ownership by exponential numbers of heirs would be to make joint tenancy with the right of survivorship the default in cases of intestacy. What objections can you imagine to such a proposal?

§2.2 Sharing Rights and Responsibilities Between Co-Owners

A. Division of Benefits and Expenses

Unless they agree otherwise by contract, co-tenants are entitled to share the benefits of the property and obligated to share its burdens. If there is a dispute regarding these, a tenant can seek a judicial **accounting**, either during co-ownership or in determining division of proceeds in a partition action or voluntary sale, to require their co-owners to pay their portions of required expenses or to force co-owners to hand over profits from the property.

Possession. The right of possession is a key benefit. Each co-owner has the right to possess the entire parcel. If one co-owner chooses to live in the commonly owned property and the other co-owner chooses not to live there, in most states the tenant in possession has no duty to pay rent to the non-possessing tenant. Joint tenants and tenants in common only have a duty to pay rent to their co-owners if they have committed **ouster**, an explicit act by which one co-owner excludes others from the jointly owned property. Note that the amount of rent owed is the fractional share of the rental value owned by the co-owners out of possession; a co-owner with a one-third interest in possession would have to pay only two-thirds of the fair rental value of the property to her co-owners out of possession.

Profits. In addition to sharing the right to possess the property, co-owners are entitled to share any rents or other profits from the property. The share of profits belonging to each co-owner is based on that owner's fractional interest in the property. For example, suppose *A* and *B* own a condominium unit as tenants in common, with a one-quarter interest in *A* and a three-quarters interest in *B*. They rent the unit to *C*. *A* has a right to one-quarter of the rents paid by *C*, and *B* has a right to three-quarters of the rents paid by *C*, unless *A* and *B* agree otherwise. Tenants also share profits on sale or partition of the property according to their respective fractional interests.

Burdens. Co-owners generally have a duty to share basic expenses needed to keep the property, including *mortgage* payments, property *taxes* and other assessments, and property *insurance*, in accordance with their respective shares. Co-owners generally also have a duty to share basic *maintenance* and *necessary repairs* of the premises. *See Palanza v. Lufkin*, 804 A.2d 1141 (Me. 2002) (approving contribution toward necessary repairs, even though some had cosmetic effects). Some jurisdictions, however, require a tenant to provide co-tenants with notice and opportunity to object to the repairs in order to demand contribution. *See Anderson v. Joseph*, 26 A.3d 1050, 1056-1057 (Md. Ct. Spec. App. 2011) (denying contribution for basement repairs to deal with "massive flooding" because of failure to provide notice). Co-owners have no duty to share the costs of *improvements* to the property unless they agree to do so.[2] Improving tenants may only claim the amount by which the improvement increases

2. Tenants making improvements, however, need not account to co-tenants for profits solely as a result of those improvements. *See* William B. Stoebuck & Dale A. Whitman, *The Law of Property* §5.9, at 208 n.5 (3d ed. 2000).

the value of the property at partition or sale. Thus tenants paying for work on a property that is determined not to be necessary may only demand contribution on sale or partition, and then only up to the amount the work is shown to improve the value of the property.

In most states, a co-owner who exclusively possesses the premises must bear the entire burden of expenses (including taxes, repairs, and mortgage payments) if the value of her occupation of the premises exceeds those payments. If the share of expenses that would ordinarily be borne by the tenants out of possession is less than the rental value belonging to the tenants out of possession, no action for contribution may be brought. *Barrow v. Barrow*, 527 So. 2d 1373 (Fla. 1988); William B. Stoebuck & Dale A. Whitman, *The Law of Property* §5.9, at 209 (3d ed. 2000). This principle substantially qualifies the rule that co-tenants who are occupying the premises have no duty to pay rent to the co-owners who are not occupying the property. Although a co-tenant out of possession cannot sue a co-tenant in possession for rent, a tenant in possession can sue her co-tenants out of possession only for their share of expenses that exceeds the fair rental value to which they would be entitled if the property were leased out to a third party. *See Esteves v. Esteves*, 775 A.2d 163 (N.J. Super. Ct. App. Div. 2001) (in accounting after house was sold, parents who occupied the house for 18 years were entitled to be reimbursed by son for one-half of expenses of mortgage and maintenance but son was allowed a credit against that amount equal to the reasonable value of his parents' sole occupancy of the property).

Problems

1. *A* and *B* own equal shares in an apartment as tenants in common. *B* lives in another state, but *A* lives in the apartment, whose rental value is $1,000 per month. *B* refuses to contribute to paying the mortgage, property taxes, and insurance on the apartment. *A* sues *B* for an accounting and contribution to these carrying costs. What result if the carrying costs are $500 per month? What result if these costs are $1,200 per month?

2. *A* and *B* live in a house in which they own equal shares as joint tenants. *B* builds a third bathroom in the house at a cost of $10,000 and seeks contribution from *A*. What result? The property is later sold for $200,000. How should the proceeds be divided if the bathroom is estimated to enhance the value of the property by $15,000? What if the bathroom only enhanced the value of the property by $8,000?

B. Conflicts over Rent and Possession

Olivas v. Olivas

780 P.2d 640 (N.M. Ct. App. 1989)

HARRIS L. HARTZ, Judge.

Respondent Sam Olivas (husband) appeals the property division in a divorce action. Petitioner Carolina Olivas (wife) and husband were divorced by a partial decree entered December 18, 1984. The district court did not enter its final order dividing property until August 31, 1987. The issues in this appeal arise, for the most part, as a consequence of the unusually lengthy delay between the divorce decree and the property division.

Husband and wife separated in June 1983, about two months before wife filed her petition for dissolution of marriage. The district court found that husband "chose to move out of the family home, and he then maintained another home where he also had his office for his business." Husband contends that the district court erred in failing to find that he had been constructively ousted from the family home. He requested findings and conclusions that the constructive ouster by his wife entitled him to half of the reasonable rental value of the home from the time of the initial separation.

Husband and wife held the family home as community property during the marriage and as tenants in common after dissolution. Although wife was the exclusive occupant of the house after the separation, ordinarily a co-tenant incurs no obligation to fellow co-tenants by being the exclusive occupant of the premises.

> [I]t is a well-settled principle of the common law that the mere occupation by a tenant of the entire estate does not render him liable to his co-tenant for the use and occupation of any part of the common property. The reason is easily found. The right of each to occupy the premises is one of the incidents of a tenancy in common. Neither tenant can lawfully exclude the other. The occupation of one, so long as he does not exclude the other, is but the exercise of a legal right. If, for any reason, one does not choose to assert the right of common enjoyment, the other is not obliged to stay out; and if the sole occupation of one could render him liable there for to the other, his legal right to the occupation would be dependent upon the caprice or indolence of his co-tenant, and this the law would not tolerate. *Williams v. Sinclair Refining Co.*, 47 P.2d 910, 912 (N.M. 1935).

The result is otherwise, however, when the occupant has ousted the other co-tenants. Although the term "ouster" suggests an affirmative physical act, even a reprehensible act, the obligation of the occupying co-tenant to pay rent may arise in the absence of "actual" ouster when the realities of the situation, without there being any fault by either co-tenant, prevent the co-tenants from sharing occupancy. 4 G. Thompson, *Real Property* §1805, at 189 (J. Grimes Repl. 1979), states:

> [B]efore a tenant in common can be liable to his co-tenants for rent for the use and occupation of the common property, his occupancy must be such as amounts to a denial of the right of his co-tenants to occupy the premises jointly with him, or *the character of the property must be such as to make such joint occupancy impossible or impracticable.* [Emphasis added.]

We believe that it was this latter type of situation — an "ouster" in effect, without any physical act and perhaps without any fault — to which the New Mexico Supreme Court was referring when it recognized the doctrine of "constructive ouster" in the marital context in *Hertz v. Hertz*, 657 P.2d 1169 (N.M. 1983). The court wrote:

> [I]f one of the parties in a divorce case remains in possession of the community residence between the date of the divorce and the date of the final judgment dividing the

> community assets, then there *may* be a form of constructive ouster, exclusion, or an equivalent act which is created as to the right of common enjoyment by the divorced spouse not in possession. This exclusion may render the divorced spouse in possession of the community residence liable to the divorced spouse not in possession for the use and occupation of the residence between the date of the divorce and the date of the final judgment. To hold otherwise would mean that both divorced spouses should have continued to live with each other during the eighteen month interim or that both should have abandoned the property. 657 P.2d at 1179.

Applying the notion of constructive ouster in the marital context is simply another way of saying that when the emotions of a divorce make it impossible for spouses to continue to share the marital residence pending a property division, the spouse who—often through mutual agreement—therefore departs the residence may be entitled to rent from the remaining spouse. Although one can say that the departing spouse has been constructively "ousted," the term should not suggest physical misconduct, or any fault whatsoever, on the part of the remaining spouse.

Common law precedents support the proposition that the remaining spouse should pay rent to the co-tenant when both cannot be expected to live together on the property. For example, when it is impractical for all co-tenants to occupy the premises jointly, it is unnecessary that those claiming rent from the co-tenant in possession first demand the right to move in and occupy the premises. *See Oechsner v. Courcier*, 155 S.W.2d 963 (Tex. Civ. App. 1941) (applying that principle when five heirs, with separate families totalling twenty-two members, were co-tenants of a five-room cottage being occupied by one of the families). The impracticality of joint occupancy by the co-tenants may result from the relations between the co-tenants becoming "so strained and bitter that they could not continue to reside together in peace and concord." *Maxwell v. Eckert*, 109 A. 730, 731 (N.J. Eq. 1920). If, however, hostility flows only from the co-tenant out of possession, ordinarily there would be no constructive ouster. *See O'Connell v. O'Connell*, 117 A. 634 (N.J. Eq. 1922) (wife left home and refused to return despite solicitation by husband). In that circumstance the departing spouse has "abandoned" his or her interest in possession, rather than being excluded.

One jurisdiction has gone so far as to create a rebuttable presumption of ouster of the spouse who moves out of the former marital residence upon divorce. *See Stylianopoulos v. Stylianopoulos*, 455 N.E.2d 477 (Mass. App. Ct. 1983).

Husband had the burden of proving constructive ouster in this case. Therefore, we must sustain the district court's ruling against husband unless the evidence at trial was such as to *compel* the district court to find ouster. Although the evidence of hostility between the spouses may have sustained a finding by the district court of constructive ouster, there was substantial evidence to support the inference that husband's purpose in leaving the community residence was to live with a girlfriend and his departure was the reason wife filed for divorce; he was not pushed out but pulled. Also, the delay of several years before husband demanded any rent from wife supports an inference of abandonment of his interest in occupancy. In short, the evidence was conflicting and did not compel a finding of constructive ouster.

We recognize the ambiguity in the district court's finding that defendant "chose to move out." Such language could be consistent with husband's departure being the result of marital friction, in which case there generally would be constructive ouster. On the other hand, the language could also be construed as referring to husband's abandoning the home to live with another woman. We choose the second construction of the finding, because "[i]n the case of uncertain, doubtful or ambiguous findings, an appellate court is bound to indulge every presumption to sustain the judgment." *Ledbetter v. Webb*, 711 P.2d 874, 879 (N.M. 1985). Moreover, it appeared from oral argument before this court that the issue of constructive ouster was framed in the district court in essentially the same manner as treated in this opinion. Therefore, we are comfortable in assuming that the district court applied the proper rule of law and in construing the district court's finding compatibly with its rejection of husband's proposed conclusion of law that there was a constructive ouster.

Notes and Questions

1. **Different approaches to occupancy after divorce.** Like the New Mexico courts, some courts adopt a version of the constructive ouster doctrine to require separated spouses to pay rent (equal to one-half the fair rental value) to the spouse who is no longer living at home. *In re Marriage of Watts*, 217 Cal. Rptr. 301 (Ct. App. 1985) (court may order husband to reimburse community for exclusive use of residence after separation); *Palmer v. Protrka*, 476 P.2d 185, 190 (Or. 1970) (when marital difficulties make co-occupancy impossible, requiring occupant to pay one-half of rental value seems closest to parties' intentions when they took title). Other courts, however, refuse to make an exception for marital property and hold that co-tenants in possession have no duty to pay rent unless they have affirmatively ousted their spouse by notifying them of an intent to exclude them from the joint property. *See Hughes v. Krueger*, 67 So. 2d 279 (Fla. 2011) (although divorced spouses "did not think highly of each other," husband never affirmatively excluded his ex-wife); *Kahnovsky v. Kahnovsky*, 21 A.2d 569 (R.I. 1941) (finding no ouster, although "separation was the result of marital difference"); *cf. Curtis v. Dorn*, 234 P.3d 682 (Haw. 2010) (absent explicit ouster, tenant who left residence after his relationship with his partner ended could not claim rent).

Which approach is preferable? As the attorney for one of the parties in a divorce setting, how can you avoid this problem?

2. **Property impracticable for occupancy by all co-tenants.** Some courts also hold that co-owners in possession have a duty to pay rent if the property is too small or otherwise impracticable to be physically occupied by all the co-owners. This situation is sometimes described as "constructive ouster" because the co-owners out of possession have been effectively excluded from the property. *See Capital Financial Co. Delaware Valley, Inc. v. Asterbadi*, 942 A.2d 21 (N.J. Super. App. Div. 2008) (bank that had become co-tenant through foreclosure with wife of defaulting mortgagor was constructively ousted from single-family residence).

3. Rent without ouster. Absent constructive ouster, most states require some affirmative act by which one party excludes the other. *Parker v. Shecut*, 562 S.E.2d 620 (S.C. 2002) (ouster shown when brother changed the locks on the door and refused to give his sister a key). A few courts, however, permit tenants out of possession to receive rent without proving ouster. *Modic v. Modic*, 633 N.E.2d 1151 (Ohio App. 1993) (construing Ohio Rev. Code §5307.21 to permit rent to co-tenant out of possession of jointly owned business); *see also Lerman v. Levine*, 541 A.2d 523 (Conn. App. 1988) (construing Conn. Gen. Stat. §52-404(b)) (mother was entitled to set off for use and occupancy by her daughter and son-in-law after she voluntarily left the property). Which is the better rule?

4. Adverse possession. Because each tenant is legally entitled to occupy the property, one co-tenant cannot obtain adverse possession against another unless the possessing tenant makes clear to the nonpossessory tenant that he is asserting full ownership rights in the property to the exclusion of the other co-tenants. The courts generally require some affirmative act by which the nonpossessory tenant is put on notice that her co-owner is claiming adversely to the nonpossessory tenant's interests. *See O'Connor v. Laroque*, 31 A.3d 1 (Conn. 2011) (no adverse possession despite 27 years of sole possession in the absence of "unequivocal" evidence of ouster).

5. Trespass. May one owner prevent another from receiving visitors in jointly owned property? Since each co-tenant possesses the whole, each is entitled to invite others onto the premises even if their co-owners object. But in *Georgia v. Randolph*, 547 U.S. 103 (2006), the Supreme Court held that the fourth amendment prohibited admission of evidence found after a wife gave the police permission to search the house for drugs, but her husband refused to allow them to enter. The Court held that the prohibition on unreasonable search and seizure prohibits entry over the objections of a physically present resident, even if his co-owner consents. Justice Souter explained:

> [I]t is fair to say that a caller standing at the door of shared premises would have no confidence that one occupant's invitation was a sufficiently good reason to enter when a fellow tenant stood there saying, "stay out." Without some very good reason, no sensible person would go inside under those conditions.
>
> Since the co-tenant wishing to open the door to a third party has no recognized authority in law or social practice to prevail over a present and objecting co-tenant, his disputed invitation, without more, gives a police officer no better claim to reasonableness in entering than the officer would have in the absence of any consent at all.

Id. at 113-114. Do you agree?

Problems

A woman lives with an abusive husband who has struck her several times.

1. The wife moves out after suffering battery at his hands. The husband asks her to return, but she refuses. They are separated for two years, then divorced. The wife

sues the husband for one-half of the fair rental value of the house during the two-year period. Is the husband obligated to pay one-half the fair rental value of the house to the wife?

2. Now assume that, instead of the wife leaving, she throws the husband out of the house after the battery and tells him not to come back. They are separated for two years, then divorced. In the divorce proceedings, the wife is awarded ownership of the house. The husband argues that he is entitled to one-half of the fair rental value of the home for the period beginning with his ouster from the home until the divorce date. Is she obligated to pay rent to him? What are the arguments on both sides of this question? What do you think? Is this case the same as the case in Problem 1 above or not? *See Cohen v. Cohen*, 746 N.Y.S.2d 22, 23 (App. Div. 2002) (ousted co-tenant has no right to rent for period covered by court protective order excluding him from the property when tenant in possession had obtained that order because of co-tenant's assaultive conduct).

C. Conflicts over Unilateral Transfers in Tenancy in Common and Joint Tenancy

Carr v. Deking

765 P.2d 40 (Wash. Ct. App. 1988)

DALE M. GREEN, Judge.

Joel Carr and his father, George Carr, now deceased, owned a parcel of land in Lincoln County as tenants in common. From 1974 through 1986 the Carrs leased the land to Richard Deking pursuant to a year-to-year oral agreement receiving one-third of the annual crop as rent. The Carrs paid for one-third of the fertilizer. In 1986, Joel Carr informed Mr. Deking he wanted cash rent beginning with the 1987 crop year. Mr. Deking was not receptive to this proposal.

In February 1987 Joel Carr wrote a letter to Mr. Deking to determine if he wanted to continue leasing the property. Mr. Deking did not respond. Instead he discussed the lease with George Carr. On February 18 Joel Carr went to his father's home and found Mr. Deking there discussing a possible 5-year lease. Joel Carr again indicated he wanted cash rent. Later that day, unbeknownst to Joel Carr, Mr. Deking and George Carr executed a written 10-year crop-share lease at the office of Mr. Deking's attorney. Under this lease, Mr. Deking agreed to pay all fertilizer costs. Joel Carr neither consented to nor ratified this lease and never authorized George Carr to act on his behalf.

In April Joel Carr gave notice to Mr. Deking that his tenancy would terminate at the end of the 1987 crop year. Mr. Deking responded that he would retain possession pursuant to the written lease with George Carr. In July Joel Carr commenced this action to declare that no valid lease existed, Mr. Deking had no right to farm the land and he should be required to vacate the land at the end of the 1987 crop year.

Joel Carr contends [that] the rights of Mr. Deking as lessee are subordinate to those of a nonjoining tenant in common. He argues public policy should prevent prospective lessees from going behind the back of one tenant in common to obtain a more favorable lease from the other.

On the other hand, it is Mr. Deking's position that George Carr could lawfully enter into a lease with respect to his own undivided one-half interest in the property, and Joel Carr was not entitled to bring an ejectment action to which George Carr did not agree. He asserts the proper remedy is partition, not ejectment.

It is well settled that each tenant in common of real property may use, benefit and possess the entire property subject only to the equal rights of cotenants. Thus, a cotenant may lawfully lease his own interest in the common property to another without the consent of the other tenant and without his joining in the lease. The nonjoining cotenant is not bound by this lease of the common property to third persons. The lessee "steps into the shoes" of the leasing cotenant and becomes a tenant in common with the other owners for the duration of the lease. A nonjoining tenant may not demand exclusive possession as against the lessee, but may only demand to be let into co-possession.

Applying these principles, we find Joel Carr is not entitled to eject Mr. Deking from the property. The proper remedy is partition and until that occurs, Mr. Deking is entitled to farm the land under the lease. There is no indication that this property is not amenable to physical partition. Joel Carr clearly has the right to that remedy. Joel Carr cites no authority and none has been found which would render the lease ineffective as between the estate of George Carr and Mr. Deking.

In view of our holding that the trial court properly denied Joel Carr's effort to eject Mr. Deking, Joel Carr is entitled to the benefit of the Deking-George Carr lease, at his election, until a partition of the property occurs. However, Joel Carr cannot claim the benefits contained in the Deking-George Carr lease without also accepting the other terms of that lease. Consequently, we remand to the trial court to determine Joel Carr's election choice [between] the prior oral lease with Mr. Deking [and] the Deking-George Carr lease.

Tenhet v. Boswell

554 P.2d 330 (Cal. 1976)

STANLEY MOSK, Justice.

A joint tenant leases his interest in the joint tenancy property to a third person for a term of years, and dies during that term. We conclude that the lease does not sever the joint tenancy, but expires upon the death of the lessor joint tenant.

Raymond Johnson and plaintiff Hazel Tenhet owned a parcel of property as joint tenants. Assertedly without plaintiff's knowledge or consent, Johnson leased the property to defendant Boswell for a period of 10 years at a rental of $150 per year with a provision granting the lessee an "option to purchase."[3] Johnson died some three

3. The lease did not disclose that the lessor possessed only a joint interest in the property. To the contrary, the "option to purchase" granted to the lessee, which might more accurately be described as a right of first refusal, implied that the lessor possessed a fee simple. It provided in part: "Lessee is

months after execution of the lease, and plaintiff sought to establish her sole right to possession of the property as the surviving joint tenant. After an unsuccessful demand upon defendant to vacate the premises, plaintiff brought this action to have the lease declared invalid.

II

An understanding of the nature of a joint interest in this state is fundamental to a determination of the question whether the present lease severed the joint tenancy. Civil Code section 683 provides in part: "A joint interest is one owned by two or more persons in equal shares, by a title created by a single will or transfer, when expressly declared in the will or transfer to be a joint tenancy." This statute, requiring an express declaration for the creation of joint interests, does not abrogate the common law rule that four unities are essential to an estate in joint tenancy: unity of interest, unity of time, unity of title, and unity of possession.

The requirement of four unities reflects the basic concept that there is but one estate which is taken jointly; if an essential unity is destroyed the joint tenancy is severed and a tenancy in common results. Accordingly, one of two joint tenants may unilaterally terminate the joint tenancy by conveying his interest to a third person. Severance of the joint tenancy, of course, extinguishes the principal feature of that estate — the *jus accrescendi* or right of survivorship. Thus, a joint tenant's right of survivorship is an expectancy that is not irrevocably fixed upon the creation of the estate; it arises only upon success in the ultimate gamble — survival — and then only if the unity of the estate has not theretofore been destroyed by voluntary conveyance, by involuntary alienation under an execution, or by any other action which operates to sever the joint tenancy.

Our initial inquiry is whether the partial alienation of Johnson's interest in the property effected a severance of the joint tenancy under these principles. It could be argued that a lease destroys the unities of interest and possession because the leasing joint tenant transfers to the lessee his present possessory interest and retains a mere reversion. Moreover, the possibility that the term of the lease may continue beyond the lifetime of the lessor is inconsistent with a complete right of survivorship.

On the other hand, if the lease entered into here by Johnson and defendant is valid only during Johnson's life, then the conveyance is more a variety of life estate *pur* [sic] *autre vie* than a term of years. Such a result is inconsistent with Johnson's freedom to alienate his interest during his lifetime.

We are mindful that the issue here presented is "an ancient controversy, going back to Coke and Littleton." Yet the problem is like a comet in our law: Though its existence in theory has been frequently recognized, its observed passages are few. Some

---

given a first exclusive right, privilege and option to purchase the house and lot covered by this lease. If so purchased, Lessor will convey title by grant deed on the usual form subject only to easements or rights of way of record and liens or encumbrances specifically agreed to by and between Lessor and Lessee.[] Lessor shall furnish Lessee with a policy of title insurance at Lessor's cost."

authorities support the view that a lease by a joint tenant to a third person effects a complete and final severance of the joint tenancy.

Others adopt a position that there is a temporary severance during the term of the lease. If the lessor dies while the lease is in force, under this view the existence of the lease at the moment when the right of survivorship would otherwise take effect operates as a severance, extinguishing the joint tenancy. If, however, the term of the lease expires before the lessor, it is reasoned that the joint tenancy is undisturbed because the joint tenants resume their original relation. The single conclusion that can be drawn from centuries of academic speculation on the question is that its resolution is unclear.

As we shall explain, it is our opinion that a lease is not so inherently inconsistent with joint tenancy as to create a severance, either temporary or permanent.

Under Civil Code sections 683 and 686 a joint tenancy must be expressly declared in the creating instrument, or a tenancy in common results. This is a statutory departure from the common law preference in favor of joint tenancy. Inasmuch as the estate arises only upon express intent, and in many cases such intent will be the intent of the joint tenants themselves, we decline to find a severance in circumstances which do not clearly and unambiguously establish that either of the joint tenants desired to terminate the estate.

If plaintiff and Johnson did not choose to continue the joint tenancy, they might have converted it into a tenancy in common by written mutual agreement. They might also have jointly conveyed the property to a third person and divided the proceeds. Even if they could not agree to act in concert, either plaintiff or Johnson might have severed the joint tenancy, with or without the consent of the other, by an act which was clearly indicative of an intent to terminate, such as a conveyance of her or his entire interest. Either might also have brought an action to partition the property, which, upon judgment, would have effected a severance. Because a joint tenancy may be created only by express intent, and because there are alternative and unambiguous means of altering the nature of that estate, we hold that the lease here in issue did not operate to sever the joint tenancy.

III

Having concluded that the joint tenancy was not severed by the lease and that sole ownership of the property therefore vested in plaintiff upon her joint tenant's death by operation of her right of survivorship, we turn next to the issue whether she takes the property unencumbered by the lease.

By the very nature of joint tenancy, . . . the interest of the nonsurviving joint tenant extinguishes upon his death. And as the lease is valid only "in so far as the interest of the lessor in the joint property is concerned," it follows that the lease of the joint tenancy property also expires when the lessor dies.

This conclusion is borne out by decisions in this state involving liens on and mortgages of joint tenancy property. In *Zeigler v. Bonnell*, 126 P.2d 118 (Cal. Ct. App. 1942), the Court of Appeal ruled that a surviving joint tenant takes an estate free from a judgment lien on the interest of a deceased cotenant judgment debtor. The court reasoned that "The right of survivorship is the chief characteristic that distinguishes a joint tenancy from other interests in property. The judgment lien of (the creditor) could attach only to the interest of his debtor. That interest terminated upon [the debtor's] death." *Id.* at 119. After his death "the deceased joint tenant had no interest in the property, and his judgment creditor has no greater rights." *Id.* at 120.

A similar analysis was followed in *People v. Nogarr*, 330 P.2d 858 (Cal. Ct. App. 1958), which held that upon the death of a joint tenant who had executed a mortgage on the tenancy property, the surviving joint tenant took the property free of the mortgage. The court reasoned that "as the mortgage lien attached only to such interest as [the deceased joint tenant] had in the real property[,] when his interest ceased to exist the lien of the mortgage expired with it."

As these decisions demonstrate, a joint tenant may, during his lifetime, grant certain rights in the joint property without severing the tenancy. But when such a joint tenant dies his interest dies with him, and any encumbrances placed by him on the property become unenforceable against the surviving joint tenant. For the reasons stated a lease falls within this rule.

Any other result would defeat the justifiable expectations of the surviving joint tenant. Thus, if *A* agrees to create a joint tenancy with *B*, *A* can reasonably anticipate that when *B* dies *A* will take an unencumbered interest in fee simple. During his lifetime, of course, *B* may sever the tenancy or lease his interest to a third party. But to allow *B* to lease for a term continuing after his death would indirectly defeat the very purposes of the joint tenancy. For example, for personal reasons *B* might execute a 99-year lease on valuable property for a consideration of one dollar a year. *A* would then take a fee simple on *B*'s death, but would find his right to use the property — and its market value — substantially impaired. This circumstance would effectively nullify the benefits of the right of survivorship, the basic attribute of the joint tenancy.

On the other hand, we are not insensitive to the potential injury that may be sustained by a person in good faith who leases from one joint tenant. In some circumstances a lessee might be unaware that his lessor is not a fee simple owner but merely a joint tenant, and could find himself unexpectedly evicted when the lessor dies prior to expiration of the lease. This result would be avoided by a prudent lessee who conducts a title search prior to leasing, but we appreciate that such a course would often be economically burdensome to the lessee of a residential dwelling or a modest parcel of property. Nevertheless, it must also be recognized that every lessee may one day face the unhappy revelation that his lessor's estate in the leased property is less than a fee simple. For example, a lessee who innocently rents from the holder of a life estate is subject to risks comparable to those imposed upon a lessee of joint tenancy property.

More significantly, we cannot allow extraneous factors to erode the functioning of joint tenancy. The estate of joint tenancy is firmly embedded in centuries of real property law and in the California statute books. Its crucial element is the right of survivorship, a right that would be more illusory than real if a joint tenant were permitted to lease for a term continuing after his death. Accordingly, we hold that under the facts alleged in the complaint the lease herein is no longer valid.

Notes and Questions

1. **Leases by one co-owner.** Should common owners have the right to lease the premises without the consent of the co-tenants? Is the rule promulgated in *Carr v. Deking* a good one?

2. **Remedies for leases by one co-tenant.** The court in *Carr v. Deking* held that George Carr had the power to lease his one-half interest without Joel's consent. But in conclusion, it suggests that the son, Joel Carr, is "entitled to the benefit of the Deking-George Carr lease, at his election" until partition. Other courts have also held that a co-owner has a right to choose to participate in the lease and obtain his proportional share of the rent. *American Standard Life & Accident Insurance Co. v. Speros*, 494 N.W.2d 599 (N.D. 1993). Doesn't this assume that the agreed-upon rent is close to the fair rental value of the premises? Suppose Joel could show that the agreed-upon rent in the Deking-George Carr lease was only two-thirds of the fair rental value and had been discounted (reduced) because Deking knew he had the consent of only one of two joint owners. Is either George or Joel entitled to an increase in the rent to make it reflect its fair rental value? Couldn't Joel force Deking to agree to such an increase by threatening to partition the property? If so, should Deking be required to pay fair rental value rather than the agreed-upon rent if he wishes to avoid partition? *Cf. George v. George*, 591 S.W.2d 655 (Ark. Ct. App. 1979) (setting aside 99-year lease for nominal rent that court found was intended to defraud the co-tenant).

3. **Leases by one joint tenant and the right of survivorship.** Courts are divided on the question of whether leases sever joint tenancies. Justice Mosk argues in *Tenhet v. Boswell* that "a lease is not so inherently inconsistent with joint tenancy as to create a severance." Isn't this circular reasoning? How does it help to ask whether a lease is consistent or inconsistent with something that the court is being asked to define? *Cf. In re Estate of Quick*, 905 A.2d 471 (Pa. 2006) (finding leases did not sever joint tenancy where they did not reflect intent to do so). Compare the analysis in *Alexander v. Boyer*, 253 A.2d 359 (Md. 1969), in which the court held, contrary to *Tenhet v. Boswell*, that a lease by one joint tenant severs the joint tenancy. Judge Barnes explained that when the joint tenant "conveyed her possessory rights in the land" to a lessee for a term of years, she "thereby chang[ed] the nature of her 'interest' in the land from a present interest to a reversionary interest." In so doing, she parted with "all of her possessory rights for the term of the lease," thereby "destroy[ing] the unities of interest and possession in the joint tenancy" and terminating it. *Id.* at 365. *Accord, Estate of Gulledge*, 673 A.2d 1278 (D.C. 1996). Is this explanation any less circular than that of Justice Mosk? What policies are relevant in answering the question whether a leasehold by one joint tenant destroys the right of survivorship of the other?

It might be argued that joint tenants have no justified expectations in their right of survivorship since it is so highly contingent on events that may not happen. After all, it can be lost if one dies first or if one's co-owner sells her interest in the property. On one hand, allowing severance may increase the alienability of property, especially if the court holds that leases given by one joint tenant do not survive the death of the lessor; few people will rent property if they know their possessory rights will end as soon as their landlord dies. On the other hand, the right of survivorship may increase the alienability of the property by decreasing the number of owners from two to one. This makes it easier for the property to be bought and sold since a potential lessee or buyer does not have to worry about obtaining the consent of more than one person. Which rule better promotes the reasonable use of property? How should the courts balance the right of each tenant to transfer her interest (a right of freedom of action) against the right of the co-owner to her right of survivorship (a right of security against loss of her property interest)?

4. Mortgages and the right of survivorship. Courts are also divided on the question of whether mortgages sever joint tenancies. Most states describe the borrower who grants the mortgage as the owner or title holder and the bank or lender who takes the mortgage as a "lienholder," with a right to possess the property only if the borrower defaults. In such states, courts typically hold that a mortgage by one tenant does not sever the joint tenancy. Foreclosure during the life of the tenant would sever the tenancy and create a tenancy in common between the non-borrowing tenant and the bank. If the borrowing tenant dies before foreclosure, however, the surviving co-tenant receives the entire property unburdened by the mortgage. *See Biggers v. Crook*, 656 S.E.2d 835 (Ga. 2008); *Harms v. Sprague*, 473 N.E.2d 930 (Ill. 1984); *Smith v. Bank of America*, 103 A.D.3d 21 (N.Y. App. Div. 2012). *But see General Credit Co. v. Cleck*, 609 A.2d 553 (Pa. Super. 1992) (holding that mortgage severed joint tenancy relying on 1806 decision from before Pennsylvania became a lien theory state).

A minority of states retain the older "title" theory, in which the lender takes title to the property, subject to an "equity of redemption" in the borrower who grants the mortgage. Some courts in title theory states consider a mortgage to be a transfer of ownership that has the effect of severing the joint tenancy, *see Schaefer v. Peoples Heritage Savings Bank*, 669 A.2d 185 (Me. 1996), although others do not. *Countrywide Home Loans, Inc. v. Reed*, 725 S.E.2d 667 (N.C. Ct. App. 2012). There is no substantive difference between "lien" theory states and "title" theory states; the difference today is merely verbal. Assuming that the question of severance should not depend on such a flimsy argument, how should the case have been decided, and why?

D. Conflicts over Unilateral Transfers in Tenancies by the Entirety

Sawada v. Endo

561 P.2d 1291 (Haw. 1977)

BENJAMIN MENOR, Justice.

This is a civil action brought by the plaintiffs-appellants, Masako Sawada and Helen Sawada, in aid of execution of money judgments in their favor, seeking to set aside a conveyance of real property from judgment debtor Kokichi Endo to Samuel H. Endo and Toru Endo, defendants-appellees herein, on the ground that the conveyance as to the Sawadas was fraudulent.

On November 30, 1968, the Sawadas were injured when struck by a motor vehicle operated by Kokichi Endo. On June 17, 1969, Helen Sawada filed her complaint for damages against Kokichi Endo. Masako Sawada filed her suit against him on August 13, 1969. The complaint and summons in each case was served on Kokichi Endo on October 29, 1969.

On the date of the accident, Kokichi Endo was the owner, as a tenant by the entirety with his wife, Ume Endo, of a parcel of real property situate at Wahiawa, Oahu, Hawai`i. By deed, dated July 26, 1969, Kokichi Endo and his wife conveyed the property to their sons, Samuel H. Endo and Toru Endo. This document was recorded in the Bureau of Conveyances on December 17, 1969. No consideration was paid by the grantees for the conveyance. Both were aware at the time of the conveyance that their father had been involved in an accident, and that he carried no liability insurance. Kokichi Endo and Ume Endo, while reserving no life interests therein, continued to reside on the premises.

On January 19, 1971, after a consolidated trial on the merits, judgment was entered in favor of Helen Sawada and against Kokichi Endo in the sum of $8,846.46. At the same time, Masako Sawada was awarded judgment on her complaint in the amount of $16,199.28. Ume Endo, wife of Kokichi Endo, died on January 29, 1971. She was survived by her husband, Kokichi. Subsequently, after being frustrated in their attempts to obtain satisfaction of judgment from the personal property of Kokichi Endo, the Sawadas brought suit to set aside the conveyance which is the subject matter of this controversy. The trial court refused to set aside the conveyance, and the Sawadas appeal.

The determinative question in this case is, whether the interest of one spouse in real property, held in tenancy by the entireties, is subject to levy and execution by his or her individual creditors. This issue is one of first impression in this jurisdiction.

A brief review of the present state of the tenancy by the entirety might be helpful. Dean Phipps, writing in 1951,[4] pointed out that only nineteen states and the District of Columbia continued to recognize it as a valid and subsisting institution in the field of property law. Phipps divided these jurisdictions into four groups. He made no mention of Alaska and Hawai`i, both of which were then territories of the United States.

In the Group I states (Massachusetts, Michigan, and North Carolina) the estate is essentially the common law tenancy by the entireties, unaffected by the *Married Women's Property Acts*. As at common law, the possession and profits of the estate are subject to the husband's exclusive dominion and control. In all three states, as at common law, the husband may convey the entire estate subject only to the possibility that the wife may become entitled to the whole estate upon surviving him. As at common law, the obverse as to the wife does not hold true. Only in Massachusetts, however, is the estate in its entirety subject to levy by the husband's creditors. In both Michigan and North Carolina, the use and income from the estate is not subject to levy during the marriage for the separate debts of either spouse.

---

4. Phipps, *Tenancy by Entireties*, 25 Temple L.Q. 24 (1951).

In the Group II states (Alaska, Arkansas, New Jersey, New York, and Oregon) the interest of the debtor spouse in the estate may be sold or levied upon for his or her separate debts, subject to the other spouse's contingent right of survivorship. Alaska, which has been added to this group, has provided by statute that the interest of a debtor spouse in any type of estate, except a homestead as defined and held in tenancy by the entirety, shall be subject to his or her separate debts.

In the Group III jurisdictions (Delaware, District of Columbia, Florida, Indiana, Maryland, Missouri, Pennsylvania, Rhode Island, Vermont, Virginia, and Wyoming) an attempted conveyance by either spouse is wholly void, and the estate may not be subjected to the separate debts of one spouse only.

In Group IV, the two states of Kentucky and Tennessee hold that the contingent right of survivorship appertaining to either spouse is separately alienable by him and attachable by his creditors during the marriage. The use and profits, however, may neither be alienated nor attached during coverture.

It appears, therefore, that Hawai`i is the only jurisdiction still to be heard from on the question. Today we join that group of states and the District of Columbia which hold that under the *Married Women's Property Acts* the interest of a husband or a wife in an estate by the entireties is not subject to the claims of his or her individual creditors during the joint lives of the spouses. In so doing, we are placing our stamp of approval upon what is apparently the prevailing view of the lower courts of this jurisdiction.

Hawai`i has long recognized and continues to recognize the tenancy in common, the joint tenancy, and the tenancy by the entirety, as separate and distinct estates. That the *Married Women's Property Act* of 1888 was not intended to abolish the tenancy by the entirety was made clear by the language of Act 19 of the Session Laws of Hawai`i, 1903 (now Haw. Rev. Stat. §509-1). The tenancy by the entirety is predicated upon the legal unity of husband and wife, and the estate is held by them in single ownership. They do not take by moieties, but both and each are seized of the whole estate.

A joint tenant has a specific, albeit undivided, interest in the property, and if he survives his cotenant he becomes the owner of a larger interest than he had prior to the death of the other joint tenant. But tenants by the entirety are each deemed to be seized of the entirety from the time of the creation of the estate. At common law, this taking of the "whole estate" did not have the real significance that it does today, insofar as the rights of the wife in the property were concerned. For all practical purposes, the wife had no right during coverture to the use and enjoyment and exercise of ownership in the marital estate. All she possessed was her contingent right of survivorship.

The effect of the *Married Women's Property Acts* was to abrogate the husband's common law dominance over the marital estate and to place the wife on a level of equality with him as regards the exercise of ownership over the whole estate. The tenancy was and still is predicated upon the legal unity of husband and wife, but the Acts converted it into a unity of equals and not of unequals as at common law. No longer could the husband convey, lease, mortgage or otherwise encumber the property without her consent. The Acts confirmed her right to the use and enjoyment of the whole estate, and all the privileges that ownership of property confers, including the right to convey the property in its entirety, jointly with her husband, during the marriage relation. They also had the effect of insulating the wife's interest in the estate from the separate debts of her husband.

Neither husband nor wife has a separate divisible interest in the property held by the entirety that can be conveyed or reached by execution. A joint tenancy may be destroyed by voluntary alienation, or by levy and execution, or by compulsory partition, but a tenancy by the entirety may not. The indivisibility of the estate, except by joint action of the spouses, is an indispensable feature of the tenancy by the entirety.

We are not persuaded by the argument that it would be unfair to the creditors of either spouse to hold that the estate by the entirety may not, without the consent of both spouses, be levied upon for the separate debts of either spouse. No unfairness to the creditor is involved here. We agree with the court in *Hurd v. Hughes*, 109 A. 418, 420 (Del. Ch. 1920): "But creditors are not entitled to special consideration. If the debt arose prior to the creation of the estate, the property was not a basis of credit, and if the debt arose subsequently the creditor presumably had notice of the characteristics of the estate which limited his right to reach the property."

We might also add that there is obviously nothing to prevent the creditor from insisting upon the subjection of property held in tenancy by the entirety as a condition precedent to the extension of credit. Further, the creation of a tenancy by the entirety may not be used as a device to defraud existing creditors.

Were we to view the matter strictly from the standpoint of public policy, we would still be constrained to hold as we have done here today.

It is a matter of common knowledge that the demand for single-family residential lots has increased rapidly in recent years, and the magnitude of the problem is emphasized by the concentration of the bulk of fee simple land in the hands of a few. The shortage of single-family residential fee simple property is critical and government has seen fit to attempt to alleviate the problem through legislation. When a family can afford to own real property, it becomes their single most important asset. Encumbered as it usually is by a first mortgage, the fact remains that so long as it remains whole during the joint lives of the spouses, it is always available in its entirety for the benefit and use of the entire family. Loans for education and other emergency expenses, for example, may be obtained on the security of the marital estate. This would not be possible where a third party has become a tenant in common or a joint tenant with one of the spouses, or where the ownership of the contingent right of survivorship of one of the spouses in a third party has cast a cloud upon the title of the marital estate, making it virtually impossible to utilize the estate for these purposes.

If we were to select between a public policy favoring the creditors of one of the spouses and one favoring the interests of the family unit, we would not hesitate to choose the latter. But we need not make this choice for, as we pointed out earlier, by the very nature of the estate by the entirety as we view it, and as other courts of our sister jurisdictions have viewed it, "[a] unilaterally indestructible right of survivorship, an inability of one spouse to alienate his interest, and, importantly for this case, a broad immunity from claims of separate creditors remain among its vital incidents." *In re Estate of Wall*, 440 F.2d 215, 218 (D.C. Cir. 1971).

Having determined that an estate by the entirety is not subject to the claims of the creditors of one of the spouses during their joint lives, we now hold that the conveyance of the marital property by Kokichi Endo and Ume Endo, husband and wife, to their sons, Samuel H. Endo and Toru Endo, was not in fraud of Kokichi Endo's judgment creditors.

H. BAIRD KIDWELL, Justice, dissenting.

The majority reaches its conclusion by holding that the effect of the *Married Women's Act* was to equalize the positions of the spouses by taking from the husband his common law right to transfer his interest, rather than by elevating the wife's right of alienation of her interest to place it on a position of equality with the husband's. I disagree. I believe that a better interpretation of the *Married Women's Acts* is that offered by the Supreme Court of New Jersey in *King v. Greene*, 153 A.2d 49, 60 (N.J. 1959):

> If, as we have previously concluded, the husband could alienate his right of survivorship at common law, the wife, by virtue of the act, can alienate her right of survivorship. And it follows, that if the wife takes equal rights with the husband in the estate, she must take equal disabilities. Such are the dictates of common equality. Thus, the judgment creditors of either spouse may levy and execute upon their separate rights of survivorship.

[R]estriction upon the freedom of the spouses to deal independently with their respective interests is both illogical and unnecessarily at odds with present policy trends. Accordingly, I would hold that the separate interest of the husband in entireties property, at least to the extent of his right of survivorship, is alienable by him and subject to attachment by his separate creditors, so that a voluntary conveyance of the husband's interest should be set aside where it is fraudulent as to such creditors, under applicable principles of the law of fraudulent conveyances.

Notes and Questions

1. **Marital property and male privileges.** In *Kirchberg v. Feenstra*, 450 U.S. 455, 456 (1981), the Supreme Court considered a Louisiana statute giving the "husband as 'head and master' of property jointly owned with his wife, the unilateral right to dispose of such property without his spouse's consent." *Id.* at 456. The Court held that the statute violated the equal protection clause of the fourteenth amendment because the classification was not substantially related to achieving an important governmental interest. *Id.* at 458-459.

2. **Creditors' rights to reach tenancy by the entirety property.** Massachusetts, Michigan, and North Carolina, the states that *Sawada v. Endo* stated still recognized the husband's exclusive dominion over property by the entirety, have now abolished the husband's prerogative. Mass. Gen. Laws ch. 209, §1; Mich. Comp. Laws §557.71; N.C. Gen. Stat. §39-13.6. Therefore the four rules *Sawada* described have collapsed into three:

(1) The substantial majority of states follow the *Sawada* rule that creditors cannot reach property held in the form of tenancy by the entirety to satisfy debts of one

spouse; even if the property is sold or the debtor spouse survives the non-debtor, the creditor has no claim on the estate.

(2) A smaller group of states, including Massachusetts, New Jersey, and New York, hold that creditors can attach the life interest of a tenant by the entirety. Creditors may not, however, defeat the non-debtor spouse's survivorship interest, and may not be able to demand partition of the property. *See, e.g., Capital Finance Co. Delaware Valley, Inc. v. Asterbadi*, 942 A.2d 21 (N.J. Super. App. Div. 2008).

(3) A few states, including Tennessee and Kentucky, hold that the creditor may only attach the debtor spouse's right of survivorship; the creditor only may possess the property if the debtor survives the non-debtor spouse. *See Robinson v. Trousdale County*, 516 S.W.2d 626, 630-631 (Tenn. 1974); *Raybro Elec. Supplies, Inc. v. Barclay*, 813 F. Supp. 1267 (W.D. Ky. 1992) (construing Kentucky law).

Which approach better protects the rights of women to gender equality?

3. Tax liens. In *United States v. Craft*, 535 U.S. 274 (2002), the wife of a delinquent taxpayer sued the United States to recover half the proceeds of the sale of tenancy by the entirety property. The United States had placed a lien on that portion of the proceeds to pay off her husband's delinquent federal taxes. The wife noted that under Michigan law, one tenant by the entirety has no interest separable from that of the spouse; state law did not allow her husband's creditors to reach his interest to satisfy his unpaid debts, and he therefore had no individual interest in the property that could be reached by the federal government to pay his unpaid taxes. The Supreme Court disagreed, holding that his interest did constitute "property" or a "right to property" within the meaning of the federal tax lien legislation. Using the legal realist metaphor of property as a "bundle of sticks," Justice O'Connor explained that the husband had a number of "the most essential property rights: the right to use the property, to receive income produced by it and to exclude others from it." *Id.* at 283. He also possessed the right to alienate the property with his wife's consent. "There is no reason to believe, however, that this one stick — the right of unilateral alienation — is essential to the category of 'property.'" *Id.* at 284. The Court noted it had previously decided that the government had the discretion to foreclose on an individual's interest in property, even though he lacked the unilateral power of alienation. This would mean that the United States could force a sale of the property over the wife's objections to satisfy the husband's unpaid taxes. However, the Internal Revenue Service has recognized that this creates "adverse consequences for the non-liable spouse of the taxpayer" and thus the use of foreclosure in such cases will be "determined on a case-by-case basis." *See Collection Issues Related to Entireties Property*, IRS Notice 2003-60, 2003-39 I.R.B. 643, 2003 WL 22100950 (Sept. 29, 2003). Once property is sold with the consent of both owners, as it was in *Craft*, the United States can take the husband's one-half share of the proceeds of the sale. This does not mean the delinquent taxpayer can *give* his property interest to his spouse and avoid paying the taxes. *Id.*

Justices Scalia, Thomas, and Stevens dissented. Justice Scalia noted that the Court "nullifies (insofar as federal taxes are concerned, at least) a form of property ownership that was of particular benefit to the stay-at-home spouse or mother [who is] overwhelmingly unlikely to be the source of the individual indebtedness against which a tenancy by the entirety protects." *Id.* at 289-290. Justice Thomas opined that state law defined the husband not to have any separate interest in the property; thus he had no individual "property" or "rights to property" to which the federal tax lien could attach. *Id.* at 292-299.

4. Presumptions. Although ambiguous conveyances are normally interpreted as tenancies in common rather than joint tenancies, jurisdictions that have the tenancy by the entirety may presume that a conveyance to a married couple is held by the entirety. *Beal Bank v. Almand & Associates*, 780 So. 2d 45 (Fla. 2001).

5. Homestead laws. Homestead laws may protect the surviving spouse's ownership and occupancy rights in the family home from demands of the decedent's creditors. Tex. Prob. Code §271. The effect of such laws may be to prevent the homeowner from transferring or encumbering her interests in the family home without the consent of both spousal owners. A few states provide unlimited protection for the value of the home, but most exempt only a certain dollar value, and these values are infrequently adjusted for inflation. Although the Endos's property was a homestead under Hawaiian law, the amount of homestead exemption at the time was very low: only $2,750 of its value was protected from creditors. Pat Cain, *Two Sisters versus a Father and Two Sons: The Story of* Sawada v. Endo, in *Property Stories* 114 (Gerald Korngold & Andrew Morris eds. 2009).

Problem

Can a couple create a tenancy by the entirety by contract? Couples who are not married may want to ensure that property is not sold or encumbered without the consent of either party. Unmarried male-female couples may wish to do this in the many states that have abolished tenancy by the entirety, and same-sex couples may wish to do this in the many states that do not recognize same-sex marriages.

Assume a gay male couple buys a house together as joint tenants. The deed is recorded with a separate document containing a covenant between the two men in which each covenants not to bring an action for partition of the property so long as both live in the house. It also provides that partition should not be allowed before the parties have reached a comprehensive property settlement in the event they break up; that settlement can either be one they voluntarily agree to or one that is imposed by a court in the context of litigation. The covenant also states that neither party may encumber, mortgage, sell, or lease his undivided 50 percent shares without the consent of the other and that neither one owns a property interest that can be attached by creditors unless both owners agree to the transaction. The couple is attempting to create the incidents of a tenancy by the entirety through a contract, even though they live in a state in which they cannot marry.

Are the covenants enforceable, including (a) the covenant limiting the right to partition, (b) the restraint on alienation, and (c) the attempt to limit the ability of creditors to reach the parties' individual interests? Or are they void, either because they constitute an attempt to create a new estate or because they constitute unreasonable restraints on alienation?

§2.3 Partition

Ark Land Co. v. Harper

599 S.E.2d 754 (W. Va. 2004)

Justice Robin Jean Davis.

This is a dispute involving approximately 75 acres of land situate in Lincoln County, West Virginia. The record indicates that "[t]he Caudill family has owned the land for nearly 100 years." The property "consists of a farmhouse, constructed around 1920, several small barns, and a garden[.]" Prior to 2001, the property was owned exclusively by the Caudill family. However, in 2001 Ark Land acquired a 67.5% undivided interest in the land by purchasing the property interests of several Caudill family members. Ark Land attempted to purchase the remaining property interests held by the Caudill heirs, but they refused to sell. Ark Land sought to purchase all of the property for the express purpose of extracting coal by surface mining.

After the Caudill heirs refused to sell their interest in the land, Ark Land filed a complaint in the Circuit Court of Lincoln County in October of 2001. Ark Land filed the complaint seeking to have the land partitioned and sold. On October 30, 2002, the circuit court entered an order directing the partition and sale of the property.

The dispositive issue is whether the evidence supported the circuit court's conclusion that the property could not be conveniently partitioned in kind, thus warranting a partition by sale. During the proceeding before the circuit court, the Caudill heirs presented expert testimony by Gary F. Acord, a mining engineer. Mr. Acord testified that the property could be partitioned in kind. Specifically, Mr. Acord testified that lands surrounding the family home did not have coal deposits and could therefore be partitioned from the remaining lands. On the other hand, Ark Land presented expert testimony which indicated that such a partition would entail several million dollars in additional costs in order to mine for coal.

We note at the outset that "[p]artition means the division of the land held in cotenancy into the cotenants' respective fractional shares. If the land cannot be fairly divided, then the entire estate may be sold and the proceeds appropriately divided." 7 *Powell on Real Property*, §50.07[1] (2004). It has been observed that, "[i]n the United States, partition was established by statute in each of the individual states. Unlike the partition in kind which existed under early common law, the forced judicial sale was an American innovation." Phyliss Craig-Taylor, *Through a Colored Looking Glass: A View of Judicial Partition, Family Land Loss, and Rule Setting*, 78 Wash. U. L.Q. 737, 752 (2000).

Partition by sale, when it is not voluntary by all parties, can be a harsh result for the cotenant(s) who opposes the sale. This is because "'[a] particular piece of real estate cannot be replaced by any sum of money, however large; and one who wants a particular estate for a specific use, if deprived of his rights, cannot be said to receive an exact equivalent or complete indemnity by the payment of a sum of money.' " Consequently, "[p]artition in kind . . . is the preferred method of partition because it leaves cotenants holding the same estates as before and does not force a sale on unwilling cotenants." Powell, §50.07[4][a]. The laws in all jurisdictions "appear to reflect this longstanding principle by providing a presumption of severance of common ownership in real property by partition in-kind[.]" Craig-Taylor, *supra* at 752.

In syllabus point 3 of *Consolidated Gas Supply Corp.*, this Court set out the following standard of proof that must be established to overcome the presumption of partition in kind:

> By virtue of W. Va. Code §37-4-3, a party desiring to compel partition through sale is required to demonstrate [(1)] that the property cannot be conveniently partitioned in kind, [(2)] that the interests of one or more of the parties will be promoted by the sale, and [(3)] that the interests of the other parties will not be prejudiced by the sale.

In its lengthy order requiring partition and sale, the circuit court addressed each of the three factors in *Consolidated Gas Supply Corp.* as follows:

> (14) [T]he subject property's nature, character, and amount are such that it cannot be conveniently, (that is "practically or justly") partitioned, or divided by allotment among its owners. Moreover, it is just and necessary to conclude that such a proposal as has been made by the [Caudill heirs], that of allotting the manor house and the surrounding "bottom land" unto the [Caudill heirs], cannot be affected without undeniably prejudicing [Ark Land's] interests, in violation of the mandatory provisions of Code §37-4-3; and,
>
> (15) [W]hile its uniform topography superficially suggests a division-in-kind, as proposed by Mr. Acord, the access road, the bottom lands and the relatively flat home site is, in fact, integral to establishing the fair market value of the subject property in its entirety, as its highest and best use as mining property, as shown by the uncontroverted testimony of [Ark Land's] experts Mr. Morgan and Mr. Terry; and,
>
> (16) [I]t is undisputed that the remaining heirs, that are [the Caudill heirs] herein, do not wish to sell, or have the Court sell, their interests in the subject property, solely due to their sincere sentiment for it as the family's "home place." Other family members, however, did not feel the same way. Given the equally undisputed testimony of [Ark Land's] experts, it is just and reasonable for the Court to conclude that the interests of all the subject property's owners will not be financially prejudiced, but will be financially promoted, by sale of the subject property and distribution among them of the proceeds, according to their respective interests. The subject property's value as coal mining property, its uncontroverted highest and best use, would be substantially impaired by severing the family's "home place" and allotting it to them separately.

We are troubled by the circuit court's conclusion that partition by sale was necessary because the economic value of the property would be less if partitioned in kind. We have long held that the economic value of property may be a factor to consider in determining whether to partition in kind or to force a sale. However, our cases do not support the conclusion that economic value of property is the exclusive test for determining whether to partition in kind or to partition by sale. In fact, we explicitly stated in *Hale v. Thacker*, 12 S.E.2d 524, 526 (1940), "that many considerations, other than monetary, attach to the ownership of land, and courts should be, and always have been, slow to take away from owners of real estate their common-law right to have the same set aside to them in kind."

Other courts have also found that monetary consideration is not the only factor to contemplate when determining whether to partition property in kind or by sale. In the case of *Eli v. Eli*, 557 N.W.2d 405 (S.D. 1997), the South Dakota Supreme Court [reversed an order of partition in kind over the objection of one of three co-owners of farmland in the Eli family for almost 100 years]: "[M]onetary considerations, while admittedly significant, do not rise to the level of excluding all other appropriate considerations. . . . The sale of property 'without [the owner's] consent is an extreme exercise of power warranted only in clear cases.' "

Similarly, in *Delfino v. Vealencis*, 436 A.2d 27 (Conn. 1980), two plaintiffs owned a 20.5 acre tract of land with the defendant. The defendant used part of the property for her home and a garbage removal business. The plaintiffs filed an action to force a sale of the property so that they could use it to develop residential properties. The trial court concluded that a partition in kind could not be had without great prejudice to the parties, and that the highest and best use of the property was through development as residential property. The trial court therefore ordered that the property be sold at auction. The defendant appealed. The Connecticut Supreme Court reversed for the following reasons:

> *It is the interests of all of the tenants in common that the court must consider; and not merely the economic gain of one tenant, or a group of tenants.* The trial court failed to give due consideration to the fact . . . that the [defendant] has made her home on the property; and that she derives her livelihood from the operation of a business on this portion of the property, as her family before her has for many years. A partition by sale would force the defendant to surrender her home and, perhaps, would jeopardize her livelihood. It is under just such circumstances, which include the demonstrated practicability of a physical division of the property, that the wisdom of the law's preference for partition in kind is evident.

Delfino, 436 A.2d at 32-33 (emphasis added).

In view of the prior decisions of this Court, as well as the decisions from other jurisdictions, we now make clear and hold that, in a partition proceeding in which a party opposes the sale of property, the economic value of the property is not the exclusive test for deciding whether to partition in kind or by sale. Evidence of longstanding ownership, coupled with sentimental or emotional interests in the property, may also be considered in deciding whether the interests of the party opposing the sale will be prejudiced by the property's sale. This latter factor should ordinarily control when it is shown that the property can be partitioned in kind, though it may entail some economic inconvenience to the party seeking a sale.

In the instant case, the Caudill heirs were not concerned with the monetary value of the property. Their exclusive interest was grounded in the longstanding family ownership of the property and their emotional desire to keep their ancestral family home within the family. It is quite clear that this emotional interest would be prejudiced through a sale of the property.

> **CONTEXT**
>
> No one lived in the Caudill house at the time of the decision, but it was used on weekends and for family events. The Mud River community in which the house was located had been decimated after Ark Land's mountaintop removal mining brought blasting, stream fill, and pollution to the area. Lorene Caudill was one of the last holdouts, leaving Mud River in 2006.

The expert for the Caudill heirs testified that the ancestral family home could be partitioned from the property in such a way as to not deprive Ark Land of any coal. The circuit court summarily and erroneously dismissed this uncontradicted fact because of the increased costs that Ark Land would incur as a result of a partition in kind. In view of our holding, the additional economic burden that would be imposed on Ark Land, as a result of partitioning in kind, is not determinative under the facts of this case.

[F]or nearly 100 years the Caudill heirs and their ancestors owned the property and used it for residential purposes. In 2001 Ark Land purchased ownership rights in the property from some Caudill family members. When the Caudill heirs refused to sell their ownership rights, Ark Land immediately sought to force a judicial sale of the property. In doing this, Ark Land established that its proposed use of the property, surface coal mining, gave greater value to the property. This showing is self-serving. In most instances, when a commercial entity purchases property because it believes it can make money from a specific use of the property, that property will increase in value based upon the expectations of the commercial entity. This self-created enhancement in the value of property cannot be the determinative factor in forcing a pre-existing co-owner to give up his/her rights in property. To have such a rule would permit commercial entities to always "evict" pre-existing co-owners, because a commercial entity's interest in property will invariably increase its value.

We are very sensitive to the fact that Ark Land will incur greater costs in conducting its business on the property as a result of partitioning in kind. However, Ark Land voluntarily took an economical gamble that it would be able to get all of the Caudill family members to sell their interests in the property. Ark Land's gamble failed. The Caudill heirs refused to sell their interests. The fact that Ark Land miscalculated on its ability to acquire outright all interests in the property cannot form the basis for depriving the Caudill heirs of their emotional interests in maintaining their ancestral family home. The additional cost to Ark Land that will result from a partitioning in kind simply does not impose the type of injurious inconvenience that would justify stripping the Caudill heirs of the emotional interest they have in preserving their ancestral family home.

In view of the foregoing, we find that the circuit court erred in determining that the property could not be partitioned in kind. We, therefore, reverse the circuit court's order requiring sale of the property. This case is remanded with directions to the circuit court to enter an order requiring the property to be partitioned in kind, consistent with the report and testimony of the Caudill heirs' mining engineer expert.

Chief Justice Elliot Maynard, concurring, in part, and dissenting, in part.

I concur with the new law created by the majority in this case. That is to say, I agree that evidence of longstanding ownership along with sentimental or emotional attachment to property are factors that should be considered and, in some instances, control the decision of whether to partition in kind or sale jointly-owned property which is the subject of a partition proceeding.

I dissent in this case, however, because I do not believe that evidence to support the application of those factors was presented here. In that regard, the record shows that none of the appellants have resided at the subject property for years. At most, the property has been used for weekend retreats. While this may have been the family "homeplace," a majority of the family has already sold their interests in the property to the appellee. Only a minority of the family members, the appellants, have refused to do so. I believe that the sporadic use of the property by the appellants in this case does not outweigh the economic inconvenience that the appellee will suffer as a result of this property being partitioned in kind.

> **CONTEXT**
>
> As the dissent suggests, coal mining is an important industry in West Virginia. West Virginia Supreme Court justices, like those in many states, are elected. An infamous election occurred in the year *Ark Land* was decided. Coal company Massey Energy spent $3 million to get Brent Benjamin elected to the court as part of a successful effort to win reversal of a $50 million judgment against it. The authors of both the majority and dissent in *Ark Land* were implicated in the resulting scandal. *See* Lawrence Leaman, *The Price of Justice: A True Story of Greed and Corruption* (2013).

I am also troubled by the majority's decision that this property should be partitioned in kind instead of being sold because I don't believe that such would have been the case were this property going to be put to some use other than coal mining. For instance, I think the majority's decision would have been different if this property was going to be used in the construction of a four-lane highway. Under those circumstances, I believe the majority would have concluded that such economic activity takes precedence over any long-term use or sentimental attachment to the property on the part of the appellants. In my opinion, coal mining is an equally important economic activity. This decision destroys the value of this land as coal mining property because the appellee would incur several million dollars in additional costs to continue its mining operations. As a result of the majority's decision in this case, many innocent coal miners will be out of work.

Notes and Questions

1. **Why partition?** Co-tenancy has many advantages. It permits parties to jointly finance purchases they could not otherwise make and divide family property among all family members. But it also may create disputes over management, profits, and expenses. Tenants who wish to end a co-tenancy may agree to divide or sell the land, so-called **voluntary partition**. When they cannot agree, one tenant can seek **involuntary** or **judicial partition**. One court has characterized involuntary partition as "nothing short of the private condemnation of private land for private purposes, a result which is abhorrent to the rights of defendant as a freeholder." *Butte Creek Island Ranch v. Crim*, 186 Cal. Rptr. 252, 256 (Dist. Ct. App. 1982). But the interests of the petitioning tenant are involved as well. In the words of another court, "'No person can be compelled to remain the owner with another of real estate . . . every owner is entitled to the

fullest enjoyment of his property, and that can come only through an ownership free from dictation by others as to the manner in which it may be exercised." *Fernandes v. Rodriguez*, 761 A.2d 128, 1288 (Conn. 2000).

2. **In kind or by sale.** **Partition in kind** divides the property itself among the co-tenants. Where the property cannot be divided in parcels of exactly proportional value, the co-tenant receiving disproportionate value must pay the other co-tenant **owelty** (OH-el-tee) to compensate for the difference. **Partition by sale** orders the property sold, on the open market or at auction, and the proceeds divided. Some jurisdictions by statute also permit forced sale of one tenant's interest to another. Although statutes in all jurisdictions express a strong preference for partition in kind, partition by sale is typical in many states. *Uniform Partition of Heirs Property Act*, §8 (2010).

Courts may order partition by sale if (1) division of the parcel is not practicable or (2) partition by kind will create "great prejudice," "substantial injury" or be "inequitable" to the tenants. Although cases like *Ark Land* sometimes reject partition by sale if there are significant identity interests in the property, more often courts simply order partition by sale if the property is worth "materially less" divided than it would be if sold as a single parcel. *See* 4 *Thompson on Real Property, Second Thomas Editions* §38.04, at 536-537 (2000); N.C. Gen. Stat. §46-22 (defining "substantial injury" justifying sale as when "the fair market value of each cotenant's share in an actual partition of the property would be materially less than the amount each cotenant would receive from the sale of the whole"); *Schnell v. Schnell*, 346 N.W.2d 713, 716 (N.D. 1984) ("Sentimental reasons, particularly in the preservation of a home, may also be considered, although they are subordinate to the pecuniary interests of the parties."); *Fike v. Sharer*, 571 P.2d 1252, 1254 (Or. 1977) ("[T]he financial interests of the owners is the primary factor to be considered for purposes of a determination of prejudice in the event of partition or sale."). Forced sales have been identified as one cause for the sharp decline in rural land ownership by African Americans. *See* Todd Lewan & Dolores Barclay, *Developers and Lawyers Use a Legal Maneuver to Strip Black Families of Land*, Associated Press, Dec. 30, 2001. The Uniform Partition of Heirs Property Act, promulgated in 2010, seeks to limit forced sales of heirs property; thus far it has been adopted only in Nevada, Georgia, and Montana, but has been introduced in other states.

Much scholarship considers the tension between market value and subjective value of the property, often concluding that the law adequately protects subjective value. *See* Abraham Bell & Gideon Parchomovsky, *A Theory of Property*, 90 Cornell L. Rev. 531, 601 (2005); Thomas J. Miceli & C.F. Stermans, *Partition of Real Estate, or, Breaking Up Is (Not) Hard to Do*, 29 J. Legal Stud. 783, 795 (2000). The price fetched at a partition sale, however, is likely to be far less than the market value. Partition sales are typically conducted at auctions with minimal advertising and few bidders; because individuals cannot usually obtain financing to bid at such auctions, the only bidders will often be realtors and others tipped off to such auctions or, as in *Ark Land*, developers who have purchased co-tenants' shares solely for the purpose of forcing a sale. *See* Thomas W. Mitchell, Stephen Malpezzi & Richard K. Green, *Forced Sale Risk: Class Race and the Double Discount*, 37 Fla. St. U. L. Rev. 589, 611-613 (2010) (noting that courts often refuse to set aside partition sales prices of less than 50 percent of market value).

3. Agreements not to partition. Co-tenants sometimes agree among themselves not to partition jointly held property; grantors also sometimes attempt to prevent partition by including restrictions against partition in a deed or will. Although such agreements were traditionally held to be void as restraints on alienation, today courts are likely to uphold them if they are reasonably limited in time and have a reasonable purpose. William B. Stoebuck & Dale A. Whitman, *The Law of Property* §5.11, at 216 (3d ed. 2000); *compare Kopp v. Kopp*, 488 A.2d 636 (Pa. Super. Ct. 1985) (upholding a separation agreement restricting the husband's right to partition so long as the wife lived and was residing in the house) *and Libeau v. Fox*, 892 A.2d 1068 (Del. 2006) (upholding agreement to give non-selling co-tenants a right of first refusal and that those purchasing the interest would be bound by rights of survivorship), *with Vinson v. Johnson*, 931 So. 2d 245 (Fla. Dist. Ct. App. 2006) (invalidating testamentary prohibition on partition of house and farm willed to testator's nine children). Statutes typically prohibit partition of common areas of condominiums.

§3 FAMILY PROPERTY

§3.1 Marital Property: Historical Background

A. Coverture, Dower, and Curtesy

Under the common law of England, a single woman (a *feme sole*) enjoyed the same rights to hold and manage property and to enter enforceable contracts as did a man. Once married, however, the husband retained the sole power to possess and control the profits of all land owned by himself and his wife. The wife was called a *feme covert*, and her status was described by the institution of *coverture*. The husband and wife were treated as one person in the eyes of the law; that person was the husband. He had the power to convey his wife's property without her consent and to control all the profits of the land. In addition, his consent was required in order to sell her land.

In contrast to the rigidity of the law courts, the equity courts created a variety of mechanisms by which some married women could exercise property rights during marriage. First, they could enforce antenuptial agreements by which some husbands voluntarily gave control over property to their wives. Second, a trust could be created for the benefit of the wife, and she could enforce the trust as the beneficiary without her husband's consent. Fathers often took this route to keep property in their daughters' control rather than allowing it to pass to their prospective sons-in-law. William B. Stoebuck & Dale A. Whitman, *The Law of Property* §2.13, at 65-66 (3d ed. 2000).

The common law did give the wife certain important property interests to take effect at the death of her husband. The common law gave the surviving spouse a life estate in all or some of the land owned by the deceased spouse at the time of his death. The wife's *dower* interest consisted of a life estate in one-third of the freehold lands of which the husband was seised at any time during the marriage and that could be inherited by the couple's children. The wife's dower interest could not be alienated by her husband without her consent; nor could it be used to satisfy the husband's debts.

The husband's equivalent *curtesy* interest consisted of a life estate in *all* the lands in which his wife owned a present freehold estate during the marriage and that was inheritable by issue of the couple. However, the husband's curtesy interest sprang into being *only* if the couple had a child capable of inheriting the property. Stoebuck & Whitman, *supra*, at 67-69.

Dower and curtesy remain in only a few states, and where they exist, the rights of husbands and wives have been equalized. The states that retain these institutions generally allow surviving spouses to choose between dower/curtesy and a statutorily defined share of marital assets owned by the decedent at the time of death.

B. *Married Women's Property Acts*

In the second half of the nineteenth century (starting with Mississippi in 1839), all common law states passed *Married Women's Property Acts*. These statutes abolished coverture and removed the economic disabilities previously imposed on married women. After passage of the statutes, married women had the same rights as single women and married men to contract, to hold and manage property, and to sue and be sued. The wife's earnings were her separate property and could not be controlled or taken by her husband without her consent; nor could her separate property be seized by her husband's creditors. At the same time, these acts failed to achieve the aims of nineteenth-century women's rights advocates who "sought to emancipate wives' labor in the household as well as in the market, and to do so, advocated 'joint property' laws that would recognize wives' claims to marital assets to which husbands otherwise had title." Reva B. Siegel, *Home as Work: The First Woman's Rights Claims Concerning Wives' Household Labor, 1850-1880*, 103 Yale L.J. 1073, 1077 (1994). They argued that wives were "entitled to joint rights in marital property by reason of the labor they contributed to the family economy." *Id.* Many women worked inside the home for no wages; the *Married Women's Property Acts* failed to grant such women any rights in marital property, while family law doctrines preserved their duties to render services inside the home. Other women engaged in labor inside the home for which wages were earned, such as taking in laundry or sewing, keeping boarders, gardening and dairying, and selling the crops or milk products for cash. Although some states gave married women property rights in such earnings, most *Married Women's Property Acts* granted the husband control over such earnings or were interpreted by courts in this fashion on the ground that these acts were not intended to alter family law doctrines requiring women to provide services inside the home. *Id.* at 1181-1188. Since most men worked outside the home and most married women worked inside the home, gender equality in access to property was a long time in coming.

§3.2 Community Property and Separate Property

Different rules define the property rights of spouses during marriage, on divorce or dissolution of the marriage, and on the death of one of the parties. Two basic systems govern marital property rights in the United States: the *separate property* system, in the majority of states, and the *community property system*, in effect in nine states.[5]

A. Separate Property

During marriage. In separate property states, spouses own their property separately, except to the extent they choose to share it or mingle it with their spouse's property. This means that each spouse owns whatever property he or she possessed before the marriage—such as a house, a car, stock, or a bank account—and is individually liable for prior debts. Creditors cannot go after a spouse's property to satisfy a debt individually undertaken by the other spouse. Property earned after the marriage, including wages and dividends, is also owned separately. A husband and wife may of course choose to share property with each other either informally, by sharing the costs of the household or giving part of individual earnings to the spouse, or formally, by having a joint bank account to which either spouse has access as a joint tenant.

It is important to note that spouses in separate property states are not perfectly free to keep all their property to themselves. Spouses have a legal duty to support each other, and this duty may require a sharing of property earned during the marriage. A spouse who fails to comply with this obligation may be forced to do so by a court order for maintenance, although this kind of lawsuit rarely happens outside of divorce or separation.

On divorce. Most legal disputes about marital property involve divorce or the death of a spouse. All states regulate the distribution of property rights between the parties on divorce. Separate property states have statutes that provide for **equitable distribution** of property owned by each of the parties on divorce, subject to a wide range of factors such as economic need (support for necessities, including child support), status (maintaining the lifestyle shared during the marriage), rehabilitation (support sufficient to allow one spouse to attain marketable skills such that support will no longer be needed), contributions of the parties (treating the marriage as a partnership and dividing the assets jointly earned from the enterprise), and, sometimes, fault. 3 *Family Law and Practice* §37.06. Some states allow marital fault to be considered and some explicitly exclude "marital misconduct" as a factor. *Id.* §37.06[1][h]. Specific factors that may be taken into account include age, health, occupation, income, vocational skills, contribution as a homemaker, dissipation of property during the marriage, income tax consequences, debts, obligations prior to marriage and contribution of one spouse to the education of the other. This system gives the trial judge great discretion in determining how the property should be shared or shifted between the parties. Often at issue are the standards to be used in dividing

5. Arizona, California, Idaho, Louisiana, Nevada, New Mexico, Texas, Washington, and Wisconsin. A tenth state, Alaska, permits parties to opt in to a community property system. Alaska Stat. §34.77.090.

property, the weight to be given different factors, and the determination of the kinds of intangible resources that constitute "property" subject to equitable distribution on divorce.

Separate property states also have provision for "alimony," or periodic payments from one spouse to support the other. Until recently, alimony was routinely awarded to wives who were thought to be dependent on their husbands for income. However, with the huge recent increase in women in the workforce, as well as the advent of no-fault divorce, alimony has become exceptional and, when awarded, is often temporary. Current policy in most states aims at financial independence for the parties.

On death. A spouse may dispose of her property by will. Notwithstanding her right to do so, separate property states may limit her ability to determine who gets her property on death. Many states provide for a statutory **forced share** of the decedent's estate, effectively allowing the widow or widower to override the will and receive a stated portion (usually one-third to one-half) of the estate. There is no obligation to leave separately owned property; spouses are generally free to give away their separate property during their lifetime. But the rules in force do protect the interests of a surviving spouse to the extent of defining an indefeasible right to receive a portion of the testator's **estate** (the property owned by the testator at the time of death). When no will is written, a spouse's separate property is inherited according to the state intestacy statute. While some states grant the surviving spouse the decedent's entire property, other states divide the property between the surviving spouse and the children.

B. Community Property

During marriage. In community property states, as in separate property states, property owned prior to the marriage, as well as property acquired after marriage by gift, devise, bequest, or inheritance, is separate property. The American Law Institute's *Principles of the Law of Family Dissolution*, adopted in 2002, favors the community property approach rather than the separate property approach. *See id.* §§4.01-4.12. All other property acquired during the marriage, including earnings, is community property and is owned equally by both spouses. In some community property states, earnings on separate property remain separate property. In several states, however, earnings from separate property, including interest, rents, and profits, become community property. Most states allow spouses to change, or "transmute," their property from separate to community property, and vice versa, by written agreement.

While community property is somewhat similar to joint tenancy since it is a form of common ownership, a better analogy can be drawn between community property and partnership. Since the 1960s, most states have granted spouses equal rights to manage community property; each spouse individually may deal with the community property without the consent of the other spouse. At the same time, managers of community property are fiduciaries; they have the duty to manage the property for the good of the community and to act in good faith to benefit the community. In addition, most states have statutes requiring *both* parties to agree to convey or mortgage interests in real property and in assets in a business in which both spouses participate. Community property states have widely divergent rules on whether community property can be reached by creditors of individual spouses. Some states protect such property from being reached by creditors of individual spouses unless both spouses consented to the transaction; others allow the community property to be used to satisfy debts incurred by one spouse; still others limit the portion of the community property reachable by such creditors.

On divorce. A few community property states allocate property on divorce relatively mechanically by giving each spouse his or her separate property and half of the community property. Cal. Fam. Code §2550. Most community property states adopt the "equitable distribution" principle now existing in separate property states. Ariz. Rev. Stat. §25-318; Tex. Fam. Code §7.001; Wash. Rev. Code §26.09.080. The main issue arising in community property states is how to characterize specific items of property as separate or community property.

On death. In community property states, a spouse may dispose of her separate property and one-half of the community property by will. Statutory forced share statutes do not generally exist in community property states, given the spouse's vested ownership of one-half of the community property.

C. Premarital Agreements

Spouses may attempt to vary their respective property rights during marriage or at divorce by signing a premarital or antenuptial agreement. Traditionally, such agreements were unenforceable on public policy grounds because they were thought to undermine stable marriages. *See* J. Thomas Oldham, *Would Enactment of the Uniform Premarital and Marital Agreements Act in All Fifty States Change U.S. Law Regarding Premarital Agreements?*, 46 Fam. L.Q. 367, 368 (2012). Today, however, both premarital and marital agreements are generally enforceable if voluntary and not otherwise against public policy, reflecting both respect for freedom of contract and belief that such agreements may encourage marriage and discourage bitter divorce disputes. *See In re Marriage of Traster*, 291 P.3d 494, 501 (Kan. Ct. App. 2012). The *Uniform Premarital Agreement Act* (UPAA) of 1983 made it extremely difficult to challenge premarital agreements, and although adopted in about half the states, about half of those made substantial changes to provide more protection for the parties. In 2012, the Uniform Laws Commission adopted the *Uniform Premarital and Marital Agreements Act* (UPMAA), seeking to provide a level of protection more in line with state statutes and decisions.

Courts differ in the standards applied to determine whether agreements are voluntary. Factors may include whether the agreement was demanded shortly before the wedding, the relative sophistication of the parties, and whether the challenging party had reasonable time and means to access independent counsel. *See Mamot v. Mamot,*

813 N.W.2d 440, 447, 452 (Neb. 2012) (summarizing tests and finding agreement involuntary when demanded a few days before wedding and prospective wife could not reasonably have consulted an attorney); UMPAA §9(a)-(c) (2012) (agreement unenforceable if party did not have time or means to access an attorney and did not knowingly waive right to independent counsel); Cal. Fam. Code §1612(c) (restrictions on spousal support allowed only if the party waiving rights consulted with independent counsel).

Most jurisdictions will not enforce agreements if they are "unconscionable" at the time of the agreement, but standards vary widely. Oldham at 379 (factors include the relative means of the parties, whether all distribution or economic support is waived, and degree of financial disclosure between the parties). Some jurisdictions will go further and consider whether agreements are equitable or fair. *See Ansin v. Craven-Ansin*, 929 N.E.2d 955, 964 (Mass. 2010) (reviewing to determine whether the terms of the agreement are "fair and reasonable"). Many states determine unconscionability or fairness as of the date of execution of the agreement. *See* Va. Code §20-151; N.J. Stat. §37:2-38(c); UPAA §6. A significant minority of states, however, may prohibit enforcement if unconscionable at the time enforcement is sought, particularly if there has been a substantial change in the circumstances of the parties. Oldham, *supra*, at 371, 380-381; *see also* UPMAA §9(f)(b) (optional provision permitting court to refuse to enforce agreement if it "would result in substantial hardship for a party because of a material change in circumstances arising after the agreement was signed"); Conn. Gen. Stat. §46b-36g(a)(2) (prohibiting enforcement if "unconscionable when it was executed or when enforcement is sought"); *Ansin*, 929 N.E.2d at 964 (agreement must be "fair and reasonable at the time of execution and at the time of divorce"); American Law Institute, *Principles of the Law of Family Dissolution* §9.05 (2008) (recommending against enforcement if it "would work a substantial injustice" and the couple has either had a child or there has been another substantial change in circumstances).

D. Homestead Laws

Almost all states have homestead laws designed to protect the interests of a surviving spouse and children in the family home from the claims of creditors of the deceased spouse. They generally allow the spouse to live in the family home as long as she lives. Some states require the property to be registered as a homestead before the protections attach, while in others probate judges have the power to set aside homestead property as exempt from creditor's claims. Many states limit the value that can be exempted from execution to pay debts; if the property is worth more than this limit, the property (or a divisible portion of the land) may be sold to pay amounts that exceed the limitation. *See* 3 *Thompson on Real Property, Second Thomas Editions* §21.04. Some states go further and allow owners to devise homestead property free from the reach of creditors even if there is no surviving spouse or minor child. *See McKean v. Warburton*, 919 So. 2d 341, 343-345 (Fla. 2005).

§3.3 Divorce: Equitable Distribution of Property

Distribution of property differs by gender and age, as well as race. Women, on average, earn less than men. In 2011, the median income of men who worked full time was $48,202, while the median income of women who worked full time was only $37,118, or 77 percent of male earnings. Carmen DeNavas-Walt, Bernadette D. Proctor & Jessica C. Smith, U.S. Census Bureau, Current Population Reports, P60-243, *Income, Poverty, and Health Insurance Coverage in the United States: 2011* (Sept. 2012), *available at* http://www.census.gov/prod/2012pubs/p60-243.pdf. The reasons for the disparities between women and men are complicated. It is clear, however, that a major factor is that women continue to undertake the bulk of the responsibility for raising children. This work not only is unpaid but also interferes with women's ability to work full time. *See* Martha Albertson Fineman, *The Illusion of Equality: The Rhetoric and Reality of Divorce Reform* (1991); Victor Fuchs, *Women's Quest for Economic Equality* (1988); Joan Williams, *Unbending Gender: Why Family and Work Conflict and What to Do About It* (2000); Vicki Schultz, *Life's Work*, 100 Colum. L. Rev. 1881 (2000).

Women also suffer disproportionately from divorce. After divorce, men's standard of living tends to go up by 10 percent, while women's standard of living declines by 27 percent. Richard R. Peterson, *A Re-evaluation of the Economic Consequences of Divorce*, 61 Am. Soc. Rev. 528, 534 (1996); Lenore J. Weitzman, *The Economic Consequences of Divorce Are Still Unequal: Comment on Peterson*, 61 Am. Soc. Rev. 537, 538 (1996).

Children are more likely to be poor than adults, and some children are very likely to be poor. Although 15.0 percent of the population fell below the poverty line in 2011, 21.9 percent of children did so; moreover, 37.4 percent of African American children and 34.1 percent of Hispanic children were living in poverty. Children who live in households without an adult male are extremely likely to be poor. While only 6.2 percent of children in families of married couples were poor in 2011, 31.2 percent of children living in female-headed households were poor. More than half of all children under six living in female-headed households (57.2 percent) were poor. Although 23.8 percent of white, non-Hispanic, female-headed households were poor, 42.5 percent of African American, female-headed households and 44.0 percent of Hispanic, female-headed households were poor. While the median income of married couples was $74,130, the median income of female-headed households was only $33,637, and the median income of male-headed households was $49,567. DeNavas-Walt, Proctor & Smith, *supra*.

Upon divorce, the property obtained during the marriage is typically divided between the parties according to principles of **equitable distribution**. Equitable distribution is governed by statute, but the statutes contain many factors and provide judges with significant discretion. Montana's equitable distribution statute, below, a version of the *Uniform Marriage and Divorce Act* (1973) adopted in eight states, is typical. The statute is followed by *O'Brien v. O'Brien*, 489 N.E.2d 712 (N.Y. 1985), which considers what can be considered property subject to division under New York's equitable distribution statute.

Montana Equitable Distribution Statute

Mont. Code §40-4-202 & 203

§40-4-202. Division of property

(1) In a proceeding for dissolution of a marriage, legal separation, or division of property following a decree of dissolution of marriage or legal separation by a court that lacked personal jurisdiction over the absent spouse or lacked jurisdiction to divide the property, the court, without regard to marital misconduct, shall, and in a proceeding for legal separation may, finally equitably apportion between the parties the property and assets belonging to either or both, however and whenever acquired and whether the title to the property and assets is in the name of the husband or wife or both. In making apportionment, the court shall consider the duration of the marriage and prior marriage of either party; the age, health, station, occupation, amount and sources of income, vocational skills, employability, estate, liabilities, and needs of each of the parties; custodial provisions; whether the apportionment is in lieu of or in addition to maintenance; and the opportunity of each for future acquisition of capital assets and income. The court shall also consider the contribution or dissipation of value of the respective estates and the contribution of a spouse as a homemaker or to the family unit. In dividing property acquired prior to the marriage; property acquired by gift, bequest, devise, or descent; property acquired in exchange for property acquired before the marriage or in exchange for property acquired by gift, bequest, devise, or descent; the increased value of property acquired prior to marriage; and property acquired by a spouse after a decree of legal separation, the court shall consider those contributions of the other spouse to the marriage, including:

(a) the nonmonetary contribution of a homemaker;

(b) the extent to which the contributions have facilitated the maintenance of this property; and

(c) whether or not the property division serves as an alternative to maintenance arrangements.

(2) In a proceeding, the court may protect and promote the best interests of the children by setting aside a portion of the jointly and separately held estates of the parties in a separate fund or trust for the support, maintenance, education, and general welfare of any minor, dependent, or incompetent children of the parties.

§40-4-203. Maintenance

(1) In a proceeding for dissolution of marriage or legal separation or a proceeding for maintenance following dissolution of the marriage by a court that lacked personal jurisdiction over the absent spouse, the court may grant a maintenance order for either spouse only if it finds that the spouse seeking maintenance:

(a) lacks sufficient property to provide for the spouse's reasonable needs; and

(b) is unable to be self-supporting through appropriate employment or is the custodian of a child whose condition or circumstances make it appropriate that the custodian not be required to seek employment outside the home.

(2) The maintenance order must be in amounts and for periods of time that the court considers just, without regard to marital misconduct, and after considering all relevant facts, including:

(a) the financial resources of the party seeking maintenance, including marital property apportioned to that party, and the party's ability to meet the party's needs independently, including the extent to which a provision for support of a child living with the party includes a sum for that party as custodian;

(b) the time necessary to acquire sufficient education or training to enable the party seeking maintenance to find appropriate employment;

(c) the standard of living established during the marriage;

(d) the duration of the marriage;

(e) the age and the physical and emotional condition of the spouse seeking maintenance; and

(f) the ability of the spouse from whom maintenance is sought to meet the spouse's own needs while meeting those of the spouse seeking maintenance.

O'Brien v. O'Brien

489 N.E.2d 712 (N.Y. 1985)

RICHARD D. SIMONS, J.

In this divorce action, the parties' only asset of any consequence is the husband's newly acquired license to practice medicine. The principal issue presented is whether that license, acquired during their marriage, is marital property subject to equitable distribution under Domestic Relations Law §236(B)(5).

I

Plaintiff and defendant married on April 3, 1971. At the time both were employed as teachers at the same private school. Defendant had a bachelor's degree and a temporary teaching certificate but required 18 months of postgraduate classes at an approximate cost of $3,000, excluding living expenses, to obtain permanent certification in New York. She claimed, and the trial court found, that she had relinquished the opportunity to obtain permanent certification while plaintiff pursued his education. At the time of the marriage, plaintiff had completed only three and one-half years of college but shortly afterward he returned to school at night to earn his bachelor's degree and to complete sufficient premedical courses to enter medical school. In September 1973 the parties moved to Guadalajara, Mexico, where plaintiff became a full-time medical student. While he pursued his studies defendant held several teaching and tutorial positions and contributed her earnings to their joint expenses. The parties returned to New York in December 1976 so that plaintiff could complete the last two semesters of medical school and internship training here. After they returned, defendant resumed her former teaching position and she remained in it at the time this action was commenced. Plaintiff was licensed to practice medicine in October 1980. He commenced this action for divorce two months later. At the time of trial, he was a resident in general surgery.

> **CONTEXT**
>
> As the court notes, the couple had few assets besides the medical license. Michael O'Brien took only a "duffel bag of clothes, his grandfather's rocking chair, his four guitars and a stereo" when he moved out of their New York apartment to move in with Patti Rossini, a nurse whom he ultimately married. Ira Mark Ellman, O'Brien v. O'Brien: *A Failed Reform, Unlikely Reformers,* in *Family Law Stories* 272 (Carol Sanger ed. 2008).

During the marriage both parties contributed to paying the living and educational expenses and they received additional help from both of their families. They disagreed on the amounts of their respective contributions but it is undisputed that in addition to performing household work and managing the family finances defendant was gainfully employed throughout the marriage, that she contributed all of her earnings to their living and educational expenses and that her financial contributions exceeded those of plaintiff. The trial court found that she had contributed 76% of the parties' income exclusive of a $10,000 student loan obtained by defendant. Finding that plaintiff's medical degree and license are marital property, the court received evidence of its value and ordered a distributive award to defendant.

Defendant presented expert testimony that the present value of plaintiff's medical license was $472,000. Her expert testified that he arrived at this figure by comparing the average income of a college graduate and that of a general surgeon between 1985, when plaintiff's residency would end, and 2012, when [plaintiff] would reach age 65. After considering Federal income taxes, an inflation rate of 10% and a real interest rate of 3% he capitalized the difference in average earnings and reduced the amount to present value. He also gave his opinion that the present value of defendant's contribution to plaintiff's medical education was $103,390. Plaintiff offered no expert testimony on the subject.

The court, after considering the life-style that plaintiff would enjoy from the enhanced earning potential his medical license would bring and defendant's contributions and efforts toward attainment of it, made a distributive award to her of $188,800, representing 40% of the value of the license, and ordered it paid in 11 annual installments of various amounts beginning November 1, 1982 and ending November 1, 1992. The court also directed plaintiff to maintain a life insurance policy on his life for defendant's benefit for the unpaid balance of the award and it ordered plaintiff to pay defendant's counsel fees of $7,000 and her expert witness fee of $1,000. It did not award defendant maintenance.

II

The Equitable Distribution Law contemplates only two classes of property: marital property and separate property (Domestic Relations Law §236(B)(1)(c), (d)). The former, which is subject to equitable distribution, is defined broadly as "all property acquired by either or both spouses during the marriage and before the execution of a separation agreement or the commencement of a matrimonial action, *regardless of the form in which title is held*" (Domestic Relations Law §236(B)(1)(c) (emphasis added)). Plaintiff does not contend that his license is excluded from distribution because it is separate property; rather, he claims that it is not property at all but represents a personal attainment in acquiring knowledge. He rests his argument on decisions in similar cases from other jurisdictions and on his view that a license does not satisfy common-law concepts of property. Neither contention is controlling because decisions in other States rely principally on their own statutes, and the legislative history underlying them, and because the New York Legislature deliberately went beyond traditional property concepts when it formulated the Equitable Distribution Law. Instead, our statute recognizes that spouses have an equitable claim to things of value arising out of the marital relationship and classifies them as subject to distribution by focusing on the marital status of the parties at the time of acquisition. Those things acquired during marriage and subject to distribution have been classified as "marital property" although, as one commentator has observed, they hardly fall within the traditional property concepts because there is no common-law property interest remotely resembling marital property. "It is a statutory creature, is of no meaning whatsoever during the normal course of a marriage and arises full-grown, like Athena, upon the signing of a separation agreement or the commencement of a matrimonial action. It is hardly surprising, and not at all relevant, that traditional common law property concepts do not fit in parsing the meaning of 'marital property'" (Florescue, *"Market Value," Professional Licenses and Marital Property: A Dilemma in Search of a Horn*, 1982 N.Y. St. Bar Assn. Fam. L. Rev. 13 (Dec.)). Having classified the "property" subject to distribution, the Legislature did not attempt to go further and define it but left it to the courts to determine what interests come within the terms of section 236(B)(1)(c).

We made such a determination in *Majauskas v. Majauskas*, 463 N.E.2d 15 (N.Y. 1984), holding there that vested but unmatured pension rights are marital property subject to equitable distribution. Because pension benefits are not specifically identified as marital property in the statute, we looked to the express reference to pension rights contained in section 236(B)(5)(d)(4), which deals with equitable distribution of marital property, to other provisions of the equitable distribution statute and to the legislative intent behind its enactment to determine whether pension rights are marital property or separate property. A similar analysis is appropriate here and leads to the conclusion that marital property encompasses a license to practice medicine to the extent that the license is acquired during marriage.

Section 236 provides that in making an equitable distribution of marital property, "the court shall consider: . . . (6) any equitable claim to, interest in, or direct or indirect contribution made to the acquisition of such marital property by the party not having title, including joint efforts or expenditures and contributions and services as a spouse, parent, wage earner and homemaker, and *to the career or career potential* of the other party [and] (9) the impossibility or difficulty of evaluating any component asset or any interest in a business, corporation or profession" (Domestic Relations Law §236(B)(5)(d)(6), (9) (emphasis added)). Where equitable distribution of marital property is appropriate but "the distribution of an interest in a business, corporation or *profession* would be contrary to law" the court shall make a distributive award in lieu of an actual distribution of the property (Domestic Relations Law §236(B)(5)(e) (emphasis added)). The words mean exactly what they say: that an interest in a profession or professional career potential is marital property which may be represented by direct or indirect contributions of the non-title-holding spouse, including financial contributions and nonfinancial contributions made by caring for the home and family.

The history which preceded enactment of the statute confirms this interpretation. Reform of section 236 was advocated because experience had proven that application of the traditional common-law title theory of property had caused inequities upon dissolution of a marriage. The Legislature replaced the existing system with equitable distribution of marital property, an entirely new theory which considered all the circumstances of the case and of the respective parties to the marriage. Equitable distribution was based on the premise that a marriage is, among other things, an economic partnership to which both parties contribute as spouse, parent, wage earner or homemaker. Consistent with this purpose, and implicit in the statutory scheme as a whole, is the view that upon dissolution of the marriage there should be a winding up of the parties' economic affairs and a severance of their economic ties by an equitable distribution of the marital assets. Thus, the concept of alimony, which often served as a means of lifetime support and dependence for one spouse upon the other long after the marriage was over, was replaced with the concept of maintenance which seeks to allow "the recipient spouse an opportunity to achieve [economic] independence."

The determination that a professional license is marital property is also consistent with the conceptual base upon which the statute rests. As this case demonstrates, few undertakings during a marriage better qualify as the type of joint effort that the statute's economic partnership theory is intended to address than contributions toward one spouse's acquisition of a professional license. Working spouses are often required to contribute substantial income as wage earners, sacrifice their own educational or career goals and opportunities for child rearing, perform the bulk of household duties and responsibilities and forego the acquisition of marital assets that could have been accumulated if the professional spouse had been employed rather than occupied with the study and training necessary to acquire a professional license. In this case, nearly all of the parties' nine-year marriage was devoted to the acquisition of plaintiff's medical license and defendant played a major role in that project. She worked continuously during the marriage and contributed all of her earnings to their joint effort, she sacrificed her own educational and career opportunities, and she traveled with plaintiff to Mexico for three and one-half years while he attended medical school there. The Legislature has decided, by its explicit reference in the statute to the contributions of one spouse to the other's profession or career (see Domestic Relations Law §236(B)(5)(d)(6),(9);(e)), that these contributions represent investments in the economic partnership of the marriage and that the product of the parties' joint efforts, the professional license, should be considered marital property.

Plaintiff's principal argument . . . is that a professional license is not marital property because it does not fit within the traditional view of property as something which has an exchange value on the open market and is capable of sale, assignment or transfer. The position does not withstand analysis for at least two reasons. First, as we have observed, it ignores the fact that whether a professional license constitutes marital property is to be judged by the language of the statute which created this new species of property previously unknown at common law or under prior statutes. Thus, whether the license fits within traditional property concepts is of no consequence. Second, it is an overstatement to assert that a professional license could not be considered property even outside the context of section 236(B). A professional license is a valuable property right, reflected in the money, effort and lost opportunity for employment expended in its acquisition, and also in the enhanced earning capacity it affords its holder, which may not be revoked without due process of law. That a professional license has no market value is irrelevant. Obviously, a license may not be alienated as may other property and for that reason the working spouse's interest in it is limited. The Legislature has recognized that limitation, however, and has provided for an award in lieu of its actual distribution (see Domestic Relations Law §236(B)(5)(e)).

Plaintiff also contends that alternative remedies should be employed, such as an award of rehabilitative maintenance or reimbursement for direct financial contributions. The statute does not expressly authorize retrospective maintenance or rehabilitative awards and we have no occasion to decide in this case whether the authority to do so may ever be implied from its provisions. It is sufficient to observe that normally a working spouse should not be restricted to that relief because to do so frustrates the purposes underlying the Equitable Distribution Law. Limiting a working spouse to a maintenance award, either general or rehabilitative, not only is contrary to the economic partnership concept underlying the statute but also retains the uncertain and inequitable economic ties of dependence that the Legislature sought to extinguish by equitable distribution. Maintenance is subject to termination upon the recipient's remarriage and a working spouse may never receive adequate consideration for his or her contribution and may even be penalized for the decision to remarry if that is the only method of compensating the contribution. As one court said so well, "[t]he function of equitable distribution is to recognize that when a marriage ends, each of the spouses, based on the totality of the contributions made to it, has a stake in and right to a share of the marital assets accumulated while it endured, not because that share is needed, but because those assets represent the capital product of what was essentially a partnership entity" (*Wood v. Wood*, 465 N.Y.S.2d 475 (Sup. Ct. 1983)). The Legislature stated its intention to eliminate such inequities by providing that a supporting spouse's "direct or indirect contribution" be recognized, considered and rewarded (Domestic Relations Law §236(B)(5)(d)(6)).

Turning to the question of valuation, it has been suggested that even if a professional license is considered marital property, the working spouse is entitled only to reimbursement of his or her direct financial contributions.

By parity of reasoning, a spouse's down payment on real estate or contribution to the purchase of securities would be limited to the money contributed, without any remuneration for any incremental value in the asset because of price appreciation. Such a result is completely at odds with the statute's requirement that the court give full consideration to both direct and indirect contributions "made to the acquisition of such marital property by the party not having title, including joint *efforts* or expenditures and *contributions and services as a spouse, parent,* wage earner and *homemaker*" (Domestic Relations Law §236(B)(5)(d)(6) (emphasis added)). If the license is marital property, then the working spouse is entitled to an equitable portion of it, not a return of funds advanced. Its value is the enhanced earning capacity it affords the holder and although fixing the present value of that enhanced earning capacity may present problems, the problems are not insurmountable. Certainly they are no more difficult than computing tort damages for wrongful death or diminished earning capacity resulting from injury and they differ only in degree from the problems presented when valuing a professional practice for purposes of a distributive award, something the courts have not hesitated to do. The trial court retains the flexibility and discretion to structure the distributive award equitably, taking into consideration factors such as the working spouse's need for immediate payment, the licensed spouse's current ability to pay and the income tax consequences of prolonging the period of payment and, once it has received evidence of the present value of the license and the working spouse's contributions toward its acquisition and considered the remaining factors mandated by the statute, it may then make an appropriate distribution of the marital property including a distributive award for the professional license if such an award is warranted. When other marital assets are of sufficient value to provide for the supporting spouse's equitable portion of the marital property, including his or her contributions to the acquisition of the professional license, however, the court retains the discretion to distribute these other marital assets or to make a distributive award in lieu of an actual distribution of the value of the professional spouse's license.

BERNARD S. MEYER, Judge (concurring).

I concur in Judge Simons' opinion but write separately to point up for consideration by the Legislature the potential for unfairness involved in distributive awards based upon a license of a professional still in training.

An equity court normally has power to " 'change its decrees where there has been a change of circumstances.' " The implication of Domestic Relations Law §236(B)(9)(b), which deals with modification of an order or decree as to maintenance or child support, is, however, that a distributive award pursuant to section 236(B)(5)(e), once made, is not subject to change. Yet a professional in training who is not finally committed to a career choice when the distributive award is made may be locked into a particular kind of practice simply because the monetary obligations imposed by the distributive award made on the basis of the trial judge's conclusion (prophecy may be a better word) as to what the career choice will be leaves him or her no alternative.

The present case points up the problem. A medical license is but a step toward the practice ultimately engaged in by its holder, which follows after internship, residency and, for particular specialties, board certification. Here it is undisputed that plaintiff was in a residency for general surgery at the time of the trial, but had the previous year done a residency in internal medicine. Defendant's expert based his opinion on the difference between the average income of a general surgeon and that of a college graduate of plaintiff's age and life expectancy, which the trial judge utilized, impliedly finding that plaintiff would engage in a surgical practice despite plaintiff's testimony that he was dissatisfied with the general surgery program he was in and was attempting to return to the internal medicine training he had been in the previous year. The trial judge had the right, of course, to discredit that testimony, but the point is that equitable distribution was not intended to permit a judge to make a career decision for a licensed spouse still in training. Yet the degree of speculation involved in the award made is emphasized by the testimony of the expert on which it was based. Asked whether his assumptions and calculations were in any way speculative, he replied: "Yes. They're speculative to the extent of, will Dr. O'Brien practice medicine? Will Dr. O'Brien earn more or less than the average surgeon earns? Will Dr. O'Brien live to age sixty-five? Will Dr. O'Brien have a heart attack or will he be injured in an automobile accident? Will he be disabled? I mean, there is a degree of speculation. That speculative aspect is no more to be taken into account, cannot be taken into account, and it's a question, again, Mr. Emanuelli, not for the expert but for the courts to decide. It's not my function nor could it be."

The equitable distribution provisions of the Domestic Relations Law were intended to provide flexibility so that equity could be done. But if the assumption as to career choice on which a distributive award payable over a number of years is based turns out not to be the fact (as, for example, should a general surgery trainee accidentally lose the use of his hand), it should be possible for the court to revise the distributive award to conform to the fact. And there will be no unfairness in so doing if either spouse can seek reconsideration, for the licensed spouse is more likely to seek reconsideration based on real, rather than imagined, cause if he or she knows that the nonlicensed spouse can seek not only reinstatement of the original award, but counsel fees in addition, should the purported circumstance on which a change is made turn out to have been feigned or to be illusory.

Notes and Questions

1. **Division of the family home.** When a married couple gets divorced, the courts face the task of dividing property acquired during the marriage. The marital home is ordinarily the most valuable asset of the parties. Spouses often attempt to work out a settlement, which may be reviewed by the court for fairness and legality. Many considerations influence the outcome. On one hand, requiring the house to be sold means that neither party can continue to live there. Having to move is especially disruptive to children. On the other hand, because both parties contribute to the joint enterprise of the marriage, they have a right to equitably share in the property acquired during the marriage. If the couple has invested in a home, it may be impossible to divide the monetary value of the home between the parties without selling it; the person to whom the home is given ordinarily does not have enough assets simply to pay off the other party. Moreover, the cost of maintaining the house may be greater than the cost of moving to more modest accommodations and may tax the limited resources of the couple, whose expenses may have risen since living separately. Finally, sale of the home may be the only way to obtain a significant source of funds to pay the added expenses of splitting up the household, allowing each of the parties to attain economic independence.

Courts have reached different conclusions in response to these conflicting pressures. In *In re Marriage of King*, 700 P.2d 591 (Mont. 1985), for example, the court awarded the family home solely to the wife over her husband's objection after finding that it would be in the best interests of the minor children to remain there, and the husband's income as a professional gambler did not permit a regular child support award. In *Ramsey v. Ramsey*, 546 N.E.2d 1280 (Ind. Ct. App. 1989), by contrast, the court ordered the house sold over the objections of *both* the husband and wife, a couple who had been married for 20 years and who wished the wife to continue living in the marital home with the five children where the father could continue to visit the children daily. The ruling was upheld on appeal as within the trial judge's discretion but was accompanied by a vigorous dissent.

In *Behrens v. Behrens*, 532 N.Y.S.2d 893 (App. Div. 1988), the court ordered the family house sold on the grounds that neither party had sufficient resources to afford the maintenance costs of the home. The wife had objected to the sale on the grounds that it would force her and the children to leave their present community, where the family had established strong ties. A dissenting opinion argued that the imagined savings of moving were illusory since the lower rents in alternative housing would increase over time, while the mortgage payments on the current home would remain constant. Similarly, in *In re Marriage of Stallworth*, 237 Cal. Rptr. 829 (Ct. App. 1987), the court held that the adverse economic, emotional, and social impact on the minor child from being forced to move out of the family home would be minimal, even though the child was under psychiatric care and in a special education program at school. The court concluded that the adverse effect on the child was outweighed by the husband's economic interest in the sale of the home.

In a variation on this theme, the court in *Stolow v. Stolow*, 540 N.Y.S.2d 484 (App. Div. 1989), ordered the sale of the family "mini-mansion" on the grounds that it was extravagant and that the wife and children could use the proceeds of the sale to buy another "fine residence." The court ordered the sale so that the husband could obtain his share of the value of the house, despite the fact that the husband was wealthy enough to be able to afford the house payments and in the face of the "well settled principle of matrimonial law that exclusive possession of a marital residence is generally awarded to a custodial spouse with minor children." *Id.* at 486.

2. "Property" divisible on divorce. Almost all states reject New York's approach in *O'Brien* and hold that graduate degrees and professional licenses are *not* "property" whose value is divisible on divorce under statutes providing for equitable distribution of property acquired during the marriage. Nonetheless, the *O'Brien* ruling has been repeatedly reaffirmed. *See Holterman v. Holterman*, 814 N.E.2d 765 (N.Y. 2004); *McSparron v. McSparron*, 662 N.E.2d 745 (N.Y. 1995); *see also Elkus v. Elkus*, 572 N.Y.S.2d 901 (App. Div. 1991) (holding that the value of the career and celebrity status of opera singer Frederica von Stade Elkus constituted property divisible on divorce to the extent her spouse contributed to and increased the value of her career).

In *Mahoney v. Mahoney*, 453 A.2d 527 (N.J. 1982), the court rejected the idea that graduate degrees constitute property, on the grounds that (a) professional degrees do not resemble traditional property interests because they cannot be transferred in any way; (b) they are the cumulative product of many years of hard work and cannot be acquired by mere expenditure of money; (c) their value cannot be readily determined because "valuing a professional degree in the hands of any particular individual at the start of his or her career would involve a gamut of calculations that reduces to little more than guesswork," including what jobs the holder will have, what specialties she will practice, the location of practice, the length of interruptions in the career; and (d) unlike alimony, awards of property are final and unmodifiable, and courts therefore have no power to correct a mistake in the valuation of the license, no matter how gross the mistake. Justice Morris Pashman further argued that "[m]arriage is not a business arrangement in which the parties keep track of debits and credits, their accounts to be settled on divorce." *Id.* at 533. *See also Hoak v. Hoak*, 370 S.E.2d 473 (W. Va. 1988) (adopting this approach). How does the New York Court of Appeals respond to these arguments?

A number of states do hold that contributions toward receipt of the license or degree and the opportunity cost of not pursuing greater earning potential to permit the other spouse's education can be reflected in either equitable divisions of marital property or in support payments. As Justice Shirley Abrahamson wrote for the Wisconsin Supreme Court,

> [I]n a marital partnership where both parties work toward the education of one of the partners and the marriage ends before the economic benefit is realized and property is accumulated, it is unfair under these circumstances to deny the supporting spouse a share in the anticipated enhanced earnings while the student spouse keeps the degree and all the financial rewards it promises. As this court has recognized, "in a sense," the degree "is the most significant asset of the marriage" and "it is only fair" that the supporting spouse be compensated for costs and opportunities foregone while the student spouse was in school.

Haugan v. Haugan, 343 N.W.2d 796, 800 (Wis. 1984); *see also Holt v. Holt*, 976 S.W.2d 25 (Mo. Ct. App. 1998) (affirming award of 78 percent of marital property to wife who had worked full time while husband completed college and two master's degrees and was primary caretaker of children and home); *Baldwin v. Baldwin*, 788 So. 2d 800 (Miss. Ct. App. 2001); *cf. Berger v. Berger*, 747 N.W.2d 336, 350 (Mich. Ct. App. 2008) (holding that although equitable claims of contribution were available, they were not proved here: "plaintiff pursued her dancing education to fulfill her dreams but simultaneously maintained her role as primary caregiver to the children and secondary financial supporter of the family. At best, defendant tolerated plaintiff's educational pursuits; he did not sacrifice his own business or employment opportunities to support plaintiff's education.").

3. Goodwill as marital property. Although few states hold that professional degrees and licenses are property that can be divided, most permit division of the value of business "goodwill," the value of a business's reputation, patronage, or other intangible assets that enable it to produce income above the value of its individual parts. 4 *Thompson on Real Property, Second Thomas Editions* §37.11(c)(1) (3d ed. 2000); *May v. May*, 589 S.E.2d 536, 541-542 (W. Va. 2003) (surveying approaches). Many of these seek to distinguish between "enterprise goodwill," which can be transferred on the market separate from the individual (such as by selling an ongoing practice), and "personal goodwill," which is associated with an individual's reputation and skill, and divide only the former. *See Gaskill v. Robbins*, 282 S.W.3d 306 (Ky. 2009) (holding that value of oral surgery practice was largely derived from reputation and skill of wife, and so could not be divided). Others do not make this distinction, reasoning that reputation has a sale value as well. *See McReath v. McReath*, 800 N.W.2d 399, 412 (Wis. 2011). A striking case of the latter comes from the divorce of former *Saturday Night Live* star Joe Piscopo, in which the court divided the value of what it called "celebrity goodwill" over objections that his value as a star was personal to him and that his future earnings were too uncertain. The New Jersey trial and appellate courts rejected these arguments:

> Plaintiff's record of past earning was undisputed. It was also undisputed that whatever plaintiff had achieved as a celebrity had taken place during the marriage. While the trial judge recognized that it would be difficult to value plaintiff's celebrity goodwill, that difficulty would not affect its includability in the marital estate.

Piscopo v. Piscopo, 557 A.2d 1040 (N.J. Super. Ct. App. Div. 1989).

4. **Modifiability of the property award.** Suppose the defendant in *O'Brien* takes a position in a clinic in which his earnings are substantially lower than estimated by the experts at trial. He petitions the court to modify the amount of the award based on his new, lower salary. The statute in question appears to allow modifications in alimony but not in property awards. Is there any way to characterize the ex-wife's property interest in the degree to allow the court to modify the award?[6]

Problems

1. In *Pascale v. Pascale*, 660 A.2d 485 (N.J. 1995), Debra and James Pascale divorced after a 13-year marriage. Although they were granted "joint legal custody" of the three children, Debra was the "primary caretaker" with "physical custody" of the children most of the time. James was ordered to pay 60 percent of the costs of supporting the children. He was granted visitation rights with the children at his home from 5:30 to 8:30 P.M. for dinner on Wednesday and Thursday evenings and would keep the children for a 24-hour period each weekend. During the summer, the children would stay with him overnight on Wednesdays and Thursdays, and the couple was ordered to alternate major holidays with the children. At the time of the divorce, Debra had a gross annual income of $52,500, and James had an income of $72,500.

The court interpreted statutory child support requirements to guarantee "the right of children of divorce to be supported at least according to the standard of living to which they had grown accustomed prior to the separation of their parents." *Id.* at 489. The court determined that the parties could not maintain two large and equal houses.

---

6. The issue never arose in *O'Brien*, because the defendant convinced the plaintiff that he could not afford to pay the award and she accepted an undisclosed lump sum settlement instead. O'Brien did not in fact become a surgeon, deciding that would be too difficult with his Mexican degree. Instead, he became an emergency room doctor and continues to practice today. *See* Ellman, *Family Law Stories, supra*.

It was faced with a choice between ordering the house sold immediately, allowing each spouse to obtain a house of equal size and quality, or allowing the primary caretaker to stay in the larger family home until the children were older, thereby forcing the husband to live in a smaller home than he could afford if he could immediately obtain his 50 percent of the equity built up in the family home. The court compromised by awarding the family house to Debra on the understanding that she had agreed to sell it in five years when the oldest child was to begin high school.

a. What arguments would you make for James that the court should order the house to be sold immediately?

b. What arguments would you make for Debra that she should be given possession of the house until the youngest child reaches 18?

c. What should the court do, and why?

2. California has addressed the problem of equitable distribution of the value of graduate degrees by statute, creating a presumption that reimbursement is appropriate for contributions to a spouse's education that substantially enhance his earning potential. However, this award will be reduced or eliminated (1) if the couple has already substantially benefited from the education (with a presumption that this has occurred after ten years of marriage), (2) if the supporting spouse was similarly supported in receiving education, or (3) if the education enables the supported spouse to obtain employment that reduces support to which the supported spouse would otherwise be entitled. *See* Cal. Fam. Code §2641. At the same time, the statute provides that contribution to education that increases a spouse's earning potential is a factor to be considered in determining whether alimony should be awarded. In determining whether one party will be required to provide support for the other, the courts are to consider a variety of additional factors, including the extent to which the earning capacity of each party is sufficient to maintain the standard of living established during the marriage, the length of the marriage, the needs of the parties, and the ability of each to support themselves and the other party. Cal. Fam. Code §§4320, 4330. The statutory language suggests that alimony is more likely to be awarded when the supporting spouse is not able to use his or her own earning power in the marketplace to obtain the standard of living established during the marriage. *Cf. Schaefer v. Schaefer*, 642 N.W.2d 792 (Neb. 2002) (graduate degree is not property divisible on divorce, but the fact that one spouse attained a degree with the aid of the other is a factor to be considered in dividing other marital assets as well as in determining whether to award alimony).

Assume a bill is introduced in the New York legislature to overrule the result in *O'Brien* and adopt the California approach. Would you favor passage of the bill? Why or why not?

§3.4 Child Support

See Chapter 2, §4.1.

§3.5 Unmarried Partners

Family property law was built around marriage. Unmarried cohabitation was shameful and even criminalized in many states. Between 1970 and 2011, however, the number of households including an unmarried partner increased more than tenfold, from 523,000 to 6,746,000. Among women born since 1965, most have lived with a sexual partner. Although most of these relationships terminate or end in marriage within five years, many last for many years and involve children. The materials in this section concern the degree to which the law should recognize distinctive property rights arising from long-term unmarried cohabitation.

Watts v. Watts

405 N.W.2d 303 (Wis. 1987)

SHIRLEY S. ABRAHAMSON, Justice.

The case involves a dispute between Sue Ann Evans Watts, the plaintiff, and James Watts, the defendant, over their respective interests in property accumulated during their nonmarital cohabitation relationship which spanned 12 years and produced two children.

The plaintiff and the defendant met in 1967, when she was 19 years old, was living with her parents and was working full time as a nurse's aide in preparation for a nursing career. Shortly after the parties met, the defendant persuaded the plaintiff to move into an apartment paid for by him and to quit her job. According to the amended complaint, the defendant "indicated" to the plaintiff that he would provide for her.

Early in 1969, the parties began living together in a "marriage-like" relationship, holding themselves out to the public as husband and wife. The plaintiff assumed the defendant's surname as her own. Subsequently, she gave birth to two children who were also given the defendant's surname. The parties filed joint income tax returns and maintained joint bank accounts asserting that they were husband and wife. The defendant insured the plaintiff as his wife on his medical insurance policy. He also took out a life insurance policy on her as his wife, naming himself as the beneficiary. The parties purchased real and personal property as husband and wife. The plaintiff executed documents and obligated herself on promissory notes to lending institutions as the defendant's wife.

During their relationship, the plaintiff contributed childcare and homemaking services, including cleaning, cooking, laundering, shopping, running errands, and maintaining the grounds surrounding the parties' home. Additionally, the plaintiff contributed personal property to the relationship which she owned at the beginning of the relationship or acquired through gifts or purchases during the relationship. She served as hostess for the defendant for social and business-related events. [P]eriodically, between 1969 and 1975, the plaintiff cooked and cleaned for the defendant and his employees while his business, a landscaping service, was building and landscaping a golf course.

From 1973 to 1976, the plaintiff worked 20-25 hours per week at the defendant's office, performing duties as a receptionist, typist, and assistant bookkeeper. From 1976 to 1981, the plaintiff worked 40-60 hours per week at a business she started with the defendant's sister-in-law, then continued and managed the business herself after the dissolution of that partnership. The plaintiff further alleges that in 1981 the defendant made their relationship so intolerable that she was forced to move from their home and their relationship was irretrievably broken. Subsequently, the defendant barred the plaintiff from returning to her business.

The plaintiff alleges that during the parties' relationship, and because of her domestic and business contributions, the business and personal wealth of the couple increased. Furthermore, the plaintiff alleges that she never received any compensation for these contributions to the relationship and that the defendant indicated to the plaintiff both orally and through his conduct that he considered her to be his wife and that she would share equally in the increased wealth.

The plaintiff asserts that since the breakdown of the relationship the defendant has refused to share equally with her the wealth accumulated through their joint efforts or to compensate her in any way for her contributions to the relationship.

IV

[Plaintiff claims] that she and the defendant had a contract to share equally the property accumulated during their relationship. The essence of the complaint is that the parties had a contract, either an express or implied in fact contract, which the defendant breached.

Wisconsin courts have long recognized the importance of freedom of contract and have endeavored to protect the right to contract. A contract will not be enforced, however, if it violates public policy. [Defendant suggests that] any contract between the parties regarding property division contravenes public policy because the contract is based on immoral or illegal sexual activity.

Courts have generally refused to enforce contracts for which the sole consideration is sexual relations, sometimes referred to as "meretricious" relationships. Courts distinguish, however, between contracts that are explicitly and inseparably founded on sexual services and those that are not. This court, and numerous other courts, have concluded that "a bargain between two people is not illegal merely because there is an illicit relationship between the two so long as the bargain is independent of the illicit relationship and the illicit relationship does not constitute any part of the consideration bargained for and is not a condition of the bargain." *In Matter of Estate of Steffes*, 290 N.W.2d 697, 709 (1980).

While not condoning the illicit sexual relationship of the parties, many courts have recognized that the result of a court's refusal to enforce contract and property rights between unmarried cohabitants is that one party keeps all or most of the assets accumulated during the relationship, while the other party, no more or less "guilty," is deprived of property which he or she has helped to accumulate.

[C]ourts recognize that their refusal to enforce what are in other contexts clearly lawful promises will not undo the parties' relationship and may not discourage others from entering into such relationships. A harsh, per se rule that the contract and property rights of unmarried cohabiting parties will not be recognized might actually encourage a partner with greater income potential to avoid marriage in order to retain all accumulated assets, leaving the other party with nothing.

The plaintiff has alleged that she quit her job and abandoned her career training upon the defendant's promise to take care of her. A change in one party's circumstances in performance of the agreement may imply an agreement between the parties.

In addition, the plaintiff alleges that she performed housekeeping, childbearing, childrearing, and other services related to the maintenance of the parties' home, in addition to various services for the defendant's business and her own business, for which she received no compensation. Courts have recognized that money, property, or services (including housekeeping or childrearing) may constitute adequate consideration independent of the parties' sexual relationship to support an agreement to share or transfer property.

According to the plaintiff's complaint, the parties cohabited for more than twelve years, held joint bank accounts, made joint purchases, filed joint income tax returns, and were listed as husband and wife on other legal documents. Courts have held that such a relationship and "joint acts of a financial nature can give rise to an inference that the parties intended to share equally." *Beal v. Beal*, 577 P.2d 507, 510 (Or. 1978). The joint ownership of property and the filing of joint income tax returns strongly implies that the parties intended their relationship to be in the nature of a joint enterprise, financially as well as personally.

We . . . conclude that public policy does not necessarily preclude an unmarried cohabitant from asserting a contract claim against the other party to the cohabitation so long as the claim exists independently of the sexual relationship and is supported by separate consideration. Accordingly, we conclude that the plaintiff in this case has pleaded the facts necessary to state a claim for damages resulting from the defendant's breach of an express or an implied in fact contract to share with the plaintiff the property accumulated through the efforts of both parties during their relationship. [W]e do not judge the merits of the plaintiff's claim; we merely hold that she be given her day in court to prove her claim.

V

The plaintiff's [next] theory of recovery involves unjust enrichment. Essentially, she alleges that the defendant accepted and retained the benefit of services she provided knowing that she expected to share equally in the wealth accumulated during their relationship. She argues that it is unfair for the defendant to retain all the assets they accumulated under these circumstances and that a constructive trust should be imposed on the property as a result of the defendant's unjust enrichment.

Unlike claims for breach of an express or implied in fact contract, a claim of unjust enrichment does not arise out of an agreement entered into by the parties. Rather, an action for recovery based upon unjust enrichment is grounded on the moral principle that one who has received a benefit has a duty to make restitution where retaining such a benefit would be unjust.

Because no express or implied in fact agreement exists between the parties, recovery based upon unjust enrichment is sometimes referred to as "quasi contract," or contract "implied in law" rather than "implied in fact." Quasi contracts are obligations created by law to prevent injustice.

In Wisconsin, an action for unjust enrichment, or quasi contract, is based upon proof of three elements: (1) a benefit conferred on the defendant by the plaintiff, (2) appreciation or knowledge by the defendant of the benefit, and (3) acceptance or retention of the benefit by the defendant under circumstances making it inequitable for the defendant to retain the benefit.

As part of his general argument, the defendant claims that the court should leave the parties to an illicit relationship such as the one in this case essentially as they are found, providing no relief at all to either party.

As we have discussed previously, allowing no relief at all to one party in a so-called "illicit" relationship effectively provides total relief to the other, by leaving that party owner of all the assets acquired through the efforts of both. Yet it cannot seriously be argued that the party retaining all the assets is less "guilty" than the other. Such a result is contrary to the principles of equity. Many courts have held, and we now so hold, that unmarried cohabitants may raise claims based upon unjust enrichment following the termination of their relationships where one of the parties attempts to retain an unreasonable amount of the property acquired through the efforts of both.

In this case, the plaintiff alleges that she contributed both property and services to the parties' relationship. She claims that because of these contributions the parties' assets increased, but that she was never compensated for her contributions. She further alleges that the defendant, knowing that the plaintiff expected to share in the property accumulated, "accepted the services rendered to him by the plaintiff" and that it would be unfair under the circumstances to allow him to retain everything while she receives nothing. We conclude that the facts alleged are sufficient to state a claim for recovery based upon unjust enrichment.

As part of the plaintiff's unjust enrichment claim, she has asked that a constructive trust be imposed on the assets that the defendant acquired during their relationship. A constructive trust is an equitable device created by law to prevent unjust enrichment. To state a claim on the theory of constructive trust the complaint must state facts sufficient to show (1) unjust enrichment and (2) abuse of a confidential relationship or some other form of unconscionable conduct. The latter element can be inferred from allegations in the complaint which show, for example, a family relationship, a close personal relationship, or the parties' mutual trust. These facts are alleged in this complaint or may be inferred. Therefore, we hold that if the plaintiff can prove the elements of unjust enrichment to the satisfaction of the circuit court, she will be entitled to demonstrate further that a constructive trust should be imposed as a remedy.

VI

The plaintiff's last alternative legal theory on which her claim rests is the doctrine of partition. The plaintiff has asserted in her complaint a claim for partition of "all real and personal property accumulated by the couple during their relationship according to the plaintiff's interest therein and pursuant to Chapters 820 and 842, Wis. Stats."

In Wisconsin partition is a remedy under both the statutes and common law. Partition applies generally to all disputes over property held by more than one party.

In this case, the plaintiff has alleged that she and the defendant were engaged in a joint venture or partnership, that they purchased real and personal property as husband and wife, and that they intended to share all the property acquired during their relationship. In our opinion, these allegations, together with other facts alleged in the plaintiff's complaint (*e.g.*, the plaintiff's contributions to the acquisition of their property) and reasonable inferences therefrom, are sufficient . . . to state a claim for an accounting of the property acquired during the parties' relationship and partition. We do not, of course, presume to judge the merits of the plaintiff's claim. Proof of her allegations must be made to the circuit court. We merely hold that the plaintiff has alleged sufficient facts in her complaint to state a claim for relief [for] statutory or common law partition.

Notes and Questions

1. **Meretricious relationship, contract, and partnership.** States have adopted three quite different approaches to the problem of property rights between unmarried cohabitants upon dissolution of the relationship. The early approach was to deny any remedy on the ground that a relationship between unmarried cohabitants violates public policy reflected in statutes encouraging marriage and prohibiting common law marriage. *Hewitt v. Hewitt*, 394 N.E.2d 1204, 1207-1208 (Ill. 1979), is illustrative:

> There are major public policy questions involved in determining whether, under what circumstances, and to what extent it is desirable to accord some type of legal status to claims arising from such relationships. Of substantially greater importance than the rights of the immediate parties is the impact of such recognition upon our society and the institution of marriage. Will the fact that legal rights closely resembling those arising from conventional marriages can be acquired by those who deliberately choose to enter into what have heretofore been commonly referred to as "illicit" or "meretricious" relationships encourage formation of such relationships and weaken marriage as the foundation of our family-based society? Does not the recognition of legally enforceable property and custody rights emanating from nonmarital cohabitation in practical effect equate with the legalization of common law marriage?

Although a few states still follow this approach, today almost all states that have considered the issue allow enforcement of some agreements between the parties to provide support in exchange for non- sexual services. As noted in the leading case of *Marvin v. Marvin*, 557 P.2d 106 (Cal. 1976), "[t]he fact that a man and woman live together without marriage, and engage in a sexual relationship, does not in itself invalidate agreements between them relating to their earnings, property, or expenses. Agreements between nonmarital partners fail only to the extent that they rest upon a consideration of meretricious sexual services." *Id.* at 113. In these cases, a central question is how explicit the agreement needs to be and whether an agreement can be inferred from the conduct of the parties.

Some jurisdictions require that such agreements be in writing. *Posik v. Layton*, 695 So. 2d 759 (Fla. App. 1997), for example, adopted this approach in enforcing a written agreement by Dr. Nancy Layton to support Emma Posik in the amount of $2,500 per month for the rest of her life in exchange for her agreeing to give up her career as a nurse at the hospital where they met, move to Brevard County with her, and maintain and take care of their home. Four years later, Layton sought to move another woman into the house and served a notice of eviction on Posik. Although the trial court refused to enforce the agreement, the court of appeals reversed:

> Certainly, even though the agreement was couched in terms of a personal services contract, it was intended to be much more. It was a nuptial agreement entered into by two parties that the state prohibits from marrying. But even though the state has prohibited same-sex marriages and same-sex adoptions, it has not prohibited this type of agreement. By prohibiting same-sex marriages, the state has merely denied homosexuals the rights granted to married partners that flow naturally from the marital relationship. But the State has not denied these individuals their right to either will their property as they see fit nor to privately commit by contract to spend their money as they choose.
>
> [A]n agreement for support between unmarried adults is valid unless the agreement is inseparably based upon illicit consideration of sexual services. . . . Because of the potential abuse in marital-type relationships, we find that such agreements must be in writing. The Statute of Frauds (section 725.01, Florida Statutes) requires that contracts made upon consideration of marriage must be in writing. This same requirement should apply to non-marital, nuptial-like agreements.

Id. at 761-762. In 2010, the New Jersey Legislature amended its statute of frauds to require contracts to provide support to unmarried partners to be in writing and signed by the promisor, abrogating earlier decisions. N.J. Stat. §25:1-5; *Maeker v. Ross*, 62 A.3d 310 (N.J. Super. Ct. App. Div. 2013) (holding that that statute barred enforcement of agreements made before its enactment even if agreement was broken post-enactment).

Other courts enforce oral agreements, but require the agreement to be express rather than implied from the conduct of the parties. The New York Court of Appeals adopted this approach in *Morone v. Morone*, 413 N.E.2d 1154, 1157 (N.Y. 1980). Justice Bernard Meyer explained,

> [I]t is not reasonable to infer an agreement to pay for the services rendered when the relationship of the parties makes it natural that the services were rendered gratuitously. As a matter of human experience personal services will frequently be rendered by two people living together because they value each other's company or because they find it a convenient or rewarding thing to do. For courts to attempt through hindsight to sort out the intentions of the parties and affix jural significance to conduct carried out within an essentially private and generally noncontractual relationship runs too great a risk of error.

Id. at 1157.

The third approach provides for property distribution even though the parties were not legally married and did not enter any agreement pertaining to support or property rights. As suggested by the Wisconsin Supreme Court in *Watts*, this may be based on either finding an implied agreement to pool resources from the conduct of the parties or by imposing a constructive trust to avoid unjust enrichment. These cases consider factors such as whether the parties held joint accounts or property in common, sacrificed paid employment for work in the home, worked in the other partner's business, and contributed financially to the purchase of property in the other partner's name. *See Sullivan v. Rooney*, 533 N.E.2d 1372 (Mass. 1989); *Pickens v. Pickens*, 490 So. 2d 872 (Miss. 1986); *Wallender v. Wallender*, 870 P.2d 232 (Or. 1994); *Connell v. Francisco*, 898 P.2d 831 (Wash. 1995); *In re Marriage of Lindsey*, 678 P.2d 328 (Wash. 1984). In *Pickens*, for example, the Mississippi Supreme Court found that the parties had created a relationship akin to a *partnership*. "Where parties such as these live together in what must at least be acknowledged to be a partnership and where, through their joint efforts, real property or personal property, or both, are accumulated, an equitable division of such property will be ordered upon the permanent breakup and separation." 490 So. 2d at 875-876. This approach rests on the assumption that the parties relied on each other and that both contributed to their ongoing relationship. Recovery is allowed based on the nature of the relationship rather than on a real or fictitious contract between the parties. Instead of finding a contract implied in fact from the conduct of the parties evidencing their actual intent to agree, the court imposed an agreement implied in law, which is binding on the parties regardless of their assent. This approach was recently proposed by the American Law Institute in the *ALI Principles of the Law of Family Dissolution* §§6.01-6.06, adopted in 2002. Some scholars have defended this approach as protective of the justified expectations of the parties to the relationship, *see* Nancy D. Polikoff, *Making Marriage Matter Less: The ALI Domestic Partner Principles Are One Step in the Right Direction*, 2004 U. Chi. Legal F. 353, while others have criticized it for imposing obligations on individuals who did not voluntarily assume them and who may have deliberately chosen to eschew such obligations. *See* Marsha Garrison, *Is Consent Necessary? An Evaluation of the Emerging Law of Cohabitant Obligation*, 52 UCLA L. Rev. 815 (2005)).

Which approach best promotes gender equality?

2. Constructive trust. In *Sullivan v. Rooney*, 533 N.E.2d 1372 (Mass. 1989), the court imposed a constructive trust on a house in which an unmarried couple with a long-term relationship had lived for several years. The trial court found that the parties thought of the purchase as a joint transaction, although the defendant placed title in his name alone, explaining to the plaintiff that this was necessary to get 100 percent Veterans' Administration financing. The court found that the defendant had repeatedly promised to place the house in both of their names, but never did. The defendant paid the mortgage obligations, taxes, utilities, and insurance on the house, while the plaintiff put all her savings and earnings as a waitress into the house, paying for the food, household supplies and furniture, and doing all the housework and entertaining the defendant's colleagues. The Supreme Judicial Court of Massachusetts upheld the trial court's order placing a constructive trust on the home:

> The judge's unchallenged findings of fact demonstrate that there was a fiduciary relationship between the parties and that the defendant violated his fiduciary duty to the plaintiff. Equitable principles impose a constructive trust on property to avoid the

> unjust enrichment of a party who violates his fiduciary duty and acquires that property at the expense of the person to whom he owed that duty. Here the plaintiff was less educated (a high school graduate) and less experienced (she is a waitress) than the defendant (a career army officer attending law school at the time of the purchase of the house). She relied on him over a long period in important matters. That reliance was reasonable, and the defendant knew of and accepted the plaintiff's trust in him.
>
> It would be unjust not to impose a constructive trust in this case. The plaintiff gave up her career as a flight attendant and undertook to maintain a home for the defendant while he advanced his career. She contributed her earnings and services to the home. The defendant's assurances to the plaintiff that they would own the property together (although title would be taken only in his name), his later promises to transfer title to joint ownership, and the plaintiff's reasonable reliance on those promises made by one in whom she reasonably placed special confidence call for the imposition of a constructive trust in the plaintiff's favor on one-half the Reading property.

Id. at 1373-1375. Five years later, in *Collins v. Guggenheim*, 631 N.E.2d 1016 (Mass. 1994), the same court considered a case in which an unmarried couple had jointly taken out loans, invested in, and labored on a rundown farm titled in the woman's name to turn it into a profitable pick-your-own business. The court refused to impose a constructive trust on the farm in favor of the man, finding that Massachusetts had refused to accord unsolemnized relationships the incidents of marriage, and that in the absence of "fraud, breach of fiduciary duty or other misconduct," a constructive trust would not be imposed. *Id.* at 1017. The court did not cite its decision in *Sullivan*. How would you explain the different results?

3. **Property rights on death.** In *Williams v. Mason*, 556 So. 2d 1045 (Miss. 1990), Roosevelt Adams promised Frances Mason in 1962 that if she would live in his home, take care of him, and "do his bidding," he would leave her all his property on his death. Mason lived with Adams for more than 20 years. When Adams died, he left a farm but, unfortunately, not a will or, indeed, any written memorandum of his promise to Mason. Adams never divorced his wife, who lived in Chicago, and he never promised to marry Mason. The court held that the promise to devise the property was unenforceable because it was not in writing, as required by the statute of frauds. Quoting Justice Oliver Wendell Holmes, the court explained:

> "We are aware that by our construction of Pub. Sts. C. 141, §1, the statute of frauds may be made an instrument of fraud. But this is always true, whenever the law prescribes a form for an obligation. The very meaning of such a requirement is that a man relies at his peril on what purports to be such an obligation without that form." *Bourke v. Callahan*, 35 N.E. 460 (Mass. 1893).
>
> Notwithstanding these well settled principles, experience has taught that gross unfairness may result where one acts in good faith and lives up to an oral agreement to provide services for another under circumstances such as today's. Our law has seen in such situations a potential for unjust enrichment, if not fraud. In recognition of these practical realities, the positive law of this state directs that a person, who provides services to another in good faith and in consequence of an oral agreement to devise property in exchange for the services, is not without enforceable rights. These rights arise

not out of the agreement but the conduct of the parties. The promisee activates the rights the law affords by performing the services in good faith reliance on the promise.

When the parties have so acted with respect one to the other, that is, when one has provided services for the other in reasonable reliance upon a promise to give consideration there for, our cases are legion that, upon the death of the promisor, the promisee may recover of and from the estate on a *quantum meruit* basis. In such cases the amount of recovery is limited to the monetary equivalent of the reasonable value of the services rendered to the decedent for which payment has not been received. Said sum becomes a charge against the assets of the estate.

Our law recognizes an additional basis upon which—assuming proper proof—a person such as Mason may recover. Where parties live together without benefit of marriage and where, through their joint efforts, [they] accumulate real property or personal property, or both, a party having no legal title nevertheless acquires rights to an equitable share enforceable at law. *Pickens v. Pickens*, 490 So. 2d 872, 875-876 (Miss. 1986).

The New Jersey Supreme Court similarly held that an unmarried companion may receive a share of the decedent's estate in *In re Estate of Roccamonte*, 808 A.2d 838 (N.J. 2002), but the legislature later abrogated this result by amending the statute of frauds to require promises of support between those in "non-marital personal relationships" to be in writing. N.J. Stat. §25:1-5(h).

Problem

The broad wording of some laws banning same-sex marriage may even affect the property rights of male-female couples. For example, the Ohio constitutional amendment reads:

> Only a union between one man and one woman may be a marriage valid in or recognized by this state and its political subdivisions. This state and its political subdivisions shall not create or recognize a legal status for relationships of unmarried individuals that intends to approximate the design, qualities, significance or effect of marriage.

Ohio Const. art. XV, §11. The amendment to the Arkansas constitution reads:

> Marriage consists only of the union of one man and one woman. Legal status for unmarried persons which is identical or substantially similar to marital status shall not be valid or recognized in Arkansas, except that the legislature may recognize a common law marriage from another state between a man and a woman.

Ark. Const. amend. LXXXIII, §§1, 2. Does the Ohio constitutional amendment prohibit Ohio courts from dividing the property of an unmarried male-female couple when they break up, as the Wisconsin court did in *Watts v. Watts*? Does the Arkansas amendment?

§3.6 Same-Sex Partners

The last 20 years have seen a sea change in the law regarding same-sex marriages and relationships. Until 2003, state laws criminalizing sodomy between persons of the same sex were deemed constitutional. *See Lawrence v. Texas*, 539 U.S. 558, 573 (2003) (overruling *Bowers v. Hardwick*, 478 U.S. 186 (1986)). When, in 1996, a trial court in Hawai`i held that denying individuals the freedom to marry others of the same sex constituted sex discrimination in violation of the Hawai`i constitution, *Baehr v. Miike*, 1996 WL 694235 (Haw. Cir. Ct., Dec. 03, 1996), *aff'd Baehr v. Miike*, 950 P.2d 1234 (Haw. 1997) (construing *Baehr v. Lewin*, 852 P.2d 44, 59 (Haw. 1993)), the reaction was sharp and swift. That year, Congress enacted the Defense of Marriage Act (DOMA), declaring that for all federal programs and laws, "the word 'marriage' means only a legal union between one man and one woman as husband and wife," and no state was required to recognize a same-sex marriage performed under the laws of any other state. 1 U.S.C. §7 (held unconstitutional by *United States v. Windsor*, 113 S. Ct. 2675 (2013)) & 28 U.S.C. §1738C. After the Hawai`i Supreme Court affirmed the trial court, Hawaiians amended their constitution to authorize prohibition of same-sex marriages. Haw. Const. art. 1, §23.

In 1999, the Supreme Court of Vermont held in *Baker v. State of Vermont*, 744 A.2d 864 (Vt. 1999) that the Vermont constitution requires the state to grant same-sex couples the legal incidents of marriage, whether or not the state chooses to call such relationships "marriages." Implementing this constitutional mandate, Vermont enacted legislation allowing "civil unions" but not "marriages" between same-sex partners. *See* Vt. Stat. tit. 15, §§1201-1206. Over the next several years, Connecticut, New Jersey, California, Colorado, the District of Columbia, Hawai`i, Illinois, Maryland, Oregon, Nevada, New Hampshire, New Jersey, Vermont, Washington, and Wisconsin all enacted statutes providing for civil unions or domestic partnerships.

On November 18, 2003, the Massachusetts Supreme Judicial Court held in *Goodridge v. Department of Public Health*, 798 N.E.2d 941 (Mass. 2003), that barring individuals from marrying each other solely because they were of the same sex violated the state constitutional guarantees of liberty and equality. Chief Justice Margaret Marshall wrote that the "Massachusetts Constitution affirms the dignity and equality of all individuals" and that "[i]t forbids the creation of second-class citizens." *Id.* at 948. The Commonwealth of Massachusetts had defended limiting marriage to male-female couples on the grounds that marriage provided a favorable setting for procreation, ensured the optimal setting for child rearing, and preserved scarce state resources. The court found none of these goals constitutionally adequate, given the fact that child rearing often occurs outside traditional marriages and that the ability to procreate was never a prerequisite to marriage. After a six-month delay to permit legislative reaction, same-sex couples began marrying in Massachusetts on May 17, 2004.

The recognition of the first same-sex marriages in the United States prompted a wave of "mini-DOMAs" across the United States, in which states enacted statutes and frequently amended their constitutions to prohibit recognition of same-sex marriages. Today the laws of more than 35 states explicitly ban same-sex marriage, and half of all states ban it in their constitutions.

More recently, *Goodridge* helped catalyze other states to recognize same-sex marriage. In 2008, by closely divided 4-3 votes, the Supreme Courts of California and Connecticut held that their state constitutional rights to equal protection of the laws grant same-sex couples the same right to marry as is enjoyed by opposite-sex couples. *In re Marriage Cases*, 183 P.2d 384 (Cal. 2008); *Kerrigan v. Commissioner of Public Health*, 957 A.2d 407 (Conn. 2008).[7] Both courts ruled that existing statutory provisions recognizing civil union or domestic partnership arrangements for same-sex couples were not equivalent to laws recognizing opposite-sex civil marriages. *Accord, Opinions of the Justices*, 802 N.E.2d 565 (Mass. 2004) (civil unions not equivalent to civil marriages).[8] In 2009, in *Varnum v. Brien*, 763 N.W.2d 862 (Iowa 2009), the Iowa Supreme Court struck down that state's law prohibiting same-sex marriage, holding that discrimination against same-sex couples was subject to heightened scrutiny and could not meet that standard.

Since then, 12 more states and the District of Columbia have formally authorized same-sex marriages. These states include (in chronological order): Vermont, New Hampshire, and the District of Columbia in 2009; New York in 2011; Washington, Maine, and Maryland in 2012; and Rhode Island, Delaware, Minnesota, New Jersey, Hawai`i, and Illinois in 2013. Same-sex marriages may also be performed in Argentina, Belgium, Brazil, Canada, Denmark, France, Iceland, the Netherlands, New Zealand, Norway, Portugal, South Africa, Spain, Sweden, England, Wales, Uruguay, and Mexico City and the Mexican state of Quintana Roo. Five Indian tribes in the United States also authorize same-sex marriages: the Coquille Indian Tribe, the Little Traverse Bay Bands of Odawa Indians, the Pokagon Band of Potawatomi Indians, the Ipsay Nation of Santa Ysabel, and the Suquamish Tribe.[9]

Despite the expansion of marriage equality, the legal effect of same-sex marriages is limited by laws prohibiting recognition of such marriages wherever they are entered into. Until 2013, DOMA also precluded recognition for any purposes under federal law. The General Accounting Office has determined that marriage is a factor in 1,138 federal laws, including many with property implications, such as joint marital filing

---

7. These courts, like other courts that have considered the issue, differed in their reasoning. The Connecticut Supreme Court held that legal classifications based on sexual orientation are subject to intermediate scrutiny as a quasi-suspect classification, while the California Supreme Court held that they are subject to strict scrutiny. The California court further held that the right to marry is a basic civil right whose denial impinges upon same-sex couples' fundamental privacy interests in having official family relationships accorded equal respect and dignity and that no compelling state interest justified the differential treatment of same-sex and opposite-sex couples.

8. The California decision was overturned when in 2008 voters approved an amendment to the California constitution, but the amendment was found to unconstitutionally burden the fundamental right to marry and discriminate against same-sex couples without a rational justification in *Perry v. Schwarzenegger*, 704 F. Supp. 2d 921, 1004 (N.D. Cal. 2010). The State of California declined to defend the amendment on appeal, and the Ninth Circuit permitted the private proponents of the initiative to defend it in their stead and affirmed the district court decision. The Supreme Court reversed, holding that the appellants did not have standing to defend the initiative, thus leaving the district court's invalidation of the initiative intact. *Hollingsworth v. Perry*, 133 S. Ct. 2652 (2013).

9. At least where one partner to a tribal marriage is a tribal member, such marriages will likely be recognized by states that recognize same-sex marriages performed outside the state.

of tax forms, estate taxation, social security and veterans benefits, bankruptcy protections, mortgage insurance, and federal land and natural resource rights. GAO, D. Shah, *Defense of Marriage Act: Update to Prior Report* 1 (GAO-04-353R, 2004). The facts of *United States v. Windsor*, 113 S. Ct. 2675 (2013), exemplify the property effects of marriage under federal law. Edith Windsor and Thea Spyer began their relationship in 1963, registered as domestic partners in New York in 1993, and married in Canada in 2007. Spyer died in 2009, leaving her entire estate to Windsor. Although New York recognized the Canadian marriage as valid, the federal government did not. The result was that Windsor was ineligible for the marital estate-tax deduction, and so owed $363,053 in estate taxes. The district court, Second Circuit, and finally the Supreme Court held that DOMA was unconstitutional. The Supreme Court declared:

> The Constitution's guarantee of equality "must at the very least mean that a bare congressional desire to harm a politically unpopular group cannot" justify disparate treatment of that group. The avowed purpose and practical effect of the law here in question are to impose a disadvantage, a separate status, and so a stigma upon all who enter into same-sex marriages made lawful by the unquestioned authority of the States.
>
> DOMA's principal effect is to identify a subset of state-sanctioned marriages and make them unequal. By creating two contradictory marriage regimes within the same State, DOMA forces same-sex couples to live as married for the purpose of state law but unmarried for the purpose of federal law, thus diminishing the stability and predictability of basic personal relations the State has found it proper to acknowledge and protect. The differentiation demeans the couple, whose moral and sexual choices the Constitution protects, *see Lawrence*, 539 U.S. 558 (2003), and whose relationship the State has sought to dignify. And it humiliates tens of thousands of children now being raised by same-sex couples. The law in question makes it even more difficult for the children to understand the integrity and closeness of their own family and its concord with other families in their community and in their daily lives.
>
> What has been explained to this point should more than suffice to establish that the principal purpose and the necessary effect of this law are to demean those persons who are in a lawful same-sex marriage. This requires the Court to hold, as it now does, that DOMA is unconstitutional as a deprivation of the liberty of the person protected by the Fifth Amendment of the Constitution. This opinion and its holding are confined to those lawful marriages.

Id. Although *Windsor* invalidates the federal DOMA, a majority of states still explicitly refuse to recognize same-sex marriages. This could leave in jeopardy the ability of legally married couples to exercise the rights and rely on the obligations that stem from marriage. *See* Joseph William Singer, *Same Sex Marriage, Full Faith and Credit, and the Evasion of Obligation*, 1 Stan. J. Civ. Rts. & Civ. Liberties 1 (2005). It remains to be seen whether *Windsor* will lead to invalidations of state laws prohibiting the recognition of same-sex marriages solemnized elsewhere. A federal district court has already relied on *Windsor* to issue a temporary restraining order directing Ohio to recognize the Maryland marriage of a man dying from amyotrophic lateral sclerosis (ALS) on his death certificate, in part to ensure his that surviving spouse could be buried beside him. *Obergefell v. Kasich*, No. 1:13-cv-501 (July 22, 2013).

Notes and Questions

1. **Contracts.** Same-sex couples may enter into agreements just as male-female couples may to share property both during their relationship and at separation. *Posik v. Layton*, 695 So. 2d 759 (Fla. Dist. Ct. App. 1997); *Crooke v. Gilden*, 414 S.E.2d 645 (Ga. 1992). However, some state laws prohibiting recognition of same-sex marriages are worded so broadly that they arguably prohibit recognition of property or contract rights arising out of such relationships.

As with male-female couples, an alternative to enforcement of an express or implicit agreement is the application of constructive trust doctrine to prevent unjust enrichment. A same-sex couple living together for a significant period may create an interdependent financial and personal relationship that would justify distributing the property acquired during the relationship between the parties when they break up, especially if the parties agree to support each other and if failure to reallocate property rights would result in unjust enrichment of one of the parties. *See, e.g., Minieri v. Knittel*, 727 N.Y.S.2d 872 (N.Y. Sup. Ct. 2001); *Doe v. Burkland*, 808 A.2d 1090 (R.I. 2002); *Gormley v. Robertson*, 83 P.3d 1042 (Wash. Ct. App. 2004).

When a party to a marriage dies without a will, intestacy statutes provide for inheritance of the surviving spouse. Imposing a constructive trust on the estate of an unmarried partner, however, poses additional problems because of the greater potential for fraud and uncertainty after one of the parties who could testify to the relationship has died. Despite this, in *Vásquez v. Hawthorne*, 33 P.3d 735 (Wash. 2001), the Washington Supreme Court authorized imposing a constructive trust on the estate of a man involved in a "long-term, stable, cohabiting relationship" if his partner could prove an implied partnership based on the relationship.

2. **Child support.** In all states, noncustodial parents are obligated to provide child support for their minor children, but establishing parentage is often more difficult for same-sex couples. Absent adoption a court may determine that a partner who is not the biological parent is not a parent for child support purposes. A non-biological parent may also adopt her spouse's children through a stepparent adoption; some states, however, do not permit so-called second parent adoptions by unmarried partners. In many states, parentage is presumed for children born during a legal marriage, although the application of the presumption to same-sex couples is uncertain. *See* Jennifer Rosato, *Children of Same-Sex Parents Deserve the Security Blanket of the Parentage Presumption*, 44 Fam. Ct. Rev. 74 (2006). If a party to a same-sex marriage is ordered to pay child support on the dissolution of her marriage based on this presumption and then moves to a state that refuses to recognize same-sex marriages, may she evade the child support order? 28 U.S.C. §1738B requires all states to extend full faith and credit to child support orders issued by the state child's "home state" at the time of the initial order. In *Miller-Jenkins v. Miller-Jenkins*, 637 S.E.2d 330 (Va. App. 2006), the Virginia Court of Appeals held that under a related law, 28 U.S.C. §1738A, Virginia courts were required to recognize Vermont's parentage and custody orders regarding a child born within a same-sex civil union despite that state's mini-DOMA.

If 28 U.S.C. §1738B is held to have a similar effect, other courts would have to recognize orders entered by the child's home state.

3. Divorce. Although many states will solemnize the marriages of couples who do not reside in the state, most will not exercise jurisdiction over a divorce unless one of the spouses has been domiciled or resided in the state for a substantial period, often six months to a year. Many states that refuse to recognize same-sex marriages also refuse to divorce same-sex couples. *See In re Marriage of J.B. and H.B.*, 326 S.W.3d 654 (Tex. App. 2010) (dismissing divorce petition for lack of subject matter jurisdiction); *Austin v. Austin*, 75 Va. Cir. 240 (2008) (same). *But see Christiansen v. Christiansen*, 253 P.3d 153 (Wyo. 2011) (holding that court had jurisdiction to divorce same-sex couple). This leaves couples who wish to dissolve their same-sex marriages in limbo: they are considered married in many states (and by the federal government), but not married, and unable to divorce, in their home states. *See* Elisabeth Oppenheimer, *No Exit: The Problem of Same-Sex Divorce*, 90 N.C. L. Rev. 73 (2011).

Problems

1. A law school friend is in a committed relationship with his same-sex partner. Upon graduating, he plans to turn down lucrative job offers in New York and San Francisco and move to Indiana where his partner has a job as a law professor. He has a job offer in Indiana, but at a far lower salary. The couple plans to buy a house together. Indiana law declares that "a marriage between persons of the same gender is void in Indiana even if the marriage is lawful in the place where it is solemnized." Ind. Code §31-11-1-1. What advice would you give your friend?

2. In *Gormley v. Robertson*, 83 P.3d 1042 (Wash. Ct. App. 2004), the court ruled that unmarried same-sex couples, like unmarried male-female couples, may be entitled to court-ordered division of their property when the couple breaks up. Would such a result be banned in a state that adopted a constitutional amendment like that in Michigan, which provides that "the union of one man and one woman in marriage shall be the only agreement recognized as a marriage or similar union for any purpose"?

§4 ENTITY PROPERTY

One traditional view of property is that ownership carries with it the right to control the thing that is owned; if the owner manages the resource well, she will benefit, and if she doesn't, she will suffer accordingly. Self-interest will therefore tend to result in the efficient management of property. *See* Harold Demsetz, *Toward a Theory of Property Rights*, 57 Am. Econ. Rev. 347 (1967). This view has its limits even when someone wholly owns property as an individual, *see* Chapter 2, §3.2, but it is particularly challenged in the increasingly common situation where people own property in the form of a stake in an entity whose size and nature can deprive them of meaningful governance rights. Corporations are the most important example of this, dividing the ownership of shares in the corporation from operational control by managers and boards of directors. Common interest developments similarly place control in the hands of owners associations in which an individual owner may have little voice. Trusts, limited partnerships, limited liability companies, and a range of other entity types likewise divide the ownership of property from control. These forms of entity ownership raise questions of efficient and just management and the public role in regulating private relationships. To understand why, consider the following reading.

Adolf A. Berle & Gardner C. Means, The Modern Corporation and Private Property

1-3, 7-8, 121, 124-125 (1932)

Corporations have ceased to be merely legal devices through which the private business transactions of individuals may be carried on. Though still much used for this purpose, the corporate form has acquired a larger significance. The corporation has, in fact, become both a method of property tenure and a means of organizing economic life. Grown to tremendous proportions, there may be said to have evolved a "corporate system" — as there was once a feudal system — which has attracted to itself a combination of attributes and powers, and has attained a degree of prominence entitling it to be dealt with as a major social institution.

In its new aspect the corporation is a means whereby the wealth of innumerable individuals has been concentrated into huge aggregates and whereby control over this wealth has been surrendered to a unified direction. The power attendant upon such concentration has brought forth princes of industry, whose position in the community is yet to be defined. The surrender of control over their wealth by investors has effectively broken the old property relationships and has raised the problem of defining these relationships anew. The direction of industry by persons other than those who have ventured their wealth has raised the question of the motive force back of such direction and the effective distribution of the returns from business enterprise.

[This new] organization of economic activity rests upon two developments, each of which has made possible an extension of the area under unified control. The factory system, the basis of the industrial revolution, brought an increasingly large number of workers directly under a single management. Then, the modern corporation, equally revolutionary in its effect, placed the wealth of the innumerable individuals under the same central control. By each of these changes the power of those in control was immensely enlarged and the status of those involved, work or property owner, was radically changed. The independent worker who entered the factory became a wage laborer surrendering the direction of his labor to his industrial master. The property owner who invests in a modern corporation so far surrenders his wealth to those in control of the corporation that he has exchanged the position of independent owner for one in which he may become merely recipient of the wages of the capital.

Outwardly the change is simple enough. Men are less likely to own the physical instruments of production. They are more likely to own pieces of paper, loosely known as stocks, bonds, and other securities, which have become mobile through the machinery of the public markets. Beneath this, however, lies a more fundamental shift. Physical control over the instruments of production has been surrendered in ever growing degree to centralized groups who manage property in bulk, supposedly, but by no means necessarily, for the benefit of the security holders. Power over industrial property has been cut off from the beneficial ownership of this property — or, in less technical language, from the legal right to enjoy its fruits. Control of physical assets has passed from the individual owner to those who direct the quasi-public institutions, while the owner retains an interest in their product and increase. We see, in fact, the surrender and regrouping of the incidence of ownership, which formerly bracketed full power of manual disposition with complete right to enjoy the use, the fruits, and the proceeds of physical assets. There has resulted the dissolution of the old atom of ownership into its component parts, control and beneficial ownership.

This dissolution of the atom of property destroys the very foundation on which the economic order of the past three centuries has rested. Private enterprise, which has molded economic life since the close of the middle ages, has been rooted in the institution of private property. Under the feudal system, its predecessor, economic organization grew out of mutual obligations and privileges derived by various individuals from their relation to property which no one of them owned. Private enterprise, on the other hand, has assumed an owner of the instruments of production with complete property rights over those instruments. Whereas the organization of feudal economic life rested upon an elaborate system of binding customs, the organization under the system of private enterprise has rested upon the self-interest of the property owner — a self-interest held in check only by competition and the conditions of supply and demand. Such self-interest has long been regarded as the best guarantee of economic efficiency. It has been assumed that, if the individual is protected in the right both to use his own property as he sees fit and to receive the full fruits of its use, his desire for personal gain, for profits, can be relied upon as an effective incentive to his efficient use of any industrial property he may possess.

In the quasi-public corporation, such an assumption no longer holds. As we have seen, it is no longer the individual himself who uses his wealth. Those in control of that wealth, and therefore in a position to secure industrial efficiency and produce profits, are no longer, as owners, entitled to the bulk of such profits. Those who control the destinies of the typical modern corporation own so insignificant a fraction of the company's stock that the returns from running the corporation profitably accrue to them in only a very minor degree. The stockholders, on the other hand, to whom the profits of the corporation go, cannot be motivated by these profits to a more efficient use of the property, since they have surrendered all disposition of it to those in control of the enterprise. The explosion of the atom of property destroys the basis of the old assumption that the quest for profits will spur the owner of the individual property to its effective use. It consequently challenges the fundamental economic principle of individual initiative in industrial enterprise. It raises for reexamination the question of the motive force back of industry, and the ends for which the modern corporation can be or will be run.

When the owner was also in control of his enterprise he could operate it in his own interest and the philosophy surrounding the institution of private property has assumed that he would do so. This assumption has been carried over to present conditions and it is still expected that enterprise will be operated in the interests of the owners. But have we any justification for assuming that those in control of a modern corporation will also choose to operate it in the interests of the owners? The answer to this question will depend on the degree to which the self-interest of those in control may run parallel to the interest of ownership and, insofar as they differ, on the checks on the use of power which may be established by political, economic, or social conditions.

The recognition that industry has come to be dominated by these economic autocrats must bring with it a realization of the hollowness of the familiar statement that economic enterprise in America is a matter of individual initiative. To the dozen or so men in control, there is room for such initiative. For the tens and even hundreds of thousands of workers and of owners in a single enterprise, individual initiative no longer exists. Their activity is group activity on a scale so large that the individual, except he be in position of control, has dropped into relative insignificance. At the same time the problems of control have become problems in economic government.

Henry N. Butler, The Contractual Theory of the Corporation

11 Geo. Mason U. L. Rev. 99, 101-102, 106, 110, 120-121 (1989)

A major intellectual theme in the study of the modern corporation is the "separation of ownership and control" thesis, which was first popularized by Adolf A. Berle and Gardiner C. Means, in 1932 in their famous book. [T]he Berle and Means thesis has provided the basis for many calls for more stringent legal controls on managerial behavior. This area of corporate policy is called "corporate governance," which refers to the manner in which the relations between the parties to the corporate contract are restrained by government regulation or private ordering.

[In contrast,] agency theory suggests that unity of ownership and control is not a necessary condition of efficient performance of a firm. This perspective stresses the voluntary, contractual nature of the corporation. [T]he contractual theory of the corporation [depends on] the Efficient Capital Markets Hypothesis. The hypothesis states, in most basic terms, that securities prices are efficient in that they accurately reflect all publicly available information about the security.

The basic mechanism of market efficiency is that information about a firm continually alters investor expectations about future returns and hence the prices at which they will sell and buy their securities. This information reaches investors in a wide variety of ways, including voluntary and mandatory disclosures by firms, stories in the media, reports by securities analysts, and disclosure of insider trades. The efficient markets hypothesis is important because it means that corporate contracts that harm investor interests will be recognized and punished by price reductions in the market. Incorporation in a state with corporation law that facilitates managerial abuse of shareholders, for example, will result in lower share prices than would be found if the same firm were incorporated in a state with a different corporation law.

From a legal perspective, where the concern is often with fairness rather than efficiency, the efficient capital markets hypothesis means that securities markets are fair in the sense that a corporate shareholder gets what he is paying for in both the terms of the contract and the substantive nature of the product, including the quality of management. The contractual theory of the corporation suggests that share prices will not only be fair, but also that corporate managers will have incentives to maximize share value.

[T]he realities of the corporate agency relationship dictate that the corporation's managers select the contractual terms that are then offered to potential investors. In order to raise capital at the lowest possible price, managers must offer contract terms — including evidence of the existence of intra-firm incentive structures — that convince investors that agency costs will be minimized. The managers of firms select the mix of legal and market governance mechanisms that is optimal given the particular circumstances of the firm. The "nexus of contracts" specifies the extent of reliance upon differing mechanisms. Managers substitute among the various governance mechanisms until the marginal net productivity of each mechanism is equal. The corporate governance mechanisms, when combined in the manner most appropriate for the particular circumstances of each firm, resolve most of the conflicts between shareholders and managers. Freedom of contract allows the parties to structure their relations in a manner that ameliorates most of the problems inherent in the large corporation.

[T]he contractual theory of the corporation offers a new perspective on the corporation and the role of corporation law. The corporation is in no sense a ward of the state; it is rather, the product of contracts among the owners and others. Once this point is fully recognized by the state legislators and legal commentators, the corporate form may finally be free of unnecessary and intrusive legal chains.

Notes and Questions

1. **The increasing importance of entity ownership.** Berle and Means were writing during the Great Depression at a time when widespread public ownership of companies was relatively novel. Today it represents a significant fraction of property that people in the U.S. own. In 2011, the total U.S. household net worth — assets minus liabilities — was about $40.2 trillion. About 25 percent of this represented equity in people's homes. At the same time, however, Americans held 15 percent of their net assets in stocks and mutual funds and another 31 percent in various forms of retirement accounts. This represents a fundamental shift even over the last generation. In 1984, over 40 percent of aggregate U.S. assets were in home equity, while only 7 percent of American's wealth was held in stocks and mutual funds, and a mere 2 percent was held in retirement accounts. Alfred Gottschalck et al., *Household Wealth in the U.S.: 2000 to 2011* (Census Bureau, March 2013), *available at www.census.gov/people/wealth/files/Wealth%20Highlights%202011.pdf.* Assets in stocks and similar investments are

very unevenly held, but more than half of Americans own some stock. *See* Catherine Rampell, *Stock Markets Rise, but Half of Americans Don't Benefit*, N.Y. Times, May 8, 2013.

2. **Splitting the atom of ownership and control.** What does it mean to "own" a portion of a corporation? Typically, shares may be sold, used as collateral for debt, devised, and passed by intestacy. But there may be thousands or even millions of other shareholders, particularly for large, public companies. Berle and Means identified a central problem with the basic structure of entity ownership that flows from this broad diffusion of ownership, which we now call **agency costs**. Berle and Means argued that the separation of ownership from control means that corporate managers and directors (the agents) are likely to have a different agenda than shareholders (the principals).

As Berle and Means noted, how serious this divergence between principal and agent is "will depend on the degree to which the self-interest of those in control may run parallel to the interest of ownership." What might lead managers to have different interests than shareholders?

There are a number of legal mechanisms designed to manage this principal-agent problem. For example, corporate law generally recognizes that officers and directors have **fiduciary duties** to act in the best interests of shareholders. *See* Hillary A. Sale, *Delaware's Good Faith*, 89 Cornell L. Rev. 456 (2004) (discussing duties of due care, loyalty, and good faith). While it can be difficult for shareholders to enforce these duties, given the deference that courts give to managerial decisions, *see* note 4, below, the obligation nonetheless serves as a norm for officers and directors.

Moreover, corporations—and business entities more generally—are subject to oversight federal and state regulation, some of which polices the relationship between management and ownership. The Securities and Exchange Commission, for example, regulates disclosure requirements for public companies and has used this authority to try to improve shareholder governance. *See, e.g.*, Securities and Exchange Commission, Final Rule, *Facilitating Shareholder Director Nominations* (Nov. 15, 2010) (codified in various parts of 17 C.F.R. pts. 200, 232, 240 and 249) (requiring public companies to include nominees of significant, long-term shareholders in the materials they provide to shareholders for voting).

However, much of corporate law is permissive, giving business entities latitude to structure investor governance rights. This has given rise to **shareholder activism**, particularly on the part of large institutional investors such as pension funds, with a focus on leveraging what has traditionally been passive investment into more meaningful oversight and even direct election of corporate board members. John H. Biggs, *Shareholder Democracy: The Roots of Activism and the Selection of Directors*, 39 Loy. U. Chi. L.J. 493 (2008).

If these mechanisms fail, what other recourse do shareholders have?

3. **Property versus contract in corporate governance.** As Professor Butler notes, the **nexus of contracts** theory of corporate governance came to dominate corporate law theory in the 1970s. The nexus of contracts theory conceives of the corporation as

an efficient conduit through which parties make and organize vast numbers of private agreements. The implication of this view is that capital markets will discipline corporate managers, leaving little justification for further legal ordering to mediate the relationship between shareholders and managers. What might undermine the ability of shareholders to price the structure of corporate management accurately? When might it be better to regulate governance rather than rely on price mechanisms, which depend on shareholders who are dissatisfied with management being able to sell their shares?

Today, scholars are revisiting the contract-based theory of the corporation, arguing that property-based perspectives are crucial. *See* John Armour & Michael J. Whincop, *The Proprietary Foundations of Corporate Law*, 27 Oxford J. Legal Stud. 429 (2007); Henry Hansmann & Reinier Kraakman, *The Essential Role of Organizational Law*, 110 Yale L.J. 387 (2000). What is at stake in the distinction? First, property rights are generally good not simply against parties and intended beneficiaries to an agreement, but against many unknown parties. For example, personal creditors of the shareholders, the directors, and the managers, may not generally reach corporate assets, and owners and creditors of the corporation have their rights prioritized against each other despite the absence of agreements between them. Second, while contract law begins from a presumption of infinite contractual forms, property law tends to limit the forms in which property may be held (the rule against creation of new estates or *numerus clausus* principle). *See* Chapter 10, §5.1. Because property rights are good against the public generally, property forms are limited to ensure that they serve public interests and provide notice to those who may be affected by them. A property-based theory therefore places more focus on the organizational form of the corporate entity and the balance of rights between owners and third parties affected by the activities of the corporation or its agents.

4. The limits of owner control. Owners who wish to enforce the fiduciary obligations of corporate management can file a shareholder derivative suit on behalf of the corporation against the corporation's directors or officers. Such suits, however, face a number of procedural hurdles, and liability is judged by the extremely deferential business judgment rule. In *Salsitz v. Nasser*, 208 F.R.D. 589 (E.D. Mich. 2002), for example, a shareholder in the Ford Motor Company alleged that board members had breached their fiduciary duty of care for three major management decisions. The court rejected these claims:

> "A basic premise of corporate governance under Delaware law is that the directors, rather than the shareholders, manage the business and affairs of the corporation." *McCall v. Scott*, 239 F.3d 808, 816 (6th Cir. 2001) (citing *Aronson v. Lewis*, 473 A.2d 805, 811 (Del. 1984)). Shareholders, thus, are permitted to challenge the propriety of decisions made by directors under their authority, only by overcoming "the powerful presumptions of the business judgment rule." *Id.*
>
> [The business judgment rule] provides that "whether a judge or jury considering [a business decision] after the fact, believes a decision substantively wrong, or degrees of wrong extending through 'stupid' to 'egregious' or 'irrational,' provides no ground for

> director liability, so long as the court determines that the process employed was either rational or employed in a good faith effort to advance corporate interests." *In re Caremark Internat'l Inc. Derivative Litigation*, 698 A.2d 959, 967 (Del. Ch. 1996). Thus, a court may not consider "the content of the board decision that leads to corporate loss, apart from consideration of the good faith or rationality of the process employed." *Id.* at 591.

Id. Accepting the allegations of the complaint as true, the court then reviewed the three alleged fiduciary breaches. The first involved something called the "TFI module":

> The TFI module is a computerized ignition system that was installed by Ford in a number of vehicle models directly onto the engine block. It is alleged that the TFI has a propensity to fail and thereby shut down the engine if overheated. Engineers began to raise warnings about TFI module overheating and malfunctioning as early as 1982. In May 1982, Ford engineers compiled a list of components that could cause a "quits on road" condition — a failure that causes the vehicle to shut down while being driven. While the document questioned whether a recall was necessary, the Company took no corrective action; it also continued to tell [the National Highway Traffic Safety Administration (NHTSA)] there was no "common pattern or cause" behind the complaints about stalling. A warranty analysis conducted in January 1984 demonstrated that the TFI — which was supposed to last for the lifetime of the vehicle — would fail at a rate of 56% at five years or 50,000 miles.
>
> Ford's Policy and Strategy Committee, which included some of the Defendants, repeatedly discussed the risks and problems inherent in the TFI mechanism. On March 12, 1985 the committee discussed problems with the TFI module and concluded in an internal document that "'stall' rates on 1985 model Tempos-Topazes were unchanged from the year earlier." The committee claimed that stalling problem was not a safety issue. The committee would have been required to report safety issues to NHTSA. NHTSA has recently obtained information regarding the TFI and has found that Ford improperly withheld this information, because it was, in fact, safety related.
>
> [A report] delivered to Ford's president on or about November 5, 1986, indicated that the total cost of correcting the TFI problems would have cost Ford approximately only $200 million more than the expected cost for one year of warranty related repairs. Ford was also aware that about 10% of TFI modules would have stalling problems in 1986. On November 13, 1986, Ford's President gave the Board a status report on the ongoing TFI problem. The Board at this time concluded that a recall was "not feasible" because the Company did not have sufficient replacement parts. The TFI issue was discussed at Board meetings held in December 1987, January 1989, and October 1991. In 1995, Ford finally stopped attaching the TFI module to the distributor.
>
> Ford settled four lawsuits involving serious injuries and deaths arising out of the TFI defect. On August 30, 2000, Judge Ballachey, a California state judge presiding over litigation arising out of the TFI defect accused Ford of engaging in an enormous cover-up by concealing the TFI design defect from regulators and consumers. That case was settled in 2001. Settlement was reported as having the potential of costing Ford as much as $2.7 billion. Judge Ballachey also blamed Ford for a corporate culture in which executives understood that their careers would be ruined if they reported design defects. The judge stated that the testimony of a top Ford engineer's reluctance to convey bad news about the ignition module reminded him of "The Emperor's New Clothes." Other actions regarding the TFI module are pending in five other states.

Id. at 593-594. The second disagreement involved allegations about Bridgestone/Firestone tires:

> In 1990, the Ford Explorer was introduced to replace the Bronco II, which had attracted unfavorable publicity after the vehicle was widely linked to rollovers. The reported problems with Bronco II should have alerted Ford to take extra precautions with the Explorer. Ford intentionally designed the Explorer with a high center of gravity to take advantage of the Bronco II's rugged SUV image. A 1990 internal Ford memorandum observed that "[t]he relative high engine position of the Explorer, unchanged from the Bronco II, prevents further significant improvement in stability."
>
> At least two tire manufacturers, Michelin and Firestone, competed to supply tires for the new Explorer. Michelin has at all times held a world-wide reputation for high safety standards; Firestone, on the other hand, has had a long history of quality and manufacturing problems, including tread separation problems that in 1978 resulted in a forced recall of 13 million Firestone "500" tires. As a result of the 1978 tire problems, which were linked to 41 deaths, Firestone faced more than 250 personal injury lawsuits, a host of class action suits, and a virtual rebellion by customers. Firestone was crippled financially by the 1978 recall and only managed to limp through the 1980's until 1988, when it was acquired by Bridgestone, a Japanese corporation. Firestone was founded by the great-grandfather of Defendant William Clay Ford, Jr., and the Ford Company has maintained a close relationship with Firestone since 1906. In 1990 Ford chose Firestone to supply the tires for its new Explorer. Ford's Board deferred all tire safety oversight and monitoring to Firestone. Ford kept no safety records on the Firestone tires installed on Explorers.
>
> In part to compensate for the SUV's high center of gravity, Ford recommended that Explorer owners under-inflate their tires to ensure a smooth ride. Ford was aware that under-inflation would result in excessive pressure on the tire belts and also contribute to heat building up in tires, both factors that could increase the occurrence of tread separation. As early as 1992, motorists in Saudi Arabia and Venezuela complained that they were experiencing blowouts while driving Ford vehicles equipped with Firestone tires. In a widely reported accident on September 5, 1996, TV reporter Stephen Gauvain was thrown from his Explorer and killed when the tread suddenly separated from one of his original-issue Firestone tires. In October 1998, Ford itself noted problems of tread separation on Firestone tires mounted on the Explorer and other light truck models in Venezuela and sent examples of the failed tires to Firestone for analysis.
>
> It was not until August 1999, that Ford quietly began replacing Firestone tires with tread separation problems on Explorers previously sold in Saudi Arabia. Ford, however, did not publicly disclose its safety concerns with the tires, and instead concealed the true purpose behind the offer to replace tires, terming it a "customer notification enhancement action." Ford also failed to inform NHTSA of its actions in Saudi Arabia. This failure to report was in response to, inter alia, the specific request of Firestone, which was concerned that reporting the Saudi recall would prompt costly regulatory scrutiny in the United States. More than a year before initiating any public education and/or recall procedures in the United States, Ford had come under fire for beginning a Firestone tire recall in 16 foreign countries. On August 9, 2000, Firestone announced a region by region recall of more than 6.5 million tires, the majority of which had been installed by Ford on its Explorer and other light truck models. As a result of the tire/rollover debacle, Ford has been named in a number of class action lawsuits.

Id. at 595-597. Finally, a third set of allegations involved the company's materials reserves.

> On January 2002, Ford disclosed that it was required to take a $1 billion write-off on the value of its stockpile of precious metals, primarily palladium. Ford left the job of acquiring palladium to the same purchasing-department employees who normally buy its steel and copper. These purchasing department personnel failed to coordinate with Ford's treasury department personnel and thus did not take the sort of basic precautions a reasonably sophisticated buyer routinely would use to hedge the inherent financial risk involved in high dollar purchases in clearly recognized potentially volatile markets. Likewise the purchasing department failed to stay in reasonable contact with Ford's engineering department, and thus was unaware of Ford's own engineering innovations which were continuing to shrink the Company's need for the metal at the same time that the Company was increasing its purchases. Consequently, not only does Ford now find itself holding a huge over-supply of palladium, but, because the prices of the metal have recently fallen drastically and Ford failed to ensure its positions in the metal were properly hedged, the Company must now take the $1 billion dollar write-off.

Id. at 599. The court rejected these claims under the business judgment rule, finding that the board had either rationally considered each decision in good faith or, in the case of the palladium write-off, was unaware of the problem.

Would private shareholder interests and public interests in well-functioning corporations be better served by a more stringent standard of review? Or would the potential for more retrospective scrutiny prevent corporate directors from acting creatively and effectively to enhance corporate productivity?

5. Who owns the corporation? It is a traditional assumption of corporate law that managers are obligated to act on behalf of shareholders as the owners of the entity. But what obligations does management have to other stakeholders in the entity, such as employees, bondholders, or even the community in which the company does business?

Professor Kent Greenfield has argued that employees should be represented on the board of directors, and that directors' fiduciary duties should extend to employees, not just shareholders. Kent Greenfield, *The Place of Workers in Corporate Law*, 39 B.C. L. Rev. 283 (1998). Professor Greenfield rejects the argument that the nature of corporate ownership dictates the obligations of management:

> The property-based justification for shareholder dominance begs the question, of course. Asking whether directors should owe fiduciary duties to workers or whether workers should have a say in electing directors is, in one sense, simply asking again whether shareholders should "own" the firm. One cannot answer this question simply by saying that the shareholders own the firm. At heart, the property-based conception attempts to answer the question of why shareholders are dominant in corporate law simply by reference to the fact that they are dominant in corporate law.

Id. at 290-291. What consequences would an expanded view of corporate ownership hold? What are the best arguments in favor and against the traditional view of the obligations of management to shareholders as owners?

6. Property in other common entity forms. The basic corporate form has a number of variations based on state law and federal tax treatment, but it is only one of an array of common types of entity ownership. Like the menagerie of common law estates, each form carries with it certain default characteristics and some latitude for the participants to vary those defaults. There are significant technical regulatory, governance, and tax implications to the selection of entity form for ownership, but property lawyers must have at least a basic familiarity with the range of options.

a. Partnerships. The partnership is a long-standing form of collective ownership. Partnerships may be either general partnerships or limited partnerships. Although a general partnership is a separate legal entity, it does not divide ownership from control. Today, all states except Louisiana govern partnerships either through the revised *Uniform Partnership Act (1997)* (RUPA) (adopted by about 40 states), or through the original *Uniform Partnership Act (1914).* A partnership is formed whenever there is "association of two or more persons to carry on as co-owners a business for profit," regardless of whether the parties recognize or intend that their actions form a partnership. RUPA §202(a). Although agreement is necessary, it need not be in writing. Rather, a partnership is created whenever individuals "place their money, assets, labor, or skill in commerce with the understanding that profits will be shared between them." *Id. Compare Swecker v. Swecker*, 360 S.W.3d 422, 426 (Tenn. App. 2011) (finding that son was entitled to a share of dairy business on his father's death as a partner with him in the business) *with Love v. Mail on Sunday*, 489 F. Supp. 2d 1100 (C.D. Cal. 2007), *aff'd Love v. Associate Newspapers, Inc.*, 611 F.3d 601 (9th Cir. 2010) (holding that Brian Wilson and Mike Love of the Beach Boys did not form a legal partnership by writing songs together without any evidence that they agreed to be co-owners of a business).

Absent other agreements, each partner has an equal right to possess the partnership property for partnership purposes and to share in the profits of the partnership. Because ownership is limited to the purposes of the partnership, partners do not have an individual interest in the partnership (as opposed to its profits or distributions of the property) that may be sold to or inherited by others or reached by personal creditors of the partners. Partners in a general partnership, however, are personally liable for all obligations of the partnership. RUPA §306.

Limited partnerships are similar to the corporate form in dividing ownership and control and affecting rights of third parties. Limited partners contribute capital in exchange for a share of profits but do not receive rights to manage or control partnership assets. In the increasingly popular limited liability partnership, partners are not personally liable for partnership debts; a creditor or tort victim may only reach partnership assets and the asset of the partner personally responsible for the debt. RUPA §306(c).

b. Limited liability companies. Limited liability companies, or LLCs, mirror many of the characteristics of limited partnerships, but allow managing members to retain limited liability while not giving up operational control.

c. Trusts. Trusts, which can also divide ownership from control through the separation of legal and beneficial ownership, are used not only for estate planning but also for business purposes as well. For example, "real estate investment trusts," or REITs, can be publicly traded trusts that have tax advantages for holding real estate if they meet requirements set by the Internal Revenue Service. Similarly, mortgage securities are often held in a trust form for investors.

Trusts are used as well to support a wide variety of nonprofit organizations and are a common way that ownership is structured for many colleges, hospitals, churches, arts organizations, and other nonprofits. Donors set up charitable trusts to generate income for charities, specifying the use to which the funds can be put in the trust documents, and can receive tax benefits in return. *See* Chapter 10, §4.3. Some of the largest philanthropies in the world are charitable trusts, including the Bill and Melinda Gates Charitable Trust, which in 2012 had assets of more than $36 billion. State attorneys general are responsible for overseeing charitable trusts, but have significant resource constraints, which can create challenges in terms of accountability. *See* Geoffrey A. Manne, *Agency Costs and the Oversight of Charitable Organizations*, 1999 Wis. L. Rev. 227, 235.

d. Condominiums, cooperatives, and other common interest developments. This increasingly common form of homeownership also significantly divides ownership from control. Such common interest developments typically have property owners associations governed by boards of directors charged with managing and enforcing the covenants governing the development. Property owners associations are often incorporated as not-for-profit corporations. Their boards of directors are usually comprised of volunteer unit owners elected by the owners, although some may be appointed by the developer during the active marketing stage of the development. Although unit owners may find it easier to influence decisions of the board of a property owners association than shareholders of corporations do, board decisions may have a much greater impact on owners' lives, perhaps determining, for example, what color they can paint their houses or whether they can have pets. Some jurisdictions apply the business judgment rule to property owner actions seeking relief from board decisions. *See* Chapter 8, §4.2.

7. Public versus private role in corporate governance. Berle and Means thought of the corporation as a quasi-public institution to be regulated. Many corporate theorists of 1980s and today take as an implication of the nexus-of-contracts perspective that willing parties who invest in corporate ownership should be given substantial freedom of contract. Does this view account for the impact of limited liability on nonconsensual creditors? The twenty-first century has seen a resurgence of insistence on the public nature of the corporation following the Enron scandal of 2001 and the financial crisis of 2008. *See, e.g.*, Simon Johnston & James Kwak, *13 Bankers: The Wall Street Takeover and the Next Financial Meltdown* (2011) (arguing that size and influence of the financial industry permits it to control both the global economy and political efforts to regulate it). What do you think is the appropriate balance between private and public control of corporations? Does taking a contract-based versus a property-based view of the corporation affect your analysis?

CHAPTER 10

Present Estates and Future Interests

§1 DIVISION OF OWNERSHIP OVER TIME

One way owners may share ownership is by dividing ownership rights *over time*, separating the present right to possess the property from the **future interest**, the right to take possession in the future under specified circumstances.

The grantor specifies the circumstances under which the property will shift in the future from the present interest holder to the future interest holder. For example, the grantor may convey property to *A* so long as she is alive and then provide that at *A*'s death, the property will transfer to *B*. The grantor in this case is not attempting to control directly what *A* does with the property; however, by deciding who will own the property at *A*'s death, the grantor often hopes to indirectly control what is done with the property—perhaps by keeping the property in the family and making sure it is available for the grandchildren to inherit. Other times, the grantor seeks to directly control use of the property; for example, the grantor may convey property to *A* so long as the property is used for residential purposes, but if it is ever used for nonresidential purposes, ownership will revert to the grantor. In this case, the potential loss of title deters and sanctions the present owner for violating the conditions of the grant.

> **Terms:**
> Technically, **heirs** are those entitled by law to inherit the property if the owner dies **intestate** (without a will), while **devisees** are those entitled to real property under a will. Intestate heirs are typically one's spouse (and any children not from that marriage); if there is no spouse, then one's children; if no spouse or children, then one's parents; if no parents, then one's siblings; if no siblings, then certain other relatives. If no relatives qualify as heirs, the property will **escheat** (es-CHEET) to the state.

Present and future interests may be created by sale, lease, will, or trust. A seller may create a future interest in a deed. A landlord necessarily creates a future interest either orally or in a written lease because the property will revert to the landlord when the lease term expires. A **testator** or **testatrix** (one who dies leaving a valid will) can create a future interest by devising or bequeathing property in a will. A grantor may also create a future interest when establishing a **trust** (a legal arrangement in which one person or entity holds title to property for the benefit of another).

Future interests may be certain to come into possession or may be **contingent** on events that may or may not happen. If *O* leases property to *A* for one year, for example, the property will automatically revert after one year (which is to say, the lease will end). If, however, *O* conveys property to *A* so long as it is used for residential purposes, the property will revert only if the property is used for nonresidential purposes, which may never happen.

Future interests exist the moment they are created even though the holder of the interest has no right to possess the property until the triggering event occurs. Suppose *O* conveys property to *A* so long as it is used for residential purposes; if the property is ever used for nonresidential purposes, the property goes automatically to *B*. The future interest in *B* comes into existence at the moment of the original conveyance to *A*; we say that *B* owns a future interest in the property, although *B* has no present right to occupy or use the property. *B* will have a right to possess, use, and control the property only if and when the condition is violated; the future interest will not become **possessory** unless and until the condition occurs.

By delegating to property owners the power to create future interests, the legal system enables people to exercise some degree of control over who owns the property in the future and what the future owner is entitled to do with it. This is an awesome power. The law of future interests raises a host of complicated policy questions. The two most pressing are the problem of dead hand control and the problem of social hierarchy.

The dead hand. Owners may seek to control who owns property long after they die, giving rise to a problem often described as "dead hand control." Allowing grantors or testators to do this may promote their interests and even enhance alienability; owners may be more willing to part with their property if they can control who owns it or how it is used in the future. However, conditions limit what owners may do with their property, thus interfering with freedom of future owners to control the property. This may undermine the autonomy of future owners and the efficient use and transfer of property. Affected persons may be able to remove archaic restrictions by contracting with the beneficiaries of the restraints to give up their rights. However, transaction costs may block such deals, especially if the persons with the right to enforce the restraint are not yet born or ascertained. Rigid enforcement of restrictions imposed long ago by grantors who could not anticipate current conditions can prevent property from being devoted to its best uses as social circumstances and needs change. The struggle for control between prior owners and current owners or between current owners and future owners requires a legal structure that balances their relative interests.

Hierarchy. A second problem associated with future interests is the possibility that imposing restraints on alienation and use will have the effect of concentrating ownership in the hands of certain groups and excluding others. Restricting ownership to one's descendants, for example, may be a useful way of securing expectations. If common, however, it would also concentrate ownership in the families of those who already own property. Such restrictions may also be even more pernicious; if property ownership could be lawfully conditioned on the property's not being occupied by a person of a particular race, for example, future interests could be used to perpetuate racial hierarchies.

To some extent, the marketplace is designed to decentralize power over social resources, dispersing them among citizens rather than concentrating them in the hands of government officials or an aristocracy. To maintain this decentralization of power, however, rules of law are necessary to prevent private owners from re-concentrating ownership by creating new monopolies or centers of power. For example, in *People ex rel. Moloney v. Pullman's Palace Car Co.*, 51 N.E. 664 (Ill. 1898), the Illinois Supreme Court required the corporate owner of a company town inhabited by 12,000 people to sell off most of the property, *id.* at 674:

> [T]he existence of a town or city where the streets, alleys, school houses, business houses, sewerage system, hotels, churches, theaters, water-works, market places, dwellings and tenements are the exclusive property of a corporation is opposed to good public policy and incompatible with the theory and spirit of our institutions. It is clearly the theory of our law, streets, alleys and public ways, and public school buildings, should be committed to the control of the proper public authorities, and that real estate should be kept as fully as possible in the channels of trade and commerce, and good public policy demands that the number of persons who should engage in the business of selling such articles as are necessary to the support, maintenance and comfort of the people of any community should not be restricted by the will of any person, natural or artificial, but should be left to be determined by the healthy, wholesome and natural operations of the rules of trade and business, free from all that which tends to stifle competition and foster monopolies.

Regulation of future interests may similarly help to maintain the dispersal of access to property so that a decentralized market system can function properly.

§2 HISTORICAL BACKGROUND: DEATH AND TAXES

Future interest law emerged from centuries of attempts to avoid the only two things said to be certain, death and taxes. Since the Middle Ages, owners have sought to control ownership and use of their property after death and, even more important, avoid estate taxes and other payments to third parties. The law governing future interests was shaped as each generation thwarted past efforts to control property after death and governments thwarted efforts to avoid estate taxes and controls over landownership. After the historical purposes of the rules ended, the rules themselves often continued, in part because of inertia, in part because they served other policy goals, and in part because of the interests of lawyers and other estate professionals in maintaining the value of their expertise. Today the law of future interests is being revised yet again, as states change

> **CONTEXT**
>
> The Norman Conquest left deep marks on legal language. Property, contract, tort, assault, battery, mortgage, covenant, court, justice, and indeed most legal terms owe their origins to French, which was for centuries the language of statutes and pleadings in England. 1 Frederick Pollock & Frederic Maitland, *History of the English Law* 80-81 (1898).

their laws to attract tax-evading dynasty trusts. The resulting rules are both a revealing historical artifact and a potentially maddening trap for the unwary.

The estates system originated with the 1066 Norman Conquest of England led by William the Conqueror. To maintain military control of the conquered country, William divided its land in fee or feudum among his supporters. In return, they pledged him loyalty and certain duties, generally the provision of a number of knights for a portion of the year. One way tenants obtained knights was by allocating land to subtenants, who pledged the tenant-in-chief loyalty and knight service in return. This process of **subinfeudation** continued down the ladder to the tenant in demesne, the one who actually occupied and worked the land. Although each tenant owed loyalty and service to the superior landowner, these tenements were considered **freehold** estates. Even below these tenants were villeins, peasants who occupied and worked the land, but had unfree tenure. The distinction between free and unfree tenure was central since those possessed of free tenements had the right to bring lawsuits, called real actions, in the central royal courts where the common law developed. Until the sixteenth century, however, the villeins holding unfree tenure were relegated to manorial courts governed by local custom and the lord's whim.

Land possession in this system embedded one in a set of relationships and obligations. "Estate," the word still used today to describe one's interest in land, can be traced to the Latin root meaning "status." Tenants owed their lords two different kinds of obligations: **services** (the periodic obligations promised by the tenant-grantee to the lord-grantor) and **incidents** (infrequent liabilities, including escheat and inheritance taxes).

Reflecting the idiosyncrasy of services owed for tenancies in land, Castle Conway, in Wales, was held at a rent of six shillings and eight pence, and "a dish of fish to the Lord of Hertford as often as he passed through town." Blount, Fragmentata Antiquitatis, at 322. Photograph by Albertran, Creative Commons License.

When the feudal system began, most services were either knight service or other military service to the crown. Land was also granted to religious persons or institutions in return for religious services, or purely economic, such as the exchange of goods or labor. But services were often more idiosyncratic, designed to symbolize the relationship between the lord and his vassal. For example, one estate was held upon the service of holding the towel for the king when he washed his hands on the day of his coronation; another estate, notoriously, was held on the service of performing each Christmas day for the King's amusement, "altogether and at once, a leap, a puff, and a fart." Thomas Blount, *Fragmentata Antiquitatis: Ancient Tenures of Land* 79 (Josiah Beckwith & H.M. Beckwith eds. 1815). Within a few centuries, however, most services were commuted to monetary payments. Obligations to provide knight service became obligations to provide scutage, essentially a form of taxation controlled by the Parliament, and obligations to provide most other services were relieved by the payment of quit-rents, moneys enabling the tenant to "quit" other service. Although feudal services were commuted to money payments, the payments did not keep pace with inflation and their importance quickly declined.

Feudal incidents, in contrast, involved possession of the land and its profits — benefits that did keep pace with inflation. Incidents initially included the obligation to pay a portion of the profits from the land in unspecified times of need; the right of the lord to appoint a new tenant at the death of the first; to act as guardian of the land (and reap its profits) if the tenant's heir was a minor when the tenant died; and to arrange the marriages of his minor children and perhaps even his widow. Efforts by noble landholders to limit incidents generated the foundational documents of English constitutional law. In 1100, the *Charter of Liberties* provided that a tenant's heir could automatically inherit his land upon the payment of relief — essentially estate taxes — and that the tenant's widow could not be forced to remarry. The *Magna Charta* of 1215, the Great Charter of Liberties, emerged from a rebellion by the barons largely in protest against feudal incidents. Two-thirds of its provisions dealt with them, limiting when tenants could be obliged to pay incidents,[1] fixing the amount of relief required before land could be inherited, and regulating the behavior of guardians appointed as wards of the estates of underage heirs. Important continuing incidents also included **escheat**, the right of the lord to regain the land if his tenant died without an heir or committed a felony, and **forfeiture**, the right of the king to retake the land if the tenant committed treason.

Royal reaction to attempts to avoid incidents ultimately led to the creation of the **fee simple**, land held without homage to any lord. The initial tenurial relationship was personal; because service from that particular landholder was key to the relationship between a vassal and his lord, it was not possible to simply buy and sell land. One could only subinfeudate, remaining a vassal to the lords above in the feudal ladder, and becoming a lord to one's own tenants in turn.

Because incidents reflected the value of the land to the person owing the incidents, however, a tenant could reduce the incidents owed to his lord by subinfeudating for a profit of little value. If *O* had a tenant *A*, and *A* subinfeudated to his son *B* in return for a pound of pepper a year, then *A*'s incidents to *O* reflected the value of that pepper. To avoid such evasion, Parliament enacted the statute *Quia Emptores* in 1290, prohibiting further subinfeudation and requiring all future transfers of interests in land to take place by substitution of one owner for another — in effect a sale of all one's interests and obligations. *Quia Emptores* created a deep paradox. Although intended to protect

1. After the *Magna Charta*, payments could only be required when ransoming the lord from captors or upon the knighting of the lord's eldest son or the marriage of his eldest daughter.

feudalism, it did so by enshrining at the core of the common law of property the key principle of promoting the alienability of property.

Efforts to avoid incidents and determine how property would descend on death created a further dance between landowners and government. Until 1540, land could not be devised by will, but only inherited by one's legal heirs. Heirs are those who inherit by operation by law; today this generally means division among one's closest relatives. For much of English history, however, this generally meant inheritance only by one's eldest living son, called **primogeniture**. Daughters would receive land only if no sons survived the landowner, and younger sons and widows could never inherit. *Quia Emptores*, however, meant that the heir could alienate the land, ending the family's connection to the land and the status it conferred. In addition, the doctrine of coverture meant that a woman's property legally became her husband's; unless specially conditioned, that could mean it would descend to her husband's heirs rather than her own or those of her family. To evade these results and payment of relief on death, landholders sought to transfer their land during their lifetimes and place conditions on who would have it after their deaths. These efforts, and the responses by heirs and Parliament, created a number of estates and rules with some relevance today. Four of these, **the Rule in Shelley's Case**, **the doctrine of worthier title**, **the trust**, and **the fee tail**, are discussed here.

The Rule in Shelley's Case. One attempt to avoid payment of relief was to create a life estate — a property interest that lasts only for the life of the grantee — in one individual with a future interest in the grantee's heirs. Because *A*'s heirs acquired the interest during *O*'s lifetime by conveyance, rather than by inheritance on *A*'s death, they did not have to pay relief. If the owner of the life estate was a woman, moreover, the conveyance could help ensure that the land went to her children, rather than what would otherwise have been a required transfer to her husband and his children by any later wife. The courts responded with what became known as the **Rule in Shelley's Case**, which treated the interest in *A*'s heir as an interest in *A*. In other words,

O to *A* for life, and then to *A*'s heirs
would be read as
O to *A*.

Although the payment of relief as such ended in England in the seventeenth century, the Rule in Shelley's Case continued in England until 1925, and was adopted in the United States as well. The Rule has now been abolished in almost all states, but may still exist in Arkansas, Colorado, Delaware, and in some form in Indiana. T.P. Gallanis, *The Future of Future Interests*, 60 Wash. & Lee L. Rev. 513, 541-542 (2003); *Restatement (Third) of Property: Wills & Donative Transfers* §16.2 (2011); *see also* John V. Orth, *The Mystery of the Rule in Shelley's Case*, 7 Green Bag 2d 45 (2003).

The doctrine of worthier title. The **doctrine of worthier title** is similar to the Rule in Shelley's case, but applies to grants in which a life estate is followed by an interest in the *grantor's*, rather than the grantee's, heirs. The interest in the grantor's heirs would be read as an interest in the grantor, so that his heirs would have to inherit rather than take without paying relief, like this:

> *O* to *A* for life, then to *O*'s heirs
> becomes
> *O* to *A* for life, then to *O*.

Like the Rule in Shelley's Case, most states have abolished the doctrine of worthier title, but it may remain viable in Mississippi, New Jersey, and Virginia, and perhaps a few other states. Gallanis, *supra*, at 546-548; *Restatement (Third) of Property: Wills & Donative Transfers* §16.3 (2011). Even in states that recognize the rule, it has become simply a rule of construction that can be defeated by clear intent of the grantor.

Although largely abolished, the rules do have some current policy justification. No one has heirs until they die. It is therefore impossible to contract regarding future ownership of the property until the death of the life estate holder, because the owners of that interest won't be identified until then. This inability to contract may interfere with the alienability of the property.

The trust. Landowners also sought to evade descent rules by granting property to one individual for the "use" of another. For example, *O* might grant property to *A* for the use of *B*. *A* would have the legal estate, but *B* would have the right to use and profit from the land. *O* might even grant land to *A* for the use of *O*. Although estates in land could not be left by will, uses could, so a use might be willed to one's younger sons, widow, or daughters. Uses could also be used to evade feudal incidents. Felony or treason by the user would not result in escheat or forfeiture. If the legal estate was vested in several people and one died, moreover, the estate would be consolidated in the survivors without inheritance, thus avoiding both relief and the possibility of escheat because of failure of heirs. Finally, because transferring uses did not require the same public formalities as transferring estates, the use could be employed to hide one's conveyances from the public. In a development reminiscent of modern trust law, the legal estates were often vested in attorneys, who received suitable compensation, creating a professional class devoted to continuing the use.

In 1536, Parliament sought to end exploitation of the use with the *Statute of Uses*, which provided that the legal estate would vest entirely in the user. Grants of uses, therefore, would have the same effect as grants of land and be subject to the same inheritance laws. Reaction against the statute was so negative that Parliament enacted the *Statute of Wills* in 1540, which for the first time allowed landowners to devise their property by will. Thereafter, owners had an easier way to avoid both primogeniture and escheat in the absence of heirs.

Hasty drafting of the Statute of Uses also created a number of loopholes, which courts were often willing to exploit. In particular, a grant of a use "in trust" for a third party, or to accomplish a particular purpose, was not affected by the statute. By 1700, the trust had filled the place the use had occupied. Today modern trusts involve a grantor, called the **settlor** or **trustor**, conveying property to some person or entity (the

trustee) for the benefit of another person or purpose or entity, called the **beneficiary**.[2] A trust may be in favor of one's family and friends, commercial, or for charitable purposes. For example:

> *O* to *A*, in trust for *B* until she reaches the age of majority, then to *B*.
> *O* in trust to *A Foundation*, to provide health care to the poor.

In both cases, *A* has *legal title*, but is bound by equitable rules to use the estate for the trust beneficiary or the purposes of the trust. As in early English practice, the trust plays an important role in tax and estate planning, in charitable giving, and in the business of lawyers and other professionals.

The fee tail. The fee tail should be familiar to anyone who has read the books of Jane Austen or watched *Downton Abbey*. The traditional words to create a fee tail are "*O* to *A* and the heirs of his body." This conveyance created ownership in *A* for life, then ownership in *A*'s lineal descendant entitled to inherit under English law for life, and so on through a series of life estates in *A*'s lineal descendants until the blood line ran out. A fee tail might be more specific, only in favor of heirs of the bodies of a married couple, in favor of female heirs, or in favor of male heirs. We see an example of the fee tail in *Pride and Prejudice*, in which Mr. Bennett's estate "was entailed, in default of heirs male, on a distant relation," the dreadful Mr. Collins. The book revolves around the efforts of his daughter and wife to avoid the resulting loss of income and social position after his death.

The fee tail was initially intended to preserve the integrity of the family estate. Because one could not contract with unborn heirs to obtain their future interests, the land could not be sold away from the family or levied to pay the life tenant's debts. By the fifteenth century, however, life tenants were able to bar, or eliminate, the entail through a procedure known as the **common recovery**, a collusive lawsuit that resulted in a default judgment awarding the land to a cooperative litigant, who would then convey the estate back to the tenant free of the entail.[3] *Pride and Prejudice* may refer to the common recovery in explaining that Mr. Bennett had expected to have a son, and "[t]his son was to join in cutting off the entail, as soon as he should be of age, and the widow and younger children would by that means be provided for."

In the United States, most states abolished the fee tail soon after the Revolution. The abolition is often described as a triumph of civic republicanism. Thomas Jefferson, for example, credited himself with the abolition of the fee tail in Virginia, declaring that the change undermined an "aristocracy of wealth," making an "opening for the aristocracy of virtue and talent." Recent scholarship by Claire Priest challenges this

2. Note that the settlor, trustee, and beneficiary need not be different people. A common estate planning scheme today is to settle property on oneself for one's own benefit, with the remainder to go to designated individuals or entities after one's death.

3. Common recoveries were clearly sham lawsuits. So why did courts allow them? While decisions and statutes at various periods restricted the common recovery, particularly when challenged by the issue in tail, in general courts respected the recovery as a means to restrain burdensome restrictions on property by the dead.

characterization. As in England, the life tenant could bar the entail and alienate the estate. Yet entailed property was fairly common in the colonies, and included humble estates as well as large ones. Why, if it was not effective in preventing alienation, was the entail so popular? Professor Priest argues that because only the landowners themselves could bar the entail, it was an effective means of protecting the homestead from creditors, who might otherwise seize the property for payment of debts. She argues that the end of the entail owes more to opposition by creditors and desire of large slaveholders to maintain a liquid market for land for plantations. *See* Claire Priest, *Creating an American Property Law: Alienability and Its Limits in American History*, 120 Harv. L. Rev. 385 (2006).

Today the fee tail is recognized in only four states, Delaware, Maine, Massachusetts, and Rhode Island, and even these permit easy barring of the entail. *See* Mass. Gen. Laws ch. 183, §45 (owner of fee tail may convert it to the fee simple by conveying it to another). States have adopted a variety of ways to treat any fee tail interests that come up. Most states interpret a fee tail as a fee simple absolute, Cal. Civ. Code §763; N.Y. Est. Powers & Trusts §6-1.2; *Restatement (Third) of Property: Wills & Donative Transfers* §24.4 (2011), while others interpret fee tails as life estates in the present owner with a remainder in fee simple in her issue. 765 Ill. Comp. Stat. 6; Ohio Rev. Code §2131.08.

§3 THE CONTEMPORARY ESTATES SYSTEM

The modern estates are largely those created during this medieval English history. For several reasons, it remains important to learn them today. First, ambiguous grants and conveyances will be interpreted as fitting into one of these existing categories. For lawyers who draft wills, trusts, leases, and conveyances, therefore, understanding the language that creates the estates and their properties is necessary to accomplish the intent of your clients. For lawyers representing clients in challenging or defending existing conveyances, understanding the traditional forms is equally important. Second, even when modern law has modified the traditional forms, wills and conveyances will usually be interpreted under the rules governing when they were created. Third, understanding how these estates work is a necessary step in tackling the rule against perpetuities, which, when it applies, may entirely defeat future interests. Finally, studying these estates has been a rite of passage for aspiring lawyers since before there were law schools. You are joining a very old club — welcome.

These materials are divided according to the potential length in time of the present estate: first, the **fee simple estates**, which could potentially last forever; and second, the **life estates**, which last only for the life of a particular person. There is a third present estate, the **term of years**, which is any estate limited not by a natural life or event but by a specific period of time, whether 6 months or 100 years. Terms of years were considered non-freehold estates under medieval law, and therefore often not subject to the same rules as other estates. They will therefore not be discussed here, but rather in Chapter 11, *Leaseholds*.

There are three interpretive rules that may be helpful in interpreting language creating future interests. First, one cannot grant more than one has. For example, if one grants a present estate limited by a future interest to another, the grantee generally receives the property limited by the future interest as well. Second, unless the grant contains limiting language, the grantor will be presumed to have given away all of the transferred interest. So, for example, a grant of a fee simple interest from grantor to grantee without specifying a future interest will be interpreted as granting the property forever. Third, whatever is not granted remains with the grantor. For example, if the grant transfers the interest only for a certain period of time, but does not specify what happens to the property after that period, the future interest is presumed to remain with the grantor.

§3.1 Fee Simple Interests

A fee simple is a present estate that could potentially last forever. "Forever" in the context of the fee simple of course does not mean that you can own property after your death, but simply that the interest does not necessarily end because of lapse of time or death. In effect, it is the right to determine who owns it in the future, whether by sale, gift, inheritance, or devise. There are four fee simple estates: the fee simple absolute; the fee simple determinable; the fee simple subject to a condition subsequent; and the fee simple subject to executory limitation.[4]

A. Fee Simple Absolute

A **fee simple absolute** (often just called a fee simple) is a fee simple without an associated future interest. Because no one owns a future interest in the property, the grantor is free to determine who owns it in the future and how. A conveyance of a fee simple interest can be accomplished by the following language:

O to *A*.
O to *A* and her heirs.
O to *A* in fee simple.

The language "*A* and her heirs" is technical in nature; it indicates a fee simple interest in *A*. The words "and her heirs" do not give *A*'s heirs any interests in the property. Of course, *A* may choose to leave the property to them in a will or, if *A* dies without a will, they may inherit the property. If, however, *A* chooses to write a will leaving the

4. The *Restatement (Third) of Property: Wills & Donative Transfers* §§24.3 & 25.1 (2011) would absorb all the defeasible fees under the term "fee simple defeasible," and their associated future interests under the terms remainder and reversion. Because no jurisdiction has yet adopted this terminology, and older grants will continue to be interpreted under the traditional rules, it remains important to learn the different names.

property to someone else or to sell the property during her lifetime, *A*'s potential heirs cannot complain; they have no ownership rights of their own.[5]

B. Defeasible Fees

Present interests that terminate at the happening of a specified event, other than the death of the current owner, are called **defeasible fees.** The categories of defeasible fees relate to two crucial distinctions: (1) whether the future interest is in the grantor or in a third party, and (2) whether the future interest becomes possessory *automatically* when the stated event occurs or becomes possessory only if the future interest holder *chooses to assert* his property rights.

1. Automatic transfer to the grantor: fee simple determinable. When the future interest reverts automatically to the grantor on the happening of the stated event, the present interest is called a **fee simple determinable** and the future interest is called a **possibility of reverter.**

A fee simple determinable is created by describing the present interest with *words of duration* (*e.g.*, so long as, during, while, until). The grant need not explicitly state the possibility of reverter. Following the general rule that whatever one does not give away one keeps for oneself, language denoting that the ownership is limited to a time period during which certain conditions are met will be interpreted to have the property revert to the grantor after that time period.

O to *A* so long as used for residential purposes.
O to *A* while used for residential purposes.
O to *A* during residential use.
O to *A* so long as used for residential purposes; if used for a nonresidential purpose, the property shall revert to *O*.

Any of these conveyances creates a fee simple determinable in *A* with a possibility of reverter in *O* or his heirs or devisees. When the condition is violated, ownership automatically shifts to *O* or her heirs or *O*'s devisees.

2. Transfer upon grantor's assertion of property rights: fee simple subject to a condition subsequent. Instead of providing for automatic transfer of the property rights upon violation of the condition, the grantor may choose to retain for herself or her heirs the right to decide, at the time the condition is violated, whether to retake the property. If the future interest owner chooses to assert her rights when the condition is violated or the stated event occurs, the property ownership shifts to her; if she does not assert her rights, ownership stays with the current owner. The current interest is called a **fee simple subject to a condition subsequent** and the future interest is

5. The language identifying the named owner *A* is referred to as *words of purchase* because it identifies who owns the property; the language "and her heirs" is referred to as *words of limitation* because it describes the kind of estate owned by *A* (a fee simple) rather than identifying who owns the property.

called a **right of entry** (sometimes also referred to as a *right of reentry* or a *power of termination*).

A fee simple subject to a condition subsequent is created using *words of condition* (*e.g.*, on condition that, but if, provided that). It generally must explicitly state the right of entry, but some courts will interpret grants made "on express condition" as implying the right of entry:

> *O* to *A* on condition that the property is used for residential purposes; in the event it is not so used, *O* shall have a right of entry.
>
> *O* to *A*, but if used for nonresidential purposes, *O* shall have the power to terminate the grant.
>
> *O* to *A*, provided that the property is used for residential purposes; if this condition is violated, *O* shall have a right of entry.

Each of these conveyances creates a fee simple subject to condition subsequent with a right of entry in *O* or her heirs. If the property is used for nonresidential purposes, *A* retains ownership unless and until *O* asserts her right to regain possession of the property.

Possibilities of reverter and rights of entry were traditionally not transferable, both because they were deemed too insubstantial to transfer, and because permitting transfer would facilitate enforcement of the restriction. In many jurisdictions, even when possibilities of reverter were alienable, rights of entry were not. *Restatement (Third) of Property: Wills & Donative Transfers* §25.2 (2011). Some states retain the traditional rule. *See* 765 Ill. Comp. Stat. 330 (possibilities of reverter and rights of entry not alienable); Neb. Rev. Stat. §76-299 (possibilities of reverter and rights of entry neither alienable nor devisable); N.D. Cent. Code §47-09-02 (rights of entry not transferrable except to possessory owner of property affected). Most states now hold that future interests are alienable as well as devisable and inheritable. *See, e.g.*, N.Y. Est. Powers & Trusts §6-5.1. Even in states that now permit alienation of possibilities of reverter and rights of entry, however, transfers made before the law changed to permit alienability will be invalid. *See Cathedral of the Incarnation in the Diocese of Long Island, Inc. v. Garden City Co.*, 697 N.Y.S.2d 56 (App. Div. 1999) (attempted transfer in 1893 destroyed right of entry).

Traditionally, a major difference between possibilities of reverter and rights of entry involved the statute of limitations for adverse possession. When a condition in a fee simple determinable is violated or occurs, the possibility of reverter kicks in automatically, giving the holder an immediate right of possession. The statute of limitations starts running immediately, and if the holder of the possibility of reverter does nothing for the statutory period, title will shift back to the current possessor. However, a right of entry does not become possessory until the holder asserts a right of possession; if the holder of the right of entry never asserts the right, the title will remain with the present estate owner. This would mean that violation of the condition in a fee simple subject to condition subsequent does not trigger the statute of limitations unless and until the holder of the right of entry demands a right of possession; before that point, no trespass has occurred. *See Swaby v. Northern Hills Regional Railroad*

Authority, 769 N.W.2d 798 (S.D. 2009) (although railroad had breached a condition subsequent by abandoning an easement in 1970, because future interest holders had not exercised their power of termination, statute of limitation had not begun to run). Under this understanding, there is a huge difference between rights of entry and possibilities of reverter.

However, the two types of future interests may now be treated similarly under one of three theories. First, **laches** may prevent the holder of a right of entry from waiting too long to assert her right of entry; laches prevents recovery when an unreasonable delay in asserting legal rights unfairly prejudices another. Relatedly, some courts require that a right of entry be exercised within a reasonable time after violation of the condition. *Sligh v. Plair*, 263 Ark. 936 (1978); *Martin v. City of Seattle*, 765 P.2d 257 (Wash. 1988). In both cases, the statute of limitations for trespass provides one measure of unreasonable delay. *Ator v. Ator*, 146 P.3d 821 (Okla. App. 2006) (8-year delay in exercising right of entry not unreasonable in light of 15-year statute of limitations for trespass). Finally, some states provide a statute of limitations for rights of entry by statute. Cal. Civ. Code §885.070 (five-year statute of limitations).

3. Transfer to a third party: fee simple subject to executory limitation. When the future interest in a defeasible fee belongs to someone other than the grantor, the present interest is called a **fee simple subject to executory limitation**, and the future interest is called an **executory interest.**[6] The condition may use either words of duration (like a fee simple determinable) or words of condition (like a fee simple subject to condition subsequent). In either case, however, ownership automatically shifts to the third party when the condition is violated:

O to *A* so long as used for residential purposes, then to *B*.
O to *A* on condition that it is used for residential purposes, then to *B*.

Each of the two conveyances above creates a fee simple subject to an executory limitation. The executory interest in *B* automatically becomes possessory if the property is used for nonresidential purposes.

§3.2 Life Estates

A. Reversions and Remainders

Present ownership rights can be held during the life of a designated individual. A conveyance from *O to A for life* creates a **life estate** in *A*. This means that *A* owns the

6. An executory interest is any interest not in the grantor that cuts short an estate before its natural termination, *i.e.*, before it necessarily ends at death, as in a life estate, or due to an expiration of a term of years. Traditionally, an executory interest that cuts short an estate in someone other than the grantor has been called a **shifting** executory interest, while an executory interest that follows an estate in the grantor has been called a **springing** executory interest. These terms are relevant for the rule of destructibility of contingent remainders, which prohibits springing but not shifting executory interests, but the rule is no longer in effect in the United States. *See* §3.2.C, *infra*.

property during his lifetime. The future interest following a life estate can be either in the grantor or in a third party. If the property reverts to the grantor when *A* dies, the future interest is called a **reversion**; if the grantor designates a third party to obtain ownership when *A* dies, the future interest in the third party is called a **remainder**.

The difference between a life estate and a fee simple is that the owner of a fee simple can choose who will own the property after her death by either writing a will or availing herself of the state intestacy statute. In contrast, a life estate owner has no right to determine who owns the property on her death since ownership automatically shifts to the reversioner or remainder holder. If a life estate owner, *A*, sells her property to a buyer, *B*, the buyer gets exactly what the seller had: an estate for the life of *A*. Thus, when *A* dies, the property will shift to the reversioner or remainder holder. *B*'s interest is called a **life estate for the life of another** or a **life estate *per autre vie***.

O to *A* for life.

This conveyance gives a life estate to *A* and automatically creates a reversion in *O*. When *A* dies, the property reverts to *O* or, if *O* is deceased, to her heirs or devisees. It is not necessary for the conveyance to mention the reversion; *O* retains whatever property rights are not given away. When *A* dies, her ownership rights terminate and ownership automatically shifts back to *O*.

O to *A* for life, then to *B*.

This conveyance creates a life estate in *A*, with a remainder in *B*. Note that an executory interest divests, or cuts short, a present estate while a reversion or remainder takes effect at the "natural" termination of the preceding estate, such as the death of a life tenant holder or the end of a term of years in a lease. A life estate may be subject to a divesting condition that would cause the interest to shift before the owner dies; if so, the future interest would be an executory interest.

B. Contingent and Vested Remainders

One final set of distinctions is important. We have seen that future interests following defeasible fees vest either in the grantor (*possibility of reverter* or *right of entry*) or in a third party (*executory interest*). Future interests following life estates also may vest either in the grantor (*reversion*) or in a third party (*remainder*). Remainders are further divided into two kinds: **contingent remainders** and **vested remainders**.

Contingent remainders. Remainders are contingent if one or both of two conditions are met: (1) if the remainder will take effect only upon the happening of an event that is not certain to happen, or (2) if the remainder will go to a person who cannot be ascertained at the time of the initial conveyance.

For example, a conveyance from "*O* to *A* for life, then to *B* if *B* has graduated from law school," creates a contingent remainder because at the time of the original conveyance from *O* to *A* it is not certain that *B* will graduate from law school. (If *B* does not graduate from law school, the property will revert to *O* on *A*'s death; if *B* later graduates from law school, the property will then spring to *B*.)

Contingent remainders often arise in the context of **class gifts**, grants to a group that is merely described but not named. For example, a class gift from "*O* to *A* for life, then to the children of *B*," creates a contingent remainder in the children of *B* if *B* has no children upon the conveyance from *O* to *A*, because the children cannot be individually identified at the time of the conveyance. Another example of a class gift creating a contingent remainder is "*O* to *A* for life, then to the heirs of *B*." If *B* is alive at the time of the conveyance from *O* to *A*, it is impossible to tell who *B*'s heirs will be until *B* dies; only persons alive at the time of *B*'s death can inherit as "heirs" under the intestacy statute.

Vested remainders. Vested remainders, conversely, are remainders to persons who are identifiable at the time of the initial conveyance and for whom no conditions must occur before the future interest becomes possessory other than the death of the life estate tenant. Vested remainders are of three kinds.

1. **Absolutely vested remainders.** This is a remainder that is not subject to change. "*O* to *A* for life, and then to *B*" for example, creates an absolutely vested remainder.

2. **Vested remainders subject to open.** Typically arising in class gifts, this is a remainder that is vested in some individuals but may be divided with others who join the class in the future. For example, a class gift from "*O* to *A* for life, then to the children of *B*," is a vested remainder if *B* has any living children at the time of the conveyance from *O* to *A*; it is **subject to open**, however, because any children of *B* born *after* the conveyance from *O* to *A* may share the property rights with the children who were alive at the time of the conveyance. Under the **rule of convenience**, most courts will, absent contrary evidence of grantor intent, close the class when *A* dies so that *B*'s children can take possession at *A*'s death and will not have to share the property with any after-born children.

3. **Vested remainders subject to divestment.** This is a vested remainder that may be lost due to an event that occurs after the original conveyance. For example, a conveyance from "*O* to *A* for life, then to *B*, but if *B* marries a lawyer, the property shall then revert to *O*," creates a vested remainder in *B* because *B* is ascertained at the time of the conveyance to *A* and there are no conditions precedent to *B*'s taking the property; however, it is **subject to divestment** because if the condition is met at any time — if *B* marries a lawyer — *B* will lose his right to obtain the property on the death of *A*.

C. Destructibility of Contingent Remainders

The law formerly provided that contingent remainders were "destroyed" in two circumstances. First, contingent remainders were destroyed if they did not vest before the preceding life estate ended. For example, in the conveyance "*O* to *A* for life, then to *B* if she has been elected president of the United States," the contingent remainder in *B* would be destroyed if *B* had not been elected president before the death of *A*. The justification for the rule was purely formal: the property would revert to *O* if the condition had not occurred by the end of the life estate, and it was believed inconsistent with the nature of the estate to have a remainder "spring" from the life estate over an interest in *O* once the condition occurred.

Second, contingent remainders were destroyed by "merger" of the present and future estates. For example, suppose *O* conveyed her property to *A* for life, and then to *A*'s children. If *A* does not have children at the time of the conveyance, then the children have a contingent remainder, and the property will revert to *O* if *A* dies without children. If *O* then conveyed her reversion to *A*, the traditional doctrine would say that the contingent remainder was destroyed, leaving *A* with a fee simple and any future children with nothing. *See Abo Petroleum Corp. v. Amstutz*, 600 P.2d 278 (N.M. 1979) (rejecting the doctrine of merger).

Almost all states have abolished the destructibility of contingent remainders by common law or statute, and the last case to apply the rule was decided in 1963. *Restatement (Third) of Property: Wills & Donative Transfers* §25.5 (2011). While it is theoretically possible that one of the few states that have not officially abolished the rule might apply it, it is extremely unlikely. It is fair to conclude with the *Restatement (Third)* that "[t]he Rule of Destructibility of Contingent Remainders is not recognized as part of American law." *Id.*

The traditional rule effectively destroyed many future interests that could have vested after the death of the current life estate holder. Applying the rule therefore resulted in freeing land from archaic restrictions. Today contingent remainders likely to vest too far into the future are regulated by the rule against perpetuities or by statutory limits on their continuation, discussed at §5.3.C, *infra*.

Estates System: Freehold Interests			
Present Interest	***Words Used to Create***	***Future Interest***	
		In grantor	***In third party***
Fee simple absolute	"to *A*" "to *A* and her heirs"		
Fee simple determinable	"as long as" "during" "until" "while"	possibility of reverter	
Fee simple subject to condition subsequent	"provided that" "on condition" "but if"	right of entry (also called right of reentry or power of termination)	
Fee simple subject to executory limitation	"until (or unless) . . . , then to . . . " "but if . . . , then to . . ."		executory interest
Life estate	"for life"	reversion	remainder (vested or contingent)

Problems

1. O *to* A *and her heirs.* What estate does *A* have? What result if *A* dies, leaving the property in her will to her friend *B*, and her heir *C* claims the property for himself? What if *A* sells the property to *D*, then dies leaving the property to *B* in her will?

2. O *to* A *for life, then to* A*'s children. A* is alive and has one child, *C*. What estates do *A* and *C* have? If *A* sells the property to *B*, then dies, who owns the property?

3. O *to* A *so long as the property is used as a school.* What estates are created? What happens if the property stops being used as a school after *O* dies?

4. *O* grants a strip of land to *A "for use as a railroad, but if the property ever ceases to be used for railroad purposes,* O *may terminate the grant."* What does *A* have? What does *O* have? What result if the property was converted to a hiking trail in 1970 and *O*'s successors file a quiet title suit in 2000?

5. O *to* A *for life, then to* B *if she graduates from law school.* What does *A* have? What does *B* have? If *A* dies before *B* graduates from law school, who gets the property? What happens if *B* later does graduate?

§4 INTERPRETATION OF AMBIGUOUS CONVEYANCES

§4.1 Presumption Against Forfeitures and the Grantor's Intent

A. Fee Simple versus Defeasible Fee

Wood v. Board of County Commissioners of Fremont County

759 P.2d 1250 (Wyo. 1988)

C. STUART BROWN, Chief Justice.

Appellants Cecil and Edna Wood, husband and wife, appeal summary judgment favoring appellee, the Board of County Commissioners for Fremont County, Wyoming. By a 1948 warranty deed appellants conveyed land in Riverton, Wyoming, to Fremont County for the construction of a county hospital. They now contend that language in the deed created either a fee simple determinable or a fee simple subject to a condition subsequent with a right of reversion in them if the land ceased to be used for the hospital. [This case presents the question whether] cessation of appellee's hospital operation by sale of public hospital facilities to a private company constituted the occurrence of an event which divested appellee of its estate in property conditionally conveyed by appellants. The trial court found that appellants retained no interest in the land surrounding and under the old county hospital as a matter of law. We affirm.

On September 1, 1948, by warranty deed, appellants conveyed

> [a] tract of land situated in the SE 1/4 SW 1/4, Sec. 26, Township 1, North Range 4 East, W.R.M., Fremont County, Wyoming, described . . . as follows: Beginning at the Southwest corner of said SE 1/4 SW 1/4, Sec. 26, aforesaid, thence east along the South line of said Section 310 feet, thence North at right angles to said South line 297 feet, thence West on a line parallel to said South line 310 feet, thence South 297 feet to the point of beginning, containing 2.1 acres. . . . Said tract is conveyed to Fremont County *for the purpose of constructing and maintaining thereon a County Hospital in memorial to the gallant men of the Armed Forces of the United States of America from Fremont County, Wyoming*. . . . (Emphasis added.)

This deed was recorded in the Fremont County Clerk's Office on December 14, 1948. Appellee constructed a hospital on the land and operated it there until November 18, 1983. At that time appellee sold the land and the original hospital facility to a private company. The buyer operated a hospital on the premises until September, 1984, at which time it moved the operation to a newly constructed facility. The private company then put the premises up for sale.

Appellants' argument boils down to whether or not the language ". . . for the purpose of constructing and maintaining thereon a County Hospital in memorial to the gallant men of the Armed Forces of the United States of America from Fremont County, Wyoming . . ." in the 1948 warranty deed is sufficient limiting language to create either 1) a fee simple determinable, or 2) a fee simple subject to a condition subsequent giving appellants title to the land. We review disputed language in a deed to determine the intent of the parties to it from the plain language in the deed considered as a whole. Also, Wyo. Stat. §34-2-101 (1977) provides, in pertinent part: "[E]very conveyance of real estate shall pass all the estate of the grantor . . . unless the intent to pass a less estate shall expressly appear or be necessarily implied in the terms of the grant."

A fee simple estate in land that automatically expires upon the happening of a stated event, not certain to occur, is a fee simple determinable. *Restatement of Property* §44, at 121 (1936). In *Williams v. Watt*, 668 P.2d 620, 627 (Wyo. 1983), we said:

> The existence of an estate in fee simple determinable requires the presence of special limitations. An estate in fee simple determinable may be created so as to be defeasible upon the occurrence of an event which is not certain ever to occur. Words such as "so long as," "until," or "during" are commonly used in a conveyance to denote the presence of this type of special limitation. The critical requirement is that the language of special limitation must clearly state the particular circumstances under which the fee simple estate conveyed might expire. Language of conveyance that grants a fee simple estate in land for a special purpose, without stating the special circumstances that could trigger expiration of the estate, is not sufficient to create a fee simple determinable.

The plain language in the 1948 deed, stating that appellants conveyed the land to Fremont County for the purpose of constructing a county hospital, does not clearly state that the estate conveyed will expire automatically if the land is not used for the stated purpose. As such, it does not evidence an intent of the grantors to convey a fee simple determinable, and we hold that no fee simple determinable was created when the land was conveyed.

Use of the language conveying the land in "memorial" similarly fails to create a fee simple determinable. "Memorial" is defined in *Webster's Third New International Dictionary* 1409 (1971) as "[s]omething that serves to preserve memory or knowledge of an individual or event." The time for which the hospital should serve to "preserve" the memory or knowledge is not stated in the deed, just as the time for maintaining the hospital is not there stated. The language of conveyance fails to designate the time at which the hospital must be constructed as well as the time during which it must be maintained or during which the indicated memory must be preserved. The omission of such limiting language evidences an intent not to convey a fee simple determinable.

Similar reasoning applies to appellants' assertion that the language of conveyance created a fee simple subject to a condition subsequent. A fee simple subject to a condition subsequent is a fee simple estate in land that gives the grantor a discretionary power to terminate the grantee's estate after the happening of a stated event, not certain to occur. This type of interest is similar to the fee simple determinable in that the language of conveyance must clearly state the grantor's intent to create a discretionary power to terminate the estate he conveys. Words commonly used in a conveyance to denote the presence of a fee simple estate subject to a condition subsequent include "upon express condition that," "upon condition that," "provided that," or "if." In *J.M. Carey & Brother v. City of Casper*, 213 P.2d 263, 268 (Wyo. 1950), we quoted 19 *Am. Jur. Estates* §65 at 527 (1939), which said:

> It is a well-settled rule that conditions tending to destroy estates, such as conditions subsequent, are not favored in law. They are strictly construed. Accordingly, no provision will be interpreted to create such a condition if the language will bear any other reasonable interpretation, or unless the language, used unequivocally, indicates an intention upon the part of the grantor or devisor to that effect and plainly admits of such construction.

That rule has not lost its potency. Applying it to this case, we hold that the plain language of the 1948 warranty deed, while articulating that the land conveyed was to be used for a county hospital, does not clearly state an intent of the grantors to retain a discretionary power to reenter the land if the land ceased to be used for the stated purpose. Appellants did not convey a fee simple subject to a condition subsequent, and we will not create one by construction some forty years after the conveyance took place.

Quick Review:
How should the Woods have written the grant if they wanted to retake the property once it was no longer used as a hospital?

B. Fee Simple versus Life Estate

Edwards v. Bradley

315 S.E.2d 196 (Va. 1984)

George M. Cochran, Justice.

In this appeal, the question presented to us is whether by certain provisions in her will a testatrix devised a fee simple estate or a life estate in real property therein described.

Viva Parker Lilliston died testate in 1969. Her will dated January 12, 1957, duly probated with a 1958 codicil irrelevant to this case, provided in part as follows:

> Item Twelve: I give and devise my farm situated on the Seaside from Locustville, in the County of Accomack, State of Virginia . . . to my daughter, Margaret Lilliston Edwards, upon the conditions, set out in Item Fourteen. . . .
>
> Item Fourteen: all gifts made to my daughter, Margaret L. Edwards, individually and personally, under Items Eleven and Twelve of this Will, whether personal estate or real estate, are conditioned upon the said Margaret L. Edwards keeping the gift or devise herein free from encumbrances of every description, and in the event the said Margaret L. Edwards shall attempt to encumber same or sell her interest, or in the event any creditor or creditors of said Margaret L. Edwards shall attempt to subject her interest in the gift or devise herein made to the payment of the debts of the said Margaret L. Edwards, then and in that event the interest of said Margaret L. Edwards therein shall immediately cease and determine, and the gift or devise shall at once become vested in her children, viz: Betty Belle Branch, Beverly Bradley, John R. Edwards, Bruce C. Edwards, Jill A. Edwards and Jackie L. Edwards, in equal shares in fee simple. . . .

Margaret L. Jones, formerly Margaret L. Edwards, qualified as executrix under her mother's will. In 1979, Jones sought to have her children and their spouses execute an agreement to consent to her selling the farm devised to her. Only a daughter, Beverly Bradley, and the latter's husband declined to execute the agreement. In 1980, Jones died testate; in her will, executed in 1979, she left Bradley $1.00, and directed that the farm be sold and the proceeds distributed equally among her other children. The executors named in the will duly qualified. Bradley filed a bill of complaint in the trial court against these personal representatives and her five brothers and sisters, alleging that under the Lilliston will a life estate was devised to Jones with remainder to Jones's children. Bradley sought to enjoin the sale or encumbrance of the farm without her consent and asked that her interest therein be determined.

After hearing evidence presented by Bradley, the trial court determined that Jones had not violated any of the conditions specified in the Lilliston will. Edwards presented no evidence. The trial judge issued a letter opinion in which he stated his conclusion that under the Lilliston will a life estate in the farm was devised to Jones with remainder to her six named children in fee simple. A final decree, incorporating the opinion by reference, was entered March 25, 1981. On appeal, Edwards argued before us that Jones had fee simple title subject to valid conditional limitations and, having not violated the conditions, could freely dispose of the farm by will as she chose. Edwards argued in the alternative on brief that if the conditions were invalid Jones was vested with fee simple title without restrictions or conditions even though such unconditional vesting would have been contrary to her mother's intent to protect the farm from Jones's creditors.

There is no conflict in the evidence. Jones was in financial difficulties when the Lilliston will was executed. The will was prepared by an experienced attorney. One provision, referring specifically to the enabling statute, established a spendthrift trust for the benefit of another child of the testatrix.

The trial judge, in his opinion, noted that the "able and experienced" draftsman had used the words "fee simple" at least seven times in the will and codicil. Apparently, the judge reasoned that if a fee simple estate had been intended for Jones, the draftsman would have used that terminology in Item Twelve. Moreover, the judge stated that under Edwards's theory that Jones died vested with fee simple title, a creditor could then bring a creditor's suit to subject the land to the satisfaction of the debt contrary to the testamentary conditions and the intent of Lilliston. The judge further stated that the conditions set forth in Item Fourteen were repugnant to a fee simple estate but not to an estate for life. For these reasons, he ruled that a life estate was created under the Lilliston will.

As a general rule, a condition totally prohibiting the alienation of a vested fee simple estate or requiring a forfeiture upon alienation is void. As an exception to the rule, conditions prohibiting alienation of land granted to corporate entities for their special purposes are valid. A conditional limitation imposed upon a life estate, however, is valid. *See also Restatement of Property* §409 (1944), where such limitations, therein classified as forfeiture restraints, are said to be valid as to life estates.

It is apparent, therefore, that if Lilliston's will vested fee simple title to the farm in Jones, the unqualified restraint on alienation would be invalid and the property from the time of vesting would be subject to sale, encumbrance, or devise by her and subject to the claims of her creditors, results contrary to the express intent of the testatrix. On the other hand, if Lilliston's will vested a life estate in Jones, the unqualified restraint on alienation imposed by the testatrix would be valid. Jones could not acquire, as Edwards suggested, a life estate which, upon compliance with the testamentary conditions, became a fee simple estate at the time of her death. Jones acquired under the Lilliston will either a fee simple estate free of conditions and thus inconsistent with the testatrix's intent or a life estate subject to conditions and thus consistent with such intent.

The draftsman of the Lilliston will carefully avoided using in either Item Twelve or Item Fourteen the words "fee simple" which he had used elsewhere in the instrument. It is true, as Edwards observed, that he also did not use the words "life estate" in those clauses of the will. Under Va. Code §55-11 it is not necessary to use the words "in fee simple" to create a fee simple estate where real estate is devised without words of limitation unless a contrary intention shall appear by the will. In the present case, however, the real estate was devised with words of limitation and a contrary intention appears in the will. Moreover, unless there is a power of disposal in the first taker, Va. Code §55-7, a life estate may be created by implication as well as by explicit language, provided the will shows the requisite intent.

Since the testatrix established a spendthrift trust in another provision of her will, she was aware of the availability of that device but did not choose to use it for the benefit of Jones. Moreover, under Va. Code §55-7, the testatrix could have devised the land to Jones for life with a power of appointment under which Jones could have disposed of the property by will. She did not do so.

The intention of the testatrix is to be upheld if the will can be reasonably construed to effectuate such intent and if it is not inconsistent with an established rule of law. In addition, the language of the will is "to be understood in the sense in which the circumstances of the case show" that the testatrix intended. *Gray v. Francis*, 124 S.E. 446,

450 (Va. 1924). Here, the testatrix intended that Jones have the use and benefit of the real estate free of the claims of her creditors. The ultimate beneficiaries were Jones's children. Although the will did not expressly designate the children as remaindermen, the conditional limitation to them indicated that they were intended to take the farm when their mother's interest terminated, whether by violation of the conditions or otherwise. Accordingly, we conclude that the trial court properly ruled that Jones acquired a life estate in the property with remainder at her death in fee simple to her six children.

Notes and Questions

1. **Estates.** We could allow owners complete freedom to create future interests as they please. This approach would protect freedom of contract or free disposition of property. This is not the way the property law system developed. A variety of rules limits the ability of owners to create future interests, both to protect the interests of current owners in using their property and having the power to transfer it and to protect social interests in efficient land use. These rules compromise between the interests of grantors and grantees. One regulatory rule is the **rule against creation of new estates**, discussed below at §5.1. This rule prohibits owners from creating ownership packages that do not fit within one of the established estates; it helps ensure that sufficient rights are consolidated in owners so that they can act like owners. This means that the courts must interpret conveyances or wills to determine which estate the grantor intended to create. The court cannot simply ask what future interest the grantor intended to create; instead, the court must fit the future interest into an established category.

2. **Interpretation and the presumption against forfeitures.** Sometimes grantors do not use traditional language to create one of the estates. Other times, grantors use conflicting language, seeming to create one estate in one phrase and another estate in another phrase. In either case, courts must interpret the conveyance to determine what types of current and future interests were created and who owns the property. Two conflicting rules of interpretation dominate court discussions of this issue. On one hand, courts often proclaim their fealty to the goal of effectuating the *grantor's intent* to the extent it can be discerned from language in the deed or will or, possibly, from the surrounding circumstances. On the other hand, when the language is ambiguous, most courts also voice a preference for a construction of the language that will avoid recognition of a future interest. This is especially so if recognition of the future interest would mean that the present possessor lost her title to the future interest holder. It is a common maxim that "the law abhors a forfeiture." *Harrison v. Morrow*, 977 So. 2d 457 (Ala. 2007). There is therefore a **presumption against forfeitures**. If it is possible to interpret the language to avoid loss of the property by the current owner, the courts will generally adopt this interpretation.

If the choice is between a future interest and mere precatory language (a statement of purpose not intended to be legally binding), the presumption is to recognize a fee simple absolute with no future interest. *Roberts v. Rhodes*, 643 P.2d 116, 118 (Kan.

1982) ("The general rule is well settled that the mere expression that property is to be used for a particular purpose will not in and of itself suffice to turn a fee simple into a determinable fee."). If the choice is either a covenant or a future interest, the presumption is against the future interest and in favor of the enforceable covenant because this will keep title with the current owner. If the choice is either a fee simple determinable or a fee simple subject to condition subsequent, the fee simple subject to condition subsequent is preferred because the current interest is not automatically forfeited when the condition is violated, thereby keeping ownership (at least for the time being) with the current owner. If the choice is between a life estate and a fee simple (defeasible or absolute), a fee simple interest is preferred. *Accord, Howson v. Crombie Street Congregational Church*, 590 N.E.2d 687 (Mass. 1992). *But see Edwards v. Bradley, supra* (finding a life estate rather than a fee simple when this will promote the grantor's intent to effectuate an enforceable restraint on alienation); *Cain v. Finnie*, 785 N.E.2d 1039 (Ill. App. Ct. 2003) (similarly interpreting a will leaving land to "Blanche Spurlock so long as she remains my widow" as a conditional life estate rather than as a fee simple determinable).

3. Policies behind the presumption against forfeitures. The choice of preferring either the interests of the current owner or the interests of the future interest holder involves a policy decision about the proper distribution of power over property between grantors and grantees. Enforcing the condition in the original conveyance by requiring a forfeiture promotes the interests of the grantor in controlling the future use and disposition of property; it also creates security for neighboring property owners who may benefit by the condition. In contrast, the presumption against forfeitures promotes the interests of current owners in controlling property in their possession, giving them greater freedom to change land uses as economic conditions and social values change; it also promotes social interests in deregulating economic activity to allow property owners the freedom to shift property to more valuable or desired uses. At the same time, the presumption against forfeitures may further the grantor's intent, on the theory that the grantor presumably intends to give away any interests she has and would be likely to make it very clear if she intended to retain a future interest.

4. Purpose language. When conveyances include language explaining the purpose of the transfer, such as in *Wood*, the vast majority of courts agree with *Wood* and will hold the language to be **precatory**—not intended to have any legal significance—and will interpret the conveyance to have transferred all the interests the grantor owned. If the grantors owned a fee simple, the courts presume that is what they intended to convey. This result follows from the presumption against forfeitures and protects the interests of the grantee, placing the burden on the grantors to be clear if they intend to retain a future interest in the property. *Accord, St. Mary's Medical Center v. McCarthy*, 829 N.E.2d 1068 (Ind. App. 2005).

The courts are not unanimous on this score and sometimes find a future interest in the absence of language clearly creating one. For example, in *Cathedral of the Incarnation in the Diocese of Long Island, Inc. v. Garden City Co.*, 697 N.Y.S.2d 56 (App. Div. 1999), the court found that a conveyance to the Cathedral of the Incarnation for purposes of the local Episcopal diocese "without any power, right, or authority to grant, convey, or mortgage the same or any part thereof in any way or manner whatsoever," created a right of entry despite the lack of any language specifying this future interest. The court found, however, that the grantors' attempt in 1893 to transfer their right of entry had destroyed it, because rights of entry were not transferable at common law at the time. Therefore the Cathedral, which was in financial distress and had filed for bankruptcy, had a fee simple free from any restrictions on sale of the land.

Although most courts are reluctant to find a future interest in the absence of clear language creating one, some courts are eager to find a future interest when the property is donated for charitable purposes. In the absence of a future interest, the owner is entitled to shift the property to a noncharitable use, thereby possibly violating the intent of the grantor and harming the public interest by ending the charitable use. Property is often more valuable if sold on the open market than when reserved for charitable purposes. There are pressures therefore to sell such property. In order to help preserve charitable uses, courts sometimes do not apply the presumption against forfeitures or future interests to charitable property.

Recognition of a future interest will not always promote charitable uses. After all, if the grantors had prevailed in *Wood* and reclaimed the property, they could have used the property for any purpose, including a noncharitable one. Finding no restriction, moreover, may permit the use of property in the way most beneficial to the charity. In *St. Mary's Medical Center v. McCarthy*, *supra*, for example, the court determined that a grant to a hospital for the purposes of building a chapel did not create a trust, permitting the chapel to be destroyed so that the hospital could expand its facilities.

When a deed states a charitable purpose for property or restricts its use to charitable purpose, courts have attempted to achieve the charitable purpose by adopting a number of different interpretations. Most hold the language to be precatory, applying the presumption against forfeitures. However, from time to time, courts have rejected this approach, granting substantial legal effect to language of purpose. William B. Stoebuck & Dale A. Whitman, *The Law of Property* §2.5, at 41 (3d ed. 2000). Some have found a future interest, as did the court in *Cathedral of the Incarnation* (either a possibility of reverter or a right of entry). Other courts have interpreted the purpose language or use restriction as an enforceable covenant, allowing the covenant to be enforced in gross at least in the context of charitable property. *Davis v. St. Joe School District*, 284 S.W.2d 635 (Ark. 1955). Still other courts have imposed a constructive trust on the property, obligating the current owner to use it for charitable purposes or transfer it to someone who will so use it. *United States v. Certain Land in Cape Girardeau*, 79 F. Supp. 558 (D. Mo. 1947).

5. Restraints on alienation. The Virginia Supreme Court in *Edwards v. Bradley* resolved what it saw as an ambiguity in the conveyance partly by reference to the fact that the property was subject to a restraint on alienation — a restraint that would be valid if attached to a life estate but void if attached to a fee simple. The presumption against forfeitures would suggest that the fee simple be chosen over the life estate, the restraint held void, and the property left with a fee simple absolute. The court refused to adopt this approach, instead focusing on the fact that the grantor intended to create a valid restraint on alienation and the only way to achieve that result was to interpret the conveyance as creating a life estate. Which of these interpretations is preferable and why?

6. **Changed conditions.** The changed conditions doctrine denying enforcement of covenants when circumstances are so drastically changed that they are no longer of benefit to the dominant estate has traditionally not applied to future interests. *Prieskorn v. Maloof,* 991 P.2d 511 (N.M. Ct. App. 1999). Some states, moreover, have statutes that remove future interests from charitable properties where the restrictions substantially impede the charitable organization in achieving its purposes or become "unlawful, impracticable, impossible to achieve, or wasteful." *See, e.g.,* Wash. Rev. Code §11.96A.127; N.Y. Real Prop. Acts Law §1955; Mich. Comp. L. §451.926. Should a court grant relief from such restrictions in the absence of a statute?

§4.2 Waste

Life tenants and owners of remainders or reversions have conflicting interests. It is in the interest of life tenants to maximize the profits and minimize the costs from the property while they have it. It is in the interest of the future interest holders to preserve the property and its value until they come into possession. The doctrine of **waste** seeks to mediate these conflicts by preventing present possessory owners from unreasonably damaging the estate. Prohibitions against waste also apply to relationships between tenants and landlords and between mortgagors and mortgagees, although the default rules vary with the different ownership interests. Applying the doctrine involves questions of efficient use of resources, the intent of the drafters, the justified expectations and rights of the future and present interest holders, and the role of property in society. For discussions of the various theories behind the doctrine of waste, *see* John Lovett, *Doctrines of Waste in Landscape of Waste,* 72 Mo. L. Rev. 1209 (2007), and Jedediah Purdy, *The American Transformation of Waste Doctrine: A Pluralist Interpretation,* 91 Cornell L. Rev. 653 (2006).

McIntyre v. Scarbrough

471 S.E.2d 199 (Ga. 1996)

HUGH P. THOMPSON, Justice.

In October 1988, plaintiffs Russell and Sally Scarbrough purchased from defendant Dillie McIntyre a 16.59 acre tract of land by warranty deed, with reservation of a life estate in Ms. McIntyre in 1.2 acres which included a mobile home, porch, and shed. The reservation provided: "[L]ife estate is for [McIntyre's] natural life and during her occupancy of this tract as a personal residence. As to this tract, [McIntyre] shall be responsible for maintenance and upkeep of the property and all improvements thereon and for payment of ad valorem taxes."

In 1994, the plaintiffs brought a petition to establish title and to terminate the life estate, and subsequently moved for summary judgment, asserting that: (1) the defendant ceased occupying the tract as a personal residence in violation of the warranty deed, and (2) committed waste by failing to maintain the property and improvements thereon. Because the evidence conclusively established that the life tenant failed to exercise ordinary care for the preservation of the property, we agree with the trial court that she forfeited her interest to the remaindermen and that they are entitled to immediate possession.

The evidence on summary judgment showed the following: The Scarbroughs both averred by affidavit that they had not seen Ms. McIntyre on the property since 1990; that there was no water or gas service to the mobile home, nor a mailbox on the property; and that the structure is in a state of dilapidation. Ms. Scarbrough further averred that ad valorem property taxes had accrued on the McIntyre property since 1990, and that she (Ms. Scarbrough) was forced to pay the arrearage to avoid injury to her remainder interest. The Scarbroughs also offered the affidavit of a fire marshall who opined that the mobile home appeared to have been vacant for some time; that it was in a general state of decay and disrepair; and that it posed fire and health hazards and was unfit for habitation.

In response, Ms. McIntyre offered her own affidavit in which she stated that she is now 90 years of age, that she had been recently unable to occupy her residence due to health problems, and that she was in the process of renovating her home to make it fit for habitation. A July 29, 1994 sheriff's entry of service form shows that Ms. McIntyre could not be located and served because she was residing in a convalescent home outside the court's jurisdiction.

Ms. McIntyre also offered the affidavit of her grandson who averred that she had been confined away from home for medical reasons, that she had always expressed her intention of returning to the home and occupying it for the remainder of her life, that she had never removed any of her personal belongings during the time she was away, and that he completed certain repairs to the mobile home making it fit for habitation.

1. The trial court found that the warranty deed required Ms. McIntyre to occupy the tract as a personal residence as a condition of her life estate, concluding that "occupy" meant to "to dwell in" according to Webster's New Universal Unabridged Dictionary. Relying on the affidavits of record, the court found as a matter of law that Ms. McIntyre failed to occupy the property. However, the court's definition of occupancy was too narrow.

"Occupy" is more expansively defined in Black's Law Dictionary as "to hold possession of; to hold or keep for use; to possess." Because one may occupy a residence by holding it or keeping it for use, the court erred in imposing a requirement that permanent physical presence was necessary to fulfill the occupancy requirement of the warranty deed. Evidence that Ms. McIntyre had never removed any of her personal belongings during the time she had been away for medical reasons, as well as her stated ongoing intent to occupy the residence until her death, raises a question of fact as to whether she continued to occupy the residence while residing elsewhere for medical recuperation.

2. The trial court, however, correctly determined that the plaintiffs were entitled to judgment as a matter of law under plaintiffs' alternative theory of recovery, that the life estate was extinguished under the doctrine of waste.

A life tenant is entitled to the full use and enjoyment of the property if in such use he or she exercises the ordinary care of a prudent person for its preservation and protection and commits no acts which would permanently injure the remainder interest. Ga. Code §44-6-83; *Graham v. Bryant*, 89 S.E.2d 640 (Ga. 1955). The unrebutted evidence shows that Ms. McIntyre had failed to pay ad valorem property taxes on the 1.2 acre tract for the years 1991 through 1993, or on the improvements for the years 1992 through 1994. In *Austell v. Swann*, 74 Ga. 278, 281 (1885), this Court stated that "a neglect to pay the burdens imposed by law upon the property during the term would be a want of such ordinary care as a prudent person should exercise for its protection and preservation, and would tend to divest the title to the fee by exposing it, or a portion of it, to sale, to raise the taxes levied on it." In the present case, not only was the defendant obligated by law to maintain taxes on her portion of the property, but she also specifically agreed to pay ad valorem taxes as a condition of the warranty deed. Although the question of waste is generally one for a jury, the undisputed facts show that the defendant failed to exercise ordinary care for the preservation of the property, and to comply with a condition of the warranty deed, resulting in forfeiture of the life estate as a matter of law.

ROBERT BENHAM, Chief Justice, joined by HUNSTEIN and CARLEY, dissenting.

I agree fully with the first division of the majority opinion, and I believe the evidence submitted on motion for summary judgment would, in a trial, support a verdict for the Scarbroughs. I do not believe, however, that they are entitled to judgment as a matter of law, so I must dissent from the majority opinion's affirmance of the trial court grant of summary judgment on the issue of waste.

As the majority opinion correctly notes, the question of waste is generally one for a jury. That is especially so in a case such as the present one where there is evidence presented in defense of the life estate to the effect that any damage to the estate has been unintentional and due to the circumstances of the holder of the life estate rather than from disregard of the estate. [In] *Roby v. Newton*, 49 S.E. 694 (Ga. 1905), this court noted that, as forfeitures are not favored, the statute must be strictly construed, as a criminal statute must be. The court went on to construe the statute as requiring a concurrence of permissive (lack of due care) and voluntary (active) waste, and held that the waste which would authorize forfeiture must be committed "in such a manner as to indicate an utter disregard of the rights of those who are thereafter to take."

In the present case, there is evidence that Ms. McIntyre has made some efforts, through the agency of her son, to reverse the deterioration of the property and that she has been ill and unable to care for the property adequately, although she has always intended to return to it. That evidence, if believed, does not show the wilful behavior required to warrant a forfeiture. The evidence offered in favor of forfeiture does not demand, as a matter of law, a finding of wilfulness. As this court noted in *Grimm v. Grimm*, 113 S.E. 91 (Ga. 1922), "if the life tenant from poverty or inability to keep the premises from falling into decay, allowed them to get in such condition, such conduct would be merely permissive, and would not be voluntary. . . ."

"The question of intent . . . fits the pattern of those issues of material fact which are not appropriate issues for summary judgment but are decided by the trier of fact." *State Farm Fire & Cas. Co. v. Morgan*, 368 S.E.2d 509 (Ga. 1988). The question of whether Ms. McIntyre's conduct with regard to the life estate she holds has been so egregiously wasteful as to warrant forfeiture of her interest in the property should be submitted to a jury. I must, therefore, dissent to the affirmance of the trial court's grant of summary judgment on that issue.

Notes and Questions

1. Voluntary and permissive waste. The dissent in *McIntyre v. Scarbrough* distinguishes between voluntary and permissive waste. **Voluntary** or **affirmative waste** is the result of deliberate acts by the possessory tenant, such as destruction or removal of structures or resources on the property. An important category of voluntary waste is the removal of natural resources, such as timber, minerals, or oil and gas. Removal of minerals or oil and gas is generally prohibited voluntary waste unless, under the "open mines" doctrine, the resource was already being mined when the life tenant came into possession. *See Galkin v. Town of Chester*, 716 A.2d 25 (Vt. 1998). Similarly, removing timber is permitted if the land was already used for timber harvesting or the removal is consistent with good husbandry of the land, but voluntary waste otherwise. **Permissive waste**, in contrast, is a matter of omission rather than commission. As in *McIntyre*, permissive waste includes failure to make ordinary repairs preventing deterioration as well as failure to pay real property taxes and other carrying charges necessary to prevent loss of the property. The distinction between voluntary and permissive waste may be important in setting remedies, as discussed below.

Natural disaster and waste. Although life tenants must make ordinary repairs to prevent deterioration, they generally have no obligation to repair damage caused by natural disasters like hurricanes. But the remainder holder has no obligation to pay for such repairs either. This leaves the life tenant whose home is catastrophically damaged with two bad choices: either pay for repairs herself, although the value will ultimately go to the remainder holder, or vacate the damaged property.

2. Remedies. A future interest holder may sue the life tenant to enjoin waste or seek damages for losses to the property or moneys spent to protect it. Suit for damages may also be brought against the life tenant's estate after death, although the suit may be barred by laches or statutes of limitations. *See Moore v. Phillips*, 627 P.2d 831 (Kan. Ct. App. 1981) (no laches where life tenant if alive could not have disputed waste); *McCarver v. Blythe*, 555 S.E.2d 680 (N.C. App. 2001) (statute of limitations barred action, which began running as soon as remainder holder noticed some deterioration). Many states by statute permit the more radical remedy of termination of the life estate. Some of these require that the waste be either voluntary or willful to result in termination, while others allow termination without a showing of intent. *See Matteson v. Walsh*, 947 N.E.2d 44 (Mass. App. 2011) (finding forfeiture for failing to pay taxes and make repairs necessary to prevent leaks and structural rot). States may also permit double or treble damages against tenants committing waste, at least where the damage is intentional. *See* N.J. Stat. §2A:65-3 (tenants committing waste will pay treble damages and lose the place wasted); *Thomas v. Thomas*, 661 N.W.2d 1, 9 (S.D. 2003) (treble damages only permitted where the waste is willful, wanton, or malicious).

3. **Ameliorating waste.** What happens if the life tenant's actions change the character of the property but *increase*, rather than decrease, the value or utility of the property? This is called variously **ameliorating, ameliorative**, or **meliorative waste**. Although the original rule was that any fundamental alteration of the property was waste, today ameliorating waste is sometimes condoned. An important case in this shift is *Melms v. Pabst Brewing Co.*, 79 N.W. 738 (Wis. 1899), which involved a claim for damages for destruction of a large house by the Pabst Brewing Co. after it was determined that Pabst had only a life estate *per autre vie* on the land. Changes to the surrounding area in the city of Milwaukee had left the house isolated and surrounded by factories and railroad tracks and undesirable as a residence, but valuable if cleared for industrial development. The court held that ordinarily a life tenant was prohibited from making any changes, even if beneficial, to the "identity of the property," but could make fundamental changes where "a complete and permanent change of surrounding conditions . . . has deprived the property of its value and usefulness as previously used." *Id.* at 741.

While some jurisdictions maintain the rule prohibiting ameliorating waste, most will approve substantial alteration that increases value if it is justified in light of changed circumstances, consistency with what a fee simple owner would do, and the intent of the parties. *See* Thomas Merrill, Melms v. Pabst Brewing Co. *and the Doctrine of Waste in American Property Law*, 94 Marq. L. Rev. 1055, 1083 (2011). The 1936 *Restatement on Property* also encouraged this shift, providing that the duty of the life tenant is not to decrease "the market value of the interests," *id.* at §138, and that alteration is only prohibited if the remainder or reversion holders would have a "reasonable ground for objection thereto." *Id.* at §141.[7] What reasonable grounds for objection might there be to fundamental changes that increase the value of a property? Would preserving a family home be a reasonable ground for objection? What about preserving a wooded area in a relatively undeveloped state? For a critique of the majority rule (and a fascinating history of *Melms*), *see* Merrill, *supra*.

4. **Sale by the life tenant.** If property is no longer economically viable or personally useful in its prior form, can the life tenant sell it rather than develop it? There is no legal obstacle to selling the life estate, but who wants to buy a life estate? Property held under a life estate is likely to be marketable only if the present and future holders can agree to a sale of a fee simple interest. Proceeds from the sale would be divided between the parties according to the value of their respective interests. Can a life tenant force the remainder holders to agree? *Baker v. Weedon*, 262 So. 2d 641 (Miss. 1972), considered a petition by an elderly life tenant who was impoverished and unable to support herself upon the meager income of $1,300 from her agricultural land. A planned highway bypass had increased the value of the land to $168,500 if it could be sold for development, but the value would double to $336,000 when the bypass

7. The rules are different for lessees and mortgagors, with lessees generally prohibited from making any fundamental alteration to the property unless contemplated by the lease, and mortgagors generally prohibited only from making changes that reduce the value of the property, unless otherwise restricted by the mortgage.

was completed in the next few years. The court held that equity included the power to order a sale of the land when it was "in the best interest of all parties," but found that the facts did not meet this test, ordering sale of only a small portion of part of the property. *Id.* at 645.[8]

Suppose on remand the trial court had found that the remainder holders are wealthy and do not need income from either sale or lease of the land; they prefer to keep the land for a summer retreat, while the life estate owner is barely getting by because the farming income from the land is almost nil. Should the court order the sale on grounds of relative hardship? Whose rights should prevail?

5. **Contracting to avoid conflicts.** Grantors may avoid the default rules limiting alteration, sale, or exploitation of the property by contracting around them. For example, a will creating a life estate in oil-producing property might permit the life tenant to create leases extending beyond her life or to receive royalties from newly drilled wells. *See Steger v. Muenster Drilling Co.*, 134 S.W.3d 359 (Tex. App. 2003) (life tenant had authority to create leases extending after her death); *Singleton v. Donalson*, 117 S.W.3d 516 (Tex. App. 2003) (life tenant had authority to receive royalties from new oil wells). Similarly, a life tenant might be expressly authorized to sell the fee or fundamentally alter structures on the property.

6. **Trust versus life estate.** More flexibility may also be created by using a trust for life rather than a legal life estate. For example, a property could be placed in trust for the benefit of the grantor's widow or widower for life, and then to the grantor's children. The trustee could be empowered to sell the property (the "trust corpus") so long as sale met the trustee's fiduciary obligations to act in the best interests of the beneficiaries. *See* Jesse Dukeminier, James E. Krier, Gregory Alexander & Michael Schill, *Property* 216 (7th ed. 2010) (arguing that "[a] legal life estate is unsuited to a modern economy that regards land as just another form of income-producing wealth, which can swiftly appreciate in value under pressure for development and which must be managed effectively"). Trusts do not, however, resolve all disputes between present and future interest holders. *See Bailey v. Delta Trust & Bank*, 198 S.W.3d 506 (Ark. 2004) (ruling on challenge to trustee's payment of expenses of life beneficiary).

7. **Duties to the community not to commit waste?** There is generally no duty for the living not to waste fee simple property. Absent nuisance, historic preservation, or other prohibitions, fee simple holders may alter and destroy their property, even if it reduces its value. But a number of courts have prohibited execution of wills that ordered destruction of valuable homes after the death of the testator, particularly when it would impact the value of surrounding properties. *See Estate of Eyerman v.*

---

8. At common law, a life estate was valued at one-third of the value of the fee. Today life estates are valued by calculating the value of receiving the going rate of interest on the fee each year for the expected life of the life tenant. *See* 26 C.F.R. §20.2031-7. In *Baker v. Weedon*, the proposal was to invest the proceeds of the sale, with the life tenant to receive the interest on the investment for the rest of her life.

Mercantile Trust Co., 524 S.W.2d 210 (Mo. Ct. App. 1975); *In re Estate of Jones*, 389 A.2d 436, 437 (N.H. 1978); *In re Will of Pace*, 400 N.Y.S.2d 488, 491 (Surr. Ct. 1977). As the court explained in *Pace*,

> There is a greater need for the protection of the community interests after the death of the testator. Although a person may wish to deal capriciously with his property, while he is alive, his self-interest will usually prevent him from doing so. After his death there is no such restraint and it is against public policy to permit the decedent to confer this power upon someone else where his purpose is merely capricious.

400 N.Y.S.2d at 491. Do such decisions inappropriately violate grantor intent, or are they appropriate restraints on the reach of the dead hand? Should the living be restrained from destroying or wasting property? *Compare* Lior Jacob Strahilevitz, *The Right to Destroy*, 114 Yale L.J. 781 (2005) (arguing in favor of a right to destroy), *with* Joseph L. Sax, *Playing Darts with a Rembrandt: Public and Private Rights in Cultural Treasures* (1999) (arguing for restrictions on destruction to conserve historic and artistic treasures), *and* Edward J. McCaffery, *Must We Have the Right to Waste?*, in *New Essays in the Legal and Political Theory of Property* 76 (Stephen R. Munzer ed. 2001) (arguing against a right to destroy for both the living and the dead).

§4.3 Charitable Trusts and the *Cy Pres* Doctrine

When a settlor establishes a charitable trust and the charitable purpose identified by the settlor becomes impracticable or impossible to achieve, courts may apply the doctrine of ***cy pres***, or equitable reformation, to modify the purpose of the trust. For example, imagine that in 1940 a donor created a trust for the treatment of polio in Maryland. Once polio was eradicated in the United States, should the trust fail and be returned to the settlor's heirs or devisees? Or should it be used for another charitable purpose, and if so, which one? To fighting polio overseas, for example, or to another similarly devastating childhood illness in Maryland? Although many nineteenth-century American courts rejected *cy pres* as impermissible governmental control of donor property, after 1900 it quickly spread with the explosion of charitable trusts in the wake of the Gilded Age. Application of *cy pres* involves difficult questions of the determination of donor intent in light of changed circumstances and the role of societal interests in modifying charitable trusts.

> **Terms:**
> Reflecting the medieval English origins of property law, ***cy pres*** comes from the old Norman French phrase, "*cy pres comme possible*," as close as possible, and may be pronounced consistently with the French as "see pray," but is more often pronounced half in English and half in French as "sigh pray."

Evans v. Abney

396 U.S. 435 (1970)

Mr. Justice Hugo Black delivered the opinion of the Court.

Once again this Court must consider the constitutional implications of the 1911 will of United States Senator A. O. Bacon of Georgia which conveyed property in trust to Senator Bacon's home city of Macon for the creation of a public park for the exclusive use of the white people of that city. As a result of our earlier decision in this case which held that the park, Baconsfield, could not continue to be operated on a racially discriminatory basis, *Evans v. Newton*, 382 U.S. 296 (1966), the Supreme Court of Georgia ruled that Senator Bacon's intention to provide a park for whites only had become impossible to fulfill and that accordingly the trust had failed and the parkland and other trust property had reverted by operation of Georgia law to the heirs of the Senator. Petitioners, the same Negro citizens of Macon who have sought in the courts to integrate the park, contend that this termination of the trust violates their rights to equal protection and due process under the Fourteenth Amendment. We granted certiorari because of the importance of the questions involved. For the reasons to be stated, we are of the opinion that the judgment of the Supreme Court of Georgia should be, and it is, affirmed.

In 1911 United States Senator Augustus O. Bacon executed a will that devised to the Mayor and Council of the City of Macon, Georgia, a tract of land which, after the death of the Senator's wife and daughters, was to be used as "a park and pleasure ground" for white people only, the Senator stating in the will that while he had only the kindest feeling for the Negroes he was of the opinion that "in their social relations the two races (white and negro) should be forever separate." The will provided that the park should be under the control of a Board of Managers of seven persons, all of whom were to be white. The city kept the park segregated for some years but in time let Negroes use it, taking the position that the park was a public facility which it could not constitutionally manage and maintain on a segregated basis.

Thereupon, individual members of the Board of Managers of the park brought this suit in a state court against the City of Macon and the trustees of certain residuary beneficiaries of Senator Bacon's estate, asking that the city be removed as trustee and that the court appoint new trustees, to whom title to the park would be transferred. The city answered, alleging it could not legally enforce racial segregation in the park. The other defendants admitted the allegation and requested that the city be removed as trustee.

Several Negro citizens of Macon intervened, alleging that the racial limitation was contrary to the laws and public policy of the United States, and asking that the court refuse to appoint private trustees. Thereafter the city resigned as trustee and amended its answer accordingly. Moreover, other heirs of Senator Bacon intervened and they and the defendants other than the city asked for reversion of the trust property to the Bacon estate in the event that the prayer of the petition were denied.

The Georgia court accepted the resignation of the city as trustee and appointed three individuals as new trustees, finding it unnecessary to pass on the other claims of the heirs. On appeal by the Negro intervenors, the Supreme Court of Georgia affirmed, holding that Senator Bacon had the right to give and bequeath his property to a limited class, that charitable trusts are subject to supervision of a court of equity, and that the power to appoint new trustees so that the purpose of the trust would not fail was clear.

The Court in *Evans v. Newton*, supra, went on to reverse the judgment of the Georgia Supreme Court and to hold that the public character of Baconsfield "requires that it be treated as a public institution subject to the command of the Fourteenth Amendment, regardless of who now has title under state law." 382 U.S., at 302. [On remand, petitioners and the Georgia Attorney General] argued that the trust should be saved by applying the *cy pres* doctrine to amend the terms of the will by striking the racial restrictions and opening Baconsfield to all the citizens of Macon without regard to race or color. The trial court, however, refused to apply *cy pres*. It held that the doctrine was inapplicable because the park's segregated, whites-only character was an essential and inseparable part of the testator's plan. Since the "sole purpose" of the trust was thus in irreconcilable conflict with the constitutional mandate expressed in our opinion in *Evans v. Newton*, the trial court ruled that the Baconsfield trust had failed and that the trust property had by operation of law reverted to the heirs of Senator Bacon. On appeal, the Supreme Court of Georgia affirmed.

We are of the opinion that in ruling as they did the Georgia courts did no more than apply well-settled general principles of Georgia law to determine the meaning and effect of a Georgia will. At the time Senator Bacon made his will Georgia cities and towns were, and they still are, authorized to accept devises of property for the establishment and preservation of "parks and pleasure grounds" and to hold the property thus received in charitable trust for the exclusive benefit of the class of persons named by the testator. Ga. Code, ch. 69-5 (1967); Ga. Code §§108-203, 108-207 (1959). These provisions of the Georgia Code explicitly authorized the testator to include, if he should choose, racial restrictions such as those found in Senator Bacon's will. The city accepted the trust with these restrictions in it. When this Court in *Evans v. Newton, supra*, held that the continued operation of Baconsfield as a segregated park was unconstitutional, the particular purpose of the Baconsfield trust as stated in the will failed under Georgia law. The question then properly before the Georgia Supreme Court was whether as a matter of state law the doctrine of *cy pres* should be applied to prevent the trust itself from failing. Petitioners urged that the *cy pres* doctrine allowed the Georgia courts to strike the racially restrictive clauses in Bacon's will so that the terms of the trust could be fulfilled without violating the Constitution.

The Georgia *cy pres* statutes upon which petitioners relied provide:

> When a valid charitable bequest is incapable for some reason of execution in the exact manner provided by the testator, donor, or founder, a court of equity will carry it into effect in such a way as will as nearly as possible effectuate his intention. Ga. Code §108-202 (1959).
>
> A devise or bequest to a charitable use will be sustained and carried out in this State; and in all cases where there is a general intention manifested by the testator to effect a certain purpose, and the particular mode in which he directs it to be done shall fail from any cause, a court of chancery may, by approximation, effectuate the purpose in a manner most similar to that indicated by the testator. Ga. Code §113-815 (1959).

The Georgia courts have held that the fundamental purpose of these *cy pres* provisions is to allow the court to carry out the general charitable intent of the testator where this intent might otherwise be thwarted by the impossibility of the particular plan or scheme provided by the testator. But this underlying logic of the *cy pres* doctrine implies that there is a certain class of cases in which the doctrine cannot be applied. Professor Scott in his treatise on trusts states this limitation on the doctrine of *cy pres* which is common to many States as follows:

> It is not true that a charitable trust never fails where it is impossible to carry out the particular purpose of the testator. In some cases . . . it appears that the accomplishment of the particular purpose and only that purpose was desired by the testator and that he had no more general charitable intent and that he would presumably have preferred to have the whole trust fail if the particular purpose is impossible of accomplishment. In such a case the *cy pres* doctrine is not applicable. 4 A. Scott, The Law of Trusts §399, at 3085 (3d ed. 1967).

In this case, Senator Bacon provided an unusual amount of information in his will from which the Georgia courts could determine the limits of his charitable purpose. Immediately after specifying that the park should be for "the sole, perpetual and unending, use, benefit and enjoyment of the white women, white girls, white boys and white children of the City of Macon," the Senator stated that "the said property under no circumstances . . . [is] to be . . . at any time for any reason devoted to any other purpose or use excepting so far as herein specifically authorized." And the Senator continued:

> I take occasion to say that in limiting the use and enjoyment of this property perpetually to white people, I am not influenced by any unkindness of feeling or want of consideration for the Negroes, or colored people. On the contrary I have for them the kindest feeling, and for many of them esteem and regard, while for some of them I have sincere personal affection.
>
> I am, however, without hesitation in the opinion that in their social relations the two races . . . should be forever separate and that they should not have pleasure or recreation grounds to be used or enjoyed, together and in common.

The Georgia courts, construing Senator Bacon's will as a whole, concluded from this and other language in the will that the Senator's charitable intent was not "general" but extended only to the establishment of a segregated park for the benefit of white people. The Georgia trial court found that "Senator Bacon could not have used language more clearly indicating his intent that the benefits of Baconsfield should be extended to white persons only, or more clearly indicating that this limitation was an essential and indispensable part of his plan for Baconsfield." Since racial separation was found to be an inseparable part of the testator's intent, the Georgia courts held that the State's *cy pres* doctrine could not be used to alter the will to permit racial integration. The Baconsfield trust was therefore held to have failed, and, under Georgia law, "[w]here a trust is expressly created, but uses . . . fail from any cause, a resulting trust is implied for the benefit of the grantor, or testator, or his heirs." Ga. Code §108-106(4) (1959). The Georgia courts concluded, in effect, that Senator Bacon would have rather had the whole trust fail than have Baconsfield integrated.

When a city park is destroyed because the Constitution requires it to be integrated, there is reason for everyone to be disheartened. We agree with petitioners that in such a case it is not enough to find that the state court's result was reached through the application of established principles of state law. No state law or act can prevail in the face of contrary federal law, and the federal courts must search out the fact and truth of any proceeding or transaction to determine if the Constitution has been violated. Here, however, the action of the Georgia Supreme Court declaring the Baconsfield trust terminated presents no violation of constitutionally protected rights, and any harshness that may have resulted from the state court's decision can be attributed solely to its intention to effectuate as nearly as possible the explicit terms of Senator Bacon's will.

The construction of wills is essentially a state-law question, and in this case the Georgia Supreme Court, as we read its opinion, interpreted Senator Bacon's will as embodying a preference for termination of the park rather than its integration. Given this, the Georgia court had no alternative under its relevant trust laws, which are long standing and neutral with regard to race, but to end the Baconsfield trust and return the property to the Senator's heirs.

A second argument for petitioners stresses the similarities between this case and the case in which a city holds an absolute fee simple title to a public park and then closes that park of its own accord solely to avoid the effect of a prior court order directing that the park be integrated as the Fourteenth Amendment commands. Yet, assuming arguendo that the closing of the park would in those circumstances violate the Equal Protection Clause, that case would be clearly distinguishable from the case at bar because there it is the State and not a private party which is injecting the racially discriminatory motivation. In the case at bar there is not the slightest indication that any of the Georgia judges involved were motivated by racial animus or discriminatory intent of any sort in construing and enforcing Senator Bacon's will. Nor is there any indication that Senator Bacon in drawing up his will was persuaded or induced to include racial restrictions by the fact that such restrictions were permitted by the Georgia trust statutes. On the contrary, the language of the Senator's will shows that the racial restrictions were solely the product of the testator's own full-blown social philosophy. Similarly, the situation presented in this case is also easily distinguishable from that presented in *Shelley v. Kraemer*, 334 U.S. 1 (1948), where we held unconstitutional state judicial action which had affirmatively enforced a private scheme of discrimination against Negroes. Here the effect of the Georgia decision eliminated all discrimination against Negroes in the park by eliminating the park itself, and the termination of the park was a loss shared equally by the white and Negro citizens of Macon since both races would have enjoyed a constitutional right of equal access to the park's facilities had it continued.

Mr. Justice William J. Brennan, Jr., dissenting.

For almost half a century Baconsfield has been a public park. Senator Bacon's will provided that upon the death of the last survivor among his widow and two daughters title to Baconsfield would vest in the Mayor and Council of the City of Macon and their successors forever. The city acquired title to Baconsfield in 1920 by purchasing the interests of Senator Bacon's surviving daughter and another person who resided on the land. Some $46,000 of public money was spent over a number of years to pay the purchase price. From the outset and throughout the years the Mayor and City Council acted as trustees, Baconsfield was administered as a public park. T. Cleveland James, superintendent of city parks during this period, testified that when he first worked at Baconsfield it was a "wilderness . . . nothing there but just undergrowth everywhere, one road through there and that's all, one paved road." He said there were no park facilities at that time. In the 1930's Baconsfield was transformed into a modern recreational facility by employees of the Works Progress Administration, an agency of the Federal Government. Other capital improvements were made in later years with both federal and city money.

I have no doubt that a public park may constitutionally be closed down because it is too expensive to run or has become superfluous, or for some other reason, strong or weak, or for no reason at all. But under the Equal Protection Clause a State may not close down a public facility solely to avoid its duty to desegregate that facility.

The Court, however, affirms the judgment of the Georgia Supreme Court on the ground that the closing of Baconsfield did not involve state action. This discriminatory closing is permeated with state action: at the time Senator Bacon wrote his will Georgia statutes expressly authorized and supported the precise kind of discrimination provided for by him; in accepting title to the park, public officials of the City of Macon entered into an arrangement vesting in private persons the power to enforce a reversion if the city should ever incur a constitutional obligation to desegregate the park; it is a public park that is being closed for a discriminatory reason after having been operated for nearly half a century as a segregated public facility; and it is a state court that is enforcing the racial restriction that keeps apparently willing parties of different races from coming together in the park. That is state action in overwhelming abundance. I need emphasize only three elements of the state action present here.

First, there is state action whenever a State enters into an arrangement that creates a private right to compel or enforce the reversion of a public facility. Whether the right is a possibility of reverter, a right of entry, an executory interest, or a contractual right, it can be created only with the consent of a public body or official, for example the official action involved in Macon's acceptance of the gift of Baconsfield. The State's involvement in the creation of such a right is also involvement in its enforcement; the State's assent to the creation of the right necessarily contemplates that the State will enforce the right if called upon to do so. Where, as in this case, the State's enforcement role conflicts with its obligation to comply with the constitutional command against racial segregation the attempted enforcement must be declared repugnant to the Fourteenth Amendment.

A finding of discriminatory state action is required here on a second ground. *Shelley v. Kraemer*, 334 U.S. 1 (1948), stands at least for the proposition that where parties of different races are willing to deal with one another a state court cannot keep them from doing so by enforcing a privately devised racial restriction. Nothing in the record suggests that after our decision in *Evans v. Newton*, *supra*, the City of Macon retracted its previous willingness to manage Baconsfield on a nonsegregated basis, or that the white beneficiaries of Senator Bacon's generosity were unwilling to share it with Negroes, rather than have the park revert to his heirs. [In addition,] the Attorney General of Georgia was made a party after remand from this Court, and, acting "as parens patriae in all legal matters pertaining to the administration and disposition of charitable trusts in the State of Georgia in which the rights of beneficiaries are involved," he opposed a reversion to the heirs and argued that Baconsfield should be maintained "as a park for all the citizens of the State of Georgia." [S]o far as the record shows, this is a case of a state court's enforcement of a racial restriction to prevent willing parties from dealing with one another. The decision of the Georgia courts thus, under *Shelley v. Kraemer*, constitutes state action denying equal protection.

Finally, a finding of discriminatory state action is required on a third ground. In *Reitman v. Mulkey*, 387 U.S. 369 (1967), this Court announced the basic principle that a State acts in violation of the Equal Protection Clause when it singles out racial discrimination for particular encouragement, and thereby gives it a special preferred status in the law, even though the State does not itself impose or compel segregation. [In 1905] prior to the enactment of §§69-504 and 69-505 of the Georgia Code "it would have been extremely doubtful" whether Georgia law authorized "a trust for park purposes when a portion of the public was to be excluded from the park." Sections 69-504 and 69-505 removed this doubt by expressly permitting dedication of land to the public for use as a park open to one race only.

In 1911, only six years after the enactment of §§69-504 and 69-505, Senator Bacon, a lawyer, wrote his will. When he wrote the provision creating Baconsfield as a public park open only to the white race, he was not merely expressing his own testamentary intent, but was taking advantage of the special power Georgia had conferred by §§69-504 and 69-505 on testators seeking to establish racially segregated public parks. This state-encouraged testamentary provision is the sole basis for the Georgia courts' holding that Baconsfield must revert to Senator Bacon's heirs. The Court's finding that it is not the State of Georgia but "a private party which is injecting the racially discriminatory motivation" inexcusably disregards the State's role in enacting the statute without which Senator Bacon could not have written the discriminatory provision.

Notes and Questions

1. **Donor intent.** In applying *cy pres* to charitable trusts, the hypothetical inquiry is whether the donor, knowing of the changed circumstances, would prefer to have the charitable donation fail altogether or modified to serve a related purpose. In *Evans v. Abney*, how should we construct this hypothesized testator? Are we asking what Senator Bacon would have wanted in 1911 had the city refused to segregate the park (unimaginable in 1911), or what he would have wanted had he lived through the changes leading to the decisions that public segregation was unconstitutional and private segregation violated federal civil rights statutes (also unimaginable in 1911)? Which inquiry better respects the donor's wishes? Which better respects the donor himself?

The *cy pres* doctrine traditionally places the burden on the party seeking reformation to prove that the donor had a "general charitable intent" beyond the specific purposes named in the bequest. *Kolb v. City of Storm Lake*, 736 N.W.2d 546, 559 (Iowa

2007). This has been the most litigated element of the *cy pres* determination. Often the trust document itself states only specific purposes and there is no other evidence of intent. Nevertheless, courts often find a general intent in such circumstances. *See id.* at 559 (finding that despite several mentions of specific location of a memorial garden, the donors had a general charitable intent permitting the city to move the garden when its location became impracticable).

The modern trend is to do away with this requirement and presume general charitable intent. The *Restatement (Third) of Trusts* (2003) provides that if the purposes of a charitable trust become impossible, impracticable, or wasteful to achieve, the trust shall be redirected to a purpose that "reasonably approximates" the stated purpose "[u]nless the terms of the trust provide otherwise." *Id.* §67; *see In re Elizabeth J.K.L. Lucas Charitable Gift,* 261 P.3d 800, 808-809 (Haw. App. 2011) (noting trend). The *Uniform Trust Code,* a model law promulgated by the National Conference of Commissioners on Uniform State Laws, provides that a charitable trust whose purposes become impossible or impracticable to accomplish "shall not fail" and "shall not revert to the settlor" and the court may modify it in a manner consistent with the settlor's charitable purposes. *Uniform Trust Code* §413 (2000). Even specific provisions for reversion to the grantor on failure of the trust shall not be enforced unless the settlor is still living or the trust has been in existence for less than 21 years. *Id.* About half the states have already adopted the provision. While other states may continue to espouse a need to find a general charitable purpose, many will likely apply it by assuming that the testator had such a purpose absent clear evidence otherwise.

Does the new test sacrifice donor intent in order to achieve public interests in charitable trusts? Or does is it appropriately attribute to the donor the motives of a reasonable generous person, who would prefer to see her bequest used effectively than fail or be devoted to an impracticable purpose? *Compare* Vanessa Laird, *Phantom Selves: The Search for General Intent in the Application of the* Cy Pres *Doctrine,* 40 Stan. L. Rev. 973 (1988) (arguing that presuming that donors would want their gifts used charitably and usefully honors donor intent), *and Restatement (Third) of Trusts* §67 cmt. b ("'[T]he dilemma of whether to enforce the testator's intent or to modify the terms of the will in accordance with changed conditions since his death is often a false one.'") (quoting Richard A. Posner, *Economic Analysis of Law* 556-557 (5th ed. 1998)), *with* Alberto V. Lopez, *An Evaluation of* Cy Pres *Redux,* 78 U. Cinn. L. Rev. 1307 (2010) (arguing that the new rules improperly elevate societal interests over donor intent). Note that (as seen in the dissent in *Evans v. Abney*) the state attorney general is often a party or even the petitioner in a *cy pres* action, with the sometimes conflicting roles of safeguarding the donor's intent and society's interests as *parens patriae* for charities.

2. Impossible or just contrary to the public interest? The traditional inquiry, maintained in many states, is whether fulfilling the purpose of the trust is actually or practicably impossible to achieve. *See Estate of Estes v. Central United Methodist Church,* 523 N.W. 2d 863 (Mich. App. 1994) (trust corpus could only be used for building a new church, although existing church was in landmarked well-constructed building, congregation was shrinking, and no plans had been made to build new church in the 21 years since the gift). The modern trend, however, is to permit reformation if the purpose is broadly impracticable, "wasteful," or unreasonable. *See Restatement (Third) of Trusts* §67 (adding "wasteful" element); *Uniform Trust Code* §413 (2000) (same); N.H. Rev. Stat. §498:4-a (*cy pres* permitted if, among other things, the trust is "prejudicial to the public interest").

3. ***Cy pres* and the reform of discriminatory trusts.** Many courts have applied *cy pres* to reform trusts that illegally restricted their benefits on the basis of race or sex. *Home for Incurables of Baltimore City v. University of Maryland Medical System Corp.*, 769 A.2d 746 (Md. 2002) (reforming trust for construction of rehabilitation center for white patients); *In re Crichfield Trust*, 426 A.2d 88 (N.J. Super. Ct. Ch. Div. 1980) (reforming trust that established a college scholarship for male graduates of a public high school); *Coffee v. William Marsh Rice University*, 408 S.W.2d 269, 271 (Tex. Ct. App. 1966) (using *cy pres* to excise racial restriction in endowment fund). *Cf. United States v. Hughes Memorial Home*, 396 F. Supp. 544 (D. W. Va. 1975) (*cy pres* doctrine applied to excise racial restriction on trust benefiting orphanage because racial exclusion from the orphanage would violate the federal *Fair Housing Act*). In *In re Certain Scholarship Funds,* 575 A.2d 1325 (N.H. 1990), for example, a testator established a charitable scholarship trust to provide a college education "for some Poor and worthy Keene boy who is a scholar in the Keene High School." A second settlor established a similar trust providing that the income be used "to provide tuition for one year for some worthy protestant boy" at Keene High School. The New Hampshire Supreme Court agreed to remove the race and gender restrictions, affirming the trial court's finding that "there was no indication that Mr. Wright or Mr. Alger would not have responded to the changes in attitudes experienced by society since the creation of these trusts." *Id.* at 1328. The court denied the Attorney General's request that it should cure the unconstitutional restrictions by substituting private trustees for the Board of Education:

> [T]he court must ask whether its first priority is to end the discrimination or to preserve it. [W]e believe that the appropriate source of values for our judgment is the constitution, which forbids the agencies of the State to act in a manner that would preserve the constitutionally impermissible desires of the testator.

Id. at 1329-1330. In a similar case, however, the New York Court of Appeals substituted private trustees for Board of Education officials in two trusts, one for scholarships for "five (5) young men who shall have graduated from the Canastota High School, three (3) of whom shall have attained the highest grades in the study of science and two (2) of whom shall have attained the highest grades in the study of chemistry" and the other for scholarships for "bright and deserving young men who have graduated from the High School of [the Croton-Harmon Union Free] School District." *Matter of Estate of Wilson*, 452 N.E.2d 1228, 1228 (N.Y. 1983). The trial court found that the donors had a specific intent to benefit men, and that gender-specific scholarships did not violate public policy. *Id.* What justifies the different approaches?

4. State action. In *Shelley v. Kraemer*, 334 U.S. 1 (1948), the Supreme Court held that judicial enforcement of a racially restrictive covenant to prevent a sale to an African American family constituted state action and so was prohibited by the fourteenth amendment. *See* Chapter 8, §5.2. *Evans v. Abney*, however, holds that the reversion required by state statute after a trust fails because of violation of the fourteenth amendment is not state action. What justifies the difference? In 1955, the North Carolina Supreme Court reached the same result, affirming the constitutionality of a possibility of reverter of land conveyed to the city of Charlotte as a public park "for use by the white race only." *Charlotte Park & Recreation Commission v. Barringer*, 88 S.E.2d 114 (N.C. 1955). The court found no state action:

> If Negroes use the Bonnie Brae Golf Course, the determinable fee conveyed to plaintiff by Barringer, and his wife, automatically will cease and terminate by its own limitation expressed in the deed. . . . The operation of this reversion provision is not by any judicial enforcement by the State Courts of North Carolina, and *Shelley v. Kraemer*, 334 U.S. 1, has no application.

Id. at 123. In contrast, in *Capitol Federal Savings & Loan Association v. Smith*, 316 P.2d 252 (Colo. 1957), a group of property owners entered into a covenant not to sell or lease their land to "any colored person or persons," and providing that if any parcel were conveyed or leased in violation of the covenant, the interest of the African American owner "shall be forfeited to and rest in such of the then owners of all of said lots and parcels of land not included in such conveyance or lease who may assert title thereto by filing for record notice of their claim." The court held that regardless of whether the restriction was a covenant or an executory interest, the policies underlying *Shelley v. Kraemer* applied:

> No matter by what ariose terms the covenant under consideration may be classified by state counsel, it is still a racial restriction in violation of the Fourteenth Amendment to the Federal Constitution. While the hands may seem to be the hands of Esau to a blind Isaac, the voice is definitely Jacob's. We cannot give our judicial approval or blessing to a contract such as is here involved.

Id. at 254-255. Which approach is correct?

Problems

1. In the 1940s and 1950s, Georgia O'Keefe donated the important art collection of her husband, Alfred Stieglitz, and several of her own paintings to Fisk University, a historically black college in Nashville, Tennessee, which at that time provided a uniquely integrated cultural and artistic center in the South. The gifts were made with numerous specific restrictions including that the works could not be sold, that the photographs could not be loaned for display elsewhere, and that the works had to be displayed as an entire collection, in a room painted in a white or off-white color selected by O'Keefe. In 2005, in dire financial straits and unable to afford to show the collection, Fisk sought permission to sell some of the paintings. What should the court do? *See In re Fisk University*, 392 S.W.3d 582 (Tenn. App. 2011).

2. In *Hermitage Methodist Homes of Virginia, Inc. v. Dominion Trust Co.*, 387 S.E.2d 740 (Va. 1990), a testator named Jack Adams died, leaving a charitable trust providing income to the Prince Edward School, "so long as Prince Edward School Foundation admits to any school, operated or supported by it, only members of the White Race." His will further provided that if the school should ever "matriculate . . . any person who is not a member of the White Race, no further payment of income shall be made" to the school, but all income should go to the Miller School. Further gifts were provided to the Seven Hills School and then to Hampden-Sydney College if the prior recipient violated the "whites-only" provision of the trust. The final beneficiary of the successive gifts over was Hermitage Methodist Homes of Virginia; this final gift had no racial restriction built in. At the time Adams wrote his will, Virginia Code §55-26 made it lawful to create a charitable trust for the education of white or "colored" persons but not of both. The statute was later repealed.

In 1987, the trustee sued the first beneficiary, Prince Edward School, because it had admitted African American students. The trial court held that all "racially discriminatory conditions of the Trust are unconstitutional and void" and determined that Prince Edward School should continue receiving the income from the trust. The Virginia Supreme Court reversed, holding that even if it were unconstitutional to enforce a restrictive condition, depriving Prince Edward of the income from the trust effected no such enforcement. The condition in the trust did not take the form of a condition subsequent but was, rather, a "special limitation" that ended Prince Edward's beneficial ownership interest automatically as soon as the condition was violated. Thus, no court action was needed to alter ownership of the income from Prince Edward. Because all of the educational institutions had admitted black students, the interests in the trust proceeds went to Heritage Methodist Homes, which alone had no restrictions in its gift.

Professor Jonathan Entin reports the history of the Prince Edward School:

> The Prince Edward School Foundation was founded in June 1955 to establish private schools for white pupils in the event that the federal courts ordered the public schools of Prince Edward County to desegregate. Such an order seemed certain because the county school board was one of the defendants in *Brown v. Board of Education*. The order finally came in 1959. Local officials responded by shutting down the public schools. At the same time, the Foundation opened a private school known as Prince Edward Academy that enrolled almost every white student in the county. The Academy continued to enroll a large majority of the county's white pupils for some years after the Supreme Court ordered the public schools reopened on a desegregated basis in 1964.

Jonathan Entin, *Defeasible Fees, State Action, and the Legacy of Massive Resistance*, 34 Wm. & Mary L. Rev. 769 (1993). Does this knowledge change your analysis of the case?

3. Section 1982 of the *Civil Rights Act of 1866*, 42 U.S.C. §1982, provides that

> [a]ll citizens of the United States shall have the same right, in every State and Territory, as is enjoyed by white citizens thereof to inherit, purchase, lease, sell, hold, and convey real and personal property.

The statute clearly prohibits any state law that would prevent persons of a particular race from inheriting property. Does it also prevent the state from enforcing a racial restriction placed by a donor in a donative transfer? If it does, does §1982 require the restriction to be stricken, leaving title with the city and thereby keeping the park open? Even if the equal protection clause of the Constitution does not prevent closure of the park to honor the donor's discriminatory intent, does §1982 prohibit enforcement of the racial restriction? *See* Florence Wagman Roisman, *The Impact of the Civil Rights Act of 1866 on Racially Discriminatory Donative Transfers,* 53 Ala. L. Rev. 463 (2002) (arguing that it does).

§5 REGULATORY ESTATES AND FUTURE INTERESTS

Future interests are regulated by both common law rules and statutes. The main structural rules include (1) the rule prohibiting the creation of new estates; (2) the rule against unreasonable restraints on alienation; (3) the rule against perpetuities; and (4) the rule against unreasonable restraints on marriage.

§5.1 Rule Against Creation of New Estates (The *Numerus Clausus* Doctrine)

The rules underlying the creation of future interests are intended to discourage the social hierarchy characteristic of feudalism and to promote a market system involving wide dispersal of property rights to prevent local monopolies. The commitment to these goals requires courts to decide which forms of property shall be recognized. We could just allow owners to create whatever future interests they want, but this is not how the law developed.

In light of this problem, courts follow a general **rule against the creation of new estates**. A conveyance that does not fit within any of the established categories (including fee simple absolute subject to covenants, defeasible fees, life estates, leaseholds, and in some states, fees tail) must be interpreted to create the most closely analogous estate.

This rule has both formal and substantive dimensions. *See* Thomas W. Merrill & Henry E. Smith, *Optimal Standardization in the Law of Property: The* Numerus Clausus *Principle,* 110 Yale L.J. 1 (2000). Formally, it means that grantors must put their conveyances in a recognizable form if they want courts to recognize the package of rights they intended to create. Substantively, it means that certain packages of rights will not be recognized. This limits the number of packages of ownership bundles that can be created, facilitating exchange both by making it easier to determine what one is buying and by ensuring that owners have certain basic rights when they acquire those standard bundles. The rule against creation of new estates also helps consolidate property rights, either immediately or over time, in a single owner. It does this by limiting the power of grantors to create particular future interests. Consider how Justice Oliver Wendell Holmes, Jr., reacted to the following estate.

Johnson v. Whiton

34 N.E. 542 (Mass. 1893)

OLIVER WENDELL HOLMES, JR., J.

This is an action to recover a deposit paid under an agreement to purchase land. The land in question passed under the seventh clause of the will of Royal Whiton to his five grandchildren, and a deed executed by them was tendered to the plaintiff, but was refused, on the ground that one of the grandchildren, Sarah A. Whiton, could not convey a fee-simple absolute, and this action is brought to try the question. The clause of the will referred to is as follows: "After the decease of all my children, I give, devise, and bequeath to my granddaughter Sarah A. Whiton and her heirs on her father's side one-third part of all my estate, both real and personal, and to my other grandchildren and their heirs, respectively, the remainder, to be divided in equal parts between them."

We see no room for doubt that the legal title passed by the foregoing clause. We think it equally plain that the words "and her heirs on her father's side" are words of limitation, and not words of purchase. The only serious question is whether the effect of them was to give Sarah A. Whiton only a qualified fee, and whether, by reason of the qualification, she is unable to convey a fee simple. By the old law, to take land by descent a man must be of the blood of the first purchaser, and descent is traced from the purchaser. For instance, if the land had been acquired in fee simple by Sarah A. Whiton's father, it could only have descended from her to her heirs on her father's side. It was no great stretch to allow a limitation in the first instance to Sarah of a fee with the same descendible quality that it would have had in the case supposed. Especially is this true if, as Mr. Challis argues, the grantee under such a limitation could convey a fee simple, just as he or she could have done if the estate actually had descended from the father. But our statute of descent looks no further than the person himself who died seised of or entitled to the estate. The analogy which lies at the foundation of the argument for the possibility of such limitations is wanting. A man cannot create a new kind of inheritance. These and other authorities show, too, that, except in the case of a grant by the king, if the words "on her father's side" do not effect the purpose intended, they are to be rejected, leaving the estate a fee simple. Certainly, it would seem that in this commonwealth an estate descending only to heirs on the father's side was a new kind of inheritance.

What we have to consider, however, is not the question of descent, but that of alienability; and that question brings a further consideration into view. It would be most unfortunate and unexpected if it should be discovered at this late day that it was possible to impose such a qualification upon a fee, and to put it out of the power of the owners to give a clear title for generations. In the more familiar case of an estate tail, the legislature has acted, and the statute has been carried to the furthest verge by construction. It is not too much to say that it would be plainly contrary to the policy of the law of Massachusetts to deny the power of Sarah A. Whiton to convey an unqualified fee.

§5.2 Rule Against Unreasonable Restraints on Alienation

See Chapter 8, §5.3.

§5.3 Rule Against Perpetuities

A. The Traditional Rule

The **rule against perpetuities** invalidates future interests that may vest too far into the future. It does so in order to protect against dead hand control, limiting the time within which the identity of who will own the property in the future may become certain. By doing so, the rule arguably promotes alienability and productive use of land by requiring that the identity of those who own the property be fixed within a certain period of time.

Under the rule, future interests are invalid unless they are certain to "vest" or fail to vest within the lifetime of someone who is alive ("in being") at the creation of the interest or no later than 21 years after her death. In John Chipman Gray's famous formulation:

> *No interest is good unless it must vest, if at all, no later than 21 years after the death of some life in being at the creation of the interest.*

John Chipman Gray, *The Rule Against Perpetuities* §201 (4th ed. 1942).

The rule is technical, complicated, and, in the minds of some, archaic. It has also been substantially modified by statute in more than half the states. At the same time, the policies underlying the rule still have substantial support among many judges, legislators, and scholars. The rule is "designed to prevent remoteness of vesting and thereby leave control of the wealth of the world more in the hands of the living than in the hands of the dead." 3 *Thompson on Real Property, Second Thomas Editions* §28.02. Although modified by statute, it has been abolished entirely only in a few states.

> **The Rule in the Movies:** *The Descendants*, an Academy Award–winning 2011 film, features a conveyance written to avoid the rule against perpetuities. George Clooney is a beneficiary of a trust of land providing that the trust will end and the land may be sold 20 years after the death of the last of the descendants living at the time of the settlor's death. For an older starring role of the rule, see *Body Heat* (1981), in which Kathleen Turner gains a fortune and lands William Hurt in prison through her knowledge of the rule.

The rule against perpetuities has been the bane of law students for generations. As Gray wrote in his foundational text,

> There is something in the subject which seems to facilitate error. Perhaps it is because the mode of reasoning is unlike that with which lawyers are most familiar. . . . [T]here are few lawyers of any practice in drawing wills and settlements who have not at some time either fallen into the net which the Rule spreads for the unwary, or at least shuddered to think how narrowly they have escaped it.

Gray, *supra*, at ix-x. In an infamous decision, the California Supreme Court even held that a lawyer could not held guilty of malpractice for drafting a will that violated the rule because it was unreasonable to expect a lawyer of "ordinary skill and capacity" to apply it correctly. *Lucas v. Hamm*, 364 P.2d 685 (1961).

How to apply the rule. The rule is difficult to apply to complicated conveyances. However, the rule is not difficult in the vast majority of cases. These materials explain the rule in detail and show how to apply it to a series of representative problems.

The rule requires four steps. First, identify the future interests created by the grant. If the interest is in the grantor, it is not subject to the rule (except for certain commercial interests discussed below). Second, identify what has to happen for the interest to fully vest, meaning that any conditions will have occurred, and no more people can be added to the class of recipients. Third, identify all the "lives in being," the people alive at the creation of the interest who can have something to do with it vesting. Fourth, see if you can imagine any way—however unlikely or in defiance of normal rules of reproductive biology—in which the future interest will vest more than 21 years after the death of all of the people identified in step three. If you can, the future interest is invalid. Let us consider these steps in more depth.

1. Identify the future interests created by the grant. *All future interests in the grantor are exempt* from the rule against perpetuities; these include reversions (following life estates and leaseholds) and possibilities of reverter and rights of entry (following defeasible fees). Interests in the grantor were conceptualized as "vested" the moment they were created. This is because an owner of a fee simple absolute who conveys a fee simple determinable is carving out a present estate from a fee simple absolute that is already vested; the possibility of reverter is part of that vested interest that was not given away. These future interests are "good" and will be enforced by the courts unless they are regulated by special statutory limitations other than the rule against perpetuities. The only interests in third parties that are similarly exempt from the rule against perpetuities are *vested remainders* that are either absolutely vested or vested subject to divestment.

Future interests that are subject to the rule against perpetuities are executory interests, contingent remainders, and vested remainders subject to open. These interests must be tested to see whether they comply with the rule. Vested remainders subject to open are subject to the rule because some of the interests to the class members are vested and some are contingent (those belonging to persons who are not born at the creation of the interest). All future interests in third parties following defeasible fees (executory interests) are subject to the rule against perpetuities. Future interests in third parties following life estates (remainders) are subject to the rule only if they are contingent, that is, if there is a condition precedent to their vesting or if they are allocated to persons unascertained at the time of the original conveyance creating them. Vested remainders subject to open are partially contingent and therefore have traditionally been held subject to the rule.

A common example of a future interest traded in the marketplace is an **option to purchase**, which is the right to buy property for a stated price at some point in the future. Because options are rights to terminate an estate, they are akin to executory interests and therefore are ordinarily subject to the rule against perpetuities. This is true whether the option is held by the original grantor of the property or by a third party. **Preemptive rights**, also called **rights of first refusal**, allow the holder to purchase property whenever the current owner decides to sell. Some courts hold that preemptive rights are not subject to the rule against perpetuities because they allow the current owner either to obtain the fair market value or to have an offer by a third party matched by the owner of the preemptive right. Either way, the property is alienable. Other courts hold that preemptive rights, like options to purchase, are subject to the rule against perpetuities. *See* §5.3.D, *infra*.

Note that the type of interest is fixed when it is created. Thus when an owner of a right of entry transfers the interest to another person, it remains a right of entry and does not change into an executory interest, even though it is held by someone other than the grantor or her heirs.

2. Identify what has to happen for the interest to fully vest. This step requires you to understand the concept of vesting. **Fully vest** means that all future interest holders are ascertained and any contingencies for their ownership are removed. In other words, we know exactly who is going to get the interest, that they are going to get it, and what fraction of the interest they are going to get.

Importantly, the question is not when the future interest becomes *possessory*, but rather when we know exactly who will own the property in the future. For example, imagine a will providing,

O to *A* for life, and then to *A*'s children.

What has to happen for this interest to vest in anybody? *A* needs to have some children! The children do not need to survive *A* for the interest to vest. Once they come into being, they have a right to at least some portion of the remainder. If any children of *A* die before *A*, the property may go to their heirs or devisees. But what needs to happen for the remainder to *fully* vest for purposes of the rule? *A* needs to die. Because *A* might have another child before he dies, until that happens the remainder is vested subject to open, and although we know that the existing children are entitled to something, we do not know whether any other children will share the remainder.

3. Identify all the lives in being at the creation of the interest. This step requires you to understand two concepts, "creation of the interest" and "lives in being."

a. "Creation of the interest." A future interest is created by conveyance (sale) at the moment of the conveyance. It is created in a will at the moment the testator dies. It is created in a trust the moment the trust document is signed and the trust created if the trust is irrevocable. If the trust is revocable, it is created at the moment it becomes irrevocable — trusts created during the life of the settlor (**inter vivos trusts**), for example, often are revocable until the settlor's death.

b. "Life in being." A life in being is a person alive (or in utero) at the creation of the interest who may have something to do with it vesting. It includes both people mentioned in the conveyance and people not mentioned who are alive and may affect vesting. A life in being includes only human beings, not corporations, animals, or other non-human entities.

To apply step 3 to the above example, imagine that *O to A for life, and then to A's children,* is part of a will. The interest is created when *O* dies. The lives in being include both *A* and any of *A*'s children alive when *O* dies.

4. See if you can imagine any way, however unlikely, in which the future interest will fully vest more than 21 years after the death of all of the lives in being identified in step 3. This is the tricky step, because it requires you to imagine not what is likely to happen, but what could possibly happen if all normal practices are suspended. The inquiry also requires you to look at the state of things when the interest is created, not as it exists at the moment you are looking at the situation. The question is whether the interest might only fully vest (or become certain not to vest) outside the "perpetuities period," the lifetime of all lives in being plus 21 years. (Actually, the period is the life in being plus 21 years and around 9 months, because periods of gestation are not counted within the 21 years.[9])

In our *O to A for life, then to A's children* example, the perpetuities period looks like this:

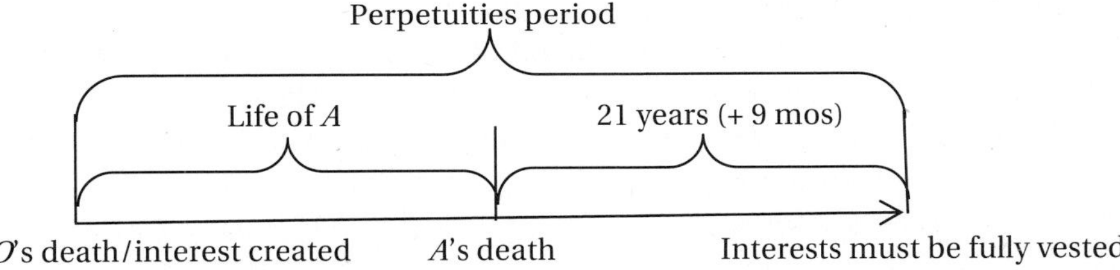

Is there any chance the remainder in *A*'s children will not fully vest within this period? No. *A* will have any children she is going to have by the time she dies—this interest has 21 years to spare.

But now imagine that the bequest is from *O to A for life, then to A's children who have graduated from college. A* could have a child just before her death. (One must ignore actual or probable fertility in applying the traditional rule against perpetuities; everyone is assumed to be able to have children until they die.) Because that child was not born when *O* died and the interest was created, he does not count as a life in being. He might not graduate from college until he is 40, more than 21 years after *A*'s death. Because of the possibility that the future interest will not fully vest until after the perpetuities period, this interest is invalid.

Remedy for violating the rule against perpetuities. The remedy for violating the rule is simply to strike, or cross out, the offending language. Thus, for example:

O to *A* for residential purposes, then to *B*.

---

9. Of course, new reproductive technologies render this traditional assumption—that people can only have children during their lifetimes or shortly thereafter—more than problematic! *See* Sharona Hoffman & Andrew P. Morriss, *Birth After Death: Perpetuities and the New Reproductive Technologies,* 38 Ga. L. Rev. 575 (2004).

If the conveyance to *B* violates the rule against perpetuities (it does — can you see why?), strike out the words "then to *B*." We are left with "*O* to *A* for residential purposes." This describes a fee simple determinable; since the possibility of reverter in *O* is not subject to the rule, the interest is valid.

O to *A*, but if the property is not used for residential purposes, then to *B*.

If the conveyance to *B* violates the rule (and, again, it does), strike out the entire phrase "but if the property is not used for residential purposes, then to *B*," leaving "*O* to *A*," creating a fee simple absolute in *A*. This is because merely striking out the words "then to *B*" leaves a conveyance that is not recognizable as a standard estate.

The different results in these two conveyances have been subject to criticism, especially because the possibility of reverter in *O* is just as pernicious a clog on title as an executory interest in *B* would be. Some courts therefore treat these conveyances alike and convert *A*'s interest to a fee simple in both cases.

Some class gifts are partially valid and partially invalid. For example, a conveyance from "*O* to *A* for life, then to the grandchildren of *A*" creates a vested remainder subject to open in the grandchildren if one grandchild is alive at the time of the conveyance to *A*. The interest in the living grandchild is vested while the interest in unborn grandchildren is contingent. If the jurisdiction applies the rule of convenience and the class closes at the death of *A*, the grandchildren's interest will be valid because their interests will vest at the death of a life in being. However, if the class does not close at the death of *A*, then the interest in unborn grandchildren may violate the rule because *A* could have another child after the conveyance from *O* to *A* and that child could have a child more than 21 years after the death of *O*, *A*, and any children or grandchildren of *A* alive at the creation of the interest. Some states invalidate the entire class gift to the grandchildren of *A* because some of the interests may violate the rule. Other states split the difference by validating the vested interests in the grandchildren who are alive at the creation of the interest while striking down the contingent remainders. *See In re Estate of Weaver*, 572 A.2d 1249, 1253 (Pa. Super. Ct. 1990) (explaining the evolution of Pennsylvania law on treatment of class gifts).

Illustrations

To illustrate how the rule is applied, we will examine a series of problems, first identifying future interests and then applying the rule against perpetuities.

Caveat: It is important to note that the following examples will provide a false sense of precision and determinacy. The rules may be applied differently in different jurisdictions. Moreover, the law changes over time, and changes in perceptions of the relative interests of grantors, present owners, and owners of future interests may lead to changes in the way the rule is interpreted and applied.

Interests in the grantor. Future interests in the grantor or her heirs are exempt from the rule against perpetuities. For example:

1. O *to* A *as long as used for residential purposes.* The possibility of reverter in *O* is exempt from the rule against perpetuities and the interest is good. (Remember

a statute may cut off possibilities of reverter if they do not vest within a certain number of years of the creation of the interest.)

2. O *to* A *for life*. The reversion in *O* is exempt from the rule against perpetuities and the interest is good.

Absolutely vested remainders. Remainders that are absolutely vested are immune from the rule.

3. O *to* A *for life, then to* B. The vested remainder in *B* is not subject to the rule. If *B* dies before *A*, then *B*'s heirs will get the property when *A* dies. If *A* dies before *B*, then *B* will get it when *A* dies.

Vested remainders subject to divestment. Remainders that are vested subject to divestment are immune from the rule.

4. O *to* A *for life, then to* B, *but if* B *marries* C, *then the property shall revert to* O. *B*'s remainder is *vested remainder subject to divestment* (or defeasance) and is valid.

Executory interests. Executory interests are subject to the rule against perpetuities. The main exception is that the rule does not apply if both the present estate owner and the future interest owner are **charities**. Because executory interests are subject to the rule, they are void unless they are certain to vest or fail to vest within 21 years of the death of some person alive at the creation of the interest. For example:

5. O *to* A *as long as used for residential purposes, then to* B. The property could be used for residential purposes for a thousand years, long after *O, A, B,* and everyone else alive at the creation of the interest has died and 21 years have passed. Because there is a possibility the executory interest in *B* may vest too far into the future, it is void. The traditional remedy is to strike out the words "then to *B*," leaving the words "O *to* A *as long as used for residential purposes.*" This is a recognizable estate (a fee simple determinable) and the possibility of reverter in *O* is immune from the rule and thus is good. Some courts, however, may strike out the whole condition, leaving *A* with a fee simple absolute.
6. O *to* A, *but if the property is ever used for nonresidential purposes, then to* B. *B*'s executory interest is invalid for the same reasons it was invalid in example 5 above. However, the remedy traditionally has been different. One cannot strike out only the words "then to *B*" because what is left is not a recognizable estate; it contains a "but if" clause but then does not say what happens if the condition is fulfilled. Therefore, the courts traditionally struck out all the language after "*O* to *A*" and *A* would be left with a fee simple absolute rather than a fee simple determinable as in example 5. The difference is a formal one and does not have any real policy justification because the two conveyances are otherwise functionally identical. For this reason, and to further the policy of reducing dead hand control, some courts may strike the interest in *B* and leave *A* with a fee simple absolute in example 5 as well.
7. O *to* A, *but if the property is used for nonresidential purposes within 21 years of this conveyance, then to* B. The executory interest in *B* is subject to the rule

against perpetuities but does not violate it because it will vest, if ever, within 21 years of the conveyance and thus within 21 years of all lives in being at the creation of the interest.

Contingent remainders and vested remainders subject to open. Contingent remainders are dependent on something occurring that will not necessarily occur, such as an individual having children or performing a certain act. When a remainder goes to all the people who meet a particular condition (*i.e.*, is a class gift), it may vest in some members of the class, but because others may join the class it is vested subject to open, and still be contingent for those who may join the class in the future. Contingent remainders and vested remainders subject to open will generally be good if the contingency depends solely on the actions of someone named in the document creating the interest—that person is a life in being, and the contingency must occur during the person's lifetime, if at all. When unnamed persons can have something to do with vesting, however, things get trickier. For example:

8. O *to* A *for life, then to* B *if* B *marries* C. The contingent remainder in *B* is good because *B* must marry *C*, if at all, during the lifetimes of both *B* and *C*, both of whom were lives in being at the creation of the interest.
9. O *to* A *for life, then to the children of* B. If *B* has no children at the time of the conveyance, they have a contingent remainder because they are not ascertainable at that time. The remainder will vest when *B* has a child, and *B* must have a child, if at all, within *B*'s lifetime (or around nine months after *B*'s death if *B* is a man). If *B* dies without children, the remainder will fail, and the property will revert to *O*.

If *B* is alive at the time of the conveyance from *O* to *A* and has children at that time, those children have a vested remainder subject to open because *B* could have more children. Their interest is subject to the rule against perpetuities but does not violate it. If the jurisdiction has adopted the rule of convenience, the class will close and their interest will vest when *A* dies. Even if the jurisdiction has not adopted the rule of convenience, the class will close when *B* dies, and so will fully vest during a life in being.

10. O *to* A *for life, then to the first child of* B *to be elected President of the United States.* Whether or not *B* has children at the time of the conveyance, *B* could have a daughter who would be born after the conveyance, so she is not a life in being at the creation of the interest; she could become president more than 21 years after the death of *O, A, B,* and any children of *B* alive at the creation of the interest, so the contingent remainder in *B*'s child violates the rule against perpetuities. Because the remainder is void, it is struck out, leaving "*O* to *A* for life"; *O* has a reversion that is not subject to the rule.

Contingent remainders give rise to some well-known and rather humorous traps that have been studied by generations of law students.

Unborn widow. The first is the "unborn widow." A conveyance from "*O* to *A* for life, remainder to *A*'s widow for life, remainder to *A*'s surviving children" creates a contingent remainder in *A*'s surviving children that violates the traditional rule against perpetuities. What has to happen for the interest to vest in *A*'s children? They have to survive *A*'s widow. Even if *A* is married at the time of the conveyance, that person will not necessarily be his widow—his wife could die, and *A* could marry someone who was born after the conveyance, and so would not be a life in being. *A*'s children as well could be born after the conveyance, so they are not necessarily lives in being either. *A*'s widow could outlive *A* for more than 21 years. So we will not necessarily know if *A*'s children survive her within the perpetuities period. Note that if the conveyance did not require them to survive *A*'s widow, their interests would vest when *A* died (even though they would not become possessory until the death of *A*'s widow). It is the requirement that they survive *A*'s widow that makes their interest invalid.

Fertile octogenarian. If *O* grants property to "*A* for life, remainder to *A*'s grandchildren," the assumption has always been that *A* could have more children until she dies, even if she is 80 years old. This assumption used to be humorous but new reproductive technologies make it perfectly plausible today; imagine a frozen embryo of hers implanted in another woman who bears her child. The contingent remainder in the grandchildren (or vested remainder subject to open if there are grandchildren at the conveyance from *O* to *A*) violates the rule because *A* could have a child after the creation of the interest and that child could have a child more than 21 years after the death of *A* (and everyone else alive at the creation of the interest). *A*'s children alive at the time of the creation of the interest could all predecease *A*, with the property going back to *O* as a reversion. If the after-born child has a child more than 21 years later, the interest will have vested too remotely. Thus the remainder violates the rule and is invalid.

The endless will contest. O to *A* for life, then to *B*'s children after *A*'s will is probated. The will contest could last forever; there is no guarantee the lawsuit will ever end, making the contingent remainder in *B*'s children void. In addition, if *B* has no children at the time of the conveyance from *O* to *A*, then their interest is contingent because they are unascertained and the will could be probated more than 21 years after the deaths of *O, A,* and *B* and all other lives in being at the creation of the interest, giving a second reason to invalidate their contingent remainder.

For other explanations of the rule, *see* Paula A. Franzese, *A Short and Happy Guide to Property* (2011); Carolyn Burgess Featheringill, *Understanding the Rule Against Perpetuities: A Step-by-Step Approach,* 13 Cumb. L. Rev. 161 (1982); and Jesse Dukeminier, *A Modern Guide to Perpetuities,* 74 Cal. L. Rev. 1867, 1884 (1986).

Problems

In answering these problems, determine (a) what is the present possessory interest; (b) what are the future interests; (c) does the future interest violate the rule against perpetuities; (d) if so, how should the interest be reformed? Unless otherwise stated, *O*, *A*, and *B* are human beings who are alive at the time the future interest is created.

1. *O* to *A*, but if the land is ever developed, then to *B*.
2. *O* to *A*, but if *A* ever seeks to develop the land, then to *B*.
3. *O* to *A* for life, then to *B* when she reaches 25. (*B* is alive but is not yet 25.)
4. *O* to *A* for life, then to *A*'s children who reach 25.
5. *O* to *A* for life, then to *A*'s grandchildren.
6. *O* to *A* for life, then to *O*'s grandchildren. (devise)
7. *O* to *A* for life, then to *A*'s first child to pass the Bar exam.
8. The first devise below is invalid, the second two are valid. Why?
   a. *O* to *A* for life, then to *A*'s widow for life, then to *A*'s children then living.
   b. *O* to *A* for life, then to *A*'s widow for life, then to *A*'s children.
   c. *O* to *A* for life, then to *B* (who is *A*'s wife) for life, then to *A*'s children then living.
9. *O* to *A* for 1,000 years, then to *B*.

Drafting Around the Rule: Savings Clauses

Because even experienced lawyers may fall into the traps laid by the rule against perpetuities, drafters often insert "savings clauses" intended to provide for validity in case an interest violates the rule. Such clauses may take different forms. Some may provide the court or a trustee corporation with the power of reforming the document if necessary to avoid invalidity. *See, e.g.*, W. Barton Leach & James K. Logan, *Perpetuities: A Standard Savings Clause to Avoid Violations of the Rule*, 74 Harv. L. Rev. 1141 (1961). Others may provide that should the interest violate the rule, it should be construed to vest only in those persons who may legally take it under the rule. *Smith v. Smith ex rel. Clarke*, 747 A.2d 85 (Del. Ch. 1999) (finding such a clause saved an option to purchase from invalidity).

Yet other clauses provide that in case of invalidity, the future interest shall vest within 21 years after the death of a particular class of people alive at the creation of the interest. The members of this class need not be beneficiaries of the interest—today, for example, it is common to have the class include the living descendants of Joseph P. Kennedy, father of John F., Robert, and Teddy. Drafters using such clauses must take care, however, to select a class whose members are reasonably ascertainable. If the class chosen is so large that determining its members would effectively be a perpetual task, then the class violates the rule. *Restatement (Second) of Property (Donative Transfers)* §1.3; *see* N.Y. Est. Powers & Trusts Law §9-1.1(b) (measuring lives must not be "unreasonably difficult to determine"); Wyo. Stat. §34-1-139 (same). *Compare State v. McGee*, 204 N.W. 408 (Iowa 1925) (holding impermissible a grant to "each and every member of American Legion of Iowa, each and every member of the Independent Order of Odd Fellows of Iowa, each and every member of the Knights of Pythias of Iowa, and each and every attorney at law in Iowa"), *with In re Villar*, 1 Ch. 243 (1929) (U.K.) (upholding interest that vested "20 years from the day of the death of the last survivor of all the lineal descendants of Her Late Majesty Queen Victoria, who shall be living at the time of [the testator's] death," although there were more than 120 descendants living in different parts of the globe), *and Bender v. Bender*, 74 A. 246 (Pa. 1909) (upholding grant in which 11 grandnephews and grandnieces were used as validating lives).

B. Modern Approaches and the Rise of the Perpetuity

The rule against perpetuities facilitated productive use of land and distribution of wealth by limiting the power of the dead hand to keep property within families and control its use. But the difficulty of applying it and the invalidation of interests that would not in practice vest outside the perpetuities period led some jurisdictions to adopt modifications to avoid its harsh results. The most popular are wait and see and *cy pres*. The *Uniform Statutory Rule Against Perpetuities* (USRAP), adopted in about half the states since 1986, uses and expands both modifications.[10] Even more significant has been the trend for states to effectively abolish the rule in an effort to compete for the profitable business of dynasty trusts. These trusts represent the antithesis of the rule: means to ensure that successive generations benefit from the trust fund, and are shielded from federal estate taxes and creditors, potentially forever.[11]

Despite these changes, the rule remains important to understand. First, even in the many states that have adopted wait and see reforms, the validity of a future interest that violates the traditional rule cannot be ascertained for many years after its creation, but interests that are good under the traditional rule can be validated immediately. Second, because the law applicable to a particular grant may change depending on the domicile of the deceased, the location of the property granted, or other factors, it makes sense to ensure validity under the laws of most states. *See CS-Lakeview at Gwinnett, Inc. v. Simon Property Group, Inc.*, 659 S.E.2d 359 (Ga. 2008) (although

---

10. Jurisdictions that have adopted the USRAP include Alabama, Arizona, Arkansas, California, Colorado, Connecticut, the District of Columbia, Florida, Georgia, Hawai`i, Indiana, Kansas, Massachusetts, Michigan, Minnesota, Montana, Nebraska, Nevada, New Jersey, New Mexico, North Carolina, North Dakota, Oregon, South Carolina, Tennessee, the Virgin Islands, Virginia, and West Virginia. Alaska initially adopted the USRAP but later repealed it, replacing it with a prohibition on restricting the power of alienation for more than a life in being plus 30 years, and a 1,000-year limit on the power of appointment. Alaska Stat. §§34.27.051 & 34.27.90

11. For an incisive critique of each of the three phases of perpetuities modification, from early wait and see and *cy pres*, to the *Uniform Statutory Rule Against Perpetuities*, to the abolition and rise of the dynasty trust, *see* a trilogy of articles by the late Jesse Dukeminier, *Perpetuities: Measuring Lives*, 85 Colum. L. Rev. 1648 (1985), *The Uniform Statutory Rule Against Perpetuities: Ninety Years in Limbo*, 34 UCLA L. Rev. 1023 (1987), and (with James Krier) *The Rise of the Perpetual Trust*, 50 UCLA L. Rev. 1303 (2003).

option to purchase would be valid under Georgia law, it was invalid under Delaware law, which was chosen by the parties in their contract). Finally, the law in this area is rapidly changing, with proposals coming from all directions. Lawyers should be able to understand its current variations, and to weigh in on the changes.

1. Traditional wait and see. Some states modify the rule by using a **wait and see** or **second look** test. Under the traditional rule, a future interest is void if a *possibility* exists that it will vest outside the perpetuities period; this can be determined on the date of the conveyance. Under the wait and see test, the courts will not hold that a future interest violates the rule until the perpetuities period has passed and they are certain that the future interest has not vested within that period. For example, in the conveyance "*O* to *A* so long as the property is used for residential purposes, then to *B*," the executory interest in *B* is void under the traditional rule because it is possible that the property will be used for residential purposes long after the deaths of *O*, *A*, and *B* plus 21 years.

In contrast, under the traditional wait and see test, the courts will wait until the condition occurs or the perpetuities period ends, whichever comes first. In this case, the perpetuities period ends 21 years after the death of the last of *O*, *A*, and *B*. (Do you see why?) If the property is used for nonresidential purposes before that period has lapsed, the executory interest is good and will be recognized; the property shifts to *B*. If, however, *O*, *A*, and *B* die and 21 years pass, and the property is still used for residential purposes, at that moment the future interest in *B* (actually *B*'s heirs or devisees since *B* is dead) is destroyed.

The advantage of the wait and see test is clear—rather than invalidating interests because of a mere possibility of remote vesting, it validates them so long as they do in fact vest within the perpetuities period. The disadvantages are more subtle. Under the old rule, the validity of the future interest could be determined immediately. Under wait and see, it remains in limbo during the perpetuities period. Traditional wait and see also requires determining exactly who were the relevant lives in being and when they died. Although a number of states had adopted some form of wait and see before 1986, most of these have now adopted the USRAP, which modifies the wait and see doctrine as discussed below.

2. *Cy pres.* The *cy pres* doctrine permits a court to modify a grant to validate it, on the presumption that this is consistent with the intent of the grantor. The most common application of *cy pres* is to reduce age contingencies that invalidate the future interest. For example, "*O* to *A* for life, then to the first child of *B* to attain 25 years of age," creates a contingent remainder in the first child of *B* to reach 25 (assuming *B* has no children at the time of the initial conveyance), which violates the rule since a child could be born after the conveyance and reach 25 more than 21 years after the deaths of *O*, *A*, and *B*. A court may invoke the *cy pres* doctrine to reduce the age contingency of 25 to 21. *See In re Estate of Chun Quan Yee Hop*, 469 P.2d 183 (Haw. 1970). Some jurisdictions may also apply *cy pres* to provide that a reference to an individual's "widow" is intended to refer to his current wife, thus eliminating the unborn widow problem, or cure other interpretive stumbling blocks under the common law rule.

3. ***Uniform Statutory Rule Against Perpetuities.*** The USRAP validates future interests in donative transfers (those created in gifts or trusts or wills) that otherwise violate the traditional rule against perpetuities if the interest vests at any time within 90 years of the date of its creation. This test applies the wait and see doctrine for interests that violate the traditional rule but limits the perpetuities period to 90 years rather than to "lives in being at the creation of the interest plus 21 years." The 90-year wait and see provision applies only to interests that would have been invalid under the traditional rule. If an interest violates the 90-year wait and see period, the statute authorizes the courts to reform the deed, will, or trust in the manner that most closely approximates the transferor's manifested plan of distribution and is within the allowable 90-year period. Although the law only applies to interests created after the passage of the statute, it also provides for *cy pres* to reform interests created earlier.

4. Abolition of the rule for family trusts. Many states have now abolished or substantially altered the rule against perpetuities, at least with respect to trusts. *See, e.g.*, Jesse Dukeminier & James T. Krier, *The Rise of the Perpetual Trust*, 50 UCLA L. Rev. 1303, 1313-1314 (2003) (listing 20 states that had abolished the rule for trusts, and anticipating that the list would grow). Some states have done so by providing that the rule only applies to suspension of the power of alienation; so long as the trustee has the ability to sell the trust assets as a fee simple absolute, the rule does not apply. *See, e.g.*, S.D. Codified Laws §43-5-1; Wis. Stat. §700.16; N.J. Stat. §46:2F-10. Other states have abolished the rule for all trusts, but left non-trust transfers untouched. *See* Del. Code tit. 25, §503 (providing that trusts are not subject to the rule, but that their assets must be distributed within 110 years after settlement). Yet other states have effectively abolished the rule by adopting very long perpetuities periods. *See* Utah Code §752-1203 (1,000 years); Wyo. Stat. §34-1-139 (1,000 years); Fla. Stat. §689.225(2)(f) (360 years).

These changes are driven by a race by banks and trust companies to act as trustees for family trusts. Tax avoidance is a big part of the story. Before 1976, no federal estate tax was levied at the end of a life estate, so testators could avoid taxation of their estates by leaving a series of life estates to their descendants. The only limitation was the rule against perpetuities, which generally meant that the trust would be distributed to the grandchildren of the testator in fee simple, and taxed then. In 1976, Congress amended the tax code to provide that a generation skipping transfer (GST) tax is due at the end of a life estate when it passes to the remainder holder. In 1986, Congress simplified the GST and added an important exclusion: $1 million of the initial settlement was exempt from the GST. This exemption has now risen to $5 million. What is more, that initial exempt trust corpus remains immune from estate taxation, even if compounding interest and prudent investments multiply its value.

The competition for trustee fees from family dynasties seeking to avoid these and other taxes has created a race to the bottom in state laws. One of the more blatant stories of legislative change comes from the Alaska Trust Company, which boasts on its website of its founding by two brothers, one an estate planning attorney from New York, who were on a fishing trip in Alaska and decided that it would be a great place to live and set up a trust company if only they could change some of the laws. They then successfully lobbied to change state laws to "make Alaska the premier location for trust services," resulting in the abolition of the rule against perpetuities for alienable personal property and several other "unique pieces of legislation." Other states that were traditional homes to the trust business, like Delaware and Florida, amended their laws to keep up. *See* Ray Madoff, *Immortality and the Law: The Rising Power of the American Dead* 80-81 (2010). A 2005 empirical study found that these legislative changes pay off. States that both abolished the rule against perpetuities and eliminated state income taxes on trusts saw the value of trust funds in their states increase by 20 percent, an average of $6 billion. Robert Sitkoff & Max Schwartzenbach, *Jurisdictional Competition for Trust Funds: An Empirical Study of Perpetuities and Taxes*, 115 Yale L.J. 356 (2005).

5. The return of the rule? Many commentators have criticized the rise of perpetual trusts and the decline of the rule against perpetuities. One potentially influential critique comes from the American Law Institute's *Restatement (Third) of Property: Wills & Donative Transfers* (2011). In the *Restatement*, the drafters point out that as each generation passes, the settlor of a family trust has less connection to the beneficiaries and the number of potential beneficiaries grows. This makes the trust both more expensive and less practicable to administer and takes it further from the legitimate scope of the settlor's interests. *Id.* at ch. 27 (Introductory Note). They propose reforming the rule against perpetuities to restore its bite and better serve its goals. They would have all interests — both vested and contingent, in the grantor and in third parties — terminate and return to fee simple absolute after the death of the beneficiaries two generations after the grantor. The generations would not need to be born at the time of the creation of the interest to count as measuring lives under the rule. *Id.* §27.1. The proposal would simplify and rationalize the application of the rule, but it is not clear that there is an incentive to adopt it with states seeking to attract dynasty trusts and lawyers glad not to have to worry about the rule at all. One scholar has critiqued the proposal, advocating eliminating the rule altogether in favor of a series of more discretionary constraints on future interests. Scott Andrew Shepard, *Which the Deader Hand: A Counter to the American Law Institute's Proposed Revival of a Dying Perpetuities Rule*, 86 Tul. L. Rev. 559 (2012).

C. Other Statutory Limits on Future Interests

Many states have passed statutes that codify the rule against perpetuities. Some states have passed other statutes that also affect future interests.

1. Statutory cut-offs. The rule against perpetuities does not apply to rights of entry or possibilities of reverter. The common law courts in England treated these interests as vested from the very beginning since they defined interests in the grantor that were reserved when the present estate was created. Yet, as a matter of public policy, it makes no sense to worry about executory interests because of the problem of dead hand control while deferring to future interests in the heirs of the grantor that could similarly vest 300 years in the future.

This is especially true in light of the ability to evade the rule against perpetuities by careful drafting. For example, a grantor who wanted to convey property to *A* so long as used for residential purposes, then to *B*, could easily do so in a two-step transaction. The grantor could convey a fee simple determinable to *A*, retaining a possibility of reverter. The grantor would then convey her possibility of reverter to *B*. The transfer of the future interest to *B* does not convert it to an executory interest. Since it was a possibility of reverter, the rule against perpetuities does not apply and the policy of restricting dead hand control has been evaded. A second way to do this is for *O* to transfer a fee simple absolute to *B*, and then for *B* to convey a fee simple determinable to *A*; since *B*'s interest is a possibility of reverter rather than an executory interest, it is immune from the rule against perpetuities.

For these reasons, some states have passed statutes that cut off interests in the grantor following defeasible fees if the condition does not occur within a stated time period, often 30 years after the initial conveyance. *See, e.g.*, Cal. Civ. Code §885.030; Ky. Rev. Stat. §381.221; Mass. Gen. Laws ch. 184A, §7; Mich. Comp. L. §554.62; *Black Mountain Energy Corp. v. Bell County Board of Education*, 467 F. Supp. 2d 715 (E.D. Ky. 2006) (holding statute voiding possibilities of reverter after 30 years did not violate the takings clause). The odd result is that while an executory interest or contingent fee may continue for 90 years under the *Uniform Statutory Rule Against Perpetuities*, a right of entry or possibility of reverter, although traditionally not subject to the rule, will terminate in only 30 years.

2. Marketable title acts. Many states have marketable title statutes requiring that future interests be re-recorded periodically in the local registry of deeds (typically every 30 or 40 years) to remain valid and enforceable. *See, e.g.*, Cal. Civ. Code §§880.020-887.090; Iowa Code §614.24. Statutes that effectively nullify future interests have often been challenged on the grounds that they violate due process or unconstitutionally take property or impair contracts. *Compare Severns v. Union Pacific Railroad Co.*, 125 Cal. Rptr. 2d 100 (Cal. App. 2002) (finding California statute valid) *with Board of Education v. Miles*, 207 N.E.2d 181 (N.Y. 1965) (holding New York statute invalid). These laws are generally upheld today if they apply prospectively and give owners enough notice of the obligation to re-record their interests.

D. Commercial Future Interests: Options to Purchase and Preemptive Rights

The rule against perpetuities was originally created in the context of so-called donative transfers, such as wills and other gifts to family and friends. It was justified both with the desire to prevent restriction of wealth to family dynasties and with the need to promote productive use of land. How do these interests apply to so-called commercial options created in the context of market transactions? The two most important kinds of commercial options are **options to purchase**, a right to acquire the property at some time in the future for a fixed price, and **preemptive rights**, or **rights of first refusal**, rights to acquire the property at the market price should it be sold in the future. Today cases involving such commercial interests are common in perpetuities litigation.

Symphony Space, Inc. v. Pergola Properties, Inc.

669 N.E.2d 799 (N.Y. 1996)

Map: 2537 Broadway at 95th Street, New York, New York

JUDITH KAYE, Chief Judge.

This case presents the novel question whether options to purchase commercial property are exempt from the prohibition against remote vesting embodied in New York's Rule against Perpetuities (N.Y. Est. Powers & Trusts §9-1.1[b]). Because an exception for commercial options finds no support in our law, we decline to exempt all commercial option agreements from the statutory Rule against Perpetuities.

Here, we agree with the trial court and Appellate Division that the option defendants seek to enforce violates the statutory prohibition against remote vesting and is therefore unenforceable.

I. Facts

The subject of this proceeding is a two-story building situated on the Broadway block between 94th and 95th Streets on Manhattan's Upper West Side. In 1978, Broadwest Realty Corporation owned this building, which housed a theater and commercial space. Broadwest had been unable to secure a permanent tenant for the theater—approximately 58% of the total square footage of the building's floor space. Broadwest also owned two adjacent properties, Pomander Walk (a residential complex) and the Healy Building (a commercial building). Broadwest had been operating its properties at a net loss.

Plaintiff Symphony Space, Inc., a not-for-profit entity devoted to the arts, had previously rented the theater for several one-night engagements. In 1978, Symphony and Broadwest engaged in a transaction whereby Broadwest sold the entire building to Symphony for the below-market price of $10,010 and leased back the income-producing commercial property, excluding the theater, for $1 per year. Broadwest maintained liability for the existing $243,000 mortgage on the property as well as certain maintenance obligations. As a condition of the sale, Symphony, for consideration of $10, also granted Broadwest an option to repurchase the entire building. Notably, the transaction did not involve Pomander Walk or the Healy Building.

The purpose of this arrangement was to enable Symphony, as a not-for-profit corporation, to seek a property tax exemption for the entire building—which constituted a single tax parcel—predicated on its use of the theater. The sale-and-leaseback would thereby reduce Broadwest's real estate taxes by $30,000 per year, while permitting Broadwest to retain the rental income from the leased commercial space in the building, which the trial court found produced $140,000 annually. The arrangement also furthered Broadwest's goal of selling all the properties, by allowing Broadwest to postpone any sale until property values in the area increased and until the commercial leases expired. Symphony, in turn, would have use of the theater at minimal cost, once it received a tax exemption.

Thus, on December 1, 1978, Symphony and Broadwest — both sides represented by counsel — executed a contract for sale of the property from Broadwest to Symphony for the purchase price of $10,010. The contract specified that $10 was to be paid at the closing and $10,000 was to be paid by means of a purchase-money mortgage.

The parties also signed several separate documents, each dated December 31, 1978: (1) a deed for the property from Broadwest to Symphony; (2) a lease from Symphony to Broadwest of the entire building except the theater for rent of $1 per year and for the term January 1, 1979 to May 31, 2003, unless terminated earlier; (3) a 25-year, $10,000 mortgage and mortgage note from Symphony as mortgagor to Broadwest as mortgagee, with full payment due on December 31, 2003; and (4) an option agreement by which Broadwest obtained from Symphony the exclusive right to repurchase all of the property, including the theater.

It is the option agreement that is at the heart of the present dispute. Section 3 of that agreement provides that Broadwest may exercise its option to purchase the property during any of the following "Exercise Periods":

> "(a) at any time after July 1, 1979, so long as the Notice of Election specifies that the Closing is to occur during any of the calendar years 1987, 1993, 1998 and 2003;
>
> "(b) at any time following the maturity of the indebtedness evidenced by the Note and secured by the Mortgage, whether by acceleration or otherwise;
>
> "(c) during the ninety days immediately following any termination of the Lease by the lessor thereof other than for nonpayment of rent or any termination of the Lease by the lessee thereof;
>
> "(d) during the ninety days immediately following the thirtieth day after Broadwest shall have sent Symphony a notice specifying a default by Symphony of any of its covenants or obligations under the Mortgage."

Section 1 states that "Broadwest may exercise its option at any time during any Exercise Period."

The following purchase prices of the property, contingent upon the closing date, are set forth in section 4: $15,000 if the closing date is on or before December 31, 1987; $20,000 if on or before December 31, 1993; $24,000 if on or before December 31, 1998; and $28,000 if on or before December 31, 2003.

Importantly, the option agreement specifies in section 5 that "Broadwest's right to exercise the option granted hereby is . . . unconditional and shall not be in any way affected or impaired by Broadwest's performance or nonperformance, actual or asserted, of any obligation to be performed under the Lease or any other agreement or instrument by or between Broadwest and Symphony," other than that Broadwest was required to pay Symphony any unpaid rent on the closing date.

Symphony ultimately obtained a tax exemption for the theater. In the summer of 1981, Broadwest sold and assigned its interest under the lease, option agreement, mortgage and mortgage note, as well as its ownership interest in the contiguous Pomander Walk and Healy Building, to defendants' nominee for $4.8 million. The nominee contemporaneously transferred its rights under these agreements to defendants Pergola Properties, Inc., Bradford N. Swett, Casandium Limited and Darenth Consultants as tenants in common.

Subsequently, defendants initiated a cooperative conversion of Pomander Walk, which was designated a landmark in 1982, and the value of the properties increased substantially. An August 1988 appraisal of the entire blockfront, including the Healy Building and the unused air and other development rights available from Pomander Walk, valued the property at $27 million assuming the enforceability of the option. By contrast, the value of the leasehold interest plus the Healy Building without the option were appraised at $5.5 million.

[In 1985, Swett and Pergola sought to terminate the lease and exercise the option to purchase. After much litigation, both the trial court and the Appellate Division held that the option was void under the rule against perpetuities.]

II. Statutory Background

The Rule against Perpetuities evolved from judicial efforts during the 17th century to limit control of title to real property by the dead hand of landowners reaching into future generations. Underlying both early and modern rules restricting future dispositions of property is the principle that it is socially undesirable for property to be inalienable for an unreasonable period of time. These rules thus seek "to ensure the productive use and development of property by its current beneficial owners by simplifying ownership, facilitating exchange and freeing property from unknown or embarrassing impediments to alienability" (*Metropolitan Transp. Auth. v. Bruken Realty Corp.*, 492 N.E.2d 379, 381 (N.Y. 1986)).

In New York, the rules regarding suspension of the power of alienation and remoteness in vesting — the Rule against Perpetuities — have been statutory since 1830. Prior to 1958, the perpetuities period was two lives in being plus actual periods of minority. Widely criticized as unduly complex and restrictive, the statutory period was revised in 1958 and 1960, restoring the common-law period of lives in being plus 21 years.

Formerly, the rule against remote vesting in New York was narrower than the common-law rule, encompassing only particular interests. A further 1965 amendment enacted a broad prohibition against remote vesting. This amendment was intended to make clear that the American common-law rule of perpetuities was now fully in force in New York.

New York's current statutory Rule against Perpetuities is found in N.Y. Est. Powers & Trusts §9-1.1. Subdivision (a) sets forth the suspension of alienation rule and deems void any estate in which the conveying instrument suspends the absolute power of alienation for longer than lives in being at the creation of the estate plus 21 years. The prohibition against remote vesting is contained in subdivision (b), which states that "[n]o estate in property shall be valid unless it must vest, if at all, not later than twenty-one years after one or more lives in being at the creation of the estate and any period of gestation involved." This Court has described subdivision (b) as "a rigid formula that invalidates any interest that may not vest within the prescribed time period" and has "capricious consequences" (*Wildenstein & Co. v. Wallis*, 595 N.E.2d 828, 831-32 (N.Y. 1992)). Indeed, these rules are predicated upon the public policy of the State and constitute non-waivable, legal prohibitions.

In addition to these statutory formulas, New York also retains the more flexible common-law rule against unreasonable restraints on alienation. Unlike the statutory Rule against Perpetuities, which is measured exclusively by the passage of time, the common-law rule evaluates the reasonableness of the restraint based on its duration, purpose and designated method for fixing the purchase price.

III. Validity of the Option Agreement

Defendants proffer three grounds for upholding the option: that the statutory prohibition against remote vesting does not apply to commercial options; that the option here cannot be exercised beyond the statutory period; and that this Court should adopt the "wait and see" approach to the Rule against Perpetuities. We consider each in turn.

A. Applicability of the Rule to Commercial Options

Under the common law, options to purchase land are subject to the rule against remote vesting. Such options are specifically enforceable and give the option holder a contingent, equitable interest in the land. This creates a disincentive for the landowner to develop the property and hinders its alienability, thereby defeating the policy objectives underlying the Rule against Perpetuities.

Typically, however, options to purchase are part of a commercial transaction. For this reason, subjecting them to the Rule against Perpetuities has been deemed "a step of doubtful wisdom" (Leach, *Perpetuities in Perspective: Ending the Rule's Reign of Terror,* 65 Harv. L. Rev. 737). As one vocal critic, Professor W. Barton Leach, has explained,

> "[t]he Rule grew up as a limitation on family dispositions; and the period of lives in being plus twenty-one years is adapted to these gift transactions. The pressures which created the Rule do not exist with reference to arms-length contractual transactions, and neither lives in being nor twenty-one years are periods which are relevant to business men and their affairs" (Leach, *Perpetuities: New Absurdity, Judicial and Statutory Correctives,* 73 Harv. L. Rev. 1318, 1321-1322).

Professor Leach, however, went on to acknowledge that, under common law, "due to an overemphasis on concepts derived from the nineteenth century, we are stuck with the application of the Rule to options to purchase," urging that "this should not be extended to other commercial transactions" (*id.*, at 1322).

It is now settled in New York that, generally, N.Y. Est. Powers & Trusts §9-1.1(b) applies to options. While defendants offer compelling policy reasons—echoing those voiced by Professor Leach—for refusing to apply the traditional rule against remote vesting to these commercial option contracts, such statutory reformation would require legislative action similar to that undertaken by numerous other State lawmakers.

Our decision in *Metropolitan Transp. Auth. v. Bruken Realty Corp.*, 492 N.E.2d 379, *supra,* is not to the contrary. In *Bruken*, we held that §9-1.1(b) did not apply to a preemptive right in a "commercial and governmental transaction" that lasted beyond the statutory perpetuities period. In doing so, we explained that, unlike options, preemptive rights (or rights of first refusal) only marginally affect transferability. Enforcement of the preemptive right in the context of the governmental and commercial transaction, moreover, actually encouraged the use and development of the land, outweighing any minor impediment to alienability. *Id.*

Here, the option agreement creates precisely the sort of control over future disposition of the property that we have previously associated with purchase options and that the common-law rule against remote vesting — and thus §9-1.1(b) — seeks to prevent. As the Appellate Division explained, the option grants its holder absolute power to purchase the property at the holder's whim and at a token price set far below market value. This Sword of Damocles necessarily discourages the property owner from investing in improvements to the property. Furthermore, the option's existence significantly impedes the owner's ability to sell the property to a third party, as a practical matter rendering it inalienable.

That defendants, the holder of this option, are also the lessees of a portion of the premises does not lead to a different conclusion here.

Generally, an option to purchase land that originates in one of the lease provisions, is not exercisable after lease expiration, and is incapable of separation from the lease is valid even though the holder's interest may vest beyond the perpetuities period. Such options — known as options "appendant" or "appurtenant" to leases — encourage the possessory holder to invest in maintaining and developing the property by guaranteeing the option holder the ultimate benefit of any such investment. Options appurtenant thus further the policy objectives underlying the rule against remote vesting and are not contemplated by §9-1.1(b).

To be sure, the option here arose within a larger transaction that included a lease. Nevertheless, not all of the property subject to the purchase option here is even occupied by defendants. The option encompasses the entire building — both the commercial space and the theater — yet defendants are leasing only the commercial space. With regard to the theater space, a disincentive exists for Symphony to improve the property, since it will eventually be claimed by the option holder at the predetermined purchase price.

Where, as here, the parties to a transaction are corporations and no measuring lives are stated in the instruments, the perpetuities period is simply 21 years. Section 1 of the parties' agreement allows the option holder to exercise the option "at any time during any Exercise Period" set forth in section three. Section 3(a), moreover, expressly provides that the option may be exercised "at any time after July 1, 1979," so long as the closing date is scheduled during 1987, 1993, 1998 or 2003.

Even factoring in the requisite notice, then, the option could potentially be exercised as late as July 2003 — more than 24 years after its creation in December 1978. Defendants' contention that section 3(a) does not permit exercise of the option beyond the 21-year period is thus contradicted by the plain language of the instrument. [Each of the other time periods provided for exercising the option could also be exercised until 2003.]

C. *"Wait and See" Approach*

Defendants next urge that we adopt the "wait and see" approach to the Rule against Perpetuities: an interest is valid if it actually vests during the perpetuities period, irrespective of what might have happened. The option here would survive under the "wait and see" approach since it was exercised by 1987, well within the 21-year limitation.

This Court, however, has long refused to "wait and see" whether a perpetuities violation in fact occurs. As explained in *Matter of Fischer*, 307 N.Y. 149, 157, 120 N.E.2d 688, "[i]t is settled beyond dispute that in determining whether a will has illegally suspended the power of alienation, the courts will look to what might have happened under the terms of the will rather than to what has actually happened since the death of the testator."

IV. Remedy

As a final matter, defendants argue that, if the option fails, the contract of sale conveying the property from Broadwest to Symphony should be rescinded due to the mutual mistake of the parties. We conclude that rescission is inappropriate and therefore do not pass upon whether Broadwest's claim for rescission was properly assigned to defendant Pergola.

A contract entered into under mutual mistake of fact is generally subject to rescission. CPLR 3005 provides that when relief against mistake is sought, it shall not be denied merely because the mistake is one of law rather than fact. Relying on this provision, defendants maintain that neither Symphony nor Broadwest realized that the option violated the Rule against Perpetuities at the time they entered into the agreement and that both parties intended the option to be enforceable.

The remedy of rescission . . . moreover, lies in equity and is a matter of discretion. Defendants' plea that the unenforceability of the option is contrary to the intent of the original parties ignores that the effect of the Rule against Perpetuities—which is a statutory prohibition, not a rule of construction—is always to defeat the intent of parties who create a remotely vesting interest.

The Rule against Perpetuities reflects the public policy of the State. Granting the relief requested by defendants would thus be contrary to public policy, since it would lead to the same result as enforcing the option and tend to compel performance of contracts violative of the Rule.

Accordingly, the order of the Appellate Division should be affirmed, with costs, and the certified question answered in the affirmative.

Notes and Questions

1. Options to purchase. Options to purchase have traditionally been considered to be executory interests and subject to the rule against perpetuities. *Arundel Corp. v. Marie*, 860 A.2d 886 (Md. 2004); *Bortolotti v. Hayden*, 866 N.E.2d 882 (Mass. 2007). As in *Symphony Space*, this is true even if the right is in the original grantor of the property, because the need to *purchase* the property to reacquire indicates

CONTEXT

As a result of the decision, Symphony Space acquired a property worth millions for $10,010. Today, Symphony Space remains a unique multimedia performing arts center, hosting over 600 events a year, including dance, music, theater performances, films, dramatic readings (including for the NPR show *Selected Shorts*), and other cultural events.

that the option is not simply the reversion of an already vested right in the property, but a new interest cutting off an existing estate. It is easy to see how an option to purchase for a fixed price at a period far in the future might hinder productive use of land. *See, e.g., Central Delaware County Authority v. Greyhound Corp.*, 588 A.2d 485 (Pa. 1991) (plaintiff sued to invalidate option to purchase created in 1941, which would permit the land to be purchased for the original sales price, $5,500, if it ever ceased to be used for public purposes). Is it true that allowing the option in *Symphony Space* would have hindered the productive use of the property?

2. Options to purchase and renew in leases. Despite the general rule, most courts hold that options to purchase in commercial leases are exempt from the rule against perpetuities. William B. Stoebuck & Dale A. Whitman, *The Law of Property* §3.18, at 123 (3d ed. 2000). As Chief Justice Ellen Peters explained in *Texaco Refining & Marketing, Inc. v. Samowitz*, 570 A.2d 170 (Conn. 1990), "[a]n option coupled with a long-term commercial lease . . . stimulates improvement of the property and thus renders it more rather than less marketable." *Id.* at 174. Similarly, many courts hold that options to renew leases during the lease term are not subject to the rule against perpetuities. *See Bleecker Street Tenants Corp. v. Bleeker Jones, LLC*, 945 N.E.2d 484 (N.Y. 2011). What if an option in a lease is exercised by a tenant who has become a month-to-month tenant after her initial term of years expires? In *Bleecker Street Tenants Corp.*, the New York Court of Appeals considered this to be still within the lease term and therefore not violative of the rule. Was this the right resolution?

3. *Uniform Statutory Rule Against Perpetuities* and commercial options. The drafters of the USRAP intended it to supersede the common law rule against perpetuities entirely and so provided in §9 of the act. Because the USRAP applies only to donative transfers, the USRAP's drafters suggested that states pass separate laws limiting executory interests such as options to purchase to a 30-year period, and some states have done so. Mass. Gen. Laws ch. 184A, §5; N.C. Gen. Stat. §41-29. *Cf.* 765 Ill. Comp. Stat. 305/4(a)(7) (40-year limit). Some states adopted the USRAP without imposing any limit on commercial options. *See, e.g., Larson Operating Co. v. Petroleum, Inc.*, 84 P.3d 626 (Kan. Ct. App. 2004) (interpreting Kan. Stat. §59-340). Some states that adopted the USRAP refused to enact §9 but did not pass any supplementary legislation concerning nondonative interests. In those states, such interests are probably still governed by the traditional rule against perpetuities. *See Buck v. Banks*, 668 N.E.2d 1259 (Ind. Ct. App. 1996). Some states adopted statutes that explicitly apply the rule against perpetuities as modified by the wait and see test to nondonative transfers. *See* Va. Code §55-13.3. Even in states that have adopted both the USRAP and a limit on commercial options, moreover, the common law rule against perpetuities may bar options created before their enactment. *Compare Bauermeister v. Waste Management Co. of Nebraska*, 783 N.W.2d 594 (Neb. 2010) (statutory abolition reflected policy regarding nondonative transfers created before enactment), *with New Bar Partnership v. Martin*, 729 S.E.2d 625 (N.C. Ct. App. 2012) (right of first refusal barred by common law rule against perpetuities).

In states that have abolished the rule against perpetuities with respect to nondonative transfers, options to purchase are still regulated by the common law rule against

unreasonable restraints on alienation. *See* Chapter 8, §5.4. Courts may refuse to enforce an option, especially if it is for a fixed price, if the option has no time limit and the option was not exercised within a reasonable period after its creation (unless the option is included in a lease). *Mr. Sign Sign Studios, Inc. v. Miguel,* 877 So. 2d 47 (Fla. Dist. Ct. App. 2004).

4. **Preemptive rights or rights of first refusal.** Some jurisdictions retain the traditional rule that preemptive rights, also called rights of first refusal, are subject to the rule against perpetuities. *See Selig v. State Highway Administration,* 861 A.2d 710 (Md. 2004) (noting that rule still generally applied to preemptive rights, although transportation statute exempted preemptive rights against state); *Hensley-O'Neal v. Metropolitan National Bank,* 297 S.W.3d 610 (Mo. Ct. App. 2009); *New Bar Partnership v. Martin,* 729 S.E.2d 625 (N.C. Ct. App. 2012). Preemptive rights give the holder the right to purchase the property if the owner chooses to sell, either by offering the market price for the property, or by matching the offer made by any bona fide purchaser. Some courts reason that preemptive rights may restrict alienability by deterring other bidders for the land, or leading sellers to accept below-market prices rather than litigate over fair market value. *Selig,* 861 A.2d at 718-719.

As *Symphony Space* discusses, an increasing number of courts hold that preemptive rights are wholly exempt from the rule against perpetuities. *See Bortolotti v. Hayden,* 866 N.E.2d 882 (Mass. 2007); *Old Port Cove Holdings v. Old Port Cove Condominium Association,* 986 So. 2d 1279 (Fla. 2008); *Hartnett v. Jones,* 629 P.2d 1357 (Wyo. 1981). As the Massachusetts Supreme Court argued in *Bortolli,* "[b]ecause the holder of a right of first refusal may only choose to purchase property on the same terms as a bona fide offer, if and when the owner decides to sell, there is no power either to compel an owner to sell the property at an unfavorable price, or to encumber an owner's ability to sell the property for a lengthy period of time. There is no casting of a cloud of uncertainty on the title to the property, and no potential to forestall a sale." 866 N.E.2d, at 889. When preemptive rights are held by owners associations to purchase units in common interest developments, moreover, they may increase the market value of the properties held by association members. *Cambridge Co. v. East Slope Investment Corp.,* 700 P.2d 537 (Colo. 1985). Courts adopting this approach may hold that preemptive rights must be exercised within a reasonable time in order to avoid invalidation as unreasonable restraints on alienation, *see Shiver v. Benton,* 304 S.E.2d 903 (Ga. 1983), or interpret them to be exercisable only during a particular person's lifetime, thereby validating them under the rule. *See Firebaugh v. Whitehead,* 559 S.E.2d 611 (Va. 2002).

5. **The *Restatement (Third)*.** The *Restatement (Third) of Property (Servitudes)* §3.3 (2000) provides that the rule against perpetuities "does not apply to servitudes or powers to create servitudes," which it defines to include options and rights of first refusal. The reason for the exemption is explained in Comment b:

> [The] vice [of the rule against perpetuities is] that it operate[s] arbitrarily, applying a time limit totally unsuited to commercial transactions. Lives in being plus 21 years is too long for some servitude arrangements and irrational in others. For example, an option

> in gross should rarely, if ever be permitted to last as long as the rule would permit. As another example, the power of a property owners association to grant easements in common areas should be limited by the duration of the association, rather than by the lives of the developer's family and friends plus 21 years, or by a fixed period of 21 or 90 years.

Instead, the "purpose of the restriction must be balanced against the harm caused by the nature of the restraint, a process that is best carried out under the rules against restraints on alienation, which permit a contextualized inquiry into the utility of the arrangement." The proposed exemption of options and preemptive rights from the rule against perpetuities applies not only to commercial transactions but to family gifts as well. The Reporter's note to §3.3 candidly admits that the *Restatement* has chosen a minority position in an attempt to influence the future course of the law. Do you agree with the *Restatement* position?

Problem

Grantor, *O*, conveys property to *A* so long as it is used for residential purposes. *A* opens a law office on the premises, and *O* sues for a declaratory judgment that title has reverted to *O*. Possibilities of reverter are, of course, viewed as "vested" and thus exempt from the rule against perpetuities. *Alby v. Banc One Financial*, 82 P.3d 675 (Wash. Ct. App. 2003) (a possibility of reverter is "immediately vested in the grantor"). *A* responds that the policies underlying the common law rule against perpetuities apply to possibilities of reverter as well as to executory interests, and that it is nonsensical to continue to exempt possibilities of reverter from the rule on the grounds that they are "vested." *A* further argues that this proposed change in the law (applying the rule against perpetuities to possibilities of reverter) should be applied retroactively, on the ground that when the rule was first developed in the *Duke of Norfolk's Case*, 22 Eng. Rep. 931 (1681), it was applied retroactively to the conveyance in that case. What arguments could you make for the plaintiff? For the defendant? What should the court do?

Consider that in *Washington State Grange v. Brandt*, 148 P.3d 1069 (Wash. Ct. App. 2006), a conveyance provided that "the land herein deeded reverts back to original plot in event it is no longer used for Grange purposes." The court interpreted "to original plot" to mean to the "current owner of the retained land at the time the condition is violated"; since this was an executory interest in a third party, the court held that it was void under the rule against perpetuities. However, this left language creating a possibility of reverter ("the land . . . reverts back . . . in the event it is no longer used for Grange purposes"). Since possibilities of reverter are not subject to the rule, the court deemed that interest valid. Does this make sense?

§5.4 Rule Against Unreasonable Restraints on Marriage

Restraints on marriage often raise public policy concerns, both as restraints on an important area of human freedom and because of public support for marriage generally. But testators not infrequently condition their gifts based on their survivors' marital choices. What should be the role of the courts in enforcing testators' efforts to control marriage choices after death?

Estate of Guidotti

109 Cal. Rptr. 2d 674 (Cal. App. 2001)

ARTHUR GILBERT, Presiding Judge

A clause in a husband's testamentary trust gives his wife the net income for life, but only if she does not remarry or live with a man as though married. Here we conclude that the clause is void as a restraint on marriage. (Cal. Civ. Code §710.)

Petitioner Darlene Guidotti appeals an order by the probate court denying a petition to reform the will of her deceased husband, Earl Guidotti, to comply with the requirements of the Internal Revenue Code concerning the marital deduction and the charitable deduction. We reverse.

On March 13, 1999, Earl Guidotti died. His last will and testament dated November 19, 1993, created a testamentary trust for the benefit of his wife, Darlene. The trust generally provided for Darlene during her lifetime and upon her death, provided for distribution to "charitable 501(c)(3) organizations" within the meaning of the Internal Revenue Code. The trust granted Darlene the power to appoint the charitable beneficiaries.

The trust gave Darlene the right to live in the family residence during her lifetime, rent-free. In the event she moved from the residence or was absent for more than 60 continuous days, without an intent to return, Darlene forfeited the right to live in the residence.[12]

The trust also provided that Darlene would receive the net income for her lifetime. However, "[i]n the event [she] should remarry, or, live with a man as though they were husband and wife, even though not married, all income payments to her shall immediately stop. . . ." The trust also permitted an invasion of the trust principal as necessary for Darlene's proper health, maintenance, and support. The power to invade principal, however, ceased in the event of Darlene's remarriage or cohabitation "with a man as though they were husband and wife, even though not married." During the probate proceedings, Darlene expressly disclaimed any interest in the trust principal by filing a written disclaimer pursuant to Probate Code section 275.

On March 13, 2000, Darlene filed a petition to reform the will in order to meet the technical requirements of the Internal Revenue Code regarding the marital and charitable deductions. Darlene asserted that the clause that terminated her income interest upon remarriage or cohabitation precluded the federal estate tax marital deduction and also prevented the charitable tax deduction because the remainder interest passing to charity would be uncertain. (26 U.S.C. §§2055, 2056.) She argued that

12. This provision prevented Darlene from selling the family residence and acquiring a condominium or a smaller home. The trial court declared this provision unenforceable for several reasons. The clause is not in issue here.

the clause regarding her remarriage or cohabitation with a man was void as a restraint on marriage. (Cal. Civ. Code §710.)

In support of the reformation petition, Darlene offered a declaration by the attorney who drafted Earl's will and testamentary trust. The attorney declared that Earl was "extremely jealous" of Darlene and "did not want Darlene to remarry nor live with another man as if married" after Earl's death. Earl instructed him to draft the will "in such a manner that Darlene would be severely penalized in the event she remarried or lived with another man as if married." The attorney stated: "[Earl] intended and specifically directed me to draft provisions which would prevent, in so far as he could control, the remarriage of Darlene or her living with another man as if married."

According to the attorney's declaration, Earl also hoped to obtain a marital deduction and a charitable deduction for federal estate tax purposes. The attorney stated: "[Earl] wished to [accomplish the estate plan] without payment of state or federal death taxes. He wanted there to be no federal or state estate taxes at his death." Indeed, the trust empowered the personal representative "to elect qualified terminable interest treatment [regarding the marital deduction] for all or for any portion" of the trust.

The probate court considered the petition for reformation and determined that the clause regarding remarriage or cohabitation was not a restraint on marriage because it fell under the exception of Civil Code section 710, "where the intent was not to forbid marriage, but only to give the use until marriage." The trial court reasoned that the clause was "harsh, unwise and somewhat punitive" but "also" reflected an intent that any new partner provide for Darlene's support. The court therefore refused to declare the clause void and reform the will to comply with federal estate tax requirements for favorable tax treatment.

Darlene appeals and contends that the clause restraining marriage is against public policy and void. Her appeal is unopposed by the Attorney General, who represents the yet unnamed charitable beneficiaries.

The interpretation of a written instrument, including a will, is a judicial function. A reviewing court may exercise its independent judgment in interpreting an instrument provided that extrinsic evidence regarding interpretation is not conflicting. (*Estate of Edwards*, 250 Cal. Rptr. 779, 781-82 (Cal. App. 1988).) Probate Code section 21102, subdivision (a), provides: "The intention of the transferor as expressed in the instrument controls the legal effect of the dispositions made in the instrument." Thus, the paramount rule in the construction of a will is the determination of the testator's intent.

Civil Code section 710 provides: "Conditions imposing restraints upon marriage . . . are void; but this does not affect limitations where the intent was not to forbid marriage, but only to give the use until marriage." Our Supreme Court has invalidated clauses in wills that either restrain marriage generally or marriage to a particular person. (*Estate of Duffill*, 183 P. 337 (Cal. 1919) (testatrix's will reduced gift to son if he married "Mrs. Alice McNamara"); *Estate of Scott*, 148 P. 221 (Cal. 1915) (testator's will limited wife's bequest if she "[s]hould . . . wish to marrie agane").)

Here Earl's will terminates payment of all trust income to Darlene "[i]n the event [she] should remarry, or, live with a man as though they were husband and wife." The declaration of the attorney who drafted the will states that Earl was jealous of Darlene and wanted to preclude her remarrying or living with another man. Indeed, the attorney states that he counseled Earl that a clause restraining her remarriage "might be unenforceable as against public policy." Our review of the wording of the will and more importantly, the evidence surrounding its execution shows that Earl intended to restrain Darlene's relationships or remarriage in violation of Civil Code section 710. His intent was not to provide for her until such time as she formed another relationship. (*Estate of Fitzgerald*, 119 P. 96 (Cal. 1919) (testator left estate to wife, but "in the event" she remarried, her gift was divided with testator's son unless he died without issue).) Unlike the circumstances in *Estate of Fitzgerald, supra*, we cannot say there is "not the slightest indication that there was any design or [the testator's] part to deter his wife from contracting another marriage, or that he had any objection whatever to her so doing." We draw the reasonable inference from the declaration of the drafting attorney that Earl intended to restrict Darlene from remarrying or living with a man.

The order is reversed and the matter remanded for further proceedings concerning reformation of the will and the charitable bequests.

Notes and Questions

1. **Restraints on remarriage of testator's spouse.** The traditional and still majority rule is that bequests to a surviving spouse conditioned on the beneficiary remaining unmarried are valid and will be enforced. In the words of the Missouri Supreme Court, "[i]t seems settled law that men have a sort of mournful property right, so to speak, in the viduity [widowhood] of their wives." *Knost v. Knost*, 129 S.W. 665, 667 (Mo. 1910). What justifies the rule? An early court stated dramatically, "[i]t would be extremely difficult to say, why a husband should not be at liberty to leave a homestead to his wife, without being compelled to let her share it with a successor to his bed, and to use it as a nest to hatch a brood of strangers to his blood." *Commonwealth v. Stauffer*, 10 Pa. 350, 355 (1849). But a testator may have other reasons for divestment on remarriage, such as preserving the estate for the testator's children by another marriage. As seen in *Guidotti*, however, these restrictions may have a drastic monetary impact. Although the federal marital deduction immunizes inheritance from a spouse from estate taxation, bequests terminable before the end of a life estate are not eligible. *See Roels v. United States*, 928 F. Supp. 812 (D. Wis. 1996) (construing I.R.C. §2056(b)(1)).

In *Guidotti*, the court followed a state statute in determining whether the restriction was mere possessiveness or was to support the widow. Other states have similar statutes. Ga. Code §44-6-68; Ind. Code §29-1-6-3; *In re Estate of Robertson*, 859 N.E.2d 772 (Ind. App. 2007) (invalidating life estate for widower "until he remarries or allows any female companion to live with him who is not a blood relative"). Should other states, by common law or statute, require review of remarriage restrictions and strike them down if they are simply demands for faithfulness from beyond the grave? The *Restatement (Second) of Property (Donative Transfers)* §6.3 (1983), while it otherwise requires review for reasonableness for restrictions on remarriage, would simply uphold without review restraints on remarriage by the testator's spouse.

2. Restraints on marriage generally. In contrast with restrictions on remarriage of a surviving spouse, restrictions on a first marriage are invalid if they unreasonably limit the opportunity to marry. *Restatement (Second) of Property (Donative Transfers)* §6.2. Thus restraints on marriage until the individual turns 21, or prohibiting marrying one particular individual, will be upheld. *See Taylor v. Rapp*, 124 S.E. 2d 271 (Ga. 1962) (upholding will prohibiting daughter from sharing in the estate should she "marry JODY TAYLOR, a boy I do not like and care for in any respects"). Bequests conditioned on the beneficiary remaining unmarried will only be upheld if the intent is to provide support to the individual when unmarried. *See Restatement (Second)* §6.1; *Lewis v. Searles*, 452 S.W.2d 153 (Mo. 1970).

3. Religious restrictions. Courts generally uphold conditions that the beneficiary must marry an individual of a particular ethnicity or religion. *See, e.g., Gordon v. Gordon*, 124 N.E.2d 228, 230 (Mass. 1955) (upholding a condition that beneficiaries must marry persons "born in the Hebrew faith"; court revoked gift to son when he married a Jew by choice (convert)); *Shapira v. Union National Bank*, 315 N.E.2d 825 (Ohio Ct. Comm. Pleas 1974) (upholding a condition that testators' son "should receive his share of the bequest only if he is married at the time of my death to a Jewish girl whose both parents were Jewish" or so married within seven years of his death); *In re Estate of Keffalas*, 233 A.2d 248 (Pa. 1967) (upholding gift to sons conditional on their marrying women of "true Greek blood and descent and of Orthodox religion").

The *Restatement (Third) of Trusts* §29(c) cmt. j, illus. 3 (2001), in contrast, provides that conditions limiting gifts if the recipient does not marry a person of a particular religion are void as against public policy because they interfere with the fundamental right to marry. The Illinois Supreme Court considered both the *Restatement (Third)* and constitutional arguments in *In re Estate of Feinberg*, 919 N.E.2d 888 (Ill. 2009), but upheld a provision that an estate be divided only among those grandchildren who, if married, were married to Jews or whose non-Jewish spouses had converted within one year of marriage. The court rejected the challenger's constitutional arguments, finding no state action in enforcement of the condition. Emphasizing the states' strong policy of respecting testator intent, the court found that public policy did not prohibit benefitting only the "grandchildren whose lives most closely embraced the values [the testators] cherished." *Id.* at 903.

A restriction will be held invalid when it effectively prohibits the beneficiary from marrying at all. Thus in *Madox v. Madox*, 52 Va. 804 (1854), the court invalidated a condition that the testator's daughter remain a member in good standing of the Society of Friends, because members were prohibited from marrying nonmembers and there were not "more than five or six marriageable male members of the society" in the county, so "the restriction imposed by the condition would have operated a virtual prohibition of her marrying." While there might have been other members outside the county, she "could not be expected, if she had the means, which it seems she had not, to go abroad in search of a helpmate; and to subject her to the doubtful chance of being sought in marriage by a stranger." Should the advent of Internet dating change the result in a similar case today?

4. Gender roles. Professor Mary Joe Frug argues that cases involving women as parties often implicate tacit assumptions about gender roles. Mary Joe Frug, *Re-Reading Contracts: A Feminist Analysis of a Contracts Casebook,* 34 Am. U. L. Rev. 1065 (1985). A donor may make a transfer of property conditional on the transferee remaining single for various reasons. The donor could hope to induce the donee not to marry, or the donor could imagine that the donee will no longer need the property once she marries. Such donors may or may not distinguish among donees based on their sex. One goal of property law is to confer freedom on donors to determine how and on which conditions to part with their property, but another is to construct rules governing property ownership in a manner that does not treat women as less worthy of owning or controlling property than men. *See Married Women's Property Acts,* Chapter 9, §3.1.B, above (giving married women right to own property); *Kirchberg v. Feenstra,* 450 U.S. 455 (1981) (finding that giving husbands the sole power to manage and control jointly owned property violated the equal protection clause). How should courts think about restraints on marriage if one goal is to promote gender equality?

5. Encouragement of divorce. Provisions in gifts of property encouraging separation or divorce are widely viewed with disfavor and generally held to violate public policy. They may be upheld if the "dominant motive of the transferor is to provide support in the event of separation or divorce, in which case the restraint is valid." *Restatement (Second) of Property (Donative Transfers)* §7.1. Thus, in a case devising $2,000 to the testator's daughter, who was married at the time of execution, if she remarried a man of "true Greek blood and descent and of Orthodox religion" was invalid as encouraging divorce, although similar conditions on his unmarried sons' receipt of their devises were valid. *In re Estate of Keffalas,* 233 A.2d 248 (Pa. 1967); *see also In re Estate of Owen,* 855 N.E.2d 603 (Ind. 2006) (voiding prohibition on daughter renting residence while married to her husband).

Problem

A testator creates a trust to be shared among his grandchildren, but his 2007 will provides that the children of his son Robert may not benefit from the trust if Robert shall "not be married to the child's mother within six months of the child's birth." Robert, who his father knew was gay, is married to a man with whom he has a child via a surrogate. New York, where the will is construed, enacted the *Marriage Equality Act* in 2011, providing in part that "marriage is a fundamental right. Same sex couples should have the same access as others to the protections, responsibilities, rights, obligations, and benefits of civil marriage." Robert challenges the restriction in the will as restricting his right to marry and encouraging a sham marriage. What arguments could you make as the attorneys challenging or defending the condition? How should the court rule? *See* Kathianne Boniello, *Manhattan Businessman's Will Ordered Gay Son to Marry Woman Who Gave Birth to Their Child,* N.Y. Post, Aug. 19, 2012 (reporting dispute, but not resolution).

CHAPTER 11

Leaseholds

§1 LEASEHOLD ESTATES

Property interests known as **leaseholds** are familiar to most law students. In a lease, the landlord agrees to transfer possession of the property for a specified period to the tenant in return for the tenant's promise to make a periodic rental payment. When the tenancy is over, possession ordinarily reverts to the landlord unless she has sold the property, conveying her interest to someone else. Landlord-tenant law therefore involves a division of property interests between the landlord and the tenant as well as a long-term relationship between them.

A lease is both a **conveyance** of an important property interest, akin in many ways to other estates such as the life estate, as well as a **contract** between the landlord and the tenant. Many of the topics in this chapter highlight this dual character. In some instances, doctrines traditionally based in property law have given way to contractual norms, and this has been an important part of the modernization of landlord-tenant law.[1]

§1.1 Categories of Tenancies

There are four major types of tenancies or leaseholds: **term of years**, **periodic tenancy**, **tenancy at will**, and **tenancy at sufferance**.

1. Term of years. A term of years lasts for a specified period of time determined by the parties. The period can be of any length. For example, a one-year lease is a term of years; so is a 10-year lease or a 60-day lease. For that matter, so is a 99-year lease. A term of years ends automatically at the agreed-upon time, but it may be terminated

1. Although leaseholds have their origins in the feudal estates system as with the estates we discussed in Chapter 10, leaseholds had elements of contract from their earliest common law development. *See* Milton R. Friedman & Patrick A. Randolph, *Friedman on Leases* 1-7 (5th ed. 2004).

CONTEXT

URLTA was approved by the National Conference of Commissioners on Uniform State Laws in 1972 and has been adopted in some form by nearly half the states. In 2011, the Uniform Law Commission authorized a committee to draft a *Revised Uniform Residential Landlord and Tenant Act*, and the drafting committee is currently considering a range of updates.

before the end of the fixed period on the happening of some event or condition stated in the lease agreement.[2] The future interest that follows the term of years, if retained by the landlord, is a **reversion**. If, at the time the lease is signed, the owner provides that the property will shift to a third party at the end of the leasehold, the third party holds a **remainder**.[3] The death of either party does not terminate the tenancy. The landlord is not entitled to evict the tenant before the end of the term; the only exception occurs when the tenant is breaching a material term of the lease, such as the covenant to pay rent.

2. Periodic tenancy. Periodic tenancies renew automatically at specified periods unless either the landlord or the tenant chooses to end the relationship. For example, a tenant may have a lease that renews annually for a year period. By statute or common law, notice is required before either party can terminate the relationship and end the periodic tenancy. Usually, the required notice for termination is the length of one period (up to some maximum, such as six months).

Many tenants have no written leases or specified end to their tenancy but pay monthly rent to the landlord. These arrangements create **month-to-month tenancies**, a form of periodic tenancy; they renew automatically each month if neither party notifies the other that he intends to end the relationship. Many states require a month's notice to end a month-to-month tenancy, while the *Uniform Residential Landlord and Tenant Act* (URLTA) §4.301(b) requires 60-day notice for such termination. The death of either the landlord or the tenant does not terminate the tenancy. Of course, the heirs or devisees of the deceased landlord or tenant may choose to end the tenancy, unless some statute or common law rule prevents this. Under this arrangement, the landlord can evict the tenant only by providing the requisite notice that the tenancy will not be renewed.

3. Tenancy at will. The tenancy at will is similar to a periodic tenancy except that it can be ended with no notice by either party. Many states have effectively abolished tenancies at will by requiring notice before a tenancy can be terminated; if the required notice is the same as that for a month-to-month tenancy, the two become virtually identical. But some differences remain. For example, traditionally, the death of either the landlord or the tenant terminates the tenancy at will. This result differs from periodic tenancies or the term of years and may have important consequences. Although the landlord still needs to give the statutorily required notice to evict, the landlord may have an absolute right to do so since the tenancy is at an end. In contrast, the landlord under a periodic tenancy may not be able to terminate

2. Legislation may require the landlord to use court proceedings to evict the holdover tenant and to provide a minimum amount of notice before the tenant can be evicted.

3. These terms are similarly used in the context of the life estate. *See* Chapter 10, §3.2.

the tenancy if the tenant has a defense to eviction, such as violation of the implied warranty of habitability.

4. Tenancy at sufferance (holdover tenant). A tenant rightfully in possession who wrongfully stays after the leasehold has terminated is called a **tenant at sufferance**, or a **holdover tenant**. The term is intended to distinguish between a tenant who wrongfully retains possession after the end of the lease term from a trespasser, who never had a right to possess the property. The legal procedures for ejecting trespassers often differ in significant ways from those for evicting holdover tenants. It may be lawful for an owner to physically eject a trespasser herself or to call on the police to do so. In contrast, an eviction proceeding and a court judgment are generally required to evict a tenant, including a tenant at sufferance. A landlord who accepts rent checks from a holdover tenant may be held to have agreed to a new tenancy calculated by the rental payment schedule (monthly checks creating a month-to-month tenancy).

§1.2 Commercial and Residential Tenancies

Courts often distinguish between **residential** and **commercial** tenancies. Residential tenancies involve renting property for the purpose of establishing a home; commercial tenancies involve any nonresidential use, including operation of a business for profit or operation of a nonprofit institution such as a church, hospital, or university. Residential leases tend to be relatively shorter than commercial leases; one-year residential leases are common, while commercial leases can last a decade or more, depending on the nature of the use.

Most rules are the same for both types of tenancy, but there are some differences. Even when the rules are the same, courts often analyze the two situations separately, on the assumption that the underlying policy considerations and the justified expectations of the parties may differ. In general, courts are more inclined to adopt common law rules regulating the terms of residential leases, on the assumption that commercial tenants are more likely to have sufficient bargaining power and expertise to shape the contractual arrangement in their best interests, while residential tenants are less likely to bargain for appropriate terms in the contract that reflect their justified expectations. *See Wesson v. Leone Enterprises*, 774 N.E.2d 611, 620 (Mass. 2002). By its own terms, ULRTA applies only to residential tenancies. The doctrines canvassed in this chapter apply to residential and commercial tenancies, although their application may differ in each context; when they do, we will make the distinctions explicit.

§1.3 Regulation of Landlord-Tenant Relationships

In most states, landlord-tenant relationships are heavily regulated by both common law and local, state, and federal statutes. **Procedural regulations**, for example, impose formal requirements for *creating* the landlord-tenant relationship. Under the **Statute of Frauds**, most states require that leases of more than one year be in writing, while leases of one year or less are enforceable whether they are written or oral. Oral periodic tenancies are generally enforceable under the Statute of Frauds so long as the period is one year or less; month-to-month tenancies satisfy this condition because, although they could last more than one year in total, the relevant period — one month — is less than a year. Oral tenancies at will are valid as well. Regulations also define the procedures required to **terminate** the relationship; these procedures ordinarily require **notice** and an **eviction proceeding** and court judgment to evict the tenant from the property. They may also provide for expedited court proceedings, often called **summary process**, to allow relatively quick evictions.

Substantive regulations define the parties' obligations to each other. For example, administrative agencies established by legislation may pass housing codes specifying the minimum requirements for conditions in an apartment, including heat, toilet and kitchen facilities, and pest control. Common law rules also govern the mutual obligations of the parties and impose implied terms in the contract. For example, all leaseholds include an implied covenant of quiet enjoyment by which the landlord promises not to disturb the tenant's use and enjoyment of the property.

Common law doctrines, and some statutes, define the circumstances under which a breach of the agreement by each of the parties entitles the other party to end her performance of her contractual obligations. For example, the landlord's failure to comply with the housing code may relieve the tenant partially or totally of the obligation to pay rent.

Some terms implied into leases are waivable by the parties, who may contract around them by agreeing to different arrangements. Other implied terms are compulsory or nonwaivable; any contractual term purporting to waive or alter the implied term is void and unenforceable.

In addition to legislation specifically regulating landlord-tenant relations, many states have passed general **consumer protection statutes**. In recent years, a number of courts have held that tenants may bring claims against landlords as **consumers of housing services**.

Why do tenants bring claims under consumer protection acts when they have remedies under a statute or the common law for issues covered, for example, by the implied covenant of quiet enjoyment? They do so because some unfair trade practices or consumer protection statutes provide for multiple damages or reimbursement for attorneys' fees or both. Multiple damages are awarded both to punish the wrongdoer and to deter wrongful conduct. Legislatures fear that compensatory damages may not be enough to deter fraudulent conduct since defendants may simply factor possible liability into their cost-benefit calculations, thus treating it as a cost of doing business. If the benefits of such conduct outweigh the costs, businesses may simply continue the unlawful conduct, thereby defeating the purpose of the legislation, which aims to protect consumers from such activity in the first place.

Various issues arise in these cases. First, courts must determine whether tenants are protected by general consumer protection statutes that prohibit "unfair" or "deceptive" trade practices in the sale of "goods" and "services" to consumers. Courts commonly hold that rental housing constitutes a "service" that is bought by tenants as consumers, thus enabling tenants to sue under these statutes, or otherwise find landlords to be covered by such statutes. *See, e.g., Sawyer v. Robson*, 915 A.2d 1298, 1304 (Vt. 2006); *People ex rel. City of Santa Monica v. Gabriel*, 112 Cal. Rptr. 3d 574, 579 (Ct. App. 2010). Some courts, however, have held that the presence of specific landlord-tenant legislation, such as the URLTA, demonstrates a legislative intent to exclude tenants from coverage under other statutes and that tenants therefore cannot obtain additional remedies under general consumer protection legislation. *State v. Schwab*, 693 P.2d 108 (Wash. 1985).

Second, courts must define what kinds of conduct constitute "unfair" or "deceptive" practices. For example, the Massachusetts Supreme Judicial Court has held that including illegal and unenforceable clauses in residential leases constitutes an unfair and deceptive practice that "injures" tenants, even if the landlord never attempts to enforce the clause and the tenant admits never having read the clause. In the absence of reliance, however, damages are nominal. *Leardi v. Brown*, 474 N.E.2d 1094 (Mass. 1985). Other kinds of conduct held to constitute unfair or deceptive trade practices include retaliatory evictions, *Hernandez v. Stabach*, 193 Cal. Rptr. 350 (Ct. App. 1983), and the failure to maintain rental housing in a habitable condition, *Dean v. Hill*, 615 S.E.2d 699, 701-702 (N.C. Ct. App. 2005); *State v. Weller*, 327 N.W.2d 172 (Wis. 1982). Another central issue is addressed in the following problem.

Problem

Consumer protection laws generally regulate those involved in "trade" or "business" or "commerce." If a landlord owns a two-unit building and rents out one unit, is she engaged in a trade or business? What arguments can be made on both sides? How should the court rule? *Compare Billings v. Wilson*, 493 N.E.2d 187 (Mass. 1986) (no), *with Stanley v. Moore*, 454 S.E.2d 225 (N.C. 1995) (yes).

§1.4 Distinguishing Tenancies from Other Property Relationships

The following case deals with the question whether migrant farmworkers who reside in facilities provided by their employer are entitled to a court hearing before being evicted. Tenants are generally entitled to such legal process; others generally are not so entitled. In addition, tenants may have a right under certain circumstances to continued occupancy over the landlord's objections. The farmworkers' relationship with their employer has many of the elements of a landlord-tenant relationship: The employer transfers possession of a portion of the employer's property by allowing the farmworkers to live there in exchange for the farmworkers' promises to convey value back to the employer. Their relationship also appears different, in ways that may be significant, from that of most tenants. Many migrant farmworkers pay no rent; instead, they work for the employer in the fields. They are compensated for these services in the form of wages. This compensation *may* be reduced to account for the rental value of the employer's property they occupy. The exchange of land for services may make the relationship seem more like a feudal one than a modern contractual one.

Whether the employees are classified as tenants or otherwise, the common law may require employers to follow certain procedures to exclude an ex-employee from the employer's property. The important question therefore centers on the real procedures required to evict fired employees who, during their employment, were legally entitled to live on the employer's property. Can the employer-landlord eject them physically? Can he call the police and have them arrested? Or must the employer provide notice and obtain a court judgment?

Vásquez v. Glassboro Service Association, Inc.

415 A.2d 1156 (N.J. 1980)

STEWART G. POLLOCK, J.

Glassboro [Service Association] is a non-profit corporation comprised of farmers who contracted with Glassboro for migrant farm labor. The farmers called Glassboro as they needed workers to pick crops, and Glassboro transported workers from its labor camp to the farms. The length of time that a worker stayed at a farm varied, depending primarily on the time needed to pick a crop. Glassboro paid the worker his wages, and the farmer paid Glassboro for those wages plus a commission for Glassboro's services.

Only men were hired; the workers' families remained in Puerto Rico. Glassboro paid a farmworker $2.40 per hour and charged him $23 per week for meals. The worker agreed to work eight hours a day for six days a week, plus overtime as mutually agreed.

[In 1976, Glassboro negotiated a contract with the Puerto Rican Department of Labor.] The contract stated that a worker was to pay for his transportation from Puerto Rico. If he completed his contract, he would be reimbursed for the cost of transportation from and provided return transportation to Puerto Rico. If the worker did not fulfill his contract, Glassboro was not obliged to reimburse him for the cost of transportation. Although the contract provided that Glassboro would furnish a non-negotiable airplane ticket to Puerto Rico for a worker who became physically unfit, there was no comparable provision for a worker who was fired. The contract period was for 28 weeks, or until December 1, whichever came first.

The contract provided that, if an employee was to be discharged, a hearing was to occur no later than five days after the employee was given notice of termination. The contract did not require a minimum amount of time to elapse between notice and termination of employment. The contract provided further for administrative review within the Puerto Rican Department of Labor whenever a worker had a complaint "regarding the breach, application, interpretation or compliance" with the contract. If the Secretary of Labor determined that Glassboro had "not adequately remedied the complaint," the Secretary could represent the worker and sue Glassboro.

Pursuant to the contract, Glassboro supplied living quarters for workers at its labor camp in New Jersey. Those quarters consisted of barracks housing up to 30 men. Each worker received a mattress, bedding, and a locker. The barracks were equipped with common toilets, showers, and lavatories. Although some farmers charged the workers for housing while the workers were at the farms, Glassboro did not impose any extra charge for housing at its labor camp. The contract did not require a migrant farmworker to live at Glassboro's labor camp. Nonetheless, the parties contemplated that the farmworker would reside at the labor camp.

In 1976, [Natividad] Vásquez was recruited in Puerto Rico and came to New Jersey to work for Glassboro. According to Glassboro's foreman, Vásquez's work was not satisfactory. On July 19, 1976, the foreman told Vásquez that he was to be discharged. A few hours later Vásquez had his "hearing" with the foreman and a field representative of the Puerto Rican Department of Labor. Thereafter the foreman decided to complete the discharge, a decision Vásquez does not challenge in this action. Although there were vacant spaces at the Glassboro barracks, Vásquez was not permitted to remain overnight. The foreman told him to gather his belongings and leave.

Unable to speak English and without funds to return to Puerto Rico, Vásquez sought the assistance of the Farmworkers Corporation, a federally funded non-profit corporation dedicated to the needs of farmworkers. A Rutgers law student returned with Vásquez to the camp and requested that Vásquez be allowed to remain overnight. The request was refused. Vásquez stayed with a friend who was participating in a job training program conducted by the Farmworkers Corporation.

The Farmworkers Rights Project filed a complaint on July 22, 1976, seeking an order permitting Vásquez to reenter his living quarters and enjoining defendants from depriving him of the use of the quarters except through judicial process. Although Vásquez has since found housing, other workers have been evicted, one at 3:00 A.M.

II

At common law, one who occupied premises as an employee of the owner and received the use of the premises as part compensation for his services or under a contract of employment was not considered a tenant.

[The *New Jersey Anti-Eviction Act,* N.J. Stat. §§2A:18-61.1 to 2A:18-61.12, prohibits eviction of tenants unless the landlord can show good cause, as defined in the statute. Section 2A:18-61.1(m) allows eviction if the "landlord or owner conditioned the tenancy upon and in consideration for the tenant's employment by the landlord or owner as superintendent, janitor or in some other capacity and such employment is being terminated."]

The initial question is whether the Legislature intended to include migrant farmworkers in the phrase "in some other capacity" in N.J. Stat. §2A:18-61.1(m). Where general words follow a specific enumeration, the principle of *ejusdem generis* requires that the general words are applicable only to the same class of things already mentioned. In N.J. Stat. §2A:18-61.1(m), the general words "in some other capacity" follow the specific enumeration of "superintendent" and "janitor." We determine that, within the meaning of the statute, a farmworker does not belong to the same class of employees as a janitor or superintendent. A farmworker who possesses a mattress and locker in an unpartitioned barracks while waiting to be sent to work on a farm is different from a superintendent or janitor residing with his or her family in an apartment house. The farmworkers are all men who come from Puerto Rico without their families. They live in large barracks with no privacy, sleeping in bunks in an unpartitioned room and sharing toilets and showers. Their occupancy of the barracks is intermittent, since it is a base camp for use while they are awaiting assignment to farms.

Our analysis of the words of the statute, the absence of any illuminating legislative history, and the application of principles of statutory construction lead to the conclusion that a migrant farmworker is not a tenant within the meaning of N.J. Stat. §2A:18-61.1(m). The special characteristics of migrant workers' housing, the absence of a contractual provision for the payment of rent, the lack of privacy, the intermittent occupancy, and the interdependence of employment and housing support this conclusion.

III

In ascertaining whether a farmworker is entitled to notice before dispossession, we turn next to the Glassboro contract. [T]he contract resulted from negotiations between the Puerto Rican Department of Labor and Glassboro. No migrant farmworker participated directly or through a labor union in the negotiations. The record does not demonstrate whether or not the Puerto Rican Department of Labor has the same interests as the migrant farmworkers. The Puerto Rican Department of Labor may have been concerned also about reducing unemployment in Puerto Rico by finding jobs for its residents on farms in New Jersey. Whatever the interests of the parties to the negotiations, a migrant farmworker was required to accept the contract as presented by Glassboro.

The contract in evidence is written in English. Although Vásquez spoke Spanish only, the record does not show that he received a Spanish translation of the contract. Nonetheless, he signed a copy of the contract.

Once a migrant farmworker came to Glassboro's labor camp in New Jersey, he depended on Glassboro for employment, transportation, food, and housing. He was separated by over 1300 miles from his home and family. Although an American citizen, he was isolated from most citizens in New Jersey by his inability to speak English. An invisible barrier separated a migrant farmworker from the rest of the State as he was shuttled from the labor camp to the farms. The lack of alternative housing emphasized the inequality between Glassboro and the migrant farmworkers. Once his employment ended, a farmworker lost not only his job but his shelter. The fear of discharge, and with it the loss of income, housing, and return passage to Puerto Rico permeated the contractual relationship. This is the setting in which we measure the contract against the public policy of the State.

Public policy eludes precise definition and may have diverse meanings in different contexts. The sources of public policy include federal and state legislation and judicial decisions.

In the past, courts in New Jersey have refused to enforce contracts that violate the public policy of the State. No contract can be sustained if it is inconsistent with the public interest or detrimental to the common good. Contracts have been declared invalid because they violate statutes, promote crime, interfere with the administration of justice, encourage divorce, violate public morality, or restrain trade. With respect to employment contracts that have an otherwise lawful purpose, courts have afforded judicial sanction to post-employment restrictive covenants only to the extent that the covenants are reasonable and comport with public policy.

The courts and Legislature of New Jersey have demonstrated a progressive attitude in providing legal protection for migrant farmworkers. [The state legislature has passed legislation regulating housing conditions and sanitation for migrant farmworkers. In 1979, the federal government, pursuant to the *Occupational Safety and Health Act of 1970*, 29 U.S.C. §651 *et seq.*, assumed responsibility for inspection of many migrant labor camps.] The constant attention accorded by Congress and the State Legislature demonstrates a legislative concern for the well-being of migrant farmworkers.

In *State v. Shack*, 277 A.2d 369 (N.J. 1971), this Court reversed convictions for trespass of a fieldworker and an attorney for organizations providing services for migrant farmworkers. Declining to characterize the migrant farmworker as either tenant or employee, Chief Justice Weintraub wrote:

> We see no profit in trying to decide upon a conventional category and then forcing the present subject into it. That approach would be artificial and distorting. The quest is for a fair adjustment of the competing needs of the parties, in the light of the realities of the relationship between the migrant worker and the operator of the housing facility. 277 A.2d at 374.

The Court weighed the property rights of the farmer against the rights of the farmworkers to information and services and found that the balance tipped in favor of the farmworker. Underlying that conclusion was recognition of the fundamental right of the farmworker to live with dignity. As in *Shack*, the appropriate result in this case arises from the status and the relationship of the parties.

The enlightened approach of the courts and the Legislature provides the context in which we assess the Glassboro contract and consider how a migrant farmworker should be dispossessed from his living quarters at a labor camp.

A basic tenet of the law of contracts is that courts should enforce contracts as made by the parties. However, application of that principle assumes that the parties are in positions of relative equality and that their consent is freely given. In recent years, courts have become increasingly sensitive to overreaching in contracts where there is an inequality in the status of the parties.

In a variety of situations, courts have revised contracts where there was an inequality in the bargaining power of the parties. The principle has been applied also to leases. In *Kuzmiak v. Brookchester*, 111 A.2d 425 (N.J. Super. Ct. App. Div. 1955), the court invalidated a clause in an apartment lease exculpating a landlord from liability for negligence. More recently the inequality of bargaining power between landlord and tenant led this Court to comment that "lease agreements are frequently form contracts of adhesion." *Trentacost v. Brussel*, 412 A.2d 436, 442 (N.J. 1980).

A migrant farmworker has even less bargaining power than a residential tenant. Although the contract did not require a migrant farmworker to live at the labor camp, the realities of his employment forced him to stay at the camp. Residence at the labor camp benefited not only the farmworker, but also Glassboro and its member farmers.

It was more convenient for them if the workers resided at the camp: the pool of labor was at hand, and the workers could be transported conveniently to the farms. The contract assured Glassboro that there would be a labor source available on its property.

Under the contract, once a worker's employment was ended, he had no right to stay at the camp. Glassboro's possible need for the bed of a discharged farmworker, particularly during the growing season, is relevant, but not persuasive. In this case, Glassboro had ample space for Vásquez, yet he was turned out of the barracks on the same day he was fired. The interest of neither the migrant farmworker nor the public is served by casting the worker adrift to fend for himself without reasonable time to find shelter.

The status of a worker seeking employment with Glassboro is analogous to that of a consumer who must accept a standardized form contract to purchase needed goods and services. Neither farmworkers nor consumers negotiate the terms of their contracts; both must accept the contracts as presented to them. In both instances, the contracts affect many people as well as the public interest.

With respect to a standardized form contract, the intention of the consumer has been described as "but a subjection more or less voluntary to terms dictated by the stronger party, terms whose consequences are often understood only in a vague way, if at all." Kessler, *Contracts of Adhesion — Some Thoughts About Freedom of Contract*, 43 Colum. L. Rev. 629, 632 (1943). A contract where one party, as here, must accept or reject the contract does not result from the consent of that party. It is a contract of adhesion:

> There being no private consent to support a contract of adhesion, its legitimacy rests entirely on its compliance with standards in the public interest. The individual who is subject to the obligations imposed by a standard form thus gains the assurance that the rules to which he is subject have received his consent either directly or through their conforming to higher public laws and standards made and enforced by the public institutions that legitimately govern him. Slawson, *Standard Form Contracts and Democratic Control of Lawmaking Power*, 84 Harv. L. Rev. 529, 566 (1971).

The absence of a provision in the contract for reasonable time to find housing after termination of his employment bespeaks Glassboro's superior bargaining position. Further, by failing to provide for a reasonable time to find alternative housing, the contract is inconsistent with the enlightened attitude of the Legislature and the courts towards migrant farmworkers.

The crux of this case thus becomes the unconscionability of the contract as it is sought to be enforced against the migrant workers. The unconscionability of the contract inheres not only in its failure to provide a worker with a reasonable opportunity to find alternative housing, but in its disregard for his welfare after termination of his employment. The inherent inequity of the contract arouses a sense of injustice and invokes the equitable powers of the courts. In the absence of any concern demonstrated for the worker in the contract, public policy requires the implication of a provision for a reasonable time to find alternative housing.

IV

At common law, on termination of employment, an employer could dispossess an employee who occupied premises incidental to his employment. Similarly, a landlord could dispossess peaceably a holdover tenant. To that extent, both an employer and landlord could use self-help to regain possession peaceably. The advantage to them was that they were assured of prompt restoration of the use of their property. However, an inherent vice in self-help is that it can lead to confrontations and breaches of the peace. In the absence of self-help, a landlord or employer at common law was remitted to an action in ejectment. The problem with ejectment is that it was slow and expensive.

With regard to real property occupied solely as a residence, the Legislature has resolved the dilemma by prohibiting entry without consent and by providing a summary dispossess proceeding. N.J. Stat. §2A:39-1 and N.J. Stat. §2A:18-53 *et seq.* Similarly, the Legislature has provided a summary dispossess proceeding for the removal of residential tenants. N.J. Stat. §2A:18-61.2. As explained above, migrant farmworkers are not tenants, and there is no comparable statute providing for their summary dispossession on termination of their employment. In fashioning a suitable remedy, we acknowledge that the realities of the relationship between the migrant worker and a farm labor service are unique and summon a judicial response unrestricted by conventional categories, such as employer-employee and landlord-tenant.

In the absence of a contractual provision or legislation addressing the plight of a migrant farmworker on termination of his employment, the courts, exercising equitable jurisdiction, should devise a remedy to fit the circumstances of each case. Depending on the circumstances, an equitable adjustment of the rights of the parties may vary from one case to another. An appropriate remedy might include time in addition to that implied in the contract, assistance in obtaining alternative housing, return passage to Puerto Rico, or some other form of relief. By abolishing self-help and requiring dispossession through a judicial proceeding, we provide a forum for an equitable resolution of a controversy between a farm labor service and a migrant farmworker on termination of the latter's employment.

We are mindful of the special considerations pertaining to migrant farmworkers and of the need for a prompt resolution of disputes between farmworkers and a farm labor service. In general, a summary action under [N.J. Rule 4:67] should be a more appropriate proceeding than a plenary action. In fact, the present case was instituted on complaint and order to show cause returnable three days later, at which time the court heard testimony, reserved decision, and rendered a written opinion seven days later. We conclude that a dispute concerning the dispossession of a migrant farmworker on termination of his employment, whether instituted by a farm labor service or, as here, by a farmworker, should proceed in a summary manner under [Rule] 4:67.

Notes and Questions

1. **Summary process versus self-help.** Owners are entitled to use self-help to remove licensees and those illegally occupying their property. *See, e.g., Harkins v. Win Corp.*, 771 A.2d 1025 (D.C. 2001) (provider of transient accommodations may use self-

help to evict non-paying lodger); *Paulino v. Wright*, 620 N.Y.S.2d 363 (App. Div. 1994) (city entitled to use self-help to evict illegal occupants of city-owned property). If they refuse to leave, the owner may even use reasonable force. Owners used to be entitled to use self-help to remove tenants as well, and the law in some states still allows this, particularly for commercial tenants. *See Brown v. State Central Bank*, 459 F. Supp. 2d 837 (S.D. Iowa 2006) (commercial landlord permitted to retake possession by changing locks). However, today almost all states outlaw self-help in removing tenants, instead obligating landlords to use court proceedings (eviction) to recover possession.

2. **Leases versus licenses and easements.** The question frequently arises whether an arrangement constitutes a lease or whether it is instead a license or an easement. This matters for purposes of determining whether a landlord may use self-help, but can be an issue in a much broader range of tenant statutory and common law rights. The characterization issue comes up in the context of department store and shopping mall concessions, students living in college dormitories, apartment complex managers and migrant farmworkers, and other contexts. Students living in dormitories and apartment managers living on the premises are explicitly exempted from the protections of the URLTA. *See* URLTA §1.202 (tenancy protections do not apply to residents at educational institutions or to "occupancy by an employee of a landlord whose right to occupancy is conditional upon employment in and about the premises"). Such residents will thus not be treated as tenants in those states that have adopted URLTA without modification on this point, *compare, e.g.*, Conn. Gen. Stat. §47a-2 (excluding the general exemption for employees in Connecticut's version of URLTA), although, as *Vásquez* shows, they may have other legal protections. If no statute answers the question, these cases are generally decided by asking whether the owner has transferred exclusive "possession" of a defined space; if so, a lease will be found. If control of a particular space is not granted, or such possession is not exclusive, a license is likely to be found. *Millennium Park Joint Venture, LLC v. Houlihan*, 948 N.E.2d 1, 18-21 (Ill. 2010). However, the cases are split, with some courts finding leases and other courts finding mere licenses.

Courts have reached differing results in the case of *students* in dormitories, in part depending on the nature of the claim at issue. *Compare Burch v. University of Kansas*, 756 P.2d 431 (Kan. 1988), *and Rhaney v. University of Maryland, Eastern Shores*, 880 A.2d 357, 367 (Md. 2005) (both holding that students in dormitories are tenants for purposes of analyzing universities' tort liability as landlords), *with Houle v. Adams State College*, 547 P.2d 926 (Colo. 1976), *and Cook v. University Plaza*, 427 N.E.2d 405 (Ill. App. Ct. 1981) (both holding that universities are not landlords in the context of security deposit requirements). In the case of *employees*, such as migrant farmworkers and apartment building managers, the cases focus on determining whether access to the apartment seems to be part of the employment relationship and intended to last only as long as the employee remains on the job. It also matters whether the employer/landlord has a particular space reserved for employees and if occupancy by a nonemployee would interfere with the owner's ability to provide the services that the employee renders. *Compare GENC Realty LLC v. Nezaj*, 860 N.Y.S.2d 106 (App. Div.

2008), *with Bigelow v. Bullard*, 901 P.2d 630 (Nev. 1995) (superintendent is a tenant). *Compare De Bruyn Produce Co. v. Romero*, 508 N.W.2d 150 (Mich. Ct. App. 1993) (migrant farmworkers are licensees, not tenants), *with State v. DeCoster*, 653 A.2d 891 (Me. 1995) (migrant farmworkers are tenants).

How should the courts distinguish between licenses and leases? In *Keller v. Southwood North Medical Pavilion, Inc.*, 959 P.2d 102 (Utah 1998), a chiropractor leased space in a shopping center pursuant to a written agreement that included the right to place a sign on a large monument located near the street. Most of the signs on the monument were small brass plaques advertising various tenants' services, but the landlord allowed the chiropractor to put up a larger sign in exchange for additional consideration. When the landlord sold the shopping center, the new owner objected to the appearance of the chiropractor's sign and removed it. The chiropractor claimed that the new owner violated the state forcible entry statute, which required landlords to use court eviction proceedings rather than self-help to recover possession of property from tenants. The court, however, found that the chiropractor only had a license, not a lease subject to the statute, because the agreement did not transfer exclusive possession of any part of the monument and did not identify any particular space on the monument that the chiropractor had a right to occupy. Does the court's focus on possession make sense? Or should it instead focus on the policies underlying the prohibition on landlord self-help? We discuss those policies in §3.1, below.

The *Vásquez* court avoided the abstract question whether the farm owner had granted "possession" to the farmworkers or whether they had the status of "tenants." In effect, the court ruled that the farmworkers were entitled to protection even if they were not tenants and even if the statutory procedures did not apply to them. Was this a good idea? Was it justified? Could the legislature have intended to allow owners to engage in self-help in cases not covered by the summary process law? *See, e.g., City of New York v. Utsey*, 714 N.Y.S.2d 410 (App. Div. 2000) (governmental owner may be obligated to use eviction proceedings against long-term squatters whose initial occupancy was nonpermissive if the owner acquiesced in their occupancy in a manner that demonstrates an intent to treat them as tenants at will).

3. Contract language. Could the issue of the character of the property interest be avoided if the parties had a written agreement? The answer depends in part on whether the policy outlawing self-help is disclaimable. If it is, then there should be no problem with the parties agreeing to call their arrangement a license, under which the licensee can be removed at will without court eviction proceedings. If it is not, then the language cannot be determinative. The cases are not uniform. Courts have interpreted "lease" arrangements as licenses and "license" arrangements as leases. *Compare Halley v. Harden Oil Co.*, 357 S.E.2d 138 (Ga. Ct. App. 1987) (although contract stated that it was a "lease," owner retained possession, use, and responsibility for maintenance of property and thus was merely a license), *and Loren v. Marry*, 600 N.Y.S.2d 369 (App. Div. 1993) (same), *with Dargis v. Paradise Park, Inc.*, 819 N.E.2d 1220 (Ill. App. Ct. 2004), *and M & I First National Bank v. Episcopal Homes Management, Inc.*, 536 N.W.2d 175 (Wis. Ct. App. 1995) (both holding that "license" arrangements were leases).

4. Freedom of contract, unequal bargaining power, and minimum standards. Landlord/tenant relationships arise from voluntary agreements between landowners and those who seek access to their land. When the agreement is ambiguous, courts must interpret the agreement to determine its terms. However, contracts involve a second, distinct issue; some contracts are illegal and some contract terms are mandatory. Statutes, regulations, and common law may, for example, require eviction procedures to remove an occupant of land, whether or not the agreement between the parties provides for this. When should contracts contain mandatory terms?

One view is that contracts should be regulated when the parties have **unequal bargaining power**. Robert Hale argued that individuals may be forced to agree to onerous contract terms if they have no reasonable alternative. They may have little market power because of their poverty, lack of marketable skills, or substantial competition from others seeking similar entitlements. "[B]y judicious legal limitation on the bargaining power of the economically and legally stronger, it is conceivable that the economically weak would acquire greater freedom of contract than they now have — freedom to resist more effectively the bargaining power of the strong, and to obtain better terms." Robert Hale, *Bargaining, Duress, and Economic Liberty*, 43 Colum. L. Rev. 603, 628 (1943). If the law prohibits certain onerous contract terms, then potential tenants will be protected from them. For example, tenants will know that, if they obtain rental housing, they cannot be evicted without court proceedings to determine whether the landlord has a right to recover possession and to ensure that the tenants have time to move. Tenants and landlords may have unequal bargaining power because housing is a necessity and because of structural disparities between landlords and tenants associated with the fact that landlords own real property and tenants do not; in addition, landlords often collude by using form leases drafted by real estate associations that include terms favorable to landlords.

However, this view has been criticized because it fails to recognize that landlords can respond to regulations either by raising the rent, changing other terms of the contract, or withdrawing from the market altogether — all of which arguably hurt the very people we hoped to help by the regulation in the first place. Thus, a second view is that contracts should hardly ever be regulated by the state; the ideal of **freedom of contract** is based on the notion that the parties should be free to make whatever arrangements suit their purposes. Limitation on freedom of contract arguably both interferes with individual autonomy and is inefficient because it makes both parties worse off in their own terms. Professor Alan Schwartz argues that "just outcomes arise when people are permitted to do the best they can, given their circumstances. This is because, the theory goes, people are the best judges of what maximizes their own utility; hence, allowing them to make unrestrained choices is most likely to maximize utility for the individual and for society as a whole." Alan Schwartz, *Justice and the Law of Contracts: A Case for the Traditional Approach*, 9 Harv. J.L. & Pub. Pol'y 107, 107 (1986). This means that people should be free to contract on any terms they like. Nor should we worry about unfair contract terms because "competition in markets prevents even very large firms from exploiting even very small consumers." *Id.* at 109.

Moreover, regulating contract terms arguably hurts the very people we are trying to protect. Schwartz explains that "not enforcing contract clauses . . . tends to make people poorer rather than richer." *Id.* at 115. He continues:

> To make a person poorer is meant here to shrink the number of options a person has available to improve his or her lot in life. Suppose a judge bans a contract clause. He has imposed a restriction on the choices available to persons who agreed to it or would have agreed to it in preference to other contract clauses that firms could offer. Poor people tend to have fewer choices than rich people because they have less money. Poor people do have free will, however. If a judge bans a contract clause on the ostensible ground of protecting the poor, the judge actually is reducing the choices of poor people and is therefore preventing poor people from doing as well as they can, given their circumstances, in the realm of contractual choice.

A third view is that contracts should be regulated to ensure that they comply with **minimum standards** compatible with the legal framework of a free and democratic society. Joseph William Singer, *Things That We Would Like to Take for Granted: Minimum Standards for the Legal Framework of a Free and Democratic Society*, 2 Harv. L. & Pol'y Rev. 139 (2008). All contracts are regulated by state or federal law in some respect. Some of these regulations ensure that contracts do not violate public policy and that they are consistent with basic standards of decency in social relationships in a just society. Other regulations take the form of **consumer protection laws** that ensure that products (including housing) are safe and meet the legitimate expectations of purchasers. On this view, freedom of contract is an important norm, but it takes place within boundaries established by minimum standards regulations. If such regulations make housing too expensive for the very poorest persons, then the appropriate remedy is not to deregulate but to adopt other means either to increase their bargaining power or to provide affordable and safe housing.

Problems

1. Two university students living in a college dormitory come to you with the following problem. Along with signing many other forms and documents, the students signed form dormitory contracts that stated "LICENSE" at the top of the first page. The contract granted the students a "license" to occupy a dormitory room in exchange for rent to be paid one semester at a time. The form stated that the university "reserved the right to cancel the license at any time for any reason with 24 hours' notice." It also stated: "This agreement is not a lease." One student placed a banner reading "SUPPORT THE LIVING WAGE CAMPAIGN" outside her window in an effort to persuade the university to raise the wages it pays to its lowest-paid employees to enable them to earn enough to live in the community without taking a second job. The other student placed a banner reading "ABORTION KILLS" outside her window. The university had a policy prohibiting students from placing any banners outside their windows. The students knew about the policy but decided to violate it on the ground that it interfered with their right to free speech. Because of their violations of the rules, they were given 24 hours to vacate their dormitory rooms. They were not suspended or

otherwise punished for their conduct. A state statute provides that "tenants" cannot be evicted without one month's notice and a court eviction proceeding.

a. What is the students' argument that they are "tenants" protected from eviction without judicial process?

b. What is the school's argument that they are licensees, rather than tenants, and can be removed with self-help and no notice?

c. How should the court rule?

2. A tenant invites her boyfriend to move in with her on the condition that he pay half the rent. Is he a tenant or a licensee? In *Kiehm v. Adams*, 126 P.3d 339 (Haw. 2006), the court held that the question should be decided by the intent of the parties but that roommate arrangements should be presumed to be licenses if the roommate does not have the "right to occupy a distinct and separate part of the premises," the right is not intended to be assignable, and the right is not for a particular term. However, a dissenting judge would have found a sublease since a state statute, Haw. Stat. §521-8, defined a "rental agreement" to mean all agreements that concern the "use and occupancy of a dwelling unit and premises." *Id.* at 350 (Acoba, J., dissenting). Who is right, and how should this question be decided? From the landlord's perspective, what are the consequences of treating a roommate who is not a signatory to the lease as a licensee?

3. A number of companies, such as Airbnb, have emerged that allow people to find short-term stays in people's homes online. In New York, it is illegal in many types of buildings for residents to have paying guests for less than 30 consecutive days, N.Y. Multiple Dwelling Law §4(8)(a), and New York has taken steps to enforce this requirement, *see* Ron Lieber, *A Warning for Hosts of Airbnb Travellers*, N.Y. Times, Dec. 1, 2012, at B-1. Why would a municipality outlaw such short-term housing arrangements? Who might benefit from such services? Who might be harmed?

§2 CONFLICTS ABOUT OCCUPANCY

It is important to understand the context in which landlord-tenant litigation tends to occur. Many disputes arise because either the landlord has interfered with the tenant's possession or what is known as "quiet enjoyment" of the property or the tenant has breached his obligation to pay rent — or both. This chapter addresses these issues in this and the next two sections.

When a landlord asserts a claim against a tenant based on the tenant's failure to pay rent or on some claimed breach of the lease agreement, the landlord may seek either (or both) (a) payment of **back rent** the tenant owes, or (b) **possession** of the premises (otherwise known as **eviction**). The landlord may also make a claim for **damages** resulting from the tenant's breach — for example, the cost of repairing facilities damaged by the tenant. The tenant may answer each of these claims by denying that he has breached the lease (he has in fact paid the rent or he did not cause the damage). Or he may raise **defenses** to these claims, admitting that he stopped paying rent but asserting that he was entitled to do so because the landlord breached the agreement first.

In response to a lawsuit by the landlord, the tenant may also be able to make **counterclaims** against the landlord. These may include claims for **damages** resulting from the landlord's breach of the lease, and courts may order a rent **abatement** (a reduction in rent) owed for the period during the breach. Some courts will also allow the tenant to recover damages if the landlord acted negligently and physical harm resulted to the tenant or an invitee on the premises; such damages also may exceed the rental value of the premises. The tenant may petition for **injunctive** relief, such as an order to the landlord to fix the apartment to comply with the local housing code.

Tenants may also sue the landlord initially with the tenant's claims. Such lawsuits ordinarily ask for either (a) damages resulting from the landlord's breach, such as a failure to maintain the premises, or compensation, for example, for injuries resulting from the landlord's failure to comply with the housing code, or (b) an injunction ordering the landlord to fix the apartment to comply with the terms of the lease or the housing code.

Keep this litigation context in mind as you work through the doctrines on occupancy, rent, habitable premises, and other materials covered in this chapter.

§2.1 Initial Occupancy: Landlord's Duty to Deliver Possession

Under the current majority rule, the landlord has the duty to deliver possession of the rented premises to the tenant at the beginning of the leasehold. *Restatement (Second) of Property (Landlord and Tenant)* §6.2 (1977); URLTA §§2.103, 4.102. If a prior tenant wrongfully holds over after his lease term expires, the landlord has an obligation in most jurisdictions to remove the prior tenant within a reasonable period of time by either instituting eviction proceedings or convincing the holdover tenant to leave. Failure to deliver actual possession of the premises to the new tenant constitutes a breach of the lease by the landlord. The tenant who has been shut out may either terminate the lease and recover damages as compensation for having to find another place to live or affirm the lease, withhold rent for the period during which she could not occupy the premises, and recover damages for the cost of temporarily renting alternative housing while the landlord undertakes eviction proceedings to remove the prior tenant.

A minority of jurisdictions follow the traditional rule, under which the landlord has only the duty to deliver the *right* to possession but no duty to deliver *actual* possession. In those states, it is the new tenant's responsibility to evict the holdover tenant by bringing ejectment or other appropriate proceedings. Since the landlord is not in default under the minority rule, the new tenant is legally obligated to pay the rent even though she is not in possession. The new tenant's remedy is to go after the holdover tenant for damages.

§2.2 During the Leasehold

Leaseholds often entail an ongoing landlord-tenant relationship, with inevitable adjustments and accommodations over the term of the lease, and the nature of this relationship can vary significantly depending on the type of parties involved. A large-scale commercial tenant is likely to have a different kind of interaction with its landlord than someone renting a room upstairs in a landlord's two-family building.

A. Landlord's Right to Inspect and Repair

Uniform Residential Landlord and Tenant Act

§3.103

§3.103. Access

(a) A tenant shall not unreasonably withhold consent to the landlord to enter into the dwelling unit in order to inspect the premises, make necessary or agreed repairs, decorations, alterations, or improvements, supply necessary or agreed services, or exhibit the dwelling unit to prospective or actual purchasers, mortgagees, tenants, workmen, or contractors.

(b) A landlord may enter the dwelling unit without consent of the tenant in case of emergency.

(c) A landlord shall not abuse the right of access or use it to harass the tenant. Except in case of emergency or unless it is impracticable to do so, the landlord shall give the tenant at least [2] days' notice of his intent to enter and may enter only at reasonable times.

(d) A landlord has no other right of access except

(1) pursuant to court order;

(2) as permitted by Sections 4.202 and 4.203(b) [giving the landlord the right to enter the dwelling to fix damage to the apartment caused by the tenant or to enter the apartment in case of extended tenant absence]; or

(3) unless the tenant has abandoned or surrendered the premises.

Problem

A tenant has a one-year lease that grants the landlord the "right to inspect the premises at the landlord's discretion." After living in the apartment for three months, the landlord notifies the tenant that he intends to inspect the property three days later at 10:00 A.M. and that she need not be present if she does not want to be there during the inspection. The tenant decides not to be present. After the inspection, she finds some papers on her desk moved around. She asks the landlord about this, and he says he was checking to see if she had too many electronic devices plugged into the socket. A similar event happens a month later. She decides to stay in the apartment during the inspection this time. When the landlord comes, he does a cursory overview of the apartment and then tries to engage the tenant in conversation. She is friendly but not interested in becoming friends with the landlord and wishes he would leave. The inspections begin to occur once a month, and when the tenant asks the landlord why he needs to inspect so often, he says "just to make sure things are safe for you." These frequent visits are not customary, and the tenant is uncomfortable with them. What advice would you give the tenant? If she complains to the landlord and the landlord calls you for legal advice, what would you tell the landlord?

B. Tenant's Right to Receive Visitors and to Marry

Problem

Tenants have a nondisclaimable right to receive visitors. *State v. DeCoster*, 653 A.2d 891, 894 (Me. 1995). Similarly, a tenant who gets married should be entitled to live with his or her new spouse. But does the tenant have a right to live with someone other than a spouse? What rights go along with the leasehold? Does the landlord have the right to control occupancy to those listed on the written lease, or does the tenant have the right to have a family member or a boyfriend or girlfriend move in with her? *Cf. Barrett Japaning, Inc. v. Bialobroda*, 892 N.Y.S.2d 35 (App. Div. 2009) (landlord entitled to injunction to limit tenant to no more than one roommate). Should it matter if the landlord has religious objections to cohabitation outside marriage? Should it matter if the couple is not legally empowered to get married, as is the case for same-sex couples in most states?

C. Tenant's Duties Not to Commit Waste or Cause a Nuisance, and the Problem of Domestic Violence

Tenants generally have a duty not to commit waste, giving landlords the right to have the premises intact and not damaged, subject to normal wear and tear. Written leases almost invariably contain a clause entitling the landlord to evict the tenant for breach of this obligation. Written leases also generally contain a clause stating that the tenant "covenants not to disturb the neighbors, interfere with their quiet enjoyment of their property, or cause a nuisance" — or other words to that effect.

Problem

A woman breaks off her relationship with a man and moves out with their two children. He repeatedly harasses her at work, calling more than ten times a day, and threatens her life. She moves to a new apartment and goes to court to obtain a restraining order on him ordering him to stop harassing her and to stay away from her. He then shows up at the new apartment, throws a brick through the window, and kicks down the front door. She calls the police, who arrest him. Then the landlord sues to evict her for violating the lease terms against "committing waste" and "causing a nuisance." Is the landlord entitled to evict her? Does she have any possible defenses? *See* Jill Barton, *The Harsh Reality of Choosing Between Safety and Housing: Solutions for Victims of Domestic Violence*, 93 Women Law. J. 21 (2008).

D. Tenant Use Restrictions and Obligations

1. Use restrictions. Many residential leases, in addition to addressing waste and nuisance, limit the use of the premises to "residential purposes" or similar terms, and questions can arise about whether home businesses violate these restrictions. As with similar covenants in the context of common interest communities, courts often read residential use restrictions in leases narrowly, although some courts have found a breach for substantial businesses. *See Park West Village v. Lewis*, 465 N.E.2d 844 (N.Y. 1984) (tenant in breach where she conducted a professional counseling practice out of an apartment rented for residential purposes).

In commercial and retail leases, particularly those involving multiple tenants in office buildings and shopping centers, restrictions on the use to which tenants can put the property are quite common and can regulate the nature of a tenant's use in detail. Can you see why?

2. Covenants to operate. Tenants may also be **affirmatively obligated** in some circumstances to continue a use contemplated in a lease. In *The College Block v. Atlantic Richfield Co.*, 254 Cal. Rptr. 179 (Ct. App. 1988), a company signed a 20-year lease for land on which it agreed to build and operate a gas station. Rent was set as a percentage of gasoline delivered, with a $1,000 monthly base amount. After operating for 17 years, the company closed the service station, but continued to pay the monthly minimum of $1,000 per month due under the lease. The landlord sued for damages, seeking the amount it asserted it would have received had the station remained in business. Despite the absence of an express provision in the lease on point, the court found that a covenant of continued operation could be implied because the bulk of the contemplated rent was to have come from operations, and remanded for a finding as to whether the base rent was substantial and provided a fair return on the landlord's investment.

Most courts refuse to interpret percentage leases to find an implied covenant to operate a business continuously if the base rent is substantial. If the base rent is nominal or is much less than the fair rental value of the premises, most courts will take the approach suggested in *The College Block* and find such an implied covenant. Is an implied duty to operate likely to be more consistent or less consistent with the actual intent of the parties at the time they contracted? Should commercial tenants be exempt from implied obligations on the grounds that commercial landlords are sufficiently sophisticated and can adequately protect themselves by including an explicit covenant to operate in their leases? Should the result depend on whether the tenant had a right to sublet or assign the lease? Why? Does a negatively phrased obligation not to use the premises for anything other than a specific purpose, such as a restaurant, imply an affirmative duty to operate? What result best promotes the efficient use of property? Most likely reflects the intent of the parties?

Courts generally will enforce express covenants to operate. However, they will not force an unprofitable business to operate and are very likely to deny injunctive relief ordering the tenant to continue operating, relegating the landlord to damages on the ground that damages are an adequate remedy for the tenant's breach and because judges are not competent to manage the tenant's business operations to ensure compliance with the operating covenant. *Summit Town Center, Inc. v. Shoe Show of Rocky Mount, Inc.*, 828 A.2d 995 (Pa. 2003) (enforcing an express covenant to operate by a damages remedy and denying injunctive relief).

3. Anchor stores. Many shopping centers include large "anchor stores" that are intended to attract large numbers of patrons and to serve as a draw to the shopping center that would enable smaller stores there to attract customers. Does an anchor store have an implied obligation to continue operating?

In *Columbia East Associates v. Bi-Lo, Inc.*, 386 S.E.2d 259 (S.C. Ct. App. 1989), the court held that it did have such an obligation despite the absence of any affirmative obligation to that effect in the lease. Defendant Bi-Lo, a popular supermarket chain, leased space in the center of plaintiff's shopping center for a term of 20 years. The lease provided that the leased premises "shall be used only for the operation of a supermarket (for the sale of groceries, meats and/or other items generally sold by supermarkets)." When another supermarket in an adjacent shopping center closed, Bi-Lo took the opportunity to take over the space because it could thereby "eliminat[e] the competitor and [prevent another] competitor from taking over the [space]." *Id.* at 261. Although it had a right to sublet the original site, Bi-Lo failed to obtain a subtenant and made only minimal efforts to do so. Instead, it continued to pay the agreed-upon fixed rent, which did not include a percentage rent. Bi-Lo argued that, under the terms of the lease, it could vacate the premises and leave the store empty so long as it continued to pay rent. The landlord, Columbia East, argued that Bi-Lo was required either to operate a supermarket or to sublet to another for operation of a retail store. The court noted that Bi-Lo was an anchor tenant whose presence in the shopping center was intended by the landlord to bring customers to the smaller shops. Allowing Bi-Lo to leave without an adequate replacement would defeat the landlord's purpose in agreeing to the lease. The court held that the lease contained an implied obligation of good faith and that this encompassed a requirement of continuous operation on an anchor store even in the absence of a percentage rent agreement. Bi-Lo breached its lease by ceasing operations and by failing to make reasonable efforts to find a subtenant. Chief Judge Sanders concurred on the ground that Bi-Lo had breached the lease by using the premises not for operation of a supermarket but "for a purpose not allowed by the lease; namely, as part of a scheme to stifle competition." *Id.* at 263.

However, some other courts have disagreed with this result. For example, in *Oakwood Village LLC v. Albertsons, Inc.*, 104 P.3d 1226 (Utah 2004), the Utah Supreme Court refused to find an implied covenant of continuous operation in circumstances somewhat similar to those in *Bi-Lo.* Despite the fact that the landlord had leased the ground to the anchor tenant (which built its own store) for up to 65 years at a very low rent, which did not rise over time, the lease did not impose any obligations on the tenant who closed the store after 21 years of operation and moved to another location nearby, leaving the other 25 stores in the center without the benefit of the anchor's business. The court refused to imply a covenant of operation either from the nominal rent or the potential 65-year duration. It focused on the fact that the lease did not have a percentage rent term and that the tenant had built its own store. It was not clear why the landlord gave a ground lease for such a low rent, but the court concluded that, if this was a bad deal, the landlord had to live with it. Moreover, the tenant had the right to sublet or assign the premises without the landlord's consent. Nor did the implied covenant of good faith and fair dealing suggest imposing obligations that could not be inferred from the language of the lease. The court concluded:

> This lease is a complete and unambiguous agreement between competent commercial parties. Long-term commercial leases, by their nature, are risky. Neither side can foretell future market conditions with any certainty. We presume that both [landlord] and [tenant] bargained for the best terms and conditions each could get. Each party took the risk that unpredictable market forces would at some later day render the contractual terms unfavorable to themselves. Despite this risk, both parties willingly agreed to the terms in the lease. It is not our role to intervene now, construing the contract's unambiguous terms to mean something different from what the parties intended them to mean at the outset.

Id. at 1241. *Accord, Daniel G. Kamin Kilgore Enterprises v. Brookshire Grocery Co.*, 81 F. App'x 827 (5th Cir. 2003) (lease clause providing that the tenant "shall use and occupy" the property "for the purpose of conduct[ing a] grocery" business does not imply a continuous operation obligation); *Giessow Restaurants, Inc. v. Richmond Restaurants, Inc.*, 232 S.W.3d 576 (Mo. Ct. App. 2007) (similar result).

Problem

In *Casa D'Angelo v. A & R Realty Co.*, 553 N.E.2d 515 (Ind. Ct. App. 1990), a restaurant, Casa D'Angelo, that leased its premises from plaintiff landlord, A & R Realty, decided to open a second restaurant within a mile of the first establishment. The tenant, whose lease stated that it "shall use the premises for the operation of a restaurant facility and for no other purpose without first obtaining the written consent of Lessor," subsequently changed its operation from offering a full-service dinner menu to a limited offering of soup, salad, and sandwiches to walk-in customers only. Gross sales fell dramatically. The base rent was $825 per month, and the court assumed that this amount was substantial. However, the percentage rent (5 percent of gross sales) was also substantial, rising from $2,500 in 1978 to $18,752 in 1981 and a total of $36,230 for 1986. Eventually, the tenant closed the restaurant entirely but continued to pay the base rent of $825 per month for the remainder of the lease term. The landlord sued the tenant for the amounts of percentage rent it would have earned had the tenant maintained its operation without interruption.

What arguments would you make on behalf of the plaintiff landlord? What arguments would you make on behalf of the defendant tenant? If you were the judge, how would you rule, and why?

§2.3 Transfers of the Landlord's Leasehold Interest

The landlord has the right to transfer her property interest. What happens if the landlord sells the property or it is inherited by the landlord's heirs? The new owner receives what the landlord was able to sell or give, that is, the landlord's reversion subject to the tenant's leasehold.[4] The new owner also receives the attendant contractual rights to collect rent and to enforce the other terms of the lease. The new owner, however, does not obtain an immediate right to possess the property; the tenant's leasehold interest survives. The new owner, of course, may end a month-to-month tenancy, just as the prior landlord could have done, but if the tenant has six months left on a one-year lease, the new owner is obligated to honor the tenant's remaining six-month possessory right. The landlord's interest may also end through equitable division of property on divorce. Because property is reallocated between the parties on divorce, a building owned partly or wholly by a husband may be granted to the wife upon divorce. Such cases are treated like sales of the property and the leases survive.

What happens if the property was mortgaged and the landlord fails to make the mortgage payments and loses the property through foreclosure? The answer depends on whether the lease or mortgage was established first. If the landlord leased the property to the tenant and then borrowed money subject to a mortgage on the building, the lease generally takes priority since it was first in time. However, if the property is subject to a mortgage and the lease follows, the mortgage takes priority. The mortgage gives the lender the power to force a sale of the property to recoup the unpaid loan; tenants who rent such properties take their apartments subject to the prior mortgage. Thus, in the absence of statute to the contrary, when the landlord's title ends through foreclosure, so does the tenant's lease. A similar situation obtains with a life estate. If the landlord owns the property for life and leases it to the tenant, then the landlord's interest ends when the landlord dies; since you can only convey what you own, and the landlord did not own the right to lease the property after her death, the tenant's lease ends automatically when the landlord dies.

The subprime mortgage foreclosure crisis that began around 2008 has led to many tenants facing eviction after foreclosure, even though the tenants were faithfully paying the rent, because their leases were entered into after the mortgage that gave rise to the foreclosure. Many banks following foreclosure immediately evict the tenants because they believe it is easier to sell property that is vacant than property that is inhabited. These tenants complain that although the landlord may have defaulted on the mortgage payments to the bank, the tenants had been paying their lease payments faithfully and should not suffer because of the landlord's default. *See generally* Creola Johnson, *Renters Evicted en Masse: Collateral Damage Arising from the Subprime Foreclosure Crisis*, 62 Fla. L. Rev. 975 (2010).

A 2009 federal statute, the *Protecting Tenants at Foreclosure Act* (PTFA), Pub. L. No 111-22, 123 Stat. 1660, codified as 12 U.S.C. §5220, note, gives tenants some protection, although the statute is currently set to expire at the end of 2014. The PTFA generally requires that the immediate successor in interest following a foreclosure, which is often the bank that made the original loan, give tenants — even tenants without a

4. One exception is that a landlord generally may not transfer an interest in a tenancy at will to a new owner. *See Restatement (Second) of Property (Landlord and Tenant)* §15.1(1) (1977).

formal lease — at least 90 days' notice to vacate. The PTFA requires the new owner to allow tenants with term leases to occupy their premises until the end of the term, unless the unit is sold to someone who will occupy it as their primary residence. The PTFA provides some additional protections to tenants in housing subsidized through a federal program known as "Section 8," after the relevant statutory provision that authorized the program.[5]

A number of state and local governments have responded to the impact of the foreclosure crisis on tenants with their own legislation. These statutes vary significantly, but some examples of their scope include requirements that tenants receive notice of foreclosure, *see, e.g.*, N.J. Ct. R. 4:65-1-4:65-2, as amended by N.J. Orders 2009-37; mandates that tenants receive notice of the identity of the new owner, which responds to the problem of tenants following foreclosure not knowing where to send their rent and then facing nonpayment evictions, *see, e.g.*, Cal. Civ. Code §1962, amended by AB 1953; and provisions that tenants in units acquired through foreclosure can only be evicted for good cause, with foreclosure itself not constituting good cause, *see* Los Angeles Municipal Code ch. IV, art. 14.1, §49.92. Several states have also sought to remedy the PFTA's sunset provision by enacting substantially the same protections into state law. *See, e.g.*, Md. Code, Real Prop. §§7-105.6, 7-105.9; Me. Rev. Stat. tit. 14, §6001.

Problem

A lease for a drug store in a shopping center provided that the landlord would not lease to a competing store in the same center. Three years into the five-year term of the lease, the landlord sells the shopping center to a new owner. A few days before the transfer, the original landlord signed a lease with a grocery store that includes a small pharmacy. When the grocery store opens, the drug store tenant complains to the new owner of the shopping center, who responds that the grocery store does not violate the non-competition provision and, even if it does, the violation occurred before the sale, so it was the original owner's responsibility. If the tenant seeks to enforce the non-competition clause against the new owner, how should a court respond? Would the situation be different if the lease obligated the landlord to provide financial statements at the end of every year detailing each tenant's charges for common areas in the shopping center, and the year before the transfer, the original owner failed to meet this obligation?

§2.4 Assigning and Subleasing

The tenant's right to transfer. A tenant can generally transfer all or a portion of her possessory interest in the premises unless the lease specifically limits this

5. The Ninth Circuit has held that although tenants may raise the PTFA as a defense to eviction, tenants may not bring an independent suit for damages or injunctive relief under the statute because the statute does not provide a private right of action. *See Logan v. U.S. Bank National Association*, 722 F.3d 1163 (9th Cir. 2013). What gaps might this leave in terms of enforcing the act's protections?

right. The tenant can do so through an **assignment** or through a **sublease**, or sublet. An assignment generally conveys *all* the tenant's remaining property interests without retaining any future rights to enter the property; under a sublease, the tenant retains some future interest or the right to control the property in the future. A sublease exists, for example, if a tenant has six months remaining on the lease and transfers possession of the apartment to someone else for four months. Since the tenant retains the right to regain possession for the last two months of the term of years, the transfer is a sublease rather than an assignment. A sublease may also exist if the tenant retains a right of entry that can be exercised if the subtenant violates one or more of the terms of the sublease agreement.

Terms:
A **sublease** generally refers to a transfer by a tenant of a portion of its possessory rights under the lease; by contrast, an **assignment** generally refers to the transfer of the tenant's entire possessory rights.

Although restraints on alienation of fee interests are generally void, a "no subletting" or "no assignment" clause in a lease agreement is generally enforceable, and violation of the prohibition on assignment will entitle the landlord to evict the tenant for breaching a material term of the lease contract. Cal. Civ. Code §1995.230 ("A restriction on transfer of a tenant's interest in a lease may absolutely prohibit transfer."); *Carma Development (California), Inc. v. Marathon Development California, Inc.*, 826 P.2d 710, 717-718 (Cal. 1992). Such a clause protects the landlord from being forced to accept a substitute tenant who may be less creditworthy. For the tenant, a clause prohibiting subletting may limit her ability to get out of the lease and move elsewhere.

In limiting sublets or assignments, leases sometimes use the general term "sublet" when what is really meant is "sublet or assign." Traditional doctrine held that, in order to promote the alienability of leaseholds, a lease that limits subletting but not assigning will be strictly construed to limit only subletting. However, the modern trend is to focus on the intent of the parties; since modern usage sometimes employs the term "subletting" to mean any transfers of the leasehold interest, a clause that provides for "no subletting" may very well be interpreted to prohibit subletting *or* assigning.

Why it matters whether the transfer is an assignment or a sublease. Why is it important to know whether the arrangement is a sublease or an assignment? Traditionally, under an assignment, the new tenant — called the assignee — is responsible directly to the landlord for all the undertakings under the original lease. In other words, the tenant's covenants — including the covenant to pay rent and other covenants in the lease agreement — run with the land. The landlord and the assignee are not in **privity of contract** since they did not reach an agreement with each other. Since the original tenant has given up all interest in the property, however, the landlord and the assignee are thought to share interests in the property; they are therefore in **privity of estate**, which makes the assignee directly liable to the landlord for the covenants made by the original tenant to the landlord. It also makes the landlord liable to the assignee for breach of the landlord's covenants, such as the covenant of quiet enjoyment, which we will discuss below.

In contrast, under a sublease, the lease covenants do *not* run with the land as **real covenants**. The landlord has no right to sue the subtenant to enforce any of the covenants in the original lease, including the covenant to pay rent, if the requested relief is damages. The only exception is when the subtenant expressly promises the tenant to pay the rent to the landlord. In that case, the landlord may be able to sue the subtenant as a **third-party beneficiary** of the contract made between the tenant and subtenant; in other words, the landlord is the intended beneficiary of the subtenant's promise to the tenant. However, lease covenants probably *can* be enforced by injunction as equitable servitudes, so long as the subtenant has notice of them. Is the subtenant bound if she has not seen the original lease and that lease is not recorded? The courts are likely to find the subtenant on inquiry notice of the covenants in the original lease; the reasonable subtenant would inquire whether the tenant had made promises to the landlord restricting use of the premises.

The difficult question is whether the landlord can sue the subtenant for an injunction ordering the subtenant to comply with the covenant to pay rent. Some courts will not grant an injunction since the payment of rent is a money payment and resembles the payment of damages. Others grant an injunction because it constitutes enforcement of an affirmative covenant, even though that covenant requires the payment of money.

If an assignee fails to pay the rent, the landlord may sue the original tenant for the unpaid rent because the original tenant remains in a contractual relationship with the landlord, which the assignment does not relieve. But the landlord may instead choose to sue the assignee directly for the unpaid rent. Since the covenant to pay rent runs with the land, the assignee is directly liable to the landlord for the unpaid rent. In a sublet, however, the landlord can only sue the original tenant (who remains contractually bound to pay the rent). Note, however, that, in a sublet, if neither the tenant nor the subtenant pays the rent, the landlord can evict the tenant (sue for possession from the tenant) and end the leasehold, thereby terminating the subtenant's right of possession. In either case, if the landlord chooses to sue the original tenant for the rent, the original tenant has a right to be reimbursed by the new tenant for the amount owed to the landlord.

The tenant may choose to sublet for a rental amount different from the amount owed to the landlord. Whether the new rent is less or more than the original rent, the tenant remains liable only for the original amount to the landlord. Thus, if the subtenant is paying less than the rent owed to the landlord, the tenant must make up the difference. If the subtenant is paying more than the rent owed to the landlord, the tenant subtenant is allowed to keep the difference.[6]

Landlord consent. Many leases provide for subletting or assignment only with the landlord's consent. These clauses may be phrased either in the negative or the

6. Distinguish subleases and assignments from roommate situations where each tenant in a given premises is directly obligated to the landlord under the lease. In such co-tenant situations, there can be an agreement as well between the roommates, which can be formal or informal, to govern matters such as occupancy and mutual obligations. If one co-tenant defaults on the obligation to pay rent, the other tenant can bring an action to recover the proportional share that is owed. *Foley v. Wilson*, No. 3D12-3055, 2013 WL 1629247 (Fla. Dist. Ct. App. 2013).

affirmative, that is, "no subletting without the landlord's consent" or "subletting allowed subject to the landlord's consent." An issue that has occasioned much litigation recently is the question whether a criterion of "reasonableness" should be implied in these clauses.

Kendall v. Ernest Pestana, Inc.

709 P.2d 837 (Cal. 1985)

Map: Norman Y. Mineta San Jose International Airport, San Jose, California

ALLEN E. BROUSSARD, Justice.

This case concerns the effect of a provision in a commercial lease[7] that the lessee may not assign the lease or sublet the premises without the lessor's prior written consent. The question we address is whether, in the absence of a provision that such consent will not be unreasonably withheld, a lessor may unreasonably and arbitrarily withhold his or her consent to an assignment. This is a question of first impression in this court.

I

The lease at issue is for 14,400 square feet of hangar space at the San Jose Municipal Airport. The City of San Jose, as owner of the property, leased it to Irving and Janice Perlitch, who in turn assigned their interest to respondent Ernest Pestana, Inc. Prior to assigning their interest to respondent, the Perlitches entered into a 25-year sublease with one Robert Bixler commencing on January 1, 1970. The sublease covered an original five-year term plus four 5-year options to renew. The rental rate was to be increased every 10 years in the same proportion as rents increased on the master lease from the City of San Jose. The premises were to be used by Bixler for the purpose of conducting an airplane maintenance business.

Bixler conducted such a business under the name "Flight Services" until, in 1981, he agreed to sell the business to appellants Jack Kendall, Grady O'Hara and Vicki O'Hara. The proposed sale included the business and the equipment, inventory and improvements on the property, together with the existing lease. The proposed assignees had a stronger financial statement and greater net worth than the current lessee, Bixler, and they were willing to be bound by the terms of the lease.

The lease provided that written consent of the lessor was required before the lessee could assign his interest, and that failure to obtain such consent rendered the lease voidable at the option of the lessor. Accordingly, Bixler requested consent from

7. We are presented only with a commercial lease and therefore do not address the question whether residential leases are controlled by the principles articulated in this opinion.

the Perlitches' successor-in-interest, respondent Ernest Pestana, Inc. Respondent refused to consent to the assignment and maintained that it had an absolute right arbitrarily to refuse any such request. The complaint recites that respondent demanded "increased rent and other more onerous terms" as a condition of consenting to Bixler's transfer of interest.

The proposed assignees brought suit for declaratory and injunctive relief and damages seeking, *inter alia,* a declaration "that the refusal of Ernest Pestana, Inc. to consent to the assignment of the lease is unreasonable and is an unlawful restraint on the freedom of alienation."

II

The law generally favors free alienability of property, and California follows the common law rule that a leasehold interest is freely alienable. Contractual restrictions on the alienability of leasehold interests are, however, permitted. "Such restrictions are justified as reasonable protection of the interests of the lessor as to who shall possess and manage property in which he has a reversionary interest and from which he is deriving income." Schoshinski, *American Law of Landlord and Tenant* §815, at 578-79 (1980).

The common law's hostility toward restraints on alienation has caused such restraints on leasehold interests to be strictly construed against the lessor.[8] This is particularly true where the restraint in question is a "forfeiture restraint," under which the lessor has the option to terminate the lease if an assignment is made without his or her consent.

Nevertheless, a majority of jurisdictions have long adhered to the rule that where a lease contains an approval clause (a clause stating that the lease cannot be assigned without the prior consent of the lessor), the lessor may arbitrarily refuse to approve a proposed assignee no matter how suitable the assignee appears to be and no matter how unreasonable the lessor's objection. The harsh consequences of this rule have often been avoided through application of the doctrines of waiver and estoppel, under which the lessor may be found to have waived (or be estopped from asserting) the right to refuse consent to assignment.

The traditional majority rule has come under steady attack in recent years. A growing minority of jurisdictions now hold that where a lease provides for assignment only with the prior consent of the lessor, such consent may be withheld only where the lessor has a commercially reasonable objection to the assignment, even in the absence

8. There are many examples of the narrow effect given to lease terms purporting to restrict assignment. Covenants against assignment without the prior consent of the lessor have been held not to affect the lessee's right to sublease, to mortgage the leasehold, or to assign his or her interest to a cotenant. Such covenants also do not prevent transfer of a leasehold interest by will, by bankruptcy, by the personal representative of a deceased tenant, or by transfer among partners, or spouses. Covenants against assignment furthermore do not prohibit transfer of the stock of a corporate tenant, or assignment of a lease to a corporation wholly owned by the tenant.

of a provision in the lease stating that consent to assignment will not be unreasonably withheld.

For the reasons discussed below, we conclude that the minority rule is the preferable position.

III

The impetus for change in the majority rule has come from two directions, reflecting the dual nature of a lease as a conveyance of a leasehold interest and a contract. The policy against restraints on alienation pertains to leases in their nature as conveyances. Numerous courts and commentators have recognized that "[i]n recent times the necessity of permitting reasonable alienation of commercial space has become paramount in our increasingly urban society." *Schweiso v. Williams*, 198 Cal. Rptr. 238, 240 (Ct. App. 1984).

Civil Code section 711 provides: "Conditions restraining alienation, when repugnant to the interest created, are void." It is well settled that this rule is not absolute in its application, but forbids only unreasonable restraints on alienation. Reasonableness is determined by comparing the justification for a particular restraint on alienation with the quantum of restraint actually imposed by it. "[T]he greater the quantum of restraint that results from enforcement of a given clause, the greater must be the justification for that enforcement." *Wellenkamp v. Bank of Am.*, 148 Cal. Rptr. 379, 382 (Ct. App. 1978).

The *Restatement Second of Property* adopts the minority rule on the validity of approval clauses in leases: "A restraint on alienation without the consent of the landlord of a tenant's interest in leased property is valid, *but the landlord's consent to an alienation by the tenant cannot be withheld unreasonably*, unless a freely negotiated provision in the lease gives the landlord an absolute right to withhold consent." (*Rest. 2d Property*, §15.2(2) (1977)) (italics added). A comment to the section explains: "The landlord may have an understandable concern about certain personal qualities of a tenant, particularly his reputation for meeting his financial obligations. The preservation of the values that go into the personal selection of the tenant justifies upholding a provision in the lease that curtails the right of the tenant to put anyone else in his place by transferring his interest, but this justification does not go to the point of allowing the landlord arbitrarily and without reason to refuse to allow the tenant to transfer an interest in leased property." (*Id.*, comment a.) Under the *Restatement* rule, the lessor's interest in the character of his or her tenant is protected by the lessor's right to object to a proposed assignee on reasonable commercial grounds. The lessor's interests are also protected by the fact that the original lessee remains liable to the lessor as a surety even if the lessor consents to the assignment and the assignee expressly assumes the obligations of the lease.

The second impetus for change in the majority rule comes from the nature of a lease as a contract. As the Court of Appeal observed in *Cohen v. Ratinoff*, 195 Cal. Rptr. 84, 88 (Ct. App. 1983), "[since the majority rule was adopted], there has been an increased recognition of and emphasis on the duty of good faith and fair dealing inherent in every contract." Thus, "[i]n every contract there is an implied covenant that neither party shall do anything which will have the effect of destroying or injuring the right of the other party to receive the fruits of the contract." *Universal Sales Corp. v. Cal. etc. Mfg. Co.*, 128 P.2d 665, 677 (Cal. 1942). "[W]here a contract confers on one party a discretionary power affecting the rights of the other, a duty is imposed to exercise that discretion in good faith and in accordance with fair dealing." *Cal. Lettuce Growers v. Union Sugar Co.*, 289 P.2d 785, 791 (Cal. 1955). Here the lessor retains the discretionary power to approve or disapprove an assignee proposed by the other party to the contract; this discretionary power should therefore be exercised in accordance with commercially reasonable standards.

Under the minority rule, the determination whether a lessor's refusal to consent was reasonable is a question of fact. Some of the factors that the trier of fact may properly consider in applying the standards of good faith and commercial reasonableness are: financial responsibility of the proposed assignee; suitability of the use for the particular property; legality of the proposed use; need for alteration of the premises; and nature of the occupancy, *i.e.*, office, factory, clinic, etc.

Denying consent solely on the basis of personal taste, convenience or sensibility is not commercially reasonable. Nor is it reasonable to deny consent "in order that the landlord may charge a higher rent than originally contracted for." This is because the lessor's desire for a better bargain than contracted for has nothing to do with the permissible purposes of the restraint on alienation — to protect the lessor's interest in the preservation of the property and the performance of the lease covenants.

In contrast to the policy reasons advanced in favor of the minority rule, the majority rule has traditionally been justified on three grounds. Respondent raises a fourth argument in its favor as well. None of these do we find compelling.

First, it is said that a lease is a conveyance of an interest in real property, and that the lessor, having exercised a personal choice in the selection of a tenant and provided that no substitute shall be acceptable without prior consent, is under no obligation to look to anyone but the lessee for the rent. This argument is based on traditional rules of conveyancing and on concepts of freedom of ownership and control over one's property.

A lessor's freedom at common law to look to no one but the lessee for the rent has, however, been undermined by the adoption in California of a rule that lessors — like all other contracting parties — have a duty to mitigate damages upon the lessee's abandonment of the property by seeking a substitute lessee. Furthermore, the values that go into the personal selection of a lessee are preserved under the minority rule in the lessor's right to refuse consent to assignment on any commercially reasonable grounds. Such grounds include not only the obvious objections to an assignee's financial stability or proposed use of the premises, but a variety of other commercially reasonable objections as well. The lessor's interests are further protected by the fact that the original lessee remains a guarantor of the performance of the assignee.

The second justification advanced in support of the majority rule is that an approval clause is an unambiguous reservation of absolute discretion in the lessor over assignments of the lease. The lessee could have bargained for the addition of a reasonableness clause to the lease (*i.e.*, "consent to assignment will not be unreasonably withheld"). The lessee having failed to do so, the law should not rewrite the parties' contract for them.

Numerous authorities have taken a different view of the meaning and effect of an approval clause in a lease, indicating that the clause is not "clear and unambiguous," as respondent suggests. As early as 1940, the court in *Granite Trust Bldg. Corp. v. Great Atlantic & Pacific Tea Co.*, 36 F. Supp. 77 (D. Mass. 1940), examined a standard approval clause and stated: "It would seem to be the better law that when a lease restricts a lessee's rights by requiring consent before these rights can be exercised, *it must have been in the contemplation of the parties that the lessor be required to give some reason for withholding consent.*" (*Id.* at 78, italics added.)

[T]he assertion that an approval clause "clearly and unambiguously" grants the lessor absolute discretion over assignments is untenable. It is not a rewriting of a contract, as respondent suggests, to recognize the obligations imposed by the duty of good faith and fair dealing, which duty is implied by law in every contract.

The third justification advanced in support of the majority rule is essentially based on the doctrine of *stare decisis*. It is argued that the courts should not depart from the common law majority rule because "many leases now in effect covering a substantial amount of real property and creating valuable property rights were carefully prepared by competent counsel in reliance upon the majority viewpoint." As pointed out above, however, the majority viewpoint has been far from universally held and has never been adopted by this court. Moreover, the trend in favor of the minority rule should come as no surprise to observers of the changing state of real property law in the 20th century. The minority rule is part of an increasing recognition of the contractual nature of leases and the implications in terms of contractual duties that flow therefrom. We would be remiss in our duty if we declined to question a view held by the majority of jurisdictions simply because it is held by a majority. As we stated in *Rodriguez v. Bethlehem Steel Corp.*, 525 P.2d 669, 676 (Cal. 1974), the "vitality [of the common law] can flourish only so long as the courts remain alert to their obligation and opportunity to change the common law when reason and equity demand it."

A final argument in favor of the majority rule is advanced by respondent and stated as follows: "Both tradition and sound public policy dictate that the lessor has a right, under circumstances such as these, to realize the increased value of his property." Respondent essentially argues that any increase in the market value of real property during the term of a lease properly belongs to the lessor, not the lessee. We reject this assertion. One California commentator has written:

> [W]hen the lessee executed the lease he acquired the contractual right for the exclusive use of the premises, and all of the benefits and detriment attendant to possession, for the term of the contract. He took the downside risk that he would be paying too much rent if there should be a depression in the rental market. Why should he be deprived of the contractual benefits of the lease because of the fortuitous inflation in the marketplace[?] By reaping the benefits he does not deprive the landlord of anything to which the landlord was otherwise entitled. The landlord agreed to dispose of possession for the limited term and he could not reasonably anticipate any more than what was given to him by the terms of the lease. His reversionary estate will benefit from the increased

> value from the inflation in any event, at least upon the expiration of the lease. Miller & Starr, *Current Law of Cal. Real Estate* §27:92 at 321 (1977 & 1984 Supp.).

Respondent here is trying to get more than it bargained for in the lease. A lessor is free to build periodic rent increases into a lease, as the lessor did here. Any increased value of the property beyond this "belongs" to the lessor only in the sense, as explained above, that the lessor's reversionary estate will benefit from it upon the expiration of the lease. We must therefore reject respondent's argument in this regard.

MALCOLM M. LUCAS, Justice, dissenting.

I respectfully dissent. In my view we should follow the weight of authority which, as acknowledged by the majority herein, allows the commercial lessor to withhold his consent to an assignment or sublease arbitrarily or without reasonable cause. The majority's contrary ruling, requiring a "commercially reasonable objection" to the assignment, can only result in a proliferation of unnecessary litigation.

The correct analysis is contained in the opinion of Justice Carl Anderson for the Court of Appeal in this case. I adopt the following portion of his opinion as my dissent:

> The plain language of the lease provides that the lessee shall not assign the lease "without written consent of Lessor first had and obtained. Any such assignment or subletting without this consent shall be void, and shall, at the option of Lessor, terminate this lease." The lease does not require that "consent may not unreasonably be withheld"; the lease does not provide that "the lessor may refuse consent only where he has a good faith reasonable objection to the assignment." Neither have the parties so contracted, nor has the Legislature so required. Absent such legislative direction, the parties should be free to contract as they see fit. . . .

Slavin v. Rent Control Board of Brookline

548 N.E.2d 1226 (Mass. 1990)

FRANCIS P. O'CONNOR, Justice.

Article XXXVIII of the Brookline rent control by-law provides in relevant part as follows:

> Section 9. *Evictions.* (a) No person shall bring any action to recover possession of a controlled rental unit unless:
>
> (2) the tenant has violated an obligation or covenant of his tenancy other than the obligation to surrender possession upon proper notice and has failed to cure such violation after having received written notice thereof from the landlord;
>
> (b) A landlord seeking to recover possession of a controlled rental unit shall apply to the board for a certificate of eviction. If the board finds that the facts attested to in the landlord's petition are valid and in compliance with paragraph (a), the certificate of eviction shall be issued.

(c) A landlord who seeks to recover possession of a controlled rental unit without obtaining such certificate of eviction shall be deemed to have violated this By-law, and the Board may initiate a criminal prosecution for such violation.

The plaintiff landlord applied to the defendant rent control board of Brookline (board) for a certificate of eviction seeking to evict the defendant tenant Barry Myers on the ground that Myers had violated an obligation of his tenancy. The lease states:

> *Occupancy of Premises*—Tenant shall not assign nor underlet any part or the whole of the premises, nor shall permit the premises to be occupied for a period longer than a temporary visit by anyone except the individuals specifically named in the first paragraph of this tenancy, their spouses, and any children born to them hereafter, without first obtaining on each occasion the assent in writing of Landlord.

After a hearing, the board found that the tenant had allowed an unauthorized person to occupy his apartment without first obtaining the landlord's written consent. Nonetheless, the board refused to issue the eviction certificate. The board based its refusal on its determination of law that, implicit in the lease provision requiring the landlord's consent prior to an assignment or a sublease or the permitting of other occupants, there is an "agreement on the part of the landlord to at least consider prospective tenants [and other permitted occupants] and not withhold consent unreasonably or unequivocally." The board found that the landlord had acted unreasonably because she had categorically refused to allow the tenant to bring in someone new after the original cotenant had moved out. Because of the landlord's unreasonable behavior, the board concluded that the tenant could not be said to have violated the lease.

The issue whether a tenant's obligation, as specified in a residential lease, to obtain the written consent of a landlord before assigning the lease or subletting or permitting other occupants implies as a matter of law an obligation on the landlord's part to act reasonably in withholding consent has not been decided by this court.

A majority of jurisdictions subscribe to the rule that a lease provision requiring the landlord's consent to an assignment or sublease permits the landlord to refuse arbitrarily or unreasonably. However, the board argues that the current trend is the other way, and cites numerous cases in support of that proposition. We note that every case cited by the board except two, which we discuss below, involved a commercial, not a residential, lease. Although the significance of the distinction between commercial and residential leases may be fairly debatable, we observe that in several of the cases cited by the board the court specifically states that its holding is limited to the commercial lease context. *See Kendall v. Ernest Pestana, Inc.*, 709 P.2d 837 (Cal. 1985).

Kruger v. Page Management Co., 432 N.Y.S.2d 295 (Sup. Ct. 1980), is the only purely residential lease case cited by the board. We get little help from that case because the reasonableness requirement in New York has been statutorily imposed.

The board argues that we should be guided by the commercial lease cases because the reasons for implying a reasonableness requirement in a residential lease are at least as compelling as in a commercial lease. Our review of the commercial lease cases, however, and particularly of the rationale that appears to have motivated the courts in those cases to adopt a reasonableness requirement, does not persuade us that we should adopt such a rule in this case, which involves a residential lease in a municipality governed by a rent control law.

Two major concerns emerge from the commercial lease cases. First, courts have exhibited concern that commercial landlords may exercise their power to withhold consent for unfair financial gain. In several of the cases cited by the board, a commercial landlord refused to consent to a proposed subtenant and then attempted to enter into a new or revised lease for the same premises at a more favorable rental rate. However, in a rent control jurisdiction like Brookline there is little economic incentive to withhold consent in the residential lease context because the landlord has such limited control over the rent that can be charged.

The second concern that appears to have motivated the commercial lease decisions is a desire to limit restraints on alienation in light of the fact that "the necessity of reasonable alienation of commercial building space has become paramount in our ever-increasing urban society." *Homa-Goff Interiors, Inc. v. Cowden*, 350 So. 2d 1035, 1037 (Ala. 1977). However, this court has previously, albeit not recently, ruled that a commercial lease provision requiring a landlord's consent prior to an assignment, with no limitation on the landlord's ability to refuse, is not an unreasonable restraint on alienation. *68 Beacon St., Inc. v. Sohier*, 194 N.E. 303 (Mass. 1935).

In light of our decision in *68 Beacon St., Inc.*, and in the absence of a demonstrable trend involving residential leases in other jurisdictions, we are not persuaded that there is such a "necessity of reasonable alienation of [residential] building space" that we ought to impose on residential landlords a reasonableness requirement to which they have not agreed. We are mindful that valid arguments in support of such a rule can be made, but there are also valid counter-arguments, not the least of which is that such a rule would be likely to engender a plethora of litigation about whether the landlord's withholding of consent was reasonable. The question is one of public policy which, of course, the Legislature is free to address. We note that the Legislature has spoken in at least four States: Alaska Stat. §34.03.060; Del. Code tit. 25, §5512(b); Haw. Rev. Stat. §516-63; N.Y. Real Prop. Law §226-b.

Notes and Questions

1. **Duty of good faith and fair dealing.** In commercial leases, the trend is toward adopting an implied reasonableness term in lease clauses that give the landlord the right to consent to sublet or assignment. *See Dick Broadcasting Co. v. Oak Ridge FM, Inc.*, 395 S.W.3d 653, 665-666 (Tenn. 2013) (the "traditional common law view that parties asked to consent to assignment may refuse arbitrarily or unreasonably refuse . . . has steadily eroded over time and is now a minority position among the courts that have considered the issue"); *Uno Restaurants, Inc. v. Boston Kenmore Realty Corp.*, 805 N.E.2d 957 (Mass. 2004) (covenant of good faith and fair dealing is implied in all leasehold agreements). This is the view taken in both URLTA and the *Restatement (Second) of Property, see* URLTA §1.302 ("every duty [under the URLTA] imposes an obligation of good faith in its performance or enforcement"); *Restatement (Second) of Property (Landlord and Tenant)* §15.2(2) (1977) ("A restraint on alienation without the consent of the landlord of the tenant's interest in the leased property is valid, but the

landlord's consent to an alienation by the tenant cannot be withheld unreasonably, unless a freely negotiated provision in the lease gives the landlord an absolute right to withhold consent"). It also echoes the *Restatement (Second) of Contracts,* which likewise provides in §205 that "[e]very contract imposes upon each party a duty of good faith and fair dealing in its performance and its enforcement." *See Warner v. Konover,* 553 A.2d 1138, 1141-1142 (Conn. 1989) (applying this to a commercial landlord's assignment clause).

In contrast, in *First Federal Savings Bank of Indiana v. Key Markets,* 559 N.E.2d 600 (Ind. 1990), the court refused to imply a reasonableness requirement into a landlord consent clause. It explained the result this way:

> [C]ourts are bound to recognize and enforce contracts where the terms and the intentions of the parties can be readily determined from the language in the instrument. It is not the province of courts to require a party acting pursuant to such a contract to be "reasonable," "fair," or show "good faith" cooperation. Such an assessment would go beyond the bounds of judicial duty and responsibility. It would be impossible for parties to rely on the written expressions of their duties and responsibilities. Further, it would place the court at the negotiation table with the parties. In the instant case, the court would decide what is "fair" or "reasonable" concerning the advantage or disadvantage of control of the leased property. The proper posture for the court is to find and enforce the contract as it is written and leave the parties where it finds them. It is only where the intentions of the parties cannot be readily ascertained because of ambiguity or inconsistency in the terms of a contract or in relation to extrinsic evidence that a court may have to presume the parties were acting reasonably and in good faith in entering into the contract.

Id. at 604. Should parties be able to contract for the standard of reasonableness that will apply to their agreements? What are the best arguments on both sides?

Note that the California legislature responded to the *Kendall* decision by adopting the implied reasonableness test for commercial leases, Cal. Civ. Code §§1995.020(b), 1995.260, but providing that it should apply prospectively only to new leases, Cal. Civ. Code §1995.270, and that the parties were substantially free to contract to the contrary, Cal. Civ. Code §1995.240 ("[a] restriction on transfer of a tenant's interest in a lease may provide that the transfer is subject to any express standard or condition, including, but not limited to, a provision that the landlord is entitled to some or all of any consideration the tenant receives from a transferee in excess of the rent under the lease").

2. What is reasonable? In *Tenet Healthsystem Surgical, L.L.C. v. Jefferson Parish Hospital Service District No. 1,* 426 F.3d 738, 743 (5th Cir. 2005), a tenant leased space for an outpatient surgical center. The lease gave the tenant the right to assign its lease with the consent of the landlord, and indicated that such consent "shall not be unreasonably withheld." Two years into the lease term, the owner of an adjacent hospital bought the property. Shortly thereafter, the tenant stopped operating and sought consent to assign the lease to a new tenant who intended to open an occupational medical clinic. The new landlord refused, and, when asked why, explained that one reason was that the proposed assignee would compete with its adjacent hospital. *Id.*

at 740. In the ensuing suit, the landlord argued that "a reasonable business person in its position would deny consent to assign a lease that would bring new competition into the immediate area where it does business." The court disagreed, stating that "[i]n determining whether a landlord's refusal to consent [is] reasonable in a commercial context, only factors that relate to the landlord's interest in preserving the leased property or in having the terms of [the] prime lease performed should be considered. Among factors a landlord can consider are the financial responsibility of the proposed subtenant, the legality and suitability of proposed use and nature of the occupancy. A landlord's personal taste or convenience are factors not properly considered. Rather the landlord's objection 'must relate to ownership and operation of leased property, not lessor's general economic interest.'" *Id.* at 743. Why is it unreasonable for a landlord to take potential competition from an assignee into account? Would it have been unreasonable for the landlord to have refused to lease to that party in the first place?

3. Commercial versus residential leases. Do the distinctions between commercial and residential leases relied on by the court in *Slavin* make sense to you? Note that Massachusetts subsequently extended *Slavin* to commercial leases, refusing to adopt the *Kendall* approach. *21 Merchants Row Corp. v. Merchants Row, Inc.*, 587 N.E.2d 788 (Mass. 1992). Do the reasons for implying a reasonableness requirement differ in the residential context? If the arguments applicable to commercial leases are inapplicable to residential leases, what other arguments could you make on behalf of the tenant? How would you argue that residential leases, but not commercial leases, should be subject to an implied duty of reasonableness?

4. Common law development. The court in *Slavin* finds the laws in other states cited by the tenant to be inapposite since they are incorporated into the statutes rather than the common law of those states. *See, e.g.*, N.Y. Real Prop. Law §226-b(2)(a) (tenants can sublet with landlord's consent; such consent cannot be unreasonably withheld). What difference does this make? On one hand, it can be argued that this question should be, and has been in other states, left to the legislature to address. On the other hand, since the theory underlying contract law is that the court should enforce the presumed intent of the parties, it might be argued that because these laws reflect changing values and expectations, the presumption underlying the common law rule no longer reflects the justified expectations of the parties. Would it have made a difference to the Massachusetts Supreme Judicial Court if the tenant could have identified another state that had modernized its law by common law ruling rather than statute? Should that make a difference? Doesn't some state have to be first?

Problems

1. A law student in Massachusetts has a one-year lease, running from September 1 through August 31, that states "no subletting or assignment without the landlord's consent." The law student wants to move out on June 1 and sublet the apartment for most of the summer so that she can move to Washington, D.C., for a summer job. The landlord refuses to let the student sublet the apartment over the summer. What are the tenant's options?

2. The tenant of property on which a grocery store is operating arranges to sublease the property to a business owned by Japanese Americans. The landlord refuses to agree because of prejudice against the sublessees. What should the courts do if the landlord refuses to approve the sublease based on racially discriminatory motives? Should a lease provision granting the landlord the absolute right to approve or disapprove any subleases be enforceable under these circumstances?

3. An office tenant has a 20-year lease with a clause requiring landlord consent to sublet, such consent not to be unreasonably withheld. The neighborhood where the office building sits has been redeveloped significantly and rents for similar office space in the area are increasing significantly. The tenant seeks permission from the landlord to sublet half of its office space, and the landlord agrees on condition that the tenant pays the landlord 25 percent of any profits that result from the higher rent the tenant can now charge to any subtenant. Is this a reasonable exercise of the landlord's discretion?

§2.5 Tenant's Right to Terminate Early

In what circumstances should tenants be able to terminate their leases before the end of the term without the consent of the landlord? Several states allow tenants who have suffered domestic violence to do so, and also provide other tenant protections for such victims. In Colorado, for example, residential tenants have the right to terminate their leases if they give their landlords notice, such as a recent police report or a protection order, if the tenant "seeks to vacate the premises due to fear of imminent danger for self or children"; residential leases also cannot include provisions that would allow landlords to penalize tenants if they seek police or emergency assistance in response to domestic violence or abuse. *See* Colo. Rev. Stat. §38-12-402. And a new Massachusetts statute that came into effect in 2013 provides tenants who are victims of domestic violence, rape, sexual assault, or stalking with the right to terminate their tenancy upon notice to their landlord, protects tenants who have invoked the statute from being barred from future tenancies, and allows victims to have their landlords change their locks; it also makes any waivers of these and the other rights provided under the statute void and unenforceable. *See* Mass. Gen. Laws ch. 186, §§23-29. Similar statutes in other states vary in terms of the notice required to be provided to landlords, the type of evidence of domestic violence required, affirmative obligations landlords have to change locks and preserve confidentiality, and protections from discrimination based on a tenant's status as a victim of domestic violence. The Uniform Law Commission is currently considering whether to include provisions on these issues in a *Revised Uniform Residential Landlord and Tenant Act.*

§2.6 The End of the Tenancy: Landlord's Right to Recover Possession versus Tenant's Right to Remain

The landlord is entitled to evict the tenant if the tenant breaches material terms of the lease. The main reason for eviction is failure to pay rent or failure to pay rent on time. Is the landlord entitled to evict the tenant who has *not* breached any terms of the leasehold? A tenant with a term of years — a one-year lease, for example — cannot be evicted before the end of the term unless the tenant has breached the lease. The landlord has no obligation, however, to *renew* a leasehold. Thus a landlord is entitled to refuse to renew a one-year lease for any reason. Landlords are also entitled to end periodic tenancies, such as month-to-month tenancies, by giving requisite notice.

There are some exceptions to the general principle that landlords may choose not to renew. First, federal and state antidiscrimination statutes prohibit landlords from not renewing leaseholds if the landlord's motivation is discriminatory. Similarly, most courts hold that tenants are protected from eviction if the landlord's motivation is to retaliate against them for asserting their right to habitable premises by calling the housing inspector, for example, to report housing code violations.

Tenants in units that are subject to statutory or local rent control ordinarily are protected from eviction and, in some cases, non-renewal unless the landlord can show just cause. The District of Columbia, New Jersey, and New Hampshire are the only jurisdictions that have adopted statutes granting some or all tenants in private housing a right to continue in possession unless the landlord has just cause to end the tenancy or refuse to renew the leasehold. *See* D.C. Code §42-3505.1; N.H. Rev. Stat. §540:2; N.J. Stat. §§2A:18-61.1 to 2A:18-61.12. *See also Aimco Properties LLC v. Dziewisz*, 883 A.2d 310 (N.H. 2005) (expiration of one-year lease is not "good cause" for eviction under N.H. Rev. Stat. §540:2). Those statutes allow eviction if the tenant is not paying rent on time, damaging the premises or violating reasonable rules in the lease. They also allow eviction if the landlord or a member of the landlord's family wants to move in or the landlord wants to convert the property to a nonrental use.

The federal government subsidizes low-income families through a program known as Section 8 housing, with the federal government paying a significant portion of the tenants' rent owed to private landlords. Under one part of the program, the tenant is given a voucher, finds the apartment, and then obtains the agreement of the landlord to participate. In 1981, the federal statute was amended to prohibit eviction of tenants in Section 8 housing without "good cause." 42 U.S.C. §1437f(d)(1)(B). Public housing owned and operated by public authorities or governmental agencies is similarly prohibited from evicting tenants in the absence of "serious or repeated violation of the terms or conditions of the lease or for other good cause." 42 U.S.C. §1437d(*l*)(5).

Many municipalities, and some states, regulate the conversion of rental housing to condominiums or cooperatives to protect tenants from eviction. Some ordinances prohibit eviction of existing tenants when apartments are converted. *See Fore L Realty Trust v. McManus*, 884 N.E.2d 994, 998 (Mass. App. Ct. 2008). Some laws protect particular classes of tenants, such as the elderly or disabled. *See Senior Citizens and Disabled Protected Tenancy Act*, N.J. Stat. §2A:18-61.22 *et seq.* (granting elderly and disabled tenants protection from eviction for up to 40 years after conversion). Other statutes give tenants preference in purchasing either the building or their particular units within the building when it is converted by granting tenants preemptive rights or rights of first refusal; these rights entitle them to match any offers made by third parties and thus acquire the building or particular units within it. *See, e.g.*, D.C. Code §45-1631 *et seq.*; *Allman v. Snyder*, 888 A.2d 1161 (D.C. 2005) (tenants may assign their statutory right of first refusal to prospective third-party purchasers).

Problem

A lease provides that the tenants in a condominium unit covenant that they will not cause "any nuisance; any offensive noise, odor or fumes; or any hazard to health." The two tenants each smoke one pack of cigarettes a day. In this older building, the smoke wafted upstairs to the neighboring condominium apartments, whose occupants complained of the secondhand smoke. After complaints by the neighbors, the landlord sues to evict the tenants for smoking in their own apartment and violating the lease terms. Before they took the apartment, the landlord had told the tenants that he had lived in and smoked in that apartment for years and received no complaints. Can the landlord evict them? *See* Stefanie Shaffer, *Lighting Up in Your Condo? Think Again*, Nat'l L.J., July 4, 2005, at 6.

§3 CONFLICTS ABOUT RENT

Most lawsuits brought by landlords against tenants are instituted because the tenant has failed to pay rent. In most of these cases, the landlord sues both for back rent owed and to regain possession (to evict the tenant). A smaller number of cases involve attempts to evict tenants for breaching other express or implied terms of the lease. These other terms may include a covenant not to damage the apartment, a covenant requiring the tenants not to interfere with the quiet enjoyment of neighboring tenants in the building, covenants not to keep pets in the apartment, and covenants not to sublet.

In some cases, the tenant breaches the lease by not paying the rent and refuses to leave. Here the landlord may seek to receive back rent and to evict the tenant. In other cases, the tenant breaches the lease by not paying rent and moves out before the end of the lease term. Here the landlord ordinarily attempts to re-rent the apartment and may sue the tenant for back rent; if the new "rental price" is less than the rent under the breached lease, the landlord may sue for the difference between the new rent and the old for the remaining period of the lease.

§3.1 Landlord's Remedies When Tenant Fails to Pay Rent

Possession and back rent. If the tenant wrongfully stops paying rent or breaches other material terms in the lease and continues to occupy the premises, the landlord may sue the tenant for back rent (rent already due but not paid) and for possession (to evict the tenant and to be able to re-rent the apartment to someone else).[9] Tenants may respond to such claims by asserting defenses, such as rights based on the implied warranty of habitability and retaliatory eviction.[10] The tenant may also argue that the

9. Eviction is generally a civil matter. Arkansas, however, has a criminal eviction statute that makes it a misdemeanor to refuse willfully to vacate leased premises after a ten-day notice by the landlord for failure to pay rent. *See* Ark. Code. §18-16-101; Human Rights Watch, *Pay the Rent or Face Arrest: Abusive Impacts of Arkansas's Draconian Evictions Law* (2013).

10. These doctrines are covered later in this chapter.

landlord's attempt to evict the tenant constitutes unlawful discrimination based on family status, disability, race, or gender.[11]

The holdover tenant and the renewal of the tenancy. What happens if the tenant wrongfully holds over after the end of the lease term and *continues* to pay rent? The landlord may choose to accept a new tenancy relationship with the holdover tenant. Most states hold that the new tenancy is a periodic tenancy based on the rent payment; if the landlord accepts a rent check for one's month rent, a new month-to-month tenancy is established. A minority of states hold that a new term is created if the landlord accepts rent from a holdover tenant who was originally occupying under a term of years. In these states, the tenant is bound to another term of the same length as the original term. The tenant who holds over wrongfully is obligated to pay rent to the landlord for the time during which she occupies the premises.

The landlord is also free to take the opposite course of action, that is, to treat the tenant as a tenant at sufferance or a holdover tenant and sue for possession. If the landlord chooses the latter course, does the landlord have the right to collect rent from the holdover tenant before the eviction proceedings are completed? Some states hold that acceptance of the rent check proffered by the holdover tenant *necessarily* creates a new tenancy—regardless of whether the landlord intends to create a new tenancy. To evict the tenant, the landlord may have to go through the procedures to evict a month-to-month tenant, including providing the requisite notice. The landlord may attempt to avoid this result by suing immediately for possession and either (a) refusing to accept the tenant's proffered checks (or returning them to the tenant) or (b) cashing the checks while writing on the back of each check that the landlord is not agreeing to renew the tenancy but is merely using the check to cover the rental value of the property from the tenant at sufferance.

Self-help. A major issue when the tenant breaches the lease and refuses to leave is whether the landlord is entitled to engage in self-help to remove the tenant. Almost all states now hold that the landlord may *not* use self-help, at least in the residential context and often in the commercial context as well. The law today is generally that the landlord must evict the tenant through court proceedings. In *Berg v. Wiley*, 264 N.W.2d 145 (Minn. 1978), the tenant operated a restaurant pursuant to a written lease. The lease contained a covenant by the tenant not to make any changes in the building structure without the landlord's consent. After observing continued violations of this provision and having made several attempts to persuade the tenant to stop remodeling the building to no avail, the landlord changed the locks on the door of the tenant's restaurant, barring the tenant from the premises. The tenant sued the landlord for wrongful eviction. The court found for the tenant, holding that the only lawful means to dispossess a tenant who continues to occupy the premises and has not voluntarily surrendered her rights under the tenancy is to resort to judicial process. In so doing, the court rejected the traditional rule allowing landlords to use self-help to regain

11. *See* Chapter 13.

possession of leased premises if the landlord is legally entitled to possession and the landlord's means of reentry are "peaceable" rather than "forcible." The court argued that the legislature had provided a summary procedure to allow landlords a relatively quick judicial process for a court order allowing the landlord to recover possession. This procedure protected the landlord's rights adequately and prevented the landlord from taking the law into his own hands. Self-help, the court argued, is likely to become violent; moreover, the landlord may be mistaken about his right to possession, and he should not be "the judge of his own rights." The court noted that the landlord could also go to court for an immediate temporary restraining order to prevent the tenant from destroying the property.

Summary process. Most states have statutes providing for a relatively fast judicial determination of the landlord's claim of a right to regain possession of her property. The statutes are called by a variety of names, including **forcible entry and detainer**, **unlawful detainer**, **summary proceedings**, and **summary ejectment**. Summary process statutes often limit the issues that can be addressed in the lawsuit; for many years they were interpreted in ways that prevented tenants from raising defenses to the landlord's claim that she was entitled to possession of the premises.

These proceedings have become considerably less "summary" in recent years, as they have been interpreted by courts or amended by legislatures to allow tenants to raise an increasingly diverse number of defenses — chief among them the implied warranty of habitability. Some states, however, still prevent the tenant from raising defenses, such as the landlord's violation of the implied warranty of habitability, in summary proceedings. The United States Supreme Court has upheld this practice, holding that treating the "undertakings of the tenant and those of the landlord as independent rather than dependent covenants" is not a fundamentally unfair procedure that would violate the tenant's rights to due process of law under the fourteenth amendment. *See Lindsey v. Normet*, 405 U.S. 56, 68 (1972).

Representation. Another challenge common in landlord-tenant cases, both at the point of termination and throughout the term of the lease, is lack of tenant representation. Many landlord-tenant disputes are handled in specialized housing courts. However, the majority of landlords in these courts are represented by counsel and the overwhelming majority of tenants are not. There is evidence that outcomes differ significantly when tenants have lawyers. *See generally* Boston Bar Association Task Force on the Civil Right to Counsel, *The Importance of Representation in Eviction Cases and Homelessness Prevention* (2012) (reporting that in two pilot programs providing free representation to tenants, representation significantly reduced the risk of eviction and improved financial outcomes compared to unrepresented tenants); *see also* D. James Greiner, Cassandra Wolos Pattanayak & Jonathan Hennessy, *The Limits of Unbundled Legal Assistance: A Randomized Study in a Massachusetts District Court and Prospects for the Future*, 126 Harv. L. Rev. 901 (2013).

The Supreme Court has recognized a right to counsel for indigent defendants in criminal cases, *see Gideon v. Wainwright*, 372 U.S. 335 (1963), but has declined to extend that right to civil cases, at least as a general matter, *see Turner v. Rogers*,

131 S. Ct. 2507, 2518 (2011). Should tenants facing eviction—which can have significant adverse consequences, including homelessness—be granted the same right if they cannot afford counsel? If not, how else might the legal system, including courts and counsel for landlords, respond to the shortage of lawyers for indigent tenants?

§3.2 Landlord's Duty to Mitigate Damages

A different set of problems ensues if the tenant breaches the lease for a term of years by ceasing rent payments and moves out before the end of the lease term. The right to sue for possession is of no use since the tenant has already given up possession. In this situation, the landlord can choose among three remedies.

1. Accept the tenant's surrender. By moving out before the end of the lease term and ceasing rent payments, the tenant makes an implied offer to the landlord to end the term of years. The landlord may, if she chooses, "accept the tenant's surrender of the lease." This means that the landlord agrees that the tenant will not be legally obligated to pay the future rent because the landlord has accepted possession of the property.

It is important to note, however, that the landlord's acceptance of the tenant's surrender does *not* mean that the tenant is relieved of *all* financial liability. The landlord may still choose to sue the tenant for **back rent** owed but not paid for the time before the tenant abandoned the premises by moving out. In addition, the landlord may sue immediately (without waiting until the end of the lease term) for **damages** for breach of the lease—which is different from the amount of the **future rent**. As in other contractual settings you may have learned about, damages are likely to be measured by an estimate of the amount the landlord lost because of the tenant's failure to perform his obligations under the contract. This amount is *not* the remaining rent, but the **agreed-upon rental price minus the fair market price**. The theory is that, because the landlord can re-rent the apartment, all the landlord loses by the tenant's breach is the difference between the amount the tenant agreed to pay and the amount the landlord can get from a replacement tenant, plus the advertising and search costs of finding a replacement tenant and lost rent in the meantime. If the rental price is the same as or below the market price, damages are zero (plus the cost of locating the new tenant). The court is likely to add to the computation of damages the reasonable cost of finding a replacement—a cost the landlord would not have had to bear if the tenant had not breached.

2. Re-let on the tenant's account. The landlord may **refuse to accept the surrender**; instead, the landlord may, after notice to the tenant, actively look for a new tenant and **re-let the apartment on the tenant's account**. When a new tenant is found, the landlord may sue the *former* tenant for the difference between the old rental price and the new rent received from the new lessee, if the new rent is lower than the original rent. The new rent must be reasonable; the landlord cannot rent the apartment to her sister for $5 a month and expect to recover the difference between the agreed-upon rent and the artificially low figure charged to her sister.

An issue that often arises in this context is how the landlord can make clear that she is refusing to accept the tenant's proffered surrender of the lease. In some states, the very act of re-letting the apartment may be taken as evidence that the landlord has accepted the surrender of the leasehold. In those states, the landlord must notify the tenant that she is re-letting on the tenant's account and that she refuses to accept the surrender in order to hold the tenant to the rent later. *See OMV Associates, L.P. v. Clearway Acquisition, Inc.*, 976 N.E.2d 185, 194 (Mass. App. Ct. 2012).

Why does it matter whether the landlord is held to have accepted the surrender? Consider a situation in which the tenant under a one-year lease moves out after six months. The landlord finds a new tenant, who agrees to a month-to-month tenancy at the old rent. But this second tenant moves out after four months, with two months left on the year lease. The landlord looks for, but is unable to find, a new tenant. If the landlord has accepted the first tenant's surrender, then the landlord cannot sue the original tenant for the last two months' rent. If the landlord has *not* accepted the tenant's surrender, then the tenant will be obligated to reimburse the landlord for the last two months' rent.

3. Wait and sue for the rent at the end of the lease term versus mitigate damages. The traditional rule is that the landlord may do nothing, wait for the end of the lease term, and then sue the tenant for the remaining unpaid back rent. Rent comes due periodically; under a one-year lease with monthly rental payments, each rental payment is not due until that month arrives. Thus, the landlord could not immediately sue for the remaining rent in the middle of the lease term. To sue the tenant immediately for monetary compensation in the middle of the lease term, the landlord must ask for damages (rental price minus fair market price); to sue for the entire rent itself, the landlord must wait until the lease term ends.

Almost all states, however, now reject this option. Instead, they apply the contract doctrine that requires the aggrieved party to **mitigate damages**. The following case explores what this duty entails.

Sommer v. Kridel

378 A.2d 767 (N.J. 1977)

MORRIS PASHMAN, J.

I

A. Sommer v. Kridel

On March 10, 1972 the defendant, James Kridel, entered into a lease with the plaintiff, Abraham Sommer, owner of the "Pierre Apartments" in Hackensack, to rent apartment 6-L in that building. The term of the lease was from May 1, 1972 until April 30, 1974, with a rent concession for the first six weeks, so that the first month's rent was not due until June 15, 1972.

One week after signing the agreement, Kridel paid Sommer $690. Half of that sum was used to satisfy the first month's rent. The remainder was paid under the lease provision requiring a security deposit of $345. Although defendant had expected to begin occupancy around May 1, his plans were changed. He wrote to Sommer on May 19, 1972, explaining

> I was to be married on June 3, 1972. Unhappily the engagement was broken and the wedding plans cancelled. Both parents were to assume responsibility for the rent after our marriage. I was discharged from the U.S. Army in October 1971 and am now a student. I have no funds of my own, and am supported by my stepfather.
>
> In view of the above, I cannot take possession of the apartment and am surrendering all rights to it. Never having received a key, I cannot return same to you.
>
> I beg your understanding and compassion in releasing me from the lease, and will of course, in consideration thereof, forfeit the 2 months' rent already paid.
>
> Please notify me at your earliest convenience.

Plaintiff did not answer the letter.

Subsequently, a third party went to the apartment house and inquired about renting apartment 6-L. Although the parties agreed that she was ready, willing and able to rent the apartment, the person in charge told her that the apartment was not being shown since it was already rented to Kridel. In fact, the landlord did not re-enter the apartment or exhibit it to anyone until August 1, 1973. At that time it was rented to a new tenant for a term beginning on September 1, 1973. The new rental was for $345 per month with a six week concession similar to that granted Kridel.

Prior to re-letting the new premises, plaintiff sued Kridel in August 1972, demanding $7,000, the total amount due for the full two-year term of the lease. Following a mistrial, plaintiff filed an amended complaint asking for $5,000, the amount due between May 1, 1972 and September 1, 1973. The amended complaint included no reduction in the claim to reflect the six week concession provided for in the lease or the $690 payment made to plaintiff after signing the agreement. Defendant filed an amended answer to the complaint, alleging that plaintiff breached the contract, failed to mitigate damages and accepted defendant's surrender of the premises. He also counterclaimed to demand repayment of the $345 paid as a security deposit.

The trial judge ruled in favor of defendant. Despite his conclusion that the lease had been drawn to reflect "the 'settled law' of this state," he found that "justice and fair dealing" imposed upon the landlord the duty to attempt to re-let the premises and thereby mitigate damages. He also held that plaintiff's failure to make any response to defendant's unequivocal offer of surrender was tantamount to an acceptance, thereby terminating the tenancy and any obligation to pay rent. As a result, he dismissed both the complaint and the counterclaim. The Appellate Division reversed in a per curiam opinion, and we granted certification.

B. Riverview Realty Co. v. Perosio

This controversy arose in a similar manner. On December 27, 1972, Carlos Perosio entered into a written lease with plaintiff Riverview Realty Co. The agreement covered the rental of apartment 5-G in a building owned by the realty company at 2175 Hudson Terrace in Fort Lee. As in the companion case, the lease prohibited the tenant from subletting or assigning the apartment without the consent of the landlord. It was to run for a two-year term, from February 1, 1973 until January 31, 1975, and provided for a monthly rental of $450. The defendant took possession of the apartment and occupied it until February 1974. At that time he vacated the premises, after having paid the rent through January 31, 1974.

The landlord filed a complaint on October 31, 1974, demanding $4,000 in payment for the monthly rental from February 1, 1974 through October 31, 1974. Defendant answered the complaint by alleging that there had been a valid surrender of the premises and that plaintiff failed to mitigate damages. The trial court granted the landlord's motion for summary judgment against the defendant, fixing the damages at $4,000 plus $182.25 interest.

The Appellate Division affirmed the trial court, holding that it was bound by prior precedents, including *Joyce v. Bauman*, 174 A. 693 (N.J. 1934). Nevertheless, it freely criticized the rule which it found itself obliged to follow:

> There appears to be no reason in equity or justice to perpetuate such an unrealistic and uneconomic rule of law which encourages an owner to let valuable rented space lie fallow because he is assured of full recovery from a defaulting tenant. Since courts in New Jersey and elsewhere have abandoned ancient real property concepts and applied ordinary contract principles in other conflicts between landlord and tenant there is no sound reason for a continuation of a special real property rule to the issue of mitigation.

We granted certification.

II

As the lower courts in both appeals found, the weight of authority in this State supports the rule that a landlord is under no duty to mitigate damages caused by a defaulting tenant.

This rule has been followed in a majority of states. Nevertheless, while there is still a split of authority over this question, the trend among recent cases appears to be in favor of a mitigation requirement.

The majority rule is based on principles of property law which equate a lease with a transfer of a property interest in the owner's estate. Under this rationale the lease conveys to a tenant an interest in the property which forecloses any control by the landlord; thus, it would be anomalous to require the landlord to concern himself with the tenant's abandonment of his own property.

For instance, in *Muller v. Beck*, 110 A. 831 (N.J. 1920), where essentially the same issue was posed, the court clearly treated the lease as governed by property, as opposed to contract, precepts.[12]

Yet the distinction between a lease for ordinary residential purposes and an ordinary contract can no longer be considered viable. As Professor Powell observed, evolving "social factors have exerted increasing influence on the law of estates for

12. It is well settled that a party claiming damages for a breach of contract has a duty to mitigate his loss.

years." 2 *Powell on Real Property* (1977 ed.), §221(1) at 180-81. The result has been that

> [t]he complexities of city life, and the proliferated problems of modern society in general, have created new problems for lessors and lessees and these have been commonly handled by specific clauses in leases. This growth in the number and detail of specific lease covenants has reintroduced into the law of estates for years a predominantly contractual ingredient. *Id.* at 181.

Thus in 6 *Williston on Contracts* §890A at 592 (3d ed. 1962), it is stated:

> There is a clearly discernible tendency on the part of courts to cast aside technicalities in the interpretation of leases and to concentrate their attention, as in the case of other contracts, on the intention of the parties.

This Court has taken the lead in requiring that landlords provide housing services to tenants in accordance with implied duties which are hardly consistent with the property notions expressed in *Muller v. Beck, supra. See Braitman v. Overlook Terrace Corp.*, 346 A.2d 76 (N.J. 1975) (liability for failure to repair defective apartment door lock); *Berzito v. Gambino*, 308 A.2d 17 (N.J. 1973) (construing implied warranty of habitability and covenant to pay rent as mutually dependent); *Marini v. Ireland*, 265 A.2d 526 (N.J. 1970) (implied covenant to repair); *Reste Realty Corp. v. Cooper*, 251 A.2d 268 (N.J. 1969) (implied warranty of fitness of premises for leased purpose).

Application of the contract rule requiring mitigation of damages to a residential lease may be justified as a matter of basic fairness.[13] Professor McCormick first commented upon the inequity under the majority rule when he predicted in 1925 that eventually

> the logic, inescapable according to the standards of a "jurisprudence of conceptions" which permits the landlord to stand idly by the vacant, abandoned premises and treat them as the property of the tenant and recover full rent, will yield to the more realistic notions of social advantage which in other fields of the law have forbidden a recovery for damages which the plaintiff by reasonable efforts could have avoided. McCormick, *The Rights of the Landlord upon Abandonment of the Premises by the Tenant*, 23 Mich. L. Rev. 211, 221-22 (1925).

Various courts have adopted this position.

The pre-existing rule cannot be predicated upon the possibility that a landlord may lose the opportunity to rent another empty apartment because he must first rent the apartment vacated by the defaulting tenant. Even where the breach occurs in a multi-dwelling building, each apartment may have unique qualities which make it attractive to certain individuals. Significantly, in *Sommer v. Kridel*, there was a specific request to rent the apartment vacated by the defendant; there is no reason to believe that absent this vacancy the landlord could have succeeded in renting a different apartment to this individual.

---

13. [W]e reserve for another day the question of whether a landlord must mitigate damages in a commercial setting.

We therefore hold that antiquated real property concepts which served as the basis for the pre-existing rule, shall no longer be controlling where there is a claim for damages under a residential lease. Such claims must be governed by more modern notions of fairness and equity. A landlord has a duty to mitigate damages where he seeks to recover rents due from a defaulting tenant.

If the landlord has other vacant apartments besides the one which the tenant has abandoned, the landlord's duty to mitigate consists of making reasonable efforts to re-let the apartment. In such cases he must treat the apartment in question as if it was one of his vacant stock.

As part of his cause of action, the landlord shall be required to carry the burden of proving that he used reasonable diligence in attempting to re-let the premises. We note that there has been a divergence of opinion concerning the allocation of the burden of proof on this issue. While generally in contract actions the breaching party has the burden of proving that damages are capable of mitigation, here the landlord will be in a better position to demonstrate whether he exercised reasonable diligence in attempting to re-let the premises.

III

The *Sommer v. Kridel* case presents a classic example of the unfairness which occurs when a landlord has no responsibility to minimize damages. Sommer waited 15 months and allowed $4658.50 in damages to accrue before attempting to re-let the apartment. Despite the availability of a tenant who was ready, willing and able to rent the apartment, the landlord needlessly increased the damages by turning her away. While a tenant will not necessarily be excused from his obligations under a lease simply by finding another person who is willing to rent the vacated premises, here there has been no showing that the new tenant would not have been suitable. We therefore find that plaintiff could have avoided the damages which eventually accrued, and that the defendant was relieved of his duty to continue paying rent. Ordinarily we would require the tenant to bear the cost of any reasonable expenses incurred by a landlord in attempting to re-let the premises, but no such expenses were incurred in this case.

In *Riverview Realty Co. v. Perosio*, no factual determination was made regarding the landlord's efforts to mitigate damages, and defendant contends that plaintiff never answered his interrogatories. Consequently, the judgment is reversed and the case remanded for a new trial. Upon remand and after discovery has been completed, the trial court shall determine whether plaintiff attempted to mitigate damages with reasonable diligence, and if so, the extent of damages remaining and assessable to the tenant. As we have held above, the burden of proving that reasonable diligence was used to re-let the premises shall be upon the plaintiff.

In assessing whether the landlord has satisfactorily carried his burden, the trial court shall consider, among other factors, whether the landlord, either personally or through an agency, offered or showed the apartment to any prospective tenants, or advertised it in local newspapers. Additionally, the tenant may attempt to rebut such evidence by showing that he proffered suitable tenants who were rejected. However, there is no standard formula for measuring whether the landlord has utilized satisfactory efforts in attempting to mitigate damages, and each case must be judged upon its own facts.

Notes and Questions

1. The duty to mitigate damages. As *Sommer* notes, the traditional rule that landlords have no duty to mitigate damages reflected the idea that a lease was considered a conveyance of a property interest for the term. Having transferred exclusive control of the property to the tenant, subject only to a reversion or remainder, the landlord was entitled to the continuing payment of rent in much the same way that an installment contract can require payments over time.

Almost all states have now changed their laws through statute or judicial decision to impose on both parties to residential leases a duty to mitigate damages that emphasize the contractual nature of the lease. *E.g.,* Alaska Stat. §34.03.230; Cal. Civ. Code §1951.2; Ky. Rev. Stat. §383.670. URLTA §§1.105, 4.203(c) imposes such a duty. Most states also now extend the duty to commercial leases. *See, e.g., Frenchtown Square Partnership v. Lemstone, Inc.,* 791 N.E.2d 417 (Ohio 2003) (commercial landlord has duty to mitigate damages); *Austin Hill Country Realty v. Palisades Plaza,* 948 S.W.2d 293 (Tex. 1997) (same).

By sitting around and waiting for the unpaid rent to accumulate, the landlord arguably increases damages that could have been avoided by re-letting the apartment to another tenant. States that require the landlord to mitigate damages place an obligation on the landlord to act reasonably in seeking another tenant and respect the tenant's interest in not being bound unfairly to the lease. If the landlord does mitigate damages, he can still recover from the tenant the reasonable costs of finding a new tenant, the rent for the premises while the premises were vacant and the landlord was looking for a new tenant, and the difference between the rental price and the new rent paid by the replacement tenant if it is lower than the original rent.

A few states retain the rule that the landlord has no duty to mitigate damages. *Bowdoin Square, L.L.C. v. Winn-Dixie Montgomery, Inc.,* 873 So. 2d 1091, 1100 (Ala. 2003); *Ferrick v. Bianchini,* 2013 Pa. Super. 116 (Super. Ct. 2013) (commercial); *Holy Properties, Ltd. v. Kenneth Cole Products, Inc.,* 661 N.E.2d 694, 696 (N.Y. 1995); *Rios v. Carillo,* 861 N.Y.S.2d 129 (N.Y. App. Div. 2008). The *Restatement (Second) of Property* also adheres to the traditional rule. *Restatement (Second) of Property (Landlord and Tenant)* §12.1(3) & cmt. i (1977).

2. Effect of the failure to mitigate. The common law duty to mitigate damages is not an enforceable obligation in the sense that the landlord *must* attempt to re-let the premises. The landlord is perfectly free to leave the premises vacant. The rule simply means that, in a lawsuit against the tenant for back rent, the landlord can recover only the difference between the market rent and the contract rent provided for in the rental agreement with the original tenant, plus the costs of finding a replacement tenant. However, URLTA goes further, providing that if a landlord fails to mitigate, "the rental agreement is deemed to be terminated" and the landlord can recover no damages past that point. *See* URLTA §4.203(c).

Landlords who want to protect themselves are well advised to attempt to re-let the premises, even in jurisdictions that retain the traditional rule, given the possibility that the law may be changed at any time and be applied retroactively. If a landlord attempts to re-let and finds a new tenant who then fails to pay part or all of the rent, the landlord may want to go after the original tenant for the unpaid rent. If, however, the landlord has accepted the original tenant's surrender of the lease, he can go after only the new tenant. How can the landlord increase the likelihood that the courts will find that the landlord did not accept the tenant's surrender of the lease?

3. Arguments for and against the duty to mitigate. Some scholars argue that the duty to mitigate damages is efficient because it encourages landlords to rent the premises rather than leaving them vacant. Because the landlord can be compensated by the tenant for all the extra costs of re-letting the premises and still obtain the economic value of the leasehold, re-renting gives the landlord the benefit of the bargain; he is in the economic position he would have been in had the tenant performed. Moreover, the old tenant has been able to get out of an arrangement that was no longer in her interest; the new tenant has obtained an apartment, thus being made better off. Placing no duty on the landlord would allow him to leave the apartment vacant, thereby wasting a scarce resource. Alternatively, it would force the tenant to give up a job opportunity elsewhere, for example, and remain locked in to the apartment. Either result creates a loss of social wealth relative to re-letting the premises.

Others argue, however, that there is no such efficiency loss. The landlord bargained for the right not to have to look for another tenant before the end of the lease term. This right is a property right that the landlord owns; the tenant has no right to take this right from the landlord without offering adequate compensation. The only compensation that is adequate is the remainder of the bargained-for rent. If the tenant wanted a nine-month lease, she could have bargained for it. If the tenant wants to breach the 12-month lease by moving out early, she should have to compensate the landlord sufficiently to induce the landlord to agree to give up his right not to have to look for a new tenant. If the tenant is unwilling to compensate the landlord for the right to terminate the lease early, the cost to the landlord outweighs the benefit to the plaintiff. And tenants in many situations are as capable of subleasing or assigning their units as landlords are at renting in the first place.

Is either of these arguments convincing? Should it make a difference whether the landlord has limited a tenant's right to sublease or assign? Why?

4. Advice for tenants. In a jurisdiction that imposes a duty on landlords to mitigate damages, what advice would you give a tenant who wanted to leave before the end of the lease term? Should she give the landlord notice before she leaves? Does the duty to mitigate damages protect her sufficiently so that she can leave in confidence that she will be relieved of rent obligations for the rest of the lease term? How can the tenant minimize her legal exposure?

5. Rent acceleration clauses. Some landlords attempt to contract around the duty to mitigate damages through an "acceleration clause," making the rest of the rent due immediately if the tenant abandons the premises or otherwise breaches the lease in a material way. This is a form of "liquidated damages," whereby the parties agree to the amount of damages due if one of them breaches. This remedy goes beyond waiting until the rent is due to sue to collect it; it allows the landlord to obtain the rest of the rent immediately upon breach and, if enforceable, would allow the landlord *also* to rent out the premises to another tenant. Some courts enforce such provisions on the ground that the parties voluntarily agreed to them; however, they generally also police the term and will not enforce the clause if it constitutes a "penalty" or if the amount owed is "unconscionable." *See, e.g., Summers v. Crestview Apartments*, 236 P.3d 586, 590 (Mont. 2010). As with other liquidated damages, they will be deemed to be an unenforceable penalty if they do not constitute a reasonable estimate of the actual damages the landlord is likely to suffer because of the breach. *Cummings Properties, L.L.C. v. National Communications Corp.*, 869 N.E.2d 617 (Mass. 2007). Most (but not all) courts will not allow such a clause to waive the duty to mitigate damages; while the remaining rent payments are what the landlord "could have expected to receive . . . over the term of the lease," the landlord is also expected to attempt to re-let the premises and the accelerated rent payments will be reduced by the damages that would have been avoided by re-letting. *HealthSouth Rehabilitation Corp. v. Falcon Management Co.*, 799 So. 2d 177, 185-186 (Ala. 2001); *Aurora Business Park Association v. Albert, Inc.*, 548 N.W.2d 153, 157-158 (Iowa 1996); *Restatement (Second) of Property (Landlord and Tenant)* §12.1 cmt. k (1977).

6. Burden of proof. *Sommer* holds that the landlord has the burden to persuade the decision maker that he tried to mitigate damages and to justify the amount lost because of the inability to mitigate. This appears to be the majority rule at least in the case of residential tenancies. However, some states impose the burden on the tenant, and this appears to be the majority rule in cases involving commercial leases, for those states that have addressed the issue. *See, e.g., Commercial Real Estate Investment, L.C. v. Comcast of Utah II, Inc.*, 285 P.3d 1193, 1204 (Utah 2012). By statute, Maine and Wisconsin have a shifting burden of proof on this issue, requiring the landlord initially to prove reasonable efforts to comply and then giving the tenant the opportunity to prove that the landlord was not reasonable. *See* Me. Rev. Stat. tit. 14, §6010-A(3); Wis. Stat. §704.29(3). Which approach is better?

Problems

1. A professional real estate company with a large portfolio of properties manages a recently developed 16-story apartment building with 80 units. Each floor in the building contains the same mix of studio, one-bedroom, and two bedroom apartments. Each apartment of a given type has the same layout and standard finishes, and the views from each are similar, although slightly better from higher floors. A tenant breaches her one-year lease on a one-bedroom apartment and moves out after only three months. At the time the landlord sets out to re-let the apartment, the building has three other one-bedroom apartments available to rent, and a handful of studio and two-bedroom apartments vacant as well. If a prospective tenant comes to the

building's leasing office seeking an apartment and does not specify any particular unit, must the landlord rent the newly vacated unit before offering any other vacant units? What if the prospective tenants are a couple with a small child?

2. A landlord who lives in a three-unit building rents two of the apartments. The building is located in an urban area with many universities and a shortage of rental housing; many prospective tenants look for housing much of the time. Most of the tenants are students, many of whom go elsewhere for the summer. Because the landlord lives in the building, she is concerned about finding tenants who will not be disruptive. Because the state imposes a duty to mitigate damages, however, tenants have started leaving at the end of the school year and stopping rent payments. This constitutes a breach of the year-long lease; however, they know that the landlord will be able to find replacement tenants and that she has a "duty to mitigate damages." Because she can easily find new tenants, she is unlikely to come after them for the money.

The landlord comes to you for advice. She would rather not have to look for new tenants twice a year, in September and again in June. Suppose she were to place a clause in the lease that states:

> If Tenant abandons or vacates the Leased Premises during the Term of this Lease, Landlord may elect to re-enter the premises and, at her option, re-let the Leased Premises. If the Landlord elects not to re-let the Leased Premises, Tenant shall be liable for the remainder of the rent due under the Lease until its expiration. Landlord has no duty to mitigate damages.

Would such a clause be enforceable? Should it be?

§3.3 Security Deposits

Many landlords protect themselves from the possibility that tenants may fail to pay rent or damage the premises by requiring a security deposit, often in the amount of one or two months' rent at the beginning of the leasehold. Some states regulate security deposits by statutes that may (1) limit the amount that can be required as a security deposit; (2) require the landlord to place the deposit in a separate account; and (3) require the landlord to repay the security deposit to the tenant with interest at the termination of the leasehold, less any amounts deducted to pay for repairs necessitated by damage caused by the tenant during the leasehold. URLTA §2.101.

§3.4 Rent Control

A few municipalities (most notably, New York City) have laws limiting the amount by which landlords can raise the rent. Such laws are intended to allow landlords to obtain a reasonable return on their investment, while protecting the rights of tenants to continue living in their homes. Rent control has been repeatedly upheld against claims that it constitutes an unconstitutional taking of the landlord's property rights. *Yee v. City of Escondido*, California, 503 U.S. 519 (1992).

Rent control laws generally allow rents to rise to market levels when the current tenant vacates the premises. This fact leads to a great deal of game-playing on both sides. Landlords may try to harass tenants to get them to move out so the landlord can raise the rent, and tenants may sublet the apartment against the wishes of the landlord. In addition, tenants are generally entitled to leave their apartments to spouses or other family members living with the tenant before the tenant's death. In the famous case of *Braschi v. Stahl Associates*, 543 N.E.2d 49 (N.Y. 1989), the court ruled that a partner in a same-sex couple was a "family member" entitled to continue living in the apartment when his partner died. The rent control ordinance was subsequently amended to reflect this result. *N.Y. City Rent & Eviction Regulations* §2204.6(d)(3). But in *Hudson View Properties v. Weiss*, 450 N.E.2d 234 (N.Y. 1983), the landlord sought to evict a tenant from a rent-controlled apartment on the ground that she had breached a term in her lease under which she covenanted not to allow anyone to occupy the premises with her who was not a member of her "immediate family." She lived with a man "with whom she [had] a loving relationship," but the court decided that because the couple was not married, the man was not a part of the tenant's immediate family.

§4 TENANT'S RIGHTS TO QUIET ENJOYMENT AND HABITABLE PREMISES

§4.1 The Covenant of Quiet Enjoyment and Constructive Eviction

Minjak Co. v. Randolph

528 N.Y.S.2d 554 (App. Div. 1988)

Map: W. 20th Street, New York, New York

MEMORANDUM DECISION.

In July of 1983 petitioner-landlord commenced the within summary non-payment proceeding against respondents [Diane] Randolph and [Masabumi] Kikuchi, tenants of a loft space on the fourth floor of petitioner's building on West 20th Street in Manhattan, alleging non-payment of rent since July 1981. The tenants' answer set forth as affirmative defenses that because they were unable to use two-thirds of the loft space due to the landlord's renovations and other conditions, they were entitled to an abatement of two-thirds of the rent, and that as to the remaining one-third space, they were entitled to a further rent abatement due to the landlord's failure to supply essential services. The tenants also counterclaimed for breach of warranty of habitability, seeking both actual and punitive damages and attorney's fees.

[At trial] it was stipulated that rent was due and owing from October 1981 through November 1983 in the amount of $12,787 ($200 due for October 1981, $450 due each month from November 1981 through December 1982, and $567 per month since January 1983).

Respondents commenced residency of the loft space in 1976 pursuant to a commercial lease. Petitioner offered a commercial lease even though at the time of the signing of the lease the building was used predominantly for residential purposes and the respondents had informed petitioner that they would use the loft as their residence. The loft space measures 1700 square feet, approximately two-thirds of which is used as a music studio for Mr. Kikuchi, where he composes, rehearses and stores his very expensive electronic equipment and musical instruments. The remainder of the space is used as the tenants' residence.

Late in 1977, the fifth-floor tenant began to operate a health spa equipment business which included the display of fully working jacuzzis, bathtubs, and saunas. The jacuzzis and bathtubs were filled to capacity with water. From November 1977 through February 1982, respondents suffered at least 40 separate water leaks from the fifth floor. At times the water literally poured into the bedroom and bedroom closets of respondents' loft, ruining their clothes and other items. Water leaked as well into the kitchen, the bathroom and onto Mr. Kikuchi's grand piano and other musical instruments. Respondents' complaints to petitioner went unheeded.

CONTEXT

Masabumi Kikuchi is a well-known New York jazz musician who has recorded with such luminaries as Miles Davis, Joe Henderson, Elvin Jones, Gil Evans, and Sonny Rollins. He continues to live in the same loft space that was at issue in *Minjak*. *See* Ben Ratliff, *Floating in Time, Hiding in Sight*, N.Y. Times, Mar. 23, 2012.

In January of 1978 the fifth-floor tenant began to sandblast the walls, causing sand to seep through openings around pipes and cracks in the ceiling and into respondent's loft. The sand, which continued to fall into the loft even as the parties went to trial, got into respondent's clothes, bed, food and even their eyes.

In September of 1981 the landlord commenced construction work in the building to convert the building into a Class A multiple building. To convert the freight elevator into a passenger elevator, petitioner had the elevator shaft on respondent's side of the building removed. The workers threw debris down the elevator shaft, raising "huge clouds of dust" which came pouring into the loft and settled everywhere, on respondents' clothes, bed, food, toothbrushes and musical equipment. The musical equipment had to be covered at all times to protect it from the dust. Respondents began to suffer from eye and sinus problems, nausea, and soreness in their throats from the inhalation of the dust. Respondents attempted to shield themselves somewhat from the dust by putting up plastic sheets, only to have the workmen rip them down.

To demonstrate the hazardous nature of some of the construction work, respondents introduced evidence that as the landlord's workers were demolishing the stairs from the seventh floor down, no warning signs were posted, causing one visitor to come perilously close to falling through a hole in the stairs. The workers jackhammered a new entrance to the loft, permitting the debris to fall directly onto the floor of respondents' loft. The workmen would mix cement right on respondents' floor. A new entrance door to the loft was sloppily installed without a door sill, and loose bricks were left around the frame. A day later, brick fragments and concrete fell on tenant Randolph's head as she closed the door.

The record contains many more examples of dangerous construction and other conduct interfering with respondents' ability to use and enjoy possession of their loft. From 1981 until the time of trial, Kikuchi was completely unable to use the music studio portion of the loft. His musical instruments had been kept covered and protected against the sand and later the dust since 1978.

The jury rendered a verdict awarding respondents a rent abatement of 80% for July 1981 through November 1983, as compensatory damages on the theory of constructive eviction from the music studio portion of the loft; a 40% rent abatement for January 1981 through November 1983, on the remainder of the rent due for the residential portion of the premises, on a theory of breach of warranty of habitability; a 10% rent abatement on the rent attributable to the residential portion of the premises for all of 1979, on a breach of warranty of habitability theory; and punitive damages in the amount of $20,000. After trial the court granted respondents' motion made pursuant to Real Property Law Sec. 234 for reasonable attorney's fees, awarding respondents $5000. The court also granted petitioner's motion to set aside the verdict and for other relief, only to the extent of reducing the award for punitive damages to $5000.

On appeal to the Appellate Term that court reversed the judgment. Holding that the doctrine of constructive eviction could not provide a defense to this non-payment proceeding, because tenants had not abandoned possession of the demised premises, the court reversed the jury's award as to the 80% rent abatement predicated on the constructive eviction theory.

We agree with the holding and reasoning of *East Haven Associates v. Gurian*, 313 N.Y.S.2d 927 (Civ. Ct. 1970), that a tenant may assert as a defense to the nonpayment of rent the doctrine of constructive eviction, even if he or she has abandoned only a portion of the demised premises due to the landlord's acts in making that portion of the premises unusable by the tenant. Indeed "compelling considerations of social policy and fairness" dictate such a result.

The evidence at trial fully supported a finding that respondents were compelled to abandon the music studio portion of the loft due to "the landlord's wrongful acts [which] substantially and materially deprive[d] the tenant[s] of the beneficial use and enjoyment" of that portion of the loft.

Petitioner does, however, correctly point out that as the constructive eviction claim was asserted as a defense to the nonpayment of rent and respondents did not request an abatement for any months other than those in which they did not pay rent, the jury's award of an 80% rent abatement as to the months July, August, September and half of October of 1981 must be stricken.

The award for punitive damages, as reduced by the Civil Court to $5000, should be reinstated as well. Although generally in breach of contract claims the damages to be awarded are compensatory, in certain instances punitive damages may be awarded when to do so would "deter morally culpable conduct." The determining factor is "the moral culpability of the defendant," and whether the conduct implies a "criminal indifference to civil obligations."

[I]t has been recognized that punitive damages may be awarded in breach of warranty of habitability cases where the landlord's actions or inactions were intentional and malicious.

[W]e are satisfied that this record supports the jury's finding of morally culpable conduct in light of the dangerous and offensive manner in which the landlord permitted the construction work to be performed, the landlord's indifference to the health and safety of others, and its disregard for the rights of others, so as to imply even a criminal indifference to civil obligations. One particularly egregious example of the landlord's wanton disregard for the safety of others was the way in which the stair demolition was performed: steps were removed and no warning sign even posted. The landlord's indifference and lack of response to the tenants' repeated complaints of dust, sand and water leak problems demonstrated a complete indifference to their health and safety and a lack of concern for the damage these conditions could cause to the tenants' valuable personal property. Such indifference must be viewed as rising to the level of high moral culpability. Accordingly, the award of punitive damages is sustained.

3000 B.C. v. Bowman Properties Ltd.

No. 1968, 2008 WL 5544414 (Pa. Com. Pl. 2008) (*aff'd in part, vacated in part, remanded by* 3000 B.C v. Bowman, 990 A.2d 33 (Table) (Pa. Super. Ct. 2009))

MARK BERNSTEIN, J.

Plaintiff, 3000 B.C., is a professional spa, offering a variety of therapeutic treatments including massage and facials. The success of their business relied on their clients' happiness and the ability to provide a serene and tranquil environment. This objective was irrevocably destroyed at 3000 B.C., when their Indian flute music was overwhelmed by hammering, sawing, colorful language of construction workers, and by the joyful sounds of gleeful children playing while awaiting their turn at the Hair Cuttery occupying the apartment above. Defendant Bowman Properties understood that 3000 B.C. required a tranquil environment to run a spa because they had leased the property to 3000 B.C. for 12 years.

A covenant of quiet enjoyment is implied into every lease in the Commonwealth of Pennsylvania. This covenant exists between the landlord and the tenant and is breached when a tenant's possession is impaired by acts of the lessor. "There is an implied covenant for the quiet enjoyment of the demised premises, and it is settled that any . . . act of the landlord which results in an interference of the tenant's possession, in whole or in part, is an eviction for which the landlord is liable in damages to the tenant." *Kelly v. Miller*, 94 A. 1055, 1056 (Pa. 1915). A breach of the covenant can be demonstrated through constructive eviction, if the tenant can establish that the utility of the premises has been substantially and fundamentally impaired. The manner in which defendant leased to the Hair Cuttery violated the covenant of quiet enjoyment.

In the case of a breach of a constructive eviction, [a] lessee may recover "for all losses which he can prove he has actually sustained, or which he will necessarily sustain, under the circumstances, as a result of the unlawful eviction. The measure of damages has been liberally extended to include . . . profits of the business." *Pollock v. Morelli*, 369 A.2d 458, 462 (Pa. Super. 1976). As in any other contract action, the purpose of damages is to restore the injured party to the financial position it would have achieved had the contract been fulfilled. This means that the injured party is "entitled to be reimbursed for the money actually paid out and for all reasonable and necessary expenses incurred on the faith of the contract." *Emerman v. Baldwin*, 142 A.2d 440, 447 (Pa. Super. 1958).

Accordingly, the court in this non-jury trial must determine what the financial position of 3000 B.C. would have been if constructive eviction had not occurred. This analysis begins with determining the length of time for which damages must be awarded. The lease from which the plaintiff was evicted expired on August 1, 2006. Although plaintiff argues that the 12-year rental history would allow the court to presume that the lease would have been repeatedly renewed and therefore calculate damages beyond the August 1, 2006 termination date, the court rejects that proposition. In Pennsylvania, a landlord can refuse to renew a lease for any good reason, for no reason, or any bad reason, as long as no constitutionally protected right is violated. Only speculation could determine the length of a new lease of the adjusted rent if the court were to calculate damages upon the leap of faith that the lease would be renewed. To determine damages upon these assumptions is to rely on speculation upon speculation. This speculation is impermissible.

[The court reviewed the proof presented as to damages. The court began with 3000 B.C.'s losses from the start of the noise, in February 2005, through 3000 B.C.'s forced evacuation in December 2005, including attorneys' fees, moving expenses, and additional rent that 3000 B.C. was required to pay. The court also awarded 3000 B.C. damages for spa credits given customers whose treatments had been destroyed as well as loss of business good will, or the value of a business' reputation, noting that "the disruption described in testimony necessarily causes consternation, hard feelings, ill will, and dismay among clients in a business which had been providing healthful therapeutic serenity to customers for over 12 years at the same location." The court declined to award damages for the expense of retraining new staff for the new location, which the court found would have occurred at the natural termination of the lease. The court also deducted from damages the rent that 3000 B.C. owed but had not paid in 2006, because that amount would have been a necessary expense if the constructive eviction had not taken place. In sum, the court awarded 3000 B.C. $236,233.45 in damages.]

Notes and Questions

1. **Express and implied terms in the landlord-tenant relationship.** The landlord-tenant relationship is governed partly by the **express terms** of any written lease. The landlord-tenant relationship is also governed by **implied terms**. These terms need not be written down or even explicitly discussed to be legally binding. They may

or may not be waivable by the parties. One important term implied in every landlord-tenant relationship by common law or statute is the **covenant of quiet enjoyment** by which the landlord impliedly promises not to disturb the tenant's quiet enjoyment of the property. Other implied terms that are frequently recognized include reasonable rights of access across land or through non-leased portions of a building, *see, e.g., Kysar v. Amoco Product Co.*, 93 P.3d 1272 (N.M. 2004), or for parking next to a retail store, *see Sierad v. Lilly*, 22 Cal. Rptr. 580 (Dist. Ct. App. 1962).

2. Actual eviction. If the landlord breaches the lease by physically barring the tenant from the property, the tenant's obligation to pay rent ceases entirely. The placement of new locks on the door constitutes actual eviction. *Olin v. Goehler*, 694 P.2d 1129 (Wash. Ct. App. 1985); *see also Sengul v. CMS Franklin, Inc.*, 265 P.3d 320, 326 (Alaska 2011). The tenant also may sue the landlord for damages for trespass and may seek an injunction ordering the landlord to reconvey possession of the premises to the tenant.

What happens if the landlord bars the tenant from only *part* of the leased property? A **partial actual eviction** constitutes a breach of the lease and provides the tenant with ample justification to move out before the end of the lease term; the tenant will not be liable for the rent after moving out. *But see Eastside Exhibition Corp. v. 210 East 86th Street Corp.*, 965 N.E.2d 246 (N.Y. 2012) (relaxing the traditional rule by holding that a commercial landlord's interference with possession of 12 square feet of space out of a total of 15,000 square feet does not constitute a partial actual eviction entitling the tenant to a full rent abatement). What happens if the tenant chooses to stay? The traditional rule relieves the tenant of the obligation to pay rent *completely* even though the tenant continues to occupy the rest of the premises. But the more recent trend seems to be to *abate* the rent (reduce it) to the fair market value of the property that remains. *Restatement (Second) of Property (Landlord and Tenant)* §6.1 (1977).

3. Constructive eviction. A "constructive" eviction occurs when the landlord substantially interferes with the tenant's quiet enjoyment of the premises. The defense of constructive eviction allows the tenant to stop rent payments and move out before the end of the lease term. The theory is that when the landlord allows the conditions in the apartment to deteriorate such that living in the apartment is either impossible or uncomfortable, her actions are functionally equivalent to physically barring the tenant from the premises.

What happens if the tenant stops paying rent and fails to move out? The traditional rule is that the tenant can raise a defense of constructive eviction only if he moves out within a reasonable period of time. To establish constructive eviction, the tenant must claim that the landlord's interference with the tenant's quiet enjoyment of the premises is so substantial that nobody in his right mind would stay there; the place is uninhabitable and, therefore, the landlord's actions are equivalent to barring the door. If, however, the tenant *stays*, then this can be used as evidence that the interference is not sufficiently serious to justify allowing the tenant to stop paying rent or ending the leasehold. *Barash v. Pennsylvania Terminal Real Estate Corp.*, 256 N.E.2d 707 (N.Y. 1970).

East Haven Associates, Inc. v. Gurian, 313 N.Y.S.2d 927 (Civ. Ct. 1970), on which the court in *Minjak* relies, held that tenants could establish a defense of **partial constructive eviction**. Under this doctrine, tenants can show that the landlord's actions have substantially deprived the tenant of the use and enjoyment of a portion of the property. The defense of partial constructive eviction may allow the tenant to continue living in the remaining part of the premises from which the tenant does not claim to have been constructively evicted. *Minjak* illustrates that the remedy for partial constructive eviction for the tenant who wants to stay is likely to be a partial, rather than complete, abatement of rent. The court in *East Haven* explained the basis for the doctrine, *id.* at 930-931:

> It cannot be seriously disputed that a major shortage in residential housing has prevailed in our metropolitan area for several decades. The clear effect has been to undermine so drastically the bargaining power of tenants in relation to landlords that grave questions as to the fairness and relevance of some traditional concepts of landlord-tenant law are presented.
>
> The very idea of requiring families to abandon their homes before they can defend against actions for rent is a baffling one in an era in which decent housing is so hard to get, particularly for those who are poor and without resources. It makes no sense at all to say that if part of an apartment has been rendered uninhabitable, a family must move from the entire dwelling before it can seek justice and fair dealing. *See Arbern Realty Co. v. Clay Craft Planters Co.,* 727 N.Y.S.2d 236 (App. Div. 2001) (applying the partial constructive eviction doctrine in the context of a commercial lease).

The *Restatement (Second) of Property (Landlord and Tenant)* §6.1 (1977) provides that "there is a breach of the landlord's obligations if, during the period the tenant is entitled to possession of the leased property, the landlord, or someone whose conduct is attributable to him, interferes with a permissible use of the leased property by the tenant." The *Second Restatement* departs from traditional law in several respects. First, it defines constructive eviction as interference that is "more than insignificant" rather than requiring the interference to be "substantial." Reporter's note 1. Second, it adopts view that the landlord is liable not only for actions the landlord takes, but also for the acts of third parties "performed on property in which the landlord has an interest, which conduct could be legally controlled by him." Cmt. d. Third, it rejects the traditional requirement that the tenant abandon the premises before taking advantage of the constructive eviction doctrine, on the ground that "it makes the law completely unavailable to tenants who for one reason or another cannot move, *e.g.*, indigent urban apartment dwellers in many cities, and available only at great risk to others, who must first deprive themselves of such benefit as they are deriving from the premises before getting a ruling on whether they were justified in doing so." Reporter's note 6.

4. Relation to the implied warranty of habitability. The warranty of habitability, considered in §4.2, below, obligates landlords to provide premises that are safe and suitable for habitation. Breach of the warranty entitles tenants to move out before the end of the lease term or to stay and either stop paying rent or pay a reduced rent until the improper conditions of the premises are fixed. Because of the development of the implied warranty, litigation about constructive eviction now tends to focus less on the physical condition of the premises and more on acts by the landlord that interfere with quiet enjoyment, such as noise or harassment attributable to the landlord. Constructive eviction applies, as well, when the landlord undertakes some activity that interferes with the tenant's beneficial use of the premises, such as legal action. *See, e.g., Kohl v. PNC Bank National Association,* 912 A.2d 237 (Pa. 2006) (landlord lawsuit against tenant that substantially impairs tenant's possessory interest in bad faith, and primarily other than to seek legal redress constitutes breach of the covenant of quiet enjoyment). Constructive eviction also remains a factor for physical conditions attributable to a landlord's actions for commercial tenants where the warranty of habitability may not apply. *See, e.g., Manhattan Mansions v. Moe's Pizza,* 561 N.Y.S.2d 331 (Civ. Ct. 1990).

5. Tenant's duties to other tenants. Many written leases contain express clauses obligating tenants not to disturb the quiet enjoyment of other tenants, and many states have statutes, like the URLTA, that require the tenant to "conduct himself and require other persons on the premises with his consent to conduct themselves in a manner that will not disturb his neighbors' peaceful enjoyment of the premises." URLTA §3.101(7). Breach of this obligation would entitle the landlord to evict the tenant. If the tenant's conduct rises to the level of a common law nuisance, such as excessive noise, others tenants may have remedies for damages or injunctive relief.

6. Landlord's liability for acts of other tenants. The traditional rule provides that constructive eviction may be shown only if the landlord or someone acting under the landlord has acted in a way that interfered with the tenant's interest in quiet enjoyment. Under this traditional rule, the landlord is not responsible for the acts of other tenants unless the lease specifically includes an obligation to control the conduct of other tenants. The trend, however, appears to be in the direction of the approach adopted by the *Second Restatement. Restatement (Second) of Property (Landlord and Tenant)* §6.1 (1977); *see, e.g., Arbern Realty Co. v. Clay Craft Planters Co., Inc.,* 727 N.Y.S.2d 236, 237 (Sup. Ct. 2001) (landlord's failure to protect tenant's access for loading and unloading of trucks and parking from another tenant's interference was a partial constructive eviction); *Blackett v. Olanoff,* 358 N.E.2d 817 (Mass. 1976); *see also Bocchini v. Gorn Management Co.,* 515 A.2d 1179, 1184 (Md. Ct. Spec. App. 1986) (noting that the traditional rule "has been increasingly abandoned").

In *Blackett, supra,* landlords who were renting apartments also leased nearby premises to a cocktail lounge that was intending to play live music. The lounge, however, played music almost daily until 1:30 or 2 in the morning that was loud enough for neighboring residents to hear through the granite walls of their building. In finding the landlord liable for violation of the residential tenants' covenant of quiet enjoyment, the court paid particular attention to the fact that the landlord had the right under its lease to the lounge to control lounge's noise.

In the absence of such a clause, should a tenant have an implied duty not to disturb his neighbors such that violation of the duty would constitute a breach of the lease and entitle the landlord to evict the tenant? Should the landlord have not only the *right* but the *obligation* to evict a noisy tenant to protect the interests of neighboring tenants? Should it be enough to find a violation of a tenant's covenant of quiet enjoyment that a landlord rents to a new tenant whose use of the premises is likely to conflict with the existing tenant's use?

Problems

1. A client comes into your office with the following story. She is a law student renting a third-floor apartment in a three-unit apartment house near the law school. She shares the apartment with two roommates; all three of them have signed the lease, which runs from September 1 to August 31. It is now November 10. Starting in October, the tenant occupying the second floor began making unwanted sexual comments to your client as she walked up to her apartment. He has never touched her and has not directly threatened to attack her. She is afraid of him because of these comments, which he now makes daily. She believes he waits for her to come home so that he can accost her on the stairway as she goes up to her apartment. If it were not for this neighbor, she would be very happy with the apartment, which is well maintained, reasonably priced, attractive, and close to both school and shopping. At the same time, she is considering moving out—something her roommates do not want her to do. She asks you for advice about her legal rights.

   a. What questions would you ask her?
   b. What options does she have?
   c. What legal advice would you give her?

2. May a tenant move out before the end of the lease term because of secondhand smoke generated by another tenant in the building? In *Poyck v. Bryant*, 820 N.Y.S.2d 774 (Civ. Ct. 2006), the court held that a tenant of a condominium unit who was allergic to tobacco smoke and recovering from cancer surgery could move out and be relieved of lease obligations because of secondhand smoke generated by neighbors in another condo when they smoked in common areas and in their condo. The court held that the landlord could have attempted to get the condominium association to stop the neighbors from smoking in common areas or he could have better ventilated the apartment to solve the problem. Was the case correctly decided?

3. Do tenants have a right to leave if a registered sex offender moves in next door? *See Knudsen v. Lax*, 842 N.Y.S.2d 341, 350 (Civ. Ct. 2007) (yes, because this "resolution approximates the terms the parties would have negotiated had they foreseen the circumstances that have given rise to the dispute").

§4.2 Warranty of Habitability

Before the 1970s, most courts held that landlords had no implied duty to repair the rented premises and that leaseholds included no implied representations that the apartment was in habitable condition. The only exception to this principle was that landlords had a duty to fix latent defects known to them and not easily discoverable by the tenant. If the tenant wanted a warranty or a contractual obligation on the landlord to maintain the apartment, she had to bargain for it.

Courts also held that the contractual obligations of the landlord and tenant were **independent** rather than **dependent**. This meant that, contrary to other kinds of contracts, the parties' obligations to perform were not contingent on the other party's performance. Thus, the tenant's obligation to pay rent was enforceable by the landlord even if the landlord herself was violating a covenant to repair the premises. The tenant's only remedy was to sue the landlord for damages. To terminate the lease, the tenant needed to show constructive eviction; thus, any defects or failures to repair that did not rise to the level of constructive eviction prevented the tenant from lawfully getting out of the lease early, even if there was a covenant to repair and the landlord was breaching the agreement.

In recent years, most states have repudiated both the lack of a duty to repair or maintain and the independent covenants rule, at least in the context of residential housing. Starting around 1970, there was a virtual revolution in residential landlord-tenant law. Before 1970, courts viewed a leasehold solely as a transfer of a property interest; the landlord granted the tenant the right to possess the premises for a specified period of time, conditional on an agreed-upon rent. The landlord's obligations were limited to transferring possession; constructive eviction was seen as a failure to comply with this duty. The tenant had a duty to pay the rent and not to commit waste by damaging the property. No other obligations attended the relationship, which was governed by *caveat emptor* or *caveat lessee*—let the buyer beware.

This tradition rapidly unraveled after the groundbreaking decision in *Javins v. First National Realty Corp.* As you read the opinion below, consider the reasons that Judge J. Skelly Wright gives to change the law. Are they convincing?

Javins v. First National Realty Corp.

428 F.2d 1071 (D.C. Cir. 1970)

Map: (Wardman Court Apartments)
1350 Clifton Street, NW,
Washington, D.C.

J. Skelly Wright, Circuit Judge:

These cases present the question whether housing code violations which arise during the term of a lease have any effect upon the tenant's obligation to pay rent.

We hold that a warranty of habitability, measured by the standards set out in the Housing Regulations for the District of Columbia, is implied by operation of law into leases of urban dwelling units covered by those Regulations and that breach of this warranty gives rise to the usual remedies for breach of contract.

I

By separate written leases, each of the appellants rented an apartment in a three-building apartment complex in Northwest Washington known as Clifton Terrace. The landlord, First National Realty Corporation, filed separate actions in the Landlord and Tenant Branch of the Court of General Sessions on April 8, 1966, seeking possession on the ground that each of the appellants had defaulted in the payment of rent due for the month of April. The tenants, appellants here, admitted that they had not paid the landlord any rent for April. However, they alleged numerous [1500] violations of the Housing Regulations as "an equitable defense or (a) claim by way of recoupment or set-off in an amount equal to the rent claim," as provided in the rules of the Court of General Sessions. Appellants conceded at trial, however, that this offer of proof reached only violations which had arisen since the term of the lease had commenced.

Clifton Terrace was built between 1914 and 1915 as luxury apartments by the prolific D.C. developer Harry Wardman. After struggling for decades, the complex was eventually taken over by the U.S. Department of Housing and Urban Development and underwent a $37 million renovation that was completed in 2004. It is now listed on the National Register of Historic Places.

Clifton Terrace in 1930. Picture courtesy of the D.C. Public Library Commons.

II

Since, in traditional analysis, a lease was the conveyance of an interest in land, courts have usually utilized the special rules governing real property transactions to resolve controversies involving leases. However, as the Supreme Court has noted in another context, "the body of private property law . . . more than almost any other branch of law, has been shaped by distinctions whose validity is largely historical." Courts have a duty to reappraise old doctrines in the light of the facts and values of contemporary life — particularly old common law doctrines which the courts themselves created and developed. As we have said before, "The continued vitality of the common law . . . depends upon its ability to reflect contemporary community values and ethics."

The assumption of landlord-tenant law, derived from feudal property law, that a lease primarily conveyed to the tenant an interest in land may have been reasonable in a rural, agrarian society; it may continue to be reasonable in some leases involving farming or commercial land. In these cases, the value of the lease to the tenant is the land itself. But in the case of the modern apartment dweller, the value of the lease is that it gives him a place to live. The city dweller who seeks to lease an apartment on the third floor of a tenement has little interest in the land 30 or 40 feet below, or even in the bare right to possession within the four walls of his apartment. When American city dwellers, both rich and poor, seek "shelter" today, they seek a well known package of goods and services — a package which includes not merely walls and ceilings, but also adequate heat, light and ventilation, serviceable plumbing facilities, secure windows and doors, proper sanitation, and proper maintenance.

Some courts have realized that certain of the old rules of property law governing leases are inappropriate for today's transactions. In order to reach results more in accord with the legitimate expectations of the parties and the standards of the community, courts have been gradually introducing more modern precepts of contract law in interpreting leases.

In our judgment the trend toward treating leases as contracts is wise and well considered. Our holding in this case reflects a belief that leases of urban dwelling units should be interpreted and construed like any other contract.

III

Modern contract law has recognized that the buyer of goods and services in an industrialized society must rely upon the skill and honesty of the supplier to assure that goods and services purchased are of adequate quality. In interpreting most contracts, courts have sought to protect the legitimate expectations of the buyer and have steadily widened the seller's responsibility for the quality of goods and services through implied warranties of fitness and merchantability.

The rigid doctrines of real property law have tended to inhibit the application of implied warranties to transactions involving real estate. Now, however, courts have begun to hold sellers and developers of real property responsible for the quality of their product. For example, builders of new homes have recently been held liable to purchasers for improper construction on the ground that the builders had breached an implied warranty of fitness. In other cases courts have held builders of new homes liable for breach of an implied warranty that all local building regulations had been complied with.

Despite this trend in the sale of real estate, many courts have been unwilling to imply warranties of quality, specifically a warranty of habitability, into leases of apartments. Recent decisions have offered no convincing explanation for their refusal; rather they have relied without discussion upon the old common law rule that the lessor is not obligated to repair unless he covenants to do so in the written lease contract. However, the Supreme Courts of at least two states, in recent and well reasoned opinions, have held landlords to implied warranties of quality in housing leases. *Lemle v. Breeden*, 462 P.2d 470 (Haw. 1969); *Reste Realty Corp. v. Cooper*, 251 A.2d 268 (N.J. 1969). In our judgment, the old no-repair rule cannot coexist with the obligations imposed on the landlord by a typical modern housing code, and must be abandoned in favor of an implied warranty of habitability. In the District of Columbia, the standards of this warranty are set out in the Housing Regulations.

IV

A

In our judgment the common law itself must recognize the landlord's obligation to keep his premises in a habitable condition. This conclusion is compelled by three separate considerations. First, we believe that the old rule was based on certain factual assumptions which are no longer true; on its own terms, it can no longer be justified.

Second, we believe that the consumer protection cases discussed above require that the old rule be abandoned in order to bring residential landlord-tenant law into harmony with the principles on which those cases rest. Third, we think that the nature of today's urban housing market also dictates abandonment of the old rule.

The common law rule absolving the lessor of all obligation to repair originated in the early Middle Ages. Such a rule was perhaps well suited to an agrarian economy; the land was more important than whatever small living structure was included in the leasehold, and the tenant farmer was fully capable of making repairs himself. These historical facts were the basis on which the common law constructed its rule; they also provided the necessary prerequisites for its application.

Court decisions in the late 1800's began to recognize that the factual assumptions of the common law were no longer accurate in some cases. For example, the common law, since it assumed that the land was the most important part of the leasehold, required a tenant to pay rent even if any building on the land was destroyed. Faced with such a rule and the ludicrous results it produced, in 1863 the New York Court of Appeals declined to hold that an upper story tenant was obliged to continue paying rent after his apartment building burned down. The court simply pointed out that the urban tenant had no interest in the land, only in the attached building.

These as well as other similar cases demonstrate that some courts began some time ago to question the common law's assumptions that the land was the most important feature of a leasehold and that the tenant could feasibly make any necessary repairs himself. Where those assumptions no longer reflect contemporary housing patterns, the courts have created exceptions to the general rule that landlords have no duty to keep their premises in repair.

It is overdue for courts to admit that these assumptions are no longer true with regard to all urban housing. Today's urban tenants, the vast majority of whom live in multiple dwelling houses, are interested, not in the land, but solely in "a house suitable for occupation." Furthermore, today's city dweller usually has a single, specialized skill unrelated to maintenance work; he is unable to make repairs like the "jack-of-all-trades" farmer who was the common law's model of the lessee. Further, unlike his agrarian predecessor who often remained on one piece of land for his entire life, urban tenants today are more mobile than ever before. A tenant's tenure in a specific apartment will often not be sufficient to justify efforts at repairs. In addition, the increasing complexity of today's dwellings renders them much more difficult to repair than the structures of earlier times. In a multiple dwelling repair may require access to equipment and areas in the control of the landlord. Low and middle income tenants, even if they were interested in making repairs, would be unable to obtain any financing for major repairs since they have no long-term interest in the property.

Our approach to the common law of landlord and tenant ought to be aided by principles derived from the consumer protection cases referred to above. In a lease contract, a tenant seeks to purchase from his landlord shelter for a specified period of time. The landlord sells housing as a commercial businessman and has much greater opportunity, incentive and capacity to inspect and maintain the condition of his building. Moreover, the tenant must rely upon the skill and bona fides of his landlord at least as much as a car buyer must rely upon the car manufacturer. In dealing with major problems, such as heating, plumbing, electrical or structural defects, the tenant's position corresponds precisely with "the ordinary consumer who cannot be expected to have the knowledge or capacity or even the opportunity to make adequate inspection of mechanical instrumentalities, like automobiles, and to decide for himself whether they are reasonably fit for the designed purpose." *Henningsen v. Bloomfield Motors, Inc.*, 161 A.2d 69, 78 (N.J. 1960).

Since a lease contract specifies a particular period of time during which the tenant has a right to use his apartment for shelter, he may legitimately expect that the apartment will be fit for habitation for the time period for which it is rented. We point out that in the present cases there is no allegation that appellants' apartments were in poor condition or in violation of the housing code at the commencement of the leases. Since the lessees continue to pay the same rent, they were entitled to expect that the landlord would continue to keep the premises in their beginning condition during the lease term. It is precisely such expectations that the law now recognizes as deserving of formal, legal protection.

Even beyond the rationale of traditional products liability law, the relationship of landlord and tenant suggests further compelling reasons for the law's protection of the tenants' legitimate expectations of quality. The inequality in bargaining power between landlord and tenant has been well documented. Tenants have very little leverage to enforce demands for better housing. Various impediments to competition in the rental housing market, such as racial and class discrimination and standardized form leases, mean that landlords place tenants in a take it or leave it situation. The increasingly severe shortage of adequate housing further increases the landlord's bargaining power and escalates the need for maintaining and improving the existing stock. Finally, the findings by various studies of the social impact of bad housing has led to the realization that poor housing is detrimental to the whole society, not merely to the unlucky ones who must suffer the daily indignity of living in a slum.

Thus we are led by our inspection of the relevant legal principles and precedents to the conclusion that the old common law rule imposing an obligation upon the lessee to repair during the lease term was really never intended to apply to residential urban leaseholds. Contract principles established in other areas of the law provide a more rational framework for the apportionment of landlord-tenant responsibilities; they strongly suggest that a warranty of habitability be implied into all contracts for urban dwellings.

B

We believe, in any event, that the District's housing code requires that a warranty of habitability be implied in the leases of all housing that it covers. The housing code — formally designated the Housing Regulations of the District of Columbia — was established and authorized by the Commissioners of the District of Columbia on August 11, 1955. Since that time, the code has been updated by numerous orders of the Commissioners. The 75 pages of the Regulations provide a comprehensive regulatory scheme setting forth in some detail: (a) the standards which housing in the District of

Columbia must meet; (b) which party, the lessor or the lessee, must meet each standard; and (c) a system of inspections, notifications and criminal penalties. The Regulations themselves are silent on the question of private remedies.

Two previous decisions of this court, however, have held that the Housing Regulations create legal rights and duties enforceable in tort by private parties. The District of Columbia Court of Appeals gave further effect to the Housing Regulations in *Brown v. Southall Realty Co.*, 237 A.2d 834 (D.C. 1968). There the landlord knew at the time the lease was signed that housing code violations existed which rendered the apartment "unsafe and unsanitary." Viewing the lease as a contract, the District of Columbia Court of Appeals held that the premises were let in violation of Sections 2304 and 2501 of the Regulations and that the lease, therefore, was void as an illegal contract. In the light of *Brown*, it is clear not only that the housing code creates privately enforceable duties, but that the basic validity of every housing contract depends upon substantial compliance with the housing code at the beginning of the lease term. The *Brown* court relied particularly upon Section 2501 of the Regulations which provides:

> Every premises accommodating one or more habitations shall be maintained and kept in repair so as to provide decent living accommodations for the occupants. This part of this Code contemplates more than mere basic repairs and maintenance to keep out the elements; its purpose is to include repairs and maintenance designed to make a premises or neighborhood healthy and safe.

By its terms, this section applies to maintenance and repair during the lease term. Under the *Brown* holding, serious failure to comply with this section before the lease term begins renders the contract void. We think it untenable to find that this section has no effect on the contract after it has been signed. To the contrary, by signing the lease the landlord has undertaken a continuing obligation to the tenant to maintain the premises in accordance with all applicable law.

This principle of implied warranty is well established. Courts often imply relevant law into contracts to provide a remedy for any damage caused by one party's illegal conduct.[14]

[T]hat the housing code must be read into housing contracts — a holding also required by the purposes and the structure of the code itself. The duties imposed by the Housing Regulations may not be waived or shifted by agreement if the Regulations specifically place the duty upon the lessor. Criminal penalties are provided if these duties are ignored. This regulatory structure was established by the Commissioners because, in their judgment, the grave conditions in the housing market required serious

---

14. As a general proposition, it is undoubtedly true that parties to a contract intend that applicable law will be complied with by both sides. We recognize, however, that reading statutory provisions into private contracts may have little factual support in the intentions of the particular parties now before us. But, for reasons of public policy, warranties are often implied into contracts by operation of law in order to meet generally prevailing standards of honesty and fair dealing. When the public policy has been enacted into law like the housing code, that policy will usually have deep roots in the expectations and intentions of most people. *See* Costigan, *Implied-in-Fact Contracts and Mutual Assent*, 33 Harv. L. Rev. 376, 383-85 (1920).

action. Yet official enforcement of the housing code has been far from uniformly effective. Innumerable studies have documented the desperate condition of rental housing in the District of Columbia and in the nation.

We therefore hold that the Housing Regulations imply a warranty of habitability, measured by the standards which they set out, into leases of all housing that they cover.

V

In the present cases, the landlord sued for possession for nonpayment of rent. Under contract principles, however, the tenant's obligation to pay rent is dependent upon the landlord's performance of his obligations, including his warranty to maintain the premises in habitable condition. In order to determine whether any rent is owed to the landlord, the tenants must be given an opportunity to prove the housing code violations alleged as breach of the landlord's warranty.

At trial, the finder of fact must make two findings: (1) whether the alleged violations[15] existed during the period for which past due rent is claimed, and (2) what portion, if any or all, of the tenant's obligation to pay rent was suspended by the landlord's breach. If no part of the tenant's rental obligation is found to have been suspended, then a judgment for possession may issue forthwith. On the other hand, if the jury determines that the entire rental obligation has been extinguished by the landlord's total breach, then the action for possession on the ground of nonpayment must fail.[16]

The jury may find that part of the tenant's rental obligation has been suspended but that part of the unpaid back rent is indeed owed to the landlord. In these circumstances, no judgment for possession should issue if the tenant agrees to pay the partial rent found to be due. If the tenant refuses to pay the partial amount, a judgment for possession may then be entered.

Notes and Questions

1. **Common law evolution and the judicial role.** The United States Court of Appeals for the District of Columbia, the federal court to which Judge J. Skelly Wright had been appointed by President Kennedy, regularly heard landlord-tenant matters in the 1960s. In a letter to Professor Edward Rabin, Judge Wright reflected on why there were such significant changes in landlord-tenant law in that period. "I was indeed influenced," Judge Wright noted, "by the fact that, during the nationwide racial turmoil of the sixties and the unrest caused by the injustice of racially selective service in Vietnam, most of the tenants in Washington, D.C. slums were poor and black and most of the landlords were rich and white. There is no doubt in my mind that these conditions

15. The jury should be instructed that one or two minor violations standing alone which do not affect habitability are *de minimis* and would not entitle the tenant to a reduction in rent.

16. As soon as the landlord made the necessary repairs rent would again become due. Our holding, of course, affects only eviction for nonpayment of rent. The landlord is free to seek eviction at the termination of the lease or on any other legal ground.

played a subconscious role in influencing my landlord and tenant decisions." Edward H. Rabin, *The Revolution in Landlord-Tenant Law: Causes and Consequences*, 69 Cornell L. Rev. 517, 549 (1984) (quoting an October 14, 1982 letter from Judge J. Skelly Wright). Were these legitimate considerations to influence Judge Wright? Would it have been possible for a judge sitting in the District of Columbia to rule on landlord-tenant matters at the time without considering them?

Allowing the tenant to raise the landlord's violation of the housing code or analogous failures to provide habitable premises makes eviction proceedings considerably more complicated, drawn out, and expensive. Because of this, the defense seems to contradict the policy underlying summary process statutes, whose purpose was to provide the landlord with relatively expeditious proceedings for eviction of tenants who were violating the terms of the lease. Is the implied warranty of habitability compatible with the policies underlying summary process statutes? If so, how?

It may (or may not) be helpful to note that many states responded to the judicial creation of the implied warranty of habitability by incorporating it into their landlord-tenant legislation. To the extent the implied warranty violated the purpose or intent of the summary process statutes, these legislative enactments explicitly or implicitly amended the summary process procedure by allowing tenants to raise the warranty as a defense to a claim for possession.

Did Judge Wright engage in illegitimate judicial activism to create a new defense to the landlord's claim for possession? Or was the *Javins* decision a legitimate implementation of the policies underlying the housing code?

2. Relation to building and housing codes. Building codes set minimum requirements for a building's structural safety, water and waste systems, mechanical equipment, electrical wiring, and other standards. Housing codes more directly regulate the safety and sanitary conditions of residential buildings, typically addressing requirements for minimum dwelling space, ventilation, and adequate services. These codes are generally administered and enforced by local government agencies. Many housing codes also provide statutory rights to tenants, such as the right to escrow rent while violations are outstanding or even to terminate the lease. *See, e.g.*, Mich. Comp. Laws §125.53; Ohio Rev. Code §5321.07B. If a condition in a rental unit fails to meet the standards of the housing code, a tenant may have distinct rights under her lease and the housing code.

3. Majority rule. The implied warranty of habitability has been adopted in almost all states for residential tenancies. However, there are still a few holdouts. *See, e.g., Harper v. Coleman*, 705 So. 2d 388 (Ala. Civ. App. 1996), *rev'd on other grounds by Ex parte Coleman*, 705 So. 2d 392 (Ala. 1997).

Is the warranty waivable or disclaimable? If so, then it is merely a **presumption** or **default** position that the courts will assume to be the agreement of the parties in the absence of language to the contrary. If the implied warranty is **nondisclaimable** or **nonwaivable**, it constitutes a **compulsory term** in the contract that the parties have no power to alter by agreement. *Javins* provided that "[a]ny private agreement to shift the duties would be illegal and unenforceable." 428 F.2d at 1082 n.58. This position is supported in most jurisdictions by statute or common law. *See, e.g., Hilder v. St. Peter*, 478 A.2d 202, 210 (Vt. 1984); Mass. Gen. Laws ch. 186, §14.

Some states measure the landlord's obligations by reference to state or local housing codes, holding that the warranty is breached when the landlord fails to comply with applicable building code provisions so as to materially impair health and safety. Other courts, however, have measured the landlord's obligations independently of the applicable housing code, holding that landlords have an obligation to conform with "general community standards of suitability for occupancy." Robert S. Schoshinski, *American Law of Landlord and Tenant* §3:17, at 128 (1980). *See Detling v. Edelbrock*, 671 S.W.2d 265, 270 (Mo. 1984) (habitability to be judged by community standards, including but not limited to local housing codes). Examples of problems that are likely to violate the implied warranty include lack of heat or hot water, broken windows, pest infestation, and leaky roofs.

If a landlord fails to provide a necessary service, such as heat or hot water, does the tenant have an immediate right to a rent reduction when the problem occurs to compensate for the lowered rental value of the premises, or does the landlord have a grace period within which to fix the problem? Many courts hold that the implied warranty is not violated until the landlord has been notified of the problem and has a reasonable opportunity to fix it. *Chiodini v. Fox*, 207 S.W.3d 174, 177 (Mo. Ct. App. 2006). However, some courts find a violation the moment the condition occurs, *Knight v. Hallsthammar*, 623 P.2d 268, 273 (Cal. 1981) (breach of warranty existed whether or not landlord had reasonable time to repair defects existing when he purchased the building), and others hold that the violation starts when the landlord is notified, *Berman & Sons, Inc. v. Jefferson*, 396 N.E.2d 981, 985-986 (Mass. 1979) (breach occurred when landlord received notice of lack of heat and hot water, even though he promptly fixed the problem). Which approach is better?

For commercial leases, most courts have adopted the modern view that the covenants in commercial leases are dependent rather than independent; some, however, have retained the older view that they are independent. *Compare Wesson v. Leone Enterprises, Inc.*, 774 N.E.2d 611 (Mass. 2002) (covenants in commercial lease are dependent), *with Universal Communications Network, Inc. v. 229 West 28th Owner, LLC*, 926 N.Y.S.2d 479, 480 (N.Y. App. Div. 2011) (covenants in commercial lease independent unless lease terms state otherwise). On the other hand, while a few states find an implied warranty of suitability for intended purposes to commercial leases, *e.g., Davidow v. Inwood N. Professional Group*, 747 S.W.2d 373 (Tex. 1988), most still do not do so, holding that commercial leases have no implied warranties unless they state so explicitly. *Pinzon v. A & G Props.*, 874 A.2d 347, 351 (D.C. 2005); *Propst v. McNeill*, 932 S.W.2d 766 (Ark. 1996); *B.W.S. Investments v. Mid-Am Restaurant, Inc.*, 459 N.W.2d 759 (N.D. 1990). And those few states that do recognize warranties for commercial leases make them disclaimable. *See Gym-N-I Playgrounds, Inc. v. Snider*, 220 S.W.2d 905 (Tex. 2007). Does it make sense to distinguish commercial from residential leases in terms of the expectations of the parties and the other grounds Judge Wright discussed in *Javins*?

4. Remedies. Various remedies are available to vindicate the tenant's rights under the implied warranty of habitability. In most states, the remedies available to tenants come from a combination of common law doctrines and specific statutory provisions, some of which may explicitly modify or limit common law remedies. *See* URLTA §§4.104-4.105. The most important remedies are discussed below.

a. Rescission, or the right to move out before the end of the lease term. The landlord's violation of his contractual obligation to provide a habitable apartment entitles the tenant to stop performance of her contractual obligations. Thus, the tenant may repudiate the contract and move out before the end of the lease term without being liable for rent for the months remaining on the lease. This is the case when breach of the warranty of habitability results in a material change in housing conditions even when that change would not amount to constructive eviction. *Wesson v. Leone Enterprises, Inc., supra* (finding this result in the case of a commercial lease). Suppose the tenant moves out five months before the end of the lease term, and the landlord sues the tenant for the remaining five months' rent. If the tenant can show that the landlord violated the implied warranty of habitability, then the tenant has a defense to the landlord's claim for the remaining rent.

b. Rent withholding. If the landlord breaches the implied warranty of habitability, the tenant ordinarily has the right to stop paying rent and continue living in the premises. If the landlord sues the tenant for back rent owed, the tenant may raise the violation of the warranty as a defense to the claim for back rent. If the landlord has breached the implied warranty, then the tenant's failure to pay rent does not constitute a breach of the tenant's contractual obligations; rather, the tenant had a legal right to stop paying rent under the circumstances. This distinguishes the implied warranty of habitability from constructive eviction, which ordinarily requires the tenant to move out to become entitled to stop paying rent before the end of the lease term.

If the landlord sues the tenant for possession on the grounds of nonpayment of rent, the tenant can raise the violation of the warranty as a defense to the eviction proceedings. If the defense is established, the landlord will not be allowed to evict the tenant, who will be able to continue living in the apartment.

It is advisable for tenants who are contemplating rent withholding to determine whether any statutes regulate their ability to withhold rent. These statutes may, for example, require that the tenant give notice to the landlord of the defect in the premises before the tenant is entitled to withhold rent. They may also limit rent withholding to situations in which the tenant has verified the complaint by calling a local housing inspector to document the existence and seriousness of the housing code violation.

It is also advisable for tenants who stop paying rent to the landlord to deposit the usual rental amount in a separate account, called an **escrow** account. If it turns out that the tenant was not entitled to withhold rent, the court will order the tenant to pay back rent to the landlord. If the tenant is unable to pay this back rent within a reasonable period of time, the tenant can be evicted. It is therefore advisable for the tenant to save, rather than spend, the money that would otherwise be going to the landlord as the monthly rent. Some states may have statutes requiring tenants to make rental payments to an escrow account. In the alternative, these statutes may allow the landlord to go to court for an order requiring the tenant to pay the rent into an escrow account held by the court clerk pending adjudication.

c. Rent abatement. When the landlord violates the implied warranty of habitability, the tenant ordinarily is entitled to a reduction in the rent, also known as **rent abatement**. The tenant can sue the landlord for a declaratory judgment that the landlord has violated the implied warranty of habitability and ask the court to order the landlord to reimburse the tenant for all or a portion of the rent previously paid to the landlord during the period of the violation.

Usually, however, the tenant withholds rent, waits to be sued by the landlord for back rent or possession, then argues that the rent should be abated for the period of the violation. When the case is adjudicated, the court ordinarily will determine what, if any, portion of the rent withheld should be paid back to the landlord. If the violation of the implied warranty is quite serious, the landlord may get nothing for the period of the violation. If the violation is less serious, the court may rule that the tenant is obligated to pay a portion of the rent, such as 25 or 50 percent.

The amount of the rent deduction depends on the test used in the jurisdiction. Some states apply a **fair market value** test. The amount of rent owed to the landlord during the period of the violation is based on the fair market value of the premises "as is" or with the defect. Most states simply reduce the rent by a percentage amount that reflects the seriousness of the violation and the amount of discomfort experienced by the tenant.

d. Repair and deduct. The tenant may be able to pay for needed repairs herself and then deduct the cost of the repairs from the rent paid to the landlord. Local statutes may regulate this practice by limiting the amount deducted or the kinds of repairs allowed.

e. Injunctive relief, or specific performance. Some states, by statute or common law, allow tenants to bring a lawsuit against the landlord for an injunction ordering the landlord to comply with the housing code by making needed repairs.

f. Administrative remedies. Finally, many states provide for administrative remedies. The local housing code may include procedures for enforcement by local housing inspectors. For example, the aggrieved tenant may be able to call the local housing inspector to ask for a rapid inspection of the apartment. If the inspector finds material violations of the housing code, the inspector may then contact the landlord herself and order repairs to be made. If the landlord fails to make repairs, the inspector may be empowered to bring a court action for injunctive relief, ordering the landlord to comply with the housing code. The inspector may also seek civil damages against the landlord as provided by statute; these damages are paid to the state rather than to the tenant.

g. Criminal penalties. Building codes may provide for criminal penalties, including fines and imprisonment, for landlords who fail to fix dangerous and unlawful conditions in their apartment buildings. Judges have even ordered recalcitrant landlords to live for a period of time in one of their substandard buildings as punishment for continued and unconscionable violations of the law. Luz Delgado, *Landlord Forced to Live in His Decrepit Property,* Boston Globe, June 10, 1992, at 50.

h. Compensatory damages. In most cases, tenants raise the implied warranty of habitability as a defense to claims by landlords for back rent or possession. Sometimes, however, tenants bring claims for compensatory damages against landlords for violation of the implied warranty either as independent lawsuits or as counterclaims to landlord suits. A claim for damages may seek an amount of money that exceeds the rent rather than merely a reduction in the rent or reimbursement for some of the rent already paid. *See Hilder v. St. Peter, supra* (tenant claim for damages). Damages might exceed the amount of the rent if the violation harms valuable personal property of the tenant, such as the expensive musical equipment owned by the tenant in *Minjak* (*see* §4.1, above), or if the tenant seeks reimbursement for the costs of staying in a hotel while the premises were uninhabitable. Ordinarily, however, courts are likely to assume that a judgment for breach of the duty of habitability cannot exceed the agreed-upon rent on the ground that the rental amount constitutes the value of what was lost by the tenant.

Damages for personal injury may require a showing of negligence on the part of the landlord, which may or may not be present in the context of a violation of the implied warranty. This issue, as well as the question of damages for infliction of severe emotional distress, is discussed below in §4.4.

5. Natural disasters and other events beyond a landlord's control. In *Park West Management Corp. v. Mitchell,* 391 N.E.2d 1288 (1979), a 17-day strike by an apartment complex owner's staff interrupted maintenance and left piles of rotting garbage, which created conditions so serious that the New York City Department of Health declared a health emergency. Some tenants withheld rent for the period of the strike and when the landlord sued for nonpayment, one tenant asserted the implied warranty of habitability as a defense. The New York Court of Appeals agreed with the tenant that the landlord was responsible for conditions in the complex notwithstanding the strike, holding that "conditions occasioned by . . . acts of third parties or natural disaster are within the scope of the warranty." *Id.* at 1294.

There is a general consensus among scientists that climate change is likely increasing the frequency and intensity of certain weather-related events such as extreme coastal high water, although there remain significant questions of measurement. *See* Sonia Seneviratne et al., *Changes in Climate Extremes and Their Impacts on the Natural Physical Environment,* in *Managing the Risks of Extreme Events and Disasters to Advance Climate Change Adaptation* 178-180 (A Special Report of Working Groups I and II of the Intergovernmental Panel on Climate Change, Cambridge University Press 2012). If this trend continues, questions of liability for natural disaster, and how best to adapt to a changing climate, are likely to loom larger in many areas of property law, including landlord-tenant. *Cf.* John A. Lovett, *Property and Radically Changed Circumstances: Hurricane Katrina and Beyond,* 74 Tenn. L. Rev. 463, 495-510 (2007).

In the wake of Hurricane Sandy in 2012, New York City experienced severe flooding, with many tenants losing electricity, heat, and other essential services. *See* Damon Howard, *Landlord-Tenant Obligations in the Aftermath of Hurricane Sandy*, 248 N.Y. L.J. 4 (2012). Should the warranty of habitability apply to these kinds of wide-scale disasters? If not, why not? Who is likely to be in a better position to respond, landlords or tenants? Or is another institutional response necessary?

6. **Impact of the implied warranty?** How important is the implied warranty of habitability in practice? The promise of the warranty—and the broader revolution in landlord-tenant law of which it was a part—requires tenants to have the resources and knowledge to assert their rights in litigation. It also requires capable advocates and courts that are institutionally equipped to resolve the often complex questions raised by issues such as failure to repair and landlord retaliation. Indeed, one reason why *Javins* was brought was that a Neighborhood Legal Services Program office was located at Clifton Terrace. *See* Richard H. Chused, *Saunders* (a.k.a. *Javins*) *v. First National Realty Corporation*, in *Property Stories* 136 (Gerald Korngold & Andrew P. Morriss eds. 2d ed. 2009).

Professor David Super argues that formal limitations in the doctrine, notably that tenants who withhold rent in many states must show that they did so solely to contest repair issues and the practice of landlords obtaining protective orders requiring tenants to deposit rent as condition of raising a warranty defense, have undermined the warranty. Super also points to a court system with few resources and a propensity to favor landlords as repeat players as factors in limiting the warranty's impact. *See* David A. Super, *The Rise and Fall of the Implied Warranty of Habitability*, 99 Cal. L. Rev. 389 (2011). How might these shortcomings be remedied? Would our legal system be better off without an affirmative obligation on the part of landlords to maintain habitable premises, even if relatively few tenants are able to succeed in pressing claims in court based on this duty?

7. **Habitability in the *Uniform Residential Landlord and Tenant Act*.** The URLTA codifies a version of the implied warranty of habitability. The excerpts below contain the primary relevant provisions. As you read them, consider the extent to which the provisions track the common law warranty or modify it.

§1.403. Prohibited Provisions in Rental Agreements

(a) A rental agreement may not provide that the tenant:

(1) agrees to waive or forego rights or remedies under this Act;

(2) authorizes any person to confess judgment on a claim arising out of the rental agreement;

(3) agrees to pay the landlord's attorney's fees; or

(4) agrees to the exculpation or limitation of any liability of the landlord arising under law or to indemnify the landlord for that liability or the costs connected therewith.

(b) A provision prohibited by subsection (a) included in a rental agreement is unenforceable. If a landlord deliberately uses a rental agreement containing provisions known by him to be prohibited, the tenant may recover in addition to his actual damages an amount up to [3] months' periodic rent and reasonable attorney's fees.

§1.404. Separation of Rents and Obligations to Maintain Property Forbidden

A rental agreement, assignment, conveyance, trust deed, or security instrument may not permit the receipt of rent free of the obligation to comply with Section 2.104(a).

§2.104. Landlord to Maintain Premises

(a) A landlord shall

(1) comply with the requirements of applicable building and housing codes materially affecting health and safety;

(2) make all repairs and do whatever is necessary to put and keep the premises in a fit and habitable condition;

(3) keep all common areas of the premises in a clean and safe condition;

(4) maintain in good and safe working order and condition all electrical, plumbing, sanitary, heating, ventilating, air-conditioning, and other facilities and appliances, including elevators, supplied or required to be supplied by him;

(5) provide and maintain appropriate receptacles and conveniences for the removal of ashes, garbage, rubbish, and other waste incidental to the occupancy of the dwelling unit and arrange for their removal; and

(6) supply running water and reasonable amounts of hot water at all times and reasonable heat [between [October 1] and [May 1]] except where the building that includes the dwelling unit is not required by law to be equipped for that purpose, or the dwelling unit is so constructed that heat or hot water is generated by an installation within the exclusive control of the tenant and supplied by a direct public utility connection.

(b) If the duty imposed by paragraph (1) of subsection (a) is greater than any duty imposed by any other paragraph of that subsection, the landlord's duty shall be determined by reference to paragraph (1) of subsection (a).

(c) The landlord and tenant of a single family residence may agree in writing that the tenant perform the landlord's duties specified in paragraphs (5) and (6) of subsection (a) and also specified repairs, maintenance tasks, alterations, and remodeling, but only if the transaction is entered into in good faith.

(d) The landlord and tenant of any dwelling unit other than a single family residence may agree that the tenant is to perform specified repairs, maintenance tasks, alterations, or remodeling only if

(1) the agreement of the parties is entered into in good faith and is set forth in a separate writing signed by the parties and supported by adequate consideration;

(2) the work is not necessary to cure noncompliance with subsection (a)(1) of this section; and

(3) the agreement does not diminish or affect the obligation of the landlord to other tenants in the premises.

§3.101. Tenant to Maintain Dwelling Unit

A tenant shall

(1) comply with all obligations primarily imposed upon tenants by applicable provisions of building and housing codes materially affecting health and safety;

(2) keep that part of the premises that he occupies and uses as clean and safe as the condition of the premises permit;

(3) dispose from his dwelling unit all ashes, garbage, rubbish, and other waste in a clean and safe manner;

(4) keep all plumbing fixtures in the dwelling unit or used by the tenant as clear as their condition permits;

(5) use in a reasonable manner all electrical, plumbing, sanitary, heating, ventilating, air-conditioning, and other facilities and appliances including elevators in the premises;

(6) not deliberately or negligently destroy, deface, damage, impair, or remove any part of the premises or knowingly permit any person to do so; and

(7) conduct himself and require other persons on the premises with his consent to conduct themselves in a manner that will not disturb his neighbors' peaceful enjoyment of the premises.

§4.101. Noncompliance by the Landlord in General

(a) Except as provided in this Act, if there is a material noncompliance by the landlord with the rental agreement or a noncompliance with Section 2.104 materially affecting health and safety, the tenant may deliver a written notice to the landlord specifying the acts and omissions constituting the breach and that the rental agreement will terminate upon a date not less than [30] days after receipt of the notice if the breach is not remedied in [14] days, and the rental agreement shall terminate as provided in the notice subject to the following:

(1) If the breach is remedial by repairs, the payment of damages or otherwise and the landlord adequately remedies the breach before the date specified in the notice, the rental agreement shall not terminate by reason of the breach.

(2) If substantially the same act or omission which constituted a prior noncompliance of which notice was given recurs within [6] months, the tenant may terminate the rental agreement upon at least [14 days'] written notice specifying the breach and the date of termination of the rental agreement.

(3) The tenant may not terminate for a condition caused by the deliberate or negligent act or omission of the tenant, a member of his family, or other person on the premises with his consent.

(b) Except as provided in this Act, the tenant may recover actual damages and obtain injunctive relief for noncompliance by the landlord with the rental agreement or Section 2.104. If the landlord's noncompliance is willful the tenant may recover reasonable attorney's fees.

(c) The remedy provided in subsection (b) is in addition to any right of the tenant arising under Section 4.101(a).

(d) If the rental agreement is terminated, the landlord shall return all security recoverable by the tenant under Section 2.101 and all prepaid rent.

§4.103. Self-Help for Minor Defects

(a) If the landlord fails to comply with the rental agreement or Section 2.104, and the reasonable cost of compliance is less than [$100], or an amount equal to [one-half] the periodic rent, whichever amount is greater, the tenant may recover damages for the breach under Section 4.101(b) or may notify the landlord of his intention to correct the condition at the landlord's expense. If the landlord fails to comply within [14] days after being notified by the tenant in writing or as promptly as conditions require in case of emergency, the tenant may cause the work to be done in a workmanlike manner and, after submitting to the landlord an itemized statement, deduct from his rent the actual and reasonable cost or the fair and reasonable value of the work, not exceeding the amount specified in this subsection.

(b) A tenant may not repair at the landlord's expense if the condition was caused by the deliberate or negligent act or omission of the tenant, a member of his family, or other person on the premises with his consent.

§4.104. Wrongful Failure to Supply Heat, Water, Hot Water, or Essential Services

(a) If contrary to the rental agreement or Section 2.104 the landlord willfully or negligently fails to supply heat, running water, hot water, electric, gas, or other essential service, the tenant may give written notice to the landlord specifying the breach and may

(1) take reasonable and appropriate measures to secure reasonable amounts of heat, hot water, running water, electric, gas, and other essential service during the period of the landlord's noncompliance and deduct their actual and reasonable cost from the rent; or

(2) recover damages based upon the diminution in the fair rental value of the dwelling unit; or

(3) procure reasonable substitute housing during the period of the landlord's noncompliance, in which case the tenant is excused from paying rent for the period of the landlord's noncompliance.

(b) In addition to the remedy provided in paragraph (3) of subsection (a) the tenant may recover the actual and reasonable cost or fair and reasonable value of the substitute housing not in excess of an amount equal to the periodic rent, and in any case under subsection (a) reasonable attorney's fees.

(c) If the tenant proceeds under this section, he may not proceed under Section 4.101 or Section 4.103 as to that breach.

(d) Rights of the tenant under this section do not arise until he has given notice to the landlord or if the condition was caused by the deliberate or negligent act or omission of the tenant, a member of his family, or other person on the premises with his consent.

§4.105. Landlord's Noncompliance as Defense to Action for Possession or Rent

(a) In an action for possession based upon nonpayment of the rent or in an action for rent when the tenant is in possession, the tenant may [counterclaim] for any amount he may recover under the rental agreement or this Act. In that event the court from time to time may order the tenant to pay into court all or part of the rent accrued and thereafter accruing, and shall determine the amount due to each party. The party to whom a net amount is owed shall be paid first from the money paid into court, and the balance by the other party. If no rent remains due after application of this section, judgment shall be entered for the tenant in the action for possession. If the defense or counterclaim by the tenant is without merit and is not raised in good faith, the landlord may recover reasonable attorney's fees.

(b) In an action for rent when the tenant is not in possession, he may [counterclaim] as provided in subsection (a) but is not required to pay any rent into court.

Problems

1. Assume your state has adopted the URLTA and imposes a warranty of habitability on residential tenancies but imposes no implied warranty of habitability or suitability in commercial tenancies. Assume the same facts as in *Minjak*. The tenants rent a loft — a large open space — pursuant to a written agreement entitled "Commercial Lease," stating that the premises are leased for "commercial purposes." The landlord knows that the tenants will be using the space for work purposes, storing and using equipment to make electronic music, but the landlord knows also that the tenants intend to live in the space, treating it as their residence. The landlord fails to maintain the premises in a safe condition, allowing hazardous conditions — such as flooding in the tenants' apartment caused by the operation of a health club with jacuzzis upstairs, the presence of huge clouds of dust caused by the landlord's renovation work in common areas, and the formation of holes in the stairway — to develop unchecked. Two questions arise.

   a. How would the courts interpret the lease — as a residential lease, a commercial lease, or a mixed residential/commercial lease?

   b. If the courts interpret the lease as a commercial or a mixed residential/commercial lease, and the tenants are using the space as their residence, is it still subject to the implied warranty of habitability, or does the "commercial" designation constitute an effective waiver by the tenant of the implied warranty?

2. Assume you are in a jurisdiction that has adopted the URLTA making the implied warranty of habitability nondisclaimable in residential leaseholds (*see* §§1.403, 1.404) but has refused to adopt §2.104(d). The legislature is considering a proposed amendment to allow tenants to waive the protections of the implied warranty, possibly by deleting §1.404 from the statute. This does not mean that the landlord would be relieved of the obligation to comply with the relevant provisions of the housing code, which regulates the conditions in rental housing. Rather, the tenant would not be able to raise the landlord's failure to maintain the apartment in a habitable condition as a defense to a claim for possession or back rent. Thus, by waiving the protection of the implied warranty, the tenant agrees to pay rent regardless of any housing code violations; also, such violations do not entitle the tenant to move out before the end of the lease term and stop paying rent.

The local real estate board, an association of landlords, argues that landlords and tenants should be free to make whatever arrangements they wish. The board argues also that continued payment of the rent is essential to provide the landlord funds to pay for repairs to the apartment. The local tenants' association, on the other hand, argues that the tenant's right to withhold rent if the landlord fails to maintain the apartment in a habitable condition is the tenant's most powerful—and perhaps her only *effective*—way to induce recalcitrant landlords to comply with the housing code.

Suppose you are testifying before a legislative committee on the proposed amendment to the statute.

a. What arguments would you make on behalf of the real estate board to allow tenants to waive the protections of the implied warranty of habitability?

b. What arguments would you make on behalf of the tenants' association to make the protections of the implied warranty of habitability nondisclaimable?

3. Tenants living in an apartment in a 20-unit building in New England in the wintertime awake to find that they have no heat. They call the building manager to fix the problem, and he says he will talk to the landlord and call them back. Two hours later, the manager calls to say that the furnace is broken and it is not clear when it will be fixed. The temperature outside the apartment is 30 degrees Fahrenheit and the temperature inside is now about 55 degrees. The tenants then read in the morning newspaper that the landlord, who owns ten buildings in the surrounding area, is in financial straits and may be forced to declare bankruptcy. The tenants call you for advice. What rights do they have under the URLTA, and how should they proceed? As the landlord's lawyer, what advice would you give?

§4.3 Retaliatory Eviction

Hillview Associates v. Bloomquist

440 N.W.2d 867 (Iowa 1989)

JAMES H. ANDREASEN, Justice.

Gracious Estates Mobile Home Park (Gracious Estates) is located in Des Moines. It is owned by Hillview Associates (Hillview), a partnership based in California. The general partner of Hillview is William Cavanaugh, a resident of California. Management of Gracious Estates has been delegated to a company known as Tandem Management Services, Inc. (Tandem), also owned by Cavanaugh and the other general partners of Hillview. Tandem employed Kathy Nitz as a regional manager, Gennie Smith as park manager and Doug Cavanaugh as property manager at Gracious Estates.

In January 1987 tenants at Gracious Estates began to meet informally to discuss their concerns over the physical condition of the trailer court and recent increases in rent. On January 28, 1987, the first meeting of a tenant's association was held in the clubhouse of Gracious Estates, and approximately 125 tenants came to the meeting. This meeting resulted in an agenda of specific concerns for the health, safety and quality of living in Gracious Estates. A volunteer leadership committee was established for the association, now known as the Gracious Estates Tenant's Association. In the course of organizing and articulating complaints, tenants contacted the Iowa Attorney General's office and their state representative.

On February 9, 1987, a meeting was held between approximately five members of the association, Ms. Nitz and the park maintenance supervisor. The tenants lodged several complaints at this meeting. This meeting lasted approximately one hour and was relatively calm. The relationship between the tenant's association and the management of Gracious Estates began to erode. The tenants were frustrated with the lack of action taken by the management of Gracious Estates.

A meeting with Ms. Nitz was scheduled for April 15, 1987. A meeting did occur on April 15 between representatives of the tenants association and Ms. Nitz. This "meeting" was held in Nitz's private office and lasted approximately five to ten minutes. The discussion quickly disintegrated into a shouting match which climaxed in a physical altercation between Nitz and one of the tenants, Kimber Davenport.

After this meeting, the management of the trailer court served ultimatums on all tenants requiring them to sign the park rules or be evicted. Management also sought out tenants not in the tenant's association in an attempt to start a rival tenants' association favorable to management. On April 22, 1987, Hillview served a thirty-day notice of termination on the following tenants: Tom and Sandra Bloomquist; Kimber and Reva Davenport; Richard and Nellie Swartz; and Donald and Judith Ray. At least one member of each of these married couples was present at the April 15 meeting. A former secretary of Ms. Nitz testified that "they'd [management] get these now, and then the rest later. That way it wouldn't look like they were doing it because they were members of an association."

Hillview later discovered that the thirty-day notice did not provide specific grounds for termination as required by statute. On June 4, 1987, Hillview again served each of these tenants with a notice of termination which provided a sixty-day period for them to leave. At the end of the sixty-day period, the tenants remained in possession. Hillview then served three-day notices to quit. The tenants remained in the park and Hillview filed a forcible entry and detainer action.

In this summary action for forcible entry and detainer, the tenants raised the defenses of retaliatory eviction and waiver.

III

The Iowa Legislature adopted remedial legislation for mobile home tenants in the *Mobile Home Parks Residential Landlord and Tenant Act.* Iowa Code §562B.32 (1987).

[The Act] prohibits retaliatory conduct by landlords:

> 1. Except as provided in this section, a landlord shall not retaliate by increasing rent or decreasing services or by bringing or threatening to bring an action for possession or by failing to renew a rental agreement after any of the following:
>
> (a) The tenant has complained to a governmental agency charged with responsibility for enforcement of a building or housing code of a violation applicable to the mobile

> home park materially affecting health and safety. For this subsection to apply, a complaint filed with a governmental body must be in good faith.
>
> (b) The tenant has complained to the landlord of a violation under section 562B.16 [requiring landlords to maintain the premises in habitable condition].
>
> (c) The tenant has organized or become a member of a tenant's union or similar organization.
>
> (d) For exercising any of the rights and remedies pursuant to this chapter.
>
> 2. If the landlord acts in violation of subsection 1 of this section, the tenant has a defense in an action for possession. In an action by or against the tenant, evidence of a complaint within six months prior to the alleged act of retaliation creates a presumption that the landlord's conduct was in retaliation. The presumption does not arise if the tenant made the complaint after notice of termination of the rental agreement. For the purpose of this subsection, "presumption" means that the trier of fact must find the existence of the fact presumed unless and until evidence is introduced which would support a finding of its nonexistence.
>
> 3. Notwithstanding subsections 1 and 2 of this section, a landlord may bring an action for possession if either of the following occurs:
>
> (a) The violation of the applicable building or housing code was caused primarily by lack of reasonable care by the tenant or other person in the household or upon the premises with the tenant's consent.
>
> (b) The tenant is in default of rent three days after rent is due.

Iowa Code §562B.32 (1987).

IV

In 1968 the United States Court of Appeals for the District of Columbia held that a landlord was not free to evict a tenant in retaliation for the tenant's report of housing code violations. As a matter of statutory construction and for reasons of public policy, such an eviction would not be permitted. *Edwards v. Habib*, 397 F.2d 687, 699 (D.C. Cir. 1968). However, a tenant who proves a retaliatory purpose is not entitled to remain in possession in perpetuity. If the illegal purpose is dissipated, the landlord can, in the absence of legislation or a binding contract, evict the tenant for legitimate reasons or even for no reason at all. The question of permissible or impermissible purpose is one of fact for the court or jury.

In 1979 the Iowa Legislature adopted the *Uniform Residential Landlord and Tenant Act* and the *Mobile Home Parks Residential Landlord and Tenant Act.* Both acts prohibit retaliatory conduct. *See* Iowa Code §§562A.36 & 562B.32. In an action by or against the tenant, evidence of a complaint within six months prior to the alleged act of retaliation creates a presumption that the landlord's conduct was in retaliation. For the purpose of the statutory subsection "presumption" means the trier of fact must find the existence of the fact presumed unless and until evidence is introduced which could support a finding of its nonexistence.

As a matter of statutory construction, we hold this statutory presumption imposes a burden upon the landlord to produce evidence of legitimate nonretaliatory reasons to overcome the presumption. The tenant may then be afforded a full and fair opportunity to demonstrate pretext. The burden of proof of the affirmative defense of retaliatory termination of the lease remains upon the tenant. If the landlord does not meet the burden of producing evidence of a nonretaliatory reason for termination, the statutory presumption would compel a finding of retaliatory lease termination. If the landlord does produce evidence of a nonretaliatory purpose for terminating the lease, then the fact-finder must determine from all the evidence whether a retaliatory termination has been proven by a preponderance of the evidence. Although the burden of producing evidence shifts to the landlord once the tenant has offered evidence of a complaint within six months of the notice of termination, the burden of proof remains with the tenant to establish the affirmative defense.

In deciding whether a tenant has established a defense of retaliatory eviction, we consider the following factors, among others, tending to show the landlord's primary motivation was not retaliatory.

(a) The landlord's decision was a reasonable exercise of business judgment;

(b) The landlord in good faith desires to dispose of the entire leased property free of all tenants;

(c) The landlord in good faith desires to make a different use of the leased property;

(d) The landlord lacks the financial ability to repair the leased property and therefore, in good faith, wishes to have it free of any tenant;

(e) The landlord was unaware of the tenant's activities which were protected by statute;

(f) The landlord did not act at the first opportunity after he learned of the tenant's conduct;

(g) The landlord's act was not discriminatory. *Restatement (Second) of Property* §14.8 comment f (1977).

V

We find the tenants have offered substantial evidence of a retaliatory termination. They were active, vocal members of a newly-formed tenant's association. They made good faith complaints about the landlord's failure to maintain the mobile home park in a clean and safe condition. An employee of the landlord testified that certain leases were terminated because the tenants were active members of the tenants association. In response, the landlord has offered substantial evidence of a nonretaliatory reason for termination. The tenants who actively participated in the disturbance and physical abuse of Ms. Nitz during the April 15 meeting were notified of lease termination, other active members of the association were not.

According to Ms. Nitz, the tenants surrounded her desk on April 15 and implored her to call California. One of the tenants, Kimber Davenport, placed both hands in the middle of Nitz's desk, leaned over the desk, shouted that Nitz had a "truck-driver's mentality" and that she wasn't a lady. Nitz asked the tenants to leave and all but Mr. and Mrs. Rathburn refused. Ms. Nitz then left her office and, after a cooling-off period, returned and demanded that the other tenants leave the office. She again demanded that they leave and threatened to call the police if they did not. The tenants began to leave. Mr. Davenport was the last to leave, and as he left he continued the verbal abuse of Ms. Nitz and gestured to her with his finger close to her face. According to Ms. Nitz, she pushed his finger away and Davenport struck her in the face, knocking her into a doorjamb. At that point, another tenant, Don Carlson, entered the room and physically removed Davenport.

Davenport's testimony concerning the April 15 meeting was very different from Ms. Nitz's testimony. Davenport testified at the forcible entry and detainer trial that he was polite and reasonable during this meeting. Further, he claimed that he did not place his hands on Nitz's desk, shout at her, or strike her. Rather, he testified that he pushed her away with an open hand. Davenport's testimony loses credibility when it is compared with his prior testimony in a criminal case concerning this incident. In his prior testimony, Davenport admitted that he placed his hands in the middle of Ms. Nitz's desk, shouted insults at her, and struck her.

Several conclusions can fairly be drawn from the evidence. First, the April 15 meeting was initiated by members of a tenant's association in an attempt to address grievances with the management of the trailer court. This meeting disintegrated into a shouting match. The tenants were told to leave three times and they left only after a threat to call the police. We, like the trial court, conclude that Davenport did strike Ms. Nitz in the face as he left the room. He was the principal agitator, quickly leaving the topic of improvements for the park and launching into a personal attack on Ms. Nitz.

Under Iowa law, tenants may organize and join a tenant's association free from fear of retaliation. The tenants may participate in activities designed to legitimately coerce a landlord into taking action to improve living conditions. The presumption of retaliatory eviction in Iowa Code §562B.32 protects legitimate activities of tenant unions or similar organizations.

The resolution of landlord-tenant grievances will normally involve some conflicts and friction between the parties. Arguments, even heated arguments with raised voices, cannot fairly be described as being in violation of proper conduct. There is, however, a limit to the type of conduct that will be tolerated. Kimber Davenport crossed beyond the line of legitimate behavior. Davenport has failed to establish by a preponderance of the evidence that the termination of his lease was retaliatory. The termination of the Davenports' lease was legitimate and thus cannot be said to be retaliation arising from his complaints or union activities.

Although the statutory presumption of retaliation has been neutralized by the evidence produced by Hillview, we find the evidence of retaliatory eviction concerning tenants Bloomquist, Swartz, and Ray, to be more convincing. Although they were present at the April 15 meeting and did participate in the arguments, they did not encourage or participate in the assault of Ms. Nitz. The landlord's response by an attempted termination of their leases can reasonably be attributed to their active membership in the tenant's organization and in response to legitimate complaints they had made.

We reject Hillview's argument that there must be specific intent to retaliate on the part of Hillview's general partner before the tenants can prevail on a defense of retaliatory eviction. The evidence reveals that the local and regional managers of Gracious

Estates made the decision to evict these tenants. The general partner ratified this decision without direct participation in the decision-making process.

The acts of an agent are attributable to the principal. In this situation, to require specific intent by the general partner of a multi-state real estate business would frustrate the intention of Iowa Code §562B.32. Hillview's interpretation would allow mid-level managers to retaliate against tenant associations and seek refuge by keeping top-level directors uninformed of specific disputes with individual tenants. Tenants Bloomquist, Swartz, and Ray have established by a preponderance of the evidence their affirmative defense of retaliatory eviction. Tenants Davenport have not.

Imperial Colliery Co. v. Fout

373 S.E.2d 489 (W. Va. 1988)

THOMAS B. MILLER, Justice:

Danny H. Fout, the defendant below, appeals a summary judgment dismissing his claim of retaliatory eviction based on the provisions of W. Va. Code §§55-3A-3(g), which is our summary eviction statute. Imperial Colliery had instituted an eviction proceeding and Fout sought to defend against it, claiming that his eviction was in retaliation for his participation in a labor strike.

This case presents two issues: (1) whether a residential tenant who is sued for possession of rental property under W. Va. Code §§55-3A-1, *et seq.*, may assert retaliation by the landlord as a defense, and (2) whether the retaliation motive must relate to the tenant's exercise of a right incidental to the tenancy.

Fout is presently employed by Milburn Colliery Company as a coal miner. For six years, he has leased a small house trailer lot in Burnwell, West Virginia, from Imperial Colliery Company. It is alleged that Milburn and Imperial are interrelated companies. A written lease was signed by Fout and an agent of Imperial in June, 1983. This lease was for a primary period of one month, and was terminable by either party upon one month's notice. An annual rental of $1.00 was payable in advance on January 1 of each year. No subsequent written leases were signed by the parties.

On February 14, 1986, Imperial advised Fout by certified letter that his lease would be terminated as of March 31, 1986. Fout's attorney corresponded with Imperial before the scheduled termination date. He advised that due to various family and monetary problems, Fout would be unable to timely vacate the property. Imperial voluntarily agreed to a two-month extension of the lease. A second letter from Fout's attorney, dated May 27, 1986, recited Fout's personal problems and requested that Imperial's attempts to oust Fout be held "in abeyance" until they were resolved. A check for $1.00 was enclosed to cover the proposed extension. Imperial did not reply.

On June 11, 1986, Imperial sued for possession of the property, pursuant to W. Va. Code §§55-3A-1, *et seq.*, in the Magistrate Court of Kanawha County. Fout answered and removed the suit to the circuit court on June 23, 1986. He asserted as a defense that Imperial's suit was brought in retaliation for his involvement in the United Mine Workers of America and, more particularly, in a selective strike against Milburn. Imperial's retaliatory motive was alleged to be in violation of the First Amendment rights of speech and assembly, and of the *National Labor Relations Act*, 29 U.S.C. §§151, *et seq*. Fout also counter-claimed, seeking an injunction against Imperial and damages for annoyance and inconvenience.

Our initial inquiry is whether retaliation by the landlord may be asserted by the tenant as a defense in a suit under W. Va. Code §55-3A-3(g).

It appears that the first case that recognized retaliatory eviction as a defense to a landlord's eviction proceeding was *Edwards v. Habib*, 397 F.2d 687 (D.C. Cir. 1968). [In that case,] the court reviewed at length the goals sought to be advanced by local sanitary and safety codes. It concluded that to allow retaliatory evictions by landlords would seriously jeopardize the efficacy of the codes. A prohibition against such retaliatory conduct was therefore to be implied, even though the regulations were silent on the matter.

Many states have protected tenant rights either on the *Edwards* theory or have implied such rights from the tenant's right of habitability. Others have utilized statutes analogous to section 5.101 of the *Uniform Residential Landlord and Tenant Act*, 7B U.L.A. 503 (1985),[17] which is now adopted in fifteen jurisdictions. Similar landlord and tenant reform statutes in seventeen other states also provide protection for tenancy-related activities.

Under W. Va. Code §37-6-30, a tenant is, with respect to residential property, entitled to certain rights to a fit and habitable dwelling. In *Teller v. McCoy*, 253 S.E.2d 114 (W. Va. 1978), we spoke at some length of the common law right of habitability which a number of courts had developed to afford protection to the residential tenant. We concluded that these rights paralleled and were spelled out in more detail in W. Va. Code §37-6-30.

The central theme underlying the retaliatory eviction defense is that a tenant should not be punished for claiming the benefits afforded by health and safety statutes passed for his protection. These statutory benefits become a part of his right of habitability. If the right to habitability is to have any meaning, it must enable the tenant to exercise that right by complaining about unfit conditions without fear of reprisal by his landlord.

After the seminal decision in *Edwards*, other categories of tenant activity were deemed to be protected. Such activity was protected against retaliation where it bore a relationship to some legitimate aspect of the tenancy. For example, some cases

17. Section 5.101 of the *Uniform Act* provides, in part:

> (a) Except as provided in this section, a landlord may not retaliate by increasing rent or decreasing services or by bringing or threatening to bring an action for possession after:
>
> (1) the tenant has complained to a governmental agency charged with responsibility for enforcement of a building or housing code of a violation applicable to the premises materially affecting health and safety; or
>
> (2) the tenant has complained to the landlord of a violation [of the requirement to maintain the premises] under Section 2.104; or
>
> (3) the tenant has organized or become a member of a tenant's union or similar organization.

provided protection for attempts by tenants to organize to protect their rights as tenants. Others recognized the right to press complaints directly against the landlord via oral communications, petitions, and "repair and deduct" remedies.

A few courts recognize that even where a tenant's activity is only indirectly related to the tenancy relationship, it may be protected against retaliatory conduct if such conduct would undermine the tenancy relationship. Typical of these cases is *Windward Partners v. Delos Santos*, 577 P.2d 326 (Haw. 1978). There a group of month-to-month tenants gave testimony before a state land use commission in opposition to a proposal to redesignate their farm property from "agricultural" to "urban" uses. The proposal was sponsored by the landlord, a land developer. As a result of coordinated activity by the tenants, the proposal was defeated. Within six months, the landlord ordered the tenants to vacate the property and brought suit for possession.

The Hawaii Supreme Court noted that statutory law provided for public hearings on proposals to redesignate property, and specifically invited the views of the affected tenants. The court determined that the legislative policy encouraging such input would be jeopardized "if . . . [landlords] were permitted to retaliate against . . . tenants for opposing land use changes in a public forum." 577 P.2d at 333.

The Legislature, in giving approval to the retaliation defense, must have intended to bring our State into line with the clear weight of case law and statutory authority outlined above. We accordingly hold that retaliation may be asserted as a defense to a summary eviction proceeding under W. Va. Code §§55-3A-1, *et seq.*, if the landlord's conduct is in retaliation for the tenant's exercise of a right incidental to the tenancy.

Fout seeks to bring this case within the *Windward* line of authority. He argues principally that Imperial's conduct violated a public policy which promotes the rights of association and free speech by tenants. We do not agree, simply because the activity that Fout points to as triggering his eviction was unrelated to the habitability of his premises.

From the foregoing survey of law, we are led to the conclusion that the retaliatory eviction defense must relate to activities of the tenant incidental to the tenancy. First Amendment rights of speech and association unrelated to the tenant's property interest are not protected under a retaliatory eviction defense in that they do not arise from the tenancy relationship. Such rights may, of course, be vindicated on other independent grounds.

Notes and Questions

1. **Retaliatory eviction.** In the famous case of *Robinson v. Diamond Housing Corp.*, 463 F.2d 853 (D.C. Cir. 1972), the landlord, Diamond Housing, had brought an earlier lawsuit against the month-to-month tenant, Mrs. Robinson, for possession on the ground of nonpayment of rent. The landlord lost that lawsuit when the tenant successfully raised the defense of the landlord's violation of the warranty of habitability, *id.* at 858:

> Specifically, Mrs. Robinson introduced evidence showing that large pieces of plaster were missing throughout the house, that there was no step from the front walk to the

front porch, that the front porch was shaky and unsafe, that there was a wall in the back bedroom which was not attached to the ceiling and which moved back and forth when pressed, that nails protruded along the side of the stairway, that there was a pane of glass missing from the living room window, and that the window frame in the kitchen was so far out of position that one could see into the back yard through the space between it and the wall.

The landlord brought a second lawsuit against the tenant, attempting to end the month-to-month tenancy by providing 30 days' notice. (Recall that periodic tenancies renew automatically unless one of the parties notifies the other that it intends to end the relationship.) The landlord hoped to evict Mrs. Robinson not because of nonpayment of rent but simply because the landlord wanted to end the periodic tenancy. The tenant argued that the landlord's attempt to end the periodic tenancy and evict her was in retaliation for her earlier assertion of her legal right to remain in the apartment because of the landlord's breach of the implied warranty of habitability. She argued that the landlord's retaliatory motivation constituted a defense to his claim for possession and that she had the right to continue to possess the property.

The landlord argued that he was unable or unwilling to make the legally required repairs on the premises necessary to put the housing in compliance with the housing code and that he intended to take the apartment off the rental market. If he were not entitled to end the month-to-month tenancy and evict the tenant under these circumstances, he would never be able to do so, and the court would have substantially transferred to the tenant the landlord's possessory rights in the property.

The court held that the tenant could successfully raise the defense of retaliatory eviction under these circumstances. Judge J. Skelly Wright argued, *id.* at 860-868:

> "In large measure, the scope and effectiveness of tenant remedies for substandard housing will be determined by the degree of protection given tenants against retaliatory actions by landlords. If a landlord is free to evict or otherwise harass a tenant who exercises his right to secure better housing conditions, few tenants will use the remedies for fear of being put out on the street." Daniels, *Judicial and Legislative Remedies for Substandard Housing: Landlord-Tenant Law Reform in the District of Columbia*, 59 Geo. L.J. 909, 943 (1971).
>
> The danger stems not from the possibility that landlords might take low-cost units off the market altogether, but rather from the possibility that they will do so selectively in order to "make an example" of a troublesome tenant who has the temerity to assert his legal rights in court.
>
> [However,] Diamond says that it intends to take the unit off the market altogether when Mrs. Robinson leaves — the very thing which this court has suggested a landlord do when he is unwilling or unable to repair the premises. Whatever limitations the law imposes on how it chooses its tenants, Diamond claims an absolute right to choose not to have any tenants.
>
> First, then, it should be noted that the *Edwards* defense deals with the landlord's subjective state of mind — that is, with his motive. If the landlord's actions are motivated by a desire to punish the tenant for exercising his rights or to chill the exercise of similar rights by other tenants, then they are impermissible.

It is commonplace, however, that a jury can judge a landlord's state of mind only by examining its objective manifestations. Thus when the landlord's conduct is "inherently destructive" of tenants' rights, or unavoidably chills their exercise, the jury may, under well recognized principles, presume that the landlord intended this result. An unexplained eviction following successful assertion of a defense [based on the landlord's breach of the implied warranty of habitability] falls within this inherently destructive category and hence gives rise to the presumption. Once the presumption is established, it is then up to the landlord to rebut it by demonstrating that he is motivated by some legitimate business purpose rather than by the illicit motive which would otherwise be presumed. We wish to emphasize, however, that the landlord's desire to remove a tenant who is not paying rent is not such a legitimate purpose. [*Brown v. Southall Realty Co.*, 237 A.2d 834 (D.C. 1968)] and the housing code guarantee the right of a tenant to remain in possession without paying rent when the premises are burdened with substantial housing code violations making them unsafe and unsanitary. The landlord of such premises who evicts his tenant because he will not pay rent is in effect evicting him for asserting his legal right to refuse to pay rent.

It does not follow, however, that mere desire to take the unit off the market is by itself a legitimate business reason which will justify an eviction. Expression of such a desire begs the further question of why the landlord wishes to remove the unit. If he wishes to remove the unit for some sound business reason, then of course he is free to do so. But a landlord who fails to come forward with a substantial business reason for removing a unit from the market — such as, for example, his financial inability to make the necessary repairs — may be presumed to have done so for an illicit reason.

None of this is to say that the landlord may not go out of business entirely if he wishes to do so or that the jury is authorized to inspect his motives if he chooses to commit economic harakiri. There would be severe constitutional problems with a rule of law which required an entrepreneur to remain in business against his will. Thus we hold that the landlord's right to discontinue rental of all his units in no way justifies a partial closing designed to intimidate the remaining tenants.

Judge Roger Robb wrote a blistering dissent, *id.* at 871-872:

I cannot accept the proposition espoused by the majority that when a landlord states under oath and without contradiction that he wishes to remove a housing unit from the market it will be presumed that his reasons are "illicit," unless he is able to prove to the satisfaction of a jury that he is financially unable to make necessary repairs or has some other "substantial business reason" for removing the unit from the market. I find no warrant in law for any such presumption or requirement of proof.

The theory of the majority seems to be that if not an outlaw a landlord is at least a public utility, subject to regulation by the court in conformity with its concept of public convenience and necessity. I reject that notion, which in practical application will commit to the discretion of a jury the management of a landlord's business and property.

The majority suggests that its decision will promote the development of more and better low-cost housing. This reasoning passes my understanding. In my judgment the majority's Draconian treatment of landlords will inevitably discourage investment in housing for rental purposes.

Which position is more convincing?

2. How long may the tenant stay? How long may the tenant stay in the premises if the landlord is denied the right to evict the tenant? Most courts hold that the landlord may not evict the tenant until the landlord can show a legitimate, nonretaliatory business reason for the eviction. They may not refuse to renew a lease (or grant a periodic tenancy in place of a term of years) for a retaliatory reason. However, the Utah Supreme Court criticized this approach. Noting that "we cannot saddle the landlord with a perpetual tenant," and requiring the landlord to show that "his actions are not the result of retaliatory motives" will be a very difficult burden for a landlord to overcome, the court held that the tenant "should be permitted to remain until the landlord has made the repairs required by law." *Building Monitoring System, Inc. v. Paxton*, 905 P.2d 1215, 1219 (Utah 1995). The court held that the tenant may be evicted any time after repairs have been made as long as the tenant is also given "sufficient time, without the pressure normally exerted in a holdover eviction proceeding, to find other suitable housing."

Although the URLTA prohibits retaliatory action by the landlord, *see* §5.101, it does not explain how long the tenant may stay. A number of states have dealt with the issue by statute. Some states expressly apply the retaliatory eviction doctrine to the landlord's refusal to renew a tenancy, including a term of years. D.C. Code §45-2552(a); 765 Ill. Comp. Stat. 720/1; N.J. Stat. §2A:42-10.10(d).

Some states have interpreted their statutes to apply to nonrenewal of a tenancy and not just eviction. *See, e.g., Houle v. Quenneville*, 787 A.2d 1258, 1263 (Vt. 2001) (interpreting 9 Vt. Stat. §4465, Vermont's statutory prohibition against retaliation, to apply to the nonrenewal of a fixed term lease). In contrast, some states have held that their statutes prohibit retaliatory eviction of month-to-month tenants but allow landlords to refuse to renew term-of-years or fixed term leases for retaliatory reasons. *Frenchtown Villa v. Meadors*, 324 N.W.2d 133 (Mich. Ct. App. 1982) (interpreting Mich. Comp. Laws §600.5720). Still other states adopt a middle position, prohibiting retaliatory eviction for a specified time. For example, California prohibits a landlord from retaliating against a tenant for exercising rights protected by the implied warranty for 180 days but allows landlords freedom to seek not to renew a periodic tenancy or to increase the rent or otherwise change the terms of the leasehold after that time. Cal. Civ. Code §1942.5. *Accord*, Conn. Gen. Stat. §47a-20 (prohibiting eviction for six months after a protected act by a tenant). New York has passed a statute that applies the retaliatory eviction doctrine to nonrenewal of a term of years but provides that "a landlord shall not be required . . . to offer a new lease or a lease renewal for a term greater than one year and after such extension of a tenancy for one year shall not be required to further extend or continue such tenancy." N.Y. Real Prop. Law §223-b(2).

3. Tenant remedies, landlord rights. Under URLTA, if a landlord violates the act by retaliating against a tenant, the tenant has several remedies. The tenant may recover possession of the premises, terminate the lease, and recover damages; the tenant also has a defense in any retaliatory action for possession of the premises. URLTA §§4.107, 5.101(b). URLTA, however, provides that a landlord may recover possession if "(1) the violation of the applicable building or housing code was caused primarily by lack of reasonable care by the tenant, a member of his family, or other person on the premises with his consent; or (2) the tenant is in default in rent; or (3) compliance with the applicable building or housing code requires alteration, remodeling, or demolition which would effectively deprive the tenant of use of the dwelling unit." URLTA §5.101(c).

4. Tenant screening. Landlords regularly screen tenants on criteria such as credit scores and criminal records. A substantial industry has emerged providing landlords with information about prospective tenants, and among the information that has become available is whether a tenant has been the subject of an eviction action (regardless of the outcome) or even appeared in housing court. *See* Motoko Rich, *A Blacklist for Renters*, N.Y. Times, Apr. 8, 2004, at F-1. Moreover, even minor disputes with landlords that result in a judgment against a tenant, for example over the amount of rent due, can have a significant impact on a tenant's credit score, even if the judgment is promptly paid. This can, in turn, impact the tenant's future ability not only to rent, but also to obtain a mortgage or any other debt.

If a conflict between a landlord and a tenant may impact a tenant's credit score or place a tenant on a landlord "blacklist," does this undermine tenant protections against retaliation? Should tenants be able to litigate against landlords in a way that would protect their anonymity when they seek to rent again? *Cf.* Lior Jacob Strahilevitz, *Pseudonymous Litigation*, 77 U. Chi. L. Rev. 1239 (2010) (noting that the failure to be able to sue under a pseudonym may deter some litigation).

Problem

A landlord owns five buildings. Two of the buildings, including Building 1, are in Cambridge, Massachusetts. The other buildings are in the nearby towns of Somerville, Arlington, and Brookline. The buildings have old furnaces that do not work well. All the tenants have month-to-month leases. Some of the tenants in each building meet to form a tenants' association to complain to the landlord about inadequate heat and hot water. The landlord promises to fix the problem but does nothing about it. The members of the tenants' association agree to stop paying rent. In Building 1, about half the tenants stop paying rent. In the other buildings, anywhere from 10 percent to 25 percent of the tenants similarly withhold rent.

The landlord responds by suing to evict all the tenants in Building 1 on the ground that the landlord intends to convert the building to nonresidential use as an office building. It is crucial to note that the landlord *does not* ask for possession on the ground that the tenants have breached their leases by not paying rent; they are legally entitled to stop paying rent. Rather, the landlord seeks only to end the periodic tenancies by providing the statutorily required one month's notice.

The tenants respond by raising the defense of retaliatory eviction. They appeal to *Hillview Associates v. Bloomquist* and to *Robinson v. Diamond Housing*, arguing that the landlord has no right to evict tenants if the landlord's *motive* is to retaliate against them for asserting rights guaranteed by the implied warranty of habitability. The landlord responds by arguing that there is an exception in both *Hillview* and *Robinson* for landlords who want to go out of business. The landlord claims that he has an absolute right to convert the building from rental housing to use as an office building, regardless of his motive. The tenants, however, argue that the landlord cannot take advantage of that exception unless the landlord goes out of the rental housing business entirely. Since the landlord is retaining four other buildings, they argue, the defense is not available. They conclude that the landlord is using the eviction of these tenants as a way to intimidate the other tenants and prevent them from complaining to the authorities or withholding rent, thus losing the right to evict them, if their allegations are proven.

What should the court do?

§4.4 Landlord's Tort Liability to Tenants

Strict liability versus negligence. Damages for the landlord's violation of the implied warranty of habitability are generally limited to the amount of the rent or less. Can the tenant sue the landlord for damages that *exceed* the amount of the rent during the period of the violation? This question raises the extent of the landlord's **tort liability** to the tenant for injuries resulting from the landlord's violation of her duty to provide habitable premises. Are landlords liable for injuries to tenants caused by defects in the premises that may or may not result from the landlord's failure to take adequate care in maintaining the habitability of the premises?

Under the traditional rule, landlords were immune from liability to tenants for injuries arising out of the condition of the premises. *See Bowles v. Mahoney*, 202 F.2d 320 (D.C. Cir. 1952). Some states retain this rule. *Isbell v. Commercial Investment Associates*, 644 S.E.2d 72 (Va. 2007). Under the current practice in most states, however, landlords *are* liable to tenants for injuries arising out of the landlord's negligence, including negligent failure to comply with housing codes or the implied warranty of habitability. *E.g., New Haverford Partnership v. Stroot,* 772 A.2d 792 (Del. 2001) (landlord may be liable for negligently caused injury from toxic mold in building).

Should landlords be liable only when tenants can prove that the landlord acted negligently (acting so as to cause a foreseeable and unreasonable risk of harm), or should a strict liability standard apply, making the landlord liable if a defect in the premises caused the plaintiff's injuries, regardless of whether the landlord could have foreseen and prevented the harm by reasonable maintenance? A negligence claim is based on an allegation that the landlord is at fault or has acted unreasonably by not taking proper precautions or investing sufficiently in safety. A strict liability claim is based on the unreasonably dangerous condition of the building or the landlord's failure to comply with the housing code, regardless of whether a reasonable landlord would have known of and corrected the defect.

California adopted a strict liability standard in *Becker v. IRM*, 698 P.2d 116 (Cal. 1985), but overruled *Becker* in *Peterson v. Superior Court*, 899 P.2d 905 (Cal. 1995). In *Becker*, a tenant was injured when he slipped and fell against a shower door made of untempered glass that shattered. The court held that the landlord was strictly liable for damages arising out of a latent defect in the premises.

> Absent disclosure of defects, the landlord in renting the premises makes an implied representation that the premises are fit for use as a dwelling and the representation is ordinarily indispensable to the lease. The tenant purchasing housing for a limited period is in no position to inspect for latent defects in the increasingly complex modern apartment buildings or to bear the expense of repair whereas the landlord is in a much better position to inspect for and repair latent defects. The tenant's ability to inspect is ordinarily substantially less than that of a purchaser of the property.
>
> The tenant renting the dwelling is compelled to rely upon the implied assurance of safety made by the landlord. It is also apparent that the landlord by adjustment of price at the time he acquires the property, by rentals or by insurance is in a better position to bear the costs of injuries due to defects in the premises than the tenants.
>
> In these circumstances, strict liability in tort for latent defects existing at the time of renting must be applied to insure that the landlord who markets the product bears the costs of injuries resulting from the defects "rather than the injured persons who are powerless to protect themselves."
>
> The cost of protecting tenants is an appropriate cost of the enterprise. Within our marketplace economy, the cost of purchasing rental housing is obviously based on the anticipated risks and rewards of the purchase, and thus it may be expected that along with numerous other factors the price of used rental housing will depend in part on the quality of the building and reflect the anticipated costs of protecting tenants, including repairs, replacement of defects and insurance. Further, the landlord after purchase may be able to adjust rents to reflect such costs. The landlord will also often be able to seek equitable indemnity for losses.
>
> We conclude that the absence of a continuing business relationship between builder and landlord does not preclude application of strict liability in tort for latent defects existing at the time of the lease because landlords are an integral part of the enterprise and they should bear the cost of injuries resulting from such defects rather than the injured persons who are powerless to protect themselves.

698 P.2d at 122-124. However, in overruling *Becker*, the *Peterson* court explained, 899 P.2d at 912-913:

> The effect of imposing upon landlords liability without fault is to compel them to insure the safety of their tenants in situations in which injury is caused by a defect of which the landlord neither knew nor should have known.
>
> A landlord or hotel owner, unlike a retailer, often cannot exert pressure upon the manufacturer to make the product safe and cannot share with the manufacturer the costs of insuring the safety of the tenant, because a landlord or hotel owner generally has no "continuing business relationship" with the manufacturer of the defective product. As one commentator has observed: "If the objective of the application of the stream of commerce approach is to distribute the risk of providing a product to society by allowing an injured plaintiff to find a remedy for injury along the chain of distribution, it will probably fail in the landlord/tenant situation. The cost of insuring risk will not be distributed along the chain of commerce but will probably be absorbed by tenants who will pay increased rents. One could argue that this was not the effect sought by the court in earlier cases which anticipated that the cost of risk would be distributed vertically in the stream of commerce." (Alice L. Perlman, Becker v. IRM Corporation: *Strict Liability in Tort for Residential Landlords*, 16 Golden Gate L. Rev. 349, 360 (1986).)

The prevailing rule is that the landlord is liable for harms to tenants only if she has acted negligently. This means that the landlord may be relieved of liability if the injury is caused by a latent defect of which the landlord could not reasonably have been aware. The South Carolina Supreme Court declined to adopt a strict liability standard in *Young v. Morrisey*, 329 S.E.2d 426, 428 (S.C. 1985), citing the "compelling reasons" of a trial court in New Jersey:

> (1) A landlord is not engaged in mass production whereby he places his product — the apartment — in a stream of commerce exposing it to a large number of customers; (2) he has not created the product with a defect which is preventable by greater care at the time of manufacture or assembly; (3) he does not have the expertise to know and correct the condition, so as to be saddled with responsibility for a defect regardless of negligence; (4) an apartment includes several rooms with many facilities constructed by many artisans with differing types of expertise, and subject to constant use and deterioration from many causes; (5) it is a commodity wholly unlike a product which is expected to leave a manufacturer's hands in a safe condition with an implied representation upon which the consumer relies; (6) the tenant may expect that at the time of letting there are no hidden dangerous defects known to the landlord of which the tenant has not been warned, but he does not expect that all will be perfect in his apartment for all the years of his occupancy; (7) to apply strict liability would impose an unjust burden on property owners; how can a property owner prevent a latent defect or repair when he has no way of detecting it? And if he can't prevent the defect, why should he be liable? [*Dwyer v. Skyline Apartments, Inc.*, 301 A.2d 463 (N.J. Super. Ct. App. Div. 1973), *aff'd mem.*, 311 A.2d 1 (1973).][18]

Damages for emotional distress. A number of courts have allowed tenants to recover damages for intentional infliction of emotional distress resulting from a landlord's violation of statutory duties and the implied warranty of habitability. *McNairy v. C.K. Realty*, 59 Cal. Rptr. 3d 429 (Ct. App. 2007); *Hilder v. St. Peter*, 478 A.2d 202 (Vt. 1984). *See also Thomas v. Goudreault*, 786 P.2d 1010, 1014-1018 (Ariz. Ct. App. 1989) (interpreting the Arizona version of the *Uniform Residential Landlord and Tenant Act* to allow the tenant to recover damages for emotional distress). These cases ordinarily involve extreme and outrageous conduct such as the sexual harassment, persistent lack of heat, and severe pest infestation present in *Haddad v. Gonzalez*, 576 N.E.2d 658 (Mass. 1991). *See also Chryar v. Wolf*, 21 P.3d 428 (Colo. App. 2000) (landlord liable for damages for emotional distress when he wrongfully put the tenant's personal belongings on the street with a sign inviting people to take them); *Rodriguez v. Cambridge Housing Authority*, 823 N.E.2d 1249 (Mass. 2005) (landlord public housing authority liable for damages for severe emotional distress suffered by tenant and her son when she was violently attacked in her apartment by trespassers after the landlord negligently failed to change the locks on her apartment after it had

---

18. *Young* was superseded in 1986 by the *South Carolina Landlord-Tenant Act* for residential tenancies. *See Byerly v. Connor*, 415 S.E.2d 796 (S.C. 1992); *Robinson v. Code*, 682 S.E.2d 495 (S.C. Ct. App. 2009).

been invaded and she had been attacked inside). *Accord, Simon v. Solomon,* 431 N.E.2d 556 (Mass. 1981).

Intervening criminal conduct. Courts have increasingly held landlords liable for negligently failing to provide sufficient security in the building, such as functioning locks on the front door to the building, when such failures have allowed intruders to enter the building and rape or otherwise attack a tenant. *See Rodriguez, supra; Hemmings v. Pelham Wood LLP,* 862 A.2d 443 (Md. 2003); *Smith ex rel. Koss v. Lagow Construction & Developing Co.,* 642 N.W.2d 187 (S.D. 2002).

Problems

1. A tenant notifies the landlord that another tenant in the building is selling drugs out of his apartment. The landlord does nothing. The tenant is held up at gunpoint and robbed in the hallway of the building by a customer of the drug dealer. The tenant sues the landlord for negligent infliction of emotional distress.

   a. What is the tenant's argument that she should be able to hold the landlord responsible for damages?

   b. What is the landlord's argument that he is not responsible for the harm?

   c. How should the court rule?

2. The problem of lead paint poisoning in children has resulted in substantial legislative activity. In 1992, Congress passed the *Residential Lead-Based Paint Hazard Reduction Act,* 42 U.S.C. §§4851-4856, which requires sellers and landlords to provide buyers or lessees of most property built before 1978 with a "lead hazard information pamphlet" and to disclose the presence of any known lead-based paint. 42 U.S.C. §4852d. *See* 40 C.F.R. §§745.101-745.107. States have also passed laws regulating lead paint in residential rental housing. Massachusetts, for example, requires landlords of families with children to remove or cover lead paint in the units. *See, e.g.,* Mass. Gen. Laws ch. 111, §197 (2011).

Assume a state statute provides that "whenever a child under six years of age resides in any premises in which any paint, plaster or other accessible structural material contains dangerous levels of lead, the owner shall remove or contain said paint, plaster or other accessible structural materials." The statute also provides that a "landlord who fails to comply with the act shall be liable to any child injured because of that failure for damages."

A landlord fails to comply with the act, and a four-year-old child becomes ill with lead poisoning after eating paint chips that fell from a window sill. The child's father sues the landlord for negligence, arguing that the landlord's failure to remove the lead paint in the apartment posed a foreseeable risk of harm to his child and caused his child's illness. The landlord seeks to reduce whatever liability may be found against her by arguing that the tenant was "contributorily negligent," *i.e.,* that if the father had been more vigilant, he would have prevented the child from ingesting the paint chips and the harm would not have occurred.

a. What is the child's argument that the statute does not allow the landlord to raise a defense of contributory negligence?

b. What is the landlord's argument that such a defense is consistent with the statute?

c. How should the court rule?

§4.5 Minimum Standards Revisited

Advocates debating the advisability and legitimacy of imposing minimum standards on landlords, particularly in the context of tenant rights such as a nonwaivable implied warranty of habitability, tenant protections against retaliatory eviction, and expanded landlord tort liability, make both rights-based and economic arguments.[19] Many of these arguments apply in the broader debate about regulating landlord and tenant relations, including rent control, regulation of security deposits, and even tenant civil rights protections.

As to **rights-based arguments**, recall the discussion of freedom of contract in §1.4, above, in the context of determining whether a given agreement creates a lease or another property relationship. Similar arguments play out for habitability and other tenant rights. On one side, advocates might argue that making particular terms nondisclaimable prevents tenants from agreeing to waive the right to withhold rent in return for lower rent, even if they wish to do so. After all, our legal system allows those accused of crime the right to waive even the most fundamental constitutional trial rights, so why not tenants? On the other side is the argument that no one would voluntarily agree to rent an apartment that did not comply with minimum standards of habitability or similarly waive other central aspects of a rented home; the fact that people agree to do so is evidence not that they affirmatively wanted to agree but that they were forced to agree because they had no legally or practically available alternatives. Consent in this context is illusory because choice is fundamentally constrained.

Another rights-based argument has to do with the fairness of imposing particular burdens on landlords. Because landlords may have a limited ability to pass along the cost of providing habitable premises to tenants and the cost of other tenant rights, the result is a redistribution of wealth from landlords to tenants. Some would argue that this targeted redistribution is unfair because it places the burden of dealing with poverty on a small subset of the population (that is, landlords) when the obligation to care for poor people should be shared by all members of the community through general taxes to support rental subsidies or welfare programs. The counterargument is that it would be unfair for landlords to make a living by providing substandard housing; in creating an ongoing relationship with their tenants, it is only fair for landlords to conduct those relationships in accordance with minimum standards of decency. Just as

---

19. Many of these arguments have been identified and categorized by Professor Duncan Kennedy. Duncan Kennedy, *Distributive and Paternalist Motives in Contract and Tort Law, with Special Reference to Compulsory Terms and Unequal Bargaining Power*, 41 Md. L. Rev. 563 (1982).

it is unlawful to enter a contract of slavery, it should be unlawful to enter a contract by which one agrees to allow someone else to live in deplorable conditions.

The debate about mandatory landlord-tenant regulations also raises important questions about individual self-determination and its limits. A concern about paternalism would suggest that individual citizens are the best judges of their own interests; the state should not prevent people from entering into voluntary agreements on the grounds that it is not in their best interest to do so. Institutionally, the argument continues, courts and legislatures are ill equipped to determine what private arrangements best satisfy people's needs, and a legal structure that begins with freedom of contract as the baseline best allows individuals to pursue their ends in their own way. Countering these propositions are the arguments that any contract by which tenants waive basic rights to habitability is unlikely to represent the actual intent of the parties and because of a variety of well-recognized cognitive limitations, people are actually relatively poor judges of their own long-term interests in many situations. More importantly, some contractual agreements are so fundamentally unfair or unconscionable that they should not be enforced even if the parties have voluntarily and knowingly agreed to them.

Economic arguments, by contrast, tend to focus less on fairness or the relationship between the state and the individual, and more on incentives and the consequences for allocative efficiency of mandatory lease terms. For example, if tenants are willing to live in less well-maintained apartments, they should be able to enter into a contract for lower rent and then have money available to use for other things such as food and clothing. Some also argue that landlords will respond to the additional legal and economic exposure created by new tenant rights by attempting to raise the rent. Either this will pass along the costs of the warranty to tenants or, if tenants are unable to pay a greater rent, may induce landlords to reduce their investment in housing or even leave the rental market, hurting tenants — the very people the change in law is meant to help.

On the other hand, substandard housing creates significant externalities — third-party effects that are not internalized by the parties — such as medical problems for residents and community blight. And predicting, *a priori*, what effects rights such as the implied warranty will have on the market depends on a host of factors affecting both demand and supply. Whether tenants are harmed or the implied warranty simply redistributes wealth between landlords and tenants without decreasing the supply of housing turns on how price sensitive is demand for housing. Landlords may not be able to pass along costs to tenants and if landlords are earning "economic rents," which exceed the minimum required to keep the investment in its current use, then other housing providers may be able to enter the market to increase supply. If supply is constrained, and landlords are earning economic rents with high profits, a reduction in those profits may allow them to stay in business while complying with the warranty and still earn more than they could in other businesses.

Which of these arguments do you find convincing, and why? Are they mutually exclusive?

PART FIVE

THE LEGAL FRAMEWORK OF THE MARKET FOR REAL ESTATE

CHAPTER 12

Real Estate Transactions

§1 REAL ESTATE TRANSACTIONS: STRUCTURE AND ROLES

The purchase and sale of real property involves a host of complex issues, whether the transaction involves a single-family house, a condominium unit, a shopping center, an office building, or undeveloped land. At the same time, many aspects of these transactions have become routinized, particularly for home sales. In many jurisdictions, such transactions are marked by the use of standardized forms and by the allocation of responsibility in relatively set ways among the parties. However, more complex real estate transactions introduce significant variations, and it is in such transactions that lawyers are now most heavily involved. This chapter introduces you to the basic structure of real estate transactions and highlights several issues that are likely to be important in any transaction.

§1.1 Attorneys' Transactional Roles

In real estate transactions, as with "deals" more generally, attorneys can play several different roles that are distinct from resolving disputes. Lawyers, of course, are often responsible for memorializing the terms of the parties' agreements and counseling their clients to understand exactly what the agreements mean. This function is increasingly less important in residential real estate, where brokers often help the parties fill the blanks on form contracts and attorneys appear to be involved in a minority of transactions. Michael Braunstein, *Structural Change and Inter-Professional Competitive Advantage: An Example Drawn from Residential Real Estate Conveyancing*, 62 Mo. L. Rev. 241, 262 (1997) (citing evidence that attorneys appear to be involved in only 40 percent of residential transactions).[1] The increasing marginalization of

1. Some form real estate contracts include an "attorney approval clause," giving the parties a specified time, such as three days, to consult with an attorney after signing the document and allowing the parties to withdraw if they wish. Alice N. Noble-Allgire, *Attorney Approval Clauses in Residential Real Estate Contracts — Is Half a Loaf Better Than None?* 48 Kan. L. Rev. 339 (2000).

lawyers in residential sales may reduce the cost of such transactions, although it may also leave the parties subject to legal vulnerabilities. If the actual understanding of the parties of the meaning and effect of their deal diverge from the provisions contained in form contracts, courts will have to respond. Some argue, however, that litigation has clarified the rights of the parties (or will do so in the future) and that ordinary home purchasers do not need the participation of an attorney in the transaction to protect their rights. Braunstein, *supra,* at 271-279. Lawyers, however, remain central to contracting in most other types of real estate transactions.

Lawyers are responsible for regulatory compliance in the transaction. Real estate conveyancing is regulated in a number of ways by federal, state, and local governments. For example, the federal *Real Estate Settlement Procedures Act* (RESPA), 12 U.S.C. §§2601-2617, requires the disclosure of all settlement costs charged to home borrowers and sellers at closing, among other things. More esoterically, an executive order issued shortly after September 11, 2001 blocks transfers of property owned by foreign persons who "have committed, or who pose a significant risk of committing, acts of terrorism that threaten the security of U.S. nationals or the national security, foreign policy, or economy of the U.S." Exec. Order No. 13,224, 66 Fed. Reg. 49,079 (Sept. 23, 2001). The order prohibits anyone in the United States from participating in transactions involving such "blocked" property. As a result, real estate lawyers must check a government watch list to ensure they do not help listed persons engage in real estate transactions. Many real estate lawyers now include clauses in purchase and sale agreements requiring buyers and sellers to warrant that they are not on the watch list, they are not entities prohibited from doing business under antiterrorism laws, and that they will not do business with anyone who is so prohibited. *See* Nora Lockwood Tooher, *Real Estate Lawyers Adding "Anti-Terrorism" Clauses to Contracts and Leases,* Lawyers USA, Aug. 28, 2006, at 5.

This is one example of how lawyers in real estate transactions work to identify and allocate risks for both sides. Common risks include both regulatory concerns and matters related to the parties, such as the capacity of a buyer to obtain sufficient financing; the physical state of the property, such as the condition of a building or the presence of environmental hazards; and questions about title to the property, such as whether the seller has the right to convey or an encumbrance limits the use of the property. Particularly in more complicated transactions, lawyers must also negotiate and structure agreements in ways that can bridge divides between the parties and ideally add value. There are a variety of tools that transactional lawyers can bring to bear to help parties reach agreement, such as contingencies, disclosure requirements, warranties, and indemnification provisions.

When you read the Offer to Purchase Real Estate and Standard Form Purchase and Sale Agreement, reproduced below, pay attention to how the agreements allocate and respond to common risks and uncertainties and creates mechanisms that may make it easier for parties to achieve their ultimate goal of closing the deal and transferring the property.

§1.2 Phases of the Transaction

From the simplest home sale to the most complex multi-phase development, most real estate transactions follow a similar structure, and it is useful to organize legal issues along a timeline that reflects that structure. The first phase of most real estate transactions is **pre-contracting**. Here, sellers typically prepare to market property while buyers engage in the search for property. **Brokers** are the dominant professionals at this stage of the transaction. If the seller and buyer reach agreement on the basic terms of an agreement, which can sometimes be memorialized in a term sheet or informal letter agreement, they will then enter into a contract called a **purchase and sale agreement**. It is at this stage that lawyers generally enter the scene.

The contract and background common law doctrines then govern what is known as the **executory period**. During this phase of the transaction, buyers primarily engage in due diligence, investigating the property and its state of title, and often work to arrange for financing. At the same time, sellers have responsibilities as well, such as preparing to lift encumbrances on the property, such as loans that will be paid off from the proceeds of the transaction, and responding to the buyer's concerns about the property.

If the parties meet their respective obligations, the fourth phase of the transaction is **closing**. It is at this crucial moment that the lender will fund the loan, the buyer will pay the purchase price, and the seller will convey the property through a **deed**. Finally, there may be legal issues between the parties **post-closing**, including liability for problems that were not known at the time of closing and title-related matters that can emerge years after the property changes hands.

Because most real estate transactions involve borrowing by the purchaser to finance the purchase, there are typically two transactions playing out in parallel. The first is the actual conveyance of the property and the second is the funding of the loan to the purchaser. These parallel tracks typically come together at the closing, but real estate attorneys must pay attention to their intersection throughout the transaction. We will address real estate financing in detail later in the chapter.

A. Pre-Contracting and the Role of Brokers

Some sales are made directly by the owner with the buyer. The owner may sell the property directly to a friend, family member, business associate, or acquaintance. In other cases, the owner advertises the property on-line and shows the place directly to prospective buyers. In most cases, however, sellers hire real estate brokers (also called agents or realtors) to help sell the property. The seller normally signs a contract with the broker by which the broker agrees to look for prospective buyers and show the property to them, perhaps for a set period of time such as six months, in exchange for a commission, which is often 5 percent to 7 percent of the sale price.

There are three basic types of broker listing agreements.

1. **Exclusive right to sell.** The broker has the right to collect the commission if the property is sold to anyone during the period of the contract, even if the sale is to a buyer that the owner found without the broker's help.
2. **Exclusive agency.** The broker gets the commission, or a share of the commission, if the property is sold by her efforts or the efforts of any other broker, but not if the property is sold by the owner.

3. **Open, or nonexclusive.** The broker is entitled to a commission only if she is the first person to procure a buyer who is ready, willing, and able to buy.

In many communities, brokers use **multiple listing services** established by the local real estate board. Each broker who is a member of the listing service registers every exclusive listing she receives with the listing service. Other brokers will then have access to that information and can attempt to sell the property as well. If any sale goes through, the commission is shared by the listing service and the broker who arranged for the sale. Any broker who finds a buyer will share the commission with the broker hired by the seller.

Disputes sometimes break out between brokers and sellers when the broker finds a buyer who makes a down payment and signs a purchase and sale agreement but then, for whatever reason, the deal falls through. It is quite clear that the seller has a duty to pay the commission if the seller himself wrongfully backs out of the deal after the broker has found a ready, willing, and able buyer. But what happens if the buyer refuses to complete the transaction by paying the rest of the purchase price?

When the buyer backs out of the deal, brokers sometimes allege that they have the right to their commission because they fulfilled their contractual obligation to find a ready, willing, and able buyer. Until the middle of the twentieth century, the prevailing rule was that the broker's commission was indeed earned and due at the time the purchase and sale agreement was signed, regardless of whether the sale was actually completed. The rule still holds in a number of jurisdictions and is often reflected in standard form brokerage agreements. *See* Roger Bernhardt & Dale Whitman, *When Is a Commission Due: Problems with Broker Listing Agreements*, ABA Prob. & Prop. (Jan.-Feb. 2013). This result does not accord with the expectations of most sellers, who contemplated that the commission would be paid only if the deal went through since the commission is normally taken out of the purchase price paid by the buyer. It can also create a problem for sellers if an offer is made at the full asking price in a market where sellers may be able to command a premium above that price. Bernhardt & Whitman, *supra* (discussing *RealPro, Inc. v. Smith Residual Co.*, 138 Cal. Rptr. 3d 255 (Ct. App. 2012)).

Although still in the minority, a substantial number of courts have changed the traditional rule, holding that the broker's commission is earned and due only if the sale is completed. *See, e.g., McCully, Inc. v. Baccaro Ranch*, 816 N.W.2d 728 (Neb. 2012); *Tristram's Landing, Inc. v. Wait*, 327 N.E.2d 727 (Mass. 1975). The seller has a duty to pay the commission if the seller defaults and backs out of the deal without a good reason, but the commission is not due if the buyer refuses to go forward. This emerging rule is based on the fact that the "owner hires the broker with the expectation of becoming liable for a commission only in the event a sale of the property is consummated, unless the title does not pass because of the owner's improper or frustrating conduct." *Ellsworth Dobbs, Inc. v. Johnson*, 236 A.2d 843, 853 (N.J. 1967). Although some courts find this rule to be nondisclaimable, *id.* at 856, others allow the parties to contract around it. *Sparks v. Fiduciary National Title Insurance Co.*, 294 F.3d 259, 266 (1st Cir. 2002). Many states, however, retain the traditional rule. 11 *Thompson on Real Property, Second Thomas Editions* §95.05(b).

Unauthorized practice of law. Every state requires lawyers to be licensed to practice law, and brokers who provide legal advice or draft complex legal documents for their clients may be subject to penalties for the unauthorized practice of law. *Toledo Bar Association v. Chelsea Title Agency of Dayton, Inc.*, 800 N.E.2d 29 (Ohio 2003) (unauthorized practice of law for title agency to prepare deed for client when not written by licensed attorney). Brokers often provide standard purchase and sale agreements for sellers and buyers to use. If they do no more than fill the blanks on such forms, these activities are thought be an "incident to the business" of providing brokerage services, and courts are unlikely to find a violation of the laws prohibiting nonlawyers from "practicing law."

However, if brokers draft deeds, mortgages, or other documents that transfer interests in real property, express opinions on the status of titles or zoning law and the like, or conduct closings, they may be found to have engaged in the unauthorized practice of law. These restrictions on the conduct of brokers are intended to "protect[] the public from the potentially severe economic and emotional consequences which may flow from erroneous advice given by persons untrained in the law." *Matrix Financial Services Corp. v. Frazer*, 714 S.E.2d 532, 534 (S.C. 2011). *Accord, Doe v. McMaster*, 585 S.E.2d 773, 776-777 (S.C. 2003) (unauthorized practice of law to prepare closing documents such as deeds and title opinions); *Ex parte Watson*, 589 S.E.2d 760 (S.C. 2003) (finding it unauthorized practice of law to examine public records and issue an opinion regarding title in connection with tax foreclosure sale).

Some states have begun to loosen these regulations to allow brokers to perform functions that used to be performed by lawyers on the ground that this serves the public interest by lowering the costs of buying and selling real estate. The Supreme Court of New Jersey, for example, authorized brokers and title companies to conduct closings in an area of the state where it was typical for neither seller nor buyer to be represented by a lawyer at the closing. *In re Opinion No. 26 of the Commission on Unauthorized Practice of Law*, 654 A.2d 1344 (N.J. 1995). While holding that they were engaged in the practice of law, their activity was not "unauthorized" because it was in the public interest for them to help owners conduct real estate transactions, and there was not sufficient warrant to force every owner and every buyer to hire a lawyer in order to buy or sell real estate. *See also Countrywide Home Loans, Inc. v. Kentucky Bar Association*, 113 S.W.3d 105 (Ky. 2003) (allowing laypersons to conduct real estate closings as long as they do not give legal advice); *Dressell v. Ameribank*, 664 N.W.2d 151 (Mich. 2003) (not unauthorized practice of law for title company to prepare leases, mortgages, and deeds).

Broker's duties to buyer. It has become increasingly common for buyers to hire their own brokers to advise them. Buyer's brokers can be paid a percentage of the sale price (often splitting the commission with the seller's broker), a fixed fee, or an hourly rate.

What duties, however, does a *seller's* agent have to the *buyer*? Although the seller's agent is formally working for the seller, many buyers feel that the broker is also working for them. Although they have no contract with the seller's broker, courts may impose certain fiduciary or other obligations toward the buyer. For example, if the seller's broker fails to reveal relevant information to the buyer, the buyer may sue the broker for fraud. *See Jackowski v. Borchelt*, 278 P.3d 1100 (Wash. 2012) (fraudulent concealment claim by purchaser against seller's broker).

Dual agency. Conflicts may arise when a real estate agency provides broker's services to both buyers and sellers, since the buyer's broker will be attempting to minimize the sale price, while the seller's agent will try to get as much as possible for the property. Unless the law prohibits it, a single person may be in the business of representing both buyers and sellers, and it is possible that the seller will deal with a buyer who has engaged the same agent. While one might argue that such an agent would facilitate the deal, she also might fail to represent one or both sides adequately. *See Estate of Eller v. Bartron*, 31 A.3d 895 (Del. 2011). Many states have passed statutes that regulate such potential conflicts of interest, mainly by requiring disclosure that a broker is acting as a dual agent. *See* Ga. Code §§10-6A-10 and 10-6A-12(a).

Many states now also allow a **designated agency**, in which one broker in the agency represents the seller, while another represents the buyer in the transaction. Ann Morales Olazábal, *Redefining Realtor Relationships and Responsibilities: The Failure of State Regulatory Responses*, 40 Harv. J. Legis. 65, 75-76 (2003). Some states are now experimenting with allowing brokers to act as **transaction brokers**, in which they do not represent either the seller or the buyer; instead, they act as professionals, giving independent advice on the transaction. *Id.* at 87-91. *See* Ga. Code §10-6A-3(14). If brokers are not the agent of either the seller or the buyer, they cannot be liable for breach of fiduciary duty. While this may relieve the broker of worry about possible liability, it may also remove incentives to promote the interest of one or both parties to the transaction, and for this reason every state that has adopted this idea has imposed some statutory duties on transaction brokers. Morales Olazábal, *supra*, at 90-91.

Buyer's duties to broker. What happens if the buyer attempts to arrange with the seller to buy the property independent of the broker to save the cost of the broker's commission? Ordinarily, the broker can sue the seller for breach of the listing agreement. But suppose the seller no longer has the money for some reason; can the broker sue the buyer as well? Some courts have held that "when a prospective buyer solicits a broker to find or to show him property which he might be interested in buying, and the broker finds property satisfactory to him which the owner agrees to sell at the price offered, and the buyer knows the broker will earn a commission for the sale from the owner, the law will imply a promise on the part of the buyer to complete the transaction with the owner." *Ellsworth Dobbs*, 236 A.2d at 859. This approach has been adopted in California, *Donnellan v. Rocks*, 99 Cal. Rptr. 692 (Ct. App. 1972), but rejected in Michigan and Virginia, *Rich v. Emerson-Dumont Distributing Corp.*, 222 N.W.2d 65 (Mich. Ct. App. 1974); *Professional Realty Corp. v. Bender*, 222 S.E.2d 810 (Va. 1976).

Brokers and consumer protection. The primary function that brokers serve in a real estate transaction is to help parties find each other and reach a mutually satisfactory agreement more efficiently than the parties could on their own. The Internet, however, has lowered information costs in searching for properties and potential purchasers and this is increasingly challenging the intermediary role that brokers have traditionally played. As brokers and their trade association, the National Association of Realtors (NAR), have sought to maintain their position, regulators have intervened to protect consumers. For example, in 2005, the U.S. Justice Department sued the NAR for antitrust violations relating to an NAR policy that limited the ability of brokers to put all multiple-listing service listings on-line for their customers. In 2008, the NAR settled the complaint, agreeing not to discriminate against Internet-based brokerage companies. *See United States v. National Association of Realtors*, Final J., Civil Action No. 05 C 5140 (Nov. 18, 2008). How would you expect brokers to react to the increasing ubiquity of real estate–related search engines?

B. Contracting: The Purchase and Sale Agreement

When a buyer finds a place that she likes and can afford, she makes an offer to buy it. The offer may be oral or in writing. The buyer may offer to pay the entire sale price set by the seller. Depending on the market, the buyer may offer some lower amount or, in so-called seller's markets, may even offer more than the asking price. The seller may accept the offer or make a counteroffer. The buyer and seller may negotiate about other terms of the transaction as well, including when the seller would be able to move out and transfer possession, who will pay back taxes, which side has the burden of repairing any known defects, and the like.[2] When the parties agree on a price and on the general terms of the transaction, they proceed to the next step in the transaction: the sales contract, often called the **purchase and sale agreement**.

In the purchase and sale agreement, the seller agrees to convey title at a date in the future when the **closing** will take place. The buyer generally makes a deposit (sometimes called **earnest money**) that can be modest or in some markets as much as 10 percent of the purchase price; the buyer also promises to pay the rest of the purchase price at the closing. Sometimes buyers will make an initial, nominal payment when an offer is made and then a larger down payment later after inspections are done. The date of the closing is negotiated by the parties, and, in residential transactions, is often one or two months after the purchase and sale agreement is signed. The contract then governs the mutual obligations of the parties during the executory period as well as the conditions that must be met for the transaction to close. We will consider in detail several issues related to the purchase and sale agreement later in the chapter.

2. In some transactions, particularly in commercial real estate, the parties may mark the general terms of an agreement through a term sheet or similar informal document. When one party decides not to complete the transaction, controversies sometimes arise as to whether these documents constitute a binding contract that meets the Statute of Frauds. *See, e.g., Triple A Supplies, Inc. v. WPA Acquisition Corp.*, 95 A.D.3d 1301 (N.Y. App. Div. 2012).

C. The Executory Period

Under the purchase and sale agreement, the buyer's obligations are normally made contingent on (1) the seller's ability to convey marketable title; (2) the buyer's ability to get adequate financing for the rest of the purchase price; and (3) inspections of the premises for structural defects, termites, and environmental hazards, such as radon and toxic waste generated by a leaking oil tank. The seller's performance is usually conditioned only on the buyer's paying the purchase price at the closing, but it may also be conditioned on the seller's finding a new place to live. As a result, during the period between the execution of the agreement and closing, the parties must arrange to remove all of these **contingencies**.

Inspections. Buyers will arrange for the various inspections of the premises. This is generally done by hiring professionals to examine the property and provide opinions on the condition of the property. In a single-family home sale, a simple home inspection may suffice; for commercial real estate transactions, a variety of experts may be engaged for what is called **due diligence**, such as structural engineers and environmental experts, and the terms and timing of inspection rights can be important aspects of the contract.

Mortgage financing. Buyers will generally also attempt to get financing, usually by seeking a loan from a bank or other lending institution. The bank and the buyer will enter into a **loan agreement** that will specify how large a down payment the buyer must make, the interest to be paid on the loan, and the time period over which the loan will be repaid. The bank is also likely to insist on a **mortgage** to accompany the loan. A mortgage constitutes an agreement by the buyer that if the buyer defaults on the loan payments or other material terms of the mortgage agreement (such as maintaining insurance on the property and keeping it in good repair), the bank will be able to **foreclose** on the property by arranging for it to be sold, with the proceeds of the sale being used to satisfy the buyer's debt to the bank.

The bank will be unwilling to lend the money without assuring itself that the buyer will be able to repay the loan and that the seller actually owns the property, meaning that no other property interests encumber the property (such as other mortgages) that would impair the value of the property as collateral for the loan. The bank will therefore ask the buyer for information about her credit history, job history, and current assets and salary. The bank will also make arrangements to assure itself that the seller has clear title to the house. It will do this by either (1) searching the title itself in the registry of deeds, (2) requiring the buyer to hire a lawyer to do this and provide evidence of a satisfactory result, or (3) requiring the buyer to buy **title insurance** from an insurance company that will research the title and agree to guarantee the seller's title in return for a fee from the buyer. We will examine title problems in greater depth later in the chapter.

If the buyer cannot obtain financing, the inspection reveals serious defects, the seller's title is not marketable, or some other contingency is not met, the buyer may be excused from the deal, although in many situations, buyers and sellers seek to remedy concerns if that is possible. If all conditions are met or waived, the parties proceed to closing.

Risk of loss during the executory period and equitable conversion. What happens if the house burns down after the purchase and sale agreement has been signed but before the closing? Who bears the **risk of loss** — the seller or the buyer — if the contract does not answer this question? Must the buyer complete the transaction despite the loss, or may the buyer rescind and get her earnest money deposit back? Many courts hold that the risk of loss is on the buyer, under the doctrine of **equitable conversion**. If the contract gives the buyer the equitable right to have the contract specifically enforced, and many real estate contracts do, it is appropriate to treat the buyer for certain purposes *as if* the transaction had already been completed. Thus, some courts treat the buyer as the equitable owner during the executory period, despite the fact that the seller may retain the right to possess the property until the closing. *See, e.g., Trustees of Zion Baptist Church v. Conservators of Estate of Peay*, 525 S.E.2d 291 (Va. 2000); *see also Jackson v. Scheible*, 902 N.E.2d 807, 813 (Ind. 2009) (buyer liable to third parties for conditions on the property after purchase and sale agreement executed).

The rule that treats buyers as equitable owners has been subject to much criticism. "To say that equity will specifically enforce the contract certainly does not compel one to disregard reality and view the contract as already performed." William B. Stoebuck & Dale A. Whitman, *The Law of Property* §10.13 at 787 (3d ed. 2000). This allocation of the risk rarely comports with the parties' expectations. Moreover, the seller is usually in a better position to exercise care to avoid the loss and to carry insurance on the property. For these reasons, some courts reject the doctrine and place the risk of loss during the executory period on the seller, thereby allowing the buyer to get out of the deal or reduce the amount of the price owed by the amount of the damage suffered. *Brush Grocery Kart, Inc. v. Sure Fine Market, Inc.*, 47 P.3d 680 (Colo. 2002) ("It is counterintuitive . . . that merely contracting for the sale of real property should not only relieve the vendor of his responsibility to maintain the property until execution but also impose a duty on the vendee to perform despite the intervention of a material, no-fault casualty loss preventing him from ever receiving the benefit of his bargain."); *Skelly Oil Co. v. Ashmore*, 365 S.W.2d 582 (Mo. 1963). This is also the approach taken by the *Uniform Vendor and Purchaser Risk Act*, which has been adopted in ten states. Stoebuck & Whitman, *supra*, at 795.

In practice, most purchase and sale agreements explicitly place the risk of loss on the vendor during the executory period and most vendors have property insurance. Even in states that force the buyer to complete the contract at the agreed-upon price, most courts will not tolerate the seller's getting both the purchase price and the insurance proceeds, while the buyer pays full market value and gets a burned-out property. Instead, the courts are likely to impose a constructive trust on the insurance proceeds and require that the purchase price be reduced by the amount of those proceeds so that the seller does not receive a windfall.

D. Closing

Closings either take place in person, where the parties gather with their representatives and execute various agreements, or through **escrow**, where the parties submit executed documents to an escrow agent with instructions to complete the closing if specified conditions are met.

At the closing, the buyer pays the remaining amount of the purchase price above the deposit. Simultaneously, the buyer executes the loan and mortgage agreements with the lender and the lender pays the amount it has agreed to fund. The buyer or the lender, or often a title company working for one of the parties, may make a last-minute check of the records in the recording office to make sure that the state of title has not changed between the time the title search was first conducted and the time of the closing.

In exchange for payment of the full purchase price, the seller delivers a **deed** to the buyer. The deed recites that the grantor (seller) conveys the property to the grantee (buyer). It describes the property and is signed by the grantor. It may contain reference to easements and covenants restricting the use of the property. The deed may also contain various **warranties** by which the seller covenants that he has good title to the property. The deed will generally be recorded immediately in the appropriate recorder's office, often by a title company involved in the closing.[3]

RESPA, 12 U.S.C. §§2601-2617, regulates closings in two primary ways. First, it requires disclosure of all settlement costs. This is intended to help the parties ensure that there are no hidden fees and that the work done in relation to closing can be matched to specific charges. Substantively, RESPA also protects real estate buyers from having to pay kickbacks or other unearned or undisclosed fees by prohibiting acceptance of fees for rendering of real estate settlement services, such as loan processing, title searches, surveys, preparation of documents, in connection with federally related mortgage loans "other than for services actually performed." 12 U.S.C. §2607(b). In *Freeman v. Quicken Loans, Inc.*, 132 S. Ct. 2034 (2012), the Supreme Court considered whether RESPA applies to unearned fees that are not split with other settlement services providers. Rejecting a policy statement from the U.S. Department of Housing and Urban Development that interpreted the statute to apply to *any* unearned fee, the Court held that RESPA only regulates settlement charges that are "divided between two or more persons." *Id.* at 2044.

Attorneys involved in closing may also be subject to federal anti-money-laundering statutes. For example, parties responsible for real estate closings must report

---

3. As with brokers, title companies involved in aspects of residential real estate closings have been challenged on the ground that such activities constitute the unauthorized practice of law. *See Real Estate Bar Association for Massachusetts, Inc. v. National Real Estate Information Services*, 946 N.E.2d 665 (Mass. 2011) (finding that ordering title abstracts, preparing closing statements, reviewing documents for valid execution, delivering documents for recording, issuing title insurance, and other services do not constitute the practice of law; drafting deeds and interpreting the state of title do).

to the Internal Revenue Service any cash payments of $10,000 or more received at a closing or connected with a transaction. 26 U.S.C. §6050I. Further, Title III of the *USA Patriot Act*, passed shortly after September 11, 2001, amended the *Bank Secrecy Act*, 31 U.S.C. §§5311-5355, to require every "financial institution" to develop internal anti-money-laundering programs designed to prevent the financing of terrorism. 31 U.S.C. §5318(h). The definition of "financial institution" includes reference to "persons involved in real estate closings and settlements," 31 U.S.C. §5312(a)(2)(U). *See* 31 C.F.R. pt. 103.

E. Post-Closing

Ordinarily, the deed replaces the purchase and sale agreement at the closing and is treated as the complete contractual arrangement between the parties. This doctrine is known as **merger**. If the parties intend the promises in the purchase and sale agreement to be enforceable post-closing, the parties must normally provide explicitly that the purchase and sale agreement (or specific terms in it) will **survive the deed**. Otherwise, the buyer will be limited to remedies associated with or contained in the deed; in that case, the buyer may sue the seller for **breach of warranties** in the deed but not for breach of the purchase and sale agreement.

Some obligations survive the deed even though they are not explicitly carved out. For example, if the seller lies to the buyer about the condition of the building, the buyer may be able to sue the seller for fraud even after the closing has taken place. Under these circumstances, the buyer may ask for damages or to rescind the deal by transferring title back to the seller and recovering the purchase price.

§2 PURCHASE AND SALE AGREEMENTS: FORM, FORMALITIES, AND REMEDIES

§2.1 The Terms of the Agreement

Review the following Offer to Purchase Real Estate and Standard Form Purchase and Sale Agreement from the Greater Boston Real Estate Board. As you do, see if you can identify the primary legal and practical risks involved in purchasing a home that the documents address, from both the buyer's perspective as well as the seller's. What mechanisms, if any, do the documents include to allocate or mitigate these risks? What important contingency discussed above is not mentioned in these agreements?

OFFER TO PURCHASE REAL ESTATE

TO ______________________________ Date: ______________________
(Seller and Spouse)
______________________________ From the Office of : ______________________
____

The property herein referred to is identified as follows: ______________________________
____

Special provisions (if any) re fixtures, appliances, etc. ______________________________
____

hereby offer to buy said property, which has been offered to me by ______________________________
______________________________ as the Broker(s) under the following terms and conditions:

1. I will pay therefore $______________________, of which

   CHECK ONE:
   - ❑ Check, subject to collection
   - ❑ Cash

   (a) $ ______________ is paid herewith as a deposit to bind this Offer
   (b) $ ______________ is to be paid as an additional deposit upon the execution of the Purchase and Sale Agreement provided for below.
   (c) $ ______________ is to be paid at the time of delivery of the Deed in cash, or by certified, cashier's, treasurer's or bank check(s).
   (d) $ ______________
   ____
   (e) $ ______________ Total Purchase Price
2. This Offer is good until ____________ A.M. P.M. on ______________________, 20____ at or before which time a copy hereof shall be signed by you, the Seller and your (husband) (wife), signifying acceptance of this Offer, and returned to me forthwith, otherwise this Offer shall be considered as rejected and the money deposited herewith shall be returned to me forthwith.
3. The parties hereto shall, on or before ____________ A.M. P.M. ______________________, 20____ execute the applicable Standard Form Purchase and Sale Agreement recommended by the Greater Boston Real Estate Board or any form substantially similar thereto, which, when executed, shall be the agreement between the parties hereto.
4. A good and sufficient Deed, conveying a good and clear record and marketable title shall be delivered at 12:00 Noon on ______________, 20____ at the appropriate Registry of Deeds, unless some other time and place are mutually agreed upon in writing.
5. If I do not fulfill my obligations under this Offer, the above mentioned deposit shall forthwith become your property without recourse to either party. Said deposit shall be held by ______________________ as escrow agent subject to the terms hereof provided however that in the event of any disagreement between the parties, the escrow agent may retain said deposit pending instructions mutually given in writing by the parties. A similar provision shall be included in the Purchase and Sale Agreement with respect to any deposit held under its terms.
6. Time is of the essence hereof.
7. Disclosures: For one to four family residences, the Buyer hereby acknowledges receipt of the Home Inspectors: Facts for Consumers brochure produced by the Office of Consumer Affairs. For residential property constructed prior to 1978, Buyer must also sign Lead Paint "Property Transfer Notification."
8. The initialed riders, if any, attached hereto are incorporated herein by reference. Additional terms and conditions, if any:
   ____
   ____

NOTICE: This is a legal document that creates binding obligations. If not understood, consult an attorney.

WITNESS my hand and seal Signed______________________
Buyer
____
Buyer

____
Address/City/State/Zip Phone Numbers (Work & Home)

This Offer is hereby accepted upon the foregoing terms and conditions at ______________ A.M. / P.M. on ______________, 20____
WITNESS my (our) hand(s) and seal(s)

______________________ ______________________
Seller (or spouse) Seller

RECEIPT FOR DEPOSIT

Date ______________

Received from ______________________ Buyer the sum of $______________ as deposit under the terms and conditions of above Offer, to be held by ______________________ as escrow agent.

Under regulations adopted pursuant to the Massachusetts license law: All offers submitted to brokers or salespeople to purchase real property that they have a right to sell shall be conveyed forthwith to the owner of such real property.

____
Agent for Seller

Form ID: RA101 PD: 08/05

EQUAL HOUSING OPPORTUNITY

This form has been made available through the courtesy of the Greater Boston Real Estate Board and is protected by copyright laws.

GREATER BOSTON REAL ESTATE BOARD

STANDARD FORM PURCHASE & SALE AGREEMENT

From the Office of:____________________

This_______________ day of_______________, 20______

1. PARTIES AND MAILING ADDRESSES *(fill in)*

hereinafter called the SELLER, agrees to SELL and

2. DESCRIPTION *(fill in and include title reference)*

hereinafter called the BUYER or PURCHASER, agrees to BUY, upon the terms hereinafter set forth, the following described premises:

3. BUILDINGS, STRUCTURES, IMPROVEMENTS, FIXTURES *(fill in or delete)*

Included in the sale as a part of said premises are the buildings, structures, and improvements now thereon, and the fixtures belonging to the SELLER and used in connection therewith including, if any, all wall-to-wall carpeting, drapery rods, automatic garage door openers, venetian blinds, window shades, screens, screen doors, storm windows and doors, awnings, shutters, furnaces, heaters, heating equipment, stoves, ranges, oil and gas burners and fixtures appurtenant thereto, hot water heaters, plumbing and bathroom fixtures, garbage disposers, electric and other lighting fixtures, mantels, outside television antennas, fences, gates, trees, shrubs, plants and, ONLY IF BUILT IN, refrigerators, air conditioning equipment, ventilators, dishwashers, washing machines and dryers; and

but excluding

4. TITLE DEED *(fill in)*
**Include here by specific reference any restrictions, easements, rights and obligations in party walls not included in (b), leases, municipal and other liens, other encumbrances, and make provision to pro-tect SELLER against BUYER's breach of SELLER's covenants in leases, where necessary.*

Said premises are to be conveyed by a good and sufficient quitclaim deed running to the BUYER, or to the nominee designated by the BUYER by written notice to the SELLER at least seven ____________ days before the deed is to be delivered as herein provided, and said deed shall convey a good and clear record and marketable title thereto, free from encumbrances, except

a. Provisions of existing building and zoning laws;
b. Existing rights and obligations in party walls which are not the subject of written agreement;
c. Such taxes for the then current year as are not due and payable on the date of the delivery of such deed;
d. Any liens for municipal betterments assessed after the date of this agreement;
e. Easements, restrictions and reservations of record, if any, so long as the same do not prohibit or materially interfere with the current use of said premises;
*f.

5. PURCHASE PRICE *(fill in); space is allowed to write out the amounts if desired*

The agreed purchase price for said premises is $

dollars, of which

$ have been paid as a deposit this day and
$
$ are to be paid at the time of delivery of the deed in cash, or by certified, cashier's,check(s).

$
$ TOTAL

6. PLANS

If said deed refers to a plan necessary to be recorded therewith the SELLER shall deliver such plan with the deed in form adequate for recording or registration.

7. REGISTERED TITLE	In addition to the foregoing, if the title to said premises is registered, said deed shall be in form sufficient to entitle the BUYER to a Certificate of Title of said premises, and the SELLER shall deliver with said deed all instruments, if any, necessary to enable the BUYER to obtain such Certificate of Title.
8. TIME FOR PERFORMANCE; DELIVERY OF DEED *(fill in)*	Such deed is to be delivered at__________o'clock (am/pm)_______on the__________day of____________________20 , at the__________________ Registry of Deeds, unless otherwise agreed upon in writing. It is agreed that time is of the essence of this agreement.
9. POSSESSION and CONDITION of PREMISE *(attach a list of exceptions, if any)*	Full possession of said premises free of all tenants and occupants, except as herein provided, is to be delivered at the time of the delivery of the deed, said premises to be then (a) in the same condition as they now are, reasonable use and wear thereof excepted, and (b) not in violation of said building and zoning laws, and (c) in compliance with the provisions of any instrument referred to in clause 4 hereof. The BUYER shall be entitled personally to enter said premises prior to the delivery of the deed in order to determine whether the condition thereof complies with the terms of this clause.
10. EXTENSION TO PERFECT TITLE OR MAKE PREMISES CONFORM *(Change period of time if desired).*	If the SELLER shall be unable to give title or to make conveyance, or to deliver possession of the premises, all as herein stipulated, or if at the time of the delivery of the deed the premises do not conform with the provisions hereof, then any payments made under this agreement shall be forthwith refunded and all other obligations of the parties hereto shall cease and this agreement shall be void without recourse to the parties hereto, unless the SELLER elects to use reasonable efforts to remove any defects in title, or to deliver possession as provided herein, or to make the said premises conform to the provisions hereof, as the case may be, in which event the SELLER shall give written notice thereof to the BUYER at or before the time for performance hereunder, and thereupon the time for performance hereof shall be extended for a period of thirty________________ days.
11. FAILURE TO PERFECT TITLE OR MAKE PERMISES CONFORM, etc.	If at the expiration of the extended time the SELLER shall have failed so to remove any defects in title, deliver possession, or make the premises conform, as the case may be, all as herein agreed, or if at any time during the period of this agreement or any extension thereof, the holder of a mortgage on said premises shall refuse to permit the insurance proceeds, if any, to be used for such purposes, then any payments made under this agreement shall be forthwith refunded and all other obligations of the parties hereto shall cease and this agreement shall be void without recourse to the parties hereto.
12. BUYER's ELECTION TO ACCEPT TITLE	The BUYER shall have the election, at either the original or any extended time for performance, to accept such title as the SELLER can deliver to the said premises in their then condition and to pay therefore the purchase price without deduction, in which case the SELLER shall convey such title, except that in the event of such conveyance in accord with the provisions of this clause, if the said premises shall have been damaged by fire or casualty insured against, then the SELLER shall, unless the SELLER has previously restored the premises to their former condition, either a. pay over or assign to the BUYER, on delivery of the deed, all amounts recovered or recoverable on account of such insurance, less any amounts reasonably expended by the SELLER for any partial restoration, or____________________ b. if a holder of a mortgage on said premises shall not permit the insurance proceeds or a part thereof to be used to restore the said premises to their former condition or tobe so paid over or assigned, give to the BUYER a credit against the purchase price, on delivery of the deed, equal to said amounts so recovered or recoverable and retained by the holder of the said mortgage less any amounts reasonably expended by the SELLER for any partial restoration.
13. ACCEPTANCE OF DEED	The acceptance of a deed by the BUYER or his nominee as the case may be, shall be deemed to be a full performance and discharge of every agreement and obligation herein contained or expressed, except such as are, by the terms hereof, to be performed after the delivery of said deed.
14. USE OF MONEY TO CLEAR TITLE	To enable the SELLER to make conveyance as herein provided, the SELLER may, at the time of delivery of the deed, use the purchase money or any portion thereof to clear the title of any or all encumbrances or interests, provided that all instruments so procured are recorded simultaneously with the delivery of said deed.

15. INSURANCE **Insert amount (list additional types of insurance and amounts as agreed)*	Until the delivery of the deed, the SELLER shall maintain insurance on said premises as follows: *Type of Insurance* — *Amount of Coverage* a. Fire & Extended Coverage — *$ b. — *$ c. — *$
16. ADJUSTMENTS *(list operating expenses, if any, or attach schedule)*	Collected rents, mortgage interest, water and sewer use charges, operating expenses (if any) according to the schedule attached hereto or set forth below, and taxes for the then current fiscal year, shall be apportioned and fuel value shall be adjusted, as of the day of performance of this agreement and the net amount thereof shall be added to or deducted from, as the case may be, the purchase price payable by the BUYER at the time of delivery of the deed. Uncollected rents for the current rental period shall be apportioned if and when collected by either party.
17. ADJUSTMENT OF UNASSESSED AND ABATED TAXES	If the amount of said taxes is not known at the time of the delivery of the deed, they shall be apportioned on the basis of the taxes assessed for the preceding fiscal year, with a reapportionment as soon as the new tax rate and valuation can be ascertained; and, if the taxes which are to be apportioned shall thereafter be reduced by abatement, the amount of such abatement, less the reasonable cost of obtaining the same, shall be apportioned between the parties, provided that neither party shall be obligated to institute or prosecute proceedings for an abatement unless herein otherwise agreed.
18. BROKER's FEE *(fill in fee with dollar amount or percentage;also name of Brokerage firm/s)*	A Broker's fee for professional services of__________________ is due from the SELLER to__________________ the Broker(s) herein, but if the SELLER pursuant to the terms of clause 21 hereof retains the deposits made hereunder by the BUYER, said Broker(s) shall be entitled to receive from the SELLER an amount equal to one-half the amount so retained or an amount equal to the Broker's fee for professional services according to this contract, whichever is the lesser.
19. BROKER(S) WARRANTY *(fill in name)*	The Broker(s) named herein__________________ warrant(s) that the Broker(s) is (are) duly licensed as such by the Commonwealth of Massachusetts.
20. DEPOSIT *(fill in name)*	All deposits made hereunder shall be held in escrow by__________________ as escrow agent subject to the terms of this agreement and shall be duly accounted for at the time for performance of this agreement. In the event of any disagreement between the parties, the escrow agent may retain all deposits made under this agreement pending instructions mutually given in writing by the SELLER and the BUYER.
21. BUYER's DEFAULT; DAMAGES	If the BUYER shall fail to fulfill the BUYER's agreements herein, all deposits made hereunder by the BUYER shall be retained by the SELLER as liquidated damages unless within thirty days after the time for performance of this agreement or any extension hereof, the SELLER otherwise notifies the BUYER in writing.
22. RELEASE BY HUSBAND OR WIFE	The SELLER's spouse hereby agrees to join in said deed and to release and convey all statutory and other rights and interests in said premises.
23. BROKER AS PARTY	The Broker(s) named herein join(s) in this agreement and become(s) a party hereto, insofar as any provisions of this agreement expressly apply to the Broker(s), and to any amendments or modifications of such provisions to which the Broker(s) agree(s) in writing.
24. LIABILITY OF TRUSTEE, SHAREHOLDER, BENEFICIARY, etc.	If the SELLER or BUYER executes this agreement in a representative or fiduciary capacity, only the principal or the estate represented shall be bound, and neither the SELLER or BUYER so executing, nor any shareholder or beneficiary of any trust, shall be personally liable for any obligation, express or implied, hereunder.
25. WARRANTIES AND REPRESENTATIONS *(fill in)*; if none, state "none"; if any listed, indicate by whom each warranty or representation was made	The BUYER acknowledges that the BUYER has not been influenced to enter into this transaction nor has he relied upon any warranties or representations not set forth or incorporated in this agreement or previously made in writing, except for the following additional warranties and representations, if any, made by either the SELLER or the Broker(s):

26.CONTINGENCY CLAUSE *(omit if not provided for in Offer to Purchase)*	In order to help finance the acquisition of said premises, the BUYER shall apply for a conventional bank or other institutional mortgage loan of $__________ at prevailing rates, terms and conditions. If despite the BUYER's diligent efforts a commitment for such loan cannot be obtained on or before__________, 20______the BUYER may terminate this agreement by written notice to the SELLER and/or the Broker(s), as agent(s) for the SELLER, prior to the expiration of such time, whereupon any payments made under this agreement shall be forthwith refunded and all other obligations of the parties hereto shall cease and this agreement shall be void without recourse to the parties hereto. In no event will the BUYER be deemed to have used diligent efforts to obtain such commitment unless the BUYER submits a complete mortgage loan application conforming to the foregoing provisions on or before__________, 20______.
27. CONSTRUCTION OF AGREEMENT	This instrument, executed in multiple counterparts, is to be construed as a Massachusetts contract, is to take effect as a sealed instrument, sets forth the entire contract between the parties, is binding upon and enures to the benefit of the parties hereto and their respective heirs, devisees, executors, administrators, successors and assigns, and may be cancelled, modified or amended only by a written instrument executed by both the SELLER and the BUYER. If two or more persons are named herein as BUYER their obligations hereunder shall be joint and several. The captions and marginal notes are used only as a matter of convenience and are not to be considered a part of this agreement or to be used in determining the intent of the parties to it.
28. LEAD PAINT LAW	The parties acknowledge that, under Massachusetts law, whenever a child or children under six years of age resides in any residential premises in which any paint, plaster or other accessible material contains dangerous levels of lead, the owner of said premises must remove or cover said paint, plaster or other material so as to make it inaccessible to children under six years of age.
29. SMOKE DETECTORS	The SELLER shall, at the time of the delivery of the deed, deliver a certificate from the fire department of the city or town in which said premises are located stating that said premises have been equipped with approved smoke detectors in conformity with applicable law.
30. ADDITIONAL PROVISIONS	The initialed riders, if any, attached hereto, are incorporated herein by reference.

FOR RESIDENTIAL PROPERTY CONSTRUCTED PRIOR TO 1978, BUYER MUST ALSO HAVE SIGNED LEAD PAINT "PROPERTY TRANSFER NOTIFICATION CERTIFICATION"

NOTICE: This is a legal document that creates binding obligations. If not understood, consult an attorney.

SELLER:__________	BUYER:__________
PRINT NAME:__________	PRINT NAME:__________
Taxpayer ID/Social Security No.__________	Taxpayer ID/Social Security No.__________
SELLER (or Spouse):__________	BUYER:__________
PRINT NAME:__________	PRINT NAME:__________
Taxpayer ID/Social Security No.__________	Taxpayer ID/Social Security No.__________

____

BROKER(S)

Problems

How do the Offer to Purchase Real Estate and the Standard Form Purchase and Sale Agreement address the following situations?

1. After signing the Offer to Purchase Real Estate, but before executing the Standard Form Purchase and Sale Agreement, the seller receives a much higher offer for the property and would like to accept it.

2. Assume the parties sign the Standard Form Purchase and Sale Agreement. The buyer is concerned about possible environmental conditions on the property and wants to have an environmental consultant conduct an inspection. What if the seller told the buyer before they signed the contract that "there is nothing to worry about" in response to a question by the buyer about these environmental concerns?

3. The seller's property is damaged in an electrical fire a week before the scheduled closing. Does it matter whether the seller had property insurance?

4. The buyer, in examining the state of the property's title, discovers a judgment lien against the property, arising from a tort suit between the seller and a third party.

5. The buyer unexpectedly loses her job shortly after signing the Standard Form Purchase and Sale Agreement and is now unable to obtain the loan that she thought she could.

6. The seller agrees to remove an old outbuilding from the property, but says that he needs another two weeks after closing to complete the project.

§2.2 Statute of Frauds versus Part Performance and Estoppel

Burns v. McCormick

135 N.E. 273 (N.Y. 1922)

Map: Hornell, New York

BENJAMIN N. CARDOZO, J.

In June, 1918, one James A. Halsey, an old man, and a widower, was living, without family or housekeeper, in his house in Hornell, New York. He told the plaintiffs, [who are husband and wife,] so it is said, that if they gave up their home and business in Andover, New York, and boarded and cared for him during his life, the house and lot, with its furniture and equipment, would be theirs upon his death. They did as he asked, selling out an interest in a little draying business in Andover, and boarding and tending him till he died, about five months after their coming. Neither deed nor will, nor memorandum subscribed by the promisor, exists to authenticate the promise.

The plaintiffs asked specific performance. The defense is the statute of frauds (Real Property Law [Consol. Laws, ch. 50] §259).

We think the defense must be upheld. Not every act of part performance will move a court of equity, though legal remedies are inadequate, to enforce an oral agreement affecting rights in land. There must be performance "unequivocally referable" to the agreement, performance which alone and without the aid of words of promise is unintelligible or at least extraordinary unless as an incident of ownership, assured, if not existing.

"An act which admits of explanation without reference to the alleged oral contract or a contract of the same general nature and purpose is not, in general, admitted to constitute a part performance." *Woolley v. Stewart,* 118 N.E. 847, 848 (N.Y. 1918).

What is done must itself supply the key to what is promised. It is not enough that what is promised may give significance to what is done. The housekeeper who abandons other prospects of establishment in life and renders service without pay upon the oral promise of her employer to give her a life estate in land must find her remedy in an action to recover the value of the service. Her conduct, separated from the promise, is not significant of ownership, either present or prospective. On the other hand, the buyer who not only pays the price, but possesses and improves his acre, may have relief in equity without producing a conveyance. His conduct is itself the symptom of a promise that a conveyance will be made. Laxer tests may prevail in other jurisdictions. We have been consistent here.

Promise and performance fail when these standards are applied. The plaintiffs make no pretense that during the lifetime of Mr. Halsey they occupied the land as owners or under claim of present right. They did not even have possession. The possession was his; and those whom he invited to live with him were merely his servants or his guests. He might have shown them the door, and the law would not have helped them to return. Whatever rights they had were executory and future. The tokens of their title are not, then, to be discovered in acts of possession or dominion. The tokens must be found elsewhere if discoverable at all. The plaintiffs did, indeed, while occupants of the dwelling, pay the food bills for the owner as well as for themselves, and do the work of housekeepers. One who heard of such service might infer that it would be rewarded in some way. There could be no reasonable inference that it would be rewarded at some indefinite time thereafter by a conveyance of the land. The board might be given in return for lodging. The outlay might be merely an advance to be repaid in whole or part. "Time and care" might have been bestowed "From a vague anticipation that the affection and gratitude so created would, in the long run, insure some indefinite reward." *Maddison v. Alderson,* L.R. 8 App. Cas. [467,] 486. This was the more likely since there were ties of kinship between one of the plaintiffs and the owner. Even if there was to be a reward, not merely as of favor, but as of right, no one could infer, from knowledge of the service, without more, what its nature or extent would be. Mr. Halsey paid the taxes. He paid also for the upkeep of the land and building. At least, there is no suggestion that the plaintiffs had undertaken to relieve him of those burdens. He was the owner while he lived. Nothing that he had accepted from the plaintiffs evinces an agreement that they were to be the owners when he died.

We hold, then, that the acts of part performance are not solely and unequivocally referable to a contract for the sale of land. Since that is so, they do not become sufficient because part of the plaintiffs' loss is without a remedy at law. At law the value of board and services will not be difficult of proof. The loss of the draying business in Andover does not permit us to disregard the statute, though it may go without requital. We do not ignore decisions to the contrary in other jurisdictions. They are not law for us. Inadequacy of legal remedies, without more, does not dispense with the requirement that acts, and not words, shall supply the framework of the promise. That requirement has its origin in something more than an arbitrary preference of one form over others. It is "intended to prevent a recurrence of the mischief" which the statute would suppress. *Maddison v. Alderson, supra*, L.R. 8 App. Cas. at 478. The peril of perjury and error is latent in the spoken promise. Such, at least, is the warning of the statute, the estimate of policy that finds expression in its mandate. Equity, in assuming what is in substance a dispensing power, does not treat the statute as irrelevant, nor ignore the warning altogether. It declines to act on words, though the legal remedy is imperfect, unless the words are confirmed and illuminated by deeds. A power of dispensation, departing from the letter in supposed adherence to the spirit, involves an assumption of jurisdiction easily abused, and justified only within the limits imposed by history and precedent. The power is not exercised unless the policy of the law is saved.

In conclusion, we observe that this is not a case of fraud. No confidential relation has been abused. No inducement has been offered with the preconceived intention that it would later be ignored. The most that can be said against Mr. Halsey is that he made a promise which the law did not compel him to keep, and that afterwards he failed to keep it. We cannot even say of his failure that it was willful. He had made a will before the promise. Negligence or mere inertia may have postponed the making of another. The plaintiffs left the preservation of their agreement, if they had one, to the fallible memory of witnesses. The law exacts a writing.

Hickey v. Green

442 N.E.2d 37 (Mass. App. Ct. 1982)

Map: Massasoit Avenue, Plymouth, Massachusetts

R. Ammi Cutter, Justice.

Mrs. Gladys Green owns a lot (Lot S) in the Manomet section of Plymouth. In July, 1980, she advertised it for sale. On July 11 and 12, Hickey and his wife discussed with Mrs. Green purchasing Lot S and "orally agreed to a sale" for $15,000. Mrs. Green on July 12 accepted a deposit check of $500, marked by Hickey on the back, "Deposit on Lot . . . Massasoit Ave. Manomet . . . Subject to Variance from Town of Plymouth." Mrs. Green's brother and agent "was under the impression that a zoning variance was needed and [had] advised Hickey to write" the quoted language on the deposit check.

It turned out, however, by July 16 that no variance would be required. Hickey had left the payee line of the deposit check blank, because of uncertainty whether Mrs. Green or her brother was to receive the check and asked "Mrs. Green to fill in the appropriate name." Mrs. Green held the check, did not fill in the payee's name, and neither cashed nor endorsed it. Hickey "stated to Mrs. Green that his intention was to sell his home and build on Mrs. Green's lot."

"Relying upon the arrangements with Mrs. Green," the Hickeys advertised their house on Sachem Road in newspapers on three days in July, 1980, and agreed with a purchaser for its sale and took from him a deposit check for $500 which they deposited in their own account. On July 24, Mrs. Green told Hickey that she "no longer intended to sell her property to him" but had decided to sell to another for $16,000. Hickey told Mrs. Green that he had already sold his house and offered her $16,000 for Lot S. Mrs. Green refused this offer.

The Hickeys filed this complaint seeking specific performance. Mrs. Green asserts that relief is barred by the Statute of Frauds contained in Mass. Gen. Laws ch. 259, §1. The trial judge granted specific performance. Mrs. Green has appealed.

The present rule applicable in most jurisdictions in the United States is succinctly set forth in *Restatement (Second) of Contracts*, §129 (1981). The section reads, "A contract for the transfer of an interest in land may be specifically enforced notwithstanding failure to comply with the Statute of Frauds if it is established that the party seeking enforcement, *in reasonable reliance on the contract* and on the continuing assent of the party against whom enforcement is sought, *has so changed his position that injustice can be avoided only by specific enforcement*" (emphasis supplied).[4] The earlier Massachusetts decisions laid down somewhat strict requirements for an estoppel precluding the assertion of the Statute of Frauds. Frequently there has been an actual change of possession and improvement of the transferred property, as well as full payment of the full purchase price, or one or more of these elements.

---

4. Comments a and b to §129, read (in part):

> a. This section restates what is widely known as the "part performance doctrine." Part performance is not an accurate designation of such acts as taking possession and making improvements when the contract does not provide for such acts, but such acts regularly bring the doctrine into play. The doctrine is contrary to the words of the Statute of Frauds, but it was established by English courts of equity soon after the enactment of the Statute. Payment of purchase-money, without more, was once thought sufficient to justify specific enforcement, but a contrary view now prevails, since in such cases restitution is an adequate remedy. Enforcement has been justified on the ground that repudiation after "part performance" amounts to a "virtual fraud." A more accurate statement is that courts with equitable powers are vested by tradition with what in substance is a dispensing power based on the promisee's reliance, *a discretion to be exercised with caution* in the light of all the circumstances [emphasis supplied].
>
> b. Two distinct elements enter into the application of the rule of this Section: first, the extent to which the evidentiary function of the statutory formalities is fulfilled by the conduct of the parties; second, the reliance of the promisee, providing a compelling substantive basis for relief in addition to the expectations created by the promise.

It is stated in Park, *Real Estate Law*, §883, at 334, that the "more recent decisions indicate a trend on the part of the [Supreme Judicial] [C]ourt to find that the circumstances warrant specific performance." This appears to be a correct perception.

The present facts reveal a simple case of a proposed purchase of a residential vacant lot, where the vendor, Mrs. Green, knew that the Hickeys were planning to sell their former home (possibly to obtain funds to pay her) and build on Lot S. The Hickeys, relying on Mrs. Green's oral promise, moved rapidly to make their sale without obtaining any adequate memorandum of the terms of what appears to have been intended to be a quick cash sale of Lot S. So rapid was action by the Hickeys that, by July 21, less than ten days after giving their deposit to Mrs. Green, they had accepted a deposit check for the sale of their house, endorsed the check, and placed it in their bank account. Above their signatures endorsing the check was a memorandum probably sufficient to satisfy the Statute of Frauds. At the very least, the Hickeys had bound themselves in a manner in which, to avoid a transfer of their own house, they might have had to engage in expensive litigation. No attorney has been shown to have been used either in the transaction between Mrs. Green and the Hickeys or in that between the Hickeys and their purchaser.

There is no denial by Mrs. Green of the oral contract between her and the Hickeys. This, under §129 of the *Restatement*, is of some significance.[5] There can be no doubt (a) that Mrs. Green made the promise on which the Hickeys so promptly relied, and also (b) she, nearly as promptly, but not promptly enough, repudiated it because she had a better opportunity. The stipulated facts require the conclusion that in equity Mrs. Green's conduct cannot be condoned. This is not a case where either party is shown to have contemplated the negotiation of a purchase and sale agreement. If a written agreement had been expected, even by only one party, or would have been natural (because of the participation by lawyers or otherwise), a different situation might have existed. It is a permissible inference from the agreed facts that the rapid sale of the Hickeys' house was both appropriate and expected. These are not circumstances where negotiations fairly can be seen as inchoate.

No public interest behind Mass. Gen. Laws ch. 259, §1 in the simple circumstances before us, will be violated if Mrs. Green fairly is held to her precise bargain by principles of equitable estoppel.

---

5. Comment d of *Restatement (Second) of Contracts*, §129, reads[:]

> d. Where specific enforcement is rested on a transfer of possession plus either part payment of the price or the making of improvements, it is commonly said that the action taken by the purchaser must be unequivocally referable to the oral agreement. But this requirement is not insisted on *if the making of the promise is admitted or is clearly proved.* The promisee *must act in reasonable reliance on the promise, before the promisor has repudiated* it, and the action must be such that the remedy of restitution is inadequate. If these requirements are met, *neither taking of possession nor payment of money nor the making of improvements is essential* [emphasis supplied].

Notes and Questions

1. **Gender roles and the construction of social reality.** In *Burns v. McCormick*, Justice Cardozo distinguished the acts of a "housekeeper who abandons other prospects of establishment in life and renders service without pay upon the oral promise of her employer to give her a life estate in land" from "the buyer who not only pays the price, but possesses and improves his acre." Cardozo explained that "[h]er conduct, separated from the promise, is not significant of ownership, either present or prospective," while "[h]is conduct is itself the symptom of a promise that a conveyance will be made." When discussing the housekeeper, Cardozo refers to "her" conduct; but when discussing a hypothetical buyer, he refers to "his" conduct. Why does he make this shift in gender? Plaintiffs were a married couple. Is there any evidence Cardozo considered the circumstances of the husband's conduct?

Why does Cardozo refer to the person providing personal services as a "housekeeper," while calling the one who improves the land a "buyer"? Doesn't the use of this language beg the question? Why is performing personal service less indicative of a contractual arrangement than payment of money? Does Cardozo assume that "housework" is normally performed by women for no compensation? Are housekeepers likely to engage in personal service in exchange for a chance of an indefinite reward, while those who work the land are unlikely to do so?

Cardozo suggests that the housekeeper's conduct is compatible with several explanations, while the "buyer's" conduct is susceptible of only one. According to Cardozo's understanding of social custom, a housekeeper might go to work for an employer, without wages, and pay for the food bills for both her employer and herself in exchange for lodging and the vague expectation of "some indefinite reward" that might be bestowed "in the long run." No "buyer," however, would pay a substantial sum of money and improve real property without having received a promise to convey the property to the buyer. Is it true that no other explanation might fit the set of facts, which includes (a) paying a large sum of money and (b) improving real property? Recall the cases about easements by estoppel and constructive trusts in Chapter 8.

2. **The family versus the market.** Consider the following descriptions of the relationship among gender roles, the family, and the market.

In upholding the decision of the Illinois Supreme Court to deny Myra Bradwell admission to the Illinois bar because she was a woman, Justice Joseph P. Bradley wrote a famous concurring opinion for the United States Supreme Court, in which he wrote:

> [T]he civil law, as well as nature herself, has always recognized a wide difference in the respective spheres and destinies of man and woman. Man is, or should be, woman's protector and defender. The natural and proper timidity and delicacy which belongs to the female sex evidently unfits it for many of the occupations of civil life. The constitution of the family organization, which is founded in the divine ordinance, as well as in the nature of things, indicates the domestic sphere as that which properly belongs to the domain and functions of womanhood.

Bradwell v. Illinois, 83 U.S. (16 Wall.) 130, 141 (1873) (Bradley, J., concurring).

and the authority to act on behalf of the parties to a transaction. *See, e.g., Leist v. Tugendhaft*, 882 N.Y.S.2d 521 (N.Y. App. Div. 2009). Does the relative informality of electronic communications undermine one of the goals of the Statute of Frauds, which is to remind the parties of the significance of the transaction before it becomes binding? On the other hand, should real property be treated differently from other types of assets, often of great value, that can be traded electronically today?

4. **General exceptions to the Statute of Frauds**

a. Part performance. The part performance doctrine allows an oral sales contract to be enforced if the buyer has substantially changed her position and taken steps to complete the transaction. *Kiernan v. Creech*, 268 P.3d 312, 317 (Alaska 2012). Justice Cardozo in *Burns* applied the traditional rule that the buyer must take steps that are "unequivocally referable" to a land sales contract. Today courts do not require this degree of certainty, instead relying on three factors that ordinarily will suggest that a contract has been made: (1) payment of all or a substantial part of the **purchase price**; (2) taking **possession** of the property; and (3) making substantial **improvements** on the land. *See, e.g., Sullivan v. Porter*, 861 A.2d 625 (Me. 2004); *Sharp v. Sumner*, 528 S.E.2d 791 (Ga. 2000). The states differ on whether all three elements are required or only one or two. Payment of part of the purchase price is generally not enough to trigger the doctrine because the buyer can be made whole by having the money returned (with interest). However, payment of the purchase price in combination with one or both of the other factors is likely to be sufficient because they ordinarily would not occur without a promise to convey. Many cases rely on a combination of payment of part of the purchase price plus the taking of possession as sufficient to take the case out of the Statute of Frauds and allow enforcement.

b. Estoppel. An alternative basis for the part performance doctrine is estoppel. "[I]f one party to the transaction induces the other to make a substantial change of position to his or her detriment in good faith reliance on the first party's actions, then the first party may be estopped from denying the transaction." 14-81A *Powell on Real Property* §81A.02[3][e]. When the seller makes a promise on which the buyer relies substantially, it is not fair to allow the seller to claim that she did not make a promise if this would cause detriment to the buyer who reasonably relied on the promise to convey. *Roussalis v. Wyoming Medical Center*, 4 P.3d 209 (Wyo. 2000); *see also Harvey v. Dow*, 11 A.3d 303, 307 (Me. 2011) (parents' "general promise to give [their daughter] land at some time" coupled with their "acquiescence, support, and encouragement" of their daughter's "construction of a house on a parcel of their land," demonstrated the parents' "intention to make a present conveyance of that property"). The buyer who has taken substantial steps to complete the transaction by taking possession or making improvements will ordinarily suffer hardship if the contract is not enforced. The seller may also seek specific enforcement of the contract if she has changed her position in reliance on the sale occurring, such as investing the proceeds in the purchase of another property.

How would *Burns v. McCormick* come out under the standard adopted in *Hickey v. Green*? Was the plaintiffs' reliance reasonable? Is the result unjust? How would *Hickey v. Green* have come out if Gladys Green had denied that she made the promise? How important should an admission of a promise be, if there is one? *See Brown v. Branch*, 758 N.E.2d 48, 53 (Ind. 2001) (finding oral promise to convey title to a house to his girlfriend not enforceable despite the fact that the girlfriend quit her job, dropped out of college, and moved back to Indiana from Missouri; refusal to enforce the promise would not inflict "an unjust and unconscionable injury and loss").

c. Constructive trust. A third method of avoiding the Statute of Frauds is the constructive trust doctrine, which may be applied to prevent unjust enrichment when "property has been acquired in such circumstances that the holder of the legal title may not in good conscience retain the beneficial interest." *Davis v. Barnfield*, 833 So. 2d 58, 64 (Ala. Ct. App. 2002); *accord Rawlings v. Rawlings*, 240 P.3d 754 (Utah 2010). This doctrine may apply if the funds of one person are used to acquire property, but title is held in the name of another.

5. Formality versus informality. Would it be better to enforce the Statute of Frauds rigidly rather than creating equitable exceptions? Do these exceptions enable the court to obtain justice in the individual case, or do they reward negligence and undermine predictability? Is it compatible with the judicial role to read exceptions into general statutes such as the Statute of Frauds? Which rule is more likely to accord with the will of the parties? Which rule is more likely to reduce the costs of transactions? Which rule is more likely to prevent fraud?

In 1996, New Jersey amended its Statute of Frauds to eliminate the requirement that a contract for the sale of real of real property must be in writing. The statute only requires "a description of the real estate sufficient to identify it, the nature of the interest to be transferred, the existence of the agreement and the identity of the transferor and the transferee are proved by clear and convincing evidence." N.J. Stat. §25:1-13. A claimant may appeal to part performance or reliance to prove the existence of the agreement by clear and convincing evidence but the statute authorizes enforcement even without part performance or reliance by the buyer as long as the evidence of the existence and terms of the agreement is sufficiently strong. *See Barron v. Kipling Woods, LLC*, 838 A.2d 490 (N.J. Super. Ct. App. Div. 2004). Is this a good change in the law?

§2.3 What Constitutes a Breach of the Contract

A. Misrepresentation and Fraudulent Nondisclosure

Johnson v. Davis

480 So. 2d 625 (Fla. 1985)

JAMES C. ADKINS, Justice.

In May of 1982, the Davises entered into a contract to buy for $310,000 the Johnsons' home, which at the time was three years old. The contract required a $5,000 deposit payment, an additional $26,000 deposit payment within five days and a closing by June 21, 1982.

Before the Davises made the additional $26,000 deposit payment, Mrs. Davis noticed some buckling and peeling plaster around the corner of a window frame in the family room and stains on the ceilings in the family room and kitchen of the home. Upon inquiring, Mrs. Davis was told by Mr. Johnson that the window had had a minor problem that had long since been corrected and that the stains were wallpaper glue and the result of ceiling beams being moved. There is disagreement among the parties as to whether Mr. Johnson also told Mrs. Davis at this time that there had never been any problems with the roof or ceilings. The Davises thereafter paid the remainder of their deposit and the Johnsons vacated the home. Several days later, following a heavy rain, Mrs. Davis entered the home and discovered water "gushing" in from around the window frame, the ceiling of the family room, the light fixtures, the glass doors, and the stove in the kitchen.

Two roofers hired by the Johnsons' broker concluded that for under $1,000 they could "fix" certain leaks in the roof and by doing so make the roof "watertight." Three roofers hired by the Davises found that the roof was inherently defective, that any repairs would be temporary because the roof was "slipping," and that only a new $15,000 roof could be "watertight."

The Davises filed a complaint alleging breach of contract, fraud and misrepresentation, and sought rescission of the contract and return of their deposit. The Johnsons counterclaimed seeking the deposit as liquidated damages.

We agree with the district court's conclusions under a theory of fraud and find that the Johnsons' statements to the Davises regarding the condition of the roof constituted a fraudulent misrepresentation entitling respondents to the return of their $26,000 deposit payment. In the state of Florida, relief for a fraudulent misrepresentation may be granted only when the following elements are present: (1) a false statement concerning a material fact; (2) the representor's knowledge that the representation is false; (3) an intention that the representation induce another to act on it; and (4) consequent injury by the party acting in reliance on the representation.

The evidence adduced at trial shows that after the buyer and the seller signed the purchase and sales agreement and after receiving the $5,000 initial deposit payment the Johnsons affirmatively repeated to the Davises that there were no problems with the roof. The Johnsons subsequently received the additional $26,000 deposit payment from the Davises. The record reflects that the statement made by the Johnsons was a false representation of material fact, made with knowledge of its falsity, upon which the Davises relied to their detriment as evidenced by the $26,000 paid to the Johnsons.

The doctrine of *caveat emptor* does not exempt a seller from responsibility for the statements and representations which he makes to induce the buyer to act, when under the circumstances these amount to fraud in the legal sense. To be grounds for relief, the false representations need not have been made at the time of the signing of the purchase and sales agreement in order for the element of reliance to be present. The fact that the false statements as to the quality of the roof were made after the signing of the purchase and sales agreement does not excuse the seller from liability when the misrepresentations were made prior to the execution of the contract by conveyance of the property. It would be contrary to all notions of fairness and justice for this Court to place its stamp of approval on an affirmative misrepresentation by a wrongdoer just because it was made after the signing of the executory contract when all of the necessary elements for actionable fraud are present. Furthermore, the Davises' reliance on the truth of the Johnsons' representation was justified and is supported by this Court's decision in *Besett v. Basnett*, 389 So. 2d 995 (Fla. 1980), where we held "that a recipient may rely on the truth of a representation, even though its falsity could have been ascertained had he made an investigation, unless he knows the representation to be false or its falsity is obvious to him."

In determining whether a seller of a home has a duty to disclose latent material defects to a buyer, the established tort law distinction between misfeasance and nonfeasance, action and inaction must carefully be analyzed. The highly individualistic philosophy of the earlier common law consistently imposed liability upon the commission of affirmative acts of harm, but shrank from converting the courts into an institution for forcing men to help one another. This distinction is deeply rooted in our case law. Liability for nonfeasance has therefore been slow to receive recognition in the evolution of tort law.

In theory, the difference between misfeasance and nonfeasance, action and inaction is quite simple and obvious; however, in practice it is not always easy to draw the line and determine whether conduct is active or passive. That is, where failure to disclose a material fact is calculated to induce a false belief, the distinction between concealment and affirmative representations is tenuous. Both proceed from the same motives and are attended with the same consequences; both are violative of the principles of fair dealing and good faith; both are calculated to produce the same result; and, in fact, both essentially have the same effect.

Still there exists in much of our case law the old tort notion that there can be no liability for nonfeasance. The courts in some jurisdictions, including Florida, hold that where the parties are dealing at arms' length and the facts lie equally open to both parties, with equal opportunity of examination, mere nondisclosure does not constitute a fraudulent concealment. The Fourth District affirmed that rule of law in *Banks v. Salina*, 413 So. 2d 851 (Fla. Dist. Ct. App. 1982), and found that although the sellers had sold a home without disclosing the presence of a defective roof and swimming pool of which the sellers had knowledge, "[i]n Florida," there is no duty to disclose when parties are dealing at arms length. *Id.* at 852.

These unappetizing cases are not in tune with the times and do not conform with current notions of justice, equity and fair dealing. One should not be able to stand behind the impervious shield of *caveat emptor* and take advantage of another's ignorance. Our courts have taken great strides since the days when the judicial emphasis was on rigid rules and ancient precedents. Modern concepts of justice and fair dealing have given our courts the opportunity and latitude to change legal precepts in order to conform to society's needs. Thus, the tendency of the more recent cases has been to restrict rather than extend the doctrine of *caveat emptor*. The law appears to be working toward the ultimate conclusion that full disclosure of all material facts must be made whenever elementary fair conduct demands it.

The harness placed on the doctrine of *caveat emptor* in a number of other jurisdictions has resulted in the seller of a home being liable for failing to disclose material defects of which he is aware. This philosophy was succinctly expressed in *Lingsch v. Savage*, 29 Cal. Rptr. 201 (Ct. App. 1963):

> It is now settled in California that where the seller knows of facts materially affecting the value or desirability of the property which are known or accessible only to him and also knows that such facts are not known to or within the reach of the diligent attention and observation of the buyer, the seller is under a duty to disclose them to the buyer.

In *Posner v. Davis*, 395 N.E.2d 133 (Ill. 1979), buyers brought an action alleging that the sellers of a home fraudulently concealed certain defects in the home which included a leaking roof and basement flooding. Relying on *Lingsch*, the court concluded that the sellers knew of and failed to disclose latent material defects and thus were liable for fraudulent concealment. Numerous other jurisdictions have followed this view in formulating law involving the sale of homes.

We are of the opinion, in view of the reasoning and results in *Lingsch*, *Posner* and the aforementioned cases decided in other jurisdictions, that the same philosophy regarding the sale of homes should also be the law in the state of Florida. Accordingly, we hold that where the seller of a home knows of facts materially affecting the value of the property which are not readily observable and are not known to the buyer, the seller is under a duty to disclose them to the buyer. This duty is equally applicable to all forms of real property, new and used.

In the case at bar, the evidence shows that the Johnsons knew of and failed to disclose that there had been problems with the roof of the house. Mr. Johnson admitted during his testimony that the Johnsons were aware of roof problems prior to entering into the contract of sale and receiving the $5,000 deposit payment. Thus, we agree with the district court and find that the Johnsons' fraudulent concealment also entitles the Davises to the return of the $5,000 deposit payment plus interest.

JOSEPH A. BOYD, JR., Chief Justice, dissenting.

I respectfully but strongly dissent to the Court's expansion of the duties of sellers of real property. This ruling will give rise to a flood of litigation and will facilitate unjust outcomes in many cases. If, as a matter of public policy, the well settled law of this state on this question should be changed, the change should come from the legislature.

Homeowners who attempt to sell their houses are typically in no better position to measure the quality, value, or desirability of their houses than are the prospective purchasers with whom such owners come into contact. Based on this and related considerations, the law of Florida has long been that a seller of real property with improvements is under no duty to disclose all material facts, in the absence of a fiduciary relationship, to a buyer who has an equal opportunity to learn all material information and is not prevented by the seller from doing so. This rule provides sufficient protection against overreaching by sellers.

I do not agree with the Court's belief that the distinction between nondisclosure and affirmative statement is weak or nonexistent. It is a distinction that we should take special care to emphasize and preserve. Imposition of liability for seller's nondisclosure of the condition of improvements to real property is the first step toward making the seller a guarantor of the good condition of the property.

Although as described in the majority opinion this change in the law sounds progressive, high-minded, and idealistic, it is in reality completely unnecessary. Prudent purchasers inspect property, with expert advice if necessary, before they agree to buy. Prudent lenders require inspections before agreeing to provide purchase money. Initial deposits of earnest money can be made with the agreement to purchase being conditional upon the favorable results of expert inspections. It is significant that in the present case the major portion of the purchase price was to be financed by the Johnsons who were to hold a mortgage on the property. If they had been knowingly trying to get rid of what they knew to be a defectively constructed house, it is unlikely that they would have been willing to lend $200,000 with the house in question as their only security.

Notes and Questions

1. **Misrepresentation.** Traditionally, the courts have differentiated misrepresentation, suppression, and nondisclosure as bases for claims of fraud in real estate transactions. An outright lie or misrepresentation of facts has always constituted fraud and may give rise to liability for damages as well as a right to rescind the sale. If the misrepresentation is about a condition of the premises that is apparent to the buyer, a fraud claim may be denied on the ground that a reasonable buyer would have inspected the premises and discovered the evident defect, and thus any reliance on the seller's statement was unreasonable. Certain statements of material fact, however, can be fraudulent even if a buyer might be able to investigate, if the seller creates a situation where a reasonable buyer would not undertake that investigation. *See, e.g., Bowman v. Presley*, 212 P.3d 1210, 1221 (Okla. 2009) (firm statement about a home's square footage can serve as a "positive assurance upon which a purchaser may rely without being compelled independently to determine the truth or falsity of the fact represented").

> ***ELEMENTS***
>
> **Fraudulent misrepresentation** generally consists of
> 1. a false statement concerning a material fact;
> 2. that the maker of the statement knows is false;
> 3. made with the intent to induce reliance; and
> 4. consequent injury to the party relying on the statement.

A recurring issue in misrepresentation cases is whether a statement constitutes a fact or an opinion. For example, the statement that "It's a great house" is often characterized as an opinion, which can shield the seller from liability for fraud. In *Ray v. Montgomery*, 399 So. 2d 230 (Ala. 1980), the court held that the statement that a house "was supported by hewn pine timbers, had good support, was 'a nice house,' was solid, and was in good condition" was an opinion and could not constitute fraud, even though the seller knew that the house was afflicted with termite damage. Do you agree? *Compare Cooper & Co., Inc. v. Lester*, 832 So. 2d 628, 633 (Ala. 2000) (opinion may be the basis for fraud claim if actual fraudulent intent in making such a representation is proven).

2. ***Caveat emptor* or obligation to disclose?** Courts traditionally held that sellers are under no obligation to disclose defects in the houses they are selling. Real estate sales were governed by the doctrine of *caveat emptor* — let the buyer beware. This traditional rule, which generally relieved sellers for liability arising from property defects, is still followed in some states. *See, e.g., Teer v. Johnston,* 60 So. 3d 253, 258 (Ala. 2010) (*caveat emptor* applies to sales of used real property); *Urman v. South Boston Savings Bank,* 674 N.E.2d 1078 (Mass. 1997) (no common law duty to disclose latent defects; exception if duty is imposed by statute).

A number of states continue to apply this rule in the context of *apparent defects.* As long as the seller does not affirmatively lie to the buyer about the condition of the premises (making a fraudulent misrepresentation), buyers are generally charged with notice of what an inspection of the premises would have revealed. *Puget Sound Service Corp. v. Dalarna Management Corp.,* 752 P.2d 1353 (Wash. Ct. App. 1988). However, some courts make exceptions to this principle if the seller acts to conceal the defect or other otherwise suppress knowledge of it by a potential buyer. *Osterhaus v. Toth,* 249 P.3d 888, 905 (Kan. 2011); *Kracl v. Loseke,* 461 N.W.2d 67 (Neb. 1990); *Restatement (Second) of Torts* §550 (1977).

ELEMENTS

Sellers generally have a **duty to disclose**
1. known facts;
2. that are material to the sale; and
3. are not within reach of diligent attention of buyer.

In recent years, there has been a trend to require sellers and brokers of real estate to disclose information about *latent defects known to the seller* and not readily discoverable by a buyer. Violation of this **duty to disclose** constitutes fraud and will entitle the buyer to rescind the sale and/or obtain damages caused by the fraud. *Hess v. Chase Manhattan Bank, USA,* 220 S.W.2d 758 (Mo. 2007); *Shapiro v. Sutherland,* 76 Cal. Rptr. 2d 101, 107 (Ct. App. 1998); *Timm v. Clement,* 574 N.W.2d 368 (Iowa 1997). Some states limit this disclosure obligation to defects that pose a danger to health or safety. *Blaylock v. Cary,* 709 So. 2d 1128 (Ala. 1997); *Conahan v. Fisher,* 463 N.W.2d 118 (Mich. Ct. App. 1990); *Restatement (Second) of Torts* §353 (1977). Some states go further and require sellers to reveal facts of which they are aware that materially affect the value or desirability of the property. *Hermansen v. Tasulis,* 48 P.3d 235 (Utah 2002) (for brokers); *Assilzadeh v. California Federal Bank,* 98 Cal. Rptr. 2d 176, 182 (Ct. App. 2000).

3. **What information must be disclosed?** A claim that a defendant fraudulently failed to disclose certain information is premised on the assumption that the defendant had a duty to disclose that information to the plaintiff. This naturally raises the question of what information must be disclosed. In general, states that impose liability for nondisclosure require disclosure of nonobvious information that a reasonable buyer would want to know about and that might affect the terms of the transaction — especially the market value of the property — or induce the buyer to back out of the deal. *Logue v. Flanagan,* 584 S.E.2d 186, 190 (W. Va. 2003) (holding that "where a vendor is aware of defects or conditions which substantially affect the value or habitability of the property and the existence of which are unknown to the purchaser and would not be disclosed by a reasonably diligent inspection, then the vendor has a duty to disclose the same to the purchaser").

Many cases imposing liability on sellers or brokers for fraudulent nondisclosure concern information about defective conditions that pose a risk of harm and that would not be apparent to a reasonable observer. For example, defendants have been found liable for fraudulent nondisclosure when they have failed to disclose that the building was infested by termites, *Obde v. Schlemeyer*, 353 P.2d 672 (Wash. 1960), that the home was built on collapsible soil, *Hess v. Canberra Development Co., LC*, 254 P.3d 161 (Utah 2011), and that the property was located next to a landfill contaminated with toxic waste and that federal environmental officials had written a report advising against use of the site for human habitation, *Strawn v. Canuso*, 657 A.2d 420 (N.J. 1995), *superseded by* N.J. Stat. §§46:3C-1 to 46:3C-12.

Failure to disclose defective conditions may give rise to liability even when they have not been proven to be dangerous but are nonetheless material to the transaction in the sense that most buyers would want to know about them. *See, e.g., Roberts v. Estate of Barbagallo*, 531 A.2d 1125 (Pa. Super. Ct. 1988) (imposing liability for fraudulent nondisclosure on both the seller and the real estate broker hired by the seller because they failed to reveal that the house was insulated with ureaformaldehyde foam insulation, a substance that had been banned in future house construction by the federal government).

Other kinds of information have also been deemed relevant. For example, in *Reed v. King*, 193 Cal. Rptr. 130 (Ct. App. 1983), the seller was held liable for failing to disclose that a woman and her four children were murdered in the house ten years prior to the sale. In holding that the disclosure of murder would be relevant to most buyers, the court argued, *id.* at 133:

> The murder of innocents is highly unusual in its potential for so disturbing buyers they may be unable to reside in a home where it has occurred. This fact may foreseeably deprive a buyer of the intended use of the purchase. Murder is not such a common occurrence that buyers should be charged with anticipating and discovering this disquieting possibility. Accordingly, the fact is not one for which a duty of inquiry and discovery can sensibly be imposed upon the buyer.

The court argued that one way to demonstrate that a fact is material is to show that knowledge of the fact would affect the market value of the property.

> Reputation and history can have a significant effect on the value of realty. "George Washington slept here" is worth something, however physically inconsequential that consideration may be. Ill-repute or "bad will" conversely may depress the value of property. Failure to disclose such a negative fact where it will have a foreseeably depressing effect on income expected to be generated by a business is tortious.

Id. Compare *Milliken v. Jacono*, 60 A.3d 133 (Pa. Super. Ct. 2013) (no duty to disclose that murder-suicide took place in a listed house); *Deptula v. Simpson*, 164 P.3d 640, 646 (Alaska 2007) (no duty to disclose that previous owner had died and partially decomposed in house).

Stambovsky v. Ackley, 572 N.Y.S.2d 672 (App. Div. 1991), involved a particularly unusual variation on the obligation to disclose. The seller of an old Victorian-style house in Nyack, New York, had promoted the house as being haunted, going as far as reporting in the local and national press that there were three ghosts on the premises. The seller, however, did not mention this to the out-of-town buyers, a couple from New York City. The court found that "the most meticulous inspection and the search would not reveal the presence of poltergeists at the premises or unearth the property's ghoulish reputation in the community," *id.* at 676, and such a reputation "goes to the very essence of the bargain between the parties, greatly impairing both the value of the property and its potential for resale." *id.* at 674. Accordingly, the seller had a duty to disclose the reputation of the house and, as a result of her failure to do so, the buyers could rescind the contract.

The house at issue in *Stambovsky* eventually sold in 1995 to new buyers, a family who knew about its haunting reputation but still found the house's "vibe" to be "warm and inviting." John Patrick Shultz, *Nyack's Legally Haunted House*, At Home in Nyack Blog (Oct. 29, 2010), *available at http://athomeinnyack.wordpress.com/2010/10/29/nyacks-legally-haunted-house/*. When the house sold again in 2012, for $1,725,000, the listing made no mention of the resident ghosts. *See http://www.randrealty.com/NY/Property/1281830/1-La-Veta-Place-Nyack-NY10960/*. If you were buying a house today, would you Google the address?

4. **Legislation.** More than half the states have passed legislation requiring sellers to disclose defects in real property to prospective buyers. *See, e.g.*, Cal. Civ. Code §§1102-1102.17; N.J. Stat. §§46:3C-1 to 46:3C-12 (*interpreted by Nobrega v. Edison Glen Associates*, 772 A.2d 368 (N.J. 2001)). However, the obligations vary widely and may not extend to commercial property. *See, e.g., Futura Realty v. Lone Star Building Centers (East) Inc.*, 578 So. 2d 363 (Fla. Dist. Ct. App. 1991). Some states allow sellers to avoid disclosure by getting the buyer to sign a contract disclaiming reliance on any information by the seller. *See* Craig W. Dallon, *Theories of Real Estate Broker Liability and the Effect of the "As Is" Clause*, 54 Fla. L. Rev. 395 (2002). Would you favor passage of disclosure legislation in your state? A number of states regulate the scope of disclosures for certain conditions, such as off-site environmental hazards. *See, e.g., The New Residential Real Estate Off-Site Conditions Disclosure Act*, N.J. Stat. §§46:3C-1 to 46:3C-12. Why might brokers be in favor of statutes regulating disclosures?

Note that in 1992 Congress passed the *Residential Lead-Based Paint Hazard Reduction Act*, 42 U.S.C. §§4851-4856, requiring sellers and landlords of housing built before 1978 to provide buyers or lessees with a "lead hazard information pamphlet" and to disclose the presence of any known lead-based paint. *Id.* §4852d. *See* 40 C.F.R. §§745.101-745.107.

5. **The duty to disclose and the problem of trust.** If contracting parties have no duty to disclose information relevant to a transaction, then they must protect themselves by undertaking an independent investigation. The question whether there is a duty to disclose therefore poses a conflict between self-reliance and reliance on others with whom one enters market relationships. It also presents questions about the extent to which the law should encourage an atmosphere of trust or distrust in contractual relationships.

For example, *Bonnco Petrol, Inc. v. Epstein*, 560 A.2d 655 (N.J. 1989), concerned the sale of a home to a commercial entity. After extended negotiations, the "buyer" agreed to lease the property from the owner with an option to purchase that could be exercised at a specified date. The "seller" entrusted the buyer to amend the written contract drafts to accord with their oral agreement. The buyer, however, included a term in the contract that varied from the oral agreement. The seller skimmed the documents before signing them, relying on the buyer's claim that he amended the documents in accord with the parties' mutual understanding. The court found that the buyer misrepresented, by his silence, that the agreement signed by the seller conformed with earlier samples. The New Jersey Supreme Court concluded: "Silence in the face of an obligation to disclose amounts to equitable fraud." Justice Marie Garibaldi explained: "[I]t matters little that [the seller] failed to read the agreement carefully before signing. 'One who engages in fraud . . . may not urge that one's victim should have been more circumspect or astute.' We find, therefore, that equitable fraud has occurred. There was an inaccurate assertion (in the form of a nondisclosure) as to a material element of the bargain, on which the [sellers] justifiably relied. Their reliance was justifiable because they entrusted the drafting of the documents to [buyer]." *Id.* at 661.

Would it be better to encourage everyone to read a contract carefully before signing? What rule would better reduce transaction costs? Which rule better discourages fraud? What arguments could you make on both sides of these questions?

6. Waiver. In *Danann Realty Corp. v. Harris*, 157 N.E.2d 597 (N.Y. 1959), plaintiff alleged that it was induced to lease a building held by defendants because of oral representations, falsely made by the defendants, as to the operating expenses of the building and as to the profits to be derived from the investment. The court quoted the following clause contained in the contract:

> The Purchaser has examined the premises agreed to be sold and is familiar with the physical condition thereof. The Seller has not made and does not make any representations as to the physical condition, rents, leases, *expenses, operation* or any other matter or thing affecting or related to the aforesaid premises, except as herein specifically set forth, and the Purchaser hereby *expressly acknowledges that no such representations have been made, and the Purchaser further acknowledges that it has inspected the premises and agrees to take the premises "as is."* It is understood and agreed that all understandings and agreements heretofore had between the parties hereto are merged in this contract, which alone fully and completely expresses their agreement, *and that the same is entered into after full investigation, neither party relying upon any statement or representation,* not embodied in this contract, made by the other. The Purchaser has inspected the buildings standing on said premises and is thoroughly acquainted with their condition.

Id. at 598 (emphasis supplied by court).

The court held that generally a merger clause stating that the written agreement embodies the whole agreement does not protect the defendant from a claim of fraud. The court distinguished this case, however, noting that the contractual language was more specific, *id.* at 599-600:

[Here] plaintiff has in the plainest language announced and stipulated that it is not relying on any representations as to the very matter as to which it now claims it was defrauded. Such a specific disclaimer destroys the allegations in plaintiff's complaint that the agreement was executed in reliance upon these contrary oral representations.

[W]here a person has read and understood the disclaimer of representation clause, he is bound by it. [We have previously held,] as a matter of law, the allegation of plaintiffs "that they relied upon an oral statement made to them in direct contradiction of this provision of the contract." *Ernst Iron Works v. Duralith Corp.*, 200 N.E. 683, 685 (N.Y. 1936). The presence of such a disclaimer clause "is inconsistent with the contention that plaintiff relied upon the misrepresentation, and was led thereby to make the contract." *Kreshover v. Berger*, 119 N.Y.S. 737, 738 (App. Div. 1909).

[T]he plaintiff made a representation in the contract that it was not relying on specific representations not embodied in the contract, while, it now asserts, it was in fact relying on such oral representations. Plaintiff admits then that it is guilty of deliberately misrepresenting to the seller its true intention. To condone this fraud would place the purchaser in a favored position. This is particularly so, where, as here, the purchaser confirms the contract, but seeks damages. If the plaintiff has made a bad bargain he cannot avoid it in this manner.

If the language here used is not sufficient to estop a party from claiming that he entered the contract because of fraudulent representations, then no language can accomplish that purpose. To hold otherwise would be to say that it is impossible for two businessmen dealing at arm's length to agree that the buyer is not buying in reliance on any representations of the seller as to a particular fact.

Justice Stanley H. Fuld dissented, *id.* at 600-602, 606:

If a party has actually induced another to enter into a contract by means of fraud, I conceive that language may not be devised to shield him from the consequences of such fraud. The law does not temporize with trickery or duplicity, and this court, after having weighed the advantages of certainty in contractual relations against the harm and injustice which result from fraud, long ago unequivocally declared that "a party who has perpetrated a fraud upon his neighbor may [not] contract with him, in the very instrument by means of which it was perpetrated, for immunity against its consequences, close his mouth from complaining of it, and bind him never to seek redress. Public policy and morality are both ignored if such an agreement can be given effect in a court of justice. The maxim that fraud vitiates every transaction would no longer be the rule, but the exception." *Bridger v. Goldsmith*, 38 N.E. 458, 459 (N.Y. 1894). "In the realm of fact it is entirely possible for a party knowingly to agree that no representations have been made to him, while at the same time believing and relying upon representations which in fact have been made and in fact are false but for which he would not have made the agreement. To deny this possibility is to ignore the frequent instances in everyday experience where parties accept and act upon agreements containing exculpatory clauses in one form or another, but where they do so, nevertheless, in reliance upon the honesty of supposed friends, the plausible and disarming statements of salesmen, or the customary course of business. To refuse relief would result in opening the door to a multitude of frauds and in thwarting the general policy of the law." *Bates v. Southgate*, 31 N.E.2d 551, 558 (Mass. 1941).

The guiding rule [is] that fraud vitiates every agreement which it touches. Contrary to the intimation in the court's opinion, the nonreliance clause cannot possibly operate

> as an estoppel against the plaintiff. Essentially equitable in nature, the principle of estoppel is to be invoked to prevent fraud and injustice, not to further them. The statement that the representations in question were not made was, according to the complaint, false to the defendant's knowledge. Surely, the perpetrator of a fraud cannot close the lips of his victim and deny him the right to state the facts as they actually exist.

The *Danann* rule continues to be the law in many jurisdictions. *See Teer v. Johnston,* 60 So. 3d 253 (Ala. 2010); *Alires v. McGehee,* 85 P.3d 1191 (Kan. 2004); *Citibank, N.A. v. Plapinger,* 485 N.E.2d 974 (N.Y. 1985) (reaffirming the *Danann* rule). *See also* Florrie Young Roberts, *Let the Seller Beware: Disclosures, Disclaimers, and "As Is" Clauses,* 31 Real Est. L.J. 303, 315 (2003).

Other courts, however, reject the *Danann* rule, holding instead that a fraud claim is still available despite an "as is" clause or a "non-reliance" clause when the seller affirmatively lies about the condition of the premises. *Bowman v. Presley,* 212 P.3d 1210 (Okla. 2009); *Engels v. Ranger Bar, Inc.,* 604 N.W.2d 241 (S.D. 2000). In *Mulkey v. Waggoner,* 338 S.E.2d 755 (Ga. Ct. App. 1985), the seller failed to deliver to the purchaser a certificate, required by the contract, declaring the property free of termites and termite damage. At the closing, buyer Sheryl Waggoner refused to go ahead unless seller Z.A. Mulkey promised to give her such a certificate to complete the transaction. The seller's broker wrote into the sales contract the words: "The sale is as is condition." After the closing, when Waggoner discovered wood beetle damage and the fact that Mulkey had hired an exterminator two years earlier, she sued Mulkey for fraud. The court rejected defendant's argument that the "as is" clause in the contract absolutely precluded plaintiff from claiming that defendant had fraudulently induced her to sell. "[W]e are satisfied that an 'as is' clause concerns itself with obvious defects or at least those which are reasonably discernible. Had Mrs. Waggoner purchased the house unseen and accepted it with a patent defect easily exposed, the arguments of Mulkey may have had more validity." The clause could not be used to immunize the seller from liability for false oral statements upon which the buyer reasonably relied. *Accord, McClain v. Octagon Plaza, L.L.C.,* 71 Cal. Rptr. 3d 885 (2008) (enforcing Cal. Civ. Code §1668); *Snyder v. Lovercheck,* 992 P.2d 1079 (Wyo. 1999). Can you distinguish the relevant facts in *Danann* and *Mulkey*?

If sellers cannot enclose a clause in the contract of sale stating that the buyer agrees to buy the property "as is" or that the buyer is not relying on any oral statements made by the seller, how can sellers protect themselves from buyers who falsely allege that the seller made an oral statement on which the buyer relied?

Problem

Sellers of a home seek to move because their ten-year old son was sexually molested by an older minor boy living next door. The older boy was found guilty of the offense in juvenile court. The sellers feel torn about whether they should disclose this fact to potential buyers. They want to protect any families that might move into the home; at the same time, they know that revealing this information may make it much harder to sell their home. They are also aware that they cannot refuse to sell their home to a family with children because the federal *Fair Housing Act*, 42 U.S.C. §3601 *et seq.*, prohibits discrimination against families with children. In addition, they know that juvenile records are supposed to be sealed to protect the identity of juvenile offenders, although they are not directly bound by that confidentiality provision and may lawfully reveal the information. Do they have an obligation to reveal the information? Should they? If they do not have such an obligation, does the broker have a duty to reveal the information?

B. Seller's Failure to Provide Marketable Title

A purchase and sale agreement ordinarily requires the seller to be able to deliver "marketable title" at the date set for the closing and if the contract is silent, courts will often imply that obligation. The seller's inability to provide marketable title will excuse the buyer from the deal. What kinds of defects in the title are sufficiently serious to justify allowing the buyer to rescind the contract or refuse to close? In *Conklin v. Davi*, 388 A.2d 598 (N.J. 1978), the validity of the title to a portion of the premises was based on the sellers' claim to have acquired the property by adverse possession. The buyers argued that they were justified in repudiating the agreement in the absence of record title, which the sellers could have acquired either by seeking a deed from the record owner or by bringing suit to quiet title to the property. The court rejected this argument, holding instead that a "marketable title" was one "free from reasonable doubt, but not from every doubt." Title based on adverse possession, the court concluded, is marketable if the adverse possession can be "clearly established."

The main defects that make the title unmarketable are **encumbrances** and **chain of title defects**. Encumbrances are property interests in persons other than the grantor that seriously affect the value or usability of the property. These include possessory interests, such as conflicting titles and leases, and nonpossessory interests, such as easements, covenants, mortgages, and liens. Because many typical encumbrances have the potential to make title unmarketable, it is common for sales contracts to include explicit exceptions for matters in the public record, as the Standard Form Purchase and Sale Agreement reproduced above in §2 does in clause 4(e). How else does the Form Agreement address questions of encumbrances that might undermine marketable title?

Chain of title defects are mistakes or irregularities in the documents or procedures by which title has been transferred or encumbered over time. For example, a prior deed may turn out to have been forged, or the present deed may misdescribe the property.

Two other standards for title can be found in purchase and sale agreements, although contracts often combine requirements. Some contracts require title to be "insurable," which shifts the standard to the state of title that a reputable title insurance company would be willing to insure. *See, e.g., 111-38 Management Corp. v. Benitez*, 70 A.D.3d 911 (N.Y. App. Div. 2010) (distinguishing marketable title from insurable title). Some purchase and sale agreements, by contrast, require that title be valid "of record," which means that not only must title be good, but also that that fact be reflected in the public records. A requirement of record validity would thus not be met by an adverse possession claim because the public record would indicate an owner other than the seller. Given the possible uncertainties of adverse possession litigation and the fact that buyers may well hesitate to buy property so acquired, should a buyer be forced to conclude the transaction?

C. Seller's Breach of Warranty of Habitability for New Residential Real Estate

In contrast to the traditional *caveat emptor* doctrine still applicable in some states to the sale of used residential housing, most states protect buyers of newly constructed residential real estate by imposing an implied **warranty of habitability**. *See, e.g.*, 2012 La. Acts 112. The implied warranty goes by many names, including "habitability," "fitness," "quality," or "good workmanship." *See, e.g., Curry v. Thornsberry*, 128 S.W.3d 438 (Ark. 2003); *Albrecht v. Clifford*, 767 N.E.2d 42 (Mass. 2002). Breach of this warranty may allow the buyer to rescind the sale or obtain damages.

D. Buyer's Failure to Make Good Faith Efforts to Obtain Financing

Does a financing contingency imply an obligation to try in good faith to get a loan? In *Bushmiller v. Schiller*, 368 A.2d 1044 (Md. Ct. Spec. App. 1977), the buyer changed her mind after signing the purchase and sale agreement and made no serious effort to obtain financing. The buyer argued that her obligations under the contract were contingent on her getting financing and that since she had not obtained financing she was free to back out of the deal and recover her $13,000 deposit. The seller claimed that the agreement contained an implied good faith term under which the buyer impliedly promised to make good faith efforts to obtain financing. Since the buyer failed to do this, the seller argued that he was entitled to keep the $13,000 deposit and to recover damages from the buyer of the difference between the contract price and the lower price at which the seller could sell the property to a third party. The court held that the buyer must undertake "reasonable efforts" to obtain financing and that the buyer was not contractually justified in simply changing her mind about the house.

§2.4 Remedies for Breach of the Purchase and Sale Agreement

A. Buyer's Remedies

A buyer whose seller has breached the purchase and sale agreement has four remedies. *See generally* 2 *Friedman on Contracts and Conveyances of Real Property* §7.2 (7th ed. 2005 & Supp. 2012).

1. Specific performance. The buyer can obtain an injunction ordering the seller to convey the property to the buyer by transferring title in exchange for the agreed-upon contract price. *Tauber v. Quann*, 938 A.2d 724 (D.C. 2007).

2. Damages. The buyer may seek damages, measured in most states by the difference between the 'property's market value at the time of breach and contract price (expectation or benefit of the bargain damages), return of the deposit, and any additional expenses occasioned by the breach. A significant number of states, however, follow the English rule of *Flureau v. Thornhill*, 96 Eng. Rep. 638 (1776), and refuse to give the buyer expectation damages if the seller acted in good faith and believed he had good title at the time he entered the agreement; in these situations, the buyer may recover only the deposit, plus expenses. The buyer is entitled to expectation damages only if the seller did not in good faith believe he had good title, willfully or arbitrarily refused to complete the sale, or failed to perfect title when it was easy to do so. On one hand, the good faith rule has been severely criticized for treating real estate contracts differently from other types of contracts without justification. On the other hand, the different treatment has been justified by the difficulties with the recording system and the fact that reasonable sellers may be mistaken about the state of their title. Does the *Flureau* rule still make sense, given the generally high quality of public records about title in the United States?

3. Rescission. The buyer may seek to rescind the deal and recover the down payment or deposit.

4. Vendee's lien. This remedy is based on the premise that the seller's breach of the purchase and sale agreement creates a debt owed by the seller to the buyer, that is, the amount of the deposit, which is secured by a lien on the property. The court can therefore order the property sold to raise the funds to pay back the deposit. A vendee's lien can also establish the buyer's priority of recovery for the deposit in a foreclosure brought by other interests, such as a bank that loans money to the seller. *See Benz v. D.L. Evans Bank*, 268 P.3d 1167 (Idaho 2012). In some states, legislation has limited the circumstances in which a vendee's lien can be established. *See Goebel v. Glover*, 881 A.2d 493, 496 (Conn. Ct. App. 2005) (equitable vendee's lien denied where purchase and sale agreement was not witnessed and acknowledged as required by statute).

B. Seller's Remedies

The seller whose buyer has breached the purchase and sale agreement also has four remedies. *See generally* Friedman, *supra*, at §7.1.

1. Specific performance. The seller may be able to sue the buyer for the purchase price in exchange for the seller's handing over to the buyer the deed to the property, thus forcing the buyer to comply with the terms of the contract. This remedy may not be available everywhere. The theory behind specific performance for the buyer is that land is unique and that a money judgment will not put the buyer in the position she would have been in had the contract been performed. While this is true, money is *not* unique; the seller should not care whether the purchase price comes from the buyer or someone else. Nonetheless, the seller may be able to get specific performance either on the ground of mutuality (each side should have the same options as to remedies) or on the ground of the seller's inability to find another buyer. *But see Kesler v. Marshall*, 792 N.E.2d 893 (Ind. Ct. App. 2003) (denying specific performance to a seller who failed to mitigate damages by attempting to find another buyer).

2. Damages. The seller may elect to sue for damages, which are generally measured by the contract price minus the market price of the parcel at the time of the breach, plus other expenses occasioned by the breach. Some courts consider this unfair to the seller in a context where the market is rapidly declining, assessing damages instead as the difference between the contract price and the price obtained in a sale to a new buyer.

3. Rescission and forfeiture of down payment. The seller may simply attempt to rescind the deal, keeping the down payment or earnest money deposit paid by the buyer. Usually, the purchase and sale agreement explicitly provides the seller with the right to keep the down payment if the buyer breaches the contract. *See, e.g., Uzan v. 845 UN Limited Partnership*, 778 N.Y.S.2d 171 (App. Div. 2004) (seller could retain a deposit that amounted to 25 percent of the purchase price and exceeded $8 million when the buyer refused to go ahead with the deal).

4. Vendor's lien. This remedy is used generally to secure unpaid amounts owed to a seller under a purchase and sale agreement. The remedy presumes that the property belongs equitably to the buyer, who is obligated to purchase the property; it also presumes that the seller has a lien on the buyer's equitable title and that the property can be sold to satisfy the buyer's obligation to pay the rest of the purchase price to the seller.

§3 DEEDS

§3.1 Essential Terms

The deed must (1) identify the parties; (2) describe the property being conveyed; (3) state the grantor's intent to convey the property interest in question; and (4) contain the grantor's signature. The deed need not be recorded to transfer title; delivery of the deed to the grantee is sufficient. Most deeds are—and should be—recorded to protect the grantee's rights. To be recorded, most states require the deed to be acknowledged by a public notary or other official and some require one or more witnesses to the transaction. Thus, although acknowledgments are not necessary to transfer title (except in a few states), they usually accompany the transfer of the deed to enable the deed to be recorded.

The land being conveyed must be described in the deed. *See Firma, Inc. v. Twillman*, 126 S.W.3d 790 (Mo. Ct. App. 2004) (deed invalid when it failed to describe the property with reasonable certainty). The description must be sufficiently precise to locate the boundaries of the property. Those boundaries may be defined by reference to official surveys, plats, or by "metes and bounds." Most of the land in the United States has been surveyed under the Government Survey System devised by Thomas

Jefferson and first adopted by the Continental Congress in 1785. The system divides the land by a series of north-south and east-west lines and defines so-called townships, which are further subdivided into "sections."[6] These sections may be further divided into halves and quarters, or even smaller divisions. Property can be located within these quarter sections by reference to these official land parcels.

Property may also be described by a plat or subdivision map. A **plat** is a map produced by a private developer (not a government official) that describes the lots being created in a subdivision. These lots are generally the ones that actually will be bought and sold; their borders are often not straight. Often the subdivision is given a name and divided into "Blocks," with each Block being further subdivided into "lots." The plat is generally approved by a local agency before being filed in the recording office. Deeds may then describe the lot being sold by reference to the plat. So, for example, a lot being conveyed might be described as Block G, Lot 1 of Gerry's Landing Subdivision, recorded at Middletown County Registry of Deeds, Plat 46, in Plat Book 114, page 75.

Property may also be described by **metes and bounds**. This system starts at a defined point (usually described by a natural or artificial "monument" such as a fence or a street edge) and identifies the direction and distance of the first border, then the second border, and so on, until returning to the original point. In effect, it describes how one would walk around the borders of the property. Direction is notated in degrees (and minutes and seconds) east or west of due north or south. The convention is to state north or south first and then describe the east or west deviation. So a border that runs in a northwesterly direction would be notated as "North 45 degrees West 30 feet." Subsequent borders take a similar form until one returns to the starting place.

If a deed contains a mistaken description of the property, either party may sue to reform the deed.

Sample Deed

Johannes Brahms, Grantor, of 24 Main Street, Unit #6, Middletown, Middlesex County, Massachusetts, for consideration paid, and in full consideration of THREE HUNDRED EIGHTEEN THOUSAND FIVE HUNDRED DOLLARS ($318,500), grants to Clara and Robert Schumann, Grantees, wife and husband, of 75 Broad Street, Middletown, Massachusetts, as joint tenants with QUITCLAIM COVENANTS, Unit #6 in the 24 Main Street Condominium (a condominium subject to Massachusetts General Laws, chapter 183A) in Middletown, Middlesex County, Massachusetts, created by Master Deed dated August 23, 2002, recorded on August 25, 2002, at the Middlesex County

---

6. William B. Stoebuck & Dale A. Whitman, *The Law of Property* §11.2, at 821-822 (3d ed. 2000). The major north-south lines are called Principal Meridians, and the major east-west lines are called Base Lines. Parallel to the Principal Meridians at 6-mile intervals are north-south lines that divide the land into "Ranges." Parallel to the base lines are east-west lines that divide the land into "Townships." This system creates 6-mile squares also referred to as "Townships." Each Township is divided into 36 "sections." *Id.* §11.2, at 774-775.

Registry of Deeds, Book 14632, page 75, together with an undivided 15.22 percent interest in said Unit and in the Common Areas of the buildings and land described in the Master Deed, being the lot marked "F" on the plan of land drawn by Wolfgang Amadeus Mozart, Civil Engineer, September 1942, which plan is filed with Middlesex Registry of Deeds, Book 10479, page 214 (being lot F on the plan filed with said Deed as filed plan No. 95) and said lot F is bounded and further described as follows: southwesterly by Main Street, by a slightly curved line, seventy-five feet; northwesterly by lot "E" on said plan one hundred twenty-six and 45/100 feet; northeasterly by land of owner unknown seventy-five feet; and southeasterly by the lot marked "G" on said plan, one hundred eighteen and 24/100 feet; containing, according to the plan, 9,315 square feet.

Being the same premises conveyed to Grantor by deed of Ludwig van Beethoven by deed dated July 31, 2000, and recorded at Book 12469, page 143.

Said premises are conveyed subject to the restrictions and conditions as set forth in paragraph 7 of said Master Deed, including:

(1) no Unit shall be used other than for residential purposes by one (1) family;
(2) the architectural integrity of the Building and the Units shall be preserved without modifications, including but not limited to the following restrictions: that no balcony, enclosure, awning, screen antenna, sign, banner or other device, and no exterior change, addition, structure, projection, decoration or other feature shall be erected or placed upon or attached to any Unit; no addition to or change or replacement (except, so far as practicable, with identical kind) of any exterior light, door knocker or other exterior hardware, exterior Unit door, or door frames shall be made and no painting or other decoration shall be done on any exterior part of surface of any Unit;
(3) no Unit shall be leased without the consent of the Condominium Association.

The restrictions set forth in paragraphs (1), (2) & (3) above shall be for the benefit of all of the Unit Owners and the 24 Main Street Condominium Association, and:

(1) shall be administered on behalf of said Owners by the Trustees of said 24 Main Street Condominium Association, duly chosen as provided for in the Master Deed;
(2) shall be enforceable by the Trustees on behalf of the Condominium Association, insofar as permitted by law;
(3) may be waived in specific cases by the Trustees; and
(4) shall, as permitted by law be perpetual and run with the land, and may be extended from time to time in such manner as permitted or required by law for the continued enforceability thereof.

Said premises are also conveyed subject to easements, rights, conditions, and restrictions of record insofar as the same may be now in force and applicable.

WITNESS my hand and seal this 6th day of December 2014.

Johannes Brahms

THE COMMONWEALTH OF MASSACHUSETTS

Middlesex, ss. December 6, 2014

Then personally appeared the above-named Johannes Brahms and acknowledged the foregoing instrument to be his free act and deed before me.

Notary Public

Print Name:

My Commission Expires:

§3.2 Delivery

A deed must be delivered to the grantee to effectuate a transfer of ownership. The purpose of the delivery requirement is to ensure that the grantor intends to part with the property and to clarify who owns it. When property is sold, this requirement usually raises no problems since few people will hand over such a large sum of money as the purchase price for real property without getting something in return. When, however, people give real property as a gift, ordinarily to family members, problems of delivery can occur.

First, a person sometimes obtains physical possession of a deed, and may even record the deed, when the owner does not intend to transfer ownership. Possession of the deed or recording it, or both, may give rise to a presumption that the grantor intended to transfer ownership of the land. Most courts hold that this presumption can be overcome by extrinsic evidence that the original owner did not intend to transfer ownership, such as oral testimony that the owner intended to transfer ownership only at her death or evidence of an installment land contract, providing that the buyer would obtain title only after all payments are made to the seller. *Stockwell v. Stockwell*, 790 N.W.2d 52 (S.D. 2010); *Salter v. Hamiter*, 887 So. 2d 230 (Ala. 2004); *Blancett v. Blancett*, 102 P.3d 640 (N.M. 2004). *See In re Estate of Hardy*, 805 So. 2d 515 (Miss. 2002) (recording deed creates presumption of delivery but no delivery was found when grantor retained deeds until her death, they were found in her purse, and there was no other evidence of intent to transfer title).

Second, someone may make out a deed in front of a notary public granting ownership of her home to her daughter, place the deed in a safety deposit box in her bank, and tell her daughter that she has given her the property on the condition that the daughter allow her to continue living in the house until her death. What happens if the woman then dies leaving a will providing that all of her property be divided equally between her daughter and her son? The son claims a half interest in the house; her daughter claims that she owns it because her mother gave it to her before she died. Has the deed been "delivered"?

Some courts are reluctant to find delivery unless the deed has been physically handed over to the donee or to a third party who has instructions to deliver the deed. *Smith v. Lockridge*, 702 S.E.2d 858, 863 (Ga. 2010). Most courts find that "delivery" can occur even if the deed is not physically delivered to the donee under a doctrine of **constructive delivery**. This doctrine holds that writing a deed and engaging in conduct that demonstrates intent to transfer ownership is sufficient to constitute delivery. Intent to transfer ownership is more likely to be established if the deed is physically deposited in a safety deposit box or with a third party. *Montgomery v. Callison*, 700 S.E.2d 507 (W. Va. 2010). Many courts hold that delivery of a deed to a third party, such as an attorney, with instructions to hand over the deed to the grantee at the grantor's death constitutes delivery of a vested remainder to the grantee, with a life estate retained by the grantor. *In re Craddock*, 403 B.R. 355 (Bankr. M.D.N.C. 2009). Which rule strikes you as the better approach?

§3.3 Title Covenants

A. Warranties of Title

Perhaps the most important elements of a real estate transaction are the seller's ability to convey title to the property to the buyer and the buyer's ability to rest assured that the buyer's ownership rights will be secure against other claimants. The buyer (or the mortgage lender's lawyer) will certainly want to search the seller's record title. But the title search may not reveal some important defects in the chain of title. For this reason, the buyer may want additional assurances.

One form of additional assurance is the **title covenant** or **warranty of title** contained in the deed. Six standard covenants have developed and are explained below.

1. Present covenants. These covenants are breached, if at all, at the time of the conveyance (the closing). That is when the statute of limitations starts to run.

a. Covenant of seisin. This covenant is the grantor's promise that he owns the property interest (the estate) he is purporting to convey to the grantee. Thus, an owner of a leasehold would breach this covenant if he purported to convey a fee simple. Similarly, an owner of a one-half interest as a tenant in common would breach the covenant if he purported to convey full ownership of the property as a sole fee simple owner.

b. Covenant of the right to convey. This constitutes the grantor's promise that he has the power to transfer the interest purportedly conveyed to the grantee. Although in most cases the same as the covenant of seisin, it might differ in several instances. For example, a life estate burdened by an enforceable restraint on alienation would violate this covenant if the owner purported to convey it to the grantee. Similarly, if the property were adversely possessed by someone other than the seller, the seller would have record title (seisin) of the property but not the right to convey it.

c. Covenant against encumbrances. This is the grantor's promise that no mortgages, leases, liens, unpaid property taxes, or easements encumber the property other than those acknowledged in the deed itself.

2. Future covenants. These covenants are breached, if at all, after the closing, when the disturbance to the grantee's possession occurs. The statute of limitations starts to run when the grantee's possession is disturbed.

a. Covenant of warranty. By this covenant, the grantor promises to compensate the grantee for any monetary losses occasioned by the grantor's failure to convey the title promised in the deed.

b. Covenant of quiet enjoyment. The grantor promises by this covenant that the grantee's possession will not be disturbed by any other claimant with a superior lawful title. This covenant is substantially the same as the covenant of warranty.

c. Covenant for further assurances. Rarely used, this covenant requires the seller to take further steps to cure defects in the grantor's title, such as paying an adverse possessor to leave the property or paying the owner of an encumbrance to release the encumbrance.

Deeds are generally classified as general warranty, special warranty, or quitclaim. A **general warranty deed** covenants against all defects in title. A **special warranty deed** limits the covenant to defects in title caused by the grantor's own acts but not by the acts of prior owners. It can also cover defects, such as the allowance of adverse possession, that were the result of the current owner's failure to act. Finally, a **quitclaim deed** contains no warranty (or covenant) of title whatsoever. It purports to convey whatever interests in the property are owned by the grantor. It does not, however, promise that the grantor *in fact* owns the property interest that the grantor claims to own—or, indeed, any interest. It suffices to transfer whatever property interests the grantor has to the grantee, but does not provide the buyer with any real assurance that the grantor has the right to convey the interest the grantor purports to convey.

Some states have standardized the covenants by statute. These covenants may be contained in the deed by reference to the statute in which they are defined. They are thereby incorporated into the deed by reference.

B. Remedies for Breach of Warranty of Title

The most widely used covenant is the covenant of warranty. If it turns out that the seller did not have the right to convey the property interest the deed purported to convey, the buyer can sue the seller for breach of the warranty of title. This covenant runs with the land and can be enforced by subsequent grantees as well. The damages for breach of the covenants of warranty, seisin, right to convey, and quiet enjoyment are generally measured by the **price** paid for the property that has been lost. This price is generally near the fair market value of the property **at the time of the closing**.

If the breach is discovered after the closing, the ousted buyer will not be able to recover the market value of the property at the time the buyer was ousted; moreover, the market value may be much higher than the original price. This result has often been criticized since it may very well not leave the buyer in the position the buyer would have been in had the original contract been performed; if the price of land has been rising since the closing, the buyer may not be able to purchase a similar piece of property for the same amount the buyer paid for the premises from which she was ousted. Stoebuck & Whitman, *supra*, at 913-914. At the same time, allowing the buyer to obtain from the seller more than the value paid places an uncertain and possibly onerous obligation on the seller for many years into the future. The availability of title insurance may suggest a better way to handle the problem.

The damages for breach of the covenant against encumbrances is either the cost of removing the encumbrance (that is, paying off the mortgage or buying out the covenant or easement) or the difference between the value of the property without the encumbrance and with it.

§4 REAL ESTATE FINANCE

§4.1 The Basic Structure of Real Estate Finance

Very few people can afford to buy property without borrowing money. Homeowners and businesses accordingly turn to lending institutions, such as banks and mortgage companies, to borrow money to finance the purchase of real estate. Traditionally, for home buyers, the lender would check out the credit history of the prospective borrower, his current employment, family assets, and other financial information to decide whether to lend money. The lender will also want information about the value of the home and how much of a down payment the borrower will be making. This is because the property will serve as **collateral** to secure repayment of the loan. In commercial real estate, this underwriting process is generally more complex, but follows the same basic structure.

Borrowing money to finance a real estate purchase usually entails two separate contracts. The first is the **note**. This constitutes the borrower's promise to repay the principal amount of the loan with interest, in the amounts and at the times specified in the note. For example, imagine that Béla Bartók borrows $270,000 to buy a $300,000 house, paying the remaining $30,000 owed to the seller of the house from his savings. Bartók would sign a note with the lender that recites the terms and conditions of the loan, for example an obligation to repay the $270,000 at 5 percent interest over 30 years. Traditionally, in a "fully amortized" loan, part of each installment payment represents interest and part represents repayment of the principal. (In the beginning, most of the payment is allocated to interest.) The note creates a personal liability in Bartók to repay the borrowed money, and the lender can sue Bartók for defaulting on Bartók's promises contained in the note.

> **Terms:**
> A real estate lender is typically called the **mortgagee**. The buyer-homeowner is called the **mortgagor**. The mortgagor (homeowner) thus grants a mortgage to the mortgagee (lender).

The second contract is the **mortgage**. To obtain greater security for the repayment of the note, the lender will require Bartók to execute a mortgage on the property Bartók is buying. The mortgage will contain a series of promises by Bartók, including the promise to pay off the note in accordance with its terms, to maintain insurance on the property, to pay property taxes when due, and to maintain the property so that it does not become dilapidated and lose its market value, thereby impairing the lender's security. The mortgage also gives the lender a security interest in the property. This means that if Bartók defaults on his loan payments or violates any other material term of the mortgage, the lender has the ability to declare the entire amount of the loan due, force the property to be sold, and use the proceeds of the sale to pay off the rest of the note. The sale may be conducted privately or under judicial supervision, depending on the rules in the jurisdiction in which the property is located. The forced sale of the property is called **foreclosure** or **foreclosing the mortgage**. We will explore a number of questions about the foreclosure process below, in §4.3, as well as how courts react to attempts by lenders to avoid the debtor protections in foreclosure altogether, in §4.4.

The terms and conditions of commercial lending, such as interest rates, the period of repayment (or amortization), and the rights that go along with a lender's security interest, can vary significantly. Financing for home purchases has been more standardized, but there is still some variation. Most home loans have traditionally been long term, often 30 years, have carried a fixed rate of interest, and require a substantial down payment by the borrower, sometimes as much as 25 percent. Richard K. Green & Susan M. Wachter, *The American Mortgage in Historical and International Context*, 19 J. Econ. Persp. 93, 99-101 (2005). In the run-up to the subprime crisis, home mortgages with more exotic terms, such as interest rates that fluctuate (called **adjustable rate mortgages**), with short terms that include **balloon payments**, which are large one-time payments that substantially exceed the regular payment amount, or loans that require little or no down payment, became more common.

Borrowers also use their property as collateral for debt that is not used for purchasing the property. In the residential context this is generally called home equity lending, where homeowners borrow money using the value in their home above what is owed on other debt as collateral. This kind of debt can be used to pay for home renovations and similar investments, but it can also be used for expenses unrelated to the property, such as medical bills, education, or even general consumer spending.[7]

§4.2 Mortgage Regulation and the Subprime Crisis

A. Regulating Mortgage Markets

Markets are structured by law, and they need regulation to function effectively. Real estate finance is no exception, and federal, state, and local laws shape many aspects of mortgage markets, which we can only touch on briefly here.[8] Beyond the consumer protections mortgagors have when they default on their mortgage and face foreclosure, there are two other primary ways in which the law structures mortgage

7. Another type of home lending is called a **reverse mortgage loan**, and is generally available only to elderly borrowers. In a reverse mortgage, a homeowner takes out a loan using the value of her house as collateral, but is not required to repay the loan until she moves or passes away. This can be a way to generate funds for older homeowners for medical expenses or even daily expenses, but can also be risky because borrowers are still required to have enough resources to pay property taxes and insurance on their homes. *See* Jessica Silver-Greenberg, *A Risky Lifeline for the Elderly Is Costing Some Their Homes*, N.Y. Times, Oct. 14, 2012, at A-1.

8. Many areas of mortgage regulation implicate both federal and state law. Where this creates a conflict, federal law can preempt state law, which can restrict the ability of the states to enforce consumer protection laws. *See, e.g., Watters v. Wachovia Bank, N.A.*, 550 U.S. 1 (2007) (state registration and inspection authority preempted for federally chartered mortgage lender and state-chartered subsidiary).

markets. First, public institutions seek to expand consumer credit, particularly for those underserved by traditional lending practices. Second, the federal government and to some extent the states regulate the terms and conditions of how individual loans are provided, a process called **origination**, as well as how loans are managed by lenders or companies working for lenders, which is called **servicing** the loan. We will turn to this avenue of regulation in §4.2.B, below.

In terms of access to credit, a number of institutions have been created, primarily at the federal level, to increase the availability, or reduce the cost, of mortgage funds. In response to the Great Depression, for example, Congress in 1932 passed the *Federal Home Loan Bank Act*, Pub. L. No. 72-304, 47 Stat. 725 (1932). The act created the Federal Home Loan Bank Board and 12 regional banks to give loans to local institutions that finance home mortgages in order to encourage them to lend money to home buyers. As a further prod to home lenders, Congress in the *National Housing Act of 1934*, Pub. L. 84-345, 48 Stat. 847 (1934), created the Federal Housing Administration (FHA), an agency that insures private mortgages.

Other federal institutions designed to spur home lending include the Federal National Mortgage Association (Fannie Mae), created in 1938, and the Federal Home Loan Mortgage Corporation (Freddie Mac), created in 1970. These **government-sponsored entities** (GSEs) buy mortgages from lenders and sell securities to investors backed by the expected payments from borrowers on those mortgages. This fosters a **secondary market** in mortgages, bringing investment from capital markets to lending institutions to allow those institutions to make more mortgage loans.[9]

The *Home Mortgage Disclosure Act of 1975* (HMDA), 12 U.S.C. §§2801-2810, was passed to respond to the problem of lenders failing in many communities "to provide adequate home financing to qualified applicants on reasonable terms and conditions" *Id.* §2801(a). The statute was intended to generate "sufficient information to enable [citizens and public officials] to determine whether depository institutions are filling their obligations to serve the housing needs of the communities and neighborhoods in which they are located." *Id.* §2801(b). HMDA requires banks to keep records of the loans they make and to disclose them publicly to facilitate the ability to determine whether banks are engaged in discriminatory lending patterns.

Similarly, the *Community Reinvestment Act of 1977* (CRA), 12 U.S.C. §§2901-2908, encourages lending institutions to provide credit in the local communities in which they operate, especially for the "credit needs [of] low- and moderate-income neighborhoods, consistent with the safe and sound operation of [the] institution." *Id.* §2903(a)(1). There are no penalties for noncompliance but banks that do not comply with the statutory requirements may be denied the right to establish new bank branches or to engage in mergers with other institutions.

9. For a long time, people argued about whether or not securities issued by the GSEs had the implicit backing of the federal government, but in 2008, early in the subprime crisis, the federal government placed Fannie Mae and Freddie Mac into federal conservatorship, effectively resolving the question.

B. Securitization and the Subprime Crisis

For many years, mortgage banking was a staid profession with a conservative outlook and a regulatory environment largely set by New Deal responses to the Great Depression. But beginning in the 1980s, a new regulatory environment emerged with less government oversight, more competition among mortgage providers, and new forms of mortgages and mortgage markets. *See generally* Financial Crisis Inquiry Commission, *The Financial Crisis Inquiry Report: Final Report of the National Commission on the Causes of the Financial and Economic Crisis in the United States* (2011); *id.* at xviii ("The sentries were not at their posts, in no small part due to the widely accepted faith in the self-correcting nature of the markets and the ability of financial institutions to effectively police themselves.").

State usury laws had traditionally regulated the interest rates that could be charged for loans financing the purchase of a home. In 1980, with interest rates at historic highs, Congress passed the *Depository Institutions Deregulation and Monetary Control Act,* 12 U.S.C. §1735f-7a(a)(1), that preempted state usury laws, allowing banks to charge whatever they wanted. Lending institutions soon realized they could induce people to buy homes even if interest rates were high by offering **adjustable rate mortgages (ARMs)** with initially low interest rate payments that increased over time. These loans appeared secure because the value of real estate was rising, borrowers hoped they could refinance before higher interest rates kicked in, and lenders could always recoup their investment by foreclosure. Over time, lenders began offering these loans to lower-income families as well as more traditional borrowers; to compensate for the added risk posed by these loans, the interest rates were very high. Some lenders decided that they could make money by giving loans to borrowers who could not pay them back when the higher interest rates kicked in. They even loaned money to people without any proof of their income or ability to pay.[10]

Lenders were willing to offer such risky loans in part because they increasingly sold the loans to other entities that took over the risk. Traditionally, lenders had often kept the mortgage and with it the risk of non-payment. The market to buy the loans increased as mortgage loans were increasingly **securitized**, which involves bundling many loans and selling shares in these bundled loans to investors. These securities were called **collateralized debt obligations (CDOs)** or **mortgage-backed securities (MBSs)** because the mortgages in the real property were collateral or security for the debts. The structure of the securities became extremely complex. A typical structure involves many different parties and multiple steps of securitization. Mortgages, which may be of different types, geographies, and origins, are pooled together into a trust, which is then divided into **tranches** that have different risk and reward characteristics.

---

10. Instead of going to banks to apply for mortgages, prospective home buyers also increasingly sought assistance from **mortgage brokers** to help find mortgages and compare rates and terms among various mortgages offered by different institutions. These brokers had incentives to induce buyers to obtain higher-cost loans because the brokers got higher fees that way. Similarly, mortgage brokers had incentives to induce homeowners to refinance their mortgages, even if there were no economic benefits to the homeowners, because brokers received fees for every refinancing.

The securities were themselves often rebundled and resold, removing them still further from essential information about the mortgages that backed the securities. Each time the mortgage pool was sliced or repackaged, informational problems occurred, creating more risk.

The market for these securities grew tremendously in the 1990s and early 2000s, both in absolute dollar terms and as a part of the national and world financial markets. In 1995, only 30 percent of mortgages were securitized, but by 2006, this number had climbed to over 80 percent. Benjamin J. Keys, Tanmoy K. Mukherjee, Amit Seru & Vikrant Vig, *Did Securitization Lead to Lax Screening? Evidence from Subprime Loans,* 125 Q. J. Econ. 307, 314 (2010). Importantly, the quality of mortgages declined during this time period. Subprime mortgages grew from 9.5 percent, or $70 billion, of total mortgage originations to 23.5 percent, or $600 billion, in 2006. *See Financial Crisis Inquiry Report, supra,* at 70. Nevertheless, as the United States experienced prolonged growth in housing prices, the real estate sector and related financial industries generated high returns, and mortgage-backed securities, together with the real estate market, experienced a boom.

Lending institutions also bought and sold a complicated form of insurance for mortgage-backed securities called **credit default swaps**, which were unregulated and not backed by any security. Companies like AIG sold this insurance because defaults on securities backed by real estate were thought to be unlikely, even if particular borrowers defaulted on their loans, because the rising value of land would recover the debts. But because many institutions were on both sides of these transactions (both insuring and being insured) and because many institutions held risky debt, any chink in the payment schedule, combined with a decrease in the value of land, had the possibility of making the whole system unravel.

And unravel it did, partly because borrowers were over their heads and could not afford to make the higher payments when their ARMs jumped to the new higher interest rates and partly because the housing bubble burst. As long as house prices continued to rise, borrowers could refinance their loans when they became too burdensome — as, for example, when ARM interest rates automatically reset and created an unmanageable monthly payment. When house prices and sales began to drop, the decline had a massive nationwide effect, eroding the security for subprime mortgages. Many borrowers now owed more on their loans than the value of the real estate securing those loans. As people began to stop making mortgage payments, foreclosures increased significantly.

A "death spiral" was in place: "Falling prices meant that firms using debt securities as collateral had to mark them to market and put up cash, requiring the sale of more securities, which caused market prices to plummet further downward." Steven L. Schwarcz, *Understanding the Subprime Financial Crisis,* 60 S.C. L. Rev. 549, 553 (2009). The impact was dramatic. In the face of huge losses on the securities, and with ongoing bankruptcies of important players in a variety of markets, fear began to seize the debt markets. Banks, which had already taken huge losses from their holdings in the mortgage sector, were unable to secure funding from capital providers, and the entire financial services industry underwent a massive reorganization. Some centrally important companies, such as Lehman Brothers, went bankrupt, and many others were reorganized, sold, or taken over by the federal government. Credit markets froze and the subprime crisis spread from mortgage-backed securities to the entire global economy. *See* Kathleen C. Engel & Patricia A. McCoy, *The Subprime Virus: Reckless Credit, Regulatory Failure, and Next Steps* (2011).[11]

The legal system has had to grapple with the fallout from the subprime crisis, as the next case illustrates.

Commonwealth v. Fremont Investment & Loan

897 N.E.2d 548 (Mass. 2008)

Botsford, Margot, J.

[Fremont Investment & Loan and its parent company, Fremont General Corporation (collectively, Fremont)] is an industrial bank chartered by the State of California. Between January, 2004, and March, 2007, Fremont originated 14,578 loans to Massachusetts residents secured by mortgages on owner-occupied homes. Of the loans originated during that time period, roughly 3,000 remain active and roughly 2,500 continue to be owned or serviced by Fremont. An estimated fifty to sixty per cent of Fremont's loans in Massachusetts were subprime.[12] Because subprime borrowers present a greater risk to the lender, the interest rate charged for a subprime loan is typically higher than the rate charged for conventional or prime mortgages. After funding the loan, Fremont generally sold it on the secondary market, which largely insulated Fremont from losses arising from borrower default.

---

11. Some commentators argue that the subprime crisis can be attributed to incentives under the *Community Reinvestment Act* (CRA) to serve low-income communities and individuals. Likewise, commentators point to the obligations that the federal government has placed on Fannie Mae and Freddie Mac since 1992 to serve low-income borrowers. These affordable housing mandates, the argument goes, distorted the market and induced lenders into taking unreasonable risks in their underwriting. *See, e.g.*, Raghuram Rajan, *Bankers have been sold short by market distortions*, Financial Times (June 2, 2010). There are several problems with this argument. First, there is a question of timing. The CRA was passed in 1977 and existed for nearly three decades before the subprime crisis. Similarly, Fannie Mae and Freddie Mac were very late to the subprime mortgage market, entering only in the immediate run-up to the crisis to compete with so-called private-label lenders. And the majority of subprime loans were made by lenders who were either not subject to supervision under the CRA, or subject to relatively little oversight. *See* Prepared Testimony of Michael S. Barr, Committee on Financial Services, U.S. House of Representatives, *The Community Reinvestment Act: Thirty Years of Accomplishments, But Challenges Remain*, Feb. 13, 2008, at 4 ("More than half of subprime loans were made by independent mortgage companies not subject to comprehensive federal supervision; another 30 percent of such originations were made by affiliates of banks or thrifts, which are not subject to routine examination or supervision."). Finally, careful empirical studies have found that the CRA and the GSE affordable housing mandates had no effect on subprime lending volumes, loan pricing, or default rates. *See, e.g.*, Rubén Hernández-Murillo et al., *Did Affordable Housing Legislation Contribute to the Subprime Securities Boom?*, Federal Reserve Working Paper 2012-005B (Aug. 2012).

12. "Subprime" loans are loans made to borrowers who generally would not qualify for traditional loans offered at the generally prevailing rate of interest for conventional mortgages.

In originating loans, Fremont did not interact directly with the borrowers; rather, mortgage brokers acting as independent contractors would help a borrower select a mortgage product, and communicate with a Fremont account executive to request a selected product and provide the borrower's loan application and credit report. If approved by Fremont's underwriting department, the loan would proceed to closing and the broker would receive a broker's fee.

Fremont's subprime loan products offered a number of different features to cater to borrowers with low income. A large majority of Fremont's subprime loans were adjustable rate mortgage (ARM) loans, which bore a fixed interest rate for the first two or three years, and then adjusted every six months to a considerably higher variable rate for the remaining period of what was generally a thirty-year loan.[13] Thus, borrowers' monthly mortgage payments would start out lower and then increase substantially after the introductory two-year or three-year period. To determine loan qualification, Fremont generally required that borrowers have a debt-to-income ratio of less than or equal to fifty per cent — that is, that the borrowers' monthly debt obligations, including the applied-for mortgage, not exceed one-half their income. However, in calculating the debt-to-income ratio, Fremont considered only the monthly payment required for the introductory rate period of the mortgage loan, not the payment that would ultimately be required at the substantially higher "fully indexed" interest rate.[14] As an additional feature to attract subprime borrowers, who typically had little or no savings, Fremont offered loans with no down payment. Instead of a down payment, Fremont would finance the full value of the property, resulting in a "loan-to-value ratio" approaching one hundred per cent. Most such financing was accomplished through the provision of a first mortgage providing eighty per cent financing and an additional "piggy-back loan" providing twenty per cent.[15]

As of the time the Attorney General initiated this case in 2007, a significant number of Fremont's loans were in default. An analysis by the Attorney General of ninety-eight of those loans indicated that all were ARM loans with a substantial increase in payments required after the first two (or in a few cases, three) years, and that ninety per cent of the ninety-eight had a one hundred per cent loan-to-value ratio.

On March 7, 2007, Fremont executed a "stipulation and consent to the issuance of an order to cease and desist" (consent agreement) with the Federal Deposit Insurance

---

13. The variable rate was based on the six month London Interbank Offered Rate (LIBOR), a market interest rate, plus a fixed margin (referred to as a "rate add") to reflect the risk of the loan. For example, the variable rate might be expressed as "LIBOR plus 5," meaning the LIBOR interest rate increased by an additional five percentage points as the rate add.

14. The "fully indexed" rate refers to the interest rate that represents the LIBOR rate at the time of the loan's inception plus the rate add specified in the loan documents. The judge noted that calculation of the debt-to-income ratio based on the fully indexed rate generally yields a ratio that exceeds fifty per cent.

15. 38.4 percent of all Fremont's loans were stated income loans without income documentation required. In addition, 12.2 per cent of Fremont's loans offered the borrower lower monthly payments based on a forty-year amortization schedule, with a balloon payment required at the end of thirty years; the usual amortization schedule was based on a thirty-year period.

Corporation (FDIC), settling charges of unsound banking practices brought by that agency. The consent agreement ordered Fremont, *inter alia,* to cease and desist from originating ARM products to subprime borrowers in ways described as unsafe and unsound, including making loans with low introductory rates without considering borrowers' ability to pay the debt at the fully indexed rate, and with loan-to-value ratios approaching one hundred per cent. In entering into the consent agreement, Fremont did not admit to any wrongdoing.

On or about July 10, 2007, Fremont entered into a term sheet letter agreement (term sheet agreement) with the Massachusetts Attorney General, agreeing to give the Attorney General ninety days' notice before foreclosing on any Massachusetts residential mortgage loan. If the Attorney General objected, Fremont agreed to negotiate in good faith to resolve the objection, possibly by modifying the loan agreement. If no resolution could be reached, the Attorney General was granted an additional fifteen days in which to determine whether to seek an injunction.

As it turned out, the Attorney General objected to every proposed foreclosure that Fremont identified except those where the home was not owner-occupied and Fremont had been unable to contact the borrower. On October 4, 2007, the Attorney General filed this action.

The judge granted a preliminary injunction in a memorandum of decision dated February 25, 2008. In his decision, the judge found no evidence in the preliminary injunction record that Fremont encouraged or condoned misrepresentation of borrowers' incomes on stated income loans, or that Fremont deceived borrowers by concealing or misrepresenting the terms of its loans. However, the judge determined that the Attorney General was likely to prevail on the claim that Fremont's loans featuring a combination of the following four characteristics qualified as "unfair" under Mass. Gen. Laws ch. 93A, §2: (1) the loans were ARM loans with an introductory rate period of three years or less; (2) they featured an introductory rate for the initial period that was at least three per cent below the fully indexed rate; (3) they were made to borrowers for whom the debt-to-income ratio would have exceeded fifty per cent had Fremont measured the borrower's debt by the monthly payments that would be due at the fully indexed rate rather than under the introductory rate; and (4) the loan-to-value ratio was one hundred per cent, or the loan featured a substantial prepayment penalty (defined by the judge as greater than the "conventional prepayment penalty" defined in Mass. Gen. Laws ch. 183C, §2) or a prepayment penalty that extended beyond the introductory rate period.

The judge reasoned that Fremont as a lender should have recognized that loans with the first three characteristics just described were "doomed to foreclosure" unless the borrower could refinance the loan at or near the end of the introductory rate period, and obtain in the process a new and low introductory rate.[16] The fourth factor, however,

16. The judge's prognosis of doom followed from the fact that the interest payments required when the introductory rate period ended and the fully indexed rate came into play would be significantly greater than the payments called for under the introductory rate (so-called "payment shock"). As a result, the borrower's debt-to-income ratio would necessarily increase, probably and foreseeably beyond the borrower's breaking point.

would make it essentially impossible for subprime borrowers to refinance unless housing prices increased, because if housing prices remained steady or declined, a borrower with a mortgage loan having a loan-to-value ratio of one hundred per cent or a substantial prepayment penalty was not likely to have the necessary equity or financial capacity to obtain a new loan. The judge stated that, "[g]iven the fluctuations in the housing market and the inherent uncertainties as to how that market will fluctuate over time . . . it is unfair for a lender to issue a home mortgage loan secured by the borrower's principal dwelling that the lender reasonably expects will fall into default once the introductory period ends unless the fair market value of the home has increased at the close of the introductory period. To issue a home mortgage loan whose success relies on the hope that the fair market value of the home will increase during the introductory period is as unfair as issuing a home mortgage loan whose success depends on the hope that the borrower's income will increase during that same period."

The judge concluded that the balance of harms favored granting the preliminary injunction, and that the public interest would be served by doing so. The injunction he granted requires Fremont to do the following: (1) to give advance notice to the Attorney General of its intent to foreclose on any of its home mortgage loans; and (2) as to loans that possess each of the four characteristics of unfair loans just described and that are secured by the borrower's principal dwelling (referred to in the injunction as "presumptively unfair" loans), to work with the Attorney General to "resolve" their differences regarding foreclosure — presumably through a restructure or workout of the loan. If the loan cannot be worked out, Fremont is required to obtain approval for foreclosure from the court. The judge made clear that the injunction in no way relieved borrowers of their obligation ultimately to prove that a particular loan was unfair and foreclosure should not be permitted, or their obligation to repay the loans they had received.

Discussion

Fremont argues that the judge committed two "fundamental" errors of law in concluding that the Attorney General was likely to prevail on the merits of her ch. 93A claim: first, the judge in effect, and improperly, applied the provisions of the Massachusetts *Predatory Home Loan Practices Act,* Mass. Gen. Laws ch. 183C, to Fremont's loans, even though the loans are not subject to ch. 183C; and second, the judge failed to recognize that under Mass. Gen. Laws ch. 93A, §3, Fremont's loans are exempt from ch. 93A because all of Fremont's challenged loan terms were permitted under the Federal and Massachusetts laws and regulatory standards governing mortgage lenders. Fremont also contends that the judge erred in determining that the public interest would be served by the preliminary injunction order. We address these arguments separately below. Before doing so, we consider a basic claim that lies underneath all of Fremont's legal challenges to the injunction.

Retroactive Application of Unfairness Standards

Fremont's basic contention is that, while the terms of its subprime loans may arguably seem "unfair" within the meaning of Mass. Gen. Laws ch. 93A, §2, if judged by current standards applicable to the mortgage lending industry, they did not violate any established concept of unfairness at the time they were originated; the judge, in Fremont's view, applied new rules or standards for defining what is "unfair" in a retroactive or ex post facto fashion — a result that is not in accord with the proper interpretation of ch. 93A, §2, and also represents "bad policy," because (among other reasons) lenders cannot know what rules govern their conduct, which will reduce their willingness to extend credit, hurting Massachusetts consumers. We do not agree that the judge applied a new standard retroactively.

General Laws ch. 93A, §2 (a), makes unlawful any "unfair or deceptive acts or practices in the conduct of any trade or commerce." Chapter 93A creates new substantive rights, and in particular cases, "mak[es] conduct unlawful which was not unlawful under the common law or any prior statute." *Kattar v. Demoulas*, 739 N.E.2d 246, 257 (Mass. 2000). The statute does not define unfairness, recognizing that "[t]here is no limit to human inventiveness in this field." *Id.* at 257. What is significant is the particular circumstances and context in which the term is applied. It is well established that a practice may be deemed unfair if it is "within at least the penumbra of some common-law, statutory, or other established concept of unfairness." *PMP Assocs., Inc. v. Globe Newspaper Co.*, 321 N.E.2d 915, 918 (Mass. 1975).

Fremont highlights the judge's statement that at the time Fremont made the loans in question between 2004 and March of 2007, loans with the four characteristics the judge identified as unfair were not considered by the industry or more generally to be unfair; Fremont argues this acknowledgment by the judge is proof that the judge was creating a new definition or standard of unfairness. The argument lacks merit. First, the judge's statement that Fremont's combination of loan features were not recognized to be unfair does not mean the converse: that the loans were recognized to be fair. More to the point, at the core of the judge's decision is a determination that when Fremont chose to combine in a subprime loan the four characteristics the judge identified, Fremont knew or should have known that they would operate in concert essentially to guarantee that the borrower would be unable to pay and default would follow unless residential real estate values continued to rise indefinitely — an assumption that, in the judge's view, logic and experience had already shown as of January, 2004, to be unreasonable. The judge concluded that the Attorney General was likely to prove that Fremont's actions, in originating loans with terms that in combination would lead predictably to the consequence of the borrowers' default and foreclosure, were within established concepts of unfairness at the time the loans were made, and thus in violation of Mass. Gen. Laws ch. 93A, §2. The record supports this conclusion.

Fremont correctly points out that as a bank in the business of mortgage lending, it is subject to State and Federal regulation by a variety of agencies.[17] Well before 2004, State and Federal regulatory guidance explicitly warned lending institutions making

17. State agencies regulating mortgage lending by banks such as Fremont and other lenders include the Massachusetts Division of Banks, and Federal agencies include the Office of the Comptroller of the Currency (OCC), the Board of Governors of the Federal Reserve System, the Federal Deposit Insurance Corporation (FDIC), and the Office of Thrift Supervision.

subprime loans that, even if they were in compliance with banking-specific laws and regulations and were "underwrit[ing] loans on a safe and sound basis, [their] policies could still be considered unfair and deceptive practices" under Mass. Gen. Laws ch. 93A. Consumer Affairs and Business Regulation Massachusetts Division of Banks, *Subprime Lending* (Dec. 10, 1997). More particularly, the principle had been clearly stated before 2004 that loans made to borrowers on terms that showed they would be unable to pay and therefore were likely to lead to default, were unsafe and unsound, and probably unfair. Thus, an interagency Federal guidance published January 31, 2001, jointly by the Office of the Comptroller of the Currency (OCC), the Board of Governors of the Federal Reserve System, the FDIC, and the Office of Thrift Supervision, stated: "Loans to borrowers who do not demonstrate the capacity to repay the loan, *as structured*, from sources other than the collateral pledged are generally considered unsafe and unsound" (emphasis supplied).[18] *Expanded Guidance for Subprime Lending Programs* at 11 (Jan. 31, 2001). On February 21, 2003, one year before the first of Fremont's loans at issue, the OCC warned that certain loans could be unfair to consumers:

> When a loan has been made based on the foreclosure value of the collateral, rather than on a determination that the borrower has the capacity to make the scheduled payments under the terms of the loan, based on the borrower's current and expected income, current obligations, employment status, and other relevant financial resources, the lender is effectively counting on its ability to seize the borrower's equity in the collateral to satisfy the obligation and to recover the typically high fees associated with such credit. Not surprisingly, such credits experience foreclosure rates higher than the norm.
>
> [S]uch disregard of basic principles of loan underwriting lies at the heart of predatory lending.

OCC Advisory Letter, *Guidelines for National Banks to Guard Against Predatory and Abusive Lending Practices,* AL 2003-2 at 2 (Feb. 21, 2003).

The record here suggests that Fremont made no effort to determine whether borrowers could "make the scheduled payments under the terms of the loan." Rather, as the judge determined, loans were made in the understanding that they would have to be refinanced before the end of the introductory period. Fremont suggested in oral argument that the loans were underwritten in the expectation, reasonable at the time, that housing prices would improve during the introductory loan term, and thus could

18. "Unsafe and unsound" refers to practices that carry too high a risk of financial harm to the lending institution, rather than to the consumer. Not all conduct that is institutionally unsafe and unsound is harmful to borrowers. However, when the lending institution's practices are deemed unsafe and unsound because they create too high a risk of default and foreclosure, the borrower, as the counterparty to the loan, obviously faces the same risk. Accordingly, such lending practices may indicate unfairness under Mass. Gen. Laws ch. 93A. *Cf.* Consumer Affairs and Business Regulation Massachusetts Division of Banks, *Subprime Lending* (Dec. 10, 1997) (warning of both safety and soundness, and consumer protection, risks from subprime lending); OCC, *Guidelines for National Banks to Guard Against Predatory and Abusive Lending Practices,* AL 2003-2 at 1 (Feb. 21, 2003) ("even where the particular attributes of a loan are not subject to a specific prohibition, loans reflecting abusive practices nevertheless can involve unfair and deceptive conduct and present significant safety and soundness, reputation, and other risks to national banks").

be refinanced before the higher payments began. However, it was unreasonable, and unfair to the borrower, for Fremont to structure its loans on such unsupportable optimism. As a bank and mortgage lender, Fremont had been warned repeatedly before 2004 (in the context of guidance on loan safety and soundness) that it needed to consider the performance of its loans in declining markets. See, e.g., *Consumer Affairs and Business Regulation, Massachusetts Division of Banks, Subprime Lending* (Dec. 10, 1997) ("[M]ost subprime loans have been originated during robust economic conditions and have not been tested by a downturn in the economy. Management must ensure that the institution has adequate financial and operational strength to address these concerns effectively"). Fremont cannot now claim that it was taken by surprise by the effects of an economic decline, or that it should not be held responsible.

Finally, the conclusion that Fremont's loans featuring the four characteristics at issue violated established concepts of unfairness is supported by the consent agreement that Fremont entered into with the FDIC on March 7, 2007, the date Fremont stopped making loans. The consent agreement contains no admission of wrongdoing by Fremont, and we do not consider it as evidence of liability on Fremont's part. However, we view it as evidence of existing policy and guidance provided to the mortgage lending industry. The fact that the FDIC ordered Fremont to cease and desist from the use of almost precisely the loan features that are included in the judge's list of presumptively unfair characteristics indicates that the FDIC considered that under established mortgage lending standards, the marketing of loans with these features constituted unsafe and unsound banking practice with clearly harmful consequences for borrowers. Such unsafe and unsound conduct on the part of a lender, insofar as it leads directly to injury for consumers, qualifies as "unfair" under Mass. Gen. Laws ch. 93A, §2.

General Laws ch. 93A, §3

Fremont argues that the Commonwealth's claim is barred by Mass. Gen. Laws ch. 93A, §3, because Fremont's actions were permitted by the law as it existed at the time it originated the loans. We disagree.

General Laws ch. 93A, §3, provides:

> "Nothing in this chapter shall apply to transactions or actions otherwise permitted under laws as administered by any regulatory board or officer acting under statutory authority of the commonwealth or of the United States. For the purpose of this section, the burden of proving exemptions from the provisions of this chapter shall be upon the person claiming the exemptions."

This provision must be read together with Mass. Gen. Laws ch. 93A, §2. That section "'created new substantive rights,'' and thus "[t]he fact that particular conduct is permitted by statute or by common law principles should be considered, but it is not conclusive on the question of unfairness." *Schubach v. Household Fin. Corp.*, 376 N.E.2d 140, 142 (Mass. 1978) (*quoting Commonwealth v. DeCotis*, 316 N.E.2d 748, 755 n.8 (Mass. 1974)). A defendant's burden in claiming the exemption is "a difficult one to meet. To sustain it, a defendant must show more than the mere existence of a related or even overlapping regulatory scheme that covers the transaction. Rather, a defendant must show that such scheme affirmatively *permits* the practice which is alleged to be unfair or deceptive" (emphasis in original). *Fleming v. Nat'l Union Fire Ins. Co.*, 837 N.E.2d 1113, 1121 (Mass. 2005).

The judge concluded, as have we, that the Attorney General is likely to succeed on her claim that Fremont's practice of originating loans bearing the particular combination of four features identified in the preliminary injunction was unfair. To carry its burden under Mass. Gen. Laws ch. 93A, §3, of demonstrating that a regulatory scheme "affirmatively *permits* the practice which is alleged to be unfair," Fremont must show that some regulatory scheme affirmatively permitted the practice of combining all of those features. Fremont has not done so. Rather, it cites authority demonstrating, it asserts, that each of the four features was permitted by statute and regulatory authorities. Assuming, without deciding, that Fremont is correct that every feature was affirmatively permitted separately, it was Fremont's choice to combine them into a package that it should have known was "doomed to foreclosure"; the relevant question is whether some State or Federal authority permitted that combination. No authority did.

Notes and Questions

1. Regulating mortgage terms. *Fremont* addressed the substantive standards that should govern home lending. Several states have passed legislation regulating the terms and conditions of subprime mortgages, attempting to prevent the kinds of abusive practices that *Fremont* addressed. Among the strongest in the nation is the Minnesota statute, passed in 2007. It prohibits (1) making a residential loan to someone without regard to the borrower's ability to pay; (2) refinancing mortgages when no economic benefit accrues to the borrowing; and (3) certain prepayment penalties. *See* Minn. Stat. §§58.13(1)(a)(24) to (26), 58.137, 609.822. *See also* N.Y. Banking Law §6(g-m) (similar provisions).

Several of the characteristics in *Fremont* that marked the loans in that case as "unfair" involved what the lenders knew about the borrowers' ability to repay when they originated the loans. The *Dodd-Frank Wall Street Reform and Consumer Protection Act*, Pub. L. No. 111-203, 124 Stat. 1376 (2010) (*Dodd-Frank Act*), which was passed in response to the subprime mortgage crisis, for the first time sets national standards to address this issue. *See* 15 U.S.C. §1639c(a)(1) ("[N]o creditor may make a residential mortgage loan unless the creditor makes a reasonable and good faith determination based on verified and documented information that, at the time the loan is consummated, the consumer has a reasonable ability to repay the loan, according to its terms, and all applicable taxes, insurance . . . and assessments."). Lenders are now required to evaluate this ability to repay through documentation about the borrower and, for adjustable rate mortgages, lenders must evaluate ability to repay based on the required payments over the life of the loan, not just an introductory "teaser" rate. 15 U.S.C. §1639c(a)(3).

The *Dodd-Frank Act* established a presumption that certain "qualified mortgages" comply with this provision, 15 U.S.C. §1639c(b), and a new agency that the statute created, the Consumer Financial Protection Bureau (CFPB), has issued regulations that spell out what constitutes a qualified mortgage. *See Ability-to-Repay and Qualified Mortgage Standards Under the Truth in Lending Act (Regulation Z)*, 78 Fed. Reg. 6407 (Jan. 30, 2013) (to be codified at 12 C.F.R. pt. 1026). The *Dodd-Frank Act* also established specific prerequisites and underwriting criteria for qualified mortgages, and these standards have also been elaborated by regulation. The *Dodd-Frank Act* generally excludes loans that are **negative amortizing**, which means that the balance increases despite regular payments; loans that require payments of interest but not principal; loans that have balloon payments; or that have terms that exceed 30 years. The act and its implementing regulations also exclude loans where lenders fail to verify the assets or income of the borrower, and loans that require borrowers to pay certain fees and "points," which are up-front payments to reduce the interest rate of a loan.

A 1994 amendment to TILA called the *Home Ownership and Equity Protection Act* (HOEPA) regulated the terms and conditions of certain loans that have particularly high interest rates or high fees, primarily loans used for refinancing or home-equity loans. Home-equity loans are loans that are not used to purchase homes but instead use a home as collateral to finance borrowing for other purposes, such as home renovation. The *Dodd-Frank Act* significantly expanded HOEPA's reach, applying it to almost all "high-cost" mortgages. 15 U.S.C. §1602. The law allows borrowers to get out of the deal within three business days of receiving a notice of their rights. It also bans certain loan terms, such as balloon payments, negative amortization, and most prepayment penalties. The law also prohibits lending to a person who is not financially able to pay back the loan and requires pre-loan consumer counseling for high-cost mortgages. *See High-Cost Mortgage and Homeownership Counseling Amendments to the Truth in Lending Act (Regulation Z) and Homeownership Counseling Amendments to the Real Estate Settlement Procedures Act (Regulation X)*, 78 Fed. Reg. 6855 (Jan. 31, 2013) (to be codified at 12 C.F.R. pts. 1024 and 1026).

2. Regulating the process of origination. A number of statutes focus on fair treatment for individual borrowers or seek to help consumers navigate the loan transaction itself. These are procedural regulations, as opposed to substantive regulations of the terms and conditions of the actual loans themselves. The *Truth in Lending Act* (TILA), 15 U.S.C. §1639, and the *Real Estate Settlement Procedures Act* (RESPA), 12 U.S.C. §§2601-2617, for example, have long required disclosure of the basic terms of lending agreements. Lenders must provide such disclosures at two stages of the transaction: first when consumers apply for financing, so that they can better shop for loans, and then again when it comes time to close the loan, in order to ensure that the terms were actually provided. The *Dodd-Frank Act* mandated that these mortgage disclosure regimes be unified. The CFPB is currently working on regulations that would do so. *See Integrated Mortgage Disclosures Under the Real Estate Settlement Procedures Act (Regulation X) and the Truth in Lending Act (Regulation Z)*, 77 Fed. Reg. 54843-01 (Sept. 6, 2012) (to be codified at 12 C.F.R. pts. 1024 and 1026).

3. Fair lending and access to credit. The *Fair Housing Act*, 42 U.S.C. §§3601-3619, prohibits discriminatory practices by real estate finance providers. Similarly, the

Equal Credit Opportunity Act of 1974, 15 U.S.C. §§1691-1691f, prohibits discriminatory practices in any "credit transaction." Anyone who is denied credit is entitled to demand a "statement of reasons" for the denial from the creditor. *Id.* §1691(d)(2). The *Fair Housing Act* and the *Equal Credit Opportunity Act* are covered in depth in Chapter 13, §5.

4. Regulating loan servicing. Another area of regulation that has taken on new urgency in the wake of the subprime crisis involves what are called **loan servicers**, which are companies that lenders hire to collect mortgage payments, pay real estate taxes on behalf of borrowers, and manage other aspects of "servicing" loans. In the wake of the subprime crisis, the role of loan servicers has garnered increasing scrutiny, given their control over the borrower-lender relationship in many instances, and a number of problems that consumers have faced with servicers. *See* Peter Swire, *What the Fair Credit Reporting Act Should Teach Us About Mortgage Servicing,* Center for American Progress (Jan. 2011). The CFPB recently issued regulations under RESPA and TILA to set national standards to govern loan servicers. The rules cover a number of topics, but most significantly require periodic billing statements and statements when borrowers pay off their loans, mandate notice before an adjustable rate mortgage first changes its interest rate, and limit the servicer's ability to charge for insurance on behalf of a borrower. The new rules, recognizing the central role that servicers play not just in managing loans but also in the process of foreclosure, require early intervention when a borrower is having difficulty repaying her loan and continuity of contact with delinquent borrowers. The regulations also set forward specific steps that servicers must take to mitigate losses for home loans, in order to keep borrowers in their homes if possible. *See Mortgage Servicing Rules Under the Real Estate Settlement Procedures Act (Regulation X)* and *Mortgage Servicing Rules Under the Truth in Lending Act (Regulation Z),* 12 C.F.R. pt. 1024; 12 C.F.R. pt. 1026.

5. Structural responses to the subprime crisis. The subprime crisis led to significant government intervention to save the banks and to help the millions of homeowners facing foreclosure. These foreclosures would affect not only the families losing their homes but neighbors as well. A neighborhood dotted with foreclosed homes lowers the property values of those who remain, and in a recession, it is difficult to find buyers for those homes. *See* Kristopher S. Gerardi et al., *Foreclosure Externalities: New Evidence,* NBER Working Paper No. 18353 (2012). Owners are also reluctant to sell at the low market values because they will suffer big losses in their wealth.

In the years after the subprime crisis hit, the federal government created a series of programs to facilitate refinancing for borrowers who owe more on their property than the property is worth or are otherwise at risk for default, *see* Peter W. Salsich, Jr., *Homeownership-Dream or Disaster?,* 21 J. Affordable Hous. & Community Dev. L. 17, 40-50 (2012), but these programs have been faulted for not more directly restructuring at-risk mortgages. *See, e.g.,* Dan Immergluck, *Too Little, Too Late, and Too Timid: The Federal Response to the Foreclosure Crisis at the Five-Year Mark,* 23 Housing Policy

Debate 199, 216 (2013).[19] The federal government, as well as state and local governments, also worked to mitigate the neighborhood-level consequences of the increase in, and concentration of, foreclosures. *Id.* at 218-222 (describing efforts such as the federal Neighborhood Stabilization Program). The other main area of regulatory response to the subprime crisis has occurred mostly at the state level, where the process of foreclosure itself has seen significant changes, both judicial and statutory. We will consider those reforms in the next section.

§4.3 Defaults and the Right to Foreclose

If a mortgagor defaults on her loan, she has the right to prevent loss of her property by paying off the debt before foreclosure; indeed, some states allow the mortgagor to prevent foreclosure by paying the arrears only. This debtor protection is called the **equity of redemption**, a name that alludes to the origin of mortgages in the courts of equity in England — and is why people often refer to the value an owner has in her property as "equity." Originally, the owner-borrower would convey title to the property to the lender with a condition subsequent, allowing the borrower to pay off the debt on a certain day and thereby get the deed back. If the borrower did not pay off the debt on the appointed day, she would lose the property forever. Since the land was usually worth more than the debt, the lender would often get a windfall.

Borrowers began to ask the equity courts for relief from this result, and the chancellor responded by granting the borrower extra time to pay off the debt, thereby redeeming the property (getting it back). In so doing, the court effectively rewrote the contract, changing the terms of the condition. At first, this was subject to the equity court's discretion, but by the seventeenth century it was a matter of right. The borrower's interest came to be called the equity of redemption, while the mortgagee held title.[20] *See* Ann M. Burkhart, *Lenders and Land*, 64 Mo. L. Rev. 249 (1999) (excellent overview of history of mortgage law and regulation).

---

19. One significant proposal that emerged early in the subprime crisis would have allowed homeowners to restructure mortgages in bankruptcy. Currently, home mortgage loans are not dischargeable in bankruptcy, unlike most other consumer debt. *See* 11 U.S.C. §1322(b)(2) (debtors may "modify the rights of holders of secured claims, other than a claim secured only by a security interest in real property that is the debtor's principal residence"). Reform of bankruptcy law would have enabled borrowers to reduce or eliminate their mortgage debt in bankruptcy in order to start over. However, this proposal has not become law.

20. Approximately ten jurisdictions retain this **title theory** of mortgages for some or all financing arrangements: Alabama, Connecticut, District of Columbia, Georgia, Maine, Massachusetts, New Hampshire, Pennsylvania, Rhode Island, and Tennessee. *Restatement (Third) of Property (Mortgages)* §4.1, Note on Mortgage Theories Followed by American Jurisdictions (1997). The number is approximate because some states are less than clear about their approach. Most states subscribe to the **lien theory**, under which the borrower retains title to the property and the lender has merely a lien on the property. A few (like Maryland) adopt an **intermediate theory**, whereby the mortgagor has title until default occurs, at which point legal title passes to the mortgagee. With minor exceptions, no practical difference remains between the title theory and the lien theory in terms of the legal rights of the parties. *Restatement (Third) of Property (Mortgages)* §4.1 cmt. a.

Allowing the borrower some extra time to get the property back by paying off the debt protected the mortgagor's interest but left the mortgagee without any clear remedy. For this reason, the equity courts put a time limit on the mortgagor's right to redeem. The equity courts began a procedure to allow the lender to cut off, or **foreclose**, the equity of redemption. At first, courts used a procedure called **strict foreclosure**, which would give the borrower extra time to pay off the debt but provide that if the debt remained unpaid by a particular date, title would vest in the mortgagee without a sale. Because of perceived unfairness of strict foreclosure, this procedure has been substantially abolished in the United States and is available in only a couple of states where it is subject to judicial discretion. *See* Conn. Gen. Stat. §§49-15, 49-24; Vt. Stat. tit. 12, §4528.

Today most foreclosures involve a sale of the mortgaged property, either through a judicial proceeding or by a private sale, depending on the contractual arrangements between the parties and state law. In a **judicial sale**, the mortgagee will bring a foreclosure action in which they must prove the existence of the mortgage, the right to foreclose, and the mortgagor's default. If the mortgagee meets these burdens, and the borrower has no other defenses, the court will issue a foreclosure decree. The decree provides for public sale of the property by a court officer, payment of the proceeds to the mortgagee and any other creditors with liens on the property, and transfer of any surplus funds to the mortgagor.

Several states allow the mortgagor to waive the protection of a judicial sale by granting the mortgagee a **power of sale**.[21] If so, the mortgagee can conduct the public sale itself or through a public official such as a sheriff, after notice to all interested parties, without the need for judicial proceedings. A similar arrangement is the **deed of trust**, which is prevalent in some states. Under this arrangement, the borrower or **trustor** conveys title to a third party (called the **trustee**) as security for the trustor's payment of its debt obligation to the lender (called the **beneficiary**). If the trustor defaults, the trustee can arrange a public nonjudicial sale of the property to satisfy the debt. In practice, unlike in an ordinary trust, the borrower who grants a deed of trust to secure real estate generally continues to act as the true owner, and the trustee's functions come into play if that owner defaults.

Some states have enacted a **statutory right of redemption**, which allows the mortgagor to buy back the property for the price bid at the foreclosure sale for a designated period (typically six months to a year) **after foreclosure**.[22] These statutes generally allow the mortgagor to remain in possession of the property in the meanwhile. The statutory right of redemption is meant to encourage market prices at the foreclosure sale on the theory that if bids are below fair market price, the mortgagor has time go to

---

21. About 30 states and the District of Columbia allow nonjudicial foreclosure, and in about two-thirds of those jurisdictions, it is the primary method of foreclosure. Grant S. Nelson & Dale A. Whitman, *Real Estate Finance Law* §§7.9, 7.19 at 801, 845 (5th ed. 2007).

22. This statutory redemption right, which is available in about half the states, *see* 4-37 *Powell on Real Property* §37.46, should not be confused with the equity of redemption, which is the mortgagor's right to pay off the rest of the debt *before* foreclosure and redeem the property.

borrow the money to buy back the property for the (artificially low) price paid at the foreclosure sale. However, the ability of the mortgagor to redeem the property after foreclosure may actually decrease the market value of the property at the time of the foreclosure sale since the buyer cannot possess the property immediately and, in fact, has no assurance it will ever be able to possess the property.

Upon a foreclosure sale, the mortgagor's equity of redemption is cut off. If the sale does not bring in enough proceeds to pay off the debt, many states allow the lender to bring an action for a **deficiency judgment** personally against the mortgagor for the rest of the debt. Some states, however, prohibit deficiency judgments or require lenders to bring any deficiency action at the same time as they bring a foreclosure action. *See, e.g.*, Cal. Civ. Proc. Code §580b.

In the wake of the subprime crisis, many aspects of foreclosure practice that had once been fairly routine have become complicated by the realities of securitization. Consider the following case.

U.S. Bank National Association v. Ibanez

941 N.E.2d 40 (Mass. 2011)

Ralph Gants, J.

On December 1, 2005, Antonio Ibanez took out a $103,500 loan for the purchase of property at 20 Crosby Street in Springfield, secured by a mortgage to the lender, Rose Mortgage, Inc. (Rose Mortgage). The mortgage was recorded the following day. Several days later, Rose Mortgage executed an assignment of this mortgage in blank, that is, an assignment that did not specify the name of the assignee. The blank space in the assignment was at some point stamped with the name of Option One Mortgage Corporation (Option One) as the assignee, and that assignment was recorded on June 7, 2006. Before the recording, on January 23, 2006, Option One executed an assignment of the Ibanez mortgage in blank.

According to U.S. Bank, Option One assigned the Ibanez mortgage to Lehman Brothers Bank, FSB, which assigned it to Lehman Brothers Holdings Inc., which then assigned it to the Structured Asset Securities Corporation, which then assigned the mortgage, pooled with approximately 1,220 other mortgage loans, to U.S. Bank, as trustee for the Structured Asset Securities Corporation Mortgage Pass-Through Certificates, Series 2006-Z. With this last assignment, the Ibanez and other loans were pooled into a trust and converted into mortgage-backed securities that can be bought and sold by investors — a process known as securitization.

According to U.S. Bank, the assignment of the Ibanez mortgage to U.S. Bank occurred pursuant to a December 1, 2006, trust agreement, which is not in the record. What is in the record is the private placement memorandum (PPM), dated December 26, 2006, a 273-page, unsigned offer of mortgage-backed securities to potential investors. The PPM describes the mortgage pools and the entities involved, and summarizes the provisions of the trust agreement, including the representation that mortgages "will be" assigned into the trust. According to the PPM, "[e]ach transfer of a Mortgage Loan from the Seller [Lehman Brothers Holdings Inc.] to the Depositor [Structured

Asset Securities Corporation] and from the Depositor to the Trustee [U.S. Bank] will be intended to be a sale of that Mortgage Loan and will be reflected as such in the Sale and Assignment Agreement and the Trust Agreement, respectively." The PPM also specifies that "[e]ach Mortgage Loan will be identified in a schedule appearing as an exhibit to the Trust Agreement." However, U.S. Bank did not provide the [lower court] judge with any mortgage schedule identifying the Ibanez loan as among the mortgages that were assigned in the trust agreement.

In June, 2007, U.S. Bank caused to be published in the Boston Globe the notice of the foreclosure sale required by Mass. Gen. Laws c. 244, §14. The notice identified U.S. Bank as the "present holder" of the mortgage. At the foreclosure sale on July 5, 2007, the Ibanez property was purchased by U.S. Bank, as trustee for the securitization trust, for $94,350, a value significantly less than the outstanding debt and the estimated market value of the property. The foreclosure deed (from U.S. Bank, trustee, as the purported holder of the mortgage, to U.S. Bank, trustee, as the purchaser) and the statutory foreclosure affidavit were recorded on May 23, 2008. On September 2, 2008, more than one year after the sale, and more than five months after recording of the sale, American Home Mortgage Servicing, Inc., "as successor-in-interest" to Option One, which was until then the record holder of the Ibanez mortgage, executed a written assignment of that mortgage to U.S. Bank, as trustee for the securitization trust. This assignment was recorded on September 11, 2008.

[A similar sequence occurred with respect to a mortgage that Mark and Tammy LaRace gave on May 19, 2005 to Option One as security for a $103,200 loan; Option One assigned the LaRace mortgage to Bank of America, who then assigned it to the Asset Backed Funding Corporation (ABFC). ABFC pooled the mortgage with others and assigned it to Wells Fargo, as trustee for the ABFC 2005-OPT 1 Trust, ABFC Asset-Backed Certificates, Series 2005-OPT 1, pursuant to a pooling and servicing agreement. In June 2007, Wells Fargo, as trustee, published a statutory notice of sale in the Boston Globe, identifying itself as the "present holder" of the mortgage. At the subsequent foreclosure sale, Wells Fargo, as trustee, purchased the LaRace property for $120,397.03, significantly below its estimated market value.]

The plaintiffs [U.S. Bank and Wells Fargo] brought actions under Mass. Gen. Laws ch. 240, §6, seeking declarations that the defendant mortgagors' titles had been extinguished and that the plaintiffs were the fee simple owners of the foreclosed properties. As such, the plaintiffs bore the burden of establishing their entitlement to the relief sought. To meet this burden, they were required "not merely to demonstrate better title . . . than the defendants possess, but . . . to prove sufficient title to succeed in [the] action." [*Sheriff's Meadow Foundation, Inc. v. Bay-Courte Edgartown, Inc.*, 516 N.E.2d 144, 146 (Mass. 1987).] There is no question that the relief the plaintiffs sought required them to establish the validity of the foreclosure sales on which their claim to clear title rested.

Massachusetts does not require a mortgage holder to obtain judicial authorization to foreclose on a mortgaged property. See Mass. Gen. Laws ch. 183, §21; Mass. Gen. Laws ch. 244, §14. Where a mortgage grants a mortgage holder the power of sale, as did both the Ibanez and LaRace mortgages, it includes by reference the power of sale set out in Mass. Gen. Laws ch. 183, §21, and further regulated by Mass. Gen. Laws ch. 244, §§11-17C. Under Mass. Gen. Laws ch. 183, §21, after a mortgagor defaults in the performance of the underlying note, the mortgage holder may sell the property at a public auction and convey the property to the purchaser in fee simple, "and such sale shall forever bar the mortgagor and all persons claiming under him from all right and interest in the mortgaged premises, whether at law or in equity." Even where there is a dispute as to whether the mortgagor was in default or whether the party claiming to be the mortgage holder is the true mortgage holder, the foreclosure goes forward unless the mortgagor files an action and obtains a court order enjoining the foreclosure.

Recognizing the substantial power that the statutory scheme affords to a mortgage holder to foreclose without immediate judicial oversight, we adhere to the familiar rule that "one who sells under a power [of sale] must follow strictly its terms. If he fails to do so there is no valid execution of the power, and the sale is wholly void." *Moore v. Dick*, 72 N.E. 967 (Mass. 1905). One of the terms of the power of sale that must be strictly adhered to is the restriction on who is entitled to foreclose. The "statutory power of sale" can be exercised by "the mortgagee or his executors, administrators, successors or assigns." Mass. Gen. Laws ch. 183, §21. Any effort to foreclose by a party lacking "jurisdiction and authority" to carry out a foreclosure under these statutes is void. *Chace v. Morse*, 76 N.E. 142 (Mass. 1905).

The plaintiffs claim that the securitization documents they submitted establish valid assignments that made them the holders of the Ibanez and LaRace mortgages before the notice of sale and the foreclosure sale. We turn, then, to the documentation submitted by the plaintiffs to determine whether it met the requirements of a valid assignment. Focusing first on the Ibanez mortgage, U.S. Bank argues that it was assigned the mortgage under the trust agreement described in the PPM, but it did not submit a copy of this trust agreement to the judge. The PPM, however, described the trust agreement as an agreement to be executed in the future, so it only furnished evidence of an intent to assign mortgages to U.S. Bank, not proof of their actual assignment. Even if there were an executed trust agreement with language of present assignment, U.S. Bank did not produce the schedule of loans and mortgages that was an exhibit to that agreement, so it failed to show that the Ibanez mortgage was among the mortgages to be assigned by that agreement. Finally, even if there were an executed trust agreement with the required schedule, U.S. Bank failed to furnish any evidence that the entity assigning the mortgage — Structured Asset Securities Corporation — ever held the mortgage to be assigned. The last assignment of the mortgage on record was from Rose Mortgage to Option One; nothing was submitted to the judge indicating that Option One ever assigned the mortgage to anyone before the foreclosure sale. Thus, based on the documents submitted to the judge, Option One, not U.S. Bank, was the mortgage holder at the time of the foreclosure, and U.S. Bank did not have the authority to foreclose the mortgage.

[Wells Fargo was similarly unable to demonstrate authority to foreclose based on the documentation relating to the securitization of the LaRace mortgage in the record.]

Where a plaintiff files a complaint asking for a declaration of clear title after a mortgage foreclosure, a judge is entitled to ask for proof that the foreclosing entity was the mortgage holder at the time of the notice of sale and foreclosure, or was one of the parties authorized to foreclose under Mass. Gen. Laws ch. 183, §21, and Mass. Gen. Laws ch. 244, §14. A plaintiff that cannot make this modest showing cannot justly proclaim that it was unfairly denied a declaration of clear title.

We do not suggest that an assignment must be in recordable form at the time of the notice of sale or the subsequent foreclosure sale, although recording is likely the better practice. Where a pool of mortgages is assigned to a securitized trust, the executed agreement that assigns the pool of mortgages, with a schedule of the pooled mortgage loans that clearly and specifically identifies the mortgage at issue as among those assigned, may suffice to establish the trustee as the mortgage holder. However, there must be proof that the assignment was made by a party that itself held the mortgage. A foreclosing entity may provide a complete chain of assignments linking it to the record holder of the mortgage, or a single assignment from the record holder of the mortgage.

Conclusion. For the reasons stated, we agree with the judge that the plaintiffs did not demonstrate that they were the holders of the Ibanez and LaRace mortgages at the time that they foreclosed these properties, and therefore failed to demonstrate that they acquired fee simple title to these properties by purchasing them at the foreclosure sale.

ROBERT CORDY, J., concurring.

I concur fully in the opinion of the court, and write separately only to underscore that what is surprising about these cases is not the statement of principles articulated by the court regarding title law and the law of foreclosure in Massachusetts, but rather the utter carelessness with which the plaintiff banks documented the titles to their assets. There is no dispute that the mortgagors of the properties in question had defaulted on their obligations, and that the mortgaged properties were subject to foreclosure. Before commencing such an action, however, the holder of an assigned mortgage needs to take care to ensure that his legal paperwork is in order. Although there was no apparent actual unfairness here to the mortgagors, that is not the point. Foreclosure is a powerful act with significant consequences, and Massachusetts law has always required that it proceed strictly in accord with the statutes that govern it.

The type of sophisticated transactions leading up to the accumulation of the notes and mortgages in question in these cases and their securitization, and, ultimately the sale of mortgage-backed securities, are not barred nor even burdened by the requirements of Massachusetts law. The plaintiff banks, who brought these cases to clear the titles that they acquired at their own foreclosure sales, have simply failed to prove that the underlying assignments of the mortgages that they allege (and would have) entitled them to foreclose ever existed in any legally cognizable form before they exercised the power of sale that accompanies those assignments. The court's opinion clearly states that such assignments do not need to be in recordable form or recorded before the foreclosure, but they do have to have been effectuated.

Notes and Questions

1. **Problems of proof and authority in foreclosure.** When a bank obtains a mortgage on a home, the Statute of Frauds requires it to be in writing, and the mortgagee generally records the mortgage. If the mortgage is assigned to another institution, the purchaser of the bank's rights should record its interest as well, although as *Ibanez* makes clear, recording is not legally required to effectuate the transfer. In some cases, the institutions that buy mortgages neither record the transaction nor obtain sufficient proof of their interest. *Ibanez* illustrates what can happen if a party seeks to foreclose on a mortgage but is unable to demonstrate that it is, in fact, authorized to do so. This has become an increasingly important aspect of foreclosure litigation in the aftermath of the housing crisis. *See generally* Bradley T. Borden, David J. Reiss & W. KeAupuni Akina, *Show Me the Note!*, 19 Bank & Lender Liab. 3 (2013) (surveying challenges to the authority to foreclose based on deficiencies in proof relating to holding the note or the mortgage); Nestor M. Davidson, *New Formalism in the Aftermath of the Housing Crisis*, 93 B.U. L. Rev. 389 (2013) (raising concerns about trends in these cases).

In *Ibanez*, U.S. Bank and Wells Fargo were both acting as a trustee for entities that purported to own the underlying mortgages. Mortgage servicers, as well, often file foreclosure lawsuits on behalf of mortgagees, but they are not the "owners" of the mortgages they service. Accordingly, servicers may be required to present proof of ownership of the mortgage for the foreclosure to proceed. Some courts have refused to allow loan servicers to bring foreclosure lawsuits on behalf of the underlying mortgagee. *See Bayview Loan Servicing, L.L.C. v. Nelson*, 890 N.E.2d 940 (Ill. App. Ct. 2008) (denying a loan servicer the power to bring a foreclosure suit).

Similar problems may arise with the **Mortgage Electronic Registration Systems, Inc. (MERS)**. In 1993, mortgage lenders who engaged in trades of mortgages established a private organization, MERS, to hold those mortgages for the benefit of the mortgagees. MERS does not actually "own" the mortgage; it has no right to the payments from the borrower; nor does it act as the loan servicer. Rather, it acts as the agent of the mortgagees, and MERS is listed as either the "nominee" of the lender or as the record owner of the mortgage in the recording office. This is designed to eliminate the need for new recordings when mortgages are transferred, allowing mortgages to be traded more cheaply and quickly. In a number of cases, borrowers have challenged the ability of MERS to initiate foreclosures, and the courts have disagreed about whether MERS is entitled to foreclose. *Compare, e.g., Brandrup v. ReconTrust Co., N.A.*, 303 P.3d 301 (Or. 2013) (MERS not eligible to serve as beneficiary under *Oregon Deed of Trust Act* and did not show authorization as an agent of lender); *Mortgage Electronic Registration Systems, Inc. v. Saunders*, 2 A.3d 289 (Me. 2010) (MERS lacks standing to initiate foreclosure), *with Mortgage Electronic Registration Systems, Inc. v. White*, 896 A.2d 797 (Conn. 2006) (upholding MERS-initiated foreclosure as nominee for lenders). MERS no longer allows foreclosures under its name, but this has not stopped challenges from arising. *See, e.g., Bucci v. Lehman Brothers Bank, FSB*, 68 A.3d 1069, 1079-1080 (R.I. 2013) (noting the policy change, but finding a challenge to

MERS's authority to act on behalf of a lender not moot); *see also Edwards v. Mortgage Electronic Registration Systems, Inc.*, 300 P.3d 43 (Ind. 2013) (the fact that MERS acts as nominee for lender does not preclude foreclosure).

2. The purpose of recording mortgage transfers. MERS raises broader questions about the function of the public records system when it comes to mortgage transfers. The New York Court of Appeals has held that the recording office is obligated to record mortgages held by MERS, even though it is not itself the mortgagee. *MERSCORP, Inc. v. Romaine*, 861 N.E.2d 81 (N.Y. 2006). Partially dissenting, Chief Judge Judith Kaye noted that MERS makes it more difficult for the recording system to achieve its purpose, which is to create a public system that puts potential buyers on notice of who owns interests in real estate. She noted that one result of MERS is that it may be difficult (or impossible) for a homeowner to determine who owns the underlying mortgage. The mortgage can be sold, and the borrower may be dealing only with the loan servicer rather than the mortgagee. The loan servicer does not see it as its job to engage in such negotiations (particularly since loan servicers often get higher fees for conducting foreclosures than for collecting routine loan payments). If so, then there is a transactional barrier to renegotiation that may lead to an unnecessary foreclosure, with the third-party effects such foreclosures engender. *Id.* at 88-89. To solve these problems, some scholars have begun to call for a public national registry. *See, e.g.*, Tanya Marsh, *Foreclosures and the Failure of the American Land Title Recording System*, 111 Colum. L. Rev. Sidebar 19 (2011).

3. Challenging judicial versus nonjudicial foreclosures. In a judicial foreclosure, there is an initial lawsuit before a sale can take place, which affords home borrowers the opportunity to contest the basis for the foreclosure and raise any affirmative defenses they might have. With a power-of-sale foreclosure or deed of trust, borrowers must affirmatively challenge the sale, or bring claims after the sale if there were infirmities in the process or result of the sale. Some borrowers in default may also file for bankruptcy, a process that includes an automatic stay of claims, including foreclosure. 11 U.S.C. §362(a)(1). *Ibanez* was somewhat unusual in that the successful bidders at the foreclosure sale, U.S. Bank and Wells Fargo, brought a quiet title action, which then allowed the original borrowers to contest the validity of the foreclosure itself. Does this procedural posture matter?

4. *Fair Debt Collection Practices Act.* A 1977 statute, the *Fair Debt Collection Practices Act*, 15 U.S.C. §§1692-1692p (FDCPA), prohibits the use of unfair or abusive practices in the collection of debts by third parties acting on behalf of lenders. Debt collectors, for example, are barred from communicating with borrowers if borrowers are represented by counsel or inform the debt collector that they do not wish to be contacted. *Id.* §1692c. And debt collectors may not use or threaten violence or use obscene or profane language. *Id.* §1692d. The FDCPA also contains a number of affirmative requirements for debt collectors, including identifying themselves as debt collectors, informing the borrower of the amount of the debt, and notifying the borrower of the right to contest the debt. *Id.* §1692g.

With the subprime crisis, borrowers are increasingly invoking the FDCPA in defending against practices related to foreclosure, and lawyers involved in foreclosures may be subject to the FDCPA. Courts have taken differing views about whether foreclosures constitute "debt collection," as opposed to the realization of a security interest. *Compare, e.g., Diessner v. Mortgage Electronic Registration Systems, Inc.*, 618 F. Supp. 2d 1184, 1188-1189 (D. Ariz. 2009), *aff'd sub nom. Diessner v. Mortgage Electronic Registration Systems, Inc.*, 384 F. App'x 609 (9th Cir. 2010), *with, e.g., Glazer v. Chase Home Finance LLC*, 704 F.3d 453, 462 (6th Cir. 2013); *Kaltenbach v. Richards*, 464 F.3d 524, 529 (5th Cir. 2006).

§4.4 Foreclosure Sales

A common problem in foreclosure sales arises with the price bid for the property. Anyone can bid on the property, including the mortgagor and the mortgagee. Although publicity should generate knowledge about the sale and offers from anyone interested in the property, it is often the case that the mortgagee is the only entity or person bidding at the foreclosure sale. Can you see why? In such a case, there is a danger that the mortgagee will make a low bid; the mortgagee will get the property for less than its fair market value but be able to sell it for fair market value and pocket the excess. If the sale price is less than the unpaid debt, the mortgagee can not only resell the property but, in many states, can file a deficiency judgment against a mortgagor who has other assets. Under what circumstances, then, should courts set aside the sale entirely? Consider the following case.

Baskurt v. Beal

101 P.3d 1041 (Alaska 2004)

WARREN W. MATTHEWS, Justice.

This case involves two parcels of land originally owned by Marion and Mortimer Moore. In 1953 Mortimer was granted a homestead patent to a forty-acre parcel which he conveyed to his wife, Marion, in 1959. The following year, Marion acquired a second parcel to the north of the homestead property, Parcel 1. In 1974 the majority of the homestead property was sold, leaving Parcel 2, which adjoined Parcel 1 to the south. The two parcels were never replatted or otherwise legally merged into a single parcel.

The Moores divorced in 1976. In 1991 Mortimer and Marion simultaneously sold their respective parcels to Charles McAlpine. The following day, McAlpine conveyed the parcels to Annette Beal by quitclaim deed. These transactions were financed by two separate promissory notes signed by McAlpine: Note A for $95,000 payable to Mortimer; and Note B for $135,000 payable to Marion. Each note was to be paid to the respective seller through its own separate escrow account.

The two promissory notes were secured by a single deed of trust covering both parcels containing the following special condition: "This deed of trust is covered by 2 Promissory Notes, and Trustor is aware that default on either of the 2 Note

[sic], will constitute default under the other Note and foreclosure laws of the State of Alaska shall apply." The deed of trust also provided that "[u]pon default by Trustor in payment of any indebtedness secured hereby . . . Trustee . . . shall," at the option of the Beneficiary, "sell said property[,] . . . either as a whole or in separate parcels and in such order as it may determine, at public auction to the highest and best bidder. . . ."

In 1994 Annette paid off the $95,000 owed on Note A for Parcel 1 to Mortimer. At that time, there was some discussion regarding paying off Note B, but Marion preferred to continue to receive monthly payments rather than being paid off in a single lump sum. Marion did agree to a reduction of the interest rate on Note B. The 1991 deed of trust was modified to reflect the payoff of the note to Mortimer and the change in interest rate on Marion's note.

In the fall of 1999, after an erratic payment history, Annette fell behind in her payments. Sarah Baskurt, the Moores' daughter [as trustee for a trust established by Marion Moore], took steps to commence foreclosure, including contacting attorney Jim Christie to conduct the foreclosure. Christie and Land Title Company of Alaska, Inc., made the arrangements for the foreclosure. At that time, Annette owed $26,780.81 on Parcel 2, having paid approximately eighty percent of the original $135,000 purchase price.

The foreclosure sale was held on April 26, 2000, inside the main entrance of the Nesbett Memorial Courthouse in Anchorage. Prior to arriving at the sale, Baskurt, who wanted to bid on the property but believed she lacked the financial strength and knowledge of property development to do so on her own, contacted friends to see if they would be interested in bidding on the property as her partner. Robert and Joyce Wainscott agreed and Baskurt and Joyce Wainscott formed a partnership for the purpose of acquiring and developing or reselling the property. Baskurt, who believed the property was worth at least $250,000, brought a check for $151,000 to the sale. The Wainscotts brought a check for $100,000 to the sale. The trio had at least $251,000 available to put toward the purchase price of the property. [They later agreed to add Baskurt's neighbor, Allen Rosenthal, whom Baskurt knew to have considerable experience in home construction, to the partnership.]

The foreclosure sale, conducted by Christie, was by public outcry. Baskurt made the opening and only bid for $26,781.81, a dollar over the remaining debt owed on the property, on behalf of the partnership. There were no other bids, and the property was sold to Baskurt, Joyce, and Rosenthal via a trustee's deed.

On May 17, 2000, Annette filed a complaint seeking to have the foreclosure sale set aside. Baskurt, Wainscott, and Rosenthal (collectively "Purchasers") subsequently moved for summary judgment, arguing there was no basis for setting aside the sale. Purchasers' motion for summary judgment was denied because a question of fact remained whether "the parties intended for both parcels to be subject to foreclosure upon default of one note when the other note had been satisfied." After a three-day bench trial, the superior court set aside the foreclosure sale as both void and voidable. Final judgment setting aside the foreclosure sale and awarding attorney's fees and costs to Annette was entered on February 28, 2003. Purchasers appeal.

Pursuant to Alaska Stat. §34.20.070 a trustee under a deed of trust executed as security for the payment of an indebtedness may, in the case of default or noncompliance with the terms of the deed, foreclose and sell the property according to the terms provided in the deed. However, defects in the mechanics of the trustee's exercise of the power to foreclose may render the foreclosure sale voidable. Generally, mere inadequacy of price is not sufficient by itself to require setting aside a foreclosure sale. However, if the inadequacy of the sale price is (1) "so gross as to shock the conscience and raise a presumption of fraud or unfairness," or (2) is coupled with other irregularities in the sale procedures, then invalidation of the sale may be justified.

Gross inadequacy is measured by reference to the fair market value of the property at the time of the sale.[23] Fair market value for these purposes has been defined as

> not the fair "forced sale" value of the real estate, but the price which would result from negotiation and mutual agreement, after ample time to find a purchaser, between a vendor who is willing, but not compelled to sell, and a purchaser who is willing to buy, but not compelled to take a particular piece of real estate.[24]

Courts determine adequacy of price by comparing the fair market value to the purchase price of the property at the foreclosure sale. Jurisdictions vary on what percentage of fair market value renders the purchase price grossly inadequate. Foreclosure sale prices of fifty percent or more of fair market value are routinely upheld. Even prices garnering less than fifty percent of fair market value are often upheld. However, several courts have upheld the invalidation of a foreclosure sale that produced a price of twenty percent of fair market value or less. The New Mexico Supreme Court has enunciated the standard that when the price falls into the ten to forty percent range, it should not be confirmed "absent good reasons why it should be."[25]

The Restatement adopts the position that although "'gross inadequacy' cannot be defined in terms of a specific percentage of fair market value," generally, "a court is warranted in invalidating a sale where the price is less than twenty percent of fair market value and, absent other foreclosure defects, is usually not warranted in invalidating a sale that yields in excess of that amount."[26] The Restatement adopts a sliding-scale approach to the cumulative effect that price and irregular procedures have on the fairness of the sale:

> Even where the foreclosure price for less than fair market value cannot be characterized as "grossly inadequate," if the foreclosure proceeding is defective under local law

23. *Restatement (Third) of Property (Mortgages)* §8.3 cmt. b, at 584, 593 (1997).

24. *Id.* at 584; *see also BFP v. Resolution Trust Corp.,* 511 U.S. 531, 537-38 (1994) ("The market value of . . . a piece of property is the price which it might be expected to bring if offered for sale in a fair market; not the price which might be obtained on a sale at public auction or a sale forced by the necessities of the owner, but such a price as would be fixed by negotiation and mutual agreement, after ample time to find a purchaser, as between a vendor who is willing (but not compelled) to sell and a purchaser who desires to buy but is not compelled to take the particular . . . piece of property.") (citing *Black's Law Dictionary* 971 (6th ed. 1990)).

25. *Armstrong v. Csurilla,* 817 P.2d 1221, 1234-35 (1991).

26. Restatement §8.3 cmt. b, at 584.

> in some other respect, a court is warranted in invalidating the sale and may even be required to do so. Such defects may include, for example, . . . selling too much or too little of the mortgaged real estate. For example, even a slight irregularity in the foreclosure process coupled with a sale price that is substantially below fair market value may justify or even compel the invalidation of the sale. . . . On the other hand, even a sale for slightly below fair market value may be enough to require invalidation of the sale where there is a major defect in the foreclosure process.[27]

In *McHugh* [*v. Church,* 583 P.2d 210, 213 (Alaska 1978)], we considered the effect of selling property in bulk as opposed to by parcel. Though we declined to adopt "a flat rule requiring the trustee to sell real property in separate lots or parcels, rather than as a whole unit," we recognized that a trustee under a deed of trust is a dual fiduciary owing duties to both the trustor and the beneficiary. Among the duties owed by the trustee is the duty to take reasonable and appropriate steps to avoid sacrifice of the debtor's property and interest.

Bearing these principles in mind, we turn to the facts of this case. Purchasers contend that there was no basis to set the foreclosure sale aside as voidable. They argue, among other things, that the sale should not have been set aside on the basis of an inadequate price since under *McHugh,* an inadequate price is an insufficient basis for setting aside a foreclosure sale. Further, they contend that the sale should not have been set aside on the ground that the parcels were sold together because under *McHugh,* the trustee was under no duty to sell the parcels separately.

We are not convinced by Purchasers' argument. The test for whether a sale is voidable based on price inadequacy is whether the price paid was *grossly* inadequate when compared to the fair market value of the property on the date of the foreclosure sale. The trial court found that the 1991 sales price of $225,000 was the best indicator of fair market value. The fact that the foreclosure purchase price of $26,781.10 was less than fifteen percent of the sale price indicates that the gross inadequacy standard was met. The trial court so found, and Purchasers identify no circumstances indicating that this finding is erroneous.

The superior court also found that the sale of either parcel alone would likely have generated sufficient proceeds to satisfy the amount due. By conducting the sale in bulk rather than selling only one parcel, the court found that the trustee failed in its duty to act reasonably to protect Beal's interests. This finding is supported by the evidence and is in accordance with our observation in *McHugh* that a trustee has a duty to take reasonable steps to act impartially and in such a way as "not to sacrifice the debtor's property." When coupled with the inadequacy of the price, the trustee's unreasonable failure to sell only one parcel initially justifies invalidating the sale.[28]

---

27. [*Id.* §8.3, at 587.]

28. Our conclusion should not be read as implying that the gross inadequacy of the sale price alone would not be a sufficient ground to set aside the sale. It is not necessary to reach that question in this case because of the additional flaw in the sale process.

We conclude that the superior court properly set aside the sale based on the grossly inadequate sale price and the trustee's failure to sell only one parcel in breach of its duty to act reasonably to protect Beal's interests.

Notes and Questions

1. **The process of foreclosure sales.** Most foreclosure sales take place by public auction, which typically involves a single opportunity for interested purchasers to come to a single location in order to bid. State law sets the terms of the required public notice of the sale and other conditions that must be met. Although this process can help borrowers in distress reduce carrying costs and market properties quickly, scholars have argued that "it would be difficult to design a sale procedure less apt to result in market prices than the usual foreclosure auction. The absence of so many features that buyers in negotiated sales have come to expect virtually ensures that below-market prices will prevail." Grant S. Nelson & Dale A. Whitman, *Reforming Foreclosure: The Uniform Nonjudicial Foreclosure Act*, 53 Duke L.J. 1399, 1423 (2004). Indeed, many institutional lenders have come to view foreclosure less as process to liquidate the property for its immediate value than as a way to transfer title to themselves so that they can sell it outside of the bidding process. *Id.*

2. **Ensuring a fair price at foreclosure sales.** States have developed several mechanisms to ensure that the price bid at the foreclosure sale is near the fair market value. First, the mortgagor has the right to bid at the foreclosure sale. This enables the mortgagor to go to another lender, which may be willing to lend the mortgagor the money so long as the property is worth more than the unpaid debt, and the property will constitute the security for *its* new loan. If the mortgagee bids too low, the mortgagor may be able to counter with a higher bid, forcing the mortgagee to bid more to get the property. Second, there must be public notice of the sale so that others can bid on the property. Third, some states prohibit deficiency judgments. This decreases the mortgagee's incentive to bid below the fair market value of the property. Fourth, many states allow a mortgagor to sue a mortgagee for unjust enrichment if the mortgagee buys the property at a low price and resells it within a short period of time for a much higher price. The mortgagee may be forced to disgorge the profits and turn them over to the mortgagor. This procedure protects the mortgagor's right to the excess proceeds and prevents the mortgagee from bidding low, reselling the property, and keeping those proceeds itself.

As the *Baskurt* court noted, when a party challenges a foreclosure based on the price obtained through the sale, courts generally require either a level of inadequacy that "shocks the conscience" sufficient to "raise a presumption of fraud or unfairness," or is coupled with other irregularities in the sale procedures. Some courts are reluctant to set aside foreclosure sales, even with very low proceeds, in the absence of some irregularity. In *Phillips v. Blazier-Henry*, 302 P.3d 349 (Idaho 2013), for example, a lower court in a foreclosure action had issued a writ of execution in the amount $87,211.07 for unpaid debt, interest, and fees. At the subsequent sheriff's sale, a bidder purchased the mortgaged property for $1,000. The lender sued to set aside the sale, arguing that a substitution of counsel prevented the lender from making a bid for the outstanding amount of the debt, something called a credit bid. The lower court agreed to set aside the sale, finding that the inadequacy of price "shocked the conscience" of the court. On appeal, the Idaho Supreme Court reversed, holding that inadequacy of price alone is insufficient to warrant setting aside a sale; "additional circumstances" even if "very slight" are required, such as an irregularity in the bidding process. *Id.* at 354.

3. Priorities in foreclosure. A lender who forecloses on a property may be the only lienholder; in such circumstances, the main questions about the use of the proceeds of the sale are whether there is any surplus after repaying the debt for the borrower to recover, and, if there is a shortfall, whether the lender may seek a deficiency judgment against the borrower. *See* §4.3, above. It is not uncommon, however, for a single property in foreclosure to have multiple liens, such as a mortgage loan taken out to purchase the property and a later home equity loan to finance renovations, or a judgment lien that has attached to the property, or a homeowners association assessment fee lien. In that situation, courts are required to decide how the proceeds of the sale should be divided among the lienholders.

In general, proceeds are paid out in full to each lienholder in turn based on their **priority**, which is usually set by the order in which the relevant security interest was **recorded** in the public records. 12 *Thompson on Real Property, Second Thomas Editions* §101.06(a). We will discuss the system of recording interests in land in detail below, *see* §5, below, but for now it is sufficient to understand that a mortgage, when recorded, will be entitled to any funds that flow from a foreclosure before any interests that are recorded later. These are called **senior** liens, and later-recorded interests are thus **junior**. When someone has a "first" mortgage and a "second" mortgage, it means that they have two mortgages recorded first and second. If the first mortgagee forecloses, the second mortgagee is only entitled to any proceeds of the sale if the first mortgagee's debt is fully paid.[29]

There are some exceptions to this first-in-time principle for determining lien priority. For example, in most states, a **purchase-money mortgage** can take priority over other liens, even those recorded beforehand (such as a judgment lien). Similarly, in many states, **mechanics' liens** may take priority over subsequently recorded mortgages. And liens to secure the payment of property taxes can also take priority over subsequently recorded mortgages.

Terms:
A **purchase-money mortgage** is one used to acquire property, rather than to use property as collateral for other purposes, such as renovations. A **mechanics'** or **materialman's lien** is a security interest in property granted to someone who provides materials or labor for that property.

Lienholders can also agree among themselves to change the order of priorities that would otherwise apply through a process called **subordination**. For example, a bank may not be willing to lend funds for the construction of a building on undeveloped land unless it has priority over the bank that financed the purchase of that land. The first lender might be willing to subordinate its lien to the later construction

29. A number of states that provide for a statutory right of redemption after foreclosure extend that right to junior lienholders.

lender because those latter funds will be used to enhance the value of the property. An owner would thus negotiate a subordination agreement between the two lenders that would reverse their priorities in the event of a foreclosure.[30]

4. Necessary parties to a foreclosure and the effects of non-joinder. For judicial foreclosures, a mortgagee is generally required to join all junior lienholders. This is because a foreclosure is meant to allow a mortgagee to sell the collateral with only claims that existed when the security interest attached. If a borrower could add additional loans and have those mortgages remain after a foreclosure, the original lender's security interest would not be very secure. By joining all junior lienholders, a senior mortgagee can discharge junior liens and sell the property free and clear of those interests. A junior lienholder who is not joined to the foreclosure action is generally not discharged through the foreclosure action.

A junior lienholder generally cannot discharge the security of a more senior mortgage, so if a junior lienholder forecloses, the property is sold subject to any senior mortgages.[31] This does not mean that the buyer is personally obligated to pay a senior mortgage, but it does mean that the new owner takes title subject to the risk that that mortgage will be foreclosed.

What about foreclosures pursuant to a power of sale in a mortgage or under a deed of trust, which do not require a court proceeding? Although such foreclosures are not supervised by the court, they generally have the same effect on liens. Mortgages that are senior to the lien being foreclosed are not discharged in a nonjudicial foreclosure sale, but junior liens generally are. The notice that senior lienholders are required to give junior lienholders before exercising a power of sale or foreclosing under a deed of trust can vary. *See* Nelson & Whitman, *supra*, at 1431.

5. Tenant eviction after foreclosure. The same principal of priorities means that tenants can face eviction from their homes when their landlords lose their properties through foreclosure, if the tenant rented after a mortgage was recorded. Banks that buy foreclosed properties often want to evict the tenants because they believe it is easier to sell unoccupied property. Although this may be true for many types of property, it is not clear that it is true for property devoted to residential tenancy purposes, especially in a time of recession when it may not be so easy to find tenants who are creditworthy and able to pay the rent on time. At the same time, mortgage providers generally are not in the business of managing property in a landlord capacity. Mortgage foreclosure laws protect the right of borrowers to stay in their homes by making good on defaulted mortgage payments. The federal *Protecting Tenants at Foreclosure Act* and its state analogues, *see* Chapter 11, §2.3, as well as some rent-control statutes, can provide similar protection for tenants from eviction.

---

30. Courts can also order one loan priority subordinated to another in some circumstances to avoid unjust enrichment. *See* §5.3, below.

31. Certain senior interests, such as judgment liens, can be discharged in foreclosure, but generally not a validly recorded mortgage. *Eastern Savings Bank, FSB v. CACH, LLC*, 55 A.3d 344 (Del. 2012).

One issue that can arise after foreclosure is whether the purchaser at a foreclosure sale can use self-help to obtain possession from the former owner. While some jurisdictions do allow self-help, most require purchasers to use statutory eviction procedures. *See Nickens v. Mount Vernon Realty Group LLC*, 54 A.3d 742, 751 n.14 (Md. 2012) (approving changing the locks while a holdover was out of town following foreclosure, but noting that only 14 jurisdictions still allow such self-help). Is there any reason to allow self-help after foreclosure if a statutory eviction process is available?

6. Reforming foreclosure process. During the Great Depression, some states passed laws protecting homeowners from foreclosure under certain circumstances. In *Home Building & Loan Association v. Blaisdell*, 290 U.S. 398 (1934), the Supreme Court upheld the constitutionality of the 1933 Minnesota *Mortgage Moratorium Act*, which temporarily authorized courts to extend periods of redemption — the time during which the homeowner-mortgagor could pay off the loan to the mortgagee — without being subject to a foreclosure sale. There has been no similar legislation broadly halting foreclosures during the subprime crisis; however, the crisis has ushered in important changes to foreclosure law in a number of states. Although the details vary, much of this reform effort has focused on giving home lenders and the servicers who work for them greater obligations to undertake loss mitigation, which involves finding alternatives to foreclosure, as well as on raising the procedural protections that homeowners have in foreclosure itself. *See* Frank S. Alexander et al., *Legislative Responses to the Foreclosure Crisis in Nonjudicial Foreclosure States*, 31 Rev. Banking & Fin. L. 341 (2011).

In 2012, for example, California passed the *Homeowners Bill of Rights*, 2012 Cal. Stat., c. 86 (A.B.278); 2012 Cal Stat. c. 87 (S.B.900). The new statutory regime bars mortgage servicers from foreclosing if a homeowner is in the process of seeking a modification of her loan, a process known as **dual tracking** that raised significant concerns following the subprime crisis. It also requires that parties filing or recording a notice of default, an affidavit in a foreclosure action, and other documents, must have "competent and reliable evidence" of the borrower's default and the lender's right to foreclose, and authorizes civil penalties for signing unverified mortgage documents. Cal. Civ. Code §2924.17. These reforms respond to a practice that came to light during the subprime crisis, called **robo-signing**, which involved servicers and others signing foreclosure-related documents, often by the thousands, without knowledge of the underlying facts.

Similarly, the Illinois Supreme Court recently issued a series of rules, which took effect in May 2013, to respond to abusive foreclosure practices. Under the rules, lenders are required to file a current copy of the note and an affidavit specifying the amounts due and owing and how the lender can identify those amounts. Lenders seeking to foreclose must also show that they informed borrowers about mortgage counseling programs, mediation, free legal representation, interpretive services for non-English speakers, and loan modification procedures. Finally, lenders have to attest to compliance with any loss mitigation requirements that apply to the loan. *See* Ill. Sup. Ct. R. 99.1, 113, and 114.

For a comprehensive overview of current foreclosure practices by state, *see* John Rao et al., *Foreclosures: Mortgage Servicing, Mortgage Modifications, and Foreclosure Defense* (4th ed. 2012).

§4.5 Alternative Financing Arrangements

A. Installment Land Contracts

An installment land contract is an alternative way to finance real estate. Under an installment land contract, the buyer makes a down payment to the seller and signs a contract promising to pay the rest of the purchase price to the seller at specified times and in specified amounts. At the end of the contract, the seller will convey title to the property to the buyer. The contract normally allows the seller to regain possession of the property on the buyer's default. It also ordinarily allows the seller to keep the payments already made by the buyer as **liquidated damages** for the buyer's breach of the agreement. Liquidated damages are damages for breach of contract set in advance by the parties themselves as part of their agreement.

This arrangement poses the same problems for the buyer as the mortgage does, but states often provide such buyer-borrowers fewer procedural protections than are granted to mortgagors. Some states implicitly or explicitly prohibit installment land contracts by making the protections of the mortgage foreclosure statute nonwaivable. Other states treat some installment land contracts like mortgages. States that allow installment land contracts may permit the seller to regain possession of the property but will examine the amounts paid by the buyer to determine whether they are grossly disproportionate to the damages suffered by the seller. Damages that are too high are considered a **penalty** or a **forfeiture**, and the court will order the seller to disgorge part of that amount back to the buyer. Another issue raised when a buyer defaults on an installment land contract is whether the buyer has a **right of redemption**. Does the buyer have the right after default to continue in possession of the property by paying off all or some of the rest of the purchase price?

Consider the following case.

Sebastian v. Floyd

585 S.W.2d 381 (Ky. 1979)

Map: Covington, Kentucky

J. Calvin Aker, Justice.

This case presents the question whether a clause in an installment land sale contract providing for forfeiture of the buyer's payments upon the buyer's default may be enforced by the seller.

The movant, Jean Sebastian, contracted on November 8, 1974, to buy a house and lot situated in Covington, Kentucky, from Perl and Zona Floyd, respondents in this motion for review. Sebastian paid $3,800.00 down and was to pay the balance of the $10,900.00 purchase price, plus taxes, insurance, and interest at the rate of 8% per annum, in monthly installments of $120.00. A forfeiture clause in the contract provided that if Sebastian failed to make any monthly payment and remained in default for 60 days, the Floyds could terminate the contract and retain all payments previously made as rent and liquidated damages.

During the next 21 months, Sebastian missed seven installments. Including her down payment, she paid the Floyds a total of $5,480.00, rather than the $6,320.00 which was called for by the terms of the contract. Of this amount, $4,300.00, or nearly 40% of the contract price, had been applied against the principal.

The Floyds brought suit in the Kenton Circuit Court against Sebastian in August, 1976, seeking a judgment of $700.00 plus compensation for payments for taxes and insurance, and seeking enforcement of the forfeiture clause. Sebastian admitted by her answer that she was in default but asked the court not to enforce the forfeiture clause.

When a typical installment land contract is used as the means of financing the purchase of property, legal title to the property remains in the seller until the buyer has paid the entire contract price or some agreed-upon portion thereof, at which time the seller tenders a deed to the buyer. However, equitable title passes to the buyer when the contract is entered. The seller holds nothing but the bare legal title, as security for the payment of the purchase price.

There is no practical distinction between the land sale contract and a purchase money mortgage, in which the seller conveys legal title to the buyer but retains a lien on the property to secure payment. The significant feature of each device is the seller's financing the buyer's purchase of the property, using the property as collateral for the loan.

Where the purchaser of property has given a mortgage and subsequently defaults on his payments, his entire interest in the property is not forfeited. The mortgagor has the right to redeem the property by paying the full debt plus interest and expenses incurred by the creditor due to default. In order to cut off the mortgagor's right to redeem, the mortgagee must request a court to sell the property at public auction. From the proceeds of the sale, the mortgagee recovers the amount owed him on the mortgage, as well as the expenses of bringing suit; the mortgagor is entitled to the balance, if any.

We are of the opinion that a rule treating the seller's interest as a lien will best protect the interests of both buyer and seller. Ordinarily, the seller will receive the balance due on the contract, plus expenses, thus fulfilling the expectations he had when he agreed to sell his land. In addition, the buyer's equity in the property will be protected.

Notes and Questions

1. **Three approaches to installment land contracts.** In addressing the scope of consumer protection in alternative financing arrangements such as installment land contracts, courts have developed a variety of approaches. The first approach handles

these questions in one fell swoop by holding that installment land contracts are equivalent to mortgages and therefore must be governed by the same rules. *See, e.g., Prue v. Royer*, 67 A.3d 895 (Vt. 2013) (discussing the growing trend of courts treating contracts for deed as mortgages); *see also Restatement (Third) of Property (Mortgages)* §3.4 (1997) (providing that a "contract for deed" — *i.e.*, an installment land contract — is a mortgage).

This gives buyers under installment land contracts the full range of protections available to mortgagors, including an equity of redemption (the right to retain the property by paying the rest of the purchase price at or before the foreclosure sale), the procedural protections of the foreclosure statutes (including notice of intent to foreclose and perhaps a judicially supervised public sale), and the right to recover any proceeds of the foreclosure sale in excess of the unpaid debt.[32] This approach, adopted by the Kentucky court in *Sebastian v. Floyd*, effectively makes the protections of mortgage foreclosure statutes nondisclaimable.

A second approach extends mortgage protections only to *some* installment land contracts. Colorado, for example, has developed a test to distinguish installment land contracts that must be treated like mortgages from those that may be enforced according to their own terms. In *Grombone v. Krekel*, 754 P.2d 777 (Colo. Ct. App. 1988), the court held that trial courts have the discretion to make this determination based on a range of factors, including "the amount of the vendee's equity in the property, the length of the default period, the willfulness of the default, whether the vendee has made improvements, and whether the property has been adequately maintained." *Id.* at 779. If the buyer has made a large down payment, occupied the property for a long time, and paid a substantial portion of the purchase price, the court is likely to provide the buyer with all the protections accorded a mortgagee, including a right to redeem, a right to notice and a foreclosure sale, and a right to recover proceeds from the foreclosure sale exceeding the unpaid debt. *See also Lewis v. Premium Investment Corp.*, 568 S.E.2d 361 (S.C. 2002); *Bean v. Walker*, 464 N.Y.S.2d 895 (App. Div. 1983).

Finally, some states hold that the buyer has no right of redemption under installment land contracts; thus, the seller has the right to get the property back on the buyer's default and to eject the buyer from the property. The only question in these states is whether the amount of payments already made by the buyer so exceeds the seller's damages as to constitute an unconscionable **forfeiture** or **penalty**. If it does, the buyer may have a right to be reimbursed for part of the down payment. The West Virginia Supreme Court of Appeals took this approach in *Stonebraker v. Zinn*, 286 S.E.2d 911 (W. Va. 1982). In that case, the buyers had occupied the property for a year and made a $1,500 down payment as well as 12 monthly payments of $189.09 each. The parties agreed that $189.09 was a fair rental payment for the property, and the court found

---

32. It is often unclear whether the courts are interpreting the mortgage foreclosure statute to apply to all land financing arrangements (thus holding that the legislature *intended* to regulate installment land contracts by its passage of the mortgage foreclosure statute) or whether the courts are changing common law rules to cohere with the policy judgments underlying the legislation addressed to mortgages.

that allowing the seller to retain the $1,500 down payment as well as the monthly payments as liquidated damages was not excessive.

2. Comparing the interests of lenders and borrowers. California Chief Justice Rose Bird has argued that all installment land contracts should be given the same protections granted to mortgages.

> The predominant use of installment land sale contracts has been to finance the purchase of housing by low-income families and individuals unable to qualify for conventional mortgage financing or government loan guarantee programs.
>
> Providing installment contract vendees the same protections that are afforded to mortgagors would eliminate some abusive practices of vendors, who have exploited the lack of legal sophistication and limited capacity to litigate of their low-income clients. Most important, defaulting vendees would be able to avoid the loss of their homes by paying only the delinquent amounts. Under the majority's holding, a wilfully defaulting vendee may avoid this fate only by paying the outstanding balance in full. This is an unjustifiably harsh burden to place on the low-income and middle-income families and individuals who will be most affected.

Petersen v. Hartell, 707 P.2d 232, 245-246 (Cal. 1985).

In the same case, Justice Stanley Mosk advocated granting the trial court discretion to "weigh the equities of the case to determine the just result":

> As the majority readily admit, the equities in the case at bar weigh heavily against the vendees. "The Petersens' monthly payments were erratic and delinquent almost from the beginning even though the seller made clear her need of the payments for her support. By April 1973 the Petersens had made only 58 out of the 65 payments then due, and their first attempt to reinstate the contract was not until 29 months later, when they tendered $250 out of the $1,800 that was by then overdue and unpaid."
>
> As between the deliberately defaulting vendees and the elderly vendor who desperately needed the modest payments on the contract for her very survival, the equities clearly favor the latter.

Id. at 248. Similarly, the Indiana Supreme Court held in *Skendzel v. Marshall*, 301 N.E.2d 641 (Ind. 1973), that the question whether an installment land contract should be treated like a mortgage should depend on case-by-case determinations of whether "forfeiture" of the buyer's accumulated equity in the property would be consistent with "generally accepted principles of fairness and equity." *Id.* at 646. The buyer who has paid most of the purchase price "has acquired a substantial interest in the property, which, if forfeited, would result in substantial injustice." *Id.* Is this argument circular? If the seller is entitled to keep the proceeds and evict the buyer, then the buyer will not have "acquired a substantial interest in the property." The buyer will have "acquired" such an interest only if the courts strike down the forfeiture provision in the contract. What then makes the forfeiture unjust?

Consider what the situation would look like if the buyer were treated like a renter or tenant. If the monthly payment to the lender is near the fair rental value of the property, isn't the only difference between a renter and a buyer the amount of the down payment? Or is there also a distinction in the sense that the buyer is entitled to treat the property as her own, renovating the property and making structural changes as she sees fit, and thus develops expectations based on considering the property as her own? Does the buyer have no right to develop a personal attachment to the property given the seller's right to end the agreement if the buyer defaults?

3. Low-income buyers. Will regulation of installment land contracts make things better or worse for low-income families who do not qualify for conventional mortgages?

B. Equitable Mortgages

Koenig v. Van Reken

279 N.W.2d 590 (Mich. Ct. App. 1979)

VINCENT J. BRENNAN, Presiding Judge.

In 1970, plaintiff [Helen Koenig] owned a home in Oakland County with a market value of $60,000 that was encumbered by three mortgages totaling $25,933.26. The real estate taxes on plaintiff's home had become delinquent and foreclosure proceedings had begun on one of the mortgages. Plaintiff was then approached by defendant, Stanley Van Reken, who proposed that for a fee of 10 percent he would "service" the mortgages and pay the delinquent taxes. Subsequently, on June 16, 1970, plaintiff and defendant Stanley Van Reken executed three documents that form the basis of this action.

The first of these documents, entitled "AGREEMENT," stated that plaintiff desired to prevent the loss of her home and provided that defendant Stanley Van Reken purchase the property, redeem it from tax sale and mortgage foreclosure, and give plaintiff an exclusive right to repurchase according to the terms of a lease-option agreement that was also executed between the parties.

The second document was a warranty deed which conveyed the property from plaintiff to defendants for a stated consideration of $28,600. Plaintiff alleges that the deed was silent as to consideration when she signed it, that the figure of $28,600 was added subsequently, and that she never received any such consideration.

The third document provided that Stanley Van Reken was to lease the premises to plaintiff for a 3-year period at a fixed monthly rent of $300. Plaintiff was also to receive an exclusive option to repurchase the premises during the term of the lease for a price of $32,318.79, with a down payment of $3,500 and monthly payments of $300 which were to include taxes, insurance, principal and interest.

At no time during the negotiations that led to the execution of these documents was plaintiff represented by an attorney, and all three documents were prepared by Stanley Van Reken.

The parties operated under the lease from June 16, 1970, to February, 1972, and during this time plaintiff made total payments of $5,800. In February, 1972, plaintiff defaulted in a monthly rental payment. Plaintiff was thereupon evicted from the home.

[Plaintiff sued to have the deed executed by her to be declared an equitable mortgage.]

The court of equity protects the necessitous by looking through form to the substance of the transaction. Although no set criterion has been established, the controlling factor in determining whether a deed absolute on its face should be deemed a mortgage is the intention of the parties. Such intention may be gathered from the circumstances attending the transaction including the conduct and relative economic positions of the parties and the value of the property in relation to the price fixed in the alleged sale. Under Michigan law, it is well settled that the adverse financial condition of the grantor, coupled with the inadequacy of the purchase price for the property, is sufficient to establish a deed absolute on its face to be a mortgage. *Ellis v. Wayne Real Estate Co.*, 97 N.W.2d 758 (Mich. 1959).

In *Ellis, supra*, plaintiffs initially sought a loan from defendant to save their home from forfeiture. After hurried negotiations, the plaintiffs executed a quitclaim deed to defendant and simultaneously entered into a land contract under which the plaintiffs were to repurchase the property. The defendant then satisfied a default and paid the delinquent taxes. In noting the discrepancy between the price paid by the defendant and the value of the property, the Court held that the transaction constituted a loan by defendant secured by a mortgage on the property.

In taking the plaintiff's well-pleaded facts in the present case as true, there is a close parallel with *Ellis, supra*. Here the plaintiff, while in financial distress, sought help from the defendants in saving her home from foreclosure. Although plaintiff was not desirous of selling her home, she entered into a transaction which conveyed her equity worth over $30,000 for less than $4,000. While financial embarrassment of the grantor and inadequacy of consideration do not provide an infallible test, they are an indication that the parties did not consider the conveyance to be absolute. We note that the lease-back arrangement entered into by the parties effectively circumvented the right to redeem, which is designed to protect purchasers such as plaintiff in times of financial crisis. In applying these facts to the aforementioned case law, it could be found without difficulty that the subject transaction constituted a mortgage to secure a loan in the amount of defendants' initial expenditure.

Notes and Questions

1. **Transfer as a security interest.** An equitable mortgage is declared when a transfer of a deed was intended merely to provide security for a loan rather than a sale of the property. The most common example is the deed of trust, which generally purports to be a conveyance from the borrower to a trustee, but actually only grants a security interest. *See Bain v. Metropolitan Mortgage Group, Inc.*, 285 P.3d 34, 38 (Wash. 2012). In other situations, however, parties attempt to circumvent mortgage law by entering into agreements that appear to convey property.

2. **Recognizing equitable mortgages.** What conduct is necessary to turn what looks like a conveyance into a security arrangement? In *Flack v. McClure*, 565 N.E.2d

131 (Ill. App. Ct. 1990), the court identified factors to consider in determining whether an equitable mortgage should be recognized.

> Six factors [should] be considered by the trial judge to determine whether an equitable mortgage exists. Those factors include whether a debt exists, the relationship of the parties, whether legal assistance was available, the sophistication and circumstances of each party, the adequacy of the consideration and who retained possession of the property.

Id. at 136. *Cf. Hudson v. Vandiver*, 810 So. 2d 617 (Miss. Ct. App. 2002) (transfer of title interpreted as intent to provide security for a promise to pay contractors for services to be rendered). *Accord, Bernstein v. New Beginnings Trustee, L.L.C.*, 988 So. 2d 90 (Fla. Dist. Ct. App. 2008). The court in *Koenig v. Van Reken* also relied on various factors in assessing whether to recognize an equitable mortgage. But what, exactly, is the ultimate standard to which the factors are relevant? Does the court in *Koenig* find that the parties *intended* to create a security arrangement rather than a sale, or is the intent of the parties irrelevant? What is the rule of law promulgated by the court in *Koenig*?

In *Johnson v. Cherry*, 726 S.W.2d 4 (Tex. 1987), plaintiff Richard Johnson purchased property for $125,000, with his grantor reserving a vendor's lien on the property. When Johnson and his wife were later divorced, Johnson purchased his ex-wife's community interest in the property with a note promising to pay over time. Johnson encountered difficulty paying all his debts, which totaled $120,000. He entered into a series of transactions with defendants F.G. Cherry and the Texas State Bank of Tatum whereby he gave a deed to the property to defendants, and they gave him a one-year lease on the land with an option to repurchase it. In return for the general warranty deed, Johnson received $120,000 from Cherry, who assumed the $38,000 remaining balance on the note to Johnson's ex-wife. The lease provided for two semiannual payments of $12,510 each; also, Johnson could exercise his option for $132,000 and reassume the note to his ex-wife. When Johnson defaulted on his lease payments, Johnson sued defendants to cancel the deed on the grounds that it was a mortgage on his homestead prohibited by the Texas constitution.

In granting Johnson's request, the Texas Supreme Court held that a transfer of a deed will be treated as a mortgage when "the parties actually intended the instrument as a mortgage." *Id.* at 5. Concluding that the evidence supported the jury's finding that the parties intended the deed as a mortgage, the court explained, *id.* at 7:

> In addition to Johnson's testimony regarding his intentions, the evidence was that the repurchase price was exactly 10% more than the original price; the land was worth almost twice as much as the original "sale" price; the lease price equaled exactly 9% interest on the balance of the note to Johnson's ex-wife assumed by Cherry and 18% interest on the alleged purchase price; Johnson was indebted to other creditors for approximately $119,000 of the $120,000 he received from Cherry; Johnson was within one week of losing the land entirely; and Johnson had told a real estate agent he was not interested in listing his property for sale.

If the parties had signed a contract stating that the "transfer of this deed is intended to be a sale and not a mortgage," would the case have come out any differently? Should it?

Problem

A bank acquires title to a house at a foreclosure sale. It wants to get around all rules about mortgages, installment land contracts, and equitable mortgages, so it adopts the simple device of asking mortgagors to waive the protection of the mortgage statute. The bank sells the property to a buyer for a purchase price of $250,000, subject to a financing arrangement with the bank. The buyer makes a $25,000 down payment with the bank, which lends the rest of the purchase price to the buyer. The buyer grants a mortgage to the bank. The mortgage contract has a waiver clause:

> Mortgagor agrees to waive the benefits of the mortgage statute. If Mortgagor defaults on any payments due under this mortgage, Mortgagee has the right to retake possession of the property without a foreclosure sale and to keep any payments already made.

The state mortgage statute merely recites that "all mortgages shall be subject to the provisions of this act." It has no language specifically stating whether the protections afforded by the statute are disclaimable or waivable by the mortgagor. Should the mortgagor have the right to waive the protections of the mortgage statute?

§5 THE RECORDING SYSTEM

§5.1 Recording Acts

A. Recording Act Fundamentals

The recording system is intended to provide buyers of real property with the security of knowing that they will really own the property interests they are buying and to let those with other interests in property, such as a lien, understand who has priority when conflicts arise. Purchasers can use the system to find out whether the person purporting to own and sell the property indeed owns it and to ensure that neither the owner nor any of his predecessors in interest has conveyed to someone else all or part of the property interests that the seller has contracted to sell to the buyer. Lenders can also use the system to understand and give notice to others of their security interest in the property.

Every state has a **recording act**, which provides for a central registry at each locality—often at the county level of government—where holders of real property interests can submit copies of deeds, mortgages, leases, easements, general plans, condominium declarations, judgment liens, and the like. Submitting a document to the registry is called **recording**. Although many recording-act disputes involve competing claims of outright ownership, the recording acts also help to establish the respective priorities and rights of lienholders, tenants, and others having interests in a given property.

The common law rule before the recording system was "first in time, first in right." This rule was based on the theory that the grantor could not convey what she did not own; once the property interest had been transferred to the first grantee, the grantor had nothing left to convey to the subsequent grantee.

Recording acts change the common law rule by defining the circumstances under which a party who has recorded his interest in the proper registry of deeds will prevail over a party who did not properly protect his interest by recording it. In general, a *subsequent interest holder who has no notice of a prior conveyance and who records his interest will prevail over any prior unrecorded interest.*

Recording acts define the property interests that may be recorded. Many statutes, for example, provide for recording leases of longer than a year. A variety of other interests may also be recorded, such as mortgages, option agreements, wills, judgments in suits affecting property, or even a *lis pendens,* which is a filing that provides notice of pending litigation. For property interests not covered by the recording act, the common law rule of "first in time, first in right" applies.

It is important to recognize that recording acts do not *require* that an instrument be recorded to be legally valid. A deed, for example, is valid against the grantor upon delivery with or without recording. When the seller delivers the deed to the buyer, the buyer becomes the lawful owner of the property—at least in the absence of conflicting claims by other grantees. The seller cannot dispossess the buyer on the ground that the seller's deed (received from the seller's grantor) was recorded but that the grantee had not yet recorded her deed. Similarly, a month-to-month tenant could not defend against an eviction proceeding brought by the new owner on the ground that the new owner had not recorded her deed and therefore did not own the property.

The recording system will not protect the grantee against all risk. In many places, the buyer may have to check other parts of the court system to determine whether a lawsuit being brought affects ownership of the property, a will being probated affects the title, or a divorce proceeding being filed by the owners results in changes in property rights. Other points to check are whether the owner has declared bankruptcy and whether the tax authorities are planning to place a lien on the property to collect unpaid property taxes. Finally, the recording system will not protect a buyer against a claim of adverse possession; for this reason, the buyer must investigate to determine whether any such claims may be in the wings.

Recording systems are increasingly moving from paper to electronic records, with a number of states having passed statutes that facilitate electronic recording.[33] New Jersey, for example, extensively revised its recording act system in 2012 for just this reason. *See Assembly Bill A-2565* P.L.2011, c.217; *see also, e.g.,* Ariz. Rev. Stat. §11-487; Ark. Code §14-2-301 *et seq.*; Wis. Stat. §706.25 *et seq.* Many recorder of deeds' offices have now made their records accessible on-line.

---

33. In 2004, the Uniform Law Commissioners promulgated the *Uniform Real Property Electronic Recording Act* (URPERA). URPERA validates electronically signed documents, applying the principals of E-SIGN and the UETA, *see* §2.2, above, to the requirements for recording. It also establishes an oversight board to set statewide standards for electronic recording practices.

B. How to Conduct a Title Search

It is impossible for a buyer to find all the interests affecting a particular parcel of land without referring to some kind of index. It also is impossible for the system to work unless the buyer can limit his search to places where conflicting deeds are likely to be found; otherwise, a search of the hundreds of thousands of documents would be endless.

The simplest way to index and research the title is to file information by **tract**. Given the mathematical precision with which physical descriptions of the geographic bounds of each parcel of property can be made, it is possible to create a tract system whereby the buyer can find, in one place, all interests that purport to affect the title to that particular tract. The problem is that this is not how the recording system started, and converting to a tract system would be quite expensive. Most places do not have a tract index.

The typical recording office uses a **grantor-grantee index**. Separate files are kept for grantors and grantees. In the **grantor index**, all instruments are listed both alphabetically and chronologically by the grantor's last name. In the **grantee index**, all instruments are listed both alphabetically and chronologically by the grantee's last name. A deed from Johann Sebastian Bach to Wolfgang Amadeus Mozart would be indexed under the name "Bach" in the grantor index and the name "Mozart" in the grantee index. Where paper records are still being used, the recording office ordinarily compiles volumes that cover particular time periods. For example, conveyances by grantors may be divided into one volume that includes conveyances made between 1950 and 1960, a second volume for the years 1960 to 1970, and so on. More recent conveyances may be grouped by year, and very recent conveyances by month and by day. The recent conveyances are later compiled in master volumes like those of the older conveyances to simplify the search process by limiting the number of places in which one must look.

The index describes the bare outlines of each transaction, including the grantor and grantee, a description of the land, the type of interest conveyed, the date recorded, and the book and page numbers where a copy of the document can be found. The title searcher must then look at each complete document.

Suppose you are planning to buy a house from J.S. Bach. You want to find out if and how Bach obtained title to the property. You would therefore start in the grantee index to find who his grantor was. You start in the present in the grantee index and go backward until you find a deed to Bach conveying the property in question. You find a reference to a deed in 1997 from Frédéric Chopin. To find out how Chopin obtained his title, you look backward in the grantee index from 1997 until you find a conveyance to Chopin. You continue this process until you have gone back far enough to assure yourself that the title will be good. The practice in each locality differs on how far back to go. It may be enough to look backward for 50 or 60 years, or until the beginning of the twentieth century, or until a title can be traced to some sovereign. In most places, the practice is not to go all the way back to the beginning of the recording system but some lesser number of years. **Marketable title acts** may describe a time period beyond which interests are lost if they are not re-recorded. *See* §5.5, below. When you are done, you have a list of grantors who are predecessors in interest of Bach.

Suppose you have gone back to 1954 to find a deed from Edward Elgar to Antonín Dvořák. You now switch to the **grantor index** and go forward in time under the name of **each grantor** you have found, starting on the date that grantor acquired her interest and going forward until you find an instrument conveying that interest to a subsequent grantee. The period for each search starts when the grantor **acquired** her interest (the date of **execution** of the first deed giving title to the grantor) and stops on the date a new conveyance of that interest is **recorded**. You would thus start with Dvořák and carry forward until the point Dvořák recorded the conveyance of his interest. It is important to note that the search in the grantor index starts at the date of **execution** rather than at the date of **recording**. This is because the grantor may have mortgaged the property or encumbered it after acquiring it (after receiving the deed at the closing) but before recording her deed.

Searching a Grantor-Grantee Index

1. Grantee Index	2. Grantor Index
Bach – present record owner ↓	*Bach – present record owner* ↑ 2011: Second mortgage from Bach to Leipzig Savings
1997: Chopin to Bach by warranty deed ↓	1997: Chopin to Bach; release of WS mortgage; mortgage from Bach to Brandenburg Bank ↑
1960: Dvořák to Chopin by quitclaim deed ↓	1960: Dvořák to Chopin; release of FBB mortgage; mortgage from Chopin to Warsaw Savings (WS) ↑ 1957: Easement from Dvořák to Franck
1954: Elgar to Dvořák by warranty deed	1954: Elgar to Dvořák; mortgage from Dvořák to First Bank of Bohemia (FBB)

C. Types of Recording Acts

As mentioned, each state has its own recording statute. The wording of the statute, as well as court interpretations of it, must be examined in detail to determine how it will apply to a particular dispute. Generally, recording acts are divided into three types: (1) race, (2) notice, and (3) race-notice.

Race statutes. Under a race statute, as between successive purchasers of Blackacre, the person who records first prevails — she has won the race to the registry.

This is true even if the person who records first *knows* about an earlier conveyance to someone else. These statutes exist for all property only in two states, North Carolina, N.C. Gen. Stat. §47-18, and Louisiana, La. Rev. Stat. §9.2721, and for certain interests, like mortgages or mineral interests, in a handful more.[34]

O conveys Blackacre to *A*, who does not record. *O* subsequently conveys Blackacre a second time to *B*. *B* knows of the earlier conveyance to *A*. *B* records the deed from *O* to *B*. In a lawsuit between *A* and *B*, *B* prevails.

An example of a race statute is N.C. Gen. Stat. §47-18:

> (a) No (i) conveyance of land, or (ii) contract to convey, or (iii) option to convey, or (iv) lease of land for more than three years shall be valid to pass any property interest as against lien creditors or purchasers for a valuable consideration from the donor, bargainor or lessor but from the time of registration thereof in the county where the land lies, or if the land is located in more than one county, then in each county where any portion of the land lies to be effective as to the land in that county. Unless otherwise stated either on the registered instrument or on a separate registered instrument duly executed by the party whose priority interest is adversely affected, (i) instruments registered in the office of the register of deeds shall have priority based on the order of registration as determined by the time of registration.

Notice statutes. Under a notice statute, a subsequent purchaser prevails over an earlier purchaser only if the subsequent purchaser did not have notice of the earlier conveyance. Further, the notice statute protects any purchaser without notice against prior unrecorded interests even if the purchaser does not record first. These statutes are in place in 23 states. For example:

O conveys Blackacre to *A*, who does not record. *O* then conveys Blackacre to *B*. *B* has no knowledge of the earlier conveyance from *O* to *A*. *B* prevails over *A* even though *B* does not record the deed from *O* to *B*. *B* also prevails over *A* even if *A* later records her deed from *O* to *A* before *B* records her deed from *O* to *B*.

An example of a notice statute is Iowa Code §558.41:

> An instrument affecting real estate is of no validity against subsequent purchasers for a valuable consideration, without notice, or against the state or any of its political subdivisions during and after condemnation proceedings against the real estate, unless the instrument is filed and recorded in the county in which the real estate is located, as provided in this chapter.

---

34. Arkansas, Delaware, and Pennsylvania have pure race rules for mortgages. *See* Ark. Code §18-40-102; 25 Del. C. §2106; Pa. Stat. tit. 42 §8141. Ohio has a pure race statute for mortgages and oil and gas leases. Ohio Rev. Code §5301.23. There is some authority to suggest that North Carolina has modified the effect of its pure race statute by judicial interpretation. 11 *Thompson on Real Property, Second Thomas Editions* §92.08(a) n.283 (citing North Carolina cases that require purchasers to have no notice to invoke the recording act).

See also Ariz. Rev. Stat. §§33-422, 33-412; Mass. Gen. Laws ch. 183, §4; Fla. Stat. §695.01.

Race-notice statutes. Under a race-notice statute, in effect in 25 states and D.C., a subsequent purchaser prevails over prior unrecorded interests only if she (1) had no notice of the prior conveyance at the time she acquired her interest and (2) records before the prior instrument is recorded. For example:

> *O* conveys Blackacre to *A*, who does not record. *O* then conveys Blackacre to *B*. *B* has no knowledge of the earlier conveyance from *O* to *A*. *A* records; then *B* records. *A* prevails over *B* because, even though *B* did not have notice of *A*'s deed, *A* recorded before *B* did.

An example of a race-notice statute is Ga. Code §44-2-2:

> (b) Deeds, mortgages, and liens of all kinds which are required by law to be recorded in the office of the clerk of the superior court and which are against the interests of third parties who have acquired a transfer or lien binding the same property and who are acting in good faith and without notice shall take effect only from the time they are filed for record in the clerk's office.

See also Cal. Civ. Code §1107; Mich. Comp. Laws §565.29; Pa. Stat. tit. 21, §351; Wash. Rev. Code §65.08.070.

D. Who Qualifies as a Bona Fide Purchaser?

Recording acts generally protect **bona fide purchasers**. In notice and race-notice jurisdictions, this requires that an interest holder purchases in good faith without notice of a conflicting interest. We will consider notice in the next section, but conflicts also often arise with respect to a second requirement for bona fide purchaser status, which is that the interest holder must have paid value for her interest. Courts generally agree that something more than nominal value is required to be considered a "purchaser," although it need not be the property's full market value. *Anderson v. Anderson*, 435 N.W.2d 687 (N.D. 1987). This requirement of payment for value excludes donees, heirs, and devisees from the protections of the recording system. Thus, if a donor gives the same property as a gift to two different people, the first donee wins under the common law first-in-time rule.

But what about a purchaser who has only made a down payment, but not yet paid the full purchase price when a conflicting interest is recorded? Or a purchaser under an installment land contract who has paid half the value of the property, but still owes the remaining half? Can they claim the protection of the recording acts? The outcome partly depends on whether the subsequent purchaser would ordinarily be expected to search the records. An ordinary purchaser would normally search title prior to closing, and courts will generally not accord purchaser status in the context of executory contracts. However, a purchaser in a long-term installment contract might not. Some courts afford subsequent purchasers partial protection, giving them a claim against the prior purchaser but only for the value they paid.

When parties other than actual purchasers seek to invoke the recording acts to protect their priority, the question of value can be complicated. For example, parties who win a lawsuit are entitled to record the judgment as a lien against the losing party's property. If the losing party has actually conveyed the property in an unrecorded transfer, can the judgment creditor claim priority against the prior purchaser who failed to record, even though winning a lawsuit is not paying value? Some recording acts explicitly protect judgment creditors in this situation. *See, e.g.*, N.J. Stat §46:26A-12(c). Where the recording act is silent, however, judgment credits are generally not able to prevail, either because they are only entitled to a lien against property that a defendant actually owns or because the recording act is interpreted to exclude them from the definition of "purchaser." William B. Stoebuck & Dale A. Whitman, *The Law of Property* §11.10, at 878-879 (3d ed. 2000).

§5.2 Chain of Title Problems

Sabo v. Horvath

559 P.2d 1038 (Alaska 1976)

ROBERT BOOCHEVER, Chief Justice.

Grover C. Lowery occupied land in the Chitna Recording District on October 10, 1964 for purposes of obtaining Federal patent. Lowery filed a location notice on February 24, 1965, and made his application to purchase on June 6, 1967 with the Bureau of Land Management (BLM). On March 7, 1968, the BLM field examiner's report was filed which recommended that patent issue to Lowery. On October 7, 1969, a request for survey was made by the United States Government. On January 3, 1970, Lowery issued a document entitled "Quitclaim Deed" to the Horvaths; Horvath recorded the deed on January 5, 1970 in the Chitna Recording District. Horvath testified that when he bought the land from Lowery, he knew patent and title were still in the United States Government, but he did not rerecord his interest after patent had passed to Lowery.

Following the sale to the Horvaths, further action was taken by Lowery and the BLM pertaining to the application for patent and culminating in issuance of the patent on August 10, 1973.

Almost immediately after the patent was issued, Lowery advertised the land for sale in a newspaper. He then executed a second document also entitled "quitclaim" to the Sabos on October 15, 1973. The Sabos duly recorded this document on December 13, 1973.

Luther Moss, a representative of the BLM, testified to procedures followed under the *Alaska Homesite Law* (43 U.S.C. §687a (1970)). After numerous steps, a plat is approved and the claimant notified that he should direct publication of his claim. In this case, Lowery executed his conveyance to the Horvaths after the BLM field report had recommended patent.

The first question this court must consider is whether Lowery had an interest to convey at the time of his transfer to the Horvaths.

[W]e hold that at the time Lowery executed the deed to the Horvaths he had complied with the statute to a sufficient extent so as to have an interest in the land which was capable of conveyance.

Since the Horvaths received a valid interest from Lowery, we must now resolve the conflict between the Horvaths' first recorded interest and the Sabos' later recorded interest.

The Sabos, like the Horvaths, received their interest in the property by a quitclaim deed. They are asserting that their interest supersedes the Horvaths under Alaska's statutory recording system. Alaska Stat. §34.15.290 provides that:

> A conveyance of real property . . . is void as against a subsequent innocent purchaser . . . for a valuable consideration of the property . . . whose conveyance is first duly recorded. An unrecorded instrument is valid . . . as against one who has actual notice of it.[35]

Quick Review:
What type of **recording act** does Alaska have?

Initially, we must decide whether the Sabos, who received their interest by means of a quitclaim deed, can ever be "innocent purchaser[s]" within the meaning of Alaska Stat. §34.15.290. Since a "quitclaim" only transfers the interest of the grantor, the question is whether a "quitclaim" deed itself puts a purchaser on constructive notice. Although the authorities are in conflict over this issue, the clear weight of authority is that a quitclaim grantee can be protected by the recording system, assuming, of course, the grantee purchased for valuable consideration and did not otherwise have actual or constructive knowledge as defined by the recording laws. We choose to follow the majority rule and hold that a quitclaim grantee is not precluded from attaining the status of an "innocent purchaser."

In this case, the Horvaths recorded their interest from Lowery prior to the time the Sabos recorded their interest. Thus, the issue is whether the Sabos are charged with constructive knowledge because of the Horvaths' prior recordation. Horvath is correct in his assertion that in the usual case a prior recorded deed serves as constructive notice pursuant to Alaska Stat. §34.15.290, and thus precludes a subsequent recordation from taking precedence. Here, however, the Sabos argue that because Horvath recorded his deed prior to Lowery having obtained patent, they were not given constructive notice by the recording system. They contend that since Horvaths' recordation was outside the chain of title, the recording should be regarded as a "wild deed."

It is an axiom of hornbook law that a purchaser has notice only of recorded instruments that are within his "chain of title." If a grantor (Lowery) transfers prior to obtaining title, and the grantee (Horvath) records prior to title passing, a second grantee who diligently examines all conveyances under the grantor's name from the date that the grantor had secured title would not discover the prior conveyance. The rule in most jurisdictions which have adopted a grantor-grantee index system of recording is that a "wild deed" does not serve as constructive notice to a subsequent purchaser who duly records.

---

35. Alaska Stat. §34.15.290 is now Alaska Stat. §40.17.080. — Eds.

Alaska's recording system utilizes a "grantor-grantee" index. Had Sabo searched title under both grantor's and grantee's names but limited his search to the chain of title subsequent to patent, he would not be chargeable with discovery of the pre-patent transfer to Horvath.

On one hand, we could require Sabo to check beyond the chain of title to look for pretitle conveyances. While in this particular case the burden may not have been great, as a general rule, requiring title checks beyond the chain of title could add a significant burden as well as uncertainty to real estate purchases. To a certain extent, requiring title searches of records prior to the date of a grantor acquired title would thus defeat the purposes of the recording system. The records as to each grantor in the chain of title would theoretically have to be checked back to the later of the grantor's date of birth or the date when records were first retained.

On the other hand, we could require Horvath to rerecord his interest in the land once title passes, that is, after patent had issued to Lowery. As a general rule, rerecording an interest once title passes is less of a burden than requiring property purchasers to check indefinitely beyond the chain of title.

It is unfortunate that in this case due to Lowery's double conveyances, one or the other party to this suit must suffer an undeserved loss. We are cognizant that in this case, the equities are closely balanced between the parties to this appeal. Our decision, however, in addition to resolving the litigants' dispute, must delineate the requirements of Alaska's recording laws.

Because we want to promote simplicity and certainty in title transactions, we choose to follow the majority rule and hold that the Horvaths' deed, recorded outside the chain of title, does not give constructive notice to the Sabos and is not "duly recorded" under the *Alaskan Recording Act*, Alaska Stat. §34.15.290. Since the Sabos' interest is the first duly recorded interest and was recorded without actual or constructive knowledge of the prior deed, we hold that the Sabos' interest must prevail.

Notes and Questions

1. **Types of notice.** In both notice and race-notice jurisdictions, only subsequent purchasers without notice of the earlier conveyance can prevail over the earlier grantee. **Actual notice**, where a party knows about an earlier instrument, obviously violates this condition. But the import of the recording system is that **constructive notice** will also deprive a subsequent purchaser of protection. Constructive notice exists when the grantee, by conducting a reasonable title search, would have discovered the earlier conveyance. This holds true whether or not the grantee actually searched the records.

Complications arise if a deed is recorded incorrectly or was not entitled to be recorded in the first place. For example, if an instrument is required to have a legal description to be validly recorded, then recording such an instrument without that description will not give subsequent interest holders constructive notice. *In re Rivera*, No. 11SA261, 2012 WL 1994873 (Colo. June 4, 2012). *But cf. Regions Bank v. Deluca*, 97 So. 3d 879 (Fla. App. Ct. 2012) (because errors in a mortgage's property description could be corrected by examining the entire document, the document still imparted constructive notice).

Similarly, a clerical error in *indexing* the deed, which is important because it is only through the index that a party may find certain interests, may result in a finding that a later purchaser was not on constructive notice of the prior conveyance. *Greenpoint Mortgage Funding, Inc. v. Schlossberg*, 888 A.2d 297 (Md. 2005). Problems may also arise if a subsequent conveyance occurs after the deed is filed with the registry office but before it is indexed. *Compare NYCTL 1998-1 Trust & the Bank of N.Y. v. Ibrahiem*, 15 Misc. 3d 294 (N.Y. Civ. Ct. 2007) (deed is considered recorded when delivered to registry office), *with Dyar v. Martinez*, 54 Cal. Rptr. 3d 907 (Ct. App. 2007) (unindexed *lis pendens* did not impart constructive notice).

Another common problem involves misspelled names in documents. If a purchaser is searching for records relating to J.S. Bach, and there is a mortgage recorded under the name J.S. Back, will that document give constructive notice? A doctrine known as *idem sonans* governs this question and generally looks to whether similar names sound alike or common usage otherwise associates them.

What about electronic recording systems, which are easier to search than paper records? Should the standard for which instruments give constructive notice then change? *See First Citizens National Bank v. Sherwood*, 879 A.2d 178 (Pa. 2005) (finding constructive notice because an electronic search would have revealed a mortgage improperly indexed under the name of the beneficiary of a trust rather than the trustee); *see also* William A. Reppy, Jr., *Some Issues Raised by Alaska's Recording Act*, 27 Alaska L. Rev. 195, 210 (2010) (arguing that because Alaska's title records have now been digitized and can be searched on-line, *Sabo* should be overruled).

Inquiry notice is a kind of constructive notice. Under this theory, notice will be imputed if the subsequent purchaser would have discovered the conveyance had she acted reasonably to investigate facts at her disposal. If the property is being occupied by someone other than the grantor, for example, a purchaser is on inquiry notice that a prior claim may be hanging around. Inquiry notice will also exist if a recorded instrument refers to another property interest, such as a lease, a life estate, a condominium declaration, or a general plan. Inquiry notice can even arise from an oral statement made by the earlier interest holder. *Swanson v. Swanson*, 796 N.W.2d 614 (N.D. 2011) (statement declaring a conflicting property interest sufficient to put subsequent purchasers on notice that they should at least investigate basis for the statement).

2. Estoppel by deed. *Sabo v. Horvath* concerns a dispute between two grantees. What would have happened if the grantor, Lowery, had claimed ownership of the property as against the first grantees, the Horvaths, when the grantor finally received the patent from the government? The doctrine of **estoppel by deed** would enable the grantees to prevail. *Ackerman v. Abbott*, 978 A.2d 1250 (D.C. 2009). If a grantor purports to convey a property interest she does not own to a grantee, and the grantor subsequently comes to own the property interest by receiving the deed, ownership is automatically vested in the grantee. Thus, if *O* purports to convey property to *A*, but *O* does not own the property, *A* gets nothing; one can convey only what one owns.

However, if *O* later obtains title to the property from *B*, the doctrine of estoppel by deed vests title immediately in *A*. *O* is estopped from asserting ownership rights as against *A*.[36]

3. **Wild deeds.** *Sabo v. Horvath* deals with a particular version of the more general problem of deeds outside the **chain of title**, the linked documents that make up a record of a property's ownership. This problem arises because it is impractical to require all buyers to search every one of the hundreds of thousands of deeds in the entire recording index. To make the search manageable, customary practice limits the search to the period between the date the grantor obtained his deed and the date a deed out from that grantor was recorded. Because it is sometimes possible that a predecessor in interest made a conveyance outside that period—either before or after—and because some buyers do not diligently record their interest, it is possible that some deeds relating to the property in question will not be found. Some deeds are recorded *too early* to appear in the chain of title (before a grantor obtained title to the property); others are recorded *too late* to be discovered (after a deed from that grantor was recorded).

a. **Recorded too early.** *O* conveys property to *A* that *O* does not own. *A* records the deed. *B*, the true owner, conveys the property to *O*. At this point, the property transfers automatically to *A* under the doctrine of estoppel by deed. However, unbeknownst to *A*, *O* then conveys title to *X*, a bona fide purchaser who has no knowledge of the conveyance from *O* to *A*. The majority of states will handle the situation just as the Alaska Supreme Court did. In these states, the first purchaser, *A*, would prevail in a contest between herself and the grantor, *O*. However, *X*, the second purchaser without notice of the earlier conveyance to *A*, would prevail in a contest with the first purchaser, *A*. This result obtains because *X* is required to search the records only so far back as the date when her grantor, *O*, acquired her interest; since *O* had purported to convey the interest to *A before O* obtained her title from *B*, *X* would not be charged with notice of the conveyance to *A*. This result, of course, protects the interests of the second bona fide purchaser, *X*, at the expense of the earlier bona fide purchaser, *A*, perhaps on the ground that *A* acted negligently in purchasing property from someone who did not in fact possess the right to convey it.

Some states require a more extended search on the part of the subsequent grantee; in these states, the doctrine of estoppel by deed is extended to apply to disputes not only between the grantor and the first grantee but between the first grantee and subsequent grantees. Under this theory, when the grantor gets the deed to the property already conveyed to the first grantee, title automatically passes to the first grantee, leaving the grantor nothing to convey to the subsequent purchaser.

---

36. This situation is analogous, but not identical, to the situation that obtained in *Sabo*. It is analogous only because the court concluded in *Sabo* that the grantor, Lowery, had undertaken sufficient acts under the federal statute to be considered the owner of the property conveyed to the first purchaser.

b. Recorded too late. *O* conveys to *A*, who does not record. *A* conveys to *B*, who records. *O* then conveys to *Z*, a bona fide purchaser without notice of the earlier conveyance from *O* to *A*. *B* then gets ahold of the deed from *O* to *A* and records it. In a contest between *B* and *Z*, *Z* would prevail because the deed from *O* to *A* was recorded too late. When *Z* bought the property, the deed from *A* to *B* had already been recorded, but since *A* had not yet recorded the deed from *O* to *A*, there is no way that *Z* could have found it. Neither *A* nor *B* was in *O*'s chain of title at the time *Z* purchased, so *Z* had no way to learn of the conveyance to *B*.

Here is a second example. *O* conveys to *A*, who does not record. *O* then conveys to *X*, who has notice of the earlier conveyance to *A*. *X* records her deed; then *A* records her deed. *X* conveys to *Z*, who has no notice of the earlier conveyance to *A*. In a contest between *A* and *Z*, *Z* would prevail because the deed from *O* to *A* was recorded too late. Can you see why?

4. Shelter doctrine. The shelter doctrine allows a bona fide purchaser to convey property to a third party even if the third party is on notice of an earlier conveyance. For example, *O* conveys to *A*, who does not record. *O* then conveys to *X*, a bona fide purchaser without notice of the conveyance to *A*; *X* records. Because *X* had no notice of the earlier conveyance to *A*, and because *X* recorded first, *X* would prevail over *A* in either a notice jurisdiction or a race-notice jurisdiction. *X* then wants to convey to *C*, but *C* has notice of the earlier conveyance to from *O* to *A*. The **shelter doctrine** allows *X* to convey the property to *C*, despite *C*'s knowledge of the earlier conveyance. This doctrine allows bona fide purchasers to convey title even if they subsequently find out, after they buy the property, of the earlier conveyance. The bona fide purchaser who records first obtains full rights in the property over the earlier buyer who did not record. Any other rule would restrict the bona fide purchaser's ability to transfer the property.

5. Favored position of bona fide purchasers. In *Matter of Edwards*, 962 F.2d 641 (7th Cir. 1992), the bona fide purchaser of property at a bankruptcy sale obtained title free and clear of a preexisting mortgage because the debtor who declared bankruptcy gave the court an old address for the mortgagee's lawyer; the mortgagee had listed its correct address, but the court clerk did not notice the discrepancy, so the mortgagee-lender was not notified of the bankruptcy sale of the property. Judge Richard Posner commented on the policies behind the protection of bona fide purchasers: "If purchasers at judicially approved sales of property of a bankrupt estate, and their lenders, cannot rely on the deed that they receive at the [bankruptcy] sale, it will be difficult to liquidate bankrupt estates at positive prices." *Id.* at 643. Yet Posner noted the unfairness of this procedure to the innocent owner:

> To take away a person's property — and a lien is property — without compensation or even notice is pretty shocking, but we have property rights on both sides of the equation here, since [the mortgagee/lender] wants to take away property that [the buyer at the bankruptcy sale] purchased and [the buyer's lender] financed, without compensating them for their loss.

Id. at 645. Does the disappointed mortgagee have any claim against the debtor who listed the wrong address for the mortgagee?

6. Statutory interpretation. Why aren't buyers on constructive notice of any deeds recorded under the names of predecessors in interest? What justifies limiting the required search to time periods associated with the chain of title? Have the courts interpreted the meaning of "notice" in recording statutes, or have they rewritten them by creating an exception for situations not contemplated by the legislature? If you believe the courts have created an exception, are the courts justified on the grounds that the legislature could not have intended to require an unlimited search, or are the courts practicing illegitimate judicial activism and ignoring the plain language of the statute?

Problems

Determine how the following cases would be resolved in a jurisdiction with (a) a race statute; (b) a notice statute; and (c) a race-notice statute:

1. *O* to *A* (*A* does not record). *O* to *B* (*B* has notice of the earlier conveyance to *A*).
B records. *A* records.
B sues *A* for title.

2. *O* to *A* (*A* does not record). *O* to *B* (*B* has no actual notice of the earlier conveyance to *A*).
B records.
A records.
B sues *A* for title.

3. *O* to *A* (*A* does not record). *O* to *B* (*B* has no actual notice of the earlier conveyance to *A*).
A records.
B records.
B sues *A* for title.

4. *O* to *A* (*A* does not record). *A* to *B* (*B* records).
O to *Z* (*Z* has no actual notice of deed from *O* to *A*; *Z* records).
B records deed from *O* to *A*.
B sues Z for title.

5. *O* to *A* (*A* does not record). *O* to *X* (*X* has notice of conveyance from *O* to *A*).
X records.
A records.
X conveys to *Z* (*Z* has no actual notice of deed from *O* to *A*).
A sues *X* and *Z* for title.

6. *O* to *A* (*A* does not record). *O* to *X* (*X* has notice of conveyance from *O* to *A*).
A records.
X records.

X conveys to *Z* (*Z* has no actual notice of deed from *O* to *A*).
A sues *X* and *Z* for title.

7. *O* to *A* (*A* does not record). *O* to *X* (*X* has no actual notice of conveyance from *O* to *A*).
X records.
A records.
X conveys to *C* (*C* has notice of conveyance from *O* to *A*).
A sues *C* for title.

§5.3 Equitable Subrogation

Property owners may take out more than one mortgage on their property. In such cases, the first mortgage has priority over later mortgages, at least if the first mortgage is recorded or the second mortgagee otherwise has notice of it. This means that if the borrower defaults on payments and the property is sold through foreclosure, the proceeds are paid to the first mortgagee; if there are assets left, they go to pay off the second mortgage, and so on down the priority list. But what happens if a borrower refinances a particular loan? In *Countrywide Home Loans, Inc. v. First National Bank of Steamboat Springs,* 144 P.3d 1224 (Wyo. 2006), an owner took out a third mortgage for the purpose of paying off the first mortgage. When the borrower defaulted on the second mortgage, the court had to determine whether the second mortgagee or the third mortgagee had priority; who would get paid first if the foreclosure sale did not yield enough proceeds to pay off both mortgages? The court applied the recording act principle of "first in time, first in right." Since the third mortgage was not only given after the second mortgage, but also recorded afterward (with notice of the second mortgage), the court held that the second mortgagee should be paid off first.

The opposite result was reached in *Columbia Community Bank v. Newman Park, LLC,* 304 P.3d 472 (Wash. 2013), because the court applied the doctrine of **equitable subrogation**. Under that doctrine, someone who assumes the rights or obligations of another steps into their shoes and assumes whatever rights or obligations they had to the extent necessary to prevent unjust enrichment. Because second mortgagees know that their mortgages are subordinate to first mortgages, they cannot not complain if the identity of the first mortgagee changes by assignment. If the refinancing of the loan and the assignment of the mortgagee's rights to a third party would mean that the second mortgage would move up and have priority over the first mortgagee, this would amount to a windfall neither earned nor deserved by the second mortgage and would constitute unjust enrichment. The *Restatement (Third) of Property (Mortgages)* §7.6 (1997) adopts this position on the ground that it serves the interests of homeowners by making refinancing cheaper and more widely available and does not hurt the interests of anyone else; the *Restatement* found it not to conflict with the spirit (if not the letter) of the state recording statute.

§5.4 Fraud and Forgery

Brock v. Yale Mortgage Corporation

700 S.E.2d 583 (Ga. 2010)

CAROL W. HUNSTEIN, Chief Justice.

Appellant Jerry Brock ("Brock") commenced this action against his ex-wife, Joyce Brock ("Joyce"), and appellee Yale Mortgage Corporation ("Yale") to, among other things, quiet title in the Suwanee residence he and Joyce once shared (the "property"); set aside a forged quitclaim deed purporting to transfer Brock's interest in the property to Joyce; and set aside a subsequent deed to secure debt Joyce executed in Yale's favor or limit the deed to a one-half undivided interest in the property.

The Brocks purchased the property jointly in 1987, financing the transaction with a loan from First Railroad Mortgage Company. In connection with the loan, the Brocks executed a security deed and promissory note in the amount of $56,000 in the lender's favor. The Brocks did not have a joint bank account. Brock maintained a checking account and gave his wife money each month to make the loan payment, but she did not always use the funds for that purpose. As a result, [the Brocks' loan went into default in 1996, but Joyce] borrowed money from a friend to bring the loan current and stop the foreclosure process. In August 2000, Joyce received a second notice of foreclosure sale [but she worked out a payment plan with the lender.]

In January 2001, Joyce received a third notice of foreclosure sale after defaulting under the payment plan. Once again, Joyce did not inform Brock of the foreclosure sale notice, but instead contacted Jerri Browning of mortgage broker Capital Lending Group ("Capital"), about obtaining a new loan. Browning assisted Joyce in procuring a loan from Yale. Browning advised Joyce that in order to secure a loan in her name only, Brock would need to convey his interest in the property to her. At Browning's suggestion, Joyce requested a blank quitclaim deed from Yale's closing attorney, who faxed the deed to her. At the February 2001 loan closing, Joyce presented an executed, unrecorded quitclaim deed by which Brock purportedly transferred his interest in the property to her. Yale does not dispute that Brock's signature on the quitclaim deed is forged. Yale loaned Joyce $60,000, of which $15,460 was used to satisfy the Brocks' [original mortgage]. Joyce received $38,085.44 in cash at closing. Joyce executed a promissory note and deed to secure debt in Yale's favor.

In May 2004, Brock discovered that his wife had spent over $200,000 from his checking account without his knowledge. He filed for divorce shortly thereafter. Around the same time, Brock learned about the 2001 foreclosure proceedings, the forged quitclaim deed, and the Yale loan. According to Brock, he called Yale after learning of the Yale loan, but the representative he spoke with told him she did not have to speak with him and terminated the call. In August 2004, the Brocks executed a settlement agreement in their divorce proceedings in which Joyce transferred "any and all of her rights, title and interest [in the property], whether legal or equitable" to her husband. In January 2005, Brock commenced this action.

[Georgia Code §23-3-40] provides that a deed may be cancelled on grounds of forgery. If the forged quitclaim deed is set aside here, however, that would not invalidate the subsequent security deed in its entirety. One holding property with another person as tenants in common cannot convey or affect that person's interest without his or her consent. Yet, a tenant in common may encumber or convey his or her own interest in property without the consent of other cotenants. Thus, if a tenant in common purports to convey an interest in the entire property, the deed will affect his or her interest although non-consenting cotenants will not be bound. It is undisputed that the Brocks acquired the property as tenants in common under a 1987 warranty deed transferring the property to both of them as grantees. Accordingly, the security deed under which Joyce purported to convey legal title to the entire property to Yale, at a minimum, effectively vested Yale with a security interest in the one-half undivided interest in the property Joyce indisputably held and was free to convey.

As a general rule, "[a] bona fide purchaser for value is protected against outstanding interests in land of which the purchaser has no notice." *Farris v. Nationsbanc Mortg. Corp.*, 493 S.E.2d 143, 145 (1997); [Georgia Code §§23-1-19, 23-1-20]. We have long held that "[a] grantee in a security deed who acts in good faith stands in the attitude of a bona fide purchaser, and is entitled to the same protection." *Roop Grocery Co. v. Gentry*, 25 S.E.2d 705, 711 (1943). But we have also long recognized that a forged deed is a nullity and vests no title in a grantee. As such, even a bona fide purchaser for value without notice of a forgery cannot acquire good title from a grantee in a forged deed, or those holding under such a grantee, because the grantee has no title to convey. [Accordingly,] Yale would not acquire a valid security interest in the entire property simply by proving its status as a bona fide purchaser for value.

Under Georgia law, a forged signature is nonetheless binding if ratified by the person whose name was signed. "A ratification may be express or implied from the acts or silence of the principal." [Georgia Code] §10-6-52. Whether ratification occurs is usually a fact question for the jury.

Yale argues, and the trial court apparently agreed, that Brock ratified "the subject loan agreement" under the divorce settlement agreement. The correct focus of the analysis, however, is whether Brock ratified the forged quitclaim deed such that his wife's security deed effectively conveyed a security interest in the entire property to Yale. The ratification doctrine does not apply to the loan agreement or security deed because Joyce did not purport to enter into them in Brock's name or under authority from him.

Yale principally relies on the following language in the settlement agreement, which appears immediately after Joyce's agreement to transfer her interest in the property to him:

> The parties acknowledge that [Joyce] has incurred a $50,000 liability on the property. The parties will seek to have said debt forgiven. If the parties are unsuccessful in having the debt forgiven, then [Joyce] shall be responsible for the repayment of said debt. [Joyce] shall further indemnify and hold [Brock] harmless from any and all liability, loss, damage, claim, demand, cost or judgment, including reasonable attorney's fees, arising out of [Joyce's] failure to pay said debt.

In acknowledging that Joyce incurred a "liability on the property," the settlement agreement appears to assume the existence of a valid encumbrance on the property but does not specify its nature. Significantly, the settlement agreement does not clarify whether the parties believed that the Yale debt encumbered the entire property or only Joyce's interest. To the extent that Brock merely acknowledged that his wife encumbered her share of the property, that acknowledgment would not evidence an election to treat the forged quitclaim deed as valid. *See Restatement (Third) of Agency* §4.01 cmt. b (2006) ("The act of ratification consists of an externally observable manifestation of assent to be bound by the prior act of another person."). Further, if Brock believed that the property interest he was accepting from his wife was encumbered, he might have wanted to clarify that he was not personally liable for the debt and to bargain for protection from any loss he might incur as the result of the debt. Given the ambiguity in the settlement agreement arising from the phrase "liability on the property," a factual issue exists regarding the intention of the parties, which should be determined in light of all the relevant evidence.

The trial court also concluded that ratification occurred by virtue of the fact that a portion of the Yale loan proceeds paid off the balance of $15,460 on the [original] note. Ratification occurs if a principal, with full knowledge of all the material facts, accepts the benefits of an unauthorized act, or retains such benefits after discovering the material facts. For example, in [*Ferguson v. Golf Course Consultants*, 252 S.E.2d 907 (Ga. 1979),] we held that the plaintiff ratified and could not set aside a warranty deed to which his business partner signed the plaintiff's name without the plaintiff's knowledge or authority when the plaintiff knowingly received and spent proceeds the partner earned from the conveyance. In concluding that "[the plaintiff] cannot accept the proceeds of the sale, keep them, use them, decline to tender them back, and then expect a court of equity to set aside the deed from which he derived a profit," *id.* [at 908], we relied, inter alia, on prior precedent that a grantor seeking to cancel a deed in equity must first restore or tender to the grantee any consideration received under the deed.

Here, Brock received nothing of value under the forged quitclaim deed. To the extent he allegedly benefitted incidentally from the payoff of the prior loan in a transaction "once removed" from the unauthorized forged quitclaim deed, he was not required to tender such benefit to Yale as a precondition to equitable relief or to avoid ratification.

For the reasons set forth above, we affirm in part, reverse in part, and remand for proceedings not inconsistent with this opinion.

McCoy v. Love

382 So. 2d 647 (Fla. 1980)

JOSEPH A. BOYD, JR., Justice.

Mary V. Nowling Elliott, now deceased, brought an action seeking the cancellation of a deed. The trial court found that Mrs. Elliott, a simple, elderly woman who could neither read nor write, owned an undivided one-fifth interest in the minerals underlying a seventy-five acre tract of land. In January 1972 B.G. Russell offered to buy her entire interest, but she refused. She orally agreed to sell Mr. Russell two of the thirteen to fifteen mineral acres she owned for $3300.00. The trial court found further: Defendant Russell prepared the mineral deed, and instead of the two acres of minerals agreed upon, fraudulently substituted the clause: "one-fifth (1/5) interest in and to all the oil, gas, and other minerals" and then inserted the legal description of the 75 acres. Obviously, one-fifth of 75 acres is 15 acres, a deal that the Plaintiff had consistently refused to make.

Mrs. Elliott lived with her daughter, who could read, write, and understand simple things. The daughter looked over the instrument Russell had prepared. Although she did not understand the deed, she advised Mrs. Elliott that she guessed it was all right.

Several days later, Russell contacted Mrs. Elliott and told her that he had made a mistake in drawing up the deed. He offered to pay her $15,000 for the interest that had been conveyed. She refused and insisted on a reconveyance of that portion of the interest which she had not intended to sell. "[O]n February 16, 1972, Russell and his wife purported to reconvey to Plaintiff the thirteen seventy-fifths (13/75ths) interest of which she had been defrauded." On February 11, 1972, however, Russell conveyed a substantial portion of the same mineral rights to C.P. McClelland, who later conveyed to respondents Messrs. Love, Harris, and Carpenter. Mrs. Elliott remained ignorant of the Russell-McClelland and subsequent transactions until October 1973 when she wanted to sell more of her mineral rights and a title search revealed them. She sued for cancellation of the deed.

A bona fide purchaser has the right to rely on the record title of his grantor, but this protection extends only to those purchasing a legal title. The recording of a void or forged deed is legally insufficient to create a legal title, and affords no protection to those claiming under it.

The trial court's findings of fact that the grantee committed fraud and that the grantor was not negligent do not compel the conclusion that there was such an alteration of documents as to be the equivalent of a forgery. The grantor knew that she was executing and delivering a deed of mineral rights. The law charged her with the responsibility of informing herself as to the legal effect of the document she was signing.

Where all the essential legal requisites of a deed are present, it conveys legal title. Fraud in the inducement renders such a legally effective deed voidable in equity. We hold that the district court was correct in holding that the deed was merely voidable, and that it conveyed a legal title to the grantee.

Because of its holding that the deed was void, the trial court granted summary judgment in favor of the plaintiff. Therefore there were no findings of fact on the issue of the good faith of the purchasers from McClelland. While the district court was correct in holding the deed voidable rather than void, there was no basis for it to conclude from the record that the defendants were bona fide purchasers. The case should be remanded for trial of this factual issue.

Notes and Questions

1. Void or voidable? When a deed has been obtained by fraud or forgery, it is classified as either void or voidable. If no further conveyances are made, a court will set aside the deed on the true owner's request. The difficult issue is determining what happens if the property has been conveyed to a bona fide purchaser, one who paid value and had no notice of the fraud or forgery. If the deed is **void**, then it conveys no title to the grantee and the grantee has no power to convey title to another; the bona fide purchaser is therefore not protected. If, however, the deed is merely **voidable** by the true owner, who was the victim of the foul play, then a subsequent bona fide purchaser will be able to obtain good title. In that case, the victim's sole remedy will be a suit for damages for fraud or conversion against the wrongdoer.

2. Forgery. Forged deeds are absolutely void and therefore transfer no interest to the grantee; nor can they be the basis of a transfer from the grantee to a subsequent bona fide purchaser even though that purchaser has no knowledge of the forgery. Thus, a bona fide purchaser who buys in reliance on the record title, which appears good, will obtain nothing. *In re Sutter*, 665 F.3d 722, 728 (6th Cir. 2012); *Special Property VI v. Woodruff*, 730 N.W.2d 753, 756 (Mich. Ct. App. 2007); *First National Bank in Albuquerque v. Enriquez*, 634 P.2d 1266, 1268 (N.M. 1981). This universally recognized rule appears to conflict with the policies underlying the recording system, which is intended to give a bona fide purchaser assurance that she receives what she pays for and that the seller has a right to convey the property. Why do you suppose courts refuse to protect bona fide purchasers from forged deeds?

In *Brock v. Yale Mortgage Corp.*, the court also considered whether Jerry Brock had **ratified** the forged deed. Ratification, as well as the equitable defenses of waiver and estoppel, can validate a void deed; ratification generally involves a party knowingly accepting the action of the forger and indicating intent to adopt the otherwise unauthorized deed. *See Erier v. Creative Finance & Investments, L.L.C.*, 203 P.3d 744, 750-752 (Mont. 2009).

3. Fraud. In contrast to forged deeds, deeds obtained through fraud are generally voidable rather than void. They are voidable by the defrauded victim — the one who was fraudulently induced to transfer the property. Once the property passes to a bona fide purchaser without notice of the fraud, however, the conveyance can no longer be rescinded. *Fallon v. Triangle Management*, 215 Cal. Rptr. 748 (Ct. App. 1985). The reason for this distinction has been explained by a Maryland court as follows:

> A deed obtained through fraud, deceit or trickery is voidable as between the parties thereto, but not as to a bona fide purchaser. A forged deed, on the other hand, is void ab initio.
>
> [A] forger can pass no better title than he has. Consequently, there can be no bona fide holder of title under a forged deed. A forged deed, unlike one procured by fraud, deceit or trickery is void from its inception. The distinction between a deed obtained by fraud and one that has been forged is readily apparent. In a fraudulent deed an innocent purchaser is protected because the fraud practiced upon the signatory to such a deed

> is brought into play, at least in part, by some act or omission on the part of the person upon whom the fraud is perpetrated. He has helped in some degree to set into motion the very fraud about which he later complains. A forged deed, on the other hand, does not necessarily involve any action on the part of the person against whom the forgery is committed.

Harding v. Ja Laur Corp., 315 A.2d 132 (Md. Ct. Spec. App. 1974). Courts seem to suggest that if the grantor has negligently participated in creating the problem, she is estopped from claiming the property from a bona fide purchaser.

Because of the fraud/forgery distinction, the courts have often had to contend with behavior that could be described as either forgery or fraud. For example, in *Harding v. Ja Laur, supra*, plaintiff Lucille M. Harding claimed that defendant Ja Laur induced her to sign a blank page that she was told would be used merely to straighten out a boundary line but that was later affixed to a deed transferring a small portion of land that she owned. Defendant Ja Laur had wanted the land because it was contiguous to land it owned and was extremely valuable because it provided access to that land. On one hand, the court could have held that the case involved fraud rather than forgery because Ms. Harding had been induced to sign on the basis of a false impression of the document. On the other hand, the court could characterize the affixing of the signature to another legal document as a forgery since it involved an alteration of her signature, *id.* at 135-136:

> So that if a person has two deeds presented to him, and he thinks he is signing one but in actuality, because of fraud, deceit or trickery he signs the other, a bona fide purchaser, without notice, is protected. On the other hand, if a person is presented with a deed, and he signs that deed but the deed is thereafter altered *e.g.* through a change in the description or affixing the signature page to another deed, that is forgery and a subsequent purchaser takes no title.

Given the possible difficulties in distinguishing fraud from forgery in some cases, does the distinction make sense?

§5.5 Marketable Title Acts and Other Ways to Clear Title

Several other statutory regimes operate in conjunction with the recording acts to determine the state of title for any given property. Statutes of limitation and adverse possession are a common way in which disputes over title are resolved, at least where physical possession is an issue. *See* Chapter 5, §1.1. This makes understanding the precise state of title from the public record more complicated.

A seemingly more bright-line approach can be found in **marketable title acts**, which exist in 18 states. 11 *Thompson on Real Property, Second Thomas Editions* §92.06. These acts try to solve the problem of defining how far back one must search in the grantor-grantee index by limiting searches to a reasonable period, often 30 to 40 years. When a person has a record title for the designated period of time, all prior claims or interests are extinguished. To preserve prior claims, owners must **re-record** their interest or file a **notice of claim** every 30 years or so after the recording of their initial deed. Some property interests are exempt from this requirement, including easements that are observable by physical inspection and mineral rights, federal and state interests, and, in some states, remainders, reversions, rights of entry, possibilities of reverter, and restrictive covenants. These various exceptions have the effect of reducing the utility of the marketable title acts as a method of reducing the cost of searching title, but serve other interests.[37]

§5.6 Title Companies and the Recording System

Originally, lawyers conducted the title searches required to determine the state of a property's title, either for a conveyance or for establishing a lender's lien priority. In some areas, this is still the case. In many places, however, title insurance companies have emerged to fulfill this function. Most lenders require the purchaser to buy title insurance as a condition for getting a mortgage loan. Even when insurance is not required, many purchasers will obtain it to protect their interests. It has therefore become standard practice for title companies to perform title searches.

Title companies can be liable for negligently performing title searches, independent of any claims under a title insurance policy, although many courts still refuse to identify such a duty. *Compare, e.g., 100 Investment LP v. Columbia Town Center Title Co.*, 60 A.3d 1 (Md. 2013) (title companies owed a duty of care to their customer in preparing a title commitment) *with Walker Rogge, Inc. v. Chelsea Title & Guaranty Co.*, 562 A.2d 208 (N.J. 1989) (limiting a title company's liability to the insurance policy and barring tort liability for negligence in searching records).

A title company will typically issue a title commitment, also known as a title binder, which indicates that the company will insure a given beneficiary under specified conditions, such as certain affidavits being provided or liens being removed. The title commitment also typically contains detailed information about the state of title, including encumbrances and defects. Title companies generally issue the actual title policy after closing. Title insurance policies provided to owners explain that the company promises, in return for a premium, to insure the purchaser against losses occasioned by defects in title to the property, defining the kinds of defects they cover and specifying exceptions to coverage. Similarly, lender policies insure a specified lien priority. The insurance company may also promise to pay the costs of defending the title through litigation.

Disputes may arise between a title insurance companies and the holder of the insurance over the interpretation of the insurance contract. These disputes involve issues such as the kinds of defects in title that are covered by the contract and the nature of exclusions and exceptions. *See, e.g., Cox v. Commonwealth Land Title Insurance Co.*, 59 A.3d 1280 (Me. 2013); *Hart v. Ticor Title Insurance Co.*, 272 P.3d 1215 (Haw. 2012).

---

37. Unlike the recording acts, a root of title under a marketable title act may be based on a wild deed or even a forged deed. That is because marketable title acts validate a root of title that is recorded within the relevant period where this is a conflict with a recorded interest that is outside the period, regardless of a prior defect in the chain. *See Marshall v. Hollywood, Inc.*, 236 So. 2d 114 (Fla. 1970).

They can also involve an insurer's obligation to defend the insured against lawsuits based on matters covered by title insurance. *See, e.g., Deutsche Bank National Association v. First American Title Insurance Co.*, 465 Mass. 741 (2013) (title insurer not obligated to defend lender against claim seeking to have a note and mortgage rescinded because of predatory lending).

§5.7 Title Registration

Some jurisdictions have partially adopted a **title registration system**, or "Torrens system," named after Sir Robert Torrens, an Irish immigrant in Australia who established the first registration system there in 1858. It has never caught on broadly in the United States, and is available only in ten states. 14-83 *Powell on Real Property* §83.01[3]. An owner who wishes to register his land must file a petition for a judicial or quasi-judicial proceeding that is similar to an action to quiet title. Notice must be given to all persons having any interest in the land. The result of the adjudication is a certificate of registration or title. The official certificate of title states the identity of the property owner and includes descriptions of all encumbrances (easements, covenants, liens, mortgages, leases, and the like) affecting the title. The certificate is conclusive as to the title and is filed in the registrar's office. If an owner transfers his land, the deed must be brought to the registry and a new certificate issued. A title examiner for a purchaser need only examine the current certificate of title and the documents referred to in the list of encumbrances on the certificate.

Although this system simplifies title problems immensely, it is expensive to institute. Either the state would have to pay for a judicial proceeding to produce a certificate of title for every parcel in the state or the individual owner would have to bear the cost, which may amount to hundreds of dollars. Because the states that have adopted it have allowed owners to register their land on a voluntary basis, most land is still unregistered and governed by the old grantor-grantee record system.

In addition, some factors militate against the absolute conclusiveness that is supposed to attach to the title. What happens, for example, if it turns out that an earlier deed was forged? If the current certificate of title is absolutely conclusive — if it cannot be challenged — then an innocent person may lose the property because of the forgery. Note, however, that forgeries are rare because the "registry will not issue a new certificate in the ordinary course of business unless the old owner's duplicate is presented for cancellation. In addition, the registries in some states maintain files of signature cards against which purported conveyances are checked." William B. Stoebuck & Dale A. Whitman, *The Law of Property* §11.15, at 928 n.20 (3d ed. 2000).

CHAPTER 13

Fair Housing Law

§1 INTRODUCTION TO FAIR HOUSING

§1.1 Sources of Fair Housing Law

The federal *Fair Housing Act*, Title VIII of the *Civil Rights Act of 1968*, 42 U.S.C. §3601 *et seq*., was the last plank in a series of civil rights statutes enacted in the 1960s, and secured passage at President Lyndon Johnson's urging a week after the assassination of Martin Luther King, Jr. The act originally prohibited discrimination on the basis of race, color, national origin, and religion. Congress added sex to the list of protected categories in 1974 and added handicap (disability) and familial status (which covers children under the age of 18 living with parents or legal custodians as well as pregnant women) in 1988.[1]

The *Fair Housing Act* prohibits discrimination in the sale or rental of housing and in a wide variety of other housing-related contexts. For example, the act covers discrimination in residential finance as well as activities by real estate brokers and appraisers. *Id.* §3605. The act also applies to land use regulation, and constitutional protections relating to takings, due process, equal protection, the free exercise of religion, and free speech are also important constraints in this context. *See* Chapter 7, §6; Chapter 14; Chapter 15. Several other federal statutes also prohibit discrimination in important aspects of the real estate market, including the *Civil Rights Act of 1866*, 42 U.S.C. §§1981-1982; *Title VI* of the *Civil Rights Act of 1964*, 42 U.S.C. §2000d *et seq*.; §504 of the *Rehabilitation Act of 1973*, 29 U.S.C. §794; and the *Equal Credit Opportunity Act*, 15 U.S.C. §§1691-1691f, all of which we will touch on in this chapter.

Almost every state and a great many local governments have some kind of fair housing law. Such laws often regulate more types of discrimination than are covered

1. The *Fair Housing Act* uses the term "handicap" but it is more common now to use the term "disability" and this chapter will generally do so. There is no distinction in legal meaning. *See Bragdon v. Abbott*, 524 U.S. 624, 631 (1998).

by federal fair housing law. For example, many state laws prohibit discrimination on the basis of marital status, age, or source of income, while an increasing number of state and local laws prohibit discrimination because of sexual orientation. In addition, state and local laws may apply to housing that is exempt from the federal *Fair Housing Act,* such as owner-occupied three-unit buildings or claims that are barred by the federal statute of limitations but timely under state or local law. Finally, as we shall see, courts also respond to discrimination in housing through the traditional tools of equity.

§1.2 The *Fair Housing Act*

Fair Housing Act

42 U.S.C. §§3601-3605, 3607, 3613, 3617, 3631

§3601. Declaration of policy

It is the policy of the United States to provide, within constitutional limitations, for fair housing throughout the United States.

§3602. Definitions

(b) "Dwelling" means any building, structure, or portion thereof which is occupied as, or designed or intended for occupancy as, a residence by one or more families, and any vacant land which is offered for sale or lease for the construction or location thereon of any such building, structure, or portion thereof.

(c) "Family" includes a single individual.

(e) "To rent" includes to lease, to sublease, to let and otherwise to grant for a consideration the right to occupy premises not owned by the occupant.

(h) "Handicap" means, with respect to a person—

(1) a physical or mental impairment which substantially limits one or more of such person's major life activities,

(2) a record of having such an impairment, or

(3) being regarded as having such an impairment, but such term does not include current, illegal use of or addiction to a controlled substance as defined in section 802 of Title 21.

(i) "Aggrieved person" includes any person who—

(1) claims to have been injured by a discriminatory housing practice; or

(2) believes that such person will be injured by a discriminatory housing practice that is about to occur.

(k) "Familial status" means one or more individuals (who have not attained the age of 18 years) being domiciled with—

(1) a parent or another person having legal custody of such individual or individuals; or

(2) the designee of such parent or other person having such custody, with the written permission of such parent or other person.

The protections against discrimination on the basis of familial status shall apply to any person who is pregnant or is in the process of securing legal custody of any individual who has not attained the age of 18 years.

§3603. Effective dates of certain prohibitions

(b) Exemptions

Nothing in section 3604 of this title (other than subsection (c)) shall apply to—

(1) any single-family house sold or rented by an owner: *Provided,* That such private individual owner does not own more than three such single-family houses at any one time: *Provided further,* That after December 31, 1969, the sale or rental of any such single-family house shall be excepted from the application of this subchapter only if such house is sold or rented (A) without the use in any manner of the sales or rental facilities or the sales or rental services of any real estate broker, agent, or salesman, or of such facilities or services of any person in the business of selling or renting dwellings, or of any employee or agent of any such broker, agent, salesman, or person and (B) without the publication, posting or mailing, after notice, of any advertisement or written notice in violation of section 3604(c) of this title, or

(2) rooms or units in dwellings containing living quarters occupied or intended to be occupied by no more than four families living independently of each other, if the owner actually maintains and occupies one of such living quarters as his residence.

§3604. Discrimination in sale or rental of housing and other prohibited practices

As made applicable by section 3603 of this title and except as exempted by sections 3603(b) and 3607 of this title, it shall be unlawful—

(a) To refuse to sell or rent after the making of a bona fide offer, or to refuse to negotiate for the sale or rental of, or otherwise make unavailable or deny, a dwelling to any person because of race, color, religion, sex, familial status, or national origin.

(b) To discriminate against any person in the terms, conditions, or privileges of sale or rental of a dwelling, or in the provision of services or facilities in connection therewith, because of race, color, religion, sex, familial status, or national origin.

(c) To make, print, or publish, or cause to be made, printed, or published any notice, statement, or advertisement, with respect to the sale or rental of a dwelling that indicates any preference, limitation, or discrimination based on race, color, religion, sex, handicap, familial status, or national origin, or an intention to make any such preference, limitation, or discrimination.

(d) To represent to any person because of race, color, religion, sex, handicap, familial status, or national origin that any dwelling is not available for inspection, sale, or rental when such dwelling is in fact so available.

(e) For profit, to induce, or attempt to induce any person to sell or rent any dwelling by representations regarding the entry or prospective entry into the neighborhood of a person or persons of a particular race, color, religion, sex, handicap, familial status, or national origin.

(f)(1) To discriminate in the sale or rental, or to otherwise make unavailable or deny, a dwelling to any buyer or renter because of a handicap of—

(A) that buyer or renter;

(B) a person residing in or intending to reside in that dwelling after it is so sold, rented, or made available; or

(C) any person associated with that buyer or renter.

(2) To discriminate against any person in the terms, conditions, or privileges of sale or rental of a dwelling, or in the provision of services or facilities in connection with such dwelling, because of a handicap of—

(A) that buyer or renter;

(B) a person residing in or intending to reside in that dwelling after it is so sold, rented, or made available; or

(C) any person associated with that person.

(3) For purposes of this subsection, discrimination includes—

(A) a refusal to permit, at the expense of the handicapped person, reasonable modifications of existing premises occupied or to be occupied by such person if such modifications may be necessary to afford such person full enjoyment of the premises except that, in the case of a rental, the landlord may where it is reasonable to do so condition permission for a modification on the renter agreeing to restore the interior of the premises to the condition that existed before the modification, reasonable wear and tear excepted;

(B) a refusal to make reasonable accommodations in rules, policies, practices, or services, when such accommodations may be necessary to afford such person equal opportunity to use and enjoy a dwelling; or

(C) in connection with the design and construction of covered multifamily dwellings for first occupancy after the date that is 30 months after September 13, 1988, a failure to design and construct those dwellings in such a manner that—

(i) the public use and common use portions of such dwellings are readily accessible to and usable by handicapped persons;

(ii) all the doors designed to allow passage into and within all premises within such dwellings are sufficiently wide to allow passage by handicapped persons in wheelchairs; and

(iii) all premises within such dwellings contain the following features of adaptive design:

(I) an accessible route into and through the dwelling;

(II) light switches, electrical outlets, thermostats, and other environmental controls in accessible locations;

(III) reinforcements in bathroom walls to allow later installation of grab bars; and

(IV) usable kitchens and bathrooms such that an individual in a wheelchair can maneuver about the space.

(7) As used in this subsection, the term "covered multifamily dwellings" means—

(A) buildings consisting of 4 or more units if such buildings have one or more elevators; and

(B) ground floor units in other buildings consisting of 4 or more units.

§3605. Discrimination in residential real estate-related transactions

(a) *In general.* It shall be unlawful for any person or other entity whose business includes engaging in residential real estate-related transactions to discriminate against any person in making available such a transaction, or in the terms or conditions of such a transaction, because of race, color, religion, sex, handicap, familial status, or national origin.

(b) *Definition.* As used in this section, the term "residential real estate-related transaction" means any of the following:

(1) The making or purchasing of loans or providing other financial assistance—

(A) for purchasing, constructing, improving, repairing, or maintaining a dwelling; or

(B) secured by residential real estate.

(2) The selling, brokering, or appraising of residential real property.

§3607. Exemption

(a) Religious organizations and private clubs

Nothing in this title shall prohibit a religious organization, association, or society, or any nonprofit institution or organization operated, supervised or controlled by or in conjunction with a religious organization, association, or society, from limiting the sale, rental or occupancy of dwellings which it owns or operates for other than a commercial purpose to persons of the same religion, or from giving preference to such persons, unless membership in such religion is restricted on account of race, color, or national origin. Nor shall anything in this subchapter prohibit a private club not in fact open to the public, which as an incident to its primary purpose or purposes provides lodgings which it owns or operates for other than a commercial purpose, from limiting the rental or occupancy of such lodgings to its members or from giving preference to its members.

(b) Numbers of occupants; housing for older persons; persons convicted of making or distributing controlled substances

(1) Nothing in this subchapter limits the applicability of any reasonable local, State, or Federal restrictions regarding the maximum number of occupants permitted to occupy a dwelling. Nor does any provision in this title regarding familial status apply with respect to housing for older persons.

(2) As used in this section, "housing for older persons" means housing—

(A) provided under any State or Federal program that the Secretary determines is specifically designed and operated to assist elderly persons (as defined in the State or Federal program); or

(B) intended for, and solely occupied by, persons 62 years of age or older; or

(C) intended and operated for occupancy by persons 55 years of age or older, and—

(i) at least 80 percent of the occupied units are occupied by at least one person who is 55 years of age or older;

(ii) the housing facility or community publishes and adheres to policies and procedures that demonstrate the intent required under this subparagraph; and

(iii) the housing facility or community complies with rules issued by the Secretary for verification of occupancy, which shall—

(I) provide for verification by reliable surveys and affidavits; and

(II) include examples of the types of policies and procedures relevant to a determination of compliance with the requirement of clause (ii). Such surveys and affidavits shall be admissible in administrative and judicial proceedings for the purposes of such verification.

(3) Housing shall not fail to meet the requirements for housing for older persons by reason of:

(A) persons residing in such housing as of the date of enactment of this Act who do not meet the age requirements of subsections (2)(B) or (C): *provided,* That new occupants of such housing meet the age requirements of subsections (2)(B) or (C); or

(B) unoccupied units: *provided,* That such units are reserved for occupancy by persons who meet the age requirements of subsections (2)(B) or (C).

(4) Nothing in this subchapter prohibits conduct against a person because such person has been convicted by any court of competent jurisdiction of the illegal manufacture or distribution of a controlled substance as defined in section 802 of Title 21.

(5)(A) A person shall not be held personally liable for monetary damages for a violation of this title if such person reasonably relied, in good faith, on the application of the exemption under this subsection relating to housing for older persons.

(B) For the purposes of this paragraph, a person may only show good faith reliance on the application of the exemption by showing that—

(i) such person has no actual knowledge that the facility or community is not, or will not be, eligible for such exemption; and

(ii) the facility or community has stated formally, in writing, that the facility or community complies with the requirements for such exemption.

§3613. Enforcement by private persons

(a) Civil action

(1)(A) An aggrieved person may commence a civil action in an appropriate United States district court or State court not later than 2 years after the occurrence or the termination of an alleged discriminatory housing practice to obtain appropriate relief with respect to such discriminatory housing practice or breach.

(b) Appointment of attorney by court

Upon application by a person alleging a discriminatory housing practice or a person against whom such a practice is alleged, the court may—

(1) appoint an attorney for such person; or

(2) authorize the commencement or continuation of a civil action under subsection (a) of this section without the payment of fees, costs, or security, if in the opinion of the court such person is financially unable to bear the costs of such action.

(c) Relief which may be granted

(1) In a civil action under subsection (a) of this section, if the court finds that a discriminatory housing practice has occurred or is about to occur, the court may award to the plaintiff actual and punitive damages, and may grant as relief, as the court deems appropriate, any permanent or temporary injunction, temporary restraining order, or other order (including an order enjoining the defendant from engaging in such practice or ordering such affirmative action as may be appropriate).

(2) In a civil action under subsection (a) of this section, the court, in its discretion, may allow the prevailing party, other than the United States, a reasonable attorney's fee and costs.

§3617. Interference, coercion, or intimidation; enforcement by civil action

It shall be unlawful to coerce, intimidate, threaten, or interfere with any person in the exercise or enjoyment of, or on account of his having exercised or enjoyed, or on account of his having aided or encouraged any other person in the exercise or enjoyment of, any right granted or protected by section 3603, 3604, 3605, or 3606 of this title.

§3631. Violations; penalties

Whoever, whether or not acting under color of law, by force or threat of force willfully injures, intimidates or interferes with, or attempts to injure, intimidate or interfere with—

(a) any person because of his race, color, religion, sex, handicap (as such term is defined in section 3602 of this title), familial status (as such term is defined in section 3602 of this title), or national origin and because he is or has been selling, purchasing, renting, financing, occupying, or contracting or negotiating for the sale, purchase, rental, financing or occupation of any dwelling, or applying for or participating in any service, organization, or facility relating to the business of selling or renting dwellings; or

(b) any person because he is or has been, or in order to intimidate such person or any other person or any class of persons from—

(1) participating, without discrimination on account of race, color, religion, sex, handicap (as such term is defined in section 3602 of this title), familial status (as such term is defined in section 3602 of this title), or national origin, in any of the activities, services, organizations or facilities described in subsection (a) of this section; or

(2) affording another person or class of persons opportunity or protection so to participate; or

(c) any citizen because he is or has been, or in order to discourage such citizen or any other citizen from lawfully aiding or encouraging other persons to participate, without discrimination on account of race, color, religion, sex, handicap (as such term is defined in section 3602 of this title), familial status (as such term is defined in section 3602 of this title), or national origin, in any of the activities, services, organizations or facilities described in subsection (a) of this section, or participating lawfully in speech or peaceful assembly opposing any denial of the opportunity to so participate—

shall be fined under Title 18 or imprisoned not more than one year, or both; and if bodily injury results from the acts committed in violation of this section or if such acts include the use, attempted use, or threatened use of a dangerous weapon, explosives, or fire shall be fined under Title 18 or imprisoned not more than ten years, or both; and if death results from the acts committed in violation of this section or if such acts include kidnapping or an attempt to kidnap, aggravated sexual abuse or an attempt to commit aggravated sexual abuse, or an attempt to kill, shall be fined under Title 18 or imprisoned for any term of years or for life, or both.

§1.3 Advertising and the Reach of the *Fair Housing Act*

Fair Housing Council of San Fernando Valley v. Roommate.com, LLC

666 F.3d 1216 (9th Cir. 2012)

ALEX KOZINSKI, Chief Judge:

There's no place like home. In the privacy of your own home, you can take off your coat, kick off your shoes, let your guard down and be completely yourself. While we usually share our homes only with friends and family, sometimes we need to take in a stranger to help pay the rent. When that happens, can the government limit whom we choose? Specifically, do the anti-discrimination provisions of the *Fair Housing Act* ("FHA") extend to the selection of roommates?

Facts

Roommate.com, LLC ("Roommate") operates an internet-based business that helps roommates find each other. Roommate's website receives over 40,000 visits a day and roughly a million new postings for roommates are created each year. When users sign up, they must create a profile by answering a series of questions about their sex, sexual orientation and whether children will be living with them. An open-ended "Additional Comments" section lets users include information not prompted by the questionnaire. Users are asked to list their preferences for roommate characteristics, including sex, sexual orientation and familial status. Based on the profiles and preferences, Roommate matches users and provides them a list of housing-seekers or available rooms meeting their criteria. Users can also search available listings based on roommate characteristics, including sex, sexual orientation and familial status.

The Fair Housing Councils of San Fernando Valley and San Diego ("FHCs") sued Roommate in federal court, alleging that the website's questions requiring disclosure of sex, sexual orientation and familial status, and its sorting, steering and matching of users based on those characteristics, violate the *Fair Housing Act*, 42 U.S.C. §3601 et seq., and the *California Fair Employment and Housing Act* ("FEHA"), Cal. Gov't Code §12955. [T]he district court held that Roommate's prompting of discriminatory preferences from users, matching users based on that information and publishing these preferences violated the FHA and FEHA, and enjoined Roommate from those activities. Roommate appeals the grant of summary judgment and permanent injunction.

If the FHA extends to shared living situations, it's quite clear that what Roommate does amounts to a violation. The pivotal question is whether the FHA applies to roommates.

I

The FHA prohibits discrimination on the basis of "race, color, religion, sex, familial status, or national origin" in the "sale or rental *of a dwelling*." 42 U.S.C. §3604(b) (emphasis added). The FHA also makes it illegal to

> make, print, or publish, or cause to be made, printed, or published any notice, statement, or advertisement, with respect to the sale or rental *of a dwelling* that indicates any preference, limitation, or discrimination based on race, color, religion, sex, handicap, familial status, or national origin, or an intention to make any such preference, limitation, or discrimination.

Id. §3604(c) (emphasis added). The reach of the statute turns on the meaning of "dwelling."

The FHA defines "dwelling" as "any building, structure, or portion thereof which is occupied as, or designed or intended for occupancy as, a residence by one or more families." *Id.* §3602(b). A dwelling is thus a living unit designed or intended for occupancy by a family, meaning that it ordinarily has the elements generally associated with a family residence: sleeping spaces, bathroom and kitchen facilities, and common areas, such as living rooms, dens and hallways.

It would be difficult, though not impossible, to divide a single-family house or apartment into separate "dwellings" for purposes of the statute. Is a "dwelling" a bedroom plus a right to access common areas? What if roommates share a bedroom? Could a "dwelling" be a bottom bunk and half an armoire? It makes practical sense to interpret "dwelling" as an independent living unit and stop the FHA at the front door.

There's no indication that Congress intended to interfere with personal relationships *inside* the home. Congress wanted to address the problem of landlords discriminating in the sale and rental of housing, which deprived protected classes of housing opportunities. But a business transaction between a tenant and landlord is quite different from an arrangement between two people sharing the same living space. We seriously doubt Congress meant the FHA to apply to the latter. Consider, for example, the FHA's prohibition against sex discrimination. Could Congress, in the 1960s, really have meant that women must accept men as roommates? Telling women they may not lawfully exclude men from the list of acceptable roommates would be controversial today; it would have been scandalous in the 1960s.

While it's possible to read dwelling to mean sub-parts of a home or an apartment, doing so leads to awkward results. And applying the FHA to the selection of roommates almost certainly leads to results that defy mores prevalent when the statute was passed. Nonetheless, this interpretation is not wholly implausible and we would normally consider adopting it, given that the FHA is a remedial statute that we construe broadly. Therefore, we turn to constitutional concerns, which provide strong countervailing considerations.

II

The Supreme Court has recognized that "the freedom to enter into and carry on certain intimate or private relationships is a fundamental element of liberty protected by the *Bill of Rights*." *Bd. of Dirs. of Rotary Int'l v. Rotary Club of Duarte*, 481 U.S. 537, 545 (1987). "[C]hoices to enter into and maintain certain intimate human relationships must be secured against undue intrusion by the State because of the role of such relationships in safeguarding the individual freedom that is central to our constitutional scheme." *Roberts v. U.S. Jaycees*, 468 U.S. 609, 617-18 (1984). Courts have extended the right of intimate association to marriage, child bearing, child rearing and cohabitation with relatives. *Id.* While the right protects only "highly personal relationships," *IDK, Inc. v. Clark Cnty.*, 836 F.2d 1185, 1193 (9th Cir. 1988) (quoting *Roberts*, 468 U.S. at 618), the right isn't restricted exclusively to family, *Bd. of Dirs. of Rotary Int'l*, 481 U.S. at 545. The right to association also implies a right *not* to associate. *Roberts*, 428 U.S. at 623.

To determine whether a particular relationship is protected by the right to intimate association we look to "size, purpose, selectivity, and whether others are excluded from critical aspects of the relationship." *Bd. of Dirs. of Rotary Int'l*, 481 U.S. at 546. The roommate relationship easily qualifies: People generally have very few roommates; they are selective in choosing roommates; and non-roommates are excluded from the critical aspects of the relationship, such as using the living spaces. Aside from immediate family or a romantic partner, it's hard to imagine a relationship more intimate than that between roommates, who share living rooms, dining rooms, kitchens, bathrooms, even bedrooms.

Because of a roommate's unfettered access to the home, choosing a roommate implicates significant privacy and safety considerations. The home is the center of our private lives. Roommates note our comings and goings, observe whom we bring back at night, hear what songs we sing in the shower, see us in various stages of undress and learn intimate details most of us prefer to keep private. Roommates also have access to our physical belongings and to our person. As the Supreme Court recognized, "[w]e are at our most vulnerable when we are asleep because we cannot monitor our own safety or the security of our belongings." *Minnesota v. Olson*, 495 U.S. 91, 99 (1990). Taking on a roommate means giving him full access to the space where we are most vulnerable.

Equally important, we are fully exposed to a roommate's belongings, activities, habits, proclivities and way of life. This could include matter we find offensive (pornography, religious materials, political propaganda); dangerous (tobacco, drugs, firearms); annoying (jazz, perfume, frequent overnight visitors, furry pets); habits that are incompatible with our lifestyle (early risers, messy cooks, bathroom hogs, clothing borrowers). When you invite others to share your living quarters, you risk becoming a suspect in whatever illegal activities they engage in.

Government regulation of an individual's ability to pick a roommate thus intrudes into the home, which "is entitled to special protection as the center of the private lives of our people." *Minnesota v. Carter*, 525 U.S. 83, 99 (1998) (Kennedy, J., concurring). "Liberty protects the person from unwarranted government intrusions into a dwelling or other private places. In our tradition the State is not omnipresent in the home." *Lawrence v. Texas*, 539 U.S. 558, 562 (2003). Holding that the FHA applies inside a home or apartment would allow the government to restrict our ability to choose roommates compatible with our lifestyles. This would be a serious invasion of privacy, autonomy and security.

For example, women will often look for female roommates because of modesty or security concerns. As roommates often share bathrooms and common areas, a girl may not want to walk around in her towel in front of a boy. She might also worry about unwanted sexual advances or becoming romantically involved with someone she must count on to pay the rent.

An orthodox Jew may want a roommate with similar beliefs and dietary restrictions, so he won't have to worry about finding honey-baked ham in the refrigerator next to the potato latkes. Non-Jewish roommates may not understand or faithfully follow all of the culinary rules, like the use of different silverware for dairy and meat products, or the prohibition against warming non-kosher food in a kosher microwave. Taking away the ability to choose roommates with similar dietary restrictions and religious convictions will substantially burden the observant Jew's ability to live his life and practice his religion faithfully. The same is true of individuals of other faiths that call for dietary restrictions or rituals inside the home.

The U.S. Department of Housing and Urban Development recently dismissed a complaint against a young woman for advertising, "I am looking for a female christian roommate," on her church bulletin board. In its Determination of No Reasonable Cause, HUD explained that "in light of the facts provided and after assessing the unique context of the advertisement and the roommate relationship involved . . . the Department defers to Constitutional considerations in reaching its conclusions." *Fair Hous. Ctr. of W. Mich. v. Tricia*, No. 05-10-1738-8 (Oct. 28, 2010) (Determination of No Reasonable Cause).

It's a "well-established principle that statutes will be interpreted to avoid constitutional difficulties." *Frisby v. Schultz*, 487 U.S. 474, 483 (1988). "[W]here an otherwise acceptable construction of a statute would raise serious constitutional problems, the Court will construe the statute to avoid such problems unless such construction is plainly contrary to the intent of Congress." *Pub. Citizen v. U.S. Dep't of Justice*, 491 U.S. 440, 466 (1989) (internal quotation marks omitted). Because the FHA can reasonably be read either to include or exclude shared living arrangements, we can and must choose the construction that avoids raising constitutional concerns. Reading "dwelling" to mean an independent housing unit is a fair interpretation of the text and consistent with congressional intent. Because the construction of "dwelling" to include shared living units raises substantial constitutional concerns, we adopt the narrower construction that excludes roommate selection from the reach of the FHA.

III

Because we find that the FHA doesn't apply to the sharing of living units, it follows that it's not unlawful to discriminate in selecting a roommate. As the underlying conduct is not unlawful, Roommate's facilitation of discriminatory roommate searches does not violate the FHA.

Notes and Questions

1. What did Congress mean by "dwelling"? The U.S. Department of Housing and Urban Development (HUD), the agency Congress tasked with interpreting the *Fair Housing Act,* has long taken the position that it does not violate the advertising provision of the act, 42 U.S.C. §3604(c), to express a preference with regard to *sex* if one is not advertising for a "separate unit." HUD apparently continues to believe that expressed preferences will violate §3604(c) if based on other categories such as race, religion, national origin, disability, or familial status. Memorandum from Roberta Achtenberg, Assistant Secy. for Fair Hous. & Equal Opportunity, U.S. Dept. of Hous. & Urban Dev., to Fair Hous. & Equal Opportunity Dirs. & Staff (Jan. 9, 1995), *available at http://portal.hud.gov/hudportal/documents/hud doc?id=DOC_11870.pdf.*

The Ninth Circuit in *Roommate.com* went further, holding that the statute does not apply at all to roommate situations because of the statute's definition of the term "dwelling." Do you find Chief Judge Kozinski's reasoning persuasive? The court does not address the portion of the statutory definition of dwelling that applies the act to "any . . . portion" of a building. Does the opinion make that language irrelevant?

In the portion of the *Roommate.com* decision addressing constitutional avoidance, the two examples that Chief Judge Kozinski gave involve gender and religion. Would the same concerns hold if someone refused to accept a paying roommate — as a tenant, subtenant, or co-tenant — because of that person's race? Does the text of the *Fair Housing Act* provide any reason to distinguish race from other protected categories?

Other types of living arrangements have also raised questions about the scope of the term "dwelling" in the *Fair Housing Act.* In *Lakeside Resort Enterprises, LP v. Board of Supervisors of Palmyra Township,* 455 F.3d 154 (3d Cir. 2006), the court considered whether a drug- and alcohol-treatment facility constituted a "dwelling" subject to the act. Citing the reference to a dwelling as including a place "intended for occupancy as . . . a residence," §3602(b), the court concluded that the issue turns on "whether the facility is intended or designed for occupants who intend to remain" there for "any significant period of time," and would view the residence "as a place to return to." 455 F.3d. at 158. Although the residents would on average stay only for slightly more than two weeks, because the facility was intended for longer stays, and the residents treated it like a home, the court found that the act applied. *Id.* at 160. Similar controversies have arisen over homeless shelters. *Compare Intermountain Fair Housing Council v. Boise Rescue Mission Ministries*, 717 F. Supp. 2d 1101 (D. Idaho 2010) (homeless shelter not a "dwelling" under §3602(b)), *with Boykin v. Gray*, 895 F. Supp. 2d 199 (D.D.C. 2012) (homeless shelter is covered by the act).

What indications are there in the text of the statute about how broadly or narrowly Congress intended the term "dwelling" to be interpreted? If a constitutionally based right of intimate association is one reason to read "dwelling" narrowly, as the court in *Roommate.com* found, what associational interests might suggest a *broader* reading of the *Fair Housing Act*?

2. Intimate association and freedom of speech. The FHA includes a number of exemptions, including for "rooms or units in dwellings containing living quarters occupied or intended to be occupied by no more than four families living independently of each other, if the owner actually maintains and occupies one of such living quarters as his residence." §3603(b)(2). This exemption, however, does not apply to §3604(c)'s restrictions on discriminatory advertisements and other statements. As a result, §3604(c) has a broader application than the remaining substantive prohibitions in §3604.

In *Chicago Lawyers' Committee for Civil Rights Under the Law, Inc. v. Craigslist, Inc.*, 519 F.3d 666 (7th Cir. 2008), Judge Easterbrook noted that many people who advertise housing for sale or rent qualify for the exemptions in §3603(b). To Judge Easterbrook, the fact that §3604(c) continues to apply independently to create liability in these circumstances raises free speech concerns. *Id.* at 668 ("[A]ny rule that forbids truthful advertising of a transaction that would be substantively lawful encounters serious problems under the first amendment"). *Compare, e.g., United States v. Space Hunters, Inc.*, 429 F.3d 416, 425 (2d Cir. 2005) (finding housing information provider's statements that violated §3604(c) to be commercial speech not protected by the first amendment).

Why do you think the *Fair Housing Act* covers a broader scope of communications in §3604(c) than its direct provisions on sale or rental of housing? Do you agree with Judge Easterbrook that the act's regulation of discriminatory speech as an independent basis for liability presents a conflict with the first amendment? *See generally* Robert G. Schwemm, *Discriminatory Housing Statements and Section 3604(c): A New Look at the Fair Housing Act's Most Intriguing Provision*, 29 Fordham Urb. L.J. 187 (2001).

3. The FHA and on-line advertising. In many parts of the country, housing transactions are increasingly advertised on the Internet. These on-line advertisements, just as with statements posted on physical bulletin boards, are generally covered by §3604(c), even if the underlying transaction falls within the FHA's exemption in §3603(b). A review of roughly 10,000 Craigslist postings in 10 cities found that "a significant number of on-line housing ads — roughly several hundred on any given day — violate [§3604(c)]." Rigel C. Oliveri, *Discriminatory Housing Advertisements On-Line: Lessons from Craigslist*, 43 Ind. L. Rev. 1125, 1127-1128 (2010). This study found that the vast majority of the postings were for roommates, and expressed preferences on the basis of familial status. Does *Roommate.com* change this conclusion?

If a newspaper prints a discriminatory advertisement from a third party, the paper is potentially liable under §3604(c). For on-line advertising, however, the *Communications Decency Act of 1996* (CDA), 47 U.S.C. §230(c)(1), states that "[n]o provider or user of an interactive computer service shall be treated as the publisher or speaker of any information provided by another information content provider." Thus, Craigslist was not liable under §3604(c) for discriminatory roommate advertisements posted on its web site. *Chicago Lawyers' Committee, supra.* The CDA's exemption does not to apply where an on-line service provider is itself "responsible, in whole or in part for the creation or development" of the discriminatory information, 47 U.S.C. §230(f)(3). In an earlier round of the *Roommate.com* case, the company was found not to come within this exception when it created questionnaires that asked users to identify themselves by sex, sexual orientation, and marital status and to express their preferences in those categories. *Fair Housing Council of San Fernando Valley v. Roommates.com, L.L.C.*, 521 F.3d 1157 (9th Cir. 2008). Moreover, the company used that information to create profiles that provided the users' relevant information and preferences, and it channeled searches and sent e-mails based on the discriminatory preferences its forms had elicited. *Id.*

4. Subtle signaling. Advertisements that limit housing to whites clearly violate §3604(c). Can a housing provider *indirectly* demonstrate an interest in customers of a certain race or other protected class?

In *Ragin v. New York Times Co.*, 923 F.2d 995 (2d Cir. 1991), the court held that a newspaper's practice of publishing real estate advertisements almost always showing white models in a city with a significant population of African Americans and other minorities might violate the *Fair Housing Act* by showing a discriminatory preference. The district court held that the ultimate issue for the fact finder was whether "[t]o an ordinary reader the natural interpretation of the advertisements published [in the newspaper] is that they indicate a racial preference in the acceptance of tenants." In affirming the lower court's opinion, the Second Circuit explained, in an opinion by Judge Ralph Winter:

> Section 3604 (c) states in pertinent part that it is unlawful: "To . . . publish . . . any . . . advertisement, with respect to the sale or rental of a dwelling that indicates any preference . . . based on race." Beginning our analysis with the statutory language, the first critical word is the verb "indicates." Giving that word its common meaning, we read the statute to be violated if an ad for housing suggests to an ordinary reader that a particular race is preferred or dispreferred for the housing in question. Moreover, the statute prohibits all ads that indicate a racial preference to an ordinary reader whatever the advertiser's intent.
>
> The next question is whether and in what circumstances the use of models may convey an illegal racial message. Advertising is a make-up-your-own world in which one builds an image from scratch, selecting those portrayals that will attract targeted consumers and discarding those that will put them off. Locale, setting, actions portrayed, weather, height, weight, gender, hair color, dress, race and numerous other factors are varied as needed to convey the message intended. A soft-drink manufacturer seeking to envelop its product in an aura of good will and harmony may portray a group

> of persons of widely varying nationalities and races singing a cheerful tune on a mountaintop. A chain of fast-food retailers may use models of the principal races found in urban areas where its stores are located. Similarly, a housing complex may decide that the use of models of one race alone will maximize the number of potential consumers who respond, even though it may also discourage consumers of other races.
>
> In advertising, a conscious racial decision regarding models thus seems almost inevitable. All the statute requires is that in this make-up-your-own world the creator of an ad not make choices among models that create a suggestion of a racial preference. The deliberate inclusion of a black model where necessary to avoid such a message seems to us a far cry from the alleged practices that are at the core of the debate over quotas. If race-conscious decisions are inevitable in the make-up-your-own world of advertising, a statutory interpretation that may lead to some race-conscious decisionmaking to avoid indicating a racial preference is hardly a danger to be averted at all costs.

Id. at 999-1001.

Professor Lior Strahilevitz has argued that as direct statements of discrimination have become less common, housing providers have turned to other methods to signal racial preferences. Strahilevitz argues that providers, thwarted by civil rights laws, have developed the strategy of providing unnecessary amenities not because they are what people actually want, but rather because they send messages to prospective residents. He cites the example of golf courses as a particularly racially polarizing amenity that signals exclusion. *See* Lior Jacob Strahilevitz, *Exclusionary Amenities in Residential Communities*, 92 Va. L. Rev. 437 (2006). How should fair housing advocates respond to this kind of subtle signaling? How, if at all, should the law address it?

5. **Other prohibited communications.** The *Fair Housing Act* regulates other communications related to housing. For example, the act makes it unlawful to misrepresent the availability of housing. 42 U.S.C. §3604(d). It likewise prohibits inducing or attempting to induce people to sell or rent "by representations regarding the entry or prospective entry into the neighborhood" of people of a particular protected category. *Id.* §3604(e). This latter provision was passed to remedy the practice of "blockbusting," where brokers would try to convince white residents to sell by invoking fears about neighborhood integration.

Problems

1. You are the lawyer for a newspaper that runs housing advertisements, some of which include pictures. Your client is worried about cases holding publishers liable for publishing advertisements with only white models. Does every advertisement have to include models of different races? Formulate a general policy for the newspaper on how to handle this issue to avoid violating the *Fair Housing Act.*

2. Two men post an advertisement seeking a third roommate who will sign the lease (upon the landlord's approval). While interviewing potential roommates, they tell a recent immigrant from Mexico who applies that they do not want to live with him because of where he comes from. Are they entitled to the exemption in §3603(b)(2)?

3. An owner places an advertisement in the newspaper stating: "Shopping center in white community looking for tenants." Has the owner violated the *Fair Housing Act*?

4. Does §3604(c) apply to a Facebook posting for a roommate? A real estate broker's Twitter feed? What else might you need to know to answer this question?

5. In *Roommate.com*, Judge Kozinski discusses reasons for allowing roommates to discriminate on the basis of sex or religion. Does banning advertising of those preferences constitute as grave an intrusion on the roommates' freedom of association as banning advertising on the basis of race, national origin, disability, or familial status?

§2 INTENTIONAL DISCRIMINATION OR DISPARATE TREATMENT

§2.1 Discrimination on the Basis of Race

Asbury v. Brougham

866 F.2d 1276 (10th Cir. 1989)

Map: 7329 Troup Avenue, Kansas City, Kansas

JAMES A. PARKER, District Judge.

Plaintiff Rosalyn Asbury brought suit under 42 U.S.C. §1982[2] and the *Fair Housing Act*, 42 U.S.C. §3601 *et seq*. (FHA), claiming that the defendants refused to rent or to allow her to inspect or negotiate for the rental of an apartment or townhouse at Brougham Estates in Kansas City. Defendants Leo Brougham, individually and doing business as Brougham Estates and Brougham Management Company, and Wanda Chauvin, his employee, appeal a jury verdict awarding Asbury compensatory damages of $7,500 against them upon a finding that the defendants discriminated against her on the basis of race and/or sex. Leo Brougham appeals from the jury verdict awarding punitive damages in the amount of $50,000 solely against him.

I. Sufficiency of Evidence Supporting a Finding of Racial Discrimination in Violation of §1982 and FHA

42 U.S.C. §1982 and the FHA both prohibit discrimination on the basis of race. In order to prevail on a claim made under these statutes, plaintiff must prove a

2. Section 1982 provides: "All citizens of the United States shall have the same right, in every State and Territory, as is enjoyed by white citizens thereof to inherit, purchase, lease, sell, hold, and convey real and personal property." — EDS.

discriminatory intent. A violation occurs when race is a factor in a decision to deny a minority applicant the opportunity to rent or negotiate for a rental, but race need not be the only factor in the decision. In addition, §3604(d) of the FHA specifically prohibits dissemination of false information about the availability of housing because of a person's race. Accordingly, failure to provide a minority applicant with the same information about availability of a rental unit or the terms and conditions for rental as is provided to white "testers," results in false information being provided and is cognizable as an injury under the FHA.

A. *Asbury's Prima Facie Case Under §1982 and FHA*

The three-part burden of proof analysis established in *McDonnell Douglas Corp. v. Green*, 411 U.S. 792 (1973), a Title VII employment discrimination case, has been widely applied to FHA and §1982 claims. Under the *McDonnell Douglas* analysis, plaintiff first must come forward with proof of a *prima facie* case of discrimination. Second, if plaintiff proves a *prima facie* case, the burden shifts to defendants to produce evidence that the refusal to rent or negotiate for a rental was motivated by legitimate, non-racial considerations. Third, once defendants by evidence articulate non-discriminatory reasons, the burden shifts back to plaintiff to show that the proffered reasons were pretextual.

The proof necessary to establish a *prima facie* case under the FHA also establishes a *prima facie* case of racial discrimination under §1982. In order to establish her *prima facie* case, plaintiff had to prove that:

(1) she is a member of a racial minority;
(2) she applied for and was qualified to rent an apartment or townhouse in Brougham Estates;
(3) she was denied the opportunity to rent or to inspect or negotiate for the rental of a townhouse or apartment; and
(4) the housing opportunity remained available.

A review of the evidence in this case shows that plaintiff established her *prima facie* case. Defendants stipulated that Asbury is black. Plaintiff testified that on February 23, 1984, she went to Brougham Estates with her daughter to obtain rental housing. At the rental office at Brougham Estates, Asbury encountered Wanda Chauvin, the manager, and explained to Chauvin that she was being transferred to Kansas City and needed to rent housing. Asbury told Chauvin that she needed to secure housing by the middle of March or the beginning of April. In response, Chauvin said there were no vacancies, but told Asbury she could call back at a later time to check on availability. Chauvin provided no information concerning availability of rental units that would assist Asbury in her efforts to rent an apartment or townhouse at Brougham Estates. Asbury asked for the opportunity to fill out an application, but Chauvin did not give her an application, again stating that there were no vacancies and that she kept no waiting list. Asbury also requested floor plans or the opportunity to view a model unit, and Chauvin refused. Instead, Chauvin suggested Asbury inquire at the Westminister Apartments, an apartment complex housing mostly black families. Although Chauvin did not ask Asbury about her qualifications, plaintiff was employed with the Federal Aviation Authority at a salary of $37,599. Based on her salary, defendants concede that Asbury would likely be qualified to rent an apartment or townhouse at Brougham Estates.

Although there was a conflict in the evidence as to the availability of housing at the time Asbury attempted to inspect and negotiate for rental, there was abundant evidence from which the jury could find that housing was available. Defendants testified that families with a child are housed exclusively in the townhouses at Brougham Estates, and that there were no townhouses available on the date Asbury inquired. Asbury introduced evidence suggesting that both apartments and townhouses were available and, in addition, that exceptions previously had been created to allow children to reside in the apartments.

On February 24, 1984, the day after Asbury inquired about renting, Asbury's sister-in-law, Linda Robinson, who is white, called to inquire about the availability of two-bedroom apartments. The woman who answered the telephone identified herself as "Wanda" and invited Robinson to come to Brougham Estates to view the apartments. The following day, February 25, 1984, Robinson went to the rental office at Brougham Estates and met with Wanda Chauvin. Chauvin provided Robinson with floor plans of available one- and two-bedroom apartments at Brougham Estates. Robinson specifically asked Chauvin about rental to families with children, and Chauvin did not tell Robinson that children were restricted to the townhouse units. Robinson accompanied Chauvin to inspect a model unit and several available two-bedroom apartments. Upon inquiry by Robinson, Chauvin indicated that the apartments were available immediately and offered to hold an apartment for her until the next week.

Asbury also provided evidence indicating that townhouses were available for rent. On February 1, 1984, Daniel McMenay, a white male, notified Brougham Estates that he intended to vacate his townhouse. On April 4, 1984, Brougham Estates rented the townhouse vacated by McMenay to John Shuminski, a white male. On March 10, 1984, Randall Hockett, a white male, also rented a townhouse at Brougham Estates. In addition, Asbury provided computer data sheets generated by Brougham Estates which indicated that a third townhouse was unoccupied at the time of her inquiry on February 23, 1984 and remained vacant as of April 10, 1984. There was also evidence that a building which included townhouse units had been closed for the winter but would be available for rent beginning in the spring. On February 22, 1984, one day prior to Asbury's inquiry into vacancies, James Vance, a white male, paid a deposit for a townhouse which he occupied when the building opened on April 10, 1984. Since Asbury testified that she told Chauvin she did not need to occupy a rental unit until the beginning of April, the jury could have concluded that at least one of the townhouses which was subsequently rented to the white males was available at the time Asbury inquired. Although defendants took the position at trial that the townhouses were closed or out of order for repair and therefore not available to rent, the jury was free to accept the evidence of availability presented by the plaintiff.

Since Asbury met her burden of proving a *prima facie* case of racial discrimination, the burden shifted to defendants to prove a legitimate, non-discriminatory reason for denial of housing.

B. Failure of Proof of Legitimate, Non-Discriminatory Reason for Rejection

Defendants claimed their legitimate, non-discriminatory reasons for rejecting Asbury arose out of the policies at Brougham Estates that families with one child could rent townhouses but not apartments, and that families with more than one child were not permitted to move into Brougham Estates. Defendants further argued that they made no exceptions to these rules. Defendants contended that in accordance with these rental policies, no appropriate housing was available for Asbury when she inquired. However, plaintiff introduced evidence indicating that exceptions to these rules had been made on several occasions; families with children had rented apartments, and families with more than one child had been permitted to move into Brougham Estates. Asbury was not provided information about the terms and conditions that gave rise to an exception to the policy concerning children being restricted to the townhouses. The jury could therefore find that defendants' reasons for denying Asbury the opportunity to negotiate for rental were not legitimate and non-discriminatory.

Defendants also argue that evidence of a high percentage of minority occupancy in Brougham Estates conclusively rebuts the claim of intentional racial discrimination. Although such statistical data is relevant to rebutting a claim of discrimination, statistical data is not dispositive of a claim of intentional discrimination. Moreover, there was other evidence from which the jury could have determined that race was a motivating factor in defendants' decision to refuse to negotiate with Asbury for a rental unit.

II. Sufficiency of Evidence Supporting Punitive Damages Award

Defendant Brougham contends that there was insufficient evidence supporting the jury's award of punitive damages against him because he never met or dealt with the plaintiff, the actions of Chauvin should not be attributed to him, and he did not promulgate any discriminatory policies or procedures.

Punitive damages may be awarded against a defendant "when the defendant's conduct is shown to be motivated by evil motive or intent, or when it involves reckless or callous indifference to the federally protected rights of others." *Smith v. Wade*, 461 U.S. 30, 56 (1983). The jury has discretion to award punitive damages to punish outrageous conduct on the part of a defendant and to deter similar conduct in the future.

Plaintiff advanced two theories supporting Brougham's liability for punitive damages: (1) Brougham's own discriminatory conduct in establishing rental policies, procedures and rules; and (2) his authorization or ratification of discriminatory conduct by Chauvin, his employee. We find sufficient evidence to establish liability under either theory.

In this case, Asbury presented evidence that Leo Brougham was the managing partner of Brougham Estates and Brougham Management Company. Brougham established all policies, rules and rental procedures for Brougham Estates. Chauvin worked for Brougham who instructed her about the rental policies and procedures. Among the policies and procedures implemented by Brougham were the requirements that

Chauvin routinely and untruthfully tell people over the phone that there were no vacancies, whether or not vacancies existed, but that Chauvin then encourage the individuals to come in, inspect the premises and discuss upcoming vacancies. Brougham established the requirement of visual observation of a prospective tenant. Although a policy that prospective tenants must be visually scrutinized is not necessarily improper, under the circumstances of this case, the jury could have inferred that the policy operated to screen prospective tenants on the basis of race and that, at a minimum, Brougham was callously indifferent to this result of his policy. Indeed, this policy had given rise to several administrative complaints by single black females prior to Asbury's inquiry about a vacancy. Brougham was aware of previous claims of discriminatory practices in the rental of units at Brougham Estates.

Another policy established by Brougham was that a family with a child could occupy only a townhouse. Chauvin was advised of this policy. Brougham testified that he made no exceptions to the policy, and he testified specifically that no tenant or prospective tenant with a child could obtain permission to be excepted from the rule. Plaintiff, however, produced evidence that exceptions had been created on occasion. Those exceptions had been authorized by Brougham and had been made on an individual basis. From the evidence presented, the jury could have determined that the policies established and implemented by defendant Brougham directly fostered the discrimination which Asbury experienced, that Brougham should have been aware that this might occur, and that Brougham was recklessly or callously indifferent to it happening.

Plaintiff also offered evidence tending to prove that Brougham ratified Chauvin's actions. [After investigating, Brougham] determined [that] Asbury had only one child and therefore fit within the residential policies of Brougham Estates. Furthermore, the jury could have drawn the inference that Brougham's failure to apologize or otherwise remedy the situation, after personally investigating Asbury's claim of discrimination at Brougham Estates, was an acceptance and ratification of Chauvin's treatment of Asbury.

Having reviewed the record in this case, we find that there was substantial evidence supporting and a reasonable basis for the jury's verdict awarding both compensatory and punitive damages, and we affirm the district court's decision to deny defendants' motion for a new trial.

Notes and Questions

1. **Who is liable and standards of liability.** Although *Asbury* states that plaintiffs must prove discriminatory intent under the *Fair Housing Act*, most courts to have considered this issue as well as the U.S. Department of Housing and Urban Development (HUD) have concluded that plaintiffs may also raise claims that assert a disparate impact on the basis of a protected category. *See generally* 24 C.F.R. §§100.1-100.500 (HUD's FHA regulations).[3] **Disparate treatment** claims involve intentionally treating

3. The Supreme Court recently granted certiorari on the question whether the *Fair Housing Act* allows for claims based on disparate impact. *See* §3.2, below.

members of the protected class differently from others so as to deny particular persons housing opportunities. **Disparate impact** claims allege that a defendant's actions have a disproportionate, exclusionary effect on members of a protected group that is not justified by legitimate government or business objectives. We will consider the standards that govern claims asserting disparate impact in §3, below.

In disparate treatment cases, if a plaintiff can demonstrate to the finder of fact sufficient direct evidence of discriminatory intent, such as a statement by a defendant expressing racial animus in the context of a housing decision, then the court need not engage in the three-part framework that *Asbury* described. *See, e.g., Lindsay v. Yates*, 498 F.3d 434, 440 n.7 (6th Cir. 2007). These kinds of cases are relatively uncommon, however, so most disparate treatment claims must rely on circumstantial evidence.

For such discriminatory intent claims, *Asbury* describes the traditional elements of a *prima facie* case under the *Fair Housing Act*.[4] If the plaintiff can produce evidence of the various elements of the *prima facie* case, the burden shifts to the defendant to show a nondiscriminatory reason for the differential treatment. If the defendant fails to assert any such justification and the fact finder is persuaded that the plaintiff has proven the *prima facie* case, the plaintiff is likely to prevail. If the defendant articulates and produces evidence of nondiscriminatory reasons for its actions, the plaintiff must then show that those reasons are pretextual. If the plaintiff does so, the jury may (but is not required) to conclude that the real reason for the denial was discriminatory. What reasons did defendant articulate in *Asbury*? Are they legitimate under the current statute as amended in 1988? How did the plaintiff attempt to show that the proffered reasons were not legitimate and nondiscriminatory?

As *Asbury* demonstrates, employers are generally vicariously liable for the acts of their employees; thus landlords or real estate brokerage firms may be liable if their agents engage in discriminatory conduct. *See Holley v. Crank*, 400 F.3d 667, 674-675 (9th Cir. 2004). However, officers of corporations are not generally personally liable unless they acted as an employee or agent of the corporation to direct or approve those discriminatory practices. *Meyer v. Holley*, 537 U.S. 280 (2003).

ELEMENTS

For disparate treatment cases without direct evidence and disparate impact cases, courts often follow a three-part framework, although the specific details at each stage vary depending on the nature of the claim: Generally, a claimant must first establish a ***prima facie* case**. If so, the party charged with discriminating has the opportunity to demonstrate **legitimate nondiscriminatory reasons** for her action. Finally, the claimant has the opportunity to show that those reasons are merely a **pretext**.

2. Remedies. Under the *Fair Housing Act*, aggrieved persons may file a lawsuit in federal court for injunctive relief and for compensatory and punitive damages, 42

4. Note that this test applies only to claims based on the defendant's "refusal to sell" or "refusal to lease" to the plaintiff. A landlord who selectively takes a particular apartment off the market, refusing to rent it to anyone so as to avoid renting it to a member of a protected class, may be violating the statute on the ground that such conduct constitutes a "refusal to deal" or "otherwise make[s] unavailable or den[ies]" housing because of race. 42 U.S.C. §3604(a).

U.S.C. §3613. Originally, there had been a $1,000 limit on punitive damages, but this cap was eliminated by the *Fair Housing Amendments Act of 1988*, which also extended the statute of limitations from six months to two years.

Aggrieved persons may choose instead to file a complaint with HUD, which has the power to investigate and mediate the dispute, as well as to hear and adjudicate the complaint. If HUD has certified a state agency as competent to adjudicate fair housing disputes, HUD will often refer the complaint to that state agency rather than handle the complaint itself. *See* §3610(f). If HUD itself investigates the complaint and finds reasonable cause to believe a violation of the law has been committed, it must issue a "charge" on behalf of the aggrieved person, explaining "the facts upon which the Secretary has found reasonable cause to believe that a discriminatory housing practice has occurred." §3610.

When a charge is filed, either the complainant or the respondent may elect to have the complaint heard in federal court rather than in an administrative proceeding held by HUD through an administrative law judge (ALJ). *See* §3612(a). If this option is chosen, HUD will authorize the United States Attorney General to file the lawsuit in federal district court, which is entitled to grant both compensatory and punitive damages, as well as injunctive relief. *See* §3612(o). If no party elects to go to federal court, HUD will conduct a hearing if the complainant so desires. *See* §3612(b). The ALJ is empowered to issue injunctive relief as well as assess damages ranging from $10,000 to $50,000 based on the timing and number of prior offenses. *See* §3610(g)(3). Either the plaintiff or the defendant may appeal the ALJ's finding to federal court. *See* §3612(i).

In addition to the foregoing, the Attorney General is empowered to bring lawsuits against persons who have engaged in a "pattern or practice of resistance to the full enjoyment of any rights" granted by the act under §3614.

Are the remedies provided by the FHA adequate? Professor Robert Schwemm, one of the leading authorities on fair housing law, notes that racial discrimination by landlords "remains at alarmingly high levels." Robert G. Schwemm, *Why Do Landlords Still Discriminate (and What Can Be Done About It)?*, 40 J. Marshall L. Rev. 455, 509 (2007). *See also* Margery Austin Turner et al., U.S. Dept. of Hous. & Urban Dev., *Housing Discrimination Against Racial and Ethnic Minorities* (2013) (national discrimination study indicates that although overall discrimination against minorities has declined compared to similar studies over four decades, subtle discrimination persists, particularly in terms of the number of units shown to minority renters and home buyers). Many discrimination victims fail to report violations or pursue claims. Moreover, the delay and expense of litigation seriously undermine the deterrent value of the FHA.

In addition, a "large amount of rental discrimination against racial minorities may be the result of unconscious bias by landlords who do not see themselves as prejudiced. To change this behavior will require efforts beyond simply more rigorous enforcement of the FHA's intent-based nondiscrimination commands." *Id.* Research by cognitive psychologists has shown that many people are influenced by unconscious racial bias. *See* Michelle Wilde Anderson & Victoria C. Plaut, *Property Law: Implicit*

Bias and the Resilience of Spatial Colorlines, in *Implicit Racial Bias Across the Law* (2012); Charles R. Lawrence III, *The Id, the Ego, and Equal Protection: Reckoning with Unconscious Racism,* 39 Stan. L. Rev. 317 (1987). *See also* Jerry Kang & Mahzarin R. Banaji, *Fair Measures: A Behavioral Realist Revision of "Affirmative Action,"* 94 Cal. L. Rev. 1063, 1066 (2006) (arguing that the presence of implicit bias creates discrimination by causing merit to be mismeasured). What avenues might work to solve the problems of explicit and implicit racial bias?

3. Racial steering. Many cases brought under the *Fair Housing Act* concern claims against realtors who have engaged in "racial steering." This practice involves showing minority customers housing in certain areas and white customers housing in other areas. It also involves not telling minority customers about the availability of housing in certain areas. Such practices violate the act by "otherwise mak[ing] unavailable" housing because of race, *United States v. Mitchell,* 580 F.2d 789, 791-792 (5th Cir. 1978), and violate the express prohibition against discrimination in "real estate-related transactions" in 42 U.S.C. §3605, which prohibits discrimination by real estate brokers. Steering may also fall afoul of the act's prohibition against "mak[ing] . . . any statement . . . with respect to the sale and rental of a dwelling that indicates any preference, limitation, or discrimination" on the basis of a protected class, 42 U.S.C. §3604(c), a prohibition that includes oral statements.

4. Testers. Gathering evidence of FHA violations often involves the use of "testers." Testers are "individuals who, without an intent to rent or purchase a home or apartment, pose as renters or purchasers for the purpose of collecting evidence of unlawful steering practices." *Havens Realty Corp. v. Coleman,* 455 U.S. 363, 373 (1982). Testing is done, for example, by using one or more persons to pose as a potential buyer in seeking assistance from a realtor. The plaintiff in *Asbury* used a form of testing when her sister-in-law approached the defendant landlord and asked for housing in the same complex in which the plaintiff had been denied housing. Testers may approach a realtor who has told an African American customer that no housing is available in a certain area; if the realtor shows houses in that area to the white buyer that were not shown to the African American buyer, it may be possible to draw an inference that the realtor was discriminating against the initial buyer on account of her race. Similarly, a white tester may approach a seller to see whether the seller offers different terms than were offered to a prior potential African American purchaser.

5. Standing. Who has **standing** to bring a lawsuit under the *Fair Housing Act*? Those who are denied housing opportunities in violation of the act clearly may sue to vindicate their rights. It is also clear that the statute protects whites who are denied housing because of their association with minorities, *Littlefield v. Mack,* 750 F. Supp. 1395 (N.D. Ill. 1990) (white plaintiff was evicted from her apartment and harassed by defendant landlord because her boyfriend was African American and because they had a child), as well as minorities who are even visiting non-minority renters, *see Lane v. Cole,* 88 F. Supp. 2d 402, 406 (E.D. Pa. 2000) (black invitee who is excluded or coerced into leaving an apartment rented by a white tenant has standing). White persons are also entitled to bring an action against a realtor who engaged in racial steering on the ground that they have been denied the "right to the important social, professional, business and economic, political and aesthetic benefits of interracial associations that arise from living in integrated communities free from discriminatory housing practices." *Havens Realty Corp. v. Coleman*, 455 U.S. at 376-377. The Supreme Court also held in *Havens* that testers have standing to bring claims in federal court under the *Fair Housing Act* against realtors and sellers who have engaged in racial discrimination. Finally, the Court held that an organization devoted to promoting equal access to housing could bring a lawsuit against a realtor who engaged in steering if it could demonstrate that the defendant's steering practices caused the organization to devote extra resources to identify available housing and counteract the defendant's steering practices. *Id.* at 379.

6. Unlawful harassment and retaliation. Section 3617 of the *Fair Housing Act* makes it "unlawful to coerce, intimidate, threaten, or interfere with any person in the exercise or enjoyment of" any "right granted or protected" by the act. Harassment and retaliation claims brought under this provision "account for a significant portion of all FHA claims." Robert G. Schwemm, *Neighbor-on-Neighbor Harassment: Does the Fair Housing Act Make a Federal Case Out of It?*, 61 Case West. Res. L. Rev. 865, 865-866 (2011). Such claims can also give rise to criminal liability. *See id.* at 866 n.11 (citing *United States v. Jackson*, No. 3:10-CR-00120-KLH (W.D. La. 2010), where a defendant pled guilty to an FHA violation after placing a hangman's noose in a home's carport).

Many cases under §3617 involve harassment or intimidation by neighbors. For a period of time, the Seventh Circuit took a narrow view of §3617 (and the FHA's primary protection under §3604), following Judge Posner's opinion in *Halprin v. Prairie Single Family Homes of Dearborn Park Association*, 388 F.3d 327 (7th Cir. 2004), on the theory that the act applies to people seeking housing, not activity that occurs after acquisition. Five years later, however, the Seventh Circuit reversed course in *Bloch v. Frischholz*, 587 F.3d 771 (7th Cir. 2009) (en banc), holding that §3617 applies to interference with rights protected by the act even after someone has obtained housing. For a discussion of neighbor harassment and the role it plays in perpetuating residential segregation, *see* Jeannine Bell, *Hate Thy Neighbor: Move-in Violence and the Persistence of Residential Segregation in American Housing* (2013).

7. The *Civil Rights Act of 1866*. *Asbury* involved claims under both the *Fair Housing Act* and §1982. Section 1 of the *Civil Rights Act of 1866*, passed pursuant to the thirteenth amendment and reenacted in 1870 after passage of the fourteenth amendment, provides that "[a]ll citizens of the United States shall have the same right, in every State and Territory, as is enjoyed by white citizens thereof to inherit, purchase, lease, sell, hold, and convey real and personal property." 42 U.S.C. §1982. For more than a century, §1982 was interpreted as prohibiting states from passing statutes that deprived African Americans of the capacity to buy or lease real property. The act was interpreted, however, not to encompass discrimination by private housing providers unless mandated by state legislation. This situation changed in 1968 with *Jones v. Alfred Mayer Co.*, 392 U.S. 409 (1968), where the Supreme Court held that §1982 applied to private acts of discrimination as well as to discriminatory state action. Today almost all cases brought under the *Fair Housing Act* also allege a violation of §1982.[5]

Problem

A landlord who owns and lives in a two-story house rents the second floor as a separate apartment. She refuses to rent to an African American family. Does the family have a claim against the landlord under §1982 or is the landlord entitled to discriminate under §3603(b)(2)? What arguments can you make on both sides of this question? *See Morris v. Cizek*, 503 F.2d 1303 (7th Cir. 1974); *Gonzalez v. Rakkas*, 1995 WL 451034 (E.D.N.Y. 1995) (§1982 claim available).

§2.2 Integration and Nondiscrimination

United States v. Starrett City Associates

840 F.2d 1096 (2d Cir. 1988)

Map: (Spring Creek Towers)
1201-1310 Pennsylvania Avenue,
Brooklyn, New York

ROGER J. MINER, Circuit Judge.

Appellants [Starrett City Associates, Starrett City, Inc., and Delmar Management Company (collectively "Starrett")] constructed, own and operate "Starrett City," the largest housing development in the nation, consisting of 46 high-rise buildings containing 5,881 apartments in Brooklyn, New York.

Starrett has sought to maintain a racial distribution by apartment of 64% white, 22% black and 8% hispanic at Starrett City. Starrett claims that these racial quotas are necessary to prevent the loss of white tenants, which would transform Starrett City into a predominantly minority complex. Starrett points to the difficulty it has had in attracting an integrated applicant pool from the time Starrett City opened, despite extensive advertising and promotional efforts. Because of these purported difficulties, Starrett adopted a tenanting procedure to promote and maintain the desired racial

5. In addition, *Title VI* of the *Civil Rights Act of 1964* provides that "[n]o person in the United States shall, on the ground of race, color, or national origin, be excluded from participation in, be denied the benefits of, or be subjected to discrimination under any program or activity receiving Federal financial assistance." 42 U.S.C. §2000d. *Title VI* is narrower than the *Fair Housing Act* in the categories it protects and covers only programs and activities, including housing benefits, considered to be Federal financial assistance. However, because *Title VI* covers areas beyond housing, there are a few areas where *Title VI* may provide broader coverage than the *Fair Housing Act. See, e.g.*, April Kuehnhoff, *Holding on to Home: Preventing Eviction and Termination of Tenant-Based Subsidies for Limited English Proficiency Tenants Living in Housing Units with HUD Rental Assistance*, 17 Geo. J. on Poverty L. & Pol'y 221, 234 (2010) (noting that *Title VI*, but not the *Fair Housing Act*, has produced regulations and guidance for language access for limited English proficient groups).

balance. This procedure has resulted in relatively stable percentages of whites and minorities living at Starrett City between 1975 and the present.

The tenanting procedure requires completion of a preliminary information card stating, *inter alia*, the applicant's race or national origin, family composition, income and employment. The rental office at Starrett City receives and reviews these applications. Those that are found preliminarily eligible, based on family composition, income, employment and size of apartment sought, are placed in "the active file," in which separate records by race are maintained for apartment sizes and income levels. Applicants are told in an acknowledgement letter that no apartments are presently available, but that their applications have been placed in the active file and that they will be notified when a unit becomes available for them. When an apartment becomes available, applicants are selected from the active file for final processing, creating a processed applicant pool. As vacancies arise, applicants of a race or national origin similar to that of the departing tenants are selected from the pool and offered apartments.

In December 1979, a group of black applicants brought an action against Starrett in the United States District Court for the Eastern District of New York. Plaintiffs alleged that Starrett's tenanting procedures violated federal and state law by discriminating against them on the basis of race. The parties stipulated to a settlement in May 1984, and a consent decree was entered subsequently. The decree provided that Starrett would, depending on apartment availability, make an additional 35 units available each year for a five-year period to black and minority applicants.

The government commenced the present action against Starrett in June 1984, "to place before the [c]ourt the issue joined but left expressly unresolved" in the consent decree: the "legality of defendants' policy and practice of limiting the number of apartments available to minorities in order to maintain a prescribed degree of racial balance." The complaint alleged that Starrett, through its tenanting policies, discriminated in violation of the *Fair Housing Act*.

Starrett maintained that the tenanting procedures [were intended to] "achieve and maintain integration and were not motivated by racial animus." To support their position, appellants submitted the written testimony of three housing experts. They described the "white flight" and "tipping" phenomena, in which white residents migrate out of a community as the community becomes poor and the minority population increases, resulting in the transition to a predominantly minority community. Acknowledging that "the tipping point for a particular housing development, depending as it does on numerous factors and the uncertainties of human behavior, is difficult to predict with precision," one expert stated that the point at which tipping occurs has been estimated at from 1% to 60% minority population, but that the consensus ranged between 10% and 20%.

Title VIII of the *Civil Rights Act of 1968* ("*Fair Housing Act*" or "the Act"), 42 U.S.C. §§3601-3631 (1982), was enacted pursuant to Congress' thirteenth amendment powers, "to provide, within constitutional limitations, for fair housing throughout the United States." 42 U.S.C. §3601. Section 3604 of the statute prohibits discrimination because of race, color or national origin in the sale or rental of housing by, *inter alia*:

(1) refusing to rent or make available any dwelling, *id.* §3604(a); (2) offering discriminatory "terms, conditions or privileges" of rental, *id.* §3604(b); (3) making, printing or publishing "any notice, statement, or advertisement that indicates any preference, limitation, or discrimination based on race, color or national origin," *id.* §3604(c); and (4) representing to any person "that any dwelling is not available for rental when such dwelling is in fact so available," *id.* §3604(d).

Housing practices unlawful under Title VIII include not only those motivated by a racially discriminatory purpose, but also those that disproportionately affect minorities. Section 3604 "is designed to ensure that no one is denied the right to live where they choose for discriminatory reasons." Although "not every denial, especially a temporary denial, of low-income public housing has discriminatory impact on racial minorities" in violation of Title VIII, an action leading to discriminatory effects on the availability of housing violates the Act.

Starrett's allocation of public housing facilities on the basis of racial quotas, by denying an applicant access to a unit otherwise available solely because of race, produces a "discriminatory effect [that] could hardly be clearer," *Burney v. Hous. Auth.*, 551 F. Supp. 746, 770 (W.D. Pa. 1982).

Both Starrett and the government cite to the legislative history of the *Fair Housing Act* in support of their positions. This history consists solely of statements from the floor of Congress. These statements reveal "that at the time that Title VIII was enacted, Congress believed that strict adherence to the anti-discrimination provisions of the [A]ct" would eliminate "racially discriminatory housing practices [and] ultimately would result in residential integration." *Burney*, 551 F. Supp. at 769. Thus, Congress saw the antidiscrimination policy as the means to effect the antisegregation-integration policy. While quotas promote Title VIII's integration policy, they contravene its antidiscrimination policy, bringing the dual goals of the Act into conflict. The legislative history provides no further guidance for resolving this conflict.

We therefore look to analogous provisions of federal law enacted to prohibit segregation and discrimination as guides in determining to what extent racial criteria may be used to maintain integration.

Although any racial classification is presumptively discriminatory, a race-conscious affirmative action plan does not necessarily violate federal constitutional or statutory provisions. However, a race-conscious plan cannot be "ageless in reach into the past, and timeless in ability to affect the future." *Wygant v. Jackson Bd. of Educ.*, 476 U.S. 267 (1986) (plurality opinion). A plan employing racial distinctions must be temporary in nature with a defined goal as its termination point. Moreover, we observe that societal discrimination alone seems "insufficient and over expansive" as the basis for adopting so-called "benign" practices with discriminatory effects "that work against innocent people," *Wygant*, 476 U.S. at 276, in the drastic and burdensome way that rigid racial quotas do. Furthermore, the use of quotas generally should be based on some history of racial discrimination or imbalance within the entity seeking to employ them. Finally, measures designed to increase or ensure minority participation, such as "access" quotas, have generally been upheld. However, programs designed to maintain integration by limiting minority participation, such as ceiling quotas, are of doubtful validity, because they "single[] out those least well represented in the political process to bear the brunt of a benign program," *Fullilove* [*v. Klutznick*, 448 U.S. 448, 519 (1980)] (Marshall, J., concurring).

Starrett's use of ceiling quotas to maintain integration at Starrett City lacks each of these characteristics. First, Starrett City's practices have only the goal of integration maintenance. The quotas already have been in effect for ten years. Appellants predict that their race-conscious tenanting practices must continue for at least fifteen more years, but fail to explain adequately how that approximation was reached. In any event, these practices are far from temporary. Since the goal of integration maintenance is purportedly threatened by the potential for "white flight" on a continuing basis, no definite termination date for Starrett's quotas is perceivable. Second, appellants do not assert, and there is no evidence to show, the existence of prior racial discrimination or discriminatory imbalance adversely affecting whites within Starrett City or appellants' other complexes. On the contrary, Starrett City was initiated as an integrated complex, and Starrett's avowed purpose for employing race-based tenanting practices is to maintain that initial integration. Finally, Starrett's quotas do not provide minorities with access to Starrett City, but rather act as a ceiling to their access. Thus, the impact of appellants' practices falls squarely on minorities, for whom Title VIII was intended to open up housing opportunities. Starrett claims that its use of quotas serves to keep the numbers of minorities entering Starrett City low enough to avoid setting off a wave of "white flight." Although the "white flight" phenomenon may be a factor "take[n] into account in the integration equation," it cannot serve to justify attempts to maintain integration at Starrett City through inflexible racial quotas that are neither temporary in nature nor used to remedy past racial discrimination or imbalance within the complex.

We do not intend to imply that race is always an inappropriate consideration under Title VIII in efforts to promote integrated housing. We hold only that Title VIII does not allow appellants to use rigid racial quotas of indefinite duration to maintain a fixed level of integration at Starrett City by restricting minority access to scarce and desirable rental accommodations otherwise available to them. We therefore affirm the judgment of the district court.

JON O. NEWMAN, Circuit Judge, dissenting.

Though the terms of the statute literally encompass the defendants' actions, the statute was never intended to apply to such actions. This statute was intended to bar perpetuation of segregation. To apply it to bar maintenance of integration is precisely contrary to the congressional policy "to provide, within constitutional limitations, for fair housing throughout the United States." 42 U.S.C. §3601.

We have been wisely cautioned by Learned Hand that "[t]here is no surer way to misread a document than to read it literally." That aphorism is not always true with respect to statutes, whose text is always the starting point for analysis and sometimes the ending point. But literalism is not always the appropriate approach even with statutes, as the Supreme Court long ago recognized: "It is a familiar rule, that a thing may be within the letter of the statute and yet not within the statute, because not within its spirit, nor within the intent of its makers."

Title VIII bars discriminatory housing practices in order to end segregated housing. Starrett City is not promoting segregated housing. On the contrary, it is maintaining integrated housing. It is surely not within the spirit of the *Fair Housing Act* to enlist the Act to bar integrated housing. A law enacted to enhance the opportunity for people of all races to live next to each other should not be interpreted to prevent a landlord from maintaining one of the most successful integrated housing projects in America.

Respected civil rights advocates like the noted psychologist, Dr. Kenneth Clark [support Starrett City's policy]. In the words of Dr. Clark: "[I]t would be a tragedy of the highest magnitude if this litigation were to lead to the destruction of one of the model integrated communities in the United States."

Because the *Fair Housing Act* does not require this tragedy to occur, I respectfully dissent.

Notes and Questions

1. **Integration as a goal of the *Fair Housing Act*.** One goal of the proponents of the *Fair Housing Act* was to achieve "truly integrated and balanced living patterns," 114 Cong. Rec. 3422 (1968) (statement of Senator Mondale), at a time of increasing concern about racial segregation. The act expressed this goal not only through its non-discrimination provisions, but also through a broad mandate to federal agencies, and more importantly the state and local governments that the federal government funds through its programs, to take affirmative steps to respond to the legacy of segregation. 42 U.S.C. §3608(e)(5) (HUD must administer its programs and activities "in a manner affirmatively to further the policies of [the *Fair Housing Act*]"); §3608(d) (same for other federal agencies); U.S. Dept. of Hous. & Urban Dev., *Fair Housing Planning Guide*, Vol. 1, at 1-1 to 1-3 (describing planning tools to implement the "affirmatively furthering" obligation to foster inclusive communities). For an excellent discussion of these mandates and similar obligations in other civil rights statutes, *see* Olatunde C.A. Johnson, *Beyond the Private Attorney General: Equality Directives in American Law*, 87 N.Y.U. L. Rev. 1339 (2012).[6]

2. **Conflicts between integration and nondiscrimination.** *Starrett City* brings to the surface the possible conflict between the *Fair Housing Act*'s goal of integration and the act's nondiscrimination mandate. The dissenting opinion in *Starrett City* cites Dr. Kenneth Clark in support of the idea of allowing the use of racial quotas to prevent "tipping" and thereby to promote the development of integrated communities. Dr. Clark's testimony provided the factual basis for the ruling in *Brown v. Board of Education*, 347 U.S. 483 (1954), which focused on the psychological harm that segregated

---

6. This "affirmatively furthering fair housing" mandate has been at issue in recent litigation against Westchester County, New York. *See United States ex rel. Anti-Discrimination Center of Metro New York, Inc. v. Westchester County*, 712 F.3d 761 (2d Cir. 2013).

schools inflicted on African American children. Another noted scholar, Professor Derrick Bell, has criticized the use of such quotas. Bell notes that it is wrong for African American citizens to be denied housing they would otherwise get simply because of white prejudice. In effect, when an exclusionary quota is used to prevent tipping, the number of housing units available to African Americans is measured by the extent of white prejudice in the housing complex; the more prejudice, the lower the tipping level and the fewer the units available to African American purchasers or renters. Bell argues that "[a] so-called benign housing quota seems invidious to the blacks excluded by its operation. They are no less victims of housing bias than are those excluded from neighborhoods by restrictive covenants." Derrick Bell, *And We Are Not Saved: The Elusive Quest for Racial Justice* 153 (1989).

Problems

1. Your client is a real estate broker with the following questions.

a. The broker tells you that, although she has no illegitimate racial animus, her customers do. If she shows potential buyers houses that she knows sellers will refuse to sell to them because of the buyer's race or ethnicity, she is wasting her time. Her competitors do not do this, and it simply costs too much to pursue sales that are not going to happen. If the owners who engage her services ask her not to show their houses to members of a particular race, and she complies with this request, has she violated the *Fair Housing Act*?

b. A buyer expresses a preference for living in an area that is predominantly white and asks the broker to explain the local racial balance in different neighborhoods. Can the broker answer this question?

c. A buyer wants to live in an "integrated" community. Can the broker give the buyer information about which neighborhoods are "integrated"? *See Hannah v. Sibcy Cline Realtors*, 769 N.E.2d 876 (Ohio Ct. App. 2001) (broker has no duty to answer questions about the racial makeup of a community when a mother wanted to live in a racially integrated community so that her children would not be the only African American children in the school, noting that some courts have held that a broker who answers such a question may be liable for unlawful racial steering, while other courts have held that a broker has not engaged in steering when the racial information is provided in response to a buyer's question). *But cf. Village of Bellwood v. Dwivedi*, 895 F.2d 1521, 1529-1531 (7th Cir. 1990) ("The statute does not require a broker to endeavor to make his customers better people by withholding information that they request about the racial composition of the communities in which the broker sells houses. It does not impose liability for failing to promote integration, or for failing to coordinate individual integrative acts that have an aggregate resegregative effect. If the broker treats all his customers the same, regardless of race, he is not liable.").

2. Can a landlord in an area dominated by African Americans actively seek white tenants to move into the complex as a means of promoting integration?

§2.3 Sex Discrimination: Sexual Harassment

Quigley v. Winter

598 F.3d 938 (8th Cir. 2010)

WILLIAM JAY RILEY, Circuit Judge.

[Dale] Winter owned more than twenty rental homes in Sioux City, Iowa. Many of Winter's tenants were low-income women who received Section 8 housing vouchers (housing vouchers) from the Sioux City Housing Authority (SCHA) to help pay their rent. In 2000, [Jaymie] Quigley, along with her then-husband and her four children, rented a home from Winter. Quigley used a housing voucher to pay her rent.

In 2002, Quigley informed Winter she was eligible to move into a larger home. Winter drove Quigley in his car to one of Winter's other properties. Quigley inspected the property, and when she returned to the car, Winter rubbed his hand down Quigley's arm and said, "[W]ell, how do you like it?" Quigley recalled this incident made her feel "[s]cared" and "yucky." Quigley, her boyfriend, and her children moved into a different rental property owned by Winter, using a housing voucher to pay the rent.

In 2004, Quigley's boyfriend moved to Louisiana to visit his ill father. After Quigley's boyfriend moved out of the house, Winter behaved inappropriately toward Quigley on several other occasions. First, Quigley learned from a neighbor that Winter had been inside Quigley's house without prior notice when Quigley was not at home. When Quigley went to her bedroom, she noticed her housecoat, which had been hanging on the back of the bedroom door when she left, was now lying on her bed. Quigley confronted Winter about entering the home without giving prior notice, and Winter claimed he had to replace the screen on Quigley's bedroom window. Quigley's screen was not damaged and had not been replaced.

One evening, Winter came to inspect Quigley's house while she was making dinner for her children. On that occasion, Winter stood very close to Quigley and rubbed his genital area. Another time, Winter came to Quigley's house for an inspection at 9:30 or 10:00 in the evening without giving Quigley prior notice. Quigley's fourteen year-old sister was staying the night with her, and they were in their pajamas getting ready for bed. While conducting his inspection, Winter followed Quigley and her sister into a bedroom and then a bathroom, which made them feel uncomfortable. Quigley and her sister were watching television, and Winter lay down on Quigley's sectional couch after he completed the inspection. Winter stayed on the couch for five or ten minutes until Quigley said, "Hey, Dale, we're going to bed." Quigley had to tell Winter to leave "at least three times" before he left. Quigley also reported receiving phone calls from Winter at inappropriate times, sometimes as late as 2:30 or 3:00 in the morning. Winter sounded intoxicated when he called, and the phone calls made Quigley feel scared and worried about protecting her children and younger sister.

Quigley wanted to move out of the house because of Winter's conduct, but she would have lost her housing voucher if she broke the lease. Quigley met with her SCHA worker and reported Winter's inappropriate actions. Quigley asked if she could change the locks on her rental home, but the housing worker told her she could not change the locks unless she gave Winter a key. The housing worker told Quigley she could get out of the lease without losing her housing voucher if Winter agreed to rescind the lease. When Quigley asked Winter to release her from the lease, Winter refused. Thereafter, Quigley changed the locks on her door without giving Winter a key.

About a month and a half before Quigley's lease ended, Winter showed up at her house while Quigley, her sister, and Quigley's friend were outside lying in the sun. Quigley approached Winter's vehicle and inquired whether she would be getting her deposit back. Winter fluttered his hand against Quigley's stomach and said, "My eagle eyes have not seen everything yet." Winter followed Quigley to the porch. Quigley observed Winter staring at Quigley's sister's chest. Quigley's sister was wearing shorts and a sport bra, so Quigley told her sister to "go get something on." Winter said to Quigley's sister, "You're really mature. How old are you?" When Quigley said her sister was "only 14," Winter said, "Well, she looks a lot more mature than you." Quigley's friend went to her car to get a cigarette, and Winter noticed the friend had a scar on her back. Winter traced the scar with his finger, without consent, pulling the friend's pants downward to see where the scar ended. Quigley moved out of the rental home, and Winter did not return her deposit.

Quigley filed a complaint with the Sioux City Human Rights Commission (SCHRC). The investigator who handled Quigley's complaint testified other single, female tenants of Winter's who were receiving housing assistance, corroborated Quigley's claims.

In June 2006, Quigley filed a complaint against Winter in the district court, alleging sexual harassment; sex discrimination; and coercion, intimidation, threats, and interference with Quigley's rights, in violation of the [*Fair Housing Act*] and the [*Iowa Civil Rights Act*]. Quigley also asserted a breach of contract claim against Winter based upon Winter's failure to return Quigley's deposit. Winter brought a breach of contract counterclaim against Quigley, insisting Quigley owed him unpaid rent and failed to leave the rental home "in a clean and satisfactory condition." The jury found in favor of Quigley, and against Winter, on Winter's counterclaim and each of Quigley's claims, and awarded Quigley $13,685.00 in compensatory damages for the housing claims, $400.00 for Quigley's breach of contract claim, and $250,000.00 in punitive damages. Following a hearing on [subsequent] motions, the district court entered an order reducing the award of punitive damages from $250,000.00 to $20,527.50.

Hostile Housing Environment Created by Sexual Harassment

As a preliminary matter, Winter questions whether a claim for hostile housing environment created by sexual harassment is actionable under the FHA. We conclude it is. *See Neudecker v. Boisclair Corp.*, 351 F.3d 361, 364 (8th Cir. 2003) (recognizing a cause of action under the FHA for hostile housing environment created by disability harassment and citing, with approval, cases from other jurisdictions recognizing an FHA claim for hostile housing environment created by sexual harassment); *see also DiCenso v. Cisneros*, 96 F.3d 1004, 1008 (7th Cir. 1996) (recognizing an FHA claim for hostile housing environment created by sexual harassment); *Honce v. Vigil*, 1 F.3d 1085, 1089-90 (10th Cir. 1993) (same).

Next, Winter insists there was insufficient evidence to support the jury's verdict in favor of Quigley on her hostile housing environment created by sexual harassment claim. In this case, there was sufficient evidence to support a hostile housing environment claim if a reasonable jury could find Quigley proved by a preponderance of the evidence Winter subjected her to unwelcome sexual harassment, and the harassment was sufficiently severe or pervasive so as to interfere with or deprive Quigley of her right to use or enjoy her home. *See DiCenso*, 96 F.3d at 1008 ("Applied to the housing context, a claim [of hostile housing environment caused by sexual harassment] is actionable 'when the offensive behavior unreasonably interferes with use and enjoyment of the premises.' " (quoting *Honce*, 1 F.3d at 1090) ("The harassment must be sufficiently severe or pervasive to alter the conditions of the housing arrangement.")).

Winter denies he subjected Quigley to sexual advances or requests for sexual favors, and, alternatively, any sexual harassment Quigley experienced was not sufficiently severe or pervasive to support the jury's verdict. Viewing the evidence in the light most favorable to Quigley, we conclude Quigley presented sufficient evidence of numerous unwanted interactions of a sexual nature that interfered with Quigley's use and enjoyment of her home. Quigley testified Winter subjected her to unwanted touching on two occasions, made sexually suggestive comments, rubbed his genitals in front of her, placed several middle of the night phone calls to her home, made repeated unannounced visits, and, on one occasion, while Winter lay on Quigley's couch, had to be told to leave her home at least three times before he complied. We emphasize that Winter subjected Quigley to these unwanted interactions in her own home, a place where Quigley was entitled to feel safe and secure and need not flee, which makes Winter's conduct even more egregious.

"Quid Pro Quo" Sexual Harassment

Winter next contends the district court erred in denying his motion for judgment as a matter of law on Quigley's "quid pro quo" sexual harassment claim. " 'Quid pro quo' harassment occurs when housing benefits are explicitly or implicitly conditioned on sexual favors." *Honce*, 1 F.3d at 1089; *cf. Ogden v. Wax Works, Inc.*, 214 F.3d 999, 1006 n.8 (8th Cir. 2000) ("To prevail on her [employment discrimination] quid pro quo claim, [plaintiff] needed to prove (1) she was a member of a protected class; (2) she was subjected to unwelcome harassment in the form of sexual advances or requests for sexual favors; (3) the harassment was based on sex; and (4) her submission to the unwelcome advances was an express or implied condition for receiving job benefits or her refusal to submit resulted in a tangible job detriment." (citation omitted)).

While the evidence of "quid pro quo" harassment was not overwhelming, after viewing the evidence in the light most favorable to Quigley, we conclude there was sufficient evidence to support the jury's verdict. Specifically, when Quigley inquired about the likelihood of receiving her deposit back from Winter, Winter fluttered his hand against Quigley's stomach and said, "My eagle eyes have not seen everything yet." The jury could reasonably infer Winter was telling Quigley the return of her deposit was conditioned upon Winter seeing more of Quigley's body or even receiving a sexual favor, which would amount to "quid pro quo" sexual harassment. We will not disturb the jury's verdict.

Coercion, Intimidation, or Interference with Housing Rights

Winter maintains the district court should not have denied Winter's post-trial motion on Quigley's coercion, intimidation, and interference claim under 42 U.S.C. §3617. Winter contends Quigley's claim was "essentially a retaliation claim" and Quigley failed to prove retaliation.

24 C.F.R. §100.400 gives the following examples of conduct prohibited by 42 U.S.C. §3617:

> (1) Coercing a person, either orally, in writing, or by other means, to deny or limit the benefits provided that person in connection with the sale or rental of a dwelling . . . because of . . . sex. . . .
>
> (2) Threatening, intimidating or interfering with persons in their enjoyment of a dwelling because of the . . . sex . . . of such persons, or of visitors or associates of such persons.
>
> . . .
>
> (5) Retaliating against any person because that person has made a complaint, testified, assisted, or participated in any manner in a proceeding under the Fair Housing Act.

In arguing there was insufficient evidence to support the jury's verdict, Winter focuses solely on the retaliation aspect of 42 U.S.C. §3617. As Quigley points out, retaliation is only one form of conduct prohibited under §3617. Viewing the evidence in the light most favorable to Quigley, we conclude there was more than sufficient evidence of coercion, intimidation, and interference with Quigley's enjoyment of her housing rights, other than retaliation, to support the jury's verdict.

Punitive Damages

We first address Winter's contention that the district court erred in allowing the jury to consider punitive damages. "The [FHA] provides for the recovery of punitive damages by victims of discriminatory housing practices." *Badami v. Flood*, 214 F.3d 994, 997 (8th Cir. 2000) (citing 42 U.S.C. §3613(c)(1) (1994)). We apply the same standard for punitive damages in [FHA] cases as we do in employment discrimination and 42 U.S.C. §1983 civil rights cases. "Punitive damages are appropriate in a federal civil rights action 'when the defendant's conduct is shown to be motivated by evil motive or intent, or when it involves reckless or callous indifference to the federally protected rights of others.' " *Id.* at 997.

The district court determined Quigley had presented sufficient evidence to justify instructing the jury on punitive damages, because Winter admitted at trial he knew sexual harassment was unlawful, he had been a landlord for many years and managed many properties, he had worked with various governmental agencies to provide subsidized housing, and his lease agreement with Quigley stated he, as the landlord, was not to discriminate on the basis of sex. We agree with the district court. The district court did not err in submitting punitive damages for the jury's consideration.

The jury found Quigley was entitled to punitive damages in the amount of $250,000.00, and the district court entered judgment. Winter then filed a motion to amend the judgment to reduce the punitive damages award. The district court noted the punitive damages award was more than eighteen times the compensatory damages award ($13,685.00) and found the award was excessive and did not comport with due process. The district court reduced the award to $20,527.50, which amounted to one and a half times the compensatory damages award, "for the simple reason that [Winter's] conduct . . . can be considered only as to what he said and did directly to [Quigley]."

Quigley challenges the district court's analysis, arguing the jury's punitive damages award complied with due process and the original award should be reinstated. To assess the reasonableness or excessiveness of a punitive damages award, we consider: (1) "the degree of reprehensibility of the defendant's conduct," (2) the ratio between punitive damages and actual harm (compensatory damages), and (3) "the civil or criminal penalties that could be imposed for comparable misconduct." *BMW of N. Am., Inc. v. Gore*, 517 U.S. 559, 575, 580-81 (1996).

Winter's conduct was reprehensible. Quigley lived alone with small children at the time of Winter's harassment, and she had few, if any, alternative housing options. Quigley's financial vulnerability was evidenced by her need for Section 8 housing vouchers. Winter held a certain level of power over Quigley and her family. Winter repeatedly subjected Quigley to inappropriate conduct during Quigley's tenancy, and Winter's conduct was unquestionably intentional and more than churlish. Most significant, Winter's conduct intruded upon Quigley's sense of security in her own home. However, as we explain below, we do not believe the degree of reprehensibility of Winter's conduct justifies the jury's large punitive damages award.

Recognizing we are not bound by a rigid mathematical formula, we nevertheless, are persuaded a single digit multiplier is appropriate in the present case. We take our guidance from the Supreme Court's assessment of single-digit multipliers. Quigley was awarded $13,685.00 in compensatory damages, which is not a nominal amount. We find the circumstances of this case and due process do not justify a punitive damages award eighteen times greater than the compensatory damages and, agreeing with the district court, conclude the jury's punitive damage award was excessive.

We turn then to the final *Gore* factor, a comparison between the punitive damages award and the civil and criminal penalties available for comparable misconduct. "[A] reviewing court engaged in determining whether an award of punitive damages is excessive should 'accord "substantial deference" to legislative judgments concerning appropriate sanctions for the conduct at issue.'" *Gore*, 517 U.S. at 583. Quigley points out 42 U.S.C. §3614 permits the Attorney General to commence a civil action against "any person . . . engaged in a pattern or practice of resistance to the full enjoyment of any of the rights granted by the [FHA]." Section 3614(d)(1)(C), as adjusted by the *Inflation Adjustment Act of 1990*, Pub. L. No. 101-410, §5(a)(4), 104 Stat. 891, and 29 C.F.R. §85.3(b)(3), states a court may grant relief for a first violation in an amount not exceeding $55,000.

While we agree with the district court that the jury's punitive damage award was excessive, we disagree with the district court's assessment that $20,527.50, which is one and a half times the compensatory award, sufficiently reflects the reprehensibility of Winter's conduct. We conclude an appropriate punitive damages award in this case is $54,750. This amount is four times greater than Quigley's compensatory damages ($13,685.00), which we find is an appropriate ratio under the circumstances of this case. This amount comports with due process, while achieving the statutory and regulatory goals of retribution and deterrence.

Notes and Questions

1. **Sex discrimination by a landlord.** Although the *Fair Housing Act* does not expressly define sexual harassment as sex discrimination, *Quigley* illustrates how courts have reached that conclusion nonetheless. *See also Williams v. Poretsky Management, Inc.*, 955 F. Supp. 490 (D. Md. 1996) (sexual harassment of tenant by building superintendent violates *Fair Housing Act*). *Cf. Meritor Savings Bank, FSB v. Vinson*, 477 U.S. 57 (1986) (interpreting Title VII of the *Civil Rights Act of 1964* to define sexual harassment as sex discrimination in the employment context). Some state laws, by contrast, explicitly define sexual harassment as a form of sex discrimination. *See Edouard v. Kozubal*, No. 98-BPR-0957, 2002 WL 977225 (MCAD) (Mass. Commn. Against Discrimination, 2002) (applying Mass. Gen. Laws ch. 151B §1(18)).

2. **How severe must the harassment be?** In *DiCenso v. Cisneros*, 96 F.3d 1004 (7th Cir. 1996), when the landlord came to the tenant's apartment to collect the rent he caressed her arm and back, and said that if she could not pay the rent, she could "take care of it in other ways"; when she slammed the door in his face, he called her a "bitch" and a "whore." The Seventh Circuit noted that employment discrimination cases had recognized sex discrimination in the context of a "hostile environment" and that those cases required the employer's conduct to be "sufficiently severe or pervasive to alter the conditions of the victim's employment," *id.* at 1008 (quoting *Harris v. Forklift Systems, Inc.*, 510 U.S. 16, 21 (1993)), and that this one incident did not rise to that level. Do you agree? *See* Michele Adams, *Knowing Your Place: Theorizing Sexual Harassment at Home*, 40 Ariz. L. Rev. 17 (1998) (arguing that housing discrimination should be subject to different standards than employment discrimination because of the importance of the home as a safe place).

Would the plaintiff in *DiCenso* have a remedy under §3604(c)? *See* Robert G. Schwemm & Rigel C. Oliveri, *A New Look at Sexual Harassment Under the Fair Housing Act: The Forgotten Role of §3604(c)*, 2002 Wis. L. Rev. 771, 814-815 (arguing in the affirmative).

3. **Domestic violence and the *Fair Housing Act*.** Victims of domestic violence can subsequently suffer housing discrimination as a result. For example, landlords sometimes evict survivors of domestic violence under "zero-tolerance" policies that mandate eviction for criminal activity or because of complaints by other tenants. *See* Lenora M. Lapidus, *Doubly Victimized: Housing Discrimination Against Victims of*

Domestic Violence, 11 J. Gender, Soc. Poly. & L. 377 (2003). A handful of cases have addressed whether such evictions constitute discrimination on the basis of sex under the *Fair Housing Act,* given that the overwhelming majority of victims of domestic violence are women. For example, in *Bouley v. Young-Sabourin,* 394 F. Supp. 2d 675 (D. Vt. 2005), a woman had called the police after her husband attacked her in the apartment they had rented with their two children upstairs from their landlord. The woman obtained a restraining order against her husband, who eventually pled guilty to criminal charges related to the incident. Three days after the assault, the landlord visited the woman, attempting to resolve the dispute, and allegedly sought to engage in a discussion of religion. The victim got upset and the landlord left. Later that day, the landlord served the victim with a notice of eviction, citing a provision of the lease that provided that the tenant "will not use or allow said premises or any part thereof to be used for unlawful purposes, in any noisy, boisterous or any other manner offensive to any other occupant of the building." Ruling on cross-motions for summary judgment, the court held that the victim had presented a *prima facie* case of sex discrimination (and discrimination on the basis of religion) under the *Fair Housing Act.*

Title VI of the *Violence Against Women Reauthorization Act of 2013,* Pub. L. No. 113-4, 127 Stat. 54 (Mar. 7, 2013), reauthorized provisions of the former *Violence Against Women Act,* 42 U.S.C. §14043e *et seq.,* that, since 2005, had provided victims of domestic violence with some protection from eviction. The 2013 *Reauthorization Act* expanded these protections to include a much wider range of federally subsidized housing programs than the earlier 2005 version.

4. Sexual orientation. It is quite clear that a landlord commits race discrimination if she refuses to rent to a white female tenant because that tenant's boyfriend is African American. By analogy, it appears clear that a refusal to rent to someone who is gay commits sex discrimination because the denial is based on the sex of the persons to whom the prospective tenant is attracted or has a relationship. In addition, such a landlord is engaged in a form of sex stereotyping by assuming that tenants should have sexual partners only of the opposite sex. *See Price Waterhouse v. Hopkins,* 490 U.S. 228 (1989) (sex discrimination in employment when employer engaged in sex stereotyping by not giving partnership to a woman who was deemed "too masculine"). However, no court has held that discrimination in the housing market on the basis of sexual orientation constitutes sex discrimination, partly because only about 20 states have statutes expressly prohibiting discrimination in public accommodations or housing on the basis of sexual orientation, *see* §2.5, below, and the courts have interpreted the antidiscrimination laws not to show evidence of a legislative intent to prohibit discrimination based on sexual orientation.

5. Enforcement and attorneys' fees. Courts may award attorneys' fees to the prevailing party in an FHA action. *See* 42 U.S.C. §3613(c). Courts usually apply the "lodestar" approach to determining attorneys' fees, which calculates the entitlement based on a determination of hours reasonably expended and reasonable hourly rates. Can you see why attorneys' fee questions are particularly important in cases like *Quigley*?

Problems

1. If a landlord excludes single males while renting to single females and married couples, has he engaged in prohibited sex discrimination?

2. If a landlord decides not to count alimony and child support in determining whether divorced women are qualified to rent, has the landlord engaged in prohibited sex discrimination?

3. An owner of a house lives in the first-floor apartment and rents the top floor as a separate apartment. The owner sexually harasses the tenant, engaging in the same kind of outrageous conduct as the landlord in *Quigley v. Winter.* What legal rights does the tenant have?

4. A gay male couple wishes to rent an apartment, and the landlord refuses because of their sexual orientation. The landlord rents other apartments to unmarried heterosexual couples. One of the two men sues the landlord under the *Fair Housing Act,* claiming that the landlord discriminated against him "because of sex," arguing that if he had been a woman, the landlord would have rented the apartment to the couple. Does the landlord's conduct constitute sex discrimination?

§2.4 Discrimination Based on Familial Status

Human Rights Commission v. LaBrie, Inc.

668 A.2d 659 (Vt. 1995)

Map: 4102 VT Route 14, Williamstown, Vermont

FREDERIC W. ALLEN, Chief Justice.

Defendants LaBrie, Inc., Linda LaBrie and Ernest LaBrie appeal from superior court orders, which held that defendants committed unfair housing practices by discriminating against persons with minor children in violation of Vt. Stat. tit. 9 §4503(a). Defendants claim that the court's findings on disparate-treatment discrimination are clearly erroneous because the evidence did not show any intent to discriminate, [and] the court committed plain error by holding Ernest LaBrie personally liable for unfair housing practices. We affirm.

On May 1, 1981, Linda and Ernest LaBrie purchased Limehurst Mobile Home Park. The Park consists of thirty-three mobile home lots. Most of the residents own their own mobile homes and rent only the lot. LaBrie, Inc. purchased the Park from Ernest and Linda LaBrie on October 30, 1987. Ernest and Linda LaBrie are the sole corporate officers and shareholders of LaBrie, Inc. Ernest LaBrie is the president, and Linda LaBrie is the vice-president and treasurer. The office of LaBrie, Inc. is in their home. The Park is managed primarily by Linda, who is responsible for renting units, collecting rent, and making all general management decisions. She also sets policies, rules, and lease terms, and approves residents for tenancy. Ernest is primarily responsible for maintenance under the direction of Linda but is aware of the decisions made by Linda.

When the LaBries purchased the Park, the lease term on occupancy stated "that only one family shall occupy a mobile home on a permanent basis." In 1982, the LaBries changed the occupancy provision to:

> Lessees, who have entered into a lease agreement after April 1, 1982, shall *not* be permitted to have *children under the age of 18 years* reside in their mobile home unit. Lessee hereby agrees that lessee shall terminate this lease and vacate the premises prior to having said children reside in their mobile home. (Emphasis added.)

In July 1988, the occupancy provision was essentially the same but stated in addition, "This age restriction applies to all lots at Limehurst Mobile Home Park based on VSA 9-4508(b)."

In April 1989, the occupancy provision was revised to state:

> Lessees who have entered into a lease agreement after July 1, 1988 shall *not* be permitted to have *more than two permanent occupants* per lease premises. Lessees prior to July 1, 1988, who have more than two permanent occupants shall be grandfathered, but the number of occupants cannot expand beyond what existed as of July 1, 1988. (Emphasis added.)

Currently, only one mobile home in the Park houses a family with a minor child. This family moved into the Park prior to 1982. No persons with minor children moved into the Park after the LaBries purchased it, even after the occupancy provision was changed from adults-only to a two-occupant maximum. The population of the Park declined from May 1981 to May 1990, from ninety-five residents to sixty residents. The LaBries also own two other mobile home parks, four homes leased as residential units, and twelve mobile homes throughout Vermont. There are minor children living in many of these homes.

Scott and Luanne McCarthy purchased a mobile home in the Park for $7,000 in August 1986. Linda LaBrie sent them a letter on August 1, 1986, accepting their application, and stating: "We remind you that Limehurst Mobile Home Park is an adult park and if you should have children in the future you will be required to vacate Limehurst Mobile Home Park prior to the arrival of said child." In July 1989, the McCarthys contacted a broker to sell their mobile home because Luanne was pregnant. The broker determined that the McCarthys should ask $18,000 for their home.

The McCarthys' son was born September 18, 1989. When they returned home from the hospital, they found a letter from Linda LaBrie informing them that they must vacate the premises "upon arrival of your third occupant." Following the letter, the McCarthys received telephone calls, visits, and additional letters from Linda LaBrie telling them to vacate the Park. On December 28, 1989, the McCarthys were served with a summons and complaint for eviction brought by the LaBries in the name of LaBrie, Inc. d/b/a Limehurst Mobile Home Park.

When the McCarthys informed the LaBries that they had accepted a deposit for the sale of their home, the LaBries delayed the sale, indicating that they would not act on the purchasers' application until the eviction action was resolved. The purchasers' application was approved February 25, 1990, and the McCarthys sold their mobile home on March 2, 1990, for $13,000. At trial, the broker testified that one-half of potential purchasers were ineligible because a minor child in the family put them over the occupancy limit. There was conflicting evidence regarding the value of the home, but the court determined that the fair market value of the home at the time of the sale was $13,000.

From September 1989 through March 1990, while living at the Park, Luanne McCarthy felt humiliated by Linda LaBrie's demands to vacate the premises. Consequently, she did not leave her home often. She was unable to sleep and had chest pains. The McCarthys moved from the Park to the home of Scott McCarthy's parents, where they had to share a family room in the basement with their newborn child. Luanne McCarthy worried about their inability to find their own housing; her chest pains increased and she was given two medications to relieve stress.

The McCarthys filed a complaint with the Human Rights Commission, which commenced this action in Washington Superior Court in October 1990, alleging that defendants LaBrie, Inc., Linda LaBrie, and Ernest LaBrie violated the *Fair Housing and Public Accommodations Act*, Vt. Stat. tit. 9 §4503(a)(1)-(3), by discriminating against persons intending to occupy a dwelling with one or more minor children. The Commission contended that the restrictive occupancy limit for the Park (1) was adopted for the purpose of discriminating against persons with minor children by either limiting or eliminating them from occupancy in the Park, and (2) although facially neutral, has an unlawful discriminatory impact because it excluded persons with minor children in significant numbers. Defendants maintained that the occupancy limit was necessary due to limited water and septic capacity.

At trial, both parties presented expert testimony on the capacity of the septic system and water supply at the Park. Defendants' expert testified that the septic system at the Park was adequate to serve a maximum of sixty-six people. The court found that the expert had not performed the tests necessary to properly assess the potential capacity of the septic system, and concluded that there was no credible evidence that the system could not support an increase in population in the Park. Similarly, the court found that there was no credible evidence that water supply or water pressure was inadequate to serve more than sixty-six people. Although the court acknowledged the LaBries' fear that problems—which had existed prior to installation of a new well and replacement of their leachfields—would reoccur, it concluded that the LaBries have less restrictive alternatives available to them than the two-person occupancy limit.

The court concluded that plaintiff had established that the McCarthys were evicted due to the presence of a minor child, and that persons with minor children were constructively denied access to housing in the Park by the two-person occupancy limit. Further, the court concluded that defendants had not established the occupancy limit as a legitimate business necessity arising from septic and water capacities of the Park.

Accordingly, the court held that defendants had violated Vt. Stat. tit. 9 §4503(a) and awarded the McCarthys $2,700 in attorney's fees for the eviction proceeding, $1,500 for the emotional distress and humiliation suffered as a result of defendants' actions, $3,000 for loss of civil rights caused by the eviction and by restricting potential purchasers, and $3,000 in punitive damages. The court also awarded the Human Rights Commission civil penalties of $6,000. In subsequent orders, the court permanently enjoined defendants from adopting or enforcing a two-person-per-lot occupancy limit at the Limehurst Mobile Home Park, and awarded plaintiff $51,072 in attorney's fees, $2,194.39 for expenses and $240 for discovery costs. Defendants appeal.

The *Vermont Fair Housing and Public Accommodations Act* (FHPA), Vt. Stat. tit. 9 §§4500-4507, prohibits discrimination in renting "a dwelling or other real estate to any person because of the race, sex, sexual orientation, age, marital status, religious creed, color, national origin or handicap of a person, or because a person intends to occupy a dwelling with one or more minor children, or because a person is a recipient of public assistance." Vt. Stat. tit. 9 §4503(a)(1). Discrimination on the basis of age, or because a person intends to occupy a dwelling with one or more minor children, has been prohibited in the rental of dwelling units in Vermont since 1986.

Mobile home lot rentals were, however, covered by a separate provision enacted in 1988, which did not strictly prohibit discrimination on the basis of age or because a person intended to occupy a dwelling with one or more minor children. The mobile-home-lot-rental provision was repealed in 1989, when the Legislature revised Vermont's housing discrimination laws to comply with the federal *Fair Housing Act* Amendments of 1988. Thus, Vermont's general housing-discrimination provision has been applicable to the rental of mobile home lots since 1989.

FHPA is patterned on Title VIII of the *Civil Rights Act of 1968 (Fair Housing Act)*, 42 U.S.C. §§3601-3631, and therefore, in construing FHPA, we consider cases construing the federal statute. Courts analyzing Title VIII, the federal housing-discrimination statute, often rely on cases analyzing Title VII, the federal employment-discrimination statute. Accordingly, we also consider Vermont and federal employment-discrimination law in analyzing the instant case.

Plaintiff alleged violations of FHPA under two theories of discrimination law: (1) disparate treatment — defendants intentionally discriminated against members of a statutorily protected category because of their membership in that group, and (2) disparate impact — defendants' facially neutral policy has a disproportionate effect on a statutorily protected category. The trial court found defendants liable for housing discrimination under both theories. We do not address defendants' challenges to the trial court's finding of disparate impact because we uphold the trial court's decision on the theory of disparate treatment.

Defendants first claim that the court erred in finding disparate treatment or intent to discriminate in the absence of any direct evidence of discrimination against persons with minor children. Intentional discrimination may be shown by circumstantial or direct evidence. Thus, the short answer to defendants' challenge is that no direct evidence is necessary to prove a disparate-treatment discrimination claim. Indeed, direct evidence of unlawful discrimination is often difficult to obtain.

In this case, however, plaintiff presented direct evidence of discrimination. [E]vidence of a discriminatory practice prior to civil rights legislation, coupled with a post-legislation pattern of maintaining the status quo, may be sufficient to establish the intent to continue the discrimination through a neutral policy. In this case, the trial court found that defendants clearly excluded minor children from the Park prior to 1989. That year, Vermont's mobile-home-lot-rental provision was repealed, and defendants changed the occupancy provision in their leases from adults-only to a two-person maximum. Although the new occupancy provision appears neutral on its face, defendants have maintained the status quo at the Park — no minor children have moved into the Park since defendants purchased it. This evidence is sufficient to infer that the two-person occupancy limit was adopted for the purpose of eliminating or limiting persons with minor children from the Park. Based on defendants' actions against the McCarthys and defendants' pattern and practice of excluding minor children from the Park, we conclude that there was no clear error in the trial court finding an intent to discriminate against persons intending to occupy a dwelling with one or more minor children.

Pursuant to Vt. Stat. tit. 9 §4504(4), defendants assert as an affirmative defense that their actions against the McCarthys were based on a legitimate, nondiscriminatory occupancy limit. Section 4504(4) provides that the unfair-housing-practices provisions do not apply "to limit a landlord's right to establish and enforce legitimate business practices necessary to protect and manage the rental property, such as the use of references. However, this subdivision shall not be used as a pretext for discrimination in violation of this section." FHPA is a remedial statute; thus, we construe it generously and read exemptions narrowly.

At trial, defendants maintained that their occupancy limit is based on legitimate septic and water capacity considerations. They presented evidence that the septic system at the Park was capable of handling a maximum of sixty-six people — or two persons per lot. They also presented evidence on the limits of the Park's water supply. The trial court rejected this defense, finding that defendants had failed to present credible evidence that an increase in the number of occupants per living unit would adversely affect the septic or water systems. It also found that there are less restrictive alternatives available to defendants. The court, therefore, concluded that the business necessity advanced by defendants was not legitimate, but rather, a mere pretext for discriminating against persons with minor children.

The federal *Fair Housing Act* has an occupancy restriction provision, which allows only reasonable local, state or federal restriction on the maximum number of occupants per dwelling. *See* 42 U.S.C.A. §3607(b)(1). Courts have found privately imposed occupancy limits, such as the limit imposed by defendants in this case, to unreasonably limit or exclude persons with minor children, and therefore, violate the *Fair Housing Act. See, e.g., United States v. Lepore*, 816 F. Supp. 1011, 1023 (M.D. Pa. 1991) (court cannot conclude two-person-per-mobile-home lot limitation is reasonable when defendants have never attempted any water-saving or septic-system alternatives). We agree that a privately enforced occupancy limit must be at minimum reasonable. Defendants failed to show that their actions against the McCarthys were reasonable or that the sixty-six-person limit was reasonable.

Notes and Questions

Familial versus marital status. The FHA prohibits discrimination based on familial status, which does not cover **marital status**. *See White v. U.S. Department of Housing and Urban Development*, 475 F.3d 898, 906 (7th Cir. 2007). However, a number of state and local antidiscrimination provisions do explicitly prohibit discrimination on the basis of marital status. In *McCready v. Hoffius*, 586 N.W.2d 723 (Mich. 1998), defendants were found to have violated the Michigan *Civil Rights Act*, Mich. Comp. Laws §37.2502(1), by refusing to rent to an unmarried couple. The court interpreted the statutory phrase "marital status" to apply to both married and unmarried individuals and rejected the argument that the defendant landlords were discriminating based on the conduct of unmarried cohabitation. The landlords' objection was primarily that their refusal to rent was constitutionally protected "free exercise" of religion. The court initially rejected this religious defense under the first amendment and the Michigan constitution, finding the statute validly to apply as a neutral law of general applicability with no religious motivation. The Court later vacated the decision and remanded the case to determine whether the statute violated the landlords' free exercise rights by requiring them to rent to a cohabiting unmarried couple, 593 N.W.2d 545 (Mich. 1999). Do you agree with the court's initial approach or does a neutral statute that requires landlords to rent in violation of their sincerely held religious beliefs unconstitutionally infringe on the free exercise of religion?

Problems

1. A landlord refused to rent to a childless married couple when they refused to sign a document stating that they would not have children while living in the apartment and would move if the wife became pregnant. *Wasserman v. Three Seasons Association No. 1, Inc.*, 998 F. Supp. 1445 (S.D. Fla. 1998). They sued the landlord under the *Fair Housing Act*, claiming discrimination because of familial status. The landlord contended that the couple is not covered by 42 U.S.C. §3602(k) because they were not yet living with a child, and the woman was not pregnant. The prospective tenants contended, however, that they were "aggrieved persons" entitled to bring a lawsuit. The *Fair Housing Act* defines "aggrieved person" to include "any person who—(1) claims to have been injured by a discriminatory housing practice; or (2) believes that such person will be injured by a discriminatory housing practice that is about to occur." §3602(i). Judge James Lawrence King ruled in favor of the landlord, ruling that plaintiffs were not "aggrieved persons" within the meaning of the FHA because their claimed injury did not bear a sufficient nexus to actual discrimination against members of a protected class. What is the plaintiffs' argument that the landlord did violate the FHA? What is the defendant's response? How should the court have ruled?

2. A lesbian couple applies for a foster parents license. Before they are licensed by the state, they notify their landlord of their intention to act as foster parents. The landlord objects and sues to evict them. The tenants argue that they are protected by the "familial status" provisions of the *Fair Housing Act* because, as foster parents, they

would be the "designee" of the children's legal guardian (the state agency in charge of the child). *See* 42 U.S.C. §3602(k)(2). The landlord contends that they are not protected by the statute since they have not yet been designated as foster parents and are not yet living with a foster child. Moreover, the landlord points to the qualification in the definition of "familial status" in §3602(k), which states that "[t]he protections against discrimination on the basis of familial status shall apply to any person who is pregnant or is in the process of securing legal custody of any individual who has not attained the age of 18 years." The landlord notes that prospective foster parents are not "pregnant"; moreover, they are not in the process of "securing legal custody" since the state is the legal guardian of foster children and foster parents are mere "designees" of the state. Are prospective foster parents protected by the *Fair Housing Act*? For one view, *see Gorski v. Troy*, 929 F.2d 1183 (7th Cir. 1991) (holding that they are protected by the FHA).

3. A landlord converts an apartment building to housing for older persons, evicting current tenants who have children. Are those tenants protected under the *Fair Housing Act*?

4. In *Hudson View Properties v. Weiss*, 450 N.E.2d 234 (N.Y. 1983), a landlord sought to evict a tenant from a rent-controlled apartment on the ground that she had breached a term in her lease under which she covenanted not to allow anyone to occupy the premises with her who was not a member of her "immediate family." She lived with a man "with whom she [had] a loving relationship," but the landlord claimed that, because the couple was not married, the man was not a part of the tenant's immediate family. The tenant argued that the lease term discriminated against her on the basis of marital status. The court found that the man was not a member of the tenant's "immediate family" and that it would not constitute marital status discrimination to enforce the covenant. Do you agree?

§2.5 Discrimination Based on Sexual Orientation

State ex rel. Sprague v. City of Madison

555 N.W.2d 409 (Wis. Ct. App. 1996)

Robert D. Sundby, J.

Ann Hacklander-Ready and Maureen Rowe appeal from a decision affirming the Madison Equal Opportunity Commission's (MEOC) Decision and Order which found that they refused to rent housing to Carol Sprague as their housemate because of her sexual orientation, in violation of §3.23(4)(a) of the *Madison General Ordinances* (MGO).[7] We conclude that the trial court correctly found that §3.23, MGO, unambiguously applied to housemates at the time this action arose.

7. Madison General Ordinances §3.23 is now §39.03. — Eds.

At all times relevant to this action Hacklander-Ready leased a four-bedroom house. She had the owner's permission to allow others to live with her and share in the payment of rent. In the fall of 1988, Maureen Rowe began living with Hacklander-Ready and paying rent. In April 1989 they advertised for housemates to replace two women who were moving out. They chose Sprague from among numerous applicants. They knew her sexual orientation when they extended their offer to her. Sprague accepted their offer and made a rent deposit on May 4, 1989. However, the following day Hacklander-Ready informed Sprague that they were withdrawing their offer because they were not comfortable living with a person of her sexual orientation.

Sprague filed a complaint with MEOC alleging that appellants discriminated against her on the basis of sexual orientation, contrary to §3.23(4)(a), MGO.

At the time of the events in issue, §3.23, MGO, provided:

> (1) *Declaration of Policy.* The practice of providing equal opportunities in housing . . . without regard to . . . sexual orientation . . . is a desirable goal of the City of Madison and a matter of legitimate concern to its government. In order that the peace, freedom, safety and general welfare of all inhabitants of the City may be protected and ensured, it is hereby declared to be the public policy of the City of Madison to foster and enforce to the fullest extent the protection by law of the rights of all its inhabitants to equal opportunity to . . . housing.
>
> (2)(b) "Housing" shall mean any building, structure, or part thereof which is used or occupied, or is intended, arranged or designed to be used or occupied, as a residence, home or place of habitation of one or more human beings.
>
> (4) It shall be an unfair discrimination practice and unlawful and hereby prohibited:
>
> > (a) For any person having the right of ownership or possession or the right of transfer, sale, rental or lease of any housing, or the agent of any such person, to refuse to transfer, sell, rent or lease, or otherwise to deny or withhold from any person such housing because of . . . sexual orientation.
> >
> > (b) Nothing in this ordinance shall prevent any person from renting or leasing housing, or any part thereof, to solely male or female persons if such housing or part thereof is rented with the understanding that toilet and bath facilities must be shared with the landlord or with other tenants.

Sprague claims that §3.23, MGO, was intended to apply to housemate arrangements.[8] Section 3.23(4), MGO, unambiguously prohibits any person having right of rental to refuse to rent to any person because of the person's sexual orientation. Hacklander-Ready concedes that she held the lease to the house and that she had the right to rent the property to others. Further, she and Rowe admit that the sole reason they withdrew their offer was Sprague's sexual orientation. Finally, the room that appellants

8. In September 1989, subsequent to the commencement of this action, the Madison City Council amended the Equal Opportunities Ordinance by adding §3.23(c), MGO, which states, "Nothing in this ordinance shall affect any person's decision to share occupancy of a lodging room, apartment or dwelling unit with another person or persons."

sought to rent falls within the definition of housing under §3.23(2)(b), MGO, as a part of a building intended as a place of habitation for one or more human beings.

While appellants correctly argue that a statute is ambiguous if it may be construed in different ways by reasonably well-informed persons, we fail to see any reasonable interpretation that would make §3.23, MGO, inapplicable in this case. Appellants also correctly note that a court may resort to construction if the literal meaning of a statute produces an absurd or unreasonable result. However, applying §3.23(4) to the rental of a room within a house with shared common areas is not unreasonable or absurd. Because we find that the ordinance clearly and unambiguously applies to the subleasing of housing by a person having the right of rental, our inquiry in this respect is at an end.

Appellants argue that to apply the ordinance to the lease of housing by a tenant to a housemate makes §3.24(4)(a), MGO, unconstitutional in its application. Appellants cite many cases which they argue support their constitutional challenge: *NAACP v. Alabama*, 357 U.S. 449 (1958); *Griswold v. Connecticut*, 381 U.S. 479 (1965); *Moore v. City of East Cleveland*, 431 U.S. 494 (1977). However, those cases deal either with the right to privacy in the home or family or the right to engage in first amendment activity free of unwarranted governmental intrusion. Appellants gave up their unqualified right to such constitutional protection when they rented housing for profit. The restrictions placed by the Madison City Council on persons who rent housing for profit are not unreasonable and do not encroach upon appellant's constitutional protections. We therefore reject appellants' challenge to the constitutionality of §3.24, MGO, as applied.

Notes and Questions

1. **Prohibiting housing discrimination on the basis of sexual orientation.** In a landmark study, the Department of Housing and Urban Development recently published the first national assessment of housing discrimination based on sexual orientation. The study used nearly 7,000 matched-pair testers to study the experience of same-sex couples searching on-line for rental housing in 50 randomly selected housing markets across the country. The study concluded that "[s]ame-sex couples are significantly less likely than heterosexual couples to get favorable responses to e-mail inquiries about electronically advertised rental housing," and that "heterosexual couples were favored over gay male couples in 15.9 percent of tests and over lesbian couples in 15.6 percent of tests." M. Davis & Co., et al., U.S. Dept. of Hous. & Urban Dev., *An Estimate of Housing Discrimination Against Same-Sex Couples* vii (2013).

The *Fair Housing Act* does not address sexual orientation, but at least 20 states have passed statutes that specifically or by judicial interpretation prohibit housing discrimination on that basis. For example, the *Wisconsin Equal Rights Law*, Wis. Stat. §106.50(1), provides that "all persons shall have an equal opportunity for housing regardless of . . . sexual orientation." Sexual orientation is defined as "having a preference for heterosexuality, homosexuality, bisexuality, having a history of such a preference or being identified with such a preference." Wis. Stat. §111.32(13m). The statute provides that it is unlawful to discriminate "[b]y refusing to sell [or] rent . . . housing," §106.50(2)(a), and "[by] engaging in the harassment of a tenant," §106.50(2)(f).

Other jurisdictions that prohibit housing discrimination on the basis of sexual orientation include California, Cal. Civ. Code §51, Cal. Govt. Code §12955; Colorado, Colo. Rev. Stat. §24-34-502; Connecticut, Conn. Gen. Stat. §§46a-81a & 46a-81e; the District of Columbia, D.C. Code §§2-1402.21; Hawai`i, Haw. Stat. §§368-1, 378-1 *et seq.*; Illinois, 775 Ill. Comp. Stat. 5/3-101 to 5/3-106; Iowa, Iowa Code §216.8; Maine, Me. Rev. Stat. tit. 5, §§4552, 4582; Maryland, Md. Code art. 20, §20-707; Massachusetts, Mass. Gen. Laws ch. 151B, §1 *et seq.*; Minnesota, Minn. Stat. §§363A.03(44) & 363A.09; New Hampshire, N.H. Rev. Stat. §§354-A:8 to 354-A:10; New Jersey, N.J. Stat. §10:5-1 *et seq.*; New Mexico, N.M. Stat. §28-1-7; New York, N.Y. Exec. Law §291; Oregon, Or. Rev. Stat. §659A.421(2); Rhode Island, R.I. Gen. Laws §§34-37-1 to 34-37-5.4; Vermont, Vt. Stat. tit. 9, §§4502, 4503; and Washington, Wash. Rev. Code §39.60.222.

More than 200 cities also have passed local ordinances prohibiting discrimination in the real estate market based on sexual orientation or gender identity. *See, e.g.*, Boston Code tit. 12, ch. 40; Chicago Mun. Code, ch. 199; Los Angeles Mun. Code, ch. IV; New York City, Admin. Code §8-102(20); Philadelphia Fair Prac. Ordinance, ch. 9-1100; and San Francisco Code, art. 33, §3301. For a review of the law on discrimination based on sexual orientation, *see* William B. Rubenstein, Jane S. Schacter & Carlos A. Ball, *Cases and Materials on Sexual Orientation and the Law* (4th ed. 2011).

2. **Housing discrimination on the basis of sexual orientation and gender identity in federal housing programs.** HUD recently issued a rule, *Equal Access to Housing in HUD Programs Regardless of Sexual Orientation or Gender Identity*, 77 Fed. Reg. 5662 (Feb. 3, 2012), "to ensure that its core programs are open to all eligible individuals and families regardless of sexual orientation, gender identity, or marital status." *Id.* Given evidence "that lesbian, gay, bisexual, and transgender (LGBT) individuals and families are being arbitrarily excluded from housing opportunities," *id.*, the rule requires that eligibility determinations for a variety of HUD-assisted housing be made without regard to actual or perceived sexual orientation, gender identity, or marital status, generally prohibits inquiries by HUD-funded providers into these issues when making housing available, and broadens the definition of family in a number of programs.

In the agency's first enforcement action under the new rule, Bank of America settled a claim brought by a lesbian couple who were denied a mortgage because they were not married. Bank of America agreed to pay a fine of $7,500 and update its fair lending training. *See* HUD Announces Agreement with Bank of America to Settle LGBT Discrimination Claim (Press Release Jan. 2, 2013). In 2012, HUD insured roughly 15 percent of all single-family home-purchase loans, *see* FHA Single Family Activity in the Home-Purchase Market Through July 2012, *available at http://portal.hud.gov/hudportal/ HUD?src=/program_offices/housing/rmra/oe/rpts/fhamktsh/fhamkt*, which means that the new rule will reach both traditional housing subsidy programs as well as a significant portion of general single-family home purchases.

3. **Housing discrimination on the basis of sexual orientation by a roommate.** The *Sprague* court found that the ordinance unambiguously applied to

choices of roommates. Do you agree? Does the Ninth Circuit's decision in *Roommate.com* (*see* §1.3, above) suggest arguments on the other side?

4. Housing discrimination on the basis of sexual orientation by a cooperative corporation. In *170 West 85 Street HDFC v. Jones*, 673 N.Y.S.2d 830 (Civ. Ct. 1998), the court held that a cooperative corporation may have engaged in unlawful discrimination because of sexual orientation when it refused to allow Vance Jones, the gay life partner of Richard Watts, an owner of a cooperative apartment who had died of AIDS, to purchase the unit and remain living there. The proprietary lease provided that the corporation could not "unreasonably withhold consent to assignment of the lease and a transfer of the Shares to a financially responsible member of the Shareholder's *family* (other than the Shareholder's spouse, as to whom no consent is required) who shall have accepted all the terms and conditions of this lease." *Id.* at 834 (emphasis in original). Both a New York City ordinance and the lease itself prohibited the corporation from discriminating on the basis of sexual orientation. Citing an earlier rent control case that defined a gay life partner to be a "family" member for the purpose of succeeding to rights in a rent-controlled apartment, *Braschi v. Stahl Associates*, 543 N.E.2d 49 (N.Y. 1989), the court noted that Jones fit within a "more comprehensive definition of family member." 673 N.Y.S.2d at 834. This would thus negate the corporation's assertion that Jones was "a licensee whose license had expired, thereby vitiating any independent non-discriminatory grounds which [it] could have asserted to obtain possession of the subject apartment." *Id.*

5. Damages. In *Application of 119-121 East 97th Street Corp. v. New York City Commission on Human Rights*, 642 N.Y.S.2d 638 (App. Div. 1996), the court upheld a damages award of $100,000 for mental anguish and imposed a civil penalty of $25,000 against landlords who had engaged in highly abusive conduct toward a gay tenant with AIDS. The defendants had burglarized the tenant's apartment, disabled his door locks, turned off his electricity, refused to accept his timely rent checks, refused to renew his lease, and commenced eviction proceedings against him. They had also verbally and physically accosted him in public, calling him a "faggot punk," "male whore," and "sicko." They knew he had AIDS and told him they hoped he died. They left threatening messages on his answering machine, distributed a notice to tenants in his building informing them of his Human Rights complaint and HIV status, and warned the tenants not to cooperate with him. The court upheld the damages award on the ground that the abuse was both "horrendous" and malicious, *id.* at 644:

> In any event, decency and justice call out for redress to this respondent. The award herein will not only compensate complainant for the mental distress he suffered but will also serve as a deterrent to others who might emulate petitioners' actions. An agenda of spite, malice and bias, acted upon over an extended period of time, resulting in the severe emotional and mental abuse of a tenant, seriously ill with AIDS, will not be met with half-hearted sanctions or "slaps on the wrist," and we concur in the award for mental anguish.

Problems

1. A lesbian couple living in a 25-unit apartment building is often taunted by teenagers living across the street whenever the couple leaves or enters the building.

   a. Does the couple have a claim against the teenagers under the Wisconsin statute?

   b. Suppose the teenagers live in the same building on another floor. The couple asks the landlord to stop the abusive conduct; the landlord does nothing. Does the couple have a claim against the landlord for violating the Wisconsin statute?

2. An owner of a three-unit building lives on the first floor with her six-year old son and rents out the apartments on the second and third floors. Her city prohibits housing discrimination on the basis of both marital status and sexual orientation.

   a. She refuses to rent to unmarried couples because she believes that her religion would count it to be a sin for her to facilitate sexual relations outside of marriage. She has therefore refused to rent the apartments either to same-sex couples or to male-female couples who are not married. She has, however, rented the second-floor apartment to a gay man under a lease that prohibits him from having long-term visitors. When an unmarried lesbian couple seeks to rent the third-floor apartment, she refuses. Her city has an ordinance prohibiting discrimination "because of" marital status and sexual orientation. Has she violated the law?

   b. Now assume she rents the second-floor apartment to an unmarried male-female couple and offers the third-floor apartment for rent. She is willing to rent to individuals regardless of their sexual orientation and to male-female couples whether or not they are married. However, she will not rent to a gay or lesbian couple and insists on a lease that would prohibit subletting and having long-term visitors. Although her religion is opposed to cohabitation outside of marriage, she does not feel it is a sin to rent to an unmarried straight couple. However, her religion strongly condemns same-sex sexual relationships, and it would violate her sincerely held religious beliefs to rent to a cohabiting same-sex couple. She is sued by a gay male couple when she refuses to rent them the open apartment. Has she violated the law?

3. A state court rules that a state statute entitles landlords to refuse to rent apartments to gay, lesbian, and bisexual persons because such rentals would substantially burden their exercise of their religion and that eradication of discrimination because of sexual orientation was not a "compelling state interest" within the meaning of the state religious freedom statute. Another landlord refuses to rent to heterosexual couples on the ground that landlords are entitled to use religious reasons to refuse to rent to gay couples. She claims that her religious beliefs support the choice to engage in a same-sex relationship and that she wants to make housing available to gay and lesbian couples who may have trouble finding housing elsewhere. Has she violated the state statute prohibiting discrimination on the basis of sexual orientation?

§2.6 Source of Income and Other Economic Discrimination

DiLiddo v. Oxford Street Realty, Inc.

876 N.E.2d 421 (Mass. 2007)

MARGARET MARSHALL, C.J.

Massachusetts law prohibits landlords from discriminating against tenants who receive public housing subsidies either "because the individual is such a recipient," or "because of any requirement" of the subsidy program. Mass. Gen. Laws ch. 151B, §4(10).[9] We consider in this case whether, consistent with that statute, a landlord may refuse to rent an apartment to a participant in a subsidy program for temporary housing because the landlord considers the termination provisions of a form lease provided by the subsidizing agency to be economically disadvantageous.

For the reasons discussed below, we conclude that the lease termination provision at issue was a "requirement" of the alternative housing voucher program (AHVP), the program that provided a housing subsidy to Lori DiLiddo. We further conclude that, where the Legislature has exercised its authority to set the balance between the protection of landlords' interests and the need for affordable housing, the defendants' refusal to agree to the provision violated the strictures of Mass. Gen. Laws ch. 151B, §4(10).

1. *Background.* [T]he AHVP subsidy program for temporary housing was established following the abolition of rent control in the Commonwealth by popular initiative. *See* 1995 Mass. Acts ch. 179, §16. The statute called on the Executive Office of Communities and Development, now the Department of Housing and Community Development (department), to "establish and administer a *transitional* rental assistance program" for "eligible and qualified handicapped persons of low income," and to promulgate rules and regulations to implement the program (emphasis added). *Id.* The statute specifies that program participants pay a monthly rent on a rental unit limited to between twenty-five and thirty per cent of their income, with the department paying the remainder of the costs of the unit. Consistent with the transitional nature of the subsidy, the statute also provides that "all participants in the program shall be *required,* as a condition of their participation to accept suitable permanent affordable housing in accordance with regulations established by [the department] once such housing becomes available" (emphasis added). *Id.*

Pursuant to the enabling statute, the department created the AHVP, limiting eligibility to nonelderly, low income, handicapped persons. *See* 760 Code Mass. Regs. §53.03. Among the requirements of program participation is that, "[w]hen a Participant

---

9. Mass. Gen. Laws ch. 151B, §4(10), provides: "It shall be an unlawful practice . . . [f]or any person furnishing credit, services or rental accommodations to discriminate against any individual who is a recipient of federal, state, or local public assistance, including medical assistance, or who is a tenant receiving federal, state, or local housing subsidies, including rental assistance or rental supplements, because the individual is such a recipient, or because of any requirement of such public assistance, rental assistance, or housing subsidy program."

chooses or is required to move, the Participant shall give a calendar month's written notice to the [local agency administering the program] and to the Owner or Owner's Agent." 760 Code Mass. Regs. §53.07.

To administer the program, the department created a standard form lease to be signed by all landlords and tenants participating in the program (AHVP lease). Under the AHVP lease, tenancy is for a term of one year and is automatically extended from year to year unless either the landlord or the tenant gives sixty days' notice of election not to renew the lease. The AHVP lease does not allow either the landlord or the tenant to terminate the lease early, except for certain enumerated reasons that constitute "good cause." In those cases, a landlord may terminate the lease on thirty days' notice, and a tenant on one month's notice. To further implement the transitional program, the department created an AHVP voucher, which every participant in the program must sign. The voucher requires participants to "[a]ttempt to locate other suitable housing for which [the] AHVP subsidy is not necessary." The voucher and standard form lease each specify that the AHVP participant must give one calendar month's notice to both the landlord and the housing authority if suitable permanent housing is found.

DiLiddo, who was disabled after an automobile accident in 1994, was issued an AHVP voucher by the Cambridge Housing Authority in April, 1998. In late May, 1998, DiLiddo viewed an apartment located at 2 Belvedere Place, in Cambridge. [After expressing interest in the apartment and informing the landlord's agent, Oxford Street Realty, Inc. (Oxford), and its principal, Jeffrey W. Indeck, that she held an AHVP voucher, Oxford initially agreed to rent her the apartment but reneged after concluding that several of the AHVP form lease provisions were "unreasonable and excessive." Specifically, Indeck objected to the provisions that would terminate the lease on one calendar month's notice "when the Tenant becomes a participant in another housing subsidy program, or when the Tenant secures Suitable Permanent Housing, as defined" in 760 Code Mass. Regs. §53.02. Indeck testified at his deposition that he believed that these provisions placed an "unreasonable" burden on landlords.]

2. *The "requirement" provision of Mass. Gen. Laws ch. 151B, §4(10).* The question presented is a narrow one of statutory interpretation: Is the one-month termination provision of the AHVP lease a "requirement" of the AHVP, and, if so, is it a requirement that a landlord may reject for purported financial reasons without running afoul of the housing antidiscrimination law?

The relevant section of Gen. Laws ch. 151B makes it unlawful for a landlord to discriminate against recipients of rental assistance or housing subsidies "because of any requirement" of the "housing subsidy program." Mass. Gen. Laws ch. 151B, §4(10). The language is unambiguous. By its plain terms, a "requirement" is "[s]omething that is required; a necessity." *American Heritage Dictionary of the English Language* 1533 (3d ed. 1992). [D]efendants suggest that the department lacked the authority to require that a landlord use the AHVP lease because neither the statute nor the regulations mandate any particular form of lease. Mass. Gen. Laws ch. 151B, §4(10), does not limit the scope of the term "requirement" to a statutory provision or regulation, and their argument misconstrues the legitimate reach of the department's authority.

The Legislature granted the department broad authority to "establish and administer" a transitional housing subsidy program. 1995 Mass. Acts ch. 179, §16. The development of a standard form AHVP lease containing clauses designed to implement the program's transitional character is well within the bounds of the department's mandate from the Legislature.

The defendants argue that, even if the termination provisions of the AHVP lease are "requirements" of the AHVP for purposes of our antidiscrimination law, they may refuse to accept those requirements so long as they had a "legitimate, nondiscriminatory reason" for doing [so]. Put another way, they contend that, because they rejected the AHVP based on a good faith attempt to serve the landlord's economic interests and not from any discriminatory "animus," they may not be held liable for housing discrimination under Mass. Gen. Laws ch. 151B, §4(10). But it is Mass. Gen. Laws ch. 151B, itself, not the defendants' conception of what should or should not constitute discrimination, that delineates what is "legitimate" and "nondiscriminatory" under the statute. The statute contains no language requiring a showing of "animus."

The defendants urge that we read into the statute an exception that would allow landlords to reject a participant in any housing subsidy program whose requirements could cause the landlord "substantial economic harm." We may not rewrite the statute's clear terms. The General Court was aware that [the statute] imposed financial burdens on landlords, and it made various policy judgments striking the balance between those burdens and the public interest in making housing accessible and affordable for disabled persons. Absent a challenge to the reach of the statute itself, or a challenge to the scope of the implementing regulations, we may not strike a different balance.

The AHVP housing subsidy program affects relatively few individuals. But if landlords or their agents are permitted to reject for their own reasons the "requirements" of the AHVP program, that could have, as the Commonwealth argues, "a potentially widespread and profound impact on the ability of residents in the Commonwealth to utilize any rental assistance voucher to locate and then actually obtain affordable housing." The General Court has spoken unambiguously. The defendants have proffered no basis for us to ignore its mandate.

Notes and Questions

1. **Source of income and economic status.** The *Fair Housing Act* does not include economic status as a protected category, and the Supreme Court generally reviews classifications by public entities based on wealth for equal protection purposes on a deferential rational basis standard. *See San Antonio Independent School District v. Rodriguez,* 411 U.S. 1 (1973). However, a number of states and local governments include "source of income" in their fair housing laws. *See* Robert G. Schwemm, *Housing Discrimination Law and Litigation,* §30:3 n.3 (at least 12 states and 18 local governments bar source-of-income discrimination in housing);

see, e.g., Feemster v. BSA Limited Partnership, 548 F.3d 1063, 1070-1071 (D.C. Cir. 2008) (applying the District of Columbia Human Rights Act's prohibition on source-of-income discrimination to a landlord who attempted to opt out of Section 8 program); *Short v. Manhattan Apartments, Inc.*, 916 F. Supp. 2d 375 (S.D.N.Y. 2012) (applying the New York City source-of-income statute to find brokers liable for refusing to show apartments to prospective tenants who receive public assistance).

2. State constitutional claims. In the *Mount Laurel* case, *Southern Burlington County NAACP v. Township of Mount Laurel*, 336 A.2d 713 (N.J. 1975), the New Jersey Supreme Court based its holding in part on "the relation of housing to the concept of general welfare" under the New Jersey constitution. *See* Chapter 7, §5. In *Mount Laurel*, the combination of the fundamental importance of housing and the exclusionary nature of the township's land use regulations on low- and moderate-income people was sufficient to violate the due process and equal protection clauses of the New Jersey constitution.

3. Affirmatively furthering fair housing. As noted above, *see* §2.2, the *Fair Housing Act* imposes an obligation on recipients of federal housing and urban development funding affirmatively to further the purposes of the act. 42 U.S.C. §3608(e)(5). In *United States ex rel. Anti-Discrimination Center of Metro New York, Inc. v. Westchester County*, 712 F.3d 761 (2d Cir. 2013), the Westchester county executive had reached a settlement in a case involving this "affirmatively to further" obligation. The settlement's consent decree required the county executive to promote "legislation currently before the [County] Board of Legislators to ban 'source-of-income' discrimination in housing." *Id.* at 768. A subsequently elected county executive vetoed such legislation. The Second Circuit held that the veto violated the consent decree. *Id.* at 771. Should affirmatively furthering the *Fair Housing Act* include local government actions that would not be directly required by the antidiscrimination provisions of the act? What are the best arguments on each side?

4. Homelessness. What other legal tools might advocates draw on to respond to economic discrimination in housing, particularly where inability to pay denies housing altogether? *See* Chapter 1, §5.

Problem

A single mother of two children with a federal housing choice voucher applies to rent an apartment from a private landlord in a small, five-unit building in which the landlord lives. The landlord tells her that he is sympathetic to her need for housing, and he gladly rents to a number of other women like her, but the voucher program involves too much red tape and is slow to make payments to landlords. As a result, he says, he cannot accept her application. What legal rights does she have to challenge this action?

§3 DISPARATE IMPACT OR DISCRIMINATORY EFFECTS CLAIMS

Fair Housing Act claims relying on disparate impact can be brought against private parties or governmental entities.[10] In all such cases, a facially neutral housing-related policy or practice is alleged to be discriminatory under the act because the effects of that policy or practice vary based on a protected category. Many disparate impact cases involve land use regulations and related laws; the standards that govern such claims are similar to those governing private-party practices, but can have some differences when it comes to evaluating whether a challenged practice or policy is justified.

§3.1 Racially Discriminatory Effects in Land Use Regulation

Huntington Branch, NAACP v. Town of Huntington

844 F.2d 926 (2d Cir.), *review declined in part and judgment aff'd sub nom. Town of Huntington v. Huntington Branch, NAACP*, 488 U.S. 15 (1988)

Map: Huntington, New York

IRVING R. KAUFMAN, Circuit Judge:

Twenty years ago, widespread racial segregation threatened to rip civil society asunder. In response, Congress adopted broad remedial provisions to promote integration. One such statute, Title VIII of the *Civil Rights Act of 1968*, 42 U.S.C. §§3601-3631 (1982 & Supp. III 1985) ("*Fair Housing Act*"), was enacted "to provide, within constitutional limitations, for fair housing throughout the United States." 42 U.S.C. §3601. Today, we are called upon to decide whether an overwhelmingly white suburb's zoning regulation, which restricts private multi-family housing projects to a largely minority "urban renewal area," and the Town Board's refusal to amend that ordinance to allow construction of subsidized housing in a white neighborhood violates the *Fair Housing Act*.

Huntington is a town of approximately 200,000 people located in the northwest corner of Suffolk County, New York. In 1980, 95% of its residents were white. Blacks comprised only 3.35% of the Town's population and were concentrated in areas known as Huntington Station and South Greenlawn. Specifically, 43% of the total black population lived in four census tracts in Huntington Station and 27% in two census tracts in the South Greenlawn area. Outside these two neighborhoods, the Town's population

10. Some courts have held that disparate impact claims are available only against government, not private, defendants, but this approach has been rejected by most courts that have addressed the issue. *See Village of Bellwood v. Dwivedi*, 895 F.2d 1521, 1533-1534 (7th Cir. 1990); *Brown v. Artery Organization, Inc.*, 654 F. Supp. 1106 (D.D.C. 1987).

was overwhelmingly white. Of the 48 census tracts in the Town in 1980, 30 contained black populations of less than 1%.

The district court found that the Town has a shortage of affordable rental housing for low and moderate-income households. The Town's Housing Assistance Plan (HAP), which is adopted by the Town Board and filed with HUD as part of Huntington's application for federal community development funds, reveals that the impact of this shortage is three times greater on blacks than on the overall population. Under the 1982-1985 HAP, for example, 7% of all Huntington families required subsidized housing, while 24% of black families needed such housing.

In addition, a disproportionately large percentage of families in existing subsidized projects are minority. In Gateway Gardens, a public housing project built in 1967, 38 of 40 units were occupied by blacks and Hispanics in 1984. Seventy-four percent of those on the project's waiting list were minority. In Whitman Village, a 260-unit HUD subsidized development built in 1971, 56% of the families were minority in 1984. Lincoln Manor, which was built in 1980, is a 30-unit HUD Section 8 project. Thirty percent of the households and 45% of those on the waiting list were minority in 1984. Under a HUD Section 8 program, lower income families can obtain certificates to supplement their rent. Each family, however, must locate its own apartment. In January 1984, 68% of families holding certificates and 61% of those on the waiting list were minority.

Although a disproportionate number of minorities need low-cost housing, the Town has attempted to limit minority occupancy in subsidized housing projects. Michael Miness, the Director of Huntington's Community Development agency and responsible for developing the Town's low-cost housing, and Angela Sutton, Executive Director of the Huntington Housing Authority, repeatedly told whites opposing the Lincoln Manor project that they would impose a racial quota on occupancy. When HUD reviewed the project's management plan which established 5% minority occupancy, however, it advised the Huntington Housing Authority that it would not permit a racial quota at Lincoln Manor. The Town similarly attempted to impose racial quotas on occupancy at a proposed 150-unit subsidized housing project in Huntington Station on the Melville Industrial Associates (MIA) site. When Alan H. Wiener, HUD's Area Director, wrote Kenneth C. Butterfield, Town Supervisor, that "limitations on minority occupancy of housing on the Huntington Station site are not justifiable and will not be permitted," the Town Board unanimously passed a resolution withdrawing its support for the project because they could not "ensure a particular ethnic mix."

Under the Town's zoning ordinance, multi-family housing is permitted only in an "R-3M Apartment District." The relevant portion of section 198-20(A) limits private construction of multi-family housing to the Town's urban renewal area, where 52% of the residents are minority. The Town's zoning ordinance also includes a special category for multi-family housing for senior citizens called "R-RM Retirement Community District." Only one such development — Paumanack Village — has been built in Huntington. It is the only multi-family housing for low income people which is situated in an overwhelmingly white neighborhood. The development itself is largely white, having a black occupancy of 3%. Only one vacant parcel of land in Huntington currently is zoned R-3M and thus would be eligible for the appellants' proposed development:

the MIA site, which is at the northeast corner of Broadway and New York Avenue, is partially zoned C-6 and partially zoned R-3M.

In response to the great need for subsidized housing in the Town, [Housing Help, Inc. (HHI)] decided to sponsor an integrated housing project for low-income families. HHI determined that the project could foster racial integration only if it were located in a white neighborhood outside the Huntington Station and South Greenlawn areas. This decision eliminated consideration of the MIA site, the only vacant R-3M property located in the urban renewal area.

After a lengthy search, HHI determined that a 14.8 acre parcel located at the corner of Elwood and Pulaski Roads in the Town was well suited for a 162-unit housing project. This flat, largely cleared and well-drained property was near public transportation, shopping and other services, and immediately adjacent to schools.

Ninety-eight percent of the population within a one-mile radius of the site is white. HHI set a goal of 25% minority occupants. The district court found that "a significant percentage of the tenants [at Matinecock Court] would have belonged to minority groups." HHI officials determined that the property was economically feasible and offered a lengthy option period. HHI obtained its option to purchase the Elwood-Pulaski parcel on January 23, 1980.

Throughout 1980, HHI sought to advance its project by gaining the approval of the Town Board to rezone the property to R-3M from its R-40 designation. Robert Ralph, a director of HHI, addressed the Town Board on February 26, 1980, at a public hearing. The district court found that he filed a document requesting "a commitment by the Town to amend the zoning ordinance to allow multi-family rental construction by a private developer." In August 1980, HHI and National Housing Partnership, an owner-manager of federally subsidized housing, filed a joint application with HUD for Section 8 funding for the project.

At the time HHI applied for the Section 8 funding, Huntington had a Housing Assistance Plan, which had been approved by HUD. Pursuant to the provisions of the *Housing and Community Development Act of 1974*, 42 U.S.C. §§5301-20 (1982 & Supp. III 1985), when a town has such a plan, HUD must refer a Section 8 application to the Town for comment. In an October 14, 1980, letter to Alan H. Weiner, HUD Area Manager, Town Supervisor Kenneth C. Butterfield set forth seven reasons why Huntington opposed the project. It reads, in pertinent part, as follows:

> The Town's professional staff in the Planning, Legal and Community Development Departments have reviewed the proposal and have submitted the following comments:
>
> 1. The HUD-approved Housing Assistance Plan (both the three-year goal submitted with the Community Development Block Grant 1979-80 application and the annual goal submitted with the 1980-1981 Community Development Block Grant) contains no "new construction" units as a program goal.
> 2. The plan for development cannot be carried out within the existing single family R-40 (1 acre) zoning.
> 3. The development is located at the intersection of two heavily trafficked streets.
> 4. The site plan presents a poor parking plan in terms of location with respect to the units, substandard in size and the lack of streets results in very poor fire protection access.

5. The development is located adjacent to both the Long Island Railroad as well as a LILCO substation. This is in addition to the heavy traffic conditions.
6. The site plan shows recreation and/or play areas very inadequate for the number and type of dwelling units being proposed.
7. The three and four-bedroom units are quite undersized; have poor layout; bedrooms are much too small; living space is unrealistic; no storage; one full and two half-baths for a family of 6 to 8 is not realistic.

In conclusion, I do not recommend HUD approval of this proposal based on the material reviewed and the comments presented above.

When the proposal became public, substantial community opposition developed. A group called the Concerned Citizens Association was formed, and a petition containing 4,100 signatures against the proposal was submitted to the Town Board. A protest meeting in November drew about 2,000 persons. Supervisor Butterfield was the principal speaker and assured the audience of his opposition to the project. Matinecock Court came before the Town Board at a meeting on January 6, 1981. The Board rejected the proposed zoning change [on the ground that the location was inappropriate due to "lack of transportation, traffic hazard and disruption of the existing residential patterns."]

[T]his case requires what has been called "disparate impact" or "disparate effects" analysis, not "disparate treatment" analysis. A disparate impact analysis examines a facially-neutral policy or practice, such as a hiring test or zoning law, for its differential impact or effect on a particular group. Disparate treatment analysis, on the other hand, involves differential treatment of similarly situated persons or groups. The line is not always a bright one, but does adequately delineate two very different kinds of discrimination claims.

Under disparate impact analysis, as other circuits have recognized, a *prima facie* case is established by showing that the challenged practice of the defendant "actually or predictably results in racial discrimination; in other words that it has a discriminatory effect." The plaintiff need not show that the decision complained of was made with discriminatory intent. The Act's stated purpose to end discrimination requires a discriminatory effect standard; an intent requirement would strip the statute of all impact on *de facto* segregation.

Practical concerns militate against inclusion of intent in any disparate impact analysis. [A]s this court noted in *Robinson v. 12 Lofts Realty, Inc.*, 610 F.2d 1032, 1043 (2d Cir. 1979), "clever men may easily conceal their motivations." This is especially persuasive in disparate impact cases where a facially neutral rule is being challenged. Often, such rules bear no relation to discrimination upon passage, but develop into powerful discriminatory mechanisms when applied.

Once a *prima facie* case of adverse impact is presented, as occurred here, the inquiry turns to the standard to be applied in determining whether the defendant can nonetheless avoid liability under Title VIII. The Third Circuit in *Resident Advisory Board v. Rizzo*, 564 F.2d 126 (3d Cir. 1977), and the Seventh Circuit in *Metropolitan Housing Development Corp. v. Village of Arlington Heights*, 558 F.2d 1283 (7th Cir.

1977) (*Arlington Heights II*), have both made useful contributions to this inquiry. Both circuits essentially recognize that in the end there must be a weighing of the adverse impact against the defendant's justification. As phrased by the Third Circuit, the defendant must prove that its actions furthered, in theory and in practice, a legitimate, bona fide governmental interest and that no alternative would serve that interest with less discriminatory effect. *Rizzo*, 564 F.2d at 148-49. We agree with that formulation. The Seventh Circuit adds two other factors that can affect the ultimate determination on the merits. One factor is whether there is any evidence of discriminatory intent on the part of the defendant. Though we have ruled that such intent is not a requirement of the plaintiff's *prima facie* case, there can be little doubt that if evidence of such intent is presented, that evidence would weigh heavily on the plaintiff's side of the ultimate balance. The other factor is whether the plaintiff is suing to compel a governmental defendant to build housing or only to require a governmental defendant to eliminate some obstacle to housing that the plaintiff itself will build. In the latter circumstance, a defendant would normally have to establish a somewhat more substantial justification for its adverse action than would be required if the defendant were defending its decision not to build.

The discriminatory effect of a rule arises in two contexts: adverse impact on a particular minority group and harm to the community generally by the perpetuation of segregation. In analyzing Huntington's restrictive zoning, however, the lower court concentrated on the harm to blacks as a group, and failed to consider the segregative effect of maintaining a zoning ordinance that restricts private multi-family housing to an area with a high minority concentration.

Seventy percent of Huntington's black population reside in Huntington Station and South Greenlawn. Matinecock Court, with its goal of 25% minorities, would begin desegregating a neighborhood which is currently 98% white. Indeed, the district court found that a "significant percentage of the tenants" at Matinecock Court would belong to minority groups. The court, however, failed to take the logical next step and find that the refusal to permit projects outside the urban renewal area with its high concentration of minorities reinforced racial segregation in housing. This was erroneous. Similarly, the district court found that the Town has a shortage of rental housing affordable for low and moderate-income households, that a "disproportionately" large percentage of the households using subsidized rental units are minority citizens, and that a disproportionately large number of minorities are on the waiting lists for subsidized housing and existing Section 8 certificates. But it failed to recognize that Huntington's zoning ordinance, which restricts private construction of multi-family housing to the largely minority urban renewal area, impedes integration by restricting low-income housing needed by minorities to an area already 52% minority. We thus find that Huntington's refusal to amend the restrictive zoning ordinance to permit privately-built multi-family housing outside the urban renewal area significantly perpetuated segregation in the Town.

On the question of harm to blacks as a group, the district court emphasized that 22,160 whites and 3,671 minorities had incomes below 200% of the poverty line, a cutoff close to the Huntington Housing Authority's qualification standards. Thus, the district court focused on the greater absolute number of poor whites compared with indigent minorities in Huntington. By relying on absolute numbers rather than on proportional statistics, the district court significantly underestimated the disproportionate impact of the Town's policy.

The parties have stipulated that 28% of minorities in Huntington and 11% of whites have incomes below 200% of the poverty line. What they dispute is the meaning of these statistics. Judge Glasser found that, as the Town contends, there is no showing of discriminatory effect because a majority of the victims are white. We disagree. Under the Huntington HAP for 1982-1985, 7% of all Huntington families needed subsidized housing, while 24% of the black families needed such housing. In addition, minorities constitute a far greater percentage of those currently occupying subsidized rental projects compared to their percentage in the Town's population. Similarly, a disproportionately high percentage (60%) of families holding Section 8 certificates from the Housing Authority to supplement their rents are minorities, and an equally disproportionate percentage (61%) of those on the waiting list for such certificates are minorities. Therefore, we conclude that the failure to rezone the Matinecock Court site had a substantial adverse impact on minorities.

In sum, we find that the disproportionate harm to blacks and the segregative impact on the entire community resulting from the refusal to rezone create a strong *prima facie* showing of discriminatory effect. Thus, we must consider the Town's asserted justifications.

Once a plaintiff has made a *prima facie* showing of discriminatory effect, a defendant [1] must present bona fide and legitimate justifications for its action [2] [and demonstrate that no less discriminatory alternative can serve those ends]. For analytical ease, the second prong should be considered first. Concerns can usually be divided between "plan-specific" justifications and those which are "site-specific." "Plan-specific" problems can be resolved by the less discriminatory alternative of requiring reasonable design modifications. "Site-specific" justifications, however, would usually survive this prong of the test. Those remaining reasons are then scrutinized to determine if they are legitimate and bona fide. By that, we do not intend to devise a search for pretext. Rather, the inquiry is whether the proffered justification is of substantial concern such that it would justify a reasonable official in making this determination. Of course, a concern may be non-frivolous, but may not be sufficient because it is not reflected in the record.

Appellants challenge both the ordinance which restricts privately-built multifamily housing to the urban renewal area and the Town Board's decision to refuse to rezone the Elwood-Pulaski site. On appeal, appellees contend that the ordinance is designed to encourage private developers to build in the deteriorated area of Huntington Station. The Town asserts that limiting multi-family development to the urban renewal area will encourage restoration of the neighborhood because, otherwise, developers will choose to build in the outlying areas and will bypass the zone. The Town's goal, however, can be achieved by less discriminatory means, by encouraging development in the urban renewal area with tax incentives or abatements.

We turn next to the Town's reasons rejecting the Elwood-Pulaski site. The 1980 letter written by Town Supervisor Butterfield detailed seven justifications for the

Town's refusal to rezone: (1) inconsistency with the Town's Housing Assistance Plan; (2) inconsistency with zoning; (3) traffic considerations; (4) parking and fire protection problems; (5) proximity to the railroad and Long Island Lighting Company substation; (6) inadequate recreation and play areas; and (7) undersized and unrealistic units. As the judge below noted, the first two beg the question because appellants are challenging the Town's zoning ordinance. More significantly, as we have already indicated, the Town simply relied on the existence of the Housing Assistance Plan and the zoning ordinance and failed to present any substantial evidence indicating why precluding plaintiff from building a multi-family housing project outside the urban renewal area would impair significant interests sought to be advanced by the HAP and the ordinance. The fourth, sixth and seventh problems are "plan-specific" issues which could presumably have been solved with reasonable design modifications at the time appellants applied for rezoning of the parcel. The fifth concern also is largely plan-specific because proper landscaping could shield the project from the railroad and substation.

Thus, only the traffic issue and health hazard from the substation are site-specific. At trial, however, none of Huntington's officials supported these objections. Accordingly, we find the reasons asserted are entirely insubstantial.

The sewage problem was first raised at trial by appellees' expert Portman. Appellees now advance it as an additional concern. The district court, however, chose not to consider it. We agree. Post hoc rationalizations by administrative agencies should be afforded "little deference" by the courts, and therefore cannot be a bona fide reason for the Town's action. Moreover, the sewage concern could hardly have been significant if municipal officials only thought of it after the litigation began. If it did not impress itself on the Town Board at the time of rejection, it was obviously not a legitimate problem. In sum, the only factor in the Town's favor was that it was acting within the scope of its zoning authority, and thus we conclude that the Town's justifications were weak and inadequate.

In balancing the showing of discriminatory effect against the import of the Town's justifications, we note our agreement with the Seventh Circuit that the balance should be more readily struck in favor of the plaintiff when it is seeking only to enjoin a municipal defendant from interfering with its own plans rather than attempting to compel the defendant itself to build housing. As the *Arlington Heights II* court explained, "courts are far more willing to prohibit even nonintentional action by the state which interferes with an individual's plan to use his own land to provide integrated housing." 558 F.2d at 1293. Bearing in mind that the plaintiffs in this case seek only the freedom to build their own project, we conclude that the strong showing of discriminatory effect resulting from the Town's adherence to its R-3M zoning category and its refusal to rezone the Matinecock Court site far outweigh the Town's weak justifications. Accordingly, to recapitulate, we find that the Town violated Title VIII by refusing to amend the zoning ordinance to permit private developers to build multi-family dwellings outside the urban renewal area. We also find that the Town violated Title VIII by refusing to rezone the Matinecock Court site. We thus reverse the district court and direct entry of judgment in appellants' favor.

Ordinarily, HHI would not be automatically entitled to construct its project at its preferred site. The Town might well have legitimate reasons for preferring some alternative site to the one preferred by HHI.

This case, however, is not ordinary. First, we recognize the protracted nature of this litigation, which has spanned over seven years. Further delay might well prove fatal to this private developer's plans. Second, other than its decision in December 1987 to build 50 units of low-income housing in the Melville section, the Town has demonstrated little good faith in assisting the development of low-income housing. After the Town began receiving federal community development funds, HUD found it necessary to pressure the Town continually to include commitments for construction of subsidized family housing in the Town's HAPs. Because of the Town's lack of progress in constructing such housing, HUD imposed special conditions on the Town's community development grants for the 1978 fiscal allocation. Thereafter, HUD continued to express its dissatisfaction with the Town's performance. This history, while it does not rise to a showing of discriminatory intent, clearly demonstrates a pattern of stalling efforts to build low-income housing.

We therefore refuse to remand this case to the district court to determine the suitability of the 63 sites outside the urban renewal area. Rather, we find that site-specific relief is appropriate in this case.

Accordingly, we direct the district court to include in its judgment provision ordering the Town to rezone the 14.8 acre Matinecock Court site located at the corner of Elwood and Pulaski Roads in Huntington Township to R-3M status. The judgment should also order the Town to strike from its R-3M zoning ordinance that portion which limits private multi-family housing projects to the urban renewal area.

Notes and Questions

1. **Applying disparate impact theory to public actors.** In dealing with public defendants, courts are often reluctant to second guess policy justifications. Indeed, once a governmental entity provides a justification for its policy, some courts have held that this ends the matter. The First Circuit decision in *Langlois v. Abington Housing Authority*, 207 F.3d 43 (1st Cir. 2000), for example, holds that if the defendant has a "valid justification" for its policy that amounts to a "legitimate and substantial goal," then the defendant should prevail. As Judge Boudin explained, "we do not think that the courts' job is to 'balance' objectives, with individual judges deciding which seem to them more worthy." *Id.* at 50-51. Most courts have agreed with *Huntington*, however, that the court must balance the justification for the policy against the disparate impact, adding another step to the analysis. Once the plaintiff has shown a disproportionate or segregatory effect, and the defendant has provided a valid justification for its policy, the court must weigh the adverse impact against the defendant's justification.

2. **Perpetuation of segregation as a basis for liability.** Early circuit court *Fair Housing Act* involving land use restrictions or decisions that impeded projects that would have provided integrated housing in predominantly white areas held that the act could be violated if municipal defendants' actions had the effect of "perpetuating

segregation." *See, e.g.*, *Huntington Branch, NAACP v. Town of Huntington*, 844 F.2d 926, 937 (2d Cir.), *aff'd per curiam*, 488 U.S. 15 (1988); *Resident Advisory Board v. Rizzo*, 564 F.2d 126, 146-149 (3d Cir. 1977); *United States v. City of Black Jack, Missouri*, 508 F.2d 1179, 1184-1187 (8th Cir. 1974). Perpetuation of segregation cases are much less common than disparate impact cases, but courts continue to distinguish these two as independent ways to establish discriminatory effects. *See, e.g.*, *Mount Holly Gardens Citizens in Action, Inc. v. Township of Mount Holly*, 658 F.3d 375, 385 (3d Cir. 2011).

3. Equal protection and the intent requirement. In *Village of Arlington Heights v. Metropolitan Housing Development Corp.*, 429 U.S. 252 (1977), a developer applied for a rezoning of a 15-acre parcel from single-family to multiple-family use, intending to build 190 clustered townhouses for low- and moderate-income tenants. The town refused to rezone and the developer sued, claiming that the failure to rezone had a discriminatory effect on African Americans because they were less likely than white persons to be able to afford single-family homes in the town and that this effect violated the equal protection clause. Only 27 of the town's 64,000 residents were African American. Applying its ruling in *Washington v. Davis*, 426 U.S. 229 (1976), the Supreme Court held that the equal protection clause of the fourteenth amendment was violated only if a state actor engaged in intentional or purposeful discrimination and that racially disproportionate impacts of neutral governmental policies did not violate the state's obligation to provide equal protection of the laws. Plaintiff had to prove that a discriminatory purpose was a "motivating factor" in the governmental decision in order to establish a constitutional violation. *Accord, City of Cuyahoga Falls v. Buckeye Community Hope Foundation*, 538 U.S. 188 (2003).

§3.2 HUD's Discriminatory Effects Rule

24 C.F.R. §100.500 — Discriminatory effect prohibited

Liability may be established under the Fair Housing Act based on a practice's discriminatory effect, as defined in paragraph (a) of this section, even if the practice was not motivated by a discriminatory intent. The practice may still be lawful if supported by a legally sufficient justification, as defined in paragraph (b) of this section. The burdens of proof for establishing a violation under this subpart are set forth in paragraph (c) of this section.

(a) *Discriminatory effect.* A practice has a discriminatory effect where it actually or predictably results in a disparate impact on a group of persons or creates, increases, reinforces, or perpetuates segregated housing patterns because of race, color, religion, sex, handicap, familial status, or national origin.

(b) *Legally sufficient justification.* (1) A legally sufficient justification exists where the challenged practice:

(i) Is necessary to achieve one or more substantial, legitimate, nondiscriminatory interests of the respondent, with respect to claims brought under

42 U.S.C. 3612, or defendant, with respect to claims brought under 42 U.S.C. 3613 or 3614; and

(ii) Those interests could not be served by another practice that has a less discriminatory effect.

(2) A legally sufficient justification must be supported by evidence and may not be hypothetical or speculative. The burdens of proof for establishing each of the two elements of a legally sufficient justification are set forth in paragraphs (c)(2) and (c)(3) of this section.

(c) *Burdens of proof in discriminatory effects cases.* (1) The charging party, with respect to a claim brought under 42 U.S.C. 3612, or the plaintiff, with respect to a claim brought under 42 U.S.C. 3613 or 3614, has the burden of proving that a challenged practice caused or predictably will cause a discriminatory effect.

(2) Once the charging party or plaintiff satisfies the burden of proof set forth in paragraph (c)(1) of this section, the respondent or defendant has the burden of proving that the challenged practice is necessary to achieve one or more substantial, legitimate, nondiscriminatory interests of the respondent or defendant.

(3) If the respondent or defendant satisfies the burden of proof set forth in paragraph (c)(2) of this section, the charging party or plaintiff may still prevail upon proving that the substantial, legitimate, nondiscriminatory interests supporting the challenged practice could be served by another practice that has a less discriminatory effect.

(d) *Relationship to discriminatory intent.* A demonstration that a practice is supported by a legally sufficient justification, as defined in paragraph (b) of this section, may not be used as a defense against a claim of intentional discrimination.

Notes and Questions

1. **Doctrinal variation.** In *Villas West II of Willowridge Homeowners Association v. McGlothin,* 885 N.E.2d 1274 (Ind. 2008), the court noted that the U.S. Supreme Court has not ruled on the standard that governs disparate impact claims under the *Fair Housing Act.* As a result, the lower courts have adopted a variety of approaches, as follows:

> In [*Metropolitan Housing Development Corp. v. Village of Arlington Heights,* 558 F.2d 1283 (7th Cir. 1977)], the Seventh Circuit held that disparate impact recovery under the FHA is proper when the defendant's conduct produces a discriminatory effect and four factors balance in favor of granting relief. The four factors are (1) the strength of the plaintiff's showing of discriminatory effect; (2) evidence of discriminatory intent, though not enough to satisfy the constitutional standard of *Washington v. Davis;* (3) the defendant's interest in the challenged conduct; and (4) whether the plaintiff seeks affirmative relief or merely to restrain the defendant from interfering with individual property owners who wish to provide housing. *Arlington Heights II,* 558 F.2d at 1290.
>
> One month after *Arlington Heights II,* the Third Circuit adopted a burden-shifting framework similar to that already in use in Title VII employment cases. [*Resident Advisory Board v. Rizzo,* 564 F.2d 126, 148 (3d Cir. 1977).] Under this approach, the plaintiff makes a *prima facie* case by showing that the defendant's action has a discriminatory effect. *Id.* The defendant can rebut this by showing a justification which "serve[s], in theory and in practice, a legitimate, bona fide interest" and by showing that "no alternative

course of action could be adopted that would enable that interest to be served with less discriminatory impact." *Id.* at 149.

A decade later, the *Huntington* court sought to merge *Rizzo* and *Arlington Heights II.* Under the *Huntington* framework, the plaintiff establishes a prima facie case by showing that the "challenged practice of the defendant actually or predictably results in racial discrimination." [*Huntington Branch, NAACP v. Town of Huntington,* 844 F.2d 926, 934 (2d Cir. 1988).] The defendant can rebut this case by showing that its "actions furthered, in theory and in practice, a legitimate, bona fide governmental interest and that no alternative would serve that interest with less discriminatory effect." The court then balances the four *Arlington Heights II* factors to determine whether to grant relief. *Id.* at 936.

These competing approaches spawned a variety of others. One source of disagreement was the role, if any, of the *Arlington Heights II* factors. A few courts have used the factors as part of the prima facie case. This approach has been widely rejected as making the plaintiff's case too difficult. Other courts applied the *Arlington Heights II* factors only in cases involving public defendants. Still others discarded the second *Arlington Heights II* factor—proof of discriminatory intent—and weighed the remaining three, reasoning that intent was relevant only in disparate treatment cases. More recently, most federal circuits have abandoned the *Arlington Heights II* factors altogether. Yet, at least one circuit and several district courts have continued to balance.

Huntington's burden-shifting framework has also morphed. Several courts changed *Huntington*'s two burdens into three. This test still requires plaintiffs to show a discriminatory effect, but rebutting defendants need to provide only a bona fide, nondiscriminatory justification. Once the defendant offers an appropriate justification, the burden shifts back to the plaintiff to show an alternative that would serve the defendant's interest with less discriminatory effect. Courts adopting this approach explain that requiring the plaintiff to propose an alternative gives the plaintiff the ultimate burden of proving a violation and has the advantage that "neither party is saddled with having to prove a negative (the nonexistence of bona fide reasons or the absence of less discriminatory alternatives)." [*Hispanics United v. Village of Addison,* 988 F. Supp. 1130, 1162 (N.D. Ill. 1997).]

Finally, a much smaller number of federal courts have applied a variant of the disparate treatment test from *McDonnell Douglas Corp. v. Green,* 411 U.S. 792 (1973), a leading employment discrimination case, to resolve disparate impact FHA claims. Under this approach, the plaintiff must prove a discriminatory effect, which the defendant may rebut by offering a legitimate, nondiscriminatory reason for its rule. Instead of the plaintiff then showing a less discriminatory alternative, the plaintiff shows the defendant's offered reason is a pretext.

Id. at 1280-1282 (some citations omitted). It is into this confusion that the U.S. Department of Housing and Urban Development stepped in 2013 when it used its authority under 42 U.S.C. §3614a to promulgate regulations under the *Fair Housing Act. See Implementation of the Fair Housing Act's Discriminatory Effects Standard,* 78 Fed. Reg. 11,460, 11,462 (Feb. 15, 2013).

How does HUD's rule, which is codified at 24 C.F.R. §100.500, resolve the variations between the standards adopted by various circuits?

2. The HUD rule's three-part framework

a. Establishing a *prima facie* case. Generally, parties challenging a policy or practice can meet their initial burden either by showing (1) statistical evidence that the policy or practice has a significantly greater impact on a class of persons protected by the *Fair Housing Act* than it does on others; or (2) the policy or practice tends to perpetuate segregation. In establishing a disproportionate effect, plaintiffs can rely on local statistics, but national statistics may be deemed relevant as well in unusual cases. Statistics focus on the relative *percentages* of people in each group affected by the policy rather than their absolute numbers. *See Graoch Associates #33, L.P. v. Louisville/Jefferson County Metro Human Relations Commission*, 508 F.3d 366, 378 (6th Cir. 2007). Moreover, the challenged discriminatory effects must be "significant." *Pfaff v. HUD*, 88 F.3d 739, 745 (9th Cir. 1996); *Simms v. First Gibraltar Bank*, 83 F.3d 1546, 1555 (5th Cir. 1996).

There is no hard and fast rule for establishing a sufficiently disproportionate burden. As HUD stated in promulgating its discriminatory effects rule, "[w]hether a particular practice results in a discriminatory effect is a fact-specific inquiry. Given the numerous and varied practices and wide variety of private and governmental entities covered by the Act, it would be impossible to specify the showing that would be required to demonstrate a discriminatory effect in each of these contexts." 78 Fed. Reg. at 11,468.

b. Legally sufficient justification for a disparate impact? Under the HUD rule, once a party establishes its *prima facie* case, the burden shifts to the party defending the challenged practice or policy to show that the policy or practice "is necessary to achieve one or more substantial, legitimate, nondiscriminatory interests," and that "[t]hose interests could not be served by another practice that has a less discriminatory effect." 24 C.F.R. §100.500(b)(1), (c)(2). As HUD has explained:

> [a]ny interest justifying a practice with a discriminatory effect must be "substantial." A "substantial" interest is a core interest of the organization that has a direct relationship to the function of that organization. The requirement that an entity's interest be substantial is analogous to the Title VII requirement that an employer's interest in an employment practice with a disparate impact be job related. [T]he more general standard of substantiality [recognizes that] there is no single objective, such as job-relatedness, against which every practice covered by the Fair Housing Act could be measured. The determination of whether goals, objectives, and activities are of substantial interest to a respondent or defendant such that they can justify actions with a discriminatory effect requires a case-specific, fact-based inquiry. The word "legitimate," used in its ordinary meaning, is intended to ensure that a justification is genuine and not false, while the word "nondiscriminatory" is intended to ensure that the justification for a challenged practice does not itself discriminate based on a protected characteristic.

78 Fed. Reg. at 11,470.

c. Less discriminatory alternatives? Under the HUD rule, if a policy or practice that has a disparate impact is legally justified, the burden shifts back to the party challenging the policy or practice to show that the "interests supporting the challenged practice could be served by another practice that has a less discriminatory effect."

In practice, how difficult is it for tenants and others challenging practices on a disparate impact theory under the *Fair Housing Act* to show that there are alternative policies that have a less discriminatory effect?

3. Are disparate impact claims available under the *Fair Housing Act?* Until recently, it appeared firmly settled that disparate impact claims may be brought under the *Fair Housing Act,* as they are in employment discrimination cases under Title VII of the 1964 *Civil Rights Act.* Although the Supreme Court has not ruled on the issue, every circuit court has so held, *see 2922 Sherman Avenue Tenants' Association v. District of Columbia*, 444 F.3d 673, 679 (D.C. Cir. 2006) (noting that "every one of the eleven circuits to have considered the issue has held that the FHA . . . prohibits not only intentional housing discrimination, but also housing actions having a disparate impact"), and HUD's discriminatory effects rule takes the same position.

However, in *Smith v. City of Jackson*, 544 U.S. 228 (2005), the Supreme Court may have opened the door to a different interpretation. In *Smith*, the Court held that the *Age Discrimination in Employment Act* (ADEA), 29 U.S.C. §623(a)(2), allows for disparate impact claims. The Court noted that §623(a)(2) contains language, similar to Title VII, that makes it unlawful for an employer to "deprive any individual of employment opportunities or *otherwise adversely affect* his status as an employee, because of such individual's race or color. Thus, the text focuses on the *effects* of the action on the employee rather than the motivation for the action of the employer." 544 U.S. at 235-236. In a footnote, the Court compared this provision to another section of the ADEA, §623(a)(1), that makes it unlawful to discriminate "because of" an employee's age, suggesting that this latter formulation does not allow disparate-impact liability. 544 U.S. at 236, n.6. The statutory language the Court cited in the *Smith* footnote is similar to the *Fair Housing Act*'s language, which likewise does not include the text "adversely affect[ing]" in its primary prohibitions in 42 U.S.C. §3604.

As a result, opponents of disparate impact liability are now seeking to have the Court limit the *Fair Housing Act* to disparate treatment claims. In 2011, the Court granted certiorari on this question in a case involving a claim against St. Paul, Minnesota, but the parties agreed to settle before the Court ruled. *See Magner v. Gallagher*, 132 S. Ct. 548 (Mem) (2011) (granting certiorari to review *Gallagher v. Magner*, 619 F.3d 823 (8th Cir. 2010)); 132 S. Ct. 1306 (Mem) (dismissing the case). The Court granted certiorari on a second case that presented the same question, but it settled as well. *See Mount Holly Gardens Citizens in Action, Inc. v. Township of Mount Holly*, 658 F.3d 375, 385 (3d Cir. 2011), *cert. granted*, 80 U.S.L.W. 3711 (U.S. June 17, 2013) (No. 11-1507), *cert. dismissed*, 2013 WL 6050174 (U.S. Nov. 15, 2013) (No. 11-1507).

How would you construct a textual argument under 42 U.S.C. §3604 and other provisions of the *Fair Housing Act* that the statute allows for disparate-impact liability? What other tools of statutory construction might you draw on to analyze this question?

Problems

1. An African American woman with two children is denied an apartment in a landlord's building. She is a welfare recipient. The landlord has historically refused to rent to welfare recipients. The woman brings a lawsuit claiming that the landlord's policy of not renting to welfare recipients has an impermissible disparate impact on three protected groups: African Americans, women (of all races), and children. As plaintiff's attorney, how would you persuade the court that the "no welfare recipients" policy has a disparate impact on the basis of race, sex, familial status, or all of those categories, that is unjustified by any legitimate interest of the landlord? What would you argue as defendant's attorney to persuade the court that the policy is consistent with the *Fair Housing Act*? What rule of law should the court promulgate to implement the statutory language and policies?

2. A homeowner rented out her home despite a real covenant prohibiting leasing. She argued that the restraint on leasing had a disparate impact on African Americans. The court in *Villas West II of Willowbridge Homeowners Association, supra,* agreed, but found the disparate impact justified by a legitimate, nondiscriminatory reason for the policy, *i.e.*, that the covenant promoted property values by limiting occupancy to resident owners. "Renters do not maintain homes which they rent as well as owners maintain their homes. Therefore, the exclusion of renters helps maintain property values." 885 N.E.2d at 1283-1284. Was the case correctly decided?

3. After Hurricane Katrina, St. Bernard Parish, located just outside New Orleans, was devastated by the flood. When a developer proposed to build four mixed-income rental apartment complexes designed to provide affordable housing, city officials at first reacted favorably, but when public opposition developed after a local editorial suggested that crime would increase if the development went forward and that the community would turn into a "ghetto with drugs, crime, vandalism, and violence," the city council reacted by passing ordinances prohibiting the construction of multi-family housing and the rental of single-family homes to anyone other than a blood relative of the owner without a special permit. In litigation challenging these ordinances as causing a disparate impact on African Americans in violation of the FHA, Judge Helen Berrigan found that African Americans were "85% more likely to live in structures with more than five units than Caucasian households." She further found that the moratorium reduced the supply of rental properties, and while only 25 percent of white families lived in rental housing with more than five units, more than 50 percent of African Americans did so. Finally, she found that African Americans were more likely than whites to come within the income guidelines making them eligible for affordable housing. The city defended the suit by citing a number of nondiscriminatory reasons for the ordinances, each of which was found by the judge to be unsupported by the evidence. *Greater New Orleans Fair Housing Action Center v. St. Bernard Parish,* Case No. 06-7185 (E.D. La., order issued Mar. 25, 2009), *available at http://www.gnofairhousing.org/pdfs/233Order_Rescinding_Ordinance_3.25.09.pdf.*

a. If you were the lawyer for the defendant municipality in this case, what advice would you have given the city when presented with this lawsuit? What justifications could be presented to defend the ordinances?

b. If you were the lawyer for the plaintiff, how would you have rebutted the defendant's justifications?

4. A group of Orthodox Jewish students sued Yale University to challenge its policy of requiring all students (other than married students or students over 21) in their first and second years to live in coeducational residence halls. They claimed that their "religious beliefs and obligations regarding sexual modesty forbid them to reside in the coeducational housing provided and mandated by Yale." *Hack v. President & Fellows of Yale College*, 16 F. Supp. 2d 183, 187 (D. Conn. 1998), *aff'd*, 237 F.3d 81 (2d Cir. 2000). They sought and were denied exemptions from the policy. The district court rejected their claim that Yale had violated the *Fair Housing Act*, noting that Yale had reserved rooms for each of the plaintiffs and had in no way denied them housing. Plaintiffs claimed that the housing offered was not of a type that they could accept because of their religious beliefs. *Id.* How could the plaintiffs argue that the university policy had a disparate impact on them because of their religion in violation of the *Fair Housing Act*? What is Yale's defense to this argument? How should the court have ruled?

5. A landlord refuses to rent to tenants who do not speak English. A tenant claims that this policy constitutes national origin discrimination because it has an unjustified disparate impact on persons born outside the United States.

a. Does the policy impose a disparate impact based on national origin?

b. If so, is it justified by a legitimate business interest?

6. A university in a state that does not recognize same-sex marriage provides housing for married couples. A gay couple sues the university, claiming that the exclusion of gay couples violates a local law that prohibits discrimination because of sexual orientation. The plaintiffs claim that the university policy has a disparate impact on gay and lesbian couples because they, unlike heterosexual couples, cannot get married even if they want to do so. What are the arguments on both sides? How should the court rule? *See Levin v. Yeshiva University*, 730 N.Y. S.2d 15 (2001) (holding that such a policy imposed a disparate impact on gay and lesbian couples under the New York City law prohibiting sexual orientation discrimination and remanding to determine whether the disparate impact bore a "significant relationship to a significant business objective").

§4 DISCRIMINATION AGAINST PERSONS WITH DISABILITIES

§4.1 Reasonable Accommodations and Modifications

Janush v. Charities Housing Development Corp.

169 F. Supp. 2d 1133 (N.D. Cal. 2000)

RONALD M. WHYTE, District Judge.

Plaintiff Brenda Janush ("plaintiff") suffers from a severe mental health disability. Plaintiff's treating psychiatrist, Dr. David Kilgore, has testified that plaintiff's pets, two birds and two cats, lessen the effects of this disability by providing her with companionship and are necessary to her mental health.

On December 6, 1999, plaintiff signed a rental agreement for an apartment in Pensione Esperanza, a low-income apartment building run by [Charities Housing Development Corp. (CHD)], a non-profit corporation affiliated with Catholic Charities of Santa Clara County. Paragraph 23 of the rental agreement contains a "no pets" clause. Plaintiff did not alert CHD to the presence of her animals prior to moving into the apartment on January 2, 2000. On January 10, 2000, a maintenance worker discovered plaintiff's animals in the apartment. Discussions ensued between plaintiff and defendants over whether plaintiff would be allowed to keep the animals in the apartment and under what conditions. The parties disagree as to what offers and counter-offers were made. Essentially, plaintiff alleges that defendants harassed her and refused to offer any reasonable accommodation. Defendants allege that they were willing to accommodate plaintiff's requests, at least in part, but plaintiff refused to provide requested documentation such as proof that the animals had been vaccinated. On February 7, 2000, defendants filed eviction proceedings against plaintiff. On March 26, 2000, plaintiff moved out of Pensione Esperanza.

Plaintiff filed suit on March 10, 2000, principally alleging discrimination based on defendants' refusal to reasonably accommodate plaintiff's disability as required by the Fair Housing Act, as well as other federal and state law causes of action. Defendants now move to dismiss, or in the alternative, for summary judgment.

To establish a prima facie case of housing discrimination based on an alleged "refusal to make reasonable accommodations in rules, policies, practices, or services, when such accommodations may be necessary to afford such person equal opportunity to use and enjoy a dwelling[,]" 42 U.S.C. §3604(f)(3), a plaintiff must show that: (1) she suffers from a handicap as defined in 42 U.S.C. §3602(h); (2) defendant knew of the handicap or should reasonably be expected to know of it; (3) accommodation of the handicap "may be necessary" to afford plaintiff an equal opportunity to use and enjoy the dwelling; and (4) defendants refused to make such accommodation.

Defendants argue that the core allegation in each of plaintiff's claims is that she was entitled to keep her animals as a reasonable accommodation. Notwithstanding the brevity of defendants' moving papers (three pages of legal argument) and the frankness of their position ("[t]his issue is important to defendants because, given the number of low-income residents they serve, there is a very real risk that the no-pet policy at Pensione Esperanza will be overrun with demands for 'accommodations' by persons who claim to need the companionship of a variety of animals."), defendants have failed to point out which elements of which causes of actions plaintiff has failed to adequately plead. Nor have defendants cited a single case in their moving papers.

The legal basis for defendants' motion appears to be the assertion that California's definition of a "service dog" should be read into the federal statute to create a bright-line rule that accommodation of animals other than service dogs is per se unreasonable. *See* Cal. Civ. Code. §54.1(b)(6)(C)(iii). Although the federal regulations specifically refer to accommodation of seeing-eye dogs, there is no indication that accommodation of other animals is per se unreasonable under the statute. In fact, the federal regulations provide a broad definition of service animals. "Service animal means any guide dog, signal dog, or other animal individually trained to do work or perform tasks for the benefit of an individual with a disability. . . ." 28 C.F.R. §36.104. Even if plaintiff's animals do not qualify as service animals, defendants have not established that there is no duty to reasonably accommodate non-service animals. As plaintiff has adequately plead that she is handicapped, that defendants knew of her handicap, that accommodation of the handicap may be necessary and that defendants refused to make such accommodation, defendants' motion to dismiss is denied.

Federal law prohibits the failure to reasonably accommodate disabled persons in residential housing. "It shall be unlawful for any person to refuse to make reasonable accommodations in rules, policies, practices, or services, when such accommodations may be necessary to afford a handicapped person equal opportunity to use and enjoy a dwelling unit, including public and common use areas." 24 C.F.R. §100.204(a). Whether a particular accommodation is reasonable under the circumstances is the type of fact-intensive, case-specific determination that will infrequently be appropriate for resolution on summary judgment. Whether it is a reasonable accommodation for this landlord to allow this disabled tenant to keep animals in an apartment where pets are not generally permitted strikes the court as inappropriate for resolution on summary judgment based on the showing made to date.

Moreover, plaintiff has not yet had the opportunity to conduct any discovery. Specifically, plaintiff has not been able to discover the likely costs or administrative burdens that would be imposed on the defendants if they were to accommodate her. Accordingly, plaintiff's request to defer resolution of summary judgment until such time as she has had an opportunity to conduct adequate discovery is well taken. Without some evidence as to the burden plaintiff's requested accommodation will impose on defendants, the court is unable to balance that burden against the benefit to plaintiff of the requested accommodation and the court is accordingly unable to make a determination that plaintiff's request is necessarily unreasonable.

The court is not unsympathetic to defendants' concerns regarding a flood of accommodation requests. However, the law imposes on defendants the obligation to consider each request individually and to grant requests that are reasonable. Defendants have no obligation to grant unreasonable requests. The court respects defendants' charitable mission, and suspects that the burden of individually considering accommodation requests from disabled tenants and granting reasonable requests will not prevent defendants from fulfilling that mission. Unless a tenant has a disability, the reasonable accommodation issue does not arise.

Notes and Questions

1. **Reasonable accommodations and modifications for persons with disabilities.** It is clearly a violation of the *Fair Housing Act* to refuse to rent or sell housing to an individual because of that individual's disability. A significant number of fair housing cases, however, turn on the statute's provisions for reasonable accommodations and

reasonable modifications.[11] Under §3604(f)(3)(B), the provision at issue in *Janush*, it is unlawful to refuse "to make reasonable accommodations in rules, policies, practices, or services when such accommodations may be necessary to afford" individuals with disabilities "equal opportunity to use and enjoy a dwelling." Under §3604(f)(3)(A), by contrast, it is unlawful to refuse "to permit, at the expense of the [disabled] person, reasonable modifications of existing premises" if such modifications may be necessary for full enjoyment of the premises, subject to a landlord's right to require restoration of the interior. Courts have noted that the obligation to *permit* tenants to pay for their own reasonable modifications can cover different activities, most notably new construction or rebuilding of facilities, than the obligation on landlords to *make* reasonable accommodations in rules, policies, practices, or services. *See, e.g., Reyes v. Fairfield Properties*, 661 F. Supp. 2d 249, 258-262 (E.D.N.Y. 2009) (not a failure to make a reasonable accommodation even though the landlord refused to pay to install a ramp and widen doors for a disabled child in a wheelchair).

As the First Circuit recently noted, refusal to make a reasonable accommodation for an individual with a disability is a third theory of liability under the *Fair Housing Act*, in addition to disparate treatment and disparate impact. *Astralis Condominium Association v. Secretary, U.S. Department of Housing & Urban Development*, 620 F.3d 62, 67 (1st Cir. 2010). For reasonable accommodation claims, courts generally require plaintiffs to demonstrate that they are disabled; that the party from whom they requested an accommodation knew, or reasonably should have known, of the disability; that a reasonable accommodation that may be necessary to afford the plaintiff an equal opportunity to use and enjoy the housing was requested; and that the reasonable accommodation was refused. *See, e.g., id.*

HUD's FHA regulations contain several examples of the landlord's obligations to permit reasonable modifications, 24 C.F.R. §100.203(c):

> Example (1): A tenant with a handicap asks his or her landlord for permission to install grab bars in the bathroom at his or her own expense. It is necessary to reinforce the walls with blocking between studs in order to affix the grab bars. It is unlawful for the landlord to refuse to permit the tenant, at the tenant's own expense, from making the modifications necessary to add the grab bars. However, the landlord may condition permission for the modification on the tenant agreeing to restore the bathroom to the condition that existed before the modification, reasonable wear and tear excepted. It would be reasonable for the landlord to require the tenant to remove the grab bars at the end of the tenancy. The landlord may also reasonably require that the wall to which the grab bars are to be attached be repaired and restored to its original condition, reasonable wear and tear excepted. However, it would be unreasonable for the landlord to require the tenant to remove the blocking, since the reinforced walls will not interfere in any way with the landlord's or the next tenant's use and enjoyment of the premises and may be needed by some future tenant.

---

11. There is, in addition, an obligation under the *Fair Housing Act* to design and construct covered multi-family dwellings to be accessible to individuals with disabilities, as specified in the statute and elaborated in HUD's regulations. *See* 42 U.S.C. §3604(f)(3)(C); 24 C.F.R. §100.200 *et seq.*; HUD, *Fair Housing Act Design Manual* (April 1998).

> Example (2): An applicant for rental housing has a child who uses a wheelchair. The bathroom door in the dwelling unit is too narrow to permit the wheelchair to pass. The applicant asks the landlord for permission to widen the doorway at the applicant's own expense. It is unlawful for the landlord to refuse to permit the applicant to make the modification. Further, the landlord may not, in usual circumstances, condition permission for the modification on the applicant paying for the doorway to be narrowed at the end of the lease because a wider doorway will not interfere with the landlord's or the next tenant's use and enjoyment of the premises.

The regulation pertinent to the landlord's duty to make reasonable accommodations in rules and practices, 24 C.F.R. §100.204, contains the following examples:

> Example (1): A blind applicant for rental housing wants to live in a dwelling unit with a seeing eye dog. The building has a "no pets" policy. It is a violation of §100.204 for the owner or manager of the apartment complex to refuse to permit the applicant to live in the apartment with a seeing eye dog because, without the seeing eye dog, the blind person will not have an equal opportunity to use and enjoy a dwelling.
>
> Example (2): Progress Gardens is a 300 unit apartment complex with 450 parking spaces which are available to tenants and guests of Progress Gardens on a "first come first served" basis. John applies for housing in Progress Gardens. John is mobility impaired and is unable to walk more than a short distance and therefore requests that a parking space near his unit be reserved for him so he will not have to walk very far to get to his apartment. It is a violation of §100.204 for the owner or manager of Progress Gardens to refuse to make this accommodation. Without a reserved space, John might be unable to live in Progress Gardens at all or, when he has to park in a space far from his unit, might have great difficulty getting from his car to his apartment unit. The accommodation therefore is necessary to afford John an equal opportunity to use and enjoy a dwelling. The accommodation is reasonable because it is feasible and practical under the circumstances.

In recent years, a number of cases have involved reasonable accommodations for assistance animals in residences that have no-pet policies. Courts have taken varying approaches to resolving these cases. Some, like *Janush*, have taken a broad view of the importance of such animals to individuals with disabilities, even when the animals might not qualify as "service animals" such as a seeing-eye dog.

A number of courts have been more skeptical, however, relying on the argument that to be a reasonable accommodation, an animal must meet the definition of a "service animal" provided in the Americans with Disabilities Act (ADA), namely that the animal be "individually trained to do work or perform tasks for the benefit of an individual with a disability." 28 C.F.R. §36.104. *See, e.g., Inle v. Association of Apartment Owners of 2987 Kalakaua*, 304 F. Supp. 2d 1245 (D. Haw. 2003), *aff'd on other grounds*, 453 F.3d 1175 (9th Cir. 2006) (assertion by resident disabled by depression, anxiety, and dizziness, that his dog was trained to provide emotional support was insufficient to make the dog a "service animal" for purposes of reasonable accommodation claim); *see also Meadowland Apartments v. Schumacher*, 813 N.W.2d 618 (S.D. 2012) (not a violation of the FHA for landlord to evict a mentally disabled tenant for, among other things, keeping a dog without notifying landlord, even though tenant had left a doctor's note about the dog with her rent). HUD has taken the position that the ADA's narrow definition of "service animal" does not control the question whether keeping a given animal might be a reasonable accommodation for purposes of the *Fair Housing Act. See* Memorandum from Sara K. Pratt, Deputy Assistant Secretary for Enforcement and Programs, to FHEO Regional Directors and Regional Counsel, *New ADA Regulations and Assistance Animals as Reasonable Accommodations Under the Fair Housing Act and Section 504 of the Rehabilitation Act of 1973* (Feb. 17, 2011).

2. The *Federal Rehabilitation Act of 1973.* In addition to the *Fair Housing Act,* the *Federal Rehabilitation Act of 1973* prohibits discrimination on the basis of disability in federally funded programs. A provision in the act, 29 U.S.C. §794, commonly referred to as Section 504 because of the statute's original bill numbering, provides in relevant part that:

> No otherwise qualified individual with a disability shall, solely by reason of her or his disability, be excluded from the participation in, be denied the benefits of, or be subjected to discrimination under any program or activity receiving Federal financial assistance.

Although disagreements and uncertainties may arise about what constitutes "federal financial assistance," the statute clearly applies to any direct transfer payments made by the government, such as those made to public housing programs and for individual tenant vouchers for use in paying for private housing. *See Housing Authority of Lake Charles v. Pappion,* 540 So. 2d 567 (La. Ct. App. 1989) (housing vouchers); *Whittier Terrace Associates v. Hampshire,* 532 N.E.2d 712 (Mass. App. Ct. 1989) (private housing subsidized by HUD).

Cases also address the issue of identifying which persons with disabilities are "otherwise qualified" for the program financed by federal funds under the *Federal Rehabilitation Act. See, e.g., Fialka-Feldman v. Oakland University Board of Trustees,* 678 F. Supp. 2d 576, 584 (E.D. Mich. 2009). In *Pappion, supra,* the court held that a paranoid schizophrenic tenant was not "otherwise qualified" to remain in a subsidized housing project because he interfered with the quiet enjoyment of other tenants by making loud noises, threatening other residents, and engaging in "bizarre" behavior. In *City Wide Associates v. Penfield,* 564 N.E.2d 1003 (Mass. 1991), however, the court found that a tenant in Section 8 housing who suffered from a mental disability manifested by her hearing voices was "otherwise qualified" despite the fact that she had responded to the auditory hallucinations by striking the walls of the apartment, causing superficial damage amounting to less than one month's rent. The court justified its holding on the ground that the tenant had not disturbed the quiet enjoyment of neighboring tenants and had promised to obtain counseling.[12]

12. One important difference between the *Fair Housing Act* and the *Rehabilitation Act* is in the area of reasonable modifications: Under the former, the tenant is required to pay for structural changes, such as ramps and grab bars, while under the latter, in many circumstances, landlords are obligated to pay. *See* Joint Statement of the Department of Housing and Urban Development and the Department of Justice, Reasonable Modifications Under the Fair Housing Act, at 2 n.4 (Mar. 5, 2008).

Problems

1. A mobile home park charges its residents a fee of $1.50 a day for the presence of long-term guests and $25 per month for guest parking. A tenant whose daughter's health condition requires a full-time attendant argues that the owner violated the *Fair Housing Act*'s reasonable accommodation provisions by refusing to waive the charges for her attendant. The Ninth Circuit has held that the regulation would violate §3604(f)(3)(B) if it had an "unequal impact" on persons with disabilities and resulted in an "exclusionary effect" so long as the financial impact on the landlord was not "unduly burdensome." *United States v. California Mobile Home Park Management Co.*, 29 F.3d 1413 (9th Cir. 1994). Do you agree with this formulation of what §3604(f)(3)(B) requires? Assume that the financial burden to the landlord is minimal and that enforcement of the policy will not cause the tenants to move. Should accommodation be required under the terms of the statute?

2. A tenant living on the first floor of a three-unit building of three stories is in a car accident and is paralyzed from the waist down. He wants, at his own expense, to install a ramp to enable him to enter the front door without assistance since his wheelchair could not negotiate the steps to the front porch. Without such a ramp, he cannot return home. The small front yard will be largely taken up by the ramp if the ramp is installed. The landlord objects to the installation of the ramp on aesthetic and economic grounds. She can demonstrate that the market value of the property will decline from $200,000 to $180,000 if the ramp is installed. The tenant argues that he will pay to have the ramp removed if he moves out of the apartment. Is the landlord required to allow the tenant to install the ramp? *See Rodriguez v. Montalvo*, 337 F. Supp. 2d 212 (D. Mass. 2004) (presumptive *Fair Housing Act* duty to allow tenant to affix permanent ramp to back entrance of building when landlord gave no proof that it would cause financial harm).

§4.2 Integration and the Example of Group Homes for Persons with Disabilities

Familystyle of St. Paul, Inc. v. City of St. Paul

923 F.2d 91 (8th Cir. 1991)

Map: St. Paul, Minnesota

ROGER L. WOLLMAN, Circuit Judge.

Familystyle [of St. Paul, Inc.] provides rehabilitative services to mentally ill persons and operates residential group homes for them in St. Paul, Minnesota. Familystyle sought special use permits for the addition of three houses to its existing campus of group homes, intending to expand its capacity from 119 to 130 mentally ill persons.

Twenty-one of Familystyle's houses, including the three proposed additions, are clustered in a one and one-half block area. On the condition that Familystyle would work to disperse its facilities, the St. Paul City Council issued temporary permits for the three additional houses. Familystyle failed to meet the conditions of the special use permits, and the permits expired. After St. Paul denied renewal of the permits, Familystyle exchanged its license for one excluding the three additional houses.

Relying upon the provisions of the *Fair Housing Amendment Act of 1988*, Familystyle challenges the city ordinance and state laws that bar the addition of these three houses to its campus.

Minnesota requires facilities that provide residential services for people with mental illness and retardation to be licensed. Minnesota seeks through the licensing of group homes to place the mentally ill in the least restrictive environment possible and to allow them "the benefits of normal residential surroundings." Minn. Stat. §245A.11, subd. 1. "Care, treatment, and deinstitutionalization of mentally ill adults [is] a matter of special state concern" in Minnesota. *Nw. Residence, Inc. v. City of Brooklyn Ctr.*, 352 N.W.2d 764, 772 (Minn. Ct. App. 1984).

An integral part of the licensing process guarantees that residential programs are geographically situated, to the extent possible, in locations where residential services are needed, where they would be a part of the community at large, and where access to other necessary services is available. Minn. Stat. §245A.11, subd. 4. This licensing requirement reflects the goal of deinstitutionalization — a philosophy of creating a full range of community-based services and reducing the population of state institutions.

Deinstitutionalization of the mentally ill is advanced in Minnesota by requiring a new group home to be located at least a quarter mile from an existing residential program unless the local zoning authority grants a conditional use or special use permit. Minn. Stat. §245A.11, subd. 4. The St. Paul zoning code similarly requires community residential facilities for the mentally impaired to be located at least a quarter of a mile apart.

Familystyle argues that the Minnesota and St. Paul dispersal requirements are invalid because they limit housing choices of the mentally handicapped and therefore conflict with the language and purpose of the 1988 Amendments to the *Fair Housing Act*. We disagree. We perceive the goals of non-discrimination and deinstitutionalization to be compatible. Congress did not intend to abrogate a state's power to determine how facilities for the mentally ill must meet licensing standards. Minnesota's dispersal requirements address the need of providing residential services in mainstream community settings. The quarter-mile spacing requirement guarantees that residential treatment facilities will, in fact, be "in the community," rather than in neighborhoods completely made up of group homes that re-create an institutional environment — a setting for which Familystyle argues. We cannot agree that Congress intended the *Fair Housing Amendment Act of 1988* to contribute to the segregation of the mentally ill from the mainstream of our society. The challenged state laws and city ordinance do not affect or prohibit a retarded or mentally ill person from purchasing, renting, or occupying a private residence or dwelling.

The state plays a legitimate and necessary role in licensing services for the mentally impaired. We agree with the district court that the dispersal requirement as part of the licensure process is a legitimate means to achieve the state's goals in the process of deinstitutionalization of the mentally ill.

Notes and Questions

1. **Disparate impact and reasonable accommodation in land use regulation.** Courts have generally held that land use restrictions having the effect of excluding group homes for people with disabilities violate the FHA both because they impose an unjustified disparate impact—making housing "unavailable" under 42 U.S.C. §3604(f)(1)—and because they fail to accord with the requirement to make reasonable accommodations for persons with disabilities, as required by §3604(f)(3)(B). However, some courts have been more deferential to the policy goals asserted by local governments. *See, e.g., Oxford House-C v. City of St. Louis,* 77 F.3d 249 (8th Cir. 1996) (ordinance limiting group homes to eight residents did not violate the *Fair Housing Act* because the city had legitimate interests in decreasing congestion, traffic, and noise in residential areas). In *Brandt v. Chebanse,* 82 F.3d 172 (7th Cir. 1996), the court held that a city did not violate the *Fair Housing Act* when it refused to grant a variance that would have allowed a property owner to establish a four-unit residence for persons with disabilities in an area restricted to single-family homes. According to Judge Frank Easterbrook, no disparate impact claim could be brought because the city agreed to allow the plaintiff to establish her multi-unit residence in another part of town and the city was not required, as a reasonable accommodation, to relax its restrictions on multi-family occupancy in the single-family home neighborhood, *id.* at 175:

> The variance is not necessary to allow handicapped persons to live in Chebanse, for those capable of independent living (the only ones who could use the proposed structure) could live as easily, if somewhat more expensively, in new or remodeled single-family houses. Brandt does not argue that the *Fair Housing Act* requires municipalities to eliminate rules that increase the expense of housing for all persons equally. Is the proposed accommodation "reasonable" in the sense that it is cost-justified? Again, not on this record. The costs include an increased potential for flooding and the loss of whatever tranquility single-family zoning offers to a neighborhood with little corresponding benefit—for the proposed multi-unit building could be built as easily in the many tracts of suburbia or rural America already open to multi-family buildings. Unless the *Fair Housing Act* has turned the entire United States into a multi-family dwelling zone, Brandt must lose. It doesn't, so she does.

Do you agree with this reasoning? What would the argument be on the other side?

2. **Segregation of individuals with disabilities.** Under HUD's regulations implementing the *Rehabilitation Act,* recipients of federal assistance are prohibited from providing "different or separate housing, aid, benefits, or services to individuals with [disabilities] or to any class of individuals with [disabilities] from that provided to others unless such action is necessary to provide qualified individuals with [disabilities] with housing, aid, benefits, or services that are as effective as those provided to

others." 24 C.F.R. §8.4(b)(1)(iv). This mandate is an attempt to balance the imperatives of integration with the recognition that some services are more effective if targeted to individuals with disabilities.

Beginning in the 1950s, a movement began to shut down state-run psychiatric facilities, which were often dehumanizing warehouses for the mentally ill. Between 1955 and 1994, the national population of severely mentally ill patients in public psychiatric hospitals was reduced from 558,239 to 71,619. E. Fuller Torrey, *Out of the Shadows: Confronting America's Mental Illness Crisis* 8-9 (1997). This deinstitutionalization was predicated on providing individuals with disabilities the ability to live in community settings, where there is a sufficient amount of supportive housing, but that has proven to be an ongoing challenge.

In *Olmstead v. L.C.*, 527 U.S. 581 (1999), a case involving the public services provision of the Americans with Disabilities Act, 42 U.S.C. §§12131-12165, the Supreme Court held that "[u]njustified isolation . . . is properly regarded as discrimination based on disability." *Id.* at 597. Accordingly, states must "provide community-based treatment for persons with mental disabilities" when such placement is clinically appropriate. *Id.* at 607. *Olmstead* has been called the *Brown v. Board of Education* of the disability rights movement, and HUD recently issued guidance to recipients of federal financial assistance on how to further the goals of the decision. *See Statement of the Department of Housing and Urban Development on the Role of Housing in Accomplishing the Goals of* Olmstead (June 4, 2013), *available at http://portal.hud.gov/hudportal/documents/huddoc?id=OlmsteadGuidnc060 413.pdf.*

Olmstead's integrationist vision, however, raises a number of questions. For example, can a housing provider design a facility to serve individuals with a particular type of disability, such as a group home for individuals with physical, but not mental, disabilities? Can individuals with disabilities themselves choose to exclude others with dissimilar disabilities? In *Beckert v. Our Lady of Angels Apartments, Inc.*, 192 F.3d 601 (6th Cir. 1999), the court held that it was permissible for a federally subsidized facility to provide housing to elderly physically disabled tenants to the exclusion of individuals with mental disabilities. *Id.* at 607. *Beckert* relied on the language of the statute authorizing the particular subsidy at issue, so it may be limited in its reach, but the issue the court faced has become a significant flashpoint. *See* Henry Korman, *Clash of the Integrationists: The Mismatch of Civil Rights Imperatives in Supportive Housing for People with Disabilities*, 26 St. Louis U. Pub. L. Rev. 3 (2007).

3. Spacing requirements for group homes. In *Horizon House Developmental Services, Inc. v. Town of Upper Southampton*, 804 F. Supp. 683 (E.D. Pa. 1992), *aff'd*, 995 F.2d 217 (3d Cir. 1993), a case similar to *Familystyle*, the court invalidated a municipal spacing requirement for group homes. A nonprofit organization leased two single-family homes, each housing three or four people with mental disabilities. The township then enacted an ordinance that (a) prohibited group homes providing permanent care or professional supervision within 3,000 feet of one another or within 3,000 feet of any educational, religious, recreational, or institutional entity; (b) required a six-foot-high fence surrounding group homes; and (c) required a conditional use permit. The ordinance also defined "single-family homes" to exclude group homes for purposes of the zoning ordinance. The ordinance was later amended, reducing the spacing requirement from 3,000 to 1,000 feet. Judge Lowell A. Reed, Jr. held that the ordinance violated the *Fair Housing Act*, rejecting the town's claim that the ordinance was rationally tailored to promote integration of persons with mental retardation into the community. Citing *United States v. Starrett City Associates*, 840 F.2d 1096 (2d Cir. 1988),[13] Judge Reed noted that "integration is not an adequate justification" under the *Fair Housing Amendments Act of 1988* for a zoning requirement that "disadvantages a class of people protected" by the act by "indefinitely limiting access of that class to housing, by setting an upper limit or cap or quota on the number of persons with handicap who may live in the Township." 804 F. Supp. at 695. *Familystyle* justified the spacing requirement, not as an effort to achieve integration, but as necessary to promote the mental health of group home residents. Is this sufficient to distinguish it from *Horizon House*? Is *Familystyle* consistent with *Starrett City Associates*? If not, which case is correctly decided?

4. Limits on the number of unrelated persons who can live together. In *Edmonds v. Oxford House, Inc.*, 514 U.S. 725 (1995), a nonprofit organization, Oxford House-Edmonds, attempted to open a group home for 10 to 12 adults recovering from drug addiction and alcoholism. Although the town zoning law allowed any number of "family" members related by "genetics, adoption, or marriage" to live together, it limited to five the number of unrelated persons who could live together. Oxford House challenged the zoning restriction as discriminatory against persons with disabilities, both because it made a dwelling "unavailable . . . because of a handicap," §3604(f)(1)(A), and because the town failed to make "reasonable accommodations" in its "rules, policies [and] practices, §3604(f)(3)(B)." The town defended by pointing to the *Fair Housing Act*'s exemption for "any reasonable local, State, or Federal restrictions regarding the maximum number of occupants permitted to occupy a dwelling." 42 U.S.C. §3607(b)(1). The Supreme Court found the exemption unavailable on the ground that the town's law did not prescribe "the maximum number of occupants" a dwelling unit could house because it did not limit the number of traditional family members who could live together. Justice Ginsburg wrote: "We hold that §3607(b)(1) does not exempt prescriptions of the family-defining kind, *i.e.*, provisions designed to foster the family character of a neighborhood. Instead, §3607(b)(1)'s absolute exemption removes from the FHA's scope only total occupancy limits, *i.e.*, numerical ceilings that serve to prevent overcrowding in living quarters." 514 U.S. at 728.

5. Homeless shelters and sex discrimination. In *Doe v. Butler*, 892 F.2d 315 (3d Cir. 1989), three women who had been victims of domestic violence charged that the city of Butler, Pennsylvania had violated the *Fair Housing Act*'s prohibition on sex discrimination when the city refused to approve a temporary shelter for abused women and children. The city's denial was based primarily on a zoning provision that limited transitional shelters to six residents plus staff, despite the argument from the shelter

13. For a discussion of *Starrett City Associates*, *see* §2.2, above.

provider that only a larger facility would be economically feasible. Rejecting a challenge to this limit on the size of shelters, the court stated that the limit's impact on women "does not alone establish discriminatory effect, because the resident limitation would have a comparable effect on males if the transitional dwelling was established for a different group, such as, for example, recovering male alcoholics." *Id.* at 323. Can you think of a counterargument to this proposition? How might the exclusion of shelters for battered women impose a disparate impact on women as compared to men?

Problems

1. Suppose the City of St. Paul experiences a sudden influx of immigrants, such as Soviet Jews or persons from Southeast Asia. To integrate these immigrants into the community more effectively, the city council passes an ordinance prohibiting all immigrants from buying or renting homes or apartments on the same block as another immigrant family. Under the reasoning of *Familystyle*, would such an ordinance be enforceable under the *Fair Housing Act*? Suppose the ordinance prohibits all African American families from living next door to another African American family as a means to combat racial segregation. Does this violate the *Fair Housing Act*?

2. An organization buys a house to set up a group home for mentally disabled persons. Opposition to the group home develops in the neighborhood. In response to community pressure, the city amends its zoning ordinance to require that all facilities housing more than four unrelated persons together have one parking space off the street for every two residents. The city council justifies the ordinance by noting that unrelated persons are more likely to have separate cars, whereas family members may share a vehicle and that residents in group homes need more parking for supervisors, visitors, and doctors. Moreover, the city is relatively built up and most houses do not have off-street parking. Streets are quite congested, and parking spaces are hard to find. The effect of the ordinance, however, is to make it financially impossible to set up the group home in the city. The organization sues the city, arguing that the new ordinance violates the *Fair Housing Act*. What arguments could you make on behalf of the plaintiffs? On behalf of the defendant city? What should the court do?

§5 FAIR LENDING

M & T Mortgage Corp. v. Foy

20 Misc. 3d 274 (N.Y. Sup. Ct. 2008)

Map: 517 Rogers Avenue, Brooklyn, New York

HERBERT KRAMER, J.

Equity abhors discrimination.

Equity will not enforce discriminatory practices.

This Court holds, for reasons set forth below, that a mortgage granted to a minority buyer for the purchase of property in a minority area which carries an interest rate that exceeds nine percent creates a rebuttable presumption of discriminatory practice.

This Court further holds that the lender who has brought this proceeding to foreclose the mortgage must demonstrate by a fair preponderance of the evidence that the mortgage was not the product of unlawful discrimination. If the lender is unable to do so, the foreclosure proceeding will be dismissed and the lender left to its remedies at law.

Major Jahn K. Foy, a reserve officer, was engaged on active duty, when foreclosure proceedings were initiated against her property, 517 Rogers Avenue in Brooklyn, which is located within a minority neighborhood. The thirty year note and mortgage dated July of 2000 carried an interest rate of nine and one half percent (9½%).

Previously, Major Foy moved to reform the mortgage pursuant to *New York Military Law* claiming, in essence, that her ability to comply with the terms of the 9½% mortgage was materially affected by her deployment on several tours of active duty over the course of the past several years. This Court granted a hearing.

Review of the post hearing submissions and additional research suggested that the defendant may have been the victim of a process called "reverse redlining."[14] Accordingly, on December 6, 2007 this Court informed the parties that it intended to continue the hearing and placed the burden on the defendant to demonstrate that she was a victim of discriminatory lending.

Thus the Court now modifies that decision so as to place the burden of proof upon the plaintiff to demonstrate that the loan in question is not a "higher priced loan" which is the product of discriminatory practices.[15] In so doing this Court is mindful of the effect of discrimination upon the larger population. Research has revealed that when minorities subjected to discrimination represent a very small percentage of the population, the cost of discrimination falls mainly upon the minority, however when they represent a larger segment of society, the cost of discrimination falls upon both the minorities and the majority as currently evidenced by the world wide subprime mortgage meltdown.[16]

---

14. "Redlining is the practice of denying the extension of credit to specific geographic areas due to the income, race, or ethnicity of its residents. The term was derived from the actual practice of drawing a red line around certain areas in which credit would be denied. Reverse redlining is the practice of extending credit on unfair terms to those same communities." *United Cos. Lending Corp. v. Sargeant*, 20 F. Supp. 2d 192, 203 n.5 (D. Mass. 1998).

15. The Court's ability to supervise lending practices that take advantage of unsophisticated borrowers is not newly minted. There is a well-established statutory and common law basis for the supervision of purchasers of streams of income to insure that the purchase of income from lotteries or settlements is not accomplished at a high rate of interest. *See e.g.*, *In re Cabrera*, 765 N.Y.S.2d 208 (Sup. Ct. 2003); *In re Settlement Capital Corp.*, 769 N.Y.S.2d 817 (Sup. Ct. 2003). This Court has found that an interest rate of nine percent which is the judgment interest rate, is reasonable and has approved those applications where all other circumstances being equal a rate no greater than that is charged.

16. Gary S. Becker, *The Economics of Discrimination* (2d ed. 1971). Gary Becker is a 1992 Nobel laureate in Economics.

In shifting the burden of proof this Court will use the *Home Mortgage Disclosure Act of 1975* (HMDA), 12 U.S.C. §2801 *et seq.*, definition of "higher priced loan" to determine whether the loan is one that may require further investigation for possible discriminatory practices. A loan is deemed

> "'higher priced'[17] [if its] rate spread [for a first tier loan] is three percentage points above the Treasury security of comparable maturity. [Moreover,] [t]hough price data [in and of itself] does not support definitive conclusions [with respect to the issue of unlawful discrimination, it] provides a useful screen, previously unavailable, to identify lenders, products, applicants, and geographic markets where price differences among racial or other groups are sufficiently large to warrant further investigation." Julia Reade, *HMDA, New Pricing Data,* (Federal Reserve Bank of Boston, Spring, 2006) (frequently asked questions about the new HMDA data); *see also Proposal to Amend Regulation Z,* 73 FR 1673.

"In fall 2005, the Board of Governors of the Federal Reserve System published its first study of the new HMDA interest-rate data." HMDA data is used by government agencies to identify, *inter alia,* loans, institutions or geographic markets that "reveal disparities in loan applications or originations by race, ethnicity or other characteristics that may warrant further investigation under the *Equal Credit Opportunity Act* (ECOA) or the *Fair Housing Act* (FHA). With the addition of price data for higher priced loans, the agencies are also able to identify in the HMDA data price disparities that may warrant further investigation."[18] Extensive national analyses of mortgage pricing patterns across racial and ethnic groups revealed that *"[t]raditionally under-served minority groups were more likely than other populations to pay higher prices for mortgages."* HMDA, *New Pricing Data, supra* (italics added)

The mortgage in the instant matter and indeed most thirty-year mortgages written after the year 2000, which call for an interest rate of nine percent, would constitute "higher priced loans" under these criteria.[19] Thus, this Court holds that an interest rate

---

17. This is to be distinguished from the *Home Ownership and Equity Protection Act* (HOEPA) which targets high cost loans and imposes substantive restrictions and special pre-closing disclosures on particularly high-cost refinancing and home equity loans where the "APR at consummation will exceed the yield on treasury securities of comparable maturity by more than 8 percentage points for first-lien loans." Board of Governors of the Federal Reserve System, *Proposal to Amend Regulation Z,* 73 FR 1677 n.23. Regulation Z implements the *Federal Truth in Lending Act* and the *Home Ownership and Equity Protection Act* in order to protect consumers in the mortgage market from unfair, abusive or deceptive lending and services practices. *See also* N.Y. Banking Law §6-l, which has comparable standards and restrictions.

18. If disparities are found to violate the *Equal Credit Opportunity Act* (ECOA) or the *Fair Housing Act* (FHA), certain federal agencies are authorized to compel lenders to cease discriminatory practices and, among other remedies, obtain monetary relief for victims. HMDA, *New Pricing Data.* "The price data take the form of a 'rate spread.' Lenders must report the spread (difference) between the annual percentage rate (APR) on a loan and the rate on Treasury securities of comparable maturity but only for loans with spreads above designated thresholds." *Id.*

19. The loan in question is a year 2000 30-year loan with an interest rate of nine and one half percent. The monthly history of the constant maturity Treasury yields reveals that since the year 2000 to date there have been only two months where the thirty year treasuries exceeded six percent.

exceeding nine percent evidences the existence of a higher priced loan and creates a rebuttable presumption of discrimination. *See also McGlawn v. Pennsylvania Human Relations Commission*, 891 A.2d 757 (Pa. Commw. 2006) (Pennsylvania Human Relations Commission relied upon expert testimony indicating that an interest rate three percent beyond that which exists in the general market is predatory and thus discriminatory).

Equity, which abhors unconscionable and unjust results, mandates a shift in the burden of proof to the plaintiff-lender to demonstrate that the loan is not discriminatory. Indeed, our decisional law has long since recognized that a litigant "seeking affirmative judicial action in equity . . . may not succeed if [the litigant] is asking [for] an inequitable or unconscionable result." *Monaghan v. May*, 273 N.Y.S. 475 (App. Div. 1934). Moreover, "[i]n the absence of legislation, courts of equity have exercised jurisdiction in suits for the foreclosure of mortgages to fix the time and terms of sale and to refuse to confirm sales upon equitable grounds where they were found to be unfair or inadequacy of price was so gross as to shock the conscience." *Home Building and Loan Ass'n v. Blaisdell*, 290 U.S. 398, 446 (1934). "As we have seen, equity will intervene in individual cases where it is palpably apparent that gross unfairness is imminent. That is the law of New York." *Gelfert v. National City Bank of New York*, 313 U.S. 221, 233 (1941). Indeed in our current climate — where this Court takes judicial notice — there are substantial amounts of undefended foreclosure proceedings in minority neighborhoods, the placement of the burden of proof upon the borrower[20] who is very much in a distaff position when it comes to protecting his or her rights, renders illusory the possibility of meaningful legal redress. *See, e.g., EquiCredit Corp. v. Turcios*, 752 N.Y.S.2d 684 (App. Div. 2002) (counterclaims alleging reverse redlining practices in claimed violation of the ECOA and the FHA dismissed for failure to show that mortgagors qualified for the loans in question as required pursuant to these statutes).

The courts are not merely automatons mindlessly processing paper motions in mortgage foreclosure actions most of which proceed on default. Where, as here, there is a presumably discriminatory rate, the court must order a hearing in a litigated action or an inquest where there is a default. This presumption may be rebutted by proof that the mortgage was given for non-discriminatory economic reasons.

Notes and Questions

1. Lending discrimination. Discrimination has long been a significant problem in mortgage markets. *See* Robert G. Schwemm & Jeffrey L. Taren, *Discretionary Pricing, Mortgage Discrimination, and the Fair Housing Act*, 45 Harv. C.R.-C.L. Rev. 375, 385-390

---

20. In a seminal decision under the *Fair Housing Act*, the Court adopted a two-prong test for discrimination: First the plaintiff must establish the defendant's lending practices and loan terms were predatory and unfair; and second the plaintiff must establish that defendant intentionally targeted them because of their race or that the defendant's lending practices had a disparate impact on the basis of race. *Hargraves v. Capital City Mortg. Corp.*, 140 F. Supp. 2d 7, 20 (D.D.C. 2000).

(2010). This discrimination can take several forms. Early in the development of modern home-finance, during the New Deal, federal policies encouraged "redlining," which is the practice of not providing loans in minority neighborhoods. The term derives from a practice originated by a federal agency created during the New Deal, the Home Owners' Loan Corporation (HOLC). HOLC, which was created in 1933 to refinance distressed mortgages, set about to examine cities across the country and create color-coded "residential security maps" that sorted urban and suburban neighborhoods into "A," "B," "C," or "D" ratings. These letter grades were used to evaluate the quality of loans that might be made in those neighborhoods. "A" neighborhoods were generally white and usually native born while the lowest rated neighborhoods, "D," were generally African American. On the HOLC maps, "D" neighborhoods were colored red, and lenders were discouraged from lending in those areas. *See* Kenneth T. Jackson, *Crabgrass Frontier: The Suburbanization of the United States* 199-203 (1985). This approach, subsequently adopted by the Federal Housing Administration, a federal agency that insures mortgages, shaped the landscape of home lending for decades in the twentieth century.

More recently, in the run-up to the subprime crisis, the outright denial of loans became less of a problem than the provision of loans on terms that were disadvantageous to minority borrowers. *See* Alan M. White, *Borrowing While Black: Applying Fair Lending Laws to Risk-Based Mortgage Pricing*, 60 S.C. L. Rev. 677, 678 (2009). Several common practices reinforced unequal access to credit. For example, some criteria in underwriting — which is the process of evaluating borrowers for loans — include factors, such as the value of property used for collateral, that reflect structural disadvantages for minority borrowers. This practice is often referred to as reverse redlining, because it makes unfair loans more, rather than less, available to particular neighborhoods. Minority borrowers have also been treated unfairly where banks have given loan officers discretion to vary the terms of loans from objective criteria. And even where underwriting is standardized and facially nondiscriminatory, minority borrowers have often been steered into subprime loan products that have higher interest rates and less favorable terms. *See* Schwemm & Taren, *supra*; White, *supra*. Many minority borrowers, moreover, were drawn into homeownership before the subprime crisis with inadequate resources to weather the subsequent downturn, leading to significantly worse outcomes for those borrowers when the crash hit. *See* Patrick Bayer et al., *The Vulnerability of Minority Homeowners in the Housing Boom and Bust* (ERID Working Paper Number 145) (Apr. 29, 2013).

In the wake of the subprime crisis, lenders have significantly tightened underwriting standards to ensure that borrowers have the ability to repay and new regulations have been implemented that focus on policing the process of origination. *See* Chapter 12, §4.2. Although these new regulations are an important corrective to the abusive practices that induced many homeowners to take out unsustainable loans, one consequence of the new standards is that mortgages are now more difficult to obtain for minority home buyers. *See* William C. Apgar, *Getting on the Right Track: Improving Low-Income and Minority Access to Mortgage Credit After the Housing Bust* (2012), *available at http://www.jchs.harvard.edu/research/publications/getting-right-track-improving-low-income-and-minority-access-mortgage-credit.*

2. Fair lending laws. Fair lending is regulated primarily through the *Equal Credit Opportunity Act of 1974* (ECOA), 15 U.S.C. §§1691-1691f, and the *Fair Housing Act.* ECOA bars discrimination in all credit transactions, including home lending, on the basis of race, color, religion, national origin, sex or marital status, or age. 15 U.S.C. §1691(a). The *Fair Housing Act* specifically bars "any person or other entity whose business includes engaging in residential real estate-related transactions," which includes the "making or purchasing of loans or providing other financial assistance secured by residential real estate," from discriminating on the basis of race, color, religion, sex, handicap, familial status, or national origin. 42 U.S.C. §3605.[21] Fair lending is also regulated under state consumer protection statutes and, as *M & T Mortgage Corp.* demonstrates, through the traditional tools of equity.

The recent *Dodd-Frank Wall Street Reform and Consumer Protection Act,* Pub. L. No. 111-203, 124 Stat. 1376 (2010) (the *Dodd-Frank Act*) (codified as amended in scattered sections of the U.S. Code) brought a number of changes to the regulatory landscape of fair lending at the federal level. The *Dodd-Frank Act* gave the new Consumer Financial Protection Bureau (CFPB) supervisory, enforcement, and rulemaking authority for ECOA and the *Home Mortgage Disclosure Act of 1975* (HMDA), 12 U.S.C. §2801 *et seq*. The *Fair Housing Act* is still enforced by HUD and the Justice Department. The *Dodd-Frank Act* also defined "fair lending" as "fair, equitable, and nondiscriminatory access to credit for consumers." 12 U.S.C. §5481(13). This definition has not yet been the subject of CFPB rulemaking or case law, but it has the potential, through CFPB oversight of lending institutions, to expand significantly the breadth of consumer protection for fair access to credit. Can you see how?

3. Enforcement and aggregation. In HMDA, Congress provided advocates an important tool to understand lenders' aggregate lending practices. *See* Carol Necole Brown, *Intent and Empirics: The Race to the Subprime,* 93 Marq. L. Rev. 907 (2010). HMDA requires lenders to track and disclose a wide variety of information not only about the loans they make, but about loan applications as well. This information includes the race, ethnicity, and gender of borrowers and applicants, which can reveal discriminatory patterns in lending practices.

Because direct evidence of lending discrimination is rare, it has been important for plaintiffs to use HMDA data and the tool of class action certification to aggregate sufficient comparative data to demonstrate either that an individual minority borrower has been treated less favorably than non-minority borrowers or that given practices have discriminatory effects. Schwemm & Taren, *supra,* at 389. However, the Supreme Court recently narrowed the interpretation of one of the factors courts use to evaluate

21. Lenders are also generally subject to the *Americans with Disabilities Act's* accessibility requirements. *See, e.g.,* Settlement Agreement Between the United States of America and Wells Fargo & Co. Under the Americans with Disabilities Act, No. 202-11-239 (DOJ May 31, 2011), *available at http://www.ada.gov/wells_fargo/wells_fargo_settle.htm* (bank refused to accept calls from individuals with hearing and speech disabilities who use telephone relay services, instead requiring those individuals to call a separate number and leave messages that were never answered; bank ordered to pay roughly $17 million in compensation and penalties as well as change its practices).

whether to grant a group of litigants class-action status. In *Wal-Mart Stores, Inc. v. Dukes*, 131 S. Ct. 2541 (2011), the Court considered a potential class of over a million female Wal-Mart employees who alleged that they suffered a disparate impact on the basis of sex because of decisions made by supervisors across the country on pay and promotion issues. Rule 23(b)(2) of the Federal Rules of Civil Procedure requires "commonality" to certify a class of plaintiffs, and the Supreme Court ruled that this requirement could not be met in *Dukes* given the individual discretion granted to supervisors. Because so much of the evidence of discriminatory lending involves statistical analysis of patterns and practices attributable to individual loan officers, the *Dukes* case makes it significantly more difficult for fair-lending plaintiffs to obtain class status. *See, e.g., In re Countrywide Finance Corp. Mortgage Lending Practices Litigation*, 708 F.3d 704 (6th Cir. 2013) (class certification denied on lack of commonality for African American and Hispanic borrowers who alleged that they were charged higher loan rates as a result of the subjective component of mortgage lender's loan-pricing policy).

What other tools can advocates for fair lending use to respond to discriminatory lending practices, if aggregate litigation is now more difficult?

4. **Fair lending and mortgage securitization.** In *Adkins v. Morgan Stanley*, No. 12 CV 7667(HB), 2013 WL 3835198 (S.D.N.Y. 2013), African American homeowners sued Morgan Stanley, arguing that its policies and practices caused a lender, New Century Mortgage Company, to target borrowers in the Detroit area for loans that had a disparate impact upon African Americans under the *Fair Housing Act*, 42 U.S.C. §3601 *et seq.* (FHA). Morgan Stanley moved to dismiss the FHA claim. Judge Harold Baer denied the motion. Judge Baer, accepting the allegations of the complaint for purposes of the motion, noted the plaintiffs' argument for how Morgan Stanley could have violated the FHA:

> From 2004 to 2007, "New Century was among the most notoriously predatory of the subprime lenders operating at that time." (Compl. ¶2.) Plaintiffs' theory here is that Morgan Stanley discriminated against African Americans when New Century issued predatory loans and that they did so as a result of Morgan Stanley's conduct. That conduct consisted of "five interrelated and centralized policies and practices" to securitize New Century's loans. (*Id.* ¶36.) First, Morgan Stanley "routinely purchased loans" with excessive debt-to-income ("DTI") ratios. (*Id.* ¶¶44-45.) High DTI ratios indicate that the loan is larger than the borrower can afford. Second, Morgan Stanley "regularly purchase[d] and securitize[d] mortgage loans from New Century where the [loan-to-value ratio] . . . exceeded 100%." (*Id.* ¶51.) High loan-to-value ratios, which compare the amount of the loan to the value of the home, are loans where the borrower faces a greater risk of delinquency or foreclosure. Third, Morgan Stanley required New Century to issue loans with adjustable rates and prepayment penalties. Morgan Stanley also "purchased and securitized large numbers of New Century mortgage loans with balloon payment features," exacerbating a borrower's financial risk. (*Id.* ¶60.) Fourth, Morgan Stanley provided necessary funding — in the form of warehouse lending, pre-commitments to purchase loans, and funding for loan closings — to New Century that allowed it to remain in business. Once New Century's funding dried up in 2007, the firm entered bankruptcy. (*Id.* ¶69.) Fifth, Morgan Stanley purchased loans that "deviated

> substantially from basic underwriting standards," going so far as to "encourage[ ] lending tactics that increased the levels of risk associated with individual loans." (*Id.* ¶¶73, 75.) According to Plaintiffs, by creating the conditions under which New Century originated toxic loans, Morgan Stanley caused African-American borrowers to fall prey to those loans at a disproportionate rate, or put another way, to make this homeowner nightmare come true.

Id. at *1. By setting the terms under which it would purchase loans from New Century, Morgan Stanley was directly responsible for setting the conditions under which New Century's predatory loans were issued. Morgan Stanley, it was alleged,

> ["]required New Century, as a condition of the companies' lucrative business relationship, to issue large volumes of Combined-Risk Loans[,]" [(Compl. ¶43, which had] at least two of the following risk-enhancing features: "(a) the loan was issued based upon the 'stated income,' rather than the verified-income, of the borrower; (b) the debt-to-income ratio exceeds 55%; (c) the loan-to-value ratio is at least 90%; (d) the loan has an adjustable interest rate; (e) the loan has 'interest only' payment features; (f) the loan has negative amortization features; (g) the loan has 'balloon' payment features; and/or (h) the loan imposes prepayment penalties." (*Id.* ¶34.) While any one of these features is both risky and costly to the borrower, combining those features in the same loan "dramatically" increases the loan's financial hazards. (*Id.* ¶35.)

Id. at *2. These high risk loans, the complaint continued, generated elevated rates of foreclosure, and disproportionately so for African American borrowers. As a result of Morgan Stanley's policies, "a high-cost loan originated by New Century was more than six times as likely to be in a 90%-plus minority neighborhood than the average loan originated in the Detroit region," *id.* (quoting Compl. ¶119), and "an African-American borrower in a minority neighborhood had a 21% greater chance of receiving a high-cost loan than a similarly-situated white borrower in a white neighborhood." *Id.* (quoting Compl. ¶122.) The resulting harms were both financial, for the plaintiffs, but also impacted the communities in which they lived.

> Detroit's recent bankruptcy filing only emphasizes the broader consequences of predatory lending and the foreclosures that inevitably result. Indeed, "[b]y 2012, banks had foreclosed on 100,000 homes [in Detroit], which drove down the city's total real estate value by 30 percent and spurred a mass exodus of nearly a quarter million people." Laura Gottesdiener, *Detroit's Debt Crisis: Everything Must Go,* Rolling Stone, June 20, 2013. The resulting blight stemming from "60,000 parcels of vacant land" and "78,000 vacant structures, of which 38,000 are estimated to be in potentially dangerous condition" has further strained Detroit's already taxed resources. Kevyn D. Orr, *Financial and Operating Plan* 9 (2013). And as residents flee the city, Detroit's shrinking ratepayer base renders its financial outlook even bleaker. *Id.* Given these conditions, it is not difficult to conclude that Detroit's current predicament, at least in part, is an outgrowth of the predatory lending at issue here. *See* Monica Davey & Mary Williams Walsh, *Billions in Debt, Detroit Tumbles Into Insolvency,* N.Y. Times, July 18, 2013, at A1 (listing Detroit's "shrunken tax base but still a huge, 139-square-mile city to maintain" as one factor contributing to the city's financial woes).

Id. All of this sufficed to deny Morgan Stanley's motion to dismiss the plaintiffs' FHA claim. As Judge Baer wrote:

> Plaintiffs here have successfully alleged a disparate impact under the FHA. [A] prima facie case under the FHA on a disparate impact theory requires only that Plaintiffs allege "that an outwardly neutral practice actually or predictably has a discriminatory effect; that is, has a significantly adverse or disproportionate impact on minorities, or perpetuates segregation." *Fair Hous. in Huntington Comm. Inc. v. Town of Huntington, N.Y.,* 316 F.3d 357, 366 (2d Cir. 2003). Plaintiffs here have met their pleading burden. First, they have identified the policy that they allege has a disproportionate impact on minorities. That policy consisted of Morgan Stanley (1) routinely purchasing both stated income loans and loans with unreasonably high debt-to-income ratios, (2) routinely purchasing loans with unreasonably high loan-to-value ratios, (3) requiring that New Century's loans include adjustable rates and prepayment penalties as well as purchasing loans with other high-risk features, (4) providing necessary funding to New Century, and (5) purchasing loans that deviated from basic underwriting standards. Plaintiffs go on to state that these policies resulted in "New Century aggressively target[ing] African American borrowers and communities . . . for the Combined-Risk Loans." (Compl. ¶81.) Indeed, Plaintiffs allege in detail the effect that New Century's lending had upon the African American community in the Detroit area. (Compl. ¶¶115-122). That lending, according to Plaintiffs, was a direct result of Morgan Stanley's policies. And while Plaintiffs do not allege that they qualified for better loans, they allege discrimination based only upon the receipt of these predatory, toxic loans that placed them at high financial risk. These risks exist regardless of Plaintiffs' qualifications. On a motion to dismiss, these allegations are sufficient to demonstrate a disparate impact.
>
> Morgan Stanley argues that the FHA does not reach Plaintiffs' theory here. But as an entity "engage[d] in residential real estate-related transactions," Morgan Stanley — as a loan purchaser and mortgage securitizer — falls within the scope of the FHA. 42 U.S.C. §3605(a). And as such, the FHA prohibits Morgan Stanley both from discriminating in "making available" real-estate related transactions as well as discriminating "in the terms or conditions of such a transaction." §3605(a); *see also* 24 C.F.R. §100.125 ("It shall be unlawful for any . . . entity engaged in the purchasing of loans or other debts or securities . . . to impose different terms or conditions for such purchases, because of race. . . .").
>
> Morgan Stanley's policies themselves resulted in Plaintiffs suffering a disparate impact. Indeed, Morgan Stanley's policies set the terms and conditions on which it would purchase loans from New Century. For example, "Morgan Stanley placed at least two employees onsite at New Century full-time when conducting due diligence on loans it would purchase for securitization." (Compl. ¶75.) When a "full documentation loan" indicated that a borrower could not afford a particular loan, "Morgan Stanley would shred the documentation and tell the originator to get a new, 'stated income' loan." (*Id.*) This stated income loan would appear less risky and permit the borrower to qualify, but would do nothing to change the fact that the borrower could not afford the loan. Thus the terms and conditions governing Morgan Stanley's loan purchases directly resulted in a disparate impact when they caused New Century to issue toxic loans to Plaintiffs.

Id. at *8-10.

Morgan Stanley's argument in *Adkins* that the FHA does not reach securitization was predicated on the idea that merely purchasing loans from a lender could not create a disparate impact under the FHA, regardless of the resulting actions a lender might take. Judge Baer rejected this argument in denying the motion to dismiss, but that does not necessarily end the case. Despite the plaintiffs' successfully alleged *prima facie* case of disparate impact, Morgan Stanley may have the opportunity to prove "that the challenged practice," which is to say its securitization practices, were "necessary to achieve one or more substantial, legitimate, nondiscriminatory interests." 24 C.F.R. §100.500(c). What business justifications might Morgan Stanley offer for why the mortgages it purchased were beneficial to consumers rather than harmful, or were otherwise legitimate? If the plaintiffs in *Adkins* were then to attempt to prove "that the substantial, legitimate, nondiscriminatory interests supporting the challenged practice could be served by another practice that has a less discriminatory effect," *id.*, what would their best arguments be? How should these competing arguments be assessed in light of the harms the plaintiffs alleged?

Problems

1. A mortgage lender allows its loan officers to use subjective criteria unrelated to a borrower's objective credit characteristics, such as credit history and income, to impose discretionary charges and interest mark-ups that increase the cost of borrowing money. Although application of these subjective criteria has a disparate impact on African Americans, banks defend these policies as necessary to their business model of assessing risk by careful consideration of the qualifications of borrowers and the likelihood that they will default on the loans. Does this practice violate the FHA and ECOA? Suppose the lender targets a relatively less well-off neighborhood to market subprime loans, leading several years later to massive foreclosures and decreases in the market value of all land in the neighborhood. Does this practice violate the FHA and ECOA?

2. Three Atlanta communities recently sued the British bank HSBC, arguing that HSBC aggressively marketed housing loans to minorities that were likely to fail and the resulting housing market collapse caused significant harm to the counties in terms of expenses and lost tax revenue. Similar suits in Kentucky and Maryland resulted in significant settlements. *See* Kate Brumback, *3 Georgia Counties Sue HSBC over Drop in Their Tax Base*, Boston Globe, Dec. 25, 2012, at A-11. Should lenders be responsible for the collateral consequences of their lending practices in the communities they serve? What are the best arguments on both sides of this question?

PART SIX

CONSTITUTIONAL PROTECTION FOR PROPERTY

CHAPTER 14

Equal Protection and Due Process

§1 PROPERTY AS A MEDIATOR BETWEEN CITIZENS AND THE STATE: DEFINING VERSUS DEFENDING PROPERTY RIGHTS

Property rights serve "twin roles — as protector of individual rights against other citizens, and as safeguard against excessive government interference." Jeremy Paul, *The Hidden Structure of Takings Law*, 64 S. Cal. L. Rev. 1393, 1402 (1991). Property rights mediate disputes by defining legal relations among people regarding control of valued resources. Property rights are not absolute because owners do not live alone; their rights are limited to protect the legitimate interests of other owners and of non-owners who may be affected by the exercise of those property rights. Because property rights must be limited to protect the property and personal rights of others, the state must have the power to *define* the scope of property rights so as to establish the basic framework of legal relationships in the market and to ensure that property rights are not exercised in ways that infringe on the legitimate interests of other owners or the public at large. Thus, the state must have the power to pass laws regulating and limiting the use of property to protect public health, safety, and welfare.

At the same time, granting the state the power to define property rights leaves individuals vulnerable to state infringement of those rights. The state may misuse its power to define property rights and go too far, thereby taking property rights away from owners to which they should be entitled. Property rights not only protect people against other persons but serve as a bulwark against state power. By delegating power to individuals and groups to control specific resources, the state attempts to decentralize power relationships. Individuals, rather than officials in a centralized state bureaucracy, have control of many of society's most valued resources. To maintain this decentralization, owners must be protected from having their property rights seized or unduly infringed by the state. Property rights must be *defended* from illegitimate encroachment by the state.

This dual role of property law creates an awful dilemma. How can the state both *define* property rights and be *limited* by them? If the state can simply redefine the incidents of property to readjust relations among private persons, then property rights cannot serve as a limit to state power. Some limits must be imposed on the state's ability to redefine property rights in order to *defend* property owners from illegitimate governmental power. But if the definition of property rights is frozen while circumstances change, the state is deprived of the ability to regulate the use of property to promote the general welfare. Professor Paul notes that "[t]o reconcile American law's double-edged reliance on property concepts, [we] must successfully distinguish between the courts' role as definers and defenders of property rights." *Id.* at 1415.

One strategy for managing the state's dual role is to impose constitutional limits on the state's power to reconfigure property rights. To that end, many legal systems specifically provide for some form of constitutional protection of property against government encroachment. In a legal system with robust judicial review, constitutionally protecting property empowers courts to police the behavior of government actors to ensure that, in carrying out their duties, they do not act in ways that violate constitutionally protected property rights. By finding some particular state action to violate the Constitution, courts place limits on the state that can only be undone through constitutional amendment. Determining the proper boundaries of this judicial review of the actions of other state actors within a democratic system is one of the deep questions of constitutional theory, one whose contours are more properly explored in a course dedicated to constitutional law. In the last two chapters of this book, our focus will be on the U.S. Constitution's protection of private property against government intrusion.

Many provisions in the U.S. Constitution interact with property rights in some way. For example, the regulation of land use can implicate both the religion and speech clauses of the first amendment. *See* Chapter 7, §6. Other provisions, such as the "right of the people to be secure in their persons, houses, papers, and effects, against unreasonable searches and seizures" in the fourth amendment, U.S. Const., amend. IV, and even the third amendment's prohibition against the quartering of troops "in any house," U.S. Const., amend. III, protect property rights against specific types of government action. The U.S. Constitution, however, more directly and broadly protects property in both the fifth and fourteenth amendments. The fifth amendment's due process clause states that "no person shall . . . be deprived of . . . property, without due process of law." The fourteenth amendment has very similar due process language. And the fifth amendment's takings clause prohibits the government from taking "private property" for "public use" without "just compensation." In this chapter, we will discuss the due process clause, as well as the very similar doctrines that courts have adopted under the rubric of the fourteenth amendment's equal protection clause. In the next chapter, we will explore the complex body of law that courts have developed under the takings clause.

Miller v. Schoene

276 U.S. 272 (1928)

Mr. Justice HARLAN FISKE STONE delivered the opinion of the Court.

Acting under the Cedar Rust Act of Virginia, Va. Code §§885-893 (1924), defendant in error, the state entomologist, ordered the plaintiffs in error to cut down a large number of ornamental red cedar trees growing on their property, as a means of preventing the communication of a rust or plant disease with which they were infected to the apple orchards in the vicinity.

The Virginia statute presents a comprehensive scheme for the condemnation and destruction of red cedar trees infected by cedar rust. By section 1 it is declared to be unlawful for any person to "own, plant or keep alive and standing" on his premises any red cedar tree which is or may be the source or "host plant" of the communicable plant disease known as cedar rust, and any such tree growing within a certain radius of any apple orchard is declared to be a public nuisance, subject to destruction. Section 2 makes it the duty of the state entomologist, "upon the request in writing of ten or more reputable freeholders of any county or magisterial district, to make a preliminary investigation of the locality . . . to ascertain if any cedar tree or trees . . . are the source of, harbor or constitute the host plant for the said disease . . . and constitute a menace to the health of any apple orchard in said locality, and that said cedar tree or trees exist within a radius of two miles of any apple orchard in said locality." If affirmative findings are so made, he is required to direct the owner in writing to destroy the trees and, in his notice, to furnish a statement of the "fact found to exist whereby it is deemed necessary or proper to destroy" the trees and to call attention to the law under which it is proposed to destroy them. Section 5 authorizes the state entomologist to destroy the trees if the owner, after being notified, fails to do so.

As shown by the evidence and as recognized in other cases involving the validity of this statute, cedar rust is an infectious plant disease in the form of a fungoid organism which is destructive of the fruit and foliage of the apple, but without effect on the value of the cedar. Its life cycle has two phases which are passed alternately as a growth on red cedar and on apple trees. It is communicated by spores from one to the other over a radius of at least two miles. It appears not to be communicable between trees of the same species, but only from one species to the other, and other plants seem not to be appreciably affected by it. The only practicable method of controlling the disease and protecting apple trees from its ravages is the destruction of all red cedar trees, subject to the infection, located within two miles of apple orchards.

The red cedar, aside from its ornamental use, has occasional use and value as lumber. It is indigenous to Virginia, is not cultivated or dealt in commercially on any substantial scale, and its value throughout the state is shown to be small as compared with that of the apple orchards of the state. Apple growing is one of the principal agricultural pursuits in Virginia. The apple is used there and exported in large quantities. Many millions of dollars are invested in the orchards, which furnish employment for a large portion of the population, and have induced the development of attendant railroad and cold storage facilities.

On the evidence we may accept the conclusion of the Supreme Court of Appeals that the state was under the necessity of making a choice between the preservation of one class of property and that of the other wherever both existed in dangerous proximity. It would have been none the less a choice if, instead of enacting the present statute, the state, by doing nothing, had permitted serious injury to the apple orchards within its borders to go on unchecked. When forced to such a choice the state does not exceed its constitutional powers by deciding upon the destruction of one class of property in order to save another which, in the judgment of the legislature, is of greater value to the public. It will not do to say that the case is merely one of a conflict of two private interests and that the misfortune of apple growers may not be shifted to cedar owners by ordering the destruction of their property; for it is obvious that there may be, and that here there is, a preponderant public concern in the preservation of the one interest over the other. And where the public interest is involved preferment of that interest over the property interest of the individual, to the extent even of its destruction, is one of the distinguishing characteristics of every exercise of the police power which affects property.

We need not weigh with nicety the question whether the infected cedars constitute a nuisance according to the common law; or whether they may be so declared by statute. For where, as here, the choice is unavoidable, we cannot say that its exercise, controlled by considerations of social policy which are not unreasonable, involves any denial of due process.

Notes and Questions

1. **The impossibility of doing nothing.** Can the government stay out of this kind of conflict? What if, instead of destroying the cedar trees, the government refused to take any action at all? In that case, the government would seem to have made a choice to let the costs of the cedar rust fall on apple orchards. How should the government go about choosing which property owner to favor? Would payment of compensation to either the cedar tree owners or the apple tree owners change the nature of the government's dilemma? If so, who should pay that compensation? The government (meaning taxpayers)? The benefited private parties?

2. **Nuisance.** If the owners of orchards brought a nuisance action against the owners of nearby cedar trees, would they be likely to prevail? If a court found the cedar trees to be a nuisance, would an injunction requiring the cedar tree owners to destroy their trees violate the property rights of the cedar tree owners? If not, should a legislature (or administrative agency) be able to make the same determination in the absence of a lawsuit?

3. **Harm prevention versus benefit conferral.** Is the government in *Miller* acting to prevent owners of cedar trees from harming apple orchards or is it harming cedar tree owners to confer a benefit on the owners of apple orchards? The apple tree owners could argue that the cedar tree owners were harming them by maintaining trees on their property that were causing great destruction on neighboring apple

orchards. The cedar tree owners could respond that they had done nothing wrong; that the problem was with the delicate nature of apple trees, and that they should not be made to pay for the costs of protecting the apple trees from disease. Indeed, in a case very similar to *Miller*, the Florida Supreme Court required compensation to be paid to owners of the state-destroyed trees. *Department of Agriculture and Consumer Services v. Mid-Florida Growers, Inc.*, 521 So. 2d 101, 103 (Fla. 1988) (holding that the state had to pay just compensation when it destroyed healthy orange trees to prevent the spread of citrus canker because "destruction of the healthy trees benefited the entire citrus industry and, in turn, Florida's economy, thereby conferring a public benefit rather than preventing a public harm"). *See also Rose Acre Farms, Inc. v. United States*, 373 F.3d 1177 (1st Cir. 2004) (egg producer entitled to compensation when more eggs were taken than necessary to respond to a salmonella outbreak). In the context of government regulation of incompatible land uses, is there any way to distinguish between harm prevention and benefit conferral?

§2 EQUAL PROTECTION

> **CONTEXT**
>
> The fourteenth amendment's equal protection clause says: "No state shall . . . deny to any person within its jurisdiction the equal protection of the laws."

All laws classify people, either explicitly or implicitly, for the purposes of achieving some regulatory goal. Do classifications of different property owners violate the equal protection clause by treating them differently from one another? Consider the typical zoning code, which permits some owners to engage only in residential use of their land while permitting others to engage in either commercial or residential uses. In assessing whether such a legal classification violates the requirements of equal protection, courts engage in a means-ends analysis that asks whether the classification chosen (the means) bears a sufficiently strong relationship to the goals the state is seeking to accomplish (the ends). How tightly the means must be tied to the ends varies based on the particular kind of classification the state is trying to use.

Certain classifications, such as racial distinctions, are deemed inherently suspect and therefore presumptively unconstitutional. They will be upheld only if they are strictly necessary to achieve a compelling governmental interest. Other classifications, such as those based on sex, are deemed to be sometimes relevant but often invalid. They are subject to an intermediate level of scrutiny. They must bear a substantial relationship to an important government objective. Classifications not included in the first two categories, such as those used in most regulation of property, are presumptively permissible. They are subject to a very deferential rational basis test. Applying these standards, differential treatment of various classes of property owners under a typical zoning law will be upheld if the classification is (at least arguably) rationally related to a legitimate government purpose. This test will almost always be satisfied.

Village of Willowbrook v. Olech

528 U.S. 562 (2000)

PER CURIAM.

Respondent Grace Olech and her late husband Thaddeus asked petitioner Village of Willowbrook to connect their property to the municipal water supply. The Village at first conditioned the connection on the Olechs granting the Village a 33-foot easement. The Olechs objected, claiming that the Village only required a 15-foot easement from other property owners seeking access to the water supply. After a 3-month delay, the Village relented and agreed to provide water service with only a 15-foot easement.

Olech sued the Village claiming that the Village's demand of an additional 18-foot easement violated the Equal Protection Clause of the Fourteenth Amendment. Olech asserted that the 33-foot easement demand was "irrational and wholly arbitrary"; that the Village's demand was actually motivated by ill will resulting from the Olechs' previous filing of an unrelated, successful lawsuit against the Village; and that the Village acted either with the intent to deprive Olech of her rights or in reckless disregard of her rights.

The District Court dismissed the lawsuit pursuant to Federal Rule of Civil Procedure 12(b)(6) for failure to state a cognizable claim under the Equal Protection Clause. Relying on Circuit precedent, the Court of Appeals for the Seventh Circuit reversed, holding that a plaintiff can allege an equal protection violation by asserting that state action was motivated solely by a "spiteful effort to 'get' him for reasons wholly unrelated to any legitimate state objective." It determined that Olech's complaint sufficiently alleged such a claim. We granted certiorari to determine whether the Equal Protection Clause gives rise to a cause of action on behalf of a "class of one" where the plaintiff did not allege membership in a class or group.

Our cases have recognized successful equal protection claims brought by a "class of one," where the plaintiff alleges that she has been intentionally treated differently from others similarly situated and that there is no rational basis for the difference in treatment. In so doing, we have explained that "the purpose of the equal protection clause of the Fourteenth Amendment is to secure every person within the State's jurisdiction against intentional and arbitrary discrimination, whether occasioned by express terms of a statute or by its improper execution through duly constituted agents." *Sioux City Bridge Co. v. Dakota County*, 260 U.S. 441, 445 (1923).

That reasoning is applicable to this case. Olech's complaint can fairly be construed as alleging that the Village intentionally demanded a 33-foot easement as a condition of connecting her property to the municipal water supply where the Village required only a 15-foot easement from other similarly situated property owners. The complaint also alleged that the Village's demand was "irrational and wholly arbitrary" and that the Village ultimately connected her property after receiving a clearly adequate 15-foot easement. These allegations, quite apart from the Village's subjective motivation, are sufficient to state a claim for relief under traditional equal protection analysis. We therefore affirm the judgment of the Court of Appeals, but do not reach the alternative theory of "subjective ill will" relied on by that court. . . .

Justice STEPHEN BREYER, concurring in the result.

The Solicitor General and the village of Willowbrook have expressed concern lest we interpret the Equal Protection Clause in this case in a way that would transform many ordinary violations of city or state law into violations of the Constitution. It might be thought that a rule that looks only to an intentional difference in treatment and a lack of a rational basis for that different treatment would work such a transformation. Zoning decisions, for example, will often, perhaps almost always, treat one landowner differently from another, and one might claim that, when a city's zoning authority takes an action that fails to conform to a city zoning regulation, it lacks a "rational basis" for its action (at least if the regulation in question is reasonably clear).

This case, however, does not directly raise the question whether the simple and common instance of a faulty zoning decision would violate the Equal Protection Clause. That is because the Court of Appeals found that in this case respondent had alleged an extra factor as well—a factor that the Court of Appeals called "vindictive action," "illegitimate animus," or "ill will."

In my view, the presence of that added factor in this case is sufficient to minimize any concern about transforming run-of-the-mill zoning cases into cases of constitutional right. For this reason, along with the others mentioned by the Court, I concur in the result.

Notes and Questions

Rational basis with teeth. Although rational basis review under the equal protection clause is very deferential, it may sometimes be possible to challenge government actions such as applications of zoning or building regulations as violations of the equal protection clause when the municipality treats similarly situated properties differently and cannot present a legitimate defense of this differential treatment. The equal protection challenge may be most likely to succeed when the facts of the case present some reason to think that the city was motivated by animus against the group in question, even where the group is not normally understood to be a "suspect classification" subject to less deferential scrutiny. *See City of Cleburne v. Cleburne Living Center*, 473 U.S. 432 (1985) (city violates equal protection clause when it requires group homes for persons with mental retardation to seek special permits to operate but does not impose this requirement on other group homes such as fraternities or nursing homes, and city can present no legitimate government justification for the differential treatment but is based solely on an "irrational prejudice against the mentally retarded"); *cf. Romer v. Evans*, 517 U.S. 620, 634 (1996) (striking down state constitutional amendment that barred local governments from enacting protections against discrimination on the basis of sexual orientation and noting that "laws of the kind now before us raise the inevitable inference that the disadvantage imposed is born of animosity toward the class of persons affected").

Problem

A town's zoning ordinance requires setbacks of ten feet in a particular area of the town. The zoning board routinely grants variances from this restriction as long as construction is kept five feet away from the boundary and none of the abutting neighbors objects. This practice violates the express terms of the zoning ordinance itself, as well as the state's zoning enabling act, both of which allow variances to be granted only if the owner can demonstrate extreme hardship. An owner applies for a variance to add a dining room onto her single-family home, seeking to build it so that it will be five feet from the boundary of her property. One of the four abutting neighbors objects, and the zoning board denies the variance. The owner sues the town, claiming that this deprives her of equal protection of the laws, citing *Willowbrook v. Olech*, 528 U.S. 562 (2000). The owner points out that two of her neighbors in the immediate neighborhood were granted variances to build structures that extended to five feet from the border of their properties. The zoning board defends the denial on the ground that it is rational to allow neighbors veto power over variances because such variances will affect their property more than that of anyone else. The owner contends that this effective delegation of discretion to the neighbors denies her equal protection of law. Who is right? What else might you need to know about the owner and her neighbors to evaluate this question?

§3 DUE PROCESS

§3.1 Procedural and Substantive Due Process

Although the notion of "due process" appears to be merely procedural, courts have interpreted the Constitution's due process clauses to provide both procedural and substantive protection for property owners. Procedurally, several issues are often at stake in litigation over whether the government has complied with due process when it deprives a person of property: (1) the adequacy of notice to the owner; (2) the quality of the decision maker (especially its neutrality); (3) the opportunity of the owner to be heard (either before or after the deprivation); (4) an opportunity to present evidence to the decision maker; (5) an opportunity to confront witnesses and evidence and cross-examine or contest them; (6) the right to have an attorney present; and (7) the right to have a formal decision rendered based on a fixed record and with a statement of the reasons for the decision that can provide a basis for appeal. *See* Ronald E. Rotunda & John E. Nowak, 3 *Treatise on Constitutional Law* §17.8 (a) (2013).

> **CONTEXT**
>
> The fifth amendment's due process clause says: "No person shall . . . be deprived of . . . property, without due process of law." The fourteenth amendment has a similar clause, which says: "nor shall any state deprive any person of . . . property, without due process of law."

The U.S. Supreme Court applies a sliding scale to determine how much process is due to an owner before the state may deprive her of property. As the

Court put it in the leading case of *Matthews v. Eldridge*, 424 U.S. 319 (1976), the law balances several factors in determining whether a deprivation satisfies the requirements of procedural due process:

> First, the private interest that will be affected by the official action; second, the risk of an erroneous deprivation of such interest through the procedures used, and the probable value, if any, of additional or substitute procedural safeguards; and finally, the Government's interest, including the function involved and the fiscal and administrative burdens that the additional or substitute procedural requisites would entail.

Substantively, the due process clause protects owners from deprivation of "property" rights by "arbitrary and capricious" government actions. *Nectow v. City of Cambridge*, 277 U.S. 183, 187-188 (1928). *Accord, Pennell v. City of San Jose*, 485 U.S. 1, 11 (1988) (due process is violated if law is "arbitrary, discriminatory, or demonstrably irrelevant to the policy the legislature is free to adopt"); *Village of Arlington Heights v. Metropolitan Housing Development Corp.*, 429 U.S. 252, 263 (1977) (owners have a "right to be free from arbitrary or irrational zoning actions"); *Town of Rhine v. Bizzell*, 751 N.W.2d 780, 793-794 (Wis. 2008) (zoning ordinance presumed valid unless "clearly arbitrary and unreasonable in the restricted sense that it has no substantial relation to the public health, safety, morals or general welfare"). As with equal protection, in determining whether a state action is arbitrary in the forbidden sense, courts usually apply a deferential means-ends analysis that asks whether the state's action (or means) is rationally related to a permissible government goal (or end). The difference is this requirement for some minimal fit between means and ends under the rubric of substantive due process applies to all government actions, and not just those involving the creation of legal categories. In a sense, courts treat rational basis review under the due process clause as defining the outer limits of state police-power action. To constitute a valid exercise of the state's police power, all state action must be minimally rational and must be directed toward some permissible public goal.

Bonner v. City of Brighton

828 N.W.2d 408 (Mich. Ct. App. 2012)[1]

JANE MARKEY, P.J.

Factual and Procedural History

Plaintiffs own two residential properties located in downtown Brighton. There is a house on one parcel of property and a house with a garage or barn on the other. According to the city, the three structures have been unoccupied and largely ignored and unmaintained for over 30 years, representing the most egregious instances of residential blight in Brighton. The city's building and code enforcement official (hereafter

1. At the time this book went to press, the Supreme Court of Michigan had granted review of this case, but had not yet rendered a decision. *See Bonner v. City of Brighton*, 832 N.W.2d 250 (Mich. 2013).

Figure 1 — One of the Bonners' houses (courtesy of Dennis B. Dubuc, the Bonners' attorney)

"building official") informed plaintiffs in a letter that the structures on the two properties constituted unsafe structures under the [Brighton Code of Ordinances (BCO)][2] and public nuisances under Michigan common law. The building official cited a litany of alleged defects and code violations in regard to the condition of the structures. Plaintiffs were further informed that it had been determined that it was unreasonable to repair the structures as defined in BCO §18-59, which provides in relevant part as follows:

> Whenever the city manager, or his designee, has determined that a structure is unsafe and has determined that the cost of the repairs would exceed 100 percent of the true cash value of the structure as reflected on the city assessment tax rolls in effect prior to the building becoming an unsafe structure, such repairs shall be presumed unreasonable and it shall be presumed for the purpose of this article that such structure is a public nuisance which may be ordered demolished without option on the part of the owner to repair.

---

2. BCO §18-46 defines an "unsafe structure," setting forth a number of qualifying criteria. BCO §18-47 makes it "unlawful for an owner or agent to maintain or occupy an unsafe structure." BCO §18-48 requires those responsible for a structure to "take all necessary precautions to prevent any nuisance or other condition detrimental to public health, safety, or general welfare from arising thereon."

Plaintiffs were ordered to demolish the structures with no option to repair within 60 days. Plaintiffs appealed the determination to the city council.

In preparation for the appeal, plaintiffs retained a structural engineer and various contractors to determine the repairs necessary to bring each structure into compliance with the applicable building codes. These individuals prepared drawings and repair plans and asserted that the structures were safe, structurally sound, and readily repairable. At a hearing before the city council, plaintiffs agreed to provide the building official with an expert's report and to allow city personnel access to the structures for purposes of exterior and interior inspections. The city council tabled the appeal pending the inspections. After inspecting the structures, the city's inspectors and experts identified extensive defects and code violations, requiring numerous repairs and the replacement of certain structural features. In communications to plaintiffs and the city council, the building official reiterated his position that the structures were unsafe, that it would be unreasonable to repair them, and that therefore, demolition was required.

The pending appeal to the city council was resumed, and hearings were conducted in which the council received the reports of inspectors, contractors, engineers, and other experts, along with written repair estimates, PowerPoint presentations, testimony, and oral arguments. The building official and his experts opined that the total cost to bring the structures up to code was approximately $158,000. The city determined the cash value of the structures at approximately $85,000. One of plaintiffs' experts opined that it would cost less than $40,000 per house to make the necessary repairs and bring the structures up to code. In Resolution 09-16, [t]he city council determined that plaintiffs' reports and cost estimates lacked credibility and that the structures had lost their status as nonconforming, single-family residential uses. The council concluded that the structures constituted "unsafe structures" under BCO §18-46, that plaintiffs were in violation of BCO §18-47 by owning and maintaining unsafe structures, and that the structures were unreasonable to repair and must be demolished under BCO §18-59. The city council ordered plaintiffs to demolish the structures within 60 days.

Shortly before the 60-day period was set to expire, plaintiffs filed the instant action against the city, alleging, in a first amended complaint, a violation of procedural and substantive due process. Plaintiffs' constitutional challenges were predicated on the United States Constitution, 42 U.S.C. §1983, and the Michigan Constitution.

Plaintiffs filed a motion for partial summary disposition with respect to their complaint, arguing that BCO §18-59 was unconstitutional. The trial court determined that BCO §18-59 violated substantive due process because it precluded property owners from having the opportunity to repair their property, which served no rational interest or purpose, was entirely arbitrary, and shocked the conscience. This Court granted the city's application for leave to appeal.

Analysis

The state and federal constitutions guarantee that no person shall be deprived of life, liberty, or property without due process of law. U.S. Const, Am XIV; Const 1963, art 1, §17; *Reed v. Reed*, 693 N.W.2d 825 (Mich. Ct. App. 2005). "Procedure in a particular case is constitutionally sufficient when there is notice of the nature of the proceedings and a meaningful opportunity to be heard by an impartial decision maker." *Id.* And, although the text of the Due Process Clauses provides only procedural protections, due process also has a substantive component that protects individual liberty and property interests from arbitrary government actions regardless of the fairness of any implementing procedures. *Gen. Motors Corp. v. Dep't of Treasury,* 803 N.W.2d 698 (Mich. Ct. App. 2010); *Mettler Walloon, L.L.C. v. Melrose Twp.,* 761 N.W.2d 293 (Mich. Ct. App. 2008). The right to substantive due process is violated when legislation is unreasonable and clearly arbitrary, having no substantial relationship to the health, safety, morals, and general welfare of the public. *Lingle v. Chevron U.S.A., Inc.,* 544 U.S. 528 (2005). In the context of government actions, a substantive due process violation is established only when "the governmental conduct [is] so arbitrary and capricious as to shock the conscience." *Mettler Walloon,* 761 N.W.2d 293.

A citizen is entitled to due process of law when a municipality, exercising its police power, enacts an ordinance that affects the citizen's constitutional rights. In determining whether an ordinance enacted by a municipality comports with due process, the test employed is whether the ordinance bears a reasonable relationship to a permissible legislative objective. When a municipal ordinance restricts the use of property, the issue is whether the exercise of authority entails an undue invasion of private constitutional rights without a reasonable justification in connection with the public welfare. We begin with the presumption that an ordinance is reasonable and thus constitutionally compliant. The property owner must demonstrate that the challenged ordinance arbitrarily and unreasonably affects the owner's use of his or her property. An ordinance does not offend the Due Process Clause when it satisfies the reasonableness test; the ordinance must be reasonable or reasonably necessary for purposes of preserving the public health, morals, or safety. An ordinance will be declared unconstitutional only if it constitutes an arbitrary fiat or a whimsical *ipse dixit,* leaving no legitimate dispute regarding its unreasonableness.

Although the trial court's ruling and the arguments of the parties are framed in the context of substantive due process, we find that the nature of the issues presented in this case also implicate procedural due process. The principle espoused by plaintiffs is that a property owner has the right, or must have the option or opportunity, to make repairs to a structure deemed unsafe by a municipality before the structure can be demolished or razed. Plaintiffs do not contend that the city lacks the general authority to demolish unsafe or dangerous structures; they instead argue that a property owner must be afforded the opportunity to repair an unsafe structure before the city orders it demolished. Plaintiffs' argument contains elements of procedural due process requiring notice, hearing, and a ruling by an impartial decision-maker, before the government infringes constitutionally protected property interests.

"In procedural due process claims, the deprivation by state action of a constitutionally protected interest in 'life, liberty, or property' is not in itself unconstitutional; what is unconstitutional is the deprivation of such an interest without due process of law." *Zinermon v. Burch,* 494 U.S. 113, 125 (1990). "'Procedural due process rules are meant to protect persons not from the deprivation, but from the mistaken or unjustified deprivation of life, liberty, or property.' " *Id.* at 125-126 (citation omitted). Procedural due process differs from substantive due process in that "procedural due process principles protect persons from deficient procedures that lead to the deprivation of cognizable [property] interests." *Bartell v. Lohiser*, 215 F.3d 550, 557 (6th Cir. 2000). A procedural due process violation occurs when the government unlawfully interferes with a protected property or liberty interest without providing adequate procedural safeguards. *Schiller v. Strangis*, 540 F. Supp. 605, 613 (D. Mass. 1982). To establish a violation of procedural due process, one must show that the action concerned a recognizable property or liberty interest, that there was a deprivation of that interest absent due process of law, and that the deprivation took place under the color of state law. *Id.* "A 'substantive due process' claim is, fundamentally, not a claim of procedural deficiency, but, rather, a claim that the state's conduct is inherently impermissible." *Id.* at 614. As the court in *Schiller*, 540 F. Supp. at 614, noted, "[T]he line dividing 'procedural due process' from 'substantive due process' is not always bright, [and] it may be difficult in some cases to determine which is the proper characterization of the plaintiff's claim." Ultimately, we conclude that the ordinance infringes on plaintiffs' due process rights, whether denominated procedural or substantive, thereby making it unnecessary to determine which due process principle is actually embodied in plaintiffs' argument.

Discussion

We first carefully examine the language of BCO §18-59 to determine and define its scope, its requirements, and its proper implementation. Once a determination is made that an unsafe structure exists and that the cost to repair exceeds the structure's value before it became unsafe, it is presumed that the repairs are unreasonable and that the structure is a public nuisance subject to demolition without the option to repair. [T]he ordinance does not definitively establish the unreasonableness of repairs, the existence of a public nuisance, and the authority to order demolition without option to abate the nuisance and repair the structure. Rather, the ordinance merely gives rise to these presumptions.

Under BCO §18-59, a property owner may, regardless of the fact that repair costs would exceed a structure's true cash value, avail himself or herself of an opportunity to overcome or rebut the presumption by showing that making repairs would nonetheless be reasonable under the circumstances. In turn, accomplishing the repairs would abate any unsafe conditions negating the presumption of public nuisance, thereby precluding a demolition order.

Even though BCO §18-59 can be interpreted to allow a property owner the opportunity to overcome or rebut the presumptions of that section, such a construction of BCO §18-59 still requires an owner to establish the reasonableness of making repairs. Stated otherwise, in order to overcome the presumption that allows the city to order demolition absent an option to repair, the property owner must show that making repairs is reasonable. We find this aspect of the ordinance to be constitutionally problematic and in violation of due process. The appeal section, BCO §18-61, does not provide its own or a different standard; therefore, the city council in addressing an appeal would be constrained to also apply the reasonableness standard that governs BCO §18-59. Such a standard prevents a property owner who has the desire and ability to make the necessary repairs in a timely fashion to render a structure safe, even when the cost of repairs exceeds the city-determined true cash value of the structure before it became unsafe, from doing so because the ordinance deems such repairs unreasonable.

We conclude that if the owner of an unsafe structure wishes to incur an expense that others might find unreasonable to repair a structure, bring it up to code, and avoid a demolition order, the city should not infringe upon the owner's property interest by forbidding it. There may be myriad reasons why a property owner would desire to repair a structure under circumstances in which it is not economically profitable to do so, including sentimental, nostalgic, familial, or historic, which may not be measurable on an economic balance sheet. Ultimately, the owner's reasons for desiring to repair a structure to render it safe when willing and able even though costly, are entirely irrelevant and of no concern to the municipality.

We note that BCO §18-59, by using the language "*may* be ordered" (emphasis added), gives the city manager or his designee the discretion to not order the demolition of a structure and to allow repairs even though the structure is unsafe and the repair costs exceed the structure's pertinent value. In other words, demolition is not mandated when it is unreasonable to make repairs. We find, however, that this discretionary language does not save the ordinance from constitutional challenge, considering that the ordinance places no constraints on the exercise of what is essentially unfettered discretion.

We hold that BCO §18-59 violates substantive due process because it is arbitrary and unreasonable, constituting a whimsical ipse dixit; it denies a property owner the option to repair an unsafe structure simply on the basis that the city deems repair efforts to be economically unreasonable. When a property owner is willing and able to timely repair a structure to make it safe, preventing that action on the basis of the ordinance's standard of reasonableness does not advance the city's interest of protecting the health and welfare of its citizens. We do not dispute that a permissible legislative objective of the city under its police powers is to protect citizens from unsafe and dangerous structures and that one mechanism for advancing that objective can entail demolishing or razing unsafe structures. But BCO §18-59 does not bear a reasonable relationship to this permissible legislative objective. There are two ways to achieve the legislative objective, demolition or repair, either of which results in the abatement of the nuisance or danger of an unsafe structure. There is simply no sound reason for prohibiting a willing property owner from undertaking corrective repairs on the basis that making such repairs is an unreasonable endeavor, given that the repairs, similar to demolition, will equally result in achieving the objective of protecting citizens from unsafe structures. If a property owner fails to make the necessary repairs within a reasonable timeframe, demolition can then be ordered. The city's restriction on plaintiffs' opportunity to repair the structures and right to protect their constitutionally recognized property interests from invasion has no reasonable relation to the public welfare. The public welfare is safeguarded by the construction repairs, and the ordinance does not afford the public greater protection or safeguards by calling for demolition over repairs when making repairs is characterized as being unreasonable. Of course, the municipality has the authority to define the repairs necessary and to set a reasonable time limit for their completion. For the reasons set forth above, we conclude that BCO §18-59 violates substantive due process.

We also determine that BCO §18-59 does not provide adequate procedural safeguards to satisfy the Due Process Clause. In addition to notice, a hearing, and an impartial decision-maker, which are provided for in §18 of the BCO, the city should have also provided for a reasonable opportunity to repair an unsafe structure, limited only by unique or emergency situations. Precluding an opportunity to repair on the basis that it is too costly in comparison with a structure's value or that making repairs is otherwise unreasonable can result in an erroneous and unconstitutional deprivation of a property interest, i.e., a deprivation absent due process of law. Giving a property owner the procedural protection of a repair option is the only way the city's ordinances could withstand a procedural due process challenge.

Due process is a flexible concept, but its essence is fundamental fairness. The procedures that are constitutionally required in a particular case are determined by examining (1) the private interest at stake or affected by the governmental action, (2) the risk of an erroneous deprivation of the interest under existing procedures and the value of additional safeguards, and (3) the adverse impact on the government of requiring additional safeguards, including the consideration of fiscal and administrative burdens. *In re Brock*, 499 N.W.2d 752 (Mich. 1993), citing *Mathews v. Eldridge*, 424 U.S. 319, 335 (1976). The nature of the private interest at stake in this case is substantial—plaintiffs' property interest as owners of three structures. Next, the risk of an erroneous deprivation of the property interest under BCO §18-59 is significant as it allows for the demolition of unsafe structures when repairs are considered unreasonable despite an owner's willingness and ability to make timely repairs. The added safeguard of a repair option would eliminate the risk of an erroneous deprivation of the property interest. Finally, adding the safeguard of a repair option would minimally affect the city's interest in the health and welfare of its citizens, as well as not cause any fiscal or administrative burdens beyond those that would be associated with demolition of the property. Under BCO §18-59, the cost to the city if it demolishes an unsafe structure may be assessed as a lien against the real property. If repairs are undertaken by a property owner pursuant to a repair option, the owner and not the city bears the cost of those repairs, and the city's only function would be to determine what repairs are necessary and monitor their timely completion. With forced demolition by the city, the city would incur the costs and then have to seek reimbursement of expenses incurred, possibly requiring lien-foreclosure proceedings. In sum, on review of the pertinent factors in the present case, we find that procedural due process requires a property owner to have an option to repair a structure determined to be unsafe except in unique and emergency situations demanding immediate action.

Court decisions in other jurisdictions, while not binding precedent, provide persuasive support for our holding. In *Washington v. City of Winchester*, 861 S.W.2d 125 (Ky. App. 1993), the appellant-owner challenged a circuit court order that required her to demolish a building that had numerous building code violations. A building inspector initially ordered demolition, which decision was appealed to a city appeals board. The appeals board delayed demolition to allow a determination regarding the value of the building and the cost of repairs necessary to bring the building into compliance with the building code. Subsequently it was determined that the estimated cost to repair the building exceeded 100 percent of the building's appraised value. On the basis of this information, the appeals board affirmed the inspector's demolition order, and the circuit court then affirmed the decision by the appeals board. On appeal to the Kentucky Court of Appeals, the appellant building owner argued that she should have been given the opportunity to bring the building into compliance with the code through repairs. *Id.* at 126.

The appellate court agreed with the building owner that she should have been given the option to repair the building within a reasonable time. *Id.* The court, citing *Johnson v. City of Paducah*, 512 S.W.2d 514, 516 (Ky. 1974), held that "the exercise of the city's police power is for the protection of the public, but the means of its implementation may extend no further than public necessity requires." *Washington*, 861 S.W.2d at 126. The court noted that the failure to provide a property owner the option of repair was arbitrary, that the government did not have absolute power over private property, and that improperly requiring demolition absent compensation constituted a taking. *Id.* at 126-127. Finally, the Kentucky court observed:

> [J]ust as the cost of . . . [code] compliance is a property owner's problem, the method of compliance is also the property owner's decision. It's his/her money and far be it from the [c]ity to say how a reasonable person should spend his/her money. . . . [A]s free men and women, we can spend our own money as we see fit, that if we want to pour endless dollars, sweat, etc., into some historic building, or personally appealing project, we may—even if the ultimate cost would be ten fold over the cost of demolition and rebuilding. So, too, with the [c]ity . . . and the appellant herein, if she wants to pour huge sums of money into her unfit building[ ], she has that option. A reasonable person may very well choose demolition, but it's her money and her choice. [*Id.* at 127.]

We agree with these sentiments and observations. While BCO §18-59 varies slightly from the code provision at issue in Washington, we adopt the principles espoused in Washington for purposes of our analysis of BCO §18-59.

Conclusion

While police powers generally allow the demolition of unsafe structures to achieve the legitimate legislative objective of keeping citizens safe, the ordinance's exclusion of a repair option when repairs are deemed economically unreasonable bears no reasonable relationship to this legislative objective. Demolition does not advance the objective of abating nuisances and protecting citizens to a greater degree than repairs, even ones more costly than the present value of the structure and which an owner is willing and able to timely incur. Therefore, we hold that the ordinance violates substantive due process. Moreover, by not providing procedural safeguards in the form of an option to repair when a property owner's desire to repair could be viewed as unreasonable and lead to the unlawful deprivation of a constitutionally protected property interest, and which safeguard would burden the city to a lesser extent than demolition, the city's ordinance also violates procedural due process.

CHRISTOPHER M. MURRAY, J. (dissenting).

The majority acknowledges that these ordinances provide persons with notice, an opportunity to be heard at a hearing before city council, and a decision from an impartial decision-maker. Recognizing that the ordinances provide notice and an opportunity to be heard before an impartial decision-maker should preclude any facial challenge to the ordinances based on procedural due process, especially when the procedures themselves are not alleged to be deficient. [T]here is no dispute that plaintiffs received proper notice of the city inspector's decision, had the opportunity to appeal that decision to city council where a full hearing was held, and received a decision from what the majority concedes was an impartial decision-maker. Considering the *Mathews* factors, the city's ordinance satisfied the requirements of due process. Plaintiffs received all the process that they were constitutionally due, and this Court should not rule to the contrary.

Unlike procedural due process, substantive due process bars "'certain government actions regardless of the fairness of the procedures used to implement them.'" *Mettler Walloon*, 761 N.W.2d 293, quoting *Co. of Sacramento v. Lewis*, 523 U.S. 833, 840 (1998). The established test that a plaintiff must prove is "'(1) that there is no reasonable governmental interest being advanced by the present zoning classification or (2) that an ordinance is unreasonable because of the purely arbitrary, capricious, and unfounded exclusion of other types of legitimate land use from the area in question.'" *Dorman v. Clinton Twp.*, 714 N.W.2d 350 (Mich. Ct. App. 2006), quoting *Frericks v. Highland Twp.*, 579 N.W.2d 441 (Mich. Ct. App. 1998). Here, no one questions that the ordinances advance a legitimate governmental interest. Thus, the sole issue on the substantive due process claim is whether the ordinances are an unreasonable means of advancing the undisputed governmental interest.

In conducting this analysis, the standard we must employ is again vitally important. Judicial review of a challenge to an ordinance on substantive due process grounds requires application of three rules:

> (1) the ordinance is presumed valid; (2) the challenger has the burden of proving that the ordinance is an arbitrary and unreasonable restriction upon the owner's use of the property; that the provision in question is an arbitrary fiat, a whimsical ipse dixit; and that there is not room for a legitimate difference of opinion concerning its reasonableness; and (3) the reviewing court gives considerable weight to the findings of the trial judge. [*Yankee Springs Twp. v. Fox*, 692 N.W.2d 728 (Mich. Ct. App. 2004), quoting *A & B Enterprises v. Madison Twp.*, 494 N.W.2d 761 (Mich. Ct. App. 1992).]

Applying this difficult and deferential standard, and recognizing that we conduct a de novo review of the trial court's decision, I would hold that BCO §18-59 survives plaintiffs' facial challenge. There are at least two reasons supporting this conclusion. First, city council's decision to implement a presumption of demolition if the repair costs exceed 100 percent of the value of the structure before it because unsafe is neither unreasonable nor arbitrary. [F]or structures that are not exempt from the presumption, the ordinance grants city council the discretion to approve repairs instead of ordering demolition. For example, city council could — as plaintiffs admit — simply decide after a hearing that the property owner should have an opportunity to repair before demolition occurs, or that repairs are only necessary. Thus, if there is a substantive due process right to repair one's property before demolition, then under this hypothetical that right is not violated. Because there are factual circumstances under which this ordinance is constitutional, under the governing standards plaintiffs cannot prevail on their facial challenge to the ordinance.

Second, it is difficult to conclude that the presumption is so arbitrary that it shocks the conscience. Although the position taken by the trial court and the majority is understandable, i.e., it might be good policy for the city to allow an owner to expend whatever resources they deem appropriate to repair their own premises, accepting that principle does not result in a conclusion that a presumption to the contrary for some unsafe structures is unconstitutional. In other words, that there may have been other reasonable means to accomplish the city's objective of removing unsafe structures from the city does not mean that the city's choice of employing these terms was arbitrary or the result of some "whimsical ipse dixit." City council is, of course, the policy-making body for the city, and we must be extraordinarily careful not to utilize somewhat vague constitutional standards to override policy decisions that are outside our authority to make.

Notes and Questions

1. **Deference.** Courts applying this means-ends, due process analysis are usually extremely deferential to the elected political branches. That deference makes substantive due process claims exceedingly difficult for property owners to win. The dissent in *Bonner* accuses the majority of extending insufficient deference to the city council's policy determination that owners should not have an option to repair dilapidated structures where the costs of repair exceed the value of the structure itself. Do you agree with the dissent that the majority is engaged in something more demanding than a search for some rational basis for the city council's policy decision? What reasons might the city council have had for determining that unsafe structures should be subject to demolition without giving owners the option to repair where the cost to repair is more than the value the structure had before it became unsafe?

2. **Due process in state courts.** Did the court in *Bonner* strike down the ordinance on state or federal constitutional grounds? Is there a difference between the two in Michigan? The Kentucky case of *Washington v. City of Winchester*, 861 S.W.2d 125 (Ky. App. 1993), on which the majority relied in *Bonner*, invalidated a similar demolition ordinance under §2 of the Kentucky constitution. That provision states that "[a]bsolute and arbitrary power over the lives, liberty and property of freemen exists nowhere in a republic, not even in the largest majority." Was the majority in *Bonner* correct in treating *Washington* as persuasive authority in a Michigan case applying the

federal due process standard? Whether applying their own state constitutional law or the federal due process standard, state courts often seem more willing to rule in favor of owners on substantive due process claims. Why do you think that might be?

3. Defining "property" for the Constitution. The text of the U.S. Constitution neither creates property interests nor defines what it means by "property." When considering federal constitutional property claims, where do courts turn in order to give content to the concept of property? This definitional puzzle actually has two different dimensions. First, as a threshold matter, courts need to determine what sorts of interests qualify as "property" in order to define the reach of the Constitution's property protections. If some valuable legal interest is not "property" for the purposes of the fifth amendment's due process clause, for example, its deprivation by a governmental actor cannot violate the requirements of due process, at least as they relate to property (as opposed to "life" and "liberty"). *See, e.g., College Savings Bank v. Florida Prepaid Postsecondary Education Expense Board,* 527 U.S. 666, 673-674 (1999) (no due process violation where the interest affected by state action did not qualify as "property"). Similarly, if an interest is not "private property" for the purposes of the fifth amendment's takings clause, its taking by the government for public use does not trigger the requirement of just compensation. *See Bowen v. Public Agencies Opposed to Social Security Entrapment,* 477 U.S. 41, 55-56 (1986); *Tee-Hit-Ton Indians v. United States,* 348 U.S. 272 (1955). *See* Chapter 15, §1.4.

While the interests that the Supreme Court considers when applying the due process and takings clauses are not themselves created by the Constitution, *see Board of Regents v. Roth,* 408 U.S. 564 (1972), the question of the reach of those provisions is one of federal constitutional law. *See Town of Castle Rock v. Gonzales,* 545 U.S. 748 (2005). The Court has not always been attentive to this threshold "reach" question, and it has employed different ways of answering it in different cases. Generally speaking, the Court seems to apply a broader definition of property for due process claims than for takings claims. *See* Thomas W. Merrill, *The Landscape of Constitutional Property,* 86 Va. L. Rev. 885, 886-894 (2000).

For due process claims, the Court has rejected the position that "all civil rights of pecuniary value" count as "property." *College Savings Bank,* 527 U.S. at 673-674. Nevertheless, the Court has embraced an extremely broad conception of "property" for due process purposes, particularly in procedural cases. As the Court put it in *Board of Regents v. Roth,* "the property interests protected by procedural due process extend well beyond actual ownership of real estate, chattels, or money." 408 U.S. at 571. According to the Court, the "hallmark" of property protected by the due process clause is an entitlement that "cannot be removed except for cause." *Logan v. Zimmerman Brush Co.,* 455 U.S. 422, 430 (1982); *see also Town of Castle Rock,* 545 U.S. at 756 ("[A] benefit is not a protected entitlement if government officials may grant or deny it in their discretion."). This means that, when considering due process claims, courts have treated as "property" a great many interests that would not be treated as such in other legal contexts. These include professional licenses, government benefits, and even certain forms of government employment. *See, e.g., Goss v. Lopez,* 419 U.S. 565 (1975) (treating the right to a public education as property for procedural due process purposes); *Perry v. Sindermann*, 408 U.S. 593, 599-600 (1972) (treating an informal tenure arrangement at a junior college as a property interest for due process purposes); *Goldberg v. Kelly*, 397 U.S. 254 (1970) (welfare benefits treated as property for procedural due process purposes); *Schware v. Board of Bar Examiners of State of New Mexico*, 353 U.S. 232 (1957) (law license is property for due process purposes); *see also* Merrill, *supra*, at 956-957.

In the takings context, on the other hand, the Court has tended to draw the circle more narrowly. *See* Merrill, *supra*, at 957. In *Eastern Enterprises v. Apfel*, 524 U.S. 498 (1998), for example, five members of the Court agreed that the "private property" protected by the takings clause was a narrower category than "property" for due process purposes. While due process "property" includes general obligations to pay money, the five Justices reasoned, to count as "private property" for takings purposes, the interest in question must constitute a discrete thing, or what Justice Kennedy called in his concurring opinion a "specific property interest," such as money contained in a specific bank account. *Id.* at 540-542 (Kennedy, J., concurring).

A second dimension of the definitional problem arises when courts need to actually apply federal constitutional standards to the specific legal interests created by state or federal law. In order to apply constitutional property norms, courts need to ascertain the precise content of an owner's legal rights. For example, in determining whether some state restriction of an owner's land use has "taken" the owner's property for public use without just compensation, a court needs to know whether the owner had the right to engage in the restricted use to begin with. In carrying out this task, courts turn to the body of law from which the property interest arises, whether that be state property law or federal statute. *See Ruckelshaus v. Monsanto Co.*, 467 U.S. 986, 1001 (1984).

4. Due process and zoning: *Nectow v. City of Cambridge*, 277 U.S. 183 (1928). In *Nectow v. City of Cambridge*, a vacant lot was bisected by a newly enacted zoning ordinance. The bulk of the parcel was zoned for industrial uses, but one vacant part of the parcel was limited to residential use. Although the vacant part was 100 feet wide, the master who heard the case found that the city might widen the street in such a manner as to reduce the depth of that lot to 65 feet and that as a result, "no practical use can be made of the land in question for residential purposes, because . . . there would not be adequate return on the amount of any investment for the development of the property." The Supreme Court held that the statute, as applied to this portion of the land, impermissibly infringed on constitutionally protected property rights. The Court explained its result, *id.* at 187-189:

> The last finding of the master is: "I am satisfied that the districting of the plaintiff's land in a residence district would not promote the health, safety, convenience, and general welfare of the inhabitants of that part of the defendant city, taking into account the natural development thereof and the character of the district and the resulting benefit to accrue to the whole city and I so find."
>
> It is made pretty clear that because of the industrial and railroad purposes to which the immediately adjoining lands to the south and east have been devoted and for which

> they are zoned, the locus is of comparatively little value for the limited uses permitted by the ordinance.
>
> We quite agree with the opinion expressed below that a court should not set aside the determination of public officers in such a matter unless it is clear that their action "has no foundation in reason and is a mere arbitrary or irrational exercise of power having no substantial relation to the public health, the public morals, the public safety or the public welfare in its proper sense." *Euclid v. Ambler Co.*, [272 U.S.] at 395.
>
> An inspection of a plat of the city upon which the zoning districts are outlined, taken in connection with the master's findings, shows with reasonable certainty that the inclusion of the locus in question is not indispensable to the general plan. The boundary line of the residential district before reaching the locus runs for some distance along the streets, and to exclude the locus from the residential district requires only that such line shall be continued 100 feet further along Henry street and thence south along Brookline street. There does not appear to be any reason why this should not be done. Nevertheless, if that were all, we should not be warranted in substituting our judgment for that of the zoning authorities primarily charged with the duty and responsibility of determining the question. But that is not all. The governmental power to interfere by zoning regulations with the general rights of the land owner by restricting the character of his use, is not unlimited, and, other questions aside, such restriction cannot be imposed if it does not bear a substantial relation to the public health, safety, morals, or general welfare. Here, the express finding of the master, already quoted, confirmed by the court below, is that the health, safety, convenience, and general welfare of the inhabitants of the part of the city affected will not be promoted by the disposition made by the ordinance of the locus in question. This finding of the master, after a hearing and an inspection of the entire area affected, supported, as we think it is, by other findings of fact, is determinative of the case. That the invasion of the property of plaintiff in error was serious and highly injurious is clearly established; and, since a necessary basis for the support of that invasion is wanting, the action of the zoning authorities comes within the ban of the Fourteenth Amendment and cannot be sustained.

The Supreme Court had just two years earlier upheld comprehensive zoning in *Village of Euclid v. Ambler Realty Co.*, 272 U.S. 365 (1926) against a facial attack on the statute, but left open the possibility that it might revisit that judgment in an as-applied challenge. *Id.* at 395 (noting that "when, if ever, the provisions set forth in the ordinance in tedious and minute detail, come to be concretely applied to particular premises . . . or to particular conditions, or to be considered in connection with specific complaints, some of them, or even many of them, may be found to be clearly arbitrary and unreasonable"). *See* Chapter 7, §1.2. Since *Nectow*, however, the Supreme Court has not found any zoning ordinances to violate substantive due process on grounds of irrationality, leaving the policing of constitutional due process in zoning primarily to the state courts.

5. Vagueness. Due process is also implicated in zoning statutes that are unconstitutionally vague. In *Cunney v. Board of Trustees of Village of Grand View, New York*, 660 F.3d 612 (2d Cir. 2011), an owner of a parcel situated between the Hudson River and a street called River Road had applied for permits to improve his house. In order to preserve views of the river, the Village's zoning ordinance limited the height of buildings that abutted River Road to no more than "four and one-half (4 1/2) feet above the easterly side of River Road." The owner obtained the requisite permits for his project based on height measurements that appeared to conform to this provision. However, the Village denied a certificate of occupancy after construction based on a report from the Village engineer, who took measurements that seemed to indicate that the height restriction had been violated. The property was on a slope running along River Road and throughout the permitting and approval process, it had been unclear where exactly on that slope compliance with the ordinance should be measured. The Second Circuit held that the statute violated the due process clause of the fourteenth amendment because it failed to give the owner "a reasonable opportunity to understand what conduct it prohibits," *id.* at 621 (quoting *Hill v. Colorado*, 530 U.S. 703, 732 (2000)), and because the statute failed to provide explicit standards for the officials charged with applying it, *id.* at 622. For a discussion of vagueness in the context of aesthetic zoning, *see* Chapter 7, §6.1.

6. Retroactivity. Whenever property rules change, lawmakers must confront the question whether to apply the new rule to property interests created prior to the change. The potential for new rules to unsettle (or even destroy) existing property rights raises potential constitutional concerns. Under the due process clause, courts evaluate the retroactive application of a new property rule according to due process standards that assess whether the state's application of the new rule to existing property entitlements is itself rationally related to a permissible government purpose. *See, e.g., American Express Travel Related Services, Inc. v. Sidamon-Eristoff*, 669 F.3d 359 (3d Cir. 2012) (retroactive application of shortened period for unclaimed property statute to existing travelers checks did not violate due process because it had a conceivable rational basis). But, while the substance of the inquiry concerning the fundamental fairness of retroactivity remains the same as due process analysis in other contexts, judges considering retroactivity questions sometimes seem to apply a more exacting scrutiny. *See, e.g., Eastern Enterprises v. Apfel*, 524 U.S. 498, 547 (1998) (Kennedy, J., concurring). *But see id.* at 557 ("[A] law that is fundamentally unfair because of its retroactivity is a law that is basically arbitrary [in violation of the usual Due Process principles].") (Breyer, J., dissenting). Can you think of a situation in which the retroactive application of an otherwise valid new property rule would not pass muster under a rational basis, due process review?

Problem

In *City of Wilmington v. Hill*, 657 S.E.2d 670 (N.C. Ct. App. 2008), the court held unconstitutional a city ordinance that prohibited owners from renting their property and effectively required owners to occupy their own homes. The owner had constructed a garage apartment, and the city interpreted the zoning law to require the owner to reside either in the main residence or in the garage apartment. The court held that the zoning enabling act did not delegate power to the city to pass such a law because it allowed municipalities to regulate the "use" of property, not their ownership or the identity of the possessor. The court then noted that the due process clause requires laws to have a "substantial relation to the public health, the public morals, the public safety or the public welfare" and that courts should defer to legislatures in debatable cases. *Id.* at 673. Suppose the court had held that a requirement that owners occupy their homes serves no legitimate public purpose and thus is invalid under the due process clause. Would that be a correct application of the due process clause?

§3.2 Property Regulations Burdening Fundamental Rights

An exception to the generally deferential approach to substantive due process review occurs when the state's action burdens what the Supreme Court has deemed to be a "fundamental right," such as privacy, association, or marriage. *See Washington v. Glucksberg*, 521 U.S. 702, 719 (1997) (discussing cases that have found a "fundamental right" whose burdening by the state triggers heightened scrutiny under the due process clause). Although often discussed in terms of "liberty interests," these fundamental rights can also relate to how people go about using their property, as the following cases illustrate.

Village of Belle Terre v. Boraas

416 U.S. 1 (1974)

Mr. Justice WILLIAM O. DOUGLAS delivered the opinion of the Court.

Belle Terre is a village on Long Island's north shore of about 220 homes inhabited by 700 people. Its total land area is less than one square mile. It has restricted land use to one-family dwellings excluding lodging houses, boarding houses, fraternity houses, or multiple-dwelling houses. The word "family" as used in the ordinance means, "[o]ne or more persons related by blood, adoption, or marriage, living and cooking together as a single housekeeping unit, exclusive of household servants. A number of persons but not exceeding two (2) living and cooking together as a single housekeeping unit though not related by blood, adoption, or marriage shall be deemed to constitute a family."

Appellees, the Dickmans, are owners of a house in the village and leased it in December 1971 for a term of 18 months to Michael Truman. Later Bruce Boraas became a colessee. Then Anne Parish moved into the house along with three others. These six are students at nearby State University at Stony Brook and none is related to the other by blood, adoption, or marriage. When the village served the Dickmans with an "Order to Remedy Violations" of the ordinance, the owners plus three tenants thereupon brought this action under 42 U.S.C. §1983 for an injunction and a judgment declaring the ordinance unconstitutional.

This case brings to this Court a different phase of local zoning regulations from those we have previously reviewed. *Euclid v. Ambler Realty Co.*, 272 U.S. 365 (1926), involved a zoning ordinance classifying land use in a given area into six categories.

The main thrust of *Euclid* in the mind of the Court was in the exclusion of industries and apartments, and as respects that it commented on the desire to keep residential areas free of "disturbing noises"; "increased traffic"; the hazard of "moving and parked automobiles"; the "depriving children of the privilege of quiet and open spaces for play, enjoyed by those in more favored localities." The ordinance was sanctioned because the validity of the legislative classification was "fairly debatable" and therefore could not be said to be wholly arbitrary.

If the ordinance segregated one area only for one race, it would immediately be suspect under the reasoning of *Buchanan v. Warley*, 245 U.S. 60 (1917), where the Court invalidated a city ordinance barring a black from acquiring real property in a white residential area by reason of an 1866 Act of Congress, 42 U.S.C. §1982, and an 1870 Act, §17, now 42 U.S.C. §1981, both enforcing the Fourteenth Amendment.

The present ordinance is challenged on several grounds: that it interferes with a person's right to travel; that it interferes with the right to migrate to and settle within a State; that it bars people who are uncongenial to the present residents; that it expresses the social preferences of the residents for groups that will be congenial to them; that social homogeneity is not a legitimate interest of government; that the restriction of those whom the neighbors do not like trenches on the newcomers' rights of privacy; that it is of no rightful concern to villagers whether the residents are married or unmarried; that the ordinance is antithetical to the Nation's experience, ideology, and self-perception as an open, egalitarian, and integrated society.

We find none of these reasons in the record before us. It is not aimed at transients. It involves no "fundamental" right guaranteed by the Constitution, such as voting, the right of association, the right of access to the courts, or any rights of privacy. We deal with economic and social legislation where legislatures have historically drawn lines which we respect against the charge of violation of the Equal Protection Clause if the law be "reasonable, not arbitrary" and bears "a rational relationship to a [permissible] state objective."

It is said, however, that if two unmarried people can constitute a "family," there is no reason why three or four may not. But every line drawn by a legislature leaves some out that might well have been included. That exercise of discretion, however, is a legislative, not a judicial, function.

It is said that the Belle Terre ordinance reeks with an animosity to unmarried couples who live together. There is no evidence to support it; and the provision of the ordinance bringing within the definition of a "family" two unmarried people belies the charge.

The ordinance places no ban on other forms of association, for a "family" may, so far as the ordinance is concerned, entertain whomever it likes.

The regimes of boarding houses, fraternity houses, and the like present urban problems. More people occupy a given space; more cars rather continuously pass by; more cars are parked; noise travels with crowds.

A quiet place where yards are wide, people few, and motor vehicles restricted are legitimate guidelines in a land-use project addressed to family needs. This goal is a permissible one. The police power is not confined to elimination of filth, stench, and unhealthy places. It is ample to lay out zones where family values, youth values, and the blessings of quiet seclusion and clean air make the area a sanctuary for people.

Mr. Justice THURGOOD MARSHALL, dissenting.

My disagreement with the Court today is based upon my view that the ordinance in this case unnecessarily burdens appellees' First Amendment freedom of association and their constitutionally guaranteed right to privacy.

The freedom of association is often inextricably entwined with the constitutionally guaranteed right of privacy. The right to "establish a home" is an essential part of the liberty guaranteed by the Fourteenth Amendment. And the Constitution secures to an individual a freedom "to satisfy his intellectual and emotional needs in the privacy of his own home." *Stanley v. Georgia*, 394 U.S. 557, 565 (1969). Constitutionally protected privacy is, in Mr. Justice Brandeis' words, "as against the Government, the right to be let alone . . . the right most valued by civilized man." *Olmstead v. United States*, 277 U.S. 438, 478 (1928) (dissenting opinion). The choice of household companions — of whether a person's "intellectual and emotional needs" are best met by living with family, friends, professional associates, or others — involves deeply personal considerations as to the kind and quality of intimate relationships within the home. That decision surely falls within the ambit of the right to privacy protected by the Constitution.

The instant ordinance discriminates on the basis of just such a personal lifestyle choice as to household companions. It permits any number of persons related by blood or marriage, be it two or twenty, to live in a single household, but it limits to two the number of unrelated persons bound by profession, love, friendship, religious or political affiliation, or mere economics who can occupy a single home. Belle Terre imposes upon those who deviate from the community norm in their choice of living companions significantly greater restrictions than are applied to residential groups who are related by blood or marriage, and compose the established order within the community. The village has, in effect, acted to fence out those individuals whose choice of lifestyle differs from that of its current residents.

Because I believe that this zoning ordinance creates a classification which impinges upon fundamental personal rights, it can withstand constitutional scrutiny only upon a clear showing that the burden imposed is necessary to protect a compelling and substantial governmental interest.

A variety of justifications have been proffered in support of the village's ordinance. It is claimed that the ordinance controls population density, prevents noise, traffic and parking problems, and preserves the rent structure of the community and its attractiveness to families. [T]hese are all legitimate and substantial interests of government. But I think it clear that the means chosen to accomplish these purposes are both overinclusive and underinclusive, and that the asserted goals could be as effectively achieved by means of an ordinance that did not discriminate on the basis of constitutionally protected choices of lifestyle. The ordinance imposes no restriction whatsoever on the number of persons who may live in a house, as long as they are related by marital or sanguinary bonds — presumably no matter how distant their relationship. Nor does the ordinance restrict the number of income earners who may contribute to rent in such a household, or the number of automobiles that may be maintained by its occupants. In that sense the ordinance is underinclusive. On the other hand, the statute restricts the number of unrelated persons who may live in a home to no more than two. It would therefore prevent three unrelated people from occupying a dwelling even if among them they had but one income and no vehicles. While an extended family of a dozen or more might live in a small bungalow, three elderly and retired persons could not occupy the large manor house next door. Thus the statute is also grossly overinclusive to accomplish its intended purposes.

There are some 220 residences in Belle Terre occupied by about 700 persons. The density is therefore just above three per household. The village is justifiably concerned with density of population and the related problems of noise, traffic, and the like. It could deal with those problems by limiting each household to a specified number of adults, two or three perhaps, without limitation on the number of dependent children. The burden of such an ordinance would fall equally upon all segments of the community. It would surely be better tailored to the goals asserted by the village than the ordinance before us today, for it would more realistically restrict population density and growth and their attendant environmental costs. Various other statutory mechanisms also suggest themselves as solutions to Belle Terre's problems — rent control, limits on the number of vehicles per household, and so forth, but, of course, such schemes are matters of legislative judgment and not for this Court. Appellants also refer to the necessity of maintaining the family character of the village. There is not a shred of evidence in the record indicating that if Belle Terre permitted a limited number of unrelated persons to live together, the residential, familial character of the community would be fundamentally affected.

By limiting unrelated households to two persons while placing no limitation on households of related individuals, the village has embarked upon its commendable course in a constitutionally faulty vessel. I would find the challenged ordinance unconstitutional. But I would not ask the village to abandon its goal of providing quiet streets, little traffic, and a pleasant and reasonably priced environment in which families might raise their children. Rather, I would commend the village to continue to pursue those purposes but by means of more carefully drawn and even-handed legislation.

Moore v. City of East Cleveland

431 U.S. 494 (1977)

Mr. Justice Lewis F. Powell announced the judgment of the Court, and delivered an opinion in which Mr. Justice Brennan, Mr. Justice Marshall, and Mr. Justice Blackmun joined.

East Cleveland's housing ordinance, like many throughout the country, limits occupancy of a dwelling unit to members of a single family. §1351.02.[3] But the ordinance contains an unusual and complicated definitional section that recognizes as a

3. All citations by section number refer to the Housing Code of the city of East Cleveland, Ohio.

"family" only a few categories of related individuals, §1341.08.[4] Because her family, living together in her home, fits none of those categories, appellant stands convicted of a criminal offense. The question in this case is whether the ordinance violates the Due Process Clause of the Fourteenth Amendment.

I

Appellant, Mrs. Inez Moore, lives in her East Cleveland home together with her son, Dale Moore Sr., and her two grandsons, Dale, Jr., and John Moore, Jr. The two boys are first cousins rather than brothers; we are told that John came to live with his grandmother and with the elder and younger Dale Moores after his mother's death.

In early 1973, Mrs. Moore received a notice of violation from the city, stating that John was an "illegal occupant" and directing her to comply with the ordinance. When she failed to remove him from her home, the city filed a criminal charge. Mrs. Moore moved to dismiss, claiming that the ordinance was constitutionally invalid on its face. Her motion was overruled, and upon conviction she was sentenced to five days in jail and a $25 fine. The Ohio Court of Appeals affirmed after giving full consideration to her constitutional claims, and the Ohio Supreme Court denied review. We noted probable jurisdiction of her appeal.

II

The city argues that our decision in *Village of Belle Terre v. Boraas*, 416 U.S. 1 (1974), requires us to sustain the ordinance attacked here. But one overriding factor sets this case apart from *Belle Terre*. The ordinance there affected only unrelated individuals. It expressly allowed all who were related by "blood, adoption, or marriage" to live together, and in sustaining the ordinance we were careful to note that it promoted "family needs" and "family values." East Cleveland, in contrast, has chosen to regulate the occupancy of its housing by slicing deeply into the family itself. This is no mere incidental result of the ordinance. On its face it selects certain categories of relatives who

4. Section 1341.08 (1966) provides:

"'Family' means a number of individuals related to the nominal head of the household or to the spouse of the nominal head of the household living as a single housekeeping unit in a single dwelling unit, but limited to the following:

"(a) Husband or wife of the nominal head of the household.

"(b) Unmarried children of the nominal head of the household or of the spouse of the nominal head of the household, provided, however, that such unmarried children have no children residing with them.

"(c) Father or mother of the nominal head of the household or of the spouse of the nominal head of the household.

"(d) Notwithstanding the provisions of subsection (b) hereof, a family may include not more than one dependent married or unmarried child of the nominal head of the household or of the spouse of the nominal head of the household and the spouse and dependent children of such dependent child. For the purpose of this subsection, a dependent person is one who has more than fifty percent of his total support furnished for him by the nominal head of the household and the spouse of the nominal head of the household.

"(e) A family may consist of one individual."

may live together and declares that others may not. In particular, it makes a crime of a grandmother's choice to live with her grandson in circumstances like those presented here.

When a city undertakes such intrusive regulation of the family, neither *Belle Terre* nor *Euclid* [*v. Ambler Realty Co.*, 272 U.S. 365 (1926)], governs; the usual judicial deference to the legislature is inappropriate. The city seeks to justify [the ordinance] as a means of preventing overcrowding, minimizing traffic and parking congestion, and avoiding an undue financial burden on East Cleveland's school system. Although these are legitimate goals, the ordinance before us serves them marginally, at best. For example, the ordinance permits any family consisting only of husband, wife, and unmarried children to live together, even if the family contains a half dozen licensed drivers, each with his or her own car. At the same time it forbids an adult brother and sister to share a household, even if both faithfully use public transportation. The ordinance would permit a grandmother to live with a single dependent son and children, even if his school-age children number a dozen, yet it forces Mrs. Moore to find another dwelling for her grandson John, simply because of the presence of his uncle and cousin in the same household. We need not labor the point. Section 1341.08 has but a tenuous relation to alleviation of the conditions mentioned by the city.

Our decisions establish that the Constitution protects the sanctity of the family precisely because the institution of the family is deeply rooted in this Nation's history and tradition. It is through the family that we inculcate and pass down many of our most cherished values, moral and cultural. Ours is by no means a tradition limited to respect for the bonds uniting the members of the nuclear family. The tradition of uncles, aunts, cousins, and especially grandparents sharing a household along with parents and children has roots equally venerable and equally deserving of constitutional recognition. Over the years millions of our citizens have grown up in just such an environment, and most, surely, have profited from it. Even if conditions of modern society have brought about a decline in extended family households, they have not erased the accumulated wisdom of civilization, gained over the centuries and honored throughout our history, that supports a larger conception of the family. Out of choice, necessity, or a sense of family responsibility, it has been common for close relatives to draw together and participate in the duties and the satisfactions of a common home. Especially in times of adversity, such as the death of a spouse or economic need, the broader family has tended to come together for mutual sustenance and to maintain or rebuild a secure home life. This is apparently what happened here.

Whether or not such a household is established because of personal tragedy, the choice of relatives in this degree kinship to live together may not lightly be denied by the State. [T]he Constitution prevents East Cleveland from standardizing its children and its adults by forcing all to live in certain narrowly defined family patterns.

Reversed.

Mr. Justice WILLIAM J. BRENNAN, with whom Mr. Justice MARSHALL joins, concurring.

I write to underscore the cultural myopia of the arbitrary boundary drawn by the East Cleveland ordinance in the light of the tradition of the American home that has been a feature of our society since our beginning as a Nation the "tradition" in the plurality's words, "of uncles, aunts, cousins, and especially grandparents sharing a household along with parents and children. . . . " The line drawn by this ordinance displays a depressing insensitivity toward the economic and emotional needs of a very large part of our society.

In today's America, the "nuclear family" is the pattern so often found in much of white suburbia. J. Vander Zanden, *Sociology: A Systematic Approach* 322 (3d ed. 1975). The Constitution cannot be interpreted, however, to tolerate the imposition by government upon the rest of us of white suburbia's preference in patterns of family living. The "extended family" that provided generations of early Americans with social services and economic and emotional support in times of hardship, and was the beachhead for successive waves of immigrants who populated our cities, remains not merely still a pervasive living pattern, but under the goad of brutal economic necessity, a prominent pattern virtually a means of survival for large numbers of the poor and deprived minorities of our society. For them compelled pooling of scant resources requires compelled sharing of a household.

The "extended" form is especially familiar among black families. We may suppose that this reflects the truism that black citizens, like generations of white immigrants before them, have been victims of economic and other disadvantages that would worsen if they were compelled to abandon extended, for nuclear, living patterns. Even in husband and wife households, 13% of black families compared with 3% of white families include relatives under 18 years old, in addition to the couple's own children. In black households whose head is an elderly woman, as in this case, the contrast is even more striking: 48% of such black households, compared with 10% of counterpart white households, include related minor children not offspring of the head of the household.

I do not wish to be understood as implying that East Cleveland's enforcement of its ordinance is motivated by a racially discriminatory purpose: The record of this case would not support that implication. But the prominence of other than nuclear families among ethnic and racial minority groups, including our black citizens, surely demonstrates that the "extended family" pattern remains a vital tenet of our society. It suffices that in prohibiting this pattern of family living as a means of achieving its objectives, appellee city has chosen a device that deeply intrudes into family associational rights that historically have been central, and today remain central, to a large proportion of our population.

Mr. Justice John Paul Stevens, concurring in the judgment.

In my judgment the critical question presented by this case is whether East Cleveland's housing ordinance is a permissible restriction on appellant's right to use her own property as she sees fit. Long before the original States adopted the Constitution, the common law protected an owner's right to decide how best to use his own property. The holding in *Euclid v. Ambler Realty Co.*, 272 U.S. 365 (1926), that a city could use its police power, not just to abate a specific use of property which proved offensive, but also to create and implement a comprehensive plan for the use of land in the community, vastly diminished the rights of individual property owners. It did not, however, totally extinguish those rights. On the contrary, that case expressly recognized that the broad zoning power must be exercised within constitutional limits.

Litigation involving single-family zoning ordinances is common. These cases delineate the extent to which the state courts have allowed zoning ordinances to interfere with the right of a property owner to determine the internal composition of his household. The intrusion on that basic property right has not previously gone beyond the point where the ordinance defines a family to include only persons related by blood, marriage, or adoption. Indeed, state courts have not always allowed the intrusion to penetrate that far. There appears to be no precedent for an ordinance which excludes any of an owner's relatives from the group of persons who may occupy his residence on a permanent basis.

[Chief Justice BURGER, in dissent, would not have reached the constitutional issue on the argument that appellant could have, but did not, apply for a variance under the ordinance, a proposition the majority rejected.]

Mr. Justice POTTER STEWART, with whom Mr. Justice REHNQUIST joins, dissenting.

In my view, the appellant's claim that the ordinance in question invades constitutionally protected rights of association and privacy is in large part answered by the *Belle Terre* decision. To suggest that the biological fact of common ancestry necessarily gives related persons constitutional rights of association superior to those of unrelated persons is to misunderstand the nature of the associational freedoms that the Constitution has been understood to protect. Freedom of association has been constitutionally recognized because it is often indispensable to effectuation of explicit First Amendment guarantees. But the scope of the associational right, until now, at least, has been limited to the constitutional need that created it; obviously not every "association" is for First Amendment purposes or serves to promote the ideological freedom that the First Amendment was designed to protect. The "association" in this case is not for any purpose relating to the promotion of speech, assembly, the press, or religion. And wherever the outer boundaries of constitutional protection of freedom of association may eventually turn out to be, they surely do not extend to those who assert no interest other than the gratification, convenience, and economy of sharing the same residence.

[A]ppellant contends that the importance of the "extended family" in American society requires us to hold that her decision to share her residence with her grandsons may not be interfered with by the State. This decision, like the decisions involved in bearing and raising children, is said to be an aspect of "family life" also entitled to substantive protection under the Constitution. Without pausing to inquire how far under this argument an "extended family" might extend, I cannot agree. When the Court has found that the Fourteenth Amendment placed a substantive limitation on a State's power to regulate, it has been in those rare cases in which the personal interests at issue have been deemed "'implicit in the concept of ordered liberty.'" *See Roe v. Wade*, 410 U.S. 113, 152 (1973), quoting *Palko v. Connecticut*, 302 U.S. 319, 325 (1937).

The interest that the appellant may have in permanently sharing a single kitchen and a suite of contiguous rooms with some of her relatives simply does not rise to that level.

Mr. Justice BYRON WHITE, dissenting.

Mrs. Moore's interest in having the offspring of more than one dependent son live with her qualifies as a liberty protected by the Due Process Clause; but, because of the nature of that particular interest, the demands of the Clause are satisfied once the Court is assured that the challenged proscription is the product of a duly enacted or promulgated statute, ordinance, or regulation and that it is not wholly lacking in purpose or utility. That under this ordinance any number of unmarried children may reside with their mother and that this number might be as destructive of neighborhood values as one or more additional grandchildren is just another argument that children and grandchildren may not constitutionally be distinguished by a local zoning ordinance.

That argument remains unpersuasive to me. Here the head of the household may house himself or herself and spouse, their parents, and any number of their unmarried children. A fourth generation may be represented by only one set of grandchildren and then only if born to a dependent child. The ordinance challenged by appellant prevents her from living with both sets of grandchildren only in East Cleveland, an area with a radius of three miles and a population of 40,000. The ordinance thus denies appellant the opportunity to live with all her grandchildren in this particular suburb; she is free to do so in other parts of the Cleveland metropolitan area. If there is power to maintain the character of a single-family neighborhood, as there surely is, some limit must be placed on the reach of the "family." Had it been our task to legislate, we might have approached the problem in a different manner than did the drafters of this ordinance; but I have no trouble in concluding that the normal goals of zoning regulation are present here and that the ordinance serves these goals by limiting, in identifiable circumstances, the number of people who can occupy a single household. The ordinance does not violate the Due Process Clause.

Notes and Questions

1. **Fundamental rights?** Which rights did the parties challenging the single-family ordinance in *Belle Terre* invoke? Did the majority in *Belle Terre* apply heightened scrutiny in light of these asserted rights? Should it have?

2. **Constitutional protection for the traditional family.** On what basis did the *Moore* Court distinguish *Belle Terre*? Does this distinction make sense to you? If constitutional protection for shared living turns on traditional conceptions of family, even broadly conceived, what kinds of families might that leave out?

In 2010, 41 percent of children were born to unmarried parents. Joyce A. Martin et al., *Births: Final Data for 2010*, 61 Natl. Vital Stats. Rep. 1, 8 (2012). And in the majority of states, same-sex couples are not legally able to marry. *See* Chapter 9, §3.6. Does that suggest that the constitutionality of zoning that restricts who may live in certain neighborhoods to people related by blood, marriage, or adoption (as many such ordinances hold) should be evaluated solely or even primarily through a prism of "tradition"?

3. **State constitutional protection of nontraditional families.** Many state courts accept the reasoning of *Belle Terre* and interpret their constitutions as lacking protection for nontraditional families. *See, e.g., McMaster v. Columbia Board of Zoning Appeals*, 719 S.E.2d 660 (S.C. 2011); *Ames Rental Property Association v. City of Ames*, 736 N.W.2d 255 (Iowa 2007).

A minority of state courts, however, have held that their state constitutions provide *greater* protection for nontraditional family access to real property than the federal constitution, as construed by the Supreme Court in *Belle Terre*. For example, *Charter Township of Delta v. Dinolfo*, 351 N.W.2d 831 (Mich. 1984), involved a challenge to a single-family ordinance that limited single-family residences to two or more persons related by blood, marriage, or adoption, and not more than one other unrelated person. Members of The Work of Christ Community had formed two "families" that each included not only a husband, wife, and children, but also six unrelated adults. Acknowledging that *Belle Terre* had affirmed the constitutionality of a nearly identical ordinance, the Michigan Supreme Court nonetheless held that the ordinance violated the due process clause of the Michigan constitution:

> Plaintiff lists the objectives of this ordinance: preservation of traditional family values, maintenance of property values and population and density control. We cannot disagree that those are not only rational but laudable goals. Where the difficulty arises, however, is when plaintiff attempts to convince us that the classification at hand — limiting to two the number of unrelated persons who may occupy a residential dwelling together or with a biological family — is reasonably related to the achievement of those goals. It is precisely this rational relationship between the means used to achieve the legislative goals that must exist in order for this deprivation of the defendants' use of their property to pass the due process test.
>
> Here, plaintiff attempts to have us accept its assumption that different and undesirable behavior can be expected from a functional family. Yet, we have been given not a single argument in support of such an assumption, only the assumption. Defendants, on the other hand, relying on decisions from other jurisdictions construing their own state constitutions, present a compelling argument that the means are not rationally related to the end sought.
>
> Those states that have rejected *Belle Terre* have stressed that a line drawn near the limit of the traditional family is both over- and under-inclusive. Unrelated persons are artificially limited to as few as two, while related families may expand without limit. Under the instant ordinance, twenty male cousins could live together, motorcycles, noise, and all, while three unrelated clerics could not. A greater example of over- and under-inclusiveness we cannot imagine. The ordinance indiscriminately regulates where no regulation is needed and fails to regulate where regulation is most needed.

Id. at 840-842.

Cases similar to *Dinolfo* include *City of Santa Barbara v. Adamson*, 610 P.2d 436 (Cal. 1980) (invalidating restrictive ordinance); *Borough of Glassboro v. Vallorosi*, 568

A.2d 888 (N.J. 1990) (invalidating restrictive ordinance); *McMinn v. Town of Oyster Bay*, 488 N.E.2d 1240 (N.Y. 1985) (invalidating an ordinance that limited occupancy to persons related by blood, marriage, or adoption, or two unrelated persons over the age of 62).

Problem

You are counsel to a municipal planning board that is seeking to zone a new neighborhood for single-family residential purposes. What advice would you have for the board in light of *Belle Terre* and *Moore* about crafting the relevant definition of family for this ordinance? If the municipality wants to limit potential harms related to groups of people living together, are there other ways to regulate those harms directly rather than through the proxy of limiting certain dwellings to a specific definition of "family"?

§3.3 Forfeiture

Bennis v. Michigan

516 U.S. 442 (1996)

Chief Justice WILLIAM REHNQUIST delivered the opinion of the Court.

Petitioner was a joint owner, with her husband, of an automobile in which her husband engaged in sexual activity with a prostitute. A Michigan court ordered the automobile forfeited as a public nuisance, with no offset for her interest, notwithstanding her lack of knowledge of her husband's activity. We hold that the Michigan court order did not offend the Due Process Clause of the Fourteenth Amendment or the Takings Clause of the Fifth Amendment.

Detroit police arrested John Bennis after observing him engaged in a sexual act with a prostitute in the automobile while it was parked on a Detroit city street. Bennis was convicted of gross indecency. The State then sued both Bennis and his wife, petitioner Tina B. Bennis, to have the car declared a public nuisance and abated as such under §§600.3801 and 600.3825 of Michigan's Compiled Laws.

Petitioner defended against the abatement of her interest in the car on the ground that, when she entrusted her husband to use the car, she did not know that he would use it to violate Michigan's indecency law. The Wayne County Circuit Court rejected this argument, declared the car a public nuisance, and ordered the car's abatement. In reaching this disposition, the trial court judge recognized the remedial discretion he had under Michigan's case law. He took into account the couple's ownership of "another automobile," so they would not be left "without transportation." He also mentioned his authority to order the payment of one-half of the sale proceeds, after the deduction of costs, to "the innocent co-title holder." He declined to order such a division of sale proceeds in this case because of the age and value of the car (an 11-year-old Pontiac sedan recently purchased by John and Tina Bennis for $600); he commented in this regard: "[T]here's practically nothing left minus costs in a situation such as this."

The gravamen of petitioner's due process claim is . . . [that she] was entitled to contest the abatement by showing she did not know her husband would use it to violate Michigan's indecency law. But a long and unbroken line of cases holds that an owner's interest in property may be forfeited by reason of the use to which the property is put even though the owner did not know that it was to be put to such use.

Our earliest opinion to this effect is Justice Story's opinion for the Court in *The Palmyra,* 12 Wheat. 1, 6 L. Ed. 531 (1827). The Palmyra, which had been commissioned as a privateer by the King of Spain and had attacked a United States vessel, was captured by a United States war ship and brought into Charleston, South Carolina, for adjudication. On the Government's appeal from the Circuit Court's acquittal of the vessel, it was contended by the owner that the vessel could not be forfeited until he was convicted for the privateering. The Court rejected this contention, explaining: "The thing is here primarily considered as the offender, or rather the offence is attached primarily to the thing." *Id.*, at 14.

In *Van Oster v. Kansas,* 272 U.S. 465 (1926), this Court upheld the forfeiture of a purchaser's interest in a car misused by the seller. Van Oster purchased an automobile from a dealer but agreed that the dealer might retain possession for use in its business. The dealer allowed an associate to use the automobile, and the associate used it for the illegal transportation of intoxicating liquor. The State brought a forfeiture action pursuant to a Kansas statute, and Van Oster defended on the ground that the transportation of the liquor in the car was without her knowledge or authority. This Court rejected Van Oster's claim:

> It is not unknown or indeed uncommon for the law to visit upon the owner of property the unpleasant consequences of the unauthorized action of one to whom he has entrusted it. . . . [C]ertain uses of property may be regarded as so undesirable that the owner surrenders his control at his peril.

Id., at 467-468.

Notwithstanding this well-established authority rejecting the innocent-owner defense, petitioner argues that we should in effect overrule it by importing a culpability requirement from cases having at best a tangential relation to the "innocent owner" doctrine in forfeiture cases. She cites *Foucha v. Louisiana,* 504 U.S. 71 (1992), for the proposition that a criminal defendant may not be punished for a crime if he is found to be not guilty. She also argues that our holding in *Austin v. United States,* 509 U.S. 602 (1993), that the Excessive Fines Clause limits the scope of civil forfeiture judgments, "would be difficult to reconcile with any rule allowing truly innocent persons to be punished by civil forfeiture."

In *Austin,* the Court held that because "forfeiture serves, at least in part, to punish the owner," forfeiture proceedings are subject to the limitations of the Eighth Amendment's prohibition against excessive fines. 509 U.S. at 618. In this case, . . . Michigan's Supreme Court emphasized with respect to the forfeiture proceeding at issue: "It is not contested that this is an equitable action," in which the trial judge has discretion to consider "alternatives [to] abating the entire interest in the vehicle." [527 N.W.2d 483, 495 (Mich. 1994).]

In any event, . . . forfeiture also serves a deterrent purpose distinct from any punitive purpose. Forfeiture of property prevents illegal uses "both by preventing further illicit use of the [property] and by imposing an economic penalty, thereby rendering illegal behavior unprofitable." *Calero-Toledo v. Pearson Yacht Leasing Co.*, 416 U.S. 663, 687 (1974). This deterrent mechanism is hardly unique to forfeiture. For instance, because Michigan also deters dangerous driving by making a motor vehicle owner liable for the negligent operation of the vehicle by a driver who had the owner's consent to use it, petitioner was also potentially liable for her husband's use of the car in violation of Michigan negligence law. Mich. Comp. Laws §257.401 (1990). "The law thus builds a secondary defense against a forbidden use and precludes evasions by dispensing with the necessity of judicial inquiry as to collusion between the wrongdoer and the alleged innocent owner." *Van Oster*, 272 U.S., at 467-468.

Petitioner also claims that the forfeiture in this case was a taking of private property for public use in violation of the Takings Clause of the Fifth Amendment, made applicable to the States by the Fourteenth Amendment. But if the forfeiture proceeding here in question did not violate the Fourteenth Amendment, the property in the automobile was transferred by virtue of that proceeding from petitioner to the State. The government may not be required to compensate an owner for property which it has already lawfully acquired under the exercise of governmental authority other than the power of eminent domain. *United States v. Fuller*, 409 U.S. 488, 492 (1973).

At bottom, petitioner's claims depend on an argument that the Michigan forfeiture statute is unfair because it relieves prosecutors from the burden of separating co-owners who are complicit in the wrongful use of property from innocent co-owners. This argument, in the abstract, has considerable appeal. Its force is reduced in the instant case, however, by the Michigan Supreme Court's confirmation of the trial court's remedial discretion, and petitioner's recognition that Michigan may forfeit her and her husband's car whether or not she is entitled to an offset for her interest in it.

We conclude today, as we concluded 75 years ago, that the cases authorizing actions of the kind at issue are "too firmly fixed in the punitive and remedial jurisprudence of the country to be now displaced." The State here sought to deter illegal activity that contributes to neighborhood deterioration and unsafe streets. The Bennis automobile, it is conceded, facilitated and was used in criminal activity. Both the trial court and the Michigan Supreme Court followed our longstanding practice, and the judgment of the Supreme Court of Michigan is therefore affirmed.

Justice Clarence Thomas, concurring.

As the Court notes, evasion of the normal requirement of proof before punishment might well seem "unfair." One unaware of the history of forfeiture laws and 200 years of this Court's precedent regarding such laws might well assume that such a scheme is lawless — a violation of due process.

This case is ultimately a reminder that the Federal Constitution does not prohibit everything that is intensely undesirable. As detailed in the Court's opinion and the cases cited therein, forfeiture of property without proof of the owner's wrongdoing, merely because it was "used" in or was an "instrumentality" of crime has been permitted in England and this country, both before and after the adoption of the Fifth and Fourteenth Amendments.

Improperly used, forfeiture could become more like a roulette wheel employed to raise revenue from innocent but hapless owners whose property is unforeseeably misused, or a tool wielded to punish those who associate with criminals, than a component of a system of justice. When the property sought to be forfeited has been entrusted by its owner to one who uses it for crime, however, the Constitution apparently assigns to the States and to the political branches of the Federal Government the primary responsibility for avoiding that result.

Justice RUTH BADER GINSBURG, concurring.

First, it bears emphasis that the car in question belonged to John Bennis as much as it did to Tina Bennis. At all times he had her consent to use the car, just as she had his. And it is uncontested that Michigan may forfeit the vehicle itself. The sole question, then, is whether Tina Bennis is entitled not to the car, but to a portion of the proceeds (if any there be after deduction of police, prosecutorial, and court costs) as a matter of constitutional right.

Second, it was "critical" to the judgment of the Michigan Supreme Court that the nuisance abatement proceeding is an "equitable action." That means the State's Supreme Court stands ready to police exorbitant applications of the statute. It shows no respect for Michigan's high court to attribute to its members tolerance of, or insensitivity to, inequitable administration of an "equitable action."

Nor is it fair to charge the trial court with "blatant unfairness" in the case at hand. That court declined to order a division of sale proceeds, as the trial judge took pains to explain, for two practical reasons: the Bennises have "another automobile," and the age and value of the forfeited car (an 11-year-old Pontiac purchased by John and Tina Bennis for $600) left "practically nothing" to divide after subtraction of costs.

Michigan, in short, has not embarked on an experiment to punish innocent third parties. Nor do we condone any such experiment. Michigan has decided to deter Johns from using cars they own (or co-own) to contribute to neighborhood blight, and that abatement endeavor hardly warrants this Court's disapprobation.

Justice JOHN PAUL STEVENS, with whom Justice SOUTER and Justice BREYER join, dissenting.

I would reverse because petitioner is entirely without responsibility for [her husband's] act. Fundamental fairness prohibits the punishment of innocent people.

In other contexts, we have regarded as axiomatic that persons cannot be punished when they have done no wrong. I would hold now what we have always assumed: that the principle is required by due process.

The unique facts of this case demonstrate that petitioner is entitled to the protection of that rule. Without knowledge that he would commit such an act in the family car, or that he had ever done so previously, surely petitioner cannot be accused of failing to take "reasonable steps" to prevent the illicit behavior. She is just as blameless as if a thief, rather than her husband, had used the car in a criminal episode.

Forfeiture of an innocent owner's property that plays a central role in a criminal enterprise may be justified on reasoning comparable to the basis for imposing liability on a principal for an agent's torts. Just as the risk of *respondeat superior* liability encourages employers to supervise more closely their employees' conduct, so the risk of forfeiture encourages owners to exercise care in entrusting their property to others. But the law of agency recognizes limits on the imposition of vicarious liability in situations where no deterrent function is likely to be served; for example, it exonerates the employer when the agent strays from his intended mission and embarks on a "frolic of his own." In this case, petitioner did not "entrust" the car to her husband on the night in question; he was entitled to use it by virtue of their joint ownership. There is no reason to think that the threat of forfeiture will deter an individual from buying a car with her husband — or from marrying him in the first place — if she neither knows nor has reason to know that he plans to use it wrongfully.

The absence of any deterrent value reinforces the punitive nature of this forfeiture law. But petitioner has done nothing that warrants punishment. She cannot be accused of negligence or of any other dereliction in allowing her husband to use the car for the wholly legitimate purpose of transporting himself to and from his job. She affirmatively alleged and proved that she is not in any way responsible for the conduct that gave rise to the seizure. If anything, she was a victim of that conduct. In my opinion, these facts establish that the seizure constituted an arbitrary deprivation of property without due process of law.

Justice ANTHONY KENNEDY, dissenting.

The forfeiture of vessels pursuant to the admiralty and maritime law has a long, well-recognized tradition, evolving as it did from the necessity of finding some source of compensation for injuries done by a vessel whose responsible owners were often half a world away and beyond the practical reach of the law and its processes. The prospect of deriving prompt compensation from *in rem* forfeiture, and the impracticality of adjudicating the innocence of the owners or their good-faith efforts in finding a diligent and trustworthy master, combined to eliminate the owner's lack of culpability as a defense.

This forfeiture cannot meet the requirements of due process. Nothing in the rationale of the Michigan Supreme Court indicates that the forfeiture turned on the negligence or complicity of petitioner, or a presumption thereof, and nothing supports the suggestion that the value of her co-ownership is so insignificant as to be beneath the law's protection.

For these reasons, and with all respect, I dissent.

Notes and Questions

1. **Tradition and due process.** One aspect of the debate between the majority and dissent in *Moore v. East Cleveland*, 431 U.S. 494 (1977), involved the role of tradition in defining the scope of constitutional rights. *See* §3.2, above. What role does tradition play in the majority and dissents in *Bennis*?

2. Public nuisance, seizure of property, and crime control. In recent years, local governments have used public nuisance ordinances to abate a wide variety of activities related to crime, including ordinances that even declare certain gang-related activities to be a public nuisance. *See People ex rel. Gallo v. Acuna*, 929 P.2d 596, 608, 615 (Cal. 1997) (upholding injunction against gang members "[s]tanding, sitting, walking, driving, gathering, or appearing anywhere in public view . . . with any other known [fellow gang] member"). The practice of civil forfeiture of property connected to alleged criminal activity has grown steadily in recent decades, with proceeds collected by the Justice Department increasing from $27 million in 1985 to nearly $4.2 billion in 2012. *See* Sarah Stillman, *Taken*, The New Yorker, Aug. 12, 2013. Advocates have raised concerns that civil forfeiture, particularly by cash-strapped local governments, is rife with abuse and that it is difficult for parties whose property is seized by the police to challenge those seizures because the costs of doing so often outstrip the value of the property. *Id.*

In *Keshbro, Inc. v. City of Miami*, 801 So. 2d 864 (Fla. 2001), the Florida Supreme Court upheld the temporary closure of a motel that had been the site of numerous drug and prostitution offenses but overturned an order closing an apartment complex for one year when it had been the site of only two illegal drug sales. The court held that the city had taken the property of the apartment complex owner without just compensation because the illegal activity was not so pervasive as to constitute either a private or public nuisance. Did the court rule correctly? Is this result consistent with *Bennis*?

3. Eviction of innocent public housing tenants. In *Department of Housing and Urban Development v. Rucker*, 535 U.S. 125 (2002), the Supreme Court interpreted a federal statute to allow eviction of innocent public housing tenants when members of their households have engaged in illegal drug use or sales on or off the housing site. *See* 42 U.S.C. §1437d(*l*)(6) (requiring public housing authorities to use leases that provide that "any drug-related criminal activity on or off such premises, engaged in by a public housing tenant, any member of the tenant's household, or any guest or other person under the tenant's control, shall be cause for termination of [the] tenancy"). *See also* 24 C.F.R. §966.4(e)(12). The Court found no constitutional problem with forfeiture of property owned by an innocent party even if that tenant had done everything possible to prevent family members from using or selling drugs on the ground that the government was acting as an owner-landlord placing conditions in the lease with which the tenants voluntarily concurred and not as a sovereign regulating the lease terms or punishing an innocent party because of the criminal acts of another. Is this holding consistent with the holding in *Keshbro*? Do you agree?

CHAPTER 15

Takings Law

§1 EMINENT DOMAIN

§1.1 The Eminent Domain Power and the Condemnation Process

As an inherent aspect of their sovereignty, the federal and state governments have the power to take property by eminent domain. The fifth amendment provides that "Nor shall private property be taken for public use, without just compensation." U.S. Const., amend. V. That clause is made applicable to the States by the fourteenth amendment, *Chicago, Burlington & Quincy Railroad Co. v. Chicago*, 166 U.S. 226 (1897), and all state constitutions have equivalent provisions. The text of the takings clause suggests several constitutional questions in eminent domain: Does a purported taking involve "private property" subject to the clause; is the taking for "public use"; and, if so, has there been payment of "just compensation"?

When the government acquires property without the owner's consent, it is usually clear that a taking has occurred and compensation must be paid. However, where governmental actions interfere with an owner's property rights but do not involve an actual transfer to the government, the question is whether there has been a "taking" at all. We will focus on that issue, which falls under the doctrinal heading of "regulatory takings," beginning in §2.

The condemnation power is regulated and defined by statute. Sometimes the legislature exercises the power directly and sometimes it delegates eminent domain authority to an agency that is empowered by the government to take property for specific purposes. For example, the Massachusetts Port Authority has the statutory power to take property for airport or harbor purposes and the U.S. Department of Transportation has the power to take property for highway purposes, as authorized by legislation. Municipalities generally are delegated eminent domain power as well for purposes such as road and school construction and condemnation of unsafe structures. In some circumstances private entities, such as railroads, utilities, and turnpike companies, are also delegated the authority to condemn private property.

Statutes define the procedures by which the condemnation process occurs. Some states have "quick-take" statutes that authorize the seizure of property immediately in certain circumstances, with the government paying what it deems to be just compensation, and placing the burden on the owner to challenge that amount. Usually, however, the condemning agency must attempt to negotiate to purchase the property from the owner for a fair price before filing a lawsuit against the owner and any occupants to condemn the property. If the parties cannot agree on a fair price, the court may appoint experts to determine the fair market value of the property, and a lawsuit with witnesses on both sides may be conducted to determine the compensation mandated by both statute and the constitution. Absent appeals, the suit ends with a condemnation decree that transfers title to the property from the owner to the condemning agency.

§1.2 Public Use

Kelo v. City of New London

545 U.S. 469 (2005)

Map: Trumbull Street, New London, Connecticut

Justice John Paul Stevens delivered the opinion of the Court, in which Kennedy, Souter, Ginsburg, and Breyer, JJ., joined.

In 2000, the city of New London approved a development plan that, in the words of the Supreme Court of Connecticut, was "projected to create in excess of 1,000 jobs, to increase tax and other revenues, and to revitalize an economically distressed city, including its downtown and waterfront areas." In assembling the land needed for this project, the city's development agent has purchased property from willing sellers and proposes to use the power of eminent domain to acquire the remainder of the property from unwilling owners in exchange for just compensation. The question presented is whether the city's proposed disposition of this property qualifies as a "public use" within the meaning of the Takings Clause of the Fifth Amendment to the Constitution.

I

The city of New London (hereinafter City) sits at the junction of the Thames River and the Long Island Sound in southeastern Connecticut. Decades of economic decline led a state agency in 1990 to designate the City a "distressed municipality." In 1996, the Federal Government closed the Naval Undersea Warfare Center, which had been located in the Fort Trumbull area of the City and had employed over 1,500 people. In 1998, the City's unemployment rate was nearly double that of the State, and its population of just under 24,000 residents was at its lowest since 1920.

These conditions prompted state and local officials to target New London, and particularly its Fort Trumbull area, for economic revitalization. To this end, respondent New London Development Corporation (NLDC), a private nonprofit entity established some years earlier to assist the City in planning economic development, was reactivated. In January 1998, the State authorized a $5.35 million bond issue to support the NLDC's planning activities and a $10 million bond issue toward the creation of a Fort Trumbull State Park. In February, the pharmaceutical company Pfizer Inc. announced that it would build a $300 million research facility on a site immediately adjacent to Fort Trumbull; local planners hoped that Pfizer would draw new business to the area, thereby serving as a catalyst to the area's rejuvenation. After receiving initial approval from the city council, the NLDC continued its planning activities and held a series of neighborhood meetings to educate the public about the process. In May, the city council authorized the NLDC to formally submit its plans to the relevant state agencies for review. Upon obtaining state-level approval, the NLDC finalized an integrated development plan focused on 90 acres of the Fort Trumbull area.

The Fort Trumbull area is situated on a peninsula that juts into the Thames River. The area comprises approximately 115 privately owned properties, as well as the 32 acres of land formerly occupied by the naval facility (Trumbull State Park now occupies 18 of those 32 acres). The development plan encompasses seven parcels. Parcel

Fort Trumball before. Photo Courtesy of the Renaissance City Development Association.

1 is designated for a waterfront conference hotel at the center of a "small urban village" that will include restaurants and shopping. This parcel will also have marinas for both recreational and commercial uses. A pedestrian "riverwalk" will originate here and continue down the coast, connecting the waterfront areas of the development. Parcel 2 will be the site of approximately 80 new residences organized into an urban neighborhood and linked by public walkway to the remainder of the development, including the state park. This parcel also includes space reserved for a new U.S. Coast Guard Museum. Parcel 3, which is located immediately north of the Pfizer facility, will contain at least 90,000 square feet of research and development office space. Parcel 4A is a 2.4-acre site that will be used either to support the adjacent state park, by providing parking or retail services for visitors, or to support the nearby marina. Parcel 4B will include a renovated marina, as well as the final stretch of the riverwalk. Parcels 5, 6, and 7 will provide land for office and retail space, parking, and water-dependent commercial uses.

The NLDC intended the development plan to capitalize on the arrival of the Pfizer facility and the new commerce it was expected to attract. In addition to creating jobs, generating tax revenue, and helping to "build momentum for the revitalization of downtown New London," the plan was also designed to make the City more attractive and to create leisure and recreational opportunities on the waterfront and in the park.

The city council approved the plan in January 2000, and designated the NLDC as its development agent in charge of implementation. *See* Conn. Gen. Stat. §8-188. The city council also authorized the NLDC to purchase property or to acquire property by exercising eminent domain in the City's name. *Id.* §8-193. The NLDC successfully negotiated the purchase of most of the real estate in the 90-acre area, but its negotiations with petitioners failed. As a consequence, in November 2000, the NLDC initiated the condemnation proceedings that gave rise to this case.

II

Petitioner Susette Kelo has lived in the Fort Trumbull area since 1997. She has made extensive improvements to her house, which she prizes for its water view. Petitioner Wilhelmina Dery was born in her Fort Trumbull house in 1918 and has lived there her entire life. Her husband Charles (also a petitioner) has lived in the house since they married some 60 years ago. In all, the nine petitioners own 15 properties in Fort Trumbull — 4 in parcel 3 of the development plan and 11 in parcel 4A. Ten of the parcels are occupied by the owner or a family member; the other five are held as investment properties. There is no allegation that any of these properties is blighted or otherwise in poor condition; rather, they were condemned only because they happen to be located in the development area.

In December 2000, petitioners brought this action in the New London Superior Court. They claimed, among other things, that the taking of their properties would violate the "public use" restriction in the Fifth Amendment. After a 7-day bench trial, the Superior Court granted a permanent restraining order prohibiting the taking of the properties located in parcel 4A (park or marina support). It, however, denied petitioners relief as to the properties located in parcel 3 (office space).[1]

After the Superior Court ruled, both sides took appeals to the Supreme Court of Connecticut. That court held, over a dissent, that all of the City's proposed takings were valid. [R]elying on cases such as *Hawai`i Housing Authority v. Midkiff*, 467 U.S. 229 (1984), and *Berman v. Parker*, 348 U.S. 26 (1954), the court held that such economic development qualified as a valid public use under both the Federal and State Constitutions.

The three dissenting justices would have imposed a "heightened" standard of judicial review for takings justified by economic development. Although they agreed that the plan was intended to serve a valid public use, they would have found all the takings unconstitutional because the City had failed to adduce "clear and convincing evidence" that the economic benefits of the plan would in fact come to pass.

We granted certiorari to determine whether a city's decision to take property for the purpose of economic development satisfies the "public use" requirement of the Fifth Amendment.

III

Two polar propositions are perfectly clear. On the one hand, it has long been accepted that the sovereign may not take the property of *A* for the sole purpose of transferring it to another private party *B*, even though *A* is paid just compensation. On the other hand, it is equally clear that a State may transfer property from one private party to another if future "use by the public" is the purpose of the taking; the condemnation of land for a railroad with common-carrier duties is a familiar example. Neither of these propositions, however, determines the disposition of this case.

As for the first proposition, the City would no doubt be forbidden from taking petitioners' land for the purpose of conferring a private benefit on a particular private party. Nor would the City be allowed to take property under the mere pretext of a public purpose, when its actual purpose was to bestow a private benefit. The takings before us, however, would be executed pursuant to a "carefully considered" development plan. The trial judge and all the members of the Supreme Court of Connecticut agreed that there was no evidence of an illegitimate purpose in this case. Therefore, as was true of the statute challenged in *Midkiff*, 467 U.S., at 245, the City's development plan was not adopted "to benefit a particular class of identifiable individuals."

On the other hand, this is not a case in which the City is planning to open the condemned land — at least not in its entirety — to use by the general public. Nor will the private lessees of the land in any sense be required to operate like common carriers,

---

1. While this litigation was pending before the Superior Court, the NLDC announced that it would lease some of the parcels to private developers in exchange for their agreement to develop the land according to the terms of the development plan. Specifically, the NLDC was negotiating a 99-year ground lease with Corcoran Jennison, a developer selected from a group of applicants. The negotiations contemplated a nominal rent of $1 per year, but no agreement had yet been signed.

making their services available to all comers. But although such a projected use would be sufficient to satisfy the public use requirement, this "Court long ago rejected any literal requirement that condemned property be put into use for the general public." *Id.* at 244. Indeed, while many state courts in the mid-19th century endorsed "use by the public" as the proper definition of public use, that narrow view steadily eroded over time. Not only was the "use by the public" test difficult to administer (*e.g.*, what proportion of the public need have access to the property? at what price?), but it proved to be impractical given the diverse and always evolving needs of society.[2] Accordingly, when this Court began applying the Fifth Amendment to the States at the close of the 19th century, it embraced the broader and more natural interpretation of public use as "public purpose." Thus, in a case upholding a mining company's use of an aerial bucket line to transport ore over property it did not own, Justice Holmes' opinion for the Court stressed "the inadequacy of use by the general public as a universal test." *Strickley v. Highland Boy Gold Mining Co.*, 200 U.S. 527, 531 (1906).[3] We have repeatedly and consistently rejected that narrow test ever since.

The disposition of this case therefore turns on the question whether the City's development plan serves a "public purpose." Without exception, our cases have defined that concept broadly, reflecting our longstanding policy of deference to legislative judgments in this field.

In *Berman v. Parker*, 348 U.S. 26 (1954), this Court upheld a redevelopment plan targeting a blighted area of Washington, D.C., in which most of the housing for the area's 5,000 inhabitants was beyond repair. Under the plan, the area would be condemned and part of it utilized for the construction of streets, schools, and other public facilities. The remainder of the land would be leased or sold to private parties for the purpose of redevelopment, including the construction of low-cost housing.

The owner of a department store located in the area challenged the condemnation, pointing out that his store was not itself blighted and arguing that the creation of a "better balanced, more attractive community" was not a valid public use. Writing for a unanimous Court, Justice Douglas refused to evaluate this claim in isolation, deferring instead to the legislative and agency judgment that the area "must be planned as a whole" for the plan to be successful. The Court explained that "community redevelopment programs need not, by force of the Constitution, be on a piecemeal basis — lot by lot, building by building." The public use underlying the taking was unequivocally affirmed, *id.* at 33:

---

2. From upholding the Mill Acts (which authorized manufacturers dependent on power-producing dams to flood upstream lands in exchange for just compensation), to approving takings necessary for the economic development of the West through mining and irrigation, many state courts either circumvented the "use by the public" test when necessary or abandoned it completely. *See* Nichols, *The Meaning of Public Use in the Law of Eminent Domain,* 20 B.U. L. Rev. 615, 619-24 (1940) (tracing this development and collecting cases).

3. *See also Clark v. Nash*, 198 U.S. 361 (1905) (upholding a statute that authorized the owner of arid land to widen a ditch on his neighbor's property so as to permit a nearby stream to irrigate his land).

> We do not sit to determine whether a particular housing project is or is not desirable. The concept of the public welfare is broad and inclusive. The values it represents are spiritual as well as physical, aesthetic as well as monetary. It is within the power of the legislature to determine that the community should be beautiful as well as healthy, spacious as well as clean, well-balanced as well as carefully patrolled. In the present case, the Congress and its authorized agencies have made determinations that take into account a wide variety of values. It is not for us to reappraise them. If those who govern the District of Columbia decide that the Nation's Capital should be beautiful as well as sanitary, there is nothing in the Fifth Amendment that stands in the way.

In *Hawai`i Housing Authority v. Midkiff*, 467 U.S. 229 (1984), the Court considered a Hawai`i statute whereby fee title was taken from lessors and transferred to lessees (for just compensation) in order to reduce the concentration of land ownership. We unanimously upheld the statute and rejected the Ninth Circuit's view that it was "a naked attempt on the part of the state of Hawai`i to take the property of A and transfer it to B solely for B's private use and benefit." Reaffirming *Berman*'s deferential approach to legislative judgments in this field, we concluded that the State's purpose of eliminating the "social and economic evils of a land oligopoly" qualified as a valid public use. Our opinion also rejected the contention that the mere fact that the State immediately transferred the properties to private individuals upon condemnation somehow diminished the public character of the taking. "It is only the taking's purpose, and not its mechanics," we explained, that matters in determining public use. *Id.* at 244.

In that same Term we decided another public use case that arose in a purely economic context. In *Ruckelshaus v. Monsanto Co.*, 467 U.S. 986 (1984), the Court dealt with provisions of the *Federal Insecticide, Fungicide, and Rodenticide Act* under which the Environmental Protection Agency could consider the data (including trade secrets) submitted by a prior pesticide applicant in evaluating a subsequent application, so long as the second applicant paid just compensation for the data. We acknowledged that the "most direct beneficiaries" of these provisions were the subsequent applicants, but we nevertheless upheld the statute under *Berman* and *Midkiff*. We found sufficient Congress' belief that sparing applicants the cost of time-consuming research eliminated a significant barrier to entry in the pesticide market and thereby enhanced competition.

Viewed as a whole, our jurisprudence has recognized that the needs of society have varied between different parts of the Nation, just as they have evolved over time in response to changed circumstances. Our earliest cases in particular embodied a strong theme of federalism, emphasizing the "great respect" that we owe to state legislatures and state courts in discerning local public needs. For more than a century, our public use jurisprudence has wisely eschewed rigid formulas and intrusive scrutiny in favor of affording legislatures broad latitude in determining what public needs justify the use of the takings power.

IV

Those who govern the City were not confronted with the need to remove blight in the Fort Trumbull area, but their determination that the area was sufficiently distressed to justify a program of economic rejuvenation is entitled to our deference. The City has carefully formulated an economic development plan that it believes will provide appreciable benefits to the community, including — but by no means limited to — new jobs and increased tax revenue. As with other exercises in urban planning and development,[4] the City is endeavoring to coordinate a variety of commercial, residential, and recreational uses of land, with the hope that they will form a whole greater than the sum of its parts. Given the comprehensive character of the plan, the thorough deliberation that preceded its adoption, and the limited scope of our review, it is appropriate for us, as it was in *Berman*, to resolve the challenges of the individual owners, not on a piecemeal basis, but rather in light of the entire plan. Because that plan unquestionably serves a public purpose, the takings challenged here satisfy the public use requirement of the Fifth Amendment.

To avoid this result, petitioners urge us to adopt a new bright-line rule that economic development does not qualify as a public use. Putting aside the unpersuasive suggestion that the City's plan will provide only purely economic benefits, neither precedent nor logic supports petitioners' proposal. Promoting economic development is a traditional and long accepted function of government. There is, moreover, no principled way of distinguishing economic development from the other public purposes that we have recognized. In our cases upholding takings that facilitated agriculture and mining, for example, we emphasized the importance of those industries to the welfare of the States in question; in *Berman*, we endorsed the purpose of transforming a blighted area into a "well-balanced" community through redevelopment;[5] in *Midkiff*, we upheld the interest in breaking up a land oligopoly that "created artificial deterrents to the normal functioning of the State's residential land market"; and in *Monsanto*, we accepted Congress' purpose of eliminating a "significant barrier to entry in the pesticide market." It would be incongruous to hold that the City's interest in the economic benefits to be derived from the development of the Fort Trumbull area has less of a public character than any of those other interests. Clearly, there is no basis for exempting economic development from our traditionally broad understanding of public purpose.

Petitioners contend that using eminent domain for economic development impermissibly blurs the boundary between public and private takings. Again, our cases

---

4. *Cf. Vill. of Euclid v. Ambler Realty Co.*, 272 U.S. 365 (1926).

5. It is a misreading of *Berman* to suggest that the only public use upheld in that case was the initial removal of blight. The public use described in *Berman* extended beyond that to encompass the purpose of developing that area to create conditions that would prevent a reversion to blight in the future. *See* 348 U.S., at 34-35 ("It was not enough, [the experts] believed, to remove existing buildings that were insanitary or unsightly. It was important to redesign the whole area so as to eliminate the conditions that cause slums. . . . The entire area needed redesigning so that a balanced, integrated plan could be developed for the region, including not only new homes, but also schools, churches, parks, streets, and shopping centers. In this way it was hoped that the cycle of decay of the area could be controlled and the birth of future slums prevented"). Had the public use in *Berman* been defined more narrowly, it would have been difficult to justify the taking of the plaintiff's nonblighted department store.

foreclose this objection. Quite simply, the government's pursuit of a public purpose will often benefit individual private parties. For example, in *Midkiff*, the forced transfer of property conferred a direct and significant benefit on those lessees who were previously unable to purchase their homes. In *Monsanto*, we recognized that the "most direct beneficiaries" of the data-sharing provisions were the subsequent pesticide applicants, but benefiting them in this way was necessary to promoting competition in the pesticide market. The owner of the department store in *Berman* objected to "taking from one businessman for the benefit of another businessman," referring to the fact that under the redevelopment plan land would be leased or sold to private developers for redevelopment.[6] Our rejection of that contention has particular relevance to the instant case: "The public end may be as well or better served through an agency of private enterprise than through a department of government — or so the Congress might conclude. We cannot say that public ownership is the sole method of promoting the public purposes of community redevelopment projects." *Id.* at 34.[7]

It is further argued that without a bright-line rule nothing would stop a city from transferring citizen *A*'s property to citizen *B* for the sole reason that citizen *B* will put the property to a more productive use and thus pay more taxes. Such a one-to-one transfer of property, executed outside the confines of an integrated development plan, is not presented in this case. While such an unusual exercise of government power would certainly raise a suspicion that a private purpose was afoot,[8] the hypothetical cases posited by petitioners can be confronted if and when they arise. They do not warrant the crafting of an artificial restriction on the concept of public use.[9]

---

6. Notably, as in the instant case, the private developers in *Berman* were required by contract to use the property to carry out the redevelopment plan.

7. Nor do our cases support Justice O'Connor's novel theory that the government may only take property and transfer it to private parties when the initial taking eliminates some "harmful property use." There was nothing "harmful" about the nonblighted department store at issue in *Berman*; nothing "harmful" about the lands at issue in the mining and agriculture cases, *see, e.g., Strickley*; and certainly nothing "harmful" about the trade secrets owned by the pesticide manufacturers in *Monsanto.* In each case, the public purpose we upheld depended on a private party's future use of the concededly nonharmful property that was taken. By focusing on a property's future use, as opposed to its past use, our cases are faithful to the text of the Takings Clause. See U.S. Const., Amdt. 5. ("Nor shall private property be taken for public use, without just compensation"). Justice O'Connor's intimation that a "public purpose" may not be achieved by the action of private parties, confuses the purpose of a taking with its mechanics, a mistake we warned of in *Midkiff*, 467 U.S., at 244. *See also Berman*, 348 U.S., at 33-34 ("The public end may be as well or better served through an agency of private enterprise than through a department of government").

8. Courts have viewed such aberrations with a skeptical eye. *See, e.g., 99 Cents Only Stores v. Lancaster Redevelopment Agency*, 237 F. Supp. 2d 1123 (C.D. Cal. 2001); *cf. Cincinnati v. Vester*, 281 U.S. 439, 448 (1930) (taking invalid under state eminent domain statute for lack of a reasoned explanation). These types of takings may also implicate other constitutional guarantees. *See Vill. of Willowbrook v. Olech*, 528 U.S. 562 (2000) (per curiam).

9. A parade of horribles is especially unpersuasive in this context, since the Takings Clause largely "operates as a conditional limitation, permitting the government to do what it wants so long as it pays the charge." *Eastern Enters. v. Apfel*, 524 U.S. 498, 545 (1998) (Kennedy, J., concurring in judgment and dissenting in part). Speaking of the takings power, Justice Iredell observed that "it is

Alternatively, petitioners maintain that for takings of this kind we should require a "reasonable certainty" that the expected public benefits will actually accrue. Such a rule, however, would represent an even greater departure from our precedent. "When the legislature's purpose is legitimate and its means are not irrational, our cases make clear that empirical debates over the wisdom of takings—no less than debates over the wisdom of other kinds of socioeconomic legislation—are not to be carried out in the federal courts." *Midkiff*, 467 U.S., at 242. Indeed, earlier this Term we explained why similar practical concerns (among others) undermined the use of the "substantially advances" formula in our regulatory takings doctrine. *See Lingle* v. *Chevron U.S.A. Inc.*, 544 U.S. 528, 544 (2005) (noting that this formula "would empower—and might often require—courts to substitute their predictive judgments for those of elected legislatures and expert agencies"). The disadvantages of a heightened form of review are especially pronounced in this type of case. Orderly implementation of a comprehensive redevelopment plan obviously requires that the legal rights of all interested parties be established before new construction can be commenced. A constitutional rule that required postponement of the judicial approval of every condemnation until the likelihood of success of the plan had been assured would unquestionably impose a significant impediment to the successful consummation of many such plans.

Just as we decline to second-guess the City's considered judgments about the efficacy of its development plan, we also decline to second-guess the City's determinations as to what lands it needs to acquire in order to effectuate the project. "It is not for the courts to oversee the choice of the boundary line nor to sit in review on the size of a particular project area. Once the question of the public purpose has been decided, the amount and character of land to be taken for the project and the need for a particular tract to complete the integrated plan rests in the discretion of the legislative branch." *Berman*, 348 U.S., at 35-36.

In affirming the City's authority to take petitioners' properties, we do not minimize the hardship that condemnations may entail, notwithstanding the payment of just compensation. We emphasize that nothing in our opinion precludes any State from placing further restrictions on its exercise of the takings power. Indeed, many States already impose "public use" requirements that are stricter than the federal baseline. Some of these requirements have been established as a matter of state constitutional law,[10] while others are expressed in state eminent domain statutes that carefully limit

---

not sufficient to urge, that the power may be abused, for, such is the nature of all power—such is the tendency of every human institution: and, it might as fairly be said, that the power of taxation, which is only circumscribed by the discretion of the Body, in which it is vested, ought not to be granted, because the Legislature, disregarding its true objects, might, for visionary and useless projects, impose a tax to the amount of nineteen shillings in the pound. We must be content to limit power where we can, and where we cannot, consistently with its use, we must be content to repose a salutory confidence." *Calder v. Bull*, 3 U.S. 386, 400 (1798) (opinion concurring in result).

10. *See, e.g., Cnty. of Wayne v. Hathcock*, 684 N.W.2d 765 (Mich. 2004).

the grounds upon which takings may be exercised.[11] As the submissions of the parties and their *amici* make clear, the necessity and wisdom of using eminent domain to promote economic development are certainly matters of legitimate public debate.[12] This Court's authority, however, extends only to determining whether the City's proposed condemnations are for a "public use" within the meaning of the Fifth Amendment to the Federal Constitution. Because over a century of our case law interpreting that provision dictates an affirmative answer to that question, we may not grant petitioners the relief that they seek.

The judgment of the Supreme Court of Connecticut is affirmed.

Justice ANTHONY M. KENNEDY, concurring.

This Court has declared that a taking should be upheld as consistent with the Public Use Clause, U.S. Const., Amdt. 5., as long as it is "rationally related to a conceivable public purpose." *Hawai`i Housing Authority v. Midkiff*, 467 U.S. 229, 241 (1984). This deferential standard of review echoes the rational-basis test used to review economic regulation under the Due Process and Equal Protection Clauses, *see, e.g., FCC v. Beach Communications, Inc.*, 508 U.S. 307, 313-314 (1993); *Williamson v. Lee Optical of Okla., Inc.*, 348 U.S. 483 (1955). The determination that a rational-basis standard of review is appropriate does not, however, alter the fact that transfers intended to confer benefits on particular, favored private entities, and with only incidental or pretextual public benefits, are forbidden by the Public Use Clause.

A court applying rational-basis review under the Public Use Clause should strike down a taking that, by a clear showing, is intended to favor a particular private party, with only incidental or pretextual public benefits, just as a court applying rational-basis review under the Equal Protection Clause must strike down a government classification that is clearly intended to injure a particular class of private parties, with only incidental or pretextual public justifications. *See Cleburne v. Cleburne Living Center, Inc.*, 473 U.S. 432, 446-47, 450 (1985); *Department of Agriculture v. Moreno*, 413 U.S. 528, 533-36 (1973).

A court confronted with a plausible accusation of impermissible favoritism to private parties should treat the objection as a serious one and review the record to see if it has merit, though with the presumption that the government's actions were reasonable and intended to serve a public purpose. Here, the trial court conducted a careful and extensive inquiry into "whether, in fact, the development plan is of primary benefit to the developer [*i.e.*, Corcoran Jennison], and private businesses which may eventually locate in the plan area [*e.g.*, Pfizer], and in that regard, only of incidental

11. Under California law, for instance, a city may only take land for economic development purposes in blighted areas. Cal. Health & Safety Code §§33030-33037. *See, e.g., Redevelopment Agency of Chula Vista v. Rados Bros.*, 115 Cal. Rptr. 2d 234 (Ct. App. 2002).

12. For example, some argue that the need for eminent domain has been greatly exaggerated because private developers can use numerous techniques, including secret negotiations or precommitment strategies, to overcome holdout problems and assemble lands for genuinely profitable projects. Others argue to the contrary, urging that the need for eminent domain is especially great with regard to older, small cities like New London, where centuries of development have created an extreme over division of land and thus a real market impediment to land assembly.

benefit to the city." The trial court considered respondents' awareness of New London's depressed economic condition and evidence corroborating the validity of this concern; the substantial commitment of public funds by the State to the development project before most of the private beneficiaries were known; evidence that respondents reviewed a variety of development plans and chose a private developer from a group of applicants rather than picking out a particular transferee beforehand; and the fact that the other private beneficiaries of the project are still unknown because the office space proposed to be built has not yet been rented.

The trial court concluded, based on these findings, that benefiting Pfizer was not "the primary motivation or effect of this development plan"; instead, "the primary motivation for [respondents] was to take advantage of Pfizer's presence." Likewise, the trial court concluded that "there is nothing in the record to indicate that [respondents] were motivated by a desire to aid [other] particular private entities." This case, then, survives the meaningful rational basis review that in my view is required under the Public Use Clause.

My agreement with the Court that a presumption of invalidity is not warranted for economic development takings in general, or for the particular takings at issue in this case, does not foreclose the possibility that a more stringent standard of review than that announced in *Berman* and *Midkiff* might be appropriate for a more narrowly drawn category of takings. There may be private transfers in which the risk of undetected impermissible favoritism of private parties is so acute that a presumption (rebuttable or otherwise) of invalidity is warranted under the Public Use Clause. This demanding level of scrutiny, however, is not required simply because the purpose of the taking is economic development.

This is not the occasion for conjecture as to what sort of cases might justify a more demanding standard, but it is appropriate to underscore aspects of the instant case that convince me no departure from *Berman* and *Midkiff* is appropriate here. This taking occurred in the context of a comprehensive development plan meant to address a serious city-wide depression, and the projected economic benefits of the project cannot be characterized as *de minimus*. The identity of most of the private beneficiaries were unknown at the time the city formulated its plans. The city complied with elaborate procedural requirements that facilitate review of the record and inquiry into the city's purposes. In sum, while there may be categories of cases in which the transfers are so suspicious, or the procedures employed so prone to abuse, or the purported benefits are so trivial or implausible, that courts should presume an impermissible private purpose, no such circumstances are present in this case.

Justice SANDRA DAY O'CONNOR, with whom THE CHIEF JUSTICE, Justice SCALIA, and Justice THOMAS join, dissenting.

Over two centuries ago, just after the Bill of Rights was ratified, Justice Chase wrote:

> An ACT of the Legislature (for I cannot call it a law) contrary to the great first principles of the social compact, cannot be considered a rightful exercise of legislative authority.

> A few instances will suffice to explain what I mean. [A] law that takes property from A. and gives it to B: It is against all reason and justice, for a people to entrust a Legislature with SUCH powers; and, therefore, it cannot be presumed that they have done it. *Calder v. Bull*, 3 U.S. 386, 388 (1798) (emphasis deleted).

Today the Court abandons this long-held, basic limitation on government power. Under the banner of economic development, all private property is now vulnerable to being taken and transferred to another private owner, so long as it might be upgraded — *i.e.*, given to an owner who will use it in a way that the legislature deems more beneficial to the public — in the process. To reason, as the Court does, that the incidental public benefits resulting from the subsequent ordinary use of private property render economic development takings "for public use" is to wash out any distinction between private and public use of property — and thereby effectively to delete the words "for public use" from the Takings Clause of the Fifth Amendment. Accordingly I respectfully dissent.

Where is the line between "public" and "private" property use? We give considerable deference to legislatures' determinations about what governmental activities will advantage the public. But were the political branches the sole arbiters of the public-private distinction, the Public Use Clause would amount to little more than hortatory fluff. An external, judicial check on how the public use requirement is interpreted, however limited, is necessary if this constraint on government power is to retain any meaning.

This case presents an issue of first impression: Are economic development takings constitutional? I would hold that they are not. We are guided by two precedents about the taking of real property by eminent domain. In *Berman*, we upheld takings within a blighted neighborhood of Washington, D.C. The neighborhood had so deteriorated that, for example, 64.3% of its dwellings were beyond repair. It had become burdened with "overcrowding of dwellings," "lack of adequate streets and alleys," and "lack of light and air." Congress had determined that the neighborhood had become "injurious to the public health, safety, morals, and welfare" and that it was necessary to "eliminate all such injurious conditions by employing all means necessary and appropriate for the purpose," including eminent domain. Mr. Berman's department store was not itself blighted. Having approved of Congress' decision to eliminate the harm to the public emanating from the blighted neighborhood, however, we did not second-guess its decision to treat the neighborhood as a whole rather than lot-by-lot. *See Midkiff*, 467 U.S., at 244 ("it is only the taking's purpose, and not its mechanics, that must pass scrutiny").

In *Midkiff*, we upheld a land condemnation scheme in Hawai`i whereby title in real property was taken from lessors and transferred to lessees. At that time, the State and Federal Governments owned nearly 49% of the State's land, and another 47% was in the hands of only 72 private landowners. Concentration of land ownership was so dramatic that on the State's most urbanized island, Oahu, 22 landowners owned 72.5% of the fee simple titles. The Hawai`i Legislature had concluded that the oligopoly in land ownership was "skewing the State's residential fee simple market, inflating land prices, and injuring the public tranquility and welfare," and therefore enacted a condemnation scheme for redistributing title.

In those decisions, we emphasized the importance of deferring to legislative judgments about public purpose. Because courts are ill-equipped to evaluate the efficacy of proposed legislative initiatives, we rejected as unworkable the idea of courts' "'deciding on what is and is not a governmental function and invalidating legislation on the basis of their view on that question at the moment of decision, a practice which has proved impracticable in other fields.'" *Id.* at 240-41.

The Court's holdings in *Berman* and *Midkiff* were true to the principle underlying the Public Use Clause. In both those cases, the extraordinary, precondemnation use of the targeted property inflicted affirmative harm on society—in *Berman* through blight resulting from extreme poverty and in *Midkiff* through oligopoly resulting from extreme wealth. And in both cases, the relevant legislative body had found that eliminating the existing property use was necessary to remedy the harm. Thus a public purpose was realized when the harmful use was eliminated. Because each taking *directly* achieved a public benefit, it did not matter that the property was turned over to private use. Here, in contrast, New London does not claim that Susette Kelo's and Wilhelmina Dery's well-maintained homes are the source of any social harm. Indeed, it could not so claim without adopting the absurd argument that any single-family home that might be razed to make way for an apartment building, or any church that might be replaced with a retail store, or any small business that might be more lucrative if it were instead part of a national franchise, is inherently harmful to society and thus within the government's power to condemn.

In moving away from our decisions sanctioning the condemnation of harmful property use, the Court today significantly expands the meaning of public use. It holds that the sovereign may take private property currently put to ordinary private use, and give it over for new, ordinary private use, so long as the new use is predicted to generate some secondary benefit for the public—such as increased tax revenue, more jobs, maybe even aesthetic pleasure. But nearly any lawful use of real private property can be said to generate some incidental benefit to the public. Thus, if predicted (or even guaranteed) positive side-effects are enough to render transfer from one private party to another constitutional, then the words "for public use" do not realistically exclude *any* takings, and thus do not exert any constraint on the eminent domain power.

Any property may now be taken for the benefit of another private party, but the fallout from this decision will not be random. The beneficiaries are likely to be those citizens with disproportionate influence and power in the political process, including large corporations and development firms. As for the victims, the government now has license to transfer property from those with fewer resources to those with more. The Founders cannot have intended this perverse result. "That alone is a *just* government," wrote James Madison, "which *impartially* secures to every man, whatever is his *own*." For the National Gazette, Property, (Mar. 29, 1792), *reprinted in* 14 Papers of James Madison 266 (R. Rutland et al. eds. 1983).

Justice CLARENCE THOMAS, dissenting.

Long ago, William Blackstone wrote that "the law of the land . . . postpones even public necessity to the sacred and inviolable rights of private property." 1 *Commentaries on the Laws of England* 134-135 (1765). The Framers embodied that principle in the Constitution, allowing the government to take property not for "public necessity," but instead for "public use." Amdt. 5. Defying this understanding, the Court replaces the Public Use Clause with a "'Public Purpose"' Clause (or perhaps the "Diverse and Always Evolving Needs of Society" Clause (capitalization added)), a restriction that is satisfied, the Court instructs, so long as the purpose is "legitimate" and the means "not irrational." This deferential shift in phraseology enables the Court to hold, against all common sense, that a costly urban-renewal project whose stated purpose is a vague promise of new jobs and increased tax revenue, but which is also suspiciously agreeable to the Pfizer Corporation, is for a "public use."

I cannot agree. The most natural reading of the [Public Use] Clause is that it allows the government to take property only if the government owns, or the public has a legal right to use, the property, as opposed to taking it for any public purpose or necessity whatsoever. At the time of the founding, dictionaries primarily defined the noun "use" as "the act of employing any thing to any purpose." 2 S. Johnson, *A Dictionary of the English Language* 2194 (4th ed. 1773). The term "use," moreover, "is from the Latin *utor*, which means 'to use, make use of, avail one's self of, employ, apply, enjoy, etc.' " J. Lewis, *Law of Eminent Domain* §165, p. 224, n.4 (1888). When the government takes property and gives it to a private individual, and the public has no right to use the property, it strains language to say that the public is "employing" the property, regardless of the incidental benefits that might accrue to the public from the private use. The term "public use," then, means that either the government or its citizens as a whole must actually "employ" the taken property.

Granted, another sense of the word "use" was broader in meaning, extending to "convenience" or "help," or "qualities that make a thing proper for any purpose." 2 Johnson 2194. Nevertheless, read in context, the term "public use" possesses the narrower meaning. Elsewhere, the Constitution twice employs the word "use," both times in its narrower sense. Claeys, *Public-Use Limitations and Natural Property Rights*, 2004 Mich. St. L. Rev. 877, 897. Article 1, §10 provides that "the net Produce of all Duties and Imposts, laid by any State on Imports or Exports, shall be for the Use of the Treasury of the United States," meaning the Treasury itself will control the taxes, not use it to any beneficial end. And Article I, §8 grants Congress power "to raise and support Armies, but no Appropriation of Money to that Use shall be for a longer Term than two Years." Here again, "use" means "employed to raise and support Armies," not anything directed to achieving any military end. The same word in the Public Use Clause should be interpreted to have the same meaning. The Constitution's text, in short, suggests that the Takings Clause authorizes the taking of property only if the public has a right to employ it, not if the public realizes any conceivable benefit from the taking.

The Constitution's common-law background reinforces this understanding. The common law provided an express method of eliminating uses of land that adversely impacted the public welfare: nuisance law. Blackstone and Kent, for instance, both carefully distinguished the law of nuisance from the power of eminent domain. Blackstone rejected the idea that private property could be taken solely for purposes of any public benefit. "So great . . . is the regard of the law for private property," he explained, "that it will not authorize the least violation of it; no, not even for the general good of the whole community." 1 *Blackstone* 135. He continued: "If a new road . . . were to be made through the grounds of a private person, it might perhaps be extensively beneficial to the public; but the law permits no man, or set of men, to do this without the consent of the owner of the land." *Id.* Only "by giving [the landowner] full indemnification" could the government take property, and even then "the public [was] now considered as an individual, treating with an individual for an exchange." *Id.* When the public took property, in other words, it took it as an individual buying property from another typically would: for one's own use. The Public Use Clause, in short, embodied the Framers' understanding that property is a natural, fundamental right, prohibiting the government from "taking *property* from A. and giving it to B." *Calder v. Bull,* 3 U.S. 386, 388 (1798).

Early American eminent domain practice largely bears out this understanding of the Public Use Clause. States employed the eminent domain power to provide quintessentially public goods, such as public roads, toll roads, ferries, canals, railroads, and public parks. Though use of the eminent domain power was sparse at the time of the founding, many States did have so-called Mill Acts, which authorized the owners of grist mills operated by water power to flood upstream lands with the payment of compensation to the upstream landowner. Those early grist mills "were regulated by law and compelled to serve the public for a stipulated toll and in regular order," and therefore were actually used by the public. J. Lewis, *Law of Eminent Domain* §178, at 246, & n.3 (1888). They were common carriers — quasi-public entities. These were "public uses" in the fullest sense of the word, because the public could legally use and benefit from them equally.

To be sure, some early state legislatures tested the limits of their state-law eminent domain power. Some States enacted statutes allowing the taking of property for the purpose of building private roads. These statutes were mixed; some required the private landowner to keep the road open to the public, and others did not. Later in the 19th century, moreover, the Mill Acts were employed to grant rights to private manufacturing plants, in addition to grist mills that had common-carrier duties. *See, e.g.,* M. Horwitz, *The Transformation of American Law 1780-1860,* at 51-52 (1977).

These early uses of the eminent domain power are often cited as evidence for the broad "public purpose" interpretation of the Public Use Clause, but in fact the constitutionality of these exercises of eminent domain power under state public use restrictions was a hotly contested question in state courts throughout the 19th and into the 20th century. The disagreement among state courts, and state legislatures' attempts to circumvent public use limits on their eminent domain power, cannot obscure that the Public Use Clause is most naturally read to authorize takings for public use only if the government or the public actually uses the taken property.

I would revisit our Public Use Clause cases and consider returning to the original meaning of the Public Use Clause: that the government may take property only if it actually uses or gives the public a legal right to use the property. The consequences of today's decision are not difficult to predict, and promise to be harmful. So-called "urban renewal" programs provide some compensation for the properties they take, but no compensation is possible for the subjective value of these lands to the individuals displaced and the indignity inflicted by uprooting them from their homes. Allowing the government to take property solely for public purposes is bad enough, but extending the concept of public purpose to encompass any economically beneficial goal guarantees that these losses will fall disproportionately on poor communities. Those communities are not only systematically less likely to put their lands to the highest and best social use, but are also the least politically powerful. If ever there were justification for intrusive judicial review of constitutional provisions that protect "discrete and insular minorities," *United States v. Carolene Products Co.*, 304 U.S. 144, 152 n.4 (1938), surely that principle would apply with great force to the powerless groups and individuals the Public Use Clause protects. The deferential standard this Court has adopted for the Public Use Clause is therefore deeply perverse. It encourages "those citizens with disproportionate influence and power in the political process, including large corporations and development firms" to victimize the weak (*see ante*, O'Connor, J., dissenting).

Those incentives have made the legacy of this Court's "public purpose" test an unhappy one. In the 1950's, no doubt emboldened in part by the expansive understanding of "public use" this Court adopted in *Berman*, cities "rushed to draw plans" for downtown development. B. Frieden & L. Sagalayn, *Downtown, Inc. How America Rebuilds Cities* 17 (1989). "Of all the families displaced by urban renewal from 1949 through 1963, 63 percent of those whose race was known were nonwhite, and of these families, 56 percent of nonwhites and 38 percent of whites had incomes low enough to qualify for public housing, which, however, was seldom available to them." *Id.* at 28. Public works projects in the 1950's and 1960's destroyed predominantly minority communities in St. Paul, Minnesota, and Baltimore, Maryland. *Id.* at 28-29. In 1981, urban planners in Detroit, Michigan, uprooted the largely "lower-income and elderly" Poletown neighborhood for the benefit of the General Motors Corporation. J. Wylie, *Poletown: Community Betrayed* 58 (1989). Urban renewal projects have long been associated with the displacement of blacks; "in cities across the country urban renewal came to be known as 'Negro removal.'" Pritchett, *The "Public Menace" of Blight: Urban Renewal and the Private Uses of Eminent Domain*, 21 Yale L. & Pol'y Rev. 1, 47 (2003). Over 97 percent of the individuals forcibly removed from their homes by the "slum-clearance" project upheld by this Court in *Berman* were black. 348 U.S. at 30. Regrettably, the predictable consequence of the Court's decision will be to exacerbate these effects.

Notes and Questions

1. **The eminent domain power and the police power.** In *Hawai`i Housing Authority v. Midkiff*, 467 U.S. 229, 240 (1984), the Supreme Court held that "[t]he 'public use' requirement is coterminous with the scope of a sovereign's police powers." This means that whatever the state may legitimately achieve through its power to regulate property under the police power, it may instead choose to do through the power to take property through eminent domain. Justice Kennedy, in a passage quoted by the

majority in *Kelo*, justified the breadth of public use on the theory that, unlike the police power, the takings clause "operates as a conditional limitation, permitting the government to do what it wants so long as it pays the charge." *Eastern Enterprises v. Apfel*, 524 U.S. 498, 545 (1998) (Kennedy, J., concurring in judgment and dissenting in part). Are there reasons to take a narrower view of public use in the power to take property by eminent domain than the full reach of the police power to regulate? Conversely, are there actions that the government might *not* be able to take through its power to regulate that it might, nonetheless, justify as public use for purposes of condemnation?

2. Detecting political process failure. As the *Kelo* majority suggests, one reason for courts to take a deferential approach to reviewing public use challenges is to respect the democratic process. However, Justice Kennedy, in his concurrence, argues that courts should nonetheless scrutinize takings for "impermissible favoritism," and take a more skeptical approach to their review where such favoritism is evident. Both the *Kelo* majority and Justice Kennedy placed some weight on the fact that there had been an extensive planning process for the redevelopment of the Fort Trumbull area. If the New London city council had passed legislation taking the property at issue in the case as part of the city council's ordinary business, but without a separate planning process, would that have made the taking more vulnerable to a public use challenge? Should it?

3. Harms and benefits. Justice O'Connor, in her *Kelo* dissent, distinguished the Supreme Court's unanimous decisions in *Berman* and *Midkiff*, the latter of which she authored, as cases that involved property arrangements that "inflicted affirmative harm on society." Is there a principled way to distinguish between exercises of the power of eminent domain that cause harm and those that seek to improve conditions or otherwise confer a benefit? Is there a reason to limit the power of eminent domain to harm prevention?

4. "Use by the public." Justice Thomas would have held that "the government may take property only if it actually uses or gives the public a legal right to use the property." There are certainly relatively easy cases under this standard, as with a government buildings, public parks, and highways. Would public housing, which is publicly funded but open only to a limited number of qualified tenants, be an acceptable "public use" under Justice Thomas's standard?

5. State constitutions. Many state supreme courts have historically interpreted their state constitutions in a manner consistent with the federal interpretation. *See, e.g., County of Hawai`i v. C & J Coupe Family LP*, 242 P.3d 1136, 1151 (Haw. 2010) ("Great weight is accorded to legislative findings and declarations of public use, and a heavy burden is on the defendant to demonstrate that the use was clearly and palpably of a private character."). However, states are entitled to grant greater protection for property than that afforded by the U.S. Constitution, and an increasing number of supreme courts have adopted a different path, interpreting their state constitutional "public use" requirements more stringently than has the U.S. Supreme Court.

First, some courts have adopted a version of the test proposed by Justice Kennedy and held that the public use test is not met unless "the public benefits and characteristics of the intended use substantially predominate over the private nature of that use." *Bailey v. Myers*, 76 P.3d 898, 904 (Ariz. Ct. App. 2003) (city could not take private property for transfer to private developers to construct a retail shopping and office center). *Accord, In re Opening Private Road for Benefit of O'Reilly*, 5 A.3d 246, 258-259 (Pa. 2010) (private roads act can only be constitutional if the public is "the primary and paramount beneficiary of the taking"); *City of Bozeman v. Vaniman*, 898 P.2d 1208 (Mont. 1995) (not a public purpose to take property for space in visitors center to be occupied by private Chamber of Commerce).

Second, some courts have adopted a version of the test proposed by Justice O'Connor and held that property cannot be taken and transferred from one owner to another unless the nature of the property itself justifies the taking. Such rulings prohibit takings for economic development purposes unless the property being taken is causing harm to others. For example, property may be taken and transferred to another owner if its condition is dangerous to occupants or neighbors and in need in demolition or if it is "blighted" and in need of redevelopment to counteract slum conditions. *See Arvada Urban Renewal Authority v. Columbine Professional Plaza Association*, 85 P.3d 1066 (Colo. 2004) (not a public purpose to take a private lake for a new Wal-Mart unless there was a recent finding that the property was blighted). *Accord, Gallenthin Realty Development, Inc. v. Borough of Paulsboro*, 924 A.2d 447 (N.J. 2007); *City of Norwood v. Horney*, 853 N.E.2d 1115 (Ohio 2006).

Third, some courts have held that the taking must be justified in the sense that the public purpose could not be achieved in any other way than through a taking of one owner's property and transfer to another. *Southwestern Illinois Development Authority v. National City Environmental*, 768 N.E.2d 1 (Ill. 2002) (not a public purpose to take a factory's property to expand a parking lot for a race track next door).

The Michigan Supreme Court combined several of these rationales in *Wayne County v. Hathcock*, 684 N.W.2d 765 (Mich. 2004), which unanimously overruled the famous 1981 decision in *Poletown Neighborhood Council v. City of Detroit*, 304 N.W.2d 455 (Mich. 1981). *Poletown* had held that the public use requirement was met when a city took private homes and other properties in a residential area and transferred those lots to General Motors Corp. to construct an automobile manufacturing plant. However, in *Hathcock*, the Michigan Supreme Court reversed course, holding that economic development was not a sufficient purpose to justify the condemnation of private lands for transfer to another private owner. Rather, the court held that transferring property from one private owner to another satisfies the public use test only when (1) "public necessity of the extreme sort" requires collective action; (2) the property will be "subject to public oversight after transfer to a private entity"; and (3) the property is selected because of "facts of independent public significance" about the property being taken, rather than advantage to the private entity to whom the property is transferred, such as a conclusion that the area is blighted and in need of redevelopment that is unlikely to occur without public action of this sort. 684 N.W.2d at 781-783.

Quick Review:
Imagine that *Poletown* was evaluated under federal law after *Kelo*. What arguments could you make on both sides?

Finally, some courts have adopted a version of the approach proposed by Justice Thomas and held that "public use" means either "public ownership" or "use by the public," thereby denying the power to take property from any private person if it is to be transferred to another and used privately rather than by the public at large. For example, in *Manufactured Housing Communities of Washington v. Washington*, 13 P.3d 183 (Wash. 2000), the Washington Supreme Court struck down a state law granting existing mobile home tenants a right of first refusal if the landlord sought to sell the property on which their mobile homes sat. As the court explained:

> Although preserving dwindling housing stocks for a particularly vulnerable segment of society provides a "public benefit," this public benefit does not constitute a public use. If it is something in which he has the actual right of property there is no rule of law nor principle of equity which would warrant a court in taking it from him against his will for the benefit of another. No amount of hardship in a given case would justify the establishment of such a precedent. The next step in the invasion of the right of property would be to invite the courts to measure the comparative needs of private parties, and compel a transfer to the one most needing and who might best utilize the property. If a man may be required to surrender what is his own, because he does not need it and cannot use it, and because another does need it and can use it, then there is no reason why he may not be required to surrender what he needs but little because another needs it much. A doctrine so insidiously dangerous should never find lodgment in the body of the law through judicial declaration.

Id. at 196. Do you agree with this reasoning?[13]

6. Statutory constraints on eminent domain for economic development. In response to *Kelo*, Congress has enacted some limitations on using federal funds for projects that involve economic development eminent domain. *See, e.g.*, 12 U.S.C. §4567(f) (2008) (prohibiting use of federal funds appropriated for affordable housing in conjunction with properties taken by eminent domain for economic development). *But see Transportation, Housing and Urban Development, and Related Agencies Appropriations Act*, 2012, Pub. L. No. 112-55, §409, 125 Stat. 552, 708-709 (2011) (exempting most transportation, utility, infrastructure, and public safety condemnations from limitations on economic development eminent domain).

Many states have passed legislation or constitutional amendments that limit the power to take property for economic development purposes. *See* Marc Mihaly & Turner Smith, Kelo*'s Trail: A Survey of State and Federal Legislative and Judicial Activity Five Years Later*, 38 Ecology L.Q. 703 (2011). The legislation limiting eminent domain powers falls into several categories; some states have passed laws in just one of these categories, and others passed more than one type of limitation. Some states repudiate *Kelo* by

---

13. Recall that *Hawai`i Housing Authority v. Midkiff*, 467 U.S. 229 (1984), involved a program that allowed tenants to convert their leasehold interest into fee title. *See also* D.C. Stat. §42-3401.01 *et seq.* (District of Columbia's Tenant Opportunity to Purchase Act, which gives tenants a right of first refusal when their landlord is selling their building); *cf.* Mass. Gen. Laws ch. 40L, §5 (granting the state a right of first refusal in certain agricultural lands in the state to prevent conversion of agricultural lands to residential or commercial use).

prohibiting the use of eminent domain to take property from one person to transfer it to another person if the taking is for economic development purposes, such as increased tax revenue or additional jobs. *See, e.g.*, Alaska Stat. §§09.55.240(d), 29.35.030; 735 Ill. Comp. Stat. 30/5-5-5(c); Me. Rev. Stat. tit. 1, §816; N.H. Rev. Stat. §162-K:2(IX-a)(b); Vt. Stat. tit. 12, §1040(a). Some states adopt Justice Thomas's literal approach by prohibiting all takings of property from one private owner for transfer to another unless the property is open for public "use," meaning public ownership or access. *See* Fla. Stat. §73.013; Iowa Code §§6A.21 to 6A.22; N.H. Rev. Stat. §162-K:2(IX-a)(a); Tenn. Code §29-17-102(2). Many states passed laws prohibiting takings unless the property being taken is "blighted," raising health or safety concerns. Ala. Code §§24-2-2, 24-3-2; Cal. Health & Safety §33030; Iowa Code §§6A.22; Mo. Rev. Stat. §523.271; Wis. Stat. §32.03(6). And some states regulate takings by procedural measures designed to increase public participation in the process through more hearings, better public notice, or through requirements that the taking authority present evidence sufficient to justify the taking. *See* 735 Ill. Comp. Stat. 30/5-5-5(d); W. Va. Code §16-18-6.

Problems

1. The original plan for the redevelopment of the Fort Trumbull neighborhood, the controversy at issue in the *Kelo* case, was for the New London Development Corporation to own the land and enter into long-term ground leases with private parties, who would then develop and own the buildings. *See Kelo v. City of New London*, 843 A.2d 500, 510 (Conn. 2004). Imagine instead that New London had decided to develop the Fort Trumbull property itself and become the landlord for the occupants of the planned residences, offices, and retail facilities. Because the government would still own the entire property outright, it would no longer be transferring to a private party, except as landlord. Would this be more or less offensive than the transfer to private parties in *Kelo*? Why do you imagine the city did not do this?

2. An economically depressed city on the Atlantic Ocean seeks to take 58 modest single-family homes located on the beach to transfer the property to a developer who will build 10-story luxury condominiums with restaurants and shops on the first floor. Most of the homes have been owned by the same families for a very long time — an average of 46 years — and about one-third of the residents are retirees. The area is on the northern end of a redevelopment area designated by the town in a comprehensive plan designed to revitalize the local tourist industry, create jobs, and increase property taxes to pay for local fire and police services and local public schools. The redevelopment would encourage greater density, create a walkable environment, and foster an enlarged base population to sustain a lively, year-round retail and residential core on the town's oceanfront. The homeowners refuse to sell their properties to the city and resist having them taken by eminent domain. *See City of Long Branch v. Anzalone*, 2008 WL 3090052 (N.J. Super. Ct. App. Div. 2008) (describing a situation like this).

   a. Assume the state constitution is worded the same as the federal constitution. Should the state supreme court allow the taking by applying the standard applied by the majority opinion in *Kelo*, or should it find the taking not to constitute a public use under the state constitution by applying some other standard? If the latter, what standard should it use?

b. Assume now the state constitution allows takings of property for transfer to another private owner only if the property is "blighted." *See* N.J. Const. art. I, ¶20; *Gallenthin Realty Development, Inc. v. Borough of Paulsboro*, 924 A.2d 447 (N.J. 2007). A study finds that 37 percent of the properties in the area are vacant, 27 percent of the homes are in fair condition, and 19 percent are in poor condition, while only 17 percent are in good condition. No construction permits had been granted in the area over the prior 5 years, as opposed to 4,725 permits issued for the rest of the city. What standard should the court adopt to define "blighted property"?

§1.3 Just Compensation

As noted, the U.S. Constitution requires payment of "just compensation" when private property is taken for public use. U.S. Const. amends. V & XIV. The Supreme Court has held that this requires payment of the **fair market value** of the property prior to the taking. In general, this means the amount the property would likely sell for on the open market. Compensation is measured by the damage suffered to the owner, not the benefit attained by the government; thus any increase in value of the property caused by the taking is not owed to the owner. By definition, fair market value is likely to undercompensate the owner. For example, any owner who is not trying to sell her property likely values it at more than fair market value because if you offered to buy her property at its market price, the owner would refuse. To induce such an owner to sell, one would have to offer more (and perhaps much more) than fair market value. If the goal is to fully indemnify the owner for the loss, then the just measure of compensation should be the owner's asking price, not market value. But the Supreme Court has rejected asking price as the constitutional measure of just compensation because it is too hard to figure out what an owner's asking price is, while market value can be determined relatively objectively. *Kimball Laundry Co. v. United States*, 338 U.S. 1, 5 (1949) ("In view of the liability of all property to condemnation for the common good, loss to the owner of nontransferable values deriving from his unique need for property or idiosyncratic attachment to it, like loss due to an exercise of the police power, is properly treated as part of the burden of common citizenship.").

The potential unfairness of paying market value may be especially acute if the property taken is a home or a small business. In such cases, the owner may have substantial emotional attachment to the property, and no amount of compensation will make up for the loss. We saw such a case with Susette Kelo, who refused to sell her house in New London. *See* §1.2 above. Our legal system allows this where such takings are necessary to collect the properties required for the common good, such as public roads. It arguably also reflects the fact that vulnerability to having one's property taken is one of the obligations imposed on citizens in a democracy. *Cf.* Brian Angelo Lee, *Just Undercompensation: The Idiosyncratic Premium in Eminent Domain*, 113 Colum. L. Rev. 593, 622 (2013) ("Each member of the community has a social duty, in his or her relationship with property, not to impose too much upon the well-being of other

seven years remained on the lease. Although the lease did not give the lessee a legally enforceable right to renew the lease, the lessor had routinely renewed the lease in the past and was likely to do so in the future. There was no question that the leasehold held by the tenant was "property" compensable when taken by the government or that the value of the improvements during the remaining years of the lease should be counted in determining the market value of the lease, but the trial court had held that there should be no compensation for the likelihood that the lease would be renewed or for the value of the buildings that would remain after the lease ended.

The Supreme Court held that just compensation should be measured by the market value of the lease and that this included the "full monetary equivalent of the property taken. The owner is to be put in the same position monetarily as he would have occupied if his property had not been taken." *Id.* at 473-474. Since "fair market value" is defined by the amount "a willing buyer would pay in cash to a willing seller," the lessee was entitled to be compensated for the value of the improvements on the land over their useful life, based on evidence that the lessor would likely have continued to renew the lease and that the lessee could have alienated the leasehold based on the ability of the purchaser to continue to use those buildings. *Id.* at 474. Four Justices dissented, arguing that the "property" taken by the government should be defined by the legal rights acquired by the government and that, in this case, the government condemned the leasehold and not the buildings or the business; because the tenant had no contractual right to renewal of the lease, it was not entitled to compensation for the mere expectation of renewal. 409 U.S. at 484-485 (Rehnquist, J, dissenting).

In *United States v. 564.54 Acres of Land, More or Less*, 441 U.S. 506 (1979), however, the Supreme Court held that the owner was not entitled to the replacement cost of the buildings on the land that was taken. The owner operated three nonprofit summer camps along the Delaware River, and although the cost of building functionally equivalent facilities elsewhere was approximately $5.8 million, the fair market value of the properties taken was only $485,400. Justice Thurgood Marshall noted that "fair market value does not include the special value of property to the owner arising from its adaptability to his particular use." *Id.* at 512. The Court acknowledged that this result might be unjust but found that "it is not at all unusual that property uniquely adapted to the owner's use has a market value on condemnation which falls far short of enabling the owner to preserve that use." *Id.* at 514. *Accord, United States v. 50 Acres of Land*, 469 U.S. 24 (1984) (public owner legally obligated to replace the facilities taken has no right to compensation for replacement costs).

Partial takings. Imagine an owner has 100 acres of farmland. If the state takes only 40 acres from the owner to build a government facility, rather than the property as a whole, it must compensate not only for the fair market value of those 40 acres but also for any reduction in value to the remaining 60 acres caused by the taking of the 40. This reduction in the value of the remaining 60 acres is called **severance damages**. *New Hampshire Department of Transportation v. Franchi*, 48 A.3d 849, 852 (N.H. 2012). For example, in *State v. Weiswasser*, 693 A.2d 864 (N.J. 1997), New Jersey took a sliver of property from a large undeveloped parcel near a major highway as part of road project. The court held that the owners were entitled to compensation not only for the physical property that was taken, but also for the diminution of value of the owners' remaining property that was specifically attributable to the fact that the property could now not be seen as easily from the nearby highway, which made marketing development on the parcel more expensive. *Id.* at 876. *Accord, Utah Department of Transportation v. Admiral Beverage Corp.*, 275 P.3d 208, 214 (Utah 2011).

However, sometimes the taking will *increase* the value of the owner's remaining property by providing a **special benefit** that will not accrue to the public at large. This can happen, for example, by placing a major road along the land in a way that will increase its attractiveness to retail business. It may be that all businesses in the area will benefit from improved traffic circulation, but some businesses will benefit specifically by being particularly close to the opportunity that new traffic creates — a benefit that derives from the taking itself. Where there are severance damages and special benefits, courts will generally reduce, or *offset,* the severance damages by the amount of the special benefit. *City of Maryland Heights v. Heitz,* 358 S.W.3d 98, 105-108 (Mo. Ct. App. 2011); *Oregon v. Fullerton,* 34 P.3d 1180 (Or. Ct. App. 2001). Some courts allow an offset for both special *and* **general benefits** accruing to the remaining property. *L.A. County v. Continental Development Corp.*, 941 P.2d 809 (Cal. 1997); *see also McCoy v. Union Elevated Railroad Co.*, 247 U.S. 354, 366 (1918) (holding that "we are unable to say that [an owner] suffers deprivation of any fundamental right when a state . . . permits consideration of actual benefits-enhancement in market value flowing directly from a public work, although all in the neighborhood receive like advantages").

Courts are divided on the question whether the government may reduce the amount it owes to an owner for property actually taken by the amount of the special benefit accruing to the land not taken. For example, assume the 40 acres taken by the government are worth $200,000 but the taking provides a special benefit that increases the value of the remaining 60 acres by $50,000. Under an old Supreme Court case, *Bauman v. Ross*, 167 U.S. 548 (1897), the increase in value from a special benefit to the remaining 60 acres would be offset against the amount due for the taking of the 40 acres; thus, the owner would receive only $150,000. A substantial number of states agree. *E-470 Public Highway Authority v. Revenig*, 91 P.3d 1038, 1043-1044 (Colo. 2004); *see also Department of Transportation v. Rowe*, 549 S.E.2d 203 (N.C. 2001). However, most states do not allow such an offset, and instead would award the owner the full $200,000 for the taken land without any reduction for the increase in the value of the retained land. *Williams Natural Gas Co. v. Perkins*, 952 P.2d 483 (Okla. 1997). Is granting an owner full value for property taken as well as the increase in value to any retained property from the taking a fair measure of compensation to an owner?

New Jersey recently changed its longstanding rule that limited any reduction in compensation for partial takings to special benefits. In *Borough of Harvey Cedars v. Karan*, 70 A.3d 524 (N.J. 2013), the borough government took part of a couple's beachfront property to construct dunes to prevent erosion or loss during storms. At the condemnation trial, the court allowed the owners to introduce evidence that the dunes had reduced the value of their home by obstructing their view, but did not allow the borough to introduce evidence that the dune had enhanced the value of the couple's home by protecting it from storms and ocean surges. The jury awarded the couple $375,000. The New Jersey Supreme Court reversed. "In a partial-takings case," the court held, "homeowners are entitled to the fair market value of their loss, not to a windfall, not to a pay out that disregards the home's enhanced value resulting from a public project." *Id.* at *1. That meant that just compensation for a partial taking "must be based on a consideration of all relevant, reasonably calculable, and non-conjectural factors that either decrease or increase the value of the remaining property," including in this case that "the dune would likely spare the Karans' home from total destruction in certain fierce storms and from other damage in lesser storms." *Id.* This eliminated the distinction between special and general benefits, and instead simply required any benefits to the owner, if reasonably quantifiable, to be measured against losses in market value caused by the partial taking.

Problem

Starting around 2006, the real estate market in the U.S. began to suffer a significant downturn. *See* Chapter 12, §4.2. In the wake of the subprime crisis, home values plummeted, leaving many owners "underwater," meaning that they owe more — sometimes multiple times more — on their mortgage loans than their homes are worth. Refinancing these mortgages would reduce the incentive to default and the risk of foreclosure, relieving the burden on communities where cascades of foreclosure have caused significant harm. However, many of these mortgages were securitized, posing significant barriers to renegotiation. Securitized mortgages are typically managed by servicers who may have no incentive to renegotiate, and often contractually cannot renegotiate without the agreement of a supermajority of the disparate investors with interests in the securities. Robert C. Hockett, *It Takes a Village: Municipal Condemnation Proceedings and Public/Private Partnerships for Mortgage Loan Modification, Value Preservation, and Local Economic Recovery*, 18 Stan. J.L. Bus. & Fin. 121, 139-142 (2012).

A private company called Mortgage Resolution Partners has proposed working with local governments to use eminent domain to solve this impasse. A local government would condemn a homeowner's loan, using funds provided by private investors to pay just compensation to the lender. The compensation for these loans would be set based on the fact that if an underwater mortgage were sold on the open market, its value should be less than its face value because the security for the loan is worth less than the outstanding debt. The local government, now the owner of the mortgage loan, would then negotiate with the borrower — the homeowner — to refinance the mortgage at a rate that more clearly reflected the home's post-crisis value. *See* Tad Friend, *Home Economics: Can an Entrepreneur's Audacious Plan Fix the Mortgage Mess?*, New Yorker, Feb. 4, 2013, at 26.

a. Would this use of eminent domain satisfy the public use requirement? What else might you need to know to answer this question?

b. Is the measure of compensation based on the discounted value of the mortgage "just"? What are the best arguments on both sides?

c. What other legal issues might this plan to use eminent domain to condemn mortgages raise?

§1.4 Expropriation Without "Taking"

In a number of contexts, courts are called upon to decide whether a claimed interest that might be considered property for some purposes is "private property" under the takings clause. *See, e.g., United States v. Rands*, 389 U.S. 121, 125-126 (1967) (state-created riparian rights that "are not assertable against the superior rights of the United States, are not property" for the takings clause even though they might be enforceable against private parties). As a general matter, the Supreme Court has noted that "[b]ecause the Constitution protects rather than creates property interests, the existence of a property interest is determined by reference to 'existing rules or understandings that stem from an independent source such as state law.' " *Phillips v. Washington Legal Foundation*, 524 U.S. 156, 164 (1998).

In the case of interests in land and most personal property, determining whether the interest is "private property" for purposes of the takings clause is not often controversial, although it can be. *Compare, e.g., Lynch v. United States*, 292 U.S. 571, 579 (1934) ("Valid contracts are property, whether the obligor be a private individual, a municipality, a State or the United States."), *with New England Estates, LLC v. Town of Branford*, 988 A.2d 229, 241-243 (Conn. 2010) (option to purchase property is a contractual right not protected by the takings clause). Takings claims are also brought in the context of intangible property. *See, e.g., Ruckelshaus v. Monsanto Co.*, 467 U.S. 986, 1001-1004 (1984) (trade secrets); *Armstrong v. United States*, 364 U.S. 40 (1960) (materialmen's liens); *West River Bridge Co. v. Dix*, 47 U.S. 507, 533 (1848) (corporate franchise); *see also City of Oakland v. Oakland Raiders*, 646 P.2d 835 (Cal. 1982) (condemnation of sports team).[14]

Are there reasons why an interest might be recognized as "property" in some constitutional (or common law) contexts, but not for purposes of the takings clause? What might interference, or even the outright expropriation, of an interest recognized as property in one context, but not for purposes of the takings clause, look like? Consider the following case.

Tee-Hit-Ton Indians v. United States

348 U.S. 272 (1955)

Map: (Tongass National Forest) Wrangell Island, Alaska

Mr. Justice Stanley Reed delivered the opinion of the Court.

This case rests upon a claim under the Fifth Amendment by petitioner, an identifiable group of American Indians of between 60 and 70 individuals residing in Alaska, for compensation for a taking by the United States of certain timber from Alaskan

14. Takings that involve the appropriation of funds or requirements to pay money raise special challenges that we will explore below. *See* §7, below.

lands allegedly belonging to the group. The area claimed is said to contain over 350,000 acres of land and 150 square miles of water. The Tee-Hit-Tons, a clan of the Tlingit Tribe, brought this suit in the Court of Claims under 28 U.S.C. §1505. The compensation claimed does not arise from any statutory direction to pay. Payment, if it can be compelled, must be based upon a constitutional right of the Indians to recover.

The Court of Claims held that petitioner was an identifiable group of American Indians residing in Alaska; that its interest in the lands prior to purchase of Alaska by the United States in 1867 was "original Indian title" or "Indian right of occupancy." It was further held that if such original Indian title survived the Treaty of 1867, 15 Stat. 539, Arts. III and VI, by which Russia conveyed Alaska to the United States, such title was not sufficient basis to maintain this suit as there had been no recognition by Congress of any legal rights in petitioner to the land in question. [W]e granted certiorari.

The Alaskan area in which petitioner claims a compensable interest is located near and within the exterior lines of the Tongass National Forest. By Joint Resolution of August 8, 1947, 61 Stat. 920, the Secretary of Agriculture was authorized to contract for the sale of national forest timber located within this National Forest "notwithstanding any claim of possessory rights." The Resolution defines "possessory rights"[15] and provides for all receipts from the sale of timber to be maintained in a special account in the Treasury until the timber and land rights are finally determined.

The Secretary of Agriculture, on August 20, 1951, contracted for sale to a private company of all merchantable timber in the area claimed by petitioner. This is the sale of timber which petitioner alleges constitutes a compensable taking by the United States of a portion of its proprietary interest in the land.

The problem presented is the nature of the petitioner's interest in the land, if any. Petitioner claims a "full proprietary ownership" of the land; or, in the alternative, at least a "recognized" right to unrestricted possession, occupation and use. Either ownership or recognized possession, petitioner asserts, is compensable. If it has a fee simple interest in the entire tract, it has an interest in the timber and its sale is a partial taking of its right to "possess, use and dispose of it." *United States v. General Motors*, 323 U.S. 373, 378 (1945).

I. Recognition

Where the Congress by treaty or other agreement has declared that thereafter Indians were to hold the lands permanently, compensation must be paid for subsequent taking. The petitioner contends that Congress has sufficiently "recognized" its possessory rights in the land in question so as to make its interest compensable. Petitioner points specifically to two statutes to sustain this contention.

We have carefully examined these statutes and the pertinent legislative history and find nothing to indicate any intention by Congress to grant to the Indians any permanent rights in the lands of Alaska occupied by them by permission of Congress.

15. "That 'possessory rights' as used in this resolution shall mean all rights, if any should exist, which are based upon aboriginal occupancy or title, or upon [the *Organic Act for Alaska of 1884* and the *Acts of 1891 and 1900*]."

II. *Indian Title*

It is well settled that in all the States of the Union the tribes who inhabited the lands of the States held claim to such lands after the coming of the white man, under what is sometimes termed original Indian title or permission from the whites to occupy. That description means mere possession not specifically recognized as ownership by Congress. After conquest they were permitted to occupy portions of territory over which they had previously exercised "sovereignty," as we use that term. This is not a property right but amounts to a right of occupancy which the sovereign grants and protects against intrusion by third parties but which right of occupancy may be terminated and such lands fully disposed of by the sovereign itself without any legally enforceable obligation to compensate the Indians.

This position of the Indian has long been rationalized by the legal theory that discovery and conquest gave the conquerors sovereignty over and ownership of the lands thus obtained. The great case of *Johnson v. M'Intosh*, 21 U.S. (8 Wheat.) 543 (1823), denied the power of an Indian tribe to pass their right of occupancy to another. It confirmed the practice of two hundred years of American history "that discovery gave an exclusive right to extinguish the Indian title of occupancy, either by purchase or by conquest." 8 Wheat. at 587.

> Conquest gives a title which the Courts of the conqueror cannot deny, whatever the private and speculative opinions of individuals may be, respecting the original justice of the claim which has been successfully asserted. 8 Wheat. at 590-591.

In *Beecher v. Wetherby*, 95 U.S. 517 (1877), a tract of land which Indians were then expressly permitted by the United States to occupy was granted to Wisconsin. In a controversy over timber, this Court held the Wisconsin title good.

> The grantee, it is true, would take only the naked fee, and could not disturb the occupancy of the Indians: that occupancy could only be interfered with or determined by the United States. It is to be presumed that in this matter the United States would be governed by such considerations of justice as would control a Christian people in their treatment of an ignorant and dependent race. Be that as it may, the propriety or justice of their action towards the Indians with respect to their lands is a question of governmental policy, and is not a matter open to discussion in a controversy between third parties, neither of whom derives title from the Indians. The right of the United States to dispose of the fee of lands occupied by them has always been recognized by this court from the foundation of the government. 95 U.S. at 525.

In 1941 a unanimous Court wrote, concerning Indian title, the following:

> Extinguishment of Indian title based on aboriginal possession is of course a different matter. The power of Congress in that regard is supreme. The manner, method and time of such extinguishment raise political, not justiciable issues. *United States v. Santa Fe Pacific R. Co.*, 314 U.S. 339, 347 (1941).

No case in this Court has ever held that taking of Indian title or use by Congress required compensation. The American people have compassion for the descendants of those Indians who were deprived of their homes and hunting grounds by the drive of civilization. They seek to have the Indians share the benefits of our society as citizens of this Nation. Generous provision has been willingly made to allow tribes to recover for wrongs, as a matter of grace, not because of legal liability.

This is true, not because an Indian or an Indian tribe has no standing to sue or because the United States has not consented to be sued for the taking of original Indian title, but because Indian occupation of land without government recognition of ownership creates no rights against taking or extinction by the United States protected by the Fifth Amendment or any other principle of law.

What has been heretofore set out deals largely with the Indians of the Plains and east of the Mississippi. The Tee-Hit-Tons urge, however, that their stage of civilization and their concept of ownership of property takes them out of the rule applicable to the Indians of the States. They assert that Russia never took their lands in the sense that European nations seized the rest of America. The Court of Claims, however, saw no distinction between their use of the land and that of the Indians of the Eastern United States. That court had no evidence that the Russian handling of the Indian land problem differed from ours. The natives were left the use of the great part of their vast hunting and fishing territory but what Russia wanted for its use and that of its licensees, it took. The court's conclusion on this issue was based on strong evidence.

In considering the character of the Tee-Hit-Tons' use of the land, the Court of Claims had before it the testimony of a single witness who was offered by plaintiff. He stated that he was the chief of the Tee-Hit-Ton tribe. He qualified as an expert on the Tlingits, a group composed of numerous interconnected tribes including the Tee-Hit-Tons. His testimony showed that the Tee-Hit-Tons had become greatly reduced in numbers. Membership descends only through the female line. At the present time there are only a few women of childbearing age and a total membership of some 65.

The witness pointed out that their claim of ownership was based on possession and use. The use that was made of the controverted area was for the location in winter of villages in sheltered spots and in summer along fishing streams and/or bays. The ownership was not individual but tribal. As the witness stated, "Any member of the tribe may use any portion of the land that he wishes, and as long as he uses it that is his for his own enjoyment, and is not to be trespassed upon by anybody else, but the minute he stops using it then any other member of the tribe can come in and use that area."

The witness learned the alleged boundaries of the Tee-Hit-Ton area from hunting and fishing with his uncle after his return from Carlisle Indian School about 1904. From the knowledge so obtained, he outlined in red on the map, which petitioner filed as an exhibit, the territory claimed by the Tee-Hit-Tons. Use by other tribal members is sketchily asserted. This is the same 350,000 acres claimed by the petition. On it he marked six places to show the Indians' use of the land: (1) his great uncle was buried here, (2) a town, (3) his uncle's house, (4) a town, (5) his mother's house, (6) smokehouse. He also pointed out the uses of this tract for fishing salmon and for hunting beaver, deer and mink.

The testimony further shows that while membership in the tribe and therefore ownership in the common property descended only through the female line, the various tribes of the Tlingits allowed one another to use their lands. Before power boats, the Indians would put their shelters for hunting and fishing away from villages. With the power boats, they used them as living quarters.

In addition to this verbal testimony, exhibits were introduced by both sides as to the land use. These exhibits are secondary authorities but they bear out the general proposition that land claims among the Tee-Hit-Tons [were] wholly tribal. It was more a claim of sovereignty than of ownership. There were scattered shelters and villages moved from place to place as game or fish became scarce. There was recognition of tribal rights to hunt and fish on certain general areas, with claims to that effect carved on totem poles. From all that was presented, the Court of Claims concluded, and we agree, that the Tee-Hit-Tons were in a hunting and fishing stage of civilization, with shelters fitted to their environment, and claims to rights to use identified territory for these activities as well as the gathering of wild products of the earth.

The line of cases adjudicating Indian rights on American soil leads to the conclusion that Indian occupancy, not specifically recognized as ownership by action authorized by Congress, may be extinguished by the Government without compensation. Every American schoolboy knows that the savage tribes of this continent were deprived of their ancestral ranges by force and that, even when the Indians ceded millions of acres by treaty in return for blankets, food and trinkets, it was not a sale but the conquerors' will that deprived them of their land.

In the light of the history of Indian relations in this Nation, no other course would meet the problem of the growth of the United States except to make congressional contributions for Indian lands rather than to subject the Government to an obligation to pay the value when taken with interest to the date of payment. Our conclusion does not uphold harshness as against tenderness toward the Indians, but it leaves with Congress, where it belongs, the policy of Indian gratuities for the termination of Indian occupancy of Government-owned land rather than making compensation for its value a rigid constitutional principle.

Mr. Justice WILLIAM O. DOUGLAS, with whom THE CHIEF JUSTICE and Mr. Justice FRANKFURTER, concur, dissenting.

The first Organic Act for Alaska became a law on May 17, 1884, 23 Stat. 24. [Section 8 provides that] "the Indians or other persons in said district shall not be disturbed in the possession of any lands actually in their use or occupation or now claimed by them but the terms under which such persons may acquire title to such lands is reserved for future legislation by Congress." Respondent contends, and the Court apparently agrees, that this provision should be read, not as recognizing Indian title, but as reserving the question whether they have any rights in the land.

[In the debates about the Act,] Senator Benjamin Harrison [said] it was the intention of the committee "to save from all possible invasion the rights of the Indian residents of Alaska . . . except in so far as it was necessary in order to establish title to mining claims in the Territory." The conclusion seems clear that Congress in the 1884 Act recognized the claims of these Indians to their Alaskan lands. [Given uncertainty about the extent of Indian claims,] Congress did the humane thing of saving to the Indians all rights claimed; it let them keep what they had prior to the new Act. The future course of action was made clear—conflicting claims would be reconciled and the Indian lands would be put into reservations.

That purpose is wholly at war with the one now attributed to the Congress of reserving for some future day the question whether the Indians were to have any rights to the land.

Notes and Questions

1. **Indian title and the takings clause.** As far back as 1835, the Supreme Court called it "a settled principle, that [American Indians'] right of occupancy is considered as sacred as the fee simple of the whites." *Mitchel v. United States*, 34 U.S. 711, 746 (1835). Since 1790, federal statutes have criminalized trespass on tribal land and required restitution for damage to tribal property. The federal government has repeatedly sued to protect or seek damages for interference with the tribal right of occupancy, regardless of whether that right was guaranteed by the federal government. *See United States v. Santa Fe Pacific Railroad Co.*, 314 U.S. 339, 345 (1941) ("Unquestionably it has been the policy of the federal government from the beginning to respect the Indian right of occupancy . . ."). Congress also enacted many laws waiving sovereign immunity so that tribes could sue the federal government for taking of tribal property. Nonetheless, *Tee-Hit-Ton* holds that Indian title is not property within the meaning of the fifth amendment's taking clause, and can instead can be abrogated by the United States without compensation. Only Indian title recognized by Congress through a treaty or statute constitutes property that cannot be taken without just compensation. What justifies this distinction?

2. **Statutory compensation after *Tee-Hit-Ton*.** Although not constitutionally compelled to do so, in 1971 Congress enacted the *Alaska Native Claims Settlement Act*, compensating native inhabitants of Alaska for the loss of their land in the amount of $962.5 million and reserving approximately 45 million acres of federal public lands to Alaska Native villages. 43 U.S.C. §1601 *et seq.*; *Cohen's Handbook of Federal Indian Law* §4.07[3][b][ii][B], at 330 (Nell Newton et al. eds. 2012 ed.). In return, the Native Alaskans agreed to extinguishment of claims to an additional 335 million acres. The act was catalyzed by the discovery of oil in Prudhoe Bay in 1968. Because Alaska Natives likely still had property claims against private individuals, oil developers pressed Congress to reach a settlement with Alaska Natives to avoid uncertainty in mineral development.

3. **Interest on past expropriations.** Perhaps the greatest practical significance of *Tee-Hit-Ton* was that it helped protect the United States from having to pay interest on claims based on seizure of Indian lands. In 1946, Congress had enacted the *Indian Claims Commission Act* (ICCA), 60 Stat. 1049, 25 U.S.C. §70 *et seq.*, which allowed Indian nations to bring claims against the United States for uncompensated (or poorly compensated) takings of their property. The ICCA granted compensation for takings of both original Indian title land and recognized title land; the amount of compensation due was measured by the value of the land at the time of the taking—in many cases, low, nineteenth-century values. Interest, however, was paid only in takings of recognized title land since only such takings were found to have violated the

fifth amendment. In a portion of the *Tee-Hit-Ton* opinion not included in the excerpt above, the Court noted that "if aboriginal Indian title was compensable without specific legislation to that effect, there were claims with estimated interest already pending under the Indian jurisdictional act aggregating $9,000,000,000." Of this $9 billion, $8 billion was interest. Nell Jessup Newton, *At the Whim of the Sovereign: Aboriginal Title Reconsidered,* 31 Hastings L.J. 1215, 1248 (1980). The *Tee-Hit-Ton* decision, in effect, saved the United States $8 billion, almost $70 billion in 2012 dollars.

4. Compensation for the taking of recognized Indian title. In 1868, the United States entered the *Fort Laramie Treaty* with the Sioux Nation, 15 Stat. 635, and pledged that the Great Sioux Reservation, including the Black Hills, would be "set apart for [their] absolute and undisturbed use and occupation," "solemnly agree[ing]" that no unauthorized persons "shall ever be permitted to pass over, settle upon, or reside in [this] territory." In return, the Sioux agreed to relinquish their rights under a prior treaty to occupy territories outside the reservation, while reserving their right to hunt on some of those lands. The treaty also provided that no agreement to cede any of the reservation "shall be of any validity or force as against the said Indians, unless executed and signed by at least three fourths of all the adult male Indians, occupying or interested in the same."

In 1874, Lieutenant Colonel George Armstrong Custer led an expedition to the Reservation, confirming the presence of gold in the region. That led to an intense popular demand for the "opening" of the Black Hills for settlement. In 1875, President Grant secretly instructed the military to stop protecting the Sioux from invasion by settlers. That winter, the military also sought to prevent the Sioux from hunting off the reservation; these efforts initially led to the Sioux victory in the Battle of Little Big Horn, but the hunters were eventually rounded up, deprived of their horses and weapons, and left dependent on government rations. In 1876, Congress sought new land cessions, threatening to stop supplying rations if they did not sign. The resulting agreement was signed by only 10 percent of the adult male Sioux population in violation of the *Fort Laramie Treaty*. It was enacted into law on Feb. 28, 1877.

United States v. Sioux Nation of Indians, 448 U.S. 371 (1980), found that the *1877 Act* constituted a compensable taking. In its opinion, the Supreme Court noted that previous cases had held that the United States may manage tribal lands as a trustee for Indian nations and had discretion to exchange tribal lands for other property so long as it made a good faith effort to provide fair compensation. But the power to manage did not extend " 'so far as to enable the Government to give the tribal lands to others, or to appropriate them to its own purposes, without rendering, or assuming an obligation to render, just compensation. Spoliation is not management.' " 448 U.S. at 408 (quoting *Shoshone Tribe v. United States,* 299 U.S. 476, 477, 478 (1937)). The question was how to distinguish between a "good faith effort" to manage tribal property and an unconstitutional taking of property without just compensation:

> [A] trustee may change the form of trust assets as long as he fairly (or in good faith) attempts to provide his ward with property of equivalent value. If he does that, he cannot be faulted if hindsight should demonstrate a lack of precise equivalence. On the other hand, if a trustee (or the government in its dealings with the Indians) does not

> attempt to give the ward the fair equivalent of what he acquires from him, the trustee to that extent has taken rather than transmuted the property of the ward.
>
> [In this case, the] only item of "consideration" that possibly could be viewed as showing an attempt by Congress to give the Sioux the "full value" of the land the government took from them was the requirement to furnish them with rations until they became self-sufficient.

Id. at 416-417. Reviewing all the evidence, the Court concluded that these rations were not viewed as fair compensation, but instead were provided as "an attempt to coerce the Sioux into capitulating to congressional demands." *Id.* at 418. The *1877 Act* was not, therefore, a good faith change in the form of investment, but a taking of tribal property implying an obligation to make just compensation to the Sioux Nation with interest.

What justifies the rule in *Sioux Nation* that when the federal government takes the recognized title lands of Indian nations, it is not liable for fair market value as long as it makes a "good faith" effort to grant "equivalent value"? Does the Supreme Court believe the U.S. government can be trusted when it deals with Indian lands but not when it deals with non-Indian lands? Is there any basis for such a conclusion?

§2 AN INTRODUCTION TO REGULATORY TAKINGS

§2.1 Historical Origins

The Supreme Court has broadly interpreted the police power to allow states to regulate property for public health, welfare, and safety. *Village of Euclid v. Ambler Realty Co.*, 272 U.S. 365 (1926). In a long line of cases, the Court held that in exercising this authority, the state was not required to compensate owners for any resulting loss in value to their property. For example, in *Mugler v. Kansas*, 123 U.S. 623 (1887), the Court held that a state statute that prohibited the manufacture and sale of alcoholic beverages did not constitute a "taking" of the plaintiff's property. It reached this result even though the brewery had been constructed solely for the purpose of manufacturing such beverages, the property had "little value" for any other purpose, and that purpose had been lawful at the time plaintiff invested in building the factory and its business. The Court declared that "[a] prohibition simply upon the use of property for purposes that are declared, by valid legislation, to be injurious to the health, morals, or safety of the community, cannot, in any just sense, be deemed a taking or an appropriation of property." *Id.* at 668-669. Two years later, *Powell v. Pennsylvania*, 127 U.S. 678 (1888), held that it was permissible to outlaw completely the manufacture of oleomargarine, even if the value of the plaintiff's buildings and equipment "would be entirely lost," so long as the legislature passed the law for the purpose of protecting public health and preventing fraud. Similarly, in *Hadacheck v. Sebastian*, 239 U.S. 394 (1915), the Court upheld a city ordinance prohibiting the operation of an established brickyard, although the owner had made excavations on the land that prevented it from being utilized for any other purpose and the brickyard was lawful when the owner started operating. The Court held that it was within the legislative power to declare the business a nuisance and that the city need not compensate even if that declaration destroyed the business.

In 1922, however, the Supreme Court for the first time suggested limits on the principle that the state may regulate under the police power without compensation.

Pennsylvania Coal Co. v. Mahon

260 U.S. 393 (1922)

Mr. Justice OLIVER WENDELL HOLMES delivered the opinion of the Court.

This is a bill in equity brought by the defendants in error to prevent the Pennsylvania Coal Company from mining under their property in such way as to remove the supports and cause a subsidence of the surface and of their house. The bill sets out a deed executed by the Coal Company in 1878, under which the plaintiffs claim. The deed conveys the surface but in express terms reserves the right to remove all the coal under the same and the grantee takes the premises with the risk and waives all claim for damages that may arise from mining out the coal. But the plaintiffs say that whatever may have been the Coal Company's rights, they were taken away by an Act of Pennsylvania, approved May 27, 1921 (P. L. 1198), commonly known there as the Kohler Act. The Court of Common Pleas found that if not restrained the defendant would cause the damage to prevent which the bill was brought but denied an injunction, holding that the statute if applied to this case would be unconstitutional. On appeal the Supreme Court of the State agreed that the defendant had contract and property rights protected by the Constitution of the United States, but held that the statute was a legitimate exercise of the police power and directed a decree for the plaintiffs. A writ of error was granted bringing the case to this Court.

The statute forbids the mining of anthracite coal in such way as to cause the subsidence of, among other things, any structure used as a human habitation, with certain exceptions, including among them land where the surface is owned by the owner of the underlying coal and is distant more than one hundred and fifty feet from any improved property belonging to any other person. As applied to this case the statute is admitted to destroy previously existing rights of property and contract. The question is whether the police power can be stretched so far.

Government hardly could go on if to some extent values incident to property could not be diminished without paying for every such change in the general law. As long recognized some values are enjoyed under an implied limitation and must yield to the police power. But obviously the implied limitation must have its limits or the contract and due process clauses are gone. One fact for consideration in determining such limits is the extent of the diminution. When it reaches a certain magnitude, in most if not in all cases there must be an exercise of eminent domain and compensation to sustain the act. So the question depends upon the particular facts. The greatest weight is given to the judgment of the legislature but it always is open to interested parties to contend that the legislature has gone beyond its constitutional power.

This is the case of a single private house. No doubt there is a public interest even in this, as there is in every purchase and sale and in all that happens within the commonwealth. Some existing rights may be modified even in such a case. But usually in ordinary private affairs the public interest does not warrant much of this kind of interference. A source of damage to such a house is not a public nuisance even if similar damage is inflicted on others in different places. The damage is not common or public. The extent of the public interest is shown by the statute to be limited, since the statute ordinarily does not apply to land when the surface is owned by the owner of the coal. Furthermore, it is not justified as a protection of personal safety. That could be provided for by notice. Indeed the very foundation of this bill is that the defendant gave timely notice of its intent to mine under the house. On the other hand the extent of the taking is great. It purports to abolish what is recognized in Pennsylvania as an estate in land — a very valuable estate — and what is declared by the Court below to be a contract hitherto binding the plaintiffs. If we were called upon to deal with the plaintiffs' position alone we should think it clear that the statute does not disclose a public interest sufficient to warrant so extensive a destruction of the defendant's constitutionally protected rights.

It is our opinion that the act cannot be sustained as an exercise of the police power, so far as it affects the mining of coal under streets or cities in places where the right to mine such coal has been reserved. As said in a Pennsylvania case, "For practical purposes, the right to coal consists in the right to mine it." *Commonwealth v. Clearview Coal Co.*, 100 A. 820 (Pa. 1917). What makes the right to mine coal valuable is that it can be exercised with profit. To make it commercially impracticable to mine certain coal has very nearly the same effect for constitutional purposes as appropriating or destroying it. This we think that we are warranted in assuming that the statute does.

It is true that in *Plymouth Coal Co. v. Pennsylvania*, 232 U.S. 531, it was held competent for the legislature to require a pillar of coal to the left along the line of adjoining property, that with the pillar on the other side of the line would be a barrier sufficient for the safety of the employees of either mine in case the other should be abandoned and allowed to fill with water. But that was a requirement for the safety of employees invited into the mine, and secured an average reciprocity of advantage that has been recognized as a justification of various laws.

The rights of the public in a street purchased or laid out by eminent domain are those that it has paid for. If in any case its representatives have been so short sighted as to acquire only surface rights without the right of support we see no more authority for supplying the latter without compensation than there was for taking the right of way in the first place and refusing to pay for it because the public wanted it very much. The protection of private property in the Fifth Amendment presupposes that it is wanted for public use, but provides that it shall not be taken for such use without compensation. When this seemingly absolute protection is found to be qualified by the police power, the natural tendency of human nature is to extend the qualification more and more until at last private property disappears. But that cannot be accomplished in this way under the Constitution of the United States.

The general rule at least is that while property may be regulated to a certain extent, if regulation goes too far it will be recognized as a taking. It may be doubted how far exceptional cases, like the blowing up of a house to stop a conflagration, go — and if they go beyond the general rule, whether they do not stand as much upon tradition as upon principle. In general it is not plain that a man's misfortunes or necessities will justify his shifting the damages to his neighbor's shoulders. We are in danger of forgetting that a strong public desire to improve the public condition is not enough to warrant achieving the desire by a shorter cut than the constitutional way of paying for the change. As we already have said this is a question of degree — and therefore cannot be disposed of by general propositions.

We assume, of course, that the statute was passed upon the conviction that an exigency existed that would warrant it, and we assume that an exigency exists that would warrant the exercise of eminent domain. But the question at bottom is upon whom the loss of the changes desired should fall. So far as private persons or communities have seen fit to take the risk of acquiring only surface rights, we cannot see that the fact that their risk has become a danger warrants the giving to them greater rights than they bought.

Mr. Justice Louis D. Brandeis dissenting.

Coal in place is land, and the right of the owner to use his land is not absolute. He may not so use it as to create a public nuisance, and uses, once harmless, may, owing to changed conditions, seriously threaten the public welfare. Whenever they do, the Legislature has power to prohibit such uses without paying compensation; and the power to prohibit extends alike to the manner, the character and the purpose of the use. Are we justified in declaring that the Legislature of Pennsylvania has, in restricting the right to mine anthracite, exercised this power so arbitrarily as to violate the Fourteenth Amendment?

Every restriction upon the use of property imposed in the exercise of the police power deprives the owner of some right theretofore enjoyed, and is, in that sense, an abridgment by the state of rights in property without making compensation. But restriction imposed to protect the public health, safety or morals from dangers threatened is not a taking. The restriction here in question is merely the prohibition of a noxious use. The property so restricted remains in the possession of its owner. The state does not appropriate it or make any use of it. The state merely prevents the owner from making a use which interferes with paramount rights of the public.

If by mining anthracite coal the owner would necessarily unloose poisonous gases, I suppose no one would doubt the power of the state to prevent the mining, without buying his coal fields. And why may not the state, likewise, without paying compensation, prohibit one from digging so deep or excavating so near the surface, as to expose the community to like dangers? In the latter case, as in the former, carrying on the business would be a public nuisance.

It is said that one fact for consideration in determining whether the limits of the police power have been exceeded is the extent of the resulting diminution in value, and that here the restriction destroys existing rights of property and contract. But values are relative. If we are to consider the value of the coal kept in place by the restriction, we should compare it with the value of all other parts of the land. That is, with the value not of the coal alone, but with the value of the whole property. The rights of an owner as against the public are not increased by dividing the interests in his property into surface and subsoil. The sum of the rights in the parts can not be greater than the rights in the whole. The estate of an owner in land is grandiloquently described as extending ab orco usque ad coelum. But I suppose no one would contend that by selling his interest above 100 feet from the surface he could prevent the state from limiting, by the police power, the height of structures in a city. And why should a sale of underground rights bar the state's power? For aught that appears the value of the coal kept in place by the restriction may be negligible as compared with the value of the whole property, or even as compared with that part of it which is represented by the coal remaining in place and which may be extracted despite the statute.

Yet it is said that these provisions of the act cannot be sustained as an exercise of the police power where the right to mine such coal has been reserved. The conclusion seems to rest upon the assumption that in order to justify such exercise of the police power there must be "an average reciprocity of advantage" as between the owner of the property restricted and the rest of the community; and that here such reciprocity is absent. Reciprocity of advantage is an important consideration, and may even be an essential [one], where the state's power is exercised for the purpose of conferring benefits upon the property of a neighborhood, as in drainage projects or upon adjoining owners, as by party wall provisions. But where the police power is exercised, not to confer benefits upon property owners but to protect the public from detriment and danger, there is in my opinion, no room for considering reciprocity of advantage . . . unless it be the advantage of living and doing business in a civilized community. That reciprocal advantage is given by the act to the coal operators.

Notes and Questions

1. **When does a regulation go "too far"?** *Pennsylvania Coal Co. v. Mahon* established the proposition that "while property may be regulated to a certain extent, if regulation goes too far it will be recognized as a taking." But Justice Holmes's opinion is clear about little else. Contemporary regulatory takings claims do not rely directly on *Mahon* for a doctrinal test, but echoes of Justice Holmes's reasoning can be heard in the modern cases.

There are several ways that one might interpret *Mahon* to discern when a regulation has gone "too far." One way is to focus on the magnitude of the harm to an owner. At some point, under this view, a restriction on property has crossed a threshold of permissible harm regardless of the importance of the public purpose at issue, and compensation must be provided. This might be so because, from an owner's perspective, such a regulation is the functional equivalence of an actual physical taking by the government, which requires compensation even though the exercise of the power of eminent domain must be for a valid public purpose.

Another interpretation of *Mahon* is that determining when a regulation has gone too far requires balancing public interest against private harm. In this view, the determinative question is not simply the diminution in an owner's value, but also the extent to which the public interest demands such diminution. Pennsylvania Coal in this case had purchased the "support estate," a distinct estate under Pennsylvania law consisting of the subsurface support needed to keep the surface from collapsing. On one view, then, Justice Holmes may have viewed the act as primarily serving private interests by shifting the support estate back to the surface estate holders. *See* William Michael Treanor, *Jam for Justice Holmes: Reassessing the Significance of* Mahon, 86 Geo. L.J. 813, 859-860 (1998).

A third way to read *Mahon* is that the case is more generally about when it is fair to *concentrate* harms as opposed to asking the general public to bear a given burden. "In general it is not plain," Justice Holmes wrote, "that a man's misfortunes or necessities will justify his shifting the damages to his neighbor's shoulders."

Professor William Treanor has argued that Justice Holmes viewed the case as involving a different concern: the role of the state not as regulator but as an interested party acquiring property for the public. According to Professor Treanor, Holmes was concerned that Pennsylvania was trying to protect public property by acquiring only surface estates and then requiring subsurface estates to be left in place without paying for that right. As Treanor noted, private risks posed by subsidence could have been protected by notice from coal companies, but there was "greater evidence of real harm with respect to public lands. The record in the case shows that, while homeowners might have avoided danger, the same was not true of people travelling on public roads and children going to school." Treanor, *supra*, at 859-860. In correspondence with then professor, later Justice, Felix Frankfurter, Holmes wrote that he regretted not "bring[ing] out more clearly the distinction between the rights of the public generally and their rights in respect of being in a particular place where they have no right to be at all except so far as they have paid for it." Letter from Oliver Wendell Holmes to Felix Frankfurter (Feb. 14, 1923), in *Holmes and Frankfurter: Their Correspondence, 1912-1934*, 150 (Robert M. Mennel & Christine L. Compston eds. 1996). In this view, then, what went "too far" in *Mahon* was the state acting to acquire property for its own purposes without paying for that property.

The Supreme Court effectively repudiated the result in *Mahon* in *Keystone Bituminous Coal Association v. DeBenedictis*, 480 U.S. 470 (1987), which upheld the constitutionality of a similar law. However, the principle *Mahon* established is settled law; regulations that "go too far" — however that line is determined — may be deemed takings of property.

2. Average reciprocity of advantage and the harm/benefit distinction. How does Justice Holmes address cases such as *Mugler* and *Powell*? What about Justice Brandeis? Should it make a difference in terms of whether a restriction on property requires compensation that the regulatory regime creates reciprocal harms and benefits, as where a rule requiring an owner to maintain a party wall also protects that owner from harm by her neighbors? One way to think about reciprocity of advantage is that certain regulations, however onerous the burden, provide a kind of implicit compensation that mitigates the unfairness of not directly compensating owners.

3. What is the extent of the property being regulated? How did Justice Holmes define the relevant property interest being regulated by the Kohler Act? How did Justice Brandeis in dissent approach this issue? Why does it matter?

How one defines the property that is being regulated has come to be called the **denominator** question, and it is crucial in determining the extent to which a regulation diminishes the value of the property, among other aspects of takings law. *See Palazzolo v. Rhode Island,* 533 U.S. 606, 631 (2001) (noting "the difficult, persisting question of what is the proper denominator in the takings fraction"). In discussing this question, Professor Margaret Jane Radin coined the term "conceptual severance," which, she says,

> consists of delineating a property interest consisting of just what the government action has removed from the owner, and then asserting that that particular whole thing has been permanently taken. Thus this strategy hypothetically or conceptually "severs" from the whole bundle of rights just those strands that are interfered with by the regulation, and then hypothetically or conceptually construes those strands in the aggregate as a separate whole thing.

Margaret Jane Radin, *The Liberal Conception of Property: Cross Currents in the Jurisprudence of Takings,* 88 Colum. L. Rev. 1667, 1676 (1988). Can you see how this idea applies to the disagreement between Justice Holmes and Justice Brandeis about how to characterize the property interest involved in *Mahon*?

§2.2 "Categorical" Regulatory Takings and the *Ad Hoc* Test

The Supreme Court has repeatedly said that the takings clause serves "to bar Government from forcing some people alone to bear public burdens which, in all fairness and justice, should be borne by the public as a whole." *Armstrong v. United States,* 364 U.S. 40, 49 (1960). A regulation of property will therefore be deemed a taking if "fairness and justice" require a court to conclude that "the public at large, rather than a single owner, must bear the burden of an exercise of state power in the public interest." *Agins v. Tiburon,* 447 U.S. 255, 260 (1980). In other words, regulations are not takings if they are "properly treated as part of the burden of common citizenship," *Kimball Laundry Co. v. United States,* 338 U.S. 1 (1949).

It is of more than passing interest that the standard the Supreme Court has adopted to determine whether a regulation has "taken" property is whether the burden the regulation imposes on the owner is just or fair. This places concepts of fairness and justice at the heart of both the takings clause and property law itself. It also assumes that owners have obligations as well as rights. Owners must live with substantial regulation designed to protect the interests of others affected by the exercise of their property rights, including other owners and non-owners, as well as the community at large. Nevertheless, fairness and justice place limits on the obligations individual owners can be forced to bear for the good of the community.

Doctrinally, the vast majority of regulatory takings cases are analyzed under the test the Supreme Court articulated in *Penn Central Transportation Co. v. New York City,* 438 U.S. 104 (1978). The *Penn Central* test requires courts to engage in "essentially *ad hoc,* factual inquiries" of the "particular circumstances" of each case, with a focus on three factors of "particular significance": (1) the "economic impact" of the regulation on the particular owner; (2) the protection of "reasonable" or "distinct" "investment-backed expectations"; and (3) the "character of the governmental action." *Id.* at 124; *Kaiser Aetna v. United States*, 444 U.S. 164, 175 (1979). Most, but by no means all, regulations will be upheld under this test as legitimate exercises of the police power despite their impact on property use or value. *See* §3, below.

While the Court normally applies this **ad hoc**, multifactor test to determine when a regulation becomes a taking, it has flirted with attempts to develop *per se* tests to identify types of regulations that constitute **categorical takings** for which compensation is required regardless of other factors. For a

while the Court appeared to be intent on identifying more *per se* takings. However, the Court has now clarified that there are only "two categories of regulatory action that generally will be deemed *per se* takings." *Lingle v. Chevron U.S.A. Inc.*, 544 U.S. 528, 538 (2005).

The two types of "categorical" takings are government-mandated "permanent physical invasions of property," *id.*; *see Loretto v. Teleprompter Manhattan CATV Corp.*, 458 U.S. 419 (1982), and regulations that "completely deprive an owner of *all* economically viable use of her property [unless] background principles of nuisance and property law independently restrict the owner's intended use of the property," *Lingle*, 544 U.S. at 538; *see Lucas v. South Carolina Coastal Council*, 505 U.S. 1003 (1992). These cases apply in "relatively narrow" circumstances and will only "generally" be deemed *per se* takings. *Lingle*, 544 U.S. at 538. Thus even these two classes of cases are not always deemed takings of property. *See* §4, below.

Terms:
Regulatory takings claims are brought through an action for **inverse condemnation**. This is a claim by a property owner against a public body alleging that a regulation has taken the owner's property without just compensation. In the usual eminent domain case, the public body brings condemnation proceedings against the property and the court sets the amount of just compensation required. Lawsuits by property owners for damages are the "inverse" of this procedure.

The *per se* categories apply the general rule; they merely identify particular circumstances that are almost certain to be classified as regulatory takings. For that reason, if a case does not qualify as a purportedly categorical taking, it may nonetheless be deemed an unconstitutional taking of property under the *Penn Central* test.

There are additional types of regulations or laws that have significantly more chance to be deemed takings of property, even if the court has not characterized these categories as *per se* takings. The first involves the deprivation of certain core property rights or estates in land, such as the right to pass on fee simple property at death. *See, e.g., Babbitt v. Youpee*, 519 U.S. 234 (1997). *See* §5.1, below. A second type of case involves retroactive deprivation of vested rights belonging to owners who invested in reasonable reliance on a prior regulatory authorization. *See, e.g., Kaiser Aetna v. United States*, 444 U.S. 164, 179-180 (1979). *See* §5.2, below.

One final doctrinal category bears mention. The Supreme Court has held that in certain circumstances, conditions on land use development permits, commonly known as exactions, can be unconstitutional when those conditions do not "substantially advance[] the *same* interests that land-use authorities asserted would allow them to deny the permit altogether." *Lingle*, 544 U.S. at 547; *see Koontz v. St. Johns River Water Management District*, 133 S. Ct. 420 (2013); *Dolan v. City of Tigard*, 512 U.S. 374 (1994); *Nollan v. California Coastal Commission*, 483 U.S. 825 (1987). As the Court explained in *Dolan*, the government "may not require a person to give up a constitutional right—[for example,] the right to receive just compensation when property is taken for a public use—in exchange for a discretionary benefit conferred by the government where the benefit has little or no relationship to the property." 512 U.S. at 385. *See* §7, below.

§2.3 Regulatory Takings and Due Process

In 1980, the Court stated that a regulatory taking would be found if a law "does not substantially advance legitimate state interests," *Agins v. City of Tiburon*, 447 U.S. 255 (1980). This formulation suggested a version of a means-end test akin to due process analysis, but possibly with a higher level of scrutiny than the deferential rational basis standard. The formulation reflected longstanding confusion in the Court's decisions about the interaction between due process and regulatory takings.

In 2005, however, the Supreme Court unanimously ruled that a regulation cannot be ruled to be an unconstitutional taking on that basis, and that it was improper to derive a test for regulatory takings based on due process precedents. *Lingle v. Chevron U.S.A. Inc.*, 544 U.S. 528 (2005). In *Lingle*, the Court upheld a Hawai`i statute that limited the rents that oil companies could charge dealers leasing company-owned stations against claims that the law was unlikely to achieve its stated purpose of helping consumers because the oil companies could recoup any reductions in their rental income by raising wholesale gasoline prices. *Id.* at 544. The Court held that the judiciary should not be in the business of "scrutiniz[ing] the efficacy [of government regulations,] a task for which courts are not well suited [and which] might often require courts to substitute their predictive judgments for those of elected legislatures and expert agencies." *Id.* A "substantially advances" inquiry, the Court noted,

> suggests a means-ends test: It asks, in essence, whether a regulation of private property is *effective* in achieving some legitimate public purpose. An inquiry of this nature has some logic in the context of a due process challenge, for a regulation that fails to serve any legitimate governmental objective may be so arbitrary or irrational that it runs afoul of the Due Process Clause. See, *e.g., County of Sacramento v. Lewis*, 523 U.S. 833, 846 (1998) (stating that the Due Process Clause is intended, in part, to protect the individual against "the exercise of power without any reasonable justification in the service of a legitimate governmental objective"). But such a test is not a valid method of discerning whether private property has been "taken" for purposes of the Fifth Amendment.

Id. at 542. The Court thus made clear that despite the doctrinal variation in approaches to regulatory takings—a landscape we will be begin to explore in the next section—each approach "aims to identify regulatory actions that are functionally equivalent to the classic taking in which government directly appropriates private property or ousts the owner from his domain." *Id.* at 539.

One area where the distinction between due process and regulatory takings continues to be unresolved involves retroactivity. It is clear that newly enacted laws that interfere with owners' reliance interests can be unconstitutional; it is not clear, however, whether those interests are most appropriately protected by the takings clause or by the due process clause. As you work through regulatory takings doctrine for the remainder of this chapter, pay attention to this tension.

§3 THE *AD HOC* TEST: FAIRNESS AND JUSTICE

§3.1 The Foundation of the *Ad Hoc* Test

Penn Central Transportation Co. v. New York City

438 U.S. 104 (1978)

Map: 100 E. 42nd Street (intersection with Park Avenue), New York, New York

Mr. Justice WILLIAM J. BRENNAN delivered the opinion of the court, in which STEWART, WHITE, MARSHALL, BLACKMUN, and POWELL, JJ., joined.

The question presented is whether a city may, as part of a comprehensive program to preserve historic landmarks and historic districts, place restrictions on the development of individual historic landmarks — in addition to those imposed by applicable zoning ordinances — without effecting a "taking" requiring the payment of "just compensation." Specifically, we must decide whether the application of New York City's Landmarks Preservation Law to the parcel of land occupied by Grand Central Terminal has "taken" its owners' property in violation of the Fifth and Fourteenth Amendments.

Façade of Grand Central Terminal[16]

16. © 2008 Free Software Foundation, Inc. *http://fsf.org/*. Photoshop work by Mira Singer.

I

Over the past 50 years, all 50 States and over 500 municipalities have enacted laws to encourage or require the preservation of buildings and areas with historic or aesthetic importance. These nationwide legislative efforts have been [based on] a widely shared belief that structures with special historic, cultural, or architectural significance enhance the quality of life for all.

Under the New York City *Landmarks Preservation Law*, the Landmarks Preservation Commission (Commission) [may] designate a building to be a "landmark," situated on a particular "landmark site," or will designate an area to be a "historic district." After the Commission makes a designation, New York City's Board of Estimate may modify or disapprove the designation, and the owner may seek judicial review of the final designation decision. Final designation as a landmark imposes a duty upon the owner to keep the exterior features of the building "in good repair" [and requires] Commission [approval of] any proposal to alter the exterior architectural features of the landmark or to construct any exterior improvement on the landmark site. Under New York City's zoning laws, owners of real property who have not developed their property to the full extent permitted by the applicable zoning laws are allowed to transfer development rights to [nearby] parcels.

CONTEXT

New York enacted its *Landmarks Preservation Law* against the backdrop of the destruction of the dramatically beautiful former Penn Station building in 1963. Of the difference between the old and the current Penn Station, Yale architectural historian Vincent Scully famously said, "One entered the city like a god; [o]ne scuttles in now like a rat." Herbert Muschamp, *Architecture View: In This Dream Station Future and Past Collide*, N.Y. Times, June 20, 1993. The demolition shocked historic preservationists into action, and the statute, and the battle over Grand Central, was the result.

This case involves the application of New York City's Landmarks Preservation Law to Grand Central Terminal (Terminal). The Terminal, which is owned by the Penn Central Transportation Co. and its affiliates (Penn Central), is one of New York City's most famous buildings. Opened in 1913, it is regarded not only as providing an ingenious engineering solution to the problems presented by urban railroad stations, but also as a magnificent example of the French beaux-arts style.

[T]he Commission designated the Terminal a "landmark" and designated the "city tax block" it occupies a "landmark site" [and the] Board of Estimate confirmed this action on September 21, 1967. Although appellant Penn Central had opposed the designation before the Commission, it did not seek judicial review of the final designation decision.

[Four months later,] appellant Penn Central entered into a [lease] with appellant UGP Properties, Inc., [under which] UGP was to construct a [50 story-high] office building above the Terminal.

The Commission rejected two different plans for the building on the ground that "balanc[ing] a 55-story office tower above a flamboyant Beaux-Arts facade seems nothing more than an aesthetic joke. Quite simply, the tower would overwhelm the Terminal by its sheer mass."

Appellants did not seek judicial review of the denial of either certificate. Instead, appellants filed suit in New York Supreme Court, Trial Term, claiming that the application of the Landmarks Preservation Law had "taken" their property without just compensation in violation of the Fifth and Fourteenth Amendments and arbitrarily deprived them of their property without due process of law in violation of the Fourteenth Amendment.

II

A

The question of what constitutes a "taking" for purposes of the Fifth Amendment has proved to be a problem of considerable difficulty. While this Court has recognized that the "Fifth Amendment's guarantee [is] designed to bar Government from forcing some people alone to bear public burdens which, in all fairness and justice, should be borne by the public as a whole," *Armstrong* v. *United States*, 364 U.S. 40, 49 (1960), this Court, quite simply, has been unable to develop any "set formula" for determining when "justice and fairness" require that economic injuries caused by public action be compensated by the government, rather than remain disproportionately concentrated on a few persons. *See Goldblatt v. Hempstead*, 369 U.S. 590, 594 (1962). Indeed, we have frequently observed that whether a particular restriction will be rendered invalid by the government's failure to pay for any losses proximately caused by it depends largely "upon the particular circumstances [in that] case." *United States v. Central Eureka Mining Co.*, 357 U.S. 155, 168 (1958); *see United States v. Caltex, Inc.*, 344 U.S. 149, 156 (1952).

In engaging in these essentially ad hoc, factual inquiries, the Court's decisions have identified several factors that have particular significance. The economic impact of the regulation on the claimant and, particularly, the extent to which the regulation has interfered with distinct investment-backed expectations are, of course, relevant considerations. So, too, is the character of the governmental action. A "taking" may more readily be found when the interference with property can be characterized as a physical invasion by government, *see, e.g., United States v. Causby*, 328 U.S. 256 (1946), than when interference arises from some public program adjusting the benefits and burdens of economic life to promote the common good.

"Government hardly could go on if to some extent values incident to property could not be diminished without paying for every such change in the general law," *Pennsylvania Coal Co. v. Mahon*, 260 U.S. 393, 413 (1922), and this Court has accordingly recognized, in a wide variety of contexts, that government may execute laws or programs that adversely affect recognized economic value.

More importantly for the present case, in instances in which a state tribunal reasonably concluded that "the health, safety, morals, or general welfare" would be promoted by prohibiting particular contemplated uses of land, this Court has upheld land-use regulations that destroyed or adversely affected recognized real property interests. Zoning laws are, of course, the classic example, *see Euclid v. Ambler Realty Co.*, 272 U.S. 365 (1926) (prohibition of industrial use); *Gorieb v. Fox*, 274 U.S. 603, 608 (1927) (requirement that portions of parcels be left unbuilt); *Welch v. Swasey*, 214 U.S. 91 (1909) (height restriction), which have been viewed as permissible governmental action even when prohibiting the most beneficial use of the property.

Zoning laws generally do not affect existing uses of real property, but "taking" challenges have also been held to be without merit in a wide variety of situations when the challenged governmental actions prohibited a beneficial use to which individual parcels had previously been devoted and thus caused substantial individualized harm. *Miller v. Schoene*, 276 U.S. 272 (1928), is illustrative. In that case, [a] unanimous Court [found no taking when the state ordered the destruction of many ornamental red cedar trees to prevent the transmission of cedar rust fatal to apple trees cultivated nearby.] The Court held that the State might properly make "a choice between the preservation of one class of property and that of the other" and since the apple industry was important in the State involved, concluded that the State had not exceeded "its constitutional powers by deciding upon the destruction of one class of property [without compensation] in order to save another which, in the judgment of the legislature, is of greater value to the public." *Id.* at 279.

Again, *Hadacheck v. Sebastian*, 239 U.S. 394 (1915), upheld a law prohibiting the claimant from continuing his otherwise lawful business of operating a brickyard in a particular physical community on the ground that the legislature had reasonably concluded that the presence of the brickyard was inconsistent with neighboring uses. *See also Walls v. Midland Carbon Co.*, 254 U.S. 300 (1920) (law prohibiting manufacture of carbon black upheld); *Reinman v. Little Rock*, 237 U.S. 171 (1915) (law prohibiting livery stable upheld); *Mugler v. Kansas*, 123 U.S. 623 (1887) (law prohibiting liquor business upheld).

Goldblatt v. Hempstead, *supra*, [upheld a 1958 city safety ordinance that] effectively prohibited the claimant from continuing a sand and gravel mining business that had been operated on the particular parcel since 1927. The Court upheld the ordinance against a "taking" challenge, although the ordinance prohibited the present and presumably most beneficial use of the property and had, like the regulations in *Miller* and *Hadacheck*, severely affected a particular owner. The Court assumed that the ordinance did not prevent the owner's reasonable use of the property since the owner made no showing of an adverse effect on the value of the land. Because the restriction served a substantial public purpose, the Court thus held no taking had occurred.

Pennsylvania Coal Co. v. Mahon, 260 U.S. 393 (1922), [found a taking when a law] forbade any mining of coal that caused the subsidence of any house, unless the house was the property of the owner of the underlying coal and was more than 150 feet from the improved property of another. Because the statute made it commercially impracticable to mine the coal, and thus had nearly the same effect as the complete destruction of rights claimant had reserved from the owners of the surface land, the Court held that the statute was invalid as effecting a "taking" without just compensation. *See generally* Michelman, *Property, Utility, and Fairness: Comments on the Ethical Foundations of "Just Compensation" Law*, 80 Harv. L. Rev. 1165, 1229-34 (1967).

Finally, government actions that may be characterized as acquisitions of resources to permit or facilitate uniquely public functions have often been held to constitute "takings." *United States v. Causby*, 328 U.S. 256 (1946), is illustrative. In holding that direct over flights above the claimant's land that destroyed the present use of the land as a chicken farm, constituted a "taking," *Causby* emphasized that Government had not "merely destroyed property [but was] using a part of it for the flight of its planes." *Id.* at 262-63 n.7.

B

Appellants urge that the Landmarks Law has deprived them of any gainful use of their "air rights" above the Terminal and that, irrespective of the value of the remainder of their parcel, the city has "taken" their right to this superjacent airspace, thus entitling them to "just compensation" measured by the fair market value of these air rights.

[T]he submission that appellants may establish a "taking" simply by showing that they have been denied the ability to exploit a property interest that they heretofore had believed was available for development is quite simply untenable. Were this the rule, this Court would have erred not only in upholding laws restricting the development of air rights, but also in approving those prohibiting both the subjacent, and the lateral development of particular parcels. "Taking" jurisprudence does not divide a single parcel into discrete segments and attempt to determine whether rights in a particular segment have been entirely abrogated. In deciding whether a particular governmental action has effected a taking, this Court focuses rather both on the character of the action and on the nature and extent of the interference with rights in the parcel as a whole — here, the city tax block designated as the "landmark site."

Secondly, appellants, focusing on the character and impact of the New York City law, argue that it effects a "taking" because its operation has significantly diminished the value of the Terminal site. Appellants concede that the decisions sustaining other land-use regulations, which, like the New York City law, are reasonably related to the promotion of the general welfare, uniformly reject the proposition that diminution in property value, standing alone, can establish a "taking," *see Euclid v. Ambler Realty Co.*, 272 U.S. 365 (1926) (75% diminution in value caused by zoning law); *Hadacheck v. Sebastian*, 239 U.S. 394 (1915) (87 1/2% diminution in value); and that the "taking" issue in these contexts is resolved by focusing on the uses the regulations permit. Appellants, moreover, also do not dispute that a showing of diminution in property value would not establish a "taking" if the restriction had been imposed as a result of historic-district legislation, but appellants argue that New York City's regulation of individual landmarks is fundamentally different from zoning or from historic-district legislation because the controls imposed by New York City's law apply only to individuals who own selected properties.

Stated baldly, appellants' position appears to be that the only means of ensuring that selected owners are not singled out to endure financial hardship for no reason is to hold that any restriction imposed on individual landmarks pursuant to the New York City scheme is a "taking" requiring the payment of "just compensation." Agreement with this argument would, of course, invalidate not just New York City's law, but all comparable landmark legislation in the Nation. We find no merit in it.

It is true, as appellants emphasize, that both historic-district legislation and zoning laws regulate all properties within given physical communities whereas landmark laws apply only to selected parcels. But, contrary to appellants' suggestions, landmark laws are not like discriminatory, or "reverse spot," zoning: that is, a land-use decision which arbitrarily singles out a particular parcel for different, less favorable treatment than the neighboring ones. In contrast to discriminatory zoning, which is the antithesis of land-use control as part of some comprehensive plan, the New York City law embodies a comprehensive plan to preserve structures of historic or aesthetic interest wherever they might be found in the city, and as noted, over 400 landmarks and 31 historic districts have been designated pursuant to this plan.

It is, of course, true that the Landmarks Law has a more severe impact on some landowners than on others, but that in itself does not mean that the law effects a "taking." Legislation designed to promote the general welfare commonly burdens some more than others. The owners of the brickyard in *Hadacheck*, of the cedar trees in *Miller v. Schoene*, and of the gravel and sand mine in *Goldblatt v. Hempstead*, were uniquely burdened by the legislation sustained in those cases.[17] Similarly, zoning laws often affect some property owners more severely than others but have not been held to be invalid on that account. For example, the property owner in *Euclid* who wished to use its property for industrial purposes was affected far more severely by the ordinance than its neighbors who wished to use their land for residences.

In any event, appellants' repeated suggestions that they are solely burdened and unbenefited is factually inaccurate. This contention overlooks the fact that the New York City law applies to vast numbers of structures in the city in addition to the Terminal — all the structures contained in the 31 historic districts and over 400 individual landmarks, many of which are close to the Terminal. Unless we are to reject the judgment of the New York City Council that the preservation of landmarks benefits all New York citizens and all structures, both economically and by improving the quality of life in the city as a whole — which we are unwilling to do — we cannot conclude that the owners of the Terminal have in no sense been benefited by the Landmarks Law. Doubtless appellants believe they are more burdened than benefited by the law, but that must have been true, too, of the property owners in *Miller, Hadacheck, Euclid,* and *Goldblatt.*

---

17. Appellants attempt to distinguish these cases on the ground that, in each, government was prohibiting a "noxious" use of land and that in the present case, in contrast, appellants' proposed construction above the Terminal would be beneficial. We observe that the uses in issue in *Hadacheck, Miller,* and *Goldblatt* were perfectly lawful in themselves. They involved no "blameworthiness, . . . moral wrongdoing or conscious act of dangerous risk-taking which [induced society] to shift the cost to a [particular] individual." Sax, *Takings and the Police Power,* 74 Yale L.J. 36, 50 (1964). These cases are better understood as resting not on any supposed "noxious" quality of the prohibited uses but rather on the ground that the restrictions were reasonably related to the implementation of a policy — not unlike historic preservation — expected to produce a widespread public benefit and applicable to all similarly situated property.

Nor, correlatively, can it be asserted that the destruction or fundamental alteration of a historic landmark is not harmful. The suggestion that the beneficial quality of appellants' proposed construction is established by the fact that the construction would have been consistent with applicable zoning laws ignores the development in sensibilities and ideals reflected in landmark legislation like New York City's.

C

We now must consider whether the interference with appellants' property is of such a magnitude that "there must be an exercise of eminent domain and compensation to sustain [it]." *Pennsylvania Coal Co. v. Mahon*, 260 U.S., at 413. That inquiry may be narrowed to the question of the severity of the impact of the law on appellants' parcel, and its resolution in turn requires a careful assessment of the impact of the regulation on the Terminal site.

[T]he New York City law does not interfere in any way with the present uses of the Terminal. Its designation as a landmark not only permits but contemplates that appellants may continue to use the property precisely as it has been used for the past 65 years: as a railroad terminal containing office space and concessions. So the law does not interfere with what must be regarded as Penn Central's primary expectation concerning the use of the parcel. More importantly, on this record, we must regard the New York City law as permitting Penn Central not only to profit from the Terminal but also to obtain a "reasonable return" on its investment.

Appellants, moreover, exaggerate the effect of the law on their ability to make use of the air rights above the Terminal in two respects. First, it simply cannot be maintained, on this record, that appellants have been prohibited from occupying *any* portion of the airspace above the Terminal. While the Commission's actions in denying applications to construct an office building in excess of 50 stories above the Terminal may indicate that it will refuse to issue a certificate of appropriateness for any comparably sized structure, nothing the Commission has said or done suggests an intention to prohibit *any* construction above the Terminal. The Commission's report emphasized that whether any construction would be allowed depended upon whether the proposed addition "would harmonize in scale, material, and character with [the Terminal]." Since appellants have not sought approval for the construction of a smaller structure, we do not know that appellants will be denied any use of any portion of the airspace above the Terminal.

Second, to the extent appellants have been denied the right to build above the Terminal, it is not literally accurate to say that they have been denied *all* use of even those pre-existing air rights. Their ability to use these rights has not been abrogated; they are made transferable to at least eight parcels in the vicinity of the Terminal, one or two of which have been found suitable for the construction of new office buildings. Although appellants and others have argued that New York City's transferable development-rights program is far from ideal, the New York courts here supportably found that, at least in the case of the Terminal, the rights afforded are valuable. While these rights may well not have constituted "just compensation" if a "taking" had occurred, the rights nevertheless undoubtedly mitigate whatever financial burdens the law has imposed on appellants and, for that reason, are to be taken into account in considering the impact of regulation.

On this record, we conclude that the application of New York City's Landmarks Law has not effected a "taking" of appellants' property. The restrictions imposed are substantially related to the promotion of the general welfare and not only permit reasonable beneficial use of the landmark site but also afford appellants opportunities further to enhance not only the Terminal site proper but also other properties.

Affirmed.

Mr. Justice REHNQUIST, with whom THE CHIEF JUSTICE and Mr. Justice STEVENS join, dissenting.

Of the over one million buildings and structures in the city of New York, appellees have singled out 400 for designation as official landmarks. The question in this case is whether the cost associated with the city of New York's desire to preserve a limited number of "landmarks" within its borders must be borne by all of its taxpayers or whether it can instead be imposed entirely on the owners of the individual properties.

Typical zoning restrictions may, it is true, so limit the prospective uses of a piece of property as to diminish the value of that property in the abstract because it may not be used for the forbidden purposes. But any such abstract decrease in value will more than likely be at least partially offset by an increase in value which flows from similar restrictions as to use on neighboring properties. All property owners in a designated area are placed under the same restrictions, not only for the benefit of the municipality as a whole but also for the common benefit of one another. In the words of Mr. Justice Holmes, speaking for the Court in *Pennsylvania Coal Co. v. Mahon*, 260 U.S. 393, 415 (1922), there is "an average reciprocity of advantage."

Where a relatively few individual buildings, all separated from one another, are singled out and treated differently from surrounding buildings, no such reciprocity exists. The cost to the property owner which results from the imposition of restrictions applicable only to his property and not that of his neighbors may be substantial — in this case, several million dollars — with no comparable reciprocal benefits. And the cost associated with landmark legislation is likely to be of a completely different order of magnitude than that which results from the imposition of normal zoning restrictions. Under the historic-landmark preservation scheme adopted by New York, the property owner is under an affirmative duty to *preserve* his property *as a landmark* at his own expense. The property has been thus subjected to a nonconsensual servitude not borne by any neighboring or similar properties.

Appellees are not prohibiting a nuisance. The record is clear that the proposed addition to the Grand Central Terminal would be in full compliance with zoning, height limitations, and other health and safety requirements. Instead, appellees are seeking to preserve what they believe to be an outstanding example of beaux arts architecture. Penn Central is prevented from further developing its property basically because *too good* a job was done in designing and building it. The city of New York, because of its unadorned admiration for the design, has decided that the owners of the building must preserve it unchanged for the benefit of sightseeing New Yorkers and tourists.

[A] multimillion dollar loss has been imposed on appellants; it is uniquely felt and is not offset by any benefits flowing from the preservation of some 400 other "landmarks" in New York City. Appellees have imposed a substantial cost on less than one one-tenth of one percent of the buildings in New York City for the general benefit of all its people. It is exactly this imposition of general costs on a few individuals at which the "taking" protection is directed.

Notes and Questions

1. Relevant factors. How do the courts determine whether "fairness and justice" require the cost of a regulatory law to be shared among taxpayers rather than being borne by the individual property owners whose interests are negatively affected by the regulation? *Penn Central* identified three factors central to this determination: "the economic impact of the regulation, its interference with reasonable investment backed expectations, and the character of the government action." *Kaiser Aetna v. United States*, 444 U.S. 164, 175 (1979).

> ***FACTORS***
>
> In evaluating the *ad hoc* analysis of fairness and justice in regulatory takings cases courts generally look to:
>
> 1. The economic impact of the regulation;
> 2. Its interference with reasonable investment backed expectations; and
> 3. The character of the governmental action.

a. Economic impact. The greater the diminution in value, the more likely the regulation will be characterized as a taking. Complete deprivation of any "economically viable use" is likely to be a taking unless the regulation denies property rights that never existed in the first place, such as the right to commit a nuisance, *Lucas v. South Carolina Coastal Council*, 505 U.S. 1003 (1992). On the other hand, no owner is guaranteed the most beneficial use of the property. Moreover, regulatory laws can be passed and applied to economic conduct even if this has the effect of depriving the parties of bargained-for contractual rights. For example, the Supreme Court has repeatedly upheld the constitutionality of rent control laws as long as they guarantee the landlord a reasonable return on her investment. *Lingle v. Chevron U.S.A. Inc.*, 544 U.S. 528 (2005); *Yee v. City of Escondido*, 503 U.S. 519 (1992); *Pennell v. City of San Jose*, 485 U.S. 1 (1988); *Block v. Hirsch*, 256 U.S. 135 (1921).

The extent of the diminution in value depends on how the courts define the relevant property interest, a question that first divided the Supreme Court in *Pennsylvania Coal v. Mahon*. *See* §2.1, above. A zoning law that prohibits construction above four stories can be understood as destroying a separate parcel of "air rights," which can, after all, be bought and sold and are valuable property interests. If, however, the property right is defined more broadly as "the right to build on one's parcel," then the ordinance will restrict a much smaller percentage of the total property value since it allows construction up to four stories.

The question is how to identify the "denominator" against which the deprivation numerator will be compared. In *Penn Central*, the Court endorsed a "parcel as a whole" rule for the denominator, which echoes Justice Brandeis's approach in his dissent in *Mahon*. But what *is* that whole parcel? In *Penn Central*, the Court considered it to be the "city tax block designated as the 'landmark site.' " The New York Court of Appeals had earlier determined the relevant parcel to include Penn Central's other property in the same vicinity as Grand Central Terminal. *See Penn*

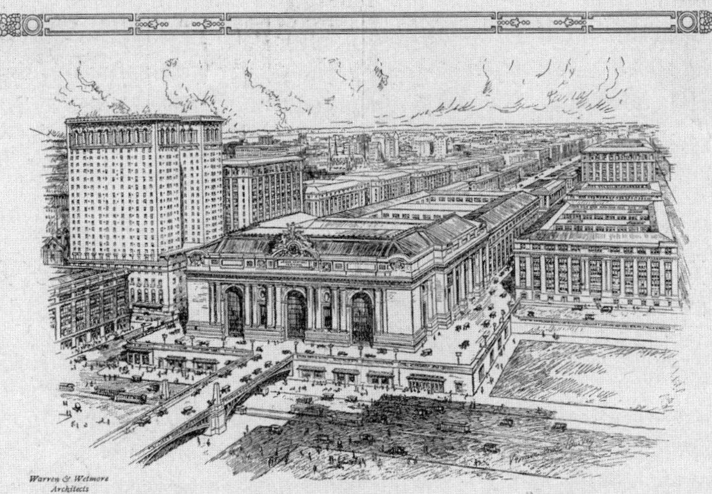

THE TERMINAL CITY

THE GREATEST CIVIC DEVELOPMENT EVER UNDERTAKEN—INCIDENT TO THE NEW GRAND CENTRAL TERMINAL IN NEW YORK CITY, WHICH WILL BE

OPENED FEBRUARY, 1913

This vast undertaking comprehends the erection of a great Terminal City, a city within a city, occupying an area of thirty blocks, in New York City.

It will embrace hotels and modern apartment houses, convention and exhibition halls, clubs and restaurants, and department stores and specialty shops. In short, practically every sort of structure or enterprise incident to the modern city.

These features are all in addition to post office, express buildings and other natural adjuncts of the up-to-date terminal—to expeditiously handle diverse traffic.

All these structures will be erected over the tracks about the terminal itself, while a plaza will surround the Terminal building, reached on the North and South by a new Boulevard, hiding all trace of the railroad yard.

THE NEWLY COMPLETED GRAND CENTRAL TERMINAL

Will provide every detail essential to the comfort and convenience of its patrons. The Terminal itself is the physical embodiment of the latest and the highest ideal of service. Its adequate description is impossible here. It must be seen to be fully appreciated—or indeed to be completely comprehended.

The Main Terminal alone is 722 feet long and 301 feet wide on the surface, and half again as wide below the street level. It will accommodate comfortably 30,000 people at one time.

Through and suburban service occupy different levels approached by inclines, avoiding stairways, so that each level may be reached without confusion. Incoming and outgoing traffic is segregated and the two currents of travel separated. Every facility is progressively arranged so that no step need be retraced, no time lost.

There are 42 tracks for through travel and 25 tracks for local trains, 33 miles in all, within the Terminal, accommodating over 1000 cars at one time. Dedicated to the Public Service, February, 1913.

Central Transportation Co. v. New York City, 366 N.E.2d 1271, 1276-1277 (N.Y. 1977). In a footnote in *Lucas v. South Carolina Coastal Council,* 505 U.S. 1003 (1992), Justice Scalia criticized the New York court's approach as "extreme" and "unsupportable." *Id.* at 1016 n.7. Was it necessarily so far off? Grand Central Terminal was built as part of a development on land reclaimed when the New York Central Railroad, Penn Central's predecessor, moved its rail yards underground. New York Central had marketed the entire development as a single "Terminal City," a 30-block "city within a city"—the very area the New York Court of Appeals had in mind for the relevant parcel.

b. Interference with "distinct" or "reasonable" investment-backed expectations.[18] A regulation is more likely to be held a taking if a citizen has already invested substantially in reasonable reliance on an existing statutory or regulatory scheme. It is less likely to be ruled a taking if the regulation prevents the owner from realizing an expected benefit in the future, imposing a mere opportunity cost, as was the case in *Penn Central.* The dilemma here is that people must have some right to rely on existing law at the time they invest; otherwise, the state could pass a general law subjecting all property in the state to being taken for public use without just compensation, thereby rendering the constitutional protection meaningless. At the same time, the legislature must have the power to change the law to impose greater restrictions on land use when circumstances change or new scientific discoveries arise concerning the importance of wetlands, navigable waters, and fragile coastland to the environment.

c. Character of the government action. The state is generally empowered to legislate to protect the public without compensating those whose property interests suffer a resultant economic impact. "Government hardly could go on if to some extent values incident to property could not be diminished without paying for every such change in the general law," *Pennsylvania Coal Co. v. Mahon,* 260 U.S. 393, 413 (1922). However, if "protecting the public welfare" is sufficient to characterize a government action as a legitimate regulation rather than an unconstitutional taking, then the government will be able to destroy property interests at will without compensation and the takings clause will be meaningless. On the other hand, by defining "nuisance" or "public welfare" narrowly, courts will interfere in the legislatures' ability to protect people from harm and to promote the general welfare; moreover, activist judges would be substituting their own judgment for that of democratically elected representatives.

One question this raises is whether a regulatory law is legitimately preventing an owner from harming others by imposing negative externalities on neighbors or the community or is illegitimately requiring the owner to contribute a benefit to the community. The dispute between the majority and minority opinions in *Penn*

---

18. In *Penn Central,* the Court described this element of the analysis as focusing on interference with "distinct investment-backed expectations," 438 U.S. at 124, but as the analysis has developed, the Court has at times uses the phrase "*reasonable* investment-backed expectations." *See, e.g., Palazzolo v. Rhode Island,* 533 U.S. 606, 617 (2001) (emphasis added). This is in recognition that not all expectations are necessary reasonable in light of existing understandings of property law.

Central revolves around this issue. It also concerns whether the law illegitimately imposes a disparate impact on a few owners or constitutes a legitimate general regulatory law affecting a class of property that is appropriately subject to restrictions. It is clear that owners have no vested right to destroy the environment and pollute neighboring property; the common law of nuisance has always limited an owner's property rights in this regard. In contrast, if the city government needs new office space and wants to take a private home to be used for that purpose, there is no question it must compensate the owner for the taking. But drawing the line between harm-preventing and benefit-conferring legislation is not an exact science. How should courts go about making this distinction?

2. **Transfer of development rights.** The Court in *Penn Central* argues that one factor militating against the finding of a taking is that the owners of Grand Central Terminal could sell their air rights. Transfer of development rights, or "TDR," regimes, are increasingly common and generally involve a kind of market created by a zoning code that allows owners of unused development rights to sell those rights to other owners. *See* Robin Finn, *The Great Air Race*, N.Y. Times, Feb. 24, 2013, at RE-1. The general idea is to hold total density of development constant, but shift where that density is placed in a given community, with the benefit of creating a valuable asset where there would otherwise only be a restriction. TDR regimes can also be used to generate funds for public purposes, in addition to compensating owners, and have been used to support goals such as preserving open space, maintaining parks, and supporting the arts. *See generally* Arthur C. Nelson, Rick Pruetz & Doug Woodruff, *The TDR Handbook: Designing and Implementing Transfer of Development Rights Programs* (2011).

Problems

1. A scientific research company builds a facility to test chemical weapons in the middle of a busy city. The company has a contract with the U.S. Department of Defense to undertake the research. Word of the purpose of the facility leaks out to the general public. A referendum is placed on the ballot to amend the zoning ordinance to prohibit the testing of chemical weapons anywhere in the city. The company explains that the facility is perfectly safe; scientific experts agree that operation of the plant poses little, if any, danger of causing public health problems. Nonetheless, the public is frightened by the prospect of the facility and votes for the referendum. The company sues the city, claiming that enforcement of the amended zoning law would interfere with its vested rights and constitute a taking of property without just compensation. The multimillion-dollar facility is not structured for other kinds of scientific research and would have to be substantially rebuilt in order to convert to other research purposes; application of the ordinance therefore would destroy millions of dollars of the company's investment. The city responds that the amendment regulates a public nuisance and protects the community from any possible contagion from the facility. Does the regulation take the company's property rights? How should the case be resolved?

2. A law school owns a student center and dormitories designed by a famous architect. Although designated as a historic monument, the student center is too small for the current student body, its internal spaces are cramped, and are unsuited to current university architectural standards. Moreover, the school has expanded both its student body and its faculty by about 50 percent, making the facilities inadequate for its current purposes. The school wants to expand its physical facilities and would like to demolish all these buildings to create a modern student and dormitory center. However, designation of the buildings as historic monuments prevents the change and requires the school to maintain the properties as is. What is the school's argument that the historic preservation law effects an unconstitutional taking of property? What is the state's response? If you were on the Supreme Court, how would you rule and what would you say in the opinion?

3. Wetlands are important to the environment in myriad ways. They prevent flooding, release vegetative matter into other waters to feed fish, help cleanse rivers by recycling nutrients, and serve as habitats for animals. *See generally* Paul A. Keddy, *Wetland Ecology: Principles and Conservation* (2010). In *Friedenburg v. N.Y. State Department of Environmental Conservation*, 767 N.Y.S.2d 451 (App. Div. 2003), the court found a taking under the *Penn Central* test when a wetlands law denied a waterfront owner the right to build anything on the land, thereby lowering the property value by 95 percent. The court acknowledged enormously important public interests in avoiding destruction of wetlands but held that such a severe impact on the owner meant that the regulation did not result in an "average reciprocity of advantage." Was the case correctly decided?

§3.2 Takings Statutes

A few states have passed statutes that go beyond the takings clause in protecting owners from uncompensated deprivation of property rights. Both the federal government and many states have passed assessment laws that require government entities to consider the impact of regulations on private property owners before promulgating them to avoid unconstitutional takings of property and to review regulations if they are challenged as regulatory takings or if they are likely to reduce property values by a set amount. *See, e.g.*, Del. Code tit. 29, §605; Fla. Stat. §70.001.[19]

A few states have passed laws that allow either injunctive relief or just compensation when regulation reduces the value of property, even if that reduction would not constitute an unconstitutional taking of property. Some states require compensation if an owner's property values are reduced by a particular percentage unless the regulation fits into an established exemption. *See* Tex. Govt. Code §§2007.001-2007.045

---

19. In 1988, President Reagan issued an executive order that is still in effect that requires all federal agencies to conduct a "takings impact analysis" of all regulations that may affect the use of private property to avoid government actions that might result in an unconstitutional taking of property. Exec. Order No. 12,630, 3 C.F.R. §554 (1988), *reprinted in* 5 U.S.C. §601.

(*Private Real Property Rights Preservation Act*) (both injunctive relief and damages available for state agency regulations that reduce property value by 25 percent or more unless the regulation fits within a list of exemptions). Other states provide relief if a regulation imposes an unfair or inordinate burden on a property owner, even if that burden would not amount to an unconstitutional taking, effectively leaving it to the courts to determine what constitutes an unfair burden. *See* Fla. Stat. §70.001(a) (*Bert J. Harris, Jr. Private Property Rights Protection Act of 1995*) (granting relief when a "new" law or regulation "unfairly affects real property" by imposing an "inordinate burden" on an existing use of real property by impairing the owner's "reasonable, investment-backed expectation for the existing use of the real property" or by leaving the owner "with existing or vested uses that are unreasonable such that the property owner bears permanently a disproportionate share of a burden imposed for the good of the public, which in fairness should be borne by the public at large").

Oregon adopted the most radical law. In 2004, the voters adopted a state law known as Measure 37 that required compensation when any regulation "restricts the use of real property" and is enacted after an owner or a family member acquires title to land if the regulation "has the effect of reducing the fair market value of property," unless the regulation restricts public nuisances, protects public health and safety, or prohibits the use of property for selling pornography or performing nude dancing. Or. Stat. §195:305; Michael C. Blumm & Erik Grafe, *Enacting Libertarian Property: Oregon's Measure 37 and Its Implications,* 85 Denv. U. L. Rev. 279 (2007). Because the law applied to any regulations passed after an owner (or a family member) acquired title, owners could go back to the laws in effect at the time their family first acquired the land — for some families, this may go back to a time before any zoning or environmental laws were in effect. This meant that zoning in a particular area would be inconsistent if acquired by different families at different times, meaning each parcel might be subject to different land use regulations.

Rather than pay compensation for land use restrictions going back to the 1970s, municipalities overwhelmingly chose to waive their zoning laws. As property owners found their neighbors planning massive development in their quiet neighborhoods or valuable agricultural land, support for the Measure turned to passionate opposition. In 2007, Oregon voters passed Measure 49, which restricted Measure 37 claims to laws regulating residential, farm, or forest uses of property, while allowing, without compensation, laws that limit commercial or industrial uses like strip malls and mines, and limited those seeking compensation for pre-enactment regulations to waivers to build a few houses on their land. For lessons from the experience of Measure 37 and its aftermath, *see* Bethany R. Berger, *What Owners Want and Governments Do: Evidence from the Oregon Experiment,* 78 Fordham L. Rev. 1281 (2009).

In 2006, Arizona passed an act similar to Measure 37, known as Proposition 207 or the *Private Property Rights Protection Act.* Ariz. Stat. §12-1134. Not surprisingly, Proposition 207 has had a chilling effect on land use regulation in Arizona. Phoenix, for example, has delayed downtown redevelopment projects, while Tucson chose to forgo regulating the proliferation of student housing in residential neighborhoods, among other consequences. *See* Jeffrey L. Sparks, Note, *Land Use Regulation in Arizona After the Private Property Rights Protection Act*, 51 Ariz. L. Rev. 211, 219-222 (2009).

§3.3 Justifying Regulatory Takings

A number of theories have been proposed to justify the exercise of identifying regulatory takings as distinct from exercises of the police power that do not require compensation. These include (a) tradition, (b) efficiency, and (c) distributive justice. Consider the extent to which these theories might apply to explain the government's power of eminent domain more generally.

Tradition. One answer looks to traditional definitions of property interests to determine which government actions other than outright transfer of property to the government constitute "takings" of "property" that must be compensated. Traditional doctrine may identify both the type of activity that constitutes a nuisance (thereby helping to distinguish harm prevention from benefit extraction) and the strands of rights that constitute core property rights. But how does one identify what property rights are traditional? Should the courts look just to the common law, or should they consider longstanding legislative alterations to common law rights? Recognizing that property law has changed over time (sometimes dramatically), one must identify both a particular time — and a particular jurisdiction — to identify the property interests to which "tradition" will refer. How should this be done? Should changes over time be recognized as evolution of the tradition or departure from it? *See* Margaret Jane Radin, *Government Interests and Takings: Cultural Commitments of Property and the Role of Political Theory* in *Reinterpreting Property* 166, 172-177 (1993) (noting that sudden large changes in property law are more likely to be held to be takings while the same changes occurring gradually over a long period of time are less likely to be seen as takings because gradual evolution alters expectations of what rights go along with ownership).

Even when the rules appear to be clear, determining their scope involves discretion and judgment; prior cases can, after all, be distinguished. Moreover, property rights have always been subject to restrictions incorporated in various equitable doctrines, such as *laches*, estoppel and the *sic utere* doctrine (use your rights so as not to injure the legitimate rights of others). Should the source of traditional property law be the relatively clear *rules* that developed over time (and at what time?) or the background *principles* that modify and condition otherwise applicable rights? *See* Frank Michelman, *Property, Federalism, and Jurisprudence: A Comment on* Lucas *and Judicial Conservatism*, 35 Wm. & Mary L. Rev. 301 (1993). A final problem is that the common law definition of property was developed by unelected judges; why should their definition of "property" have greater legitimacy than the definition embodied in statutes promulgated by elected legislators who are responding to public needs and contemporary social values? *See* Louise A. Halper, *Why the Nuisance Knot Can't Undo the Takings Muddle*, 28 Ind. L. Rev. 329 (1995).

Efficiency. In an important article, Frank Michelman argued that compensation should be required when it will help to promote efficient (that is, welfare-maximizing) legislation. Frank Michelman, *Property, Utility, and Fairness: Comments on the Ethical Foundations of "Just Compensation" Law*, 80 Harv. L. Rev. 1165, 1184 (1967). Michelman explained that a utilitarian should be concerned about weighing the gains from public projects against three kinds of costs: (1) the harms to uncompensated victims resulting from the project, (2) the settlement or administrative costs of arranging for compensation for those victims, and (3) the "demoralization" costs that would accrue if the victims were not compensated and people believed that this lack of compensation was unfair. He argued that from a utilitarian perspective, compensation should be awarded when the demoralization costs of failing to compensate are greater than the settlement costs of arranging for compensation. Other scholars have similarly used efficiency analysis to argue for and against compensation for the effects of particular changes in regulatory laws. *See, e.g.*, Daniel Farber, *Economic Analysis and Just Compensation*, 12 Intl. Rev. L. & Econ. 125 (1992); William A. Fischel, *Introduction: Utilitarian Balancing and Formalism in Takings*, 88 Colum. L. Rev. 1581 (1988); Louis Kaplow, *An Economic Analysis of Legal Transitions*, 99 Harv. L. Rev. 509 (1986).

The efficiency argument that would justify requiring compensation when regulatory laws impinge on property rights rests on the proposition that legislation is welfare maximizing if its benefits outweigh its costs. Legislatures may pass statutes that cause more harm than good because they are responding to special interest groups. Requiring compensation for those whose property interests are harmed by legislation tests the proposition that the legislation benefits the public welfare by requiring those who benefit from the policy to compensate those who lose. If the winners win more than the losers lose, the winners should be willing to raise taxes to pay for the program since they will gain more from the legislation than it costs them in taxes; if winners are not willing to pay for the program by compensating those who lose, we have evidence that the program benefits them less than it harms the property owners adversely affected by it. In this case the legislation is not efficient and should not have been passed in the first place; requiring compensation will prevent legislators from passing an inefficient law. This can serve to reduce the incentive for corruption and align the actions of the government more closely to the general public good. *See* Abraham Bell & Gideon Parchomovsky, *The Hidden Function of Takings Compensation*, 96 Va. L. Rev. 1673 (2010); *cf.* Jed Rubinfeld, *Usings*, 102 Yale L.J. 1077, 1080 (1993) (arguing that governmental action should require compensation only "when government conscripts someone's property for state use").

On the other hand, there are a number of efficiency arguments that would justify *not* compensating owners when regulatory laws impinge on their property rights.[20] First, the administrative costs of compensating everyone injured by any regulation are enormous and may outweigh any benefit derived from the regulation. Second, requiring compensation may mean that efficient legislation, which benefits the public

20. Moreover, it is not clear that governmental actors weigh costs and benefits in the same way that private actors do — or that they necessarily should. Daryl J. Levinson, *Making Government Pay: Markets, Politics, and the Allocation of Constitutional Costs*, 67 U. Chi. L. Rev. 345 (2000).

by preventing activities whose social costs outweigh their benefits, will not be passed; this may happen when people irrationally underestimate the risks of current conduct (for example, people seek the short-run benefits of industrial development and fail to take into account the long-run harm to the environment). If government fails to adopt welfare-maximizing policies, government policy will lower social welfare by adopting an inefficiently low level of regulation. Third, requiring compensation creates a "moral hazard" by removing incentives for economic actors to foresee both the effects of their conduct on others and the likelihood that their conduct will be regulated in the future. Providing compensation for changes in regulatory law creates insurance against adverse changes in land use regulation, causing developers to over-invest in socially harmful activities. In contrast, if no compensation is provided, developers will discount the profitability of activity that is likely to be regulated in the future, decreasing the likelihood that they will engage in socially destructive conduct. *See* Kaplow, *supra*.

Distributive justice. A third justification for compensation recognizes that takings doctrine in many respects rests on distributive concerns. The central question is whether the regulation causes a loss that the individual property owner should, in all fairness and justice, bear as a member of society for the good of the community as a whole.

The distributive argument for requiring compensation is that this ensures that the costs of public programs benefiting the community are borne by taxpayers as a group rather than unfairly imposed on individual property owners. When particular owners suffer unique burdens from regulation, there is no average reciprocity of advantage; therefore, they should be compensated unless their use of the property is morally wrongful.

The distributive argument against requiring compensation is that regulations prevent owners from engaging in activities that harm the public welfare. Because individuals have no right to commit a nuisance or to engage in activities that cause substantial negative externalities, they have no right to be compensated when those regulations impinge on their property interests; they have not lost anything to which they were entitled in the first place. Regulations generally create an "average reciprocity of advantage"; those harmed by the regulation are also benefited by it because it regulates not only their activities but their neighbors' as well. The distributive effect is therefore fair because the burdens of the regulation are balanced by a compensating benefit.

Individuals are not generally expected to pay for public goods that benefit them disproportionately, what can be called "givings" as opposed to takings. *See* Abraham Bell & Gideon Parchomovsky, *Givings*, 111 Yale L.J. 547 (2001). A property owner whose property greatly increases in value because the government decides to build a golf course or an off ramp nearby need not pay for the related giving to her property; does distributive justice demand that she share some of this unearned benefit with the community that created it?

§4 *"PER SE"* TAKINGS

§4.1 Physical Invasions

PruneYard Shopping Center v. Robins

447 U.S. 74 (1980)

Map: 1875 S. Bascom Avenue, Campbell, California

Mr. Justice WILLIAM H. REHNQUIST delivered the opinion of the Court.

Appellant PruneYard is a privately owned shopping center in the city of Campbell, Cal. It covers approximately 21 acres — 5 devoted to parking and 16 occupied by walkways, plazas, sidewalks, and buildings that contain more than 65 specialty shops, 10 restaurants, and a movie theater. The PruneYard is open to the public for the purpose of encouraging the patronizing of its commercial establishments. It has a policy not to permit any visitor or tenant to engage in any publicly expressive activity, including the circulation of petitions, that is not directly related to its commercial purposes. This policy has been strictly enforced in a nondiscriminatory fashion. The PruneYard is owned by appellant Fred Sahadi.

Appellees are high school students who sought to solicit support for their opposition to a United Nations resolution against "Zionism." On a Saturday afternoon they set up a card table in a corner of PruneYard's central courtyard. They distributed pamphlets and asked passersby to sign petitions, which were to be sent to the President and Members of Congress. Their activity was peaceful and orderly and so far as the record indicates was not objected to by PruneYard's patrons.

Soon after appellees had begun soliciting signatures, a security guard informed them that they would have to leave because their activity violated PruneYard regulations. The guard suggested that they move to the public sidewalk at the PruneYard's perimeter. Appellees immediately left the premises and later filed this lawsuit in the California Superior Court of Santa Clara County. They sought to enjoin appellants from denying them access to the PruneYard for the purpose of circulating their petitions.

The California Supreme Court [held] that the California Constitution protects "speech and petitioning, reasonably exercised, in shopping centers even when the centers are privately owned." It concluded that appellees were entitled to conduct their activity on PruneYard property.

Before this Court, appellants contend that their constitutionally established rights under the Fourteenth Amendment to exclude appellees from adverse use of appellants' private property cannot be denied by invocation of a state constitutional provision or by judicial reconstruction of a State's laws of private property.

Appellants contend that a right to exclude others underlies the Fifth Amendment guarantee against the taking of property without just compensation and the Fourteenth Amendment guarantee against the deprivation of property without due process of law.

It is true that one of the essential sticks in the bundle of property rights is the right to exclude others. *Kaiser Aetna v. United States*, 444 U.S. 164, 179-80 (1979). And here there has literally been a "taking" of that right to the extent that the California Supreme Court has interpreted the State Constitution to entitle its citizens to exercise free expression and petition rights on shopping center property. But it is well established that "not every destruction or injury to property by governmental action has been held to be a 'taking' in the constitutional sense." *Armstrong v. United States*, 364 U.S. 40, 48 (1960). Rather, the determination whether a state law unlawfully infringes a landowner's property in violation of the Taking Clause requires an examination of whether the restriction on private property "forc[es] some people alone to bear public burdens which, in all fairness and justice, should be borne by the public as a whole." *Id.* at 49. This examination entails inquiry into such factors as the character of the governmental action, its economic impact, and its interference with reasonable investment-backed expectations. When "regulation goes too far it will be recognized as a taking." *Pennsylvania Coal Co. v. Mahon*, 260 U.S. 393, 415 (1922).

Here the requirement that appellants permit appellees to exercise state-protected rights of free expression and petition on shopping center property clearly does not amount to an unconstitutional infringement of appellants' property rights under the Taking Clause. There is nothing to suggest that preventing appellants from prohibiting this sort of activity will unreasonably impair the value or use of their property as a shopping center. The PruneYard is a large commercial complex that covers several city blocks, contains numerous separate business establishments, and is open to the public at large. The decision of the California Supreme Court makes it clear that the PruneYard may restrict expressive activity by adopting time, place, and manner regulations that will minimize any interference with its commercial functions. Appellees were orderly, and they limited their activity to the common areas of the shopping center. In these circumstances, the fact that they may have "physically invaded" appellants' property cannot be viewed as determinative.

This case is quite different from *Kaiser Aetna v. United States, supra. Kaiser Aetna* was a case in which the owners of a private pond had invested substantial amounts of money in dredging the pond, developing it into an exclusive marina, and building a surrounding marina community. The marina was open only to fee-paying members, and the fees were paid in part to "maintain the privacy and security of the pond." *Id.* at 168. The Federal Government sought to compel free public use of the private marina on the ground that the marina became subject to the federal navigational servitude because the owners had dredged a channel connecting it to "navigable water."

The Government's attempt to create a public right of access to the improved pond interfered with Kaiser Aetna's "reasonable investment backed expectations." We held that it went "so far beyond ordinary regulation or improvement for navigation as to amount to a taking." *Id.* at 178. Nor as a general proposition is the United States, as opposed to the several States, possessed of residual authority that enables it to define "property" in the first instance. A State is, of course, bound by the Just Compensation Clause of the Fifth Amendment, but here appellants have failed to demonstrate that the "right to exclude others" is so essential to the use or economic value of their property that the state-authorized limitation of it amounted to a "taking."

Mr. Justice HARRY A. BLACKMUN joins the opinion of the Court except that sentence thereof, which reads: "Nor as a general proposition is the United States, as opposed to the several States, possessed of residual authority that enables it to define 'property' in the first instance."

Mr. Justice THURGOOD MARSHALL, concurring.

Appellants' claim in this case amounts to no less than a suggestion that the common law of trespass is not subject to revision by the State, notwithstanding the California Supreme Court's finding that state-created rights of expressive activity would be severely hindered if shopping centers were closed to expressive activities by members of the public. If accepted, that claim would represent a return to the era of *Lochner v. New York*, 198 U.S. 45 (1905), when common-law rights were also found immune from revision by State or Federal Government. Such an approach would freeze the common law as it has been constructed by the courts, perhaps at its 19th-century state of development. It would allow no room for change in response to changes in circumstance. The Due Process Clause does not require such a result.

On the other hand, I do not understand the Court to suggest that rights of property are to be defined solely by state law, or that there is no federal constitutional barrier to the abrogation of common-law rights by Congress or a state government. The constitutional terms "life, liberty, and property" do not derive their meaning solely from the provisions of positive law. They have a normative dimension as well, establishing a sphere of private autonomy which government is bound to respect. Quite serious constitutional questions might be raised if a legislature attempted to abolish certain categories of common-law rights in some general way. Indeed, our cases demonstrate that there are limits on governmental authority to abolish "core" common-law rights, including rights against trespass, at least without a compelling showing of necessity or a provision for a reasonable alternative remedy. That "core" has not been approached in this case.

Mr. Justice LEWIS F. POWELL, JR., with whom Mr. Justice WHITE joins, concurring in part and in the judgment.

The State may not compel a person to affirm a belief he does not hold. A property owner may be faced with speakers who wish to use his premises as a platform for views that he finds morally repugnant. Numerous examples come to mind. A minority-owned business confronted with distributors from the American Nazi Party or the Ku Klux Klan, a church-operated enterprise asked to host demonstrations in favor of abortion, or a union compelled to supply a forum to right-to-work advocates could be placed in an intolerable position if state law requires it to make its private property available to anyone who wishes to speak. The strong emotions evoked by speech in such situations may virtually compel the proprietor to respond.

On the record before us, I cannot say that customers of this vast center would be likely to assume that appellees' limited speech activity expressed the views of the PruneYard or of its owner.

Loretto v. Teleprompter Manhattan CATV Corp.

458 U.S. 419 (1982)

Map: 303 W. 105th Street, New York, New York

Justice THURGOOD MARSHALL delivered the opinion of the Court.

This case presents the question whether a minor but permanent physical occupation of an owner's property authorized by government constitutes a "taking" of property for which just compensation is due under the Fifth and Fourteenth Amendments of the Constitution. New York law provides that a landlord must permit a cable television company to install its cable facilities upon his property. N.Y. Exec. Law §828(1). In this case, the cable installation occupied portions of appellant's roof and the side of her building. The New York Court of Appeals ruled that this appropriation does not amount to a taking. Because we conclude that such a physical occupation of property is a taking, we reverse.

[Appellant Jean Loretto purchased a five-story rental apartment building located at 303 West 105th Street, New York City in 1971. The previous owner had granted appellees Teleprompter Corp. and Teleprompter Manhattan CATV (collectively Teleprompter) permission to install a crossover cable on the building (serving other property but not the Loretto property) and the exclusive privilege of furnishing cable television (CATV) services to the tenants at some point in the future. The cable measured slightly less than one-half inch in diameter and ran approximately 36 feet in length along the side of the building; Teleprompter also installed two directional taps measuring 4 inches by 4 inches by 4 inches and two cable boxes measuring 18 inches by 12 inches by 6 inches for a total displaced volume of about one and a half cubic feet. On January 1, 1973, New York state adopted a law that required residential landlords to allow cable television companies to install cable boxes and cables on their property to enable tenants to get access to cable television, N.Y. Exec. Law §828. The state commission established by that law later ruled that landlords were entitled to a nominal fee of $1 when such cables are installed.]

Appellant [Loretto] did not discover the existence of the cable until after she had purchased the building. She brought a class action against Teleprompter in 1976 on behalf of all owners of real property in the State on which Teleprompter has placed CATV components, alleging that Teleprompter's installation was a trespass and, insofar as it relied on §828, a taking without just compensation. [The Supreme Court and the Court of Appeals both upheld the constitutionality of the statute. We reverse.] We conclude that a permanent physical occupation authorized by government is a taking without regard to the public interests that it may serve.

[T]he Court has often upheld substantial regulation of an owner's use of his own property where deemed necessary to promote the public interest. At the same time, we have long considered a physical intrusion by government to be a property restriction of an unusually serious character for purposes of the Takings Clause. Our cases further establish that when the physical intrusion reaches the extreme form of a permanent physical occupation, a taking has occurred. In such a case, "the character of the government action" not only is an important factor in resolving whether the action works a taking but also is determinative.

When faced with a constitutional challenge to a permanent physical occupation of real property, this Court has invariably found a taking. As early as 1872, in *Pumpelly v. Green Bay Co.*, 13 Wall. 166, this Court held that the defendant's construction, pursuant to state authority, of a dam which permanently flooded plaintiff's property constituted a taking.

In *Kaiser Aetna v. United States*, 444 U.S. 164 (1979), the Court held that the Government's imposition of a navigational servitude requiring public access to a pond was a taking where the landowner had reasonably relied on Government consent in connecting the pond to navigable water. The Court emphasized that the servitude took the land-owner's right to exclude, "one of the most essential sticks in the bundle of rights that are commonly characterized as property." *Id.* at 176. The Court explained [that] "the imposition of the navigational servitude in this context will result in an *actual physical invasion* of the privately owned marina." *Id. Kaiser Aetna* reemphasizes that a physical invasion is a government intrusion of an unusually serious character.

Another recent case underscores the constitutional distinction between a permanent occupation and a temporary physical invasion. In *PruneYard Shopping Center v. Robins*, 447 U.S. 74 (1980), the Court upheld a state constitutional requirement that shopping center owners permit individuals to exercise free speech and petition rights on their property, to which they had already invited the general public. The Court emphasized that the State Constitution does not prevent the owner from restricting expressive activities by imposing reasonable time, place, and manner restrictions to minimize interference with the owner's commercial functions. Since the invasion was temporary and limited in nature, and since the owner had not exhibited an interest in excluding all persons from his property, "the fact that [the solicitors] may have 'physically invaded' [the owners'] property cannot be viewed as determinative." *Id.* at 84.

In short, when the "character of the governmental action" is a permanent physical occupation of property, our cases uniformly have found a taking to the extent of the occupation, without regard to whether the action achieves an important public benefit or has only minimal economic impact on the owner.

The historical rule that a permanent physical occupation of another's property is a taking has more than tradition to commend it. Such an appropriation is perhaps the most serious form of invasion of an owner's property interests. To borrow a metaphor, *cf. Andrus v. Allard*, 444 U.S. 51, 65-66 (1979), the government does not simply take a single "strand" from the "bundle" of property rights: it chops through the bundle, taking a slice of every strand.

Property rights in a physical thing have been described as the rights "to possess, use and dispose of it." *United States v. General Motors Corp.*, 323 U.S. 373, 378 (1945). To the extent that the government permanently occupies physical property, it effectively destroys *each* of these rights. First, the owner has no right to possess the occupied space himself, and also has no power to exclude the occupier from possession and use of the space. The power to exclude has traditionally been considered one of the most treasured strands in an owner's bundle of property rights. Second, the permanent physical occupation of property forever denies the owner any power to control the use of the property; he not only cannot exclude others, but can make no nonpossessory use of the property. Although deprivation of the right to use and obtain a profit from property is not, in every case, independently sufficient to establish a taking, it is clearly relevant. Finally, even though the owner may retain the bare legal right to dispose of the occupied space by transfer or sale, the permanent occupation of that space by a stranger will ordinarily empty the right of any value, since the purchaser will also be unable to make any use of the property.

Moreover, an owner suffers a special kind of injury when a *stranger* directly invades and occupies the owner's property. [P]roperty law has long protected an owner's expectation that he will be relatively undisturbed at least in the possession of his property. To require, as well, that the owner permit another to exercise complete dominion literally adds insult to injury. *See* Michelman, *Property, Utility, and Fairness: Comments on the Ethical Foundations of "Just Compensation" Law*, 80 Harv. L. Rev. 1165, 1228, and n.110 (1967). Furthermore, such an occupation is qualitatively more severe than a regulation of the *use* of property, even a regulation that imposes affirmative duties on the owner, since the owner may have no control over the timing, extent, or nature of the invasion.

The traditional rule also avoids otherwise difficult line-drawing problems. Few would disagree that if the State required landlords to permit third parties to install swimming pools on the landlords' rooftops for the convenience of the tenants, the requirement would be a taking. If the cable installation here occupied as much space, again, few would disagree that the occupation would be a taking. But constitutional protection for the rights of private property cannot be made to depend on the size of the area permanently occupied.

Teleprompter's cable installation on appellant's building constitutes a taking under the traditional test. The installation involved a direct physical attachment of plates, boxes, wires, bolts, and screws to the building, completely occupying space immediately above and upon the roof and along the building's exterior wall.

Teleprompter notes that the law applies only to buildings used as rental property, and draws the conclusion that the law is simply a permissible regulation of the use of real property. We fail to see, however, why a physical occupation of one type of property but not another type is any less a physical occupation. Insofar as Teleprompter means to suggest that this is not a permanent physical invasion, we must differ. So long as the property remains residential and a CATV company wishes to retain the installation, the landlord must permit it.[21]

Finally, we do not agree with appellees that application of the physical occupation rule will have dire consequences for the government's power to adjust landlord-tenant relationships. This Court has consistently affirmed that States have broad power to regulate housing conditions in general and the landlord-tenant relationship in particular without paying compensation for all economic injuries that such regulation entails. *See, e.g., Heart of Atlanta Motel, Inc. v. United States,* 379 U.S. 241 (1964) (discrimination in places of public accommodation); *Home Building & Loan Assn. v. Blaisdell,* 290 U.S. 398 (1934) (mortgage moratorium); *Block v. Hirsh,* 256 U.S. 135 (1921) (rent control). In none of these cases, however, did the government authorize the permanent occupation of the landlord's property by a third party. Consequently, our holding today in no way alters the analysis governing the State's power to require landlords to comply with building codes and provide utility connections, mailboxes, smoke detectors, fire extinguishers, and the like in the common area of a building. So long as these regulations do not require the landlord to suffer the physical occupation of a portion of his building by a third party, they will be analyzed under the multifactor inquiry generally applicable to nonpossessory governmental activity. *See Penn Central Transp. Co. v. New York City,* 438 U.S. 104 (1978).

Our holding today is very narrow. We affirm the traditional rule that a permanent physical occupation of property is a taking. In such a case, the property owner entertains a historically rooted expectation of compensation, and the character of the invasion is qualitatively more intrusive than perhaps any other category of property regulation. We do not, however, question the equally substantial authority upholding a State's broad power to impose appropriate restrictions upon an owner's *use* of his property. The issue of the amount of compensation that is due, on which we express no opinion, is a matter for the state courts to consider on remand.

Justice HARRY BLACKMUN, with whom Justice BRENNAN and Justice WHITE, join, dissenting.

The Court of Appeals found, first, that §828 represented a reasoned legislative effort to arbitrate between the interests of tenants and landlords and to encourage development of an important educational and communications medium. Second, the court concluded that the statute's economic impact on appellant was *de minimis* because §828 did not affect the fair return on her property. Third, the statute did not

21. It is true that the landlord could avoid the requirements of §828 by ceasing to rent the building to tenants. But a landlord's ability to rent his property may not be conditioned on his forfeiting the right to compensation for a physical occupation. Teleprompter's broad "use-dependency" argument proves too much. For example, it would allow the government to require a landlord to devote a substantial portion of his building to vending and washing machines, with all profits to be retained by the owners of these services and with no compensation for the deprivation of space. It would even allow the government to requisition a certain number of apartments as permanent government offices. The right of a property owner to exclude a stranger's physical occupation of his land cannot be so easily manipulated.

interfere with appellant's reasonable investment-backed expectations. When appellant purchased the building, she was unaware of the existence of the cable. Thus, she could not have invested in the building with any reasonable expectation that the one-eighth cubic foot of space occupied by the cable television installment would become income-productive.

The Court's recent Takings Clause decisions teach that *nonphysical* government intrusions on private property, such as zoning ordinances and other land-use restrictions may diminish the value of private property far more than minor physical touchings. Nevertheless, as the Court recognizes, it has "often upheld substantial regulation of an owner's use of his own property where deemed necessary to promote the public interest."

Surprisingly, the Court draws an even finer distinction today—between "temporary physical invasions" and "permanent physical occupations." When the government authorizes the latter type of intrusion, the Court would find "a taking without regard to the public interests" the regulation may serve. Yet the newly created distinction is even less substantial than the distinction between physical and nonphysical intrusions that the Court already has rejected.

First, what does the Court mean by "permanent"? As the Court itself concedes, §828 does not require appellant to permit the cable installation forever, but only "[so] long as the property remains residential and a CATV company wishes to retain the installation." This is far from "permanent."

The Court reaffirms that "States have broad power to regulate housing conditions in general and the landlord-tenant relationship in particular without paying compensation for all economic injuries that such regulation entails." Thus, §828 merely defines one of the many statutory responsibilities that a New Yorker accepts when she enters the rental business. If appellant occupies her own building, or converts it into a commercial property, she becomes perfectly free to exclude Teleprompter from her one-eighth cubic foot of roof space. But once appellant chooses to use her property for rental purposes, she must comply with all reasonable government statutes regulating the landlord-tenant relationship.

The Court's talismanic distinction between a continuous "occupation" and a transient "invasion" finds no basis in either economic logic or Takings Clause precedent. In the landlord-tenant context, the Court has upheld against takings challenges rent control statutes permitting "temporary" physical invasions of considerable economic magnitude. *See, e.g., Block v. Hirsh*, 256 U.S. 135 (1921) (statute permitting tenants to remain in physical possession of their apartments for two years after the termination of their leases). Moreover, precedents record numerous other "temporary" officially authorized invasions by third parties that have intruded into an owner's enjoyment of property far more deeply than did Teleprompter's long-unnoticed cable. *See, e.g., PruneYard Shopping Center v. Robins*, 447 U.S. 74 (1980) (leafletting and demonstrating in busy shopping center).

Setting aside history, the Court also states that the permanent physical occupation authorized by §828 is a *per se* taking because it uniquely impairs appellant's powers to dispose of, use, and exclude others from, her property. In fact, the Court's discussion nowhere demonstrates how §828 impairs these private rights in a manner *qualitatively* different from other garden-variety landlord-tenant legislation.

As a practical matter, the regulation ensures that tenants living in the building will have access to cable television for as long as that building is used for rental purposes, and thereby likely increases both the building's resale value and its attractiveness on the rental market. In any event, §828 differs little from the numerous other New York statutory provisions that require landlords to install physical facilities "permanently occupying" common spaces in or on their buildings. As the Court acknowledges, the States traditionally — and constitutionally — have exercised their police power "to require landlords to . . . provide utility connections, mailboxes, smoke detectors, fire extinguishers, and the like in the common area of a building." Like §828, these provisions merely ensure tenants access to services the legislature deems important, such as water, electricity, natural light, telephones, intercommunication systems, and mail service.

The Court also suggests that §828 unconstitutionally alters appellant's right to control the *use* of her one-eighth cubic foot of roof space. But other New York multiple dwelling statutes not only oblige landlords to surrender significantly larger portions of common space for their tenants' use, but also compel the *landlord* — rather than the tenants or the private installers — to pay for and to maintain the equipment. For example, New York landlords are required by law to provide and pay for mailboxes that occupy more than five times the volume that Teleprompter's cable occupies on appellant's building. If the State constitutionally can insist that appellant make this sacrifice so that her tenants may receive mail, it is hard to understand why the State may not require her to surrender less space, *filled at another's expense*, so that those same tenants can receive television signals.

Notes and Questions

1. **The physical invasion "rule."** The Supreme Court often repeats that a *per se* taking occurs when a law authorizes a permanent physical invasion of property. *See Arkansas Game and Fish Commission v. United States*, 133 S. Ct. 511, 518 (2012) ("[A] permanent physical occupation of property authorized by government is a taking"); *Stop the Beach Renourishment, Inc. v. Florida Department of Environmental Protection*, 130 S. Ct. 2592, 2601 (2010) ("[I]t is a taking when a state regulation forces a property owner to submit to a permanent physical occupation"). Although *Loretto* tries to establish a clear rule, not all physical invasions of property authorized by the state are takings of property and the *per se* rule announced in *Loretto* "is very narrow." 458 U.S. at 441. The Court has taken varying approaches, at times *per se* and often *ad hoc*, to the question whether a forced physical invasion is a taking.[22]

22. In *Arkansas Game and Fish Commission v. United States*, 133 S. Ct. 511 (2012), the Court faced the question whether the fact that a physical invasion was temporary created an exemption from takings liability, and held that there is no such exemption. Temporary physical invasions, the Court held, must be evaluated under the *Penn Central* test, with the duration of the invasion "a factor

2. Parsing the physical invasion cases. The *Loretto* opinion attempts to distinguish *PruneYard.* Consider the cases described below in this note. Is the Court successful in distinguishing the two cases? If not, which one is correct?

a. Cases finding a taking on the basis of a physical invasion by a stranger. Besides *Loretto,* a few other cases are routinely cited for the proposition that forced physical invasion or occupation of property by a stranger constitutes a *per se* taking. Here are the most widely cited cases.

Pumpelly v. Green Bay Co., 80 U.S. 166 (1872). When a statute authorized a canal company to build a dam and flood the plaintiff's land, the Supreme Court had no trouble in finding that this constitutes a *per se* taking of plaintiff's property. The court found that it would be "a very curious and unsatisfactory result" if the state could "destroy [the] value [of property] entirely," or "inflict irreparable and permanent injury" to it or even cause its "total destruction" and avoid paying compensation merely because the government did not formally "take" title to the land. *Id.* at 177-178. "Such a construction would pervert the constitutional provision[]." *Id.* at 178.

United States v. Causby, 328 U.S. 256 (1946). Military aircraft flew so close to the ground and caused such extreme noise over plaintiffs' property near an airport that it both rendered plaintiffs' home uninhabitable and made it impossible for them to operate their chicken farm because the noise frightened the chickens and caused them to fly into the walls, killing many of them. Although owners own the airspace over their land, and the passage of planes overhead is technically a trespass, all land ownership is subject to an airspace servitude that allows this. But because the planes were flying so low to the ground, the Court found that this exceeded the scope of the public servitude and thus the entry and passage of the planes constituted a forced taking of a public easement over the plaintiffs' land. Although the "airspace is a public highway, it is obvious that if the landowner is to have full enjoyment of land, he must have exclusive control of the immediate reaches of the enveloping atmosphere. Otherwise buildings could not be erected, trees could not be planted, and even fences could not be run." *Id.* at 264.

Kaiser Aetna v. United States, 444 U.S. 164 (1979). In *Kaiser Aetna,* the owner and lessee of a shallow, private lagoon invested substantial amounts of money in developing the property, connecting it to navigable waters in the ocean, and creating a marina that was to be open only to fee-paying members. Navigable waters are subject to a servitude that allows public access for navigation purposes. The federal government tried to force the owners to grant public access to the lagoon once it had been converted into navigable waters. Although upholding the navigational servitude doctrine, the Supreme Court noted that the owners had invested in developing the marina and connecting the lagoon to the ocean in the expectation that they would continue to be able to control access to the lagoon and charge its members fees to pay for maintenance of the lagoon; the property

---

in determining the existence *vel non* of a compensable taking." 133 S. Ct. at 522. The Court also clarified that "the degree to which the invasion is intended or is the foreseeable result of authorized government action" can influence the *Penn Central* analysis. *Id.*

became included in the navigable waters of the United States only because of the owner's investment. A public access requirement would have converted at least some of the property from land controlled by a private fee-paying club into land freely open to the public. The owners would therefore have lost "one of the most essential sticks in the bundle of rights that are commonly characterized as property — the right to exclude others." *Id.* at 176.

b. Cases finding no taking despite a forced physical invasion by a stranger. Besides *PruneYard,* the most important cases authorizing the physical invasion of land are those upholding the constitutionality of antidiscrimination laws, including public accommodation, fair housing, and employment discrimination laws. No takings claims have reached the Supreme Court to challenge either the employment discrimination laws or the fair housing laws. Both require owners to suffer the physical invasion of property by strangers they would rather exclude. In the case of the *Fair Housing Act,* 42 U.S.C. §§3601-3631, owners and landlords covered by the act can be compelled by injunction to transfer their property to a prospective buyer or tenant when the reason for refusing to sell or rent is the potential occupant's race, color, national origin, religion, sex, familial status, or handicap.

Heart of Atlanta Motel, Inc. v. United States, 379 U.S. 241 (1964). Title II of the *Civil Rights Act of 1964,* 42 U.S.C. §2000a, requires, among other things, that hotels and motels accept customers regardless of race. Since the statute provides for injunctive relief alone, it authorizes courts to issue injunctions mandating that owners allow strangers to stay in their premises that those owners would rather exclude. Besides finding the statute to be properly enacted pursuant to Congress's power to regulate interstate commerce, the Supreme Court held, with no analysis whatsoever, that it did not "find any merit in the claim that the Act is a taking of property without just compensation." *Id.* at 261.

c. Physical invasions by those in contractual relationships with the owner. The Supreme Court has repeatedly upheld anti-eviction laws that grant tenants the right to continue renting their apartments as long as they pay the agreed-upon rent and do not damage the property or violate other material terms of the lease, even if these laws authorize occupation beyond the end of the lease term. A similar result has obtained in the case of mortgage moratorium statutes.

Block v. Hirsh, 256 U.S. 135 (1921). In *Block v. Hirsh,* the Court upheld against a takings challenge a statute that permitted tenants to remain in physical possession of their apartments after the termination of their leases at rents set by a rent control commission. The owner could evict the tenant only if the tenant were in breach of the lease or if the owner sought to regain possession for occupancy by herself or her family. Justice Holmes noted that the statute guaranteed the owner a "reasonable rent" and that the statutory eviction controls were justified by the emergency conditions of a housing shortage in Washington, D.C., brought on by an influx of people during World War I. *Accord, Edgar A. Levy Leasing Co. v. Siegel,* 258 U.S. 242 (1922) (upholding a similar New York law).

Home Building & Loan Association v. Blaisdell, 290 U.S. 398 (1934). In the midst of the Great Depression, Minnesota passed a mortgage moratorium law giving courts discretion to postpone foreclosure on homes whose mortgages were in default and giving borrowers an extension of the period of redemption during which they could pay their delinquent mortgage charges and thus keep their homes. The effect of the law was to allow the borrower/homeowner to remain in her home and to delay transfer of title to the property at foreclosure sale to a buyer (who often would be the bank that loaned the money in the first place). The statute thus authorized a forced physical occupation of the premises by the homeowner in a manner that was inconsistent with the mortgage agreement and the mortgagee's foreclosure rights. The Supreme Court unanimously upheld the statute against challenges that it violated both the due process clause and the constitutional clause prohibiting the impairment of contracts, U.S. Const. art. I, §10, because the moratorium was temporary and the bank was entitled to rent to compensate for the extended occupation of the premises.

Yee v. City of Escondido, California, 503 U.S. 519 (1992). The Supreme Court reaffirmed *Block v. Hirsh* in *Yee,* holding that an anti-eviction law that allowed mobile home owners to continue renting the land in the mobile home park on which their homes sat, even after the end of the lease term, did not amount to a forced physical invasion of the park owner's property. The statute allowed the park owner to give six months' notice and then go out of business, evict the mobile home tenants, and convert the property to other uses. It did not matter to the Court that the effect of the anti-eviction law, when combined with the applicable rent control statute, allowed the mobile home owner to sell the home in place and transfer the tenancy to the new owner of the mobile home (at the rent-controlled rent) without the consent of the park owner. The buyer of the mobile home who would become the new tenant would of course be a stranger to the park owner. In effect, the law gave the tenants an absolute right to assign their leasehold even if assignment was prohibited by the lease. Such a buyer/assignee would pay more to buy such mobile homes because they were located in a rent-controlled environment; the mobile home owner, rather than the landlord, would reap the economic benefit of this one-time premium.

None of this was relevant to the question of whether the law constituted a taking even though it imposed a forced physical occupation by a stranger. Rather, the Court concluded that what mattered was the initial "invitation" to occupy the land. *Id.* at 532. "Because they voluntarily open their property to occupation by others, petitioners cannot assert a *per se* right to compensation based on their inability to exclude particular individuals." *Id.* at 531. The statutes here did "not authorize an unwanted physical occupation" of the park owners' land; rather, they were "a regulation of [the park owners'] use of their property, and thus [did] not amount to a *per se* taking [under *Loretto*]." *Id.* at 532. However, the Court did note that the ordinance allowed the owner to go out of business and that "[a] different case would be presented were the statute, on its face or as applied, to compel a landowner over objection to rent his property or to refrain in perpetuity from terminating a tenancy." *Id.* at 528.

3. **Does the landlord have a right to occupy her own land?** State courts have generally upheld anti-eviction laws against takings challenges even when those laws prevent the landlord from converting the property to another use. In *Flynn v. City of*

Cambridge, 418 N.E.2d 335 (Mass. 1981), for example, the court upheld a condominium conversion law that prohibited landlords from evicting a tenant so they could convert the building into condominiums and move into the property themselves. The court found that the law did not effect an unconstitutional taking because the owners retained their "primary expectation concerning the use of the property" and they were still able to "obtain a reasonable return on [their] investment." *Id.* at 339-340; *see also Rent Stabilization Association of New York City v. Higgins*, 630 N.E.2d 626, 632 (N.Y. 1993) ("That a rent-regulated tenancy might itself be of indefinite duration . . . does not, without more, render it a permanent physical occupation of property."). Some courts, however, have struck down similar statutes as unconstitutional takings of property when they prevent the landlord from evicting a tenant so the landlord can move into the property herself. *Cwynar v. City & County of San Francisco*, 109 Cal. Rptr. 2d 233 (Ct. App. 2001).

4. **Does the landlord have a right to go out of business?** Most anti-eviction laws have exceptions that allow the landlord to go out of business and devote the property to uses other than residential rental uses. But some laws do not allow eviction for this purpose. In *Nash v. City of Santa Monica*, 688 P.2d 894 (Cal. 1984), *appeal dismissed*, 470 U.S. 1046 (1985), the California Supreme Court upheld a rent-control ordinance prohibiting removal of rental units from the housing market by conversion or demolition without a removal permit.[23] The court sustained the ordinance against a takings challenge by an owner who was prevented from evicting his tenants and tearing the building down. Although he was earning a fair return on his investment, the landlord claimed a right to "go out of business" as a landlord, demolish the building, and wait for the value of the property to appreciate before selling or developing it. The California Supreme Court disagreed, noting that the property had no "personal or sentimental value to him," that he did not plan to live there, and that "adverse economic effects of land use regulation do not give rise to a constitutional claim so long as the property retains value." *Id.* at 900 n.6.

In contrast, the New York Court of Appeals struck down an anti-warehousing law that prohibited owners of single room occupancy (SRO) hotels from shutting down and going out of business. In *Seawall Associates v. City of New York*, 542 N.E.2d 1059 (N.Y. 1989), the City of New York had imposed a moratorium on conversion of SRO properties, requiring owners of SRO properties to rehabilitate all vacant units and offer them for rent. The ordinance imposed heavy penalties for violations, but allowed owners to purchase exemptions if they were able either (a) to pay roughly $45,000 per vacant unit, (b) to replace the units taken off the market with other units, (c) to demonstrate hardship, or (d) to show that there was no reasonable possibility that they could earn a reasonable rate of return (defined as a net annual return of 8 percent of the assessed value of the property as an SRO multiple dwelling). The New York Court of Appeals found the ordinance to be a taking of property under both the federal and state constitutions, *id.* at 1063-1065, partly on the ground that it required owners to

23. California has since passed a law allowing landlords to go out of business. *Ellis Act*, Cal. Govt. Code §7060.

rent their rooms to strangers. Unlike anti-eviction laws that require owners to keep renting to existing tenants, this law compelled the owners "to admit persons as tenants" and "to surrender the most basic attributes of private property, the rights of possession and exclusion." *Id.* This constituted a forced physical invasion by third parties, akin to the takings found in *Loretto* and *Causby*. "Where, as here, owners are forced to accept the occupation of their properties by persons not already in residence, the resulting deprivation of rights in those properties is sufficient to constitute a physical taking for which compensation is required." *Id.* Can this ruling be reconciled with *Heart of Atlanta Motel*? With *Yee*?

Problems

1. A New Jersey statute grants low-income elderly persons and persons with disabilities a protected tenancy of up to 40 years after an apartment building is converted to a condominium. *Senior Citizens and Disabled Protected Tenancy Act,* N.J. Stat. §§2A:18-61.22 to 2A:18-61.39. This means that the landlord cannot evict such a tenant even if the landlord intends to occupy the unit herself or make it available to a member of her family. This statute was upheld against a takings challenge in *Troy v. Renna,* 727 F.2d 287 (3d Cir. 1984). Assume a takings challenge to the law reaches the Supreme Court. A landlord wishes to evict a tenant so the landlord can move into the apartment herself. The tenant has a disability and therefore the statutory right to remain for up to 40 years. Does the New Jersey statute take the landlord's property without just compensation?

2. Most states now have restraining order statutes that allow victims of domestic violence to obtain emergency injunctions on an *ex parte* basis (meaning without prior notice to the other party) to exclude from the home a household member who has allegedly beaten or otherwise assaulted them. *See, e.g.,* Wis. Stat. §813.12 (judge or family court commissioner may temporarily or permanently order a respondent in a domestic violence case to avoid the victim's residence). Assume an unmarried heterosexual couple has lived together in the man's house for five years. He begins to beat her and she obtains a restraining order excluding him from the house. The order stays in effect for three months while she looks for a new place to live. He brings a lawsuit claiming that, because the title to the house is in his name and the couple is not married, she has no property interest in the house; to exclude him from his own home, even for a short period of time, without a criminal conviction, constitutes a taking of property without just compensation. Is he right? What arguments could you make on both sides? How would you resolve the issue? *Cf. Cote v. Cote,* 599 A.2d 869 (Md. Ct. Spec. App. 1992) (no taking where husband accused of domestic violence was barred from the marital home during the pendency of a divorce proceeding, on the ground that the husband still derived some benefit from the home in the form of not having to provide for an alternative home for his wife during that period).

3. In *Loretto,* Justice Marshall distinguishes the cases that allow substantial regulation of landlord-tenant relationships. "In none of these cases," he explains, "did the government authorize the permanent occupation of the landlord's property by a third party." 458 U.S. at 440. The federal *Fair Housing Act* prohibits discrimination in the sale of real property and provides for injunctive relief. *See* Chapter 13, §1. Consider an owner who is subject to this law who refuses to sell her house to an African American family. The family sues, and the court orders the owner to sell the property to them for its fair market value. The court order effects a permanent physical occupation of the property by strangers. Is this case distinguishable from *Loretto*?

§4.2 Deprivation of All Economically Viable Use

Lucas v. South Carolina Coastal Council

505 U.S. 1003 (1992)

Map: Isle of Palms, South Carolina

Justice Antonin Scalia delivered the opinion of the Court.

In 1986, petitioner David H. Lucas paid $975,000 for two residential lots on the Isle of Palms in Charleston County, South Carolina, on which he intended to build single family homes. In 1988, however, the South Carolina Legislature enacted the *Beachfront Management Act*, S.C. Code §§48-39-250 *et seq.* (Act), which had the direct effect of barring petitioner from erecting any permanent habitable structures on his two parcels. A state trial court found that this prohibition rendered Lucas's parcels "valueless." This case requires us to decide whether the Act's dramatic effect on the economic value of Lucas's lots accomplished a taking of private property under the Fifth and Fourteenth Amendments requiring the payment of "just compensation." U.S. Const., Amdt. 5.

I

A

South Carolina's expressed interest in intensively managing development activities in the so-called "coastal zone" dates from 1977 when, in the aftermath of Congress's passage of the federal *Coastal Zone Management Act of 1972*, 86 Stat. 1280, as amended, 16 U.S.C. §§1451 *et seq.*, the legislature enacted a *Coastal Zone Management Act* of its own. *See* S.C. Code §§48-39-10 *et seq.* (1987). In its original form, the South Carolina Act required owners of coastal zone land that qualified as a "critical area" (defined in the legislation to include beaches and immediately adjacent sand dunes) to obtain a permit from the newly created South Carolina Coastal Council (respondent here) prior to committing the land to a "use other than the use the critical area was devoted to on [September 28, 1977]."

In the late 1970's, Lucas and others began extensive residential development of the Isle of Palms, a barrier island situated eastward of the City of Charleston. Toward the close of the development cycle for one residential subdivision known as "Beachwood East," Lucas in 1986 purchased the two lots at issue in this litigation for his own account. No portion of the lots, which were located approximately 300 feet from the beach, qualified as a "critical area" under the 1977 Act; accordingly, at the time Lucas acquired these parcels, he was not legally obliged to obtain a permit from the Council in advance of any development activity. His intention with respect to the lots was to do what the owners of the immediately adjacent parcels had already done: erect single-family residences. He commissioned architectural drawings for this purpose.

The *Beachfront Management Act* brought Lucas's plans to an abrupt end. Under that 1988 legislation, the Council was directed to establish a "baseline" connecting the landward-most "point[s] of erosion . . . during the past forty years" in the region of the Isle of Palms that includes Lucas's lots. In action not challenged here, the Council fixed this baseline landward of Lucas's parcels. That was significant, for under the Act construction of occupable improvements was flatly prohibited seaward of a line drawn 20 feet landward of, and parallel to, the baseline. The Act provided no exceptions.

B

Lucas promptly filed suit in the South Carolina Court of Common Pleas, contending that the *Beachfront Management Act*'s construction bar effected a taking of his property without just compensation. Lucas did not take issue with the validity of the Act as a lawful exercise of South Carolina's police power, but contended that the Act's complete extinguishment of his property's value entitled him to compensation regardless of whether the legislature had acted in furtherance of legitimate police power objectives. Following a bench trial, the court agreed.

The Supreme Court of South Carolina reversed. The Court ruled that when a regulation respecting the use of property is designed "to prevent serious public harm," no compensation is owing under the Takings Clause regardless of the regulation's effect on the property's value. We granted certiorari.

III

A

Prior to Justice Holmes' exposition in *Pennsylvania Coal Co. v. Mahon*, 260 U.S. 393 (1922), it was generally thought that the Takings Clause reached only a "direct appropriation" of property, *Legal Tender Cases*, 12 Wall. 457, 551 (1871), or the functional equivalent of a "practical ouster of [the owner's] possession." *Transportation Co. v. Chicago*, 99 U.S. 635, 642 (1879). Justice Holmes recognized in *Mahon*, however, that if the protection against physical appropriations of private property was to be meaningfully enforced, the government's power to redefine the range of interests included in the ownership of property was necessarily constrained by constitutional limits. If, instead, the uses of private property were subject to unbridled, uncompensated qualification under the police power, "the natural tendency of human nature [would be] to extend the qualification more and more until at last private property disappear[ed]." *Id.* at 415. These considerations gave birth in that case to the oft-cited maxim that, "while property may be regulated to a certain extent, if regulation goes too far it will be recognized as a taking." *Id.*

Nevertheless, our decision in *Mahon* offered little insight into when, and under what circumstances, a given regulation would be seen as going "too far" for purposes of the Fifth Amendment. In 70-odd years of succeeding "regulatory takings" jurisprudence, we have generally eschewed any "set formula" for determining how far is too far, preferring to "engag[e] in . . . essentially ad hoc, factual inquiries," *Penn Central Transp. Co. v. New York City*, 438 U.S. 104, 124 (1978). We have, however, described at least two discrete categories of regulatory action as compensable without case-specific inquiry into the public interest advanced in support of the restraint. The first encompasses regulations that compel the property owner to suffer a physical "invasion" of his property. In general (at least with regard to permanent invasions), no matter how minute the intrusion, and no matter how weighty the public purpose behind it, we have required compensation. For example, in *Loretto v. Teleprompter Manhattan CATV Corp.*, 458 U.S. 419 (1982), we determined that New York's law requiring landlords to allow television cable companies to emplace cable facilities in their apartment buildings constituted a taking, even though the facilities occupied at most only 1 1/2 cubic feet of the landlords' property.

The second situation in which we have found categorical treatment appropriate is where regulation denies all economically beneficial or productive use of land. *See Agins v. Tiburon*, 447 U.S. 255, 260 (1980). As we have said on numerous occasions, the Fifth Amendment is violated when land-use regulation "does not substantially advance legitimate state interests *or denies an owner economically viable use of his land*." *Id.* (emphasis added).[24]

We have never set forth the justification for this rule. Perhaps it is simply, as Justice Brennan suggested, that total deprivation of beneficial use is, from the land-owner's point of view, the equivalent of a physical appropriation. Surely, at least, in the extraordinary circumstance when no productive or economically beneficial use of land is permitted, it is less realistic to indulge our usual assumption that the legislature is

---

24. Regrettably, the rhetorical force of our "deprivation of all economically feasible use" rule is greater than its precision, since the rule does not make clear the "property interest" against which the loss of value is to be measured. When, for example, a regulation requires a developer to leave 90% of a rural tract in its natural state, it is unclear whether we would analyze the situation as one in which the owner has been deprived of all economically beneficial use of the burdened portion of the tract, or as one in which the owner has suffered a mere diminution in value of the tract as a whole. The answer to this difficult question may lie in how the owner's reasonable expectations have been shaped by the State's law of property — i.e., whether and to what degree the State's law has accorded legal recognition and protection to the particular interest in land with respect to which the takings claimant alleges a diminution in (or elimination of) value. In any event, we avoid this difficulty in the present case, since the "interest in land" that Lucas has pleaded (a fee simple interest) is an estate with a rich tradition of protection at common law, and since the South Carolina Court of Common Pleas found that the *Beachfront Management Act* left each of Lucas's beachfront lots without economic value.

David Lucas's lots and surrounding beachfront. Photo courtesy of William A. Fischel.

simply "adjusting the benefits and burdens of economic life," *Penn Central Transp. Co.*, 438 U.S., at 124, in a manner that secures an "average reciprocity of advantage" to everyone concerned. *Pennsylvania Coal Co. v. Mahon*, 260 U.S., at 415. And the functional basis for permitting the government, by regulation, to affect property values without compensation — that "Government hardly could go on if to some extent values incident to property could not be diminished without paying for every such change in the general law," *id.* at 413 — does not apply to the relatively rare situations where the government has deprived a landowner of all economically beneficial uses.

On the other side of the balance, affirmatively supporting a compensation requirement, is the fact that regulations that leave the owner of land without economically beneficial or productive options for its use — typically, as here, by requiring land to be left substantially in its natural state — carry with them a heightened risk that private property is being pressed into some form of public service under the guise of mitigating serious public harm. The many statutes on the books, both state and federal, that provide for the use of eminent domain to impose servitudes on private scenic lands preventing developmental uses, or to acquire such lands altogether, suggest the practical equivalence in this setting of negative regulation and appropriation.

We think, in short, that there are good reasons for our frequently expressed belief that when the owner of real property has been called upon to sacrifice all economically beneficial uses in the name of the common good, that is, to leave his property economically idle, he has suffered a taking.

B

The trial court found Lucas's two beachfront lots to have been rendered valueless by respondent's enforcement of the coastal-zone construction ban. Under Lucas's theory of the case, which rested upon our "no economically viable use" statements, that finding entitled him to compensation. Lucas believed it unnecessary to take issue with either the purposes behind the *Beachfront Management Act,* or the means chosen by the South Carolina Legislature to effectuate those purposes. The South Carolina Supreme Court, however, thought otherwise. In its view, the *Beachfront Management Act* was no ordinary enactment, but involved an exercise of South Carolina's "police powers" to mitigate the harm to the public interest that petitioner's use of his land might occasion. By neglecting to dispute the findings enumerated in the Act or otherwise to challenge the legislature's purposes, petitioner "concede[d] that the beach/dune area of South Carolina's shores is an extremely valuable public resource; and that discouraging new construction in close proximity to the beach/dune area is necessary to prevent a great public harm." In the court's view, these concessions brought petitioner's challenge within a long line of this Court's cases sustaining against Due Process and Takings Clause challenges the State's use of its "police powers" to enjoin a property owner from activities akin to public nuisances. *See Mugler v. Kansas,* 123 U.S. 623 (1887) (law prohibiting manufacture of alcoholic beverages); *Hadacheck v. Sebastian,* 239 U.S. 394 (1915) (law barring operation of brick mill in residential area); *Miller v. Schoene,* 276 U.S. 272 (1928) (order to destroy diseased cedar trees to prevent infection of nearby orchards); *Goldblatt v. Hempstead,* 369 U.S. 590 (1962) (law effectively preventing continued operation of quarry in residential area).

It is correct that many of our prior opinions have suggested that "harmful or noxious uses" of property may be proscribed by government regulation without the requirement of compensation. For a number of reasons, however, we think the South Carolina Supreme Court was too quick to conclude that that principle decides the present case. The "harmful or noxious uses" principle was the Court's early attempt to describe in theoretical terms why government may, consistent with the Takings Clause, affect property values by regulation without incurring an obligation to compensate — a reality we nowadays acknowledge explicitly with respect to the full scope of the State's police power. We made this very point in *Penn Central Transportation Co.,* where, in the course of sustaining New York City's landmarks preservation program against a takings challenge, we rejected the petitioner's suggestion that *Mugler* and the cases following it were premised on, and thus limited by, some objective conception of "noxiousness":

> [T]he uses in issue in *Hadacheck, Miller,* and *Goldblatt* were perfectly lawful in themselves. They involved no "blameworthiness, . . . moral wrongdoing or conscious act of dangerous risk-taking which induce[d society] to shift the cost to a pa[rt]icular individual." Sax, *Takings and the Police Power,* 74 Yale L.J. 36, 50 (1964). These cases are better understood as resting not on any supposed "noxious" quality of the prohibited uses but rather on the ground that the restrictions were reasonably related to the implementation of a policy — not unlike historic preservation — expected to produce a widespread public benefit and applicable to all similarly situated property. 438 U.S., at 133-34 n.30.

"Harmful or noxious use" analysis was, in other words, simply the progenitor of our more contemporary statements that "land-use regulation does not effect a taking if it 'substantially advance[s] legitimate state interests.'" *Nollan, supra,* at 834.

The transition from our early focus on control of "noxious" uses to our contemporary understanding of the broad realm within which government may regulate without compensation was an easy one, since the distinction between "harm-preventing" and "benefit-conferring" regulation is often in the eye of the beholder. It is quite possible, for example, to describe in either fashion the ecological, economic, and aesthetic concerns that inspired the South Carolina legislature in the present case. One could say that imposing a servitude on Lucas's land is necessary in order to prevent his use of it from "harming" South Carolina's ecological resources; or, instead, in order to achieve the "benefits" of an ecological preserve. *Compare, e.g., Claridge v. New Hampshire Wetlands Board,* 485 A.2d 287, 292 (N.H. 1984) (owner may, without compensation, be barred from filling wetlands because landfilling would deprive adjacent coastal habitats and marine fisheries of ecological support), *with, e.g., Bartlett v. Zoning Comm'n of Old Lyme,* 282 A.2d 907, 910 (Conn. 1971) (owner barred from filling tidal marshland must be compensated, despite municipality's "laudable" goal of "preserv[ing] marshlands from encroachment or destruction"). Whether one or the other of the competing characterizations will come to one's lips in a particular case depends primarily upon one's evaluation of the worth of competing uses of real estate. A given restraint will be seen as mitigating "harm" to the adjacent parcels or securing a "benefit" for them, depending upon the observer's evaluation of the relative importance of the use that the restraint favors. Whether Lucas's construction of single-family residences on his parcels should be described as bringing "harm" to South Carolina's adjacent ecological resources thus depends principally upon whether the describer believes that the State's use interest in nurturing those resources is so important that any competing adjacent use must yield.[25]

When it is understood that "prevention of harmful use" was merely our early formulation of the police power justification necessary to sustain (without compensation) any regulatory diminution in value; and that the distinction between regulation that "prevents harmful use" and that which "confers benefits" is difficult, if not impossible, to discern on an objective, value-free basis; it becomes self-evident that noxious-use logic cannot serve as a touchstone to distinguish regulatory "takings" — which require compensation — from regulatory deprivations that do not require compensation. A fortiori the legislature's recitation of a noxious-use justification cannot be the basis for departing from our categorical rule that total regulatory takings must be compensated. If it were, departure would virtually always be allowed. The South Carolina Supreme Court's approach would essentially nullify *Mahon*'s affirmation of limits to the noncompensable exercise of the police power. Our cases provide no support for this: None of them that employed the logic of "harmful use" prevention to sustain a regu-

25. In Justice Blackmun's view, even with respect to regulations that deprive an owner of all developmental or economically beneficial land uses, the test for required compensation is whether the legislature has recited a harm-preventing justification for its action. Since such a justification can be formulated in practically every case, this amounts to a test of whether the legislature has a stupid staff. We think the Takings Clause requires courts to do more than insist upon artful harm-preventing characterizations.

lation involved an allegation that the regulation wholly eliminated the value of the claimant's land.

Where the State seeks to sustain regulation that deprives land of all economically beneficial use, we think it may resist compensation only if the logically antecedent inquiry into the nature of the owner's estate shows that the proscribed use interests were not part of his title to begin with. This accords, we think, with our "takings" jurisprudence, which has traditionally been guided by the understandings of our citizens regarding the content of, and the State's power over, the "bundle of rights" that they acquire when they obtain title to property. It seems to us that the property owner necessarily expects the uses of his property to be restricted, from time to time, by various measures newly enacted by the State in legitimate exercise of its police powers; "[a]s long recognized, some values are enjoyed under an implied limitation and must yield to the police power." *Pennsylvania Coal Co. v. Mahon*, 260 U.S., at 413. And in the case of personal property, by reason of the State's traditionally high degree of control over commercial dealings, he ought to be aware of the possibility that new regulation might even render his property economically worthless (at least if the property's only economically productive use is sale or manufacture for sale), *see Andrus v. Allard*, 444 U.S. 51, 66-67 (1979) (prohibition on sale of eagle feathers). In the case of land, however, we think the notion pressed by the Council that title is somehow held subject to the "implied limitation" that the State may subsequently eliminate all economically valuable use is inconsistent with the historical compact recorded in the Takings Clause that has become part of our constitutional culture.[26]

Where "permanent physical occupation" of land is concerned, we have refused to allow the government to decree it anew (without compensation), no matter how weighty the asserted "public interests" involved — though we assuredly would permit the government to assert a permanent easement that was a pre-existing limitation upon the landowner's title. *Compare Scranton v. Wheeler*, 179 U.S. 141, 163 (1900) (interests of "riparian owner in the submerged lands . . . bordering on a public navigable water" held subject to Government's navigational servitude), *with Kaiser Aetna v. United States*, 444 U.S., at 178-80 (imposition of navigational servitude on marina created and rendered navigable at private expense held to constitute a taking). We

26. After accusing us of "launch[ing] a missile to kill a mouse," Justice Blackmun expends a good deal of throw-weight of his own upon a noncombatant, arguing that our description of the "understanding" of land ownership that informs the Takings Clause is not supported by early American experience. That is largely true, but entirely irrelevant. The practices of the States prior to incorporation of the Takings and Just Compensation Clauses, *see Chicago, B. & Q. R. Co. v. Chicago*, 166 U.S. 226 (1897) — which, as Justice Blackmun acknowledges, occasionally included outright physical appropriation of land without compensation — were out of accord with any plausible interpretation of those provisions. Justice Blackmun is correct that early constitutional theorists did not believe the Takings Clause embraced regulations of property at all, but even he does not suggest (explicitly, at least) that we renounce the Court's contrary conclusion in *Mahon*. Since the text of the Clause can be read to encompass regulatory as well as physical deprivations (in contrast to the text originally proposed by Madison) ("No person shall be . . . obliged to relinquish his property, where it may be necessary for public use, without a just compensation"), we decline to do so as well.

believe similar treatment must be accorded confiscatory regulations, *i.e.*, regulations that prohibit all economically beneficial use of land: Any limitation so severe cannot be newly legislated or decreed (without compensation), but must inhere in the title itself, in the restrictions that background principles of the State's law of property and nuisance already place upon land ownership. A law or decree with such an effect must, in other words, do no more than duplicate the result that could have been achieved in the courts — by adjacent landowners (or other uniquely affected persons) under the State's law of private nuisance, or by the State under its complementary power to abate nuisances that affect the public generally, or otherwise.[27]

On this analysis, the owner of a lake bed, for example, would not be entitled to compensation when he is denied the requisite permit to engage in a landfilling operation that would have the effect of flooding others' land. Nor the corporate owner of a nuclear generating plant, when it is directed to remove all improvements from its land upon discovery that the plant sits astride an earthquake fault. Such regulatory action may well have the effect of eliminating the land's only economically productive use, but it does not proscribe a productive use that was previously permissible under relevant property and nuisance principles. The use of these properties for what are now expressly prohibited purposes was always unlawful, and (subject to other constitutional limitations) it was open to the State at any point to make the implication of those background principles of nuisance and property law explicit. In light of our traditional resort to "existing rules or understandings that stem from an independent source such as state law" to define the range of interests that qualify for protection as "property" under the Fifth (and Fourteenth) amendments, this recognition that the Takings Clause does not require compensation when an owner is barred from putting land to a use that is proscribed by those "existing rules or understandings" is surely unexceptional. When, however, a regulation that declares "off-limits" all economically productive or beneficial uses of land goes beyond what the relevant background principles would dictate, compensation must be paid to sustain it.[28]

The "total taking" inquiry we require today will ordinarily entail (as the application of state nuisance law ordinarily entails) analysis of, among other things, the degree of harm to public lands and resources, or adjacent private property, posed by the claimant's proposed activities, the social value of the claimant's activities and their suitability to the locality in question, and the relative ease with which the alleged harm can be avoided through measures taken by the claimant and the government (or adjacent private landowners) alike. The fact that a particular use has long been engaged in by

27. The principal "otherwise" that we have in mind is litigation absolving the State (or private parties) of liability for the destruction of "real and personal property, in cases of actual necessity, to prevent the spreading of a fire" or to forestall other grave threats to the lives and property of others. *Bowditch v. Boston*, 101 U.S. 16, 18-19 (1880).

28. Of course, the State may elect to rescind its regulation and thereby avoid having to pay compensation for a permanent deprivation. *See First English Evangelical Lutheran Church of Glendale v. Cnty. of Los Angeles*, 482 U.S. 304, 321 (1987). But "where the [regulation has] already worked a taking of all use of property, no subsequent action by the government can relieve it of the duty to provide compensation for the period during which the taking was effective." *Id.*

similarly situated owners ordinarily imports a lack of any common-law prohibition (though changed circumstances or new knowledge may make what was previously permissible no longer so). So also does the fact that other landowners, similarly situated, are permitted to continue the use denied to the claimant.

It seems unlikely that common-law principles would have prevented the erection of any habitable or productive improvements on petitioner's land; they rarely support prohibition of the "essential use" of land. The question, however, is one of state law to be dealt with on remand. We emphasize that to win its case South Carolina must do more than proffer the legislature's declaration that the uses Lucas desires are inconsistent with the public interest, or the conclusory assertion that they violate a common-law maxim such as *sic utere tuo ut alienum non laedas*. As we have said, a "State, by *ipse dixit*, may not transform private property into public property without compensation." *Webb's Fabulous Pharmacies, Inc. v. Beckwith*, 449 U.S. 155, 164 (1980). Instead, as it would be required to do if it sought to restrain Lucas in a common-law action for public nuisance, South Carolina must identify background principles of nuisance and property law that prohibit the uses he now intends in the circumstances in which the property is presently found. Only on this showing can the State fairly claim that, in proscribing all such beneficial uses, the *Beachfront Management Act* is taking nothing.[29]

The judgment is reversed and the cause remanded for proceedings not inconsistent with this opinion.

Justice ANTHONY M. KENNEDY, concurring in the judgment.

The South Carolina Court of Common Pleas found that petitioner's real property has been rendered valueless by the State's regulation. The finding appears to presume that the property has no significant market value or resale potential. This is a curious finding, and I share the reservations of some of my colleagues about a finding that a beach front lot loses all value because of a development restriction. While the Supreme Court of South Carolina on remand need not consider the case subject to this constraint, we must accept the finding as entered below. Accepting the finding as entered, it follows that petitioner is entitled to invoke the line of cases discussing regulations that deprive real property of all economic value.

The finding of no value must be considered under the Takings Clause by reference to the owner's reasonable, investment-backed expectations. The Takings Clause, while conferring substantial protection on property owners, does not eliminate the police power of the State to enact limitations on the use of their property. The rights

29. Justice Blackmun decries our reliance on background nuisance principles at least in part because he believes those principles to be as manipulable as we find the "harm prevention benefit"/ "conferral" dichotomy. There is no doubt some leeway in a court's interpretation of what existing state law permits — but not remotely as much, we think, as in a legislative crafting of the reasons for its confiscatory regulation. We stress that an affirmative decree eliminating all economically beneficial uses may be defended only if an objectively reasonable application of relevant precedents would exclude those beneficial uses in the circumstances in which the land is presently found.

conferred by the Takings Clause and the police power of the State may coexist without conflict. Property is bought and sold, investments are made, subject to the State's power to regulate. Where a taking is alleged from regulations which deprive the property of all value, the test must be whether the deprivation is contrary to reasonable, investment-backed expectations.

There is an inherent tendency towards circularity in this synthesis, of course; for if the owner's reasonable expectations are shaped by what courts allow as a proper exercise of governmental authority, property tends to become what courts say it is. Some circularity must be tolerated in these matters, however, as it is in other spheres. The definition, moreover, is not circular in its entirety. The expectations protected by the Constitution are based on objective rules and customs that can be understood as reasonable by all parties involved.

In my view, reasonable expectations must be understood in light of the whole of our legal tradition. The common law of nuisance is too narrow a confine for the exercise of regulatory power in a complex and interdependent society. The State should not be prevented from enacting new regulatory initiatives in response to changing conditions, and courts must consider all reasonable expectations whatever their source. The Takings Clause does not require a static body of state property law; it protects private expectations to ensure private investment. I agree with the Court that nuisance prevention accords with the most common expectations of property owners who face regulation, but I do not believe this can be the sole source of state authority to impose severe restrictions. Coastal property may present such unique concerns for a fragile land system that the State can go further in regulating its development and use than the common law of nuisance might otherwise permit.

The Supreme Court of South Carolina erred, in my view, by reciting the general purposes for which the state regulations were enacted without a determination that they were in accord with the owner's reasonable expectations and therefore sufficient to support a severe restriction on specific parcels of property. The promotion of tourism, for instance, ought not to suffice to deprive specific property of all value without a corresponding duty to compensate. Furthermore, the means as well as the ends of regulation must accord with the owner's reasonable expectations. Here, the State did not act until after the property had been zoned for individual lot development and most other parcels had been improved, throwing the whole burden of the regulation on the remaining lots. This too must be measured in the balance.

Justice HARRY A. BLACKMUN, dissenting.

Today the Court launches a missile to kill a mouse. The Court creates its new taking jurisprudence based on the trial court's finding that the property had lost all economic value. This finding is almost certainly erroneous. Petitioner still can enjoy other attributes of ownership, such as the right to exclude others, "one of the most essential sticks in the bundle of rights that are commonly characterized as property." *Kaiser Aetna v. United States*, 444 U.S. 164, 176 (1979). Petitioner can picnic, swim, camp in a tent, or live on the property in a movable trailer. State courts frequently have recognized that land has economic value where the only residual economic uses are recreation and camping. Petitioner also retains the right to alienate the land, which would have value for neighbors and for those prepared to enjoy proximity to the ocean without a house.

The Court [has] create[d] a new scheme for regulations that eliminate all economic value. From now on, there is a categorical rule finding these regulations to be a taking unless the use they prohibit is a background common-law nuisance or property principle.

This Court repeatedly has recognized the ability of government, in certain circumstances, to regulate property without compensation no matter how adverse the financial effect on the owner may be. More than a century ago, the Court explicitly upheld the right of States to prohibit uses of property injurious to public health, safety, or welfare without paying compensation: "A prohibition simply upon the use of property for purposes that are declared, by valid legislation, to be injurious to the health, morals, or safety of the community, cannot, in any just sense, be deemed a taking or an appropriation of property." *Mugler v. Kansas*, 123 U.S. 623, 668-669 (1887). On this basis, the Court upheld an ordinance effectively prohibiting operation of a previously lawful brewery, although the "establishments will become of no value as property." *Id.* at 664.

Mugler was only the beginning in a long line of cases. In *Powell v. Pennsylvania*, 127 U.S. 678 (1888), the Court upheld legislation prohibiting the manufacture of oleomargarine, despite the owner's allegation that "if prevented from continuing it, the value of his property employed therein would be entirely lost and he be deprived of the means of livelihood." *Id.* at 682. In *Hadacheck v. Sebastian*, 239 U.S. 394 (1915), the Court upheld an ordinance prohibiting a brickyard, although the owner had made excavations on the land that prevented it from being utilized for any purpose but a brickyard. In *Miller v. Schoene*, 276 U.S. 272 (1928), the Court held that the Fifth Amendment did not require Virginia to pay compensation to the owner of cedar trees ordered destroyed to prevent a disease from spreading to nearby apple orchards. The "preferment of [the public interest] over the property interest of the individual, to the extent even of its destruction, is one of the distinguishing characteristics of every exercise of the police power which affects property." *Id.* at 280.

More recently, in *Goldblatt v. Hempstead*, 369 U.S. 590 (1962), the Court upheld a town regulation that barred continued operation of an existing sand and gravel operation in order to protect public safety. "Although a comparison of values before and after is relevant," the Court stated, "it is by no means conclusive." *Id.* at 594. In *First Lutheran Church v. Los Angeles County*, 482 U.S. 304 (1987), the owner alleged that a floodplain ordinance had deprived it of "all use" of the property. The Court remanded the case for consideration whether, even if the ordinance denied the owner all use, it could be justified as a safety measure.[30] And in *Keystone Bituminous Coal [Association v. DeBenedictis*, 480 U.S. 470 (1970)], the Court summarized over 100 years of

30. On remand, the California court found no taking in part because the zoning regulation "involves this highest of public interests — the prevention of death and injury." *First Lutheran Church v. Los Angeles*, 258 Cal. Rptr. 893 (Ct. App. 1989), *cert. denied*, 493 U.S. 1056 (1990).

precedent: "the Court has repeatedly upheld regulations that destroy or adversely affect real property interests." 480 U.S. at 489, n.18.

These cases rest on the principle that the State has full power to prohibit an owner's use of property if it is harmful to the public. "[S]ince no individual has a right to use his property so as to create a nuisance or otherwise harm others, the State has not 'taken' anything when it asserts its power to enjoin the nuisance-like activity." *Keystone Bituminous Coal*, 480 U.S., at 491, n.20. It would make no sense under this theory to suggest that an owner has a constitutionally protected right to harm others, if only he makes the proper showing of economic loss.

Ultimately even the Court cannot embrace the full implications of its *per se* rule: it eventually agrees that there cannot be a categorical rule for a taking based on economic value that wholly disregards the public need asserted. Instead, the Court decides that it will permit a State to regulate all economic value only if the State prohibits uses that would not be permitted under "background principles of nuisance and property law."

Until today, the Court explicitly had rejected the contention that the government's power to act without paying compensation turns on whether the prohibited activity is a common-law nuisance. The brewery closed in *Mugler* itself was not a common-law nuisance, and the Court specifically stated that it was the role of the legislature to determine what measures would be appropriate for the protection of public health and safety. In upholding the state action in *Miller*, the Court found it unnecessary to "weigh with nicety the question whether the infected cedars constitute a nuisance according to common law; or whether they may be so declared by statute." 276 U.S., at 280. Instead the Court has relied in the past, as the South Carolina Court has done here, on legislative judgments of what constitutes a harm.

The Court rejects the notion that the State always can prohibit uses it deems a harm to the public without granting compensation because "the distinction between 'harm-preventing' and 'benefit-conferring' regulation is often in the eye of the beholder." Since the characterization will depend "primarily upon one's evaluation of the worth of competing uses of real estate," the Court decides a legislative judgment of this kind no longer can provide the desired "objective, value-free basis" for upholding a regulation. The Court, however, fails to explain how its proposed common law alternative escapes the same trap.

The threshold inquiry for imposition of the Court's new rule, "deprivation of all economically valuable use," itself cannot be determined objectively. As the Court admits, whether the owner has been deprived of all economic value of his property will depend on how "property" is defined. The "composition of the denominator in our 'deprivation' fraction," is the dispositive inquiry. Yet there is no "objective" way to define what that denominator should be. "We have long understood that any land-use regulation can be characterized as the 'total' deprivation of an aptly defined entitlement. Alternatively, the same regulation can always be characterized as a mere 'partial' withdrawal from full, unencumbered ownership of the landholding affected by the regulation." Michelman, *Takings, 1987*, 88 Colum. L. Rev. 1600, 1614 (1988).

Even more perplexing, however, is the Court's reliance on common-law principles of nuisance in its quest for a value-free taking jurisprudence. In determining what is a nuisance at common law, state courts make exactly the decision that the Court finds so troubling when made by the South Carolina General Assembly today: they determine whether the use is harmful.

Common-law public and private nuisance law is simply a determination whether a particular use causes harm. There is nothing magical in the reasoning of judges long dead. They determined a harm in the same way as state judges and legislatures do today. If judges in the 18th and 19th centuries can distinguish a harm from a benefit, why not judges in the 20th century, and if judges can, why not legislators? There simply is no reason to believe that new interpretations of the hoary common law nuisance doctrine will be particularly "objective" or "value-free." Once one abandons the level of generality of *sic utere tuo ut alienum non laedas*, one searches in vain, I think, for anything resembling a principle in the common law of nuisance.

Finally, the Court justifies its new rule that the legislature may not deprive a property owner of the only economically valuable use of his land, even if the legislature finds it to be a harmful use, because such action is not part of the "long recognized" "understandings of our citizens." These "understandings" permit such regulation only if the use is a nuisance under the common law. Any other course is "inconsistent with the historical compact recorded in the Takings Clause." It is not clear from the Court's opinion where our "historical compact" or "citizens' understanding" comes from, but it does not appear to be history.

The principle that the State should compensate individuals for property taken for public use was not widely established in America at the time of the Revolution. "The colonists . . . inherited . . . a concept of property which permitted extensive regulation of the use of that property for the public benefit — regulation that could even go so far as to deny all productive use of the property to the owner if, as Coke himself stated, the regulation 'extends to the public benefit . . . for this is for the public, and every one hath benefit by it.'" F. Bosselman, D. Callies & J. Banta, *The Taking Issue* 80-81 (1973), quoting *The Case of the King's Prerogative in Saltpetre*, 12 Co. Rep. 12-13 (1606).

Although, prior to the adoption of the Bill of Rights, America was replete with land use regulations describing which activities were considered noxious and forbidden, the Fifth Amendment's Taking Clause originally did not extend to regulations of property, whatever the effect. Most state courts agreed with this narrow interpretation of a taking. Even when courts began to consider that regulation in some situations could constitute a taking, they continued to uphold bans on particular uses without paying compensation, notwithstanding the economic impact, under the rationale that no one can obtain a vested right to injure or endanger the public.

Nor does history indicate any common-law limit on the State's power to regulate harmful uses even to the point of destroying all economic value. Nothing in the discussions in Congress concerning the Taking Clause indicates that the Clause was limited by the common-law nuisance doctrine. In short, I find no clear and accepted "historical compact" or "understanding of our citizens" justifying the Court's new taking doctrine.

Justice JOHN PAUL STEVENS, dissenting.

The Court's new [categorical] rule is wholly arbitrary. A landowner whose property is diminished in value 95% recovers nothing, while an owner whose property is diminished 100% recovers the land's full value. Moreover, because of the elastic nature of property rights, the Court's new rule will also prove unsound in practice. In response to the rule, courts may define "property" broadly and only rarely find regulations to effect total takings.

On the other hand, developers and investors may market specialized estates to take advantage of the Court's new rule. The smaller the estate, the more likely that a regulatory change will effect a total taking. Thus, an investor may, for example, purchase the right to build a multi-family home on a specific lot, with the result that a zoning regulation that allows only single-family homes would render the investor's property interest "valueless." In short, the categorical rule will likely have one of two effects: Either courts will alter the definition of the "denominator" in the takings "fraction," rendering the Court's categorical rule meaningless, or investors will manipulate the relevant property interests, giving the Court's rule sweeping effect. To my mind, neither of these results is desirable or appropriate, and both are distortions of our takings jurisprudence.

Like many bright-line rules, the categorical rule established in this case is only "categorical" for a page or two in the U.S. Reports. No sooner does the Court state that "total regulatory takings must be compensated," than it quickly establishes an exception to that rule. The exception provides that a regulation that renders property valueless is not a taking if it prohibits uses of property that were not "previously permissible under relevant property and nuisance principles." The Court's holding today effectively freezes the State's common law, denying the legislature much of its traditional power to revise the law governing the rights and uses of property. Arresting the development of the common law is not only a departure from our prior decisions; it is also profoundly unwise. The human condition is one of constant learning and evolution — both moral and practical. Legislatures implement that new learning; in doing so they must often revise the definition of property and the rights of property owners. Thus, when the Nation came to understand that slavery was morally wrong and mandated the emancipation of all slaves, it, in effect, redefined "property." On a lesser scale, our ongoing self-education produces similar changes in the rights of property owners: New appreciation of the significance of endangered species, the importance of wetlands, and the vulnerability of coastal lands, shapes our evolving understandings of property rights.

Of course, some legislative redefinitions of property will effect a taking and must be compensated — but it certainly cannot be the case that every movement away from common law does so. There is no reason, and less sense, in such an absolute rule. We live in a world in which changes in the economy and the environment occur with increasing frequency and importance. If it was wise a century ago to allow Government "the largest legislative discretion" to deal with "the special exigencies of the moment," *Mugler*, 123 U.S., at 669, it is imperative to do so today. The rule that should govern a decision in a case of this kind should focus on the future, not the past.[31]

[Justice David H. Souter stated that he would have dismissed the writ of certiorari as improvidently granted. The factual conclusion of the trial court—that Lucas had been deprived of any economically viable use of his property—was "questionable" but was not reviewed by the state supreme court; thus it could not be reviewed by the Supreme Court.]

Palazzolo v. Rhode Island

533 U.S. 606 (2001)

Map: Atlantic Avenue and Winnapaug Pond, Westerly, Rhode Island

Anthony Palazzolo was denied permits to develop his waterfront property in Rhode Island by a state agency charged with enforcing laws regulating construction on the coast. After several unsuccessful attempts to obtain approval to fill in his coastal marshlands and develop 74 homes there, Palazzolo sued the State of Rhode Island, seeking $3,150,000 in compensation for a taking of his property. He argued, on the authority of *Lucas*, that he had been denied all economically viable use of his property because it appeared that the Rhode Island Coastal Resources Management Council would not allow him to build anything on the waterfront property. It did appear that the agency would allow him to develop the upland part of the property away from the water; that development was worth $200,000.

The Rhode Island Supreme Court rejected his takings claim for three reasons. First, the court held that his claim was not ripe for decision; the state agency had merely rejected several development proposals and had not issued a final ruling that clearly denied any right to develop the marshland area. Second, the court held that Palazzolo had not been deprived of all economic value because he could develop the upland property away from the water. Third, the court noted that at the time Palazzolo acquired title to the property from the prior owner (a corporation in which he had held shares and eventually became the sole shareholder), the law regulating coastal development was already in place. The court held that Palazzolo could have no "reasonable" investment-backed expectations at the time he acquired title if existing laws at the time he acquired title made his intended use of the property illegal. In effect,

31. Even measured in terms of efficiency, the Court's rule is unsound. The Court today effectively establishes a form of insurance against certain changes in land-use regulations. Like other forms of insurance, the Court's rule creates a "moral hazard" and inefficiencies: In the face of uncertainty about changes in the law, developers will overinvest, safe in the knowledge that if the law changes adversely, they will be entitled to compensation. *See generally* Farber, *Economic Analysis and Just Compensation*, 12 Int'l Rev. of Law & Econ. 125 (1992).

the state court created a safe haven rule that would have protected the state from any takings claim by an owner who obtained title after a regulatory law restricting the use of that property came into effect.

The Supreme Court reversed the first and third findings and reserved judgment on the second. Over the objections of three dissenters, the Court found, first, that the evidence was sufficiently clear that the coastal agency would not allow any of the marshland to be filled in; thus the scope of the permitted development was clear and the takings claim was ripe for decision. *See also MacDonald, Sommer & Frates v. Yolo County*, 477 U.S. 340, 351 (1986); *Williamson County Regional Planning Commission v. Hamilton Bank of Johnson City*, 473 U.S. 172 (1985) (both holding that a takings claim is not ripe for decision unless the state has made a final decision on the scope of the permitted development).

Second, the Supreme Court refused to define the constitutional standard for determining whether Palazzolo had been denied all economically viable use of his land. Because it appeared that he could develop some of his land, but not all of it, the Court was confronted with the "denominator" question reserved in *Lucas*. Was the development ban a 100 percent taking of the portion of his land that could not be developed or only a partial taking of his whole parcel (the upland land that could be developed combined with the marshland that could not be developed)? Palazzolo had argued that it was irrelevant that he was allowed to develop 18 acres in the upland part of his property; because the wetlands law prevented him from building on his substantial waterfront property, that law had effectively converted a substantial portion of his property into a "nature reserve," denying him 100 percent of the value of that land. In deciding whether this was a partial taking or a total taking, he argued that the relevant denominator was the developable tract or some subset of his whole property. The fact that he was allowed to develop part of his property did not alter the fact that he was denied the right to develop most of his land; the land he could not develop had been deprived of all economically viable use. The Supreme Court found that Palazzolo had effectively waived this argument below. However, Justice Kennedy observed that "[s]ome of our cases indicate that the extent of deprivation effected by a regulatory action is measured against the value of the parcel as a whole, but we have at times expressed discomfort with the logic of this rule." 533 U.S. at 631.

Third, the Supreme Court reversed the ruling that states are insulated from taking claims merely because an owner has acquired title after a regulatory law went into effect. The fact that the owner took title with notice of the regulation did not, by itself, immunize the state from facing a challenge to the regulation as a taking of property. Justice Kennedy explained, *id.* at 627-630:

> The right to improve property, of course, is subject to the reasonable exercise of state authority, including the enforcement of valid zoning and land-use restrictions. The Takings Clause, however, in certain circumstances allows a landowner to assert that a particular exercise of the State's regulatory power is so unreasonable or onerous as to compel compensation. Just as a prospective enactment, such as a new zoning ordinance, can limit the value of land without effecting a taking because it can be understood as reasonable by all concerned, other enactments are unreasonable and do not

> become less so through passage of time or title. Were we to accept the State's rule, the postenactment transfer of title would absolve the State of its obligation to defend any action restricting land use, no matter how extreme or unreasonable. A State would be allowed, in effect, to put an expiration date on the Takings Clause. This ought not to be the rule. Future generations, too, have a right to challenge unreasonable limitations on the use and value of land.
>
> Nor does the justification of notice take into account the effect on owners at the time of enactment, who are prejudiced as well. Should an owner attempt to challenge a new regulation, but not survive the process of ripening his or her claim (which, as this case demonstrates, will often take years), under the proposed rule the right to compensation may not be asserted by an heir or successor, and so may not be asserted at all. The State's rule would work a critical alteration to the nature of property, as the newly regulated landowner is stripped of the ability to transfer the interest which was possessed prior to the regulation. The State may not by this means secure a windfall for itself.
>
> We have no occasion to consider the precise circumstances when a legislative enactment can be deemed a background principle of state law or whether those circumstances are present here. It suffices to say that a regulation that otherwise would be unconstitutional absent compensation is not transformed into a background principle of the State's law by mere virtue of the passage of title.

Because the lower court had found that this was not a 100 percent taking of the property's value, the *Lucas* rule did not apply. However, the general multifactor *Penn Central* test did apply and the Supreme Court remanded the case to be addressed under that standard.

Justice O'Connor concurred, agreeing that the acquisition of title after a regulatory law was passed did not protect the state from a takings claim. She explained, *id.* at 632-633 (O'Connor, J., concurring):

> The more difficult question is what role the temporal relationship between regulatory enactment and title acquisition plays in a proper *Penn Central* analysis. Today's holding does not mean that the timing of the regulation's enactment relative to the acquisition of title is immaterial to the *Penn Central* analysis. Indeed, it would be just as much error to expunge this consideration from the takings inquiry as it would be to accord it exclusive significance. Our polestar instead remains the principles set forth in *Penn Central* itself and our other cases that govern partial regulatory takings. Under these cases, interference with investment-backed expectations is one of a number of factors that a court must examine. Further, the regulatory regime in place at the time the claimant acquires the property at issue helps to shape the reasonableness of those expectations.
>
> If investment-backed expectations are given exclusive significance in the *Penn Central* analysis and existing regulations dictate the reasonableness of those expectations in every instance, then the State wields far too much power to redefine property rights upon passage of title. On the other hand, if existing regulations do nothing to inform the analysis, then some property owners may reap windfalls and an important indicium of fairness is lost. As I understand it, our decision today does not remove the regulatory backdrop against which an owner takes title to property from the purview of the *Penn Central* inquiry. It simply restores balance to that inquiry. Courts properly consider the effect of existing regulations under the rubric of investment-backed expectations

> in determining whether a compensable taking has occurred. As before, the salience of these facts cannot be reduced to any "set formula." The temptation to adopt what amount to *per se* rules in either direction must be resisted. The Takings Clause requires careful examination and weighing of all the relevant circumstances in this context.

Justice Scalia concurred but disagreed strongly with Justice O'Connor on this point, *id.* at 636 (Scalia, J., concurring):

> In my view, the fact that a restriction existed at the time the purchaser took title (other than a restriction forming part of the "background principles of the State's law of property and nuisance") should have no bearing upon the determination of whether the restriction is so substantial as to constitute a taking. The "investment-backed expectations" that the law will take into account do not include the assumed validity of a restriction that in fact deprives property of so much of its value as to be unconstitutional.

Justices Ginsburg, Souter, and Breyer dissented, disagreeing with the majority's conclusion that the state agency had come to a final ruling with regard to the extent of development permitted on the property.

On remand, the Rhode Island trial court found that development of Palazzolo's salt marsh land south of a shallow, tidal pond would constitute a public nuisance because it would inhibit the "valuable filtering system regarding water runoff containing pollutants and nitrogen from adjacent land." *Palazzolo v. State,* No. WM 88-0297, 2005 WL 1645974, at *3 (R.I. Super. Ct. 2005). The court also found that half of the property was below the mean high water line, making it tidal land subject to the public trust doctrine, which defines such lands as owned by the public and not subject to private development at all. Finally, the court found that although one upland site could be developed, almost no lower lots could ever have been profitably developed because of the extraordinary engineering costs involved in draining the site and preparing the site to support structures. Thus, there was no taking of property.

Tahoe-Sierra Preservation Council, Inc. v. Tahoe Regional Planning Agency

535 U.S. 302 (2002)

Map: Lake Tahoe, California

A regional planning agency placed a temporary moratorium on construction around Lake Tahoe. The moratorium officially lasted for 32 months, but a court injunction effectively extended the ban on construction for as much as 6 years. The construction ban was intended to allow the agency time to develop a plan to limit construction around the lake to prevent the loss of Lake Tahoe's "exceptional clarity." Unlike most lakes, Lake Tahoe lacked algae that obscures the water clarity; the district court found that undue development could change runoff patterns in a manner that would not only destroy this clarity, but that it would be impossible to fix for 700 years, if at all. Petitioners were owners of land around the lake who claimed that the temporary building moratorium took all economically viable use of their property for the period in which it was in effect and that this amounted to a categorical (although temporary) taking of their property for which they were entitled to compensation under the rule in *Lucas*.

The Court disagreed, refusing to find that a temporary building moratorium was a *per se* taking of property. Justice Stevens explained that, despite the attempts in *Loretto* and *Lucas* to develop some rules that could identify categorical takings, the Court has "'generally eschewed' any set formula" for identifying regulatory takings, instead engaging in "essentially *ad hoc*, factual inquiries." *Id.* at 326. "Indeed," wrote Justice Stevens, "we still resist the temptation to adopt *per se* rules in our cases involving partial regulatory takings, preferring to examine 'a number of factors' rather than a simple 'mathematically precise' formula." *Id.* The majority opinion went on to quote Justice O'Connor's concurring opinion in *Palazzolo* at some length, agreeing with her inclination to "resist[] the temptation to adopt what amount to *per se* rules in either direction." *Id.* at 321.

The Court acknowledged that a prior case, *First English Evangelical Lutheran Church of Glendale v. County of Los Angeles*, 482 U.S. 304 (1987), had held that owners are entitled to sue for compensation for temporary takings of their property. When a regulation is determined to be a taking, the government may either enforce the regulation and pay compensation for the loss of property rights or decide to forgo enforcing the regulation and pay compensation for the temporary loss of property rights during the time the regulation limited the use of the property. However, Justice Stevens explained that *First English* merely held that compensation should be paid when a taking is found; it did not hold that a temporary limit on construction necessarily constituted a taking.

The Court clarified that it meant what it said in *Lucas*: Only a 100 percent diminution in value of the property — a "complete elimination of value" — triggered the *Lucas* rule. *Id.* at 330. Any lesser deprivation of value is governed by the multifactor *Penn Central* test. *See also Lingle v. Chevron U.S.A.*, 544 U.S. 528, 538 (2005) (*Lucas* applies to regulations that "completely deprive an owner of *all* economically beneficial use of her property"). Because ownership extends over time as well as space, a temporary moratorium, by definition, does not result in a complete elimination of value, *id.* at 334-335:

> [T]he extreme categorical rule that any deprivation of all economic use, no matter how brief, constitutes a compensable taking surely cannot be sustained. [Such a rule] would apply to numerous "normal delays in obtaining building permits, changes in zoning ordinances, variances, and the like," as well as to orders temporarily prohibiting access to crime scenes, businesses that violate health codes, fire-damaged buildings, or other areas that we cannot now foresee. Such a rule would undoubtedly require changes in numerous practices that have long been considered permissible exercises of the police power. As Justice Holmes warned in *Mahon*, "government hardly could go on if to some extent values incident to property could not be diminished without paying for every such change in the general law." 260 U.S. at 413. A rule that required compensation for

> every delay in the use of property would render routine government processes prohibitively expensive or encourage hasty decisionmaking. Such an important change in the law should be the product of legislative rulemaking rather than adjudication.

Chief Justice Rehnquist dissented, along with Justices Scalia and Thomas. They argued that the development ban, as extended by court injunction, had actually lasted for six years and that such a long moratorium was not reasonably related to legitimate land use planning needs. The functional effect of the moratorium was to temporarily deny the owners all economically viable use of their land, *id.* at 348 (Rehnquist, C.J., dissenting):

> The regulation in *Lucas* was the "practical equivalence" of a long-term physical appropriation, *i.e.*, a condemnation, so the Fifth Amendment required compensation. The "practical equivalence," from the landowner's point of view, of a "temporary" ban on all economic use is a forced leasehold. For example, assume the following situation: Respondent is contemplating the creation of a National Park around Lake Tahoe to preserve its scenic beauty. Respondent decides to take a 6-year leasehold over petitioners' property, during which any human activity on the land would be prohibited, in order to prevent any further destruction to the area while it was deciding whether to request that the area be designated a National Park. Surely that leasehold would require compensation.

Notes and Questions

1. **Rules, standards, and the "denominator" problem.** The *Lucas* rule applies when an owner has been deprived of "economically viable use," but this seemingly bright line rule raises a variation on the denominator problem that first emerged in the debate between Justice Holmes and Justice Brandeis in *Mahon.* Consider a developer who seeks to develop 50 acres. Does a regulation prohibiting development of 5 acres constitute a 100 percent taking of the 5 acres or only a 10 percent taking of the 50 acres? Is the denominator 5 or 50? This can have a great deal of practical significance, because a regulation that falls within the *Lucas* rule is generally more vulnerable than one that is evaluated based on *Penn Central*'s *ad hoc* approach.

The Supreme Court has emphasized that the inquiry "must focus on 'the parcel as a whole,"' 535 U.S. at 327. But what does this mean? In *Loveladies Harbor, Inc. v. United States,* 28 F.3d 1171 (Fed. Cir. 1999), the Federal Circuit held that the courts must use a "flexible approach, designed to account for factual nuances" to determine the appropriate "denominator" for calculating whether a *Lucas* total deprivation has occurred. *See also Dunes W. Golf Club, LLC v. Town of Mount Pleasant,* 737 S.E.2d 601, 614-618 (S.C. 2013) (discussing the "Gordian Knot" of the denominator question).

One possibility is the "whole property" owned by the developer — in this case, the entire 50 acres. The trial judge on remand in *Palazzolo* used this measure: "This Justice finds that the denominator or 'parcel as a whole' is that property in which Palazzolo invested that is subject to the regulations." 2005 WL 1645974, at *3. Another possibility is the "developable tract" or the area that could have been developed under reasonable zoning laws — in this case the five acres. When air rights are at issue, the courts have consistently held that a height limit does not constitute a 100 percent taking of air rights over that limit; the denominator is the tract as a whole. However, the Federal Circuit has sometimes held that, in the context of wetlands regulations, the denominator is the developable tract. *Palm Beach Isles Associates v. United States*, 208 F.3d 1374 (Fed. Cir. 2000) (relevant parcel was a 50.7-acre tract out of an original 311.7-acre purchase); *Loveladies Harbor, Inc. v. United States, supra* (relevant parcel was a 12.5-acre tract out of an original 51-acre purchase). The Federal Circuit continues to vacillate on this issue. *Compare Norman v. United States*, 429 F.3d 1081, 1091 (Fed. Cir. 2005) (proper denominator is the entire 2,280 acres held for development purposes, not the individual parcels), *with Lost Tree Village Corp. v. United States*, 707 F.3d 1286, 1294 (Fed. Cir. 2013) (citing *Loveladies* and finding that an individual plat rather than the larger property originally purchased as one contiguous lot that included that plat, was the relevant parcel). Should the denominator be the individual lots that zoning and land use law allow to be separately developed? Which definition of the "denominator" is correct?

2. Background principles of property law. Many owners have brought inverse condemnation cases challenging the application of environmental protection statutes to their property. Many statutes designed to protect the environment also severely restrict the development of particular types of land, such as wetlands and habitats for endangered species. The courts have traditionally upheld these regulations, even when they have severely limited land development, by analogy to nuisance laws, which prevent owners from using their land in a way that will injure the community. *See, e.g., Gardner v. N.J. Pinelands Commission*, 593 A.2d 251 (N.J. 1991); *Presbytery of Seattle v. King County*, 787 P.2d 907 (Wash. 1990); *Just v. Marinette County*, 201 N.W.2d 761 (Wis. 1972). The Federal Circuit and the Court of Federal Claims have suggested or ruled that compensation is required when wetlands or endangered species act regulations have prevented all development of land. *Palm Beach Isles Associates v. United States*, 231 F.3d 1354 (Fed. Cir. 2000) (wetlands); *Laguna Gatuna, Inc. v. United States*, 50 Fed. Cl. 336 (2001) (*Clean Water Act* regulations); *Tulare Lake Basin Water Storage District v. United States*, 49 Fed. Cl. 313 (2001) (*Endangered Species Act*); *Florida Rock Industries, Inc. v. United States*, 45 Fed. Cl. 21 (1999) (wetlands).

The question in these cases is whether laws that deprive owners of "economically viable use" are constitutional because they "inhere in the title itself, in the restrictions that background principles of the State's law of property and nuisance already place upon land ownership background principles of the State's law of property and nuisance" and thus regulate conduct that was never part of the owner's title in the first place? On remand in *Palazzolo*, the court found that development of Palazzolo's salt marsh land south of a shallow, tidal pond would constitute a public nuisance because it would inhibit the "valuable filtering system regarding water runoff containing pollutants and nitrogen from adjacent land" and thus his property rights never included the power to engage in this proposed development. *Palazzolo v. State*, No. WM 88-0297, 2005 WL 1645974, at *3 (R.I. Super. Ct. 2005). In contrast, on remand in *Lucas*, the South Carolina Supreme Court held that construction of housing on the coast would not have constituted a public or private nuisance under the common law existing before the regulatory laws limited such development. *Lucas v. South Carolina Coastal Council*, 424 S.E.2d 484 (S.C. 1992).

Can "background principles" evolve? Justice Stevens, in his *Lucas* dissent, argued that the decision "effectively freezes the State's common law," but is there any reason why judges in evaluating common law nuisances cannot recognize new harms? In *Prah v. Maretti*, 321 N.W.2d 182 (Wis. 1982), the Wisconsin Supreme Court recognized that interference with solar panels can be a private nuisance, *see* Chapter 6, §3. Does this suggest that the harm principle is no longer relevant?

3. Public nuisance and legislative latitude to define "background principles." Legislatures have traditionally had wide latitude to define public nuisance in order to address harms that would not necessarily constitute private nuisances. In his *Lucas* concurrence and again in his majority opinion in *Palazzolo*, Justice Kennedy raised — but did not answer — the question whether and in what way a legislative enactment can become a "background principle" of a state's law of property. One way this may happen is when regulatory regimes become widespread enough that they become part of the reasonable expectations of most owners. Comprehensive zoning codes were considered innovative at the time the Supreme Court validated that approach to regulating property in *Village of Euclid v. Ambler Realty Co.*, 272 U.S. 365 (1926). Today few owners would question the idea that zoning is not a part of the background principles of every state. *Cf. Tahoe-Sierra Preservation Council, Inc. v. Tahoe Regional Planning Agency*, 535 U.S. 302, 351 (2002) (Rehnquist, C.J., dissenting) (noting that legislative zoning regulations are background principles of property law).

Public nuisance has also become increasingly important in the context of criminal activity, which again raises the question of the latitude allowed for abating public nuisances without compensation. In *City of Seattle v. McCoy*, 4 P.3d 159 (Wash. Ct. App. 2000), the court found a regulatory taking when a restaurant was temporarily closed as a drug nuisance when the owner had acted reasonably and done as much as possible to prevent the drug use. The court found a total taking under *Lucas* and that the nuisance exception to *Lucas* did not apply because it interpreted state law not to impose absolute liability for nuisance on an owner who took all reasonable steps to prevent illegal activity on the property. The court held that abatement of a business could not be based on illegal acts of business patrons when the owners were not aware of or involved in the illegal activity.

4. Destruction and necessity. In a footnote in *Lucas*, Justice Scalia indicated that the destruction of "real and personal property, in cases of actual necessity" need not be compensated. This issue arises commonly when property is damaged pursuant to police activities. A car may be hit in a chase; a building may be damaged in pursuit of a criminal. Most courts hold that no compensation is required when such injuries occur. In *Eggleston v. Pierce County*, 64 P.3d 618 (Wash. 2003), the court found no taking when a home was rendered uninhabitable because of damage that occurred when police executed a search of the house pursuant to a valid search warrant. The police came to the house to arrest the owner's son for drug dealing; he engaged in an exchange of fire with the police and killed a police officer. The search warrant authorized the police to take evidence from the home; that evidence included two walls, one of which was load bearing. Its removal made the house unstable and uninhabitable. The court held that the seizure of evidence for a criminal trial can never be a taking; nor was the damage to the home pursuant to the police efforts to apprehend a criminal. *Accord, Kam-Almaz v. United States*, 682 F.3d 1364 (Fed. Cir. 2012) (finding no taking from seizure and examination of laptop at an airport immigration and customs station resulting in damage to the hard drive and the loss of irretrievable business records); *Johnson v. Manitowoc County*, 635 F.3d 331 (7th Cir. 2011) (destruction of a concrete garage floor with a jackhammer during a murder investigation was not a taking). In contrast, in *Steele v. City of Houston*, 603 S.W.2d 786 (Tex. 1980), the court found a taking when police had burned down an innocent person's home to eject suspects. *Accord, Wegner v. Milwaukee Mutual Insurance Co.*, 479 N.W.2d 38 (Minn. 1991).

Are governments liable for takings of property when they inadvertently or negligently cause damage to property? *Pumpelly v. Green Bay Co.*, 80 U.S. 166, 179, 181 (1872), holds that a taking has occurred if government constructs a dam that floods property, thereby invading it and inflicting "a serious interruption to the common and necessary use of property" in a manner that "effectually destroy[s] or impair[s] its usefulness." In *Pacific Bell v. City of San Diego*, 96 Cal. Rptr. 2d 897 (Ct. App. 2000), the court held that a city had taken property when a pipe leading to a fire hydrant corroded and burst, flooding a house, because the "city's water delivery system was deliberately designed, constructed, and maintained without any method or program for monitoring the inevitable deterioration of cast iron pipes other than waiting for a pipe to break." And in *Richards v. Washington Terminal Co.*, 233 U.S. 546 (1914), the Supreme Court held that government may legislatively authorize a railroad to commit what would otherwise be a nuisance without any requirement of paying compensation for the lost value of property but that if a particular owner suffers "special and peculiar damage" then compensation may be due. *See* Carlos A. Ball, *The Curious Intersection of Nuisance and Takings Law*, 86 B.U. L. Rev. 819 (2006).

Hurricane Katrina led to the destruction of much of New Orleans, and it has been argued that the damage was partly caused by negligent construction of levees and the water drainage system, as well as design flaws in the canal system in the city that caused the erosion of wetlands and channeled water into particular areas of the city. If the homeowners in New Orleans could prove that the flooding that destroyed most of the property in the city would not have occurred if the flood control system had been designed, built, and maintained better, do they have a takings claim against the federal government that designed the flood control system in the city? *Nicholson v. United States*, 77 Fed. Cl. 605 (2007), answered this question in the negative on the ground that a taking occurs only if the government intends to invade a property interest or the harm is the "direct, natural, or probable result of an authorized activity and not the incidental or consequential injury inflicted by the action." *Id.* at 617. Do you agree with that approach?

5. Temporary takings and the temporal denominator. As *Tahoe-Sierra* notes, the Court in *First English Evangelical Lutheran Church of Glendale v. County of Los Angeles*, 482 U.S. 304 (1987), held that owners might be able to obtain damages for a **temporary taking** if they were prevented from using their property for any period. A court judgment that a regulation constitutes a taking of property leaves the regulatory body with the choice of enforcing the regulation (in which case compensation must be paid for a permanent taking) or rescinding the regulation (in which case the owner may have a claim for damages for a temporary taking for the period when the regulation was enforced against him). However, *Tahoe-Sierra* explained that a building ban does not necessarily constitute a taking, especially if it is temporary. *Tahoe-Sierra* approached the question of how long the period of a ban must be to give rise to a taking the same way that the Court had approached the question of the appropriate physical "denominator" for takings claims. Just as the owner of Grand Central in the *Penn Central* case could not legitimately isolate the physical area over which it had air rights as a distinctive "parcel," the Court in *Tahoe-Sierra* held that an owner cannot isolate the *slice of time* over which it had the right to build as a distinctive (temporal) piece of property. The parcel-as-a-whole rule prohibits this kind of conceptual severance.

Problems

1. Justice Blackmun, in his *Lucas* dissent, notes that cases such as *Miller v. Schoene*, 276 U.S. 272 (1928), have traditionally held that a state could destroy property to prevent harm without paying compensation without regard to whether it was a common law nuisance. After *Lucas*, does it matter whether the property would have constituted a common law private nuisance or not?

2. In *Keshbro, Inc. v. City of Miami*, 801 So. 2d 864 (Fla. 2001), the Florida Supreme Court upheld the temporary closure of a motel that had been the site of numerous drug and prostitution offenses but overturned an order closing an apartment complex for one year when it had been the site of only two illegal drug sales. The court held that the city had taken the property of the apartment complex owner without just compensation because the illegal activity was not so pervasive as to constitute either a private or public nuisance. Did the court rule correctly? *See also Dallas v. Stewart*, 361 S.W.3d 562, 569-570 (Tex. 2012) (evaluating nuisance for purposes of determining that there was no taking when property is demolished is a judicial, not administrative, responsibility).

3. A developer who owns 50 acres of property subdivides it and sells 45 single-family homes on single-acre lots. One 5-acre parcel remains but is designated as wetlands; under state law, the owner is prohibited from building anything on it. The developer sues the state, arguing that the wetlands regulation deprives her of any economically viable use for the 5 acres of wetlands; the diminution in value for this parcel is 100 percent. The state claims that the parcel represents 10 percent of the total area that the developer had owned and that since the developer had sold 45 homes, she was not deprived of economically viable use for her property. How should the court

analyze this question? Is this a 100 percent taking of the 5 acres or a 10 percent taking of the 50 acres? Should the owner be entitled to compensation for her inability to develop the 5-acre parcel?

4. In *Hunziker v. State*, 519 N.W.2d 367 (Iowa 1994), a lot owner was prevented from building a house on his lot when excavators discovered an American Indian burial mound made between 1,000 and 2,500 years ago in the middle of his property. A state statute in effect at the time the developer purchased the land authorized the state archeologist to prohibit owners from disinterring human remains found on private land if they had historic significance. The archeologist so found and required a buffer zone around the mound to protect its continued existence. The original developers of the subdivision refunded the purchase price and took back title and then sued the state, claiming that their inability to develop the lot deprived them of all economically viable use and that the statute, as applied to the lot, constituted a taking of property. The court held that the *Lucas* rule did not apply because the restriction on developing property where human beings are buried was part of the law of Iowa at the time the owner purchased the land and thus "inhered in the title." Because state law did not allow development in these circumstances, the owner could not have had a legitimate expectation of being able to so develop the property. The case is appealed to the Supreme Court. Should it affirm or reverse? It should be noted that state laws have traditionally regulated and required the preservation of marked cemeteries but only recently have states passed laws protecting older unmarked graves of American Indians. *See* Chapter 3, §7.2. Does this historical fact matter?

A Note on Regulatory Takings Procedures

Facial versus "as applied" challenges to regulations. A facial challenge to a regulation is a claim that enforcement of the regulation would *necessarily* constitute a taking of private property *in every case*; thus, under *no* circumstances would the application of the statute be constitutional. In contrast, a challenge to a regulation "as applied" argues that the *effect* of the regulation on a *particular* parcel or parcels of property owned by the plaintiff constitutes a taking of the plaintiff's property. Facial challenges are likely to succeed only in cases where a law imposes a permanent physical invasion of property, *Loretto v. Teleprompter Manhattan CATV Corp.*, 458 U.S. 419 (1982), or completely extinguishes a core property right, such as the right to pass on fee simple property at death, *Babbitt v. Youpee*, 519 U.S. 234 (1997). Otherwise, the owner must demonstrate the individual impact on a particular parcel of property to show that a law effects a taking as applied to that property.

Ripeness and preclusion. As the Supreme Court noted in *Palazzolo v. Rhode Island*, 533 U.S. 606 (2001), a claim that one's property has been unconstitutionally taken without just compensation is premature (not "ripe") if the agency empowered to regulate the land use has not made a final decision on the scope of the permitted development. In general, this means that an owner must apply for a permit to develop the land and be denied that right in a manner that suggests that further applications will be fruitless. *MacDonald, Sommer & Frates v. Yolo County*, 477 U.S. 340 (1986); *Williamson County Regional Planning Commission v. Hamilton Bank of Johnson City*, 473 U.S. 172 (1985). Moreover, the owner must exhaust all appeals and administrative remedies available under state law before challenging the state's development limitation as a taking. *Suitum v. Tahoe Regional Planning Agency*, 520 U.S. 725 (1997). *Accord, City of Monterey v. Del Monte Dunes at Monterey, Ltd.*, 526 U.S. 687, 721 (1999) (a takings claim is not ripe until the owner has "been denied an adequate postdeprivation remedy").[32]

An owner who wishes to make a facial challenge to a regulatory law may do so by choosing to sue in federal court; however, owners may not bring "as-applied" takings claims in federal court before exhausting all state remedies, and those remedies include bringing suit in state court to argue that the regulation constitutes a taking of property. Moreover, once an owner goes to state court to argue that a regulatory law constitutes a taking of property as applied to that owner's property, and the state courts rule on the owner's takings claim, the only way to attain federal court review is by appealing through the state court system and then seeking a writ of *certiorari* from the Supreme Court. The owner is not entitled to bring an action in federal district court to challenge the ruling of a state supreme court as effecting an unconstitutional taking because the federal full faith and credit statute, 28 U.S.C. §1738, requires federal courts to give preclusive effect to final state court judgments. *San Remo Hotel L.P. v. City & County of San Francisco*, 545 U.S. 323 (2005). As a practical matter, this means that almost all takings claims against states and local governments are brought in state court in the first instance.

In *City of Monterey, supra*, the Supreme Court found that a city could not avoid a takings challenge by repetitive and unfair procedures that never seem to result in a final determination of the scope of the permitted land use. *Palazzolo* reaffirmed the conclusion that, when a local government has repeatedly denied development permits, a court may conclude that further applications would have been fruitless and that the scope of the permitted development is known with sufficient finality and certainty to entertain the takings challenge.

Civil rights. Section 1983 authorizes a party who has been deprived of a federal right under the color of state law to seek relief through "an action at law, suit in equity, or other proper proceeding for redress." 42 U.S.C. §1983. *City of Monterey, supra*, held that an owner may sue the city under §1983 for violating its civil rights by taking its property through repeatedly rejecting development proposals over a five-year period, thus arguably denying the owner economically viable use of the property. The Supreme Court affirmed the trial court's finding that the city had both taken the owner's

32. Takings claims against the federal government, as opposed to claims against states or local governments, can be brought in the Court of Federal Claims under a statute called the Tucker Act, 28 U.S.C. §1491(a)(1). Generally, such claims *must* be brought in the Court of Federal Claims, unless Congress has withdrawn Tucker Act jurisdiction in the context of another statutory regime. *See Horne v. Department of Agriculture*, 133 S. Ct. 2053 (2013) (slip op. at 12-13).

property and denied plaintiff equal protection by treating the owner differently from other similarly situated owners without adequate reason. *City of Monterey* approved the use of §1983 as a remedy for a takings claim even though the effect of the ruling was to allow a jury rather than the judge to decide whether a taking had occurred. The Supreme Court held that this was permissible in that the jury's discretion was constrained by proper instructions limiting them to determining whether the "the city's particular decision to deny Del Monte Dunes' final development proposal was reasonably related to the city's proffered justifications." *Id.* at 706. *But see Wilkie v. Robbins*, 551 U.S. 537 (2007) (holding that the plaintiff could not assert a constitutional claim seeking damages from the government for its decade-long harassment and retaliation against him for not granting it an easement over his property).

§5 SPECIAL CASES

§5.1 Deprivation of Core Property Rights

In the United States, individuals are generally free to write a will determining who will own their property when they die. Statutes require wills to be in writing and to be witnessed (generally by two persons). Individuals are free to sell or give away their property before death so as to leave nothing to their family members when they pass on. Family members have no right to inherit property. U.S. law generally allows parents to disinherit their children. Every state does provide some protection for surviving spouses, however. Most states allow a surviving spouse to reject the will and recover a set portion of the decedent's estate (**statutory forced share statutes**). Many states also protect the right of a surviving spouse to continue living in the marital **homestead**. Other states provide for joint ownership of property acquired during marriage and give the surviving spouse half the **community property** acquired during the marriage on the death of the spouse. The property of those who die without a valid will is distributed to the decedent's **heirs** as specified in the state **intestacy statute**. Some intestacy laws divide the decedent's property between a surviving spouse and the children, while others leave everything to the surviving spouse. If the decedent leaves no spouse and no children, then other relatives are entitled to inherit, such as parents, uncles and aunts, and cousins. If the decedent leaves no heirs, the property will **escheat** to the state.

Could the state completely abolish the power to pass on one's property when one dies? Consider the following case.

Babbitt v. Youpee

519 U.S. 234 (1997)

Justice Ruth Bader Ginsburg delivered the opinion of the Court.

In this case, we consider for a second time the constitutionality of an escheat-to-tribe provision of the *Indian Land Consolidation Act* (ILCA). 96 Stat. 2519, *as amended*,

25 U.S.C. §2206. Specifically, we address §207 of the ILCA, as amended in 1984. Congress enacted the original provision in 1983 to ameliorate the extreme fractionation problem attending a century-old allotment policy that yielded multiple ownership of single parcels of Indian land. Amended §207 provides that certain small interests in Indian lands will transfer — or "escheat" — to the tribe upon the death of the owner of the interest. In *Hodel v. Irving*, 481 U.S. 704 (1987), this Court held that the original version of §207 of the ILCA effected a taking of private property without just compensation, in violation of the Fifth Amendment to the United States Constitution. We now hold that amended §207 does not cure the constitutional deficiency this Court identified in the original version of §207.

I

In the late Nineteenth Century, Congress initiated an Indian land program that authorized the division of communal Indian property. Pursuant to this allotment policy, some Indian land was parceled out to individual tribal members. Lands not allotted to individual Indians were opened to non-Indians for settlement. *See Indian General Allotment Act of 1887*, ch. 119, 24 Stat. 388. Allotted lands were held in trust by the United States or owned by the allottee subject to restrictions on alienation. On the death of the allottee, the land descended according to the laws of the State or Territory in which the land was located. In 1910, Congress also provided that allottees could devise their interests in allotted land.

The allotment policy "quickly proved disastrous for the Indians." *Irving*, 481 U.S. at 707. The program produced a dramatic decline in the amount of land in Indian hands. And as allottees passed their interests on to multiple heirs, ownership of allotments became increasingly fractionated, with some parcels held by dozens of owners. A number of factors augmented the problem: Because Indians often died without wills, many interests passed to multiple heirs; Congress' allotment Acts subjected trust lands to alienation restrictions that impeded holders of small interests from transferring those interests; Indian lands were not subject to state real estate taxes, which ordinarily serve as a strong disincentive to retaining small fractional interests in land. The fractionation problem proliferated with each succeeding generation as multiple heirs took undivided interests in allotments.

The administrative difficulties and economic inefficiencies associated with multiple undivided ownership in allotted lands gained official attention as early as 1928. *See* L. Meriam, *Institute for Government Research, The Problem of Indian Administration* 40-41 (1928). Governmental administration of these fractionated interests proved costly, and individual owners of small undivided interests could not make productive use of the land. Congress ended further allotment in 1934. *See Indian Reorganization Act*, 25 U.S.C. §§461 *et seq*. But that action left the legacy in place. As most owners had more than one heir, interests in lands already allotted continued to splinter with each generation. In the 1960's, congressional studies revealed that approximately half of all allotted trust lands were held in fractionated ownership; for over a quarter of allotted trust lands, individual allotments were held by more than six owners to a parcel.

In 1983, Congress adopted the ILCA in part to reduce fractionated ownership of allotted lands. Section 207 of the Act—the "escheat" provision—prohibited the descent or devise of small fractional interests in allotments. Instead of passing to heirs, such fractional interests would escheat to the tribe, thereby consolidating the ownership of Indian lands. Congress defined the targeted fractional interest as one that both constituted 2 percent or less of the total acreage in an allotted tract and had earned less than $100 in the preceding year. Section 207 made no provision for the payment of compensation to those who held such interests.

In *Hodel v. Irving*, this Court invalidated §207 on the ground that it effected a taking of property without just compensation, in violation of the Fifth Amendment. The appellees in *Irving* were, or represented, heirs or devisees of members of the Oglala Sioux Tribe. But for §207, the appellees would have received 41 fractional interests in allotments; under §207, those interests would escheat to the Tribe. This Court tested the legitimacy of §207 by considering its economic impact, its effect on investment-backed expectations, and the essential character of the measure. Turning first to the economic impact of §207, the Court in *Irving* observed that the provision's income-generation test might fail to capture the actual economic value of the land. The Court next indicated that §207 likely did not interfere with investment-backed expectations. Key to the decision in *Irving*, however, was the "extraordinary" character of the Government regulation. As this Court noted, §207 amounted to the "virtual abrogation of the right to pass on a certain type of property." Such a complete abrogation of the rights of descent and devise could not be upheld.

II

In 1984, while *Irving* was still pending in the Court of Appeals for the Eighth Circuit, Congress amended §207. Amended §207 differs from the original escheat provision in three relevant respects. First, an interest is considered fractional if it both constitutes 2 percent or less of the total acreage of the parcel and "is incapable of earning $100 in any one of the five years [following the] decedent's death"—as opposed to one year before the decedent's death in the original §207. 25 U.S.C. §2206(a). If the interest earned less than $100 in any one of five years prior to the decedent's death, "there shall be a rebuttable presumption that such interest is incapable of earning $100 in any one of the five years following the death of the decedent." *Id.* Second, in lieu of a total ban on devise and descent of fractional interests, amended §207 permits devise of an otherwise escheatable interest to "any other owner of an undivided fractional interest in such parcel or tract" of land. 25 U.S.C. §2206(b). Finally, tribes are authorized to override the provisions of amended §207 through the adoption of their own codes governing the disposition of fractional interests; these codes are subject to the approval of the Secretary of the Interior. 25 U.S.C. §2206(c). In *Irving*, "we express[ed] no opinion on the constitutionality of §207 as amended." 481 U.S. at 710, n.1.

Under amended §207, the interests in this case would escheat to tribal governments. The initiating plaintiffs, respondents here, are the children and potential heirs of William Youpee. An enrolled member of the Sioux and Assiniboine Tribes of the Fort Peck Reservation in Montana, William Youpee died testate in October 1990. His will devised to respondents, all of them enrolled tribal members, his several undivided interests in allotted trust lands on various reservations in Montana and North Dakota. These interests, as the Ninth Circuit reported, were valued together at $1,239. Each interest was devised to a single descendant. Youpee's will thus perpetuated existing fractionation, but it did not splinter ownership further by bequeathing any single fractional interest to multiple devisees.

III

In determining whether the 1984 amendments to §207 render the provision constitutional, we are guided by *Irving*.[33] The United States maintains that the amendments, though enacted three years prior to the *Irving* decision, effectively anticipated the concerns expressed in the Court's opinion. As already noted, amended §207 differs from the original in three relevant respects: It looks back five years instead of one to determine the income produced from a small interest, and creates a rebuttable presumption that this income stream will continue; it permits devise of otherwise escheatable interests to persons who already own an interest in the same parcel; and it authorizes tribes to develop their own codes governing the disposition of fractional interests. These modifications, according to the United States, rescue amended §207 from the fate of its predecessor. The Government maintains that the revisions moderate the economic impact of the provision and temper the character of the Government's regulation; the latter factor weighed most heavily against the constitutionality of the original version of §207.

The narrow revisions Congress made to §207, without benefit of our ruling in *Irving*, do not warrant a disposition different from the one this Court announced and explained in *Irving*. Amended §207 still trains on income generated from the land, not on the value of the parcel. The Court observed in *Irving* that "even if . . . the income generated by such parcels may be properly thought of as *de minimis*," the value of the land may not fit that description. The parcels at issue in *Irving* were valued by the Bureau of Indian Affairs at $2,700 and $1,816, amounts we found "not trivial." The value of the disputed parcels in this case is not of a different order; as the Ninth Circuit reported, the value of decedent Youpee's fractional interests was $1,239. In short, the economic impact of amended §207 might still be palpable.

Even if the economic impact of amended §207 is not significantly less than the impact of the original provision, the United States correctly comprehends that *Irving* rested primarily on the "extraordinary" character of the governmental regulation. *Irving* stressed that the original §207 "amount[ed] to virtually the abrogation of the right to pass on a certain type of property—the small undivided interest—to one's heirs." 481 U.S. at 716. The *Irving* Court further noted that the original §207 "effectively abolish[ed] both descent and devise [of fractional interests] even when the passing of

33. In *Irving* we relied on *Penn Central Transp. Co. v. New York City*, 438 U.S. 104 (1978). Because we find *Irving* dispositive, we do not reach respondents' argument that amended §207 effects a "categorical" taking, and is therefore subject to the more stringent analysis employed in *Lucas v. South Carolina Coastal Council*, 505 U.S. 1003 (1992).

the property to the heir might result in consolidation of property." 481 U.S. at 716. As the United States construes *Irving,* Congress cured the fatal infirmity in §207 when it revised the section to allow transmission of fractional interests to successors who already own an interest in the allotment.

Congress' creation of an ever-so-slight class of individuals equipped to receive fractional interests by devise does not suffice, under a fair reading of *Irving,* to rehabilitate the measure. Amended §207 severely restricts the right of an individual to direct the descent of his property. Allowing a decedent to leave an interest only to a current owner in the same parcel shrinks drastically the universe of possible successors. And, as the Ninth Circuit observed, the "very limited group [of permissible devisees] is unlikely to contain any lineal descendants." Moreover, amended §207 continues to restrict devise "even in circumstances when the governmental purpose sought to be advanced, consolidation of ownership of Indian lands, does not conflict with the further descent of the property." *Irving,* 481 U.S. at 718.

The third alteration made in amended §207 also fails to bring the provision outside the reach of this Court's holding in *Irving.* Amended §207 permits tribes to establish their own codes to govern the disposition of fractional interests; if approved by the Secretary of the Interior, these codes would govern in lieu of amended §207. *See* 25 U.S.C. §2206(c). The United States does not rely on this new provision to defend the statute. Nor does it appear that the United States could do so at this time: Tribal codes governing disposition of escheatable interests have apparently not been developed.

Justice John Paul Stevens, dissenting.

Section 207 of the *Indian Land Consolidation Act,* 25 U.S.C. §2206, did not, in my view, effect an unconstitutional taking of William Youpee's right to make a testamentary disposition of his property. As I explained in *Hodel v. Irving,* 481 U.S. 704 (1987) (opinion concurring in judgment), the Federal Government, like a State, has a valid interest in removing legal impediments to the productive development of real estate. For this reason, the Court has repeatedly "upheld the power of the State to condition the retention of a property right upon the performance of an act within a limited period of time." *Texaco, Inc. v. Short,* 454 U.S. 516, 529 (1982). I remain convinced that "Congress has ample power to require the owners of fractional interests in allotted lands to consolidate their holdings during their lifetimes or to face the risk that their interests will be deemed to be abandoned." *Hodel,* 481 U.S. at 732 (Stevens, J., concurring in judgment). The federal interest in minimizing the fractionated ownership of Indian lands—and thereby paving the way to the productive development of their property—is strong enough to justify the legislative remedy created by §207, provided, of course, that affected owners have adequate notice of the requirements of the law and an adequate opportunity to adjust their affairs to protect against loss.

In my opinion, William Youpee did have such notice and opportunity. More than six years passed from the time §207 was amended until Mr. Youpee died on October 19, 1990 (this period spans more than seven years if we count from the date §207 was originally enacted). During this time, Mr. Youpee could have realized the value of his fractional interests (approximately $1,239) in a variety of ways, including selling the property, giving it to his children as a gift, or putting it in trust for them. I assume that he failed to do so because he was not aware of the requirements of §207. This loss is unfortunate. But I believe Mr. Youpee's failure to pass on his property is the product of inadequate legal advice rather than an unconstitutional defect in the statute.

Notes and Questions

1. **Was allotment a taking of property?** As Justice Ginsburg notes, the *General Allotment Act of 1887* provided for the breakup of communally held tribal property into allotments held by individual tribal members. Congress took property owned by Indian nations and transferred title over that land to individual tribal members, who then owned bits of what had been tribal land. The act was intended to destroy tribal culture, and eventually tribal sovereignty, and to speed the assimilation and Christianization of American Indians by giving them individual property rights. The allotment acts provided compensation to the tribes, but the compensation was frequently far below market value.

In *Lone Wolf v. Hitchcock*, 187 U.S. 553 (1903), the Supreme Court upheld allotment of Kiowa, Comanche, and Apache land against challenges based on the fifth amendment and prior treaties. "We must presume that Congress acted in perfect good faith in the dealings with the Indians," the Court declared, and "as Congress possessed full power in the matter, the judiciary cannot question or inquire into the motives which prompted the enactment of this legislation." *Id.* at 568. *But cf. United States v. Sioux Nation of Indians*, 448 U.S. 371 (1980) (permitting a limited takings claim for taking treaty land without a good faith attempt to give compensation).

Was it fair for the Supreme Court to uphold the legislation that created the problem of fractionated shares (the *General Allotment Act*) but to strike down the legislation passed to correct the problems created by the act? If the original allotment policy effected an unconstitutional taking of tribal property, should this have affected the result in *Babbitt*?

2. **Another attempt to address fractionation.** The first two versions of the *Indian Land Consolidation Act* (ILCA) were held unconstitutional in *Hodel v. Irving* and *Babbitt v. Youpee.* Congress tried again, passing a third version of the law in 2000, which it then amended in the *American Indian Probate Reform Act of 2004. See* 25 U.S.C. §2206. It authorizes the Indian nations to pass their own probate laws, and it prescribes a federal probate code to determine devise and descent if the tribe does not enact its own code. In general, the property of an allottee who dies intestate will go to the decedent's surviving spouse, with the remainder in the decedent's children, grandchildren, or great-grandchildren, or the decedent's parents or siblings, and if the decedent leaves no such relatives, the interest will go to the tribe (unless a co-owner buys the interest for its fair market value). If the interest is less than 5 percent of the total undivided ownership of the property, the remainder can go only to one person — the oldest eligible child, grandchild, great-grandchild, parent, or sibling, with the tribe as heir of last resort. The allottee can get around these restrictions by writing a valid will. If there is no tribal probate code regulating devise, the allottee may

devise the interest to lineal descendants, any co-owner of the allotment, the tribe, or any Indian. The owner may also give a life estate to any person (such as a non-Indian spouse or child), with the remainder interest to be held by the tribe. The statute also gives the Secretary of the Interior the power to partition highly fractionated allotments (with more than 100 owners or 50 to 99 owners if none owns more than a 10 percent interest). At such a partition sale, the only eligible buyers would be the tribe, the tribe's members, descendants of the original allottee, or co-owners of the interest if they are members of another tribe.

3. **Right to alienate property.** Can the law prohibit an owner from alienating her property without compensation? Consider the following cases.

Buchanan v. Warley, 245 U.S. 60 (1917). Twenty-one years after the Supreme Court approved "separate but equal" public accommodations, thereby approving state-mandated racial segregation in *Plessy v. Ferguson*, 163 U.S. 537 (1896), it struck down a local zoning law that promoted racial segregation in housing. The Louisville city ordinance in *Buchanan* prohibited both white persons and African Americans from purchasing homes on a street that included a majority of owners of the opposite race. Justice Day explained: "Property is more than the mere thing which a person owns. It is elementary that it includes the right to acquire, use, and dispose of it. The Constitution protects these essential attributes of property." *Id.* at 74. While reaffirming state-mandated racial segregation in public accommodations, *id.* at 81, the Court found zoning laws that prohibit the sale of real property on the basis of race deny "property rights . . . by due process of law" and therefore are "not a legitimate exercise of the police power" because they "annul[] . . . the civil right of a white to dispose of his property if he saw fit to do so to a person of color and of a colored person to make such disposition to a white person," *id.* at 81-82. Thus, although the Court mentioned the "right to acquire" property, its focus in striking down the ordinance was denial of the "right to sell."

Andrus v. Allard, 444 U.S. 51 (1979). The *Eagle Protection Act* and the *Migratory Bird Treaty Act* were designed to protect various species of birds from extinction. The statutes prohibited the sale of eagle feathers, including those acquired before the act was passed. In the Court held that the statute did not effect a taking of property without just compensation despite the total ban on sale, *id.* at 65-66:

> The regulations challenged here do not compel the surrender of the artifacts, and there is no physical invasion or restraint upon them. Rather, a significant restriction has been imposed on one means of disposing of the artifacts. But the denial of one traditional property right does not always amount to a taking. At least where an owner possesses a full "bundle" of property rights, the destruction of one "strand" of the bundle is not a taking, because the aggregate must be viewed in its entirety. Regulations that bar trade in certain goods have been upheld against claims of unconstitutional taking. For example, the Court has sustained regulations prohibiting the sale of alcoholic beverages despite the fact that individuals were left with previously acquired stocks.

Is *Andrus v. Allard* consistent with *Babbitt*? *Cf. Lucas v. South Carolina Coastal Council*, 505 U.S. 1003, 1027-1028 (1992), (citing *Andrus* as a case about the high degree of state control over personal property as opposed to land).

4. Future interests and covenants. Courts and legislatures have often changed the rules regulating the estates system. Some of these changes have allowed individuals to create future interests that had previously been illegal. For example, the *Uniform Statutory Rule Against Perpetuities*, adopted in more than half the states, validates some future interests that violate the traditional rule against perpetuities. Other changes have invalidated future interests that had previously been lawful. For example, some states limit possibilities of reverter and options to purchase property to a set period, such as 30 years. Other states require future interests to be re-recorded every 30 or 40 years to remain viable. Can these changes in law be applied retroactively to property interests created before they were passed?

Some courts allow time limits to be placed on contingent future interests created before passage of the statute on the ground that the owner had "no more than an expectation, a possibility" that an interest might accrue in the future. *Trustees of Schools of Township No. 1 v. Batdorf*, 130 N.E.2d 111 (Ill. 1955) (upholding a marketable title act that retroactively limited possibilities of reverter and rights of entry created before passage of the act to 50 years). However, these courts usually find it important that owners of previously created interests are given a limited time to re-register the interest. *See id.* (one year to re-record interest was sufficient to permit retroactive application of statute). *Accord, Black Mountain Energy Corp. v. Bell County Board of Education*, 467 F. Supp. 2d 715 (D. Ky. 2006); *Town of Brookline v. Carey*, 245 N.E.2d 446 (Mass. 1969); *see also Walton v. City of Red Bluff*, 3 Cal. Rptr. 2d 275 (Ct. App. 1991) (upholding retroactive application of a statute converting a possibility of reverter into a right of entry when owner had five years to re-record the interest). However, some courts have held that some statutory changes in the rule against perpetuities cannot constitutionally be retroactively applied to property interests created before passage of the statute. *Lake of the Woods Association, Inc. v. McHugh*, 380 S.E.2d 872 (Va. 1989) (holding that the statutory wait and see test could not retroactively be applied to preserve a preemptive right invalid under the traditional rule against perpetuities).

Most of the cases abolishing male privileges associated with tenancy by the entirety apply the statutes retroactively to tenancies created before the effective date of the statute. Retroactive application is arguably legitimate here because the unequal property rights associated with tenancies by the entirety probably violate the equal protection clause. *Kirchberg v. Feenstra*, 450 U.S. 455 (1981). *But see West v. First Agricultural Bank*, 419 N.E.2d 262 (Mass. 1981) (refusing to apply retroactively a change in tenancy by the entirety law granting women equal management powers over property).

Courts ordinarily do not find a taking when statutes retroactively alter the enforceability of covenants by modifying the changed conditions or relative hardship doctrines. *Blakeley v. Gorin*, 313 N.E.2d 903 (Mass. 1974); *see also Barrett v. Dawson*, 71 Cal. Rptr. 2d 899 (Ct. App. 1998) (statute that retroactively precluded enforcement of restrictive covenants limiting family day care homes in residential neighborhoods was not a taking). However, some courts have found takings when a statute retroactively increases or decreases the time period during which a covenant will be enforceable. *Compare Appalachee Entertainment v. Walker*, 463 S.E.2d 896 (Ga. 1995) (unconstitutional to apply a statute allowing covenants to last for 30 years when the developer purchased the property in reliance on a prior statute that limited covenants to 20 years), *with Bickford v. Yancey Development Co.*, 585 S.E.2d 78 (Ga. 2003) (statute can apply to property purchased after the statute was in effect and the covenants had been in existence for 20 years).

Problems

1. A state adopts a statute extending the rule against perpetuities to possibilities of reverter and rights of entry on the ground it never made any sense to strike down an executory interest in a third party under the rule against perpetuities while enforcing an identical possibility of reverter held by a descendant of the grantor. If the statute applies to conveyances made prior to the effective date of the statute, would this constitute a taking of property without just compensation?

2. Does the state have to compensate an owner if it acquires the owner's property by adverse possession? What are the arguments on both sides of this question? *Compare Pascoag Reservoir & Dam, L.L.C. v. Rhode Island*, 217 F. Supp. 2d 206 (D.R.I. 2002), *aff'd on other grounds*, 337 F.3d 87 (1st Cir. 2003) (holding that compensation is constitutionally required), *with Weidner v. State*, 860 P.2d 1205 (Alaska 1993); *Stickney v. City of Saco*, 770 A.2d 592, 2001 ME 69 (Me. 2001) (both holding that no compensation is due).

3. In *Bormann v. Board of Supervisors in and for Kossuth County*, 584 N.W.2d 309 (Iowa 1998), a state law authorized the creation of "agricultural areas" in which particular owners were entitled to immunity from certain nuisance claims by neighbors. Similar "right-to-farm" statutes have been enacted in many states. Neighbors challenged the statute because it deprived them of rights they had under prior law to be protected against nuisances committed on neighboring property. The Iowa Supreme Court held the statute unconstitutionally took the right to be free from nuisances from owners in the affected areas and granted farmers a kind of easement — a right to commit a nuisance affecting neighboring property. Because property law traditionally gave owners the right to be free from unreasonable and substantial interferences with their use or enjoyment of their property, the Iowa Supreme Court concluded that the statute authorizing farmers to commit nuisances effectuated an unconstitutional taking of the property rights of those affected by what would otherwise have constituted an actionable nuisance. Assume the Supreme Court agrees to hear the case on appeal. Should the court's ruling be affirmed or reversed?

4. Massachusetts has a statute that gives the municipality where property is located a right of first refusal to purchase land of five acres or more used and zoned for agricultural purposes. The municipality has the right to match a bona fide third-party offer and take title to the land for that price. It also has the option to purchase the land for its fair market value if the owner discontinues the agricultural use. The act applies only if the owner has applied to the municipality and been granted the right to have the land assessed as agricultural land for property tax purposes, resulting in much lower than normal property taxes on the land. Mass. Gen. Laws ch. 61A, §14. Does the statute violate the takings clause?

A local condominium conversion ordinance gives tenants a right of first refusal to purchase their units if the landlord chooses to convert the apartment building to condominiums. Does the ordinance violate the takings clause? If so, on what grounds?

§5.2 Vested Rights and Transitional Relief

A lot is zoned for institutional use and, in reliance on that zoning designation, a university obtains a building permit, complying with all applicable construction regulations, and builds a classroom building. Two years after the building is completed, the city completes a "downzoning" project and rezones much of the land in the city to limit the placement and development of institutional and commercial uses and increase areas zoned for housing. The land on which the classroom building sits is now placed in a district limited to residential uses. Is the university obligated to tear down the building and construct an apartment building in its place? The answer is no, partly because it is likely the state zoning enabling act and the city zoning ordinance itself have provisions to grandfather prior nonconforming uses and partly because any such requirement would almost certainly constitute a taking of property without just compensation.

Once an owner invests substantially in reliance on applicable zoning and building requirements, the owner acquires a "vested right" to the existing use that cannot be changed retroactively unless the regulatory law is designed to prevent the owner from committing a nuisance or otherwise harming individuals or the public. In *Dobbins v. Los Angeles*, 195 U.S. 223 (1904), the Supreme Court held that a zoning law prohibiting the use of a parcel of land for a gasworks could not be retroactively applied to an owner unless just compensation was paid when the use was lawful at the time the owner bought the property, the owner had already invested substantially in the project, and the owner had begun construction. However, it also held that retroactive regulations are lawful without compensation when the legislating body could have rationally believed that the regulation was needed to prevent the owner from committing a public or private nuisance or otherwise causing harm to individuals or to property. In *Dobbins*, however, the Court found that, because the property was located in an industrial district, there was no indication that the law had been changed to prevent a nuisance or other harm to neighboring owners or the public.

In contrast, *Mugler v. Kansas*, 123 U.S. 623 (1887), upheld a state constitutional amendment prohibiting the manufacture and sale of alcoholic beverages on the ground that it promoted the public health, welfare, safety, and morals by outlawing a public nuisance and thus did not unconstitutionally take the property of a brewery owner. *See also Keystone Bituminous Coal Association v. DeBenedictis*, 480 U.S. 470 (1970) (upholding a regulatory law requiring substantial amounts of coal to be left in place under the ground to support the surface and prevent subsidence of surface structures); *Goldblatt v. Hempstead*, 369 U.S. 590 (1962) (upholding a law that prevents continued operation of a quarry in residential area); *Miller v. Schoene*, 276 U.S. 272 (1928) (upholding an order to destroy diseased cedar trees to prevent infection of nearby orchards); *Hadacheck v. Sebastian*, 239 U.S. 394 (1915) (upholding a law barring operation of brick mill in a residential area).

The vested rights principle was applied in *Kaiser Aetna v. United States*, 444 U.S. 164 (1979), when the Supreme Court found that a private, fee-paying marina club could not be forced to provide free public access to its lagoon when it invested in an expensive construction project to connect the lagoon to public navigable waters. The Supreme Court held that requiring the club to allow access to its property by non-paying members of the public would interfere with its "reasonable investment backed expectations" as well as imposing a forced physical invasion by strangers to its land. *Id.* at 175, 179-180.[34] Laws that adjust the burdens of economic life, such as consumer protection laws, workplace regulations, and changes in tort laws that require compensation when one causes harm to others, have almost never been ruled to be unconstitutional takings of property. However, some such changes so alter established expectations that they have been challenged as unconstitutional takings of property; although such claims generally fail, the courts do take them seriously. Retroactivity is also an issue under the due process clause. *See* Chapter 14, §3.1.

Problems

1. In *Mann v. Georgia Department of Corrections*, 653 S.E.2d 740 (Ga. 2007), the Georgia Supreme Court held that a state statute prohibiting registered sex offenders from living or working within 1,000 feet of any facility where minors congregate, *see* Ga. Code §42-1-15, constituted a taking of property as applied to a sex offender who was forced to move after a child care center opened a facility within 1,000 feet of his home. The court noted that "it is apparent that there is no place in Georgia where a registered sex offender can live without being continually at risk of being ejected." 653 S.E.2d at 755. Moreover, the effect of the statute "is to mandate appellant's immediate physical removal from his . . . residence." The court noted "the strong governmental interests that are advanced by the residency restriction" on sex offenders, but also found that the law effectively allowed "private third parties" to establish child-centered uses and thereby "force a registered sex offender . . . to forfeit valuable property rights in his legally-purchased home." Was the case correctly decided?

2. In the 1960s, the federal government promoted the construction of low-income housing by private developers by providing mortgage insurance that allowed the developers to obtain funds from private lenders for 40-year low-interest mortgages. In return, the developers consented to extensive government regulation of the properties. The terms of the mortgages provided that they could be prepaid without government approval after 20 years and that doing so would lift the restrictions arising from the regulations. In 1990, to stop a mass withdrawal of properties from the program through prepayment, Congress enacted statutes that effectively nullified the prepayment right.

34. This topic is further explored in Chapter 7 in the sections discussing prior nonconforming uses (§2.1) and vested rights in zoning law (§2.2).

Although Congress reinstated the prepayment rights in 1996, in *Cienega Gardens v. United States*, 331 F.3d 1319 (Fed. Cir. 2003), the Federal Circuit held that the developers had a vested property right to "buy out" of the program. The repeal of this right constituted a temporary taking under the *ad hoc* test for the four plaintiffs for whom the trial court had made findings of fact. However, when on remand the trial court held that the measure took property of the other developers, the Federal Circuit reversed, holding that the court had to consider the impact of the measure on the value of the property as a whole, the benefits that the developers received from participation in the program, and the extent of reliance on the prepayment option. *Cienega Gardens v. United States*, 503 F.3d 1266 (Fed. Cir. 2007). How should the court on remand analyze the question of whether denying prepayment rights constituted a taking of property that interfered with the owner's reasonable investment-backed expectations? *See CCA Associates v. United States*, 667 F.3d 1239, 1244-1248 (Fed. Cir. 2011).

3. Massachusetts passed a law requiring tobacco companies to reveal the components in their cigarette products. Such disclosure was intended to ensure that potential users knew what ingredients they would be ingesting. However, those ingredients were also trade secrets, and the First Circuit held the state law to constitute a taking of property without just compensation. What are the arguments on both sides of this case? *Philip Morris, Inc. v. Reilly*, 312 F.3d 24 (1st Cir. 2002).

4. Assume a community property state has a law that allows courts to grant alimony on divorce. The law divides property acquired during the marriage equally and in a mechanical fashion, with half going to each spouse. The legislature adopts a statute providing for "equitable distribution of the property" acquired during the marriage on the ground that mechanical division does not account for a number of factors relevant to the property distribution, as the overwhelming majority of states now recognize. A court awards a wife 60 percent of the property acquired during the marriage rather than 50 percent pursuant to its determination that this is the most equitable result. The husband argues that the statute cannot be constitutionally applied to marriages that were celebrated before the statute was passed; to do so would constitute a taking of 10 percent of the property from the husband to be transferred to the wife. How should the case be decided? *Cf. In re Marriage of Heikes*, 899 P.2d 1349 (Cal. 1995) (statute allowing a divorcing spouse to be reimbursed for the value of separate property used during marriage to purchase community property jointly owned by both spouses cannot be constitutionally applied to divorces filed before passage of the statute).

§6 JUDICIAL TAKINGS

Stop the Beach Renourishment, Inc. v. Florida Department of Environmental Protection

130 S. Ct. 2592 (2010)

Justice ANTONIN SCALIA announced the judgment of the Court and delivered the opinion of the Court with respect to Parts I, IV, and V, and an opinion with respect to Parts II and III, in which THE CHIEF JUSTICE, Justice THOMAS, and Justice ALITO join.

We consider a claim that the decision of a State's court of last resort took property without just compensation in violation of the Takings Clause of the Fifth Amendment, as applied against the States through the Fourteenth.

I

A

Generally speaking, state law defines property interests, including property rights in navigable waters and the lands underneath them. In Florida, the State owns in trust for the public the land permanently submerged beneath navigable waters and the foreshore (the land between the low-tide line and the mean high-water line). Fla. Const., Art. X, §11; *Broward v. Mabry*, 50 So. 826, 829-30 (Fla. 1909). Thus, the mean high-water line (the average reach of high tide over the preceding 19 years) is the ordinary boundary between private beachfront, or littoral[35] property, and state-owned land.

Littoral owners have, in addition to the rights of the public, certain "special rights" with regard to the water and the foreshore, *Broward*, 50 So., at 830, rights which Florida considers to be property, generally akin to easements. These include the right of access to the water, the right to use the water for certain purposes, the right to an unobstructed view of the water, and the right to receive accretions and relictions to the littoral property. This is generally in accord with well-established common law, although the precise property rights vary among jurisdictions.

At the center of this case is the right to accretions and relictions. Accretions are additions of alluvion (sand, sediment, or other deposits) to waterfront land; relictions are lands once covered by water that become dry when the water recedes. (For simplicity's sake, we shall refer to accretions and relictions collectively as accretions, and the process whereby they occur as accretion.) In order for an addition to dry land to qualify as an accretion, it must have occurred gradually and imperceptibly—that is, so slowly that one could not see the change occurring, though over time the difference became apparent. When, on the other hand, there is a "sudden or perceptible loss of or addition to land by the action of the water or a sudden change in the bed of a lake or the course of a stream," the change is called an avulsion. [*Board of Trustees of Internal Improvement Trust Fund v. Sand Key Associates, Ltd.*, 512 So. 2d 934, 936 (Fla. 1987).]

In Florida, as at common law, the littoral owner automatically takes title to dry land added to his property by accretion; but formerly submerged land that has become dry land by avulsion continues to belong to the owner of the seabed (usually the State). *See, e.g., Sand Key, supra*, at 937; 2 W. Blackstone, *Commentaries on the Laws of England* 261-62 (1766) (hereinafter *Blackstone*). Thus, regardless of whether

35. Many cases and statutes use "riparian" to mean abutting any body of water. The Florida Supreme Court, however, has adopted a more precise usage whereby "riparian" means abutting a river or stream and "littoral" means abutting an ocean, sea, or lake. *Walton Cty. v. Stop the Beach Renourishment, Inc.*, 998 So. 2d 1102, 1105, n.3 (2008). When speaking of the Florida law applicable to this case, we follow the Florida Supreme Court's terminology.

an avulsive event exposes land previously submerged or submerges land previously exposed, the boundary between littoral property and sovereign land does not change; it remains (ordinarily) what was the mean high-water line before the event. It follows from this that, when a new strip of land has been added to the shore by avulsion, the littoral owner has no right to subsequent accretions. Those accretions no longer add to *his* property, since the property abutting the water belongs not to him but to the State.

B

In 1961, Florida's Legislature passed the *Beach and Shore Preservation Act,* 1961 Fla. Laws ch. 61-246, as amended, Fla. Stat. §§161.011-161.45 (2007). The Act establishes procedures for "beach restoration and nourishment projects," §161.088, designed to deposit sand on eroded beaches (restoration) and to maintain the deposited sand (nourishment). §§161.021(3), (4). A local government may apply to the Department of Environmental Protection for the funds and the necessary permits to restore a beach, *see* §§161.101(1), 161.041(1). When the project involves placing fill on the State's submerged lands, authorization is required from the Board of Trustees of the Internal Improvement Trust Fund, see §253.77(1), which holds title to those lands, §253.12(1).

Once a beach restoration "is determined to be undertaken," the Board sets what is called "an erosion control line." §§161.161(3)-(5). It must be set by reference to the existing mean high-water line, though in theory it can be located seaward or landward of that.[36] See §161.161(5). Much of the project work occurs seaward of the erosion-control line, as sand is dumped on what was once submerged land. See App. 87-88. The fixed erosion-control line replaces the fluctuating mean high-water line as the boundary between privately owned littoral property and state property. §161.191(1). Once the erosion-control line is recorded, the common law ceases to increase upland property by accretion (or decrease it by erosion). §161.191(2). Thus, when accretion to the shore moves the mean high-water line seaward, the property of beachfront landowners is not extended to that line (as the prior law provided), but remains bounded by the permanent erosion-control line. Those landowners "continue to be entitled," however, "to all common-law riparian rights" other than the right to accretions. §161.201.

C

In 2003, the city of Destin and Walton County applied for the necessary permits to restore 6.9 miles of beach within their jurisdictions that had been eroded by several hurricanes. The project envisioned depositing along that shore sand dredged from further out. It would add about 75 feet of dry sand seaward of the mean high-water

36. We assume that in this case the erosion-control line is the pre-existing mean high-water line. Respondents concede that, if the erosion-control line were established landward of that, the State would have taken property.

line (to be denominated the erosion-control line). The Department issued a notice of intent to award the permits, and the Board approved the erosion-control line.

The petitioner here, Stop the Beach Renourishment, Inc., is a nonprofit corporation formed by people who own beachfront property bordering the project area (we shall refer to them as the Members). [After losing an administrative challenge to the proposed project, Stop the Beach brought an action in state court. The District Court of Appeal for the First District concluded that the order had eliminated the Members' littoral rights (1) to receive accretions to their property; and (2) to have the contact of their property with the water remain intact. It certified the following question to the Florida Supreme Court: "On its face, does the Beach and Shore Preservation Act unconstitutionally deprive upland owners of littoral rights without just compensation?"] The Florida Supreme Court answered the certified question in the negative. It faulted the Court of Appeal for not considering the doctrine of avulsion, which it concluded permitted the State to reclaim the restored beach on behalf of the public. It described the right to accretions as a future contingent interest, not a vested property right, and held that there is no littoral right to contact with the water independent of the littoral right of access, which the Act does not infringe. Petitioner sought rehearing on the ground that the Florida Supreme Court's decision itself effected a taking of the Members' littoral rights contrary to the Fifth and Fourteenth Amendments to the Federal Constitution. The request for rehearing was denied. We granted certiorari.

II

A

The Takings Clause — "nor shall private property be taken for public use, without just compensation," U.S. Const., Amdt. 5 — applies as fully to the taking of a landowner's riparian rights as it does to the taking of an estate in land. The Takings Clause (unlike, for instance, the Ex Post Facto Clauses, see Art. I, §9, cl. 3; §10, cl. 1) is not addressed to the action of a specific branch or branches. It is concerned simply with the act, and not with the governmental actor ("nor shall private property *be taken*" (emphasis added)). There is no textual justification for saying that the existence or the scope of a State's power to expropriate private property without just compensation varies according to the branch of government effecting the expropriation. Nor does common sense recommend such a principle. It would be absurd to allow a State to do by judicial decree what the Takings Clause forbids it to do by legislative fiat.

In sum, the Takings Clause bars *the State* from taking private property without paying for it, no matter which branch is the instrument of the taking. To be sure, the manner of state action may matter: Condemnation by eminent domain, for example, is always a taking, while a legislative, executive, or judicial restriction of property use may or may not be, depending on its nature and extent. But the particular state *actor* is irrelevant. If a legislature *or a court* declares that what was once an established right of private property no longer exists, it has taken that property, no less than if the State had physically appropriated it or destroyed its value by regulation. "[A] State, by *ipse dixit,* may not transform private property into public property without compensation." *Webb's Fabulous Pharmacies, Inc. v. Beckwith,* 449 U.S. 155, 164 (1980).

C

Justice Kennedy says that we need not take what he considers the bold and risky step of holding that the Takings Clause applies to judicial action, because the Due Process Clause "would likely prevent a State from doing by judicial decree what the Takings Clause forbids it to do by legislative fiat." *Post.* The first problem with using Substantive Due Process to do the work of the Takings Clause is that we have held it cannot be done. Where a particular Amendment provides an explicit textual source of constitutional protection against a particular sort of government behavior, that Amendment, not the more generalized notion of "substantive due process," must be the guide for analyzing these claims. The second problem is that we have held for many years (logically or not) that the "liberties" protected by Substantive Due Process do not include economic liberties. Justice Kennedy's language ("If a judicial decision . . . eliminates an established property right, the judgment could be set aside as a deprivation of property without due process of law") propels us back to what is referred to (usually deprecatingly) as "the *Lochner* era." See *Lochner v. New York,* 198 U.S. 45, 56-58 (1905). That is a step of much greater novelty, and much more unpredictable effect, than merely applying the Takings Clause to judicial action.

We do not grasp the relevance of Justice Kennedy's speculation that the Framers did not envision the Takings Clause would apply to judicial action. They doubtless did not, since the Constitution was adopted in an era when courts had no power to "change" the common law. *See* 1 *Blackstone* 69-70 (1765). Where the text they adopted is clear, however ("nor shall private property be taken for public use"), what counts is not what they envisioned but what they wrote. Of course even after courts, in the 19th century, did assume the power to change the common law, it is not true that the new "common-law tradition . . . allows for incremental modifications to property law," so that "owners may reasonably expect or anticipate courts to make certain changes in property law." *Post.* In the only sense in which this could be relevant to what we are discussing, that is an astounding statement. We are talking here about judicial elimination of established private property rights. If that is indeed a "common-law tradition," Justice Kennedy ought to be able to provide a more solid example for it than the only one he cites, a state-court change (from "noxious" to "harmful") of the test for determining whether a neighbor's vegetation is a tortious nuisance. *Fancher v. Fagella,* 650 S.E.2d 519, 522 (Va. 2007). But perhaps he does not really mean that it is a common-law tradition to eliminate property rights, since he immediately follows his statement that "owners may reasonably expect or anticipate courts to make certain changes in property law" with the contradictory statement that "courts cannot abandon settled principles." If no "settled principl[e]" has been abandoned, it is hard to see how property law could have been "change[d]," rather than merely clarified.

Justice Kennedy [asserts] that "it is unclear what remedy a reviewing court could enter after finding a judicial taking," post, at 2617. Justice Kennedy worries that we may only be able to mandate compensation. That remedy is even rare for a legislative or executive taking, and we see no reason why it would be the exclusive remedy for a judicial taking. If we were to hold that the Florida Supreme Court had effected an uncompensated taking in the present case, we would simply reverse the Florida Supreme Court's judgment that the Beach and Shore Preservation Act can be applied to the property in question. These, and all the other "difficulties," "difficult questions," and "practical considerations," *post*, that Justice Kennedy worries may perhaps stand in the way of recognizing a judicial taking, are either nonexistent or insignificant.

IV

We come at last to petitioner's takings attack on the decision below. Petitioner argues that the Florida Supreme Court took two of the property rights of the Members by declaring that those rights did not exist: the right to accretions, and the right to have littoral property touch the water (which petitioner distinguishes from the mere right of access to the water). Under petitioner's theory, because no prior Florida decision had said that the State's filling of submerged tidal lands could have the effect of depriving a littoral owner of contact with the water and denying him future accretions, the Florida Supreme Court's judgment in the present case abolished those two easements to which littoral property owners had been entitled. This puts the burden on the wrong party. There is no taking unless petitioner can show that, before the Florida Supreme Court's decision, littoral-property owners had rights to future accretions and contact with the water superior to the State's right to fill in its submerged land. Though some may think the question close, in our view the showing cannot be made.

Two core principles of Florida property law intersect in this case. First, the State as owner of the submerged land adjacent to littoral property has the right to fill that land, so long as it does not interfere with the rights of the public and the rights of littoral landowners. Second, if an avulsion exposes land seaward of littoral property that had previously been submerged, that land belongs to the State even if it interrupts the littoral owner's contact with the water. The issue here is whether there is an exception to this rule when the State is the cause of the avulsion. Prior law suggests there is not. In *Martin v. Busch*, 112 So. 274 (Fla. 1927), the Florida Supreme Court held that when the State drained water from a lakebed belonging to the State, causing land that was formerly below the mean high-water line to become dry land, that land continued to belong to the State. This is not surprising, as there can be no accretions to land that no longer abuts the water. Thus, Florida law as it stood before the decision below allowed the State to fill in its own seabed, and the resulting sudden exposure of previously submerged land was treated like an avulsion for purposes of ownership. The right to accretions was therefore subordinate to the State's right to fill.

The Florida Supreme Court decision before us is consistent with these background principles of state property law. *Cf. Lucas v. South Carolina Coastal Council*, 505 U.S. 1003, 1028-29 (1992). It did not abolish the Members' right to future accretions, but merely held that the right was not implicated by the beach-restoration project, because the doctrine of avulsion applied. The Florida Supreme Court's opinion describes beach restoration as the reclamation by the State of the public's land, just as *Martin* had described the lake drainage in that case. Although the opinion does not cite *Martin* and is not always clear on this point, it suffices that its characterization of the littoral right to accretion is consistent with *Martin* and the other relevant principles of Florida law we have discussed.

Even if there might be different interpretations of *Martin* and other Florida property-law cases that would prevent this arguably odd result, we are not free to adopt them. The Takings Clause only protects property rights as they are established under state law, not as they might have been established or ought to have been established. We cannot say that the Florida Supreme Court's decision eliminated a right of accretion established under Florida law.

V

Because the Florida Supreme Court's decision did not contravene the established property rights of petitioner's Members, Florida has not violated the Fifth and Fourteenth Amendments. The judgment of the Florida Supreme Court is therefore affirmed.

Justice JOHN PAUL STEVENS took no part in the decision of this case.

Justice ANTHONY M. KENNEDY, with whom Justice SOTOMAYOR joins, concurring in part and concurring in the judgment.

This case does not require the Court to determine whether, or when, a judicial decision determining the rights of property owners can violate the Takings Clause of the Fifth Amendment of the United States Constitution. This separate opinion notes certain difficulties that should be considered before accepting the theory that a judicial decision that eliminates an "established property right," constitutes a violation of the Takings Clause.

The Court would be on strong footing in ruling that a judicial decision that eliminates or substantially changes established property rights, which are a legitimate expectation of the owner, is "arbitrary or irrational" under the Due Process Clause. Thus, without a judicial takings doctrine, the Due Process Clause would likely prevent a State from doing "by judicial decree what the Takings Clause forbids it to do by legislative fiat." The objection that a due process claim might involve close questions concerning whether a judicial decree extends beyond what owners might have expected is not a sound argument; for the same close questions would arise with respect to whether a judicial decision is a taking.

The evident reason for recognizing a judicial takings doctrine would be to constrain the power of the judicial branch. Of course, the judiciary must respect private ownership. But were this Court to say that judicial decisions become takings when they overreach, this might give more power to courts, not less. Consider the instance of litigation between two property owners to determine which one bears the liability and costs when a tree that stands on one property extends its roots in a way that damages adjacent property. *See, e.g., Fancher v. Fagella*, 650 S.E.2d 519 (Va. 2007). If a court deems that, in light of increasing urbanization, the former rule for allocation of these costs should be changed, thus shifting the rights of the owners, it may well increase the value of one property and decrease the value of the other. This might be the type of incremental modification under state common law that does not violate due process, as owners may reasonably expect or anticipate courts to make certain changes in property law. The usual due process constraint is that courts cannot abandon settled principles.

But if the state court were deemed to be exercising the power to take property, that constraint would be removed. Because the State would be bound to pay owners for takings caused by a judicial decision, it is conceivable that some judges might decide that enacting a sweeping new rule to adjust the rights of property owners in the context of changing social needs is a good idea. Knowing that the resulting ruling would be a taking, the courts could go ahead with their project, free from constraints that would otherwise confine their power. The resulting judgment as between the property owners likely could not be set aside by some later enactment. And if the litigation were a class action to decide, for instance, whether there are public rights of access that diminish the rights of private ownership, a State might find itself obligated to pay a substantial judgment for the judicial ruling. Even if the legislature were to subsequently rescind the judicial decision by statute, the State would still have to pay just compensation for the temporary taking that occurred from the time of the judicial decision to the time of the statutory fix.

If and when future cases show that the usual principles, including constitutional principles that constrain the judiciary like due process, are somehow inadequate to protect property owners, then the question whether a judicial decision can effect a taking would be properly presented. In the meantime, it seems appropriate to recognize that the substantial power to decide whose property to take and when to take it should be conceived of as a power vested in the political branches and subject to political control.

Justice Stephen G. Breyer, with whom Justice Ginsburg joins, concurring in part and concurring in the judgment.

I agree that no unconstitutional taking of property occurred in this case, and I therefore join Parts I, IV, and V of today's opinion. I cannot join Parts II and III, however, for in those Parts the plurality unnecessarily addresses questions of constitutional law that are better left for another day.

Property owners litigate many thousands of cases involving state property law in state courts each year. Each state-court property decision may further affect numerous nonparty property owners as well. Losing parties in many state-court cases may well believe that erroneous judicial decisions have deprived them of property rights they previously held and may consequently bring federal takings claims. [S]uch cases can involve state property law issues of considerable complexity. Hence, the approach the plurality would take today threatens to open the federal court doors to constitutional review of many, perhaps large numbers of, state-law cases in an area of law familiar to state, but not federal, judges. And the failure of that approach to set forth procedural limitations or canons of deference would create the distinct possibility that federal judges would play a major role in the shaping of a matter of significant state interest — state property law.

[W]hen faced with difficult constitutional questions, we should "confine ourselves to deciding only what is necessary to the disposition of the immediate case." *Whitehouse v. Illinois Central R. Co.*, 349 U.S. 366, 373 (1955). There is no need now to decide more than what the Court decides in Parts IV and V, namely, that the Florida Supreme Court's decision in this case did not amount to a "judicial taking."

Notes and Questions

1. **Judiciary as the state actor for takings.** Almost all claims that property has been unlawfully "taken" without compensation involve challenges to legislative or administrative actions. Barton H. Thompson, Jr., in a well-known article, *Judicial Takings*, 76 Va. L. Rev. 1449 (1990), argued that judicial interpretations of the common law or changes in common law rules could constitute a taking of property, and Justice Scalia embraced this proposition in his plurality opinion in *Stop the Beach Renourishment.* The plurality's approach raises important questions about takings law and the role of the judiciary.

On one hand, there is no inherent reason why a state supreme court's interpretation of the common law could not unfairly divest owners of rights they had assumed belonged to them, thereby unjustly interfering with investment-backed expectations. And it is certainly not unheard of for the Supreme Court to recognize the judiciary as the relevant state actor in constitutional cases. *See, e.g., Shelley v. Kraemer*, 334 U.S. 1 (1948).

On the other hand, interpreting the law is not necessarily the same thing as enforcing private agreements, and courts often define the rights that go along with property ownership through the common law process. If changes in common law rules can represent takings of property, the courts could be significantly curtailed in modernizing the law. They might even be disempowered from holding that a prior case was distinguishable from the current case.

2. **Takings versus due process, again.** Justice Kennedy, in concurrence, argues that there are limits to the judiciary's ability to redefine property rights, but that this limitation is a question of due process, not takings. He had earlier stated a similar view as the deciding Justice in his concurrence in *Eastern Enterprises v. Apfel*, 524 U.S. 498 (1998). *Apfel* involved a statute that required Eastern Enterprises to contribute funds for health benefits for retired coal miners who had worked for it before 1966 even though the company had left the coal business in 1966. The company had previously signed labor agreements obligating it to contribute certain amounts to trust funds established for this purpose, but the statute obligated it to contribute an additional $50 to $100 million. A four-Justice plurality would have held this to be a taking of property, arguing that legislation is unconstitutional "if it imposes severe retroactive liability on a limited class of parties that could not have anticipated the liability, and the extent of that liability is substantially disproportionate to the parties' experience." 524 U.S. at 528-529. In this case, the plurality found this standard met because Eastern Enterprises' new liability was not proportional to its experience with the plan and substantially interfered with its investment-backed expectations by imposing obligations based on events that had

happened 30 years earlier. In addition, no pattern of regulation would have placed Eastern on notice that such large, disproportionate, retroactive obligations might be forthcoming.

However, a five-Justice majority took a different approach, all agreeing that the case should not be resolved under the takings clause. Justice Kennedy voted with the four- Justice plurality to hold the statute unconstitutional as applied to Eastern, but did so under the due process clause, arguing that the problem with the law was not that it "took" property but was unfairly retroactive. "If retroactive laws [of great severity] change the legal consequences of transactions long closed, the change can destroy the reasonable certainty and security which are the very objects of property ownership." *Id.* at 548-549. (Kennedy, J., concurring in the judgment and dissenting in part). The four other dissenting Justices agreed that the statute should be evaluated under the due process clause, but would have held that it was not unfair retroactive legislation both because Eastern had led its employees to expect that it would take care of them and because it was not unfair to require Eastern to compensate its own workers for medical problems caused by their exposure to coal dust on the job.

Is due process a better constitutional framework than the takings clause for evaluating state actions that retroactively upset investment-backed expectations? What are the arguments on both sides? For one approach, *see* Eduardo Moisés Peñalver & Lior Jacob Strahilevitz, *Judicial Takings or Due Process?*, 97 Cornell L. Rev. 305 (2012) (arguing that the takings clause is more appropriate where judicial decisions intentionally seize private property to achieve legitimate public ends, but due process better serves to analyze cases where there is no intent to appropriate or the judicial action is claimed to serve no legitimate public purpose).

3. Practical difficulties with judicial takings. Because only four members of the Court endorsed the theory of judicial takings, it may not be necessary to work out the range of difficult procedural questions the doctrine poses any time soon. Those questions include how to join the state if the suit initially involves only private parties; what remedies should be available and, if compensation is required, how to compel the state to pay for the results of a judicial decision; and how to address the claims of owners whose property may be "taken" by a judicial decision to which they are not a party, among others. *See generally* D. Benjamin Barros, *The Complexities of Judicial Takings*, 45 U. Rich. L. Rev. 903 (2011).

4. Custom and beach access. One area where judicial takings has been an issue is in public access to beaches. *See* Chapter 1, §4. In *McBryde Sugar Co. v. Robinson*, 504 P.2d 1330 (Haw. 1973), the Hawai`i Supreme Court overruled a Territorial Court decision holding that two sugar plantation owners possessed certain water rights in their land. *Territory v. Gay*, 31 Haw. 376, 387-388, *aff'd*, 52 F.2d 356 (9th Cir. 1930). The Hawai`i Supreme Court held that this pre-statehood decision had unlawfully divested native Hawaiians of their traditional customary rights of access to water and that the state had the exclusive right to control the flow of the river in question. The property owners whose water rights were divested sued state officials, claiming that the court's decision in *McBryde* effectuated a taking of their property rights. The state defended on the grounds that the *McBryde* court overruled a prior decision in an effort to correct an error, that the overruled decision had itself effectuated a taking of native Hawaiians' property, and that the sugar companies never had rights to the land free of preexisting water easements. The Ninth Circuit ruled, in *Robinson v. Ariyoshi*, 753 F.2d 1468 (9th Cir. 1984), *aff'g* 441 F. Supp. 559 (D. Haw. 1977), *vacated on other grounds*, 477 U.S. 902 (1986), that the *McBryde* decision unconstitutionally took the "vested" property rights of the plantation owners without compensation.

By comparison, in *Stevens v. City of Cannon Beach*, 854 P.2d 449 (Or. 1993), Oregon beachfront owners unsuccessfully charged that the Oregon Supreme Court had effected a taking of their property when it applied the common law doctrine of custom to rule that the public had a right of access to dry sand areas of beaches for recreational purposes in *State ex rel. Thornton v. Hay*, 462 P.2d 671 (Or. 1969). The U.S. Supreme Court denied *certiorari*, 510 U.S. 1207 (1994), but Justices Scalia and O'Connor dissented from that denial, Justice Scalia writing that although "the Constitution leaves the law of real property to the States," a state may not "deny" property rights "by invoking nonexistent rules of state substantive law." Justice Scalia argued that the Oregon Supreme Court had misapplied the English doctrine of custom. "It is by no means clear that the facts — either as to the entire Oregon coast, or as to the small segment at issue here — meet the requirements for the English doctrine of custom." *See also Esplanade Properties, L.L.C. v. City of Seattle*, 307 F.3d 978 (9th Cir. 2002) (restriction on construction in tidelands area is not a taking because the public trust doctrine had always prohibited such uses to preserve public access).

What does it mean to say that the Oregon Supreme Court misapplied the English doctrine of custom? Isn't the issue the definition of the *Oregon* doctrine of custom? How could the Oregon Supreme Court get that wrong, if it is the final arbiter of what Oregon law is? Does it matter that the Oregon Supreme Court viewed the case as one of first impression?

§7 EXACTIONS AND LINKAGE REQUIREMENTS

Koontz v. St. Johns River Water Management District

133 S. Ct. 2586 (2013)

Justice Samuel A. Alito delivered the opinion of the Court.

In 1972, petitioner purchased an undeveloped 14.9-acre tract of land on the south side of Florida State Road 50, a divided four-lane highway east of Orlando. The property is located less than 1,000 feet from that road's intersection with Florida State Road 408, a tolled expressway that is one of Orlando's major thoroughfares.

A drainage ditch runs along the property's western edge, and high-voltage power lines bisect it into northern and southern sections. The combined effect of the ditch, a 100-foot wide area kept clear for the power lines, the highways, and other construction on nearby parcels is to isolate the northern section of petitioner's property from any other undeveloped land. Although largely classified as wetlands by the State, the northern section drains well; the most significant standing water forms in ruts in an unpaved road used to access the power lines. The natural topography of the property's southern section is somewhat more diverse, with a small creek, forested uplands, and wetlands that sometimes have water as much as a foot deep. A wildlife survey found evidence of animals that often frequent developed areas: raccoons, rabbits, several species of bird, and a turtle. The record also indicates that the land may be a suitable habitat for opossums.

The same year that petitioner purchased his property, Florida enacted the Water Resources Act, which divided the State into five water management districts and authorized each district to regulate "construction that connects to, draws water from, drains water into, or is placed in or across the waters in the state." 1972 Fla. Laws ch. 72-299, pt. IV, §1(5), pp. 1115, 1116 (codified as amended at Fla. Stat. §373.403(5) (2010)). Under the Act, a landowner wishing to undertake such construction must obtain from the relevant district a Management and Storage of Surface Water (MSSW) permit, which may impose "such reasonable conditions" on the permit as are "necessary to assure" that construction will "not be harmful to the water resources of the district." 1972 Fla. Laws §4(1), at 1118 (codified as amended at Fla. Stat. §373.413(1)).

In 1984, in an effort to protect the State's rapidly diminishing wetlands, the Florida Legislature passed the *Warren S. Henderson Wetlands Protection Act,* which made it illegal for anyone to "dredge or fill in, on, or over surface waters" without a Wetlands Resource Management (WRM) permit. 1984 Fla. Laws ch. 84-79, pt. VIII, §403.905(1), pp. 204-205. Under the Henderson Act, permit applicants are required to provide "reasonable assurance" that proposed construction on wetlands is "not contrary to the public interest," as defined by an enumerated list of criteria. See Fla. Stat. §373.414(1).

Petitioner decided to develop the 3.7-acre northern section of his property, and in 1994 he applied to the District for MSSW and WRM permits. Under his proposal, petitioner would have raised the elevation of the northernmost section of his land to make it suitable for a building, graded the land from the southern edge of the building site down to the elevation of the high-voltage electrical lines, and installed a dry-bed pond for retaining and gradually releasing stormwater runoff from the building and its parking lot. To mitigate the environmental effects of his proposal, petitioner offered to foreclose any possible future development of the approximately 11-acre southern section of his land by deeding to the District a conservation easement on that portion of his property.

The District considered the 11-acre conservation easement to be inadequate, and it informed petitioner that it would approve construction only if he agreed to one of two concessions. First, the District proposed that petitioner reduce the size of his development to 1 acre and deed to the District a conservation easement on the remaining 13.9 acres. In the alternative, the District told petitioner that he could proceed with the development as proposed, building on 3.7 acres and deeding a conservation easement to the government on the remainder of the property, if he also agreed to hire contractors to make improvements to District-owned land several miles away. When the District asks permit applicants to fund offsite mitigation work, its policy is never to require any particular offsite project, and it did not do so here. Instead, the District said that it "would also favorably consider" alternatives to its suggested offsite mitigation projects if petitioner proposed something "equivalent." App. 75.

Believing the District's demands for mitigation to be excessive in light of the environmental effects that his building proposal would have caused, petitioner filed suit in state court. Among other claims, he argued that he was entitled to relief under Fla. Stat. §373.617(2), which allows owners to recover "monetary damages" if a state agency's action is "an unreasonable exercise of the state's police power constituting a taking without just compensation."

After considering testimony from several experts who examined petitioner's property, the trial court found that the property's northern section had already been "seriously degraded" by extensive construction on the surrounding parcels. App. to Pet. for Cert. D-3. In light of this finding and petitioner's offer to dedicate nearly three-quarters of his land to the District, the trial court concluded that any further mitigation in the form of payment for offsite improvements to District property lacked both a nexus and rough proportionality to the environmental impact of the proposed construction. It accordingly held the District's actions unlawful under our decisions in *Nollan v. California Coastal Comm'n*, 483 U.S. 825 (1987) and *Dolan v. City of Tigard*, 512 U.S. 374 (1994).

The Florida District Court affirmed, but the State Supreme Court reversed. Recognizing that the majority opinion rested on a question of federal constitutional law on which the lower courts are divided, we granted the petition for a writ of certiorari, and now reverse.

II

A

We have said in a variety of contexts that "the government may not deny a benefit to a person because he exercises a constitutional right." *Regan v. Taxation With Representation of Wash.*, 461 U.S. 540, 545. In *Perry v. Sindermann*, 408 U.S. 593 (1972), for example, we held that a public college would violate a professor's freedom of speech if it declined to renew his contract because he was an outspoken critic of the college's administration. And in *Memorial Hospital v. Maricopa County*, 415 U.S. 250 (1974), we concluded that a county impermissibly burdened the right to travel by extending healthcare benefits only to those indigent sick who had been residents of the county for at least one year. Those cases reflect an overarching principle, known as the unconstitutional conditions doctrine, that vindicates the Constitution's enumerated rights by preventing the government from coercing people into giving them up.

Nollan and *Dolan* "involve a special application" of this doctrine that protects the Fifth Amendment right to just compensation for property the government takes when owners apply for land-use permits. Our decisions in those cases reflect two realities of the permitting process. The first is that land-use permit applicants are especially vulnerable to the type of coercion that the unconstitutional conditions doctrine prohibits because the government often has broad discretion to deny a permit that is worth far more than property it would like to take. By conditioning a building permit on the owner's deeding over a public right-of-way, for example, the government can pressure an owner into voluntarily giving up property for which the Fifth Amendment would otherwise require just compensation. So long as the building permit is more valuable than any just compensation the owner could hope to receive for the right-of-way, the owner is likely to accede to the government's demand, no matter how unreasonable. Extortionate demands of this sort frustrate the Fifth Amendment right to just compensation, and the unconstitutional conditions doctrine prohibits them.

A second reality of the permitting process is that many proposed land uses threaten to impose costs on the public that dedications of property can offset. Where a building proposal would substantially increase traffic congestion, for example, officials might condition permit approval on the owner's agreement to deed over the land needed to widen a public road. Respondent argues that a similar rationale justifies the exaction at issue here: petitioner's proposed construction project, it submits, would destroy wetlands on his property, and in order to compensate for this loss, respondent demands that he enhance wetlands elsewhere. Insisting that landowners internalize the negative externalities of their conduct is a hallmark of responsible land-use policy, and we have long sustained such regulations against constitutional attack. See *Village of Euclid v. Ambler Realty Co.*, 272 U.S. 365 (1926).

Nollan and *Dolan* accommodate both realities by allowing the government to condition approval of a permit on the dedication of property to the public so long as there is a "nexus" and "rough proportionality" between the property that the government demands and the social costs of the applicant's proposal. *Dolan, supra,* at 391; *Nollan,* 483 U.S., at 837. Our precedents thus enable permitting authorities to insist that applicants bear the full costs of their proposals while still forbidding the government from engaging in "out-and-out . . . extortion" that would thwart the Fifth Amendment right to just compensation. *Ibid.* Under *Nollan* and *Dolan* the government may choose whether and how a permit applicant is required to mitigate the impacts of a proposed development, but it may not leverage its legitimate interest in mitigation to pursue governmental ends that lack an essential nexus and rough proportionality to those impacts.

B

The principles that undergird our decisions in *Nollan* and *Dolan* do not change depending on whether the government approves a permit on the condition that the applicant turn over property or denies a permit because the applicant refuses to do so. We have often concluded that denials of governmental benefits were impermissible under the unconstitutional conditions doctrine. In so holding, we have recognized that regardless of whether the government ultimately succeeds in pressuring someone into forfeiting a constitutional right, the unconstitutional conditions doctrine forbids burdening the Constitution's enumerated rights by coercively withholding benefits from those who exercise them.

A contrary rule would be especially untenable in this case because it would enable the government to evade the limitations of *Nollan* and *Dolan* simply by phrasing its demands for property as conditions precedent to permit approval. [A] government order stating that a permit is "approved if" the owner turns over property would be subject to *Nollan* and *Dolan*, but an identical order that uses the words "denied until" would not. Our unconstitutional conditions cases have long refused to attach significance to the distinction between conditions precedent and conditions subsequent. To do so here would effectively render *Nollan* and *Dolan* a dead letter.

The Florida Supreme Court puzzled over how the government's demand for property can violate the Takings Clause even though "'no property of any kind was ever taken,'" 77 So. 3d, at 1225, but the unconstitutional conditions doctrine provides a ready answer. Extortionate demands for property in the land-use permitting context run afoul of the Takings Clause not because they take property but because they impermissibly burden the right not to have property taken without just compensation. As in other unconstitutional conditions cases in which someone refuses to cede a constitutional right in the face of coercive pressure, the impermissible denial of a governmental benefit is a constitutionally cognizable injury.

Nor does it make a difference, as respondent suggests, that the government might have been able to deny petitioner's application outright without giving him the option of securing a permit by agreeing to spend money to improve public lands. *See Penn Central Transp. Co. v. New York City*, 438 U.S. 104 (1978). Virtually all of our unconstitutional conditions cases involve a gratuitous governmental benefit of some kind. Yet we have repeatedly rejected the argument that if the government need not confer a benefit at all, it can withhold the benefit because someone refuses to give up constitutional rights. Even if respondent would have been entirely within its rights in denying the permit for some other reason, that greater authority does not imply a lesser power to condition permit approval on petitioner's forfeiture of his constitutional rights. See *Nollan*, 483 U.S., at 836-37 (explaining that "[t]he evident constitutional propriety" of prohibiting a land use "disappears . . . if the condition substituted for the prohibition utterly fails to further the end advanced as the justification for the prohibition").

That is not to say, however, that there is no relevant difference between a consummated taking and the denial of a permit based on an unconstitutionally extortionate demand. Where the permit is denied and the condition is never imposed, nothing has been taken. While the unconstitutional conditions doctrine recognizes that this burdens a constitutional right, the Fifth Amendment mandates a particular remedy—just compensation—only for takings. In cases where there is an excessive demand but no taking, whether money damages are available is not a question of federal constitutional law but of the cause of action—whether state or federal—on which the landowner relies. Because petitioner brought his claim pursuant to a state law cause of action, the Court has no occasion to discuss what remedies might be available for a *Nollan/Dolan* unconstitutional conditions violation either here or in other cases.

C

Respondent contends that we should affirm because petitioner sued for damages but is at most entitled to an injunction ordering that his permit issue without any conditions. But we need not decide whether federal law authorizes plaintiffs to recover damages for unconstitutional conditions claims predicated on the Takings Clause because petitioner brought his claim under state law. Florida law allows property owners to sue for "damages" whenever a state agency's action is "an unreasonable exercise of the state's police power constituting a taking without just compensation." Fla. Stat. §373.617. Whether that provision covers an unconstitutional conditions claim like the one at issue here is a question of state law that the Florida Supreme Court did not address and on which we will not opine.

For similar reasons, we decline to reach respondent's argument that its demands for property were too indefinite to give rise to liability under *Nollan* and *Dolan*. The Florida Supreme Court did not reach the question whether respondent issued a demand of sufficient concreteness to trigger the special protections of *Nollan* and *Dolan*. It relied instead on the Florida District Court of Appeals' characterization of respondent's behavior as a demand for *Nollan/Dolan* purposes. Whether that characterization is correct is beyond the scope of the questions the Court agreed to take up for review. If preserved, the issue remains open on remand for the Florida Supreme Court to address.

Finally, respondent argues that we need not decide whether its demand for offsite improvements satisfied *Nollan* and *Dolan* because it gave petitioner another avenue for obtaining permit approval. Specifically, respondent said that it would have approved a revised permit application that reduced the footprint of petitioner's proposed construction site from 3.7 acres to 1 acre and placed a conservation easement on the remaining 13.9 acres of petitioner's land. We agree with respondent that, so long as a permitting authority offers the landowner at least one alternative that would satisfy *Nollan* and *Dolan*, the landowner has not been subjected to an unconstitutional condition. But respondent's suggestion that we should treat its offer to let petitioner build on 1 acre as an alternative to offsite mitigation misapprehends the governmental benefit that petitioner was denied. Petitioner sought to develop 3.7 acres, but respondent in effect told petitioner that it would not allow him to build on 2.7 of those acres unless he agreed to spend money improving public lands. Petitioner claims that he was wrongfully denied a permit to build on those 2.7 acres. For that reason, respondent's offer to approve a less ambitious building project does not obviate the need to determine whether the demand for offsite mitigation satisfied *Nollan* and *Dolan*.

III

We turn to the Florida Supreme Court's alternative holding that petitioner's claim fails because respondent asked him to spend money rather than give up an easement on his land. A predicate for any unconstitutional conditions claim is that the government could not have constitutionally ordered the person asserting the claim to do what it attempted to pressure that person into doing. For that reason, we began our analysis in both *Nollan* and *Dolan* by observing that if the government had directly seized the easements it sought to obtain through the permitting process, it would have committed a *per se* taking.

We note as an initial matter that if we accepted this argument it would be very easy for land-use permitting officials to evade the limitations of *Nollan* and *Dolan*. Because the government need only provide a permit applicant with one alternative that satisfies the nexus and rough proportionality standards, a permitting authority wishing to exact an easement could simply give the owner a choice of either surrendering an easement or making a payment equal to the easement's value. Such so-called "in lieu of" fees are utterly commonplace, Rosenberg, *The Changing Culture of American Land Use Regulation: Paying for Growth with Impact Fees*, 59 S.M.U. L. Rev. 177, 202-03 (2006), and they are functionally equivalent to other types of land use exactions. For that reason and those that follow, we reject respondent's argument and hold that so-called "monetary exactions" must satisfy the nexus and rough proportionality requirements of *Nollan* and *Dolan*.

A

In *Eastern Enterprises v. Apfel*, 524 U.S. 498 (1998), the United States retroactively imposed on a former mining company an obligation to pay for the medical benefits of retired miners and their families. A four-Justice plurality concluded that the statute's imposition of retroactive financial liability was so arbitrary that it violated the Takings Clause. *Id.* at 529-37. Although Justice Kennedy concurred in the result on due process grounds, he joined four other Justices in dissent in arguing that the Takings Clause does not apply to government-imposed financial obligations that "d[o] not operate upon or alter an identified property interest." *Id.* at 540 (opinion concurring in judgment and dissenting in part); *see id.* at 554-56 (Breyer, J., dissenting) ("The 'private property' upon which the [Takings] Clause traditionally has focused is a specific interest in physical or intellectual property"). Relying on the concurrence and dissent in Eastern Enterprises, respondent argues that a requirement that petitioner spend money improving public lands could not give rise to a taking.

Respondent's argument rests on a mistaken premise. Unlike the financial obligation in *Eastern Enterprises*, the demand for money at issue here did "operate upon . . . an identified property interest" by directing the owner of a particular piece of property to make a monetary payment. *Id.* at 540 (opinion of Kennedy, J.). In this case, unlike *Eastern Enterprises*, the monetary obligation burdened petitioner's ownership of a specific parcel of land. In that sense, this case bears resemblance to our cases holding that the government must pay just compensation when it takes a lien — a right to receive money that is secured by a particular piece of property. *See Armstrong v. United States*, 364 U.S. 40, 44-49 (1960); *Louisville Joint Stock Land Bank v. Radford*, 295 U.S. 555, 601-02 (1935); *United States v. Security Industrial Bank*, 459 U.S. 70, 77-78 (1982). The fulcrum this case turns on is the direct link between the government's demand and a specific parcel of real property.[37] Because of that direct link, this case implicates the central concern of *Nollan* and *Dolan*: the risk that the government may use its

37. Thus, because the proposed offsite mitigation obligation in this case was tied to a particular parcel of land, this case does not implicate the question whether monetary exactions must be tied to a particular parcel of land in order to constitute a taking. That is so even when the demand is considered "outside the permitting process." *Post* (Kagan, J., dissenting). The unconstitutional conditions analysis requires us to set aside petitioner's permit application, not his ownership of a particular parcel of real property.

substantial power and discretion in land-use permitting to pursue governmental ends that lack an essential nexus and rough proportionality to the effects of the proposed new use of the specific property at issue, thereby diminishing without justification the value of the property.

In this case, moreover, petitioner does not ask us to hold that the government can commit a regulatory taking by directing someone to spend money. As a result, we need not apply *Penn Central*'s "essentially ad hoc, factual inquir[y]," 438 U.S., at 124, at all, much less extend that "already difficult and uncertain rule" to the "vast category of cases" in which someone believes that a regulation is too costly. *Eastern Enterprises*, 524 U.S., at 542 (opinion of Kennedy, J.). Instead, petitioner's claim rests on the more limited proposition that when the government commands the relinquishment of funds linked to a specific, identifiable property interest such as a bank account or parcel of real property, a "*per se* [takings] approach" is the proper mode of analysis under the Court's precedent. *Brown v. Legal Foundation of Wash.*, 538 U.S. 216 (2003).

B

Respondent and the dissent argue that if monetary exactions are made subject to scrutiny under *Nollan* and *Dolan*, then there will be no principled way of distinguishing impermissible land-use exactions from property taxes. We think they exaggerate both the extent to which that problem is unique to the land-use permitting context and the practical difficulty of distinguishing between the power to tax and the power to take by eminent domain.

It is beyond dispute that "[t]axes and user fees . . . are not 'takings.' " *Brown v. Legal Foundation of Wash.*, 538 U.S. 216, 243 n.2 (2003) (Scalia, J., dissenting). This case therefore does not affect the ability of governments to impose property taxes, user fees, and similar laws and regulations that may impose financial burdens on property owners. At the same time, we have repeatedly found takings where the government, by confiscating financial obligations, achieved a result that could have been obtained by imposing a tax. Most recently, in *Brown, supra*, at 232 we were unanimous in concluding that a State Supreme Court's seizure of the interest on client funds held in escrow was a taking despite the unquestionable constitutional propriety of a tax that would have raised exactly the same revenue. Our holding in *Brown* followed from *Phillips v. Washington Legal Foundation*, 524 U.S. 156 (1998), and *Webb's Fabulous Pharmacies, Inc. v. Beckwith*, 449 U.S. 155 (1980), two earlier cases in which we treated confiscations of money as takings despite their functional similarity to a tax. Perhaps most closely analogous to the present case, we have repeatedly held that the government takes property when it seizes liens, and in so ruling we have never considered whether the government could have achieved an economically equivalent result through taxation. *Armstrong*, 364 U.S. 40; *Louisville Joint Stock Land Bank*, 295 U.S. 555.

Two facts emerge from those cases. The first is that the need to distinguish taxes from takings is not a creature of our holding today that monetary exactions are subject to scrutiny under *Nollan* and *Dolan*. Rather, the problem is inherent in this Court's long-settled view that property the government could constitutionally demand through its taxing power can also be taken by eminent domain.

Second, our cases show that teasing out the difference between taxes and takings is more difficult in theory than in practice. *Brown* is illustrative. Similar to respondent in this case, the respondents in *Brown* argued that extending the protections of the Takings Clause to a bank account would open a Pandora's Box of constitutional challenges to taxes. But also like respondent here, the *Brown* respondents never claimed that they were exercising their power to levy taxes when they took the petitioners' property. Any such argument would have been implausible under state law; in Washington, taxes are levied by the legislature, not the courts.

The same dynamic is at work in this case because Florida law greatly circumscribes respondent's power to tax. *See* Fla. Stat. §373.503 (authorizing respondent to impose ad valorem tax on properties within its jurisdiction); §373.109 (authorizing respondent to charge permit application fees but providing that such fees "shall not exceed the cost . . . for processing, monitoring, and inspecting for compliance with the permit"). If respondent had argued that its demand for money was a tax, it would have effectively conceded that its denial of petitioner's permit was improper under Florida law. Far from making that concession, respondent has maintained throughout this litigation that it considered petitioner's money to be a substitute for his deeding to the public a conservation easement on a larger parcel of undeveloped land.

We need not decide at precisely what point a land-use permitting charge denominated by the government as a "tax" becomes "so arbitrary . . . that it was not the exertion of taxation but a confiscation of property." *Brushaber v. Union Pacific R. Co.*, 240 U.S. 1, 24-25 (1916). For present purposes, it suffices to say that despite having long recognized that "the power of taxation should not be confused with the power of eminent domain," *Houck v. Little River Drainage Dist.*, 239 U.S. 254, 264 (1915), we have had little trouble distinguishing between the two.

C

Finally, we disagree with the dissent's forecast that our decision will work a revolution in land use law by depriving local governments of the ability to charge reasonable permitting fees. Numerous courts—including courts in many of our Nation's most populous States—have confronted constitutional challenges to monetary exactions over the last two decades and applied the standard from *Nollan* and *Dolan* or something like it. *See, e.g., Northern Ill. Home Builders Assn. v. County of Du Page*, 649 N.E.2d 384, 388-389 (Ill. 1995); *Home Builders Assn. v. Beavercreek*, 729 N.E.2d 349, 356 (Ohio 2000); *Flower Mound v. Stafford Estates Ltd. P'ship*, 135 S.W.3d 620, 640-641 (Tex. 2004). Yet the "significant practical harm" the dissent predicts has not come to pass. That is hardly surprising, for the dissent is correct that state law normally provides an independent check on excessive land use permitting fees.

The dissent's argument that land use permit applicants need no further protection when the government demands money is really an argument for overruling *Nollan* and *Dolan*. After all, the Due Process Clause protected the Nollans from an unfair allocation of public burdens, and they too could have argued that the government's demand for property amounted to a taking under the *Penn Central* framework. See *Nollan*, 483 U.S., at 838. We have repeatedly rejected the dissent's contention that other constitutional doctrines leave no room for the nexus and rough proportionality requirements of *Nollan* and *Dolan*. Mindful of the special vulnerability of land use permit applicants to extortionate demands for money, we do so again today.

Justice ELENA KAGAN, with whom Justice GINSBURG, Justice BREYER, and Justice SOTOMAYOR join, dissenting.

Claims that government regulations violate the Takings Clause by unduly restricting the use of property are generally "governed by the standards set forth in *Penn Central Transp. Co. v. New York City*, 438 U.S. 104 (1978)." *Lingle v. Chevron U.S.A. Inc.*, 544 U.S. 528, 538. Our decisions in *Nollan* and *Dolan* are different: They provide an independent layer of protection in "the special context of land-use exactions." *Lingle*, 544 U.S., at 538. In that situation, the "government demands that a landowner dedicate an easement" or surrender a piece of real property "as a condition of obtaining a development permit." *Id.* at 546. If the government appropriated such a property interest outside the permitting process, its action would constitute a taking, necessitating just compensation. *Id.* at 547. *Nollan* and *Dolan* prevent the government from exploiting the landowner's permit application to evade the constitutional obligation to pay for the property. They do so, as the majority explains, by subjecting the government's demand to heightened scrutiny: The government may condition a land-use permit on the relinquishment of real property only if it shows a "nexus" and "rough proportionality" between the demand made and "the impact of the proposed development." *Dolan*, 512 U.S., at 386, 391. *Nollan* and *Dolan* thus serve not to address excessive regulatory burdens on land use (the function of *Penn Central*), but instead to stop the government from imposing an "unconstitutional condition" — a requirement that a person give up his constitutional right to receive just compensation "in exchange for a discretionary benefit" having "little or no relationship" to the property taken. *Lingle*, 544 U.S., at 547.

Accordingly, the *Nollan-Dolan* test applies only when the property the government demands during the permitting process is the kind it otherwise would have to pay for — or, put differently, when the appropriation of that property, outside the permitting process, would constitute a taking. Only if that is true could the government's demand for the property force a landowner to relinquish his constitutional right to just compensation.

Here, Koontz claims that the District demanded that he spend money to improve public wetlands, not that he hand over a real property interest. I assume for now that the District made that demand (although I think it did not.) The key question then is: Independent of the permitting process, does requiring a person to pay money to the government, or spend money on its behalf, constitute a taking requiring just compensation? Only if the answer is yes does the *Nollan-Dolan* test apply.

But we have already answered that question no. *Eastern Enterprises v. Apfel*, 524 U.S. 498 (1998), as the Court describes, involved a federal statute requiring a former mining company to pay a large sum of money for the health benefits of retired employees. Five Members of the Court determined that the law did not effect a taking, distinguishing between the appropriation of a specific property interest and the imposition of an order to pay money. Justice Kennedy acknowledged in his controlling opinion that the statute "impose[d] a staggering financial burden" (which influenced his conclusion that it violated due process). *Id.* at 540 (opinion concurring in judgment and dissenting in part). Still, Justice Kennedy explained, the law did not effect a taking because it did not "operate upon or alter" a "specific and identified propert[y] or property right[ ]." *Id.* at 540-41. Justice Breyer, writing for four more Justices, agreed. He stated that the Takings Clause applies only when the government appropriates a "specific interest in physical or intellectual property" or "a specific, separately identifiable fund of money"; by contrast, the Clause has no bearing when the government imposes "an ordinary liability to pay money." *Id.* at 554-55 (dissenting opinion).

Thus, a requirement that a person pay money to repair public wetlands is not a taking. Such an order does not affect a "specific and identified propert[y] or property right[ ]"; it simply "imposes an obligation to perform an act" (the improvement of wetlands) that costs money. *Id.* at 540-41 (opinion of Kennedy, J.). To be sure, when a person spends money on the government's behalf, or pays money directly to the government, it "will reduce [his] net worth" — but that "can be said of any law which has an adverse economic effect" on someone. *Id.* at 543.

The majority tries to distinguish *Apfel* by asserting that the District's demand here was "closely analogous" (and "bears resemblance") to the seizure of a lien on property or an income stream from a parcel of land. But the majority's citations succeed only in showing what this case is not. When the government dissolves a lien, or appropriates a determinate income stream from a piece of property — or, for that matter, seizes a particular "bank account or [the] accrued interest" on it — the government indeed takes a "specific" and "identified property interest." *Apfel*, 524 U.S., at 540-41 (opinion of Kennedy, J.). But nothing like that occurred here. The District did not demand any particular lien, or bank account, or income stream from property. It just ordered Koontz to spend or pay money (again, assuming it ordered anything at all). Koontz's liability would have been the same whether his property produced income or not — e.g., even if all he wanted to build was a family home. And similarly, Koontz could meet that obligation from whatever source he chose — a checking account, shares of stock, a wealthy uncle; the District was "indifferent as to how [he] elect[ed] to [pay] or the property [he] use[d] to do so." *Id.* at 540.

The majority thus falls back on the sole way the District's alleged demand related to a property interest: The demand arose out of the permitting process for Koontz's land. But under the analytic framework that *Nollan* and *Dolan* established, that connection alone is insufficient to trigger heightened scrutiny. As I have described, the heightened standard of *Nollan* and *Dolan* is not a freestanding protection for land-use permit applicants; rather, it is "a special application of the doctrine of unconstitutional conditions, which provides that the government may not require a person to give up a constitutional right — here the right to receive just compensation when property is taken" — in exchange for a land-use permit. *Lingle*, 544 U.S., at 547. As such, *Nol-*

lan and *Dolan* apply only if . . . the demand would have constituted a taking when executed outside the permitting process. And here, under *Apfel*, it would not.[38]

The majority's approach, on top of its analytic flaws, threatens significant practical harm. By applying *Nollan* and *Dolan* to permit conditions requiring monetary payments — with no express limitation except as to taxes — the majority extends the Takings Clause, with its notoriously "difficult" and "perplexing" standards, into the very heart of local land-use regulation and service delivery. 524 U.S., at 541. Cities and towns across the nation impose many kinds of permitting fees every day. Some enable a government to mitigate a new development's impact on the community, like increased traffic or pollution — or destruction of wetlands. Others cover the direct costs of providing services like sewage or water to the development. Still others are meant to limit the number of landowners who engage in a certain activity, as fees for liquor licenses do. All now must meet *Nollan* and *Dolan*'s nexus and proportionality tests. The Federal Constitution thus will decide whether one town is overcharging for sewage, or another is setting the price to sell liquor too high. And the flexibility of state and local governments to take the most routine actions to enhance their communities will diminish accordingly.

That problem becomes still worse because the majority's distinction between monetary "exactions" and taxes is so hard to apply. The majority acknowledges, as it must, that taxes are not takings. But once the majority decides that a simple demand to pay money — the sort of thing often viewed as a tax — can count as an impermissible "exaction," how is anyone to tell the two apart? How to separate orders to pay money from . . . well, orders to pay money, so that a locality knows what it can (and cannot) do. Because "[t]here is no set rule" by which to determine "in which category a particular" action belongs, *Eastern Diversified Properties, Inc. v. Montgomery Cty.*, 570 A.2d 850, 854 (Md. 1990), courts often reach opposite conclusions about classifying nearly identical fees. *Compare, e.g., Coulter v. Rawlins*, 662 P.2d 888, 901-904 (Wyo. 1983) (holding that a fee to enhance parks, imposed as a permit condition, was a regulatory exaction), *with Home Builders Assn. v. West Des Moines*, 644 N.W.2d 339, 350 (Iowa 2002) (rejecting *Coulter* and holding that a nearly identical fee was a tax). Nor does the majority's opinion provide any help with that issue: Perhaps its most striking feature is its refusal to say even a word about how to make the distinction that will now determine whether a given fee is subject to heightened scrutiny. [T]he majority's refusal "to say more" about the scope of its new rule now casts a cloud on every

38. The majority's sole response is that "the unconstitutional conditions analysis requires us to set aside petitioner's permit application, not his ownership of a particular parcel of real property." That mysterious sentence fails to make the majority's opinion cohere with the unconstitutional conditions doctrine, as anyone has ever known it. That doctrine applies only if imposing a condition directly — i.e., independent of an exchange for a government benefit — would violate the Constitution. Here, *Apfel* makes clear that the District's condition would not do so: The government may (separate and apart from permitting) require a person — whether Koontz or anyone else — to pay or spend money without effecting a taking. The majority offers no theory to the contrary: It does not explain, as it must, why the District's condition was "unconstitutional."

decision by every local government to require a person seeking a permit to pay or spend money.[39]

By extending *Nollan* and *Dolan*'s heightened scrutiny to a simple payment demand, the majority threatens the heartland of local land-use regulation and service delivery, at a bare minimum depriving state and local governments of "necessary predictability." *Apfel,* 524 U.S., at 542 (opinion of Kennedy, J.). That decision is unwarranted — and deeply unwise. I would keep *Nollan* and *Dolan* in their intended sphere and affirm the Florida Supreme Court.

II

A

Nollan and *Dolan* apply only when the government makes a "demand[ ]" that a landowner turn over property in exchange for a permit. *Lingle,* 544 U.S., at 546. A *Nollan-Dolan* claim therefore depends on a showing of government coercion, not relevant in an ordinary challenge to a permit denial. Before applying *Nollan* and *Dolan,* a court must find that the permit denial occurred because the government made a demand of the landowner, which he rebuffed. And unless *Nollan* and *Dolan* are to wreck land-use permitting throughout the country — to the detriment of both communities and property owners — that demand must be unequivocal. If a local government risked a lawsuit every time it made a suggestion to an applicant about how to meet permitting criteria, it would cease to do so; indeed, the government might desist altogether from communicating with applicants. That hazard is to some extent baked into *Nollan* and *Dolan*; observers have wondered whether those decisions have inclined some local governments to deny permit applications outright, rather than negotiate agreements that could work to both sides' advantage. See W. Fischel, *Regulatory Takings* 346 (1995). But that danger would rise exponentially if something less than a clear condition — if each idea or proposal offered in the back-and-forth of reconciling diverse interests — triggered *Nollan-Dolan* scrutiny. At that point, no local government official with a decent lawyer would have a conversation with a developer.

[Here,] the District never made a demand or set a condition — not to cede an identifiable property interest, not to undertake a particular mitigation project, not even to write a check to the government. Instead, the District suggested to Koontz several non-exclusive ways to make his applications conform to state law. The District's only hard-and-fast requirement was that Koontz do something — anything — to satisfy the relevant permitting criteria. Koontz's failure to obtain the permits therefore did not result from his refusal to accede to an allegedly extortionate demand or condition;

39. Our *Penn Central* test protects against regulations that unduly burden an owner's use of his property: Unlike the *Nollan-Dolan* standard, that framework fits to a T a complaint (like Koontz's) that a permitting condition makes it inordinately expensive to develop land. And the Due Process Clause provides an additional backstop against excessive permitting fees by preventing a government from conditioning a land-use permit on a monetary requirement that is "basically arbitrary." *Eastern Enters. v. Apfel,* 524 U.S. 498, 557-58 (1998) (Breyer, J., dissenting).

rather, it arose from the legal deficiencies of his applications, combined with his unwillingness to correct them by any means. *Nollan* and *Dolan* were never meant to address such a run-of-the-mill denial of a land-use permit. As applications of the unconstitutional conditions doctrine, those decisions require a condition; and here, there was none.

B

And finally, a third difficulty: Even if (1) money counted as "specific and identified propert[y]" under *Apfel* (though it doesn't), and (2) the District made a demand for it (though it didn't), (3) Koontz never paid a cent, so the District took nothing from him. The majority remands that question to the Florida Supreme Court, and given how it disposes of the other issues here, I can understand why. As the majority indicates, a State could decide to create a damages remedy not only for a taking, but also for an unconstitutional conditions claim predicated on the Takings Clause. And that question is one of state law, which we usually do well to leave to state courts.

But as I look to the Florida statute here, I cannot help but see yet another reason why the Florida Supreme Court got this case right. That statute authorizes damages only for "an unreasonable exercise of the state's police power constituting a taking without just compensation." Fla. Stat. §373.617 (2010). In what legal universe could a law authorizing damages only for a "taking" also provide damages when (as all agree) no taking has occurred? I doubt that inside-out, upside-down universe is the State of Florida. Certainly, none of the Florida courts in this case suggested that the majority's hypothesized remedy actually exists; rather, the trial and appellate courts imposed a damages remedy on the mistaken theory that there had been a taking (although of exactly what neither was clear). So I would, once more, affirm the Florida Supreme Court, not make it say again what it has already said — that Koontz is not entitled to money damages.

Notes and Questions

1. **Linkage ordinances and exactions.** Municipalities regularly enact ordinances that require developers to mitigate the impact of new development, or authorize local agencies to negotiate for such mitigation in the permitting process. This mitigation can come either through specific improvements or dedications or through payments in lieu of such mitigation, also called impact fees.

For example, new construction may exacerbate local shortages in low-income housing by increasing employment, and therefore the demand for housing, in the locality. If the increased demand is not entirely met by new construction, competition for existing housing both raises rents and pushes out lower-income tenants. It is not profitable to build low-income housing in the absence of governmental subsidies since poor persons cannot afford to pay even the minimum costs for housing; for this reason, the market does not respond to housing shortages by constructing new low-income housing. New development is therefore thought to create externalities — exacerbating shortages in low-income housing or pushing low-income persons out of the city or into undesirable neighborhoods. Linkage programs are intended to internalize these costs by requiring developers to account to the community for those externalities, again either by dedicating a portion of new development to affordable housing or by paying for such development off site. Linkage programs and exactions have been applied to a wide variety of negative externalities from development, including child care shortages, new demand for public education, increased use of public infrastructure such as roads and transit, and other burdens on existing community amenities.

Land use regulation in recent years has increasingly shifted to a model of negotiation, *see* Chapter 7, §1.5, and exactions that seek to mitigate the negative impact of new development have been an important aspect of such negotiations. *Koontz* suggests that a proposal by a local agency in the context of negotiations over permit approval can give rise to liability under the doctrine announced in *Nollan v. California Coastal Commission,* 483 U.S. 825 (1987), and *Dolan v. City of Tigard,* 512 U.S. 374 (1994). As Justice Kagan's dissent in *Koontz* points out, this has the potential to deter what might be mutually beneficial agreements between developers and public officials and may lead local governments to make permitting a less discretionary, and thus more blunt, process.

2. Impact fees and individualized determinations. Prior to *Koontz,* some courts had held that the *Nollan-Dolan* unconstitutional conditions doctrine did not apply to impact fees because both cases had involved required dedications of land. *See, e.g., Garneau v. City of Seattle,* 147 F.3d 802 (9th Cir. 1998). *Koontz* has now settled the general question whether *Nollan-Dolan* applies to monetary exactions, but leaves open whether it applies only to individualized decisions or also applies to general legislative judgments about impact.

In *Koontz, Nollan,* and *Dolan,* a government agency made an individualized determination about a particular owner in the context of permit review. There was no general law or regulation requiring all owners to take similar steps. Many linkage laws, however, provide pre-set conditions that developers must meet. Such general laws may mitigate some concern over the risk of abuse by local officials and may also represent a general law affecting many or all parcels of land in an area. They may therefore create an "average reciprocity of advantage" like a general zoning law rather than an expropriation of property from an individual owner that is out of proportion to any harms caused by that owner.

Some courts have held that it is sufficient for a local government to make a general determination that particular types of development have particular impacts and impose fees reasonably related to those impacts. For example, a city might commission a study that demonstrates that new commercial development increases the need for housing and this need increases demand on the existing housing supply, bidding up prices and pushing out low-income families who cannot find affordable housing because the market does not find it profitable to build low-income housing. *San Remo Hotel L.P. v. City & County of San Francisco,* 41 P.3d 87, 102-103 (Cal. 2002), *aff'd on other grounds,* 545 U.S. 323 (2005) (*Nollan-Dolan* test applies to a housing replacement fee that is determined on an *ad hoc* or individualized or "adjudicative" basis but not to general legislatively determined fees); *Home Builders Association of Dayton & Miami Valley v. City of Beaver Creek,* 729 N.E.2d 349 (Ohio 2000) (upholding legislatively determined impact fee under *Nollan-Dolan* test); *Holmdel Builders Association v. Holmdel,* 583 A.2d 277 (N.J. 1990) ("We find a sound basis to support a legislative judgment that there is a reasonable relationship between unrestrained nonresidential development and the need for affordable residential development.").

Other courts have disagreed, noting that, because *Dolan* requires individualized determinations that impact fees bear a "rough proportionality" to the externalities of the development, studies might have to be conducted for each parcel subjected to the exaction. They have struck down impact fees that could not be shown to be related to the particular impacts of the development of particular parcels of land. *See, e.g., Volusia County v. Aberdeen at Ormond Beach, L.P.,* 760 So. 2d 126 (Fla. 2000) (uniform impact fee to fund schools was unconstitutional as applied to mobile home park only open to persons over 55).

3. Essential nexus and rough proportionality. *Nollan* and *Dolan* established two central federal constitutional requirements for any exaction: that there be an "essential nexus" between the exaction and the mitigation sought by the government and, if that threshold is crossed, that the mitigation have some reasonable relationship to the impact of the new development. Because the phrase "reasonable relationship," which had been common in the state courts, was too similar to the term "rational basis" used in equal protection cases, the Supreme Court in *Dolan* adopted the phrase "rough proportionality." 512 U.S. at 391. In *Nollan,* the Court found no essential nexus between the government's interest in protecting the public's view of a beach and the beach access that would facilitate and a requirement that beachfront owners applying for a building permit provide a right of way for the public to reach the beach. 483 U.S. at 836-837. In *Dolan,* a city was able to satisfy the threshold nexus requirement when it sought to condition an expansion of an owner's commercial property on requirements that the owner dedicate land in a flood plain for a public greenway to facilitate storm drainage and allow a bike and pedestrian path on her property to offset the increased traffic the development would generate. 512 U.S. at 387. However, the owner prevailed because the city could not demonstrate the required relationship between the impact of the new building and the specific conditions imposed.

It can be difficult to evaluate "proportionality," which, as the Utah Supreme Court has pointed out, is a term that does not suggest any particular ratio of harm and mitigation. *B.A.M. Development, L.L.C. v. Salt Lake County,* 196 P.3d 601 (Utah 2008) ("Of course, the [U.S. Supreme] Court did not mean rough *proportionality* at all. While 1 to 1 is a proportion, so is 1 to 1000, as any fifth-grade student will be happy to tell you. Any two numbers, measured by the same units, form a proportion. So to be roughly proportional literally means to be roughly related, not necessarily roughly *equivalent,* which is the concept the Court seemed to be trying to describe."). As a result, exactions are often accompanied by studies, sometimes quite extensive, about the relationship between development impact and required mitigation.

4. Unconstitutional conditions and takings. Most unconstitutional conditions cases involve situations where someone is being asked to give up a constitutional right in exchange for some government benefit. *See, e.g., United States Agency for International Development v. Alliance for Open Society International, Inc.*, 133 S. Ct. 2321 (2013) (requirement that aid recipients have an anti-prostitution policy was an unconstitutional burden on free speech). However, the *Koontz* majority does not hold, although it appears to assume, that the underlying suggestion regarding funding offsite improvements to mitigate the harm of the proposed development would necessarily have been a taking if the District had imposed it directly as a regulatory requirement. This may signal an attempt by the Court to expand takings doctrine. The Court may alternatively have viewed its holding as a preventative measure to forestall even the threat of potentially unconstitutional action. If so, is that an appropriate role for the Court to take?

5. Money and takings. The *Koontz* majority and dissent disagree about whether an obligation to pay a fungible amount of money can give rise to takings liability. The Court had previously addressed takings cases involving specific and identifiable funds. In *Webb's Fabulous Pharmacies, Inc. v. Beckwith*, 449 U.S. 155 (1980), for example, a company called Eckerd's of College Park, Inc., had agreed to purchase Webb's Fabulous Pharmacies, Inc. for over $1.8 million. When it came time to close on the purchase, however, it appeared that the pharmacy's debts were greater than the purchase price. Eckerd's filed an interpleader, which is an action to resolve claims to a limited pool of funds, bringing in the pharmacy and its numerous creditors. Eckerd's deposited the amount of the purchase price with the court, which the court's clerk then deposited in an interest-bearing account. Nearly a year later, the court appointed a receiver to process claims against this fund, which the court ordered transferred to the receiver. Interest on the fund by that point totaled more than $100,000, but was not included in the transfer. The receiver filed a motion seeking to have the court clerk transfer the interest, which the court granted. On appeal, however, the Florida Supreme Court reversed, relying on a state statute that provided that "[a]ll interest accruing from moneys deposited shall be deemed income of the office of the clerk of the circuit court investing such moneys," Fla. Stat. §28.33.

The Supreme Court in turn reversed, reasoning that:

> The principal sum deposited in the registry of the court plainly was private property, and was not the property of Seminole County. The deposited fund was the amount received as the purchase price for Webb's assets. It was property held only for the ultimate benefit of Webb's creditors, not for the benefit of the court and not for the benefit of the county. And it was held only for the purpose of making a fair distribution among those creditors. Eventually, and inevitably, that fund, less proper charges authorized by the court, would be distributed among the creditors as their claims were recognized by the court. The creditors thus had a state-created property right to their respective portions of the fund.
>
> What would justify the county's retention of that interest? It is obvious that the interest was not a fee for services, for any services obligation to the county was paid for

> and satisfied by [a separate] fee and described specifically in that statute as a fee "for services" by the clerk's office. Section 28.33, in contrast, in no way relates the interest of which it speaks to "services rendered." Indeed, if the county were entitled to the interest, its officials would feel an inherent pressure and possess a natural inclination to defer distribution, for that interest return would be greater the longer the fund is held; there would be, therefore, a built-in disincentive against distributing the principal to those entitled to it.
>
> This Court has been permissive in upholding governmental action that may deny the property owner of some beneficial use of his property or that may restrict the owner's full exploitation of the property, if such public action is justified as promoting the general welfare. Here, however, Seminole County has not merely "adjust[ed] the benefits and burdens of economic life to promote the common good." [*Penn Central Transportation Co. v. New York City*, 438 U.S. 104, 125-129 (1978).] Rather, the exaction is a forced contribution to general governmental revenues, and it is not reasonably related to the costs of using the courts. No police power justification is offered for the deprivation. Neither the statute nor appellees suggest any reasonable basis to sustain the taking of the interest earned by the interpleader fund.
>
> Neither the Florida Legislature by statute, nor the Florida courts by judicial decree, may accomplish the result the county seeks simply by recharacterizing the principal as "public money" because it is held temporarily by the court. The earnings of a fund are incidents of ownership of the fund itself and are property just as the fund itself is property. The state statute has the practical effect of appropriating for the county the value of the use of the fund for the period in which it is held in the registry. To put it another way: a State, by *ipse dixit*, may not transform private property into public property without compensation, even for the limited duration of the deposit in court. This is the very kind of thing that the Taking Clause of the Fifth Amendment was meant to prevent. That Clause stands as a shield against the arbitrary use of governmental power.

449 U.S. at 160-164.

In *Phillips v. Washington Legal Foundation*, 524 U.S. 156 (1998), a public interest organization challenged a Texas practice, used by almost every state, that requires lawyers to place client funds held by lawyers into a common pool managed by the state in order to generate interest on those funds so that the interest (so-called Interest on Lawyers' Trust Accounts or IOLTAs) could be used to help fund legal services for the poor. Texas had argued that the interest earned on the pooled account was not the client's "property" because it was only earned as a result of the state mandating the pooling of funds and thus the client lost nothing that she would ever have earned. The Supreme Court held that interest earned on such accounts was "property" belonging to the client whose funds generated the interest even if the client's account was so small and held for so short a time that it would not have generated any interest unless it were pooled with other such accounts.

In a follow-up case several years later, *Brown v. Legal Foundation of Washington*, 538 U.S. 216 (2003), the Supreme Court addressed the issue of whether IOLTA programs constitute unconstitutional takings of property. On remand in *Phillips*, the trial court had held that, even though the interest was *property* of the client, the IOLTA program did not constitute a *taking* of property because the program applied only to client funds that would not have earned interest absent the program and that the clients therefore "lost nothing of economically realizable value." *Washington Legal Foundation v. Texas Equal Access to Justice*, 86 F. Supp. 2d 624, 643 (D. Tex. 2000). The Supreme Court affirmed but on a different theory. It held by a 5-4 vote that the IOLTA program had indeed "taken property" belonging to the clients; on the other hand, the Court ruled that it had not done so "without just compensation." Justice Stevens explained that no compensation was due because the clients would not have earned any interest on their funds absent the IOLTA program; thus their loss of this interest caused them no economic loss and just compensation is measured "by the property owner's loss rather than the government's gain," *id.* at 235-236. Further, no compensation is due for the "nonpecuniary consequences" of using the interest for purposes other than those that might have been chosen by the owner. *Id.* at 236-237.

These cases all involve some identifiable fund but, as the *Koontz* majority and dissent both note, *Eastern Enterprises v. Apfel*, 524 U.S. 498 (1998), had seemed to resolve the question whether the takings clause applies to the obligation to pay money beyond that context. Five members of the Court agreed that the takings clause applies only to takings of specific property interests, such as interests in real property or interests in a particular identifiable fund of money; it does not apply to general obligations to pay money from whatever funds one possesses. Justice Alito distinguishes this approach by arguing that the demand for money in *Koontz* in fact operated on an identifiable property interest — not the funds themselves, but "petitioner's ownership of a specific parcel of land." Is that a meaningful distinction or is the *Koontz* dissent more convincing when it comes to *Apfel*?

If takings claims are not limited to specific funds, courts will be required to adjudicate not only the point at which a fee violates *Nollan-Dolan*, but also when fees and taxes more generally might constitute a taking. All taxation by its very nature arguably can be thought to "take" property by requiring payments of money to the government but if every tax were a taking of property then the taxing power would be meaningless. The Court in *Koontz* argued that it will not be difficult to distinguish between taxes and claims for fund that trigger takings liability. Is that argument convincing?

6. The denominator in another guise? *Koontz* does not explicitly discuss the Court's varying approaches since *Mahon* to determining the relevant parcel for purposes of the takings clause. The majority, however, appears to find that the right to build on a 3.7-acre portion of Koontz's property to be a distinct property interest. The Court indicates that:

> respondent's suggestion that we should treat its offer to let petitioner build on 1 acre as an alternative to offsite mitigation misapprehends the governmental benefit that petitioner was denied. Petitioner sought to develop 3.7 acres, but respondent in effect told petitioner that it would not allow him to build on 2.7 of those acres unless he agreed to spend money improving public lands. Petitioner claims that he was wrongfully denied a permit to build on those 2.7 acres.

If this were a straightforward takings claim, would the denial of the right to build on a portion of an owner's property be treated as a distinct property interest?

7. Government benefits. *Koontz* holds that *Nollan-Dolan* applies even where the underlying governmental benefit is entirely discretionary, given that the Water District would have been entitled to deny the permit outright. In *Ruckelshaus v. Monsanto Co.*, 467 U.S. 986 (1984), the Supreme Court held that the takings clause was not violated by a federal law requiring that businesses applying for government permission to use an insecticide disclose trade secrets to the government and consent to government use and disclosure of those trade secrets. In a footnote in *Nollan*, Justice Scalia distinguished *Monsanto* by arguing that a right to register and sell an insecticide was a "valuable government benefit" and not an established property right, whereas the "right to build on one's own property — even though its exercise can be subjected to legitimate permitting requirements — cannot remotely be described as a 'government benefit.'" *Nollan*, 483 U.S. at 833 n.2. Thus, Justice Scalia concluded, the "announcement that the application for (or granting of) the permit will entail the yielding of a property interest cannot be regarded as establishing the voluntary 'exchange,' that we found to have occurred in *Monsanto*." *Id.* Justice Brennan disagreed, arguing that *Nollan* was indistinguishable from *Monsanto*, 483 U.S. at 860 n.10:

> Both Monsanto and the Nollans hold property whose use is subject to regulation; Monsanto may not sell its property without obtaining government approval and the Nollans may not build new development on their property without government approval. Obtaining such approval is as much a "government benefit" for the Nollans as it is for Monsanto. If the Court is somehow suggesting that "the right to build on one's own property" has some privileged natural rights status, the argument is a curious one. By any traditional labor theory of value justification for property rights. *See, e.g.*, J. Locke, *The Second Treatise of Civil Government* 15-26 (1947 ed.), Monsanto would have a superior claim, for the chemical formulae which constitute its property only came into being by virtue of Monsanto's efforts.

Does *Koontz* change this analysis?

Problems

1. Imagine that you are counsel to a local agency charged with reviewing a permit application for development that did not meet existing state requirements, but that could do so with some modifications to mitigate the impacts of the development. After *Koontz*, what advice would you give your client about whether and how to negotiate permit conditions? If you were representing the developer, how would you approach such negotiations?

2. In *Wyman v. James*, 400 U.S. 309 (1971), the Supreme Court held that the fourth amendment's prohibition against unreasonable searches and seizures was not violated by a New York law requiring that welfare recipients agree, as a condition of receiving benefits, to home inspections. The Court concluded that the home visits were not coerced because the family could avoid them by declining to agree to accept welfare benefits. *See Sanchez v. San Diego*, 464 F.3d 916 (9th Cir. 2006) (mandated home

visits are reasonable under fourth amendment). Suppose Barbara James, the public assistance recipient in *Wyman*, had characterized the home visits as a taking of her property rights rather than a violation of the fourth amendment. Is *Wyman* covered by *Monsanto* or by the *Nollan-Dolan* line of cases? Is welfare simply a "government benefit" rather than a vested property right or does the condition in *Wyman* constitute a physical invasion of property (the home visit)? Consider further than the "permanent" invasion of the cable box in *Loretto* was required by law only so long as the property was held for residential rental purposes. Is greater coercion involved in *Wyman* or in *Dolan*? Is the intrusion greater in *Wyman* or in *Loretto*? Can you reconcile all these cases? *See* Steven D. Schwinn, *Reconstructing the Constitutional Case Against Mandatory Welfare Home Visits*, Clearinghouse Rev., May-June 2008, at 42 (arguing that such visits violate the takings clause).

3. In *Home Builders Association of Northern California v. City of Napa*, 108 Cal. Rptr. 2d 60 (Ct. App. 2001), the court upheld a city's inclusionary zoning law against the claim that it violated the takings clause when it required 10 percent of all newly constructed residential units to be "affordable." What are the arguments on both sides of this question and who should have won the case?

4. In *San Remo Hotel L.P. v. City & County of San Francisco*, 41 P.3d 87, 102-103 (Cal. 2002), *aff'd on other grounds*, 545 U.S. 323 (2005), the California Supreme Court upheld against a takings challenge the application of an ordinance that required the San Remo Hotel in San Francisco to pay a $567,000 fee for converting rooms that had been rented to longer-term residents to rooms for tourists (with stays of seven days or less) and daily renters. The ordinance prohibited the conversion of residential hotels to tourist hotels without replacing the lost units on a one-for-one basis or paying a fee to the city to allow it to replace the lost units. The ordinance was intended to "benefit the general public by minimizing adverse impact on the housing supply and on displaced low income, elderly, and disabled persons resulting from the loss of residential hotel units through their conversion and demolition." It was accompanied by findings that the city had recently lost thousands of such units, that many low-income, elderly, and disabled persons reside in such units, and these conversions had created a low-income housing "emergency" in San Francisco.

Upholding the law against a takings claim, Justice Kathryn Mickle Werdegar wrote for the court that the ordinance was not subject to *Nollan-Dolan* analysis because it constituted generally applicable legislation with set terms that gave owners the choice of one-to-one replacement of converted units or payment of a legislatively determined fee to offset the costs of the lost units. *Id.* at 102-103. She further noted that the taking of money is always treated differently under the takings clause because all taxes constitute takings of money and the courts defer to legislative determinations of appropriate taxes. *Id.* at 106. She finally noted that even if the *Nollan-Dolan* test applied, the law would be constitutional because "the housing replacement fees bear a reasonable relationship to loss of housing." *Id.* at 107.

Justice Janice Rogers Brown wrote a blistering dissent, *id.* at 120-128.

Americans are a diverse group of hard-working, confident, and creative people molded into a nation not by common ethnic identity, cultural legacy, or history; rather, Americans have been united by a dream—a dream of freedom, a vision of how free people might live. The dream has a history. The idea that property ownership is the essential prerequisite of liberty has long been "a fundamental tenet of Anglo-American constitutional thought." (Ely, *The Guardian of Every Other Right* (1998) p. 43.) "Indeed, the framers saw property ownership as a buffer protecting individuals from government coercion. Arbitrary redistribution of property destroyed liberty, and thus the framers hoped to restrain attacks on property rights." (*Ibid.*) "Property must be secured, or liberty cannot exist" (Adams, *A Balanced Government* (1790) *in Discourses on Davila* (1805), *reprinted in* 6 *The Works of John Adams* (1851 ed.) p. 280), because property and liberty are, upon examination, one and the same thing.

But private property, already an endangered species in California, is now entirely extinct in San Francisco. The City and County of San Francisco has implemented a neo-feudal regime where the nominal owner of property must use that property according to the preferences of the majorities that prevail in the political process or, worse, the political powerbrokers who often control the government independently of majoritarian preferences. San Francisco has redefined the American dream. Where once government was closely constrained to increase the freedom of individuals, now property ownership is closely constrained to increase the power of government. Where once government was a necessary evil because it protected private property, now private property is a necessary evil because it funds government programs.

The express purpose of the [ordinance] was to preserve the City's stock of low-income residential housing by requiring hotel owners to continue leasing their rooms as residences, or to replace those residential units if they chose to convert the rooms to tourist use. Obviously, the [ordinance] is facially unconstitutional. If a person took my car and asked a ransom for its return, he or she would be guilty of theft. But what if the City, seeking to provide transportation to the poor, orders me to operate an informal carpool, or if I prefer, to buy the City a replacement car?

Here, the City has essentially said to 500 unlucky hotel owners: We lack the public funds to fill the need for affordable housing in San Francisco, so you should solve the problem for us by using your hotels to house poor people. The City might as well have ordered the owners of small grocery stores to give away food at cost.

Once again a majority of this court has proved that "If enough people get together and act in concert, they can take something and not pay for it." *Landgate, Inc. v. California Coastal Com.*, 953 P.2d 1188, 1207 n.1 (Cal. 1998) (dis. opn. of Brown, J.), *quoting* O'Rourke, *Parliament of Whores* 232 (1991). But theft is still theft. Theft is theft even when the government approves of the thievery. Turning a democracy into a kleptocracy does not enhance the stature of the thieves; it only diminishes the legitimacy of the government. The right to express one's individuality and essential human dignity through the free use of property is just as important as the right to do so through speech, the press, or the free exercise of religion. Nevertheless, the property right is now—in California, at least—a hollow one.

Who is right—the majority or the dissent?